Oxford Business English Dictionary

for learners of English

Edited by Dilys Parkinson
Assisted by Joseph Noble

OXFORD

UNIVERSITY PRESS

OXFORD
UNIVERSITY PRESS

Great Clarendon Street, Oxford OX2 6DP

Oxford University Press is a department of the University of Oxford.
It furthers the University's objective of excellence in research, scholarship,
and education by publishing worldwide in

Oxford New York

Auckland Cape Town Dar es Salaam Hong Kong Karachi
Kuala Lumpur Madrid Melbourne Mexico City Nairobi
New Delhi Shanghai Taipei Toronto

With offices in

Argentina Austria Brazil Chile Czech Republic France Greece
Guatemala Hungary Italy Japan Poland Portugal Singapore
South Korea Switzerland Thailand Turkey Ukraine Vietnam

OXFORD and OXFORD ENGLISH are registered trade marks of
Oxford University Press in the UK and in certain other countries

© Oxford University Press 2005

Database right Oxford University Press (maker)

First published 2005

2016 2015 2014 2013
13 12 11 10 9 8

The British National Corpus is a collaborative project involving
Oxford University Press, Longman, Chambers, the Universities of
Oxford and Lancaster and the British Library

ISBN-13: 978 0 19 431584 5 (BOOK)
ISBN-13: 978 0 19 431617 0 (BOOK AND CD-ROM PACK)

Typeset by Data Standards Ltd.

Printed in China

ACKNOWLEDGEMENTS
Cover photography by Corbis and Image Source
Kitemark symbol (p305) reproduced by permission of the British Standards Institution

Illustrations: David Eaton (pp 215, 371, 390, 420, 533, 576); Julian Baker (p S4-5)

Advisory Board: Dr Keith Brown, Prof Guy Cook, Dr Alan Cruse, Ruth Gairns, Moira Runcie,
Prof Gabriele Stein, Dr Norman Whitney, Prof Henry Widdowson

Contents

Preface

This completely new dictionary of Business English has been specially written to be of practical use for students of business and experienced business people who need to read, write and speak English in their work, and for those who give them language training and advice.

It is intended for learners of English at intermediate to advanced level. The definitions have been written using the Oxford 3000™ so that they are simple and clear, but accurate and detailed.

To ensure that the material included in the dictionary is as up-to-date and authentic as possible, a new 50 million word corpus of business English was used. This is a collection of written and spoken British and American English taken from various sources such as the business sections of newspapers, business journals and textbooks, and interviews with business people. It has enabled a wide range of business areas to be covered in the dictionary in addition to terms that are of more general use in communicating in English in a business context.

As people studying English for business need to know how to use words correctly as well as what they mean, detailed grammar information has been included and examples that show how a term is used in typical contexts. In addition, for terms that are commonly used there is extensive information about collocation, for example verbs that can be used with a particular noun.

1 000 words in the dictionary are marked with a star to show that they are particularly important in Business English. These are words that are frequent on our business corpus and are essential in most areas of business or combine with many others to make compounds.

During the writing of the dictionary we have been advised by teachers of Business English and by people involved in the world of business. I should like to thank the members of the Said Business School in Oxford who helped us in an advisory capacity on various areas of business, especially Burcu Hacibedel (Banking, Finance and Economics) and Doris Schedlitzki (Management and Human Resources). I am also grateful to the other people who gave us their expert advice, including Tony Ereira (Stock Exchange and Finance), Richard Spraggett (Accounting) and Roberta Wedge (Finance and Management).

I would also like to acknowledge the invaluable work of the large team of people who have been involved in the dictionary at various stages, both before and after the text was complete.

Dilys Parkinson
August 2005

How to use this dictionary

A typical entry

the headword

parts of speech

Numbers show the different meanings.

shows where the information on each part of speech begins

grammatical information

subject label indicating the area of business for this meaning

pronunciation, with American pronunciation where this is different

meaning

example of use

quarterly /ˈkwɔːtəli; AmE ˈkwɔːrtərli/

adjective, adverb, noun

● *adjective* [only before noun]
1 relating to a period of three months: *quarterly earnings/income/profits* ◇ *This is an 80% reduction on the previous quarterly dividend.*
2 produced or happening every three months: *Managers attend quarterly planning meetings.*
● *adverb*
every three months: *We meet quarterly with our accountants.*
● *noun*
1 [C] a magazine, etc. published four times a year: *The magazine is a quarterly aimed at people working in advertising.*
2 (*Accounting*) **quarterlies** [pl.] in the US, the financial results that large companies publish

How to find a word

All words are listed in alphabetical order whether they are written as one word or two or with a hyphen. If the headword is two or more words, such as **added value**, it is listed according to the first word in the compound (i.e. **added**).

This shows you phrases in the dictionary that contain this headword. These can be found at their alphabetical place.

The headword is replaced with a tilde (~).

etc. shows this is not the full list.

★**value** /ˈvæljuː/ *noun, adjective, verb*
● *noun*
  SEE ALSO **added value, agreed ~, assessed ~, asset ~, book ~, break-up ~, capital ~,** etc.
1 [U,C] how much sth is worth in money or other goods for which it can be exchanged:

Many words have alternative forms or alternative spellings. The most common form is usually given as the main entry and the less frequently used term redirects you to the main entry.

This shows an alternative term with the same meaning.

The alternative headword redirects you to the main entry.

ˈmission ˌstatement (*also* ˌstatement **of ˈpurpose**) *noun* [C]

ˌstatement of ˈpurpose = MISSION STATEMENT

American English forms are treated in the same way:

labourer (*AmE spelling* **laborer**) /ˈleɪbərə(r)/

laborer = LABOURER

Many headwords also have an abbreviated form:

ˌread-ˈwrite *adjective* (*abbr* **RW**)

This indicates an abbreviation.

Sometimes the abbreviation is used more frequently than the full form, in which case the abbreviation is the main headword.

★**GDP** /ˌdʒi: di: ˈpi:/ abbr
(*Economics*) **gross domestic product** the total value of all the goods and services produced by a

The full form is shown afterwards in **bold type**.

Derivatives are words whose meaning can be understood from another word (the **root** word). They do not have their own entry in the dictionary but are given at the same entry as the root word, in a specially marked section:

illicit /ɪˈlɪsɪt/ adjective
not allowed by the law: *the illicit trade in tobacco products* SYN ILLEGAL ▶ il**ˈlicitly** adverb

The triangle shows where the derivatives section starts.

Idioms and phrasal verbs are placed in specially marked sections within the entry. Idioms are at the entry for their first important word (= nouns, verbs, adjectives or adverbs) that is in the dictionary or at their first word. The examples below can be found at the entry for **tick**:

IDM indicates the beginning of the idioms section.

PHR V shows the beginning of the phrasal verbs section.

IDM have ˌticks in all the right ˈboxes (*informal*)
PHR V ˌtick sb/sth ˈoff (*BrE*)

Understanding and using the word

The star shows that this is an important word.

★**vendor** (*AmE spelling also* **vender**) /ˈvendə(r)/
noun [C] (*formal*)

information to show that the word is used in particular situations

Stress marks show stress on phrases.

ˌbank ˈholiday noun [C] (*BrE*)

Geography labels indicate whether the word is used in British or American English.

verb patterns

bleed /bli:d/ verb (**bled, bled** /bled/)
1 [+ obj *or no* obj] (*used especially in the continuous tenses*) (about a company) to lose a large amount

extra grammatical information

irregular forms of verbs, with their pronunciations

Irregular plurals of nouns are also shown.

irregular spelling for present and past participles and past tense

strip /strɪp/ verb, noun
● *verb* [+ obj] (**-pp-**)
1 strip sth from sb/sth | strip sb/sth of sth to remove sth from sth/sb: *They were found guilty of*

prepositions, adverbs and structures that are frequently used with this word

information on the use of adjectives

steep /sti:p/ adjective (**steeper, steepest**)
1 [usually before noun] (about a rise or fall in an amount) sudden and very big: *The steep decline in*

comparatives and superlatives of adjectives

Building your vocabulary

The dictionary also contains a lot of information that is designed
to help you increase your vocabulary.

fixed form of the noun

★statistic /stə'tɪstɪk/ *noun*
1 statistics (*also* **stats**, *informal*) [pl.] a collection
of information shown in numbers: *economic/
employment/unemployment statistics* ◇ *Official
statistics show that people in the north of the
country are the highest earners.*

alternative forms

☉ indicates that the
following words are
common phrases
and patterns.

☉ *current/monthly/new/official/recent* statistics ◆
accurate/gloomy/reliable/surprising statistics ◆
to **analyse/collect/prepare/produce/release**
statistics ◆ *statistics* **tell sb/indicate/prove/show** *sth*

statistically /stə'tɪstɪkli/ *adverb*: *The level of the
customer complaints was not* **statistically significant**.

common or fixed
phrases in **bold type**
in examples

Definitions use vocabulary from the Oxford 3000™ unless a specific term
is needed that is not in the Oxford 3000™, when it is written
in SMALL CAPITALS.

'book ˌequity *noun* [U]
(*Accounting*) the value of a company as shown in its
financial records (**books**) , which is its assets minus
its LIABILITIES (= the money it owes)

a word in a definition
that is not in the
Oxford 3000™

Words in **bold type**
with (brackets) give
the correct term for the
preceding description.

(=…) gives the meaning of
the preceding word or phrase.

Cross references direct you to other related words in the dictionary.
There are a number of notes and illustrations giving extra
information about important words.

pallet /'pælət/ *noun* [C]
a flat wooden frame used for storing and moving
goods; the frame and its contents: *Each shelf
contains two pallets and each pallet contains
60 bags.* → SKID – Picture at TRANSPORT

→ directs you to a
related word.

This directs you to
a picture illustrating
this word.

British English and American English spelling

Words that end in -*ize*, -*ization*, etc. can also be spelled -*ise*,
-*isation*, etc. in British English.

alternative British
English spelling

legalize, -ise /'li:gəlaɪz/ *verb* [+ obj]
to make sth legal: *The government has legalized
irradiation for many types of food.*

Words that are spelled differently in British English and American
English but which are only actually used in one of these varieties
of English have information to show these differences.

'colour ˌsupplement (*AmE spelling* **color ~**)
noun [C] (*BrE only*)

the American English
spelling

This indicates that the
word or phrase is only
used in British English.

Numbers

@ *symbol (only used in written English)* **at**
1 the symbol used in email addresses: *jsmith@oup.com*
2 used to show a rate or price for something, especially on a bill: *15 boxes @ $12 per box: $180*

10 000-foot view /ˌten ˈθaʊznd ˈfʊt ˈvjuː/ *noun* [C] *(informal)*
a broad general view or description of a problem
SYN HELICOPTER VIEW, OVERVIEW

16PF™ /ˌsɪkstiːn ˌpiː ˈef/ *abbr*
(HR) **16 personality factors** a test used, especially by employers, to find out about a person's character by asking questions which are designed to judge 16 different aspects of their character
→ PSYCHOMETRIC TEST

2+2=5 /ˈtuː plʌs ˈtuː iːkwəlz ˈfaɪv/ *phrase*
two plus two equals five a phrase used to express the idea that when two organizations work together or when two companies join together (**merge**), more can be achieved than if they are working separately → SYNERGY

24/7 /ˌtwenti fɔː ˈsevən; *AmE* fɔːr/ *adverb*
twenty-four hours a day, seven days a week (used to mean 'all the time'): *The web store is open 24/7.*
NOTE 24/7 is also used as an adjective: *a 24/7 schedule* and a noun: *Our business needs 24/7.*

24-hour /ˌtwenti fɔːr ˈaʊə(r)/ *adjective* [only before noun]
1 used to describe sth that is open or available all day and night: *a 24-hour store* ◊ *24-hour telephone banking*
2 used to describe sth that relates to one day or happens only on one day: *a 24-hour strike*

24-hour clock /ˌtwenti fɔːr aʊə ˈklɒk; *AmE* aʊər ˈklɑːk/ *noun* [sing.]
the system of using twenty-four numbers to talk about the hours of the day, rather than dividing the day into two units of twelve hours

24-hour society /ˌtwenti fɔːr aʊə səˈsaɪəti; *AmE* aʊər/ *noun* [U; sing.]
the fact that people can now work, play, shop, etc. all night as well as all day: *The 24-hour society may*

let people shop at midnight and buy shares on the Internet at dawn, but it could damage our health.

2G /ˌtuː ˈdʒiː/ = SECOND-GENERATION (2)

360-degree feedback /ˌθriː ˌsɪksti dɪˌɡriː ˈfiːdbaek/ *(also* ˌ360-degree apˈpraisal, ˌfull-circle ˈfeedback) *noun* [U]
(HR) information or criticism about sb's work from all the types of people they work with, including their manager, people on the same level, the people they manage, customers, etc.; a judgement of the value of their work based on this

3G /ˌθriː ˈdʒiː/ = THIRD-GENERATION (1)

401(k) /ˌfɔː(r) əʊ ˈwʌn (ˈkeɪ); *AmE* oʊ/ *noun* [C] *(plural* **401(k)s** *or* **401(k)'s**)
in the US, a way of saving money for your retirement in which a percentage of your wage is paid into an investment fund chosen by your employer, to which employers sometimes add a similar amount. Tax is only charged when you take money out of the fund: *a 401(k) plan/contribution*

the 4 Ps *(also spelled* **four Ps**) /ˌfɔː ˈpiːz; *AmE* ˌfɔːr/ *noun* [pl.]
(Marketing) **product**, **price**, **promotions** and **place**, which together form the MARKETING MIX, and which should be carefully planned if a product is to be sold successfully

the 5 Ss *(also spelled* **Five Ss**) /ˌfaɪv ˈesɪz/ *noun* [pl.]
a method of making and keeping an office or workplace clean and well organized. The 5 Ss are: **sort** (= organize and decide what to keep or throw away), **systematize** (= arrange things according to a system), **scrub** (= clean thoroughly), **standardize** (= make these activities regular and normal) and **sustain** (= continue to do it).

the 80/20 rule /ˌeɪti ˈtwenti ruːl/ *(also* **the** ˌ80/ '20 ˌprinciple) *noun* [sing.]
a theory that 80% of results come from 20% of effort or causes: *According to the 80/20 rule, 80% of your revenue comes from just 20% of your customers.* **SYN** PARETO'S PRINCIPLE—Picture at PARETO ANALYSIS

A a

A1 /ˌeɪ ˈwʌn/ *adjective*
1 *(Finance)* used to describe a company that is considered to be able to pay its debts and to be safe to lend money to: *The company is rated A1 by Moody's and A+ by Standard and Poor's.* → TRIPLE-A
2 used to describe sth such as a ship, or a person, that is in the best possible condition

AAA /ˌtrɪpl ˈeɪ/ = TRIPLE-A

AA rating /ˌeɪ ˈeɪ/ = AVERAGE AUDIENCE RATING

★abandon /əˈbændən/ *verb* [+ obj]
1 to stop doing sth, especially before it is finished; to stop having or using sth: *The group has been forced to abandon its plan to raise capacity by 8%.* ◊ *The company was abandoned by many of its customers.*

2 *(Insurance)* to give up the legal ownership of sth, such as a ship or cargo that has been damaged, to an insurance company in exchange for an insurance payment, especially when the cost of repairing it is more than its total value
3 *(Law)* to stop trying to make a claim in a court: *The claim was abandoned with the permission of the court.*
► **abandonment** /əˈbændənmənt/ *noun* [U]
→ idiom at SHIP

abate /əˈbeɪt/ *verb* [+ obj *or* no obj]
to become less strong; to make sth less strong: *The three-year recession showed no signs of abating.*
► **aˈbatement** *noun* [U]

abˌbreviated acˈcounts *noun* [pl.] *(BrE)*
(Accounting) a type of financial record that contains

less detail than normal, which small companies can produce for official records

ABC1 /ˌeɪ biː siː 'wʌn/ *noun* [U] (*BrE*)
(*Marketing*) the top three social and economic groups in a society, used to refer to these groups as possible customers for particular products: *41% of ABC1 women aged between 15 and 24 read a weekly women's magazine.* → C2DE

'A/'B/'C share (*also* **class 'A/'B/'C share**) *noun*
[C, usually pl.]
(*Finance*) in the UK, different types of shares that give the owners different rights or have different restrictions. People who own **A shares** usually do not have a vote at meetings of shareholders.
→ ORDINARY SHARE

★ **ability** /ə'bɪləti/ *noun* (*plural* **abilities**)
1 [sing.] the fact that sb is able to do sth: *Candidates must have the ability to work in a team under pressure.*
2 [C,U] a level of skill or intelligence: *I want an opportunity to prove my abilities.*

a,bility-to-'pay ,principle *noun* [sing.]
(*Economics*) a theory that states that people who earn more money should pay more tax, so that there are higher rates of tax on higher incomes
→ BENEFIT PRINCIPLE

★ **abolish** /ə'bɒlɪʃ; *AmE* ə'bɑːl-/ *verb* [+ obj]
to officially end a law, a system or an institution: *Instead of abolishing the estate tax, why not reform it?* ▶ **abolition** /ˌæbə'lɪʃn/ *noun* [U]: *the abolition of exchange controls*

a,bove 'par *adjective*
(*Finance*) (used about the price of a share, bond, etc.) higher than the price at which it was first made available for sale (the **nominal price**): *The gilts achieved a price above par.* ◇ *above-par securities*

a,bove the 'fold *adverb*
(*IT*) in the top part of a web page that you see first on the screen: *Your ads are always shown above the fold.* ▶ **a,bove the 'fold** *adjective*: *above-the-fold ads* → BELOW THE FOLD

a,bove-the-'line *adjective* [usually before noun]
1 (*Accounting*) relating to the normal business costs and income that form a company's total profit: *Raw materials are usually recorded as above-the-line costs.*
2 (*Accounting*) in the US, relating to costs that everyone can take away from their income to calculate their total (**gross**) income before they pay tax: *an above-the-line deduction for college tuition expenses*
3 (*Marketing*) relating to advertising that uses one of the main ways of telling large numbers of people about a product, for example advertisements on television, in newspapers or outdoors: *A budget of over $10 million has been allocated to above-the-line advertising.* ◇ *The marketing mix includes above-the-line promotion.*
▶ **a,bove-the-'line** *adverb*: *Property costs will be taken above-the-line.* → BELOW-THE-LINE

ABS /ˌeɪ biː 'es/ *abbr*
(*Finance*) asset-backed securities; asset-backed securitization: *The rise of the ABS market continues.*
→ ASSET-BACKED

absence /'æbsəns/ *noun*

SEE ALSO: **leave of absence**

1 [U,C] the fact of sb not being at work or at a meeting when they should be; the occasion or period of time when sb is away: *her repeated*

absences from work ◇ *The decision was made in my absence* (= while I was not there).
2 [U] the fact of sb/sth not existing or not being available; a lack of sth: *We may have to sell the business to them in the absence of a higher offer.* ◇ *the absence of any women on the board of directors*

absentee /ˌæbsən'tiː/ *noun* [C]
(*HR*) a person who is not at work when they should be: *Why are there so many absentees today?* ◇ *an astonishingly low 2% absentee rate*

absenteeism /ˌæbsən'tiːɪzəm/ *noun* [U]
(*HR*) staying away from work, especially often and without good reasons: *Absenteeism costs the industry millions of dollars every year.* ◇ *There is a high level of absenteeism in this department.*
→ PRESENTEEISM

,absolute ad'vantage *noun* [C, usually sing.]
(*Economics*) the ability to make a product more cheaply than other countries can → COMPARATIVE ADVANTAGE, COMPETITIVE ADVANTAGE

,absolute 'auction *noun* [C] (*AmE*)
(*Commerce*) an **auction** in which there is no fixed price that must be reached before the item can be sold, so that sth is simply sold to the person who offers the most money

absorb /əb'sɔːb; -'zɔːb; *AmE* -'sɔːrb; -'zɔːrb/ *verb* [+ obj]
1 (*often* **be absorbed**) to take a smaller business into a larger one so that it becomes part of it; to take unemployed workers from other businesses into a company: *Several large clothing chains were absorbed into the group.* ◇ *a scheme to absorb workers from failing industries*
2 to be able to deal with high costs, losses or changes without showing any bad effects: *The company has absorbed the higher manufacturing costs rather than pass them on to its customers.*
3 (about a market) to accept and be able to sell a product: *It would take the market three or four years to absorb the increase in the number of hotel rooms.*
→ ACCEPT (6)
4 to use up a large supply of sth, especially money or time: *The new proposals would absorb $80 million of the federal budget.*

absorption /əb'sɔːpʃn; -'zɔːp-; *AmE* -'sɔːrp-; -'zɔːrp-/ *noun* [U]
the act of a larger company taking in a smaller company so that it becomes part of it: *The mergers they planned included the absorption of two small banks.*

ab'sorption ,costing *noun* [U]
(*Accounting*) a way of calculating the cost of a product by including all costs involved in producing it and running the business, such as raw materials, rent, electricity or wages [SYN] FULL COSTING

abstract /'æbstrækt/ *noun* [C]
a short piece of writing containing the main ideas in a talk, an article, a report, etc: *The search engine searches through 13 million abstracts from marketing journals.* [SYN] SUMMARY

a/c = ACCOUNT

ACAS /'eɪkæs/ *abbr* **Advisory Conciliation and Arbitration Service** in the UK, an organization that helps employers and employees settle disagreements: *to refer a dispute to ACAS*

accelerate /ək'seləreɪt/ *verb*
1 [+ obj or no obj] to happen or to make sth happen faster or earlier than expected: *Technological change is accelerating.* ◇ *The company has announced it is accelerating its cost-cutting programme.* [OPP] DECELERATE
2 [no obj] (about the economy) to increase in activity so that demand for goods increases: *Will*

consumption slow before the global economy starts to accelerate? [OPP] DECELERATE

3 (Finance) [+ obj] to demand that a debt is paid back at once or more quickly than first agreed, because the person who has borrowed the money has failed to make regular payments: Their major investor is now seeking to accelerate the loan.

▸ **acceleration** /ək‚selə'reɪʃn/ noun [sing; U]: a sharp acceleration in the rate of economic growth

ac‚celerated 'cost recovery ‚system noun [U] (abbr **ACRS**)
(Accounting) in the US, a way of calculating the value of assets in a company's financial records, where the value of an asset is reduced over a particular period of time fixed by the tax rules, rather than over its full useful life

ac‚celerated depreci'ation noun [U]
(Accounting) a way of calculating the value of a particular asset in a company's accounts by reducing its value over a shorter period of time than usual or by larger amounts than usual in the first few years. This is a form of TAX RELIEF (= a reduction in the amount of tax you have to pay) and is intended to help a business to develop and grow larger.

ac‚celerated 'payment noun [C,U]
(Finance) a payment that a person makes to pay back a debt or a loan at once or more quickly than was first agreed, often because they have failed to make regular payments

accelerator /ək'seləreɪtə(r)/ noun [C]
a company that helps new companies get started by giving them such things as office space, legal help and marketing services in exchange for payment

★ **accept** /ək'sept/ verb [+ obj]
1 to agree to take sth such as an offer, a job or money: The unions voted to accept a pay increase of 6%. ◇ He accepted a position as vice-president of corporate development. [OPP] REJECT
2 to agree to or approve of sth: They accepted the court's decision. ◇ The company has accepted a $5 billion takeover bid. [OPP] REJECT
3 to be willing or able to receive payment in a particular form: Will you accept a cheque? ◇ All major credit cards are accepted.
4 to agree to be responsible for sth; to agree that you are responsible for sth wrong or illegal that has happened: The auditors have accepted responsibility for failing to spot the mistake.
5 (Law) to agree to take goods or services from a seller, which means that the buyer must then pay for them: The buyer can refuse to accept the goods if they arrive later than the agreed date. [OPP] REJECT
6 (Marketing) to be willing to buy a product, a technology or a service: Our products are *well/widely accepted* in the local and international market.
7 (Law) to agree to what is stated in a contract, for example particular rules or decisions: to accept the terms of an agreement
8 (Insurance) to agree to provide payments if sb loses sth or has a serious accident, for example: The insurance company may refuse to accept the whole risk.
9 (Finance) to agree to pay the amount of money stated on a BILL OF EXCHANGE by signing it

★ **acceptance** /ək'septəns/ noun

SEE ALSO: **banker's acceptance, documents against ~, non-~, partial ~**

1 [U] the act of agreeing to sth such as a plan, an idea or an offer: Union leaders recommended acceptance of the pay offer. ◇ New ideas may have a hard time **gaining** acceptance. ◇ a *letter of acceptance*
2 (Finance) [C] the agreement of people who hold shares in a company to the offer of a TAKEOVER by

another company: They had received acceptances from 60% of the company's shareholders.
3 (Law) [U] the act of agreeing to accept sth that is offered, for example when a buyer agrees to take goods or services from a seller at a particular price: Once acceptance has taken place, the buyer cannot reject the goods.
4 [U] the willingness of people to buy or use a product, technology or service: The product has **gained** acceptance in more than fifteen countries worldwide.
● **consumer/customer/market/public** acceptance of sth • **brand/product** acceptance
5 (Insurance) [U] the act of an insurance company agreeing to provide payments if sb loses sth or has a serious accident, for example: Your acceptance into the plan is guaranteed if you apply by the end of this month.
6 (Finance) [U,C] the act of signing a document (a **bill of exchange**) to say that you promise to pay the amount of money mentioned on it; the words that are written on the document to say that you agree to pay it; the document that has been signed

ac'ceptance ‚bonus noun [C] (AmE)
(HR) an amount of money that is paid to a very difficult employee when they agree to do a very difficult task

ac'ceptance ‚sampling noun [U]
(Production) testing a small number of a total amount of items in order to decide whether the quality of the whole amount is good enough to accept or not: Acceptance sampling is usually carried out at the customer's premises.

acceptor (AmE spelling also **accepter**) /ək'septə(r)/ noun [C]
(Finance) the person or bank that signs a BILL OF EXCHANGE and promises to pay it

★ **access** /'ækses/ noun, verb
● **noun** [U]

SEE ALSO: **wheelchair access**

1 the chance or right to use or have sth: Customers can easily get access **to** information about our products. ◇ Do you have access to the Internet? ◇ increased access to the South American market
● **to gain/get/have** access • **to give/offer/provide/** access
2 the right to remove some of the money that you are keeping in an account: We don't want to limit people's access **to** their own savings.
3 permission, especially legal or official, to see sth or sb: Someone gained unauthorized access to the personnel files.
● **to gain/get/have** access to sb/sth • **to deny** sb access to sb/sth
4 a way of entering or reaching a place, especially for DISABLED people (= people who are unable to use a part of their body completely or easily): There is good access to all our stores. ◇ new legislation over disability access
● **verb** [+ obj]
1 to find information on a computer: Your electronic ID is needed to access your email account.
2 to remove some of the money that you are keeping in an account: Savers need to be able to access their accounts.
3 to be able to obtain, reach or use sth: How can we access the capital we need?

accessible /ək'sesəbl/ adjective
1 able to be reached, used or seen: This information is accessible **to** everyone.
2 (about a person) easy to talk to: A good manager should be accessible.

3 (about a place) possible to be reached or entered: *Employers must ensure that their workplaces are accessible to the disabled.*
4 easy to understand or use: *The report is accessible to non-economists.*
▶ **accessibility** /ək‚sesə'bɪləti/ *noun* [U]

accessory /ək'sesəri/ *noun* [C, usually pl.] (*plural* **accessories**)
1 an extra piece of equipment that you can add to sth and is useful or attractive but not essential: *The company is a leading manufacturer of computer accessories.*
2 a thing that you can wear or carry that matches your clothes, for example a belt or a bag: *fashion accessories*
3 small items that are sold to be used for a particular purpose or in a particular place: *kitchen/office/bathroom accessories*

'accident in‚surance *noun* [U]
a type of insurance in which money is paid for injury or death caused by an accident

accommodate /ə'kɒmədeɪt; *AmE* ə'kɑːm-/ *verb* [+ obj]
1 to have enough space for sb/sth: *There is a seven-level garage that accommodates 1400 cars.*
2 to help sb by doing or providing what they want: *The company refused to accommodate her by moving her work closer to her home.*
3 to consider sth and be influenced by it when you are designing sth or deciding what to do: *Most cubicles fail to accommodate computers in their design.*

accommodation /ə‚kɒmə'deɪʃn; *AmE* ə‚kɑːm-/ *noun*
1 [U] (*BrE*) (*AmE* **a‚ccommo'dations** [pl.]) a place to live, work or stay in (*BrE*): *We have moved to temporary accommodation.* ◇ (*AmE*) *There is a shortage of good office accommodations in the area.*
2 (*formal*) [U; C, usually sing.] a satisfactory agreement or arrangement between people or groups with different opinions: *We hope to **arrive at/reach** an accommodation with the trade unions.*
3 (*Finance*) [sing.] (*especially AmE*) money that is lent for a short time, especially because sb has an urgent need for it, before a formal arrangement is made

accommodations = ACCOMMODATION (1)

★**account** /ə'kaʊnt/ *noun, verb*
●*noun* [C]

SEE ALSO: **adjustment account, appropriation ~, approved ~, asset ~, bank ~, banking ~,** etc.

1 (*abbr* **a/c**) an arrangement that sb has with a bank or BUILDING SOCIETY to keep money there and take some out: *I would like to open a business account.* ◇ *We have an account **with/at** Barclays.* ◇ *I paid the cheque into my bank account.*
◑ *to* **close/have/hold/open** *an account* ◆ *to* **pay/put** *sth into an account* ◆ *to* **take sth out of/withdraw sth from** *an account* ◆ *to* **credit/debit** *an account*
2 (*Commerce*) (*BrE also* **'credit ac‚count**) (*AmE also* **'charge ac‚count**) an arrangement with a shop/store or business to pay bills for goods or services at a later time, for example in regular amounts every month: *We have an account with a taxi firm.* ◇ *Most customers settle their account in full* (= pay all the money they owe) *at the end of each month.* ◇ *Please charge it to* (= record the cost to be paid on) *my account.* ◇ *The amount now due on your account is $364.27.*
◑ *to* **close/have/hold/open** *an account* ◆ *to* **settle** *an account* ◆ *to* **charge sth to/put sth on** *an account*
3 (*Accounting*) a statement of money paid, received or owed over a period of time: *You will need to keep*

an account of your expenses. ◇ *an itemized account*
→ ACCOUNTS
4 (*Marketing*) a regular customer who does a lot of business with a company, especially a company working in advertising, marketing or PUBLIC RELATIONS: *the agency's pitch for the Pepsi account* ◇ *a sales rep who's chasing a million-dollar account*
◑ *to* **chase/land/lose/pitch for/win** *an account*
5 (*IT*) an arrangement that sb has with a company that allows them to use the Internet or to receive, store and send emails: *You will need to set up an account with an Internet Service Provider.*
◑ *to* **get/have/set up/sign up for** *an account* ◆ *to* **access/log onto** *your account*
IDM **on ac'count 1** to be paid for later: *Can I buy the printer on account?* **2** as part of the full amount you need to pay: *You could pay some of your tax bill on account.*
●*verb*
PHR V **ac'count for sth 1** to form or be the source of a particular amount: *Sales to Europe accounted for 80% of our total sales last year.* **2** to give an explanation of sth; to be the explanation or cause of sth: *We cannot account for the sudden fall in the company's share price.* ◇ *The low inflation rate is accounted for by the falling prices of goods.*
3 (*Accounting*) to record an amount in a company's financial records in a particular way: *The capital gain has been accounted for in the profit and loss account.* → UNACCOUNTED FOR

★**accountable** /ə'kaʊntəbl/ *adjective* [not usually before noun]
expected to explain your decisions or actions; responsible: *procedures to make companies more accountable **to** shareholders* ◇ *I am directly accountable **to** management **for** the work of my team.* ▶ **accountability** /ə‚kaʊntə'bɪləti/ *noun* [U]: *We need to **improve** the accountability of the board to shareholders.*

★**accountancy** /ə'kaʊntənsi/ *noun* [U] (*especially BrE*)

SEE ALSO: **creative accountancy**

1 the work or profession of an accountant: *He works for a top **accountancy firm** in Paris.*
◑ *the accountancy* **industry/profession** ◆ *an accountancy firm*
2 the training you need in order to become an accountant: *Applicants should have a professional qualification in accountancy.*
SYN ACCOUNTING

★**accountant** /ə'kaʊntənt/ *noun* [C]

SEE ALSO: **certified management accountant, certified public ~, chartered ~, chartered certified ~**

a person whose job is to keep or check the financial records of a person, a company or an organization and give financial advice: *She's a **qualified** accountant.* ◇ *He's the organization's **chief** accountant.* ◇ *a firm of accountants* → AUDITOR See note at PROFESSION

ac'count books = BOOKS (1)

ac'count e‚xecutive *noun* [C]
an employee of a company, especially one working in advertising, who is responsible for dealing with one of the company's regular customers: *She's an assistant account executive for Grey Advertising.* → ACCOUNT MANAGER

★**accounting** /ə'kaʊntɪŋ/ *noun* [U]

SEE ALSO: **accrual accounting, budgetary ~, cash ~, cost ~, creative ~, equity ~, false ~,** etc.

1 (*especially AmE*) the work or profession of an accountant **SYN** ACCOUNTANCY
◑ *the accounting* **industry/profession** ◆ *an accounting firm*

2 the work of keeping and checking the financial records of a person, a company or an organization: *Shareholders lost money as the result of accounting errors.* → BOOKKEEPING
○ accounting **errors/irregularities/scandals** ◆ accounting **methods/practices/procedures**
3 (*especially AmE*) the training you need in order to become an accountant: *to study accounting*
SYN ACCOUNTANCY

the ac'counting ˌcycle *noun* [sing.]
(*Accounting*) the series of steps that are used to follow what has happened in a business and to report the financial effect of those things NOTE The **accounting cycle** begins with a financial TRANSACTION and ends when the account books are closed at the end of each accounting period.

the ac'counting eˌquation (*also* the 'balance-sheet eˌquation) *noun* [sing.]
(*Accounting*) the basic principle used by accountants to make the totals of the amounts in both parts of a BALANCE SHEET equal each other NOTE The **accounting equation** can be written as 'assets = liabilities + capital'.

ac'counting ˌperiod (*also* 'trading ˌperiod) *noun* [C]
(*Accounting*) the regular period of time over which a business prepares a set of financial records; the time between two BALANCE SHEETS: *preliminary results for the eight-month accounting period ending 31 December 2005* → ACCOUNTING YEAR

ac'counting ˌprinciple *noun* [C, usually pl.]
(*Accounting*) one of a group of rules or ideas that an accountant must follow when preparing a company's financial records, so that the records are an accurate and true description of the company's financial status NOTE An example of an **accounting principle** is that financial items must be recorded in the accounts in the same way from one period to another. These rules or ideas can also be called **accounting concepts** or **accounting conventions**. → GAAP

ac'counting 'rate of re'turn *noun* [C] (*plural* **accounting rates of return**) (*abbr* **ARR**)
(*Accounting*) a percentage calculated by taking the amount of profit you expect to get from a particular investment each year and dividing it by the amount you have invested in it. It is used to help a company decide whether to invest a large amount of money in a particular project, business, etc. → INTERNAL RATE OF RETURN , PAYBACK, RETURN ON CAPITAL EMPLOYED

ac'counting ˌratio = FINANCIAL RATIO

ac'counting ˌstandard (*also* ac'counting ˌrule) *noun* [C]

SEE ALSO: **International Accounting Standards**

(*Accounting*) a law that describes the way in which amounts must be recorded in a company's financial records: *Under accounting standard FRS 17, companies must adjust their profits for changes in the value of their pension fund.*

ac'counting ˌsystem *noun*
1 [C] a particular way of keeping and preparing reports of a company's financial records; a computer system used to do this: *the benefits of installing a computerized accounting system*
2 [sing.] the practice and methods of keeping and checking financial records for businesses: *He claims that the problems with the whole financial accounting system make it difficult for investors to judge companies.*

ac'counting 'year (*BrE*) (*AmE* ˌnatural 'business year) *noun* [C]
(*Accounting*) the period of twelve months over which a business prepares a set of financial

records: *Our accounting year runs from July 1st to June 30th.* → ACCOUNTING PERIOD, FINANCIAL YEAR

ac'count ˌmanager *noun* [C]
an employee of a company who is responsible for one or more of the company's regular customers, especially in a bank or an advertising agency
→ ACCOUNT EXECUTIVE

acˌcount pa'yee *noun* [sing.] (*abbr* **a/c payee**)
words written across a cheque to mean that the cheque must only be paid into the bank account of the person or company named on the cheque NOTE The phrase 'account payee only' is also used.

★**accounts** /ə'kaʊnts/ *noun*

SEE ALSO: abbreviated accounts, final ~, financial ~, note to the ~

1 (*Accounting*) [pl.] a set of records for a business over a period, showing all the money received and paid out and how much profit has been made: *a set of accounts* ◇ *This transaction is not shown in the annual accounts.* ◇ *a computer program that takes the hard work out of doing the accounts* ◇ *The company failed to **file** its accounts* (= send them to the tax authorities) *for the 2002 financial year.* ◇ *The accounts are all **in order**.* SYN BOOKS, BOOKS OF ACCOUNT
○ to audit/do/keep (the) accounts ◆ annual/monthly/quarterly accounts
2 [U with sing./pl. verb] the department in a company where money spent and owed is recorded: *the accounts department* ◇ *She works in accounts.*

acˌcounts 'payable *noun* [pl.; U]
(*Accounting*) the amounts of money that a business owes to its suppliers or to people who have made loans (its **creditors**), shown as a LIABILITY on its BALANCE SHEET; the department of a business that deals with this: *When an invoice comes in you send it to the guy in accounts payable to deal with.*
→ CREDITOR (2)

acˌcounts re'ceivable *noun* [pl.; U] (*also* 'book debt* [C,U])
(*Accounting*) the amounts of money that are owed to a business by its customers (**debtors**), shown as an asset on its BALANCE SHEET; the department of a business that deals with this: *For many smaller businesses, accounts receivable are their most valuable asset.* → DEBTOR (2)

ac'count terms *noun* [pl.]
(*Commerce*) the arrangement that is made between a seller and a buyer that states that the buyer does not have to pay immediately but must pay in an agreed time and in the agreed way: *Open account terms are available to customers with an established credit history.* → OPEN ACCOUNT

accreditation /ə,kredɪ'teɪʃn/ *noun* [U,C]
the act of officially recognizing that sb/sth has achieved a required standard; the act of being recognized in this way: *The company is applying for official accreditation to prove the quality of its products and service.*

accredited /ə'kredɪtɪd/ *adjective* [usually before noun]
officially recognized, especially as being of a required standard: *accredited training programmes*

accretion /ə'kriːʃn/ *noun* [C,U]
(*Accounting*) an increase or growth in the amount or value of sth: *The merger resulted in a 13% accretion in the value of shares.* ▸ **accretive** /ə'kriːtɪv/ *adjective* [not usually before noun]: *The deal will be immediately accretive **to** the company's earnings.*

accrual /əˈkruːəl/ noun
(Accounting)
1 [C,U] a gradual increase in an amount of money: the accrual of interest
2 (also ac,crued 'charge, ac,crued ex'pense, ac,crued lia'bility) [C] an estimated amount of money that a business owes for goods or services that have been supplied to it but for which no request for payment has been received. This amount is recorded in the accounts at the end of the accounting period.
→ ACCRUE

ac'crual ac,counting (also ac'cruals ac,counting) noun [U]
(Accounting) a system of keeping accounts where amounts of money are written down at the time when sth is bought or sold, and before the money has been paid or received → CASH ACCOUNTING

ac'crual ,basis = ACCRUALS BASIS

ac'crual ,method = ACCRUALS BASIS

ac'cruals ac,counting = ACCRUAL ACCOUNTING

ac'cruals ,basis (BrE) (also ac'crual ,basis, AmE, BrE) (AmE also ac'crual ,method) noun [sing.]
(Accounting) the rule of accounting that ACCRUAL ACCOUNTING is based on: The effects of transactions can be recognized on an accruals basis (when the transactions take place), or on a cash basis (when money is paid or received). ◇ accruals basis accounts → CASH BASIS

accrue /əˈkruː/ verb (accruing, accrued, accrued)
(Accounting)
1 [no obj] to increase over a period of time: Interest accrues from the first of the month.
2 [+ obj] to allow an amount of money or debts to grow over a period of time: The firm had accrued debts of over $10 m. [SYN] ACCUMULATE
3 [no obj] (about a payment or a benefit) to be received by sb over a period of time: economic benefits accruing to the country from tourism → ACCRUAL

ac,crued 'benefits noun [pl.]
the money that is owed to an employee as a pension

ac,crued 'charge = ACCRUAL (2)

ac,crued depreci'ation noun [U,C]
(Accounting) the amount by which an asset has reduced in value at a particular point in time

ac,crued ex'pense = ACCRUAL (2)

ac,crued 'income noun [U]
(Accounting) income that a business earns during an accounting period but which it does not receive before the period ends

ac,crued 'interest noun [U]
(Accounting) interest earned in a particular period of time that has not yet been received

ac,crued lia'bility = ACCRUAL (2)

★accumulate /əˈkjuːmjəleɪt/ verb
1 [no obj] to gradually increase over a period of time: The deadline for repayment passed, and interest charges began to accumulate.
2 [+ obj] to gradually get more of something over a period of time: My savings are accumulating interest. [SYN] ACCRUE
▶ **accumulation** /əˌkjuːmjəˈleɪʃn/ noun [U,C]: the accumulation of wealth

ac,cumulated depreci'ation noun [sing.]
(Accounting) (in a company's accounts) the total amount taken off the value of machinery, a vehicle, etc. up to a particular time because it is old or less useful

ac,cumulated 'dividend noun [C, usually pl.]
(Accounting) part of a company's profit owed but not yet paid to shareholders

ac,cumulated 'profit noun [C, usually sing.]
(Accounting) (in a company's accounts) the profit that a company has kept for itself and not paid to shareholders as DIVIDENDS

ac,cumu'lation ,unit noun [C]
(Finance) an amount invested in an INVESTMENT TRUST that does not pay regular DIVIDENDS, but adds the amount earned to the original investment

accuse /əˈkjuːz/ verb [+ obj]
to say that sb has done sth wrong or is guilty of sth: The union accused the company of racial discrimination. ◇ A businessman appeared in court yesterday accused of stealing $2 million from his company.

acetate /ˈæsɪteɪt/ noun [C]
a thin piece of clear plastic on which you can write or print text or pictures to show on a screen using an OVERHEAD PROJECTOR → TRANSPARENCY (3)— Picture at PRESENTATION

★achieve /əˈtʃiːv/ verb [+ obj]
to succeed in reaching a particular goal, status or standard, especially by making an effort for a long time: The company achieved its target of a 15% increase in sales this year.
● to achieve a goal/an objective/a target
▶ **achievable** /əˈtʃiːvəbl/ adjective: Profits of $20 m look achievable. [OPP] UNACHIEVABLE

achievement /əˈtʃiːvmənt/ noun
1 [C] a thing that sb has done successfully, especially using their own effort and skill: To keep within the budget was a great achievement.
2 [U] the act or process of achieving sth: She felt a great sense of achievement every time she negotiated a deal.

a'chievement moti,vation noun [U]
(HR) a desire to be successful or to reach a very high standard: to have high achievement motivation

achiever /əˈtʃiːvə(r)/ noun [C]
a person who is extremely successful in their job: Many of the country's top achievers have studied abroad. → HIGH ACHIEVER

'acid-test ,ratio (also 'current ,ratio, 'liquid ,ratio, 'quick ,ratio) noun [C]
(Accounting) a way of measuring how much cash a company has available by comparing the total amount of money that it has in cash and is owed by customers with the total amount of money that it owes → LIQUIDITY RATIO

acknowledge /əkˈnɒlɪdʒ; AmE əkˈnɑːl-/ verb [+ obj]
to tell sb that you have received sth that they sent to you: All applications will be acknowledged.

acknowledgement (also spelled **acknowledgment**) /əkˈnɒlɪdʒmənt; AmE əkˈnɑːl-/ noun [C,U]
a letter saying that sth has been received: I didn't receive an acknowledgement of my application. ◇ a letter of acknowledgement → FUNCTIONAL ACKNOWLEDGEMENT

a/c payee = ACCOUNT PAYEE

★acquire /əˈkwaɪə(r)/ verb [+ obj]
1 (about a company) to buy a company or part of a company's business; to buy shares in a company: Last year the company acquired its smaller rival for $6.9 bn. ◇ It announced that it would acquire a 22 per cent stake in RTL from the UK media group. → MERGE

O *to acquire an **asset**/a **business**/a **company**/**shares**/a **stake***

2 to obtain the legal right to use sth or perform an activity: *The company has **acquired the rights** to assemble and market the new range of farm tractors.*
3 to gain sth that is valuable to you or important for your business: *By acquiring new skills you can increase your wages substantially.*
→ ACQUISITION

acquirer /ə'kwaɪərə(r)/ *noun* [C]
a company that wants to buy and take control of another company : *The media group is seen as a likely acquirer of the two television channels.*
→ TARGET COMPANY

★ **acquisition** /ˌækwɪ'zɪʃn/ *noun*

SEE ALSO: **compulsory acquisition, customer acquisition**

1 [C] a company that has been bought by another company: *The company has made 20 acquisitions since 1998.* ◇ *the recent decline in **mergers and acquisitions*** → MERGER
O *to complete/finalize/look for/make an acquisition • a planned/potential/proposed acquisition (of sth) • a big/large/major/strategic acquisition • a number/ series/string of acquisitions*
2 [U] the activity of buying another company: *the company's proposed $21.9bn acquisition of Compaq Computer* ◇ *They are seeking new **acquisition targets*** (= companies they want to buy).
O *an acquisition programme/strategy/target*
3 [U] the act of getting sth: *the acquisition of new skills* ◇ *The company spent more than $1.5 billion on subscriber acquisition when going online.*
→ ACQUIRE

ˌacquiˈsition cost *noun* [C]
1 (*Accounting*) the total cost of buying an asset, including both the price and any transport costs, professional fees, money that is taken off the price (**discounts**), etc.
2 (*Marketing*) (*also* **ˌcustomer acquiˈsition cost**) the total cost of getting a new customer

acrimonious /ˌækrɪ'məʊniəs; *AmE* -'moʊ-/ *adjective* (*formal*)
(about an argument or a disagreement) angry and full of strong bitter feelings and words: *The agreement marks the end of an acrimonious takeover battle.*

acronym /'ækrənɪm/ *noun* [C]
a word formed from the first letters of several words: *WAP is the acronym for Wireless Application Protocol.* **NOTE** **Acronyms** are pronounced as single words. For example, the acronym BASIC is pronounced /'beɪsɪk/.

aˌcross the ˈboard *phrase*
involving everyone or everything in a company or an industry: *The editorial staff took a 10 per cent pay cut across the board.* ▶ **aˌcross-the-ˈboard** *adjective* [usually before noun]: *an across-the-board wage increase*

ACRS /ˌeɪ siː ɑːr 'es/ = ACCELERATED COST RECOVERY SYSTEM

★ **act** /ækt/ *noun, verb*
● *noun* [C]
1 (*usually* **Act**) a law that has been made by a parliament: *Many companies could be **in breach of** the Data Protection Act.* → REGULATION
O *to amend/pass/repeal an act*
2 (*Law*) something that sb does that is harmful to sb else: *The auditors had been warned of possible illegal acts within the company.*
O *to commit a criminal/an illegal act*
IDM **be/get ˌin on the ˈact** (*especially BrE*) (*AmE usually* **get ˌinto the ˈact**) (*informal*) to be/become involved in an activity that sb else has started, especially to get some benefit for yourself **get your**

ˈact together (*informal*) to behave in a more effective or responsible way: *The EU needs to get its act together to enforce the new law.* → idiom at CLEAN *verb*
● *verb* [no obj]
to do sth for a particular purpose or to deal with a particular situation: *We have acted in the shareholders' best interests.* ◇ *The management has realized its mistake and has acted quickly to avoid disaster.* ◇ *The broker acted honestly and **in good faith*** (= believing he was doing the right thing).
PHRV **ˈact for sb/sth**; **ˌact on beˈhalf of sb/sth**
1 to deal with sb's/sth's affairs for them: *accountants acting for a number of trusts* **2** (*Law*) to represent sb/sth in a court **ˈact as sth** to perform a particular function; to do a particular job, especially one that requires special skills or is very responsible: *Ms Nelson will continue to act as a consultant for six other companies.* **ˈact upon sth** (*also* **ˈact on sth**, *especially formal*) to do sth as a result of advice, information, instructions, etc. that you have received: *The board **failed to** act on the takeover offer.*

acting /'æktɪŋ/ *adjective* [only before noun]
doing an important job that is usually done by sb else : *Ms Bruce will serve as acting chief executive until a successor to Mr Gray is appointed.*

★ **action** /'ækʃn/ *noun, verb*
● *noun*

SEE ALSO: **affirmative action, class ~, direct ~, disciplinary ~, group ~, industrial ~, job ~,** etc.

1 [U,C] something that you do to deal with a problem or a difficult situation: *We need to **take** urgent action to control costs.* ◇ *to decide on the best **course of action*** ◇ *a 15-point **action plan*** ◇ *His task was to propose a **plan of action**.* ◇ *The board will take tough action against certain employees.*
2 (*Law*) [C,U] a legal process to stop a person or company from doing sth, to make sb pay for a mistake or to settle a disagreement: *Where the sale involves fraud, the buyer can **bring** an action **for** damages **against** the seller.*
3 [U] the important things that happen over a particular period of time, for example, changes in the price of shares: *The big action this week will be in the US, with several companies announcing their financial results.*
IDM **convert/put/turn sth into 'action** to start doing sth in order to make an idea or plan happen or work: *You need to put your plan into action.* **a piece/slice of the 'action** (*informal*) a share or role in an interesting or exciting activity; a share in the profits: *When the company joined Wall Street, investors rushed to get a piece of the action.*
● *verb* [+ obj]
to take appropriate steps to make sure that sth is done or dealt with: *Your request will be actioned.*

actionable /'ækʃənəbl/ *adjective*
1 (*especially AmE*) if an idea is **actionable**, it is practical and can actually be done: *providing actionable advice on how to build a healthier company*
2 (*Law*) giving you a good reason to bring a claim against sb in a court: *Our lawyer advised us that the breach of contract was actionable.*

ˈaction group *noun* [C]
(often used in the name of an organization) a group that represents the interests of its members in a firm and clear way, especially one that works for social or political change: *a shareholder action group*

ˈaction ˌitem = ACTION POINT

'action ,learning noun [U]
(HR) a method of training in which small groups of people (**sets**) come together to help each other learn from real problems from the work situation

'action-,oriented adjective
1 (about a person or an organization) very active; likely to do sth in response to a situation rather than just think and plan: *creative and action-oriented staff*
2 that involves particular actions; that helps you in a practical way to achieve sth: *an action-oriented training programme*

'action plan noun [C]
a description of a set of things you need to do in order to achieve an aim or to solve a problem: *Develop an action plan for your first year in business.*

'action point (also **'action ,item**, *especially in AmE*) noun [C]
a job or task that is mentioned at a meeting and noted down to be done or dealt with by a particular person later

★ **active** /'æktɪv/ adjective
1 making a determined effort and not leaving sth to happen by itself: *playing an active role in the board of the company*
2 [not before noun] (about a company) doing a particular type of business; operating in a particular place: *The bank is active in raising finances for public agencies.* ◇ *The company is active in more than 60 countries.*
3 operating or working; being used: *The company has several million active customer accounts.*
4 doing sth frequently; having a lot of activity: *The company has been extremely active recently, with several major acquisitions.*
5 (*Finance*) if shares, bonds, etc. or a market is **active**, there is a lot of buying and selling: *Stock prices closed lower in active trading on the London Stock Exchange.*
6 (*Finance*) used to describe a way of investing in which shares, bonds, etc. are bought and sold according to changes in value: *active fund management*
7 (*IT*) being used at a particular time: *Pressing the 'cmd' and 'W' keys together closes the active window.*
→ INACTIVE, PASSIVE

,active 'partner (also **,working 'partner**) noun [C]
a member of a PARTNERSHIP who is involved in running the business as compared to one who only invests money in it (a **sleeping/silent partner**)

★ **activity** /æk'tɪvəti/ noun (plural **activities**)
1 [U] a situation in which sth is happening or a lot of things are being done: *a rise in the level of economic activity* ◇ *Manufacturing activity fell in March.*
⊕ *business/commercial/economic* activity ◆ *construction/industrial/manufacturing/trading* activity ◆ *to boost/stimulate* activity
2 [C, usually pl.] the things done by an organization or a person, especially in order to make money: *The group's activities include food retailing and travel agencies.* ◇ *a review of the company's commercial activities*
⊕ *business/commercial/day-to-day/economic* activities ◆ *core/non-core* activities ◆ *to be involved in/engage in/focus on/limit* activities

ac'tivity ,sampling = WORK SAMPLING

,act of 'bankruptcy noun [C]
(*Law*) something that you do that shows you are BANKRUPT (= that you do not have enough money to pay your debts)

actual /'æktʃuəl/ adjective [only before noun]
real; that happened, as opposed to what was expected to happen: *Total actual sales have gone up by 8.9 per cent.* ◇ *We will pay you up to 80% of your actual loss of earnings.*

,actual 'damages = COMPENSATORY DAMAGES

actuals /'æktʃuəlz/ noun [pl.]
(*Accounting*) real costs, sales, etc. that have happened, rather than ones that were estimated or expected: *Compare the targets with the actuals in Table 3.* → OUT-TURN (2) **NOTE** The word **actuals** is often used in financial reports.

actuary /'æktʃuəri; *AmE* -eri/ noun [C] (plural **actuaries**)
a person whose job involves calculating insurance risks and payments for insurance companies and PENSION FUNDS by studying how frequently accidents, fires, deaths, etc. happen See note at PROFESSION ▶ **actuarial** /ˌæktʃu'eəriəl; *AmE* -'eriəl/ adjective: *an actuarial calculation of pension benefits*

acumen /'ækjəmən; *AmE* ə'kjuːmən/ noun [U]
the ability to judge things quickly and clearly: *business/commercial/financial acumen*

★ **ad** /æd/ noun (informal)

SEE ALSO: banner ad, button ~, classified ~, display ~, small ~, teaser ~, want ~

1 [C] an advertisement: *newspaper/TV/online ads* ◇ *to put an ad in the paper* ◇ *The company ran ads in several college newspapers.* ◇ *You should post your ads on more than one website.*
⊕ *to run* an ad ◆ *to post/place/put* an ad in sth
2 [U] advertising: *an ad agency/campaign* ◇ *Our ad budget has been cut this year.* ◇ *TV ad sales are down 6.9% this year.*

'ad ,agency = ADVERTISING AGENCY

★ **adapt** /ə'dæpt/ verb
1 [+ obj] to change sth in order to make it suitable for a new use or situation: *The cars are produced in Europe and specially adapted for the American market.* **SYN** MODIFY
2 [+ obj *or* no obj] to change your behaviour in order to deal more successfully with a new situation: *A large organization can be slow to adapt to change.* **SYN** ADJUST
▶ **adaptability** /əˌdæptə'bɪləti/ noun [U]
adaptable /ə'dæptəbl/ adjective: *Successful businesses are highly adaptable to economic change.*

add /æd/ verb [+ obj]
1 add A to B | add A and B (together) to put numbers or amounts together to get a total: *Add together the total cost of the goods for the month.* **OPP** SUBTRACT
2 to put sth/sb together with sth/sb else so as to increase the size, number or amount: *Increased sales will add $1 million a year to turnover.*
3 add sth (to sth) (used about shares, bonds, etc.) to increase in value by a particular amount; to make sth do this: *Shares in Philips rose 0.7%, while Nokia added 2.2%.* ◇ *Oil shares added 8 points to the FTSE.*
▶ **addition** /ə'dɪʃn/ noun [U,C]: *the latest addition to our range of cars*
PHR V **,add sth 'on** to include or attach sth extra: *You need to add on a few dollars for delivery.* → ADD-ON ,**add 'up (to sth)** to increase by small amounts until there is a large total: *The cost of videoconferencing sessions added up.* ,**add sth 'up**; ,**add 'up** to calculate the total of two or more numbers or amounts; to make a total number or amount: *The company added up the figures wrongly.* ◇ *The figures don't add up* (= make a sensible total). ,**add 'up to sth 1** to make a particular total or amount: *Their combined income adds up to $10 000 per month.* **2** to lead to a particular result:

,added 'value *noun* [U]
1 an improvement or an extra feature that is added to a product or service to make it more useful and attractive to buyers: *E-commerce will work only if it can offer users added value.* ◇ *Mobile phone users are prepared to pay each month for added-value services.*
2 (*Economics*) the amount by which the value of a product increases at each stage of the production process, not including the cost of the basic materials
SYN VALUE ADDED

addendum /ə'dendəm/ *noun* [C] (*plural* **addenda** /-də/) (*formal*)
a section of extra information that is added to sth such as a letter or a report

'add-on *noun* [C]
1 a piece of equipment or a program that can be added to a computer system to improve its performance: *Most PC companies offer digital cameras as an add-on.* ◇ *Control your PC's interaction with add-on devices.*
❍ *add-on* **devices/hardware/memory/software**
2 an extra part or service that can be joined to a product, system or service to improve it, especially sth extra that can be sold to a customer: *People pay extra for add-ons to basic insurance cover.*
❍ *add-on* **device/module/package**

,add-on 'interest *noun* [U]
interest that is added to the original amount of money that sb has borrowed when they pay it back

★ address *noun, verb*
● *noun* /ə'dres; AmE 'ædres/

SEE ALSO: **forwarding address, public ~, web ~**

1 [C] details of where sb lives or works, where an organization is, etc. and where mail can be sent: *What's your name and address?* ◇ *The business is no longer at this address.*
❍ *a business/contact/home/private address*
2 [C] a set of words, letters, symbols and/or numbers that tells you where you can find a business, an organization, etc. on the Internet, where you can send an email, etc: *Our website address has changed.* ◇ *What's your email address?* → URL
3 (*IT*) [C] the number that states where a piece of information is stored in a computer memory
4 [C] a formal speech: *The Chairman made his annual address to the staff.*
5 [U] **a form/mode of address** the correct, polite title to use when you speak or write to sb
● *verb* /ə'dres/ [+ obj]
1 (*usually* **be addressed**) to write on an envelope or a package the name and address of the person, company, etc. that you are sending it to: *The letter was addressed to 'The Personnel Manager'.* → SAE, SASE
2 to make a formal speech to a group of people: *The Chairman addressed the meeting.*
3 to use a particular name or title for sb when you speak or write to them: *Staff are trained to address customers as 'sir' or 'madam'.*

addressee /,ædre'si:/ *noun* [C]
a person, a business or an organization that a letter is addressed to

adhere /əd'hɪə(r); AmE əd'hɪr/ *verb*
PHRV **ad'here to sth** (*formal*) to behave according to a particular law, rule, set of instructions, etc: *All managers must adhere to company rules and practices.*

adherence /əd'hɪərəns; AmE əd'hɪr-/ *noun* [U]
the fact of behaving according to a particular law,

rule, set of instructions, etc: *strict adherence to the rules*

ad hoc /,æd 'hɒk; AmE 'hɑːk/ *adjective* [usually before noun]
not planned in advance: *The meetings will be held on an ad hoc basis* (= when they are necessary). ◇ *Leading companies set up an ad hoc group to discuss the changes in the law.* ▶ **,ad 'hoc** *adverb* **NOTE** Ad hoc is a Latin phrase.

adhocracy /,æd'hɒkrəsi/ *noun* [U]
(*HR*) a form of management in which groups of people deal with specific projects and urgent problems, rather than with planning for the future of the business as a whole

★ adjourn /ə'dʒɜːn; AmE ə'dʒɜːrn/ *verb* [+ obj or no obj]
to stop a meeting or an official process for a period of time, especially in a court: *The meeting adjourned for lunch.* ◇ *The trial has been adjourned until next week.* See note at MEETING
▶ **ad'journment** *noun* [C,U]

adjudicate /ə'dʒuːdɪkeɪt/ *verb* [+ obj or no obj]
(*Law*) **adjudicate (on/upon/in) sth | adjudicate between A and B** to make an official decision about who is right in a disagreement between two groups or organizations: *A special committee adjudicates on planning applications.* ◇ *Their purpose is to adjudicate disputes.* ◇ *When was he adjudicated bankrupt* (= judged by a court of law to be unable to pay the money he owed)? ▶ **adjudication** /ə,dʒuːdɪ'keɪʃn/ *noun* [U]: *The case was referred to a higher court for adjudication.* **a'djudicator** /ə'dʒuːdɪkeɪtə(r)/ *noun* [C]: *An independent adjudicator has been appointed to deal with complaints.*

adjunct /'ædʒʌŋkt/ *noun* [C] (*formal*)
a thing that is added or attached to sth larger or more important: *The company uses its website as an adjunct to its stores.*

★ adjust /ə'dʒʌst/ *verb*
1 [+ obj] to change sth slightly to make it more suitable or more accurate: *We must adjust our prices to meet demand.* ◇ *When incomes are adjusted for inflation, many families are poorer today than 10 years ago.*
2 [+ obj or no obj] **adjust (yourself) to sth** to get used to a new situation by changing the way you behave and/or think: *It took staff time to adjust to the new working practices.* **SYN** ADAPT
→ ADJUSTED

adjustable /ə'dʒʌstəbl/ *adjective*
that can be changed slightly, especially to become better or more suitable: *Your chair should have an adjustable back and seat.* ◇ *an adjustable-rate mortgage* → VARIABLE

ad,justable 'peg *noun* [C]
(*Economics*) a way of controlling the EXCHANGE RATE (= the price of a currency in relation to other currencies) by fixing the value of currencies in relation to another currency, such as the dollar, but changing it from time to time if necessary
→ CRAWLING PEG

adjusted /ə'dʒʌstɪd/ *adjective* [usually before noun]

SEE ALSO: **inflation-adjusted**

changed slightly in a particular way or for a particular purpose: *an adjusted operating profit/loss* ◇ *Production fell 0.8 per cent on an adjusted basis from the previous month.*

a'djusted 'gross 'income *noun* [U] (*abbr* AGI)
(*Accounting*) in the US, your total income after you

have taken away particular costs, used when the amount of tax you have to pay is calculated

adjuster (also spelled **adjustor**, especially in AmE) /ə'dʒʌstə(r)/ = LOSS ADJUSTER

★ **adjustment** /ə'dʒʌstmənt/ noun [C,U]

SEE ALSO: cost-of-living adjustment, debt adjustment

1 a small change made to sth in order to correct or improve it: We'll have to **make** a few adjustments to the design. ◇ adjustments **in** the exchange rate ◇ Wages have fallen by 10% in real terms (after adjustment **for** inflation).

○ a **fine/minor/slight/small** adjustment ◆ an **important/a major/significant** adjustment
2 a process of changing to meet a new situation: The company's adjustment **to** the new markets has been successful.
3 (Insurance) the agreement reached between an insurance company and a person making a claim about how much money that person will receive
4 (Insurance) the amount of money paid to the person who makes the claim

ad'justment ac,count = CONTROL ACCOUNT

ad'justment ,factor noun [C]
(Technical) a figure that is used to correct the result of a calculation

adland /'ædlænd/ noun [U] informal)
used to refer to the advertising industry

ad litem /,æd 'laɪtem; AmE 'laɪtəm/ adjective
(Law) used about a person who represents sb, especially a child, who cannot represent themselves in a legal case: The court must appoint a guardian ad litem. **NOTE** Ad litem is a Latin phrase.

adman /'ædmæn/ noun [C] (plural admen) /-men/ (informal)
a person who works in advertising: Our adman has come up with a new slogan.

admin /'ædmɪn/ noun [U] (BrE) (informal)
administration: She works in admin. ◇ admin staff

★ **administer** /əd'mɪnɪstə(r)/ verb [+ obj]
1 (also **administrate**) (often **be administered**) to manage and organize the affairs of a company, an organization or a country: The pension funds are administered by commercial banks. **SYN** MANAGE
2 to organize the way that sth is done: The questionnaire was administered by trained interviewers.
3 (formal) to make sure that sth is done fairly and in the correct way: It is a judge's duty to administer justice quickly and fairly.

★ **administration** /əd,mɪnɪ'streɪʃn/ noun

SEE ALSO: business administration, Federal Aviation Administration

1 (BrE also **'admin**, informal) [U] the activities that are done in order to plan, organize and run a business or other institution: the day-to-day administration of a company ◇ the Sales Administration department ◇ administration costs
○ **day-to-day/general/office/routine** administration
2 [U] the process or act of organizing the way that sth is done: the administration of the new tax
3 [C] the people who plan, organize and run a business or an institution: the national telecommunications administrations
4 (often **Administration**) [C] the government of a country, especially the US: Successive administrations have failed to solve the country's economic problems.
5 (Law) [U] the management of the financial affairs of a business that cannot pay its debts by an

independent person: The company will **go into administration** if it cannot find extra funds.

admini'stration ,order noun [C]
(Law) in the UK, an order made by a court for sb to take over the management of a business that cannot pay its debts: If the administration order is granted the company has three months to find a solution to its problems.

★ **administrative** /əd'mɪnɪstrətɪv; AmE -streɪtɪv/ adjective
connected with organizing the work of a business or an institution: We managed to cut administrative costs by 30%. ◇ Staff received their salaries late due to an **administrative error**. ◇ The company lost key senior administrative staff to its main competitor.
○ administrative **charges/costs/expenses** ◆ administrative **duties/procedures/tasks/work**

ad,ministrative as'sistant noun [C]
a person who works in an office, dealing with letters and telephone calls, keeping records, etc.

ad,ministrative 'leave noun [U,C] (AmE)
(HR) a time that you are allowed to be away from work with pay for special reasons, such as if you are needed to be on a JURY, or when there is an urgent problem: She was placed on administrative leave last week.

ad,ministrative 'management noun [U]
(HR) the traditional view of management that is concerned with how a business should be organized and what a good manager should do

★ **administrator** /əd'mɪnɪstreɪtə(r)/ noun [C]
1 a person whose job is to manage and organize the public or business affairs of a company or an institution: a pensions administrator
2 (Finance) a person chosen, often by a court, to manage the financial affairs of a business that does not have enough money to pay its debts
○ to **appoint/call in** an administrator

admissible /əd'mɪsəbl/ adjective
(Law) that can be allowed or accepted, especially in a court: Photographs are usually admissible **as/in** evidence provided it can be proved that they are authentic. **OPP** INADMISSIBLE
▶ **admissibility** /əd,mɪsə'bɪləti/ noun [U]

admission /əd'mɪʃn/ noun
1 [U,C] the act of accepting sb into an institution, an organization, etc.; the right to enter a place or to join an institution or organization: countries applying for admission **to** the European Union ◇ a 38% reduction in hospital admissions
2 [C] a statement in which sb admits that sth is true, especially sth wrong or bad that they have done: The sale of the company was an admission **of** failure.
3 [U] the amount of money that you pay to go into a building or an event: a €10 admission charge

ad,mission of lia'bility noun [C]
(Law) a statement or an act admitting legal responsibility for sth

admit /əd'mɪt/ verb (-tt-)
1 [+ obj or no obj] to say that you have done sth wrong or illegal: He admitted theft. ◇ The directors refused to admit **to** any wrongdoing.
2 (Law) [+ obj] **admit liability (for sth)** to say that you are legally responsible for sth: Both companies have admitted liability for the crash.
3 [+ obj] to allow sb to enter a place, an organization or an institution: China was admitted **to** the World Trade Organization in 2001.

adopt /ə'dɒpt; AmE ə'dɑːpt/ verb [+ obj]
1 to accept and use a particular idea, system or proposal, especially a new one: Business will move to other centres if we do not adopt modern business methods.

2 (*Marketing*) to buy and use a product or service as the normal or official one: *a campaign to persuade households to adopt digital television*
3 to support, or partly support, a public place or institution, for example a school, by giving money, usually to make good relations between the company and the local community → SPONSOR *verb*

adopter /əˈdɒptə(r); AmE əˈdɑːptər/ *noun* [C, usually sing.]

SEE ALSO: **early adopter**

(*Marketing*) a company, an organization or a person who accepts and uses a product, service or system as the normal or official one: *The government is a keen adopter of new technologies.*

adoption /əˈdɒpʃn; AmE əˈdɑːpʃn/ *noun*
1 [U] the act of accepting and using a particular idea, system or proposal, especially a new one: *the adoption of a new marketing strategy ◇ the adoption of the euro by 12 European nations*
❍ *the adoption of a method/practice/proposal/ strategy*
2 (*Marketing*) [U,C] the wide use of a new product or service; the product or service that is used: *the relationship between the market adoption of a product and its price ◇ Improved security on mobile phones would help customer adoption rates.*

a'doption curve *noun* [C]
(*Marketing*) a graph showing the rate at which people buy a piece of new technology for the first time: *The adoption curve for the cellphone, as for most technologies, follows an S-shape.*

ADR /ˌeɪ diː ˈɑː(r)/ = AMERICAN DEPOSITORY RECEIPT, ALTERNATIVE DISPUTE RESOLUTION

ADSL /ˌeɪ diː es ˈel/ *abbr*
(*IT*) **asymmetric digital subscriber line** technology that allows large amounts of data to be carried over an ordinary phone line in such a way that data travels faster to the customer than from the customer: *high-speed ADSL Internet access*
→ BROADBAND

adultescent /ˌædʌlˈtesnt/ *noun* [C] (*informal*)
an adult who is no longer young, but who dresses and behaves like a young person: *The video game is aimed at smart kids and adultescents.*

ad valorem /ˌæd vəˈlɔːrem/ *adjective* [usually before noun]
(*Economics*) (about a tax) calculated as a percentage of the value of the goods: *VAT is an ad valorem tax.*
→ SPECIFIC
❍ *an ad valorem duty/tariff/tax*
▸ **ˌad vaˈlorem** *adverb*
NOTE Ad valorem is a Latin phrase.

advance /ədˈvɑːns; AmE -ˈvæns/ *noun, verb, adjective*
●*noun*

SEE ALSO: **bank advance**

1 [C, usually sing.] money paid for work before it has been done; money paid earlier than expected: *They offered an advance of 10 000 euros after the signing of the contract. ◇ She asked for an advance on her wages.*
2 [C] an increase in the price or value of sth: *These companies have seen significant advances in their share prices.*
3 [C,U] progress or a development in technology or a particular area of knowledge: *advances in the processing power of chips ◇ We live in an age of rapid technological advance.*
IDM **in advance (of sth)** before the time that is expected; before sth happens: *The rent is due one month in advance. ◇ The Director would not discuss the report in advance of its release.* → IN ARREARS

●*verb*
1 [+ obj] **advance (sb) sth** | **advance sth (to sb)** to give sb money before the time it would usually be paid: *We are willing to advance the money to you. ◇ They advanced her $2 million for five novels.*
2 [no obj] if knowledge or technology **advances**, it develops and improves: *As medical technology advances, health-care costs rise.*
3 [no obj] (about prices, costs, profits, etc.) to increase: *Inflation has advanced sharply over the last two years. ◇ Vodafone (= its shares) advanced 1.8 per cent to 179p.*
4 [+ obj] to change the time or date of an event so that it takes place earlier: *The date of the meeting has been advanced by one week.* **SYN** BRING STH FORWARD **OPP** POSTPONE
5 [+ obj] to help sth to succeed: *Studying for new qualifications is one way to advance your career.*
●*adjective* [only before noun]
done or given before sth is going to happen: *He received an advance payment for developing the new computer game. ◇ Please give us advance warning of any changes to the schedule.*

adˌvance ˈcopy *noun* [C]
(*Production*) a book, a magazine, etc. that is sent to sb to look at before it is published and becomes available to everyone

advanced /ədˈvɑːnst; AmE -ˈvænst/ *adjective*
1 having the most modern and recently developed ideas, methods, etc: *advanced technology ◇ advanced industrial societies*
2 (about a course of study) at a high or difficult level: *advanced training*
3 having been happening for some time; almost finished: *The talks are at an advanced stage.*

advancement /ədˈvɑːnsmənt; AmE -ˈvæns-/ *noun*
1 [U] progress in a job or position: *There are good opportunities for advancement if you have the right skills.*
2 [U,C] the process of helping sth to make progress or succeed; the progress that is made: *the advancement of knowledge/technology*

adˌvance ˈorder *noun* [C]
(*Commerce*) an order for a product which is made before the product is available for sale: *The company already has more than 5 000 advance orders for the new phone.*

advancer /ədˈvɑːnsə(r); AmE ədˈvænsər/ *noun* [C, usually pl.]
(*Stock Exchange*) (used in newspapers) a share whose value has risen: *Activity was quiet on the New York stock exchange, with advancers beating decliners 3 to 2.* **SYN** GAINER **OPP** DECLINER

★advantage /ədˈvɑːntɪdʒ; AmE -ˈvæn-/ *noun* [C,U]

SEE ALSO: **absolute advantage, comparative ~, competitive ~**

1 a thing that helps you to be better or more successful than other people: *Familiar brands have an advantage over less well known brands. ◇ Staff with a good command of a second language are at an advantage. ◇ Much of our business is becoming Internet-based, which has a lot of cost advantages.*
❍ *a big/definite/great/huge/tremendous advantage ◆ a commercial/cost/an economic/a financial/price advantage ◆ to be/gain/give (sb)/have an advantage*
2 a quality of sth that makes it better or more useful: *Their new sun cream has the added advantage of smelling unattractive to insects. ◇ Each of these systems has its advantages and disadvantages.*
IDM **be/work to your adˈvantage** to give you an advantage; to change a situation in a way that gives you an advantage: *Eventually, the new*

regulations may work to our advantage. → idioms at TAKE, TURN verb

adverse /'ædvɜːs; əd'vɜːs; AmE -vɜːrs/ adjective
[usually before noun]
negative; not likely to produce a good result:
adverse market conditions ◇ the adverse effects of a
high exchange rate

,**adverse 'balance** noun [C] (BrE)
(Accounting) an amount of debt shown in an
account: Your account shows an adverse balance of
€630.00. **SYN** UNFAVOURABLE BALANCE → DEFICIT

,**adverse 'trade ,balance** (also 'adverse
'balance of 'trade) noun [sing.]
(Economics) a situation when a country spends more
on imports than it earns from exports
SYN UNFAVOURABLE TRADE BALANCE

advert /'ædvɜːt; AmE -vɜːrt/ noun [C] (BrE)
(informal)
an advertisement: radio/TV/press adverts ◇ an
advert for jeans ◇ We placed a full-page advert in a
magazine.

★**advertise** /'ædvətaɪz; AmE -vərt-/ verb
1 [+ obj or no obj] to tell the public about a product
or a service in order to encourage more people to buy or
use it: If you want to attract more customers, try
advertising in the national press. ◇ to advertise a
product/business/service ◇ The company's new
Internet service has been **heavily** advertised on
television. ◇ Something advertised **as** a toy is likely to
be used by children. ◇ I bought the camera and case
as advertised in the catalogue. → PROMOTE,
PUBLICIZE
2 [no obj] to tell people about a job that is
available: We are currently advertising **for** a new
sales manager.

★**advertisement** /əd'vɜːtɪsmənt; AmE
,ædvər'taɪz-/ noun [C]

SEE ALSO: **banner advertisement, button ~,
classified ~, display ~**

1 a notice, picture or short film telling people
about a company, product or service: cigarette
advertisements ◇ advertisements for cigarettes ◇ to
take out a full-page/half-page advertisement in a
glossy magazine ◇ The product became a best-seller
through costly print and television advertisements. ◇
The advertisement appeared on TV last night. ◇ One
advertisement shows a man driving a car on a golf
course. → AD, ADVERT See note at ADVERTISING
○ newspaper/online/print/television advertisements ◆
to place/put/run/take out an advertisement ◆ the
advertisement features/shows sb/sth
2 a notice telling people about a job that is
available: an advertisement **for** a job/post/position ◇
a job advertisement
○ to place/put/take out an advertisement (in a
newspaper) ◆ to answer/reply to/respond to an
advertiser

★**advertiser** /'ædvətaɪzə(r); AmE -vərt-/ noun [C]
a company or a person that advertises a product or
a service: She claims that tobacco advertisers target
teenagers.

★**advertising** /'ædvətaɪzɪŋ; AmE -vərt-/ noun [U]

SEE ALSO: **brand advertising, comparative ~,
consumer ~, corporate ~, direct ~, direct response ~,
drip ~, etc.**

1 the act of making a company, a product or a
service known to the public; the notices, pictures
and short films that a company uses to tell people
about itself and its products: cigarette advertising ◇
How much did we spend on advertising last year? ◇
Are you easily persuaded by television advertising? ◇

The company has a huge advertising budget. ◇ Only
ten per cent of **recruitment advertising** (=
advertising for people to fill jobs) is online.
→ COLUMN INCH, PROMOTION, PUBLICITY
○ Internet/online/point-of-sale/press/radio/
television advertising ◆ an advertising **campaign** ◆
advertising **revenue(s)/sales**
2 the industry of advertising things to people on
television, in newspapers and magazines, etc:
people who work in advertising ◇ He's one of the
world's most powerful advertising executives. See
note at MARKETING
○ the advertising **business/industry/sector** ◆ an
advertising **company/executive/group/manager**

GRAMMAR POINT

advertising/advertisement

Advertising is an uncountable noun and refers to
the activity of telling customers about products
and services, or the materials that companies use
in general to do this, such as notices in magazines
or newspapers: They do a lot of advertising on
television.

Advertisement is a countable noun. It refers to a
particular piece of advertising, such as a notice or
short film/movie about a particular product. In
more informal language the words **ad** (BrE and
AmE) and **advert** (BrE) are used.

● I am replying to your advertisement in the
Guardian.
● I am replying to your advertising.

'**advertising ,agency** (also 'ad ,agency, informal)
noun [C]
a company that plans and designs advertisements
for other companies: She is an executive at a leading
New York advertising agency.

'**advertising mix** noun [U]
(Marketing) the different methods that a business
uses to advertise a product, such as television,
newspapers, radio, etc: The regional press is a vital
part of the national advertising mix. ◇ The Internet
makes up 2% of the company's advertising mix.

advertorial /,ædvə'tɔːriəl; AmE -vərt-/ noun [C,U]
(Marketing) an advertisement in a newspaper or a
magazine that is like a written article and seems to
be giving facts rather than advertising a product:
write an advertorial **about/on** your company's
products → INFOMERCIAL **NOTE** Advertorial is a
combination of the words advertisement and
editorial (= an article in a magazine or newspaper
that expresses the editor's opinion about sth).

★**advice** /əd'vaɪs/ noun

SEE ALSO: **careers advice, credit ~, letter of ~**

1 [U] an opinion or a suggestion about what sb
should do in a particular situation: The bank
provides financial advice **about** starting your own
company. ◇ We offer advice to businesses on
computer security problems. ◇ I have one **piece of
advice**: push yourself as hard as you can.
○ career/financial/legal/tax/technical advice ◆ to
give/provide/offer advice ◆ to follow/seek/take sb's
advice
2 (Accounting) [C] a formal notice about some
financial business: a remittance advice → ADVICE
NOTE
→ idiom at TAKE

ad'vice note noun [C] (BrE)
(Commerce) a document that is sent to a customer to
tell them that goods they have ordered have been
sent or are ready to send → DELIVERY NOTE,
DISPATCH NOTE

'**ad view** = IMPRESSION

★ **advise** /əd'vaɪz/ verb
1 [+ obj or no obj] to tell sb what you think they should do: *We advise our customers **against** sending cash.*
2 [+ obj or no obj] to give sb help and information on a subject that you know a lot about: *We employ an expert to advise **on** new technology.*
3 (*formal*) [+ obj] to officially tell sb sth; to inform sb: *Please advise us **of** any changes in your personal details.*

★ **adviser** (*also spelled* **advisor**, *especially in AmE*) /əd'vaɪzə(r)/ noun [C]

SEE ALSO: **independent financial adviser**

a person who gives advice to a company, government, etc., especially sb who knows a lot about a particular subject: *He briefly worked as an adviser **to** the Bank of Italy.* ◇ *the CBI's chief economic adviser*
○ *an economic/investment* adviser **◆** *a financial/ mortgage/policy* adviser

ad'vising bank noun [C]
(*Finance*) a bank in the country of an exporter that informs the exporter about a DOCUMENTARY CREDIT and receives documents on behalf of the buyer's bank

advisor = ADVISER

advisory /əd'vaɪzəri/ adjective
giving professional advice; not having the power to make decisions: *She has a position on the firm's **advisory board.*** ◇ *He is acting **in an advisory capacity** only.*

ad'visory ˌservice noun [C]
part of an organization that gives expert information on a particular subject: *the director of advisory services* ◇ *The bank provides a financial advisory service for all its clients.*

AEI /ˌeɪ iː 'aɪ/ = AVERAGE EARNINGS INDEX

AER /ˌeɪ iː 'ɑː(r)/ abbr
(*Finance*) **annual equivalent rate** a rate of interest on investments and money you save that shows how much you would receive in one year if each interest payment was added to the deposit before the next payment was calculated → APR

aeronautics /ˌeərə'nɔːtɪks; AmE ˌerə-/ noun [U]
the science or practice of building and flying aircraft: *the company's aeronautics business*
▶ **aero'nautic** adjective: *the European aeronautic sector* **aeronautical** /-'nɔːtɪkl/ adjective: *an aeronautical engineer*

aerospace /'eərəʊspeɪs; AmE 'eroʊ-/ noun [U]
(*often used as an adjective*)
the industry of building aircraft and the vehicles and equipment to be sent into space: *jobs in aerospace and defence* ◇ *the aerospace industry*

affiliate noun, verb
● *noun* /ə'fɪliət/ [C]
a company or an organization that is connected with or controlled by another larger one: *Our organization has 32 overseas affiliates.* ◇ *Airbus is an EADS affiliate.* See note at GROUP
● *verb* /ə'fɪlieɪt/ [+ obj or no obj] (*usually* **be affiliated**)
1 (about a company or an organization) to be connected to a larger one: *All three major rail unions are affiliated to the Trades Union Congress.*
2 (about a person) to have a close professional connection with an organization: *He is an independent consultant affiliated with McKinsey & Co.*
▶ **affiliation** /əˌfɪli'eɪʃn/ noun [U,C]: *The affiliation with the plastics giant (= large company) gives the business many advantages.* ◇ *Please put your name, address and affiliation (= the organization that you work for or represent) on the form.*

afˌfiliated 'company noun [C]
a company that is closely connected to or controlled by another larger company or organization: *There are 33 000 people working in our wholly owned and affiliated companies.*
SYN SUBSIDIARY

afˌfiliate 'marketing noun [U]
(*E-commerce*) the use of other websites to advertise and market the products and services of your website. The other websites receive a payment for this.

af'finity card noun [C]
a credit card that has the name of a particular charity (in the UK) or an organization (in the US) that receives an amount of money from the card company every time you use the card

afˌfirmative 'action noun [U] (*AmE*)
a practice or policy intended to make sure that everyone has the same chances of education or employment and to correct the fact that people from some groups are often treated unfairly because of their race or sex **SYN** POSITIVE DISCRIMINATION (*BrE*) → POSITIVE ACTION

affluent /'æfluənt/ adjective
having a lot of money and a good standard of living: *an energetic and affluent city* ◇ *a young, affluent professional couple* **SYN** PROSPEROUS
▶ **'affluence** noun [U]: *Increased exports have brought new affluence.*

★ **afford** /ə'fɔːd; AmE ə'fɔːrd/ verb [+ obj] (*not used in the passive.*) **HELP** Usually used with **can, could** or **be able to** especially in questions or negative sentences.
1 to have enough money to be able to buy sth: *Buy the most powerful system you can afford.* ◇ *How much can you afford (**to** spend)?* ◇ *Mobile phone operators said they could not afford the €4.95 bn fee set for each licence.*
2 (*usually used in negative sentences*) if you can't **afford sth/to do sth** you are not able to do sth or let sth happen because it would have a bad result for you: *We can't afford any more delays.* ◇ *I couldn't afford to lose the goodwill of my customers.* ◇ *Can you afford any more time off work?*

★ **affordable** /ə'fɔːdəbl; AmE ə'fɔːrd-/ adjective
that people can afford; that does not cost a lot of money: *We offer high quality at an **affordable price**.* ◇ *Luxury cars became affordable in the 1990s for millions of customers.* ◇ *There is a lack of affordable housing in the area.* ▶ **affordability** /əˌfɔːdə'bɪləti; AmE əˌfɔːrd-/ noun [U]: *the affordability of property in the area*

AFL-CIO /ˌeɪ ef ef 'el ˌsiː aɪ 'əʊ; AmE 'oʊ/ abbr
American Federation of Labor and Congress of Industrial Organizations in the US, an organization that represents a large number of labor unions → TUC

afloat /ə'fləʊt; AmE ə'floʊt/ adjective [not before noun]
(about a business, an economy, etc.) having enough money to pay debts; able to survive: *The company is trying to raise £15 million, just to **stay afloat**.* ◇ *He has been struggling to keep his business afloat.*

aforementioned /əˌfɔː'menʃənd; AmE əˌfɔː'r'm-/ (*also* **aforesaid** /ə'fɔːsed; AmE ə'fɔːrsed/) adjective [only before noun] (*formal, only used in written English*)
mentioned before, in an earlier sentence: *with reference to the aforementioned points*

'after-hours adjective [only before noun]
happening after a business or financial market has officially closed for the day: *a telephone answering*

service for after-hours calls ◇ Shares fell 64 cents to $7.25 *in* after-hours trading. ▶ **,after 'hours** adverb: We do have voicemail after hours.

,after-hours 'price noun [C]
(Stock Exchange) the price of shares that have been bought or sold after the official hours of trading are over: sell at a low after-hours price

aftermarket /'ɑːftəmɑːkɪt; AmE 'æftərmɑːrkɪt/ noun [C, usually sing.]
1 (Marketing) (especially AmE) the opportunities to sell other things that a customer needs after buying a particular product, such as new parts and extra pieces of equipment: the automotive aftermarket ◇ aftermarket sales and services
2 (Stock Exchange) the time when new shares that have just been made available are bought and sold: the range of prices at which the stock trades in the aftermarket

'after-sales adjective [only before noun] (BrE)
providing help to a customer after they have bought a product, such as doing repairs or giving advice on how to use the product: Their computers are good value and they offer an excellent after-sales service.
● after-sales *assistance/service/support*

,after 'sight adverb (abbr A/S, a/s)
(Finance) written on a BILL OF EXCHANGE to show that the bill should be paid within a particular period after it has been given to the person who has to pay it: The letter of credit is *payable* 30 days after sight. → AT SIGHT

,after-'tax adjective [only before noun]
(Accounting) after the tax has been paid or taken away: after-tax earnings ◇ The most recent results showed after-tax profits falling 6.8%.
● an after-tax *charge/loss/profit* • after-tax *earnings*

AG /,eɪ 'dʒiː/ abbr
used in the names of some companies in German-speaking countries: Volkswagen AG See note at LTD

'age discrimi,nation noun [U]
unfair treatment of people because they are considered too old: He accused them of age discrimination in their recruitment policy.
[SYN] AGEISM

'age group noun [C]
people of a similar age or within a particular range of ages: consumers in the 20–24 age group ◇ What is your target age group?

ageism (AmE spelling usually **agism**) /'eɪdʒɪzəm/ noun [U]
unfair treatment of people because they are considered too old: legislation aimed at tackling ageism in the workplace [SYN] AGE DISCRIMINATION
▶ **ageist** /'eɪdʒɪst/ adjective: ageist attitudes about life after 40 **'ageist** noun [C]

★ **agency** /'eɪdʒənsi/ noun (plural **agencies**)

SEE ALSO: ad agency, advertising ~, collection ~, commercial ~, commercial collection ~, credit ~, credit rating ~, etc.

1 (Commerce) [C] a business that provides a particular service, especially to other businesses: an ad/advertising/marketing agency ◇ He is employed **through** an agency. ◇ a reduction in the number of contract and **agency workers** (= employees provided by an employment agency) See note at BUSINESS
2 (often **Agency**) [C] a government department that provides a particular service; an international organization that provides a service to several countries: a regulatory agency ◇ the European Space Agency

3 (Law) [U] the situation that exists where sb (the **agent**) agrees to sth or does sth as the representative of sb else (the **principal**): The clause states that no partnership or **agency relationship** was created. ◇ the law of agency

'agency ,broker noun [C] (AmE)
(Property; Stock Exchange) a person or an organization that buys or sells shares or property for sb else → BROKER

'agency ,labour (AmE spelling ~ **labor**) noun [U] (especially AmE)
(HR) workers in a company or an organization who have been employed through an EMPLOYMENT AGENCY (= a business that finds workers for companies), usually for temporary work

★ **agenda** /ə'dʒendə/ noun [C]

SEE ALSO: hidden agenda

1 a list of topics to be discussed at a meeting: The next item **on the agenda** is the publicity budget. ◇ The meeting has no formal agenda. See note at MEETING
2 the things that sb thinks are important and wants to achieve; a plan of action: In our company, quality is **high on the agenda**. ◇ Some managers **pursue their own agenda** without considering their staff.

★ **agent** /'eɪdʒənt/ noun [C]

SEE ALSO: bargaining agent, business ~, buying ~, change ~, commercial ~, commission ~, customs ~, etc.

1 a person or a company that is paid by another person or company to do business for them, especially in discussing a contract, buying or selling, or finding work in entertainment or publishing: The director was **acting as** agent for the shareholders in trying to sell their shares. ◇ You can hire an agent to negotiate on your behalf.
→ PRINCIPAL
2 a person who sells a service or product for one or more companies: an independent insurance agent ◇ The company has 31 overseas agents and distributors. ◇ There have been complaints over the methods of some of their sales agents.

WHICH WORD?

agent/broker/sales representative/ dealer

All these people have jobs that involve buying or selling things.

An **agent** is given authority to carry out a particular piece of business on somebody's behalf. For example, an **estate agent** (AmE **real estate agent**) is given authority to sell a house for somebody.

A **broker** is usually a person who buys and sells investments or financial products on behalf of others: Ask your broker to explain the difference between the mortgages.

Both agents and brokers work independently or as part of their own companies (called **agencies** and **brokerages**) and receive a fee for their services.

Dealers usually buy and sell a particular type of product: an art/a car/diamond dealer.

A **sales representative** (often shortened to **representative**, or more informally, a **sales rep** or **rep**) works as an employee of a company, selling their goods or services to people in a particular area: We have representatives in over 50 countries.

'agent bank *noun* [C]

(Finance)

1 *(also* **'lead bank)** a bank that organizes a loan for a person or a company and represents the group of banks who lend the money

2 a bank in a foreign country that an investor has an account with in order to be able to make cash payments in a foreign currency

,agent of 'change *(plural* **agents of change)** = CHANGE AGENT

,agent of ne'cessity *noun* [C, usually sing.]

(Law) a person who acts for sb else in an emergency but does not have a formal right to do so

'age ,profile *noun* [C, usually sing.]

(HR; Marketing) a description of the number of people of different ages who buy a particular product or who work in an organization: *The female workforce had a different age profile from that of the male.*

aggregate *noun, adjective, verb*

●*noun* /'ægrɪgət/ [C, usually sing.]

the total number or amount made up of smaller amounts that are collected together: *She has now purchased* **an aggregate of** *16% of the company's shares.*

IDM in (the) 'aggregate *(formal)* added together as a total or single amount: *Businesses are, in the aggregate, deeper in debt than ever before.*

●*adjective* /'ægrɪgət/ [only before noun]

(Technical) made up of several amounts that are added together to form a total number: *The aggregate cost of the equipment was about $1 million.* ◇ *aggregate figures/profits*

●*verb* /'ægrɪgeɪt/ [+ obj]

(Technical) to combine different items or amounts into a single group or total: *This website aggregates hundreds of thousands of sales and promotions.*

▶ **aggregation** /,ægrɪ'geɪʃn/ *noun* [U,C]: *the aggregation of data*

'aggregate ,planning *noun* [U]

a method of planning the best way to produce the right amount of goods at the right time and at the lowest cost, based on the total number of items that need to be produced and the total amount of equipment and number of workers available

★ **aggressive** /ə'gresɪv/ *adjective*

1 (used especially about a company's policies) strong and determined to make sure that the company succeeds: *an aggressive advertising campaign* ◇ *an aggressive approach to cost-cutting* ◇ *The rival store responded with aggressive price cuts.*

○ *aggressive* **competition/cost-cutting/expansion/ pricing** ◆ *aggressive* **campaigns/price cuts/ promotions**

2 (about a person or company) behaving in a firm and determined way in order to succeed: *an aggressive seller/buyer*

▶ **ag'gressively** *adverb*: *The new snacks were aggressively marketed.*

ag,gressive 'growth fund *(also* **per'formance fund)** *noun* [C]

(Finance) a type of investment fund that buys shares that are expected to increase in value very quickly but have a high risk, in the hope of making large profits

AGI /,eɪ dʒiː 'aɪ/ = ADJUSTED GROSS INCOME

agile /'ædʒaɪl; *AmE* 'ædʒl/ *adjective*

(used especially about new, small companies) able to adapt quickly to changing situations: *The market was filling up with young, agile companies, as well as established competitors.* ▶ **agility** /ə'dʒɪləti/ *noun* [U]

'aging ,schedule *noun* [C, usually sing.] *(AmE)*

(Accounting) a list of amounts of money owed to a business, shown in the order of the dates they are due to be paid. The list is usually prepared every

month to show how quickly money is being paid and which money might not be paid.

agio /'ædʒiəʊ; *AmE* 'ædʒioʊ/ *noun* [C, usually sing.]

(plural **agios)**

(Finance) the charge that a bank makes for changing one form of money into another, for example changing coins into notes or changing one currency into another

agism = AGEISM

AGM /,eɪ dʒiː 'em/ = ANNUAL GENERAL MEETING

a,greed 'bid *noun* [C]

the situation when most shareholders in a company agree to the offer that another company makes to buy it

a,greed 'value *noun* [U]

(Insurance) the amount that a vehicle, boat, etc. is worth that is agreed with the insurance company when the insurance is arranged. This amount will be paid if the item is destroyed or stolen: *You can choose agreed value and we'll pay you the sum you chose at the start of the policy.* ◇ *an agreed-value policy* → MARKET VALUE

WHICH WORD?

agreement/arrangement/contract/ deal/deed

These words are used to describe agreements between companies or between people and companies.

Agreement and **arrangement** tend to be used about business relationships that last over a long period of time: *a worldwide marketing agreement* ◇ *a financing arrangement.*

Deal usually describes an agreement to buy or sell sth: *They've secured a €5 million deal to supply computer equipment.*

Agreement, **arrangement** and **deal** are also used to describe an agreement that is reached through much discussion: *They came to an arrangement with their bank to repay the debt over 5 years.* ◇ *We are close to reaching a deal.*

Contract is normally used about agreements contained in formal legal documents: *She broke the terms of her employment contract.*

A **deed** is a special type of written contract that is used in limited circumstances: *The owner of the land is indicated in the title deeds.* ◇ *a deed of partnership*

★ **agreement** /ə'griːmənt/ *noun*

SEE ALSO: collective agreement, framework ~, gentleman's ~, heads of ~, licence ~, purchase ~, repurchase ~, etc.

1 [C] an arrangement, a promise or a contract that two people, groups or organizations have made together: *An agreement was finally reached* **between** *management* **and** *employees.* ◇ *They had made a verbal agreement to sell.* ◇ *The agreement* (= the document recording the agreement) *was signed during the meeting.* ◇ *The company has just announced a partnership agreement* **with** *a software producer.*

○ *to* **conclude/make/reach/sign** *an agreement* ◆ *a* **formal/an informal/a legal/verbal/written** *agreement*

2 [U; sing.] the state of having the same opinion; a state of understanding between people, organizations or countries: *The Board was* **in**

complete **agreement** about the need to review the budget. ◇ The two sides failed to reach agreement.
➊ to **reach** agreement ◆ to **arrive at/come to** an agreement ◆ **broad/complete/general/total** agreement

a͵greement of 'sale = CONTRACT OF PURCHASE

agribusiness /'ægrɪbɪznəs/ noun
1 [U] farming that uses modern technology to produce high profits: Money will be directed away from agribusiness to family farmers. ◇ an agribusiness company/worker
2 [C] an organization that is involved in this: a list of the top agribusinesses in Australia

͵agricultural 'bank noun [C]
(Finance) a bank that helps farmers, especially by lending money for longer periods than other banks
→ LAND BANK

͵agricultural co'operative noun [C]
a business that sells food produced by small farmers

agriculture /'ægrɪkʌltʃə(r)/ noun [U]
the science or practice of farming: 50% of the country's population depend on agriculture.
▸ **agricultural** /͵ægrɪ'kʌltʃərəl/ adjective: agricultural exports/products/workers

agrochemical /͵ægrəʊ'kemɪkl; AmE ͵ægroʊ-/ noun [C]
a chemical used in farming, such as one for killing insects (a **pesticide**) or for helping crops grow (a **fertilizer**): an agrochemicals company
▸ **͵agro'chemical** adjective [only before noun]

'agro-͵industry noun [U]
1 the industry of farming
2 industry connected with farming
▸ **͵agro-in'dustrial** adjective [only before noun]

agronomy /ə'grɒnəmi; AmE ə'grɑːn-/ noun [U]
the science and study of crop production and the best ways of using the soil ▸ **a'gronomist** noun [C]: He works as an agronomist, advising farmers on fertilizer use.

ahead /ə'hed/ adverb
SEE ALSO: go-ahead

1 higher or greater than a previous level: Sales were 5.6% ahead in the 16 weeks up to the end of January. ◇ The Dow Jones Industrial Average closed 150 points ahead at 9 270.
2 further advanced: You need to work hard to **keep** ahead.

a'head of preposition
1 at an earlier time than sth; before an event: The project was finished **ahead of schedule**. ◇ Trading was light as many offices were closed ahead of next Tuesday's holiday.
2 further advanced than sb/sth: We will have to work hard to **stay** ahead of the competition.
IDM **to stay/be ahead of the 'game** to stay/be the most successful in an industry, activity, etc: We need more capital to stay ahead of the game.

AI /͵eɪ 'aɪ/ = ARTIFICIAL INTELLIGENCE

aid /eɪd/ noun, verb
● noun [U]
SEE ALSO: legal aid, visual aid

1 money, food, etc. that is sent to help countries or people in difficult situations: An extra $100 million in foreign aid has been promised. ◇ **aid agencies** (= organizations that provide help)
➊ **development/economic/emergency/humanitarian** aid ◆ **foreign/international/overseas/regional** aid ◆

to **give/provide/send** aid ◆ to **appeal for/get/receive** aid
2 help that is given to sb: The company's request for financial aid has been approved. ◇ The government **came to the aid of** the airline.
➊ **financial/government/state** aid ◆ to **ask for/request** aid
● verb [+ obj or no obj]
to help sb/sth to do sth, especially by making it easier: The computers was an aid to help in the move to online banking. ◇ The small increase in profits was aided by strong sales of trucks.
IDM **aid and a'bet** (Law) to help sb to do sth illegal or wrong: She was accused of aiding and abetting fraud.

AIDA /͵eɪ aɪ diː 'eɪ/ abbr
(Marketing) **awareness/attention, interest, desire, action** a description used by advertisers to try to explain how people make decisions about buying products and services

ailing /'eɪlɪŋ/ adjective
(about a business, etc.) having financial problems and getting weaker: measures to help the ailing economy ◇ an ailing software company

AIM /eɪm/ = ALTERNATIVE INVESTMENT MARKET

★**aim** /eɪm/ noun, verb
● noun [C]
the purpose of doing sth; sth that you are trying to achieve: The aim of the changes is to save money. ◇ Our main aim is to increase sales in Asia. ◇ He set out the company's **aims and objectives** in his speech.
→ OBJECTIVE
➊ a **key/long-term/strategic** aim ◆ the **main/primary/principal** aim ◆ to **achieve/fulfil/meet** an aim
● verb
1 [no obj] to try or plan to achieve sth: We are aiming **at/for** 2 000 new customers by next year. ◇ They aim to increase sales by 20%.
2 [+ obj] **be aimed at** to have sth as an aim: The proposals are aimed at reducing debt.
3 [+ obj] **aim sth at sb** (usually **be aimed**) to produce sth that meets the needs of a particular group of customers or tries to influence them: The new airfares are aimed at business travellers. ◇ a marketing campaign aimed at teenagers **SYN** TARGET

aircraft /'eəkrɑːft; AmE 'erkræft/ noun [C] (plural aircraft)
any vehicle that can fly and carry goods or passengers: the leading European aircraft manufacturer
➊ **cargo/civil/commercial/passenger** aircraft

airfare /'eəfeə(r); AmE 'erfer/ noun [C]
the money that you pay to travel by plane: an airline offering cheap/low airfares → LOW-FARE

airfreight /'eəfreɪt; AmE 'erf-/ noun [U]
goods that are carried on a plane; the system of carrying goods in this way: The company provides shipping that is faster than airfreight.

airline /'eəlaɪn; AmE 'erl-/ noun [C]
a company that provides regular flights to take passengers and goods to different places: international airlines ◇ an airline pilot ◇ an expansion in Europe's **no-frills** airline sector ◇ The airline operates about 250 flights a day.
➊ **domestic/international/national** airlines ◆ **commercial/private/state/state-owned** airlines ◆ a **charter/scheduled** airline ◆ an airline **employee/operator/passenger/pilot** ◆ the airline **business/industry**

airliner /'eəlaɪnə(r); AmE 'erl-/ noun [C]
a large plane that carries passengers

airmail /'eəmeɪl; AmE 'erm-/ noun [U]
the system of sending letters and packages by air: Send it **by** airmail. ◇ Send it airmail. ◇ an airmail envelope/letter

'Air Miles™ *noun* [pl.]
points that you collect by buying plane tickets and other products, which you can then use to pay for air travel, hotels, etc.

airport /'eəpɔːt; *AmE* 'erpɔːrt/ *noun* [C]

SEE ALSO: **international airport**

a place where planes land and take off and that has buildings for passengers to wait in: *We will be landing at Narita Airport in approximately 30 minutes.*
○ *to arrive at/land at/touch down at* an airport **◦** *to depart from/fly from/take off from* an airport **◦** *an airport building/lounge/terminal*

airtime /'eətaɪm; *AmE* 'ert-/ *noun* [U]
1 the amount of time that is given to a particular subject, or to an advertisement, on radio or television
2 the amount of time that a mobile phone/cellphone is used in a particular period of time for sending or receiving calls that you usually pay for: *This deal gives you 180 minutes free airtime a month.*

airway /'eəweɪ; *AmE* 'erweɪ/ *noun* [C]
(often used in names of airlines) a route regularly used by planes: *British Airways*

aisle /aɪl/ *noun* [C]
1 a passage between rows of shelves in a supermarket; the shelves on either side of the passage: *Coffee and tea are in the next aisle.* ◇ *The aisles are stocked with food from all over the world.*
2 a passage between rows of seats in a plane, train, theatre, etc: *Would you like an aisle seat or a window seat (= on a plane)?*

alienation /ˌeɪliə'neɪʃn/ *noun* [U]
(*HR*) a feeling that some employees have that their work is not important and they are not a valuable part of their company or organization

align /ə'laɪn/ *verb* [+ obj]
to change sth slightly so that it is in the correct relationship with sth else: *Domestic prices have been aligned with those in world markets.*
PHR V **align yourself with sb/sth** to publicly support an organization, a set of opinions or a person that you agree with

alignment /ə'laɪnmənt/ *noun* [U,C]
the correct position or relationship of things with each other: *The text and the graphics are slightly out of alignment.* ◇ *My own values were no longer in alignment with those of the company.*

A-list /'eɪ lɪst/ *noun* [C]
the most successful and popular people or companies, etc: *the magazine's A-list of high-return investments* ◇ *The firm's clients include such A-list companies as Intel and Disney.*

all-'cash *adjective* [only before noun]
(*Finance*) (used about an offer to buy a company) consisting only of money: *The company preferred the all-cash offer to a cash and stock deal of the same value.*

allegation /ˌælə'geɪʃn/ *noun* [C]
a public statement that is made without giving proof, accusing sb of doing sth that is wrong or illegal: *He will be forced to resign if the allegations made against him are true.* ◇ *serious allegations of corruption*

allege /ə'ledʒ/ *verb* [+ obj] (*often* be alleged)
to say that sb has done sth wrong or illegal, but without giving proof: *The lawsuit alleges that directors acted illegally to affect the company's share price.*

allfinanz /ˌɔːl'faɪnæns; ˌɔːlfə'næns/ *noun* [sing.]
(*BrE*)
(*Finance*; *Insurance*) the combination of banking and insurance services that is offered by many major banks SYN BANCASSURANCE

all-'hands *adjective* [only before noun]
that involves all the people who work in a company or an organization: *an all-hands meeting/session*

★ **alliance** /ə'laɪəns/ *noun* [C]

SEE ALSO: **strategic alliance**

1 an agreement between countries, companies, etc. to work together in order to achieve sth that they all want: *The two companies formed an alliance to improve shipping and distribution networks.* ◇ *The proposed alliance between the two airlines has been widely criticized.* ◇ *The training department runs the course, in alliance with the university.*
○ *to enter into/form/make* an alliance
2 a group of countries, companies, etc. who work together in order to achieve sth that they all want: *There are eight members of the alliance.* ◇ *The organization is a broad alliance of many different groups.*

all-'in *adjective* [only before noun] (*BrE*)
including everything, especially all the costs: *an all-in price of €800 with no extras to pay* ▶ **all 'in** *adverb*: *The boat trip, dinner and drinks only cost €50 all-in.* → PACKAGE

all-in'clusive *adjective*
including everything: *an all-inclusive package*

all-'loss = ALL-RISK

all-'nighter *noun* [C] (*informal*)
a period of work that lasts for a whole night: *The staff had to pull all-nighters so that the company could be launched on time.*

★ **allocate** /'æləkeɪt/ *verb* [+ obj] **allocate sth (to sb/sth)** | **allocate (sb/sth) sth** | **allocate sth (for sth)**
1 to decide officially that sth will be used for a particular purpose; to give sth officially to a particular person or thing: *The company will allocate more capital to its wholesale business.* ◇ *A large sum has been allocated for new equipment.* ◇ *Jobs have now been allocated to all new staff.* ◇ *All new staff have now been allocated jobs.*
2 (*Accounting*) to decide which department, product, etc. (**cost centre**) a particular cost relates to: *Each item of income and expenditure must be allocated to the appropriate finance code.*
▶ **allocation** /ˌælə'keɪʃn/ *noun* [C,U]: *We have spent our entire allocation for the year.* ◇ *The allocation of resources must be made more efficient.*

allot /ə'lɒt; *AmE* ə'lɑːt/ *verb* [+ obj] (**-tt-**)
allot sth (to sb/sth) | **allot (sb/sth) sth** to give time, money, tasks, etc. to sb/sth as a share of what is available: *How much money has been allotted to us?* ◇ *How much money have we been allotted?*

allotment /ə'lɒtmənt; *AmE* ə'lɑːt-/ *noun* [C,U]

SEE ALSO: **letter of allotment**

1 an amount of sth that sb is given or allowed to have; the process of giving sth to sb: *a monthly allotment of free minutes on the phone plan*
2 (*Stock Exchange*) a method of giving new company shares to people who apply for them; the number of shares given to each person who applies: *the allotment of shares to company employees*

allottee /ˌælɒ'tiː; *AmE* ˌæle'tiː/ *noun* [C]
a person who has been **allotted** sth, especially new shares

all-out 'strike *noun* [C]
(*HR*) a strike in which all employees of a company or all members of a union stop work

★ **allow** /ə'laʊ/ *verb* [+ obj]
  1 to make sth possible; to make it possible for sb to do sth: *The software allows instant comparison of sales in different regions.*
  2 to give enough time for a particular purpose: *Allow 28 days for delivery.*
  3 (*Commerce*) to take an amount of money off the price of sth, for example in exchange for another item: *How much will you allow me for my old PC?*
  4 (*Accounting*) to take an amount off an amount of money before tax is calculated: *Having allowed an expense for the last eight years, the tax office are now asking me to pay tax on it.*
  5 to accept sth; to agree that sth is true or correct: *The court allowed the claim for compensation.*
  PHR V **al'low for sb/sth** to include sb/sth when calculating sth: *All these factors must be allowed for.*

★ **allowance** /ə'laʊəns/ *noun* [C]

SEE ALSO: **capital ~, cost-of-living ~, depreciation ~, display ~, investment ~, personal ~,** etc.

  1 an amount of money that is paid to someone regularly or on particular occasions by their employer or by the state, to help them pay for travel, food, somewhere to live or other expenses: *The company gives me a travel allowance.* ◇ *a low-income allowance for child care* → WEIGHTING
  ❍ *a car/clothing/an entertainment/a housing/relocation/travel allowance* ◆ *to* **give sb/pay** *an allowance* ◆ *to* **be entitled to/claim** *an allowance*
  2 (*Accounting*) (*especially BrE*) an amount of money that you can take away from your income when calculating the amount of tax you have to pay: *The party wants to reintroduce a married couples' tax allowance.* **SYN** TAX ALLOWANCE (*BrE*)
  3 (*Accounting*) an amount of money that a business can take away from its profit when calculating the amount of tax it must pay: *the capital allowance for investment in plant and machinery*
  4 a possible future expense or change in circumstances that a person or a company pays or plans for now: *The insurance premium includes an allowance for the effects of future inflation.* ◇ *You need to* **make** *proper allowance for marketing costs.*
  → PROVISION (1)

,**all-'risk** (*also* ,**all-'risks,** ,**all-'loss**) *adjective* [only before noun]
  (*Insurance*) that pays for all types of loss or damage, except in the circumstances mentioned: *All-risk policies often have a war and related risks exclusion.*
  ◇ *to take out all-risks insurance*

,**all-'share** (*especially BrE*) (*AmE usually* ,**all-'stock**) *adjective* [only before noun]
  (*Finance*) used to describe the situation where a company buys another company by giving some of its own shares to the members of the other company, rather than paying money: *The company has agreed to buy the business in an all-share deal worth $2 billion.*

,**All-'Share ,index** (*also* ,**All-'Share,** *less frequent*) (*both especially BrE*) (*AmE usually* ,**All-'Stock ,index**) *noun* [C]

SEE ALSO: FTSE All-Share index

  an average of changes in share prices of most companies on a stock exchange, used to measure how a market is performing

,**all-'stock** = ALL-SHARE

,**All-'Stock ,index** (*also* ,**All 'Stock,** *less frequent*) = ALL-SHARE INDEX

,**all-'time** *adjective* [only before noun]
  the best or worst that has ever been recorded: *New car sales reached an all-time high of almost 2.46 million last year.*
  ❍ *an all-time high/low/peak/record*

alpha /'ælfə/ = ALPHA TEST

alphanumeric /,ælfənju:'merɪk; *AmE* -nu:'mer-/ (*also* **alphanumerical** /,ælfənju:'merɪkl; *AmE* -nu:'mer-/) *adjective*
  having both letters and numbers: *Your login name must be a four-character alphanumeric code.*

'**alpha test** (*also* '**alpha**) *noun* [C,U]
  (*IT; Marketing*) the first stage of testing a new product, especially computer software, which is done by the manufacturer under controlled conditions: *The software is currently under alpha test.*
  ❍ *to* **run/conduct** *alpha tests*
  ▶ '**alpha-test** *verb* [+ obj] *We haven't alpha-tested the business software yet.* ▶ '**alpha-,testing** (*also* '**alpha**) *noun* [U] → BETA TEST

Alt /ɔːlt/ = ALT KEY

alter /'ɔːltə(r)/ *verb*
  1 [+ obj *or* no obj] to make sb/sth different; to become different: *The company has since altered its accounting policies.*
  2 (*Law*) [+ obj] to change part of a legal agreement after it has been prepared or signed → AMEND

alteration /,ɔːltə'reɪʃn/ *noun* [C,U]
  1 changes that are made to sth, usually to improve it: *The designers have had to* **make** *major alterations to the engine.*
  2 (*Law*) a change that is made to a legal document after it has been prepared or signed

alternate /ɔː'lɜːnət; *AmE* 'ɔːltərn-/ *noun* [C] (*AmE*)
  a person who is chosen to do sb else's job when that person is ill/sick or away from their office, etc: *Four delegates and four alternates were selected.* ◇ *She is* **alternate director** *to Mr Xue, the deputy managing director.*

al,ternative dis'pute reso,lution (*also* '**dispute**) *noun* [U] (*especially AmE*) (*abbr* **ADR**)
  (*Law*) the name used to describe various methods of ending a legal disagreement without using a court **NOTE** Two popular methods are ARBITRATION and MEDIATION.

al,ternative in'vestment *noun* [C,U]
  ways of investing large amounts of money that are different from the traditional method of investing money only in shares and bonds: *Property is still regarded as the safest of alternative investments.*

Al,ternative In'vestment ,Market *noun* [sing.] (*abbr* **AIM**)
  a stock market at the LSE (= London Stock Exchange) that is designed for smaller or newer companies

'**Alt key** *noun* [C, usually sing.] (*also* **Alt** [U])
  a button on a computer keyboard that you press with other buttons for particular commands or symbols: *Hold down the Alt key and press the F4 function key.* ◇ *To exit the database press Alt + Q.*

,**always-'on** *adjective* [only before noun]
  (*IT*) (about a computer system or service) giving continuous access to the Internet: *Broadband is an always-on, high-speed Internet connection.*
  → DIAL-UP

amalgamate /ə'mælɡəmeɪt/ [+ obj *or* no obj]
  amalgamate (sth) (with sth) | **amalgamate sth into sth** if two or more organizations **amalgamate** or are **amalgamated**, they join together to form one large organization: *The firm amalgamated with several others to form a new electronics group.* ◇ *There will be job losses when the sales teams are*

amalgamated. ▶ a'malgamated *adjective* [only before noun] (*often used in the names of organizations*): *the Amalgamated Engineering Union*
amalgamation /ə,mælɡə'meɪʃn/ *noun* [U,C]: *an amalgamation of several unions*

amass /ə'mæs/ *verb* [+ obj]
to collect a large amount of sth, especially money or debt: *The company has amassed $1.4 billion in debt.*

ambiguity /,æmbɪ'ɡjuːəti/ *noun* (*plural* **ambiguities**)
1 (*Law*) [U,C] (about a legal document) the state of having more than one possible meaning; words or phrases that can be understood in more than one way: *Agreements should be drafted clearly so as to avoid ambiguity.* ◊ *ambiguities in the terms of the contract*
2 [U] the state of not being certain about the best way to do sth or to deal with sth: *the ways in which managers cope with ambiguity*

ambition /æm'bɪʃn/ *noun*
1 (*often used in the plural*) sth that you want to achieve: *He has ambitions for his group to become one of the world's top ten retailers.* ◊ *She believes the new drug will help the company achieve its ambition to increase profits by 40%.* ◊ *the group's global/international ambitions*
2 [C,U] the desire to be successful, powerful, etc. in your job: *We have been disappointed with your lack of ambition.*

ambitious /æm'bɪʃəs/ *adjective*
1 impressive but difficult to achieve because a lot of work or effort is needed: *They have an ambitious five-year plan to double the size of the business.*
2 determined to be successful in your career: *a fiercely ambitious young manager*

amend /ə'mend/ *verb* [+ obj]
to make a small change to sth such as a law or legal document, especially in order to make it better or more correct: *The pension plan should be amended to allow early retirement.* ◊ *the company's amended tax return* → ALTER ▶ a'**mendment** *noun* [C,U]: *I would like to make some slight amendments to clause 3.*

amenity /ə'miːnəti; *AmE* ə'menəti/ *noun* [C, usually pl.] (*plural* **amenities**)
a feature of sth, especially a house, hotel, etc. that makes it pleasant or more comfortable: *The hotel's amenities include a gym, a terrace and two restaurants.*

A'merican De'positary Re'ceipt *noun* [C] (*abbr* **ADR**)
(*Stock Exchange*) a certificate issued by a US bank that represents a number of shares in a foreign company and is bought and sold on stock exchanges in the US: *This is the second German company to offer shares on the New York Stock Exchange in the form of ADRs.* → EUROPEAN DEPOSITARY RECEIPT

A,merican 'Eagle = EAGLE

AMEX /'æmeks/ *noun* [sing.] (*also spelled* **Amex**)
American Stock Exchange the second largest stock exchange in the US after the New York Stock Exchange. It is based in New York and deals in the shares of new and smaller companies and many foreign organizations: *At the Amex, the market value index closed at 298.25.*

amortize, **-ise** /ə'mɔːtaɪz; *AmE* 'æmərtaɪz/ *verb* [+ obj]
1 (*Accounting*) to reduce the cost of an asset in a company's accounts over a period of time, especially an INTANGIBLE ASSET (= one you cannot touch): *Goodwill was amortized against profits every quarter for up to 20 years.* → DEPRECIATE (2), WRITE OFF

2 (*Finance*) to pay back a debt by making small regular payments over a period of time
▶ **amortizable**, **-isable** /ə'mɔːtaɪzəbl; *AmE* 'æmərt-/ *adjective*: *the amortizable assets/costs* ◊ *an amortizable loan* **amortization**, **-isation** /ə,mɔːtaɪ'zeɪʃn; *AmE* ,æmərtə'z-/ *noun* [U,C]: *Excluding goodwill amortization, pre-tax profits fell to $16.7 million.* ◊ *The lenders agreed to an improved amortization schedule.* → DEPRECIATION, WRITE-OFF

a,**mortizing 'loan** *noun* [C]
(*Accounting*) a loan which is paid back in small regular payments

★ **amount** /ə'maʊnt/ *noun, verb*
● *noun* [C,U]
SEE ALSO: face amount
1 a quantity of money: *You will receive a bill for the full amount.* ◊ *The insurance company will refund any amount due to you.* ◊ *Small amounts will be paid in cash.*
❶ *to* **pay/receive/refund** *an amount* • *to* **increase/lower/reduce** *an amount* • **large/small** *amounts* • *the* **full/right/total** *amount*
2 (*used especially with uncountable nouns*) a quantity of sth: *The amount of time shoppers spend in a store affects how much they will buy.* ◊ *We want to double the amount of business that we do in London.* ◊ *The company has huge amounts of debt.*
→ AMOUNTS DIFFER
● *verb*
PHR V a'**mount to sth** to add up to sth; to be equal to or the same as sth: *Total payments for the consulting work amounted to $13.3 million.* ◊ *Their actions amount to a breach of contract.*

a'**mount falling 'due after one 'year** *noun* [C, usually pl.]
(*Accounting*) in a company's financial records, the money which it will not have to pay back within the next year, for example money borrowed for a long period of time → LONG-TERM LIABILITIES

a'**mount falling 'due within one 'year** *noun* [C, usually pl.]
(*Accounting*) in a company's financial records, the money which it will have to pay back within the next year, for example interest on money borrowed SYN CURRENT LIABILITY

a,**mounts 'differ** *phrase*
(*Accounting, only used in written English*) if a bank returns a cheque with the phrase **amounts differ** written on it, it means that the amount written on the cheque in words is different from the amount written in figures SYN WORDS AND FIGURES DIFFER → AMOUNT

analogue (*AmE spelling usually* **analog**) /'ænəlɒɡ; *AmE* -lɔːɡ; -lɑːɡ/ *adjective*
using a continuously changing range of physical quantities to measure or store data: *a cellphone that works on both analog and digital phone systems* ◊ *The government aims to switch off the analogue television signal by 2010.* → DIGITAL

★ **analyse** (*AmE spelling* **analyze**) /'ænəlaɪz/ *verb* [+ obj]
to examine the nature or structure of sth, especially by separating it into its parts, in order to understand or explain it: *The job involves gathering and analysing data.* ◊ *We need to analyse what went wrong.* ▶ '**analyser** (*AmE spelling* **analyzer**) *noun* [C]

★ **analysis** /ə'næləsɪs/ *noun* [C,U] (*plural* **analyses** /ə'næləsiːz/)
SEE ALSO: benefit-cost analysis, break-even ~, certificate of ~, cluster ~, competitive ~, competitor ~, cost-benefit ~, etc.

the detailed study or examination of sth, in order to find answers to particular questions; the results of the study: *a detailed analysis of each customer's buying habits* ◇ *We have carried out a preliminary analysis of potential takeover targets.* ◇ *She is head of economic analysis at a top investment bank.*
→ FINANCIAL ANALYSIS at FINANCIAL ANALYST
O *(a) detailed/in-depth/thorough* analysis ◆ *business/ economic/industry/market* analysis ◆ *to* **carry out/ do/undertake** *(an)* analysis

★**analyst** /'ænəlɪst/ *noun* [C]

SEE ALSO: business analyst, business systems ~, computer ~, financial ~, market ~, systems ~, technical ~

a person whose job involves examining facts, systems, companies, markets, etc. in order to give an opinion on them
O *an* **industry/investment/a market/retail** *analyst*

analytical /ˌænə'lɪtɪkl/ *(also* **analytic** /ˌænə'lɪtɪk/*) adjective*
using a logical method in order to understand or find out about sth: *She's a respected researcher with strong analytical skills.* ◇ *an analytic approach to the problem* ◇ *analytical software/tools* ▶ **analytically** /ˌænə'lɪtɪkli/ *adverb*

'analyze,'analyzer = ANALYSE

'anchor ,tenant *noun* [C]
(Property) a very important TENANT (= a person or an organization that pays rent) in a building or on a piece of land, especially one that will attract others: *The store signed a 99-year lease to become an anchor tenant in the mall.*

ancillary /æn'sɪləri; *AmE* 'ænsəleri/ *adjective*
1 providing necessary support to the main work or activities of an organization: *ancillary workers in the health service such as cleaners and cooks* ◇ *industries ancillary* **to** *car manufacture*
O *ancillary* **equipment/services/staff/workers**
2 in addition to sth else but not as important: *ancillary rights under the law*
▶ **an'cillary** *noun* [C] *(plural* **ancillaries***): The company and its ancillaries could cost the taxpayer $1.5 billion.*

,and 'Company *(also* **and 'Co, & 'Co,** *only used in written English) phrase*
used with the name of a company that is owned by more than one person: *Levi Strauss & Co*

,angel in'vestor *noun* [C]
(Finance, informal) a private person who invests their own money in a project, especially a new business: *The majority of small businesses receive money from friends, family and angel investors.*
→ VENTURE CAPITALIST
▶ **,angel in'vestment** *noun* [U,C]

annex *(BrE spelling also* **annexe***)* /'æneks/ *noun* [C]
a section attached to the end of a document or report: *The information is given in annex B of the report.*

★**annual** /'ænjuəl/ *adjective* [usually before noun]
1 happening or done once a year: *He can earn an annual bonus of 70% of his basic pay.*
O *an annual* **bonus/fee/increase/wage** ◆ *an annual* **conference/event/meeting**
2 relating to a period of one year: *Annual earnings rose 3%.* ◇ *an average annual growth rate of 8%* ◇ *Your basic annual leave entitlement is 20 days.* ◇ *the annual budget*
O *annual* **costs/earnings/income/losses/profits/ revenue** ◆ *annual* **growth/output/sales/turnover**

▶**'annually** *adverb: The company's earnings have grown annually by 15% over the last five years.*
→ BIANNUAL

,annual ,general 'meeting *(abbr* AGM*) (BrE) (AmE* ,annual 'meeting*) noun* [C]
1 an important meeting of the shareholders or members of a company, held once a year, to present the accounts and discuss important topics: *The shareholders proposed breaking up the group at the last AGM.*
2 a meeting of the members of any organization, held once a year

,annual 'hours ,contract *noun* [C]
(HR) a contract in which employees agree to work for a particular number of hours per year rather than per week or per month, in exchange for an annual salary (= money you are paid regularly for work): *Staff with annual hours contracts work longer hours during busier periods of the year.*

annualized , -ised /'ænjuəlaɪzd/ *adjective* [only before noun]
(Accounting) (about rates of interest, INFLATION, etc.) calculated for the period of a year, using figures for a shorter period: *Inflation is currently running at an* **annualized rate** *of 10%.*

,annual 'meeting *(also* 'annual 'meeting of 'stockholders*) (also* ,annual 'stockholders' ,meeting, *less frequent)* = ANNUAL GENERAL MEETING

,annual re'port *(also* re'port*) noun* [C]
(Accounting) a financial report that a company must by law present each year to its shareholders: *The company's problems are reflected in its annual report.*

,annual re'turn *noun* [C]
(Law) in the UK, a formal statement that a company must make each year for government records, giving details of the company, its directors, its shares and its assets
O *to* **make/file** *an annual return*

,annual 'stockholders' ,meeting = ANNUAL MEETING

annuitant /ə'njuːɪtənt; *AmE* -'nuː-/ *noun* [C]
(Insurance) a person who receives an ANNUITY

annuity /ə'njuːəti; *AmE* -'nuː-/ *noun* [C] *(plural* **annuities***)*
(Finance)
1 an amount of money paid to sb every year, usually for the rest of their life
2 a type of investment that you can buy from an insurance company, usually with one large amount of money, that pays an amount of money each year: *Should I use the whole sum to buy an annuity?* ◇ *a life annuity*
3 (a payment made from this type of investment: *an annuity of $2 000 a year*

annul /ə'nʌl/ *verb* [+ obj] *(-ll-)*
(Law) to state officially that sth is no longer legally valid: *The contract was annulled.* ▶ **an'nulment** *noun* [C,U]

ANSI /'ænsi/ *abbr* **American National Standards Institute** an organization in the US that sets standards of quality and safety for manufactured items: *ANSI has devoted a standard to the proper use of safety signs.* ◇ *Our sunglasses pass the ANSI Standard Z80.3-1996.* → ISO

,Ansoff 'matrix /'ænzɒf; *AmE* -zɔːf/ *noun* [C]
(Marketing) a way of analysing the possible strategies that a company could use to increase its business

	existing product	new product
existing market	market penetration strategy	product development strategy
new market	market extension strategy	diversification strategy

'answering ma,chine (*BrE also* **'answerphone**) *noun* [C]
a machine which you connect to your telephone to answer your calls and record any message left by the person calling: *I called several times, but only got the answering machine.*

'answering ,service *noun* [C]
1 a business that receives telephone calls for people or organizations and records messages for them to listen to
2 (*especially BrE*) a service that provides recorded information when you telephone or allows you to record a message: *For timetable information please call the 24-hour answering service.*

answerphone /'ɑːnsəfəʊn; *AmE* 'aensərfoʊn/ = ANSWERING MACHINE

ante /'ænti/ *noun* [sing.]
IDM **raise/up the 'ante** to increase the level of sth, especially sums of money or competition between businesses: *Quickbuy upped the ante in the battle for customers by slashing 5% off its prices.*

anti /'ænti/ *preposition* (*informal*)
if sb is **anti** sb/sth, they do not like or agree with that person or thing: *I'm not anti the plan—I just want to go slowly.*

anti- /'ænti/ *prefix*
1 opposed to; against: *anti-euro campaigners* ◇ *anti-business*
2 the opposite of: *anticlockwise*
3 preventing: *anti-discrimination laws*

,anticipatory 'breach *noun* [C]
(*Law*) the breaking of a contract in advance by sb who says they will not be able to do what the contract says they must do: *They accepted the anticipatory breach and immediately claimed damages.*

,anti-com'petitive *adjective*
(*Economics*) not allowing other companies to compete in a fair way: *The company was penalized for anti-competitive behaviour by distributing its software free to schools.* ◇ *alleged anti-competitive practices*

,anti-'dumping *adjective* [only before noun]
(*Economics*) aimed at protecting the economy of a country by preventing other countries from selling goods there at prices that are unfairly low: *These cheap cars were regarded in Europe as unfair competition and attracted anti-dumping duties.*
→ COUNTERVAILING DUTY

,anti-in'flation *adjective* [only before noun]
aimed at lowering INFLATION or preventing it from rising, for example by controlling increases in wages or interest rates: *anti-inflation policies*

,anti-'spam *adjective* [only before noun]
(*IT*) aimed at preventing the sending of advertising by email that people do not want to receive: *anti-spam software/tools*

,anti-'takeover *adjective* [only before noun]
aimed at preventing a company from taking over another one that does not want it or agree to it: *anti-takeover provisions/insurance*

antitrust /,ænti'trʌst/ *adjective* [only before noun]
(*Economics*) aimed at preventing groups of companies from working together illegally to reduce competition, control prices, etc: *The merger has received antitrust clearance* (= official permission).

,anti'virus /,ænti'vaɪrəs/ *adjective* [only before noun]
(*IT*) that prevents and removes computer VIRUSES (= parts of a program that cause faults in the computer): *antivirus software packages*

,any ,other 'business *phrase* (*abbr* AOB)
a part of a meeting when subjects not mentioned on the AGENDA (= list of items to be discussed) can be discussed: *Is there any other business?* ◇ *Any AOB?* See note at MEETING

APACS /'eɪpæks/ *noun* [sing.]
Association for Payment Clearing Services
an organization in the UK for banks and other financial institutions which provide payment services, such as for cheques and credit cards
→ BACS, CHAPS

Apex (*also spelled* **APEX**) /'eɪpeks/ *noun* [U]
a system of cheap tickets for train or air travel if you buy your ticket a particular number of days before you travel: *Apex fares/tickets* **NOTE** Apex is the short form for 'advance purchase excursion'.

apology /ə'pɒlədʒi; *AmE* ə'pɑː-/ *noun* (*plural* **apologies**)
1 [C,U] a word or statement saying sorry for sth that has been done wrong or that causes a problem: *We offer our sincere apologies for any inconvenience caused.* ◇ *a letter of apology*
O *to* **accept/demand/make/offer** *an apology*
2 [C, usually pl.] information that you cannot go to a meeting or must leave early: *The meeting started with apologies* (= the names of people who could not go to the meeting). See note at MEETING
O *to* **present/send** *your apologies*

app /æp/ *noun* [C]

SEE ALSO: **killer app**

(*IT, informal*) a short way of saying **application** (= a computer program designed to do a particular job): *This is the perfect app for someone who is new to databases.*

apparel /ə'pærəl/ *noun* [U] (*especially AmE*)
clothing, when it is being sold in shops/stores: *winter/sports apparel* ◇ *the apparel industry*

ap,parent 'damage *noun* [U]
(*Transport*) damage to goods that is noticed and reported when they are delivered or unloaded

appeal /ə'piːl/ *noun, verb*
● *noun*
1 [C,U] a formal request to a court or to sb in authority to change a judgement or a decision made in a lower court: *She got her job back when she won an appeal against her dismissal.* ◇ *His prison sentence was reduced on appeal.*
2 [U] a quality that makes a product attractive or interesting: *The car had mass appeal and was cheap*

to run. ◇ *advertising techniques that are designed to enhance* (= improve) *a product's appeal*
⊕ *mass/popular/universal/wide/youth appeal*
● *verb*
1 [+ obj *or* no obj] to make a formal request to a court or to sb in authority to change a judgement or a decision: *All the newspapers are appealing* **against** *the judgement.* ◇ *The company said it would appeal the decision.*
2 [no obj] to attract or interest sb: *This design appeals* **strongly to** *the Japanese consumer.*

ap'peal board = APPEALS BOARD

ap'peal bond *noun* [C]
(*Law*) an amount of money that a person who appeals (= asks for a decision made in a court to be changed) may have to leave with the court, which they will lose if the appeal fails

ap'peals board (*also* **ap'peal board**) *noun* [C]
a group of officials who are appointed to listen to and judge cases where there is a dispute about an official decision that has been made

appellant /ə'pelənt/ *noun* [C]
(*Law*) a person who appeals to a court to change a judgement or a decision made in a lower court

appellate /ə'pelət/ *adjective* [only before noun]
(*Law*) concerned with appeals to change a judgement or decision made by a court or by sb in authority: *An* **appellate** *court can decide whether the decision under appeal was right or wrong.*

append /ə'pend/ *verb* [+ obj]
to add sth to the end of a piece of writing: *The signatures of all group members should be appended* **to** *the contract.*

appendix /ə'pendɪks/ *noun* [C] (*plural* **appendices** /-dɪsiːz/)
a section giving extra information at the end of a report, a book or other document: *Full details are given in appendix 3.*

appliance /ə'plaɪəns/ *noun* [C]
an electrical machine that is designed to do a particular thing in the home, such as preparing food, heating or cleaning: *They sell a wide range of domestic appliances.*

applicant /'æplɪkənt/ *noun* [C]
a person who applies for sth, especially a job, shares, etc: *There were over a hundred applicants for the job.* ◇ *Successful applicants were entitled to purchase up to 1 000 shares each.*

★ **application** /ˌæplɪ'keɪʃn/ *noun*
___
SEE ALSO: enterprise application, letter of ~, multiple ~, share ~, speculative ~
___
1 [C,U] a formal written request for sth, such as a job or permission to do sth: *I am pleased to tell you that your application* **for** *the post has been successful.* ◇ *All planning applications should be submitted to the local council.*
⊕ *to* **file/make/send in/submit** *an application* ◆ *to* **grant/reject/turn down** *an application* ◆ *to* **consider/examine/process** *an application*
2 [C] = APPLICATION FORM
3 [U,C] the practical use of sth, especially a theory, discovery, etc: *The new invention would have wide application in industry.* ◇ *a wide range of applications*
4 [U] the act of making a rule, etc. operate or become active: *strict application of the law*
5 (*IT*) (*also* **appli'cation program**) (*also* **app**, *informal*) [C] a program designed to do a particular job; a piece of software: *You can run several applications at the same time.* ◇ *software*

applications for the travel industry
SYN APPLICATION SOFTWARE

appli,cation for 'listing (*also* appli,cation for quo'tation) *noun* [C]
(*Stock Exchange*) a request by a company to be listed on a stock exchange

appli'cation form (*also* ,appli'cation) *noun* [C]
a document with spaces for writing in personal information, used for making a formal request for sth: *You will be asked to complete an application form and attend an interview.*
⊕ *to* **complete/fill in/fill out/send off** *an application form*

appli,cation for quo'tation = APPLICATION FOR LISTING

appli,cation for 'shares = SHARE APPLICATION

appli'cation ,letter = LETTER OF APPLICATION

appli'cation ,money *noun* [U]
(*Stock Exchange*) the money paid by sb who asks for new shares that are being sold

appli'cation ,program = APPLICATION (5)

appli,cation 'software *noun* [U]
(*IT*) a program designed to do a particular job: *business application software* SYN APPLICATION

★ **apply** /ə'plaɪ/ *verb* (**applies, applying, applied, applied**)
1 [no obj] **apply (to sb/sth) (for sth)** to make a formal written request for sth: *The company has applied for planning permission to build a factory on the site.* ◇ *Four people applied for the post of Assistant Manager.* ◇ *Please apply in writing with full CV to the Human Resources Manager.* ◇ *I decided to apply to business school.*
2 [+ obj] **apply sth (to sth)** to use sth or make sth work in a particular situation: *When you start work you must apply what you have learned at college.* ◇ *As the new technology was applied to farming, fewer workers were needed.*
3 [+ obj *or* no obj] (*not used in the continuous tenses*) **apply (sth) (to sb/sth)** to concern or have an effect on sb/sth: *Special conditions apply to people who are under 21.* ◇ *The tax will be applied to all new cars from next year.*

★ **appoint** /ə'pɔɪnt/ *verb* [+ obj]
1 to choose sb for a job or a position of responsibility: *He has recently been appointed* **to** *the board.* ◇ *A French woman has been appointed* **as** *head of Switzerland's largest bank.* ◇ *We are* **looking to** *appoint a financial advisor as soon as possible.* ◇ *A private bank was appointed* **to** *handle the sale.* See note at EMPLOY
2 (*formal*) to arrange or decide on a time or place for doing sth: *I arrived ten minutes before the* **appointed** *time.*

appointee /ə,pɔɪn'tiː/ *noun* [C]
(*HR*) a person who has been chosen for a job or a position of responsibility: *the new appointee to the post*

★ **appointment** /ə'pɔɪntmənt/ *noun*
___
SEE ALSO: letter of appointment
___
1 [C] a formal arrangement to meet or visit sb at a particular time, especially for a reason connected with work: *She had an urgent appointment* **with** *a client.* ◇ *I made an appointment to see the Sales Manager.* ◇ *Tours of the factory can be arranged* **by appointment** (= at a time that has been arranged in advance).
⊕ *to* **arrange/book/fix/have/make** *an appointment* ◆ *to* **keep/miss** *an appointment*
2 (*HR*) [C,U] the act of choosing a person for a job or a position of responsibility: *the appointment of a*

new administrative assistant ◊ her recent *appointment to* the post of Head of Finance
3 (*HR*) [C] a job or a position of responsibility: *promotion to a more senior appointment*

ap'pointment book (*also* **ap'pointments book**, *less frequent*) = DIARY (1)

ap'pointment ,letter = LETTER OF APPOINTMENT

ap'pointments book = APPOINTMENT BOOK

apportion /əˈpɔːʃn; *AmE* əˈpɔːrʃn/ *verb* [+ obj] **apportion sth (among/between/to sb)** to divide sth among people; to give a share of sth to sb: *Profits are apportioned among employees.* ◊ *The report gave the facts of the case but did not apportion blame.*

apportionment /əˈpɔːʃnmənt; *AmE* əˈpɔːrʃn-/ *noun* [U,C]
1 the sharing of sth among people: the amount that each person gets when sth is shared: *The contract defines the apportionment of risks between employer and contractor.* ◊ *an apportionment of land*
2 (*Accounting*) (*also* **'cost ap,portionment**) the division of a cost between accounts in as fair a way as possible; the amount put in each account: *Where parts of a business share a building, floor area can used as a basis of apportionment to share costs between appropriate cost centres.*
3 (*Law*) **apportionment of blame/liability** a method of dividing payment between people involved in an accident, or their insurance companies, according to how responsible each person was for the accident; the amount that each has to pay: *The Court of Appeal revised the apportionment of liability, finding the driver 80% liable.*
4 (*Property*) an agreement between the present owner and the future owner of a property to share expenses connected with the property until the sale is complete; the amount that each agrees to pay

★**appraisal** /əˈpreɪzl/ *noun* [C,U]

SEE ALSO: credit appraisal, self-appraisal

1 (*HR*) (*also* **per'formance ap,praisal**, **per'formance as,sessment**, **per'formance evalu,ation**, **per'formance re,view**) a meeting between an employee and their manager to discuss the quality of the employee's work and to plan future tasks: *The company introduced its staff appraisal scheme ten years ago.* → 360-DEGREE FEEDBACK
2 a judgement of the value, performance or nature of sb/sth: *He was asked to give a critical appraisal of the facilities.*

★**appraise** /əˈpreɪz/ *verb* [+ obj]
1 (*HR*) to make a formal judgement about the value of a person's work, usually after a discussion with them about it: *Each member of staff is appraised annually by his or her manager.*
2 (*formal*) to consider or examine sb/sth and decide how much it is worth: *the company's appraised value*

appraisee /ə,preɪˈziː/ *noun* [C]
(*HR*) an employee whose work is **appraised** by their manager

appraiser /əˈpreɪzə(r)/ *noun* [C]
1 (*AmE*) a person whose job is to estimate the value of sth: *The Appraiser valued the painting at $2 million.* → VALUER
2 (*HR*) a manager who **appraises** an employee's work

appreciate /əˈpriːʃieɪt/ *verb* [no obj]
to increase in value over a period of time: *The currency has appreciated by 10% against the dollar since April.* OPP DEPRECIATE See note at CURRENCY

---

appreciation /ə,priːʃiˈeɪʃn/ *noun* [U; sing.]

SEE ALSO: asset appreciation, capital appreciation

(*Economics*) increase in value over a period of time: *share price appreciation* ◊ *an appreciation in the value of land* ◊ *an appreciation of the euro against sterling* OPP DEPRECIATION

apprentice /əˈprentɪs/ *noun* [C]
(*HR*) a young person who works for an employer for a fixed period of time in order to learn the particular skills needed in their job: *She's now taken on three young apprentices.* ◊ *He started work at sixteen as an apprentice chef.*

apprenticeship /əˈprentɪʃɪp/ *noun* [C,U]
(*HR*) a period of time working as an **apprentice**: *a two-year apprenticeship in a private bank* ◊ *He had served his apprenticeship as a plumber.* ◊ *apprenticeship schemes/training*

appropriate /əˈprəʊprieɪt; *AmE* əˈproʊ-/ *verb* [+ obj]
1 (*Finance*) to keep or save money for a particular purpose: *€8 000 has been appropriated for a new training scheme.*
2 to take sth for your own use, especially illegally or without permission: *He was accused of appropriating company funds.*

appropriation /ə,prəʊpriˈeɪʃn/ *noun*
1 (*Finance*) [U] the act of keeping or saving money for a particular purpose: *a meeting to discuss the appropriation of funds*
2 (*Finance*) [C] an amount of money to be used for a particular purpose, especially by a government or a company: *an appropriation of €20 000 for payment of debts*
3 [U; sing.] the act of taking sth that belongs to sb else: *dishonest appropriation of property*

ap,propri'ation ac,count *noun* [C]
(*Accounting*)
1 a financial account that shows how the profits of a business, especially a PARTNERSHIP, have been shared between its owners
2 in the UK, an account that shows how the money that a government department has been given has been used

approval /əˈpruːvl/ *noun*
1 [U,C] official agreement to, or permission for sth, especially a plan or request: *The plan will be submitted to the committee for official approval.* ◊ *The Board of Directors has given its approval for the new branch.* ◊ *The offer is subject to approval from the AGM.* ◊ *The company is seeking marketing approval for* (= permission to sell) *a new drug.*
2 (*Commerce*) [U] if you buy goods, or if goods are sold, **on approval**, you can use them for a time without paying, until you decide if you want to buy them or not: *The goods were sent on approval and were later returned.*

★**approve** /əˈpruːv/ *verb*
1 [+ obj] to officially agree to or give permission for sth, especially a plan or request: *The committee unanimously approved the plan.* ◊ *The drug has now been approved for use in Europe.*
2 [+ obj] (*often* **be approved**) to say that sth is good enough to be used, or is correct: *The accounts were formally approved by the board.*
3 [no obj] to think that sb/sth is good or acceptable; to have a positive opinion of sb/sth: *I very much approve of his decision.*

ap,proved ac'count *noun* [C]
(*Accounting*)
1 [usually pl.] a financial account that has been officially accepted by a company or an

organization: *The figures are taken from the audited and approved accounts for last year.*
2 a CREDIT ACCOUNT held by a customer who is known to be reliable: *Our terms are cash with order, except approved accounts.*

ap,proved con'tractor *noun* [C]
a company or person that is officially recognized as doing good, reliable work for other companies: *A building company must provide detailed financial information when applying to join a list of approved contractors.*

ap,proved 'vendor = PREFERRED VENDOR

approx *abbr* (*only used in written English*)
approximate; approximately: *approx price: €200*

★ **approximate** *adjective, verb*
● *adjective* /ə'prɒksɪmət; *AmE* ə'prɑ:k-/ (*abbr* **approx**)
almost correct or accurate, but not completely so; not exact: *The cost given is only approximate.* ◇ *an approximate calculation of the overall cost*
● *an approximate* **calculation/cost/estimate/ number/total**
▶ **ap'proximately** *adverb*: *I spend approximately 60% of my working day on the phone.*
● *verb* /ə'prɒksɪmeɪt; *AmE* ə'prɑ:k-/
1 [+ obj *or* no obj] to be similar or close to sth in amount, nature, quality, etc: *The total cost will approximate 15 million dollars.* ◇ *Output from the plant approximates* **to** *one quarter of national requirements.*
2 [+ obj] to calculate or estimate sth fairly accurately: *The time required can be approximated by the following formula.*

approximation /ə,prɒksɪ'meɪʃn; *AmE* ə,prɑ:k-/ *noun* [C]
1 an estimate of a number or an amount that is almost correct, but not exact: *That's just an approximation, you understand.*
2 a thing that is similar to sth else, but is not exactly the same: *Our results should be a good approximation* **to** *the true state of affairs.*

APR /,eɪ pi: 'ɑ:(r)/ *abbr*
(*Finance*) **annual percentage rate** the total amount of money that is charged in one year for borrowing money compared with the amount of money borrowed, used when interest is normally paid more often than once a year; the amount received from money invested: *The bank offers an APR of 21% on its credit card.* → AER, EAR

aptitude /'æptɪtju:d; *AmE* -tu:d/ *noun* [U,C]
natural ability or skill at doing sth: *She showed a natural aptitude* **for** *the work.* ◇ *His aptitude for motivating people has got him to his current position.*

'aptitude test *noun* [C]
(*HR*) a test designed to show whether sb has the natural ability for a particular job: *Two candidates scored well on the aptitude test.*

arable /'ærəbl/ *adjective, noun*
● *adjective*
connected with growing crops such as wheat or corn: *Only 44% of the world's arable land* (= land suitable for growing crops) *is cultivated.* ◇ *arable farms*
● *noun* [U]
arable land or crops

arbiter /'ɑ:bɪtə(r); *AmE* 'ɑ:rb-/ *noun* [C]
a person who settles a dispute or who has the power to decide what will be done or accepted: *The union representative agreed to* **act as** *arbiter between the employee and her manager.* ◇ *the arbiter of domain name disputes*

arbitrage /'ɑ:bɪtrɑ:ʒ; -trɪdʒ; *AmE* 'ɑ:rbətrɑ:ʒ/ *noun* [U]
(*Finance*) the practice of buying sth (for example shares or foreign money) in one place and selling it immediately in another place where the price is higher: *investors hoping to exploit an arbitrage opportunity* → RISK ARBITRAGE ▶ **'arbitrage** *verb* [no obj]

arbitrageur /,ɑ:bɪtrɑ:'ʒɜ:(r); *AmE* ,ɑ:rbətrɑ:'ʒɜ:r/ (*also* **arbitrager** /'ɑ:bɪtrɑ:dʒə(r); *AmE* 'ɑ:rbətrɑ:dʒər/) *noun* [C]
(*Finance*) a person whose job is ARBITRAGE: *Shares rose unexpectedly, leaving arbitrageurs facing losses.*

★ **arbitrate** /'ɑ:bɪtreɪt; *AmE* 'ɑ:rb-/ *verb* [+ obj *or* no obj]
(*Law*) to officially settle an argument or a disagreement between two people or groups: *to arbitrate* **in/on** *a dispute* ◇ *A committee arbitrated* **between** *management and unions.* ◇ *They could request a judge to arbitrate the dispute.* → MEDIATE

★ **arbitration** /,ɑ:bɪ'treɪʃn; *AmE* ,ɑ:rb-/ *noun* [U]
(*Law*) the official process of settling a legal disagreement by sb who is not involved rather than by a court: *Both sides in the dispute have agreed to* **go to arbitration.** ◇ *They called for arbitration to resolve the strike.* → MEDIATION
● *an arbitration* **board/hearing/panel/system**

arbitrator /'ɑ:bɪtreɪtə(r); *AmE* 'ɑ:rb-/ *noun* [C]
(*Law*) a person who is chosen to settle a dispute: *The disputed insurance claim was referred to an independent arbitrator.* → MEDIATOR

arcade /ɑ:'keɪd; *AmE* ɑ:r'k-/ *noun* [C] (*BrE*)
a large building with a number of shops/stores in it: *a shopping arcade*

architect /'ɑ:kɪtekt; *AmE* 'ɑ:rk-/ *noun* [C]

SEE ALSO: **systems architect**

1 a person whose job is designing buildings, etc. See note at PROFESSION
2 a person who is responsible for planning or creating an idea, an event or a situation: *He was one of the chief architects of the reform.*

architecture /'ɑ:kɪtektʃə(r); *AmE* 'ɑ:rk-/ *noun* [U]

SEE ALSO: **information architecture**

1 the art and study of designing buildings: *a degree in architecture*
2 the design or style of a building or buildings: *modern architecture*
3 (*IT*) the design or structure of a computing system and the way the different parts work together: *the architecture of the Internet* ◇ *a client-server architecture*
4 the structure of an organization and the way the different parts and different people affect each other: *the social architecture of a company*
▶ **architectural** /,ɑ:kɪ'tektʃərəl; *AmE* ,ɑ:rk-/ *adjective*: *architectural innovation*

archive /'ɑ:kaɪv; *AmE* 'ɑ:rk-/ *noun, verb*
● *noun*
1 [C, usually pl.] a collection of historical records kept by an organization; the place where these records are stored: *account books stored in the company's archives*
2 (*IT*) [C] a part of a computer system, a tape or disk where data that is not often needed is stored → BACKUP
3 (*IT*) [C] a set of files and information that people can look at on the Internet
● *verb* [+ obj]
1 to put or store a document or other material in an **archive**: *archived documents/articles*
2 (*IT*) to move data that is not often needed to a tape, disk or another part of a computer system to store it: *archiving important files on CD-ROM* ◇ *archived emails* → BACK STH UP at BACK *verb*

★area /'eəriə; AmE 'eriə/ noun [C]

SEE ALSO: assisted area, catchment ~, core ~, development ~, dollar ~, euro ~, sales ~

1 a part of a town, a country or the world: *an industrial/a residential area* ◇ *She has been appointed **area manager** for south Wales.*
→ TERRITORY (1)
2 part of a room, building or particular space that is used for a special purpose: *a parking area* ◇ *the hotel reception area*
3 a particular subject or activity, or an aspect of it: *the areas of training and development* ◇ *Solar energy is one of our core business areas.* ◇ *My **area of expertise** (= what I have expert knowledge of and skill in) is computer-aided design.* → TERRITORY (2)

'area code noun [C] (*especially AmE*)
the numbers for a particular area or city, that you use when you are making a telephone call from outside the local area: *For long distance calls dial '1' followed by the area code and number.* → DIALLING CODE

,area 'franchise, ,area franchi'see
= MASTER FRANCHISE

arena /ə'ri:nə/ noun [C]
1 a particular market or an area of business: *The wholesale market is a highly **competitive** arena.*
2 an area of activity that concerns the public, especially one where there is a lot of opposition between different groups or countries: *The company's problems are now **in the public arena** (= are known and discussed by people in general).*

,arithmetic 'mean = MEAN noun

arm /ɑːm; AmE ɑːrm/ noun [C]
a part of a large organization which is responsible for one area of its business: *the research arm of the company*

,arm's-'length adjective [only before noun]
between companies or people that do not have close contact or any financial connections: *an arm's-length transaction/relationship*

ARR /,eɪ ɑːr 'ɑː(r)/ = ACCOUNTING RATE OF RETURN

★arrange /ə'reɪndʒ/ verb [+ obj]
arrange sth (with sb) | **arrange for sb to do sth** | **arrange to do sth** to organize sth; to make plans for sth to happen: *Will you arrange it with my secretary?* ◇ *I must arrange a meeting for next week.* ◇ *We will arrange for somebody to meet you at the airport.* ◇ *The company has arranged a $3.5 billion loan facility with its bankers.*
◑ to arrange an **appointment/interview/a meeting** ✦ to arrange a **facility/loan'**

VOCABULARY BUILDING

Making arrangements

● Can we **arrange** a time to discuss this?
● They **called** a meeting of the committee.
● (formal) The annual general meeting is **convened** by the company secretary.
● We're **organizing** a sales conference for later this year.
● (when the date/time might change) I've **pencilled** you **in** for two hours on Thursday.
● The elections were **fixed** for May 1.
● The company **scheduled** an afternoon news conference.
● All conference calls are **set up** ahead of time.

See note at POSTPONE

★arrangement /ə'reɪndʒmənt/ noun

SEE ALSO: deed of arrangement, scheme of ~, voluntary ~

1 [C, usually pl.] plans or preparations for sth that will happen in the future: *travel arrangements*
2 [C,U] a way of doing or organizing things, especially one that is formally agreed by two people or organizations, etc: *More open trading arrangements should increase investment in the country.* ◇ *You can cash cheques here **by prior arrangement** with the bank.*
3 [C] a formal relationship between two companies, etc. that provides some benefit to them both, usually over a long period of time: *The company has set up a new distribution arrangement with a Canadian publisher.* See note at AGREEMENT
4 (*Finance*) [C, usually sing.] a formal agreement made between sb who owes money but cannot pay it all back and the person or organization that they owe money to, so that only part of the money will be paid
5 [U] the act of arranging sth: *arrangement fees*

array /ə'reɪ/ noun [C]
a group or collection of products, often one that is large or impressive: *a vast array of goods to choose from* SYN RANGE
◑ a **broad/vast/wide** array of sth

arrears /ə'rɪəz; AmE ə'rɪrz/ noun [pl.]
money that sb/sth owes that they should have paid earlier: *rent/tax arrears* ◇ *The airline has now paid its arrears in landing fees.* ◇ *The country has accumulated debt arrears of $715 million.*
IDM **be in arrears (with sth)**; **fall/get into arrears (with sth)** to be late in paying money that you owe: *Wages are already more than two months in arrears.* ◇ *The tenant fell into arrears with the rent.* **in arrears** after the time that work is done, items supplied, etc: *Passengers pay in advance, but the holiday company pays its suppliers in arrears.*
OPP IN ADVANCE

arrival /ə'raɪvl/ noun
1 [U,C] the act of coming or being brought to a place: *We record the date and time of arrival of all deliveries.* ◇ *the arrivals hall (= at an airport)*
→ DEPARTURE
2 [C] a person or a thing that comes to a place: *late arrivals* ◇ *welcoming new arrivals on their first day*
3 [U] the time when sb starts a new job: *Since her arrival as chief executive, sales have increased by 19%.*
4 [U] the time when sth new starts, especially a new product or technology coming into the market: *the arrival of colour-screen mobile phones*

article /'ɑːtɪkl; AmE 'ɑːrt-/ noun
1 [C] a piece of writing in a newspaper or magazine: *an article in the Wall Street Journal*
2 (*Law*) [C] (often used about international laws) a section of a law, an agreement or other legal document that deals with a particular point
3 (*Law*) **articles** [pl.] (*BrE*) a period of practical training that has to be completed before sb can become a SOLICITOR: *She's doing her articles with a firm in London.* **NOTE** Articles is an abbreviation of **articles of clerkship.**

,articled 'clerk = TRAINEE SOLICITOR

,articles of as,soci'ation noun [pl.] (*usually* **Articles of Association**) (*BrE*)
(*Law*) one of the legal documents that is created when a company is formed. It contains rules about how the company must be managed, what rights shareholders have, what the directors can do and what formal meetings must be held: *Several restrictions on the transfer of shares are listed in the*

articles of association. **SYN** BY-LAW (*AmE*)
→ MEMORANDUM OF ASSOCIATION

,articles of in,corpo'ration *noun* [pl.] (*usually*
Articles of Incorporation) (*AmE*)
(*Law*) one of the legal documents that is created
when a company is formed. It states the name and
address of the company, its purpose and the
amount of money it can raise by selling shares.
SYN MEMORANDUM OF ASSOCIATION → ARTICLES OF
ASSOCIATION

,artificial in'telligence *noun* [U] (*abbr* AI)
(*IT*)
1 the study of how to make computers function in
an intelligent way like humans
2 technology that allows a computer to do
something in an intelligent way, similar to the way
in which a human would do it: *The software
incorporates the latest in artificial intelligence.*

,artificial 'person = LEGAL PERSON

A/S (*also spelled* **a/s**) = AFTER SIGHT

as /əz/ *or, in the strong form,* /æz/ *preposition, adverb,
conjunction*
IDM '**as at ... /'as of ...** (*Accounting*) used to show
the exact date on which sth is correct or to which
sth relates: *All prices are correct as at 1 July 2004.* ◇
Consolidated Balance Sheet as of 31 March 2005 '**as
from ... /'as of ...** (*formal*) used to show the time or
date from which sth starts: *Our fax number is
changing as from May 12.* **,as 'is** (*BrE also* **,as 'seen**)
(*Commerce*) used to mean that sth is being sold in its
present condition and that the person selling it
does not make any promises about its quality: *All
used equipment is sold as is.* → idiom at PER

asap (*also spelled* **ASAP**, *especially in AmE*) /,eɪ es eɪ
'piː ; *AmE also* 'eɪsæep/ *abbr*
as soon as possible: *Please return the completed
questionnaire asap.*

ASCII /'æski/ *abbr*
(*IT*) **American Standard Code for Information
Interchange** a system that allows data to be
moved between computers that use different
programs: *Save the text as an ASCII file.*

,Asian 'tiger *noun* [C]
a term used especially in newspapers for any
South-East Asian country whose economy is
growing very fast → TIGER

ask /ɑːsk; *AmE* æsk/ *verb* [+ obj]
to say the price that you want for sth that you are
selling: *He's asking €5 000 for the car.*
IDM ,**ask sb to 'leave** (*often* **be asked to leave**) to
ask sb to leave their job; to dismiss sb: *The chief
executive has been asked to leave.* **NOTE** This is a
polite way to say 'fire sb' or, in British English, 'sack
sb'.
PHRV ,**ask sb 'back** to ask sb to attend a further
job interview: *They asked back four people for in-
depth interviews.*

'asking price *noun* [C]
1 (*Commerce*) the price that sb/sth wants to sell sth
for: *The company seems willing to pay the asking
price for the business.* ◇ *an asking price of $110 a
share*
2 (*Stock Exchange*) (*also* '**asked price**, '**ask price**, *less
frequent*) = OFFER PRICE (2)

aspi'rational brand *noun* [C]
(*Marketing*) a brand which people admire because
they believe it is high quality and will give them a
higher social position if they use it

★assemble /ə'sembl/ *verb*
1 [+ obj *or no* obj] to bring people or things
together as a group; to come together as a group:

*The chairman has begun to assemble a new
management team.* ◇ *Before making a bid for a
company, we assembled detailed information on the
business.* ◇ *The delegates are assembling in the
conference room.*
2 [+ obj] to fit together all the separate parts of a
product: *We assemble and ship each computer within
five days of order.* ◇ *The car is assembled in the UK.*
3 (*Finance*) [+ obj] if a financial institution
assembles a loan, it gets a group of banks, etc. to
provide money: *The Fund has assembled a $10
billion emergency loan package .*

★assembly /ə'sembli/ *noun* (*plural* **assemblies**)

SEE ALSO: self-assembly

1 [U] the process of fitting together the parts of a
product: *The new model is being launched at the UK
assembly plant.* ◇ *We plan to begin car assembly at
the plant in 2006.* ◇ *easy-to-follow assembly
instructions*
2 [C] a large group of people who come together
for a particular purpose: *an assembly of over 200
people*

★ as'sembly line (*also* **pro'duction line**)
noun [C]
a line of workers and machines in a factory that fit
the parts of a product together in a fixed order:
working on an assembly line ◇ *An engine rolls off
the assembly line every 72 seconds.* ◇ *Assembly line
automation has reduced error rates in
manufacturing.*
☉ *assembly line* **methods/problems/robots/workers**

as'sembly point *noun* [C]
a place where people must meet if there is an
emergency

as'sembly ,worker *noun* [C]
a person who works in a factory producing goods:
car/electronics assembly workers ◇ *Assembly workers
were retrained to handle the new electronic
technology.*

assent /ə'sent/ *noun, verb* (*formal*)
● *noun* [U]
official agreement to sth
● *verb* [no obj]
to agree to a request, an idea or a suggestion: *By
using this website you assent to the conditions of use.*

assertive /ə'sɜːtɪv; *AmE* ə'sɜːrtɪv/ *adjective*
expressing opinions and desires in a strong
confident way so that people notice you or do what
you want: *Working abroad has made her more
confident and assertive.* ◇ *an assertive management
style* ▶ **as'sertiveness** *noun* [U]

as'sertiveness ,training *noun* [U]
(*HR*) teaching people, for example employees, to be
firm and more confident when dealing with people

★assess /ə'ses/ *verb* [+ obj]
1 to judge sb/sth or form an opinion about sb/sth
after looking carefully at all the information: *The
task assesses candidates' strengths and weaknesses.* ◇
*It is difficult to assess the impact of advertising on
sales.* ◇ *The training needs of staff are assessed every
year.* **SYN** EVALUATE
2 to calculate the amount or value of sth: *Damage
to the building was assessed at €10 000.*
3 (*Accounting; Law*) (*often* **be assessed**) **assess sb/
sth for sth | assess sb/sth on/upon sb/sth** to decide
how much money sb/sth must pay as a tax or a
fine: *The company tax is assessed on the previous
year's activities.*

as,sessed 'value *noun* [U,C]
(*Accounting*) especially in the US, the value of land
and buildings that is used to calculate how much
tax has to be paid

★ **assessment** /əˈsesmənt/ *noun*

SEE ALSO: **performance assessment, risk ~, self-~, tax ~**

1 [C,U] an opinion or a judgement about sb/sth made after all the information has been looked at carefully: *What's your assessment of the situation?* ◇ *We need to make a detailed assessment of all the risks involved.*

🔾 **to give/make** an assessment • a **detailed/thorough** assessment

2 (*Accounting*) [C,U] an amount of money, especially tax, that has been calculated and must be paid; the process of calculating this amount: *I have appealed against my income tax assessment.* ◇ *In the year of assessment 2004/2005 the trust had an income of €48 000.*

3 [C] a calculation of the amount or value of sth: *The insurance company carried out an assessment of the damage.*

🔾 **to carry out/make** an assessment

4 (*HR*) [C,U] the process of testing sb's knowledge and abilities, how well a system works, etc: *Many colleges now use continuous assessment.* ◇ *Our employees take assessment tests to see what training they need.* ◇ *Who is responsible for the safety assessment of new crops?*

🔾 **to carry out/do/use** assessment

as'sessment ˌcentre (*AmE spelling* ~ **center**) *noun* [C]
(*HR*) an event where people applying for a job are given a number of tests and interviews to find out what their strengths and weaknesses are; the place where this happens: *All job applicants will be expected to participate in an assessment centre.*

assessor /əˈsesə(r)/ *noun* [C]

SEE ALSO: **loss assessor, tax assessor**

1 a person who is an expert in sth who looks at all the information and judges how good sb/sth is: *The product got a good rating from a team of independent assessors.*

2 (*Property*) a person who decides the amount of tax you have to pay for the buildings and land that you own: *According to tax assessors' records, the estate was assessed at $1.4 million in 2005.*

3 (*Insurance*) a person whose job is to help you make a claim against an insurance company: *We called in insurance assessors after part of the building was damaged by fire.* ◇ *a claims assessor* [SYN] LOSS ASSESSOR → LOSS ADJUSTER

4 (*Law*) an expert in a particular subject who is asked by a court or other official group to give advice

★ **asset** /ˈæset/ *noun* [C, usually pl.]

SEE ALSO: **capital asset, chargeable ~, charge on ~, circulating ~, current ~, financial ~, fixed ~,** etc.

a thing of value that a person or a company owns, such as money or property or the right to receive payment of a debt: *The group has total assets of €1.2 billion.* ◇ *The vehicle is recorded as an asset in the company accounts.* ◇ *Foreign companies were prevented from buying local media assets* (= media businesses). ◇ (*figurative*) *Our staff are our most valuable asset.* → LIABILITY

🔾 **to have/hold/own/possess** assets • **to acquire/buy/ dispose of/increase/reduce/sell** assets • **to record/ show sth as** an asset • **to freeze/release/unfreeze** assets

'asset acˌcount *noun* [C]
(*Accounting*) a part of a company's financial records that shows the value of money, investments or other things which the company owns

ˌasset appreciˈation = CAPITAL APPRECIATION

'asset-ˌbacked *adjective*
(*Finance*) used to describe a type of investment that

---

a financial institution sells to investors. The company buys debts, such as car loans, and then sells investors the right to receive payments that the people who owe the money make: *asset-backed bonds/issue/debt* ◇ *the asset-backed securities market* → ABS

'asset ˌbacking *noun* [U]
(*Accounting*) a measure of the value of a company's assets, calculated by dividing the total value of its assets by the number of shares issued (= sold): *The company has strong asset backing, worth €3 per share.* [SYN] ASSET VALUE PER SHARE

'asset base *noun* [C]
(*Accounting; Finance*) the total value of the assets that a company has: *The business needs to widen its asset base.* ◇ *an asset base of $3.6 billion*

'asset ˌcoverage *noun* [U]
(*Accounting*) a measure of how easily a company can pay its debts, calculated by dividing the total value of the company's assets by its debts: *a company with limited net asset coverage*

'asset deˌflation *noun* [U]
(*Economics*) a fall in the value of assets, for example property, compared to the rate of economic growth: *Japan's two-year process of asset deflation* ◇ *the erosion of confidence created by asset deflation*

'asset inˌflation *noun* [U,C]
(*Economics*) a rise in the value of assets, for example property, compared to the rate of economic growth: *The international economy was kept going by an amazing asset inflation and a US consumer boom.*

'asset ˌmanagement *noun* [U]
(*Finance*)
1 the act of managing a company's financial assets in order to get the highest amount of profit from them: *a London-based asset management firm/ company* ◇ *Asset management revenue rose 3% to $368 million.*
2 a service offered by banks and some other financial institutions that gives advice to customers on investments
▶ **'asset ˌmanager** *noun* [C]: *a US investment bank and asset manager*

'asset mix = INVESTMENT MIX

'asset-ˌstripping *noun* [U]
(*Finance*) the practice of buying a company which is in financial difficulties at a low price and then selling everything that it owns in order to make a profit, without thinking about the future of the company: *The new chairman said he was not in the business of asset-stripping.* ▶ **'asset-ˌstripper** *noun* [C]

ˌassets under 'management *noun* [U] (*abbr* **AUM**)
(*Accounting*) the total value of the shares, cash, etc. that an investment company manages for its customers: *The fund has $30 billion of assets under management.*

ˌasset 'turnover *noun* [U,C] (*also* **ˌasset 'turnover ˌratio** [C, usually sing.])
(*Accounting*) the total amount of goods or services sold by a company compared to the value of its assets, used as a measure of how efficiently the company uses its assets: *A typical grocery store has an asset turnover of 2.5 to 3.*

'asset ˌvalue *noun* [C,U]

SEE ALSO: **net asset value**

(*Accounting*) the value of a company calculated by adding together the value of all its assets: *Most*

water companies are trading below their asset value.
▶ **'asset valu₁ation** *noun* [U]

'asset 'value per 'share *noun* [U]

SEE ALSO: net asset value per share

(*Accounting*) the total value of the assets that a company has, divided by the number of shares issued (= sold): *an increase in asset value per share* [SYN] ASSET BACKING

★ **assign** /əˈsaɪn/ *verb* [+ obj]
1 assign sth (to sb) | assign (sb) sth to give money, equipment, etc. to sth/sb for a particular purpose: *We have assigned 20% of our budget to the project.* ◇ *New employees are assigned a mentor.*
2 assign sth to sb | assign sb sth to give sb a particular job to do: *He's been assigned **the task of** creating an online magazine.*
3 (*often* be assigned) to send sb to work for a particular person or in a particular place: *I've been assigned **to** your team.*
4 to say that sth has a particular value or function: *You need to assign priority levels **to** different tasks.*
5 (*Law*) to officially arrange for your property or legal rights to belong to sb else: *The author assigns the copyright **to** the publisher.*

★ **assignment** /əˈsaɪnmənt/ *noun*
1 [C] a piece of work that sb is given to do, usually as part of their job: *The project started out as a fairly routine assignment.* ◇ *She has been given a tough assignment.*
○ to **accept/refuse/reject/take (on)/turn down** an assignment ◆ to **give sb** an assignment ◆ to **carry out/complete/work on/finish** an assignment
2 [U] the act of giving sb a particular task or sending them to work somewhere for a time: *He has requested assignment to other duties in the company.* ◇ *I was **on assignment** in Germany.*
3 (*Law*) [U,C] the act of officially arranging for your property or legal rights to belong to sb else: *an assignment of leasehold property*

as'signment clause *noun* [C]
(*Law*) a part of an insurance agreement or a contract that allows sb to pass their rights to sb else: *He transferred the policy to the bank under an assignment clause.*

as'signment work *noun* [U] (*AmE*)
(*HR*) work done by people who do not have a permanent contract with a company
[SYN] CONTINGENT WORK ▶ **as'signment ₁worker** *noun* [C]

★ **assist** /əˈsɪst/ *verb*
1 [+ obj or no obj] to help sb to do sth, especially by doing a share of the work: *You will be employed to assist the manager with his duties.* ◇ *The chairman of the committee is assisted by a technical director.*
2 [+ obj] (*often* be assisted) to help sth to happen more easily: *Development was assisted by government loans.*

★ **assistant** /əˈsɪstənt/ *noun, adjective* (*abbr* asst)
● *noun* [C]

SEE ALSO: administrative assistant, bank ~, executive ~, personal ~, sales ~, shop ~

1 a person who is below a senior person and helps them in their work: *the managing director and his assistant* ◇ *His first job in the company was as an assistant **to** the marketing director.*
2 (*BrE*) a person whose job is to serve customers in a shop/store: *The assistants price the items as they stack them on the shelves.* → SALES CLERK See note at CHAIRMAN
● *adjective* [only before noun] (*often used in titles*) having a rank below a senior person and helping them in their work, often doing the senior person's

work when they are not there: *the assistant manager* ◇ *the Assistant Director*

as₁sisted 'area *noun* [C]
in the UK, a region that receives financial support from the government in order to encourage new industries

assistive /əˈsɪstɪv/ *adjective*
providing help for people whose physical condition makes it difficult for them to use computers and other equipment: *assistive aids such as screen readers for people who are blind* ◇ *the development of **assistive-technology** products for disabled people*

assn. (*also spelled* **Assn.**) *abbr* (*especially AmE*) (*only used in written English*)
a short way of writing **association**: *a survey from the American Management Assn.*

Assoc. *abbr* (*plural* **Assoc.** *or* **Assocs.**) (*only used in written English*)
1 (used in titles) a short way of writing **Association**: *the Assoc. of British Travel Agents*
2 (used in names of companies, etc.) a short way of writing **Associate** or **Associates**: *L. Horton and Assocs.*

★ **associate** /əˈsəʊʃiət; -siət; AmE əˈsoʊ-/ *noun, adjective*
● *noun* [C]
1 a person that you work with or do business with; a business partner: *one of my **business** associates* ◇ *a senior associate*
2 Associates used in the name of an organization to show there are a number of professional partners: *Carver & Associates*
3 a member of an organization who does not have all the rights of ordinary members: *Some MBA students are summer associates at the company.*
● *adjective* [only before noun]
1 (often used in titles) having a similar job as sb else but of a lower rank: *New Zealand's associate finance minister*
2 used to describe a member of an organization who does not have all the rights of ordinary members: *associate membership of the European Union*

as₁sociate 'company (*also* as₁sociated 'company) *noun* [C]
a company of which more than 20% but less than 51% of the shares are held by another company

Associated /əˈsəʊʃieɪtɪd; -sieɪt-; AmE əˈsoʊ-/ *adjective*
used in the name of a business company that is made up of a number of smaller companies: *Associated Newspapers*

as₁sociated 'company = ASSOCIATE COMPANY

★ **association** /əˌsəʊʃiˈeɪʃn; -siˈeɪ-; AmE əˌsoʊ-/ *noun*

SEE ALSO: articles of association, brand ~, building and loan ~, freedom of ~, industry ~, memorandum of ~, savings and loan ~, etc.

1 [C with sing./pl.verb] (*abbr* Assoc.) a group of people or organizations who have joined together for a particular purpose: *Do you belong to any professional associations?* ◇ *the National Association of Pension Funds* ◇ *AIRMIC, an association that represents corporate buyers of insurance* [HELP] You will find the names of particular associations at their initials. For example, you will find the 'Association for Payment Clearing Services' at APACS. [SYN] SOCIETY
○ *a business/consumer/employers'/professional/ staff* association
2 [C,U] the act of joining or working with another person, company or group: *She has had a long and productive association **with** the firm.* ◇ *We work **in** association with our New York office.*

asst *(also spelled **Asst**) abbr*
a short way of writing **assistant**: *sales asst wanted* ◇
asst managers

assume /ə'sjuːm; *AmE* ə'suːm/ *verb* [+ obj *or* no obj]
1 to think or accept that sth is true but without
having proof of it: *It is reasonable to assume (that)
sales will improve.* ◇ *These fuels are assumed to be
non-polluting.* ◇ *Our forecasts assume an average oil
price of $55 a barrel.*
2 to take or begin to have power or responsibility:
She will assume the role of chairperson on July 1. ◇
*Under the deal, RT Group assumes full control of
Ultramast.*

as,sumed 'debt *noun* [C,U] *(also* **as,sumed
lia'bilities** [pl.])
(Accounting) the debts that a company has that
another company agrees to be responsible for
paying when it buys the first company: *They bought
the business for $2.9 bn in cash and $2.3 bn in
assumed debt.*

assurance /ə'ʃɔːrəns; -'ʃʊər-; *AmE* ə'ʃʊr-/ *noun* [U]
(BrE)

SEE ALSO: **life assurance, quality ~, term ~**

(Insurance) a type of insurance in which an amount
of money is always paid out, for example when sb
dies or after a fixed period of time: *the business
assurance division* ◇ *an assurance policy*
→ INSURANCE See note at INSURANCE

assure /ə'ʃɔː(r); -'ʃʊə(r); *AmE* ə'ʃʊr/ *verb* [+ obj]
(BrE)
(Insurance) (usually be assured*)*
to insure sb/sth, so that money will be paid out, for
example when sb dies or after a fixed period of
time: *You can assure your life for 10, 15 or 20 years.* ◇
*We will pay your dependants double the original sum
assured.* → ASSURED (2)

assured /ə'ʃɔːd; -'ʃʊəd; *AmE* -'ʃʊrd/ *adjective*
1 certain to happen or to be available: *assured coal
supplies* ◇ *The quality of the product range is assured.*
☉ *assured* **income/market/profit/supply**
2 *(Insurance)* **the assured** *noun* [C] *(plural* **the
assured**) *(BrE)* the person who is insured in a
contract with an insurance company: *A tax-free sum
is guaranteed if the* **life assured** *dies within the
specified period.* SYN INSURED → ASSURE

assurer /ə'ʃɔːrə(r); -'ʃʊər-; *AmE* ə'ʃʊr-/ *noun* [C]
(BrE)
(Insurance) a person or company that provides
people with ASSURANCE: *Prudential, the* **life** *assurer*

,at 'best *adverb*
(Stock Exchange) **sell/buy sth at best** to sell or buy
shares at the best possible price

,at 'call *adverb*
(Finance) used to describe money that has been lent
but must be paid back immediately if the person
who lent the money asks for it back: *The sum will be
lent at call.*

,at-'home *adjective* [only before noun]
1 used to describe people who work at home or
parents who do not work outside their home: *At-
home employees may lack the proper space or
equipment.*
2 happening in the home rather than from outside: *at-
home training*

ATM /ˌeɪ tiː 'em/ *noun* [C]
automated teller machine a machine in or
outside a bank, etc., from which you can get money
from your bank account using a special plastic card:
Where's the nearest ATM? ◇ *to withdraw money from
an ATM* ◇ *an ATM card* SYN CASH MACHINE

,at-risk 'pay *(also* **,at-risk compen'sation**, *less
frequent) noun* [U] *(also* **,at-risk 'salary** [C])
(HR) a percentage of the pay of some employees

that is linked to how well they are doing or how
successful their company is. It can go up or down:
*The 20% at-risk salary component aims to provide
an incentive to perform well.* → BONUS,
PERFORMANCE-RELATED PAY

at 'sight *adverb*
(Finance) written on a BILL OF EXCHANGE to show
that the bill should be paid immediately: *We only
accept payment at sight.* → AFTER SIGHT

★**attach** /ə'tætʃ/ *verb*
1 [+ obj] to fasten or join one thing to another: *an
alarm that can be attached* **to** *laptops* ◇ *(figurative)
They have attached a number of conditions to the
agreement.* → DETACH
2 [+ obj *or* no obj] to connect computer
equipment together: *You can log in from any
computer attached to the network.* SYN CONNECT
3 [+ obj] to send a document to sb using email:
*I attach the full conference timetable for your
information.* → ENCLOSE
4 [+ obj *or* no obj] to be connected with sb/sth: *to
connect sth to sth: No one is suggesting that any
health risks attach to this product.* ◇ *She will be
attached to this department for two months.*

★**attachment** /ə'tætʃmənt/ *noun*
1 *(IT)* [C] a document that you send to sb using
email: *The document can be sent as an email
attachment.*
2 *(Law)* [U] an order by a court for money or
property to be taken from sb who owes money in
order to pay their debt: *When an* **attachment** *of
earnings order is made by the court, the money is
deducted from the debtor's pay.*
3 [C,U] the act of joining one thing to another; a
thing that joins one thing to another: *attachment
points for seatbelts* ◇ *(figurative) the attachment of
new conditions to the contract*
4 [C] an object or a device that you can fix onto a
machine to make it do a particular job: *a video
attachment for a microscope*
5 *(HR)* [C,U] a short period of time when sb is
connected to a particular company, department,
etc: *Most students on the course have a 'Week in
Industry' attachment.*

★**attend** /ə'tend/ *verb* [+ obj *or* no obj]
to go to an event: *The meeting was attended by 90%
of shareholders.* ◇ *All members of staff are invited to
attend.*
PHR V **at'tend to sb/sth** to deal with sb/sth; to
take care of sb/sth: *I have some urgent business to
attend to.*

attendance /ə'tendəns/ *noun*

SEE ALSO: **certificate of attendance**

1 [U,C] the act of being present at a place or an
event: *All staff are invited to the talk but attendance
is voluntary.*
2 [C,U] the number of people present at an
organized event: *falling attendances at conferences*

at'tendance ,bonus *noun* [C]
(HR) extra pay that some companies give their
workers for coming to work regularly

at'tendance ,record *noun* [C]
a record of how often sb has been present at a
place, especially work or school: *His attendance
record showed that he had missed six weeks through
illness.*

attendee /ˌə,ten'diː/ *noun* [C]
a person who is present at an organized event:
Attached is a list of attendees at the conference.

★ **attention** /əˈtenʃn/ *noun* [U] (*only used in written English*) (*also* **atˈtention of, fao**)

SEE ALSO: selective attention

written on a business letter to show who it is intended for: *I would be grateful if you could invoice the amount due **for the attention of** Emma Walton at the above address.* → ATTN

attest /əˈtest/ *verb*
1 (*Law*) [+ obj] to state that you believe that sth is true or genuine, for example in a court: *to attest a will* ◇ *The signature was attested by two witnesses.*
2 (*formal*) [+ obj *or no obj*] **attest (to) sth** to show, prove or give evidence that sth is true: *They have a large client list of users who will attest to the effectiveness of their products.*
▶ **attestation** /ˌætesˈteɪʃn/ *noun* [C,U] **attestor** /əˈtestə(r)/ *noun* [C]

atˌtested ˈcopy = CERTIFIED COPY

attitude /ˈætɪtjuːd; *AmE* ˈætɪtuːd/ *noun* [C,U]
the way that sb thinks and feels about sb/sth, and behaves towards sb/sth: *Industry has been affected by the public's changing attitude **to** environmental issues.* ◇ *Above all, candidates must show the right attitude for the job.*

ˈattitude reˌsearch *noun* [U]
(*Marketing*) an investigation into how people think and feel towards an organization or its products: *They **conducted** public attitude research for a major oil company to measure the likely response to a new industrial development.*

attn *abbr* (*only used in written English*)
a short way of writing **attention** on a business letter to show who it is intended for: *Fax 7028674 (attn Tony Kale)*

attorney /əˈtɜːniː; *AmE* əˈtɜːrni/ *noun* [C]

SEE ALSO: district attorney, letter of ~, power of ~

(*Law*)
1 (*especially AmE*) a lawyer, especially one who can act for sb in a court See note at PROFESSION
2 a person who is given the power to act on behalf of another in business or legal matters

atˌtorney-at-ˈlaw *noun* [C] (*plural* **attorneys-at-law**) (*AmE*)
(*Law*) a lawyer who is qualified to represent sb in a court: *Michael C. Potter, Attorney-at-Law*

atˌtorney ˈgeneral *noun* [C] (*plural* **attorneys general** *or, less often,* **attorney generals**)
(*Law*)
1 the most senior legal officer in some countries or states, who also advises the government on legal matters
2 the Attorney General the head of the US Department of Justice and a member of the group of senior politicians who advise the President

★ **attract** /əˈtrækt/ *verb* [+ obj]
1 to make sb/sth go somewhere or become involved in sth: *The exhibition attracted more than 10 000 visitors.* ◇ *The company has found it difficult to **attract and keep** talent (= good staff).* ◇ *What attracted you **to** information technology?*
2 to make sb interested in a product or a business and want to spend money on it: *We are struggling to attract new customers.* ◇ *The company has attracted $10 million in investment.*
3 (*only used in written English*) (*BrE*) to be linked with sth, such as a particular rate of interest or tax, or a punishment: *Large loans usually attract a lower interest rate than small loans.*

attraction /əˈtrækʃn/ *noun* [C]

SEE ALSO: tourist attraction

an interesting or enjoyable place to go or thing to do: *The **main** attraction at Giverny is Monet's garden.*

attributable /əˈtrɪbjətəbl/ *adjective* [not before noun]
caused or explained by the thing mentioned: *The success of the business is **directly** attributable **to** our marketing strategy.*

atˌtributable ˈprofit *noun* [U,C]
(*Accounting*) (in a company's accounts) part of the profit from a contract that lasts for a long period of time, for example for building work, that is related to the amount of work that has been completed at the date of the accounts. It is part of the estimated total profit from the project after estimated costs have been taken away.

attribute *noun, verb*
● *noun* [C] /ˈætrɪbjuːt/
1 a quality that sb has: *Enthusiasm and flexibility are essential attributes for the job.*
2 a feature of a product that a customer thinks is important when deciding whether or not to buy it: *Consumers often consider quality to be the most important attribute when choosing a product.* ◇ *Price is only one of many **product attributes** that affect sales.*
● *verb* /əˈtrɪbjuːt/ [+ obj] (*often* **be attributed**)
to say or believe that sth is the result of a particular thing: *The sales boom is attributed **to** low unemployment.*

attrition /əˈtrɪʃn/ *noun* [U]
1 (*HR*) the process of reducing the number of people who are employed by an organization by not replacing people who leave their jobs: *We will lose 150 jobs through attrition and retirement over the next six months.* [SYN] NATURAL WASTAGE → LAY-OFF
2 (*Marketing*) the loss of customers, especially when they start buying another company's products: *The health club is trying to lower the rate of customer attrition.*

at ˈwarehouse *adjective, adverb*
(*Trade*) used to describe goods that can be delivered immediately, with the buyer paying a price for delivery that includes loading the goods onto road or rail transport: *All prices given are at warehouse.* ◇ *an at-warehouse price* → EX WAREHOUSE

★ **auction** /ˈɔːkʃn; ˈɒk-; *AmE* ˈɔːk-/ *noun, verb*
(*Commerce*)
● *noun* [C,U]

SEE ALSO: absolute auction, Dutch ~, reverse ~, uniform price ~

a public event at which things are sold to the person who offers the most money for them: *The stores will be **put up for** auction by the parent company.* ◇ *The painting was sold **at auction** for $50 000.* ◇ *to bid **in** an auction* → idiom at PUT *verb*
❍ *to be up for/come up for/go up for/put sth up for auction*
● *verb* [+ obj]
to sell sth at an **auction**: *The rights to use these routes were auctioned to bus companies.*
[PHRV] **ˌauction sth ˈoff** to sell sth at an **auction**, especially sth that is no longer needed or wanted: *Employees were made redundant and buildings and vehicles auctioned off.*

auctioneer /ˌɔːkʃəˈnɪə(r); ˌɒk-; *AmE* ˌɔːkʃəˈnɪr/ *noun* [C]
a person whose job is to direct an AUCTION and sell the goods

audience /ˈɔːdiəns/ noun [C]

SEE ALSO: cumulative audience, secondary ~, target ~

a number of people or a particular group of people who watch, read or listen to the same thing: *Many regard TV advertising as the best way of reaching mass audiences.* ◇ *The magazine will target a core audience of 14-year-old girls.* ◇ *The drama had a 29% audience share between 9 and 10.30 p.m.*
○ *a declining/large/mass/small/wide audience* ◆ *a female/male/young audience* ◆ *sth has/is aimed at/ reaches/targets an audience*

ˌaudience ˈflow noun [C, usually sing., U]
(*Marketing*)
1 the change in the number of people watching a television station before, during and after a particular programme: *Audience flow diagrams show where an audience went after watching a programme.*
2 the number of people who continue to watch the same television station after a particular programme has finished: *If a new show follows a very popular show, the new one will benefit from audience flow.*

ˌaudience reˈsearch noun [U]
(*Marketing*) research that is carried out on people who watch television or listen to the radio, in order to find out how popular particular shows, advertisements, etc. are and the kind of people who watch or listen to them: *Audience research showed the programme was very popular with children.*

audio- /ˈɔːdiəʊ; AmE ˈɔːdioʊ/ combining form
(in nouns, adjectives and adverbs) connected with hearing or sound: *audio-visual aids for the classroom*

ˌaudio ˈconferencing noun [U]
a system that allows people in different places to discuss something at the same time by telephone; the activity of doing this: *Benefits can be gained from audio conferencing.* ◇ *an audio conferencing facility* ▶ **ˌaudio ˈconference** noun [C]
→ TELECONFERENCING, VIDEOCONFERENCING

ˌaudio-ˈvisual (*AmE spelling* **audiovisual**)
adjective (*abbr* **AV**)
using both sound and pictures: *audio-visual technology*

★ audit /ˈɔːdɪt/ noun, verb
● **noun** [C,U]

SEE ALSO: continuous audit, green ~, internal ~, management ~, non-~, position ~, retail ~, etc.

1 (*Accounting*) an official examination of business and financial records to see that they are true and correct: *The company was in the middle of an annual audit.* ◇ *a tax audit* ◇ *fees paid to audit firms*
○ *an annual/a year-end audit* ◆ *an external/ independent audit* ◆ *to carry out/complete/ conduct an audit* ◆ *an audit committee/firm/group/ team*
2 an official examination of the quality or standard of sth: *The company paid a consultant to carry out an audit of its software.*
● **verb** [+ obj]
1 (*Accounting*) to officially examine the financial accounts of a company: *We have just had our accounts audited.* ◇ *audited accounts/financial statements* → UNAUDITED
2 to officially examine the quality or standard of sth: *Safety improvements need to be constantly tested and audited.*

ˈaudit ˌfailure noun [C,U]
(*Accounting*) the situation when an **audit** does not find a problem that exists in a business's financial

---

accounts: *Any fraud not uncovered will be considered an audit failure.*

★ auditor /ˈɔːdɪtə(r)/ noun [C]
a person who officially examines the business and financial records of a company to see that they are true and correct: *the firm of accountants that has been appointed auditors to the company* ◇ *The auditor said the mistakes were 'honest errors'.* See note at PROFESSION
○ *an external/independent/internal/outside auditor* ◆ *company auditors*

auditorium /ˌɔːdɪˈtɔːriəm/ noun [C] (*plural* **auditoriums** *or* **auditoria** /ˌɔːdɪˈtɔːriə/)
1 (*AmE*) a large building or room in which public meetings, concerts, etc. are held
2 the part of a theatre, concert hall, etc. in which the audience sits

ˈaudit reˌport noun [C]
(*Accounting*) a report written by an **auditor** for the members of a company after examining a company's financial records: *The company received a clean audit report for the year ended 31 March 2004.* ◇ *The auditors had only been able to prepare a qualified audit report* (= one that they cannot agree with completely) *due to lack of information.*

ˈaudit trail noun [C]
1 (*Accounting*) a series of documents and records that shows the history of a company's financial records. An AUDITOR can check these to see how true and correct the accounts are: *The company had destroyed large parts of the audit trail.*
2 (*IT*) a record kept by a computer of a series of events or actions

augˌmented ˈproduct noun [C, usually sing.]
(*Marketing*) a product that has extra features or services that make it more attractive than the typical product of its kind; the extra features and services that are provided: *Customer service is a valuable part of the augmented product.*

AUM /ˌeɪ juː ˈem/ = ASSETS UNDER MANAGEMENT

austerity /ɒˈsterəti; ɔːˈster-; AmE ɔːˈster-/ noun [U,C] (*plural* **austerities**)
a situation when people do not have much money to spend because there are bad economic conditions: *Protesters demanded better pay and a relaxation of austerity measures* (=official actions to reduce the amount of money that government or people spend).

authenticate /ɔːˈθentɪkeɪt/ verb [+ obj]
to prove that sth is genuine, real or true: *Digital codes are used to authenticate the user's identity.*
▶ **authentication** /ɔːˌθentɪˈkeɪʃn/ noun [U]: *The signature was sent to the solicitor for authentication.*

authenticity /ˌɔːθenˈtɪsəti/ noun [U]
the quality of being real and genuine: *The company uses holograms to guarantee the authenticity of its products.*

authoring /ˈɔːθərɪŋ/ noun [U]
(*IT*) creating MULTIMEDIA computer products with special software, without using programming language: *authoring packages/software/tools*

★ authority /ɔːˈθɒrəti; AmE əˈθɔːr-; əˈθɑːr-/ noun

SEE ALSO: Civil Aviation Authority, classification ~, Financial Services ~, line ~, Securities and Futures ~

1 [U] the official power to give orders to people, make decisions, etc: *in a position of authority* ◇ *Nothing will be done because no one in authority* (= who has a position of power) *takes the matter seriously.* ◇ *Only the manager has the authority to sign cheques.*

2 [U] official permission to do sth: *He was dismissed for signing documents without the authority of his manager.*
3 [U] the power to influence people because they respect your knowledge or official position: *As the author of six books on marketing, she speaks with authority on the subject.*
4 [C, usually pl.] the people or an organization who have the power to make decisions or who have a particular area of responsibility in a country or region: *The health authorities are investigating the problem.*
5 [C] a person with special knowledge: *She's an authority on trade law.*

★ **authorization**, **-isation** /ˌɔːθəraɪˈzeɪʃn; AmE ˌɔːθərəˈzeɪʃn/ *noun*
1 [U,C] official permission or power to do sth; the act of giving permission: *Who gave the authorization to release the data?* ◇ *He had acted without authorization.*
◊ *to* **give/grant/refuse** *(sb) authorization* ◆ *to* **ask for/ get/have/need/obtain/require** *authorization*
2 [C] a document that gives sb official permission to do sth

authori'zation code *noun* [C]
a secret set of numbers or letters that allows sb to do sth such as use a website, accept payment with a bank card, etc. → PASSWORD

★ **authorize**, **-ise** /ˈɔːθəraɪz/ *verb* [+ obj]
to give official permission for sth, or for sb to do sth: *I can authorize payments of up to $5 000.* ◇ *authorized dealers* → UNAUTHORIZED

ˌ**authorized 'capital** *(BrE also* ˌauthorized **'share** ˌcapital) *(also spelled* **authorised** ~) *noun* [U]
(Finance) the maximum amount of money that a company is allowed to raise by selling shares
SYN NOMINAL CAPITAL, REGISTERED CAPITAL
→ ISSUED CAPITAL

ˌ**authorized 'shares** *noun* [pl.] *(also* ˌauthorized **'stock** [U]) *(also spelled* **authorised** ~)
(Finance) the maximum number of shares that a company can offer for sale

auto /ˈɔːtəʊ; AmE ˈɔːtoʊ/ *noun* [C] *(plural* **autos)**
(AmE)
a car: *the auto industry*
◊ *auto* **companies/dealers/manufacturers/retailers/ workers** ◆ *auto* **production/sales**

auto- /ˈɔːtəʊ; AmE ˈɔːtoʊ/ *combining form*
1 by itself without a person to operate it: *automatic* ◇ *autopilot*
2 of or by yourself: *autonomous* ◇ *The project is auto-financing* (= it operates without borrowing money).

autocratic /ˌɔːtəˈkrætɪk/ *adjective*
expecting to be obeyed and not caring about the feelings and opinions of others: *an autocratic management style*

automaker /ˈɔːtəʊmeɪkə(r); AmE ˈɔːtoʊ-/ *noun* [C]
(AmE)
a company that makes cars

★ **automate** /ˈɔːtəmeɪt/ *verb* [+ obj] *(usually be automated)*
to use machines and computers instead of people to do a job or task: *The entire manufacturing process has been automated.* ◇ *The factory is now **fully** automated.* ◇ *an automated production line*
SYN MECHANIZE

automatic /ˌɔːtəˈmætɪk/ *adjective*
1 (about a machine, device, etc.) having controls that work without needing a person to operate them: *automatic doors* ◇ *an automatic gearbox/ transmission* (= in a car, etc.)

2 always happening as a result of a particular action or situation: *There is an automatic fine for late payment.* ◇ *A further drop in the share price would trigger automatic sell orders.*
▶ **automatically** /ˌɔːtəˈmætɪkli/ *adverb:* *The system automatically deletes any viruses attached to emails.*

ˌ**automatic 'pilot** *(also* **'autopilot)** *noun* [U]
a device in an aircraft or a ship that keeps it on a fixed course without the need for a person to control it: *The aircraft was set on automatic pilot.*
IDM **be on** ˌautomatic **'pilot** to do sth without thinking because you have done the same thing many times before: *For the first hour at work I'm on automatic pilot.*

automation /ˌɔːtəˈmeɪʃn/ *noun* [U]
the use of machines to do work that was previously done by people: *Automation using programmable machine tools meant the loss of many factory jobs.* ◇ *office automation* (= the use of computers in the office)

automobile /ˈɔːtəməbiːl/ *noun* [C] *(especially AmE)*
a car: *The organization set the standard for the production of automobiles.*
◊ *the automobile* **business/industry** ◆ *automobile* **manufacturers/workers**

automotive /ˌɔːtəˈməʊtɪv; AmE -ˈmoʊ-/ *adjective*
[only before noun] *(usually used in written English)*
connected with motor vehicles
◊ *the automotive* **industry** ◆ *automotive* **products/ sales**

ˌ**automotive engi'neer** *noun* [C]
a person whose job is to design, develop and test cars and other motor vehicles

autonomous /ɔːˈtɒnəməs; AmE ɔːˈtɑːn-/ *adjective*
1 (about a country, a region or an organization) able to govern itself or control its own affairs: *The company's hotels are run as autonomous units.* ◇ *an autonomous region of Spain*
2 (about a person or a group of people) able to do things and make decisions without help from anyone else: *autonomous team working*
SYN INDEPENDENT
▶ **au'tonomously** *adverb:* *Each bank acts autonomously.*

auˌtonomous in'vestment *noun* [U]
1 *(Economics)* an increase in the level of investment for reasons other than a high interest rate
2 *(Finance)* investment that a company or an organization makes for reasons other than to increase production

'auto parts *(also spelled* **autoparts** /ˈɔːtəʊpɑːts; AmE ˈɔːtoʊpɑːrts/) *noun* [pl.]
the pieces used to make cars: *the auto parts industry*

autopilot /ˈɔːtəʊpaɪlət; AmE ˈɔːtoʊ-/ = AUTOMATIC PILOT

AV /ˌeɪ ˈviː/ = AUDIO-VISUAL

av *abbr* (only used in written English)
average: *av number of pages*

available /əˈveɪləbl/ *adjective*
1 (about things) that you can get, buy or use: *The shoe is now available in sports stores around the country.* ◇ *The new service will be available to customers next month.*
◊ **freely/generally/readily/widely** *available* ◆ *available* **facilities/resources/supplies**
2 (about a person) free to see or talk to: *Will she be available this afternoon?* ◇ *The director was not available for comment.*
▶ aˌvaila'bility *noun* [U]: *the availability of cheap flights* ◇ *This offer is subject to availability.*

★ **average** /'ævərɪdʒ/ *adjective, noun, verb*
● *adjective*
1 calculated by adding several amounts together and dividing the total by the number of amounts: *Average earnings are around €35 000 per annum.* ◇ *households with a **below-average** income*
2 typical or normal: *Forty hours is a fairly average working week for most people.* ◇ *We can expect **above-average** financial returns.*
● *noun* [C,U]

SEE ALSO: **moving average, weighted average**

1 the result of adding several amounts together and dividing the total by the number of amounts: *The average of 4, 5 and 9 is 6.* ◇ *Food prices have risen by **an average of** about 5%.*
2 a level which is usual: *Employees' pay is above average for the industry.* ◇ *On average, wages have gone up 2%.*
3 (*Insurance*) = PARTIAL LOSS

WHICH WORD?

mean/median/mode

These words are used to describe different types of **averages**. Consider the following series of numbers:

4   4   4   5   6   6   7

The **mean** (also called the **arithmetic mean**) is calculated by adding all the numbers together and dividing by how many numbers there are: $(4+4+4+5+6+6+7)/7 = 5.14$

The **median** can only be found if the numbers are arranged in order of size. It is the number in the middle of the series: 5

The **mode** is the most common number: 4

● *verb*
1 [+ obj] (*not used in the passive*) to be equal to a particular amount as an average: *Economic growth is expected to average 2% next year.*
2 [+ obj *or* no obj] to calculate the average of sth: *Earnings are averaged over the whole period.*
PHR V ,average 'out to result in an average or equal amount over a period of time or after several occasions: *The costs of translation should average out at about €20 per page.* ,average sth 'out (at sth) to calculate the average of sth: *If you average out the seasonal earnings of a tourist guide, they are similar to those of an office worker.* ,average 'out at sth to have a particular amount as the average over a period of time: *Sales growth has averaged out at 20% over the last three years.*

'average ad,juster *noun* [C]
(*Insurance*) a person whose job is to calculate how much the insurance companies should pay when a ship or its cargo has been lost or damaged, especially when the payment is shared between several companies

,average 'audience ,rating *noun* [C] (*abbr* **AA rating**)
(*Marketing*) especially in the US, the percentage of homes that were watching or listening to a particular programme on television or radio during an average minute of the programme: *The average audience rating for the show was only 6%.*

,average 'earnings *noun* [pl.]
(*Economics*) in a particular economy, the total amount of money that people earn for work divided by the number of people who are working

,average 'earnings ,index *noun* [sing.] (*abbr* **AEI**)
(*Economics*) an official measurement in the UK that shows the increase in the average amount of money earned by a worker in a year, sometimes

within a particular industry: *The Average Earnings Index (AEI) is Great Britain's key indicator of how fast earnings are growing.* ◇ *the average earnings index for the services sector*

,average 'revenue *noun* [C]
(*Accounting*) the total money received from the sale of goods divided by the number of items sold: *a decrease/an increase in the average revenue per customer*

,average 'stock *noun* [U]
(*Accounting*) a method of calculating the average value of goods held during a particular period by adding the total value of goods held at the beginning and at the end of the period and dividing by two

aviation /,eɪvi'eɪʃn/ *noun* [U]

SEE ALSO: **civil aviation**

the designing, building and flying of aircraft: *the crisis in the aviation and travel industry*
O *the aviation **industry/sector** • **civil/commercial/ world** aviation*

avionics /,eɪvi'ɒnɪks; *AmE* -'ɑːn-/ *noun*
1 [U] the science of electronics when used in designing and making aircraft
2 [pl.] the electronic devices in an aircraft, etc.

avoid /ə'vɔɪd/ *verb* [+ obj]
1 to prevent sth bad from happening: *They are looking for funds to avoid the company going bankrupt.* ◇ *The name was changed to **avoid** confusion with another firm.*
2 to try not to do sth; to keep away from sb/sth: *The insurance company tried everything to avoid paying the claim.*

avoidance /ə'vɔɪdəns/ *noun* [U]

SEE ALSO: **tax avoidance**

not doing sth; preventing sth from existing or happening: *to remove opportunities for the avoidance of tax* ◇ *risk avoidance*

★ **award** /ə'wɔːd; *AmE* ə'wɔːrd/ *noun, verb*
● *noun* [C]
1 (*HR*) a decision about an increase in the amount of money sb earns: *The union is unhappy with this year's pay award.*
2 (*HR*) in some countries, a written document that gives details of the conditions of employment in a company or an industry that are stated in law: *Staff work under a number of awards and agreements that specify employment conditions.*
3 (*HR*) = AWARD WAGE
4 (*Law*) the amount of money that a court decides should be given to sb who has won a case; the decision to give this money: *The appeal court upheld the €100 000 damages award against the company.*
5 (often in names of particular awards) a prize such as money, etc. for sth that sb has done
● *verb* [+ obj]
award (sb) sth | award sth (to sb) to make an official decision to give sth to sb as a payment, prize, etc: *The firm has been awarded a five-year contract to supply parts to a leading manufacturer.* ◇ *The jury awarded $30 million in damages against the newspaper.*

a'ward wage (*also* a'ward) *noun* [C]
(*HR*) in some countries, the amount of money that an employer must pay by law for a particular kind of work: *increases in the award wage* ◇ *Some people with disabilities do not earn full award wages.*
→ MINIMUM WAGE

a'ward-,winning *adjective*
having won a prize: *an award-winning design*

awareness /ə'weənəs; AmE ə'wer-/ noun [U; sing.]

SEE ALSO: **brand awareness, consumer ~, product ~**

knowing sth; knowing that sth exists and is important: *What all companies are looking for is an awareness of the brand and what it stands for.* ◇ *consumers' growing awareness of Internet shopping* ● **growing/increasing** awareness • **high/low** awareness • *to* **build/heighten/increase/raise** awareness

axe (*AmE spelling also* **ax**) /æks/ noun, verb (*informal*)
● **noun** [sing.] **the axe** used especially in newspapers to describe strong measures that are taken to reduce costs, such as removing workers from their jobs, closing parts of a company, etc: *Up to 300 workers are* **facing** *the axe at the struggling company.* ◇ *The company has not announced which of its factories will* **get** *the axe.*
● **verb** [+ obj]
to take strong measures to reduce costs, such as removing workers from their jobs, closing parts of a company, etc: *Other less profitable services are to be axed later this year.*

axis /'æksɪs/ noun [C] (*plural* **axes** /'æksiːz/)
a fixed line against which the positions of points are measured, especially points on a graph: *The horizontal axis measures the level of unemployment.* ● *the* **horizontal/vertical** axis • *the axis is/measures/ shows...*

B b

B2B (*also spelled* **b2b, B-to-B**) /ˌbiː tə 'biː/ adjective [only before noun]
(*E-commerce*) **business-to-business** used to describe the buying, selling and exchanging over the Internet of products, services or information between companies, rather than between companies and consumers: *B2B solutions for e-commerce* ◇ *business-to-business advertising* **NOTE** It can also be used as a noun: *Business to business accounts for 75% of all Internet revenue.* → B2C, B2E

B2'B ex,change noun [C] (*abbr* **B2X, B2BX**)
(*E-commerce*) a network or website on the Internet that allows businesses to buy and sell goods and services directly between each other

B2BX /ˌbiː tə biː 'eks/ = B2B EXCHANGE

B2C (*also spelled* **b2c, B-to-C**) /ˌbiː tə 'siː/ adjective [only before noun]
(*E-commerce*) **business-to-consumer, business-to-customer** used to describe the selling of products, services or information to consumers over the Internet: *B2C e-commerce* ◇ *business-to-consumer transactions* **NOTE** It can also be used as a noun: *B2C has been a big disappointment so far.* → B2B, B2E

B2E (*also spelled* **b2e, B-to-E**) /ˌbiː tu 'iː/ adjective [only before noun]
1 (*IT*) **business-to-employee** used about a website that all employees of a company use to enter the Internet, and which brings together all the information they need to do their job whether in the office or away from it → INTRANET
2 (*HR*) **business-to-employee** used to describe ways in which some companies try to help employees feel happy in their job and to develop their skills and education, so that the company will attract and keep good staff
3 (*E-commerce*) **business-to-employer** used to describe the selling over the Internet of products or services that help companies provide sth for employees or find new employees → B2B, B2C

B2X /ˌbiː tu 'eks/ = B2B EXCHANGE

B&B (*also spelled* **B and B, b and b**) /ˌbiː ən 'biː/ = BED AND BREAKFAST

'baby boom noun [C]
a time when the population of a country increases rapidly, especially used to refer to a time in the UK and the US between 1948 and 1964

'baby ,boomer noun [C]
a person born during a **baby boom**, especially between 1948 and 1964 in the UK or the US: *Their traditional customers are ageing baby boomers.*

'babysitting ,service noun [C]
a service provided by a hotel in which sb takes care of your children while you go out

back /bæk/ adjective, adverb, verb
● **adjective** [only before noun]

SEE ALSO: **buy-back, dial-~, write-~**

1 owed for a time in the past: *The company owed $2 million dollars in back taxes.*
● *back* **pay/rent/taxes**
2 of or from a past time: *back issues of a magazine*
IDM **on the back 'burner** (*informal*) (about an idea, a plan, etc.) left for the present time, to be done or considered later → idiom at FRONT adj.
take a back 'seat (to sth) 1 to be given less importance than sth else: *Safety has taken a back seat to the need for cost reduction.* **2** to let other people play a more active and important role in a particular situation than you do: *Mr Clark has decided to take a back seat and be a non-executive director.* → idiom at QUEUE noun
● **adverb**
in return or reply: *Could you call back later, please?* ◇ *I emailed them back to confirm the booking.* ◇ *I can't give you an answer now. Can I get back to you on that?*
● *to* **call/email/report/write** back (to sb) • *to* **fight/hit** back
IDM **(go/get) back to 'basics** to think about the simple or most important ideas within a subject or an activity instead of new ideas or complicated details: *The future of marketing is about getting back to basics.* ◇ *a back-to-basics approach* → idiom at CLAW
● **verb** [+ obj]
to give support or help to sb/sth: *Leading businesses have backed plans to reduce VAT.* ◇ *union-backed candidates* See note at FINANCE
PHRV **,back 'out (of sth)** to decide that you are no longer going to take part in sth that has been agreed: *The company is still for sale after a prospective buyer backed out of the deal.* **,back sth 'up 1** (*IT*) to prepare a second copy of a file, program, etc. that can be used if the main one fails or needs extra support: *I back up all my files on CD-ROM once a week.* → BACKUP **2** to provide support for sb/sth: *The sales manager is backed up by an experienced team of reps.* → BACKER

backbone /'bækbəʊn; AmE -boʊn/ noun [C]
1 the most important part of a system, an organization, etc: *Small and medium-sized businesses are the backbone of the economy.*

2 (*IT*) the system of connections that carries information long distances over the Internet: *The high-speed **Internet backbone** has to deal with more and more traffic every day.*

ˌback 'catalogue (*also* 'catalogue) (*AmE spelling also* **catalog**) *noun* [C, usually sing.]
the designs, films/movies or music that a company has produced or bought in the past and that it can still produce. *A **back catalogue** can be sold to make money.*

backdate /ˌbæk'deɪt/ *verb* [+ obj]
1 to write an earlier date on a cheque or other document than the date at the time of writing
2 (*BrE*) (*usually* **be backdated**) to make sth, especially a payment, take effect from an earlier date: *Postal workers are getting a 5% pay rise, backdated to March.*
[OPP] POST-DATE

'back end *noun, adjective*
● *noun* [C]
1 the part of a business that does not meet and deal directly with customers: *They outsource much of the back end of their business.*
2 the end of a project, a process, an investment, a period of time, etc: *Your bank may add extra payments on the back end of a loan.* ◇ *Sales have improved since the back end of last year.*
3 (*IT*) the part of a computer system that processes data → SERVER
● *adjective* [only before noun]
1 connected with the end of a project, a process, an investment, a period of time, etc: *back-end royalties* ◇ *back-end charges*
2 (*IT*) used to describe a program or part of a computer system that is not seen or used by the user, especially in e-commerce: *a back-end database* → FRONT END

ˌback-end 'load (*especially AmE*) (*BrE usually* 'exit charge) *noun* [C]
(*Finance*) the fee an investor pays when they sell their shares in an investment fund, which is taken from the final payment they receive → FRONT-END LOAD ▶ˌback-end 'loaded *adjective*

ˌback-end 'loading *noun* [U]
(*Finance; Insurance*) an arrangement in which higher amounts are paid at the end of a financial agreement, such as a loan, than at the beginning → BACKLOAD

backer /'bækə(r)/ *noun* [C]
(*Finance*) a person or company that gives support to sth/sb, especially financial support: *The company is searching for **financial** backers.* See note at FINANCE
● *a corporate/key/financial backer*

background /'bækɡraʊnd/ *noun* [C]
1 the details of a person's experience, education, family, etc: *The job would suit somebody with a publishing background.*
2 the circumstances or past events which help explain why sth is how it is; information about these: *Gather plenty of background information on the company before your interview.*
3 (*IT*) the part of a computer where a program can continue to operate while the user is working with another program: *programs running **in the background***

backhander /'bækhændə(r)/ *noun* [C]
a secret and illegal payment made to sb in exchange for a favour: *He was found to be **taking** backhanders from suppliers.* [SYN] BRIBE

backhaul /'bækhɔːl/ *noun* [C]
(*Transport*) the return journey of a vehicle that transports goods after it has delivered its load: *backhaul loads/prices*

backing /'bækɪŋ/ *noun* [U]
help; support: *The merger deal has **the full backing** of the board.* ◇ *They have won financial backing from the EU.* → ASSET BACKING See note at FINANCE
● *to **get/have/receive/win** backing* ● *financial/legal/political* backing

backload /'bækləʊd; *AmE* -loʊd/ *verb, noun*
● *verb* [+ obj *or no obj*]
1 (*Finance*) to arrange for higher amounts to be paid at the end of a financial agreement than at the beginning: *a backloaded insurance policy* → BACK-END LOADING
2 (*Transport*) to arrange for a vehicle to carry a load on its return journey after delivering sth
▶ 'backloading *noun* [U]
● *noun* [C]
(*Transport*) a load that a vehicle carries on its return journey after delivering sth: *The company arranges backloads for hauliers so that they can earn money in both directions.*

backlog /'bæklɒg; *AmE* -lɔːg; -lɑːg/ *noun* [C]
a quantity of work that should have been done already, but has not yet been done: *The insurance company is still working to clear the backlog of claims.* ◇ *A huge backlog of work had built up.*
● *to **clear/reduce** a backlog* ● *a backlog **builds up/develops/grows*** ● *a **huge/large/mounting** backlog*

ˌback 'office *noun* [C]
the part of a company which does not deal directly with the public: *He runs the airline's back office.* ◇ *500 back-office and administrative jobs will be lost.* → FRONT OFFICE

'back ˌorder *noun* [C]
(*Commerce; Production*) an order for goods that have not yet been produced or supplied: *It is our aim to **fill** back orders as soon as the merchandise is available.* ▶ ˌback 'order *verb* [+ obj *or no obj*]

ˌback 'room *noun* [C]
a place where secret, administrative or other important work is done: *deals made in back rooms* ◇ *back-room staff*

'back shift (*BrE*) (*AmE* 'swing shift) *noun* [C,U]
(*HR*) a period of work from the middle of the afternoon until late at night, between the day and the night periods; the group of people who work during this period: *to work (the) back shift*

backslash /'bækslæʃ/ *noun* [C]
a symbol (\) used in computer commands → FORWARD SLASH

backspace /'bækspeɪs/ *noun, verb*
● *noun* [C]
the key on a computer keyboard which you press to move back towards the beginning of the line of text and which removes the last letter that you typed; the act of using this key
● *verb* [no obj]
to use the **backspace** key on a keyboard

ˌback-to-back 'loan (*also* ˌparallel 'loan) *noun* [C]
(*Finance*) an arrangement where companies in different countries lend money to each other at the same time in different currencies, in order to avoid high interest rates, restrictions on changing currency, etc.

backup /'bækʌp/ *noun* [C]
1 (*IT*) a copy of a file, program, etc. that can be used if the original is lost or damaged: *Always make a backup of your work.* ◇ *a backup copy*
2 extra help, ideas, equipment, etc. that you can use if the first fails: *We have a **backup plan** if the merger falls through.*
→ BACK SB/STH UP at BACK *verb*

backwardation /ˌbækwəˈdeɪʃn; AmE -wərˈdeɪʃn/ noun [U] (*also* inˌverted ˈmarket [sing.])
(*Finance*) a situation where prices for goods that will be delivered in the future are lower than prices for goods that will be delivered immediately: *A shortage of supplies has caused a state of backwardation on the coffee futures market.*
→ CONTANGO

ˌbackward inteˈgration noun [U]
(*Economics*) a situation where a company buys a company which supplies it or begins to do the same work as that company → VERTICAL INTEGRATION, FORWARD INTEGRATION—Picture at INTEGRATION

backyard /ˌbækˈjɑːd; AmE -ˈjɑːrd/ noun
IDM in your (own) backˈyard in or near the place where you live or work: *Local residents didn't want the new factory in their own backyard.* → NIMBY

BACS /bæks/ abbr
Bankers' Automated Clearing System a company owned by the UK banks that uses an electronic system to make payments between accounts in member banks. It is often used by companies to pay their employees. → APACS

ˌbad ˈdebt noun [C,U]
(*Accounting*) a debt that will not be paid: *The company has **written off** over $500 million of bad debts.*

ˌbad ˈdebt reˌcovery noun [U]
1 (*Law*) legal action to force sb to pay a debt which should have been paid already: *bad debt recovery consultants*
2 (*Accounting*) payment of a debt which seemed unlikely to be paid

ˌbad ˈfaith noun [C,U]
an intention to deceive sb: *The judge decided that the garage owner had **acted in** bad faith.* → GOOD FAITH

ˌbad ˈloan noun [C]
(*Finance*) a loan that is not being paid back as arranged and may never be: *plans to use public funds to help banks dispose of their bad loans*

baggage /ˈbæɡɪdʒ/ noun [U]

SEE ALSO: **excess baggage, hand baggage**

bags, cases, etc. that you carry your clothes and things in when you are travelling: *excess baggage* (= weighing more than the limit allowed on a plane) SYN LUGGAGE

ˈbaggage reˌclaim (*BrE*) (*AmE* ˈbaggage claim) noun [U]
the place at an airport where you get your suitcases, etc. again after you have flown

ˈbaggage room = LEFT LUGGAGE

bail /beɪl/ noun, verb
●noun [U]
(*Law*) money that sb agrees to pay if a person accused of a crime does not appear at their trial. When **bail** has been arranged, the accused person is allowed to go free until the trial: *She was released **on bail**. ◇ The judge granted bail.*
○ to allow/deny/give/grant/refuse (sb) bail
●verb [+ obj]
(*Law*) to release sb on **bail**: *He was **bailed to appear** in court on 15 March.*
PHR V ˌbail ˈout (of sth) (*BrE spelling also* **bale out (of sth)**) (*also* bail, *especially in AmE informal*) (*Law*) to stop doing or taking part in sth because it is difficult or unpleasant: *When the companies merged, several key people decided to bail (out).* ˌbail sb ˈout to pay sb's **bail** for them ˌbail sb/sth ˈout (of sth) (*BrE spelling also* **bale sb/sth out (of sth)**) to rescue sb/sth from a difficult situation: *The government*

had to bail the company out of financial difficulty.
→ BAILOUT

bailiff /ˈbeɪlɪf/ noun [C]
(*Law*)
1 (*BrE*) a law officer whose job is to take the possessions and property of people who cannot pay their debts
2 (*AmE*) an official who keeps order in a court, takes people to their seats, watches prisoners, etc.

bailout /ˈbeɪlaʊt/ noun [C]
an act of giving money to a company, a foreign country, etc. that has very serious financial problems: *The airline's shareholders voted in favour of a government bailout. ◇ The country has received an international bailout package worth $48 billion.*
→ BAIL SB/STH OUT at BAIL verb

ˌbait-and-ˈswitch noun [C,U]
(*Marketing*) a selling method where advertisements for products with low prices are used to attract customers, who are then persuaded to buy something more expensive in the range: *Salespeople can pressure you with **bait-and-switch tactics** unless you know what to look out for.* **NOTE** This term is often used in a disapproving way, as the method can be illegal.

★ **balance** /ˈbæləns/ noun, verb
●noun

SEE ALSO: **adverse balance, adverse trade ~, bank ~, closing ~, compensating ~, competitive ~, credit ~,** etc.

1 [C, usually sing.] the difference in a bank account between the total amount of money coming in and the total amount going out at a particular time: *The company's cash balance increased to $4.5 billion this quarter. ◇ Enter your password to check your account balance online.* → BANK BALANCE
2 (*Accounting*) [C, usually sing.] in a company's financial records, the difference between the total DEBITS and total CREDITS in a particular account: *The balance on the profit and loss account at 31st March 2005 was $75 738. ◇ transferring a balance from a revenue or expense account to a profit and loss account*
3 [C, usually sing.] the amount of money still owed after sb has paid part of the total: *A 10% deposit is required, with the balance payable on completion of the work.*
4 [C] an amount of money that sb owes to the bank, etc. at a particular time, because they have bought things using a credit card: *The average consumer has an outstanding balance of $1 500 on his or her credit card. ◇ I try to pay off my monthly credit-card balance in full.*
5 [U] what remains of sth after part of it has been used or taken: *The balance of your order will be supplied when we have new stock.*
6 [U; sing.] a situation in which different things exist in equal, correct or good amounts: *Try to keep a balance **between** work **and** relaxation.*
IDM on ˈbalance after considering all the information: *On balance, we have had a good year.* → idioms at REDRESS verb, STRIKE verb
●verb
1 (*Accounting*) [+ obj] **balance sth (off)** in a company's financial records, to compare the total DEBITS and the total CREDITS in an account and calculate the amount needed to make them equal: *It only needs an hour or so a month to organize and balance **the accounts**. ◇ All the accounts should have been balanced off correctly.*
2 (*Accounting*) [no obj] if an account **balances**, the DEBIT and CREDIT sides are equal: *These figures don't balance. There must be a mistake somewhere.*
3 [+ obj] to spend only the money that is available; to make the money available equal to the amount of money spent: *The spending cuts are part of the government's plan to balance its **budget**. ◇ We have*

4 [+ obj *or* no obj] **balance (sth) (out)** to be equal in value, amount, etc. to sth else that has the opposite effect: *This year's profits will balance our previous losses.* ◇ *The advantages and disadvantages seem to balance out.*

5 [+ obj] **balance A against B** to compare the relative importance of two contrasting things: *The cost of bringing in consultants needs to be balanced against the benefits.*

,balance brought 'down (*abbr* balance b/d)
(*also* ,balance brought 'forward *abbr* balance b/f, balance b/fwd) *noun* [C]
(*Accounting*) the amount that you use to start an account for a new period, which is equal to the BALANCE (= the difference between the total DEBITS and the total CREDITS) at the end of the previous period → BALANCE CARRIED DOWN **NOTE** This is usually written as an abbreviation in accounts.

,balance carried 'down (*abbr* balance c/d)
(*also* ,balance carried 'forward *abbr* balance c/f, balance c/fwd) *noun* [C]
(*Accounting*) the BALANCE at the end of one accounting period that will then become the BALANCE BROUGHT DOWN for the beginning of the next period **NOTE** This is usually written as an abbreviation in accounts.

,balanced 'budget *noun* [C, usually sing.]
(*Economics*) a plan by a government to spend the same amount of money as it receives in a particular year

,balanced 'fund (*also* ,balanced 'mutual fund)
(*both especially AmE*) *noun* [C]
(*Finance*) a type of fund that invests its customers' money in a way that makes a good profit but does not involve a lot of risk, by investing in both shares and bonds

,balanced 'scorecard *noun* [C, usually sing.]
a method of measuring how well a company's plans are helping it to achieve its aims by looking at a variety of areas of activity including finance, how efficient it is, and relations with customers: *The balanced scorecard is a tool for turning strategy into action.*

,balance of 'payments *noun* [sing.]
(*Economics*) the difference between the amount of money one country pays to other countries, especially for imports, and the amount it receives, especially from exports; the official record of this over a particular period: *An increase in exports would help Britain's balance of payments.* ◇ *a balance of payments surplus* (= profit) ◇ *The country recorded a £9.5 billion balance of payments deficit* (= debt) *for the year.* See note at BALANCE OF TRADE

WHICH WORD?

balance of trade/balance of payments

A country's **balance of trade** includes imports and exports of *goods only*. Its **balance of payments** considers *all business* with other countries: imports and exports of goods, and money earned from or paid for services and investments, such as tourism or shares in companies.

,balance of 'trade (*also* 'trade ,balance, ,visible 'balance) *noun* [C, usually sing.]
(*Economics*) the difference in value between imports and exports of goods over a particular period: *If we sell more than we buy, we have a favourable balance of trade.* ◇ *a balance-of-trade deficit* (= when a

country spends more on imports than it earns from exports) **NOTE** The **balance of trade** is an important part of a country's BALANCE OF PAYMENTS. → VISIBLE TRADE

★'balance sheet *noun* [C]
(*Accounting*) a written statement that shows the financial state of a company at a particular time. It lists the company's assets and all money owed (**liabilities**): *At present, the airline has zero debt on its balance sheet.* ◇ *dependable companies with strong balance sheets* → OFF-BALANCE-SHEET
○ *a healthy/strong balance sheet* ◆ *to improve/strengthen* your balance sheet

the 'balance-sheet e,quation = THE ACCOUNTING EQUATION

bale /beɪl/ *noun, verb*
● *noun* [C]
a large amount of a light material pressed tightly together and tied up: *bales of hay/straw/cotton/wool* ◇ *cotton exports of 9.8 million bales*—Picture at TRANSPORT
● *verb* [+ obj]
to make sth into BALES: *The waste paper is baled, then sent for recycling.*
PHR V ,bale 'out (of sth); ,bale sb/sth 'out (of sth) (*BrE*) = BAIL OUT (OF STH), BAIL SB/STH OUT (OF STH)

balloon /bəˈluːn/ *noun* [C]
(*Finance*) used to describe a type of loan where the final payment is much larger than the rest: *The mortgage is payable in 83 monthly instalments of $720 and a balloon payment of $112 000 at the end of the seventh year.*
○ *a balloon loan/maturity/mortgage/payment*

ballot /ˈbælət/ *noun, verb*
● *noun*
1 [U,C] the system of voting in writing and usually in secret; an occasion on which a vote is held: *The union cannot call a strike unless it holds a ballot of members.*
○ *to have/hold a ballot* ◆ *a postal/secret/strike ballot*
2 (*also* 'ballot ,paper) [C] the piece of paper or card on which sb marks who or what they are voting for: *To be approved, 75% of policyholders need to cast their ballots in favour of the scheme.*
3 (*Finance*) [U,C] a fair way of choosing who to sell shares, bonds, etc. to, in situations where there are not enough new shares, bonds, etc. for everyone who wants to buy them
● *verb*
1 [+ obj] to ask sb to vote in writing and secretly about sth: *The union is balloting its members on strike action.*
2 [no obj] to vote secretly about sth: *The workers balloted for a strike.*

'ballpark /ˈbɔːlpɑːk; *AmE* -pɑːrk/ *noun*
IDM in the (right) 'ballpark (*informal*) (used about a price, an amount, etc.) approximately right or acceptable: *If you said five million you'd be in the right ballpark.* ◇ *A price tag of around $20 million is in the ballpark.* in the wrong/same 'ballpark (*informal*) (used about a price, an amount, etc.) wrong or almost the same: *The offers for the contract were all in the same ballpark.* a 'ballpark figure/estimate/price (*informal*) a number, an amount, etc. that is approximately correct: *How much will the project cost? Give me a ballpark figure.*

the ,Baltic Ex'change *noun* [sing.]
(*Trade*) an organization in London that arranges agreements for the transport of raw materials between countries, especially by ship **NOTE** The full name of the Baltic Exchange is the 'Baltic Mercantile and Shipping Exchange'.

★ **ban** /bæn/ *verb, noun*
● *verb* [+ obj] (**-nn-**)
 1 to officially say that sth is not allowed, often by law: *They decided to ban company-wide emails.* ◇ *The government has banned the import of all meat and dairy products for health reasons.*
 2 (*usually* **be banned**) to officially say that sb is not allowed to do sth or go somewhere: *She was banned from holding public office.*
● *noun* [C]
 an official rule that says that sth is not allowed: *a ban on overtime/on tobacco advertising* ◇ *Congress has been urged to impose a ban on all cloning research.*
 ❍ to **impose/lift** a ban

bancassurance /'bæŋkəʃɔːrəns; -ʃʊər-; *AmE* -əʃʊr-/ *noun* [U] (*BrE*)
 (*Finance*; *Insurance*) the combination of banking and insurance services that is offered by many major banks SYN ALLFINANZ ▶ **'bancassurer** *noun* [C]: *a well-known high street bancassurer*

bandwagon /'bændwægən/ *noun*
 IDM **climb/jump on the 'bandwagon** to become involved in an activity or idea which is becoming popular or fashionable in order to become popular or successful yourself: *This is another major publishing house to jump on the e-books bandwagon.*

bandwidth /'bændwɪdθ; -wɪtθ/ [U,C]
 (*IT*) a measurement of the amount of information that a particular computer network or Internet connection can send in a particular time: *We need greater bandwidth.* ◇ *The server has a permanent connection to the Internet with a bandwidth of 128 Kbps* (= kilobits per second). ◇ (*figurative*) *He doesn't have enough personal bandwidth* (= time; mental ability) *to manage the project.*

the Bank /bæŋk/ *noun* [sing.]
 the Bank of England → CENTRAL BANK

★ **bank** /bæŋk/ *noun, verb*
● *noun* [C]

SEE ALSO: **advising bank, agent ~, agricultural ~, banker's ~, cash at ~, central ~, clearing ~,** etc.

 1 an organization that provides various financial services to people and businesses, for example keeping or lending money; a local office or a particular **bank**: *The company has £13.5 million cash in the bank.* ◇ *I need to get some money out of the bank.* ◇ *My salary is paid directly into the bank.* ◇ *I need to go to the bank today.* ◇ *Full details are available from any branch of Barclays Bank.*
 ❍ a **domestic/foreign/global/international** bank ◆ a **big/high-street/large/major/small** bank
 2 *often* **Bank, the Bank of ...** = CENTRAL BANK
 3 an amount or a number of sth collected together; a place where sth is stored ready for use: *a bank of knowledge* ◇ *a bank of 12 TV screens* ◇ *names stored in the computer's memory bank* → DATABANK
 → idiom at BREAK *verb*
● *verb*
 1 [+ obj] to put money into a bank account: *Have you banked the cheque yet?*
 2 [no obj] **bank (with/at ...)** to have an account with a particular bank: *The company banks with Coutts and HSBC.*

bankable /'bæŋkəbl/ *adjective*
 1 (*informal*) likely to make money for sb/sth: *The company's name is its most bankable asset.*
 2 (*Finance*) acceptable to a bank: *bankable documents/checks*

★ **'bank ac,count** (*also* **'banking ac,count**) *noun* [C]
 an arrangement that you have with a bank that

allows you to keep your money there, to pay in or take out money, etc: *You can open a bank account with as little as €100.* ◇ *Do we have enough funds in our bank account to pay the bills?* ◇ *The money will be paid directly into your bank account.* → ACCOUNT *noun* (1)
 ❍ to **close/have/hold/open** a bank account ◆ to **pay money into/ take money out of** a bank account

'bank ad,vance *noun* [C]
 money which a bank lends to a customer

'bank as,sistant *noun* [C] (*especially AmE*)
 a person who works in a bank but is not a manager → BANK TELLER, CASHIER

'bank ,balance *noun* [C]
 the amount of money that sb has in their bank account at a particular time: *My bank balance is always low at the end of the month.* → BALANCE *noun* (1)

'bank bill *noun* [C]
 1 (*Finance*; *Trade*) (*BrE*) (*also* **,banker's ac'ceptance,** *BrE, AmE*) a type of BILL OF EXCHANGE that is signed by a bank, which means that it agrees to pay the amount stated on the **bill** → TRADE BILL
 2 (*AmE*) = BANKNOTE

,bank 'borrowing *noun*
 1 [U] the act of taking money from a bank and agreeing to pay it back over a period of time; the amount of money that sb borrows in this way: *Small companies often have to rely on bank borrowing.*
 2 **bank borrowings** [pl.] the amount of money that is borrowed from banks: *They have sold several stores to try to pay back bank borrowings.*

'bank card (*also* **'banker's card**) *noun* [C]
 a plastic card provided by your bank that you can use to pay for sth or to get money from your account out of a machine: *We accept cheques supported by a bank card for payments over £50.* → CHEQUE CARD, CREDIT CARD, DEBIT CARD

,bank-certified 'cheque (*AmE spelling* **~ check**) *noun* [C]
 a cheque that a bank has officially said can be used, as the person who has written the cheque has enough money in their account to pay the amount on the cheque

'bank charge *noun* [C, usually pl.]
 the amount that a customer pays their bank for the services it provides: *There are no bank charges if your account stays in credit.* ◇ *to incur bank charges* (= do sth so that you have to pay them) → SERVICE CHARGE

'bank cheque (*AmE spelling* **~ check**) (*BrE also* **'banker's cheque**) *noun* [C]
 a cheque signed by your bank that you buy and use to pay sb who will not accept an ordinary cheque SYN BANK DRAFT

'bank clerk *noun* [C]
 a person who works in a bank, receiving and paying out money, helping customers, keeping records of accounts, etc. → CASHIER, BANK TELLER

'bank ,credit *noun* [U,C]
 (*Finance*) money that a bank makes available either as a loan or an OVERDRAFT; money that banks in general lend: *periods when bank credit is restricted* ◇ *a bank credit agreement/facility*

'bank debt *noun* [U]
 money that a company, an organization, etc. owes to a bank: *The airline is aiming to pay off its $100 million bank debt within six months.* ◇ *€40 million of bank debt*

'bank de,posit *noun* [C]
 1 an amount of money that you leave (**deposit**) in a bank

2 (*Economics*) **bank deposits** [pl.] the total amount of money that has been paid into one bank or all banks in a particular area or country: *Bank deposits rose to €135 billion.*

'bank draft *noun* [C]
1 (*BrE also* **'banker's draft**) a cheque signed by your bank that you buy and use to pay sb who will not accept an ordinary cheque ~~SYN~~ BANK CHEQUE, DRAFT
2 (*AmE*) = DIRECT DEBIT

★ **banker** /'bæŋkə(r)/ *noun* [C]
1 a person who owns a bank or who has an important job in a bank: *The bank is looking at ways of retaining its senior bankers.*
○ *a central/merchant/private/senior banker*
2 an organization that lends money or provides the services of a bank: *The company's bankers are aiming to sell the studio for $7 bn.*
○ *central/merchant/private bankers*

banker's ac'ceptance = BANK BILL (1)

'banker's bank *noun* [C]
(*Finance*) a bank that provides financial services to other banks: *The Central Bank acts as a banker's bank, making loans to banks.*

'banker's card = CHEQUE CARD, BANK CARD

'banker's cheque = BANK CHEQUE

'banker's draft = BANK DRAFT (1)

'banker's hours *noun* [pl.] (*informal*)
short working hours, often with a long lunch break: *You're late today! Do you think you're working banker's hours?*

banker's 'order = STANDING ORDER

'banker's reference = BANK REFERENCE

'bank fa,cility *noun* [C]
(*Finance*)
1 [usually sing.] an arrangement with a bank to borrow a particular amount of money: *a $100 million short-term bank facility*
2 a bank

the 'Bank for Inter'national 'Settlements *noun* [sing.] (*abbr* **BIS**)
an international organization in Switzerland that encourages central banks from different countries to work together and provides them with financial services

bank giro 'credit *noun* [C]
a method of payment, usually used for paying bills, etc., in which a printed form is used to tell a bank to put a particular amount of money into a particular account at that branch; the form that is used

bank guaran'tee *noun* [C]
(*Finance*) a promise by a bank to pay money owed by a customer who cannot pay a debt or who fails to provide an agreed service to sb (**defaults**): *Lenders will not risk financing a project without a bank guarantee.*

bank 'holiday *noun* [C] (*BrE*)
a public holiday, for example New Year's Day, when banks, businesses, government offices, etc. are officially closed: *a bank holiday weekend* (= a weekend followed by a Monday which is a bank holiday)

bank identifi'cation number = SORT CODE

★ **banking** /'bæŋkɪŋ/ *noun* [U]

SEE ALSO: consumer banking, home ~, retail ~

1 the business activity of banks: *a career in banking* ◇ *You may find it difficult to get to a bank during banking hours.*

○ *business/corporate/personal* banking ◆ the banking *industry/sector* ◆ banking *facilities/hours/services*
2 the activity of using the services that a bank offers: *About 20% of our customers use online banking.* ◇ *Where do you do your banking?*
○ *electronic/Internet/telephone banking*

'banking ac,count = BANK ACCOUNT

'banking ,system *noun* [C]
all the institutions that provide banking services in a country or region, and the way that they work together: *measures to maintain public confidence in the banking system*

'bank ,interest *noun* [U]
the interest that a bank charges a customer for borrowing money

,bank 'lending *noun* [U]
(*Economics*) the amount of money lent to people by banks within a country over a period of time: *Bank lending rose by 4% last month.*

,bank 'mandate *noun* [C]
a written instruction that sb gives to a bank, for example to start a new account or make regular payments from their account

banknote /'bæŋknəʊt; *AmE* -noʊt/ (*AmE also* **'bank bill**) *noun* [C]
a piece of paper money: *There had been a high demand for banknotes from ATMs.* ◇ *a 500 peso banknote* ◇ *euro banknotes and coins* ◇ *used banknotes* ~~SYN~~ NOTE

the ,Bank of 'England (*also* **the Bank**) *noun* [sing.] (*abbr* **B/E, B of E**)
the central bank of the UK → THE FEDERAL RESERVE

,bank of 'issue *noun* [C]
a bank that has the legal right to make its own notes and coins

,bank 'overdraft = OVERDRAFT

'bank rate *noun* [C]
(*Finance*) another name for BASE RATE that is not used very much now

,bank reconcili'ation (*also* **,bank reconcili'ation ,statement**) *noun* [C,U]
(*Accounting*) a regular check that a company makes to make sure that its own financial records agree with the bank's record of its BANK BALANCE, for example by considering payments that have been made but not yet recorded by the bank; a document that explains the differences: *Complete regular bank reconciliations of the management bank accounts.*

'bank ,reference (*also* **'banker's ,reference**) *noun* [C]
a statement that a bank can be asked to give about whether a customer is likely to be able to pay back a loan → STATUS ENQUIRY

,bank re'serves *noun* [pl.]
(*Economics*) the amount of money that banks must keep in the central bank, equal to a percentage of the money paid into their accounts (**deposits**): *By increasing bank reserves, the Federal Bank increases the amount of money that banks have to lend.*
→ RESERVE *noun*

bankroll /'bæŋkrəʊl; *AmE* -roʊl/ *verb, noun*
● *verb* [+ obj] (*especially AmE*) (*informal*)
to support sb or a project financially: *investors who bankroll start-ups* See note at FINANCE
▶ **'bankroller** *noun* [C]
● *noun*
1 (*especially AmE*) a supply of money: *The company has used some of its bankroll to bring in talented designers.*

2 a roll of paper money

'bank run noun [C]
(*Economics*) a time when too many people want to take their money out of the banks at the same time, so the banks cannot pay them all: *The government froze deposits to prevent a bank run.* → RUN noun (5)

★**bankrupt** /'bæŋkrʌpt/ adjective, verb, noun
•*adjective*
1 without enough money to pay what you owe, especially when this has been officially decided by a court: *a bankrupt software company* ◇ *Her husband went bankrupt two years ago.* ◇ *The company was declared bankrupt in the High Court.*
[SYN] INSOLVENT
❍ to go/be declared bankrupt
2 (*formal*) [not usually before noun] not having something that has value: *a government bankrupt of new ideas*

VOCABULARY BUILDING

When a company fails

Technical words
- to **be/go insolvent** (= to be unable to pay debts)
- to **liquidate/wind up** a company (= to sell its assets, pay its debts, etc.)
- a company is **put/goes into liquidation**

Neutral Words
- to **be/go bankrupt**
- to **go out of business**

Informal/idiomatic words
a company
- **goes under**
- **goes bust**
- **goes belly up**
- **goes to the wall**

•*verb* [+ obj]
to make sb **bankrupt**: *The company was almost bankrupted by legal costs.*
•*noun* [C]

SEE ALSO: **undischarged bankrupt**

(*Law*) a person who has been judged by a court to be unable to pay their debts

★**bankruptcy** /'bæŋkrʌptsi; -rʌpsi/ noun [U,C] (plural **bankruptcies**)

SEE ALSO: **act of bankruptcy, involuntary ~, trustee in ~, voluntary ~**

(*Law*) the state of being BANKRUPT: *They would face bankruptcy if they had to repay the loan.* ◇ *There could be further bankruptcies among small farmers.* ◇ *The company filed for bankruptcy* (= asked to be officially bankrupt) *earlier this year.* → INSOLVENCY, BANKRUPT
❍ to be on the brink of/be on the verge of/face bankruptcy ◆ to be forced into/collapse into bankruptcy ◆ to declare/file for/seek bankruptcy ◆ to avert/avoid/stave off bankruptcy ◆ a bankruptcy court/judge

'bankruptcy-law pro,tection = BANK-RUPTCY PROTECTION

'bankruptcy ,notice noun [C]
(*Law*) an official letter that tells a person or company who owes money that if they do not pay it within a particular number of days, they will be made BANKRUPT

'bankruptcy ,order noun [C]
(*Law*) an order by a court that makes a person or

company officially BANKRUPT, and allows their property to be taken and used to pay their debts: *The court made a bankruptcy order against the debtor.*

'bankruptcy pe,tition noun [C]
(*Law*) a request made to a court by a person or company who is owed money to make the person or company that owes them money BANKRUPT: *The High Court dismissed a bankruptcy petition filed against the company.*
❍ to file/issue/present/serve a bankruptcy petition

'bankruptcy pro,ceedings noun [pl.]
(*Law*) the legal process of asking the court to make a person or company BANKRUPT

'bankruptcy pro,tection (also 'bankruptcy-law pro,tection) noun [U]
(*Law*) laws that limit the amount that a person or company has to pay when they are made BANKRUPT
❍ to file for/seek bankruptcy protection ◆ to emerge from bankruptcy protection

'bank ,statement (also 'statement) noun [C]
a printed record of all the money paid into and out of a customer's bank account within a particular period: *The monthly bank statement showed a balance of $400.*
❍ to receive/request a bank statement ◆ an amount appears on/is shown on a bank statement

'bank ,teller (also 'teller) noun [C]
a person whose job is to receive and pay out money in a bank → BANK CLERK, CASHIER

'bank ,transfer noun [C]
the sending of money from an account in one bank to an account in any branch of the same bank or another: *You should allow five to seven working days for a bank transfer to be made.* ◇ *Payment may be made by bank transfer to the following account ...* → BANK GIRO CREDIT
❍ to arrange/make a bank transfer ◆ to pay by bank transfer

'banner ad (also banner /'bænə(r)/) (also 'banner ad,vertisement, formal) noun [C]
(*Marketing*) an advertisement in the form of a box with a design or symbol in that is spread across a web page, usually at the top: *a banner ad on a popular website* → BUTTON AD
▶ **'banner ,advertising** noun [U]

'banner ,towing noun [U]
(*Marketing*) a method of advertising which uses a small plane to fly over an area pulling a long sign attached to the back with an advertisement on it

the Bar /bɑː(r)/ noun [sing.]
(*Law*) (often **the bar**)
1 (*BrE*) the profession of a BARRISTER (= a lawyer in a higher court): *to be called to the bar* (= to be allowed to work as a qualified barrister)
2 (*AmE*) the profession of any kind of lawyer; lawyers as a group

bar /bɑː(r)/ noun, verb
•*noun*

SEE ALSO: **menu bar, navigation ~, scroll ~, space ~**

1 (*IT*) [C] a narrow box at the top of a computer screen that contains words or pictures of the common things that a computer can do for you to choose: *a menu/task bar* → TOOLBAR
2 [sing.] **a bar (to sth)** a thing that stops sb from doing sth: *a two-year bar on selling the company* ◇ *At that time, being a woman was a bar to promotion in most professions.*
•*verb* [+ obj] (**-rr-**)
to not allow or to prevent sb from doing sth: *He is now barred from entering the country.*

'bar chart (AmE also **'bar graph**) noun [C]
a diagram which uses bands of different heights and equal widths to show different amounts, so that they can be compared easily: *The bar chart* **shows** *the relationship between each year's sales.*
→ HISTOGRAM

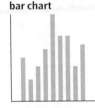

★ **'bar code** noun [C]
a pattern of thick and thin lines that is printed on things that you buy in a shop/store. It contains information that a computer can read: *The cashier uses a light pen to read the bar codes.* ◇ *a bar code reader* SYN UPC—Picture at PACKAGING
○ *to read/scan a bar code*
▶ **'bar ,coding** noun [U]

★ **bargain** /'bɑːgən; AmE 'bɑːrgən/ noun, verb
● **noun** [C]
1 something that is bought or sold at a lower price than usual: *I picked up a few good bargains in the sale.* ◇ *I managed to get the shares at a bargain price.* ◇ *bargain fare offers*
2 an agreement between two or more people or groups to do sth: *I'll make a bargain with you.* ◇ *I assure you we will keep our side of the bargain* (= do what we agreed to do).
3 (Commerce) an agreement, often a spoken agreement, between two or more people to exchange sth for a particular price: *Buyer and seller strike a bargain with each individual purchase.*
4 (Stock Exchange) a single act of buying or selling on the London Stock Exchange: *The average daily volume traded for July was 180 684 bargains.*
→ idiom at HARD adjective
● **verb** [no obj]
bargain (with sb) (about/over/for sth) to discuss prices, pay or conditions with sb in order to reach an agreement that suits everyone: *It's better to bargain for wages as a group.* ◇ *Employers sometimes have to bargain with trade unions.*

,bargain 'basement noun [C]
a part of a large shop/store, usually on the floor below street level, where goods are sold at lower prices than usual: *They are selling off their assets at* **bargain-basement prices** (= very cheaply).

'bargain ,hunter noun [C]
a person who is looking for goods that are being sold at a lower price than usual: *Share prices rose as bargain hunters rushed back into the market.*
▶ **'bargain ,hunting** noun [U] → BOTTOM FISHING

bargaining /'bɑːgənɪŋ; AmE 'bɑːrg-/ noun [U]
SEE ALSO: collective bargaining, enterprise ~, free collective ~, workplace ~

discussion of prices, pay, or conditions to try to reach an agreement that suits everyone: *pay/wage bargaining* ◇ *Many employees are in a weak* **bargaining position.** ◇ *The agreement is the result of* **hard bargaining** *on both sides for 18 months.* ◇ *Unions are ready to* **return to the bargaining table** (= start discussing again) *today.*

'bargaining ,agent noun [C]
(HR) in the US, a union that a particular group of workers choose to belong to and that represents them in discussions about wages, etc.
→ BARGAINING UNIT

'bargaining ,counter (BrE) (also **'bargaining chip**, AmE, BrE) noun [C]
a fact or a thing that you can use to get an advantage for yourself when you are trying to reach an agreement with another person or group

'bargaining ,power noun [U]
the amount of control a person or group has when

trying to reach an agreement with another group in a business or political situation: *As a cash buyer, you'll have greater bargaining power.*

'bargaining ,unit noun [C]
(HR) in the US, a group of workers who are recognized as a separate part of a union in discussions about wages, etc. → BARGAINING AGENT

'bar graph = BAR CHART

barista /bɑːˈriːstə; -ˈrɪs-; bæ-/ noun [C]
a person who works in a bar, especially a coffee bar, serving drinks to customers

barometer /bəˈrɒmɪtə(r); AmE -ˈrɑːm-/ noun [C]
something that shows the changes that are happening in an economic, social or political situation: *Retail sales figures act as a barometer of the country's economic health.*

baron /'bærən/ noun [C]
a person who owns or controls a large part of a particular industry
○ *a media/newspaper/oil/press/tobacco baron*

VOCABULARY BUILDING

baron/magnate/mogul/tycoon

Newspapers tend to use limited combinations of words to describe people in particular industries who are very powerful and wealthy. The most common include:

- a media/newspaper/press **baron**
- a media/property/shipping **magnate**
- a media/movie/TV **mogul**
- a media/an oil/a property **tycoon**

★ **barrel** /'bærəl/ noun [C]
1 a large, round container, usually made of wood or metal, with flat ends and, usually, curved sides; the amount that such a container holds—Picture at TRANSPORT
2 a unit of measurement in the oil industry equal to between 120 and 159 litres: *Oil prices rose to $60 a barrel.* ◇ *The forecast for global oil demand is 76 m barrels a day.*
3 a unit of measurement used in the beer-making (**brewing**) industry equal to about 164 litres

★ **barrier** /'bæriə(r)/ noun [C]
SEE ALSO: entry barrier, exit ~, non-tariff ~, trade ~

1 a problem, rule or situation that prevents sb from doing sth, or that makes sth impossible: *The policy protected farmers by setting up barriers* **against** *imports.* ◇ *The company denied that there are any artificial barriers to promotion.*
2 something that exists between one thing or person and another and keeps them separate: *We need to remove unnecessary barriers* **between** *management* **and** *the workforce.*

,barrier to 'entry (plural **barriers to entry**) (also **'entry ,barrier**) noun [C]
(Economics) something that makes it difficult for a company to start competing in a particular kind of business, for example high cost or advanced technology: *E-commerce is an industry with relatively low barriers to entry* (= it is simple and cheap to start doing it).

,barrier to 'exit (plural **barriers to exit**) (also **'exit ,barrier**) noun [C]
1 (Economics) something that makes it difficult for a company to leave an area of business, for example government rules or the cost of stopping employing staff: *high barriers to exit* ◇ *The presence*

of a variety of barriers to exit influenced the timing and selection of plants that were closed.
2 something that makes it difficult for a customer to stop using a particular brand of goods or for sb to change their job, etc: *We can create an experience for our customers that creates barriers to exit and keeps them loyal.*

barrister /'bærɪstə(r)/ *noun* [C]
(*Law*) a lawyer in the UK who has the right to argue cases in the higher courts See note at PROFESSION

barter /'bɑːtə(r); *AmE* 'bɑːrt-/ *verb, noun*
(*Commerce; Economics*)
● *verb* [+ obj *or no obj*]
to exchange goods, property, services, etc. for other goods without using money: *The farmers try to sell or barter whatever they grow.*
● *noun* [U]
the exchange of goods, property, services, etc. for other goods without using money: *The two countries have agreed to exchange certain goods on a barter system.* → COUNTERTRADE

★ **base** /beɪs/ *noun, verb*
● *noun* [C]

SEE ALSO: asset base, client ~, consumer ~, cost ~, customer ~, installed ~, knowledge ~, etc.

1 the main place where a business operates from: *The company has its base in Paris, and branch offices all over the world.*
2 the people, activity, etc. from which sb/sth gets most of their support, income, power, etc: *an economy with a solid **manufacturing** base* ◇ *Our firm needs to build up its consumer base.*
3 a situation, an idea, a fact, etc. from which sth is developed: *A new company must have a strong financial base if it is to survive.*
→ idiom at TOUCH *verb*
● *verb* [+ obj]
to use a particular city, town, etc. as the main place where you do business: *They based the new company in Belgrade.*
PHR V '**base sth on/upon sth** to use a fact, a situation, an idea, etc. as the point from which sth can be developed: *What are you basing this theory on?*

★ **based** /beɪst/ *adjective* [not before noun]

SEE ALSO: broad-based, competency-~, fee-~, knowledge-~, paper-~, screen-~

1 if one thing is **based on** another, it uses it or is developed from it: *The report is based on figures from six countries.* ◇ *a broadly based technology and entertainment company* (= one with a wide range of products)
2 (*also used in compounds*) working or doing business in or from a particular place: *I'm based in Osaka but spend most of my time travelling.* ◇ *a Prague-based company* ◇ *web-based training courses*
3 -based (*used in compounds*) having sth as an important feature or part: *oil-based paint*

'**base pay** = BASIC PAY
'**base price** = BASIC PRICE
'**base rate** *noun* [C]
(*Finance*) the lowest rate of interest at which the central bank lends money to other banks and financial institutions. This is used by banks, etc. to calculate how much interest they will charge to customers that they lend money to. **SYN** BANK RATE, PRIME RATE (*AmE*)

'**base ,salary** = BASIC SALARY
'**base wage** = BASIC WAGE

,**basic 'industry** *noun* [C,U]
1 (*Economics*) an industry that produces goods and services to be sold outside the region where they are produced.
2 (*Manufacturing*) an industry that supplies materials to other industries

,**basic 'pay** (*especially BrE*) (*AmE usually* '**base pay**) *noun* [U]
(*HR*) the normal amount that sb is paid, usually every week, without extra payments: *The agreement includes a 15% increase in basic pay over five years.* → BASIC SALARY, BASIC WAGE

,**basic 'price** (*AmE also* '**base price**) *noun* [C]
(*Commerce*) the lowest price of a product without extra charges for additional features, tax, etc.

'**basic rate** *noun* [C] (*BrE*)
(*Accounting*) **basic rate (of tax/income tax)** the normal level of income tax, that most people or companies pay: *a cut of 2p in the basic rate of income tax* ◇ *The current basic rate of company tax is 30% of taxable income.*

basics /'beɪsɪks/ *noun* [pl.]
1 the most important and necessary facts, skills, ideas, etc. from which other things develop: *the basics of computer programming*
2 the simplest and most important things that people need in a particular situation: *We need to buy a few basics like paper and envelopes.*
→ idiom at BACK *adv*

,**basic 'salary** (*especially BrE*) (*AmE usually* '**base ,salary**) *noun* [C]
(*HR*) the normal amount that sb is paid in a year, without any extra payments: *She joined the company on a basic salary of €40 000.*

,**basic 'wage** (*especially BrE*) (*AmE usually* '**base wage**) *noun* [C]
(*HR*) the normal amount that sb is paid, usually every week, without extra payments: *The basic wage is $10 an hour.* ◇ *workers on basic wages of €500 per week*

★ **basis** /'beɪsɪs/ *noun* (*plural* **bases** /'beɪsiːz/)

SEE ALSO: accruals basis, cash basis

1 [sing.] the reason why people take a particular action: *They employed him **on the basis of** his experience rather than his qualifications.*
2 [sing.] the way things are done, organized or arranged: *He was only employed **on a** temporary basis.* ◇ *Decisions are made on a case-by-case basis* (= considering each situation separately).
3 [C, usually sing., U] the important facts, ideas or events that support sth and that it can develop from: *Marketing strategy is likely to **form the basis for** discussions at next month's conference.*
4 [sing.] the number that is used to calculate sth from: *On a three-year accounting basis, losses were €1.5 bn for the year.*
→ idiom at CONTINGENCY

'**basis point** *noun* [C]
(*Finance*) one hundredth of one per cent. This is often used to express the interest rate on bonds: *Yields on Treasury notes were roughly 30 basis points (0.3%) higher than last month.*

'**basket case** *noun* [C, usually sing.] (*AmE*) (*informal*)
(used especially in newspapers) a country or an organization whose economic or financial situation is very bad: *The company he had built up was reduced to a basket case four years after he retired.*

,**basket of 'currencies** *noun* [C, usually sing.]
(*Economics*) a fixed group of different currencies which some countries use to set a value for their own currency; the value that is calculated for this group: *The dollar fell **against** a basket of currencies including the yen, the euro and the Canadian dollar.*

★**batch** /bætʃ/ *noun, verb*
●*noun* [C]
a number of things or tasks that are dealt with as a group: *a batch of letters/emails/bills* ◇ *We deliver the goods in batches.* ◇ *All products with this* **batch number** (= that were manufactured at the same time) *have been recalled.*
●*verb* [+ obj]
to put things into groups in order to deal with them: *The program will batch and sort orders as they come in.*

'batch ,costing *noun* [U]
(*Accounting*) a way of expressing the cost of a product based on the cost of producing a group (**batch**) rather than on an individual item → JOB COSTING

'batch ,processing *noun* [U]
(*IT*) a way of getting a computer to do a long series of jobs all at the same time automatically
→ TRANSACTION PROCESSING

'batch pro,duction *noun* [U]
(*Production*) a way of manufacturing a product by making small or large groups of the items rather than producing them continuously: *We specialize in batch production which we tailor to each customer's requirements.* → JOB PRODUCTION, MASS PRODUCTION

battery /'bætri; -təri/ *noun* [C] (*plural* **batteries**)
1 a device that is placed inside a car engine, clock, radio, etc. and that produces the electricity that makes it work: *I need to recharge the batteries in my laptop.* ◇ *battery-powered/-operated*
2 a large number of things of the same type: *a battery of aptitude tests*
→ idiom at RECHARGE

battle /'bætl/ *noun, verb*
●*noun*
1 [C] **a battle (between A and B)** | **a battle (with sb) (for/over sth)** a competition, an argument or a struggle between people or groups of people trying to win power or control: *a battle between the old and the new* ◇ *Several senior executives quit after a boardroom battle over the future of the company.* ◇ *He is involved in a bitter legal battle with his former employers for compensation.*
● *a bitter/fierce/hard-fought/long-running battle* • *a bid/boardroom/legal/takeover battle*
2 [C, usually sing.] a determined effort that sb makes to solve a difficult problem or succeed in a difficult situation: *It's an uphill battle to persuade customers to buy new phone handsets.* ◇ *Many firms are facing a battle for survival.*
● *a tough/an uphill battle*
IDM do 'battle (with sb) (for/over sth) to argue or be in competition with sb
●*verb* [+ obj or no obj]
battle (with/against sb/sth) (for/over sth) to try very hard to achieve sth difficult or to deal with sth unpleasant or dangerous: *The industry is battling with low demand.* ◇ *The two companies battled for market share.*

battleground /'bætlgraʊnd/ *noun* [C]
a subject or thing that people are arguing about or competing for: *Japan is the next battleground for big international supermarket operators.*

BBA /ˌbiː ˌbiː ˈeɪ/ *abbr*
1 (*AmE*) Bachelor of Business Administration, a university degree
2 British Banker's Association

bcc *abbr*
(*IT, only used in written English*) **blind carbon copy** a copy of an email message sent to sb without showing their name, so that the main person that the email is addressed to does not know that the message has also been sent to the other person
→ CARBON COPY

BDI /ˌbiː diː ˈaɪ/ *abbr* (*AmE*)
(*Marketing*) ,**brand de'velopment ,index** a measure of how well a particular type (**brand**) of product sells in a particular area compared to the whole country: *Where there is a low BDI, there may be an opportunity to build the brand.*

B/E = BILL OF EXCHANGE, BANK OF ENGLAND

beachhead /'biːtʃhed/ *noun* [C, usually sing.]
a strong position that a company has gained in a new field or place: *The chain has opened 30 new stores in an ambitious plan to establish a beachhead in Europe.*

'bean ,counter *noun* [C] (*informal*)
a humorous word for an accountant. It is used in a disapproving way to show that the speaker thinks the person is too interested in controlling costs and making a profit.

★**bear** /beə(r); *AmE* ber/ *noun* [C]
(*Finance; Stock Exchange*)
1 a person who sells shares, a particular currency, etc., hoping to buy them back later at a lower price because they think prices are going to fall rather than rise
2 = BEAR MARKET
→ BULL

bearer /'beərə(r); *AmE* 'berər/ *noun* [C]
(*Finance*)
1 a person who presents a document, such as a cheque or a share, bond, etc., for payment
2 used to describe a document, such as a cheque or a share, bond, etc. which can be presented for payment by anyone, not only by a named person: *Bearer bonds can be stolen, and should therefore be treated in the same way as cash.*
→ PAYABLE TO BEARER

'bear hug *noun* [C]
(*Finance*) a public offer to buy a company in order to try to force the company to accept it. A high price is offered so that the company has to accept it in order to avoid protests from its shareholders.

bearish /'beərɪʃ; *AmE* 'ber-/ *adjective*
(*Finance; Stock Exchange*) showing or expecting a fall in the prices of shares, etc: *a bearish market* ◇ *Japanese banks remain bearish.* ◇ *Many analysts are bearish on the stock.* **OPP** BULLISH

'bear ,market (*also* **bear**) *noun* [C]
(*Finance; Stock Exchange*) a period during which people are selling shares, etc. rather than buying, because they expect the prices to fall **OPP** BULL MARKET

'bear po,sition *noun* [C]
(*Finance; Stock Exchange*) a situation in which an investor sells shares, etc. that he/she has borrowed but does not own yet, hoping to be able to buy them at a cheaper price later and return them to the owner **SYN** SHORT POSITION → BULL POSITION
● *to establish/take a bear position*

'bear raid *noun* [C]
(*Finance; Stock Exchange*) an attempt by a dealer to make the price of a share, etc. go down by selling it in large numbers

'bear run *noun* [C]
(*Finance; Stock Exchange*) a situation where the value of shares, etc. is falling: *Buyers think the end of the bear run might be here.* → BULL RUN

beat /biːt/ *verb* [+ obj] (**beat, beaten** /'biːtn/)
1 to defeat sb/sth: *The way to beat the big companies is to specialize.* ◇ *a strategy to beat the competition*

2 to do or be better than sth: *Nobody beats our prices!* ◊ *Last year's sales beat the previous record achieved in 2002.*

IDM **beat sb at their own 'game** to do better than sb in an activity in which they think they are strong: *They're trying to beat the low-cost airlines at their own game.* **beat a path to sb's 'door** if a lot of people **beat a path to sb's door**, they are all interested in sth that person has to sell or to offer **if you can't beat them, 'join them** if you cannot defeat sb or be as successful as they are, then it is more sensible to join them in what they are doing and perhaps get some advantage for yourself by doing so

PHR V **,beat sb/sth 'down (to sth)** to persuade sb to reduce the price at which they are selling sth: *I beat down the price to $6 000.* **,beat 'off sth/sb/sth** to force sb/sth away: *They have managed to beat off competition from two large energy groups.* **HELP** A noun goes after **off**, but a pronoun comes between the verb and **off**.

'beauty pa,rade (*BrE also* **'beauty ,contest**) *noun* [C] (*informal*)
an occasion when several competing companies or people try to persuade sb to use their services: *Ireland is to award four telecommunications licences in a beauty parade next year.*

,bed and 'breakfast *noun* (*BrE*) (*abbr* **B&B**)
1 [U] a service that provides a room for the night and breakfast the next morning: *Do you do bed and breakfast?*
2 [C] a place that provides this service: *There are several good bed and breakfasts in the area.*

beef /biːf/ *verb*
PHR V **,beef 'up sth (with sth)** to make sth bigger, better, more interesting, etc: *Staff numbers will be beefed up by 10%.* ◊ *We need to beef up our customer care.* **HELP** A noun must always follow up, but a pronoun comes between the verb and **up**.

be'ginning ,inventory = OPENING STOCK

be,ginning of 'year *noun* [sing.] (*abbr* **BOY**)
(*Accounting*) the start of the FINANCIAL YEAR: *balance at beginning of year: $570 000*

behemoth /bɪˈhiːmɒθ; ˈbiːhɪmɒθ; *AmE* -məːθ/ *noun* [C]
a very big and powerful company or organization: *a multinational corporate behemoth*

'Beige Book *noun* [sing.]
(*Economics*) in the US, one of the regular reports on the state of the economy in the regions of the US, published by the central bank: *The Beige Book notes that some companies in Atlanta have seen increases in orders.*

beleaguered /bɪˈliːɡəd; *AmE* -ɡərd/ *adjective*
1 experiencing great financial problems: *There are signs that the beleaguered manufacturing sector may be recovering.*
2 experiencing a lot of criticism and difficulties: *The beleaguered chairman was forced to resign.*

the bell /bel/ *noun* [sing.]
(*Stock Exchange*) the sound used to signal when business starts and ends at a stock exchange: *Stocks* (= *their prices*) *are expected to drop after the opening bell on Wall Street.*
IDM **a'larm/'warning bells** used in expressions to mean that people are starting to feel worried and suspicious about sth: *The publisher set alarm bells ringing when it warned that its profits had fallen dramatically.*

'bell curve *noun* [C]
a line on a graph, shaped like a bell, that shows the normal way that measurements are spread when

there are a large number of cases chosen without any particular method

,bells and 'whistles *noun* [pl.] (*informal*)
(used especially about computers, cameras, etc.) extra features that are not really necessary but make a product more attractive to buyers: *This digital camera has all the latest bells and whistles.*

bellwether /ˈbelweðə(r)/ *noun* [C, usually sing.]
1 sth that helps you to see what will happen in the future: *London house prices are seen as a bellwether of consumer confidence.* ◊ *The company is a bellwether of global industrial trends.*
2 (*Stock Exchange*) especially in the US, a share, bond, etc. whose changes in price are a good guide to what will happen to the prices of other shares, bonds, etc: *Technology bellwether Sony rose 7.2% to 6 420 yen.* ◊ *a bellwether stock*

belly /ˈbeli/ *noun*
IDM **go belly 'up** (*informal*) if a project or a business **goes belly up**, it fails: *Many Internet start-ups went belly up because of poor business plans.* See note at BANKRUPT

be,low 'par *adjective*
(*Finance*) (used about the price of a share, bond, etc.) lower than the price at which it was first made available for sale (the **nominal price**): *bonds bought below par and repaid at par* ◊ *below-par securities*

be,low the 'fold *adverb*
(*IT*) in the middle and bottom part of a web page that you cannot see on the screen until you move down in the text: *Don't put important information below the fold.* ► **be,low the 'fold** *adjective* [usually before noun]: *below-the-fold advertising* → ABOVE THE FOLD

be,low-the-'line *adjective* [usually before noun]
1 (*Accounting*) relating to unusual costs or income after a company's total profit has been calculated that show its final profit: *It is rare for something to be treated as a below-the-line item in modern accounts.*
2 (*Accounting*) in the US, relating to further costs that you can take away from your total (*gross*) income to calculate the final income that you must pay tax on: *Some interest payments qualify as below-the-line deductions.*
3 (*Marketing*) relating to advertising activities that do not involve using television, newspapers, etc., such as direct mail or exhibitions: *The marketing mix incudes both advertising and below-the-line promotions such as merchandising.*
► **be,low-the-'line** *adverb* (*Accounting*): *Can you quantify what costs were taken below-the-line in the first half?* → ABOVE-THE-LINE

'belt-,tightening *noun* [U]
the act of spending less money because there is less available: *an increase in wages after years of belt-tightening* ◊ *We are going into a period of corporate belt-tightening.* → TIGHTEN YOUR BELT at TIGHTEN

★benchmark /ˈbentʃmɑːk; *AmE* -mɑːrk/ *noun, verb*
● *noun* [C]
1 a standard, usually of quality or performance, that other things can be compared to: *Revenue per available room is the key benchmark in the hotels sector.* ◊ *A performance benchmark has been established for the team.*
→ BEST PRACTICE
2 (*Finance*) (*also* **benchmark ,index**) a set of share prices that are used to judge the performance of other shares: *The FTSE 100 is London's benchmark index.*
3 (*IT*) a set of computer programs that can be used to measure what a computer can do and how fast it can do it
● *verb* [+ obj]
to find the best performance or process and use

this as a standard to improve performance or processes in a company: *Many companies benchmarked Motorola.* ◇ *Benchmark your skills against the standard of excellence in your field.*
▶ **'benchmarking** *noun* [U]

beneficial 'interest *noun* [U,C]
(*Law*) a right to benefit from sth, such as a right to receive the income from property or the profits that are made from selling sth: *to have a beneficial interest in property/shares*

beneficial 'owner *noun* [C]
(*Law*) the owner of an investment, a property, etc. who has the right to benefit from it, for example, by receiving the profits that are made from it. This person may not be the legal owner and another person or company may keep or look after the investment, etc. for them. ▶ **beneficial 'ownership** *noun* [U]

beneficiary /ˌbenɪˈfɪʃəri; *AmE* -ˈfɪʃieri/ *noun* [C] (*plural* **beneficiaries**)
1 a person who gains an advantage as a result of sth: *Who will be the main beneficiary of the cuts in income tax?*
2 (*Law*) a person who receives money or property when sb dies: *She is the sole beneficiary under her father's will.*
3 (*Law*) the person that a TRUST keeps and looks after property or money for → TRUSTEE
4 (*Finance*) a person or company that receives a payment of money: *the beneficiary of a cheque*

★ **benefit** /ˈbenɪfɪt/ *noun, verb*
● *noun*

SEE ALSO: **accrued benefits, cafeteria ~, cost ~, death ~, defined ~, flexible ~, fringe ~,** etc.

1 [C,U] a helpful and useful effect that sth has: *Internet shopping has real benefits for both the consumer and the environment.* ◇ *We want our shareholders to derive* (= get) *full benefit from the deal.* ◇ *The new regulations will be of benefit to everyone concerned.* ◇ *Consumers in Europe are reaping the benefits* (= enjoying the results) *of the single currency.*
❍ *a potential/real/tangible benefit ✦ a big/great/huge/significant benefit ✦ an immediate/a long-term/short-term benefit ✦ economic/financial/tax benefits ✦ to derive/get/receive a benefit*
2 [U,C] money that is paid to people who are unemployed, ill, etc., by the government or through a system of insurance **HELP** In American English the plural **benefits** is often used in this meaning: *He receives social security benefits as a result of an accident at work.* ◇ (*BrE*) *Are you entitled to claim unemployment benefit?* ◇ (*AmE*) *The number of Americans claiming jobless benefits has risen sharply.* → WELFARE
❍ *disability/pension/retirement benefits ✦ to apply for/claim/get/qualify for/receive benefits*
3 (*HR*) [C, usually pl.] the advantages that you get from your company in addition to the money you earn: *The company offers a competitive benefits package.* ◇ *We are finding it difficult to continue to provide the same level of employee benefits*
● *verb* (**-t-** *or* **-tt-**)
1 [no obj] to be in a better position because of sth: *Small businesses have benefitted from the changes in the law.*
2 [+ obj] to have a helpful or useful effect on sb/sth: *The new tax laws will benefit people on low wages.*

benefit-'cost aˌnalysis = COST-BENEFIT ANALYSIS

'benefit ˌdollar *noun* [C]
(*HR*) in the US, a unit of tax-free money that a company gives to its employees in addition to their pay so that they can buy a range of benefits such as

medical care: *The leaflet shows you the annual amount of benefit dollars you will receive.*

benefit in 'kind *noun* [C, usually pl.] (*plural* **benefits in kind**)
(*Accounting*) in the UK, a benefit, such as a car, that a person receives from their company in addition to the money they earn, and for which they have to pay tax.

'benefit ˌprinciple *noun* [sing.]
(*Economics*) a theory that states that the people who benefit more from a government product or service should pay more tax for it than those who benefit less. For example, drivers should pay more tax for roads. → ABILITY-TO-PAY PRINCIPLE

'benefits coˌordinator *noun* [C]
(*HR*) a person whose job is to develop and manage the system of benefits that a company offers its employees

bequeath /bɪˈkwiːð/ *verb* [+ obj]
(*Law, formal, only used in written English*) **bequeath sth (to sb)** | **bequeath (sb) sth** to say in a WILL that you want sb to have your property, money, etc. after you die: *He bequeathed his entire estate to his daughter.* → BENEFICIARY, BEQUEST

bequest /bɪˈkwest/ *noun* [C]
(*Law or formal*)
money or property that you ask to be given to a particular person when you die: *The school received a bequest of $300 000.*

bespoke /bɪˈspəʊk; *AmE* bɪˈspoʊk/ *adjective* [usually before noun] (*especially BrE*)
1 designed and made for a particular customer: *bespoke software/solutions* ◇ *bespoke shoes* **SYN** CUSTOM-MADE, TAILOR-MADE
2 making products or providing services specially, according to the needs of an individual customer: *a bespoke ad agency*

the best /best/ *noun*
IDM **the ˌbest and (the) 'brightest** the most intelligent and skilful people: *the best and brightest on Wall Street*

best-beˈfore date (*BrE*) (*AmE* ˌbest-if-'used-by date*) *noun* [C]
the date by which you are advised to use some types of food and drink, printed on the container or package. Food will be safe after this date, but the quality may not be so good: *The flour is not yet past its best-before date.* See note on next page.—Picture at PACKAGING

best ˌbuy *noun* [C]
a product that has been tested and compared with others of the same type and has been found to be the best product and most worth the money you pay for it: *the best buy in a range of washing machines*

best 'efforts *noun* [pl.]
1 (*Law, only used in written English*) (*also* ˌbest enˈdeavours*) (often used in contracts) all the possible actions that you can take in order to achieve sth: *We will use our best efforts to deliver the goods on time.* ◇ *The software is supported on a best-efforts basis.*
2 (*Finance*) in the US, if a financial institution (such as an INVESTMENT BANK) uses a **best-efforts** method to sell the shares in a new company, they agree to sell as many shares as they can, but do not promise they will sell them all. Any that are not sold will be returned to the company.

ˌbest enˈdeavours (*AmE spelling* ~ **endeavors**) = BEST EFFORTS (1)

ˌbest-if-'used-by date = BEST-BEFORE DATE

WHICH WORD?

Dates on products

Many goods, especially foods, have a date on them giving information about their **shelf life** (= how long you can keep them).

Dates that give information about quality

Foods that have been frozen, dried, packed in cans, etc. often have a **best-before date** (*BrE*) or **best-if-used-by date** (*AmE*). This tells the consumer how long the product is expected to remain fresh: *Best before end FEB 2006.*

Fresh foods often have a **sell-by date** (*BrE* and *AmE*) or **pull date** (*AmE*). This tells the staff of the shop/store how long they should display the product: *Sell by 14 Nov. 06.* Usually food can be eaten for a period of time after this date, although it may not taste as good.

Often shops/stores sell products that are near their **sell-by-date**, **best-before date**, etc. more cheaply.

Dates that give information about safety

Some products, for example milk, meat or medicines, must have a **use-by date** or an **expiry date** (*BrE*)/**expiration date** (*AmE*). This is the date up to which you can safely eat or use the product. It is often illegal for shops/stores to sell products that have passed this date: *Display until 20 Oct. 06. Use by 27 Oct. 06.*

---

best in 'class *adjective* [usually before noun] (often used about a company, product or service) the best or most successful of its kind: *Our digital camera has been named best in class by 'PC Magazine'.* ◇ *best-in-class software/technology*

best 'practice *noun* [U,C] the best way of doing a particular task or activity, often recorded by companies or organizations in formal documents: *strategies to achieve best practice in health and safety* ◇ *We need to identify the current best practices in IT management.* ◇ *a code of best practice for training providers* → BENCHMARK *noun*

best 'price *noun* [C] the lowest price that a buyer can buy sth for; the highest price that a seller can sell sth for: *How do you get the best insurance policy at the best price?* ◇ *These are the best-price flights for those dates.*

best-'seller (*AmE spelling* **best seller**) *noun* [C] a product, especially a book, that is bought by large numbers of people: *The book became an instant best-seller with more than 5 million copies in print.*
▶ **best-'selling** *adjective* [only before noun]: *a best-selling book/medicine/car*

bet /bet/ *noun, verb*
● *noun* [C]

SEE ALSO: spread bet

1 an act of risking money on an investment: *The company is making a big bet on e-commerce.* ◇ *Investors have placed their bets on* (= invested all their money in) *the companies they think will recover quickest.* ◇ *Their bet has paid off* (= been successful).
2 a good/safe/sure/fair bet an investment that is likely to be successful; sth that is likely to happen or be suitable: *Property is always a safe bet.* ◇ *It's a sure bet that a piece of equipment will break down when you need it most.*
→ idioms at HEDGE *verb*
● *verb* [+ obj *or no obj*] (**betting**, **bet**, **bet**) to risk money on an investment, especially because

you think sth is likely to happen: *Investors have been betting that an economic recovery will come in the second half of the year.* ◇ *Management is betting the company's future on the new technology.*
→ GAMBLE

beta /'bi:tə; *AmE* 'beɪtə/ *noun* [C, usually sing.]
1 (*IT; Marketing*) (*often used as an adjective*) a new product, especially computer software, that is in the second or final stage of testing, in which a few customers try it before the public buy or use it: *The beta users said they liked the product, but not enough to pay a high price for it.* ◇ *a beta version of the software*
✪ *a beta copy/site/version*
2 (*Stock Exchange*) (*often used as an adjective*) = BETA COEFFICIENT
3 (*IT, informal*) = BETA TEST

'beta coef,ficient (*also* '**beta**) *noun* [C] (*Stock Exchange*) a measurement of how much the price of a share has changed in a particular period of time, compared with the average change in the price of all shares in the market. A share with a high **beta coefficient** is likely to rise or fall more than the average: *A fund with a beta coefficient of 1.0 will move exactly like the market.*

'beta test *noun, verb* (*IT; Marketing*)
● *noun* [C] (*also* '**beta**, *informal*) the second or final test of a product, especially a new piece of computer software, by a few customers before the final version is sold to or used by the public: *Beta tests are scheduled to start in October.*
● *verb* [+ obj]
beta-test to test a product for the second or final time by giving it to a few customers to try before the final version is sold to or used by the public: *The software was created and beta-tested in 2004.*
▶ '**beta ,testing** (*also* '**beta**, *informal*) *noun* [U]
→ ALPHA TEST

better-than-ex'pected *adjective* [usually before noun]
better-than-expected sales, profits, results etc. are higher than had been predicted previously: *The company reported better-than-expected sales in the first quarter.* → LOWER-THAN-EXPECTED

beverage /'bevərɪdʒ/ *noun* [C] (*formal*) any drink that is produced and sold to people: *laws governing the sale of alcoholic beverages* ◇ *Femsa is Latin America's largest beverage company.*

b/f (*also spelled* **b/fwd**) = BROUGHT FORWARD

BFOQ /'bi: ef əʊ 'kju:; *AmE* əʊ/ = BONA FIDE OCCUPATIONAL QUALIFICATION

bi- /baɪ/ *combining form* (*in nouns and adjectives*) two; twice; double: *bilingual* ◇ *bimonthly* **NOTE** Bi- with a period of time can mean either 'happening twice' in that period of time, or 'happening once in every two' periods.

biannual /baɪ'ænjuəl/ *adjective* [only before noun] happening twice a year: *a biannual meeting* **NOTE** Twice-yearly can be used with the same meaning: *a twice-yearly meeting.* ▶ **bi'annually** *adverb* → ANNUAL, BIENNIAL

bias /'baɪəs/ *noun, verb*
● *noun* [U; C, usually sing.] (*plural* **biases**)

SEE ALSO: gender bias

1 bias (against/for/towards/in favour of sb/sth) if sb/sth has a **bias**, they are likely to prefer or dislike one thing, person or group rather than another, in an unfair way: *Some institutions still have a strong bias against women.* ◇ *Unions have accused the company of racial and cultural bias.*
✪ *to avoid/have/show (a) bias* ✦ *(an) age/(a) racial bias*

2 if sb/sth has a **bias** towards sth, they usually choose that course of action rather than another because they believe it is better: *The Bank of England currently has a bias* **towards** *lower interest rates.* ◇ *We're looking for people with a bias* **for** *action.*

● *to* **have/show** *a bias*

3 (*Finance*) the way that prices tend to either increase or decrease: *The market bias is positive* (= prices are rising).

● *a* **negative/positive** *bias* • *a* **downward**/*an* **upward** *bias* • *an* **easing**/*a* **neutral** *bias*

4 (*Marketing*) mistakes in the results of market research tests or interviews, caused by problems with the number or type of people questioned, the type of questions asked, the attitude of the person doing the research, etc: *Avoid bias in your research by random sampling.*

● *verb* [+ obj] (**biasing, biased** *or* **biassing, biassed**)

1 bias sb/sth (**towards/against/in favour of sb/sth**) to influence sb's opinions or decisions in an unfair way: *The newspaper reports have biassed people against the company.*

2 (*Marketing*) to produce market research results that are not accurate: *The size of the sample may bias the results.*

★ **bid** /bɪd/ *noun, verb*

● *noun* [C]

SEE ALSO: **agreed bid, closed ~, conditional takeover ~, counter-~, open ~, paper ~, sealed ~,** etc.

1 (*Commerce*; *Finance*) an offer to buy sth, especially a company or its shares; the price that is offered: *Make a bid in our online auction by clicking the button.* ◇ *A Scandinavian cooperative will launch a $150 million cash bid for the company.* ◇ *The company is likely to become a* **bid target** (= is likely to be bought). ◇ *the continuing* **bid battle** *for P&O Princess*

● *to* **accept/launch/make/reject/withdraw** *a bid* • *to* **increase/raise** *a bid* • *a* **failed/rival/successful** *bid* • *an* **all-cash/all-share/a cash/share** *bid*

2 (*Commerce*) an offer to do work or provide a service for a particular price, in competition with other companies: *The company submitted a bid for the contract to clean the hospital.* ◇ (*especially AmE*) *He's putting in a bid* **on** *a construction job.*

[SYN] TENDER

● *to* **make/put in/submit/win** *a bid*

3 [usually sing.] (used especially in newspapers) an attempt to do sth or to get sth: *to make a bid for power* ◇ *The government has reduced interest rates in a* **bid to** *increase public spending.*

● *verb* [+ obj or no obj] (**bidding, bid, bid**)

1 (*Commerce*; *Finance*) to offer to pay a particular price for sth, especially a company or its shares: *The company has said it may bid for South African Breweries.* ◇ *How much did they bid?* See note at TENDER

2 (*Commerce*) to offer to do work or provide a service for a particular price, in competition with other companies: *A French firm will be bidding for the contract.* ◇ *They are bidding to build the refinery.* ◇ (*especially AmE*) *We are ready to bid* **on** *three contracts.* [SYN] TENDER

[PHR V] **bid sth 'up/'down** to pay or offer more/less money for sth than it is worth at the time, with the result that the price increases/decreases: *There are people willing to buy several million shares and bid the price up.*

,**bid and 'asked** (*also* ,**bid and 'ask,** *especially in AmE*) *adjective*

(*Stock Exchange*) used to describe the price a dealer will pay when buying particular shares, bonds, etc. (the **bid price**) and accept when selling them (the **asked price**): *Prices are quoted as bid and asked.*
→ ASKED PRICE, BID PRICE

'**bid/'ask spread** = BID-OFFER SPREAD

'**bid bond** *noun* [C]

(*Law*) an amount of money that a company that wins a contract agrees to pay if it does not do the work

bidder /'bɪdə(r)/ *noun* [C]

(*Commerce*)

1 a person or group that offers to pay an amount of money to buy sth: *The company's assets will be sold to the highest bidder.*

2 a person or group that offers to do work or to provide a service for a particular price, in competition with others: *The group is one of six bidders competing for the $500 million contract.*

bidding /'bɪdɪŋ/ *noun* [U]

(*Commerce*) the act of offering an amount of money to buy sth, especially at an AUCTION: *Several companies remain in the bidding.* ◇ *Online bidding allows bidders all over the world to participate.*

,**bid-'offer spread** (*also spelled* ,**bid/'offer spread**) (*also* ,**bid/'ask spread, spread**) *noun* [C]

(*Stock Exchange*) the difference between the price a dealer will pay when buying particular shares, bonds, etc. (the **bid price**) and accept when selling them (the **offer price**)

'**bid price** *noun* [C]

(*Stock Exchange*) the amount that a dealer will pay when buying particular shares, bonds, etc. → ASKED PRICE, OFFER PRICE

'**bid ,rigging** *noun* [U]

(*Commerce*)

1 when two or more businesses who are competing to do work or provide services for a company, an organization, etc. secretly work together to gain an advantage for themselves and deceive the company buying the work or services. This is an illegal practice.

2 when two or more people agree not to bid against each other at an AUCTION in order to keep the price of the item lower than it should be. This is an illegal practice.

biennial /baɪ'eniəl/ *adjective* [usually before noun] happening once every two years: *a biennial convention* ▸ **bi'ennially** *adverb* → ANNUAL, BIANNUAL

BIFFEX /'bɪfeks/ *abbr*

the Baltic International Freight Futures Exchange a market in London where people buy and sell contracts relating to the cost of transporting particular amounts of raw materials on specific dates in the future (**futures contracts**)

big /bɪg/ *adjective, adverb*

● *adjective*

[IDM] **a ,big 'cheese** (*informal*) a humorous way of referring to an important and powerful person in an organization **the big enchi'lada** (*AmE*) (*informal*) a humorous way of referring to the most important and powerful person, department, etc. in an organization: *Customer Service is the big enchilada.* **a big 'gun** (*informal*) a person in a particular organization or area who has a lot of influence or power: *They're bringing in the big guns.* **a big 'noise/'shot** (*informal*) an important person: *We can't just wait for some big shot to come and save the company.* **the ,big 'picture** (*informal*) the situation as a whole: *We need to look at the big picture before focusing on the details.* **the big 'three, 'four, etc.** the three, four, etc. most important countries, companies, people, etc.

● *adverb* → idioms at HIT *verb*, MAKE *verb*

,**Big 'Bang** *noun* [sing.]

(*Stock Exchange*) the major changes that were made to the London Stock Exchange in 1986 in order to improve it (*figurative*): *The management adopted a*

big bang approach to introducing the new computer system (= made the changes suddenly and all at the same time).

the ˌBig ˈBoard noun [sing.]
an informal name for the New York Stock Exchange: *Prices fell on the Big Board.* ◇ *Big Board prices/stock*

ˌbig ˈbucks noun [pl.] (*AmE*) (*informal*)
a large amount of money: *She'll be earning big bucks soon!*

ˌbig ˈbusiness noun [U]
1 large companies which have a lot of power and influence, considered as a group: *links between politics and big business*
2 something that has become important because people are willing to spend a lot of money on it: *Health and fitness have become big business.*

ˌbig ˈhitter = HEAVY HITTER

the ˈbig league noun [C, usually sing.]
the most important companies, people, etc. in a particular field: *His past experience suggests that he will be able to take the company into the big league.*

ˌbig ˈname noun [C]
a famous company, person, product, etc. in a particular field: *one of the biggest names in sports retailing* ◇ *We want to attract a big-name CEO.*

ˌBig ˈSteel noun [U] (*informal*)
a group name for the most important steel companies in a country, especially the US: *Big Steel has been a powerful influence in US politics.*

ˌbig-ˈticket adjective [only before noun] (*especially AmE*) (*informal*)
costing a lot of money: *Demand for big-ticket items, such as homes and cars, remains healthy.*

ˈbig-time adjective [only before noun] (*informal*)
1 successful and important: *a big-time lawyer*
2 big: *The company has taken on some big-time risks.*

bilateral /ˌbaɪˈlætərəl/ adjective
involving two groups of people or two countries: *The two countries signed a bilateral trade agreement.*
O bilateral *agreements/relations/talks/trade*
▶ **biˈlaterally** adverb → MULTILATERAL

biˌlateral ˈcontract noun [C]
(*Law*) an agreement in which both parties agree to do sth for the other → UNILATERAL CONTRACT

biˌlateral ˈcredit noun [U]
an agreement between two people or groups to allow time for debts to be paid

biˌlateral moˈnopoly noun [C]
(*Economics*) a situation in which a particular service or particular goods are only supplied by one company or organization and there is only one customer, so the price must be agreed between the two

★ **bill** /bɪl/ noun, verb
• noun [C]

SEE ALSO: **bank bill, commercial ~, due ~, period ~, sight ~, T-bill, term ~,** etc.

1 a piece of paper that shows how much you owe sb for goods and services; the amount of money that you owe: *The company could now face higher fuel bills.* ◇ *I've just got a huge tax bill.* See note at INVOICE
O *a big/high/huge/large bill* • *a monthly/quarterly/ weekly bill* • *outstanding/unpaid bills* • *to face/get/ receive/send (out) a bill* • *to pay/settle a bill*
2 (*especially BrE*) (*AmE usually* **check**) a piece of paper that shows how much you have to pay for food and drinks that you have had in a restaurant;

the amount that you must pay: *Can I have the bill, please?* ◇ *Our hosts insisted on picking up the bill* (= paying) *for the meal.* See note at INVOICE
O *a big/huge/large bill* • *to ask for/have/pay/settle the bill*
3 (*especially AmE*) = NOTE (1)
4 (*Finance*; *Trade*) (*BrE*) = BILL OF EXCHANGE
→ idioms at CLEAN adj., FOOT verb
• verb [+ obj]
1 to send sb a bill for sth: *You will be billed monthly for the service.* → INVOICE verb
2 to advertise or describe sb/sth in a particular way: *It is billed as the world's smallest video camera.*

billboard /ˈbɪlbɔːd; *AmE* -bɔːrd/ noun, verb
• noun [C]
a large board on the outside of a building or at the side of the road, used for putting advertisements on: *billboard advertising* SYN HOARDING
• verb [+ obj] (*often* **be billboarded**)
1 to advertise sth on a **billboard**: *Cheap flights are often billboarded on the London underground.*
2 (*especially AmE*) to advertise sth: *the most billboarded game of the season*

ˈbill ˌbroker (*BrE also* **ˈdiscount ˌbroker**) noun [C]
(*Finance*) a person or business that buys BILLS OF EXCHANGE and sells them to banks or keeps them until they are paid

billing /ˈbɪlɪŋ/ noun

SEE ALSO: **reverse billing**

1 (*Accounting*) [U] the act of preparing and sending bills to customers: *a billing clerk* ◇ *customer billing software*
2 (*Accounting*) **billings** [pl.] the total amount of business that a company does in a particular period of time, especially in advertising or insurance: *The agency generates annual billings of around $72 million.* ◇ *The company is worth $125 million in billings.*
3 [U] the way sb/sth is advertised or described: *Their latest gaming machine is living up to* (= is as good as) *its billing as the hottest on the market.*

ˈbilling ˌcycle noun [C]
(*Accounting*) the period of time between the bills that a company sends to a customer: *Your billing cycle begins on the day you sign up for the service.*
O *an annual/a bi-monthly/monthly/quarterly billing cycle*

billion /ˈbɪljən/ number (*abbr* **bn**)
1 000 000 000; one thousand million **HELP** **Billion** and **billions** are always used with a plural verb, except when an amount of money is mentioned. You say *a, one, two, several, etc.* **billion** without a final 's' on 'billion'. **Billions (of ...)** can be used if there is no number or quantity before it: *Worldwide sales reached $2.5 billion.* ◇ *half a billion dollars* ◇ *tens of billions of yen* ◇ *They have spent billions on the problem* (= billions of dollars, etc.).

ˌbill of ˈentry noun [C]
(*Trade*) a list giving details of goods that are being brought into or taken out of a country: *Customs officials will check the bill of entry and calculate the duty to be paid.*
O *to file/prepare/present/submit a bill of entry*

ˌbill of exˈchange noun [C] (*abbr* **B/E**) (*BrE also* **bill**)
(*Finance*; *Trade*) a written order for a person or an organization to pay a particular amount of money to sb/sth when asked or at a particular time, used especially in international trade: *If the buyer accepts the bill of exchange, they will sign their name on it and date it.* ◇ *An exporter may obtain payment on an accepted bill of exchange before its due date by presenting it to his bank.* → PROMISSORY NOTE
O *to accept/discount/draw/make out/sign a bill of exchange*

,bill of 'lading *noun* [C] (*abbr* **BOL, B/L, b/l**)
(*Trade*) a list giving details of the goods that a ship, etc. is carrying. It shows that the company transporting the goods has received them and allows the buyer to collect them: *a paper-based/ electronic bill of lading* ◇ *The ship owner issued a* **clean** *bill of lading, acknowledging that the goods were received in good order.* ◇ *a* **dirty/foul/unclean** *bill of lading* (= one that states that the goods were damaged or some were missing when they were put on the ship)

,bill of ma'terials (*also* ,bill of ma'terial) *noun* [C] (*abbr* **BOM**)
1 (*Manufacturing*) a list giving details of the materials and parts that are needed for a particular project → MATERIAL REQUIREMENT PLANNING
2 (*Property*) = BILL OF QUANTITIES

,bill of 'quantities (*also* ,bill of 'quantity) (*abbr* **BOQ, BQ**) (*also* ,bill of ma'terials) *noun* [C]
(*Property*) a list giving details of the materials that are needed for a particular building project, with the prices and the cost of doing the work

,bill of 'sale *noun* [C] (*abbr* **BS**)
(*Law*) a legal document showing that sb has sold an item to sb else and that the buyer has become the new owner

'bill rate = DISCOUNT RATE (1)

,bills 'payable *noun* [U; pl.]
(*Accounting*) part of the financial records of a company that shows the BILLS OF EXCHANGE that the company has not yet paid → CURRENT LIABILITY

,bills re'ceivable *noun* [U; pl.]
(*Accounting*) part of the financial records of a company that shows the BILLS OF EXCHANGE that the company will receive money for later → CURRENT ASSETS

BIN /bɪn/ = BANK IDENTIFICATION NUMBER

binary /'baɪnəri/ *adjective*
1 (*IT*) using only 0 and 1 as a system of numbers: *the binary system*
2 (*Technical*) based on only two numbers; consisting of two parts: *binary codes/numbers*
▶ **binary** *noun* [U]: *The computer performs calculations in binary and converts the results to decimal.*

bind /baɪnd/ *verb* [+ obj] (**bound, bound** /baʊnd/)
(*Law*) (*usually* **be bound**) to force sb to do sth by a legal agreement, a law or an official decision: *A person who signs a document will normally be bound by its terms.* → BOUND

binder /'baɪndə(r)/ *noun* [C]
1 a hard cover for holding loose sheets of paper together: *a ring binder*—Picture at FILE
2 (*Law*) (*AmE*) an agreement that you sign, which, together with a first payment (**deposit**), gives you the right to buy a property for a limited period of time
3 (*Insurance*) (*AmE*) a written or spoken agreement that an insurance company will provide insurance until a permanent document is provided → COVER NOTE

binding /'baɪndɪŋ/ *adjective*
that must be obeyed because it is accepted in law: *a* **legally** *binding agreement* ◇ *The decision is binding* **on** *both parties.*
❍ *a binding* **agreement/contract/decision/promise**

biodegradable /,baɪəʊdɪ'greɪdəbl; *AmE* ,baɪoʊ-/ *adjective*
(*Technical*) (about a product or material) that will naturally change back into harmless natural substances and so will not damage the environment when it is thrown away

biomass /'baɪəʊmæs; *AmE* 'baɪoʊ-/ *noun* [U]
animal and plant material, for example agricultural waste, that is used as fuel in order to produce heat, electricity, etc: *Biomass is one of the world's most important sources of energy.*

biometric /,baɪəʊ'metrɪk; *AmE* ,baɪoʊ-/ *adjective, noun*
(*IT*)
● *adjective*
using measurements of human features or characteristics, such as fingers, eyes or voices, in order to identify people: *biometric passwords such as fingerprints or facial recognition* ◇ *biometric technology*
● *noun* [C]
a measurement of a particular human feature

biometrics /,baɪəʊ'metrɪks; *AmE* ,baɪoʊ-/ *noun* [U]
(*IT*) the use of measurements of human features or characteristics, such as fingers, eyes or voices, in order to identify people: *experiments in using biometrics to identify and charge shoppers*

biopharma /,baɪəʊ'fɑːmə; *AmE* ,baɪoʊ'fɑːrmə/ *adjective, noun* (*informal*)
● *adjective* [only before noun]
biopharmaceutical: *biopharma companies*
● *noun* [U]
biopharmaceutics: *global trends in biopharma*

biopharmaceutical /,baɪəʊfɑːmə'sjuːtɪkl; -'sjuː-; *AmE* ,baɪoʊfɑːrmə'suː-/ *adjective, noun*
● *adjective* [only before noun]
connected with the making and selling of drugs and medicines that are produced using living cells: *at the forefront of biopharmaceutical research* ◇ *a biopharmaceutical company*
● *noun* [C, usually pl.]
a drug or medicine that is produced using living cells: *developing biopharmaceuticals* ◇ *the international biopharmaceuticals company* → PHARMACEUTICAL

biopharmaceutics /,baɪəʊfɑːmə'suːtɪks; -'sjuː-; *AmE* ,baɪoʊfɑːrmə'suː-/ *noun* [U]
the study and development of the production of drugs and medicine using living cells: *The ideal candidate will have a masters degree in biopharmaceutics.* → BIOTECHNOLOGY

biotech /'baɪəʊtek; *AmE* 'baɪoʊtek/ *adjective, noun* (*informal*)
● *adjective* [only before noun]
relating to BIOTECHNOLOGY: *a biotech company/ firm/group* ◇ *the patenting of biotech drugs*
● *noun*
1 [U] biotechnology: *The company is investing heavily in biotech.*
2 [C] a BIOTECHNOLOGY company: *Many biotechs become profitable through a single successful drug.*

biotechnology /,baɪəʊtek'nɒlədʒi; *AmE* ,baɪoʊtek'nɑːl-/ *noun*
1 [U,C] the use of living cells in industrial and scientific processes: *the rapidly growing field of biotechnology* ◇ *companies in the biotechnology sector*
2 [U] (*AmE*) = ERGONOMICS (1)
▶ **biotechnological** /,baɪəʊ,teknə'lɒdʒɪkl; *AmE* ,baɪoʊ,teknə'lɑːdʒ-/ *adjective*: *biotechnological research* → BIOPHARMACEUTICS

BIS /,biː aɪ 'es/ = BANK FOR INTERNATIONAL SETTLEMENTS

bit /bɪt/ *noun* [C]
(*IT*) the smallest unit of information that is stored in a computer's memory: *The data is transferred at a rate of about 9 000 bits per second.* → BYTE

bite /baɪt/ verb, noun
● *verb* [no obj] (**bit** /bɪt/ **bitten** /'bɪtn/)
to have an unpleasant effect: *The recession is beginning to bite.*
PHRV ˌbite 'into sth to reduce sth: *Poor trading conditions have bitten into our profits.*
● *noun* [C]
1 [usually sing.] an unpleasant effect: *companies feeling the bite of the bear market*
2 a very short statement that is easy to remember (a **sound bite**): *Politicians have to learn to speak in 30-second bites.*
→ idiom at TAKE *verb*

biz /bɪz/ noun [sing.] (*informal*)
a business, especially one related to entertainment or fashion; a company: *She's involved in the music biz.* ◇ *We might even start a biz.*

B/L (*also spelled* **b/l**) = BILL OF LADING

black /blæk/ noun, adjective
● *noun*
IDM be, remain, etc. in the 'black; move into, return to, etc. the 'black **1** to be making a profit; to start to make a profit: *The company is back in the black after a year of heavy losses.* **2** (*Stock Exchange*) if markets or shares are in **the black**, they are higher in value than they were previously: *Technology stocks have been trading in the black.* **OPP** BE, REMAIN, ETC. IN THE RED, MOVE INTO, RETURN TO, ETC. THE RED
● *adjective* [only before noun]
used to describe days on which sth terrible occurs, especially days when there is a sudden large decrease in the prices of shares: *the disaster of Black Wednesday in 1992*

ˌblack 'box *noun* [C, usually sing.]
a complicated piece of equipment or process that you know produces particular results, but that you do not completely understand: *The decision-making process is seen as a black box—things go in and decisions come out.* ◇ *black-box economic models*

the ˌblack e'conomy (*BrE*) (*AmE* ˌunderground e'conomy) *noun* [sing.]
(*Economics*) business activity or work that is done without the knowledge of the government or other officials so that people can avoid paying tax on the money they earn: *Experts believe the black economy is 40% the size of the official economy.* → SHADOW ECONOMY

ˌblack 'hole *noun* [C, usually sing.]
something that costs you a lot of money or effort but does not provide any real benefit: *The company viewed the venture as a financial black hole.*

ˌblack 'knight *noun* [C]
(*Finance*) a company that tries to buy (**take over**) another company that does not want to be bought or offers too low a price → GREY KNIGHT, WHITE KNIGHT

blackleg /'blækleg/ noun [C] (*BrE*) (*informal*)
an offensive way of referring to a worker who refuses to join a strike or who works instead of sb on strike **SYN** SCAB

blacklist /'blæklɪst/ noun, verb
● *noun* [C]
a list of the people, companies, products or countries that an organization or a government cannot trust and tries to avoid
● *verb* [+ obj] (*often* be blacklisted)
to put a person, company or country on a blacklist: *No one will give him credit—he's been blacklisted by the banks.*

ˌblack 'market *noun* [C, usually sing.]
an illegal form of trade in which goods that are

difficult to get or foreign money are bought and sold: *Dollars are being sold on the black market.* ◇ *There is a huge black market in stolen cars.*
→ SHADOW MARKET ▶ ˌblack marke'teer *noun* [C]
ˌblack marke'teering *noun* [U]: *severe penalties for black marketeering*

ˌBlack 'Monday *noun* [sing.]
Monday 28 October 1929, when prices on the New York Stock Exchange fell to a very low level; Monday 19 October 1987, when there was a sudden large decrease in the prices of shares (a **crash**) on the New York Stock Exchange. Both caused similar falls in other markets around the world.

ˌBlack 'Thursday *noun* [sing.]
Thursday 24 October 1929, when there were signs that a severe CRASH (= a sudden large decrease in the prices of shares) was about to occur in the New York Stock Exchange

ˌBlack 'Tuesday *noun* [sing.]
Tuesday 29 October 1929, when there was a very large decrease in the prices of shares (a **crash**) in the US, which was the start of the Great Depression

ˌBlack 'Wednesday *noun* [sing.]
16 September 1992, when the British pound stopped being part of the EXCHANGE RATE MECHANISM and decreased in value by a large amount

ˌblank 'cheque (*AmE spelling* ~ **check**) *noun*
1 [C] a cheque that is signed but which does not have the amount of money to be paid written on it (*figurative*): *The board has been given a blank cheque to buy new assets.* **SYN** OPEN CHEQUE
2 [sing.] permission or authority to do anything that you think is necessary in order to achieve a particular result: *These laws do not give companies a blank cheque to pollute without paying.*

blanket /'blæŋkɪt/ adjective [only before noun]
1 that includes or affects all possible cases, situations or people: *a blanket ban on tobacco advertising*
2 (*Insurance*) (used about insurance contracts) that pays for damage to different items or for injury to different people, but has only one total sum insured and no particular sums for individual items or people: *While travelling on company business, you are covered under a blanket policy for injury.* ◇ *blanket cover for all machinery* → ALL-RISK, UMBRELLA

bleak /bliːk/ adjective (**bleaker, bleakest**)
not encouraging or giving any reason to have hope: *bleak sales figures* ◇ *Economists say the outlook for* (= the future of) *the economy is bleak.*

bleed /bliːd/ verb (**bled, bled** /bled/)
1 [+ obj or no obj] (*used especially in the continuous tenses*) (about a company) to lose a large amount of sth, especially money or jobs: *The business is bleeding cash at the rate of about $1 million a day.* ◇ *The fishing industry has been bleeding jobs for years.*
2 [+ obj] to take away a large amount of sb's money or resources: *The banking system has been bled of resources by the government this year.*
IDM bleed sb 'dry/'white to take away all sb's money

ˌblind 'test *noun* [C]
1 = BLIND TRIAL
2 (*Marketing*) a way of deciding which product out of a number of competing products is the best or most popular, or how a new product compares with others. People are asked to try the different products and to say which one/ones they prefer, but they are not told the names of the products: *In blind tests, consumers chose our cola over more established brands.*
→ DOUBLE-BLIND

,blind 'trial (*also* ,blind 'test) *noun* [C]
a type of research that is done to see the effects of a new product, especially a new medicine. Two groups of people believe that they are testing the product but one group is given a substance that does not contain any of it in order to compare the results with the group who are testing the real product. → DOUBLE-BLIND

blip /blɪp/ *noun* [C]
a change in a process or situation, usually when it gets worse for a short time before it gets better; a temporary problem: *The drop in sales was only a temporary blip.*

'blister pack (*also* 'bubble pack) *noun* [C]
a packet in which small goods such as pills are sold, with each individual item in its own separate cover on a piece of card: *The capsules come in a blister pack of 100.*—Picture at PACKAGING

'blister ,packaging (*also* 'bubble ,packaging, *less frequent*) *noun* [U]
materials used to protect small goods such as pills in their own separate covers on a piece of card; the process of wrapping goods in this way: *child-proof blister packaging* ◇ *blister-packaging machines*

blitz /blɪts/ *noun* [C, usually sing.]
something that involves a lot of activity and is done over a short period of time: *an advertising blitz*

bloated /'bləʊtɪd; *AmE* 'bloʊ-/ *adjective*
1 too big and costing or using too much money: *Many sectors of the economy remain bloated and uncompetitive.* ◇ *the company's bloated workforce*
2 (*IT, informal*) (about software, etc.) not efficient and needing too much computer memory: *Software programs become more bloated every week.* ◇ *bloated applications that take too long to download*

bloatware /'bləʊtweə(r); *AmE* 'bloʊtwer/ (*also* 'fatware) *noun* [U]
(*IT, informal*) software that needs too much computer memory and does not work efficiently: *Continually adding new features to a product often results in bloatware.* ◇ *a 100 megabyte piece of bloatware*

bloc /blɒk; *AmE* blɑːk/ *noun* [C]
1 a group of countries that work closely together because they have similar political or financial interests: *the former Soviet bloc* ◇ *a trade/trading bloc*
2 (*Economics*) = CURRENCY BLOC

block /blɒk; *AmE* blɑːk/ *noun, verb*
● *noun* [C]

SEE ALSO: **building blocks, office block**

1 a quantity of sth or an amount of sth that is considered as a single unit, especially a large quantity or amount: *a block of seats* ◇ *a block of text in a document* ◇ *The airline gives a discount for* **block bookings** (= a large number of tickets bought at the same time).
2 (*Finance*) a very large number of shares or bonds: *The foundation holds a large block of shares in the electronics company.* ◇ *The company has sold 40 million of its shares in a* **block trade** *worth €1 billion.*
→ BLOCKING MINORITY
IDM **be/go on the 'block** to be sold, especially by AUCTION: *The group's European assets are on the block.* **put/lay your head/neck on the 'block** to risk losing your job, damaging your reputation, etc. by doing or saying sth: *He was prepared to put his head on the block and say the bank would be profitable within one year.*
● *verb* [+ obj]
(*Finance*) to stop sb from being able to remove money from their bank account: *A joint account is usually blocked if one of you informs the bank that it is no longer needed.* ◇ *a blocked account* → FREEZE

blockade /blɒ'keɪd; *AmE* blɑː'k-/ *noun, verb*
● *noun* [C]
1 an organized action to stop people or goods from leaving or entering a particular place, often as a form of protest: *Truck drivers have begun a blockade of oil depots to protest against high fuel prices.*
☉ *to impose/lift a blockade*
2 a barrier that stops people or vehicles entering or leaving a place
● *verb* [+ obj]
to physically stop people or goods from leaving or entering a particular place, often as a form of protest: *Farmers have threatened to blockade the supermarket's distribution centres.*

blockbuster /'blɒkbʌstə(r); *AmE* 'blɑːk-/ *noun* [C]
(*Marketing*) something that has great financial success, especially a successful book, film/movie or medicine: *Amgen's blockbuster drug, Epogen* ◇ *The company relies too heavily on a single blockbuster product.* ▶ **'blockbusting** *adjective* [only before noun]: *a blockbusting arthritis drug* ◇ *a blockbusting $38 million deal*

'block ,diagram *noun* [C]
a drawing that shows how the different parts of a machine, a system or a process are linked. The parts are shown as squares, or similar shapes, with labels.

'blocking mi,nority (*also* 'blocking stake) *noun* [C]
a large number of shares in a company that give their owner the power to stop other companies from buying or controlling the company
→ CONTROLLING INTEREST

,block in'surance *noun* [U] (*BrE*)
a type of insurance that a company or an organization buys for all its employees or members: *The university has negotiated a block insurance policy to cover students' personal possessions.*
→ BLANKET (2)

,block re'lease *noun* [U]
(*HR*) in the UK, a way of studying or receiving training at a college, etc. while you are working in a job, that involves attending regular short courses: *a four-week period of block release* ◇ *The course can be studied on a block-release basis.* → DAY RELEASE

,block 'vote *noun* [C]
in the UK, a voting system in which each person who votes represents the members of their organization; the votes themselves: *the power of union leaders with hundreds of thousands of block votes*

bloodletting /'blʌdletɪŋ/ *noun* [U]
1 (*usually used in newspapers*) a situation where a company removes lots of employees from their jobs because of serious financial problems: *In the first round of bloodletting, 17 000 will lose their jobs.*
2 (*usually used in newspapers*) a situation where the prices of shares on the stock exchange decrease by a large amount: *The bloodletting on Wall Street continues as investors rush to sell their stocks.*

blow /bləʊ; *AmE* bloʊ/ *verb* (**blew** /bluː/ **blown** /bləʊn; *AmE* bloʊn/)
IDM **blow the 'whistle (on sb/sth)** (*informal*) to try to stop sth wrong or illegal that sb is doing by telling sb in authority about it: *The auditors have a duty to blow the whistle on their clients.*
→ WHISTLE-BLOWER

blowout /'bləʊaʊt; *AmE* 'bloʊ-/ *noun, adjective*
(*especially AmE*) (*informal*)
● *noun* [C, usually sing.]
1 a period of great economic difficulty; a sudden

decrease in value: *a stock-market blowout*
→ MELTDOWN
2 (*Stock Exchange*) a situation when new shares that
are being offered are all sold very quickly and the
price is high
3 a sudden large increase: *The government has
blamed poor economic conditions for the deficit
blowout.*
● *adjective* [only before noun]
very successful and making a large profit; very
large: *The company expects a blowout fourth
quarter.* ◇ *a blowout end-of-year sale*

'Blue Book *noun* [sing.]
(*Economics*) a report on the economic state of the
UK that is published every year

,blue 'chip *noun* [C, usually pl.]
(*Stock Exchange, informal*) the shares of the best-
known companies on the stock market, which are
considered to be a safe investment: *US blue chips
rose 0.2% in morning trade yesterday.* ▸ **'blue-chip**
adjective [only before noun]: *blue-chip companies/
shares/stocks* See note at STOCK

'blue-chipper *noun* [C]
a BLUE-CHIP company

,blue-'collar *adjective* [only before noun]
connected with workers who do physical work in
industry → PINK-COLLAR, WHITE-COLLAR
● *blue-collar* **jobs/labour/work/workers**

blueprint /'bluːprɪnt/ *noun* [C]
1 a plan that shows what can be achieved and how
it can be achieved: *The scheme is being tested in one
region, and may become a blueprint for the rest of
the country.*
● *to* **draft/draw up/have/provide** *a blueprint*
2 a print of a plan for a building or a machine,
with white lines on a blue background: *blueprints
of a new aircraft*
● *to* **draw up/make/produce** *a blueprint*

'blue-sky *adjective* [only before noun] (*informal*)
used to describe new and different ways of
thinking about and solving problems, although the
ideas produced may not yet be possible or
practical: *The government has been doing some* **blue-
sky thinking** *on how to improve public transport.*

,blue-sky 'laws *noun* [pl.]
(*Stock Exchange*) state laws in the US that prevent
the dishonest buying and selling of shares

Bluetooth™ /'bluːtuːθ/ *noun* [U]
a technology that allows data to be transferred
between mobile phones/cellphones, mobile
computers and other devices over short distances
without the use of wires

blurb /blɜːb; *AmE* blɜːrb/ *noun* [C, usually sing.]
(*Marketing*) a short description of a book, a new
product, etc., written by the people who have
produced it, that is intended to attract your
attention and make you want to buy it: *'This is a
diet that really works', according to the book's cover
blurb.*

bn *abbr* (only used in written English)
a billion

★ **board** /bɔːd; *AmE* bɔːrd/ *noun, verb*
● *noun*

─────────────────────────────
SEE ALSO: **across the board, appeals ~, Big ~,
bulletin ~, circuit ~, currency ~, Federal Reserve ~,**
etc.
─────────────────────────────

1 [C with sing./pl. verb] a BOARD OF DIRECTORS: *She
has a seat on the board.* ◇ *The board is/are unhappy
about falling sales.* ◇ *members of the board* ◇

discussions at board level ◇ *A* **board meeting** *was
held to discuss the offer.*
● *to* **be on/have a seat on/join/sit on** *the board* ◆ *to*
appoint/elect *sb to the board* ◆ *to* **dismiss/remove**
sb from the board
2 [C] used in the name of some organizations: *the
Welsh Tourist Board*
3 [U] the meals that are provided when you stay in
a hotel, for example; what you pay for the meals
4 [C,U] a large flat piece of wood, plastic or other
material: *The lecturer wrote his key points up on the
board.*
5 [C] = NOTICEBOARD
IDM **be above 'board** (especially about a business
arrangement) to be honest and open: *We were
assured that the deal was completely above board.*
**be, come, stay, etc. on 'board; bring, have,
keep, etc. sb on 'board** to be, become, stay, keep,
etc. sb, involved in sth: *It's good to have you on
board* (= working with us). ◇ *They wanted to bring
someone more mature on board to help with sales
and marketing.* **on 'board** on a ship, an aircraft or a
train → idiom at TAKE *verb*
● *verb*
1 [+ obj *or* no obj] to get on a plane, bus, train, etc:
The passengers are waiting to board.
2 [no obj] **be boarding** when a plane or ship **is
boarding**, it is ready for passengers to get on: *Flight
BA193 to Paris is now boarding at gate 37.*

'boarding card (*also* **'boarding pass**) *noun* [C]
a card that you show before you get on a plane or
boat

,board of di'rectors *noun* [C with sing./pl. verb]
the group of people chosen by shareholders to
control a company, decide its policies and appoint
senior officers: *The board of directors is/are
considering the takeover bid.* ◇ *She was elected to the
board of directors in 2004.* ◇ *He will continue to serve
as chairman of the board of directors.*

boardroom /'bɔːdruːm; -rʊm; *AmE* 'bɔːrd-/
noun [C]
a room in which the meetings of the BOARD of a
company (= the group of people who decide on its
policies) are held: *decisions made in the boardroom*
◇ *A senior executive quit today after a boardroom
battle* (= a disagreement between directors) *over
the future structure of the company.*
● *a boardroom* **battle/coup/dispute/power struggle/
row** ◆ *a boardroom* **shake-up/upheaval** ◆
boardroom **pay/salaries**

bobo /'bəʊbəʊ; *AmE* 'boʊboʊ/ *noun* [C] (*plural
bobos*)
a young professional who has lots of money and
probably works in an Internet company, but who
has ideas and attitudes that are different from what
is considered normal by most people **NOTE** Formed
from the first part of the words 'bourgeois
bohemian' (= a middle class person who lives in an
informal and unusual way).

'body ,copy *noun* [U]
the main section of text in an article, an
advertisement, a web page, etc: *You will need at
least one font for the title and one for the body copy.*

,body 'corporate *noun* [C] (*plural* **bodies
corporate**)
(*Law*) a group of people, for example an association
or a business, that is treated as having its own legal
status

'body ,language *noun* [U]
the process of communicating what you are feeling
or thinking by the way you place and move your
body rather than by words: *The course trains
salespeople in reading the customer's body language.*

'body shop *noun* [C]
(*Manufacturing*)
1 the part of a car factory where the main bodies of the cars are made → PAINT SHOP
2 a place where repairs are made to the main bodies of cars

the ,B of 'E (*also* ,Bo'E) *abbr* (*only used in written English*)
the Bank of England

BOGOF /'bɒɡɒf; *AmE* 'bɔːɡɔːf, -ɡɑːf/ *abbr*
(*Marketing, usually used in written English*) **buy one get one free** used in a shop/store to tell customers that they can buy two of a particular item and only pay for one

'boilerplate /'bɔɪləpleɪt; *AmE* -lər-/ *noun* [U]
(*especially AmE*)
a standard piece of writing or computer code that can be copied and used in different situations: *This boilerplate wording is used in most employment contracts.*

'boiler room *noun* [C]
1 (*Stock Exchange, informal*) a place where people sell shares by telephone, in an unfair and dishonest way: *a high-pressure salesman from a boiler-room operation*
2 a room where the heating for a building is produced

BOL /ˌbiː əʊ 'el; *AmE* oʊ/ = BILL OF LADING

'bolt-on *adjective* [only before noun]
something that can be easily added to a machine, a website, a company, etc. to enable it to do sth new: *They have added bolt-on e-commerce software to their website to enable customers to order direct.*

BOM /ˌbiː əʊ 'em; *AmE* oʊ/ = BILL OF MATERIALS

bona fide /ˌbəʊnə 'faɪdi; *AmE* ˌboʊnə/ *adjective*
[usually before noun]
(*Law*) genuine, real or legal; not false: *Is it a bona fide, reputable organization?* **NOTE** Bona fide is a Latin phrase meaning 'in good faith'.

'bona ˌfide occuˈpational qualifiˈcation *noun* [C,U] (*abbr* BFOQ)
(*HR; Law*) in the US, a reason that employers can give for employing a worker only from a particular group of people if they can prove that other people would not be able to do the job

bona fides /ˌbəʊnə 'faɪdiːz; *AmE* ˌboʊnə/ *noun* [U]
(*Law*) evidence showing that sb is what they claim to be or that what they say is true: *The firm asked for a reference to check the candidate's bona fides.*
SYN GOOD FAITH **NOTE** Bona fides is a Latin phrase meaning 'good faith'.

★bond /bɒnd; *AmE* bɑːnd/ *noun* [C]

SEE ALSO: **appeal bond, bid ~, corporate ~, customs ~, debenture ~, fidelity ~, foreign ~,** etc.

1 (*Finance*) an agreement by a government or an organization to pay back the money an investor has lent plus a fixed amount of interest on a particular date; a document containing this agreement: *Government bonds are usually considered to be a safe investment.* ◇ *The company are to issue bonds backed by its revenue from travel insurance.* ◇ *They will launch a €2 bn bond issue to cut their debt.* ◇ *the bond market* See note at FOREIGN BOND
○ *to buy/hold/invest in/issue/redeem/sell/trade bonds* • *high-yield/long-term/twenty-year bonds* • *a bond broker/investor/trader*
2 (*Law*) (*especially AmE*) an amount of money that sb pays in case they fail to do what they have agreed to do: *He was released on a $5 000 bond* (= if he did not appear in court on a particular day he would lose the money). → BAIL
3 (*Law*) a legal written agreement or promise
○ *to make/sign a bond*

4 (*Insurance*) a word used for certain kinds of insurance policy that protect companies from loss
IDM **in 'bond** (*Trade*) (about imported goods) being held until the buyer pays any necessary import taxes and other charges → BONDED WAREHOUSE

bonded /'bɒndɪd; *AmE* 'bɑːn-/ *adjective*
1 (*Trade*) (about imported goods) held until the buyer pays any necessary import taxes: *bonded goods* → BONDED WAREHOUSE
2 (*Insurance*) (*BrE*) (about a travel company) having insurance that protects the customer in case anything goes wrong: *We recommend that you use an ABTA bonded travel agent.*
3 (*Insurance*) (*AmE*) (especially about a person or company providing a service) having a type of insurance that promises the customer that the job will be done and will be done well: *a bonded electrician*

ˌbonded 'factory *noun* [C]
(*Manufacturing; Trade*) a factory that uses imported raw materials to produce goods only for export, and so does not need to pay import taxes

ˌbonded 'warehouse (*also* ˌCustoms 'warehouse, *less frequent*) *noun* [C]
(*Trade*) a building where imported goods are stored until import taxes are paid on them

'bond fund *noun* [C]
(*Finance*) a fund where the money is invested in government or company bonds. It pays regular, fixed interest and has a low risk.

bondholder /'bɒndhəʊldər; *AmE* 'bɑːndhoʊldər/ *noun* [C]
(*Finance*) a person who has bought government or company bonds

'bond note *noun* [C]
(*Trade*) a document that must be signed by CUSTOMS AND EXCISE (= the government department that collects taxes on imports) before BONDED goods can be collected by an importer or exported again

'bond ˌrating *noun* [U,C]
(*Finance*) a system of giving a grade to a bond according to how good and safe an investment it is considered to be; the grade that is given: *A triple-A bond rating guarantees a safe investment.*

★bonus /'bəʊnəs; *AmE* 'boʊ-/ *noun* [C] (*plural* **bonuses**)

SEE ALSO: **acceptance bonus, attendance bonus**

1 an extra amount of money that is added to a payment, especially to sb's wages as a reward: *If he had stayed on as CEO, he would have received a $1 million bonus.* ◇ *Productivity bonuses are paid to staff meeting agreed targets.* ◇ *bonus payments* See note at SALARY
○ *to earn/get/receive a bonus* • *to award/pay (sb) a bonus* • *merit/performance/productivity bonuses* • *an annual/end-of year/a year-end bonus* • *a loyalty/retention/signing bonus*
2 (*Finance*) a payment in money or shares that a company makes to its shareholders: *The company will issue one bonus share for every share held.*
○ *bonus dividends/shares/stock*
3 (*Insurance*) (*also* ˌcapital 'bonus) a share of its profits that a LIFE INSURANCE company pays to its customers (**policyholders**): *Terminal bonuses* (= an extra payment made at the end of a life insurance contract) *are being cut completely.*

'bonus ˌissue *noun* [C] (*especially BrE*)
(*Finance*) a situation in which a company uses its spare profits (**reserves**) to create new shares, which are then given free to the shareholders in proportion to the number of shares that they

already own: *The company has proposed a 1–for–2 bonus issue* (= shareholders get 1 extra share for every 2 shares that they own). **SYN** CAPITALIZATION ISSUE, SCRIP ISSUE

'bonus shares *noun* [C]
(*Finance*) shares that a company gives free to people who already hold its shares, for example in a CAPITALIZATION ISSUE

★ **book** /bʊk/ *noun, verb*
● *noun* [C]

SEE ALSO: **appointment book, Blue ~, cash ~, double-~, off-the-~, order ~, paying-in ~,** etc.

1 a document that forms an official record or list: *a chequebook ◇ a phone book* (= a list of the names, addresses and telephone numbers of people and businesses)
2 a piece of writing published in printed or electronic form: *an e-book*
3 (*Commerce*; *Finance*) a list of clients and/or investments that a person or a company looks after: *You will learn the skills required to* ***manage*** *a book of accounts for one or more pension funds.*
IDM **by the 'book** following rules and instructions in a very strict way: *Doing things by the book doesn't always work in the real world.* → idiom at THROW → BOOKS

● *verb*
1 [+ obj *or* no obj] (*especially BrE*) to arrange with a hotel, restaurant, etc. to have a room, table, seat, etc. on a particular date: *I'd like to book a table for six for 8 o'clock tonight. ◇ I'm sorry—we're* ***fully booked.*** → RESERVE
2 [+ obj] to arrange for sb to have a seat on a plane: *Can you book me on the 6 o'clock flight?*
3 (*Accounting*) [+ obj] to record or show sth in a company's accounts: *Last year the company booked a $150 million gain.*
PHR V **,book 'in/'into sth** to arrive at a hotel and arrange to stay there: *I arrived at ten and booked straight into a hotel.* **,book sb 'in/'into sth** to arrange for sb to have a room at a hotel

bookbuilding /'bʊkbɪldɪŋ/ *noun* [U]
(*Stock Exchange*) a way of deciding the price of new shares by first asking important investors how many they would be willing to buy and at what price: *Bookbuilding will open immediately and close tomorrow, with prices and allocations expected on Friday.*

'book debt = ACCOUNTS RECEIVABLE

'book depreci,ation *noun* [U]
(*Accounting*) how much value an asset loses each year, as written in a company's financial records (**books**) → TAX DEPRECIATION

'book ,entry *noun* [U,C]
(*Finance*) a record kept on a computer system of the names of people who have bought a bond, share, etc. With this method, certificates are not given to buyers.

'book ,equity *noun* [U]
(*Accounting*) the value of a company as shown in its financial records (**books**), which is its assets minus its LIABILITIES (= the money it owes) **SYN** BOOK VALUE

'book gain = BOOK PROFIT

booking /'bʊkɪŋ/ *noun* [C,U]
an arrangement that you make in advance to buy a ticket to travel somewhere, go to the theatre, etc: *Can I make a booking for Friday afternoon?* → RESERVATION (1)

★ **bookkeeping** /'bʊkkiːpɪŋ/ *noun* [U]

SEE ALSO: **double-entry bookkeeping, single-entry bookkeeping**

the work of keeping an accurate record of the accounts of a business: *bookkeeping entries/errors* ▶ **'bookkeeper** *noun* [C]: *He started off as a bookkeeper in the firm.*

bookmark /'bʊkmɑːk; *AmE* -mɑːrk/ *noun* [C]
(*IT*) the address of a web page, file, etc. that you store on your computer so that you can find it quickly ▶ **'bookmark** *verb* [+ obj]: *Bookmark this site!*

'book of 'final 'entry *noun* [C, usually pl.]
(*Accounting*) an account book or computer record which contains a summary of all a business's financial records for a period of time → GENERAL LEDGER

'book of 'prime 'entry *noun* [C, usually pl.] (*also* 'book of 'first 'entry, 'book of o'riginal 'entry)
(*Accounting*) an account book or computer record in which a company's financial TRANSACTIONS are first recorded

'book ,profit (*also* 'book gain) *noun* [C,U]
(*Accounting*) a profit that has been made but not taken as real money yet, for example shares that have risen in value but have not yet been sold **SYN** PAPER PROFIT

'book ,runner = MANAGING UNDERWRITER

books /bʊks/ *noun* [pl.]

SEE ALSO: **statutory books**

1 (*Accounting*) (*also* **ac'count books**) the written record of the financial affairs of a business: *People who run their own business often do the books themselves. ◇ a bid to balance the books ◇ The bank is aiming to* ***clear*** *all bad loans* ***off*** *its books over the next year.* **SYN** ACCOUNTS
O *to* ***audit/do/keep*** *the books • to* ***balance*** *the books*
2 a record of the customers, orders and stock that a company has: *There are no other large orders* ***on the books.*** → BOOK *noun* (3)
IDM **,cook the 'books** (*informal*) to put false information in a company's accounts: *The books were cooked to make profits seem much higher than they were.* **(be) on sb's 'books** (*HR*) (to be) on an organization's list, for example the list of people who work for a company, or a list of people who are available for a particular type of work: *It's the largest security firm in the UK with 10 000 staff on its books.*

,books of ac'count *noun* [pl.]
(*Accounting*) the written financial records of a business **SYN** ACCOUNTS → BOOKS (1)

'book ,transfer *noun* [C]
(*Finance*) a record kept on a computer system of a change in the ownership of shares, bonds, etc. without using certificates

'book ,value *noun* [U; C, usually sing.] (*abbr* **BV**)
(*Accounting*)
1 (*also* ,**written-down 'value**) the value that a business gives to an asset in its financial records (**books**), which is the original cost of the asset minus DEPRECIATION (= its decrease in value over a period of time): *The old photocopier is still useful, although its book value is almost nothing.* → MARKET VALUE
2 the value of a company as shown in its financial records, which is its assets minus its LIABILITIES (= the money it owes): *The group is hoping to sell the business for more than its current book value.* **SYN** BOOK EQUITY, SHAREHOLDER EQUITY → MARKET VALUE

★ **boom** /buːm/ *noun, verb*
(*Economics*)
● *noun* [C]

SEE ALSO: **baby boom**

a sudden increase in trade and economic activity; a

period of wealth and success: *a boom in sales* ◇ *The sales boom is attributed to low unemployment and low interest rates.* ◇ *the Internet boom of the 1990s* ◇ *a boom year (for trade, exports, etc.)* OPP SLUMP—Picture at BUSINESS CYCLE
➊ *a consumer/credit/an economic/investment/a sales/spending boom* ✦ *a property/retail boom* ✦ *a boom period/year* ✦ *boom times/years*
IDM **,boom and 'bust** a feature of an economic system or an industry where a period of success and wealth is followed by a period of difficulty, then by another period of success, and so on in a repeated pattern: *IT is a highly competitive industry, prone to boom and bust.* ◇ *the **boom-and-bust cycle** of agriculture*
● *verb* [no obj]
(about a business or an economy) to have a period of rapid growth; to become bigger, more successful, etc: *Use of the Internet has boomed in recent years.* ◇ *Business is booming!* ▶ **'booming** *adjective* [usually before noun]: *a booming housing market* ◇ *booming exports*

boomlet /'bu:mlət/ *noun* [C]
(*Economics*) a short period of sudden trade and economic activity and growth

★ **boost** /bu:st/ *verb, noun*
● *verb* [+ obj]
1 to increase sth in strength, number or value: *The company aims to boost earnings by 18%.* ◇ *Sales are being boosted by consumers' growing confidence in Internet shopping.*
2 to take actions that will make an economy stronger and encourage business activity: *Low interest rates are finally boosting the economy.*
● *noun* [C, usually sing.]
1 something that helps to increase or improve sth else: *Low interest rates should give a major boost to home sales.* ◇ *Intel received a boost* (= its share price increased) *from positive comments made by analysts.*
➊ *to give/provide* a boost (to sb/sth) ✦ *to get/receive a boost (from sth)* ✦ *a big/huge/major/much-needed/ welcome boost*
2 an increase: *The company has announced a boost in exports.*
➊ *to announce/enjoy/experience* a boost ✦ *a big/ dramatic/huge boost*

boot /bu:t/ *verb*
1 [+ obj] **boot sth (up)** to start a computer or a piece of software and wait for it to become ready to use: *Boot up your Web browser and type in 'www.oup.com/elt'.*
2 [no obj] (about a computer or a piece of software) to prepare itself for use: *waiting for the machine to boot up* ◇ *The system won't boot because of an error.* → REBOOT

bootable /'bu:təbl/ *adjective*
(*IT*) (about a computer disk) that contains the basic software that is necessary to start (**boot**) a computer

bootleg /'bu:tleg/ *adjective, verb, noun*
● *adjective* [only before noun]
made and sold illegally: *a bootleg cassette* ◇ *bootleg computer software* → PIRATE
● *verb* [+ obj] (**-gg-**)
to make and sell an illegal copy of sth: *bootlegging copies of the program* ▶ **'bootlegger** *noun* [C]: *Life will be getting tougher for bootleggers.* **'bootlegging** *noun* [U]
● *noun* [C]
a copy of a music recording, film/movie, book or piece of software that is made and sold illegally See note at COPY

bootstrapping /'bu:tstræpɪŋ/ *noun* [U]
the act of building a business with very little outside investment, but with a lot of imagination and effort

BOQ /ˌbi: əʊ 'kju:; *AmE* oʊ/ = BILL OF QUANTITIES

★ **borrow** /'bɒrəʊ; *AmE* 'bɑːroʊ; 'bɔːr-/ *verb* [+ obj or no obj]
to take money from a person, a bank, etc. and agree to pay it back within a particular period of time, usually with an amount of interest added: *The group has borrowed €4 billion from banks.* ◇ *She borrowed **heavily** to set the company up.* ◇ *borrowing **at** a low rate of interest* See note at LEND
PHR V **,borrow a'gainst sth; ,borrow sth a'gainst sth** to borrow money by using sth valuable as COLLATERAL (= sth that you promise to give to sb/ sth if you do not pay back the money that you owe them): *The amount of money that people are borrowing against their homes reached a very high level.*

★ **borrower** /'bɒrəʊə(r); *AmE* 'bɑːroʊ-; 'bɔːr-/ *noun* [C]
a person or company that borrows money, especially from a bank: *We offer the same rates of interest to new and existing borrowers.* ◇ *The bank has lost a lot of money from lending to high-risk borrowers.* ◇ *borrowers with a good credit history* (= people who have always paid their debts)
OPP LENDER
➊ *corporate/creditworthy/existing/high-risk/new* borrowers

★ **borrowing** /'bɒrəʊɪŋ; *AmE* 'bɑːroʊɪŋ; 'bɔːr-/ *noun*

SEE ALSO: bank borrowing, consumer ~, net ~

1 [U] the money that a company, person or government borrows; the act of borrowing money: *If it's cheap for people to borrow, borrowing and spending will increase.* ◇ *Household borrowing* (= money borrowed by families) *has reached alarming levels.* ◇ *lower borrowing costs* OPP LENDING
➊ *consumer/corporate/household* borrowing ✦ *foreign/government/public-sector* borrowing ✦ *borrowing costs/facilities/requirement(s)* ✦ *to curb/ cut/increase/reduce* borrowing
2 borrowings [pl.] the amount of money that a company has borrowed: *The car manufacturer has total borrowings of €7.5 billion.*
➊ *to cut/increase/reduce/repay* borrowings ✦ *bank/ foreign currency/long-term/short-term* borrowings

---

VOCABULARY BUILDING

Words for bosses

TOP MANAGEMENT
● *directors*
● *executives*
● *senior managers*

MIDDLE MANAGEMENT
● *junior/middle managers*
● *line managers*
● *team leaders*
● *supervisors*

Note: The word **direct report** is used to describe a person that you are directly responsible for, at any level of an organization: *Line managers should set targets with their direct reports.* The phrase **immediate boss/supervisor** can be used to describe the person that you are responsible to.

See note at RESPONSIBILITY

★ **boss** /bɒs; *AmE* bɔːs/ *noun* [C]
1 a person who is in charge of other people at work and tells them what to do: *I'll have to ask my boss about that.* ◇ *Her **immediate** boss* (= the person who tells her what to do) *is the marketing*

manager. ◇ *I like **being my own boss*** (= working for myself and making my own decisions).
2 (*informal*) (often used in newspapers) the person in charge of a company: *He's the new boss at J Sainsbury.*
→ HONCHO

the ˌBoston ˈMatrix /ˈbɒstən; *AmE* ˈbɔːs-/ (*also* **ˌgrowth-share ˈmatrix**) *noun* [C, usually sing.]
(*Marketing*) a way of analysing how successful a range of a company's products or services are by looking at the percentage of sales it has in the market and how fast the sales are growing

Boston Matrix

bot /bɒt; *AmE* bɑːt/ *noun* [C]
SEE ALSO: **shopping bot**

(*IT, informal*) a piece of software that a computer uses for ordinary or very long tasks, especially searching for particular information on the Internet **NOTE Bot** is an abbreviation of 'robot'.

bottleneck /ˈbɒtlnek; *AmE* ˈbɑːtl-/ *noun* [C]
anything that slows down development or progress, particularly in business or industry: *eliminating bottlenecks in the manufacturing process*
O major/potential/severe bottlenecks ◆ **to cause/create** a bottleneck ◆ **to clear/eliminate/remove** a bottleneck

bottler /ˈbɒtlə(r); *AmE* ˈbɑːtlər/ *noun* [C]
(*Manufacturing*) a company that puts drinks into small containers such as bottles and cans, to sell to the public: *the second largest bottler of Pepsi drinks* ◇ *a soft-drinks bottler* ▶ **ˈbottling** *noun* [U]: *new bottling plants in Southeast Asia*

bottom /ˈbɒtəm; *AmE* ˈbɑːtəm/ *noun, adjective, verb*
● *noun*
SEE ALSO: **false bottom, race to the ~, rock ~**

1 [sing.] the lowest or worst level of sth: *You have to be prepared to start **at** the bottom in the company and work your way up.* ◇ *Analysts believe this is the bottom of the cycle for mobile phone makers.* ◇ *The decline in demand for the products has now **hit bottom**.*
2 [C] the lowest part of sth: *A message should appear **at** the bottom of the screen.*
IDM the ˌbottom drops/falls ˈout of sth people stop buying or using the products of a particular industry: *The bottom has dropped out of the travel market.* **from the ˌbottom ˈup** relying on the ideas and support of the people who have lower positions in an organization: *She believes that authority comes from the bottom up, not the top down.* [OPP] FROM THE TOP DOWN → BOTTOM-UP
→ idiom at TOUCH

● *adjective* [only before noun]
in the lowest, last or furthest place or position: *Double-click on the icon in the bottom left-hand corner of your screen.* ◇ *The firm ranked in the bottom 25% of all those surveyed.* ◇ *The insurer has focused on **the bottom end of the market*** (= on selling to people who cannot afford to spend much).
● *verb* [no obj] **bottom (out)** to stop getting lower or worse: *The number of people unemployed has risen by 67 000 since bottoming in April.* ◇ *There are signs that the country's economy is bottoming out.*
▶ **ˈbottoming, ˌbottoming ˈout** *noun* [U; sing.]: *a bottoming out in energy prices*

ˈbottom ˌfishing *noun* [U] (*especially AmE*)
(*Stock Exchange, informal*) the activity of buying shares or businesses when the prices are unusually low and are not likely to fall much further: *Some people start bottom fishing too early, before the lowest prices have been reached.* ▶ **ˈbottom ˌfisher** *noun* [C] **NOTE** The use of this word often shows that the speaker disapproves of people who buy shares in this way. → BARGAIN HUNTER

★ **ˌbottom ˈline** *noun* [C, usually sing.]
1 (*Accounting*) the amount of money that is a profit or a loss after everything has been calculated: *The drop in sales had a big impact on our bottom line.* ◇ *The bottom line for 2005 was a pre-tax profit of €60 million.* ◇ *a bottom-line loss of $281 million*
O to affect/have an impact on/improve the bottom line ◆ *a bottom-line **loss/profit***
NOTE The term **bottom line** originally referred to the line at the bottom of a PROFIT AND LOSS ACCOUNT where the total amount of profit or loss was written.
2 the bottom line the most important thing that you have to consider or accept; the essential point in a discussion, etc: *The bottom line is that we have to make a decision today.*
3 the lowest price that sb will accept: *Two thousand—and that's my bottom line!*

ˌbottom-ˈup *adjective*
1 from or involving the people who have lower positions in an organization or their ideas: *a bottom-up approach to management*
2 starting from the beginning of a process: *bottom-up analysis*
[OPP] TOP-DOWN

ˌbought ˈdeal *noun* [C]
(*Stock Exchange*) a way of selling new shares or bonds that involves selling all of them to one bank, BROKER, etc., that then sells them to other investors

ˈbought ˌledger = PURCHASE LEDGER

bounce /baʊns/ *verb, noun*
● *verb*
1 [+ obj *or* no obj] (*informal*) if a cheque **bounces**, or a bank **bounces** it, the bank refuses to pay it because there is not enough money in the account: *The cheque will bounce if your salary doesn't reach your account today.* ◇ *a bounced cheque*
→ DISHONOUR, RD, RETURN
2 [+ obj *or* no obj] to increase suddenly in value or level: *The retailer's shares bounced 2.7 per cent to €55.5.*
O prices/sales/shares/the market bounced
3 [no obj] **bounce around/up and down** to repeatedly increase and decrease in value or level: *The stock price has been bouncing up and down as much as 10% a day.*
4 [+ obj *or* no obj] if an email **bounces** or the system **bounces** it, it returns to the person who sent it because it cannot be delivered.
PHR V ˌbounce ˈback (from sth) to become successful again or start to increase again after a period of difficulty: *The airline's shares have bounced back from two days of heavy losses.*
● *noun* [C]
SEE ALSO: **dead cat bounce**

a rapid increase: *She predicts a 21% bounce in the FTSE next year.* ◊ *We had expected a bounce back in sales.*

bound /baʊnd/ *adjective* [not before noun]

SEE ALSO: **strike-bound**

(*Law*) having a legal duty to do sth: *A parent is legally bound to feed, clothe and arrange education for his or her own children.* ◊ *The appeal court said it was not bound to follow its previous decision.* → BIND

bourse /bʊəs; *AmE* bʊrs/ *noun* [C]
(*Stock Exchange*) used especially in newspapers to refer to the stock exchanges of particular countries, especially France and other countries in Europe: *Wanadoo's shares rose 5 per cent to €6.31 on the Paris bourse.* **NOTE** **La Bourse** is the French term for 'stock exchange'.

boutique /buːˈtiːk/ *noun, adjective*
● *noun* [C]
1 a small shop, often with a particular style, selling, for example, fashionable clothes: *Last spring they opened their own exclusive boutique.*
● *a baby/designer/fashion boutique*
2 (*Finance*) = INVESTMENT BOUTIQUE
● *adjective* [only before noun]
small and offering a particular or special service
● *a boutique hairdresser/hotel/investment bank*

box /bɒks; *AmE* bɑːks/ *noun, verb*
● *noun* [C]

SEE ALSO: **black box, cash ~, dialog ~, drop ~, in-~, list ~, out-~**, etc.

1 a container made of wood, cardboard, metal, etc., with a flat stiff base and sides, often with a lid, that is used especially for holding solid things: *The goods will be shipped in cardboard boxes.*—Picture at PACKAGING
2 a box and its contents: *a box of chocolates*
3 a small square or similar shape on a page or a computer screen in which you write information or which you use to make a choice: *Please tick the box if you do not wish to receive any advertising from us.* ◊ (*BrE*) *Please tick the box if you do not wish to receive any advertising from us.* ◊ (*AmE*) *check the box* → CHECKBOX
4 = BOX NUMBER
5 a computer system for storing messages: *The information will be sent directly to your email box.* → INBOX
6 (*informal*) = SET-TOP BOX
7 a small area in a court or a theatre separated from where other people sit
8 an area of seats in a sports ground that is kept for a particular group of people and is separate from the seats that the public use: *a corporate box* → idioms at OUT *adj.*, THINK, TICK *verb*
● *verb* [+ obj]
box sth (up) to put sth in a box

'box file *noun* [C]
a container for letters, and other documents in the shape of a box—Picture at FILE

'box ,number (*also* **box**) *noun* [C] (*abbr* **Box no**)
a number used as an address to which letters can be sent, especially one that a company uses or one given in newspaper advertisements → PO BOX
● *to reply/write to a box number*

BOY /ˌbiː əʊ ˈwaɪ; *AmE* oʊ/ = BEGINNING OF YEAR

boycott /ˈbɔɪkɒt; *AmE* -kɑːt/ *verb, noun*
● *verb* [+ obj]
to refuse to buy, use or take part in sth as a way of protesting: *Motorists have threatened to boycott the gas stations in protest at price rises.*
● *to decide/plan/threaten/vow to boycott sth*
● *noun* [C]

SEE ALSO: **secondary boycott**

an act of **boycotting** sth; the period of time when people **boycott** sth: *a trade boycott of British goods*
● *to call for/encourage a boycott*

bpd /ˌbiː piː ˈdiː/ *abbr* **barrels per day** a way of measuring how much oil a country or a region produces

BPO /ˌbiː piː ˈəʊ; *AmE* ˈoʊ/ = BUSINESS PROCESS OUTSOURCING

BPR /ˌbiː piː ˈɑː(r)/ = BUSINESS PROCESS RE-ENGINEERING

BQ /ˌbiː ˈkjuː/ = BILL OF QUANTITIES

bracket /ˈbrækɪt/ *noun* [C]

SEE ALSO: **bulge-bracket, tax bracket**

1 **age, price, income, etc. bracket** ages, prices, etc. within a particular range: *the 25–35 age bracket* (= people aged between 25 and 35) ◊ *people in the lower income bracket* ◊ *PCs in the $1 500–$2 500 price bracket*
2 = TAX BRACKET

'bracket creep *noun* [U] (*especially AmE*)
(*Economics*) a situation in which the small pay increases that you receive because INFLATION has risen result in you paying higher amounts of tax → FISCAL DRAG, TAX BRACKET

BRAD /bræd/ = BRITISH RATE AND DATA

brain /breɪn/ *noun*
1 [C, usually pl.] (*informal*) an intelligent person: *a meeting of the best brains in the industry*
2 **the brains** [sing.] the person who is responsible for thinking of and organizing sth: *She was the brains behind London Fashion Week.*

brainchild /ˈbreɪntʃaɪld/ *noun* [sing.]
the brainchild of sb the idea or invention of a particular person or group of people: *The website is the brainchild of a team in the cosmetic department.*

'brain drain *noun* [sing.] (*informal*)
the movement of highly skilled people from one country, area or industry to another, where they can earn more money or work in better conditions: *Academics are complaining that low pay is causing a brain drain to industry.*

★ **brainstorming** /ˈbreɪnstɔːmɪŋ; *AmE* -stɔːrm-/ *noun* [U]
a way of solving problems or creating good ideas in which a group of people think about sth at the same time and then discuss all the suggestions: *No idea is ruled out during the period of the brainstorming.* ◊ *Members had a brainstorming session to identify the causes of the problem.*
▶ **'brainstorm** *verb* [+ obj or no obj]: *an opportunity to brainstorm ideas* ◊ *The team are brainstorming about marketing ideas.*

'brains trust *noun* [C] (*BrE*) (*AmE* **'brain trust**)
a group of experts that provide new ideas and advice to an organization or a government: *directors, investors and advisers acting as the company's brains trust* → THINK TANK

★ **branch** /brɑːntʃ; *AmE* bræntʃ/ *noun, verb*
● *noun* [C]
1 a local office or shop/store belonging to a large organization or company, especially a bank: *The retail bank has 170 branches in Brazil.* ◊ *Our New York branch is dealing with the matter.* ◊ *Where's the nearest branch of Tesco?* ◊ *He's been promoted to assistant branch manager.*
● *to close/establish/set up/have/open a branch* ◆ *a central/domestic/high street/local/overseas/regional branch* ◆ *a branch network/office*
2 a part of a government or other large organization that deals with one particular aspect

of its work: *The company has two branches: one for production and one for sales.* [SYN] DEPARTMENT
● *verb*
[PHR V] ,branch 'out (into sth) to start to do a new business activity: *We want to branch out into sports goods.*

★ **brand** /brænd/ *noun, verb*
● *noun*
SEE ALSO: **aspirational brand, consumer ~, family ~, house ~, manufacturer's ~, name-~, national ~,** etc.

1 [C] a type of product or group of products sold using a particular name, which is often the name of the company that produces them; the name that is given to the products: *People tend to go on buying the same brand of breakfast cereal.* ◇ *He helped to build two of the world's best-known brands: Nike and Starbucks.* ◇ *The company has strong core brands.* ◇ *She was responsible for creating the company's 'Learn it Well' brand.* → BRAND IMAGE, BRAND NAME
● *a world-class/favourite/leading/major/principal/ top brand* ● *big/core/famous/global/popular/ strong/well-known brands* ● *to build/create/ develop/establish a brand*
2 [C, usually sing.] a particular type or kind of sth: *the company's particular brand of project management* ◇ *a unique brand of humour*

WHICH WORD?

brand/label/make

These words are used to refer to names of products.

A **brand** or **label** is a name that a company gives to its products, which can also be the name of the company itself.

Brand is used about all kinds of goods and services and especially in the context of marketing: *What brand of toothpaste do you use?* ◇ *brands like Nike and Starbucks* ◇ *We invested heavily in promoting the brand.*

Label is used especially about food, clothing and music. It is mainly used in fixed word combinations or as part of the names of products: *Most supermarkets sell a range of own-label products.* ◇ *Chris would only wear designer/luxury labels.* ◇ *We decided to call it Red Label tonic water.*

A product's **make** is the name of the company that makes it. The word is usually used about cars and electrical goods: *What's the car's make and model?* ◇ *a Swiss make of watch*

● *verb* [+ obj]
(*Marketing*) (*often* **be branded**)
to give a particular name, design, etc. to a type of product or group of products that you sell: *The phone is branded with the name of the service provider.* ◇ *They are going to brand all their products under one name.* → BRANDED, BRANDING, REBRAND

,brand 'advertising *noun* [U]
(*Marketing*) advertising that aims to make people aware of and loyal to a particular brand of goods: *brand advertising of chocolate* → PRODUCT ADVERTISING

,brand associ'ation *noun* [U,C]
(*Marketing*) what people think of when they see or hear the name of a particular product: *Safety is Volvo's brand association.* ◇ *The company wants to strengthen its brand association with football.*
● *to build/create/strengthen brand association* ● *positive/powerful/strong brand association*

,brand a'wareness *noun* [U]
(*Marketing*) to what extent people know about and recognize a particular product: *The campaign is designed to build brand awareness.* → PRODUCT AWARENESS

'brand-,conscious *adjective*
(*Marketing*)
1 (about people) aware of the most fashionable or famous products and wanting to buy them: *Teenagers are highly brand-conscious.*
2 (about companies) particularly concerned about what people think about the name and image of the company and its products: *brand-conscious companies like Nike and Apple*

branded /'brændɪd/ *adjective* [only before noun]
(about a product) having a label or name that shows it is made by a particular company, usually a well-known one: *Another car manufacturer has started selling branded luggage and clothing.*
→ GENERIC, OWN BRAND
● *branded drugs/goods/products*

,brand 'equity *noun* [U]
(*Marketing*) the financial value of a particular brand to the company that sells the product, based on how good people think it is, what people connect it with, etc: *Strong brand equity allows us to keep our customers and increase our profits.* ◇ *We use a range of marketing tools to build brand equity.*
● *to build/increase/measure/track brand equity* ● *high/positive/strong brand equity*

,brand ex'tension *noun*
(*Marketing*)
1 [U] using a successful brand name to sell new types of products: *The telephone company's new strategy includes brand extension into IT products.*
→ BRAND STRETCHING
2 [C] a new product that is sold using an existing brand name: *'Fashion' magazine was such a success that it launched its own brand extension: 'Teen Fashion'.*

,brand 'image *noun* [C,U]
what people think or feel about a particular product, company name or symbol (**logo**), etc: *The company is trying to create a stronger brand image.*
→ BRAND PERSONALITY
● *to build/create/establish/improve a brand image* ● *a poor/strong brand image*

★ **branding** /'brændɪŋ/ *noun* [U]
(*Marketing*) the use of a particular name, symbol (**logo**) and design for a company's products so that people will recognize them: *Do you use the corporate branding on all your leaflets?* ◇ *They've run branding campaigns on buses and billboards.*

'brand ,label = BRAND NAME

,brand 'leader *noun* [C]
(*Marketing*) the brand of product that has the largest number of sales among products of the same type: *'Lego' is the brand leader in construction toys.* ◇ *We have lost market share to the US brand leader.*
▶ ,brand 'leadership *noun* [U]: *achieving brand leadership in a highly competitive market*

,brand 'loyalty *noun* [U,C]
(*Marketing*) the support that people give to a particular brand of product by continuing to buy it rather than changing to other brands: *They had to spend a lot on advertising to create brand loyalty.*
→ BRAND SWITCHING
● *to build/create/develop/encourage brand loyalty* ● *powerful/strong/total brand loyalty*

,brand 'management *noun* [U]
(*Marketing*) the way that a company controls how a particular type of product or group of products (a **brand**) is advertised and sold to customers: *Our brand management is based on clearly expressing the*

,**brand 'manager** noun [C]
(*Marketing*) a person at a company who is in charge of developing and selling a particular group of products (a **brand**): *She was senior brand manager for 'Jungle Instant Breakfast'.*

★ **'brand name** (*also* **'brand ,label**) noun [C]
the name given to a type of product or group of products by the company that produces or sells them, so that people will recognize them: *The company has a strong brand name—its most valuable asset.* ◇ *They will distribute the music under the brand name 'Hit Parade'.* ◇ *When buying a computer, go for a brand name* (= buy one made by a well-known company). ◇ *The store has been prevented from selling brand-name jeans at low prices.*
O to **develop/have/protect/retain** a brand name ◆ an **established/a leading/strong/well-known** brand name

,**brand perso'nality** noun [C]
(*Marketing*) the attractive and special human qualities that a company wants a product or group of products to suggest to people. A famous person, an animal or a well-known character is often used to advertise the product: *Our task was to create a new brand personality that was younger, livelier and healthier.* → BRAND IMAGE
O to **create/develop/establish** brand personality ◆ a **distinctive/lively/strong/unique** brand personality

,**brand recog'nition** noun [U]
(*Marketing*) the extent to which people recognize and value a particular brand: *Big companies can put their logo on a new product for instant brand recognition.* ◇ *Our website provides a unique opportunity to build brand recognition among teachers.* → BRAND AWARENESS
O to **build/create/have/lack** brand recognition ◆ **instant/powerful/strong** brand recognition

,**brand 'share** noun [U,C]
(*Marketing*) the amount that a company sells of a particular brand of product compared with other companies that sell the same thing: *We expect our brand share to be about 60% by 2005.* ◇ *The company has been investing heavily in advertising to build brand share.* → MARKET SHARE
O **high/low** brand share ◆ to **build/increase/lose** brand share

,**brand 'stretching** noun [U]
(*Marketing*) (often used in a disapproving way) using a successful brand name to sell new types of products → BRAND EXTENSION (1)

'**brand ,switching** noun [U]
(*Marketing*) when a customer buys a different brand of a product from the one they have usually bought in the past, or often buys different products: *Brand switching between different types of shampoo is common.* → BRAND LOYALTY
O to **encourage/generate/prevent** brand switching

brass /brɑːs; AmE bræs/ = TOP BRASS

★ **breach** /briːtʃ/ noun, verb
● **noun** [C,U]

SEE ALSO: **anticipatory breach**

(*Law*) a situation when sb does not do sth that is required by an agreement, by a promise or by law, or does sth that is not allowed: *Their actions constituted a serious breach of the guidelines.* ◇ *We are suing the company for breach of contract.* ◇ *The firm could be in breach of European Union law on insurance.* → idiom at STEP verb
O (a) **clear/serious** breach of sth ◆ (a) breach of **agreement/contract/copyright/discipline/duty/promise** ◆ sth **amounts to/constitutes** a breach

● **verb** [+ obj]
1 (*Law*) to fail to do what is required by an agreement, a promise or a law: *The group has been accused of breaching competition rules.*
2 (about a figure) to become higher than a particular amount or level: *The financial index has breached the 2 000 mark.*

,**breach of 'confidence** noun [U,C]
(*Law*) the act of giving people information that you should keep secret

,**breach of 'trust** noun [C,U]
(*Law*) a failure to take good care of sth that you have been trusted to look after, such as sb else's money or secret information

,**bread and 'butter** noun [U] (*informal*)
a person or company's main source of income: *Developing new companies is the bread and butter of Silicon Valley.* ◇ *the bread-and-butter business of the company*

breadwinner /'bredwɪnə(r)/ noun [C]
a person who supports their family with the money they earn: *She is the main breadwinner in the family.*

★ **break** /breɪk/ verb, noun
● **verb** (**broke** /brəʊk/; AmE broʊk/ **broken** /'brəʊkən; AmE 'broʊkən/) [+ obj]
1 to do sth that is against the law; to not do what you have agreed or promised to do: *The group has been accused of breaking accounting rules.* ◇ *They have broken the contract.*
2 to end a dispute or difficult situation, often by using strong action: *The company broke the strike by getting managers to work in the factory.*
3 to reach a higher level or standard than has been done before: *A number of companies have broken $100 million in sales.* → RECORD-BREAKING
4 (*especially AmE*) to exchange a piece of paper money for coins: *Can you break a twenty-dollar bill?*
IDM **break 'even** (*Finance*) if a company or a piece of business **breaks even**, it earns just enough money to pay for its costs: *The company expects to break even by the end of 2006.* → BREAK-EVEN ,**break 'ground** (*especially AmE*) (*Property*) when you **break ground** on a new building or the building **breaks ground**, you start building it: *The company will break ground on the plant by August 1 and begin production by February 1.* ,**break new 'ground** to make a new discovery or do sth that has not been done before → GROUNDBREAKING ,**make or 'break sb/sth** to be the thing that makes sb/sth either a success or a failure: *Transport costs can make or break a business.* ◇ *The demand for higher pay became the make-or-break issue in the talks.*
PHR V ,**break a'bove/be'low sth** to become slightly higher or lower than a particular figure or level: *The euro failed to break above its $1.82 high of the day before.* ,**break 'down 1** (about a machine or a vehicle) to stop working because of a fault: *The telephone system has broken down.* **2** to fail: *The partnership between the firms is breaking down.* → BREAKDOWN ,**break 'down; ,break sth 'down** to separate into parts that are easier to analyse; to divide sth into parts in order to make it easier to analyse or to do: *Each task is broken down into step-by-step procedures.* ◇ *Her approach to management breaks down into four principles.* → BREAKDOWN ,**break 'into sth 1** to start to operate in a particular area of business: *We're trying to break into the Japanese market.* **2** to reach a particular level of success: *The company should break into profit for the first time this year.* ,**break sth 'off** to end sth suddenly: *The company has broken off merger talks.* ,**break 'through sth** to succeed in going beyond a particular level; to succeed in dealing with a difficult problem: *The firm's income*

has broken through the $10 million barrier. ,**break 'up (into sth)**; ,**break sth 'up (into sth)** to be divided into smaller parts; to divide sth in this way: *Tyco plans to break up into smaller companies.* ◇ *The company will be broken up or sold.* → BREAK-UP

●*noun* [C]

SEE ALSO: **career break, page ~, tax ~**

1 a short period of time when you stop what you are doing and rest, eat, etc: *a coffee/lunch/tea break* ◇ *a break for lunch* ◇ *You should take a one-minute break from the computer every 30 minutes.*
O *to* **have/take** *a break*
2 a short holiday/vacation; a short time when an activity stops before it starts again: *The markets resumed trading after a three day break.*
3 a pause for advertisements in the middle of a television or radio programme: *More news after the break.* ◇ *a commercial break*
4 (*AmE*) a reduction in an amount that you have to pay: *Customers who download the software from the Internet will get a price break.*
O *to* **get/be given** *a break*
5 (*AmE*) a TAX BREAK

'**break clause** *noun* [C]
(*Law*) especially in the UK, a part of an agreement that allows you to end the agreement early, used especially in agreements that allow you to use a building, piece of land, etc. for a particular period of time (**leases**)

breakdown /'breikdaʊn/ *noun* [C]
1 the failure or end of sth: *The breakdown of the talks means that a strike is likely.* ◇ *a breakdown of investor confidence*
2 (*AmE also* '**breakdown**) [usually sing.] a list of all the details of sth: *Let's look at a breakdown of the costs.*
→ BREAK DOWN at BREAK *verb*

,**break-'even** *noun* [U]
(*Finance*) a time when a company or a piece of business earns just enough money to pay for its costs; the state of not making a profit or a loss: *The company expects to* **reach** *break-even next year.* ◇ *The group has promised a break-even performance in the second quarter.* → BREAK EVEN at BREAK *verb*

break-even

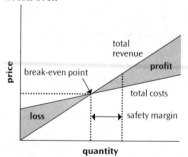

quantity

,**break-'even a,nalysis** *noun* [U,C]
(*Finance*) a way of finding out or studying when a new business or product will start earning enough money to pay for its costs: *You will need to* **do** *a break-even analysis before you approach a bank for finance.* → BREAK EVEN at BREAK *verb*

,**break-'even chart** *noun* [C]
(*Finance*) a diagram that shows how the profits and costs of a company will increase or decrease according to how much business it does, and when the business or product will reach BREAK-EVEN

,**break-'even point** *noun* [C,U]
(*Finance*) the level of sales at which a company or a piece of business earns just enough money to pay for its costs and does not make a profit or a loss: *We estimate it will take a year to* **reach** *break-even point.* ◇ *Revenues for 2005 are well below the estimated break-even point of €1 billion.*

'**break fee** *noun* [C]
(*Law*)
1 (*also* '**break-up fee**) especially in the US, an amount of money that a company must pay if it breaks an agreement to be sold to another company: *A break fee of $60 million is payable if the company pulls out of the sale.*
2 (*AmE*) an amount of money that you must pay if you end a legal agreement before the agreed time: *There is a break fee of several thousand dollars if the loan is repaid early.*

'**breaking point** *noun* [U,C] (*usually uncountable in British English and countable in American English*)
the time when problems become so great that a person, an organization or a system can no longer deal with them: *The economy is close to breaking point.* ◇ *The country's health-care system has* **reached** *a breaking point.*

breakout /'breikaʊt/ *noun, adjective*
●*noun* [C] (*AmE*)
1 [usually sing.] = BREAKDOWN (2)
2 an increase or decrease that is bigger than normal: *The price may go higher and show a breakout above 110 rupees.* ◇ *We expect a big breakout in new orders next year.*
3 a meeting of a smaller group of people away from the main meeting: *You can attend several breakouts.*
●*adjective* [only before noun]
1 that is very successful and brings fame to sb/sth: *We believe this is the breakout product we've been looking for.*
2 (*AmE*) that takes place separately from a main meeting and involves a smaller group of people: *a number of breakout sessions on specific topics*

breakthrough /'breikθruː/ *noun* [C]
an important discovery or development: *Intel has achieved a major breakthrough in chip design.* ◇ *a significant breakthrough in the negotiations*
O *to* **achieve/make** *a breakthrough* ◆ *a* **big/historic/ major/significant** *breakthrough* ◆ *a* **scientific/ technological** *breakthrough*

'**break-up** (*AmE spelling* **breakup**) *noun* [C]
the separation of a large company or group of companies into smaller parts: *The government has announced the break-up of China Telecom.* ◇ *the company's break-up plans*

'**break-up fee** = BREAK FEE (1)
'**break-up ,value** (*BrE*) *noun* [C]
(*Accounting*) an estimate of the value a company would have if it was sold in separate parts rather than as a single active company: *The break-up value is twice the current market price.* ◇ *a break-up value of €630 million* → BREAK UP at BREAK *verb*, GOING CONCERN

bribe /braɪb/ *noun, verb*
●*noun* [C]
money, etc. that you give or offer to sb to persuade them to help you, especially by doing sth dishonest: *The company paid bribes to government officials to win the contract.* → SWEETENER
O *to* **accept/offer/pay/take** *a bribe*
●*verb* [+ obj]
to give or offer sb money, etc. to persuade them to help you, especially by doing sth dishonest: *He bribed them to stay* **with** *a pay rise.* ◇ *She was bribed* **into** *handing over secret information.*
O *to* **attempt/try** *to bribe sb*

bribery /ˈbraɪbəri/ noun [U]
the giving or taking of BRIBES: *allegations of
bribery and corruption*

brick /brɪk/ noun
IDM **come up against/hit/run into a brick 'wall**
to be unable to make any progress because there is
a difficulty that stops you: *The group has hit a brick
wall in negotiations with its lenders.*

ˌbricks and 'mortar noun [U]
buildings, especially when you are thinking of
them in connection with how much they cost to
build or how much they are worth: *We own our
own buildings and consider bricks and mortar to be a
key part of our business strategy.* ◇ *a new Internet
company without a lot of bricks-and-mortar
businesses* (= businesses with buildings that
customers go to) ◇ (*AmE*) *brick-and-mortar
businesses* → idiom at CLICK

bridge /brɪdʒ/ = BRIDGING

bridging /ˈbrɪdʒɪŋ/ (*BrE*) (*AmE* **bridge**) adjective
[only before noun]
(*Finance*) used about money that you borrow for a
short time until you can arrange a longer loan
O *bridging finance/financing/funds/loans*

★ brief /briːf/ noun, verb
● noun [C]

SEE ALSO: watching brief

1 the instructions that a person is given explaining
what their job is and what their duties are: *I was
given the brief of reorganizing the department.* ◇ *a
design brief for a new product* ◇ *We've prepared a
brief for the architect.* ◇ *to stick to your brief* (= to
do only what you are asked to do)
O *to give sb a brief ◆ to prepare/produce/write a brief
(for sb)*
2 (*Law*) (*BrE*) a legal case that is given to a lawyer to
argue in court; a piece of work for a BARRISTER:
preparing a brief for counsel (= the lawyer who will
represent sb in court)
O *to accept/prepare a brief*
3 (*Law*) (*AmE*) a written summary of the facts
supporting one side of a legal case, that will be
presented to a court: *The organization has filed a
brief with the Indiana Supreme Court.*
O *to file/submit a brief*
● verb [+ obj]
1 to give sb information about sth or instructions
to do a particular job: *The director has been briefed
on what questions to expect.*
2 (*Law*) (*BrE*) to give a lawyer, especially a
BARRISTER, the main facts of a legal case so that it
can be argued in a court

briefcase /ˈbriːfkeɪs/ noun [C]
a flat case used for carrying papers and documents

briefing /ˈbriːfɪŋ/ noun
1 [C] a meeting in which people are given
instructions or information: *a daily briefing* ◇ *a
media/press briefing*
2 [C,U] the detailed instructions or information
that are given at such a meeting: *Details of the
project were included in briefing papers.*

bring /brɪŋ/ verb [+ obj] (**brought, brought** /brɔːt/)
1 bring sth to an end/a close/a conclusion to end
sth: *She brought the meeting to a close with thanks
to all who had attended.*
2 to make sb/sth come to a particular place, level,
etc: *December's figures brought overall sales for the
year to 3.97 million vehicles.* ◇ *We cannot afford
mistakes if we are to bring our products to market
on time.*
IDM **bring sth into 'force** to cause a law, rule, etc.
to start being used → idioms at CONTROL noun,
QUESTION noun
PHRV **'bring sb/sth before sb** (*formal*) to present
sb/sth for discussion or judgement: *The case will be

brought before the bankruptcy judge today.* **ˌbring
sb/sth 'down** to end sb/sth's period of success or
power: *Shareholders' loss of confidence finally
brought down the company.* **ˌbring sth 'down** to
reduce sth: *We need to look at ways to bring down
costs.* **ˌbring sth 'forward 1** to move sth to an
earlier date or time: *The board meeting was brought
forward by two days to discuss the crisis.* See note at
POSTPONE **2** to suggest sth for discussion: *The
environment minister brought forward new
proposals to reduce pollution.* **3** (*Accounting*) to
move a total sum from the bottom of one page or
column of numbers to the top of the next. **ˌbring sb
'in** to ask sb to do a particular job or to be involved
in sth, especially to help or advise: *The CEO brought
in a team of consultants to sort out the company's
problems.* **ˌbring sth 'in 1** to make a new product
or service available to people for the first time: *We
plan to bring in a new range of vans next year.*
SYN INTRODUCE **2** to introduce a new law, rule,
etc: *They are bringing in limits on overtime from
June.* **SYN** INTRODUCE **3** to attract sb/sth to a place
of business: *Our new website should bring in a lot of
new business.* **4** (*Law*) to give a decision in a court:
The jury brought in a verdict of guilty. **ˌbring 'in sth**;
ˌbring sb 'in sth to make or earn a particular
amount of money: *The marketing campaign brought
in over €6 million in sales.* **ˌbring sth 'out 1** to
produce sth; to publish sth: *They are bringing out
the next version of the software next month.* **2** to
make sth appear: *A good manager is able to bring
out the best in people.* **ˌbring sth 'up 1** to mention
a subject or start to talk about it: *Bring it up at the
meeting.* **SYN** RAISE **2** to make sth appear on a
computer screen: *Typing in 'Portugal industries'
brought up over 350 000 links on one search engine.*

brink /brɪŋk/ noun [sing.]
if you are **on the brink of sth**, you are almost in a
very new, dangerous or exciting situation: *The
company was on the brink of bankruptcy.* ◇ *He's
pulled the firm back from the brink* (= he has
saved it from disaster).
O *on the brink of bankruptcy/collapse/disaster/
failure/recession*
IDM **teeter on the 'brink/'edge of sth** to be very
close to a very unpleasant or dangerous situation:
The company is teetering on the brink of bankruptcy.

brisk /brɪsk/ adjective (**brisker, briskest**)
quick; busy, with a lot of activity: *The shop is doing
brisk business in umbrellas today.* ◇ *Trading was
brisk, with almost two million shares changing
hands.*

ˌBritish Rate and 'Data noun [sing.] (*abbr*
BRAD)
(*Marketing*) in the UK, a book published every
month that contains information about all the
newspapers, magazines and other media that have
advertising, such as how many are sold, how much
they charge for advertising, etc. → STANDARD RATE
AND DATA SERVICE

BRM /ˌbiː ɑːr ˈem/ abbr (*AmE*)
business reply mail → BUSINESS REPLY SERVICE

broadband /ˈbrɔːdbænd/ noun [U]
(*IT*) a system that can send large amounts of
electronic data at a very fast speed: *a campaign to
teach consumers the benefits of broadband* → ADSL
▶ **'broadband** adjective: *the country's leading
provider of broadband Internet services*

ˌbroad 'banding noun [U]
(*HR*) a way of dividing the jobs and ranges of pay in
a company into only a small number of levels with
a big difference between the lowest and highest
pay in each level

'broad-based (*also* **'broadly-based**) *adjective*
based on a wide variety of people, things or ideas; not limited: *She managed to develop broad-based support for her project.* ◇ *a broadly-based training and employment programme*

broadcast /'brɔːdkɑːst; *AmE* -kæst/ *verb, noun*
• *verb* (**broadcast, broadcast**)
1 [+ obj *or* no obj] to send out programmes on television, radio, etc: *The channel broadcasts to millions of homes in the south of the country.*
2 [+ obj] to tell a lot of people about sth: *I don't want to broadcast our mistake.*
▶ **'broadcaster** *noun* [C]: *a terrestrial/satellite broadcaster* ◇ *a crowd of journalists and broadcasters* **'broadcasting** *noun* [U]: *She works in broadcasting.*
• *noun*
1 [C] a programme on radio, television, etc: *a live broadcast of the speech*
2 [U] (*only used before another noun*) the activity or business of making programmes for television, radio, etc: *More viewers means more revenue for the broadcast industry.*
O *the broadcast* **business/industry** ◆ *a broadcast* **business/division/network**

'broadly-based = BROAD-BASED

'broad ,money *noun* [U]
(*Economics*) a term used in the measurement of a country's MONEY SUPPLY, that includes more than just notes and coins and the money that people have in ordinary bank accounts: *The large increase in broad money growth will lead to a rise in spending.* → Mo, M1, ETC., NARROW MONEY

★ **brochure** /'brəʊʃə(r); *AmE* broʊ'ʃʊr/ *noun* [C]
(*Marketing*) a small magazine or book that contains pictures and information about sth or advertises sth: *See our brochure for more details.* ◇ *a marketing team writing product brochures*
O *a* **marketing/product** *brochure* ◆ *to* **produce/publish/write** *a brochure*

broke /brəʊk; *AmE* broʊk/ *adjective* [not before noun] (*informal*)
having no money: *During the recession thousands of small businesses* **went broke.**
IDM **go for 'broke** (*informal*) to risk everything in one determined effort to do sth

,broken-'line graph *noun* [C]
a graph that shows data as points joined by lines

★ **broker** /'brəʊkə(r); *AmE* 'broʊ-/ *noun, verb*
• *noun* [C]

SEE ALSO: **agency broker, bill ~, commission ~, customs ~, discount ~, insurance ~, money ~, real estate ~**

1 (*Commerce*) a person or company that buys and sells things, for example shares, bonds, etc., for other people: *Luis works for a firm of insurance brokers.* ◇ *He watches how the brokers work when they are on the phone to customers.* See note at AGENT
O *an* **insurance/money/mortgage** *broker*
2 (*Stock Exchange*) = STOCKBROKER
• *verb* [+ obj] to arrange the details of an agreement: *The airline has brokered a joint marketing deal with the city tourist board.*

brokerage /'brəʊkərɪdʒ; *AmE* 'broʊ-/ *noun*

SEE ALSO: **discount brokerage**

(*Commerce*)
1 [U] the business of being a BROKER; the work a BROKER does: *brokerage services/fees* ◇ *a brokerage firm/house*
2 [C] a company whose business is buying and selling things, for example, shares, bonds, etc, for

other people: *Brokerages reported a steep fall in earnings.*
3 [C,U] an amount of money charged by a BROKER for the work done: *a sales brokerage of $25*

,broker-'dealer (*also spelled* **broker/dealer**) *noun* [C]
(*Stock Exchange*) a person or company that sells shares, bonds, etc. for other people and for themselves

broking /'brəʊkɪŋ; *AmE* 'broʊ-/ *noun* [U] (*BrE*)
the business or service of buying and selling things, for example shares, bonds, etc., for other people: *The bank is hoping to break into the online broking market.*
O *the broking* **industry/market/sector** ◆ *a broking* **company/firm/house**

Bros (*also spelled* **Bros.**, *especially in AmE*) *abbr* (*only used in written English*)
(used in the names of companies) brothers: *Moss Bros*

,brought 'forward (*abbr* **b/f, b/fwd**) (*also* **,brought 'down** *abbr* **b/d**) *adverb, adjective*
(*Accounting*) used to describe an amount that has been copied from a previous period or page of accounts: *Then enter the amount brought forward.* ◇ *Put that figure in the brought forward column.*
→ BALANCE BROUGHT DOWN **NOTE** This is usually written as an abbreviation in accounts.

brownfield /'braʊnfiːld/ *adjective, noun*
(*Property*)
• *adjective* [only before noun]
used to describe an area of land in a city that was used by industry or for offices in the past and that may now be cleared for new building development
O *a brownfield* **site** ◆ **brownfield** *development/land*
• *noun* [C]
1 (*especially AmE*) (*BrE usually* **'brownfield site**) an area of land in a city that was used by industry or for offices in the past and that may now be cleared for new building development
2 an area of land that was used by industry and that could be used for new development, but may be affected by dangerous substances → GREENFIELD

'brown goods *noun* [pl.]
(*Commerce*) small electrical items such as televisions, radios, music and video equipment
→ GREY GOODS, WHITE GOODS

browse /braʊz/ *verb* [+ obj *or* no obj]
1 (*IT*) to look for information on a computer, especially on the Internet: *I spent an hour browsing competitors' websites.*
2 to look at a lot of things in a shop/store rather than looking for one particular thing
▶ **browse** *noun* [sing.]: *I went into a bookstore for a browse.*

browser /'braʊzə(r)/ *noun* [C]
1 (*IT*) a program that lets you look at or read documents on the Internet: *Click the 'back' button on your browser.* ◇ *an Internet/a Web browser*
2 a person who looks at things in a shop/store but may not seriously intend to buy anything: *The sale brought in a steady stream of browsers.*

BRS /ˌbiː ɑːr 'es/ = BUSINESS REPLY SERVICE

BS /ˌbiː 'es/ *abbr*
1 **British Standard** a number given to a particular standard of quality set by the British Standards Institution: *BS 5750, the British Standard of excellence in quality management*
2 (*Law*) (*BrE*) = BILL OF SALE

'B-school *noun* [C]
(usually used in newspapers) a business school

'B share (*also* **class 'B share**) → A/B/C SHARE

BSI /ˌbiː es 'aɪ/ *abbr* **British Standards Institution**
an organization formed in the UK that sets and

tests quality and safety standards for industry, especially for building, engineering, chemical, TEXTILE and electrical products → KITEMARK

,B-to-'B = B2B

,B-to-'C = B2C

,B-to-'E = B2E

BTW *abbr*
used in writing for 'by the way', a way of introducing a comment or question that is not directly related to what you have been talking about

bubble /'bʌbl/ *noun* [C, usually sing.]
(*Economics*) a situation that cannot last in which prices rise very quickly and many people make a lot of money: *the bubble sectors of technology, media and telecommunications* ◇ *They went out of business when the Internet bubble **burst*** (= ended, causing people to lose a lot of money).

'bubble e,conomy *noun* [C]
(*Economics*) a temporary situation when businesses grow very fast, the prices of shares and homes, etc. rise and employment increases: *The central bank failed to put up interest rates and a bubble economy developed.*

'bubble pack = BLISTER PACK, BUBBLE WRAP

'bubble ,packaging = BLISTER PACKAGING, BUBBLE WRAP

'bubble wrap (*AmE spelling also* **Bubble Wrap™**) (*also* **'bubble pack**, **'bubble ,packaging**) *noun* [U]
plastic material containing small bubbles of air, used to protect goods that are easily damaged— Picture at PACKAGING

buck /bʌk/ *noun, verb*
• *noun*
1 (*informal*) [C] (*especially AmE*) a US or an Australian dollar: *They cost ten bucks.* ◇ *We're talking **big bucks*** (= a lot of money) *here.*
2 the buck [sing.] used in some expressions to refer to the responsibility or blame for sth: *It was my decision. **The buck stops here*** (= nobody else can be blamed). ◇ *Everyone was trying to **pass the buck*** (= not accept responsibility).
IDM **bang for your/the 'buck** (*AmE*) (*informal*) value for the money that you spend: *You get more bang for your buck with a desktop than with a laptop.* **make a (quick, fast, etc.) 'buck** (*informal*) to make a lot of money quickly and easily: *investors who just want to make a quick buck*
• *verb* [+ obj]
to resist or oppose sth: *Most share prices fell, but one or two companies managed to buck **the trend** with a small rise.* ◇ *Her attempts to buck **the system*** (= to oppose authority or rules) *caused problems with her manager.*

'bucket shop *noun* [C] (*informal*)
1 (*Stock Exchange*) a company that buys and sells shares without having a licence and often deals in a dishonest way
2 (*BrE*) a company that only provides very cheap air tickets for travellers: *We booked through a bucket shop.* ◇ *bucket-shop tickets*

★budget /'bʌdʒɪt/ *noun, verb, adjective*
• *noun*

SEE ALSO: balanced budget, capital ~, cash ~, sales ~, variable ~

1 (*Accounting*) [C,U] a plan for a particular period of time of the income and spending of a company, an organization or part of a company, etc: *Each department sets its own budget.* ◇ *Revenues are approximately in line with the budget.* ◇ *Sales have exceeded budget expectations this year.*
O *an* **annual**/*a* **departmental/draft** *budget* ♦ *to* **agree/ approve/balance/draw up/present/set** *a budget* ♦

below/in line with/on/over/under/within budget ♦ *budget* **constraints/cuts**
2 (*Economics*) (*BrE spelling also* **Budget**) [C] the official statement made by a government of the country's income from taxes, etc. and how it will be spent: *tax cuts in this year's Budget* ◇ *The budget deficit widened to 2.6% of GDP.*
O *the* **annual/draft/federal/government** *budget* ♦ *a* **balanced** *budget* ♦ *an* **austere/a tax-cutting/tough** *budget* ♦ *a budget* **deficit/shortfall/surplus**
3 [C,U] an amount of money that a person or a company can spend on particular activities, equipment, etc: *He was given a budget of $1 billion to buy assets.* ◇ *We had to furnish the offices **on a** tight budget* (= without spending too much money). ◇ *Is there any money left **in** the advertising budget?* ◇ *They **went over** budget* (= spent too much money). ◇ *The project came in **under** budget* (= did not spend all the money available).
O *a* **generous/large/low/small/tight** *budget* ♦ *to be* **given/have/keep to** *a budget* ♦ *to be/come in* **below/ over/under/within** *budget* ♦ *to* **cut/trim** *a budget*
• *verb*
1 (*Accounting*) [+ obj *or no* obj] **budget (sth) (for sth)** | **budget sth (at sth)** to plan to spend an amount of money for a particular purpose: *I budgeted for two new members of staff.* ◇ *Ten million euros has been budgeted for the project.* ◇ *The project has been budgeted at ten million euros.*
2 [no obj] to be careful about the amount of money you spend: *If we budget carefully we'll be able to afford the trip.*
▶ **'budgeting** *noun* [U]: *We train our employees in time management and budgeting.*
• *adjective* [only before noun]
(used in advertising, etc.) low in price; selling things that are low in price
O *a budget* **flight/hotel** ♦ *a budget* **airline/carrier**

'budget ac,count *noun* [C] (*BrE*)
(*Accounting*) a type of account, usually at a bank, that you put fixed regular amounts of money into in order to be able to pay large bills when they are due; an arrangement with a shop/store or company to pay your bills in fixed regular amounts

budgetary /'bʌdʒɪtəri; *AmE* -teri/ *adjective* [only before noun]
(*Accounting; Economics*) connected with a budget: *He doesn't find it easy to work within budgetary constraints* (= limits on the amount of money he can spend).

,budgetary ac'counting *noun* [U]
(*Accounting*) a type of accounting that records how a budget is spent and how much of it is left

,budgetary con'trol *noun* [U]
(*Accounting*) the process by which an organization plans how much money can be spent on each one of its activities or costs during the next accounting period and then continuously compares the actual amounts with the planned amounts to see if any changes are necessary: *to develop a budgetary control system*

buffer /'bʌfə(r)/ *noun* [C]
1 (*IT*) a temporary memory in a computer or a device connected to a computer that is used for storing information when data is being sent between two machines that work at different speeds
2 a thing or person that reduces a shock or protects sb/sth against difficulties: *The extra stock acts as a buffer **against** any problem with supplies.* ◇ *The personnel officer often has to act as a buffer **between** workers and management.*
→ idiom at HIT *verb*

'buffer stock noun [U,C]
1 (*Commerce*; *Production*) an extra quantity of goods that is kept in case it is needed: *We have now increased our buffer stocks, and should not have any shortages.*
2 (*Economics*) an amount of a product or raw material (a **commodity**), owned, for example, by a government, that is stored or sold in order to keep the supply and price of the product level

bug /bʌg/ noun [C]
(*IT*) a problem in a computer system or program: *The software company has posted a bug fix* (= a program that will remove the problem) *on its website.* → VIRUS

★ **build** /bɪld/ verb, noun
● *verb* (**built, built** /bɪlt/)
1 [+ obj *or* no obj] to make sth, especially a building, by putting parts together: *They have permission to build 200 new houses.* ◇ *We are looking for a suitable site to build on.* ◇ *The cars are built in the company's Detroit factory.*
2 [+ obj] to create or develop sth: *They have built a website that generates big sales.* ◇ *She's building a new career.* ◇ *We built a 50-person software company in under a year.* → BUILD STH UP
3 (*IT*) [+ obj] to write a set of instructions for a computer
PHR V ,build sth 'in; ,build sth 'into sth (*often be built in/into sth*) to make sth a permanent part of a system, plan, etc: *The computer comes with a CD-writer built in.* 'build on sth to use sth as a basis for further progress: *We aim to build on our success in the coming year.* ,build 'up (to sth) to become greater, more powerful or larger in number: *All the pressure built up and he was off work for weeks with stress.* → BUILD-UP ,build sth 'up to create or develop sth: *She's built up a very successful business.* → BUILD (2)
● *noun*
1 [C] the way that sth such as a vehicle is made
2 [C] an increase in the size, amount or degree of sth over a period of time: *a large build in product stocks* **SYN** BUILD-UP
3 (*IT*) [C] the process of developing a computer program; the program that is being developed: *We did the builds at night and tested them the next day.*
4 (*Manufacturing*) [U,C] the process of building sth; sth that is built: *The company has enough cash for the build.*

builder /'bɪldə(r)/ noun [C]
1 a person or company whose job is to build or repair houses or other buildings
2 (*usually used in compounds*) a person or thing that builds, creates or develops sth: *a shipbuilder* ◇ *She's a good team builder.*

building /'bɪldɪŋ/ noun

SEE ALSO: **team building**

1 [C] a structure such as a house or school that has a roof and walls: *office buildings*
2 [U] the process or work of building: *a building company* ◇ *building materials* See note at CONSTRUCTION

,building and 'loan associ,ation = SAVINGS AND LOAN ASSOCIATION

'building blocks noun [pl.]
parts that are joined together in order to make a large thing: *Chips are the tiny electrical circuits that are the building blocks of computers.*

'building code noun [C, usually sing.]
official rules that must be followed when building: *The materials used comply with the building code.*

'building ,permit (*especially BrE*) (*AmE usually* con'struction ,permit) noun [C]
official permission to build sth: *They were granted a building permit to construct offices on the site.*

'building regu,lation noun [C, usually pl.]
in the UK, an official rule that must be followed when building: *They installed smoke detectors in every room to comply with building regulations.*

'building so,ciety noun [C] (*BrE*)
(*Finance*) in the UK, an organization like a bank that lends money to people who want to buy a home. People also save money with a **building society**: *interest on savings held in banks and building societies* → SAVINGS AND LOAN ASSOCIATION

,build-to-'order adjective [usually before noun]
(*Manufacturing*) made for a particular customer, who chooses what parts, functions, features, etc. the product will have: *build-to-order computer systems*

,build-to-'stock adjective [usually before noun]
(*Manufacturing*) made with the same parts, functions, features, etc. for all customers

'build-up noun
1 [sing; U] an increase in the amount of sth over a period of time: *a worrying build-up of household debt* ◇ *a build-up in stocks of crude oil* → BUILD STH UP at BUILD *verb*
2 [C, usually sing.] the time before an important event, when people are preparing for it: *the build-up to the conference*

built /bɪlt/ combining form (*used after adverbs and in compound adjectives*)

SEE ALSO: **custom-built**

made in the particular way or place that is mentioned: *American-built cars* ◇ *newly built houses*

,built-'in (*also* ,in-'built, *less frequent*) adjective [only before noun]
included as part of sth and not separate from it: *a mobile phone with a tiny built-in camera*

,built to 'flip adjective
used to describe companies that people create just to make money quickly by selling them soon after they start, rather than with the intention of developing them over a period of years: *Built-to-flip Internet businesses have created many millionaires.*

,built to 'last adjective
created or manufactured so that it will last for a long time: *Their toys are expensive but they are built to last.* ◇ *They are a built-to-last company in a built-to-flip environment.*

'bulge-,bracket adjective [only before noun]
(*used about* INVESTMENT BANKS) largest and most successful: *The City is dominated by Wall Street's bulge-bracket firms.*

bulk /bʌlk/ noun, adjective
● *noun* [U]
1 the bulk (of sth) the main part of sth; most of sth: *The cosmetics division accounts for the bulk of group profits.* ◇ *The bulk of the savings will come from stopping all overtime.*
2 (*used about goods such as grain, oil or milk*) loose; not packed: *Grain is often transported in bulk.*
IDM buy/order/sell (sth) in 'bulk to buy, order or sell sth in large amounts, usually at a reduced price: *Companies will buy tickets and hotel rooms in bulk to get a better price.*
● *adjective* [only before noun]
(*Commerce*) in large amounts: *bulk orders of over 100 copies* ◇ *They offer bulk quantities of low-price products.*

'bulk ,cargo noun [C,U]
(*Transport*) a large amount of goods carried in a ship

loose and not packed in bags or boxes: *a bulk cargo of 30 000 tonnes of grain*

'bulk ,carrier *noun* [C]
(*Transport*) a company or a large ship that carries large amounts of goods loose and not packed in bags or boxes

,bulk 'cash *noun* [U]
a large amount of money in the form of coins and notes/bills: *Our bulk cash collection service is a convenient and safe way of depositing your takings.*

,bulk 'discount *noun* [C,U]
(*Commerce*) a reduction in the price of goods when you buy a large amount: *A 20% bulk discount applies on all orders of 20 or more items.*
SYN VOLUME DISCOUNT

,bulk 'freight *noun* [U]
(*Transport*) a large amount of goods such as wheat, metals, etc. carried in a train, lorry/truck, ship or plane loose or in very large containers

'bulk goods *noun* [pl.]
1 (*Transport*) items that are transported in large amounts and not packed in bags or boxes: *Coal, grain and sand are bulk goods. ◇ We transport most kinds of bulk goods for our customers.*
2 large items, for example pieces of furniture: *We will collect bulk goods for disposal on Wednesday mornings.*

'bulk mail *noun* [U] (*especially AmE*)
advertisements and other notices that are sent to large numbers of people either by post or by email: *Many groups are discussing ways to help reduce unsolicited bulk mail.* → JUNK MAIL

,bulk 'shipping *noun* [U]
(*Transport*) the activity of moving large amounts of goods such as grain or coal, usually loose and not packed, in a large ship: *There are losses in the group's container and bulk shipping ventures.*
▶ **,bulk 'shipment** *noun* [C]: *The ship unloads the bulk shipment immediately upon arrival.*

★ **bull** /bʊl/ *noun* [C]
(*Finance*; *Stock Exchange*)
1 a person who buys shares, a particular currency, etc., hoping to sell them soon afterwards at a higher price because they think prices are going to rise rather than fall
2 = BULL MARKET
→ BEAR

bulletin /'bʊlətɪn/ *noun* [C]
1 a printed report that gives news about an organization or a group: *the European Central Bank's monthly bulletin*
2 a short news report: *a television news bulletin*

'bulletin board *noun* [C]
1 (*IT*) a place in a computer system where any user can write or read messages: *Post a note on the central bulletin board.*
2 = NOTICEBOARD

'bullet point (*also* **bullet** /'bʊlɪt/) *noun* [C]
a black circle, square, etc. at the beginning of each item in a printed list; an item marked in this way: *Limit your bullet points to four per slide.*

bullion /'bʊliən/ *noun* [U]
gold or silver in large amounts or in the form of bars: *the market for gold bullion ◇ Bullion rose to $322 an ounce.*

bullish /'bʊlɪʃ/ *adjective*
1 (*Finance*; *Stock Exchange*) connected with, causing or expecting an increase in the price of shares, etc: *a bullish market ◇ Analysts are bullish on the company.* **OPP** BEARISH
2 confident about the future: *The Chief Executive is bullish about the company's outlook. ◇ a bullish forecast*

'bull ,market (*also* **bull**) *noun* [C]
(*Finance*; *Stock Exchange*) a long period during which the prices of shares, etc. are rising and people are buying them: *We've been in a 25-year bull market. ◇* (*figurative*) *It's a bull market for talent.*
→ BEAR MARKET

'bull po,sition *noun* [C]
(*Finance*; *Stock Exchange*) a situation in which a dealer has bought shares, etc. and plans to sell them later at a higher price **SYN** LONG POSITION
→ BEAR POSITION
O *to establish/take a bull position*

'bull run *noun* [C]
(*Finance*; *Stock Exchange*) a situation where the value of shares, etc. is rising because they are being bought in large numbers: *The stock market was on a spectacular bull run.* → BEAR RUN

'bull ,session *noun* [C] (*AmE*) (*informal*)
an informal discussion

bumper /'bʌmpə(r)/ *adjective* [only before noun]
unusually large; producing an unusually large amount: *Bumper sales may not mean bumper profits.*
O *bumper profits/sales ◆ a bumper crop/harvest/season/year*

bumpy /'bʌmpi/ *adjective* (**bumpier, bumpiest**)
1 (about a journey) uncomfortable with a lot of unpleasant movement: *a bumpy flight*
2 (about a surface) not even; with a lot of raised parts: *a bumpy road ◇* (*figurative*) *US shares are on the bumpy road to recovery* (= there are a lot of problems and difficulties on the way).
IDM **to have/give sb a bumpy 'ride** to have a difficult time; to make a situation difficult for sb: *The company's shares have had a bumpy ride* (= they have gone up and down in price several times) *this week.*

bundle /'bʌndl/ *noun, verb*
● *noun*
1 [C] a number of things that belong or are sold together: *a bundle of graphics applications for your PC ◇ A company is more than a bundle of assets.*
2 a bundle [sing.] (*informal*) a lot of money: *He retired after making a bundle in investment banking. ◇ An MBA can cost a bundle.*
● *verb* [+ obj]
to supply a product, a service or a piece of extra equipment with another product or service at no extra cost: *A further nine applications are bundled with the system.* **OPP** UNBUNDLE (2)

buoy /bɔɪ; *AmE also* 'buːi/ *verb* [+ obj] **buoy sth (up)**
(*usually* **be buoyed**) to keep prices or figures at a high or satisfactory level: *Demand for mortgages has been buoyed up by low interest rates.*

buoyant /'bɔɪənt/ *adjective*
(about prices, business activity, etc.) tending to increase or stay at a high level, usually showing financial success: *buoyant consumer spending*
O *buoyant prices/sales/spending ◆ a buoyant economy/market*
▶ **buoyancy** /'bɔɪənsi/ *noun* [U]: *the buoyancy of the market*

burden /'bɜːdn; *AmE* 'bɜːrdn/ *noun, verb*
● *noun* [C]
1 a duty, responsibility, etc. that causes difficulty or hard work: *Business customers will bear most of the burden of the rise in postage rates.*
O *to bear/carry a burden ◆ to cut/ease/lighten/reduce/relieve a burden*
2 the fact of having to pay an amount of money; the amount of money that you owe: *concern about the burden of debt being taken on by households*
SYN LOAD

➋ *a* debt/tax *burden* • *to* cut/ease/reduce *the burden* •
to take on *a burden*

● verb [+ obj] (*often* be burdened)
to give sb a duty, responsibility, etc. that causes
difficulty or hard work: *The company is burdened
with debts of over $10 million.*

,burden of 'proof *noun* [sing.]
(*Law*) the task or responsibility of proving that sth is
true: *The burden of proof lies with companies to
show that they have been harmed by an online critic.*

bureau /'bjʊərəʊ; AmE 'bjʊroʊ/ *noun* [C] (*plural*
bureaux *or* **bureaus** /-rəʊz; AmE -roʊz/)

SEE ALSO: **credit bureau, service bureau**

1 an office or organization that provides
information on a particular subject: *an employment
bureau*
2 in the US and other countries, a government
department or part of a government department:
the Australian Bureau of Statistics

bureaucracy /bjʊə'rɒkrəsi; AmE bjʊ'rɑːk-/
noun [U]
the system of official rules and ways of doing
things that an organization or a government has,
especially when these seem to be too complicated:
*Importers have to deal with high taxes and complex
bureaucracy.* SYN RED TAPE

bureaucrat /'bjʊərəkræt; AmE 'bjʊr-/ *noun* [C]
an official working in an organization or a
government department, especially one who
follows the rules of the department too strictly:
big-company bureaucrats who make bad decisions

bureaucratic /,bjʊərə'krætɪk; AmE ,bjʊr-/
adjective
connected with BUREAUCRACY or BUREAUCRATS
and involving complicated official rules which may
seem unnecessary: *The management has been
criticized for being bureaucratic and slow-moving.*
▶ **bureaucratically** /,bjʊərə'krætɪkli; AmE ,bjʊr-/
adverb

bureau de change /,bjʊərəʊ də 'ʃɑːnʒ ; AmE
,bjʊroʊ/ *noun* [C] (*plural* **bureaux de change**
/,bjʊərəʊ; AmE ,bjʊroʊ/)
an office at a hotel, in an airport, etc., where you
can exchange one currency for another NOTE This
is a French phrase.

burgeon /'bɜːdʒən; AmE 'bɜːrdʒən/ *verb* [no obj]
to begin to grow or develop rapidly: *The leisure
industry has burgeoned over the last ten years.*
▶ **'burgeoning** *adjective* [usually before noun]: *They
are developing new production methods to meet the
burgeoning demand.*

burn /bɜːn; AmE bɜːrn/ *verb, noun*
● verb (**burnt, burnt** /bɜːnt; AmE bɜːrnt/) *or* (**burned,
burned** /bɜːnd; AmE bɜːrnd/)
1 (*informal*) [+ obj or no obj] to spend a lot of money
in a careless way: *The company was burning
(through) cash at a rate of $2 million a day.*
2 (*IT, informal*) [+ obj] to put information onto a
computer disk: *to burn a CD*
3 (*informal*) [+ obj] be/get burned to cause sb to
lose money because they do sth without realizing
the possible bad results: *Many companies were
badly burnt by the rise in fuel tax.*
IDM **get your 'fingers burnt; burn your 'fingers**
to lose money as a result of doing sth without
realizing the possible bad results: *Many investors
got their fingers burnt when the Internet bubble
burst.* → idiom at CRASH *verb*
PHR V **,burn 'out; ,burn sth 'out** to stop working
or make sth stop working because it gets too hot or
is used too much: *The machines will burn out if they
are left running all night.* **,burn 'out; ,burn**

yourself/sb 'out to become extremely tired or ill/
sick by working too hard over a period of time: *The
daily demands of her job eventually burned her out.*
→ BURNOUT
● noun [U,C] (*informal*)
the process of a company spending money: *The
company's cash burn is still running at $4 million a
quarter.* ◇ *a burn rate of $7 million a month*

burnout /'bɜːnaʊt; AmE 'bɜːrnaʊt/ *noun*
1 [U,C] the state of being extremely tired or sick,
either physically or mentally, because you have
worked too hard: *He gives advice to companies about
preventing burnout among their employees.*
2 [C] (*especially AmE*) a person who is suffering
from **burnout**
→ BURN OUT, BURN YOURSELF/SB OUT at BURN *verb*

★**business** /'bɪznəs/ *noun*

SEE ALSO: **any other business, big ~, e-business, first
order of ~, organizing ~, small ~, volume ~**

1 [U] the activity of making, buying, selling or
supplying goods or services for money: *She works
in the computer business.* ◇ *She has set up in business
as a hairdresser.* ◇ *He has business interests on both
sides of the Atlantic.* ◇ *The prime minister addressed
the audience of business leaders and economists.* ◇ *It's
been a pleasure to do business with you.*
→ COMMERCE, TRADE
➋ *to* go into/set up in *business* • *business* activities/
affairs/dealings/interests • *a business* analyst/
consultant/executive/guru/leader/manager • *a
business* deal/transaction • *a business* contact/
partner/relationship • *a business* idea/investment/
proposition/venture
2 [U] work that is part of your job: *Is your trip
business or pleasure?* ◇ *Mr Castorri is away on
business.* ◇ *business travel* → BUSINESS LUNCH,
BUSINESS TRIP
3 [U] the amount of work done by a company, etc.;
the rate or quality of this work: *Business was bad.* ◇
Business was booming. ◇ *Her job was to drum up
(= increase) business.* ◇ *The opportunity to grow
business in Europe would be slow and challenging.*
➋ *business is* bad/booming/brisk/slow • *to* drum up/
grow/increase *business* • *to* attract/encourage/
generate/seek/win *new business*
4 [C] a commercial organization such as a
company, shop/store or factory: *They run their own
catering business.* ◇ *She didn't want to work in the
family business.* ◇ *It has taken ten years to build up
the business to its current size.* ◇ *business premises*
See note at TRADE
➋ *to* have/manage/run/set up/start *a business* • *to*
build up/expand/grow *a business*
5 [U] important matters that need to be dealt with
or discussed: *the main business of the meeting* → ANY
OTHER BUSINESS
6 [U] the fact of being a customer: *We're grateful
for your business.* SYN CUSTOM
7 [U] something that concerns a particular person
or organization: *She made it her business to
improve the general atmosphere in the office.*
IDM **business as 'usual** a way of saying that
things will continue as normal in spite of a difficult
situation: *We're under new management, but it's
business as usual for our workers.* **,business is
'business** a way of saying that financial and
commercial matters are the important things to
consider and you should not be influenced by
friendship, etc. **get down to 'business** to start
dealing with the matter that needs to be dealt
with, or doing the work that needs to be done **go/
put sb out of 'business** to stop or to make sb stop
operating as a business because there is no more
money or work available: *The new regulations will
put many small firms out of business.* See note at
BANKRUPT **in 'business 1** to be operating as a
business: *The loan will help the company remain in
business.* **2** to have everything that you need in

order to be able to start sth immediately: *All we need is a van and we'll be in business.* → idioms at LAND OFFICE, ORDER *noun*

business/agency/company/ consultancy/firm/house

Business is used especially to mean a business that is owned by an individual or family: *to start your own business* ◇ *a small family business*

Company is the general word for a business with a number of managers and employees: *to join a company* ◇ *the director of the company.* The word is often combined with other nouns: *an insurance/ oil/a phone company*

Firm is the general word for a business that provides a professional service: *an accountancy/a law firm*

Other words, such as **consultancy**, **agency** and **house**, are used in fewer contexts. Nouns that are often combined with these words include:

• *a design/IT/management consultancy*
• *an advertising/employment agency*
• *a publishing/software house* ◇ *an auction house*

See note at TRADE

,business admini'stration *noun* [U]
the study or practice of planning, organizing and running a business → MBA

'business ,agent *noun* [C]
1 a person whose job is to represent another person in business matters: *We are looking for a business agent in China.*
2 (*HR*) in the US, a member of a union who represents all the members from one company

'business ,analyst, 'business a,nalysis
= COMPUTER ANALYST

'business ,angel *noun* [C] (*BrE*)
(*Finance, informal*) an investor who helps new companies develop by lending them their own money, which may involve a lot of risk → VENTURE CAPITALIST

★'business card (*also* **card**) *noun* [C]
a small card printed with sb's name and the details of their job and company: *I exchanged business cards with everyone I spoke to at the conference.*
ⵔ to exchange/swap business cards

'business case *noun* [C]
(*Finance*) a document that presents the reasons that show why a product, project, etc. would be successful and make money, used to try to get people to invest in the project: *The website teaches you how to build a business case for a new product range.*

'business ,centre (*AmE spelling* ~ **center**) *noun* [C]
a place that people can pay to use for work, meetings, etc. away from their usual place of work: *The hotel's business centre offers videoconferencing facilities and a full range of business services.*

'business class *noun* [U]
the part of a plane, etc. where passengers have a very high level of comfort and service, designed for people travelling on business ▶ **'business class** *adverb*: *I always fly business class.* → ECONOMY CLASS, FIRST CLASS

'business ,college *noun* [C]
a college where students can learn basic business skills, such as accounting, management and managing an office

'business combi,nation *noun* [U,C]
the act of joining or working together with another company after a TAKEOVER or a MERGER: *Shareholders will vote on the company's proposed business combination with AXL Enterprises.*

,business conti'nuity *noun* [U]
the process of making sure that the important parts of a business continue working if there is a disaster: *Computer viruses may be a greater threat to business continuity than fires and floods.* ◇ *business continuity planning/management* ◇ *business continuity services/plans* → DISASTER RECOVERY

'business ,cycle *noun* [C]
(*Economics*) the usual pattern of a country's economy over a period of time, with periods of success (**growth**) and periods of difficulty (**recession**) happening regularly one after another
SYN ECONOMIC CYCLE, TRADE CYCLE

business cycle

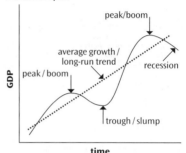

'business day *noun* [C]
a day when stock exchanges and banks are open

'business debt (*also* **'trade debt**) *noun* [U,C]
(*Accounting*) money that a company owes to other companies

'business ,entity *noun* [C]
a business of a particular type, for example a CORPORATION, a PARTNERSHIP, a LIMITED COMPANY, etc.

,business 'entity ,concept *noun* [C]
(*Accounting*) the idea that a business is separate from the people who own it, so that the financial records only show the activities of the business, not the owners

'business game (*also* **'management game**) *noun* [C]
(*HR*) a way of training people, especially managers, in business skills that asks teams, sometimes competing with each other, to deal with situations that could exist in reality: *a management game for team building, communications and leadership*

'business gift *noun* [C]
(*Accounting; Marketing*) a small item that a company gives free to people in order to advertise itself; an amount of money that a company gives to a charity. **NOTE** These gifts may be used to obtain a reduction in the amount of tax a company has to pay.

'business hours *noun* [pl.]
the times of day when a shop/store, an office, a bank, etc. is open: *Normal business hours are between 9 a.m. and 5 p.m.*

,business inter'ruption *noun* [U]
(*Insurance*) a situation where a company loses money when it has to stop work because of a

disaster: *Tens of millions of dollars were paid out in business interruption insurance claims as a result of the computer virus.*

businesslike /'bɪznəslaɪk/ *adjective*
(about a person) working in an efficient and organized way and not wasting time or thinking about personal things: *She has a brisk and businesslike manner.*
➊ *a businesslike* **approach/manner/voice/way**

'**business lunch** *noun* [C]
a meeting with lunch to talk about business or to entertain customers
➊ *to* **attend/have/speak at** *a business lunch*

★**businessman** /'bɪznəsmæn; -mən/,
businesswoman /'bɪznəswʊmən/ *noun* [C]
(*plural* **businessmen** /-men; -mən/ **businesswomen** /-wɪmɪn/)
1 a person who works in business, especially at a high level: *She had a distinguished career as a businesswoman.*
➊ *a* **high-powered/leading/prominent/self-made/ successful/wealthy** *businessman*
2 a person who is skilful in business and financial matters: *I should have got a better price for the car, but I'm not a very shrewd businessman.*
➊ *an* **astute/a good/shrewd** *businessman •* *a* **hard-nosed/tough** *businessman*
[SYN] BUSINESS PERSON

'**business mix** *noun* [C]
the types of product and/or customer that form a company's business: *We need to adapt our business mix to the current economic climate.*

'**business park** *noun* [C]
an area of land, usually outside a town or city, that is specially designed for offices and small factories
→ INDUSTRIAL ESTATE

★'**business ,person** (*also spelled*
businessperson, *especially in AmE*) *noun* [C] (*plural* **business people** *or, especially in formal use,* **business persons**)
1 a person who works in business, especially at a high level: *a group of Japanese business people*
2 a person who is skilful in business and financial matters: *As an artist, I'm not much of a business person.* [NOTE] **Business people** is usually used to talk about a group of men and women, or to avoid having to say 'businessmen' or 'businesswomen'. **Business person/business people** is also used in more formal language.

'**business plan** *noun* [C]
(*Finance*) a written document that states what a company, or part of a company, aims to do to sell its products, develop new products, etc. within a particular period, and how it will get the money it needs: *They spent a month preparing a business plan to present to the board.*
➊ *to* **draft/draw up/develop/put together/prepare/ write** *a business plan*

,**business 'process** *noun* [C]
the systems, the way things are organized and the order in which things are done inside a company in order to produce a product or service

'**business 'process out'sourcing** *noun* [U]
(*abbr* **BPO**)
the practice of giving the responsibility for running a particular system or a service to people outside the company

'**business 'process ,re-engi'neering** (*AmE spelling also* ~ **reengineering**) (*also* '**business 'process ,rede'sign**) *noun* [U] (*abbr* **BPR**)
a method of improving a business and its value to customers by organizing its systems and the way

things are done in a completely new and different way, especially in order to make full use of computer systems
➊ *to* **apply/embark on/implement/introduce** *business process re-engineering*

,**business re'ply ,service** *noun* [C] (*BrE*) (*abbr* **BRS**) (*AmE* ,**business re'ply mail** [U] (*abbr* **BRM**)
a service that allows a company to supply cards or envelopes with its address on that people can use for replying without paying the cost of a stamp. The company only pays for the ones that are sent back.

'**business school** *noun* [C,U]
a college, or part of a college or university, that teaches BUSINESS STUDIES: *She graduated from a business school in 2002.* ◇ *They don't teach you that in business school.*
➊ *to* **apply to/enrol at/in/go to** *(a) business school •* *to* **graduate from/leave** *(a) business school*

'**business sense** *noun*
1 [U] action that may help to make a business make money, be efficient, etc: *It makes good business sense to make sure your employees are happy.*
2 [sing., U] a good understanding and judgement of business: *He has a sharp business sense.*

'**business ,strategy** *noun* [C]
a plan for what a business wants to achieve and how they will do it that joins together all the different parts of the business
➊ *to* **develop/implement/plan** *a business strategy*

'**business ,studies** *noun* [pl.]
the study of subjects connected with money and managing a business: *a degree in Business Studies* ◇ *All students take Business Studies in their first year.*
➊ *to* **do/graduate in/take** *business studies*

,**business 'systems ,analyst** , ,**business 'systems a,nalysis** = SYSTEMS ANALYST

'**business trip** *noun* [C]
a journey to a place and back again in order to do business: *He's gone on a business trip to Greece.*
➊ *to* **be away on/be on/go on** *a business trip •* *to* **come back from/return from** *a business trip*

'**business trust** *noun* [C]
(*Finance*) (in the US) an association that manages investments, property, etc. for businesses and people involved in them

★**bust** /bʌst/ *adjective, noun, verb*
● *adjective* (*informal*)
(about a business or a person) failed because of a lack of money: *If the company does not cut its workforce it will* **go bust.** See note at BANKRUPT
● *noun*
1 (*Economics, informal*) [C, usually sing., U] a time when a period of economic success ends suddenly: *Hundreds of companies went under (= failed) in the dot-com bust.* → BOOM
2 (*informal*) [C] (*especially AmE*) (a person or thing that fails: *The plan turned out to be a bust.*
→ idiom at BOOM *noun*
● *verb* [+ obj] (*informal*)
to make sth fail; to break sth: *The government's proposed tax cuts could bust the budget.*

,**busted 'flush** *noun* [C] (*informal*)
a person, company, etc. that did not improve or become as successful as expected

busy /'bɪzi/ *adjective* (**busier, busiest**)
1 having a lot of work to do; not free to do sth else because you are working on sth: *I'm afraid Mr Endo is busy at the moment. Can I get him to call you back?* ◇ *I'm too busy to go to the meeting.*
2 spending a lot of time on sth: *This month the team have been busy making presentations to potential investors.*

3 full of people, activity, vehicles, etc: *one of Europe's busiest airports*
4 full of work and activity: *Have you had a busy day? ◇ Summer is our busiest season. ◇ I've got a busy schedule this week.*
5 = ENGAGED

button /ˈbʌtn/ *noun* [C]
1 a small part of a machine that you press to make it work: *You can control the temperature at the touch of a button.*
O *to hit/press/push* a button
2 (*IT*) a small place on a computer screen that you click on to make it work: *To reply to an email, click on the 'reply' button.*
3 (*Marketing*) = BUTTON AD

'button ad (*also* **'button ad,vertisement, 'button**) *noun* [C]
(*Marketing*) an advertisement in the form of a small square or circle on a web page → BANNER AD

'buttoned-down (*also* **'button-down**) *adjective*
[only before noun] (*both especially AmE*)
used to describe a traditional approach to business: *He is seen as a conventional, button-down, corporate type. ◇ a company with a buttoned-down culture*

★buy /baɪ/ *verb, noun*
●*verb* [+ obj *or no obj*] (**bought, bought** /bɔːt/) buy sth (for sb) | buy sb sth
1 to obtain sth by paying money for it: *Many people buy airline tickets online. ◇ Interbrew bought the company for $3 billion. ◇ Let me buy you lunch. ◇ If you're thinking of getting a new car, now is a good time to buy. ◇ We always buy in bulk* (= buy large numbers of things at one time).
2 (used about money) to be enough to pay for sth: *In December 2001, €1 would buy you $1.65.*
→ idiom at BULK *noun*
PHR V ,buy sth 'in 1 (*BrE*) (used about a company that produces or sells things) to buy sth from another company because you cannot produce it yourself or because you want to increase your supplies: *The power company couldn't meet demand and was forced to buy in electricity.* **2** to buy shares or bonds in a company, especially when you are putting money into that company for the first time: *With bonds, you stay with the interest rate you buy in at.* ,buy 'into sth 1 to buy shares in a company, especially in order to gain some control over it: *The company paid $1.5 billion to buy into its rival.* **2** to invest in something: *The broker advised its clients to buy into the stock.* **3** to believe that an idea is good or that a plan will be successful: *Many companies have bought into the idea of hiring a chief knowledge officer.* ,buy sb 'out to pay money for someone to be freed from a contract ,buy sb/sth 'out to buy sb's share in a company, usually in order to get total control of it for yourself: *He was bought out by his partners.* → BUYOUT ,buy sth 'up to buy all or as much as possible of sth, especially because it is cheap
●*noun*

SEE ALSO: **best buy, impulse ~, make-or-~**

1 [C] something that is bought or that is for sale: *The 17-inch monitor is a good buy* (= is worth the money you pay for it) ◇ *The company denies it is looking for a big buy* (= a company to buy that will cost a lot of money).
2 (*Stock Exchange*) [U; sing.] = BUY RATING
3 (*Stock Exchange*) [C] = BUY ORDER

'buy-back (*also spelled* **buyback**) *noun* [U,C]
1 (*Commerce*) an act of buying sth from the person that you previously sold it to: *The book store operates a book buy-back at the end of the semester.*
2 (*Finance*) a situation where a company buys its shares back from the people who own them, in order to reduce the number of its shares available, to reduce its debt, etc: *Even after a 15% share buy-*

back, the company will have plenty of cash left to make acquisitions. ◇ *buy-back contracts* SYN BUY-IN
3 (*Finance*) a situation when a government reduces its country's debt to foreign banks by buying some of it back: *a debt buy-back plan*
SYN REPURCHASE

★buyer /ˈbaɪə(r)/ *noun* [C]

SEE ALSO: **materials buyer, target ~, trade ~**

1 a person or company that buys sth, especially something valuable like a business or a home: *The company is trying to find a buyer for its toiletries business. ◇ A majority of car buyers browse the Internet for information.* → PURCHASER
O *possible/potential/prospective buyers • car/ computer/home buyers*
2 the person or company that buys sth, rather than the person who sells it (the **seller**): *foreign exchange brokers who link buyers and sellers of foreign currency*
3 (*Commerce*) a person in a company who chooses the goods, equipment or materials that the company buys: *He works as a buyer for a department store.*
IDM **buyer be'ware** (*also* **let the buyer be'ware**) (*Law*) used to say that when you are buying something it is your responsibility to check that there is nothing wrong with what you are buying
NOTE 'Buyer beware' is the meaning of the Latin phrase 'caveat emptor'.

'buyer concen,tration *noun* [C,U]
(*Economics*) the extent to which a large percentage of an industry's products are bought by only a small number of buyers: *High buyer concentration* (= only a few buyers) *increases buyers' bargaining power. ◇ The lower the buyer concentration* (= the more buyers there are) *the better it is for your industry.*
O *to increase/reduce buyer concentration*

'buyer ,power *noun* [U]
(*Economics*) the amount that buyers are able to influence price, for example because they buy in large quantities or can choose particular suppliers: *The supermarket chain's excessive buying power forced some wholesalers out of business.*

'buyer risk (*also* **'buyer's risk**) *noun* [U]
(*Commerce*) the risk that sb takes when buying sth, for example that the goods will not be supplied or will be of poor quality

,buyer's 'market *noun* [C, usually sing.]
a situation where the price of a particular item is low and people have a choice, because there are more people selling the item than people who want to buy it: *It's a buyer's market in the car industry.*
OPP SELLER'S MARKET

,buyer's 'risk *noun* [U]
1 (*Trade*) if goods are sent **at buyer's risk**, the buyer has to insure the goods during transport
2 (*Commerce*) = BUYER RISK

,buyer's 'surplus = CONSUMER SURPLUS

'buy-in *noun*

SEE ALSO: **management buy-in**

1 (*Finance*) [C] a situation where a group of people from outside a company buy more than 50% of its shares because they want to take over the management of the company → BUYOUT
2 [U] support for an idea from other people: *She spent months getting buy-in from management for her proposal.*
3 (*Finance*) [C] a situation where a company buys its shares back from the people who own them: *The buy-in was part of the company's strategy to protect itself against a hostile takeover.* SYN BUY-BACK

★ buying /'baɪɪŋ/ *noun* [U]

SEE ALSO: **media buying**

1 the activity of getting sth by paying money for it: *online buying* ◇ *the buying habits of customers* ◇ *peak buying periods*
2 the activity of choosing the goods, equipment or materials that a company or shop/store buys: *I did all my own buying for my store.*

'buying ,agent *noun* [C]
(*Trade*) a person or company whose job is to find and buy sth for sb else: *They sell their textiles through a buying agent.*

'buying be,haviour (*AmE spelling* ~ **behavior**)
= BUYING HABITS

'buying ,centre (*AmE spelling* ~ **center**) *noun* [C]
1 the group of people who make decisions about buying things for a company SYN DECISION-MAKING UNIT
2 (*Commerce*) (*often used with another noun*) a place where a lot of a particular product can be bought: *The city is the country's leading diamond buying centre.*

'buying de,cision *noun* [C]
the process involved in deciding to buy a particular product

'buying ,habits *noun* [pl.] (*also* **'buying be,haviour** [U]*)
(*Marketing*) the way that people buy things, for example how they decide what to buy, where they buy it, how much they are willing to spend, etc.

'buying ,order = BUY ORDER

'buying ,power *noun* [U]
1 the amount of money that a person or business has available for buying goods and services: *Cuts in interest rates increase consumer buying power.*
2 the amount of goods and services that a currency can buy at a particular time: *the dollar's buying power*
SYN PURCHASING POWER

'buying price *noun* [C, usually sing.]
1 (*Commerce*) the price at which you can buy sth: *We will require a downpayment of 10% of the buying price of the vehicle.*
2 (*Finance*) the price at which an investor or a dealer will or can buy particular shares, bonds, etc.: *The spread between the buying price and the selling price of the company's shares is half a percentage point.*
SYN PURCHASE PRICE → SELLING PRICE

'buying ,signals *noun* [pl.]
words, movements or actions that show that sb is ready to buy sth

'buy limit ,order *noun* [C]
(*Stock Exchange*) an instruction to a BROKER to buy a number of shares, bonds, etc. at a particular price or lower → SELL LIMIT ORDER
❍ to *execute/place* a buy limit order

'buy ,order (*also* buy, **'buying ,order**) *noun* [C]
(*Stock Exchange*) an instruction to a BROKER to buy a particular number of shares, bonds, etc. → SELL ORDER
❍ to *execute/place* a buy order

buyout /'baɪaʊt/ *noun* [C]

SEE ALSO: **employee buyout, management buyout**

(*Finance*) a situation in which a person or group gains control of a company or a particular part of it by buying all or most of its shares: *The management*

are considering a buyout of the company. ◇ *The publishing group approached the company with a buyout offer worth over $400 million.* ◇ *We are attempting a leveraged buyout of a much larger company.*
❍ to *accept/fund/lead/reject* a buyout • a buyout *bid/deal/offer*

'buy ,rating *noun* [C] (*also* **buy** [U; sing.])
(*Stock Exchange*) a statement made by a bank, a dealer, etc. that a particular company's shares are worth buying: *Our analyst has put a strong buy rating on the stock.*
❍ to *have/put* a buy rating on sth

'buy ,signal *noun* [C]
(*Stock Exchange*) a situation where the pattern of recent movements in a share price indicates that it is a good time to buy shares → SELL SIGNAL
❍ to *generate/give* a buy signal

'buzz group *noun* [C]
(*Marketing*) one of the small groups of people that a large group can be divided into in order to talk about and have ideas about a particular subject: *The buzz groups came up with some creative ideas for a marketing campaign.*

'buzz ,marketing *noun* [U]
(*Marketing*) a form of marketing where a company creates interest in a new product by persuading interested users or websites to pass on the message about it to other people or websites SYN VIRAL MARKETING

buzzword /'bʌzwɜːd; *AmE* -wɜːrd/ (*also* **buzz-phrase**) *noun* [C]
a word or phrase, especially one connected with a particular subject, that has become fashionable and popular and is used a lot in newspapers: *B2E has become a buzzword in business.*

BV /,biː 'viː/ = BOOK VALUE

'by-law *noun* [C]
(*Law*)
1 (*AmE spelling also* **bylaw**) (*BrE spelling also* **bye-law**) an official rule made by an organization for its members
2 (*usually* **Bylaws**) [pl.] (*AmE*) one of the legal documents that is created when a company is formed. It contains rules about how the company must be managed, what rights shareholders have, what the directors can do and what formal meetings must be held. SYN ARTICLES OF ASSOCIATION
3 (*especially BrE*) a law that is made by a local authority and that applies only to that area

byline /'baɪlaɪn/ *noun* [C]
a line at the beginning or end of a piece of writing in a newspaper or magazine that gives the writer's name

bypass /'baɪpɑːs/ *verb* [+ obj]
to ignore a system, a rule, or sb in authority: *Coffee growers are now bypassing the middlemen and dealing directly with consumers.*

'by-,product (*also spelled* **byproduct**, *especially in AmE*) *noun* [C]
1 a substance that is produced during the process of making or destroying sth else: *When burnt, plastics produce dangerous by-products.*
2 a thing that happens, often unexpectedly, as the result of sth else: *The cut in workforce has been a by-product of the company's investment in new technology.*

byte /baɪt/ *noun* [C]
(*IT*) a unit of information stored in a computer, equal to 8 BITS. A computer's memory is measured in **bytes**.

C c

C2C (*also spelled* **c2c**, **C-to-C**) /ˌsiː tə ˈsiː/ *adjective* [only before noun]
(*E-commerce*) **consumer-to-consumer** used to describe the buying, selling and exchanging over the Internet of products, services or information between individuals: *C2C commerce* ◇ *consumer-to-consumer auctions on the Internet* → B2C

C2DE /ˌsiː ˌtuː diː ˈiː/ *noun* [U] (*BrE*)
(*Marketing*) the lower three social and economic groups in a society, used to refer to these groups as possible customers for particular products: *C2DE men have a fairly strong interest in designer clothing.* → ABC1

cable /ˈkeɪbl/ *noun*
___
SEE ALSO: **pay cable**
___
1 [C,U] a set of wires, covered in plastic or rubber, that carries electricity, telephone signals, etc: *Connect the printer cable to your PC.* ◇ *fibre-optic cable*
2 (*IT*) [U] = CABLE TELEVISION
3 (*IT*) [U] a way of connecting a computer to the Internet using a **cable**: *Cable and DSL connections are much faster than a standard modem.*
→ FAX, TELEX, WIRE

'cable ˌcompany *noun* [C]
a company that provides services such as television, the Internet, etc. by using underground cables

ˌcable 'television (*also* **cable**, **ˌcable T'V**) (*AmE also* **comˌmunity an'tenna ˌtelevision**) *noun* [U]
a service that uses a system of wires to broadcast television programmes instead of radio waves: *the UK's biggest cable television operator* ◇ *Around 80% of homes in the country are equipped with cable.*

ˌcable 'transfer = WIRE TRANSFER

ˌcable T'V = CABLE TELEVISION

cabotage /ˈkæbətɑːʒ/ *noun* [U]
(*Economics; Transport*)
1 the activity of moving people or goods by plane, ship, etc. within a particular country or area; the right of foreign ships, planes, etc. to do this: *airline cabotage* ◇ *The law allowed unlimited cabotage rights within the EU.*
2 a policy that a country has preventing foreign ships, planes, etc. from transporting people or goods within the country

CAC 40 /ˌkæk ˈfɔːti; ˌsiː eɪ siːː; *AmE* ˈfɔːrti/ *noun* [sing.]
a measurement of how well the Paris stock exchange is performing, calculated using the share prices of the 40 largest companies on the stock exchange: *In Paris, the CAC 40 closed up 1.5 per cent.* → INDEX

cache /kæʃ/ *noun* [C]
(*IT*) a part of a computer's memory that stores copies of data so that the data can be found very quickly ► **cache** *verb* [+ obj]: *cached data*

CAD *abbr*
1 /kæd/ (*IT*) computer-aided design; computer-assisted design
2 /ˌsiː eɪ ˈdiː/ (*Trade*) cash against documents

CAE /ˌsiː eɪ ˈiː/ *abbr*
(*Manufacturing*) computer-aided engineering; computer-assisted engineering

C & F *abbr*
(*Trade, only used in written English*) carriage and freight → COST AND FREIGHT

cafeteria /ˌkæfəˈtɪəriə; *AmE* -ˈtɪr-/ *noun* [C]
a restaurant, especially one for staff or workers, where people choose and collect their meals themselves and carry them to their tables → CANTEEN

cafe'teria plan *noun* [C] (*also* **cafe'teria ˌbenefits** [pl.])
(*HR*) a system that allows employees to choose the benefits, such as health insurance, use of a car, etc. that they receive in addition to their pay, up to a particular amount of money: *We offer a cafeteria plan to provide for the individual and changing needs of our employees.* → FLEXIBLE BENEFITS

★ **calculate** /ˈkælkjuleɪt/ *verb* [+ obj]
1 to use numbers to find out a total number, amount, distance, etc: *Use the formula to calculate the interest on the loan.* ◇ *The figure was calculated by dividing the costs by the number of products we expect to sell.*
2 to guess sth or form an opinion by using all the information available: *We calculated that the advantages would be greater than the disadvantages.*

calculator /ˈkælkjuleɪtə(r)/ *noun* [C]
1 a small electronic device used for **calculating** with numbers: *to use a pocket calculator*
2 (*IT*) a piece of software used for **calculating** difficult things, such as how much income tax you have to pay: *Use the loan calculator to find out what your monthly repayments will be.*

VOCABULARY BUILDING

Calendars and diaries

A **calendar** shows the days, weeks and months of a year and is usually hung on the wall. It is used for finding out the date or keeping a brief record of an event. A **diary** (*especially BrE; AmE usually* **datebook**) is a book with spaces for each day of the year, used for writing down appointments or recording events in more detail.

Calendar, **diary** and **datebook** are also used to describe some computer programs that perform the same function as the paper versions.

A **personal organizer** or **Filofax**™ is a small book with loose sheets of paper in which you can write down addresses, appointments and other information. **Diary** and **personal organizer** can also be used to describe a small computer used for the same purpose, although these are usually called **electronic/handheld organizers** or **PDAs** (= personal digital assistants).

Note: An **agenda** is not a diary but a list of items to be discussed at a meeting.

---

calendar /ˈkælɪndə(r)/ *noun* [C]
1 a page or series of pages showing the days, weeks and months of a particular year, especially one that you hang on a wall: *a calendar for 2006* → DIARY
2 (*AmE*) a record of what you have to do each day; the book or computer system where you keep this: *The device has a built-in calendar.* SYN DIARY, APPOINTMENT BOOK

3 [usually sing.] a list of important events or dates of a particular type during the year: *the busiest day in the City's calendar*
4 calendar 2006, 2007, etc. (*AmE*) = CALENDAR YEAR

‚calendar 'month *noun* [C]
1 one of the 12 months of the year: *We finalize the accounts on the last day of each calendar month.*
2 a period of time from a particular date in one month to the same date in the next one: *Payment must be received within one calendar month from date of invoice.*

‚calendar 'year (*AmE also* **calendar 2006, 2007, etc.**) *noun* [C]
the period of time from 1 January to 31 December in the same year: *We expect to see more growth next calendar year.* ◇ *The government plans to spend €60 billion on health care in calendar 2006.* **SYN** YEAR

★ call /kɔːl/ *verb, noun*
● *verb*
1 [+ obj *or no* obj] to telephone sb: *You can call him on his cellphone.* ◇ *I called the office to tell them I'd be late.*
2 [no obj] (*especially BrE*) **call (on sb/in)** to make a short visit to a person or place: *I was out when the sales rep called.*
3 [+ obj] to order sth to happen; to announce that sth will happen: *I've called a meeting of the management team to try resolve the problem.* ◇ *The union has called a national strike.* See note at ARRANGE
4 [+ obj] to predict what will happen to sth: *She believes that analysts have called the bottom of the market* (= predicted that the prices of shares, etc. will begin to rise) *too early.*
5 [+ obj] (*often* **be called**) to order sb to come to a place: *Several candidates were called for a second interview.*
6 (*Finance*) [+ obj] **call sth (back/in)** to demand that sb immediately pays back the money they owe: *The bank has threatened to call a €460 million loan.*
7 (*Finance*) [+ obj] **call a bond | call in a bond** to pay back the money that was borrowed with a bond: *The bond can be called after five years for a price of $1 100.*
8 (*Law*) [+ obj] to require sb to give evidence to a court or to government officials: *to call a witness*
IDM ‚**call (sb) col'lect** (*AmE*) to make a telephone call which is paid for by the person that you are telephoning → REVERSE-CHARGE **call in the re'ceivers** to appoint an independent person to manage the financial affairs of a business because it is unable to pay its debts: *The company has called in the receivers after losing the support of its bankers.*
call sb/sth to 'order to ask people in a meeting to be quiet so that the meeting can start or continue
‚**call the 'shots/'tune** (*informal*) to be the person who controls a situation → idioms at PLAY *noun*, QUESTION *noun*
PHR V ‚**call 'back** to visit sb again for a particular purpose: *I'll call back for your order this evening.*
‚**call 'back;** ‚**call sb 'back** to telephone sb again or to telephone sb who telephoned you earlier **'call for sth;** '**call for sb to do sth** to publicly ask for sth to happen; to need sth: *The business plan calls for further cost reductions.* ‚**call 'in** to telephone a place, especially the place where you work: *Several people have called in sick today.* ‚**call sb 'in** to ask for the services of sb: *We called in Ernst & Young as consultants.* ‚**call sth 'in** (*Commerce*) to order or ask for the return of sth: *Cars with serious faults have been called in by the manufacturers.* **SYN** RECALL
‚**call sth 'off** to cancel sth; to decide that sth will not happen: *The deal was called off after the buyer reduced its offer.* See note at POSTPONE **'call on sb**
1 (*also* **'call upon sb** *formal*) to ask or demand that

sb do sth: *The unions have called on government to support their demands.* **2** to visit sb for a short time: *Her job is to call on schools to talk to teachers about the material.* **3** (*also* **'call upon sb** *formal*) to formally invite or ask sb to speak: *I now call upon the chairman to address the meeting.* ‚**call 'up;** ‚**call sb 'up** to telephone sb ‚**call sth 'up** to use sth that is stored or kept available: *I called up his address on the computer.*
● *noun*

SEE ALSO: **at call, cash ~, conference ~, courtesy ~, covered ~, margin ~, money at ~, wake-up ~**

1 (*also* **'phone call**) [C] the act of speaking to sb on the telephone: *I got a call from our supplier.* ◇ *Were there any calls for me while I was out?* ◇ *I'll take* (= answer) *the call in my office.* ◇ *This is a courtesy call from your bank.*
○ *to* **give sb/make/return** *a call* ✦ *to* **get/have/receive** *a call from sb* ✦ *an* **international/a local/long-distance** *call*
2 [C] a short visit to sb's house: *I've got five calls to make this morning.* ◇ *He* **paid a call on** *three of his clients yesterday.*
3 [C] a request, an order or a demand for sb to do sth or to go somewhere: *The Bank has resisted calls for a cut in interest rates.*
4 [sing.] **a call on sth | no call for sth** the demand for sth; no demand for sth: *Warmer temperatures have reduced the call on heating oil.* ◇ *There isn't a lot of call for small specialist stores these days.*
5 [C] a decision; an act of predicting sth: *It's your call!* ◇ *Traders have made a number of bad calls in recent months.*
6 (*Finance*) [C] = CALL OPTION
7 (*Finance*) [C] a situation in which a company asks shareholders to pay part of the money that they owe for their shares: *The directors have made a call of 10 cents a share.* → CALLABLE (2)
IDM **at/on 'call** if your money is **at/on call** with a bank, you can have it when you like, but you have to warn the bank before you can take it out. Banks invest money that is **at/on call** and pay you a higher rate of interest. → CALL ACCOUNT, ON DEMAND at DEMAND

callable /'kɔːləbl/ *adjective*
(*Finance*)
1 if a bond or a similar investment is **callable**, the company or government that sold it can buy it back early (before the **maturity date**) at an agreed price: *The bond is callable after 5 years.* **OPP** NON-CALLABLE → REDEEMABLE
○ *a callable* **bond/debenture/note/security**
2 if a company's shares are **callable**, they are not completely paid for and the company can require the shareholders to pay more money for them in the future

'call ac‚count (*also* ‚**call de'posit ac‚count**) *noun* [C] (*BrE*)
a type of bank account used for investing money that pays a higher rate of interest than a normal bank account. You can have your money when you like, but you may have to warn the bank a short time before you want it. → AT/ON CALL at CALL *noun*

callback /'kɔːlbæk/ *noun*
1 (*HR*) [C] (*especially AmE*) an occasion when sb is asked to return somewhere, especially for a second interview for a job; a second interview: *Students receiving callbacks should prepare thoroughly for the interview.* ◇ *a callback interview* → FLYBACK
2 [C] a telephone call which you make to sb who has just called you or to sb you have called earlier: *Does the company offer callbacks when they are busy?*
3 [C] an occasion when people are asked to return goods that they have bought, usually because they are not safe

4 [C] (*AmE*) an occasion when sb is asked to go back to work, especially to deal with a sudden serious or dangerous situation
5 (*IT*) (*also* '**dial-back**) [U] a process in which sb LOGS ON to a company computer system which then calls their computer back, used for security or to reduce telephone costs

'**callback pay** = CALL-IN PAY

'**call ,centre** (*AmE spelling* ~ **center**) *noun* [C]
an office in which a large number of people work using telephones, for example arranging insurance for people, doing market research or taking customers' orders and answering questions for a large organization: *We operate a 24-hour call centre for customer support.* → CONTACT CENTRE

,**call de'posit ac,count** (*also* '**call de,posit**) = CALL ACCOUNT

,**called-up 'capital** (*also* ,**called-up 'share ,capital**) *noun* [U] (*BrE*)
(*Finance*) the amount of money that a company has asked shareholders to pay for their shares (has **called up**) at a particular time, when the full payment is made over a period of time: *Called-up share capital now forms 79% of the total share capital.* → PAID-UP CAPITAL

caller /'kɔːlə(r)/ *noun* [C]
a person who is making a telephone call: *US callers pay 8¢ a minute to Australia.*

,**caller dis'play** (*BrE*) (*AmE* ,**caller I'D**) *noun* [U]
a system that uses a device on your telephone to identify and display the telephone number of the person who is calling you

'**call ,feature** = CALL PROVISION (1)

,**call 'forwarding** *noun* [U]
the ability of a telephone system to transfer a call to another telephone automatically: *You can use the call forwarding facility to divert calls to your mobile.*

'**calling card** *noun* [C] (*especially AmE*)
1 a card that you buy in order to make telephone calls from public telephones, etc. It allows you to make calls up to the amount that you have paid: *an international pre-paid calling card*
2 a card that you use to make telephone calls from public telephones, hotels, etc. and pay for them later with your home telephone bill → CHARGE CARD
→ PHONECARD

'**call-in pay** (*also* '**callback pay, re'porting pay**) *noun* [U] (*all AmE*)
(*HR*) an amount of money paid to workers who are asked to go to work outside their usual hours, even if there is no work for them to do

'**call loan** = DEMAND LOAN

'**call ,money** *noun* [U]
(*Finance*) money that a bank invests for short periods of time and can get back whenever it demands → AT CALL at CALL

'**call ,option** (*also* '**call**) *noun* [C]
(*Finance*) a right to buy sth, such as a number of shares in a company or a quantity of raw materials, at a particular price within a fixed period or on a particular date: *a call option to purchase 10 000 pounds of sugar at $0.50 per pound* → PUT OPTION
O *to* **buy/exercise/hold/purchase/use** *a call option*

'**call pro,vision** *noun* [C]
(*Finance*)
1 (*also* '**call ,feature**) a section (**clause**) in a bond contract that allows the seller to buy the bond back early: *Most corporate bonds have a call provision.* ◇ *The issuing company can usually exercise the call provision at any time after a specified date.*
2 part of an arrangement for a loan that allows the bank to demand full payment early if payments

have not been made, or if a business has not achieved the results it expected

'**call ,routing** *noun* [U] (*IT*)
1 the process by which a customer is connected to a particular place or person through a single central number
2 the ability to transfer calls from one telephone to another

'**call ,waiting** *noun* [U]
the ability of a telephone system to keep a person calling you waiting (**on hold**) while you deal with another telephone call

CAM /kæm/ *abbr* [U]
(*IT; Manufacturing*) computer-aided manufacturing; computer-assisted manufacturing

c & m = CARE AND MAINTENANCE

★ **campaign** /kæm'peɪn/ *noun, verb*
● *noun* [C]

SEE ALSO: **sales campaign**

a series of planned activities to persuade people to buy or to do something: *They launched a campaign to block the merger.* ◇ *We spent $15 million on an advertising campaign to raise awareness of the brand name.*
O *to* **build/fund/launch** *a campaign* ✦ *an* **advertising/cost-cutting/marketing** *campaign* ✦ *a campaign* **aimed at sb/sth/designed to do sth**
● *verb* [no obj] **campaign for/against sth** to lead or take part in a series of planned activities designed to persuade sb to do sth: *They were campaigning for better working conditions.*

campus /'kæmpəs/ *noun* [C,U]
1 the area of land where the main buildings of a college or university are: *the college campus* ◇ *She lives on campus.*
2 (*AmE*) an area of land where a company has many buildings: *The conference will take place at Cisco's San José Campus.*

can /kæn/ *verb* [+ obj] (-nn-)
1 (*especially AmE*) to preserve food by putting it in a metal container (a **can**)
2 (*informal*) (*AmE*) to dismiss sb from their job

★ **cancel** /'kænsl/ *verb* (-**ll**-, *AmE* -**l**-)
1 [+ obj] to decide that sth that has been planned or arranged will not happen: *The meeting has been cancelled.* ◇ *All flights have been cancelled because of the bad weather.* See note at POSTPONE
2 (*Law*) [+ obj *or* no obj] to say that you no longer want to continue with an agreement, especially one that has been legally arranged: *If the goods don't arrive on time, you can cancel the order.* ◇ *The US has agreed to cancel debts* (= say that they no longer need to be paid) *totalling $10 million.*
3 [+ obj] to mark a ticket, a cheque or an official document in order to show that it has been used or that it must not be used; to stop using these items: *The media group will buy back and cancel 33 million shares.* ◇ *The cancelled cheque is proof that the payment was made.*
4 [+ obj] if you **cancel** a cheque, you stop it being paid: *I realized the deal was a scam* (= a trick for making money) *so I phoned the bank and cancelled the cheque.* SYN STOP
5 [+ obj] to stop an instruction to a machine, especially a computer

★ **cancellation** (*AmE spelling also* **cancelation**) /,kænsə'leɪʃn/ *noun* [U,C]
1 a decision to stop sth that has already been arranged from happening; a statement that sth will not happen: *We have been badly affected by the*

cancellation of orders. ◇ Cancellations must be made in writing. ◇ a $200 cancellation charge
○ to cause/make (a) cancellation
2 (Law) the fact of making sth no longer valid: the cancellation of the contract
3 the act of marking a document, cheque, ticket, etc. or to show it has been used or can no longer be used; a decision to stop using these items

★ **candidate** /'kændɪdət; -deɪt/ noun [C]
a person who is applying for a job: We have some very good candidates for the post. ◇ The HR department screens job candidates carefully (= checks they are suitable for the job).
○ to evaluate/interview/screen a candidate ◆ to choose/find/hire/recruit/reject a candidate ◆ a good/ an ideal/ a successful/ an unsuccessful candidate

'**can-do** adjective [only before noun]
willing to try new things and expecting that they will be successful: Her can-do attitude got her to the top of the organization.

cannibalize, **-ise** /'kænɪbəlaɪz/ verb [+ obj]
1 (Marketing) (used about a company) to reduce the sales of one of its products by introducing a similar new product: We believe the two perfumes appeal to different buyers and won't cannibalize one another's sales.
2 (Manufacturing) to use the parts of a machine or a vehicle to repair or build another: They only keep the helicopters flying by cannibalizing others.
▶ **cannibalization**, **-isation** /ˌkænɪbəlaɪ'zeɪʃn; AmE -lə'z-/ noun [U]: the risk of sales cannibalization of existing products ◇ the cannibalization of aircraft for parts

canteen /kæn'tiːn/ noun [C] (especially BrE)
a place where food and drink are served in a factory, an office, etc: I usually grab a sandwich in the staff canteen.
○ a company/an office/a staff canteen ◆ canteen food/lunches/prices ◆ to eat in/go to/use the canteen

canvass /'kænvəs/ verb
1 (Marketing) [+ obj] to ask people about sth in order to find out what they think about it: The market research team has been canvassing young people about their attitudes to computers.
2 [+ obj or no obj] to try and get support from a group of people: The management have been canvassing support for the merger among shareholders.
3 [+ obj] to discuss an idea thoroughly: The proposal is currently being canvassed.
▶ '**canvass** noun [C]: to carry out a canvass '**canvassing** noun [U]

cap /kæp/ noun, verb
● noun

SEE ALSO: large cap, mid ~, small ~

1 [C] an upper limit on an amount of money that can be spent, borrowed or charged: The government has put a cap on local council spending. ◇ Domestic electricity consumers (= families that use electricity) are protected by a price cap.
○ to impose/put/set a cap on sth
2 (Stock Exchange, informal) [U; sing.] a short way of saying or writing capitalization (= the amount of money that shareholders have invested in a company by buying shares): The company has a market cap of $30 million.
● verb [+ obj] (-pp-)
1 (often be capped) to put a top limit on sth, for example, the amount of money that can be spent, lent, charged, etc: The government's new plan involves cutting public spending and capping the

price of goods and services. ◇ For the first year the service is offered at a capped rate of $200 a month.
→ CAPPED-RATE
2 to finish sth, such as a process or a period of time, in a particular way: The company capped a very bad year by reporting a $3 billion loss for the final quarter.

capability /ˌkeɪpə'bɪləti/ noun [C,U] (plural capabilities)
the ability or qualities necessary to do sth: The task is well within her capabilities. ◇ They tried to expand beyond their distribution capabilities and ran into problems.

★ **capacity** /kə'pæsəti/ noun (plural capacities)

SEE ALSO: excess capacity, installed ~, legal ~

1 [U; C, usually sing.] the number of things or people or the amount of sth that a container or space can hold: a fuel tank with a capacity of 50 litres ◇ large-capacity disk drives
2 (Manufacturing) [U; sing.] the quantity of goods that a factory, machine, etc. can produce; the number of people that a company can provide a service to: The factory is working at full capacity. ◇ The Renault plant near Paris had lots of spare capacity (= it had the equipment, etc. to produce more vehicles). ◇ The new car factory will open in 2006, with a capacity of 300 000 units a year
○ full/spare/total capacity ◆ manufacturing/ production capacity ◆ to cut/expand/increase/ reduce capacity
3 [C, usually sing., U] the ability to understand or to do sth: She has an enormous capacity for hard work. ◇ Limited resources are restricting our capacity to develop new products.
4 [C, usually sing.] the official position or function that sb has: acting in her capacity as manager ◇ He works for several banks in an advisory capacity.

,**cap and 'collar** noun [sing.]
(Finance) an upper and a lower limit between which an interest rate or a share price is fixed for a period of time: Under the takeover deal, the shares issued will be subject to a cap and collar of $20 to $28.
▶ ,**cap and 'collar** verb [+ obj]: You have the option to cap and collar the lending rate on our loans.

capex abbr
(Accounting) a short way of writing capital expenditure

★ **capital** /'kæpɪtl/ noun

SEE ALSO: authorized capital, authorized share ~, called-up ~, circulating ~, core ~, customer ~, etc.

1 (Accounting; Finance) [U] the total value of the land, buildings, machinery, shares in other companies, etc. (assets) that a company owns, minus its debts: Our capital is all tied up in property (= it can not easily be turned into money). ◇ The trust sold its shareholdings in other companies to release capital.
○ to free up/release/tie up/unlock capital
2 (Finance) [U; sing.] an amount of money that is invested in or is used to start a business: They help start-up companies in business planning and raising capital. ◇ The company badly need an injection of capital. ◇ They set up the business with a starting capital of €100 000. → LOAN CAPITAL, SHARE CAPITAL
○ to attract/borrow/generate/have/raise capital ◆ to put up/provide capital ◆ initial/starting/start-up capital ◆ foreign/private capital
3 (Finance) [U] money that is lent or borrowed on which interest is paid: Investors want an immediate return on their capital.
○ to borrow/invest/lend capital ◆ foreign/private capital
4 (Economics) [U] something of value that a company or an organization has, such as

machinery or money, that can be used to produce wealth: *Raw materials, land, labour and capital are used to produce finished goods.*

'capital ac,count *noun* [C]
1 (*Economics*) a record of the money coming into and going out of a country in the form of investments and loans: *The capital account surplus is due to the increase in foreign investment over the last year.* → BALANCE OF PAYMENTS, CURRENT ACCOUNT (2)
2 (*Accounting*) a record of how much owners, shareholders or partners have invested in a company
3 (*Accounting*) a record of how much a company is worth at a particular time, minus its debts
4 (*Accounting*) a record of the money that a company spends on land, buildings, machinery, shares in other companies, etc: *The capital account shows that the company invested heavily in new machine tools.* → REVENUE ACCOUNT

'capital accumu,lation (*also* **'capital for,mation**) *noun* [U]
(*Economics*) the process of getting more and more land, buildings, machinery, etc. that can be used to increase wealth; the process of getting more and more money to save or to invest in these things: *For employers, a cheap labour supply contributes to capital accumulation.*

,capital 'adequacy *noun* [U]
(*Finance*) the fact of a bank, a BROKER, etc. having enough to cover possible losses and to pay debts: *Securities firms have to pass a capital adequacy test that reflects the risks they face.*

,capital 'adequacy ,ratio (*abbr* **CAR**) (*also* **'capital ,ratio**) *noun* [C]
(*Accounting*) the amount of money or shares, bonds, etc. that can easily be changed into money (**liquid assets**) that a bank has, expressed as a percentage of the money it has lent and therefore risks losing: *The government recommends banks to have a minimum capital adequacy ratio of 8%.* → SOLVENCY RATIO

,capital al'lowance (*also* **in,vestment al'lowance**) *noun* [C]
(*Accounting*) an amount of money invested in a new building, machine, etc. that a company can take away from profits before calculating its tax: *The government is to raise capital allowances in order to encourage greater capital investment.*
→ TAX DEPRECIATION

,capital appreci'ation (*also* **,capital 'growth, ,asset appreci'ation**) *noun* [U]
(*Economics*) an increase in the value of the land, buildings, machinery, investments, etc. (**assets**) that a company or a person owns: *During the long bull market, investors could depend on steady capital appreciation.*

,capital 'asset (*also* **,fixed 'asset**) *noun* [C, *usually pl.*]
(*Accounting*) an item of value that a company owns and will keep, such as buildings, machinery, vehicles, shares in other companies, etc: *The company must include an inventory and valuation of its capital assets in the financial statement.*
→ CURRENT ASSET

,capital 'bonus = BONUS (3)

,capital 'budget *noun* [C]
(*Finance*) the plan that a company or an organization makes for buying buildings, machinery, equipment, etc. over a period of time

,capital con'sumption *noun* [U]
(*Economics*) the loss or decrease in value over a particular period of money, buildings, machines, equipment, etc. that are used to produce goods and services in a country SYN DEPRECIATION

,capital em'ployed *noun* [U]

SEE ALSO: return on capital employed

(*Accounting*) the amount of money invested in a business by its shareholders, equal to the total value of assets minus the total value of LIABILITIES

,capital e'quipment *noun* [U]
the machinery, equipment, buildings, etc. that a company or an organization uses to produce goods or services: *Some businesses are unwilling to invest in capital equipment.*

,capital exp'enditure *noun* [U] (*also* **,capital ex'pense** [C,U]) (*abbr* **capex**)
(*Accounting*) money that is spent on valuable items such as buildings, machines or vehicles, which are used for longer than the accounting period in which they are bought: *The group needs $500 million to finance its capital expenditure programme.* SYN CAPITAL OUTLAY
→ REVENUE EXPENDITURE

'capital flight *noun* [U]
(*Economics*) the sudden movement of money out of a country where it is invested to another, in order to reduce risk or to increase profit: *The capital flight that followed the stock market crash caused several banks to fail.* → FLIGHT CAPITAL

'capital flow (*also* **'capital ,movement**) *noun* [C,U]
(*Economics*) the movement of money for investment from one country to another: *A small change in interest rates can cause a large capital flow.*

'capital for,mation = CAPITAL ACCUMULATION

,capital 'gain *noun* [C,U]
(*Accounting*) a profit that is made from the sale of property or an investment: *The sale of the land and buildings generated a capital gain of $2.3 billion.*
→ CAPITAL LOSS
O *to generate/make/realize a capital gain*

,capital 'gains tax *noun* [C,U] (*abbr* **CGT**)
a tax that a person or company must pay when they have made a profit above a particular level on the sale of a CAPITAL ASSET (= buildings, machinery, vehicles, shares, etc.). In the UK companies do not pay this tax, but in the US they do.

'capital ,gearing = GEARING

'capital goods (*also* **in'vestment goods**) *noun* [pl.]
(*Economics*) items such as machines, equipment or buildings that are used to produce goods or services: *Companies should start investing heavily in capital goods.* → CONSUMER GOODS
O *to invest in/purchase/supply capital goods*

,capital 'growth = CAPITAL APPRECIATION

,capital 'growth share = CAPITAL SHARE

,capital-in'tensive *adjective*
used to describe an industry or a company in which the cost of raw materials, equipment, machinery, etc. is much higher than the cost of workers: *In capital-intensive industries such as paper production, maintenance costs can be up to 50% of production costs.* → LABOUR-INTENSIVE

,capital in'vestment *noun* [U,C]
(*Finance*) the act of spending money on machines, equipment, etc. for producing goods or services; money that is spent in this way: *The water industry has a huge capital investment programme.*
O *big/heavy/high/major/small capital investment • a capital investment plan/programme*

capitalism /ˈkæpɪtəlɪzəm/ noun [U]

SEE ALSO: **crony capitalism**

an economic system in which a country's businesses and industry are controlled and run for profit by private owners rather than by the government: *the growth of industrial capitalism in the West* → SOCIALISM

capitalist /ˈkæpɪtəlɪst/ noun, adjective
●**noun** [C]

SEE ALSO: **venture capitalist**

1 a person who supports CAPITALISM
2 a person who controls a lot of wealth and uses it to produce more wealth
●*adjective* (*also* **capitalistic** /ˌkæpɪtəˈlɪstɪk/ less frequent)
based on the principles of CAPITALISM
❍ *a capitalist economy/society/system/*

capitalization, **-isation** /ˌkæpɪtəlaɪˈzeɪʃn; AmE -ləˈz-/ noun [U; sing.]
1 (*Finance*) the act of starting to function as a company; the act of providing a company, etc. with the money it needs to function: *The paper planned to go straight to capitalization as a commercial company.*
2 (*Finance*) = CAPITAL STRUCTURE
3 (*Stock Exchange*) (*abbr* **cap**) = MARKET CAPITALIZATION

capitali'zation ˌissue noun [C] (*especially BrE*)
(*Finance*) a situation in which a company uses its spare profits (**reserves**) to create new shares, which are then given free to the shareholders in proportion to the number of shares that they already own: *The total share capital of the company was increased through a capitalization issue.*
[SYN] BONUS ISSUE, SCRIP ISSUE

capitaliˌzation of re'serves noun [C]
(*Finance*) a situation in which a company uses the spare profits that it has saved to create new shares in the company: *The shareholders have approved an increase of share capital through a capitalization of reserves.*

capitali'zation ˌrate noun [C] (*abbr* **'cap rate**)
(*Accounting*) a rate of interest that is used to help estimate the present value of an investment that will provide an income over a long period of time, such as a business or a property: *It is important to choose an appropriate capitalization rate when valuing the land.*

★**capitalize**, **-ise** /ˈkæpɪtəlaɪz/ verb
1 (*Finance*; *Stock Exchange*) [+ obj or no obj] (*often* **be capitalized at**) to get enough money to start to function as a company; to provide a company with the money it needs to function: *The company could not sell enough shares and so failed to capitalize.* ◇ *The firm is being capitalized at about €3.5 billion.*
2 (*Accounting*) [+ obj] to record money spent on machines, equipment, buildings, etc. as an asset in a company's financial records rather than as an expense: *It is company policy to capitalize assets over €5 000.*
→ CAPITALIZED
[PHR V] **'capitalize on/upon sth** to gain an advantage for yourself from a situation: *The company have capitalized on their successes by putting up prices.*

capitalized, **-ised** /ˈkæpɪtəlaɪzd/ adjective
(*Finance*) having the amount of money (**capital**) mentioned to operate as a company: *a highly capitalized industry* (= one with a lot of money) ◇ *a thinly capitalized company* (= one without enough money) → OVERCAPITALIZED, UNDERCAPITALIZED

ˌcapital 'levy = CAPITAL TAX

ˌcapital 'loss noun [C,U]
(*Accounting*) a loss that is made when an asset is sold: *Those who bought homes before prices fell have incurred a capital loss.* ◇ *a capital loss of 5% per year* → CAPITAL GAIN

'capital ˌmarket noun [C]
(*Finance*) the group of markets and stock exchanges where companies and governments sell shares, bonds, etc. in order to obtain the money they need: *The government aims to borrow $3 billion on the international capital market.* ◇ *Smaller companies can find it difficult to gain access to the capital markets.*
❍ to **borrow/raise** (money) **in/on** the capital market ◆ to **invest in/on** the capital market

'capital ˌmovement = CAPITAL FLOW

ˌcapital 'outlay noun [C]
(*Finance*) money that is spent to buy valuable items that will be kept, such as buildings, machines or vehicles: *The project requires an initial capital outlay of $1.5 million.* [SYN] CAPITAL EXPENDITURE

ˌcapital 'project noun [C]
(*Finance*) a large project that involves building or improving factories, buildings, roads, etc. : *One cereal manufacturer has undertaken a major capital project that will double its output.*

'capital ˌratio = CAPITAL ADEQUACY RATIO

ˌcapital 'rationing noun [U]
(*Finance*) the policy of a company limiting the amount of money that it uses to finance new projects and only investing in the ones most worth doing: *Under capital rationing, a company has a fixed investment budget.*

ˌcapital re'demption reˌserve noun [C]
(*Accounting*) a supply of money that a company must keep and not give to shareholders when it buys back (**redeems**) its own shares

ˌcapital re'quirement noun [C]
(*Finance*) an amount of CAPITAL that a company is legally required to have; the rule that sets this amount: *The government wants to increase the capital requirements for financial institutions.* ◇ *Banks are subject to **minimum** capital requirements.*
→ CAPITAL ADEQUACY

ˌcapital re'serve noun [C, usually pl.]
(*Accounting*)
1 (*also* **ˌundis'tributable reˌserve**, **ˌnon-dis'tributable reˌserve**, *both especially BrE*) profits, such as the increased value of a building, etc., that a company keeps as part of its CAPITAL and which cannot be paid to shareholders: *The profit on the sale of the shares was transferred to capital reserves.*
→ RESERVE noun (3), RETAINED EARNINGS, REVENUE RESERVE
2 a supply of money that a company or an organization keeps for an expected future cost, such as repairing property or buying new equipment: *We have built up capital reserves to replace the roof in five years' time.*

'capital ˌshare (*also* ˌcapital 'growth ˌshare) noun [C] (*especially BrE*)
(*Finance*) a type of share in an INVESTMENT TRUST (= a company that invests money on behalf of its shareholders). The owners of **capital shares** gain from any increase in value of the investments but do not receive regular payments from the company's profits. → INCOME SHARE, PROFIT SHARE

ˌcapital 'stock noun [U,C]
1 (*Economics*) the total value of the buildings, equipment and materials that a company owns and uses to produce goods or services: *Companies adjust their capital stock in response to changes in demand.*

2 (*Finance*) (*AmE*) all the shares a company can make available; the value of those shares: *The group will buy all the capital stock of the company for $212 million.* ◇ *The corporation has a capital stock of $500 million.* [SYN] SHARE CAPITAL, STOCK

,capital 'structure (*also* fi,nancial 'structure, ,capitali'zation) *noun* [C,U]
(*Finance*) the way in which a company obtains money for its business activities: *Their capital structure consists of 200 000 ordinary shares of five euros each.* ◇ *The company has a fairly complex share and loan capital structure.*

,capital 'sum *noun* [C]
(*Finance*) a single payment that you receive, for example from an insurance policy, a gift or an investment: *Under the terms of the plan, you will receive an initial capital sum and regular monthly payments.* → LUMP SUM

'capital tax (*also* ,capital 'levy) *noun* [C]
(*Economics*) a tax that is based on the value of the land, buildings, investments, etc. owned by a person or a company, rather than their income: *The government imposed a capital tax on corporate assets.* → CAPITAL GAINS TAX
▶ ,capital tax'ation *noun* [U]

,capital 'turnover *noun* [C, usually sing.]
(*Accounting*) the value of a company's sales for a year in relation to the total amount of money invested in the business, used as a measure of how well a company uses its assets to create sales: *We hope to improve capital turnover by closing down our old plants.* ◇ *The capital turnover **rate** for the group increased from 3.07 to 3.64.*

,capital 'value *noun* [C, usually sing., U]
(*Accounting*) the total worth of a company's assets, as recorded in its financial accounts: *The company has a capital value of about $50 million.*

'capped-rate *adjective* [only before noun] (*BrE*)
(*Finance*) a **capped-rate** loan has a rate of interest that can change but will not increase above the level that has been set → CAP *verb*

'cap rate = CAPITALIZATION RATE

,captain of 'industry *noun* [C]
used in newspapers, etc. to describe a person who manages a large company: *He is one of the most influential captains of industry in the US.*

captive /'kæptɪv/ *adjective* [only before noun]
1 not free to leave a particular place or to choose what you want do to: *A salesman loves to have a captive audience* (= who listen because they have no choice). ◇ *As the only supplier of electricity in the country they have a captive market* (= people have to buy from them).
❍ *a captive **audience/customer/market***
2 (*Marketing*) only being able to sell the products of a particular company: *Many insurance companies sell their policies through captive agents.*
❍ *a captive **agent/dealer***

capture /'kæptʃə(r)/ *verb* [+ obj]
1 to succeed in making people buy your products or services rather than those of other companies: *We have captured 25% of the US market for refrigerators* (= we produce 25% of all the refrigerators sold).
2 (*IT*) to put sth into a computer in a form it can use: *We capture the **data** using a document scanner.* → DATA CAPTURE

CAR /,si: eɪ 'ɑː(r)/ = CAPITAL ADEQUACY RATIO

carbon /'kɑːbən; *AmE* 'kɑːrb-/ *noun* [U]
1 a chemical substance that is found in all living things, and also diamonds, coal, petrol, etc: *The body of the car is made from **carbon fibre**.*

2 used to refer to gases, such as CARBON DIOXIDE, that are produced from burning fuels and can harm the planet if they are produced in large amounts: *Britain wants to reduce its carbon **emissions** by 60 per cent by 2050.* ◇ *proposals for a carbon tax* → CARBON DIOXIDE

,carbon 'copy *noun* [C]
1 a copy of a document, letter, etc. made with CARBON PAPER: *I kept a carbon copy of the form for the file.* ◇ (*figurative*) *He's a carbon copy of my former boss.*
2 (*IT*) (*abbr* **cc**) a copy of an email message: *Add additional names in the cc box if you want to send copies to other people.* → BCC

'carbon ,credit *noun* [C, usually pl.]
a right to send out a measured amount of harmful gases such as CARBON DIOXIDE into the air: *Countries that fail to reduce their emissions sufficiently will have to buy carbon credits.*
[NOTE] The word **carbon** is used because the harmful gases are measured in standard units (**carbon dioxide equivalents**) based on the damage caused to the environment by CARBON DIOXIDE. See note at EMISSION UNIT

,carbon di'oxide *noun* [U] (*abbr* CO$_2$)
a gas that is produced by burning CARBON and which can harm the planet if it is produced in large amounts: *targets for reducing carbon dioxide emissions*

,carbon mo'noxide *noun* [U]
a poisonous gas formed when CARBON burns partly but not completely. It is produced when petrol/gas is burnt in car engines.

,carbon-'neutral *adjective*
used to describe an activity where other action is taken to cancel the amount of CARBON gases produced by the activity: *The company has become carbon-neutral after planting more than 26 000 trees.*

'carbon ,paper *noun* [U]
thin paper with a dark substance on one side, that is used between two sheets of paper for making copies of written or typed documents

★ card /kɑːd; *AmE* kɑːrd/ *noun* [C]

SEE ALSO: affinity card, bank ~, banker's ~, boarding ~, business ~, calling ~, cash ~, etc.

1 a small piece of plastic, especially one given by a bank or a shop/store, used for buying things, obtaining money or using a telephone or computer system: *I put the meal on* (= paid for it with) *my card.* ◇ *Please swipe your card* (= pass it through a machine that reads the information) *to pay for your purchase.* ◇ *There has been an increase in card fraud.*
❍ *to buy sth with/pay by/pay with/put sth on/use a card* ♦ *to insert/remove/swipe a card* ♦ *to apply for/issue/withdraw a card*
2 = BUSINESS CARD
3 a small piece of stiff paper or plastic with information on it, especially information about sb's identity: *a membership card* ◇ *an appointment card* ◇ *a laminated identity card* (= one that is covered with plastic)
4 (*IT*) a small device containing an electronic CIRCUIT that is part of a computer or added to it, enabling it to perform particular functions: *a graphics card with 8 MB of memory* ◇ *installing a memory card*
❍ *a graphics/memory/modem/sound/video card* ♦ *to install/remove a card*

'card ,catalog (*BrE spelling* ~ **catalogue**) = CARD INDEX

cardholder /ˈkɑːdhəʊldə(r); AmE ˈkɑːrdhoʊl-/ noun [C]
a person who has a credit card from a bank, etc: *a Cardholder Not Present transaction* (= when you pay by card by mail, phone or over the Internet)

ˈcard ˌindex (*also* ˈindex) (*both especially BrE*) (*AmE usually* ˈcard ˌcatalog) noun [C]
a box of cards with information about an item on each one, arranged in alphabetical order: *We keep a card index of our client's details.*—Picture at OFFICE

care /keə(r); AmE ker/ noun [U]

SEE ALSO: customer care, health ~, personal ~

the process of caring for sb and providing what they need, for example for their health or protection: *a contract to provide employee care services*
IDM ˌcare and ˈmaintenance (*abbr* c & m)
(*Manufacturing*) a situation in which a building, mine, machine, etc. that is no longer in use, is kept in good condition so that it can be used again in the future: *The mine was closed and placed under care and maintenance.* 'care of sb (*AmE also* in 'care of sb) (*abbr* c/o) used when writing to sb at another person's address: *Write to him care of his lawyer.*

★ **career** /kəˈrɪə(r); AmE kəˈrɪr/ noun [C]

SEE ALSO: dual career, portfolio career

the series of jobs that a person has in a particular area of work, usually involving more responsibility as time passes: *She began her working career as an engineer at IBM.* ◇ *He left teaching to take up a career in the music industry.* ◇ *It's an interesting job but has limited career prospects.* See note at JOB
❍ to begin/build/pursue/take up/start a career (in sth) ◆ to change/end/give up your career ◆ career goals/opportunities/prospects ◆ careers advice/management

caˈreer adˌvice = CAREERS ADVICE

caˈreer break noun [C]
a period of time when you do not do your usual job, either with or without the support of your employer, for example because you have children to care for or want to study: *He has taken a career break to do further studies.* ◇ *women returning to employment after a career break*
❍ to be on/need/take a career break

caˈreer change noun [C, usually sing.]
the act of changing to a different type of job or profession: *He's thinking about making a career change.* → CAREER MOVE

caˈreer ˌcounselling (*also* caˈreers ˌcoun-selling, *less frequent*) (*AmE spelling* ~ counseling) noun [U]
(*HR*) the activity of giving people information and advice to help them choose or develop their career

caˈreer ˌcounsellor (*also* caˈreers ˌcounsellor, *less frequent*) (*AmE spelling* ~ counselor) noun [C]
(*HR*)
1 (*especially AmE*) a person whose job is to give students advice and information about jobs and careers **SYN** CAREERS OFFICER
2 a person whose job is to give people advice and information about how to change or develop their career

caˈreer fair = CAREERS FAIR

caˈreer ˌguidance = CAREERS ADVICE

caˈreer ˌladder noun [C, usually sing.]
a series of jobs from junior to senior level in a company, an organization or a profession, that have increasing amounts of responsibility: *Success was measured in terms of climbing the career ladder.*

◇ *She's reached the top of her career ladder.*
→ CORPORATE LADDER

caˈreer move noun [C]
the act of changing your job for one that you think is better and will bring the chance of more responsibility: *She's thinking about making a major career move.* ◇ *Staying in the company wouldn't have been a smart career move.*

caˈreer path noun [C, usually sing.]
a planned series of jobs in one or more professions: *We help our staff map out a career path in the company.*
❍ to decide on/follow/have/map out a career path

caˈreer ˌpattern noun [C]
(*HR*) the series of jobs that sb has during their working life; the series of jobs that a group of people in a particular profession or industry are likely to have: *There is a great variety of work in the organization and each person's career pattern is different.* ◇ *a study of typical career patterns of men and women*

caˈreers adˌvice (*also* caˈreers ˌguidance) (*both BrE*) (*AmE* caˈreer adˌvice, caˈreer ˌguidance) noun [U]
(*HR*) advice about what career to choose or how to develop your career: *The college's careers service offers careers advice and counselling.*

caˈreers adˌviser = CAREERS OFFICER

caˈreers ˌcounselling = CAREER COUNSELLING

caˈreers ˌcounsellor = CAREER COUNSELLOR

caˈreers fair (*AmE* caˈreer fair) = JOB FAIR

caˈreers ˌguidance = CAREERS ADVICE

caˈreers ˌofficer (*also* caˈreers adˌviser) noun [C] (*both BrE*)
(*HR*) a person whose job is to give students advice and information about jobs and careers: *the school careers officer* **SYN** CAREER COUNSELLOR

caˈreer ˌstructure noun [C, usually sing., U]
(*HR*) the planned way in which people move to higher levels of responsibility in a particular company or profession: *The profession has no clear career structure.*
❍ to build/develop/establish a career structure

caˈreer ˌwoman noun [C]
a woman who has a career or whose career is more important to her than getting married and having children

careline /ˈkeəlaɪn; AmE ˈkerl-/ noun [C]
(*Marketing*) a telephone service that you can call to get help, advice or information on a company's products: *Call our customer careline for advice.*

caretaker /ˈkeəteɪkə(r); AmE ˈkert-/ (*BrE*) (*AmE* cusˈtodian, ˈjanitor) noun [C]
a person whose job is to take care of a building such as a school, offices or a block of flats/an apartment building

cargo /ˈkɑːgəʊ; AmE ˈkɑːrgoʊ/ noun [C,U] (*plural* cargoes or cargos, especially in AmE)

SEE ALSO: bulk cargo, dry cargo

(*Transport*) the goods carried in a ship, plane or lorry/truck: *a cargo of sugar* ◇ *The ship can carry 40 passengers plus cargo.* ◇ *a decline in passenger and cargo volumes*
❍ to carry/deliver/load/unload (a) cargo ◆ a cargo plane/ship/vessel ◆ cargo traffic/volumes

ˈcargo ˌhandling noun [U]
(*Transport*) the process of moving goods onto and off ships, aircraft and lorries/trucks: *There is a risk that goods will be damaged during cargo handling.* ◇ *The port offers the most up-to-date cargo-handling facilities.*

carmaker /'kɑːmeɪkə(r); AmE 'kɑːrm-/ noun [C]
(AmE)
a company that makes cars: *Toyota, Japan's largest carmaker*

carnet /'kɑːneɪ; AmE 'kɑːrneɪ/ noun [C]
(Trade) a document that allows you to take goods into a country temporarily for your work without paying taxes (**import duties**) on them: *A carnet can be used for importing goods for exhibitions.* ◇ *Apply to the Chamber of Commerce for a carnet.* **NOTE** One important type of **carnet** is the **ATA carnet**. The letters 'ATA' are an abbreviation of the French and English words 'Admission Temporaire—Temporary Admission'.

'carpet-bomb verb [+ obj or no obj]
(Marketing) to send an advertisement to a very large number of people, especially by email or to their computer screen: *They carpet-bombed the public with commercials for their product.* → SPAM
▶ **'carpet-,bombing** noun [U]

'car pool
● *noun* [C]
1 (BrE) (also **'motor pool**, AmE, BrE) a group of cars owned by a company, that its staff can use
2 carpool a group of car owners who take turns to drive everyone in the group to work, so that only one car is used at a time
● *verb* (also spelled **carpool**) /'kɑːpuːl; AmE 'kɑːrp-/ [no obj]
(used about a group of people) to take turns to drive everyone in the group to work

carr. fwd. abbr
(Trade) a short way of writing **carriage forward**

carriage /'kærɪdʒ/ noun [U] (BrE)
(Trade; Transport) the act or cost of transporting goods from one place to another: *€25 including all taxes and carriage* ◇ *We charge €15 for carriage and insurance to anywhere in Europe.* **SYN** HANDLING

,carriage and 'freight = COST AND FREIGHT

'carriage and in'surance 'paid to phrase
(abbr **CIP**)
(Trade) a term meaning that the seller pays for the transport and insurance of goods to the place mentioned: *CIP Athens* → INCOTERM

,carriage 'forward phrase (BrE) (abbr **carr. fwd.**)
(Trade) a term meaning that the buyer pays for the transport of goods

,carriage 'paid to phrase (abbr **CPT**)
(Trade) a term meaning that the seller pays for the transport of goods to the place mentioned
→ INCOTERM

,carried 'forward adjective (abbr **c/f, c/fwd**) (also **,carried 'down**)
(Accounting) used to describe an amount at the end of one accounting period or page of accounts that will be copied at the start of the next: *an amount carried forward* **NOTE** This is usually written as an abbreviation in accounts. → BALANCE CARRIED FORWARD

,carried 'over adjective (abbr **c/o**)
(Accounting) used to describe an amount at the end of a page in an account that will be moved to the start of the next page **NOTE** This is usually written as an abbreviation in accounts.

★ carrier /'kæriə(r)/ noun [C]

SEE ALSO: **bulk carrier, common ~, contract ~, free ~, insurance ~, public ~**

1 a company that carries goods or passengers from one place to another, especially by air: *The airline aims to become Europe's biggest carrier.*
❍ *a budget/low-cost/no-frills carrier*

2 (IT) a company that provides access to a communications network: *the leading wireless Internet carrier*

,carrier's 'risk noun [U,C]
(Trade) if goods are sent **at carrier's risk**, the transport company has to insure the goods during transport

carryback /'kæribæk/ noun [U,C]
(Accounting) a system which allows you to treat the current year's profit or loss as if it happened in an earlier year; the amount of money that you use in this way: *A company which is making a loss can use carryback to claim back taxes paid in the three previous years.*

carryforward /,kæri'fɔːwəd; AmE -'fɔːrwərd/ noun [U,C]
(Accounting) a system which allows you to treat the current year's profit or loss as if it happened in a later year; the amount of money that you use in this way: *The company has an operating loss carryforward of $74 million for income tax purposes.*

'carrying charge noun [C]
1 (Accounting) (also **'carrying cost, 'holding cost**) the cost to a business of storing goods or holding assets rather than using them to earn income
2 (Commerce) (especially AmE) money that you pay as interest and charges when you buy sth using credit

'carry-,over (AmE spelling usually **carryover**) noun
1 [C] something that is transferred from the previous period, situation, owner, etc. to the present one: *The slow trading was a carry-over from the big losses of last week.*
2 (Accounting) [U] the amount that is moved to the next part of the accounts or the next accounting period: *The funds were approved for carry-over from one budget period to the next.*

cartel /kɑː'tel; AmE kɑːr'tel/ (also **'price ring**) noun [C with sing./pl. verb]
(Economics) a group of separate companies that agree to increase profits by fixing prices and not competing with each other: *Ten companies were fined for taking part in a cartel to control the vitamins market.* ◇ *an oil/coffee cartel*
❍ *to* **form/have/join/take part in a** *cartel* ◆ *an illegal/ a price-fixing cartel*

carton /'kɑːtn; AmE 'kɑːrtn/ noun [C]
1 a light cardboard or plastic box or pot for holding goods, especially food or liquid; the contents of a **carton**: *a milk carton* ◇ *a carton of milk*—Picture at PACKAGING
2 (especially AmE) a box in which goods are packed, often in smaller containers: *Machines load bottles of ketchup into cartons before they go to the stores.* ◇ *Most online vendors sell cigarettes* **by the carton**.

case /keɪs/ noun [C]

SEE ALSO: **basket case, business ~, display ~, test ~**

1 (Law) a question to be decided in court: *The case was settled out of court.* ◇ *A group of foreign creditors has* **brought** *a bankruptcy case* **against** *the company.*
2 [usually sing.] a set of facts or arguments that support one side in a court, discussion, etc: *Customers who lost money have a good case for compensation.*
3 a container or covering used to protect or store things; a container with its contents or the amount that it contains: *a packing case* (= a large wooden box for packing things in) ◇ *a case of champagne* (= 12 bottles in a box)
4 a suitcase

'case ˌstudy *noun* [C]
1 a detailed account of the development of a person, a group of people or a situation over a period of time, especially for teaching or training: *The results are based on case studies of 27 leading companies.* ◇ *a business school case study* ◇ *case study interviews*
O *to offer/present/provide/teach/write up* a case study
2 a particular example of sth that is used to explain a theory, a rule, an idea, a method, etc: *The agency's success is a case study of/in leadership in a difficult situation.*
O *to be/provide* a case study (of/in sth)

★ cash /kæʃ/ *noun, verb*
● *noun* [U]

SEE ALSO: **all-cash, bulk ~, digital ~, e-cash, hard ~, non-~, petty ~,** etc.

1 money in the form of coins or notes/bills: *We offer discounts for customers paying (in) cash.* ◇ *I'll give you the rest of the money in cash.* ◇ *You can make cash withdrawals of up to $500 a day.*
O *to have/hold/pay/withdraw* cash
2 money generally, especially if it is immediately available: *Telecoms companies are known for generating (= producing) cash.* ◇ *Shareholders have accepted a $10 share cash offer.*
O *to be short of/generate/need/raise/run out of* cash
IDM **cash 'down** (*BrE*) (*also* **ˌcash up 'front,** *AmE, BrE*) (*Commerce*) with immediate payment of cash: *We paid $100 cash down and then 10 monthly installments of $20.* **ˌcash in 'hand 1** (*informal*) if you pay for goods and services **cash in hand,** you pay in cash, especially so that the person being paid can avoid paying tax on the amount: *He took his payments cash in hand.* ◇ *cash-in-hand jobs* **2** (*AmE also* **ˌcash on 'hand**) (*Accounting*) money that you have and can use immediately: *Our reserves consist of cash in hand and deposits at the bank.* **ˌcash up 'front** = CASH DOWN
● *verb* [+ obj]
to exchange a cheque, share, bond, etc. for money: *Traveller's cheques can be cashed at most hotels.* → UNCASHED
PHRV **ˌcash 'in (on sth)** to gain an advantage for yourself from a situation: *Sports retailers are cashing in on the interest generated by the World Cup.* **ˌcash sth 'in** to exchange sth, such as an insurance policy, for money before the date on which it would normally end: *She cashed in her shares just before their price fell.* **ˌcash 'out; ˌcash sth 'out** (*AmE*) to sell an asset or an investment in order to make a profit: *I planned to sell the company and cash out after two years.* **ˌcash 'up** (*BrE*) (*AmE* **ˌcash 'out**) to add up the amount of money that has been received in a shop/store, club, etc., especially at the end of the day: *The men broke into the office while staff were cashing up.*

cashable /ˈkæʃəbl/ *adjective*
that can be changed into cash: *These bonds are cashable without penalty after 90 days.*

'cash acˌcount *noun* [C]
1 (*Accounting*) a financial account where a record is kept of money spent and received in cash
2 (*especially AmE*) = CURRENT ACCOUNT (1)
3 (*Stock Exchange*) an account with a BROKER where a customer buying shares, bonds, etc. has to pay immediately in cash

'cash acˌcounting *noun* [U]
(*Accounting*) a system of keeping accounts where amounts of money are written down at the time when they are paid or received → ACCRUALS ACCOUNTING

ˌcash against 'documents *phrase* (*abbr* **CAD**)
(*Trade*) a way of paying for imports where the buyer must first pay for the goods at the bank or agent to which the SHIPPING DOCUMENTS have been sent, and can then collect the goods when they arrive

ˌcash and 'carry *noun* [C,U]
(*Commerce*) a large WHOLESALE shop/store that sells goods in large quantities at low prices to customers from other businesses who pay in cash and take the goods away themselves; the system of buying and selling goods in this way: *We buy huge packs of coffee from the local cash and carry.* ◇ *a cash-and-carry store/chain* → WAREHOUSE CLUB

ˌcash at 'bank (*also spelled* **Cash at Bank**) *noun* [U]
(*Accounting, usually used in written English*) used in financial records to show the total amount of money that a company has in the bank: *Every month the Cash at Bank account must be reconciled with the bank statement.*

cashback /ˈkæʃbæk/ *noun* [U]
(*Commerce*)
1 (*AmE spelling* **cash-back**) cash that is given to customers who buy a product or service, offered as a way of persuading people to buy it: *Take out a mortgage now and receive 2% cashback.* ◇ *big cash-back offers* See note at REDUCTION
2 (*BrE*) money from your bank account that you can get when you pay for sth in a shop using a DEBIT CARD: *Would you like cashback?*

'cash ˌbasis *noun* [sing.]
(*Accounting*) the principle that CASH ACCOUNTING is based on: *The effects of transactions can be recognized on a cash basis (= when money is paid or received).* → ACCRUALS BASIS

ˌcash before de'livery *phrase* (*abbr* **CBD**)
(*Trade*) an arrangement where a buyer must pay for goods before they are sent

'cash book *noun* [C]
(*Accounting*) a record of money spent and received: *The cheque had been credited in the cash book but not yet presented to the bank.*

'cash box (*AmE spelling* **cashbox**) *noun* [C]
a strong box with a lock in which cash is kept

'cash ˌbudget *noun* [C]
(*Accounting*) an estimate of how much money will be paid and received over a particular period of time: *A large surplus was forecast for March in the cash budget.* **SYN** CASH-FLOW FORECAST

'cash call *noun* [C]
(*Finance*) a request by a company to its shareholders for more money: *The struggling company announced a cash call to raise €200 million.*

'cash card *noun* [C] (*especially BrE*)
a plastic card used to get money from a CASH MACHINE → CHEQUE CARD, DEBIT CARD

ˌcash con'version *noun* [U]
(*Accounting*) the process by which a business changes the raw materials that it buys into money received from the sale of the finished goods: *calculating the cash conversion cycle (= the number of days that this process takes)*

'cash cow *noun* [C] (*informal*)
1 (*Finance*) the part of a business or a product that always makes a profit and that provides money for the rest of the business
2 (*Marketing*) in the BOSTON MATRIX, a product that has a large market share in a market that is growing very little—Picture at BOSTON MATRIX

'cash crop *noun* [C]
a crop grown for selling, rather than for use by the person who grows it

'cash deal = CASH SETTLEMENT

,cash-de'posit ,ratio = CASH RATIO (1)

,cash 'discount *noun* [C]
(*Commerce*) a price reduction that is given if a buyer pays immediately or in cash

'cash dis,penser = CASH MACHINE

,cash 'dividend *noun* [C]
(*Finance*) money, rather than shares, that is given to shareholders as part of a company's profits

,cash e'quivalent *noun* [C]
(*Accounting*)
1 an asset or an investment that can easily be sold or changed into money: *The company said it had cash and cash equivalents of over $90 000.*
2 an amount of money that is estimated to be equal to the value of sth: *The cash equivalent of employee benefits such as company cars must be calculated for tax purposes.*

★ **'cash flow** *noun* [C,U]

SEE ALSO: discounted cash flow, free cash flow

(*Accounting*) the movement of money into and out of a business as goods are bought and sold; the difference between the amount of money a business receives and the amount it pays during a particular period of time: *We expect to return to profitability and positive cash flow in the current fiscal year.* ◇ *cash-flow problems*
O *a good/healthy/negative/positive/steady/strong/weak* cash flow • *to generate/improve* cash flow • *a cash-flow crisis/problem*

'cash-flow ,forecast (*also* **'cash-flow pro,jection**) *noun* [C]
(*Accounting*) an estimate of how much money will be paid and received over a particular period of time SYN CASH BUDGET

'cash gene,ration *noun* [U]
(*Finance*) the process of a company making extra money that can be invested after costs have been paid: *The aim of our central strategy is to increase earnings and improve cash generation.* ◇ *strong cash generation*

cashier /kæˈʃɪə(r); *AmE* -ˈʃɪr/ *noun* [C]
1 a person whose job is to receive and pay out money in a bank, shop/store, hotel, etc: *a cashier at a petrol/gas station*
2 (*Accounting*) a person in a company or an organization who is responsible for paying out and receiving money and for keeping records of this: *She was promoted to Head Cashier of the Manchester property company.*

ca,shier's 'cheque (*AmE spelling* ~ **check**) *noun* [C]
a cheque written by a bank against its own bank account: *Payment must be made with cash or by cashier's cheque.*

'cash ,issue *noun* [C]
(*Finance*) new shares that a company offers to existing shareholders in order to raise extra money → RIGHTS ISSUE

cashless /ˈkæʃləs/ *adjective*
that works without using cash; done without using cash: *We are moving towards the cashless society.* ◇ *cashless transactions*

'cash ma,chine (*BrE also* **'cash dis,penser**, **'Cashpoint™**) *noun* [C]
a machine in or outside a bank, etc., from which you can get money from your bank account using a special plastic card SYN ATM
O *to withdraw money from/use* a cash machine

'cash ,management (*also* **'treasury ,management**) *noun* [U]
(*Accounting*) the activity of controlling the money

that comes in and goes out of a company in order to maintain a good CASH FLOW: *Cost control and effective cash management are our priorities for the coming year.*

'cash ,market = SPOT MARKET

'cash pile (*also* **'cash ,mountain**) *noun* [C, usually sing.]
a large amount of money that a company has available for investment: *The company used its $3.2 billion cash pile to make several acquisitions.*

Cashpoint™ /ˈkæʃpɔɪnt/ = CASH MACHINE

'cash po,sition *noun* [C, usually sing.]
(*Accounting*) the amount of money that a company has immediately available: *We have reduced our debt levels and have a strong cash position.* ◇ *What is your current cash position?*
O *a good/strong/weak* cash position

'cash price *noun* [C]
1 (*Commerce*) the price that a seller will accept if payment is made immediately: *The cash price and the price if you pay by credit are the same.*
2 (*Finance*) = SPOT PRICE
3 (*Finance*) the price that a company will pay in cash to shareholders when it buys another company: *A cash price of €15 per share has been agreed.*

'cash ,ratio *noun* [C]
(*Accounting*)
1 (*also* **,cash-de'posit ,ratio**) the relationship between the amount of money a bank holds in cash and the total amount it holds in deposits (= money that customers have paid into their accounts) and investments: *The higher the cash ratio, the less money the bank has available to lend.* SYN RESERVE REQUIREMENT
O *to have/keep/maintain* a cash ratio
2 the relationship between the amount of money that a company holds in cash, in the bank, etc. and its LIABILITIES (= the money that it owes): *If a company has a low cash ratio, it may not be able to pay its future liabilities.* SYN LIQUIDITY RATIO
O *a cash ratio drops/falls/rises*
→ ACID-TEST RATIO

,cash ratio de'posits *noun* [pl.] (*abbr* CRD)
(*Economics*) the amount of money that banks must keep in the country's central bank

'cash ,register (*AmE also* **'register**) *noun* [C]
a machine used in shops/stores, restaurants, etc. that has a drawer for keeping money in, and that shows and records the amount of money received for each thing that is sold SYN TILL
—Picture at STORE

,cash 'rich *adjective*
(*Accounting*) (especially about a company) having a lot of money available immediately: *The company has little debt and is cash rich.* ◇ *the cash-rich telecoms group* ◇ *cash-rich, time-poor family shoppers*

'cash sale *noun* [C]
(*Commerce*) a sale where payment is made immediately: *Smaller shops are dependent on cash sales.* ◇ *If you can't make a cash sale, take a deposit.*

'cash ,settlement (*also* **'cash deal**) *noun* [C]
(*Finance*) an act of buying or selling shares, FUTURES, etc. where they are exchanged immediately for cash: *When a grain futures contract expires, either the grain is delivered or ownership is transferred in a cash settlement.*

'cash shell = SHELL COMPANY

'cash-starved adjective [only before noun]
without enough money, usually because another organization, such as the government, has failed to provide it: *cash-starved public services*

'cash-strapped adjective [only before noun]
not having enough money → STRAPPED

,casting 'vote noun [C, usually sing.]
the vote given by the person in charge of an official meeting to decide an issue when there are an equal number of votes on each side: *The chairman has the casting vote.*
O *to give/have/use a casting vote*

★ **casual** /ˈkæʒuəl/ adjective, noun
● *adjective*
1 (*HR*) (about work or workers) not done regularly, or not doing sth regularly, but only when needed: *Students looking for casual work come to the coast in summer.* ◇ *They are employed on a casual basis* (= they do not have a permanent job with the company). SYN TEMPORARY
2 not formal: *We're supposed to wear casual clothes for the conference.*
▶ **'casually** adverb: *Half their staff are employed casually.* ◇ *dressed casually in jeans and a sweater*
● *noun*
1 (*HR*) [C] a **casual** worker (= one who does not work permanently for a company): *They use casuals to supplement the basic staff in the restaurant.*
SYN TEMP
2 **casuals** [pl.] informal clothes or shoes: *dressed in casuals*

'casualty in,surance noun [U]
a type of insurance in which money is paid for injury or death or damage to property caused by a company's product or by the lack of care of the company's employees

★ **catalogue** (*AmE spelling usually* **catalog**)
/ˈkætəlɒg; *AmE* -lɔːg; -lɑːg/ noun, verb
● *noun* [C]

SEE ALSO: **back catalogue**

1 (*Marketing*) a complete list of items that a company sells, often with pictures of the items and prices: *She ran up a huge bill with a mail-order catalogue.* ◇ *The company sells home furnishings through/via an online catalogue.* → BROCHURE
O *a home shopping/mail-order/an online catalogue* • *a catalogue business/company/retailer* • *catalogue prices/shopping* • *to look at/produce/send for/send out a catalogue*
2 [usually sing.] = BACK CATALOGUE
3 (*IT*) a website that has lists of other sites in groups according to their type or subject, and has links to them → SEARCH ENGINE
● *verb* [+ obj]
to arrange a list of things in order in a **catalogue**; to record sth in a **catalogue**: *The website catalogues everything that the company makes.*

catch /kætʃ/ verb, noun
● *verb* (**caught, caught,** /kɔːt/)
IDM **have/be caught with your 'hand/'fingers in the till** used to describe a situation when sb is stealing money from their employer
PHRV **,catch 'on 1** (used about a product or an idea) to become popular with people: *Electronic greetings cards are catching on quickly.* ◇ *The idea never really caught on.* **2** (*informal*) to understand or realize sth: *Consumers have caught on to the superior quality of DVDs.* **,catch 'up (with sb/sth)** (*BrE also* **,catch sb/sth 'up**) to reach the same level or standard as sb/sth that was bigger, better or more advanced: *The supermarket chain is rapidly catching up with its rivals.*

● *noun* [C, usually sing.]
a hidden difficulty or disadvantage: *The service was so cheap that I thought there must be a catch.*

'catchment ,area noun [C] (*BrE*)
the area from which a business gets its customers, a hospital its patients, etc.

catchphrase /ˈkætʃfreɪz/ noun [C]
a popular phrase that is connected with the person, company, advertisement, etc. that used it and made it famous: *Audi's catchphrase: Vorsprung durch Technik*

'catch-up noun [U]
the process of trying to reach sb who is more advanced or better: *We are in a state of constant catch-up.* → idiom at PLAY verb

catchy /ˈkætʃi/ adjective
(about words or music used to advertise sth) easy to remember
O *a catchy name/phrase/slogan/tune*

categorize , -ise /ˈkætəgəraɪz/ verb [+ obj]
to put people or things into groups according to what type they are: *Organizations can be categorized into the following groups.*
SYN PIGEONHOLE

category /ˈkætəgəri; *AmE* -gɔːri/ noun [C] (*plural* **categories**)

SEE ALSO: **product category**

a group of people or products with particular features in common: *Our customers fall into two broad categories.* ◇ *Their software can be divided into two categories: business and general applications.*

,category 'killer noun [C]
(*Marketing*) a big company that sells a large collection of a particular type of BRANDED goods, such as toys or books, at low prices and puts smaller companies out of business

,category 'leader noun [C]
(*Marketing*) the company that sells the most of a particular type of product: *McVitie's is the category leader of the biscuit market.*
O *to establish yourself as/be/become category leader*

'category ,management noun [U] (*abbr* **CM**)
(*Marketing*) the process of manufacturers and businesses who sell to the public working together using data about what customers want in order to increase the sales of types of products (**categories**)
→ BRAND MANAGEMENT

,category 'manager (*also* ,**product line 'manager**) noun [C]
(*Marketing*) a person at a company who is in charge of developing and selling a group of related products or a type of product → BRAND MANAGER

cater /ˈkeɪtə(r)/ verb [+ obj or no obj]
to provide the food and drinks for an organization, a meeting or a social event: *Who's catering for the conference?* ◇ (*AmE*) *We have catered 950 functions this year.* ◇ *a catered lunch*
PHRV **'cater for/to sb/sth** to provide the things that a particular type of person or situation needs or wants: *a website that caters for health-care professionals* ◇ *The service caters mainly to business travellers.*

caterer /ˈkeɪtərə(r)/ noun [C]

SEE ALSO: **contract caterer**

a person or company whose job is to provide food and drinks for organizations, meetings or social events: *They brought in an outside caterer for the conference.*

catering /ˈkeɪtərɪŋ/ noun [U]
the work of providing food and drinks for

organizations, meetings or social events: *an airline catering business*
➊ *a catering business/company* ⬩ *catering services*

CATV /ˌsiː eɪ tiː ˈviː/ = COMMUNITY ANTENNA TELEVISION

ˌcause and efˈfect ˌdiagram = FISHBONE DIAGRAM

cautious /ˈkɔːʃəs/ *adjective*
being careful about what you say or do, especially in order to avoid mistakes; not taking any risks: *Investors stayed cautious* (= were unwilling to buy) *in the face of uncertain stock markets.* ◇ *a cautious forecast*

caveat /ˈkæviæt/ *noun* [C] (*formal*)
a warning that particular things need to be considered before sth can be done: *If you are thinking about buying this type of keyboard there is one important caveat: some PCs might not recognize the keyboard.* NOTE **Caveat** is a Latin word meaning 'Let a person be careful'.

caveat emptor /ˌkæviæt ˈemptɔː(r)/ *phrase*
(*Law*) used to say that when you are buying something it is your responsibility to check that there is nothing wrong with what you are buying → BUYER BEWARE at BUYER NOTE **Caveat emptor** is a Latin phrase that means 'Let the buyer be careful'.

CBA /ˌsiː biː ˈeɪ/ = COST-BENEFIT ANALYSIS

CBD /ˌsiː biː ˈdiː/ = CASH BEFORE DELIVERY, CENTRAL BUSINESS DISTRICT

CBT /ˌsiː biː ˈtiː/ = COMPUTER-BASED TRAINING

CBU /ˌsiː biː ˈjuː/ = COMPLETELY BUILT-UP

CC = CARBON COPY (2)

CCTV /ˌsiː siː tiː ˈviː/ = CLOSED-CIRCUIT TELEVISION

CD /ˌsiː ˈdiː/ *noun* [C]
1 a small disc on which sound or information is recorded. NOTE **CD** is an abbreviation for 'compact disc'.
2 (*Finance*) = CERTIFICATE OF DEPOSIT

c/d *abbr*
(*Accounting, only used in written English*) carried down

CD-ROM /ˌsiː diː ˈrɒm; *AmE* ˈrɑːm/ *noun* [C,U]
a plastic disc on which large amounts of information, sound and pictures can be stored, for use on a computer: *The software package contains five CD-ROMs.* ◇ *The encyclopedia is available on CD-ROM.* ◇ *a computer with a CD-ROM drive*—Picture at OFFICE. NOTE **CD-ROM** is an abbreviation of 'compact disc read-only memory'.

cede /siːd/ *verb* [+ obj]
to give sb control of sth or give them power, a right, etc., especially unwillingly: *It is difficult to cede **control** of projects to people who might make mistakes.*

ceiling /ˈsiːlɪŋ/ *noun* [C]

SEE ALSO: **glass ceiling, price ceiling**

the greatest amount of sth that is allowed; the top limit: *They have put a 10% ceiling on wage increases.* ◇ *Have house prices hit their ceiling?* ◇ *setting a ceiling price for oil* OPP FLOOR
➊ *to **place/put** a ceiling on sth* ⬩ *to **impose/lift/set** a ceiling (on sth)* ⬩ *to **exceed/hit/reach** a ceiling* ⬩ *a **lending/** an **output/** a **price/production/wage** ceiling*

★cellphone (*AmE spelling also* **cell phone**) /ˈselfəʊn; *AmE* -foʊn/ (*also* ˌcellular ˈphone) (*also* **cell**, *informal*) *noun* [C] (*all especially AmE*)
a telephone that does not have wires and works by radio, that you can carry with you and use anywhere SYN MOBILE PHONE

cellular /ˈseljələ(r)/ *adjective* [only before noun]
(often used in the names of companies) connected with a telephone system that works by radio instead of wires: *the country's largest cellular provider* ◇ *The service uses cellular technology to provide users with road maps.* ◇ *BellSouth Cellular (Corporation)*
➊ *a cellular **carrier/company/operator/provider*** ⬩ *a cellular **network/system/telephone***

ˌcellular ˈphone = CELLPHONE

center = CENTRE

-centered = -CENTRED

centi- /ˈsentɪ-/ *combining form* (*in nouns*)
(often used in units of measurement) one hundredth (= 0.01): *a centimetre*

ˌcentral ˈbank (*also* ˌnational ˈbank, reˈserve **bank**) *noun* [C]
the institution that controls the supply of money in a country and provides financial services to the government and other banks: *The central bank has cut interest rates to try to stimulate economic growth.*

ˌcentral ˈbusiness ˌdistrict *noun* [C] (*especially AmE*) (*abbr* **CBD**)
the part of a town or city where most of the offices are: *The hotel is situated in the heart of* (= near the centre of) *the central business district.*

ˌcentral ˈcounterparty *noun* [C]
(*Finance*) an organization that transfers and pays for investments on behalf of buyers and sellers so that they avoid dealing with each other directly and reduce risk: *The London Clearing House acts as a central counterparty for trades on London's futures and options markets.*

★centralize, **-ise** /ˈsentrəlaɪz/ *verb* [+ obj]
to control the different parts of sth or operate sth from one particular place; to give control of sth to one group of people: *Most banks have centralized their telephone services.* ◇ *His first move was to centralize training.* OPP DECENTRALIZE

★centralized, **-ised** /ˈsentrəlaɪzd/ *adjective*
that controls the different parts of sth or operates from one particular place: *The company uses a centralized computer system.* ◇ *We have a centralized human resources department for the group of companies.*

ˌcentral ˈprocessing ˌunit (*abbr* **CPU**) (*also* ˌcentral ˈprocessor) *noun* [C]
(*IT*) the part of a computer that controls all the other parts of the system SYN PROCESSOR

centre (*AmE spelling* **center**) /ˈsentə(r)/ *noun, adjective*
● *noun* [C]

SEE ALSO: **assessment centre, business ~, buying ~, call ~, contact ~, cost ~, data ~,** etc.

1 a building or place used for a particular purpose or activity: *He's the director of the company's research centre.* ◇ *She's a researcher **at** the Centre for International Studies.*
2 a place where a lot of business activity takes place: *London is a centre for international finance.* ◇ *New York is a world financial centre.*
➊ *a **commercial/economic/financial/industrial** centre*
3 (*especially BrE*) (*AmE usually* ˈdowntown [U,C]) the main part of a town or city where there are a lot of shops/stores and offices: *Most of our stores are situated in the **city/town centre**.* ◇ *the centre of town*
● *adjective*
IDM **take centre ˈstage** to be considered the most

important subject, person, etc. at a particular time: *Manufacturing techniques took centre stage at the conference.*

-centred (*AmE spelling* **-centered**) /'sentə:d; *AmE* -ərd/ *combining form* (*in adjectives*)
having the person mentioned as the centre of attention: *a user-centred approach to software design* ◊ *a client-centred organization*

,centre of 'excellence (*AmE spelling* **center ~**) *noun* [C]
a place where a particular kind of work is done extremely well: *The company is Europe's centre of excellence for producing aircraft engines.*

CEO /,si: i: 'əʊ; *AmE* 'oʊ/ = CHIEF EXECUTIVE OFFICER

cert. *abbr*
a short way of writing **certificate**

★ **certificate** *noun, verb*
● *noun* /sə'tɪfɪkət; *AmE* sər't-/ [C]

SEE ALSO: **deposit certificate, doctor's ~, fire ~, gift ~, insurance ~, medical ~, practising ~,** etc.

an official document that can be used to prove sth, for example, that facts are true, that you own sth or have a particular qualification: *Some shareholders will not be able to vote as they have not received their share certificates.* ◊ *a certificate of registration as a pharmacist*
● *to* **get/issue/obtain/provide/receive/require** *a certificate* ◆ *a* **bond/share/stock** *certificate* ◆ *a* **birth/ death/marriage** *certificate* ◆ *a certificate of* **membership/ownership/registration**
● *verb* /sə'tɪfɪkeɪt; *AmE* sər't-/ [+ obj] (*BrE*) (*usually* **be certificated**)
to give a person, a course, etc. an official document to show that a particular standard has been reached: *The qualifications are certificated by SCOTVEC.*

certificated /sə'tɪfɪkeɪtɪd; *AmE* sər't-/ *adjective* [usually before noun] (*BrE*)
(*HR*) having the certificate which shows that the necessary qualification for a particular job has been done or a particular standard has been reached: *a certificated teacher/notary* ◊ *a certificated vessel/ aircraft*

cer,tificate of a'nalysis *noun* [C]
(*Manufacturing*) a certificate provided by a company that produces chemicals or raw materials, to show what the products contain and that they have a particular quality: *All our products are thoroughly tested and supplied with a certificate of analysis.*

cer,tificate of at'tendance *noun* [C]
an official document that states that you have attended a training course or series of lessons

cer,tificate of de'posit (*abbr* CD) (*also* **de'posit cer,tificate**) *noun* [C]
(*Finance*) a type of investment offered by banks and other financial institutions in which money is lent to the bank, etc. for a fixed period of time with a fixed rate of interest: *Investing in a certificate of deposit will earn you more interest than a savings account.* → TIME DEPOSIT

cer,tificate of e'xistence *noun* [C]
1 (*Law*) (*AmE*) a document provided by a government office that an organization can show to people to prove that it legally exists: *Foreign companies must submit an original certificate of existence.*
2 (*Insurance*) (*BrE*) an official document that proves that sb is still alive and can claim a pension

cer,tificate of in,corpo'ration *noun* [C] (*Law*)
1 an official document that states that a company has officially been created: *Before a company can do business it must obtain a certificate of incorporation from the Registrar of Companies.*
2 (*AmE*) in some states in the US, another name for ARTICLES OF INCORPORATION: *preparing and filing the certificate of incorporation* → CHARTER (1,2)

cer,tificate of in'surance (*also* **in'surance cer,tificate**) *noun* [C]
(*Insurance*) a document that you get from an insurance company that proves you have insurance and gives the details: *Your insurance cover begins when you receive your certificate of insurance.*

cer,tificate of 'occupancy *noun* [C]
(*Law; Property*) especially in the US, a document that proves that a building has been carefully checked and is suitable for the kind of business that will use it: *A certificate of occupancy is required for all commercial spaces.*

cer,tificate of 'origin *noun* [C]
(*Trade*) an official document that states where sth was produced and who produced it, used especially for importing goods into a country: *A certificate of origin is required where the item is worth more than $1 000.*

cer,tificate of 'posting *noun* [C] (*BrE*)
a document that you can get from the post office that proves when you posted sth: *A certificate of posting can be used to prove that you sent off your tax return in time.* → RECORDED DELIVERY

certification /,sɜːtɪfɪ'keɪʃn; *AmE* ,sɜːrt-/ *noun* [U]
the process of checking whether sb/sth has reached a particular standard and giving them an official document to show this; the qualification that is given: *We are authorized to carry out certification of fire safety equipment.* ◊ *The software is tested thoroughly before certification is awarded.*
● *to* **award/grant** *certification* ◆ *to* **achieve/attain/ gain** *certification* ◆ *a certification* **authority/body** ◆ *certification* **procedures** ◆ *a certification* **programme/scheme**

,certified 'cheque (*AmE spelling* **~ check**) *noun* [C]
a cheque that a bank promises to pay by writing 'Good for payment' on it: *Payment must be made by certified cheque or bank draft.*

,certified 'copy (*also* **at,tested 'copy**) *noun* [C]
(*Law*) a copy of a document that has been signed by a legal official who has examined it and believes it to be genuine

,certified 'mail = RECORDED DELIVERY

,certified 'management ac'countant *noun* [C] (*abbr* CMA)
(*Accounting*) in the US, a person who has received a qualification from the Institute of Management Accountants. **Certified management accountants** have training and experience in managing the finances of companies and put CMA after their names.

,certified 'public ac'countant *noun* [C] (*abbr* CPA)
(*Accounting*) in the US, a person who is qualified to work as a professional accountant in a particular state. They put the letters CPA after their names.

★ **certify** /'sɜːtɪfaɪ; *AmE* 'sɜːrt-/ *verb* [+ obj] (**certifies, certifying, certified, certified**)
1 (*usually* **be certified**) to give sth an official document proving that it has reached a particular standard of quality: *All our products are certified 100% organic.*

2 (*usually* **be certified**) to give sb an official document proving that they are qualified to do a particular job: *She's certified to work on jet engines.* ◇ *a certified consultant/accountant*
3 to state officially, especially in writing, that sth is true: *The accounts were certified (as) correct by the finance department.*

c/f *abbr*
(*Accounting, only used in written English*) carried forward

cf. *abbr* (*only used in written English*)
a short way of writing **compare with** when you want the reader to look at sth else in the same document or in another one: *The shareholders own the company (cf. point 5, p 109).*

CFO /ˌsiː ef ˈəʊ; *AmE* ˈoʊ/ = CHIEF FINANCIAL OFFICER

CFR /ˌsiː ef ˈɑː(r)/ = COST AND FREIGHT

CGT /ˌsiː dʒiː ˈtiː/ = CAPITAL GAINS TAX

chaebol /ˈtʃeɪbɒl; *AmE* ˈkaɪbɑːl, -boːl/ *noun* [C]
(*plural* **chaebol** *or* **chaebols**)
a very large group of companies in South Korea that is involved in many kinds of business

★ **chain** /tʃeɪn/ *noun* [C]

SEE ALSO: **distribution chain, supply ~, value ~**

1 a group of shops/stores, hotels, etc. owned by the same company: *The company sells its products through retail chains.* ◇ *a chain of book stores*
❍ *a fast-food/grocery/hotel/retail/supermarket chain* ◆ *a chain of chemists/clubs/restaurants/stores/supermarkets*
2 a series of things or people that are connected: *Most organizations have a formal chain of command* (= a system by which instructions are passed down from one person to another). ◇ *a chain of events that led to the collapse of the company*

ˌ**chain of distriˈbution** = DISTRIBUTION CHAIN

ˈ**chain store** *noun* [C]
a shop/store that is one of a series of similar shops/stores in many different towns and cities owned by the same company: *an electrical/clothing chain store* ◇ *In most towns, you will find branches of chain stores such as Marks and Spencers, Gap and Virgin.* ◇ *Chain store sales fell last month.* SYN MULTIPLE

★ **chair** /tʃeə(r); *AmE* tʃer/ *noun, verb*
● *noun*
1 (*usually* **the chair**) [sing.] the position of being in charge of a meeting or committee; the person who holds this position: *She takes the chair in all our meetings.* ◇ *Please address comments to the chair.*
2 [C] the person who is in charge of a company or an organization: *She's vice chair of the group.*
→ CHAIRPERSON
● *verb* [+ obj *or* no obj]
to act as the CHAIRPERSON of a meeting, discussion, etc: *Who's chairing the meeting?*

★ **chairman** /ˈtʃeəmən; *AmE* ˈtʃer-/ *noun* [C] (*plural* **chairmen** /-mən/)

SEE ALSO: **executive chairman**

1 (*also* ˌ**chairman of the** ˈ**board**) the person who leads a company's BOARD OF DIRECTORS : *She was the founder, chairman and CEO of the company.* ◇ *He serves as non-executive chairman* (= he is not involved in running the company on a daily basis). ◇ *the outgoing chairman* (= the one who is about to leave the company) ◇ *He stepped down as Vivendi's vice chairman.* → PRESIDENT (1)
❍ *to be promoted to/serve as chairman* ◆ *to appoint sb (as)/elect sb/make sb chairman* ◆ *to resign/retire/step down as chairman*

2 the head of an official committee or organization: *the chairman of the British Medical Association*
❍ *to appoint sb (as)/elect sb/make sb/serve as chairman* ◆ *to resign/retire/stepdown as chairman* ◆ *an acting chairman*
3 the person in charge of a meeting, who tells people when they can speak, etc: *The chairman opened the meeting by welcoming those present.* ◇ *She was elected chairman at the committee's first meeting.*
❍ *to appoint sb (as)/make sb chairman*

MORE ABOUT

Referring to men and women in job titles

Neutral words like **assistant**, **worker**, **representative** or **person** are now used instead of *-man* and *-woman* in the names of jobs. For example, you can refer to a person who sells things in a shop/store as a **sales assistant** rather than a *saleswoman* or a *salesman*, and you can use **chairperson** instead of *chairman* or *chairwoman*.

chairperson /ˈtʃeəpɜːsn; *AmE* ˈtʃerpɜːrsn/ *noun* [C] (*plural* **chairpersons** *or, less frequent,* **chairpeople**)
a chairman or a chairwoman → CHAIR *noun* See note at MEETING

★ **chairwoman** /ˈtʃeəwʊmən; *AmE* ˈtʃer-/ *noun* [C] (*plural* **chairwomen** /-wɪmɪn/)
a woman in charge of a meeting, a committee, an organization or a company's BOARD OF DIRECTORS → CHAIR *noun*, CHAIRMAN

chalk /tʃɔːk/ *verb*
PHR V ˌ**chalk** ˈ**up sth** (*informal*) to have or record a success or a failure: *The company chalked up profits of $600 million last year.*

★ **challenge** /ˈtʃæləndʒ/ *noun, verb*
● *noun* [C]
1 a new or difficult task that tests sb/sth's ability and skill: *Managers in the IT industry are facing some real challenges.* ◇ *How will the government meet the challenge of rising unemployment?* ◇ *Do you enjoy a challenge?*
❍ *a big/huge/major/real/tough challenge* ◆ *a competitive/management/technical challenge* ◆ *to be/pose a challenge* ◆ *to accept/face/take on/meet a challenge*
2 an act of testing the authority or the strength of sb/sth: *The group is facing a legal challenge from its shareholders.*
❍ *to face a challenge* ◆ *to launch/mount a challenge (to sb/sth)*
● *verb* [+ obj]
1 to question whether sth is right, legal, etc: *The government's policies have been challenged by the unions.* ◇ *He does not like anyone challenging his authority.*
2 to compete with sb/sth for the highest position: *The group is trying to challenge Korea Telecom for market leadership.*
3 to test sb's ability and skills, especially in an interesting way: *The job doesn't really challenge her.* ◇ *He always challenges his staff to find new solutions to problems.*

ˌ**Chamber of** ˈ**Commerce** (*also spelled* **chamber of commerce**) *noun* [C] (*abbr* **C. of C.**)

SEE ALSO: **International Chamber of Commerce**

1 (*BrE*) a group of business people in a particular town or area who work together to help their trade

and provide information and training in business: *a training centre operated by the local Chamber of Commerce* ◊ *the Birmingham Chamber of Commerce*
2 a national organization that encourages trade between its own country and foreign companies: *the US Chamber of Commerce in Japan*

,champion of 'change *noun* [C]
1 somebody who is enthusiastic about change in an organization, a company, etc. and tries to get others to support it: *He has a reputation in the group as a champion of change.*
2 a person who is chosen to lead a CHANGE PROGRAMME (= a project to change the way a company, an organization, etc. operates): *She was appointed as a champion of change in management's drive to modernize the company.* **SYN** CHANGE AGENT

,Chancellor of the Ex'chequer *(also* **chancellor** /ˈtʃɑːnsələ(r); *AmE* ˈtʃæns-/) *noun* [C]
in the UK, the government minister who is responsible for financial affairs: *The chancellor announced a new tax on luxury goods.*

★change /tʃeɪndʒ/ *verb, noun*
● *verb* [+ obj]
1 to exchange money into the money of another country: *Where can I change my traveller's cheques?* ◊ *to change dollars into yen*
2 to exchange money for the same amount in different coins or notes: *Can you change a £20 note?* ◊ *to change a dollar bill for four quarters*
3 *(BrE)* to exchange sth that you have bought for sth else, especially because there is sth wrong with it; to give a customer a new item because there is sth wrong with the one they have bought: *This shirt I bought's too small—I'll have to change it for a bigger one.* ◊ *Of course we'll change it for a smaller size for you.* See note at EXCHANGE
IDM **change 'hands** *(also* **ex,change 'hands)** to pass to a different owner: *The company has changed hands several times.*
● *noun*

SEE ALSO: **agent of change, bureau de ~, career ~, champion of ~, pocket ~, short-~, step ~**

1 [C,U] the act or result of sth becoming different: *important changes to the tax system* ◊ *a change in interest rates* ◊ *people who resist change* ◊ *Technology creates economic and social change.*
○ *economic/social/structural/technological* change
2 [C] the process of replacing sth with sth new or different; a thing that is used to replace sth: *We must notify the bank of our change of address.* ◊ *The company has announced a number of management changes.*
3 [U] the money that you get back if you pay more than the amount sth costs: *Don't forget your change!* ◊ *The ticket machine gives change.*
4 coins rather than paper money: *I need some change for the phone.* ◊ *a dollar in change* (= coins that together are worth one dollar) ◊ *Have you got change for a twenty-euro note* (= coins or notes that are worth this amount)?

'change ,agent *(also* **,agent of 'change,** *less frequent) noun* [C]
a person who organizes and looks after change in a company, for example changes in the way the company operates **SYN** CHAMPION OF CHANGE

'change con,trol *noun* [U]
(IT; Production) the process of controlling the changes that are made to a system, design or plan: *Change control is a vital part of the repair, maintenance, and development of software.* ◊ *A formal change control process has been adopted.*

'change ,management *noun* [U]
(HR) the process of organizing the way in which a new method of working is introduced into a business or an organization: *Change management is the most challenging process facing organizations.* ◊ *The introduction of new technology requires a change management strategy.* ◊ *a change management consultant* ▶ **'change ,manager** *noun* [C]

changeover /ˈtʃeɪndʒəʊvə(r); *AmE* -oʊvər/ *noun* [C]
a change from one system or method of working to another: *the changeover from a manual to a computerized system* ◊ *a changeover period*

'change ,programme *(AmE spelling ~* **program)** *noun* [C]
a project to change the way sth operates, especially a company or an organization: *implementing a change programme in an organization* ◊ *a major change programme to improve the quality of the company's service*

channel /ˈtʃænl/ *noun, verb*
● *noun* [C]

SEE ALSO: **distribution channel, pay channel**

1 a television station: *The programme was shown on Channel 4.* ◊ *a free-to-air* channel (= one that you don't have to pay for) ◊ *a cable channel*
2 a method or system that people use to get information or to communicate: *Complaints should be made through the proper channels.*
3 *(Marketing)* (also **'sales ,channel**) a way in which a company makes its products available to customers: *developing new marketing channels* ◊ *Banks often act as a channel for selling insurance.*
● *verb* [+ obj] **(-ll-,** *AmE usually* **-l-)**
to direct money or effort towards a particular purpose; to do this using a particular route: *Most of our income is channelled into research and development.* ◊ *The government is accused of channeling funds away from health care.*

,channel of distri'bution = DISTRIBUTION CHANNEL

CHAPS /tʃæps/ *abbr* **Clearing House Automated Payment System** in the UK, a computer system that is used when a customer of one bank needs to pay a large amount of money to a customer of another bank: *The payments are made through CHAPS.* → CHIPS

chapter /ˈtʃæptə(r)/ *noun* [C]
1 *(Law)* a separate section of a written law or contract, usually with a number and title: *The bill of rights is found in chapter 2 of the constitution.* → CHAPTER 7, CHAPTER 11
2 *(especially AmE)* a local branch of a society, club, etc.

,Chapter '11 *noun* [U]
(Law) in the US, a section of the law dealing with BANKRUPTCY (=being unable to pay debts), that allows companies to stop paying their debts in the normal way while they try to find a solution to their financial problems: *The company has filed for* (= applied for) *Chapter 11 bankruptcy protection.* ◊ *Their US operations remain in* (= are being dealt with under) *Chapter 11.* ◊ *trying to help the airline out of Chapter 11* → ADMINISTRATION

,Chapter '7 *noun* [U]
(Law) in the US, a section of the law dealing with BANKRUPTCY (= being unable to pay debts) that allows a court to take assets belonging to a company or a person which are then sold to pay their debts: *The firm has filed for* (= applied for) *Chapter 7 bankruptcy.* ◊ *The case has been converted from Chapter 11 to Chapter 7.*

character /ˈkærəktə(r)/ *noun* [C]
a letter, sign, mark or symbol used in writing,

printing or on computers: *You can send a text message of up to 150 characters in length.* → OPTICAL CHARACTER RECOGNITION

★ **charge** /tʃɑːdʒ; AmE tʃɑːrdʒ/ *noun, verb*
● *noun*

SEE ALSO: **accrued charge, bank ~, carrying ~, cover ~, finance ~, floating ~,** etc.

1 [C,U] the amount of money that sb asks for goods or services; the amount of money that you pay regularly for a service: *bank/interest/telephone charges* ◇ *a charge of $50* ◇ *a $50 charge* ◇ *They are going to introduce charges for special deliveries.* ◇ *There's no charge for the service.* ◇ *You can download the software free of charge* (= without paying for it). → FEE See note at PRICE
  ○ to **impose/introduce/levy/make/waive** a charge (for sth) • an **additional/a fixed** charge
2 (*Accounting*) [C] a large cost that a company has to pay, which affects its financial results (*BrE*): *a one-off charge* ◇ (*AmE*) *a one-time charge* ◇ *The company said it would take* (= pay) *a $280 million charge to cover two new acquisitions.*
  ○ an **exceptional/a one-off/special** charge
3 (*Law*) [C,U] a formal claim that sb has committed a crime or done sth wrong: *No criminal charges will be brought against the company directors.* ◇ *After a few hours, she was released without charge.* ◇ *The manager has rejected the charge of favouritism.*
  ○ to **bring/file/lay/press** charges (against sb) • to **admit/deny** a charge/the charges
4 [U] responsibility for a group of people, a job or a task: *Nokia's vice-president in charge of Internet security products* ◇ *The profits have improved sharply since she took charge as chief executive.* ◇ *Who's in charge here?* See note at RESPONSIBILITY → CHARGE ON ASSETS
● *verb*
1 [+ obj *or* no obj] **charge (sb) (for sth)** | **charge (sb) sth (for sth)** to require payment for goods or services: *They have begun to charge for access to their website.* ◇ *We charge a 1% commission for changing traveller's cheques.* ◇ *Do you charge on an hourly basis?* ◇ *They charge clients a monthly fee of $25.* → OVERCHARGE, UNDERCHARGE
2 [+ obj] to record the cost of sth as an amount that sb has to pay: *The subscription price will be charged to your account annually.* ◇ (*AmE*) *Can I charge it* (= pay by credit card)?
3 (*Accounting*) [+ obj] to record that a cost belongs to a particular financial account: *The interest is charged to the profit and loss account.* SYN DEBIT
4 (*Law*) [+ obj] to accuse sb formally of committing a crime or doing sth wrong: *The committee charged her with professional misconduct.* NOTE In the US, **indict** is used instead of **charge** for a serious crime.
5 (*formal*) [+ obj] (*usually* **be charged with sth**) to give sb a job or a task: *The team has been charged with developing new computer applications.*

chargeable /ˈtʃɑːdʒəbl; AmE ˈtʃɑːrdʒ-/ *adjective*
(*Accounting*)
1 (used about an amount of money) that must be paid by sb: *Any expenses you may incur will be chargeable to the company.* ◇ *VAT is not chargeable on this service.* ◇ *They work 35-40 chargeable hours* (= that they must be paid for) *per week.*
2 (used about income or other money that you earn) that you must pay tax on

ˌ**chargeable 'asset** *noun* [C] (*BrE*)
(*Accounting*) an asset on which tax must be paid if it is sold

'**charge ac,count** = ACCOUNT *noun* (2)

'**charge card** *noun* [C]
1 (*Commerce*) a small plastic card provided by a shop/store which you use to buy goods there, paying for them later

2 (*BrE*) a small plastic card with a special number on it that you can use to make calls from public phones, hotels, etc. which you pay for later with your home telephone bill → CALLING CARD, PHONECARD

ˌ**charge on 'assets** *noun* [C]
(*Law*) the legal right to have some of a company's assets if the company fails to pay a debt

charitable /ˈtʃærətəbl/ *adjective*
connected with a charity or charities (*BrE*): *Amateur sports clubs are to be given charitable status* (= will become official charities). ◇ *The bank gives €170 m of its profits to charitable causes every year.* → NON-PROFIT
  ○ a charitable **foundation/group/organization/trust**

charity /ˈtʃærəti/ *noun* (*plural* **charities**)
1 [C] an organization for helping people in need: *The company makes donations to several local charities.*
2 [U] the aim of giving money, food, help, etc. to people who are in need: *The concert raised millions of dollars for charity.*

★ **chart** /tʃɑːt; AmE tʃɑːrt/ *noun, verb*
● *noun* [C]

SEE ALSO: **bar chart, break-even ~, flip ~, flow ~, Gantt ~, operation process ~, organization ~, pie ~**

1 a page or sheet of information in the form of diagrams, lists of figures, etc: *a sales chart* (= showing the level of a company's sales) ◇ *The chart shows the growth of exports and imports over the last 30 years.* See note at GRAPH
  ○ to **draw/make/produce** a chart • the chart **depicts/shows** sth
2 (*especially AmE*) = GRAPH
● *verb* [+ obj]
1 to record or follow the progress or development of sb/sth: *The software allows you to chart how a particular product is selling at any given moment.*
2 to plan a course of action: *We must chart a new course to win more customers.*

★ **charter** /ˈtʃɑːtə(r); AmE ˈtʃɑːrt-/ *noun, verb*
● *noun* [C]

SEE ALSO: **time charter, voyage charter**

1 (*HR*) a formal written statement of the principles and aims of an organization: *Under the new charter all employees must sign a contract of employment.*
2 (*Law*) (*also* ˌ**corporate 'charter**) (*both AmE*) in some US states, the name used for the ARTICLES OF INCORPORATION (= one of the legal documents that is created when a company is formed): *Shareholders voted on an amendment to the company charter.*
3 a written statement describing the rights that a particular group of people should have: *the European Union's Social Charter of workers' rights*
4 (*Transport*) the system of hiring/renting a plane, boat, etc. for use by a group of people; a vehicle used in this way: *a yacht available for charter* ◇ *a charter airline* ◇ *a charter flight* (= where a travel agency buys all the seats and sells them to its customers)
● *verb* [+ obj]
(*Transport*) to hire/rent a plane, boat, etc. for your own use: *chartered ships*

★ **chartered** /ˈtʃɑːtəd; AmE ˈtʃɑːrtərd/ *adjective*
[only before noun]
1 (*BrE*) qualified according to the rules of a particular professional organization: *a chartered surveyor/engineer*
2 (*AmE*) that has a CHARTER allowing it to operate: *the offices of a newly chartered bank*

3 (about an aircraft, a ship or a boat) hired for a particular purpose: *a chartered plane* → CHARTER verb

,**chartered ac'countant** *noun* [C]
(*Accounting*) in the UK, a fully trained and qualified accountant who is a member of one of the Institutes of Chartered Accountants

'**chartered 'certified ac'countant** *noun* [C]
(*Accounting*) in the UK, a person who is a member of the Association of Chartered Certified Accountants (ACCA). **Certified accountants** are qualified to do all types of accounting work and can become AUDITORS.

'**chartered 'life 'underwriter** *noun* [C] (*abbr* CLU)
(*Insurance*) in the US, a person who is fully qualified to sell and give advice on LIFE INSURANCE

charterer /'tʃɑːtərə(r); *AmE* 'tʃɑːrt-/ *noun* [C]
(*Transport*) a company or person that hires/rents or hires out a ship, an aircraft, etc.

,**charter 'member** = FOUNDER MEMBER

'**charter ,party** *noun* [C]
(*Transport*) a contract in which the owner of a ship allows another company to use the ship to transport goods → CHARTER

chartist /'tʃɑːtɪst; *AmE* 'tʃɑːrt-/ = TECHNICAL ANALYST

chat /tʃæt/ *noun* [U,C]
(*IT*) communication, usually about one particular topic, between people in a special area on the Internet: *The website hosts a **chat room** for freelancers.* ◇ *There will be a live **chat session** on web design at 9 pm.*

cheap /tʃiːp/ *adjective, adverb*
●*adjective* (**cheaper, cheapest**)
1 costing little money or less money than you expected: *Domestic farmers have been harmed by cheap imports.* ◇ *Cheap financing deals have boosted sales of new cars.* ◇ *immigrant workers used as a source of cheap labour* → INEXPENSIVE
2 charging low prices: *a cheap airline/supermarket* → INEXPENSIVE
3 low in price and quality: *cheap jewellery*
▶'**cheapness** *noun* [U]
IDM on the 'cheap (*informal*) spending less money than you usually need to spend to do sth: *They are getting the company's PC operations on the cheap.*
●*adverb* (**cheaper** no superlative) (*informal*)
for a low price: *You may get it cheaper on the Internet.*
IDM be ,going 'cheap to be offered for sale at a lower price than usual **sth does not come 'cheap** something is expensive: *Conference facilities like this don't come cheap.*

cheaply /'tʃiːpli/ *adverb*
without spending or costing much money: *The product was developed very quickly and cheaply.* ◇ *He hoped to buy the shares back more cheaply later.*

,**cheap 'money** *noun* [U]
(*Economics*) money that can be borrowed at a low rate of interest: *Cheap money and easy credit led to record growth in high-street sales.* **SYN** EASY MONEY

cheat /tʃiːt/ *verb, noun*
●*verb*
1 [+ obj] to trick or deceive sb: *Customers felt cheated by the sudden rise in price.*
2 [no obj] to act in a dishonest way in order to gain an advantage: *Some farmers are cheating by producing more than their quotas.* ◇ *opportunities for tax cheating*
PHRV '**cheat sb of sth**; '**cheat sb ('out) of sth** to

prevent sb from having sth, especially in a way that is not honest or fair: *The broker is accused of cheating wealthy clients out of tens of millions of dollars.*
●*noun* [C] (*especially BrE*)
1 (*also* '**cheater**, *especially AmE*) a person who cheats: *The government has promised to clamp down on tax cheats.*
2 something that seems unfair or dishonest, for example a way of doing sth with less effort than it usually needs: *By using a simple cheat, it was possible to avoid paying for phone calls.*

★ **check** /tʃek/ *noun, verb*
●*noun* [C]

SEE ALSO: credit check, sales ~, spot ~

1 (*AmE*) = CHEQUE **HELP** You will find some words formed with **check** at the spelling **cheque**.
2 an act of making sure that sth is safe, correct or in good condition by examining it: *All our machines are given regular checks.* ◇ *My job is to **keep a check** on each stage of the production process.* ◇ *You should run a virus check on your laptop.*
○ *a regular/routine/security check* ◆ *to be given/get/ have a check* ◆ *to do/run a check (on sth)*
3 something that slows down the progress of sth else or stops it from getting worse: *The new measures should **keep a check on** inflation.* ◇ *Public opinion can act as a check on the power of the executive.*
○ *to act as/serve as a check on sth*
4 (*especially AmE*) = BILL (2)
5 (*AmE*) = TICK *noun* (1)
IDM hold/keep sth in 'check to keep sth under control so that it does not spread or get worse: *The bank may raise interest rates to keep prices in check.*
●*verb*

SEE ALSO: double-check

1 [+ obj or no obj] to examine sth to see if it is correct, safe or satisfactory, or to see if it contains sth: *Get someone to check your application form.* ◇ *Have you checked the program for errors?*
2 [+ obj or no obj] to find out if sth is correct or true or if sth is how you think it is: *You'd better check with Ken what time he's expecting us.* ◇ *checking the time*
3 [+ obj] to control sth; to stop sth from increasing or getting worse: *The government is determined to check the growth of public spending.*
4 (*AmE*) [+ obj] to leave bags or cases with an official so that they can be put on a plane or train: *You must check your luggage at the airport ticket counter.*
5 (*AmE*) [+ obj] = TICK *verb*
PHRV ,**check 'in (at …)**; ,**check 'into …** to go to a desk in a hotel, an airport, etc. and tell an official there that you have arrived: *Please check in at least an hour before departure.* → CHECK-IN ,**check sth 'in** (*BrE*) to leave bags or cases with an official to be put on a plane or train: *We checked in our luggage and went through to the departure lounge.* → CHECK-IN ,**check sb/sth 'off** (*AmE*) = TICK SB/STH OFF '**check on sb/sth** to look to see how sb/sth is : *I phoned to check on my order* (= to find out how it was progressing). ,**check 'out** (*especially AmE*) if facts, etc. **check out**, they can be shown to be correct or true: *Most of the claims they make for the product do check out.* ,**check 'out (of …)** to pay your bill and leave a hotel, etc: *Guests should check out of their rooms by 11am.* → CHECKOUT ,**check sth 'out 1** to find out if sth is correct, true or acceptable: *They check out all new employees to make sure they don't have a criminal record.*
2 (*informal*) to look at or examine sth that seems interesting or attractive: *Check out the prices at our new store!* ,**check 'over/'through sth** to examine sth carefully to make sure that it is correct or acceptable: *We spent several days checking over the*

contract before signing. ˌcheck 'up on sth to find out if sth is true or correct: *I just need to check up on a few facts before the presentation.*

checkbook /'tʃekbʊk/ = CHEQUEBOOK

checkbox /'tʃekbɒks; AmE -bɑːks/ (BrE also 'tickbox) noun [C]
(*IT*) a small square on a computer screen that you click on with the mouse to choose whether a particular function is switched on or off

'**check card** = DEBIT CARD

checker /'tʃekə(r)/ noun [C]
1 (*AmE*) a person who works at the CHECKOUT in a supermarket: *a supermarket checker*
2 (*IT*) (*used in compounds*) a computer program that you use to check sth, for example the spelling and grammar of sth you have written
○ *a grammar/spelling/virus checker*

ˌcheck guaran'tee card = CHEQUE CARD

'**check-in** noun
1 [C,U] the place where you go first when you arrive at an airport, to show your ticket, etc: *The Airline apologizes for long delays at check-ins today.* ◇ *the check-in counter*
2 [U] the act of showing your ticket, etc. when you arrive at an airport: *Do you know your check-in time?*

'**checking ac,count** = CURRENT ACCOUNT (1)

'**check ,kiting** (BrE spelling cheque ~) noun [U] (AmE only)
the illegal activity of writing cheques between one bank account and another in order to get credit or take out more money than you have available in the accounts

'**check mark** = TICK noun (1)

checkoff /'tʃekɒf/ noun [U] (AmE)
(*HR*) in the US, money that an employee agrees can be taken from their wages to pay for being a member of a particular union

checkout /'tʃekaʊt/ noun
1 [C] the place where you pay for the things that you are buying in a supermarket: *to pay at the checkout* ◇ (AmE) *standing in line at the checkout counter* SYN TILL (BrE)
○ *a checkout assistant/operator ◆ checkout staff ◆ checkout delays/lines/queues*
2 [U] the time when you leave a hotel at the end of your stay: *At checkout, your bill will be printed for you.*

cheerleader /'tʃɪəliːdə(r); AmE 'tʃɪrl-/ noun [C] (informal)
a person who supports a particular person, idea, or way of doing sth: *The cheerleaders of the new technology say it will completely change the way companies use information technology.*

chemical /'kemɪkl/ adjective, noun
● *adjective*
1 connected with chemistry: *the chemical industry* ◇ *a chemical element* ◇ *Eastman Chemical Co.*
2 produced by or using processes which involve changes to atoms, etc.
○ *chemical processes/reactions*
▶ **chemically** /'kemɪkli/ adverb: *Caffeine can be removed chemically from coffee.*
● *noun* [C]
a substance obtained by or used in a chemical process: *toxic chemicals* ◇ *a US chemicals group*

ˌchemical engi'neering noun [U]
the study of the design and use of machines in industrial chemical processes ▶ ˌchemical engi'neer noun [C]

★ **cheque** (AmE spelling **check**) /tʃek/ noun [C]
SEE ALSO: bank-certified cheque, bank ~, banker's ~, blank ~, cashier's ~, certified ~, dividend ~, etc.

(*Finance*) a printed form that you can write on and sign as a way of paying for sth instead of using money: *a cheque for £100* ◇ *Will you take a cheque* (= can I pay by cheque)? ◇ *Who shall I make the cheque out to* (= what name shall I write on it)? ◇ *Cheques should be made payable to Toyland plc.* ◇ *He drew a large cheque on his company's account.* ◇ *to cash a cheque* (= to get or give money for a cheque) ◇ *I am afraid your cheque bounced* (= was not paid by your bank because there was not enough money in your account).
○ *to pay (for) sth by cheque ◆ to draw/issue/make out/sign/write sb/write (out) a cheque ◆ to deposit/ pay in a cheque ◆ to accept/clear/honour/take a cheque ◆ to bounce/cancel/stop a cheque*

'**cheque ac,count** (AmE spelling check ~) = CURRENT ACCOUNT (1)

chequebook (AmE spelling **checkbook**) /'tʃekbʊk/ noun [C]
a book of printed cheques

'**cheque card** (also ˌcheque guaran'tee card) (AmE spelling check ~) (also 'banker's card) noun [C] (all especially British)
a plastic card that you must show when you pay by cheque to prove that the bank where you have your account will pay the amount on the cheque → BANK CARD, CREDIT CARD, DEBIT CARD

'**cheque ,kiting** = CHECK KITING

'**cheque run** (AmE spelling check ~) noun [C]
the process of using a computer to record payments to be made and print cheques

'**cherry-pick** verb [+ obj or no obj]
to choose the best things or people from a group and leave those which are not so good: *Competitors may cherry-pick the most profitable mail services.* ◇ *He cherry-picked the phone industry for the best people to work with him.* ▶ '**cherry ,picker** noun [C] '**cherry-,picking** noun [U]

chief /tʃiːf/ adjective, noun
● *adjective* [only before noun]
1 most important; main: *They have fallen behind their chief competitor in recent months.*
2 highest in rank: *former chief technology officer*
● *noun* [C]
a person with a high rank or the highest rank in a company or an organization: *Industry chiefs are meeting today to discuss the latest tax rise.*

★ ˌchief e'xecutive ,officer (also ˌchief e'xecutive, especially in BrE) noun [C] (abbr CEO)
the person in a company who has the most power and authority and is responsible for managing its daily affairs under the authority of the BOARD OF DIRECTORS: *He is the chairman and chief executive officer.*
○ *to appoint sb (as)/make sb/name sb (as)/promote sb to chief executive officer ◆ to be/become/retire as/serve as chief executive officer*
NOTE The **chief executive officer** is usually a member of a company's board of directors. In the US (but not the UK) the CEO is often also the chairman of the board. → MANAGING DIRECTOR

ˌchief fi'nancial ,officer (also ˌchief 'finance ,officer) noun [C] (abbr CFO)
the person in charge of the financial department of a company NOTE The **chief financial officer** is often a member of a company's board of directors.

chief infor'mation ,officer noun [C] (abbr CIO)
1 the person in an organization who is responsible for the computer systems and technology
2 the person in an organization who is responsible for giving information about it to the public

chief 'operating ,officer (also ,chief ope'rations ,officer) noun [C] (abbr COO)
a person who is employed to manage the daily affairs of a company, usually under the authority of a CHIEF EXECUTIVE OFFICER

childcare (AmE spelling **child care**) /'tʃaɪldkeə(r); AmE -ker/ noun [U]
the job of taking care of children, especially while their parents are at work: the problems of finding good childcare ◇ Better **childcare provision** would encourage mothers back to work.

child 'labour (AmE spelling ~ **labor**) noun [U]
the use of children to do work: products produced by child labour

childrenswear /'tʃɪldrənzweə(r); AmE -wer/ noun [U]
(used especially in shops/stores) clothes for children: Childrenswear is on the first floor. ◇ the childrenswear market → MENSWEAR, WOMENSWEAR

Chinese 'wall (also 'firewall) noun [C, usually sing.]
1 something that makes it difficult or impossible to do sth, especially for people to communicate with each other: He was accused of erecting a Chinese wall between shareholders and the board.
➊ to **create/erect/raise** a Chinese wall
2 (Stock Exchange) a set of strict rules that prevent one department of a stock exchange business passing secret information to another department that could result in the information being used illegally in order to gain money: Wall Street insists that a Chinese Wall separates its research and its investment banking activities. → INSIDER TRADING
➊ to **create/erect/raise** a Chinese wall

chip /tʃɪp/ = MICROCHIP

'chip card noun [C]
a small plastic card, for example a credit card, on which a large amount of information is stored in electronic form: Chip cards will help prevent fraud as they can't be copied. [SYN] SMART CARD

chipmaking /'tʃɪpmeɪkɪŋ/ noun [U]
the business or process of making MICROCHIPS: a chipmaking plant ▶ **chipmaker** noun [C]

CHIPS /tʃɪps/ abbr
Clearing House Interbank Payments System in the US, a computer system that is used for making large payments between banks: The payments will be processed **through** CHIPS. ◇ CHIPS handles about 240 000 transactions a day. → CHAPS

choice /tʃɔɪs/ noun, adjective
●noun [sing; U]
the number or range of things that you can choose from: We are now able to offer our customers an even greater choice of products. ◇ There wasn't much choice of colour. → SELECTION (3)
➊ an **extensive/ a good/great/huge/large/wide** choice • a **limited/restricted** choice
[IDM] **of 'choice (for sb/sth)** (used after a noun) that is chosen by a particular group of people or for a particular purpose: It's the software of choice for business use. **of your 'choice** (used after a noun) that you have chosen: Passengers can enjoy the movie of their choice on their personal screen.
●adjective [only before noun]
(used especially about food) of very good quality: choice farm-fresh produce

churn /tʃɜːn; AmE tʃɜːrn/ noun, verb
●noun [U]
1 (Marketing) the situation when customers stop using a particular make of goods or services or change to another: A reduction in customer churn is our marketing priority. → LOYALTY
2 (HR) the situation of employees leaving a company and being replaced by other people: the management churn within organizations
→ TURNOVER
3 (HR) the situation when a company or an organization moves workers or equipment from one job or place to another
→ CHURN RATE
●verb
1 (Marketing) [+ obj or no obj] (used about customers) to stop using a particular make of goods or services or change to another: attempts to win back customers who had churned
2 (Stock Exchange) [+ obj] (used about BROKERS) to buy and sell shares, bonds, etc. for investors more than necessary in order to earn more COMMISSION (= money that is paid for buying and selling shares, etc.): The fees are an incentive to churn the portfolio of shares.
3 (HR) [+ obj] to move employees to another job or place: Office arrangements only last weeks as tasks change and staff are churned.
[PHR V] **,churn sth 'out** (informal) to produce sth quickly and in large amounts: The plant churns out over half a million vehicles a year. See note at PRODUCE

'churn rate noun [C]
1 (Marketing) the number of customers who stop using a particular make of goods or services or change to another: The phone company said that its churn rate was half that of other UK networks.
2 (HR) the number of people who leave jobs in an organization and are replaced by others: Most people here have come straight from college and stayed—the churn rate is very low.

CIF /,si: aɪ 'ef/ = COST, INSURANCE AND FREIGHT

CIM /,si: aɪ 'em/ = COMPUTER-INTEGRATED MANUFACTURING, RAIL CONSIGNMENT NOTE
[NOTE] CIM is formed from the first letters of the words in a French phrase.

CIO /,si: aɪ 'əʊ; AmE 'oʊ/ = CHIEF INFORMATION OFFICER

CIP abbr
(Trade, only used in written English) carriage and insurance paid to...

circuit /'sɜːkɪt; AmE 'sɜːrkɪt/ noun [C]
the complete path of wires and equipment along which an electric current flows: an electrical circuit ◇ a circuit diagram (= one showing all the connections in the different parts of the circuit)

'circuit board noun [C]
(IT) a board that holds electrical CIRCUITS inside a piece of electrical equipment

'circuit-,breaker (AmE spelling **circuit breaker**) noun
1 (Technical) a device that can automatically stop an electric current if it becomes dangerous
2 (Stock Exchange) a rule that automatically stops or slows trading on a stock exchange when prices rise and fall too quickly or too far: circuit-breaker trading ◇ How many times can the circuit breaker be **triggered** during the day?

circular /'sɜːkjələ(r); AmE 'sɜːrk-/ noun, adjective
●noun [C]
a printed letter, notice or advertisement that is sent to a large number of people at the same time: The details of the agreement will be released in a circular to shareholders.

●*adjective*
(about a letter) sent to a large number of people: *a circular letter*

circulate /'sɜːkjəleɪt; *AmE* 'sɜːrk-/ *verb* [+ obj *or* no obj]
if an idea, information, a document, etc. **circulates** or if you **circulate it**, it is passed from one person to another: *Rumours began to circulate about their financial problems.* ◇ *This document will be circulated to all members.*

,**circulating 'asset** = CURRENT ASSET

,**circulating 'capital** = WORKING CAPITAL

circulation /,sɜːkjə'leɪʃn; *AmE* ,sɜːrk-/ *noun*

SEE ALSO: **velocity of circulation**

1 [U] the passing or spreading of sth from one person or place to another: *the circulation of information/ideas*
2 [U] the use of coins and notes as money: *There is a large amount of forged money **in** circulation.* ◇ *The notes were **taken out of** circulation.*
3 [C, usually sing.] the usual number of copies of a newspaper or magazine that are sold each day, week, etc: *a daily circulation of more than one million*

cite /saɪt/ *verb* [+ obj]
to mention sth as a reason or an example, or in order to support what you are saying: *Bertelli resigned as Chief Executive last month, citing personal reasons.* ◇ *Microsoft is often cited **as** one of the world's largest businesses.*

the City /'sɪti/ *noun* [sing.]
Britain's financial and business centre, in the oldest part of London: *a City stockbroker* ◇ *What is the City's reaction to the cut in interest rates?* ◇ *the newspaper's City desk* (= the department dealing with financial news) → SQUARE MILE

civil /'sɪvl/ *adjective* [only before noun]
1 (*Law*) involving legal matters between individuals, companies, etc. and not criminal law: *Many shareholders have filed civil lawsuits to try to recover their money.* → CIVIL LAW (1)
 ➊ *a civil **action/case/claim/lawsuit*** ◆ civil **charges/ liability/litigation**
2 connected with the state rather than with the armed forces or with religion: *civil aircraft*

,**civil avi'ation** *noun* [U]
the designing, building and flying of aircraft that carry ordinary and not military passengers: *the civil aviation industry*

,**civil 'damages** *noun* [pl.]
(*Law*) money that a court forces sb/sth to pay to sb for harming them or damaging their property: *The court ordered the manufacturer to pay nearly €500 000 in fines and civil damages.*

,**civil engi'neer** *noun* [C]
a person whose job involves designing, building and repairing roads, bridges, etc. ▸,**civil engi'neering** *noun* [U]

,**civil 'law** *noun* [U]
(*Law*)
1 law that deals with commercial issues and the relationships between individuals, companies, etc., rather than with crime: *The store will seek damages from thieves under civil law.* → CRIMINAL LAW
2 a system of law that is used in many countries, especially in Europe, that is based on the law of ancient Rome (**Roman law**) and uses laws recorded in large written documents (called **codes**): *a civil law country/system* → COMMON LAW

,**civil 'servant** *noun* [C]
a person who works in the CIVIL SERVICE

the ,**civil 'service** *noun* [sing.]
the government departments in a country, (except the armed forces), and the people who work for them: *She had a long career in the civil service.*

CKD /,siː keɪ 'diː/ = COMPLETELY KNOCKED-DOWN

★**claim** /kleɪm/ *noun, verb*
●*noun* [C]

SEE ALSO: **counterclaim, baggage ~, expenses ~, pay ~, priority ~, small ~, statement of ~**

1 (*Insurance*) (*also* in'surance claim) a request that you make to an insurance company for an amount of money to be paid for loss or damage for which you are insured: *You can make a claim **on** your insurance policy.* ◇ *We're putting in an insurance claim **for** flood damage.* ◇ *The insurer has decided to settle* (= pay) *the claim.*
 ➊ *to **make/put in/submit** a claim* ◆ *to **pay/refuse/ settle** a claim*
2 a request for money that you believe you have a legal right to from the government, an official organization or a company: *claims **for** unemployment benefits* ◇ *Make sure your claims for expenses* (= money you have spent while working for your company) *are submitted by the end of the month.*
 ➊ *disability/jobless/unemployment claims* ◆ *to **file/ make/submit** a claim* ◆ *to **deal with/pay/refuse** a claim*
3 (*Law*) a demand for sth that you make by starting a court case: *She has filed a claim **against** the company for breach of contract.* ◇ *a claim **for** unfair dismissal* (= from a job) ◇ *They have offered to settle the claim* (= agree on the amount to be paid without going to court).
 ➊ *to **bring/file/make** a claim* ◆ *to **allow/uphold** a claim* ◆ *to **dismiss/reject/strike out** a claim*
4 a legal right that sb believes they have to sth, especially property, land, etc: *The company's claim **to** the oil fields has been contested.*
 ➊ *to **have** a claim on/to sth*
5 (*Marketing*) a statement about the nature or quality of a product, that may not be true: *The company has been ordered to correct its false and misleading **advertising** claims.*
 ➊ *to **make** a claim*
●*verb* [+ obj *or* no obj]
1 to ask for sth from sb/sth, especially money, because you think it is your legal right to have it: *He's not entitled to claim unemployment benefit.* ◇ *Both companies have claimed rights to the trademark.* ◇ *You can claim **on** your insurance **for** that coat you left on the train.*
2 to say that a product has a particular nature or quality although this may not be true

'**claim ad,juster** = CLAIMS ADJUSTER

claimant /'kleɪmənt/ *noun* [C]
1 a person who is receiving money from the state because they are unemployed, etc: *sickness benefit claimants*
2 (*Insurance*) a person or company that claims an amount of money from an insurance company: *Section E of the form must be signed by all claimants.*
3 (*Law*) (*BrE*) a person or company that starts a court case against sb/sth: *The claimants are seeking compensation for their injuries.* SYN PLAINTIFF → DEFENDANT
4 (*Law*) a person who believes they have a legal right to sth, especially property: *rival claimants to the land*

'**claim form** *noun* [C]
1 a form that you complete in order to claim money from an insurance company or the government

2 (*Law*) in England and Wales, an official document that you complete in order to start a court case NOTE In the past, this document was called a SUMMONS.

'claims ad,juster (*also* 'claim ad,juster, 'claims as,sessor) (*also spelled* **adjustor**) *noun* [C] (*all especially AmE*)
(*Insurance*) a person who investigates an insurance claim on behalf of an insurance company and decides how much money the insurance company should pay: *Do not start the repairs until a claims adjuster has assessed the damage.* SYN LOSS ADJUSTER (*BrE*)

'claims as,sessor = LOSS ASSESSOR, CLAIMS ADJUSTER

clampdown /'klæmpdaʊn/ *noun* [C, usually sing.] sudden action that is taken in order to stop an activity that is illegal or seen as harmful: *a clampdown on tax evasion*

class /klɑːs; *AmE* klæs/ *noun*

SEE ALSO: best in class, business ~, economy ~, first ~, second ~

1 [C, usually pl.] a series of lessons on a particular subject: *The institute holds classes in/on accounting throughout the year.* SYN COURSE
O *to attend/go to/take* classes • *to have/hold/offer/ teach a class*
2 [C with sing./pl. verb] one of the groups of people in a society that are thought of as being at the same social or economic level: *The new taxes will hurt all classes of society.* ◇ *the professional classes*
3 [C] a group of things that have similar characteristics or qualities: *The painkiller is part of a new class of drugs.* ◇ *It's the best computer available in its class.*
4 [C] each of several different levels of comfort that are available to travellers in a plane, etc.

,class 'A/'B/'C share = A/B/C SHARE

,class 'action *noun* [C] (*especially AmE*)
(*Law*) a type of court case in which one person or a small group of people make a claim on behalf of a larger group of people who have the same legal problem: *Hundreds of class actions have been filed against the investment bank.* ◇ *a class action lawsuit brought by consumers* → GROUP ACTION, PERSONAL ACTION

,classifi'cation so,ciety (*AmE also* ,classifi'cation au,thority) *noun* [C]
(*Insurance*) an official organization that checks whether a ship meets particular standards of design, safety, etc. and provides a certificate as proof of this

classified /'klæsɪfaɪd/ *adjective, noun*
● *adjective* [usually before noun]
1 containing or connected with CLASSIFIED ADVERTISEMENTS: *the New York Times classified section* ◇ *classified advertising*
2 with information arranged in groups according to subjects: *a classified catalogue*
● *noun* [pl.]
classifieds the part of a newspaper, magazine, etc. or an Internet site that contains CLASSIFIED ADVERTISEMENTS: *The job was advertised in the classifieds.*

,classified 'ad (*AmE also* 'want ad) *noun* [C, usually pl.] (*informal*)
a classified advertisement: *You can email us to place a classified ad.* SYN SMALL AD

,classified ad'vertisement *noun* [C, usually pl.] a small advertisement that you put in a newspaper, magazine, etc. or on an Internet site, if you want to

buy or sell sth, employ sb, etc: *Our rates for classified advertisements are $10 for the first 10 words and 50¢ for each additional word.* ◇ *the classified advertisement section of the daily paper*
O *to reply to/place/submit/read a classified advertisement*

,classified di'rectory *noun* [C]
a list of the names, addresses and telephone numbers of businesses in a particular area, arranged in groups according to the type of business → YELLOW PAGES

classify /'klæsɪfaɪ/ *verb* [+ obj] (**classifies, classifying, classified, classified**)
to put sb/sth into a group with other people or things of a similar type: *Taxes may be classified as either direct or indirect.* ◇ *For insurance purposes, cars are classified into five types.* ◇ *The report classifies companies according to annual income.*

★clause /klɔːz/ *noun* [C]

SEE ALSO: assignment clause, break ~, escalation ~, escalator ~, escape ~, gag ~, gagging ~, etc.

a sentence or group of sentences in a contract or legal document that has a number and deals with a particular topic, item or condition: *The clause allows you to return the items if you are unsatisfied.* ◇ *They have put in a penalty clause which specifies that late delivery will be fined.* ◇ *Under clause 8, the employer is responsible for the safety of employees.*
O *to add/include/insert/put in a clause* • *to delete/ take out/remove a clause* • *a clause allows/ provides for/states/specifies sth* • *a clause excludes/ limits sth*

claw /klɔː/ *verb*
IDM **claw your way 'back; claw your way into/ out of/to sth** to gradually achieve sth by using a lot of determination and effort: *The group is clawing its way out of financial crisis.*
PHR V **,claw sth 'back 1** (*also* ,claw 'back (from sth)) to get back sth that has been lost, usually by using a lot of effort: *The company is trying to claw back its share of the market.* **2** (*Finance*) (about a government) to get money back from people who have received a benefit, usually by taxing them: *The Chancellor is expected to claw back £2.8 billion in the budget.* → CLAWBACK **3** (*Finance*) (*BrE*) (about a company) to offer existing shareholders the right to buy a proportion of the shares that have already been offered to new investors: *Some of the shares placed with institutional investors had to be clawed back to satisfy the demand of existing shareholders.* → CLAWBACK

clawback /'klɔːbæk/ *noun* [C,U]
(*Finance*)
1 the act of getting money back from people, especially in tax, to pay for a benefit they have received; the money that is paid back: *They want the basic pension to be increased, with a tax clawback from wealthier pensioners.*
2 (*BrE*) the act of offering existing shareholders the right to buy a proportion of the shares that have already been offered to new investors: *The shares are being placed with institutional investors subject to a right of clawback by existing shareholders.*

clean /kliːn/ *adjective, verb, adverb*
● *adjective* (**cleaner, cleanest**)
1 free from harmful or unpleasant substances: *clean air/water* ◇ *the search for cleaner technologies* → GREEN
2 not showing or having any record of doing sth dishonest or against the law: *He is hoping to maintain the company's clean record on safety.* ◇ (*AmE*) *a clean driver's license*
3 (*Finance*) financially strong; having little or no debt: *The firm has a strong cash flow and a clean balance sheet.* ◇ *They are the country's biggest and cleanest bank.*

IDM **a clean bill of 'health** a report that says sth is reliable, safe or in good condition: *The auditors gave the company a clean bill of health.* **clean 'hands** if sb has **clean hands** they are not guilty of any illegal or dishonest acts: *The bank is in crisis and needs a leader with clean hands.*
→ CLEAN BILL OF LADING at BILL OF LADING
● *verb*
IDM **clean 'house** to make a company, an organization, etc. more honest and efficient, for example by removing people or things that are not necessary or not wanted ,**clean up your 'act** (*informal*) to start behaving in a moral or responsible way: *The call centre industry is trying to clean up its act and improve working conditions for staff.*
PHR V ,**clean sb 'out** (*informal*) to use all of sb/sth's money: *Paying the fine cleaned me out.* ,**clean sth 'out** to make the inside of sth very clean or empty, for example by removing things you do not want or need: *Staff were given no time to clean out their desks.* ◇ (*figurative*) *She's cleaned out her bank account* (= taken all the money out of it). ,**clean sth 'up 1** to remove crime and immoral behaviour from a place or an activity: *The industry needs to clean up its image.* **2** (*Finance*) to make sth financially stronger; to reduce the amount of debt: *He cleaned up the group by getting rid of loss-making activities.* **3** to remove harmful substances from a river, piece of land, building, etc: *cleaning up chemical spills* → CLEAN-UP
● *adverb*
IDM **come 'clean (with sb) (about sth)** to admit and explain sth that you have kept as a secret: *It's time for the chairman to come clean about the group's illegal dealings.*

'clean-out (*AmE spelling usually* **cleanout**) *noun* [C, usually sing.]
an act of making sth very clean, for example by removing things that you do not want or need: *a cleanout of huge grain surpluses*

'clean-up (*AmE spelling usually* **cleanup**) *noun* [C, usually sing.]
1 the process of removing POLLUTION: *The clean-up of the river is going to take months.* ◇ *40 000 volunteers took part in the cleanup effort on the beaches.*
● *a clean-up* **campaign/effort/operation/programme**
2 (*Finance*) the act of making a company, an industry, etc. financially stronger, especially by reducing the amount of debt: *a clean-up of bank and corporate debt*

clear /klɪə(r); *AmE* klɪr/ *verb*
1 [+ obj] to give or get official approval for sth to be done: *His appointment had been cleared by the board.* ◇ *I'll have to* **clear it with** *the manager before I can refund your money.* ◇ *The drug has been cleared for use in the US.*
2 [+ obj] to prove that sb is innocent: *She has been cleared of all charges against her.*
3 (*Commerce*) [+ obj] **clear (out) sth** to sell all the goods that you have available: *The store is trying to clear its stock of winter clothes.* ◇ *The company has dropped its prices in an attempt to clear out its* **inventory** (= its supply of products).
4 [+ obj] to remove sth that is not wanted from a place (*figurative*): *clearing bad debts from the company's books* (= financial records) ◇ *Clear the screen* (= computer screen) *and start again.*
5 [+ obj *or* no obj] if a cheque that you pay into your bank account **clears**, or a bank **clears** it, the money is available for you to use: *Cheques usually take three working days to clear.*
6 (*Finance*) [+ obj] to calculate the total amount of money and the numbers of shares, etc. that investors have agreed to exchange on a particular date, in order to arrange the transfer of the money, shares, etc. between them: *Only certain members of*

the stock exchange are authorized to clear **trades.**
→ CLEARING, SETTLE
7 (*Trade*) [+ obj] to give official permission for goods to leave or enter a place: *to clear goods through customs*
8 [+ obj] to gain or earn an amount of money as profit: *She cleared €2 000 on the deal.*
9 (*Finance*) [+ obj] if you **clear** a debt or a loan, you pay all the money back
10 [+ obj] to decide officially, after finding out information about sb, that they can be given special work or allowed to see secret papers: *She hasn't been cleared by security.*
IDM **clear your 'desk 1** (*also* **clear out your 'desk**) to remove everything from your desk at work because you are leaving your job: *She was fired on the spot and given an hour to clear her desk.* **2** to finish the work that you need to do: *He was desperately trying to clear his desk so he could get home.*

clearance /'klɪərəns; *AmE* 'klɪr-/ *noun*
1 [U,C] official permission that is given to sb before they can work somewhere, have particular information, or do sth they want to do: *The company has been given clearance to market the drug.* ◇ *I need clearance* **from** *my supervisor before I can make such a large payment.*
● *to* **be given/get/need/obtain/receive/require** *clearance*
2 (*Transport*) [U] official permission for a person, a vehicle or goods to enter or leave an airport or a country: *The pilot was waiting for clearance for take-off.* ◇ *How long will* **customs clearance** *take?*
● *to* **be given/get/need/obtain/receive/require** *clearance*
3 [U,C] the process of a cheque being paid by a bank: *Allow four working days for cheque clearance.*
4 (*Commerce*) [C] = CLEARANCE SALE

'clearance sale (*also* **'clearance**) *noun* [C]
(*Commerce*) an occasion when a shop/store sells goods cheaply in order to make space for new goods: *The department store is* **holding** *its end-of-season clearance sale.*

clearing /'klɪərɪŋ; *AmE* 'klɪrɪŋ/ *noun* [U]
(*Finance*) the activity of exchanging payments that customers of different banks make to each other: *the cheque clearing* **system** ◇ *an* **automated** *clearing system* (= one that uses a computer system to deal with payments)

'clearing bank *noun* [C]
(*Finance*)
1 in the UK, a bank that is a member of a CLEARING HOUSE (= an organization that exchanges payments between customers of different banks): *The country has eight main clearing banks.*
2 in the UK, one of the major banks that people use

'clearing house *noun* [C]
1 (*Finance*) an organization that exchanges payments between customers of different banks: *The clearing house exchanges cheques worth over $20 billion every day.* ◇ *an* **automated** *clearing house* (= one that uses a computer system to deal with payments)
2 (*Finance*) an organization that manages the exchange of FUTURES (= a contract to buy or sell a particular amount of sth at a particular time in the future and for a particular price), currencies, etc. between buyers and sellers: *All trades are cleared and guaranteed by the clearing house.*

clerical /'klerɪkl/ *adjective*
connected with office work, especially the regular tasks and activities such as dealing with documents or putting information into a computer: *We need another clerical assistant to deal with the paperwork.*

◇ *Owing to a clerical error, the document was wrongly filed.*
○ clerical **assistants/officers/staff/workers** • clerical **jobs/work**

clerk /klɑːk; *AmE* klɜːrk/ *noun* [C]

SEE ALSO: **articled clerk, bank ~, file ~, filing ~, ledger ~, wages ~**

1 a person whose job is to keep the records or accounts in an office, shop/store etc: *She is working as an office clerk while studying interior design.* ◇ *an invoice clerk*
○ an **office**/a **ticket/wages** clerk
2 (*AmE*) = SALES ASSISTANT
3 (*also* **'desk clerk**) (*both AmE*) a person whose job is dealing with people arriving at or leaving a hotel
[SYN] RECEPTIONIST
4 an official in charge of the records of a council, court, etc: *the Clerk of the Court*

click /klɪk/ *verb, noun*
● *verb* [+ obj or no obj]
to press one of the buttons on a computer mouse: *When I'd finished the email, I quickly clicked 'send'.* ◇ *I clicked **on** the link to the customer service website.*
→ DOUBLE-CLICK
● *noun* [C]
the act of pressing a button on a computer mouse: *You can book your flights with just a few clicks of the mouse* (= very quickly).
[IDM] **,clicks and 'mortar** (*also* **,clicks and 'bricks**) (*E-commerce*) that uses the Internet as well as physical shops/stores, etc. to sell products: *a clicks-and-mortar business/retailer/company* → BRICKS AND MORTAR → COST PER CLICK

'click rate = CLICK-THROUGH RATE

clickstream /'klɪkstriːm/ *noun* [C]
(*IT; Marketing*) a record of a person's activities when spending time on the Internet, including the websites they visit, how long they spend on each one, emails they send or receive, etc: *Marketing companies find it useful to analyse clickstream data.*

'click-through (*also spelled* **clickthrough**) *noun* [C,U]
(*IT; Marketing*) an occasion when sb visits a particular website because they clicked on an advertisement on another web page; the extent to which this happens: *When someone clicks on a banner ad it registers as a click-through.* ◇ *improving click-through*

'click-through rate (*also spelled* **clickthrough ~**) (*also* **'click rate**) *noun* [C]
(*IT; Marketing*) the number of people who visit a website by clicking on an advertisement on another web page, compared to the number of people who visit the web page on which the advertisement appears: *Our banner ads have a click-through rate of between 1.5% and 9%.*

★ **client** /'klaɪənt/ *noun* [C]
1 a person who uses the services or advice of a professional person or organization: *She advises clients on their investments.* ◇ *The consulting firm acts for several large corporate clients* (= companies). ◇ *The agency's client list includes Gucci and British Airways.* See note at CUSTOMER
○ a **big/big-name/large**/an **important** client • a **corporate/private** client • a **new/potential/ prospective** client • to **act for/advise/represent/ serve** a client • to **attract/find/get/keep/lose/retain** a client
2 a person who buys goods or services in a shop/ store: *A good hairdresser never lacks clients.*
3 (*IT*) a computer that is linked to a SERVER: *The data is processed on the server and then delivered to the client.* ◇ *a client machine/computer*

'client ac,count *noun* [C]
a bank account that a professional person or company, such as a law firm, keeps for a client, so that money paid or received on behalf of the client is separate from the company's own money

'client base *noun* [C, usually sing.]
the group of regular customers that a business has: *We are trying hard to expand our client base.*
○ to **broaden/expand/increase** a client base

clientele /ˌkliːənˈtel; *AmE* ˌklaɪənˈtel/ *noun* [sing. with sing./pl. verb]
all the customers or clients of a shop/store, restaurant, an organization, etc: *The boutique has an exclusive clientele.* ◇ *The restaurant's regular clientele were mostly young business people.*
See note at CUSTOMER
○ an **exclusive/international**/a **regular/young** clientele • to **attract/build up/have** a clientele

'client-,server *adjective* [only before noun]
(*IT*) used to describe a computer system in which a powerful central computer (the **server**) provides data to a number of smaller computers (**clients**) connected together in a network: *Only two-thirds of their employees were on the client-server system.*
→ ARCHITECTURE (3)

climb /klaɪm/ *verb, noun*
● *verb* [no obj]
1 to increase in value or amount: *Their profits climbed from $12.7 million to $185.7 million.* ◇ *The index has climbed 5% in the last week.*
2 to move to a higher position by your own effort: *In a few years she had climbed to the top of her profession.*
[PHRV] **,climb 'back** to return to a particular value or amount: *The unemployment rate has climbed back to last year's level.* → idiom at BANDWAGON
● *noun* [C, usually sing.]
1 an increase in value or amount: *the dollar's climb against the euro*
2 progress to a higher standard or position: *the long slow climb out of the recession*

clinch /klɪntʃ/ *verb* [+ obj]
to succeed in getting or achieving sth: *We clinched the **deal** by lowering our price.*

,clinical 'trial (*also* **,clinical 'study**) *noun* [C]
a test of a new medicine/drug that is carried out on a small number of people, in order to see whether the drug is effective and safe to sell to the public: *We are **conducting** the final round of clinical trials.*

'clip art *noun* [U]
(*IT*) pictures and symbols that are stored in computer programs or on websites for computer users to copy and add to their own documents

clipboard /'klɪpbɔːd; *AmE* -bɔːrd/ *noun* [C]
1 a small board with a part that holds papers at the top, used by sb who wants to write while standing or moving around
2 (*IT*) a place where information from a computer file is stored for a short time until it is added to another file

CLM /ˌsiː el 'em/ *abbr* (*informal*) **career-limiting move** something you do that has a bad effect on your career, for example making mistakes, being rude to your boss, etc.

clock /klɒk; *AmE* klɑːk/ *verb*
[PHRV] **,clock 'in/'on** (*BrE*) (*AmE* **,punch 'in**) to record the time at which you arrive at work, especially by putting a card into a machine: *Staff should clock in on arrival.* **,clock 'out/'off** (*BrE*) (*AmE* **,punch 'out**) to record the time at which you leave work, especially by putting a card into a machine: *She clocks off at 5.15.* **,clock 'up sth** (*informal*) to reach a particular amount or number, especially one that is very large or high: *The*

company has clocked up nearly $400 million in losses. ◇ *clocking up record profits*

'clock speed *noun* [C]

(*IT*) the speed of a computer's CENTRAL PROCESSING UNIT (= the part that controls all the other parts of the computer), which is used as a measure of how fast the computer operates: *The new chip has a clock speed of 2.2 gigahertz.*

clone /kləʊn; *AmE* kloʊn/ *noun* [C]

1 (*IT*) a computer designed to work in exactly the same way as another more expensive one made by a different company: *a company producing IBM clones*
2 used in a disapproving way to say that a thing or a person seems to be an exact copy of sth or sb else: *He's just a clone of the boss.*

★ **close** /kləʊz; *AmE* kloʊz/ *verb, noun*
● *verb*
1 [+ obj *or* no obj] (about a shop/store, business, etc.) to finish business for the day; to not be open for people to use: *What time do the banks close?* ◇ *The storm closed the airport.* OPP OPEN
2 [+ obj *or* no obj] if a company, shop/store, etc. **closes**, or if you **close** it, it stops operating as a business: *Four of the manufacturer's plants are to close.* ◇ *The retailer said it would close 12 stores and cut 2 000 jobs.* ◇ *The factory has closed its doors for the last time.* OPP OPEN → CLOSE DOWN, CLOSE STH DOWN
3 [+ obj] to end an activity or event: *I took out all my money and closed my account.* ◇ *The company closes its books* (= completes its financial records) *on a quarterly basis.* OPP OPEN
4 [+ obj *or* no obj] to close a computer program that has been running; to stop operating: *Click on the 'X' in the top right-hand corner to close the window.* OPP OPEN
5 [no obj] if shares, currencies, etc. **close** at a particular price, they are worth that amount when people stop trading them at the beginning of the day: *a closing price of €19 a share* ◇ *The shares closed at $3.67.* SYN FINISH OPP OPEN
6 [+ obj *or* no obj] to agree to sth after having discussed it for a period of time; to be agreed: *The company is only days away from closing the deal.* ◇ *We hope the deal will close on Friday.*
7 [+ obj *or* no obj] if a meeting **closes** or sb **closes** it, it ends: *The meeting closed at 5.30.* OPP OPEN
8 [+ obj] to make it impossible for goods, people, etc. to come through: *Neighbouring countries have closed their borders.* OPP OPEN
9 (*Stock Exchange*) [+ obj] **close (out/off) sth** to sell all the shares in a particular collection, or to buy back shares you have borrowed and sold in order to return the shares, resulting in a final profit or loss: *Many investors closed out their positions ahead of the New Year's holidays.* → COVER *verb* (6)
PHR V **close 'down**; **close sth 'down** if a company, shop/store, etc. **closes down**, or if you **close it down**, it stops operating as a business: *The company is closing down two of its manufacturing plants.* OPP OPEN STH UP, OPEN UP → CLOSE *verb* (2), CLOSE-DOWN **close sth 'out** (*AmE*) to sell goods very cheaply in order to get rid of them quickly
● *noun* [C, usually sing.]

SEE ALSO: **complimentary close**

the end of the day of trading, especially on a stock exchange; the price of a share, bond, etc. at this time: *By the close of London trading, Wall Street was up 9.78 points.* SYN FINISH OPP OPEN
⊕ *a flat/low/weak close* ◆ *a firm/high/strong close*

close-circuit 'television = CLOSED-CIRCUIT TELEVISION

close 'company /kləʊs; *AmE* kloʊs/ (*also* **closed**

'company), (*both BrE*) (*AmE also* **close corpo'ration**, **closed corpo'ration**) *noun* [C]
a company whose shares are not bought and sold publicly but are owned by a small number of investors, especially the directors of the company

closed /kləʊzd; *AmE* kloʊzd/ *adjective*
1 [not before noun] shut, used especially about a shop/store or public building that is not open for a period of time: *The stock market will be closed on Monday for a national holiday.*
2 [usually before noun] limited to a particular group of people; not open to everyone: *The CEO spoke to union representatives in a closed meeting.*
IDM **behind closed 'doors** with only particular people being allowed to attend or know what is happening; in private: *The merger was discussed behind closed doors.*

closed 'bid *noun* [C]
(*Commerce*) a situation where companies compete to supply work or goods, or to buy sth, by offering a particular price or amount of money. The offers are kept secret until a particular time when they are all opened and the best offer is chosen: *All closed bids have to be in by 1 June.* → OPEN BID, SEALED BID

closed-circuit 'television (*also* **close-circuit 'television**, *less frequent*) *noun* [U] (*abbr* CCTV)
a television system that works within a limited area, for example a public building, to protect it from crime

closed 'company = CLOSE COMPANY
closed corpo'ration = CLOSE COMPANY

closed-'door *adjective* [only before noun]
used to describe work, a meeting, etc. that takes place privately: *closed-door meetings with selected investors*

closed-'door ,policy *noun* [C]
1 (*Trade*) the practice of making it difficult for foreign companies to do business in your country, for example by taxing their goods, in order to protect your own industry → PROTECTIONISM
2 the practice of keeping things secret and not allowing the media or anyone else to know anything about them

closed-'end *adjective* [only before noun]
(*Finance*)
1 (used about a contract or a loan) that must finish or be paid back at a fixed time in the future
2 (*AmE*) used to describe a type of investment company that can only issue a fixed number of shares: *a closed-end fund*
OPP OPEN-ENDED

closed 'market *noun* [C]
(*Economics*) a market in which foreign companies are not allowed to sell their goods or services

'close-down *noun* [C] (*BrE*)
when a company, shop/store, etc. stops operating, usually permanently: *Serious unemployment followed the close-down of many state-owned businesses.* ◇ *planned close-downs of plants for maintenance* → SHUTDOWN

closed 'shop (*AmE also* **'union shop**) *noun* [C]
(*HR*) a factory, business, etc. in which employees must all be members of a particular union → OPEN SHOP
⊕ *to abolish/enforce/establish/operate a closed shop*

closely held 'company (*BrE*) (*AmE* **closely-held corpo'ration**) *noun* [C]
a public company where five or fewer people own more than half of the shares

closeout /'kləʊzaʊt; *AmE* 'kloʊz-/ *noun* [C] (*AmE*)
(*Commerce*) an occasion when all the goods in a

shop/store that is going to stop operating are sold cheaply in order to get rid of them quickly
[SYN] CLOSING-DOWN SALE → CLOSE STH OUT at CLOSE

★ **closing** /'kləʊzɪŋ; AmE 'kloʊzɪŋ/ noun, adjective
● **noun**
1 [U,C] the act of shutting sth such as a factory, hospital, school, etc. permanently: *The plan includes the closing of some of the company's factories.* ◇ *jobs lost because of plant closings*
2 [U,C] the act of finishing business for the day, especially on a stock market: *The Nikkei stock index reached a record high at Friday's closing.* ◇ *The Dow Jones was down 3.6% an hour before the closing bell.*
3 [U] the state of being closed: *The factory will remain open except for the regular New Year closing.*
4 [U] the final stage in a sale, the arranging of a loan, etc. when all the details have been agreed: *a sale progressing from cold call to closing*
[OPP] OPENING → CLOSURE
● **adjective** [only before noun]
coming at the end of sth: *the closing stages of the deal* [OPP] OPENING

,**closing 'balance** noun [C, usually sing.]
(*Accounting*) the **balance** shown in an account at the end of an accounting period → OPENING BALANCE

'**closing date** noun [C]
the last date by which sth must be done, such as applying for a job or entering a competition: *The closing date for applications is 31 March.*

,**closing-'down sale** noun [C] (BrE)
(*Commerce*) an occasion when all the goods in a shop/store that is going to stop operating are sold cheaply in order to get rid of them quickly
[SYN] CLOSEOUT → CLOSE DOWN at CLOSE verb

,**closing 'entry** noun [C]
(*Accounting*) a final amount that is written in an account at the end of an accounting period, before moving the BALANCE to the account for the next period

,**closing 'stock** noun [U]
(*Accounting*) the amount of goods that a shop/store has available for sale at the end of a particular period of time; the value of these goods

'**closing time** noun [C,U]
the time when a pub, shop/store, bar, etc. ends business for the day and people have to leave

closure /'kləʊʒə(r); AmE 'kloʊ-/ noun [C,U]
the situation when a factory, school, hospital, etc. shuts permanently: *The company is hoping to avoid plant closures and lay-offs.* ◇ *factories earmarked for closure*
● **branch/plant/store** closures • to **avoid/face/force/ lead to/prevent** closure(s)

clothing /'kləʊðɪŋ; AmE 'kloʊðɪŋ/ noun [U]
clothes, especially a particular type of clothes: *Protective clothing must be worn at all times.* ◇ *the country's leading retailer of men's clothing*
● **an item/a piece/an article** of clothing • a clothing **company/factory/manufacturer/store** • the clothing **business/industry/trade**

CLU /,si: el 'ju:/ = CHARTERED LIFE UNDERWRITER

'**cluster a,nalysis** noun [U,C]
(*Marketing*) a way of analysing large amounts of data to find groups of people, things, etc. that are similar to each other in some way: *A cluster analysis of 10 000 customers found that 95% fell into seven groups (clusters).*

CLV /,si: el 'vi:/ abbr
(*Marketing*) customer lifetime value → LIFETIME VALUE

CM /,si: 'em/ = CATEGORY MANAGEMENT

CMA /,si: em 'eɪ/ = CERTIFIED MANAGEMENT ACCOUNTANT

CMR /,si: em 'ɑ:(r)/ = ROAD CONSIGNMENT NOTE
[NOTE] CMR is formed from the first letters of the words in a French phrase.

Co. /kəʊ; AmE koʊ/ abbr (usually used in written English)
(often used in names) company: *the Consett Iron Co.* ◇ *Pitt, Briggs and Co.* See note at LTD

co- /kəʊ; AmE koʊ/ prefix (used in nouns, adjectives, adverbs and verbs)
together with: *co-founder of the company* ◇ *co-chief/ co-director* ◇ *cooperatively* ◇ *coexist*

c/o abbr (only used in written English)
1 (*Accounting*) = CARRIED OVER
2 care of used to address a letter to sb at an address that is not their own home: *Mr S R Brown c/o Ms D A Philips*

coach /kəʊtʃ; AmE koʊtʃ/ noun, verb
● **noun** [C]
1 (*HR*) a person who trains sb to do sth or gives lessons or advice: *Coaches can help you become a better business leader.*
● **a business/career/executive/team** coach
2 (*BrE*) a comfortable bus for carrying passengers over long distances: *Travel is by coach to Berlin.*
3 (*AmE*) the cheapest seats in a plane: *to fly coach*
● **coach fares/passengers/seats**
● **verb** [+ obj or no obj]
(*HR*) to give sb training, lessons or advice: *She coaches people on how to get their ideas across effectively.* ▶ '**coaching** noun [U]: *a one-on-one coaching session* ◇ *The training programme uses group exercises and coaching pairs.* → MENTOR

coalface /'kəʊlfeɪs; AmE 'koʊl-/ (also **face**) noun [C]
the place deep inside a mine where the coal is cut out of the rock
[IDM] **at the 'coalface** (BrE) where the real work is done, not just where people talk about it: *Some managers would benefit from spending a few weeks at the coalface.*

coalition /,kəʊə'lɪʃn; AmE ,koʊə-/ noun
1 [C with sing./pl. verb] a group formed by people from several different groups agreeing to work together for a particular purpose: *They have formed a coalition to protect the future of manufacturing in the region.* ◇ *coalition partners*
● **to build/create/form/join/lead** a coalition
2 [U] the act of two or more groups joining together: *their planned coalition with the American airline*

COBOL (also spelled **Cobol**) /'kəʊbɒl; AmE 'koʊbɑ:l; -bɔ:l/ noun [U]
(*IT*) **Common Business Oriented Language** a computer language designed to write programs for use in business: *a program in Cobol*

COD /,si: əʊ 'di:; AmE oʊ/ abbr
(*Trade*) ,**cash on de'livery** or in American English **col,lect on de'livery** payment for goods will be made when the goods are delivered: *Most people will offer a discount for cash on delivery.* ◇ *to pay COD*

★ **code** /kəʊd; AmE koʊd/ noun

SEE ALSO: **area code, authorization ~, bar ~, building ~, colour-~, dialling ~, dress ~,** etc.

1 [C,U] (often used in compounds) a system of words, letters, numbers or symbols that represent information about sth: *Tap your code number into the machine.* ◇ *In the event of the machine not operating correctly, an error code will appear.*
● **an access/error/a log-in/product/reference/security** code

2 [C] a set of standards that members of a particular profession, or people who do a particular activity, agree to follow or are recommended to follow: *The Department has issued an approved code of practice for the management of noise in the workplace.* ◇ *They failed to observe the banks' voluntary code of conduct.*
✪ *to approve/draft/draw up/produce* a code of practice, etc. **♦** *to adhere to/break/comply with/ follow/observe* a code of practice, etc.
3 *(IT)* [U] a system of computer programming instructions: *to write code*
4 [C] = DIALLING CODE

coder /ˈkəʊdə(r); *AmE* ˈkoʊdər/ *noun* [C]
(IT) a person whose job is writing computer code

ˈcode-ˌsharing *noun* [U]
an arrangement between airlines that allows them to carry each other's passengers and use their own set of letters and numbers for flights provided by another airline: *a code-sharing agreement between KLM and British Airways*

ˌco-determiˈnation *noun* [U]
(HR) a system where workers as well as managers are involved in making decisions in a company, especially when workers have representatives on boards of management

C. of C. = CHAMBER OF COMMERCE

coffers /ˈkɒfəz; *AmE* ˈkɔːfərz; ˈkɑːfərz/ *noun* [pl.]
(usually used in written English)
(usually used in newspapers) a way of referring to the money that a government, an organization, etc. has available to spend: *The new taxes will contribute over $60 billion to government coffers.*

ˌcognitive ˈdissonance *noun* [U]
(Marketing) a feeling of worry and disappointment that people often feel after they have bought sth, for example if they feel that it is not as good as they expected or that another product might suit them better: *Almost all major purchases result in cognitive dissonance.*

COGS = COST OF GOODS SOLD

coˈhesion fund *(also spelled* **Cohesion Fund***)* *noun* [sing.]
(Economics) money that the European Union uses to help the economic development of its poorer members

coin /kɔɪn/ *noun, verb*
● *noun*
1 [C] a small flat piece of metal used as money: *a 2-euro coin*
2 [U] money made of metal: *notes and coin*
● *verb* [+ obj]
to make coins out of metal
IDM **be ˈcoining it (in)**; **be ˈcoining money** *(both BrE)* *(informal)* to earn a lot of money quickly or easily: *He has a huge expenses allowance and must be coining it in.*

coinage /ˈkɔɪnɪdʒ/ *noun* [U]
(Economics) the coins or the system of money used in a particular country: *gold/silver/bronze coinage*

coˌincident ˈindicator *(also* **coˈincident ecoˈnomic ˈindicator***, less frequent) noun* [C]
(Economics) a factor that is a direct result of a country's economic situation at a particular time, and can therefore be used as one of the measures of the state of the economy at that time: *Coincident indicators like industrial production, personal income and GNP all go up when the economy is going well.* → LAGGING INDICATOR, LEADING INDICATOR

col. *abbr*
a short way of writing **column** (= a series of numbers or words arranged one under the other)

COLA /ˈkəʊlə; *AmE* ˈkoʊlə/ = COST-OF-LIVING ADJUSTMENT, COST-OF-LIVING ALLOWANCE

ˌcold-ˈcalling *noun* [U]
(Marketing) the practice of telephoning or visiting sb that you do not know in order to sell them sth: *One million people have said no to junk mail and cold-calling.* ◇ *a course for professionals who want to improve their cold-calling skills* ▸ **ˌcold-ˈcall** *verb* [+ obj or no obj]: *I cold-called 500 companies.* ▸ **ˌcold ˈcall** *noun* [C]: *I've just spent three hours making cold calls.* ▸ **ˌcold-ˈcaller** *noun* [C]

ˌcold-ˈcanvassing *noun* [U]
(Marketing) the practice of asking sb that you do not know if they are interested in sth, for example employing you or buying a product

ˌcold ˈcash = HARD CASH

★ collaborate /kəˈlæbəreɪt/ *verb* [no obj]
to work together with sb in order to produce or achieve sth : *We have collaborated on many projects over the years.* ◇ *They are collaborating closely with two other companies in this research.*

★ collaboration /kəˌlæbəˈreɪʃn/ *noun*
1 [U,C] the act of working with another person or group of people to create or produce sth: *Four firms have been involved in technical collaboration on this project.* ◇ *Many of their products are designed in collaboration with customers.* ◇ *close collaboration between schools and industry*
2 [C] a piece of work produced by two or more people or groups of people working together

collaborative /kəˈlæbərətɪv; *AmE* -reɪtɪv/ *adjective* [only before noun]
involving, or done by, several people or groups of people working together
✪ *collaborative projects/research/studies/ventures*

colˌlaborative ˈworking *noun* [U]
(HR) a method of working in which people in different places or in different organizations work together using email, VIDEOCONFERENCING, etc.

★ collapse /kəˈlæps/ *verb, noun*
● *verb* [no obj]
1 to fail suddenly or completely: *Talks between management and unions have collapsed.* ◇ *Investors lost their money when the company collapsed.*
2 to decrease suddenly in amount or value: *The company's stock market value has collapsed to under $10 million in the last year.*
● *noun* [C,U]
1 a sudden failure of sth, such as an institution, a business or a course of action: *the collapse of two important companies* ◇ *This breakdown in trust led to the collapse of the deal.* ◇ *a wave of corporate collapses*
2 a sudden fall in value: *the collapse in technology prices* ◇ *the collapse of the Nasdaq index* ◇ *share price collapses*

collate /kəˈleɪt; *AmE* ˈkoʊl-/ *verb* [+ obj]
1 to collect information together from different sources in order to examine and compare it: *to collate data/information/figures*
2 to collect pages and arrange them in the correct order, especially pages of a document when printing or copying it
▸ **collation** /kəˈleɪʃn/ *noun* [U]: *the collation of information*

collateral /kəˈlætərəl/ *noun* [U]
1 *(Finance)* property or sth valuable that you promise to give sb if you cannot pay back money that you borrow: *The company cannot sell its assets as they act as collateral for its loans.*
2 *(Marketing)* *(AmE)* = COLLATERAL MATERIAL

collateralize , **-ise** /kə'lætərəlaɪz/ verb [+ obj] (Finance) (usually **be collateralized**) to provide COLLATERAL for a loan, bonds, etc: *The loan is collateralized by the company's plant and equipment.*

col,lateral ma'terial noun [U] (also **col,lateral ma'terials** [pl.]) (also **col'lateral** [U]) (all AmE) (Marketing) printed information about a product, service or company, such as BROCHURES or LEAFLETS, that is usually sent or given directly to individual customers: *We designed a logo for use on the company's website, business cards and other collateral material.*

★ **colleague** /'kɒliːɡ; AmE 'kɑː-/ noun [C] a person who works at the same place as you, especially in a profession or a business: *a colleague of mine from the office* ◊ *an email from one of my colleagues* ◊ *swapping ideas with colleagues* ✪ *a former/junior/new/senior colleague*

VOCABULARY BUILDING

Colleagues and rivals

People in the same organization
● *If I'm not here, one of my colleagues will be able to help you.*
● *(especially AmE) Most of my co-workers are older than me.*

People in the same job but in a different organization
● *She immediately informed her counterpart in the US.*
● *(used especially in newspapers) the director of BMW and his opposite number at Volvo*

People that you are competing with
● *We're constantly developing new products to stay ahead of the competition.*
● *They are concerned about competitors stealing their ideas.*
● *Our biggest rivals are the budget airlines.*
● *If we lose the case, we have to pay the other side's legal fees.*

★ **collect** /kə'lekt/ verb
1 [+ obj] to obtain money that is owed; to be paid: *The rent is collected from tenants at the end of each month.* ◊ *The dealer collects a small fee for every trade.*
✪ *to collect debts/fees/payments/rent/taxes*
2 [+ obj] to bring things together from different people or places: *We collected the data from interviews with customers.*
✪ *to collect data/evidence/information/statistics*
3 (Finance) [+ obj] (about a bank) to receive a cheque and arrange for the money to be paid from the bank account of the person or company who wrote it: *The bank collected the cheque without checking the name of the payee.* ◊ *the collecting bank*
4 (informal) [no obj] to get sb/sth to pay back the money that they owe: *He's come to collect.* ◊ *Creditors often find it hard to collect on their debts.*

★ **collection** /kə'lekʃn/ noun

SEE ALSO: **debt collection, documentary collection**

1 [U,C] the activity of obtaining money that is owed; the amount of money that is obtained: *My work ranged from small debt collection to large acquisitions.* ◊ *Many states are facing declining tax collections.*
✪ *debt/tax/rent/revenue collection* ● *to improve/speed up collection*

2 [C] a group of objects that has been collected; a group of objects or people: *They have built up a rich collection of resources to help small businesses.*
3 [C,U] an act of taking sth away from a place; an act of bringing things together into one place: *The last collection from this mailbox is at 5.15 p.m.* ◊ *data collection*
4 (Finance) [U,C] the act of a bank arranging for a cheque, STANDING ORDER, etc. to be paid from a bank account: *You can make a simple call to the bank asking it to suspend collection so that no money is transferred.*

col'lection ,agency (also **com,mercial col'lection ,agency**) noun [C] (Finance) a business whose work is to obtain payment of money that has been owed to a company or an organization for a long time: *a debt collection agency*

collective /kə'lektɪv/ adjective, noun
● **adjective** [usually before noun] done or shared by all members of a group of people; involving a whole group of society: *It was a collective effort to get the project finished on time.*
✪ *a collective effort/decision* ● *collective action/decision-making/management/ownership/responsibility*
▶ **col'lectively** adverb: *The management board is collectively responsible for all decisions.*
● **noun** [C] a group of people who own a business or a farm and run it together; the business that they run: *an independent collective making films for TV*

col,lective a'greement noun [C,U] (HR) a signed agreement made between two groups of people, especially an agreement made by a union and an employer about the pay and working conditions of the union members; the process of making the agreement: *Working hours and rest periods should only be changed by collective agreement.*

col,lective 'bargaining noun [U]

SEE ALSO: **free collective bargaining**

(HR) discussions between a union and an employer about the pay and working conditions of the union members: *Job losses will be dealt with through collective bargaining.*
✪ *a collective bargaining agreement/deal/system* ● *collective bargaining rights/rules*

col,lective re'dundancy noun [U,C] (HR) the situation when a number of workers have to leave their jobs within a short period of time because there is no more work available for them

collector /kə'lektə(r)/ noun [C] a person who obtains money that is owed
✪ *debt/rent/tax collectors*

collision /kə'lɪʒn/ noun [C,U] an accident in which two vehicles crash into each other and there is damage or injury: *The vehicle is insured for collision damage.*
IDM **be on a col'lision course (with sb/sth)** to be in a situation which is almost certain to cause a disagreement: *The government is on a collision course with farmers over subsidies.*

collusion /kə'luːʒn/ noun [U] (formal) secret agreement especially in order to do sth dishonest or harmful: *The airline suspects collusion between insurance companies in setting the new rates.* ▶ **collusive** /kə'luːsɪv/ adjective: *a collusive agreement to reduce production*

'**color-code** = COLOUR-CODE

'**color ,supplement** = COLOUR SUPPLEMENT

'**colour-code** (AmE spelling **color-~**) noun [C] a system of marking things with different colours so that you can easily identify them: *Follow the colour code carefully on all electrical wiring.*

▶ **'colour-,coded** (*AmE spelling* **color-**) *adjective*: *Each type of material has a colour-coded label.*

'colour ,supplement (*AmE spelling* **color ~**) *noun* [C] (*BrE only*)
(*Marketing*) a magazine printed in colour and forming an extra part of a newspaper, particularly on Saturdays or Sundays: *advertising in the colour supplements*

column /'kɒləm; *AmE* 'kɑːləm/ *noun* [C]
1 (*also* **col.**) one of the vertical sections into which the printed page of a book, newspaper, etc. is divided: *a column of text* → COLUMN INCH
2 a part of a newspaper or magazine which appears regularly and deals with a particular subject or is written by a particular writer: *the financial columns*
3 a series of numbers or words arranged one under the other: *adding up a column of figures* ◇ *The data is arranged in rows and columns.*

,column 'inch *noun* [C]

SEE ALSO: **single column inch**

(*Marketing*) the amount of text or pictures that fits into 2.5 centimetres (one **inch**) of a column in a newspaper, magazine, etc., used especially to measure the length of advertisements: *Our advertising rates are $12 per column inch.*

,co-'manager *noun* [C]
(*Finance*) a bank or other financial institution that works with the LEAD MANAGER in order to help a company sell new shares, bonds, etc. A **co-manager** agrees to buy a particular amount of the shares, bonds, etc. and sell them to investors: *Morgan Stanley and Alex Brown & Sons acted as co-managers for the offering.*

★ **combination** /,kɒmbɪ'neɪʃn; *AmE* ,kɑːm-/ *noun* [C,U]

SEE ALSO: **business combination**

two or more things joined together; the act of joining two or more things together: *The combination of the two producers would create the world's largest chemical company.* ◇ *The firm is working on a new product* **in combination with** *several overseas partners.*

★ **combine** *verb, noun*
● *verb* /kəm'baɪn/
1 [+ obj *or* no obj] to join two or more things or groups together to form a single one; to come together to form a single thing or group: *plans to combine the two firms* ◇ *The three oil companies* **combined forces** (= joined together) **to form** *LevelSeas.*
2 [+ obj] to have two or more different features or characteristics; to put two or more different things, features or qualities together: *The device combines a computer and mobile phone.* ◇ *We are still looking for someone who combines all the necessary qualities.*
▶ **com'bined** *adjective* [only before noun]: *The companies had combined sales of £30 million last year.*
● *noun* /'kɒmbaɪn; *AmE* 'kɑːm-/ [C]
a group of people or organizations acting together in business: *He heads a combine that covers both the traditional media and the Internet world.*

com,bined 'ratio *noun* [C]
(*Insurance*) a way of measuring how successful an insurance company's business is by comparing the amount of money the company receives from its customers (**premiums**) with the amount it pays out in claims and expenses: *Their combined ratio has improved from 140% to 105%.*

come /kʌm/ *verb* [no obj] (**came** /keɪm/ **come**)
NOTE Most idioms containing **come** are at the

entries for the nouns, verbs or adjectives in the idioms, for example, **come due** is at **due**.
IDM **come under 'fire** to be criticized strongly: *She has come under fire from shareholders for her management of the company.* → idiom at DELIVER
PHR V **,come 'down** to become lower in value or amount: *Our costs have come down.* ◇ *Gas is coming down in price.* **,come 'in 1** (about money) to be earned or received regularly: *We can't go on much longer without any money coming in.* **2** (about a law or rule) to be introduced; to begin to be used: *The act came in in 2001.* **,come 'in (at/before, etc. sth)** to be calculated as a final amount: *Sales for 2005 will come in at around $6.8 billion.* ◇ *Revenues came in below estimates.* **,come 'in (on sth)** to become involved in sth: *If you want to come in on the deal, you need to decide now.* **,come 'off** (*informal*) to be successful; to happen: *The deal failed to come off.* **,come 'off sth; ,come 'off** (*not used in the passive*) (about prices, etc.) to start to change, especially to start to decrease after increasing for a period of time: *The shares have just come off an all-time high of 570 cents* (= the price is starting to fall). **,come 'off sth** (*not used in the passive*) to start to recover from sth: *The country was just coming off a recession.* **,come 'out at/to sth** (*not used in the passive*) to add up to a particular cost or sum: *The total bill comes out at €500.* **,come 'out of sth** (*not used in the passive*) to reach the end of a difficult period: *The economy is coming out of recession.* **,come 'out with sth** (*not used in the passive*) to create sth and make it available to people: *The company has come out with a new type of telephone.* **,come 'through (with sth)** to successfully do or provide sth that people expect or that you have promised to do: *The bank finally came through with the money.* **'come to sth** (*not used in the passive*)
1 to add up to sth: *The retailer's annual sales come to €70 million.* **2** to reach a particular state or situation: *The contract came to an end in March.* **,come 'up for sth** (*not used in the passive*) to reach the time when a decision must be made about the future of sb/sth: *The contract is coming up for renewal.* **,come 'up with sth** (*not used in the passive*) to find or produce an answer, an amount of money, etc: *She came up with a new idea for increasing sales.* ◇ *How soon can you come up with the money?*

COMEX /'kɒmeks; *AmE* 'kɑːm-/ (*also* **COMEX di,vision**) *noun* [sing.]
the part of the New York Mercantile Exchange that deals with metals such as gold and silver: *On the Comex, silver rose to $7.26 an ounce.* → NYMEX

'comfort ,letter *noun* [C]
(*Finance*)
1 = LETTER OF COMFORT
2 a statement made by an AUDITOR when a company is planning to sell new shares, to say that they have found no problems in the company's financial records

'comfort zone *noun* [C]
1 a situation in which sb feels safe, relaxed and confident: *New challenges can push you outside your comfort zone.*
2 if a person is **in the comfort zone**, he or she does not work very hard and so does not produce the best possible results

command /kə'mɑːnd; *AmE* kə'mænd/ *noun* [C]
(*IT*) an instruction given to a computer: *Use the 'ls' command to get a list of the files on the disk.*

com,mand and con'trol *noun* [U]
a way of managing a company or country in which a single leader or small group makes all the decisions and gives people detailed instructions on

what to do: *The new economy relies on cooperation, not command and control.*

com,mand e'conomy *(also* con,trolled e'conomy*) noun* [C]
(Economics) a type of economic system in which a government controls its country's industries and decides what goods should be produced and in what amounts: *the former command economies of Eastern Europe and the Soviet Union* SYN PLANNED ECONOMY OPP MARKET ECONOMY

'comment card *noun* [C]
(Marketing) a small piece of stiff paper on which customers answer questions to give their opinions about a company's products or services: *We invite all our passengers to fill out comment cards.*

★ **commerce** /'kɒmɜːs; *AmE* 'kɑːmɜːrs/ *noun* [U]

SEE ALSO: **chamber of commerce, e-commerce, Internet ~, m-commerce, Net ~, t-commerce**

the business of buying and selling things; trade: *leaders of industry and commerce* ◇ *trade figures produced by the Commerce Department* ◇ *More and more commerce is moving to the Internet.*

'Commerce Clause *noun* [sing.]
(Law) a part of the US CONSTITUTION (= the basic law of the country) that allows the national parliament (**Congress**) to control trade between the US and foreign countries and between the different states within the US

★ **commercial** /kə'mɜːʃl; *AmE* kə'mɜːrʃl/ *adjective, noun*
● *adjective*
1 [usually before noun] connected with the buying and selling of goods and services: *the commercial heart of the city* ◇ *Tesco's commercial director* ◇ *He owns hotels and property and has a range of commercial interests.* ◇ *commercial flights* (= ones that carry passengers)
2 [only before noun] connected with businesses or the process of carrying out business: *commercial insurance companies* ◇ *legislation controlling the noise level from industrial and commercial premises* ◇ *a downturn in the commercial property market* ◇ *The group has a fleet of 38 000 commercial vehicles for hire.*
3 [only before noun] making or intended to make a profit: *the commercial use of genetically-modified crops* ◇ *The new product was not a commercial success* (= it did not make much money).
4 (about television or radio) paid for by the money charged for broadcasting advertisements: *a commercial radio station/TV channel*
▶ **commercially** /kə'mɜːʃəli/ *adverb*: *commercially produced/grown/developed* ◇ *The product will be commercially available next year.*
● *noun* [C]
1 an advertisement on television or on the radio: *TV commercials* ◇ *a commercial break* (= a time during or between programmes when advertisements are shown)
2 *(Stock Exchange)* **commercials** [pl.] shares in companies that buy and sell goods to individual customers: *In the City today, commercials rose slightly but there was little interest in industrials.*

com,mercial 'agency *noun* [C,U]
1 *(Property)* a business whose work is to buy and sell property, such as office buildings, for businesses to use: *We have to cut 65 jobs in our residential and commercial agency divisions.*
2 *(Finance)* *(BrE)* a business whose work is to collect information about the financial position of a person or a business, especially whether they would be able to pay back any money that they borrow
SYN CREDIT REFERENCE AGENCY

3 *(Commerce)* a business that provides a service to other businesses and intends to make a profit: *We work independently, not through a commercial agency or a tourist board.*

com,mercial 'agent *noun* [C]
1 *(Trade)* an independent person who works on behalf of a company to find business for it, especially abroad: *The company needs a commercial agent for Chile.*
2 *(Property)* a person or a business whose work is to buy and sell property, such as office buildings, for businesses to use: *a commercial agent specializing in business, commercial/industrial leasing and property investment*

com,mercial 'art *noun* [U]
the activity of designing advertisements, the materials used to pack products, etc: *She trained at commercial art school.* ▶ **com,mercial 'artist** *noun* [C]: *We have a large team of graphic designers, commercial artists and copywriters.*

com,mercial 'bank *noun* [C]
a bank with branches in many different places, that provides a range of services, especially related to CURRENT ACCOUNTS, loans and saving money, for people and businesses: *big commercial banks, such as Barclays and NatWest* ◇ *the Commercial Bank of New York* ▶ **com,mercial 'banking** *noun* [U]

com'mercial bill = TRADE BILL

com,mercial col'lection ,agency = COLLECTION AGENCY

com,mercial corres'pondence *noun* [U]
business letters, emails, and other documents, especially as a subject of study

Com,mercial 'Counsellor *(AmE spelling ~* **counselor***) noun* [C]
(Trade) a government official who works in a foreign country and helps to develop trade between that country and their home country: *the Commercial Counsellor at the Australian embassy in Washington* → TRADE REPRESENTATIVE

commercialize , **-ise** /kə'mɜːʃəlaɪz; *AmE* -'mɜːrʃl-/ *verb* [+ obj]
1 to develop a product into sth that can be produced and sold widely: *They research, develop and commercialize vaccines for cancer and other diseases.*
2 to produce sth to try to make as much profit as possible: *Their music has become very commercialized in recent years.*
▶ **commercialization** , **-isation** /kə,mɜːʃəlaɪ'zeɪʃn; *AmE* -,mɜːrʃlə'z-/ *noun* [U]: *moving projects to commercialization quickly* ◇ *the commercialization of sport*

com,mercial 'law *noun* [U]
(Law) the collection of laws that deal with all aspects of business and trade, including contracts, buying, selling, storing and transporting goods, etc. SYN MERCANTILE LAW

com,mercial 'loan *noun* [C]
(Finance) a loan made to a business

com,mercial 'manager *noun* [C]
the person who is in charge of the part of a company that deals with selling goods or services

com,mercial mo'nopoly *noun* [C]
(Economics) a situation where one buyer or supplier can fix the price of a product, a raw material, or a service: *In the UK, air traffic services are provided by a commercial monopoly.*

com,mercial 'paper *noun* [U]
(Finance) a method that a large company, bank, etc. can use to borrow money from investors, usually for a period of less than a year. The lender cannot take the assets of the company if the loan is not

repaid: *222 companies had issued sterling commercial paper*.

➕ to **default on/issue** commercial paper

com'mercial ˌsector *noun* [sing.]

(*Economics*) the part of a country's economy that consists of businesses that are not involved in manufacturing or transport, for example, hotels, restaurants, offices, shops/stores and other businesses that offer services, and government organizations, health and education institutions, etc.

comˌmercial 'set *noun* [C]

(*Trade*) the documents that are required when exporting goods, usually including a BILL OF EXCHANGE, a BILL OF LADING, an INVOICE and an insurance certificate

comˌmercial 'traveller (*AmE spelling ~* **traveler**) *noun* [C] (*BrE only, old-fashioned*)

a person who sells a company's goods or services by visiting possible customers, usually receiving a COMMISSION on what they sell

SYN SALES REPRESENTATIVE

comˌmercial 'treaty = TRADE AGREEMENT

commingle /kə'mɪŋgl/ *verb* [+ obj or no obj]

to mix different things together: *Each company's data can be stored separately or commingled* **with** *the data of the other companies in the group.* ◇ *commingled fibres* ▶ **com'mingling** *noun* [U]: *the commingling of expired produce with fresh produce* ◇ *the commingling of funds*

★ **commission** /kə'mɪʃn/ *noun, verb*

● *noun*

SEE ALSO: **Equal Employment Opportunities Commission, Equal Opportunities ~, overriding ~, Securities and Exchange ~**

---

1 (*Commerce*) [U,C] an amount of money that is paid to sb for selling goods or services and which usually increases with the quantity they sell: *You get a 10% commission on everything you sell.* ◇ *They work* **on commission** (= they are paid according to how much they sell) *and so they try to sell you more.* See note at PRICE, SALARY

➕ to **earn/get/pay** (a) commission

2 [U,C] an amount of money that is charged by a bank, for example, for providing a particular service: *Agents charge their clients 2% commission on the sale of a house.* ◇ *The two banks have similar commission rates.*

➕ to **charge/pay** a commission

3 (*often* **Commission**) [C] a group of people who are officially asked to find out about a problem and suggest some actions in a report: *The Commission will investigate the number of jobs created.* ◇ *She is to head a commission to look into working conditions in the industry.* ◇ *a commission of enquiry*

➕ to **appoint/head/set up** a commission ◆ a commission **investigates/reports on/studies** sth

4 (*often* **Commission**) [C] an official organization with a particular purpose that manages sth or makes sure that the law is obeyed: *the Equal Opportunities Commission* → EUROPEAN COMMISSION

➕ to **appoint/head/set up** a commission ◆ a commission **investigates/reports on/studies** sth

5 [C] a formal request to an artist or a writer, for example, to produce a piece of work: *I received a commission to write an article.*

➕ to **accept/be given/get/receive** a commission

IDM **in/out of com'mission** available/not available to be used: *Several planes are temporarily out of commission and undergoing safety checks.*

● *verb* [+ obj]

to officially ask sb to write, make or create sth or to do a task for you: *The survey on consumer taste was commissioned by local stores.*

comˈmission ˌagent *noun* [C]

(*Trade*) a person or company who sells goods for sb in another country and is paid a percentage of the value of the goods for this service: *We are looking for somebody to act as a commission agent in the region.*

comˈmission ˌbroker *noun* [C]

(*Stock Exchange*) a person who buys and sells shares, bonds, etc. for other people and is paid a percentage of their value for this service

SYN BROKER

commissioner /kə'mɪʃənə(r)/ *noun* [C]

the person in charge of, or a member of, a COMMISSION (= an official group of people who are responsible for finding out about sth or for controlling sth): *the EU Transport Commissioner*

commitment /kə'mɪtmənt/ *noun*

1 [C,U] a promise to do sth or to behave in a particular way; a promise to support sb/sth; the fact of committing yourself: *The company's commitment to providing quality at low prices has been vital to its success.* ◇ *a commitment to excellence*

➕ a **clear/firm/formal/serious/strong** commitment ◆ a **continuing/long-term** commitment ◆ to **give/make** a commitment

2 [C,U] **commitment (of sb/sth) (to sth/sb)** the willingness to give time, money, effort, etc. in order to achieve sth; complete loyalty to one organization, person, etc: *Developing a new product requires a major commitment of time and money.* ◇ *He demands total commitment from his staff.*

➕ to **demand/lack/need/require** commitment ◆ **employee/personal/total** commitment

3 [C] a thing that you have promised or agreed to do; something that you have to do: *The company became unable to meet its financial commitments and went bankrupt.* ◇ *Mr Castorri has a prior commitment and is unable to attend.*

➕ **business/contractual/family/financial** commitments ◆ to **fulfil/honour/meet** a commitment

comˈmitment fee *noun* [C]

(*Finance*) a charge made by a bank for keeping a loan available for a customer to use later

comˈmitment ˌletter *noun* [C]

(*Finance*) a document formally offering to lend money to sb: *All lenders issue a commitment letter in connection with a mortgage loan.*

committed /kə'mɪtɪd/ *adjective*

willing to work hard and give your time and energy to sth; believing strongly in sth: *a highly committed workforce*

★ **committee** /kə'mɪti/ *noun* [C with sing./pl. verb]

SEE ALSO: **creditors' committee, management ~, steering ~**

---

a group of people who are chosen, usually by a larger group, to make decisions or to deal with a particular subject: *She's on the management committee.* ◇ *The Monetary Policy Committee has/have voted to keep interest rates unchanged.* ◇ *a committee member/a member of the committee* ◇ *a committee meeting*

➕ to **create/establish/form/set up** a committee ◆ to **be/serve/sit** on a committee ◆ to **be appointed to/be elected to/chair** a committee ◆ a committee **meets/votes**

comˈmodities ˌmarket = COMMODITY MARKET

★ **commodity** /kə'mɒdəti; AmE -'mɑːd-/ noun [C] (plural **commodities**)

SEE ALSO: dry commodities, hard ~, soft ~

1 (Finance) a product or a raw material, such as grain, coffee, cotton or metals, that can be bought and sold in large quantities, especially between countries: rice, flour and other basic commodities ◊ a drop in commodity prices
○ to deal/invest/trade in commodities • commodity exports/prices/trading
2 a thing that is useful or has a useful quality: Time is a precious commodity.

com'modity ex,change noun [C]
(Finance) an organization, a system or a place for business or trade in **commodities**: the Tokyo Commodity Exchange

com,modity 'futures noun [pl.]
(Finance) **commodities** that are bought at an agreed price to be delivered at a date in the future: trading/investing in commodity futures

com'modity ,market (also **com'modities ,market**) noun [C]
(Finance) business or trade in **commodities**; a place where this is done: The price of cotton collapsed on the world commodity market.

com'modity ,product noun [C]
(Marketing) a product that looks the same, functions in the same way, etc., whoever produces it: Customers are now aware that car tyres are not a commodity product. ◊ Price is the key to competition in commodity product markets. → DIFFERENTIATED PRODUCT

commonality /,kɒmə'næləti; AmE ,kɑːm-/ noun [U,C] (plural **commonalities**)
the state of sharing features or qualities; a feature or quality that is shared: There is little commonality between the systems used by the different departments. ◊ The three aircraft share 98% parts and systems commonality (= they use the same parts in their production).

,**common 'carrier** (also ,**public 'carrier**) noun [C]
1 (IT) a company that provides TELECOMMUNICATIONS services to the public: the common carrier network
2 (Law; Transport) a company that transports people or goods for the general public

,**common 'law** noun [U]
(Law) (in England, the US, Australia and some other countries) a system of laws that have been developed from customs and from decisions made by judges, not created by Parliament: Giving false information to police officers is against common law. ◊ a common law crime → CIVIL LAW

,**common 'market** noun [C, usually sing.]
(Economics)
1 a group of countries that have agreed on low taxes on goods traded between countries in the group, and higher fixed taxes on goods imported from countries outside the group: the Central American Common Market
2 Common Market a former name of the European Union

,**common 'ownership** (also ,**ownership in 'common**) noun [U]
(Law)
1 the fact of sth, such as a piece of land, a building or a company, being owned equally by more than one person or group: land in common ownership
2 the fact of one or more companies being owned by the same person or group: The directive allows common ownership of track and rail operators by a single group.

,**common 'pricing** = PRICE-FIXING

,**common 'share** = ORDINARY SHARE

,**common 'stock** (BrE also ,**ordinary 'stock**, less frequent) noun [C,U]
(Finance) shares in a company that give the owner the right to a DIVIDEND (= money paid to shareholders) according to how much profit the company has made, and the right to vote at meetings of shareholders: The price of a share of a company's common stock generally changes daily. → ORDINARY SHARE, PREFERRED STOCK See note at SHARE

comms /kɒmz; AmE kɑːmz/ noun [pl.]
(IT) used to refer to communications between different computers, and the equipment that makes this possible
○ comms packages/programs/software
NOTE Comms is a short form of the word communications.

★ **communication** /kə,mjuːnɪ'keɪʃn/ noun

SEE ALSO: corporate communication, non-verbal ~, open ~, organizational ~

1 [U] the activity or process of expressing ideas and feelings or of giving people information: She has excellent communication skills. ◊ We are in regular communication by email. ◊ Effective communication is the key to good sales.
○ external/internal communication
2 [U] (often **communications** [pl.]) methods of sending information, especially telephones, radio, computers, etc: They were quick to adopt video conferencing as a communication tool.
○ communication(s) devices/equipment/technology/tools • the communications business/industry/sector
3 communications [pl.] the road, rail, aircraft, sea, etc. systems that allow goods and passengers to be transported from one place to another: The new airport will improve communications between the islands.
○ a communications infrastructure/network/system
4 (formal) [C] a message, letter or telephone call: This letter is to confirm our recent telephone communication.

communicator /kə'mjuːnɪkeɪtə(r)/ noun [C]
a person who is able to describe their ideas and feelings clearly to others
○ an effective/a good/skilled/successful communicator

communism /'kɒmjənɪzəm; AmE 'kɑːmjə-/ noun [U]
a political movement that believes in an economic system in which the state controls the means of producing everything on behalf of the people. It aims to create a society in which everyone is treated equally. → CAPITALISM ▶ **communist** /'kɒmjənɪst; AmE 'kɑːmjə-/ noun, adjective: communist ideology

community /kə'mjuːnəti/ noun (plural **communities**)

SEE ALSO: bedroom community, European community

1 [sing.] all the people who live in a particular area, country, etc. when talked about as a group: the international community (= the countries of the world as a group) ◊ The new factory is great news for the local community.
2 [C with sing./pl. verb] a group of people who share the same race, religion, job, etc: ethnic communities ◊ The business community has/have doubts about the budget proposals.

com,munity an'tenna ,television (abbr **CATV**) = CABLE TELEVISION

com‚munity in'vestment *noun* [U,C]
the act of giving money for schools, hospitals, etc. in order to help a community improve its standard of living: *Many businesses have community investment programmes.*

commutation /‚kɒmjuˈteɪʃn; *AmE* ‚kɑːm-/ *noun* [C,U]
1 (*Insurance*) the right to exchange a series of future payments for one large sum that you receive now: *The scheme provides for full commutation of pension benefits.*
2 (*AmE*) the act of travelling regularly by bus, train, car, etc. between your place of work and your home: *Commutation times for city residents have lengthened considerably over the last ten years.*

commute /kəˈmjuːt/ *verb, noun*
● *verb*
1 [no obj] to travel regularly by bus, train, car, etc. between your place of work and your home: *She commutes from Oxford to London every day.* ◇ *The plant is within easy commuting distance of Brussels.*
2 (*Law*) [+ obj] to replace one punishment with another that is less severe: *They had their death sentences commuted to life imprisonment.*
● *noun* [C] (*especially AmE*)
the journey that a person makes when they **commute** to work: *Her daily commute takes 90 minutes.*

commuter /kəˈmjuːtə(r)/ *noun* [C]
a person who travels into a city to work each day, usually from quite far away: *Rail commuters have been badly affected by train delays.* ◇ (*BrE*) *London's* **commuter belt** (= the area around the city where lots of commuters live)

comp /kɒmp; *AmE* kɑːmp/ *noun, adjective, verb* (*AmE*)
● *noun*
1 (*informal*) [U] a short way of writing or saying **compensation**: *Workmen's comp data shows a 15% increase in construction injuries.*
2 (*informal*) [C] something that you give or receive free of charge
● *adjective* [only before noun] (*informal*)
free of charge: *Donors will receive ten comp tickets to all productions.* SYN COMPLIMENTARY
● *verb* [+ obj] (*informal*)
to give sb sth free of charge: *When I complained, the manager comped us a meal.*

‚Companies 'House *noun* [sing.]
(*Law*) in the UK, the government organization that by law holds the names of all companies in the UK and the details of their directors, shareholders and accounts: *The company must* **file** *its accounts* **with** *Companies House by Thursday.*

‚companies 'register (*also* ‚register of 'companies) *noun* [C]
(*Law*) an official list of the companies that have been created (**registered**) in a country. It includes information about a company's directors, shareholders, etc: *We searched the companies register to find the names of the shareholders.* ◇ *They are registered* **in** *the companies register as a private limited company.*

‚Companies 'Registry (*also* ‚Registry of 'Companies) *noun* [C, usually sing.]
(*Law*) in the UK and some other countries, the official organization that keeps records of the companies that are created (**registered**) in the country and to which companies must send information about their names, directors, financial results, etc. It also makes sure that laws relating to companies are obeyed: *Audited accounts must be* **filed with** *the Companies Registry.*

★ **company** /ˈkʌmpəni/ *noun* [C] (*plural* companies)

SEE ALSO: affiliated company, associate ~, associated ~, cable ~, close ~, closed ~, closely held ~, etc.

a business organization selling goods or services, especially one that has been officially created (**registered**) in a particular country and is owned by shareholders: *They are a large insurance and investment company.* ◇ *The company was founded in 1995.* ◇ *She's been working for the same company for 15 years.* ◇ *Four directors have resigned from the company.* ◇ *The company* **is listed** (= its shares are traded) *on the Johannesburg Stock Exchange.* ◇ *the Tata group of companies*
See note at BUSINESS, CORPORATION

● *a big/large/medium-sized/small* company ✦ *to create/establish/found/set up/start (up)* a company ✦ *to manage/operate/own/run* a company ✦ *to join/leave/resign from/work for* a company ✦ *to acquire/buy/sell/take over* a company ✦ *to dissolve/liquidate* a company ✦ *a company expands/grows/fails* ✦ *a company goes bankrupt/ goes out of business/goes under*

IDM take a company 'public; a company goes 'public if you **take** a company **public** or a company **goes public**, it becomes part of a stock exchange and its shares can be bought and sold by the public: *Since the company went public, its stock price has soared from $12 to $75.* → idiom at PART *verb*

MORE ABOUT

Forms of businesses

Most countries allow you to run a business in at least three different ways:
- as a **sole trader** (*especially BrE*) / **sole proprietorship** (*AmE*)
- as a **partnership**
- as a **company** (*BrE*) / **corporation** (*especially AmE*)

Important characteristics

SOLE TRADERS/SOLE PROPRIETORSHIPS
- few or no official procedures to follow
- the person starting the business is responsible for its debts

PARTNERSHIPS
- they can usually be established without following a formal procedure, although there is often a written agreement between the partners
- each partner is personally responsible for the debts of the business
- each partner can act as a representative of the business

COMPANIES/CORPORATIONS
- a number of official procedures to follow
- the company exists independently of its members and can last for ever
- the people who run the business can be different from those who own it
- the owners are responsible for a limited amount of the company's debts, equal to the value of their investment

See note at CORPORATION

‚company 'car *noun* [C]
a car that a company provides for an employee to use: *The perks* (= extra benefits of a job) *include a yearly bonus and company car.* See note at SALARY

‚company di'rector = DIRECTOR (1)

ˌcompany ˈdoctor noun [C]
1 a specialist who is employed to manage a company during a period of financial difficulty: *As Britain's top company doctor he is brought in to rescue failing firms.*
2 (*HR*) a medical doctor employed by a company to look after its employees

ˈcompany ˈlimited by guaranˈtee noun [C]
(*plural* **companies limited by guarantee**)
(*Law*) a type of company that does not sell shares to obtain funds, but is supported by a group of people who each promise to pay (**guarantee**) its debts up to a particular amount if it fails

ˈcompany ˈlimited by ˈshares noun [C] (*plural* **companies limited by shares**)
(*Law*) a type of company in which each shareholder pays debts up to the amount of the shares they have bought if it fails. Most companies in the UK are of this type.

ˌcompany ˈmeeting noun [C]
1 (*Law*) a meeting of the shareholders and directors of a company → GENERAL MEETING
2 a meeting of some or all of the employees of a company

ˌcompany ˈofficer (*AmE also* ˌcorporate ˈofficer) noun [C]
(*Law*) a person who has an official position in a company and represents the company in its activities: *The form must be signed by a company officer, such as a director or company secretary.*

ˌcompany ˈpresident = PRESIDENT (1)

ˌcompany ˈsecretary (*BrE*) (*also* ˈsecretary, *AmE*, *BrE*) (*AmE also* ˌcorporate ˈsecretary) noun [C]
(*Law*) a person in a company, usually chosen by the directors, who has various legal duties, such as looking after the company's official documents and arranging company meetings: *He was appointed company secretary last year.*

ˌcompany ˈunion noun [C]
(*HR*) an organization that a company forms for its employees to represent them when dealing with the managers. **Company unions** are not independent organizations like normal unions.

comparable /ˈkɒmpərəbl; *AmE* ˈkɑːm-/ noun [C, usually pl.] (*AmE*)
something with a known price or value and that is similar to sth you want to buy or sell: *Real estate professionals look at comparables in deciding the current market value of a property.*

ˌcomparable-store ˈsales (*also* **comps**, *informal*) = SAME-STORE SALES

ˌcomparable ˈworth noun [U] (*AmE*)
(*HR*) the principle that men and women doing jobs that have the same value to their employer should get the same wage; the right of an employee to receive a wage that relates to the value of their work: *the goal of achieving comparable worth for women*

comˌparative adˈvantage noun [C,U]
(*Economics*) the ability of a country to make a particular product or supply a particular service better and more cheaply than others: *Australia has a comparative advantage in agricultural products.*
→ ABSOLUTE ADVANTAGE

comˌparative ˈadvertising noun [U]
(*Marketing*) advertising that claims that the product being advertised is better or cheaper than a competitor's product: *Comparative advertising is common in the car industry.* **NOTE** **Comparative advertising** is illegal in some countries.
→ KNOCKING COPY

comˌpassionate ˈleave noun [U]
(*HR*) time that you are allowed to be away from work with pay because sb in your family is suddenly ill/sick or has died, or for other personal reasons: *She was granted compassionate leave to attend her father's funeral.* → PERSONAL DAY, PERSONAL LEAVE

compatibility /kəmˌpætəˈbɪləti/ noun [U]
compatibility (with sb/sth) | **compatibility (between A and B)** the ability of machines, especially computers, and computer programs to be used together: *There is no compatibility between the machines.* ◇ *Check your system compatibility before installing the software.*

compatible /kəmˈpætəbl/ adjective, noun
● *adjective*
(about equipment, especially computers or programs) able to be used together; standard: *compatible software* ◇ *The new system will be compatible with existing equipment.* ◇ *Are the web pages that you want to view WAP compatible?*
OPP INCOMPATIBLE
● *noun* [C]
(*IT*) a computer that is designed to work in exactly the same way as another type or make and use the same software: *an IBM compatible*

★ **compensate** /ˈkɒmpənseɪt; *AmE* ˈkɑːm-/ verb
1 [+ obj] to pay sb money because they have suffered some damage, loss, injury, etc: *Her lawyers say she should be compensated for her injuries.*
2 (*AmE*) [+ obj] to pay sb for work that they have done: *The positions on the boards and commissions are compensated at a daily rate.*
3 [no obj] to provide sth good to balance or reduce the bad effects of damage, loss, etc: *The savings resulting from improved efficiency will help compensate for the increase in expenses.*

ˌcompensating ˈbalance noun [C] (*especially AmE*)
(*Finance*) the amount of money a bank requires a customer to keep in an account in order to receive the bank's services free or to receive a loan

★ **compensation** /ˌkɒmpənˈseɪʃn; *AmE* ˌkɑːm-/ noun [U,C]

SEE ALSO: unemployment compensation

1 something, especially money, that sb gives you because they have hurt you, or damaged sth that you own; the act of giving this to sb: *to pay compensation for injuries received at work* ◇ *She received $10 000 in compensation.* ◇ *The bank was judged to be liable for compensation payments to customers who received poor advice.* → COMP
O *to award/give/offer/pay compensation* • *to accept/ get/obtain/receive compensation* • *to be eligible for/ be entitled to/claim/demand/seek compensation*
2 (*AmE*) the money or other benefits that an employee receives for the work that they do: *falling profits but rising employee compensation* → COMP
O *to get/give/pay/receive compensation*

compenˈsation ˌpackage noun [C]
1 a set of things, including money, that is given to sb because they have been hurt in some way, for example when sb loses their job: *The CEO received a compensation package worth over $2 million when he was removed from his job.*
2 (*HR*) (*AmE*) everything that an employee receives from their employer including pay, benefits and other rewards: *Good compensation packages can attract top executives.*

compenˌsatory ˈdamages (*also* ˌactual ˈdamages) (*both AmE*) noun [pl.]
(*Law*) an amount of money that a court orders sb to pay you to help pay for the injury they have caused you or the damage to your property, not to punish them → PUNITIVE DAMAGES

to try to be more successful or better than sb else who is trying to do the same as you: *Several companies are competing* **for** *the contract.* ◇ *We can't compete* **with** *them on price.* ◇ *Small traders cannot compete in the face of cheap foreign imports.* ◇ *competing companies/products*

competence /'kɒmpɪtəns; *AmE* 'kɑːm-/ *noun*
1 (*also* '**competency**, *less frequent*) [U,C] the ability to do sth well: *He shows a high level of competence* **in** *English.* ◇ *professional/technical competence* ◇ **competence-based pay** (= pay that goes up as the employee's level of ability and skill rises)
2 (*formal*) (*also* '**competency**, *less frequent*) [C] a skill that you need in a particular job or for a particular task: *The seminars are designed to develop specific management competences.*
3 [C] the power that a court, an organization or a person has to deal with sth: *What employees do after work is outside the firm's area of competence.*

'**competence ,profiling** = COMPETENCY PROFILING

competency /'kɒmpɪtənsi; *AmE* 'kɑːm-/ (*plural* **competencies**) = COMPETENCE (1,2)

'**competency-based** *adjective*
(*HR*) that involves looking at the skills that an employee has or needs: *a competency-based approach to performance appraisal* ◇ *competency-based training*

'**competency ,profiling** (*also* '**competence ,profiling**) *noun* [U]
(*HR*) a method of discovering the skills, knowledge and behaviour necessary for a particular task, job or career: *to undertake competency profiling*
▶'**competency ,profile** (*also* '**competence ,profile**) *noun* [C]

competent /'kɒmpɪtənt; *AmE* 'kɑːm-/ *adjective*
1 (about a person) having enough skill or knowledge to do sth well or to the necessary standard: *Make sure the firm is competent* **to** *carry out the work.* ◇ *He's very competent in his job.* ◇ *a competent worker*
2 (about a piece of work) done well or to the necessary standard: *He wrote a very competent report.*
OPP INCOMPETENT
▶'**competently** *adverb*: *to perform competently*

★ **competition** /ˌkɒmpə'tɪʃn; *AmE* ˌkɑːm-/ *noun*

SEE ALSO: **free competition, imperfect ~, perfect ~, price ~**

1 [U] a situation in which people or organizations compete with each other for sth that not everyone can have: *He really wants the job, but he will be facing stiff competition.* ◇ *We are* **in competition with** *four other companies* **for** *the contract.* ◇ *They are under pressure to cut costs amid growing competition from foreign firms.*
● **aggressive/fair/fierce/stiff/tough/unfair** competition ◆ **growing/increasing/intensifying** competition
2 the competition [sing. with sing./pl. verb] the people who are competing against sb: *We'll be able to assess the competition at the conference.* ◇ *a strategy to beat the competition* See note at COLLEAGUE
● *to* **beat/keep ahead of/out-think** *the competition*

compe'tition law *noun* [U]
(*Law*) the branch of law that deals with fair competition between companies and the control of MONOPOLIES

★ **competitive** /kəm'petətɪv/ *adjective*

SEE ALSO: **anti-competitive**

1 used to describe a situation in which people or organizations compete against each other: *a highly competitive market*
2 as good as or better than others: *We have a wide range of electrical goods at competitive prices.* ◇ *We need to work harder to remain competitive* **with** *other companies.*
3 (about a person) trying hard to be better than others: *George is very competitive and wants to be number one in the department.*
OPP UNCOMPETITIVE
▶ **com'petitively** *adverb*: *competitively priced goods* **com'petitiveness** (*also* **competitivity** /kəmˌpetə'tɪvəti/ *less frequent*) *noun* [U]: *an attempt to improve the competitiveness of British industry*

com,petitive ad'vantage *noun* [C,U]
a situation where a company is in a position to be more successful than its competitors; something that helps a company be in this position: *In the new economy, knowledge is the major source of competitive advantage.* ◇ *Their easy access to the road and rail networks gives them a huge competitive advantage* **over** *other firms.* SYN COMPETITIVE EDGE
● *to* **create/gain/have** (a) competitive advantage ◆ *to* **strengthen/weaken** *a competitive advantage* ◆ *a* **huge/key/significant/sustainable** competitive advantage

com,petitive a'nalysis (*also* **com,petitor a'nalysis, com,petitor 'profiling,** *less frequent*) *noun* [C,U]
(*Marketing*) a detailed study of a company's competitors that looks for areas where the company has or could gain an advantage: *a competitive analysis of online products and services*

com,petitive 'balance *noun* [C,U]
(*Economics*) a situation where none of the companies competing in a market has a very great or an unfair advantage: *attempts to preserve a competitive balance in national music markets*

com,petitive 'edge *noun* [sing.]
an advantage that a company has over its competitors: *Their early investment in the Internet gave them a competitive edge* **over** *their main rivals.* SYN COMPETITIVE ADVANTAGE
● *to* **gain/have/lose** *your competitive edge*

com,petitive in'telligence (*also* **com,petitor in'telligence,** *less frequent*) *noun* [U]
(*Marketing*) the ability to get and use information about competitors; the information obtained

com,petitive 'strategy (*also* **com,petitor 'strategy,** *less frequent*) *noun* [C,U]
a plan that is intended to gain an advantage for a company over its competitors; the process of making such a plan: *Research and development is a key element of their competitive strategy.*

competitivity = COMPETITIVENESS at COMPETITIVE

★ **competitor** /kəm'petɪtə(r)/ *noun* [C]

SEE ALSO: **direct competitor**

a business, person, product, etc. that competes against others: *We need to win market share from our competitors.* ◇ *The web authoring software promises to be a strong competitor* **to** *the market leaders.* SYN RIVAL See note at COLLEAGUE
● *our* **biggest/largest/main/major/nearest** competitor ◆ *a* **fierce/strong/tough** competitor

com,petitor a'nalysis = COMPETITIVE ANALYSIS

com,petitor in'telligence = COMPETITIVE INTELLIGENCE

com,petitor 'profiling = COMPETITIVE ANALYSIS

com,petitor 'strategy = COMPETITIVE STRATEGY

compile /kəm'paɪl/ *verb* [+ obj]
1 to produce a list, report, book, etc. by bringing together different items, articles, data, etc: *The report is based on statistics compiled by the Treasury.*
2 (*IT*) to translate instructions from a computer language into a form that can be read directly by the computer: *You can install the security updates without having to compile source code.*
▶ **compilation** /ˌkɒmpɪ'leɪʃn; *AmE* ˌkɑːm-/ *noun* [C,U]

compiler /kəm'paɪlə(r)/ *noun* [C]
1 a person who **compiles** sth: *the compilers of the report*
2 (*IT*) a program that translates instructions from one computer language into another for a computer to understand

complainant /kəm'pleɪmənt/ *noun* [C]
(*Law*) a person who makes a complaint, usually to the police, that somebody has harmed them or committed a crime → PLAINTIFF

★ **complaint** /kəm'pleɪnt/ *noun*
1 [C] a reason for not being satisfied; a statement that sb makes saying that they are not satisfied: *I'd like to make a complaint.* ◇ *The most common complaint is **about** poor service.* ◇ *We have received a number of complaints **from** customers.* ◇ *to lodge an official complaint*
○ *to have/make/receive* a complaint • *common/ consumer/customer* complaints • *a formal/an official* complaint • *to deal with/handle/ investigate/respond to* a complaint
2 [U] the act of complaining: *I can see no grounds for complaint.* ◇ *a letter of complaint*
3 (*Law*) [C] a statement that gives the reasons why sb is bringing a case or making a claim in a court
4 (*Law*) [C] a formal statement that sb has committed a crime

com'plaints ,management *noun* [U]
the system of analysing and responding to customers' complaints

complementary /ˌkɒmplɪ'mentri; *AmE* ˌkɑːm-/ *adjective*
two things or people that are **complementary** are different but together form a useful or attractive combination of skills, qualities or physical features: *The acquisition of the bus company is complementary to their travel business.* ◇ *a team of people with complementary skills*

,complementary 'goods *noun* [pl.]
(*Marketing*) goods that are sold separately but that are used together, for example cars and petrol/ gasoline

com,pletely built-'up *adjective* (*abbr* CBU)
(*Manufacturing*) (about a machine, etc. that is made from parts) that has been manufactured and put together: *the import of completely built-up cars*

com,pletely knocked-'down *adjective* (*abbr* CKD)
(*Manufacturing*) (about a machine, etc. that is made from parts) that has been manufactured but not put together: *The vehicle leaves the factory completely knocked-down for assembly elsewhere.*

★ **completion** /kəm'pliːʃn/ *noun* [U,C] (*BrE*)
(*Property*) the formal act of completing the sale of property, for example the sale of a house: *The keys will be handed over on completion.*

com'pletion date *noun* [C]
1 the date on which a project, especially a building project, is expected to be finished. This date is often included in the contract for the work.
2 (*BrE*) the date on which the ownership of something, especially a piece of property, is legally transferred from one person to another

com'pletion ,statement *noun* [C] (*BrE*)
(*Property*) a statement that says how much sb buying a property has to pay to the seller when the sale is completed

compliance /kəm'plaɪəns/ *noun* [U] (*usually used in written English*)
the practice of obeying rules or requests made by people in authority: *All our products are **in** compliance with existing safety laws.* ◇ *We have a Health and Safety Department to ensure **strict** compliance to labor laws.* ◇ *the bank's legal and compliance departments* OPP NON-COMPLIANCE
→ COMPLY

com'pliance ,officer *noun* [C]
a person working in a financial organization whose job is to make sure that the company is obeying the laws and rules that apply to it

compliant /kəm'plaɪənt/ *adjective*
1 in agreement with the rules: *Some of the bank's practices were not compliant **with** the law.*
2 (*Technical*) (about technical equipment, software, systems, etc.) that can be used with a particular system or set of rules: *The application is compliant **with** the industry standard.* ◇ *fully Internet compliant*
→ COMPLY

complimentary /ˌkɒmplɪ'mentri; *AmE* ˌkɑːm-/ *adjective*
1 given free of charge: *The hotel offers a complimentary cellphone for business travellers.*
2 expressing admiration, praise, etc: *She was extremely complimentary **about** his work.*

compli,mentary 'close (*also* compli,mentary 'closing) *noun* [sing.] (*AmE*)
the word or words that you write at the end of a business letter just before you sign your name, for example 'sincerely' or 'regards'

'compliments slip (*also* 'compliment slip) *noun* [C] (*both BrE*)
a small piece of paper printed with the name of a company, that is sent out together with information, goods, etc.

★ **comply** /kəm'plaɪ/ *verb* [no obj] (**complies, complying, complied, complied**)
to obey a rule, an order, etc: *Three employees refused to comply with the new regulations.*
→ COMPLIANCE, COMPLIANT

★ **component** /kəm'pəʊnənt; *AmE* -'poʊ-/ *noun* [C]
one of several parts of which sth is made: *the components of a machine* ◇ *one of the leading makers of components for cellphones* ◇ *Petroleum is a key component of their economy.*
○ *car/computer/vehicle* components • *a component maker/manufacturer/supplier* • *an essential/a key/an important/a vital* component (*of sth*)
▶ **com'ponent** *adjective* [only before noun]: *to break sth down into its component parts*

composite /'kɒmpəzɪt; *AmE* kəm'pɑːzət/ *adjective* [only before noun]
made of different parts or materials: *These composite materials are stiffer and lighter than most metals.* ◇ *the Nasdaq Composite Index*

composition /ˌkɒmpə'zɪʃn; *AmE* ˌkɑːm-/ *noun*
1 [U] the different parts which sth is made of; the way in which the parts are organized: *There were disagreements about the composition of the new board* (= about the people who would be on it).

2 (*Manufacturing*) [U] an artificial material made of several different substances, often used instead of a natural material: *composition floors*
3 (*Law*) [C, usually sing.] a legal agreement by which a person who is owed money by sb who cannot pay it all agrees to accept a percentage of the money; the agreed percentage that will be paid: *The defendant had been released by deed on **making** a composition **with** the creditors.*

compound *adjective, noun, verb*
● *adjective* /'kɒmpaʊnd; AmE 'kɑːm-/
 1 (*Accounting*) that pays or charges interest on an amount of money that includes any interest already earned or charged: *Revenues have grown at a compound annual rate of 50%.*
 2 (*Technical*) [only before noun] formed of two or more parts: *a compound lens*
● *noun* /'kɒmpaʊnd; AmE 'kɑːm-/ [C]
 a thing consisting of two or more separate things combined together: *Management requires a compound of skills.*
● *verb* /kəm'paʊnd/ [+ obj]
 (*Accounting*) to keep adding interest, profit, etc. to an amount of money as it is earned, so that the amount used as a basis for calculations keeps growing: *compounded earnings on investments*

com‚pounded 'rate = COMPOUND RATE

‚**compound 'entry** *noun* [C]
 (*Accounting*) an item in an account book that involves more than one amount of money to be recorded

‚**compound 'growth rate** *noun* [sing.]
 (*Accounting*) a rate at which an economy, a company, an investment, etc. must grow in each of a number of years in order to reach a particular size

‚**compound 'interest** *noun* [U]
 (*Accounting*) interest that is calculated on an amount of money to which all previous interest that has not yet been paid has been added
 → SIMPLE INTEREST

‚**compound 'rate** (*also* com‚pounded 'rate) *noun* [C]
 (*Accounting*) the percentage of interest on an amount of money which includes interest that has already been added

comprehensive /ˌkɒmprɪ'hensɪv; AmE ˌkɑːm-/ *adjective*
 (*Insurance*) that pays for all types of loss or damage, except in the circumstances mentioned: *comprehensive insurance* ◊ *Fully comprehensive cover is expensive for young drivers.* → ALL-RISK

compress /kəm'pres/ *verb* [+ obj]
 (*IT*) to make computer files, etc. smaller so that they use less space on a disk, etc. **SYN** ZIP
 OPP DECOMPRESS ▶ **compression** /kəm'preʃn/ *noun* [U]: *current developments in data compression*

comprise /kəm'praɪz/ *verb* [+ obj] (*not used in the continuous tenses*)
 1 (*also* be com'prised of) to have sb/sth as parts or members; to consist of sb/sth: *The Internet comprises more than 4 billion IP addresses.* ◊ *The committee is comprised of representatives from both the public and private sectors.*
 2 to be the parts or members that form sth: *Overseas sales comprise 52% of our total sales.*
 SYN MAKE UP STH
 NOTE Although this verb is not used in the continuous tenses in some meanings, it is common to see the present participle form **comprising**.

★ **compromise** /'kɒmprəmaɪz; AmE 'kɑːm-/ *noun, verb*
● *noun*
 1 [C,U] an agreement made between two people or groups in which each side gives up some of the things they want so that both sides are happy at the

end; the process of reaching this agreement: *We came to a compromise **on** the exact amount to be paid.* ◊ *The company has reached a compromise with its creditors.*
 Ο *to* **agree on/arrive at/come to/make/reach** *a compromise* ◆ *a compromise* **deal/plan/proposal/ scheme**
 2 [C] a solution to a problem where two or more things cannot exist together as they are, in which each thing is changed slightly so that they can exist together: *This model represents the best compromise **between** price and quality.*
● *verb*
 1 [no obj] to give up some of your demands in a dispute with sb, in order to reach an agreement: *Neither side is prepared to compromise.* ◊ *They might compromise **with** the union **on** the timing of the pay increase.*
 2 [+ obj] to allow the standard of sth to become lower: *They have managed to make the car more comfortable without compromising its performance.*
 3 [+ obj] **compromise sb/sth/yourself** to put sb/ sth/yourself in danger or at risk: *He compromised his career by refusing to carry out his boss's instructions.*

comps /kɒmps; AmE kɑːmps/ = COMPARABLE-STORE SALES

'**comp time** *noun* [U] (*AmE*)
 (*HR*) extra time away from work that employees can have if they have worked extra hours: *When can you give your employees comp time instead of overtime pay?* **SYN** TIME OFF IN LIEU (*BrE*)
 → OVERTIME

comptroller /kən'trəʊlə(r); kəmp-; AmE -'troʊ-/ = CONTROLLER (2)

compulsory /kəm'pʌlsəri/ *adjective*
 that must be done because of a law or a rule: *The training is compulsory for all new staff.*
 SYN OBLIGATORY

com‚pulsory acqui'sition = COMPULSORY PURCHASE

com‚pulsory liqui'dation (*also* ‚forced liqui'dation) *noun* [U,C]
 (*Law*) a situation where a company is forced to stop doing business so that it can pay its debts
 SYN INVOLUNTARY LIQUIDATION **OPP** VOLUNTARY LIQUIDATION

com‚pulsory 'purchase (*also* com‚pulsory acqui'sition) *noun* [U,C] (*BrE*)
 (*Law*) a situation in which sb has the legal right to force sb to sell sth, for example when the government needs to buy land in order to build a road: *The Council obtained a **compulsory purchase order** on the land (= legal permission to buy it).*

com‚pulsory re'tirement *noun* [U,C]
 (*HR*) the law or rule that people must retire at a particular age: *Your contract does not include a compulsory retirement age.*

★ **computer** /kəm'pjuːtə(r)/ *noun* [C]

SEE ALSO: **desktop computer, microcomputer**

an electronic machine that can store, organize and find information, do calculations and control other machines: *The data is all held on (the) computer.* ◊ *My computer crashed (= stopped working) and I lost the work I was doing.* ◊ *The computers are down (= not working).*
 Ο *to* **boot up/log onto/reboot/restart/start up** *a computer* ◆ *to* **log off/shut down** *a computer* ◆ *computer* **applications/files/games/hardware/ programs/software** ◆ *a computer* **network/system**

com‚puter-ˈaided (*also* com‚puter-asˈsisted)
adjective [only before noun]
that uses a computer to do most of the work
○ *computer-aided design/engineering/learning/manufacture*

com‚puter ‚analyst (*also* ˈbusiness ‚analyst)
noun [C]
a person whose job is to analyse the needs of a
business company or an organization and then
design processes for working efficiently using
computer programs **SYN** SYSTEMS ANALYST
▶ **com‚puter a‚nalysis** (*also* ˈbusiness a‚nalysis)
noun [U]

com‚puter-asˈsisted = COMPUTER-AIDED

computerate /kəmˈpjuːtərət/ = COMPUTER-
LITERATE

com‚puter-based ˈtraining *noun* [U] (*abbr*
CBT)
training that uses computers as the main means of
teaching

com‚puter-ˈgenerated *adjective*
produced by a computer after data or instructions
are put into it: *a computer-generated image of a
bridge* ◇ *Computer-generated presentations are
becoming very popular.*

com‚puter ˈgraphics (*also* ˈgraphics) *noun* [pl.]
pictures that are made using a computer: *the use of
computer graphics to design products*

com‚puter-integrated manuˈfacturing
noun [U] (*abbr* **CIM**)
the use of computers to link and control all the
stages of the design and manufacturing processes
in a company

★ **computerize** , **-ise** /kəmˈpjuːtəraɪz/ *verb* [+ obj]
1 to use computers to run sth: *The factory has been
fully computerized.* ◇ *a computerized factory/
machine/system*
2 to store information on a computer: *The firm has
computerized its records.* ◇ *computerized databases/
information.*
▶ **computerization**, **-isation** /kəm‚pjuːtəraɪˈzeɪʃn;
AmE -rəˈz-/ *noun* [U]

com‚puter ‚language (*also* ˈprogramming
‚language) *noun* [C,U]
a set of words, symbols and rules that is used to
write computer programs

com‚puter-ˈliterate (*also* comˈputerate)
adjective
able to use computers well ▶ **com‚puter ˈliteracy**
noun [U]

comˈputer ‚program = PROGRAM *noun* (1)
com‚puter ˈprogrammer = PROGRAMMER
com‚puter ˈprogramming = PROGRAMMING
com‚puter ˈscience *noun* [U]
the study of computers and how they can be used:
a graduate in computer science

computing /kəmˈpjuːtɪŋ/ *noun* [U]
the fact of using computers; the use or
development of computers of the type mentioned:
to work in computing ◇ *The company played an
important role in handheld computing.* ◇ *It's better to
have more computing power than a bigger monitor.*
○ *computing devices/services/skills/systems* ◆
handheld/mobile/personal computing

con /kɒn; *AmE* kɑːn/ *noun*, *verb* (*informal*)
● *noun* (*BrE also* ˈconfidence trick, *formal*) [C, usually
sing.] (*informal*)
a trick; an act of cheating sb: *The so-called bargain
was just a big con!* ◇ (*BrE*) *a con trick* ◇ (*AmE*) *a con
game*
● *verb* [+ obj] (**-nn-**) **con sb** (**into doing sth/out of sth**)
to trick sb, especially in order to get money from
them or persuade them to do sth for you: *I was
conned into buying a useless car.* ◇ *He conned his
way into the job using false references.*

concentration /‚kɒnsnˈtreɪʃn; *AmE* ‚kɑːn-/ *noun*

SEE ALSO: **buyer concentration, market concentration**

1 [C] a lot of sth in one place: *insurance premiums
for commercial buildings with high concentrations of
visitors or workers* ◇ *This area has the highest
concentration of industry in the country.*
2 [U] the act of bringing things together, or of
coming together, to form a group: *Concentration of
investments in a single company's shares was foolish.*
◇ *There is concern about the concentration of
ownership in the regional press* (= a small number of
people or groups own most of the newspapers).
3 [U] the ability to direct all your effort and
attention on one thing, without thinking of other
things: *The job demands total concentration.*
4 [U] the process of people directing effort and
attention on a particular thing: *Their concentration
on developing new markets is starting to bring
profits.*

concept /ˈkɒnsept; *AmE* ˈkɑːn-/ *noun* [C]

SEE ALSO: **business entity concept, consistency ~,
high-~, marketing ~, production ~, sales ~, selling ~**

1 an idea for a new product or to help sell a
product: *He has experience in bringing high-tech
equipment from concept to market.* ◇ *a new concept
in corporate hospitality*
2 an idea or principle that is connected with sth: *a
course to teach key business concepts*

ˈconcept ‚testing *noun* [U]
(*Marketing*) a way of finding out if an idea for a new
product or for advertising a product is a good one
by asking a number of people for their opinions
○ *to do/engage in/undertake concept testing*

concern /kənˈsɜːn; *AmE* -ˈsɜːrn/ *noun*, *verb*
● *noun* [C]

SEE ALSO: **going concern**

a business: *a major publishing concern*
● *verb* [+ obj]
1 (*often* **be concerned**) to affect sb; to involve sb:
The matter doesn't concern us. ◇ *The closure of the
firm was upsetting to all concerned* (= everyone
involved).
2 (*also* **be concerned with sth**) to be about sth: *The
report's criticism concerns the way the company
manages its pension fund.*
IDM **To whom it may concern** … (only used in
written English) used, for example, at the beginning
of a public notice or of a job reference, when you
do not know the name of the person you are
writing to

★ **concession** /kənˈseʃn/ *noun*
1 [C,U] something that you allow or do, or allow sb
to have, in order to end an argument or to make a
situation less difficult: *The firm will be forced to
make concessions if it wants to avoid a strike.* ◇ *to
win a concession from sb*
○ *to demand/seek/win concessions* ◆ *to make/offer
concessions*
2 [C, usually pl.] (*BrE*) a reduction in an amount of
money that has to be paid for sth; a ticket that is
sold at a reduced price to a particular group of
people: *tax concessions* ◇ *tickets €20, concessions
€12*
○ *to get/give/offer concessions*
3 (*Commerce*) [C] (*especially AmE*) the right to sell
sth in a particular place; the place where you sell it,
sometimes an area which is part of a larger

building or store: *They run a burger concession at the stadium.* ◇ *airport/hotel concessions*
→ FRANCHISE
⊕ *to* **open/operate/take** *concessions*
4 (*Commerce*) [C] a right to trade or operate that is given to a company or a person, especially by a government: *The government* **granted** *mining concessions covering 22 million hectares.*
⊕ *to* **award/grant/offer** *a concession*

concessionaire /kənˌseʃəˈneə(r); *AmE* -ˈner/ (*also* **concessioner** /kənˈseʃənə(r)/) *noun* [C]
(*Commerce*) a company or a person that has been given a CONCESSION to trade or operate in a particular place: *Some department stores include concessionaires or 'shops within shops'.*

concierge /ˌkɒnsiˈeəʒ; *AmE* ˌkɑːnsiˈerʒ/ *noun* [C]
a person who is employed, for example by a hotel, to provide services to a person or a group, such as booking accommodation and travel, shopping, finding out information, etc: *We provide personal and corporate concierge services for visitors to London.*

conciliation /kənˌsɪliˈeɪʃn/ *noun* [U]
a process of helping two sides in a dispute, usually employers and employees, to find a way to meet and discuss the problem and reach an agreement: *A conciliation service helps to settle disputes between employers and workers.* → ACAS

conˌcurrent engiˈneering (*also* **simulˌtaneous engiˈneering**) *noun* [U]
(*Production*) a systematic method of developing new products in which people involved in designing, manufacturing, selling and using the products work together from the beginning

★ condition /kənˈdɪʃn/ *noun*
1 [U,C] the state that sth is in: *a used car* **in** *perfect condition*
⊕ *in* **excellent/fair/good/perfect/reasonable** *condition* • *in* **bad/poor** *condition*
2 conditions [pl.] the circumstances or situation in which people live, work or do things: *a campaign to create better working conditions* ◇ *difficult market conditions* ◇ *a strike to improve* **pay and conditions**
⊕ **bad/difficult/harsh/poor** *conditions* • **favourable/ good** *conditions* • **business/economic/employment/ living/market/trading** *conditions* • **living/working** *conditions* • *to* **change/create/improve** *conditions*
3 [C] a rule or decision that you must agree to, sometimes forming part of a contract or an official agreement: *Congress can impose strict conditions on the bank.* ◇ *The offer is* **subject to** *certain conditions.* ◇ *the* **terms and conditions** *of employment* ◇ *This product is sold* **under the condition that** *it cannot be returned under any circumstances.*
⊕ **strict/stringent/tough** *conditions* • **lending/licence/ loan/membership** *conditions* • *to* **accept/ease/ impose/meet/set** *conditions*
4 [C] a situation that must exist in order for sth else to happen: *a* **necessary condition for** *economic growth* ◇ *A good training programme is one of the conditions for successful industry.*
→ idiom at MINT *noun*

conditional /kənˈdɪʃənl/ *adjective*
that only happens if sth else is done or happens first: *Payment is conditional* **upon/on** *delivery of the goods.* ◇ *She received a conditional offer of appointment to the post.* ⟨OPP⟩ UNCONDITIONAL
⊕ *conditional* **acceptance/approval** • *a conditional* **agreement/offer**
▸ conditionally /kənˈdɪʃənəli/ *adverb*

conˌditional 'sale *noun* [C]
(*Commerce*) a type of sale where there is a contract with particular conditions, usually that the buyer can pay in INSTALMENTS (= a series of regular payments) but will not legally own the goods until full payment has been made

---

conˌditional 'takeover bid *noun* [C]
(*Finance*) an offer to buy a company's shares at a particular price if particular conditions are met, for example that the buyer can buy enough shares to have control of the company → UNCONDITIONAL TAKEOVER BID

conˌditions of 'sale *noun* [pl.]
(*Commerce*) details concerning how goods will be sold, which the seller decides and the buyer must accept, for example how the goods will be paid for and delivered and what the buyer has the right to do with them

★ conduct *verb, noun*
● verb /kənˈdʌkt/ [+ obj]
1 to organize and/or do a particular activity: *The company conducted in-depth interviews with potential users in three states.*
2 conduct yourself to behave in a particular way: *The article gives advice on how to conduct yourself in an interview.*
● noun /ˈkɒndʌkt; *AmE* ˈkɑːn-/ [U]
1 the way in which a business or an activity is organized and managed: *Partners have equal responsibility for the conduct of the firm's affairs.*
2 a person's behaviour in a particular place or a particular situation: *improving standards of training and professional conduct*

confederation /kənˌfedəˈreɪʃn/ *noun* [C]
an organization consisting of countries, businesses, etc. that have joined together in order to help each other: *the Confederation of British Industry*

confer /kənˈfɜː(r)/ *verb* [no obj] (**-rr-**)
to discuss sth with sb, especially in order to exchange opinions or get advice: *She conferred* **with** *her colleagues before making a decision.*

★ conference /ˈkɒnfərəns; *AmE* ˈkɑːn-/ *noun* [C]

SEE ALSO: **news conference, press ~, sales ~, shipping ~**

1 a large official meeting, usually lasting for a few days, at which people with the same work or interests come together to discuss their views: *She is attending a two-day conference on electronic commerce in Munich.* ◇ *I've been invited to speak at the annual conference.* ◇ *125 of the 400 delegates* **at** *the conference were women.* ⟨SYN⟩ CONVENTION
⊕ *to* **attend/go to/participate in** *a conference* • *to* **hold/organize** *a conference* • *to* **speak at/address** *a conference* • *a conference* **centre/hall/room/suite** • *a conference* **attendee/delegate/participant**
2 a meeting at which a small number of people have formal discussions: *She was* **in conference** *with her lawyers all day.* ◇ *It was difficult to get all the parties around the* **conference table**.
→ TELECONFERENCE, VIDEOCONFERENCING

'conference call *noun* [C]
a telephone call in which three or more people take part: *We hold a weekly conference call* **with** *the design team.*
⊕ *to* **have/hold** *a conference call*

conferencing /ˈkɒnfərənsɪŋ; *AmE* ˈkɑːn-/ *noun* [U]

SEE ALSO: **audio conferencing**

(*IT*) the act of taking part in discussions with two or more other people by using telephones, video equipment, etc: *software for conferencing on the Web* ◇ *Courses are offered via online conferencing.*
→ TELECONFERENCE, VIDEOCONFERENCE
⊕ **Internet/online/web** *conferencing*

★ **confidence** /ˈkɒnfɪdəns; AmE ˈkɑːn-/ noun [U]

SEE ALSO: breach of confidence, consumer ~, vote of ~, vote of no ~

1 the feeling that you can trust, believe in and be sure about the abilities or good qualities of sb/sth: *We have complete confidence in our products.* ◇ *The management have lost the confidence of their employees* (= their employees do not trust them). ◇ *attempts to restore confidence in financial advice* ○ *to express/have/lose confidence in sth* ◆ *to build (up)/destroy/improve/rebuild/restore confidence*
2 a feeling that things will get better and not get worse: *Business confidence has fallen sharply.* ◇ *Confidence among American consumers has risen this month.* ◇ *The company has been hit by a crisis of confidence* (= investors do not believe it will be successful). [SYN] SENTIMENT
○ *business/investor/public confidence* ◆ *confidence declines/falls/grows/returns/rises*
3 a feeling of trust that sb will keep information private: *He told me about the project in confidence.*

'**confidence trick** (BrE) (AmE '**confidence game**) = CON noun

★ **confidential** /ˌkɒnfɪˈdenʃl; AmE ˌkɑːn-/ adjective
meant to be kept secret: *This information is strictly confidential.* ◇ *The details of the report were kept confidential.*
○ *highly/strictly confidential* ◆ *to be/be kept/remain confidential*

★ **confidentiality** /ˌkɒnfɪˌdenʃiˈæləti; AmE ˌkɑːn-/ noun [U]
the need to keep particular information secret: *There is a right of confidentiality between lawyer and client.* ◇ *Most contracts of employment have a confidentiality clause.*

configure /kənˈfɪɡə(r); AmE -ˈfɪɡjər/ verb [+ obj]
(IT; Technical) to organize or arrange sth, especially computer equipment, for a particular task: *The machine is configured to run on a network.*
→ RECONFIGURE
▶ **configuration** /kənˌfɪɡəˈreɪʃn; AmE -ˌfɪɡjəˈr-/ noun [C,U]

★ **confirm** /kənˈfɜːm; AmE -ˈfɜːrm/ verb [+ obj]
1 to say or show that sth is definitely true or correct: *The date of the meeting has not yet been confirmed.* ◇ *Please write to confirm your reservation* (= say that it is definite). ◇ *The company confirmed that it would cut 6 000 jobs.*
2 (HR) to make a position more definite or official: *After a six-month probationary period, her position was confirmed.* ◇ *Joseph Bull is likely to be confirmed as finance director.*

★ **confirmation** /ˌkɒnfəˈmeɪʃn; AmE ˌkɑːnfərˈm-/ noun [C,U]
a statement, letter, etc. that shows that sth is true, correct or definite: *We are waiting for confirmation of the report.* ◇ *I need email confirmation before I can process the order.* ◇ *to receive order/shipping confirmation*

confiscate /ˈkɒnfɪskeɪt; AmE ˈkɑːn-/ verb [+ obj]
to officially take sth away from sb, as a punishment or because they are doing sth illegal: *They had their passports confiscated on entering the country.* ◇ *confiscated property* → IMPOUND
▶ **confiscation** /ˌkɒnfɪˈskeɪʃn; AmE ˌkɑːn-/ noun [C,U]

★ **conflict** noun, verb
● noun /ˈkɒnflɪkt; AmE ˈkɑːn-/ [C,U]
1 a situation in which people, groups or countries are involved in a serious disagreement or argument: *The bank has run into conflict with the authorities.* ◇ *a conflict between two members of the*

team ◇ *They found themselves in conflict over the future of the firm.* ◇ *HR managers need to be skilled in conflict resolution* (= settling disagreements).
○ *to come into/create/run into (a) conflict* ◆ *to avoid/manage/prevent/resolve (a) conflict* ◆ *conflict management/resolution*
2 a situation in which there are opposing ideas, opinions, feelings or wishes and it may be difficult to choose: *There is often a conflict between long working hours and the demands of family life.*
[IDM] **conflict of 'interest(s)** a situation in which there are two jobs, aims, roles, etc. and it is not possible for both of them to be treated equally and fairly at the same time: *There was a conflict of interest between his business dealings and his political activities.* **conflict of 'law(s)** (Law) a situation in which a court must decide which country's laws apply to a dispute
● verb /kənˈflɪkt/ [no obj] **A and B conflict | A conflicts with B** if two ideas, beliefs, stories, etc. conflict, it is not possible for them to exist together or for them both to be true: *The statements of the two witnesses conflict.* ◇ *These results conflict with earlier findings.* ◇ *The government is accused of sending out conflicting messages on the state of the economy.*

conform /kənˈfɔːm; AmE -ˈfɔːrm/ verb [no obj]
to obey a rule or a law: *This building does not conform with fire regulations.* ◇ *The modem conforms to the V.90 industry standard.*

confrontation /ˌkɒnfrʌnˈteɪʃn; AmE ˌkɑːnfrən-/ noun [U,C]
confrontation (with sb)/(between A and B) a situation in which there is an angry disagreement between people or groups who have different opinions: *confrontation between employers and unions*

confrontational /ˌkɒnfrʌnˈteɪʃənl; AmE ˌkɑːnfrən-/ adjective
that involves or causes conflict: *a confrontational style of leadership*

conglomerate /kənˈɡlɒmərət; AmE -ˈɡlɑːm-/ noun [C]
a large organization formed by joining together a group of companies often with different business activities: *Bertelsmann, the media conglomerate*
○ *an engineering/a financial/an industrial/a media conglomerate* ◆ *to build (up)/create/form a conglomerate*

congress /ˈkɒŋɡres; AmE ˈkɑːŋɡrəs/ noun [C with sing./pl. verb]
a large formal meeting or series of meetings: *an international congress of trades unions* ◇ *a medical congress*

'**con man** noun [C] (informal)
a man who tricks other people into giving him money, etc: *Have nothing to do with that company—they're a bunch of con men!*

★ **connect** /kəˈnekt/ verb
1 [+ obj or no obj] **connect (sth) (up) (to/with sth)** to join together two or more things; to be joined together: *She connected up the two computers.* ◇ *I can connect to the office computer via a modem.*
[OPP] DISCONNECT
2 (IT) [+ obj or no obj] to link or be linked to the Internet: *Our business is connecting people to the Internet.* ◇ *Sometimes the phone lines are so busy that it's impossible to get connected* (= to the Internet). [OPP] DISCONNECT
3 [+ obj] to join telephone lines so that people can speak to each other: *Hold on please, I'm trying to connect you.* [SYN] PUT SB THROUGH [OPP] DISCONNECT
4 [no obj] (used about a bus, plane, train, etc.) to arrive at a particular time, so that passengers can

change to another bus, train, plane, etc: *a connecting flight*
→ RECONNECT

IDM **connect the 'dots** (*also* **join the 'dots**, *especially in BrE*) to find or show the relationships between different things: *In your training session, connect the dots for your audience—relate the training to real business demands.* → CONNECT-THE-DOTS

★ **connection** (*BrE spelling also* **connexion**, *less frequent*) /kəˈnekʃn/ *noun* [C]
1 (*IT*) a link to the Internet, telephone system, etc: *You pay €20 a month for their high-speed Internet connection.* ◇ *I'm having trouble establishing a connection to the network.* ◇ *There is a €150 connection fee* (= when you start receiving the service).
2 [usually pl.] a person or an organization that you know and that can help or advise you in your social or professional life: *One of my business connections gave them my name.*
3 a bus, train, plane, etc. that leaves soon after another arrives: *Our plane was so late that we missed our connection.*
4 [usually pl.] a means of travelling to another place: *There are good bus and train connections between the conference centre and the city.*
IDM **in con'nection with sb/sth** (*only used in written English*) about or concerning: *I am writing to you in connection with your application.*

connectivity /ˌkɒnekˈtɪvəti; kəˌnekˈtɪvəti; AmE ˌkaːn-/ *noun* [U]
(*IT*) the ability to be connected to the Internet or another computer: *The basic service includes email and Internet connectivity.*

con,nect-the-'dots *adjective* [only before noun]
1 that brings together facts and information from different places and shows the relationships between them: *a connect-the-dots article*
2 easy to do or understand; not complicated: *connect-the-dots instructions*

connexion = CONNECTION

connotation /ˌkɒnəˈteɪʃn; AmE ˌkaːn-/ *noun* [C]
an idea suggested by a word in addition to its main meaning: *It wasn't easy to choose a name for the company without negative connotations.*

conscientious /ˌkɒnʃiˈenʃəs; AmE ˌkaːn-/ *adjective*
taking care to do things carefully and correctly: *Her pleasant personality and conscientious work made her a valued member of staff.* ▶ **,consci'entiously** *adverb*: *He performed all his duties conscientiously.* **,consci'entiousness** *noun* [U]

consensual /kənˈsenʃuəl/ *adjective* (*formal*)
that involves getting everyone's agreement: *a consensual approach to management*

★ **consensus** /kənˈsensəs/ *noun* [sing; U]
1 agreement among a group of people: *trying to reach a consensus on an issue* ◇ *There is a growing consensus **among** experts that interest rates will rise.* ◇ *All the board's decisions are made **by** consensus.* ◇ *the process of consensus building*
○ *to **achieve/build/reach/seek** (a) consensus*
2 (*Finance*) the general view among experts of how well a company, an industry and an economy will perform: *Their quarterly sales figures beat consensus by 25%.* ◇ *The consensus forecast for growth is now 1.7%.*
○ *a consensus **estimate/forecast***

conse,quential 'loss (*also* **,indirect 'loss**) *noun* [U,C]
(*Law*) money that a business loses as an indirect result of being harmed by sb, for example a loss of profits because its factory was damaged by them

conservatism /kənˈsɜːvətɪzəm; AmE -ˈsɜːrv-/ *noun* [U]
1 the tendency to avoid unnecessary risks: *the conservatism of investors*
2 (*Accounting*) (*especially AmE*) = PRUDENCE (1)

conservative /kənˈsɜːvətɪv; AmE -ˈsɜːrv-/ *adjective*
1 not taking or involving unnecessary risk: *We have always had a conservative approach to financing our business.*
2 lower than what is probably the real amount or number: *At a conservative **estimate**, she'll be earning €80 000.* ◇ *The company's forecasts were conservative.*

conservator /kənˈsɜːvətə(r); ˈkɒnsəveɪtə(r); AmE kənˈsɜːrvətər/ *noun* [C] (*AmE*)
(*Law*) a person chosen by a court to look after sb or their finances, because they are too old, ill/sick, etc. to do so themselves: *The judge **appointed** a conservator to manager her assets.*

consignee /ˌkɒnsaɪˈniː; AmE ˌkaːn-/ *noun* [C]
(*Transport*) a person or an organization that goods are sent to: *We have informed the consignee of the delivery date.* → CONSIGNOR

consignment /kənˈsaɪnmənt/ *noun*
1 (*Transport*) [C] a quantity of goods that are sent or delivered somewhere: *a consignment of books*
SYN SHIPMENT
2 (*Commerce*) [C,U] goods that you deliver to sb, for them to sell on your behalf or return if they cannot sell them: *These pieces are being offered **on consignment**.* ◇ *imports made on a **consignment account** basis*

con'signment note *noun* [C]
(*Transport*) a document that gives details of goods that have been sent or delivered somewhere and is sent with them

con'signment store *noun* [C]
especially in the US, a type of shop/store where you can take items to be sold on your behalf or returned to you if they are not sold

consignor /kənˈsaɪnə(r)/ *noun* [C]
1 (*Commerce*) a person who delivers an item to sb for them to sell on their behalf
2 (*Transport*) a person or an organization that sends goods to sb/sth: *The package must be marked with the consignor's name and address.* **SYN** SENDER
→ CONSIGNEE
See note at EMPLOYER

con'sistency ,concept *noun* [sing.]
(*Accounting*) one of the principles used in accounting that says that similar items should be treated in the same way within each accounting period and from one period to the next, and that the organization's rules for accounting should always be followed

consolidate /kənˈsɒlɪdeɪt; AmE -ˈsaːl-/ *verb*
1 [+ obj *or* no obj] to join things, especially businesses, together into one; to be joined into one: *The two companies consolidated for greater efficiency.* ◇ *consolidated companies* ◇ *a loan to help you consolidate your debts* (= replace smaller debts with one big debt) → UNCONSOLIDATED
2 (*Accounting*) [+ obj] to combine the financial results of a group of companies into one set of figures: *There was a rise in consolidated sales.* ◇ *The parent company is required to prepare a set of consolidated accounts.* → UNCONSOLIDATED
3 [+ obj *or* no obj] to make a position of power or success stronger so that it is more likely to continue: *The merger will consolidate the group's position in the market.*

4 (*Transport*) [+ obj] to combine separate items into one load to transport them

consolidation /kənˌsɒlɪˈdeɪʃn; AmE -ˌsɑːl-/ *noun* [U,C]

SEE ALSO: **debt consolidation**

1 (*Economics*) the situation when companies of the same type join together: *the rapid consolidation of the industry into a few large companies* ◇ *2 500 jobs have been lost as part of the consolidation.*
2 the act of joining two or more things together: *The consolidation of the two production sites into one will strengthen our competitiveness.*
3 the act of making your power, success, knowledge, etc. stronger: *The training focuses on the consolidation of skills.*
4 (*Transport*) (*AmE*) = GROUPAGE

consolidator /kənˈsɒlɪdeɪtə(r); AmE -ˈsɑːl-/ *noun* [C]

1 (*Economics*) a company that takes control of several others in the same industry to form a single business: *The group has ambitions to act as a consolidator of European broadcasters.*
2 (*Commerce*) a travel company that buys travel tickets, rents hotel rooms, etc. in large numbers and offers them to the public at TRAVEL AGENCIES at low prices: *We offer consolidator airfares to Southern Africa.* → BUCKET SHOP
3 (*Transport*) a transport company that receives goods from different suppliers and packs them so that they can be transported together: *For small shipments a freight consolidator is used.*

Consols /ˈkɒnsɒlz; kənˈsɒlz; AmE ˈkɑːnsɑːlz; kənˈsɑːlz/ *noun* [pl.]
(*Finance*) in the UK, government bonds that have a fairly low fixed interest rate but do not have a fixed date for when the loan will be paid back
NOTE Consols is an abbreviation of the words 'Consolidated Stock' or 'Consolidated Annuities'.

consortium /kənˈsɔːtiəm; AmE -ˈsɔːrt-/ *noun* [C] (*plural* **consortiums** or **consortia** /-tiə/)
(*Finance*) a group of companies, banks, organizations, etc. working together on a particular project: *The company has been rescued by a consortium of banks.* ◇ *The consortium is led by BP.*
☉ to **form/join/lead** a consortium

constituent /kənˈstɪtjuənt; AmE -tʃu-/ *adjective, noun*
●*adjective* [only before noun]
forming a whole; being a part of a whole: *the group's two constituent companies*
●*noun* [C]
one of the parts that forms sth: *the constituents of the FTSE 100 index*

constitute /ˈkɒnstɪtjuːt; AmE ˈkɑːnstətuːt/ *verb*
1 [+ obj] (*usually* **be constituted**) to form a group legally or officially: *a properly constituted company with a proper balance sheet*
2 (*linking verb*) (*not used in the continuous tenses*) to be the parts that together form sth: *In the UK, women constitute 30% of managers.* **SYN** MAKE UP
3 (*formal, usually used in written English*) (*linking verb*) (*not used in the continuous tenses*) to be considered to be sth: *Does such an activity constitute a criminal offence?*
NOTE Although this verb is not used in the continuous tenses in some meanings, it is common to see the present participle form **constituting**: *Management has to fix a maximum number of hours as constituting a day's work.*

★ constitution /ˌkɒnstɪˈtjuːʃn; AmE ˌkɑːnstə-ˈtuːʃn/ *noun* [C]
the basic law or rules of a country or an organization: *A director must act according to the company's constitution.* ◇ *A two-thirds majority is needed to amend the club's constitution.* → CHARTER *noun* (1)
☉ to **adopt/amend/draft/violate** a constitution ◆ a constitution **allows sth/forbids sth/guarantees sth/states that ...**

constitutional /ˌkɒnstɪˈtjuːʃənl; AmE ˌkɑːnstəˈtuː-/ *adjective*
connected with or allowed by a **constitution**: *Do corporations have a constitutional right to tell untruths?* ◇ *It is not constitutional to imprison somebody without trial.*

construct /kənˈstrʌkt/ *verb* [+ obj]
1 construct sth (**from/out of/of sth**) (*often* be **constructed**) to build or make sth large, such as a road, building or machine: *The building was constructed in 1972.* ◇ *The frame is constructed from steel and plastic.* ◇ *a newly constructed hotel* → BUILD *verb* (1)
2 to create sth by putting different things or parts together: *I've constructed my own homepage on the Web.* ◇ *a carefully constructed letter* → BUILD *verb* (2) → RECONSTRUCT

★ construction /kənˈstrʌkʃn/ *noun*
1 [U] the process or method of building or making sth large, especially roads, buildings, bridges, etc: *Construction of the new offices has now been completed.* ◇ *This web page is currently under construction* (= being built). ◇ *He was working as a labourer on a construction site.* → MANUFACTURING
☉ to **begin/complete/start** construction ◆ **bridge/pipeline/plant/road** construction ◆ a construction **site/yard/worker** ◆ construction **costs/materials/methods/techniques**
2 [U] the business of building roads, buildings, etc: *His businesses range from shipping and construction to motels.*
☉ the construction **industry/sector** ◆ a construction **business/company/firm/group**
3 [U] the process or method of creating sth by putting different things or parts together: *the construction of rules/agreements*
4 [U,C] the way that sth has been built or made: *walls of solid construction*
5 (*formal*) [C] a thing that has been built or made: *massive constructions of bamboo and paper* → RECONSTRUCTION

WHICH WORD?

construction/building

Both **building** [U] and **construction** [U] can be used to describe the making of any structure or large, complicated piece of equipment: *the building/construction of a new hospital/pipeline/runway.*

Construction is slightly more formal and commonly used about industrial buildings or structures used for transport, such as roads or bridges.

Building [U], especially when combined with other nouns, usually describes the process of building structures for living or working in: *cement, bricks and other building materials* ◇ *The houses failed to meet local building regulations.*

---

conˈstruction ˌpermit = BUILDING PERMIT

conˌstructive disˈmissal *noun* [U; C, usually sing.] (*BrE*)
(*HR*) the situation when an employer makes an employee's working conditions so difficult or unpleasant that they have to leave their job: *The court held that the reduction in pay amounted to constructive dismissal.* → UNFAIR DISMISSAL

consul /'kɒnsl; AmE 'kɑ:nsl/ noun [C]
a government official working in a foreign city who helps people from his/her own country who are living or visiting there and encourages trade between the two countries: *the Indian consul in Toronto* ▶ **consular** /'kɒnsjələ(r); AmE 'kɑ:nsələr/ adjective

★ **consultancy** /kən'sʌltənsi/ noun (*plural* **consultancies**)

SEE ALSO: **internal consultancy**

1 [C] a company that gives expert advice on a particular subject: *Accenture, a management consultancy firm* See note at BUSINESS
O *a design/an IT/a* **management/marketing/ recruitment** *consultancy* ◆ *a consultancy* **business/ company/firm/group**
2 [U] expert advice that an independent company or person is paid to provide on a particular subject: *She's doing consultancy work with the IMF.* ◇ *He is working on a consultancy basis* (= he is not an employee).
O *consultancy* **costs/fees/work**

★ **consultant** /kən'sʌltənt/ noun [C]

SEE ALSO: **management consultant**

a person who knows a lot about a particular subject and is paid to give advice about it to other people: *a firm of business consultants* ◇ *She acts as a consultant* **to** *start-ups.* ◇ *a consultant* **on** *business ethics* See note at PROFESSION
O *a* **career/design/financial/marketing** *consultant* ◆ *an* **independent/outside** *consultant* ◆ *to* **bring in/ call in/hire/use** *a consultant*

★ **consultation** /ˌkɒnsl'teɪʃn; AmE ˌkɑ:n-/ noun

SEE ALSO: **joint consultation**

1 [U] the act of discussing sth with sb or with a group of people before a decision is made: *The plant was closed* **without** *any consultation with workers.* ◇ *The decision was taken* **in** *close consultation with* all the departments involved.
O **after/following/in/without** *consultation (with sb)* ◆ **close/full/further/proper** *consultation* ◆ **public/ wide/worker** *consultation* ◆ *a consultation* **document/paper/period/process**
2 [C] a formal meeting to discuss sth: *The firm will hold consultations with the local council before plans are finalized.*
O *to* **have/hold** *a consultation*
3 [C] a meeting with an expert to get advice: *A 30-minute consultation will cost €60.*
O *to* **book/have** *a consultation (with sb)* ◆ *to* **conduct/ do** *consultations*

★ **consulting** /kən'sʌltɪŋ/ noun [U]
(often used in the names of companies) the activity and business of providing expert advice, especially about how a business can be improved: *She works in consulting.* ◇ *Most of the large accountancy firms provide consulting services.* ◇ *Deloitte Consulting*
O *a consulting* **business/company/firm/group/ practice** ◆ *the consulting* **business/industry** ◆ *consulting* **services/work**

consume /kən'sju:m; AmE -'su:m/ verb
1 [+ obj or no obj] to buy goods and services to use yourself: *There is an index that measures how content we are with the goods and services we consume.* ◇ *the consuming public*
2 [+ obj] to use sth such as fuel, energy, time or money: *The system consumes only 5 watts of power.* ◇ *Such projects consume 20% of the country's budget.*

★ **consumer** /kən'sju:mə(r); AmE -'su:-/ noun [C]

SEE ALSO: **direct-to-consumer, end ~, ultimate ~**

1 a person who buys goods or services for their own use: *Interest rate cuts have persuaded consumers to spend more.* ◇ *Videophones are still too*

---

expensive for the average consumer. ◇ *Consumer spending will be up 2.4% this year.* ◇ *The new service has been slow to take off* (= become popular) *among consumers.* ◇ *Low interest rates were responsible for the* **consumer boom** (= period when people spend a lot). → END-USER See note at CUSTOMER
O **average/individual/rural/urban** *consumers* ◆ **domestic/foreign/online** *consumers* ◆ *consumer* **attitudes/choice/habits/needs/tastes** ◆ *consumer* **activity/expenditure/spending/trends**
2 a person, a group, a country, etc. that uses sth such as fuel or energy: *He said that America was the world's largest consumer of natural resources per head of population.* ◇ *Mexicans are believed to be the biggest consumers of soft drinks.*
O *a* **big/great/large** *consumer (of sth)* ◆ **commercial/ industrial** *consumers (of sth)* ◆ **electricity/energy** *consumers*

conˌsumer ˈadvertising noun [U]
(*Marketing*) advertising that is aimed at individual people and families, not businesses

conˌsumer aˈwareness noun [U]
(*Marketing*) how far buyers know that a product or service exists: *We are trying to strengthen consumer awareness of our brand.* → BRAND AWARENESS

conˌsumer ˌbanking = RETAIL BANKING

conˈsumer base = CUSTOMER BASE

conˌsumer beˈhaviour (*AmE spelling* **~ behavior**) noun [U]
(*Marketing*) the way in which individuals or families decide what product or service to buy and where and how to buy it: *The company sent out millions of emails to try to influence consumer behaviour.* ◇ *changes in consumer behaviour* **NOTE** This is also known as **consumer buying behaviour**.

conˌsumer ˈborrowing noun [U]
(*Economics*) the amount of money that people have borrowed, for example by using credit cards, in order to buy things: *New consumer borrowing reached €1.53 billion in October.* **SYN** CONSUMER DEBT

conˈsumer brand noun [C]
(*Marketing*) a **brand** that members of the public buy regularly: *The company has concentrated on building a strong consumer brand.* ◇ *leading consumer brands, such as Nike and Benetton*

conˌsumer ˈconfidence noun [U]
1 (*Economics*) (*also* **conˌsumer ˈsentiment**, *especially in AmE*) a measure of how willing people are to spend money, because they feel that the economy will get better or worse: *a strong increase in consumer confidence* ◇ *the link between rising unemployment and falling consumer confidence* ◇ *the* **consumer confidence index**
2 the fact that people trust and are willing to buy particular products: *The company is trying to* **restore** *consumer confidence after a scandal involving its products.* ◇ *consumer confidence* **in** *the food industry*

conˌsumer coˈoperative (*also spelled* **~ co-operative**) (*also* **conˌsumers' coˈoperative**, **ˌretail coˈoperative**) noun [C]
(*Finance*) a business that is formed, owned and controlled by a group of customers, who also share the profits

conˌsumer ˈcredit (*also* **ˌpersonal ˈcredit**) noun [U]
(*Economics; Finance*) loans made by banks and shops/stores to customers, that allow them to buy sth now and pay for it later: *In order to restrict consumer credit, the government is forced to raise*

interest rates. ◇ *Consumer credit fell by $82 million in October.* ◇ *a consumer credit agreement*

con,sumer 'credit in,surance = CREDIT INSURANCE (2)

con,sumer 'debt *noun* [U]
(*Economics*) the amount of money that people owe to shops/stores or banks for the things they have bought but not yet paid for: *Consumer debt grew $1.8 billion in September.* ◇ *One of the main risks for the economy is the high level of consumer debt.*
SYN CONSUMER BORROWING

con,sumer de'mand *noun* [U,C]
the desire or need of customers for particular goods or services: *Orders for motor vehicles rose 5%, aided by strong consumer demand.* ◇ *consumer demand for housing/flights/organic food*

con,sumer 'durables (*BrE*) (*AmE* **'durable goods**) (*also* **'durables**, *BrE*, *AmE*) *noun* [pl.]
(*Economics*; *Marketing*) goods such as cars, televisions, computers, furniture, etc. that last for a long time after you have bought them
OPP CONSUMER NON-DURABLES

con,sumer elec'tronics *noun* [pl.]
electronic goods, such as radios, televisions and music systems, that are bought and used by members of the public: *Europe's largest consumer electronics manufacturer*

con,sumer 'finance *noun* [U]
(*Finance*) the business of lending money to customers so that they can buy goods and pay for them later: *The retailer wants to sell off its consumer finance unit.*
○ *a consumer finance company/operation/unit*

con'sumer goods (*also* **con'sumer ,products**) *noun* [pl.]
(*Economics*; *Marketing*) goods such as food, clothing, etc. bought and used by individual customers: *There has been a steady increase in the demand for consumer goods.* ◇ *Unilever, the world's largest consumer goods company* SYN CONSUMPTION GOODS → CAPITAL GOODS, INDUSTRIAL GOODS

con'sumer group *noun* [C]
1 an organization that protects the rights of people who buy particular products or services: *The consumer group Energywatch criticized the gas price rise.* SYN CONSUMER WATCHDOG
2 (*Marketing*) one of a number of groups that individual buyers belong to and that influence their behaviour, such as a family group, a work group or a professional group: *consumer groups ranging from milk drinkers to motorcycle riders*

consumerism /kən'sjuːmərɪzəm; *AmE* -'suː-/ *noun* [U]

SEE ALSO: **green consumerism**

1 (*Marketing*) the activity of protecting the interests of customers or of influencing the way manufacturers make and sell goods: *The growth of consumerism has led to companies improving the service to customers after they have bought a product.*
2 (*Economics*) the buying and using of goods and services; the belief that it is good for a society or an individual person to buy and use a large quantity of goods and services: *We are living in an age of mass consumerism.*
▶ **con'sumerist** *adjective* [usually before noun]: *a consumerist society* **con'sumerist** *noun* [C]: *Advertising has been under attack by government and consumerists.*

con,sumer 'loan *noun* [C] (*especially AmE*)
a loan that a bank makes to a person for a

particular purpose, for example, to buy a car or improve their house

con'sumer maga,zine *noun* [C]
a magazine that is sold to members of the public
→ TRADE MAGAZINE

con'sumer ,market *noun* [sing.]
1 the buying and selling of goods for individual and personal use: *Sales in the consumer market are beginning to improve.*
2 the buying and selling of a particular product or service: *an expanding consumer market for leisure goods*

con'sumer 'market re'search = CONSUMER RESEARCH

con,sumer non-'durables (*also* ,non-'durables, ,non-'durable goods, dis'posables) *noun* [pl.]
(*Economics*; *Marketing*) goods such as food, drinks, newspapers, etc. that only last for a short time and need to be replaced often: *These small factories make consumer non-durables—products ranging from shoes to shampoo.* ◇ *investment in consumer non-durables* (= in companies producing these goods) OPP CONSUMER DURABLES

con'sumer ,panel (*also* **'customer ,panel**, *especially in BrE*) *noun* [C]
(*Marketing*) a carefully chosen group of customers used by a company or an organization to give their opinions or advice on particular products, services or issues, often over a long period of time: *We conduct a consumer panel in five European countries to ask people what sports shoes they buy, why they buy them, etc.*

con'sumer 'preference *noun* [U; sing.]
(*Marketing*) the desire buyers have for one product or feature rather than another: *a shift in consumer preference from white sports shoes to brown* ◇ *a strong consumer preference for one brand of soft drink*

con'sumer price *noun* [C, usually pl.]
(*Economics*) the price that the public pays for various ordinary goods and services: *Consumer prices having been falling at a rate of about one per cent a year.* ◇ *consumer prices for dairy products*

con,sumer 'price ,index *noun* [sing.] (*abbr* **CPI**)
(*Economics*) in the US and some other countries, a list of the prices of some ordinary goods and services which shows how much these prices change each month, used to measure the rate of INFLATION (= a general rise in the prices of goods and services): *The consumer price index rose 0.3 per cent in May.* SYN COST-OF-LIVING INDEX, RETAIL PRICE INDEX

con,sumer price in'flation *noun* [U]
(*Economics*) a rise in the prices that people pay for ordinary goods and services over a period of time; the rate at which this happens: *Consumer price inflation fell to only 2.1 per cent in November.*

con'sumer ,products = CONSUMER GOODS

con,sumer 'profile = CUSTOMER PROFILE (1)

con,sumer pro'motion *noun* [U,C]
(*Marketing*) activities done in order to encourage people to try or to buy a product or service: *The most widely used consumer promotion is the price reduction.* ◇ *We ran a major consumer promotion.*

con,sumer pro'tection *noun* [U]
(*Law*) the act of using laws to protect customers from dishonest businesses, products that are not safe or are too expensive, etc: *There is a need for greater consumer protection in e-commerce.* ◇ *consumer protection legislation*

con,sumer re'search (*also* **con'sumer 'market**

re'search) (also ,customer re'search, less frequent) noun [U]
(Marketing) a study of the needs and opinions of customers, especially in connection with a particular product or service: Consumer research showed that people were unwilling to pay higher prices for organic food. ◇ a consumer research group/centre/company

con,sumer re'sistance (also ,customer re'sistance, less frequent) noun [U]
(Marketing) when people are unwilling to buy a particular product or service, or dislike an aspect of it: There is growing consumer resistance to genetically modified foods. ◇ overcoming consumer resistance to shopping online
❍ to break down/ease/overcome consumer resistance

con,sumers' co'operative = CONSUMER COOPERATIVE

con,sumer 'sentiment = CONSUMER CONFIDENCE

con,sumer so'ciety noun [C]
(Economics) a society in which the buying and selling of goods and services is the most important social and economic activity: We live in a consumer society and people are used to choosing what they use and how they use it.

con,sumer 'surplus (also ,buyer's 'surplus, less frequent) noun [C]
(Economics) the difference between the highest amount that a buyer is willing to pay for sth and the lower price that he/she in fact pays

con,sumer 'watchdog noun [C] (informal)
an independent organization that checks that companies are not doing anything illegal and protects the rights of individual customers
SYN CONSUMER GROUP

★ **consumption** /kən'sʌmpʃn/ noun [U]

SEE ALSO: capital consumption

the act of using goods, services, energy, food or materials; the amount used: Consumption of soft drinks has grown by about 4 per cent this year. ◇ the country with the highest fuel consumption in the world ◇ The region produces crops for domestic consumption (= to be used in the country).
→ CONSUME
❍ average/high/low/total consumption • household/mass/personal consumption • domestic/home/local consumption • to increase/reduce consumption • consumption declines/falls/increases/rises

con'sumption ex,penditure noun [U; pl.]
(Economics) the amount of money that is spent on the goods and services that people use during a particular period of time: During the quarter, total consumption expenditure grew by 6.7%. ◇ Housing and rent accounted for 33% of personal consumption expenditures.

con'sumption goods noun [pl.]
(Economics) goods that are designed to be used by individual customers, for example clothes, food, cars, etc: Poorer countries use up most of their resources in producing consumption goods and services. SYN CONSUMER GOODS

con'sumption tax noun [C,U]
(Economics) a tax that is added to the price of goods and services: Most countries levy (= charge) consumption taxes, such as VAT or sales tax.
→ EXPENDITURE TAX, INCOME TAX, VAT

cont. abbr (only used in written English)
continued: cont. on p 18

★ **contact** /'kɒntækt; AmE 'kɑːn-/ noun, verb
●noun
1 [U] the act of communicating with sb, especially regularly: I finally made contact with (= succeeded in meeting) him in Frankfurt. ◇ They put us in contact with (= helped us to meet) an investment banker. ◇ My contact details are on my business card.
→ EYE CONTACT
❍ to get into/make contact with sb • a contact address/name/number
2 [C] a person that you know, especially sb who can be helpful to you in your work: She has some good business contacts. ◇ building up a network of contacts
❍ to build up/have/make contacts • a business/good/personal/useful contact
→ idiom at POINT noun
●verb [+ obj]
to communicate with sb, for example by telephone or letter: I've been trying to contact you all day. ◇ You can contact me on/at the following number...

'contact ,centre (AmE spelling ~ center) noun [C]
an office in which a large number of people work using telephones and email for communicating with customers, for example taking orders and answering questions → CALL CENTRE

,contact-to-'order ,ratio noun [C]
(Commerce; Marketing) the number of times a customer contacts a company before placing an order, compared to the number of orders the company receives. The contact-to-order ratio is used as a measure of how efficiently a company's ordering system works.

container /kən'teɪnə(r)/ noun [C]
1 a box, bottle, etc. in which sth can be stored or transported: drinks in plastic and glass containers
2 (Transport) a large metal box that is used for transporting goods by sea, road or rail: UK ports expect a 5% annual increase in container traffic (= the number of containers transported).
—Picture at TRANSPORT
❍ a container lorry/port/ship/truck • to load/unload containers
▶ **containerized, -ised** /kən'teɪnəraɪzd/ adjective [only before noun]: containerized cargo/shipping
containerization, -isation /kən,teɪnəraɪ'zeɪʃn; AmE -rə'z-/ noun [U]

contango /kən'tæŋɡəʊ; AmE -ɡoʊ/ noun [U]
(Finance) a situation where the price of a COMMODITY (= for example, an agricultural product, a metal, oil, etc.) that will be delivered in the future is higher than its price if it were delivered immediately: Gold is generally in contango. → BACKWARDATION

★ **content** /'kɒntent; AmE 'kɑːn-/ noun

SEE ALSO: local content

1 contents [pl.] the things that are contained in sth: Fire has caused severe damage to the contents of the building.
2 [U; pl.] the ideas in sth or the subject that sth deals with: We met to decide on the content of our presentation. ◇ She hadn't read the letter so was unaware of its contents.
3 [U] the information or other material contained on a website, a CD-ROM, etc: How do we know if our Web content meets customers' needs? ◇ the company's strength as a content provider
4 [sing.] (used after another noun) the amount of a substance that is contained in sth else: iron with a high carbon content
5 (Manufacturing) [U] the parts that make up a product: The car manufacturer is aiming for 100%

local content (= all the parts made within the country).

'content 'theory of moti'vation *noun* [C]
(*HR*) a formal idea that tries to explain why employees behave in a particular way

contingency /kənˈtɪndʒənsi/ *noun* [C] (*plural* **contingencies**)
an event that you hope will not happen, but for which you plan in case it does: *We must consider all possible contingencies.*
IDM on a conˈtingency basis if you provide services to sb/sth on **a contingency basis**, you are only paid if your services help them to achieve a particular aim, for example, winning money in a court case: *Personal injury lawyers will often work on a contingency basis.*

con'tingency ac,count = CONTINGENCY FUND

con'tingency fee (*AmE also* **con'tingent fee**) *noun* [C]
(*Law*) an arrangement by which a client pays a lawyer only if the lawyer wins money for the client in court

con'tingency fund (*also* **con'tingency ac,count, con'tingency re,serve**) *noun* [C]
(*Accounting*) an amount of money that sb keeps to pay for a possible future expense or loss: *We have a contingency fund for unexpected emergencies.*
O *to establish/have/set up* a contingency fund

con,tingency lia'bility = CONTINGENT LIABILITY

con'tingency plan *noun* [C]
a plan a business makes that will be followed if a particular disaster or other event happens: *We have a contingency plan to deal with a strike.* ◇ *contingency plans for possible breakdowns*
→ BUSINESS CONTINUITY, DISASTER RECOVERY
O *to draft/have/prepare* a contingency plan
▶ **con'tingency ,planning** *noun* [U]

con'tingency re,serve = CONTINGENCY FUND

contingent /kənˈtɪndʒənt/ *adjective* (*formal*)
that will only take place if a particular event happens: *The acquisition is contingent on/upon shareholder approval.*

con'tingent fee = CONTINGENCY FEE

con,tingent lia'bility (*also* **con,tingency lia'bility,** *less frequent*) *noun* [C]
(*Accounting*) a debt shown in a company's financial records that does not exist now but may exist in the future if a particular event happens: *The company has a number of possible contingent liabilities arising from lawsuits.*

con'tingent work *noun* [U]
(*HR*) work done by people who do not have a permanent contract with a company
SYN ASSIGNMENT WORK ▶ **con'tingent ,worker** *noun* [C]

con,tinuous 'audit *noun* [U,C]
1 (*Accounting*) a system of keeping a constant check on a company's financial records at all times rather than checking them once a year
2 (*HR*) a system of keeping a constant check on how well part of a business or a system works: *a system of staff appraisal and development that is subject to continuous audit*

con,tinuous em'ployment *noun* [U]
(*HR*) the fact of working for a company for a period of time with no breaks: *two years' continuous employment*

con,tinuous im'provement *noun* [U]
the process of continuing to make a company, its products or services better by making frequent small changes to deal with problems rather than fewer very large changes → KAIZEN

con,tinuous 'inventory (*also* **per,petual 'inventory**) *noun* [U,C]
(*Accounting*) a system of keeping a constant check on the type and quantity of products that a business has to sell

con,tinuous pro'duction (*also* **con,tinuous 'processing**) = FLOW PRODUCTION

'contra ac,count /ˈkɒntrə *AmE* ˈkɑːntrə/ *noun* [C]
(*Accounting*) a financial account that forms a pair with another account. When money goes out of one of the accounts, it goes into the other.

contraband /ˈkɒntrəbænd; *AmE* ˈkɑːn-/ *noun* [U]
goods that are illegally taken into or out of a country: *contraband goods* ◇ *to smuggle contraband*

★ **contract** *noun, verb*
● *noun* /ˈkɒntrækt; *AmE* ˈkɑːn-/ [C]

SEE ALSO: annual hours contract, bilateral ~, forward ~, futures ~, labor ~, personal ~, rolling ~, etc.

1 an official written agreement: *a contract for the supply of vehicles* ◇ *These clauses form part of the contract between buyer and seller.* ◇ *I had to draw up and cost a cleaning contract for the offices.* ◇ *The shipbuilding firm has won a contract to build two cruise liners.* ◇ *I was on a three-year contract which expired last week.* ◇ *Under the terms of the contract the job should have been finished yesterday.* ◇ *They were sued for breach of contract* (= for not keeping to a contract). See note at AGREEMENT
O *to draw up/enter into/make/sign* a contract ◆ *to be awarded/bid for/get/tender for/win* a contract ◆ *a casual/fixed-term/long-term/permanent* contract ◆ *a big/lucrative/major* contract
2 (*Finance*) an agreement to buy or sell a fixed quantity of sth at a fixed price by a fixed date in the future: *The March cocoa contract closed $46 lower.*
● *verb* /kənˈtrækt/
1 [+ obj *or* no obj] to become less or smaller; to make sth less or smaller: *a contracting market*
2 [+ obj] to make a legal agreement with sb for them to work for you or provide you with a service: *Several computer engineers have been contracted to the finance department.*
3 [no obj] to make a legal agreement to work for sb or to provide them with a service: *She has contracted to work 20 hours a week.*
PHRV con,tract 'in (to sth) (*BrE*) to formally agree that you will take part in sth **con,tract 'out (of sth)** (*BrE*) to formally agree that you will not take part in sth: *Many employees contracted out of the pension plan.* **con,tract sth 'out (to sb)** to arrange for work to be done by another company or by sb outside your company: *The maintenance and cleaning of the building has been contracted out.*

'contract bond (*also* **per'formance bond**) *noun* [C]
(*Law*) a guarantee provided by a bank or an insurance company that their customer, for example a supplier or a building company, who has a contract to supply sth or do some work for sb will complete the work. If they do not, a sum of money will be paid: *The contractor must provide a contract bond.* ◇ *A performance bond is a financial guarantee that you will honour a business contract.*

,contract 'carrier *noun* [C]
(*Transport*) a transport company that has a contract to carry goods or people for an organization
→ COMMON CARRIER

a company that has a contract to provide food for the employees of an organization

,**contract** '**labour** (AmE spelling ~ **labor**) noun [U]
(HR) workers who are employed by a business, often through another organization, for a fixed period of time, for example in order to work on a particular project

'**contract note** noun [C]
(Stock Exchange) a document that gives details of the shares, bonds, etc. that a BROKER has bought or sold for a customer

,**contract of em**'**ployment** (also ,contract of 'service) noun [C]
(HR) a formal agreement made between an employer and an employee, giving details of pay, holidays, hours of work, etc: Under her contract of employment, she is entitled to three months' pay in lieu of notice. → EMPLOYMENT (1), SERVICE CONTRACT

,**contract of in**'**surance** = INSURANCE POLICY

,**contract of** '**purchase** (also 'purchase a,greement) noun [C]
(Law) a document that gives details of the conditions under which sth is sold

,**contract of** '**service** = CONTRACT OF EMPLOYMENT

★ **contractor** /kən'træktə(r); AmE 'kɑːntræktər/ noun [C]

SEE ALSO: approved contractor, general ~, independent ~

a person or company that has a contract to do work or provide goods or services for another company: They have employed outside contractors to install the new computer system. ◇ a building/haulage contractor → SUBCONTRACTOR
O an approved/independent/outside/a recognized contractor

contractual /kən'træktʃuəl/ adjective
(Law) connected with the conditions of a legal written agreement; agreed in a contract: The company failed to meet its contractual commitments. ◇ Mr Ronson exercised his contractual right to give six months' notice.
O a contractual commitment/duty/obligation/relationship/responsibility ◆ a contractual agreement/requirement/right

'**contract** ,**worker** noun [C]
(HR) a person who works for a company for a fixed period of time, for example in order to work on a particular project, but is not an employee of the company

'**contra** ,**entry** /'kɒntrə; AmE 'kɑːntrə/noun [C]
(Accounting) an amount recorded in a financial account that forms a pair with another amount. Both amounts have the same value but one is a CREDIT and the other a DEBIT.

contrarian /kən'treəriən; AmE -'trer-/ noun [C]
(Stock Exchange) an investor who does the opposite of what everybody else is doing, for example, buying shares when other investors are selling
▶ **con**'**trarian** adjective

con,**tributing** '**shares** = PARTLY PAID SHARES

contribution /,kɒntrɪ'bjuːʃn; AmE ,kɑːn-/ noun

SEE ALSO: defined contribution

1 (HR) [C, usually pl.] an amount of money that sb or their employer pays for benefits such as health insurance, a pension, etc: You can increase your monthly contributions **to** the pension scheme.

2 [C] an amount of money that is given to a person or an organization in order to help pay for sth: Environmental taxes make only a small contribution **to** government revenues.
3 (Accounting) [C, usually sing., U] the amount of money that an individual product or service pays towards a company's FIXED COSTS, based on its sales and VARIABLE COSTS: We looked at how much contribution each product made in order to make decisions about future products.
4 (Insurance) [C,U] a share of a payment made for an item that is lost or damaged when it is insured with two or more companies; the act of sharing payments between insurance companies: If your coat is stolen from your car, your household insurer may seek a contribution from your car insurer.

contributor /kən'trɪbjətə(r)/ noun [C]
1 (HR) a person who makes regular payments to pay for benefits such as health insurance or a pension: pension-fund contributors
2 a person or thing that gives money to help pay for sth, or provides support for a project: Older people are important contributors **to** the economy.

contributory /kən'trɪbjətəri; AmE -tɔːri/ adjective
[usually before noun]
1 helping to cause sth: The bad weather was a contributory **factor** in the fall in sales.
2 involving payments from the people who will benefit: a contributory **pension plan/scheme** (= paid for by employees as well as employers) OPP NON-CONTRIBUTORY

★ **control** /kən'trəʊl; AmE -'troʊl/ noun, verb
● **noun**

SEE ALSO: budgetary control, change ~, command and ~, cost ~, credit ~, damage ~, exchange ~, etc.

1 [U] the power to make decisions about how an organization, an area, a country, etc. is run: The family has sold most of its shares and will lose control **of** the company. ◇ Workers were given more control **over** the company's management. ◇ The railway network is **under** public control.
O to acquire/assume/be given/gain/get/take control of sth ◆ to give up/hand over/keep/lose/relinquish control of sth
2 [U] the ability to make sb/sth do what you want: We have no control **over** the situation. ◇ I fear the company has lost control **of** its future. ◇ Owing to circumstances beyond our control, this service will not be available today.
O to have/keep/lose control of/over sth
3 (Finance) [U] the fact of owning sth such as shares: He claims he knows nothing about the control of shares (= who owns the shares) held through the trust.
4 [U,C] the act of restricting, limiting or managing sth; a method of doing this: Poor cost control led to the company's problems. ◇ The government has imposed tough controls **on** steel imports.
O strict/stringent/tight/tough controls ◆ to impose/introduce/relax/remove/tighten controls
5 [C, usually pl.] the switches and buttons, etc. that you use to operate a machine or a vehicle: the controls of an aircraft ◇ the control panel
6 (Technical) [C] a person, thing, group or test that you use as a standard of comparison when doing an experiment, in order to check your results: One group was treated with the new drug, and the control group was given a sugar pill.
7 [U] (also con'trol key [sing.]) (abbr Ctrl) a button on a computer keyboard that you press with other buttons when you want to perform particular operations: Press control + S to save the document.
IDM be in con'trol (of sth) to direct or manage an organization, an area or a situation be/get/run

out of con'trol to be or become impossible to manage or to control: *Consumer spending has been allowed to get out of control.* **be under con'trol** to be being dealt with successfully: *The situation's under control.* **bring/get/keep sth under con'trol** to succeed in dealing with sth so that it does not cause any harm: *attempts to keep inflation under control*

● **verb** (-ll-) [+ obj]
1 to have power over a person, company, country, etc. so that you are able to decide what they must do or how it is run: *By the age of 21 he controlled the company.* ◊ *One oil company controls 60% of the country's petrol stations.*
2 (*Finance*) to own sth such as shares: *The family still controls almost half the shares in the company.*
3 to limit sth or make it happen in a particular way: *legislation to control drug prices*
4 to stop sth from getting worse: *a rise in interest rates to control inflation*
5 to make sth, such as a machine or system, work in the way that you want it to: *The temperature is controlled by sensors.*

con'trol ac,count (*also* **ad'justment ac,count**) *noun* [C]
(*Accounting*) an account that is kept in addition to official accounts, in order to check that the official accounts are accurate

con'trol key = CONTROL *noun* (7)

con,trolled e'conomy = COMMAND ECONOMY

controller /kən'trəʊlə(r); *AmE* -'troʊ-/ *noun* [C]
1 a person who manages or directs sth, especially a large organization or part of an organization: *She's been appointed controller of their US operations.*
2 (*also* **comp'troller**, *especially in AmE*) a person who is in charge of the finances of a business or government department: *He joined the group in 2002 as a financial controller.*

con,trolling 'interest *noun* [C, usually sing.]
(*Finance*) when a person or an organization owns enough shares in a company to be able to make decisions about what the company should do; a number of shares that are bought in order to achieve this: *He has a 51% controlling interest in the new company.* → BLOCKING MINORITY

con,trolling 'shareholder (*especially BrE*)
(*AmE usually* **con,trolling 'stockholder**) *noun* [C]
(*Finance*) a person or a company that owns enough shares in a company to be able to make decisions about what the company's activities and policies should be: *She is the company's founder and controlling shareholder.*

con,trolling 'stockholder = CONTROLLING SHAREHOLDER

convene /kən'viːn/ *verb* (*formal*)
1 [+ obj] to arrange for people to come together for a formal meeting: *A special board meeting has been convened.* ◊ *He convened a team of top managers to work on improving customer service.* **NOTE** The verb **call** can be used as a less formal way of saying **convene** when talking about arranging a meeting: *A special board meeting has been called.*
2 [no obj] to come together for a formal meeting: *The committee will convene at 11.30 next Thursday.* See note at ARRANGE

convenience /kən'viːniəns/ *noun*
IDM at sb's con'venience (*formal*) at a time or a place which is suitable for sb: *Can you telephone me at your convenience to arrange a meeting?*

con'venience food *noun* [C,U]
food that is sold as a prepared meal or product, that you can cook or use very quickly and easily: *We manufacture convenience foods for the retail and catering markets.*

con'venience store *noun* [C] (*especially AmE*) a small shop/store that sells food, newspapers, etc. and often stays open all or most of the day and night: *The company operates a chain of convenience stores at gas stations.* See note at SHOP

convention /kən'venʃn/ *noun* [C]
a large meeting of the members of a profession, an organization, etc: *The industry has its annual convention in Cannes.* SYN CONFERENCE
● to **arrange/have/hold/organize** a convention ♦ to **attend/go to** a convention ♦ a convention **centre/delegate/hall**

conversion /kən'vɜːʃn; *AmE* -'vɜːrʒn; -ʃn/ *noun* [U,C]

SEE ALSO: **cash conversion**

1 the act or process of changing sth from one form, use or system to another: *the conversion of the business into a public company* ◊ *the conversion of dollars to pesos* ◊ *No conversion is needed to run this software.*
2 (*Finance*) the act of exchanging special bonds or shares for ordinary shares in a company: *The company is considering the conversion of 103 million preference shares into ordinary shares.* ◊ *The new bond has a conversion price of $10.*

con'version cost *noun* [C, usually sing.]
1 (*Accounting*) the cost of the work, the wages and other regular expenses (**overheads**) involved in producing finished goods from raw material or in changing material from one stage of production to the next: *a profit margin of 3% on direct materials cost and $10 on conversion cost*
2 (*Marketing*) the relationship between the cost of advertising products on the Internet and the number of items sold: *If we spend $1 000 on our advertising campaign and sell 20 items, the conversion cost per sale is $50.*

★ **convert** /kən'vɜːt; *AmE* -'vɜːrt/ *verb*
1 [+ obj or no obj] to change or make sth change from one form, purpose, system, etc. to another: *The software converts files from Macintosh format to Windows format.* ◊ *converting ideas into actions* ◊ *Our offices are on the second floor of a converted warehouse.* ◊ *Many TV companies are converting to digital.*
2 (*Finance*) [+ obj] to change an amount of one type of money, investment, unit, etc. into another type: *What rate will I get if I convert my dollars into euros?* ◊ *The bonds can be converted into common shares.* → idiom at ACTION

convertibility /kən,vɜːtə'bɪləti; *AmE* -,vɜːrt-/ *noun* [U]
(*Economics*) the fact that the money of a particular country can easily be changed into the money of another country: *He said that China will steadily promote the full convertibility of its currency.* → CONVERTIBLE CURRENCY

convertible /kən'vɜːtəbl; *AmE* -'vɜːrt-/ *adjective, noun*
(*Finance*)
● *adjective*
(about bonds or shares) that can be exchanged for another type of investment in a company, usually ordinary shares: *The bonds are convertible into France Telecom shares.* ◊ *The company issued €1 billion in convertible bonds.* → EXCHANGEABLE
● *noun* [C] (*also* **con,vertible se'curity**)
a special type of bond or share that can be exchanged for another investment in the company

that sold it, usually ordinary shares: *The company raised $302 million selling convertibles.*

con,vertible 'currency *noun* [C,U]
(*Economics*; *Finance*) money of one country that can easily be changed into the money of another country, especially into a strong currency such as the dollar or the euro: *All payments shall be made in freely convertible currency.* → CONVERTIBILITY

con,vertible 'note *noun* [C]
(*Finance*) a loan made to a company that has a fixed rate of interest and can either be paid back in cash or changed into ordinary shares: *The group has announced a $100 million offering (= sale) of convertible notes.*

con,vertible se'curity = CONVERTIBLE *noun*

conveyancer /kən'veɪənsə(r)/ *noun* [C]
(*Law*) a person, especially a lawyer, who is an expert in CONVEYANCING: *Ask a licensed conveyancer to check the title deeds of the house.*

conveyancing /kən'veɪənsɪŋ/ *noun* [U]
(*Law*) the work done in legally moving property from one owner to another; the branch of law that is concerned with this: *We did our own conveyancing.*

con'veyor belt (*also* **conveyor** /kən'veɪə(r)/) *noun* [C]
a continuous moving band for transporting goods from one part of a building to another, for example products in a factory or suitcases in an airport: *As the bottles move **along** the conveyor belt, tubes drop the right medicine into the right bottle.*—Picture at TRANSPORT

COO /ˌsiː əʊ 'əʊ; *AmE* oʊ 'oʊ/ = CHIEF OPERATING OFFICER

cookie /'kʊki/ *noun* [C]
(*IT*) a computer file that an Internet site sends to your computer, which is used to store information about how you use the site: *To use this website you will have to **turn cookies on** (= set your computer so that it receives them).*

,cooling-'off ,period *noun* [C]
1 a period of time during which two sides in a dispute try to reach an agreement before taking further action, for example going on strike: *If talks fail, there is a 30-day cooling-off period before the union can strike.*
2 (*Law*) a period of time after sb has agreed to buy sth, such as an insurance plan, during which they can change their mind: *You have a 14-day cooling-off period during which you can cancel the contract.*

'co-op *noun* [C] (*informal*)
a COOPERATIVE shop/store, business or farm: *Many farmers formed agricultural co-ops to obtain better prices.*

cooperative (*also spelled* **co-operative**) /kəʊ'ɒpərətɪv; *AmE* koʊ'ɑːp-/ *noun, adjective*
• *noun* [*BrE also* ,workers' co'operative] [C]

SEE ALSO: **agricultural cooperative, consumer ~, credit ~, retail ~, retailer ~, savings and credit ~, wholesale ~**

a business or other organization that is owned and run by the people involved, who work together and share the profits: *They formed a cooperative for marketing their vegetables.* ◇ *The factory is now a workers' cooperative.*
• *adjective* [usually before noun]
owned and run by the people involved, with the profits shared by them: *a cooperative association/organization/society* ◇ *a cooperative bank/farm/store*

co,operative 'marketing (*also spelled* **co-operative ~**) *noun* [U]
(*Marketing*) the activity of two or more businesses working together to advertise and sell each other's

products: *The software company has announced a cooperative marketing agreement with IBM.*

★ **coordinate** (*also spelled* **co-ordinate**) /kəʊ'ɔːdɪneɪt; *AmE* koʊ'ɔːrd-/ *verb* [+ obj]
to organize the different parts of an activity and the people involved in it so that it works well: *It is her job to coordinate the work of the teams.* ◇ *We need to develop a coordinated approach to the problem.* ◇ *a coordinating committee* ▶ **coordination** (*also spelled* **co-ordination**) /kəʊˌɔːdɪ'neɪʃn; *AmE* koʊˌɔːrd-/ *noun* [U]: *a need for greater coordination between departments* **co'ordinator** (*also spelled* **co-ordinator**) *noun* [C]: *She is the campaign's coordinator.* ◇ *a project coordinator*

copier /'kɒpiə(r); *AmE* 'kɑːp-/ = PHOTOCOPIER

★ **copy** /'kɒpi; *AmE* 'kɑːpi/ *noun, verb*
• *noun* (*plural* **copies**)

SEE ALSO: **advance copy, attested ~, body ~, carbon ~, certified ~, hard ~, knocking ~, proof ~**

1 [C] one of a number of books, newspapers, pieces of software, etc. that have been produced and are the same: *a copy of 'The Financial Times'* ◇ *The book has sold more than 8 million copies worldwide.*
2 [C] a document or computer file that is the same as an original from which it is made: *Please make two copies of the letter for the files.* ◇ *a **backup** copy of the disk (= to be used if you lose the original)* **SYN** DUPLICATE → PHOTOCOPY *noun*
○ *to keep/make/print (out) a copy*
3 [C] a product that is made to be the same as or very similar to another product, especially when this is done illegally: *a bootleg copy of a CD* → BOOTLEG, PIRATE
4 (*Marketing*) [U] written material that is to be printed or used in an advertisement: *This will make great copy for the ad.* → COPYWRITER

VOCABULARY BUILDING

Copies of products

Products that are similar to popular brands

• *They're developing a **copycat** version of the drug.*
• *It's difficult to compete in a crowded market with a **me-too** product.*
• *a **knock-off** designer handbag*

Illegal copies of software, CDs, videos, etc.

• *a stall selling **bootleg** CDs*
• ***pirated/pirate** copies of American movies*
• ***illegal/unauthorized/unlicensed** copies of the software*

• *verb* [+ obj] (**copies, copying, copied, copied**)
1 to make another document, computer file, etc. that is the same as the original: *Copy the CD **onto** your hard disk.* ◇ *illegally copied software* → PHOTOCOPY *verb* (1)
2 to do sth or try to do sth the same as sb/sth else: *Competitors are quick to copy good ideas.*
PHRV **,copy sb 'in (on sth)** to make sure that sb receives a copy of a letter, an electronic message, etc. that you are sending to sb else: *Please copy me in on all correspondence.*

copycat /'kɒpikæt; *AmE* 'kɑːp-/ *adjective* [only before noun]
that copies sb else's successful idea, design, etc: *strong sales of established and copycat drugs* ◇ *The insurer faces a host of copycat claims if it loses this case.*
○ *a copycat claim/drug/medicine/product/version*
▶ **'copycat** *noun* [C]: *copycats of the successful diabetes drug* See note at COPY

★ **copyright** /ˈkɒpiraɪt; AmE ˈkɑːp-/ noun,
adjective, verb
● **noun** [C,U]
the right to be the only person who may publish,
broadcast, make copies of, etc. an original piece of
work, such as a book, film/movie or computer
program and give other people permission to use it
or any part of it: *This software is protected by
copyright.* ◇ *The publisher has the copyright on all
his books.* ◇ *Copyright expires seventy years after the
death of the author.* ◇ *It is an infringement of
copyright to photocopy a book.*
  ❍ *to* **have/hold/own/retain** copyright *in/on* sth • *a*
  breach of/an infringement *of copyright* • *the*
  copyright **holder/owner** • *be* **in/out of/under**
  copyright

MORE ABOUT

copyright/patent/trademark

Copyright

If you produce an original piece of work such as a
book or computer program, you own the
copyright on it. This gives you the right to stop
other people from copying the work without
permission.

The right is created automatically—you do not
need to apply to the authorities.

The © symbol is used to remind people that the
work is copyright. It is not a legal requirement.

Patent

If you design a new product, device or method, for
example a new medicine, you can apply for a
patent. The patent gives you a limited period of
time, usually 20 years, in which to sell the
invention without other people copying it.

Trademarks

If you have a unique name or symbol that you use
for your products, you can apply to register it as a
trademark.

Once a trademark has been registered, other
people cannot use it in connection with similar
products.

The ® and ™ symbols are used to show that a
trademark is protected.

● *adjective*
protected by **copyright**; not allowed to be copied
without permission: *a copyright work*
● **verb** [+ obj]
to have the **copyright** for sth: *copyrighted material*
→ PATENT

ˈcopy ˌtesting *noun* [U]
(*Marketing*) the process of testing an advertisement
with a small group of people to see how effective it
is before it is used publicly: *We carried out copy
testing to see which heading attracted the most
response.* ▶ ˈcopy test *verb* [+ obj *or no obj*]: *The ads
were copy tested before the campaign and the scripts
changed.* ˈcopy test *noun* [C]: *She questions whether
copy tests can really predict sales results.*

copywriter /ˈkɒpiraɪtə(r); AmE ˈkɑːp-/ *noun* [C]
a person whose job is to write the words (**copy**) to
be used in advertisements: *She works as a
copywriter at a London ad agency.*

cordless /ˈkɔːdləs; AmE ˈkɔːrd-/ *adjective*
not connected to a power supply or another device
by wires
  ❍ *a cordless* **drill/mouse/telephone/tool**

★ **core** /kɔː(r)/ *noun, adjective*
● *noun* [C, usually sing.]
the centre of sth; the most important or essential
part of sth: *One brand will form the company's core.*
◇ *The customer is* **at the core** *of our business.* ◇ *We
have a core of experienced staff.*
● *adjective*
most important, main or essential; making the
most profit: *The manufacturer's core brands include
Zanussi and AEG.* ◇ *We moved away from our core PC
business to build a consulting firm.* ◇ *The programme
is run by a core team of researchers.* OPP NON-CORE
→ DIVERSIFY, HARD-CORE
  ❍ *a core* **brand/product** • *a core* **business/division/
  market/operation** • *core* **activities/skills** • *core*
  customers/employees/workers • *to* **focus on/
  develop/strengthen** *core brands, etc.*

ˌcore ˈarea *noun* [C]
1 the main part of a particular activity where most
of the work or business is done; the place where
most work or business is done: *The school offers
courses in three core areas: business reasoning, social
knowledge and interpersonal skills.* ◇ *We have more
readers in our core area than any other newspaper.*
2 (*HR*) one of the essential parts of a particular job:
*In your appraisal your work will be evaluated in five
core areas.*

ˌcore ˈcapital *noun* [U]
(*Finance*) the main part of a bank's funds that comes
from the money that shareholders have invested in
it and spare profits that it has kept: *Banks are
required to keep core capital at 4% of assets.*
SYN TIER I CAPITAL

ˌcore ˈcompetency (*also* ˌcore ˈcompetence)
noun [C]
1 an important ability or strength that a company
has that makes it successful and gives it an
advantage over its competitors: *Manufacturing was
their core competency.* ◇ *They decided to cut costs and
just* **focus** *on their strategic core competencies.*
2 (*HR*) an important skill that is essential for a
particular job: *The company has identified five core
competencies for executives.*

ˌcore deˈposits *noun* [pl.]
(*Finance*) the part of a bank's funds that comes from
customers who generally leave money in their bank
accounts: *The bank has found it difficult to attract
core deposits.* → RETAIL DEPOSITS

ˌcore ˈearnings *noun* [pl.]
(*Accounting*) the profit that a company makes from
its main business activities: *The company has
announced a 95% increase in core earnings.* ◇ *We
only invest in companies with strong core earnings.*

ˌcore inˈflation *noun* [U]
(*Economics*) the rate at which the prices of goods
and services rise over a period of time, measured
without considering prices that change a lot, such
as the cost of energy and some foods: *approaches to
measuring core inflation* ◇ *Core inflation rose by
2.4% in April.*

ˌcore ˈvalues *noun* [pl.]
1 the ideas and beliefs of an organization that
managers and employees share and practise in
their work: *We have nine core values and beliefs that
govern how we operate.* ◇ *to adhere to core values*
→ CORPORATE CULTURE
2 the ideas and beliefs that a person has that
influence what they do and help them make
important decisions: *I have changed, but my core
values haven't.*

ˈcorner shop (*BrE*) (*also* ˈcorner store, *BrE, AmE*)
noun [C]
a small shop/store that sells food, newspapers,
cigarettes, etc., especially one near people's houses
See note at SHOP

★ **Corp.** *abbr* (*especially AmE*)
a short way of writing **corporation**: *Sony Corp*. See
note at LTD

★ **corporate** /ˈkɔːpərət; *AmE* ˈkɔːrp-/ *adjective,
noun*

● *adjective* [only before noun]
1 connected with a company or a group, or with
business in general: *His corporate clients include 3M
and Nabisco*. ◇ *Corporate profits have grown less
than analysts expected*. ◇ *The big hotels are suffering
from cutbacks in corporate travel*.
2 (*often* **Corporate**) **corporate America, Britain,
etc.** used especially in newspapers to talk about the
people and organizations that control a country's
business: *The stock market continues to suffer as
corporate America struggles to make a profit*.
3 involving or shared by all the members of a
group: *The success of the project wasn't due to one
person—it was a corporate effort*.

● *noun* [C]

SEE ALSO: **body corporate**

1 a company, especially a large one: *The bank will
focus on corporates and financial markets*. ◇ *Asia's
leading corporates*
2 (*Finance*) = CORPORATE BOND

,**corporate ˈadvertising** *noun* [U]
(*Marketing*) advertising that tells the public about a
company, rather than particular products that it
sells, and tries to create a good image for it: *Our
corporate advertising is designed to create a strong
and desirable corporate brand image*.
→ INSTITUTIONAL ADVERTISING

,**corporate ˈbond** (*also* ˈ**corporate**) *noun* [C]
(*Finance*) a bond that is issued (= sold) by a
company

,**corporate ˈcharter** = CHARTER *noun* (2)

,**corporate communiˈcation** (*also*
,**organizational communiˈcation**) *noun* [U; C, usually
pl.]
(*HR; Marketing*) the things that a company does to
share information with its employees or with its
customers and the public, in order to keep a good
relationship with them and give a clear idea of
what it is: *Effective PR and corporate communication
will build awareness of your organization's brands
and products*. → PUBLIC RELATIONS

,**corporate ˈculture** (*also* ,**organizational
ˈculture**) *noun* [U,C]
the ideas, beliefs and values of a particular
company or organization: *We are trying to make our
corporate culture more international*.

,**corporate ˈdebt** *noun* [U]
(*Economics*) money that companies borrow from
investors, banks, etc.; investments that involve
lending money to companies: *The economy has been
burdened by heavy corporate debt*. ◇ *the corporate
debt market* → CONSUMER DEBT

,**corporate ˈfinance** *noun* [U]
the activity of helping companies to get the money
they need in order to run and develop their
businesses: *He followed a career in corporate
finance*. ◇ *the corporate finance arm* (= business/
department) *of KPMG* ▶ ,**corporate fiˈnancier** *noun*
[C]: *Senior corporate financiers were handling the
sale*.

,**corporate ˈgovernance** *noun* [U]
the way in which directors and managers control a
company and make decisions, especially decisions
that have an important effect on shareholders: *a set
of guidelines for good corporate governance*
→ GOVERNANCE

,**corporate hospiˈtality** *noun* [U]
(*Marketing*) when companies entertain customers,
business partners, their staff, etc. for example at a

big sports event, in order to help develop good
business relationships: *Corporate hospitality often
plays an important role in achieving marketing
goals*.

,**corporate iˈdentity** *noun* [C, usually sing., U]
(*Marketing*) the features, qualities or personality of a
company that make it different from others, often
expressed in its name, in symbols, in its
advertisements, etc: *The airline has developed a new
corporate identity for the 2000s*. ◇ *Your corporate
identity can create pride and motivation in your
employees*.
⊙ *to* **build/create/develop/establish** *a corporate
identity*

,**corporate ˈimage** *noun* [C, usually sing., U]
(*Marketing*) what people think or feel about a
particular company; the way that a company
presents itself to the public: *Creating a positive
corporate image is an important part of marketing
strategy*.
⊙ *to* **build/create/develop/project/promote** *a
corporate image*

,**corporate ˈincome tax** = CORPORATION TAX

,**corporate ˈladder** *noun* [C, usually sing.]
a series of jobs from junior to senior level by which
you can make progress in a company: *After several
years successfully* **climbing** *the corporate ladder, I
left to start my own business*. → CAREER LADDER

,**corporate ˈmarketing** *noun* [U]
the activity of planning and controlling a
company's marketing, to make sure that it uses the
same styles, messages, etc. and creates a particular
image for the whole company: *As vice-president of
corporate marketing, she will oversee the use of the
company's brand worldwide*.
⊙ *a corporate marketing* **plan/programme/strategy**

,**corporate ˈofficer** = COMPANY OFFICER

,**corporate ˈraider** *noun* [C]
(*Finance*) a person or company that regularly buys
large numbers of shares in other companies against
the company's wishes, either to control the
company or to sell the shares again for a large
profit: *corporate raiders, whose motto is 'Get in, get
out, get rich'* (= buy a company and then sell it
quickly for a large profit)

,**corporate reˈnewal** *noun* [U,C]
the act of making changes to a company in order to
make it more successful; the process of becoming
more successful in this way: *a programme of
corporate renewal*

,**corporate responsiˈbility** *noun* [U]
the fact of companies being concerned about social,
political or environmental issues

,**corporate ˈsecretary** = COMPANY SECRETARY

ˈ**corporate ,sector** *noun* [C, usually sing.]
the part of a country's economy that is made up of
all the public and private companies in the country:
*The corporate sector is still struggling, even as the
consumer economy booms*.

ˈ**corporate social responsiˈbility** *noun* [U,C]
(*abbr* **CSR**)
the process of running a business in a way that
helps people in society to improve their quality of
life

,**corporate ˈstrategy** *noun* [U,C]
the things a company plans to do in order to
become more successful; the activity of planning
these actions: *Our corporate strategy is to increase
the size of both of our core businesses*. ◇ *He went on
to become head of corporate strategy*.

corporate 'structure noun [C,U]
the way in which the different parts of a company or group of companies are connected with each other and managed: *We have a flat corporate structure* (= management is shared between lots of people). → HIERARCHY

corporate 'veil noun [sing.]
(*Law*) the principle that a company's shareholders or employees are not personally responsible for its debts: *What you want to avoid is anything that might pierce the corporate veil* (= would destroy this protection).

corporate 'venturing noun [U]
(*Finance*) the activity of a larger company investing in a smaller business in order to develop new products, markets, etc. as well as get a share of the profits: *Corporate venturing can bring strategic advantages to a firm.* ▶ **corporate 'venture** noun [C]: *The company is involved in a number of corporate ventures.* ◇ *a corporate venture fund*

★ **corporation** /ˌkɔːpəˈreɪʃn; *AmE* ˌkɔːrp-/ noun [C]

SEE ALSO: **closely held corporation, development ~, public ~**

1 a large company or group of companies: *the rise of giant corporations* See note at COMPANY
○ *a big/giant/large/major corporation* ◆ *a global/ multinational/transnational corporation*
2 (*Law*) (*abbr* **Corp.**) a business organization that has been officially created (**incorporated**) and is owned by shareholders: *the IBM Corporation* ◇ *They formed a corporation to buy and develop the property.*
○ *to create/form/set up a corporation* ◆ *to dissolve/ liquidate a corporation*
3 a large organization that is created by the government, in order to provide a particular service to the public: *the British Broadcasting Corporation*

WHICH WORD?

corporation/company

In both *BrE* and *AmE*, the word **company** can refer to any type of business organization, but it usually refers to a business that has been **incorporated** (= created according to a particular set of laws). The laws of different countries allow for different types of companies to be created. The type of company is shown by an abbreviation after its name (See note at LTD).

In *AmE*, but not *BrE*, the word **corporation** is used after the name of a business to show that it has been incorporated.

In *BrE*, the word corporation is usually used for foreign or international companies or public organizations: *a multinational corporation* ◇ *the British Broadcasting Corporation (BBC)*

---

corpo'ration tax (*BrE*) (*AmE* ˌcorporate 'income tax**) noun [U,C] (*abbr* **CT**)
(*Accounting*) a tax that companies pay on their profits: *Charities are not subject to corporation tax.* ◇ *The rate of corporation tax was cut from 35% to 34%.*

correction /kəˈrekʃn/ noun [C,U]

SEE ALSO: **error correction**

1 a change in prices, for example on a stock market, especially a sudden temporary fall after they have been too high: *Share prices could rise until next week, but after that there should be a*
correction. ◇ *She predicts a sharp correction in consumer spending.*
2 a change that makes a calculation more accurate than it was before: *a note indicating corrections to be made to the annual accounts* ◇ *account corrections*

correspondence /ˌkɒrəˈspɒndəns; *AmE* ˌkɔːrəˈspɑːn-; ˌkɑː-/ noun

SEE ALSO: **commercial correspondence**

1 [U,C] the activity of writing letters: *The organization has been in correspondence with the bank about the matter.* ◇ *a long correspondence*
2 [U] the letters a person sends and receives: *email correspondence* ◇ *Address all correspondence to ...*

corre'spondence course noun [C]
a course of study that you do at home, using books and exercises sent to you by post/mail: *Much of the training is done by correspondence course.*
→ DISTANCE LEARNING

correspondent /ˌkɒrəˈspɒndənt; *AmE* ˌkɔːrəˈspɑːn-; ˌkɑː-/ noun [C]
1 a person who reports news from a particular country or on a particular subject for a newspaper or a television or radio station: *a report from our Employment Correspondent*
2 a person who writes letters to another person: *email correspondents*
3 = CORRESPONDENT BANK

correspondent 'bank (*also* ˌcorres'pondent) noun [C]
(*Finance*) a bank that provides services for a bank in another place, especially one in another country: *The exporter's bank sends the bill of exchange to its correspondent bank in the importer's country.*
▶ ˌcorrespondent 'banking noun [U]

corresponding /ˌkɒrəˈspɒndɪŋ; *AmE* ˌkɔːrə- ˈspɑːn-; ˌkɑː-/ adjective
matching or connected with sth that you have just mentioned: *Fourth-quarter profits fell 10 per cent compared with the corresponding period last year.* ◇ *Although consumer spending improved, there was no corresponding increase in manufacturing activity.*
▶ ˌcorres'pondingly adverb: *a period of high demand and correspondingly high prices*

corrupt /kəˈrʌpt/ adjective, verb
● *adjective*
1 (about people) willing to use their power to do dishonest or illegal things in return for money or to get an advantage: *Corrupt employees had passed on confidential information.*
2 (about behaviour) dishonest or immoral: *The firm is notorious for its corrupt practices.*
3 (*IT*) containing changes or faults, and no longer in the original state: *software that restores corrupt files* ◇ *The text on the disk seems to be corrupt.*
● *verb*
1 to make sb/sth start behaving in a dishonest or immoral way: *He was accused of trying to corrupt a judge.* ◇ *the corrupting influence of money*
2 (*IT*) to cause mistakes to appear in a computer file, etc. with the result that the information in it is no longer correct: *It seems the virus has corrupted the file.* ◇ *rescuing a corrupted disk*

corruption /kəˈrʌpʃn/ noun [U]
1 dishonest or illegal behaviour, especially of people in authority: *allegations of bribery and corruption* ◇ *Two of the partners were charged with corruption.*
○ *to combat/eliminate/fight (against)/root out corruption*
2 (*IT*) damage to or loss of data caused by a computer, a disk, etc. not working correctly: *data corruption*

CO₂ /ˌsiː əʊ ˈtuː; *AmE* oʊ/ = CARBON DIOXIDE

cosmeceutical /ˌkɒzməˈsuːtɪkl; -ˈsjuː-; AmE ˌkɑːzməˈsuː-/ *noun* [C, usually pl.]
a COSMETIC (= a substance that you put on your face or body to make it more attractive) that also has the qualities of a medicine/drug: *skin-care cosmeceuticals ◇ the new cosmeceuticals market*
▶ **ˌcosmeˈceutical** *adjective* [only before noun]: *a cosmeceutical product ◇ The US cosmeceutical industry is growing rapidly.* **NOTE** Cosmeceutical is formed from the words **cosmetic** and **pharmaceutical**.

cosmetic /kɒzˈmetɪk; AmE kɑːz-/ *noun, adjective*
● *noun* [C, usually pl.]
a substance that you put on your face or body to make it more attractive: *She found a job selling cosmetics. ◇ the cosmetics industry ◇ cosmetic products*
● *adjective*
1 [usually before noun] connected with a substance, medical treatment, etc. that is intended to improve a person's appearance: *cosmetic surgery*
2 improving only the outside appearance of sth and not its basic character: *These reforms appear mainly cosmetic. ◇ cosmetic changes*

★ **cost** /kɒst; AmE kɔːst/ *noun, verb*
● *noun*

SEE ALSO: **acquisition cost, conversion ~, current ~, customer acquisition ~, depreciated ~, direct ~, employment ~,** etc.

1 [C,U] the amount of money that you need in order to buy, make or do sth: *The airport was built* **at a cost of** *$5.3 billion. ◇ the high cost of fuel ◇ Business should bear the full cost of developing greener energy sources. ◇ The total cost* **to** *you is €2 000. ◇ proposals to cut the costs of calling mobile phones* See note at PRICE
  ● an **additional/average/a high/low** *cost* • the **budgeted/estimated/full/gross/net/total** *cost(s)* • an **annual/a monthly** *cost* • to **absorb/bear/cover/ incur/meet/pay** *the cost(s) (of sth)* • to **cut/increase/ raise/reduce** *the cost(s) (of sth)* • to **calculate/weigh up** *the cost(s) (of sth)*
2 costs [pl.] the amount of money that a business needs to spend regularly: *The company plans to cut costs by 30%. ◇ They have stopped manufacturing in the UK due to high labour costs. ◇ the costs associated with launching a new line of clothing* → COST-CUTTING
  ● to **cut/lower/reduce/slash** *costs* • to **contain/ control/pay** *costs* • to **keep** *costs* **down/low/under control** • **high/escalating/increasing/mounting/ rising** *costs* • **falling/low** *costs* • **labour/ manufacturing/production** *costs*
3 (*Accounting*) [C] a large amount of money that a company has to pay, which affects its financial results: *The figure will be treated as an* **extraordinary** *cost* (= not connected with normal business activities) *in the profit-and-loss account for 2005. ◇ Profits fell by 7%* **before** (= without considering) *exceptional costs.*
4 [U] the amount of money that is paid to produce sth; the price that sb pays for goods they are going to sell: *Sales of computers dropped 30% and manufacturers were forced to sell their products* **below** *cost. ◇ The group has offered to provide the drugs to developing nations* **at cost.** **SYN** COST PRICE
5 (*Law*) **costs** (*also* **'court costs**) [pl.] the amount of money that sb is ordered or agrees to pay for lawyers, etc. in a legal case: *The defendant was ordered to* **pay** *€5 000* **in** *costs.*
● *verb* [+ obj] (**cost, cost**) **HELP** In meaning 3 **costed** is used for the past tense and the past participle.
1 cost (sb) sth if something **costs** a particular amount of money, you have to pay that amount in order to buy, make or do it: *The hotel costs €90 a night. ◇ How much does it cost? ◇ These delays cost small businesses well over €1 billion. ◇ These reforms will* **cost money** (= be expensive).

---

cost

total cost

variable cost

cost

fixed cost

output

2 cost (sb) sth to make sb/sth lose sth: *The rise in interest rates could cost thousands of jobs. ◇ The merger has cost the company its independence.*
3 (*Accounting*) (**costed, costed**) **cost sth (out)** (*often* **be costed**) to calculate how much money is needed to make or do sth: *Calls are costed per unit. ◇ The programme was first costed* **at** *$23 billion.*
IDM **cost a 'bomb** (*BrE*) (*informal*) to be very expensive: *An MBA can cost a bomb.* → BUNDLE (2)
cost sb 'dear to make sb lose a lot of money or suffer a lot: *Public ownership of the phone company has cost taxpayers dear.* **cost the 'earth; cost a (small) 'fortune; cost sb a (small) 'fortune** (*informal*) to be very expensive: *Office space in London costs the company a small fortune.*

'cost ac,counting *noun* [U]

SEE ALSO: **historic cost accounting**

(*Accounting*) the process of calculating and recording the detailed costs of producing goods or providing services in order to help managers control and plan a company's work: *We implemented a cost accounting system for our factory, to help make better financial decisions.*
→ MANAGEMENT ACCOUNTING
▶ **'cost ac,countant** *noun* [C]: *We abandoned the project on the advice of our cost accountant.*

'cost allo,cation *noun* [U,C]
(*Accounting*) the act of recording in a company's financial records that a cost relates to a particular department, product, etc. (a **cost centre**)

,cost and 'freight (*abbr* **CFR**) (*also* **,carriage and 'freight**) *phrase*
(*Trade*) a term meaning that the seller pays for the goods to be transported by ship to the port mentioned, but the buyer is responsible for insuring them while they are on the ship: *Our prices are quoted CFR Hamburg.* **NOTE** The abbreviation **C&F** is sometimes used for this.
→ INCOTERM

'cost ap,portionment = APPORTIONMENT (2)

'cost base *noun* [C, usually sing.]
(*Accounting*) all the things that a business pays for in order to produce and sell its products: *The firm is seeking to cut its cost base by renegotiating salaries.*
  ● a **high/low** *cost base* • to **adjust/control/cut/lower/ reduce** *a cost base*

'cost ,benefit *noun* [U,C]
(*Economics*) the relationship between the cost of doing sth and the profit or advantages that result from it: *analyzing the cost benefits of different types of industry ◇ a cost-benefit approach to decision-making*

,cost-'benefit a,nalysis (*abbr* **CBA**) (*also* **,benefit-'cost a,nalysis**) *noun* [C,U]
(*Economics*) the activity of comparing the cost of

doing sth with the profit or advantages that result from it, in order to see whether it is worth doing: *A cost-benefit analysis was carried out before the new harbour was built.*

'cost centre (*AmE spelling* ~ **center**) *noun* [C]
(*Accounting*) a part of a business that a company uses as a unit for accounting so that all the costs related to it can be calculated: *Manufacturing and distribution is our largest cost centre.* ◊ *Expenses are allocated to the appropriate cost centre.* ◊ *Equipment costs were shared between cost centres.* → PROFIT CENTRE
○ *to **allocate/charge** sth to a cost centre*

'cost-,conscious *adjective*
careful not to spend more money than is necessary

'cost con,tainment *noun* [U]
(*Accounting*) the process by which a company controls and limits how much money it spends: *The company's financial results were helped by strong cost containment.*

'cost con,trol *noun* [U,C]
(*Accounting*) the process of making sure that the different parts of a company do not spend too much money; a particular method used to achieve this: *The company suffered from overstaffing and poor cost control.* ◊ *The bank is maintaining **tight** cost controls and is cutting some management jobs.*

'cost-,cutting *noun* [U] (*often used like an adjective*)
a reduction in the amount of money a company spends: *Three thousand jobs could go as part of a cost-cutting drive.*
○ *a cost-cutting **drive/exercise/measure/plan/ programme***
▶ **'cost cut** *noun* [C]: *The company has announced $20 million of cost cuts.*

,cost-ef'fective *adjective*
giving the best possible profit or benefits for the money that is spent: *Printing the books locally is not cost-effective.* ◊ *We need a more cost-effective way to distribute our products.* ▶ **,cost-ef'fectiveness** *noun* [U]

,cost-ef'ficiency *noun*
1 [U] another way of saying COST-EFFECTIVENESS: *She has promised to improved the company's cost-efficiency.*
2 [C] a way of saving money or wasting less money in a business: *key areas where cost-efficiencies can be achieved*

,cost-ef'ficient *adjective*
another way of saying COST-EFFECTIVE: *a cost-efficient project*

,cost in'flation (*also* ,cost-'push in,flation) *noun* [U]
(*Economics*) when a cost such as wages or raw materials increases and businesses then increase their prices in order to keep their profits → DEMAND INFLATION

costing /'kɒstɪŋ; *AmE* 'kɔːst-/ *noun* [C,U]

SEE ALSO: absorption costing, batch ~, direct ~, full ~, job ~, marginal ~, standard ~, variable ~

(*Accounting*) an estimate of how much money will be needed for sth: *A team of consultants has been asked to prepare a detailed costing for the plan.* ◊ *You'd better do some costings.* ◊ *Accurate costing of the work is essential.*
○ *to **prepare/do/produce/provide** a costing*

'cost, in'surance and 'freight *phrase* (*abbr* CIF)
(*Trade*) a term meaning that the seller pays for the goods to be transported by ship to the port mentioned, and pays for basic insurance of the goods while they are on the ship: *CIF Singapore* → INCOTERM

'cost ,leader (*also* 'low-cost ,leader) *noun* [C]
(*Marketing*) a company that can make a particular product at a lower cost than its competitors: *They have positioned themselves as the cost leader **in** digital telephones.* ◊ *adopting a low-cost leader strategy*
○ *to **be/become/establish yourself as/(re)position yourself as** a cost leader*

,cost of goods 'sold (*abbr* COGS) (*also* ,cost of 'sales) *noun* [U]
(*Accounting*) the total amount of money that a business spends on obtaining and producing the goods that it sells in a particular accounting period, for example the cost of raw materials, workers, etc.: *The strike led to an increase in cost of goods sold.*

the ,cost of 'living *noun* [sing.]
the amount of money that people need to pay for ordinary goods and services, such as food, clothing and somewhere to live: *The city has the highest cost of living in the EU.*
○ *a **high/low** cost of living ◆ an **increase/a rise/fall** in the cost of living*

,cost-of-'living ad,justment *noun* [C] (*abbr* COLA)
(*Economics; HR*) in the US, an increase that is made once a year to a wage, pension, etc. because the cost of living has increased: *The Act provides for an annual cost-of-living adjustment to workers' compensation* (= for getting injured at work).

,cost-of-'living al,lowance *noun* [C, usually sing.] (*abbr* COLA)
(*Economics; HR*) extra money that an organization pays to its employees as part of their wages, because the cost of living has increased: *All nurses living in London will qualify for the new cost-of-living allowance.*

,cost-of-'living ,index *noun* [C, usually sing.]
(*Economics*) especially in the UK, a list of the prices of some ordinary goods and services which shows how much these prices change in a particular period of time: *The cost-of-living index rose by more than six per cent between May and July.*
SYN CONSUMER PRICE INDEX, RETAIL PRICE INDEX

,cost of re'placement = REPLACEMENT COST

,cost of 'sales = COST OF GOODS SOLD

,cost 'overrun *noun* [C,U]
a situation in which a manufacturer, building company, etc. spends more money on a project than was planned (**budgeted**); the extra amount that is spent: *They had huge cost overruns **on** building the factory.*

,cost per 'click *noun* [U] (*abbr* CPC)
(*Marketing*) the amount an advertiser pays to the owner of a website each time a visitor to the site clicks on their advertisement → COST PER IMPRESSION, COST PER THOUSAND

,cost per im'pression *noun* [U] (*abbr* CPI)
(*Marketing*) the cost of an advertisement or an advertising item divided by the number of times it is seen → COST PER THOUSAND

,cost per 'thousand *noun* [U] (*abbr* CPM)
(*Marketing*)
1 the cost of showing an advertisement to a thousand people using a particular form of advertising, such as television or newspapers: *Media costs are usually compared in terms of cost per thousand.* ◊ *On a cost-per-thousand basis, newspapers tend to be a cheap way of advertising.*
2 the amount an advertiser pays to the owner of a website for every thousand people who see or click on their advertisement

NOTE The **M** in the abbreviation **CPM** represents *mille*, the Latin word for a thousand.

ˌcost-'plus *adjective* [only before noun]
used to describe a way of deciding on a price for sth that involves adding a fixed extra amount to the costs for profit or to cover an unexpected increase in costs: *We offer a wide variety of goods to members at cost-plus prices.* ◇ *The work will be charged on a cost-plus basis.* → FIXED-PRICE

ˈcost price *noun* [C]
the amount of money that is paid to produce sth; the price that sb pays for goods they are going to sell: *Higher prices of raw materials have added to the manufacturer's cost price.* ◇ *Superstores often sell items such as bread and milk at below cost price.*
SYN COST → SELLING PRICE

ˌcost-'push in'flation = COST INFLATION

ˈcost ˌsaving *noun* [C, usually pl.] (*often used like an adjective*)
an amount of money that a business manages not to spend, for example by becoming smaller or more efficient: *The restructure of the company could achieve annual cost savings of $45 million.* ◇ *$45 million cost savings* ◇ *The company's cost-saving measures include reducing salaries.*
● *to achieve/make cost savings* ◆ *expected/potential/ substantial cost savings* ◆ *cost-saving initiatives/ measures/programmes/targets*

ˈcost ˌstructure *noun* [C, usually sing.]
(*Accounting*) the relationship between the different types of costs that a company has, which make up its total costs: *Your competitors may sell at lower prices because they have a different cost structure.*
● *a high/low cost structure* ◆ *to improve/lower/ maintain/manage/reduce your cost structure*

ˌcottage 'industry *noun* [C]
a small business in which the work is done by people in their homes: *Desktop publishing has become a modern cottage industry.* ◇ *She transformed the business from a cottage industry into a telecommunications giant.*

cough /kɒf; *AmE* kɔːf/ *verb*
PHRV ˌcough 'up; ˌcough sth 'up (*informal*) to give sth, especially money, unwillingly: *Unless they can convince investors to cough up more cash, the company will close.*

council /'kaʊnsl/ *noun* [C]

SEE ALSO: works council

1 (used especially in names) a group of people, especially politicians or officials, that are chosen to give advice, make rules, do research, provide money, etc: *the governing council of the European Central Bank* ◇ *She is the chairman of the Council for Economic Planning.* ◇ *a council meeting*
● *the executive/governing/ruling council (of sth)* ◆ *to form/set up a council* ◆ *to be elected to/be on/serve on/sit on a council* ◆ *a council meeting/member*
2 a group of people who are elected to govern an area such as a city or county: *She was on the Boston City Council for 20 years.*
● *to be elected to/be on/serve on/sit on/ a council* ◆ *a council meeting/member*

counsel /'kaʊnsl/ *noun* [U,C] (*plural* counsel)

SEE ALSO: general counsel

(*Law*)
1 a lawyer or group of lawyers representing sb in a court case: *to be represented by counsel* ◇ *the counsel for the defence/prosecution* ◇ *defence/prosecuting counsel* → BARRISTER
2 (*AmE*) a person or group of people that provides legal advice to an organization: *He worked as in-house counsel at CBS Records.*

counselling (*AmE spelling* counseling) /'kaʊnsəlɪŋ/ *noun* [U]

SEE ALSO: career counselling, debt counselling

professional advice that is given to sb about a problem → MENTORING at MENTOR

counsellor (*AmE spelling usually* counselor) /'kaʊnsələ(r)/ *noun* [C]

SEE ALSO: career counsellor, Commercial counsellor

1 a person whose job is to give advice: *Have you considered seeing a debt counsellor?*
● *a debt/guidance/stress counsellor* ◆ *to be referred to/see/talk to a counsellor*
2 (*Law*) (*AmE*) a lawyer

counter /'kaʊntə(r)/ *noun* [C]

SEE ALSO: bargaining counter, bean ~, over-the-~, trade ~

a long flat surface in a shop/store, bank, etc. where customers are served: *Please ask at the information counter for a free brochure.* ◇ *the assistant behind the counter* ◇ *goods displayed on a counter*—Picture at STORE
IDM under the 'counter goods that are bought or sold under the counter are sold secretly and sometimes illegally: *under-the-counter deals*

counteract /ˌkaʊntər'ækt/ *verb* [+ obj]
to do sth to reduce or prevent the bad or harmful effects of sth: *These exercises aim to counteract the effects of stress and tension at work.*

counterbid (*also spelled* counter-bid) /'kaʊntə-bɪd; *AmE* -tərb-/ (*also* 'counter-offer) *noun* [C]
(*Commerce; Finance*) an offer to buy sth, especially a company, that is higher than an offer made by sb else: *We improved our offer for the company following a counterbid from a rival Internet company.* ◇ *a counterbid for the company*

ˈcounterclaim /'kaʊntəkleɪm; *AmE* -tərk-/ *noun* [C]
(*Law*) a legal claim that sb (the **defendant**) makes against sb else who has started a legal case against them (the **claimant** or **plaintiff**): *The tenant put forward a counterclaim, in which she claimed she was wrongfully evicted.* ▶ 'counterclaim *verb* [+ obj or no obj]

countercyclical (*also spelled* counter-cyclical) /ˌkaʊntə'sɪklɪkl; *AmE* ˌkaʊntər-/ *adjective*
1 (*Economics*) used to describe actions or policies that are intended to balance or limit the effects of natural business patterns: *the government's countercyclical policy of keeping full employment despite the depression*
2 (*Finance*) used to describe shares, businesses, ways of investing, etc. that do not follow the normal pattern of business activity: *countercyclical stocks* (= for example, that rise when the economy is getting weaker)

counterfeit /'kaʊntəfɪt; *AmE* -tərf-/ *adjective, verb*
● *adjective*
(especially about money and goods for sale) made to look exactly like the real thing, in order to trick people: *Are you aware these notes are counterfeit?* ◇ *It is a crime to knowingly buy counterfeit products.*
▶ 'counterfeit *noun* [C]: *trademark counterfeits* → FORGERY
● *verb* [+ obj]
to make an exact copy of sth in order to trick people into thinking that it is the real thing: *The dollar is still the most counterfeited currency in the world.* → FORGE
▶ 'counterfeiting *noun* [U] 'counterfeiter *noun* [C]

counterfoil /ˈkaʊntəfɔɪl; AmE -tərfɔɪl/ noun [C]
(especially BrE)
the part of a cheque, ticket, etc. that you keep as a
record when you give the other part to sb else: Keep
the counterfoil as a record of your payment.
[SYN] STUB
○ to fill in/keep/tear off the counterfoil ◆ to complete/
detach/retain the counterfoil

,counter-in'flationary adjective
(Economics) that reduces or tries to reduce
INFLATION (= a general rise in the prices of goods
and services): Governments had to take counter-
inflationary measures to try to cope with the effects
of the increase in oil prices.

'counter-,offer (AmE spelling counteroffer)
noun [C]
1 (Commerce; Finance) = COUNTERBID
2 (Law) if sb trying to make an agreement or a
contract with sb makes a counter-offer, they
suggest new conditions because they cannot accept
the ones the other person has suggested
3 (HR) if a company makes a counter-offer to an
employee who has been offered a job in another
company, they offer better pay and conditions in
order to try to keep the employee

counterpart /ˈkaʊntəpɑːt; AmE -tərpɑːrt/
noun [C]
a person or thing that has a similar position or
function in a different country or organization: Our
engineering teams called their counterparts at IBM to
help resolve the problem. See note at COLLEAGUE

counterparty /ˈkaʊntəpɑːti; AmE -tərpɑːrti/ noun
[C] (plural counterparties)

SEE ALSO: central counterparty

(Finance) one of the people, companies or
organizations that are involved in a contract or
some financial business: an agreement between two
counterparties

counterproductive /ˌkaʊntəprəˈdʌktɪv; AmE
-tərp-/ adjective [not usually before noun]
having the opposite effect to the one that was
intended: It's counterproductive to put too much
pressure on your staff. → PRODUCTIVE

countersign /ˈkaʊntəsaɪn; AmE -tərs-/ verb [+ obj
or no obj]
to sign a document that has already been signed,
usually by another person, in order to show that it
is valid: All orders must be countersigned by one of
the directors.

countertrade /ˈkaʊntətreɪd; AmE -tərt-/ noun [U]
(Economics) international trade that involves
exchanging goods or services for goods or services,
rather than for money: Producer countries resort to
countertrade when they do not have enough foreign
exchange for imports. ▶ 'countertrader noun [C]
'countertrading noun [U]

,countervailing 'duty noun [C] (BrE)
(Economics) an extra tax that must be paid on
particular imports that can be produced very
cheaply in the country they come from, in order to
protect local producers → ANTI-DUMPING

,country 'risk (also ,sovereign 'risk) noun [U,C]
(Economics) the possibility that political events,
financial problems, etc. in a particular country will
decrease the value of investments in that country
or make the government, etc. unable to pay its
debts: There is still a lot of country risk to doing
business there.

coupon /ˈkuːpɒn; AmE -pɑːn; ˈkjuː-/ noun [C]

SEE ALSO: international reply coupon

1 (Marketing) a small piece of printed paper which
you can use to buy goods at a lower price or to get
sth free; a printed form that you fill in in order to
enter a competition, order goods, etc: She had saved
enough coupons to get a free flight. ◇ money-off
coupons ◇ Fill in and return the coupon below for
your free T-shirt. → VOUCHER
○ to collect/redeem/save coupons ◆ to cut out/fill in/
return/send (off) a coupon
2 (Finance) the rate of interest that is paid to sb
who invests in a bond: The bonds mature in 2010
and carry a 7% coupon.
○ to carry/have a coupon ◆ a high/low coupon

★**courier** /ˈkʊriə(r)/ noun, verb (especially BrE)
●noun [C]
1 a person or company whose job is to take
packages or important papers somewhere: We sent
the documents by courier. ◇ They operate a same-day
courier service.
2 a person who is employed by a travel company to
give advice and help to a group of tourists on
holiday
●verb [+ obj]
to send a package or an important document
somewhere by courier: Courier that letter—it needs
to get there today.

course /kɔːs; AmE kɔːrs/ noun [C]

SEE ALSO: correspondence course, refresher ~,
sandwich ~

a complete series of lessons or talks on a particular
subject: They offer a short course on management
accounting. ◇ He took a course in how to give good
presentations. ◇ All new employees attended a training
course on company policy. → idioms at COLLISION,
DUE
○ to develop/offer/run/teach a course ◆ to attend/do/
enrol on/go on/take a course ◆ to complete/fail/
pass a course ◆ a full-time/an intensive/a part-
time/short-time course

courseware /ˈkɔːsweə(r); AmE ˈkɔːrswer/ noun [U]
(IT) computer software that is designed to teach
people about a particular subject or train them in a
particular activity: courseware that helps you
prepare for the exam

★**court** /kɔːt; AmE kɔːrt/ noun

SEE ALSO: labour court, law ~, out-of-~

1 [U,C] the group of people, led by a judge, a group
of judges or another official, who listen to legal
cases and make decisions on them: We would have
to go to court in order to stop the merger. ◇ They
took the directors to court over the decision. ◇ The
firm offered $20 million to settle out of court (=
end the case without the court making a decision).
→ TRIBUNAL
○ a court hears/orders/rules/says sth ◆ a court
decision/ruling ◆ a court action/case/hearing/trial
2 [C,U] the place where legal cases are listened to
and decided: Her lawyer made a statement outside
the court. [SYN] LAW COURT → COURTROOM
3 [C] the group of people, led by a judge or
another official, who deal with a particular type of
legal case or with cases from a particular area; the
place where these cases are listened to and
decided: The sale of the company must be approved
by the bankruptcy court.
○ a bankruptcy/divorce court ◆ a county/federal/
state court
[IDM] rule/throw sth out of 'court to say that sth
is completely wrong or not worth considering,
especially in a court: The charges were thrown out of
court. ◇ Well that's my theory ruled out of court.

'court costs = COST noun (5)

courtesy /'kɜːtəsi; AmE 'kɜːrt-/ noun, adjective
● **noun** [U]
polite and pleasant behaviour that shows respect for people: *I was treated with great courtesy.*
IDM courtesy of sb/sth (*also* **by courtesy of sb/ sth**) **1** (*usually used in written English*) with the official permission of sb/sth and as a favour: *The pictures have been reproduced by courtesy of the British Museum.* **2** given as a prize or provided free by a person or an organization, often as a way of advertising: *Win a holiday in Milan, courtesy of Fiat.*
● **adjective** [only before noun]
provided free, at no cost to the person using it: *There is a courtesy bus that runs between the hotel and the airport.*

'courtesy call noun [C]
a telephone call from a bank or company that you are a customer of, to see if you are satisfied with their service

court of 'law (BrE also **'law court**) noun [C]
(*formal*)
the group of people, led by a judge or another official, who deal with legal cases; the place where cases are listened to and decided: *You can only be forced to leave your home by a court of law.* ◇ *They should be put on trial in a court of law.* ◇ *an office in the law courts*

court 'order noun [C,U]
(*Law*) a decision by a court about a legal case; the official document in which the decision is written: *We sought a court order to stop them using our trademark.* ◇ *A copy of the court order must be attached to the form.*
○ *to* **apply for/get/obtain/seek/win** *a court order* ◆ *to* **enforce/grant/issue** *a court order* ◆ *to* **break/comply with/defy/disobey** *a court order*

courtroom /'kɔːtruːm; -rʊm; AmE 'kɔːrt-/ noun [C]
a room in which trials or other legal cases are held

covenant /'kʌvənənt/ noun, verb
● **noun**
1 (*Law*) [C,U] a promise that is part of a formal written contract (a **deed**) to take particular actions or avoid particular situations: *The lease contains a covenant given by the tenant to maintain the property.* ◇ *They have committed a serious breach of covenant.*
○ *to* **breach/enforce/give/perform/relax** *a covenant*
2 (*Finance*) [C] a written promise to take particular actions or avoid particular situations which is made by sb borrowing money, so that the lender knows that the loan will be paid back: *The covenants require the company to keep a certain ratio between debt and earnings.*
○ *a* **bank/banking/debt/financial/loan** *covenant* ◆ *to* **breach/maintain/negotiate** *a covenant*
● **verb** [no obj]
(*Law*) to promise sth in a formal written contract: *Under the agreement, they covenanted to repay the loan over two years.*

★ **cover** /'kʌvə(r)/ verb, noun
● **verb**
1 [+ obj] to include sth; to deal with sth: *Do the rules cover* (= apply to) *a case like this?* ◇ *We are covered by* (= included in) *a confidentiality agreement.*
2 [+ obj] to provide a service to people or businesses in a particular area or market: *a distribution network that covers 70 countries*
3 [+ obj] to be or provide enough money for sth: *The cost covers two weeks of training.* ◇ *The show barely covered its costs.*
4 (*Insurance*) [+ obj] to protect sb/sth against loss, injury, damage, etc. by insurance: *The policy covers you and your family against personal injury.* ◇ *You are fully covered for emergency treatment abroad.*

5 [no obj] to do sb's work or duties while they are away: *Who's covering for Joan while she's on leave?*
6 (*Finance*; *Stock Exchange*) [+ obj] to buy the shares, currency, etc. that you have already agreed to sell to sb, especially so that you will not lose money if the price rises: *The Korean market saw significant gains as investors scrambled to cover their short positions.* → CLOSE verb (9)
7 [+ obj] **cover yourself (against sth)** to take action in order to protect yourself against being blamed for sth: *Companies can use performance reviews to cover themselves against lawsuits.*
● **noun**

SEE ALSO: **dividend cover, forward ~, insurance ~, interest ~**

1 [C] the outside of a book or a magazine: *the front/back cover*
2 (*Insurance*) (AmE **'coverage**) [U] protection that an insurance company provides by promising to pay you money if a particular event happens: *They took out additional cover for accidental damage.* ◇ *The policy includes cover of up to €50 000 against legal expenses.* **SYN** INSURANCE COVER
○ *to* **get/obtain/take out** *cover* ◆ *to* **arrange/provide/ withdraw** *cover* ◆ **additional/extended/standard** *cover* ◆ **accident/fire/health/life/medical** *cover* ◆ **full/restricted** *cover*
3 (*Finance*) [U] (BrE) an amount of money that is large enough to meet a debt, loss, expense, etc.
4 (*HR*) [U] when sb does another person's job when they are away or when there are not enough staff: *It's the manager's job to organize cover for staff who are absent.*
IDM under separate 'cover if a document, book or other item is sent **under separate cover**, it is sent in another envelope or package

coverage /'kʌvərɪdʒ/ noun [U]
1 (*Insurance*) (AmE) = COVER noun (2)
2 (*Commerce*) the area where a particular service is provided: *Mobile-phone coverage is limited to the big cities.* ◇ *The deal gives the airline coverage across the whole country.*
3 (*Marketing*) the percentage of a possible audience for an advertisement, etc. who see it at least once
4 (*Accounting*) = INTEREST COVER

coveralls /'kʌvərɔːlz/ = OVERALL noun (2)

'cover charge noun [C, usually sing.]
an amount of money that you pay to get into some clubs, or that you pay in addition to the cost of your meal in some restaurants

covered 'call (*also* **covered 'call option, covered 'option**) noun [C]
(*Finance*) a type of investment in which sb has the right to buy shares, bonds, etc. for a fixed price on or before a particular date (a **call option**) from a seller who owns those shares, bonds, etc. and has them ready to sell: *to write* (= sell) *a covered call*

covering 'letter (BrE) (AmE **'cover ,letter**) noun [C]
a letter that you send with a document, package, etc. that gives more information about it: *Applicants should send a covering letter* (= giving more information about themselves) *and a CV to the following address ...*

'cover note noun [C] (BrE)
(*Insurance*) a document that an insurance company provides until it sends the full insurance policy, so that you can prove you have bought insurance → BINDER (3)

'cowboy /'kaʊbɔɪ/ noun [C] (BrE) (*informal*)
a dishonest person in business, especially sb who produces work of bad quality or charges too much: *a cowboy builder/tradesman*

'co-,worker (*AmE spelling* **coworker**) *noun* [C]
a person that sb works with, doing the same kind of job: *95% of our employees know their co-workers on a first-name basis.* See note at COLLEAGUE

CPA /,si: pi: 'eɪ/ = CERTIFIED PUBLIC ACCOUNTANT, CRITICAL PATH ANALYSIS

CPC /,si: pi: 'si:/ = COST PER CLICK

CPI /,si: pi: 'aɪ/ = CONSUMER PRICE INDEX, COST PER IMPRESSION

CPM /,si: pi: 'em/ = COST PER THOUSAND, CRITICAL PATH METHOD

CPT *abbr*
(*Trade, only used in written English*) carriage paid to: *CPT Osaka*

CPU /,si: pi: 'ju:/ = CENTRAL PROCESSING UNIT

Cr (*AmE spelling* **cr**) *abbr*
(*Accounting, only used in written English*) a short way of writing **credit** in financial records

craft /krɑːft; *AmE* kræft/ *noun* [C,U]
a job or an activity for which you need skill with your hands; the objects that are made: *traditional crafts like basket-weaving ◊ a craft fair ◊ The shop sells local crafts.*

craftsman /'krɑːftsmən; *AmE* 'kræf-/ *noun* [C]
(*plural* **craftsmen** /-mən/) (*also* **'craftsperson**)
a skilled person, especially one who makes things by hand: *The furniture is built by a team of highly skilled craftsmen.*

craftsmanship /'krɑːftsmənʃɪp; *AmE* 'kræf-/ *noun* [U]
1 the skill used by sb to make sth of high quality with their hands: *Their designs combine traditional craftsmanship and the latest technology.*
2 the quality of design and work shown by sth that has been made by hand: *the superb craftsmanship of the interior of the car*

craftsperson /'krɑːftspɜːsn; *AmE* 'kræftspɜːrsn/ (*plural* **craftspeople** /-piːpl/) = CRAFTSMAN

craftswoman /'krɑːftswʊmən; *AmE* 'kræf-/ *noun* [C] (*plural* **craftswomen** /-wɪmɪn/)
a skilled woman, especially one who makes things by hand

crane /kreɪn/ *noun* [C]
a tall machine with a long arm, used to lift and move building materials and other heavy objects: *They used a crane to lower the bridge into position.* —Picture at TRANSPORT

★ crash /kræʃ/ *noun, verb*
● *noun* [C]
1 a sudden serious fall in the price or value of sth; the occasion when a business, etc. fails: *a crash in share prices ◊ the dot-com crash*
❍ *a bank/financial/property/stock market* crash
2 (*IT*) a sudden failure of a computer or software: *We believe the system crash was caused by disk failure.*
● *verb*
1 [no obj] to lose value or fail suddenly and quickly: *Share prices crashed to an all-time low yesterday. ◊ The business crashed with debts of €80 million.*
2 (*IT*) [+ obj or no obj] (about a computer or software) to suddenly stop or be stopped from working because there is a fault: *The virus crashed our computer network. ◊ The system keeps crashing.*
IDM **,crash and 'burn** (*informal*) to fail in a dramatic way: *Why do some teams fly and other crash and burn?*

crate /kreɪt/ *noun* [C]
1 a large wooden, metal or plastic box in which goods are carried or stored: *a crate of bananas* —Picture at TRANSPORT
2 the amount of sth contained in a **crate**: *They drank two crates of soft drinks at the meeting.*

,crawling 'peg (*also* **,sliding 'peg**) *noun* [C]
(*Economics*) a way of controlling the EXCHANGE RATE (= the price of a currency in relation to other currencies) by changing it by small amounts at regular intervals: *They abandoned a fixed exchange rate in favour of a crawling peg.* → ADJUSTABLE PEG

CRD /,si: ɑ: 'di:; *AmE* ɑːr/ = CASH RATIO DEPOSITS

★ creative /kri'eɪtɪv/ *adjective, noun*
● *adjective*
1 involving the use of skill and imagination to make or do new things: *a creative solution to the problem ◊ We encourage employees to engage in creative thinking. ◊ the creative process*
2 having the skill and imagination to make or do new things: *creative people*
▶ **creative** *adverb* **creativity** /,kriːeɪ'tɪvəti/ *noun* [U]: *Creativity and originality are more important than technical skill.*
● *noun* [C]
(*Marketing, informal*)
1 a person in an advertising agency who designs advertisements, rather than sb who manages the agency or sells advertising: *ad agency creatives*
2 an advertisement, especially on the Internet: *They developed 200 creatives in order to establish a memorable campaign.*

cre,ative ac'counting (*also* **cre,ative ac'countancy**) *noun* [U]
(*Accounting, informal*) recording a company's financial activities in a way that hides the true situation: *The benefits of the merger were exaggerated through creative accounting.*

cre,ative di'rector *noun* [C]
(*Marketing*) a person in a company or an advertising agency who is responsible for planning and managing the imaginative work of advertising and selling products

cre,ative 'financing *noun* [U]
unusual or imaginative ways of obtaining money to buy sth, especially a home, or to finance a business: *We offer creative financing for low-income families wanting to buy homes.*

crèche (*also spelled* **creche**) /kreʃ/ *noun* [C] (*BrE*)
a place where babies and small children are looked after while their parents are working, studying, etc: *plans for more workplace creches*

credentials /krə'denʃlz/ *noun* [pl.]
the qualities, training or experience that make you suitable to do sth: *She doesn't have the right credentials for the job. ◊ He has impeccable credentials as a researcher.*
❍ *impeccable/impressive/strong* credentials

★ credit /'kredɪt/ *noun, verb*
● *noun*

SEE ALSO: **bank credit, bank giro ~, bilateral ~, carbon ~, consumer ~, deferred ~, documentary ~,** etc.

1 (*Commerce*) [U] an arrangement that you make with a bank, shop/store, etc., to be able to buy things now and pay for them later: *I bought it on credit. ◊ The supplier won't give her credit because she's a new customer. ◊ We offer you six months' interest-free credit* (= without an extra charge for interest) *on purchases over €800.*
❍ *to get/have/use* credit ◆ *to extend/give/offer/ provide* credit ◆ *to deny/refuse* credit ◆ *a credit agreement/limit* ◆ *credit facilities/terms*

2 (*Finance*) [U] money that financial institutions lend to businesses, governments and people: *It is unlikely that the bank will extend additional credit to the firm.* ◇ *Credit costs have risen sharply for smaller businesses.*
❍ to **gain access to/have access to/get/obtain/seek** credit • to **extend/provide** credit • **domestic/ international** credit
3 [U] the fact that there is money in a bank account: *Your account is in credit.* → BE, REMAIN, ETC. IN THE BLACK at BLACK, OVERDRAWN
4 [C] an amount that is paid into a bank account; a record of this: *a credit of €100* OPP DEBIT
5 (*Accounting*) [C] (*abbr* **Cr**) (*AmE spelling* **cr**) an amount that is written in a company's financial account to show an increase in money that the company owes or a decrease in the value of its assets: *Produce a trial balance to ensure that credits equal the debits.* ◇ *the credit side of an account* OPP DEBIT—Picture at T-ACCOUNT NOTE The **credits** are recorded on the right side of a traditional T-account.
6 [C,U] a reduction in an amount of money you have to pay; a payment that you have a right to receive: *The government's tax plans included expanding the existing credit for small businesses.*
7 (*Accounting*) [C,U] an amount of money that is paid back or owed to you, because you paid too much; a record of the amount: *We will issue you with a credit for any damaged goods that you return.* ◇ *a credit of €60*
8 [U] the status of being trusted to pay back money to sb who lends it to you: *Her credit isn't good anywhere now.* → CREDIT HISTORY, CREDIT RATING
● *verb* [+ obj]
1 to put an amount of money into a bank account: *The funds will be credited **to** your cheque account today.* ◇ *Your account has been credited **with** $50 000.*
2 (*Accounting*) to write an amount in a company's financial account to show an increase in the money the company owes or a decrease in the value of its assets: *The cash received was debited in the cash book and credited to the sales account.*
OPP DEBIT NOTE You **credit** a traditional T-account by writing amounts on the right side.

'credit ac,count = ACCOUNT *noun* (2)

'credit ad,vice *noun* [C]
a message from a bank to a customer, telling them that a payment has been made into their bank account

'credit ,agency = CREDIT RATING AGENCY

'credit a,nalysis *noun* [U,C]
(*Finance*) the activity and business of calculating the risks of lending money to particular companies or governments: *a firm specializing in credit analysis* ◇ *conducting a credit analysis of a company* ▸ **'credit ,analyst** *noun* [C]

'credit ap,praisal *noun* [U,C]
(*Finance*) an examination of how much money a person or a company can afford to borrow; an opinion about their ability to pay their debts: *All new accounts will be subject to credit appraisal.* ◇ *The firm has an overall 'fair' credit appraisal.*

'credit ,balance *noun* [C]
1 the amount of money that is left in a bank account at a particular time: *The bank is offering 4% interest on credit balances.* ◇ *The bank statement shows a credit balance of €274.* OPP DEBIT BALANCE
2 (*Accounting*) in a company's financial records, the amount by which the total CREDITS are greater than the total DEBITS in a particular account: *A credit balance of $127 was carried forward from the previous year.*

'credit ,bureau = CREDIT REFERENCE AGENCY

★'credit card *noun* [C]
a small plastic card that you can use to buy goods and services and pay for them later: *Can I pay by credit card?* ◇ *I'll **put it on** (= use) my credit card.* ◇ *We accept all major credit cards.* ◇ *Please fill in your name and credit-card number.* → DEBIT CARD
❍ to **pay by/use** a credit card • to **accept/take** credit cards • a credit-card **payment/transaction** • a credit-card **bill/receipt/slip/statement**

'credit check *noun* [C]
an act of checking how well sb has paid their debts in the past, to see if they are a reliable person: *We **run** credit checks on all loan applicants.* ▸ **'credit ,checking** *noun* [U]: *a credit checking business*

'credit ,company *noun* [C]
1 a company that lends money for people or companies to buy things: *the Ford Motor Credit Company* ◇ *a credit company specializing in truck leasing and hire-purchase* → FINANCE COMPANY
2 a company that provides (**issues**) credit cards to people

'credit con,trol *noun* [C,U]
1 (*Accounting*) the way that a business manages the money it is owed, for example checking whether its customers can pay, making sure that payments are made on time, etc: *A lack of credit control led to large bills going unpaid.* ◇ *developing a credit control policy*
2 (*Finance*) the way that a bank controls the money it lends, for example checking who it lends money to and how much it can safely lend them: *The bank has **tightened** credit controls in response to the worsening economy.*
3 (*Economics*) the actions of a government to limit the amount of money that people or companies can borrow or spend using credit: *The government **imposed** credit controls in an attempt to reduce inflation.*

'credit co,operative (*also* ,savings and 'credit co,operative) *noun* [C]
(*Finance*) in some countries, a group of people, especially from a particular profession, who create a fund of money from which they can borrow at low rates of interest SYN CREDIT SOCIETY, CREDIT UNION

'credit cre,ation *noun* [U]
(*Economics*) the fact of banks making more money available for borrowers, so increasing the MONEY SUPPLY

'credit ex,posure *noun* [U]
(*Finance*) money that an organization has lent to sb and so risks losing if it is not paid back: *The bank incurred heavy losses as a result of its credit exposure to the failing company.* SYN DEBT EXPOSURE

'credit fa,cility *noun* [C]
(*Finance*) an arrangement that a business has with a bank, company, etc. to be able to borrow money up to an agreed limit for a particular period of time: *The company has secured a 5-year credit facility worth $350 million.* SYN CREDIT LINE

'credit ,history *noun* [C, usually sing.]
a record of the loans and credit that sb has received and whether they have paid back the amounts that they owe in the right way: *Getting a mortgage requires a good credit history.* ◇ *The rate of interest will be based on your credit history.* → CREDIT RATING
❍ a **good/bad/poor** credit history • **little/no** credit history • to **build/create/establish/have** a credit history

'credit infor,mation *noun* [U]
details about the financial state of a company or a

person that is used to judge how much credit they can be given and are likely to be able to pay back: *We supply up-to-date credit information on companies you may be considering doing business with.*

'credit in,surance *noun* [U,C]
1 insurance that a company buys to protect themselves against financial losses if customers do not pay their bills: *The company has taken out credit insurance to guard against bad debt.*
2 (*also* con,sumer 'credit in,surance) insurance that sb buys that will make payments on a loan, credit card, etc. if they cannot make them, for example because they are ill/sick and cannot work

'credit ,limit (*also* ,credit line) *noun* [C, usually sing.]
the highest amount of money that a customer is allowed to owe, for example to a bank or on a credit card: *She has a credit limit of $6 500 on her Visa card.* ◇ *There is a fee for exceeding your credit limit.* ◇ *The country's credit limit for buying grain has been doubled.*
❍ *to be at/exceed/have a credit limit ◆ to impose/increase/raise/reduce/set sb's credit limit*

'credit line *noun* [C]
1 (*Finance*) (*also* ,line of 'credit) an amount of credit that a bank, company, etc. makes available to a person or a company for a particular period: *We negotiated an arrangement with a new bank that gave us a $250 000 credit line.* ◇ *The company was forced to draw on credit lines as its finances worsened.* SYN CREDIT FACILITY
❍ *to arrange/get/have/open/secure/set up a credit line ◆ to give sb/provide a line of credit ◆ to cut off/extend/increase a credit line ◆ to draw (down) on/overdraw/pay down/use a line of credit*
2 = CREDIT LIMIT

'credit loss *noun* [C,U]
(*Accounting*) money that a business loses because its customers have not paid the money they owe: *The bank reported credit losses of $67 million.* ◇ *credit loss protection/provision*

'credit ,market *noun* [C]
(*Economics*) the business of financial institutions lending money to people, companies or governments: *Poor households have limited access to credit markets.* ◇ *The financial crisis had a massive effect on the credit market.*

'credit note *noun* [C] (*BrE*)
(*Commerce*) a document that a shop/store gives you when you have returned sth, that allows you to have goods of the same value in exchange

★creditor /'kredɪtə(r)/ *noun*

SEE ALSO: general creditor, preferential ~, trade ~

1 [C] a person, company, country, etc. that sb/sth owes money to: *The property will be sold to pay off their creditors.* ◇ *a meeting of the company's creditors* ◇ *Japan, the worlds biggest creditor nation* (= it has invested more in other countries than other countries have invested in it)
2 (*Accounting*) **creditors** [pl.] (*BrE*) the amounts that a business owes to its suppliers or to people who have made loans, shown as LIABILITIES on its BALANCE SHEET: *creditors falling due within one year* (= debts that must be paid within a year) SYN ACCOUNTS PAYABLE
→ DEBTOR (2)

,creditors' com'mittee *noun* [C]
(*Law*) a group of people representing the **creditors** of a BANKRUPT company or person, that help decide how the debts will be paid back: *The*

agreement reached by the creditors' committee still has to be approved by the court.

'creditors' ,ledger *noun* [C]
(*Accounting*) in a company's financial records, the group of accounts in which amounts owed to suppliers are recorded SYN PURCHASE LEDGER

'credit ,policy *noun* [U,C]
1 (*Economics*) the decisions that a government makes about how easy or expensive it will be for people and businesses to borrow money: *The government has adopted a tight credit policy and high interest rates.* → CREDIT CONTROL
2 (*Finance*) the decisions a business has made about the way it will lend money or give credit; a document that describes these decisions: *A business should have a credit policy before extending any credit.*

'credit ,quality *noun* [U]
(*Finance*)
1 how likely or unlikely it is that people or businesses will pay back money they borrow: *The bank has seen a decline in consumer credit quality.*
2 how likely or unlikely it is that a company issuing (= selling) a bond will be able to make regular payments of interest and repay the value of the bond: *stocks with good credit quality*

'credit ,rating (*also* 'rating) *noun* [C,U]
(*Finance*) a measurement of the ability of a company, person or government to pay their debts; the process of estimating this: *The company's credit rating has been downgraded to 'junk' status.* ◇ *People with no credit rating can find it difficult to take out a loan.* SYN DEBT RATING → CREDIT SCORE
❍ *to downgrade/lower/raise/upgrade a credit rating ◆ to be given/have a credit rating ◆ a good/low/poor credit rating*

'credit ,rating ,agency (*also* 'credit ,ratings ,agency, 'credit ,agency) *noun* [C]
(*Finance*) an organization that provides scores (**credit ratings**) for how likely companies, people or governments are to pay their debts: *The credit rating agency has now lowered the company's credit rating.* SYN RATING AGENCY → CREDIT REFERENCE AGENCY

'credit ,rationing *noun* [U]
(*Economics*) when lenders limit the amount of money available for borrowers or the rate of interest is very high

,credit 'reference ,agency (*BrE*) (*also* 'credit ,bureau, *especially in AmE*) *noun* [C]
(*Finance*) an organization that keeps information about whether people have paid their debts and provides this information to banks or companies: *You can ask a credit reference agency for a copy of your report.* ◇ *Debts not repaid may be registered with credit reference agencies.* → CREDIT RATING AGENCY

'credit re,pair *noun* [U]
(*Finance*) the activity of helping a person or a company to improve their CREDIT RATING, so that they will be able to borrow money or get credit: *a guide to successful credit and credit repair*

'credit re,port *noun* [C]
(*Finance*) a document that gives information about a borrower's financial position and how they have paid back loans in the past: *Credit bureaus must provide you with a free copy of your credit report if you've been turned down for credit.* ▶ **'credit re,porting** *noun* [U]: *a campaign for fair credit reporting* ◇ *credit reporting agencies*

'credit re,search *noun* [U]
(*Finance*) studying the financial state of particular companies and their ability to pay their debts: *She's a member of the credit research team at JP Morgan.*

'credit risk *noun*
(*Finance*)
1 [U,C] how likely it is that sb/sth will be able to pay their debts: *The interest rate charged reflects the credit risk of the borrower.*
2 [C] a particular person or company who is likely not to be able to pay their debts: *The company is not a serious credit risk.*

'credit sale *noun*
1 (*Commerce*; *Law*) [C,U] an act of selling sth where the price will only be paid in the future but the buyer becomes the owner as soon as the goods are received: *To protect our cash we limited credit sales and charged interest on every credit sale.* ◇ *a credit sale agreement* → HIRE PURCHASE
2 (*Accounting*) **credit sales** [pl.] the amount of money that a business receives in an accounting period for goods or services sold in this way: *Total credit sales invoiced for March were $90 000.*

'credit score (*also* **'credit ,scoring**) *noun* [C]
(*Finance*) a number that is a measurement of a person's ability to pay their debts: *Before offering you a loan, a lender will check your credit score.* → CREDIT RATING

'credit ,scoring *noun*
(*Finance*)
1 [U] the activity of calculating a CREDIT SCORE for sb before deciding whether or not to give them a loan or credit
2 [C] = CREDIT SCORE

'credit so,ciety *noun* [C]
(*Finance*) a group of people, especially from a particular profession, who create a fund of money from which they can borrow at low rates of interest: *an agricultural credit society* SYN CREDIT UNION

'credit squeeze *noun* [C, usually sing.]
(*Economics*) a period of time during which it becomes difficult and expensive to borrow money; actions taken by a government to achieve this: *Consumer demand collapsed as a result of the credit squeeze.*

'credit ,standing (*also* **'credit ,status**) *noun* [sing.]
the reputation that a person or an organization has for paying their debts: *The country has managed to restore its international credit standing.* ◇ *a satisfactory credit standing*
SYN CREDITWORTHINESS

'credit terms *noun* [pl.]
(*Commerce*) the conditions on which a business is prepared to give credit to sb/sth, such as the time limit for paying the debt, the amount that can be spent, etc: *Our standard credit terms are full payment within 30 days.* ◇ *All their business is cash; they don't offer credit terms.* ◇ *buying goods on credit terms*
➊ *easy/favourable/standard* credit terms • *to agree/ grant/negotiate/offer* credit terms

'credit ,transfer *noun* [U,C] (*BrE*)
the process of sending money from one person's bank account to another's: *Your salary will be paid monthly by automated credit transfer.* → BACS

'credit ,union *noun* [C]
(*Finance*) an organization whose members create a fund of money from which they can borrow at low rates of interest

creditworthy /ˈkredɪtwɜːði; AmE -wɜːrði/ *adjective*
able to be trusted to pay back money that is owed; safe to lend money to: *The bank will lend only to the most creditworthy borrowers.* ▶ **'creditworthiness** *noun* [U] SYN CREDIT STANDING

creep /kriːp/ *verb*, *noun*
● *verb* [no obj]
to change very slowly or by a small amount, especially to increase or rise in this way: *Unemployment has crept back to 9%.* ◇ *Exports crept up 0.6% to $77.3 billion.* ◇ *House prices continue to creep upwards.*
● *noun* [U]

SEE ALSO: **bracket creep, mission creep**

slow, steady movement, especially an increase: *the gradual creep of inflation*

creeping /ˈkriːpɪŋ/ *adjective* [only before noun]
happening or increasing gradually and not easily noticed: *The move is part of the government's creeping financial reforms.* ◇ *their attempt to gain creeping control of the company*
➊ creeping *control/expenses/inflation/privatization*

crew /kruː/ *noun* [C with sing./pl. verb]

SEE ALSO: **flight crew**

1 all the people working on a ship, plane, etc: *There were 85 passengers and crew on the flight.*
2 all the people working on a ship, plane, etc. except the officers who are in charge: *the pilot and cabin crew*
3 a group of people with special technical skills working together: *a camera/an ambulance crew*

crime /kraɪm/ *noun*
1 [C] an illegal act that can be punished by law: *No bank employee has been charged with a crime.* ◇ *In some countries tax evasion is not a crime.*
➊ *to carry out/commit* a crime • *to accuse sb of/ charge sb with* a crime
2 [U] illegal activities: *an increase in violent crime* ◇ *the government's fight against computer crime* ◇ *reducing the crime rate*
➊ *non-violent/petty/serious/violent* crime • *computer/corporate/financial/white-collar* crime

criminal /ˈkrɪmɪnl/ *adjective*, *noun*
● *adjective*
1 [usually before noun] connected with or involving crime: *It is a criminal offence to bribe a public official.* ◇ *There was no evidence of criminal wrongdoing.*
➊ *a criminal act/conviction/offence* • *criminal activity/behaviour/conduct/wrongdoing* • *criminal damage/injury/liability/negligence*
2 [only before noun] connected to the laws and institutions that deal with crime: *He could face criminal charges for obstruction of justice.* ◇ *the criminal justice system*
➊ *a criminal case/charge/prosecution/trial* • *a criminal inquiry/investigation*
● *noun* [C]
a person who commits a crime: *websites and Internet programs targeted by criminals*

,criminal 'law *noun* [U]
(*Law*) law that deals with crimes, rather than with commercial issues and the relationships between individuals, companies, etc: *Such actions are punishable under criminal law.* ◇ *a breach of the criminal law* → CIVIL LAW
▶ **,criminal 'lawyer** *noun* [C]

crisis /ˈkraɪsɪs/ *noun* [C,U] (*plural* **crises** /ˈkraɪsiːz/)
a time of great danger or difficulty when problems must be solved or important decisions must be made: *The country's economic crisis has deepened.* ◇ *The business is still in crisis.* ◇ *The global car industry was in one of its most serious crises ever.*
➊ *a major/serious/the worst* crisis • *an economic/a corporate/financial/political* crisis • *a banking/ cash/currency/debt/an energy* crisis • *a crisis arises/ deepens/is over/worsens* • *to face/avert/resolve/*

suffer/tackle a crisis • sth *causes/creates/triggers* a crisis

'crisis-hit adjective [only before noun]
experiencing a **crisis**, especially a financial one: *The crisis-hit firm will have to make redundancies.*
O a crisis-hit *company/country/industry*

'crisis ,management noun [U]
actions taken by an organization to deal with a very difficult or unexpected situation: *Market crises can develop very quickly and crisis management needs to be adapted to each situation.*

criterion /kraɪˈtɪəriən; AmE -ˈtɪr-/ noun [C] (plural **criteria** /-riə/)
a standard that you use when you make a decision or form an opinion about sb/sth: *What criteria do you use for hiring new staff?* ◊ *Each investment must meet a set of financial criteria.*
O to *establish/set/use* criteria (for sth) • to *fulfil/meet/satisfy* criteria

,critical 'incident noun [C]
(HR) an example of the way a person doing a job behaves that has a good or bad effect: *identifying the critical incidents that distinguish satisfactory workers from unsatisfactory workers*

,critical 'incident ,method (also ,critical 'incidents ,method) noun [C]
(HR) a way of deciding what abilities are needed to do a particular job and discovering how well sb is doing their job, by looking at real examples of the way people have behaved in the job that have had good or bad effects: *The critical incidents method can be used to decide on training needs for managers.*

,critical 'mass noun [U] [sing.]
the number of customers, amount of resources, etc. needed to allow a business, an industry, etc. to make a profit and continue without outside help: *We need five or six stores to achieve critical mass.* ◊ *They lack critical mass in their core markets.*
O to *achieve/create/have/reach* (a) critical mass

,critical 'path noun [sing.]
(Economics; Production) the series of tasks in a project that must be completed on time in order for the project to finish on time—Picture at PERT

,critical 'path a,nalysis (abbr CPA) (also ,critical 'path ,method abbr CPM) (also **'network a,nalysis**) noun [U,C]
(Economics; Production) a way of planning a project and calculating how long it will last by examining which order of tasks will have the fewest delays and complete the project in the fastest and cheapest way: *They use critical path analysis for scheduling complex jobs.* ◊ *The critical path method is a key tool for managing project schedules.*—Picture at PERT

,critical suc'cess ,factor noun [C, usually pl.]
one of the areas of a business that are most important for it to be successful: *Customer service is a critical success factor for any retailer.* ◊ *identifying the critical success factors of a business*

CRM /ˌsiː ɑːr ˈem/ = CUSTOMER RELATIONSHIP MANAGEMENT

,crony 'capitalism noun [U] (informal)
a system in some CAPITALIST countries in which business contracts, bank loans, etc. are given to the family and friends of the government and business leaders

crop /krɒp; AmE krɑːp/ noun [C]

SEE ALSO: **cash crop**

1 a plant that is grown in large quantities, especially as food: *Sugar has always been an*

important crop on the island. ◊ *concerns over* **GM** (= genetically modified) *crops*
2 the amount of grain, fruit, etc. that is grown in one season: *a fall in this year's coffee crop* ◊ *We are looking forward to a* **bumper** (= very large) *crop.*

cross /krɒs; AmE krɔːs/ verb [+ obj] (BrE)
if you **cross** a cheque, you draw two lines across it to show that it must be paid into sb's bank account and not exchanged for cash: *a crossed cheque* ◊ *Make sure you cross the cheque and write 'account payee only' between the lines.* → ACCOUNT PAYEE, UNCROSSED CHEQUE
IDM a crossed 'line a situation in which you can hear another telephone call when you are making a call, because a connection has been wrongly made

,cross-'border adjective [only before noun]
that takes place between people or businesses in different countries, especially ones that are next to or near each other: *The number of cross-border mergers has increased in recent years.* ◊ *cross-border trade/trading*

,cross-e'xamine verb [+ obj or no obj]
to question sb carefully and in a lot of detail about answers that they have already given, especially a witness for the other side in a court case: *They always cross-examine applicants* (= ask them a lot of questions) *on their previous experience.* ▸ **,cross-exami'nation** noun [U,C]: *He confessed to the crime under* (= during) *cross-examination.*

,cross-'functional adjective
(HR) that involves people, departments, etc. with different jobs or skills working together: *We use cross-functional* **teams** *to develop new products.*

,cross guaran'tee noun [C]
(Finance) a promise made by members of a particular group of companies to pay back the debts of a company in the group if it fails to do so, in order to help the company borrow money: *The company's subsidiaries have provided cross guarantees to secure the loan.* ◊ *cross guarantees between subsidiaries* ▸ **,cross-guaran'tee** verb [+ obj]

'cross-,holding (also ,cross-'shareholding) noun [C] (especially BrE)
(Finance) a situation in which two companies or groups own some of each other's shares; the shares that each company or group owns in the other: *a cross-holding of shares between Fiat's car division and General Motors* ◊ *Investors generally dislike cross-holdings as they reduce the chances of a takeover.*

,cross-'media adjective
involving or using different types of media such as television, radio, etc: *We have a cross-media strategy, using television, radio and print for our advertising.* ◊ *cross-media publishing*

,cross-media 'ownership noun [U] (especially BrE)
(Economics) the fact that a single organization controlling several different kinds of media company such as newspapers, television stations, etc: *The new cross-media ownership rules would still prevent the owner of a large newspaper business from buying a large TV channel.*

,cross-'merchandising noun [U]
(Marketing) the activity of displaying related products together in a shop/store to encourage customers to buy several items instead of just one: *the cross-merchandising of swimwear* **with** *sunglasses* ◊ *We use cross-merchandising to encourage multiple sales.* ▸ **,cross-'merchandise** verb [+ obj or no obj]: *Apples can be cross-merchandised* **with** *other lunch box suggestions.*
→ CROSS-PROMOTION, CROSS-SELLING

,cross-'ownership noun [U]
(*Economics*) the fact of a single organization controlling companies with related interests, especially in the area of newspapers and television: *Legislation prevented cross-ownership of a newspaper and television station in the same city.*

,cross-'platform adjective [usually before noun]
(*IT*) that can be used with or involves different types of computer systems (**platforms**): *There are a few cross-platform problems with the software.* ◇ *cross-platform compatibility*

,cross-'posting noun [U]
1 (*IT*) when the same message is sent to more than one news or discussion group on the Internet at the same time
2 (*HR*) (*BrE*) when an employee is moved to a different department, country or company

,cross-pro'motion noun [C,U]
(*Marketing*)
1 a set of advertisements or other activities that are designed to help two companies sell their products or services together: *The two TV networks have agreed to an extensive cross-promotion.*
2 a situation where a company advertises one of its products, such as a newspaper or a book, in another
→ CROSS-MERCHANDISING, CROSS-SELLING
▶ **,cross-pro'motional** adjective [only before noun]: *cross-promotional opportunities* ◇ *a cross-promotional deal/partnership* **,cross-pro'mote** verb [+ obj or no obj]

'cross-rate noun [C]
(*Finance*) an EXCHANGE RATE for two currencies that is calculated by comparing the value of each currency to a third currency (especially the US dollar): *the cross-rate between the yen and the krone*

,cross-'selling noun [U]
(*Marketing*) the activity of selling other products or services that your company or another company provides at the same time as a customer is buying one product or service: *cross-selling opportunities/ activities* ◇ *The inquiry will examine the cross-selling of banking products.* ▶ **,cross-'sell** verb [+ obj]
→ CROSS-MERCHANDISING, CROSS-PROMOTION

,cross-'shareholding = CROSS-HOLDING

,crowded 'market noun [C]
a situation where there are a lot of companies all trying to sell similar products: *The new beauty magazine is being launched into an already crowded market.* ◇ *competing in a crowded market*

,crown 'jewel noun [C]
the most valuable part of sth, especially of a business or an industry: *The company needs to raise cash and is selling off its crown jewels.* **NOTE** Jewel **in the crown** has the same meaning: *Harvey Nichols regard the Edinburgh store as the jewel in their crown.*

crude /kruːd/ adjective, noun
• *adjective*
1 (about oil and other natural substances) in its natural state, before it has been treated with chemicals: *the refining of crude oil*
❶ *crude* **oil/petroleum/iron/metal/steel/sugar**
2 (**cruder, crudest**) simple and not very accurate but giving a general idea of sth: *We produced a crude estimate of our spending for the next four years.*
❶ *a crude* **calculation/estimate/measure** (*of sth*)
• *noun* (*also* ,crude 'oil) [U]
oil in its natural state, before it has been treated with chemicals: *50 000 barrels of crude* ◇ *a rise in crude prices*

crunch /krʌntʃ/ noun, verb
• *noun* [C, usually sing.]
a situation in which there is suddenly not enough

of sth, especially money: *The company is facing a severe cash crunch.*
❶ *a* **cash/credit/liquidity/supply** *crunch* ◆ *an* **energy/a labour** *crunch* ◆ *to* **avoid/ease/experience/face** *a crunch*
• *verb* [+ obj]
(*IT*) to deal with large amounts of data very quickly: *Today's processors can crunch* **numbers** *at an incredible rate.* → NUMBER CRUNCHER

'C share (*also* **class 'C share**) → A/B/C SHARE

CSR /ˌsiː es ˈɑː(r)/ = CORPORATE SOCIAL RESPONSIBILITY

'C-suite noun [C, usually sing.] (*often* **the C-suite**) the most important managers in a company: *senior executives at the C-suite level* ◇ *C-suite executives*
NOTE The letter C in **C-suite** may refer to the word 'corporate', or to 'chief', which is found in some job titles.

CT /ˌsiː ˈtiː/ = CORPORATION TAX

,C-to-'C = C2C

Ctrl = CONTROL *noun* (7)

cu. *abbr*
a short way of writing **cubic**: *a volume of 15 cu. m* (= 15 cubic metres)

'cube farm noun [C] (*informal*)
an office that is divided into CUBICLES

cubic /ˈkjuːbɪk/ adjective [only before noun] (*abbr* **cu.**)
used to show that a measurement is the volume of sth, that is the height multiplied by the length and the width: *The plant processes 7 million cubic metres of gas a day.*

cubicle /ˈkjuːbɪkl/ noun [C] (*especially AmE*)
a small office that is made by separating off part of a larger room: *She shares a cubicle with three team members.* ◇ *working* **in** *a cubicle*

culture /ˈkʌltʃə(r)/ noun [C,U]

SEE ALSO: **corporate culture, organizational ~, safety ~**

the ways in which people in an organization relate to each other and deal with their work: *Team meetings are part of the company's culture.* ◇ *We have a culture in which staff work quickly.* ◇ *developing a culture of innovation*
❶ *to* **create/develop/have/promote** *a culture (of sth)* ◆ **business/company/management/workplace** *culture*

cum /kʌm/ preposition
(*Finance*) used to show that the buyer of a share, bond, etc. is getting the right to claim the thing mentioned: *The shares will trade cum bonus until 15 March 2005.* ◇ *The bonds were acquired on a cum-interest basis.* **NOTE** Cum is the Latin word for 'with'. OPP EX

,cum 'dividend (*also* ,cum 'div., *informal*) adverb, adjective
(*Finance*) (about a share that is sold) giving the buyer the right to claim the next payment (**dividend**) arranged: *buying shares cum dividend* ◇ *the cum-dividend price* OPP EX-DIVIDEND

cume /kjuːm/ = CUMULATIVE AUDIENCE

cumulative /ˈkjuːmjələtɪv; *AmE* -leɪtɪv/ adjective
(about a figure) that includes all the amounts that have been added previously: *We predict that cumulative sales will exceed 2 million units by 2006.* ◇ *That gives a cumulative* **total** *of 4 103.*

,cumulative 'audience (*also* **cume**, *informal*) noun [C, usually sing.]
(*Marketing*) the number of different people who

watch a particular television channel, hear a radio programme, etc. over one or more periods of time: *We reach an estimated weekly cumulative audience of 1 million viewers.* ◊ *the cumulative audience for the evening news* → CIRCULATION, REACH

ˌcumulative 'dividend *noun* [C]
(*Finance*) the regular payment that is made to sb who owns a CUMULATIVE PREFERENCE SHARE: *The shares were issued with a cumulative dividend of 9.25%, payable quarterly.*

ˌcumulative 'preference share *noun* [C]
(*BrE*) (*AmE* **ˌcumulative preferred 'stock** [U])
(*Finance*) a type of share that a company issues (= sells) that gives its owner the right to receive regular payments (**dividends**) from the company. If the company cannot afford to make a payment on time, it has to pay the amount later when it can afford to: *5% cumulative preference shares* (= ones for which you receive a 5% dividend)

curb /kɜːb; *AmE* kɜːrb/ *verb, noun*
●*verb* [+ obj]
to control or limit sth, especially sth bad: *raising interest rates to curb inflation* ◊ *A new resolution has curbed the power of the board.*
●*noun* [C]
a control or limit on sth: *a curb on local government spending* ◊ *The local steel industry is protected through import curbs.* [SYN] LIMITATION

'curb ˌmarket = KERB MARKET

VOCABULARY BUILDING

Describing what happens to currencies

Deciding the value of a currency
- *Many developing economies have their currencies **pegged** to the dollar.*
- *The government allowed the peso to **float** freely.*
- *Countries **devalued** their currencies to encourage exports.*
- *They **revalued** the currency to reflect the change in economic growth.*

Increases in value
- *The yen has **appreciated** around 7.5% against the dollar so far this year.*
- *The Swiss franc is **strengthening** against the euro.*

Decreases in value
- *The central bank cannot afford to defend a **depreciating** currency.*
- *The rand **weakened** by 5% to the euro.*

See note at INCREASE

★ **currency** /ˈkʌrənsi; *AmE* ˈkɜːr-/ *noun* (*plural* **currencies**)

SEE ALSO: **basket of currencies, convertible ~, digital ~, dual ~, e-currency, fixed ~, hard ~,** etc.

1 [C,U] the system of money that a country uses; the value of the country's money: *Brazil's currency, the real* ◊ *trading in foreign currencies* ◊ *I had to change my euros into local currency.* ◊ *A weaker currency would help our exports.* ◊ *The government has devalued the national currency by 29%.* ◊ *The dollar rose against European currencies but fell against the Japanese yen.* See note at INCREASE
  ➕ **common/domestic/foreign/local/national** currency ◆ a **stable/strong/volatile/weak** currency ◆ to **buy/ change/exchange/sell** currency ◆ to **devalue/ depreciate/peg/prop up** a currency ◆ currency **devaluation/fluctuation/movement** ◆ a currency **dealer/speculator/trader**

2 [U] the period of time during which sth is valid or is used: *The facts must remain true and accurate during **the currency of** the advertisement.*

'currency acˌcount (*also* ˌforeign 'currency acˌcount) *noun* [C]
(*Finance*) a type of CURRENT ACCOUNT for businesses that is available in a wide range of foreign currencies

'currency bloc (*also* **bloc**) *noun* [C]
(*Economics*) a group of countries that use the same type of money: *the creation of the euro currency bloc*

'currency board *noun* [C]
(*Economics*) in some countries, a government institution that controls the value of the country's money, for example, by deciding its EXCHANGE RATE

'currency efˌfect *noun* [C, usually pl.]
(*Accounting*) the way that changes in the value of currency can change a financial result: *Sales were up 5%—or 1% excluding currency effects.* ◊ *positive/ negative currency effects*

'currency exˌposure (*also* ˌforeign 'currency exˌposure) *noun* [U,C]
(*Finance*) the amount of an investment that is in a foreign currency and could be affected by changes in the value of the currency; the state of being at risk in this way: *The company manages its currency exposure by keeping dollar reserves.* ◊ *Our main currency exposures are in the Canadian dollar and the yen.* [SYN] CURRENCY RISK

'currency ˌfuture *noun* [C, usually pl.]
(*Finance*) a type of investment that involves agreeing to buy or sell a fixed amount of a foreign currency on a specific date in the future at a fixed price (which is usually stated in US dollars)

'currency hedge *noun* [C]
(*Finance*) a way of trying to protect investments from problems caused by changes in the value of foreign currency; an investment that reduces this risk

'currency ˌmarket *noun* [C]
(*Finance*) a market in which traders buy and sell currencies: *The euro weakened against the dollar on the currency markets.* ◊ *the star performers in the currency market* [SYN] FOREIGN EXCHANGE MARKET

'currency note *noun* [C, usually pl.]
money of a particular system in the form of BANKNOTES: *The old currency notes have been taken out of circulation.*

'currency ˌoption *noun* [C]
(*Finance*) a type of investment that allows you to exchange an amount of one currency for another at an agreed EXCHANGE RATE within a particular period of time: *We use currency options to guard against foreign exchange risk.*

'currency pair *noun* [C]
(*Finance*) the relation in value between two particular currencies: *the EUR/USD currency pair* (= the euro and the United States dollar)

'currency peg *noun* [C]
(*Economics*) an economic policy in which the value of a country's currency is linked to that of a foreign currency: *The government was forced to abandon the one-to-one currency peg with the dollar.* ◊ *a fixed currency peg* → ADJUSTABLE PEG

'currency rate *noun* [C]
the relation in value between one currency and another: *the currency rate between the yen and the pound* [SYN] EXCHANGE RATE

'currency reˌserves = FOREIGN CURRENCY RESERVES

'currency risk (also ˌforeign 'currency risk) noun
[U,C; usually pl.]
(Finance) the possibility that an investment that is in
a foreign currency could lose value because of
changes in the value of the currency; the state of
being at risk in this way: The group **is exposed to**
currency risk from its international business. ◇ to
hedge (against) (= protect against) currency risk
SYN CURRENCY EXPOSURE

current /'kʌrənt; AmE 'kɜːr-/ adjective [only before
noun]
happening now; of the present time: current
economic conditions ◇ your current employer ◇ a
budget for the current year

'current acˌcount noun [C]
1 (BrE) (AmE 'checking acˌcount) (also 'cash
acˌcount, AmE, BrE) (BrE also 'cheque acˌcount) a
bank account that you use to receive payments and
pay bills, for example by cheque or BANK
TRANSFER: When you **open** a current account, you
will be issued with a chequebook. ◇ The monthly
interest will be **paid** directly **into** your current
account. ◇ Some banks will pay interest on current
accounts.
2 (Economics) (also exˌternal ac'count) a record of
the money coming into and going out of a country
as a result of imports and exports of goods and
services, income from investments, etc: Declining
car exports were responsible for the €2 billion current
account **deficit** (= the amount by which money
received from exports, etc. was less than money
spent on imports, etc.). → BALANCE OF TRADE,
CAPITAL ACCOUNT

ˌ**current 'asset** (also ˌcirculating 'asset) noun [C,
usually pl.]

SEE ALSO: net current assets

(Accounting) an asset that a company holds for a
short period of time, including cash or sth that can
easily provide cash, such as products to be sold; the
value of these assets: The firm has $1.2 billion in
current assets, of which $800 million is held in cash.
◇ If current liabilities are greater than current assets,
it becomes difficult to finance day-to-day operations.
→ CAPITAL ASSET, CURRENT LIABILITY

ˌ**current 'cost** noun [C]
(Accounting) the present value of sth, calculated by
increasing its original cost to include a sum for
INFLATION (= a general rise in the price of goods
and services), or by considering the cost of buying
or producing the same item today: The accounts are
modified to maintain the current costs of assets.
→ HISTORICAL COST, REPLACEMENT COST

ˌ**current ˌliaˈbility** noun [C, usually pl.] (also
ˌshort-term liaˈbilities [pl.])
(Accounting) a debt that must be paid within a year;
the value of these debts in a company's financial
records: Total current liabilities were $149 million. ◇
The bank overdraft is repayable within three months
and thus a current liability. SYN AMOUNT FALLING
DUE WITHIN ONE YEAR → CURRENT ASSET, LONG-
TERM LIABILITIES, NON-CURRENT LIABILITIES

ˌ**current 'prices** noun [pl.]
(Accounting; Economics)
1 the prices that are being paid today for similar
things: At current prices, the company is worth
around €23 billion.
2 the original amount increased to include a sum
for INFLATION (= a general rise in the price of
goods and services): The 1992 hurricane cost the
state almost $20 billion in current prices.

'current ˌratio = ACID-TEST RATIO

ˌ**current 'yield** noun [C, usually sing.]
(Finance) the amount of interest paid on an
investment that compares the annual interest
payment to the current price of the investment: The

current yield **on** the bond is 5.2%. → REDEMPTION
YIELD

curriculum vitae /kəˌrɪkjələm 'viːtaɪ/ = CV

cursor /'kɜːsə(r); AmE 'kɜːrs-/ noun [C]
a small mark on a computer screen that can be
moved and that shows the place, for example,
where text will appear when typing: **Move** the
cursor to the bottom of the screen. → POINTER

curtail /kɜːˈteɪl; AmE kɜːrˈt-/ verb [+ obj] (formal)
to limit or reduce sth: There is pressure on the
company to curtail spending. ◇ Union powers have
been curtailed. ▶ **curˈtailment** noun [U]

curve /kɜːv; AmE kɜːrv/ noun

SEE ALSO: adoption curve, bell ~, demand ~,
experience ~, J-curve, learning ~

1 [C] a line on a graph that shows the relationship
between two things: the unemployment-income
curve (= showing the relationship between the
number of unemployed people and national
income) ◇ The new range of clothing has made their
sales curve steeper.
☉ a flat/shallow/steep curve ∘ a curve **flattens/
steepens** ∘ to **plot** a curve (on a graph)
2 the curve [sing.] the general level of skill,
knowledge, etc. that exists in a particular industry
or area of activity: We invest a lot in research to try
to stay **ahead of** the curve.

cushion /'kʊʃn/ verb, noun
● **verb** [+ obj]
to reduce the unpleasant effects of sth: The south of
the country has been cushioned **from** the worst
effects of the recession. ◇ The government is expected
to reduce taxes to **cushion the blow** of higher
unemployment (= make the effects less bad).
● **noun** [C]
something that protects you against sth unpleasant
that might happen: Their €59 million cash reserve
should provide a comfortable cushion if their
expansion plans fail. ◇ They need a **cash cushion** to
survive the difficulties ahead.

custodial /kʌˈstəʊdiəl; AmE -'stoʊ-/ adjective
[usually before noun]
1 that involves spending time in prison: The judge
gave him a custodial sentence.
2 (Finance) relating to the work of a CUSTODIAN (2):
the custodial fees charged for holding securities

cuˈstodial acˌcount noun [C]
(Finance) in the US, a collection of money, property
or shares, etc. that sb (a **custodian**) manages on
behalf of a child; the account in which these items
are recorded: She opened a custodial account for her
daughter at the bank. ◇ Almost any kind of property
can be transferred to a custodial account.

custodian /kʌˈstəʊdiən; AmE -'stoʊ-/ noun [C]
1 a person who is responsible for taking care of or
protecting sth: the museum's custodians ◇ He sees his
role as custodian of the corporate culture.
2 (Finance) a financial institution that looks after
shares, bonds, etc. and their certificates on behalf
of investors: The trust has appointed Kleinwort
Benson to act as custodian of the securities. ◇ a
custodian bank
3 (Law) (AmE) in the US, a person or company that
is given the responsibility of looking after property
or money on behalf of a child
4 (AmE) = CARETAKER

custody /'kʌstədi/ noun [U]
1 the legal right or duty to take care of or keep sb/
sth; the act of taking care of sth/sb: The bank
provides **safe custody** for valuables. ◇ The records
are **in the custody of** the National Archives.

2 (*Finance*) the activity of keeping shares, bonds, etc. and their certificates on behalf of investors: *The bank holds millions of pounds' worth of assets in custody for pension funds.* ◇ *a custody bank/account*

custom /'kʌstəm/ *noun, adjective*

●*noun*

1 [U] (*especially BrE*) the fact of being a customer: *They have cut their prices to attract custom.* ◇ *Thank you for your custom. Please call again.* SYN BUSINESS
2 [C,U] an accepted way of behaving or of doing sth in a particular company or industry: *The payment of a commission was a trade custom.* ◇ *It is the employer's custom and practice* (= it has been done like this for so long it is now like a law) *for full-time workers to work a 37-hour week.*

●*adjective* [only before noun] (*especially AmE*)
= CUSTOM-BUILT, CUSTOM-MADE: *a company making custom furniture*

,**custom-'built** (*also* '**custom**, *especially in AmE*) *adjective*
built according to a special design, usually for a particular person or company: *The computers are custom-built for each client.* ◇ *a custom-built Ferrari*
→ BESPOKE

★ **customer** /'kʌstəmə(r)/ *noun* [C]

SEE ALSO: **internal customer, target customer**

a person or an organization that buys a product or service from a shop/store or a business: *The company has around 7 million customers worldwide.* ◇ *They had no problem finding customers for their new service.* ◇ *one of the store's biggest customers* ◇ *Can you serve the next customer?* → CLIENT See note at SUPPLY CHAIN
● *to acquire/attract/find/get/have/keep/lose customers* ◆ *a big/good/large/loyal/regular customer* ◆ *an awkward/a demanding/difficult customer* ◆ *existing/future/new/potential customers* ◆ *customer feedback/preferences*

WHICH WORD?

customer/client/clientele/consumer

Customer and **client** can be used to refer to either people or companies that buy things, while **consumer** and **clientele** are used about people.

The word **customer** is usually used when the thing being sold is a standard product or service: *Phone companies are competing to sign up domestic customers.*

Client is preferred when the thing being sold is specially prepared or designed, for example professional advice: *They had advised their clients to buy the shares.*

It is now common for organizations providing public services, for example hospitals or bus companies, to refer to the people who use their services as **customers** or **clients** rather than patients, passengers, etc. This is because the words customer and client are thought to present a more professional image.

The word **consumer** is used to describe any member of the public who buys things rather than a customer of a particular company: *changes in consumer behaviour* ◇ *consumer demand for cheap flights*

The word **clientele** describes all the people who use a particular shop/store, restaurant or service: *The restaurant attracts a younger clientele.*

,**customer acqui'sition** *noun* [U]
(*Marketing*) the activity of getting new customers for a business: *They spent nearly €1.5 on customer acquisition.* ◇ *They are suffering from poor customer acquisition rates.*

,**customer acqui'sition cost** = ACQUISITION COST (2)

'**customer base** (*also* con'sumer base, *less frequent*) *noun* [C, usually sing.]
all the people who buy or use a particular product or service: *We need to appeal to a wider customer base.* → INSTALLED BASE

,**customer 'capital** *noun* [U]
(*Economics*; *HR*) the value of a company's relationship with its customers and the businesses that it sells good or services to

,**customer 'care** = CUSTOMER SERVICE

,**customer-'centric** *adjective*
that is organized around the needs of customers: *building a customer-centric organization* ◇ *a customer-centric approach*

,**customer-'focused** *adjective*
giving all your attention and effort to the needs of customers: *They have changed from a sales-oriented to a customer-focused business.* ▶ ,**customer 'focus** *noun* [U; C, usually sing.]

'**customer 'lifetime 'value** = LIFETIME VALUE

,**customer 'loyalty** *noun* [U]
the fact that a customer prefers to use a particular shop/store, etc. or continues to buy a particular type of product: *We send 'thank-you letters' to all our clients as a way of strengthening customer loyalty.*
● *to build/develop/increase/strengthen customer loyalty*

,**customer 'management** *noun* [U]
a system of collecting and analysing information about customers in order to provide them with the products or services they need: *customer management technology*

'**customer ,panel** = CONSUMER PANEL

,**customer 'profile** *noun* [C]
(*Marketing*)
1 (*also* con,sumer 'profile) a detailed description of the type of person who buys a particular product or service, shops at a particular store, etc: *We may need to adjust the style of clothes we sell to suit our customer profile.*
2 a detailed description of a particular customer: *The software instantly displays the customer profile that corresponds to the caller's phone number.*

,**customer re'lations** *noun*
(*Marketing*)
1 [pl.] the way in which a company deals with its customers: *trying to improve customer relations* ◇ *a customer relations manager*
● *excellent/good customer relations* ◆ *to improve customer relations*
2 [U with sing./pl. verb; pl.] the department of a company that is responsible for dealing with customers: *Contact us at Customer Relations if you have a problem.*

,**customer re'lationship** *noun* [C] (*often* the customer relationship) the way in which a company and its customers behave towards each other: *Managing the customer relationship is critical to long-term success.* ◇ *the importance of maintaining healthy customer relationships*

,**customer re'lationship ,management**, ,**customer re'lationship ,marketing** (*abbr* **CRM**) (*also* re'lationship ,management) *noun* [U]
(*IT*; *Marketing*) a system in which a business aims to develop a good relationship with customers, for

example by keeping information about their needs, in order to sell as many goods or services as possible and keep customers satisfied; software that helps businesses do this: *Customer relationship management has become a top priority for companies seeking a competitive advantage in today's economy.* ◇ *The software company is the market leader in CRM.* ◇ *CRM solutions/software*
▶ **customer re'lationship ,manager** *noun* [C]

,customer re'search = CONSUMER RESEARCH

,customer re'sistance = CONSUMER RESISTANCE

,customer ,satis'faction *noun* [U]
the extent to which customers are happy with a particular product or service: *Our staff work as a team to achieve customer satisfaction.* ◇ *The firm did well in a recent customer-satisfaction survey.*
❍ *to* **achieve/create/improve/increase/measure** *customer satisfaction* • *a customer-satisfaction* **index/rating/survey**

★ **,customer 'service** (*also* ,customer 'care [U]) *noun*
1 [U,C] the way in which a company treats its customers and answers their questions, complaints, etc: *How you handle complaints is an important part of customer service.* ◇ *changes in the way some customer services are delivered* ◇ *You can now contact our customer-service centre by email.*
❍ **excellent/good/poor** *customer service* • *to* **deliver/improve/provide** *customer service* • *a customer-service* **adviser/centre/department/manager/representative**
2 ,customer 'services [U with sing./pl. verb; pl.] the department in a company that deals with customers' questions, complaints, etc: *A copy of the brochure is available from customer services.* ◇ *She is head of customer services.* ◇ *Customer Services has/have improved its/their efficiency.*

customize , -ise /ˈkʌstəmaɪz/ *verb* [+ obj]
to make or change sth to meet the needs of the customer or user: *We customize our training courses to fit the needs of your staff.* ◇ *You can customize the software in several ways.* ▶ **'customized, -ised** *adjective: a customized version of the software* **,customi'zation, -isation** *noun* [U]

,custom-'made (*also* 'custom) *adjective* (*both especially AmE*)
designed and made for a particular person: *custom-made shoes* SYN BESPOKE

★ **customs** /ˈkʌstəmz/ *noun* [pl.]
1 (*usually* **Customs**) the government department that gives permission for goods to be imported and charges taxes on them (**import duties**); the officials at an airport, etc. that work for this department: *The Customs have seized large quantities of cigarettes and tobacco.* ◇ *obtaining customs* **clearance** *for the goods* (= permission to import them)
HELP American English uses a singular verb with **customs** in this meaning. → CUSTOMS AND EXCISE, CUSTOMS OFFICER
2 the place at an airport, etc. where your bags are checked as you come into a country: *to* **go through** *customs and passport control*
3 (*Trade*) = CUSTOMS DUTY

'customs ,agent = CUSTOMS OFFICER, CUSTOMS BROKER

,Customs and 'Excise *noun* [U]
in the UK, the government department that collects taxes on goods bought and sold and on goods brought into the country, and that checks what is brought in, now part of HM REVENUE AND CUSTOMS

'customs bond *noun* [C,U] (*especially AmE*)
(*Trade*) a type of insurance that an importer must buy, which promises that all taxes on goods that they import will be paid and all the rules obeyed:

You are required to **post** (= provide) *a customs bond for the goods.* ◇ *goods shipped* **under** *customs bond*

'customs ,broker (*also* 'customs ,agent) *noun* [C]
(*Trade*) a person or company that is paid to arrange for goods to be brought into a country (to **clear customs**) on behalf of an importer

'customs decla'ration *noun* [C]
(*Trade*) an official description of the goods that you want to send to another country or bring into a country: *A fully completed customs declaration must be attached to the package.* ◇ *On entering the country, all tourists must fill in a customs declaration form.*

'customs ,duty *noun* [C, usually pl., U] (*also* 'customs [pl.])
(*Trade*) taxes that must be paid to the government when goods are imported: *the customs duties* **on** *foreign cars* ◇ **paying** *customs duties* ◇ *Fruit imported from these countries* **is subject to** *customs duty of 20%.*

'customs ,entry *noun* [C,U]
(*Trade*) an official record that must be made of goods that are brought into or taken out of a country; the process of bringing goods into or taking goods out of a country in the official way: *You are required to complete a separate customs entry for each shipment of goods.* ◇ *following the formal customs entry procedures*

'customs ,officer (*also* 'customs ,of,ficial) (*also* 'customs ,agent, *especially in AmE*) *noun* [C]
a government official that works at an airport, etc., whose job involves checking for illegally imported goods

'customs ,union *noun* [C]
(*Economics*) a group of countries that have agreed not to charge taxes (**import duties**) on goods they trade with each other, and to charge the same taxes on goods imported from other countries: *Andorra joined the EC customs union in July 1990.*

,Customs 'warehouse = BONDED WAREHOUSE

cut /kʌt/ *verb, noun*
● *verb* [+ obj] (**cutting, cut, cut**)
1 to reduce sth, especially by a large amount: *The airline is to cut 2 500 more jobs.* ◇ *The number of factories has been cut* **from** *13* **to** *6.* ◇ *His salary has been cut* **by** *ten per cent.* ◇ *Forecasts for their 2005 profits have been cut.*
2 to remove text or images from one place on a computer screen, in order to put them somewhere else: *You can cut and paste between the programs.*
IDM **cut a 'deal (with sb); cut (sb) a 'deal** (*informal*) to make an arrangement with sb: *She cut a deal with the boss who allowed her to work on the project if she raised half the funds.* **a cut and 'paste job** (*informal*) a document that sb has created quickly by taking ideas or sections of text from other documents, rather than sth original that they have worked hard on
PHR V ,cut 'back (on sth); ,cut sth 'back to reduce sth: *There is no evidence that shoppers were cutting back* (= on spending) *over the holiday season.* ◇ *to cut back on spending* ◇ *If we don't sell more we'll have to cut back production.* → CUTBACK ,cut 'down (on sth); ,cut sth 'down (to sth) to reduce the size, amount or number of sth: *She wants to cut her travel load down to two days a week.* ,cut sb 'in (on sth) (*informal*) to give sb a share of the profit in a business or an activity ,cut sb 'off to interrupt sb who is speaking on the telephone by breaking the connection: *We were cut off in the middle of our conversation.* ,cut 'off sb/sth (*often* be cut off) to stop the supply of sth to sb/sth: *The bank has threatened to cut off their credit.*

●noun [C]

SEE ALSO: **price cut**

1 a reduction in the amount or number of sb/sth: *making a cut **in** interest rates* ◊ *an interest-rate cut* ◊ *The aircraft maker announced a further 1 000 cuts (= in the number of employees) last week.* ◊ *The managers had to take a 20% cut in pay.*
○ *interest-rate/tax* cuts • *budget/cost/expenditure/ spending* cuts • *job/pay/wage* cuts • *a big/deep/ dramatic* cut • *to announce/implement/make/ propose* cuts
2 (*informal*) [usually sing.] a share in a profit or money: *We take a cut of any sales to customers that we refer to them.*
○ *to get/take* a cut (of sth)

cutback /ˈkʌtbæk/ *noun* [C, usually pl.]
a reduction in sth: *cutbacks **in** production* ◊ *staff cutbacks* → CUT BACK (ON STH) at CUT *verb*

'cut-off *adjective, noun*
●adjective [only before noun]
forming a limit at which sth must stop: *The union has set a cut-off **point** for the negotiations.* ◊ *When is the cut-off **date**?*
●noun [C, usually sing.]
a point or limit when you stop sth: *The government announced a cut-off in overseas aid.* ◊ *Mortgage lending should have an upper limit cut-off.*

'cut-off score *noun* [C]
(*HR*) the number of points on a test below which sb will not be considered for employment

cutover /ˈkʌtəʊvə(r); *AmE* -oʊ-/ *noun* [C]
a time when an organization stops using one type of system, especially a computer system, and immediately starts using a new one: *The cutover is planned for 31 May 2006.* ◊ *the cutover **from** a mainframe **to** an Internet-based network*

ˌcut-'price (*especially BrE*) (*AmE usually* **'cut-rate**) *adjective* [usually before noun]
1 sold at a reduced price
○ *cut-price **deals/fares/goods/offers***
2 selling goods or services at a reduced price
○ *a cut-price **airline/store/supermarket***

'cut-throat *adjective* [usually before noun]
(about an activity) in which people compete with each other in aggressive and unfair ways: *rival companies engaged in cut-throat competition* ◊ *They are struggling to compete in the cut-throat world of IT services.*

ˌcutting 'edge *noun* [sing.]
1 the cutting edge (of sth) the newest, most advanced stage in the development of sth: *They are **at** the cutting edge of scientific research.* ◊ *operating **on** the cutting edge of technology* ◊ *cutting-edge designs* SYN LEADING EDGE
2 a quality or feature that gives sb/sth an advantage: *This qualification will give you a cutting edge **over** other candidates when you apply for a job.*

★ CV /ˌsiː ˈviː/ *abbr* **curriculum vitae** a written record of your education and employment that you send when you are applying for a job: *Applicants should send a full CV and covering letter to ...* ◊ *Voluntary work will look good on your CV (= give a good impression).* SYN RÉSUMÉ (*AmE*)

c.w.o. (*also spelled* **CWO**) /ˌsiː ˌdʌbljuː ˈəʊ; *AmE* ˈoʊ/ *abbr*
(*Trade*) **cash with order** payment for goods will be made when the goods are ordered: *Our normal terms of business are c.w.o.*

cwt. *abbr* (*plural* **cwt.**)
a short way of writing **hundredweight**

---

cyber- /ˈsaɪbə(r)/ *combining form* (*in nouns and adjectives*)
connected with electronic communication networks, especially the Internet: *a cybershop* ◊ *a cybercafe* ◊ *cybersales* ◊ *cybermarketing*

'cyber mall (*also* ˌelectronic 'mall) *noun* [C]
(*E-commerce*) a website that is shared by two or more businesses: *A fashion retailer is launching a cyber mall that will enable Internet users to buy products from a number of high street retailers.*

cyberslacker /ˈsaɪbəslækə(r); *AmE* ˈsaɪbər-/ *noun* [C] (*informal*)
an employee who uses the Internet in work time to send personal emails, shop, play games, etc. when they should be working

cyberspace /ˈsaɪbəspeɪs; *AmE* -bərs-/ *noun* [U]
the imaginary place where electronic messages, Internet pages, etc. exist while they are being sent between computers: *Some people are reluctant to transfer money **through** cyberspace.*

cybersquatting /ˈsaɪbəskwɒtɪŋ; *AmE* ˈsaɪbərskwɑːtɪŋ/ *noun* [U]
the illegal activity of buying and officially recording an address on the Internet that is the name of an existing company or a well-known person, with the intention of selling it to the owner in order to make a profit: *a victim of cybersquatting* ◊ *a cybersquatting lawsuit* ▶ **'cybersquatter** *noun* [C]

★ cycle /ˈsaɪkl/ *noun* [C]

SEE ALSO: **accounting cycle, billing ~, business ~, economic ~, family life ~, Kondratieff ~, life ~,** etc.

1 a regular pattern of events: *a vicious (= very bad) cycle of reduced spending, lower production and unemployment* ◊ *Fashions tend to go **in** cycles.* ◊ *breaking the cycle of five working days and two leisure days*
2 a pattern that an economy, an industry, a market, etc. tends to follow, with periods of success and periods of difficulty happening regularly one after another: *The market is at **the bottom of** the cycle and should start improving soon.* ◊ *The IT industry has been through many **boom-and-bust** cycles.*
3 a single period of success, failure, etc. that forms part of a regular series: *The economy appears to be moving into a **down** cycle.* ◊ *a **growth** cycle*
4 a regular period of time during which sb/sth completes a particular activity: *We are trying to shorten our product-development cycle.* ◊ *We tend to work **in** 12-month cycles.*

'cycle time *noun* [U,C]
(*Production*) the time between starting and completing a production process: *There has been a dramatic reduction in manufacturing cycle time.* ◊ *In one work area, cycle time was cut by 15 seconds by adding another worker.* → LEAD TIME

cyclical /ˈsaɪklɪkl; ˈsɪk-/ *adjective, noun*
●adjective

SEE ALSO: **countercyclical**

(*Economics; Finance*)
1 that follows a regular pattern of success and failure, increase and decrease, etc: *History has shown that economic markets are cyclical.* ◊ *the cyclical demand for steel products* ◊ *a cyclical downturn (= period of difficulty) in the advertising industry*
○ *a cyclical **downturn/peak/recovery***
2 easily affected by the success or failure of the general economy: *Improved economic conditions have benefitted cyclical stocks.* ◊ *cyclical unemployment* → DEFENSIVE

✪ *cyclical* **shares/stocks** ◆ *a cyclical* **company/industry**
● **noun** [C, usually pl.]
(*Finance*) an investment whose value is easily affected by the success or failure of the general economy: *Consumer cyclicals, like technology and industrial stocks, offer good value for investors right now.* → DEFENSIVE

D d

D/A = DOCUMENTS AGAINST ACCEPTANCE, DEPOSIT ACCOUNT

DA /ˌdiː ˈeɪ/ = DISTRICT ATTORNEY

DAF /ˌdiː eɪ ˈef/ = DELIVERED AT FRONTIER

the 'Daily Of'ficial 'List *noun* [sing.]
(*Stock Exchange*) a detailed record that gives information about the shares that are traded on a stock exchange on a particular day, especially the London Stock Exchange

★ **damage** /ˈdæmɪdʒ/ *noun, verb*
● **noun**

SEE ALSO: **actual damages, apparent ~, civil ~, compensatory ~, liquidated ~, nominal ~, non-economic ~, punitive ~**

1 [U] physical harm caused to sth which makes it less valuable or for which sb can claim money from an insurance company: *The storm didn't do much damage.* ◇ *The cost of the damage is estimated at $30 million.* ◇ *The policy covers the building for accidental damage.*
✪ *to* **cause/do** *damage (to sb/sth)* ◆ *to* **suffer** *damage* ◆ *to* **assess/prevent/repair** *damage* ◆ **considerable/ extensive/irreparable/permanent/serious/severe** *damage* ◆ **accidental/environmental/structural** *damage* ◆ **bomb/fire/flood/smoke/storm** *damage*
2 [U] harmful effects on sb/sth: *damage* **to** *a person's reputation* ◇ *This could cause serious damage* **to** *the country's economy.*
✪ *to* **cause/do** *damage (to sb/sth)* ◆ **inflict** *damage (on sb/sth)* ◆ *to* **suffer** *damage* ◆ *to* **assess/repair** *damage* ◆ **considerable/irreparable/long-term/serious** *damage* ◆ **financial/political** *damage*
3 (*Law*) **damages** [pl.] money that a court orders a person, company, etc. to pay to sb, because they have caused them harm, injury or loss: *He was ordered to* **pay** *damages of €50 000.* ◇ *The jury awarded the plaintiff $505 million* **in** *damages.*
✪ *to* **be awarded/receive/recover/win** *damages* ◆ *to* **claim/seek/sue for** *damages* ◆ *a damages* **action/ award/claim**

WHICH WORD?

damage/damages

Damage [U] refers to the harm that is done to something:

● *Did the fire cause much damage?*
● ~~The fire caused terrible damages.~~

Damages [plural] has a different meaning. It refers to the money paid to someone as part of a legal case: *She is suing the company for damages.* *He was awarded damages of €100 000.*

The word **injury** [C/U], not damage, is used to describe harm done to a person's body:

● *The driver suffered serious injuries.*
● ~~The driver suffered serious damage.~~

● **verb** [+ obj]
to harm or spoil sb/sth: *The fire badly damaged the offices.* ◇ *Investor confidence has been seriously damaged by the scandal.* ◇ *Her strategies are damaging the company.*

'damage limi,tation (*also* **'damage con,trol,** *especially in AmE*) *noun* [U]
the process of trying to limit the amount of damage that is caused by a particular event or situation

'danger ,money (*BrE*) (*AmE* **'hazard pay**) *noun* [U]
(*HR*) extra money which is paid to sb who works in a dangerous situation: *The miners have argued that they should be paid danger money.*

★ **data** /ˈdeɪtə; *BrE also* ˈdɑːtə; *AmE also* ˈdætə/ *noun*

SEE ALSO: **hard data, secondary ~, soft ~**

1 [U; pl.] (*used as a plural noun in technical English, when the singular is* **datum**) facts or information, especially when examined and used to find out things or to make decisions: *This data was collected from 73 countries.* ◇ *They have found some interesting things* **in** *the data.* ◇ **raw data** (= data that has not been studied yet) ◇ (*Technical*) *Recent economic data show that more than 2 500 jobs are created each month.*
✪ *to* **collect/get/obtain** *data* ◆ *to* **analyse/interpret/ look at/use** *data* ◆ *the* **analysis/interpretation** *of data* ◆ *data* **indicate(s)/show(s)/suggest(s)** *sth* ◆ **economic/financial/scientific/technical** *data*
2 (*IT*) [U] information that is stored by a computer: *Once we have checked the stock, we enter the data into the computer.* ◇ *a data-storage system*
✪ *to* **access/enter/process/retrieve/store** *data* ◆ *data* **management/processing/retrieval/storage**

databank (*also spelled* **data bank,** *especially in AmE*) /ˈdeɪtəbæŋk; *AmE also* ˈdætə-/ *noun* [C]
(*IT*) a large amount of data on a particular subject that is stored in a computer: *establishing a databank of customers* ◇ *a pay databank*

★ **database** /ˈdeɪtəbeɪs; *AmE also* ˈdætə-/ *noun* [C]
(*IT*) an organized set of data that is stored in a computer and can be looked at and used in various ways: *We maintain a database of all our clients.* ◇ *The details of each call are stored in a database.* ◇ *We have more than 10 000 CVs* **on** *our database.*
✪ *to* **build/create/establish/set up** *a database* ◆ *to* **add to/store sth in/maintain/manage/update/use** *a database* ◆ *database* **marketing** ◆ *a* **client/customer** *database* ◆ *a* **central/**an **online** *database*

'data ,capture *noun* [U]
(*IT*) the process of putting information into a computer system: *We use a portable bar-code scanner for the data capture.* ◇ *a data-capture system*

'data ,centre (*AmE spelling* **~ center**) *noun* [C]
1 an organization that collects scientific information about a particular subject; the place or system where the data is stored: *the World Data Centre for Greenhouse Gases* → DATABANK
2 (*IT*) a safe place at which a number of computers that store or process data are kept: *Backups of all our data are transferred to a secure data centre.*

'data ,entry *noun* [U]
(*IT*) the work of putting information into a computer, for example from paper documents: *I've*

*got a new job doing data entry for a mail-order
company.* ◇ *Data entry clerks were paid by how fast
they could key data.*

'data ˌmining *noun* [U]
(*IT; Marketing*) using software to look at large
amounts of information that has been collected on
a computer and find new patterns, etc: *Credit-card
companies can use data mining to detect fraud, by
looking for unusual spending patterns.*

ˌdata 'processing *noun* [U]
(*IT*) a series of actions that a computer performs on
data to analyse and organize it; the part of a
company where this is done: *the people in
accounting and data processing*

ˌdata pro'tection *noun* [U]
(*Law*) legal restrictions that keep information stored
on computers private and that control who can
read it or use it: *In terms of the data protection laws,
you can find out what information the company has
about you.* ◇ *a breach of the Data Protection Act*

ˌdata 'warehouse *noun* [C]
(*IT*) a collection of business information, for
example about costs and profits, that a company
keeps on a single computer system, so that it can be
analysed and used to make decisions: *The firm built
a data warehouse to help improve financial
management.* ▸ **ˌdata 'warehousing** *noun* [U]

date /deɪt/ *noun, verb*
● *noun*
─────────
SEE ALSO: best-before date, best-if-used-by ~,
closing ~, completion ~, delivery ~, drop-dead ~,
due ~, etc.
─────────
1 [C] a particular day of the month given in
numbers and words: *today's date* ◇ *We need to fix a
date for the next meeting.* ◇ *The building must be
finished by the date agreed.*
❍ *to agree (on)/arrange/decide (on)/fix/set a date*
2 [sing.] a time in the past or future that is not a
particular day: *The work will be carried out at a
future date.*
IDM **to 'date** up to the present time: *The new plant
is their largest to date.* ◇ *The stock has dropped 30%
in the year to date.*
● *verb* [+ obj]
to write or print the date on sth: *Thank you for your
letter dated 24th March.* → UNDATED

'datebook /'deɪtbʊk/ = DIARY (1)

ˌdated se'curity *noun* [C, usually pl.]
(*Finance*) an investment, such as a bond, that has a
fixed MATURITY (= when the lender must pay back
the amount borrowed) → UNDATED

'date stamp *noun, verb*
● *noun* [C]
1 a date that is printed on sth, especially an
envelope or a food product: *The date stamp shows
the letter was posted yesterday.*
2 a device for printing the date on a document
—Picture at OFFICE
● *verb* [+ obj] **date-stamp** to print the date on a
document, an envelope or a food product: *Food
items must be date-stamped to make sure the oldest
stock is used first.* ▸ **'date-ˌstamping** *noun* [U]

datum /'deɪtəm/ *noun* [C] (*plural* **data**)
(*Technical*) a fact or piece of information → DATA

'daughter ˌcompany *noun* [C]
a company that is owned completely or partly by
another company (a **parent company**): *They are a
large group, with 15 daughter companies across
Europe.* SYN SUBSIDIARY

ˌdawn 'raid *noun* [C] (*especially BrE*)
(*Stock Exchange*) a situation when a company

suddenly and unexpectedly buys a large number of
shares in another company at the beginning of a
day's business on the stock exchange: *The firm
mounted a dawn raid on shares in the retailer, and
is now likely to make a full takeover bid.*

the DAX (*also spelled* **Dax**) /dæks/ *noun* [sing.]
Deutsche Aktienindex a SHARE INDEX of shares in
30 of the most important companies on the
Frankfurt stock market: *Frankfurt's DAX index
gained 0.2% in late trade.* See note at INCREASE

daybook /'deɪbʊk/ *noun* [C]
(*Accounting*) a printed or an electronic record of the
sales made and the goods bought by a business
each day: *Enter the invoice number in the daybook.* ◇
a purchase/sales daybook

ˌday 'off *noun* [C] (*plural* **days off**)
a day on which you do not have to work: *When was
the last time you had a day off?* ◇ *She took a few days
off.* ◇ *a day off in lieu* (= in return for working
during a holiday)
❍ *to ask for/have/take a day off* • *be due for/be owed
a day off*

'day ˌorder *noun* [C]
(*Stock Exchange*) an order to buy or sell shares,
bonds, etc. that is only valid on the day it is made

'day rate *noun* [C]
the amount sb is paid or charges to do a day's work:
What is your day rate? ◇ *She sets a minimum day
rate of £200.*

ˌday re'lease *noun* [U] (*BrE*)
(*HR*) a system of allowing an employee days away
from work in order to study at a college: *She goes to
college on day release.* ◇ *a day-release course*

ˌday-to-'day *adjective* [only before noun]
involving the usual events or tasks of each day: *He
has recently handed over the day-to-day running of
the business.* ◇ *the day-to-day work of the
department* ◇ *She will continue to run the group on a
day-to-day basis.*

'day ˌtrading *noun* [U]
(*Stock Exchange*) the process of buying and selling
shares very quickly using the Internet in order to
take advantage of small price changes and so make
small quick profits: *The company struggled as
enthusiasm for the Internet and day trading
decreased.* ▸ **'day ˌtrader** *noun* [C] **'day-trade** *verb*
[+ obj *or no obj*]

dba *abbr* (*especially AmE*)
a short way of writing **doing business as** in the
name of a business, especially one owned by a SOLE
PROPRIETOR: *Kim Winton, dba Winton Tractor
Spares*

DBR /ˌdiː biː 'ɑː(r)/ = DRUM-BUFFER-ROPE

DC /ˌdiː 'siː/ = DOCUMENTARY CREDIT

DCF /ˌdiː siː 'ef/ = DISCOUNTED CASH FLOW

DDI /ˌdiː diː 'aɪ/ *abbr* (*BrE*)
Direct Dial Inwards a system where an office
building, a hotel, etc. can have a large range of
telephone numbers sharing one or a small number
of direct lines. Calls go directly to an EXTENSION
without being connected by an OPERATOR or
RECEPTIONIST. → DID

DDP /ˌdiː diː 'piː/ = DELIVERED DUTY PAID

DDU /ˌdiː diː 'juː/ = DELIVERED DUTY UNPAID

dead /ded/ *adjective*
1 [not before noun] no longer thought likely to be
successful or no longer being aimed for: *Investors
believe the controversial deal is all but dead.* ◇ *The
restructuring plan now appears to be dead.*
2 [not before noun] no longer used, fashionable or
important: *Who says e-commerce is dead?* ◇ *Analysts
say the issue is dead and buried.*

3 without activity; with nobody buying or selling anything: *The market is absolutely dead this morning.* ◊ *Since the beginning of the year the economy has been dead.*
4 (*informal*) (about machines or equipment) not working, especially because of a lack of power: *The hard disk seems to be dead.* ◊ *The phone's gone dead.*

deadbeat /'dedbiːt/ *noun* [C] (*AmE*) (*informal*)
a person or company that tries to avoid paying money that they owe: *We keep a database on deadbeats who pass bad checks.*

dead cat 'bounce *noun* [sing.]
(*Stock Exchange*) a temporary and small upward movement in share prices after a large fall, often before they start to fall again: *Traders described the recovery as nothing more than a dead cat bounce.*

dead-'end *adjective* [only before noun]
in which no more progress or development is possible: *a dead-end task/project* ◊ *He is stuck in a dead-end job* (= one with low wages and no chance of getting a better job).

★ **deadline** /'dedlaɪn/ *noun* [C]
a time or date by which sth must be done or completed: *The deadline for applications is next Friday.* ◊ *She gave herself a two-year deadline to reverse the group's decline.* ◊ *It is critical that we meet the 30 April deadline.* ◊ *The people here work under tight deadlines and intense pressure.* ◊ *You must be able to work to deadlines.*
○ to *extend/impose/set* a deadline • to *hit/make/meet/miss* a deadline • *strict/tight* deadlines • a deadline *approaches/looms/nears/passes*

dead 'load → DEADWEIGHT (1)

deadlock /'dedlɒk; *AmE* -lɑːk/ *noun* [sing; U]
a complete failure to reach agreement or settle a dispute: *The two sides met to try to break* (= end) *the deadlock on/over funding for a pay deal.* ◊ *The strike has reached a deadlock.* ◊ (*BrE*) *The negotiations appear to have reached deadlock today.*
○ to *break/resolve* a deadlock • to *end in/reach* (a) deadlock
▶ **deadlocked** /'dedlɒkt; *AmE* -lɑːkt/ *adjective*
[usually before noun]: *Pay talks remained deadlocked for weeks.*

'dead ,season *noun* [sing.]
the time of year when the level of demand is at its lowest point: *Stock markets usually experience a dead season in August.* ◊ *dead-season prices*

'dead time *noun* [U,C]
(*Production*) time that is not being used: *Bosses should take advantage of periods of dead time to rethink jobs, and tune up departments.*

deadweight (*also spelled* **dead weight**, *especially in AmE*) /,ded'weɪt/ *noun* [C,U]
1 (*Technical*) (*abbr* **dwt**) (*also* ,dead 'load) the weight of a structure or a vehicle that has no load or is empty: *These oil tankers measure 70 000 to 110 000 deadweight tonnes.*
2 (*Transport*) (*abbr* **dwt**) a measure of the total goods, fuel, passengers, etc. that a ship can carry
○ *deadweight capacity/tonnage*
3 (*Economics*) (*used as an adjective*) a financial cost or loss that is the result of money, materials, etc. not being shared out in an efficient way, for example because of the tax system: *Job creation schemes can be associated with high deadweight costs.* ◊ *a deadweight burden*

dead 'wood (*AmE spelling* **deadwood**) *noun* [U]
people or things that have become useless or unnecessary in an organization: *Her first task was to clear out the dead wood from the department.*
○ to *clear out/cut away/cut out/get rid of/sweep away* the dead wood

★ **deal** /diːl/ *noun, verb*
● *noun*

SEE ALSO: **bought deal, cash ~, new ~, package ~, sweetheart ~**

(*Commerce*)
1 [C] a formal business agreement, especially an agreement to buy or sell goods or provide a service: *The board of directors have approved the deal.* ◊ *The two companies signed a deal worth $1.7 billion.* ◊ *The deal fell through* (= no agreement was reached). ◊ *The board reached a deal with a large Chinese conglomerate.* ◊ *We did a deal with the management on overtime.* ◊ *They were hoping for a better pay deal.* ◊ (*only used in spoken English*) *It's a deal!* (= I agree to your terms) See note at AGREEMENT
○ to *agree/make/reach/sign* a deal • to *clinch/close/conclude/strike* a deal • to *block/call off/oppose/reject* a deal • a *bad/big/good/large/lucrative* deal • a deal *falls through/goes ahead/goes through*
2 a reduction in the price of a product, usually for a short period of time only: *The airline is offering deals on flights this month.* ◊ *I got a good deal on the car* (= I bought it cheaply). ◊ *The website gives advice on how to get the best deal.*
○ to *get/offer* a deal • an *excellent/a good* deal
→ idioms at CUT *verb*, DONE
● *verb* (**dealt, dealt** /delt/)
IDM **deal sb/sth a (serious, severe, etc.) 'blow; deal a (serious, severe, etc.) 'blow to sb/sth** to be very harmful to sb/sth: *The oil spill has dealt a severe blow to the area's fishing industry.*
PHRV **'deal in sth** (*Commerce*; *Finance*) to buy or sell a particular product; to trade: *The company deals in computer software.* ◊ *a trader dealing in futures and options* **'deal with sb** to talk or behave in an appropriate way according to who you are talking to, managing, etc: *You need to be good at dealing with the public.* **'deal with sb/sth** to do business regularly with a person, a company or an organization: *I usually deal with the sales manager.* ◊ *We want our customers to know they're dealing with the same firm.* **'deal with sth 1** to take action to solve a problem, carry out a task, etc., especially as part of your job: *I have to deal with 300 emails a day.* ◊ *Your order was dealt with yesterday.* **2** to be concerned with a particular subject: *This report deals with our sales prospects for the coming year.*

★ **dealer** /'diːlə(r)/ *noun* [C]

SEE ALSO: **broker-dealer, primary ~**

1 (*Commerce*) a person or shop/store whose business is buying and selling a particular product: *Britain's biggest car dealer* ◊ *She is a dealer in antiques.* ◊ *Here's how to find a dealer near you.* ◊ *the company's US dealer network*
→ WHEELER-DEALER at WHEELING AND DEALING
2 (*Finance*; *Stock Exchange*) (*BrE*) (*AmE* **'trader**) a person who buys and sells shares, bonds, currencies, etc. without using a BROKER or an agent: *She is a dealer in the financial futures market.* ◊ *a senior UK equity dealer* ◊ *Wall Street dealers* See note at AGENT
3 (*Finance*; *Stock Exchange*) a bank employee who buys and sells shares, bonds, etc. or foreign currency on behalf of the bank

dealership /'diːləʃɪp; *AmE* -lərʃ-/ *noun* [C]
(*Commerce*) a business that sells products, especially cars, for a particular company; the position of being a dealer who can buy and sell sth: *a car/an auto/a Mercedes dealership*

dealing /'di:lɪŋ/ *noun*

SEE ALSO: fair dealing, insider ~, self-~, wheeling
and ~

1 dealings [pl.] business activities between people
or organizations: *I have **had** no dealings **with*** (=
done no business with) *this company recently.* ◇ *an
investigation into the group's financial dealings*
2 (*Finance; Stock Exchange*) [C,U] (*especially BrE*)
buying and selling shares, foreign currencies, etc:
*Dealings **in** the company's shares have been
suspended.* ◇ *The rules relating to directors' share
dealings are being tightened.* → TRADING
3 [U] a way of doing business with sb: *He has a
reputation for fair/honest dealing.* ◇ *dodgy/shady
dealing* (= that seems to be dishonest or illegal)

'dealing floor = TRADING FLOOR

dealmaker (*also spelled* **deal maker**)
/'di:lmeɪkə(r)/ *noun* [C]
a person who is skilled at making financial deals or
taking part in NEGOTIATIONS: *one of Wall Street's
most aggressive dealmakers* ◇ *a City deal maker*
▶ **'dealmaking** (*also spelled* **deal making**) *noun*
[U]: *the result of intense last-minute dealmaking*

dear /dɪə(r); *AmE* dɪr/ *adjective, adverb*
● *adjective*
1 (**dearer, dearest**) costing a lot of money or more
money than you expected: *The company was hit
hard by dearer oil prices.*
2 Dear used at the beginning of a letter before the
name or title of the person that you are writing to:
Dear Sir or Madam ◇ *Dear Mrs Jones*
● *adverb*
at a high price: *to buy cheap and sell dear* → idiom at
COST *verb*

,dear 'money *noun* [U]
(*Economics*) a situation when money is difficult to
borrow and can only be borrowed at a high rate of
interest SYN TIGHT MONEY

,dear 'money ,policy *noun* [C,U]
(*Economics*) a government policy of raising interest
rates in order to make it more expensive to borrow
money and so reduce the level of spending
SYN TIGHT MONEY POLICY

dearth /dɜːθ; *AmE* dɜːrθ/ *noun* [sing.]
a lack of sth; the fact of there not being enough of
sth: *There is **a** real **dearth of** candidates with the
right experience for the job.* ◇ *a dearth of public
sector investment* → GLUT

'death ,benefit *noun* [C,U]
(*Insurance*) money that is paid to the family of an
insured person who dies

'death ,duty = INHERITANCE TAX (1)
'death tax = ESTATE TAX, INHERITANCE TAX (2)

deb (*also spelled* **deb.**) *abbr*
1 (*Accounting*) (*also* **Deb**) a short way of writing
debit
2 (*Finance*) a short way of writing **debenture**

debenture /dɪ'bentʃə(r)/ *noun* [C, usually pl.]
(*abbr* **deb**) (*AmE also* **de'benture bond**)

SEE ALSO: naked debenture

(*Finance*) a loan for a long period of time on which a
company promises to pay a fixed rate of interest;
the official document that is given to the lender
NOTE In Britain, debentures are always SECURED
on the company's assets (= the lender will get
property or items of value if the company cannot
pay back the money). In the US, debentures are not
secured in this way: *The company **issued** debentures
to certain shareholders.* ◇ *The debentures yielded
10% a year in interest.* ◇ *a debenture holder*

de'benture stock *noun* [C,U]
(*Finance*) a type of share in a company that pays
fixed amounts at fixed times: *The company used
cash reserves to pay back €10 m of bank debt and
debenture stock.*

★ **debit** /'debɪt/ *noun, verb*
● *noun*

SEE ALSO: direct debit

1 [C] an amount that is taken from a bank account;
a record of this: *a debit of €100* ◇ *The total debits on
the account were £2 000 last month.*
OPP CREDIT
2 [U] the fact that there is no money in a bank
account: *Your account is €200 **in** debit.* → BE,
REMAIN, ETC. IN THE RED at RED, OVERDRAWN
3 (*Accounting*) [C] (*abbr* **Deb, deb**) an amount that is
written in a company's financial account to show a
decrease in money that the company owes or an
increase in the value of its assets: *on the **debit side**
of an account* ◇ *Every debit must have a
corresponding credit.* OPP CREDIT—Picture at T-
ACCOUNT NOTE The **debits** are recorded on the left
side of a traditional T-account.
● *verb* [+ obj]
1 to take an amount of money from an account,
especially a bank account: *Premiums will be debited
monthly **from** your account.* ◇ *Please debit my credit
card.* ◇ *Your account has been debited **with** $50 000.*
2 (*Accounting*) to write an amount in a company's
financial account to show a decrease in the money
the company owes or an increase in the value of its
assets NOTE You **debit** a traditional T-account by
writing amounts on the left side: *The cash received
was debited in the cash book and credited to the sales
account.*
OPP CREDIT → CHARGE *verb* (3)

'debit ac,count *noun* [C]
(*Commerce*) an arrangement with a bank, shop/
store or business to pay for the cost of goods or
services using money that you already have or have
paid: *You can dial this number to find out how much
you have left in your debit account.* → CREDIT
ACCOUNT at ACCOUNT *noun* (2)

'debit ,balance *noun* [C]
1 the amount by which the money paid out of a
bank account is greater than the amount paid into
it at a particular time: *There is an outstanding debit
balance on your account.* OPP CREDIT BALANCE
2 (*Accounting*) in a company's financial records, the
amount by which the total DEBITS are greater than
the total CREDITS in a particular account: *The
calculation of minority interest gives rise to a debit
balance in the balance sheet.*

'debit card (*AmE* **'check card**) *noun* [C]
a plastic card that can be used to take money
directly out of your bank account when you pay for
goods and services: *Can I pay by debit card?* ◇ *the
growth of debit-card use in the UK and abroad*
→ CREDIT CARD

'debit note (*BrE*) (*AmE* **'debit re,ceipt**) *noun* [C]
(*Commerce*)
1 a note sent to a customer showing that they owe
money: *We realized we had undercharged the
customer and **raised** a debit note.*
2 a note sent by a customer to a supplier showing
the amount that will be taken away from the total
bill, for example because goods supplied were not
correct: *A debit note must accompany the returned
goods, stating the reasons for rejection in full.*

debriefing /,di:'bri:fɪŋ/ *noun* [C,U]
a meeting where sb gives a report about a task that
they have just completed: *a debriefing session*

SEE ALSO: assumed debt, bad ~, bank ~, book ~, business ~, consumer ~, corporate ~, etc.

1 [C] an amount of money that a person, a company, a country, etc. owes: *The group has debts of $3 billion.* ◇ *It took her years to pay off all her debts.* ◇ *interest payments on an outstanding* (= not paid) *debt* ◇ *He had run up huge credit-card debts* (= let them reach a very large amount).* → LIABILITY
○ *a big/crippling/huge/massive debt •* to *amass/ have/incur/run up debts •* to *clear/pay back/pay off/repay/settle a debt •* to *default on a debt*
2 [U] the situation of owing money, especially when you cannot pay: *The business is heavily in debt.* ◇ *The company is $17 m in debt.* ◇ *I've been afraid of getting into debt.* ◇ *We had to borrow to stay out of debt.*
○ *to be in/get into/go into/run into/slip into debt •* to *get out of/keep sb/sth out of/stay out of debt •* to *be deeply/heavily in debt*
3 (*Finance*) [U,C] CAPITAL (= money used for business activities) that a company or a government borrows, on which interest is paid: *Some analysts were worried about the company's debt.* ◇ *Sales proceeds would be used to pay down debt* (= reduce the amount of debt that is owed). ◇ *the burden of servicing a debt* (= paying interest on it) ◇ *The government would not default on its debt repayments.*
○ *to cut/pay down/reduce* (a) *debt •* to *cancel/default on/write off a debt •* to *refinance/reschedule/ restructure a company's debt • long-term/short- term debt*

'**debt ad,justment** *noun* [U,C]
1 the process in which sb who owes money agrees to make regular payments to a person or business, who takes this money and arranges with the businesses who are owed money how the debt will be paid: *We are fully licensed to deal in debt adjustment and counselling.*
2 (*Law*) a legal process that a person who is BANKRUPT (= unable to pay their bills) can use to reduce the amount of their debts and the period of time over which they must be paid: *The court must confirm the debt adjustment plan.*
▶ '**debt ad,juster** *noun* [C] '**debt ad,justing** *noun* [U]

'**debt ,capital** *noun* [U]
(*Finance*) CAPITAL (= money used for business activities) that a company gets by borrowing from banks, investors, etc: *The bond issue and loan will give the firm access to about $1.65 billion of debt capital.* ◇ *the debt capital markets* SYN LOAN CAPITAL

'**debt col,lection** *noun* [U]
the activity of obtaining money from people who owe money for goods or services they have received, often by going to their homes to get it: *If you are late with a payment, your account may be handed over to a debt collection agency.* ▶ '**debt col,lector** *noun* [C] → COMMERCIAL COLLECTION AGENCY

,**debt consoli'dation** *noun* [U,C]
the act of borrowing a larger amount of money from one lender in order to pay back several smaller debts to other lenders: *Debt consolidation can help lower your monthly payments.* ◇ *a debt consolidation loan* ▶ ,**debt con'soli,dator** *noun* [C]: *You will need to make one monthly payment to the debt consolidator.*

'**debt ,counselling** (*AmE spelling ~ counseling*) *noun* [U]
the activity of providing advice to people about how they can pay back the money that they owe
▶ '**debt ,counsellor** (*AmE spelling ~ counselor*) *noun* [C]

debt-'equity ,ratio (*also spelled* **debt/equity ratio**) (*also* ,**debt-to-'equity ,ratio**) *noun* [C]
(*Accounting*) a measure of how much debt (= loans, bonds, etc.) a company uses in order to finance its activities, compared to money invested by shareholders: *a debt-equity ratio of 3:1* (= for every dollar invested by shareholders, the company borrows another 3 dollars) ◇ *A high debt-equity ratio results in high returns for shareholders, but potentially big losses if the company fails.*
SYN GEARING

debt-'equity swap (*also spelled* **debt/equity swap**) (*also* ,**debt-for-'equity swap**, '**debt swap**) *noun* [C]
(*Finance*) an arrangement in which a lender reduces the amount of a company's debt, in exchange for receiving shares in the company: *The debt-equity swap will give creditors a 30% stake in the company.*

'**debt ex,posure** *noun* [U]
(*Finance*) money that an organization has lent to sb/ sth and so risks losing if it is not paid back: *The company's shares fell because of anxiety about its debt exposure.* SYN CREDIT EXPOSURE

'**debt ,finance** *noun* [U]
(*Finance*) money that a company borrows from banks, investors, etc. in order to finance its activities; the business of providing this money to companies: *The company has secured debt finance from Royal Bank of Scotland to fund the deal.* ◇ *She is head of the bank's debt finance division.* → EQUITY FINANCE, LOAN CAPITAL
▶ '**debt-,financed** *adjective*: *a debt-financed acquisition* '**debt ,financing** *noun* [U,C]: *sources of debt financing* ◇ *a debt financing of $250 000*

,**debt-for-'equity swap** = DEBT-EQUITY SWAP

'**debt-,laden** *adjective* [usually before noun]
(used especially in newspapers) having a lot of debt; badly affected by debt: *The debt-laden group is selling assets in an attempt to avoid bankruptcy.* ◇ *a debt-laden balance sheet*

'**debt ,leverage** *noun* [U] (*especially AmE*)
(*Finance*)
1 the relationship between the amount of money that a company owes (**debt**) and the value of its shares (**equity**): *The subsidiary has received $4.5 billion to help reduce its debt leverage.*
2 using borrowed money to buy an investment or to add to the amount invested, in order to try to increase possible profits from the investment

★ **debtor** /'detə(r)/ *noun*

SEE ALSO: sundry debtor

1 [C] a person, a country or an organization that owes money: *It is becoming too easy for debtors to default on their loans.* ◇ *They are the world's biggest debtor nation* (= many countries have invested in it). → CREDITOR (1)
2 (*Accounting*) **debtors** [pl.] (*BrE*) the amounts of money that are owed to a company, which are recorded as assets on its BALANCE SHEET: *During the period under review, debtors increased from €44 million to €57 million.* SYN ACCOUNTS RECEIVABLE → CREDITOR (2)

,**debtor-in-pos'session ,financing** *noun* [U]
(*abbr* **DIP Financing**)
(*Finance*) in the US, a type of loan that a company can get while it remains officially BANKRUPT (= unable to pay its debts): *The $1.5 billion debtor-in-possession financing will allow the airline to continue operating in the event of a bankruptcy filing.*

'**debtors' ,ledger** *noun* [C] (*BrE*)
(*Accounting, old-fashioned*) in a company's financial

records, a group of accounts that is used to record the amounts owed by particular customers: *All sales are recorded in the debtors' ledger.* SYN SALES LEDGER → CREDITORS' LEDGER

'debt ,overhang *noun* [C, usually sing., U]
(*Economics*) a situation in which the debts that a government, an organization or a person has are larger than they can pay back in the agreed time: *an initiative to remove the debt overhang of poor countries*

'debt ,payment *noun* [C]
an amount of money that a government or an organization must pay back to a lender: *The company must **meet** (= pay) a debt payment on Monday.* ◇ *The government has suspended foreign debt payments.*

'debt ,rating *noun* [C]
(*Finance*) a measurement of the ability of a government or an organization to pay its debts and interest on them; the process of estimating this: *The company's debt rating has been downgraded to 'junk' status.* ◇ *a debt-rating agency* SYN CREDIT RATING
O *to cut/downgrade/lower/raise/upgrade a debt rating* ♦ *to **be given/have** a debt rating*

'debt ,ratio *noun* [U] (*AmE*)
(*Accounting*) a figure that is equal to a company's total debts divided by its total assets, used as a measure of a company's ability to pay back its loans and other debts → DEBT-EQUITY RATIO

'debt re,structuring (*also* **'debt re,scheduling**) *noun* [U]
(*Finance*) the act of finding a new way for an organization or a government to pay back money that they have borrowed and are having difficulty paying back: *The company needs fresh funding and debt restructuring in order to survive.* ◇ *a debt rescheduling agreement/plan*

'debt re,tirement *noun* [U]
(*Finance*) the fact of a debt being paid back completely: *a charge for early debt retirement*

'debt-,ridden *adjective* [usually before noun]
(used especially in newspapers) having a lot of debt; badly affected by debt: *merger talks to save the debt-ridden company*

'debt ,service (*also* **'debt ,servicing**) *noun* [U]
(*Finance*) the act of making regular payments to a lender; the payments that are made: *The company has the necessary funds to cover immediate debt service.*

'debt service ,ratio *noun* [C] (*abbr* DSR)
1 (*Economics*) the amount of money that a government needs to pay to foreign lenders every year, compared to the amount of money received from exporting goods and services: *The country's debt service ratio has jumped to 31%.*
2 (*Finance*) the amount of money that a company or a person needs to pay to lenders, compared to the amount of particular types of income: *Lenders usually insist that a company maintains a certain debt service ratio or else risk penalties.*

'debt swap *noun* [C]
(*Finance*)
1 = DEBT-EQUITY SWAP
2 an arrangement between a government and a foreign lender. The lender agrees to reduce the amount of the government's debt in exchange for the government spending money on developing the country: *The debt swap will generate funds for local conservation programmes.*

,debt-to-'equity ,ratio = DEBT-EQUITY RATIO

debug /ˌdiːˈbʌg/ *verb* [+ obj] (**-gg-**)
(*IT*) to look for and remove the faults in computer software or equipment: *The software still needs to be written and debugged.*

debut (*also spelled* **début**) /ˈdeɪbjuː; ˈdebjuː; *AmE* deɪˈbjuː/ *noun, verb*
● *noun* [C]
the first time that sb/sth appears in public; the first time that sth is available to buy: *The new car **makes** its debut in the UK this weekend.* ◇ *Shares in the company soared 40% **on** their stock market debut.* ◇ *a debut bond issue*
● *verb* [+ obj *or* no obj]
to become or make sth available to the public for the first time; to start selling sth or being sold: *They recently debuted a phone incorporating a digital camera.* ◇ *The shares debuted at €15.25.*

deceased /dɪˈsiːst/ *adjective*
1 dead: *If the policyholder is deceased, the funds will be paid to their heir.*
2 the deceased *noun* [C] (*plural* **the deceased**)
a person who has died, especially recently

decelerate /ˌdiːˈseləreɪt/ *verb*
1 [+ obj *or* no obj] to happen or make sth happen more slowly: *Prices have decelerated rapidly.* ◇ *decelerating consumer spending* OPP ACCELERATE
2 (*Economics*) [no obj] (about the economy) to decrease in activity so that demand for goods decreases: *Economic growth decelerated sharply in January.* OPP ACCELERATE
▶ **deceleration** /ˌdiːseləˈreɪʃn/ *noun* [C,U]: *We have seen a sharp deceleration **in** consumer spending.*

★ **decentralize**, **-ise** /ˌdiːˈsentrəlaɪz/ *verb* [+ obj *or* no obj]
to give some of the power of a central organization to smaller organizations in different areas or countries; to divide the responsibilities of running an organization between many different people, departments, etc: *The company is decentralizing its corporate structure.* ◇ *Firms are decentralizing in search of reserves of labour.* OPP CENTRALIZE
▶ **decentralization**, **-isation** /ˌdiːsentrəlaɪˈzeɪʃn; *AmE* -lə'z-/ *noun* [U; sing.] **decentralized**, **-ised** /ˌdiːˈsentrəlaɪzd/ *adjective*: *Our recruitment process is decentralized, with each manager doing their own hiring.*

de'cision-,maker *noun* [C]
a person in an organization or a government who has authority to make important decisions: *The campaign was targeted at **key** decision-makers.*

de'cision-,making *noun* [U]
the process of deciding about sth important, especially in a group of people or in an organization: *Management excluded the union from decision-making.* ◇ *simplifying the decision-making process*
O *corporate/executive/management decision-making* ♦ *consensus/consensus-based decision-making*

de'cision-making ,unit *noun* [C] (*abbr* DMU)
(*Marketing*) the group of people in an organization who help to make a decision about whether to buy sth: *Key members of decision-making units include buyers, users and influencers.* SYN BUYING CENTRE

de,cision sup'port ,system *noun* [C] (*abbr* DSS)
(*IT*) a computer program that analyses business data so that users can make decisions more easily → EXECUTIVE INFORMATION SYSTEM

de'cision tree *noun* [C]
a diagram that is used to help decide the best action to take in a particular situation. Possible actions and their results are represented using lines, boxes and circles: *We developed a decision tree to compare options for funding.*

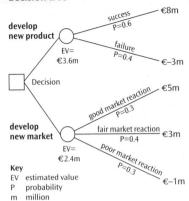

Key
EV estimated value
P probability
m million

---

declaration /ˌdeklə'reɪʃn/ noun [C,U]

SEE ALSO: customs declaration, tax declaration

1 an official or formal statement, especially about the plans of an organization or a government; the act of making such a statement: *Insurers traditionally make their annual bonus declarations in the first three months of the year.*
O to adopt/issue/make/sign a declaration
2 (*Law*) an official statement by a court about the legal rights or status of sb/sth: *They are seeking a court declaration that the contract no longer applies.*
O to grant/make/seek a declaration
3 an official written statement giving information or stating that sth is true: *You will need to sign a declaration that you are an EU resident.* ◇ *a declaration of income*
O to complete/make/sign/submit a declaration

★ declare /dɪ'kleə(r); AmE dɪ'kler/ verb [+ obj]
1 to say sth officially or publicly: *They declared their intention to buy a 25% stake in the company.* ◇ *The company was declared insolvent* (= by a court). ◇ (*BrE*) *The firm declared itself insolvent.* ◇ (*AmE*) *The company declared bankruptcy last December.*
2 to announce that a share of company's profits (a **dividend**) will be paid to shareholders: *The Board declared a dividend of 7.5 cents a share.*
3 to tell the tax authorities how much money you have earned, etc: *The group declared a loss of $187 million.*
4 to tell customs officers (= at the the border of a country) that you are carrying goods on which you should pay tax: *Do you have anything to declare?*
IDM declare an 'interest (in sth) to tell people that you have a connection with sth that could affect the decisions you make, because you may benefit in some way: *Directors are required to declare their interest in any contract with the company.*

★ decline /dɪ'klaɪn/ noun, verb
● **noun** [C, usually sing., U]
a process or period of becoming weaker, smaller or less good: *The country suffered a sharp decline in exports.* ◇ *She has failed to reverse the company's decline.* ◇ *The rate of decline is now slowing.* ◇ *The currency has been in decline since the 1980s.*
—Picture at PRODUCT LIFE CYCLE
O a dramatic/rapid/sharp/steep decline ✦ a gradual/slight/slow decline ✦ a continued/continuing/steady decline ✦ to halt/reverse/stop/suffer a decline
● **verb** [no obj]
to become weaker, smaller or less good: *The number of tourists to the resort declined by 10% last*

---

year. ◇ *The group has been hit by declining sales.* See note at INCREASE
O to decline dramatically/sharply/steeply ✦ to decline gradually/slowly/steadily

decliner /dɪ'klaɪnə(r)/ (*also* de,clining 'stock)
noun [C, usually pl.]
(*Stock Exchange*) (used in newspapers) a company whose shares have decreased (**declined**) in value in a particular period: *Technology stocks were the biggest decliners on the London Stock Exchange today.* **SYN** FALLER **OPP** ADVANCER

de,clining 'balance ,method = REDUCING BALANCE METHOD

de,clining 'stock (*also* de,clining 'share) = DECLINER

decompress /ˌdiːkəm'pres/ verb [+ obj]
(*IT*) to return computer files, etc. to their original size after they have been COMPRESSED (= made smaller): *decompressed data* **SYN** UNZIP **OPP** COMPRESS

decontrol /ˌdiːkən'trəʊl; AmE -'troʊl/ verb [+ obj]
(-**ll**-) (*especially AmE*)
(*Economics*) (*often* be decontrolled)
to remove official rules or controls from sth, especially prices or rents: *a debate over whether gas prices should be totally decontrolled* → DEREGULATE
▶ **decon'trol** noun [U]

decouple /ˌdiː'kʌpl/ verb [+ obj or no obj]
to break the connection between two activities or systems: *Their country's economy has decoupled from the problems of its neighbours.* ◇ *the need to decouple economic growth from environmental destruction*

decoy /'diːkɔɪ/ = SEED noun (2)

decrease verb, noun
● **verb** /dɪ'kriːs/ [+ obj or no obj]
to become or make sth become smaller in size, number, etc: *Profits decreased by 9.4%, from €1.17 million to 1.05 million.* ◇ *People's savings have decreased in value.* ◇ *decreasing costs*
See note at INCREASE
O to decrease considerably/dramatically/sharply/significantly ✦ to decrease gradually/slightly/steadily ✦ to decrease in number/size/value
▶ **de'creased** adjective [only before noun]: *decreased productivity*
● **noun** /'diːkriːs/ [C,U]
the process of reducing sth; the amount that sth is reduced by: *There has been a slight decrease in consumer spending this year.* ◇ *a decrease of nearly 6% in the number of visitors* **OPP** INCREASE
O a large/marked/sharp/slight decrease ✦ a price/revenue/sales/tax decrease

decree /dɪ'kriː/ noun, verb
● **noun**
1 (*Law*) [C] a decision that is made in a court: *The court granted a decree of divorce.*
2 [C,U] an official order from a ruler or a government that becomes the law: *a presidential decree*
● **verb** [+ obj] (**decreeing, decreed, decreed**)
to decide, judge or order sth officially: *The government decreed a national holiday.*

decrypt /diː'krɪpt/ verb [+ obj]
(*IT*) to change text or a message that is written in code into a form that can be understood by anyone **OPP** ENCRYPT ▶ **decryption** /diː'krɪpʃn/ noun [U,C]: *decryption programs and tools*

dedicated /'dedɪkeɪtɪd/ adjective [only before noun]
designed to do only one particular type of work; used for one particular purpose only: *They*

recommend that you use a dedicated server for the software. ◇ We have our own dedicated warehouse.

★ **deduct** /dɪˈdʌkt/ verb [+ obj or no obj] (often **be deducted**)

to take away money, a number, etc. from a total amount: Pension contributions will be deducted **from** your salary each month. ◇ Income tax is deducted **at source** (= from your pay, before you receive it).

deductible /dɪˈdʌktəbl/ adjective, noun
● adjective

SEE ALSO: **tax-deductible**

(Accounting) that can be taken away from an amount on which you must pay tax: These costs are deductible **from** profits. ▶ **de,ducti'bility** noun [U]: the deductibility of training expenses
● noun [C] (AmE)
(Insurance) a fixed charge that you must pay before an insurance company will pay the costs of sth: Medicare will cover half of the drug costs after a $600 deductible is paid. **SYN** EXCESS (BrE)

★ **deduction** /dɪˈdʌkʃn/ noun [C,U]

SEE ALSO: **standard deduction, tax deduction**

the process of taking an amount of sth, especially money, away from a total; the amount that is taken away: The payment was made **without** deduction **of** tax. ◇ The deductions **from** your salary are **made** directly by your employer. → TAX CREDIT
See note at REDUCTION

deed /diːd/ noun [C]

SEE ALSO: **title deed, transfer ~, trust ~**

a type of written agreement that is made and signed in a formal way. **Deeds** are required in particular circumstances, for example when a house is sold: the deeds of the house See note at AGREEMENT

,**deed of ar'rangement** noun [C]
(Law) in the UK, a formal written agreement between a failing company and the people it owes money to (its **creditors**), in which it agrees to pay its debts in a particular way

,**deed of 'partnership** noun [C]
(Law) a legal agreement to form a PARTNERSHIP that gives the details of the arrangement

,**deed of 'transfer** = TRANSFER DEED

,**deed of 'trust** = TRUST DEED

deep /diːp/ adjective, adverb (**deeper, deepest**)
● adjective
extreme or serious: The market is in a deeper recession than expected. ◇ We are having to make deep **cuts** in our operating costs. ◇ The weak economy forced retailers to offer **deep discounts** (= big reductions in price).
IDM ,deep '**pockets** if sb/sth has **deep pockets** they have a lot of money available to spend on sth: corporate buyers with deep pockets **jump/be thrown in at the 'deep end** (informal) to start or be made to start a new and difficult activity that you are not prepared for: She was just thrown in at the deep end on her first day and had to deal with a difficult client.
● adverb
to an extreme or serious degree: The company is being dragged deeper and deeper into debt.

,**deep-'discount** adjective [only before noun]
(Commerce; Marketing) very much reduced in price; selling at a very low price: deep-discount brands

deepen /ˈdiːpən/ verb [+ obj or no obj]
to become worse; to make sth worse: Third-quarter losses deepened. ◇ a deepening economic crisis

de facto /ˌdeɪ ˈfæktəʊ; ˌdiː:; AmE -toʊ/ adjective [usually before noun], adverb
(Law or formal)
(about an authority, a system, etc.) that exists because of the circumstances, rather than because it was created officially: For a while he was the de facto plant manager. ◇ The situation was accepted de facto. **NOTE** De facto is a Latin phrase. → DE JURE

defamation /ˌdefəˈmeɪʃn/ noun [U]
(Law or formal)
the act of causing harm to sb by saying or writing bad or false things about them: He has threatened to **sue** the newspaper **for** defamation. ◇ a defamation case ▶ **defame** /dɪˈfeɪm/ verb [+ obj]

★ **default** /dɪˈfɔːlt; ˈdiːfɔːlt/ noun, verb
● noun

SEE ALSO: **judgement by/in default**

1 (Law) [U,C] failure to do sth that is required by an agreement or by law, especially paying a debt: The country is trying to avoid a default **on** its foreign debt. ◇ They are **in default** of their obligations. ◇ The risk of default is very high. ◇ loan defaults
2 (IT) [U,C] what happens or appears if you do not make any other choice or change: The default option is to save your work every five minutes. ◇ What do you use as your default browser?
IDM **by de'fault** if something happens **by default** it happens because nothing has been done to make things happen differently or because sb has not done what they should have done: He became Chief Executive of the merged company almost by default. ◇ They won their lawsuit by default.
● verb [no obj]
1 (Law) to fail to do sth that you are legally required to do, especially by not paying a debt: The company defaulted **on** a $5 million loan repayment. ◇ a defaulted bond (= one for which the investors did not receive a payment) ◇ defaulting tenants
2 (IT) to happen when you do not make any other choice or change: The browsers default **to** the internal home page.
▶ **de'faulter** noun [C]: loan defaulters

de,fault 'judgement (also ,judgement by/in de'fault) (also spelled **judgment**) noun [C]
(Law) a decision that a court makes against sb/sth because they do not defend a claim that is brought against them

defect noun, verb
● noun /ˈdiːfekt; dɪˈfekt/ [C]

SEE ALSO: **latent defect, zero defect**

a fault in sth or in the way it has been made which means that it is not perfect: Engineers found several defects **in** the design of the vehicle. ◇ The factory has a **defect rate** of 1 per 4 engines produced.
○ an important/a major/minor/serious/slight defect • a design/mechanical/safety/structural defect
● verb /dɪˈfekt/ [no obj]
1 to stop using a particular supplier, product, etc. and use a competing one: Many of their customers defected **to** rival firms.
2 to leave an employer, political party, etc. to join another that is considered to be a competitor or enemy: Several presenters have defected **from** radio to TV.
▶ **defection** /dɪˈfekʃn/ noun [U,C]: the defection of business travellers **to** low-fare airlines **de'fector** noun [C]

defective /dɪˈfektɪv/ adjective
having a fault or faults; not perfect or complete: The manufacture offered to repair or replace any defective products. ◇ The car's tyres were defective. ◇ defective workmanship/equipment

defence (*AmE spelling* **defense**) /dɪ'fens/ *noun*
1 (*Law*) [C] (in a legal case) the reasons that sb/sth gives for not being guilty of a crime or of doing sth wrong; the act of presenting this argument in a court: *Their defence was that they were prevented from finishing the work on time.* ◇ *He wanted to conduct his own defence.*
2 (*Law*) **the defence** [sing. with sing./pl. verb] the lawyer or lawyers whose job is to prove in a court that sb/sth did not commit a crime or do sth wrong: *The defence has tried to discredit the witness.* → PROSECUTION
3 [C] (*used in compounds*) a particular method by which a company tries to avoid a TAKEOVER (= being bought by another company): *preparing a bid defence*

de'fence ,document (*AmE spelling* **defense ~**) *noun* [C] (*BrE only*)
a document that is written by a company to its shareholders, explaining why they should reject an offer to buy the company (a **takeover bid**)

★ **defend** /dɪ'fend/ *verb*
1 [+ obj *or no* obj] to protect sb/sth against an attack or harm: *The firm is prepared to defend (itself) against a hostile takeover bid.* ◇ *They have been struggling to defend market share.*
2 [+ obj] to say or write sth in support of sb/sth that has been criticized: *They have defended their decision to close the plant.*
3 (*Law*) [+ obj] to resist a legal claim that is brought against you: *You need to inform the court if you intend to defend the claim.*
4 (*Law*) [+ obj] to act as a lawyer for sb who has been charged with a crime: *She hired one of the UK's top lawyers to defend her.*

defendant /dɪ'fendənt/ *noun* [C]
(*Law*) the person in a court who is being SUED by another person or who is accused of committing a crime: *The three defendants have pleaded not guilty.* → PLAINTIFF

defense = DEFENCE

defensive /dɪ'fensɪv/ *adjective, noun*
● *adjective*
1 (*Finance*) (about an investment) safe in times of economic difficulty, because the price or value is not easily affected by circumstances: *There has been a move to defensive sectors, such as health care and food.* → CYCLICAL See note at STOCK
○ *defensive* **shares/stocks** • *a defensive* **industry/ investment/sector**
2 that tries to protect sb/sth from attack or harm: *The job cuts were a defensive move against decreasing sales.*
● *noun* [C, usually pl.]
(*Finance*) an investment that is not easily affected by times of economic difficulty: *Investors have been buying defensives, like utility and food stocks.*

defer /dɪ'fɜː(r)/ *verb* [+ obj] (**-rr-**)
to delay sth until a later time: *The lenders agreed to defer the first debt repayment.* ◇ *The department deferred the decision for six months.* ◇ *a deferred payment* ▸ **de'ferment** (*also* **deferral** /dɪ'fɜːrəl/) *noun* [C,U]: *payment deferrals* ◇ *a 90-day deferral period* → TAX-DEFERRED

de,ferred 'credit *noun* [C] (*also* **de,ferred 'income** [U])
(*Accounting*) an amount written in a company's financial records which represents money received that has not yet been earned, for example for goods or services that will be provided during a later accounting period. These amounts are shown as LIABILITIES: *Payments for orders not yet delivered are dealt with as deferred credits.*

de,ferred ,lia'bility *noun* [C]
(*Accounting*) an amount written in a company's financial records which represents money that the

---

company will pay back during a future accounting period: *Money should be set aside for deferred liabilities.*

de,ferred 'share *noun* [C]
(*Finance*) a type of share for which a company can delay the payment of a DIVIDEND (= money paid to shareholders) See note at SHARE

de,ferred tax'ation *noun* [U] (*also* **de,ferred 'tax** [U,C])
(*Accounting*) tax on profits made during a particular accounting period which only needs to be paid during a later period. Companies keep an amount of money separate in their financial records to pay for this: *Provision has been made for deferred taxation.* ◇ *The effect of deferred taxation was to reduce after-tax profit by £6.5 million.*

deficiency /dɪ'fɪʃnsi/ *noun* [C] (*plural* **deficiencies**)

SEE ALSO: notice of deficiency

1 the amount by which sth, especially income, is less than it should be: *a budget deficiency of $96 billion* SYN DEFICIT
2 (*Accounting*) (*AmE*) a situation in which sb owes more tax than they have shown on their tax forms; the amount they owe: *The IRS assessed a deficiency of $40 000 against the estate.*

de'ficiency ,judgment (*BrE spelling ~* **judgement**) *noun* [C] (*AmE only*)
(*Law*) a court decision that forces sb to finish paying a debt for which they did not give enough SECURITY (= valuable items that will be lost if the money is not paid back): *The lender has the right to obtain a deficiency judgment against you.*

de'ficiency ,notice = NOTICE OF DEFICIENCY

★ **deficit** /'defɪsɪt/ *noun* [C]

SEE ALSO: structural deficit, trade deficit

1 (*Accounting*; *Economics*) the amount by which money that a government or business spends or owes is greater than money received in a particular period of time: *Germany was running a budget deficit of 3.75 per cent.* ◇ *The trade balance is in deficit.* ◇ *an annual operating deficit* ◇ *the government/federal deficit* ○ SURPLUS
○ *a* **high/large/low/modest/small** *deficit* • *to* **face/ have/run/show** *a deficit (of sth)* • *to* **cut/eliminate/ make up/reduce** *a deficit* • *a deficit* **grows/narrows/ shrinks/widens** *(from/to sth)* • *to* **finance/fund** *a deficit*
2 [usually sing.] the amount by which sth, especially an amount of money, is too small or smaller than sth else: *The group claims it can make up the $47 million deficit in its pension fund.* ◇ *The industry has shown a deficit of creativity and innovation.*

'deficit ,financing *noun* [U]
(*Economics*) the practice of a government borrowing money in order to pay for things not paid for by the money received from taxes, etc: *The government tried to stimulate the economy through deficit financing.* → DEFICIT SPENDING

'deficit ,spending *noun* [U]
(*Economics*) money that a government spends which it needs to borrow, because it does not receive enough tax, etc: *Deficit spending was seen as a way of reducing unemployment.* → DEFICIT FINANCING

define /dɪ'faɪn/ *verb* [+ obj]
1 to say or explain what the meaning of a word or phrase is: *The Act defines 'small companies' as firms with fewer than 25 employees.*

2 to describe sth accurately: *They define success in terms of financial gain.* ◊ *A project needs to have clearly defined objectives.*
▶ **definition** /ˌdefɪˈnɪʃn/ *noun* [C,U]

de,fined 'benefit *noun* [C]
a fixed amount of money that will be paid by a PENSION PLAN: *The plan offers guaranteed defined benefits to retiring employees.* ◊ *a defined-benefit pension scheme*

de,fined contri'bution *noun* [C]
fixed payments that are made to a PENSION PLAN where the amount that will be paid out can change: *a new scheme based on defined contributions rather than final salary* ◊ *a defined-contribution pension plan*

deflate *verb* [+ obj or no obj]
1 (*Economics*) /ˌdiːˈfleɪt/ to reduce the amount of money being used in a country so that prices fall or stay steady: *The government raised interest rates in an attempt to deflate the economy.* → INFLATE, REFLATE
2 /ˌdiːˈfleɪt; dɪˈfleɪt/ to become or make sth less valuable, expensive or active: *Food prices are deflating by 1.5% a year.* ◊ *a badly deflated share price*

★ **deflation** /ˌdiːˈfleɪʃn/ *noun* [U]

SEE ALSO: **asset deflation**

1 (*Economics*) a reduction in the amount of money in a country's economy so that prices fall or remain the same: *The government is introducing measures to combat deflation.* ◊ *Companies are still laying off employees as deflation continues to reduce their revenue.* → DISINFLATION, INFLATION, REFLATION at REFLATE
2 a situation in which prices continuously become lower: *the deflation of raw materials prices* ◊ *The retailer experienced price deflation of 2% last year.*
▶ **deflationary** /ˌdiːˈfleɪʃənri; AmE -neri/ *adjective*: *deflationary policies* ◊ *the deflationary pressures on the economy*

deflator /ˌdiːˈfleɪtə(r); dɪˈ-/ *noun* [C]
(*Economics*) a figure that is used to reduce the current price of sth, so that it can be compared fairly with a price in the past: *Current prices were converted to constant prices using a price deflator.*

defraud /dɪˈfrɔːd/ *verb* [+ obj or no obj]
to get money illegally from a person or an organization by tricking them: *They were accused of defrauding the company of $600 million.* ◊ *The five men are charged with conspiracy to defraud.*

defray /dɪˈfreɪ/ *verb* [+ obj] (*formal*)
to provide money to pay or help pay for the cost of sth: *a grant to help the company defray the cost of its technology upgrade*
➲ to defray **charges/costs/expenses**

defunct /dɪˈfʌŋkt/ *adjective*
no longer existing or being used: *The routes were operated by the now defunct Sabena Airlines.*

degrade /dɪˈɡreɪd/ *verb* [+ obj or no obj]
(*Technical*) to become or to make sth become worse, especially in quality: *The software tends to degrade the performance of other programs.*

de jure /ˌdeɪ ˈdʒʊəri; ˌdiː; AmE ˈdʒʊri/ *adjective*
[usually before noun], *adverb*
(*Law*) according to the law; official: *The takeover has now been cleared and the group will take de jure control of the company on Monday.* NOTE De jure is a Latin phrase. → DE FACTO

Del *abbr* (*only used in written English*)
delete; delete key

delayering /ˌdiːˈleɪərɪŋ; AmE -ˈleər-/ *noun* [U]
(*HR*) the act of reducing the number of levels of staff in a company, especially by removing a level of managers from their jobs: *the delayering of middle management* ▶ **de'layer** *verb* [+ obj or no obj] See note at DISMISS

,del 'credere ,agent /ˌdel ˈkreɪdəri/ *noun* [C]
(*Trade*) a person or company that sells goods for another and who agrees to pay for them if the customers fail to do so, receiving an extra COMMISSION for this risk

★ **delegate** *noun, verb*
●*noun* /ˈdelɪɡət/ [C]
a person who is chosen to speak and take decisions for a group of people, especially at a meeting: *More than 300 delegates from 60 countries attended the conference.*
●*verb* /ˈdelɪɡeɪt/ [+ obj or no obj]
to give part of your work, power or authority to sb or a group of people, usually in a lower position than you: *Some managers find it hard to delegate.* ◊ *She delegated responsibility for the project to the marketing department.*
➲ to delegate **authority/responsibility/tasks/work**

delegation /ˌdelɪˈɡeɪʃn/ *noun*

SEE ALSO: **trade delegation**

1 [C] a group of people who represent the views of an organization, a country, etc: *He will lead the country's delegation to the trade fair next month.* ◊ *They are sending a delegation of business people to the talks.*
2 [U] the process of giving sb work or responsibilities that would usually be yours: *the delegation of authority*

delete /dɪˈliːt/ *verb, noun*
●*verb* [+ obj]
1 to remove sth that has been written or printed, or that has been stored on a computer: *Your name has been deleted from the list.* ◊ *I accidentally deleted your email.* → INSERT
2 to stop making or selling a particular product, especially a CD, video, etc: *The recording has been deleted in the UK, but is still available in the US.*
▶ **deletion** /dɪˈliːʃn/ *noun* [C,U]: *We publish a monthly list of additions and deletions to the products in this catalogue.* ◊ *the deletion of incorrect data*
●*noun* [U] (*also* **de'lete key** [C]) (*abbr* **Del**)
a button on a computer keyboard that you press to remove text or images: *Select the text and hit delete.*

deleveraging /ˌdiːˈliːvərɪdʒɪŋ; AmE ˈlev-/ *noun* [U]
(*Finance*) a method of changing how a company funds its activities in which it reduces the amount of money that it borrows: *the group's deleveraging and refinancing programme* ◊ *Money from the sale of the asset has helped the deleveraging of the company.*
▶ **de'leverage** *verb* [+ obj or no obj]: *The company is under pressure to deleverage.* → LEVERAGING at LEVERAGE

delinquency /dɪˈlɪŋkwənsi/ *noun* [C] (*plural* **delinquencies**) (*especially AmE*)
(*Accounting*) an act of failing to pay money that you owe to a bank or business: *Higher interest rates have led to an increase in credit-card delinquencies.* ◊ *The delinquency rate on personal loans rose to 2.3 per cent in March.* ▶ **delinquent** /dɪˈlɪŋkwənt/ *adjective* [usually before noun]: *Customers with delinquent accounts will not receive any further credit.*

delist /ˌdiːˈlɪst/ *verb* [+ obj or no obj]
(*Stock Exchange*) to remove a company from the official list of a stock exchange so that its shares are no longer traded there: *Their shares have been delisted from the Tokyo stock market.* ◊ *The group revealed that it was planning to delist.* ▶ **de'listing**

noun [U,C]: *They have applied to the stock exchange for delisting.*

★ **deliver** /dɪˈlɪvə(r)/ *verb*

1 [+ obj *or* no obj] to take goods, letters, etc. to the person or people they have been sent to: *Leaflets have been delivered to every household.* ◇ *We promise to deliver within 48 hours.*
2 [+ obj *or* no obj] to make and supply sth that has been requested by a customer: *The manufacturer delivered 112 new aircraft last year.* ◇ *The challenge is for the company to deliver on time and on budget.*
3 [+ obj] to provide a service: *They deliver exceptional customer service.*
4 [+ obj *or* no obj] to produce, provide or achieve sth that people expect or that will benefit sb/sth: *The company delivered strong financial results last year.* ◇ *We are committed to delivering real value (= profits) to shareholders.* ◇ *We are delivering on all the targets we set ourselves.* ◇ *The website looked promising, but failed to deliver.*
5 [+ obj] to give a speech, talk, etc. or make an official statement: *His talk was delivered in a clear, interesting way.* ◇ *The company has delivered a profit warning.*
→ idiom at GOODS

★ **deliverable** /dɪˈlɪvərəbl/ *noun, adjective*
● *noun* [C, usually pl.]
(*Commerce; Production*) a piece of work that must be completed, especially as part of a long project: *The development team have agreed on dates for all deliverables, including the final product.* ◇ *tracking project deliverables with software* → MILESTONE
● *adjective* [not usually before noun]
that can be achieved, provided or delivered: *Is the proposal deliverable?* ◇ *The futures contract becomes deliverable on January 31.* ◇ *deliverable results*

de,livered at 'frontier *phrase* (*abbr* DAF)
(*Trade*) (*usually used as an adjective or adverb*)
a term meaning that the seller delivers the goods to the border of the country mentioned. The buyer collects the goods and is responsible for bringing them into the country in the official way.
→ INCOTERM

de'livered 'duty 'paid *phrase* (*abbr* DDP)
(*Trade*) (*usually used as an adjective or adverb*)
a term meaning that the seller delivers the goods to the place mentioned, in the buyer's country, and pays for any IMPORT DUTIES (= taxes on goods brought into a country) → INCOTERM

de'livered 'duty un'paid *phrase* (*abbr* DDU)
(*Trade*) (*usually used as an adjective or adverb*)
a term meaning that the seller delivers the goods to the place mentioned, in the buyer's country. The buyer arranges for the goods to be brought into the country in the official way, and pays for any IMPORT DUTIES (= taxes on goods brought into a country). → INCOTERM

de,livered ex 'quay *phrase* (*abbr* DEQ)
(*Trade*) (*usually used as an adjective or adverb*)
a term meaning that the seller delivers the goods by ship to the port in the buyer's country that is mentioned. The buyer collects the goods from the port and is responsible for bringing them into the country in the official way. → INCOTERM

de,livered ex 'ship *phrase* (*abbr* DES)
(*Trade*) (*usually used as an adjective or adverb*)
a term meaning that the seller delivers the goods by ship to the port in the buyer's country that is mentioned. The buyer collects the goods from the ship and is responsible for bringing them into the country in the official way. → INCOTERM

de'livered price *noun* [C]
(*Commerce*) a price that includes all the costs for packing and transporting the goods as far as the place where they are going

★ **delivery** /dɪˈlɪvəri/ *noun* (*plural* **deliveries**)

SEE ALSO: cash before delivery, nearby ~, non-~, part ~, recorded ~, special ~, spot ~

1 [U,C] the act of taking goods, letters, etc. to the people they have been sent to: *They offer guaranteed next-day delivery to any home in the UK.* ◇ *Please pay for the goods on delivery (= when you receive them).* ◇ *Allow 28 days for delivery.* ◇ *Is there a delivery charge?* ◇ *The airline will take delivery of (= receive) 11 new planes in 2006.* ◇ *We do all our deliveries in the morning.* See note at DISTRIBUTION
○ *express/fast/next-day/overnight/same-day* delivery
• *to do/make* a delivery • *a delivery boy/business/man/van*
2 [C] a load of goods that is received: *The store receives one delivery of books a week.*
○ *to get/receive/wait for a delivery*
3 [U] the act of supplying sth or providing a service to sb/sth: *improving the delivery of public services* ◇ *a new training delivery system*
4 (*Law*) [U,C] the act of sb receiving or getting control of sth they have bought: *Delivery will take place at the seller's place of business.*

de'livery date *noun* [C]
1 (*Production*) the date on which a manufacturer or supplier agrees to deliver goods or raw materials that have been bought: *We need a firm delivery date.* ◇ *The plant missed the delivery date on two new aircraft (= it did not deliver them at the agreed time).*
○ *a firm/an estimated/a guaranteed/promised/revised* delivery date • *to miss/agree/change/meet a delivery date*
2 (*Production*) the date on which a new product will be available and ready for use: *The six-month delivery date on the new system did not give us time to develop it from scratch.*
3 (*Finance*) the date on which an investment, such as a FUTURES CONTRACT, must be finally completed: *The delivery date for the futures contract is 30 June.*

de'livery note (*especially BrE*) (*AmE usually* de'livery re,ceipt*) noun* [C]
(*Transport*) a form that you sign when goods, documents, etc. are delivered: *Record any shortages on the delivery note before signing it.* → ADVICE NOTE, DISPATCH NOTE

de'livery ,order *noun* [C] (*abbr* DO)
(*Trade*) a written document that a seller of goods gives to a buyer, to allow them to collect the goods from the place where they are being stored: *The goods must be collected within 7 days of the receipt of the delivery order.*

de'livery re,ceipt = DELIVERY NOTE

'Delphi tech,nique (*also* 'Delphi ,method)
/ˈdelfi; *AmE* ˈdelfaɪ/ *noun* [C, usually sing.]
a method of getting a group of experts to agree about sth, but without them discussing it. The experts write down their opinions in response to a set of questions and then in response to the results based on the opinions of all the experts. A group leader decides when the written opinions show that the experts have reached an agreement: *We used the Delphi technique to gain insights into future development of IT.*

★ **demand** /dɪˈmɑːnd; *AmE* dɪˈmænd/ *noun, verb*
● *noun*

SEE ALSO: consumer ~, derived ~, elasticity of ~, excess ~, final ~, on ~, etc.

1 [U,C] the desire or need of customers for goods or services which they want to buy or use: *Demand for new cars has fallen.* ◇ *a sharp fall in car demand*

◇ *The plant has increased production in order to meet demand.* ◇ *Demand for the aircraft has outstripped* (= has been greater than) *supply.* ◇ *The price is determined by the balance between* **demand and supply.** ◇ *Traders reported a strong demand from investors.* → SUPPLY noun (3)

⊕ demand **falls/drops/slows down/weakens** ◆ demand **grows/picks up/recovers/rises** ◆ *to* **meet/ keep up with/satisfy** demand ◆ *to* **boost/create/ increase/reduce/stimulate** demand ◆ demand **outstrips/exceeds** supply ◆ *(a)* **strong/growing/ huge/rising** demand ◆ *(a)* **declining/falling/poor/ low/weak** demand ◆ **domestic/external/global/ world** demand ◆ **consumer/investor/market** demand

2 [C] a very firm request for sth; sth that sb needs or asks for: *Management has rejected the union's demand for a 40 per cent pay rise.* ◇ *The firm is struggling to satisfy the demands of its shareholders.*
⊕ *to* **accept/agree to/meet/reject/satisfy** *a demand*
3 [C] a written request to pay money that is owed: *You will receive a demand for the extra tax owing.*
⊕ *to* **get/ignore/issue/receive** *a demand*
IDM **on de'mand 1** as soon as requested: *The loan is repayable on demand.* **2** *(usually used with a noun)* when you want it: *The company website offers employees information on demand.* ◇ *on-demand computing*
● **verb** [+ obj]
to ask for sth very firmly: *She demanded an apology from him.* ◇ *They are demanding €1.6 million in compensation.* ◇ *I demand to see the manager.*

de'mand curve *noun* [C, usually sing.] *(usually* **the demand curve)**
(Economics) a line on a graph that shows the relationship between the price of a product or service and the quantity of it that people buy: *Each point on the demand curve represents the quantity demanded at a particular price.* ◇ *An increase in incomes caused a shift in the demand curve for automobiles.*

de'mand de₁posit = SIGHT DEPOSIT

de'mand draft = DEMAND NOTE (1)

de'mand in₁flation *(also* de₁mand-'pull in₁flation) *noun* [U]
(Economics) an increase in prices due to the fact that the demand for goods and services rises quicker than the amount of goods and services that can be supplied → COST INFLATION

de'mand loan *(also* 'call loan) *noun* [C] *(both especially AmE)*
(Finance) a type of loan which a borrower agrees to pay back as soon as the lender asks: *Until a repayment date is decided, the loan will be treated as a demand loan.* → TERM LOAN

de'mand note *noun* [C]
(Finance)
1 *(also* **de'mand draft)** *(both especially AmE)* a document in which sb agrees to pay an amount of money to sb else whenever they ask for it: *A lot of small business loans are, in fact, demand notes, meaning that the banks have the right to ask for full payment at any time.*
2 a written demand for a debt to be paid: *an income tax demand note*

de'mand price *noun* [C, usually sing.]
(Economics) the price that customers are willing to pay when a particular amount of a product or service is available: *The demand price for a product decreases with every increase in the amount offered.*

de₁mand-'pull in₁flation = DEMAND INFLATION

de'mand side *noun* [sing.] *(usually* **the demand side)**
(Economics) the part of an economy that relates to the buying or using of goods and services, rather than their production: *On the demand side, the government has lowered taxes to encourage people to spend.* → SUPPLY SIDE
▶ **de'mand-side** *adjective* [only before noun]: *the demand-side effects of a change in income tax rates* ◇ *demand-side policies* (= that try to control the demand for goods and services)

demarcation /₁diːmɑːˈkeɪʃn; *AmE* -mɑːˈrk-/ *noun* [U] *(BrE)*
(HR) when a company can give particular types of jobs only to members of particular unions: *By working as a machine operator, the cleaner had broken the demarcation rules.* ◇ *a rigid system of job demarcation*

₁demar'cation dis₁pute *noun* [C] *(BrE)*
(HR) a disagreement between different unions about who should do particular jobs in a company

dematerialized , -ised /₁diːməˈtɪəriəlaɪzd; *AmE* -ˈtɪr-/ *adjective*
(Stock Exchange) used to describe shares, bonds, etc. that only exist in electronic records: *An investor can hold his shares in either physical or dematerialized form.*

demerge /₁diːˈmɜːdʒ; *AmE* -ˈmɜːrdʒ/ *verb* [+ obj or no obj]
to make a new company out of part of a larger business; to split from a larger business and become a separate company: *The group intends to demerge the advertising division into a separate business.* ◇ *The mobile phone company demerged from the BT group in 2001.* ◇ *head of the demerged retail business*

demerger /₁diːˈmɜːdʒə(r); *AmE* -ˈmɜːrdʒ-/ *noun* [C]
the act of separating a company from a larger company or business, especially when they had been joined together (**merged**) earlier: *The restaurant chain has struggled since its demerger from its former parent company.* ◇ *a proposed demerger of the group/business/division* → MERGER, DEMERGE

★ **demo** /ˈdeməʊ; *AmE* -moʊ/ *noun, verb*
● **noun** [C] *(plural* **demos)** *(informal)*
1 a demonstration
2 *(informal)* = DEMONSTRATION VERSION
● **verb** [+ obj] *(***demos, demoing, demoed, demoed)**
(Marketing) to show or be shown the features of a piece of equipment or software: *They will demo the phone at this year's technology fair.* ◇ *Click here to demo the software.* → DEMONSTRATE

democracy /dɪˈmɒkrəsi; *AmE* -ˈmɑːk-/ *noun* [U]
fair and equal treatment of everyone in an organization, etc., and their right to take part in making decisions: *the need to promote democracy in the workplace*

democratic /₁deməˈkrætɪk/ *adjective*
based on the principle that all members have an equal right to be involved in running an organization, etc: *The decision-making process should be more open and democratic.* ◇ *a democratic organization* ▶ **democratically** /₁deməˈkrætɪkli/ *adverb*: *The decision was taken democratically.*

demographic /₁deməˈɡræfɪk/ *noun, adjective*
● **noun**
1 **demographics** [pl.] the basic features of the members of a group of people, such as how old, rich, etc. they are, how many males and females there are, etc: *We chose the city for our first store as its demographics were young and wealthy.* ◇ *analysing customer demographics*
2 *(Marketing)* [sing.] a group of customers who are of a similar age, sex, etc: *The publication is popular within the 15 to 24-year-old male demographic.*

1 connected with the features of a population, especially as these change over a period of time: *Demographic changes have led to an increased demand for health care.*
2 (*Marketing*) connected with a particular group of people who are of a similar age, sex, etc: *Younger professionals are one of the most attractive consumer demographic groups.*
▶ **demographically** /ˌdeməˈgræfɪkli/ *adverb*: *a demographically representative audience*

‚demographic 'profile *noun* [C]
(*Marketing*) a description of the age, sex, income, etc. of people in a particular group: *They developed a demographic profile of the restaurant's customers.*

demography /dɪˈmɒgrəfi; *AmE* -ˈmɑːg-/ *noun* [U]
1 the changing number of births, deaths, diseases, etc. in a community over a period of time; the scientific study of these changes: *Demography is a useful starting point for looking at future economic developments.*
2 the basic features of a particular population: *The mobility and demography of the workforce is changing.*

'demo ‚model = DEMONSTRATION MODEL

demonetize, -ise /ˌdiːˈmʌnɪtaɪz/ *verb* [+ obj]
to decide officially that particular notes, coins, etc. can no longer be used as money: *The government demonetized silver in 1873.* ◇ *These demonetized notes are no longer exchangeable.*
▶ **de‚moneti'zation, -i'sation** *noun* [U]

★demonstrate /ˈdemənstreɪt/ *verb* [+ obj]
to show and explain how sth works or how to do sth: *The chief engineer demonstrated the features of the new videophone.* ◇ *people demonstrating how to use a product and giving free samples* → DEMO *verb*

★demonstration /ˌdemənˈstreɪʃn/ *noun* [C,U]
(*Marketing*) an act of showing or explaining a product or service, especially a new one: *They invited us to give a product demonstration.* ◇ *We are promoting the camera through in-store demonstration.* → DEMO *noun*
O *to give/provide a demonstration* • *a customer/ product/sales demonstration* • *(an) in-store/a practical/working demonstration*

‚demon'stration ef‚fect *noun* [C, usually sing.]
(*Economics*) the way that people, businesses, etc. are likely to copy the actions of others that they see are successful or to use sth that they can see is useful; an influence on sb to copy or avoid sth: *Through the demonstration effect, one successful start-up can lead to many new businesses.*

‚demon'stration ‚model (*also* **'demo ‚model**, *informal*) *noun* [C]
one example of a product that is used to show to possible customers: *We sometimes offer demonstration models for sale at lower prices.*

‚demon'stration ‚version (*also* **'demo ‚version, 'demo,** *informal*) *noun* [C]
(*IT*) a form of a computer program that you can try before deciding whether you want to buy the complete program: *You can download the demonstration version of the software by clicking here.*

★demote /ˌdiːˈməʊt; *AmE* -ˈmoʊt-/ *verb* [+ obj]
(*often* **be demoted**)
1 (*HR*) to move sb to a lower position in an organization, often as a punishment: *She was demoted from chief executive to sales director.*
2 (*Finance*) to move a company to a lower position within a particular system, such as a stock exchange index: *The airline has been demoted from the FTSE 100 Index.*
→ DOWNGRADE OPP PROMOTE

▶ **demotion** /ˌdiːˈməʊʃn; *AmE* -ˈmoʊ-/ *noun* [U,C]: *She had to work unpaid overtime or risk demotion.* ◇ *The company faces a demotion from the index following the drop in its share price.*

demotivate /ˌdiːˈməʊtɪveɪt; *AmE* -ˈmoʊ-/ *verb*
[+ obj] (*often* **be demotivated**)
(*HR*) to make sb not want to work or study: *If you hire bright people you don't want to demotivate them.* OPP MOTIVATE ▶ **de'motivated** *adjective*: *a demotivated workforce* **,de'motivating** *adjective*: *Too many assessments can be demotivating for staff.* **demotivation** /ˌdiːˌməʊtɪˈveɪʃn; *AmE* -ˌmoʊ-/ *noun* [U]: *the problems of staff demotivation* **‚demoti'vational** *adjective,* **de'motivator** *noun* [C]: *Continually correcting someone's mistakes can be a big demotivator.*

'demo ‚version (*also* **'demo**) = DEMONSTRATION VERSION

demutualize, -ise /ˌdiːˈmjuːtʃuəlaɪz/ *verb* [+ obj or no obj]
(*Finance*) to change a MUTUAL organization (= one that is run on behalf of the people who use its services) into a company with shareholders; to be changed in this way: *a demutualized building society* ◇ *The life insurer demutualized and listed on the London Stock Exchange last year.*
▶ **demutualization, -isation** /ˌdiːˌmjuːtʃuəlaɪˈzeɪʃn; *AmE* -lə'z-/ *noun* [U,C]

denationalize, -ise /ˌdiːˈnæʃnəlaɪz/ *verb* [+ obj]
(*Economics*) to sell a company or an industry so that it is no longer owned by the government: *The country is seeking to denationalize its railways.*
SYN PRIVATIZE OPP NATIONALIZE
▶ **denationalization, -isation** /ˌdiːˌnæʃnəlaɪˈzeɪʃn; *AmE* -lə'z-/ *noun* [U]

denominate /dɪˈnɒmɪneɪt; *AmE* -ˈnɑːm-/ *verb*
[+ obj] (*usually* **be denominated**)
to measure or state the value of sth using a particular currency: *Most of the country's foreign debt is denominated in dollars.*

denominated /dɪˈnɒmɪneɪtɪd; *AmE* -ˈnɑːm-/
combining form (*used in adjectives*)
expressed in the unit of money mentioned: *Thirty per cent of our sales are dollar denominated* ◇ *euro-denominated bonds/products* (= that pay interest, etc. in euros)

denomination /dɪˌnɒmɪˈneɪʃn; *AmE* -ˌnɑːm-/
noun [C]
the value stated on a note, coin, stamp, etc: *The new banknotes are being printed in denominations of 10, 20, 50 and 100.* ◇ *The central bank is considering higher denomination coins.*
O *a high/large/low/small denomination*

★department /dɪˈpɑːtmənt; *AmE* -ˈpɑːrt-/ *noun* [C]
a section of a large organization, store or government: *She heads the company's legal department.* ◇ *He works in the finance department.* ◇ *Do people outside your department ask you to help on projects?* ◇ *the home furnishings/jewellery department* ◇ *the Department of the Environment*
O *to head/manage/run a department* • *department heads/managers/staff*
IDM **be sb's department** (*only used in spoken English*) to be sth that sb is responsible for or knows a lot about: *That's not my department—let me transfer you* (= said on the telephone).

departmental /ˌdiːpɑːtˈmentl; *AmE* -pɑːrt-/
adjective [only before noun]
connected with a department rather than with the whole organization or government
O *a departmental budget/manager/meeting*

the **De'partment of 'Trade and 'Industry** noun [sing.] (abbr **DTI**)

the name in some countries, for example the UK, for the government department that supports the development of businesses and helps them trade with foreign companies

de'partment store noun [C]
a large shop/store that is divided into several parts, each part selling a different type of goods: *She works as a fashion buyer for an upmarket London department store.* ◇ *a struggling department store chain*

departure /dɪ'pɑːtʃə(r); AmE -'pɑːrt-/ noun
1 [C,U] the act of leaving a job; an example of this: *She has announced her departure from the company.* ◇ *The sudden departure of top executives has left the group in crisis.*
O *an abrupt/early/a sudden/an unexpected departure* • *a forced/planned/voluntary departure* • *executive/management/staff departures*
2 [U,C] the act of leaving a place; a plane, train, etc. leaving a place at a particular time: *Passengers must check in at least two hours before departure.* ◇ *There are 30 daily departures on the route between London and Edinburgh.* ◇ *the departures board* (= which shows when planes, etc. are leaving)
O *a departure gate/lounge/time*
→ idiom at POINT noun

deplete /dɪ'pliːt/ verb [+ obj] (usually **be depleted**)
to reduce sth by a large amount so that there is not enough left: *Production has fallen and stocks have become severely depleted.* ◇ *Their cash is being depleted by spending on investments and unprofitable trading.* ◇ *A rights issue would shore up our depleted capital base.* ▶ **depletion** /dɪ'pliːʃn/ noun [U]: *stock depletion* ◇ *the depletion of international reserves*

★ deposit /dɪ'pɒzɪt; AmE -'pɑːz-/ noun, verb
● *noun*

SEE ALSO: **bank deposit, cash ratio ~, certificate of ~, core ~, demand ~, direct ~, fixed ~,** etc.

1 [C] an amount of money that is paid into a bank or SAVINGS ACCOUNT: *Deposits can be made at any branch.* ◇ *I wish to **make** a deposit of $5 000.* ◇ *Payments are placed **on deposit** to earn interest.*
[OPP] WITHDRAWAL
2 (Economics) **deposits** [pl.] the total amount of money that has been paid into bank accounts in a particular area or country: *The combined banks would have deposits of more than $22 billion.* ◇ *The government fears **a run** on deposits.* ◇ *the ratio of deposits to gross domestic product* ◇ *dollar/sterling deposits*
3 (Commerce) [C, usually sing.] an amount of money that is given as the first part of a larger payment, especially to prevent the goods being sold to sb else: *You pay a $250 deposit now and the balance within 30 days.* ◇ *We've put down a deposit on a house.* ◇ *If you cancel the agreement after signature, you lose your deposit.* [SYN] DOWN PAYMENT
O *to ask for/require/take a deposit* • *to pay/put down a deposit* • *to forfeit/lose a deposit* • *to reclaim/ repay/return a deposit* • *a refundable/returnable/ non-refundable deposit*
4 (Property) [C, usually sing.] an amount of money that is paid by sb when they rent sth and that is returned to them if they do not lose or damage the thing they are renting: *Rent is £500 per month, plus a deposit of £300.* ◇ *Tenants need to pay a deposit of one month's rent.* ◇ *You claim back your deposit when you return the car.*
O *to ask for/require/take a deposit* • *to leave/pay a deposit* • *to forfeit/lose a deposit* • *to reclaim/ repay/return a deposit*

● *verb* [+ obj]
1 to put money into a bank or SAVINGS ACCOUNT: *At a bank you can deposit money or take out a loan.* ◇ *You can arrange to have your salary deposited directly into your bank account* ◇ *the banks' income from cash deposited **with** them in current accounts*
[OPP] WITHDRAW (1)
2 to put documents, money or sth valuable into a bank or other safe place: *We deposited the title deeds of the house at the bank.* ◇ *Full company accounts are deposited with Companies House.*

de'posit ac,count (abbr **d/a**) (BrE also **'notice ac,count**) (AmE also **'time ac,count**) noun [C] (BrE)
a type of account at a bank or BUILDING SOCIETY that pays interest on money that is left in it. You have to warn the bank a few days before you want to take the money out: *The deposit account offers a high rate of interest.* → CURRENT ACCOUNT

depositary /dɪ'pɒzɪtri; AmE dɪ'pɑːzəteri/ noun [C] (plural **depositaries**)
1 (also spelled **depository**) a person or company with whom money or documents can be left
2 = DEPOSITORY (1)

de,positary re'ceipt (also spelled **depository ~**) noun [C]
(Stock Exchange) a certificate that represents a number of shares in a foreign company. These certificates are bought and sold instead of the shares themselves, in the currency of the investor's stock exchange: *Marks and Spencer depositary receipts are traded on Euronext in Brussels and Amsterdam.* → ADR, EDR

de'posit cer,tificate = CERTIFICATE OF DEPOSIT

de'posit in,surance noun [U]
(Economics) insurance payments made by banks to a central organization. The money would be used to pay people with money in accounts at a bank if the bank went BANKRUPT (= was unable to pay its debts): *a deposit insurance system* ◇ *New Zealand has scrapped deposit insurance altogether.*

deposition /,depə'zɪʃn/ noun [C]
(Law) a formal statement, taken from sb and used in a court

de'posit lia,bilities noun [pl.]
(Finance) money that is paid into a bank, thought of as money that the bank owes and will have to pay back at some time: *Canadian banks increased their deposit liabilities with their foreign affiliates.*

depositor /dɪ'pɒzɪtə(r); AmE -'pɑːz-/ noun [C]
a person or an organization that puts money in a bank account: *The government has sought to reassure depositors that the country's banks are in no danger of collapse.*

depository /dɪ'pɒzɪtri; AmE dɪ'pɑːzətɔːri/ noun [C] (plural **depositories**)

SEE ALSO: **night depository**

1 (also spelled **depositary**) a place where things, especially money or official documents, can be stored or kept safely: *The documents are stored in a public UK depository.* ◇ *satellites acting as depositories for digital cash* ◇ *a furniture depository*
2 = DEPOSITARY (1)

de'pository insti,tution noun [C]
a DEPOSIT-TAKING financial institution

de,pository re'ceipt = DEPOSITARY RECEIPT

de'posit slip (also **de'posit re,ceipt**) noun [C]
(both especially AmE)
a printed form on which you record the amount of money, the date, etc. when you put money into your bank account [SYN] PAYING-IN SLIP (BrE)

de'posit-,taking adjective [only before noun]
(about a financial institution) which accepts

deposits, for which it pays interest or provides services: *new legislation governing deposit-taking financial institutions such as commercial banks, merchant banks, and building societies*

depot /'depəʊ; *AmE* 'di:pəʊ/ *noun* [C]
1 (*Commerce*) a place where large amounts of goods or equipment are stored, especially before being sent somewhere else: *an oil/food depot* ◇ *French hauliers are blockading **fuel** depots.* ◇ *a distribution/storage depot*
2 (*Transport*) (*BrE*) a place where vehicles, for example buses, are kept and repaired: *a bus depot*
3 (*Transport*) (*AmE*) a small station where trains or buses stop: *The train left the depot on time.*

depreciable /dɪ'pri:ʃəbl/ *adjective*
(*Accounting*) able to be DEPRECIATED over a period of time: *Baseball players should be treated as depreciable **assets** with a fixed useful life.*

de,preciable 'life *noun* [C]
(*Accounting*) the period of time over which an asset is DEPRECIATED: *An item of equipment might have a depreciable life of five years but actually be used for two years longer.*

depreciate /dɪ'pri:ʃieɪt/ *verb*
1 (*Economics*) [+ obj *or* no obj] (about a currency) to decrease in value, compared to the currencies of other countries: *Sterling is expected to depreciate **against** the US dollar.* ◇ *The Brazilian real depreciated (by) 28% against the euro.* ◇ *the country's rapidly depreciating currency*
[OPP] APPRECIATE See note at CURRENCY
2 (*Accounting*) [+ obj] to gradually reduce the value of machinery, a vehicle or other asset over a particular period of time, as stated in a company's accounts: *Fixed assets are depreciated over four years.* → AMORTIZE (1), WRITE OFF
3 [no obj] to decrease in value over a period of time: *Shares continued to depreciate on the stock markets today.* ◇ *New cars start to depreciate as soon as they are on the road.* ◇ *a depreciating asset*

de,preciated 'cost *noun* [C, usually sing.]
(*Accounting*) the cost of an asset with the amount that is being claimed against tax for DEPRECIATION taken away: *You are reimbursed for the depreciated cost of your computer only.* → NET BOOK VALUE

★ **depreciation** /dɪ,pri:ʃi'eɪʃn/ *noun*

SEE ALSO: accelerated depreciation, accrued ~, accumulated ~, book ~, rate of ~, tax ~

1 (*Economics*) [U; sing.] a fall in the value of a country's currency, compared to the currencies of other countries: *a 22% depreciation **in** the South African rand* ◇ *a **sharp** depreciation in Brazil's currency, the real* ◇ *The decline reflects the depreciation of the euro **against** sterling.*
[OPP] APPRECIATION
2 (*Accounting*) [U] a gradual reduction in the value of machinery, a vehicle or other asset over a particular period of time, as stated in a company's accounts: *the calculation of depreciation on business furniture and equipment* ◇ *a sharp rate of depreciation* → AMORTIZATION
3 [U] a gradual reduction in the value of sth over a period of time: *the depreciation of house prices*

de,preci'ation ac,count *noun* [C]
(*Accounting*) a financial record in which the amount of **depreciation** on an asset is recorded: *the balance in the depreciation account*

de,preci'ation al,lowance *noun* [C]
(*Accounting*) an amount of money that a business can take away from its profit when calculating the amount of tax it must pay, based on the fact that an asset such as machinery or a vehicle has lost part of its value over a period of time: *The government has raised depreciation allowances for small and medium-sized companies.*

depreciation
straight-line method

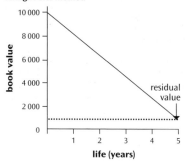

reducing balance method

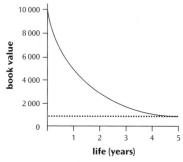

de,preci'ation fund *noun* [C]
(*Accounting*) an amount of money made available by a company to buy new assets. The money comes from investing an amount of money equal to the DEPRECIATION ALLOWANCE on an asset that the company already has.

de,preci'ation ,method *noun* [C]
(*Accounting*) any of the methods used to calculate the **depreciation** of an asset over the time it is expected to be in use: *Which depreciation method would you use if you were trying to minimize taxes?* → ACCELERATED DEPRECIATION

de,preci'ation rate (*also* ,rate of depreci'ation, *less frequent*) *noun* [C]
(*Accounting*) the rate at which a company's asset is calculated as reducing in value each year in the accounts: *a depreciation rate of 20%*

★ **depress** /dɪ'pres/ *verb* [+ obj]
1 to make an economy or market less active: *The recession has depressed the housing market.* ◇ *Lowering spending would depress the economic climate.*
2 to reduce the value of prices, wages, sales, etc: *Profits were depressed by reorganization costs.* ◇ *Warm weather has depressed sales of winter clothing.*

depressed /dɪ'prest/ *adjective*
1 without enough economic activity or employment: *The manufacturing sector remains firmly depressed.* ◇ *the depressed economic climate* ◇ *the depressed state of the global economy*
2 having a lower amount or level than usual: *Many people are buying computers at today's depressed prices.* ◇ *Car sales remain depressed.* ◇ *depressed consumer demand*

de,pressed 'market noun [C]
a market where there is not much demand for the
products and services being offered for sale: *The
break-up value of the company in the current
depressed market would be limited.* ◇ *the depressed
market for IT stocks*

★ **depression** /dɪˈpreʃn/ noun
1 (*Economics*) [C,U] a long period when there is
little economic activity, many businesses fail and
many people are poor or without jobs: *The collapse
of investment and consumption can often lead to
depression.* ◇ *We have been through a global
economic depression.* ◇ *Is the country sliding into
depression?* → BOOM, RECESSION, SLUMP
● *to sink into/slide into/tip sth into depression* • *(a)
full-scale/major/severe depression* • *a depression
deepens/ends*
2 the Depression (*also* **the ,Great De'pression**)
[sing.] the period from 1929 to 1934 when large
numbers of people in the US and Europe were
unemployed and poor because there was so little
economic activity
3 [sing.] the lowering or reducing of sth: *a
continued depression in travel demand* ◇ *the
depression of energy prices*

Dept (*also spelled* **dept**) (*AmE spelling* **Dept.**, **dept.**)
abbr (*only used in written English*)
department: *Dept of Economic Development*

'depth ,interview noun [C]
(*Marketing*) an interview in which one person is
asked detailed questions in order to find out their
opinions about a particular product ▶ **'depth
,interviewing** noun [U]

deputize , **-ise** /ˈdepjutaɪz/ verb [no obj]
to do sth that sb in a higher position than you
would usually do: *Ms Green has asked me to
deputize for her at the meeting.* [SYN] STAND IN

deputy /ˈdepjuti/ noun [C] (*plural* **deputies**)
a person who is immediately below the head of an
organization, a department, etc. in rank and who is
officially in charge when that person is not there:
Tesco's deputy chairman ◇ *The chairman is away
today, but I'm acting as his deputy.*
● *a deputy chairman/chief executive/governor/
manager/managing director*

DEQ /,di: i: 'kju:/ = DELIVERED EX QUAY

derail /dɪˈreɪl/ verb [+ obj]
to prevent a plan, an agreement, etc. from
continuing or succeeding: *This announcement
threatened to derail the deal.* ◇ *Spending plans have
been derailed by the slowdown in the economy.*

deregulate /,di:ˈregjuleɪt/ verb [+ obj] (*usually* **be
deregulated**)
to remove government rules and controls from an
industry, a business activity, etc: *The
telecommunications market is being deregulated.* ◇
Congress deregulated the airline industry in 1978.
[OPP] REGULATE → DECONTROL ▶ **,de'regulated**
adjective [only before noun]: *Power generation is a
deregulated, competitive industry.* **deregulatory**
/,di:ˈregjələtəri; *AmE* -tɔːri/ *adjective* [only before
noun]

deregulation /,di:ˌregjuˈleɪʃn/ noun [U]
(*Economics*) the removing of government rules and
controls from an industry, a business activity, etc:
the deregulation of US financial services ◇ **Under
deregulation, power companies can sell electricity
anywhere in the nation.** [OPP] REGULATION

derivative /dɪˈrɪvətɪv/ (*also* **de,rivative 'instrument**, **de,rivative 'product**) noun [C, usually pl.]
(*Finance*) a financial investment such as an OPTION
(= that gives you the right to buy or sell sth in the

future) or a FUTURE (= a contract to buy or sell sth
in the future) whose price depends on the value of
the shares, bonds, raw materials, etc. that it relates
to: *trading in energy derivatives* ◇ *the Swiss
derivatives market* ◇ *Revenues from derivatives
trading rose 2.5%.* ◇ *Liffe, London's derivatives
exchange*
● *a derivatives broker/business/deal/transaction* •
the derivatives industry/market • *energy/equity/
gold/property derivatives*

de,rivative 'instrument   = DERIVATIVE

de,rivative 'product noun [C]
1 (*Finance*) = DERIVATIVE
2 (*Marketing*) a new product based on changes
made to some of the features of an existing product
to improve it or make it suitable for different
customers: *developing derivative products*

de,rived de'mand noun [U,C]
(*Economics*) the idea that the demand for sth, such
as a natural material used to produce sth, depends
on the demand for the final goods produced: *A car
manufacturer has a derived demand for
manufacturing equipment, components, steel, etc. so
that it can satisfy its customers.*

derrick /ˈderɪk/ noun [C]
1 a tall machine used for moving or lifting heavy
weights, especially on a ship
2 a tall structure over an oil WELL for holding the
drill (= the machine that makes the hole in the
ground for getting the oil out)

DES /,di: i: 'es/ *abbr*
1 (*IT*) **data encryption standard** a popular
method for protecting business information
2 (*Trade*) = DELIVERED EX SHIP

★ **design** /dɪˈzaɪn/ noun, verb
● *noun*

SEE ALSO: job design, graphic ~, industrial ~, web ~

1 [C,U] the general arrangement of the different
parts of sth that is made, such as a building,
machine etc.; a drawing or plan that shows how to
make it: *They have created a design for a solar-
powered car.* ◇ *The building suffers from poor design.*
◇ *The architects can refine their designs on screen.*
● *to create/produce/use a design* • *to change/
improve/modify the design (of sth)* • *(a)bad/good/
new/poor/unique design* • *a basic/preliminary/
standard design* • *a design feature/flaw/problem*
2 [U] the art or process of deciding how sth will
look, work, etc: *a course in art and design* ◇ *the
design and development of new products* ◇ *Most of
the design work was done by outside studios.* ◇ *We
use computers at each stage of the design process.*
● *a design agency/company/consultancy/firm/studio*
• *a design department/team*
→ CAD
● *verb* [+ obj]
1 to decide how sth will look, work, etc: *They have
won a contract to design and build two new ships.* ◇ *a
well-designed computer desk*
2 to think of and plan a system, a way of doing sth,
etc: *We allow staff to design their own work
schedules.* ◇ *designing a solution to meet customers'
needs*
3 (*usually* **be designed**) to make, plan or intend sth
for a particular purpose or use: *The phone is
specially designed for use in wet conditions.* ◇ *a
marketing strategy designed to improve the
company's image*

designate *verb, adjective*
● *verb* /ˈdezɪgneɪt/ [+ obj] (*usually* **be designated**)
1 to say officially that sth has a particular name or
purpose: *The area has been designated as 'industrial
land'.* ◇ *The money has been designated for creating
new jobs.* ◇ *You may only park in the designated
areas.*

2 to choose or name sb for a particular job or position: *The director is allowed to designate a deputy.* ◇ *Who has she designated **as** her successor?* ◇ *Someone should be designated to answer queries.*
●*adjective* /ˈdezɪgneɪt; -nət/ [after noun]
chosen to do a job but not yet having officially started it: *the chief executive designate*

designation /ˌdezɪgˈneɪʃn/ *noun*
1 [U] the action of choosing a person or thing for a particular purpose, or of giving them or it a particular status: *They met the criteria for designation as a 'certified organic grower'.*
2 [C] a name, title or description: *Designations such as 'Champagne' and 'Parma ham' are protected by law.*

★designer /dɪˈzaɪnə(r)/ *noun, adjective*
●*noun* [C]
a person whose job is to decide how things will look or work and to make drawings or plans showing this; a business that makes designs for a particular type of product: *He worked as chief designer at Alfa Romeo.* ◇ *a designer of jewellery* ◇ *a fashion/games/software designer* ◇ *a Canadian clothing designer and manufacturer*
●*adjective* [only before noun]
made by a famous **designer**; expensive and having a famous brand name: *Fashion and designer brands have been selling well.* ◇ *designer clothes/furniture/ water*

deˌsigner ˈlabel *noun* [C]
a famous company that makes expensive clothes, bags, belts, etc. and puts a label with its name on them; the clothing, etc. that such a company makes: *Advertisers include high-profile designer labels such as Prada and Versace.* ◇ *an increase in demand for designer labels* ◇ *designer-label jeans*

deˈsign proˌtection *noun* [U] (*especially BrE*) (*AmE usually* **deˈsign ˌpatent** [C])
(*Law*) the way that the law protects how sth looks, so that it cannot be copied or used by anyone else: *Design protection is primarily of importance for consumer goods such as mobile phones.*
→ COPYRIGHT

desk /desk/ *noun* [C]

SEE ALSO: **cash desk, front ~, help ~**

1 a piece of furniture like a table that you sit at to work, use your computer, etc. *All staff have to be at their desks* (= working) *by nine o'clock.* ◇ *Have the report **on** my desk* (= finish it and give it to me) *by Monday.*—Picture at OFFICE
2 the part of an organization where a particular type of work is done: *Our dealing desks provide market updates and analysis.*
3 a place where you can get information or be served at an airport, a hotel, etc: *the person behind the reception desk* ◇ *Would Ben Potter please report to the check-in desk?*
→ idiom at CLEAR

ˈdesk clerk = CLERK (3)

deskfast /ˈdeskfast/ *noun* [C,U]
used to refer to the first meal of the day (**breakfast**) when you eat it at your desk at work

deskill /ˌdiːˈskɪl/ *verb* [+ obj]
(*HR*)
1 to change the form of a job so that sb needs less special knowledge and training to do it: *He claims that most office work has become deskilled.*
2 (*often* **be deskilled**) to reduce the skills that a worker has, or that workers in general have, by giving them less skilled work to do: *Technological advances have led to an increase in the number of workers who have become deskilled.*
▶ˌde**ˈskilled** *adjective*: *the development of a deskilled labour force in restaurants, hotels and domestic service* ˌde**ˈskilling** *noun* [U]: *The*

introduction of new technology can lead to deskilling. ◇ *the deskilling of workers*

ˈdesk job *noun* [C]
a job that involves working for long periods of time at a desk: *working at a tedious desk job* ◇ *She left her desk job to take up photography.*

ˈdesk ˌjockey *noun* [C] (*informal*)
a person whose job involves spending a long time sitting at a desk

ˈdesk rage *noun* [U]
a situation in an office when sb who works there becomes very angry or violent: *Long hours and stress can lead to desk rage.*

ˈdesk reˌsearch *noun* [U]
(*Marketing*) a form of MARKET RESEARCH that is done using data that already exists and is easy to collect, such as company records or research results that have been published

desktop /ˈdesktɒp; *AmE* -tɑːp/ *noun* [C]
1 the top of a desk: *a desktop machine/PC* ◇ *desktop tools, such as computers and telephones*
2 = DESKTOP COMPUTER
3 (*IT*) a screen on a computer which shows the ICONS of the programs and files that can be used: *Click on the file and drag it to your desktop.*

ˌdesktop comˈputer (*also* **ˈdesktop**) *noun* [C]
a computer with a keyboard, screen and main processing unit, that fits on a desk: *The software runs on standard desktop computers.* ◇ *transferring data from your desktop computer to your notebook*
→ LAPTOP—Picture at OFFICE

ˌdesktop ˈpublishing *noun* [U] (*abbr* **DTP**)
the use of a small computer and a printer to produce a small book, a magazine or other printed material: *Desktop publishing has made in-house ad services more affordable.* ◇ *desktop publishing software/systems* ▶ˌdesktop **ˈpublisher** *noun* [C]

despatch = DISPATCH **HELP** You will find words formed with **despatch** at the spelling **dispatch**.

destination /ˌdestɪˈneɪʃn/ *noun* [C]
1 (*abbr* **destn**) a place where sb/sth is going or being sent: *Spain is the most popular tourist destination for Britons.* ◇ *The goods are inspected when they arrive at the port of destination.*
◐ *to **arrive at/reach** a destination* ✦ *an **attractive/a favourite/popular** destination* ✦ *a **business/an investment** destination* ✦ *a **holiday/tourist** destination* ✦ *the **final/ultimate** destination*
2 a place that an airline flies passengers to: *The airline flies out of London to 10 destinations around Europe.*
◐ *to **fly to/serve** a destination* ✦ *a **long-haul/short-haul** destination* ✦ *a **domestic/foreign/overseas** destination*

destiˈnation site *noun* [C]
(*IT*)
1 a website that people often visit as it has a strong image in their minds because of the amount of new information and other features that they can find there **SYN** PORTAL
2 a website that sb visits by clicking on a BANNER AD or other link

destiˈnation store *noun* [C]
a store that has a strong image in customers' minds because of features such as the variety or quality of goods, the prices, etc. and is the place they choose to go for a particular item or when they want to shop: *Harrods' reputation as London's top destination store*

destn *abbr*
a short way of writing **destination**: *destn address*

destock /ˌdiːˈstɒk; *AmE* -ˈstɑːk/ *verb* [+ obj or no obj]
(*Commerce*) to reduce the amount of goods that are kept available for customers to buy; to reduce the amount of materials that are kept available for making new products, etc: *A new range was launched and a number of products were destocked.* ◇ *Many manufacturers were forced to destock after a downturn in demand.* ▸ ˌde'stocking *noun* [U]: *a decline in orders due to heavy customer destocking*

detach /dɪˈtætʃ/ *verb* [+ obj or no obj]
detach (sth) (from sth) to remove sth from sth larger; to become separated from sth: *Detach the coupon and return it as soon as possible.* ◇ *The device detaches from the computer completely when not in use.*

detailer /ˈdiːteɪlə(r); *AmE also* dɪˈteɪlər/ *noun* [C] (*especially AmE*)
1 (*Marketing*) a person whose job is to visit shops/stores and inform them about a company's products, especially drugs and medicines, and make sure the products are displayed well
2 a person whose job is to clean a car thoroughly and carefully in order to protect it and keep it in good condition: *a professional auto detailer*

deteriorate /dɪˈtɪəriəreɪt; *AmE* -ˈtɪr-/ *verb* [no obj]
to become worse: *Economic conditions have deteriorated rapidly.* ◇ *deteriorating business and consumer confidence*
○ to deteriorate **dramatically/rapidly/sharply/significantly**
▸ **deterioration** /dɪˌtɪəriəˈreɪʃn; *AmE* -ˌtɪr-/ *noun* [U,C]: *a sharp deterioration in the group's financial position*

determination /dɪˌtɜːmɪˈneɪʃn; *AmE* -ˌtɜːrm-/ *noun*

SEE ALSO: **co-determination, pay determination**

1 [U] the quality that makes you continue trying to do sth even when this is difficult: *We need people with enthusiasm, drive and determination.* ◇ *I admire the company's determination* **to** *deliver the best value for customers.*
2 (*formal*) [C,U] an official decision or judgement; the process of deciding sth officially: *A final determination will have to be made by a court.*

determine /dɪˈtɜːmɪn; *AmE* -ˈtɜːrm-/ *verb* [+ obj] (*formal*)
1 to discover the facts about sth; to calculate sth exactly: *A team of experts is trying to determine the cause of the accident.* ◇ *We produced a business plan to determine how much capital we would need.*
2 to make sth happen in a particular way or be of a particular type: *Price is determined by supply and demand.* ◇ *Age and experience will be* **determining** **factors** *in our choice of candidate.*
3 to officially decide sth: *A date for the meeting has yet to be determined.*

devalue /ˌdiːˈvæljuː/ *verb*
1 (*Economics*) [+ obj or no obj] to reduce the value of the money of one country when it is exchanged for the money of another country; to become a less valuable currency compared to another: *The authorities devalued the peso* **against** *the US dollar by nine per cent.* ◇ *The country could be forced to devalue.* ◇ *a devalued currency* OPP REVALUE See note at CURRENCY
2 [+ obj] to make sth seem less important or valuable than it should be: *They fear that selling the car alongside cheaper vehicles will devalue their brand.* ◇ *The skill of selling has become devalued.*
▸ **devaluation** /ˌdiːˌvæljuˈeɪʃn/ *noun* [C,U]: *a*

currency devaluation ◇ *The company's profits were affected by the sharp devaluation of the rand.*

★**develop** /dɪˈveləp/ *verb*
1 [+ obj or no obj] to gradually grow or become bigger, more advanced, stronger, etc.; to make sth do this: *It developed* **from** *a small family business* **into** *a multinational group.* ◇ *We have developed close relationships with our suppliers.*
2 [+ obj] to think of or produce a new idea, product, etc. and make it successful: *He helped develop our best-selling brand.* ◇ *The company develops and markets new software.*
3 [+ obj or no obj] to start to have a skill, an ability, a quality, etc. that becomes better and stronger; to become better and stronger: *What new skills have you developed in the last six months?* ◇ *His confidence as a negotiator has developed.*
4 (*Property*) [+ obj] to build new houses, factories, etc. on an area of land, especially land that was not being used effectively before: *The site is being developed as an airport.*
5 [+ obj] to start using an area of land, a mine, etc. as a source of natural materials

developed /dɪˈveləpt/ *adjective*
1 (used about a country, society, etc.) having many industries and an advanced economic system: *financial aid to less developed countries* → DEVELOPING
2 in an advanced state: *people with highly developed business skills*

★**developer** /dɪˈveləpə(r)/ *noun* [C]
1 (*Property*) a person or company that buys land or buildings in order to build new houses, shops/stores, etc., or to improve the old ones, and makes a profit from doing this: *The site has been sold to a local property developer.*
○ a **commercial/property/real-estate/residential** developer
2 a person or a company that designs and creates new products: *She was a product developer in the Womenswear division.*
○ a **drug/product/software/website** developer

developing /dɪˈveləpɪŋ/ *adjective* [only before noun]
(used about a country, society, etc.) poor, and trying to make its industry and economic system more advanced: *opening markets to goods from developing nations* ◇ *reducing poverty in* **the developing world** → DEVELOPED

★**development** /dɪˈveləpmənt/ *noun*

SEE ALSO: **human resource development, management ~, new product ~, personal ~, product ~, property ~, research and ~**, etc.

1 [U] the gradual growth of sth so that it becomes more advanced, stronger, etc: *key stages in the company's development* ◇ *Work continues on development of the brand across a number of markets.*
2 [U,C] the process of producing or creating sth new or more advanced; a new or advanced product: *a contract for the development of new computer systems* ◇ *The software is still* **in/under** *development* (= being designed). ◇ *The new car will be a joint development between the two companies.* ◇ *Development costs for the drug were high.*
○ **drug/product/software/website** development ♦ *a* development **department/division/team** ♦ *to* **finance/lead/oversee** the development (of sth)
3 (*HR*) [U] the process of getting new skills or knowledge, especially so that you can do a job more effectively: *The job offers great opportunities for career development.* ◇ *an employee training and development programme*
○ **career/personal/professional/staff** development
4 (*Property*) [U,C] the process and business of building new houses, offices, etc. in order to make

a profit; a piece of land with new buildings on it: (*AmE*) *a company specializing in real-estate development* ◇ *The piece of land will be turned into a new housing development.*
❶ (*a*) **commercial/property/real-estate/residential** *development*
5 [U] the process of preparing an area of land, a mine, etc. so that it can be a source of natural materials: *The development of the oil field could create a thousand jobs.*

de'velopment ,area *noun* [C]
in the UK, an area where new industries are encouraged in order to create jobs: *The government offered lower taxes to companies willing to move into development areas.*

de'velopment bank *noun* [C]
(often used in names) a bank that gives loans to help improve or protect the economy of a country or an area, for example by lending money to create new industries there: *a $2 bn infrastructure programme backed by the Asian Development Bank*

de'velopment corpo,ration *noun* [C]
(often used in names) an organization created by a government or a group of organizations or people in order to provide money for starting new businesses, developing local economies, etc: *the state-owned Industrial Development Corporation*

de'velopment eco,nomics *noun* [U]
(*Economics*) the branch of economics that is concerned with the economic problems of less developed countries and how they can grow and change

de'velopment grant *noun* [C]
an amount of money that a government or public organization gives for a project that will improve the economy of a particular area, such as a project to build a new factory

de'velopment land *noun* [U]
land that can be used for building new houses, offices, etc: *a shortage of development land in the south of England*

deviation /ˌdiːviˈeɪʃn/ *noun* [C,U]

SEE ALSO: standard deviation

1 a difference from what is normal, expected or required: *The loss represents a 20% deviation from our financial targets.* ◇ *Any deviation from company policy is unacceptable.*
2 (*Technical*) the amount by which a single measurement is different from the average

device /dɪˈvaɪs/ *noun* [C]
1 an object or a piece of equipment that has been designed to do a particular job: *a handheld device that functions as a mobile phone and an electronic map*
2 a method of doing sth that produces a particular result or effect: *Sending advertising by mail is very successful as a marketing device.*

devolve /dɪˈvɒlv; *AmE* -ˈvɑːlv/ *verb* [+ obj or no obj]
devolve (sth) (from sb/sth) (to sb/sth) if a duty, responsibility, power, etc. **devolves** or sb **devolves** it, it passes to a more local group or to sb who has less authority: *Decision-making will devolve to a local level.* ◇ *Control of the website can now be devolved from specialist staff to the marketing department.* ▶ **de'volved** *adjective*: *devolved decision-making*
PHRV de,volve sth 'into sth to divide sth into smaller parts: *The group was devolved into dozens of smaller businesses.*

diagnostic /ˌdaɪəgˈnɒstɪk; *AmE* -ˈnɑːs-/ *adjective*, *noun*
(*Technical*)
● *adjective* [usually before noun]
connected with identifying sth, such as an illness or

a problem with a computer system: *diagnostic software that discovers minor computer faults*
❶ diagnostic **devices/instruments/tests/tools**
● *noun* [C]
1 a device or system that is used to identify a problem, an illness or a problem with a piece of equipment or software: *a detailed, in-depth diagnostic of the company* ◇ *Your car is hooked up to a computer to run diagnostics.*
2 a message on a computer screen giving information about a fault

diagram /ˈdaɪəgræm/ *noun* [C]

SEE ALSO: block diagram, cause and effect ~, fishbone ~, Ishikawa ~, scatter ~

a simple drawing using lines to explain where sth is, how sth works, etc: *a diagram of the wiring system* ◇ *The results are shown in the diagram below.* ◇ *As you can see from the diagram, younger men are less likely to be self-employed than older men.*
See note at GRAPH
❶ to **draw** a diagram • a diagram **depicts/indicates/represents/shows** sth
▶ **diagrammatic** /ˌdaɪəgrəˈmætɪk/ *adjective*: *The manufacturing process is represented in diagrammatic form.* **diagrammatically** /ˌdaɪəgrəˈmætɪkli/ *adverb*

dial /ˈdaɪəl/ *verb* [+ obj or no obj] (-ll-, *AmE* -l-)
to use a telephone, for example by pushing buttons: *Dial 0032 for Belgium.* ◇ *mobile phones with features such as cameras and voice dialling*
PHRV ,dial 'in (to sth); ,dial 'into sth; ,dial sb/sth 'in (*IT*) to make a temporary connection between your computer and the Internet or another computer system using a telephone line and a MODEM: *The system allows customers to dial in to our network and check their accounts.* ◇ *a dialled-in computer* → DIAL-IN ,dial 'up; ,dial sb/sth 'up
1 (*IT*) to make a temporary connection between your computer and the Internet or another computer system using a telephone line and a MODEM: *Dial up and log in.* ◇ *The software lets you dial up your office computer.* → DIAL-UP **2** (*informal*) to call a particular phone number: *I found the number and dialled it up.*

'dial-back = CALLBACK (5)

'dial-in = DIAL-UP

'dialling code (*BrE*) (*also* **code**, *AmE*, *BrE*) *noun* [C]
the numbers for a particular area or city, that you use when you are making a telephone call from outside the local area: *international dialling codes* → AREA CODE

'dialog box (*BrE spelling also* **dialogue ~**) *noun* [C]
(*IT*) a box that appears on a computer screen asking the user to choose what they want to do next: *Select an option from the dialog box.* ◇ *Clicking on 'Save as' brings up a dialogue box.*
❶ a dialogue box **appears/opens/pops up** • to **bring up/close/open** a dialogue box

'dial-up (*also* **'dial-in**) *adjective* [only before noun]
(*IT*) (about a computer system or service) temporarily connected to another system or to the Internet by a telephone line: *Most of their subscribers use dial-up connections to access their email.* → ALWAYS-ON, BROADBAND
❶ a dial-up **connection/modem/service**
▶ **'dial-up** (*also* **'dial-in**) *noun* [U]: *Their broadband service is up to 25 times faster than dial-up.*

diary /ˈdaɪəri/ *noun* [C] (*plural* **diaries**)
1 (*especially BrE*) (*AmE usually* **'datebook**) (*also* **ap'pointment book**, *BrE*, *AmE*) a book with spaces for each day of the year in which you write down things you have to do; an electronic device or

program that you use in the same way: *My diary is full until June.* ◇ *Can you find space in your diary* (= do you have time) *for a meeting on the 23rd?*
→ ORGANIZER See note at CALENDAR
○ *to make a note of sth/put sth/write sth* in a diary • a **desk/**an **electronic/**a **pocket** diary
2 a book in which you can write down the events that occur each day: *I kept a diary of the project* (= wrote down what happened each day).

Dictaphone™ /ˈdɪktəfəʊn; AmE -foʊn/ *noun* [C]
a small machine used to record what you want to say in a letter, report, etc., so that sb can listen later and type the document

dictate *verb, noun*
● *verb* /dɪkˈteɪt; AmE ˈdɪkteɪt/
1 [+ obj or no obj] to say words for sb else to write down or type: *She dictated a letter to her secretary.*
2 [+ obj or no obj] to decide sth or tell sb what to do, especially in a way that seems unfair: *Carmakers have enormous power to dictate how and where their cars are sold.*
3 [+ obj] to control or influence sth: *The price is dictated by market forces.*
PHRV dic'tate to sb (*often* be dictated to) to give orders to sb, often in a rude or aggressive way: *A regional office may feel it's being dictated to by a central office that doesn't understand local needs and conditions.*
● *noun* /ˈdɪkteɪt/ [C, usually pl.]
an order, a rule or a command that you must obey: *following the dictates of the marketplace*

dic'tating ma,chine = DICTATION MACHINE

dictation /dɪkˈteɪʃn/ *noun* [U,C]
the act of speaking or recording a letter, report, etc. so that it can be written down or typed; the words that are spoken: *to take dictation* (= write/type words that are being spoken) ◇ *The digital organizer can record up to 45 minutes of dictation.*

dic'tation ma,chine (*especially BrE*) (*AmE usually* dic'tating ma,chine) *noun* [C]
a machine, especially an electronic one, used for recording what you want to say in a letter, report, etc., so that sb can listen to your words later and type the document

DID /ˌdiː aɪ ˈdiː/ *abbr* (*AmE*) **Direct Inward Dialing**
a system where an office building, a hotel, etc. can have a large range of telephone numbers sharing one or a small number of direct lines. Calls go directly to an EXTENSION without being connected by an OPERATOR or RECEPTIONIST. → DDI

differential /ˌdɪfəˈrenʃl/ *noun, adjective*
● *noun* [C]

SEE ALSO: **duty differential, earnings ~, wage ~**

a difference in the amount, value or size of sth, especially the difference in rates of pay for people doing different work in the same industry or profession: *They found that the differential between men's and women's pay has narrowed slightly.* ◇ *the interest rate differential between the US and the eurozone* ◇ *a differential in prices*
○ *to create/increase/narrow/reduce/widen* a differential • *income/pay* differentials • *interest rate/price* differentials
● *adjective* [only before noun]
that treats different people or things differently; not equal: *The tax is unfair in its differential effect on large and small businesses.* ◇ *Unions are objecting to differential pay levels for similar skills.* ◇ *Their policy of **differential pricing** (= supplying the same product to different markets at different prices) means poorer countries can also afford the medicines.*

differentiate /ˌdɪfəˈrenʃieɪt/ *verb*
1 (*Marketing*) [+ obj] to make your product or service seem different from other similar products or services, for example to attract a particular group of customers: *We differentiate ourselves from our rivals by offering a higher standard of customer service.* ◇ *They have differentiated their vehicles with new interior designs.*
2 [+ obj] to be the particular thing that shows that things or people are not the same: *Our reputation for quality differentiates us from our competitors.* ◇ *Customer service has become an important differentiating factor.*
3 [+ obj or no obj] **differentiate (between) A and B** | **differentiate A (from B)** to recognize or show that two things are not the same: *As a lender we need to differentiate between high and low risk borrowers.*

differentiated 'product *noun* [C]
(*Marketing*) a product that is similar to other products but is different in design, quality or the way it is presented or advertised, for example to attract a particular group of customers: *They have developed a differentiated product for low-price markets.* → COMMODITY PRODUCT

differentiation /ˌdɪfəˌrenʃiˈeɪʃn/ *noun* [U]
(*Marketing*) the process of making your product or service seem different from other similar products or services that it is competing with: *Firms making similar products compete through a combination of price and product differentiation.*
○ *price/product* differentiation • *to increase/introduce/use* differentiation

digerati /ˌdɪdʒəˈrɑːti/ *noun* [pl.] (*informal*)
(often used in newspapers) people who are considered to be, or who think they are, experts or important in the area of computers and the Internet: *The digerati regarded the company as boring and chained to old technology.*

digit /ˈdɪdʒɪt/ *noun* [C]
1 any of the ten numbers from 0 to 9: *a seven-digit telephone number*
2 used with a number or an adjective to describe an amount of money or the amount by which a number has increased or decreased: *Sales have grown from six digits* (= $100 000 or more) *to $6 million* (= seven digits) *since 2001.* ◇ ***double-digit** rises* (= 10% or more) *in sales and earnings* ◇ (*especially AmE*) *an increase in the mid-single digit range* (= about 4–6%)
○ *double-single/triple* digits • *high-single/low-single/mid-single* digits

★ **digital** /ˈdɪdʒɪtl/ *adjective, noun*
● *adjective*
1 that uses a series of numbers in order to store, send or deal with information: *converting from analogue to digital technology* ◇ *Digital content is so easily stored and distributed that it is difficult to protect.* → ANALOGUE
○ *a digital camera/phone/television* • *a digital broadcast/image/photograph/signal* • *digital broadcasting/technology*
2 that relies on computer technology or the Internet: *The company has several digital brands* (= products sold on the Internet). ◇ *People need more computer skills to compete in today's digital economy.*
○ *a digital brand/business/company/strategy* • *digital marketing/publishing*
→ ELECTRONIC
IDM the ,digital di'vide the difference between communities that have computer equipment and can use the Internet and those that do not
● *noun* [U]
digital television: *The government wants to switch all viewers from analogue to digital by 2010.*

digital 'cash = E-CASH

,digital 'currency = E-CURRENCY

★ **digitally** /ˈdɪdʒɪtəli/ adverb
using DIGITAL technology: *The shows will be
broadcast digitally.*

,digital 'money = E-MONEY

,digital 'rights ,management = DRM

,digital 'signature (also ,electronic 'signature)
noun [C]
(IT) a unique number that is added to a computer
file in order to show who has created it, sent it, etc:
*The system allows you to attach a digital signature to
your emails.*

,digital 'wallet noun [C]
(E-commerce) software that can store details of your
name, bank account, address, etc. and provide
them automatically whenever you make a payment
on the Internet

diligence /ˈdɪlɪdʒəns/ noun [U]
careful and thorough work or effort: *His colleagues
respect his diligence and commitment.* → DUE
DILIGENCE

dilute /daɪˈluːt; BrE also -ˈljuːt/ verb [+ obj]
1 to make sth less valuable or effective: *Our strong
sales in the US were diluted by the weakness of the
dollar.* ◊ *The car manufacturer will not dilute its
brand image with cheaper models.*
2 (Finance) to make shares less valuable by creating
(**issuing**) more of them without increasing assets,
which reduces the amount of profits that each
shareholder can claim; to reduce the percentage of
a company's shares that sb owns by doing this: *The
share issue is likely to dilute the value of existing
shares.* ◊ *After the merger our stake in the enlarged
company will be diluted to 35%.*
▶ **dilutive** /daɪˈluːtɪv; BrE also -ˈljuːtɪv/ adjective: *the
dilutive effect of the new share issue* ◊ *The merger
would be dilutive to earnings per share.* **dilution**
/daɪˈluːʃn; BrE also -ˈljuːʃn/ noun [sing; U]: *There has
been a dilution of demand for these vehicles in Japan.*
◊ *brand/trademark dilution* ◊ *a substantial dilution
of share value*

diluted /daɪˈluːtɪd; BrE also -ˈljuːtɪd/ adjective
(Accounting) used about a figure that is based on the
number of shares that a company has issued plus
the shares that it may need to issue in the future,
for example because it has sold CONVERTIBLE
bonds (= bonds that can be exchanged for shares):
*Net income was $344 million, or 38 cents per diluted
share.* ◊ *Diluted earnings per share rose by 30
Canadian cents.*

dime /daɪm/ noun [C]
a coin of the US and Canada worth ten cents: *He
developed a marketing plan that didn't cost him a
dime.*

dimension /daɪˈmenʃn; dɪ-/ noun [C]
1 a measurement in space, for example the height,
width or length of sth: *First we need to measure the
dimensions of the room.* ◊ *computer design tools that
work in three dimensions*
2 (Marketing) an important aspect of a product or
service: *The 24-hour help desk adds a new dimension
to the product.* ◊ *the customer-service dimension of e-
commerce*

-dimensional /daɪˈmenʃənl; dɪ-/ combining form
(used in adjectives)
having the number of **dimensions** mentioned: *We
work with three-dimensional models on-screen.*

di,minishing 'balance ,method =
REDUCING BALANCE METHOD

di,minishing re'turns noun [pl.]
(Economics) a situation where you gain less and less
benefit or profit from sth, even though you spend
more time or money on it: *Our increased efforts*

were producing diminishing returns. ◊ *The law of
diminishing returns applies to physical products: at
some point unit cost increases with volume.*

dip /dɪp/ verb, noun
● **verb** [no obj] (-**pp-**)
dip (from sth) (to/below sth) to go down in value or
level, especially by a small amount or for a short
period of time: *Sales of furniture have started to dip.*
◊ *Profits dipped slightly to $5.4 million from $5.7
million.* ◊ *The share price dipped 4.5%.*
IDM **dip into your 'pocket** (informal) to spend
some of your money on sth **dip a 'toe in/into sth**;
dip a 'toe in/into the water to start doing sth
very carefully to see if it will be successful or not:
*Some investors are now prepared to dip a toe in
riskier markets.*
PHR V **,dip 'into sth** to take an amount from
money that has been saved: *The government has
had to dip into emergency funds.*
● **noun** [C]

SEE ALSO: **double-dip**

a decrease in the amount or success of sth, usually
for only a short period: *They reported a 5% dip in
profits from £8.1 million to £7.7 million.* ◊ *The
survey reveals a slight dip in consumer confidence.* ◊ *I
always try to **buy on the dips** (= buy shares, bonds,
etc. when prices fall).*
● *a **big/brief/sharp/slight/small/an unexpected** dip*

'DIP ,Financing /dɪp/ = DEBTOR-IN-POSSESSION
FINANCING

direct /dəˈrekt; dɪ-; daɪ-/ adjective, verb, adverb
● **adjective** [usually before noun]
1 happening or done without involving other
people or actions in between: *Mr Dolan will take
direct responsibility for the team.* ◊ *We have direct
access to the central computer system.*
2 happening as an immediate result of sth,
without the influence of sth else: *They want to see a
direct connection between performance and pay.*
● **verb** [+ obj]
1 **direct sth to/towards sb/sth | direct sth at/
against sb/sth** to aim sth in a particular direction or
at a particular person: *We are directing our efforts
towards expanding the business.*
2 to control or be in charge of sb/sth: *A new
manager has been appointed to direct the project.*
3 to send a letter, etc. to a particular place or to a
particular person: *Enquiries should be directed to the
Customer Services department.*
● **adverb**
without involving other people or businesses: *I
prefer to deal with them direct.* ◊ *selling direct to
consumers*

di,rect 'action noun [U,C]
(HR) the use of strikes, protests, etc. in order to
achieve a political or social aim: *The drivers' union
has so far opposed the campaign of direct action.*

di,rect 'advertising noun [U]
(Marketing) advertising that uses normal methods,
such as magazine or television advertisements:
*There has been an increase in direct advertising of
prescription drugs to consumers.* → INDIRECT
ADVERTISING, DIRECT RESPONSE ADVERTISING

di,rect com'petitor noun [C]
a business or product that is competing for the
same group of customers as your business or
product: *We have no direct competitor in the UK.* ◊
*The new chocolate drink is a direct competitor to the
market leader.* ▶ **di,rect compe'tition** noun [U]:
*The new games console will be in direct competition
with Sony's Playstation 3.*

di‚rect 'cost *noun* [C, usually pl.]
(*Accounting*) the cost of raw materials and workers involved in making a particular product or providing a particular service: *They have modernized the production line in an attempt to cut direct costs.* ◊ *The project manager's salary is a direct cost.* **SYN** PRIME COST → DIRECT LABOUR (1), DIRECT OVERHEAD, INDIRECT COST

di‚rect 'costing = VARIABLE COSTING

di‚rect 'debit (*AmE also* '**bank draft**) *noun* [U,C]
especially in the UK, an instruction to your bank to allow sb else to take an amount of money from your account on a particular date, especially to pay bills: *They give you a discount if you pay by direct debit.* → STANDING ORDER
❶ *to cancel/set up a direct debit*

di‚rect de'posit *noun* [U,C]
the system of paying sb's wages, etc. straight into their bank account

di‚rect 'dialling (*AmE spelling* ~ **dialing**) *noun* [U]
the ability to make telephone calls without needing to be connected to the OPERATOR or a RECEPTIONIST: *international direct dialling tariffs* ◊ *All our rooms have direct dialling telephones.*
▶ **di‚rect-'dial** *adjective*: *Your direct-dial number replaces your old extension number.* → DDI

di‚rect 'export *noun* [C, usually pl., U]
(*Economics*; *Trade*) goods that are sold directly to customers in another country; this method of selling goods: *Most of their revenue comes from direct exports from the UK.* ◊ *If economic conditions do not favour direct exports, we get local companies to manufacture for us.* → INDIRECT EXPORT
▶ **di‚rect ex'porting** *noun* [U]

di‚rect 'import *noun* [C, usually pl., U]
(*Economics*; *Trade*) goods that are bought directly from producers in another country; this method of buying goods ▶ **di‚rect im'porting** *noun* [U]

di‚rect in'vestment = FOREIGN DIRECT INVESTMENT

directive /dəˈrektɪv; dɪ-; daɪ-/ *noun* [C]
an official instruction: *The EU has issued a new set of directives on data protection.* ◊ *a draft directive*

di‚rect 'labour (*AmE spelling* ~ **labor**) *noun* [U]
1 (*Accounting*) the people who work to produce a particular product or supply a particular service; the money that is spent on their wages: *Direct labour is a major element of product costs for manufacturing companies.* ◊ *The direct labour costs are about 80% of the cost of producing one unit.* → DIRECT COST (1), DIRECT MATERIALS, DIRECT OVERHEAD
2 (*HR*) people who are employed directly by a company or an organization to build or produce sth, rather than by an independent business that is paid to find people to do the work: *Most of the construction work is done by direct labour rather than by sub-contractors.* → INDIRECT LABOUR

di‚rect 'mail *noun* [U]
(*Marketing*) advertisements that are sent in the post/mail usually to people who might be interested in buying the products or services: *UK consumers buy over €30 bn worth of goods through direct mail each year.* ◊ *a direct mail campaign targeting new users* ◊ *We plan to use direct mail to promote our new magazine.* → JUNK MAIL
❶ *to buy/market/sell sth by/through direct mail* ◆ *to use direct mail* ◆ *direct mail advertising/marketing/selling* ◆ *direct mail advertisers/marketers* ◆ *direct mail buyers/customers*

▶ **di‚rect 'mailing** *noun* [U,C]: *There was a good response to the initial direct mailing.* ◊ *a direct mailing campaign*

di‚rect 'marketing *noun* [U]
(*Marketing*) the business of selling products or services directly to customers by contacting them by mail or telephone, by visiting their homes or through online computer shopping: *Direct marketing cuts out the costs of supplying shops and enables customers to buy at lower prices.* ▶ **di‚rect 'marketer** *noun* [C]

di‚rect ma'terials *noun* [pl.]
(*Accounting*) the basic things that a business uses in order to produce a particular product or provide a particular service; money that is spent on these: *Cost of production is calculated as direct materials and labour plus a share of manufacturing overheads.* ◊ *Direct materials costs for each unit were €4.30.* → INDIRECT MATERIALS

★**director** /dəˈrektə(r); dɪ-; daɪ-/ *noun* [C]

SEE ALSO: board of directors, creative ~, executive ~, independent ~, managing ~, non-executive ~, outside ~, worker ~

1 (*also* ‚**company di'rector**) one of a group of people who are chosen by shareholders to run a company and decide its policies: *Three new directors have been appointed to the board.* ◊ *The bank has reduced the number of executive directors on its board to six.* See note at BOSS
❶ *to be appointed (as)/become/be elected/be made (a) director* ◆ *to act as/serve as a director* ◆ *to resign as/step down as director* ◆ *an acting/an assistant/a deputy director*
2 a person who is in charge of a particular activity or department in a company, an organization, etc: *He was appointed finance director of British Aerospace in 1992.* ◊ *She became director of finance at the company.* ◊ *He is taking up the newly created post of group creative director.* → VICE-PRESIDENT
❶ *to be appointed (as)/become/be made (a) director* ◆ *to act as/serve as a director* ◆ *to resign as/retire as/step down as director* ◆ *a finance/commercial/marketing/production/research/sales director* ◆ *acting/an assistant/a deputy director*

directorate /dəˈrektərət; dɪ-; daɪ-/ *noun* [C]
1 a section of a government department in charge of one particular activity: *the EU's Competition Directorate*
2 the group of directors who run a company

di‚rector 'general (*AmE spelling also* **director-general**) *noun* [C] (*plural* **directors general**)
the head of a large organization, especially a public organization: *the director general of the BBC* ◊ *They have appointed a new director general.*

directorship /dəˈrektəʃɪp; dɪ-; daɪ-; *AmE* -tərʃ-/ *noun* [C]
the position of a company director; the period during which this is held: *He has been disqualified from holding company directorships.* ◊ *Under her directorship, the firm nearly doubled in size.*
❶ *to hold/resign/take up a directorship* ◆ *an executive/a non-executive directorship*

di‚rector's 'interest *noun* [C, usually pl.]
(*Law*) the fact that a company director benefits in a personal way from a contract, deal, etc. with the company: *The company is obliged to keep a record of all of its directors' interests.* **NOTE** Two plural forms are possible: 'director's interests', referring to one director, or 'directors' interests', referring to several or all the directors.

di‚rectors' re'port *noun* [C]
a report that a company's directors must write for shareholders every year, giving a summary of the company's activities, details about the DIVIDEND that will be paid and the names of the directors

and what they earned: *The directors' report for the year to June 30 lists the chairman as owner of 29% of the company's share capital.*

directory /dəˈrektəri; dɪ-; daɪ-/ *noun* [C] (*plural* **directories**)

SEE ALSO: **classified directory, ex-~, telephone ~**

1 a book or series of Internet pages containing lists of information, usually in alphabetical order, for example people's telephone numbers or the names and addresses of businesses in a particular area: *They publish a directory of law firms.* ◇ *creating an online business directory* ◇ *They have decided to sell their directories business.*
◐ an **online/a printed** directory • a **business/ telephone/trade** directory • to **compile/create/ publish** a directory • to **be listed in** a directory • to **consult/look sb up in/search** a directory
2 (*IT*) a file containing a group of other files or programs in a computer: *Create a directory called 'DATA' on your hard disk and copy the files to it.*
◐ to **create/delete** a directory • to **copy** sth **from/into/ to** a directory • a **current/default/root** directory

di,rectory en'quiries (*BrE*) (*AmE also* **di'rectory as,sistance, ,infor'mation**) *noun* [U with sing./pl. verb]
a telephone service that you can use to find out a person's telephone number: *I got the number from directory enquiries.* ◇ *They are expanding their directory-enquiries service to include mobile-phone numbers.*

di,rect 'overhead *noun* [C]
(*Accounting*) a share of **overheads** (= money that a business spends on equipment, electricity, rent, etc.) that are considered to be part of the cost of producing a particular product or supplying a particular service: *We have a system for allocating direct overheads between the different production units.* ◇ *the direct overhead **costs** associated with the project* → INDIRECT OVERHEAD

di,rect par,tici'pation *noun* [U]
(*HR*) a system in which managers in an organization provide opportunities for individual employees to take part in decision-making

di,rect re'port *noun* [C]
a person who has a position directly below someone else in an organization: *the relationship between manager and direct report* ◇ *I try to have regular meetings with my direct reports.* → LINE MANAGER See note at BOSS

di,rect res'ponse ,advertising (*also* **di,rect res'ponse ,marketing**) *noun* [U]
(*Marketing*) advertising that asks people to reply to the company in some way in order to buy a product, for example by making a telephone call or sending an email: *A coupon or a free phone number are the most common forms of direct response advertising.* ◇ *direct response TV advertising*
→ DIRECT ADVERTISING, IMAGE ADVERTISING, INSTITUTIONAL ADVERTISING
▶ **di,rect res'ponse ad** *noun* [C]: *Our direct response ads generated hundreds of enquiries.*

di,rect 'sale *noun*
(*Marketing*)
1 [C, usually pl., U] (*also* **di,rect 'selling** [U]) the practice of selling goods or services directly to customers, rather than through a system of suppliers or shops/stores: *The new law could allow the direct sale of certain medicines.* ◇ *Direct sales rose by nearly 11%.*
2 [C] an item sold in this way: *We are trying to increase direct sales to small businesses.* ◇ *The car was a direct sale from the factory.*
→ INDIRECT SALE

di,rect 'tax *noun* [C,U]
(*Economics*) tax which is collected directly from the person or company who pays it, for example income tax: *The government has reduced direct taxes but raised taxes on spending.* → INDIRECT TAX
▶ **di,rect tax'ation** *noun* [U]

di,rect-to-con'sumer *adjective* [only before noun] (*abbr* **DTC**)
(*Marketing*) aimed at or involving members of the public directly: *Direct-to-consumer advertising for prescription drugs is allowed in the US.* ◇ *a direct-to-consumer product/sale*

dirigisme /ˈdɪrɪʒɪzəm/ *noun* [U]
(*Economics*) the control of a country's economy by the government → LAISSEZ-FAIRE ▶ **dirigiste** /ˈdɪrɪʒɪst/ *adjective*

dirty /ˈdɜːti; *AmE* ˈdɜːrti/ *adjective* (**dirtier, dirtiest**)
1 unpleasant or dishonest: *dirty fighting in the boardroom* ◇ *Small airlines have accused the national carrier of using **dirty tricks** to steal their customers.*
2 causing POLLUTION; containing substances that may be harmful: *Energy production today relies on dirty fuels, such as coal, oil and gas.* OPP CLEAN
IDM **(do sb's) 'dirty work** (to do) the unpleasant or dishonest jobs that sb else does not want to do: *They hired an external consultant to do the dirty work of firing people.* **,quick and 'dirty** (*informal*) **quick and dirty** methods or systems provide fast, simple solutions to problems but may not last or be effective for a long time

,dirty 'money *noun* [U]
money that sb gains from dishonest or illegal activities: *preventing the banking system from attracting dirty money*

disability /ˌdɪsəˈbɪləti/ *noun* (*plural* **disabilities**)
1 [C] a physical or mental condition that means that you cannot use a part of your body completely or easily or carry out some normal day-to-day activities: *making computers easier to use for people with disabilities* ◇ *Almost all of the company's employees have a physical disability.*
2 [U] the state of not being able to use a part of your body completely or easily or carry out some normal day-to-day activities: *He qualifies for help on the grounds of disability.* ◇ *Small employers need support to comply with disability legislation* (= that states that people with a disability must not be treated less fairly than others).
3 [U,C] the state of not being able to work because of an injury or an illness; the injury or illness itself: *insuring against unemployment and disability* ◇ *people on disability **benefit(s)/pensions***
4 [U] (*AmE*) money that is paid to sb who cannot work because of an injury, illness, etc: *He had back surgery and has been **on** disability since 2003.* ◇ *She lives on her monthly disability check.*

disabled /dɪsˈeɪbld/ *adjective*
1 unable to use a part of your body completely or easily because of a physical condition, illness, injury, etc: *Grants are available for the changes firms need to make to employ disabled workers.*
2 **the disabled** *noun* [pl.] people who are disabled: *facilities for the disabled*

disallow /ˌdɪsəˈlaʊ/ *verb* [+ obj]
to officially refuse to accept sth or give permission for sth: *Their claim for a tax deduction was disallowed.* ◇ *The Commission disallowed the merger because it might hurt the consumer.*

disaster /dɪˈzɑːstə(r); *AmE* -ˈzæs-/ *noun*
1 [C] an unexpected event such as a very bad accident, a flood or a fire that kills a lot of people or

causes a lot of damage: *an air/ferry/rail disaster* ◇ *a* **natural disaster** (= one caused by nature)
2 [U,C] a very bad situation that causes problems; a failure: *The company's expansion into the US proved to be a financial disaster.* ◇ *The scheme ended in disaster.*

di'saster ˌmanagement *noun* [U]
the actions that a business takes before, during and after a disaster to reduce the effects on the business
→ BUSINESS CONTINUITY, DISASTER RECOVERY

di'saster reˌcovery *noun* [U] (*abbr* DR)
(*IT*) (*often used as an adjective*)
the process of making sure that the computer systems of a business operate again as quickly as possible after a disaster such as a flood, a fire or an explosion, etc., and that as little data as possible is lost: *It is essential to plan thoroughly for disaster recovery.* ◇ *Every business needs to have a disaster recovery plan.* ◇ *disaster recovery services/software/ systems* → BUSINESS CONTINUITY

disburse /dɪsˈbɜːs; *AmE* -ˈbɜːrs/ *verb* [+ obj]
to pay money to sb from a large amount that has been collected for a purpose: *The funds were disbursed in two instalments.* ◇ *The current aid programme disburses about €150 million to farmers every year.*

disbursement /dɪsˈbɜːsmənt; *AmE* -ˈbɜːrs-/ *noun*
1 [U,C] money that is paid to sb/sth from a large fund; the act of paying it: *the disbursement of funds* ◇ *aid disbursements*
2 (*Accounting*) [C] a payment that a professional person makes on behalf of a customer while performing services for them, such as a payment of court fees by a lawyer : *We can only provide you with an estimate of our fees and disbursements.*

disc (*also spelled* **disk**, *especially in AmE*) /dɪsk/ *noun* [C]
1 a thin flat circular device that is used for storing information: *a blank disc*
2 (*BrE*) a disk for a computer: *The computer comes with a built-in disc drive.*
→ CD, DVD

discharge *verb, noun*
●*verb* /dɪsˈtʃɑːdʒ; *AmE* -ˈtʃɑːrdʒ/ [+ obj]
1 (*usually* **be discharged**) to give sb official permission to leave a place or job; to make sb leave a job: *She was discharged from the police force for bad conduct.*
2 (*formal*) to do everything that is necessary to perform and complete a particular duty or task: *to discharge your duties/obligations/responsibilities* ◇ *to discharge a debt/liability* (= to finish paying back money you owe)
3 (*formal*) to free sb from a particular duty or responsibility: *The judge discharged the jury from reaching a decision.*
4 (*Law*) to officially allow a BANKRUPT person to stop paying back their debts and do business again: *First-time bankrupts are discharged automatically after three years.*
●*noun* /ˈdɪstʃɑːdʒ; *AmE* -tʃɑːrdʒ/
1 [U,C] the act of officially allowing sb, or of telling sb, to leave a job or a place (*AmE*): *The fired employees sued for unlawful discharge.*
2 (*formal*) [U] the act of performing a task or a duty or of paying an amount of money that is owed: *the discharge of a contract* (= doing everything that you were required to do) ◇ *the discharge of debts/ liabilities/duties*
3 (*Law*) [U] the official act of allowing a person who is BANKRUPT to stop paying their debts and do business again: *applying to court for the discharge of a bankrupt*

4 [C,U] an act of releasing a substance such as a liquid or gas into the environment: *a project to reduce discharges of hazardous waste* ◇ *the discharge of chemicals into rivers*
5 (*Transport*) [U] the act of removing goods or passengers from a ship that has arrived at a port: *the port of discharge* (= where the goods are being sent)

disciplinary /ˈdɪsəplɪnəri; ˌdɪsəˈplɪnəri; *AmE* ˈdɪsəplənəri/ *adjective*
(*HR*) connected with punishing people who break the rules of an organization or society, especially employees or professional people: *Information on disciplinary matters can be found in the staff handbook.* ◇ *Disciplinary measures were taken but no one was fired.* ◇ *It is a disciplinary offence to send offensive emails to other employees.*
🔾 *a disciplinary* **enquiry/investigation** • *disciplinary* **measures/proceedings** • *a disciplinary* **committee/ tribunal**

ˌdisciplinary ˈaction *noun* [U,C]
(*HR*) ways in which an employer or an authority can punish sb who does not meet the required standards of the organization or who breaks the rules: *The company will* **take** *disciplinary action* **against** *any employee who violates* (= breaks) *workplace safety rules.*

ˌdisciplinary ˈhearing *noun* [C]
(*HR*) a meeting like a court trial, at which senior people decide if an employee or a member of the organization has broken the rules and, if so, how they should be punished: *They were wrong to fire her without* **holding** *a formal disciplinary hearing.*

ˌdisciplinary proˈcedure *noun* [C, usually pl.]
(*HR*) the formal process that an employer or authority must follow if sb has broken the rules of the organization; action that is taken against sb according to this process: *If the employee's behaviour does not improve it may be necessary to start disciplinary procedures.* ◇ *They did not follow the internal disciplinary procedure in firing him.*

disclaimer /dɪsˈkleɪmə(r)/ *noun* [C]
(*Law*) a statement in which sb says that they are not connected with or responsible for sth, or that they do not have any knowledge of it: *The report included a disclaimer that the writers accepted no responsibility for the accuracy of the data.*
🔾 *to* **issue/make/publish/use** *a disclaimer*

★**disclose** /dɪsˈkləʊz; *AmE* -ˈkloʊz/ *verb* [+ obj]
to tell sb sth; to make sth known publicly: *Management refused to disclose details of the takeover* **to** *the press.* ◇ *The company disclosed* **that** *it had overstated its profits by \$11 million.*

★**disclosure** /dɪsˈkləʊʒə(r); *AmE* -ˈkloʊ-/ *noun* [C,U]
1 the act of making sth known or public; the facts that are made known: *the disclosure of confidential information* ◇ *He resigned following disclosures about his private life.*
2 information that a company is required to make public about its financial position, important events, etc.; the act of doing this: *Privately owned companies make only limited financial disclosures.* ◇ *rules requiring the disclosure of directors' salaries*
OPP NON-DISCLOSURE

disconnect /ˌdɪskəˈnekt/ *verb, noun*
●*verb*
1 [+ obj *or no obj*] to separate two things that were joined together: *Disconnect the modem* **from** *the computer.*
2 (*IT*) [+ obj *or no obj*] to end a connection to the Internet: *I keep getting disconnected when I'm on the Web.* ◇ *My computer crashes every time I disconnect* **from** *the Internet.*

3 [+ obj] (*usually* **be disconnected**) to break the contact between two people who are talking on the telephone: *We were suddenly disconnected.*
OPP CONNECT
▸ **discon'nection** *noun* [U,C]
● *noun* [C]
a situation where there is no connection between sb/sth: *There can be a disconnect between boardrooms and IT departments when it comes to technology.*

discontinue /ˌdɪskənˈtɪnjuː/ *verb* [+ obj]
to stop doing sth, especially making a particular product: *They have discontinued their adult line of clothing.* ◇ *Operations at the plant were discontinued in 2002.* ◇ *a discontinued product*

★ **discount** *noun, verb*
● *noun* /ˈdɪskaʊnt/

SEE ALSO: **bulk discount, cash ~, deep-~, frequency ~, trade ~, volume ~**

1 (*Commerce*) [C,U] an amount of money that is taken off the usual cost of sth: *We give a 15% discount **on** large orders.* ◇ *They were forced to sell their old stock **at a discount** (= at reduced prices).* ◇ *Retailers are offering deep discounts to get shoppers into stores.* ◇ *a discount **for** paying within 30 days* ◇ *a discount airline (= one that sells tickets at low prices)* See note at REDUCTION
  ◐ *to **get/give/offer** a discount ◆ a **big/deep/heavy** discount ◆ discount **airlines/carriers/fares/tickets** ◆ a discount **brand/chain/retailer/store**
2 (*Finance*) [C, usually sing.] if a share, etc. is bought or sold at a **discount**, its price is lower than sth, such as its price at an earlier time or its PAR VALUE (= the value shown on the share, etc.): *The company should continue trading **at a discount to** the rest of the industry.* ◇ *The new shares were issued at 131¢, at a discount of 14.5¢ to yesterday's closing price.* ◇ *The gilts were offered at a discount of 10%.*
● *verb* /dɪsˈkaʊnt; *AmE also* ˈdɪskaʊnt/
1 (*Commerce*) [+ obj *or no obj*] to take an amount of money off the usual cost of sth; to sell sth at a **discount**: *The airline has discounted its fares by 20%.* ◇ *They have discounted **heavily** in order to attract orders.* ◇ *Shops achieved higher sales through aggressive price discounting.*
2 (*Finance*) [+ obj] (*often* **be discounted**) (about a price) to include the effect of what investors expect to happen: *Analysts believe the publisher's share price already discounts lower profits for next year.* ◇ *A lot of the bad news is already discounted in the share price (= the price had already fallen because people expected the bad news).*
3 (*Finance*) [+ obj] to buy or sell a BILL OF EXCHANGE before its payment date for less than the amount that will be paid on it in the future: *The bank discounts the bill of exchange and advances the money to the seller.*
▸ **discountable** /dɪsˈkaʊntəbl/ *adjective*

'discount ˌbroker *noun* [C]
1 (*Stock Exchange*) a type of BROKER that charges low fees but does not provide extra services, such as advice on what shares, bonds, etc. to buy
2 (*Finance*) (*BrE*) = BILL BROKER

'discount ˌbrokerage *noun* [C] (*especially AmE*)
(*Stock Exchange*) a business that buys and sells shares, bonds, etc. on behalf of investors for low fees, but does not provide extra services such as advice on the best investments

disˌcounted 'cash flow *noun* [U; C, usually sing.] (*abbr* **DCF**)
(*Accounting*) a method of comparing how much profit investments will make by calculating what the future income would be worth now
→ DISCOUNT RATE

discounter /ˈdɪskaʊntə(r)/ *noun* [C]
(*Commerce*)
1 a shop/store that sells things very cheaply, often in large quantities or from a limited range of goods: *Discounters have stolen market share from department stores.* SYN DISCOUNT STORE
2 a business that offers its products at very low prices: *They have established themselves as a deep discounter of computer hardware.*

'discount house *noun* [C]
1 (*Finance*) a financial institution that buys and sells BILLS OF EXCHANGE before their payment date for less than the value shown on them: *The exporter can overcome problems of cash flow by discounting the bill with a discount house.*
2 (*Commerce*) (*AmE*) = DISCOUNT STORE

discounting /ˈdɪskaʊntɪŋ/ *noun* [U]
1 (*Commerce*) taking an amount of money off the usual cost of sth: *a period of aggressive discounting by retailers*
  ◐ **aggressive/heavy/widespread** discounting ◆ **fare/price** discounting
2 (*Finance*) = INVOICE DISCOUNTING
3 (*Finance*) the act of buying a BILL OF EXCHANGE for less than the amount that will be paid on it in the future

'discount loan *noun* [C]
(*Finance*) an amount of money that sb borrows from which the interest and other charges have been taken away before they receive the money

'discount ˌmarket *noun* [C, usually sing.]
1 (*Finance*) the part of the financial market that deals in the buying and selling of BILLS OF EXCHANGE
2 (*Commerce*) the part of a market in which goods or services are sold at low prices: *The airline cannot be a genuine competitor in the discount market until its cost base matches its fares.*

'discount price *noun* [C]
a price that is lower than the normal price: *We offer a wide selection of products at discount prices.*

'discount rate *noun* [C]
1 (*Finance*) (*also* **'bill rate**) the amount that the price of a BILL OF EXCHANGE is reduced by when it is bought before it reaches its payment date
2 (*Finance*) in the US and other countries, the rate of interest at which banks can borrow money from the Federal Reserve Bank
3 (*Accounting*) a rate of interest that is used to calculate how much an amount of money that will be paid or received in the future is worth now

'discount store (*also* **'discount house**) *noun* [C]
a shop that sells goods at prices that are much lower than normal: *a chain of high-street discount stores* ◇ *Discount stores thrive even in the current sluggish economy.* SYN DISCOUNTER

ˌdiscount 'warehouse *noun* [C]
a large DISCOUNT STORE: *Profit warnings have been pouring in from discount warehouses.*

'discount ˌwindow *noun* [C]
(*Finance*) in the US, a time when banks are able to borrow money from the central bank at low rates of interest: *The Fed has to closely monitor discount window borrowing.*

discrepancy /dɪsˈkrepənsi/ *noun* [C,U] (*plural* **discrepancies**)
a difference between two or more numbers or amounts that should be the same: *The investigation uncovered numerous discrepancies **in** the company's accounts.* ◇ *Why is there a discrepancy **between** these two figures?*
  ◐ a **growing/large/minor/small** discrepancy ◆ **accounting/price** discrepancies

discretion /dɪˈskreʃn/ *noun* [U]
the freedom or power to decide what should be done in a particular situation: *I leave it to your discretion.* ◇ *Managers should use their own discretion to arrange schedules.* ◇ *Firms have a lot of discretion about the wage rates they set.*
IDM **at sb's disˈcretion** according to what sb decides or wishes to do: *Bonuses may be paid to employees at their manager's discretion.*

discretionary /dɪˈskreʃənəri; *AmE* -neri/
adjective [usually before noun]
1 decided according to the judgement of a person in authority about what is necessary in each particular situation, rather than being decided by a set of rules: *Each member of staff is eligible for a discretionary bonus.*
O *a discretionary* **award/bonus/grant/payment**
2 (*Finance*) relating to investment funds placed with a BROKER or manager who is free to make decisions about how to invest them on the investor's behalf: *a discretionary portfolio manager*

disˌcretionary acˈcount *noun* [C]
(*Finance*) an investor's account where the BROKER or manager is given the freedom to make decisions about what shares, bonds, etc. to buy and sell on the investor's behalf

disˌcretionary ˈincome *noun* [U]
(*Economics*) the income sb is left with to spend or save as they want after taxes, etc. and necessary living expenses have been taken away from it: *The rise in energy costs is taking a big bite out of discretionary income.* → DISPOSABLE INCOME

disˈcretionary ˌorder *noun* [C]
(*Stock Exchange*) a piece of financial business in which the BROKER can decide when to buy or sell in order to get the best price for the investor

disˌcretionary ˈspending *noun* [U]
1 (*Economics*) the amount of money that consumers spend on things they want rather than on things they need: *Increases in taxes eat into discretionary spending by consumers.*
2 (*Accounting*) the amount of money that a company spends that can easily be controlled: *The company slashed discretionary spending such as travel and delayed raises.*

disˈcretionary trust *noun* [C]
(*Law*) a TRUST in which the person managing it is able to decide what kind of investments to make or how the money should be shared out

discriminate /dɪˈskrɪmɪneɪt/ *verb*
1 (*Law*) [no obj] to treat one person or group differently from another in an unfair way: *He has been accused of discriminating **in favour of** female candidates.* ◇ *It is illegal to discriminate on grounds of race, sex or religion.*
2 [+ obj or no obj] to recognize that there is a difference between people or things; to show a difference between people or things: *These regulations do not discriminate a large company **from** a small one.* ◇ *The Web does not discriminate **between** Macs and PCs.*

disˌcriminating ˈduty (*also* **disˌcriminating ˈtariff**) *noun* [C,U]
(*Trade*) a tax charged on imported goods which varies depending on the country that the goods come from: *A discriminating duty of 10% of the value is imposed on goods imported from foreign countries.*

discrimination /dɪˌskrɪmɪˈneɪʃn/ *noun* [U]

SEE ALSO: age discrimination, genetic ~, positive ~, price ~, reverse ~

(*Law*) the practice of treating a person, a particular group of people or a particular class of things differently from another in an unfair way: *The company has been accused of discrimination against people with disabilities.* ◇ *This is a clear case of discrimination.* ◇ *discrimination **on the grounds of** age* ◇ *Accusations of race and gender discrimination accounted for a majority of the complaints.*
O **gender/race/racial/sex/sexual** *discrimination* • *discrimination* **against/in favour of** *sth*

discriminatory /dɪˈskrɪmɪnətəri; *AmE* dɪˈskrɪmɪnətɔːri/ *adjective*
(*Law*) treating a person or one group of people worse than others, in an unfair way: *He claimed his treatment was discriminatory under human rights law.* ◇ *sexually/racially discriminatory laws*
O *discriminatory* **laws/measures/practices/rules**

disˈcriminatory tax *noun*
1 (*Economics*) [C,U] a tax that is charged only on a particular group of producers or goods, for example producers from other countries, so that other groups can compete more easily: *discriminatory taxes on foreign alcohol products* ◇ *Magazine publishers are fighting the discriminatory tax of 25% on magazines and zero on newspapers.*
2 [C] a particular tax that some people think is unfair as it does not affect everyone equally
▶ **disˌcriminatory taˈxation** *noun* [U]

diseconomy /ˌdɪsɪˈkɒnəmi; *AmE* -ˈkɑːn-/ *noun* [C, usually pl., U] (*plural* **diseconomies**)
(*Economics*) a financial or economic disadvantage such as increases in cost; sth that produces an increase in cost: *Urban diseconomies are the financial and social burdens arising from location in a major urban area.*

ˌdiseconomy of ˈscale *noun* [C, usually pl., U]
(*Economics*) an economic disadvantage, such as an increase in the average cost of producing goods, that may happen when an organization becomes larger: *Some firms become too large and reach a point where diseconomies of scale occur.*—Picture at ECONOMY OF SCALE

disequilibrium /ˌdɪsiːkwɪˈlɪbriəm; ˌdɪsˌek-/ *noun* [U]
(*Economics*) a loss or lack of balance in a situation, especially in relation to supply, demand and prices: *a high disequilibrium between market demand and supply of the product* ◇ *A surplus or a shortage indicates market disequilibrium.*

dishoarding /dɪsˈhɔːdɪŋ; *AmE* -ˈhɔːrd-/ *noun* [U]
(*Economics*) spending or investing money rather than keeping or saving it, especially the selling of gold by investors: *The dramatic rise in local currency gold prices led to high levels of dishoarding.* → HOARD *verb*

dishonour (*AmE spelling* **dishonor**) /dɪsˈɒnə(r); *AmE* -ˈɑːn-/ *verb* [+ obj]
1 (used about a bank) to refuse to pay a cheque, usually because there is not enough money in the account: *If the account is overdrawn, the cheques are automatically dishonoured.* **SYN** BOUNCE
2 (*Finance*) to fail to accept a BILL OF EXCHANGE or fail to pay it after accepting it
3 to fail to keep an agreement or promise that you have made: *The union claims the firm dishonoured an agreement to improve working conditions.*
→ HONOUR

disincentive /ˌdɪsɪnˈsentɪv/ *noun* [C]
something that makes sb less willing to do sth: *removing financial disincentives **for** people to work after the age of 55* ◇ *Such a tax would **act as** a major disincentive to companies expanding by taking over other companies.* **OPP** INCENTIVE

disinflation /ˌdɪsɪnˈfleɪʃn/ *noun* [U]
(*Economics*) a gradual reduction in the rate of INFLATION in a country's economy, without

increasing unemployment. This is done by such measures as restricting consumers' spending by raising interest rates, restricting credit agreements and introducing price controls on goods that are in short supply: *We may have already moved beyond disinflation into a period of full-scale deflation.* ◇ *the government's policy of disinflation* → DEFLATION, INFLATION, REFLATION at REFLATE
▶ **disinflationary** /ˌdɪsɪnˈfleɪʃənri; AmE -neri/ adjective

disintegration /dɪsˌɪntɪˈɡreɪʃn/ noun [U]
the breaking up of a company or group of companies: *This takeover is likely to trigger the total disintegration of the century-old firm.* → VERTICAL DISINTEGRATION

disintermediation /ˌdɪsɪntəˌmiːdiˈeɪʃn; AmE -tər,m-/ noun [U]
(*Economics*)
1 a reduction in the use of banks and other financial institutions to arrange business between borrowers and lenders, or between buyers and sellers of investments, etc. → INTERMEDIATION
2 a reduction in the use of a person or an organization to arrange business between producers and customers
→ INTERMEDIARY

disinvest /ˌdɪsɪnˈvest/ verb [no obj]
(*Economics*) to stop investing money in a company, an industry or a country; to reduce the amount of money invested: *The recession has caused many companies to disinvest.* ▶ **disinˈvestment** noun [U,C]: *He blamed the huge backlog in repairs on disinvestment in the railways over many years.*

disk /dɪsk/ noun [C]

SEE ALSO: fixed disk, floppy ~, hard ~

1 (*especially AmE*) = DISC
2 (*also* **magˌnetic ˈdisk**) a flat piece of metal or plastic used for storing information on a computer: *Can you read this disk?* ◇ *I'm running out of disk space.* ◇ *I'll send you a copy of the report on disk.*

ˈdisk drive noun [C]
(*IT*) a device in a computer that passes data between a disk and the memory of the computer or from one disk or computer to another: *a disk drive manufacturer*

diskette /dɪsˈket/ = FLOPPY DISK

dislocation /ˌdɪsləˈkeɪʃn; AmE -loʊ-/ noun [U,C]
(*Economics*) the state of no longer being in the usual place or continuing in the usual way; the process of making this happen: *a period of economic dislocation* ◇ *the dismissal and dislocation of thousands of workers*

★ **dismiss** /dɪsˈmɪs/ verb [+ obj]
1 (*HR*) to officially remove an employee from their job: *She claims she was unfairly dismissed from her post.* ◇ *He was dismissed for breach of contract.* ◇ *to be summarily dismissed* (= without paying attention to the normal process that should be followed)
2 (*Law*) to refuse to say that a trial or legal case should not continue, usually because there is not enough evidence: *After a five-day hearing the case was dismissed.*

★ **dismissal** /dɪsˈmɪsl/ noun [U,C]

SEE ALSO: constructive dismissal, unfair ~, wrongful ~

1 (*HR*) the act of removing an employee from their job; an example of this: *Six employees face possible dismissal.* ◇ *The dismissals followed the resignation of the chairman.* ◇ *Going over budget can be grounds for dismissal.* ◇ *dismissal with/without notice*
2 (*Law*) the act of not allowing a trial or legal case to continue, usually because there is not enough evidence: *the dismissal of the appeal*

VOCABULARY BUILDING

Getting rid of employees

When employees do something wrong
● to **dismiss** sb – *She was dismissed for misuse of company property.*
● to **fire** sb (*more informal*) – *We fired him for dishonesty.*
● to **remove** sb (*used especially about people with important jobs*) – *He has been removed from the company's board.*
● to **sack** sb (*BrE; used informally or in newspapers*) – *The company sacked its chief executive after a series of poor results.*

When employees are no longer needed or a company needs to save money
● to make sb **redundant** (*BrE*) – *More than 100 workers have been made redundant.*
● to **lay** sb **off** – *The company has laid off 200 of its employees.*
● to **terminate** sb (*especially AmE*) – *They are obliged to compensate terminated employees.*
● to **downsize** – *Big companies are downsizing and increasing their temporary workforce.*
● to **delayer** (= to reduce the number of levels of management) – *Restructuring and delayering have meant redundancies for many experienced people.*

See note at EMPLOY

---

dispatch (*also spelled* **despatch**, *especially in BrE*) /dɪsˈpætʃ/ verb [+ obj]
1 to send sb somewhere, especially for a special purpose: *A courier was dispatched to collect the documents.*
2 (*Commerce*) to send a letter, parcel/package or message somewhere: *Goods are dispatched within 24 hours of your order reaching us.*
▶ **disˈpatch** (*also spelled* **despatch**, *especially in BrE*) noun [U]: *The goods are ready for dispatch.* ◇ *the central dispatch office*
See note at DISTRIBUTION

dispatcher /dɪsˈpætʃə(r)/ noun [C]
1 (*Transport*) (*especially AmE*) a person whose job is to control a group of vehicles such as lorries/trucks or taxis and send them to where they are needed: *The new technology means that dispatchers always know the exact location of every truck.* ◇ *cab dispatchers*
2 (*Transport*) a person whose job is to see that planes, trains or buses leave on time: *flight dispatchers*
3 (*Commerce*) a person or a company that has sent goods to customers

disˈpatch note (*also spelled* **despatch ~**) noun [C]
(*Commerce*) a document that is sent to a customer, either with goods or separately, giving details of the items that have been sent: *When returning items, please include a copy of the dispatch note.*
→ ADVICE NOTE, DELIVERY NOTE

disˈpatch ˌrider (*also spelled* **despatch ~**) noun [C] (*BrE only*)
a person who delivers urgent business documents using a motorcycle

dispense /dɪsˈpens/ verb
1 [+ obj] to provide sth or give it out to people: *The machine dispenses a range of drinks and snacks.* ◇ *The organization has dispensed over $35 million in small business grants.*

2 [+ obj or no obj] to prepare medicine and give it to people, as a job: *About 115 million prescriptions were dispensed through July of this year.* ◇ *(BrE) a dispensing chemist*

PHRV **di'spense with sb/sth** to stop using sb/sth because you no longer need them or it: *Debit cards dispense with the need for cash altogether.* ◇ *He has dispensed with the services of management consultants.*

dispenser /dɪ'spensə(r)/ *noun* [C]

SEE ALSO: **cash dispenser**

1 (*usually used with another noun*) a machine or container holding money, drinks, paper towels, etc., that you can obtain quickly, for example by pulling a handle or pressing buttons: *a drinks/tape dispenser*
2 a person who prepares medicine and gives it to people, as a job
3 a person or thing that provides sth

display /dɪ'spleɪ/ *noun, verb*
●*noun*

SEE ALSO: **caller display, island display**

1 [C] an arrangement of goods for people to look at or buy, often in a shop/store: *an attractive display of merchandise* ◇ *Our window displays are changed weekly.* ◇ *a point-of-sale display*—Picture at STORE
2 (*IT*) [C] a computer screen or other piece of equipment that shows information: *a 17-inch flat-panel display* ◇ *There is a miniature display at the bottom of my mobile phone.* ◇ *a display panel/screen*
3 (*IT*) [U] the words, pictures, etc. shown on a computer screen; the way in which these appear on the screen: *There are some display problems with this model.* ◇ *Double-click on the 'Display' icon and select the 'Settings' tab.*
IDM **on di'splay** put in a place where people can see it: *All the goods on display are in the sale.*
●*verb* [+ obj]
1 to arrange sth in a place where people can see it easily, especially sth that is for sale: *We are looking at new ways to display our products.* ◇ *Their merchandise is attractively displayed in the window.* ◇ *The posters will be displayed for three weeks.*
2 (*IT*) to show information on a computer screen: *This column displays the title of the mail message.* ◇ *The date and time are displayed on the screen.*

di'splay ad (*also* **di'splay ˌadvert, di'splay adˌvertisement**) *noun* [C]
(*Marketing*) an advertisement that is designed in a way that will attract people's attention: *The volume of display ads being booked in national newspapers has been in decline.* ▶ **di'splay ˌadvertising** *noun* [U]: *Display advertising is expected to fall 9% in the full year.*

di'splay alˌlowance *noun* [C]
(*Marketing*) a fee that a manufacturer pays to a shop/store to put their goods in a place where people will easily see them

di'splay bin = DUMP BIN

di'splay case (*also* **di'splay ˌcabinet**) *noun* [C]
a special container, made all or partly of glass, used for showing items in a shop/store: *display cases for cosmetics*—Picture at STORE

di'splay ˌmedium *noun* [C]
1 (*Marketing*) a thing, such as a POSTER, sign, card, etc., that attracts people's attention to goods on sale: *specialists in the fields of print, broadcast and display media advertising*
2 a way of showing information to people: *The Web is mainly a display medium, like television.* ◇ *display media such as graphs, letters, lines, and drawings*

di'splay pack *noun* [C]
(*Marketing*) a box that is designed to show goods that are on sale and attract people's attention: *a front-of-counter display pack*

di'splay type *noun* [U]
(*Marketing*) large printed letters that are designed to be immediately noticeable, used especially in advertisements

disposable /dɪ'spəʊzəbl; AmE -'spoʊ-/ *adjective, noun*
●*adjective*
1 [usually before noun] (about goods, etc.) produced cheaply and intended to be thrown away after use: *a disposable camera/razor/bottle* **SYN** THROWAWAY → SINGLE-USE
2 [only before noun] available for use
O *disposable* **assets/capital/resources**
●*noun* **disposables** [pl.]
(*Economics; Marketing*) = CONSUMER NON-DURABLES

diˌsposable 'income (*also* **exˌpendable 'income**, *especially in AmE*) *noun* [U,C]
(*Economics*)
1 income left after taxes, etc. have been taken away from it and that you are free to spend or save: *Higher fuel costs reduce people's disposable income.* ◇ *Interest payments stand at 7% of disposable income.*
→ DISCRETIONARY INCOME, TAKE-HOME PAY
2 in a particular country, the total amount of money that people have to spend or save, after taxes, etc. has been paid

★disposal /dɪ'spəʊzl; AmE -'spoʊ-/ *noun*
1 [C,U] the sale of part of a business, property, etc: *the disposal of the company's chemical services division* ◇ *The disposal is expected to raise around $50 m.* ◇ *The sale is part of an* **asset** *disposal to shore up the company's finances.*
2 [U] the act of getting rid of sth that you do not want or cannot keep: *Disposal of industrial waste is a serious problem.* ◇ *waste disposal*
IDM **at sb's dis'posal** available for sb to use: *Larger companies have larger resources at their disposal.*

dispose /dɪ'spəʊz; AmE dɪ'spoʊz/ *verb*
PHRV **di'spose of sth 1** to sell part of a business, property, etc: *The company has pledged to dispose of its non-core* **assets.** ◇ *He is disposing of his stake in the company.* **2** to get rid of sth that you do not want or cannot keep: *Chrome is difficult to dispose of safely.* ◇ *We need to reduce the amount of toxic waste disposed of in landfill sites.*

dispute *noun, verb*
●*noun* /dɪ'spjuːt; 'dɪspjuːt/ [C,U]

SEE ALSO: **demarcation dispute, industrial ~, labour ~, trade ~**

an argument or a disagreement between two people, groups or countries; discussion about a subject where there is disagreement: *They are making renewed efforts to settle the pay dispute.* ◇ *The union is* **in dispute with** *management over working hours.* ◇ *There is no sign of an end to the long-running dispute* **between** *the two executives.*
O *to be involved in/have/resolve/settle a dispute* ◆ *industrial/labour/pay disputes* ◆ *a bitter/damaging dispute*
●*verb* /dɪ'spjuːt/ [+ obj]
to question whether sth is true and valid: *These figures have been disputed.*

di'spute proˌcedure (*also* **'dispute ~**) = DISPUTES PROCEDURE

di'spute resoˌlution (*also* **'dispute ~**) *noun* [U]

SEE ALSO: **alternative dispute resolution**

(*Law*) the process of settling disputes, for example by using a court or an ARBITRATOR (= a person chosen to settle the dispute): *The study recommends* arbitration as a cheaper alternative to more traditional forms of dispute resolution. ◇ a dispute resolution procedure/process

di'sputes pro,cedure (also **di'spute proc,edure, 'dispute(s)** ~) noun [C]
(Law) an official process that is followed in order to settle a dispute, especially one involving members of an organization: *Management and employees should use the disputes procedure where there is a possibility of a strike.*

disqualify /dɪsˈkwɒlɪfaɪ; AmE -ˈkwɑːl-/ verb [+ obj] (**disqualifies, disqualifying, disqualified, disqualified**)
to prevent sb from doing sth because they have broken a rule or are not suitable: *She has been disqualified from practising as a lawyer.* ◇ *He was disqualified as a director after being declared bankrupt.* ▶ **disqualification** /dɪsˌkwɒlɪfɪˈkeɪʃn; AmE -ˌkwɑːl-/ noun [C,U]: *Directors can face fines or disqualification if they allow an insolvent company to go on trading.*

disrupt /dɪsˈrʌpt/ verb [+ obj]
to make it difficult for sth to continue in the normal way: *The strike could disrupt oil supplies.* ◇ *Train services have been severely disrupted by the storm.*
▶ **disruption** /dɪsˈrʌpʃn/ noun [U,C]: *We have tried to minimize the disruption to our services.* ◇ *a disruption in operations/production/supply*
disruptive /dɪsˈrʌptɪv/ adjective: *disruptive protests and strikes*

dis,ruptive tech'nology noun [C,U]
(Technical) any new technology that completely changes the way people and businesses work: *What will be the next disruptive technology after the Internet?*

dissaving /dɪsˈseɪvɪŋ/ noun
(Economics)
1 [U,C] the act of spending more money than you earn during a particular period of time: *The act of borrowing money from a bank is a form of dissaving.* ◇ *a dissaving of £8 million* ◇ *government/public/private dissaving*
2 dissavings [pl.] the amount by which the money spent is more than the money earned
→ SAVING
▶ **dis'save** verb [+ obj or no obj]: *Governments dissave by spending more money than they receive in taxes.* ◇ *The study found that households in the 65+ age group dissaved €3 000 a year.* → SAVE

dissolution /ˌdɪsəˈluːʃn/ noun [U; C, usually sing.]
the act of officially ending a contract or business relationship; the act of breaking up an organization, etc: *The board of directors approved the dissolution of the company and the disposal of its assets.*

dissolve /dɪˈzɒlv; AmE -ˈzɑːlv/ verb [+ obj or no obj]
to officially end a contract or business relationship; to come to an end: *The airline is seeking to dissolve its contract with the union.* ◇ *The partnership dissolved in 2004.*

'distance ,learning (also **,open 'learning**) noun [U]
a system of education or training in which people study at home, at the place where they work, etc. with the help of special Internet sites and/or television and radio programmes, and send or email work to their teachers: *an MBA by distance learning* ◇ *web-based distance learning*

distress /dɪˈstres/ noun [U]
(Law) when the goods of a person or a company are legally taken in order to pay money that they owe: *The distress sale is unlikely to raise enough to repay all the loans.*

distressed /dɪˈtrest/ adjective (especially AmE)
1 (Law) used to describe property or goods that have been legally taken from sb who cannot pay money that they owe, and are offered for sale cheaply: *buyers and sellers of distressed assets*
2 used to describe goods that have been damaged or used

dis,tributable 'profit noun [C, usually pl., U]
(Accounting) the amount of profit from normal business activities that a company has left at the end of an accounting period, which it can pay to shareholders as DIVIDENDS: *The company's distributable profits are not sufficient to pay any dividends.* ◇ *a distributable profit after tax of $3.48 million* → DISTRIBUTED PROFIT

dis,tributable re'serve noun [C, usually pl.]
(Accounting) a fund of money that a company keeps which it can use to make payments to shareholders; the money in this fund, which comes, for example, from profits left at the end of an accounting period: *An extra dividend can only be paid if sufficient distributable reserves are available.* ◇ *a transfer to distributable reserves*
→ NON-DISTRIBUTABLE RESERVE

★ **distribute** /dɪˈstrɪbjuːt; AmE ˈdɪstrɪbjuːt/ verb
1 (Marketing) [+ obj or no obj] to make a product available to customers, for example, by supplying it to shops/stores and businesses: *Who distributes our products in the UK?* ◇ *The magazine is distributed through restaurants and clubs.* ◇ *We distribute worldwide.* → DISTRIBUTION, DISTRIBUTOR
2 [+ obj] to share money, goods or property between a group of people; to give things to a large number of people: *The company distributes most of its profits to investors as dividends.* ◇ *The firm's assets will be distributed among creditors.* ◇ *The newspaper is distributed free.*

dis,tributed 'profit noun [C, usually pl.]
(Accounting) the amount of the profits that a company has left at the end of an accounting period and has paid to shareholders: *Domestic companies are liable to an income tax of 10% on distributed profits.* → DIVIDEND

★ **distribution** /ˌdɪstrɪˈbjuːʃn/ noun

SEE ALSO: **channel of distribution, retail** ~, **selective** ~

1 (Marketing) [U] the activity of making a product available to customers, for example by supplying it to shops/stores; the system of transporting and delivering a product to shops/stores or customers: *marketing, sales and distribution* ◇ *European distribution is handled from our centre in the Netherlands.* ◇ *high distribution costs caused by poor transport systems* ◇ *We have secured exclusive distribution rights for the product in the UK.*
→ DISTRIBUTE, DISTRIBUTOR See note on next page.
⊕ *to control/handle/improve/organize distribution* • *broad/international/limited/local/wide distribution* • *a distribution agreement/deal* • *a distribution network/operation/system* • *a distribution facility/warehouse* • *a distribution business/company*
2 [U,C] the act of sharing money, goods or property between a group of people or giving people things; the money or goods that people receive: *the distribution of leaflets* ◇ *The board has approved a cash distribution to stockholders of $2.50 a share.*

,distri'bution ,centre (AmE spelling ~ **center**) noun [C]
a large WAREHOUSE that receives goods from factories and suppliers and sends them to shops/stores or customers: *They have opened a new distribution centre north of Mexico City.*

distribution/delivery/dispatch/logistics

These words are all used about sending goods to customers.

Distribution involves arranging for a product to pass from one place to another until it reaches somewhere, for example a shop/store, where people can buy it. The series of businesses is the **distribution chain** and a particular business or place where the goods are finally sold is a **distribution channel**: *Our main distribution channels are convenience stores and the Internet.*

Logistics involves physically collecting, transporting and delivering goods. These responsibilities are often given to a transport company: *FedEx handle the logistics.*

Delivery involves giving the goods to the customer: *Allow up to 3 weeks for delivery.* ◇ *Our terms are cash on delivery* (= you pay when the goods arrive).

Dispatch refers to the process of goods leaving a factory or office: *We check all orders before dispatch.* ◇ *the date of dispatch*

See note at SUPPLY CHAIN

---

distri'bution chain (*also* ,chain of distri'bution, *less frequent*) *noun* [C]
(*Marketing*) the series of businesses that deal with a product between when it is produced and the time that customers receive it: *pushing products through the distribution chain* ◇ *By supplying direct we cut out an entire level of the distribution chain.*
→ SUPPLY CHAIN See note at DISTRIBUTION

distri'bution ,channel (*also* ,channel of distri'bution, *less frequent*) *noun* [C]
(*Marketing*) the way that products are made available to customers: *The Internet is a new distribution channel for us.*
See note at DISTRIBUTION

★ **distributor** /dɪˈstrɪbjətə(r)/ *noun* [C]
a person or business that supplies goods produced by other companies to shops/stores or directly to the public: *Japan's largest software distributor* ◇ *the largest US distributor of canned fruit and vegetables* ◇ *We have been appointed sole distributor for these products in Australia and New Zealand.* ◇ *Most of our sales are through distributors.* ◇ *a wholesale distributor* (= one that only sells to shop/stores, etc.) See note at SUPPLY CHAIN
O *to act as/appoint (sb as)/use* a distributor ◆ *an authorized/exclusive/a sole* distributor ◆ *a foreign/local* distributor
▶ **dis'tributorship** *noun* [C]: *The group has won an exclusive distributorship for the range in Singapore.*

district at'torney *noun* [C] (*abbr* DA)
in the US, a government lawyer in a particular area or state who decides whether to accuse sb of a crime and start a court case against them

div /dɪv/ *abbr*
1 Div. a short way of writing **division** (= a part of a large company): *IBM's Microelectronics Div.*
2 (*Finance*) a short way of writing or saying **dividend**: *shares traded **cum div** (= the buyer receives the next dividend)*

dive /daɪv/ *verb, noun*
● *verb* [no obj] (**dived, dived,** *AmE also* **dove** /dəʊv; *AmE* doʊv/; **dived**)
(about a price, figure, etc.) to fall suddenly: *The share price dived 11.8% **to** an all-time low of 455¢.* ◇ *They have seen their sales dive **by** 28%.*
See note at INCREASE
● *noun* [C, usually sing.]
a sudden drop in a price, figure, etc: *a dive in the company's share price* → idiom at TAKE *verb*
→ NOSEDIVE

diverge /daɪˈvɜːdʒ; *AmE* -ˈvɜːrdʒ/ *verb* [no obj]
1 if two things **diverge**, or one thing **diverges** from another, they become different and the difference between them increases: *The speeds of growth in the manufacturing and consumer sectors are diverging.* ◇ *The country's interest rates have diverged further **from** those in Europe.* ◇ *the diverging economic fortunes of the two countries*
2 (about opinions, decisions, etc.) to be different: *Opinions diverge greatly on this issue.* ◇ *diverging policies*
3 to be or become different from what is expected, planned, etc: *Inflation has diverged **from** the central bank's target.* ◇ *to diverge from the norm*
▶ **divergence** /daɪˈvɜːdʒəns; *AmE* -ˈvɜːrdʒ-/ *noun* [C,U]: *a continuing divergence **between** the prices of goods and services* ◇ *a divergence **in/of** opinion* ◇ *a divergence **from** objectives* **divergent** /daɪˈvɜːdʒənt; *AmE* -ˈvɜːrdʒ-/ *adjective*: *The US and Japanese economies show divergent trends.* ◇ *divergent views*

diversify /daɪˈvɜːsɪfaɪ; *AmE* -ˈvɜːrs-/ *verb* [+ obj or no obj] (**diversifies, diversifying, diversified, diversified**)
(about a business, an investor, etc.) to develop a wider range of products, markets, investments, etc. in order to be more successful or reduce risk: *The company has grown and diversified.* ◇ *The trust wants to diversify its investments.* ◇ *Many investors are diversifying **from** shares **into** bonds and commodities.* ◇ *We want to diversify **away from** traditional phone services.* ▶ **diversification** /daɪˌvɜːsɪfɪˈkeɪʃn; *AmE* -ˌvɜːrs-/ *noun* [U,C]: *Toyota's diversification **into** housing and telecommunications* ◇ *the diversification of risk* **di'versified** *adjective*: *We continue to benefit from our diversified business mix.*

diversion /daɪˈvɜːʃn; *AmE* -ˈvɜːrʒn/ *noun* [C,U]
1 diversion (from sth) (into/to sth) the act of changing what sth is used for or of using sth for a different purpose from what was intended: *the diversion of revenue away from product research*
2 (*Economics; Marketing*) (*also* ,product di'version) the situation when goods that are supplied to be sold in a particular area or place are sold in a different area or place, more cheaply than when they are bought from an official local supplier: *Many big clothing brands suffer from diversion of their products.* ◇ *the diversion of cheap drugs intended for poor countries to rich countries*

diversity /daɪˈvɜːsəti; *AmE* -ˈvɜːrs-/ *noun* [U; C, usually sing.]
the quality or fact of including a range of many people or things, especially people's different skills and qualities; a range of different people or things: *Valuing and managing diversity in an organization leads to more satisfied employees.* ◇ *Use the diversity of jobs that you've had to emphasize your skills.*

divert /daɪˈvɜːt; *AmE* -ˈvɜːrt/ *verb* [+ obj]
1 divert sb/sth (from sth) (into/to sth) to use money, materials, etc. for a different purpose from their original purpose or for sth new: *diverting resources away from research and development* ◇ *The company is diverting its savings into improving facilities.*
2 (*Economics; Marketing*) to sell goods outside the area or place where they were intended to be sold: *There are things you can do to avoid having your products diverted.* ◇ *Our distributors are required to buy back any diverted product that can be traced to them.*

3 (*Transport*) to change the place that a load of goods is going to or the way that it is being sent: *Instructions were received to divert the shipment from motor to air transportation.*
▶ **di'verter** *noun* [C]

divest /daɪˈvest/ *verb* [+ obj] (*formal*)
to sell part of a business or assets; to get rid of sth you own: *He said that the company is not planning to divest its auto-parts business.* ◇ *The government is seeking to divest itself of a 72% stake in the manufacturer.*
O to divest **assets/businesses/brands/products**
▶ **di'vestment** *noun* [C,U]: *The company has identified non-core assets for divestment.* ◇ *They have announced divestments worth $5bn.* ◇ *a divestment programme* **divestiture** /daɪˈvestɪtʃə(r)/ *noun* [C,U]: *the possible divestiture of one or more product lines* ◇ *mergers, acquisitions and divestitures*

divi /ˈdɪvi/ *noun* [C] (*plural* **divis**) (*BrE*)
(*Finance*) an informal word for DIVIDEND: *The final divi will depend on our cash position in March.*
SYN DIVVY

★ **divide** /dɪˈvaɪd/ *verb*
1 [+ obj] to find out how many times one number is contained in another: *The bond's yield is the interest payment divided by the price.*
2 [+ obj or no obj] to separate or make sth separate into parts: *The work process was divided into different tasks.*

★ **dividend** /ˈdɪvɪdend/ (*abbr* **div**) (*also* '**share** ˌdividend**) *noun* [C]

SEE ALSO: accumulated dividend, cash ~, cum ~, cumulative ~, ex-~, extra ~, etc.

(*Finance*) an amount of the profits that a company pays to shareholders: *The company will pay a dividend of 10 cents a share.* ◇ *The board declared* (= announced) *a quarterly dividend of $0.125.* ◇ *They increased the dividend payout for the year from 7¢ to 9¢.* → idioms at PAY *verb*, PASS *verb*
O to **declare/pay/propose/receive** a dividend ◆ to **increase/maintain/raise** a dividend ◆ to **cut/omit/ pass/scrap/suspend** a dividend ◆ a dividend **forecast/payment/payout**

'**dividend cheque** (*AmE spelling* ~ **check**) (*BrE also* '**dividend** ˌwarrant**) *noun* [C]
(*Finance*) a cheque that a shareholder receives as payment of a **dividend**, that also gives details of the tax paid

'**dividend ˌcover** *noun* [sing; U]
(*Accounting*) the number of times a company's profits would pay the **dividend**: *Our policy is to keep the group's dividend cover within a range of 2.5 to 3 times.*

ˌ**dividend rein'vestment plan** *noun* [C] (*abbr* **DRIP**)
(*Finance*) in the US, an investment plan that some companies offer in which shareholders can buy more shares in the company instead of receiving regular cash **dividends**

'**dividend ˌwarrant** (*BrE*) = DIVIDEND CHEQUE

ˌ**dividend 'yield** *noun* [C,U]
(*Finance*) the **dividend** that a company pays on each share, compared to the current price of the share: *It's an attractive stock, offering a dividend yield of over 5%.*

★ **division** /dɪˈvɪʒn/ *noun* [C] (*abbr* **div**)
a large and important unit or section of an organization that has responsibility for a particular market or area of activity: *The company's electronics division reported a 8.4 per cent drop in sales.* ◇ *He works in the marketing division.* ◇ *the finance/ research/sales/service division* ◇ *the chemicals/ software/truck division* ▶ **divisional** /dɪˈvɪʒənl/

adjective [only before noun]: *a divisional head/ manager* ◇ *divisional results/revenue/profits*

diˌvision of 'labour (*AmE spelling* ~ **labor**) *noun* [U,C]
1 (*HR*) the way in which different people do different tasks in a process in order to make the best use of time and money and produce as many goods as possible: *He believes that division of labour improves productivity as people specialize in what they do best.* → MULTISKILLING
2 a way of arranging a society, an organization or a group so that each type of work is done by a particular group of people: *the division of labour between member states and the EU*

divvy /ˈdɪvi/ *verb, noun*
● *verb* (**divvies, divvying, divvied, divvied**)
PHRV ˌ**divvy sth 'up** (*informal*) to divide sth, especially sth valuable, into two or more parts: *a dispute over how to divvy up the assets* ◇ *The profits have been divvied up **to** shareholders.* ◇ *Complex computing tasks are divvied up **among** several PCs.*
● *noun* [C] (*plural* **divvies**) (*BrE*)
(*Finance*) an informal word for DIVIDEND **SYN** DIVI

DIY /ˌdiː aɪ ˈwaɪ/ *abbr* (*especially BrE*)
do-it-yourself (*used as an uncountable noun*)
the activity of making, repairing or decorating things in the home yourself, instead of paying sb to do it: *These tools are available from most DIY stores.* ◇ *Castorama, the French DIY chain* **SYN** HOME REPAIR
▶ ˌ**DI'Y'er** *noun* [C]

DJIA™ /ˌdiː dʒeɪ aɪ ˈeɪ/ = Dow Jones Industrial Average: *a fall of 4.7% in the DJIA*

DLC /ˌdiː el ˈsiː/ *abbr*
1 (*Trade*) documentary letter of credit
→ DOCUMENTARY CREDIT
2 (*Stock Exchange*) = DUAL-LISTED COMPANY

DMU /ˌdiː em ˈjuː/ = DECISION-MAKING UNIT

DO /ˌdiː ˈəʊ; *AmE* ˈoʊ/ = DELIVERY ORDER

doable /ˈduːəbl/ *adjective*
that is possible and likely to be achieved: *Decide on a few small doable changes.* ◇ *The price increases seem doable.*

dock /dɒk; *AmE* dɑːk/ *noun, verb*
● *noun*
1 [C] a part of a port where ships are repaired or where goods are put onto or taken off them: *dock workers* ◇ *a dock strike* ◇ *The ship is **in dock**.*
2 docks [pl.] a group of **docks** in a port and the buildings around them that are used for repairing ships, storing goods, etc: *He works at the docks.*
3 [C] (*AmE*) a raised platform for loading vehicles or trains
4 [C] the part of a court where the person who has been accused of a crime stands or sits during a trial
IDM be in the '**dock** (**over sth**) (*used especially in newspapers*) to be heavily criticized for sth; to be asked questions that are difficult to deal with: *The company is in the dock over its poor safety record.*
● *verb*
1 [+ obj or no obj] if a ship **docks** or you **dock** a ship, it sails into a harbour and stays there: *The ship is expected to dock in Durban at 14.00 tomorrow.*
2 [+ obj] to take away part of sb's wages, etc: *Employers have threatened to dock the strikers' wages.* ◇ *They've docked 15% **off** my pay for this week.*
3 (*IT*) [+ obj] to connect a computer to a DOCKING STATION: *I docked my portable and started work.*

docker /ˈdɒkə(r); *AmE* ˈdɑːk-/ *noun* [C] (*BrE*)
a person whose job is moving goods on and off ships **SYN** STEVEDORE (*AmE*)

docket /'dɒkɪt; AmE 'dɑːk-/ noun [C]
1 a document or label that shows what is in a package, which goods have been delivered, which jobs have been done, etc: *a delivery docket*
2 (*AmE*) a list of items to be discussed or things to be done

'**docking ,station** noun [C]
(*IT*) a device to which a LAPTOP computer can be connected so that it can be used like a DESKTOP computer

dockyard /'dɒkjɑːd; AmE 'dɑːkjɑːrd/ noun [C]
an area with DOCKS (= the place where ships are loaded and unloaded in a port) and equipment for building and repairing ships

'**doctor's cer,tificate** = MEDICAL CERTIFICATE

★ **document** noun, verb
● *noun* /'dɒkjumənt; AmE 'dɑːk-/ [C]

SEE ALSO: **defence document, offer document**

1 an official paper or book that gives information about sth, or that can be used as evidence or proof of sth: *The company has published a 29-page document outlining the proposed merger.* ◇ *a consultation document on boardroom pay* ◇ *Have you received your tickets and travel documents?* ◇ *Copies of the relevant documents must be filed at court.*
○ *a* **formal/legal/an official/a written** *document* ◆ *a* **consultation/discussion/policy/strategy** *document* ◆ *to* **draft/draw up/publish/sign** *a document* ◆ *to* **destroy/shred/tear up** *documents* ◆ *a document* **details/outlines/says/states** *sth*
2 a computer file that contains text that has a name that identifies it: *To create a new document, select 'New' from the File menu.* ◇ *scrolling through a document*
○ *to* **create/edit/save** *a document* ◆ *to* **close/ download/open/print (out)** *a document*
● *verb* /'dɒkjument; AmE 'dɑːk-/ [+ obj]
to record the details of sth in writing: *a project to document manufacturing procedures* ◇ *The country's economic problems have been well documented.*

,**documentary col'lection** noun [C,U]
(*Trade*) a way of arranging payment for exports, especially by ship, in which the seller gives the documents that are needed to collect the goods to the buyer's bank, which keeps them until it receives payment for the goods

,**documentary 'credit** noun [U,C] (*abbr* **DC**) (*also* '**documentary 'letter of 'credit** [C])
(*Trade*) a LETTER OF CREDIT in which a bank promises to pay an exporter for goods when documents are provided that prove the goods have been sent

documentation /,dɒkjumen'teɪʃn; AmE ,dɑːk-/ noun [U]
1 the documents that are required for sth, or that give evidence or proof of sth: *I couldn't enter the country because I didn't have all the necessary documentation.* ◇ *They have insufficient documentation to support their claims.*
2 the act of recording sth in a document; the state of being recorded in a document: *the documentation of accounting decisions* ◇ *an electronic documentation system*
3 the documents that describe how sth works or how to operate it: *the technical documentation for a computer system*

,**document of 'title** noun [C]
(*Law; Trade*) a document, such as a BILL OF LADING, that allows sb to claim the goods that are described in it: *The agent presented the documents of title at the airport.*

,**documents a,gainst ac'ceptance** phrase (*abbr* **D/A**)
(*Trade*) a way of paying for imports where the buyer must sign a document (**bill of exchange**) promising to pay for the goods within a particular amount of time before the bank gives them the documents needed to collect the goods: *The method of payment shall be documents against acceptance, within 120 days after sight* (= the time when the importer signs the bill of exchange). → DOCUMENTS AGAINST PAYMENT

,**documents a,gainst 'payment** phrase (*abbr* **D/P**)
(*Trade*) a way of paying for imports in which the buyer pays for the goods when the bank gives them the documents that are needed to collect the goods → DOCUMENTS AGAINST ACCEPTANCE

'**document ,sharing** noun [U]
(*IT*) the ability that some computer systems have that allows people in different places to look at and work on the same computer document at the same time

dodge /dɒdʒ; AmE dɑːdʒ/ noun, verb
● *noun* [C]
a clever and dishonest trick, done in order to avoid sth: *Many people bought the pensions as a form of tax dodge.*
● *verb* [+ obj]
to avoid doing sth, especially in a dishonest way: *She tried to dodge paying her taxes.*

dodger /'dɒdʒə(r); AmE 'dɑːdʒ-/ noun [C] (*informal*)
a person who dishonestly avoids doing sth: *tax dodgers*

dodgy /'dɒdʒi; AmE 'dɑːdʒi/ adjective (**dodgier**, **dodgiest**) (*BrE*) (*informal*)
seeming or likely to be dishonest: *rumours about dodgy accounting* ◇ *I don't want to get involved in anything dodgy.*

dog /dɒg; AmE dɔːg/ noun [C]

SEE ALSO: **top dog**

1 (*Marketing*) in the BOSTON MATRIX, a product that has a small market share in a market that is growing very little—Picture at BOSTON MATRIX
2 (*informal*) used to describe sth that is very bad or a failure, especially an investment that always does badly: *If you have bought a dog fund, be brave and get out!* ◇ *It's been a dog of a year.*
IDM (**a case of**) ,**dog eat 'dog** a situation in business, politics, etc. where there is a lot of competition and people are willing to harm each other in order to succeed: *I'm afraid in this line of work it's a case of dog eat dog.* ◇ *We're operating in a dog-eat-dog world.* **eat your own 'dog food** (*IT, informal*) when a company tests or uses its own software products in the organization **go to the** '**dogs** (*AmE also* **go to hell in a 'handbasket**) (*informal*) to get into a very bad state: *This firm's gone to the dogs since the new management took over.* **that dog won't 'hunt** (*AmE*) (*informal*) used to say that an idea will not work

,**dog and 'pony show** noun [C] (*AmE*) (*informal*)
a complicated presentation, event or display that is designed, for example, to persuade people to invest in a company → ROAD SHOW

dogsbody /'dɒgzbɒdi; AmE 'dɔːgzbɑːdi/ noun [C] (*plural* **dogsbodies**) (*BrE*) (*informal*)
a person who does all the boring jobs that nobody else wants to do, and who is treated as being less important than other people **SYN** GOFER

,**do-it-your'self** = DIY: *a do-it-yourself chain/ retailer/store*

dol. abbr
a short way of writing **dollar** or **dollars**: *a cost of 7 dol. per day*

doldrums /'dɒldrəmz; AmE 'doʊl-/ noun [pl.]
a lack of activity or improvement: *The media sector
remains **in the doldrums** as companies advertise
less.* ◇ *There are signs that the country is climbing out
of its economic doldrums.*

dole /dəʊl; AmE doʊl/ noun [sing.] (*usually* **the dole**)
(*BrE*) (*informal*)
money paid by the state to unemployed people: *The
number of people **on the dole** (= without a job) is
the highest for 19 years.* ◇ *The government is
changing the rules for claiming (the) dole.*
SYN WELFARE (*AmE*)

'dole queue (*BrE*) (*AmE* **,unem'ployment line**)
noun [C]
used especially in newspapers to describe the
group of unemployed people in a society: *the
country's lengthening dole queues* ◇ *Thousands more
workers could join the dole queue next year.*

dollar /'dɒlə(r); AmE 'dɑːl-/ noun, adjective
● *noun*

SEE ALSO: **benefit dollar, top dollar**

1 [C] (*abbr* **dol.**, **$**) the unit of money in the US,
Canada, Australia and several other countries: *All
prices are quoted in dollars.* ◇ *converting dollars into
pesos* ◇ *an investment worth millions of dollars* ◇ *a
multi-million dollar investment* → BUCK (1)
2 **the dollar** [sing.] the value of the US dollar
compared with the value of the money of other
countries: *The dollar closed two cents down.* ◇ *The
strong dollar has made US goods expensive overseas.*
◇ *The currency fell to a two-week low **against**
(= compared to) the dollar.* ◇ *an exchange rate of
two pesos to the dollar* → GREENBACK
3 [C] dollars that are spent on a particular activity
or come from a particular source: *They spent their
research dollars* (= money intended to be spent on
research) *in other areas of the business.* ◇ *competing
for investment dollars*
4 [C] a BANKNOTE or coin worth one dollar: *Do you
have a dollar?* ◇ *a dollar bill*
See note at INCREASE
● *adjective* [only before noun]
having a price or value that is measured in US
dollars: *dollar assets/bonds/debts*

the 'dollar ,area noun [sing.]
(*Economics*) the area of the world where the US
dollar is used as the main currency or where the
currency is linked to the dollar

,dollar-cost 'averaging noun [U]
(*Finance*) in the US, a method of investing money
that involves investing a fixed amount of money
regularly in particular shares, whatever their price

dollarization , **-isation** /,dɒləraɪ'zeɪʃn; AmE
,dɑːlərə-/ noun [U,C]
(*Economics*)
1 the process of a country or group of countries
starting to use the US dollar in addition to or
instead of their national currency: *He has predicted
a dollarization of the Americas.*
2 the process of linking the value of a country's
currency with the value of the US dollar
▶ **'dollarize, -ise** verb [+ obj or no obj]: *Ecuador's
decision to dollarize was taken in January 2000.* ◇ *a
dollarized economy*

domain /də'meɪn; dəʊ-; AmE doʊ-/ noun [C]

SEE ALSO: **public domain, top-level domain**

1 (*IT*) a set of Internet addresses that end with the
same group of letters: *.com is the most popular
domain on the Internet, with over 21 million names.*
◇ *You will need to register a **domain name** (= an
individual Internet address).*
2 an area of knowledge or activity, especially one
that sb is responsible for: *a collection of documents

relating to the domain of banking* ◇ *Sometimes
things outside your domain go wrong.*

★**domestic** /də'mestɪk/ adjective
1 [usually before noun] of or inside a particular
country; not foreign or international: *One carmaker
reported a 13% drop in domestic sales of new
vehicles.* ◇ *They hope the reforms will attract new
investment, both foreign and domestic.* ◇ *They
produce cheap cars for domestic **consumption** (= to
be sold in the country where they are produced).* ◇
a domestic flight/route/service (= to and from places
within a country) **SYN** INTERNAL → HOME adj. (4)
2 [only before noun] used in the home; connected
with the home or family: *domestic appliances*
▶ **domestically** /də'mestɪkli/ adverb: *domestically
produced goods* → GROSS DOMESTIC PRODUCT

dominant /'dɒmɪnənt; AmE 'dɑːm-/ adjective
more important or powerful than other things: *The
firm has established a dominant market position.* ◇
*There are four dominant players in the banking
industry.* ▶ **dominance** /'dɒmɪnəns; AmE 'dɑː-/
noun [U]: *They have lost their market dominance.*

★**dominate** /'dɒmɪneɪt; AmE 'dɑːm-/ verb
1 [+ obj or no obj] to control or have a lot of
influence over sth: *The mobile phone market is
dominated by a handful of very large companies.* ◇ *a
male-dominated industry* (= one in which there are
more men than women and they have more
influence)
2 [+ obj] to be the most important or noticeable
feature of sth: *an economy dominated by oil exports*
▶ **domination** /,dɒmɪ'neɪʃn; AmE ,dɑː-/ noun [U]:
*companies fighting for domination of the software
market* ◇ *economic/political domination*

'domino ef,fect noun [C, usually sing.]
a situation in which one event causes a series of
similar events to happen one after the other:
Employers fear the strike could cause a domino effect
(= that there will be many other strikes as a result).

donate /dəʊ'neɪt; AmE 'doʊneɪt/ verb [+ obj or
no obj]
to give money, equipment, etc. to sb/sth to help
them: *They donate 1% of their sales **to** charity.* ◇ *The
school's computers were donated by IBM.*
▶ **donation** /dəʊ'neɪʃn; AmE doʊ-/ noun [C,U]: *They
made a €50 000 donation **to** charity.*

done /dʌn/ adjective, exclamation
● *adjective*
IDM **a ,done 'deal** (*especially AmE*) a plan, an
agreement or a project that has been completely
arranged and agreed: *The takeover is not yet a done
deal.*
● *exclamation* (*only used in spoken English*)
used to show that you accept an offer: *'I'll give you
$800 for it.' 'Done!'*

,door to 'door adverb
1 (*Marketing*) visiting all the homes or offices in an
area, especially to try to sell sth: *They sell household
goods door to door and through catalogues.*
2 if sth is delivered **door to door**, it is brought
directly from the factory or supplier to the
customer: *We deliver door to door anywhere in
the US.*
▶ **,door-to-'door** adjective [only before noun]: *a
door-to-door salesman/sales force* ◇ *door-to-door
package delivery*

dormant /'dɔːmənt; AmE 'dɔːrm-/ adjective
1 not active or growing now but able to become
active or to grow in the future: *a dormant company*
◇ *Inflation has remained dormant.*
● *to **be/become/lie/remain/sit** dormant*

2 (about a bank account) that has not been used for a long time: *a dormant account*
○ *to be/become/lie/remain/sit dormant*

DOS /dɒs; AmE dɑːs/ *abbr*
(*IT*) **disk operating system** a set of programs that control the way a computer works and runs other programs

dossier /'dɒsieɪ; AmE 'dɔːs-; 'dɑːs-/ *noun* [C]
a collection of documents that contain information about a person, an event or a subject: *He has prepared a dossier on a number of potential partners.* ◇ *a dossier of information* **SYN** FILE
○ *to compile/keep/prepare/publish a dossier*

dot /dɒt; AmE dɑːt/ *noun* [C]

SEE ALSO: **connect-the-dots**

a small symbol (.) that is used to separate different parts of an email or Internet address: *Please email us at enquiry@oup.com.* **NOTE** The email address in this example would be said as 'enquiry at o u p dot com'.
IDM **on the 'dot** (*informal*) exactly on time or at the exact time mentioned: *The cab showed up on the dot.* ◇ *Please tell him I'll call him on the dot of twelve.*
→ idiom at CONNECT

dotcom (*also spelled* **dot-com, dot.com**) /,dɒt 'kɒm; AmE ,dɑːt 'kɑːm/ *noun* [C]
a company that sells goods and services on the Internet, especially one whose address ends '.com': *The weaker dotcoms have collapsed.* ◇ *a dotcom millionaire* ◇ *the bursting of the dotcom bubble* (= when many dotcoms failed)
○ *a dotcom business/company/start-up* • *the dotcom boom/bubble/collapse/crash*

dot 'matrix ˌprinter *noun* [C]
(*IT*) a machine that prints letters, numbers, etc. formed from very small dots

ˌdotted 'line *noun* [C] (*informal*)
a line made of dots, especially the place in a legal agreement where you sign your name → idiom at SIGN *verb*

ˌdouble 'bind *noun* [C, usually sing.]
a situation in which it is difficult to choose what to do because whatever you choose will have negative results

ˌdouble-'blind (*also* ˌdouble-'blinded) *adjective* [usually before noun]
used to describe a type of research that tests the effects of a new product, especially a new medicine. Neither the testers nor the people testing the product know who has received the real product and who has received a substance that does not contain any of it: *a double-blind trial/study* → BLIND TRIAL

ˌdouble-'book *verb* [+ obj] (*often be double-booked*)
to promise the same room, seat, table, etc. to two different people at the same time: *I'm afraid that the room has been double-booked.* → OVERBOOK
▶ ˌdouble-'booking *noun* [C,U]

ˌdouble-'check *verb* [+ obj *or no obj*]
to check sth for a second time or with great care: *I'll double-check the figures.* ▶ ˌdouble-'check *noun* [C]

ˌdouble-'click *verb* [+ obj *or no obj*]
to press one of the buttons on a computer mouse twice quickly in order to open a computer file, program, etc: *Just double-click on the icon to open the file.* ◇ *Double-click the 'My Documents' folder.*
▶ ˌdouble-'click *noun* [C]

ˌdouble-declining 'balance ˌmethod *noun* [sing.]
(*Accounting*) a way of reducing the value of (**depreciating**) an asset in a company's financial records in which the amount taken from the asset's value decreases each year. The value of the asset (its **book value**) is reduced at a fixed rate each year, calculated as the difference between the original value of the asset and its final (**residual**) value, divided by a particular number of years and multiplied by two. → REDUCING BALANCE METHOD, STRAIGHT-LINE METHOD, SUM OF THE DIGITS METHOD

ˌdouble 'digits = DOUBLE FIGURES

ˌdouble 'dip *noun* [C]
a situation where there is a second decrease in prices, the growth of an economy, etc. after a short period of improvement: *The stock market is recovering but the chances of a double dip remain high.* ◇ *a double-dip recession*

ˌdouble-'dip *verb* [no obj] (-**pp**-) (*especially AmE*) (*informal*)
to obtain two incomes, pensions, etc. in an illegal or unfair way; to be paid twice for sth: *He had been double-dipping in that he had claimed a pension while still receiving a salary.* ▶ ˌdouble-'dipper *noun* [C], ˌdouble-'dipping *noun* [U]

ˌdouble-entry 'bookkeeping *noun* [U]
(*Accounting*) the usual way of keeping a company's financial records, in which each amount spent, received, etc. is recorded with a credit in one account and a DEBIT in another. For example, if a company paid €1 000 in cash for a new computer, this amount would be recorded as a credit in the cash account and as a debit in an asset account.

ˌdouble 'figures (*especially BrE*) (*AmE usually* ˌdouble 'digits) *noun* [pl.]
used to describe a number that is not less than 10 and not more than 99: *Inflation is in double figures.*
→ SINGLE FIGURES
▶ ˌdouble-'figure (*especially BrE*) (*AmE usually* ˌdouble-'digit) *adjective* [only before noun]: *a double-figure pay rise*

ˌdouble in'demnity *noun* [U,C] (*AmE*)
(*Insurance*) an arrangement in which an insurance company will pay twice the normal amount in particular circumstances, for example if the person who is insured is injured or dies in an accident: *The policy pays double indemnity for accidental death.* ◇ *a double-indemnity clause/policy*

ˌdouble in'surance *noun* [U,C]
(*Insurance*) a situation in which sb has bought insurance to protect themselves against sth from more than one company

ˌdouble ta'xation *noun* [U]
(*Accounting*)
1 a situation in which sb must pay tax on the same income, etc. to two different governments: *The two countries have signed a treaty for the avoidance of double taxation.* ◇ *a double-taxation agreement* (= between two countries, so that people living in one and earning money in the other avoid paying tax in both)
2 a situation in which the authorities charge tax twice on the same income, etc: *the double taxation of dividends* (= when a government taxes companies for paying dividends and taxes shareholders for receiving them)

ˌdouble 'time *noun* [U]
(*HR*) twice sb's normal pay, that they earn for working at times which are not normal working hours: *We are paid time and a half for extra hours on weekdays and double time for public holidays.*
→ TIME AND A HALF

double-'witching noun [U]
(*Stock Exchange*) a situation where people buy and sell more shares, bonds, etc. than normal on a particular day, because sales of two types of OPTIONS or FUTURES must be completed: *Friday was a double-witching day, with futures and options expiring.* → TRIPLE-WITCHING

doubtful 'debt noun [C]
(*Accounting*) a debt that is not likely to be paid: *a provision against doubtful debts*

dough /dəʊ; AmE doʊ/ noun [U] (*slang*)
money: *They made a pile of dough on the deal.*

Dow 'Jones™ /ˌdaʊ 'dʒəʊnz; AmE 'dʒoʊnz/ noun
1 (*usually* **the Dow Jones™**) (*also* **the Dow™**)
[sing.] used to refer to the Dow Jones Industrial Average: *The Dow Jones slipped below the 10 000 level yesterday.* ◇ *the Dow Jones average/index*
2 [U] a company in the US that publishes measures (**indexes**) of the share prices of important companies. Its most famous measure is the Dow Jones Industrial Average: *the Dow Jones Stoxx Index of shares in European companies* ◇ *Dow Jones Averages™*

the 'Dow 'Jones In'dustrial 'Average noun [sing.] (*abbr* DJIA™)
a measure of the share prices of the 30 most important companies that are traded on the New York Stock Exchange: *By late morning, the Dow Jones Industrial Average was up 57 points to 8 455.*

'Dow 'Jones in'dustrials noun [pl.]
(*Stock Exchange*) the 30 companies whose share prices make up the Dow Jones Industrial Average; the Dow Jones Industrial Average: *The Dow Jones industrials fell to their lowest level in 5 months.* ◇ *The Dow Jones industrials climbed above the 9 000 level.*

down /daʊn/ adverb, verb, adjective
● *adverb* ᴴᴱᴸᴾ For the special uses of **down** in phrasal verbs, look at the entries for the verbs. For example, **break down** is in the phrasal verb section at **break**.

SEE ALSO: **balance carried down, buttoned-~, close-~, completely knocked-~, drop-~, knock-~**, etc.

1 at a lower level or rate: *Prices have gone down recently.* ◇ *Output was down by 20%.*
See note at INCREASE
2 having lost the amount of money mentioned: *At the end of the day we were $200 down.*
3 if you pay an amount of money **down**, you pay that to start with, and the rest later: *You can buy this car with no money down.* ◇ *a cash-down payment*
ᴵᴰᴹ **be down to sth** to have only a little money left: *I'm down to my last dollar.* → idiom at CASH noun
● *verb*
ᴵᴰᴹ **down 'tools** (*BrE*) (about workers) to stop work; to go on strike
● *adjective* [not before noun]
if a computer or a computer system is **down**, it is not working: *The system was down all morning.* → DOWNTIME

downbeat /'daʊnbiːt/ adjective
not feeling much hope about the future: *The group remained downbeat about the outlook for next year.* ◇ *a downbeat assessment of the group's trading prospects* ᴼᴾᴾ UPBEAT

downgrade /ˌdaʊn'ɡreɪd/ verb [+ obj]
1 (*Economics; Finance*) to give sth a lower grade, value or status: *They have now downgraded the group's credit rating* (= the group is now less likely to pay its debts). ◇ *The share price fell after analysts downgraded the stock.* ◇ *The Bank has downgraded its forecast for economic growth.*
2 (*HR*) to give sb a less important job; to make a job less important: *They plan to make six managers*

redundant and downgrade three others. ◇ *Some jobs had gradually been downgraded from skilled to semi-skilled.*
→ DEMOTE
▶ **downgrade** /'daʊnɡreɪd/ noun [C]: *A credit-rating downgrade could increase borrowing costs for the company.* ◇ *a downgrade from AAA to A*
downgrading /ˌdaʊn'ɡreɪdɪŋ/ noun [U,C]
→ UPGRADE

★ **download** verb, noun
(*IT*)
● *verb* /ˌdaʊn'ləʊd; AmE -'loʊd/ [+ obj or no obj]
to move data to a smaller computer system from a larger one; to be moved in this way: *data downloaded from the Internet* ◇ *You can look at one site while another is downloading.* ᴼᴾᴾ UPLOAD
▶ **downloadable** /ˌdaʊn'ləʊdəbl; AmE -'loʊd-/ adjective: *The software is downloadable for free on the Web.*
● *noun* /'daʊnləʊd; AmE -loʊd/
1 [U,C] the act or process of copying data from a larger computer system to a smaller one
2 [C] data copied from a larger computer system to a smaller one: *a popular download from bulletin boards*

downmarket /ˌdaʊn'mɑːkɪt; AmE -'mɑːrk-/ (*AmE also* '**downscale**) adjective [usually before noun]
1 designed for or used by large numbers of customers who have less money; cheap and of poor quality: *a downmarket fashion chain* ◇ *The company is starting to lose its downmarket image.*
○ *a downmarket* **brand/hotel/image/product/store**
2 used to describe people who have less money and cannot afford expensive products and services: *downmarket customers*
▶ ˌ**down'market** (*AmE also* ˌ**down'scale**) adverb: *To get more viewers the TV station will have to move downmarket.* ᴼᴾᴾ UPMARKET

down 'payment noun [C]
(*Commerce*) an amount of money that is given as the first part of a larger payment when you buy sth over a period of time or invest in sth: *saving money for a down payment on a house* ◇ *The company has made a €30 million down payment on developing the new drug.* ˢʸᴺ DEPOSIT → PAY STH DOWN at PAY verb

downscale /'daʊnskeɪl; ˌdaʊn'skeɪl/ verb, adjective (*AmE*)
● *verb* [+ obj]
to reduce the size or extent of sth: *We had to downscale the programme due to lack of funds.*
● *adjective* [usually before noun] = DOWNMARKET

downshift /'daʊnʃɪft/ verb [+ obj or no obj]
1 to change to a job where you may earn less but which puts less pressure on you and involves less stress: *He decided to downshift to spend more time with his family.* ◇ *Since downshifting her career she only works four days a week.*
2 to reduce sth; to become or make sth less active or important: *The union has downshifted its demands.* ◇ *a downshifting economy*
▶ '**downshift** noun [C,U]: *a career downshift* ◇ *the downshift in economic growth* '**downshifter** noun [C] '**downshifting** noun [U]

downside /'daʊnsaɪd/ noun
1 (*Economics; Finance*) [sing; U] the possibility that sth will decrease in price or value: *She claims that there is little downside to the oil price at the moment.* ◇ *The shares carry downside protection.* ◇ *The takeover bid means that there is limited* **downside risk**. ◇ *Analysts warn that these stocks could see a further downside* (= decrease in value).
2 [C] the disadvantages or less positive aspects of sth: *The major downside to the new model is that it*

uses more fuel. ◇ *I enjoy the freedom of working from home.* **On the downside**, *I miss the contact with colleagues.*
OPP UPSIDE

downsize /'daʊnsaɪz/ *verb* [+ obj *or* no obj]
1 (*HR*) to reduce the number of people who work in a company, business, etc. in order to reduce costs: *Several of their smaller offices are being downsized.* ◇ *The company has downsized to eight employees.* ◇ *downsized organizations/workers*
See note at DISMISS
2 (*especially AmE*) to make sth smaller; to produce sth in a smaller size: *downsized cars*
▸'**downsizing** *noun* [U,C]: *the downsizing of the manufacturing division* ◇ *He lost his job in a corporate downsizing.* ◇ *the downsizing of food portions*

downstream /ˌdaʊn'striːm/ *adjective*
(*Economics*; *Production*) at a late stage in an industrial or commercial process: *downstream activities, such as refining* ◇ *They have decided to sell their downstream gas business.* OPP UPSTREAM
● *downstream **assets/businesses/earnings/operations***
▸ˌ**down'stream** *adverb*: *Many manufacturers are moving downstream into retailing.*

downswing /'daʊnswɪŋ/ = DOWNTURN
OPP UPSWING

downtick /'daʊntɪk/ (*also* '**minus tick**) *noun* [C, usually sing.] (*both AmE*)
(*Economics*; *Finance*) a small decrease in the level or value of sth, especially in the price of shares: *a downtick **in** unemployment/the economy* ◇ *stocks bought **on a downtick** (= when their prices have started to decrease)* OPP UPTICK

downtime /'daʊntaɪm/ *noun* [U]
1 (*IT*) the period of time when a machine, especially a computer, is not working and cannot be used: *A high percentage of system downtime is caused by software failure.* ◇ *The downtime resulted in lost production.*
2 (*Production*) a period of time when a factory is not working, for example because a machine needs to be repaired or there is not enough demand for goods: *There is scheduled downtime from 5.00 p.m Friday until 8.00 a.m. Monday.*
3 (*especially AmE*) the time when sb stops working and is able to relax: *Everyone needs a little downtime.*
→ IDLE TIME, UPTIME

downtown /ˌdaʊn'taʊn/ *adverb* (*especially AmE*)
in or towards the centre of a city, especially its main business area: *to go/work downtown*
▸'**downtown** *adjective* [only before noun]: *a downtown hotel* ◇ *Their headquarters are in downtown Toronto.* ◇ *Hong Kong's downtown area*
'**downtown** *noun* [U,C] = CENTRE *noun* (3)

downtrend /'daʊntrend/ *noun* [sing.] (*especially AmE*)
a situation in which business activity or performance decreases over a period of time: *a global downtrend **in** the car market* OPP UPTREND

★**downturn** /'daʊntɜːn/ *AmE* -tɜːrn/ (*also* '**downswing**) *noun* [C, usually sing.]
a time when an economy, industry, etc. is weaker than normal; a fall in the amount of business that is done: *There are signs that the economy is recovering from last year's downturn.* ◇ *We experienced a sharp downturn **in** sales last month.* SYN TURNDOWN
OPP UPTURN → TURN DOWN at TURN *verb*
● *a **dramatic/prolonged/severe/sharp/steep** downturn* ◆ *a **business/global/market** downturn* ◆ *an **economic/industry** downturn*

dowry /'daʊri/ *noun* [C] (*plural* **dowries**) (*figurative*)
(used especially in newspapers) an extra amount of money that a company offers in order to encourage another company to agree to a TAKEOVER (= where one company buys another): *The merger has been consummated (= completed) with a dowry of more than $8 billion.* NOTE When journalists use the word **dowry** in this way they are comparing the process of buying a company to getting married. In some cultures, a wife or her family must give money and/or property (a dowry) to her husband when they get married.

doz. *abbr*
a short way of writing **dozen**: *price: €8 per doz.*

dozen /'dʌzn/ *noun* [C] (*plural* **dozen**)

SEE ALSO: half a dozen

1 (*abbr* **doz.**) a group of twelve of the same thing: *two dozen eggs*
2 a group of approximately twelve people or things: *several dozen/a few dozen people*
→ idiom at DIME

D/P = DOCUMENTS AGAINST PAYMENT

dpi /ˌdiː piː 'aɪ/ *abbr*
(*IT*) **dots per inch** a measure of how clear the images produced by a printer, SCANNER, etc. are: *a 600 dpi laser printer* → RESOLUTION

DPS /ˌdiː piː 'es/ *abbr*
(*Finance, usually in written English*) **dividend per share** the amount of profits (the **dividend**) that a company pays to each shareholder: *a DPS of $2*

DR /ˌdiː 'ɑː(r)/ = DISASTER RECOVERY, OVERDRAWN

★**draft** /drɑːft; *AmE* dræft/ *noun, verb*
● *noun* [C]

SEE ALSO: banker's draft, demand ~, exposure ~, sight ~

1 a rough written version of a document that is not yet in its final form: *the first draft of the report* ◇ *The committee has drawn up a draft action plan.* ◇ *a draft agreement/letter*
● *to **draw up/prepare/produce/write** a draft* ◆ *an **early/the final/latest** draft*
2 (*Finance*) a written order to a bank to pay money to sb: *Please pay by draft or cheque.* ◇ *She presented a draft **on** a bank in New York.* SYN BANK DRAFT
● *verb* [+ obj] (*also spelled* **draught**, *especially in BrE*) to write the first rough version of a document: *to draft a contract* ◇ *I'll draft a letter and show it to you.*
▸'**drafter** (*also spelled* **draughter**, *especially in BrE*) *noun* [C]: *legal drafters*
PHR V ˌ**draft sb 'in**; ˌ**draft sb 'into sth** to choose sb or a group of people and send them somewhere for a special task: *He has been drafted in to try to repair the group's finances.*

drag /dræg/ *verb, noun*
● *verb* (-gg-)
1 [+ obj] to move some text, an ICON, etc. across the screen of a computer using the mouse: *Click on the file and drag it across.* ◇ *You can **drag and drop** text between the two windows (= move it from one window and put it in the other).* → DROP *verb* (4)
2 [+ obj *or* no obj] (*used with an adverb or a preposition*) to make an economy, a market, etc. decrease in size or grow more slowly; to bring sth to a lower level: *Low consumer demand is dragging the economy down.* ◇ *Poor sales dragged the firm to a loss of $659 million.*
3 [+ obj] (*used with an adverb or a preposition*) to use a lot of effort to make sb/sth go in a particular direction: *The store is offering big discounts to drag shoppers in.* ◇ *These policies are aimed at dragging the country out of recession.*

SEE ALSO: **fiscal drag**

something that causes an economy, a market, etc. to decrease in size or value or to grow more slowly: *Rising oil prices are a potential drag **on** growth.*

drain /dreɪn/ *noun, verb*
● *noun* [sing.]

SEE ALSO: **brain drain**

1 a thing that uses a lot of the time, money, etc. that could be used for sth else: *The training programme proved to be a huge drain **on** the company's resources.* ◇ *Our Canadian operations have become a **cash drain**.*
2 a process by which people with important skills, etc. leave an organization or a place in order to work somewhere else: *There has been a drain of top talent from the company.*
→ idiom at MONEY
● *verb*
1 [+ obj] to make sth/sb poorer, weaker, etc. by gradually using up their money, supplies, strength, etc: *Going into new markets has drained our resources.* ◇ *The fund has become drained **of** capital.* ◇ *They accuse the government of draining skilled workers **from** poorer countries.* ◇ *Her work has left her physically and emotionally drained.*
2 [no obj] (about money, supplies, strength, etc.) to gradually disappear: *The firm's cash started to drain away.*

draught ,**'draughter** = DRAFT *verb*

draw /drɔː/ *verb, noun*
● *verb* [+ obj] (**drew** /druː/ **drawn** /drɔːn/)
1 (*Finance*) **draw sth out (of sth)** | **draw sth from sth** to take money from a bank account: *He's gone to the bank to draw out some money.* ◇ *to draw $500 from/out of an account* ◇ *You can use your credit card to draw cash from an ATM.* [SYN] WITHDRAW
2 (*Finance*) (*often* **be drawn**) to write out a cheque or BILL OF EXCHANGE: *Please draw cheques **in** favour of 'Highland Glassware'.* ◇ *The cheque was drawn on his personal account.*
3 to receive a regular income or a pension: *He draws a €40 000 salary.* ◇ *The number of people drawing a pension has increased.*
4 (*Finance*) = DRAW STH DOWN (FROM STH), DRAW DOWN ON STH
[PHR V] **draw sth 'down; draw 'down** (*especially AmE*) to reduce a supply of sth that has been created over a period of time; to be reduced: *There are many life events that can unexpectedly draw down savings.* ◇ *If we don't cut costs, our reserves will draw down.* → DRAWDOWN (1), DRAW ON/UPON STH
draw sth 'down (from sth); **draw 'down on sth** (*especially AmE*) (*BrE usually* **draw**) (*Finance*) to take money from a fund that a bank, etc. has made available: *The company has already drawn down €600 million of its €725 million credit line.* ◇ *They can draw down on the loan at any time.*
→ DRAWDOWN (2) **'draw sth from sth** to get sth from a particular source: *The country draws most of its revenue from exports.* **'draw on/upon sth** to start using a supply of sth that has been created over a period of time: *Countries may be forced to draw on their oil reserves.* ◇ *I'll have to draw on my savings.* → DRAW STH DOWN, DRAW DOWN ,**draw sth 'out** (*Finance*) = DRAW (1) ,**draw sth 'up** to make or write sth that needs careful thought or planning: *to draw up a plan/list/contract*
● *noun* [C]
1 a person, a thing or an event that attracts a lot of people: *Picture messaging on cellphones will be a big draw for consumers.*
2 [usually sing.] (*especially AmE*) the act of using part of a supply that has been created over a period of time, especially a supply of oil or gas; the amount

that is used: *Increased use of oil by refineries accounted for some, but not all, of the **stock draw**.*

drawback /'drɔːbæk/ *noun*
1 [C] a disadvantage or problem that makes sth a less attractive idea: *The main drawback **to** the plan is the cost.* ◇ *This is the one major drawback of the new system.*
2 (*Trade*) [U,C] (*AmE*) = DUTY DRAWBACK

drawdown /'drɔːdaʊn/ *noun* [C,U]
1 the act of reducing a supply of sth that has been created over a period of time; the amount used: *The cold winter has led to a larger-than-expected drawdown on oil stocks.*
2 (*Finance*) the act of using money that is available to you; the amount used : *a drawdown of cash from the company's reserves* ◇ *The interest rate is fixed at drawdown.*

drawee /ˌdrɔːˈiː/ *noun* [C]
(*Finance*)
1 (*also* ,**drawee 'bank**) the bank of the person or organization that has written a cheque, which is therefore asked to pay the amount written on it to the person named: *The cheque was dishonoured* (= not paid) *by the drawee* (*bank*) *because there were insufficient funds in the account.* → DRAWER, PAYEE
2 the bank or company that agrees to pay the amount written on a BILL OF EXCHANGE

drawer /'drɔːə(r)/ *noun* [C]

SEE ALSO: **refer to drawer**

(*Finance*) a person who writes a cheque or BILL OF EXCHANGE that asks for a payment to be made to sb: *Any correction on the cheque must be signed in full by the drawer.* ◇ *the drawer of a bill* → DRAWEE

'drawing ac,count *noun* [C] (*AmE*)
1 (*Accounting*) an account in which the money that the owners of a company take for their personal use is recorded
2 a company account that a company's SALESPEOPLE can use when they are spending money doing their job

drayage /'dreɪɪdʒ/ *noun* [U] (*AmE*)
(*Transport*) the process of moving goods a short distance by lorry/truck; the charge made for this: *For exhibitors requiring drayage, please ensure that all boxes are packed and ready.*

dress /dres/ *noun, verb*
● *noun* [U]
clothes for men or women: *We have a policy of casual dress in the office.* ◇ *formal business dress*
● *verb*
[PHR V] ,**dress 'down** (*often used as an adjective*) to wear clothes that are more informal than those you usually wear: *Staff are allowed to dress down on Fridays.* ◇ *The company has a **dress-down Friday**.*

'dress code *noun* [C]
a set of rules that an organization has about what people must or must not wear: *The company has an informal dress code.*

drift /drɪft/ *verb, noun*
● *verb* [no obj]
(about a share price, figure, etc.) to change slowly, especially to a lower level and in a way that does not seem to be controlled: *The Nikkei average drifted lower yesterday.* ◇ *Inflation rates have drifted below 2 per cent.*
● *to drift **higher/lower*** • *to drift **above/below** sth* • *to drift **down/up** (by sth)*
● *noun* [sing; U]

SEE ALSO: **wage drift**

a gradual change or development from one

situation to another, especially to sth bad; a slow, steady movement from one place to another: *a downward period of drift* in *inflation* ◇ *a long period of drift or decline in the markets* ◇ *a drift* **to** *the cities*

drill /drɪl/ *verb* [+ obj *or no obj*]
to make a deep hole in the ground using a machine, in order to look for valuable natural substances, especially oil or gas: *They're drilling* **for** *oil off the Irish coast.* ▶**drilling** *noun* [U]
PHRV ,drill 'down *(IT)* to go to deeper and deeper levels of an organized set of data on a computer or a website in order to find more and more detail: *You can view orders by customer and date and then drill down to view individual order details, invoices and payments.*

DRIP /drɪp; ,di: ɑːr aɪ 'piː/ = DIVIDEND REINVESTMENT PLAN

'drip ,advertising *noun* [U]
(Marketing) a continuous small amount of advertising for a product over a long period of time

'drip ,marketing *noun* [U]
(Marketing) the activity of trying to sell products to customers by contacting them often over a long period of time: *an email drip marketing campaign* → DRIP ADVERTISING

drive /draɪv/ *verb, noun*
● *verb* [+ obj] (**drove** /drəʊv; *AmE* droʊv/ **driven** /'drɪvn/)
1 *(often* **be driven***)* to cause sth; to be the main influence on sth: *Our products are driven by customers' needs.* → -DRIVEN (1)
2 drive sth (forward) to make sth grow stronger, develop or progress: *Exports have helped to drive economic growth.* ◇ *Profits rose 38 per cent, driven by strong sales in Asia.*
3 *(used with an adverb or a preposition)* to force a price, figure, etc. to go up or down or move to a particular level: *The conflict is driving oil prices higher.* ◇ *Management is under pressure to drive down costs.*
4 to force sb to act in a particular way: *Fears about unemployment drove consumers to cut back on spending.* ◇ *You're driving yourself too hard* (= you're making yourself work too much).
IDM be in the 'driving seat *(also* be in the 'driver's seat*)* to be the person in control of a situation: *The workshop will put you firmly in the driving seat of change in your company.* → idioms at GROUND *noun,* HARD *adj.*
PHRV ,drive sb/sth 'out (of sth) to make sb/sth disappear or stop doing sth: *The supermarkets are driving small shopkeepers out of business.*
● *noun* [C]
SEE ALSO: **disk drive, economy ~, flash ~, hard ~, sales ~, tape ~, test ~**

1 an organized effort by a group of people to achieve sth: *They cut their staff by 400 in a drive* **to** *reduce costs.* ◇ *a drive* **for** *greater efficiency*
● *a cost-cutting/marketing/recruitment* drive
2 *(IT)* the part of a computer that reads and stores information on disks or tapes: *a CD-ROM drive* ◇ *a DVD drive*

'drive-in *noun* [C]
a place where you can buy food or other goods, watch films/movies, etc. without leaving your car: *We stopped at a drive-in for a hamburger.* ◇ *a drive-in bank*

★-driven /'drɪvn/ *combining form (used to form adjectives)*
1 influenced or caused by a particular thing or person: *a customer-driven approach to marketing* ◇ *a results-driven sales team* ◇ *15% of car sales will be*

Internet-driven by 2005. → DRIVE (1)
2 *(about machines, computer systems, etc.)* operated, moved or controlled by a particular thing: *a petrol-driven engine*

driver /'draɪvə(r)/ *noun* [C]
1 a person who drives a vehicle: *a bus/cab/truck driver* ◇ *High-risk drivers pay more in insurance premiums.*
2 an important influence on sth, especially sth that makes it grow, develop or progress: *Consumer spending has been one of the main drivers of economic growth.* ◇ *Technology is a key business driver.*
3 *(IT)* software that controls the sending of data between a computer and a piece of equipment that is attached to it such as a printer
IDM be in the 'driver's seat = BE IN THE DRIVING SEAT at DRIVE *verb*

'drive-through *(AmE spelling also* -thru, *informal) noun* [C] *(especially AmE)*
a restaurant, bank, etc. where you can be served without leaving your car: *The drive-through is open 24 hours a day.* ◇ *The bank has a drive-through window.*

'drive time *noun* [U]
(Marketing) a time during the day when many people are driving their cars, for example to or from work, considered to be a good time to put an advertisement on the radio ▶'drive-time *adjective*: *an ad on a drive-time radio show*

'drive-up *noun* [C] *(especially AmE)*
a place at a bank, restaurant, etc. where you can be served without leaving your car

'driving force *noun* [C]
a person or an event with a very strong influence on sth and that causes a big change: *New flavours are a driving force in the soft-drinks trade.* ◇ *Who was the driving force* **behind** *the company's growth?*

DRM /,di: ɑːr 'em/ *abbr*
(E-commerce) **digital rights management** actions and devices that are designed to prevent people from illegally copying software or other electronic material from the Internet: *The songs you purchased are DRM protected.*

drop /drɒp; *AmE* drɑːp/ *verb, noun*
● *verb* (-pp-)
1 [+ obj *or no obj*] to become or make sth weaker, lower or less: *The price of the shares dropped by 14¢.* ◇ *The shares dropped* **in price** *by 14¢.* ◇ *Inflation dropped 0.5 per cent in November.* ◇ *He had to drop his price by $300.*
● *to drop* **dramatically/sharply/slightly/steeply**
2 [+ obj] to not continue with sth; to stop using sb/sth: *They have dropped their plans to build a new factory.* ◇ *Dropping that supplier was a good decision.*
3 [+ obj] to lose money: *I dropped $3 000 in salary when I changed jobs.*
4 [+ obj] to place text, a file, etc. in a particular place on a computer screen by using the mouse button: *Drag the file and drop it in the recycling bin.* → DRAG *verb* (1)
IDM ,drop the 'ball (on sth) *(AmE) (informal)* to be responsible for sth going wrong or for doing sth badly; to stop taking responsibility for sth: *I want to know who dropped the ball on this project.* → idiom at BOTTOM
PHRV ,drop a'way = DROP OFF ,drop 'back (to sth) to return to a lower level or amount: *The price of gold dropped back to $378 an ounce.* ,drop 'off *(BrE) (also* ,drop a'way, *AmE, BrE)* to decrease in level or amount, especially after being high for a long time: *Consumer spending dropped off sharply in February.* → DROP-OFF ,drop 'out (of sth) to no

longer take part in or be part of sth: *Some investors want to drop out of the deal.*
• *noun* [C, usually sing.]

SEE ALSO: leaflet drop

a fall or reduction in the amount, level or number of sth: *The airline has seen a steep drop in ticket sales.* ◊ *Manufacturing activity showed a drop of 1.2%. in July.* ◊ *a 15% drop in profits*
O *a big/dramatic/large/sharp/slight/steep drop* • *to expect/forecast/report/suffer a drop (in sth)*

'drop box *noun* [C] (*especially AmE*)
a box in which you can safely leave sth for sb to collect later, such as a payment, the keys of a car, etc: *Payments made by cheque can be deposited in the drop box.*

,drop-'dead date *noun* [C] (*AmE*) (*informal*)
a final date by which sth must be done, especially one fixed in a contract or by someone in authority: *We got the job done two hours before the drop-dead date.* → DEADLINE

'drop-down (*also* **'pull-down**) *adjective* [only before noun]
(*IT*) used to describe a list of choices that appears on a computer screen below the place where you click: *Choose the 'New picture' option from the drop-down menu.* → POP-UP *adj.*

'drop-off *noun*
1 [C, usually sing., U] a decrease in the level or amount of sth, especially after being high for a long time: *The industry has seen a sharp drop-off in sales.* ◊ *We are expecting some drop-off in demand.* → DROP OFF at DROP *verb*
O *a massive/sharp/slight/steep drop-off*
2 [C] the act of delivering sth/sb to a particular place; the place where sb/sth is delivered or the thing or person that is delivered: *They've increased the size of the trucks and the number of drop-offs that drivers have to make.*
→ PICKUP

'drop ,shipment *noun*
(*Commerce*; *Transport*)
1 [U] = DROP SHIPPING
2 [C] an amount of goods that is advertised and sold by a business but is delivered directly from the producer to the customer: *There is an additional charge for each drop shipment.*

'drop ,shipping (*also* **'drop ,shipment**, *less frequent*) *noun* [U]
(*Commerce*; *Transport*) an arrangement in which a business advertises and sells goods, but they are delivered directly from the producer to the customer: *We offer drop shipping at an additional charge.* ▶ **'drop-ship** *verb* [+ obj *or no obj*] (**-pp-**): *We can drop-ship at any location in the US and Canada.*

drug /drʌg/ *noun* [C]
1 a substance used as a medicine or used in a medicine: *They are the world's largest **drug company**.* ◊ *a **blockbuster** drug* (= one that sells very well) ◊ *sales of prescription drugs* (= drugs you can only buy with a written order from a doctor)
→ COPYCAT, DRUGMAKER
2 an illegal substance that people use to give them pleasant or exciting feelings: *Drugs have been seized with a street value of two million dollars.*

drugmaker (*also spelled* **drug maker**) /'drʌgmeɪkə(r)/ *noun* [C]
a company that manufactures medicines

drugstore /'drʌgstɔː(r)/ *noun* [C] (*AmE*)
a shop/store that sells medicines and also other types of goods, for example COSMETICS

drum /drʌm/ *noun*, *verb*
• *noun* [C]
a tall metal or plastic container with round ends

that is used for oil or chemicals: *an oil drum* ◊ *a 50-gallon drum* → BARREL—Picture at TRANSPORT
• *verb* (**-mm-**)
PHR V **,drum sth 'up** to try hard to get support or business: *They are running promotions to try to drum up support for the product.*
O *to drum up business/interest/support*

,drum-'buffer-rope *adjective* [only before noun] (*abbr* **DBR**)
(*Production*) using a method of planning a production process which makes sure that there is always an efficient flow of work by considering possible problems and delays
O *a drum-buffer-rope system/technique/model* • *drum-buffer-rope production management/scheduling*

dry /draɪ/ *verb* (**dries, drying, dried, dried**)
PHR V **,dry 'up** if a supply of sth **dries up**, there is gradually less of it until there is none left: *Their sources of finance are drying up.* ◊ *Manufacturers have suffered as orders have dried up.*

,dry 'cargo *noun* [U]
(*Transport*) goods that are not liquid that are transported on ships, especially goods that are transported in large quantities, such as coal, wood, metals, etc: *The port handles both containerized and dry cargo.* ◊ *a dry-cargo vessel/ship*

'dry goods *noun* [pl.]
1 (*Trade*) (*also* **'dry com,modities**) goods such as coffee, sugar, cloth, etc. that are not liquid and must be kept in dry conditions → WET GOODS
2 (*Commerce*) (*AmE*) goods such as cloth and things that are made out of cloth, materials for sewing, etc. → SOFT GOODS

'dry lease *noun* [U,C]
an arrangement that allows a company to use another company's aircraft, but not people to fly them, for a period of time

'dry spell *noun* [C]
(*Stock Exchange*) a time when there is little buying or selling or business activity: *a two-month dry spell in the IPO market*

DSL /,di: es 'el/ *abbr*
(*IT*) **digital subscriber line** a telephone line which can carry data, for television, video and Internet access, at high speed → ADSL

DSR /,di: es 'ɑː(r)/ = DEBT SERVICE RATIO

DSS /,di: es 'es/ = DECISION SUPPORT SYSTEM

DTC /,di: ti: 'si:/ = DIRECT-TO-CONSUMER

DTI /,di: ti: 'aɪ/ = DEPARTMENT OF TRADE AND INDUSTRY

DTP /,di: ti: 'pi:/ = DESKTOP PUBLISHING

dual /'djuːəl; *AmE* 'duːəl/ *adjective* [only before noun]
having two parts or aspects: *She has taken on the dual role of chairman and chief executive.* ◊ *The rooms serve a dual purpose as offices and main meeting rooms.*

,dual ca'reer *noun* [C, usually pl., U]
1 the situation when a husband and wife or other couple both have careers: *couples trying to manage dual careers and children's activities* ◊ *dual-career families/couples*
2 the situation when one person has two careers

,dual 'currency *noun* [C,U]
(*Economics*) when two valid currencies are used for accounts, trading, etc: *a dual currency system in which sterling and the euro operate alongside each other*

dual e'conomy noun [C]
(*Economics*) an economy that has two clearly different parts: *We have the problems of managing a dual economy, where manufacturing output is at record lows but the service sector output was up almost 4.5 per cent last year.*

dual-listed 'company noun [C] (*abbr* **DLC**)
(*Stock Exchange*) a business that is made of two companies whose shares are traded on stock exchanges in different countries: *The dual-listed company will be traded in London and New York.*

dual 'listing noun [C]
(*Stock Exchange*) a situation in which a company sells its shares on two different stock exchanges; the shares that are sold in this way: *The company is seeking a dual listing in London and Dublin.* ▶ **dual-'listed** adjective: *dual-listed stocks*

dual 'pricing noun [U]
1 (*Economics*) the act of selling the same goods or services for different prices in different markets: *Dual pricing sets different prices for domestic markets and export markets.*
2 (*Finance*) when there is one price for people who are selling sth, such as shares, and a different, higher one for people who are buying: *Unit Trusts often operate a dual-pricing system.*
3 (*Commerce*) when prices are given in two different currencies: *Retailers were told to stop using dual pricing—in euros and pounds.*

dual-'purpose adjective
that can be used for two different purposes: *a dual-purpose vehicle* (= for carrying passengers or goods)

dual 'sourcing noun [U]
(*Production*) when a company, especially a manufacturer, buys its supplies of a particular product from two different suppliers: *A strategy of dual-sourcing can be expensive, but there is less risk of having a shortage of materials.* ▶ **dual-'source** verb [+ obj or no obj]

dud /dʌd/ noun [C]
a thing that is useless, especially because it does not work correctly or provide any benefit: *What we thought was a good investment turned out to be a dud.* ▶ **dud** adjective [only before noun]: *a dud cheque* (= written by sb who has not enough money in their bank account)

due /djuː; AmE duː/ adjective

SEE ALSO: **past due**

1 [not usually before noun] (about a payment or debt) that must be paid immediately or at the time mentioned: *Payment is due on 1 October.* ◇ *The company has $9 billion in debt coming due this year.* ◇ *If you miss a repayment the full amount of the loan becomes due and payable.*
○ *a payment, etc.* **becomes/comes/falls/is** due
2 [not before noun] arranged or expected: *The committee is due to meet on Tuesday.* ◇ *The pipeline is due for completion in January 2006.*
3 [not before noun] owed sth; deserving sth: *I'm still due 15 days' leave.* ◇ *She's due for promotion soon.*
→ **DUES**
IDM **in ,due 'course** at the right time and not before: *Your request will be dealt with in due course.*
in ,due 'form (*Law*) in the legally correct way: *Applications for funding must be submitted in writing in due form.*

'due bill noun [C] (AmE)
a document that shows what sb owes **SYN** IOU

'due date noun [C, usually sing.]
the date on or by which sth, especially an amount

of money, is owed or expected: *If payment is not made by the due date, 10% will be added to the bill.*

due 'diligence noun
1 [U] the process of taking great care in doing sth or deciding sth, especially in buying or selling sth: *We try to exercise due diligence in selecting employees.* ◇ *She believes brokers are not doing enough due diligence on investment funds.*
○ *to act with/conduct/do/exercise/undertake due diligence*
2 (*Law*) [U,C] a process in which sb examines the financial records, documents, etc. of a business in order to decide whether they want to buy it and how much money to offer: *The deal is subject to due diligence.* ◇ *An exact sale price will be set after a due diligence is completed in May.* ◇ *doing due diligence on a company*
○ *to carry out/complete/conduct/do/undertake (a) due diligence (on sth)* • *a due diligence exercise/procedure/process*

dues /djuːz; AmE duːz/ noun [pl.]
1 money that you pay regularly to belong to an organization, especially a union: *paying union dues*
2 (*Commerce*; *Production*) orders accepted for goods that cannot be supplied immediately: *When the new stock arrives all dues will be given priority.*
3 (*Transport*) money that the owner of a ship pays for using a port: *Dock dues are charged for each ton of cargo shipped.*

dummy /ˈdʌmi/ noun, adjective
● noun [C] (plural **dummies**)
1 a thing that seems to be real but is only a copy of the real thing: *The bottles of perfume on display are all dummies.* → MOCK-UP
2 a model of a person, used especially when making clothes or for showing them in a shop window: *clothes displayed on dummies*
● adjective [only before noun]
1 made to look real, or used instead of sth real: *a dummy edition of the newspaper* ◇ *I put dummy numbers in the spreadsheet when I didn't know the real figures.*
2 created to deceive people, especially about where money came from or who it was paid to: *He set up a dummy company through which stolen funds were passed.*

dump /dʌmp/ verb [+ obj]
1 to get rid of sth you do not want, especially in a place which is not suitable: *Too much toxic waste is being dumped at sea.* ◇ *dumped cars/PCs*
2 to sell sth that is not worth keeping, especially in large quantities and at low prices: *Worried investors dumped 8 million shares in the company at just 40¢ each.*
3 (*Economics*) to sell your goods in another country at very low prices, with the result that local companies cannot compete fairly: *They claim the company is dumping fish in the US at below fair prices.*
4 to get rid of sb/sth that is no longer useful or helpful: *They have dumped the firm as their auditors.* ◇ *They dumped the 'BakeMax' name in favour of 'Jo's Bakery Supplies'.*
→ DUMPING

'dump bin (BrE) (also **dis'play bin**, AmE, BrE) noun [C]
(*Marketing*) a container like a box in a shop/store for displaying goods, especially goods whose prices have been reduced—Picture at STORE

dumping /ˈdʌmpɪŋ/ noun [U]

SEE ALSO: **anti-dumping**

1 (*Economics*) the practice of selling large amounts of goods in a particular country at prices that are unfairly low: *They claim the dumping of steel below the cost of production is harming the domestic industry.*

2 the act of getting rid of sth you do not want, especially dangerous substances: *a ban on the dumping of radioactive waste at sea*

'dumping ground *noun* [C, usually sing.]
a place where sth that is not wanted is **dumped**: (*figurative*) *Auction houses are being used as a dumping ground for used or out-of-date PCs.*

Dumpster™ /'dʌmpstə(r)/ = SKIP—Picture at TRANSPORT

'DUNS™ ,number /dʌnz/ *abbr* **Data Universal Numbering System number** a unique number given to a business by D&B™, (an organization that supplies financial information about companies), that is used to identify an individual business

duopoly /dju:'ɒpəli; *AmE* du:'ɑ:-/ *noun* [C] (*plural* **duopolies**)
(*Economics*) a situation in which an industry is controlled by two companies; the two companies themselves: *The two companies have a duopoly in the heavy aircraft market.* ◇ *The business is one half of a duopoly.* → MONOPOLY

★**duplicate** *verb, adjective, noun*
●*verb* /'dju:plɪkeɪt; *AmE* 'du:-/ [+ obj]
1 (*often* **be duplicated**) to make an exact copy of sth: *a duplicated form/letter*
2 to do sth again, especially when it is unnecessary: *The two departments are duplicating each other's efforts.*
  ▶ **duplication** /,dju:plɪ'keɪʃn; *AmE* ,du:-/ *noun* [U,C]
●*adjective* /'dju:plɪkət; *AmE* 'du:-/ [only before noun]
exactly like sth else; made as a copy of sth else: *Make sure you keep a duplicate copy of the letter.* ◇ *a duplicate invoice*
●*noun* /'dju:plɪkət; *AmE* 'du:-/ [C]
one of two or more things that are the same in every detail: *Is this a duplicate or the original?*
SYN COPY
IDM **in duplicate** (about documents, etc.) as two copies that are exactly the same in every detail: *The form must be completed in duplicate.* → TRIPLICATE

durable /'djʊərəbl; *AmE* 'dʊr-/ *adjective*
SEE ALSO: **consumer durables, consumer non-~, semi-~**
likely to last for a long time without breaking or getting weaker: *durable plastics/fabrics* ◇ *He claims their software is more durable and reliable.* ◇ *creating a durable economy* OPP NON-DURABLE
  ▶ **durability** /,djʊərə'bɪləti; *AmE* ,dʊr-/ *noun* [U]: *She doubts the durability of the economic recovery.*

'durable goods (*also* **'hard goods**) = CONSUMER DURABLES

durables /'djʊərəblz; *AmE* 'dʊr-/ = CONSUMER DURABLES

duress /dju'res; *AmE* du-/ *noun* [U]
(*Law*) threats or force that are used to make sb do sth: *She claims the payment was made **under** duress.*

,Dutch 'auction *noun* [C]
1 (*Commerce*) a type of **auction** in which the price of the item being sold is gradually reduced until sb offers to buy it
2 (*Commerce*) (*also* **,uniform 'price ,auction**) a way of selling a number of similar items in which people offer to buy a particular number at a particular price. The seller accepts as many of the highest offers as are needed to sell all the items and the selling price is set at the price of the lowest successful offer: *The company is selling $1.5 million of bills in a Dutch auction.* ◇ *He believes a Dutch auction achieves fairer results than a traditional IPO.*
3 (*Finance*) in the US, a method by which a company can buy back shares from its shareholders. Shareholders offer to sell a particular number of shares to the company at a particular price, which they choose from a range of prices

that the company sets. The company then accepts as many of the highest offers as are needed to reach the number of shares it wants to sell. The buying price is set at the price of the lowest successful offer.

dutiable /'dju:tiəbl; *AmE* 'du:-/ *adjective*
(*Trade*) (about goods brought into a country) on which tax (**import duty**) must be paid: *dutiable goods/imports* ◇ *If the parcel contains items that are dutiable you must complete a customs form.*

★**duty** /'dju:ti; *AmE* 'du:ti/ *noun* (*plural* **duties**)
SEE ALSO: **countervailing duty, customs ~, death ~, discriminating ~, heavy-~, import ~, light-~**, etc.
1 (*Economics; Trade*) [C,U] a tax that you pay on things that you buy, especially those that you bring into a country: *They have put higher duties on steel imports.* ◇ *$500 m was paid to the government in duty.* ◇ *There is no increase in the duty on fuel.*
2 [U] the work that is your job: *Report for duty at 8 a.m.* ◇ *I'm on night duty this week.*
3 **duties** [pl.] tasks that are part of your job: *Your duties will include setting up a new computer system.*

'duty diffe,rential *noun* [C]
(*Economics*)
1 a difference in the rate of tax that is charged on two similar types of imported goods or materials: *There is a huge duty differential between crude (65%) and refined oils (92.5%).*
2 a difference in the rate of tax that one country charges on particular imported goods compared to another country: *The duty differential between the UK and France has led to smuggling of alcohol and cigarettes.*

,duty 'drawback (*AmE also* **'drawback**) *noun* [U,C]
(*Trade*) all or part of a tax paid on imported goods that is paid back when the goods are exported again or used to make new goods for export: *Exporters can now claim duty drawback on locally purchased raw materials.*

,duty-'free *adjective, noun*
●*adjective*
(*Trade*) used to describe goods that can be brought or sent into a country without paying tax on them: *duty-free cigarettes/alcohol* (= bought at an airport, etc.) ◇ *Under the scheme, imports of farm products from the area will be made duty-free.* ◇ *Duty-free exports to the US grew by 83%.* ▶ **,duty-'free** *adverb*: *They can sell some goods into the US market duty-free.*
●*noun* (*plural* **duty-frees**) (*informal*)
1 [U; pl.] (*BrE*) goods that can be brought into a country without paying tax on them: *We bought a load of duty-frees at the airport.*
2 [C] = DUTY-FREE SHOP

,duty-'free shop (*also* **,duty-'free**) *noun* [C]
a shop/store in an airport or on a ship, etc. that sells goods such as cigarettes, alcohol, jewellery, etc. without tax on them

,duty-'paid *adjective* [usually before noun]
(*Trade*) used to describe goods being imported on which taxes have been paid: *There are no limits on the import of duty-paid goods, if they are for personal use.*

DVD /,di: vi: 'di:/ *noun* [C]
a disk on which large amounts of information, especially photographs and video, can be stored, for use on a computer or **DVD-player**: *a DVD-ROM drive* NOTE **DVD** is short for 'digital videodisc' or 'digital versatile disc'.

'dwell time *noun* [U,C]

1 (*Marketing*) the amount of time that people spend at a shop/store, website, etc. or looking at sth such as a piece of advertising: *The site gets over 10 000 visitors a month and the average dwell time is 12 minutes.* ◇ *Dwell time at the tills is longer than in the aisles.*

2 (*Production*) the amount of time that sth spends in a particular stage of a process

dwindle /'dwɪndl/ *verb* [no obj]

to become gradually less or smaller: *dwindling audiences/profits/supplies* ◇ *Jobs in the clothing industry have dwindled from about 500 000 to 175 000.*

dwt *abbr*

(*Transport*) a short way of writing **deadweight** or

deadweight tonnes/tonnage: *14 vessels were over 175 000 dwt.*

dynamic /daɪ'næmɪk/ *adjective, noun*

● *adjective*

1 always changing; always adapting to new circumstances and making progress: *It's difficult to set prices in such a dynamic market.* OPP STATIC

2 having a lot of energy and a strong personality: *a dynamic boss*

● *noun*

1 dynamics [pl.] the way in which people or things behave and react to each other in a particular situation: *group dynamics* (= the way in which members of a group react to each other) ◇ *Market dynamics are working in the company's favour.*

2 [sing.] a force that produces change, action or effects: *a changing dynamic in the communications industry*

E e

★ **e-** /iː/ *combining form* (*used to form nouns and verbs*)

1 connected with the use of electronic communication, especially the Internet, for sending information, doing business, etc: *e-banking* ◇ *e-marketing* ◇ *an e-poll* ◇ *Last year our e-sales totalled $91 billion.*

2 stored in electronic form on a disk, MICROCHIP, etc: *an e-book/e-document* ◇ *e-money*

ea. *abbr*

a short way of writing **each**, used especially when giving prices: *T-shirts €20 ea.*

Eagle /'iːgl/ (*also* A,merican 'Eagle) *noun* [C]

in the US, a coin made from gold, silver or PLATINUM that you can buy as an investment: *Statistics from the US Mint indicate strong sales of Silver Eagles.* ◇ *an American Eagle gold coin*

EAI /,iː eɪ 'aɪ/ = ENTERPRISE APPLICATION INTEGRATION

E&OE *abbr*

(*Commerce*) **errors and omissions excepted** written in a document, for example a list of prices, to show that the writer is not responsible for any mistakes it contains, nor for leaving out any information: *All prices are correct as of today's date, E&OE.*

EAP /,iː eɪ 'piː/ = EMPLOYEE ASSISTANCE PROGRAMME, EMPLOYMENT ASSISTANCE PROGRAMME

EAR /,iː eɪ 'ɑː(r)/ *abbr*

(*Finance*) **effective annual rate** the amount of interest paid in one year for borrowing money compared with the amount of money borrowed, used when interest is normally paid more often than once a year; the amount of interest received from money invested: *Interest is charged at an EAR of 10%.* → APR

early /'ɜːli; *AmE* 'ɜːrli/ *adjective* (**earlier**, **earliest**)

IDM **at your earliest con'venience** (*only used in written English*) as soon as possible: *Please telephone at your earliest convenience.*

,**early a'dopter** *noun* [C]

(*Marketing*) a person or an organization that starts using a new product, especially a new piece of technology, as soon as it becomes available: *The company was an early adopter of the new technology.*

,**early ma'jority** *noun* [sing.]

1 (*Marketing*) the group of customers who will start to use a new product once some people (**early adopters**) have tried it and shown it is successful, but before many other people use it

2 (*HR*) the people in an organization who start to use a new method, process or system after some people in the organization have tested it, but before many others

→ LATE MAJORITY

,**early re'tirement** *noun* [U]

(*HR*) the act of stopping work before the usual age: *The chief executive took early retirement for health reasons.*

'early-stage *adjective* [only before noun]

used to describe sth that is being developed or that began not very long before: *Several early-stage products have been dropped.* ◇ *investing in small, early-stage companies*

,**early-stage 'financing** *noun* [U]

(*Finance*) the first stages of investment in a young company, including START-UP investment, SEED money and FIRST-ROUND FINANCING

earmark /'ɪəmɑːk; *AmE* 'ɪrmɑːrk/ *verb* [+ obj] (*usually* **be earmarked**)

to decide that sth will be used for a particular purpose; to state that sth will happen to sb/sth in the future: *The factory has been earmarked for closure.* ◇ *They earmarked €8 million of their budget for new stores.* ◇ *He has been earmarked to take over as president.*

★ **earn** /ɜːn; *AmE* ɜːrn/ *verb*

1 [+ obj *or no obj*] to get money for work that you do: *She earned about €40 000 last year in pay and bonuses.* ◇ *You will earn a basic salary of $2 000 a month.* ◇ *He earns a living from selling second-hand books.* ◇ *She must earn a fortune* (= earn a lot of money)! ◇ *I only have to pay back the loan when I start earning.*

➊ to earn a **fee**/an **income**/a **salary/wage** ◆ to earn **money** ◆ to earn a **bonus/raise/rise**

2 [+ obj] to obtain money from business activities: *In the last quarter the company earned $1.16 billion, or 47 cents a share.* ◇ *The firm earns most of its money from renting out property.* ◇ *There are special tax rates on income earned from exports.*

➊ to earn an **income**/a **profit/return** ◆ to earn **income/money/profits/revenue(s)**

3 [+ obj] to get money as a profit or interest on money that you invest, lend, etc: *How much interest do you earn on your savings?* ◇ *The shares earned a 17% return.*
◆ *to earn interest ◆ to earn a dividend/return*
4 [+ obj] to get a benefit because you buy sth from a particular shop/store, etc. or use a particular credit card: *Shoppers will be able to earn points on all credit-card purchases.*
IDM **earn your 'keep** to be worth the amount of time or money that is being spent: *He felt he no longer deserved such a high salary. He just wasn't earning his keep.*

,earned 'income *noun* [U]
(*Accounting*) money that you receive from the work that you do, not from investments, etc: *You must enter the amount of earned income on your tax form.* **OPP** UNEARNED INCOME

earner /'ɜːnə(r); *AmE* 'ɜːrn-/ *noun* [C]

SEE ALSO: wage earner

1 a person who earns money for a job that they do: *The survey revealed that top earners in the country tended to be men.*
◆ *a high/low earner ◆ income/salary/wage earners*
2 an activity or a business that makes a profit: *Tourism is the country's biggest foreign currency earner.* ◇ (*BrE*) (*informal*) *Her new business has turned out to be a nice little earner.*
◆ *a big/steady earner ◆ a dollar/an export/a foreign currency earner*

'earnest ,money *noun* [U] (*also* **earnest** /'ɜːnɪst; *AmE* 'ɜːrn-/ [C]) (*both especially AmE*)
(*Commerce*) an amount of money that you pay to show sb that you are serious about doing business with them, especially when you are buying a home

'earning ,power *noun* [U]
the ability of sb to earn money from doing work; the ability of sth to make a profit: *The study found that the earning power of men was twice that of women.* ◇ *the earning power of an investment*

★ earnings /'ɜːnɪŋz; *AmE* 'ɜːrn-/ *noun* [pl.]

SEE ALSO: average earnings, core ~, headline ~, loss of ~, retained ~, statement of ~, undistributed ~

1 the money that you earn for the work that you do; the money that people earn in a particular industry or during a particular time: *She* **has earnings of $60 000 per year.** ◇ *compensation for loss of earnings caused by the accident*
◆ *annual/hourly/weekly earnings ◆ gross/net/pre-tax/taxable earnings ◆ high/low earnings*
2 the profit that a country, a company, an industry or an investment makes: *Germany's earnings from exports rose by 2%.* ◇ *The company has reduced its 2005 earnings forecast.* See note at INCOME
◆ *annual/full-year/quarterly earnings ◆ expected/strong earnings ◆ corporate/export/operating earnings ◆ to boost/grow/have/report earnings*

'earnings before 'interest and 'tax(es)
= EBIT

'earnings before 'interest, 'tax(es), depreci'ation and amorti'zation
= EBITDA

'earnings diffe,rential *noun* [C]
(*Economics*) the amount of money that one group of people in society generally earn compared to another group: *The earnings differential between skilled and unskilled workers has increased.* ◇ *the male-female earnings differential* → WAGE DIFFERENTIAL

,earnings per 'share *noun* [pl.] (*abbr* EPS)
(*Accounting*) the amount of profit that a company has made during a particular period, divided by the number of ORDINARY SHARES (= shares that give

their owners the right to a share of the company's profits) that people own: *Earnings per share were 15 cents, down from 22 cents a year ago.* ◇ *The company expects annual earnings-per-share growth of 12 per cent.* ◇ *an earnings-per-share estimate/forecast* ◇ *The company expects EPS growth of 15 per cent next year.*
HELP This phrase can also be used as a singular noun: *an earnings per share of 121 cents.* **NOTE** This is also sometimes called **earnings per common share** in American English and **earnings per ordinary share** in British English.

'earnings-re,lated *adjective* [usually before noun] (*BrE*)
(about payments, etc.) connected to the amount of money that you earn and changing as that amount does: *an earnings-related pension scheme*

'earnings re,port *noun* [C] (*AmE*)
(*Accounting*) a record that a company publishes of its income and expenses for a particular period that shows if it has made a profit: *Nissan's shares went up after it issued a positive earnings report.*
SYN PROFIT AND LOSS ACCOUNT

'earnings ,statement = STATEMENT OF EARNINGS

'earnings yield *noun* [C]
(*Accounting*) a financial measure that compares the amount of profit that a company has available to pay on each share (the **earnings per share**) with the current share price: *In the UK the average earnings yield is near 5 per cent, which is very close to the average bond yield.* → PRICE-EARNINGS RATIO

'earn-out *noun* [C]
(*Finance*) an extra payment that is made to the seller of a company, in addition to the original price, if the company's income goes above a fixed level after the company has been sold but before the new owner has control: *earn-out payments/deals*

ease /iːz/ *verb* [+ obj or no obj]
1 to become or to make sth less unpleasant, severe, etc: *They have started importing fuel to ease the shortage.* ◇ *He believes the pressure on the economy is easing.*
2 to become or make sth lower in value or level: *Share prices eased back from yesterday's levels.* ◇ *The shares eased 10¢ to $27.70.*
3 if a central bank **eases**, or **eases** interest rates, the rates become slightly lower: *There is a strong chance the Fed will ease rates by a quarter point.*
▶ easing /'iːzɪŋ/ *noun* [U,C]: *an easing of the tax rules* ◇ *We can expect to see an easing in inflation.* ◇ *an easing bias/policy*
PHR V **,ease 'off**; **,ease 'off sth** to start to become lower in value or level: *There is evidence that consumer spending may be easing off.* **,ease 'up 1** to do sth in a more reasonable and less extreme way: *Directors were urged to ease up on pay* (= not take such large pay rises). ◇ *You seem very tired—you should ease up a bit* (= not work so hard). **2** to become less strong, unpleasant, etc: *The rate at which budgets are being cut is easing up.*

easy /'iːzi/ *adjective* (**easier, easiest**)
IDM **be, close, finish, etc. 'easier** (*Stock Exchange*) to be, close, etc. slightly lower in price or level: *The index was 0.4% easier at 2 627 points.* **(be, live) on 'easy street** (*AmE*) (to be) enjoying a comfortable way of life with plenty of money

,easy 'monetary ,policy (*also* ,easy 'money ,policy) *noun* [C,U]
(*Economics*) a policy of making it cheap and easy for people to borrow money, so that they will invest more money in business activities and help the economy to grow

ˌeasy ˈmoney *noun* [U]

1 money that you get without having to work very hard for it: *She says there's no easy money to be made on the stock exchange any more.*
2 (*Economics*) money that can be borrowed at a low rate of interest SYN CHEAP MONEY

ˌeasy ˈterms *noun* [pl.] (*especially BrE*)
(*Commerce*; *Finance*) a way of borrowing money to pay for sth at a low rate of interest and paying it back in small amounts: *loans on easy terms.*

EBIT (*also spelled* **ebit**) /ˈebɪt/ *abbr*
(*Accounting*) **earnings before interest and tax(es)** (*used as a singular or an uncountable noun*) the amount of profit that a company makes during a particular period, without taking away the tax that it owes or the interest that it has paid to its lenders: *an EBIT of €151 million ◇ an EBIT loss/profit* HELP The full phrase is sometimes used with a singular verb.
→ OPERATING PROFIT

EBITDA (*also spelled* **ebitda**) /ˈebɪtdə/ *abbr*
(*Accounting*) **earnings before interest, tax(es), depreciation and amortization** (*used as a singular or an uncountable noun*) the amount of profit that a company makes during a particular period, without taking away the tax that it owes, the interest that it has paid to its lenders, or the amount by which its assets have become less valuable: *EBITDA is expected to reach €2 billion this year. ◇ The company's goal is to keep its debt below three times EBITDA. ◇ the debt to EBITDA ratio ◇ an EBITDA loss/profit* HELP The full phrase is sometimes used with a singular verb.

ˈe-ˌbusiness (*also* ˌelectronic ˈbusiness, *less frequent*) *noun* [U,C]
any business activity that is done using the Internet, such as selling goods and services or linking parts of a business together; a company that uses the Internet in this way: *The company has decided to move into e-business. ◇ our e-business strategy manager ◇ E-businesses can fail if they don't have the right kind of security.*

EC /ˌiː ˈsiː/ = EUROPEAN COMMUNITY, EUROPEAN COMMISSION

ˈe-cash (*also* ˌelectronic ˈcash, *less frequent*) (*also* ˌdigital ˈcash) *noun* [U]

1 (*E-commerce*) a system for paying for goods or services on the Internet without using a credit card. You store a small amount of money in electronic form which is used whenever you need to pay for sth.
2 a way of paying for small items without using cash. You store money in electronic form on a plastic card (a **smart card**), which you use in a similar way to a BANK CARD

ECB /ˌiː siː ˈbiː/ = EUROPEAN CENTRAL BANK

echelon /ˈeʃəlɒn; *AmE* -lɑːn/ *noun* [C, usually pl.]
a rank or position of authority in an organization or a society; the people who have that rank or position: *people in the top echelons of organizations*

ECN /ˌiː siː ˈen/ *abbr*
(*Stock Exchange*) **electronic communications network** (*used as a countable noun*)
an electronic system that allows people to buy and sell shares privately at any time without using a BROKER

★ˈe-ˌcommerce (*also* ˌelectronic ˈcommerce, *less frequent*) (*also* **Internet ˌcommerce**) *noun* [U]
the business of buying and selling things using the Internet: *E-commerce has completely changed the way we buy goods and services. ◇ The mail-order firm launched an e-commerce operation last year. ◇*

Our e-commerce sales have increased significantly.
→ M-COMMERCE
⊕ to **be involved in/expand into/move into** e-commerce ◆ an e-commerce **initiative/operation/ strategy** ◆ an e-commerce **business/company** ◆ e-commerce **software/solutions/systems**

econometrics /ɪˌkɒnəˈmetrɪks; *AmE* ɪˌkɑːn-/ *noun* [U]
(*Economics*) the branch of economics that uses mathematical methods (**statistics**) in order to understand how economies operate: *using econometrics to measure the return on investment*
▸ **econoˈmetric** *adjective*: *econometric methods/ models/techniques* **econometrician** /ɪˌkɒnəmə-ˈtrɪʃn; *AmE* ɪˌkɑːn-/ *noun* [C]

★economic /ˌiːkəˈnɒmɪk; ˌekə-; *AmE* -ˈnɑːm-/ *adjective*

1 [only before noun] connected with the trade, industry and development of wealth of a country, an area or a society: *social, economic and political issues ◇ Exports account for two-thirds of our economic activity. ◇ He blamed the drop in sales on the global economic downturn. ◇ The economic outlook remains positive.*
⊕ economic **activity/development/growth/reform/ weakness** ◆ an economic **boom/recovery/upturn** ◆ an economic **crisis/downturn/slowdown** ◆ the economic **climate/conditions/environment/ outlook/situation** ◆ economic **data/figures/reports/ research**
2 (about a process, a business or an activity) producing enough profit to continue: *The company will have to get rid of staff if it is to remain economic.* SYN PROFITABLE OPP UNECONOMIC
3 that costs less money or uses less time, materials or effort: *In this case, trains would be more economic for transporting the goods. ◇ an economic use of resources* SYN ECONOMICAL OPP UNECONOMIC

WHICH WORD?

economic/economical

These two adjectives are often confused.

Economical relates to the cost of things. Something is economical if it provides good value for the amount of money you spend on it: *It was more economical to hire the vehicles than to buy them.*

In its most common sense, **economic** only appears *before* nouns and its meaning is connected with the word **economy** and the subject of **economics**. It is used mainly when describing the financial situation of a country: *the region's gradual economic recovery ◇ economic reforms*

Less commonly, **economic** is used to mean 'making enough profit' or as a synonym of **economical**. In these senses the word can appear before or after the noun.

ˌeconomic ˈagent *noun* [C]
(*Economics*) any person or organization that influences an economy by making or spending money: *The government is usually the largest economic agent in a country.*

★economical /ˌiːkəˈnɒmɪkl; ˌekə-; *AmE* -ˈnɑːm-/ *adjective*

1 providing good value, profit or service in relation to the amount of time or money spent; not wasting time or money: *We are looking for the most economical production methods. ◇ It is not economical to sell these chemicals in small quantities.* OPP UNECONOMICAL See note at ECONOMIC
2 using no more of sth than is necessary: *an economical use of space*

1 in a way that is connected with the trade, industry and development of wealth of a country, an area or a society: *The country is facing a crisis, both economically and socially.*
2 in a way that provides good value, profit or service in relation to the amount of time or money spent: *If we can show that the project is **economically viable**, the bank has agreed to finance it.*
3 in a way that uses no more of sth than is necessary: *The design is intended to use space as economically as possible.*
→ UNECONOMICAL

ˌeconomic ˈcycle *noun* [C, usually sing.]
(*Economics*) the usual pattern of a country's economy over a period of time, with periods of success (**growth**) and periods of difficulty (**recession**) happening regularly one after another: *The improvement in sales could mean we have passed the low point in the economic cycle.* **[SYN]** BUSINESS CYCLE

ˌeconomic ˈgood *noun* [C, usually pl.]
(*Economics*) anything that people want and are willing to pay a price for, rather than sth that is available freely: *the transformation of natural resources into economic goods for the household*

ˌeconomic ˈindicator *noun* [C, usually pl.]
(*Economics*) a figure, such as the level of employment or prices, that is seen as a measure of the success of an economy: *Gold* (= its price) *remains an important economic indicator.* ◇ *an index of **leading** economic indicators* (= ones that change before the economy improves or gets worse)

ˌeconomic ˈlife *noun* [C, usually sing.]
(*Accounting*) the period of time that you can use an asset such as a machine or vehicle before it is worth buying a new one to replace it: *The period of the loan will depend on the economic life of the asset being financed.* **[SYN]** USEFUL LIFE

ˌeconomic ˈorder ˌquantity *noun* [C,U] (*abbr* EOQ)
(*Accounting*) the best amount of sth to order that is enough for what you need and keeps all the costs involved, such as the cost of storing items, as low as possible: *We calculate the economic order quantity for each stock item.*

★ **economics** /ˌi:kəˈnɒmɪks; ˌekə-; *AmE* -ˈnɑːm-/ *noun*

SEE ALSO: **development economics, industrial economics**

1 [U] the study of the production, DISTRIBUTION and use of goods and services; the study of how a society organizes its money, trade and industry: *a degree in politics and economics* ◇ *Keynesian/ Marxist/market economics*
2 [pl.; U] the financial aspects of a business, a project, etc., especially the relationship between money spent and the benefits or profit produced: *The economics of the project are very encouraging.*

ˌeconomic ˈvalue *noun* [U,C]
(*Accounting*) the value of sth, such as a business, a product or an asset, that is based on the future income it will produce: *The firm's fair economic value, based on long-term prospects, is estimated at €1.1 billion.*

★ **economist** /ɪˈkɒnəmɪst; *AmE* ɪˈkɑːn-/ *noun* [C]
a person who studies or writes about economics; a person whose job involves studying particular economies and predicting their future progress: *an academic/business economist* ◇ *The bank's chief economist has reduced her forecast for growth in the eurozone to 0.5%.*

economize, **-ise** /ɪˈkɒnəmaɪz; *AmE* ɪˈkɑːn-/ *verb* [no obj]
to use less money, time, etc. than you normally use: *We need to economize **on** electricity costs.* ◇ *They centralized their operations in an attempt to economize.*

★ **economy** /ɪˈkɒnəmi; *AmE* ɪˈkɑːn-/ *noun* (*plural* **economies**)

SEE ALSO: **black economy, bubble ~, command ~, controlled ~, dual ~, exchange ~, experience ~,** etc.

1 (*often* **the economy**) [C] the relationship between production, trade and the supply of money in a particular country or region: *The economy is in recession.* ◇ *While exports have improved the domestic economy remains weak.* ◇ *The US is moving from a manufacturing economy to a service one.* ◇ *A further interest-rate cut may help to boost the economy.*
🔾 *to* **control/handle/manage/run** *the economy* ◆ *to* **boost/strengthen/weaken** *the economy* ◆ *a* **booming/sluggish/strong/weak** *economy* ◆ *the economy* **expands/grows/recovers** ◆ *the economy* **contracts/slows (down)/weakens**
2 [C] a country, when you are thinking about its economic system: *China is one of the world's fastest-growing economies.*
3 [U,C] the use of the time, money, etc. that is available in a way that avoids waste: *The diesel version of the car has better fuel economy.* ◇ *economy of effort in the handling of loads*
4 [C, usually pl.] a reduction in the amount of money that you spend: *We need to make substantial economies.* ◇ *It's a **false economy** to buy cheap tools* (= it seems cheaper but it is not really since they do not last very long). ◇ *Tough economy **measures** in every area of the company should halve the losses.*
5 [U] (*used as an adjective*) offering good value for the money that you spend: *a regular pack of 30 tablets or an economy pack of 60* ◇ *an economy fare* (= the cheapest)
6 [U] = ECONOMY CLASS

eˈconomy class (*also* eˈconomy) *noun* [U]
the cheapest class of air travel; the part of a plane where people with the cheapest tickets sit: *Fares start from €597 for economy class.* ◇ *an economy-class fare/ticket/seat* ◇ *I always fly economy class.*
→ BUSINESS CLASS

eˈconomy drive *noun* [C, usually sing.]
an organized effort to reduce costs and avoid wasting money: *We're **on** an economy drive.*

economies of scale

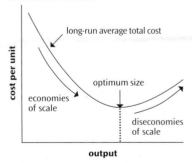

long-run average total cost

cost per unit

economies of scale

optimum size

diseconomies of scale

output

eˌconomy of ˈscale (*also* ˈscale eˌconomy, *less frequent*) *noun* [C, usually pl., U]
(*Economics*) the fact that as the amount of goods or services produced increases, the cost decreases: *To **achieve** economies of scale, many retailers have*

merged. ◇ *These manufacturers benefit from economies of scale by using the same parts in all their products.* → DISECONOMY OF SCALE

e'conomy-size *(also* **e'conomy-sized)** *adjective*
[usually before noun]
used to describe sth that you buy that offers a larger quantity than usual, especially when it is the best value for money of the sizes available: *an economy-size bottle of ketchup*

ecotourism /ˌiːkəʊˈtʊərɪzəm; -ˈtɔːr-; *AmE* ˌiːkoʊˈtʊr-/ *noun* [U]
organized holidays/vacations to places that not many people have the chance to see, designed so that the tourists damage the environment as little as possible, especially when some of the money they pay is used to protect the local environment and animals: *Ecotourism is financing rainforest preservation.* ▶ **eco'tourist** *noun* [C]

ECR /ˌiː siː ˈɑː(r)/ = EFFICIENT CONSUMER RESPONSE

'e-ˌcurrency *(also* ˌelectronic 'currency, *less frequent)* *(also* ˌdigital 'currency) *noun* [C,U]
(E-commerce) one of the electronic forms of money (**e-money**) that you can buy from particular companies on the Internet and use for making and receiving payments on the Internet: *We accept payment by bank transfer or any of the following e-currencies ...* ◇ *They offer a service to exchange cash into e-currency.*

ED /ˌiː ˈdiː/ = EXPOSURE DRAFT

edge /edʒ/ *noun, verb*
●*noun* [sing.]

SEE ALSO: **competitive edge, cutting ~, leading ~**

1 a slight advantage over sb/sth: *They have the edge in car design.* ◇ *This technology gives us an edge over our rivals.*
☉ *to* **gain/have/keep/lose/maintain** *an edge (on/over sth/sb)* • *sth* **gives** *you an edge (on/over sth/sb)*
2 *(usually* **the edge)** the point at which sth, especially sth bad, may begin to happen: *The country is on the edge of financial collapse.*
IDM **be on 'edge; put sb/sth on 'edge** to be nervous or uncertain: *The increasing oil price has* **put** *markets on edge.* → idiom at BRINK
●*verb* [no obj] *(used with an adverb or a preposition)* (used especially in newspapers) to increase or decrease slightly in value or level: *The share price edged up 1% to ¥5 350.* ◇ *Inflation has edged below the 2% target.* See note at INCREASE

EDI /ˌiː diː ˈaɪ/ = ELECTRONIC DATA INTERCHANGE

EDR /ˌiː diː ˈɑː(r)/ = EUROPEAN DEPOSITARY RECEIPT

edutainment /ˌedjuˈteɪnmənt/ *noun* [U,C]
products such as computer software, books and television programmes that both educate and entertain; the activity of using a form of entertainment in order to teach sb sth ▶ **edu'tain** *verb* [+ obj *or no* obj]: *These games are designed to edutain people.*

EEA /ˌiː iː ˈeɪ/ = EUROPEAN ECONOMIC AREA

EEC /ˌiː iː ˈsiː/ = EUROPEAN ECONOMIC COMMUNITY

'e-eˌnabled *adjective*
using the Internet to do business, to communicate with other people, companies, etc: *an e-enabled business/company*

EEO /ˌiː iː ˈəʊ; *AmE* ˈoʊ/ = EQUAL EMPLOYMENT OPPORTUNITY

EEOC /ˌiː iː iː ˈsiː; *AmE* oʊ/ = EQUAL EMPLOYMENT OPPORTUNITIES COMMISSION

★**effect** /ɪˈfekt/ *noun, verb*
●*noun*

SEE ALSO: **currency effect, demonstration ~, domino ~, halo ~, Hawthorne ~, income ~, price ~,** etc.

1 [C,U] a change that sb/sth causes in sb/sth else; a result: *The fall in tourism is having an adverse effect on business.* ◇ *What are the long-term effects of this strategy?* ◇ *We are still feeling the effects of the stock-market crash.* ◇ *Excluding the effect of exchange rates, profits grew 9.7% last year.*
☉ *to* **have/produce** *an effect (on sth)* • *a* **big/dramatic/ significant** *effect* • **little/no** *effect* • *an* **adverse/a damaging/harmful/negative** *effect* • *a* **beneficial/ positive** *effect* • *to* **feel/suffer** *the effects (of sth)* • *to* **counter/offset/reverse** *the effects (of sth)*
2 effects [pl.] *(formal, only used in written English)* your personal possessions: *The insurance policy covers all baggage and personal effects.*
IDM **bring/put sth into ef'fect** to cause sth to come into use: *The recommendations will soon be* **put** *into effect.* **come into ef'fect** to come into use; to begin to apply: *New controls come into effect next month.* **in ef'fect** (about a law or rule) in use: *These laws are in effect in twenty states.* **take ef'fect** to come into use; to begin to apply: *The new pricing structure will take effect from 1 July.* **to the effect that ...; to this/that ef'fect** *(formal)* used in formal or legal documents to say that what has been written has a particular meaning, purpose or result **with immediate ef'fect; with effect from ...** starting now; starting from ...: *She has resigned as chairman with immediate effect.* ◇ *With effect from 1 August, there will be an extra €2 charge on all deliveries.*
●*verb* [+ obj] *(formal)*
to make sth happen: *You may* **effect payment** *for your order in several currencies.*

★**effective** /ɪˈfektɪv/ *adjective*

SEE ALSO: **cost-effective**

1 producing the result that is wanted or intended; producing a successful result: *training managers to be more effective leaders* ◇ *The ad was simple but highly effective.* ◇ *Promotions can be effective* **in** attracting new customers.
2 (about laws, contracts, etc.) officially starting to apply: *The law becomes effective on 1 March.* ◇ *The price increase, effective from 15 July, has received a lot of criticism.* → EFFECTIVE DATE
3 [only before noun] in reality, although not officially intended: *The deal gives the bank effective control of the company.*
▶ **ef'fectiveness** *noun* [U]: *assessing the effectiveness of the marketing campaign*

efˌfective 'age *noun* [C,U]
(Accounting) the age of an asset plus or minus a number of years depending on how bad or good its condition is judged to be

ef'fective date *noun* [C] *(usually* **the effective date** [sing.])
(Law)
1 the date on which a law or rule comes into use: *The effective date of the court order has been delayed for two weeks.*
2 a date chosen in a legal contract for when sth will happen or when sth must be done: *These changes to your policy apply from the effective date shown below.*

efˌfective 'tax rate *noun* [C] *(abbr* **ETR)**
(Accounting) the total amount of tax that a business pays in a particular period of time divided by its total profit

SEE ALSO: **cost-efficiency, technical ~, x-~**

1 [U] the ability to do sth well with no waste of time or money: *improvements in efficiency at the factory* ◇ *I was impressed by the speed and efficiency with which my order was processed.* ◇ *The increase in profits was mainly due to efficiency gains.*
O *to* **achieve/boost/improve/increase/maximize** efficiency ◆ efficiency **gains/savings** ◆ *an* efficiency **drive/programme**
2 efficiencies [pl.] ways of wasting less time and money or of saving time and money: *We are looking at our business to see where efficiencies can be made.*
3 (*Technical*) [U] the relationship between the amount of energy that goes into a machine or an engine, and the amount that it produces: *The generator is running at only 40% efficiency.*

★ **efficient** /ɪˈfɪʃnt/ *adjective*

SEE ALSO: **cost-efficient**

doing sth well and thoroughly with no waste of time, money or energy: *an efficient organization/ manager/service* ◇ *ensuring money is used in the most efficient way* ◇ *a* **fuel-efficient** *car* (= that does not use much fuel) [OPP] INEFFICIENT
▶ **efficiently** /ɪˈfɪʃntli/ *adverb*: *They did the job quickly and efficiently.* ◇ *an efficiently run company*

efˈficient conˈsumer resˈponse *noun* [U; sing.] (*abbr* **ECR**)
(*Marketing; Production*) (used especially in the food industry) a process in which manufacturers, suppliers and RETAILERS (= businesses that sell goods directly to the public) work together to reduce costs and give the public a better, faster service

efˌficient ˈmarket *noun* [C]
(*Economics*) a market in which the prices of shares, bonds, etc. are set by buyers and sellers who know all the current information that affects their value, with the result that prices are always accurate: *In an efficient market, news of financial difficulties will have an immediate effect on a company's share price.*

EFT /eft; ˌiː ef ˈtiː/ *abbr*
(*Finance*) **electronic ˈfund(s) ˌtransfer** a system for making payments to and from bank accounts using computers; a payment that is made in this way: *Payment must be made by EFT.* ◇ *an EFT payment*

EFTPOS /ˈeftpɒs; *AmE* -pɑːs/ *abbr*
(*Commerce*) **electronic funds transfer at point of sale** a system used in shops/stores to allow people to pay for goods or services using a bank card or credit card. The money is paid directly from the customer's account by a computer link.

e.g. /ˌiː ˈdʒiː/ *abbr*
for example: *direct investments e.g. shares and bonds* NOTE e.g. is formed from the first letters of a Latin phrase meaning 'for example'.

egalitarian /iˌɡælɪˈteəriən; *AmE* -ˈter-/ *adjective*
based on, or holding, the belief that everyone is equal and should have the same rights and opportunities: *egalitarian companies/workplaces*

EGM /ˌiː dʒiː ˈem/ = EXTRAORDINARY GENERAL MEETING

ˈe-goods *noun* [pl.]
(*E-commerce*) products that you can buy on the Internet and transfer to your computer (**download**), such as software or electronic books

EHO /ˌiː eɪtʃ ˈəʊ; *AmE* ˈoʊ/ = ENVIRONMENTAL HEALTH OFFICER

EI /ˌiː ˈaɪ/ = EMPLOYEE INVOLVEMENT

EIS /ˌiː aɪ ˈes/ *abbr*
1 **environmental impact statement** in the US, a written document that describes the good and bad effects on the environment of proposed projects, based on a scientific study
2 (*IT*) = EXECUTIVE INFORMATION SYSTEM

ˈe-lance *adjective*
used to describe a way of earning money by using the Internet to sell your work or services to different organizations anywhere in the world: *e-lance work/workers* ◇ *the new e-lance economy*
▶ **ˈe-lance** *verb* [no obj]: *Are you ready to e-lance?*
ˈe-lancer *noun* [C] NOTE **E-lance** is formed from 'e-' (electronic) and 'freelance'.

elastic /ɪˈlæstɪk/ *adjective*
(*Economics*) used to describe the situation when a small change in one thing, such as the price of a product or service, or a change in people's incomes, results in a larger change in another thing, such as the amount that people want to buy: **Demand** *for oil is not very elastic.* ◇ *The broadsheet market is less* **price elastic** *than the tabloid market.*
[OPP] INELASTIC—Picture at ELASTICITY OF DEMAND

elasˌticity of ˈdemand (*also* ˈprice elasˈticity of deˈmand) *noun* [C, usually sing., U]
(*Economics*) the extent to which people want to buy more or less of a product or service when its price changes: *The elasticity of demand for luxury goods tends to be* **higher** *than for necessities* (= a small change in price results in a large change in the number of people buying them). → INCOME ELASTICITY OF DEMAND

elasticity of demand
inelastic demand

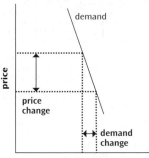

elastic demand

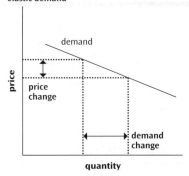

'e-,learning *noun* [U]

the process of learning sth using the Internet or an INTRANET: *E-learning helps workers develop new knowledge and skills.* ◇ *a company-wide e-learning programme* → COMPUTER-AIDED

★ **elect** /ɪˈlekt/ *verb, adjective*

● *verb* [+ obj]

elect sb (to sth) | **elect sb (as) sth** (*often* **be elected**) to choose sb to do a particular job by voting for them: *elected directors/officials/representatives* ◇ *He has been elected to the management committee.* ◇ *She was elected chief executive by the board of directors.*

● *adjective*

used after nouns to show that sb has been chosen for a job, but is not yet doing that job: *the chairman elect*

election /ɪˈlekʃn/ *noun*

1 [U,C] the process of choosing a person or a group of people for a position by voting: *the election of directors to the board* ◇ *They plan to hold elections in November.*

○ *to* **call/have/hold** *an election* ◆ *to* **lose/win** *an election*

2 [U] the fact of being chosen for a position by **election**: *We welcome his election as president.* ◇ *They have proposed her election to the board.*

e,lectrical engi'neering *noun* [U]

the design and building of machines and systems that use or produce electricity; the study of this subject ▶ **e,lectrical engi'neer** *noun* [C]

electrician /ɪˌlekˈtrɪʃn/ *noun* [C]

a person whose job is to connect, repair, etc. electrical equipment

electronic /ɪˌlekˈtrɒnɪk; *AmE* -ˈtrɑːnɪk/ *adjective* [usually before noun] **HELP** You will find most words formed with **electronic** at the form e-.

1 (about a device) having many small parts, such as MICROCHIPS, that control and direct a small electric current: *an electronic calculator* ◇ *electronic equipment/products* ◇ *a manufacturer of electronic components/parts*

2 (about information) stored in electronic form on a disk, computer or MICROCHIP: *an electronic book/ document* ◇ *They are developing an electronic form of cash.* → DIGITAL, E-

3 using an electronic system of communication, especially the Internet, in order to exchange information, do business, etc: *the rise of electronic banking* ◇ *a system for making electronic payments* → E-

,electronic 'cottage *noun* [C]

(*HR; IT*) a home, usually in the country, where sb has the necessary computer and telephone equipment, so that they can work there instead of travelling to an office in a town or city → TELECOTTAGE

,electronic 'data ,interchange *noun* [U] (*abbr* EDI)

(*IT*) the activity of exchanging standard business documents, such as order forms and INVOICES, electronically rather than on paper: *Many companies use electronic data interchange to link their systems with those of their suppliers.*

,electronic 'mail = EMAIL *noun* (1)

,electronic 'mall = CYBER MALL

,electronic 'purse *noun* [C]

a small amount of money that is stored in electronic form, for example on a SMART CARD, and can be used to pay for sth instead of cash: *You can top up your electronic purse at any automatic teller machine.*

★ **electronics** /ɪˌlekˈtrɒnɪks; *AmE* -ˈtrɑːn-/ *noun*

SEE ALSO: **consumer electronics**

1 [U] the branch of science and technology that studies electronic currents in electronic equipment

2 [U] the use of electronic technology, especially in developing new equipment: *the electronics industry/sector* ◇ *Samsung Electronics*

3 [pl.] the electronic CIRCUITS and COMPONENTS (= parts) used in electronic equipment: *There may be a fault in the electronics.* ◇ *an electronics maker/ manufacturer*

4 [pl.] electronic goods, such as CD players, televisions, etc: *Stores reported strong demand for clothing, electronics, books and toys.*

,electronic 'signature = DIGITAL SIGNATURE

elephant /ˈelɪfənt/ *noun* [C] (*informal*)

SEE ALSO: **white elephant**

a way of referring to a company that is very large and employs a lot of people, but creates very few new jobs → GAZELLE, MOUSE

elevator /ˈelɪveɪtə(r)/ = LIFT *noun* (2)

'elevator pitch *noun* [C]

a very short, clear summary of a business idea or company for possible investors, that should last only the few minutes that a ride in an **elevator** would take

★ **eligible** /ˈelɪdʒəbl/ *adjective*

having the right to have sth or to do sth, because you have the right qualifications, are the right age, etc: *About a million people are eligible for the new tax credit.* ◇ *All shareholders are eligible to vote on the scheme.* **OPP** INELIGIBLE

▶ **eligibility** /ˌelɪdʒəˈbɪləti/ *noun* [U]: *eligibility requirements/criteria*

★ **email** (*also spelled* **e-mail**) /ˈiːmeɪl/ *noun, verb*

● *noun*

1 (*also* **,electronic 'mail**, *formal*) [U] a way of sending messages and data to other people by means of computers connected together in a network: *You can contact us by email.* ◇ *Do you have email* (= a system to send and receive emails)? ◇ *They offer a free email service from their website.*

○ *to* **have/use** *email* ◆ *an email* **program/service/ system**

2 [C,U] a message sent by email: *We will send you an email confirming your order.* ◇ *I need to check my email* (= see if I have received any emails). ◇ *an email attachment* (= a document that is sent together with an email)

○ *to* **fire off/forward/send** *an email (to sb)* ◆ *to* **get/ receive** *an email (from sb)* ◆ *to* **check/delete/read** *emails*

● *verb* [+ obj or no obj]

email sth (to sb) | **email (sb) (sth)** to send a message to sb by email: *I'll email the documents to her.* ◇ *I'll email her the documents.* ◇ *I sent him an email last week but he hasn't emailed me back yet.* ◇ *How much time do you spend emailing?*

'email ac,count *noun* [C]

an arrangement with a company that allows you to receive, store and send emails: *Do you have an email account?* ◇ *You can set up an email account on the Internet.* → MAILBOX

EMAS /ˈiːmæs/ *abbr*

Eco-Management and Audit Scheme in the EU, a system that organizations can join if they want to reduce the harmful effects of what they do on the environment

embargo /ɪmˈbɑːɡəʊ; *AmE* ɪmˈbɑːrɡoʊ/ *noun* [C] (*plural* **embargoes**)

(*Economics*) an official order that prevents trade with another country: *The government has put an* embargo **on** oil exports. ◇ a trade embargo **against/on** certain countries → BOYCOTT

O to **enforce/impose** an embargo (on sth) • to **place/put** an embargo **on** sth • to **end/lift** an embargo • an **arms/oil/a trade** embargo

▶ **em'bargo** verb [+ obj] (**embargoes, embargoing, embargoed, embargoed**): All grain sales were embargoed. → BOYCOTT

embattled /ɪmˈbætld/ adjective [only before noun] (used especially in newspapers) surrounded by problems and difficulties: The embattled chief executive has been advised to cut his pay, not raise it.

embed (also spelled **imbed**) /ɪmˈbed/ verb [+ obj] (-dd-)
(IT) (usually **be embedded**)
1 to fix electronic parts or a computer system inside a product so that it can perform a special function: a washing machine with an embedded computer ◇ embedded chips/software/systems
2 to include text, a piece of computer code or a computer program as part of a file, an Internet page, an email, etc: an email with an embedded hyperlink

embezzle /ɪmˈbezl/ verb [+ obj or no obj] to steal money that you are responsible for or that belongs to your employer: He admitted embezzling nearly $2 million from his clients' accounts.
▶ **em'bezzlement** noun [U]: She was found guilty of embezzlement. **embezzler** /ɪmˈbezlə(r)/ noun [C]

emerge /iˈmɜːdʒ; AmE iˈmɜːrdʒ/ verb [no obj]
1 to appear or become known; to start to gain influence, power or wealth: Amazon has emerged as a leader in e-commerce. ◇ the emerging markets of East Asia
2 (about facts, ideas, etc.) to become known: More evidence has emerged that sales growth during the holiday season was very weak.
3 to return to a normal state after a period of difficulty: The company should emerge **from** bankruptcy in September.
▶ **emergence** /iˈmɜːdʒəns; AmE iˈmɜːrdʒ-/ noun [U]: the emergence of new technologies/evidence

emergency /iˈmɜːdʒənsi; AmE iˈmɜːrdʒ-/ noun (plural **emergencies**)
1 [C,U] a sudden serious event or situation which needs immediate action: Staff are trained on what to do **in** an emergency.
2 [U] (used as an adjective) used or done in an emergency: They maintain emergency stocks of oil. ◇ The company called an emergency board meeting to discuss the offer.

emission /iˈmɪʃn/ noun
1 [C, usually pl.] harmful gas, etc. that is sent out into the air: emissions from vehicles/power stations ◇ They aim to reduce carbon dioxide emissions by 20% by 2010.
2 [U] the production or sending out of harmful gas, etc: low emission cars

e'mission ˌcredit (also e'missions ˌcredit, polˈlution ˌcredit) noun [C, usually pl.]
a right to send out a measured amount of harmful gases into the air: Companies that beat their sulphur dioxide targets can sell emission credits to those that exceed them. See note at EMISSION UNIT

e'missions ˌtrading noun [U]
the activity of buying and selling EMISSION CREDITS or EMISSION UNITS: a scheme for emissions trading across Europe

e'mission ˌunit noun [C, usually pl.]
a right to send out a measured amount of harmful gases such as CARBON DIOXIDE into the air: The Kyoto Protocol permits trading of emission units between countries. → CARBON CREDIT

Emission units

Under the Kyoto Protocol, countries are given a number of **emission units** equal to the maximum amount of harmful gases they are allowed to produce. Countries that produce a smaller amount than their limit can sell units to countries that produce more than their limit. Countries can also earn units, for example by planting trees or helping other countries to use technologies that use energy more efficiently.

All units are the same size and can be traded in the same way. But some people distinguish units that are earned from those that are given by calling them carbon **credits** or emission **credits** rather than emission **units**.

Emission credit is also used to describe the units of systems other than the Kyoto Protocol, for example the system in the US to reduce sulphur dioxide pollution.

emolument /iˈmɒljumənt; AmE iˈmɑːl-/ noun [C, usually pl.]
(Accounting, formal) the total amount of money that sb gets for the job they do or the position they hold, including any extra benefits that they receive, especially when this is a lot of money: He received an €800 000 bonus last year, which took his total emoluments to €1.82 million.

'e-ˌmoney (also ˌelectronic 'money, ˌdigital 'money) noun [U]
money that is stored in electronic form, for example on a SMART CARD or in the memory of a computer, and can be used to make electronic payments: Under the system, you will be able to store e-money in your mobile-phone account.

emoticon /iˈməʊtɪkɒn; AmE iˈmoʊtɪkɑːn/ noun [C]
a short set of keyboard symbols that represents the expression on sb's face, used in email, etc. to show the feelings of the person sending the message. For example, :-) represents a smiling face.

eˌmotional 'capital noun [sing; U]
(HR) the feelings, beliefs and values of a company's employees that make good relationships possible and help a business to be successful

eˌmotional inˈtelligence noun [U]
(HR) the ability of a person to understand, control and use their feelings and to understand the feelings of others → EQ

empire /ˈempaɪə(r)/ noun [C]
a group of commercial organizations controlled by one person or company: The company is part of the Virgin empire. ◇ She rapidly built her business empire by investing in start-ups.
O to **break up/build (up)/control/expand/run** an empire • an empire **collapses/grows** • a **business/media/publishing/retail** empire

★ **employ** /ɪmˈplɔɪ/ verb, noun
● verb [+ obj]
1 to give sb a job to do for payment: How many people does the company employ? ◇ For the past three years he has been employed **as** a systems analyst. ◇ The number of people employed **in** manufacturing has fallen. ◇ IT workers employed **to** install new computer systems
2 (formal) to use sth such as a skill, method, etc. for a particular purpose: the accounting practices employed by large companies
● noun
IDM in sb's emˈploy; in the emˈploy of sb
(formal) working for sb; employed by sb: How long has she been in your employ?

Employing people

- to **recruit** sb – *Many businesses are having trouble recruiting workers with adequate skills.*
- to **hire** sb (*especially AmE*) – *If you want to keep growing, hire more salespeople.*
- to **take on** sb – *She was taken on as a trainee last year.*
- to **appoint** sb – *A new head of the Environment Agency was appointed last year.*
- to **headhunt** sb – *He was headhunted by a major US law firm.*

See note at DISMISS

employable /ɪmˈplɔɪəbl/ *adjective*
having the skills and qualifications that will make sb want to employ you: *training schemes that aim to make young people more employable*
OPP UNEMPLOYABLE ▶ **employability**
/ɪmˌplɔɪəˈbɪləti/ *noun* [U]

employed /ɪmˈplɔɪd/ *adjective*

SEE ALSO: self-employed

1 having a job: *employed people/adults/workers* ◇ *a fully employed economy* SYN WORKING
2 **the employed** *noun* [pl.] people who are employed: *Factory-floor workers account for almost 50% of the employed.*
→ UNEMPLOYED

★ **employee** /ɪmˈplɔɪiː/ *noun* [C]

SEE ALSO: public employee

a person who is paid to work for sb: *The firm has over 500 employees.* ◇ *In addition to a competitive salary, the company offers attractive employee benefits.*
➕ *full-time/part-time/permanent/temporary employees* ◆ *hourly/salaried employees* ◆ *key/junior/senior/valued employees* ◆ *to have/hire/recruit/retain/train employees* ◆ *to dismiss/fire/lay off employees* ◆ *to empower/motivate employees* ◆ *employee benefits/relations/rights/status*

em,ployee as'sistance ,programme (*also* em,ployment as'sistance ,programme) (*AmE spelling* ~ **program**) *noun* [C] (*abbr* EAP)
(*HR*) a service that employers offer that helps employees with problems that may affect the way they do their job: *Our employee assistance programme provides advice, counselling, training and support.*

em,ployee 'buyout *noun* [C]
(*Finance*) a situation in which the employees gain control of a company, or a particular part of it, by buying most of its shares: *She led an employee buyout of the plant.*

em,ployee in'volvement *noun* [U] (*abbr* EI)
(*HR*) ways of making employees feel that they are an important part of a company so that they will work better, especially by allowing them to take part in making decisions on things that affect them: *The survey showed that many workers want a higher level of employee involvement.* → EMPLOYEE PARTICIPATION

em,ployee 'leasing *noun* [U]
(*HR*)
1 an arrangement in which workers are supplied to work in a company for a short period of time
2 an arrangement in which a business that has special skill in employing people takes responsibility for some or all of the employees of a company and pays them, arranges their benefits, etc.

em,ployee 'ownership *noun* [U]
(*HR*) the situation when workers own some or all of the shares in the company they work for: *a sense of partnership created by the employee ownership structure*

em,ployee partici'pation (*also* ,worker partici'pation) *noun* [U]
(*HR*) a system where employees take part in making decisions in a company: *proposals to encourage employee participation in management* → EMPLOYEE INVOLVEMENT

em,ployee re'ferral ,programme (*AmE spelling* ~ **program**) *noun* [C]
(*HR*) especially in the US, a policy of encouraging employees to suggest people that they know for a job, usually by offering money

em,ployee re'lations *noun* [pl.] (*abbr* ER)
(*HR*) ways in which managers exchange information and ideas with their employees, involve them in making decisions and encourage them to want to work well; the department of a company that is responsible for this: *Flexible working arrangements can lead to improved employee relations.* ◇ *head of employee relations at the bank*

em,ployee self 'service *noun* [U] (*abbr* ESS)
(*HR*) a system in which employees can use the Internet to do administrative tasks connected with their pay, benefits, personal information, etc. that used to be done by managers or office staff

em,ployee 'share ,ownership plan (*BrE*) (*AmE* em,ployee 'stock ,ownership plan) *noun* [C] (*abbr* ESOP)
(*Finance*; *HR*) a system in which a company gives its employees shares, or allows them to buy shares, so that when the company makes a profit they will receive part of it SYN SHARE INCENTIVE PLAN

em,ployee 'stock ,option *noun* [C] (*abbr* ESO)
(*Finance*; *HR*) the right given to some employees in a company to buy shares in the company at a fixed price

em,ployee 'stock ,ownership plan
= EMPLOYEE SHARE OWNERSHIP PLAN

★ **employer** /ɪmˈplɔɪə(r)/ *noun* [C]
a person or company that pays people to work for them: *They're very good employers* (= they treat the people that work for them well). ◇ *one of the largest employers in the area* ◇ *How long have you worked for your current employer?*
➕ *a big/large/major/small employer* ◆ *a private sector/public sector employer* ◆ *a current/former/potential/previous/prospective employer* ◆ *to work for/have an employer*

Words ending in -or, -er and -ee

Nouns ending in **-or/-er** often refer to a person who gives or sends something to somebody. Nouns ending in **-ee** refer to the person who receives the thing. For example:

- an *employer* gives a job to an *employee*
- a *consignor* sends goods to a *consignee*
- a *franchiser* gives the right to operate a business to a *franchisee*
- a *lessor* gives a *lessee* the use of a building
- a *licensor* gives a *licensee* the right to use sth

em,ployer of 'record *noun* [C] (*AmE*)
(*HR*; *Law*) the person or company who is legally responsible for employees' pay, taxes, benefits, etc.

SEE ALSO: continuous employment, contract of ~, lifetime ~, precarious ~

1 [U,C] work, especially when it is done to earn money; the state of being employed: *to be in paid employment* ◇ *Graduates are finding it more and more difficult to find employment.* ◇ *conditions/ terms of employment* ◇ *She has negotiated a five-year employment contract with the company.* → WORK
● *casual/full-time/part-time/seasonal/temporary employment* • *to be in/get/have/take up employment* • *to find/look for/seek employment* • *employment opportunities/prospects* • *an employment agreement/contract*
2 [U] the situation in which people have work: *The government is aiming at full employment* (= when nobody is unemployed). ◇ *Changes in farming methods have badly affected employment in the area.* ◇ *school-leavers entering the employment market* OPP UNEMPLOYMENT
● *falling/full/high/low/total employment* • *to boost/ create/cut/increase/reduce employment* • *employment data/figures/growth/records*
3 [U] the act of employing sb: *The expansion of the factory will mean the employment of sixty extra workers.*

emˈployment ˌagency *(BrE also* ˈstaff ˌagency*) noun* [C]
(*HR*) a business that helps people to find work and employers to find workers: *Many people find jobs very quickly by going to private employment agencies.* ◇ *You must register with a government employment agency.*

emˌployment asˈsistance ˌprogramme
= EMPLOYEE ASSISTANCE PROGRAMME

emˌployment costs *noun* [pl.]
the amount of money that a business spends on employing people, including wages, payments for health insurance, pensions, etc: *Introducing a 35-hour week would mean a rise in employment costs.*

emˌployment ˈequity *noun* [U]
the policy of giving everyone the same chances of employment, especially by helping groups that are often treated unfairly because of their race, sex, etc.

emˈployment law *noun* [U]
the collection of laws that deal with all aspects of employment and the rights of people who are employed SYN LABOUR LAW

emˈployment proˌtection *(also* ˈjob proˌtection*) noun* [U]
(*HR*) a group of laws that protect the rights of workers in a company, including pay, time away from work, etc.; the rights that are protected: *The most important aspect of employment protection is the unfair dismissal scheme.*

emˌployment reˈlations *noun* [pl.]
(*HR*) the rights of employees, employers, unemployed and SELF-EMPLOYED people and the relations between individuals, organizations and the government; the laws that deal with this: *the 1999 Employment Relations Act* → INDUSTRIAL RELATIONS

emˌployment reˈlationship *noun* [sing.]
(*Law*) the situation that exists when an employer pays an employee in exchange for work or services, usually with written conditions: *reasons to terminate an employment relationship*

emˌployment seˈcurity *(also* seˌcurity of emˈployment*) noun* [U]
a situation where a job is likely to last for a long time and you will keep the job if you do what you are expected to: *These jobs offer low pay, few benefits and less employment security.* SYN JOB SECURITY

emˈployment tax *noun* [U,C] *(AmE)*
(*Accounting*) the amount of money that you pay to the government according to how much you earn, which is taken out of your pay by your employer

emˌployment triˈbunal *(also* inˌdustrial triˈbunal, *old-fashioned) noun* [C]
(*HR*) in the UK, a type of court that can deal with disagreements between employees and employers: *She took her case to an employment tribunal, who decided she had been unfairly dismissed.* → LABOUR COURT

emporium /emˈpɔːriəm/ *noun* [C] *(plural* **emporiums** *or* **emporia** /emˈpɔːriə/)
1 a shop/store where you can buy a wide variety of a particular type of goods: *a fashion emporium*
2 *(old-fashioned)* a large shop/store

empower /ɪmˈpaʊə(r)/ *verb* [+ obj] *(often* be empowered)
1 to give sb the ability and confidence to control the situation they are in: *The Internet empowers consumers to shop efficiently.* ◇ *A successful business requires an empowered workforce.*
2 *(formal)* to give sb the power or authority to do sth: *Congress has empowered a committee to investigate the claims.* SYN AUTHORIZE

empowerment /ɪmˈpaʊəmənt; *AmE* -ˈpaʊər-/ *noun* [U]
(*HR*) when managers give employees more responsibility to control their own work, make their own decisions, etc: *Companies that take empowerment and training seriously tend to perform better.*

ˌempty ˈnester /ˌempti ˈnestə(r)/ *noun* [C, usually pl.]
a parent whose children have grown up and left home: *an ideal smaller home for first-time buyers or empty nesters*

EMS /ˌiː em ˈes/ *noun, abbr*
● *noun*
1 [U] **enhanced message service** a system for sending pictures, music and long written messages from one mobile phone/cellphone to another
2 [C] a message sent by **EMS**
→ SMS, MMS
● *abbr* = ENVIRONMENTAL MANAGEMENT SYSTEM

EMU /ˈiːmjuː; ˌiː em ˈjuː/ *abbr* **European Monetary Union** an arrangement by which countries in Europe use similar economic policies and a single currency (the **euro**); the group of countries who use the euro: *EMU entry/membership* NOTE This is also sometimes referred to as **Economic and Monetary Union**.

-enabled /ɪˈneɪbld/ *combining form (used in compound adjectives)*

SEE ALSO: e-enabled, web-enabled

that can be used with a particular system or technology, especially the Internet: *Your browser is not Java-enabled.* ◇ *Internet-enabled business is like any other business.*

enabling /ɪˈneɪblɪŋ/ *adjective*
giving sb/sth new powers or abilities to do particular things: *We are developing an enabling technology for wireless Internet.* ◇ *Good feedback can be very enabling.*

enc. = ENCL.

encash /ɪnˈkæʃ/ *verb* [+ obj] *(BrE) (formal)*
1 *(Finance; Insurance)* to exchange an investment for money: *You will receive a lump sum when the policy is encashed.* SYN CASH STH IN at CASH
2 *(Finance)* to exchange a cheque, etc. for money: *Most banks impose a charge for encashing foreign cheques.* SYN CASH

▶ **en'cashment** noun [U,C]: Policyholders will have to pay a 10 per cent charge on early encashment (= if they want the policy paid early).

encl. (also spelled **enc.**) abbr
a short way of writing **enclosed** or **enclosure** on business letters to show that another document is being sent in the same envelope: draft agenda encl.

enclose /ɪnˈkləʊz; AmE ɪnˈkloʊz/ verb [+ obj]
to put sth in the same envelope, parcel/package, etc. as sth else: Please return the completed form, enclosing a stamped addressed envelope. ◇ (formal) Please **find enclosed** a cheque for €300.

enclosure /ɪnˈkləʊʒə(r); AmE -ˈkloʊ-/ noun [C]
something that is placed in an envelope with a letter: Always state the number of enclosures at the bottom of your letter.

encrypt /ɪnˈkrɪpt/ verb [+ obj]
(IT) to put information into a special code, especially in order to prevent people from looking at it without permission: The system encrypts your email so that only the intended receiver can read it. ◇ encrypted data OPP DECRYPT
▶ **encryption** /ɪnˈkrɪpʃn/ noun [U,C]: encryption programs/software/technology

end /end/ noun, verb
●**noun**

SEE ALSO: back end, closed-~, dead-~, ~-to-~, front ~, high-~, low-~, etc.

1 [sing.] the final part of a period of time, an event or an activity: They plan to cut 2 500 jobs by the end of the year. ◇ There will be a chance to ask questions at the end. ◇ an end-of-season sale
2 [C] a point or level that is the highest or lowest in a particular range: These two products are from opposite ends of the price range. ◇ We are aiming at the premium (= very expensive) end of the market. **○** the bottom/high/low/top/upper end • the budget/cheap/expensive/premium end
3 [sing.] a situation in which sth does not exist any more: Her contract **comes to an end** (= finishes) in June. ◇ The two sides finally reached a deal, bringing the ten-day strike **to an end**.
4 [C, usually sing.] a part of an activity with which sb is concerned, especially in business: We need somebody to handle the marketing end of the business. ◇ I have kept my end of the bargain.
5 [C, usually sing.] either of two places connected by a telephone call, journey, etc: I answered the phone but there was no one **at the other end**.
IDM **make (both) ends 'meet** to earn just enough money to be able to buy the things you need, pay what you owe, etc: Many small businesses are struggling to make ends meet. → idioms at DEEP adjective, SHARP
●**verb** [+ obj or no obj]
to finish; to make sth finish : The meeting ended on a positive note. ◇ They reported a €16 million loss for the year ending 31 August.

end con'sumer noun [C]
a member of the public who buys and uses a product: We want to give end consumers an easy way to buy online. ◇ creating the best product for the end consumer

end-of-'year adjective [only before noun]
relating to the end of December; relating to the end of a FINANCIAL YEAR: The company's end-of-year results will be released in February. ◇ End-of-year spending by consumers has lifted sales of mobile phones. → YEAR END

endorse (AmE spelling also **indorse**) /ɪnˈdɔːs; AmE ɪnˈdɔːrs/ verb [+ obj]
1 to say publicly that you support a person, statement or course of action: I strongly endorse the directors' plans.
2 (Marketing) to say in an advertisement that you use and like a particular product or service so that other people will want to buy or use it: We decided to use a celebrity to endorse our restaurant. ◇ products endorsed by loyal customers
3 (Finance) to sign the back of a cheque or BILL OF EXCHANGE so that it can be paid to sb else; to sign the back of a cheque in order to receive cash from the bank: You must endorse the cheque before we can deposit it.
4 (Insurance) to add conditions to a standard insurance policy so that it applies to particular circumstances: Policies that refer only to employees should be endorsed to include volunteer workers.

endorsement (AmE spelling also **indorsement**) /ɪnˈdɔːsmənt; AmE -ˈdɔːrs-/ noun [C,U]
1 a public statement or action showing that you support sb/sth; official approval of sth: The chairman's comments were a **ringing** (= powerful) endorsement of the senior management team. ◇ The plan will now go to the bankruptcy court for endorsement.
2 (Marketing) a statement made in an advertisement, usually by sb famous or important, saying that they use and like a particular product or service: They are looking for a **celebrity endorsement** (= one given by a famous person) of their new line of T-shirts. ◇ She has signed an endorsement deal with Nike.
3 (Finance) the act of signing the back of a cheque or BILL OF EXCHANGE; the signature and the words that are written: The trader will transfer the bill of exchange to his bank through endorsement.
4 (Insurance) conditions that are added to a standard insurance policy in order to make it apply to particular circumstances: This endorsement should be applied where the building to be insured is a farmhouse. ◇ a policy endorsement

endorser /ɪnˈdɔːsə(r); AmE ɪnˈdɔːrs-/ noun [C]
1 (Marketing) a person, usually sb famous or important, who says in an advertisement that they use and like a particular product or service: There is no money for a celebrity endorser.
2 (Finance) the person who signs the back of a cheque, a BILL OF EXCHANGE, etc.

endowment /ɪnˈdaʊmənt/ noun
1 [C,U] money that is given to a school, a college or another institution to provide it with an income; the act of giving this money: The university has a $10.5 billion endowment fund. ◇ a fund for the endowment of the performing arts
2 (Finance; Insurance) [C] a type of investment that you can buy from an insurance company in which you make regular payments over a period of time, or until you die, after which the company pays out an amount of money: to buy/sell an endowment ◇ Final payouts on 25-year **endowment policies** have fallen by 9 per cent in the past year.

en'dowment ,mortgage noun [C] (BrE)
a type of **mortgage** (= a loan to buy property) in which money is regularly paid into an **endowment**. At the end of a particular period of time this money is then used to pay back the money that was borrowed.

end 'product noun [C]
something that is produced by a particular activity or process: This report is the end product of two years of market research. ◇ Parts are assembled by hand and the end products are exported.

end-to-'end adjective [usually before noun]
connected with all the stages of a process or an activity: It's an end-to-end solution—from product

design to production. ◊ *end-to-end testing of the system*

,end-'user (*AmE spelling also* **end user**) *noun* [C]
a person who actually uses a product rather than one who makes or sells it, especially a person who uses a product connected with computers: *They sell their computers directly to businesses and individual end-users.* ◊ *end-user demand* [SYN] ULTIMATE CONSUMER → CONSUMER

energy /'enədʒi; *AmE* -ərdʒi/ *noun* [U]
a source of power, such as fuel, used for driving machines, providing heat, etc: *solar/wind/nuclear energy* ◊ *We have suffered from disappointing sales and higher energy costs.* ◊ *energy-saving equipment* ◊ *an energy company/supplier*

★ **enforce** /ɪn'fɔːs; *AmE* ɪn'fɔːrs/ *verb* [+ obj]
1 to make sure that people obey a particular law or rule: *The legislation will be difficult to enforce.* ◊ *The rules were strictly enforced.*
2 to make sth happen or force sb to do sth: *The company has said there will be no enforced redundancies.*
▶ **enforceable** /ɪn'fɔːsəbl; *AmE* -'fɔːrs-/ *adjective*: *legally enforceable contracts* **en'forcement** *noun* [U]

engage /ɪn'geɪdʒ/ *verb* [+ obj] (*formal*)
to employ sb to do a particular job: *He is currently engaged* **as** *a consultant.* ◊ *They engaged a young designer* **to** *create a new corporate identity.*

engaged /ɪn'geɪdʒd/ (*BrE*) (*also* **'busy**, *AmE, BrE*) *adjective*
(about a telephone line) being used: *I couldn't get through—the line's engaged.* ◊ *I phoned earlier but you were engaged* (= using your phone). ◊ *the engaged tone/signal*

engagement /ɪn'geɪdʒmənt/ *noun*

SEE ALSO: **letter of engagement, without engagement**

1 [C] an arrangement to do sth at a particular time, especially sth official or sth connected with your job: *I had to refuse because of a* **prior** *engagement.* ◊ *She has a number of* **speaking** *engagements next month.* ◊ *an engagement book/ diary*
2 (*HR*) [U,C] an arrangement to employ sb; the process of employing sb: *The terms of engagement are to be agreed in writing.*

en'gagement ,letter = LETTER OF ENGAGEMENT

engine /'endʒɪn/ *noun* [C]

SEE ALSO: **search engine**

1 the part of a vehicle that produces power to make the vehicle move: *a diesel/petrol engine* ◊ *an aircraft/car engine*
2 a thing that makes sth happen or has a very strong influence: *He believes that China will become the engine of growth for Asia.*
3 (*IT*) the part of a computer program that is designed to keep performing a particular task: *Each charge is processed through the payment engine.* ◊ *You can use the shopping engine to find the best prices on the net.*

★ **engineer** /,endʒɪ'nɪə(r); *AmE* -'nɪr/ *noun, verb*
● *noun* [C]

SEE ALSO: **automotive engineer**, CHEMICAL ENGINEER at **chemical engineering, civil ~, product ~, project ~, re-~, sales ~, software ~**

1 a person whose job involves designing and building engines, machines, roads, bridges, etc. See note at PROFESSION
2 a person who is trained to repair machines and electrical equipment: *They're sending an engineer to fix the phone.*

3 a person whose job is to control and repair engines, especially on a ship or an aircraft: *a flight engineer* ◊ *the chief engineer on a cruise liner*
● *verb* [+ obj]
1 to design and build sth: *The car is beautifully engineered and a pleasure to drive.*
2 to arrange for sth to happen or take place, especially when this is done secretly in order to give yourself an advantage: *He is trying to engineer a merger of two leading department store groups.*

★ **engineering** /,endʒɪ'nɪərɪŋ; *AmE* -'nɪr-/ *noun* [U]

SEE ALSO: **chemical engineering, concurrent ~, electrical ~, financial ~, genetic ~, heavy ~, human factors ~**, etc.

the activity of applying scientific knowledge to the design, building and control of machines, roads, bridges, electrical equipment, etc: *The engine is an impressive piece of engineering.* ◊ *We try to focus on engineering and production rather than on marketing.* ◊ *an engineering company/firm/group*

engi'neering in,surance *noun* [U]
a type of insurance in which money is paid if electrical equipment or machinery stops working because of a fault

enhance /ɪn'hɑːns; *AmE* -'hæns/ *verb* [+ obj]
to improve the good quality, value or status of sb/ sth: *This is an opportunity to enhance the reputation of the company.* ◊ *The acquisition has enhanced earnings.* ▶ **en'hanced** *adjective*: *enhanced productivity* ◊ *enhanced software* **en'hancement** *noun* [U,C]: *Formal training leads to skill enhancement.* ◊ *software enhancements*

enlargement /ɪn'lɑːdʒmənt; *AmE* -'lɑːrdʒ-/ *noun* [U; sing.]
the process or result of sth becoming or being made larger: *the enlargement of the company's overseas business activities* ◊ *EU enlargement* (= the fact of more countries joining the EU)

enquire (*also spelled* **inquire**, *especially in AmE*) /ɪn'kwaɪə(r)/ *verb* [no obj]
to ask sb for some information: *Several people telephoned to enquire* **about** *the new service.* ◊ *Someone was enquiring* **whether** *the business was for sale.* ▶ **en'quirer** (*also spelled* **inquirer**, *especially in AmE*) *noun* [C]: *Take down the name and telephone numbers of any enquirers.*
[PHR V] **en'quire into sth** to find out more information about sth: *A committee was appointed to enquire into the complaints.* [SYN] INVESTIGATE

★ **enquiry** (*also spelled* **inquiry**, *especially in AmE*) /ɪn'kwaɪəri; *AmE usually* 'ɪnkwəri/ *noun* (*plural* **enquiries**)

SEE ALSO: **status enquiry**

1 [C] ~ **(from sb) (about sb/sth)** a request for information about sb/sth; a question about sb/sth: *a telephone enquiry* ◊ *We received over 300 enquiries about the job.* ◊ *I'll have to* **make** *a few* **enquiries** (= try to find out about it) *and get back to you.* ◊ *enquiries from prospective buyers*
● *to* **make/receive** *an enquiry* • *to* **answer/deal with/ handle/respond to** *an enquiry*
2 [C] an official process to find out the cause of sth or to find out information about sth: *The organization has launched an internal enquiry into the matter.* ◊ *a merger enquiry* (= to see if it should happen or not)
● *to* **conduct/hold/launch** *an enquiry* • *to* **call for/ demand/order** *an enquiry*
3 [U] the act of asking questions or collecting information about sb/sth: *scientific enquiry* ◊ *a committee of enquiry*

4 enquiries [pl.] (*BrE*) a place where you can get information: *Ask at enquiries to see if your bag has been handed in.*
5 (*IT*; *Production*) [C,U] the act of finding information, for example about orders, costs or stock, that is stored in electronic form: *using SAP for a basic stock enquiry*

enter /'entə(r)/ *verb* [+ obj]
1 to begin taking part in an activity or a situation, especially to start competing in a particular kind of business: *As more manufacturers enter the market, price falls sharply. ◇ A new company has entered the bidding for the supermarket chain.*
2 (**be entered** *is not used*) (used about people or products) to arrive in a country or region: *He has called for a ban on new GM products entering the EU. ◇ tariffs on steel entering the US market*
3 to begin or reach a particular period of time in a process: *Our economy is entering a phase of recovery. ◇ The strike is entering its seventh month.*
4 (**be entered** *is not used*) to start working in a profession or career: *What advice would you give to anyone entering the industry? ◇ the number of young people entering the workforce ◇ She entered management as a young graduate.*
5 enter sth (in/into/on sth) to put information into a set of accounts, a list, a computer file, etc: *Enter your username and password. ◇ a system for entering and retrieving data ◇ I enter all my travel expenses on a spreadsheet.* → DATA ENTRY
IDM **enter/join the 'fray** to join in a situation in which people or companies are competing with each other for sth: *Several more companies have entered the fray to win the contract.* **enter 'service** to start to be used for the first time: *The new aircraft will be ready to enter service in 2009.* → idiom at FORCE *noun*
PHRV **'enter into sth (with sb)** to begin sth or become involved in sth, especially an official discussion or agreement: *Management has agreed to enter into discussions with the unions.*

★ enterprise /'entəpraɪz; *AmE* -tərp-/ *noun*

SEE ALSO: **free enterprise, private ~, small and medium-sized ~**

1 [C] a company or business: *a thriving fast-food enterprise ◇ How do you turn a loss-making enterprise into a profitable concern? ◇ The country has been selling off its state enterprises.*
○ *a family/multinational/private/public/state-owned enterprise ◆ a large/medium-sized/small enterprise ◆ to control/invest in/manage/run an enterprise ◆ an enterprise expands/grows/fails/succeeds*
2 [C] a business project or activity, especially one that is difficult or involves taking risks: *a joint enterprise between French and Japanese companies ◇ his latest business enterprise ◇ I have some concerns about the whole enterprise.* SYN VENTURE
○ *a business/commercial/new enterprise ◆ an ambitious/a difficult/an exciting enterprise ◆ to embark on/start/undertake an enterprise ◆ an enterprise fails/succeeds*
3 [U] the activity of starting and developing businesses: *grants to encourage enterprise in the region ◇ an enterprise culture (= in which people are encouraged to develop small businesses)*
○ *to encourage/promote enterprise*
4 [U] the ability to think of new projects and make them successful, especially by taking risks: *Its profits can be seen as a reward for enterprise and innovation. ◇ a man of enterprise*
○ *great enterprise ◆ to show enterprise*

'enterprise appli,cation *noun* [C]
(*IT*) software that is designed to help an organization manage an important part of the

business, such as the payment of staff (**payroll**), human resources and supplies of goods (**stock**), and is used by many different parts of the organization

,enterprise appli,cation inte'gration *noun* [U] (*abbr* **EAI**)
(*IT*) a central service that links other pieces of software within an organization so that information can easily be shared

,enterprise 'bargaining = WORKPLACE BARGAINING

'enterprise ,centre (*AmE spelling* ~ **center**) *noun* [C]
an office where people who want to start or develop a small business can get information, advice and help

,enterprise re'source ,planning *noun* [U] (*abbr* **ERP**)
(*Production*) a software system that links together all the aspects of a company's activities, such as finance, manufacturing, human resources and DISTRIBUTION, designed to help the business manage and control its work most efficiently

'enterprise ,union *noun* [C]
(*HR*) in some countries, a union for employees in one business or company

'enterprise zone *noun* [C]
(*Economics*) an area of a country which the government helps by encouraging companies to open new offices and factories there, usually by offering them financial benefits such as lower taxes

enterprising /'entəpraɪzɪŋ; *AmE* -tərp-/ *adjective*
able to think of new projects or new ways of doing things and make them successful: *Six enterprising college students decided to start their own business.*

entertainment /,entə'teɪnmənt; *AmE* -tər't-/ *noun* [C]

SEE ALSO: **home entertainment**

1 (*HR*) the act of taking a company's customers out for meals, drinks, etc.; the money spent on this: *We are specialists in corporate entertainment. ◇ an entertainment budget*
2 the business of making films/movies, television programmes, records, etc. to entertain people: *the entertainment industry*

entitle /ɪn'taɪtl/ *verb* [+ obj] (*usually* **be entitled**)
to give sb the right to do or to have sth: *If you are over 65 years of age you are entitled to a reduction. ◇ A clause in his contract entitles him to two years' salary if the company is taken over.*

entitlement /ɪn'taɪtlmənt/ *noun*
1 [U] the official right to have or do sth: *This may affect your entitlement to the full pension.*
2 [C] something that you have an official right to; the amount that you have the right to receive: *Staff must use their full holiday entitlement. ◇ Some people regard huge pay rises as an entitlement.*
3 [C] (*AmE*) a government system that provides financial support to a particular group of people: *a reform of entitlements ◇ Medicaid, Medicare and other entitlement programs*

entity /'entəti/ *noun* [C] (*plural* **entities**)

SEE ALSO: **business entity, legal entity**

(*Accounting*; *Law*) a business that exists as a separate unit and has its own legal identity: *The unit has become part of a larger department and no longer exists as a separate entity. ◇ We have to compete with giant corporate entities.*
○ *an independent/a legal/new/separate/single entity*

entrant /'entrənt/ *noun* [C]
1 (*Marketing*) a company that starts to sell goods or services in a particular market: *Competition would*

be fierce even without a new entrant in the market. ◇ a late entrant **to** the industry ◇ Two recent entrants offer competing services.
2 a person who has recently joined a profession, university, etc: new entrants **to** the teaching profession

entrepôt /'ɒntrəpəʊ; AmE 'ɑːntrəpoʊ/ noun [C]
(Trade) a port or other trading centre where goods are brought for import and export and are stored before being sent somewhere else: Dubai now serves as the main entrepôt of the Persian Gulf. **NOTE** Entrepôt is a French word.

★ **entrepreneur** /,ɒntrəprə'nɜː(r); AmE ,ɑːn-/ noun [C]

SEE ALSO: **serial entrepreneur**

a person who makes money by starting or running businesses, especially when this involves taking financial risks: a dotcom/fashion/high-tech/an Internet/a media entrepreneur ▶ **entrepreneurial** /,ɒntrəprə'nɜːriəl; AmE ,ɑːn-/ adjective: entrepreneurial skills/flair **entrepreneurialism** /,ɒntrəprə'nɜːriəlɪzm; AmE ,ɑːn-/ noun [U]: Our competitive advantage lies in our innovation, creativity and entrepreneurialism.
entrepreneurship /,ɒntrəprə'nɜːʃɪp; AmE ,ɑːntrəprə'nɜːr-/ noun [U]: fostering entrepreneurship in inner cities

entry /'entri/ noun (plural **entries**)

SEE ALSO: **barrier to entry, bill of ~, book ~, book of final ~, book of first ~, book of original ~, book of prime ~,** etc.

1 [U] the right or opportunity to take part in sth or become a member of an organization, a profession or a group: The government has ruled out early entry **into** the single currency. ◇ the five economic tests for euro entry ◇ More young people are postponing their entry into full-time work. ◇ We have 30 remaining graduate entry positions.
O early/late entry • to delay/gain/negotiate (sb's) entry • to oppose/support (sb's) entry
2 (Marketing) [U] when a company starts competing in a particular kind of business: Shell's entry **into** Japan's retail gas market ◇ Restrictions on **market entry** are soon to be abolished altogether.
O early/first/late entry • to announce/gain/plan entry (into sth)
3 (Accounting; IT) [C] an item, for example a piece of information, that is written or printed in a set of accounts, a computer file, a diary, etc: an accounting entry ◇ He faces charges of bank fraud and making false entries. ◇ There is no entry **in** his diary for that day. → DOUBLE-ENTRY BOOKKEEPING, SINGLE-ENTRY BOOKKEEPING
O to check/make/write an entry • accounting/ledger entries • calendar/diary/journal entries
4 (IT) [U] the act of putting information into a computer: The manual entry of some information led to errors.
O to do/handle/speed up entry
5 [U] the right of people or goods to enter a place; the act of entering a place: We were refused entry to the building. ◇ an entry visa ◇ new entry points for goods
O to be denied/be granted/be refused/gain entry • an entry charge/fee

'entry ˌbarrier = BARRIER TO ENTRY

'entry ˌlevel (also spelled **entry-level**, especially in AmE) noun [C,U]
1 (HR) (especially AmE) the lowest level of job in a particular profession, company, etc: Not enough good people are being recruited at the entry level.
2 the most basic of a group of similar products, suitable for new users who may later move on to a more advanced product

▶ **'entry-ˌlevel** adjective [usually before noun]: an entry-level job ◇ an entry-level computer

envelope /'envələʊp; 'ɒn-; AmE 'envəloʊp; 'ɑːn-/ noun [C]

SEE ALSO: **padded envelope, pre-addressed envelope**

1 a flat paper container used for sending letters in: an airmail/a padded/prepaid envelope → SAE, SASE
2 a flat container made of plastic for keeping papers in
→ idiom at PUSH verb

environment /ɪn'vaɪrənmənt/ noun

SEE ALSO: **marketing environment**

1 [C,U] the conditions that affect the behaviour and development of sb/sth; the physical conditions that sb/sth exists in: a pleasant working/learning environment ◇ We need to respond quickly to the changing business environment.
O the business/economic/political environment
2 the environment [sing.] the natural world in which people, animals and plants live: measures to protect the environment ◇ pollution of the environment
3 (IT) [C] the complete structure within which a user, computer or program operates: a desktop development environment
▶ **environmental** /ɪn,vaɪrən'mentl/ adjective [usually before noun]: the environmental effect of tourism **environmentally** /ɪn,vaɪrən'mentəli/ adverb: an environmentally sensitive area (= one that is easily damaged or that contains rare animals, plants, etc.)

en,vironmental a'nalysis = ENVIRONMENTAL SCANNING

en,vironmental 'health noun [U]
the activity of making sure that people are not damaged by the conditions in which they live or work: If you provide food, register with the local environmental health department for food hygiene training.

en,vironmental 'health ,officer noun [C] (abbr **EHO**)
a person who is responsible for making sure that people are not damaged by the conditions in which they live or work

en,vironmental 'impact noun [C, usually sing., U]
the effect that sth such as a new development, a business activity, etc. has on the environment: examining the environmental impact of adopting the new technology ◇ an environmental impact policy/study

environmentalist /ɪn,vaɪrən'mentəlɪst/ noun [C]
a person who is concerned about the natural environment and wants to improve and protect it
▶ **en,viron'mentalism** noun [U]

en,vironmentally-'friendly (also en,vironment-'friendly) adjective
(about products) not harming the environment: environmentally-friendly cars/energy/fuel/packaging

en,vironmental 'management ,system noun [U] (abbr **EMS**)
the way in which a business plans to manage and control its activities in order to protect and preserve natural resources such as clean air and water, the countryside, etc.

en,vironmental 'marketing = GREEN MARKETING

en,vironmental 'scanning noun [U] (also en,vironmental a'nalysis [U,C])
the process of obtaining and using information about current events, developments, changes, etc. that may affect an organization, so that the managers of the organization can plan its future

en,vironment-'friendly = ENVIRON-MENTALLY-FRIENDLY

EOC /,i: əʊ 'si:; AmE oʊ/ = EQUAL OPPORTUNITIES COMMISSION

EoI /,i: əʊ 'aɪ; AmE oʊ/ = EXPRESSION OF INTEREST

EOQ /,i: əʊ 'kju:; AmE oʊ/ = ECONOMIC ORDER QUANTITY

EPOS /'i:pɒs; AmE -pɑ:s/ abbr
(Commerce) **electronic point of sale** the electronic machines and computer systems used in shops/stores to record information about the goods sold: suppliers of cash tills, EPOS and scanning systems for supermarkets ◇ Stock control and financial data is updated directly from the EPOS terminal.

e-pro'curement noun [U]
(Production) the process of businesses obtaining supplies of goods or services using the Internet

EPS (AmE spelling usually **eps**) /,i: pi: 'es/
= EARNINGS PER SHARE, EXTENSIVE PROBLEM SOLVING

EQ /,i: 'kju:/ abbr
(HR) **emotional quotient** (used as a countable noun) a measurement of a person's EMOTIONAL INTELLIGENCE, sometimes calculated from the results of special tests: Employees with a high EQ are much more productive than those with a low EQ.

equal /'i:kwəl/ adjective, verb
● adjective
1 the same in size, quantity, value, etc. as sth else: You will get a commission equal **to** 5% of the selling price. ◇ The four companies are broadly equal in size. ◇ We have an equal number of men and women working here.
2 having the same rights or being treated the same as other people: I was never treated as an equal partner in the business. ◇ campaigning for equal treatment for all employees
IDM on ,equal 'terms (with sb) having the same advantages and disadvantages as sb else: Can our industry compete on equal terms with its overseas rivals?
● verb [+ obj] (-ll-, AmE -l-)
to be the same in size, quantity, value, etc. as sth else: two plus two equals four (2+2=4) ◇ Profits this quarter rose 50%, equalling the profits made in the whole of last year.

,Equal Em'ployment Oppor,tunities Com,mission noun [sing.] (abbr **EEOC**)
(HR) the organization in the US that tries to make sure that everyone has the same chances of employment, and is treated the same way at work, without differences of race, colour, religion or sex being considered

,equal em'ployment oppor,tunity (abbr **EEO**) = EQUAL OPPORTUNITY

equality /i'kwɒləti; AmE i'kwɑ:-/ noun [U]
the fact of being equal in rights, status, advantages, etc: equality of opportunity ◇ We are committed to promoting equality in the workplace. ◇ Women were working to achieve economic equality with men.
● economic/gender/social equality ◆ to achieve/demand/promote equality

,Equal Oppor'tunities Com,mission noun [sing.] (abbr **EOC**)
the organization in the UK that tries to make sure that women have the same chances of employment and the same pay as men, and that men and women are treated fairly at work

,equal oppor'tunity (also ,equal em'ployment oppor,tunity) noun [U,C; usually pl.]
(HR) the idea that everyone should have the same chances of employment, without differences such as race, religion, sex or age being considered: The company has a policy of equal opportunity. ◇ She advises banks and other large companies on equal opportunities. ◇ We are an **equal opportunity employer.**

,equal 'pay noun [U]
(HR) the idea that men and women should receive the same pay for doing the same work: Women are gaining access to the best jobs and winning equal pay. ◇ equal pay cases/claims/legislation

equation /ɪ'kweɪʒn/ noun [C]

SEE ALSO: **accounting equation**

a statement showing that two amounts or values are equal

★ **equilibrium** /,i:kwɪ'lɪbriəm; ,ek-/ (also ,market equi'librium) noun [U; sing.]

SEE ALSO: **partial equilibrium**

(Economics) a situation in which the amount of particular goods or services that people want to buy (**demand**) at a particular price equals the amount that businesses want to supply (**supply**): He believes that the steel market is **reaching** an equilibrium. ◇ The market is **in** equilibrium. ◇ the equilibrium rate of employment (= the supply of work and the demand for work are equal)—Picture at SUPPLY AND DEMAND

equi'librium price noun [C]
(Economics) the price at which the amount of a particular product or service being supplied equals the amount demanded → MARKET PRICE—Picture at SUPPLY AND DEMAND

equi'librium ,quantity noun [C]
(Economics) the amount of a particular product or service being bought or sold at the EQUILIBRIUM PRICE—Picture at SUPPLY AND DEMAND

equip /ɪ'kwɪp/ verb [+ obj] (-pp-) (often be equipped)
to supply sb/sth with what is needed for a particular purpose or task: We needed €650 000 to build and equip the manufacturing plant. ◇ a **fully** equipped office ◇ The phone **comes equipped with** a built-in digital camera.

★ **equipment** /ɪ'kwɪpmənt/ noun [U]

SEE ALSO: **capital equipment**

the machines, tools, etc. that are needed for a particular purpose or activity: They supply equipment for the food industry. ◇ Spending on computer equipment has decreased. ◇ This **piece of equipment** is used to label the bottles. See note at INFORMATION
⊕ to install/provide/supply/use equipment ◆ business/computer/industrial/office/telecoms equipment ◆ heavy/high-tech/obsolete/standard equipment

★ **equity** /'ekwəti/ noun

SEE ALSO: **book equity, brand ~, employment ~, external ~, home ~, horizontal ~, internal ~,** etc.

1 (Finance) [U] the money for business activities (**capital**) that a company obtains by selling shares rather than from loans: The company has raised €7 million of fresh equity. ◇ holding equity **in** a company ◇ *We have decided to reduce our* **equity capital**. ◇ *They have taken a large equity stake in the airline.* → DEBT

○ *to* **issue/raise** *equity* • *an equity* **interest/stake** *(in sth)* • *equity* **holdings/investments** • *equity* **markets/prices/values** • *an equity* **analyst/investor/trader**

2 (*Finance*; *Stock Exchange*) **equities** [pl.] shares in companies, especially ORDINARY SHARES; the business of trading shares: *Investing in equities carries a fairly high risk.* ◇ *Many investors are switching from equities to bonds.* ◇ *Equities fell 8.4% in June.* ◇ *the equities market*

○ *to* **buy/hold/invest in/sell/trade** *equities*

3 (*also* '**home** ,**equity**, *especially in AmE*) [U] the value of a property after all debts have been paid: *They have 10 years of mortgage payments left and about $75 000 equity in their home.*

○ *to* **have/take out/use** *equity*

'**equity ac,counting** *noun* [U] (*also* '**equity ,method** [sing.])
(*Accounting*) the practice of recording in your company's financial records the share of profits that you could claim from another company because you own part of it

'**equity ,finance** *noun* [U]
(*Finance*) money that a company gets by selling shares in order to finance its activities; the business of helping companies get money in this way: *It is now easier for smaller companies to attract investors and raise equity finance.* ◇ *the bank's equity finance division* → DEBT FINANCE

▶'**equity-,financed** *adjective*: *The firm is entirely equity-financed.* '**equity ,financing** *noun* [U,C]

'**equity fund** *noun* [C]
(*Finance*) an investment company that invests the money that people pay into it in shares: *Investors have withdrawn $80 billion from equity funds in the last four months.* ◇ *an equity fund manager*

'**equity ,gearing** = GEARING

'**equity ,kicker** *noun* [C]
(*Finance*)
1 a right to buy shares, often at a lower price than usual, that a company gives to sb as extra payment for receiving a loan: *By offering an equity kicker they can borrow at lower rates of interest.*
2 (*especially AmE*) a share of the profits from a property that you promise to sb who lends you money to buy it

the '**equity ,method** = EQUITY ACCOUNTING

'**equity share** *noun* [C]
(*Finance*) a share in a company that gives its owner the right to receive payments from profits (**dividends**) and vote in company meetings; a number of these that sb owns: *The company issued 12 000 equity shares of 12 rupees each.* ◇ *They have bought a 50% equity share in the company.*

ER /ˌiː ˈɑː(r)/ = EMPLOYEE RELATIONS

erase /ɪˈreɪz; *AmE* ɪˈreɪs/ *verb* [+ obj]
1 to remove or destroy sth completely: *The share price dropped 5% today, erasing yesterday's gains.*
2 to remove a recording from a tape or information from a computer's memory: *The files have been erased from the disk.* → DELETE *verb* (1)

'**e-re,cruitment** *noun* [U]
(*HR*) the practice of using the Internet to find new people to join a company or an organization

ergonomic /ˌɜːgəˈnɒmɪk; *AmE* ˌɜːrgəˈnɑːm-/ *adjective*
designed to be used or operated in a safe, comfortable and efficient way: *an ergonomic chair/keyboard* ◇ *the ergonomic design of workplaces*

▶ˌ**ergo'nomically** /ˌɜːgəˈnɒmɪkli; *AmE* ˌɜːrgəˈnɑːm-/ *adverb*

ergonomics /ˌɜːgəˈnɒmɪks; *AmE* ˌɜːrgəˈnɑːm-/ *noun*
1 (*AmE also* ˌ**biotech'nology**) [U] the study of how offices, equipment, furniture, etc. can be made more comfortable, safe and efficient for working people to use
2 [pl.] the aspects of the design of sth that make it comfortable, safe and efficient to use: *the ergonomics of the workstation*

ergonomist /ɜːˈgɒnəmɪst; *AmE* ɜːrˈgɑːn-/ *noun* [C]
a person who studies how offices, equipment, furniture, etc. can be made more comfortable, safe and efficient for working people to use

ERISA /eˈrɪsə/ *abbr*
Employee Retirement Income Security Act in the US, a law that protects the rights of people who take part in employee benefit and pension plans

ERM /ˌiː ɑːr ˈem/ = EXCHANGE RATE MECHANISM (1)

erode /ɪˈrəʊd; *AmE* ɪˈroʊd/ *verb* [+ obj or no obj]
(*often* **be eroded**)
to gradually destroy sth or make it weaker over a period of time; to be destroyed or made weaker in this way: *Unemployment is eroding consumer confidence.* ◇ *By the early 2000s the chain's brand identity had eroded.* ▶ **erosion** /ɪˈrəʊʒn; *AmE* ɪˈroʊʒn/ *noun* [U]: *the erosion of consumer confidence* ◇ *brand/price erosion*

ERP /ˌiː ɑː ˈpiː; *AmE* ɑːr/ = ENTERPRISE RESOURCE PLANNING

erratic /ɪˈrætɪk/ *adjective*
not following any plan or regular pattern; that you cannot rely on: *The share price has been erratic over the last year.* ◇ *erratic swings in price*

error /ˈerə(r)/ *noun* [C,U]

SEE ALSO: **margin of error**

a mistake, especially one that causes problems or affects the result of sth: *The auditors found several errors* **in** *the accounts.* ◇ *He believes the company made a strategic error in cutting staff.* ◇ *The payment was made* **in error** (= by mistake).

○ *to* **correct/discover/find/make** *an error* • *to* **check for/look for** *errors (in sth)* • *an* **accounting/a clerical/typing** *error* • *a* **computer/factual/pricing** *error* • *a* **fatal/serious/small** *error*

'**error cor,rection** *noun* [U]
(*IT*) a process by which a computer automatically corrects mistakes in data

'**error ,message** *noun* [C]
(*IT*) a message that appears on a computer screen which tells you that you have done sth wrong or that the program cannot do what you want it to do

Esc = ESCAPE

escalate /ˈeskəleɪt/ *verb*
1 [+ obj or no obj] to become or to make sth greater, more serious, etc: *The organization is faced with escalating costs and decreasing revenue.* ◇ *The management's action could escalate the dispute.*
2 [+ obj] to increase a price, charge, etc. in order to pay for a rise in the cost of materials, wages, etc: *Our management fees are escalated* **at** *3% a year.*
▶ **escalation** /ˌeskəˈleɪʃn/ *noun* [C,U]: *an escalation in food prices*

ˌ**esca'lation clause** *noun* [C]
a condition in a contract that allows sb to charge extra in order to pay for an increase in the cost of materials, wages, etc.

'**escalator clause** (*also* **escalator** /ˈeskəleɪtə(r)/) *noun* [C] (*both especially AmE*)
a condition in a contract that allows wages, prices,

etc. to increase or decrease in particular circumstances, for example when costs rise or fall: *The pension includes an escalator clause that raises payments in line with inflation.*

escape /ɪˈskeɪp/ noun [U] (also **esˈcape key** [C]) (abbr **Esc**)
(*IT*) a button on a computer keyboard that you press to stop a particular operation or leave a program: *Press escape to get back to the menu.*

eˈscape clause noun [C]
a condition in a contract that allows you to break part of the contract in particular circumstances

esˈcape key = ESCAPE

escrow /ˈeskrəʊ; AmE ˈeskroʊ/ noun [U,C]
(*IT; Law*) an arrangement in which sth valuable, such as a document, an amount of money, etc. is held by an independent person or organization until a particular condition has been met, when it is transferred to the person or organization who has a right to claim it; a document or other valuable item held in this way: *The shares will be held in escrow pending completion of the sale.* ◊ *The company has paid 1.5 million into an escrow account to cover potential tax liabilities.* ▶ **ˈescrow** verb [+ obj]

ESO /ˌiː es ˈəʊ; AmE ˈoʊ/ = EMPLOYEE STOCK OPTION

ESOP /ˈiːsɒp; AmE ˈiːsɑːp/ = EMPLOYEE SHARE OWNERSHIP PLAN, EMPLOYEE STOCK OWNERSHIP PLAN

espionage /ˈespiənɑːʒ/ noun [U]
the activity of finding out secret information about a country or an organization for another country or organization: *Two former research staff were arrested on charges of **industrial** espionage.*

ESS /ˌiː es ˈes/ = EMPLOYEE SELF SERVICE

est. abbr
1 a short way of writing **established** to show when a company was formed: *Grove's Tea Merchants, est. 1982*
2 a short way of writing **estimated** to show that a figure is not exact: *Est. total cost: $47 million*

establish /ɪˈstæblɪʃ/ verb [+ obj]
1 to start or create an organization, a system, etc. that is meant to last for a long time: *The group was established in 1934.* ◊ *The treaty established a free trade zone across Europe.*
2 **establish sb/sth/yourself (in sth) (as sth)** to become successful, especially in a new business: *It has quickly established itself as one of the top computer systems companies.*

establishment /ɪˈstæblɪʃmənt/ noun
1 [C] an organization, a large institution, a hotel or a restaurant: *a fast-food establishment* ◊ *The hotel is a comfortable and well-run establishment.* ◊ *a survey of business establishments used to calculate the number of people in work*
2 (*usually* **the establishment**) [sing. with sing./pl. verb] the people in a society or a profession who have influence and power and who usually do not support change: *the banking establishment*
3 [U] the act of starting or creating sth that is meant to last for a long time: *Since its establishment in 2001, the firm has enjoyed rapid growth.* ◊ *the establishment of a pension scheme*

estate /ɪˈsteɪt/ noun

SEE ALSO: industrial estate, real ~, trading ~

1 [C] (*BrE*) an area of land with a lot of houses, office buildings or factories of the same type on it: *There are several office buildings empty on the estate.* ◊ *a housing estate*

2 (*Law*) [C,U] all the money and property that a person owns, especially everything that is left when they die: *Her estate was left to her daughter.* ◊ *a bankrupt estate*
3 [C, usually sing., U] (*BrE*) a group of small businesses, especially places where people go to drink alcohol (**pubs**), that are owned and controlled by a single organization: *The company plans to sell its estate of 108 coffee bars.* ◊ *a pub estate*

eˈstate ˌagent (*BrE*) (also **ˈreal estate ˌagent**, AmE, BrE) (AmE also **ˈRealtor™**) noun [C]
a person or business that sells or rents houses, buildings and land for the owners, usually in return for a fee that is a percentage of the price of the property: *a national network of estate agents*
▶ **eˈstate ˌagency** (*BrE*) (also **ˈreal estate ˌagency**, AmE, BrE) noun [C]: *an estate agency chain/network*

eˈstate tax (also **ˈdeath tax**, informal) noun [C,U]
in the US, tax that must be paid on the value of the money and property of sb who has died
→ INHERITANCE TAX

★ **estimate** noun, verb
● *noun* /ˈestɪmət/
1 a judgement that you make without having the exact details or figures about the size, amount, cost, etc. of sth: *Can you give me a rough estimate of the time involved?* ◊ *Estimates of inflation range from 4 to 6 per cent.* ◊ *We had to cut our sales estimate by 5%.* ◊ *Earnings are in line with our estimates.*
❍ *a final/an initial/a preliminary estimate ♦ a best/careful/rough estimate ♦ to cut/lower/raise/revise an estimate ♦ sth is in line with/above/below an estimate*
2 (*Commerce*) a statement of how much a piece of work will probably cost: *We got estimates from three firms and accepted the lowest.* See note at QUOTE
❍ *to give (sb)/prepare/provide (sb with)/submit an estimate ♦ to accept/ask for/get an estimate*
→ idiom at BALLPARK
● *verb* /ˈestɪmeɪt/ [+ obj] (*often* **be estimated**)
to form an idea of the cost, size, value etc. of sth, but without calculating it exactly: *They estimate that the oil price could increase to $27 by 2025.* ◊ *Sales this year are estimated at £6 billion.* ◊ *a contract estimated to be worth €100 million* ◊ *The contract is worth an estimated €100 million.* ◊ *The costs were more than originally estimated.*
▶ **estimation** /ˌestɪˈmeɪʃn/ noun [C]: *Estimations of our total world sales are around 50 million.*

estimator /ˈestɪmeɪtə(r)/ noun [C]
a person whose job involves calculating the cost, price or value of sth: *She works as an estimator at a construction company.*

ˈe-ˌtailer noun [C]
(*E-commerce*) a business that sells goods to the public on the Internet: *a furniture e-tailer*
NOTE E-tailer is formed from 'e-' (electronic) and 'retailer'. ▶ **ˈe-ˌtailing** noun [U]: *an e-tailing business/site*

etc. /ˌet ˈsetərə; ˌɪt/ abbr
et cetera used after a list to show that there are other things that you could mention: *We talked about the contract, the pay, etc.* **NOTE** Et cetera is a Latin phrase meaning 'and the rest'.

Ethernet /ˈiːθənet; AmE -θərn-/ noun [sing.]
(*IT*) a system for connecting a number of computer systems to form a network

ethic /ˈeθɪk/ noun
1 ethics [pl.] moral principles that control or influence a person's behaviour: *professional/business/corporate ethics* ◊ *The company has drawn up a code of ethics for its managers.*

2 [sing.] a system of moral principles or rules of behaviour: *There is a strong work ethic among the staff.*

ethical /'eθɪkl/ *adjective*
1 morally correct or acceptable: *Is it ethical to read employees' emails? ◇ an ethical investment fund* (= that invests in companies, etc. whose actions are considered morally acceptable) OPP UNETHICAL
2 connected with beliefs and principles about what is right and wrong: *an ethical issue/problem/ question*
▶ **ethically** /'eθɪkli/ *adverb*

ethnic 'monitoring *noun* [U]
(*HR*) the activity of collecting and analysing information about the race of all the employees in a company or an organization to check that all races are present in a fair way

ethos /'i:θɒs; *AmE* 'i:θɑːs/ *noun* [sing.]
the moral ideas and attitudes that belong to a particular group, organization or society: *Our company ethos is based on being totally reliable.*

'e-ticket (*also* ,electronic 'ticket) *noun* [C]
1 a series of numbers, letters or symbols that you receive instead of a paper ticket when you pay on the Internet or by telephone for a service, especially to travel on a plane, go to a theatre, etc. It is recorded on the computer of the business that provides the service: *Customers who book online will be issued with an e-ticket.*
2 a ticket, for example, one to travel on a train or bus, which is stored electronically on a small plastic card (a **smart card**)
▶ **'e-ticketing** (*also* ,electronic 'ticketing) *noun* [U]: *They have introduced e-ticketing for all local flights.*

etiquette /'etɪket; *AmE* -kət/ *noun* [U]
the rules of polite and correct behaviour: *Punctuality is an important aspect of business etiquette.* → NETIQUETTE

ETR /,iː tiː 'ɑː(r)/ = EFFECTIVE TAX RATE

EU /,iː 'juː/ = EUROPEAN UNION

Euribor /'jʊəribɔː(r); *AmE* 'jʊribɔːr/ *abbr*
(*Finance*) **Euro Interbank Offered Rate** the average rate of interest that the largest European banks charge each other for borrowing an amount of euros for a particular period of time: *Interest on the loan is charged at 2 per cent over Euribor.*

Euro /'jʊərəʊ; *AmE* 'jʊroʊ/ *adjective* (*informal*)
1 (used especially in newspapers) connected with Europe or the European Union: *Euro laws/leaders*
2 (*Finance*) used to describe a currency or an investment that is traded in the EUROMARKETS: *Euro commercial paper*

euro /'jʊərəʊ; *AmE* 'jʊroʊ/ *noun* (*plural* **euros**)
1 [C] the unit of money of some countries of the European Union; €: *The price is given in dollars or euros. ◇ In New York, the US currency rose half a cent against the euro. ◇ the introduction of euro coins and banknotes* See note at INCREASE
2 (*often* **the euro**) [sing.] the system of using the euro as a national currency: *He believes that Denmark will join the euro.*

Euro- /'jʊərəʊ; *AmE* 'jʊroʊ/ *combining form*
1 (*used to form nouns and adjectives*) connected with Europe or the European Union: *a Euro-MP*
2 (*Finance*) used with the name of a currency or an investment to indicate that it is traded in the EUROMARKETS: *Euro-Yen*

'euro ,area = EUROZONE

Eurobond /'jʊərəʊbɒnd; *AmE* 'jʊroʊbɑːnd/ (*also* 'global bond) *noun* [C]
(*Finance*) a type of bond in a particular currency that governments and large organizations sell to international investors outside the country that uses that currency: *The bank plans to issue*

---

eurobonds worth €200 million with a term of five years. ◇ a five-year dollar-denominated eurobond → FOREIGN BOND NOTE The word **Euro** in **Eurobond** does not refer to Europe or the euro. Eurobonds can be sold in any country and have a price in any currency.

Eurocurrency /'jʊərəʊkʌrənsi; *AmE* 'jʊroʊkɜːr-/ *noun* [C,U] (*plural* **Eurocurrencies**)
(*Finance*) a form of money that is held or bought and sold outside its home country: *London has become the major centre for Eurocurrency business.* NOTE The word **Euro** in **Eurocurrency** does not refer to Europe or the euro. A Eurocurrency can be from any country in the world.

Eurodollar /'jʊərəʊdɒlə(r); *AmE* 'jʊroʊdɑːl-/ *noun* [C]
(*Finance*) a US dollar that is held in a bank account or borrowed by an organization outside the US: *The price of Eurodollars has been falling.*

Euroland (*also spelled* **euroland**) /'jʊərəʊlænd; *AmE* 'jʊroʊ-/ *noun* [U] (*informal*)
(used especially in newspapers) the countries in the European Union that use the euro as a unit of money → EUROZONE

Euromarket /'jʊərəʊmɑːkɪt; *AmE* 'jʊroʊmɑːrk-/ *noun* [C]
(*Finance*)
1 an international market in which banks and large organizations buy and sell EUROBONDS, EUROCURRENCIES, etc: *A group of 10 international banks will underwrite and sell the bonds in the Euromarkets.*
2 [sing.] the European Union considered as a single financial or commercial market

the 'European 'Central 'Bank *noun* [sing.] (*abbr* **ECB**)
a central bank for the countries in Europe who use the euro as their national currency (the **eurozone**)

the 'European Com'mission *noun* [sing.] (*abbr* **EC**)
a group of officials, led by a president, who run the European Union and apply its laws. Its members are chosen by the governments of the countries in the European Union.

the 'European Com'munity *noun* [sing.] (*abbr* **EC**)
a group of countries in Europe that have developed common rules on many political and economic matters, for example on what taxes to charge on imported goods and on how companies may compete fairly with each other NOTE The **European Community** is now part of the **European Union**. The term **European Community** is still sometimes used to refer to the **European Union**.

'European De'positary Re'ceipt *noun* [C] (*abbr* **EDR**)
(*Stock Exchange*) a type of DEPOSITARY RECEIPT that is bought and sold on stock exchanges in Europe

the 'European 'Economic 'Area *noun* [sing.] (*abbr* **EEA**)
an agreement between many countries in Europe. People living in one of these countries can work in any of the other countries, and goods, money, etc. can be moved between the countries without having to pay taxes.

the 'European 'Economic Com'munity *noun* [sing.] (*abbr* **EEC**)
an organization of European countries that was formed in 1957 in order to reduce trade restrictions in Europe. It developed into the EUROPEAN COMMUNITY.

'European 'Monetary 'Union = EMU

the ‚European 'Union noun [sing.] (abbr **EU**)
an economic and political organization that many
European countries belong to

Eurostocks /'jʊərəʊstɒks; AmE 'jʊroʊstɑːks/
noun [pl.]
(used especially in newspapers) shares that are
traded on European stock exchanges

Eurozone (also spelled **eurozone**) /'jʊərəʊzəʊn;
AmE 'jʊroʊzoʊn/ (also '**euro ‚area**) noun [sing.]
the countries in the European Union that use the
euro as a unit of money: a cut in interest rates in the
Eurozone → EUROLAND

evade /ɪ'veɪd/ verb [+ obj]
to find a way of not doing sth, especially sth you
legally or morally should do: He has been
charged with evading sales tax on $15 million of
purchases. ▶ **evasion** /ɪ'veɪʒn/ noun [C,U]: plans to
fight fare evasion on public transport → TAX EVASION

★ **evaluate** /ɪ'væljueɪt/ verb [+ obj]

SEE ALSO: re-evaluate

to study all the available information about sb/sth
and then form an opinion about them/it: We use
written tests and interviews to evaluate job
candidates. ◊ The bids will be evaluated by an
independent committee. [SYN] ASSESS
▶ **evaluative** /ɪ'væljuətɪv/ adjective: They have
developed a set of evaluative criteria for websites.

evaluation /ɪ,vælju'eɪʃn/ noun

SEE ALSO: job evaluation, performance evaluation

1 [U] the process of studying all the available
information about sb/sth and forming an opinion
about them/it: Ongoing training and evaluation of
employees should be a priority.
2 [C] a spoken or written opinion about the
quality, value, importance, etc. of sb/sth: All
employees will have an annual performance
evaluation. ◊ We conducted a thorough evaluation of
the system.

e'vent ‚management noun [U]
1 (Marketing) the activity of organizing events such
as concerts, sports competitions and parties for
companies as part of their marketing activities: The
company specializes in event management and
corporate hospitality.
2 (Production) = SUPPLY CHAIN EVENT
MANAGEMENT

e'vent ‚marketing noun [U]
1 the activity of showing and advertising products
or services to people in public places or at special
events such as TRADE SHOWS or sports
competitions: We set up stalls in several shopping
malls as part of an event marketing campaign.
2 the activity of advertising and attracting people
to a special event

evict /ɪ'vɪkt/ verb [+ obj]
(Law) to force sb to leave a house or land, especially
when you have the legal right to do so: A number of
tenants have been evicted for not paying the rent.
▶ **eviction** /ɪ'vɪkʃn/ noun [U,C]: to face eviction
from your home

evidence /'evɪdəns/ noun [U]
the information that is used in a court to try to
prove sth: You cannot be forced to give evidence
(= say what you know, describe what you have
seen, etc. in a court) against your spouse. ◊ The
investigation found no evidence of wrongdoing.
❍ to give/present (sb with)/produce evidence ◆ to
consider/examine/hear/study evidence ◆ to admit/
allow/exclude evidence

evolve /ɪ'vɒlv; AmE ɪ'vɑːlv/ verb [+ obj or no obj]
to develop gradually, especially from a simple to a
more complicated form; to develop sth in this way:
The company has evolved into a major electronics
manufacturer. ◊ Their business evolved from a series
of mergers. ◊ We constantly evolve our products to
meet the changing needs of customers.

EVP /,i: vi: 'pi:/ = EXECUTIVE VICE-PRESIDENT

ex /eks/ preposition
1 (BrE) not including sth: The price is €2 000 ex VAT.
→ EXCLUDING
2 (Trade) used to show that a price or contract
includes the cost of delivering goods to the place
mentioned: All prices are ex dock New York.
→ DELIVERED EX QUAY, DELIVERED EX SHIP
3 (Trade) used to show that a price or contract does
not include transport from the place mentioned
→ EX WAREHOUSE, EX WORKS
4 (Finance) used to show that the buyer of a share,
bond, etc. will not receive the right to claim the
thing mentioned: As of 11 May, the shares will be
traded ex bonus. ◊ The bonds will be issued on an ex-
interest basis. [OPP] CUM

★ **exceed** /ɪk'siːd/ verb [+ obj]
1 to be greater than a particular number or
amount: Total sales are expected to exceed
€250 million. ◊ While demand exceeds supply, prices
will continue to rise. ◊ We have exceeded our
earnings target this year.
2 to do more than the law or an order, etc. allows
you to do: There is a charge for exceeding your
overdraft limit.

excellence /'eksələns/ noun [U]

SEE ALSO: centre of excellence

the quality of being extremely good: an award for
excellence in design and engineering ◊ efforts to
achieve manufacturing excellence

except /ɪk'sept/ preposition, verb
● **preposition** (also ex'cept for)
not including: We are open every day except Sunday.
● **verb** [+ obj] (usually be excepted)
to not include sb/sth: Some types of advertisements
are excepted from the regulations.

exception /ɪk'sepʃn/ noun [C]

SEE ALSO: management by exception

1 (Insurance) in an insurance policy, particular risks
that you are not protected for: The policy exceptions
include claims for sports injuries.
2 (IT) the fact that a computer cannot process an
instruction in the normal way: The software
generates a daily exception report of sales that cannot
be processed. → ERROR

exceptional /ɪk'sepʃənl/ adjective, noun
● **adjective**

SEE ALSO: pre-exceptional

1 unusually good: 2005 was an exceptional year for
the business.
2 very unusual: We reserve the right to close the
account in exceptional circumstances.
3 (Accounting) used to describe an amount of
money in a company's financial records that is
connected with a company's normal business
activities but is much larger than usual and will
have an important effect on profits: The cost of
cancelling the contract will be accounted for as an
exceptional charge.
● **noun** [C] (usually **exceptionals** [pl.])
(Accounting) = EXCEPTIONAL ITEM

ex‚ceptional 'item (also ex'ceptional) noun [C,
usually pl.]
(Accounting) (in a company's financial records) an
amount of money that is paid or received as part of
normal business activities but which is unusually

large and has an important effect on profits: *Net profit before* (= not including) *exceptional items fell by 5.9%.* → EXTRAORDINARY ITEM

★ **excess** *noun, adjective*
● *noun* /ɪk'ses/
1 [sing; U] more than is necessary or acceptable: *There is an excess of diamonds in the marketplace.* ◇ *Growth in sales is expected to be in excess of* (= more than) *five per cent.*
2 [C,U] an amount by which sth is larger than sth else: *We cover costs up to €800 and then you pay the excess.*
3 (*Insurance*) [C,U] the part of an insurance claim that you must pay while the insurance company pays the rest: *All claims are subject to an excess of €100.*
● *adjective* /'ekses/ [only before noun]
in addition to an amount that is necessary or that can be used: *The excess office space has been rented to another company.* ◇ *We have cut our prices in an attempt to reduce excess stock.*

,**excess 'baggage** *noun* [U]
bags, cases, etc. taken on to a plane that weigh more than the amount each passenger is allowed to carry without paying extra

,**excess ca'pacity** *noun* [U]
(*Economics; Production*) the ability to produce or supply more of a product or service than is needed; the extra quantity that could be produced or supplied: *Some aircraft and telecoms companies are still struggling with excess capacity.*

,**excess de'mand** *noun* [U]
(*Economics*) a situation in which more of a product or service is wanted by buyers at a particular price than the industry can supply: *Because there is excess demand for energy, we can expect the price to rise.*

,**excess sup'ply** *noun* [U,C]
(*Economics*) a situation in which more of a product or service is supplied by an industry than buyers want at the price; the extra goods or services available: *Prices have fallen as a result of excess supply.*

★ **exchange** /ɪks'tʃeɪndʒ/ *noun, verb*
● *noun*

SEE ALSO: B2B exchange, bill of ~, commodity ~, foreign ~, futures ~, information ~, International Securities ~, etc.

1 [C,U] an act of giving sth to sb or doing sth for sb and receiving sth in return: *an exchange of emails* ◇ *Workers agreed to a pay cut in exchange for shares in the company.*
2 (*Commerce; Finance*) [C] an organized system that allows traders to buy and sell currencies, investments, goods, etc.; a place where this takes place: *The company's shares are traded on the Euronext exchange in Paris.* ◇ *the floor of the exchange* (= where traders deal with each other) ◇ *They have set up an electronic trading exchange* (= for example, using an Internet site) *for wood products.*
3 [U] the process of changing an amount of one currency for an equal value of another: *The government plans to introduce controls on currency exchange.* → EXCHANGE RATE, FOREIGN EXCHANGE
4 [C] an arrangement when two people or groups from different countries visit each other's homes or do each other's jobs for a short time: *a 12-month work exchange for recent graduates* ◇ *an exchange student*
5 [C] = TELEPHONE EXCHANGE
● *verb* [+ obj]
1 to give sth to sb and receive sth else from them: *We exchanged business cards.* ◇ *The bank will exchange €2 million of debt for shares in the company.*

2 to change an amount of one currency for another: *They exchanged their dollars for pesos.*
3 if you **exchange** sth you have bought, or a shop/store **exchanges** it, you return it and get sth different or better instead: *Can I exchange this shirt for a larger size?* ◇ *Sale goods cannot be exchanged.*
4 (*Law*) (*BrE*) **exchange contracts** to sign a contract with the person that you are buying a building or piece of land on from: *They have just exchanged contracts on the purchase of a new warehouse.*
IDM ex,**change 'hands** = CHANGE HANDS at CHANGE *verb*

───────────────────

WHICH WORD?

exchange/change/return

If you are unhappy with goods you have bought from a shop/store, you can usually **exchange** or **change** them.

If you **return** something, you take it back to the seller and get your money back.

───────────────────

exchangeable /ɪks'tʃeɪndʒəbl/ *adjective*
1 that can be exchanged: *These vouchers are not exchangeable for cash.*
2 (*Finance*) (about bonds) that can be exchanged for shares in another company at a particular time in the future: *The bonds are exchangeable into shares of Thomson Multimedia.* → CONVERTIBLE

ex'change con,trol *noun* [C, usually pl., U]
(*Economics*) a set of rules that a government uses to limit the amount of local currency that people can sell or the price at which they can sell it: *The government has implemented exchange controls to protect the bolivar currency.* ◇ *exchange control regulations*
O *to* **impose/introduce/tighten** *exchange controls* ✦ *to* **lift/relax** *exchange controls*

ex'change e,conomy *noun* [C]
(*Economics*) an economy in which people trade goods with each other or buy goods using money

ex'change ,market = FOREIGN EXCHANGE MARKET

ex,change of 'shares (*BrE*) (*AmE* ex,change of 'stock) *noun* [C,U]
(*Finance*) when a company buys or joins with another company by using some of its shares to pay for shares in the other company: *The merger will be financed by an exchange of shares.*

ex'change rate (*also* ,rate of ex'change) *noun* [C]

SEE ALSO: floating exchange rate, real exchange rate

the relation in value between one currency and another: *The current exchange rate is 50 rupees to the euro.* ◇ *the rupee/euro exchange rate* ◇ *The euro has a high exchange rate against the yen.* ◇ *movements/fluctuations in the exchange rate*
SYN CURRENCY RATE
O *a* **high/low/stable/strong/weak** *exchange rate* ✦ *a* **competitive/favourable** *exchange rate* ✦ *the exchange rate* **drops/falls/rises** ✦ *an exchange rate* **regime/system**

ex'change rate ex,posure *noun* [U,C]
(*Finance*) the fact that a business may lose money in the future by needing to change one currency for another less valuable one: *Our high percentage of foreign sales means we face significant exchange rate exposure.* ◇ *We have a large exchange rate exposure to the yen.* ◇ *to* **hedge (against)** (= protect against) *exchange rate exposure*

ex'change rate ,mechanism *noun*
(*Economics*)
1 Exchange Rate Mechanism (*abbr* **ERM**) [sing.] a
way of linking the currencies of some European
Union countries and controlling their EXCHANGE
RATES, before the euro was introduced in 1999
2 [C] any system in which the values of different
currencies are linked together: *She predicts that
Asian economies will set up an exchange rate
mechanism.*

excise /'eksaɪz/ *noun* [U]

SEE ALSO: **Customs and Excise**

a tax on particular goods and services that are sold
within a country, such as alcohol and cigarettes:
The government has decided to freeze the excise **on**
fuel. ◇ (*BrE*) *a reduction in* **excise duties** *on beer* ◇
(*AmE*) *a proposal to increase the* **excise tax** *on
cigarettes* → CUSTOMS DUTY

excl. *abbr* (*only used in written English*)
excluding: *Price: $15 each (excl. GST)*

★ **exclude** /ɪk'skluːd/ *verb* [+ obj]
1 to deliberately not include sth in what you are
doing or considering: *The price of the trip excludes
insurance.* ◇ *The cost of borrowing has been excluded
from the inflation figures.* OPP INCLUDE
2 to prevent sb/sth from entering a place or taking
part in sth: *The public were excluded from the board
meeting.*

excluding /ɪk'skluːdɪŋ/ *preposition* (*abbr* **excl.**)
not including: *Lunch costs $25 per person, excluding
drinks.* ◇ *Excluding unusual charges, income was up
by 54%.* → EX (1)

★ **exclusion** /ɪk'skluːʒn/ *noun*
1 [U] the act of preventing sb/sth from entering a
place or taking part in sth: *The company faces
exclusion from the FTSE 100.* ◇ *Focus on your career,
but not* **to the exclusion of** *everything else.*
2 (*Law*) [C] a particular person, thing or situation
that a contract, law, tax, etc. does not apply to:
Check the list of exclusions in the insurance policy. ◇
There are several exclusions **to** *the trade tariff.*

exclusive /ɪk'skluːsɪv/ *adjective*
1 only given to one particular person, group or
organization; not involving others: *The CEO has
exclusive use of a company car.* ◇ *We have exclusive
rights to distribute the products in the UK.* ◇ *These
travel products are exclusive* **to** *our company* (= no
one else sells them).
2 being the only official one or ones: *We are the
exclusive distributor of the products worldwide.*
3 of a high quality and expensive and therefore
not often bought or used by most people: *an
exclusive hotel* ◇ *exclusive designer stores/clothes*
4 exclusive of sb/sth not including sb/sth: *The
price quoted is exclusive of VAT.*

exclusivity /,eksklu:'sɪvəti/ *noun* [U]
1 the right to be the only person or organization to
do sth: *Agents are given exclusivity to trade in certain
areas.* ◇ *The retailer has exclusivity deals with several
suppliers* (= they do not supply others).
○ *to give/grant exclusivity to sb/sth* • *an exclusivity
agreement/clause/contract/deal*
2 (*also* **exclusiveness** / ɪk'skluːsɪvnəs/ *less frequent*)
the fact that people see a product or service as
being of high quality and expensive and therefore
only a small group buy or use it: *a designer whose
clothes have not lost their exclusivity*

excuse /ɪk'skjuːs/ = SICK NOTE

,ex-di'rectory *adjective* (*BrE*)
(about a person or telephone number) not listed in
the public telephone book, at the request of the
owner of the telephone. Telephone services will

not give these numbers to people who ask for
them: *an ex-directory number* SYN UNLISTED

,ex-'dividend (*also* ,**ex-'div.**, *informal*) *adverb*,
adjective (*abbr* **xd**)
(*Finance*) (about a share that is sold) that does not
give the buyer the right to claim the next payment
(**dividend**): *The shares will trade ex dividend from
June 18.* ◇ *the ex-dividend price* ◇ *The shares begin
trading xd as from next Friday.* OPP CUM DIVIDEND

exec /ɪg'zek/ *noun* [C] (*informal*)
an **executive** in a business: *the company's chief exec*
◇ *the high salaries paid to top execs*

execute /'eksɪkjuːt/ *verb*
1 [+ obj] to do a piece of work, perform a duty, put
a plan into action, etc: *We can execute most orders in
just one week.* ◇ *to execute a plan/strategy/project* ◇
All trades (= in shares, etc.) *are executed through a
broker.*
2 [no obj] to achieve a particular business goal; to
be successful as a business: *Our success is due to our
managers' ability to execute.* ◇ *Their online travel
company is executing well and showing impressive
growth.*
3 (*IT*) [+ obj] to make a computer perform an
action: *To execute a program, type the program
name.* ◇ *execute a command/an instruction/a query*
SYN RUN
PHR V **'execute on sth** to complete a task or
perform an activity properly: *The firm now has the
necessary skills and funding to execute on its business
plan.*

execution /,eksɪ'kjuːʃn/ *noun* [U]

SEE ALSO: **writ of execution**

1 the act of doing a piece of work, performing a
duty, or putting a plan into action: *There are doubts
about the company's execution of its business
strategy.* ◇ *The idea was good, but the execution was
poor.*
2 the act of achieving a particular business goal or
being successful as a business: *Most CEOs fail due to
a lack of execution.*
3 (*Finance*) the act of transferring money and
shares, bonds, etc. between buyers and sellers in a
market: *They have set up an online execution service.*

exe'cution risk *noun* [U,C]
the risk that a new business, project, etc. will fail
because it is not managed or carried out in the
right way: *the execution risks associated with
expanding into a new region*

★ **executive** /ɪg'zekjətɪv/ *noun*, *adjective*
● *noun*

SEE ALSO: **account executive**

1 [C] (*abbr* **exec**) a person who has an important
job as a manager of a company or an organization:
Several top executives have left the company. ◇ *Our
executives are judged on how well they manage
people and look after the company's reputation.* See
note at BOSS
○ *high-ranking/key/senior/top executives* • *business/
company/corporate/industry executives* • *an
advertising/a marketing/media/an oil/a sales
executive*
2 [C with sing./pl. verb] a group of people who run a
company or an organization: *The union's executive
has/have yet to reach a decision.*
● *adjective* [only before noun]
1 connected with managing a business or an
organization, and with making plans and decisions:
She has an executive position in a finance company. ◇
the executive management team
○ *executive decisions/duties/jobs/positions* •
executive bonuses/pay/perks
2 having the power to put important laws and
decisions into effect; connected with this: *The
executive board have approved the redundancies.* ◇

○ an executive **board/committee/officer**
3 for the use of sb who is important; expensive and of good quality: *the executive lounge* (= at an airport)

○ an executive **jet/lounge/suite** ◆ executive **cars/housing**

e,xecutive as'sistant *noun* [C]

a person whose job is to help a senior manager or **executive** in a company by organizing their affairs, dealing with letters, etc: *He was appointed executive assistant to the managing director.* [SYN] EXECUTIVE SECRETARY

e,xecutive 'chairman *noun* [C]

a person who is the most senior member of the BOARD of a large company and is also involved in running it: *He moved from being executive chairman to chief executive.*

e,xecutive di'rector *noun* [C]

a member of the BOARD that controls a company who is also employed as a senior manager of the company → NON-EXECUTIVE DIRECTOR

e,xecutive infor'mation ,system *noun* [C]

(*abbr* **EIS**)
(*IT*) computer software that contains all the data and information that senior managers need to make decisions → DECISION SUPPORT SYSTEM

e'xecutive search *noun* [C,U]

(*HR*) the process of finding sb who is suitable for a very senior job in a company by looking at people working in other companies who have the right skills and experience: *They carried out an executive search for a new chief executive.* ◇ *an executive search firm* → HEADHUNT

e,xecutive 'secretary *noun* [C]

1 a person who works as secretary for a senior manager or an **executive** in a company: *an executive secretary to the HR director*
[SYN] EXECUTIVE ASSISTANT, PA
2 the leader of some types of public or government organizations; a senior official in some businesses: *She has been appointed (as) executive secretary of the Economic Commission for Europe.*

e,xecutive 'summary (*also* ,management 'summary, *less frequent*) *noun* [C]

a short statement that gives the important facts, conclusions and suggestions of a report, usually printed at the beginning of the report

e,xecutive ,vice-'president *noun* [C]

(*especially AmE*) (*abbr* **EVP**)
an important person who is in charge of a particular part of a business and who works closely with the CHIEF EXECUTIVE OFFICER

e,xemplary 'damages = PUNITIVE DAMAGES

★ exempt /ɪgˈzempt/ *adjective, verb*

● *adjective*
1 if sb/sth is **exempt** from sth, they are not affected by it, do not have to do it, pay it, etc: *Payments into a pension fund are exempt from tax.* ◇ *Larger companies will have to pay the charge, but small businesses are exempt.*
2 (*used with a noun to form adjectives*) not having to do, pay, etc. the thing mentioned: *tax-exempt*
● *verb* [+ obj]
to decide officially that a rule or law, especially one concerning payment of tax, will not apply to particular people or things: *The government may exempt various products from the import tax.*

★ exemption /ɪgˈzempʃn/ *noun*

SEE ALSO: **personal exemption, tax exemption**

1 [U,C] official permission not to do sth or pay sth that you would normally have to do or pay:

Graduates in accounting may qualify for exemption from some professional examinations. ◇ *The law contains a small-business exemption* (= it does not apply to small businesses).

○ to **apply for/claim/qualify for/seek** (an) exemption ◆ to **enjoy/secure/win** (an) exemption ◆ to **give/grant** (an) exemption (to sb)

2 [C] an amount of income, profit, etc. on which you do not have to pay tax; a product or service on which tax is not charged: *a $4 000 personal exemption on income tax*

○ to **apply for/claim/qualify for/seek** an exemption ◆ to **give/grant** an exemption (to sb)

exercise /ˈeksəsaɪz; *AmE* -sərs-/ *noun, verb*

● *noun*
1 [C] an activity or series of activities that is designed to achieve a particular result: *a training exercise* ◇ *The company has undertaken a rebranding exercise.* ◇ *an exercise in public relations*

○ to **carry out/conduct/undertake** an exercise
2 [U] the use of power or a right to make sth happen: *The Internet has made the exercise of choice by consumers easy.*

○ to **encourage/justify/limit** the exercise of sth
3 (*Finance*) [U] **the exercise of an option** an act of using an OPTION, especially in order to buy or sell shares in a company: *revenues from the exercise of share options*
● *verb* [+ obj]
1 to use your power or rights in order to achieve sth: *We are continuing to exercise tight control over costs.* ◇ *to exercise a veto*
2 (*Finance*) if you **exercise** an OPTION you use it, especially in order to buy or sell shares in a company: *The company has exercised an option to sell its remaining shares in the business.*

'exercise price (*also* 'strike price, 'striking price) *noun* [C]

(*Finance*) the price at which sb/sth can buy or sell shares in a company for which they own OPTIONS: *The options have an exercise price of 26 Canadian dollars per share.*

,ex 'factory = EX WORKS

,ex 'gratia /ˌeks ˈgreɪʃə/ *adjective* (*only used in written English*)

given or done as a gift or favour, not because there is a legal duty to do it: *ex gratia payments* ◇ *The bonus was made on an ex gratia basis.* ▶ **ex 'gratia** *adverb*: *The sum was paid ex gratia.* [NOTE] Ex gratia is a Latin phrase.

exhaust /ɪgˈzɔːst/ *verb* [+ obj]

to use all of sth so that there is none left: *The trust had exhausted its funds.* ◇ *Don't give up until you have exhausted all the possibilities.*

exhibit /ɪgˈzɪbɪt/ *verb, noun*

● *verb* [+ obj or no obj]
to show sth in a public place for people to enjoy or to give them information: *They will be exhibiting their new designs at the trade fairs this spring.* ◇ *Over sixty companies are exhibiting at the food festival.*
● *noun* [C]
1 (*especially AmE*) = EXHIBITION
2 an object or a collection of objects put in a public place for people to see

exhibition /ˌeksɪˈbɪʃn/ (*especially BrE*) (*AmE usually* ex'hibit) *noun* [C]

SEE ALSO: **trade exhibition**

a collection of things, for example products produced by different companies, that are shown to the public; an event at which these things are shown: *an exhibition of photographs* ◇ *You are invited to join us at our exhibition stand in hall 9.* ◇

The hotel has space for conferences and exhibitions. ◇ *the cost of exhibit space* → EXPO, FAIR, SHOW

◒ *to* **have/hold/host** *an exhibition* ◆ *to* **organize/put on/set up** *an exhibition* ◆ *to* **attend/visit** *an exhibition* ◆ *an exhibition* **centre/hall/space/stand**

exhibitor /ɪgˈzɪbɪtə(r)/ *noun* [C]
a business or an organization that shows their products or services at an exhibition: *The agricultural show has attracted over 1 000 exhibitors from 33 countries.*

Eximbank (*also spelled* **Exim bank, Ex·Im bank**) /ˈeksɪmbæŋk/ = EXPORT-IMPORT BANK

exit /ˈeksɪt; ˈegzɪt/ *noun, verb*
● *noun* [C]

SEE ALSO: **barrier to exit**

1 a way out of a public building or vehicle: *If the alarm sounds, leave by the nearest fire exit.*
2 an act of leaving, especially when sb leaves a job, or a business or an investor leaves a market: *Her exit has been a blow to the company.* ◇ *the group's exit from the insurance business*

◒ *to* **find/look for/make** *an exit (from sth)* ◆ *sth* **provides** *an exit (from sth)*

3 a way of ending an agreement, a contract, a loan, etc.; an act of doing so: *We must make sure that we have an exit from the contract.* ◇ *You pay a 25% exit penalty if you cash in the policy early.*

◒ *an exit* **charge/cost/fee/penalty**
● *verb*

1 [+ obj *or* no obj] to go out; to leave a building, vehicle, etc: *We exited via the fire escape.*
2 [+ obj] to leave a job; to stop being involved in sth, such as a type of business or an investment: *He is the latest in a series of senior executives to exit the company.* ◇ *The group is considering exiting television.*
3 (*IT*) [+ obj] to finish using a computer program or a part of it: *Press 'Esc' to exit the program.*

ˈexit ˌbarrier = BARRIER TO EXIT

ˈexit charge = BACK-END LOAD

ˈexit ˌinterview *noun* [C]
(*HR*) a meeting between an employer and an employee who is leaving the company to find out why they are leaving: *Small companies may not have the time to carry out exit interviews and employee-satisfaction surveys.*

exodus /ˈeksədəs/ *noun* [C, usually sing.]
a situation in which many people or businesses leave a place, an activity, etc. at the same time: *the exodus of companies from the region* ◇ *preventing a mass exodus of staff to rival firms*

ˌex of·ˈficio /ˌeks əˈfɪʃiəʊ; *AmE* -ʃioʊ/ *adjective* (*formal*)
included or allowed because of your job, position or rank: *an ex officio member of the committee* ▶ **ˌex of·ˈficio** *adverb*: *He was present at the meeting ex officio.* **NOTE** Ex officio is a Latin phrase.

exorbitant /ɪgˈzɔːbɪtənt; *AmE* -ˈzɔːrb-/ *adjective*
(about a price) much too high: *exorbitant prices/ fees/costs* ◇ *It is a nice building but the rent is exorbitant.* ▶ **eˈxorbitantly** *adverb*: *They charge exorbitantly high rates of interest.*

★ expand /ɪkˈspænd/ *verb* [+ obj *or* no obj]
1 to become greater in size, number or value; to make sth greater in size, number or value: *an expanding range of products* ◇ *The company recently expanded its board from 11 to 15 members.*
2 if a business **expands** or **is expanded**, new branches are opened, it makes more money, etc: *Our business has expanded rapidly, from 16 to 30 stores in a year.* ◇ *The group wants to expand its*

presence in the Balkan region. ◇ *ambitious plans to develop the business and expand* **into** *new markets*

★ expansion /ɪkˈspænʃn/ *noun* [U,C]

SEE ALSO: **horizontal expansion, margin ~, vertical ~**

an act of increasing or making sth increase in size, amount or value: *There was little expansion* **in** *business investment last year.* ◇ *a period of rapid economic expansion* ◇ *The company has announced plans for a major expansion of its retail business.*

◒ *an expansion* **drive/plan/programme/project/ strategy** ◆ *to* **continue/halt/slow/stop** *expansion* ◆ *to* **finance/fund** *(an) expansion*

expatriate /ˌeksˈpætriət; *AmE* -ˈpeɪt-/ (*also* **expat** /ˌeksˈpæt/ *informal*) *noun* [C]
a person living in a country that is not their own: *helping expatriates adjust to life in another country* ◇ *Australian expats living in Europe* ▶ **ˌexˈpatriate** (*also* **ˌexˈpat**, *informal*) *adjective* [only before noun]: *expatriate workers*

exˈpectancy ˌtheory *noun* [sing.]
(*HR*) the idea that employees will want to work hard if they feel that they will be successful and that there are likely to be good results for them that they think are important

ˌexpectation of ˈlife = LIFE EXPECTANCY (1)

expedite /ˈekspədaɪt/ *verb* [+ obj] (*formal*)
to make a process happen more quickly: *We have developed rapid order processing to expedite deliveries to customers.* ◇ *expedited delivery*

expendable /ɪkˈspendəbl/ *adjective*
1 that you believe you can get rid of without causing yourself or your business harm: *He was seen as expendable to the organization.* ◇ *They sold all their expendable assets.*
2 **expendable** supplies are items that have little value and are used in such a way that they cannot be used again or there is little or none left afterwards: *expendable office supplies such as paper, pens, paper clips, staples, etc.*
3 made to be used for a limited period of time and then replaced: *The warranty does not included expendable items such as tyres and batteries.*
▶ **exˈpendable** *noun* [C]: *the cost of chemicals and other expendables* → DISPOSABLE

exˌpendable ˈincome = DISPOSABLE INCOME

★ expenditure /ɪkˈspendɪtʃə(r)/ *noun* [U,C]

SEE ALSO: **capital expenditure, consumption ~, operating ~, revenue ~**

(*Accounting; Economics*) the act of spending or using money; an amount of money that sb/sth spends during a particular period of time: *a reduction in government/corporate expenditure* ◇ *The group has been aggressive in cutting expenditure.* ◇ *Expenditure* **on** *advertising was 2.3 per cent higher this year.* ◇ *IT expenditure* (= money spent on computers, etc.) ◇ *The budget provided for a total expenditure of $27 billion.* → INCOME See note at SPENDING

◒ **heavy/high/huge/low/major** *expenditure* ◆ *to* **cut (back)/limit/reduce/trim** *expenditure* ◆ *to* **increase/ raise** *expenditure* ◆ *expenditure* **decreases/doubles/ drops/falls/rises**

exˈpenditure tax *noun* [C,U]
(*Economics*) a tax that is based on the amount of money that people spend rather than on their income: *They argue that an expenditure tax would promote savings.* ◇ *In effect, VAT is a consumer expenditure tax.* → CONSUMPTION TAX, INCOME TAX

★ expense /ɪkˈspens/ *noun*

SEE ALSO: **accrued expense, capital ~, fixed ~, interest ~, operating ~**

1 (*Accounting*) [C,U] money that a business spends on supplies, workers, services, etc. in order to operate **NOTE** Expenses are taken away from **profits** in a company's financial records: *Labour is the airline industry's biggest expense.* ◇ *marketing/ sales expenses* ◇ *The cost of the insurance can be deducted as a business expense.* ◇ *Even after expenses, healthy profit margins remain.*

O *to **bear/incur** an expense ◆ to **cover/meet** an expense ◆ to **deduct sth/treat sth/write sth off** as an expense ◆ to **control/cut/reduce/trim** expenses ◆ **big/ high/large/low** expenses ◆ an **extra/unexpected/ unnecessary** expense*

2 expenses [pl.] money that you spend while doing a job that your employer or the person you are working for will pay back to you later : *We will cover your travel expenses.* ◇ *I charge $200 an hour plus expenses.* ◇ *(BrE) to take a client out for a meal* **on expenses** ◇ *an **all-expenses-paid** trip*
→ EXPENSES CLAIM

O *basic/out-of-pocket* expenses ◆ to *incur* expenses ◆ to *cover/pay/refund/reimburse* sb's expenses ◆ to *claim (back)/recover* your expenses

3 [U] the money that you spend on sth: *The factory was rebuilt **at** considerable expense.* ◇ *He arranged everything, **no expense spared*** (= he spent as much as was needed).

IDM at sb's expense paid for by sb/sth: *We were taken for a meal at the company's expense.*

ex'pense ac,count *noun* [C]
an arrangement by which money spent by sb while they are at work is later paid back to them by their employer; a record of money spent in this way: *Put the cost of the petrol/gas on your expense account.*

ex'penses claim *(BrE) (AmE* **ex'pense re,port)** *noun* [C]
a list of amounts that you spend while you are working that your employer will pay back: *Your manager must approve the expenses claim before you submit it.* ◇ *Employees now **file** their expense reports by email.*

★ **expensive** /ɪk'spensɪv/ *adjective*
costing a lot of money: *expensive equipment/tools* ◇ *expensive hotels/restaurants/stores* (= that charge high prices) ◇ *What is the least expensive option?* ◇ *The new model is less expensive **to** produce.* ◇ *Restructuring the company could prove expensive.*
OPP INEXPENSIVE

O *to **be/become/look/prove/sound** expensive ◆ extremely/hugely/prohibitively/relatively/very** expensive*

► **ex'pensively** *adverb*: *expensively priced* ◇ *The private sector can produce these products less expensively than the government.*

experience /ɪk'spɪəriəns; *AmE* -'spɪr-/ *noun*

SEE ALSO: **work experience**

1 [U] the knowledge and skill that you have gained through doing sth for a period of time; the process of gaining this: *Do you have any previous experience of this type of work?* ◇ *Consultants should have a college degree and at least 10 years' business experience.*

O *practical/previous/prior/relevant/valuable* experience ◆ *considerable/extensive/little* experience ◆ *business/financial/industry/ management* experience ◆ to *have/gain/lack* experience

2 [C] an event or activity that affects you in some way: *We have to provide a better customer experience.*

O *a/the **customer/learning/shopping** experience ◆ a **negative/positive** experience ◆ to **have** an experience*

3 [U] the things that have happened to you that influence the way you think and behave: ***Based on past experience,** most visitors to the website will fill out the form.*

O *direct/first-hand/personal* experience

ex'perience curve *(also* **'learning curve)** *noun* [C, usually sing.]
the rate at which the cost of producing sth falls as the number produced increases, as a result of the knowledge and skill that a company and its workers gain

experienced /ɪk'spɪəriənst; *AmE* -'spɪr-/ *adjective*
having knowledge or skill in a particular job or activity: *an experienced management team* ◇ *We need someone experienced **in** marketing.*

ex'perience e,conomy *noun* [C]
(Economics) an economy in which companies aim to sell their products by telling people not about what a particular product can do, but about the way buying or using it will affect them and their lives

★ **expert** /'ekspɜːt; *AmE* -pɜːrt/ *noun, adjective*
● *noun* [C]
a person with special knowledge, skill or training in sth: *a legal/financial/tax expert* ◇ *a leading expert **on/in** tax law* ◇ *an expert **at** designing web pages* ◇ *Industry experts predict that oil prices could rise even higher.*
● *adjective*
done with, having or involving great knowledge or skill: *to seek expert advice/help* ◇ *I need an expert opinion on this.* ◇ *We are expert **at** planning and running corporate events.*

expertise /ˌekspɜː'tiːz; *AmE* -pɜːr't-/ *noun* [U]
expert knowledge or skill in a particular subject, activity or job: *We have the expertise to help you run your business.* ◇ *the group's expertise **in** developing new products*

O *great/little* expertise ◆ *business/financial/ management/technical* expertise ◆ to *gain/have/ lack* expertise

,expert 'system *noun* [C]
(IT) a computer system that can provide information and expert advice on a particular subject. The program asks users a series of questions about their problem and gives them advice based on its store of knowledge: *We use an expert system to decide whether to lend money to a client.*

expiration /ˌekspə'reɪʃn/ = EXPIRY
,expi'ration date = EXPIRY DATE

★ **expire** /ɪk'spaɪə(r)/ *verb* [no obj]
1 (about a document, an agreement, a right to buy or sell shares, etc.) to be no longer valid because the period of time for which it could be used has ended: *Our lease on the property expires next month.* ◇ *The offer to buy the company expired without a deal being finalized.* ◇ *The August crude oil contract expires today* (= today is the last day you can buy or sell contracts to have oil delivered in August).
SYN RUN OUT
2 (about a period of time, especially one during which sb holds a position of authority) to end: *The chairman's three-year term is due to expire in March.*

expiry /ɪk'spaɪəri/ *(plural* **expiries)** *(especially BrE) (AmE usually* **,expi'ration)** *noun* [U,C]
1 an ending of the period of time when an official document can be used, or when an agreement or contract is valid: *The licence can be renewed on expiry.*
2 *(Finance)* the end of the period of time when an OPTION can be used or a FUTURES CONTRACT is valid: *The oil futures contract reached $30 a barrel before its expiry at the end of the day.*

ex'piry date *(especially BrE) (AmE usually* **,expi'ration date)** *noun* [C]
1 the date after which an official document, agreement, etc. is no longer valid: *What is the expiry date on your credit card?*

2 (*Finance*) the final or only day on which you can use your right to buy or sell particular shares, bonds, etc. (an **option**)
3 the date, printed on a container or package, by which an item of food, a medicine, etc. should be eaten or a product should be used. The items must not be sold after this date: *Do not take medicine after its expiry date.* See note at BEST-BEFORE DATE

ex‚plicit 'knowledge *noun* [U]
(*HR*) information that can be described and written down, for example in books, documents, reports, etc: *Explicit knowledge can be easily communicated and shared.* → TACIT KNOWLEDGE

exploit /ɪkˈsplɔɪt/ *verb* [+ obj]
1 to treat sb unfairly by making them work and not giving them much in return: *Some employers exploit young workers, making them work long hours for low pay.*
2 to use sth as an opportunity to gain an advantage for yourself: *He exploited his father's name to get himself a job.*
3 to develop or make the best use of sth for business or industry: *to exploit an oil field ◊ exploiting opportunities for growth ◊ finding ways to fully exploit the potential of the brand*
▸ **exploitation** /ˌeksplɔɪˈteɪʃn/ *noun* [U]: *the exploitation of cheap labour ◊ commercial exploitation of the mineral resources in Antarctica*

expo /ˈekspəʊ; *AmE* -poʊ/ *noun* [C]
1 (*Trade*) **Expo** a large international event at which representatives from different countries show the products, machinery, buildings, etc. that their countries are producing, building, etc: *Shanghai will host the 2010 World Expo.*
2 (*Marketing*) a public event at which one company or many different companies producing related products show and sell their new products and services: *a toy industry expo ◊ the expo hall*
[SYN] TRADE SHOW
[NOTE] The word **expo** is a short form of **exposition**.

exponential /ˌekspəˈnenʃl/ *adjective*
(about a rate of increase) becoming faster and faster: *China's economy has seen exponential growth. ◊ Since the mid 1990's, e-commerce has grown at an exponential rate.* ▸ **exponentially** /ˌekspəˈnenʃəli/ *adverb*: *Our sales in Russia are increasing exponentially.*

★ **export** *noun*, *verb*
● *noun* /ˈekspɔːt; *AmE* ˈekspɔːrt/

SEE ALSO: **direct export, import-~, indirect ~, re-~, visible ~**

1 [C, usually pl.] a product or service that is sold and sent or supplied to another country: *Copper is Chile's biggest export. ◊ Demand for Asian exports has grown.*
2 exports [pl.] the amount or value of goods and services that are sold and sent or supplied to other countries over a period of time: *oil/steel/wheat exports ◊ Exports account for around 40 per cent of the country's GDP. ◊ A weaker dollar would boost exports.*
3 [U] the selling and sending of goods or services to another country: *There are strict controls on the export of certain chemicals. ◊ Most of what we produce is for export. ◊ export earnings/revenue ◊ Europe remains the UK's largest export market. ◊ an export licence for the sale of chemicals*
[OPP] IMPORT
● *verb* /ɪkˈspɔːt; *AmE* ɪkˈspɔːrt/
1 [+ obj or no obj] to sell and send goods or services to another country: *Nigeria exports around two million barrels of crude oil a day. ◊ 90% of the engines are exported to Europe. ◊ an exporting country/nation*

2 [+ obj] to introduce an idea or activity to another country or area: *The retailer has exported its marketing expertise to the US.*
3 (*IT*) [+ obj] to change data into a form that allows it to be used with a different type of software: *Can you export it as an ASCII file?*
[OPP] IMPORT
▸ **exportability** /ɪkˌspɔːtəˈbɪləti; *AmE* -ˌspɔːrt-/ *noun* [U] **exportable** /ɪkˈspɔːtəbl; *AmE* -ˈspɔːrt-/ *adjective*: *quality standards for exportable coffee* **exportation** /ˌekspɔːˈteɪʃn; *AmE* -spɔːrˈt-/ *noun* [U,C]

'export ‚credit *noun* [U,C]
(*Trade*) an arrangement by which an importer can buy foreign goods or services now and pay for them later: *The bank provides international buyers with export credits to buy US goods. ◊ an export credit agency* (= that helps exporters to sell goods in this way)

‚export 'credit guaran‚tee *noun* [C]
(*Trade*) a promise, often by a government, to pay for goods that are exported if the importer does not pay (often used in the names of institutions that give these promises): *The construction firm has applied for export credit guarantees from the British government. ◊ the Export Credit Guarantee Company of Egypt*

★ **exporter** /ekˈspɔːtə(r); *AmE* ekˈspɔːrt-/ *noun* [C]

SEE ALSO: **net exporter**

1 a business, country or person that sells goods or services to another country: *A stronger yen hurts Japanese exporters because it makes their goods more expensive abroad. ◊ Ecuador is the world's largest banana exporter.*
2 a country whose people or businesses invest money (**capital**) in companies, funds, etc. in other countries: *The country has moved from being a supplier of cheap goods to an exporter of capital.*
→ IMPORTER

'export ‚factoring *noun* [U]
(*Trade*) a financial arrangement in which a bank (a **factor**) takes responsibility for collecting payments for goods that an exporter sends abroad, so that the exporter can borrow money from the bank before customers pay their debts

‚Export-'Import Bank (*also* 'Eximbank) *noun* [C]
(*Trade*) in some countries, a bank that is created by the government to provide loans, etc. so that foreign companies and governments can buy goods and services that are exported by local businesses: *Exports to Malaysia can be supported by the US Export-Import Bank.*

exposed /ɪkˈspəʊzd; *AmE* ɪkˈspoʊzd/ *adjective*
(*Finance*) likely to experience financial losses: *The decision to invest only in shares left a number of investors exposed. ◊ The UK economy is highly exposed to consumer spending* (= it is likely to suffer if people stop spending).

exposition /ˌekspəˈzɪʃn/ *noun* [C]
(*Marketing, formal*) a public event at which many different companies producing related products show and sell their new products and services: *an annual exposition of computer technology*
[SYN] TRADE SHOW → EXPO

★ **exposure** /ɪkˈspəʊʒə(r); *AmE* -ˈspoʊ-/ *noun* [U,C]

SEE ALSO: **credit exposure, currency ~, debt ~, exchange rate ~**

1 (*Finance*) the fact that a business, an investor, etc. risks losing money, for example if customers do not pay their bills, or if investments fail; the amount that could be lost: *The company has plans to reduce their high exposure to bad debt. ◊ The bank has a €3 billion exposure* (= the bank has lent €3 billion) *to the Brazilian economy.*

◐ to **have** (an) exposure • to **avoid/increase/limit/ reduce** exposure • **heavy/high/large** exposure
2 (*Finance*) the opportunity to invest money in sth: *It's hard to **gain** exposure **to** property with small amounts of money.*
3 (*Marketing*) opportunities for people to see advertisements and information about a company or its products on television, in the newspapers, on the Internet, etc: *gaining media exposure for your products* ◇ *We are trying to increase our brand exposure on the Internet.*
◐ to **gain/have/increase** exposure

ex'**posure draft** *noun* [C] (*BrE*) (*abbr* **ED**)
(*Accounting*) a document that is produced for discussion before a final document is published, especially one produced by the Financial Accounting Standards Board before an accounting rule (**standard**) is completed

express /ɪk'spres/ *verb, adjective, adverb, noun*
● *verb* [+ obj]
1 to describe an amount, a quantity, etc. using a particular unit of measurement: *On the income statement, costs are expressed **as** a percentage of sales.* ◇ *Expressed **in** dollars, sales increased by 23%.*
2 to send sth by **express** post/mail: *As soon as I receive payment I will express the book to you.*
● *adjective* [only before noun]
1 travelling very fast; sent or delivered very quickly: *an express bus* ◇ *The parcel was sent by express mail.* ◇ *We offer an **express delivery** service.*
2 (about a piece of business, etc.) that can be done very quickly: *express clearance through customs* ◇ *Use the express checkout if you are buying five items or fewer.*
3 (*Law*) (about a part of a contract) that is stated or put in writing and agreed: *It was an express term of the contract that their employment was for a period of four years.* → IMPLIED
● *adverb*
using a special fast service: *I'd like to send this package express, please.*
● *noun*
1 [C] a fast train or bus that does not stop at many places
2 [U] a service for sending or transporting things quickly; a company that provides this: *The books were sent by express.* → SPECIAL DELIVERY

ex,**pression of** '**interest** *noun* [C] (*abbr* **EoI**)
(*Commerce*) a formal statement in which a company or person says that they would be interested in doing sth, such as making an offer to supply sth or do a piece of work, buying shares, joining sth, etc: *The company has made an expression of interest in a motor business.* ◇ *She said it was an expression of interest, not a formal bid.* ◇ *The government has received 23 expressions of interest from developers interested in building the stadium.* → LETTER OF INTENT
◐ to **make/submit** an expression of interest • to **set a deadline for/invite/receive** expressions of interest

ex'**press lane** *noun* [C] (*AmE*)
a place in a shop/store where particular customers can go to avoid waiting for a long time: *Customers with ten items or fewer can use the express lane.* ◇ *express lanes at fast-food restaurants*

,ex-'**rights** *adverb, adjective*
(*Finance*) (about a share) that is sold without giving the buyer the right to buy any new shares that the company may offer: *The shares **go ex rights** on 9 August* (= if you buy them after this date you will not receive the right to buy new shares). ◇ *an ex-rights price of €1*

,ex '**stock** *adverb, adjective*
(*Commerce*; *Production*) used to describe goods that can be delivered immediately because the seller has a supply of them available: *Most standard sizes*

are available ex stock. ◇ *We offer ex-stock delivery on a wide range of products.*

ext. *abbr* (*only used in written English*)
extension (used with a telephone number)

★ **extend** /ɪk'stend/ *verb*
1 [+ obj *or* no obj] to make sth last longer: *The deadline has been extended to next Friday.* ◇ *The lease runs for two years with an option to extend for a further two.* ◇ *supermarkets with extended trading hours* (= that are open longer than normal)
2 [+ obj] to make a business, a law, etc. cover more areas or operate in more places: *The company plans to extend its operations into Asia.* ◇ *The law is being extended to all businesses that employ more than ten people.*
3 [+ obj] to offer or give sth to sb: *The bank refused to extend any further credit **to** the company* (= to lend them any more money). ◇ *The company extended an invitation to shareholders to visit the factory.*
4 (*Marketing*) [+ obj] if a business **extends** a brand, it uses a successful brand name to sell new products: *an attempt to extend the Easy brand beyond EasyJet* ◇ *They have extended their brand into the mobile phone market.*
→ EXTENSION

ex,**tended** '**credit** *noun* [U]
an arrangement by which you can spend as much money as you wish using your credit card, if you do not spend more than the limit you are allowed and if you pay back a particular amount every month

ex,**tended** '**warranty** (*also* ex,**tended guaran'tee**, *less frequent*) *noun* [C]
a type of insurance that shops/stores sell to customers that increases the period of time during which a product will be repaired or replaced if it breaks

★ **extension** /ɪk'stenʃn/ *noun*
SEE ALSO: **brand extension, line extension**
1 [C,U] the act of making sth longer, larger, more complicated, etc.; the thing that is added to do this: *The extension of the subway will take several months.* ◇ *We see the website as an extension **of** our telephone service.* ◇ *The bank plans various extensions **to** its credit facilities.*
2 [C] an extra period of time allowed for sth: *He's been granted an extension **of** the contract for another year.* ◇ *a 14-month extension **to** the loan facility*
3 [C] a new part that is added to a building: *They are planning a $60 million extension **to** the airport terminal.*
4 [C] (*abbr* **ext.**) one of many telephone lines that are connected to a SWITCHBOARD in a large building, each with its own number: *What's your extension number?* ◇ *Can I have extension 1125 please?*
5 (*IT*) [C] the set of letters that are placed after a dot at the end of the name of a file and that show what type of file it is: *The file must be saved with a .htm extension.*

ex'**tension** ,**strategy** *noun* [C]
(*Marketing*) a plan for reaching new customers for an existing product by making small changes to it, finding new uses for it, etc.—Picture at PRODUCT LIFE CYCLE

ex,**tensive** '**problem** ,**solving** *noun* [U] (*abbr* **EPS**)
(*Marketing*) the situation when a customer must find information about a new product or service and think carefully before deciding which brand to buy

external /ɪk'stɜːnl; *AmE* ɪk'stɜːrnl/ *adjective*
1 coming from outside an organization: *An external auditor will verify the accounts.* ◇ *The company has interviewed both internal and external candidates for the job.*
2 used to describe the situation when a company increases in size by buying or joining with other companies: *They expect to use about €3.5 billion for external growth over a three-year period.*
→ INORGANIC
3 connected with foreign countries: *an increase in external trade* ◇ *Japan's economy has been supported largely by external demand.*
4 (*IT*) that is not built into the main computer or device but must be connected to it: *an external modem/disk drive*
OPP INTERNAL

ex,ternal ac'count = CURRENT ACCOUNT (2)

ex,ternal a'nalysis *noun* [C,U]
(*Marketing*) the study of the things outside a company that are important for its success, such as customers, competition and social change

ex,ternal com'petitiveness *noun* [U]
1 (*Economics*) the ability to sell goods and services to foreign customers at an attractive (= good) price
2 (*HR*) = EXTERNAL EQUITY

ex,ternal 'debt *noun* [U]
(*Economics*) money that the government and organizations in a particular country owe to lenders in other countries: *The country has $90 billion of external debt.* SYN FOREIGN DEBT

ex,ternal 'equity (*also* ex,ternal com'petitiveness) *noun* [U]
(*HR*) a situation in which the basic pay that employees in an organization receive is similar to the pay for the same type of work in other organizations: *achieving external equity in pay*
→ INTERNAL EQUITY

ex,ternal 'labour ,market (*AmE spelling* ~ **labor** ~) *noun* [C]
(*HR*) the people who are available for work in the area outside an organization that an employer is likely to get new workers from: *The skills that a particular employer needs may be in short supply on the external labour market.* → INTERNAL LABOUR MARKET

ex,ternal ,lia'bility *noun* [C, usually pl., U]
1 (*Accounting*) the money that an organization owes that is not owed to its shareholders: *A company's net worth is the value of its assets minus its external liabilities.*
2 (*Economics*) the money that a country owes to foreign lenders: *Their exports are sufficient to cover external liabilities.*

extinguish /ɪk'stɪŋgwɪʃ/ *verb* [+ obj]
to stop sth from continuing or developing: *to extinguish a debt/liability/right* ◇ *If a currency becomes too strong it can extinguish growth in exports.*

extinguisher /ɪk'stɪŋgwɪʃə(r)/ = FIRE EXTINGUISHER

extort /ɪk'stɔːt; *AmE* ɪk'stɔːrt/ *verb* [+ obj]
to make sb give you sth, especially money, by threatening them: *Some people have tried to extort money from companies for a domain name.*
▶ **extortion** /ɪk'stɔːʃn; *AmE* ɪk'stɔːrʃn/ *noun* [U,C]: *She was arrested and charged with extortion.*

extra /'ekstrə/ *adjective, noun, adverb*
● *adjective*
more than is usual, expected, or than exists already: *Breakfast is provided at no extra charge.* ◇ *The conference is going to be a lot of extra work.* ◇

They said they would need to borrow an extra $500 million.
● *noun* [C]
1 a thing that is added to sth that is not usual, standard or necessary and that costs more: *The monthly fee is fixed and there are no hidden extras* (= unexpected costs). ◇ *The CD player is an optional extra.*
2 (*Finance*) = EXTRA DIVIDEND
● *adverb*
1 in addition; more than is usual, expected or exists already: *You pay a little extra for their overnight delivery service.* ◇ *The rate for a room is €50, but breakfast is extra.*
❍ to **charge/cost/pay** extra
2 (*used with an adjective or adverb*) more than usually: *an extra-large T-shirt*

extract *verb, noun*
● *verb* /ɪk'strækt/ [+ obj] **extract sth (from sth)**
1 to remove or obtain a substance from sth, for example by using an industrial or a chemical process: *The gas is extracted from coal.* ◇ *We should be able to extract 80 million barrels of oil from the site.*
2 to get money, information, etc., especially from sb who is unwilling to give it: *The government is confident it can extract an emergency loan from the IMF.*
3 to find information in a computer file, a document, etc. to use for a particular purpose: *The program extracts email addresses from websites.*
● *noun* /'ekstrækt/ [C]
a substance that has been obtained from sth else using a particular process: *yeast extract* ◇ *face cream containing natural plant extracts*

extractor /ɪk'stræktə(r)/ *noun* [C]
1 (*also* **ex'tractor fan**) a device that removes hot air, unpleasant smells, etc. from a room: *the noise of the factory's extractor fan* ◇ *fume extractor equipment*
2 a device or machine that removes sth from sth else
3 (*IT*) software that finds and collects particular information from a computer file, web page, etc: *an email extractor*

,extra 'dividend (*also* 'extra) = SPECIAL DIVIDEND

extranet /'ekstrənet/ *noun* [C]
(*IT*) a type of INTRANET (= a computer network used within a company) which a company's customers and suppliers can link to using the Internet in order to obtain or provide information: *We have set up extranets with our 51 top suppliers.* ◇ *communicating with customers via an extranet*

extraordinary /ɪk'strɔːdnri; *AmE* ɪk'strɔːrdəneri/ *adjective*
1 not normal or ordinary; greater or better than usual: *These bonds pay an extraordinary rate of interest.* ◇ *What we have achieved is extraordinary.*
2 (*Accounting*) [only before noun] (about a cost) that is unusual for a company to pay and does not relate to its normal business activities: *extraordinary costs relating to repairing flood damage* → EXCEPTIONAL
3 [only before noun] arranged for a special purpose and happening in addition to what normally or regularly happens: *An extraordinary meeting was held to discuss the problem.*

ex'traordinary 'general 'meeting *noun* [C]
(*BrE*) (*abbr* **EGM**)
a meeting of the shareholders or members of a company that is held to discuss an urgent issue that cannot be left until the next ANNUAL GENERAL MEETING: *The deal has been approved by shareholders at an extraordinary general meeting.*

ex‚traordinary 'item noun [C, usually pl.]
(*Accounting*) (in a company's financial records) an amount of money paid that is unusual for a company and does not relate to its normal business activities: *Profits are expected to be an improvement on last year, excluding extraordinary items.*
→ EXCEPTIONAL ITEM

extravagant /ɪk'strævəgənt/ adjective
spending or costing too much money: *an extravagant pay package* ◇ *It seemed extravagant for a young firm to have such large offices.* → FRUGAL

EXW = EX WORKS

‚ex 'works (*abbr* EXW) (*also* ‚ex 'factory, ‚ex 'warehouse*) adverb, adjective (*BrE*)
(*Trade*) a term meaning that goods are delivered to the buyer at the factory or the place where they are made or stored, and the buyer pays for transporting and insuring the goods from there: *Prices start at £9 000 ex works.* ◇ *All stock is sold ex warehouse.* ◇ *ex-factory prices* → INCOTERM

eyeballs /'aɪbɔːlz/ noun [pl.]
(*Marketing, informal*) people who watch a particular television channel or visit a particular website: *The more eyeballs you can claim, the more you can charge advertisers.* ◇ *a pair/set of eyeballs* (= one person)
IDM **(be) up to your eyeballs (in sth)** to have a lot of sth to deal with: *They're up to their eyeballs in work.*

'eye ‚contact noun [U]
if you make **eye contact** with sb, you look at them at the same time as they look at you: *To hold the attention of your customers, you need to make eye contact with them.*
☉ to **avoid/have/make** eye contact (with sb)

'eye ‚tracking noun [U]
(*Marketing*) a research method that studies which parts of an advertisement people look at by watching how their eyes move

'e-zine noun [C]
a magazine published in electronic form on the Internet or sent by email

F f

F2F (*also spelled* **f2f, F-to-F**) /‚ef tuː 'ef/ adjective
[only before noun] (*informal*) **face-to-face** used to describe a situation where people meet together in order to discuss sth: *We can discuss this at our F2F meeting next week.* **NOTE** It can also be used as a noun: *'F2F is indispensable for many business activities.'*

FA /‚ef 'eɪ/ = FUNCTIONAL ACKNOWLEDGEMENT

the FAA /‚ef eɪ 'eɪ/ = FEDERAL AVIATION ADMINISTRATION

fab /fæb/ noun [C]
(*Manufacturing*) a factory where MICROCHIPS are made See note at FABRICATE ▶ **fab** verb [+ obj] (**-bb-**): *The chips are fabbed by IBM.* **NOTE** The word **fab** was formed from the words 'fabrication (plant)' and 'fabricate'.

fabricate /'fæbrɪkeɪt/ verb [+ obj]
(*Manufacturing*) (*often* **be fabricated**)
to build or make equipment, structures, etc., especially by putting together different parts or materials: *The firm fabricates all kinds of rubber products.* ◇ *The structure is fabricated from standard steel sections.* ▶ **fabrication** /‚fæbrɪ'keɪʃn/ noun [U]: *the fabrication of computer chips* **fabricator** /'fæbrɪkeɪtə(r)/ noun [C]: *a steel fabricator*

WHICH WORD?

fabrication/fab/fabricator/factory

Fabrication is an uncountable noun and refers to the process of manufacturing something, not to the place where it is made, which is often called a **factory** [C]: *the fabrication of computer circuits* ◇ *to open a new factory*

The word **fabricator** refers to a business that has special skills in building things: *The work was done by specialist fabricators.* ◇ *a fabricator of steel structures*

A **fab** is a factory where microchips are produced: *a chip fab*

See note at FACTORY

---

face /feɪs/ = COALFACE

'face a‚mount noun [C,U] (*especially AmE*)
1 (*Insurance*) the amount of money stated in an insurance policy to be paid if the person who is insured dies or the contract ends (**matures**) → SUM ASSURED
2 (*Finance*) = FACE VALUE

facelift /'feɪslɪft/ noun [C, usually sing.]
changes made to a building, product, service, etc. to make it more attractive to customers: *They have given the flagship Paris store a €50 million facelift.*

‚face 'out adverb
used to describe the way books are placed on a shelf in a shop/store so that their covers can be seen: *Books that are face out on the shelves sell much better than books that are spine out.*

'face-‚saving adjective [only before noun]
intended to protect sb's reputation and to avoid embarrassment: *a face-saving solution/compromise* → SAVE (SB'S) FACE at SAVE

'face time noun [U]
(*HR, informal*)
1 time that you spend talking to sb in the same room rather than sending them emails, talking to them on the telephone, etc: *Managers are encouraged to give employees plenty of face time.* ◇ *getting more face time with clients*
2 the amount of time that sb spends at work, especially beyond their normal working hours: *People here work incredibly long hours because there is a strong face time culture.*

‚face-to-'face adjective, noun
● *adjective*
involving people in the same room or place: *a face-to-face meeting/interview* ▶ **face-to-'face** adverb: *The discussions will take place face-to-face.* → F2F
● *noun* [C] (*plural* **face-to-faces**) (*informal*)
a **face-to-face** meeting: *There often isn't time to have a face-to-face with the boss.*

‚face 'value (*also* **'face a‚mount**, *especially in AmE*)
noun [C,U]
(*Finance*) the value that is shown on a coin, a note, a financial document, etc: *The bond is trading at only half of its face value.* → MARKET VALUE, PAR VALUE

facia = FASCIA

★**facilitate** /fə'sɪlɪteɪt/ *verb* [+ obj]
  1 to make an action or a process possible or easier: *She used her contacts at the company to facilitate a deal.* ◇ *a website that facilitates online payments*
  2 to help people work together or reach an agreement
  ▶ **facilitation** /fə,sɪlɪ'teɪʃn/ *noun* [U; sing.]: *the facilitation of trade* ◇ *team facilitation*

facilitator /fə'sɪlɪteɪtə(r)/ *noun* [C]
  a person who helps sb or a group of people to do sth more easily or reach an agreement about sth by discussing problems, giving advice, etc. rather than by telling them what to do: *They brought in an outside facilitator to lead the discussions.*

fa'cilities ,management *noun* [U]
  the activity of looking after or operating a building, factory, equipment, etc., often on behalf of another organization: *The company has won a 40-year contract to provide facilities management to hospitals.*

★**facility** /fə'sɪləti/ *noun* (*plural* **facilities**)
  SEE ALSO: **bank facility, credit facility**

  1 [C] a factory or a set of buildings where particular goods are produced or particular work is done: *They built a new facility to produce the drug.* ◇ *an oil storage facility* See note at FACTORY
  ○ *a distribution/manufacturing/production/research/storage facility* • *to build/close/open a facility*
  2 facilities [pl.] buildings, services, equipment, etc. that are provided for a particular purpose: *Does the hotel have conference facilities?* ◇ *The airport provides good facilities for business travellers.* ◇ *All rooms have private facilities* (= a private bathroom).
  ○ *conference/cooking/leisure/parking/sports facilities* • *to improve/provide/use facilities*
  3 (*Finance*) [C] an arrangement that a person, a business, etc. has with a bank or a company to be able to borrow money during a particular period of time up to an agreed amount: *We have sufficient borrowing facilities to fund the purchase.* ◇ *to draw down on* (= borrow money using) *a facility* ◇ *The facility runs until next December.* See note at LOAN
  ○ *to arrange/have/(re)negotiate/obtain/secure a facility* • *a bank, etc. extends/grants/increases/provides/withdraws a facility* • *a facility ends/expires/matures/runs* • *to draw (down) on/have access to/use a facility*
  4 [C] a special feature of a machine, piece of software, etc. that makes it possible to do sth extra: *The program has a facility for checking spelling.*

facsimile /fæk'sɪməli/ = FAX

factor /'fæktə(r)/ *noun, verb*
● *noun*
  SEE ALSO: **adjustment factor, critical success ~, load ~, wow ~**

  1 [C] one of several things that cause or influence sth: *You need to take economic factors into account.* ◇ *Training is a big factor in the success of a company.*
  ○ *a big/critical/crucial/an important/a key/significant factor* • *the deciding/decisive/determining/main/major factor* • *factors affect/cause/contribute/influence sth*
  2 [sing.] **the ... factor** a quality or feature that has an important influence on whether sb/sth is popular, successful, etc: *The hassle factor of extra security checks has stopped many business people from flying.*

  3 [C] the amount by which sth increases or decreases: *The real wage of the average worker has increased by a factor of over ten* (= by more than ten times) *in the last 70 years.*
  4 (*Finance*) [C] a business that buys the right to collect payments that are owed to a manufacturer: *A factor can take anything between two and eight per cent of an invoice as their fee.* ◇ *a debt/invoice factor* → FACTORING
  5 (*Commerce*) [C] a person or business that acts as an agent in particular trades, usually receiving a fee based on the amount of sales achieved. **Factors** hold the goods and sell them in their own name.
  → idiom at FEEL-GOOD
● *verb* [+ obj]
  (*Finance*) to sell the right to collect payments from customers to a bank, company, etc: *The company was forced to raise money by factoring its accounts receivable.* ◇ *to factor an invoice* → FACTORING
  PHR V ,**factor sth 'in**; ,**factor sth 'into sth** (*Technical*) to include a particular fact or situation when you are calculating sth or when you are thinking about or planning sth: *Remember to factor in staffing costs when you are planning the project.*
  ,**factor sth 'out**; ,**factor sth 'out of sth** (*Technical*) to not include a particular fact or situation when you are calculating sth or when you are thinking about or planning sth: *You have to factor out newly opened or closed stores when comparing sales between one year and the next.*

'**factor cost** *noun* [C,U]
  (*Economics*) the cost of producing goods and services based on the cost of what is needed to produce it, such as labour, land and CAPITAL: *It is preferable to measure the value of total output at factor cost rather than in market prices.*

factoring /'fæktərɪŋ/ *noun* [U]
  SEE ALSO: **export factoring**

  (*Finance*) a financial arrangement in which a bank or other business (a **factor**) buys the right to collect payments that are owed to a manufacturer. The **factor** pays the debts and then collects the money, receiving a percentage of the money owed for doing this: *They sold their debts to a bank under a factoring arrangement in order to raise cash.* ◇ *debt/invoice factoring* ◇ *a factoring company/agent*

,**factor of pro'duction** *noun* [C]
  (*Economics*) any person or thing that is involved in producing goods or providing services: *Land, labour and capital are the main factors of production.* **SYN** INPUT

★**factory** /'fæktri; -təri/ *noun* [C] (*plural* **factories**)
  SEE ALSO: **bonded factory, ex factory**

  a building or group of buildings where goods are made: *a car factory* ◇ *to work in a factory* ◇ *factory workers* ◇ *a fall in factory output*
  ○ *to build/close/open a factory*

VOCABULARY BUILDING

Types of factories

General Words

• a **factory** – *an aircraft/a clothing/large/small factory*
• a **plant** – *an assembly/a car/chemical plant*

Words with more limited use

• *a production/research* **facility**
• *a flour/paper/steel/wood* **mill**
• *an industrial/a manufacturing/production* **site**
• *a cement/chemical/gas/steel* **works**

See note at FABRICATION

'factory cost noun [C, usually sing.]
(*Accounting*) the cost of manufacturing a product, including labour and raw materials but not costs such as transport, etc.

'factory farm noun [C] (*BrE*)
a type of farm in which animals are kept inside in small spaces and are fed special food so that a large amount of meat, milk, etc. is produced as quickly and cheaply as possible ▶ **'factory farming** noun [U]

factory 'floor noun [sing.]
(*often* **the factory floor**) the part of a factory where the goods are actually produced: *He believes executives should spend more time with workers on the factory floor.*

factory 'gate noun [C]
(*Economics*) the entrance to a factory, used to describe the time when a finished product leaves a factory: *Manufacturers were only able to raise prices at the factory gate* (= the basic price paid to the manufacturer before transport or any profits have been added) *by 0.1% over the month.* ◇ *a fall in factory-gate prices*

'factory ,outlet = FACTORY SHOP

'factory price noun [C, usually pl.]
the price at which a manufacturer sells goods, used especially in advertising to show that a shop/store is selling sth at a very low price: *Designer clothing at near factory prices!* → FACTORY GATE

'factory shop (*BrE*) (*AmE* **'factory store**) (*also* **'factory ,outlet**, *AmE*, *BrE*) noun [C]
a shop/store in which goods, especially goods that are slightly damaged or not needed, are sold directly by the company that produces them at a cheaper price than normal

'fact sheet noun [C] (*especially BrE*)
a piece of paper or a small book giving information about a product or service

fail /feɪl/ verb, noun
● *verb*
1 [no obj] to not be successful in achieving sth: *Their marketing strategy failed to increase sales.* ◇ *They failed in their bid to buy the company.* ◇ *So far, negotiations have failed.*
2 [no obj] to not do sth: *She failed to keep the appointment.* ◇ *They claim that the government has failed in its duties.*
3 [no obj] (about a business) to be unable to continue: *Statistics show that 80% of businesses fail within the first five years.* ◇ *a failing company*
4 [no obj] (about a machine or system) to stop working: *The idea is that if one part of the system fails, the others continue to run.*
5 [+ obj] to not pass a test or an exam; to decide that sb/sth has not passed a test or an exam: *She failed her professional exams.* ◇ *190 units failed inspection last month.* OPP PASS
● *noun* [C]
the result of a test or an exam when sb/sth is not successful
IDM **without 'fail 1** when you tell sb to do sth without fail, you are telling them that they must do it: *I want you here by two o'clock without fail.* **2** always: *She attends board meetings without fail.*

failed /feɪld/ adjective [only before noun]
1 not successful: *a failed attempt to merge the companies* ◇ *a failed bid*
2 (about a business) that has stopped operating: *a failed airline*

'fail-safe adjective [usually before noun]
(about machinery or equipment) designed to stop working if anything goes wrong: *a fail-safe device/mechanism*

failure /'feɪljə(r)/ noun
SEE ALSO: audit failure
1 [U] lack of success in doing or achieving sth: *The company's failure to meet sales targets resulted in serious problems.* ◇ *the failure of the company's marketing strategy*
2 [C] somebody or something that is not successful: *He was a failure as a manager.* ◇ *The project suffered from too many mistakes and failures.*
3 [U,C] an act of not doing sth, especially sth that you are expected to do: *Failure to comply with the regulations will result in prosecution.*
4 [C,U] a situation in which a business has to close because it is not successful: *Business failures dropped by 6% last year.* ◇ *New companies suffer from a high failure rate.*
5 [U,C] (about a machine or system) the state of not working correctly or as expected; an occasion when this happens: *The crash was caused by engine failure.* ◇ *a systems/technical failure*

★**fair** /feə(r)/; *AmE* fer/ adjective, adverb, noun
● *adjective* (**fairer, fairest**)
1 acceptable and appropriate in a particular situation: *a fair deal/price* ◇ *a fair estimate of the company's value* ◇ *We believe our offer is fair and reasonable.*
2 treating everyone equally and according to the rules or law: *demands for a fairer tax system* ◇ *My manager is always very fair.*
OPP UNFAIR
IDM **(give sb/get) a fair hearing** (to allow sb) the opportunity to give their opinion of sth before deciding if they have done sth wrong: *I'll see that you get a fair hearing.* **(give sb/get) a fair 'shake** (*AmE*) (*informal*) (to give sb/get) fair treatment that gives you the same chance as sb else: *Are older people getting a fair shake in the workplace?*
● *adverb*
according to the rules; in a way that is considered to be acceptable and appropriate: *He claims they didn't play fair in winning the contract* (= they did sth dishonest in order to get it).
IDM **set fair (to do sth/for sth)** (*BrE*) having the necessary qualities or conditions to succeed: *The company looks set fair for growth.*
● *noun* [C]
SEE ALSO: careers fair, job ~, recruitment ~, trade ~
an event at which people, businesses, etc. show and sell their goods: *Fewer foreign exhibitors took part in the fair this year.* ◇ *a technology/agricultural fair* → EXHIBITION, SHOW

fair 'average 'quality noun [U] (*abbr* **FAQ**)
(*Trade*) used to describe goods, especially crops, that are sold on the understanding that the quality will be the same as the average quality of goods produced in the same country in the same period of time, or the average quality of several samples: *The contract was for goods of fair average quality.*

fair 'dealing noun [U]
(*Law*)
1 ways of doing business that are honest and fair to your customers and the people you do business with: *Financial advisers should have a reputation for fair dealing.*
2 (*especially BrE*) (*AmE usually* **fair 'use**) conditions under which you are allowed to use or copy an original piece of work, such as part of a book, a song, etc: *Fair dealing covers activities such as quoting a passage from a book for a review.*

fair 'market 'value = FAIR VALUE

fair 'trade noun [U]
1 trade which supports producers in developing countries by paying fair prices and making sure

that workers have good working conditions and fair pay: *Our aim is to support fair trade by giving the cocoa growers a fair price for their beans.* ◇ *We buy 10% of our bananas from fair-trade sources.* **2** trade that is fair to customers: *fair trade laws to prevent misleading advertising*

fair 'trading *noun* [U]
1 buying and selling activities that are honest and fair to businesses, producers, sellers and customers: *The company is committed to a policy of fair trading.* ◇ *a fair trading agreement*
2 (*Economics*) a system of international trade where the countries involved agree not to put taxes on particular items they import from each other: *Some state subsidies could pose a threat to fair trading conditions.* → FREE TRADE

fair 'use = FAIR DEALING (2)

fair 'value (*also* **fair 'market 'value**) *noun* [C,U]
1 a price paid for an item that is fair to both the buyer and the seller: *A fair value for crude oil would be around $32 a barrel.* ◇ *a fair value price*
2 (*Accounting*) a method of valuing the assets of a business based on the price at which they could be sold: *Some analysts thought a fair value for the assets would be $500 million.*

fair 'wage *noun* [C]
(*HR*) an amount of money paid to a worker that is equal to the work done: *fair wages for coffee farmers*

faithfully /ˈfeɪθfəli/ *adverb*
IDM **Yours faithfully** (*BrE*) (*only used in written English*) used at the end of a formal letter before you sign your name, when you have addressed sb as 'Dear Sir/Dear Madam', etc. and not by their name

fake /feɪk/ *adjective, noun, verb*
●*adjective*
1 not genuine; appearing to be sth it is not: *The fake DVDs were of poor quality.* ◇ *fake designer clothing* → COUNTERFEIT, PIRATE
2 made to look like sth else: *a jacket in fake fur*
●*noun* [C]
a product, work of art, piece of jewellery, etc. that is not genuine but has been made to look as if it is: *The trade in fakes costs industry billions of pounds a year.*
●*verb* [+ obj]
to make sth false appear to be genuine, especially in order to deceive sb: *She had faked her supervisor's signature on the document.*

fall /fɔːl/ *verb, noun*
●*verb* [no obj] (**fell** /fel/ **fallen** /ˈfɔːlən/)
1 to decrease in amount, value or level: *Orders for new products have continued to fall.* ◇ *Their profits fell (by) nearly 30 per cent.* ◇ *The company's shares fell sharply on Tuesday.* ◇ *a period of falling prices* ◇ *Our market share has fallen to its lowest level ever.* See note at INCREASE
2 to pass into a particular state; to begin to be sth: *The company fell into bankruptcy with debts of $12 billion.* ◇ *The first interest payment falls due* (= must be paid) *in January.*
IDM **fall foul of sb/sth** to be guilty of not obeying sb/sth: *Companies risk heavy penalties if they fall foul of the new accounting rules.* **fall from 'grace** to become less popular and successful, especially after doing sth wrong and losing people's trust: *After the collapse of the Internet bubble, he quickly fell from grace and later left the company.* **fall on your 'sword** to take responsibility for sth bad that has happened, especially by leaving your job: *If the company's profits don't improve this year, the CEO will be forced to fall on his sword.* **fall 'short of sth** to fail to reach the standard that you expected or

need: *We're going to fall short of our sales targets for this year.* → idioms at ARREARS, PREY *noun*, STAND *verb*
PHR V **fall a'part 1** to be in very bad condition so that parts break off: *The machines are falling apart.* **2** to have so many problems that it is no longer possible to exist or function: *The merger plans fell apart last week.* → FALL THROUGH **fall a'way** to become gradually fewer or smaller; to disappear: *The market for their products fell away to almost nothing.* **fall 'back** to decrease in value or amount: *Share prices fell back after brisk early trading.* **fall 'back on sth** (*not used in the passive*) to have sth to use when you are in difficulty or if other things fail: *Many households have no savings to fall back on.* ◇ *The company can fall back on its classic brands.* → FALLBACK **fall be'hind**; **fall be'hind sb/sth** to fail to keep level with sb/sth: *All too often, companies fall behind technologically.* ◇ *The project has fallen behind schedule.* **fall be'hind with sth** to not pay or do sth at the right time: *They had fallen behind with their loan repayments.* **fall 'off** to decrease in quantity or level: *We expect sales to fall off in the new year.* → FALL-OFF **fall 'out of sth** to no longer be part of a particular group or have a particular status: *The group is in danger of falling out of the FTSE 100.* **fall 'through** to not be completed, or not happen: *The deal fell through when they could not agree on price.* → FALL APART
●*noun* [C]

SEE ALSO: free fall

a decrease in size, number, rate or level: *The firm announced a five per-cent-fall in profits.* ◇ *a dramatic fall in unemployment*
⊕ *a big/dramatic/sharp/slight/steep fall (in sth)*
IDM **sb's fall from 'grace** a situation in which a person or a company becomes less popular and successful, especially after doing sth wrong and losing people's trust: *The company suffered a dramatic fall from grace and most of its directors were replaced.* → idiom at RIDE *verb*

fallback /ˈfɔːlbæk/ *noun* [C]
1 a plan or course of action that is ready to be used in an emergency if other things fail: *Each stage of the plan has a fallback.* ◇ *We need a fallback position if they don't accept our offer.* → FALL BACK ON STH at FALL *verb*
2 a reduction or decrease in sth: *a fallback in energy prices* **SYN** FALL → FALL BACK at FALL *verb*

fallen 'angel *noun* [C]
(*Finance, informal*) a company whose bonds were once a good investment but have now dropped in value

faller /ˈfɔːlə(r)/ *noun* [C]
(*Stock Exchange*) (used in newspapers) a company whose shares have decreased in value: *The airline was the biggest faller in FTSE 100 index today, dropping 7.6 per cent.* **SYN** DECLINER **OPP** GAINER

'fall guy *noun* [C] (*especially AmE*)
a person who is blamed or punished for sth wrong that sb else has done: *He was made the fall guy for the company's failure.*

falling 'market *noun* [C]
1 a market in which most investments are decreasing in value: *They were forced to sell the shares in a falling market.*
2 a situation in which the demand for a particular type of product is decreasing: *a falling market for IT products and services.*

falling-'off = FALL-OFF

'fall-off (*AmE spelling* **falloff**) (*BrE also* **falling-'off**, *less frequent*) *noun* [sing.]
a reduction in the amount, level or quality of sth: *a recent fall-off in demand for exports* → FALL OFF at FALL *verb*

fallout /'fɔːlaʊt/ *noun* [U]
the bad results of a situation or an action: *The banks were hit by the fallout from the economic crisis.*

false /fɔːls/ *adjective*
1 wrong; not correct or true: *She gave false information to the insurance company.* ◇ *false marketing claims*
2 not genuine, but made to look real to deceive people: *a false passport*
3 wrong, because it is based on sth that is not true or correct: *Buying a cheap computer is a false economy* (= will not actually save you money).
▶ **'falsely** *adverb*: *to be falsely accused of sth*
IDM **by/under/on false pre'tences** (*AmE* spelling **~ pretenses**) by claiming that sth is true which is not, especially in order to gain some advantage for yourself: *She was accused of obtaining money by false pretences.*

false ac'counting *noun* [U]
the crime of reporting information about a company's financial state that is not true, so that people believe it has less debt, more profit, etc. than it really has

false 'bottom *noun* [C]
(*Economics*) if a market in which share prices are falling has a **false bottom**, it seems as if prices have reached their lowest level because they begin to rise, but then they fall even lower

false 'dawn *noun* [C]
a situation in which you think that sth good is going to happen but it does not: *a false dawn for the economy*

falsify /'fɔːlsɪfaɪ/ *verb* [+ obj] (**falsifies, falsifying, falsified, falsified**)
to change a written record or information so that it is no longer true: *to falsify data/documents/records* ◇ *The directors had falsified the accounts.*
▶ **falsification** /ˌfɔːlsɪfɪ'keɪʃn/ *noun* [U,C]: *the deliberate falsification of the company's records*

falter /'fɔːltə(r)/ *verb* [no obj]
to become weaker or less effective; to stop increasing or improving: *The business faltered and then collapsed.* ◇ *The economy shows no signs of faltering.* ▶ **faltering** /'fɔːltərɪŋ/ *adjective*: *the country's faltering economy*

'family brand *noun* [C]
(*Marketing*) a name that a company uses to sell a range of different products: *Each product line is sold under a different family brand.* ▶ **'family ˌbranding** *noun* [U]: *a strong family branding*

family-'friendly *adjective*
(*HR*) suitable for workers who have children: *family-friendly policies/working hours*

family 'life ˌcycle *noun* [C, usually sing.]
(*Marketing*) the different stages of family life that depend on the age of the parents and children, and how many children are living at home: *Clothing needs differ throughout the family life cycle.*

fancy /'fænsi/ *adjective* (**fancier, fanciest**)
1 unusually complicated, often in an unnecessary way: *The program has a lot of fancy graphics.*
2 [only before noun] (especially about small things) attractive, with a lot of decorations or bright colours: *fancy goods* (= things sold as gifts or for decoration)
3 (sometimes disapproving) expensive or connected with an expensive way of life: *fancy restaurants with fancy prices*

Fannie Mae™ /ˌfæni 'meɪ/ *noun* (*Finance, informal*)
1 [sing.] (*abbr* **FNMA**) in the US, the Federal National Mortgage Association, a private company supported by the government that supplies money

for MORTGAGES: *Fannie Mae leads the market to expand home ownership.*
2 [C, usually pl.] the bonds that are issued by **Fannie Mae**: *Fannie Maes with a yield of 4.05%* ◇ *a fund that invests in Fanny Maes*
→ FREDDIE MAC, GINNIE MAE

fao /ˌef eɪ 'əʊ; *AmE* 'oʊ/ *abbr* (*BrE*)
for the attention of; written on a business letter or document to say who should deal with it

FAQ /ˌef eɪ 'kjuː; *AmE also* fæk/ *abbr, noun*
● *abbr*
1 (*IT, usually used in written English*) also /fæk/ frequently asked questions: *The site has a list of FAQs on the new tax law.*
2 (*Trade*) = FAIR AVERAGE QUALITY
● *noun* [C, usually pl.] (*plural* **FAQs**)
(*IT*) an Internet page on which there are answers to questions that people often ask about the site or a special topic: *Please check our FAQs before contacting the customer support centre.* ◇ *an FAQ page/section*

fare /feə(r); *AmE* fer/ *noun*

SEE ALSO: low-fare

1 [C,U] the money that you pay to travel by bus, plane, taxi, etc: *Bus fares will go up by 7% next week.* ◇ *Children over 16 pay full fare.* ◇ *a 7% fare increase* ◇ *The price of walk-up fares* (= that you do not book before you travel) *has been cut.* → AIRFARE
O *a one-way/single fare ◆ a return/round-trip fare ◆ full/half fare ◆ cheap/discount/high/low fares ◆ off-peak/peak fares ◆ last-minute/standby/walk-up fares*
2 [C] a passenger in a taxi: *The taxi driver picked up a fare at the station.*

farm /fɑːm; *AmE* fɑːrm/ *noun, verb*
● *noun* [C]

SEE ALSO: cube farm, fish ~, non-~, server ~, wind ~

1 an area of land, and the buildings on it, used for growing crops and/or keeping animals: *a 40-hectare farm* ◇ *a farm labourer/worker* ◇ *farm buildings/machinery* ◇ *an increase in jobs in the farm sector*
2 a place where particular fish or animals are bred: *a cattle/chicken/fish farm* → FACTORY FARM
● *verb* [+ obj or no obj]
to use land for growing crops and/or keeping animals: *The family has farmed in the area for generations.* ◇ *organically farmed produce*
PHR V **ˌfarm sth 'out to sb** (*BrE*) to send out work for other people to do: *Most of the engineering work is farmed out to independent firms.*

farmer /'fɑːmə(r); *AmE* 'fɑːrm-/ *noun* [C]
a person who owns or manages a farm

farmer's 'market (*also spelled* **farmers' ~**) *noun* [C]
a market where farmers sell their fruit and vegetables

farming /'fɑːmɪŋ; *AmE* 'fɑːrm-/ *noun* [U]
the business of managing or working on a farm: *to take up farming* ◇ *sheep/fish/organic farming* ◇ *farming systems/techniques* ◇ *a farming community*

FAS /ˌef eɪ 'es/ = FREE ALONGSIDE SHIP

FASB /'fæsbi/ = FINANCIAL ACCOUNTING STANDARDS BOARD

fascia (*BrE* spelling *also* **facia**) /'feɪʃə/ *noun* [C] (*BrE*)
1 a board above the entrance of a shop/store, with the name of the shop/store on it; the name of a shop/store: *Some stores will continue to operate under the Safeway fascia.*
2 the hard cover on a mobile phone/cellphone

fashion /'fæʃn/ noun
  1 [U,C] a popular style of clothes, hair, etc. at a particular time or place: *dressed in the latest fashion* ◊ *new hair fashions* ◊ *Black is always in fashion.* ◊ *a store selling shoes and fashion accessories*
  ➋ current/the latest/new *fashions* • to be in/out of *fashion*
  2 [U] the business of making or selling clothes, shoes, etc., especially in new and different styles: *the world of fashion* ◊ *a career in the fashion industry*
  ➋ a fashion business/chain/house/retailer • a fashion designer/magazine/show

'fashion goods noun [pl.]
  (*Commerce*) items such as clothes, shoes, etc. that manufacturers need to change often as styles, etc. change: *Its fashion goods now range from watches to shoes.*

fast /fɑːst; *AmE* fæst/ adjective, adverb
  ● *adjective* (**faster, fastest**)
  1 happening quickly or without delay: *the fastest rate of increase for several years* ◊ *a fast response time* ◊ *a fast Internet connection*
  2 moving quickly; producing or allowing quick movement: *a fast train service* ◊ *the fastest route between two cities*
  → idiom at HARD *adj.*
  ● *adverb* (**faster, fastest**)
  1 quickly: *Exports are growing faster than GDP.*
  2 in a short time; without delay: *We want to get our new products on the shelves as fast as possible.*

,fast-'changing adjective
  changing quickly: *satisfying fast-changing consumer demands*

,fast 'food noun [U]
  hot food that is served very quickly in special restaurants, and often taken away to be eaten in the street: *We intend to offer quality fast food.* ◊ *the world's largest fast-food chain*

,fast-'forward verb, adjective
  ● *verb*
  1 [+ obj or no obj] to wind a tape or video forward without playing it
  2 [no obj] to think about a point later in time: *If we can fast-forward two years, let's have a look at our sales projections.*
  3 (*informal*) [+ obj or no obj] to grow or progress quickly; to make sth do this: *We will fast-forward the product and bring it to the market by 2008.*
  ● *adjective* (*informal*)
  growing or progressing very quickly: *a fast-forward company/marketplace*

,fast-'growing adjective [only before noun]
  getting bigger quickly: *a fast-growing business* ◊ *Portables make up the fastest-growing segment of the computer market.*

'fast lane noun [sing.]
  1 a very busy life, where a lot is happening, that often also has a lot of stress and worry: *Life in the fast lane can have long-term effects on health and family life.*
  2 (*HR*) = FAST TRACK

,fast-'moving adjective [usually before noun]
  1 growing, developing or changing quickly: *fast-moving technology companies* ◊ *the fast-moving world of computer gaming*
  2 selling quickly: *fast-moving consumer goods*
  → FMCG

,fast-'paced adjective [usually before noun]
  developing or changing quickly: *a fast-paced marketplace*

'fast track (*also* **'fast lane**) noun [sing.]
  (*HR*) a plan or path that brings success in your career and more important jobs more quickly than normal: *The company put him on a fast track to higher management.* ◊ *a fast-track career/executive*
  ▶ **'fast-track** verb [+ obj]: *Exceptional employees can be fast-tracked into positions of greater responsibility.* **'fast-,tracking** noun [U]

'fat cat noun [C] (*informal*)
  a person who earns, or who has, a lot of money (especially when compared to people who do not earn so much): *corporate/industry fat cats*

fatware /'fætweə(r); *AmE* -wer/ = BLOATWARE

fault /fɔːlt/ noun
  1 [C] something that is wrong or not perfect with sth; something that is wrong with a machine or system that stops it from working correctly: *a technical fault* ◊ *faults in design*
  2 [U] the responsibility for sth wrong that has happened or been done: *She lost her job through no fault of her own.*

'fault-,finding noun [U]
  the act of looking for faults in sth: *We provide computer servicing, fault-finding and repair.*

'fault ,tolerance noun [U]
  (*IT*) the ability of a computer or a network to continue to work even when there is an unexpected problem with the HARDWARE or software ▶ **'fault-,tolerant** adjective [usually before noun]

faulty /'fɔːlti/ adjective
  1 not perfect; not working or made correctly: *faulty goods/workmanship* ◊ *The product was recalled because a part was faulty.*
  2 (about a way of thinking) wrong or containing mistakes, often resulting in bad decisions: *faulty analysis*

favourable (*AmE spelling* **favorable**) /'feɪvərəbl/ adjective
  1 good for sth/sb and making it/them likely to be successful or have an advantage: *Conditions are not favourable for private investors at the moment.* ◊ *favourable economic conditions*
  2 fairly good and not too expensive: *Because of its size, the company can buy supplies on favourable terms.*
  OPP UNFAVOURABLE

★ fax /fæks/ noun, verb
  ● *noun* (*also* **fac'simile**, *formal*)
  1 (*also* **'fax ma,chine**) [C] a machine that sends and receives documents in an electronic form along telephone wires and then prints them: *Do you have a fax?*
  2 [U] a system for sending documents using a **fax** machine: *Can you send it to me by fax?* ◊ *What's your fax number?*
  3 [C] a letter or message sent by **fax**: *Did you get my fax?* ◊ *You can send faxes by email from your computer.*
  ➋ an incoming/outgoing *fax* • to get/receive/send a *fax*
  ● *verb* [+ obj or no obj]
  to send sb a document, message, etc. by **fax**: *Could you fax me the latest version?* ◊ *Could you fax it to me?* ◊ *The printer can also fax, scan and copy.*

faxback /'fæksbæk/ noun [U,C]
  a system in which sb can automatically receive information by **fax** from a website, or, when they ask, from a fax machine or a telephone

'fax ma,chine = FAX noun (1)

FCA /,ef siː 'eɪ/ = FREE CARRIER

FCL /,ef siː 'el/ = FULL CONTAINER LOAD

FCM /,ef siː 'em/ = FUTURES COMMISSION MERCHANT

fco /,ef siː 'əʊ; *AmE* 'oʊ/ = FRANCO

ˌfeasiˈbility ˌstudy (also ˌfeasiˈbility reˌport, less frequent) noun [C]
an examination of every detail of a new project, such as the costs, benefits and risks, in order to decide if it is possible and likely to be achieved; the document that is produced: We are doing a feasibility study on building a factory in France.

feasible /ˈfiːzəbl/ adjective
that is possible and likely to be achieved: It is not feasible to complete the project in under 3 months.
● a feasible idea/plan/suggestion
▶ **feasibility** /ˌfiːzəˈbɪləti/ noun [U]: The directors are examining the feasibility of a management buyout. ◇ a feasibility test

ˌfeather-ˈbedding (AmE spelling **featherbedding**) noun [U]
(HR) the activity of limiting the production of goods or of using too many workers, in order to save or create jobs, especially because of a contract with a union

★ **feature** /ˈfiːtʃə(r)/ noun, verb
● noun [C]

SEE ALSO: **call feature**

1 something important, interesting or typical of a thing or place: Ease of use is a key feature of all their products. ◇ The new computer system is much more powerful and has more safety and security features.
● a distinguishing/key/major/standard/striking/unique feature ◆ a handy/an interesting/a useful feature ◆ design/safety/security features
2 (in newspapers, on television, etc.) a special article or programme about sth/sb: There's a special feature on Japan in next week's issue.
● verb
1 [+ obj] to include a particular thing or person as a special feature: The latest models of notebook computers feature a 30 cm screen. ◇ The company is featured in the current edition of the magazine.
2 [no obj] to be included as an important part of sth: The plant does not feature in the company's plans for the future. SYN FIGURE

the Fed /fed/ = FEDERAL RESERVE BOARD, FEDERAL RESERVE BANK, FEDERAL RESERVE SYSTEM

federal /ˈfedərəl/ adjective
1 having a system of government in which the individual states of a country have control over their own affairs, but are controlled by a central government for national decisions, etc: a federal republic
2 within a federal system, especially the US, connected with national government rather than the local government of an individual state: state and federal income taxes ◇ a federal court ◇ federal funding/grants
▶ **ˈfederally** adverb

the ˌFederal Aviˈation Adminiˌstration noun [sing. with sing./pl. verb] (abbr FAA)
the department of the US government that is responsible for non-military air travel

ˌFederal ˈfunds (also **ˈfed funds**) noun [pl.]
money that is put into FEDERAL RESERVE BANKS by other banks that can be used for short, temporary loans to banks that need it. The rate of interest charged on such loans is an important sign of what the economy is doing: a cut in the 3.5 per cent Federal funds rate

the ˌFederal Reˈserve = FEDERAL RESERVE SYSTEM

the ˈFederal Reˈserve ˈBank (also the Fed, informal) noun [C] (abbr FRB)
one of the 12 banks that form the central bank of the US

the ˌFederal Reˈserve Board (also the ˈFederal Reˈserve ˈBoard of ˈGovernors) (also the Fed, informal) noun [sing. with sing./pl. verb] (abbr FRB)
a group of seven people who are named by the US President and elected politicians (the **Senate**) to manage the Federal Reserve System

the ˌFederal Reˈserve ˌSystem (also the ˌFederal Reˈserve) (also the Fed, informal) noun [sing.] (abbr FRS)
the banking system in the US that lends money to banks and to the government and issues (= makes available) notes and coins

ˌFederal ˈTrade Comˌmission noun [sing. with sing./pl. verb] (abbr FTC)
in the US, an independent government organization that makes sure that business is done in a legal and fair way and protects the rights of consumers, etc: The Federal Trade Commission has conditionally approved the merger. → OFFICE OF FAIR TRADING

federated /ˈfedəreɪtɪd/ adjective
(about states, organizations, etc.) united under a central government or organization but keeping some local control

federation /ˌfedəˈreɪʃn/ noun [C]

SEE ALSO: **labour federation**

1 a group of companies, unions, clubs, etc. that have joined together to form an organization: the European Chemical Industry Federation
2 a country consisting of a group of individual states that have control over their own affairs but are controlled by a central government for national decisions, etc.

★ **fee** /fiː/ noun [C]

SEE ALSO: **break fee, break-up ~, commitment ~, contingency ~, contingent ~, licence ~, no-win no-~, user ~**

1 (Commerce) an amount of money that you pay for professional advice or services: legal fees ◇ Does the bank charge a fee for setting up the account? ◇ There's an upfront fee of €50 and a small annual charge. ◇ a pool of fee income from advisory work See note at PRICE
● to charge/collect/earn/pay a fee ◆ a fat/high/huge/low/nominal fee ◆ an annual/hourly/a monthly fee ◆ a fixed/flat/one-off/an upfront fee ◆ consultancy/management/transaction/transfer fees
2 an amount of money that you pay to join an organization or to do sth: a membership fee
● access/entry/membership/registration/subscription fees ◆ to charge/collect/pay a fee

ˈfee-based adjective
(Commerce) (about a service) that you have to pay a fee to use: a fee-based information service

feed /fiːd/ verb, noun
● verb (fed, fed /fed/) [+ obj]
1 feed A (with B) | feed B into A to supply sth to sb/sth: The electricity line is fed with power through an underground cable.
2 feed A (with B) | feed B into/through A to put or push sth into or through a machine: You have to feed the sheets into the printer one at a time.
PHR V **ˌfeed ˈback (into sth)** to have an influence on the development of sth; to help to improve sth: The goodwill feeds back into increased store sales. **ˌfeed sth ˈback (into sth)** to return sth, especially money, to an organization, etc. so that it can be used to help improve it: Our profits are usually fed back into the company to keep it growing. **ˌfeed sth ˈback (to sb)** to give sb information, advice or

opinions about sth such as how good a product or sb's work is, especially so that it can be improved: *The results of our research will be fed back to the teams.* → FEEDBACK **'feed into sth**; **,feed 'through into sth** (about information, an opinion, etc.) to affect sth; to help to form or develop sth: *The report's findings will feed into company policy.* ◇ *Increases in public spending will feed through into higher employment.* **,feed 'through (to sb/sth)** to reach sb/sth after going through a process or system: *It will take time for the higher rates to feed through to investors.* → FEED INTO STH

●*noun*

SEE ALSO: **sheet feed**

1 [C] a pipe, device, etc. which supplies a machine with sth: *The printer has an automatic paper feed.*
2 [U,C] material supplied to a machine: *a feed pipe*
3 [U] (*AmE*) television programmes that are sent from a central station to other stations in a network; the system of sending out these programmes

★ **feedback** /'fi:dbæk/ *noun* [U]

SEE ALSO: **full-circle feedback, 360-degree feedback**

1 (*HR*) advice or information that is given to an employee about how good their work is so that they can improve
O *constructive/immediate/negative/positive/useful feedback* • *to get/give/offer/provide/receive feedback*
2 (*Marketing*) information that is given by users to a business about how useful a product or service is so that it can be improved: *They offered free product samples in return for customer feedback.*
O *consumer/customer/investor feedback* • *good/ immediate/negative/positive/useful feedback* • *to get/give/offer/provide/receive/solicit feedback*

'feeding ,frenzy *noun* [C] (*informal*)
a situation in which a lot of people compete with each other to buy or get sth for themselves: *Shortages of the toys created a feeding frenzy.*

feedstock /'fi:dstɒk; *AmE* -sta:k/ *noun* [C,U]
(*Manufacturing*) a raw material used in the process of manufacturing a product, or as fuel for a machine

'feel-good (*also spelled* **feelgood**) *adjective* [only before noun]
making you feel happy and pleased about life: *The social events organized for staff are important for their feel-good effect.*
IDM **the/a 'feel-good factor** (*BrE*) a feeling of confidence in the future that is shared by many people

,felt-tip 'pen (*also* **'felt tip, ,felt-tipped 'pen**) *noun* [C]
a pen that has a point made of a soft, thick material

feminization, -isation /,femɪnaɪ'zeɪʃn; *AmE* -nə'z-/ *noun* [U]
(*HR*) the fact that more women than before are involved in a particular activity: *the feminization of management*

ferry /'feri/ *noun, verb*
●*noun* [C] (*plural* **ferries**)
a boat that carries goods, people and vehicles across a river or across a narrow part of the sea: *the cross-Channel ferry service*
O *a ferry business/company/operator/service*
●*verb* [+ obj or no obj] (**ferries, ferrying, ferried, ferried**)
(*usually used with an adverb or a preposition*)
to carry goods, people or vehicles from one place to

another, often for a short distance and as a regular service: *Barges ferry the gas and heating oil to regional distributors.*

fertilizer, -iser /'fɜ:tɪlaɪzə(r); *AmE* 'fɜ:rt-/ *noun* [C,U]
a substance added to soil to make plants grow more successfully: *artificial/chemical /liquid fertilizers*

FEU /,ef i: 'ju:/ *noun* [C]
(*Transport*) **forty-foot equivalent unit** a standard container for transporting goods, that is approximately twelve metres long

ff. *abbr* (*only used in written English*)
following pages

FHLMC /,ef eɪtʃ el em 'si:/ = FREDDIE MAC

fiber optics, fiber-optic = FIBRE OPTICS

fibre (*AmE spelling* **fiber**) /'faɪbə(r)/ *noun*
1 [C,U] a material that is made from a mass of natural or artificial threads: *nylon and other man-made fibres*
2 [C] one of the many thin threads that form natural materials, such as wood and cotton: *cotton fibres*

,fibre 'optics (*AmE spelling* **fiber ~**) *noun* [U]
(*IT*) the use of thin **fibres** of glass, etc. for sending information in the form of light signals ▶ **,fibre-'optic** (*AmE spelling* **fiber-~**) *adjective*: *fibre-optic cables*

fickle /'fɪkl/ *adjective*
1 changing often and suddenly: *the notoriously fickle fashion sportswear market*
2 (about a person) often changing their mind so you cannot rely on them: *fickle consumers/investors* ▶ **'fickleness** *noun* [U]: *the fickleness of financial markets*

fiddle /'fɪdl/ *verb, noun*
(*informal*)
●*verb* [+ obj]
to change the details or figures of sth in order to try to get money dishonestly, or gain an advantage: *to fiddle the accounts* ◇ *She **fiddled the books** (= changed the company's financial records) while working as an accountant.*
●*noun* [C]
something that is done dishonestly to get money: *an insurance/a tax fiddle*

fi'delity bond *noun* [C] (*also* **fi'delity in,surance** [U])
(*Insurance*) protection that a company can have to pay for losses caused by an employee doing sth dishonest or making a mistake

fiduciary /fɪ'dju:ʃəri; -'du:ʃ-; *AmE also* fɪ'du:ʃieri/ *adjective, noun*
(*Law*)
●*adjective*
used to describe the relationship based on trust between the people who manage money or property for sb, and the person/people they manage it for: *The company's directors were accused of breaching their **fiduciary duty** to the shareholders.*
●*noun* [C] (*plural* **fiduciaries**)
a person or an organization that is responsible for managing money or property for another person or group of people SYN TRUSTEE

field /fi:ld/ *noun, verb*
●*noun*

SEE ALSO: **gold field, playing field**

1 [sing. with sing./pl. verb] all the people or products competing in a particular area of business: *They **lead** the field in home entertainment systems.* ◇ *The company is recognized as a world leader **in** its field.*

2 [C] a particular subject or activity that sb works in or is interested in: *What field of business are you in?*

3 [sing.] (*often used as an adjective*) used to describe work or study that is done outside the office, factory or LABORATORY and the people who do this work: *We get vital customer information from our agents* **in the field.** ◇ *We carried out field research on people's shopping habits.* → FIELD-TEST

4 (*IT*) [C] a space for a separate item of data: *You will need to create separate fields for first name, surname and address.*

● *verb* [+ obj]
to receive and deal with questions or comments: *I had to field some difficult questions after the presentation.*

'field sales *noun* [U; pl.]
(*Marketing*) the business of selling things outside a company's offices; the people who do this work: *jobs in field sales* ◇ *Our experienced field sales force cover all areas of the UK.* ◇ *the field sales manager*

'field-test *verb* [+ obj]
to test sth, such as a product or a piece of equipment, in the place where it will be used
▶ **'field test** *noun* [C]: *The cards are undergoing field tests and could be available next year.*

FIFO /'faɪfəʊ; *AmE* -foʊ/ = FIRST IN, FIRST OUT

,fifty-'fifty *adjective, adverb* (*informal*)
divided equally between two people, groups or possibilities: *I think our bid has a better than fifty-fifty chance of success.* ◇ *Let's split the money fifty-fifty.*

fig. *abbr* (*only used in written English*)
a figure: *See fig. 34.*

★ **figure** /'fɪgə(r); *AmE* 'fɪgjər/ *noun, verb*
● *noun* [C]

SEE ALSO: **double figures, sales ~, single ~, trade ~**

1 a number representing a particular amount, especially one given in official information: *Profits were well below last year's figure of $58 million.* ◇ *The latest figures show that prices are still rising.* ◇ *Unemployment rose to 4.1 million last month according to official figures.* ◇ *rising jobless figures* ◇ *a decline in listening/viewing figures* (= the number of people who listen to or watch a programme on the radio or TV)
O *a high/low* figure • *an average/exact/a rough* figure • *final/interim/preliminary* figures • *current/official/recent* figures
2 a symbol rather than a word representing one of the numbers between 0 and 9: *a six-figure salary* (= over 100 000 dollars, euros, etc.)
3 a person of the type mentioned: *a leading figure in the music industry*
O *an important/a leading/key/respected/senior* figure • *corporate/government/industry/public* figures
4 (*abbr* **fig.**) a picture, diagram, etc. in a book, that is referred to by a number: *The results are illustrated in figure 3 opposite.*
IDM **put a 'figure on sth** to say the exact price or number of sth → idiom at BALLPARK

● *verb*
1 [+ obj] (*AmE*) to calculate an amount or the cost of sth: *We've figured the cost of moving offices at about $10 000.*
2 [no obj] **figure (as sth) (in/among sth)** to be part of a process, situation, etc. especially an important part: *The factory doesn't figure in the company's future plans.* **SYN** FEATURE
PHRV **figure sth 'out 1** to calculate an amount or the cost of sth: *Have you figured out how much it will cost?* **2** to find the answer to sth; to solve sth: *We have to figure out how to improve cash flow.* **3** to plan or think of sth: *Have you figured out what to do next?* **SYN** WORK STH OUT

★ **file** /faɪl/ *noun, verb*
● *noun* [C]

SEE ALSO: **box file, lever arch ~, log ~, Pay and ~, rank and ~, sig ~, suspension ~,** etc.

1 (*IT*) a collection of information stored together in a computer, under a particular name: *You'll find the document on the C-drive in a file called 'Zambia'.*
O *to access/copy/create/delete/save a* file • *a computer/data/text* file
2 a box or folded piece of card for keeping loose papers together and in order: *Put that letter in the file marked 'Urgent'.*
3 a **file** and the information it contains, for example about a particular person or subject: *They have vast files on markets, clients and competitors.* ◇ *Your application will be kept on* file.
O *to have/keep/maintain a* file (*on sb/sth*) • *to consult/have access to/read/refer to a* file
● *verb*
1 [+ obj] to put and keep documents, etc. in a particular place and in a particular order so that you can find them easily: *I filed the letters* **away** *in the drawer.* ◇ *The forms should be filed alphabetically.*
2 [+ obj *or* no obj] to present sth so that it can be officially recorded and dealt with: *to file* **for** *bankruptcy* ◇ *to file a claim/a lawsuit* ◇ *The company filed its accounts last week.* → LODGE

'file ,cabinet = FILING CABINET

'file clerk = FILING CLERK

'file ,manager *noun* [C]
(*IT*) a computer program that is used to organize, arrange and find files and DIRECTORIES (= groups of files)

'file ,server = SERVER

'file ,transfer *noun* [C,U]
(*IT*) an act or the process of sending an electronic file from one computer to another: *You can use the cable to connect two computers for a file transfer.*

filing /'faɪlɪŋ/ *noun*

SEE ALSO: **regulatory filing**

1 [U] the act of putting documents, letters, etc. into a file: *We hired an assistant to do all the filing.* ◇ *a centralized filing system*
2 [U] the act of presenting sth so that it can be officially recorded and dealt with: *There are penalties for late filing of accounts.* ◇ *the filing of*

files

file

lever arch file

box file

binder   folder

lawsuits/criminal charges ◇ *tax filing software*
3 [C] (*especially AmE*) an act of presenting documents to a court or government department; a document that is presented in this way: *The company is required to* **make** *filings* **to/with** *the Securities and Exchange Commission.* ◇ *In a court filing, he claims the firm acted legally.* ◇ *bankruptcy/regulatory/tax filings*

'filing ˌcabinet (*AmE also* **'file ˌcabinet**) *noun* [C]
a piece of office furniture with deep drawers for storing files: *All the records are stored in a metal filing cabinet.*
→ SUSPENSION FILE—Picture at OFFICE

'filing clerk (*BrE*) (*AmE* **'file clerk**) *noun* [C]
a person whose job is to **file** letters, etc. and do general office tasks

fill /fɪl/ *verb* [+ obj]
1 to appoint sb to a job: *The vacancy has already been filled.*
2 to do a job, have a role or position, etc: *He fills the post satisfactorily* (= performs his duties well). ◇ *The team needs someone to fill* **the role of** *manager very soon.*
3 to make or sell sth that is not yet available: *The managing editor thinks the new magazine will fill a gap in the market.*
4 to provide sth that will stop people from continuing to want or need sth: *The hardware store has devoted itself to filling customers' needs.*
5 if a company **fills** an order, it gives the customer the goods they have asked for: *They have a reputation for filling orders quickly.*
6 if sb **fills** a SHORTFALL, they provide sth so that there will be as much as is needed or expected: *plans to train staff in order to fill the shortfall of skills*
IDM **fill your 'pockets** to make or take a lot of money for yourself: *There were rumours that the bosses had filled their pockets at the expense of shareholders.* **fill sb's 'shoes/'boots** to do sb's job in a satisfactory way when they are not there: *When she leaves it will not be easy to find somebody to fill her shoes.*
PHR V **ˌfill 'in (for sb/as sth)** to do sb's job for a short time while they are not there; **ˌfill sth 'in** (*also* **ˌfill sth 'out**) to complete a form, etc. by writing information on it: *You can fill out the application online.* **ˌfill sb 'in (on sth)** to tell sb about sth that has happened: *Can you fill me in on what happened in the meeting?* **ˌfill sth 'out** = FILL STH IN **ˌfill 'up (with sth)**; **ˌfill sth 'up (with sth)** to become completely full; to make sth completely full: *Our order books are beginning to fill up.*

ˌfill or 'kill ˌorder (*also* **ˌfill or 'kill**, *less frequent*) *noun* [C] (*abbr* **FOK**)
(*Stock Exchange*) an instruction to a BROKER to buy or sell a particular number of shares at a particular price immediately or else not at all: *The trade was carried out on a fill or kill basis.* ◇ *to submit an FOK*
NOTE The plural is usually **fill or kill orders**.

Filofax™ /'faɪləʊfæks; *AmE* -loʊ-/ *noun* [C]
a small book with pages that can be added or removed easily, used for writing notes, addresses, etc. in → PERSONAL ORGANIZER See note at CALENDAR

filter /'fɪltə(r)/ *noun, verb*
● *noun* [C]
(*IT*) a computer program that receives data and processes it according to particular rules before displaying it, or sending it somewhere to stop particular things from being seen: *You can set up filters to manage your incoming and outgoing emails.* ◇ *We use a web filter to block access to certain websites.*

● *verb*
1 (*IT*) [+ obj] (*about a computer program*) to process data according to particular rules before displaying it or sending it somewhere, for example in order to stop particular figures, text, etc. from being seen: *The program filters web pages for unsuitable contents.* ◇ *Incoming emails are filtered into different mail boxes based on their subject.*
2 [no obj] (*used with an adverb or a preposition*) to have an effect on sth, especially in small amounts over a period of time: *The economic recovery is beginning to filter through to the job market.*
PHR V **ˌfilter sth 'out** to remove sth that you do not want using a special device or system: *The system filters out all junk emails.* ◇ (*figurative*) *The test is used to filter out candidates who may be unsuitable.*

filtering /'fɪltərɪŋ/ *noun* [U]
(*IT*) using a computer program to decide whether particular emails, Internet pages, data, etc. should be displayed or sent somewhere: *an email filtering program*

fin. *abbr*
1 a short way of writing **financial**: *fin. statements*
2 a short way of writing **finance**: *the International Lease Fin. Corp.*

★final /'faɪnl/ *adjective, noun*
● *adjective*
1 [only before noun] being or happening at the end of a series of events, actions, statements, etc: *Sales increased by 5% in the final quarter of the year.* ◇ *a final report/draft/payment* ◇ *The project is in its final stages/phase.*
2 [only before noun] being the result of a particular process: *the final product* ◇ *The parts are made in China and shipped to Scotland for final assembly.*
3 that cannot be argued with or changed: *The judge's decision is final.* ◇ *The deal still needs final approval from the bankruptcy court.* ◇ *€12 000 is our best and final offer.*
▶ **finally** /'faɪnəli/ *adverb*: *The matter was not finally settled until later.*
● *noun* **finals** [pl.]
(*Accounting, informal*) a short way of writing or saying **final results**: *Finals are expected from several companies this week.* → INTERIMS

ˌfinal ac'counts *noun* [pl.]
(*Accounting*) the set of accounts that a business produces at the end of the FINANCIAL YEAR: *The final accounts were prepared by a firm of local accountants.* ◇ *to sign the final accounts*

ˌfinal de'mand *noun*
1 (*Economics*) [U] the extent to which people and businesses are buying goods and services; a measure of this: *An increase in final demand leads to an increase in production.* ◇ *Final demand grew by 2.5% last year.*
2 (*Accounting*) (*also* **ˌfinal re'minder**) [C] (*both BrE*) the last request for payment of a bill or a debt before court action is taken; the document that states this: *The council issued a final demand and threatened legal action.*

ˌfinal 'dividend *noun* [C]
(*Finance*) a **dividend** that is paid at the end of the FINANCIAL YEAR and must be approved by the shareholders at the AGM: *Analysts believe it will pass* (= not pay) *its final dividend.* → INTERIM DIVIDEND

★finalize , **-ise** /'faɪnəlaɪz/ *verb* [+ obj]
to complete the last part of a plan, a project, an agreement, etc: *We have now finalized the deal.* ◇ *The details of the contract have not yet been finalized.* ◇ *to finalize yourarrangements/ plans*
▶ **finalization, -isation** /ˌfaɪnəlaɪ'zeɪʃn; *AmE* -lə'z-/ *noun* [U]

ˌfinal re'minder = FINAL DEMAND (2)

(HR) especially in the UK, an arrangement in which employees receive a pension when they retire based on how long they have worked for the company and the amount of money they were earning when they stopped: *Many big-name companies have closed their final salary pension schemes to new staff.*

★ **finance** /'faɪnæns; faɪ'næns; fə'næns/ *noun, verb*
● *noun*

> SEE ALSO: **consumer finance, corporate ~, debt ~, equity ~, high ~, mezzanine ~, mortgage ~,** etc.

1 [U] money that sb/sth borrows from a bank, receives from investors, etc. in order to run a business, complete an activity or buy sth: *The project will only go ahead if they can raise the necessary finance.* ◇ *A group of banks will provide finance **for** the takeover.* ◇ *international sources of finance*
○ *to **apply for/get/obtain/raise/secure** finance • to **arrange/provide** finance • **long-term/short-term** finance • a finance **business/group***
2 [U] the activity of managing money, especially by a commercial organization or a government: *the company's new finance chief* ◇ *She works in the finance department.* ◇ *a diploma in banking and finance* ◇ *the company's consumer finance arm* (= that provides loans, etc. to customers) ◇ *The government's poor management of public finance lost it the election.* → CHIEF FINANCE OFFICER
○ *a finance **chief/director** • a finance **committee/ department/team** • **company/corporate/personal/ public** finance*
3 finances [pl.] the money available to a person, an organization or a country; the way this money is managed: *The company is battling to put its finances in order.* ◇ *Buying new premises put a strain on our finances.* ◇ *Her personal finances are in a mess.*
○ *to **sort out/handle/manage** your finances • **company/corporate/government/household/ public** finances • **healthy/sound/strong** finances • **deteriorating/shaky/weak** finances • sth **boosts/ strengthens** your finances*

VOCABULARY BUILDING

Providing finance

VERB	NOUN	PERSON
finance	financing	financier
invest	investment	investor
fund	funding	funder
sponsor	sponsorship	sponsor
back	backing	backer

• *The organization is **financed** by the government.*
• *They **invested** $50 000 in the trust.*
• *Extra **funding** will be needed to pay for the project.*
• *The company has agreed to **sponsor** a TV show.*
• *They are struggling to win financial **backing** for their plans.*

● *verb* [+ obj]
to provide or obtain money for a project, or for a business or government to operate: *We have sufficient funds to finance operations for another year.* ◇ *The deal was largely financed by/with/ through a share issue.* SYN FUND

'finance charge noun [C]
the amount you must pay when you arrange a loan; the amount of interest you pay on the money you borrow: *He has huge credit-card debt and pays hundreds of dollars a month in finance charges.*

'finance ,company (also **'finance house,** *especially in BrE*) noun [C]
a company that lends money to people or

---

businesses so that they can buy expensive items, such as vehicles, pieces of equipment, etc. and pay the money back over a period of time: *a consumer finance company* (= that lends money to consumers) ◇ *Many car manufacturers operate their own finance companies.*

'finance house noun [C] *(especially BrE)*
1 = FINANCE COMPANY
2 (*Finance*) a company that arranges loans, investors, etc. for business projects: *a finance house that specializes in securing funding for start-up technology companies*

'finance lease noun [C]
an arrangement in which a financial institution buys a vehicle, piece of machinery, etc. and lets a business use it for an agreed period of time in exchange for regular payments: *The aircraft were acquired under a finance lease.* → OPERATING LEASE

★ **financial** /faɪ'nænʃl; fə'næn-/ *adjective, noun*
● *adjective*
1 [usually before noun] connected with money and finance: *a financial transaction/arrangement* ◇ *financial institutions* ◇ *a financial adviser/ consultant/planner* ◇ *They offer independent financial advice on all types of mortgages.* ◇ *The firm has run into financial difficulties.* ◇ *Tokyo and New York are major financial centres.* **NOTE** The word **financial** is sometimes used in the names of companies that provide loans, advice about money, etc.: *Capital One Financial, the credit-card issuer.*
2 [only before noun] interested in making a profit; intended to make a profit: *A group of financial buyers is interested in acquiring the business* (= because they want to make a profit, not run the business). ◇ *Our stake in the company is a financial investment rather than central to our business strategy.*
▸ **financially** /faɪ'nænʃəli; fə'næn-/ *adverb*: *Financially, the firm is better off than a year ago.* ◇ *a financially sound company* ◇ *Such projects are not financially viable without government funding.*
● *noun*
1 (*Stock Exchange*) [C, usually pl.] a company that provides **financial** services whose shares are traded on a stock exchange, for example, a bank: *Technology stocks and financials recorded strong gains on the market today.*
2 (*Accounting*) **financials** [pl.] (*informal*) a way of referring to a company's **financial results**: *The company's financials for the six months to 30 June are disappointing.*

fi,nancial ac'counting noun [U]
(*Accounting*) the branch of accounting concerned with preparing accurate records of the activities and state of a business (**financial statements**), rather than with looking at the profit and costs of different parts of the business

Fi'nancial Ac'counting 'Standards Board noun [sing.] (*abbr* FASB)
in the US, the organization that decides on accounting standards

fi,nancial ac'counts noun [pl.]
(*Accounting*) the written records of an organization's assets, debts, profits, etc.; a summary of these that is prepared for shareholders, lenders, etc. and describes the financial activity during a particular period of time: *to prepare a set of financial accounts* ◇ *The annual financial accounts will be presented to shareholders next week.*

fi,nancial 'analyst noun [C]
a person whose job involves studying the financial state of particular companies and advising people whether to buy or sell those shares: *Financial*

analysts forecast pre-tax profits of £40 billion this year. ▶ **fi͵nancial a'nalysis** *noun* [U,C]

fi͵nancial 'asset *noun* [C]
(*Accounting*) an asset that is not physically useful but has a financial value, for example money, an investment or a right to claim payments: *The firm has financial assets of $18.4 billion.*

fi͵nancial engi'neering *noun* [U]
(*Finance*) (often used in a disapproving way) the practice of changing the way in which a company borrows money, owns assets, pays debts, etc., especially in order to make its profits seem greater: *The firm used complex financial engineering to remove debt from its balance sheet.* ◇ *techniques of financial engineering, such as reporting profits from future business*

fi͵nancial 'indicator *noun* [C]
a figure that is seen as a measure of the success of a company, an economy, a market, etc: *The company has improved its key financial indicators, including profitability and the debt-equity ratio.* ◇ *It is clear that on every financial indicator the country is doing well.* → ECONOMIC INDICATOR

fi͵nancial insti'tution *noun* [C]
an organization such as a bank that offers financial services, such as accepting deposits, making loans or investing customers' money

fi͵nancial 'instrument *noun* [C]
(*Finance*) any investment that has a cash value and can be bought and sold in an organized system, such as shares, bonds, FUTURES (= contracts to buy or sell a particular amount of sth at a particular time in the future for a particular price), etc: *In the city there are banks which trade in all types of financial instruments.* ◇ *New financial instruments, such as credit derivatives, are continually being created.* [SYN] INSTRUMENT

fi͵nancial inter'mediary *noun* [C]
(*Finance*) a financial organization such as a bank that holds money from lenders in order to make loans to borrowers: *banks and non-bank financial intermediaries*

fi͵nancial 'market (*also* 'market) *noun* [C]
(*Finance*) the activity of buying and selling shares, bonds, currencies, etc.; the organized structure for doing this or the place where it happens: *Brazil's financial markets* ◇ *a single financial market for Europe* ◇ *Financial markets reacted positively to the cut in interest rates.* ◇ *They offered their shares to be traded on the financial market.*

fi͵nancial 'ratio (*also* ac'counting ͵ratio) *noun* [C]
(*Accounting*) the result of comparing two figures that describe a company's financial state, for example its share price and the amount of profit each shareholder can claim, used by managers or investors to decide how well a company is performing: *Smaller companies can offer greater value in terms of key financial ratios, such as price-earnings.*

fi͵nancial re'porting *noun* [U]
(*Accounting*) the act of giving investors and authorities regular financial information about a company's profits, debts, assets, etc: *good/inaccurate/fraudulent financial reporting* ◇ *Auditors have a critical role in the financial reporting process.* ◇ *financial reporting rules/standards*

fi͵nancial re'sults = RESULTS (1)

fi͵nancial 'services *noun* [pl.]
(*Finance*) the business of dealing with money for people or providing advice about money and investments: *They offer a broad range of financial services, from credit cards to travel insurance.* ◇ *The economy is heavily dependent on financial services.* ◇ *the financial services industry/market/sector*

the Fi͵nancial 'Services Au͵thority *noun* [sing.] (*abbr* **FSA**)
in the UK, the public organization that controls companies that provide financial services, for example insurance companies and banks

★ **fi͵nancial 'statement** *noun* [C, usually pl.]
(*Accounting*) a document that a company, etc. must prepare regularly, showing its financial performance during a particular period of time. It usually includes the PROFIT AND LOSS ACCOUNT, the BALANCE SHEET and other information: *The trust is required to publish audited financial statements by April 30.* ◇ *The auditors refused to sign off the financial statements.*
O *to **prepare/publish** financial statements* ◆ *to **file/submit** financial statements* ◆ *to **approve/certify/sign/sign off** financial statements* ◆ *annual/half-year/quarterly/year-end financial statements*

fi͵nancial 'structure = CAPITAL STRUCTURE

fi͵nancial 'supermarket *noun* [C]
(used in newspapers) a bank or company that provides many kinds of financial services, such as loans, insurance policies, investments, etc: *The bank aims to become a financial supermarket, with divisions operating in insurance and share trading.*

fi͵nancial 'year (*BrE*) (*also* ͵fiscal 'year, *AmE, BrE*) *noun* [C] (*abbr* **FY**)
(*Accounting*) a period of twelve months that a company chooses as the time over which it will complete a full set of financial records: *They forecast sales of ¥1.5 billion for the current financial year, ending 30 June.* ◇ *the 2006/2007 financial year* (= for example, that starts on 1 April 2006 and ends on 31 March 2007) ◇ *the first/second half of the financial year* → TAX YEAR

financier /faɪˈnænsiə(r); fə-; *AmE* ˌfɪnənˈsɪr/ *noun* [C]
(*Finance*) a person who is an expert in financial matters and who lends money to businesses or manages large amounts of money for a business: *George Soros, the billionaire financier* ◇ *The financiers will have to struggle to make the firm's books balance.* → CORPORATE FINANCIER at CORPORATE FINANCE See note at FINANCE

★ **financing** /ˈfaɪnænsɪŋ; faɪˈnænsɪŋ; fəˈnænsɪŋ/ *noun* [U]

SEE ALSO: creative financing, debtor-in-possession ~, deficit ~, early-stage ~, first-round ~, self-~, takeout ~

(*Finance*) money that is made available to sb/sth in order to buy sth or run a business or activity; the process of obtaining this money or making it available: *We need to secure additional financing for the project.* ◇ *They will provide $120 million in financing to help the firm reduce its debt.* ◇ *This firm has shown a preference for debt over equity financing* (= it prefers to borrow money rather than sell shares). ◇ *Car manufacturers have been offering cheap financing deals* (= with a low rate of interest) *to attract customers.* See note at FINANCE
O *to **get/raise/secure** financing* ◆ *to **arrange/offer/provide** financing* ◆ ***long-term/short-term** financing* ◆ ***bank/bond/debt/equity** financing* ◆ *a financing **arrangement/deal/facility/package*** ◆ *a financing **plan/strategy*** ◆ *financing **charges/costs***

find /faɪnd/ *verb* (**found, found** /faʊnd/)
1 [+ obj] to have sth available so that you can use it: *How are we going to find €1 million for the new equipment?* ◇ *They have not yet found the financial backing they need.*
2 (*Law*) [+ obj or no obj] to make a particular decision in a court: *The jury found him guilty of*

fraud. ◊ *The court found for* (= supported the claims of) *the plaintiff.* → HOLD *verb* (9)
🔾 *to find against/for/in favour of* sb

finding /'faɪndɪŋ/ *noun*

SEE ALSO: **fault-finding**

1 [C, usually pl.] information that is discovered as the result of research into sth: *What were the main findings from the survey?* ◊ *The committee will issue its initial findings tomorrow.*
🔾 *to issue/present/publish/release/report findings* ◆ *initial/preliminary findings*
2 (*Law*) [C] a decision made by a court, etc. concerning a dispute: *They reached a finding of professional misconduct.*
🔾 *to make/reach a finding* ◆ *to overturn/uphold a finding* ◆ *a finding against/in favour of* sb/sth

fine /faɪn/ *noun, verb*

● *noun* [C]
an amount of money that must be paid as punishment for breaking a law or rule: *a parking fine* ◊ *Offenders will be liable to a heavy fine* (= one that costs a lot of money). ◊ *The firm has been ordered to pay a fine of $7.5 million for misleading customers.*
🔾 *to impose/levy a fine* ◆ *to avoid/be liable to/face/pay a fine* ◆ *a heavy/hefty/large/an unlimited fine*
● *verb* [+ obj]
to make sb pay money as an official punishment: *The five banks were fined $100 000 for fixing prices.* ◊ *He was fined heavily for insider trading.*

the ,**fine 'print** = SMALL PRINT

,**fine-'tune** *verb* [+ obj]
to make very small changes to sth so that it is as good as it can possibly be: *We need to fine-tune the marketing concept.* ▶ ,**fine-'tuning** *noun* [U]: *The system is set up but it needs some fine-tuning.*

finish /'fɪnɪʃ/ *verb, noun*

● *verb* [+ obj or no obj]
to be at a particular price or level at the end of a period of trading on a stock exchange: *The Nikkei stock average finished 2% higher yesterday.* ◊ *China Telecom* (= its share price) *finished the morning session at HK$1.45.* SYN CLOSE
● *noun*
1 [sing.] the end of a period of trading on a stock exchange; the level of share prices, etc. at this time: *At London's finish, the Dow Jones was down 0.8 per cent.* ◊ *The share price rose to $1.94 from a finish of $1.81 yesterday.* SYN CLOSE
2 [C] the final details that are added to sth to make it complete: *The packaging gives the product a stylish finish.*

finished /'fɪnɪʃt/ *adjective* [usually before noun]

SEE ALSO: **semi-finished**

(about a product) that has been put together from different parts or materials and is fully completed: *Manufacturers are trying to lower their stocks of finished goods.* ◊ *transforming raw materials into finished products*

,**finite ca'pacity ,scheduling** *noun* [U]
(*Production*) the process, using computer software, that organizes tasks in a production process so that the best and most efficient way of producing what is needed at the right time is achieved using the available resources

★ **fire** /'faɪə(r)/ *verb* [+ obj]
(*HR*) to force sb to leave their job: *'You're fired!'* ◊ *She got fired from her first job for always being late.* ◊ *Who is responsible for hiring and firing staff?*
SYN SACK See note at DISMISS
PHRV **fire a'way** (*usually used in spoken English, informal*) used to tell sb to begin to speak or ask a question: *'Can I ask you a question?' 'Fire away!'*
,**fire sth 'off 1** to write or say sth to sb very

---

quickly, often when you are angry: *He fired off a letter of complaint.* **2** if you **fire off** an email, you send it ,**fire sth 'up** (*informal*) to start a machine, piece of equipment, computer program, etc: *Let me just fire up my laptop.*

'**fire a,larm** *noun* [C]
a bell or other device that gives people warning of a fire in a building: *to set off the fire alarm*

'**fire cer,tificate** *noun* [C]
a legal document that shows that a building meets the official standards for keeping workers safe in case of fire and gives details of safety measures, ways of escape, etc: *to apply for a fire certificate*

'**fire door** *noun* [C]
a heavy door that is used to prevent a fire from spreading in a building

'**fire drill** (*BrE also* '**fire ,practice**) *noun* [C,U]
a practice of what people must do in order to escape safely from a fire in a building

'**fire es,cape** *noun* [C]
metal stairs, etc. on the outside of a building, which people can use to escape from a fire

'**fire ex,tinguisher** (*also* ex'**tinguisher**) *noun* [C]
a metal container with water or chemicals inside for putting out small fires

firefighting /'faɪəfaɪtɪŋ; *AmE* 'faɪərf-/ *noun* [U]
the activity of dealing with problems in a company or an organization as they happen: *Most of the CEOs were focused on daily firefighting rather than strategy.*

'**fire in,surance** *noun* [U]
insurance that pays for goods, vehicles, etc. that are damaged by fire

'**fire ,marshal** = FIRE SAFETY OFFICER

firepower /'faɪəpaʊə(r); *AmE* 'faɪərp-/ *noun* [U]
the amount of money, power or influence that an organization has available: *The company has enormous financial firepower.* ◊ *The merger will give us more firepower to compete with our bigger rivals.*

'**fire ,practice** = FIRE DRILL

'**fire safety ,officer** (*also* '**fire ,marshal**) *noun* [C]
an employee in an organization who is responsible for equipment, activities, etc. to keep places of work and workers safe in case of fire

'**fire sale** *noun* [C]
1 an occasion when a company sells goods cheaply because they have been damaged in a fire
2 a situation in which a company sells its machinery, parts of its business, etc. cheaply because it needs money quickly: *The store may be forced to conduct a fire sale in order to stay alive.* ◊ *selling key assets at fire-sale prices*

firewall /'faɪəwɔːl; *AmE* 'faɪərw-/ *noun* [C, usually sing.]
1 (*IT*) a part of a computer system that is designed to prevent people from getting at information without authority but still allows them to receive information that is sent to them: *firewall programs/software* ◊ *The program sits behind a firewall, and cannot be accessed by Internet users directly.*
🔾 *to build/install a firewall*
2 (*Stock Exchange*) = CHINESE WALL

'**firing line** *noun*
IDM **be in the** '**firing line** (*BrE*) (*AmE* **be on the** '**firing line**) to be in a position where people can criticize or blame you: *The employment secretary found himself in the firing line over recent job cuts.*
→ idiom at LINE *noun*

★ **firm** /fɜːm; AmE fɜːrm/ noun, adjective, verb
● **noun** [C]

SEE ALSO: **search firm**

---

a business or company, especially one that provides a professional service: *an accounting/engineering/investment firm* ◇ *a law firm* ◇ *She hired a firm of management consultants to study the problems.* ◇ *The firm was founded in 1996.* ◇ *new tax breaks for small firms* See note at BUSINESS
　○ to **create/found/set up/start (up)** a firm ◆ to **manage/run** a firm ◆ to **close (down)/shut (down)** a firm
● **adjective**
1 (not used in the form **firmer, firmest**) that cannot be changed after it has been decided or agreed: *The airline has placed firm orders for 10 new planes.* ◇ *We need a firm date for delivery.*
　○ a firm **bid/date/offer/order** ◆ a firm **agreement/commitment/decision/promise**
2 (**firmer, firmest**) at a good or high price or level; steady: *The pound remained firm **against** (= compared to) the dollar.* ◇ *Shares in oil companies were firmer.* [OPP] SOFT
● **verb** [no obj]
(about shares, prices, etc.) to become steady or rise steadily: *Philips' shares firmed 5.8 per cent to €18.19.* ◇ *The Canadian dollar firmed **against** (= compared to) the US currency today.* ▶ **'firmness** noun [U]: *the recent firmness in share prices*
[PHRV] **firm 'up** to become stronger or more stable: *Prices are firming up.* ◇ *Sales growth needs to firm up before we expand further.* **firm 'up sth** to make sth stronger, more stable or fixed: *The company has not yet firmed up its plans for expansion.* ◇ *The precise details still have to be firmed up.*

firmware /'fɜːmweə(r); AmE 'fɜːrmwer/ noun [U]
(IT) a type of software that is stored in such a way that it cannot be changed or lost: *downloading a firmware upgrade* ◇ *mobile phone/cellphone firmware*

,**first 'class** noun, adverb
● **noun** [U]
1 the best and most expensive seats or accommodation on a train, ship, etc: *You can upgrade to first class for €50.* ◇ *first-class travel* → BUSINESS CLASS
2 in the UK, the class of mail that is delivered most quickly: *First class costs more.* ◇ *A book of first-class stamps, please.*
3 in the US, the class of mail that is used for letters and cards
● **adverb**
1 using the best and most expensive seats or accommodation in a train, ship, etc: *to travel first class*
2 by the quickest form of mail: *Orders within the UK are sent first class.*

,**first 'cost** = PRIME COST

,**first-gene'ration** adjective [only before noun]
used to describe the first type of a machine to be developed: *the first-generation personal computers* → SECOND-GENERATION, THIRD-GENERATION

,**first 'half** noun [C, usually sing.]
1 (Accounting) (also ,**fiscal first 'half**, especially in AmE) the first six months of a company's FINANCIAL YEAR: *The company had a good first half.* ◇ *First-half profits were up 21 per cent compared with the same period last year.*
2 the period of six months between 1 January and 30 June: *Exports to Asia rose steeply in **the first half of** the year.*
→ SECOND HALF

,**first 'in, first 'out** phrase
1 (Production) (abbr **FIFO**) a method of STOCK CONTROL in which the first goods or raw materials bought or produced are the first ones used or sold
2 (Accounting) (abbr **FIFO**) a method of valuing supplies of goods or units of raw materials based on the idea that the first goods bought or produced are the first ones used or sold. The value of goods left at the end of the year is based on the most recent prices.
3 (HR) used, for example in a situation when people are losing their jobs, to say that the first people to be employed will be the first to go
4 (IT) used to describe a system where the data that is received first is the first to be processed
→ LAST IN, FIRST OUT

,**first-line 'manager** noun [C]
(HR) the lowest level of manager in an organization → SUPERVISORY MANAGEMENT

,**first 'mover** noun [C]
(Marketing) a business that is the first to offer a new product or service or to use a new technology: *In new industries, such as the Internet, the first movers have a great advantage over new entrants.* ◇ *We have first-mover **advantage** in this market.*

,**first order of 'business** noun [C]
the most important task that sb must deal with: *His first order of business was making the company solvent.*

,**first re'fusal** = RIGHT OF FIRST REFUSAL

,**first-round 'financing** noun [U]
(Finance) the first investment in a young company that is made by investors who are not closely connected with the company or its managers, to help the company develop manufacturing, marketing and selling → EARLY-STAGE FINANCING

,**first 'section** noun [sing.]
the part of the Tokyo Stock Exchange on which the shares of the largest and most successful companies are traded: *first-section shares/stocks* → BLUE CHIP, SECOND SECTION

,**first 'tier** noun [C]
the first level of sth or the top level of sth: *the first tier of local government* ◇ *first-tier companies/stock* (= the biggest, most important companies)

,**first-tier sup'plier** noun [C]
(Production) a company that is responsible for delivering raw materials or goods directly to the customer's factory → SECOND-TIER SUPPLIER

,**first-'time** adjective [only before noun]
doing or experiencing sth for the first time: *a computer program designed for first-time users* ◇ *First-time buyers are finding it increasingly difficult to get into the housing market.*

★ **fiscal** /'fɪskl/ adjective, noun
● **adjective**
1 (Economics) connected with government or public money, especially taxes: *a package of fiscal reforms* ◇ *The fiscal deficit is running at 7 per cent of GDP.* ◇ *The government must impose fiscal discipline and reduce spending.* → FISCAL POLICY
　○ fiscal **austerity/discipline/prudence/restraint** ◆ fiscal **loosening/tightening** ◆ a fiscal **deficit/surplus**
2 (Finance) (especially AmE) connected with financial matters: *More and more companies are facing a fiscal crisis.*
3 (Accounting) (especially AmE) connected with the period of twelve months over which a government or a company prepares a full set of financial records, or part of this period: *Orders in the company's fiscal third quarter dropped by 12%.*
▶ **fiscally** /'fɪskəli/ adverb (Economics): *The government has become more fiscally responsible.* ◇ *fiscally conservative/prudent*

● **noun** [C] fiscal 2006, 2007, etc. (*AmE*) (*Accounting*) = FISCAL YEAR: *Fiscal 2006 is likely to be our best year ever.*

ˌfiscal ˈdrag *noun* [U]
(*Economics*) a situation in which a government takes an increasing proportion of people's wages in income tax because it does not increase the levels of income at which tax is charged at the same rate as INFLATION → BRACKET CREEP

ˌfiscal first ˈhalf = FIRST HALF (1)

ˌfiscal ˈpolicy *noun* [C,U]
(*Economics*) the way in which a government charges taxes or spends money in order to manage the economy: *Loose fiscal policy* (= low taxes and/or high government spending) *could lead to high inflation.* → MONETARY POLICY
⊙ *loose/tight fiscal policy* ◆ *to loosen/tighten fiscal policy*

ˌfiscal second ˈhalf = SECOND HALF

ˌfiscal ˈyear (*abbr* FY) (*AmE also* fiscal 2006, 2007, etc.) *noun* [C]
1 (*Accounting*) (*especially AmE*) = FINANCIAL YEAR
2 (*Economics*) the period of twelve months over which a government prepares a full set of financial records: *Parliament has approved the budget for the 2006-07 fiscal year.* **NOTE** In the UK, the **fiscal year** runs from 6 April of one year to 5 April of the next. In the US it runs from 1 October to 30 September.

ˈfishbone ˌdiagram (*also* ˌcause and efˈfect ˌdiagram, ˌIshiˈkawa ˌdiagram) *noun* [C]
a diagram that is used to analyse the different causes of a particular effect or problem

fishbone diagram

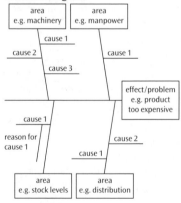

fishery /ˈfɪʃəri/ *noun* (*plural* fisheries)
1 [C] a part of the sea or a river where fish are caught in large quantities: *a herring/tuna fishery* ◇ *The oil spill is threatening one of Spain's richest fisheries.*
2 [C] = FISH FARM
3 [U; pl.] the business or industry of catching fish: *EU fishery ministers* ◇ *the North Atlantic Fisheries College*

ˈfish farm (*also* ˈfishery) *noun* [C]
a place where fish are bred as a business

fit /fɪt/ *verb, noun, adjective*
● *verb* (fitting, fitted, fitted) (*AmE usually* fitting, fit, fit *except in the passive*)
1 [+ obj] (*often* be fitted) to put or fix sth somewhere: *Several expensive features are fitted as standard on these vehicles.*
2 [+ obj or no obj] (*used with an adverb or a preposition*) to put or join sth in the right place: *The*

---

parts must be machined accurately in order to fit together properly.
3 [+ obj or no obj] (*not used in the continuous tenses*) to agree with, match or be suitable for sth: *choosing software that fits your company's needs* ◇ *Expanding into new areas doesn't fit with our plans.* → FIT IN (WITH SB/STH)
4 [+ obj] (*especially BrE*) to make sb/sth suitable for a particular job: *His experience fitted him perfectly for the job.* ◇ *His experience fitted him to do the job.* → idiom at SIZE *noun*
PHR V ˌfit sb/sth ˈin; ˌfit sb/sth ˈin/ˈinto sth to find time to see sb or to do sth: *I'll try and fit you in after lunch.* ˌfit ˈin (with sb/sth) **1** to work in an easy and natural way with sb/sth: *We tried to decide how well each candidate would fit in.* **2** to agree with, match or be suitable for sth: *It was a nice offer but it didn't fit in with our main business.* → FIT *verb* (3) ˌfit sb/sth ˈout/ˈup (with sth) to supply sb/sth with all the equipment, clothes, etc. that they need: *The cost of fitting out the coffee shop was nearly $200 000.*
● *noun* [C, usually sing., U]

SEE ALSO: **strategic fit**

the way in which things or people match each other or are suitable for each other: *We need to work out the best fit between the staff needed and the people available.* ◇ *These brands are an excellent fit with our core business.* ◇ *She is a good fit for the job.* ◇ *She and the company make a good fit.*
IDM by/in ˌfits and ˈstarts frequently starting and stopping again; not continuously: *Economic recovery is proceeding in fits and starts.*
● *adjective* (fitter, fittest)
healthy and strong: *The government aims to make British industry leaner and fitter* (= employing fewer people and with lower costs).

fitness /ˈfɪtnəs/ *noun* [U]
1 the state of being physically healthy and strong: *They operate a chain of fitness clubs.* ◇ *the health and fitness sector/industry* ◇ *We need to ensure the company's financial fitness.*
2 the state of being suitable or good enough for sth: *There were doubts about her fitness for the position.*

fitter /ˈfɪtə(r)/ *noun* [C]
1 a person whose job is to put together or repair equipment: *a pipe/gas fitter*
2 a person whose job is to cut and fit clothes or carpets, etc: *carpet fitters*

ˌfive ˈnines *noun* [U]
(*IT*) 99.999 per cent, which is the percentage of the time that some computer systems are expected to work properly: *Most telephone companies are able to offer the five nines—or 99.999% reliability.* ◇ *a server with five nines availability*

★ fix /fɪks/ *verb, noun*
● *verb*
1 [+ obj] to decide on a date, a time, an amount, etc. for sth: *Has the date of the next meeting been fixed?* ◇ *Interest on the loan is fixed at 4.5% for the first three years* (= will not change during that time). **SYN** SET See note at ARRANGE
2 [+ obj] fix sth (up) to arrange or organize sth: *I'll fix up a meeting with the supplier.* ◇ *How are you fixed* (= do you have any plans) *for Thursday?*
3 [+ obj] to repair or correct sth: *Our engineers are trying to fix the problem.*
4 (*Economics*) [+ obj] fix prices to decide with other businesses that you will sell particular goods or services at the same prices and not compete with each other. This is illegal in many countries: *The companies were fined over $20 million for fixing toy prices.* → PRICE-FIXING

5 (*Finance*) [+ obj *or* no obj] (*usually* **be fixed**) to decide on the official price of sth, especially gold, at a particular time of the day, based on supply and demand: *Gold was fixed at $318.70 an ounce on Wednesday afternoon in London.* → FIXING

• **noun** [C]

1 (*informal*) a solution to a problem, especially an easy or temporary one: *There is no* **quick fix** *for the steel industry.*

2 (*IT*) a small computer program that is used to repair a problem with a larger piece of software: *a bug fix* ◇ *You can download a temporary fix from their website.*

3 (*Finance*) the official price of sth, especially gold, at a particular time of the day, based on supply and demand; the process of deciding this price: *Gold's lowest fix this week was below $354 per ounce.* → FIXING

fixed /fɪkst/ *adjective*
staying the same; not changing or able to be changed: *fixed prices* ◇ *a fixed rate of interest* ◇ *The money has been invested for a fixed period.* ◇ *You can either pay a fixed monthly fee or per minute.*

fixed 'asset = CAPITAL ASSET

fixed 'capital *noun* [U]
(*Accounting*) money that a company has invested in its buildings, machinery, etc. (**capital assets**)

fixed 'cost (*also* **fixed ex'pense**) *noun* [C, usually pl.]
(*Accounting*) an amount of money used to run a business that remains the same whatever quantity of goods is produced: *Rent is a fixed cost.* ◇ *They are used to buying goods from the Far East, where the fixed costs are much lower.* → VARIABLE COST— Picture at COST

fixed 'currency *noun* [C]
(*Economics*) a currency whose value is fixed compared to sth else, especially units of another currency

fixed de'posit *noun* [C,U]
an arrangement where you leave an amount of money in a bank account for a particular period of time or longer in order to get a better rate of interest: *a fixed-deposit account*

fixed ex'pense = FIXED COST

fixed 'income *noun* [C,U]
(*Finance*)
1 money that sb receives from an investment or a pension that does not change or increase: *retired people living on fixed incomes* ◇ *fixed-income investments/securities*
2 investments that offer an income that does not change over a period of time: *They invest about $18 billion in fixed income.* ◇ *fixed-income trading*

fixed-interest se'curity *noun* [C, usually pl.]
(*Finance*) an investment that pays you agreed regular amounts of income that do not change: *Many investors have switched from shares to fixed-interest securities, such as government bonds.*

fixed in'vestment *noun* [U,C]
(*Economics*) money that a business invests in machinery, buildings, vehicles, etc. that will be used over a long period of time (**capital equipment**)

fixed 'line (*also* **'landline**) *noun* [C]
a series of wires carried on poles or under the ground that joins a home, an office, etc. to a telephone network: *Many of their customers have switched from fixed lines to mobile phones.* ◇ *Calls to fixed-line phones are charged at 12¢ a minute.*

fixed 'network *noun* [C]
(*IT*) a series of wires and devices that permanently joins together telephones, computers, etc. that are in different places

fixed 'parity *noun* [C,U]
(*Economics*) a fixed price at which a unit of a currency can be bought; a system in which there is a fixed relationship between the value of two currencies: *The US dollar was convertible to gold at a fixed parity.* ◇ *The currency has fixed parity against the euro.*

fixed 'phone = FIXED TELEPHONE

fixed-'price *adjective* [only before noun]
a **fixed-price** contract, deal, etc. is one in which a particular fee is agreed which does not change even if there is an increase in costs: *Fixed-price contracts can give the manufacturer an unfair share of risks and costs.* → COST-PLUS

'fixed-rate *adjective* [only before noun]
charging or paying a particular fixed rate of interest, etc: *fixed-rate bonds/debt/loans/mortgages* → FLOATING RATE

fixed 'tax (*BrE also* **flat 'tax, pro,portional 'tax**) *noun* [C, usually sing.]
(*Accounting; Economics*) a system in which tax is paid at the same rate, however much you earn or spend: *an annual fixed tax on vehicle ownership* → PROGRESSIVE, REGRESSIVE

fixed 'telephone (*also* **fixed 'phone**) *noun* [C]
a telephone that is permanently attached to a network using wires → MOBILE PHONE

fixed 'term *noun* [C]
(*Commerce*) an agreed or limited period of time: *employees taken on for a fixed term* ◇ *The policy will pay a lump sum at the end of a fixed term.* ◇ *workers employed on* **fixed-term contracts** *for specific assignments*

fixed 'wireless *noun* [U]
(*IT*) a system or device that does not use wires to connect to other telephones, computers, etc. and is situated in one place, such as a home or an office: *Fixed wireless is ideal for people living in remote areas.* ◇ *fixed-wireless broadband* (= that allows a fast connection to the Internet)

fixer /ˈfɪksə(r)/ *noun* [C]
a person who arranges business deals, especially illegal or dishonest ones

fixing /ˈfɪksɪŋ/ *noun* [C]

SEE ALSO: **price-fixing**

(*Finance*) the process of deciding on the official price of sth, especially gold, at a particular time of the day, based on supply and demand: *Gold was $341.50 an ounce at London's afternoon fixing.* → FIX *noun* (3)

flag /flæg/ *verb, noun*
• **verb** (-gg-)
1 [no obj] to become tired, weaker or less enthusiastic: *It's been a long day and I'm starting to flag.* ◇ *Support for the deal is flagging.* ◇ *flagging sales/demand/confidence*
2 [+ obj] to put a special mark next to information, an email, etc. that you think is important: *I've flagged the paragraphs that we need to look at in more detail.*
3 [+ obj] **flag (up) sth** to announce or draw attention to sth: *The group flagged 15% growth in the first half of the year.* ◇ *We have flagged up various problems with the deal.*
• **noun** [C]
a special mark that you put next to information, an email, etc. that you think is important

flag of con'venience *noun* [C]
(*Transport*) a flag of a foreign country that is used by

flagship /ˈflæɡʃɪp/ *noun* [C, usually sing.]
1 the most important product, service, building, etc. that an organization owns or produces: *They are opening a new flagship store in Madrid.* ◇ *The software will continue to be our flagship.*
○ *a flagship* **brand/product/store**
2 the most important company in an industry or economy: *They were once the flagship of the chocolate industry.* ◇ *UBS, Switzerland's banking flagship*
○ *a flagship* **airline/company/fund**

flame /fleɪm/ *noun, verb*
● *noun* [C]
a rude, offensive or unacceptable message sent by email: *flames about inexperienced users posting stupid messages*
● *verb* [+ obj]
to send sb a **flame**; to criticize sb in a **flame**: *They flamed him on chat rooms across the Internet.*

ˈflame mail *noun* [C,U]
rude, offensive or unacceptable messages sent by email; a message of this type: *Some people have been so upset by flame mail that they have left their jobs.*

flash /flæʃ/ *noun*
1 (*Marketing*) [C] a band of colour or writing across a book, pack, etc.
2 (*IT*) Flash™ [U] a program which creates moving images for websites

ˈflash drive (*also* **ˈflash ˌmemory drive**, **ˌflash memory ˈpen drive**) *noun* [C]
(*IT*) a small device that you can connect to a computer and use to store data and move it from one computer to another

flat /flæt/ *adjective* (**flatter**, **flattest**)
1 not very successful because very little is being sold: *The housing market has been flat for months.* ◇ *Profits rose last year, despite flat sales.*
2 (about prices, numbers, etc.) increasing only a small amount; not increasing or falling: *Shares were flat at €53.* ◇ *Staff numbers will remain broadly flat next year.* ◇ *flat profits*
3 (*not used in the forms* **flatter**, **flattest**) (about a payment) fixed; without any extra payments or charges: *She charges a flat fee for her services rather than an hourly rate.*
4 (*HR*) used to describe an organization where there are fewer levels between the top and the bottom: *They plan to introduce a flatter organizational structure, eliminating middle managers and increasing the need for knowledgeable workers.* → HORIZONTAL, TALL

ˌflatbed ˈscanner (*also* **flatbed** /ˈflætbed/) *noun* [C]
(*IT*) a SCANNER (= device for copying pictures and documents so that they can be stored on a computer) on which the picture or document can be laid flat for copying—Picture at OFFICE

ˌflat-ˈpanel = FLAT-SCREEN

ˌflat ˈrate *noun* [C, usually sing.]
a price for sth that is fixed at a particular amount and does not change; an amount paid or charged that is the same for everyone: *Repayments on the loan are made at a flat rate of interest.* ◇ *Employees contribute a flat rate of 5% of income to the fund.* ◇ *a flat-rate tax system* (= in which everyone pays the same percentage of tax)

ˌflat-ˈscreen (*also* **ˌflat-ˈpanel**) *adjective* [only before noun] (*both especially BrE*)
(especially about televisions or computer screens) not curved and usually in a thin case: *A flat-screen monitor would save you a lot of desk space.*—Picture at OFFICE

ˌflat ˈtax = FIXED TAX

flatten /ˈflætn/ *verb* [+ obj *or no obj*]
1 if a price or number **flattens** or sb/sth **flattens** it, it stops increasing or continues to increase at a slower rate: *Sales of its portable computers have flattened.* ◇ *There has been a flattening trend in industrial production.*
2 (*HR*) if sb/sth **flattens** an organization or it **flattens**, the number of levels between the top and the bottom are reduced: *We flattened the organization by removing several layers of management.* ◇ *As a business flattens, it tends to become more productive.*
PHR V **ˌflatten ˈout/ˈoff** to stay at a steady level of development or progress after a period of sharp rises or falls: *Oil prices are now flattening out.* ◇ *There are signs that the economy has hit bottom or flattened out.* SYN LEVEL OFF/OUT

flaw /flɔː/ *noun* [C]
a mistake in sth that means that it is not correct or does not work correctly: *They found a flaw in the software's security system.* ◇ *a fatal* (= extremely serious) *design flaw* ◇ *The business plan has fundamental* (= very serious) *flaws.*
○ **fatal/fundamental/serious** *flaws* ◆ **design/security/ structural** *flaws*

flawed /flɔːd/ *adjective*
having a **flaw**: *We are trying to reduce the number of flawed products that reach customers.* ◇ *We believe that the report is fundamentally flawed.*
○ **deeply/fatally/fundamentally/seriously** *flawed*

ˈflea ˌmarket *noun* [C]
an outdoor market at which goods are sold at cheap prices, especially SECOND-HAND goods (= ones that are old or used)

fledgling (*also spelled* **fledgeling**) /ˈfledʒlɪŋ/ *noun* [C] (*usually used before another noun*)
a person, an organization or a system that is new and without experience: *a fledgling business/ company/start-up* ◇ *protecting fledgling industries*

fleece /fliːs/ *verb* [+ obj] (*informal*)
to take a lot of money from sb by charging them too much: *He claims that banks are fleecing their small business clients.*

fleet /fliːt/ *noun* [C]

SEE ALSO: **rental fleet**

1 a group of planes, vehicles, ships, etc. travelling together or owned by the same organization: *the company's new fleet of vans* ◇ *The airline plans to cut its long-haul fleet by a quarter.*
2 (*used before another noun*) a **fleet** customer, business, etc. is one that uses the same supplier, insurance company, etc. for all its vehicles: *We can offer a range of discounts to fleet customers.*
3 a group of ships fishing together: *a fishing/ whaling fleet*

ˈfleet ˌmanagement *noun* [U]
the activity of looking after, repairing, etc. a **fleet** of vehicles on behalf of a company: *We offer fleet management for companies with both big and small fleets.* ◇ *a fleet management company/service*
▶ **ˈfleet ˌmanager** *noun* [C]

ˈFleet Street *noun* [U]
a street in central London where many national newspapers used to have their offices (now used to mean British newspapers and journalists in general)

flexecutive /flekˈsekjətɪv/ *noun* [C]
a manager whose hours or place of work can change easily because of new technology; a professional worker who has many skills and can

change jobs or tasks easily: *Flexecutives can choose where they live and still remain connected to the business world.* **NOTE** Flexecutive is formed from the words 'flexible' and 'executive'.

★ **flexible** /'fleksəbl/ *adjective*
able to change or be changed to suit new conditions or situations: *Our plans need to be flexible enough to cater for the needs of everyone.* ◇ *a flexible approach to clients' requirements*
OPP INFLEXIBLE → STIFF (3)
▶ **flexibility** /,fleksə'bɪləti/ *noun* [U]: *Computers offer a much greater degree of flexibility in the way work is organized.* ◇ *greater flexibility **on** pay and duties* '**flexibly** *adverb*: *We allow our staff to work flexibly—when they want and where they want.*

,**flexible 'benefits** *noun* [pl.]
(*HR*) benefits, such as health insurance, use of a car, etc. that employees receive in addition to their pay and can choose themselves: *flexible benefits packages* → CAFETERIA PLAN

,**flexible 'hours** (*also* ,**flexible 'working hours**) *noun* [pl.]
(*HR*) a system in which an employee can choose what time he or she will start or finish work each day: *Parents with young children can ask for flexible hours.* → FLEXITIME See note at SALARY

,**flexible 'working** (*also* ,**flexible 'work**) *noun* [U]
(*HR*) a way of organizing work in a company or an organization that is different from the traditional way and may not have fixed times or places of work, for example: *We now offer flexible working. Staff can work part-time or only in the school terms.* ◇ *increased part-time working and the introduction of flexible working practices*

,**flexible 'working hours** = FLEXIBLE HOURS

flexing /'fleksɪŋ/ *noun* [U]
(*HR*) changing the hours that employees work to suit the changing needs of the company: *the flexing of working days/hours* ▶ **flex** /fleks/ *verb* [+ obj]: *Buyers can flex their start time and occasionally work from home.*

flexitime /'fleksitaɪm/ (*especially BrE*) (*AmE usually* **flextime** /'flekstaɪm/) *noun* [U]
(*HR*) a system in which employees work a particular number of hours each week or month but can choose when they start and finish work each day: *She works flexitime.* ◇ *flextime schedules*

flier = FLYER

flight /flaɪt/ *noun*

SEE ALSO: **capital flight, top flight**
---

1 [C] a journey made by air, especially in a plane; a plane making a particular journey: *Did you have a good flight?* ◇ *They operate 78 daily flights between the UK and US.* ◇ *I'd like to catch an earlier flight.*
○ *to **cancel/operate/overbook** a flight* • *a **domestic/ an international**/a **long-haul/short-haul** flight* • *a **charter/scheduled** flight* • ***cheap/low-cost** flights*
2 (*Economics*; *Finance*) [U; sing.] a situation in which people quickly move their money from one country to another or from one type of investment to another in order to avoid risk or to improve profits: *There has been a flight of capital away from the stock market.* ◇ *Investors have made a **flight to quality*** (= they have begun to buy more expensive and safer shares, bonds, etc.).

'**flight at,tendant** *noun* [C]
a person whose job is to take care of passengers on a plane, bring them meals, etc.

'**flight ,capital** *noun* [U]
(*Economics*) money that people move out of a country to avoid taxes or because they believe there is too much financial risk there: *This country is one of the largest sources of flight capital, with an annual flow of $2.8 billion.* → CAPITAL FLIGHT

'**flight crew** *noun* [C with sing./pl. verb]
the people who work on a plane during a flight

flighting /'flaɪtɪŋ/ *noun* [U]
(*Marketing*) a pattern of advertising a product during a period of time in which there is more advertising at some times and less or none at others → PULSING

'**flip chart** *noun* [C]
large sheets of paper fixed at the top to a stand so that they can be turned over, used for presenting information at a talk or meeting—Picture at PRESENTATION

★ **float** /fləʊt; *AmE* floʊt/ *verb, noun*
● *verb*
1 (*Stock Exchange*) [+ obj *or* no obj] to sell a company's shares on a stock exchange for the first time: *The business was floated on the stock market in 1992.* ◇ *We plan to float by the end of June.* ◇ *The shares floated **at** $14.50.* ◇ *The shares were floated at $14.50.*
2 (*Economics*) [+ obj *or* no obj] if a government **floats** its currency or allows it to **float**, it removes controls on the price so that its value is decided by what people are willing to pay for it: *Investors have praised the decision of the central bank to float the currency.* ◇ *The peso is now freely floating alongside the dollar.* ◇ *a floating currency/regime/system* ◇ *the floating of the Thai baht* See note at CURRENCY
3 [+ obj] to suggest an idea or a plan for other people to consider: *The idea of the merger was floated several months ago.*
PHR V ,**float 'off/'out sth** (*Stock Exchange*) (*often* **be floated off/out**) to form a new company from part of a business and sell its shares on a stock exchange: *The joint venture may be floated off as a new company.* **HELP** A pronoun comes between the verb and **off/out**
● *noun*
1 (*Stock Exchange*) [C,U] = FLOTATION
2 (*Economics*) [C, usually sing.] a situation where a government stops controlling the price of its currency and allows it to be bought and sold freely: *The currency fell by 40% against the dollar on the first day of the float.* → FREE-FLOATING
3 [C] (*especially BrE*) an amount of money consisting of coins and notes of low value that is given to sb before they start selling things so that they can give customers CHANGE
4 (*Finance*) [C, usually sing.] the number of a company's shares that are owned by the public and are available to be bought and sold

floatation = FLOTATION

floater /'fləʊtə(r); *AmE* 'floʊ-/ *noun* [C] (*AmE*)
1 (*Finance, informal*) = FLOATING-RATE NOTE
2 (*Insurance*) insurance you can buy that pays for items that are lost, damaged, etc. wherever they are: *You can purchase a floater to cover movable property such as tools and equipment.* ◇ *a personal articles floater*
3 a person who is employed to do a variety of jobs as needed: *I have been working as a floater secretary in different departments of the firm.*

floating /'fləʊtɪŋ; *AmE* 'floʊ-/ *adjective* [usually before noun]

SEE ALSO: **free-floating**
---

not fixed permanently at a particular level or value: *They use a combination of fixed and floating prices.*

,**floating 'charge** *noun* [C]
(*Law*) in the UK and some other countries, an arrangement where all the assets of a business can be claimed or sold if a debt is not paid

floating ex'change rate (*also* '**floating rate**)
noun [C]
(*Economics*) an **exchange rate** for a currency that is not controlled by the government but changes as the demand for the currency changes: *a floating exchange rate system/regime*

floating popu'lation noun [C]
used to describe people who frequently move from one place to another: *a floating population of migrant workers*

'**floating rate** noun [C]
1 (*Finance*) a percentage of interest that you pay or receive that changes because it is linked to the cost of borrowing money in a market: *Most mortgages sold in the UK have floating rates.* ◇ *a floating-rate mortgage/bond/loan*
2 (*Economics*) = FLOATING EXCHANGE RATE

floating-rate 'note (*abbr* FRN) (*also* '**floater,** *informal*) noun [C]
(*Finance*) a type of bond that pays interest at a rate which can vary, for example when the rate at which banks lend money to each other changes: *The company is selling $1.5 billion of two-year floating-rate notes.*

flog /flɒg; *AmE* flɑːg; flɔːg/ verb [+ obj] (-**gg**-) (*informal*)
to sell sth to sb: *The airline plans to flog the tickets over the Internet.*
PHR V **,flog sth 'off** **1** to sell all or part of an industry, a company, etc., often at a low price in order to get rid of it **2** to sell things cheaply because you want to get rid of them or because you need the money

★**flood** /flʌd/ noun, verb
●noun [C]
a very large number or amount of sth that appears at the same time: *a flood of complaints* ◇ *There has been a flood of cheap imports into the market.* ◇ *The trickle of bankruptcies has become a flood.*
●verb
1 [no obj] **flood in/into/out of sth** to arrive or go somewhere in large numbers or amounts: *Investment has flooded into the country.* ◇ *Shoppers are flooding to the High Street stores.* ◇ *Telephone calls came flooding in from customers.*
2 [+ obj] (*usually* **be flooded**) to send sth somewhere in large numbers: *The office was flooded with applications for the job.* ◇ *We've been flooded with complaints.*
3 [+ obj] to become or to make sth become available somewhere in large numbers or amounts: *Cheap imported goods are flooding the market.* ◇ *Investors normally flood the stock market with cash early in the year.*

floor /flɔː(r)/ noun
SEE ALSO: **dealing floor, factory ~, ground ~, shop ~, trading ~**

1 [C, usually sing.] the area in a factory, shop/store, stock exchange, etc. where things are made, displayed or traded: *The new stores will increase our floor space by 45%.* ◇ *trading on the floor of the New York Stock Exchange*
2 [C, usually sing.] a level below which it is difficult for a price, number, etc. to fall; the lowest price, number, etc. that is possible: *The market could lose 500 points before reaching a floor.* ◇ *an attempt to put a floor under falling share prices* ◇ *They set a floor price of $1.7 million for the bidding.* ◇ *Sales are falling through the floor.*
● to **find/hit/reach** a floor **●** to **keep/put** a floor **under** sth **●** to **set** a floor to/for sth
3 the floor [sing.] the group of people who attend a formal talk or discussion: *Are there any questions from the floor?* ◇ *to take the floor* (= to make a statement or ask a question)
IDM **get/be given/have the 'floor** to get/be

given/have the right to speak during a formal discussion → idiom at HOLD verb

'**floor ,broker** noun [C]
(*Stock Exchange*) a person who is employed to buy and sell shares, OPTIONS, etc. on behalf of others on an EXCHANGE

'**floor ,limit** noun [C]
(*Commerce*) the value of goods or services that you can buy with a bank or credit card without the shop/store having to get permission from the bank, etc. to accept the payment: *If the sale exceeds the merchant's floor limit, she must phone the credit-card company for authorization.*

'**floor ,manager** noun [C] (*AmE*)
(*Commerce*) a person who works in a large store and who is in charge of one floor or department

'**floor plan** noun [C]
a drawing of the shape of a room or building, as seen from above, showing the position of the furniture, etc.

'**floor ,trader** noun [C]
(*Stock Exchange*) an individual investor who is allowed to buy and sell shares, OPTIONS, etc. on an EXCHANGE

flop /flɒp; *AmE* flɑːp/ noun, verb
●noun [C]
a plan, project, product, etc. that fails badly: *Their new sports magazine proved a costly flop.*
●verb [no obj] (-**pp**-)
to be a complete failure: *The business flopped and investors lost all their money.*

floppy /'flɒpi; *AmE* 'flɑːpi/ (*plural* **floppies**)
= FLOPPY DISK

,floppy 'disk (*also* **dis'kette,** '**floppy**) noun [C]
(*IT*) a flat disk inside a plastic cover, that is used to store data in the form that a computer can read, and that can be removed from the computer: *to save files on/onto a floppy disk* → HARD DISK

flotation (*also spelled* **floatation**) /fləʊ'teɪʃn; *AmE* floʊ-/ (*also* **float**) (*both especially BrE*) noun [C,U]
(*Stock Exchange*) the act of selling shares in a company on a stock exchange for the first time: *plans for flotation on the stock exchange* ◇ *a stock-market flotation* ◇ *They have announced the partial flotation* (= only a percentage of the total shares are sold) *of their luxury fashion brand.* ◇ *The shares have fallen far below their 160¢ flotation price.*
SYN IPO
● to **announce/consider/plan/seek** a flotation **●** to **abandon/cancel/pull** a flotation **●** to **handle/launch/manage** a flotation **●** a **partial/successful** flotation

flounder /'flaʊndə(r)/ verb [no obj]
(often used in newspapers) to have a lot of problems and to be in danger of failing completely: *The stock market is floundering at all-time lows.* ◇ *The drop in business travel left the airline floundering.*

flourish /'flʌrɪʃ; *AmE* 'flɜːrɪʃ/ verb [no obj]
to develop quickly and be successful or common: *Few businesses are flourishing in the present economic climate.* ◇ *a flourishing black market*
SYN THRIVE

★**flow** /fləʊ; *AmE* floʊ/ noun, verb
●noun [C, usually sing., U]
SEE ALSO: **audience flow, capital ~, cash ~**

the continuous movement of sth from one person, place or thing to another; the thing that moves: *There has been a constant flow of investment into the region.* ◇ *We need to improve the flow of information*

up, down and across our organization. ◇ The strike
has interrupted the flow of goods. ◇ the flow of work
through the factory
➊ a **constant/continuous/free/steady** flow of sth • to
control/improve/increase/manage/speed (up) the
flow • to **disrupt/prevent/reduce/reverse/stop** the
flow
• **verb** [no obj]
1 (usually used with an adverb or a preposition) to
move or pass continuously from one place or
person to another, especially in large numbers or
amounts: More than €60 billion flowed out of these
funds last year. ◇ Capital is flowing back into the
country. ◇ We try to keep information flowing
between the different departments.
➊ to flow **easily/freely/smoothly**
2 to be available easily and in large amounts: Once
demand improves, profits will start to flow.
PHRV '**flow from sth** (formal) to come or result
from sth: These changes flowed from the
reorganization of the company. ,**flow** '**through to
sth** to reach sb/sth or have an effect on them/it: It
will take time for the drop in manufacturing costs to
flow through to consumers.
'**flow chart** (also spelled **flowchart**) (also '**flow
,diagram,** '**flowsheet**) noun [C]
a diagram that shows the connections between the
different stages of a process or parts of a system: a
flow chart showing what happens to the product
between manufacture and final delivery

flow chart

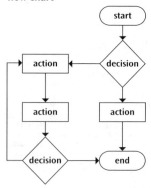

,**flow of** '**funds** noun [C, usually sing.]
(Economics) the way in which money moves from
one country to another or between different parts
of the economy, for example by people giving and
receiving loans: The Federal Reserve's 'flow of funds'
report shows a decrease in the wealth of households.
'**flow pro,duction** (also con,**tinuous
pro'duction**) noun [U]
(Production) a way of manufacturing a product in
large quantities in which each unit moves
continuously through the stages of production one
after the other → BATCH PRODUCTION, JOB
PRODUCTION, MASS PRODUCTION
flowsheet /'fləʊʃiːt; AmE 'floʊ-/ = FLOW CHART
★ **fluctuate** /'flʌktʃueɪt/ verb [no obj]
to change frequently in size, amount, level, etc.,
especially from one extreme to another: The price of
cocoa can fluctuate wildly on world markets. ◇
Workers can move between factories as the workload
fluctuates. ◇ fluctuating prices
➊ to fluctuate **dramatically/widely/wildly**

fluctuation /ˌflʌktʃu'eɪʃn/ noun [C,U]
frequent changes in the size, amount, level, etc. of
sth, especially from one extreme to another: We
saw wild fluctuations **in** sales from week to week.
➊ **day-to-day/monthly/seasonal/short-term/weekly**
fluctuations

flush /flʌʃ/ adjective, verb
• **adjective** [not before noun] (informal)
having a lot of money, usually for a short time:
companies flush **with** cash/funds/money ◇ With the
high cost of borrowing, consumers are no longer
feeling flush.
• **verb**
PHRV ,**flush sb** '**out** to force sb who is planning or
doing sth secretly, especially sth dishonest, to say
what they are planning or who they are: Their offer
is likely to flush out any rival bidders.

flutter /'flʌtə(r)/ noun [C, usually sing.] (BrE)
(informal)
a small amount of money that you risk on a bet, an
investment, etc: to have a flutter **on** the stock
market **SYN** BET, GAMBLE

fly /flaɪ/ verb (**flies, flying, flew** /fluː/ **flown** /fləʊn;
AmE floʊn/)
1 [+ obj] to transport goods or passengers in a
plane: The airline flew nearly a million passengers
last month. ◇ The replacement parts had to be flown
in specially.
2 (AmE) [no obj] to be successful: It remains to be
seen whether his project will fly.
IDM fly '**standby** to travel by plane using a ticket
that cannot be bought in advance and is only
available a very short time before the plane leaves
(a **standby** ticket): One in ten business travellers flies
standby. → idiom at SHELF

flyback /'flaɪbæk/ noun [C] (AmE)
(HR) a very thorough and detailed job interview
that sb, especially a student, has in an employer's
office, generally after a first more general
interview with the employer: Getting a flyback
shows that the firm thinks you are qualified for the
job. ◇ a flyback interview **SYN** CALLBACK (1)

'**fly-by-night** adjective [only before noun]
(about a person or business) dishonest and only
interested in making money quickly: There are
plenty of fly-by-night operators who enter the trade
looking for easy money. ▶ '**fly-by-night** noun [C]

flyer (also spelled **flier**) /'flaɪə(r)/ noun [C]

SEE ALSO: **frequent flyer, high-flyer**

(Marketing) a small sheet of paper that advertises a
product or an event, copies of which are given to a
large number of people: to hand out flyers for a new
club ◇ We put out a flyer promoting our product range.
IDM take a '**flyer (on sb/sth)** (also spelled ~ **flier**)
(especially AmE) (informal) to risk your money,
reputation, etc. on sb/sth that you are not sure of:
Are you ready to throw away your success and take a
flyer on something new?

FMCG /ˌef em siː 'dʒiː/ abbr
(Marketing) **fast-moving consumer goods** goods
that sell quickly because people use them in large
quantities every day, especially food and drinks:
the FMCG sector/industry ◇ Unilever, the FMCG giant

FNMA /ˌef en em 'eɪ/ = FANNIE MAE

FOB /ˌef əʊ 'biː; AmE oʊ/ = FREE ON BOARD

★ **focus** /'fəʊkəs; AmE 'foʊ-/ verb, noun
• **verb** [+ obj or no obj] (**-s-** or **-ss-**)
to give attention, effort, etc. to one particular
subject, situation or person rather than another:
They need to focus more **on** marketing the products.
◇ We are going to focus our resources on our most
promising products.
➊ to focus your **attention/efforts/energy/resources** on
sb/sth

1 [C, usually sing., U] the thing or person that is most important to a business or a group of people; the act of paying special attention to a particular aim or activity: *The focus will remain **on** improving sales.* ◇ *The company is shifting its focus from manufacturing to distribution.* ◇ *We have tried to develop a **customer focus*** (= to concentrate on treating customers well).

⊙ *to **develop/have** a focus* ✦ *to **lack** (a) focus* ✦ *to **change/keep/lose/maintain/shift** your focus*

2 [U] the quality of being able to give all your attention to a particular aim or activity and not spend time and energy on other things

focused (*also spelled* **focussed**) /'fəʊkəst; *AmE* 'foʊ-/ *adjective*

with very clear aims; with your attention directed to what you want to do or to a particular thing: *adopting a more focused approach to marketing* ◇ *The challenge is to keep staff focused and productive.*

→ CUSTOMER-FOCUSED

'focus group *noun* [C]

1 (*Marketing*) a small group of people, specially chosen to represent different social classes, etc., who are asked to discuss and give their opinions about a particular subject. The information obtained is used by people doing MARKET RESEARCH, for example about new products or advertisements: *Feedback from focus groups suggested the advertisement made people feel they could talk to the bank.* ◇ *focus-group research*

⊙ *to **conduct/do/hold/run/use** a focus group*

2 (*HR*) a small group of employees who are asked to discuss and give their opinions about aspects of company policy such as management or changes: *She formed a focus group composed of representatives from every department.*

⊙ *to **conduct/do/hold/run/use** a focus group*

'focus list *noun* [C]

(*Stock Exchange*) a list of companies whose shares are worth buying or selling, according to a particular bank, etc: *a focus list of poor performers*

focussed = FOCUSED

FOK /,ef əʊ 'keɪ; *AmE* oʊ/ = FILL OR KILL ORDER

fold /fəʊld; *AmE* foʊld/ *verb* [+ obj *or* no obj] (about a business) to close because it is not successful: *The company will fold unless it gets more financing.* ◇ *Some of the smaller funds are at risk of folding.*

PHRV ,fold sth 'into sth to make a smaller business, service, etc. part of a larger one; to join different businesses, services, etc. together: *The company is being folded into GM's European operations.*

-fold /fəʊld; *AmE* foʊld/ *combining form* (*used in adjectives and adverbs*)

multiplied by; having the number of parts mentioned: *Interware reported a fourfold increase in pre-tax profits.* ◇ *The company's share price has climbed nearly tenfold in three years.*

★ **folder** /'fəʊldə(r); *AmE* 'foʊld-/ *noun* [C]

SEE ALSO: **square cut folder**

1 a cardboard or plastic cover for holding loose papers, etc: *a folder of invoices*—Picture at FILE

⊙ *to **keep/put** sth **in/take** sth **out of** a folder* ✦ *to **close/open** a folder*

2 (*IT*) (in some computer systems) a way of organizing and storing computer files: *Create a new folder for each project.* ◇ *The program allows you to organize your emails into folders.* ◇ *Click on the files and drag them into the 'set-up' folder.*

⊙ *to **create/delete/name/rename** a folder* ✦ *to **close/open** a folder*

'fold-out (*AmE spelling* **foldout**) *adjective* [only before noun]

used to describe a page in a book, magazine, etc. that is designed to be opened out to make a larger page ▶ **'fold-out** (*AmE spelling* **foldout**) *noun* [C]

follow /'fɒləʊ; *AmE* 'fɑːloʊ/ *verb*

1 [+ obj *or* no obj] to come after sth/sb else in time or order; to happen as a result of sth: *The share price fell dramatically following the company's poor results.* ◇ *Our opening hours are **as follows**...*

2 [+ obj] to accept advice, instructions, etc. and do what you have been told or shown to do: *We are required to follow certain rules on hygiene and safety.*

3 [+ obj *or* no obj] to act or behave in the same way that sb else has just done; to copy sb/sth: *If the insurer cuts its dividend others will surely follow.* ◇ *They **followed the lead** of other carmakers and reduced their product range.*

4 [+ obj] to develop or happen in a particular way: *Inflation is likely to follow a downward trend until next year.*

PHRV ,follow 'through (on/with sth); ,follow sth 'through to finish sth that you have started: *They failed to follow through on their commitments.*

→ FOLLOW-THROUGH ,follow sth 'up; ,follow 'up on sth/sb to find out more about sth/sb that sb has told you about or suggested to you: *Remember to follow up on all sales leads* (= information about possible customers). → FOLLOW-UP ,follow sth 'up with sth to add to sth that you have just done by doing sth else: *You should follow up your phone call with an email or a letter.* → FOLLOW-UP

follower /'fɒləʊə(r); *AmE* 'fɑːloʊ-/ *noun* [C]

1 a company that only produces new products, uses new technologies, etc. once others have tried to do so; a company that enters a market after others: *Their company is a follower rather than an innovator.* ◇ *They entered the electronics industry as a market follower, producing cheap versions of established products.*

2 a person who is very interested in a particular activity and is aware of all the recent news about it: *Followers of the company think that it is heading for good results.*

→ LEADER

,follow-'through *noun* [U]

the actions that sb takes in order to complete a plan: *The project could fail if there is inadequate follow-through.* → FOLLOW STH THROUGH at FOLLOW

'follow-up *noun* [C,U]

an action or a thing that continues sth that has already started or comes after sth similar that was done earlier: *The call will be a follow-up **to** the email sent to customers last week.* ◇ *There had been no follow-up after the initial training.* → FOLLOW STH UP, FOLLOW UP ON STH/SB at FOLLOW

⊙ *a follow-up **call/letter/meeting/report***

food /fuːd/ *noun*

SEE ALSO: **convenience food, fast ~, non-~, spider ~**

1 [U] things that people eat: *the food industry* ◇ *Imports of food products have exceeded exports.*

2 [C,U] a particular type of food **NOTE** This is sometimes used, especially in the plural, in the names of organizations that produce or deal with food: *packaged/frozen/chilled foods* ◇ *The market for fast food has shrunk.* ◇ *Iberia Foods*

→ idiom at DOG

'food ,service *noun* [U, C]

the business of making, transporting and serving food, for example in schools, stores, airports or companies: *food service businesses* ◇ *working in food service management* → CATERING

foodstuff /ˈfuːdstʌf/ *noun* [C, usually pl.]
(*Economics*) any substance that is used as food:
There is no sales tax on basic foodstuffs.

foot /fʊt/ *noun, verb*
● *noun* [C] (*plural* **feet** /fiːt/ *or* **foot**)
a unit for measuring length equal to 12 inches or
30.48 centimetres
IDM **be run/rushed off your ˈfeet** to be
extremely busy; to have too many things to do **get
your ˈfeet wet** (*especially AmE*) (*informal*) to start
doing sth new: *This is a good way of getting your feet
wet in e-commerce.* **get/have a/your ˌfoot in the
ˈdoor** to manage to enter an organization, a field of
business, etc. that could bring you success: *They
wanted to get a foot in the door of the developing
telecoms industry.* **on your ˈfeet** in a normal state
again after a period of trouble or difficulty: *The new
chairman hopes to get the company back on its feet
within six months.*
● *verb*
IDM **foot the ˈbill** (*informal*) to be responsible for
paying the cost of sth: *Manufacturers will have to
foot the bill for recycling their products.*

footer /ˈfʊtə(r)/ *noun* [C]
a line or block of text that is automatically added to
the bottom of every page that is printed from a
computer: *The page number and heading appear in
the footer.* → HEADER

footfall /ˈfʊtfɔːl/ (*especially BrE*) (*AmE usually* **ˈfoot
ˌtraffic**) *noun* [C,U]
(*Marketing*) the number of people that visit a
particular shop/store, shopping centre, etc. over a
period of time: *The centre has an average weekly
footfall of 600 000 visitors.* ◇ *a campaign to increase
footfall*

foothold /ˈfʊthəʊld; *AmE* -hoʊld/ *noun* [C,
usually sing.]
a strong position in a business, profession, etc. from
which sb can make progress and achieve success:
*The deal will give us a foothold in the competitive
Australian market.* → BEACHHEAD
○ *to* **establish/gain/have/obtain/secure** *a foothold* ◆
sth **gives** *you a foothold*

footing /ˈfʊtɪŋ/ *noun*
1 [sing; U] the state of being strong and steady: *The
economy has struggled to regain its footing.* ◇ *The
loan has put the company back on a sound financial
footing.*
○ *to* **find/gain/lose/regain** *your footing* ◆ *to* **be on/put
sb/sth on** *a ... footing* ◆ *a* **firm/good/solid/
stable/strong** *footing*
2 [sing.] the position or status of sb/sth in relation
to others; the relationship between two or more
people or groups: *We are competing on an equal
footing with foreign firms.* ◇ *The new law puts
temporary staff on the same footing as long-term
employees.*
○ *to* **be on** *a ... footing* ◆ *a* **competitive/an equal/the
same** *footing*

footprint /ˈfʊtprɪnt/ *noun* [C]
1 the amount of space on a desk that a computer
or other piece of equipment fills: *This model has a
smaller footprint than anything else on the market.*
2 (*IT*) the area on the earth in which a signal from a
communications SATELLITE can be received

Footsie /ˈfʊtsi/ = FTSE 100 INDEX

ˈfoot ˌtraffic *noun* [U]
1 (*Marketing*) (*especially AmE*) = FOOTFALL
2 the movement of people from one place to
another

footwear /ˈfʊtweə(r); *AmE* -wer/ *noun* [U]
(used especially in shops/stores) things that people
wear on their feet, especially shoes or boots: *Sales*

of clothing and footwear climbed by 11%. ◇ *the
footwear market/industry*

foray /ˈfɒreɪ; *AmE* ˈfɔː-; ˈfɑː-/ *noun* [C]
(often used in newspapers) an attempt to become
involved in a different business activity or market:
The bank has made its first foray into Brazil. ◇ *the
company's disastrous foray into telecommunications*
○ *to* **end/launch/make** *a foray (into sth)*

force /fɔːs; *AmE* fɔːrs/ *noun, verb*
● *noun*

SEE ALSO: **driving force, labour ~, sales ~, task ~**

1 [C] a person or thing that has a lot of power or
influence: *The company has become a major force in
the cellphone industry.* ◇ *He is seen as a powerful
force for change.* → MARKET FORCES
○ *a* **dominant/driving/major/powerful** *force* ◆
competitive/economic *forces*
2 [U] the authority of sth: *These guidelines do not
have the force of law.*
3 (*HR*) [C with sing./pl. verb] a group of people who
have been organized for a particular purpose
→ WORKFORCE
IDM **come/enter into ˈforce** (about a law, rule,
etc.) to start being used: *New accounting rules come
into force next year.* **in ˈforce** (about a law, rule,
etc.) being used or applied: *the environmental
standards in force in Europe* **join/combine ˈforces
(with sb)** to work together in order to achieve a
shared aim: *They hoped to join forces with Fiat to
develop new vehicles.* → idiom at BRING
● *verb* [+ obj]
1 (*often* **be forced**) to make sb/sth do sth that they
do not want to do: *The president was forced into
resigning.* ◇ *She was forced out of her job.* ◇ *The
economic downturn has forced us to cut jobs.* ◇ *to be
forced into bankruptcy*
2 (*often used with an adverb or a preposition*) to make
sth happen, especially sth bad or sth other people
do not want: *They have collected enough signatures
to force a vote.* ◇ *Fierce competition has forced down
the cost of telephone services.*

forced /fɔːst; *AmE* fɔːrst/ *adjective*
used to describe sth that happens or is done when
sb does not want it: *a forced sale of his property* ◇
*the forced departure/resignation of the chief
executive* → COMPULSORY

ˌforced liquiˈdation = COMPULSORY
LIQUIDATION

ˌforced ˈselling *noun* [U]
(*Finance*) a situation in which an investment fund
must sell particular shares, bonds, etc. in order to
follow its own rules, for example, rules about the
quality of investments it can keep ▶ **ˌforced ˈseller**
noun [C]

ˌforce field aˈnalysis *noun* [C,U]
(*HR*) a way of making change more acceptable in an
organization by analysing the positive and negative
aspects and working to increase the positive and
decrease the negative

force majeure /ˌfɔːs mæˈʒɜː(r); *AmE* ˌfɔːrs/
noun [U]
(*Law*) unexpected circumstances, such as war, that
can be used as an excuse when they prevent sb
from doing sth that is written in a contract: *a force
majeure clause* (= in a written contract) **NOTE** Force
majeure is a French phrase.
○ *to* **accept/challenge/declare** *force majeure*

★ **forecast** /ˈfɔːkɑːst; *AmE* ˈfɔːrkæst/ *noun, verb*
● *noun* [C]

SEE ALSO: **cash-flow forecast**

a statement about what will happen in the future,
based on information that is available now: *It is
difficult to give an accurate forecast of sales.* ◇ *We
have raised our forecast for growth by 2 per cent.* ◇

Profits are in line with our previous forecast of €6.4 billion.

○ *an economic/a financial forecast ◆ an earnings/ inflation/a growth/profit/sales forecast ◆ to give/ make/provide a forecast ◆ to change/revise a forecast ◆ to increase/raise a forecast ◆ to downgrade/lower/reduce a forecast ◆ to beat/ exceed/meet/miss a forecast*

● *verb* [+ obj] (**forecast, forecast** *or* **forecasted, forecasted**)
to say what you think will happen in the future based on information that you have now: *Experts are forecasting a recovery in the economy. ◇ Rice exports are forecast to fall sharply. ◇ Sales were lower than forecast.* [SYN] PREDICT ▶ **'forecasting** *noun* [U]: *forecasting models/techniques*

forecaster /'fɔːkɑːstə(r); AmE 'fɔːrkæstər/ *noun* [C]
a person or an organization that studies an economy, industry, etc. and says what they think will happen to it in the future: *Most independent forecasters expect the economy to grow by under 1.5 per cent this year. ◇ an economic/a financial forecaster*

foreclose /fɔː'kləʊz; AmE fɔːr'kloʊz/ *verb*
1 (*Finance*) [+ obj *or no obj*] (especially about a bank) to take control of sb's property because they have not paid back money that they have borrowed: *to foreclose on a mortgage/property ◇ The bank has threatened to foreclose on the company.*
2 (*formal*) [+ obj] to reject sth as a possibility: *We cannot foreclose any of the options at this stage.* [SYN] EXCLUDE

foreclosure /fɔː'kləʊʒə(r); AmE fɔːr'kloʊ-/ *noun* [U,C]
(*Finance*) the act of FORECLOSING on money that has been borrowed or the right to do this; an example of this: *Mortgage foreclosures reached their highest level in April. ◇ The bank applied to the court for an order for foreclosure.*

forefront /'fɔːfrʌnt; AmE 'fɔːrf-/ *noun* [sing.]
at/in/to the 'forefront (of sth) in or into an important or leading position in a particular group or activity: *The group was then at the forefront of new drug development.*

★**foreign** /'fɒrən; AmE 'fɔːrən; 'fɑːrən/ *adjective*
1 in or from a country that is not your own: *earning foreign currency from exporting goods ◇ Developing countries need to attract foreign capital/ investment. ◇ a foreign-owned company*
→ OFFSHORE
2 [only before noun] dealing with or involving other countries: *foreign affairs/policy/trade*

,foreign 'bond *noun* [C]
(*Finance*) a bond that investors in a particular country can buy in their own currency but which is issued by a foreign company: *Canadians invested $2.5 billion in foreign bonds during the quarter.*
→ EUROBOND

> **MORE ABOUT**
>
> ### Foreign bonds
>
> There are different names for **foreign bonds** that are sold in particular countries. For example, a foreign bond that is sold in the US can be called a **Yankee bond**, one sold in Japan a **Samurai bond** and one sold in the UK a **Bulldog bond**.

,foreign 'currency ac,count = CURRENCY ACCOUNT

,foreign 'currency ex,posure = CURRENCY EXPOSURE

,foreign 'currency re,serves (*also* **'currency re,serves**) *noun* [pl.]
(*Economics*) supplies of foreign money, and assets such as gold that can easily be exchanged for money, that a government keeps to buy its own currency when it needs to protect its value compared to other currencies [SYN] FOREIGN EXCHANGE RESERVES

,foreign 'currency risk = CURRENCY RISK

,foreign 'debt *noun* [C,U]
(*Economics; Finance*) money that the government and organizations in a particular country owe to lenders in other countries: *The country owes more than $100 billion in foreign debt. ◇ foreign debt payments/repayments* [SYN] EXTERNAL DEBT

'foreign di'rect in'vestment (*abbr* **FDI**) (*also* **di,rect in'vestment**) *noun* [U; C, usually sing.]
(*Economics*) money that people or companies of one country invest in another by buying property, building factories, buying businesses, etc: *The continued flow of foreign direct investment is critical for developing countries.*

★**,foreign ex'change** *noun*
(*Economics; Finance*)
1 [U] (*abbr* **forex**) the system of exchanging the money of one country for that of another: *Controls on foreign exchange limit the amount of money you can take out of the country. ◇ a country's foreign exchange policy*
2 [U] money that is obtained using this system: *Tourism is our largest source of foreign exchange. ◇ a foreign exchange trader/dealer ◇ Oil exports account for 70% of the country's foreign exchange earnings.*
→ FOREX
3 [C] a place where money of different countries is exchanged: *The pound fell on the foreign exchanges yesterday.*

,foreign ex'change ,market (*also* **ex'change ,market**, *less frequent*) *noun* [C]
(*Finance*) the system in which organizations, governments and investors buy and sell currencies; anywhere that this happens: *The foreign exchange market is the largest financial market in the world with a daily turnover of over $1.3 trillion. ◇ By midday the dollar was trading at 121.92 yen on the Tokyo foreign exchange market.* [SYN] CURRENCY MARKET → FOREX

,foreign ex'change re,serves (*also* **,foreign re'serves**, **,international re'serves**) *noun* [pl.]
(*Economics*) supplies of foreign money and assets such as gold that can easily be exchanged for money, which a government keeps to buy its own currency when it needs to protect its value compared to other currencies: *The central bank holds most of its foreign exchange reserves in US dollars and Treasury bills.* [SYN] FOREIGN CURRENCY RESERVES

,foreign 'trade zone *noun* [C] (*abbr* **FTZ**) (*AmE*)
(*Trade*) an area in the US where you can receive, work with and store imported goods without paying taxes on them → FREE ZONE

foreman /'fɔːmən; AmE 'fɔːrmən/, **forewoman** /'fɔːwʊmən; AmE 'fɔːrw-/ *noun* [C] (*plural* **foremen** /-mən/ **forewomen** /-wɪmɪn/)
1 a worker who is in charge of a group of other factory or building workers: *a foreman on a building site ◇ a factory/drilling foreman*
2 a person who acts as the leader of a JURY in a court

fo,rensic ac'counting /fə'rensɪk; -'renzɪk/ *noun* [U]
(*Accounting*) the activity of investigating financial records in order to find evidence of illegal

payments, stolen money, etc: *auditors trained in forensic accounting* ▶ **forensic ac'countant** *noun* [C]

forestry /'fɒrɪstri; AmE 'fɔːr-; 'fɑːr-/ *noun* [U]
the science or industry of planting and taking care of trees and forests: *a forestry company* ◇ *forestry products such as timber and paper*

forex (*also spelled* **Forex**) /'fɒreks; AmE 'fɔːr-; 'fɑːr-/ (*also* **FX**) *abbr*
(*Finance*) a short way of saying or writing **foreign exchange**: *trading in the forex market* ◇ *forex trading* ◇ *a forex dealer/trader*

forfeit /'fɔːfɪt; AmE 'fɔːrfət/ *verb* [+ obj]
1 to lose sth or have sth taken away from you because you have done sth wrong: *If you cancel your flight, you will forfeit your deposit.*
2 to agree not to receive sth that you have a right to: *She forfeited her salary for an extended period of leave.*

forfeiture /'fɔːfɪtʃə(r); AmE 'fɔːrfətʃər/ *noun* [U,C]
an act of FORFEITING sth: *the forfeiture of property*

forge /fɔːdʒ; AmE fɔːrdʒ/ *verb* [+ obj]
1 to put a lot of effort into making sth successful or strong so that it will last: *We have tried to forge closer links with our suppliers.*
○ *to forge* **links/ties** (*with sb*) • *to forge an* **alliance**/*a* **partnership/relationship** • *to forge a* **deal/merger**
2 to make an illegal copy of sth in order to deceive people: *They had been passing forged notes.* ◇ *a forged signature* → COUNTERFEIT
○ *to forge a* **banknote/document/passport/signature**
PHRV **forge a'head** (about a price, number, etc.) to increase, especially by a large amount within a short period of time: *Sales have forged ahead (by) 7%.* **forge a'head (with sth)** to move forward quickly; to make a lot of progress quickly: *They are forging ahead with their merger plans.* **forge 'higher** if the value of a share, a currency, etc. **forges higher**, it rises by a large amount within a short period of time: *The dollar forged higher against (= compared to) the euro yesterday.*

forgery /'fɔːdʒəri; AmE 'fɔːrdʒ-/ *noun* (*plural* **forgeries**)
1 [U] the crime of copying money, documents, etc. in order to deceive people
2 [C] something, for example a document, piece of paper money, etc., that has been copied in order to deceive people: *The signature was a forgery.*

forgive /fə'gɪv; AmE fər'gɪv/ *verb* [+ obj] (**forgave** /fə'geɪv; AmE fər'g-/ **forgiven** /fə'gɪvn; AmE fər'g-/) (*formal*)
(about a bank, company, etc.) to say that sb does not need to pay back money that they have borrowed: *The company has forgiven a $15 million loan to its former chairman.* ◇ *forgiving developing countries' debt* ▶ **forgiveness** /fə'gɪvnəs; AmE fər'g-/ *noun* [U]: *debt forgiveness*

fork /fɔːk; AmE fɔːrk/ *verb*
PHRV **fork 'out (for sth)**; **fork 'out sth (for/on sth)** (*AmE also* **fork 'over sth (for sth)**) (*informal*) to spend a lot of money on sth, especially unwillingly: *We doubt whether consumers will fork out for such an expensive service.* ◇ *They forked over $60 000 for legal fees.* **SYN** SHELL OUT

forklift /'fɔːklɪft; AmE 'fɔːrk-/ (*also* **forklift 'truck**) *noun* [C]
a vehicle with special equipment on the front for moving and lifting heavy objects—Picture at TRANSPORT

★ **form** /fɔːm; AmE fɔːrm/ *noun, verb*
● *noun* [C]
SEE ALSO: **application form**, **claim ~**, **I-9 ~**, **order ~**, **substance over ~**, **tax ~**
an official paper or electronic document containing questions and spaces for answers or information: *Use form 8E if you are renewing your passport.* ◇ *You can submit your form by email.* → idiom at DUE
○ *to* **complete/fill in/fill out/sign** *a form* • *to* **file/return/submit** *a form* • *a* **booking/an entry/a registration/reservation** *form*
● *verb* [+ obj or no obj]
to start a group of people, such as an organization, a committee, etc.; to come together in a group of this kind: *The group was formed from the merger of two engineering firms.* ◇ *They have formed an alliance with a British bank.* ◇ *a newly formed company* ◇ *The partnership formed in 1996.* See note at FOUND

★ **formal** /'fɔːml; AmE 'fɔːrml/ *adjective*
1 (about a style of dress, speech, writing, behaviour, etc.) very correct and suitable for official or important occasions: *Legal firms may have a policy of formal dress.* ◇ *You should use a formal style of writing in the report.*
2 official; following an agreed or official way of doing things: *formal legal processes* ◇ *A formal announcement of the appointment is expected today.* ◇ *No formal agreement has yet been reached.*
3 (*Economics*) [only before noun] used to describe the part of an economy that involves businesses which are officially established or recognized and employment in these businesses: *Only 15% of the labour force are employed in the formal sector.* → SHADOW ECONOMY
▶ **formally** /'fɔːməli; AmE 'fɔːrm-/ *adverb*: *Dress formally for your interview.* ◇ *The accounts were formally approved by the board.*

formality /fɔː'mæləti; AmE fɔːr'm-/ *noun* (*plural* **formalities**)
1 [C, usually pl.] a thing that you must do as a formal or an official part of a legal process, a social situation, etc: *It takes a month to complete the legal formalities of the sale.* ◇ *Let's skip the formalities and get down to business.* ◇ *lengthy customs formalities*
○ *to* **complete/deal with/follow/go through** (*the*) *formalities* • *to* **dispense with/skip** (*the*) *formalities*
2 [C, usually sing.] a thing that you must do as part of an official process, but which has little meaning and will not affect what happens: *He already knows he has the job so the interview is a mere formality.*
3 [U] correct and formal behaviour

formalize, **-ise** /'fɔːməlaɪz; AmE 'fɔːrm-/ *verb* [+ obj]
1 to give sth a fixed structure or form by introducing rules: *Entry to jobs at all levels has become more formalized.*
2 to make an arrangement, a plan, etc. legal or official: *They have now formalized the investigation.*
▶ **formalization**, **-isation** /ˌfɔːməlaɪ'zeɪʃn; AmE ˌfɔːrmələ'z-/ *noun* [U]

format /'fɔːmæt; AmE 'fɔːrmæt/ *noun, verb*
● *noun* [C]
1 the arrangement, plan, design, etc. that is chosen for sth: *About half the stores are being converted into a convenience store format.* ◇ *The document uses a question-and-answer format.*
2 the way in which information is stored on a computer, disk, tape, etc: *The images are stored in a digital format.* ◇ *the increasing popularity of the DVD format* ◇ *Convert the document into HTML format.*
3 (*Marketing*) the shape and size of a book, magazine, etc: *The magazine is being relaunched in a new format.* ◇ *advertising on large-format billboards*

●*verb* [+ obj] (-tt-)
1 to arrange text or numbers in a particular way on a page or a screen: *Format the document in two columns.* ◇ *The data is automatically formatted into the report.*
2 (*IT*) to prepare a computer disk so that data can be recorded on it SYN INITIALIZE

formation /fɔːˈmeɪʃn; *AmE* fɔːrˈm-/ *noun* [U,C]

SEE ALSO: **capital formation**

the action of establishing or developing sth; sth that is established or developed: *She has been in charge of the firm since its formation in 1998.* ◇ *the formation of corporate strategy* ◇ *The country has a high rate of new business formation(s).*

formatting /ˈfɔːmætɪŋ; *AmE* ˈfɔːrm-/ *noun* [U,C]
the way in which you arrange text and numbers on the screen in an electronic document, a SPREADSHEET, etc: *You will lose some of the formatting when viewing the document in another program.* ◇ *paragraph formatting*

former /ˈfɔːmə(r); *AmE* ˈfɔːrm-/ *adjective* [only before noun]
1 that used to have a particular position or status in the past: *my former boss/colleague*
2 that used to exist in earlier times: *the former Soviet republics*

'form ,letter *noun* [C]
a letter with standard content that can be sent to a large number of people, especially one produced in large numbers using a computer program → PRO FORMA

formula /ˈfɔːmjələ; *AmE* ˈfɔːrm-/ *noun* [C] (*plural* **formulas** *or, especially in scientific use,* **formulae** /ˈfɔːmjəliː; *AmE* ˈfɔːrm-/)

SEE ALSO: **golden formula**

1 (*Technical*) a series of letters, numbers or symbols that represent a rule or law: *They use complex mathematical formulas to calculate the insurance premium.*
2 a particular method of doing or achieving sth: *There's no simple formula for the success of a business.*

'formula in,vesting *noun* [U]
(*Finance*) a way of investing money by following a particular set of rules

★**formulate** /ˈfɔːmjuleɪt; *AmE* ˈfɔːrm-/ *verb* [+ obj]
to create or prepare sth carefully, giving particular attention to the details: *to formulate a plan/policy/strategy* ◇ *The patent covers the way in which the drug is formulated.* ▶ **formulation** /ˌfɔːmjuˈleɪʃn; *AmE* ˌfɔːrm-/ *noun* [U,C]: *the formulation of new policies* ◇ *new formulations of existing drugs*

,for-'profit *adjective* [only before noun]
used to describe a company or an organization that is run with the aim of making a profit: *They operate a for-profit hospital chain.* → NON-PROFIT

fortune /ˈfɔːtʃuːn; *AmE* ˈfɔːrtʃ-/ *noun*
1 [C] a large amount of money: *She made a fortune in real estate.* ◇ *He built his fortune selling computers in Latin America.*
O *to amass/build (up)/make a fortune* ◆ *to lose/pay/spend a fortune* ◆ *a considerable/large/substantial fortune* ◆ *a family/personal fortune*
2 [C, usually pl.] the good and bad things that happen to a person, business, country, etc: *The company's financial fortunes are closely linked to those of Mexico.* ◇ *the changing fortunes of the film industry* ◇ *a plan to restore the group's fortunes*
O *changing/declining/flagging/mixed fortunes* ◆ *to restore/reverse/revive sb's/sth's fortunes*
→ idiom at COST *verb*

Fortune '500 /ˌfaɪv ˈhʌndrəd/ *noun* [sing.]
a list that is published every year of the 500 US companies that have the largest income: *The company ranks 33rd on/in the Fortune 500.* ◇ *a Fortune 500 company*

★**forum** /ˈfɔːrəm/ *noun* [C]
a place where people can exchange opinions and ideas on a particular issue; a meeting organized for this purpose: *an electronic discussion forum* ◇ *Our weekly meetings provide a forum for debating important issues.*

★**forward** /ˈfɔːwəd; *AmE* ˈfɔːrwərd/ *adverb, adjective, verb*
●*adverb*

SEE ALSO: **brought forward, carriage ~, carried ~**

1 towards a good result: *She felt she needed to move forward in her career.* ◇ *technologies that will drive the industry forward* ◇ *The project will go forward (= continue) as planned.*
2 in or concerning the future: *Looking forward, we expect sales to increase significantly.*
3 (*Commerce*; *Finance*) if sth is sold or bought forward, the seller agrees to provide it for a fixed price at a particular time in the future, when they have produced or obtained it: *Growers can currently sell forward cotton to be picked in 2006 for about A$540 a bale.*
IDM **going 'forward** in the future: *The competition will be less intense going forward.* ◇ *Going forward, we expect to see increased profit growth.*
●*adjective*
1 relating to the future: *A little forward planning could have saved us a lot of expense.* ◇ *forward economic growth*
2 (*Commerce*) relating to sth that will be provided or delivered in the future: *We hold stocks equivalent to 90 days of forward demand.* ◇ *the forward market for crude oil* → FORWARD CONTRACT, FORWARD SALE
●*verb* [+ obj]

SEE ALSO: **fast-forward, store-and-forward**

1 to send or pass goods, information, an email, etc. to sb: *We will be forwarding our new catalogue to you next week.* ◇ *The message is automatically forwarded to your email account.* SYN SEND STH ON → CALL FORWARDING
2 to send a letter, etc. received at the address a person used to live or work at to their new address: *Could you forward any mail to us in Shanghai?* SYN SEND STH ON NOTE The words 'Please forward' or 'to be forwarded' are usually written on the envelope.

'forward ,contract *noun* [C]
(*Finance*) an agreement to supply sth for a fixed price at a particular time in the future, when it has been produced or obtained, especially an amount of a COMMODITY (= an agricultural product, oil, a metal, etc.) or a currency: *a forward contract to supply oil and gas* ◇ *Forward contracts can provide a hedge (= protection) against future changes in the exchange rate.* → FUTURE

,forward 'cover *noun* [U,C]
(*Finance*) a right to buy or sell an amount of currency for a fixed price at a particular time in the future. Businesses buy **forward cover** to protect against changes in the value of currencies they will need in the future: *We obtain forward cover on all export orders.*

forwarder /ˈfɔːwədə(r); *AmE* ˈfɔːrwərdər/
= FREIGHT FORWARDER

,forward ex'change rate *noun* [C]
(*Finance*) the price agreed for buying an amount of currency at a particular time in the future

forwarding /ˈfɔːwədɪŋ; AmE ˈfɔːrwərd-/ noun [U]

SEE ALSO: **call forwarding**

(*Trade; Transport*) the process of arranging for goods to be transported and/or exported on behalf of others: *forwarding instructions*

forwarding ad,dress noun [C]
a new address to which letters should be sent from an old address that sb has moved away from: *She left no forwarding address.*

forwarding ,agent noun [C]
(*Trade; Transport*) a company that is paid to arrange for goods to be transported and often exported on behalf of others: *Your order will be delivered by our US forwarding agent.* **SYN** FREIGHT FORWARDER

,forward inte'gration noun [U]
(*Economics*) a situation where a company buys a business that it normally supplies goods or services to, or starts doing the same work as that business: *Forward integration into retailing should bring us a competitive advantage.* ◇ *an aggressive forward-integration strategy* → BACKWARD INTEGRATION —Picture at INTEGRATION

'forward-,looking adjective
planning for the future; willing to consider modern ideas and methods: *a forward-looking company* ◇ *We need someone dynamic and forward-looking to grow the company.*

'forward price noun [C]
(*Finance*) the price agreed for goods, currencies, etc. which will be delivered at a particular time in the future → SPOT PRICE

'forward sale noun [C]
(*Finance*) a type of sale where sb agrees to supply sth for a fixed price at a particular time in the future, when they have produced or received it: *Mining companies have reduced their forward sales of gold.* ◇ *matching forward sales with future production*

'forward ,selling noun [U]
(*Finance*) the practice of agreeing to supply sth for a fixed price at a particular time in the future, when it has been produced or obtained: *the forward selling of yet-to-be-mined gold*

'forward slash noun [C]
the symbol (/) used in computer commands and in Internet addresses to separate the different parts → BACKSLASH

★**found** /faʊnd/ verb [+ obj]
to start sth, such as an organization or an institution, especially by providing money: *Fiat was founded in 1899 by the Agnelli family.* ◇ *She was one of the founding members of the firm.*

VOCABULARY BUILDING

Starting a business

- *The company has a long history, being **founded** in 1904.*
- *The group was **created** in 2001 through a merger of three banks.*
- *They are **forming** a joint venture with a Canadian manufacturer.*
- *She **set herself up** as a management consultant.*
- *We **set up** a company to market the products.*
- *He had always wanted to **start up** his own business.*

★**foundation** /faʊnˈdeɪʃn/ noun
1 [C] an organization that is established to provide money for a particular purpose, for example

charity, or that does research on a particular subject: *a report published by the Foundation for International Business and Economic Research*
2 [U] the act of starting a new institution or organization: *The organization has grown enormously since its foundation in 2002.*

★**founder** /ˈfaʊndə(r)/ noun, verb
● *noun*
a person who starts an organization, a company, etc: *He is the group's founder and chief executive.* ◇ *a founder shareholder* (= who invests money in shares to help start a company)
● *verb* [no obj]
(about a plan, business, etc.) to fail because of a particular problem or difficulty: *The project foundered after problems with funding.* ◇ *Negotiations foundered on the issue of pay.*

,founder 'member (*BrE*) (*AmE* ,charter 'member) noun [C]
one of the first members of a society, an organization, etc., especially one who helped start it

foundry /ˈfaʊndri/ noun [C] (*plural* **foundries**)
1 a factory where metal or glass is melted and made into different shapes or objects: *an iron foundry*
2 a factory where MICROCHIPS are made: *a chip/silicon foundry*

,four-colour 'process (*AmE spelling* ~ color ~) noun [C]
a system used in printing in which the colours blue, red, yellow and black are combined to create a wide range of colours

'four-pack noun [C]
a set of four things wrapped and sold together

fraction /ˈfrækʃn/ noun [C]
a small part or amount of sth: *These investments are now worth only a fraction of their original value.* → SAMPLING FRACTION

fractional /ˈfrækʃənl/ adjective
1 (*formal*) very small; not important: *a fractional decline in earnings*
2 [only before noun] forming or connected with a part of sth larger: *They sold most of the business but kept the fractional part that was profitable.*
▶ **fractionally** /ˈfrækʃənəli/ adverb: *Passenger numbers were fractionally higher in February.*

,fractional 'ownership noun [U]
(*Finance; Law*) a situation where different people or companies buy and share an asset; the right that they each have to use, keep, etc. the asset: *Many aircraft manufacturers now offer fractional ownership programs.* ◇ *selling fractional ownership in a property* ▶ **,fractional 'owner** noun [C]

'framework a,greement noun [C]
a formal arrangement between two or more groups, companies, countries, etc. to behave in a particular way or do particular things. It also suggests future actions or discussions: *a framework agreement on the voluntary reduction of greenhouse gas emissions*

★**franchise** /ˈfræntʃaɪz/ noun, verb
● *noun*

SEE ALSO: **area franchise, master franchise**

1 (*Commerce*) [C,U] a right that sb buys from a company that allows them to do particular business activities, such as selling the company's goods and services in a particular area; formal permission given by a government to sb that wants to operate a public service as a business: *They won the franchise to operate outlets in the UK.* ◇ *to operate a business **under franchise*** ◇ *In the reorganization, Southern Television lost their franchise.*

❶ to **buy/have/hold/lose/own/win** *a franchise* ✦ to **award/give sb/grant sb/sell** *a franchise* ✦ *a* **catering/fast food/rail/television** *franchise* ✦ *a franchise* **business/company/operation** ✦ *a franchise* **agreement/holder/owner**
2 (*Commerce*) [C] a business or service run under **franchise**: *The restaurant chain has 257 franchises across Europe.* ◇ *a burger franchise*
3 (*Marketing*) [C] the group of people within a population that buy a particular product or service: *The young-male franchise generally consider it to be their brand.* ◇ *We needed to widen the brand's franchise.*
4 (*Marketing*) [C] the right to sell a particular film/movie, television show, computer program, etc. and use the name to market other products; the group of products that have the name: *They own the Tomb Raider franchise.* ◇ *a new movie in the Harry Potter franchise*
● *verb* [+ obj]
(*Commerce*) (*usually* **be franchised**) to give or sell a **franchise** to sb: *Catering has been franchised (out) to a private company.* ◇ *The group has 9 000 franchised restaurants.* ▶ **'franchising** *noun* [U]: *They intend to expand through franchising agreements.*

franchisee /ˌfræntʃaˈziː/ *noun* [C]
(*Commerce*) a person or company that has been given a **franchise** → MASTER FRANCHISE

franchiser (*also spelled* **franchisor**) /ˈfræntʃaɪzə(r)/ *noun* [C]
(*Commerce*) a company or an organization that gives sb a **franchise** See note at EMPLOYER

franco /ˈfræŋkəʊ; *AmE* -oʊ/ *adverb* (*abbr* **fco**)
(*Trade*) used to say that goods will be delivered to a particular place without any charge for transport: *The goods will be delivered franco to your warehouse.*

frank /fræŋk/ *verb* [+ obj] (*often* **be franked**)
to stamp a mark on an envelope, etc. to show that the cost of posting it has been paid or does not need to be paid: *a franked envelope* ◇ *a franking machine*

★ **fraud** /frɔːd/ *noun* [U,C]
the crime of deceiving sb in order to get money or things illegally: *property that has been obtained by fraud* ◇ *Investigators have uncovered a $12 million accounting fraud.* ◇ *She was accused of committing fraud against her clients.*
● *a* **complex/massive/serious** *fraud* ✦ **accounting/bank/credit-card/tax** *fraud* ✦ **corporate/financial** *fraud* ✦ *to* **commit/engage in/perpetrate** *fraud* ✦ *a fraud* **case/investigation/trial**

fraudulent /ˈfrɔːdjələnt; *AmE* -dʒə-/ *adjective*
intended to deceive sb, usually in order to make money illegally: *He had made several fraudulent insurance claims.* ◇ *Statistics show that 33% of job applications contain fraudulent information.*
▶ **fraudulently** /ˈfrɔːdjələntli; *AmE* -dʒə-/ *adverb*: *charged with fraudulently obtaining a bank loan*

FRB /ˌef ɑː ˈbiː; *AmE* ɑːr/ = FEDERAL RESERVE BANK, FEDERAL RESERVE BOARD

Freddie Mac™ /ˌfredi ˈmæk/ *noun*
(*Finance*)
1 [sing.] (*abbr* **FHLMC**) in the US, the Federal Home Loan Mortgage Corporation, a private company supported by the government that supplies money for MORTGAGES: *Freddie Mac sold a total of $3 billion of one-month bills on Monday.*
2 [C, usually pl.] the bonds that are issued by Freddie Mac: *Freddie Macs with a yield of 4.10%*
→ FANNIE MAE, GINNIE MAE

★ **free** /friː/ *adjective, verb, adverb*
● *adjective* (**freer** /ˈfriːə(r)/ **freest** /ˈfriːɪst/)

SEE ALSO: duty-free, hands-~, interest-~, post-~, smoke-~, tax-~, toll-~

1 costing nothing: *Drug companies regularly give out* **free** *samples of their products.* ◇ *The website is free for personal use (but companies pay to use it).*
2 able to move or be exchanged between people without restrictions: *There is free movement of capital and labour within the European Union.* ◇ *a free flow of information*
3 not containing or affected by sth harmful or unpleasant: *Our products are completely free* **from** *harmful chemicals.* ◇ *Benefits received under the policy are free* **of** *tax.*
4 -**free** (*in adjectives*) without the thing mentioned; not affected by the thing mentioned: *a risk-free investment*
5 available to be used: *The software requires about 20 megabytes of free hard-disk space.*
6 (about a person or a time) without particular plans or arrangements; not busy: *Keep Monday morning free for a meeting.*
IDM **there's no such ˌthing as a free ˈlunch** used to say that it is not possible to get sth for nothing
● *verb* [+ obj]
free sb/sth (up) to make sb/sth available for a particular purpose: *Selling these assets will free up capital to invest in our core business.*
● *adverb*
without payment: *Children under five travel free.* ◇ *You can download the booklet free of charge.*

ˌfree ˈagent *noun* [C]
(*Commerce*) a person who is independent and works for several different companies or organizations: *Free agents often work longer hours and under greater pressure than their colleagues inside companies.* ▶ **ˌfree ˈagency** *noun* [U]

ˈfree aˈlongside ˈship *phrase* (*abbr* **FAS**)
(*Trade*) a term meaning that the seller delivers the goods to a ship at a particular port and gets official permission for them to be exported. The buyer is responsible for having the goods loaded onto the ship and transported: *We deliver FAS Tokyo.* → INCOTERM

freebie /ˈfriːbi/ *noun* [C] (*informal*)
something that is given to sb without payment, usually by a company: *They always put some freebies in with the orders.* ◇ *a freebie holiday*

ˌfree ˈcarrier *noun* [U] (*abbr* **FCA**)
(*Trade*) a term meaning that the seller gets official permission for the goods to be exported and delivers them to the person or company (**carrier**) who will then transport them on behalf of the buyer: *Our delivery terms are FCA Stockholm airport.* → INCOTERM

ˌfree ˈcash flow *noun* [U,C]
(*Accounting*) income that a business has left at the end of an accounting period after paying for its supplies, workers, etc. and any assets that it has bought, such as machinery or property; the state of having this income available to spend: *The group is anxious to generate free cash flow in order to repay debt.* ◇ *We expect to achieve free cash flow by the end of the year.*

ˌfree collective ˈbargaining *noun* [U] (*BrE*)
(*HR*) formal talks between unions and employers, about pay and working conditions, that are not limited by the law or government

ˌfree compeˈtition *noun* [U]
(*Economics*) a system in which prices, incomes, etc. are controlled by supply and demand and businesses compete freely with each other

freedom of associ'ation noun [U]
(*Law*) the right to join or form an organization, especially a union

free 'enterprise noun [U]
an economic system in which private businesses compete with each other without much government control → PRIVATE ENTERPRISE

free 'fall noun [U]
a sudden drop in the value of sth that cannot be stopped: *The share price went into free fall after the firm announced poor year-end results.*

free-'floating adjective
able to move freely; not controlled by anything: *a free-floating exchange rate*

Freefone™ = FREEPHONE

'free-for-all noun [sing.]
a situation in which there are no rules or controls and everyone acts for their own advantage: *The lowering of trade barriers has led to a free-for-all among exporters.* ◇ *a price-cutting free-for-all*

free 'gift noun [C]
(*Marketing*) a gift that a shop/store, a business, etc. offers people to encourage them to do sth, especially to buy a product or service: *Subscribe to the magazine and receive a free gift!*

freehold /'fri:həʊld; *AmE* -hoʊld/ noun [C,U] (*also* **freehold e'state** [C] *less frequent*) (*both especially BrE*)
(*Law*; *Property*) the fact of owning a building or piece of land for a period of time that is not limited: *Private tenants in flats have the right to buy the freehold from their landlord.* ▶ **'freehold** adjective **'freehold** adverb → LEASEHOLD

freeholder /'fri:həʊldə(r); *AmE* -hoʊld-/ noun [C]
(*especially BrE*)
(*Law*; *Property*) a company, person, etc. who owns the **freehold** of a building or piece of land → LEASEHOLDER

'free ,issue = SCRIP ISSUE

freelance /'fri:lɑ:ns; *AmE* -læns/ adjective, noun, verb
● *adjective*
used to describe a way of earning money by selling your work or services to several different organizations rather than being employed by one particular organization: *a freelance writer/journalist/executive* ◇ *freelance work/income* ◇ *I work for the company on a freelance basis.*
▶ **'freelance** adverb: *She went* (= started to work) *freelance in 2005.*
● *noun* (*also* **freelancer** /'fri:lɑ:nsə(r); *AmE* -lænsər/) [C]
a person who works **freelance**: *They have two full-time employees and 100 freelances around the world.*
● *verb* [no obj]
to earn money by selling your work to several different organizations: *He freelances for several companies.*

★ **,free 'market** noun [C]
(*Economics*) an economic system in which the price of goods and services is affected by supply and demand rather than controlled by a government: *to compete in a free market* ◇ *The new law will create a free market for electricity.* ◇ *free-market policies*

free-market e'conomy = MARKET ECONOMY

free marke'teer noun [C]
a person who believes that countries should have FREE MARKETS ▶ **free marke'teering** noun [U]

free on 'board phrase (*abbr* **FOB**)
(*Trade*) a term meaning that the seller delivers the goods to a ship at a particular port and gets official permission for them to be exported. The buyer is responsible for the goods once they are put on the

ship: *All our prices are FOB Rotterdam.* → FREE CARRIER, INCOTERM

Freephone (*also spelled* **Freefone™**) /'fri:fəʊn; *AmE* -foʊn/ noun [U]
in the UK, a system in which the cost of a telephone call is paid for by the organization being called, rather than by the person making the call: *Call now on Freephone 0800 89216 for further details.* → TOLL-FREE

free 'port noun [C]
(*Trade*) a port at which tax is not paid on goods that have been brought there temporarily before being sent to a different country

Freepost /'fri:pəʊst; *AmE* -poʊst/ noun [U]
in the UK, a system in which the cost of sending a letter is paid for by the organization receiving it, rather than by the person sending it: *Send the completed form to the Freepost address given below.*

free 'rider noun [C]
a person or an organization that accepts a benefit or service that other people pay for or have worked to get: *There are about 3 million free riders in Britain who benefit from collective bargaining but are not union members.* ▶ **free 'ride** noun [C, usually sing.]: *people getting a free ride by viewing news on the Web rather than buying newspapers* **'freeride** verb [no obj]

freesheet /'fri:ʃi:t/ noun [C] (*BrE*)
a free newspaper, especially one that is delivered to all the homes in a particular area and is paid for by advertising

free-standing 'insert noun [C] (*abbr* **FSI**)
(*Marketing*) a printed advertisement of one or more pages that is put inside a newspaper or magazine, but is not attached to it

free 'television = FREE TV

free-to-'air adjective [usually before noun]
(about television programmes) that you do not have to pay to watch: *a free-to-air television channel*
▶ **free-to-'air** adverb: *The games are being shown free-to-air.*

free 'trade noun [U]
(*Economics*) a system of international trade in which there are no restrictions or taxes on imports and exports: *The pact encourages free trade in the region.* ◇ *The EU is negotiating a free-trade agreement with Chile.*
❍ *a free-trade* **agreement/area/zone**

free 'trial noun [C]
(*Marketing*) the chance to use a product or service for a short period without paying anything before you decide whether to buy it or not: *The service costs $100 a year, but there is a 30-day free trial.* ◇ *a free trial offer/period*

free T'V (*also* **,free 'television**) noun [U]
a system of television broadcasting in which you do not pay to watch programmes: *a free-TV broadcaster* → PAY TV

freeware /'fri:weə(r); *AmE* -wer/ noun [U]
(*IT*) software that is offered free for anyone to use → SHAREWARE

★ **freeze** /fri:z/ verb, noun
● *verb* (froze /frəʊz; *AmE* froʊz/ frozen /'frəʊzn; *AmE* 'froʊzn/)
1 [+ obj] to hold costs, wages, prices, etc. at a fixed level for a period of time: *Salaries have been frozen for the current year.* SYN PEG
2 [+ obj] to prevent money, a bank account, etc. from being used, especially by getting a court order: *The company's assets have been frozen.* ◇ *a government decision to freeze bank deposits*
3 [no obj] when a computer screen **freezes**, you cannot move any of the images, etc. on it, because there is a problem with the system

PHR V ,freeze sb 'out (of sth) to deliberately try to prevent other businesses from competing in a particular market, for example by selling goods very cheaply: *The high tariffs were intended to freeze out foreign companies.* ◇ *Small producers are being frozen out of the health food market.* → FROZEN

• *noun* [C]

1 the act of keeping costs, wages, prices, etc. at a particular level for a period of time: *The firm announced an immediate spending freeze to cut costs.* ◇ *The pay freeze has now been lifted* (= stopped). ◇ *a freeze on income tax rates*

○ *a pay/price/salary/wage freeze* ◆ *a hiring/recruitment freeze* ◆ *to implement/impose/introduce a freeze* ◆ *to end/lift a freeze*

2 the act of stopping sth: *The company has put a freeze on all recruitment.* ◇ *a freeze on exports*

○ *to impose/put a freeze on sth* ◆ *to end/lift a freeze*

3 an official rule or order that prevents sb/sth from using their bank account, selling their assets, etc: *The sanctions involve a freeze on the government's foreign assets.*

○ *to impose/put a freeze on sth* ◆ *to end/lift a freeze*

'free zone *noun* [C] (*AmE*)
(*Trade*) an area in a country where goods can be imported and stored without paying taxes on them: *Free zones are considered to be outside the US Customs territory.* → FOREIGN TRADE ZONE

★ **freight** /freɪt/ *noun, verb*
(*Transport*)

• *noun* [U]

SEE ALSO: **bulk freight, carriage and ~, cost and ~, cost, insurance and ~**

1 goods that are transported by ships, planes, trains or lorries/trucks; the system of transporting goods in this way: *Firms are being encouraged to shift freight off the roads and onto rail.* ◇ *Freight was organized by our distributor.* → AIRFREIGHT

○ *ocean/rail/road freight* ◆ *a freight ship/train* ◆ *a freight depot/terminal/yard* ◆ *to carry/haul/move/ship/transport freight* ◆ *to load/unload freight* ◆ *a freight carrier/handler/hauler/haulier/operator*

2 the amount charged to transport a load of goods by ship, plane, train or lorry/truck: *The buyer pays the freight.*

• *verb* [+ obj]
to send or carry goods by air, sea or train: *The goods were freighted by air.* ▶ **'freighting** *noun* [U]

freightage /'freɪtɪdʒ/ *noun* [U]
(*Transport*) the amount charged to transport a load of goods by ship, plane, train or lorry/truck

freight col'lect (*also* ,freight 'forward, *especially in BrE*) *phrase*
(*Trade*) a term meaning that the person or company receiving the goods pays the delivery costs when they receive the goods from the transport company: *The delivery will be on a freight collect basis.* ◇ *All shipments are freight collect.*

freighter /'freɪtə(r)/ *noun* [C]
a large ship or plane that carries goods

,freight 'forward = FREIGHT COLLECT

'freight ,forwarder (*also* 'forwarder) *noun* [C]
(*Trade; Transport*) a company that is paid to arrange for goods to be transported and often exported on behalf of others **NOTE** The **freight forwarder** often arranges insurance for the goods and completes the official procedures to allow the exporter to be paid. **SYN** FORWARDING AGENT
▶ **'freight ,forwarding** *noun* [U]: *a freight forwarding company*

,freight ,pre'paid *phrase* (*especially AmE*)
(*Trade*) a term meaning that the person or company sending the goods pays for the delivery costs before giving them to the transport company: *Our terms of sale are freight prepaid.*

'frequency ,discount *noun* [C]
(*Marketing*) a reduced price offered to advertisers who publish an advertisement a particular number of times during a particular period of time

,frequent 'flyer *noun* [C]
a person who uses a particular airline a lot, especially sb who belongs to a club which allows them to receive free flights or special advantages from the airline: *A free transfer service is available to our frequent flyers.* ◇ *Earn frequent-flyer miles each time you fly.*

,fresh 'money *noun* [U]
(*Finance*) money for investments that has not been invested before: *They may be forced to raise fresh money from shareholders.*

,frictional unem'ployment (*also* ,search unem'ployment) *noun* [U]
(*Economics*) the number of people who are not doing paid employment because they are moving between jobs and have not yet found another one, although there are jobs available → SEASONAL UNEMPLOYMENT, STRUCTURAL UNEMPLOYMENT

friendly /'frendli/ *adjective* (**friendlier, friendliest**)

SEE ALSO: **environmentally-friendly, family-~, user-~**

1 (*often used in compound adjectives*) that is helpful and easy to use; that helps sb/sth or does not harm them/it: *This software is much friendlier than the previous version.* ◇ *child-friendly instructions*

2 (*Finance*) (about an attempt to buy or gain control of a company) that the directors of the company that is to be bought want and are willing to accept or consider: *The bank has launched a friendly bid for Credit Lyonnais worth 19.5 billion euros.* → HOSTILE

○ *a friendly bid/offer/takeover* ◆ *a friendly acquisition/approach/deal* ◆ *a friendly acquirer/bidder*

frills /frɪlz/ *noun* [pl.]

SEE ALSO: **no-frills**

things that are not necessary but are added to make sth more attractive or interesting: *They offer cheap flights with no frills.*

fringe /frɪndʒ/ *noun* [C]
the outer or less important part of an area or a group: *offices on the fringe of the City* ◇ *He is more of a fringe player than a decision maker.*

'fringe ,benefit *noun* [C, usually pl.]
(*HR*) extra things that an employer gives you as well as your wages: *The fringe benefits include free health insurance.*

FRN = FLOATING-RATE NOTE

front /frʌnt/ *noun, adjective, verb*
• *noun*

1 [sing.] behaviour that is not genuine, done in order to hide your true feelings or opinions: *We need to present a united front at the negotiations* (= show the others that we have the same views and demands).

2 [C, usually sing.] a person or an organization that is used to hide an illegal or secret activity: *They used front companies to import goods into Europe without paying duties.*

3 [C] the front side of a building: *a shop/store front*

IDM ,front of 'mind (*also* ,top of 'mind) (*Marketing*) if a brand or product is **front of mind**, it is one that people are very aware of and will name first when thinking about a particular type of product: *A newsletter will help to keep the product (at) front of mind.* ◇ *front-of-mind awareness* → SHARE OF MIND at SHARE *noun* (,out) ,in 'front leading a particular industry: *In certain areas of aircraft engine* manufacture Rolls Royce is now out in front. **,up 'front** (informal) as payment in advance: They wanted three months' rent up front. ◇ We'll pay you half up front and the other half when you've finished the job. → UPFRONT → idioms at CASH, LEAD verb, QUEUE noun

● **adjective**

IDM **on the front 'burner** (especially AmE) (informal) (about an issue, a plan, etc.) being given a lot of attention because it is considered important: In a recession you need to put cost-cutting on the front burner. → idiom at BACK adj

● **verb** [+ obj] to lead or represent a company, an organization, etc., especially in a particular activity or project: He fronts a multinational company. ◇ She will front the presentation to shareholders on Monday.

PHRV **'front for sb/sth** to represent a group or an organization and try to hide its secret or illegal activities: He fronted for them in several illegal property deals.

frontage /ˈfrʌntɪdʒ/ noun [C,U] (Property) the front of a building such as a shop/ store, especially when this faces a road or river: The warehouse also has retail shop frontage.

'frontage road = SERVICE ROAD

,front 'desk noun [C, usually sing.] the place where visitors go to introduce themselves or get information when they enter a hotel, an office building, etc: There's a parcel waiting for you at the front desk.

'front end noun, adjective

● **noun** [C]

1 the part of a business that meets and deals with customers: The website serves as the front end of the supply chain.

2 the beginning of a project, a process, an investment, a period of time, etc: You may have to pay a fee at the front end of the loan.

3 (IT) the part of a computer program that a user sees and uses to operate other parts of the program or system: a graphical front end → INTERFACE → BACK END

● **adjective** [only before noun]

1 connected with the beginning of a project, a process, an investment, a period of time, etc: The front-end design takes six to nine months. ◇ The policy has a front-end fee and exit charges.

2 (IT) that allows the user to operate other parts of a computer program or system

,front-end 'load noun [C] (Finance) the fee an investor pays when they buy shares in an investment fund, an insurance policy, etc., which is included in the first payment → BACK-END LOAD ▶ **,front-end 'loaded** adjective

,front-end 'loading noun [U] (Finance) the practice of a fund, bank, etc. taking most of its fees and expenses from payments that are made at the beginning of the period of an investment, a loan, etc.; the fees and expenses taken in this way: Front-end loading puts all the charges onto the early years of the policy. → FRONT-LOAD

,front 'line (also spelled **frontline**) noun [C] (usually the front line)

1 the area of greatest activity, where you can have an important effect on sth: The company is in the front line of the global telecoms industry.

2 the group of employees in a company who deal directly with customers or who physically produce sth; the work that they do: Managers weren't giving feedback to the people on the front line.

'front-line (also spelled **frontline**) adjective [only before noun] (HR)

1 used to describe an employee who deals directly with customers or physically makes a product: Front-line staff should know all the products on sale.

2 used to describe a manager who deals directly with a group of workers: The frontline manager has an important role in supporting the team.

,front-'load verb [+ obj] (Finance) (usually **be front-loaded**) to charge or pay for sth at or near the beginning: Most of the project's costs will be front-loaded in the first few years. ◇ the front-loaded costs of acquiring a new business ▶ **,front-'loading** noun [U]

,front 'office noun [sing.] (especially AmE) the part of a business concerned with managing things or dealing with the public: He worked at all levels of the firm, from the boardroom to the front office.

,front of 'house noun [U] the part of a hotel, restaurant or other business that involves dealing directly with customers: I cooked and my wife did front of house. ◇ a front-of-house manager/worker

,front 'runner noun [C] a person or an organization that seems most likely to win a race or competition: They have emerged as the front runners in the race to buy the airline.

'front-,running noun [U] (Stock Exchange) the activity of buying particular shares after obtaining secret information that sb is about to buy a large number of them, which will probably make their value rise **NOTE** Front-running is usually illegal.

frozen /ˈfrəʊzn; AmE ˈfroʊzn/ adjective

1 (about food) kept at a very low temperature in order to preserve it: frozen desserts/meals/vegetables ◇ a chain of frozen food stores

2 (about money, assets, etc.) not available to be used or sold because of an official rule or order: People's savings remain frozen in bank accounts. → FREEZE verb

FRS /ˌef ɑːr ˈes/ = FEDERAL RESERVE SYSTEM

frugal /ˈfruːgl/ adjective using only as much money or food as is necessary: Frugal shoppers are waiting for bargains. **OPP** EXTRAVAGANT ▶ **frugality** /fruˈgæləti/ noun [U]: consumer frugality **frugally** /ˈfruːgəli/ adverb

FSA /ˌef es ˈeɪ/ = FINANCIAL SERVICES AUTHORITY

FSI /ˌef es ˈaɪ/ = FREE-STANDING INSERT

FT /ˌef ˈtiː/ abbr

1 in the UK, Financial Times

2 (only used in written English) = FULL-TIME

FTA /ˌef tiː ˈeɪ/ abbr (Economics) a FREE TRADE agreement: negotiations for a bilateral US-Australia FTA

FTC /ˌef tiː ˈsiː/ = FEDERAL TRADE COMMISSION

FTSE™ /ˈfʊtsi/ noun [sing.]

1 a company that publishes INDICES (= average prices for groups of shares, bonds, etc.) for particular markets: The main FTSE indices enjoyed strong gains. **NOTE** FTSE is a short form of Financial Times-Stock Exchange.

2 an average of the share prices of particular companies traded on the London Stock Exchange, usually the 100 largest companies: On Friday, the FTSE closed down 11 points at 3 567. ◇ The FTSE has fallen to its lowest level since November. ◇ FTSE stocks (= companies whose share price are included in the average)

FTSE '100 ,Index (also ,FTSE '100) /ˌfʊtsi wʌn ˈhʌndrəd/ (also **'Footsie**, informal) noun [sing.]
an average of the share prices of the 100 largest companies traded on the London Stock Exchange: *The FTSE 100 Index fell 11 points to 3567.* ◇ *FTSE 100 companies/stocks*

FTZ /ˌef ti: 'zed; AmE 'zi:/ = FOREIGN TRADE ZONE

fuel /'fju:əl/ noun, verb
• **noun** [U,C]
any material that produces heat or power, usually when it is burnt: *fossil/nuclear fuels* ◇ *Airlines are suffering with higher fuel costs.*
• **verb** [+ obj] (**-ll-**) (AmE **-l-**)
1 to supply sth with material that can be burnt to produce heat or power: *Natural gas is used to fuel the plant.* ◇ *oil-fuelled power stations*
2 to increase sth; to make sth stronger: *Higher salaries helped to fuel inflation.* ◇ *Job cuts have fuelled workers' fears that the factory will soon close.*

★ **fulfil** (AmE spelling **fulfill**) /fʊl'fɪl/ verb [+ obj] (**fulfilling, fulfilled, fulfilled**)
1 to do or have what is required or necessary: *to fulfil the terms/conditions of an agreement* ◇ *He was accused of not fulfilling his duties as a director.* ◇ *No candidate fulfils all the criteria for this position.*
 ○ to fulfil a **duty/an obligation/a pledge/promise** ◆ to fulfil **demands/expectations/instructions/needs/requirements**
2 to do or achieve what was hoped for or expected: *The deal has fulfilled the company's ambition to expand into wider financial services.* ◇ *helping employees to fulfil their potential*
 ○ to fulfil an **ambition**/a **dream** ◆ to fulfil your **potential/promise**
3 to have a particular role or purpose: *The 'touch screen' fulfils the function of a keyboard.*
 ○ to fulfil **the function/role** of sb/sth
4 (Commerce) if a business **fulfils** an order, they supply the full amount of sth that has been asked for: *the processes involved in taking and fulfilling orders over the Web*
5 if a job **fulfils** you or you **fulfil** yourself, you feel happy and satisfied with what you are doing or what you have done: *I need a job that really fulfils me.*

fulfilled /fʊl'fɪld/ adjective
feeling happy and satisfied that you are doing sth useful with your life: *He doesn't feel fulfilled in his present job.*

fulfilling /fʊl'fɪlɪŋ/ adjective
causing sb to feel satisfied and useful: *I'm finding the work much more fulfilling now.*

fulfilment (AmE spelling **fulfillment**) /fʊl'fɪlmənt/ noun [U]
1 the act of doing what is required or necessary: *The offer is subject to the fulfilment of certain conditions.*
2 (Commerce) the act of supplying the full amount of sth that sb has asked for: *The software tracks every stage of **order fulfilment** and billing. ◇ He has 20 full-time employees in the fulfillment warehouse.*
3 the feeling of being happy and satisfied with what you are doing or have done: *The most common reason for leaving a job is lack of **personal fulfillment**.*
4 the act of doing or achieving what was hoped for or expected: *the fulfilment of expectations*

ful'filment house noun [C]
(Commerce) an organization that is paid to deal with mail, requests for information or orders for another company: *She has delegated order-taking to an outside fulfillment house so that she can focus on design and marketing.*

full-circle 'feedback = 360-DEGREE FEEDBACK

Full Con'tainer Load noun [C] (abbr **FCL**)
(Transport) an amount of goods being transported for sb that fills one whole container: *Rates for Full Container Load depend on the size of the container needed.* ◇ *full-container-load shipments* → LESS THAN CONTAINER LOAD

full 'costing noun [U]
(Accounting) a way of calculating the cost of a product by including all costs involved in producing it and running the business, such as raw materials, rent, electricity or wages: *Under the full costing method, fixed overheads are allocated evenly to the units produced.* SYN ABSORPTION COSTING → MARGINAL COSTING

full-'page adjective [only before noun]
filling a complete page of a newspaper or magazine: *a full-page ad*

full-'service adjective [only before noun]
providing a complete range of services for customers: *a full-service bank/brokerage* ◇ *The full-service airlines have found it difficult to compete with no-frills operators.*

full-'size (also ,full-'sized) adjective [usually before noun]
not made smaller; of the usual size: *full-size trucks* ◇ *The laptop has a full-sized keyboard.*

full-'time adjective, adverb (abbr **FT**)
for all the hours of a week during which people normally work, rather than just for a part of it: *a full-time employee* ◇ *a full-time job* ◇ *He was hired on a full-time basis.* ◇ *We need somebody to work on the project full-time.* → PART-TIME, REGULAR adj. (6)

full-'timer noun [C]
a person who works **full-time**: *She has a staff of 14 full-timers.*

full-'year adjective [only before noun]
(Accounting) relating to a complete FINANCIAL YEAR (= a period of 12 months over which a company prepares a full set of financial records): *full-year results/profits/forecasts* ◇ *He said that full-year 2005 earnings would be disappointing.*

★ **function** /'fʌŋkʃn/ noun, verb
• **noun**
1 [C,U] a special activity or purpose of a person or thing: *to fulfil/perform a useful function* ◇ *Smartphones combine the functions of cellphones and handheld computers.* ◇ *Your function is to run your department efficiently.*
2 [C] the part of a company that is responsible for a particular area: *accounting, manufacturing, sales and marketing and other corporate functions* ◇ *We considered splitting up our key business functions so that they were not all in one place.*
3 (IT) [C] a part of a program, etc. that carries out a basic operation: *the function keys*
4 [C] a social event or official ceremony: *The staff are allowed two social functions a year.*
5 [sing.] **a function of sth** if one thing is **a function of** another, its value depends on the varying values of the other thing: (figurative) *Salary is a function of age and experience.*
• **verb** [no obj]
to work in the correct way: *The fire alarm system is now functioning again.* ◇ *a fully functioning market economy* SYN OPERATE
PHR V **'function as sb/sth** to perform the action or the job of the thing or person mentioned: *The sofa also functions as a bed.* ◇ *The managers had already been functioning as owners of the company.*

functional /ˈfʌŋkʃənl/ adjective

SEE ALSO: **cross-functional**

1 having a special purpose: *Any project can be broken down into different functional roles.*
2 (HR) connected with a particular area of activity or skill, especially within a business: *The main functional areas of a business are finance, production, personnel and marketing.* ◇ *a functional team* (= of accountants, engineers, etc.) ◇ *In a functional structure, employees are grouped according to work activity.*
3 practical and useful, often with little or no decoration: *The design is simple and functional.*
4 working; able to do the job for which it is intended: *The device is a **fully** functional computer.* ◇ *The system is only 80% functional.*
▸ **functionally** /ˈfʌŋkʃənəli/ adverb: *Both versions of the software are visually and functionally similar.*

functional ackˈnowledgement noun [C]
(abbr **FA**)
(E-commerce) an electronic message sent to sb to say that their electronic order, INVOICE, etc. has been received

functional flexiˈbility noun [U]
(HR) the policy of training workers so that they have more skills and abilities and can do a greater variety of tasks

★ **functionality** /ˌfʌŋkʃəˈnæləti/ noun (plural functionalities)
1 (IT) [U,C] the range of functions that a computer or other electronic system can perform: *People generally use only 10% of a program's functionality.* ◇ *a phone with email functionality*
2 [U] the quality in sth of being very suitable for the purpose it was designed for: *We carry out extensive tests to prove the functionality and reliability of the system.*

functional organiˈzation noun [C]
(HR) an organization where employees are put into different departments depending on the type of work that they do: *We changed from a functional organization into a team-based operation.*

★ **fund** /fʌnd/ noun, verb
(Finance)
● **noun**

SEE ALSO: **balanced fund, bond ~, cohesion ~, contingency ~, depreciation ~, equity ~,** etc.

1 [C] an amount of money that is saved or collected for a particular purpose, especially for investing in companies, projects, etc.; an organization that controls this money: *We set up a fund **for** technological research.* ◇ *a $7.5 billion investment fund* ◇ *The fund went down in value by 13% this year.* ◇ *the International Monetary Fund* ◇ *a fund company/group* (= that manages investments) → FUND MANAGER at FUND MANAGEMENT
  ○ to **create/establish/set up/start** a fund ◆ to **invest in/manage/run** a fund
2 funds [pl.] money that sb/sth has available to spend: *We have limited funds available for research.* ◇ *The company will need to raise fresh funds from its shareholders.* ◇ *They ran out of funds before they could finish the building work.* ◇ *We decided to allocate more funds to advertising.* → FUND-RAISING
  ○ to **borrow/obtain/raise/secure** funds ◆ to **have/use** funds ◆ to **be short of/run out of** funds ◆ to **allocate/provide** funds ◆ **insufficient/limited/sufficient** funds ◆ **private/public** funds
● **verb** [+ obj]
fund sth (by/with/from sth) (often **be funded**)
to provide money for sth: *The group is seeking partners to fund a new €2 billion production plant.* ◇

The acquisition will be entirely funded by debt. ◇ *The company claims its business plan is fully funded.* ◇ *a government-funded programme* → OVERFUNDED, UNDERFUNDED See note at FINANCE
  ○ to fund **expansion/growth/operations** ◆ **fully/well** funded ◆ **privately/publicly** funded

fundamentals /ˌfʌndəˈmentlz/ noun [pl.]
(Economics) the important aspects of an economy, an industry or a business, which lead to its success or failure over a long period of time; measures of these: *The economic fundamentals remain weak—high inflation, high interest rates and low productivity.*

funder /ˈfʌndə(r)/ noun [C]
a person or an organization that provides money for a particular purpose: *The start-up failed after its main funders withdrew support.* See note at FINANCE

★ **funding** /ˈfʌndɪŋ/ noun [U]
money for a particular purpose; the act of providing money for such a purpose: *There have been large cuts in government funding for scientific research.* ◇ *We secured €5 million in funding from our shareholders.* ◇ *finding alternative sources of funding* ◇ *The group faces a $2.2 billion funding gap* (= they still need this amount). See note at FINANCE
  ○ to **find/look for/seek** funding ◆ to **attract/get/raise/secure** funding ◆ to **cut/provide/withdraw** funding ◆ **government/private/public/state** funding ◆ a funding **crisis/deficit/gap/problem/shortfall**

ˈfund ˌmanagement noun [U]
(Finance) the act of managing an amount of money which is used to buy and sell shares, bonds, etc. on behalf of investors in order to make as much profit as possible: *the fund management industry*
SYN INVESTMENT MANAGEMENT
▸ **ˈfund ˌmanager** noun [C]: *Many fund managers believe that share prices are likely to rise in the next few months.*

fund of ˈfunds noun [C]
(Finance) a type of investment fund, especially a UNIT TRUST, that invests money in a range of other investment funds

ˈfund-ˌraising noun
1 (Finance) [C,U] the act or activity of obtaining money from investors, lenders, etc: *The group has launched a €150 million fund-raising.* ◇ *a fund-raising exercise/plan*
2 [U] the activity of collecting money for a charity or organization: *a fund-raising campaign/dinner/event*

fungible /ˈfʌndʒəbl/ adjective, noun
● **adjective**
(Finance; Law) that can be replaced or exchanged with sth of the same kind without changing the quality, characteristics or value: *Oil is a fungible commodity: if one producer stops supplying you, you can simply go to another.* ◇ *These bonds are fungible with those already listed.*
● **noun** [C, usually pl.]
1 (Finance; Law) shares, bonds, etc. that can replace or be exchanged with others without losing their value: *Fungibles have been issued by several multinational companies to raise funds from different markets at the same time.*
2 (Commerce; Law) goods that are valued and sold by their number or weight: *Grain and flour are typical fungibles.*

ˈfunny ˌmoney noun [U]
1 money with little or no value, such as money that has been printed illegally or is in an unusual currency
2 an unusual type of shares, bonds, etc. that a company issues, whose value often moves up and down rapidly

furnish /ˈfɜːnɪʃ; *AmE* ˈfɜːrnɪʃ/ *verb* [+ obj]
1 to put furniture in an office, a room, etc: *The room is furnished* **with** *a desk, chair and bookshelf.* ◇ *furnished accommodation* (= with furniture)
2 (*formal*) **furnish sb/sth with sth** | **furnish sth to sb**: to supply or provide sb/sth with sth; to supply sth to sb: *Please furnish us with the correct information.*

'further to *preposition* (*formal*)
used in letters, emails, etc. to refer to a previous letter, email, conversation, etc: *Further to our conversation of last Friday, I would like to book the conference centre for 26 June.*

future /ˈfjuːtʃə(r)/ *noun* [C, usually pl.] (*also* **'futures ˌcontract** [C])

SEE ALSO: **commodity futures, currency future**

(*Finance*) a contract to buy or sell a particular amount of sth, such as a raw material, currency or shares, at a particular time in the future and for a particular price. **Futures** are traded in organized markets (**futures exchanges**): *coffee/gold/oil/energy futures* ◇ *bond/commodity/stock futures* ◇ *Futures prices* **for** *natural gas are up 130% from last year.*
→ FORWARD CONTRACT → idiom at HITCH *verb*
❍ *to* **buy/offer/sell/trade (in)** *futures* • *futures* **expire/trade** • *a futures* **broker/trader**

ˌfutures comˈmission ˌmerchant *noun* [C] (*abbr* **FCM**)
(*Finance*) a person or an organization that tries to get or accepts orders from people who want to buy or sell **futures**

'futures ˌcontract = FUTURE

'futures exˌchange *noun* [C]
(*Finance*) a market at a particular place where **futures** are traded: *The Chicago Mercantile Exchange is the world's second-largest futures exchange.*

'futures ˌmarket *noun* [C]
(*Finance*) the buying and selling of **futures**; a particular place where this type of trading occurs: *The price of cocoa has shot up on the futures market.* ◇ *LIFFE, the London futures market*

fwd (*AmE spelling* **fwd.**) *abbr*
a short way of writing **forward**

FX /ˌef ˈeks/ = FOREX

FY /ˌef ˈwaɪ/ = FINANCIAL YEAR, FISCAL YEAR

FYI *abbr* (*informal*)
a short way of writing **for your information**: *FYI, I have attached our programme for next year.*

G g

G /dʒiː/ *abbr* (*informal*)
a short way of saying or writing **grand** (= one thousand dollars, etc.)

the G10 /ˌdʒiː ˈten/ *abbr*
Group of Ten the eleven nations whose central banks meet and work together to support the international finance and currency system and who lend money to the IMF **NOTE** It is called the **G10** because originally there were only ten members. The members now are: Belgium, Canada, France, Germany, Italy, Japan, Netherlands, Sweden, Switzerland, the UK and the USA. It is also known as the **Paris Club**.

the G7 /ˌdʒiː ˈsevn/ *abbr*
Group of Seven the seven leading industrial nations whose finance officers meet regularly to discuss economic and financial matters **NOTE** The **G7** are: Canada, France, Germany, Italy, Japan, the UK and the USA.

the G8 /ˌdʒiː ˈeɪt/ *abbr*
Group of Eight the eight leading industrial nations that meet regularly to discuss political and economic issues **NOTE** The **G8** are: Canada, France, Germany, Italy, Japan, Russia, the UK and the USA.: *Third-world debt is a major theme of the G8 summit this year.*

G&A /ˌdʒiː ənd ˈeɪ/ *abbr*
general and administrative (*also* **G&AE** /ˌdʒiː ənd eɪ ˈiː/ **general and administrative expenses**)
(*Accounting*) used to describe the general costs of running a business, such as those of employing accountants or lawyers, rather than those connected with a particular product or service: *G&A costs are expected to be 23% of sales.*

GAAP /ɡɑːp/ = GENERALLY ACCEPTED ACCOUNTING PRINCIPLES

gadget /ˈɡædʒɪt/ *noun* [C]
a small tool or device that does sth useful: *electronic gadgets*

'gag clause = GAGGING CLAUSE

gage = GAUGE

'gagging clause (*BrE*) (*AmE* **'gag clause**) *noun* [C]
(*HR*) a part of a contract of employment that prevents an employee from giving information about the company to journalists, politicians, union officers, etc. → WHISTLE-BLOWER

'gagging ˌorder (*BrE*) (*AmE* **'gag ˌorder**) *noun* [C]
(*Law*) an order made by a court, a government, etc. that prevents sth being discussed in public or reported by journalists: *The chief executive sought a gagging order preventing the two former employees from talking to the press or passing on information about the company.* ◇ *A gag order was imposed while the jury considered how much compensation to award.*

★ gain /ɡeɪn/ *verb, noun*
● *verb*
1 [+ obj] to gradually get more of sth: *I have gained a lot of experience in the job.* ◇ *The economy is out of recession now and gaining strength.*
2 [+ obj or no obj] (about a currency, share price, etc.) to increase in value: *The shares gained 5 per cent to $14.70.* ◇ *The Canadian dollar gained* **against** (= compared to) *the yen today.* OPP LOSE
See note at INCREASE
3 [+ obj or no obj] **gain (sth) (by/from sth)** to obtain an advantage or a benefit from sth or from doing sth: *There may be no advantage to be gained from lowering prices.* ◇ *Who* **stands to gain** *most from the sale of the company?*
→ idiom at GROUND *noun*
● *noun*

SEE ALSO: **book gain, capital ~, paper ~**

1 [C] an increase or an improvement in the amount, value or level of sth: *The company reported a 16% gain* **in** *market share.* ◇ *Media shares enjoyed strong gains this week.* ◇ *Increased spending on new*

technology resulted in a dramatic gain in productivity. ◇ efficiency/productivity gains OPP LOSS
○ a **big/dramatic/an impressive/a significant/strong** gain • a **modest/small/slight** gain • to **bring/make** a gain • to **enjoy/show** a gain • to **expect/forecast** a gain • to **post/record/report** a gain • to **erase/lose/ reverse/wipe out** a gain
2 [C] an advantage, benefit or profit that is achieved from doing sth: This figure includes a €1.7 million one-off gain **from** sale of assets. ◇ The potential gains of doing business online are great, but so are the challenges.
○ to **bring/have/make/result in** a gain
3 [U] financial profit, especially when this benefits only yourself: They sold the company purely **for** short-term gain. ◇ He only seems to be interested in personal gain.
○ to **be motivated by/do sth for/seek** gain

gainer /ˈɡeɪnə(r)/ noun [C]
1 (used in newspapers) shares, a currency, an investment, etc. that increases (**gains**) in value over a period of time: The Swiss franc was the biggest gainer in early trade. ◇ the FTSE 100 gainers
SYN WINNER OPP LOSER
2 a person, an organization, etc. that benefits from sth: The biggest gainers from the new rules will be high-rate taxpayers.

gainful /ˈɡeɪnfl/ adjective (formal)
used to describe useful work that you are paid for: gainful employment ▶ **gainfully** /ˈɡeɪnfəli/ adverb: gainfully employed

gainsharing (also spelled **gain sharing**) /ˈɡeɪnʃeərɪŋ; AmE -ʃer-/ noun [U]
(HR) a system in which employees receive part of the increased profit that has been made by improvements in the rate, the amount or the cost of producing goods that they have helped to make: The company's gainsharing program ties bonuses directly to team performance.

gal. abbr (only used in written English)
gallon(s)

galleria /ˌɡæləˈriːə/ noun [C]
a collection of small shops/stores under a single roof → ARCADE

gallon /ˈɡælən/ noun [C] (abbr **gal.**)
a unit for measuring liquid. In the UK it is equal to about 4.5 litres; in the US it is equal to about 3.8 litres. The UK measure is often referred to as an **imperial gallon**: In the US, oil is measured in barrels of about 42 gallons, or 159 litres.

galloping /ˈɡæləpɪŋ/ adjective [only before noun]
increasing or growing rapidly: Galloping **inflation** pushed the economy into chaos.

Gallup poll™ /ˈɡæləp pəʊl; AmE poʊl/ noun [C]
a way of finding out public opinion by asking a typical group of people questions: A recent Gallup poll showed that 25% of people intend to spend less on clothing this year.

gamble /ˈɡæmbl/ verb, noun
● verb [+ obj or no obj]
1 to take a risk with sth, hoping that you will be successful: He's gambling his reputation **on** the deal. ◇ We gambled **that** consumers would pay more for an online service.
2 to risk money on a card game, horse race, etc: He gambled all his money **on** the race.
▶ **gambler** /ˈɡæmblə(r)/ noun [C]
PHR V **gamble sth a'way** to lose sth such as money, possessions, etc. by gambling: They found their funds had been gambled away on the stock market.

● noun [C, usually sing.]
an action that you take when you know there is a risk but when you hope that the result will be a success: They **took a gamble on** the yen going up in value. ◇ Entering the sports car market was a huge gamble for us, but it **paid off** (= was successful).

game /ɡeɪm/ noun [C] (informal)
SEE ALSO: **business game, confidence ~, management ~, positive-sum ~, zero-sum ~**

a type of activity or business: How long have you been in this game? ◇ We decided to get back into the marketing game.
IDM **the only, best, biggest, etc. game in 'town** (especially AmE) the only, best, biggest, etc. thing or person that is available or worth dealing with: At that time, bonds were the only game in town. **raise/ lift/up your 'game** to improve the way that you perform an activity or do business: She believes the train operator should raise its game and offer cut-price deals. → idioms at AHEAD OF, BEAT, RULE noun

game plan noun [C]
a plan for success in the future: Our game plan is to buy property now, while the market is weak. ◇ to **develop** a game plan for the business

game ˌtheory noun [U]
an economic theory in which situations where people, businesses, etc. compete with each other are analysed as a type of game, with each person, business, etc. choosing the best action from a limited set of actions, based on what the others are likely to do

gaming /ˈɡeɪmɪŋ/ noun [U]
1 the business of taking bets from people or providing games, activities, etc. that allow people to bet money: regulation of the gaming industry ◇ gaming laws
2 playing computer games: online gaming

Gantt chart /ˈɡænt/ noun [C]
a chart used for managing the tasks involved in a project that shows when each stage should start and end and compares the amount of work done with the amount planned

Gantt chart

	Jan	Feb	Mar	Apr	May	Jun	Jul	Aug
Task 1	■■■							
Task 2		■■■						
Task 3			■■					
Task 4			■■■					
Task 5					■■■			
Task 6							■■■	

★ **gap** /ɡæp/ noun [C]
SEE ALSO: **gender pay gap, trade ~, wage ~**

1 a difference that separates two people, groups or things: The gap **between** men's and women's pay has narrowed. ◇ The country is closing the technology gap **with** (= between it and) its economic rivals.
○ to **bridge/close/narrow** a gap • a gap **grows/ narrows/opens/widens** • a **big/growing/small/ wide/widening** gap
2 a space where sth is missing: They took a $1 million loan to plug the gap in their finances. ◇ We need to fill the gaps in our top management. ◇ a €1.5 billion financing gap
○ a **big/crucial/major/significant** gap • to **bridge/ close/fill/plug** a gap
3 an area of business in which few or no companies operate but where profits could be made: We saw a **gap in the market** for low-cost pensions. ◇ They aim to fill the gap left by the large manufacturers that moved overseas. → NICHE
○ to **fill/identify/leave/see** a gap

'gap a,nalysis *noun* [C,U]
(*Marketing*) a comparison between the products, skills, etc. that are available and what is needed, used to decide what products, skills, etc. to develop: *Gap analysis can help the retailer to re-evaluate their product range.*

garbage /ˈɡɑːbɪdʒ; *AmE* ˈɡɑːrb-/ *noun*
IDM garbage ,in, garbage 'out (*abbr* **GIGO**) (*IT*) used to express the idea that if wrong or poor quality data is put into a computer, wrong or poor quality data will come out of it

'gardening leave (*also* **'garden leave**) *noun* [U] (*both BrE*)
(*HR*) a period when an employee, especially a senior person, who is going to leave a company is not allowed to work but is sent home on full pay, so that they will not be able to compete with the company or pass important information to a competitor: *She has been put* **on** *gardening leave until the end of her contract.*

garnish /ˈɡɑːnɪʃ; *AmE* ˈɡɑːrnɪʃ/ (*also* **,garni'shee**) *verb* [+ obj]
(*Law*) to take away part of sb's income or money and pay it to a person or an organization that they owe money to: *He agreed to pay off his debt by having his wages garnished.* ▶ **'garnishment** *noun* [U,C]: *He paid the debt in cash to avoid garnishment.* ◇ *wage garnishments*

garnishee /,ɡɑːnɪˈʃiː; *AmE* ,ɡɑːrn-/ *noun, verb* (*Law*)
● *noun* [C]
a company, bank, etc. that is ordered by a court to keep or to GARNISH sb's income or money
● *verb* [+ obj] (**garnishees, garnisheeing, garnisheed**)
1 to make sb a **garnishee**
2 = GARNISH

gas /ɡæs/ *noun* (*plural* **gases** *or* **gasses** *less frequent*)

SEE ALSO: natural gas

1 [C,U] any substance like air that is neither a solid nor a liquid: *CFC gases* ◇ *The pipeline could carry up to 700 billion cubic feet of gas a year.*
2 [U] a particular type of **gas** or mixture of **gases** used as fuel for heating, cooking, etc: *a gas cooker/furnace* ◇ *a gas-fired power station*

gate /ɡeɪt/ *noun* [C]

SEE ALSO: factory gate, stage-gate

the door or area at an airport, a bus station, etc. where passengers leave or arrive: *a departure gate* ◇ *The flight to Jakarta is now boarding at gate 12.*

gatefold /ˈɡeɪtfəʊld; *AmE* -foʊld/ *noun* [C,U]
an extra large page in a book, magazine, etc. that is folded to be the same size as the other pages so that you open it out to look at it; a sheet of paper that is folded from left and right to make three or more pages: *an advertising gatefold*

gatefold

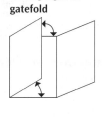

gatekeeper /ˈɡeɪtkiːpə(r)/ *noun* [C]
a person in an organization who controls access to information, goods or services, or to the people in the organization who make the important decisions: *He told me you've got to get past the gatekeeper to the decision-maker before you can make a sale.*

gateway /ˈɡeɪtweɪ/ *noun*
1 [C, usually sing.] a place through which you can go to reach another larger place: *The port is an important gateway* **to/into** *southern Africa.*

---

2 [C, usually sing.] a means of getting or achieving sth: *A good education is the gateway* **to** *success.*
3 (*IT*) [C] a device that is used to connect two computer networks together, especially a connection to the Internet

gauge (*AmE spelling also* **gage**) /ɡeɪdʒ/ *noun, verb*
● *noun* [C]
1 [usually sing.] a fact or an event that can be used to estimate or judge sth: *The retail sector is closely watched as a key gauge of consumer spending.* ◇ *Question-and-answer interviews may not be a good gauge of a candidate's abilities.*
2 a system that is used to calculate or measure the level, size, etc. of sth: *the consumer price index, the main US inflation gauge*
3 (*often used in compounds*) an instrument for measuring the amount or level of sth: *a fuel/petrol/temperature gauge*
● *verb* [+ obj]
1 to estimate or measure the level, size, etc. of sth: *We rely on previous sales figures to gauge demand.* ◇ *gauging the strength of the economy*
2 to make a judgement about sth/sth: *It's too early to gauge* **whether** *the scheme was a success.*
3 (*Technical*) to measure sth accurately using a special instrument: *precision instruments that can gauge the diameter to a fraction of a millimetre*

gazelle /ɡəˈzel/ *noun* [C] (*informal*)
a way of referring to a company that is growing very quickly → ELEPHANT, MOUSE

gazette /ɡəˈzet/ *noun* [C]
1 a newspaper or magazine published by an organization, a government, etc. containing official notices and information: *a stock-exchange gazette*
2 **Gazette** used in the titles of some newspapers: *the Montreal Gazette*

gazump /ɡəˈzʌmp/ *verb* [+ obj] (*BrE*)
(*Property*) (*usually* **be gazumped**) when sb who has made an offer to pay a particular price for sth, and who has had this offer accepted, is **gazumped**, their offer is no longer accepted by the seller, because sb else has made a higher offer: *The merger failed when their bid was gazumped by a larger US firm.* ▶ **gazumping** /ɡəˈzʌmpɪŋ/ *noun* [U]

GB (*also spelled* **Gb**) /,dʒiː ˈbiː/ = GIGABYTE

★ **GDP** /,dʒiː diː ˈpiː/ *abbr*
(*Economics*) **gross domestic product** the total value of all the goods and services produced by a country in one year: *Tourism contributes about 5% of GDP.* ◇ *GDP grew by 0.5 per cent in the fourth quarter.*

gear /ɡɪə(r)/; *AmE* ɡɪr/ *verb, noun*
● *verb* [+ obj]
gear sth for/to/towards sth (*usually* **be geared**) to make, change or prepare sth so that it is suitable for a particular purpose or for particular people: *The magazine is geared* **towards** *women over 35.* ◇ *The economy is now geared* **to** *growth.*
PHRV **'gear sth/yourself for sth** to make sth/yourself ready for sth: *The company is gearing itself for future success.* **'gear sth/yourself to sth** to depend on sth; to be connected with sth: *Salary adjustments are geared to the cost of living.* ◇ *Life assurance companies are heavily geared to stock market performance.* **,gear 'up (for/to sth)**; **,gear sb/sth 'up (for/to sth)** to prepare yourself/sb/sth to do sth: *The country is gearing up for elections.*
● *noun*
1 [U] (*informal*) a piece of equipment or a system: *computer/networking/telecom gear*
2 [U] equipment or clothing used for a particular purpose: *sports/protective gear* ◇ *They carry all their gear (files, phones and laptops) to a new desk every day.*

3 (*informal*) [U,C] the speed at which sth takes place; the effort involved in doing sth (*BrE*): *Sales growth has moved into top gear.* ◇ (*AmE*) *The tax-cut plans are shifting into high gear.*
IDM **get, kick, swing, etc. into 'gear; get, kick, etc. sth into 'gear** to start working, or to start sth working, in an efficient way: *If you fill in the form, within 24 hours the service will kick into gear.*

geared /gɪəd; *AmE* gɪrd/ *adjective* (*BrE*)
(*Finance*)
1 (about a company or an organization) using borrowed money in order to operate, in addition to money from shareholders: *The firm is about 88% geared.* ◇ *The company is highly geared, with borrowings of €1.5 million compared with physical assets of €3 million.*
2 (about an investment) using borrowed money: *a geared investment*
→ LEVERAGED

gearing /'gɪərɪŋ; *AmE* 'gɪrɪŋ/ (*also* **'capital ,gearing, 'equity ,gearing**) (*all especially BrE*) *noun* [U]
(*Finance*) the relationship between the amount of money that a company owes (**debt**) and the value of its shares (**equity**): *There is concern about the company's high gearing* (= it has borrowed a large amount compared to the value of its shares). ◇ *It is important for the company to maintain a low gearing ratio* (= to borrow a small amount compared to the value of its shares). ◇ *The group hopes to reduce gearing from 121 per cent to a more manageable 100 per cent.* **SYN** DEBT-EQUITY RATIO, LEVERAGE

gender /'dʒendə(r)/ *noun* [U]
the fact of being male or female: *Employers are not allowed to discriminate on the basis of gender.*

'gender ,bias *noun* [U; C, usually sing.]
(*HR*) the situation where men and women are not treated in the same way, often in a way that is unfair to women: *evidence of gender bias in the ICT sector* ▶ **'gender-,biased** (*also spelled* ~ **biassed**) *adjective*: *The construction industry is no longer a gender-biased profession.*

,gender 'pay gap *noun* [sing.]
(*HR*) the difference in the average amount of money that men and women earn: *The increases paid to the highest-earning men have widened the gender pay gap.*

general /'dʒenrəl/ *adjective*

SEE ALSO: **attorney general, director general**

1 used in some job titles to indicate that the person is the head of the organization or business, or part of it: *She is the general director for human resources.* ◇ *the director general of the World Trade Organization*
2 not limited to one thing, aspect, subject, etc: *Sales of general merchandise, including clothing, shoes and gifts, went up 10.4%.*

,general con'tractor *noun* [C] (*especially AmE*)
(*Property*) a person or company that takes responsibility for building sth, such as an office, a factory, etc. and hires other businesses (**subcontractors**) to do the work

,general 'counsel *noun* [U,C] (*especially AmE*)
(*Law*) an organization's senior lawyer, who usually works as an employee of the organization: *She became general counsel of Lotus in 1996.*
→ COUNSEL (2)

,general 'creditor *noun* [C] (*especially AmE*)
(*Law*) a person, company, etc. that lends money to sb without an agreement that they will receive some of the borrower's assets if the borrower does not pay back the money → SECURED (2), UNSECURED (2)

,general ex'penses *noun* [pl.]
(*Accounting*) money that is spent on managing and organizing a business rather than on any one activity such as producing goods, selling services, etc: *We have cut costs by lowering our general expenses.* ◇ *Administrative and general expenses are rising.*

,general in'surance *noun* [U]
insurance that you buy to protect any kind of property or goods: *The company provides both life and general insurance.* ▶ **,general in'surer** *noun* [C]

generalist /'dʒenrəlɪst/ *noun* [C]
a person who has knowledge of several different subjects or activities; a business that is involved in a range of activities, investments, etc: *We have one technician in the team and the rest of us are generalists.* ◇ *generalist knowledge/training* ◇ *generalist firms* → SPECIALIST

,general 'ledger (*also* **,nominal 'ledger**) *noun* [C]
(*Accounting*) a set of financial accounts in which a company records all the amounts it pays, receives, etc: *The sales are first recorded in a journal and then posted to* (= written in) *a general ledger.*

'Generally Ac'cepted Ac'counting ,Principles *noun* [pl.] (*abbr* GAAP)
(*Accounting*) in the US, a set of rules and principles that accountants must follow when keeping financial records and preparing financial reports: *The financial statements were prepared in accordance with GAAP.*

,general 'manager *noun* [C]
a person who is responsible for running a business, or part of it, on a daily basis: *She is general manager of marketing and advertising.* ◇ *assistant general manager for supply-chain planning*

,general 'meeting *noun* [C]

SEE ALSO: **annual general meeting, extraordinary general meeting**

(*Law*) a meeting of the shareholders of a company, at which important decisions about the company are made: *The company will be holding an emergency general meeting for shareholders to vote on the merger.*

,general 'offer *noun* [C]
(*Finance*) an offer to buy all the shares in a company: *The law requires a shareholder to make a general offer if their shareholding goes above 30%.*

,general 'partner *noun* [C]
a member of a business PARTNERSHIP who shares its profits and can be made to pay all its debts if it fails → LIMITED PARTNER at LIMITED PARTNERSHIP

,general 'partnership *noun* [C] (*especially AmE*)
a type of business **partnership** in which members share profits and any member can be made to pay all the debts if the business fails See note at COMPANY

,general 'practice *noun* [U,C] (*especially AmE*)
(*Law*) the work of a lawyer who deals with all kinds of legal cases and who is not a specialist in one particular area of law; the place where a lawyer like this works

the ,general 'public *noun* [sing. with sing./pl. verb]
ordinary people who are not members of a particular group or organization: *The general public has/have a right to know about the safety of food.*

,general 'retailer *noun* [C]
(*Commerce*) a shop/store, or a group of shops/stores, that sells a wide variety of goods

,general 'store *noun* [C] (*BrE also* **,general 'stores** [pl.])
a shop/store that sells a wide variety of goods,

especially one in a small town or village: *She runs the post office and general store.*

,general 'strike *noun* [C]
a period of time when most of the employees in a country stop working because of a disagreement over pay or conditions: *Union leaders called a general strike over rises in fuel prices.*

,general 'union *noun* [C]
(*HR*) especially in the UK, a union that organizes workers from different industries and jobs

★ generate /'dʒenəreɪt/ *verb* [+ obj]
1 to produce or create sth: *to generate cash/cost savings/income* ◇ *The proposal has generated a lot of interest.* ◇ *Around 80% of our sales are generated by 30 stores.*
2 to produce energy, especially electricity: *to generate electricity/power* ◇ *a generating plant/station*

generation /,dʒenə'reɪʃn/ *noun*

SEE ALSO: **cash generation, first-~, next-~, second-~, third-~**

1 [C, usually sing.] a stage in the development of a product or system, usually a technical one: *the latest generation of handheld computers*
2 [U] the production of sth: *They are focusing on the generation of free cash flow.* ◇ *methods of income generation*
3 [U] the production of energy, especially electricity: *the generation of electricity*

,Generation 'X *noun* [U]
the group of people who were born between the early 1960s and the middle of the 1970s, who are often thought to lack a sense of direction in life and not feel an important part of society: *We wanted to associate the brand with things that would appeal to Generation X.* ▶ **Generation Xer** /- 'eksə(r)/ *noun* [C] → BABY BOOMER

generative /'dʒenərətɪv/ *adjective*
that can produce sth: *The company is well run and strongly cash generative.*

generator /'dʒenəreɪtə(r)/ *noun* [C]
1 a machine or series of machines for producing electricity: *a nuclear/wind generator* (= one that uses nuclear/wind power to produce electricity)
2 a person, company, product, etc. that produces or creates sth: *the role of small companies as generators of jobs* ◇ *Mobile-phone messaging has been a major cash generator for the group.*
3 (*BrE*) a company that produces and sells electricity: *the UK's major electricity generator*

generic /dʒə'nerɪk/ *adjective, noun*
• *adjective*
1 (about products, especially drugs) produced as a standard type of product, that does not have a brand name or is not protected by a TRADEMARK: *generic copies of patented drugs* ◇ *Seven of their drugs now face generic competition.*
2 typical of or connected with a whole group of things; not specific: *A name like 'service provider' is too generic to trademark.* ◇ *They argued that 'feta' is a generic term and should not be reserved for use by Greek producers.*
• *noun* (*also* ge,neric 'drug) [C]
a drug that is sold with a name that is not protected by a TRADEMARK: *The drug went off patent and is now available as a cheap generic.* ◇ *generic makers/manufacturers/competitors*

ge,netically 'modified = GM (1)

ge,netic discrimi'nation *noun* [U]
unfair treatment of people because they are likely to develop a particular disease that their parents or other members of their family have: *laws to prevent genetic discrimination in health insurance*

ge,netic ,engi'neering *noun* [U]
the science of changing how a living creature or plant develops by changing the information in its cells

ge,netic modifi'cation = GM (1)

,gentleman's a'greement (*also* ,gentlemen's a'greement) *noun* [C]
an informal agreement between people who trust each other, which is not written down and does not have legal status

get /get/ *verb* [+ obj] (**getting, got, got** /gɒt/; *AmE* gɑːt/) (*not used in the passive*) HELP In spoken American English the past participle **gotten** is almost always used.
1 to receive sth: *She gets* (= earns) *€50 000 a year.* ◇ *We got more than a hundred responses to the questionnaire.*
2 to obtain sth: *He just got a new job.* ◇ *You can get the basic model for $100.*
3 to obtain or receive an amount of money by selling sth: *We got a good price for the van.*
4 to buy sth, for example a newspaper or magazine, regularly: *Which newspaper do you get?* → idiom at ARREARS
PHR V **,get a'cross (to sb)**; **,get sth a'cross (to sb)** to be communicated or understood; to succeed in communicating sth: *He's not very good at getting his ideas across.* **,get a'head (of sb)** to make progress (further than others have done): *She wants to get ahead in her career.* **,get 'back to sb** to speak or write to sb again later, especially in order to give a reply: *I'll find out the price and get back to you.* **,get be'hind (with sth)** to fail to make enough progress or to produce sth at the right time: *We're getting behind with the project.* ◇ *She got behind with her loan repayments.* **,get 'by (on/in/with sth)** to manage to live or do a particular thing using the money, knowledge, equipment, etc. that you have: *How does she get by on such a small salary?* **,get 'down to sth** to begin to do sth; to give serious attention to sth: *Let's get down to business.* **,get 'into sth** to start a career in a particular profession: *How did you get into programming?* **,get 'off**; **,get 'off sth** to leave work with permission: *What time do you get off* (work) *on Friday?* **,get 'on to sb (about sth)** to contact sb by telephone, letter or email: *The money should have been paid yesterday; I'll get on to our accounts department.* **,get 'on with sth** used to talk or ask about how well or fast sb is doing a task: *I'm not getting on very fast with this job.* **,get 'out (of sth)** to stop being involved in sth; to escape a difficult situation: *We wanted to make a quick profit and then get out* (= of the market, deal, etc.). **,get sth 'out** to produce or publish sth: *We are determined to get the new model out by the end of the year.* **,get 'through sth** to manage to do or complete sth: *Let's start the meeting—there's a lot to get through.* **,get 'through (sth)**; **,get sth 'through (sth)** to be officially accepted; to make sth be officially accepted: *The firm will still need to get the drug through the US approval process.* **,get 'through (to sb)** to make contact with sb by telephone: *I couldn't get through on the number you gave me.* **,get 'through to sb** to make sb understand or accept what you say, especially when you are trying to help them: *Her views have finally got through to the directors.*

'get-out clause *noun* [C, usually sing.] (*BrE*)
a way of avoiding sth, especially a responsibility or duty: *a get-out clause in the contract* → ESCAPE CLAUSE

giant /'dʒaɪənt/ *noun, adjective*
• *noun* [C]
a very large and powerful organization: *a banking/*

oil/retail/software giant ◇ *There is room in the PC market for two or three giants.*

● *adjective* [only before noun]
very large; much larger or more important than similar things usually are: *a giant poster* ◇ *services offered by giant banks* ◇ *Three giant stores have opened in the area.*

'giant-sized (*also* **'giant-size**) *adjective* [usually before noun]
(*Commerce*) used to describe sth that you buy that is very large or the largest you can get: *a giant-size box of tissues*

GIF™ (*also spelled* **gif**) /gɪf/ *abbr*
(*IT*) **Graphic Interchange Format** (*used as a countable noun*) a type of computer file that contains images and is used a lot on the Internet: *Send it as a GIF.* ◇ *animated gifs*

gift /gɪft/ *noun, verb*
● *noun* [C]

─────────────────────────
SEE ALSO: **business gift, free gift**
─────────────────────────

1 a thing, an amount of money, etc. that you give to sb: *We are not allowed to accept gifts from clients.* ◇ *Thank you for your generous gift.*
2 (*Law*) property or money that is given to sb and recognized as a present in law: *She **made a gift of** her property to charity.*
3 (*informal*) [usually sing.] a thing that is very easy to do or cheap to buy: *At €17 a share, this stock is a gift.*
● *verb* [+ obj]
to give money or property to sb, especially in order to help them financially: *The government had gifted the company more than $1 billion in loans and support.*

'gift card *noun* [C]
1 a small plastic card that is worth a particular amount of money and that can be used to buy goods in a particular shop/store up to that amount: *Many retailers now issue wallet-sized gift cards rather than paper certificates.* → GIFT VOUCHER
2 a piece of stiff paper that is folded in the middle and has a picture on the front of it, used for sending sb a GIFT VOUCHER

'gift cer,tificate = GIFT VOUCHER

'gift ,coupon = GIFT VOUCHER

'gift pack *noun* [C]
a small attractive container with several products inside, usually sold to be given to people as presents: *We also sell gift packs containing a selection of beauty products.*

'gift shop (*also* **'gift store**, *especially in AmE*) *noun* [C]
a shop/store that sells small goods that are suitable for giving as presents

'gift tax *noun* [U,C]
tax that is charged on gifts made by people who are still alive that are worth more than a particular amount: *Shares given to children may be subject to gift tax.* → ESTATE TAX, INHERITANCE TAX

'gift ,voucher (*also* **'gift ,token**, **'gift ,coupon**) (*all especially BrE*) (*AmE usually* **'gift cer,tificate**) *noun* [C]
a piece of paper that is worth a particular amount of money and that can be exchanged for goods in a particular shop/store: *Join today and receive a free €20 gift voucher.* ◇ *to **redeem** a gift voucher* (= to exchange it for goods)

'gift wrap *noun* [U]
attractive coloured or patterned paper used for wrapping presents in ▶ **'gift-wrap** *verb* [+ obj] (-**pp**-) (*often* **be gift-wrapped**): *Would you like the*

chocolates gift-wrapped? ◇ *The store offers a gift-wrapping service.*

gig /gɪg/ *noun* [C]
1 (*IT, informal*) = GIGABYTE
2 (*informal*) (*AmE*) a temporary job or task: *She is making a career out of different projects and consulting gigs.* ◇ *Time to get a new gig.*

gigabyte /'gɪgəbaɪt/ (*also* **gig**, *informal*) *noun* [C] (*abbr* **GB**)
(*IT*) a unit of computer memory, equal to 2^{30} (or about a billion) BYTES: *an 80 gigabyte hard drive*

GIGO /'gaɪgəʊ; *AmE* -goʊ/ = GARBAGE IN, GARBAGE OUT at GARBAGE

gilt /gɪlt/ *noun* [C, usually pl.]
(*Finance*) bonds paying a fixed amount of interest that are sold by the British government to obtain funds: *It is likely that the government will issue new gilts to finance its spending plans.* ◇ *The yield on the 10-year gilt has fallen to 4.2 per cent.* ◇ *long-dated/ short-dated gilts* (= that pay interest over a long/ short period of time)
➋ *to **buy/issue/sell/trade (in)** gilts*

,gilt-'edged *adjective*
(*Finance*)
1 [usually before noun] (used especially about investments) very safe: *The country has raised its credit rating to a gilt-edged AAA.* ◇ *These investments enjoy a gilt-edged reputation.*
2 [only before noun] connected with GILTS: *gilt-edged securities/stock* ◇ *the gilt-edged market*

gimmick /'gɪmɪk/ *noun* [C]
an unusual trick or unnecessary device that is intended to attract attention or to persuade people to buy sth: *The free gift is just a gimmick to get you to buy the magazine.* ◇ *It's a competitive business and you've got to have a gimmick.*
➋ *to **have/rely on/use** gimmicks* ● *a **marketing/ promotional/sales** gimmick*
▶ **gimmicky** /'gɪmɪki/ *adjective*: *a gimmicky title*

Ginnie Mae™ /,dʒɪni 'meɪ/ *noun* (*AmE*)
(*Finance*)
1 [sing.] (*abbr* **GNMA**) **Government National Mortgage Association** a US government organization that is responsible for helping to provide MORTGAGES (= loans to buy homes) for people with low incomes
2 [C, usually pl.] the bonds that are issued by **Ginnie Mae**
→ FANNIE MAE, FREDDIE MAC

giro /'dʒaɪrəʊ; *AmE* -roʊ/ *noun* [U,C] (*plural* **giros**)
a system in which money can be moved from one bank or post office account to another by a central computer: *to pay by giro* ◇ *giro banking* ◇ *a giro credit/payment/transfer*

GIS /,dʒiː aɪ 'es/ *abbr*
(*IT*) **geographical information system** software and other tools that are used to collect and analyse information about the earth's surface, physical features, divisions, products, population, etc.

gismo = GIZMO

giveaway /'gɪvəweɪ/ *noun, adjective*
● *noun* [C]
something that a company or an organization gives free, usually with sth else that is for sale; an occasion when things are given in this way: *There's a giveaway with our magazine next month—a free CD!* ◇ *the airline's latest ticket giveaway*
● *adjective* [only before noun] (*informal*)
(about prices) very low: *They were offering giveaway prices on furniture.*

giveback /'gɪvbæk/ *noun* [C,U] (*AmE*)
(*HR*) a situation in which employees agree to accept lower wages or fewer benefits than had been agreed, usually in return for new benefits later:

Workers were asked for givebacks on the wage increases they had won. ◇ *The airline is negotiating a giveback plan with its unions.*

gizmo (*also spelled* **gismo**) /'gɪzməʊ; *AmE* -moʊ/ *noun* [C] (*plural* **gizmos**) (*informal*)
a general word for a small piece of equipment, often one that does sth in a new and clever way: *a new electronic gizmo for storing telephone numbers*

'glamour ˌstock (*AmE spelling* **glamor ~**) *noun* [C]
(*Stock Exchange*) a company whose shares become very popular with investors at a particular time: *the glamour stocks of the telecoms sector*

ˌglass 'ceiling *noun* [sing.]
(*HR*) the imaginary barrier that stops women, or other groups, from getting the best jobs in a company, etc. although there are no official rules to prevent them from getting these jobs: *the first woman to break through the glass ceiling in engineering*

ˌglass 'wall *noun* [C]
(*HR*) the imaginary barrier that stops women, or other groups, from being employed outside particular industries or jobs, although there are no official rules to prevent this: *Women at the radio station were confined to office jobs—the glass wall— and to lower administrative levels—the glass ceiling.*

glitch /glɪtʃ/ *noun* [C] (*informal*)
a small problem or fault that stops sth working successfully: **Technical** *glitches delayed the launch of the service.*

★ **global** /'gləʊbl; *AmE* 'gloʊbl/ *adjective*
1 [usually before noun] covering or affecting the whole world: *Global demand for oil is increasing.* ◇ *a global network of accounting firms* ◇ *We are trying to build a global brand* (= that will be sold everywhere). ◇ *In the last few years the business has* **gone global** (= started operating in different countries across the world).
2 considering or including all parts of sth: *We need to take a more global approach to the problem.* ◇ *They sent a global email to all staff.*
▶ **globally** /'gləʊbəli; *AmE* 'gloʊb-/ *adverb*: *We have increased our market share both domestically and globally.* ◇ *The group employs 50 000 staff globally.*

'global bond = EUROBOND

★ **globalization**, **-isation** /ˌgləʊbəlaɪ'zeɪʃn; *AmE* ˌgloʊbələ'z-/ *noun* [U]
1 the process by which businesses and organizations grow and start to operate in countries all over the world, which has been made easier by new technology and political developments: *Globalization may not be a viable strategy for most US steelmakers.* ◇ *As a result of the globalization of business, a broad range of skills will now be needed for professional success.*
2 the fact that different cultures and economic systems around the world are becoming connected with and similar to each other because of the influence of large MULTINATIONAL companies and of improved communication: *the globalization of world markets*

★ **globalize**, **-ise** /'gləʊbəlaɪz; *AmE* 'gloʊ-/ *verb* [+ obj *or* no obj]
if something, for example a business, **globalizes** or **is globalized**, it operates all around the world: *If companies hope to grow, then their only choice is to globalize.* ◇ *Our advertising will globalize the brand so it is recognized in every country.* ▶ **'globalized**, **-ised** *adjective*: *As the economy becomes more globalized, individual governments have less power.* ◇ *They run a globalized operation with factories all round the world.*

ˌglobal 'market *noun* [C]
the world population who might buy goods: *They are building several new factories so they can supply the global market with their products.*

ˌglobal 'marketing *noun* [U]
presenting, advertising and selling a product all over the world: *A strong brand image can be the key to global marketing success.*

ˌglobal 'village *noun* [sing.]
the whole world, looked at as a single community that is connected by electronic communication systems: *Television helped to create a global village.*

globe /gləʊb; *AmE* gloʊb/ *noun* [sing.]
the world, especially when considered as a commercial unit: *The bank operates across the globe.* ◇ *From a computer, anyone can now do business with companies on the other side of the globe.*

globetrotting /'gləʊbtrɒtɪŋ; *AmE* 'gloʊbtrɑ:tɪŋ/ *adjective* (*informal*)
travelling often to many different places around the world: *The sales job is a globetrotting post as we have customers in several countries.* ▶ **'globetrotter** *noun* [C] **'globetrotting** *noun* [U]

glocalization, **-isation** /ˌgləʊkəlaɪ'zeɪʃn; *AmE* ˌgloʊkələ'z-/ *noun* [U]
(*Marketing*) a strategy where a company is operating all round the world but adapts its products or services and its manufacturing methods to make them suitable for local conditions **NOTE** This word is formed from the words 'globalization' and 'local'.

gloom /glu:m/ *noun* [U; sing.]
a feeling that things will not get better; a situation without much hope: *Lower interest rates will lift the economic gloom as companies recover.* ◇ *It is not all* **doom and gloom** *for shareholders as sales improved slightly last month.* → PESSIMISM

gloomy /'glu:mi/ *adjective* (**gloomier**, **gloomiest**)
without much hope of success for the future: *Retail stores said sales were down in January and the outlook was gloomy as customers were staying at home.* → BUOYANT

glut /glʌt/ *noun, verb*
● *noun* [C, usually sing.]
a situation where there is a greater supply of sth than there is demand: *Prices fell because of a glut of steel on world markets.* ◇ *a global banana glut*
SYN SURPLUS **OPP** SHORTAGE → DEARTH
O *an* **inventory/supply** *glut*
● *verb* [+ obj] (**-tt-**)
(*usually* **be glutted**) to supply or provide sth, usually a market, with too much of sth: *The market was glutted* **with** *small cars so production was shut down.* **SYN** SATURATE

GM /ˌdʒi: 'em/ *abbr*
1 (*Technical*) **genetically modified, genetic modification** (about food, animals, etc.) having had units in their cells deliberately changed to make them able to resist insects or disease; the process of doing this: *GM crops/food*
2 (*Accounting*) = GROSS MARGIN

GmbH /ˌdʒi: em bi: 'eɪtʃ/ *abbr* (*only used in written English*)
used in the names of some companies in German-speaking countries: *Mertz GmbH* See note at LTD

GNMA /ˌdʒi: en em 'eɪ/ = GINNIE MAE (1)

Gnomes of Zurich /ˌnəʊmz əv 'zjʊərɪk; 'zʊərɪk; *AmE* ˌnoʊmz əv 'zʊrɪk/ *noun* [pl.]
Swiss BANKERS who control foreign money **NOTE** This phrase is often used to suggest that these bankers are powerful in a secret way. You can also refer to bankers in any city who control foreign money as **gnomes**: *the gnomes of Brussels.*

GNP /ˌdʒiː en 'piː/ abbr
(Economics) **gross national product** the total value of all the goods and services produced by a country in a particular period including the income from investments in foreign countries: Today farming produces only about 2–4% of GNP. → GDP

go /ɡəʊ; AmE ɡoʊ/ verb, noun
● verb [no obj] (**goes** /ɡəʊz; AmE ɡoʊz/ **went** /went/ **gone** /ɡɒn; AmE ɡɔːn; ɡɑːn/)
1 when money **goes**, it is spent or used for sth: 5% of the profits went **on** repairs. ◇ I don't know where the money goes!
2 to be sold: The firm went **to** an Italian group for €400 m.
3 (about jobs, opportunities, etc.) to disappear or no longer exist: If the merger happens then 250 jobs will go.
4 (informal) **be going** to be available: There just aren't any jobs going in this area.
5 (about a machine, an economy, etc.) to work or function properly: They're trying to get the economy going again.
6 to leave a place or an organization: The current chief executive has finally agreed to go (= to leave his job).
7 (usually used with an adjective) to become different in a particular way: to go global/national ◇ to go bankrupt ◇ We've gone **from** being a loss-maker to being a money-maker.
IDM **NOTE** Most idioms containing **go** are at the entries for the nouns, verbs or adjectives in the idioms, for example **go from strength to strength** is at **strength**.
go all 'out for sth; **go all out to 'do sth** to make a very great effort to get sth or do sth: We continue to go all out to meet our own higher expectations. **go it a'lone** to do sth without help from anyone: Andrew decided to go it alone and start his own business. **go 'plural** (informal) to leave an important job that you do for all the hours of the working week and take several less important jobs for shorter hours → DOWNSHIFT **go through the 'roof** (about prices, etc.) to rise or increase very quickly: House prices here have gone through the roof.
PHR V **go 'after sb/sth** to try to get sb/sth: We're both going after the same job. **go a'head** to happen; to be done: The building of the new offices will go ahead as planned. **SYN** PROCEED → GO-AHEAD **go a'head (with sth)** to begin to do sth, especially when sb has given permission or has expressed doubts or opposition: 'May I start now?' 'Yes, go ahead.' **go a'long with sb/sth** to agree with sb/sth: I do not go along with his views on the EU. **go 'down 1** to become lower or smaller: The price of oil is going down. ◇ Oil is going down in price. See note at INCREASE **2** to stop working temporarily: The system is going down in ten minutes. → CRASH **'go for sth 1** to try hard to get or achieve sth: It sounds a great idea. Go for it! **2** to choose sth; to be persuaded that sth is a good idea: Shoppers are going for the cheap options. **go 'forward (with sth)** to continue with a plan, project, etc: Prices will rise if either of the deals goes forward. **go 'in with sb** (informal) to join sb in starting a business: My brothers are opening a garage and they want me to go in with them. **go 'into sth 1** to start working in a particular field or for a particular organization, especially in order to have a career in it: After graduating, she went into corporate law. **2** to examine sth carefully: We need to go into the question of costs. **3** (about money, time, effort, etc.) to be spent on sth or used to do sth: A lot of money has gone into the project. **go 'on to sth** to pass from one item to the next: Let's go on to the next item on the agenda. **go 'over sth** to examine or check sth carefully: We went over the contract several times in case we had forgotten

something. **go 'through** if a law, contract, etc. goes through, it is officially accepted or completed: If both deals go through, Citibank would become the single largest shareholder. **go 'through sth 1** to look at or examine sth carefully, especially in order to find sth: She went through the company's accounts, looking for evidence of fraud. **2** to perform a series of actions; to follow a method or procedure: All new staff go through an orientation program. **3** to experience or suffer sth: We are going through an economic downturn. **go 'through with sth** to do what is necessary to complete a course of action, especially one that is difficult or unpleasant: They decided not to go through with the planned merger. **'go to sb/sth** to be given to sb/sth: All the proceeds from the concert (= the money received from selling tickets, etc.) will go to charity. **'go towards sth** to be used as part of the payment for sth: The money will go towards developing the business. **go 'under** (informal) to become BANKRUPT (= be unable to pay what you owe): The firm will go under unless business improves. See note at BANKRUPT **go 'up 1** to become higher or larger: The price of cigarettes is going up. ◇ Cigarettes are going up in price. See note at INCREASE **2** to be built: New offices buildings are going up everywhere. **'go with sth 1** to be included with or as part of sth: A car goes with the job. **2** to accept or choose sth, for example a plan or an offer: You're offering $5 000? I think we can go with that.
● noun [C] (plural **goes** /ɡəʊz/)

SEE ALSO: go-go, pay-as-you-~, stop-~

IDM **be a 'go** (AmE) (informal) to be planned and possible or allowed: We're still not sure if the project is a go. **make a 'go of sth** (informal) to be successful in sth: We've had a few problems, but we're both determined to make a go of this business.

'go-ahead noun, adjective
● noun [sing.]
permission for sb to start doing sth: The project has finally got the go-ahead. ◇ The local council has given the go-ahead **for** the development.
● adjective [usually before noun]
willing to try new ideas, methods, etc. and therefore likely to succeed: a go-ahead company

★ **goal** /ɡəʊl; AmE ɡoʊl/ noun [C]
something that you hope to achieve: The company has set itself some long-term organizational goals. ◇ Our goal is to increase market share this year. ◇ Team members are committed to achieving common goals. ◇ A goal should be thought of as an agreement between a manager and an employee.
SYN OBJECTIVE, TARGET
✪ to **define/establish/set** a goal ♦ to **achieve/meet/ pursue/reach** a goal ♦ your **long-term/short-term/ ultimate** goal ♦ a **measurable/ realistic** goal ♦ a **clear/main/primary/specific** goal ♦ **business/career/financial/profit/strategic** goals

'goal-di,rected (also **'goal-,oriented**) adjective
1 (about a person or a group) working hard because they want to achieve the tasks that have been set: We found that the successful people were self-motivated and goal-directed.
2 (about a plan, an activity, etc.) that aims to achieve particular things: goal-directed training

'goal ,setting noun [U]
(HR) the process of deciding and agreeing on what you will try to achieve: The most important part of goal setting is that the people who have to reach the goals also take part in setting them. ◇ a consultant who assists executive teams with goal setting

'go-be,tween noun [C,U]
a person or an organization that takes messages between one group and another: to act as (a) go-between ◇ Sumitomo, the trading house, was the go-between in the Wal-Mart/Seiyu deal.

godown /'gəʊdaʊn; AmE 'goʊ-/ noun [C]
a word used in India and some other countries to mean a WAREHOUSE (= a building where goods are stored)

gofer (also spelled **gopher**) /'gəʊfə(r); AmE 'goʊ-/ noun [C] (informal)
a person whose job is to do small boring tasks for other people in a company: He's the office gofer who runs errands for us. [SYN] DOGSBODY

'go-,getter noun [C] (informal)
a person who is determined to succeed, especially in business: Older employees have just as much talent as the young go-getters.

'go-go adjective [usually before noun]
1 (about an investment, shares, etc.) expected to make a lot of money quickly: the go-go stock of the hi-tech boom
2 used to describe a period of time when businesses are growing and people are making money fast: the go-go 1990s

,going con'cern noun [C]
1 a business or an activity that is making a profit and is expected to continue: He sold the cafe **as a** going concern.
2 (Accounting) a method of valuing an asset, a project or a business that assumes that the business will continue to operate for a long period of time: the going concern concept

,going 'rate noun [C] **the going rate** (Technical) the usual amount of money paid for goods or services at a particular time: They pay slightly more than the going rate **for** freelance work.

gold /gəʊld; AmE goʊld/ noun [U]
a chemical element. Gold is a yellow substance used for making coins, jewellery, etc. and kept by central banks as part of their FOREIGN EXCHANGE RESERVES: safe investments like gold and bonds
→ BULLION → idiom at STRIKE verb

,golden fare'well = GOLDEN GOODBYE

,golden 'formula noun [sing.]
(HR) in the UK, a rule that says that strikes organized by unions are only legal if they are about matters that are connected with employment rather than about political matters, and that workers involved in legal strikes should not lose their jobs

,golden good'bye (also ,golden fare'well) noun [C]
(HR) a large amount of money given by a company to a senior employee when they are forced to leave their job before they want to: moves to stop companies paying golden goodbyes to get rid of underperforming directors

,golden 'handcuffs noun [pl.]
(HR) a large amount of money and other financial benefits that are given to sb to persuade them to continue working for a company rather than leaving to work for another company: Benefit schemes that become more attractive the longer employees stay with the company act as golden handcuffs tying them to the company. ◇ a golden handcuffs contract/deal

,golden 'handshake (also 'handshake) noun [C]
(HR) a large amount of money given by a company to an employee when they retire or when they are forced to leave their job: The company has asked people over 50 if they would like to leave in return for a golden handshake of a year's pay.

,golden hel'lo noun [C]
(HR) a large amount of money or other financial benefits given by a company to some new employees in order to attract good people

,golden 'parachute noun [C]
(HR, informal) a part of a contract in which a company promises to give a large sum of money to a very senior employee if they have to leave their job, for example if the company is bought by another company; the money that is given

,golden 'share noun [C] (BrE)
a share in a company that gives the holder, usually the government, the power to stop any changes to the company that they do not approve of
→ CONTROLLING INTEREST

goldfield /'gəʊldfiːld; AmE 'goʊld-/ noun [C]
an area of land where gold is dug out of the ground

'gold mine noun [C]
1 a place where gold is dug out of the ground
2 a business or an activity that makes a large profit: Air conditioner companies see India as a potential gold mine.

'gold re,serve noun [C, usually pl.]
an amount of gold kept by a country's central bank in order to support the supply of money: plans to sell some of the country's gold reserves

'gold rush noun [C, usually sing.]
a situation in which a new opportunity to make money appears and a lot of people try to take advantage of it: a pioneer of the Internet gold rush

'gold ,standard noun [sing.] (usually **the gold standard**)
1 (Economics) an economic system in which the value of money is based on the value of gold: Britain left the gold standard in 1931.
2 something that is considered to be the best in a particular field and that other similar things are compared to: This system is considered the gold standard for 3-D computer games.

Goliath (also spelled **goliath**) /gə'laɪəθ/ noun [C, usually sing.]
a person or company that is very large or powerful: The company is the Goliath of the computer industry. ◇ a telecoms goliath [NOTE] This comes from **Goliath**, a giant in the Bible who was killed by the boy David with a stone.

gondola /'gɒndələ; AmE 'gɑːn-; gɑːn'dəʊlə/ noun [C]
1 (Commerce) (BrE) a set of shelves in a shop/store or supermarket with goods on all sides—Picture at STORE
2 (Transport) (also **'gondola car**) (both AmE) a long, low open section of a train that is used to transport heavy goods

'gone-a,way noun [C]
(Marketing) people on a company's MAILING LIST (= a list of the names and addresses of people who are regularly sent information, advertising material, etc.), who no longer live at the address on the list; items that are sent to these people: Our lists will be regularly cleaned of gone-aways.
[NOTE] From the words 'gone away' that are written on items of mail that have to be returned to the sender as the person no longer lives at the address.

good /gʊd/ noun [sing.]

SEE ALSO: **economic good**

(Economics) a thing that is made to be used or sold: a graph of the demand for a good against income
→ GOODS → idiom at REPAIR noun

,good 'faith noun [U]

SEE ALSO: **utmost good faith**

the intention to be honest and helpful: a gesture of good faith ◇ They reached a good faith agreement on the value of the business. ◇ *He acted in good faith.* ◇ *Customers buy our product in good faith* (= they trust us). → BAD FAITH, BONA FIDES

★ **goods** /gʊdz/ *noun* [pl.]

SEE ALSO: **brown goods, bulk ~, capital ~, complementary ~, consumer ~, consumption ~, dry ~,** etc.

1 physical things that are produced to be sold, including things that are manufactured or prepared and raw materials: *agricultural/electrical/household/sporting goods* ◇ *a French luxury goods company* ◇ *a rise in the price of basic goods* ◇ *New orders for costly manufactured goods are falling.* ◇ *Customers feel more confident about buying goods and services on the Internet.* ◇ *There is a time lag between invoicing a client and delivery of the goods.*
  ○ *cheap/low-priced/mass-produced* goods ◆ *branded/brand-name/own-label* goods ◆ *to* **make/manufacture/produce** goods ◆ *to* **buy/export/import/sell** goods ◆ *to* **deliver/supply/transport** goods
2 (*BrE*) (*often used before a noun*) things (not people) that are transported by rail, road, ship, etc: *a goods train* ◇ *a heavy goods vehicle* → CARGO, FREIGHT
  ○ *a goods* **train/van/vehicle** ◆ *a goods* **depot/yard**
  IDM **deliver/come up with the 'goods** (*informal*) to do what you have promised to do or what people expect or want you to do: *The company looks good on paper, and its shares could go higher if it delivers the goods.*

,**good-till-'cancelled ,order** (*AmE spelling* **good-til-canceled ~**) *noun* [C] (*abbr* **GTC order**) (*Stock Exchange*) an order to a BROKER to buy or sell shares, FUTURES, etc. at a particular price that remains valid until it is completed or until it is cancelled by the investor

★ **goodwill** /ˌgʊdˈwɪl/ *noun* [U] (*Accounting*) assets that a company has that do not exist physically but are calculated as part of its value, such as a good relationship with its customers, its name, the knowledge and skill of its workers, etc. **NOTE** Only **goodwill** that a company pays for when it buys a business is recorded in the financial accounts: *Goodwill is the amount a buyer pays above a company's assets.* ◇ *Earnings before goodwill amortization and exceptional items rose 32%.*
  ○ *to* **build (up)/keep/lose/value** goodwill ◆ *to* **amortize/write off** goodwill ◆ goodwill **accounting/amortization/impairment** ◆ *a goodwill* **charge/write-down/write-off**

good'will ,payment *noun* [C] an amount of money that a company believes it should pay to sb even though they may not have a legal right to it, for example a payment to a customer who has experienced problems: *Goodwill payments were made by the electricity company to 9 000 customers affected by power cuts.*

gopher = GOFER

,**go-'slow** (*BrE*) (*AmE* '**slowdown**) *noun* [C] (*HR*) a protest that workers make by doing their work more slowly than usual: *Roads were blocked as 200 cab drivers staged a go-slow.* See note at STRIKE
  ○ *to* **resort to/stage/start** *a go-slow* ◆ *to* **be on** *a go-slow*

'**go-to** *adjective* [only before noun] (*informal*) used to refer to the person, place, system, etc. that is the best person, place, etc. to go to if you need help, advice or information: *This is the go-to site for researching companies.*

govern /ˈgʌvn; *AmE* ˈgʌvərn/ *verb*
1 [+ obj *or no obj*] to legally control a country or its people and be responsible for introducing new laws, organizing public services, etc: *The country is governed by elected representatives of the people.* ◇ *the governing party*
2 [+ obj] (*often* **be governed**) to control or influence sb/sth or how sth happens, etc: *Prices are governed by market demand.* ◇ *The company has a new policy governing the use of computers and email in the workplace.*

governance /ˈgʌvənəns; *AmE* -vərn-/ *noun* [U]

SEE ALSO: **corporate governance**

the activity of controlling a company, an organization, or a country; the way in which this is done: *They wish to change the governance of the rail industry.* ◇ *the group's governance structure*

,**government-'backed** *adjective*
1 (*Finance*) used to describe credit, debt, loans, etc. that the government has promised to pay if the borrower is unable to do so: *government-backed bonds/insurance* ◇ *The airline has got about $380 million in government-backed loans.*
2 a plan, project, etc. that receives money and support from the government: *government-backed research*

,**government 'bond** *noun* [C] (*Finance*) a bond that is sold by a government: *Japanese government bond prices rose sharply.* ◇ *The yield on a 10-year government bond is less than 1%.*

,**government se'curity** *noun* [C, usually pl.] (*also* ,**government 'stock** [C,U])
(*Finance*) a bond that is issued (= sold) by a government in order to raise money: *In the bond market, government securities rose sharply.* ◇ *a government securities dealer* → GILT, GILT-EDGED, TREASURY BOND

governor /ˈgʌvənə(r); *AmE* -vərn-/ *noun* [C]
1 a person who is in charge of an institution such as the Central Bank: *the governor of the Bank of England* ◇ *the new Bank of Japan governor*
2 a member of a group of people who are responsible for controlling an institution such as a school, hospital, etc: *a BBC governor*

GPM /ˌdʒiː piː ˈem/ = GROSS PROFIT MARGIN

GPRS /ˌdʒiː piː ɑːr ˈes/ *abbr*
General Packet Radio Service a system that allows you to send and receive information such as emails using a mobile phone/cellphone: *GPRS networks/phones/technology*

gr (*also spelled* **gr.**) = GROSS (1,2)

grace /greɪs/ *noun* [U] extra time that is given to sb to enable them to pay a bill, finish a piece of work, etc: *The banks have given him a month's grace to pay the amount.* ◇ *The seller had allowed a **period of grace** for late payment.* → idiom at FALL *verb*

grade /greɪd/ *noun, verb*
● *noun* [C]

SEE ALSO: **high-grade, investment ~, low-~**

1 the quality of a particular product or material: *All the materials used were of the highest grade.*
2 (*HR*) a level in a system of pay or employment in an organization: *salary grades* (= levels of pay) ◇ *She's still only on a secretarial grade.*
3 (*Finance*) a measurement of how good or safe sth such as an investment is: *The company has been downgraded to non-investment grade.*
  IDM **make the 'grade** to reach the necessary standard; to succeed: *About 10% of trainees fail to make the grade.*
● *verb* [+ obj] (*often* **be graded**) to arrange people or things in groups according to

● *verb* [+ obj] (*often* **be graded**)
to arrange people or things in groups according to their ability, quality, size, etc: *The containers are graded according to size.* ◇ *Employees are constantly graded* **for** *performance.* ◇ *the highest-graded hotel in the area*

grading /ˈɡreɪdɪŋ/ *noun* [U,C]

SEE ALSO: **job grading**

1 the process of examining a product, a company, etc. and giving it a label to show its quality, size, etc: *regulations covering vegetable grading* ◇ *a six-level grading system for corn* ◇ *gradings of companies' creditworthiness*
2 (*HR*) the process of giving a grade to an employee that shows how well they are doing their job; the grade that is given: *There are clear limits on how employers can use pay and grading to reward achievement.* ◇ *She received a grading of 'Excellent'.*

graduated /ˈɡrædʒueɪtɪd/ *adjective*
divided into groups or levels on a scale: *Our income tax is based on a graduated tax scale* (= the more you earn, the higher the rate of tax you pay).

graft /ɡrɑːft; *AmE* ɡræft/ *noun, verb*
● *noun* [U]
1 (*especially AmE*) the use of illegal or unfair methods, especially giving or taking BRIBES, in order to gain advantage in business, etc.; money obtained in this way: *He promised an end to graft and corruption in public life.* ◇ *a multi-million dollar graft scandal*
2 (*BrE*) (*informal*) hard work: *Their success was the result of years of* **hard graft**.
● *verb*
1 [+ obj] **graft sth (onto sth)** to make one idea, system, etc. become part of another one: *The new regulations are being grafted onto the old.*
2 [no obj] (*BrE*) (*informal*) to work hard: *She's been grafting all day.*

grain /ɡreɪn/ *noun* [U]
food crops such as corn and rice: *a record grain harvest of 85 million tons* ◇ *grain imports/exports* ◇ *US grain and livestock futures prices rose yesterday.*

grandfather /ˈɡrænfɑːðə(r)/ *verb* [+ obj] (*AmE*)
(*Law, informal*) **grandfather sb/sth (in)** to give sb official permission not to do sth that is required by a new law, or to continue doing sth that is now illegal: *The new zoning law grandfathered in existing buildings.* ◇ *a grandfathered activity*

'grandfather clause (*also* **'grandfather pro,vision**) *noun* [C] (*also* **'grandfather rights** [pl.]) (*all AmE*)
(*Law, informal*) a part of a new law that allows those who already do the activity that is controlled or made illegal by the new law to continue to do so: *The new law does not allow any retail outlets in this zone but the grandfather clause exempts existing retail outlets.*

'grandfather rights *noun* [pl.] (*AmE*) (*informal*)
1 (*Law*) = GRANDFATHER CLAUSE
2 (*Transport*) the rights of airlines that have operated at an airport for a long time to keep the same times for landing or taking off that they have always had

,grand 'total *noun* [C]
the final total when a number of other totals have been added together: *That makes a grand total of 11 000 dollars.*

grant /ɡrɑːnt; *AmE* ɡrænt/ *verb, noun*
● *verb* [+ obj]
1 **grant sth (to sb/sth)** | **grant (sb) sth** to agree to give sb what they ask for, especially formal or legal permission to do sth: *The bank finally granted the company a loan.* ◇ *The bank finally granted a loan to the company.* ◇ *Local officials grant and revoke*

(= take away) *licences.* ◇ *The plant has not yet been granted permission to operate at full power.*
2 (*Law*) to transfer the legal right to own particular property or a piece of land from one person to another
● *noun*

SEE ALSO: **development grant**

1 [C] an amount of money that is given by the government or by another organization to be used for a particular purpose: *The study was supported by a $70 000 grant from a research group.* ◇ *They were awarded grants* **to** *develop new methods of crop production.*
2 [U,C] the action of formally giving sb sth, or giving them legal permission to do sth

grantee /ɡrɑːnˈtiː; *AmE* ɡrænˈtiː/ *noun* [C]
1 a person who receives an amount of money (a **grant**) to pay for research, a project, etc.
2 (*Law*) a person who receives the right to own a particular property or an area of land
See note at EMPLOYER

grantor /ɡrɑːnˈtɔː(r); *AmE* ɡrænˈt-/ *noun* [C]
1 a person or an organization that gives an amount of money (a **grant**) to sb to pay for research, a project, etc.
2 (*Law*) a person who transfers the right to own a particular property or an area of land to sb
3 (*formal*) a person or an organization that agrees to give sb what they ask for such as permission to do sth: *credit grantors such as credit-card companies and banks*
See note at EMPLOYER

the grapevine /ˈɡreɪpvaɪn/ *noun* [C, usually sing.]
an informal way in which information and news is spread simply by people talking to each other: *I heard* **on** *the grapevine* (= by talking to other people) *that you're leaving.*

WHICH WORD?

graph/chart/diagram/graphic

A **graph** (*BrE* and *AmE*) or **chart** (*especially AmE*) uses lines and regular shapes to illustrate numbers: *This graph shows how sales have been declining steadily.* ◇ *The largest slice of the pie chart represents customers under the age of 25.* **Graphic** is a related adjective: *The guide summarizes the year's results in a graphic format.*

In both *BrE* and *AmE*, a **chart** can also be a list of figures: *Income for the last three years is displayed in the following chart.* **Graph** is not used in this way.

A **diagram** uses lines and symbols to illustrate a concept or system: *The next diagram shows how the responsibilities of the two departments overlap.* ◇ *a wiring diagram*

As a noun, **graphic** [C] is used to mean a diagram or picture, especially one that appears on a computer screen or in a newspaper or book: *We use the same graphic on each page to make the design more consistent.*

★ **graph** /ɡræf; *BrE also* ɡrɑːf/ *noun, verb*
● *noun* [C] (*also* **chart**, *especially in AmE*)

SEE ALSO: **bar graph, broken-line ~, line ~**

a planned drawing, usually consisting of a line or lines, showing how two or more sets of numbers are related to each other: *to plot a graph of price against earnings* ◇ *The graph shows the company's net profits over the past ten years.*

➍ *to draw/plot* a graph ◆ *to show sth in/on* a graph ◆ *a graph shows sth*
● *verb* [+ obj]
to present information on a **graph**: *The computer program uses statistical techniques to graph different financial scenarios.*

★ **graphic** /ˈɡræfɪk/ *adjective, noun*
● *adjective*
1 connected with diagrams or pictures used on a computer screen: *graphic images/software* See note at GRAPH
2 shown in the form of a graph: *graphic information*
3 connected with drawings, printing and design, especially in the production of books, magazines, etc: *a graphic artist* → GRAPHIC DESIGN
● *noun* [C]
a diagram or picture, especially one that appears on a computer screen or in a newspaper or book: *This Java-based graphic fits in the upper right corner of the screen.* → COMPUTER GRAPHICS

graphical /ˈɡræfɪkl/ *adjective*
1 [only before noun] connected with art or computer **graphics**: *The system uses an impressive graphical interface.*
2 in the form of a diagram or graph: *a graphical presentation of results*

graphic deˈsign *noun* [U]
the process of arranging text and pictures in a magazine, an advertisement, etc. in a clear and effective way; the result of this process: *She runs a graphic design and publishing company.* ◇ *poor graphic design* ▸ **graphic deˈsigner** *noun* [C]

graphics /ˈɡræfɪks/ = COMPUTER GRAPHICS

ˈgraphics card *noun* [C]
(*IT*) a device that can be put into a computer to allow the use of video and other images on the screen

graphology /ɡræˈfɒlədʒi; *AmE* -ˈfɑːl-/ *noun* [U]
(*HR*) the study of the way sb writes (their **handwriting**), sometimes used to find out more about a person who has applied for a job

grassroots (*also spelled* **grass roots**) /ˌɡrɑːsˈruːts; *AmE* ˈɡræsruːts/ *noun* [pl.]
the ordinary people in an organization or in society, rather than the leaders or people who usually make the decisions: *Change begins at the grassroots of an organization.* ◇ *a grassroots campaign/initiative/movement* ▸ **ˈgrassroot** *adjective* [only before noun]: *people working at grassroot level*

gratis /ˈɡrætɪs; ˈɡreɪtɪs; ˈɡrɑːtɪs/ *adverb*
done or given without having to be paid for: *She agreed to work gratis (= for no money) for the first few months.* ▸ **ˈgratis** *adjective*: *Gratis software can be downloaded.*

gratuity /ɡrəˈtjuːəti; *AmE* -ˈtuː-/ *noun* [C] (*plural* **gratuities**)
1 money that you give to sb who has provided a service for you: *Our staff are not permitted to accept gratuities.* SYN TIP
2 (*BrE*) money that is given to employees when they leave their job: *a retirement gratuity*

ˈgraveyard ˌmarket *noun* [C]
(*Stock Exchange*) a BEAR MARKET (= a market in which prices are falling) in which owners of shares who have already lost a lot of money want to sell their shares but buyers do not want to buy until the market improves

ˈgraveyard shift *noun* [C, usually sing.]
(*HR*) a period of time worked late at night or in the very early morning, especially the hours between midnight and 8 a.m.; the people who work these hours: *She went to college during the day and then worked the graveyard shift at the plant.*

ˈgravy train *noun* [sing.] (*informal*)
a way of getting a lot of money easily without much work: *Investors are trying to jump on the gravy train.*

gray = GREY **HELP** You will find most words formed with **gray** at the spelling **grey**.

the ˌGreat Deˈpression = DEPRESSION (2)

green /ɡriːn/ *adjective* (**greener, greenest**)
not harming the environment; concerned with the protection of the environment, often as a political principle: *green energy/products* ◇ *The company has decided to go green (= start using green policies).*

ˌgreen ˈaudit *noun* [C]
an official examination of the effect of a company or an industry on the environment: *Businesses in the city were asked to carry out a green audit.*

greenback /ˈɡriːnbæk/ *noun* [C, usually sing.] (*AmE*) (*informal*)
an American dollar note or other note; the dollar when it is traded on currency markets: *Employees may need greenbacks for cab fares or parking.* ◇ *The greenback rose to 124.6 yen.*

ˌgreen ˈbelt (*also spelled* **Green Belt**) *noun* [U; C, usually sing.] (*especially BrE*)
an area of open land around a city where new building is not usually allowed: *A large area of green belt will be lost if a new airport is built.*

ˌgreen ˈcard (*also spelled* **Green Card**) *noun* [C]
1 a document that legally allows sb to live and work in a country that is not their own
2 (*also* ˌInternational ˈMotor Inˌsurance Cerˌtificate*) in the UK, an insurance document that you need when you drive a car, motorcycle, truck, etc. in another country

ˌgreen conˈsumerism *noun* [U]
when customers choose to buy and use products that cause the least harm to the environment: *a national survey regarding your level of green consumerism*

greenfield /ˈɡriːnfiːld/ *adjective, noun* (*Property*)
● *adjective* [only before noun]
used to describe an area of land that has not yet had buildings on it, but for which building development may be planned
➍ *a greenfield site* ◆ *greenfield development/land*
● *noun* [C] (*especially AmE*) (*BrE usually* ˌgreenfield ˈsite*)
an area of land that has not yet had buildings on it, but for which building development may be planned → BROWNFIELD

ˌgreen ˈlight *noun* [sing.]
permission for a project, etc. to start or continue: *The company has decided to give the plan the green light.* ▸ **ˈgreen-light** *verb* [+ obj] (*especially AmE*): *The managing director decided to green-light the idea.*

ˌgreen ˈmarketing (*also* enˌvironmental ˈmarketing) *noun* [U]
marketing that tries to present a product or company as not harmful to the environment: *Green marketing often uses terms like 'recyclable', 'refillable' and 'biodegradable'.*

the ˌGreen Revoˈlution *noun* [sing.]
1 the dramatic increase in the quantity of crops such as rice and wheat produced, which happened in the second half of the twentieth century as the result of more scientific methods of agriculture
2 a dramatic rise in concern about the environment in countries with developed industries

grey (*AmE spelling* **gray**) /greɪ/ *adjective* [only before noun]

1 (*Economics*) used to describe the situation when goods are not bought from an official supplier but are bought in another country and then imported to be sold at a lower price than the official price: *the grey trade in drugs through the Internet* ◇ *There has been a range of action in the courts against grey goods.* → GREY MARKET (2), PARALLEL (1)
2 belonging to or aimed at the older section of the population: *US advertisers are competing for the gray dollar* (= the money that older people can spend on goods). ◇ *An increase in life span causes an increase in grey power* (= the economic and political power of older people). → GREY MARKET (3)

'grey goods (*AmE spelling* **gray ~**) *noun* [pl.]
(*Commerce*) computer equipment: *The market for brown and grey goods grew by 2.4%.* → BROWN GOODS, WHITE GOODS

,grey 'knight (*AmE spelling* **gray ~**) *noun* [C]
(*Finance*) a third company or person that is a possible buyer for another company. They are 'grey' because it is not known if they will be good or bad for the company. → BLACK KNIGHT, WHITE KNIGHT

,grey 'market (*AmE spelling* **gray ~**) *noun* [C, usually sing.]
1 (*Stock Exchange*) the buying and selling of new shares before they are officially issued on the stock market: *The unofficial grey market initially priced the shares between €2.89 and €2.96.*
2 (*Economics*) the buying and selling of goods that have not been obtained from an official supplier, usually at a lower price than the official price: *Grey market buyers can obtain goods up to 40% cheaper than through authorized channels.* → GREY (1), BLACK MARKET, PARALLEL (1) **NOTE** The grey market is legal but secret; the black market is illegal.
3 (*also* **,silver 'market**) older people, when they are thought of as customers for goods; the goods that are produced for them or that they buy: *The grey market is worth €46.4 billion and accounts for 12.3% of total retail spending.*

grid /grɪd/ *noun* [C]
1 a system of cables, pipes, etc. for sending electricity, gas or water over a large area: *the national power grid* (= the electricity supply in a country)
2 (*IT*) a number of computers that are linked together using the Internet so that they can share power, data, etc. in order to work on difficult problems: *Grid computing allows widely dispersed organizations to share applications, data and resources.*
3 a pattern of straight lines, usually crossing each other to form squares: *Results are shown on a grid showing a candidate's strengths and weaknesses.*

grievance /ˈɡriːvəns/ *noun* [C,U]
1 (*HR*) a complaint that an employee or a union makes to an employer about sth at work that they feel is unfair: *The employee should first send the employer a written statement of the grievance.* ◇ *Does the company have a formal grievance procedure* (= a formal way of telling sb your complaints)?
2 the feeling that you have been treated unfairly: *He had been nursing a grievance against the boss for months.*

grind /ɡraɪnd/ *noun, verb*
● *noun* [sing.]
an activity, especially work, that is tiring or boring and takes a lot of time: *the daily grind of work—phone calls, emails, meetings*
● *verb* (ground, ground /ɡraʊnd/)
IDM **grind to a 'halt; come to a grinding 'halt** to go slower gradually and then stop completely: *Production ground to a halt during the strike.* ◇ *If*

---

consumers stop spending, the economy will come to a grinding halt.

grocer /ˈɡrəʊsə(r); *AmE* ˈɡroʊ-/ *noun* [C]
1 (*also* **grocer's**) (*plural* **grocers**) a shop/store or company that sells food and some other things used in the home; a supermarket: *the supermarket chain that is the UK's leading grocer*
2 a person who owns, manages or works in a shop/store selling food and other things used in the home

grocery /ˈɡrəʊsəri; *AmE* ˈɡroʊ-/ *noun* (*plural* **groceries**)
1 (*especially BrE*) (*AmE usually* **'grocery store**) [C] a shop/store that sells food and other things used in the home **HELP** In American English 'grocery store' is often used to mean 'supermarket': *She had a job at a grocery.* ◇ *The average grocery store stocks around 30 000 items.*
2 **groceries** [pl.] food and other goods sold by a grocer or at a supermarket: *low prices on groceries* ◇ *People are buying groceries online.*
▶ **'grocery** *adjective* [only before noun]: *grocery chains* ◇ *the grocery business/industry*

★ **gross** /ɡrəʊs; *AmE* ɡroʊs/ *adjective, adverb, verb, noun*
● *adjective*
1 (*Accounting*) (*abbr* **gr**) (about an amount of money) being the total before tax or other costs are taken away: *She has a gross income of $55 000.* ◇ *Our gross revenues rose 5% last year.* ◇ *It will soon be easier for overseas investors to receive gross interest.* → NET
○ gross **earnings/income/revenue/salary/wages** ◆ gross **interest/returns/yields**
2 (*abbr* **gr**) (about a weight) including everything such as the container or wrapping as well as the contents: *The regulations do not apply to goods vehicles with a maximum gross weight* (= including the vehicle and the contents) *of less than 3 500 kg.*
3 (*Law, formal*) [only before noun] (about behaviour) very bad and unacceptable: *The firm had suffered from years of gross mismanagement.* ◇ *The finance director was dismissed for gross misconduct.*
● *adverb*
in total, before tax or any other costs are taken away: *He earns $30 000 a year gross.* → NET
● *verb* [+ obj]
to earn a particular amount of money before tax and other costs are taken away: *He predicted that the company would gross $20 million in 2005.* ◇ *It is one of the highest grossing movies of all time.*
PHR V **,gross sth 'up** (*Accounting*) to calculate a total amount by adding the amount that is usually taken off in taxes, etc. to a NET amount (= with taxes taken off): *You must gross it up by 30% to give you the equivalent amount of gross income.* → GROSS-UP
● *noun* [C]
1 (*plural* **grosses**) (*especially AmE*) a total amount of money earned by sb/sth, especially a film/movie, before any costs are taken away
2 (*plural* **gross**) (*abbr* **gr.**) a group of 144 things: *to sell sth by the gross*

'gross do'mestic 'product = GDP

,gross in'vestment *noun* [U,C, usually sing.]
(*Accounting; Economics*) the total amount spent in a particular period on buying new equipment and structures, and repairing and replacing old ones: *Gross investment in plant and machinery for that year was over $60 billion.*

,gross 'loss = TRADING LOSS

,gross 'margin (*abbr* **GM**) (*also* **,gross 'profit ,margin** *abbr* **GPM**) *noun* [U,C]
(*Accounting*) a percentage showing the relationship between a business's profits before OVERHEADS are

company's gross margin reached a record 61.4%. ◇ *The store needs a gross margin of 25% to become profitable.* → GROSS PROFIT, NET MARGIN

'gross 'national 'product (*also* ,national 'product) = GNP

,gross 'profit = TRADING PROFIT

,gross 'profit ,margin = GROSS MARGIN

,gross 'rating point *noun* [C] (*abbr* **GRP**)
(*Marketing*) a measurement of the number of people who see a particular TV programme or advertisement, used to show if it is good at reaching the group of people that a business wants to sell its products to. It is equal to the percentage of the possible audience who see it multiplied by the number of times it is shown: *The strength of a television schedule is measured in terms of Gross Rating Points (GRPs).* ◇ *An average GRP goal for a typical packaged product is 1 000 to 5 000 in a year.*

,gross 'sales *noun* [pl.]
(*Accounting*) the total amount of money that is received from selling goods or services before taking away money for goods returned by customers, price reductions (**discounts**), etc: *The company generates gross sales of €1 million a month.* → NET SALES

'gross-up *noun* [C,U]
(*Accounting*) the act of calculating a total amount by adding the amount that is usually taken off in taxes, etc. to a NET amount (= with taxes taken off): *a 25% gross-up of the amount received* → TO GROSS STH UP at GROSS *verb*

ground /graʊnd/ *noun, verb*
● *noun* [C, usually pl.]

SEE ALSO: **dumping ground**

a good or true reason for saying, doing or believing sth: *You have no grounds for complaint.* ◇ *He retired from the job* **on health grounds**. ◇ *Employers cannot discriminate* **on grounds of** *age.*
IDM **drive/run/work sb/yourself into the 'ground** to work sb/yourself so hard that they or you become extremely tired and unable to work **gain/make up 'ground 1** to rise in value: *The yen has gained ground* **against** *the euro.* **2** to gradually become more powerful or successful in relation to a competitor: *The supermarket chain is determined to* **gain ground** *on its main rival.* **get (sth) off the 'ground** to start happening successfully; to make sth start happening successfully: *Without more money, the project is unlikely to get off the ground.* ◇ *to get a new company off the ground* **give/lose 'ground (to sb/sth)** to allow sb to have an advantage; to lose an advantage for yourself: *They are not prepared to give ground on tax cuts.* ◇ *The company has lost a lot of ground to its rival.* **run/ drive sth into the 'ground** to use sth so much that it is broken or damaged: *The country has been overtaxed and almost run into the ground.* → idioms at BREAK *verb*, HIT *verb*, LOSE *verb*
● *verb* [+ obj]
to prevent an aircraft from taking off: *All planes out of Heathrow have been grounded by the strikes.*

'groundbreaking /'graʊndbreɪkɪŋ/ *adjective*
[only before noun]
making new discoveries; using new methods: *a groundbreaking piece of research* → BREAK NEW GROUND at BREAK *verb*
▶ **'groundbreaker** *noun* [C]: *These programs were groundbreakers in their time.*

grounded /'graʊndɪd/ *adjective*
IDM **(be) 'grounded (in/on sth)** (to be) based on sth such as facts, an idea, etc: *His views are grounded on a belief in the free market.* ◇ *a well-grounded claim/theory*
→ GROUND *verb*

,ground 'floor *noun*
IDM **be/get in on the ground 'floor** to become involved in a plan, project, etc. at the beginning and so gain an advantage over those who follow later: *This is a chance for investors to get in on the ground floor of a new industry.*

grounding /'graʊndɪŋ/ *noun*
1 [sing.] knowledge of, or training in, the basic parts of a subject: *The course will give you a good grounding* **in** *advertising.*
2 [U,C] the act of keeping a plane on the ground or a ship in a port: *The airline collapsed, resulting in the grounding of its fleet for lack of cash.*

'ground rules *noun* [pl.]
the basic rules on which sth is based: *The new code of conduct lays down the ground rules for management-union relations.*

'ground transpor,tation *noun* [U] (*especially AmE*)
ways in which passengers travel between a town or the place where they are staying and an airport, a ship, etc.

groundwork /'graʊndwɜːk; *AmE* -wɜːrk/ *noun* [U]
work that is done as preparation for sth else: *They are* **laying** *the groundwork* **for** *a possible takeover bid.*

★ group /gruːp/ *noun* [C with sing./pl. verb]

SEE ALSO: **action group, age ~, buzz ~, consumer ~, focus ~, income ~, investor ~,** etc.

1 (*also* ,group of 'companies) a number of companies that are owned by the same person or organization: *a media group* ◇ *the chief executive of Vodafone Group* ◇ *The group's shares fell 11% yesterday.* ◇ *the group sales director* ◇ *an external audit of the* **group accounts** (= accounts showing the costs, profit, etc. for each part of the group)
2 a number of people or things that are together in the same place or that are connected in some way: *A small group of us got together and started a business.* ◇ *A group of 10 banks will provide the new loan.* ◇ *a group discussion/interview*

VOCABULARY BUILDING

Subsidiaries and groups of companies

A **subsidiary** is a company that is controlled by another company, called a **holding company** or a **parent company**. (See note at HOLDING COMPANY)

Companies that are subsidiaries of the same holding/parent company are often called **sister companies**, **related companies** or **affiliates**: *We share customer information with our affiliates.*

A holding/parent company and its subsidiaries are called a **group** or **group of companies**.

Often the word **Holdings** or **Group** is used in the names of holding/parent companies: *InterContinental Hotels Group, parent company of Holiday Inn*

,group 'action *noun* [C]
(*Law*) a type of court case in which a large number of claims against the same person or organization, or resulting from the same event, are dealt with together → CLASS ACTION

groupage /ˈgruːpɪdʒ/ (BrE) (AmE **con,soli'dation**)
noun [U,C]
(*Transport*) the action of putting items from different exporters together into one load in order to transport them; a load consisting of different items of this kind: *a UK company specializing in groupage and full loads to Europe* ◇ *If your shipment does not fill a container, you can save money by sending it groupage.* ◇ *a groupage company/service/load*

,group in'centive noun [C] (BrE)
(*HR*) a reward given to a group or team of employees based on the group's achievements: *Group incentives have a very positive impact on performance.* ◇ *group incentive wages*

,group in'surance noun [U]
a single insurance contract that protects a group of people such as all the people who work for a particular company: *The company arranges group insurance for its employees.*

,group of 'companies (*also spelled* **Group of Companies**) = GROUP (1)

groupthink /ˈɡruːpθɪŋk/ noun [U] (*especially AmE*)
a process in which bad decisions are made because the different members of a group do not express their individual opinions about a plan, proposal, etc. but only say what they think the rest of the group would agree with

groupware /ˈgruːpweə(r); AmE -wer/ noun [U]
(*IT*) software that is designed to help a group of people on different computers to work together

grow /grəʊ; AmE groʊ/ verb (**grew** /gruː/ **grown** /grəʊn; AmE groʊn/)
1 [no obj] to increase in size, number, strength or quality: *Profits grew by 5% last year.* ◇ *The company's turnover grew from $1.56 billion to $1.58 billion.* ◇ *The economy failed to grow in the final quarter.* ◇ *The company is growing bigger all the time.* ◇ *the challenges of running a growing business* ◇ *the fastest-growing sector of the aviation industry*
2 [+ obj] to increase the size, quality or number of sth: *We are trying to grow the business.* ◇ *The savings were used to grow market share.*
HELP Grow and **grow up** are sometimes confused. **Grow up** only means 'to become an adult'. It does not mean 'to increase'.
IDM **it/money doesn't grow on 'trees** (*informal*) used to tell sb not to use sth or spend money carelessly because you do not have a lot of it
PHRV **,grow 'into sth** to become more confident in a new job, etc. and learn to do it better: *He needed time to grow into the job.* **,grow 'out of sth** to develop from sth: *The introduction of job-sharing grew out of a desire for more flexible working hours.*

★ **growth** /grəʊθ; AmE groʊθ/ noun [U]

SEE ALSO: **capital growth, high-growth**

1 an increase in the size, amount or degree of sth: *Sales showed 0.3 per cent growth in the first quarter.* ◇ *rapid growth in consumer spending* ◇ *Online travel is the company's biggest growth area* (= a part of the business where sales are growing fast). ◇ *Internet companies are on a steep growth curve.* ◇
❍ **fast/rapid/slow/steady/strong** growth • **earnings/ profit/revenue/sales** growth **companies/ industries/markets/stocks**
2 (*Economics*) an increase in economic activity: *a disappointing year of little growth in Britain and America* ◇ *the impact of weak economic growth and falling tax revenues* ◇ *an annual growth rate of 10%* ◇ *Growth forecasts were cut for Japan and Europe.*
❍ **fast/high/rapid/steady/strong/sustainable** growth • **low/slow/sluggish/weak** growth

'growth fund noun [C]
(*Finance*) a fund that invests in shares that are likely to increase in value quickly, rather than those

which pay large DIVIDENDS: *The average large company growth fund has declined in value by 30 per cent.* → AGGRESSIVE GROWTH FUND

'growth share = GROWTH STOCK

,growth-share 'matrix (*also spelled* **growth/ share ~**) = BOSTON MATRIX

'growth stock noun [U,C] (BrE *also* **'growth share** [C, usually pl.])
(*Stock Exchange*) shares in companies that grow more quickly than average companies and are likely to continue to grow fast because they invest in order to do so: *The fund focuses on low-risk growth stocks.* ◇ *A growth stock usually pays no dividends but increases in value.* → GLAMOUR STOCK
See note at STOCK

GRP /ˌdʒiː ɑː ˈpiː; AmE ɑːr/ = GROSS RATING POINT

grubstake /ˈɡrʌbsteɪk/ noun [U,C] (AmE)
(*Finance, informal*) money or materials given to sb to start a business, project, etc. in return for part of the future profits: *Venture capital firms raised nine-figure grubstakes from institutional investors.*
▶ **'grubstake** verb [+ obj]

gr. wt. (*also spelled* **GR. Wt.**) abbr
a short way of writing **gross weight**

GSM /ˌdʒiː es ˈem/ abbr
Global System for Mobiles a system that allows you to use a mobile phone/cellphone in different countries

GST /ˌdʒiː es ˈtiː/ abbr
(*Accounting*) **Goods and Services Tax** in Australia, Canada, New Zealand and some other countries, a general tax on the supply of almost all goods and services → VAT

GTC order /ˌdʒiː tiː ˈsiː ˌɔːdə(r); AmE ˈɔːrd-/ = GOOD-TILL-CANCELLED ORDER

★ **guarantee** /ˌɡærənˈtiː/ noun, verb (abbr **guar.**)
● noun

SEE ALSO: **bank guarantee, company limited by ~, cross-~, export credit ~, money-back ~**

1 [C,U] a written promise given by a company that sth you buy will be replaced or repaired without payment if it goes wrong within a particular period: *We provide a 5-year guarantee against manufacturing faults.* ◇ *The watch is still under guarantee.* ◇ *The television comes with a year's guarantee.* ◇ *a money-back guarantee*
SYN WARRANTY
❍ **to offer/provide** a guarantee • sth **carries/comes with/has** a guarantee
2 (*Finance*; *Law*) (*also* **'guaranty**) [C,U] money or sth valuable that you give or promise to a bank, for example, to make sure that you will pay back money that you borrow: *We had to offer our house as a guarantee when getting the loan.* ◇ *guarantees against bad loans* → COLLATERAL
❍ **to give/offer/provide** (sth as) a guarantee
3 (*Finance*; *Law*) (*also* **'guaranty**) [C] an agreement to be legally responsible for sth, especially for paying sb's debts if they cannot pay them: *The airline is seeking government loan guarantees of $1.8 billion to avoid bankruptcy.*
❍ **to give/provide** a guarantee • **to get/seek** a guarantee
4 [C] a firm promise that you will do sth or that sth will happen: *He wanted written guarantees of the package before accepting.* ◇ *They have given a guarantee that the business will not be sold.*
❍ **to give/offer/provide** a guarantee • **to ask for/get/ want** a guarantee

● *verb* [+ obj]
1 to promise to do sth; to promise that sth will happen: *We guarantee to deliver your goods within a week.*
2 to give a written promise to replace or repair a product free if it goes wrong: *The toaster is guaranteed for a year against faulty workmanship.*
3 (*Finance; Law*) to agree to be legally responsible for sth or for doing sth such as paying back a loan: *The loan will be guaranteed by the German government.* ◇ *to guarantee to pay somebody's debts*

,**guaranteed 'wage** *noun* [sing.] (*also* ,**guaranteed 'wages** [pl.]) (*also* ,**guaranteed 'pay** [U])
(*HR*) the level of pay that employees are promised in their contract during a particular period of time, even if there is little or no work to do

,**guaran'tee fund** *noun* [C]
(*Finance*) an amount of money that can be used to pay back a loan if the borrower is unable to do so, or to pay sb for a financial loss

guarantor /ˌɡærənˈtɔː(r)/ *noun* [C]
1 (*Finance; Law*; *AmE also* **guaranty**) a person or an organization that agrees to pay back a loan or a debt, etc. if the person or company that borrowed the money is not able to do so: *a mortgage guarantor* ◇ *The company had to act as guarantor for a loan of $750m.*
2 (*Law*) a person who agrees to be responsible for sb or sth: *In Japan, you may need a guarantor in order to rent an apartment.*

guaranty /ˈɡærənti/ (*plural* **guaranties**) = GUARANTEE (2), GUARANTEE (3), GUARANTOR (1)

guardian /ˈɡɑːdiən/ *AmE* /ˈɡɑːrd-/ *noun* [C]
1 a person who is responsible for protecting sth: *Board members are the guardians of shareholders' interests.*
2 (*Law*) a person who is legally responsible for the care of another person

guer'rilla ,marketing (*also spelled* **guerilla** ~) *noun* [U]
a type of marketing that uses different and unusual methods to achieve the greatest effect for the smallest amount of money ▶ **guer'rilla ,marketer** (*also spelled* **guerilla** ~) *noun* [C]

guesstimate (*also spelled* **guestimate**) /ˈɡestɪmət/ *noun* [C] (*informal*)
an attempt to calculate sth that is based more on guessing than on real information ▶ **guesstimate** (*also spelled* **guestimate**) /ˈɡestɪmeɪt/ *verb* [+ obj or no obj] **NOTE** Guesstimate is formed from the words 'guess' and 'estimate'.

guest /ɡest/ *noun* [C]
1 a person who is visiting a place, for example sb else's home, company, or country, usually after being invited to go there: *They are here as guests of our company.* ◇ *Make sure he's on the guest list.* ◇ *She was invited as the guest speaker.*
2 a customer in a hotel or restaurant: *Guests should vacate their rooms by 10.30 a.m.*

guestimate = GUESSTIMATE

'**guest ,worker** *noun* [C]
a person who is allowed to come and work in a country which is not their own country for a period of time

GUI /ˌdʒiː juː ˈaɪ/ *abbr*
(*IT*) **graphical user interface** a way of giving

instructions to a computer using things that can be seen on the screen such as symbols, windows and MENUS

★ **guidance** /ˈɡaɪdns/ *noun* [U]
1 help or advice: *Managers need to monitor progress and offer guidance.*
2 the act of managing or guiding sb/sth: *The fund was set up under the guidance of the finance director.*
3 written instructions which tell you what you may or must do when dealing with a particular thing: *Revised guidance was issued.* ◇ *guidance on employment rights* **SYN** GUIDELINE

guide /ɡaɪd/ *noun, verb*
● *noun* [C]
1 something that indicates what may happen or what is happening: *Investors know that past performance is no guide to future returns.*
2 something that helps you to form an opinion or make a decision: *These figures are just a rough guide.* → GUIDELINE
3 a book or document which tells you about sth: *a restaurant/hotel/city guide* ◇ *You can download the site's 10-step guide to investing.*
4 = GUIDE PRICE
● *verb* [+ obj]
1 to help sb/sth to move in a particular direction: *He guided the company to sales of more than $60 million.* ◇ *The company has been guiding down investor expectations.*
2 to explain to sb how to do sth, especially sth complicated or difficult: *The health and safety officer will guide you through the safety procedures.*

guideline /ˈɡaɪdlaɪn/ *noun*
1 **guidelines** [pl.] written instructions which tell you what you may or must do when dealing with a particular thing: *The organization issued a set of guidelines for builders.* ◇ *Some companies have breached government guidelines on pollution.* **SYN** GUIDANCE
◐ *to draw up/give/issue/publish guidelines • to breach/follow/stick to guidelines • clear/revised/strict guidelines*
2 **guidelines** [pl.] advice: *Here are some basic guidelines to help you delegate more effectively.*
3 [C] something that helps you to form an opinion or make a decision: *The figure of $30 per person is just a guideline.*

'**guide price** (*also* **guide**, *less frequent*) *noun* [C]
a price which is approximately the amount that you will have to pay for sth such as property or shares: *The building is for sale at a guide price of €5 million.*

gulf /ɡʌlf/ *noun* [C, usually sing.]
an extremely large difference between people, ideas or things: *attempts to bridge the gulf between management and employees*

gun /ɡʌn/ *verb, noun*
● *verb*
PHRV be '**gunning for sth** to be trying very hard to achieve sth or to get sth: *The board is gunning for a price of €40 per share.* ◇ *She's definitely gunning for the top job.*
● *noun* → idiom at BIG *adj.* → HIRED GUN, LASER GUN, STAPLE GUN

guru /ˈɡʊruː/ *noun* [C] (*informal*)
an expert on a particular subject who shares his or her knowledge through books, articles and training: *She is one of the highest paid management gurus in the world.*
◐ *a business/design/an investment/a management/technology guru*

H h

hack /hæk/ *verb, noun*
● *verb* [+ obj *or* no obj]
1 (*IT*) to use a computer to steal, change or look at data on sb else's computer system without permission: *He hacked into the bank's computer.* ◇ *They had hacked secret data.*
2 (*often used with an adverb or a preposition*) to reduce jobs, costs, etc. in a very severe way: *To curb costs, he is planning to hack back bonuses.*
▶ **'hacker** *noun* [C] **'hacking** *noun* [U]
● *noun* [C]
a writer or journalist who does a lot of low-quality work and does not get paid much

haemorrhage (*AmE spelling* **hemorrhage**)
/'heməridʒ/ *noun, verb*
● *noun* [C, usually sing.]
a serious loss of people or money from a company or an organization: *The haemorrhage of senior staff has continued.*
● *verb* [+ obj *or* no obj]
if a company or an organization **haemorrhages** money, people or jobs, it loses a large amount: *Our immediate task is to stop the company haemorrhaging cash.*
IDM **haemorrhage red 'ink** (*often used in newspapers*) to lose a large amount of money: *In the timber industry, mills are closing, unemployment is rising and companies are haemorrhaging red ink.*

haggle /'hægl/ *verb* [no obj]
haggle (with sb) (over sth) to argue with sb in order to reach an agreement, especially about the price of sth: *They were haggling over the price.* ▶ **'haggle** *noun* [C]

the 'Hague Rules /'heɪg/ *noun* [pl.]
a set of international rules relating to the transport of goods by ship

haircut /'heəkʌt; *AmE* 'herkʌt/ *noun* [sing.]
1 a reduction, especially in an amount of money: *Most of the Internet-related stocks took a haircut* (= lost value) *yesterday.*
2 (*Finance*) an amount of money that dealers take off the price that they pay for shares, bonds, etc. or add to the price that they sell them for, which pays their fee: *A haircut of 2.5 per cent is applied to each buy/sell-back transaction.*
▶ **'haircut** *verb* [+ obj]

half a 'dozen = HALF-DOZEN

half 'day *noun* [C]
a day on which people work only in the morning or in the afternoon: *Tuesday is her half day.*

'half-day *adjective* [only before noun]
lasting for either the morning or the afternoon: *a half-day trading session* ◇ *Workers staged a half-day strike.*

half-'dozen (*also* **half a 'dozen**) *noun* [sing.]
a set or group of six: *a half-dozen companies* ◇ *We hope to have about half a dozen new products in the shops by December.*

half-'page *adjective* [only before noun]
using or covering half a page: *a half-page advertisement*

half 'point *noun* [C]
(*Finance*) one of two equal divisions of a unit of measurement, especially half of one per cent: *Rates were cut by a half point.* ◇ *a half-point cut in interest rates*

half-'price *adjective* [only before noun]
costing half the usual price: *a half-price ticket*
▶ **half-'price** *adverb*: *Children aged under four go half-price.* **half 'price** *noun* [U]: *We have many items at half price or less.*

half-'year *adjective* [only before noun]
relating to a period of six months: *Half-year figures showed a 20% rise in pre-tax profits.* ◇ *half-year losses/profits* ▶ **half-'year** *noun* [sing.]: *We returned to profit in the half-year ending Feb 28th.*

half-'yearly *adjective* [only before noun]
happening every six months; happening after the first six months of the year: *a half-yearly meeting* ◇ *the half-yearly sales figures* ▶ **half-'yearly** *adverb*: *Interest will be paid half-yearly in June and December.*

hallmark /'hɔːlmɑːk; *AmE* -mɑːrk/ *noun, verb*
● *noun* [C]
1 a feature or quality that is typical of sth: *Cooperation has been the hallmark of the entire project.* ◇ *The award is the hallmark of excellence* (= a sign of high quality) *for business communication.*
2 in the UK, a mark put on a gold, silver or PLATINUM object, showing the quality of the metal and where and when the object was made
● *verb* [+ obj]
to put a **hallmark** on an object made from gold, silver or PLATINUM

'hall test *noun* [C]
(*Marketing*) a form of MARKET RESEARCH in which a group of people are asked to come into a room and give their opinions about a product, an advertisement, etc.

'halo ef,fect *noun* [sing.]
the way that a good feeling or opinion about one thing, or about one aspect of a person, is likely to give you a good feeling about other things or about the whole person: *The new sports car has provided a halo effect for the whole brand.* ◇ *Beware of the halo effect when you are interviewing candidates for a job.*

hammer /'hæmə(r)/ *noun, verb*
● *noun*
IDM **be/come/go under the 'hammer** (*Commerce*) to be sold at an AUCTION (= a sale where items are sold to the person who offers the highest price)
● *verb* [+ obj]
to reduce the amount or value of sth in a sudden or extreme way: *Shares have been hammered by the recent news.* ◇ *The cold weather hammered ice cream sales.*
PHR V **hammer a'way at sth** to keep working on sth or emphasizing sth: *People will continue to hammer away at this issue.* **hammer sth 'down** to reduce prices, costs, etc. by a large amount: *All our goods are at hammered-down prices.* **hammer sth 'out** to discuss a plan or a deal until all the details are agreed: *Final details have yet to be hammered out.*

hammering /'hæmərɪŋ/ *noun* [C, usually sing.]
a sudden and extreme reduction in value or strength: *Shares have taken a hammering.*

hand /hænd/ *noun, verb*

●*noun*

SEE ALSO: **second-hand, stock in hand**

1 (*informal*) **a hand** [sing.] help in doing sth: *Do you need a hand* **with** *those invoices?*
2 (*used in adjectives and verbs*) by a person rather than a machine: *hand-painted pottery*
3 [C] a person who does physical work, especially on a farm or in a factory
IDM **be good with your 'hands** to be skilful at making or doing things with your hands **by 'hand 1** by a person rather than a machine: *The vases are painted by hand.* **2** if a letter is delivered **by hand**, it is delivered personally rather than sent by post/mail **get your 'hands on sth/sb** to find or get sb/sth: *They want to get their hands on the company's assets.* **in 'hand 1** if you have sth **in hand**, it is available to be used: *We have the money in hand to begin the work now.* → ON HAND **2** if you have a particular situation **in hand**, you are in control of it: *Don't worry about the travel arrangements— everything is in hand.* **3** the job or task **in hand** is the one that you are dealing with: *She likes to dedicate herself 100% to the job in hand.* **in the hands of sb; in sb's 'hands 1** owned or controlled by a particular person or group: *The airline will remain in UK hands.* **2** being dealt with by sb; being taken care of by sb: *I'll leave that in your hands.* **on 'hand 1** available: *Staff are on hand to give you help and advice.* ◊ *We still have 12 000 of the older models on hand.* **2** (*AmE*) = TO HAND **,out of your 'hands** no longer your responsibility: *I'm afraid the matter is now out of my hands.* **put your ,hand in your 'pocket** (*BrE*) to provide the money for sth, usually unwillingly: *The government has put its hand in its pocket to rescue the fishing industry.* **to 'hand** (*BrE*) (*AmE* **on 'hand**) available immediately; easy to reach: *Do you have the figures to hand?* → idioms at CASH *noun*, CATCH *verb*, CHANGE *verb*, CLEAN *adj.*, EXCHANGE *verb*, HOLD *verb*, MONEY, SHOW

●*verb*

PHRV **,hand sth 'down (to sb) 1** to give or leave sth to a younger member of your family: *These skills used to be handed down from father to son.* **2** (*Law*) (*especially AmE*) to officially give a decision, statement, etc: *A judgement may be handed down within days.* **,hand sth 'in (to sb)** to give sth to sb in authority, especially a piece of work, a plan, etc: *Please make sure all proposals are handed in by Friday.* ◊ *I heard she had handed in her* **notice/ resignation** (= had formally told her employer that she wanted to stop working for them). **,hand sth 'off (to sb)** (*AmE*) to give sb else your responsibility for sth: *handing off the project to your successor* **,hand sth 'on (to sb)** to give or leave sth to sb else: *The company is not obliged to hand this benefit on to customers.* **SYN** PASS STH ON **,hand sth 'out (to sb)** to give a number of things to members of a group: *Copies of the report will be handed out at the meeting.* **SYN** DISTRIBUTE → HANDOUT **,hand sth 'over (to sb); ,hand 'over (to sb)** to give sb else your position of power or the responsibility for sth: *She will hand over the day-to-day running of the division to Mr Butler.*

'hand ,baggage = HAND LUGGAGE

handbill /'hændbɪl/ *noun* [C]
a small printed advertisement that is given to people by hand

handbook /'hændbʊk/ *noun* [C]

SEE ALSO: **service handbook**

a book that contains information or instructions on a particular subject: *a practical handbook for*

managers ◊ *All new staff will receive an employee handbook.* → MANUAL

handcraft /'hændkrɑːft; *AmE* -kræft/ = HANDICRAFT

hand-held *adjective, noun*
●*adjective* **,hand-'held** [usually before noun] small enough to be held in the hand while being used: *a hand-held camera*
●*noun* **'hand-held** [C]
a small computer that can be used in the hand

'hand-,holding *noun* [U]
the act of giving sb a lot of help and support (often used in a disapproving way): *Some customers require a tremendous amount of hand-holding and follow-up service.*

handicraft /'hændɪkrɑːft; *AmE* -kræft/ (*AmE also* **'handcraft**) *noun* [C, usually pl., U]
the activity of making things with your hands using technical skill and artistic ability; things made in this way: *traditional activities such as farming and handicrafts*

★**handle** /'hændl/ *verb, noun*
●*verb* [+ obj]
1 to deal with sth, especially products, money or customers: *Banks are used to handling large amounts of cash.* ◊ *The UK's seven airports handle about 10 million passengers a month.* ◊ *We can't handle orders for less than 500.* ◊ *The system handles huge amounts of data.*
2 to manage, organize or be responsible for sth: *Eddie handles marketing, sales and finance.* ◊ *The launch of the new website was handled by an outside agency.*
3 (*Transport*) to store, pack or move goods: *We handle merchandise for several well-known firms.* → HANDLING
4 to touch, hold or move sth with your hands: *The package was marked: 'Fragile. Handle with care.'*
5 to deal with a difficult situation or person: *The crisis was handled very badly.* ◊ *Can you give me some advice about handling difficult customers?*
●*noun*
IDM **get/have a 'handle on sth** (*informal*) to get/ have the information that you need in order to deal with sth: *online tools to help employees get a handle on their finances*

handler /'hændlə(r)/ *noun* [C]
1 a company that moves, stores or packs goods: *grain/freight handlers*
2 a person who carries or touches sth as part of their job: *food handlers*

handling /'hændlɪŋ/ *noun* [U]

SEE ALSO: **cargo handling, manual ~, materials ~, shipping and ~**

1 (*Transport*) the act or cost of storing, packing and moving goods: *a $2 charge for postage and handling* ◊ *moves to cut handling costs* ◊ *The company plans to sell its handling division.* **SYN** CARRIAGE (*BrE*)
⊕ *handling* **charges/costs/expenses/fees** • *a handling* **agent/company**
2 (*Commerce*) the cost of dealing with an order, booking tickets, etc: *There is a small handling charge for advance bookings.*
3 the way that sb deals with a situation: *I was impressed by his handling* **of** *the recent buy-out.*
⊕ **assured/careful/firm/poor** *handling*
4 the act of touching, carrying or moving sth: *products that can stand up to rough handling* ◊ *baggage handling* ◊ *In the manufacturing industries heavy materials handling is often done by robots.*
⊕ **baggage/food/materials** *handling* • **careful/rough** *handling*
5 (*IT*) the activities of storing, moving, and processing data; the ability to do this

6 the process of dealing with sth: *the firm's cash handling operations* ◇ *The airport has limited passenger handling facilities.*

'hand ,luggage (*also* **'hand ,baggage,** *less frequent*) *noun* [U] (*both especially BrE*)
small bags that you can carry with you onto a plane

handmade /,hænd'meɪd/ *adjective*
made by a person using their hands rather than by machines: *handmade shoes and bags* → MACHINE-MADE

,hand-'operated *adjective*
(about a machine) controlled by a person rather than working automatically

handout /'hændaʊt/ *noun* [C]
1 money or goods given to sb who needs help: *to rely on handouts*
2 money that is given to a person or an organization by the government, etc., for example to encourage commercial activity: *The company needed another massive state handout to keep going.*
3 a document that is given out at a meeting or other event
→ HAND STH OUT (TO SB) at HAND *verb*

handover /'hændəʊvə(r); *AmE* -oʊvər/ *noun* [C,U]
an act of giving sth to sb else, for example control of an organization or country; the period when this is done: *He agreed to remain as CEO until the handover was complete.* ◇ *Everything is in place for a smooth handover.*

,hand-'picked *adjective*
1 chosen very carefully, often by a particular person: *a hand-picked team*
2 picked by people rather than by machines: *All our fruit is hand-picked.* ▶ **hand-'pick** *verb* [+ obj]: *She was able to hand-pick her own team.*

'hands-free *adjective* [usually before noun]
(about a telephone) able to be used without needing to be held in the hand: *hands-free phones/headsets*

handshake /'hændʃeɪk/ *noun* [C]
1 an act of shaking sb's hand, used especially to say hello or goodbye or when you have made an agreement: *Everything was agreed on a handshake.*
2 **handshake deal/agreement** a deal which has been agreed in a conversation or an email, although there is not yet a formal written agreement: *He is determined to get them to stick to their handshake deal.*
3 = GOLDEN HANDSHAKE
4 (*IT*) an instance of **handshaking**

handshaking /'hændʃeɪkɪŋ/ *noun* [U]
(*IT*) the process of your computer connecting with another computer, for example when you use the Internet; the sound of this happening

,hands-'off *adjective* [usually before noun]
dealing with people or a situation by not becoming directly involved and by allowing people to do what they want: *He has a hands-off **approach** to managing the company.* → HANDS-ON

,hands-'on *adjective* [usually before noun]
1 dealing with sth by becoming directly involved, rather than leaving other people to do it: *his hands-on **approach** to running the business* ◇ *I'm a hands-on manager.* → HANDS-OFF
2 doing something rather than just talking about it: *They both have hands-on **experience** of marketing.* ◇ *hands-on training*

'hang-out loan *noun* [C] (*AmE*)
(*Finance*) the amount of money that you still have to pay at the end of the period of time that you have borrowed the money for

the ,Hang 'Seng ,Index (*also* **the Hang Seng**) /,hæŋ 'seŋ/ *noun* [sing.]
a figure which shows the average price of shares on the Hong Kong stock exchange: *The Hang Seng Index was up 35.81 points.*

,happy 'camper *noun* [C] (*informal*)
a customer, an employee, etc. who has no complaints: *'We are not exactly happy campers',* one employee said after the job cuts.

harass /'hærəs; hə'ræs/ *verb* [+ obj] (*often* **be harassed**)
to annoy, worry or threaten sb by putting pressure on them or saying or doing unpleasant things to them: *She claims she has been **sexually** harassed at work.* ◇ *harassing phone calls*

harassment /'hærəsmənt; hə'ræsmənt/ *noun* [U]
behaviour which is deliberately unpleasant or frightening, and which causes sb to feel upset: *claims of bullying and harassment in the workplace* ◇ *He had been subjected to continual racial harassment* (= harassment because of his race) *by colleagues.*
O *to be subjected to/be subject to/suffer* harassment
• *racial/sexual* harassment

hard /hɑːd; *AmE* hɑːrd/ *adjective, adverb*
• *adjective* (**harder, hardest**)
1 [only before noun] definite; based on information that can be proved: *Is there any hard evidence that the company is recovering?* ◇ *We think about 90% of the email is internal, but we have no hard figures.*
O *hard evidence/facts/figures/numbers*
2 [usually before noun] if the market is **hard**, or if prices are **hard**, prices remain high: *We expect the hard market to be sharp and brief.*
→ SOFT
IDM **drive/strike a hard 'bargain** to argue in an aggressive way to try to force sb to agree on the best possible price or arrangement **,hard and 'fast** (*used especially after* **no, not,** *etc.*) that cannot be changed in any circumstances: *There are no hard and fast **rules** about this.*
• *adverb*
IDM **be hard 'up for sth** to have too few or too little of sth: *We're hard up for good ideas.* → HARD UP → idiom at HIT *verb*

,hard 'asset *noun* [C, usually pl.]
(*Finance*) an investment in physical things such as gold, silver, coins and art → INTANGIBLE ASSET

hardball /'hɑːdbɔːl; *AmE* 'hɑːrd-/ *noun* [U]
a way of behaving which shows that you are very determined to get what you want and will not let sb else gain an advantage: *BA is prepared to **play** hardball.* ◇ *This is management hardball.* ◇ *a hardball negotiator*

,hard 'cash (*BrE*) (*AmE* **,cold 'cash**) *noun* [U]
money, especially in the form of coins and notes, that you can spend: *hard cash on the balance sheet* ◇ *turning your equity into hard cash*

,hard-'charging *adjective*
working very hard and being very determined to get what you want: *hard-charging managers/executives*

,hard-'code *verb* [+ obj]
(*IT*) to write data so that it cannot easily be changed

,hard com'modity *noun* [C, usually pl.]
(*Finance*) a raw material such as metal, chemicals, oil, etc. that can be bought and sold to make a profit: *trading in hard commodities* ◇ *hard-commodity prices* → SOFT COMMODITY

,hard 'copy *noun* [C,U]
text, pictures, etc. on paper rather than in a computer file: *Do you keep hard copies of your emails?*

'hard-core adjective [usually before noun]
1 particularly active or enthusiastic: *Early Xbox sales were mainly to hard-core gamers.*
2 involving people who are unlikely to change their opinions or behaviour: *the hard-core unemployed* (= who have had no work for a long time and are not very likely to find a job)

'hard costs noun [pl.]
(*Accounting*) money that is spent on physical equipment and materials → SOFT COSTS

,hard 'currency noun [U,C]
(*Economics*) money which is easy to exchange for money from another country because it is not likely to lose its value: *Expatriate workers are paid in hard currency.* → SOFT CURRENCY

,hard 'data noun [U]
information that can be measured or proved: *The business plan is full of hard data in the form of tables and graphs.* → SOFT DATA

,hard 'disk (*also* **'hard drive**) noun [C]
(*IT*) the part inside a computer on which data and programs are stored: *Save it to the hard disk.*

,hard-'earned adjective [only before noun]
that you get only after a lot of work and effort: *their hard-earned cash*

harden /'hɑːdn; AmE 'hɑːrdn/ verb [no obj]
if prices **harden**, or if the market **hardens**, prices rise and stay high: *Gold hardened to around $347 an ounce.*

'hard goods = DURABLE GOODS

,hard 'hat noun [C]
1 a hat worn for safety in areas where building work is being done, or in factories
2 (*informal*) (*especially AmE*) a worker in the building trade: *We need to get the hard hats back on the job.*

,hard HR'M /,eɪtʃ ɑːr 'em/ noun [U]
(*HR*) **hard human resources management** an approach to managing people that regards them as assets that must be used for the benefit of the business → SOFT HRM

,hard 'landing noun [C, usually sing.]
(*Economics, informal*) a situation when the economy, or part of it, experiences a rapid decrease in trade and activity after a long period when it has been growing: *The government has lowered interest rates to try to avoid a hard landing for the economy.* → SOFT LANDING

,hard 'loan noun [C]
(*Finance*) a loan to a person or country at a normal rate of interest and which must be paid back in HARD CURRENCY → SOFT LOAN

,hard 'sell noun
(*Marketing*)
1 [sing; U] the process of trying very hard to persuade sb to buy sth, in a way that puts pressure on them: *Customers don't like the hard sell.* ◇ *There's no hard sell here.* ◇ *hard-sell advertising*
2 [sing.] (*AmE*) a product that is not easy to sell: *The shares will be a hard sell in the current market.* → SOFT SELL

,hard 'selling noun [U]
(*Marketing*) the activity of trying very hard to persuade sb to buy sth, in a way that puts pressure on them ▶ **,hard-'selling** adjective [only before noun]: *hard-selling salespeople*

hardship /'hɑːdʃɪp; AmE 'hɑːrd-/ noun [sing; U]
a situation that is difficult or unpleasant because you do not have enough money or are working in difficult conditions: *a hardship allowance for doctors working in unpleasant conditions*

,hard 'up adjective (*informal*)
not having enough money: *The company's now so hard up, it can't afford to pay its staff.* ◇ *hard-up students* → idiom at HARD *adv*

★ **hardware** /'hɑːdweə(r); AmE 'hɑːrdwer/ noun [U]
1 (*IT*) the machinery and electronic parts of a computer system: *computer hardware and software suppliers* → SOFTWARE
2 electronic or mechanical equipment: *suppliers of machinery, trucks, hardware and other items*

,hard-'wired adjective
1 (*IT*) being part of a computer system, rather than being provided by software
2 (about behaviour) that happens automatically and that cannot be changed: *We are hard-wired to communicate verbally.*
▶ **,hard-'wire** verb [+ obj]

,hard-'working adjective
putting a lot of effort into your work: *She's open, hard-working and a good team member.*

harmonization, **-isation** /,hɑːmənaɪ'zeɪʃn; AmE ,hɑːrmənə'z-/ noun [U; sing.]
1 the activity of making systems, rules or standards the same in different areas, countries, parts of an organization, etc: *global harmonization*
2 (*HR*) the process of giving all of your employees the same status or conditions, for example by removing the difference between workers and managers, or by making everyone wear the same uniform

harmonize, **-ise** /'hɑːmənaɪz; AmE 'hɑːrm-/ verb
1 [+ obj *or* no obj] to successfully combine different ideas, systems or people; to combine successfully: *The leader's role is to put together and harmonize such views.*
2 [+ obj] to make systems, rules or standards the same in different parts of an organization or area: *the need to harmonize tax levels across the European Union*

harness /'hɑːnɪs; AmE 'hɑːrnɪs/ verb [+ obj]
to use energy, skills or resources in order to achieve sth: *There are many ways to harness the power of the Net.* ◇ *We must harness the skill and creativity of our workforce.*

harvesting /'hɑːvɪstɪŋ; AmE 'hɑːrv-/ noun [C,U]
(*Marketing*) the practice of no longer investing in a product but continuing to sell it, so that profits increase. This usually happens in the period before the product is removed from the market.

'hatchet man noun [C] (*informal*)
a person in an organization who is responsible for telling people that they have lost their jobs or for making other changes which are not popular

haul /hɔːl/ verb, noun
● *verb* [+ obj]
(*Transport*) to transport or move goods by road or rail: *a trucking business that hauls containers to and from the ports* ◇ *a waste hauling company*
IDM **haul sb over the 'coals** (*BrE*) (*AmE* **rake sb over the 'coals**) to criticize sb severely because they have done sth wrong: *I was hauled over the coals by my boss for being late.*
● *noun* [C]

SEE ALSO: **short-haul**

1 (*Transport*) the distance covered in a particular journey: *The truck's last haul was less than 75 miles.* → BACKHAUL
2 a quantity of fish caught at one time

haulage /'hɔːlɪdʒ/ (*especially BrE*) (*AmE usually* **'hauling**) noun [U]

SEE ALSO: **heavy haulage, road haulage**

(*Transport*) the activity or business of transporting goods by road or rail; money charged for this: *the* road haulage industry ◇ a haulage firm/contractor ◇ How much is haulage?

haulier /ˈhɔːliə(r)/ (BrE) (AmE **hauler** /ˈhɔːlə(r)/) noun [C]

SEE ALSO: **road haulier**

(Transport) a company or person whose business is transporting goods by road or rail SYN CARRIER

hauling /ˈhɔːlɪŋ/ = HAULAGE

have /hæv/ verb
IDM be 'had (informal) if you **have been had**, you have been cheated or tricked: You've been had—it's not worth that much.

haven /ˈheɪvn/ noun [C]

SEE ALSO: **safe haven, tax haven**

a safe place: Gold stocks are a haven for investors in difficult times.

the 'Hawthorne ef,fect noun [sing.]
(HR) the fact that people's behaviour changes if they believe they are being observed or studied

the 'Hay ,system noun [sing.]
(HR) a system for measuring the knowledge and skills that are needed or used in a particular job

hazard /ˈhæzəd; AmE -ərd/ noun [C]

SEE ALSO: **moral hazard, occupational hazard**

a thing that can be dangerous or cause damage: This would not **pose** a safety hazard. ◇ The aim is to make employees aware of potential hazards.

,hazardous 'substances noun [pl.]
types of solids, liquids or gases which may be present where people work and are dangerous to their health

'hazard pay = DANGER MONEY

★ **head** /hed/ noun, verb
● noun [C,U]

SEE ALSO: **head-to-head**

the person in charge of a group of people or an organization: I am the head of a small company. ◇ a meeting of department heads ◇ She resigned as head of marketing. ◇ the head buyer of women's wear See note at RESPONSIBILITY
IDM a/per 'head for each person: The meal worked out at $50 a head. get your 'head around/round sth to be able to understand sth: Once we've got our heads around this problem, we can start to suggest solutions. have/get/keep your 'head down to start/continue to work very hard: Let's just get our heads down and finish the project. have a 'head for sth to be good at sth: a hardworking manager with a good head for business have/get/give sb a head 'start (in sth/on sb/over sb) to have or give sb an advantage at the beginning of sth: This course will give you a head start in your career. ◇ The competition had a one-year head start on us (= they produced the product one year before we did). heads will 'roll (informal) used to say that some people will be punished because of sth that has happened (be) in over your 'head (be) involved in sth that is too difficult for you to deal with: After a week in the new job, I soon realized that I was in over my head. keep your 'head above water to deal with a difficult situation, especially one in which you have financial problems, and just manage to survive: The French company is struggling to keep its head above water. over sb's 'head 1 too difficult or complicated for sb to understand: Much of the technical information was over my head. 2 to a higher position of authority than sb: I'm not happy that you went over my head to ask for this time off. put our/your/their 'heads together to think about or discuss sth as a group two heads are better than 'one used to say that two people can

achieve more than one person working alone
→ idioms at BLOCK noun, TURN verb
● verb
1 [+ obj] to lead or be in charge of sth: She has been appointed to head a team of 50 sales staff. ◇ a committee headed by an outside lawyer SYN HEAD UP STH
2 [no obj] (also **be headed**, especially in AmE) (used with an adverb or a preposition) to move in a particular direction: Can you forecast where the economy is heading? ◇ The manufacturing sector may be heading back towards recession. ◇ Prices are already headed higher. ◇ 100 000 copies of the new game are headed **for** the US.
3 [+ obj] (usually **be headed**) to put a word or words at the top of a page or section of a book or an article as a title: a section of the report headed 'Strengths and weaknesses of the company' ◇ Print the letter on **headed paper** (= paper with the company's name and address on it).
IDM head 'north/'south (about share prices, currencies, etc.) to rise/fall in value: The country's currency headed south for the second day, weakening 1.4%.
PHRV ,head sth 'off to take action in order to prevent sth from happening: trying to head off job losses ,head 'up sth to lead or be in charge of a department, part of an organization, etc: They are searching for someone to head up the new department. HELP A noun must always follow up, but a pronoun comes between the verb and up
SYN HEAD See note at RESPONSIBILITY

headcount (AmE spelling usually **head count**) /ˈhedkaʊnt/ noun [C,U]
an act of counting the number of people who are employed by an organization, are at an event, etc.; the number of people that have been counted in this way: The company is cutting its headcount to about 45 000.
● to **cut/lower/reduce** (the) headcount • the headcount **drops/falls** • to **do/make/take** a headcount

header /ˈhedə(r)/ noun [C]
a line or block of text that is automatically added to the top of every page that is printed from a computer: The header gives the page number and date of the document. → FOOTER

headhunt /ˈhedhʌnt/ verb [+ obj]
(HR) (usually **be headhunted**)
to find sb who has the right skills and experience for a senior job in a company or an organization and persuade them to leave their present job: I was headhunted by a marketing agency. See note at EMPLOY ▶'**headhunter** noun [C]: Headhunters have been brought in to search for a successor to the chairman. '**headhunting** noun [U]: a headhunting firm

heading /ˈhedɪŋ/ noun [C]
1 a title printed at the top of a page or at the beginning of a section of a book, report, etc.
2 the subject of each section of a speech or piece of writing: The company's aims can be grouped under three main headings.

★ **headline** /ˈhedlaɪn/ adjective (BrE)
1 (Economics) used to describe a number, figure, rate, etc. that includes everything: The unadjusted headline figure for unemployment is 4.2 million.
2 (Finance) used to describe a figure that does not include profits or losses related to unusual events: Headline pre-tax profits before goodwill rose 32% to $98 m.
→ UNDERLYING

headline 'earnings noun [pl.] (BrE)
(Finance) the profit that a company makes, not including profits or losses related to unusual events such as the sale of assets, emergency payments, etc: The company reported a sharp fall in headline earnings. ◇ Regular earnings per share may have collapsed but headline EPS are up 1.5%.

headline in'flation noun [U] (also 'headline 'rate of in'flation [C, usually sing.]) (both BrE)
(Economics) the rate at which the prices of goods and services rise over a period of time, including costs which are likely to change, such as food and fuel and, in the UK, the cost of MORTGAGES (= loans to buy a home): Headline inflation rose by 2.9%. → UNDERLYING INFLATION, RETAIL PRICE INDEX

★ **head 'office** (abbr HO) (also ,main 'office) noun [C; U with sing./pl. verb]
the main office of a company; the managers who work there: Their head office is in New York. ◇ I don't know what head office will think about this proposal.

head-'on adjective [only before noun]
in which people compete or deal with sb/sth in a direct and determined way: The store is trying to avoid head-on competition with the supermarkets. ◇ There was a head-on confrontation between management and unions. ▶ ,head-'on adverb: We must tackle the problem head-on (= without trying to avoid it).

headquartered /,hed'kwɔ:təd; AmE 'hed-kwɔ:rtərd/ adjective [not before noun]
having headquarters in the place mentioned: The business will be headquartered in London.

★ **headquarters** /,hed'kwɔ:təz; AmE 'hed-kwɔ:rtərz/ noun [U with sing./pl. verb; C] (plural headquarters) (abbr HQ)
the place from where an organization is controlled; the people who work there: The company's headquarters is/are in Cambridge. ◇ Several companies have their headquarters in the area. ◇ I'm now based at headquarters.

headset /'hedset/ noun [C]
equipment worn on the head, for example when using a telephone or computer: hands-free headsets for mobile phones/cellphones

heads of a'greement noun [C,U] (plural heads of agreement) (BrE)
(Law) a document that states the main points in a deal or an agreement that two organizations are discussing, before a full legal contract is written: The two companies have signed a non-binding heads of agreement to merge.

'heads-up noun [C, usually sing.]
1 a warning about sth: Thanks for the heads-up about business etiquette!
2 a short report giving the most recent information, especially about what is going to happen: Let me give you a quick heads-up on the new design.

head-to-'head adjective [only before noun]
in which two people or groups face each other directly in order to decide the result of a dispute or competition: a head-to-head battle between the low-fares airlines ▶ ,head-to-'head adverb: The two banks will go head-to-head in a battle to win the deal.

headway /'hedweɪ/ noun
IDM make 'headway to rise in value: The pound made headway against the euro. ◇ In the food retail sector Tesco made headway, rising 0.8%.

health /helθ/ noun [U]
1 how successful or strong sth is: There were fears about the health of the US economy. ◇ Investors were misled about the company's financial health.
2 the work of providing medical services: The job includes pension and health benefits.
3 the condition of a person's body or mind: Health and beauty sales were up by 3.3%.
→ idiom at CLEAN adjective

★ **health and 'safety** noun [U]
(HR) activities connected with recognizing risks and dangers to health in places of work and protecting employees from these risks: We are committed to improving health and safety standards for all our employees. ◇ She's head of Health and Safety at the Fire Brigades Union.
● health and safety laws/policies/regulations/requirements/rules/standards
NOTE In the UK, health and safety regulations are based on the Health and Safety Act of 1974 and the 1992 Health and Safety at Work Regulations and are an important part of an employee's contract of employment.

'health care (also spelled **healthcare**) noun [U]
1 the service of providing medical care: providers of private health care ◇ There was a dispute over employee health-care benefits.
● health-care benefits/costs • health-care personnel/professionals/workers
2 medical products and services: The group has split into three divisions—health care, chemicals and agrochemicals. ◇ reductions on beauty and health-care products
● a health-care business/company/group/market • health-care products

'health in,surance noun [U]
a type of insurance in which a person receives money to pay for medical treatment if they are ill/sick or injured, often provided by employers: Many companies offer private health insurance as part of their employment packages. **SYN** MEDICAL INSURANCE See note at SALARY

'health ,warning noun [C]
a notice on particular products, required by law, that warns people that using the items can damage their health: Cigarette packets are required to carry a health warning. ◇ (figurative) These investments come with a health warning that their value can go up or down.

healthy /'helθi/ adjective (healthier, healthiest)
large or successful, working well, etc: a healthy economy ◇ The telecom group have made a healthy profit. ◇ We are in a much healthier position now than we were last year. ▶ healthily /'helθɪli/ adverb

hearing /'hɪərɪŋ; AmE 'hɪr-/ noun [C]

SEE ALSO: disciplinary hearing

an official meeting at which the facts about a crime, complaint, etc. are presented to the person or group of people who will have to decide what action to take: A court hearing ruled that the directors had acted illegally. ◇ There was a hearing into the causes of the accident. → idiom at FAIR adj.
● to conduct/have/hold a hearing • to attend a hearing • a committee/court/tribunal hearing • a full/private/public hearing

heartland /'hɑːtlænd; AmE 'hɑːrt-/ noun [C] (also heartlands [pl.])
1 an area where an activity or an organization is especially successful, popular or important: the industrial heartlands of Germany ◇ the heartland of the automobile business
● the agricultural/industrial/manufacturing heartland

2 a place which is considered to be at the centre of a country or region: *a dairy company in America's heartland*

heatseeker /ˈhiːtsiːkə(r)/ *noun* [C] (*informal*)
a customer who always buys the newest version of a product as soon as it is available

heavy /ˈhevi/ *adjective* (**heavier, heaviest**)
1 more or worse than usual in amount, degree, etc: *Trading was heavy at 818 million shares.* ◇ *The bank faces heavy losses.* ◇ *Competition from cheap imports is now heavier than ever.*
2 (about machines, vehicles, etc.) large and powerful: *The company manufactures a wide range of heavy machinery.* ◇ *heavy trucks*
3 (*BrE*) **heavy on sth** having or using a lot of sth: *We're light on stocks and heavy on bonds.*
4 [usually before noun] involving a lot of work or activity; very busy: *a heavy schedule*
5 needing a lot of physical strength: *I have been advised to avoid heavy lifting.*
▶ **heavily** /ˈhevɪli/ *adverb*: *Microsoft has invested heavily in China.* ◇ *heavily indebted telecoms firms* (= with large amounts of debt) ◇ *a heavily loaded van* → LIGHT

heavy-'duty *adjective* [only before noun]
very strong and suitable for hard physical work or to be used all the time: *heavy-duty trucks* (= strong and large) ◇ *For business use you need a heavy-duty word-processing program.* [OPP] LIGHT-DUTY
→ MEDIUM-DUTY

heavy engi'neering *noun* [U]
businesses that design and produce large things such as ships, machinery and vehicles; the activities of these businesses → LIGHT ENGINEERING

heavy 'goods ,vehicle = HGV

heavy half *noun* [sing.]
(*Marketing*) the group of customers which are half or less than half of the total number, who buy more than half of the total goods sold

heavy 'haulage *noun* [U]
(*Transport*) the activity or business of transporting heavy goods or materials; the vehicles or systems used for this

heavy 'hitter (*also* **big 'hitter**) *noun* [C]
1 (often used in newspapers) a person who has a lot of influence in business, politics or public life: *A heavy hitter has been brought in as chairman.*
2 (often used in newspapers) a product or business which is very successful: *The business has decided to focus on their heavy hitters.*

heavy 'industry *noun* [U,C]
businesses that use large amounts of raw materials and large machines to produce metal, coal, vehicles, etc: *The area has been hit by the decline of heavy industry.* → LIGHT INDUSTRY ▶ **heavy in'dustrial** *adjective*: *heavy industrial facilities*

heavyweight /ˈheviweit/ *noun* [C]
1 a successful or important person, company or thing, that has a lot of influence: *technology/software/oil heavyweights* ◇ *He transformed the company into a global gas and power heavyweight.* ◇ *the appointment of several heavyweights to the Board*
2 a thing, material, etc. that weighs more than usual
→ LIGHTWEIGHT
▶ **heavyweight** *adjective* [only before noun]: *heavyweight stocks*

hectic /ˈhektɪk/ *adjective*
full of activity; extremely busy: *a hectic day's trading* ◇ *I have a hectic schedule.* ◇ *It's been hectic in the store this morning.*

hecto- /ˈhektəʊ; *AmE* -toʊ/ *combining form* (*used in nouns; often used in units of measurement*)
one hundred: *hectolitre*

hedge /hedʒ/ *verb, noun*
● *verb* [+ obj *or* no obj] (*Finance*)
to protect yourself against the risk of losing money in the future because of changes in the value of shares, currencies, raw materials, etc., for example by buying or selling FUTURES (= contracts to buy or sell a particular amount of sth for a fixed price at a particular time in the future), OPTIONS (= the right to buy or sell sth for a fixed price in the future), etc: *They want to hedge their exposure to interest-rate risk.* ◇ *The airline has hedged 77% of its expected fuel requirements next quarter at 79¢ a gallon.* ◇ *He prefers companies that choose not to hedge.*
▶ **hedging** *noun* [U]: *There's a balance between the cost of hedging and running an acceptable risk.* ◇ *hedging strategies/techniques*
[IDM] **hedge your 'bets** to reduce the risk of losing or making a mistake by supporting more than one side in a competition, an argument, etc., or by having several choices available to you: *She hedged her bets by applying for several jobs.*
[PHRV] **'hedge against sth** to do sth to protect yourself against problems, especially against losing money: *The news encouraged investors to hedge against a fall in the dollar.*
● *noun* [C]

SEE ALSO: **currency hedge**

a way of reducing the risk of losing money in the future because of changes in the value or price of sth such as shares, currencies, raw materials, rates of interest, etc: *Real estate can be a hedge **against** inflation* (= property will rise in value more than the rate of inflation).

'hedge fund *noun* [C]
(*Finance*) a type of UNREGULATED investment fund used by people or organizations with large amounts of money to invest and not open to the general public, that tries to gain maximum profit by using a variety of investment strategies, including some with very high risk: *Hedge funds have invested $29 bn in Japan.* ◇ *a hedge fund manager*

hefty /ˈhefti/ *adjective* (**heftier, heftiest**)
large; in large quantities: *They sold it easily and made a hefty profit.* ◇ *Interest rates have gone up to a hefty 12%.*

'helicopter view *noun* [C] (*informal*)
a broad general view or description of a problem
[SYN] OVERVIEW → 10 000-FOOT VIEW

helm /helm/ *noun*
[IDM] **at the 'helm (of sth)** in charge of an organization or a project: *With Mr Munro at the helm, the company has continued to grow.* **take the 'helm (of/at sth)** to take charge of an organization or a project: *He took the helm at the bank in 1999.*

'help desk *noun* [C]
a service, usually in a company, that gives people information and help, especially if they are having problems with a computer

helpline /ˈhelplaɪn/ *noun* [C] (*BrE*)
a telephone service that provides advice and information about particular problems: *a 24-hour telephone helpline* ◇ *a health helpline*

'help ,menu *noun* [C]
(*IT*) a list of subjects shown on a computer screen that you can click on when you need help with a computer program

hemorrhage = HAEMORRHAGE

heritage /ˈherɪtɪdʒ/ *noun* [C, usually sing.]
the history, traditions and qualities that a country, society or company has had for many years and

that are considered an important part of its character: *Aston Martin's prestigious brand heritage*

'heritage ˌindustry *noun* [C with sing./pl.verb]
organizations that are involved in the history, traditions and culture of a place; the people, places and activities connected with these organizations: *a managerial role in the heritage industry*

HFE /ˌeɪtʃ ef 'iː/ = HUMAN FACTORS ENGINEERING

HGV /ˌeɪtʃ dʒiː 'viː/ *abbr* (*BrE*)
heavy goods vehicle a large lorry/truck: *an HGV licence* ◇ *HGV drivers*

ˌhidden aˈgenda *noun* [C]
the thing that sb is really trying to achieve, rather than the thing that they say they are trying to achieve: *Analysts should be trusted advisers, not salesmen with a hidden agenda.*

ˌhidden unemˈployment *noun* [U]
(*Economics*) people who have no work or very little work but who are not officially recorded as unemployed, for example people who are ill/sick or who are caring for sb: *The country suffers from severe hidden unemployment, with the official jobless count a fraction of the real total.* ▶ **ˌhidden unemˈployed** *noun* [pl.]: *The number of hidden unemployed had risen 130 000 since 2002.*

★hierarchy /ˈhaɪərɑːki; *AmE* -rɑːrki/ *noun* (*plural* **hierarchies**)
1 [C,U] the different levels at which people or things are organized, depending on how much authority, responsibility or importance they have: *the highest levels of the corporate hierarchy* ◇ *She's quite high up in the management hierarchy.*
2 [C with sing./pl. verb] the group of people in control of a large organization or institution ▶ **hierarchical** /ˌhaɪəˈrɑːkɪkl; *AmE* -ˈrɑːrk-/ *adjective*: *hierarchical organizations* **hierarchically** /ˌhaɪəˈrɑːkɪkli; *AmE* -ˈrɑːrk-/ *adverb*

ˌhierarchy of ˈneeds = MASLOW'S HIERARCHY OF NEEDS

high /haɪ/ *adjective, adverb, noun*
● *adjective* (**higher, highest**)
1 greater or better than normal in quantity, size or degree: *high prices* ◇ *a high rate of inflation* ◇ *a demand for higher wages* ◇ *Sales were 5.9% higher than last year.* ◇ *Unemployment is at its highest level for eight years.* ◇ *The job needs a high degree of accuracy.*
2 [usually before noun] above other people or things in importance or status: *She has reached the highest rank for a woman ever at the company.* ◇ *We place a high priority on employees' development.*
3 containing a lot of a particular substance: *foods which are high in fat*
4 above the usual or expected standard: *Our customers expect the highest quality of service.*
OPP LOW → idioms at PLAY *verb*, RIDE *verb*
● *adverb* (**higher, highest**)
at or to a large cost, value or amount: *high-priced products* ◇ *Prices are expected to rise even higher this year.* OPP LOW
● *noun* [C]

SEE ALSO: **historic high, sky-high**

the highest level or amount: *The share price has fallen from a high of 773¢ to 95¢.* ◇ *Unemployment hit record highs.* OPP LOW
○ **an all-time/a record high** • **to hit/reach/rise to a high of …**
IDM **on ˈhigh** used in a humorous way to refer to the people in senior positions in an organization: *An order came down from on high that lunch breaks were to be half an hour and no longer.*

ˌhigh aˈchiever *noun* [C]
a person who is very successful in their work or studies: *The women were all high achievers in their fields.* → HIGH-FLYER

ˌhigh-ˈconcept *adjective* [usually before noun]
used to describe sth that has a very interesting, attractive and clear idea: *high-concept designer stores*

ˌhigh-ˈcost (*also* ˌhigher-ˈcost) *adjective* [usually before noun]
involving high costs; expensive: *the higher-cost airports* ◇ *The firm is located in a high-cost area.*
OPP LOW-COST

'high-end *adjective* [usually before noun]
having the highest price, quality or importance: *a high-end product* ◇ *high-end retailers* ◇ *buying high-end PCs* ▶ **'high-end** *noun* [sing.] OPP LOW-END

ˌhigher-ˈcost = HIGH-COST

ˌhigher-ˈincome = HIGH-INCOME (1)

ˌhigher-ˈup (*especially AmE*) (*BrE usually* ˌhigh-ˈup) *noun* [C] (*informal*)
a person with a high position in a company or an organization: *improving the way higher-ups communicate with employees*

ˌhigh ˈfinance *noun* [U]
business activities which involve very large amounts of money: *the world of high finance* ◇ *They're a big name in high finance.*

ˌhigh-ˈflyer (*AmE spelling usually* **-flier**) *noun* [C]
1 a person who has the desire and the ability to be very successful in their job: *high-flyers in retail banking* → HIGH ACHIEVER
2 a company or an investment that is or has been very successful: *The company was a stock market high-flyer during the Internet boom.*
▶ **ˌhigh-ˈflying** *adjective*: *a high-flying career in advertising*

ˌhigh-ˈgrade *adjective* [usually before noun]
1 having a high level or quality: *The plans were printed on high-grade waste paper.* ◇ *high-grade workers/specialists*
2 (*Finance*) not likely to lose money: *high-grade bonds*
OPP LOW-GRADE

ˌhigh-ˈgrowth *adjective* [usually before noun]
growing quickly in value or importance; likely to do this: *The bank has concentrated on high-growth areas.* ◇ *high-growth stocks*

ˌhigh-ˈimpact *adjective* [usually before noun]
making a strong impression; having a strong influence: *a high-impact ad campaign* OPP LOW-IMPACT

ˌhigh-ˈincome *adjective* [usually before noun]
1 (*also* ˌhigher-ˈincome) having or earning a lot of money: *high-income countries/households* ◇ *higher-income earners/taxpayers*
2 earning a high level of interest: *high-income bonds*
OPP LOW-INCOME

ˌhigh-inˈvolvement ˌproduct *noun* [C]
(*Marketing*) a product that customers are willing to spend a lot of time and effort looking for and buying → LOW-INVOLVEMENT PRODUCT

ˌhigh-ˈlevel *adjective* [only before noun]
1 involving senior people: *high-level meetings* ◇ *a series of high-level management changes*
2 (*IT*) (about a computer language) similar to an existing language such as English, making it fairly simple to use: *written in a high-level language like BASIC*
OPP LOW-LEVEL

highlight /ˈhaɪlaɪt/ verb, noun
● verb [+ obj]
1 to make sth very obvious so that people give it more attention: *The figures highlighted the need for reforms to the market.* ◇ *The dollar's problems were highlighted by its weakness against the yen.*
2 to emphasize parts of a text with colour, using a pen or a computer: *Highlight the section that you want to delete.*
● noun
1 highlights [pl.] the most important information about sth; a document containing this information: *sales highlights* ◇ *Here are some highlights of the survey.*
2 [C] the best or most important part of an activity or event: *the highlight of his career*

highly /ˈhaɪli/ adverb
1 at or to a high standard, level or amount: *a highly paid job* ◇ *highly trained workers*
2 very: *a highly successful business woman* ◇ *a highly skilled workforce*

high-ˈmargin adjective [usually before noun]
(Accounting; Marketing) providing a high profit: *Greater sales of higher-margin products had helped the company to meet the target earlier than expected.* → LOW-MARGIN

high net ˈworth adjective [only before noun]
having a large amount of money; involving a large amount of money: *high net worth customers/clients/investors* → HNWI

high-ˈpaid adjective [usually before noun]
1 earning a lot of money: *high-paid accountants and lawyers*
2 the high-paid noun [pl.] people who are paid a lot of money
OPP LOW-PAID

high-perˈformance adjective [only before noun]
that can go very fast or do complicated things: *high-performance organizations/companies* ◇ *high-performance computers*

high-perˈforming adjective [usually before noun]
working to a very high standard: *a high-performing company/team*

high-ˈpowered adjective
1 (about people) having a lot of power and influence; full of energy: *high-powered executives*
2 (about a job) important; with a lot of responsibility: *She has an extremely high-powered job in London.*
3 (also high-ˈpower) (about machines) very powerful: *a high-powered computer/laser*

high-ˈpressure adjective [only before noun]
1 that involves aggressive ways of persuading sb to do sth or to buy sth: *high-pressure selling techniques*
2 that involves a lot of worry and anxiety: *a high-pressure job* SYN STRESSFUL
OPP LOW-PRESSURE

high-ˈpriced (also high-ˈprice) adjective [usually before noun]
expensive: *high-priced housing/hotel rooms* ◇ *high-price advertising space* OPP LOW-PRICED

high-ˈprofile adjective [usually before noun]
receiving a great deal of attention in the media; well-known: *high-profile events such as boxing matches* ◇ *high-profile companies* OPP LOW-PROFILE

high-ˈquality adjective
of a high standard: *high-quality products* ◇ *high-quality, committed workers*

high-ˈranking adjective [usually before noun]
senior; important: *the highest-ranking executives* ◇ *a high-ranking post*

high-resoˈlution (also hi-res, high-res) /ˌhaɪ ˈrez/) adjective [usually before noun]
showing a lot of clear, sharp detail: *high-resolution cameras* ◇ *high-resolution photographs* OPP LOW-RESOLUTION

ˈhigh-rise adjective [only before noun]
a high-rise building is very tall, with many levels: *a high-rise apartment building* ◇ *the company's new high-rise headquarters* ▶ **ˈhigh-rise** noun [C]: *the city's most expensive high-rise*

ˈhigh road noun [sing.]
(HR) a method of gaining an advantage in business which involves developing workers' skills, paying them high wages, giving them good conditions, etc. and producing goods of high value: *encouraging corporations to* **take** *the high road* ◇ *a high-road company* → LOW ROAD

high ˈroller noun [C] (AmE) (informal)
1 a person who gambles very large amounts of money, either on the stock exchange or in clubs where you play games for money (**casinos**): *City high rollers* ◇ *the high rollers that flock to Las Vegas*
2 an important person who earns or spends a great deal of money: *a meeting of high-tech high rollers*
▶ **high-ˈrolling** adjective

the ˌhigh ˈseas noun [pl.] (formal)
areas of the oceans that are not under the legal control of a particular country

high ˈseason noun [U; sing.] (especially BrE)
the time of year when a hotel or tourist area receives most visitors: *Hotels usually raise their prices in (the) high season.* ◇ (figurative) *It's high season for bankers in the region as they compete for clients who are eager to move their funds.* OPP LOW SEASON

high-ˈspeed adjective [only before noun]
fast: *high-speed Internet access* ◇ *a high-speed connection to the Internet* ◇ *a high-speed rail link*

ˈhigh street noun [C, usually sing.] (BrE)
the main road in a town, where the shops/stores, banks, etc. are: *They have a store in the High Street.* ◇ *Sales were stronger in out-of-town centres than on the high street* (= the businesses in the centre of a town). ◇ *high-street stores/retailers* ◇ *High-street sales have been poor.*

★high-ˈtech (also spelled hi ~) adjective, noun
● adjective
1 using the most modern methods, machines or devices, especially electronic ones: *high-tech equipment/systems* ◇ *Today's clothing industry is very high-tech and computerized.*
2 (about objects, designs, etc.) very modern in appearance; using modern materials: *a high-tech table made of glass and steel*
3 [usually before noun] producing things that include very modern technologies: *the high-tech boom of the late 1990s*
→ LOW-TECH
● noun [U] (informal) = HIGH TECHNOLOGY

high techˈnology (formal) (also high-ˈtech) noun [U]
areas of business which provide or use very advanced computers and methods; the computers and methods involved: *the number of people working in high technology* ◇ *high-technology stocks/exports*

high ˈtouch adjective [usually before noun]
involving a lot of human contact or activity, rather than relying on machines: *a process that maintains a high-touch, personal feel* ▶ **high ˈtouch** noun [U]: *The focus is on high touch rather than high tech.*

high-'up = HIGHER-UP

high 'volume *noun* [C,U]
a large quantity of sth: *We need to make a high volume of calls around the world every day.* ◊ *We are ready to start high-volume production.* OPP LOW VOLUME

high-'yield (*also* high-'yielding) *adjective* [only before noun]
(*Finance*) used to describe investments that produce a high income but may have some risk: *high-yield bonds/funds/debt* ◊ *high-yielding currencies/stocks* ◊ *the European high-yield* **market** → JUNK BOND, LOW-YIELD
▶ **high-'yielder** *noun* [C]

hijack /'haɪdʒæk/ *verb* [+ obj]
1 to take over a meeting, an idea or a system in a way that other people do not like, in order to achieve what you want: *Its annual meeting was hijacked by critics.*
2 to take control of sth, especially sb's computer, without their agreement: *A hacker had hijacked their email system.*

hike /haɪk/ *noun, verb* (*informal*)
● *noun* [C] (*especially AmE*)
a large or sudden increase in prices, costs, etc: *a 16% hike* **in** *profits* ◊ *Another hike in interest rates has been announced.* ◊ *a tax/rate/price hike*
● *verb* [+ obj or no obj]
hike sth (up) to increase prices, taxes, etc. suddenly or by a large amount: *He is not planning to hike interest rates.* ◊ *They will not hike up prices.*

hinterland /'hɪntəlænd; *AmE* -tərl-/ *noun* [C, usually sing.]
1 the areas of a country that are away from the coast, from the banks of a large river or from the main cities
2 the area around a major town or port: *Who is buying property in London's green hinterland?*

★ **hire** /'haɪə(r)/ *verb, noun*
● *verb*
1 (*HR*) [+ obj or no obj] (*especially AmE*) to give sb a job: *She was hired three years ago.* ◊ *He does the* **hiring and firing** *in our company.* ◊ *We're not hiring right now.*
2 [+ obj] to employ sb for a short time to do a particular job: *to hire a lawyer* ◊ *They hired a firm of consultants to design the new system.*
3 [+ obj] (*especially BrE*) to pay money to borrow sth for a short time: *to hire a car/room/DVD* → RENT
PHR V **,hire sth 'out** (*Commerce*) to let sb use sth for a short time, in return for payment: *The rooms are hired out for corporate meetings.* **,hire yourself 'out (to sb)** to arrange to work for sb: *He hired himself out to whoever needed his services.* See note at EMPLOY
● *noun*
1 (*Commerce*) [U] (*especially BrE*) the act of paying to use sth for a short time: *Mobile phones are available* **for** *hire.* ◊ *The price includes the hire of the hall.* ◊ *a hire car* ◊ *a car hire firm* SYN RENTAL → RENT *noun*
2 (*HR*) [C] (*especially AmE*) a person that a company has recently given a job to: *New hires get raises after a set period of time.* SYN RECRUIT

,hired 'gun *noun* [C] (*AmE*) (*informal*)
1 an expert who is brought into a company to solve difficult legal or financial problems, for example during a TAKEOVER
2 a person who works for different companies as they are needed: *There will be core workers and hired guns.*

,hire 'purchase *noun* [U] (*abbr* **h.p.**) (*BrE*) (*also* **in'stalment plan** [C] *AmE, BrE*)
(*Commerce*) a way of paying for goods gradually over a long period. You have the goods immediately, but legally you do not own them until you have finished paying: *They bought it* **on** *hire purchase.* ◊ *a hire purchase* **agreement/contract**

hirer /'haɪərə(r)/ *noun* [C]
1 (*especially AmE*) a person who employs other people: *Her company has a reputation as a skilled hirer.*
2 (*BrE*) a person who hires sth such as a tool or vehicle
3 (*Commerce*) (*BrE*) a person who buys sth by HIRE PURCHASE

hi-'res = HIGH RESOLUTION

'hiring hall *noun* [C] (*AmE*)
(*HR*) an EMPLOYMENT AGENCY, managed by a union, which provides skilled workers as employers need them

histogram /'hɪstəɡræm/ *noun* [C]
a diagram which uses bands of different heights to show the rate at which sth happens and different widths to show a range, so that they can be compared → BAR CHART

histogram

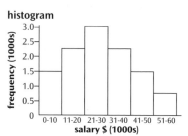

his,torical 'cost = HISTORIC COST
his,torical 'cost ac,counting = HISTORIC COST ACCOUNTING
his,torical 'high = HISTORIC HIGH
his,torical 'low = HISTORIC LOW

his,toric 'cost (*also* his,torical 'cost) *noun* [U,C]
(*Accounting*) the original price or value of an item: *Companies report on derivatives at market values rather than historic cost.*

his,toric 'cost ac,counting (*also* his,torical 'cost ac,counting) *noun* [U]
(*Accounting*) a method of accounting that uses the original price or value of items

his,toric 'high (*also* his,torical 'high, *less frequent*) *noun* [C]
a time when a value or amount is higher than at any other time; this value or amount: *Job creation was* **at** *a historic high.* ◊ *The dollar hit a historic high of 760 pesos.*

his,toric 'low (*also* his,torical 'low, *less frequent*) *noun* [C]
a time when a value or amount is lower than at any other time; this value or amount: *Interest rates are* **at** *historic lows.* ◊ *The yield on the bond fell to a historic low of 0.7%.*

history /'hɪstri/ *noun* [C] (*plural* **histories**)

SEE ALSO: **credit history, sales history**

a record of the things that a person has done or that have happened to them: *We always check candidates' education, employment history and references.*

★ **hit** /hɪt/ *verb, noun*
● *verb* (**hitting, hit, hit**)
1 [+ obj or no obj] to have a bad effect on sb/sth: *The industry has been hit by a series of strikes.* ◊ *We*

were hit **with** a 10% tax penalty. ◇ A global recession hit and markets plunged.

2 [+ obj] to reach a particular price or level, especially one that is very high or low: Unemployment has hit a 10-year high. ◇ He believes crude oil could hit $40 a barrel. ◇ There are signs that the economy has **hit bottom** and will start to improve.

3 (informal) [+ obj] to experience sth difficult; to stop making progress with sth: We hit a problem installing the system. ◇ The economy hit a **rough patch** (= a difficult period) this year.

4 (informal) [+ obj] if a product **hits** the shelves, stores, etc. it becomes available and starts being sold: The camera should hit the shelves in early May. ◇ The shares hit the market at $4.

IDM be hit 'hard (by sth); be hard 'hit (by sth) to be affected very badly by sth: The area has been hard hit by a decline in manufacturing. ◇ the hard-hit steel industry **hit (it) 'big** (informal) to be very successful: We all know some company owners who have hit it big and made lots of money. **hit the 'buffers** (especially BrE) (informal) if sth **hits the buffers** it suddenly stops happening or being successful: Consumer spending has hit the buffers. **,hit the ground 'running** (informal) to start doing sth and continue very quickly and successfully: We need people who are trained properly and can hit the ground running. **hit a 'wall** if a company, a person, a price, etc. **hits a wall**, they reach a point where they are unable to make any further progress: After years of booming sales and profits, the company has hit a wall. **hit the 'wall** if a company **hits the wall**, it starts to fail or fails completely: If your company hit the wall and fired all of its employees tomorrow, how long would it take you to find a new job? → idiom at BRICK

PHRV ,hit sb 'up (for sth); 'hit sb for sth (AmE) (informal) to ask sb for money: When launching their new companies they hit up friends and family.

● noun [C]

1 (IT) a result of a search on a computer, especially on the Internet; a person who visits an Internet page: You can limit the number of search hits. ◇ The site had 20 000 hits on just one day.

2 a person or thing that is very popular: The drink is proving a big hit **with** young consumers.

3 something that has a bad effect on sb/sth: The legislation will limit the hit to taxpayers.

IDM take a 'hit **1** to be damaged or badly affected by sth: The airline industry took a hit last year. ◇ The economy has taken a big hit from high energy costs.

2 if a company's profits **take a hit**, they are reduced by the amount mentioned, especially because the company has had to pay an unusual cost: The company has taken a €170 million hit **to** its earnings.

hitch /hɪtʃ/ noun, verb

● noun [C]

a problem or difficulty that causes a short delay: The introduction of the new currency went ahead without a hitch. ◇ a last-minute/legal/technical hitch

● verb

IDM hitch your 'wagon/'fortunes/'future to sb/ sth (especially AmE) to rely on a particular person or thing for your success: The firm had hitched its fortunes to the US technology boom. ◇ They chose the wrong leader to hitch their wagon to.

PHRV ,hitch 'up (with sb/sth) (informal) (about two businesses) to join together: It is fifteen years since the two companies hitched up.

,hi-'tech = HIGH-TECH

'hit list noun [C] (informal)

a list of people, organizations, etc. against whom some action is being planned or is needed: They publish an annual hit list of poorly performing shares.

---

hive /haɪv/ verb

PHRV ,hive sth 'off (into/to sth) (especially BrE) (often be hived off) to separate one part of a group from the rest; to sell part of a business: The retail business is being hived off into a separate company. ◇ We decided to hive off the research departments and run them as a separate company.

'HM 'Revenue and 'Customs noun [U] (abbr **HMRC**)

the government organization in the UK that is responsible for collecting all taxes, paying some benefits, protecting borders, etc.

HNWI /,eɪtʃ en ,dʌblju: 'aɪ/ abbr (informal) **high net worth individual** a very rich person

HO /,eɪtʃ 'əʊ; AmE 'oʊ/ = HEAD OFFICE

Ho. = HOUSE (2)

hoard /hɔːd; AmE hɔːrd/ noun, verb

● noun [C]

a collection of money, supplies, food, etc. that is kept safe to be used in the future: They have a huge hoard of investments.

● verb [+ obj or no obj]

to collect and keep large amounts of money, supplies, food, etc., especially secretly: The group has traditionally hoarded any spare cash rather than returning it to shareholders. ▶ '**hoarder** noun [C]: cash hoarders

hoarding /'hɔːdɪŋ; AmE 'hɔːrd-/ noun [C] (BrE) (Marketing) a large board on the outside of a building or at the side of the road, used for putting advertisements on: a 20 x 10 foot advertising hoarding **SYN** BILLBOARD

★ **hold** /həʊld; AmE hoʊld/ verb, noun

● verb (held, held /held/)

1 [+ obj] to have or own sth: The government holds a 55% stake in the firm. ◇ a **privately/publicly held** company ◇ Most of our funds are held in cash.

2 [+ obj] to organize or have a meeting, a discussion, an event, etc: The board will hold a meeting on Tuesday to discuss the proposals.

3 [+ obj] to have a particular job or position, especially an important or official one: Few women hold top executive jobs.

4 [+ obj] to have enough space for sth/sb; to contain sth/sb: This barrel holds 25 litres.

5 [+ obj] to keep a price, cost, etc. at a particular level: The central bank has decided to hold interest rates at 4.0 per cent.

6 [+ obj or no obj] to remain the same: How long can these prices hold? ◇ These stocks tend to **hold their value**.

7 [+ obj] to keep sth so that it can be used later: records held on computer ◇ We can hold your reservation for three days. ◇ stocks of finished goods held by manufacturers

8 [+ obj or no obj] to wait until you can speak to the person you have telephoned: That extension is busy right now. Can you hold?

9 (Law) [+ obj or no obj] to make a judgement about sb/sth in a court: The judge held (**that**) she had been negligent. → FIND (2)

IDM be in a 'holding pattern to be in a situation where there is not much change or activity: The market will be in a holding pattern until after the holiday. **hold sb's 'hand** to give sb a lot of support and help (often used in a disapproving way): A qualified employee shouldn't need anyone to hold their hand. → HAND-HOLDING **,hold the 'floor** to speak during a formal discussion, especially for a long time so that nobody else can speak **,hold the 'purse strings** to be in control of how money is spent → idioms at CHECK noun, GROUND noun

PHRV ,hold sb/sth 'back to limit or slow down the progress of sb/sth: High interest rates are holding back growth. **,hold sth 'down 1** to keep sth at a low level: *The rate of inflation must be held down.* ◇ *holding down costs* **2** to keep a job for some time: *He finds it difficult to hold down a job.* **,hold 'on** used on the telephone to ask sb to wait until they can talk to the person they want: *Can you hold on? I'll see if he's here.* **,hold 'on to sth/sb**; **,hold 'onto sth/sb** to keep sth/sb that is valuable or that provides an advantage; to not give or sell sth to sb else: *You should hold on to your oil shares.* ◇ *the difficulty of holding on to skilled employees* **,hold 'out for sth** to cause a delay in reaching an agreement because you hope you will gain sth: *The union is holding out for a higher pay offer.* → HOLDOUT **,hold sth 'over** (*usually* be held over) to not deal with sth immediately; to leave sth to be dealt with later: *This matter will be held over until the next meeting.* **,hold 'up** to remain strong; to work well: *Sales for the third quarter held up better than expected.* **,hold sb/sth 'up** to delay or block the movement or progress of sb/sth: *Differences of opinion over price could hold up a deal.* → HOLD-UP

● *noun*
1 [sing.] influence, power or control over sb/sth: *The merger will allow them to increase their hold* **on** *the domestic market.* ◇ *The management still have a strong hold* **over** *the company.*
● *to* **gain/increase/loosen/lose/maintain/tighten** *a hold*
2 (*Stock Exchange*) [U; sing.] = HOLD RATING: *Deutsche Bank downgraded the stock from 'hold' to 'sell'.*
3 (*Transport*) [C] the part of a ship or plane where the goods being carried are stored: *The goods were loaded into the ship's hold.*
IDM **on 'hold 1** delayed until a later time or date: *The project has been* **put** *on hold due to lack of funding.* **2** (especially about interest rates) remaining the same: *The committee voted to* **keep/leave** *interest rates on hold.* **3** if a person on the telephone is put **on hold**, they have to wait until the person that they want to talk to is free: *Do you mind if I* **put** *you on hold?* **take 'hold** to start to have an effect; to become strong: *A new idea about management took hold in boardrooms and business schools.*

★ **holder** /ˈhəʊldə(r); *AmE* ˈhoʊ-/ *noun* [C]
――――――――――――――――
SEE ALSO: **title-holder**
――――――――――――――――
a person who has or owns the thing mentioned: *a licence/patent holder* ◇ *a holder of bonds/debt/equity/shares* ◇ *an account holder* ◇ *This form must be signed by the credit-card holder.* ◇ *previous holders of the post* ◇ *job holders*

,holder of 'record = SHAREHOLDER OF RECORD

★ **holding** /ˈhəʊldɪŋ; *AmE* ˈhoʊ-/ *noun*
――――――――――――――――
SEE ALSO: **cross-holding, hand-holding**
――――――――――――――――
(*Finance*)
1 [C, usually pl.] an amount of sth that a company, fund, etc. owns as an asset: *The group has large holdings* **in/of** *government bonds.* ◇ *Central banks have increased their euro holdings.* ◇ *a cash holding of 1.76 billion pounds* → SHAREHOLDING (2)
● **bond/equity/property/real estate** *holdings*
2 [C] a share of the ownership of a company; the number or value of the shares owned: *They have a 27% holding* **in** *the company.* ◇ *The chairman increased his holding to 670 000 shares.* ◇ *The fund's holdings include Samsung Electronics Co. and SK Telecom Corp* (= shares in these companies).
SYN SHAREHOLDING (1)
● *to* **build (up)/have/increase/raise/reduce/sell** *a holding* ◆ *a* **majority/minority** *holding*
3 Holdings [pl.] used especially in the names of companies to show that the company is a HOLDING COMPANY: *HSBC Holdings PLC*

'holding ,company *noun* [C]
(*Finance*) a company that is formed to buy shares in other companies which it then controls: *Electro Investments is the holding company* **of/for** *the group.* ◇ *The group consists of a holding company and three subsidiaries.* → HOLDING (3), PARENT COMPANY

――――――――――――――――
WHICH WORD?

holding company/parent company

Both words are used about companies that own other companies (called **subsidiaries**).

Parent company is more common when referring to a company that is the main owner of a subsidiary and operates in the same type of business: *Citigroup, the parent company of Citibank.*

Holding company often describes a company that owns shares in different types of businesses and may or may not carry out its own business activities: *The holding company owns 25% of each of the regional banks.* ◇ *Zest Ventures is a holding company for the family's publishing and property interests.*

See note at GROUP
――――――――――――――――

'holding cost = CARRYING CHARGE (1)

'holding ope,ration *noun* [C]
a series of actions that are taken so that a particular situation stays the same or does not get any worse: *They are engaged in a holding operation, designed to keep the company afloat* (= with enough money to survive).

holdout /ˈhəʊldaʊt; *AmE* ˈhoʊld-/ *noun* [C]
(*especially AmE*)
a person who resists or delays accepting sth; an act of resisting sth: *The last holdouts were the engineers, who refused to accept pay cuts.* → HOLD OUT FOR STH at HOLD *verb*

'hold ,rating *noun* [C] (*also* **hold** [U; sing.])
(*Stock Exchange*) a statement by a bank, a dealer, etc. that investors should keep a particular company's shares rather than buy or sell them: *Most analysts have a hold rating on the shares.*
● *to* **have/put** *a hold rating on sth*

'hold-up *noun* [C]
a situation in which sth is prevented from happening for a short time: *The fault caused a hold-up in production.* ◇ *technical hold-ups* → HOLD SB/STH UP at HOLD *verb*

,hole in the 'wall *noun* [C] (*BrE*) (*informal*)
a CASH MACHINE (= a machine from which you can get money using a bank card)

holiday /ˈhɒlədeɪ; *AmE* ˈhɑːl-; *BrE also* -di/ *noun*
――――――――――――――――
SEE ALSO: **bank holiday, legal ~, package ~, public ~, tax ~**
――――――――――――――――
1 [U] (*also* **holidays** [pl.]) (*both BrE*) (*AmE* **va'cation**) a period of time when you are not at work. Employees are allowed a particular number of days of paid **holiday**: *I'm afraid Mr. Walsh is away on* **holiday** *this week.* ◇ *The package includes 20 days' paid holiday a year.* ◇ *My holiday entitlement is 25 working days.*
2 [C] (*BrE*) (*AmE* **va'cation**) a period of time spent travelling or resting away from home: *An increasing number of people are booking holidays on the Internet.* ◇ *a bad year for holiday companies*
3 [C] a day when most people do not go to work or school, especially because of a religious or national celebration: *Financial markets were closed for the New Year's holiday.* ◇ *The store has had its busiest holiday shopping season for some years.*

4 holidays [pl.] (*AmE*) the time in December and early January that includes Christmas, Hanukkah and New Year: *the last trading day before the year-end holidays*
5 [C] (*BrE*) a period of time when you do not need to make a particular payment: *As there was a surplus in the pension fund, the employer took a contribution holiday*
○ *a contribution/payment/pension* holiday

'holiday rep = REPRESENTATIVE *noun* (3)

holidays = HOLIDAY (1,4)

home /həʊm; *AmE* hoʊm/ *adjective, adverb*
●*adjective* [only before noun]

SEE ALSO: at-home, in-~, stay-at-~

1 connected with the place where sb lives: *a person's home address/town* ◇ *They offer free home delivery on all their products.*
2 connected with the place where a business or an organization is established: *We established excellent distribution networks in our home state of North Carolina.*
3 used or made at home: *a home computer*
4 (*especially BrE*) connected with your own country or region rather than foreign countries or regions: *products for the home market* SYN DOMESTIC
●*adverb*
IDM **bring home the 'bacon** (*informal*) to earn money for your company, your family, etc.; to be successful at sth: *The quality of your product is what is going to bring home the bacon.* **take/bring home sth** to earn the amount mentioned: *The directors took home an additional $5 million in bonuses.*
→ TAKE-HOME PAY

home 'banking *noun* [U]
a system for controlling a bank account from your home, for example, giving instructions to the bank by telephone

home 'country *noun* [C]
the country where an organization that operates in many countries is based: *The manufacturer earns more than 50% of its revenue outside its home country.* → HOST COUNTRY

home enter'tainment *noun* [U]
all the electronic equipment, movies/films, music recordings, etc. that people use in their homes for entertainment; the business of selling these things: *a supplier of home entertainment equipment* ◇ *the home entertainment sector*

'home ,equity = EQUITY (3)

home 'equity loan (*also spelled* **home-equity ~**) *noun* [C]
a loan that you can get by using the value of your home after all debts have been paid as COLLATERAL (= sth that you will lose if you do not pay back the loan)

home im'provement *noun* [U] (*also* **home im'provements**, *plural*)
making changes to your home, for example by adding a new room, better windows, etc.; the business of providing equipment, tools, supplies, etc. for this: *a home improvement chain/retailer/store* ◇ *a home improvement loan*

home 'loan *noun* [C]
a loan that you get from a bank or similar financial organization to buy a house, flat/apartment, etc: *A record number of home loans were approved in December.* → MORTGAGE See note at LOAN

home 'office *noun* [C]
a part of your home that you use regularly for business: *She works out of her home office in Chicago.*

homeowner /'həʊməʊnə(r); *AmE* 'hoʊmoʊ-/ *noun* [C]
a person who owns their house or flat/apartment: *Many homeowners are selling their properties and renting.*

★**'home page** *noun* [C]
(*IT*)
1 the main page created by a company, an organization, etc. on the Internet from which connections to other pages can be made
2 a page on the Internet that you choose to appear first on your screen whenever you make a connection to the Internet

'home ,product *noun* [C, usually pl.]
goods that are used in the home, such as items for the kitchen and bathroom, sheets, furniture, etc: *The new store combines upmarket food retail with home products.*

home re'pair *noun* [U]
the activity of repairing or decorating things in the home yourself, instead of paying sb to do it: *Because of the national passion for home repair, DIY sales have risen almost 7%.* SYN DIY

home 'shopping *noun* [U]
a way of choosing goods at home and buying them by ordering by telephone, email, or on the Internet and having them delivered to your home: *The supermarket operates a successful home-shopping service.*

homeshoring /'həʊmʃɔ:rɪŋ; *AmE* 'hoʊm-/ *noun* [U]
(*HR, informal*) the act of moving part of your company's operations to smaller towns in your own country or to people working from their homes → OFFSHORE *verb*

homeworker /'həʊmwɜ:kə(r); *AmE* 'hoʊmwɜ:rk-/ *noun* [C]
(*HR*) a person who works for a company at home rather than in an office ▸ **'homeworking** *noun* [U]

Hon (*also spelled* **Hon.**, *especially in AmE*) *abbr* (*BrE*)
a short way of writing **Honorary** in official titles of jobs: *Hon Treasurer: K Scott*

honcho /'hɒntʃəʊ; *AmE* 'hɑ:ntʃoʊ/ *noun* [C] (*plural* **honchos**) (*especially AmE*) (*informal*)
the person who is in charge of: *the company's head honcho* → BOSS

hone /həʊn; *AmE* hoʊn/ *verb* [+ obj]
to develop and improve sth, especially a skill, over a period of time: *She's a finance expert who has honed her skills working for top accounting firms.*

honor = HONOUR

honorarium /,ɒnə'reəriəm; *AmE* ,ɑ:nə'rer-/ *noun* [C] (*plural* **honoraria** /,ɒnə'reəriə; *AmE* ,ɑ:nə'rer-/)
(*HR, formal*) a payment made for sb's professional services HELP Use **an**, not **a** before **honorarium**.

honorary /'ɒnərəri; *AmE* 'ɑ:nəreri/ *adjective* (*abbr* **Hon**)
(about a position in an organization) not paid: *an honorary chairman*

honour (*AmE spelling* **honor**) /'ɒnə(r); *AmE* 'ɑ:nər/ *verb, noun*
●*verb* [+ obj]
1 to do what you have agreed or promised to do: *The company was advised that they were not obliged to honour the contract.* ◇ *The bank refused to honour the cheque* (= keep an agreement to pay it). ◇ *The store has a policy of honouring all cards* (= allowing them to be used).
○ *to honour a* **commitment/contract/obligation/pledge** ◆ *to honour a* **card/cheque/ticket**

2 to pay money that you owe: *They think the group will be unable to honour its debts.*
O *to honour a* **commitment/debt/payment**
→ DISHONOUR
● *noun* **HELP** Use **an**, not **a**, before **honour**.
1 [U] great respect and admiration for sb: *the guest of honour* (= the most important one)
2 [C] an award, official title, etc. given to sb as a reward for sth that they have done: *Two European companies took top honours for best car and truck.*

hook /hʊk/ *noun, verb*
● *noun* [C] (*informal*)
something interesting, clever, strange, etc. that is used to attract people's attention: *The promotion is a hook to attract consumers.*
IDM **be on the 'hook (for sth/to do sth)** (*informal*) (*AmE*) to be legally responsible for paying sth or for doing sth: *Unless you report the theft of your credit card immediately you may be on the hook for $500.*
get (sb) off the 'hook; let sb off the 'hook (*informal*) to free yourself or sb else from a difficult situation or a punishment → idiom at RING *verb*
● *verb* [+ obj] (*informal*)
to attract and keep sb's attention: *The show hooked around 2.4 million viewers.*
PHR V **hook 'in; hook 'into sth; hook sth 'into sth** (*IT*) to be connected or to connect sth to a computer or telephone system, etc: *Our customers can still hook in from America.* **hook 'up (with sb)** (*informal*) to start working with sb: *She hooked up with a partner to start a children's clothing company.* **hook 'up (to sth); hook sth 'up (to sth)** to connect sb/sth to a piece of electronic equipment or to a power supply: *Check that the modem is hooked up to the phone line.* → HOOK-UP **hook sb 'up (with sb/sth)** (*informal*) to arrange for sb to meet sb or to do sth: *I can hook you up with their chief buyer.*

'hook-up (*also spelled* **hookup**) *noun* [C]
a connection between two or more pieces of equipment, especially electronic equipment: *Each room has a high-speed Internet hook-up.*

HOQ /ˌeɪtʃ əʊ ˈkjuː; *AmE* oʊ/ = HOUSE OF QUALITY

horizontal /ˌhɒrɪˈzɒntl; *AmE* ˌhɔːrəˈzɑːntl; ˌhɑːr-/ *adjective*
1 (*HR*) having few levels of management or control between the top and the bottom: *changing from a vertical to a horizontal organization* ◇ *a horizontal management structure* → FLAT
2 (*HR*) having the same level in a group or an organization; involving people or jobs at the same level: *Her transfer to the marketing department was a horizontal move rather than a promotion.* ◇ *Horizontal communication in a company is far more informal and social than vertical communication.*
SYN LATERAL
3 (about a line, etc.) flat and level; going across and parallel to the ground rather than going up and down: *the horizontal axis of the graph* → VERTICAL

horizontal 'equity *noun* [U]
(*Economics*) the principle that people with the same characteristics should be treated in the same way, for example that people with a similar level of income should pay the same rate of tax → VERTICAL EQUITY

hori,zontal inte'gration (*also* hori,zontal ex'pansion, ,lateral inte'gration) *noun* [U,C]
(*Economics*) a situation where different companies that are involved in the same stage of producing or selling sth join together → HORIZONTAL MERGER— Picture at INTEGRATION

horizontal 'loading *noun* [U]
(*HR*) the fact of giving sb more tasks to do in their job, but no more responsibility → VERTICAL LOADING

horizontal 'merger *noun* [C]
(*Economics*) a situation where a company joins with another company that produces similar goods or provides similar services → HORIZONTAL INTEGRATION

horizontal segre'gation *noun* [U]
(*HR*) used to describe the fact that there are more men than women in some kinds of jobs or industry, and more women than men in others → VERTICAL SEGREGATION

'horse-,trading *noun* [U]
(often used in newspapers) the activity of discussing business with sb using clever or strong methods in order to reach an agreement that suits you

hospitality /ˌhɒspɪˈtæləti; *AmE* ˌhɑːs-/ *noun* [U]
SEE ALSO: corporate hospitality
1 food, drink or services that are provided by an organization for guests, customers, etc: *the hospitality industry* (= hotels, restaurants, etc.)
2 friendly and generous behaviour towards guests: *Thank you for your kind hospitality.*

host /həʊst; *AmE* hoʊst/ *noun, verb*
● *noun* [C]
1 a country, a city or an organization that provides the space, services, etc. for a special event and may also arrange it: *The business school is **playing host** to the conference this year.*
2 a country, a city or an area where an organization operates, especially an organization that is based in another country or city: *The country is now host to 96 multinationals.* → HOST COUNTRY
3 (*IT*) a computer that provides information or services to other computers that are connected to it: *transferring files from the host to your local computer* ◇ *a host computer*
● *verb* [+ obj]
1 to act as a **host** for an event, an organization, etc: *to host a conference/an event/a meeting* ◇ *Japan hosts the biggest proportion of the world's major multinationals.*
2 (*IT*) to store a website on a computer connected to the Internet, usually in exchange for a fee: *a company that builds and hosts e-commerce sites* ◇ *You pay a monthly charge for the hosting service.*
→ WEB HOSTING

host 'country *noun* [C]
a country where an organization that is based in another country operates: *Smaller firms may need to find a partner to work with in the host country.* ◇ *Many of the senior posts go to host-country nationals.* → HOME COUNTRY

hostile /ˈhɒstaɪl; *AmE* ˈhɑːstl; -taɪl/ (*also* un'friendly, *less frequent*) *adjective*
(*Finance*) (about an attempt to buy or gain control of a company) not wanted by the directors of the company that is to be bought: *a hostile attempt to acquire the company* ◇ *They are trying to fight off a $1.2 billion hostile bid from a rival travel operator.* ◇ *The falling share price makes the company vulnerable to a hostile takeover.* → FRIENDLY
O *a hostile* **bid/offer/takeover** • *a hostile* **acquisition/ approach/deal** • *a hostile* **acquirer/bidder**
IDM **to go/turn 'hostile** (*Finance*) to try to force the sale of a company against the wishes of its directors, by offering to buy large enough quantities of shares from its shareholders: *The firm has threatened to go hostile if the board refuses the takeover offer.*

hot-'desking *noun* [U]
(*HR*) the practice in an office of giving workers an available desk when they need one, rather than giving each worker their own desk: *cutting costs by promoting teleworking and hot-desking*
→ HOTELLING
▶ **hot-'desk** *verb* [no obj]: *Some workers such as sales people have traditionally hot-desked.*

hotel /həʊˈtel; AmE hoʊ-/ *noun* [C]
a building where people stay, usually for a short time, paying for their rooms and meals: *to stay at/in a hotel* ◇ *to book a hotel room* ◇ *a budget/luxury/five-star hotel* ◇ *The group is Europe's largest hotel operator.*

hotelier /həʊˈteliə(r); -lier; AmE hoʊˈteljər; ˌoʊtelˈjeɪ/ *noun* [C]
a person who owns or manages a hotel

hotelling (*also spelled* **hoteling**, *especially in AmE*) /həʊˈtelɪŋ; AmE hoʊ-/ *noun* [U] (*especially AmE*)
(*HR*) a system in which employees who normally work outside the company offices, or employees of another company, can arrange to have office space when they need it: *We used hotelling for our audit staff, who spend most of their time with clients.*
→ HOT-DESKING ▶ **hotel** /həʊˈtel; AmE hoʊ-/ *verb* [+ obj *or* no obj] (**-ll-**, *AmE* **-l-**)

'hot key *noun* [C]
(*IT*) one key, or a group of two or three keys, on a computer keyboard that you can press to make a program perform a particular task quickly

hotline /ˈhɒtlaɪn; AmE ˈhɑːt-/ *noun* [C]
a special telephone line that people can use in order to get information or to talk about sth: *They set up a telephone hotline for customers with questions or complaints.*

hotlink /ˈhɒtlɪŋk; AmE ˈhɑːt-/ *noun* [C]
(*IT*) a place in an electronic document that you can click on to move from there to another place in the document or to another electronic document **SYN** HYPERLINK ▶ **'hotlink** *verb* [+ obj]

'hot ˌmoney *noun* [U]
1 (*Finance*) money that is moved quickly between countries in order to make profits from changes in interest rates or in the value of currencies
2 used to say what people who know a lot think will happen: *The hot money is on an outsider as the new CEO.*

the 'hot seat *noun* [sing.] (*informal*)
being in a difficult or unpleasant position where you have to take responsibility for decisions and actions that people may not like: *He has resigned as chief executive after four years in the hot seat.*

hotshot /ˈhɒtʃɒt; AmE ˈhɑːtʃɑːt/ *noun* [C] (*informal*)
a person who is extremely successful in their career: *Wall Street is filled with hardworking young hotshots.* ▶ **'hotshot** *adjective* [only before noun]: *a hotshot lawyer*

'hot spot (*also spelled* **hotspot**) *noun* [C]
(*IT*)
1 an area on a computer screen that you can click on to start an operation such as loading a file
2 a place in a hotel, restaurant, station, etc. that is fitted with a special device that enables you to connect a computer to the Internet without using wires: *a wireless/wi-fi hot spot*

ˌhourly 'rate *noun* [C]
the amount paid for each hour worked: *All store employees are paid an hourly rate.*

house /haʊs/ *noun* (*plural* **houses** /ˈhaʊzɪz/)

SEE ALSO: **clearing house, Companies ~, discount ~, finance ~, front of ~, fulfilment ~, in-~,** etc.

1 [C] (*with other nouns*) a company involved in a particular kind of business; an institution of a

particular kind: *a fashion/banking/publishing house* ◇ *a house magazine/journal* (= for the people who work in that company or business) See note at BUSINESS
2 **House** [sing.] (*BrE*) (*abbr* **Ho.**) used in the names of office buildings: *Their offices are on the second floor of Chester House.*
3 [C] (*with other nouns*) a restaurant: *a coffee house* → idiom at CLEAN *adj.*

'house brand (*also* **'house ˌlabel**) *noun* [C] (*both especially AmE*)
(*Commerce; Marketing*) a product that a shop/store sells with its own name on: *Tesco's successful house brands* ◇ *house-brand products* **SYN** OWN BRAND, PRIVATE BRAND, STORE BRAND

household /ˈhaʊshəʊld; AmE -hoʊld/ *noun, adjective*
● *noun*
all the people living together in a single house or flat/apartment, considered as a unit: *This report is based on a survey of around 5 000 households.* ◇ *How much does the average household spend on food each week?*
❶ *high-income/low-income/middle-income/single-earner* households • *rural/urban* households
● *adjective* [only before noun]
1 connected with looking after a house or flat/apartment and the people living in it: *There has been a sharp increase in household debt.*
2 designed for use in the home: *Sales of durable household goods, such as televisions and washing machines, were strong.* → HOUSEWARES

householder /ˈhaʊshəʊldə(r); AmE -hoʊld-/ *noun* [C] (*formal*)
a person who owns or rents the home that they live in; the person who is in charge of a **household**

ˌhousehold 'name (*also* **ˌhousehold 'word**, *less frequent*) *noun* [C]
a name or brand that has become very well known: *The Electrolux group includes household names such as AEG, Zanussi and Frigidaire.*

ˌhousehold 'product *noun* [C, usually pl.]
a small item that is used in the home, especially for cleaning: *household products such as cleaning liquids, glue and paints*

ˌhousehold 'word = HOUSEHOLD NAME

housekeeping /ˈhaʊskiːpɪŋ/ *noun* [U]
1 jobs that are done to enable an organization or a computer system to work well: *A spending review is simply good housekeeping.*
2 the work involved in taking care of a hotel, an office building, etc. especially cleaning the rooms; the department that is responsible for this: *Call housekeeping and tell them to bring us some clean towels.*

ˌHouse of 'Quality *noun* [C,U] (*abbr* **HOQ**)
(*Production*) a technique used when new products are being planned, that collects information from customers about what they want and need, information about competing products, and technical information → QUALITY FUNCTION DEPLOYMENT

houseware /ˈhaʊsweə(r); AmE -wer/ *noun* [U] (*also* **'housewares** [pl.] *especially AmE*)
small things that are used in the home, especially kitchen equipment and electrical items **NOTE** The term **household goods** is also used, especially in British English.

housing /ˈhaʊzɪŋ/ *noun*
1 [U] houses, flats/apartments, etc. that people live in, especially when referring to their type, price or condition: *There is a shortage of affordable*

housing in the city. ◇ a boom/slowdown in the **housing market** (= the activity of buying and selling houses, etc.)
2 [U] the job of providing houses, flats/apartments, etc. for people to live in: a housing committee/department/officer
3 [C] a hard cover that protects part of a machine or a piece of equipment: There was a small crack in the plastic housing.

'housing start noun [C]
(Economics) a new home that has started to be built **NOTE** The number of **housing starts** in a particular period is used as an important sign of the state of the economy: Housing starts rose 2.4% in November as low mortgage rates attracted buyers.

'how-to adjective, noun
● **adjective** [only before noun]
used to describe a book, course, etc. that gives you detailed and practical advice: a how-to guide to building a business plan
● **noun** [C] (plural **how-tos**)
a piece of detailed and practical advice; a book, etc. containing this kind of advice: Now we come to the how-tos of web design.

h.p. (also spelled **HP**) /ˌeɪtʃ ˈpiː/ = HIRE PURCHASE

HQ /ˌeɪtʃ ˈkjuː/ = HEADQUARTERS

HR /ˌeɪtʃ ˈɑː(r)/ = HUMAN RESOURCES (2)

HRD /ˌeɪtʃ ɑː ˈdiː; AmE ɑːr/ = HUMAN RESOURCE DEVELOPMENT

HRIS /ˌeɪtʃ ɑːr aɪ ˈes/ = HUMAN RESOURCE INFORMATION SYSTEM

HRM /ˌeɪtʃ ɑːr ˈem/ = HUMAN RESOURCE MANAGEMENT

HRP /ˌeɪtʃ ɑː ˈpiː; AmE ɑːr/ = HUMAN RESOURCE PLANNING

★ **HTML** /ˌeɪtʃ tiː em ˈel/ abbr
(IT) **Hypertext Mark-up Language** a system used to mark text for WORLD WIDE WEB pages in order to obtain colours, style, pictures, etc: an HTML document/file/version

HTTP /ˌeɪtʃ tiː tiː ˈpiː/ abbr
(IT) **Hypertext Transfer Protocol** the set of rules that control the way data is sent and received over the Internet

hub /hʌb/ noun [C, usually sing.]
1 the central and most important part of a particular place or activity: the commercial hub of the city ◇ Mumbai, India's financial hub ◇ He's a man who likes to feel he's **at the hub of things** (= where things happen and where important decisions are made).
2 (IT; Transport) in a system of transport or communication, a central place to which passengers, messages, etc. go before going on to another place: All international flights are via our hub at Schipol airport. ◇ a distribution/transportation/network hub ◇ a hub airport

hub-and-'spoke ˌsystem noun [C]
(Transport) a system of transport in which passengers or cargo go from local airports, stations, etc. to a central one (a **hub**), from where flights, etc. go to other places; any organization, system of communication, etc. with this structure

ˌhuman 'capital noun [U]
(Economics; HR) people, when considering the value of their skills, knowledge and experience to an organization or a country: Financial capital means little to a company without human capital. ◇ to invest in human capital (= to provide better education, training, etc.)

ˌhuman 'factors engiˌneering noun [U] (abbr HFE)
the use of scientific knowledge in designing systems, equipment, tools, etc. for work so that people can use them in the safest and most effective way → ERGONOMICS

ˌhuman reˈlations noun
(HR)
1 [pl.] the way in which employees treat and deal with each other in an organization
2 [U] the study of how to improve this in order to make an organization more friendly, efficient, etc.

ˌhuman reˈsource deˌvelopment noun [U] (abbr HRD)
(HR) the process of encouraging employees to gain new skills and knowledge through training, courses, etc.

ˈhuman reˈsource inforˈmation ˌsystem noun [C] (abbr HRIS)
(HR) a computer system that is used to collect, store and provide information about employees that will be used in HUMAN RESOURCE MANAGEMENT

ˌhuman reˈsource ˌmanagement noun [U] (abbr HRM)
(HR) the activities involved in choosing, training, etc. and taking care of employees in an organization, especially in helping them develop their skills and abilities in a way that will help the organization → HARD HRM, SOFT HRM

ˌhuman reˈsource ˌplanning noun [U] (abbr HRP)
(HR) the activity of deciding what skills, knowledge and abilities an organization needs and how these can be met by existing and new employees

★ **ˌhuman reˈsources** noun
(HR)
1 [pl.] the people who work for a particular organization; their skills and abilities, seen as sth the organization can use: investing in human resources ◇ the human resources manager
2 [U with sing./pl. verb] (abbr **HR**) the department in a company that deals with employing and training people: the human resources director ◇ HR executives/managers/professionals **SYN** PERSONNEL
▶ **ˌhuman reˈsource** adjective [only before noun]: a human resource policy/strategy ◇ human resource managers/professionals/consultants

hundredweight /ˈhʌndrədweɪt/ noun [C] (plural **hundredweight**) (abbr **cwt.**)
a unit for measuring weight equal to 112 pounds in the UK and 100 pounds in the US. There are 20 **hundredweight** in a ton.

hurdle /ˈhɜːdl; AmE ˈhɜːrdl/ noun [C]
a problem or difficulty that must be solved or dealt with before you can achieve sth: There are several legal hurdles to **overcome** before the merger can go ahead.

'hush ˌmoney noun [U]
money that is paid to sb so that they do not tell others about sth secret or dishonest

hybrid /ˈhaɪbrɪd/ noun [C]
something that is the product of mixing two or more different things: The new magazine is a hybrid between a consumer and a customer magazine. ◇ a hybrid vehicle (= for example, one that has both a petrol engine and an electric motor)

hygiene /ˈhaɪdʒiːn/ noun [U]

SEE ALSO: industrial hygiene, occupational hygiene

the practice of keeping yourself and your working areas clean in order to prevent illness and disease: food hygiene ◇ In the interests of hygiene, please wash your hands. ◇ The factory failed to meet hygiene standards.

hype /haɪp/ *noun, verb*
● *noun* [U]
advertisements and discussion on television, radio, etc. telling the public about a product, service, etc. and about how good or important it is: *marketing/ media hype* ◇ *Despite all the hype **about/ surrounding** electronic books, sales have been slow.*
● *verb* [+ obj] (*informal*)
hype sth (up) to advertise sth a lot and exaggerate its good qualities, in order to get a lot of attention for it: *Brokers were accused of hyping certain stocks during the technology boom.*

hyper- /ˈhaɪpə(r)/ *prefix* (*used in adjectives and nouns*)
more than normal; too much: *a hypercompetitive industry* ◇ *a period of hypergrowth*

hypercompetition /ˌhaɪpəˌkɒmpəˈtɪʃn; *AmE* ˌhaɪpərˌkɑːm-/ *noun* [U]
(*Economics*) a situation in which all the companies producing particular goods or services continue to compete with each other in order to try to make the way they produce them as cheap and efficient as possible ▶ **hypercompetitive** /ˌhaɪpə kəm-ˈpetətɪv; *AmE* ˌhaɪpər-/ *adjective*

hyperinflation /ˌhaɪpərɪnˈfleɪʃn/ *noun* [U]
(*Economics*) a situation in which prices and wages rise very fast, causing damage to a country's economy

hyperlink /ˈhaɪpəlɪŋk; *AmE* -pərl-/ *noun* [C]
(*IT*) a place in an electronic document, for example an Internet page, that you can click on in order to show another document or a different part of the same document: *There are hyperlinks **to** our partners' websites.* ◇ *an email with embedded hyperlinks* SYN HOTLINK ▶ **ˈhyperlink** *verb* [+ obj]: *a hyperlinked set of web pages*

hypermarket /ˈhaɪpəmɑːkɪt; *AmE* -pərmɑːrk-/ *noun* [C]
a very large shop/store, usually outside a town, that sells a wide range of goods: *The company plans to open 15 hypermarkets in Japan.* ◇ *a chain of hypermarkets* See note at SHOP

hypertext /ˈhaɪpətekst; *AmE* -pərt-/ *noun* [U]
(*IT*) text stored in a computer system that contains links that allow the user to move from one piece of text or document to another: *a hypertext link on the Internet* → HTML

I i

I-9 form /aɪ ˈnaɪn/ *noun* [C]
(*HR*) an official document that an employer must have which shows that an employee has the right to work in the US

IAS /ˌaɪ eɪ ˈes/ = INTERNATIONAL ACCOUNTING STANDARDS

IASB /ˌaɪ eɪ es ˈbiː/ = INTERNATIONAL ACCOUNTING STANDARDS BOARD

IATA /aɪˈɑːtə/ *abbr*
International Air Transport Association the organization that most of the world's airlines belong to, which helps them to operate efficiently and sets standards for how tickets are sold, the safety of aircraft, etc: *an IATA approved travel agency*

IC /ˌaɪ ˈsiː/ = INDEPENDENT CONTRACTOR

ICAO /ˌaɪ si: eɪ ˈəʊ; *AmE* ˈoʊ/ = INTERNATIONAL CIVIL AVIATION ORGANIZATION

ICC /ˌaɪ siː ˈsiː/ = INTERNATIONAL CHAMBER OF COMMERCE

icon /ˈaɪkɒn; *AmE* -kɑːn/ *noun* [C]
1 (*IT*) a small picture on a computer screen that represents a program or a file: *Click on the printer icon.*
2 a famous person, organization or thing that people admire and see as a symbol of a particular idea, style, way of doing things, etc: *Fiat became an icon of Italian industry.*
▶ **iconic** /aɪˈkɒnɪk; *AmE* -ˈkɑːnɪk/ *adjective*: *The Body Shop achieved iconic status in the 1980s.*

ICT /ˌaɪ siː ˈtiː/ *abbr* (*BrE*)
information and communication technology/ technologies the use of computers, the Internet, video, and other technology in an organization to collect, store and send information; the computers and other equipment that are used for this

ID /ˌaɪ ˈdiː/ *noun, verb*
● *noun* [U,C]
an official way of showing who you are, for example a document with your name, date of birth and often a photograph on it: *You must carry ID at all times.* ◇ *an ID card/badge/number* NOTE ID is a short form of 'identity' or 'identification'.
● *verb* [+ obj] (**ID's, ID'ing, ID'd, ID'd**) (*informal*)
to ask sb to show an official document that shows who they are, how old they are, etc: *You can't get into the building without being ID'd.*

IDD /ˌaɪ di: ˈdiː/ *abbr*
International Direct Dialling a system that allows you to telephone people in other countries without needing to be connected by the OPERATOR

identification /aɪˌdentɪfɪˈkeɪʃn/ *noun*
1 [U,C] the process of showing, proving or recognizing who or what sb/sth is: *Each part has a number for easy identification.* ◇ *an identification number*
2 [U] official papers or a document that can prove who you are: *Can I see some identification, please?* → ID *noun*

identifier /aɪˈdentɪfaɪə(r)/ *noun* [C]
1 a number, name, etc. that is used to identify a person or thing: *Your social security number serves as a personal identifier.*
2 (*IT*) a series of characters used to refer to a program or set of data within a program

identify /aɪˈdentɪfaɪ/ *verb* [+ obj] (**identifies, identifying, identified, identified**)
1 to find or discover sb/sth: *As yet they have not identified a buyer for the company.* ◇ *The group identified €16 million in possible cost savings.* ◇ *We think we have identified a gap in the market.*
2 to recognize sb/sth and be able to say who or what they are: *The machine identifies you by scanning your fingerprint.*

i'dentity theft *noun* [U]
using somebody else's name to obtain credit cards in their name or to take money out of their account: *victims of identity theft* ▶ **i'dentity thief** *noun* [C]

ideology /ˌaɪdiˈɒlədʒi; AmE -ˈɑːl-/ noun [C,U] (plural **ideologies**)

a set of beliefs, especially one held by a particular group, that influences the way people behave: *Key decisions are in line with the core ideology of the organization.* ▶ **ideological** /ˌaɪdiəˈlɒdʒɪkl; AmE -ˈlɑːdʒ-/ adjective **ideologically** /ˌaɪdiəˈlɒdʒɪkli; AmE -ˈlɑːdʒ-/ adverb

idle /ˈaɪdl/ adjective, verb

● *adjective*

1 (about machines, factories, etc.) not being used: *Many of the factories lie idle during the holiday season.* ◇ *an increase in idle capacity* (= machines, factories, etc. that are not being used) ◇ *Recent research shows there is a lot of idle money in the banking system.*
○ to **lie/remain/sit/stand** idle
2 (about people) not working; without work: *Over ten per cent of the workforce is now idle.*
→ UNEMPLOYED

● *verb* [+ obj] (AmE)

to close a factory, etc. or stop providing work for the workers, especially temporarily: *The strikes have idled nearly 4 000 workers.*

'idle time noun [U]

(*IT*) the time that a machine, especially a computer, is not being used although it is available to use: *The service may be automatically disconnected after 10 minutes of idle time.* → DOWNTIME, UPTIME

i.e. /ˌaɪ ˈiː/ abbr

used to explain exactly what the previous thing that you have mentioned means **NOTE** i.e. is formed from the first letters of a Latin phrase meaning 'that is'.

IFA /ˌaɪ ef ˈeɪ/ = INDEPENDENT FINANCIAL ADVISER

IFRS /ˌaɪ ef ɑːr ˈes/ = INTERNATIONAL FINANCIAL REPORTING STANDARDS

IHT /ˌaɪ eɪtʃ ˈtiː/ = INHERITANCE TAX

★ **illegal** /ɪˈliːɡl/ adjective

not allowed by the law: *They claimed that illegal payments had been made to executives.* ◇ *The legislation will make it illegal to use personal information for marketing purposes.* **OPP** LEGAL
○ illegal **activities/payments/practices/trading** ◆ to **declare/judge/make/rule** sth illegal
▶ **illegally** /ɪˈliːɡəli/ adverb: *The company had acted illegally in fixing the price of its product.* ◇ *illegally copied CDs* See note at COPY

illegality /ˌɪliˈɡæləti/ noun (plural **illegalities**)
1 [U] the state of being illegal: *There was no illegality in their actions.*
2 [C] an illegal act
→ LEGALITY

illicit /ɪˈlɪsɪt/ adjective

not allowed by the law: *the illicit trade in tobacco products* **SYN** ILLEGAL ▶ **il'licitly** adverb

illiquid /ɪˈlɪkwɪd/ adjective

(*Accounting*; *Finance*)
1 (about assets) that cannot easily be sold and changed into cash: *Property is a highly illiquid investment.*
2 (about a company, an investor, etc.) having little cash or few assets that can easily be changed into cash: *Much of their money is tied up in a small, illiquid company.*
3 an illiquid market is one where there is little buying and selling: *In an illiquid market the only way to sell shares fast is to accept a lower price.*
OPP LIQUID—Picture at LIQUIDITY
▶ **illiquidity** /ˌɪlɪˈkwɪdəti/ noun [U]

ILM /ˌaɪ el ˈem/ = INTERNAL LABOUR MARKET

ILO /ˌaɪ el ˈəʊ; AmE ˈoʊ/ = INTERNATIONAL LABOUR ORGANIZATION

IM /ˌaɪ ˈem/ = INFORMATION MANAGEMENT, INSTANT MESSAGING

image /ˈɪmɪdʒ/ noun

SEE ALSO: **brand image, corporate image**

1 [C,U] the impression that a person, an organization or a product, etc. gives to other people or to the public: *The advertisements are intended to improve the product's image.* ◇ *We are trying to convey an image of a reliable, safe brand.* ◇ *In today's business environment, image sells.* ◇ *The industry suffers from an image problem.*
○ to **create/develop/have/present** an image ◆ to **change/improve/promote/shed** an image ◆ sth **damages/tarnishes** sb's/sth's image ◆ a **good/positive/strong** image ◆ a **negative/poor** image
2 [C] a picture of sb/sth seen through a camera or on a television or computer: *The camera produces sharp, high-resolution images.*
○ to **capture/display/produce/scan/store** an image ◆ a **black-and-white/colour/digital** image

'image ˌadvertising noun [U]

(*Marketing*) advertising that creates an attractive impression of a company or a product, so that people will want to buy the product: *Television is the best medium for image advertising.* ◇ *a brand/corporate image advertising campaign* ▶ **'image adˌvertisement** noun [C] → INSTITUTIONAL ADVERTISING, PRODUCT ADVERTISING

'image ˌmarketing noun [U]

(*Marketing*) the activity of trying to sell products by creating an attractive image for a company or a product: *Selling sports shoes through image marketing is more successful than selling through need or usefulness.*

imaging /ˈɪmɪdʒɪŋ/ noun [U]

(*IT*) the use of computers and electronic equipment to obtain, store and display images of objects, documents, pictures, etc: *imaging software/systems/technology*

imbalance /ɪmˈbæləns/ noun [C,U]

a situation in which two or more things are not the same size or are not treated the same, in a way that is unfair or that causes problems: *an imbalance in/of supply and demand* ◇ *Attempts are being made to redress* (= put right) *the imbalance between our export and import figures.* ◇ *the growing trade imbalance between China and the US* → BALANCE
○ to **cause/correct/create/redress** (an) imbalance

imbed = EMBED

IMC /ˌaɪ em ˈsiː/ = INTEGRATED MARKETING COMMUNICATIONS

IMF /ˌaɪ em ˈef/ abbr

International Monetary Fund an organization within the United Nations which encourages trade and economic development. It lends money to countries that are having economic problems and sometimes tells governments to change their economic policies

imˌmediate posˈsession noun [U] (especially AmE)

(*Property*) if a house, flat/apartment, etc. is offered for sale with **immediate possession**, you can move into it as soon as the sale is complete

impact noun, verb

● *noun* /ˈɪmpækt/ [C, usually sing., U]

SEE ALSO: **environmental impact**

the powerful effect that sth has on sb/sth: *What impact will a strong currency have on the economy?*

• **verb** /ɪmˈpækt/ [+ obj or no obj]
to have an effect on sth, usually a bad one: *The high cost of labour will impact **on/upon** business growth.*

impairment /ɪmˈpeəmənt; AmE -ˈperm-/ noun [U]
(*Accounting*) a situation where an asset becomes less valuable and a company must show this by reducing its value in the financial records: *a charge for goodwill impairment* ◇ *An impairment charge will have to be taken* (= paid) *to cover the drop in value of their properties.*

impeach /ɪmˈpiːtʃ/ verb [+ obj]
(about a court or other official body, especially in the US) to charge an important person with a serious crime ▶ **imˈpeachment** noun [U,C]: *the impeachment process/trial*

imperfect /ɪmˈpɜːfɪkt; AmE -ˈpɜːrf-/ adjective
containing mistakes or faults: *All our sale items are slightly imperfect.* ◇ *Flawed or imperfect goods are sold at reduced prices.*

imp,erfect compeˈtition noun [U]
(*Economics*) a situation where there are a limited number of sellers, each with a lot of control over prices and little information about what the others are doing → PERFECT COMPETITION

imperfection /ˌɪmpəˈfekʃn; AmE -pərˈf-/ noun [C,U]
a fault or weakness in sb/sth: *Rapid cooling can cause imperfections in the glass.* ◇ *the imperfections of the international trading system*

im,perfect ˈmarket noun [C, usually sing.]
(*Economics*) a situation where individual buyers and sellers can influence the price of goods, for example if there are only a few sellers, buyers do not have enough information about products and prices, or there are not enough goods of the same type produced: *Health care is an imperfect market, and does not follow the classic rules of supply and demand.*

★**implement** /ˈɪmplɪmənt/ verb [+ obj]
1 to make sth that has been officially decided start to happen or be used: *The banks have agreed to implement measures to improve customer information.* ◇ *These changes will be implemented over a five-year period.*
○ to implement *changes/measures/reforms* • to implement a *decision/plan/policy/strategy* • to implement sth *extensively/fully/successfully*
2 (*IT*) to introduce or start to use a new system: *We have implemented the software across our distribution network.*
▶ **implementation** /ˌɪmplɪmenˈteɪʃn/ noun [U,C]: *the successful implementation of new technology* ◇ *software implementations*

im,plicit ˈknowledge = TACIT KNOWLEDGE

implied /ɪmˈplaɪd/ adjective [only before noun]
(*Law*)
1 an **implied** condition is one that becomes part of an agreement automatically because of the law and does need to be stated: *In a contract for sale of goods there is an implied condition that the goods are of satisfactory quality.*
2 (about a legal agreement) that is believed to exist because of people's behaviour rather than agreed in a formal way: *They argued that they had an implied licence to use the software.*
→ EXPRESS
▶ **imˈpliedly** adverb: *an expressly or impliedly authorized act*

implode /ɪmˈpləʊd; AmE ɪmˈploʊd/ verb [no obj]
(about an organization, a system, etc.) to fail suddenly and completely: *The stock market imploded, losing a quarter of its value in two hours.*
▶ **implosion** /ɪmˈpləʊʒn; AmE -ˈploʊ-/ noun [C,U]

★**import** noun, verb
• **noun** /ˈɪmpɔːt; AmE ˈɪmpɔːrt/

SEE ALSO: **direct import, visible imports**

1 [C, usually pl.] a product or service that is brought into one country from another: *Our largest agricultural import is wheat.* ◇ *food imports from abroad* ◇ *Some domestic producers had been harmed by cheap imports.*
2 imports [pl.] the amount or value of goods and services that are brought from one country into another over a period of time: *an $11 billion increase in imports of goods and services in October* ◇ *Exports fell while imports rose.*
3 [U] the act of buying a product or service from another country and bringing it into a country: *There are strict controls on the import of meat and plants.* ◇ *products approved for import into the EU* ◇ *The import market for organic foods has grown rapidly.* ◇ *an import licence*
OPP EXPORT
• **verb** /ɪmˈpɔːt; AmE ɪmˈpɔːrt/
1 [+ obj or no obj] to bring a product or service into one country from another: *The country has to import most of its raw materials.* ◇ *goods imported from Japan into the US* ◇ *Sales of imported cars have increased.* ◇ *importing countries/nations*
2 [+ obj] to introduce an idea or activity from another country or area: *They are using management ideas imported from the business world.*
3 (*IT*) [+ obj] to move data into one computer file, program or system from another: *Click on the button to import the table into your document.*
OPP EXPORT
▶ **importable** /ɪmˈpɔːtəbl; AmE -ˈpɔːrt-/ adjective: *importable goods* ◇ *importable file formats*
importation /ˌɪmpɔːˈteɪʃn; AmE -pɔːrˈt-/ noun [U,C]: *The government has banned the importation of these foods.*

ˈimport ,duty noun [C,U]
(*Trade*) a tax that is paid on particular goods or services that are brought into a country: *The government imposes import duties on tea of up to 30 per cent.* ◇ *Uncut diamonds are no longer subject to import duty.* → TARIFF

★**importer** /ɪmˈpɔːtə(r); AmE -ˈpɔːrt-/ noun [C]
1 a business, country or person that buys and brings in goods or services from another country: *a London-based importer of Italian goods* ◇ *China* (= its businesses, etc.) *became the second-largest importer of Japanese steel.* ◇ *The country is a **net importer** of oil* (= it imports more than it exports).
2 a country whose government or businesses borrow money or receive investment from other countries: *Traditionally, the country was an importer of capital to finance industrial growth.*
→ EXPORTER

,import-ˈexport adjective [usually before noun]
(*Trade*)
1 an **import-export** company, business, etc. is one that buys goods from foreign suppliers to sell to local companies, as well as supplying local goods to foreign buyers
2 connected with goods and services that are brought into or sent out of a country: *import-export statistics* ◇ *the import-export market*

ˈimport ,surcharge noun [C]
(*Economics*) an extra tax charged on goods being brought into a country in addition to the normal tax (**import duty**)

impose /ɪmˈpəʊz; AmE ɪmˈpoʊz/ verb [+ obj]
to introduce a new law, rule, tax, etc.; to order that a rule, punishment, etc. be used: *A new tax was imposed on fuel.* ◇ *The court can impose fines of up*

to two million euros. ▶ **imposition** /ˌɪmpəˈzɪʃn/ noun [U]: *the imposition of tax on domestic fuel*

impound /ɪmˈpaʊnd/ verb [+ obj]
to officially take sth away from sb, so that they cannot use it: *Customs agents impounded the goods at the docks.* → CONFISCATE

impression /ɪmˈpreʃn/ (also **'ad view**) noun [C]

SEE ALSO: **cost per impression, page impression**

(*Marketing*)
1 the number of times a web page or a BANNER AD is shown: *What is the cost per thousand impressions?*
2 the number of times that one person sees an advertisement
→ PAGE VIEW

imprest /ˈɪmprest/ noun [C]
(*Accounting*)
1 a fund that is used by a business for making regular small payments: *Each office holds an imprest for its running expenses.* ◇ *an imprest account/fund* → FLOAT, PETTY CASH
2 an amount of money that is given in advance to sb for a particular purpose

imprint /ˈɪmprɪnt/ noun [C]
1 a brand name under which books are published: *They publish under several imprints.*
2 the name of the PUBLISHER of a book, usually printed below the title on the first page

improper /ɪmˈprɒpə(r); AmE -ˈprɑːp-/ adjective
dishonest; against the rules: *improper accounting practices* ◇ *She was sued for making improper use of company funds.* ▶ **im'properly** adverb

impropriety /ˌɪmprəˈpraɪəti/ noun [U,C] (plural **improprieties**) (*formal*)
behaviour or actions that are dishonest or not appropriate for a person in a position of responsibility: *allegations of financial impropriety* ◇ *The bank has denied any impropriety in the way it managed the accounts.*

improve /ɪmˈpruːv/ verb [+ obj or no obj]
to become better than before; to make sth/sb better than before: *Market conditions have improved considerably.* ◇ *The shares improved 5¢ to 542¢.* ◇ *We aim to improve efficiency at all our plants.* ◇ *I need to improve my French.* ◇ *an improved quality of service*
✪ *sb/sth begins/continues/fails/starts to improve* ✦ *to aim/attempt/try/work to improve sth* ✦ *to improve (sth) considerably/greatly/dramatically/significantly* ✦ *to improve (sth) continuously/slowly/steadily*
PHR V **im'prove on/upon sth** to achieve or produce sth that is of a better quality than sth else: *We've certainly improved on last year's figures.*

improvement /ɪmˈpruːvmənt/ noun

SEE ALSO: **continuous improvement, home improvement**

1 [U] the act of making sth better; the process of sth becoming better: *The economy is showing signs of improvement.* ◇ *Although we have made progress with quality standards, there is still room for improvement.* ◇ *Retailers saw some improvement in sales this year.*
✪ *to expect/report/see improvement (in sth)* ✦ *sth shows improvement*
2 [C] **improvement (from/on/over sth)** a change in sth that makes it better; sth that is better than it was before: *These figures are a big improvement from a year ago.* ◇ *We have made improvements to the design of many of our products.* ◇ *benefits from cost-cutting and productivity improvements*
✪ *to achieve/expect/make/report/see an improvement* ✦ *sth shows an improvement* ✦ *a big/*

dramatic/major/significant improvement ✦ *a modest/slight/steady improvement*

imprudent /ɪmˈpruːdnt/ adjective (*formal*)
not wise or sensible: *It would be imprudent to invest all your money in one company.* ◇ *imprudent purchases* OPP PRUDENT ▶ **imprudence** /ɪmˈpruːdns/ noun [U] **im'prudently** adverb

'impulse buy (also **'impulse ˌpurchase**) noun [C]
(*Marketing*) a product that you see in a shop/store, etc. and suddenly decide to buy without planning to do so: *One out of every two books sold is an impulse buy.* ◇ *The shelves next to the tills are reserved for impulse buys.* ▶ **'impulse ˌbuyer** (also **'impulse ˌpurchaser**) noun [C]**'impulse ˌbuying** (also **'impulse ˌpurchasing**) noun [U]: *The layout of a supermarket is designed to encourage impulse buying.*

in. (*plural* **in.** *or* **ins.**) = INCH

inactive /ɪnˈæktɪv/ adjective
1 not doing anything; not active: *inactive customers* ◇ *The stock market is likely to remain inactive this week.*
2 not in use; not working: *an inactive bank account* ◇ *an inactive oil well*
▶ **inactivity** /ˌɪnækˈtɪvəti/ noun [U]: *The financial markets have suffered a long period of inactivity.*

inadmissible /ˌɪnədˈmɪsəbl/ adjective
(*Law*) that cannot be allowed or accepted, especially in court: *inadmissible evidence* OPP ADMISSIBLE

inappropriate /ˌɪnəˈprəʊpriət; AmE -ˈproʊ-/ adjective
not suitable or appropriate in a particular situation: *inappropriate actions/behaviour/language* ◇ *It would be inappropriate for me to comment on the situation.* ▶ **ˌinap'propriately** adverb**ˌinap'propriateness** noun [U]

'in-ˌbasket = INBOX (2)

inbound /ˈɪnbaʊnd/ adjective
going towards a place rather than leaving it: *inbound flights/passengers* ◇ *The centre handles over 6 000 inbound calls a week from all around the world.* ◇ *attempts to attract inbound investment* (= from abroad) OPP OUTBOUND → INCOMING (2)

ˌinbound ˌtele'marketing noun [U]
(*Marketing*) selling goods or services by inviting people to telephone the company selling the product → OUTBOUND TELEMARKETING

★ **inbox** /ˈɪnbɒks; AmE -bɑːks/ noun [C]
1 (*IT*) the place in a computer where email messages are shown when they arrive: *Keep the number of messages in your inbox to a minimum.* → OUTBOX
2 (*also spelled* **in-box**, *AmE also* **'in-ˌbasket**) = IN TRAY

ˌin-'built = BUILT-IN

Inc. (*also spelled* **inc**) /ɪŋk/ abbr
used in the names of companies in the US as a short way of writing **Incorporated** (= officially created as a company): *Microsoft Inc.* See note at LTD

inc. = INCL.

inca'pacity ˌbenefit noun [U,C]
in the UK, money that the government pays to people who cannot work because they are ill, injured, etc: *The number of young people on incapacity benefit has risen.*

★ **incentive** /ɪnˈsentɪv/ noun [C,U]

SEE ALSO: **group incentive, sales ~, tax ~**

something that encourages people to do sth, especially to work harder, spend more money, etc: *generous incentives for small businesses to invest in new equipment* ◇ *They are trying to increase their market share by offering customers big financial*

incentives. ◇ *creating an incentive plan to retain key workers* [SYN] INDUCEMENT [OPP] DISINCENTIVE
○ *big/generous/powerful/real/strong incentives • to create/offer/provide incentives • an incentive package/payment/plan/system*

in'centive ,marketing *noun* [U]
a way of selling more goods or services by offering rewards such as low prices, gifts, etc. to customers to persuade them to buy

in'centivize, -ise /ɪn'sentɪvaɪz/ *verb* [+ obj]
to encourage sb to do sth, especially to work harder or to buy sth, by offering them a reward for doing it: *We set up a system of bonuses to incentivize sales staff.* ◇ *incentivizing the purchase of energy-efficient vehicles*

inch /ɪntʃ/ *noun, verb*
● *noun* [C] (*abbr* **in.**)
SEE ALSO: column inch
a unit for measuring length, equal to 2.54 centimetres: *a screen measuring 3.4 inches by 1.8 inches* ◇ *a 14-inch monitor*
● *verb* [no obj] (*used with an adverb or a preposition*)
to move slowly towards a particular level or position: *The euro inched higher to 122.69 against the yen.*

incidental /ˌɪnsɪ'dentl/ *adjective, noun*
● *adjective*
happening in connection with sth else, but not as important as it: *We regarded the delivery service as incidental to our main business.* ◇ *You can claim up to €30 for incidental expenses* (= small costs related to your main activity).
● *noun* [C, usually pl.]
something that happens in connection with sth else, but is less important: *You'll need money for incidentals such as tips and taxis.*

incl. (*BrE also* inc.) *abbr*
1 a short way of writing **including** or **included**, especially in advertisements: *breakfast not incl.* ◇ *€170 inc. all taxes*
2 a short way of writing **inclusive**: *The exhibition runs from 9 to 16 June incl.*

★ include /ɪn'kluːd/ *verb* [+ obj]
1 (*not used in the continuous tenses*) if one thing **includes** another, it has the second thing as one of its parts: *Does the price include tax?* ◇ *Their clients included Unilever and Coca-Cola.* ◇ *Your duties include receiving guests and answering the telephone.*
2 include sb/sth (as/in/on sth) to make sb/sth part of sth: *We haven't included February's sales in these figures.* [OPP] EXCLUDE

including /ɪn'kluːdɪŋ/ *preposition* (*abbr* incl.)
having sth as part of a group or set: *a fare of €79, including taxes* ◇ *How much time do you spend using the Internet for work, not including email?*
[OPP] EXCLUDING

inclusive /ɪn'kluːsɪv/ *adjective*
SEE ALSO: all-inclusive
1 having the total cost, or the cost of the thing mentioned, contained in the price: *Prices are inclusive of all packaging and delivery.* ◇ *a VAT-inclusive price* [OPP] EXCLUSIVE
2 (*BrE*) (*abbr* incl.) including all the days, months, numbers, etc. mentioned: *An extra charge applies for the period (from) 1 to 14 July inclusive.*
3 including a wide range of people, not only the people with power or authority: *The company takes an inclusive approach to decision making* (= it includes the workers in the process).

★ income /'ɪnkʌm; -kəm/ *noun* [C,U]
SEE ALSO: accrued income, adjusted gross ~, deferred ~, discretionary ~, disposable ~, earned ~, expendable ~, etc.
the money that a person, a region, a country, etc. earns from work, from investing money, from business, etc: *people on high/low incomes* ◇ *a weekly income of €400* ◇ *They receive a proportion of their income from the sale of goods and services.* ◇ *Tourism is a major source of income for the area.*
→ EXPENDITURE See note at INCREASE
○ *an annual/a monthly/quarterly/weekly income • family/household/national/personal income • gross/net income • after-tax/pre-tax/post-tax/taxable income • dividend/investment/rental/retirement income • to earn/generate/have/provide/receive (an) income*

WHICH WORD?

income/earnings/revenue
These words all describe money that is earned.

Income is used to describe money earned by a person, an organization or a country, especially on a regular basis. It is usually used in the singular or as an uncountable noun: *an income of $10 000 a year* ◇ *a drop in income*. In the plural, it refers only to money earned by individuals: *The research shows that families on low incomes are struggling with debts.*

Earnings is a plural noun and is used mainly in the context of calculating or reporting amounts that are earned by people or businesses: *Full-year earnings rose by 15%.* ◇ *You must declare all earnings to the tax office.* It is also used to describe money that a country earns from exporting goods: *export earnings*

Revenue [U] or **revenues** [plural] are used about money earned by a business: *A product generates revenue for the business.* ◇ *Over half the company's revenues are in dollars.*

Income [U] or **revenue** [U or plural], not earnings, are used when describing the way in which money is earned: *fee/investment/sales income* (= money earned from fees/investments/sales) ◇ *licence/sales/tax revenues*

,income and ex'penditure ac,count
noun [C]
(*Accounting*) a financial account used by NON-PROFIT organizations such as charities, universities, etc. to record income and expenses; a report of the income and expenses for a particular period: *Donations are credited to the income and expenditure account.* ◇ *The society's income and expenditure account for the year end 31 December shows a surplus of £3.7 million.* → PROFIT AND LOSS ACCOUNT

'income bond *noun* [C]
(*Finance*)
1 in the UK, a type of bond that pays the investor an amount of interest regularly, for example every month: *Many pensioners buy income bonds with part of their pension fund to boost their income.*
2 in the US, a bond that pays interest at a rate which is related to the amount of money earned by the company selling it

'income ef,fect *noun* [C]
(*Economics*) the way in which a change in the price of a product or service results in a change in the quantity demanded because the consumer is able to buy more or less with their money as a result of the price change → SUBSTITUTION EFFECT

'income elas'ticity of de'mand noun [C,U]
(*Economics*) the extent to which people buy more or less of a product or service when the amount of money that they earn changes → ELASTICITY OF DEMAND

'income fund noun [C]
(*Finance*) a type of fund that invests in shares, bonds, etc. that are safe and pay a regular income → GROWTH FUND

'income group noun [C]
(*Economics*) a group of people within the population who earn similar wages: *There is a high percentage of part-time workers within Britain's lowest income group.*
○ *high/low/middle* income groups

'income in,surance (*also* ,**income pro'tection in,surance**) noun [U,C]
a type of insurance in which you receive money if you are unable to work, because you are ill/sick, etc.

'income share noun [C, usually pl.] (*also* '**income stock** [U,C])
(*Finance*) a share in a company that is likely to provide investors with high, regular DIVIDENDS (= payments from company profits)

'income ,statement noun [C] (*AmE*)
(*Accounting*) an official financial record that gives details of all a company's income and expenses for a particular period and shows if it has made a profit or a loss [SYN] PROFIT AND LOSS ACCOUNT

'income stock = INCOME SHARE

'income stream noun [C]
(*Finance*)
1 regular payments that sb receives from an investment or a property, especially over a long period of time: *The investment will bring a steady income stream.*
2 the money that a business produces: *Our research services continue to provide a substantial income stream.*

'income tax noun [U,C]
the amount of money that you pay to the government according to how much you earn or receive from some other sources. In the US, businesses also pay income tax: *cuts in the rate of income tax* ◇ *the agency collecting federal income tax*
○ *corporate/personal* income tax ◆ to *avoid/evade/pay* income tax ◆ to *collect/levy* income tax ◆ to *cut/increase/raise/reduce* income tax

incoming /'ɪnkʌmɪŋ/ adjective [only before noun]
1 recently elected or chosen: *the incoming chairman/chief executive/president*
2 arriving somewhere, or being received: *an incoming flight* ◇ *incoming mail/messages/orders* → INBOUND
[OPP] OUTGOING

incomings /'ɪnkʌmɪŋz/ noun [pl.] (*BrE*) (*informal*)
income [OPP] OUTGOINGS

,**in-'company** = IN-HOUSE

incompatible /,ɪnkəm'pætəbl/ adjective, noun
● *adjective*
(about equipment, especially computers or programs) not able to be used together; not standard: *New software is often incompatible with older computers.* ◇ *These two systems are incompatible.* [OPP] COMPATIBLE ▶ **incompatibility** /,ɪnkəm,pætə'bɪləti/ noun [U,C] (*plural* **incompatibilities**)
● *noun* [C, usually pl.]
something, such as a piece of equipment, a computer program, a drug, a chemical, etc. that cannot be used with something else

incompetence /ɪn'kɒmpɪtəns; *AmE* -'kɑːm-/ noun [U]
the lack of skill or ability to do a job as it should be done: *managerial/professional incompetence* ◇ *She was fired for incompetence.*

incompetent /ɪn'kɒmpɪtənt; *AmE* -'kɑːm-/ adjective, noun
● *adjective*
not having the skill or ability to do a job as it should be done: *incompetent managers/workers* ◇ *his incompetent handling of the company's finances* [OPP] COMPETENT
▶ **in'competently** adverb
● *noun* [C]
a person who does not have the skill or ability to do a job as it should be done

★**incorporate** /ɪn'kɔːpəreɪt; *AmE* -'kɔːrp-/ verb (*often* **be incorporated**)
1 [+ obj or no obj] to form a legal company or organization, for example by obtaining a certificate from the authorities: *The business was incorporated as a limited liability company.* ◇ *The firm incorporated in Delaware in 1997.*
2 [+ obj] incorporate sth (in/into/within sth) to include sth as part of sth else: *Many of your suggestions have been incorporated into the plan.* ◇ *a phone incorporating a digital camera*

★**incorporated** /ɪn'kɔːpəreɪtɪd; *AmE* -'kɔːrp-/ adjective
formed into an official company or organization with legal status: *an incorporated company* ◇ *the Incorporated Society of British Advertisers* ◇ *Wal-Mart Stores Incorporated* → INC. See note at CORPORATION

incorporation /ɪn,kɔːpə'reɪʃn; *AmE* -,kɔːrp-/ noun [U,C]

SEE ALSO: **articles of incorporation, certificate of incorporation**

an act of forming a legal company or organization: *Delaware is the most popular state in the US for incorporation.* ◇ *The rate of new incorporations is a good measure of business activity.* ◇ *The company moved its incorporation from the US to Bermuda for tax purposes* (= it changed its legal home to Bermuda).

Incoterm /'ɪnkəʊtɜːm; 'ɪŋ-; *AmE* -koʊtɜːrm/ noun [C]
(*Trade*) (used in contracts between exporters, importers, etc.) one of a list of standard phrases that show who is responsible for the delivery and insurance of goods being sent between countries
[NOTE] **Incoterm** is formed from the phrase **International Commercial Term**. The **Incoterms** are created by the International Chamber of Commerce and are changed from time to time. They are referred to in contracts by their abbreviations, such as **CIF** (*cost, insurance, freight*) and **FOB** (*free on board*). Note on page S6

★**increase** verb, noun
● *verb* /ɪn'kriːs/ [+ obj or no obj]
to become or to make sth greater in amount, number, value, etc: *Revenues increased 4.5 per cent to ¥3 537 billion.* ◇ *The rate of inflation increased by 2%.* ◇ *Oil has increased in price.* ◇ *concerns over increasing unemployment* ◇ *We need to increase productivity.* ◇ *They've increased the price by 50%.*
[OPP] DECREASE
○ to increase *considerably/dramatically/sharply/significantly* ◆ to increase *gradually/slightly/steadily* ◆ to increase in *number/size/value*
▶ **in'creased** adjective [only before noun]: *increased demand*
● *noun* /'ɪnkriːs/ [C,U]
a rise in the amount, number or value of sth: *The company reported a 12 per cent increase in costs.* ◇ *We expect sales to show a significant increase from/*

over last year. ◇ a year-on-year increase (= between this year and the previous year) ◇ They demanded a wage increase of 3 per cent. ◇ Industrial activity is on the increase. ◇ The rate of increase has slowed.
OPP DECREASE
O a big/dramatic/large/sharp/significant increase • a pay/salary/wage increase • a cost/(an interest) rate/price/tax increase

increment /ˈɪŋkrəmənt/ noun [C]
1 (HR) a regular increase in the amount of money that sb is paid for their job: *The pay system contains automatic annual increments in the early years.*
2 an increase in a number or an amount, especially one in a series: *The bids rose in increments of $1000.*

incremental /ˌɪŋkrəˈmentl/ adjective
1 used to describe sth that happens gradually, a little at a time: *incremental changes/improvements to existing products* ◇ *slow incremental growth*
2 used to describe an increase in a number or amount: *The factory then begins production runs in incremental jumps, from 1000 to 10000 and on up.*
3 (HR) used to describe a system in which the amount of money that sb is paid for their job increases regularly: *After three months you will move to the next point on the incremental scale.*
4 (Accounting) used to describe the total change in income, sales, costs, etc. that results from an extra activity, product, service, customer, employee, etc: *If 12% of possible new customers upgrade their PCs, that could mean tens of millions of dollars in incremental revenue.* ◇ *The incremental cost of delivering one more page of data is zero.*
▶ **incrementally** /ˌɪŋkrəˈmentəli/ adverb: *The number of employees has grown incrementally over the last decade.*

incubator /ˈɪŋkjubeɪtə(r)/ noun [C]
a company that helps people to start businesses, especially ones connected with modern technology or the Internet: *They set up an incubator for biotechnology start-ups.* ◇ *an Internet incubator* (= that helps to start Internet companies)

ˈincubator space noun [C,U]
offices, buildings, etc. that are provided free or at low cost to small, new businesses: *The university provides an incubator space for emerging technology companies.*

incumbent /ɪnˈkʌmbənt/ noun, adjective
● **noun** [C]
1 a person who has an official position: *They are looking for a new chief executive, the previous incumbent having left suddenly.*
2 a company that has a large share of a particular market: *the Swedish telecoms incumbent*
● **adjective**
1 [only before noun] having an official position: *the incumbent manager/chief executive*
2 [only before noun] having a large market share: *incumbent operators without a real threat of competition*
3 (formal) [not before noun] necessary as part of sb's duties: *It was incumbent on/upon them to attend.*

★ **incur** /ɪnˈkɜː(r)/ verb [+ obj] (-rr-)
1 to do sth that means you lose or have to pay an amount of money: *You risk incurring bank charges if you exceed your overdraft limit.* ◇ *The group incurred a €3 million loss on the sale of the business.*
O to incur **charges/costs/debts/expenses/losses**
2 to do sth that means you have to deal with sth unpleasant: *At busy times, orders may incur delays.* ◇ *They incurred the wrath of their customers* (= made them angry) *by putting up their prices again.*
O to incur **delays/risks**

indebted /ɪnˈdetɪd/ adjective (formal)
(about companies, governments, etc.) owing money to other countries or organizations: *The scheme provides relief for heavily indebted countries.* ◇ *Several insurance companies are indebted to the bank.* ▶ **inˈdebtedness** noun [U]: *The board has focused on reducing the level of indebtedness of the group.* ◇ *a rise in consumer indebtedness*

indemnify /ɪnˈdemnɪfaɪ/ verb [+ obj] (indemnifies, indemnifying, indemnified, indemnified)
(Law) to promise to pay sb an amount of money if they suffer any damage or loss: *The contract indemnifies them against loss of earnings.* ◇ *You are indemnified for the legal costs of defending a claim.*
▶ **indemnification** /ɪnˌdemnɪfɪˈkeɪʃn/ noun [U,C]

indemnity /ɪnˈdemnəti/ noun [U,C] (plural indemnities)
SEE ALSO: **double indemnity, letter of indemnity**
(Law)
1 protection against damage or loss, especially in the form of a promise to pay for any that happens; a payment that is made for damage or loss: *an indemnity clause/fund/policy* ◇ *indemnity insurance/cover* ◇ *The parcel service only paid a small indemnity for loss of the two packages.*
2 an agreement not to make sb legally responsible for sth: *She has gained indemnity from prosecution.*

indenture /ɪnˈdentʃə(r)/ noun [C]
(Finance) a legal document that states the conditions that apply to a particular bond: *The*

dates for payment of interest are specified in the **bond indenture.**

★ **independent** /ˌɪndɪˈpendənt/ *adjective, noun*
● *adjective*
1 not part of a larger company or group of companies: *small independent retailers* ◇ *an independent bookstore*
2 not connected with or controlled by sb/sth; not connected with each other: *The marketing team is independent of the sales department.* ◇ *Two independent reports reached the same conclusions.* ◇ *a review by independent auditors*
3 done or given by sb who is not involved in a situation and so is able to judge it fairly: *You should seek independent legal advice.* ◇ *an independent inquiry*
4 supported by private money rather than government money: *independent television/schools* ◇ *the independent sector*
▶ **inde'pendently** *adverb*: *a small independently owned airline* ◇ *The two departments work independently of each other.*
● *noun* [C]
a business that is not connected with a larger company or group of companies: *The group has been buying up smaller independents and converting them into brands.*

inde,pendent con'tractor *noun* [C] (*abbr* **IC**)
a person or business that has a contract with a company to do particular work **NOTE** The company controls what is done, but not how it is done: *The company employs 6 full-time employees and 17 independent contractors.*

inde,pendent di'rector = NON-EXECUTIVE DIRECTOR

inde'pendent fi'nancial ad'viser *noun* [C] (*abbr* **IFA**) (*BrE*)
a person who gives advice about different companies' insurance policies, investments, etc. and helps people to buy them: *Most of their products are sold through independent financial advisers.* → TIED AGENT

★ **index** /ˈɪndeks/ *noun, verb*
● *noun* [C]

SEE ALSO: **All-Share index, All-Stock ~, average earnings ~, card ~, consumer price ~, cost-of-living ~, FTSE 100 ~,** etc.

1 (*Economics*; *Finance*) (*plural* **indices** /ˈɪndɪsiːz/ *or* **indexes**, *especially in AmE*) a system that shows the level of prices, wages, etc. so that they can be compared with those of a previous day or time: *the cost-of-living index* ◇ *an index measuring consumer confidence* ◇ *an index of business activity* ◇ *In the US, all three major indices—the Dow, the Nasdaq and S&P 500—fell today.* ◇ *The manufacturing sector index jumped to 4.9 in December.* → SHARE INDEX See note at INCREASE
2 (*plural* **indices** /ˈɪndɪsiːz/) a sign or measure that sth else can be judged by: *The number of new houses being built is a good index of a country's prosperity.* → INDICATOR
3 (*plural* **indexes**) (*especially BrE*) = CARD INDEX
● *verb* [+ obj]
(*Economics*; *Finance*) (*usually* **be indexed**) to link wages, payments, etc. to the level of prices of particular items, so that they both increase at the same rate: *Salaries are indexed to the rate of inflation.* ◇ *Interest on the bond is indexed to the price of oil.*

indexation /ˌɪndekˈseɪʃn/ *noun* [U]
the practice of linking increases in wages, pensions, etc. to increases in prices

'index card *noun* [C]
a small card used for recording information, kept with others in a box (a **card index**)

-indexed /ˈɪndekst/ *combining form*
(*Finance*) (about investments) having a value or payments that are linked to the thing mentioned: *inflation-indexed securities*

,indexed 'bond *noun* [C]
(*Finance*) a bond whose value or interest payments vary according to changes in a particular index, especially one that measures the general level of prices (**inflation**)

'index fund = TRACKER FUND

,index-'linked *adjective* (*especially BrE*)
(*Economics*; *Finance*) if a bond, pension, wage, etc. is **index-linked**, its value or payments vary according to the rate of INFLATION (= a general rise in the price of goods and services): *We offer an index-linked policy where the sum insured is adjusted in line with general rises in costs.* ▶ **,index-'linking** *noun* [U]

'index ,option *noun* [C]
(*Finance*) a type of investment which involves buying the right to receive or pay an amount of money in the future that is based on the change in value of a particular SHARE INDEX (= a system for showing the average value of a chosen group of shares)

indicative /ɪnˈdɪkətɪv/ *adjective*
1 (*Finance*) [usually before noun] an **indicative** offer, price, etc. shows the amount you expect to pay, charge, etc., but is not decided definitely: *The bank has received an indicative bid for its car leasing business.* ◇ *She said the profit targets were indicative rather than a firm commitment.*
2 showing or suggesting sth: *These results are not indicative of future sales trends.*

★ **indicator** /ˈɪndɪkeɪtə(r)/ *noun* [C]

SEE ALSO: **coincident indicator, economic ~, financial ~, key performance ~, lagging ~, leading ~, performance ~, technical ~**

a sign or figure that shows you what sth is like or how a situation is changing: *January sales are closely watched as an early indicator of consumer confidence.* ◇ *All the indicators are pointing towards further weakness in the economy.*
❶ *a good/an important/a key/reliable indicator* • *sth is considered (as)/seen as/watched as an indicator (of sth)* • *indicators point towards/show/signal/ suggest/tell us sth*

indices = plural of INDEX

indict /ɪnˈdaɪt/ *verb* [+ obj] (*especially AmE*)
(*Law*) (*usually* **be indicted**) to officially charge sb with a serious crime: *He was indicted for failing to pay taxes.* → CHARGE *verb* (4)

indictment /ɪnˈdaɪtmənt/ *noun* [C,U]
(*Law*)
1 (used in connection with serious crimes) a formal document that accuses sb of committing a crime: *The indictment charges him with 14 counts of fraud.*
2 in the US, a decision by a JURY to accuse sb of committing a crime: *Prosecutors are seeking an indictment against the firm.*

indie /ˈɪndi/ *noun* [C] (*informal*)
a small independent company, especially one producing films/movies, books, music CDs, etc.

,indirect 'advertising *noun* [U]
(*Marketing*) advertising that a company uses to make people aware of a product often without them realizing it, for example putting a name on clothing, paying for a sports event or a concert, or giving the product to people free: *In some countries*

there is a ban on direct and indirect advertising of
alcohol and tobacco. → DIRECT ADVERTISING

indirect 'cost *noun* [C, usually pl.]
(*Accounting*) costs that are not directly connected
with making a particular product or providing a
particular service, for example training, heating,
rent, etc: *The move to a single office reduced indirect
costs by 13%. ◇ The software enables us to measure
the exact cost of a customer order, including indirect
costs.* → OVERHEAD OPP DIRECT COST

indirect 'export *noun* [C, usually pl., U]
(*Economics; Trade*)
1 goods or services that are sold to another
country through another company, sometimes in a
different country, rather than sold directly to
customers; this method of selling goods: *The figure
for exports includes indirect exports from third
countries via our ports.*
2 parts, materials, etc. that are sent from one
producer to another before being made into goods
that are exported; this method of exporting goods:
*Most of our products are supplied to furniture
manufacturers for indirect export to North America.*
→ DIRECT EXPORT
▶ **,indirect ex'porting** *noun* [U]

indirect 'labour (*AmE spelling* ~ **labor**) *noun* [U]
1 (*Accounting; HR*) the people in a business who are
not directly involved in producing goods or
providing services, for example senior managers,
secretaries, etc.; the money that is spent on these
people: *As technology advanced, labour costs
decreased and indirect labour increased. ◇ We aim to
reduce indirect labour costs by removing some layers
of supervision.* → INDIRECT COST, INDIRECT
MATERIALS, INDIRECT OVERHEAD
2 (*HR*) people who work for a company or an
organization but are employed by an independent
business that provides their services under a
contract
→ DIRECT LABOUR

indirect 'loss = CONSEQUENTIAL LOSS

indirect 'materials *noun* [pl.]
(*Accounting*) things such as electricity, gas, etc. that
are used when making a product but that do not
form part of the finished product: *Indirect materials
normally represent just 20% of corporate purchasing.*
→ DIRECT MATERIALS

indirect 'overhead *noun* [C]
(*Accounting*) a share of the **overheads** (= money
that a business spends on equipment, electricity,
rent, etc.) that are not connected to a particular
project but form part of the general cost of running
a business: *Indirect overhead costs are often
overlooked when preparing a project budget.*
→ DIRECT OVERHEAD

indirect partici'pation *noun* [U]
(*HR*) the system of workers taking part in making
important decisions through a representative

indirect 'sale *noun*
(*Marketing*)
1 [C, usually pl., U] (*also* **,indirect 'selling** [U]) the
practice of using another company's shops/stores,
salespeople, etc. in order to sell your product
rather than selling it yourself; goods that are sold
in this way: *the indirect sale of financial assets ◇ An
indirect sales channel can be more costly than the
direct approach.*
2 [C] an item sold in this way
→ DIRECT SALE

indirect 'tax *noun* [C,U]
(*Economics*) tax which is collected from businesses
on the goods and services that people buy from
them: *The government raises most of its revenue
from indirect taxes such as VAT and duty on fuel.*
→ DIRECT TAX ▶ **,indirect tax'ation** *noun* [U]

individual /ˌɪndɪˈvɪdʒuəl/ *adjective, noun*
● *adjective* [only before noun]
1 connected with one person; designed for one
person: *individual income tax ◇ individual investors
◇ We set team and individual goals.*
2 considered separately rather than as part of a
group: *Our products are designed for individual
markets. ◇ We can't discuss individual cases.*
● *noun* [C]
a person considered separately rather than as part
of a group: *The tests are used to assess the
individual's strengths and weaknesses.*

indorse = ENDORSE

indorsement = ENDORSEMENT

inducement /ɪnˈdjuːsmənt; *AmE* ɪnˈduːs-/ *noun*
[C,U]
inducement (to sb) (to do sth) something that is
given to sb to persuade them to do sth: *She was
offered a large block of shares as an inducement to
take the job. ◇ With interest rates so low there is little
inducement to save.* SYN INCENTIVE

induction /ɪnˈdʌkʃn/ *noun* [U,C]
(*HR*) the process of introducing sb to a new job,
skill, organization, etc: *induction **into** an
organization's culture ◇ an induction course/
programme ◇ Your induction is tomorrow.*

★ **industrial** /ɪnˈdʌstriəl/ *adjective, noun*
● *adjective* [usually before noun]
1 connected with industry: *an expansion in
industrial activity ◇ industrial development/
production/output ◇ a large industrial business/
conglomerate/group*
2 used by industries: *chips designed for
communications and industrial applications ◇
industrial chemicals/equipment*
3 connected with businesses rather than
individuals: *industrial advertising* (= advertising to
businesses) *◇ industrial consumers*
4 having many industries: *an industrial area ◇ the
world's leading industrial nations*
5 (*HR*) connected with the work that you do: *a
report on industrial injuries ◇ an industrial accident/
disease* SYN JOB-RELATED, WORK-RELATED
● *noun* **industrials** [pl.]
(*Stock Exchange*) manufacturers whose shares are
bought and sold on the stock exchange: *Industrials
showed strong earnings growth in the fourth quarter.
◇ the industrials sector*

in,dustrial 'action (*BrE*) (*AmE* **'job ,action**) *noun*
[U,C]
(*HR*) action that workers take, especially stopping
work, to protest to their employers about sth:
Unions took industrial action over wage demands.
○ *to call (for)/organize/take/threaten industrial
action • to avert/avoid/call off industrial action*

**in'dustrial and ,organi'zational
psy'chology** *noun* [U] (*abbr* I/O psychology)
(*especially AmE*)
(*HR*) the study of how people behave at work and
what influences their attitudes and behaviour, in
order to make organizations better places to work
in and more successful → OCCUPATIONAL
PSYCHOLOGY ▶ **in'dustrial and ,organi'zational
psy'chologist** *noun* [C] (*abbr* I/O psychologist)

in'dustrial base = MANUFACTURING BASE (1)

in,dustrial con'trol *noun* [C]
(*Manufacturing*) an electronic or a mechanical
device that is used to control machinery

in,dustrial de'sign *noun* [U]
the job or skill of designing the shape and
appearance of manufactured products such as

furniture, electronic equipment, etc. ▸ **in,dustrial de'signer** noun [C]

in,dustrial dis'pute noun [C] (BrE) (HR)
1 a disagreement between workers and employers about pay or conditions: *attempts to resolve the industrial dispute*
2 a strike: *The ports were closed because of an industrial dispute.*
SYN LABOUR DISPUTE, TRADE DISPUTE See note at STRIKE

in,dustrial eco'nomics noun [U]
the branch of economics that studies how businesses operate and compete with each other within industries

in,dustrial engi'neering noun [U]
the branch of engineering that studies and designs the most efficient ways that organizations can use people, processes, technology, materials, information, etc. to make or process a product
→ ERGONOMICS ▸ **in,dustrial engi'neer** noun [C]

in,dustrial es'tate (BrE) (AmE **in,dustrial 'park**) (BrE also **'trading es,tate**) noun [C]
an area especially for factories, on the edge of a town: *The plant is located on a nearby industrial estate.*

in'dustrial goods (also **in'dustrial ,products**) noun [pl.]
(Economics) machines, tools, parts, etc. that are produced for use in industry rather than by the public: *They want to eliminate import duties on most consumer and industrial goods.* → CAPITAL GOODS, CONSUMER GOODS, CONSUMPTION GOODS

in,dustrial 'hygiene (also **,occupational 'hygiene**) noun [U]
(HR) the study and practice of protecting and improving the safety and health of people at work

industrialist /ɪn'dʌstriəlɪst/ noun [C]
a person who owns or runs a large factory or industrial company: *Alfred Nobel, the Swedish industrialist* ◇ *a leading/prominent/wealthy industrialist*

★ **industrialize**, **-ise** /ɪn'dʌstriəlaɪz/ verb [+ obj or no obj]
if a country or an area is **industrialized** or if it **industrializes**, industries are developed there: *The southern part of the country was slow to industrialize.* ◇ *a meeting of the world's largest industrialized nations* ◇ *The country has the highest level of public debt in the industrialized world.*
▸ **industrialization**, **-isation** /ɪn,dʌstriəlaɪ'zeɪʃn; AmE -lə'z-/ noun [U]

in,dustrial 'marketing noun [U]
the activity of selling goods and services to other businesses or organizations rather than the public
NOTE This is sometimes called **B2B marketing**.

in,dustrial 'park = INDUSTRIAL ESTATE

in,dustrial pro'duction noun [U]
1 (Economics) the total amount that factories, mines, gas and electricity industries, etc. in a country produce during a particular period: *the industrial production index for October*
2 (Manufacturing) the process of making sth in large amounts in a factory: *the industrial production of iron*

in'dustrial ,products = INDUSTRIAL GOODS

in,dustrial re'lations noun [pl.] (abbr IR)
(HR) relations between employers and employees in an organization or an industry, particularly through trade/labor unions: *laws on labour and industrial relations* ◇ *The company is attempting to*

improve its industrial relations. ◇ *an industrial relations breakdown* SYN LABOUR RELATIONS

in'dustrial-strength adjective (often used in a humorous way)
very strong or powerful: *an industrial-strength cleaner* ◇ *industrial-strength coffee*

in,dustrial tri'bunal = EMPLOYMENT TRIBUNAL

industrious /ɪn'dʌstriəs/ adjective
working hard; busy: *an industrious labour force* SYN HARD-WORKING
▸ **in'dustriously** adverb

★ **industry** /'ɪndəstri/ noun (plural **industries**)
SEE ALSO: agro-industry, basic ~, captain of ~, cottage ~, Department of Trade and ~, heavy ~, heritage ~, etc.

1 [U] the production of goods from raw materials, especially in factories: *They raised import duties to protect local industry.* ◇ *the problems of British industry* ◇ *He left college and went into industry.*
○ **domestic/local/traditional** industry • **to be in/go into/enter** industry
2 [C] the people and activities involved in producing a particular thing, or in providing a particular service: *the banking/car/steel industry* ◇ *We're in an industry that's growing at 14% a year.* ◇ *We're in a growth industry.* ◇ *Sales fell across the industry.* See note at TRADE
○ a **global/growing/growth/key/mature** industry • **domestic/global/local/traditional** industries • **communications/manufacturing/service** industries • **to create/dominate/lead** an industry • **to regulate/restructure** an industry • an industry **analyst/expert/observer**

'industry associ,ation noun [C]
an organization for companies in the same industry, that provides advice, information and other services for its members: *the Computer & Communications Industry Association* SYN TRADE ASSOCIATION

,industry 'leader noun [C]
1 a company which is the most successful in its area of business: *They built the company up into an industry leader.*
2 a successful and important business person: *Industry leaders have criticized the proposals.*

industrywide /,ɪndəstri'waɪd/ adjective
through all of an area of business: *the industrywide drop in advertising* ▸ **industry'wide** adverb: *Revenue fell 1.5% industrywide in November.*

★ **ine'fficiency** /,ɪnɪ'fɪʃənsi/ noun [C,U] (plural **inefficiencies**)
SEE ALSO: technical inefficiency

failure to use time, money, resources or people in the best way; an example of this: *The organization has been criticized for inefficiency and corruption.* ◇ *Reorganization has reduced operating inefficiencies.* → X-INEFFICIENCY

★ **inefficient** /,ɪnɪ'fɪʃnt/ adjective
not using time, money, resources or people in the best way: *The industry remains highly inefficient.* ◇ *an inefficient way of working* OPP EFFICIENT

inelastic /,ɪnɪ'læstɪk/ adjective
(Economics) used to describe the situation when a change in one thing, such as the price of a product or service, or a change in people's incomes, results in only a small change in another thing, such as the amount that people want to buy: *Demand for their product is inelastic.* ◇ *Some products such as petrol/gas are price inelastic—even when prices go up demand doesn't fall.* OPP ELASTIC—Picture at ELASTICITY OF DEMAND

ineligible /ɪnˈelɪdʒəbl/ *adjective*
not having the right to do sth or have sth, because you do not have the necessary qualifications, are not the right age, etc: *She was ineligible for the grant because her business was too small.* OPP ELIGIBLE ▶ **ineligibility** /ˌɪnˌelɪdʒəˈbɪləti/ *noun* [U]

inertia /ɪˈnɜːʃə; *AmE* -ɜːrʃə/ *noun* [U]
lack of action or change; lack of desire to act or to change things: *Banks can no longer rely on customer inertia as people become less loyal.* ◇ *inertia in consumer prices*

inexpensive /ˌɪnɪkˈspensɪv/ *adjective*
not costing a lot of money: *simple, inexpensive software* SYN CHEAP OPP EXPENSIVE

inflate /ɪnˈfleɪt/ *verb*
1 [+ obj] to deliberately make a number, an amount, etc. appear higher or be higher, often in a dishonest way: *He knowingly inflated sales figures.* ◇ *An employee claimed that earnings had been inflated by accounting tricks.*
2 [+ obj *or no obj*] to increase in price; to increase the price of sth: *Oil prices were inflated by the threat of war.* ◇ *Food prices are no longer inflating at the same rate as last year.*
→ DEFLATE, REFLATE

inflated /ɪnˈfleɪtɪd/ *adjective* [usually before noun]
(especially about prices) very high; much higher than normal or reasonable: *Customers no longer want to pay highly inflated prices for designer clothes.* ◇ *the chairman's grossly inflated pay packet*

★ **inflation** /ɪnˈfleɪʃn/ *noun* [U]

SEE ALSO: anti-inflation, asset ~, consumer price ~, core ~, cost ~, cost-push ~, demand ~, etc.

a rise in the general prices of goods and services in a particular country over a period of time, resulting in a fall in the value of money; the rate at which this happens: *Inflation rose again this year.* ◇ *the current low rate of inflation* ◇ *an annual inflation rate of 3%* ◇ *Wage increases must be in line with inflation.* ◇ *The price of food, adjusted for inflation, has fallen by around 1% annually.* ◇ *a 3% inflation target* ◇ *the November inflation report*
● *inflation falls/rises* • *falling/rising inflation* • *a jump/rise/surge in inflation* • *a decline/drop/fall in inflation* • *high/low/stable/zero inflation* • *galloping/rapid/runaway/spiralling inflation* • *to bring down/control/curb/reduce inflation*

inˈflation acˌcounting *noun* [U]
(*Accounting*) a method of keeping a company's financial records which considers the general increase in prices, and values assets according to how much it would cost to buy them today

inˈflation-adˌjusted *adjective* [usually before noun]
(*Economics*) (about prices, income, etc.) that takes into account a general increase in prices and a general decrease in the value of money: *inflation-adjusted interest rates* ◇ *Spending fell an inflation-adjusted 0.3%.*

inflationary /ɪnˈfleɪʃənri; *AmE* -neri/ *adjective* [usually before noun]

SEE ALSO: counter-inflationary

causing or connected with a general increase in prices and a general decrease in the value of money: *the inflationary effects of the government's spending* ◇ *Higher economic growth will increase inflationary pressure.* ◇ *inflationary pay awards*

inˈflection point *noun* [C]
a time of very noticeable change in a business or an industry; a time when sth important happens: *Last spring we hit an inflection point.* ◇ *The software industry is at an inflection point.*

★ **inflexible** /ɪnˈfleksəbl/ *adjective*
1 that cannot change or be changed to suit new conditions or situations: *an inflexible attitude/routine/system* ◇ *an inflexible retirement age*
2 (about a material) difficult or impossible to bend OPP FLEXIBLE
▶ **inflexibility** /ɪnˌfleksəˈbɪləti/ *noun* [U]

inflow /ˈɪnfləʊ; *AmE* -floʊ/ *noun* [U,C]
the movement of money or assets into a business or a country; the amount of money or assets coming in: *Cash inflow for the half year was $3.5 m.* ◇ *inflows of foreign funds into the region* OPP OUTFLOW → INFLUX

influencer /ˈɪnfluənsə(r)/ *noun* [C]
(*Marketing*) a person or a group that can directly affect the opinions and behaviour of those who make decisions

influx /ˈɪnflʌks/ *noun* [C, usually sing.]
a sudden arrival of many things or people at the same time: *the influx of jobs brought in by new investment* ◇ *the influx of wealth into the region* → INFLOW

info /ˈɪnfəʊ; *AmE* ˈɪnfoʊ/ *noun*
1 (*informal*) [U] information: *I shall send info to all dept heads asap.* ◇ *For prices and stockists email: info@ouptext.com.*
2 info- (*in nouns*) connected with information: *an infosheet* ◇ *We send all potential clients an infopack.*

infobahn /ˈɪnfəʊbɑːn; *AmE* ˈɪnfoʊ-/ =
INFORMATION SUPERHIGHWAY

infomediary /ˌɪnfəˈmiːdiəri/ *noun* [C] (*plural* infomediaries)
(*E-commerce*) a website that collects and provides information for businesses and their customers NOTE **Infomediary** is formed from the words 'information' and 'intermediary'.

infomercial /ˌɪnfəʊˈmɜːʃl; *AmE* ˌɪnfoʊˈmɜːrʃl/ (*also* ˌinforˈmercial*) *noun* [C]
(*Marketing*) a long advertisement on television or the Internet that tries to give a lot of information about a subject, so that it does not appear to be an advertisement: *We produced a 30-minute infomercial for our new range of products.*
→ ADVERTORIAL NOTE **Infomercial** is formed from the words 'information' and 'commercial'.

★ **inform** /ɪnˈfɔːm; *AmE* ɪnˈfɔːrm/ *verb* [+ obj]
1 inform sb (of/about sth) to tell sb about sth, especially in an official way: *The employer must inform the employee of its decision.* ◇ *I am pleased to inform you that you have been selected for interview.* ◇ *It's vital to keep staff informed.* → NOTIFY
2 to influence sth; to be the basis for sth: *This belief has always informed the board's decisions.*

the inˌformal eˈconomy = SHADOW ECONOMY

informant /ɪnˈfɔːmənt; *AmE* -ˈfɔːrm-/ *noun* [C]
(*Marketing*) a person who answers questions in a survey or gives information about their attitudes, opinions, etc: *a representative group of informants* ◇ *informant interviews* → RESPONDENT

★ **information** /ˌɪnfəˈmeɪʃn; *AmE* ˌɪnfər'm-/ *noun*

SEE ALSO: credit information, inside ~, insider ~

1 [U] facts or details about sth or sb: *information about employees* ◇ *For further information, call ...* ◇ *This information is confidential.* ◇ *The leaflet is produced for the information of (= to inform) our customers.* ◇ *a piece of information* ◇ *an information desk/bureau/office* → INFO
● *to collect/gather/obtain/receive information* • *to give/pass on/provide information* • *company/competitor/financial information*

2 (*AmE*) [U with sing./pl. verb] = DIRECTORY ENQUIRIES

▸ **informational** /ˌɪnfəˈmeɪʃənl; *AmE* -fərˈm-/ *adjective* [only before noun]: *informational advertising* ◇ *They launched an informational site last year.*

IDM **for information ˈonly** written on documents that are sent to sb who needs to know the information in them but does not need to deal with them → FYI

Uncountable nouns

Many nouns in English are uncountable, they are not used with *a* or *an*, and do not have plural forms, for example **information**: *I need some information.*

In order to refer to a particular number of an uncountable noun, especially one, you can join the noun to a word that is countable, or use a countable synonym instead.

Uncountable noun	A particular number
equipment	a *piece of* equipment
machinery	a *piece of* machinery
	a *machine*
software	a *piece of* software
	an *application*
	a *program*
training	a *training course*
	a *training programme*

ˌinformation ˈarchitecture *noun* [U]
(*IT*) the process of designing the way websites are organized and used, in order to help users find and manage information more successfully

ˌinforˈmation exˌchange *noun* [C,U]
the act of giving and receiving information, especially electronically; a system, an opportunity or a place for doing this: *protocols for information exchange between publishers and agencies* ◇ *the need for information exchange agreements*

ˌinforˈmation ˌmanagement *noun* [U] (*abbr* IM)
the collection, control and use of data in an organization; a system for organizing and using data: *We increased the use of computers for information management.* ◇ *the development of information management systems for manufacturers*

ˌinformation reˈtrieval *noun* [U]
(*IT*) the process of finding particular data that is stored in a computer

inforˈmation ˌscience *noun* [U]
the study of processes for storing and obtaining data electronically

ˌinformation superˈhighway (*also* ˌsuperˈhighway, ˈinfobahn*) noun* [C, usually sing.]
(*IT*) a large electronic network such as the Internet, used for sending information such as sound, pictures and video quickly

ˌinformation techˈnology = IT (1)

informercial /ˌɪnfɔːˈmɜːʃl; *AmE* ˌɪnfɔːrˈmɜːr-/ = INFOMERCIAL

infraction /ɪnˈfrækʃn/ *noun* [C,U]
an act of breaking a rule or law: *minor infractions of company regulations*

★infrastructure /ˈɪnfrəstrʌktʃə(r)/ *noun* [C,U]
1 (*Economics*) the basic systems and services that are necessary for a country to run smoothly, for example buildings, transport, and water and power supplies: *They need to attract foreign investment to improve the country's infrastructure.*
2 the systems or equipment that an organization needs in order to be able to operate efficiently: *a leading supplier of IT infrastructure*
▸ **infrastructural** /ˌɪnfrəˈstrʌktʃərəl/ *adjective* [usually before noun]: *infrastructural development*

infringe /ɪnˈfrɪndʒ/ *verb* [+ obj or no obj]
to break a law or rule: *The material can be copied without infringing copyright.* ▸ **infringement** /ɪnˈfrɪndʒmənt/ *noun* [U,C]: *copyright infringement* ◇ *an infringement of copyright/patent*

infusion /ɪnˈfjuːʒn/ *noun* [C,U]
infusion (of sth) (into sth) the act of adding sth to sth else in order to make it stronger or more successful: *a cash infusion into the business* ◇ *The company needs an infusion of new blood* (= new employees with new ideas).

ingot /ˈɪŋgət/ *noun* [C]
a solid piece of metal, especially gold or silver, usually shaped like a brick

ingredient /ɪnˈgriːdiənt/ *noun* [C]
1 one of the things from which sth is made: *The only active ingredient in this medicine is aspirin.* ◇ *A food safety agency has been set up to approve new food ingredients.*
2 one of the things or qualities that are necessary to make sth successful: *Customer loyalty is one of the key ingredients in business success.*

inˌherent ˈvice *noun* [C]
(*Insurance*) a natural tendency that particular goods, such as foods, have to become damaged or be destroyed, especially when they are being transported **NOTE** This is not usually covered by insurance policies: *The court found the shortage was caused by an inherent vice in the cargo.*

inherit /ɪnˈherɪt/ *verb*
1 [+ obj or no obj] to receive money, property, etc. from sb when they die: *She inherited the company from her father.* ◇ *the tax on inherited wealth*
2 [+ obj] if you **inherit** a particular situation from sb, you are now responsible for dealing with it, especially because you have replaced that person in their job: *I inherited a number of problems from my predecessor.* ◇ *He's inherited a very motivated and talented team.*
▸ **inˈheritor** *noun* [C]

inheritance /ɪnˈherɪtəns/ *noun* [C, usually sing., U]
the money, property, etc. that you receive from sb when they die; the fact of receiving sth when sb dies: *She decided to invest her inheritance.*
SYN LEGACY

inˈheritance tax *noun* [C,U] (*abbr* IHT)
1 (*BrE also* ˈdeath ˌduty, *old-fashioned*) in the UK, tax that is paid on the total value of the money and property of sb who has died → ESTATE TAX
2 (*AmE also* ˈdeath tax, *informal*) tax that you must pay on the value of the money or property that you receive from sb when they die

ˌin-ˈhome *adjective* [only before noun]
happening in sb's home: *in-home selling* ◇ *an in-home demonstration of a product*

ˌin-ˈhouse (*also* ˌin-ˈcompany) *adjective* [only before noun]
existing or happening within a company or an organization: *an in-house magazine* ◇ *in-house lawyers/design teams* ◇ *in-company training* ▸ **in-ˈhouse** *adverb*: *The software was developed in-house.*
→ OUT-OF-HOUSE

initial /ɪˈnɪʃl/ *adjective, noun, verb*
●*adjective* [only before noun]
happening at the beginning; first: *an initial payment of €75 and ten instalments of €30* ◇ *The initial estimate for the project was ¥12 bn.*

1 initials [pl.] the first letters of all of a person's names: *Just write your initials.*
2 [C] the first letter of a person's first name
● *verb* (**-ll-**, *AmE usually* **-l-**) [+ obj]
to mark or sign sth with your initials: *Please initial each page and sign in the space provided.*

initialize , **-ise** /ɪˈnɪʃəlaɪz/ *verb* [+ obj]
(IT)
1 to make a computer program or system ready for use → BOOT (1)
2 to prepare a computer disk so that data can be recorded on it SYN FORMAT
▶ **initialization, -isation** /ɪˌnɪʃəlaɪˈzeɪʃn; *AmE* -lə'z-/ *noun* [U]

i,nitial 'price *noun* [C]
1 *(Finance)* the price that a new share, bond, etc. is sold for SYN ISSUE PRICE
2 the first or original price that sth is sold for

i'nitial 'public 'offering *(also* i'nitial 'public 'offer) = IPO

i,nitial 'yield *noun* [C]
(Finance)
1 the amount of profit that an investment makes within the first financial period, that compares the income to the original cost
2 the amount of interest that a bond offers when it is first issued: *a 10-year bond with a face value of $1 000 and an initial yield of 6.5%*

initiative /ɪˈnɪʃətɪv/ *noun*
1 [C] a new plan for dealing with a particular problem or for achieving a particular purpose: *In a new initiative, the company is targeting local advertisers.* ◇ *The CEO announced a series of cost-cutting initiatives.*
2 the initiative [sing.] the power or opportunity to act and gain an advantage before other people do: *Several leading companies took the initiative to establish an independent business school.* ◇ *to seize/lose the initiative*
3 [U] the ability to decide and act on your own without waiting for sb to tell you what to do: *I encourage my employees to use their judgement and initiative right from the start.*

injunction /ɪnˈdʒʌŋkʃn/ *noun* [C]
SEE ALSO: **interim injunction, preliminary injunction**
(Law) an official order given by a court which demands that sth must or must not be done: *They are seeking an injunction to prevent the sale of the product in the UK.* ◇ *The court issued a temporary injunction against the takeover.*
O to **apply for/obtain/seek** an injunction • to **grant/issue/refuse/uphold** an injunction • to **lift/withdraw** an injunction • a **permanent/temporary** injunction

injure /ˈɪndʒə(r)/ *verb* [+ obj]
1 to harm yourself or sb else physically, especially in an accident: *No one was injured in the fire at the factory.* ◇ *Injured workers are entitled to medical care.*
2 to damage sb's reputation, pride, etc: *This could seriously injure the company's reputation.*

injury /ˈɪndʒəri/ *noun* (*plural* **injuries**)
SEE ALSO: **personal injury, repetitive strain injury**
1 [C,U] harm done to a person's body, for example in an accident: *They cannot afford to insure staff against injuries at work.* ◇ *We need to reduce the number of workdays lost because of injury.* See note at DAMAGE
2 [U] harm that is done to a company, an industry, a person's career or reputation, etc: *Unfairly dismissed employees can sue for injury to feelings.* ◇ *Imported products could cause serious injury to the domestic industry.*

ink /ɪŋk/ *noun, verb*
● *noun* [U,C]
SEE ALSO: **red ink**
coloured liquid for writing, drawing and printing: *Dell sells its own line of ink and toner cartridges.* ◇ *(figurative) The ink was hardly dry on the deal* (= it had only just been arranged). → idiom at HAEMORRHAGE *verb*
● *verb* [+ obj] *(informal)*
to sign a document, especially a contract: *The group has just inked a $10 million deal.*
PHRV **,ink sth/sb 'in** to decide on a definite date for an appointment, a meeting, etc: *The company has inked in June 1st for the launch.* → PENCIL SB/STH IN at PENCIL

inland *adjective, adverb*
● *adjective* /ˈɪnlænd/ [usually before noun]
1 used to describe mail, transport, etc. that only goes within one country rather than to another country: *Your inland mail is delivered within two working days.* ◇ *inland cargo transport*
→ INTERNATIONAL, OVERSEAS
2 located in or near the middle of a country, not near the edge or on the coast: *Business is booming in both inland and coastal resorts.*
● *adverb* /ˌɪnˈlænd/ in a direction towards the middle of a country; away from the coast: *The airport lies a few kilometres inland.*

the ,Inland 'Revenue *(also* the 'Revenue) *noun* [sing.] *(abbr* IR)
the government department in the UK that is responsible for collecting taxes, now part of HM REVENUE AND CUSTOMS → INTERNAL REVENUE SERVICE

,in-'line *adjective*
(Finance; Stock Exchange) used to describe sth that is making as much profit as expected or the same amount as other similar things: *Goldman Sachs upgraded the stock to 'in-line' from 'underperform'.* ◇ *Retail sales were in-line or weaker.* → OUTPERFORM, UNDERPERFORM

★ **innovate** /ˈɪnəveɪt/ *verb* [+ obj or no obj]
to introduce new things, ideas or ways of doing sth: *We must constantly adapt and innovate to ensure success in a growing market.* ◇ *to innovate new products* ▶ **innovator** /ˈɪnəveɪtə(r)/ *noun* [C]

★ **innovation** /ˌɪnəˈveɪʃn/ *noun*
SEE ALSO: **product innovation**
1 [U] the introduction or development of new things, ideas or ways of doing sth: *We have a passion for quality, innovation and value for money.* ◇ *They have been the leaders in product innovation.* ◇ *scientific and technological innovation*
2 [C] a new idea, way of doing sth, etc: *recent innovations in steel-making technology*

innovative /ˈɪnəveɪtɪv/ *BrE also* ˈɪnəvətɪv/ *(also* **innovatory**, *less frequent* /ˌɪnəˈveɪtəri/; *AmE also* ˈɪnəvətɔːri/) *adjective*
introducing or using new ideas, ways of doing sth, etc: *The company's dedicated to developing innovative new products.* ◇ *an innovative approach to training* ▶ **innovatively** *adverb*

inoperative /ɪnˈɒpərətɪv; *AmE* ɪnˈɑːp-/ *adjective*
1 (about a rule, system, etc.) not valid or able to be used: *Your insurance policy will become inoperative if your circumstances change.*
2 (about a machine) not working: *The inoperative pump was sent back to the manufacturer.*

inorganic /ˌɪnɔːˈɡænɪk; *AmE* ˌɪnɔːrˈɡ-/ *adjective*
[usually before noun]
used to describe the situation when a company

increases in size by buying or joining with other companies: *She sees inorganic growth as the way forward for the bank in the coming days.* ◇ *inorganic expansion/development* → EXTERNAL (2)

,in-'pack *adjective* [only before noun]
(*Marketing*) inside the container that goods are sold in: *in-pack promotions*

,in-'person *adjective* [usually before noun]
involving a direct meeting with another person rather than communicating by letter, telephone, etc: *an in-person interview* ◇ *The training would be both in-person and online.*

★input /'ɪmpʊt/ *noun, verb*
● *noun*
1 (*Economics*) [U,C, usually pl.] any person or thing that is involved in producing goods or providing services: *Women provide 25% of the labour input in farming.* ◇ *Inputs of labour, capital and energy are becoming more costly.* ◇ *The increase in input costs was largely due to the rise in oil prices.* SYN FACTOR OF PRODUCTION → OUTPUT
2 [U,C] advice, ideas, knowledge, etc. that you give to a project, meeting, etc. in order to make it succeed; the act of doing this: *I'd appreciate your input on this.* ◇ *Do your employees have an input into the decision-making process?* ◇ *We get customer input early in the development of new products.*
3 (*IT*) [U] the act of putting information into a computer; the information that you put in: *data input* ◇ *This program accepts input from most word processors.* → OUTPUT
4 [C] a place or means for electricity, data, etc. to enter a machine or system: *Is there an audio input on the PC?*
→ OUTPUT
● *verb* (**inputting, input, input**) *or* (**inputting, inputted, inputted**) [+ obj]
(*IT*) to put information into a computer: *to input text/data/figures* ◇ *She is responsible for inputting customer information into the database.* → OUTPUT

,input/'output *adjective*
1 (*IT*) (*abbr* **I/O**) relating to information passing into and out of a computer, computer system, etc. or the devices that control this process: *the basic input/output system of your computer*
2 (*Economics*) used to describe a method of analysing the economy of an area that considers the relationships between different parts of the economy and how changes in the amount that one part produces affects what happens in others: *an economic input/output model of the United States*
▶ **,input/'output** *noun* [U] (*IT*)

'input tax *noun* [C,U]
(*Accounting*) the tax (**VAT**) that a company pays on goods and services that it buys → OUTPUT TAX

inquire, inquirer → ENQUIRE

inquiry = ENQUIRY

inquisitorial /ɪn.kwɪzə'tɔːriəl/ *adjective*
(*Law*) (about a trial or legal system) in which a judge examines the evidence and questions people involved in the case

inroad /'ɪnrəʊd; *AmE* -roʊd/ *noun* [C]
something that is achieved, especially by reducing the power or success of sth else: *This deal is their first major inroad into the American market.*
IDM make inroads (into/on sth) if one thing makes inroads into another, it has an important effect on the second thing, especially by reducing it, or influencing it: *They are likely to make further inroads into the UK market.*

insert *verb, noun*
● *verb* [+ obj] /ɪn'sɜːt; *AmE* ɪn'sɜːrt/
1 insert sth (in/into/between sth) to put sth into sth else or between two things: *I inserted the disk into my computer.* ◇ *Our leaflets will be inserted in the next issue of the magazine.*
2 to add sth to a piece of writing: *Position the cursor where you want to insert a word.* OPP DELETE
▶ **insertion** /ɪn'sɜːʃn; *AmE* ɪn'sɜːrʃn/ *noun* [U,C]: *She suggested the insertion of an extra clause in the contract.* ◇ *full-page colour insertions*
● *noun* /'ɪnsɜːt; *AmE* 'ɪnsɜːrt/ (*also* **'inset**, *less frequent*) [C]

SEE ALSO: **free-standing insert**

an extra section added to a book, newspaper or magazine, especially to advertise sth: *an 8-page insert on the new car models*

,in-'service *adjective* [only before noun]
(*HR*)
1 (about training, courses of study, etc.) done while sb is working in a job, in order to learn new skills: *in-service training*
2 used to describe sb who is working or sth that is being used for a particular purpose: *pre-service and in-service teachers* ◇ *The ship has a scheduled in-service date of 2011.*

,in-service with'drawal *noun* [U,C]
when an employee leaves a company pension plan while they are still employed by the company

inset /'ɪnset/ = INSERT

inside /,ɪn'saɪd/ *adjective* [only before noun]
known or done by sb in a group or an organization: *He has an extensive inside knowledge of the telecoms industry.*

,inside infor'mation (*also* **in,sider infor'mation**) *noun* [U]
(*Finance*) secret information which is known by people who work for a company or an organization but which is not known by the public NOTE It is usually illegal to make use of this information when buying or selling shares, bonds, etc.: *She is accused of relying on inside information when she sold nearly 4 000 shares.* → INSIDER TRADING

insider /ɪn'saɪdə(r)/ *noun* [C]
1 a person who knows a lot about a group or an organization, because they are part of it: *The situation was described by one insider as 'absolute chaos'.* ◇ *Industry insiders predict a merger within the next year.*
2 (*Finance*) the directors, senior officers, lawyers, accountants, etc. of a company and anyone who owns more than ten per cent of the company's voting shares: *company/corporate insiders* ◇ *Insider buying of shares is a positive sign of a company's future.*

in,sider 'dealing = INSIDER TRADING

in,sider infor'mation = INSIDE INFORMATION

in,sider 'trade *noun* [C, usually pl., U]
(*Stock Exchange*) the buying and selling of a company's shares, OPTIONS, etc. by directors or senior managers of the company: *Executives must report insider trades within two days.* ◇ *an analysis of insider trade behavior* SYN INSIDER TRADING

in,sider 'trading (*also* **in,sider 'dealing**) *noun* [U]
(*Stock Exchange*)
1 the crime of buying or selling shares, bonds, etc. in a company with the help of secret information about the company that is not available to the public: *He was convicted of insider trading and fined $2.2 million.*
2 the buying and selling of a company's shares, bonds, etc. by directors or senior managers of the company SYN INSIDER TRADING

ˌinside 'track *noun* [sing.] (*especially AmE*)
a position in which you have an advantage over sb else or know about sth before other people do: *This is a good way to get on the inside track for future career opportunities.*

ˌinside 'worker *noun* [C]
(*HR*) an employee who works in a company's offices, factory, etc. → OUTSIDE WORKER

★ **insolvency** /ɪnˈsɒlvənsi; *AmE* -ˈsɑːl-/ *noun* [U,C]
(*plural* **insolvencies**)
(*Accounting*; *Law*) the state of not having enough money to pay what you owe: *The company is close to insolvency.* ◇ *The government may support the firm, which said it could file for insolvency at any time.* ◇ *a wave of corporate insolvencies* ◇ *Its European carrier business is expected to start insolvency **proceedings** soon.* OPP SOLVENCY → BANKRUPTCY, INSOLVENT
  ● *to **face/file for/go into** insolvency* • *to **avoid/be rescued from/stave off** insolvency* • *an insolvency **expert/lawyer/specialist***

inˌsolvency pracˈtitioner *noun* [C] (*BrE*)
in the UK, a person or company that is legally qualified to manage the affairs of a company that is INSOLVENT (= does not have enough money to pay its debts)

★ **insolvent** /ɪnˈsɒlvənt; *AmE* -ˈsɑːl-/ *adjective*
(*Accounting*; *Law*) not having enough money to pay what you owe: *The company has been declared insolvent.* ◇ *plans to take over insolvent private banks* ◇ *The bank's liabilities exceed its assets, making it **technically** insolvent.* OPP SOLVENT → INSOLVENCY
See note at BANKRUPT
  ● *to **become/be declared** insolvent* • *to **be/declare yourself** insolvent*

insourcing /ˈɪnsɔːsɪŋ; *AmE* -sɔːrs-/ *noun* [U]
(*HR*) the process of producing goods or providing services within a company rather than buying them from outside: *The cooperative has benefited from the insourcing of products previously purchased from outside suppliers.* ▶ **'insource** *verb* [+ obj *or* no obj]:
We insource our training. ◇ *We are providing an insourced telesales solution for the company's call centre in Scotland.*

inspect /ɪnˈspekt/ *verb* [+ obj]
1 to look closely at sth/sb, especially to check that everything is as it should be: *Make sure you inspect the goods before signing for them.* ◇ *Samples of the products are inspected **for** quality and consistency.*
2 to officially visit a factory, restaurant, etc. in order to check that laws are being obeyed and that standards are acceptable: *Public health officials were called in to inspect the premises.*

inspection /ɪnˈspekʃn/ *noun* [U,C]
1 an official visit to a factory, restaurant, etc. in order to check that rules are being obeyed and that standards are acceptable: *Regular inspections are carried out at the factory.* ◇ *Banks were hit by concern over inspections by the Financial Services Agency.*
  ● *to **carry out/conduct/make** an inspection* • *to **fail/pass** an inspection* • *a **full/regular/routine/surprise** inspection*
2 the act of looking closely at sth/sb, especially to check that everything is as it should be: *The documents are available **for** inspection.* ◇ *On closer **inspection**, the notes proved to be forgeries.*
  ● *to **carry out/make** an inspection* • *a **close/detailed/thorough** inspection*

inspector /ɪnˈspektə(r)/ *noun* [C]
1 a person whose job is to visit factories, restaurants, etc. to check that laws are being obeyed and that standards are acceptable: *Her role as a factory inspector is to enforce health and safety legislation.*

  ● *a **factory/quality/safety** inspector* • *a **government/an independent** inspector*
2 (*AmE*) = SURVEYOR (2)

inspectorate /ɪnˈspektərət/ *noun* [C with sing./pl. verb] (*especially BrE*)
an official group of INSPECTORS who work together on the same subject or at the same kind of institution: *A member of the company inspectorate was sent into the firm.*

inˌspector of 'taxes (*also* **'tax inˌspector**)
noun [C]
in the UK, a person who is responsible for collecting the tax that people must pay on the money they earn SYN TAXMAN

inst. *abbr*
1 (*old-fashioned*) a short way of writing **instant**, used in business letters to mean 'of this month': *We acknowledge receipt of your letter of 14 inst.*
2 a short way of writing **institute** or **institution**

★ **install** /ɪnˈstɔːl/ *verb* [+ obj]
1 (*IT*) to put a new program into a computer: *I'll need some help installing the software.* ◇ *The new software was installed **on** 850 desktops.*
2 to fix equipment on to sth or into position so that it can be used: *They plan to install motion detectors on many appliances.* ◇ *The hotel has had terminals installed in every room.*
3 to put sb in a new position of authority: *He was installed **as** CEO last May.* ◇ *The company has installed its own management team in Toulouse.*

installation /ˌɪnstəˈleɪʃn/ *noun*
1 [U,C] the act of fixing equipment or furniture in position so that it can be used: *Installation of the security system will take several days.* ◇ *We offer free installation and free service.* ◇ *installation costs*
2 (*IT*) [U] the act of putting a new program into a computer: *the installation of the SAP software*
3 [C] a piece of equipment or machinery that has been fixed in position so that it can be used: *a heating installation*
4 [C] a place where specialist equipment is kept and used: *a chemical/nuclear/oil installation*
5 [U] the act of placing sb in a new position of authority: *the installation of a new chief executive*

inˈstalled base *noun* [C, usually sing.]
(*IT*; *Marketing*) the total number of a particular product, especially equipment such as computers, that have been sold and are still used by customers: *The installed base of PCs in India rose to 5 million units last month.* → CUSTOMER BASE

inˌstalled caˈpacity *noun* [U; C, usually sing.]
(*Technical*) the full amount of energy that a particular power station, machine, etc. could supply: *China's installed capacity exceeds 400 million kw.*

installer /ɪnˈstɔːlə(r)/ *noun* [C]
1 (*IT*) a piece of software that helps you to put another larger piece of software onto your computer: *I downloaded the software and ran the installer.*
2 a person or company that fixes equipment or furniture in position so that it can be used: *an installer of security systems* ◇ *phone installers*

★ **instalment** (*AmE spelling usually* **installment**)
/ɪnˈstɔːlmənt/ *noun* [C]
(*Commerce*) one of a number of payments that are made regularly over a period of time until sth has been paid for or an agreed amount has been paid: *We paid for it **by/in** instalments.* ◇ *The loan can be repaid in 24 monthly instalments.* ◇ *The final instalment on the loan is due next week.* ◇ *They were unable to keep up (= continue to pay) the instalments.*

❂ *to keep up/pay/repay (the) instalments*

in'stalment plan *(AmE spelling usually* **installment ~**) = HIRE PURCHASE

in'stalment sale *(AmE spelling usually* **installment ~**) *noun* [U,C]
(Commerce) an arrangement in which the seller of goods, assets, etc. receives the money in regular payments over a fixed period of time → HIRE PURCHASE

instant /ˈɪnstənt/ *adjective*
happening immediately: *This connection gives you instant access to the Internet.* ◇ *Don't expect instant results.*

ˌinstant ˈaccess acˌcount *noun* [C] *(BrE)*
a bank account that allows you to take your money out at any time you like without paying a fee

ˌinstant ˈmessaging *noun* [U] *(abbr* IM)
(IT) a system on the Internet that allows people to exchange written messages with each other very quickly ▶ **ˌinstant ˈmessage** *noun* [C]

instigate /ˈɪnstɪɡeɪt/ *verb* [+ obj]
1 *(especially BrE)* to make sth start or happen, usually sth official: *The council has instigated an independent inquiry.*
2 to cause sth bad to happen: *The company has been blamed for instigating the price war.*

institute /ˈɪnstɪtjuːt; *AmE* -tuːt/ *noun, verb*
● *noun* [C]
an organization that has a particular purpose, especially one that is connected with education or a particular profession; the building used by this organization: *the senior economist at Nomura Research Institute* ◇ *the Institute of Chartered Accountants*
● *verb* [+ obj]
to introduce a system, policy, etc. or start a process: *The new management intends to institute a number of changes.* ◇ *to institute criminal proceedings against sb*

★ **institution** /ˌɪnstɪˈtjuːʃn; *AmE* -ˈtuːʃn/ *noun*

SEE ALSO: **depository institution, financial ~, thrift ~**

1 [C] a large important organization that has a particular purpose, for example a bank: *a banking/an investment/a lending institution* ◇ *The sale has already been accepted by the big* **City institutions** (= the banks and finance companies in London). ◇ *the Royal Institution of Chartered Surveyors*
2 [C] a custom or system that has existed for a long time among a particular group of people: *The Web as an institution seems more important than ever.*
3 [U] the act of starting or introducing sth such as a system or a law: *the institution of new safety procedures*

institutional /ˌɪnstɪˈtjuːʃənl; *AmE* -ˈtuː-/ *adjective*
[usually before noun]
connected with an institution, especially a large financial organization: *institutional buyers/clients/investors/shareholders* ◇ *There is a strong institutional demand for government bonds.*
▶ **institutionally** /ˌɪnstɪˈtjuːʃənəli; *AmE* -ˈtuː-/ *adverb*

ˌinstitutional ˈadvertising *noun* [U]
(Marketing) advertising that tells the public about an organization, a company or a product in general (for example, coffee), rather than about particular products. It usually tries to create an attractive image and is used by large well-known companies: *an institutional advertising campaign for the water industry* → IMAGE ADVERTISING, PRODUCT ADVERTISING
▶ **ˌinstitutional adˈvertisement** *noun* [C]

ˌinstitutional ˈfund *noun* [C]
(Finance) an investment fund that is only open to large financial organizations: *an institutional fund manager*

ˌin-ˈstore *adjective* [only before noun]
1 within a large shop/store: *in-store marketing/promotions* ◇ *The Internet will reduce in-store sales.* ◇ *The company uses signs and in-store displays to grab consumer attention.*
2 belonging to a particular shop/store: *special discounts for shoppers who use in-store credit cards* ◇ *the supermarket's in-store magazine*
▶ **ˌin-ˈstore** *adverb*: *His focus has turned to products being sold in-store.*

★ **instruct** /ɪnˈstrʌkt/ *verb* [+ obj]
1 to tell sb to do sth, especially in a formal or an official way: *Some mechanics were instructed* **to** *do jobs that they weren't qualified to do.* ◇ *My boss instructed me not to spend too much time on the task.*
2 to teach sb sth, especially a practical skill: *We instructed managers* **(on)** *how to use the online hiring system.* ◇ *instructing new employees* **in** *the use of the equipment*
3 *(Law) (especially BrE)* to employ sb to represent you in a legal situation, especially as a lawyer, and give them information or orders: *He must indicate which of the firms he wishes to instruct.*

★ **instruction** /ɪnˈstrʌkʃn/ *noun, adjective*
● *noun*
1 **instructions** [pl.] detailed information on how to do or use sth: *You should follow the instructions given by the manufacturer.* ◇ *It comes with* **step-by-step** *instructions* (= that tell you exactly what to do at each stage).
❂ *to follow/read (the) instructions* • *clear/detailed/full instructions* • *assembly/installation/operating instructions*
2 [C, usually pl.] something that sb tells you to do: *Have you given the payment instructions to the bank?* ◇ *Salespeople were given instructions to offer a reduced price.*
❂ *to give sb/issue/receive instructions* • *to carry out/ignore sb's instructions* • *clear/firm/strict/written instructions*
3 *(IT)* [C] a piece of information that tells a computer to perform a particular operation: *This computer can carry out 400 million instructions per second.*
❂ *to carry out/execute instructions*
● *adjective* [only before noun]
giving detailed information on how to do or use sth: *an instruction book/manual*

instructional /ɪnˈstrʌkʃənl/ *adjective* [usually before noun]
that teaches people sth: *instructional materials/videos*

instrument /ˈɪnstrəmənt/ *noun* [C]

SEE ALSO: **derivative instrument, financial ~, trust ~**

1 *(Finance)* any investment such as shares, bonds, OPTIONS, FUTURES, etc. that is bought and sold in an organized system: *We have had to replace our investments with lower-yielding instruments.* ◇ *fixed-income instruments* ◇ *equity/liquid/low-risk instruments* SYN FINANCIAL INSTRUMENT
2 a tool or device used for a particular task, especially for delicate or scientific work: *optical/precision/surgical instruments*
3 a device used for measuring speed, distance, temperature, etc. in a vehicle or on a piece of machinery: *the flight instruments* ◇ *the instrument panel*
4 *(Law)* a formal legal document: *an instrument of transfer* (= that shows that property has been passed to sb else)

insufficient /ˌɪnsəˈfɪʃnt/ *adjective*
not large, strong or important enough for a
particular purpose: *insufficient time* ◇ *His salary is
insufficient to meet his needs.* → N.S.F.
▶ **insufficiency** /ˌɪnsəˈfɪʃənsi/ *noun* [U; sing.]
ˌinsufˈficiently *adverb*

★ **insurable** /ɪnˈʃɔːrəbl; -ˈʃʊər-; AmE -ˈʃʊr-/
adjective
able to be **insured**: *$3.5 billion is the maximum
payout for a single insurable incident.* ◇ *The
challenge is to work out what risks are insurable.*
OPP UNINSURABLE
➕ *insurable events/incidents/risks*

★ **insurance** /ɪnˈʃɔːrəns; -ˈʃʊər-; AmE -ˈʃʊr-/ *noun*
SEE ALSO: **accident insurance, block ~, casualty ~,
certificate of ~, consumer credit ~, contract of ~,
credit ~,** etc.

1 [U,C] an arrangement with a company in which
you pay them regular amounts of money or make a
single payment and they agree to pay the costs, for
example if you die or are ill/sick, or if you lose or
damage sth: *car/travel/home/unemployment
insurance* ◇ *Make sure you take out adequate
insurance to cover your possessions.* ◇ *Can you claim
for the loss **on** your insurance?* ◇ *Many people have
insurance **against** sickness and unemployment.* ◇ *It's
time to renew your motor insurance.* NOTE There are
four main classes of insurance: **accident, fire, life**
and **marine.**
➕ *to **arrange/have/renew/take out** insurance ◆ to
buy/sell insurance ◆ to **offer/provide/refuse**
insurance ◆ insurance **covers/pays for** sth ◆
insurance **contributions/payments/premiums**
2 [U] (often used in the names of companies) the
business of providing people with insurance: *She
works **in** insurance.* ◇ *The insurance industry is one
of the country's biggest employers.* ◇ *Cox Insurance*
3 [U] money paid to an insurance company;
money paid by an insurance company: *Some people
just cannot afford to pay insurance.* ◇ *After the
accident he received €15 000 in insurance.*
4 (*Stock Exchange*) [pl.; U] used to refer to shares in
insurance companies: *Insurances did well,
recovering some of last week's losses.*

WHICH WORD?

insurance/assurance

In *BrE*, insurance that pays out a sum of money
when a person dies or reaches a particular age is
called **life assurance** or **life insurance**. The term
used in *AmE* is **life insurance**.

In both *BrE* and *AmE*, **insurance** is used to
describe types of insurance that protect you
against uncertain future events, such as injuries,
car crashes, thefts or natural disasters: *car/house/
medical insurance.*

---

inˈsurance adˌjuster (*also spelled ~ adjustor,
especially in AmE*) *noun* [C] (*AmE only*)
an independent person or company that decides
whether insurance claims are valid and how much
should be paid SYN CLAIMS ADJUSTER, LOSS
ADJUSTER (*BrE*)

inˈsurance ˌagent *noun* [C]
a person or company whose job is to give advice
about and sell insurance on behalf of one or more
companies: *I contacted several life insurance agents.*
◇ *The San Francisco-based insurance agent was
founded in 1994.*

inˈsurance ˌbroker *noun* [C]
an independent person or company that gives
people advice about insurance and arranges
insurance for them: *Speak to your insurance broker
regularly to make sure you are getting the best deal.*

inˈsurance ˌcarrier = INSURANCE COMPANY

inˈsurance cerˌtificate = CERTIFICATE OF
INSURANCE

inˈsurance claim = CLAIM *noun* (1)

inˈsurance ˌcompany (*AmE also* **inˈsurance
ˌcarrier**) *noun* [C]
an organization whose business is providing
insurance: *Insurance companies have been badly hit
by the recent storms and floods.* SYN INSURER

inˈsurance ˌcover (*also* inˈsurance ˌcoverage)
noun [U]
protection that an insurance company provides by
promising to pay you money if a particular event
happens: *Many mortgage lenders will require you to
take out full insurance cover.* SYN COVER
➕ *adequate/full insurance cover ◆ to **take out/get/
obtain** insurance cover ◆ to **arrange/provide/
withdraw** insurance cover*

inˈsurance ˌpolicy (*also* ˌcontract of inˈsurance)
noun [C]
a written agreement between a person or company
and an insurance company: *One in fifteen
holidaymakers who took out a travel insurance
policy last year made a claim.*
➕ *to **take out/apply for/have** an insurance policy ◆ an
accident/a life/travel insurance policy*

inˈsurance ˌpremium *noun* [C]
a payment made to an insurance company in return
for which the company agrees to pay for loss,
damage or expenses, usually up to a particular
amount: *Insurance premiums are expected to
continue rising.* ◇ *You can pay your car insurance
premiums annually or monthly.* SYN PREMIUM

inˈsurance ˌrating = RATING (5)

inˈsurance risk *noun* [C]
the possibility of loss or damage that sth is insured
against: *Airlines were given help to cover insurance
risks.* SYN RISK

inˈsurance ˌunderwriter *noun* [C]
1 (*Insurance*) a person whose job is to estimate the
risks involved in a particular activity or in insuring
a particular client and decide how much sb must
pay for insurance
2 a company or person that agrees to accept all the
risks involved in an insurance contract: *He used to
work for Lloyd's, the insurance underwriters.*
SYN UNDERWRITER

★ **insure** /ɪnˈʃɔː(r); -ˈʃʊə(r); AmE -ˈʃʊr/ *verb*
1 [+ obj *or* no obj] **insure (sth/yourself) (for/against
sth)** to make an arrangement with a company in
which you pay them regular amounts of money or
make a single payment and they agree to pay you
money, for example if you die or are ill/sick, or if
you lose or damage sth: *The painting is insured for
$10 million.* ◇ *Companies are required to insure
against accidents in the workplace.* ◇ *Are you
adequately insured?*
2 [+ obj] to sell insurance to sb for sth: *The
company insures high-risk drivers.*

insured /ɪnˈʃɔːd; -ˈʃʊəd; AmE -ˈʃʊrd/ *adjective*
SEE ALSO: **sum insured**

1 having insurance: *Her life was insured **for**
$250 000.* ◇ *The buildings were insured **against** fire
damage.* ◇ *Are you insured to drive this car?*
2 the insured *noun* [C] (*plural* **the insured**) the
person who has made an agreement with an
insurance company and who receives money if, for
example, they are ill/sick or if they lose or damage
sth: *The insured had made a claim against the
insurers.* → ASSURED (2)

★ **insurer** /ɪnˈʃɔːrə(r); -ˈʃʊər-; AmE -ˈʃʊr-/ noun [C]
a company that provides insurance: *Allianz is the world's number two insurer.* ◇ *The insurers* (= the particular company that has a contract to provide insurance) *are refusing to pay the full claim.*
[SYN] INSURANCE COMPANY

intangible /ɪnˈtændʒəbl/ adjective, noun
● *adjective* [usually before noun]
1 that exists but is not physical: *Everything is changing—some of the change is intangible, some very physical.*
○ intangible **benefits/changes/ideas/rewards**
2 that does not exist physically, but represents a cost or a benefit to a company: *My work involves developing intangible success factors such as trust, commitment and competitive advantage.*
○ intangible **capital/expenses/liabilities/property/ value**
[OPP] TANGIBLE adj.
● *noun*
1 [C] a thing that exists but is not physical
2 (*Accounting*; *Finance*) [C, usually pl.] = INTANGIBLE ASSET
[OPP] TANGIBLE noun

in,tangible 'asset (*also* in'tangible) noun [C, usually pl.]
(*Accounting*; *Finance*) something that a company has and that benefits it but does not exist physically, for example a brand or the company's reputation: *The most important intangible asset is the company's brand.* ◇ *the value of goodwill and other intangible assets* [OPP] TANGIBLE ASSET

★ **integrate** /ˈɪntɪɡreɪt/ verb [+ obj or no obj]
integrate (A) (into/with B) | integrate A and B to combine two or more things so that they work together; to combine with sth else in this way: *These programs will integrate with your existing software.* ◇ *These programs can be integrated with your existing software.* ◇ *the problems involved in integrating the two businesses*

integrated /ˈɪntɪɡreɪtɪd/ adjective [usually before noun]
1 in which several different parts are closely connected and work successfully together: *an integrated print and online recruitment strategy*
2 (about a company or a business) that does everything connected with producing and selling its products: *an integrated oil company that digs for and refines crude oil and natural gas products*
3 included as part of a product, not supplied separately: *phones with integrated cameras*

,integrated 'marketing noun [U]
the process of organizing all the different areas of marketing, for example the way things are advertised (**promotion**), the way they are wrapped (**packaging**), the way they are sent to shops/stores to be sold (**distribution**) and the price, so that they all work well together: *developing an integrated marketing strategy* ◇ *an integrated marketing campaign*

,integrated ,marketing communi-'cations noun [U; pl.] (*abbr* IMC)
a way of managing a company's marketing so that all forms of information about products or the company are carefully linked: *She emphasized the importance of integrated marketing communications in achieving customer loyalty.*

,integrated pro'ducer noun [C]
(*Manufacturing*) a company producing goods that owns more than one stage in the process

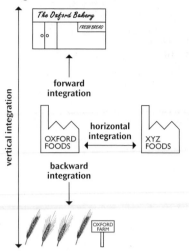

★ **integration** /ˌɪntɪˈɡreɪʃn/ noun [U]

SEE ALSO: **backward integration, enterprise application ~, forward ~, horizontal ~, lateral ~, vertical ~**

1 a process of combining two or more companies, organizations or systems so that they work together well: *The aim is to promote closer economic integration.* ◇ *The new technology will mean better integration of the company's existing computer systems.*
2 (*Economics*) a situation in which a company gains control of its competitors, customers or suppliers, so that there are fewer companies operating in a particular area: *The airline has now completed the integration of its rival.* ◇ *Recent years have seen increasing integration in the car industry.*

integrator /ˈɪntɪɡreɪtə(r)/ noun [C]
1 (*IT*) (*also* '**systems ,integrator, 'system ,integrator**) a person or company that puts together computers and programs to make a complete system for a particular customer, especially a business: *Our aim was to rebuild IBM as the premier integrator of total solutions.* ◇ *the systems integrators who worked on our supply chain*
2 a person who is skilled at making the different parts of a business or different businesses work well together: *He has little experience as an integrator of businesses.*

,intel,lectual 'assets noun [pl.]
(*HR*) the knowledge and skills of a company's employees that can be used to make the business more successful: *We need to find more ways to extract value from our intellectual assets.*

,intel,lectual 'capital noun [U]
(*HR*) anything that is not physical that can be used to make a business more successful, for example its relationships with its customers, its brands, ideas or designs for new products, the knowledge and skills of employees, etc: *The company is putting emphasis on intellectual capital over bricks and mortar.*

,inte,llectual 'property noun [U]
(*Law*) an idea, a design, a piece of writing, etc. that belongs to a person or an organization and cannot be sold or copied without the owner's permission: *Awareness of the need to protect intellectual property*

rights is growing. ◊ *Theft of intellectual property is threatening many American companies.*

inter- /ˈɪntə(r)/ *prefix (used in verbs, nouns, adjectives and adverbs)*
between; from one to another: *interaction* ◊ *inter-company loans* ◊ *interfirm collaboration*

★ **interactive** /ˌɪntərˈæktɪv/ *adjective*
interactive technology allows information to be passed continuously and in both directions between the user and the piece of technology, allowing the user to control what happens: *View our interactive map by clicking here.* ◊ *Grey Interactive TV has developed a series of interactive adverts for the bank.*
○ interactive **media/software/television**
▶ **inter'actively** *adverb* **interactivity** /ˌɪntəræk'tɪvəti/ *noun* [U]: *Each episode will be broadcast with added interactivity.*

ˌinteractive ˈmarketing *noun* [U]
the use of a website and the Internet to sell products in a way that allows the customer and the seller to influence what happens and what information is exchanged: *the brand manager in charge of interactive marketing*

ˌinteractive ˈwhiteboard *noun* [C]
a piece of equipment using a computer linked to a large screen like a **whiteboard** that you can write on or use to control the computer by touching it or pointing at it with a pen. It can be used for teaching or for giving talks.

inter alia /ˌɪntər ˈeɪliə/ *adverb (formal)*
among other things: *The report is concerned, inter alia, with the reform of the tax system.* **NOTE** This is a Latin phrase.

interbank /ˈɪntəbæŋk; *AmE* -terb-/ *adjective* [only before noun]
happening between banks: *The three-month interbank interest rate is currently 3%.* ◊ *the interbank lending trade*

ˌinter-ˈcompany (*also spelled* **intercompany**) *adjective* [only before noun]
happening between companies, especially linked companies: *inter-company meetings* ◊ *The company was owed $1.2 billion of inter-company debt.*

★ **interest** /ˈɪntrəst; -trest/ *noun*

SEE ALSO: **accrued interest, add-on ~, bank ~, beneficial ~, compound ~, controlling ~, expression of ~,** etc.

1 [U] the extra money that you have to pay when you borrow money: *You'll have to pay interest on the loan.* ◊ *The money was repaid with interest.* ◊ *The company is set to default on (= fail to pay) its interest payments.* → INTEREST RATE
○ to **charge/pay** interest ◆ interest **charges/payments** ◆ **annual/monthly** interest
2 [U] the extra money that you receive when you invest money: *Their business account pays 3% interest.* ◊ *That cash could be earning interest in a bank account.* ◊ *Bond interest is fixed, but earnings per share are growing.* → INTEREST RATE See note at PROFIT
○ **earn/pay** interest ◆ interest **payments** ◆ **annual/monthly** interest
3 (*Finance*) [C, usually pl.] a share in a business or company and a legal right to a share of its profits: *The group has extensive interests in China.* ◊ *She has business interests in France.* ◊ *American interests in Europe (= money invested in European countries)* → HOLDING
○ **business/commercial/economic** interests ◆ **energy/mining/oil** interests
4 [C,U] a connection with sth which affects your attitude to it, especially because you may benefit from it in some way: *Organizations have an*

interest in ensuring that employee motivation is high. ◊ *I should, at this point, **declare my interest**.*
5 [C, usually pl.] a group of people who are in the same business or who share the same aims which they want to protect: *powerful farming interests* ◊ *relationships between local government and business interests*
6 (*Law*) [C] a legal right to land or property: *You must give the names and addresses of anyone you know who has an interest in the land.*
→ idioms at CONFLICT *noun*, DECLARE

ˈinterest-ˌbearing *adjective* [usually before noun]
(*Finance*) used to describe loans, etc. on which interest is paid: *They are cutting their workforce and reducing their interest-bearing debt.* ◊ *interest-bearing deposits*

ˈinterest ˌcover (*also* ~coverage) *noun* [U]
(*Accounting*) a company's profit in relation to the amount of interest it has to pay on loans: *The company has interest cover of seven times its operating profits.* ◊ *Interest cover remains very comfortable.*

ˌinterested ˈparty *noun* [C]
a person or an organization that is in a position to gain from a situation or to be affected by it, especially one with a financial interest in a company: *The financier will deliver his rescue plan for the company to interested parties this week.*

ˈinterest exˌpense *noun* [U,C, usually pl.]
(*Accounting*) the amount that a company has to pay in interest on money it has borrowed: *They reported a drop in profits, largely due to a sharp rise in interest expense.* ◊ *Interest expenses rose almost 10%.*

ˌinterest-ˈfree *adjective*
used to describe loans on which the borrower does not have to pay **interest**: *Ford said on Monday it was extending interest-free loans on some models.* ◊ *You should always pay the loan off at the end of the interest-free period.*
○ interest-free **credit/financing** ◆ an interest-free **loan/period**

★ ˈinterest rate (*also* ˌrate of ˈinterest) *noun* [C]
the cost of borrowing money, usually expressed as a percentage of the amount borrowed: *Interest rates are low and unlikely to be raised soon.* ◊ *The Bank of England has cut interest rates by half a percentage point.* ◊ *Interest rates of 2.75% are low by past standards.* ◊ *Stocks rose on hopes of an interest-rate cut this week.*
○ **high/low** interest rates ◆ to **cut/increase/raise/reduce/slash** interest rates ◆ interest rates **fall/rise**

ˈinterest-rate risk *noun* [U]
(*Finance*) the risk that the value of an investment or an asset will fall if rates of interest change, for example that the value of a bond will fall as rates of interest rise: *The group may have trouble managing its exposure to interest rate risk.*

ˈinterest-rate swap *noun* [C]
(*Finance*) an agreement between two organizations that have borrowed money at different rates of interest, for example one at a fixed rate and the other at a rate that changes. In order to reduce INTEREST-RATE RISK, they agree to exchange regular payments based on the rates of interest at which they have borrowed.

★ **interface** /ˈɪntəfeɪs; *AmE* -tərf-/ *noun, verb*
● *noun* [C]
1 the point where two systems, subjects, etc. meet and affect each other: *He is interested in the interface **between** big business and small communities.* ◊ *We work at the interface **with** the public.*

2 (*IT*) the way a computer program presents information to a user or receives information from a user: *The software has a standard Windows™ interface.* ◇ *Customers have suggested improvements to our user interface.* → GUI
3 (*IT*) a connection between one device or system and another: *the interface **between** the computer and the printer*
● *verb*
1 [no obj] to come into contact with a person, product, system, etc. and to affect them or be affected by them in some way: *How users actually interface **with** the product is very important.* ◇ *We thought people would interface with call centres only at peak times.*
2 (*IT*) [+ obj or no obj] **interface (sth) (with sth)** | **interface A and B** to connect sth using an **interface**; to be connected in this way: *The system interfaces with many different financial software packages.*

★ **interim** /ˈɪntərɪm/ *adjective* [only before noun]
1 (*Accounting*) **interim** results, figures, etc. are calculated before the final figures are known, often after half a FINANCIAL YEAR: *Interim figures released yesterday show strong growth.* ◇ *a 21% increase in interim pre-tax profits*
O interim **accounts/figures/losses/profits/results**
2 intended to last for only a short time, until sth/sb more permanent is found: *He will take over the running of the company on an interim basis.* ◇ *The union agreed to an interim 4% pay offer.*

‚interim 'dividend *noun* [C]
(*Finance*) a **dividend** that is paid half way through the FINANCIAL YEAR → FINAL DIVIDEND

‚interim in'junction (*BrE*) (*AmE* pre‚liminary in'junction) *noun* [C]
(*Law*) an official order from a court that a person or company must not do sth until a dispute has been resolved: *They asked the court to issue an immediate interim injunction against the company.*

‚interim 'management *noun* [U]
a situation where a company is temporarily controlled by managers who do not normally control it, usually because of serious problems; the managers who are in charge of a company in this way: *The company has been **under** interim management since the CEO resigned last month.*

‚interim 'payment *noun* [C]
1 a payment that is made before full payment, or while the size of the full payment is being decided: *Our insurer was prepared to make an interim payment.*
2 (*Finance*) an INTERIM DIVIDEND

interims /ˈɪntərɪmz/ *noun* [pl.]
(*Accounting*) results or figures that are calculated before the final figures are known: *International Greetings announces its interims tomorrow.*

intermediary /ˌɪntəˈmiːdiəri; *AmE* ˌɪntərˈmiːdieri/ *noun* [C] (*plural* **intermediaries**)

SEE ALSO: financial intermediary

a person or an organization that helps other people or organizations who are unable or unwilling to deal with each other directly to reach an agreement: *The company acts as an intermediary **between** buyers and growers.* SYN MIDDLEMAN
▶ **‚inter'mediary** *adjective*: *a small intermediary company* ◇ *an intermediary role*

inter'mediate goods *noun* [pl.]
(*Manufacturing*) partly finished goods that are used in the manufacture of other goods: *Orders for intermediate goods rose 3.5%.*

‚intermediate tech'nology *noun* [C,U]
1 technology that is suitable for use in developing countries, because it is cheap and simple and can use local materials
2 a technology that comes between early and later versions, and is less successful than either

intermediation /ˌɪntəˌmiːdiˈeɪʃn; *AmE* -tərˈm-/ *noun* [U]
(*Finance*) an arrangement where a bank or similar financial institution helps two people or groups (**parties**) to borrow and lend money, bearing all or part of the risk → DISINTERMEDIATION (1)

intern (*also spelled* **interne**) /ˈɪntɜːn; *AmE* ˈɪntɜːrn/ *noun* [C] (*AmE*)
a student, or a person who has recently finished studying, who is getting practical experience in a job: *She spent last summer as an intern at a software company.* ▶ **internship** /ˈɪntɜːnʃɪp; *AmE* -tɜːrn-/ *noun* [C] → WORK EXPERIENCE

internal /ɪnˈtɜːnl; *AmE* ɪnˈtɜːrnl/ *adjective*
1 [usually before noun] involving or concerning only the people who are part of a particular organization rather than people from outside it: *an internal inquiry* ◇ *internal emails/memos* ◇ *Internal recruitment gives staff opportunities for promotion and new challenges.*
2 used to describe the situation when a company develops its existing business rather than growing by buying other companies, etc: *We have tripled our sales through internal growth and acquisitions.* → ORGANIC (1)
3 [only before noun] connected with a country's own affairs rather than those that involve other countries: *internal affairs/trade/markets* ◇ *an internal flight* (= within a country) SYN DOMESTIC OPP EXTERNAL
▶ **internally** /ɪnˈtɜːnəli; *AmE* ɪnˈtɜːrn-/ *adverb*: *It is too early to say whether the positions will be filled internally or externally.*

in‚ternal 'audit *noun* [C,U]
(*Accounting*) an examination that an organization does of its own activities, especially to see if its own controls and systems are working properly: *The theft was uncovered by an internal audit last year.*
▶ **in‚ternal 'auditor** *noun* [C]

in‚ternal con'sistency = INTERNAL EQUITY

in‚ternal con'sultancy *noun* [C,U]
(*HR*) a situation where one department with special skills in an organization sells its services to other departments, who can choose to use outside experts instead: *IT consultants and staff who provide internal consultancy* ▶ **int‚ernal con'sultant** *noun* [C]

in‚ternal 'customer *noun* [C]
(*HR*) the idea that an employee working on one stage of a process is a customer of employees working on the stage before. This encourages employees to produce work of a good quality at each stage of a process: *good relationships with external and internal customers* ◇ *a facilities manager serving and supporting the company's internal customers*

in‚ternal 'equity (*also* in‚ternal con'sistency) *noun* [U]
(*HR*) a situation in which the pay that employees in an organization receive is related to the type of job they do in the organization: *Internal equity is achieved if the employee's pay corresponds to their responsibilities.* → EXTERNAL EQUITY

in‚ternal 'labour ‚market (*AmE* spelling ~ **labor ~**) *noun* [C] (*abbr* ILM)
(*HR*) in an **internal labour market**, employers find people for senior positions from employees within the organization, rather than looking outside: *The employer is building an internal labour market, with*

a view to retaining skilled workers. → EXTERNAL
LABOUR MARKET

in.ternal 'market *noun* [C, usually sing.]
(*Economics*)
1 = SINGLE MARKET
2 a situation in which different departments in the
same organization buy goods and services from
each other

in'ternal 'rate of re'turn *noun* [C,U] (*abbr* **IRR**)
(*Accounting*) a way of comparing the value of
different investments based on the income they
will produce and the amount spent on them. A rate
of interest is calculated for which the value of the
income from each investment equals the amount
spent on it. → PRESENT VALUE

In.ternal 'Revenue Code *noun* [sing.] (*abbr*
IRC)
the tax laws of the US

In.ternal 'Revenue .Service *noun* [sing.]
(*abbr* **IRS**)
the branch of government in the US that is
responsible for collecting most taxes, including
INCOME TAX → HM REVENUE AND CUSTOMS

in.ternal 'search *noun* [C,U]
(*Marketing*) the process by which consumers use
information from their own experiences and
memory when they make a decision about buying a
product or service

★ **international** /,ɪntəˈnæʃnəl; *AmE* -tərˈn-/
adjective [usually before noun]
connected with or involving two or more countries:
*The group has seen strong growth in its international
business.* ◇ *a violation of the rules for international
trade* ◇ *The number of passengers on international
flights fell last year by 4.4%.* → DOMESTIC (1)
▶ **internationally** /,ɪntəˈnæʃnəli; *AmE* -tərˈn-/
*adverb: Holiday Inn is an internationally recognized
name.*

Inter.national Ac'counting .Standards
noun [pl.] (*abbr* **IAS**)
a set of rules for accounting, produced by the
International Accounting Standards Board. Firms
can choose whether or not to follow them.

**Inter.national Ac'counting .Standards
Board** *noun* [sing.] (*abbr* **IASB**)
an independent organization that decides on rules
for accounting that can be used all over the world
NOTE This has replaced the International
Accounting Standards Committee (IASC).

inter.national 'airport *noun* [C]
a large airport that has flights to and from many
different countries: *Tokyo International Airport*

Inter'national 'Chamber of 'Commerce
noun [sing.] (*abbr* **ICC**)
an international association of business people
based in Paris that aims to encourage, support and
protect world business and trade → INCOTERM

**Inter'national 'Civil Avi'ation
Organi.zation** *noun* [sing.] (*abbr* **ICAO**)
an international organization that advises airlines
and sets safety standards for air travel

**Inter'national Fi'nancial Re'porting
.Standards** *noun* [pl.] (*abbr* **IFRS**)
a set of rules for accounting, produced by the
International Accounting Standards Board

the **.International 'Labour
Organi.zation** (*AmE spelling* ~ **Labor** ~) *noun*
[sing.] (*abbr* **ILO**)
an organization formed by the United Nations to
improve working conditions in all parts of the
world

inter.national 'labour .standards (*AmE
spelling* ~ **labor** ~) *noun* [pl.]
a set of instructions for employment conditions
produced by the International Labour
Organization. Countries can choose whether or not
to follow them.

.international 'law *noun* [U]
the system of laws that are recognized by most
states as controlling their relations with each other
and their treatment of each other's citizens: *The
proposed action would be illegal under international
law.* ◇ *The company said its claim was in line with
international law.*

.international 'management *noun*
1 [U; C with sing./pl. verb] the process of running a
business that operates in several different countries
(a **multinational**); the people who do this
2 [U] the process of developing an organization's
production or marketing activities across national
borders

inter.national 'monetary .system *noun*
[sing.]
the system which controls the sale and exchange of
different currencies → IMF

**.International 'Motor In.surance
Cer.tificate** = GREEN CARD (2)

.International Re'ply .Coupon *noun* [C]
(*abbr* **IRC**)
a printed form that can be bought from a post
office and sent with a letter to another country and
is then exchanged for the cost of sending a reply by
air from that country

.international re'serves = FOREIGN
EXCHANGE RESERVES

.International Se'curities Ex.change *noun*
[sing.] (*abbr* **ISE**)
in the US, a system that allows people to use a
computer to trade OPTIONS (= the right to buy or
sell a fixed quantity of shares, bonds, etc. for a
particular price within a particular period)

interne = INTERN

Internesia /,ɪntəˈniːziə; *AmE* ,ɪntərˈn-/ *noun* [U]
(*informal*)
an inability to remember on which website you saw
a particular piece of information or to find it again
NOTE Internesia is formed from **Internet** and
amnesia (= a medical condition in which sb loses
their memory).

★ **Internet** /ˈɪntənet; *AmE* -tərn-/ (*usually* **the
Internet**) (*also* **the Net**, *informal*) *noun* [sing.]

SEE ALSO: wireless Internet

(*IT*) an international computer network that
connects other networks and computers all over
the world: *The company is trying to build a strong
presence on the Internet.* ◇ *You can download the
software from the Internet.* ◇ *We aim to build a truly
global Internet company.* → EXTRANET, INTRANET

.Internet 'cafe *noun* [C]
a place with computers where customers can use
the Internet and buy drinks and food: *The Internet
cafe is open from 8 a.m. to midnight.*

'Internet .commerce (*also* **'Net .commerce**, *less
frequent*) = E-COMMERCE

interoperable /,ɪntərˈɒpərəbl; *AmE* -ˈɑːp-/
adjective
(*IT*) (about computer systems or programs) able to
exchange information or be used together
▶ **interoperability** /,ɪntər,ɒpərəˈbɪləti; *AmE* -ˈɑːp-/
noun [U]

interpersonal /ˌɪntəˈpɜːsənl; *AmE* -tərˈpɜːrs-/ *adjective* [only before noun]
connected with relationships between people: *We always look for people with good interpersonal skills.*

interpreter /ɪnˈtɜːprɪtə(r); *AmE* -ˈtɜːrp-/ *noun* [C]
1 a person whose job is to translate what sb is saying while they are speaking: *The chairman spoke through an interpreter.*
2 (*IT*) a computer program that changes the instructions of another program into a form that the computer can understand and use

interruption /ˌɪntəˈrʌpʃn/ *noun* [C,U]

SEE ALSO: **business interruption**

1 the act of stopping sb from speaking or doing sth: *The constant interruptions make it hard to concentrate.*
2 an event that temporarily stops an activity or a process; a time when an activity is stopped: *an interruption to/in the power supply* ◇ *Credits will be given to any customer who experienced an interruption of service.*

intersect /ˌɪntəˈsekt; *AmE* -tərˈs-/ *verb* [no obj]
if two areas of activity **intersect**, they come into contact and affect each other: *Traditional business practices can cause problems when they intersect with the world of the Internet.* ◇ *The institute explores ways in which technology and human issues intersect.* ► **intersection** /ˌɪntəˈsekʃn; *AmE* -tərˈs-/ *noun* [C,U]

interstate /ˈɪntəsteɪt; *AmE* -tərs-/ *adjective* [only before noun]
between states, especially in the US: *interstate commerce*

intervene /ˌɪntəˈviːn; *AmE* -tərˈv-/ *verb* [no obj]
to become involved in a situation in order to improve it: *It is not the government's role to intervene in companies' problems.* ◇ *The Central Bank said it would intervene again to prop up the currency.* ► **intervention** /ˌɪntəˈvenʃn; *AmE* -tərˈv-/ *noun* [U,C]: *an argument about state intervention in industry* ◇ *Officials threatened intervention to push down the yen.*

interventionism /ˌɪntəˈvenʃənɪzəm; *AmE* -tərˈv-/ *noun* [U]
(*Economics*) the policy or practice of a government influencing the economy of its own country ► **interventionist** /ˌɪntəˈvenʃənɪst; *AmE* -tərˈv-/ *adjective, noun* [C]

interˈvention price *noun* [C]
(*Economics*) the minimum price for a product, especially an agricultural product, set by a government or an organization such as the European Union. If the market price falls below this price, the government, etc. pays the difference to the producer, or buys the product at the agreed price: *The goal is to move the EU's intervention prices downwards.*

★ **interview** /ˈɪntəvjuː; *AmE* -tərv-/ *noun, verb*
● *noun* [C]

SEE ALSO: **depth interview, exit ~, screening ~, semi-structured ~, situational ~**

1 a formal meeting at which sb is asked questions to see if they are suitable for a particular job: *a job interview* ◇ *He has an interview next week for the manager's post.* ◇ *I've got an interview with United Biscuits.* ◇ *We're about to start the second round of interviews.* ◇ *to be invited for (an) interview*
● *to* **carry out/conduct/do/hold** *an interview* • *to* **attend/be called for/have** *an interview* • *an interview* **board/panel**

2 a way of finding out sb's opinion about products or services by asking them questions in a private meeting: *Interviews and questionnaires are the most important tools of market research.* ◇ *The survey team carried out over 200 interviews with retired people.*
● *a* **face-to-face/telephone** *interview* • *to* **carry out/conduct/do** *an interview*

3 a meeting (often a public one) at which a journalist asks sb questions in order to find out their opinions: *The interview with the new CEO was published last Friday.*
● *a* **newspaper/press/radio/television** *interview* • *to* **carry out/conduct/do** *an interview* • *to* **do/give (sb)/grant (sb)** *an interview*

● *verb*
1 [+ obj *or* no obj] to talk to sb and ask them questions at a formal meeting to find out if they are suitable for a job, etc: *We interviewed ten people for the job.* ◇ *Which post are you being interviewed for?*
2 [no obj] (*especially AmE*) to talk to sb and answer questions at a formal meeting to get a job, etc: *If you don't interview well you are unlikely to get the job.*
3 [+ obj] to ask sb questions at a private meeting, especially to find out what they think about particular products or services: *We interviewed over 500 teenagers to find out what young people want in a magazine.*
4 [+ obj] to ask sb questions about their life, opinions, etc., especially on the radio or television or for a newspaper or magazine: *The directors declined to be interviewed.*
► **ˈinterviewing** *noun* [U]: *The research involves in-depth interviewing.* ◇ *interviewing skills/techniques*

interviewee /ˌɪntəvjuːˈiː; *AmE* -tərv-/ *noun* [C]
the person who answers the questions in an interview

interviewer /ˈɪntəvjuːə(r); *AmE* -tərv-/ *noun* [C]
the person who asks the questions in an interview

ˌin-the-ˈtrenches *adjective* [only before noun]
in-the-trenches employees and managers are directly involved in the most active part of the business: *Many in-the-trenches leaders blame the people above them when they fail to make progress.*

intra- /ˈɪntrə/ *prefix* (*used in adjectives and adverbs*)
inside; within: *intra-departmental* (= within a department) ◇ *intraday* ◇ *intracompany communication*

intraday /ˈɪntrədeɪ/ *adjective* [only before noun]
(*AmE*)
(*Finance*) happening within one day: *The rand recovered after a five per cent intraday fall against the dollar.* ◇ *The yield on the ten-year Japanese bond fell to a four-year low in intraday trade yesterday.*

★ **intranet** /ˈɪntrənet/ *noun* [C, usually sing.]
(*IT*) a computer network that is private to a company or an organization but is connected to and uses the same software as the Internet: *You need a password to access the company intranet.* ◇ *intranet learning resources* → EXTRANET

intrapreneur /ˌɪntrəprəˈnɜː(r)/ *noun* [C]
an employee in a large company who develops new products or services, starts SUBSIDIARY businesses, etc. for the company rather than leaving to form their own company → ENTREPRENEUR
► **intrapreneurial** /ˌɪntrəprəˈnɜːriəl/ *adjective*
intrapreneurship /ˌɪntrəprəˈnɜːʃɪp; *AmE* -ˈnɜːrʃɪp/ *noun* [U]

ˈin tray (*also* **ˈinbox**) *noun* [C]
a container on your desk for letters and other documents that are waiting to be read or answered: *I've read through everything in my in tray.* → OUT TRAY

intrinsic /ɪn'trɪnsɪk; -zɪk/ *adjective*
belonging to or part of sth: *Change is intrinsic **to** (= an essential part of) business today.* ◇ *With intrinsic motivation (= doing sth because you want to) the reward is the activity itself.*

in,trinsic 'value *noun* [C,U]
(*Finance*) the real value that a company, an asset, etc. has, rather than the current value as shown, for example, by share prices or its market value. **Intrinsic value** can be calculated by experts: *Concentrate on building intrinsic value over time.* ◇ *The company's intrinsic value is well above $25 per share.*

★ **introduce** /,ɪntrə'djuːs; AmE 'duːs/ *verb* [+ obj]
1 to make a new product or service available to people for the first time: *Earlier this year the manufacturer introduced the product **to** the general market.* ◇ *The new service will be introduced next year.* SYN BRING STH IN
2 to start to use a new system or a new method of doing sth: *We've introduced a computerised system to deal with orders.* SYN BRING STH IN
3 introduce A (to B) | introduce A and B | introduce yourself (to sb) to tell two or more people who have not met before what one another's names are; to tell sb what your name is: *Can I introduce my wife?* ◇ *Participants get one minute to introduce themselves.*
4 (*often* be introduced (to sth/sb)) to help sb find out about sth/sb or do sth for the first time: *Jones was introduced to the firm by a business associate.* ◇ *The course introduces students to drafting business plans.*
5 to formally suggest a new law so that it can be discussed: *The government has introduced a bill to reform pensions.*

★ **introduction** /,ɪntrə'dʌkʃn/ *noun*
1 [U] the act of bringing a product, service, system, etc. into use for the first time: *the introduction of new manufacturing methods*
2 [C] a product, service, etc. that is brought into use for the first time: *We have begun the biggest wave of new product introductions in our history.*
3 [C,U] the act of making one person formally known to another: *Shall I **do** the introductions (= tell people one another's names)?* ◇ *a **letter of introduction** (= a letter which tells sb who you are, written by sb who knows both you and the person who will read the letter)*

introductory /,ɪntrə'dʌktəri/ *adjective*
1 offered for a short time only, when a product or service is first on sale or when a new customer buys it: *This introductory offer is for three days only.* ◇ *credit cards offering a 0% introductory rate*
○ an introductory **discount/offer/package/price/rate**
2 written or said at the beginning of sth as an introduction to what follows
○ introductory **chapters/paragraphs/remarks**
3 intended as an introduction to a subject or an activity for people who have never done it before
○ an introductory **book/class/course**

invalid /ɪn'vælɪd/ *adjective*
1 not legally or officially acceptable: *The contract was invalid because parts were added after it was signed.*
2 (*IT*) of a type that a computer cannot recognize: *The URL is invalid.*
3 not based on all the facts and therefore not correct: *an invalid argument*
OPP VALID
▶ **invalidity** /,ɪnvə'lɪdəti/ *noun* [U]

invalidate /ɪn'vælɪdeɪt/ *verb* [+ obj]
to make a document, contract, etc. no longer legally or officially valid: *Putting the TV channel up for sale would invalidate this contract.* SYN NULLIFY
OPP VALIDATE ▶ **invalidation** /ɪn,vælɪ'deɪʃn/ *noun* [U]

invaluable /ɪn'væljuəbl/ *adjective*
invaluable (to/for sb/sth) | invaluable (in sth) extremely useful: *This information is invaluable.* ◇ *She has made an invaluable contribution to the company.* ◇ *His energy will be invaluable in driving the business forward.* SYN VALUABLE
HELP Invaluable means 'very valuable or useful'. The opposite of **valuable** is **worthless**.

invent /ɪn'vent/ *verb* [+ obj]
to design or produce a product or method that has not existed before: *Inventing new products and services is my first love.* ◇ *Who invented the Internet?* ◇ *Companies are inventing new ways of doing business together.*

invention /ɪn'venʃn/ *noun*
1 [C] a thing or an idea that has been invented: *What was Henry Ford's greatest invention?* ◇ *The best inventions are the simplest and most obvious.*
2 [U] the act of inventing a product, method, etc: *the 100th anniversary of the invention **of** air conditioning*

inventor /ɪn'ventə(r)/ *noun* [C]
a person who has invented sth or whose job is inventing things: *Dick Morley is the inventor of the floppy disk.*

★ **inventory** /'ɪnvəntri; AmE -tɔːri/ *noun, verb*
● *noun*

SEE ALSO: beginning inventory, continuous inventory

1 (*Commerce; Production*) [C,U] (*especially AmE*) the goods that a business has for sale at a particular time: *We will carry a large inventory of candy.* ◇ *Crude oil inventories are running low.* ◇ *What do you do when you're stuck with inventory you can't sell?* SYN STOCK
○ to **buy (in)/order/replenish** inventory ◆ to **carry/have/hold** inventory ◆ to **control/get rid of/reduce/run down/sell off** inventory
2 (*Accounting; Production*) [U,C] (*especially AmE*) all the goods owned by a business, including raw materials, parts, work not yet finished and finished products: *The company has no factories, no inventory, no delivery trucks and no sales force.* ◇ *The software can improve inventory management and cash flow.* ◇ *a drive to cut costs and reduce inventory levels in manufacturing* SYN STOCK, STOCK-IN-TRADE
○ to **build (up)/maintain/order/replenish/store** inventory ◆ to **control/get rid of/reduce/run down/sell (off)** inventory
3 [C] a complete list of something, especially of all the goods and property owned by a person, a company, an organization, etc: *She keeps a full inventory of company assets and updates it every six months.* ◇ *They made/took an inventory of all the goods in the shop.*
● *verb* [+ obj] (**inventories, inventorying, inventoried, inventoried**)
to make a complete list of sth: *The equipment was rarely inventoried.*

'inventory con,trol (*also* 'inventory ,management) *noun* [U] (*especially AmE*)
(*Commerce; Production*) the process of making sure that a suitable quantity of goods, materials or parts are stored and available at any time while keeping the costs of doing this as low as possible; the department in a company that is responsible for this process: *The industry has become much better at inventory control.* ◇ *They have cut costs by adopting stricter inventory control practices.* SYN STOCK CONTROL
▶ **'inventory con,troller** (*also* 'inventory ,manager) *noun* [C]

'inventory count noun [C]
(*Accounting*) an act of checking how many items a shop/store or business has available for sale [SYN] STOCK COUNT

,inventory on 'hand noun [U] (*especially AmE*)
(*Accounting*; *Commerce*) the materials, parts, finished products, etc. that a company holds ready to be used [SYN] STOCK IN HAND

'inventory risk noun [U]
(*Commerce*; *Production*) the risk that the goods and materials that a business has will fall in value, costing the business money: *State-of-the-art IT systems reduce inventory risk.*

,inventory-to-'sales ,ratio noun [C]
(*Economics*) a measure of the demand for goods or of how well supplies are being managed, calculated by dividing the value of the supply of goods that a business or an industry has by the sales in a particular period: *The drop in inventory-to-sales ratios are positive for the economy.*

,inventory 'turnover (*also* ,inventory 'turn)
noun [C,U] (*also* ,inventory 'turnover ,ratio [C])
(*Accounting*) the relationship between the value of goods that a business sells in a particular period, usually 12 months, and the average value of the goods it has available to sell: *An inventory turnover of 40 to 60 times means that, on average, the entire stock is replaced each week.* ◇ *They wanted to achieve 14 inventory turns a year.* [SYN] STOCK TURNOVER

'inventory valu,ation noun [U,C]
(*Accounting*) the process of calculating the value of all the goods, finished or not finished, and materials that a company, shop/store, etc. has stored and available for use or sale at the end of a particular period; the value that is calculated [SYN] STOCK VALUATION

inverse /,ɪn'vɜːs; *AmE* ,ɪn'vɜːrs/ adjective [only before noun]
opposite in amount or position to another thing: *There is an inverse **relationship** between shares and the dollar* (= the value of one goes up as the value of the other goes down). ▸ **inversely** /,ɪn'vɜːsli; *AmE* -'vɜːrs-/ adverb: *The gold price often moves inversely to the dollar.*
[IDM] **in inverse pro'portion to** if one thing is **in inverse proportion to** another, the more of one thing there is, the less there is of the other: *The attractiveness of a city tends to be in inverse proportion to its economic productivity.*

in,verted 'market = BACKWARDATION

★ **invest** /ɪn'vest/ verb
1 [+ obj or no obj] to buy property, shares, etc. in order to sell them again and make a profit: *Now is a good time to invest **in** the property market.* ◇ *We have invested €100 000 in the business.* ◇ *More individuals are investing.*
2 [+ obj or no obj] (about a company, government, etc.) to spend money on sth in order to make it better or more successful: *The government has invested **heavily** in public transport.* ◇ *The company will invest $160 million **on** new plant and equipment this year.* See note at FINANCE
3 [+ obj] to save money in a bank account, an insurance policy, etc. in order to receive interest: *You have to decide how best to invest your savings.* ◇ *She invested $10 000 **in** a high interest savings account.*
▸ **investable** (*also spelled* **investible**, *less frequent*)
/ɪn'vestəbl/ adjective: *The bank has about 300 000 customers with $1 million or more in investable assets.*

in,vested 'capital noun [U]
(*Accounting*) the amount of money invested in a business by its owners or shareholders

investible = INVESTABLE at INVEST

investigate /ɪn'vestɪɡeɪt/ verb
1 [+ obj or no obj] **investigate (sth)** | **investigate how/what/whether** etc. to carefully examine the facts of a situation, an event, a crime, etc. to find out the truth about it or how it happened: *Inspectors were asked to investigate possible instances of insider dealing in the City.* ◇ *The Board hired a law firm to investigate.*
2 [+ obj] **investigate sb (for sth)** to try to find out the truth about the activities of a person or company suspected of having done sth wrong or illegal: *He has been investigated for fraud.*
▸ **investigation** /ɪn,vestɪ'ɡeɪʃn/ noun [C,U]: *The company faces an investigation **into** its accounting practices.* ◇ *The firm is **under** investigation by the U.S. Justice Department.*
investigator /ɪn'vestɪɡeɪtə(r)/ noun [C]

★ **investment** /ɪn'vestmənt/ noun

SEE ALSO: alternative investment, autonomous ~, capital ~, community ~, direct ~, fixed ~, foreign direct ~, etc.

1 [U] the action or process of using money in order to make a profit or earn interest, for example by buying shares, bonds, property, etc: *We need to attract foreign investment.* ◇ *Investment **in** these savings plans is expected to grow rapidly.* ◇ *Why is the company an attractive investment opportunity?* ◇ *Investment income is liable to tax.* ◇ *the bank's chief investment officer*
● **domestic/foreign/private/public** investment
2 [C] the amount of money that a person or business invests: *There is a minimum investment of $10 000.* ◇ *I have had a high return on my original investment.* ◇ *The company wishes to sell its entire investment.* See note at FINANCE
● **an initial/a maximum/minimum/one-off** investment ♦ **to make** an investment
3 [C] the thing that a person or business invests in: *Our investments are not doing well.* ◇ *You should think of equities as a medium- to long-term investment.* ◇ *The value of an investment can go down as well as up.*
● **a good/low-risk/profitable/safe** investment ♦ **a bad/ high-risk/risky/speculative** investment ♦ **long-term/ medium-term/short-term** investments ♦ **to have/ hold** investments ♦ **to buy/sell** investments
4 [C,U] the act or process of buying materials, machines, etc. to make goods to sell: *The area must attract new industrial investment.* ◇ *Investment **in** manufacturing has fallen dramatically.* ◇ *The company has announced a $5 million investment in new technology.* ◇ *higher investment spending*
● **business/corporate** investment ♦ **heavy/major/new** investment (in sth) ♦ **industrial/infrastructure/ technology** investment ♦ **to attract/boost/ encourage/stimulate** investment (in sth)

in,vestment al'lowance = CAPITAL ALLOWANCE

in'vestment bank noun [C] (*especially AmE*)
(*Finance*) a bank that provides finance for companies by buying their shares and selling them to the public. It also advises on TAKEOVERS and MERGERS (= when one company buys or joins with another) and on ways of raising money: *The sale was handled by investment bank Merrill Lynch.*
→ MERCHANT BANK
▸ **in'vestment ,banker** noun [C] **in'vestment ,banking** noun [U]

in'vestment bou,tique (*also* bou'tique)
noun [C]
(*Finance*) a small business that offers advice and

help about a particular industry or area to people or organizations that want to invest money

in'vestment ,company (*also* **in'vestment trust, in'vestment trust ,company**) *noun* [C] (*Finance*) a company that invests its money in other companies' shares, bonds, etc. It makes its profits from the money made on these investments: *a Hong Kong-based investment company*

in'vestment goods = CAPITAL GOODS

in'vestment grade *adjective* [only before noun] (*Finance*) used to describe companies, bonds, etc. that are fairly safe to invest in because they have a low risk: *The company's credit rating is now investment grade.* ◇ *investment-grade debt* (= that is likely to be paid back) ◇ *More than $28 billion of new investment-grade bonds have been sold in the past two weeks.*

in'vestment ,management *noun* [U] (*Finance*) the act of managing an amount of money which is used to buy and sell shares, bonds, etc. on behalf of investors in order to make as much profit as possible: *He is chief executive of Rostrum, an investment management group.* ◇ *The new company will offer investment management services to Japanese pension funds.* [SYN] FUND MANAGEMENT, MONEY MANAGEMENT
▸ **in'vestment ,manager** *noun* [C]: *She began her career as investment manager for Mercury Asset Management.*

in'vestment mix (*also* **'asset mix**) *noun* [C, usually sing., U] (*Finance*) a combination of different investments that are put together in order to get the highest amount of profit from them: *A good planner will help come up with a good investment mix for your retirement savings.*

in'vestment re,search *noun* [U] (*Finance*) the study of different types of investments, in order to decide which ones are good to invest in: *Investment banks produce investment research mainly for the benefit of their investment clients.*

in'vestment trust = INVESTMENT COMPANY

in'vestment trust ,company = INVESTMENT COMPANY

★ **investor** /ɪnˈvestə(r)/ *noun* [C]

SEE ALSO: angel investor, small ~, value ~

a person or an organization that invests money in order to make a profit or receive interest: *Investors in the fund lost all their money.* ◇ *Foreign investors have traditionally been welcome in Germany.* ◇ *Efforts are being made to restore investor confidence.* See note at FINANCE
❍ *institutional/large/major* investors • *individual/private* investors • *foreign/international/overseas* investors

in'vestor group *noun* [C] (*Finance*) a group of investors acting together, especially to take over a company: *He led an investor group that acquired a $40 million department store chain.*

in,vestor pro'tection *noun* [U] systems and rules designed to make sure that financial institutions treat investors fairly and do not cheat them: *We have to strike a balance between investor protection and market efficiency.*

in,vestor re'lations *noun* [U] (*abbr* **IR**) the process by which a company communicates with investors and possible investors, providing them with accurate information about the company and how successful it is likely to be in the future: *the director of investor relations* ◇ *Effective investor relations can help a company build a shareholder base and hold onto them.*

invisibles /ɪnˈvɪzəblz/ *noun* [pl.] (*Economics*) services such as banking, education, TOURISM, etc. that countries sell to and buy from each other → VISIBLES

in,visible 'trade *noun* [U] (*Economics*) services such as education, banking, TOURISM, etc. that countries sell to and buy from each other → VISIBLE TRADE

★ **invitation** /ˌɪnvɪˈteɪʃn/ *noun* [C] an invitation (to sth/to do sth) a spoken or written request to sb to do sth or to go somewhere: *an invitation to a product demonstration* ◇ *He accepted the invitation to join the board.*
❍ *to extend/issue/withdraw* an invitation • *to accept/decline/turn down/reject* an invitation

★ **invite** /ɪnˈvaɪt/ *verb* [+ obj]
1 (*formal*) **invite sth** | **invite sb to do sth** | **invite sb (to/for sth)** to offer sb the opportunity to do sth: *The company is inviting bids for a stake in the business.* ◇ *We invite customers to call for a prospectus.* ◇ *Applications are invited from suitably qualified persons.*
❍ *invite bids/offers/tenders* • *invite comments/debate/questions/suggestions*
2 (*formal*) **invite sb (to/for sth)** | **invite sb to do sth** to ask sb formally to go somewhere: *Successful candidates will be invited for interview.* ◇ *I was invited to their meetings.*
3 invite sb (to sth/to do sth) to ask a person to come to a social event: *We were invited to lunch.* ◇ *He invited me to visit him if I were ever in Huston.*

★ **invoice** /ˈɪnvɔɪs/ *noun, verb* (*Accounting*)
● *noun* [C]

SEE ALSO: purchase invoice, sales ~, tax ~

a list of goods that have been sold, work that has been done, etc. showing what you must pay: *If you pay the invoice within 15 days, you get a 5% discount off your next purchase.* ◇ *When you confirm your booking, an invoice will be automatically raised and sent to you.*
See note on next page
❍ *to generate/issue/raise/send/submit* an invoice • *to pay/settle* an invoice
● *verb* [+ obj]
invoice sb (for sth) | **invoice sth (to sb/sth)** to write or send a bill for work you have done or goods you have provided: *You will be invoiced for these items at the end of the month.* ◇ *Invoice the goods to my account.* ▸ **'invoicing** *noun* [U]

'invoice ,discounting (*also* **'discounting**) *noun* [U] (*Finance*) a financial arrangement in which a bank or other business buys the right to receive payments that are owed to a company. The bank pays the debts immediately, receiving a percentage of the money owed for doing this, and then gets the money when the company has collected it. → FACTORING ▸ **'invoice ,discounter** *noun* [C]

'invoice price *noun* [C] the price for goods or services that is shown on an invoice

invoke /ɪnˈvəʊk; AmE ɪnˈvoʊk/ *verb* [+ obj]
1 to mention or use a law, rule, etc. as a reason for doing sth: *They delayed their payment, invoking a ten-day grace period* (= extra time) *allowed under the terms of the deal.*
2 (*IT*) to begin to run a program, etc: *This command will invoke the HELP system.*

invoice/bill/check/receipt/statement of account/voucher

Before you pay for something you receive a piece of paper telling you how much you owe. This is called by different names:

- **Bill** is often used about goods and services provided to individuals: *I can't afford to pay my credit card bills.*

- In *BrE*, **bill** is also used in the context of a restaurant: *Can we have **the bill**, please?* The *AmE* word is **check**: *I asked the waiter to bring **the check**.*

- **Invoice** is the word that an accountant would use: *In order to be paid, you must submit an invoice.*

After you pay for something you receive a **receipt** telling you how much you have paid: *Keep your receipt in case you want to return the goods.* In accounting, this is often called a **voucher**: *Supporting vouchers should be attached to the claim form.*

A **statement of account** is used when several payments are made over a period of time. It tells a customer what money has been paid and what is owing: *We send you a monthly statement of account.*

involuntary /ɪnˈvɒləntri; *AmE* ɪnˈvɑːlənteri/ *adjective*
happening without the person concerned wanting it to: *involuntary unemployment* ◇ *There has been an increase in involuntary part-time work* (= when people are unable to get a job for the normal working hours). OPP VOLUNTARY

in,voluntary 'bankruptcy *noun* [U]
(*Law*) a situation in which a person's CREDITORS (= the people or companies who are owed money) ask a court to officially declare that person BANKRUPT → VOLUNTARY BANKRUPTCY

in,voluntary liqui'dation *noun* [U,C]
(*Law*) a situation where a company is forced to stop doing business so that it can pay its debts SYN COMPULSORY LIQUIDATION OPP VOLUNTARY LIQUIDATION

inward /ˈɪnwəd; *AmE* -wərd/ *adjective*
1 coming into a particular place rather than going out of it: *Scotland has little inward immigration.* ◇ *the inward flow of cash and resources*
2 towards the centre or the inside of sth: *The industry is becoming inward-looking and conservative.* OPP OUTWARD

,inward in'vestment *noun* [U,C]
(*Finance*) investment in one country or area that is made by another country or area: *Inward investment into the UK plunged last year.* ◇ *inward investment projects* ► **,inward in'vestor** *noun* [C]: *The plant was opened by inward investors from Japan in the 1980s.* → OUTWARD INVESTMENT

I/O = INPUT/OUTPUT (1)

,I/'O psy,chology, ,I/'O psy,chologist = INDUSTRIAL AND ORGANIZATIONAL PSYCHOLOGY

IOU /,aɪ əʊ ˈjuː; *AmE* -oʊ-/ *noun* [C] (*informal*)
a written promise that you will pay sb the money that you owe them: *I wrote him an IOU for $200.* ◇ *Corporate bonds are IOUs issued by companies.* NOTE 'IOU' is a way of writing 'I owe you'.

IPO /,aɪ piː ˈəʊ; *AmE* ˈoʊ/ *abbr*
(*Stock Exchange*) **initial public offering, initial public offer** the act of selling shares in a company on a stock exchange for the first time: *The company had its IPO in September 2004.* ◇ *There have been 14 IPOs since January.* ◇ *The investment bankers set an IPO price of $17 per share.* ◇ *IPO shares* SYN FLOTATION, PUBLIC ISSUE
O *to* **announce/launch/make/plan/seek** *an IPO* ◆ *to* **complete/do/have/subscribe (to)** *an IPO* ◆ *to* **handle/manage** *an IPO* ◆ *to* **abandon/cancel/withdraw** *an IPO* ◆ *a* **big/hot/large/lucrative/successful** *IPO* ◆ *a* **partial** *IPO*

IR /,aɪ ˈɑː(r)/ = INDUSTRIAL RELATIONS, INLAND REVENUE, INVESTOR RELATIONS

IRC /,aɪ ɑː ˈsiː; *AmE* ɑːr/ = INTERNAL REVENUE CODE, INTERNATIONAL REPLY COUPON

iron /ˈaɪən; *AmE* ˈaɪərn/ *noun* [U]
a hard metal that is used to make steel: *an iron and steel works*

IRR /,aɪ ɑːr ˈɑː(r)/ = INTERNAL RATE OF RETURN

irrecoverable /,ɪrɪˈkʌvərəbl/ *adjective*
irrecoverable debts, losses, etc. will never be paid back: *The bank has to make provision for ¥480 billion in irrecoverable loans.* OPP RECOVERABLE

irredeemable /,ɪrɪˈdiːməbl/ *adjective*
(*Finance*) used to describe bonds or other forms of loans that pay interest but have no date when they must be paid back → UNDATED (2)
► **,irre'deemables** *noun* [pl.]

irregular /ɪˈreɡjələ(r)/ *adjective*
1 not according to the usual rules or laws: *The inquiry found there was no evidence of irregular trading.* ◇ *An employee claims that the firm's accounting has been irregular.*
2 not happening regularly: *Many contract workers have irregular incomes.* OPP REGULAR

irregularity /ɪ,reɡjəˈlærəti/ *noun* [C, usually pl., U]
(*plural* **irregularities**)
an activity or a practice that is not according to the usual rules: *The company admitted to significant accounting irregularities.*
O **massive/serious/significant** *irregularities* ◆ **accounting/financial/management** *irregularities* ◆ *to* **allege/deny/find/investigate** *irregularities*

irretrievable /,ɪrɪˈtriːvəbl/ *adjective*
that you can never make right or get back: *an irretrievable situation* ◇ *The money already paid is irretrievable.* → RETRIEVE
► **irretrievably** /,ɪrɪˈtriːvəbli/ *adverb*

IRS /,aɪ ɑːr ˈes/ = INTERNAL REVENUE SERVICE

ISBN /,aɪ es biː ˈen/ *abbr*
International Standard Book Number a number that identifies an individual book, that you can use when ordering the book: *Can you give me the ISBN?*

ISDN /,aɪ es diː ˈen/ *abbr*
(*IT*) **integrated services digital network** a system that uses telephone connections to send sound, images and data between computers at high speed: *an ISDN Internet connection*

ISE /,aɪ es ˈiː/ = INTERNATIONAL SECURITIES EXCHANGE

,Ishi'kawa ,diagram /,ɪʃɪˈkɑːwə/ = FISHBONE DIAGRAM

ISIC /,aɪ es aɪ ˈsiː/ *abbr* **International Standard Industrial Classification of all economic activities** an international list in which industries and services are given a code of letters and numbers to show which type of economic activity they are involved in, for reference and research purposes → NACE, NAICS

'island dis,play *noun* [C]
(*Marketing*) a type of structure for displaying goods with shelves on all four sides

'island po,sition *noun* [C]
(*Marketing*) a place for an advertisement with no other advertisements near it, in a newspaper or magazine, or on television or radio

ISO /ˌaɪ es 'əʊ; 'aɪsəʊ; *AmE* 'oʊ; 'aɪsoʊ/ *abbr*
1 International Organization for Standardization the organization that sets international quality and safety standards for industry and business: *All ISO standards are voluntary.*
2 (*E-commerce*) **Independent Service Organization** a company that offers to deal with credit-card payments made on the Internet

ISO '14000 /-ˌfɔːtiːn 'θaʊznd; *AmE* ˌfɔːrtiːn/ *noun* [sing.]
(*Production*) a set of standards to ensure that businesses do not use processes that harm the environment: *All facilities must reach the ISO 14001 standard.*

ISO '9000 /-naɪn 'θaʊznd/ *noun* [sing.]
(*Production*) a set of standards connected with the processes organizations use to ensure the quality of their products and services: *More than 90 countries have adopted ISO 9000 as their national standard.*

ISP /ˌaɪ es 'piː/ *abbr*
(*IT*) **Internet service provider** a company that provides you with an Internet connection and services such as email, etc.

issuance /'ɪʃuəns; *BrE also* 'ɪsjuː-/ *noun* [C, usually sing., U]
1 (*Finance*) the act of issuing shares, bonds, etc.; the shares, bonds, etc. that are issued: *The company said it would postpone the issuance of new stock.* ◇ *This past year has been a record year for bond issuances.*
2 the act of making sth available: *the preparation and issuance of audit reports*
SYN ISSUE

★ issue /'ɪʃuː; *BrE also* 'ɪsjuː/ *noun, verb*
● *noun* [C]

SEE ALSO: **bank of issue, bonus ~, capitalization ~, cash ~, free ~, new ~, note ~,** etc.

1 (*Finance*) the act of offering shares, bonds, etc. for sale: *The bank plans to raise $1.37 bn through a new share issue.* ◇ *The company has announced an issue of bonds in the coming weeks.*
SYN ISSUANCE
2 (*Finance*) the number of shares that a company offers for sale at one time: *The new issue was heavily oversubscribed* (= more people wanted to buy shares than could have them). ◇ *There was strong demand for new corporate bond issues in January.*
3 the act of producing coins and paper money and making them available to the public; the coins and paper money produced: *a new issue of banknotes*
● *verb* [+ obj]
1 (*Finance*) to offer shares, bonds, etc. for sale: *The engineering group issued $105 million of bonds.* ◇ *Several large euro-zone companies have recently issued 30-year securities.*
2 to produce coins and paper money and make them available to the public: *Three institutions in Hong Kong are allowed to issue banknotes.*
3 issue sb with sth | issue sth (to sb) to give or supply sth to sb; to make sth available: *New employees will be issued with a temporary identity card.* ◇ *They found that payroll checks had been issued to dead or non-existent employees.*
4 to announce sth formally or officially: *Yesterday the group issued a fresh profits warning.* ◇ *The board will issue a statement on Thursday.*

issued 'capital (*also* sub,scribed 'capital, *less frequent*) (*BrE also* ,issued 'share ,capital) *noun* [U]
(*Finance*) the amount of money that a company has raised from the sale of its shares: *The company is offering to buy back up to 10% of its issued capital.*
→ AUTHORIZED CAPITAL

'issue price (*also* 'issued price, *less frequent*) *noun* [C]
(*Finance*) the price that a new share, bond, etc. is sold for: *On Monday the shares were well below their issue price of €27.75.* **SYN** INITIAL PRICE

issuer /'ɪʃuːə(r); *BrE also* 'ɪsjuːə(r)/ *noun* [C]
1 a person or an organization that supplies sth to sb: *Credit-card issuers lose billions each year to fraud.*
2 (*Finance*) a company or government that offers shares, bonds, etc. for sale: *Vehicle manufacturers are among the largest corporate issuers of dollar bonds.*

'issues ,management *noun* [U]
the process of considering how a business's plans might cause problems for members of the public, the government, etc. in the future, and then making plans to deal with this if it happens

'issuing bank *noun* [C]
(*Finance*)
1 a bank or other financial institution that supplies sb with a credit card and is responsible for their account
2 a bank that supplies sth such as a cheque or a LETTER OF CREDIT (= a letter from a bank promising to pay sb on behalf of a customer): *It takes about five days for the issuing bank to pay off the letter of credit.* → ADVISING BANK

'issuing house *noun* [C] (*BrE*)
(*Finance*) a financial institution, especially a MERCHANT BANK (= a bank that deals mainly with businesses) that sells a company's shares to the public: *The issuing house buys the shares from the issuing company and places them with investors.*

★ IT /ˌaɪ 'tiː/ *noun* [U]
1 information technology the study or use of electronic systems and equipment, especially computers, for storing, sending and receiving information: *The company has invested a lot in IT.* ◇ *Mary works in IT.* ◇ *The job requires good IT skills*
2 a company that deals in computers, software, computer services, the Internet, etc: *IT stocks were the worst performers last year.*
3 the department in a company or an organization that runs the computer systems: *Marketing, sales and IT are being merged to cut costs.*

item /'aɪtəm/ *noun* [C]

SEE ALSO: **action item, exceptional ~, extraordinary ~**

1 a single article or object, especially one that you buy: *The supermarket chain is reducing the prices of about 1 000 items.* ◇ *The camera-phone quickly became a must-have item.*
2 (*Accounting*) a single piece of information in a set of accounts: *Fuel formed one of the biggest items in the accounts.* ◇ *Excluding one-off items, the company reported earnings of $4 billion.*
3 a single thing on a list, especially on a list of things to be discussed at a meeting (an **agenda**): *Shall we move on to the next item on the agenda?* ◇ *We queried several items on the bill.* See note at MEETING

itemize , **-ise** /'aɪtəmaɪz/ *verb*
1 [+ obj] to produce a detailed list of things: *The report itemizes 23 different faults.* ◇ *an itemized*

phone bill (= each call is shown separately) ◊ *Bar codes mean customers can have itemized receipts.* **2** [+ obj or no obj] (*especially AmE*) to list separately on a tax form all the amounts that you can take away from your income before tax is calculated: *If you want to itemize instead of taking the standard deduction, you need to use the longer form.*
→ STANDARD DEDUCTION

itinerant /aɪˈtɪnərənt/ *adjective* [usually before noun]
travelling from place to place, especially to find work: *itinerant workers*

J j

jackpot /ˈdʒækpɒt; *AmE* -pɑːt/ *noun* [C]
a large amount of money that is the most valuable prize in a game of chance: *She won the lottery jackpot.* ◊ (*figurative*) *Investors are unlikely to* **hit the jackpot** (= make a large profit) *with these shares.*

janitor /ˈdʒænɪtə(r)/ = CARETAKER

jargon /ˈdʒɑːɡən; *AmE* ˈdʒɑːrɡən/ *noun* [U]
words or expressions that are used by a particular profession or group of people, and are difficult for others to understand: *computer/legal/industry jargon*

Jasdaq /ˈdʒæzdæk/ *noun* [sing.]
a type of stock market in Japan that deals with the shares of young successful companies: *The publisher listed on the Jasdaq last year.*

J-curve /ˈdʒeɪ kɜːv; *AmE* -kɜːrv/ *noun* [C]
(*Technical*) any curve in the shape of the letter 'J', which shows sth first decrease slightly then rapidly increase to a much higher level **NOTE** In economics, the **J-curve** is used to show the change in level of a country's imports compared to exports (its **balance of trade**) after a decrease in the value of the national currency.

JE /ˌdʒeɪ ˈiː/ = JOB EVALUATION

jettison /ˈdʒetɪsn/ *verb* [+ obj]
1 to get rid of sth/sb that you no longer need or want: *They jettisoned 217 staff when the recession hit.*
2 to reject an idea, a belief, plan, etc. that you no longer think is useful or likely to be successful

Jiffy™ /ˈdʒɪfi/ *noun* [C] (*plural* **Jiffies**)
used to describe a thick soft envelope for sending things that might break or tear easily: *a Jiffy bag/envelope/mailer* → PADDED ENVELOPE

jingle /ˈdʒɪŋɡl/ *noun* [C]
(*Marketing*) a short song or tune that is easy to remember and is used as part of an advertisement on radio, television, etc: *a catchy advertising jingle* ◊ *to write a jingle*

JIT /ˌdʒeɪ aɪ ˈtiː/ = JUST-IN-TIME

jitters /ˈdʒɪtəz; *AmE* -tərz/ *noun* [pl.]
(used in newspapers) feelings of being anxious about whether sth bad is about to happen: *The threat of further strikes has added to investor jitters.*

jittery /ˈdʒɪtəri/ *adjective*
(used in newspapers) anxious and uncertain: *Shoppers are already jittery* **about** *job security.* ◊ *a jittery market*

★**job** /dʒɒb; *AmE* dʒɑːb/ *noun, verb*
● *noun* [C]
SEE ALSO: desk job, off-the-~, on-the-~

1 work for which you receive regular payment: *She applied for a job* **as** *director of marketing.* ◊ *Who is likely to get the top job at the bank?* ◊ *jobs in the auto industry* ◊ *He's been* **out of a job** (= unemployed) *for six months now.* ◊ *The plan involves about 10 000 job losses.*

○ *to* **apply for/look for** *a job* ◆ *to* **find/get/have/keep/take** *a job* ◆ *to* **leave/lose/quit** *a job* ◆ *to* **offer sb/fill** *a job* ◆ *a* **full-time/part-time/permanent/steady/temporary** *job* ◆ *to* **create/cut/shed** *jobs* ◆ *job* **cuts/losses** ◆ *job* **offers/openings/opportunities**

WHICH WORD?

job/career/position/post/vocation/work

Your **job** is what you do in order to receive a regular income. The word is often used when describing how your work meets your personal or financial requirements: *a boring/an interesting/a well-paid job*

Work is an uncountable noun and is used to describe what you do in your job: *What work do you do?* ◊ *full-time/manual/skilled work.* It is also often used when speaking about the relationship between your personal life and time spent working: *the difficulties of balancing work and family*

Both **job** and **work** are used to describe the state of having work: *to* **look for/find** *work/a job* ◊ *to* **be out of** *work/a job* (= not doing any paid work)

A **career** is a series of jobs in a particular area of work, especially one for which you need a qualification or special training: *a career in business/law*

A **vocation** describes a career that you believe is particularly suitable for you, even though it may be difficult or badly paid: *He found his vocation in teaching.*

Post and **position** are both fairly formal and are often found in advertisements. **Post** is often used about academic or government jobs: *a teaching post.* **Position** often refers to a job in a company with a lot of responsibility: *a managerial/senior position*

---

2 a particular task or piece of work: *Fighting inflation is the bank's main job.* ◊ *Two men have been given the job of pushing up the company's sales and profits.* ◊ *They have done a couple of design jobs for us.* ◊ *Clients pay professional advisers by the hour, not by the job.*
3 a responsibility or duty: *The broker's job is to act in the best interests of their investors.* ◊ *It's not my job to lock up!*
4 (*IT*) an item of work which is processed by a computer as a single unit: *The job can be processed overnight.* **SYN** TASK
IDM **do a good, great, bad, etc. 'job (on sth)**; **make a good, bad, etc. job of sth** to do sth well, badly, etc: *They did a very professional job.* ◊ *The authors make an excellent job of summarizing their approach to management.* **don't give up the 'day job** used to tell sb in a humorous way that you do not think they are very good at sth they are doing that is not their real job **a job of 'work** (*BrE*

old-fashioned or formal) work that you are paid to do or that must be done **jobs for the 'boys** (BrE) (informal) people use the expression **jobs for the boys** when they are criticizing the fact that sb in power has given work to friends or relatives **more than your 'job's worth (to do sth)** (BrE) (only used in spoken English) not worth doing because it is against the rules or because it might cause you to lose your job **on the 'job** while doing a particular job: No sleeping on the job! ◇ on-the-job training
→ idiom at WALK verb
● verb (-bb-) [no obj]
to do work for different people that is not regular or permanent: He jobbed **as** a truck driver for some time.
PHR V **job sth 'out** (especially AmE) to arrange for work to be done by another company rather than your own: Some of the work was jobbed out to other printers. **SYN** CONTRACT STH OUT

'job ,action = INDUSTRIAL ACTION

'job a,nalysis noun [C,U]
(HR) a detailed study of a job and its relation to other jobs in the organization, especially in order to see what skills are needed for the job

'job bank noun [C] (AmE)
(HR)
1 a collection of job advertisements or details of people looking for work: Search our online job bank for a position that matches your requirements.
2 an arrangement by which workers who lose their jobs continue to receive wages and sometimes training while waiting for a new job to become available; the fund of money from which they are paid: Workers will be placed in a job bank for future hire by the company.

jobber /'dʒɒbə(r); AmE 'dʒɑːb-/ noun [C]
1 (Stock Exchange) in the UK in the past, a person who earned money on the stock exchange by buying shares, bonds, etc. from BROKERS and selling them to other BROKERS
2 (Commerce; AmE) a business that buys large amounts of particular goods and sells them to other businesses: We purchase our books from jobbers, usually at a substantial discount.
SYN WHOLESALER

jobbing /'dʒɒbɪŋ; AmE 'dʒɑːb-/ adjective [only before noun]
1 (BrE) used to describe sb who does work for different people that is not regular or permanent: a jobbing builder
2 (Commerce; Stock Exchange) used to describe a company that buys and sells goods, shares, etc. as an agent: a jobbing company with quality products and competitive prices

jobcentre (AmE spelling **jobcenter**) /'dʒɒbsentə(r); AmE 'dʒɑːb-/ noun [C] (BrE only)
a government office where people can get advice in finding work and where jobs are advertised: advertising vacancies in local jobcentres
→ EMPLOYMENT AGENCY

'job ,costing noun [U]
(Accounting) the practice of calculating a separate cost for each piece of work, project or order that is done by a business: Producers of custom-built goods, such as heavy machinery, generally use job costing.
→ BATCH COSTING

'job cre,ation noun [U]
(Economics) the process of providing opportunities for paid work, especially for people who are unemployed: Cutting taxes should encourage investment and job creation.

'job des,cription noun [C]
(HR) a written description of the exact work and responsibilities of a job, its position in the organization, the conditions of employment and

the pay: to write a formal job description ◇ Make sure you have an up-to-date job description. ◇ She never said 'That isn't in my job description' (= about sth she was asked to do that was not part of her normal job). → JOB SPECIFICATION

'job de,sign noun [U,C]
(HR) the process of putting together the tasks that need to be done in an organization to form jobs that individual people will do: Poor job design or conditions can cause stress.

'job en,richment noun [U]
(HR) a way of increasing the variety of tasks that an employee does by giving them more difficult tasks to do or more responsibility

'job evalu,ation noun [U,C] (abbr **JE**)
(HR) a method of studying jobs and their relation to each other in an organization in order to give them a position on a scale and decide on the rate of pay for each level; an occasion when this is done

'job fair (BrE also **ca'reers fair, re'cruitment fair**) noun [C]
(HR) an event where people who are looking for a job can meet companies who are looking for new employees: Companies attending the job fair will be looking for graduates in all subjects.

'job ,family noun [C]
(HR) a group of jobs in an organization that have similar activities and need similar skills but have different levels on a scale: Each job family contains different levels of responsibility and has an individual pay structure.

,job for 'life noun [C] (plural **jobs for life**)
the idea that once you had a job with a company, you could keep it until you retired: Employees must now be more flexible and mobile and not expect jobs for life.

'job ,grading noun [U]
(HR) a system of arranging similar jobs in an organization in order according to the type of tasks, amount of responsibility, etc. that they have; the rank that a particular job has: a job grading structure based on skills and abilities

jobholder (also spelled **job holder**) /'dʒɒbhəʊldə(r); AmE 'dʒɑːbhoʊldər/ noun [C]
(HR) a person who has a particular job; a person who has a regular job: How can the jobholder improve his/her performance? ◇ There is a decline in the number of people looking for work, not an increase in the number of jobholders.

'job ,hopping noun [U]
(HR) the practice of changing jobs very often ▶ **'job ,hopper** noun [C]

'job-,hunter noun [C]
a person who is trying to find a job: The number of job-hunters rose to 3.5 million in January. ▶ **'job-hunt** verb [no obj]: A third of the unemployed have been job-hunting for more than a year. **'job-hunt** noun [C]: I've got to go **on a job-hunt**. **'job-,hunting** noun [U]: I'd used the Web for job-hunting. ◇ job-hunting costs

jobless /'dʒɒbləs; AmE 'dʒɑːb-/ adjective
(HR)
1 unemployed; without a job: The closure left 500 people jobless.
2 the jobless noun [pl.] people who are unemployed
▶ **'joblessness** noun [U]: Joblessness among young men is on the increase.

'job lock noun [U,C]
(HR, informal) in the US, the situation where employees cannot leave their jobs because they are

afraid they will lose their health benefits: *One effect of employer-provided health insurance is job lock.*

job 'lot *noun* [C] (*BrE*)
(*Commerce*) a collection of different things that are sold together, usually at a low price: *a job lot of car parts*

'job ,market = LABOUR MARKET

'job ,order *noun* [C]
1 (*Production*) an order for a particular piece of work, quantity of items, etc. for a particular customer
2 (*HR*) information that an employer provides to an EMPLOYMENT AGENCY when they are looking for sb for a particular job, including details of the job and the qualifications and experience needed

'job pro,duction *noun* [U]
(*Production*) a way of producing things in which products are made one at a time for individual customers → BATCH PRODUCTION

job-protected 'leave *noun* [U]
(*HR*) a longer period of time when you are officially allowed to be away from your work for a special reason and will not lose your job: *a law that guarantees up to 12 weeks of unpaid, job-protected leave for certain employees, for example to care for a family member*

'job pro,tection = EMPLOYMENT PROTECTION

'job-re,lated *adjective* [usually before noun]
(*especially AmE*)
connected with the work that you do: *83 out of every 1 000 workers experienced some kind of job-related illness or injury last year.* ◇ *job-related skills/activities* → INDUSTRIAL (5)

'job ro,tation *noun* [U,C]
(*HR*) the practice of regularly changing the job that a particular person does so that they have a variety of tasks and become experienced in different areas: *Job rotation between different tasks was introduced to reduce physical and mental fatigue.*

'job satis,faction *noun* [U]
the feeling of achievement and enjoyment that a worker gets from their job: *When employees take full responsibility for their work, this can lead to higher job satisfaction.* ◇ *a job satisfaction survey*
● **high/low/poor** job satisfaction • a **high/an increased/a low** level of job satisfaction • to **give/improve/obtain/provide** job satisfaction

'job se,curity *noun* [U]
a situation where a job is likely to last for a long time and you will keep the job if you do what you are expected to: *Consumers have cut back on their spending because of worries about job security.*
SYN EMPLOYMENT SECURITY → JOB STABILITY
● a **high/low level of** job security • to **have/improve/increase/provide** job security

'job ,seeker (*also spelled* **jobseeker**) *noun* [C]
often used in official language in the UK to describe a person without a job who is trying to find one: *claiming the job seeker's allowance* ▸ **'job-,seeking** *noun* [U]

'job-,sharing (*also* **'work-,sharing**, *less frequent*) *noun* [U]
(*HR*) an arrangement where two or more people do one job, dividing the hours between them: *Rather than lay off staff, the company introduced a job-sharing scheme.* ▸ **'job-share** *verb* [no obj]: *We have been job-sharing for three months.* **'job-share** *noun* [C]: *We arrange job-shares and part-time working for women with children.* **'job-sharer** *noun* [C]

'job shop *noun* [C]
(*Manufacturing*) a small factory that makes small quantities of goods, often designed for a particular customer

'job specifi,cation *noun* [C]
(*HR*) a written statement about a job that includes a JOB DESCRIPTION and the skills, experience and personal qualities that sb needs in order to do the job, used when an organization is looking for a new person for a job

'job sta,bility *noun* [U]
(*HR*)
1 how long workers or groups of workers keep the same job: *Years ago job stability was a reality and people stayed with the same company until retirement.* → JOB SECURITY
2 how long sb has kept the jobs they have had: *A loan officer will consider your salary, job stability (two years in the same line of work is preferred) and disposable income.*

'job stress *noun* [U,C]
(*HR*) pressure or worry caused by your work: *A recent survey showed that job stress is the most common cause of depression.* ◇ *identifying and managing job stress*

'job ,tenure *noun* [U]
(*HR*) how long sb keeps a particular job: *Average job tenure has remained stable in recent years.*

★ join /dʒɔɪn/ *verb, noun*
● *verb*
1 [+ obj or no obj] to become a member of an organization, a company, a club, etc: *She joined the company as a trainee three years ago.* ◇ *It costs €100 to join.* ◇ *to join a pension/union scheme* ◇ (*figurative*) *to join the ranks of the unemployed*
2 [+ obj] to take part in sth that sb else is doing or to go somewhere with them: *Will you join us for lunch?* ◇ *Do you mind if I join you?* ◇ *Over 200 members of staff joined the strike.* ◇ *Join our online discussion.*
3 [+ obj or no obj] **join A to B** | **join A and B (together/up)** to fix or connect two or more things together: *Join one section of pipe to the next.* ◇ *Join the two sections of pipe together.* ◇ *How do these two pieces join?*
4 [+ obj or no obj] if you **join** a train, plane, etc. you get on it: *joining passengers boarding the plane in Brisbane*
→ idioms at BEAT, ENTER, FORCE *noun*
PHRV **,join 'in (sth/doing sth); ,join 'in (with sb/sth)** to take part in an activity with other people: *Several banks have joined in the bidding.* **,join 'up (with sb); 'join sb/sth up** to combine with sb else to do sth: *The company has joined with two others in its industry to form a new corporation.*
● *noun* [C]
a place where two things are fixed together: *The two pieces were stuck together so well that you could hardly see the join.*

,joined-'up *adjective* [usually before noun]
(*often used in newspapers*) intelligent and involving good communication between different parts so that they can work together effectively: *We need more joined-up thinking in our approach to the environment.*

joint /dʒɔɪnt/ *adjective* [only before noun]
involving two or more people, organizations, etc. together: *The two firms will take joint control of the fund.* ◇ *They are joint owners of the property* (= they own it together). → CO-
● a joint **bid/initiative/offer/project/undertaking**
▸ **'jointly** *adverb*: *a jointly owned company*

,joint ac'count *noun* [C]
a bank account that is used by two or more people, for example a husband and wife

joint consul'tation noun [C,U]
(HR) in the UK, a formal arrangement for managers and union representatives in an organization to meet to discuss matters that affect both sides before decisions are made

joint-stock 'company noun [C] a business organization that is owned by a group of people (shareholders) who provide its funds, appoint its managers and share its profits and debts

joint 'venture noun [C]
a new business that is started by two or more companies, often in the form of an independent company whose shares they own; the product or service that the business sells or provides: *The French company has a joint venture with Dongfeng Motor in China.* ◇ *The two firms plan to launch a 50-50 joint venture* (= one which they each own half of).
○ *to create/form/have/launch/set up a joint venture (with sb/sth)* • *a joint venture agreement/company/ partner*

jolt /dʒəʊlt; AmE dʒoʊlt/ noun, verb
● noun [C, usually sing.]
a sudden shock or event that causes a change in the price, value, etc. of sth: *News of falling sales delivered a nasty jolt to the company's share price.* ◇ *The tax cuts will give the economy a much-needed jolt.*
● verb [+ obj]
to give sb/sth a sudden shock, especially so that they start to take action or deal with a situation: *The government was jolted into action by the sudden rise in inflation.*

journal /'dʒɜːnl; AmE 'dʒɜːrnl/ noun [C]

SEE ALSO: **trade journal**

1 a newspaper or magazine that deals with a particular subject or profession: *a business/ professional journal*
2 used in the title of some newspapers: *the Wall Street Journal*
3 (Accounting) a written record that is used to move amounts from one financial account to another: *The journal entry consists of three parts: a debit entry, a credit entry and a short explanation.*

judge /dʒʌdʒ/ noun, verb
● noun [C]
1 a person who has authority to decide legal cases: *a High Court judge* ◇ *A federal judge awarded the company $1.2 million in damages.* → MAGISTRATE
2 a person who decides who has won a competition: *The judges' decision is final.*
● verb
1 [+ obj or no obj] to form an opinion about sb/sth, based on the information you have: *Each project is judged on the profits it could generate.* ◇ *You need to judge our results against those of our competitors.*
2 [+ obj] to decide the result of a competition; to be the judge in a competition: *He was asked to judge the design competition.*
3 [+ obj] to decide whether sb/sth has committed a crime or is legally responsible for sth: *The company was judged guilty of price-fixing.*

judgement (also spelled **judgment**, especially in AmE) /'dʒʌdʒmənt/ noun **HELP** Judgement is the usual spelling in BrE, but **judgment** is used in legal situations. **Judgment** is also the normal spelling in AmE.

SEE ALSO: **default judgement, deficiency ~, value ~**

1 [U] the ability to make sensible decisions after carefully considering the best thing to do: *good/ poor/sound judgement* ◇ *I trust your judgement in these matters.*

2 [C,U] an opinion that you form about sth after thinking about it carefully; the act of making this opinion known to others: *We need to make a judgement on/about this.* ◇ *I would like to reserve judgement until I have seen the report.*
3 (usually **judgment**) [C,U] a decision of a court or a judge; the reasons given for the decision: *The court will hand down* (= give) *its judgment on Friday.* ◇ *The court has yet to pass judgment* (= make a decision) *in the case.*

judgement by/in de'fault (also spelled **judgment**) (plural judgements by/in de'fault)
= DEFAULT JUDGEMENT

judgment = JUDGEMENT **HELP** You will find words formed with **judgment** at at the spelling **judgement**.

judiciary /dʒu'dɪʃəri; AmE -ʃieri/ noun [C with sing./pl. verb] (plural **judiciaries**) (usually **the judiciary**) (Law) the judges of a country or a state, when they are considered as a group: *an independent judiciary*

juggernaut /'dʒʌɡənɔːt; AmE -ɡərn-/ noun [C]
1 a very large lorry/truck
2 a large and powerful force or institution that cannot be controlled: *They have created a multimedia juggernaut.*

juggle /'dʒʌɡl/ verb [+ obj or no obj]
1 to try to deal with two or more important jobs or activities at the same time so that you can fit all of them into the time available: *We have to juggle four or five projects at a time.* ◇ *As a mother of three, she is used to juggling work and home life.*
2 to organize information, figures, the money you spend, etc. in the most useful or effective way: *They were accused of juggling finances to make growth and profits look better than they were.*

jumbo /'dʒʌmbəʊ; AmE -boʊ/ noun, adjective
● noun [C] (plural **jumbos**) (also **jumbo 'jet**)
a large plane that can carry several hundred passengers, especially a Boeing 747
● adjective [only before noun] (informal)
very large; larger than usual: *a jumbo pack of cornflakes*

jump /dʒʌmp/ verb, noun
● verb [no obj] (usually used with an adverb or a preposition)
(about a price, level, etc.) to rise suddenly by a large amount: *The yen jumped to its highest level against the dollar for six months.* ◇ *Investment from abroad has jumped sharply.* See note at INCREASE
IDM jump 'ship to change the organization that you are loyal to, especially the company you work for: *Their finance director announced he was jumping ship to take a position in a rival firm.*
→ idioms at BANDWAGON, DEEP adjective, SHIP noun
PHRV 'jump at sth to respond to sth quickly and with enthusiasm: *He jumped at the chance of working for the company.* ◇ *Consumers have jumped at these new phones.* **jump 'in; jump 'into sth** to become involved in sth: *The company is keen to jump into the profitable US market.*
● noun [C]
a sudden increase in a price, cost, level, etc: *We've seen a 17% jump in insurance costs.* ◇ *unusually large price jumps*
○ *a big/huge/large/sharp jump* • *a surprise/an unexpected jump*
IDM get/have a 'jump on sb (AmE) (informal) to get or have an advantage over sb, because you have acted quickly

'jump-start verb [+ obj]
to put a lot of energy into starting a process or an activity or into making it start more quickly: *The*

Fed has cut interest rates to jump-start the economy.
▶ **'jump-start** *noun* [C] → KICK-START

jumpy /'dʒʌmpi/ *adjective* (**jumpier, jumpiest**)
(*informal*)
nervous and anxious: *Financial markets are extremely jumpy* (= prices may go up and down quickly).

★ **junior** /'dʒuːniə(r)/ *adjective, noun*
● *adjective*
1 [usually before noun] having a lower rank in an organization or profession than others: *junior lawyers/analysts/bankers* ◇ *He is junior to me.* ◇ *I am the most junior member of the design team.* ◇ (*figurative*) *The bank fears it would be the junior partner in any merger with Lloyds.* OPP SENIOR See note at BOSS
● *a junior* **employee/executive/manager** • *a junior* **associate/partner** • *a junior* **position/post**
2 (*Finance*) used to describe a debt that will only be paid after all other debts have been paid if the borrower has financial problems
SYN SUBORDINATED
● *junior* **bonds/debentures/debt** • *junior* **creditors/lenders**
● *noun* [C]

SEE ALSO: **office junior**

a person with a lower level of job or status than others: *The firm's senior lawyers are allocated work that could be done by juniors.* OPP SENIOR

junk /dʒʌŋk/ *noun* [U]
1 (*Finance*) used to show that a company or government has a low CREDIT RATING or that there is a lot of risk involved in buying their bonds: *The company's long-term debt is now rated as junk.* ◇ *Moody's dropped its rating on the firm to one grade above 'junk' status.* ◇ *a junk-rated company* → INVESTMENT-GRADE
2 used to describe sth that is of little value: *There's so much junk in my office!* ◇ *filtering out* **junk email** (= emails advertising sth, sent to people who have not asked for them) → JUNK MAIL

'junk bond *noun* [C]
(*Finance*) a type of bond that pays a high rate of interest because there is a lot of risk involved, often used if a company wants to raise money quickly in order to buy the shares of another company: *The company plans to sell $925 million of junk bonds to fund the acquisition.* ◇ *investing in high-yield junk bonds*

'junk mail *noun* [U]
advertising material that is sent either by post or by email to people who have not asked for it → BULK MAIL, JUNK (2), SPAM

jurisdiction /ˌdʒʊərɪs'dɪkʃn; *AmE* ˌdʒʊr-/ *noun* (*Law*)
1 [U,C] the authority that an official organization has to make legal decisions about sb/sth: *The commission has no jurisdiction over foreign companies.* ◇ *This sector does not come under the jurisdiction of the World Trade Organization.*
● *to* **exercise/have** *jurisdiction* **over** *sth* • *sth comes/falls/is* **outside/under/within** *the jurisdiction of sb/sth*
2 [C] an area or a country in which a particular system of laws has authority: *The tax rules are different in each jurisdiction.*
● *a* **foreign/local/an offshore** *jurisdiction*

jurist /'dʒʊərɪst; *AmE* 'dʒʊr-/ *noun* [C] (*formal*)
a person who is an expert in law

juˌristic 'person = LEGAL PERSON

juror /'dʒʊərə(r); *AmE* 'dʒʊr-/ *noun* [C]
a member of a JURY: *The jurors decided that company had acted illegally.*

jury /'dʒʊəri; *AmE* 'dʒʊri/ (*plural* **juries**) (*also* **'panel, 'jury ˌpanel,** *both especially AmE*) *noun* [C with sing./pl. verb]
a group of members of the public who listen to the facts of a case in a court and decide who the winner is or whether sb is guilty of a crime: *The jury awarded the plaintiffs $14 billion in damages.* ◇ *The jury has/have returned a verdict of guilty.*
● *to* **be on/serve on/sit on** *a jury* • *a jury* **acquits/convicts** *sb*
IDM **the jury is (still) 'out on sth** used when you are saying that sth is still not certain: *The jury is out on whether the ad campaign will lead to greater market share.*

ˌjust-in-'time *adjective* [only before noun] (*abbr* JIT) (*Production*) used to describe a system, especially one for manufacturing goods, where things are done, supplied, made, etc. only when they are needed: *We prefer suppliers who are able to deliver on a just-in-time basis.* ◇ *The aim of just-in-time manufacturing is to keep stocks of parts and finished goods to a minimum.* ◇ *JIT delivery of products to customers*
● *just-in-time* **delivery/manufacturing/production**
▶ **ˌjust-in-'time** *noun* [U] (*abbr* JIT): *Before the industry adopted just-in-time, many electronics firms held large stocks of components.*

K k

K /keɪ/ *abbr*
1 (*informal*) (*used especially about an amount of money*) a thousand: *He earns nearly 100K* (= 100 thousand pounds/dollars per year).
2 (*IT*) kilobyte(s)
3 (*IT*) kilobit(s): *a 56K modem*

kaizen /ˌkaɪ'zen/ *noun* [U]
the practice of continuously improving the way in which a company operates: *Companies that adopt kaizen can boost their productivity by as much as 30%.* → CONTINUOUS IMPROVEMENT NOTE Kaizen comes from the Japanese words for 'improvement'.

kai'zen eˌvent *noun* [C]
a series of activities, usually over a number of days, in which a team of managers and workers decide how to improve a particular process within a

company and then take the actions needed to do so: *We held a week-long kaizen event to redesign the factory floor.*

KAM /ˌkeɪ eɪ 'em/ = KEY ACCOUNT MANAGEMENT

kanban /'kænbæn/ *noun* (*Production*)
1 (*also* **'kanban ˌsystem**) [U,C] a system of manufacturing in which the production of parts and their movement around the factory is controlled using instructions, usually written on cards, that are sent to the relevant group of workers whenever the parts are needed → JUST-IN-TIME
2 [C] in this type of manufacturing system, a card with information about the type and number of

parts needed **NOTE** Kanban comes from a Japanese term meaning 'sign' or 'billboard'.

Kb (also spelled **KB**) abbr
(*IT, only used in written English*) kilobyte(s): *The device has a 512 Kb memory.*

Kbps abbr
(*IT*) a short way of writing **kilobits per second** (= a unit for measuring the speed at which data is sent or received, for example along a telephone line): *a 56 Kbps modem*

KD /ˌkeɪ ˈdiː/ = KNOCK-DOWN (2)

keen /kiːn/ adjective (**keener, keenest**)
1 (*especially BrE*) if prices are **keen**, they are kept low to compete with other prices: *We are aiming to provide better quality at keener prices.*
2 involving people, businesses, etc. competing very hard with each other: *They are facing keen competition from larger companies.*
▸ **'keenly** adverb: *keenly priced fashions* ◇ *Our products are keenly competitive.*

keep /kiːp/ verb (**kept, kept** /kept/)
1 [+ obj or no obj] to stay in a particular condition, or at a particular level; to make sb/sth do this: *Our job is to keep the customer happy.* ◇ *Competition is keeping down prices.* ◇ *keeping up-to-date with changes*
2 [+ obj] to continue to have sth and not lose it or give it back: *There will be some new top people, but the CEO is keeping his job.* ◇ *Here's a ten euro note— please keep the change.*
3 [+ obj] to have a supply of sth; to store sth in a particular place: *We keep a large supply of popular items.*
4 [+ obj] to write down sth as a record: *We keep a record of all telephone conversations.* ◇ *She keeps the books (= the financial records) for the family business.*
5 [+ obj] to do what you should do or what you have agreed to do: *I agreed to see her but she didn't keep the appointment.*
6 [no obj] (about food) to remain in good condition: *Once it's been opened it won't keep more than a few days.*
7 [+ obj] (*BrE*) to own and manage a shop/store or restaurant: *Her father kept a grocer's shop.*
→ SHOPKEEPER **NOTE** Idioms containing **keep** are at the entries for the nouns or adjectives in the idioms, for example **keep your head above water** is at **head**.
PHR V ˌkeep sb 'on to continue to employ sb: *If the company is sold, some of the staff will be kept on.* ˌkeep to sth to do what you have promised or agreed to do: *to keep to an agreement* ˌkeep 'up (with sb/sth) to move, make progress or increase at the same rate as sb/sth: *The company is is not keeping up with demand.* ˌkeep 'up with sth to continue to pay or do sth regularly: *If you do not keep up with the payments you could lose your home.* ˌkeep sth 'up to continue to do sth at the same, usually high, level: *We're having difficulty keeping up our mortgage payments.* ◇ *Good work—keep it up!*

keiretsu /keɪˈretsuː/ noun [C] (*plural* **keiretsu**)
in Japan, a group of companies that own large numbers of shares in each other, with the result that it is difficult for companies outside the group to gain control of any of them

'kerb ˌmarket (also **kerb**) (*AmE spelling* **curb ~**) /kɜːb; *AmE* kɜːrb/ noun [C]
(*Finance*) trading of shares that takes place outside the official system of stock markets: *The American Stock Exchange developed from an informal kerb market.*

★ **key** /kiː/ adjective, noun, verb
● **adjective** [usually before noun]
most important; essential: *Japan is a key market for us.* ◇ *We identified five key areas for investment.* ◇

They emerged as a key player in the pharmaceuticals market. ◇ *This project is key to our financial success.*
● **noun**
SEE ALSO: Alt key, control ~, escape ~, hot ~, scroll ~, shift ~
1 [C, usually sing.] a thing that makes you able to achieve or understand sth: *In our industry, the key to success is minimizing costs.* ◇ *This plan holds (= is) the key to development in the region.* ◇ (*especially AmE*) *The key is to work as a team.*
2 [C] any of the buttons that you press to operate a computer: *Press the escape key to quit the program.*
● **verb** [+ obj] **key sth (in)** | **key sth (into sth)**
to put information into a computer using a keyboard: *Key (in) your password.* **SYN** ENTER
PHR V 'key sth to sth (*usually* be keyed to) to link sth closely to sth else: *Pricing is keyed to value.*

ˌkey ac'count noun [C]
one of the most important customers that a company has: *She will oversee a number of key accounts.*

ˌkey ac'count ˌmanagement noun [U] (*abbr* KAM)
the work of maintaining and developing a company's relationship with its most important customers ▸ ˌkey ac'count ˌmanager noun [C]

keyboard /ˈkiːbɔːd; *AmE* -bɔːrd/ noun, verb
● **noun** [C]
the set of keys for operating a computer, etc.
→ NUMERIC KEYPAD—Picture at OFFICE
● **verb** [+ obj]
to type information into a computer
▸ **'keyboarding** noun [U]

keyboarder /ˈkiːbɔːdə(r); *AmE* -bɔːrd-/ noun [C]
a person whose job is to type data into a computer

keynote /ˈkiːnəʊt; *AmE* -noʊt/ noun [C]
a keynote speech, speaker, etc. is an important one that introduces a meeting or its subject: *Steve Dobbs will deliver the keynote address at the conference.*
▸ **'keynoter** noun [C]: *She is known as a dynamic keynoter and business consultant.*

keypad /ˈkiːpæd/ noun [C]
a small set of buttons with numbers, etc. on used to operate a telephone, television, etc.; the buttons on the right of a computer keyboard: *Please press star on your keypad.*

ˌkey per'formance ˌindicator noun [C, usually pl.] (*abbr* KPI)
1 a measure that shows if a company has reached the necessary standard in one of the factors that are essential for its success: *Traditionally in our industry the key performance indicators were price, quality and delivery.* ◇ *The company's key performance indicators showed slowing growth in subscriber numbers.* → METRIC noun
2 (*HR*) a measure that shows if a person, a team or a department has achieved a particular standard and is often connected with rates of pay: *Bonuses are offered for outstanding employees who meet key performance indicators and complete 100 hours training.*

ˌkey 'prospect noun [C]
(*Marketing*) a person, company, etc. that could develop or be developed into a customer: *Identify your key prospects and invite them to your stand at the show.*

'key rate noun [C]
(*Finance*) the rate of interest at which a central bank lends money to other banks and financial institutions: *The National Bank of Hungary has cut its key rate to 8.5 per cent.* → BASE RATE

keyword /'ki:wɜːd; AmE -wɜːrd/ noun [C]
(IT) a word or phrase that you type on a computer keyboard to give an instruction or to search for information about sth: *Type in the keyword 'hotels' and click on Search.* ◇ *You can search by keyword, company name or business type.*

ˌkeyword 'advertising noun [U]
(Marketing) a system of advertising on the Internet in which a business pays for an advertisement and a link to a website to be displayed when a user searches for particular words ► ˌkeyword 'ad (also ˌkeyword ad'vertisement, less frequent) noun [C]: *You'll pay around $50 CPM (cost per thousand impressions) for your keyword ads on most search engines.*

kg abbr (plural **kg** or **kgs**) (only used in written English)
kilogram(s): *10kg*

kick /kɪk/ verb
IDM kick the 'tyres (AmE spelling ~ **tires**) (especially AmE) (informal) to test the quality of sth; to see if sth is suitable for you: *We now spend longer kicking the tyres before investing in start-ups.* → TYREKICKER
PHRV ˌkick sth a'bout/a'round (informal) to discuss a plan, a plan, etc. in an informal way: *We'll kick some ideas around and make a decision tomorrow.* ˌkick 'back; ˌkick 'back sth (AmE) (often be kicked back) to pay money illegally to sb who has helped you do sth or gain an advantage: *In order to get the contract, they agreed to kick back 5% of their fees to the project manager.* **HELP** A noun or phrase must always follow **back**, but a pronoun is placed between the verb and **back**. → KICKBACK ˌkick 'off (with sth/by doing sth) (informal) to start: *The year kicked off with lower sales than expected.* → KICK-OFF ˌkick 'off sth to start a discussion, a meeting, an event, etc: *The discounts are likely to kick off a price war with other supermarkets.* → KICK-OFF ˌkick sb/sth 'out (of sth) (informal) to make sb leave a job or position or go away from somewhere; to remove sth: *They kicked out their chief executive.* ◇ *The firm has been kicked out of the index of top-performing companies.*

kickback /'kɪkbæk/ noun [C, often pl.]
money paid illegally to sb who has helped you do sth or gain an advantage: *They accuse her of accepting kickbacks in exchange for helping the firm win state contracts.* → BRIBE

'kick-off noun [sing.]
the start of an activity: *the kick-off of the holiday season* ◇ *a kick-off meeting* → KICK OFF at KICK, KICK OFF STH at KICK

'kick-start verb [+ obj]
to do sth to help a process or project start more quickly: *These reforms were aimed at kick-starting the failing economy.* ► 'kick-start noun [C, usually sing.]: *The project should give a kick-start to regional tourism.*

kidult /'kɪdʌlt/ noun, adjective (informal)
● noun [C]
an adult who enjoys films/movies, books, games, television programmes, etc. that are intended for children and young people: *Many of our customers are 25- to 55-year-old kidults with good incomes and they like toys.*
● adjective [only before noun]
intended for adults and children: *the market for kidult movies*

kill /kɪl/ verb [+ obj]
to spoil or destroy sth; to stop or end sth: *Too many features can kill a product.* ◇ *They didn't like the terms and conditions and killed the deal.*
PHRV ˌkill sth 'off to stop or get rid of sth: *They have killed off several of their brands.*

'killer app (also spelled ~ ap, less frequent) (also 'killer appli,cation) noun [C]
1 (IT, informal) a computer program that is so popular that it encourages people to buy or use the computer system, OPERATING SYSTEM, etc. that it runs on: *Email remains the killer app of the Internet.*
2 (Marketing) a special feature of a product that is presented as being essential or much better than competitors' products: *There is no killer application to excite consumers into buying these expensive products and services.*

killing /'kɪlɪŋ/ noun
IDM ˌmake a 'killing (informal) to make a lot of money quickly: *The company made a killing by inventing the CD.*

kilo /'ki:ləʊ; AmE 'ki:loʊ/ noun [C] (plural **kilos**)
a kilogram

kilo- /'kɪləʊ; AmE 'kɪloʊ/ combining form (used in nouns; often used in units of measurement)
one thousand: *kilogram* ◇ *kilometre*

kilobit /'kɪləbɪt/ noun [C] (abbr **K**)
(IT) a unit for measuring computer memory or information, equal to 1 024 BITS

kilobyte /'kɪləbaɪt/ noun [C] (abbr **Kb, K**)
(IT) a unit for measuring computer memory or information, equal to 1 024 BYTES

kind /kaɪnd/ noun
IDM in 'kind (about a payment) consisting of goods or services, not money: *As well as his salary, he gets benefits in kind.*

king /kɪŋ/ noun [C]
a person, an organization or a thing that is thought to be the best or most successful of a particular type: *Nokia, king of the mobile phone industry*
IDM sb/sth is 'king the person or thing mentioned is the most important part of sth and should be considered carefully: *In this industry, the customer is king.* ◇ *The first rule of web development is that content is king.*

kingmaker /'kɪŋmeɪkə(r)/ noun [C]
(used especially in newspapers) a person or an organization with power or influence who is able to make sb/sth powerful or successful: *He will play the role of kingmaker in any merger between the companies.*

'king-size (also 'king-sized) adjective [usually before noun]
very large; larger than normal when compared with a range of sizes: *a king-size bed*

kiosk /'ki:ɒsk; AmE -ɑːsk/ noun [C]
1 a small shop/store, open at the front, where newspapers, drinks, etc. are sold. In some countries kiosks also sell food and things used in the home.
2 a small machine consisting of a computer and screen, that is fixed in a particular place and that members of the public can use, for example to get information about sth: *Passengers can check in using the self-service kiosks.* ◇ *an information kiosk with a touch-sensitive screen*

kit /kɪt/ noun

SEE ALSO: press kit

1 [C,U] a set of tools, equipment, materials, etc. that you use for a particular purpose: *a tool kit* ◇ *The printer is an expensive piece of kit.* ◇ *The computer comes with a starter kit of software* (= one to help you start using the computer).
2 [C] a set of parts ready to be made into sth: *The car is designed to be assembled from a kit.* ◇ *selling furniture in kit form*

kite /kaɪt/ verb [+ obj] (AmE) (informal)
to use an illegal cheque to obtain money or credit dishonestly: *to kite checks* → CHECK KITING

Kitemark™
/'kaɪtmɑːk; *AmE* -mɑːrk/
noun [C, usually sing.]
in the UK, an official
mark that is put on
products to show that
they have been
approved by the British
Standards Institution
because they are of
good quality and safe to
use

kitty /'kɪti/ *noun* [C]
(*plural* **kitties**) (*informal*)
an amount of money that a person, a group of
people, an organization, etc. has available to
spend: *We don't have enough money in the kitty to
keep the project going.*

KM /ˌkeɪ 'em/ = KNOWLEDGE MANAGEMENT

knock /nɒk; *AmE* nɑːk/ *verb, noun*
● *verb* [+ obj] (*often used with an adverb*)
to affect sb/sth badly: *Scandals like this are
knocking investor confidence.* ◇ *A decline in sales
knocked profits back 67% to €7.7 million.*
IDM **come ˈknocking** (*informal*) if sb **comes
knocking** they speak to or visit you because they
want sth: *You can't rely on existing customers to
come knocking when they need something.* **knock
on/at sb's/the ˈdoor; knock on ˈdoors** (*informal*)
to talk to or visit sb because you want sth from
them: *Investment bankers have been knocking on
our door once a month* (= wanting to invest).
PHRV **ˌknock sb/sth ˈback** (*usually* **be knocked
back**) **1** to have a bad effect on sb/sth; to prevent
sb/sth from achieving sth or making progress: *The
economy was knocked back by last year's recession.*
2 (*informal*) (*especially BrE*) to reject sb/sth: *They
remain optimistic, although their takeover bid has
been knocked back.* **ˌknock sb ˈdown (from sth) (to
sth)** (*informal*) to persuade sb to reduce the price of
sth: *I managed to knock him down to $400.*
→ KNOCK-DOWN **ˌknock sth ˈdown (from sth) (to
sth)** (*informal*) to reduce the price of sth: *They
knocked down the price from €400 to €300.*
→ KNOCK-DOWN **ˈknock sth from sth** to cause the
value of sth to fall by the amount mentioned: *The
weakness of the currency knocked $30 million from
our profits.* **ˌknock ˈoff; ˌknock ˈoff sth** (*informal*)
to stop doing sth, especially work: *Do you want to
knock off early today?* **ˌknock ˈoff sth** (*informal*) to
produce a product that is a cheap copy of sb else's
design, often illegally **HELP** A noun or phrase must
follow **off**, but a pronoun is placed between the
verb and **off.** → KNOCK-OFF **ˌknock sth ˈoff;
ˌknock ˈoff sth** to reduce the price, value,
length, etc. of sth: *They knocked off €50 because
there was a scratch.* ◇ *The news knocked 13% off the
company's shares.*
● *noun*
IDM **take a (hard, severe, etc.) ˈknock** (*informal*)
to have an experience that makes sb/sth less
confident or successful; to be harmed or damaged:
*Confidence in the industry took a severe knock from
the crisis.*

ˈknock-down (*AmE spelling also* **knockdown**)
adjective [only before noun]
1 (*informal*) (about prices, etc.) much lower than
usual: *They were forced to sell the business at a
knock-down price.* **SYN** ROCK-BOTTOM → KNOCK STH
DOWN at KNOCK *verb*
2 (*AmE*) (*abbr* **KD**) used to describe furniture that
can easily be put together and taken apart, and is
sold in separate pieces

ˈknocking ˌcopy *noun* [U] (*BrE*)
(*Marketing, informal*) advertising in which an
opponent's product is criticized → COMPARATIVE
ADVERTISING

ˈknock-off (*AmE spelling also* **knockoff**) *noun* [C]
a copy of a product, especially an expensive
product: *inexpensive knock-offs of well-known
perfumes* → KNOCK OFF STH See note at COPY

ˈknock-on *adjective* [only before noun] (*especially
BrE*)
causing other events to happen one after another
in a series: *The increase in the oil price will have a
knock-on effect on airfares.* ◇ *knock-on costs/benefits*

ˈknow-how *noun* [U]
knowledge of how to do sth and experience in
doing it: *We do not have the technical know-how to
design this type of structure.* ◇ *business/financial/
marketing know-how*

knowledge /'nɒlɪdʒ; *AmE* 'nɑːl-/ *noun* [U,C]

SEE ALSO: **explicit knowledge, implicit ~, tacit ~**

the information, understanding and skills that
people gain through education or experience: *The
job allowed me to apply the knowledge I had acquired
at college.* ◇ *We have specialist tools and materials
and a vast body of knowledge to draw on* (= use). ◇ *A
working* (= basic) *knowledge of French is essential.* ◇
*How long does it take to master the skills and
knowledge to do the job?*
● to acquire/gain/have/lack knowledge ◆ to apply/
draw on/use knowledge ◆ a deep/an extensive/in-
depth/intimate knowledge (of sth) ◆ a detailed/
thorough/working knowledge (of sth) ◆ business/
specialist/technical knowledge

ˈknowledge ˌasset *noun* [C, usually pl.] (*also*
ˈknowledge ˌcapital [U])
a collection of information, for example in the form
of data or documents, or a set of skills that an
organization has and that helps it to succeed:
*Knowledge assets include knowledge of markets,
products and technologies.* ◇ *The real strength of an
organization lies in its knowledge assets.*
→ INTELLECTUAL CAPITAL

ˈknowledge base *noun* [C]
a collection of information or rules that can be
used to perform tasks or solve problems, especially
one that forms part of a computer system: *We are
creating a knowledge base of our products, systems
and customers.*

ˈknowledge-based *adjective* [usually before
noun]
1 making particular use of information, ideas, or
modern technology, especially computer systems:
*the change from an industrial to a knowledge-based
economy*
2 (*IT*) (about a computer system) that uses a
collection of information or rules (a **knowledge
base**) to solve problems: *knowledge-based software/
systems*

ˈknowledge ˌcapital = KNOWLEDGE ASSET

ˈknowledge eˌconomy *noun* [C]
(*Economics*) an economy in which information and
modern technology produces economic benefits

ˈknowledge ˌmanagement *noun* [U] (*abbr*
KM)
ways of organizing, keeping and sharing important
information in a company, for example about work
methods, customers, suppliers, etc. in order to
make the company more successful: *One of the
main challenges of knowledge management is
keeping track of who knows what.* ◇ *knowledge
management software/systems*

ˈknowledge ˌofficer *noun* [C]
a person who is responsible for how a company
keeps important information and makes it available
to staff: *She was appointed chief knowledge officer.*

'knowledge ,worker *noun* [C]
a person whose job involves working with information rather than producing goods: *Nearly all knowledge workers use a computer in their jobs, most of them all the time.*

Kon'dratieff ,cycle (*also* **Kon'dratieff wave**) (*also* **Kondratiev**) /kɒnˈdrɑːtjef; *AmE* kɑːn-/ *noun* [C] (*Economics*) a pattern in a country's economy that lasts 50–60 years in which a long period of economic success (**growth**) is followed by a long period of difficulty (**recession**) → BUSINESS CYCLE

KPI /ˌkeɪ piː ˈaɪ/ = KEY PERFORMANCE INDICATOR

L l

L /el/ *abbr*
(especially for sizes of clothes) large: *S, M and L* (= small, medium and large)

lab /læb/ = LABORATORY

★ **label** /ˈleɪbl/ *noun, verb*
● *noun* [C]

SEE ALSO: brand label, designer ~, own ~, private ~, store ~

1 a piece of paper, etc. that is attached to sth and gives information about it: *price/address labels* ◇ *The washing instructions are on the label.* ◇ *Foods containing the substance must carry a warning label.* → TAG *noun* (1), TICKET
2 a name that is used to sell a range of goods to the public, especially food, clothes or music; the goods themselves: *She sells the foods under the label Zest.* ◇ *He only buys famous labels.* See note at BRAND
3 a company that produces and sells goods under a particular name: *One of the country's biggest labels has merged with an Australian drinks giant.*
● *verb* [+ obj] (-ll-, *AmE* -l-) (*often* **be labelled**)
to fix a label on sth or write information on sth: *We carefully label each item with the contents and date.* ◇ *The document was labelled 'Confidential'.*
▶ **'labelling** (*AmE spelling* **labeling**) *noun* [U]: *new rules for food labelling* ◇ *They were forced to change the labelling on their products.* ◇ *labelling laws/regulations/requirements*

labor = LABOUR ⓗⓔⓛⓟ You will find most words formed with **labor** at the spelling **labour**.

'labor a,greement = LABOR CONTRACT

laboratory /ləˈbɒrətri; *AmE* ˈlæbrətɔːri/ *noun* [C] (*plural* **laboratories**) (*also* **lab**, *informal*) (sometimes used in the plural in the names of companies) a room or building used for scientific research, experiments, testing, etc: *We are carrying out a number of tests in the laboratory.* ◇ *Abbott Laboratories discovers, develops, manufactures and sells health-care products.*

'labor ,contract (*also* **'labor a,greement**) (*BrE spelling* **labour ~**) *noun* [C] (*AmE only*) (*HR*) an agreement between a union and a company about the pay, benefits, etc. that workers will receive: *The new three-year labor contract, agreed on Friday, will raise mechanics' pay by 18 per cent.* → COLLECTIVE AGREEMENT

laborer = LABOURER

'labor ,union = TRADE UNION

★ **labour** (*AmE spelling* **labor**) /ˈleɪbə(r)/ *noun, verb*
● *noun* [U]

SEE ALSO: agency labour, child ~, contract ~, direct ~, division of ~, indirect ~, mobility of ~, organized ~

1 work, especially physical work: *The price will include labour and materials.* ◇ **manual labour** (= work using your hands) ◇ (*BrE*) *The workers voted to withdraw their labour* (= to stop work as a way of protesting).
2 the people who work or are available for work in a country or a company: *a shortage of skilled labour* ◇ *countries with good supplies of raw materials and cheap labour* ◇ *The company wants to keep down labour costs.*
● *verb* [no obj]
to try very hard to do sth difficult or to deal with a difficult problem: *He was still labouring away over some papers in his office.* ◇ *The group is labouring under €5 bn of debt.*

'labour court (*AmE spelling* **labor ~**) *noun* [C]
a type of court that can deal with disagreements between employees and employers: *The labour court has ruled against the company.* → EMPLOYMENT TRIBUNAL
🅞 *to bring sth before/go to/refer sth to/take sb/sth to a labour court*

'labour dis,pute (*AmE spelling* **labor ~**) *noun* [C] (*HR*)
1 a disagreement between workers and employers about pay or conditions: *a bitter labour dispute between dock workers and port operators*
2 a strike
ⓢⓨⓝ INDUSTRIAL DISPUTE

labourer (*AmE spelling* **laborer**) /ˈleɪbərə(r)/ *noun* [C]
a person whose job involves hard physical work that is not skilled, especially work that is done outdoors: *finding work as an agricultural labourer* ◇ *immigrant day laborers*

'labour ,federation (*AmE spelling* **labor ~**) *noun* [C]
a union or a group of unions

'labour force (*AmE spelling* **labor ~**) *noun* [C with sing./pl. verb]
all the people who work for a company or country: *a skilled/an unskilled labour force* ◇ *Only 17% of the labour force in the UK is educated to degree level.*
ⓢⓨⓝ WORKFORCE

,labour-in'tensive (*AmE spelling* **labor ~**) *adjective*
(about a type of work) needing a lot of people to do it; involving a lot of workers: *Tourism is a labour-intensive industry.* ◇ *They are looking for ways to cut costs on labour-intensive production lines.* → CAPITAL-INTENSIVE

'labour law (*AmE spelling* **labor ~**) *noun* [U]
the collection of laws that deal with all aspects of employment and the rights of people who are employed ⓢⓨⓝ EMPLOYMENT LAW

'labour ,market (*AmE spelling* **labor ~**) (*also* **'job ,market**) *noun* [C]
the number of people who are available for work in relation to the number of jobs available: *young people about to enter the labour market* ◇ *the external labour market* (= the number of possible employees outside an organization)
🅞 *a flexible/an inflexible/a strong/tight/weak labour market* • *labour market conditions/flexibility*

ˌlabour moˈbility (*AmE spelling* **labor ~**) (*also* **moˌbility of ˈlabour**) *noun* [U]
(*Economics*; *HR*) the ability and willingness of workers to move from one place or job to another: *In theory there is full labour mobility within the EU.* ◇ *legal and cultural barriers to labour mobility*

ˈlabour reˌlations (*AmE spelling* **labor ~**) *noun* [pl.]
(*HR*) relations between employers and employees: *The company has a history of poor labour relations.* **SYN** INDUSTRIAL RELATIONS

ˈlabour-ˌsaving (*AmE spelling* **labor~**) *adjective* [usually before noun]
designed to reduce the amount of work or effort needed to do sth: *a labour-saving device/gadget* ◇ *Investment in labour-saving technology became the key to economic growth.*

ladder /ˈlædə(r)/ *noun* [C, usually sing.]

SEE ALSO: **career ladder, corporate ladder**

a series of stages by which sb/sth makes progress: *She worked her way up the ladder to become CEO.* ◇ *climbing the technology ladder*

laden /ˈleɪdn/ *adjective*
1 heavily loaded with sth: *The tanker was laden* **with** *520 000 barrels of oil.* ◇ *a **fully/heavily** laden truck* **OPP** UNLADEN
2 having a lot of sth, especially sth unpleasant: *The company is laden* **with** *debts of $13 billion.*
3 -laden used to form adjectives showing that sth has a lot of, or is loaded with, the thing mentioned: *a debt-laden company*

lading /ˈleɪdɪŋ/ *noun* [U,C]

SEE ALSO: **bill of lading**

(*Trade*) the act of loading a ship with goods; the cargo

lag /læg/ *verb, noun*
● *verb* (-gg-)
1 [+ obj *or* no obj] to grow, increase, develop, etc. more slowly than sb/sth else: *Economic growth in Europe has lagged* **behind** *the US this year.* ◇ *Demand for the chips doubled, but production lagged* **far/well behind**. ◇ *The company lags Tesco in terms of market share.*
2 [no obj] to grow, increase, etc, more slowly than normal: *Business investment continues to lag.* ◇ *They continued to open new stores despite lagging sales.* → LAGGING INDICATOR
● *noun* [C] = TIME LAG

laggard /ˈlægəd; *AmE* -gərd/ *noun* [C]
1 (used especially in newspapers) a company, an economy, etc. that is slow to improve or grow compared to others: *They are the laggards in the technology sector.*
2 (*Marketing*) a person or an organization that is among the last to start using a new product or service

ˌlagging ˈindicator (*also* **ˈlagging ecoˈnomic ˈindicator**, *less frequent*) *noun* [C]
(*Economics*) a measure of economic activity that changes after the economy has already begun to follow a particular pattern and shows the result of previous actions: *Many economists claim unemployment is a lagging indicator; first, the economy needs to improve and then employment follows.* → COINCIDENT INDICATOR, LEADING INDICATOR

ˌlaid-ˈoff *adjective* [only before noun]
(*HR*) (used about workers) told to stop work for a short period or permanently because there is not enough work in the company: *payments to laid-off workers* → LAY SB OFF at LAY, REDUNDANT

laissez-faire (*also spelled* **laisser-faire**, *less frequent*) /ˌleseɪ ˈfeə(r); *AmE* ˈfer/ *noun* [U]
(*Economics*) the policy of allowing businesses and the economy to develop without government control: *We live in an age of laissez-faire.* ◇ *laissez-faire economics/capitalism* → DIRIGISME
NOTE Laissez-faire is a French phrase.

ˌlame ˈduck *noun* [C]
1 a person or an organization that is not very successful and that needs help: *The government gives too much support to lame ducks.* ◇ *lame-duck industries*
2 a politician, a government or an official whose period of office will soon end and who will not be elected again or kept in the same position: *Her replacement has already been named, making her a lame duck until she steps down.* ◇ *a lame-duck chairman*

LAN /læn/ *abbr*
(*IT*) **local area network** a number of computers and other devices, in the same building or in buildings next to each other, that are connected together so that equipment and information can be shared → WAN

land /lænd/ *verb*
1 [no obj] to arrive somewhere in a plane or a boat: *We will shortly be landing at Narita International Airport.* → TAKE OFF at TAKE *verb*
2 (*Trade*) [+ obj *or* no obj] to put sth/sb on land from an aircraft, a boat, etc: *It cost over $25 000 just to land the goods* (= pay for their transport, taxes, etc.).
3 [+ obj] to succeed in getting a job, piece of work, etc., especially one that is seen as very valuable: *She landed a top job at Microsoft.* ◇ *The company has landed a €350 million contract to construct the rail line.*
4 [no obj] (*used with an adverb or a preposition*) (about a piece of work, document, etc.) to arrive somewhere and cause difficulties that have to be dealt with: *Why do complaints always land* **on my desk**?

ˈland bank *noun*
1 [U; sing.] an amount of land that a person or a company owns and is waiting to build on: *The company will develop its prime land bank when economic conditions are right.*
2 (*Finance*) (*often* **Land Bank**) [C] (often used in names) a bank that helps farmers or people who live in the countryside, especially by lending money for longer periods than other banks: *Texas Land Bank*

landed /ˈlændɪd/ *adjective* [only before noun]
(*Trade*) including all taxes and transport costs connected with bringing goods into a country: *The landed* **cost/price** *of oil has risen by 30% in the last year.*

landfill /ˈlændfɪl/ *noun*
1 [C,U] an area of land where large amounts of waste material are buried under the earth: *Old tyres often end up* **in** *a landfill.* ◇ *landfill sites*
2 [U] the process of burying large amounts of waste material: *the choice of landfill or incineration* ◇ *landfill taxes*
3 [U] waste material that will be buried

landing /ˈlændɪŋ/ *noun* [C]

SEE ALSO: **hard landing, soft landing**

1 the moment when an aircraft comes down to the ground after a journey: *a perfect/safe/smooth landing* **OPP** TAKE-OFF

2 (*Transport*) an act of taking goods off a ship or plane onto land; the amount of goods taken off: *Landings of fish have been good recently.*

'landing card *noun* [C]
a card recording personal details that some passengers must complete when they arrive in a country

'landing charge (*also* **'landing fee**, *less frequent*) *noun* [C, usually pl.]
(*Transport*) a fee charged for using an airport or a harbour

'landing page *noun* [C]
(*IT*) the first page of a website that sb sees: *How many readers have clicked on the hyperlink in the email and got to your landing page?*

landlady /ˈlændleɪdi/ *noun* [C] (*plural* **landladies**)
1 a woman from whom you rent a room, a house, etc.
2 (*BrE*) a woman who owns or manages a small hotel or a pub
→ LANDLORD

landline /ˈlændlaɪn/ = FIXED LINE

landlord /ˈlændlɔːd; *AmE* -lɔːrd/ *noun* [C]
1 a person or company that rents a building or land to sb: *The lease requires the landlord to carry out repairs to the premises.* ◊ *the law of landlord and tenant* (= that controls how people can rent property) → LESSOR
2 a person from whom you rent a room, a house, etc: *Her landlord threatened to throw her out if she didn't pay the rent.* → LANDLADY
3 (*BrE*) a man who owns or manages a small hotel or a pub → LANDLADY

landmark /ˈlændmɑːk; *AmE* -mɑːrk/ *noun* [C]
an event, achievement, etc. that is seen as very important, especially one that is the first of its kind: *The introduction of wind power is an important landmark for the industry.* ◊ *This is a landmark agreement that will promote freer world trade.* ◊ *a landmark court case/decision/ruling*

'land ˌoffice *noun* [C, usually sing.]
in the US, a government office that keeps records of sales of public land
IDM **do (a) 'land-office business** to do a lot of successful business: *They are doing a land-office business selling music online.*

the 'Land ˌRegistry *noun* [sing.]
a government office that keeps records of who owns land in England and Wales

language /ˈlæŋɡwɪdʒ/ *noun*

SEE ALSO: **body language, computer ~, programming ~**

1 [C] the system of communication in speech and writing that is used by people of a particular country: *the Japanese language* ◊ *This manual is available in five different languages.* ◊ *good/poor language skills*
○ to **learn/speak/understand/use** a language ♦ to **translate** sth **into** a language
2 [U] a particular style of speaking or writing: *scientific/technical language* ◊ *the language of business/law*
○ to **understand/use** language
3 (*IT*) [C,U] a system of symbols and rules that is used to operate a computer: *Web pages are written in HTML.* → COBOL, HTML
○ to **learn/use/write** (a) language ♦ to **write** sth **in** (a) language
IDM **speak/talk the same 'language** to be able to communicate easily with another person because you share similar experience or knowledge: *Our*

production and IT people don't speak the same language.

languish /ˈlæŋɡwɪʃ/ *verb* [no obj]
(used especially in newspapers) to become weaker or fail to make progress: *The oil price was languishing below $20 a barrel.* ◊ *Our economy continues to languish.*

lapse /læps/ *verb, noun*
● *verb* [no obj]
(about a contract, an offer, an agreement, etc.) to be no longer valid because the period of time that it lasts has come to an end or because payments have not been made: *The patent on the drug lapses in 2009.* ◊ *We must decide whether to renew the lease or allow it to lapse.* ◊ *A life insurance policy lapses when you stop paying the premiums.* ▶ **lapsed** *adjective* [only before noun]: *a lapsed offer/subscription*
PHR V **'lapse into sth** to gradually pass into a worse or less active state: *The economy has lapsed into a mild recession.*
● *noun* [C]
1 a small mistake, especially one that is caused by forgetting sth or by being careless: *The bank admitted there had been a serious lapse in security.* ◊ *The mistake was caused by a lapse of judgement.*
2 a period of time between two things that happen: *a time lapse of 30 minutes*

★laptop /ˈlæptɒp; *AmE* -tɑːp/ (*also* ˌlaptop com'puter) *noun* [C]
a small computer that can work without wires and be easily carried: *I have a copy of the file on my laptop.* → DESKTOP COMPUTER, NOTEBOOK, PALMTOP—Picture at PRESENTATION

larceny /ˈlɑːsəni; *AmE* ˈlɑːrs-/ *noun* [U,C] (*plural* **larcenies**) (*AmE or BrE old-fashioned*)
the crime of stealing property or money from sb; an occasion when this takes place: *He was charged with three counts of grand/petty larceny* (= stealing things that are valuable/not very valuable).

'large cap *noun* [C]
(*Stock Exchange*) a company that has a high total value of shares (**market capitalization**) on the stock exchange: *Their research shows that small caps usually outperform large caps.* ◊ *They invest heavily in large-cap stocks.* → MID CAP, SMALL CAP

'large-scale *adjective* [usually before noun]
(about an organization or an activity) involving many people or things, especially over a wide area: *large-scale job cuts/layoffs/redundancies* ◊ *They are planning large-scale trials of the drug.* ◊ *the most efficient large-scale car manufacturers in the world*
OPP SMALL-SCALE

'large-sized (*also* **'large-size**) *adjective* [usually before noun]
large; important: *large-sized companies* ◊ *PCs with large-size screens* → MEDIUM-SIZED, SMALL-SIZED

largesse (*also spelled* **largess**) /lɑːˈdʒes; *AmE* lɑːrˈdʒes/ *noun* [U] (*often formal*)
(used especially in newspapers, in a humorous or disapproving way) the act or quality of being generous with money: *The industry has attracted criticism for relying on government largesse.*

laser /ˈleɪzə(r)/ *noun* [C]
a device that produces a very strong line of controlled light (a **ray**) that can be used as a tool: *a laser beam* ◊ *The holes in the metal are cut with a laser.* ◊ *a laser bar-code reader*

'laser gun *noun* [C]
a piece of equipment which uses a very strong line of controlled light to read BAR CODES

'laser ˌprinter *noun* [C]
(*IT*) a printer that produces good quality printed material by means of a **laser**

,last-'ditch *adjective* [only before noun]
used especially in newspapers to describe a final attempt to achieve sth, when there is not much hope of succeeding: *Union leaders met with government officials in a last-ditch attempt/effort to avoid a strike.*

,last 'in, ,first 'out *phrase*
1 (*Commerce; Production*) (*abbr* **LIFO**) a method of STOCK CONTROL in which the last goods or raw materials bought or produced are the first ones used or sold → FIRST IN, FIRST OUT
2 (*Accounting*) (*abbr* **LIFO**) a method of valuing supplies of goods or units of raw materials based on the idea that the last goods bought or produced are the first ones used or sold. The value of goods left at the end of the year is based on the earliest price paid: *The production costs were calculated on a last in, first out basis.* ◇ *The LIFO cost is lower than the actual cost of goods when there is inflation.*
→ FIRST IN, FIRST OUT
3 (*HR*) used, for example in a situation when people are losing their jobs, to say that the last people to be employed will be the first to go
4 (*IT*) used to describe a system where data received last is the first to be processed

,late ma'jority *noun* [sing.]
1 (*Marketing*) the group of customers who will only start to use a new product after many other people are using it: *Late majority people are sceptical about new products and eventually adopt them because of economic necessity or social pressure.*
2 (*HR*) the people in an organization who will only start to use a new method, process or system after most people in the organization are using it
→ EARLY MAJORITY

,late-'night *adjective* [only before noun]
happening or available late at night: *late-night meetings/talks* ◇ *Evening and late-night shopping is becoming more common.*

latent /'leɪtnt/ *adjective* [usually before noun]
existing, but not yet very noticeable, active or well-developed: *a latent market* ◇ *Look for latent management skills in your staff.* ◇ *We estimate a huge latent demand for electronic dictionaries.*

,latent 'defect *noun* [C,U]
(*Law*) a fault in a product that you notice only after you have bought it: *The seller will not be liable for any latent defects.* → PATENT DEFECT

lateral /'lætərəl/ *adjective* [usually before noun]
having the same level of status or authority; involving people or jobs at the same level: *He decided to make a lateral career move from production manager to head of marketing.*
[SYN] HORIZONTAL
▶ **laterally** /'lætərəli/ *adverb*: *sharing information laterally throughout the company*

,lateral inte'gration = HORIZONTAL INTEGRATION

★ **launch** /lɔːntʃ/ *verb, noun*
● *verb* [+ obj or no obj]
1 to start an activity, especially an organized one: *an advertising campaign launched by the British Tourist Authority* ◇ *He has launched a bid for control of the supermarket chain.* ◇ *The business launched last year with 15 employees.*
2 to start selling a product or service for the first time; to make sth available so that it can be bought and sold: *The company is launching a new telephone service in Japan this year.* ◇ *They are planning to launch a $2 billion bond issue.*
[PHR V] **,launch 'out** to do sth new in your career, especially sth more exciting: *It's time I launched out on my own.*

● *noun* [C,U]
SEE ALSO: product launch
the action of **launching** sth; an event at which sth is **launched**: *the successful launch of euro notes and coins* ◇ *The official launch date is in June.* ◇ *The channel has attracted an audience of two million since its launch a month ago.* ◇ *This is the first of a number of new launches from the company.* ◇ *The new drug is scheduled for launch next month.*
● *to announce/oversee/plan a launch* • *to bring forward/delay/postpone/put back a launch* • *a commercial/formal/an official launch* • *a launch campaign/date/party*

launder /'lɔːndə(r)/ *verb* [+ obj]
to move money that has been obtained illegally into foreign bank accounts or legal businesses so that it is difficult for people to know where the money came from: *$8 million had been laundered through the firm.* → MONEY LAUNDERING
▶ **launderer** *noun* [C] **laundering** *noun* [U]: *the laundering of drug money through casinos*

'laundry list *noun* [C]
a long list of people or things: *a laundry list of problems* ◇ *There is a laundry list of prohibited investments.*

★ **law** /lɔː/ *noun*
SEE ALSO: attorney-at-law, blue-sky laws, by-~, civil ~, commercial ~, common ~, competition ~, court of ~, criminal ~, employment ~, international ~, labour ~, maritime ~, mercantile ~, Moore's ~, Parkinson's ~, private ~, public ~

1 (*also* **the law**) [U] the whole system of rules that everyone in a country or society must obey: *You would be breaking the law by not paying health insurance.* ◇ *It is against the law to discriminate against someone because of their race or sex.* ◇ *Employers are required by law to provide a safe working environment.*
● *to break/enforce/respect/violate the law* • *the law allows/forbids/prohibits/requires/says sth*
2 [U] *usually* ... **law** a particular branch of the law; the laws of a particular country or area: *company/ intellectual property/contract law* ◇ *international/ federal/local law* ◇ *The company denies any liability under Indian law.* ◇ *The merger would be in breach of EU competition law.* ◇ *the law governing competition*
● *to breach/break/enforce/infringe/violate... law* • *... law allows/forbids/prohibits/requires/says sth*
3 [C] a rule that deals with a particular crime, agreement, etc: *Existing laws on store opening hours should be relaxed.* ◇ *They passed* (= officially introduced) *a law against sending 'spam' emails.* ◇ *a law banning the sale of cigarettes by mail order* ◇ *strict new anti-fraud laws*
● *to enact/introduce/pass a law* • *to amend/change/ relax/strengthen a law* • *a law allows/bans/ prohibits/requires/says sth* • *to break/enforce/ implement/violate a law* • *strict/tough laws* • *international/local/national/state laws*
4 [U] the study of the law as a subject at university, etc.; the profession of being a lawyer: *Chris is studying law.* ◇ *What made you go into law?* ◇ *Hong Kong is home to some of the world's top international law firms.*
● *to go into/practise/study law* • *a law firm/practice/ school*
5 [C] the fact that sth always happens in the same way in an activity or in nature: *the law of supply and demand* [SYN] PRINCIPLE → idioms at CONFLICT *noun*, LETTER *noun*

'law-a,biding *adjective*
obeying and respecting the law: *law-abiding companies/citizens*

'law court = COURT OF LAW

lawful /'lɔːfl/ *adjective*
allowed or recognized by law; legal: *It was judged to be lawful for the company to monitor employees' emails.* OPP UNLAWFUL
▶ **lawfully** /'lɔːfəli/ *adverb* **'lawfulness** *noun* [U]

'law of 'one 'price *noun* [sing.]
(*Economics*) the rule that without trade restrictions, transport costs, etc. the same goods would cost the same in all countries

lawsuit /'lɔːsuːt; *BrE also* -sjuːt/ (*also* **suit**) *noun* [C]
a claim or complaint against sb that a person or an organization can make in court: *He filed a lawsuit against the company for breach of contract.* ◇ *a string of product liability lawsuits*
○ *to bring/file/settle* a lawsuit

★ **lawyer** /'lɔːjə(r)/ *noun* [C]
a person who is trained and qualified to advise people about the law, to represent them in court, and to write legal documents: *Seek advice from your lawyer before you finalize the contract.* ◇ *corporate lawyers* ◇ *a bankruptcy lawyer* → BARRISTER, SOLICITOR

lay /leɪ/ *verb* [+ obj]
1 to put something down: *to lay a cable/pipe*
2 to present a proposal, some information, etc. to sb for them to think about and decide on: *Proposals will be laid before the committee at the next meeting.*
IDM **,lay it on the 'line** (*informal*) to tell sb clearly what you think, especially when they will not like what you say: *The manager laid it on the line—some people would have to lose their jobs.* → idioms at MARKER, BLOCK *noun*
PHRV **,lay sth 'down** if you **lay down** a rule or a principle, you state officially that people must obey it or use it: *The Department of Health lays down guidelines for safety at work.* **,lay sb 'off** (*HR*) to stop employing sb because there is not enough work for them to do: *Although they wanted to cut costs, they promised they would not lay anyone off.* ◇ *About 1 000 workers at the factory will be laid off.* → LAID-OFF, LAY-OFF See note at DISMISS **,lay 'out (for/on sth)**; **,lay sth 'out (for/on sth)** (*informal*) to spend money on sth: *People do not want to have to lay out for a new computer every year.*

layaway /'leɪəweɪ/ *noun* [U] (*AmE*)
(*Commerce*) a system of buying goods in a store, where the customer pays a small amount of the price for an item and the store keeps the goods until the full price has been paid: *All our furniture can be bought over 90 days on layaway.* ◇ *If you want to extend payments over time, you can put your purchase on a layaway plan.*
○ *a layaway agreement/order/payment/plan/ program*

layer /'leɪə(r); 'leə(r); *AmE* 'ler/ *noun, verb*
● *noun* [C]
1 a level or part within a system or set of ideas: *There were too many layers of management in the company.*
2 a quantity or thickness of sth that lies over a surface or between surfaces: *Finally, three layers of protective coating are sprayed onto the wood.*
● *verb* [+ obj]
to arrange sth in levels or layers: *a big layered company* ◇ *Layering new technology on top of existing computer systems can cause problems.*

'lay-off *noun* [C] (*plural* **lay-offs**)
1 an act of making people unemployed because there is no more work left for them to do; an example of this: *They announced the temporary lay-off of 8 000 car workers.* ◇ *There may be more lay-offs at the factory.*
2 a period of time when sb is not working or not doing sth that they normally do regularly: *an eight-week lay-off with a broken leg*

layout /'leɪaʊt/ *noun* [C, usually sing.]
the way in which the parts of sth such as the page of a book, a building or a town are arranged: *We need a more attractive page layout for our brochure.* ◇ *The new store layout is very popular with customers.*

layover /'leɪəʊvə(r); *AmE* -oʊ-/ = STOPOVER

lb (*AmE spelling* **lb.**) (*plural* **lb** *or* **lbs**) = POUND (3)

LBO /,el biː 'əʊ; *AmE* 'oʊ/ *abbr*
(*Finance*) **leveraged buyout** when a person or an organization buys a company with a large amount of borrowed money, using the assets of the company they are buying as COLLATERAL in order to obtain the money

l.c. (*also spelled* **L/C**) = LETTER OF CREDIT

LCD /,el siː 'diː/ *abbr* **liquid crystal display** a way of showing information in electronic equipment such as LAPTOP computers, etc. An electric current is passed through a thin layer of liquid and images can be seen on a small screen: *an LCD monitor* ◇ *a pocket calculator with LCD*

LCL /,el siː 'el/ = Less than Container Load

LDC /,el diː 'siː/ = LESS-DEVELOPED COUNTRY

★ **lead** /liːd/ *verb, noun*
● *verb* (**led**, **led** /led/)
1 [+ obj *or* no obj] to be the best at sth; to be in first place: *They have a reputation for leading the market with creative advertising ideas.* ◇ *We have led the field in magazine publishing for many years.*
2 [+ obj] to be in control of sth; to be the leader of sth: *Daniel Snell leads the marketing team.*
IDM **lead from the 'front** to take an active part in what you are telling or persuading others to do: *Good managers lead from the front.*
PHRV **'lead to sth** to have sth as a result: *We are hoping that the contacts we made at the trade show will lead to future business.* **,lead 'up to sth** to be an introduction to or the cause of sth: *The weeks leading up to the sales conference are always busy.*
● *noun*
1 [sing.] the position ahead of everyone else in a competition or race; the amount that sb/sth is ahead: *Hyundai is determined to maintain its lead in a competitive industry.* ◇ *We have the highest market share and we need to look at ways to stay in the lead.* ◇ *They have now lost their market lead.* ◇ *They have a lead of 12% of market share over their closest competitor.*
○ *to have/increase/lose/maintain/take* a lead
2 (*usually used as an adjective*) the most important person, product, etc: *the lead engineer on the project* ◇ *Two of its lead products failed in clinical trials.*
3 [sing.] an example or action for people to copy or follow: *If one bank raises interest rates, all the others will follow their lead.* ◇ *They have taken the lead in attracting younger consumers.*
4 (*Marketing*) [C] a piece of information that may help you find new customers: *We offer quality information to help you generate business leads.* ◇ *I prefer not to source leads from the Web.*
○ *to follow up/generate/have/source* leads • *business/customer/sales* leads
5 (*Insurance*) [C] the group (**syndicate**) of Lloyd's UNDERWRITERS that accepts the most responsibility for an insurance policy

★**leader** /'liːdə(r)/ noun [C]

SEE ALSO: brand leader, category ~, cost ~, industry ~, loss-~, low-cost ~, market ~, etc.

1 a company, a thing, a person, etc. that is the best, or in first place in a business, competition, etc: *The company is a world leader in electrical goods.* ◇ *Our new product is a leader in its field.*
2 a person who leads a group of people, especially the head of a country, an organization, etc: *The changes are supported by a growing number of business leaders.* ◇ *The team leader has called a meeting for 3 p.m.* ◇ *Most organizations have at least one person who is a natural leader.* See note at BOSS

★**leadership** /'liːdəʃɪp/ AmE -dərʃ-/ noun

SEE ALSO: transactional leadership, transformational leadership

1 [U] the state or position of being a leader: *The company had its most successful period under the leadership of Michael C. Potter.* ◇ *They claim world leadership in the chip-making sector.*
2 [U] the ability to be a leader; the qualities a good leader should have: *leadership qualities/skills* ◇ *The company needs strong leadership to get it through this difficult phase.* ◇ *Their problems may be due to a lack of leadership.*
3 [C with sing./pl.verb] a group of leaders of a particular organization, etc: *The leadership of the union was accused of not listening to ordinary members.*

leading /'liːdɪŋ/ adjective [only before noun]
most important or most successful: *We are Europe's leading provider of business information.* ◇ *The magazine contains articles by leading analysts.* ◇ *a leading player in the European market*

,**leading 'edge** noun [sing.]
the leading edge (of sth) the most important and advanced position in an area of activity, especially technology: *We operate at/on the leading edge of technology.* ◇ *leading-edge technologies*
SYN CUTTING EDGE

,**leading 'indicator** noun [C]
(*Economics*) a measure of economic activity that changes before the economy begins to follow a particular pattern and helps to show what the economy is going to do: *Jobs figures are closely watched as they are considered a good leading indicator of consumer demand.* → COINCIDENT INDICATOR, LAGGING INDICATOR

,**lead 'manager** (also ,**lead 'underwriter**, ,**managing 'underwriter**) noun [C]
(*Stock Exchange*) the main bank or financial organization that is responsible for organizing an INITIAL PUBLIC OFFERING (= an act of selling shares in a company for the first time), the sale of bonds, etc: *The company selected Salomon as lead manager for its $5 billion bond offering.* ▶ ,**lead-'manage** verb [+ obj]: *Three major banks are competing to secure the right to lead-manage the sale of the company.*

,**leads and 'lags** noun [pl.]
(*Finance*) the process of making payments to suppliers abroad or sending bills to foreign customers more quickly than usual (**leads**) or later than usual (**lags**) when a change in the EXCHANGE RATE is expected

'**lead time** noun [U,C]
(*Production*) the time between receiving an order and delivering the product or service to the customer: *The lead time for the motorcycle is two months.* ◇ *For small orders she's brought the lead time down from ten days to three.* → CYCLE TIME

,**lead 'underwriter** = LEAD MANAGER

,**lead 'user** noun [C]
(*Marketing*) a company, person, etc. that is the first to experience a particular need, and therefore adapts an existing product or service to meet this need or is the first to use a new service or product: *Lead users are a valuable source of new product ideas.*

leaflet /'liːflət/ noun, verb
●**noun** [C]
a printed sheet of paper or a few printed pages that are given free of charge to advertise or give information about sth: *We have hired a team to hand out promotional leaflets in the street.*
●**verb** [+ obj or no obj]
to give out **leaflets** to people: *We did a lot of leafleting in the area.*

'**leaflet drop** noun [C]
(*Marketing*) a method of advertising by delivering **leaflets** to a large number of houses

leak /liːk/ verb, noun
●**verb**
1 [+ obj or no obj] to allow liquid or gas to get in or out through a small hole or crack: *a leaking pipe*
2 [+ obj] to give secret information to the public, for example by telling a newspaper: *The contents of the report were leaked to the press.* ◇ *a leaked document*
●**noun** [C]
1 a small hole or crack that lets liquid or gas flow in or out of sth by accident: *a leak in the gas pipe* ◇ *oil leaks*
2 a deliberate act of giving secret information to the newspapers, etc: *a leak to the press about the government plans on tax*

leakage /'liːkɪdʒ/ noun
1 [C,U] an amount of liquid or gas escaping from a container that has a fault; an occasion when this happens: *a leakage of toxic waste into the sea* ◇ *Check bottles for leakage before use.* ◇ *(figurative) the continuing leakage of deposits from the banking system*
2 (*Commerce*) = SHRINKAGE (2)

lean /liːn/ adjective (**leaner, leanest**)
1 used to describe a method of production that aims to cut costs while keeping quality high by producing only the quantity of goods that has been ordered and by reducing the amount of time and space that the production process uses: *By focusing on the elimination of waste, the plant has become a model of lean manufacturing.* ◇ *They have cut costs through leaner processes and more efficient logistics.*
2 (about costs, quantities, etc.) very low; as low as possible: *Companies are trying to keep their workforces lean, so jobs are hard to find.* ◇ *If sales fall, dealers will cut back their lean inventories of new cars even further.*
3 (about organizations, etc.) strong and efficient, especially because the number of employees has been reduced: *The closure of the factory is difficult but will produce a leaner, fitter business.*
4 [usually before noun] used to describe a difficult period of time that does not produce much money, etc: *The company has recovered well after several lean years.* ◇ *This is the leanest time of year for the tourist industry.*
▶ **leanness** /'liːnnəs/ noun [U]: *We are aiming to improve the leanness of the production process.*

leap /liːp/ verb (**leapt, leapt** /lept/ or **leaped, leaped**) [+ obj or no obj]
to increase suddenly and by a large amount: *Shares leapt in value from 476¢ to close at 536¢.* ▶ **leap** noun [C]: *a leap in profits/productivity*

leapfrog /ˈliːpfrɒg; *AmE* -frɔːg; -frɑːg/ *verb* (**-gg-**)
[+ obj *or no obj*]
to get to a higher position or rank by going past sb else or by missing out some stages: *We're looking at how to leapfrog the competition.* ◇ *They have leapfrogged back to the top of the airline industry.*

learning /ˈlɜːnɪŋ; *AmE* ˈlɜːrnɪŋ/ *noun* [U]

SEE ALSO: **action learning, distance ~, e-learning, lifelong ~, organizational ~, workplace ~**

the process of learning sth: *computer-assisted learning*

'learning curve *noun* [C, usually sing.]
1 the rate at which you learn a new subject or a new skill; the process of learning from the mistakes you make: *Mastering this new equipment requires a steep learning curve* (= there is a lot to learn in a short time).
2 = EXPERIENCE CURVE

★ **lease** /liːs/ *noun, verb*
(*Law; Property*)
• *noun* [C]

SEE ALSO: **dry lease, finance ~, operating ~, wet ~**

a legal agreement that allows you to use a building, a piece of equipment or some land for a period of time, usually in return for rent: *The current lease expires on 31 March.* ◇ *Under the terms of the lease, you are liable for any repairs to the building.*
❍ *to take on/take out* a lease • *a lease expires/runs out*
• *verb* [+ obj] **lease sth (from sb)** | **lease sth (out) (to sb)** | **lease sb sth** to use, or to let sb use sth, especially property or equipment, in exchange for rent or a regular payment: *We lease all our photocopy equipment.* ◇ *Parts of the building are leased out to tenants.* ◇ *the dealer that leased them the vehicles* → LESSEE, LESSOR
▶ **'leasing** *noun* [U]: *car leasing* ◇ *a leasing company*
PHR V **,lease sth 'back (to sb)** to sell property or a valuable asset and continue to use it by paying rent to the new owner; to buy property or an asset and allow the seller to continue using it in exchange for rent: *At one stage they had to sell and lease back their head office to raise cash.* ◇ *The trust has agreed to lease the property back to them for 40 years.*

leaseback /ˈliːsbæk/ *noun* [U,C]

SEE ALSO: **sale and leaseback**

(*Property*) the process of selling property or another valuable asset and continuing to use it by paying rent to the new owner; a legal agreement where this happens: *The firm used a leaseback on its factories to raise the cash it needed.*

leasehold /ˈliːshəʊld; *AmE* -hoʊld/ *noun, adjective*
(*Law; Property*)
• *noun* [C,U] (*also* **,leasehold e'state** [C] *less frequent*)
the right to use a building or a piece of land according to the arrangements in a LEASE: *We hope to acquire a long leasehold on the property.* ◇ *leasehold possession of property* → FREEHOLD
• *adjective*
(about property or land) that can be used for a limited period of time, according to the arrangements in a LEASE: *The group owns leasehold properties worth over €50 million.* ▶ **'leasehold** *adverb*: *to purchase land leasehold* → FREEHOLD

leaseholder /ˈliːshəʊldə(r); *AmE* -hoʊld-/ *noun* [C]
(*Law; Property*) a company, person, etc. who has the right to use a building or a piece of land according to the arrangements in a LEASE → FREEHOLDER

,leasehold e'state = LEASEHOLD *noun*

★ **leave** /liːv/ *noun* [U]

SEE ALSO: **administrative leave, compassionate ~, gardening ~, job-protected ~, maternity ~, parental ~, paternity ~,** etc.

1 (*HR*) a period of time when you are allowed to be away from work for a holiday/vacation or for a special reason: *to take a month's paid/unpaid leave* ◇ *Mr. Alden is on leave this week.* ◇ *Your basic annual leave entitlement is 20 days.* ◇ *a period of paid educational leave* (= for formal study or training)
HELP In this meaning, **leave** is uncountable in British English but can be uncountable or countable in American English.
❍ *to be entitled to/get/have* leave • *to go on/save/take/use (up)* leave • *to apply for/be given/be granted* leave • *paid/unpaid* leave
2 official permission to do sth: *to be absent without leave* ◇ *The court granted him leave to appeal against the sentence.*
❍ *to ask/obtain/request* leave (to do sth) • *to give/grant/refuse sb* leave

,leave of 'absence *noun* [U,C] (*plural* **leaves of absence**)
(*HR*) permission to have time away from work for a particular period; the period of time that you are allowed: *I wish to apply for leave of absence on medical grounds.* ◇ *She had four months' leave of absence.*
❍ *to apply for/be given/be granted/take* leave of absence

-led /led/ *combining form* (*used to form adjectives*)
1 having the thing mentioned as its main influence: *consumer-led product development* ◇ *a market-led economy* (= one controlled by markets rather than by the government) ◇ *stimulating demand-led growth in the economy*
2 organized or controlled by the person or organization mentioned: *manager-led discussions* ◇ *a government-led financial rescue for the firm*

ledger /ˈledʒə(r)/ *noun* [C]

SEE ALSO: **bought ledger, creditors' ~, debtors' ~, general ~, nominal ~, purchase ~, sales ~**

(*Accounting*) a book or computer file in which a bank, a business, etc. records the money it has paid and received: *balancing a ledger* ◇ *A company director was accused of falsifying entries in the company ledger.*

'ledger clerk *noun* [C]
a person whose job is to make and check entries in a company **ledger**

,left 'luggage *noun* [U,C] (*also* **,left-'luggage ,office** [C]) (*both BrE*) (*AmE* **'baggage room** [C])
a place where you can pay to leave bags for a short time, for example at a train station

leg /leg/ *noun*
IDM **have, gain, grow 'legs** (*informal*) if you say that sth **has legs**, you mean that it will continue, or people will be interested in it, for a long time: *Some investors think the rally (in share prices) still has legs.* ◇ *It's too early to tell if this idea has legs.*

legacy /ˈlegəsi/ *noun, adjective*
• *noun* [C] (*plural* **legacies**)
1 a situation that exists now because of events, actions, etc. that took place in the past: *The failed project left the company with a legacy of massive debt.*
2 money or property that is given to you by sb when they die SYN INHERITANCE
• *adjective*
1 (*IT*) used to describe a system, product, etc. that is no longer generally available, but that is still used: *legacy software such as Windows 98* ◇ *The cost of replacing a legacy computer system can be huge.*

Study Pages

Idiomatic language in Business English

As you use this dictionary, you will see many explanations of idioms that are used frequently in Business English. When we use the term 'idiom', people often think of colourful expressions such as *sell like hot cakes* or *bring home the bacon*. However, the English language also includes many thousands of less obviously colourful expressions. We use these expressions every day in speech and writing, often without even noticing them. The language of business is no exception to this. Consider the following examples of Business English:

▶ *Investors are worried about the health of the economy.*

▶ *The company is at risk of going under.*

▶ *The dollar has gained ground against the euro.*

These examples all use idiomatic language. In the first example, the economy is being seen as a human body, which can be healthy or unhealthy. In the second, a company that is failing is seen as a sinking ship, going under the waves. And in the third, it is as though the currencies are in a race, with the euro being ahead but the dollar catching up.

Common themes

If we look at the language people use when speaking and writing about business, we can see that certain themes are repeated over and over again.

Sport, games and war

The themes of sport, games and war are some of the most frequent. This is not surprising. Business is all about competition, so it is natural that when people speak and write about businesses competing they should select expressions related to other areas of human activity that involve success and failure, victory and defeat.

Companies compete with rival companies to be the best and most successful in their field, just as athletes and sportsmen and women compete to win a race or a match. If competition is fierce, rival businesses are even seen as being like opposing countries or armies, where the survival of one seems to require the destruction of another. Businesses and the people in charge of them are often described as players, and business leaders are portrayed as captains or generals, developing strategy, directing operations, attacking the enemy, or encouraging their troops. The themes of war and sport run through the following piece about competition between supermarket companies (some of the idiomatic expressions are explained below):

Supermarket giants battle for top place

Britain's two biggest supermarkets are playing for high stakes in their battle to control the nation's shopping trolleys. The food retailing giants have targeted some of their smaller rivals, with one or more hostile takeovers predicted in the coming months. Control of one or more of the smaller regional chains would allow either group to comfortably outstrip their rivals and claim the top spot in British retailing.

- **to play for high stakes**: to risk a lot of money on being the most successful
- **the nation's shopping trolleys**: the retail industry
- **to target**: to choose to attack somebody
- **to outstrip**: to become faster, better or more successful than a competitor
- **the top spot**: the first position in a competition

Vehicles and machines

Another theme that occurs frequently in Business English is that of businesses being described in terms of vehicles or machines. Again, these seem to be quite natural images. Like many machines, businesses are complicated things made up of many different parts that all have to work well at the same time. They have to move forwards in order to survive, and movement is the defining characteristic of vehicles. Have a look at the following text:

Train parts manufacturer back on track

Troubled train parts manufacturer Railparts is *back on track*. The company, which makes high-tech components for high-speed trains, has *had a bumpy ride* over the past few years. Already under pressure from foreign competitors, the company *hit the buffers* when a prolonged industrial dispute saw production at its Scottish plant *grind to a halt* late last year. Now, with a new productivity agreement in place and new management *in the driving seat*, the business looks to be *on track* to return to profitability by the third quarter of this year.

The writer has used several idioms relating to vehicles and machinery to describe the company's problems and recovery. When the company was having problems it was like a train that had left the tracks as the result of an accident; like a car on a bad road it was *having a bumpy ride*.
Its activities then suddenly stopped: when a train *hits the buffers*, it hits the barrier at the end of a railway line. Production *ground to a halt* like a machine that stops working or a vehicle that stops moving. Now it has recovered, it is *back on track*. Business leaders are often described in terms of pilots or drivers, directing and controlling the progress of the business, and here the management team is *in the driving seat*, firmly in control.

Health

The theme of health also features strongly in Business English. People will often describe a business, an industry or an economy as if it were a living thing with a state of health. Its condition is seen to improve or worsen in the same way that a person's health does, and it often needs a particular treatment in order to regain its health. The following examples use the theme of health:

▶ *We're a **leaner, fitter** business than we were a year ago.*
▶ *She admits that the company is **bleeding** cash on the project.*
▶ *If banks tighten their lending policies, **healthy** firms may be **starved of** credit.*
▶ *The risks of the economy **suffering** a **relapse** are high.*
▶ *An urgent plan is needed to **revive** the **ailing** manufacturing industry.*
▶ *The airline is seeking an **injection of funds** from shareholders.*

When you are reading or listening to people talking about business in English, look out for the kinds of themes and idioms we have discussed here. It will make your studies more interesting, and help increase your understanding of what Business English is all about.

Computers and the Internet

In order to be able to run programs, a computer uses an **operating system**, such as Windows or Linux. Once this is **installed**, applications can be **loaded** to perform particular functions, such as:

- a **word processesor** for working with text
- a **spreadsheet** for working with figures
- a **database** for working with details of customers, products, etc.
- a **CAD** program for design
- a **desktop publishing** program for creating brochures, posters, etc.

If your computer is on a **network**, you will have to **enter** your **username** and **password** before you can use it. You will then see the **programs** on your computer displayed as **icons** on the **desktop**.

To open a program, **click** (or **double-click**) on the **icon**, and the program will open in a new **window**. Use the **drop-down menu** on the menu **toolbar** to open an existing document or to create a new one. If you create a new document, save it to your **hard disk** so that you won't lose it if the computer **crashes**.

When you have **entered** text or **data** in the program, you can edit or **format** it in a number of ways:

- You can use the menus or icons at the top of the screen to **delete** it, to **cut** and **paste** it, etc.
- You can **right-click** (= click the right-hand button on your mouse) and select an option from the **pop-up menu**.
- You can also use keyboard shortcuts to perform many functions, such as Ctrl-C to copy text, or Ctrl-P to **print out** a document.

To move text around, you can **highlight** it, then click and **drag** it with the mouse. To move to another part of a document, use the **scroll bar** to **scroll** up or down, and click to position the **cursor** where you want it.

When you have a lot of files on your computer, you should **back** them **up**, for example by **uploading** them onto a **server**, or by **burning** them onto a CD-ROM. In order to take up less space, you may want to **zip/compress** the files first.

workstation

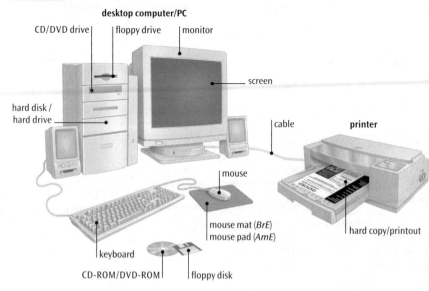

desktop computer/PC

CD/DVD drive | floppy drive | monitor

screen

hard disk / hard drive

cable

printer

mouse

mouse mat (*BrE*)
mouse pad (*AmE*)

hard copy/printout

keyboard

CD-ROM/DVD-ROM | floppy disk

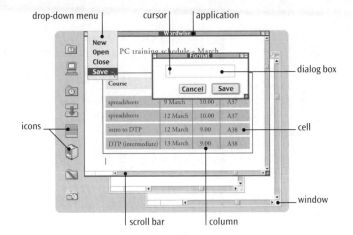

drop-down menu | cursor | application

icons —

— dialog box

— cell

— window

scroll bar | column

Email

To send an email, write the address of the **recipient** in the *To:* **field**, or click on an address from your address book. If you want to **copy** someone **in** on the email, put their address in the *Cc:* (carbon copy) field, or in the *Bcc:* (blind carbon copy) field if you don't want the recipient to know who is copied in. If you need to **attach** a document to the email, select *Attach file* from the menu, or click on the paperclip icon, and then **browse** your computer for the document you want to attach.

To say the email address:
j_martin@martin-wood.com
you would say 'j underscore martin at martin hyphen wood dot com'

The Internet

In order to search for information on the Internet, open your **browser** (for example Microsoft Internet Explorer, Netscape or Mozilla), and type some keywords into the *Search* box of whatever **search engine** you use (for example Yahoo! or Google). If you want to find the names of interpreters who work in New York, for example, you could type in the keywords *interpreters* and "*New York*" (in double quotes to keep these words together), and then click on one of the websites that the search brings up.

To open a web page, click on a **link**, or type the page's **URL** into the address **bar** at the top of the screen, and the page will **download**.

If you want to save the address of a website that you have **searched for** or just come across by chance, you can **bookmark** it.

The URL of a company's **home page** is often something like:
▶ http://www.martinwood.com

To read this URL to somebody over the phone, you would say:
▶ 'h-t-t-p colon, two forward slashes, double-u double-u double-u dot, martinwood (all one word), dot com'

The *.com* in the example above is called a **top-level domain**. Common ones include:

.com /ˌdɒt 'kɒm/ (*AmE* /ˌdɑːt 'kɑːm/)
– this is used by businesses

.org /ˌdɒt 'ɔːg/ (*AmE* /ˌdɑːt 'ɔːrg/)
– used by organizations that are not businesses

.edu /ˌdɒt 'edjuː/ (*AmE* ˌdɑːt 'edjuː/)
– used by colleges, universities, etc.

.gov /ˌdɒt 'gʌv/ (*AmE* /ˌdɑːt 'gʌv/
– used by government bodies

.net /ˌdɒt 'net/ (*AmE* /ˌdɑːt 'net/)
– used especially by Internet service providers

Most countries have their own domain ending, and this is usually pronounced as separate letters, for example Bulgaria is **.bg** /ˌdɒt biː 'dʒiː/, and China is **.cn** /ˌdɒt siː 'en/.

Common UK domain names include:
.co.uk /ˌdɒt ˌkəʊ dɒt juː 'keɪ/
– this is often used by companies

.ac.uk /ˌdɒt ˌæk dɒt juː 'keɪ /
– used by universities

Incoterms

A number of standard conditions of sale have come to be used in International Trade. Perhaps the most popular are the International Commercial Terms or Incoterms, which were decided by the International Chamber of Commerce (ICC). They are used both in writing and negotiating contracts. For example, a seller in Brazil might say that they can sell you an amount of coffee *FOB Santos* for a particular price. As you will see from the table below, this means that for

the stated price they will deliver the goods to the port of Santos, load them onto a ship and get permission for them to be exported, but you must pay for the shipping costs and get permission to import them into your country. The table below gives a summary of the main features of the Incoterms (2000 edition). **Note:** You should contact the ICC for a full description of the Incoterms if you want to use them in a contract. The ICC updates the Incoterms from time to time.

Incoterm	Place of delivery *	Responsibility for transport costs	Responsibility for damage to the goods	Dealing with officials	Form of transport
EXW ex works… (named place)	at the seller's **factory** or **warehouse**	the **buyer** pays for the goods to be collected	the **buyer** is responsible once the goods have been collected	everything is done by the **buyer**	any
FCA free carrier… (named place)	where the **carrier** (chosen by the **buyer**) receives the goods	the **buyer** is responsible once the goods have been delivered to the **carrier**	the **buyer** is responsible once the goods have been delivered to the **carrier**	the **seller** gets permission to send the goods from their country and the **buyer** gets permission to bring the goods into theirs	any
FAS free alongside ship… (named port)	at the **port of departure**, next to a particular ship	the **buyer** is responsible once the goods have been delivered to the **port**	the **buyer** is responsible once the goods have been delivered to the **port**		ship
FOB free on board… (named port)	on board a particular **ship** at the **port of departure**	the **buyer** is responsible once the goods are **on the ship**	the **buyer** is responsible once the goods are **on the ship**		ship
CFR cost and freight… (named destination port)	on board a particular **ship** at the **port of departure**	the **seller** pays for shipping to the **destination port** (the buyer pays for transport after that)	the **buyer** is responsible once the goods are **on the ship**		ship
CIF cost, insurance and freight… (named destination port)	on board a particular **ship** at the **port of departure**	the **seller** pays for shipping to the **destination port** (the buyer pays for transport after that)	the **buyer** is responsible once the goods are **on the ship** (but the seller pays for basic insurance while the goods are at sea)		ship

Increasing risk/cost for seller →

Term		the seller pays for transport / is responsible	the buyer/seller responsible	export/import	transport type
CPT carriage paid to… (named destination)	where the **carrier** (chosen by the **seller**) receives the goods	the **seller** pays for transport to the **named destination**	the **buyer** is responsible once the goods have been delivered to the carrier		any
CIP carriage and insurance paid to… (named destination)	where the **carrier** (chosen by the **seller**) receives the goods	the **seller** pays for transport to the **named destination**	the **buyer** is responsible once the goods have been delivered to the carrier (but the seller pays for basic insurance while the goods are being transported)		any
DAF delivered at frontier… (named place)	a **named border** between the countries of the buyer and the seller	the **seller** pays for transport to the **border** (the buyer pays to collect goods from the train, truck, etc.)	the **seller** is responsible until the goods reach the **border**		any (but not where delivery is at a port or on a ship)
DES delivered ex ship… (named destination port)	**on the ship**, at the **destination port**	the **seller** is responsible until the goods reach the **destination port** (the buyer pays to collect the goods from the ship)	the **seller** is responsible until the goods reach the **destination port**		ship
DEQ delivered ex quay … (named destination port)	**off the ship**, in the **destination port** (on the quay)	the **seller** is responsible until the goods are **off the ship** in the port (the buyer pays to collect the goods from the port)	the **seller** is responsible until the goods are **off the ship**		ship
DDU delivered duty unpaid… (named destination)	at a named **place**	the **seller** is responsible until the goods reach the **destination** (the buyer pays to collect the goods from the train, truck, etc.)	the **seller** is responsible until the goods reach the **destination**		any (but not where delivery is at a port or on a ship)
DDP delivered duty paid… (named destination)	at a named **place**	the **seller** is responsible until the goods reach the **destination** (the buyer pays to collect the goods from the train, truck, etc.)	the **seller** is responsible until the goods reach the **destination**	the **seller** gets export and import permission and pays the taxes	any (but not where delivery is at a port or on a ship)

*(where the buyer takes legal responsibility for the goods)

increasing risk/cost for seller →

Writing letters, emails and memos

Business **letters** are written in a formal style: you should avoid short forms and informal expressions. A lot of modern business communication takes place by **email**. Emails are generally less formal in style than letters, but emails to customers and suppliers are more formal than emails between colleagues. **Memos** are used for communication within companies and range from formal to informal depending on the subject. Business **faxes** use a similar style to formal letters.

Formal letters

❈ York Designs

❶ 10 Turf Street • York • YO27 7QR
Telephone +44 (0)1632 523499 • Fax +44 (0)1632 523500
Email: joe@yorkdesigns.co.uk • www.yorkdesigns.co.uk

❷ Your ref: 10/06/05
Our ref: JG/EW

❸ 26 June 2005

❹ Ms E Wedgwood
Wedgwoods Furniture
High Street
Raleigh
Essex SS3 5TU

❺ Dear Ms Wedgwood

❻ **Sales enquiry**

Thank you for your recent enquiry concerning the possibility of selling our traditional handmade wooden furniture through your stores.

I am **❼** pleased to enclose a copy of our catalogue and current price list. In addition to the designs shown, we will shortly be producing a range of storage units, for which a catalogue will be available next month. Each item is made to order, so there is usually a period of four to six weeks between ordering and delivery.

❽ Please let me know if you require any further information or if I can be of assistance in any way. If you are in the area and would like to visit us, I would be delighted to show you around our workshop.

I look forward to hearing from you.

❾ Yours sincerely

❿ *Joe Goodfellow*

Joseph Goodfellow
⓫ Managing director

⓬ Encl.

❶ Often there is a letterhead printed on the paper, which can appear anywhere at the top of the page. Otherwise, the sender's address and other details (phone number, fax, email address, etc.) usually go on the right-hand side.

❷ If the letter to which you are replying has a reference, often made up of initials, a date, an account number, etc., this can be included at *Your ref*. Include any reference that you want to be used in the response to your letter at *Our ref*. The references can go either on the right- or left-hand side.

❸ The date can also go on the right or the left. British style is to put the day, then the month, then the year. American style is to have the month before the day (*June 26, 2005* or *6-26-2005*). In order to avoid confusion, it is best to write the month out in full rather than use figures.

❹ The address of the person receiving the letter goes on the left of the page. If you know their name and job title, put them before the address. Alternatively, you can put the name or job title on a new line after the address and use the expression *for the attention of* (often shortened to *fao*): *For the attention of the Marketing Director*

❺ There are various ways of starting a letter. If you know the name of the person you are writing to, start with *Dear Mr/Mrs/Ms/Dr…* and the person's surname. If you do not have the name of a specific person, you can address the letter: *Dear Sir/Madam, Dear Sir or Madam* (in British English) or *To whom it may concern* (in American English). *Dear Sirs* is used, especially in British English, when addressing a company rather than a particular person. In American English, a letter to a company usually starts with

Gentlemen. In British English, you can choose whether to put a comma after the name (*Dear Ms Wedgwood,* or *Dear Ms Wedgwood*). In American English, it is usual to put a colon (*Dear Mr Smith:*).

6 You can mention the subject of your letter in a title. It is not necessary to begin the title with *Re* (short for 'concerning').

7 Avoid using short forms: use *I am* rather than *I'm*.

8 It is usual to separate paragraphs with a line space.

9 If the letter starts with *Dear Sir/Madam* or *Dear Sirs*, the usual ending in British English is *Yours faithfully*. If you write to a named person it is *Yours sincerely*. In American English, the endings *Sincerely* or *Sincerely yours* can be used, whether or not you write to a named person. You can choose whether to put a comma after this (*Yours sincerely,* or *Yours sincerely*).

10 Your signature is followed by your printed name. If the letter is signed by one person on behalf of another, *pp* is used before the printed name.

11 It is a good idea to include your job title, especially if you have not dealt with the person you are writing to before.

12 *Encl.* stands for *Enclosed* or *Enclosure(s)*: it means that there are other documents sent with the letter.

Formal emails

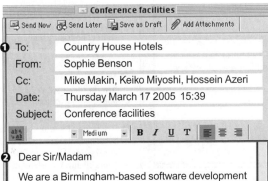

1 **Header information:** This includes who the message is to and from, and what it is about. Cc ('carbon copies') is for the email addresses of anyone you want to send copies to.

2 **Message text:** Even formal emails are often less formal than letters. Sometimes there is no opening greeting, and phrases like *Many thanks* or *Regards* are often used instead of the more formal *Yours faithfully* or *Yours sincerely*, especially after the initial exchange of emails. Although a more informal tone may be appropriate, particularly when writing to someone you deal with regularly, you should still use correct spelling, grammar and punctuation. Avoid using whole words in capitals (URGENT), which may be interpreted as shouting. If you want to stress a word you can use asterisks on either side of it: *urgent*

3 **Signature:** this often includes the name and address of the sender's company, their phone/fax number, email address and the company's website.

Informal emails

❶ You can start an email with *Hi* or *Hello* (with or without the person's name) or just with their first name: *Janie*. People often start with no greeting at all, especially if they have emailed each other recently and are continuing the same topic.

❷ In an email to someone you know well it is appropriate to use informal language and a tone similar to that of conversation. Short forms are acceptable (*I'm* instead of *I am*).

❸ Informal emails can be fairly free in their punctuation, although it still advisable to write full sentences with initial capital letters and full stops. An email without basic punctuation may be seen as rushed or unprofessional.

❹ Abbreviations such as **btw** (*by the way*), **fyi** (*for your information*) are commonly used.

❺ *Best* is short for *Best wishes*. Other possible ways to end are *Regards*, *All the best*, or *Yours* (slightly more formal).

Send Now Send Later Save as Draft Add Attachments

To:	Jane Mathews
From:	Frances Jones
Cc:	
Date:	Friday 24/06/05
Subject:	Lunch

Hi ❶ Janie

I'm ❷ going to be in Bristol next Wednesday and thought maybe we could meet up for lunch (and to discuss the stand at the Milan fair…) - are you free? ❸ My train gets in about 11.30.

Btw ❹ I ran into Kabir at a meeting last week and he said he was looking forward to working with you on the new range - he seems really nice and very keen.

Hope to see you next week.

Best ❺

Fran

Writing letters, emails and memos

A formal fax

Fax

Beth's Bags
1472 Grant Ave
Tuscon, AZ 17601
Fax: 717 3784166

To:	Gino Conte, Prima Fashions
Fax no:	0039 055 295783
From:	Beth Daly
Date:	5.30.05
Subject:	Order for 50 leather purses

No of pages including this one: 2

Please note that your invoice no: 2753 of 4.22.05 was paid directly into your bank account last Monday, as shown by the accompanying deposit slip. Please make the goods available for collection immediately as we have customers waiting for them.

Beth Daly

A formal memo

Confidential Memo
Bright Sky Productions

From:	Frank Burgess
To:	All staff
Subject:	New head of marketing
Date:	September 15 2005

I am pleased to announce that we have appointed a new head of marketing, Stephanie Collins, to replace Jim Laird. Stephanie comes to us from Greymont Media, where she has been director of marketing for the past three years. She will be joining us on October 3. Please note that the appointment is currently confidential and should not be discussed with anyone outside the company until it has been officially announced.

I am sure you will all wish to join me in welcoming Stephanie to the company.

Frank

Frank Burgess
CEO

Applying for a job

Job adverts and applications

Here are some useful phrases for
a cover letter:

1 say what job you are applying for
and when you saw the advertisement
  ▶ *I am writing to apply for the post of sales
    manager advertised in the Publishing
    Times of 6 November.*
  ▶ *I am writing in response to your
    advertisement in the Publishing Times
    of 6 November for a sales manager.*

2 say who you are and why your experience
and qualifications make you the right
person for the job
  ▶ *I believe my long experience in selling
    magazine advertising and managing
    sales teams makes me a strong candidate
    for the job.*

3 describe how the job is right for you
  ▶ *I am looking for a challenging position
    with a leading magazine, which makes
    the advertised job ideal.*
  ▶ *I am extremely interested in this position
    as I am looking to join a company in which
    I can fulfil my potential.*

4 say when you would be available for
interview and to begin work
  ▶ *I am available for interview any
    day of the week.*
  ▶ *My notice period for my current job
    is 6 weeks.*

Hi! magazine

Sales Manager

**Leading magazine publisher
wishes to recruit a highly motivated
professional with a proven track
record in magazine publishing,
to extend its revenues and sales.**

You will be responsible for:
- researching and developing
  new leads
- managing and motivating
  an experienced sales team
- identifying and building
  new business relationships

You will be a goal-oriented and
results-driven individual with
outstanding analytical and
communicative skills, together
with a sound understanding
of current market trends.

Attractive benefits package.

Send CV and cover letter with details
of current salary to

The Human Resources Director
Hi! Magazine
4 Albion Road
London SE1 8DD

Closing date 10 February 2006

**Only shortlisted candidates will
be notified**

In newspaper adverts, abbreviations and foreign
terms are often used. Here is an example:

Wntd PA PT 20 hrs/wk sml mkt co. Slry circa 25k p.a.
neg pro rata. Apply with CV and cover letter.
Interviews w/c 24/8.

The full version of this advert might read as follows:
  ▶ *Wanted, personal assistant (part-time) to work
    20 hours a week in a small marketing company.
    Good salary in the region of £25 000 per year, pro rata*
    (negotiable). Apply with a CV and cover letter.
    Interviews are in the week commencing 24 August.*

* This is the full-time salary on which the part-time salary
  will be based.

Other abbreviations you
may see include:

appt	appointment
comm	commission
exp	experience
FT	full-time
incl.	including
pref	preferred
p.w.	per week
qual	qualified
reqd	required
temp	temporary
w/e	weekends
yrs	years

Writing a CV or résumé

The principal differences between a CV and a résumé are:

- A CV is a complete record of your professional and academic history, together with a summary of your skills; a résumé is a summary of the experience and strengths that you have that are relevant to the particular job you are applying for.
- A résumé is usually one page, except for very senior posts; a CV can be longer than this.

- It is unusual to include personal information such as your birth date, marital status, etc. on a résumé; this information is optional on a CV.
- It is common to include the names and contact details of your referees on a CV, but rare to do so on a résumé.

CVs are moving closer to the model of the US résumé, in that it is now becoming common to summarize your experience and strengths in the Profile (also called the Career summary) section.

CV (curriculum vitae) – British Style

Name: Julie Warwick
Date of birth: 12/10/72
Nationality: British
Address: 131 Fernley Road, London, H17 9QT
Tel: 0207 946 0277
Email: julie@jswarwick.net

Profile

A goal-oriented and motivational retail manager with excellent problem-solving and leadership skills.

Education and Qualifications

- 1982–1989
  Tatfield Comprehensive School, East Ham, London:
  10 GCSEs and 3 A levels in English, French, and Economics
- 1990–1993
  University of Surrey:
  BSc Hons Retail Management (2:1)

Employment

- 2000–present
  Mackson & Peters Retail Co., East London

  Regional Manager
  Responsible for managing operations, refitting stores, negotiating contracts, controlling budgets and liaising with internal and external clients and customers, collating information from stores, as well as dealing with all health and safety issues.

[1]

- 1995–1999
  Hennford's Supermarket, Ealing, London

  General Store Manager
  Responsible for profit and loss, customer service and the training and development of staff.

- 1993–1994
  Hennford's Supermarket, North Cheam, Surrey

  Graduate Trainee Manager
  Introduction to all areas of store management by shadowing a manager and then working under the manager's supervision.

Skills

- Competent user of standard office-suite computer programs
- Fluent speaker of Spanish; some knowledge of French

Interests

Golf, travel, cooking

Referees

- Michael Page, Regional Director, Mackson & Peters Retail Co. 61–63 Cotley Business Park, Station Road, Reading, Berkshire RG1 8TZ , Tel: 01632 261 085
- Jenny Norman, Area Manager, Hennford's Supermarkets, Head Office, 311 Caesar Hill, London SE7 6ES, Tel: 0207 946 0932

[2]

Thomas D. Lanow

1252 Gains Street
Greyfield, PA 15904
thomaslanow@spacevision.com
telephone 814-266-9772

Objective

A challenging position in marketing
that allows me to utilize my creative
skills and critical thinking and to widen
my professional experience.

Summary of qualifications

- Four years' experience in
  managing major business projects
- Strong record of success in
  achieving targets
- Excellent team management skills
- Dynamic, articulate, analytical and
  results-oriented

Professional Experience

2002-
Callphone
Deputy Marketing Manager
- Developed campaign for highly
  successful XV-200 range
- Recruited and managed 30-strong
  sales team.

2000–02
Vista Handheld Computers
Marketing Assistant
- Handled Internet component
  of major marketing campaigns
- Assisted in development of
  campaigns for full range of products

Education

Pennsylvania State University, Bachelor
of Science, Business Administration

Referees

Available on request

Other useful phrases for a CV or resumé:

- *Native French speaker*
- *Near-native command of English*
- *Good spoken and written German*
- *Computer literate*
- *Familiar with HTML*
- *Experienced trainer and facilitator*

- *Baccalauréat, série C (equivalent of
  A levels in Maths and Physics)*
- *The qualifications described below do not
  have exact equivalents in the American
  system.*
- *I enclose photocopies of my certificates
  with English translations.*
- *Four weeks' work experience at a leading
  software house*
- *Summer internship at a marketing firm*

- *Team player*
- *Work well as part of a team*
- *Work well under pressure*
- *Welcome new challenges*
- *Highly motivated*
- *Can-do attitude*

- *Interests include music and photography*

Describing graphs

Here are some phrases you can use to refer to a graph:

▶ *If we look at the graph, we can see this year's sales.*
▶ *If you look at this chart, you can see how sales have gone over the past year.*
▶ *This graph shows/illustrates sales against time for the last year.*
▶ *The y-axis shows unit sales in thousands.*
▶ *Unit sales are shown on the vertical axis.*
▶ *Values refer to thousands of units sold.*

Some common verbs to describe movements are:

↑ *climb, go up, grow, increase, rise*
↓ *decrease, dip, drop, go down, fall (away/off), sink*
→ *level out, plateau, remain steady/unchanged*
⤳ *fluctuate*
⤴ *peak*
⤵ *bottom out*

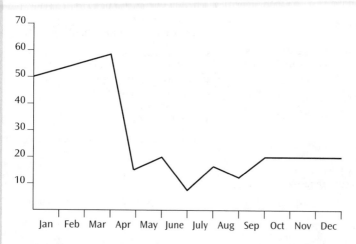

Use adverbs to describe changes in more detail:

▶ *gradually, slightly, steadily; dramatically, rapidly, sharply, significantly, steeply*

Note how prepositions are used to describe the levels and time periods shown in the graph:

▶ *Sales rose gradually **between** January **and** March **to just short of** 60 000.*
▶ *In April, sales fell sharply **from just under** 60 000 **to around** 15 000.*
▶ *They then recovered slightly **in** May **to about** 20 000.*
▶ ***From** May **to** October, sales fluctuated **between** 20 000 **and** 8 000.*
▶ *From October onwards, sales remained steady **at slightly more than** 20 000.*

▶ *Sales increased **by** about 17% **over** the first quarter.*
▶ *Sales peaked **at** almost 60 000 in March, and bottomed out in June **at** 8 000.*

Nouns can be used instead of verbs. Again, note the prepositions used:

▶ *There was a significant fall **in** sales in April.*
▶ *Sales reached a peak **of** almost 60 000 in March.*
▶ *In June, sales hit a low **of** around 8 000.*
▶ *Between March and May there was a four-fold decrease **in** sales.*
▶ *There was an overall upward trend **between** June and October.*

Adjectives you can use include:

▶ *dramatic, marked, sharp, steep, sudden, significant, rapid; moderate, slight, steady*

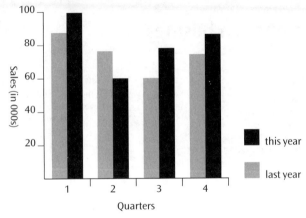

Phrases for comparing sales this year with last year include:
▶ *Sales for the last quarter were up **on** last year.*
▶ ***Like-for-like** sales for the second quarter were down by 20%.*
▶ *The **year-on-year** increase for the first quarter was around 15%.*

To compare results with predictions you can use:
▶ ***In line with** predictions, sales peaked in the first quarter.*
▶ *Results for the second quarter were **much lower than expected**.*
▶ *Sales grew by a **better-than-expected** 20% in the third quarter.*

Pie charts

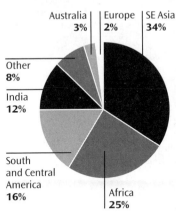

Here are some useful phrases for describing
pie charts:
▶ *In this pie chart, sales **are broken down** by region.*
▶ *This pie chart **breaks** sales **down** by region.*
            *—— shows how the sales **break down**
                regionally.*
            *—— **illustrates** the distribution of sales
                across regions.*
            *—— **compares** percentage sales in
                different regions.*
▶ *Total sales **are divided into** 7 regions.*
▶ *The combined sales in SE Asia and Africa **comprise**
over half total sales.*
▶ *Other parts of the world **make up** less than
50% of the total.*
▶ *SE Asia **accounts for** 34% of total sales,
while Europe **represents** just 2%.*
▶ *Percentages **range from** 2% in Europe,
to 34% in SE Asia.*

The development of a business

Planning

- decide on a product: a new type of fruit juice
- develop the product and do market research
- decide on a brand name: **Forest Fruits**
- develop a business plan
- decide on a form of business: sole trader/sole proprietorship, partnership, company
- raise the finance: founder's own funds; loans; look for backers or partners

RISKS

⚠ the founder cannot get a loan:
  — poor credit rating
  — insufficient collateral
⚠ the founder is unable to attract investors

↓

Start-up

- form a company: **Forest Fruits Ltd**
- rent premises, purchase equipment and supplies, employ and train staff
- start producing and marketing the product

RISKS

⚠ the company fails to achieve a critical mass of customers
⚠ bad debts
⚠ lenders recall their loans

 EXIT STRATEGIES
- sell the company's assets
- offer shares to other members of the company

Growth

- the number of customers grows; the company gains a share of the fruit-juice market
- turnover increases; the company breaks even
- the company employs more staff and divides into different functions: management, accounting, sales and marketing, production
- the company develops a network of suppliers and customers
- the **Forest Fruits** brand becomes well-known
- the company needs fresh capital to buy production facilities: it decides to sell shares to the public to obtain the finance

RISKS

⚠ competition from other producers
⚠ fruit juices fall out fashion
⚠ insufficient capital; poor management of cash flow
⚠ the founder finds it difficult to delegate authority

EXIT STRATEGIES
- sell the business as a going concern
- sell the brand name and customer list to a competitor

Going public/flotation

- Forest Fruits Ltd is converted into a public company: **Forest Fruits plc**
- an investment bank draws up a prospectus giving details of the shares to be sold, the value of the company, past earnings and future profits
- the company's shares are offered to private and institutional investors
- the shares are listed on the stock exchange

EXIT STRATEGY
sell shares to other investors on the stock exchange

Maturity

- the company continues to grow:
  — organically, by developing its range of products
  — through joint ventures with other producers
  — by buying the brands of other businesses and integrating them into the company's portfolio
  — by acquiring other companies, using cash or shares
- the company uses an employee share/stock ownership plan to attract and keep talent
- the company maintains a stable management structure
- shareholders receive regular dividends; the share price grows

RISKS

⚠ the share price is affected by market volatility
⚠ hostile takeover bids
⚠ failure to integrate businesses that are acquired; management struggles
⚠ poor media and investor relations
⚠ succession: who will lead the company when the founder leaves?

2 used to describe something that took place in the past but still affects the present: *The company's difficulties are the result of poor legacy decisions.*

★ **legal** /'li:gl/ *adjective*
1 [only before noun] connected with the law: *the legal profession/system ◇ to take/seek legal advice ◇ a legal adviser/expert ◇ legal costs ◇ They are currently facing a long legal battle in the US courts. ◇ the company's legal department*
2 allowed or required by law: *Full-time employees are entitled to four weeks' leave as a legal minimum. ◇ the legal rights of shareholders ◇ legal currency ◇ Their actions were entirely legal.* OPP ILLEGAL
▶ **legally** /'li:gəli/ *adverb: You are legally entitled to a full refund. ◇ The business has been conducted perfectly legally. ◇ a **legally binding** contract* (= that must be obeyed because it is accepted in law)

,**legal 'action** *noun* [U] (*also* ,**legal pro'ceedings** [pl.])
the act of using the legal system to settle a disagreement, etc: *He threatened to take legal action against the hospital.* → ACTION *noun* (2)

,**legal 'aid** *noun* [U]
money that is given by the government or another organization to sb who needs help to pay for legal advice or a lawyer

,**legal ca'pacity** *noun* [U]
(*Law*) the right or ability to make legal arrangements, to make legal decisions about your property or affairs, to be legally responsible for sb/sth, etc: *reaching the age of legal capacity*

'**legal costs** (*also* '**legal ex,penses**) *noun* [pl.]
money that sb who is involved in a legal case has to pay

,**legal 'entity** *noun* [C]
(*Law*) an organization or a person that has the right to make contracts, to use the legal system to settle disputes, and to make other legal arrangements: *The company is a separate legal entity that can sue and be sued.*

legalese /,li:gə'li:z/ *noun* [U] (*informal*)
the sort of language used in legal documents that is difficult to understand: *If insurance policies are written in legalese, people tend not to read them.*

'**legal ex,penses** = LEGAL COSTS

,**legal 'holiday** *noun* [C]
in the US, a public holiday that is fixed by law
→ BANK HOLIDAY

,**legal in'vestment** *noun* [C]
(*Finance*) in the US, a type of investment that is suitable for a person or an organization that is looking after money for sb else

legality /li:'gæləti/ *noun* (*plural* **legalities**)
1 [U] the fact of being legal: *Shareholders challenged the legality of the merger.*
2 [C] the legal aspect of an action or a situation: *You need a lawyer to explain all the legalities of the contracts.*
→ ILLEGALITY

legalize, -ise /'li:gəlaɪz/ *verb* [+ obj]
to make sth legal: *The government has legalized irradiation for many types of food.* ▶ **legalization, -isation** /,li:gəlaɪ'zeɪʃn; *AmE* ,li:gələ'z-/ *noun* [U]: *the legalization of electronic signatures*

,**legal 'list** *noun* [C]
(*Finance*) in the US, a list of LEGAL INVESTMENTS

,**legal mo'nopoly** *noun* [C]
(*Economics*)
1 a situation in which only one company has the legal right to provide a particular service or product in a particular area: *The Bank of England has a legal monopoly on the issue of banknotes in England and Wales.*

2 a company that has this right: *The national postal service has been a legal monopoly until now, but is about to be privatized.*

'**legal pad** *noun* [C] (*AmE*)
a book of writing paper, which is usually yellow and has lines for writing on

,**legal 'person** (*also* ,**artificial 'person**, ju,**ristic 'person**) *noun* [C] (*plural* ~ **persons**)
(*Law*) an organization or company that has its own legal status and is treated in law as a person, separate from the people who run and own it: *The benefit of the Act extends to both natural and legal persons.*

,**legal pro'ceedings** = LEGAL ACTION

,**legal re'serve** *noun* [C]
(*Accounting*) the smallest amount of money that a bank, an insurance company, etc., is legally required to keep in case it is needed in the future

'**legal ,system** *noun* [C]
the institutions and laws that exist in a particular country to deal with legal cases

,**legal 'tender** *noun* [U]
money that can legally be used to pay for things in a particular country: *These coins are no longer legal tender.*

legible /'ledʒəbl/ *adjective*
(about written or printed words) clear enough to read: *a legible signature ◇ Both handhelds are compact and have legible screens.* ▶ **legibility** /,ledʒə'bɪləti/ *noun* [U] **legibly** /'ledʒəbli/ *adverb*

★ **legislation** /,ledʒɪs'leɪʃn/ *noun* [U]
1 a law or a set of laws passed by a parliament: *an important piece of legislation on working hours ◇ The conference will discuss the impact of new legislation on the IT industry.*
❍ *to* **draft/draw up** *legislation* ◆ *to* **amend/approve/ introduce/pass** *legislation* ◆ *to* **comply with** *legislation*
2 the process of making and passing laws: *Legislation will be difficult and will take time*

legit /lɪ'dʒɪt/ *adjective* (*informal*)
legal, or acting according to the law or the rules: *The business seems legit.* NOTE *Legit* is a short form of 'legitimate'.

legitimate *adjective, verb*
● *adjective* /lɪ'dʒɪtɪmət/
1 allowed and acceptable according to the law: *We are operating a perfectly legitimate business.* SYN LEGAL
2 for which there is a fair and acceptable reason: *It seemed a perfectly legitimate question.* SYN VALID
▶ **legitimacy** /lɪ'dʒɪtɪməsi/ *noun* [U]: *I intend to challenge the legitimacy of his claim.* **le'gitimately** *adverb: legitimately recorded music*
● *verb* /lɪ'dʒɪtɪmeɪt/ [+ obj] (*less frequent*) = LEGITIMIZE

legitimize, -ise /lɪ'dʒɪtəmaɪz/ *verb* (*also* **le'gitimate**, *less frequent*) *verb* [+ obj]
1 to make sth legal: *It is a simple matter to legitimize your home business.* SYN LEGALIZE
2 to make sth that is wrong or unfair seem acceptable: *The union said that the tribunal's decision legitimized discrimination.*

leisure /'leʒə(r); *AmE* 'li:ʒər/ *noun* [U]
time that is spent doing what you enjoy when you are not working or studying: *These days we have more money and more leisure to enjoy it. ◇ The airline relies more on business travellers than the **leisure market*** (= people who travel or buy products for pleasure).

'leisure ,industry *noun* [C]
the people and activities involved in providing goods and services for things that people do in their free time: *the hotel and leisure industry* ◇ *Sporting events and the leisure industry have been hit by the bad weather.*

lemon /'lemən/ *noun* [C] (*informal*)
a product, especially a car, that is useless and does not work as it should; a poor investment

★ **lend** /lend/ *verb* (**lent, lent** /lent/)
1 [+ obj *or no obj*] **lend (sth) (to sb/sth)** | **lend sb sth** (about a bank or financial institution) to give money to sb on condition that they pay it back over a period of time and pay interest on it: *The bank refused to lend the money to us.* ◇ *They refused to lend us the money.* ◇ *30 financial institutions lent $2 billion to the project.* ◇ *Some banks have stopped lending to small businesses.*
2 [+ obj] to give sth to sb or allow them to use sth that belongs to you, which they have to return to you later: *Can you lend me a pen?* ◇ *Security cards should not be lent to other employees.*
[SYN] LOAN → BORROW

> **WHICH WORD?**
>
> ### lend/borrow/loan
>
> You **borrow** something **from** somebody but **lend** something **to** somebody: *I borrowed Dave's laptop.* ◇ *Dave lent me his laptop.*
>
> In the context of money, the verb **loan** is often used instead of lend or borrow, especially in American English: *We **loaned** the money **from** the bank* ◇ *The bank was willing to **loan** us the money.*
>
> The person or organization that **borrows** something or **receives a loan** is called the **borrower**, and the person or organization that **lends** something or **gives a loan** is called the **lender**.
>
> See note at LOAN

★ **lender** /'lendə(r)/ *noun* [C]

SEE ALSO: **mortgage lender**

a person or an organization that lends money: *The bank is Europe's biggest lender.* ◇ *The company is in rescue talks with its lenders.* [OPP] BORROWER → MONEYLENDER

'lender of 'last re'sort *noun* [C]
(*Economics*) the role of a country's central bank when it lends money in a time of great difficulty to a bank that does not have enough to cover what its customers are taking out and cannot borrow money from anywhere else

★ **lending** /'lendɪŋ/ *noun* [U]

SEE ALSO: **bank lending, predatory lending**

the act of lending money; the amount of money that is lent: *Lending by banks and building societies rose to €4.9 billion last year.* ◇ *the consumer lending market* [OPP] BORROWING
● *commercial/consumer/mortgage/personal* lending ◆ *an increase/a rise/surge* in lending ◆ *a decrease/downturn* in lending ◆ *a lending bank/institution/service*

'lending rate *noun* [C]

SEE ALSO: **prime lending rate**

(*Finance*) the rate of interest that you must pay when you borrow money from a bank or another financial organization → BASE RATE

less /les/ *preposition*
used before a particular amount that must be taken away from the amount just mentioned: *a monthly salary of €2 500 less tax and insurance* ◇ *Send a cheque for the catalogue price, less 10% discount.* [SYN] MINUS → PLUS

,less-developed 'country *noun* [C] (*abbr* LDC)
(*Economics*) a country that is poor and trying to make its industry and economic system more advanced → DEVELOPING

lessee /le'si:/ *noun* [C]
(*Law; Property*) a person who has use of a building, an area of land, etc. on a LEASE → TENANT

lessor /le'sɔ:(r)/ *noun* [C]
(*Law; Property*) a person who gives sb the use of a building, an area of land, etc. on a LEASE → LANDLORD See note at EMPLOYER

'Less than Con'tainer 'Load *noun* [C] (*abbr* LCL)
(*Transport*) an amount of goods being transported for sb that does not fill one whole container so will be transported with other goods: *We offer a less-than-container-load service to and from Europe.* → FULL CONTAINER LOAD

let /let/ *verb, noun*
● *verb* [+ obj] (**letting, let, let**) (*especially BrE*) **let sth (out)** (**to sb**) to allow sb to use rooms, a building, etc. in return for regular payments: *They decided to let out the smaller offices at low rents.*
[IDM] **let sb 'go** (*informal*) to make sb have to leave their job: *They're having to let 100 employees go because of falling profits.* ◇ *I'm going to have to let you go* (=dismiss you).
● *noun* [C] (*BrE*)
an act of renting a home, etc: *We have three industrial units available on a short-term let.*

letter /'letə(r)/ *noun, adjective*
● *noun* [C]

SEE ALSO: **comfort letter, commitment ~, cover ~, covering ~, form ~**

1 a message that is written down or printed on paper and usually put in an envelope and sent to sb: *a letter of complaint* ◇ *Who is the letter addressed to?* ◇ *You will be notified by letter.* ◇ *guidelines for writing effective sales letters* (= to possible customers)
● to *mail/post/send* a letter ◆ to *draft/write* a letter ◆ to *get/open/receive* a letter ◆ to *acknowledge/answer/reply to* a letter ◆ *a business/personal/formal/informal* letter
2 a written or printed sign representing a sound used in speech: *Your business card looks more impressive if you have letters after your name* (= showing your qualifications).
[IDM] **the ,letter of the 'law** the exact words of a law or rule rather than its general meaning: *Although the company sticks to the letter of the law, its employment practices are clearly unfair.* **to the 'letter** exactly what sb/sth says, paying attention to every detail: *I followed your instructions to the letter.*
● *adjective* (*AmE*) = LETTER-SIZE

letterhead /'letəhed; *AmE* 'letər-/ *noun* [C]
the name and address of a business that is printed at the top of the paper it uses for letters: *The logo appears in the company letterhead.*

,letter of ad'vice *noun* [C]
(*Commerce*) a letter that is sent to sb giving them some information or telling them of sth that the sender has done

,letter of appli'cation (*also* appli'cation ,letter, *less frequent*) *noun* [C]
(*HR*) a letter written by sb who is asking to be considered for a job, usually one that has been advertised: *Send your CV, a letter of application and*

the names and addresses of two referees to the Director of Personnel Services.

,letter of ap'pointment (also ap'pointment ,letter, less frequent) noun [C]
(HR) a letter from an employer offering sb a job and giving details of pay and conditions: The salary and salary scale are as stated in individual letters of appointment.

,letter of at'torney = POWER OF ATTORNEY

,letter of 'comfort (also 'comfort ,letter) noun [C]
(Finance) a letter that a company writes to a bank to support a SUBSIDIARY company (= a company that it owns) that needs to borrow money: A letter of comfort has been provided by the parent company in order to secure the $100 000 loan.

,letter of 'credit noun [C] (abbr l.c., L/C)
(Finance; Trade) a letter that a bank prepares for a customer in which it agrees to pay sb an amount of money under particular circumstances, used especially as a way of paying for imported goods: The importer asks the bank to **issue** a letter of credit on his behalf. → DOCUMENTARY CREDIT

,letter of en'gagement (also en'gagement ,letter) noun [C]
(HR) a letter which states the conditions under which sb is employed to do work for a company

,letter of in'demnity noun [C]
(Law) a letter from one person, company, etc. to another in which they agree to be responsible for particular damage, loss, etc. if it happens

,letter of in'tent noun [C]
(Law, formal) a formal letter in which sb states what they intend to do about sth. It is not a promise or a legal contract but shows that they are serious about doing sth: They have signed a letter of intent to buy 10% of the company.

,letter of 'licence (AmE spelling ~ license) noun [C]
(Law) a letter in which sb who is owed money agrees to allow the person who owes the money more time in which to pay

,letter of re'gret (also re'gret ,letter) noun [C]
a letter that is sent to a person who has had an interview, a company that has tried to win a contract, etc., to tell them that they have not been successful

lettershop /'letəʃɒp; AmE 'letərʃɑːp/ noun [C]
(Marketing) a company that organizes and sends letters or advertisements to large numbers of people for other companies

'letter-size (also 'letter) adjective (both AmE)
used to describe paper that is 8½ inches (215.9 mm) wide and 11 inches (279.4 mm) long

letting /'letɪŋ/ noun [U,C]
(Property) the act of allowing sb to use a building or part of a building in return for regular payments; a period of time when this is done or a building that is used in this way: an office letting agency ◇ evening/weekend lettings

★ level /'levl/ noun, adjective, verb
● noun

SEE ALSO: entry level, high-~, price ~, top-~

1 [C] the amount of sth that exists in a particular situation at a particular time: low levels of investment ◇ a high level of risk ◇ attempts to raise production levels ◇ Profits were at the same level as the year before.
❍ a high/low level of sth ◆ to control/improve/ increase/lower/raise the level of sth ◆ a level rises/ falls/stays the same/varies

2 [C,U] a particular standard or quality: We offer the highest level of customer service. ◇ This research will take technology to another level.
❍ a high/low level (of sth) ◆ an advanced/a basic/an elementary level ◆ to achieve/reach a level

3 [C,U] a position on a scale of quantity or value: The euro has dropped to its lowest level since 2003.
❍ a high/low level ◆ to break above/drop below/drop to/fall below a level

4 [U,C] a position or rank in an organization or a system: a decision taken **at** board level ◇ Employees at every level will be affected by the changes.
❍ a high/low level ◆ a junior/senior level ◆ an international/a local/national level ◆ to reach/rise to a level

IDM on the 'level (AmE also on the ,up and 'up) (informal) honest; legal: Are you sure this deal is on the level?
● adjective

1 having a flat surface that does not slope
2 having the same value or position as sth: This latest rise is intended to keep wages level **with** inflation.
→ idiom at PLAYING FIELD
● verb [+ obj] (-ll-, AmE -l-)
to make sth equal or similar: New technology has a levelling effect on industries.
PHRV ,level 'down; ,level sth 'down to become the same low or lower level as sth; to make standards, amounts, etc. be of the same low or lower level: The company is aiming to level down the salaries of its executives to cut costs. ,level 'off/'out to stay at a steady level of development or progress after a period of sharp rises or falls: Sales have levelled off after a period of rapid growth.
SYN FLATTEN OFF/OUT ,level sth 'up to make standards, amounts, etc. be of the same high or higher level: We need to level up our after-sales service to the standard of our products.

lever /'liːvə(r); AmE 'levər/ noun, verb
● noun [C]
1 a handle used to operate a piece of machinery or a vehicle: Pull the lever towards you to start the machine.
2 an action or thing that is used to persuade sb to do sth: The company used every possible lever to secure the deal. ◇ a powerful lever **for** change
● verb [+ obj]
to move sth with a **lever**: (figurative) The government is hoping to lever money from private investors for the project.

★ leverage /'liːvərɪdʒ; AmE 'lev-/ noun, verb
● noun [U]

SEE ALSO: debt leverage

1 the ability to influence sth: Large stores use their size as leverage to lower suppliers' prices.
2 (Finance) (especially AmE) the relationship between the amount of money that a company owes (**debt**) and the value of its shares (**equity**)
SYN GEARING
3 (Finance) (especially AmE) using borrowed money to buy an investment or to add to the amount invested, in order to try to increase possible profits from the investment: The buyout provided a high return on investment and excellent leverage.
● verb [+ obj]
1 to get as much advantage or profit as possible from sth that you have: A consultant can advise you on leveraging the skills of your workforce.
2 (Finance) to use borrowed money to buy an investment or to add to the amount invested, in order to try to increase possible profits from the investment: a leveraged takeover bid

3 to attract money or other advantages: *The design award we won leveraged large loans from several sources.*

▶ **'leveraging** *noun* [U]

PHR V **,leverage 'up**; **,leverage sth 'up 1** (*Finance*) if a company or an investor **leverages up**, they borrow more money in order to try to increase profits: *For years companies have leveraged up to boost shareholder returns.* **2** to increase or improve sth: *Our software will leverage up your efficiency.*

leveraged /'liːvərɪdʒd; *AmE* 'lev-/ *adjective*

SEE ALSO: **over-leveraged**

(*Finance*)
1 (about a company or an organization) having borrowed a large amount of money in relation to the value of the shares it has sold: *Businesses such as banks and credit-card companies are highly leveraged.*
2 (about an investment) involving a large amount of borrowed money: *a highly-leveraged transaction* ◇ *a leveraged buyout/takeover*
→ GEARED, LBO

'lever arch file *noun* [C]
a type of file for holding papers in which metal rings that are opened and closed with a **lever** go through the edges of the pages, holding them in place—Picture at FILE

levy /'levi/ *noun*, *verb*
• *noun* [C] (*plural* **levies**)

SEE ALSO: **capital levy**

(*Finance*) an extra amount of money that has to be paid, especially as a tax to the government: *The government has imposed a levy of 20% on most imports.*
O *to be exempt from/pay* a levy • *to impose/ introduce/put* a levy *on* sth • *to abolish/end* a levy
• *verb* [+ obj] (**levies**, **levying**, **levied**, **levied**)
to demand and collect a payment, tax, etc: *A tax of 15% is levied on the sale of shares.*

LFL /,el ef 'el/ = LIKE-FOR-LIKE

★ **liability** /,laɪəˈbɪləti/ *noun* (*plural* **liabilities**)

SEE ALSO: **accrued liability, admission of ~, contingency ~, contingent ~, current ~, deferred ~, deposit liabilities**, etc.

1 (*Accounting*; *Finance*) [C, usually pl.] the amount of money that a company or a person owes: *The company is reported to have liabilities of nearly €90 000.* ◇ *We need to make sure we have enough money set aside to meet future liabilities.* **SYN** DEBT
→ ASSET
O *to have/take on* liabilities • *to cover/match/meet/ reduce* liabilities • *future/long-term/potential/ short-term* liabilities • *insurance/pension/tax* liabilities
2 (*Law*) [U] the state of being legally responsible for sth: *The company cannot accept liability for any damage caused by natural disasters.* → LIABLE
O *to accept/admit/deny/have* liability (*for sth*) • *full/ legal* liability

lia'bility in,surance (*also* lia'bility ,cover) *noun* [U]
insurance that a person or an organization buys to protect them against legal claims made by others, for example by people who suffer an injury while on their property: *The company must display a copy of their certificate of employer's liability insurance.*

★ **liable** /'laɪəbl/ *adjective* [not before noun]
(*Law*)
1 legally responsible for paying the cost of sth: *Are the manufacturers liable for any damage their products do?* ◇ *The partners were held personally*

liable *for the debts of the firm.* See note at RESPONSIBLE
2 likely to be punished by law for sth: *Offenders are liable to fines of up to $500.*
3 having to do sth by law: *The supply of services is liable to VAT.*

liaise /li'eɪz/ *verb* [no obj]
1 (*especially BrE*) to work closely with sb and exchange information with them: *I have been liaising closely with the marketing department.*
2 to act as a link between two or more people or groups: *His job is to liaise between the staff and management.*

liberalize, **-ise** /'lɪbrəlaɪz/ *verb* [+ obj]
to make the rules that apply to an activity, an industry, etc. less strict; to make it easier for more people to take part: *plans to liberalize world trade* ◇ *The country's energy market has been fully liberalized for some time.* ▶ **liberalization, -isation** /,lɪbrəlaɪ'zeɪʃn; *AmE* -lə'z-/ *noun* [U]: *economic/ market/trade liberalization*

LIBOR /'laɪbɔː(r)/ = LONDON INTER-BANK OFFERED RATE

★ **licence** (*AmE spelling* **license**) /'laɪsns/ *noun* [C]

SEE ALSO: **letter of licence, practicing license**

(*Law*) an official document that shows that permission has been given to do, own or use sth: (*BrE*) *a driving licence* ◇ *a licence for the software* ◇ *The company won a licence to operate a mobile phone network.* ◇ *a licence holder* (= a person who has been given a licence)
O *to have/hold/get/own* a licence • *to apply for/ renew* a licence • *to grant/issue/refuse/suspend/ take away* a licence • *a licence expires/runs out*
IDM **a licence to print 'money** (*informal*) used to describe a business which makes a lot of money with little effort **under 'licence** (about a product) made with the permission of a company or an organization: *The vehicles are manufactured under licence from Toyota.*

'licence a,greement (*AmE spelling* **license ~**) *noun* [C]
(*Law*) a legal document with a piece of software that states it can be used and how many people can use it

'licence fee (*AmE spelling* **license ~**) (*also* **'licensing fee**, *especially in AmE*) *noun* [C]
an amount of money paid to a business or an authority in order to obtain a licence: *They are charging a licence fee of $100 per user of the software.*

★ **license** /'laɪsns/ *verb*, *noun*
• *verb* [+ obj]
(*Commerce*; *Law*) to give a person or an organization official permission to do, own, or use sth, often in exchange for a fee: *The drug has not yet been licensed in Europe.* ◇ *We license the technology to other manufacturers.* ◇ *They had licensed the firm to produce the drug.* ◇ *They rely heavily on licensing income.*
• *noun* [C] (*AmE*)
(*Law*) = LICENCE **HELP** You will find words formed with **license** at the spelling **licence**.

licensed /'laɪsnst/ *adjective*
(*Commerce*)
1 having official permission to do, make or use sth: *licensed dealers* ◇ *We are licensed to make the toys.*
2 that you have official permission to make, own or use: *licensed products* ◇ *licensed cabs*

licensee /,laɪsənˈsiː/ *noun* [C]
(*Law*) a person or company who has been given official permission to do, make, own or use sth
→ LICENSOR

'licensing fee = LICENCE FEE

licensor (*also spelled* **licenser**) /ˈlaɪsənsə(r)/ *noun*
[C]
(*Law*) a person or an organization that gives a
licence to sb: *the licensor of the software* → LICENSEE
See note at EMPLOYER

lien /ˈliːən; liːn/ *noun* [C]

SEE ALSO: **tax lien**

(*Law*) a right to keep property belonging to sb else
until they pay what they owe: *A mechanic may
claim a lien **over** a car he is repairing.* ◇ *They hold a
lien **on** the shares as security for the debt.* ◇ *The
mortgage lender will check for liens **against** the
property.*
➊ *to claim/exercise/have/hold a lien*
▶ **lienee** /ˌliːəˈniː; ˌliːˈniː/ *noun* [C] **lienor**
/ˈliːənɔː(r); ˈliːnɔː(r)/ *noun* [C]

lieu /luː; *BrE also* ljuː/ *noun*
IDM **in lieu (of sth)** (*formal*) instead (of sth): *She
received six months' salary in lieu of notice.*
→ TIME OFF IN LIEU

life /laɪf/ *noun*

SEE ALSO: **depreciable life, economic ~, expectation
of ~, job for ~, non-~, shelf ~, useful ~,** etc.

1 [C] the period of time when sth exists or works,
is good enough to use, etc: *You will pay the same
interest rate over the life of the loan.* ◇ *The restaurant
began life as a factory canteen.* ◇ *methods of
prolonging the storage life of fresh fruit* (= the time it
can be stored)
2 [U,C] (*often used with an adjective*) the activities
and experiences that are typical of a particular way
of living or working: *city life* ◇ *Internal competition
is a natural part of corporate life.*
3 [C] (*often used with an adjective*) the period of time
that sb spends in a particular situation: *She was
looking for a better balance between her personal life
and her business life.*
→ idiom at WALK *noun*

'life as‚surance = LIFE INSURANCE

'life-‚balance *adjective* [only before noun]
(*HR*) used to describe the relationship between your
work and the rest of your life

lifeblood /ˈlaɪfblʌd/ *noun* [U]
the thing that keeps sth strong and healthy and
allows it to continue successfully: *Money is the
lifeblood of any company.* ◇ *The disaster is
threatening the area's economic lifeblood.*

lifeboat /ˈlaɪfbəʊt; *AmE* -boot/ *noun* [C]
(*Finance*) (used in newspapers) financial help given
to a company that is in trouble: *The troubled
company is hoping for a financial lifeboat from the
banks.* **NOTE** A **lifeboat** is a special boat that is sent
out to rescue people who are in danger at sea.

'life ‚cycle *noun* [C]

SEE ALSO: **product life cycle**

the period during which a product, a project, or an
organization exists; the developments and changes
which occur during this period: *the natural life cycle
of new businesses* ◇ *The tasks will vary over the life
cycle of the project.* ◇ *These models are nearing the
end of their life cycles.*

'life ex‚pectancy *noun* [U,C]
1 (*also* ‚**expectation of 'life**) the number of years
that a person is likely to live: *Pension fund managers
have to cope with longer life expectancy and new
pension regulations.*
2 the length of time that sth is likely to exist or
continue for: *the short life expectancy of dotcoms*
3 the length of time that an asset is likely to be
used for

'life fund *noun* [C]
money that is paid to insurance companies for LIFE

INSURANCE and invested by them. Claims are paid
from this money: *The present value of the life fund is
about $18 billion.* ◇ *a with-profits life fund*

'life in‚surance (*BrE also* **'life as‚surance**) *noun*
[U]
a type of insurance in which you make a single
payment or regular payments so that you receive a
sum of money when you are a particular age, or so
that your family will receive a sum of money when
you die: *Sales of life insurance and annuities have
increased.* ◇ *life insurance companies* ◇ *payouts on
life insurance policies*

lifeline /ˈlaɪflaɪn/ *noun* [C, usually sing.]
help given to a person or an organization that is in
trouble; sth that sb/sth depends on: *The
government **threw** a financial lifeline to the industry.*
◇ *The deal will offer a much-needed lifeline to the
firm.*

‚lifelong 'learning *noun* [U]
(*HR*) the idea that employees need to keep
developing their knowledge and skills throughout
their working lives: *Universities are working with
businesses and local people to promote lifelong
learning.*

lifespan /ˈlaɪfspæn/ *noun* [C]
the length of time that sth will last, will be useful,
or will be wanted: *The product has a 10-year
lifespan.* ◇ *the lifespan of the software*

lifestyle /ˈlaɪfstaɪl/ *noun* [C,U]
the way in which a person or a group of people
lives and works: *They borrowed heavily to support
their lavish lifestyle* (= they spent a lot of money). ◇
*The food and health magazine is aimed at people
with busy lifestyles.* ◇ *Are you living a healthy
lifestyle?*
➊ *a comfortable/healthy/lavish/outdoor lifestyle* •
lifestyle brands/changes/choices/magazines

'life ‚tables (*also* mor'tality ‚tables) *noun* [pl.]
(*Insurance*) lists that show how many years people
in particular groups are expected to live, used in
calculating insurance risks

‚lifetime em'ployment *noun* [U]
(*HR*) when employees in an organization are
promised a job until they retire: *There is no
guarantee of full lifetime employment.* ◇ *the concept
of lifetime employment in Japan* → TENURE

‚lifetime 'value (*abbr* **LTV**) (*also* **'customer
'lifetime 'value** *abbr* **CLV**) *noun* [U]
(*Marketing*) the total amount of profit that a
company expects to make from each customer
during the period of time that they buy the
company's products

‚life-work 'balance (*also spelled* **life/work ~**)
= WORK-LIFE BALANCE

LIFFE /laɪf/ *abbr* **London International Financial
Futures and Options Exchange** a market for
buying and selling FUTURES and OPTIONS

LIFO /ˈlaɪfəʊ; *AmE* -oʊ/ = LAST IN, FIRST OUT
→ FIFO

lift /lɪft/ *verb, noun*
● *verb*
1 [+ obj] to make an amount or level of sth greater:
*The number of new jobs this year helped lift
consumer confidence and incomes.*
2 [+ obj *or no obj*] to become or to make sth
become more valuable or successful: *efforts to lift
the economy out of recession* ◇ *Some stocks lifted
yesterday.*
3 [+ obj] to remove or end a restriction, policy or
threat: *The ban was later lifted.* ◇ *efforts to lift
economic sanctions*

4 [+ obj] to raise sth to a higher position or level: *There are special ways of lifting large, heavy objects.* ▸ **'lifting** *noun* [U]: *a partial lifting of the ban* ◇ *Who will do the **heavy lifting**?*

● *noun*
1 [C, usually sing.] an increase in sth; an improvement in sth: *We recorded a 3% lift in sales in April.*
2 (*BrE*) (*AmE* **'elevator**) [C] a machine that carries people or goods up and down to different levels in a building or a mine: *It's on the sixth floor—let's take the lift.*

light /laɪt/ *adjective* (**lighter, lightest**)
1 not great in amount or degree: *Trading was light as many offices were closed.* ◇ *The job losses were lighter than at other banks.*
2 [only before noun] used to describe smaller vehicles, machines, etc. that are not of the most powerful type: *The plant will build light vehicles.* ◇ *Light truck sales were up 6 per cent.* ◇ *light manufacturing companies*
3 (*BrE*) **light on sth** not having a large amount or enough of sth: *It's a service company, very light on assets.*
3 [usually before noun] not involving a lot of work or activity; not very busy: *My schedule is much lighter this week.*
4 not needing a lot of physical strength: *After his accident he was moved to lighter work.*
→ HEAVY
IDM **make light 'work of sth** to do sth quickly and with little effort: *The big six-cylinder engines made light work of the load.*

,light-'duty *adjective* [only before noun]
designed to carry or operate with normal or small loads: *small, light-duty trucks* [OPP] HEAVY-DUTY
→ MEDIUM-DUTY

,light engi'neering *noun* [U]
businesses that design and build machinery or equipment which is small or light; the activities of these businesses: *In the region there are light industries such as clothing, electronics and light engineering.* → HEAVY ENGINEERING

,light 'industry *noun* [U,C]
businesses that produce small or light goods, such as things used in the house, using small machines and factories: *the shift towards light industry and service activities* → HEAVY INDUSTRY
▸ **,light in'dustrial** *adjective*: *light industrial goods/property*

,lightning 'strike *noun* [C] (*BrE*)
(*HR*) a strike by a group of workers that happens very suddenly → WILDCAT *adj.* (1)

'light pen *noun* [C]
(*IT*)
1 a piece of equipment, shaped like a pen, that is sensitive to light and can be used to pass information to a computer when it touches the screen
2 a similar piece of equipment that is used for reading BAR CODES

lightweight /'laɪtweɪt/ *adjective*
1 not heavy: *lightweight materials like aluminium* ◇ *lightweight laptops*
2 not as powerful or successful as other people or things
→ HEAVYWEIGHT
▸ **'lightweight** *noun* [C]: *He is considered a lightweight.*

,like-for-'like *adjective* [only before noun] (*abbr* LFL)
(*Accounting*) used to describe figures that are adjusted to allow comparison with a similar period,

excluding for example any new stores or businesses or any unusual activities: *Warm weather helped trading in August, with like-for-like sales up 5.9%.* ◇ *Full-year like-for-like growth was 4.8%.* ◇ *Operating profits fell 11.2 per cent on a like-for-like basis.*
→ SAME-STORE SALES
ⓞ *like-for-like* **figures/growth/revenues/sales**
▸ **,like-for-'like** *adverb*: *Sales grew by 1.7%, but fell by 1.5% like-for-like.*

,like-for-'likes *noun* [pl.]
(*Accounting, informal*) figures that have been adjusted so that they can be compared with figures for a similar period, excluding for example any new stores or businesses or any unusual activities: *They have seen like-for-likes slip in the past year due to increased competition and falling sales.* ◇ *Hotels had reported an 8% increase in like-for-likes for the beginning of the year.*

limit /'lɪmɪt/ *noun, verb*
● *noun* [C]

SEE ALSO: **credit limit, floor ~, time ~**

the greatest or smallest amount of sth that is possible or allowed: *Some banks set a daily limit on cash withdrawals.* ◇ *to keep government spending within acceptable limits*
● *verb* [+ obj]
1 to stop sth from increasing beyond a particular amount or level: *The agreement with the union limits the number of layoffs to 400.*
2 **limit yourself/sb (to sth)** to restrict or reduce the amount of sth that you or sb can have or use: *Employees are limited to two short breaks a day.*
PHRV **'limit sth to sb/sth** (*usually* **be limited to**) to make sth exist or happen only in a particular place or within a particular group: *The service will be limited to the US market.*

limitation /ˌlɪmɪ'teɪʃn/ *noun* [C]

SEE ALSO: **damage limitation**

a rule, fact or condition that limits sth: *to impose limitations on imports* ◇ *Make clear the budget available and any budgetary limitations.* [SYN] CURB, RESTRAINT

limi,tation of lia'bility *noun* [U,C]
(*Law*) the fact that sb's responsibility for sth such as damage, loss, etc., especially their financial responsibility, is limited

Limited /'lɪmɪtɪd/ *adjective*
used in the UK after the name of a LIMITED COMPANY: *LW Investments Limited* → LTD

limited /'lɪmɪtɪd/ *adjective*
1 restricted; only for a particular time, particular numbers, etc: *This offer is for a limited period only.*
2 not great in amount or extent; small: *a limited product range* ◇ *He has limited experience in this area.* ◇ *We are doing our best with the limited resources available.*

,limited 'company *noun* [C]

SEE ALSO: **public limited company**

in the UK, a company whose owners have responsibility for paying only a limited amount of the company's debt → PRIVATE COMPANY

,limited lia'bility *noun* [U]
(*Law*) the legal position in which shareholders of a company are only responsible for the money they have given if the company cannot pay its debts: *The firm is a limited liability partnership.*

,limited 'partnership *noun* [C] (*abbr* LP)
a business owned by two or more people who are responsible only for the amount that they have invested in the business if it is unable to pay its debts: *He set up a limited partnership.* ▸ **,limited 'partner** *noun* [C]

SEE ALSO: **buy limit order, sell limit order**

(*Stock Exchange*) an order not to sell shares below a particular price, or not to buy shares above a particular price

linchpin (*also spelled* **lynchpin**) /'lɪntʃpɪn/ *noun* [C, usually sing.]
the person or thing that an organization or a project depends on; the most important person or thing: *Consumers are the linchpin of the economy.*

★**line** /laɪn/ *noun, verb*
● *noun*

SEE ALSO: **above-the-line, assembly ~, below-the-~, bottom ~, credit ~, dotted ~, firing ~,** etc.

1 [C] a type of product made or sold by the same company: *We sell an exclusive line of children's clothing.* ◇ *Dell has recently moved to expand its line of products.* SYN RANGE
2 [C] a system of making sth in a factory, in which the product moves from one worker to the next until it is finished: *A new car rolled off the line every 49 seconds.* ◇ *teams of line workers*
3 [C] a telephone connection; a particular telephone number: *If you hold the line* (= stay on the telephone and wait), *I'll see if she is available.* ◇ *Your bill includes line rental.* → HELPLINE, HOTLINE
4 [C, usually sing.] a series of people in order of importance: *a line of command* ◇ *He is second in line to the chairman.* ◇ *Orders came down the line from the very top.* → LINE MANAGER
5 [sing.] a type or area of business, activity or interest: *My line of work pays pretty well.*
→ SIDELINE
6 [C] a supply of sth such as credit: *The company has already put in place new lines of credit to cover about $100 m.*
7 [C] (*AmE*) = QUEUE (1,2)
8 [C] (*often used in names*) a company that provides transport for people or goods: *The two cruise lines said they remained confident of success.*
→ AIRLINE
9 (*Finance*) [C] a number or group of a particular share, bond, etc: *a line of 1.9 m shares*
IDM **be, come, etc. on 'line 1** to start to operate; to become available: *The new working methods will come on line in June.* **2** using or connected to a computer or the Internet; communicating with other people by computer: *All our offices are now on line.*
→ ONLINE **be in the line of 'fire** to be in a position where people can criticize or blame you **bring sb/sth, come, get, fall, etc. into 'line (with sb/sth)** to behave or make sb/sth behave in the same way as other people or how they should behave: *We need to bring capacity into line with demand.* **in 'line** under control or at an appropriate or expected level: *It takes some time for a big company to get expenses in line.* **in 'line (for sth)** likely to get sth: *She is in line for promotion.* **in 'line with sth** similar to sth or so that one thing is closely connected with another: *Annual pay increases will be in line with inflation.* **(put sth) on the 'line** (*informal*) at risk: *The proposed cutbacks have put 5 000 jobs on the line.* **toe the 'line** (*AmE also* **toe the 'mark**) to do what sb in authority tells or orders you to do, even if you do not think it is right
→ idioms at CROSS, FIRING LINE, LAY, OUT, SIGN *verb*
● *verb*
IDM **line your (own)/sb's 'pockets** to get richer or make sb richer, especially by taking unfair advantage of a situation or by being dishonest: *Why should I work 16 hours a day to line someone else's pockets?*
PHR V **line 'up** to stand in a line or row; to form a QUEUE: *We've had people lining up outside the store since 4 a.m.* **line 'up (behind sb/sth)** to support sb/sth on a particular issue: *Other Board members appear to have lined up behind the CEO.* **line sb/sth 'up** to arrange for an event or activity to happen, or arrange for sb to be available to do sth: *They had lined up a manufacturer to fill the order.*

lineage /'laɪnɪdʒ/ *noun* [U]
(*Marketing*) the total amount of space used by an advertisement

'line au,thority *noun* [U]
(*HR*) the power that managers have to control and give orders to the people that they are responsible for, in order to achieve the things that their own managers expect

'line chart = LINE GRAPH

'line ex,tension *noun* [C,U]
(*Marketing*) a new product that is closely related to existing products and is sold using an existing brand name; the practice of marketing products in this way: *We are developing two new apple flavours as a line extension of our best-selling classic apple juice.*

'line ,filling *noun* [U]
(*Marketing*) the activity of adding new products to an existing range in order to make the range more complete: *Line filling closes gaps in the market and keeps competitors out.*

'line graph (*also* **'line chart**) *noun* [C]
a type of graph which displays data by means of a series of points connected by a line: *This line graph shows sales trends over the five-year period.*

line graph

'line ,management *noun* (*BrE*)
(*HR*)
1 [U] a system of organizing a company in which information and instructions are passed from each employee or manager to the person one rank above or below them: *Newly-qualified staff start out at the bottom of a system of line management.*
2 [U with sing./pl. verb] the managers in a company who are responsible for the main activities of the company, such as manufacturing, sales, etc: *Line management is/are responsible for ensuring that production targets are met.*

'line ,manager *noun* [C]
(*HR*)
1 a person who has a number of employees working under them and who is responsible for giving them work and checking how they develop: *I have regular one-to-one meetings with my line manager.* → DIRECT REPORT See note at BOSS
2 a manager who is involved in running the main business activities of a company

,line of 'credit = CREDIT LINE

'line ,stretching (*also* **'product line ,stretching**) *noun* [U]
(*Marketing*) the activity of adding new products to an existing range that are higher or lower in price, in order to attract a different group of customers: *For the luxury car manufacturer, line stretching means producing a car for the middle range of the market.*

★**link** /lɪŋk/ *noun, verb*
● *noun* [C]
1 a relationship between two or more people, countries or organizations: *to establish/maintain trade links* **with** *Asia* ◇ *The project will strengthen links between the two companies.*

2 a means of travelling or communicating between two places: *a high-speed rail link* ◇ *a link road* ◇ *a telephone/video link*
3 (*IT*) a place in an electronic document which connects one part of the document to another part or connects the document to a different one and moves you there if you click on it: *Click here for related links.* ◇ *The site has links to a list of search engines.*
● *verb* [+ obj] (*often* be **linked**)
1 link A to/with B ǀ link A and B (**together**) to make a connection between people, places, or things: *The Channel Tunnel links Britain with the rest of Europe.* ◇ *The computers are linked together in a network.*
2 link A to/with B to say that there is a connection or relationship between two or more things or people: *The company is being linked with a bid to take over a rival supermarket chain.* ◇ *He had been linked to the vacant post of chief executive.*
3 (*Finance*) if the value of an investment, a currency, or a payment **is linked** to something else, it changes in the same way that the other thing does: *All our investments were linked to the stock market.* ◇ *The country's currency is linked to the US dollar.* → INDEX-LINKED
4 (*IT*) link A to/with B to connect websites or parts of a web page so that a user can move to another website or part of a document by clicking: *Link your site to ours.*
PHR V ,link 'up (with sb/sth) to work with another company or organization to achieve something: *The designers have linked up with Britain's largest furniture maker.* → LINK-UP

linkage /'lɪŋkɪdʒ/ *noun*
1 [U] the act of linking things; the state of being linked: *We examine proposals to ensure linkage with company policy.*
2 [C] a connection between things: *The study identified important linkages between economic and political change.*
3 [C] an agreement to work with another company or organization to achieve something: *We have established a linkage with a local college to provide training for new recruits.*
4 [U] the act of making one part of an agreement depend on another: *the linkage of pay to productivity*

'**link-up** *noun* [C]
a connection formed between two things, for example two companies or two broadcasting systems: *There are rumours of a link-up between the two big carmakers.* ◇ *a video link-up with the conference* → LINK UP (WITH SB/STH) at LINK *verb*

the '**lion's share** *noun* [sing.] (*BrE*)
the largest or best part of something when it is divided: *Software sales account for the lion's share of the company's profits.*

liquid /'lɪkwɪd/ *adjective*
(*Accounting*; *Finance*)
1 (about assets) that can easily be sold and changed into cash: *The company has $2.8 billion in cash and other liquid assets.* ◇ *highly liquid shares*
2 (about a company, an investor, etc.) having cash or assets that can easily be changed into cash: *They have a strong position and are among the most liquid companies in the industry.*
3 a **liquid** market is one in which there is a lot of buying and selling: *In this highly liquid market, prices are relatively stable.*
OPP ILLIQUID—Picture at LIQUIDITY

★ **liquidate** /'lɪkwɪdeɪt/ *verb*
1 (*Law*) [+ obj *or* no obj] to sell a company's assets and pay its debts in order to close it: *The bankruptcy court has ordered the company to liquidate.* ◇ *If the deal falls through, the tour operator is likely to be liquidated.* **SYN** WIND UP See note at BANKRUPT
2 (*Accounting*; *Finance*) [+ obj] to sell sth in order to get money or to avoid losing money: *The group announced plans to liquidate its assets.* **SYN** REALIZE
3 (*Accounting*) [+ obj] to pay a debt: *This land was sold for the purpose of liquidating debts.*

,liquidated 'damages *noun* [pl.]
(*Law*) in a contract, a fixed amount of money that sb agrees to pay if they do not do what they have promised: *If the building is not completed in time, the contractors must pay liquidated damages.*

★ **liquidation** /ˌlɪkwɪ'deɪʃn/ *noun* [U]

SEE ALSO: compulsory liquidation, forced ~, involuntary ~, voluntary ~

1 (*Law*) the process of closing a company, selling its assets and paying its debts. *The firm has gone into liquidation.* ◇ *Shareholders are worried that the group will be put into liquidation.* **SYN** WINDING UP See note at BANKRUPT
2 (*Accounting*; *Finance*) the action of selling sth to get money or to avoid losing money: *Falling prices may lead to further liquidation of stocks.* → BANKRUPTCY, RECEIVERSHIP

liquidator /'lɪkwɪdeɪtə(r)/ *noun* [C]
(*Law*) a person responsible for selling a company's assets and paying its debts, so that it can be closed: *The board has appointed liquidators to wind up the company.* → ADMINISTRATOR (2), RECEIVER (1)
❍ to **appoint/call in** liquidators

liquidity

more ↑   **cash**

         current accounts

         shares, bonds, etc.

liquid   **high interest deposit accounts**

         certificates of deposit

         loans

less ↓   **physical assets, property, machinery, etc.**

liquidity /lɪ'kwɪdəti/ *noun* [U]
(*Finance*)
1 the state of owning cash or things of value that can easily be exchanged for cash in order to pay debts, etc: *Asset sales are intended to improve the company's liquidity.* ◇ *The commercial banks' liquidity is recovering.* ◇ *The airline is facing a liquidity crisis.*
2 the quality of being easy to exchange for cash: *Shareholders will benefit from an increase in liquidity of their investment.*
3 the amount of trading that takes place in a market: *Investors are concerned about market liquidity.*
→ ILLIQUID

li'quidity ,preference *noun* [U]
(*Economics*) the way that people, especially investors, prefer to have money or assets that can easily be exchanged for cash

li'quidity ,ratio *noun* [C]
(*Accounting*) a way of measuring a company's ability to pay its debts by comparing the amount of money that it holds in cash or assets that can easily be

changed into cash and its LIABILITIES (= the amount of money it owes): *The bank is required to have a liquidity ratio of 25%.* SYN CASH RATIO

li'quidity risk *noun* [C,U]
(*Finance*) the possibility that a person or company will not be able to pay the money they owe because they do not have enough cash or assets that can easily be exchanged for cash

'liquid ,ratio = ACID-TEST RATIO

list /lɪst/ *noun, verb*
● *noun* [C]

SEE ALSO: A-list, Daily Official ~, focus ~, hit ~, laundry ~, legal ~, Lloyd's ~, etc.

a series of names, items, figures, etc., especially when they are written or printed: *We'll send you a list of current prices.* ◇ *His name is on the list of candidates for the post.* → SHORTLIST
❍ *to* **compile/draw up/make** *a list*
● *verb*
1 [+ obj] to provide a list of things in a particular order: *The directory lists more than 900 000 lawyers and law firms.*
2 (*Stock Exchange*) [+ obj or no obj] to make shares in a company available for trading on a stock exchange: *The company has applied to list its shares on the New York Stock Exchange.*
3 [+ obj or no obj] (*AmE*) to advertise sth for sale at a particular price; to be advertised for sale at a particular price: *There has been an increase in the number of homes listed at $750 000 or higher.* ◇ *The new model lists for $28 105.*

'list box *noun* [C]
(*IT*) a list of choices in a box on a computer screen

listed /'lɪstɪd/ *adjective*
(*Stock Exchange*)
1 a **listed** company is one whose shares may be bought and sold on a stock exchange: *the government's holdings in listed companies* ◇ *The target of the takeover bid is a firm which is not listed.*
◇ *a London-listed bank*
❍ *a listed* **business/company/firm/subsidiary**
2 that may be bought and sold on a stock exchange: *The value of listed stocks has fallen sharply.*
❍ *listed* **equity/securities/shares/stocks**
SYN QUOTED OPP UNLISTED

listener /'lɪsənə(r)/ *noun* [C]
someone who listens to a particular radio programme or station → VIEWER

listing /'lɪstɪŋ/ *noun* [C]

SEE ALSO: application for listing, dual listing

1 (*Stock Exchange*) a place on the official list of companies whose shares can be bought and sold on a stock exchange: *The company is seeking a stock exchange listing.* ◇ *They face losing their listings on the New York Stock Exchange and NASDAQ.*
2 a list, especially an official or published list of people or things, often arranged in alphabetical order: *a comprehensive listing of all airlines*

listless /'lɪstləs/ *adjective*
developing or happening more slowly than usual: *Retail sales were listless during the summer months.*

'list price (*AmE also* **'sticker price**) *noun* [C]
(*Commerce*) the advertised or published price for sth, especially a car: *The store offers savings of as much as 70% off the manufacturer's list price.* ◇ *These cars carry a sticker price of under $13 000.*

'list ,rental *noun* [U]
(*Marketing*) an arrangement in which the owner of a list of the names and addresses of possible customers allows it to be used on a temporary basis by another organization in exchange for a fee:

Email list rental can be an excellent way to reach new customers. ▶ **'list ,renting** *noun* [U]

lite /laɪt/ *adjective*
(often used in the names of food or drink) light; containing less fat or sugar than other similar food or drink and therefore less likely to make you fat: *lite ice cream*

literature /'lɪtrətʃə(r)/ *AmE also* -tʃʊr/ *noun* [U]
pieces of writing or printed information on a particular subject, such as a product or a company: *promotional/sales literature*

litigant /'lɪtɪɡənt/ *noun* [C]
(*Law*) a person who is making or defending a claim in court: *Unsuccessful litigants have the right to appeal.*

★ **litigate** /'lɪtɪɡeɪt/ *verb* [+ obj or no obj]
(*Law*) to take a claim or disagreement to court: *The workers obtained reasonable compensation without having to litigate.* ◇ *The lawyer can tell you how long it will take to litigate the case.*
❍ *to litigate a* **case/claim/issue**

litigation /,lɪtɪ'ɡeɪʃn/ *noun* [U]
(*Law*) the process of making or defending a claim in court: *The company is* **in** *litigation over copyright issues.*

litigator /'lɪtɪɡeɪtə(r)/ *noun* [C] (*AmE*)
(*Law*) a lawyer who presents or defends a claim in a court of law: *an international trade litigator*

litigious /lɪ'tɪdʒəs/ *adjective* (*formal*)
too ready to take disputes to a court of law: *Dissatisfied consumers are becoming increasingly litigious.* ▶ **li'tigiousness** *noun* [U]

livelihood /'laɪvlihʊd/ *noun* [U; C, usually sing.]
a means of earning money in order to live: *Many people depend on agriculture for their livelihood.* ◇ *Hundreds of workers may* **lose** *their livelihoods.*

livery /'lɪvəri/ *noun* [C,U] (*plural* **liveries**) (*BrE*)
(*Marketing*) the colours used by a particular company for its vehicles or products: *aircraft painted in the new British Airways livery* ◇ *their distinctive gold and green livery*

livestock /'laɪvstɒk; *AmE* -stɑːk/ *noun* [U; pl.]
the animals kept by farmers as a source of income, for example cows or sheep: *The severe weather poses a threat to both crops and livestock.*

living /'lɪvɪŋ/ *noun*

SEE ALSO: cost of living, standard of living

1 [C, usually sing.] money to buy the things that you need in life: *She earns her living as a freelance journalist.* ◇ *What do you* **do for a living**?
❍ *to* **earn/make** *a living* • *a* **good/decent/modest** *living*
2 [U] a way or style of life: *People are moving away because of the high costs of urban living.* ◇ *a period of economic growth and rising living standards*
❍ **daily/day-to-day/everyday** *living* • **rural/urban** *living* • *living* **conditions/standards**

,living 'trust *noun* [C]
(*Law*) an arrangement which allows sb to transfer their assets to sb else while they are alive but keep control of them, used in order to avoid the legal process of dealing with a WILL when they die

,living 'wage *noun* [sing.]
a wage that is high enough for sb to buy the things they need in order to live: *The people who grow the coffee now get something like a living wage.* ◇ *unions fighting for a living wage*
❍ *to* **be paid/earn/receive** *a living wage* • *to* **offer/pay** *a living wage*

LLC /ˌel el ˈsiː/ *abbr* (*AmE*) (*usually used in written English*)
limited liability company (used after the name of a company or business) See note at LTD

Lloyd's /lɔɪdz/ (*also* ˌLloyd's of ˈLondon) *noun* [U]
(*Insurance*) an organization consisting of groups of insurance UNDERWRITERS (= people who provide insurance, agreeing to pay if there is any loss or damage), providing insurance especially for ships and large risks: *a Lloyd's insurance syndicate* ◇ *Lloyd's underwriters* → NAME (2)

ˌLloyd's ˈList *noun* [sing.]
(*Transport*) a daily newspaper providing information about ships and businesses associated with ships

ˌLloyd's of ˈLondon = LLOYD'S

ˌLloyd's ˈRegister (*also* ˈLloyd's ˈRegister of ˈShipping) *noun* [sing.] (*abbr* LR)
(*Transport*) a list of ships arranged in groups according to their size, with detailed information about them, published once a year; the organization that produces the list and sets the standards for the groups

LME /ˌel em ˈiː/ *abbr* **London Metal Exchange** a market for trading metals that are bought at agreed prices but delivered and paid for at a later time: *Copper prices on the LME fell sharply.*

load /ləʊd; *AmE* loʊd/ *noun, verb*
● *noun* [C]

> SEE ALSO: **back-end load, dead ~, front-end ~, Full Container ~, Less than Container ~**

1 something that is being carried, especially in large amounts: *The trucks waited at the warehouse to pick up their loads.* ◇ *These planes are designed to carry heavy loads.* → CARGO
> ○ *to* **carry/deliver/pick up/transport** *a load* ◆ *a* **heavy/large** *load*
2 (*often used to form a noun with another noun*) the total amount of sth that sth can carry or contain: *a busload of tourists* ◇ *They ordered three truckloads of sand.* ◇ *The plane took off with a full load.*
3 an amount of work that a person or machine has to do: *He hired some more employees to lighten his load.* ◇ *Sharing the load makes work less stressful.*
> → WORKLOAD
> ○ *to* **lighten/reduce** *a load* ◆ *to* **share/spread** *the load*
4 the fact of having to pay an amount of money, especially a large amount; the amount of money that you owe: *Many companies were already struggling with high debt loads.* SYN BURDEN
> ○ *a* **debt/tax** *load*
5 (*Finance*) a fee that is charged when an investor buys or sells shares in an investment fund, an insurance policy, etc: *The fund carries a 5.75% load.*
● *verb*
1 [+ obj *or* no obj] **load sth (into/onto sth)** to put goods into or onto sth: *The dockers had begun loading the ship.* ◇ *He finished loading and drove off.* ◇ *a fully loaded tanker* OPP UNLOAD → LOAD UP, LOAD STH UP
2 [no obj] to receive a load: *The tankers were still loading.* OPP UNLOAD
3 [+ obj *or* no obj] **load (sth) (up)** to put data or a program into the memory of a computer: *Have you loaded the software?* ◇ *Wait for the program to load.*
> → DOWNLOAD
> PHRV ˌload ˈup (with sth); ˌload sth ˈup (with sth) to put a large amount of goods onto a vehicle: *Men were loading up a truck with timber.* → LOAD *verb* (1,3), ˌload ˈup on sth to get or buy a large amount of sth: *Consumers have loaded up on credit-card debt.*

loader /ˈləʊdə(r); *AmE* ˈloʊdər/ *noun* [C]
1 a person who puts goods into or onto sth: *weekly bonuses for dock loaders*
2 a lorry/truck of the type mentioned: *He operates a seven tonne loader.*

ˈload ˌfactor *noun* [C]
1 (*Transport*) the number of seats on an aircraft, etc. that have been sold, expressed as a percentage of the total number of seats: *The airline reported a load factor of 80% last month.*
2 (*Technical*) the relationship between the actual amount of sth and the total possible amount: *the cargo load factor*

ˈload fund *noun* [C]
(*Finance*) a type of fund, especially a UNIT TRUST, that charges a fee when investors buy or sell → NO-LOAD FUND

loading /ˈləʊdɪŋ; *AmE* ˈloʊd-/ *noun* [C,U]

> SEE ALSO: **back-end loading, front-end ~, vertical ~**

1 an extra amount added to the basic cost of sth such as insurance: *If you are a young or inexperienced driver, a loading will be added to your insurance premium.* ◇ *The 2% loading for using the card abroad has been removed.*
2 (*HR*) especially in Australia and New Zealand, extra money that sb is paid for their job because they have special skills or qualifications

ˈload line (*also* ˈPlimsoll line, ˈPlimsoll mark) *noun* [C]
(*Transport*) a line on the side of a ship showing the highest point that the water can safely reach when the ship is loaded

> **WHICH WORD?**
>
> ### loan/facility/home loan/mortgage/overdraft
>
> All these words are used to describe money that banks lend to customers.
>
> **Loan** is the most general word and is used about money lent both to individuals and businesses. Loans can be paid back over short or long periods of time and can be small or large.
>
> **Mortgages** or **home loans** are used by individuals to buy homes. The amount borrowed is large and paid back over a number of years.
>
> **Overdrafts** are used by individuals and businesses. An overdraft differs from a loan in that there is not a particular amount of money that is lent at a particular time. It is an arrangement to borrow up to an agreed amount whenever you need it. You obtain the money through your bank account.
>
> **Facility** is used to describe any arrangement in which a person or company can borrow money during a particular period of time up to an agreed amount. This can be an overdraft, or it may have special conditions and be established for a particular purpose: *The company has secured a short-term facility to fund the purchase.*
>
> See note at LEND

★ **loan** /ləʊn; *AmE* loʊn/ *noun, verb*
● *noun* [C]

> SEE ALSO: **amortizing loan, back-to-back ~, bad ~, call ~, commercial ~, consumer ~,** etc.

money that an organization such as a bank lends and sb borrows: *The government offers low-interest loans to small companies.* ◇ *Many people take out a loan to buy a new car.* ◇ *The loans should be repaid within ten years.* ◇ *The company had breached the terms of its loan agreement.* ◇ *The banks have*

refused to extend (= give) *more loans to the company.* ◇ *Lower interest rates have made it easier for companies to* **service** (= pay interest on) *their loans.* → LOAN SERVICING See note at LEND
  ➊ *a high-interest/an interest-free/a low-interest/no-interest loan* ◆ *a long-term/short-term loan* ◆ *consumer/corporate/personal loans* ◆ *to* **apply for/ arrange/take out** *a loan* ◆ *to* **get/give sb/make sb** *a loan* ◆ *to* **pay back/pay off/repay** *a loan* ◆ *a loan* **agreement/facility/repayment**
● *verb* [+ obj] (*especially AmE*) **loan sth (to sb)** | **loan (sb) sth** to lend sth to sb, especially money: *The bank loaned the business more than $200 000.* ◇ *Lenders are reluctant to loan money to those they consider to be a financial risk.* [SYN] LEND

'loan ,capital *noun* [U]
  (*Finance*) money used to start and run a business that comes from borrowing rather than selling shares [SYN] DEBT CAPITAL → SHARE CAPITAL

'loan loss *noun* [C,U]
  (*Accounting*) money that is lost by a bank because a borrower does not pay back a loan: *The bank has set aside $800 million to cover loan losses.* ◇ *loan loss provisions* → BAD LOAN

'loan note *noun* [C]
  (*Finance*) a written agreement to pay a sum of money that you owe [NOTE] **Loan notes** are sometimes preferred to cash because tax is not paid until the money is received: *The acquisition was funded by a mixture of shares, loan notes and cash.*

'loan ,servicing *noun* [U]
  (*Finance*) the process of collecting and managing the regular payments made to pay back a loan → SERVICE *verb* (1,2)

'loan shark *noun* [C] (*informal*)
  a person who lends money at very high rates of interest: *Loan sharks were charging 30% a month.* → SHARK

'loan stock *noun* [C,U]
  (*Finance*) investments in the form of loans to a company for a fixed period of time that receive a fixed rate of interest: *Methods of financing include borrowing from banks and issuing loan stock.* → DEBENTURE

local /'ləʊkl; *AmE* 'loʊkl/ *adjective, noun*
● *adjective* [usually before noun]
  belonging to or connected with the particular place or area that you are talking about or with the place where you live: *Foreign oil companies began to compete in the local market.* ◇ *Decisions are made at local rather than national level.* ◇ *Some cable companies offer free local calls* (= phone calls to a place that is near). ◇ *We reach Delhi at 8.30 a.m. local time.* → DOMESTIC
  ▶ **locally** /'ləʊkəli; *AmE* 'loʊkəli/ *adverb*: *to advertise/work/shop locally* ◇ *locally grown fruit*
● *noun* [C]
  1 (*AmE*) a local branch of an organization, especially a trade union
  2 (*AmE*) a bus or train that stops at all the places on the route
  3 (*Stock Exchange, informal*) a trader at a stock exchange who buys and sells shares, etc. for themselves rather than for other investors

,local area 'network = LAN

,local 'content *noun* [U]
  (*Manufacturing*) the part of a manufactured product that is made or supplied within a particular country or area: *The target for local content in the Nigerian oil industry was 45%.*

localize , -ise /'ləʊkəlaɪz; *AmE* 'loʊ-/ *verb* [+ obj]
  1 (*Marketing*) to adapt a product or service to make it more suitable for a particular region or country: *This is a US product and no attempt has been made to localize it for European markets.*

2 if a company **localizes** its activities, they happen in particular areas rather than in a central area: *Localized control at our five plants had cost us money.*

locate /ləʊ'keɪt; *AmE* 'loʊkeɪt/ *verb*
  1 [+ obj] to put or build sth in a particular place: *They located their headquarters in Brussels.* → RELOCATE
  2 [no obj] (*especially AmE*) (*used with an adverb or a preposition*) to start a business in a particular place: *There are tax breaks for businesses that locate in rural areas.*

located /ləʊ'keɪtɪd; *AmE* 'loʊkeɪ-/ *adjective* [not before noun]
  if sth is **located** in a particular place, it exists there or is based there: *Most of the fastest-growing companies are located near the largest cities.*

location /ləʊ'keɪʃn; *AmE* loʊ-/ *noun*
  1 [C] a place where sth happens or exists; the position of sth: *Ratings are based on the quality and location of hotels.* ◇ *Coffee shops need to be in high street locations.*
  2 [U] the act of finding a place for sth or of placing sth somewhere: *Location of a suitable site may take some time.*

lock /lɒk; *AmE* lɑːk/ *verb, noun*
● *verb* [+ obj] **be locked in/into sth** to be involved in a discussion or an argument that continues for a long time: *The company is still locked in talks with its bankers.* ◇ *The two sides are locked in a bitter legal dispute.*
  ➊ *be locked in* **discussions/negotiations/talks** ◆ *be locked in an* **argument/a battle/conflict/dispute**
  [IDM] **lock 'horns (with sb) (over sth)** to get involved in an argument or a dispute with sb
  [PHR V] **,lock sth a'way** (*also* ,**lock sth 'up**) to put money into an investment that you cannot easily turn into cash: *Investors should think carefully before locking up their money in a long-term annuity.* ,**lock 'into sth** (*Finance*) to agree to pay or receive a fixed rate of interest for a fixed period of time: *We were able to lock into a very good interest rate.* ,**lock sb/sth/yourself 'into sth** to involve sb, sth or yourself in a situation that cannot easily be changed: *It is not advisable to lock yourself into a lease agreement that is longer than necessary.* ,**lock sb 'out (of sth)** **1** (*HR*) (*about an employer*) to refuse to allow workers into their place of work until they agree to particular conditions: *Employers have locked striking workers out of the factory.* → LOCKOUT **2** to stop sb from doing a particular activity or becoming involved in sth: *those now locked out of the job market* ,**lock sth 'up** = LOCK STH AWAY
● *noun*
  [IDM] **get/have a 'lock on sth** (*especially AmE*) to get or have complete control, possession or use of sth: *These dealers had a lock on a small section of the market.*

lockbox /'lɒkbɒks; *AmE* 'lɑːkbɑːks/ *noun* [C] (*AmE*)
  1 a strong box with a lock that is used for keeping mail or valuable items safe
  2 (*also* '**lockbox ,service**) a bank or another business that receives a fee for dealing with payments sent to a company by mail

lockout /'lɒkaʊt; *AmE* 'lɑːk-/ *noun* [C]
  (*HR*) a situation when an employer refuses to allow workers into their place of work until they agree to various conditions: *The 10-day lockout of dockworkers shut down 29 major ports.* ◇ *a lockout by employers* → LOCK SB OUT at LOCK See note at STRIKE

'lock-up noun [C]

1 (Finance) an agreement not to sell or exchange shares for a particular period of time: The shares will be subject to a lock-up for 180 days.

2 (BrE) a small shop/store that the owner does not live in; a small building for cars (a **garage**) that is usually separate from other buildings and is rented to sb

▶ **'lock-up** adjective [only before noun]: A lock-up agreement prevented the shares from being sold for six months. ◇ a lock-up garage/shop/warehouse

lodge /lɒdʒ; AmE lɑːdʒ/ verb [+ obj]

1 **lodge sth (with sb) (against sb/sth)** to make a formal statement about sth to a public organization or authority: It is expected that the company will lodge an appeal against the decision. **SYN** FILE
○ to lodge an **appeal**/a **claim**/**complaint**

2 (Law) (BrE) to present sth so that it can be officially recorded and dealt with: Copies of the audited results were lodged with the stock exchange last week. **SYN** FILE

3 **lodge sth with sb/in sth** to leave money or sth valuable in a safe place: Your will should be lodged with your lawyer.

▶ **'lodgement** noun [U]

log /lɒg; AmE lɔːg; lɑːg/ verb, noun

● verb [+ obj] (-gg-)

1 to put information in an official record or write a record of events: The system is designed to help trainees log their progress. ◇ All incoming support calls are logged. **SYN** RECORD

2 to do or get a large amount of sth: They logged about $60 million in sales last year.

PHR V **,log 'in/'on**; **,log 'into/'onto sth** to perform the actions that allow you to begin using a computer system: You need a password to log on. **,log 'off/'out**; **,log 'off/'out of sth** to perform the actions that allow you to finish using a computer system: Log out before switching the computer off.

● noun [C]

1 (also **'logbook**) a record of events during a particular period of time: At the end of the month, the accountant receives copies of the weekly logs.

2 (HR) in Australia, a set of demands for better pay or conditions, especially claims made by a trade union to an INDUSTRIAL TRIBUNAL (= a type of court that deals with disagreements between employers and employees)

logbook /'lɒgbʊk; AmE 'lɔːg-; 'lɑːg-/ noun [C]
1 = LOG noun (1)
2 (Transport) (BrE) a document that records official details about a vehicle, especially a car, and its owner → REGISTRATION

'log file noun [C]
(IT) a computer file that keeps a record of tasks performed by a computer. It can be used for dealing with problems in the system or for collecting information about users of a website: The log file tells you which search terms someone used to find your website.

logic /'lɒdʒɪk; AmE 'lɑːdʒɪk/ noun
1 [U; sing.] sensible reasons for doing sth: a strategy based on sound commercial logic
2 (IT) [U] a system or set of principles used in preparing a computer to perform a particular task

logistics /lə'dʒɪstɪks/ noun [U with sing./pl. verb]

SEE ALSO: reverse logistics

1 (Production) the work of planning and organizing the supply of materials, goods and staff: The company provides an excellent service in the areas of logistics and distribution. ◇ A logistics firm was hired to organize deliveries.

2 **the logistics of sth** the practical organization that is needed to make a complicated plan successful: We had to think carefully about the logistics of opening a new branch. See note at DISTRIBUTION

▶ **lo'gistic** (also **logistical** /lə'dʒɪstɪkl/) adjective: a postal and logistic group ◇ There are serious logistical problems involved in introducing the new computer system.

logjam /'lɒgdʒæm; AmE 'lɔːg-; 'lɑːg-/ noun
1 [C, usually sing.] a complete failure to make progress, reach agreement or settle sth: The agreement on working hours is seen as a way of breaking the logjam. → DEADLOCK
2 [C] a large amount of work that has not been done because there are too many things to do: logjams of paperwork → BACKLOG, BOTTLENECK

★ **logo** /'ləʊgəʊ; AmE 'loʊgoʊ/ noun [C] (plural **logos**)
a printed design or symbol that a company or an organization uses as its special sign: All over the world there are red and white paper cups bearing the company logo. ◇ Putting logos on clothes is another form of indirect advertising.

'London 'Inter-Bank 'Offered Rate noun [sing.] (abbr **LIBOR**)
the rate of interest at which London banks lend money to each other: The interest rate is 1% above the London Inter-Bank Offered Rate.

long /lɒŋ; AmE lɔːŋ/ adjective

SEE ALSO: year-long

(Finance; Stock Exchange) if somebody is **long** on/in shares, currencies, etc., they have bought them, intending to sell them later at a profit when their value rises **HELP** The forms **longer** and **longest** are not usually used in this meaning: Traders feel it is unwise to be long **on** stocks. ◇ Investors did not want to be long **in** dollars due to political uncertainties. **OPP** SHORT

▶ **long** adverb: We believe that technology stocks have reached their lowest point, so now is a good time to go long on these shares.

IDM **work/have long 'hours/'days** to work more hours in the day than usual: Managers often expect staff to work very long hours. → idiom at LONG RUN

'long bond noun [C]
(Finance)
1 an investment in the form of an agreement to lend a sum of money for ten years or more to a company or government who will pay it back with interest: Long bonds are affected more by interest rate changes than short-term bonds.
2 a thirty-year bond issued by the US Treasury

,long-'dated adjective [usually before noun]
(Finance) used to describe investments that will be paid back after a long period of time: Long-dated government bonds were badly hit by inflation.
→ LONGS

'long-haul adjective [only before noun]
that involves transporting people or goods over long distances: The company cut its loss-making long-haul route to Australia. ◇ long-haul passengers → SHORT-HAUL

'long po,sition noun [C]
(Finance; Stock Exchange) a situation in which a dealer or an investor has bought shares, currencies, etc. and holds them intending to sell them later at a profit as they expect their value to rise: Speculative traders held long positions in the currency. **SYN** BULL POSITION → SHORT POSITION

,long-'range adjective [only before noun]
made for a period of time that will last a long way into the future: long-range planning/goals

,long 'run (*also* **,long 'term**) *noun* [sing.]
(*Economics*) a period of time long enough for a
business or an industry to change everything that
can be changed: *In the long run, the industry can
build new factories and produce new products.* ◇ *The
long run trend is one of modest growth.*
→ SHORT RUN
IDM in/over the 'long run; in the 'long term
over a long period in the future: *Shares are a good
investment in the long run.* ◇ *The business should
make a profit in the long term.*

'long-run = LONG-TERM (1)

longs /lɒŋz; *AmE* lɔːŋz/ *noun* [pl.]
(*Finance*)
1 investments such as government bonds that will
be paid back after a long period of time, for
example 15 years: *A balance of longs and shorts
offers less risk than a traditional portfolio.*
2 shares, bonds, currency, etc. that a dealer or an
investor holds and is intending to sell later at a
profit when the value rises → LONG POSITION,
SHORTS

,long-'serving *adjective* [only before noun]
having had the same job or position or worked for
the same employer for a long time: *Three long-
serving members of staff are retiring.*

longshoreman /'lɒŋʃɔːmən; *AmE* 'lɔːŋʃɔːrmən/
(*plural* **longshoremen** /-mən/) = STEVEDORE

,long 'term = LONG RUN

'long-term *adjective* [usually before noun]
1 (*also* **'long-run**) that will continue or have an
effect for a long period of time: *Bevan negotiated a
long-term contract with one of his clients.* ◇ *a new
strategy for dealing with long-term unemployment*
2 (*Accounting*) relating to a period of one year or
longer: *Rates on long-term financing, which
companies use to fund capital expenditure, are rising.*
3 (*Finance*) (about money) that is borrowed, lent or
invested for a long period of time, usually more
than five years: *expensive short-term debt and
cheaper long-term loans* ◇ *The stock is expected to be
a good long-term investment.*
→ SHORT-TERM

,long-term lia'bilities *noun* [pl.]
(*Accounting*) debts that do not need to be paid until
after a particular period of time, usually 12 months
SYN NON-CURRENT LIABILITIES → CURRENT
LIABILITY

,long 'ton *noun* [C] (*especially BrE*) (*abbr* **lt.**)
a unit for measuring weight, equal to 2 240 pounds
or 1 016.05 kilograms → SHORT TON, TON

look /lʊk/ *verb*
IDM be just 'looking (*BrE*) used in a shop/store to
say that you are not ready to buy sth: *'Can I help
you?' 'I'm just looking, thank you.'* **be looking to
do sth** (often used in newspapers) to be trying to
find ways of doing sth; to be planning to do sth:
*The firm is looking to sell its car and home insurance
unit.* **look 'good** to show success or that sth good
might happen: *This year's sales figures are looking
good.*
PHRV look 'after sth/sb to be responsible for sth/
sb: *She looks after export sales.* **,look 'into sth** to
examine sth: *The committee is looking into whether
the company gave out secret information.* **,look 'up**
(*informal*) to improve: *The economy is starting to
look up.* ◇ *Things are looking up for the IT
industry.*

loom /luːm/ *verb* [no obj]
to appear important or threatening and likely to
happen soon: *There was a staffing crisis looming.*

loop /luːp/ *noun* [C]
(*IT*) a set of instructions that is repeated again and
again until a particular set of conditions is satisfied
IDM in the 'loop (*informal*) part of a group of

people who know what is happening and are
dealing with important matters: *Do you feel you're
in the loop at work?* **out of the 'loop** (*informal*) not
informed about important matters and so unable to
help make decisions about them

loophole /'luːphəʊl; *AmE* -hoʊl/ *noun* [C]
a small mistake in the way a law or contract has
been written that allows people to legally avoid sth
that the law or contract intended them to do: *The
authorities will pursue companies that abuse tax
loopholes* (= ways of paying less tax).
○ *a legal/tax loophole* • *to close/plug a loophole*

loose /luːs/ *adjective* not tied together; not held in
position by anything or contained in anything
HELP The forms **looser** and **loosest** are not used in
this meaning: *The potatoes are sold loose, not in
bags.* ◇ *loose tea* ◇ *The promotional leaflet will be a
loose insert in a weekly magazine.*

,lo-'res = LOW-RESOLUTION

lorry /'lɒri; *AmE* 'lɔːri/ *noun* [C] (*plural* **lorries**) (*BrE*)
a large motor vehicle for carrying heavy loads by
road: *Goods are delivered to shops by a fleet of
lorries.* ◇ *a lorry driver* ◇ *Sixty-five per cent of Brazil's
freight is carried by lorry.* **SYN** TRUCK—Picture at
TRANSPORT

lose /luːz/ *verb* (**lost, lost** /lɒst; *AmE* lɑːst; lɔːst/)
1 [+ obj *or no obj*] **lose (sth) (on sth)** | **lose sb sth** to
fail to keep money; to cause sb to fail to keep
money: *The business is losing money.* ◇ *The firm has
lost $176 million in the past six quarters.* ◇ *We lost on
that deal.*
2 [+ obj] **lose sth (to sb)** | **lose sb sth** to have sth
taken away by sb; to fail to keep sth: *Singapore has
lost business to ports in Malaysia.* ◇ *You will lose your
deposit if you cancel the order.* ◇ *He lost his job as a
result of the incident.*
3 [+ obj] (about a currency, share price, etc.) to fall
to a lower level or price: *The FTSE 100 lost a quarter
of its value last year.* ◇ *Royal Dutch Petroleum lost 0.3
per cent.* **OPP** GAIN See note at INCREASE
IDM lose 'face to be less respected or look stupid
because of sth you have done → LOSS OF FACE at
LOSS, SAVE (SB'S) FACE at SAVE **lose 'ground** to
fall in value: *Tokyo shares lost ground on
Wednesday.* **lose your 'shirt** (*informal*) to lose
everything you have: *If you just put your money in
the bank, at least you can't lose your shirt.*
PHRV ,lose 'out (on sth) to not get sth that you
expected or wanted: *Thousands of investors lost out
on the plans.* ◇ *The firm has lost out on yet another
important contract.* **,lose 'out to sb/sth** to not get
sth that you expected to get or used to get, because
someone else has taken it: *They lost out to a rival
group in the bidding war.*

loser /'luːzə(r)/ *noun* [C]

SEE ALSO: **money loser**

1 (*Stock Exchange*) (used especially in newspapers) a
company whose shares lose value in trading on a
stock exchange: *The day's biggest loser was Sage
Group.* **OPP** GAINER
2 a person or company that loses or suffers in a
particular situation: *The real losers here are the
taxpayers.* **OPP** WINNER

★loss /lɒs; *AmE* lɔːs/ *noun*

SEE ALSO: **all-loss, capital ~, credit ~, gross ~, loan ~,
operating ~, paper ~,** etc.

1 [C] money that has been lost by a business or an
organization: *The company has announced losses of
$324 million.* ◇ *The group made a loss of €29
million.* ◇ *The airline is reeling from two years of
heavy losses.* ◇ *We are now operating at a loss.*
OPP PROFIT → GAIN—Picture at BREAK-EVEN

➊ *to announce/make/post/record/report a loss* ♦ *to face/stem/suffer a loss* ♦ *heavy/huge/pre-tax/ significant/substantial losses*

2 [C,U] the state of no longer having sth or as much of sth; the process that leads to this: *The closure of the factory will lead to the loss of 2 000 jobs.* ◇ *The loss of one of its biggest customers is a damaging blow to the company.*

3 [U] property that has been damaged or stolen and that an insurance company will pay you money to replace: *This type of policy does not cover loss of or damage to your own vehicle.*

IDM **loss of 'face** a situation when sb is less respected or looks stupid because of sth they have done → LOSE FACE at LOSE

'loss a,djuster (also **a'djuster**) noun [C]
(*Insurance*) an independent person or company that decides whether insurance claims are valid and how much should be paid **SYN** INSURANCE ADJUSTER (*AmE*), CLAIMS ADJUSTER (*AmE*)

'loss as,sessor (also **'claims as,sessor**) noun [C] (*both BrE*)
(*Insurance*) a person who helps sb who has an insurance policy to make a claim **SYN** ASSESSOR

'loss-,leader noun [C]
(*Marketing*) a product or service that is sold at a very low price in order to attract customers, who will then buy goods or services that produce more profit: *Supermarkets use bread and milk as their most important loss-leaders.* ◇ *In promotional pricing, the company must decide on loss-leader pricing.*

'loss-,making (also spelled **lossmaking**) adjective
1 a loss-making company, business, or part of a business does not make a profit: *The group is to sell its loss-making computer assembly business.* ◇ *Research departments are generally loss-making.*
2 a loss-making period of time is a period in which a company does not make a profit: *The aim is to break even next year after several loss-making years.*
▶ **'loss-,maker** noun [C]: *The division has been a heavy loss-maker.*

,loss of 'earnings noun [U]
a situation in which a person or company does not earn money that they expected to earn, as a result of illness, an accident, sb's actions, etc: *I want to buy an accident policy that includes loss of earnings cover.*

,lost 'time noun [U]
working time that is lost, for example because workers are injured or because machines are broken: *The average lost time per employee due to on-the-job accidents has fallen by about 20 per cent.*

lot /lɒt; *AmE* lɑːt/ noun [C]

SEE ALSO: **job lot, round lot**

1 (*Commerce*) an item or a group of items that is sold at an AUCTION (= a sale where items are sold to the person who offers the most money): *Lot 183 is a document shredder.*
2 (*Production*) a quantity of goods that are produced or sold together: *The trend in some industries is towards making smaller lots in greater varieties.* ◇ *The products bear the lot number L32891.*
3 an area of land used for a particular purpose: *a parking lot* ◇ *a vacant lot* (= one available to be built on or used for sth)

low /ləʊ; *AmE* loʊ/ adjective, adverb, noun
● *adjective* (**lower, lowest**)
1 below the usual or average amount, level or value: *The brand offers high value at low prices.* ◇ *a low level of unemployment* ◇ *Inflation is at its lowest*

level for ten years. ◇ *Annual profits were lower than expected.* **OPP** HIGH
2 having a reduced amount or not enough of sth: *Our money is running low* (= we do not have much left). ◇ *Many supermarkets are now low on staples such as bread and bottled water.*
3 below the usual or expected standard: *Customers complained that the quality of the goods was low.* **OPP** HIGH
4 below other people or things in importance or status: *jobs with low status* ◇ *Training was given a very low priority.* **OPP** HIGH
● *adverb* (**lower, lowest**)
at a level below what is usual or expected: *a low-powered PC*
● *noun* [C]

SEE ALSO: **historic low**

a low level, point or figure: *The pound fell to a new low against the euro.* ◇ *The company's shares are at an all-time low.* **OPP** HIGH
➊ *an all-time/a record low* ♦ *to fall to/hit a low*

lowball /'ləʊbɔːl; *AmE* 'loʊ-/ verb [+ obj] (*AmE*) (*informal*)
to deliberately make an estimate of the cost, value, etc. of sth that is too low: *He lowballed the cost of the project in order to obtain federal funding.*
▶ **'lowball** noun [C] (*usually used as an adjective*): *a lowball bid/price*

,low-'cost (also **,lower-'cost**) adjective [usually before noun]
costing or charging less than others: *Which is Europe's largest low-cost airline?* ◇ *Sony has switched assembly to lower-cost countries.* **OPP** HIGH-COST

,low-cost 'leader = COST LEADER

'low-end adjective [usually before noun]
low-end goods are among the cheapest available: *The low-end model will be priced at around $300.* ◇ *low-end phones* ▶ **'low-end** noun [sing.]: *Many of our competitors are not present in the low-end.* **OPP** HIGH-END

lower /'ləʊə(r); *AmE* 'loʊ-/ verb [+ obj or no obj]
to reduce sth, or to become less in value, quality, etc: *The Fed lowered interest rates again yesterday.* ◇ *Shipping merchandise directly to the customer lowers costs.* **SYN** CUT **OPP** RAISE

,lower-'cost = LOW-COST

,lower-'income = LOW-INCOME (1)

,lower-than-ex'pected adjective [usually before noun]
lower-than-expected sales, profits, results etc. are smaller than had been predicted previously: *The company reported lower-than-expected sales in the first quarter.* → BETTER-THAN-EXPECTED

,low-'fare (also **,low-'fares**, *less frequent*) adjective [only before noun]
(about an airline) that sells very cheap tickets: *British Airways is facing increasing competition from low-fare airlines.*

,low-'grade adjective [usually before noun]
1 of poor quality or status: *Millions of bags of low-grade coffee need to be destroyed.* ◇ *people in low-grade jobs*
2 (*Finance*) low-grade investments carry a high risk of failing: *low-grade debt* **OPP** HIGH-GRADE

,low-hanging 'fruit noun [U]
a term used by some managers to refer to easy ways of increasing profits, cutting costs, etc: *A lot of the low-hanging fruit has already been picked.*

,low-'impact adjective [usually before noun]
not having a strong influence or making many changes: *The team worked hard but remained a low-impact team.* **OPP** HIGH-IMPACT

low-'income *adjective* [usually before noun]
1 (*also* ,lower-'income) not having or earning much money: *new businesses in low-income areas* ◇ *financial services for lower-income customers*
2 earning a low level of interest: *Many pensioners prefer to put their savings into no income or low-income investments.*
OPP HIGH-INCOME

low-in'volvement ,product *noun* [C]
(*Marketing*) a product that customers buy often and do not spend a lot of time and effort looking for and buying OPP HIGH-INVOLVEMENT PRODUCT

low-'level *adjective* [usually before noun]
1 involving people at a junior level: *a low-level job*
2 (*IT*) (about a computer language) similar to MACHINE CODE
OPP HIGH-LEVEL

low-'margin *adjective* [usually before noun]
(*Accounting*; *Marketing*) **low-margin** products cost almost as much to produce as they can be sold for, so they do not provide big profits: *When you fill capacity with low-margin sales, you leave no room for high-margin sales.* OPP HIGH-MARGIN

low-'paid *adjective* [usually before noun]
1 earning very little money; providing very little money: *low-paid local government workers* ◇ *It suits some people to take part-time or lower-paid jobs.*
2 the low-paid *noun* [pl.] people who are low-paid: *A scheme to help the low-paid.*
OPP HIGH-PAID

'low-,pressure *adjective* [only before noun]
1 (*Marketing*) that involves encouraging people to do or to buy sth rather than using aggressive methods to persuade them: *We are proud of our reputation for low-pressure selling and excellent service.*
2 that involves little worry and anxiety: *We have friendly staff and a low-pressure work environment.*
OPP HIGH-PRESSURE

low-'priced (*also* ,low-'price) *adjective* [usually before noun]
not expensive; cheap: *low-priced goods/fashion* ◇ *the low-price end of the market* OPP HIGH-PRICED

low-'profile *adjective* [usually before noun]
receiving or involving very little attention in the media; not very well-known: *a low-profile company*
OPP HIGH-PROFILE

low-'ranking *adjective* [usually before noun]
junior; not very important

low-reso'lution (*also* lo-res, low-res /,ləʊ 'rez; AmE /,loʊ/) *adjective* [usually before noun]
not showing a lot of clear detail: *a low-resolution scan* OPP HIGH-RESOLUTION

'low road *noun* [sing.]
(*HR*) a method of trying to gain an advantage in business which involves paying workers low wages, giving them poor working conditions and producing goods of low value: *He has built a high road tyre company in an industry known for taking the low road.* ◇ *a low-road company* → HIGH ROAD

low 'season *noun* [U; sing.] (*especially BrE*)
the time of year when a hotel or tourist area receives fewest visitors: *A deluxe room costs $193 in (the) low season.* SYN OFF SEASON OPP HIGH SEASON
▶ **,low-'season** *adjective* [only before noun]: *low-season prices*

low-'tech *adjective*
not involving the most modern technology or methods: *Initially production was low-tech.* ◇ *low-tech toys for kids* OPP HIGH-TECH

low 'volume *noun* [C,U]
a small quantity of sth: *The questionnaire brought*

only a low volume of responses. ◇ *low-volume trading* OPP HIGH VOLUME

low-'yield (*also* ,low-'yielding) *adjective* [only before noun]
(*Finance*) used to describe investments that do not produce a high income but also have a low level of risk: *low-yield government bonds* ◇ *They have borrowed funds in a low-yielding currency.* → HIGH-YIELD

loyal /'lɔɪəl/ *adjective*
1 a **loyal** customer tends to buy the same products all the time, rather than trying different ones: *The company has 34 million loyal customers.* ◇ *Many shareholders remained loyal to us in difficult times.*
2 a **loyal** employee works for the same company for a long time: *The secret of our success is our high-quality, loyal workforce.*

loyalty /'lɔɪəlti/ *noun* [U]

SEE ALSO: **brand loyalty, customer loyalty**

the quality of being faithful to a particular product, company, etc.

'loyalty card *noun* [C]
(*Marketing*) a card given to customers by a shop/store to encourage them to shop there regularly. Each time they buy sth they collect points which will allow them to have an amount of money taken off goods they buy in the future: *The store has a loyalty-card scheme.*

LP /,el 'piː/ = LIMITED PARTNERSHIP

LR /,el 'ɑː(r)/ = LLOYD'S REGISTER

LSE /,el es 'iː/ *noun* [sing.] **London Stock Exchange plc** a market for buying and selling company shares, bonds, etc: *The company is listed on the London Stock Exchange.*

lt. = LONG TON

Ltd (*AmE spelling* **Ltd.**) *abbr* (*only used in written English*)
limited, used after the names of particular types of companies in some countries: *Oxford Cameras Ltd*
See note on page 328

LTV /,el tiː 'viː/ = LIFETIME VALUE

lucrative /'luːkrətɪv/ *adjective*
producing a large amount of money; making a large profit: *The US has proved to be our most lucrative market.* ◇ *The deal proved highly lucrative for the company.*
➊ a lucrative **business/contract/deal/market** ◆ **extremely/highly/hugely/potentially** lucrative
▶ **'lucratively** *adverb*

Luddite /'lʌdaɪt/ *noun* [C] (*BrE*)
a word used in a disapproving way to describe sb who is opposed to new technology or working methods NOTE Named after Ned **Lud**, one of the workers who destroyed machinery in the cotton and wool factories in the early 19th century, because they believed it would take away their jobs.

luggage /'lʌgɪdʒ/ *noun* [U]

SEE ALSO: **hand luggage, left luggage**

bags, cases, etc. that you carry your clothes and things in when you are travelling: *Passengers are allowed to have up to three pieces of luggage.*
SYN BAGGAGE

lull /lʌl/ *noun* [C, usually sing.]
a quiet period between times of activity: *There was an increase in trading this week after the usual summer lull.* ◇ *a lull in consumer spending*

lumber /'lʌmbə(r)/ = TIMBER (2)

Company abbreviations

Abbreviations like **Ltd** or **Corp.** often appear after the names of businesses. They are usually required by law and tell you something about the type of company that has been established.

IN THE UK

Ltd (= limited) a company that is owned by a small number of people, often members of a family, and can be run by a single person

plc (= public limited company) a large company that can sell its shares to the public and has a board of directors

IN THE US

Corp. (= corporation); **Co.** (= company); **Inc.** (= incorporated). These abbreviations indicate that a business is a company but give no information about its size, number of shareholders or management.

LLC (= limited liability company) a company owned by a group of people who usually also run the business

OTHER COUNTRIES

AG in Germany, a large company that can sell shares to the public and is run by a group of managers

GmbH in Germany, a company with one or a number of shareholders. It cannot sell shares to the public.

Pty (= proprietary) used in Australia and South Africa for companies that are owned by a small number of people

SA in France and Spain, a large company that can sell shares to the public and is run by a board of directors

SARL in France, a company with a small number of shareholders

SpA in Italy, a company with one or a number of shareholders. It can sell shares to the public and is run by a board of directors or group of managers.

See note at CORPORATION

lump /lʌmp/ *noun* [C] (*informal*) = LUMP SUM
IDM **take your 'lumps** (*AmE*) (*informal*) to accept bad things that happen to you without complaining: *If you can't solve the problem, take your lumps and figure out how to avoid it next time.*

,lump 'sum (*also* ,lump sum 'payment) (*also* lump, *informal*) *noun* [C]
a single payment of money: *Workers can receive their vacation pay **in** a lump sum.* ◇ *You can take up to 25% of your pension as a tax-free lump sum.*

lunch /lʌntʃ/ *noun, verb*
● *noun* [U,C]

SEE ALSO: **business lunch, power lunch**

a meal eaten in the middle of the day: *I had lunch with their marketing director.* ◇ *She isn't back from lunch yet.* ◇ *Let's discuss the contract **over** lunch.* ◇ *a 30-minute **lunch break** → idiom at FREE adj.*
❍ *to be at/go out for/go to/have lunch • to buy sb/meet sb for/take sb to lunch • a working lunch*
● *verb* [no obj or + obj]
to have lunch, especially at a restaurant: *He often lunches with leading figures in the industry.*

'lunch hour *noun* [C]
the time around the middle of the day when you stop work to eat lunch: *I often work through my lunch hour.*

lure /lʊə(r); ljʊə(r); *AmE* lʊr/ *verb, noun*
● *verb* [+ obj] (*usually used with an adverb or a preposition*)
to persuade sb to go somewhere or do sth by promising them a reward or making it seem exciting: *Many retailers are lowering their prices to lure customers into the shops.* ◇ *Young people are lured to the city by the prospect of a job and money.*
● *noun* [C, usually sing.]
the attractive qualities of sth: *The lure of cheap credit has proved too strong for consumers.*

luxury /'lʌkʃəri/ *noun, adjective*
● *noun* (*plural* **luxuries**)
1 [C] a thing that is expensive and enjoyable but not essential: *An in-house IT consultant is a luxury few small businesses can afford.* ◇ *Consumers are cutting down on luxuries like eating out.* ◇ *a well-known luxury store* (= that sells expensive items)
2 [U] the enjoyment of special and expensive things, particularly food and drink, clothes and surroundings: *My wages don't allow us to live **in** luxury.*
3 [U; sing.] a pleasure or an advantage that you do not usually have: *We had the luxury of being able to choose from four good candidates for the job.*
● *adjective* [only before noun]
expensive and of high quality; not essential: *There has been a decline in the demand for luxury goods.* ◇ *There are plans to build two new luxury hotels in the city.* **SYN** PRESTIGE
❍ *luxury brands/goods/items/products • a luxury apartment/car/hotel*

lynchpin = LINCHPIN

M m

M /em/ *abbr*
(especially for sizes of clothes) medium: *S, M and L* (= small, medium and large)

m (*also spelled* **m.**) *abbr*
1 million(s): *a profit of €16 m*
2 male: *Please tick m or f.*
3 married

M0, M1, etc. /,em 'zɪərəʊ, ,em 'wʌn; *AmE* 'zɪroʊ; 'ziː-/ *noun* [U]
(*Economics*) different ways of measuring the amount of money being used or that is available in an economy (the **money supply**): *In the UK, M0*

includes all notes and coins in circulation plus banks' balances with the central bank. → MONEY SUPPLY

M & A /,em ənd 'eɪ/ *abbr*
a short way of writing **mergers and acquisitions** (= the activity of buying and selling companies): *an investment bank specializing in M & A* ◇ *Why do most M & As fail?*

★**machine** /mə'ʃiːn/ *noun, verb*
● *noun* [C]

SEE ALSO: **answering machine, cash ~, dictation ~, tape ~, ticker-tape ~, vending ~**

1 (*often used in compounds*) a piece of equipment with moving parts that is designed to do a particular job and uses electricity, gas, wind power, etc. in order to operate: *a drilling/copying machine* ◊ *How does this machine work?* ◊ *The machine runs on solar power.* ◊ *The stone is cut* **by** *machine.* ◊ *a machine operator* → FAX *noun* (1)

⊕ *a* **heavy/large/powerful** *machine* ◆ *to* **install/service** *a machine* ◆ *to* **operate/run/start/stop/use** *a machine* ◆ *a machine* **breaks down/runs/works**

2 a particular machine, when you do not refer to it by its full name, especially a computer: *The software will run on most desktop machines.*

3 [usually sing.] a group of people that control an organization or part of an organization: *the company's marketing machine*

● *verb* [+ obj]
(*Manufacturing*) to make or shape sth with a machine: *This material can be cut and machined easily.* ▶ **ma'chining** *noun* [U]: *the precision machining of aircraft parts*

ma'chine code (*also* **ma'chine ˌlanguage**) *noun* [U]
(*IT*) the basic language that is used to write instructions that can be read directly by a computer, consisting only of numbers

maˌchine-'made *adjective*
made by a machine: *machine-made carpets* → HANDMADE

maˌchine-'readable *adjective*
(*IT*) (about data) in a form that a computer can understand: *machine-readable passports*

★ machinery /məˈʃiːnəri/ *noun* [U]

SEE ALSO: **office machinery**

machines as a group, especially large ones: *investing in new machinery and equipment* ◊ *a piece of machinery* ◊ *The machinery is housed in a special building.* See note at INFORMATION

⊕ **agricultural/electrical/heavy/industrial** *machinery* ◆ *to* **install/maintain/service/set up** *machinery* ◆ *to* **control/operate/use** *machinery* ◆ *to* **drive/run** *machinery* ◆ *machinery* **breaks down/operates/works** ◆ *a machinery* **maker/manufacturer**

ma'chine shop *noun* [C]
(*Manufacturing*) a room or building in which there are machines for making things, especially out of metal: *They created a prototype of the bike in their machine shop.*

ma'chine tool *noun* [C]
(*Manufacturing*) a tool for cutting or shaping metal, wood, etc., driven by a machine

machinist /məˈʃiːnɪst/ *noun* [C]
(*Manufacturing*)
1 a person whose job is operating a machine, especially machines used in industry for cutting and shaping things, or a sewing machine
2 a person whose job is to make or repair machines

macro /ˈmækrəʊ; *AmE* ˈmækroʊ/ *noun* [C] (*plural* **macros**)
(*IT*) a single instruction in a computer program that automatically causes a complete series of instructions to be put into effect, in order to perform a particular task: *You can set up a macro to type the ending of a letter in one keystroke.*

macro- /ˈmækrəʊ; *AmE* ˈmækroʊ/ *combining form*
(*used to form nouns, adjectives and adverbs*) large; on a large scale: *macroeconomics* ◊ *At a macro-level, the economy has performed well.*
OPP MICRO-

macroeconomics /ˌmækrəʊˌiːkəˈnɒmɪks; *AmE* -kroʊˌekəˈnɑːm-/ *noun*
(*Economics*)
1 [U] the study of large economic systems, such as those of whole countries or areas of the world

2 [pl.; U] the features or state of such a system: *The city is affected by the macroeconomics of the region.*
→ MICROECONOMICS

▶ ˌmacroˌecoˈnomic *adjective*: *macroeconomic policies* **macroeconomist** /ˌmækrəʊˈkɒnəmɪst; *AmE* -kroʊˈkɑːn-/ *noun* [C]

macromarketing /ˌmækrəʊˈmɑːkɪtɪŋ; *AmE* ˌmækroʊˈmɑːrk-/ *noun* [U]
(*Marketing*) the study of the system of producing and selling goods and services in a country or an economy, including the effects of cultural, political, social and economic conditions

madam /ˈmædəm/ *noun* [sing.] (*formal*)
used when speaking or writing to a woman in a formal or business situation: *Can I help you, madam?* ◊ *Dear Madam* (= in a letter)

made /meɪd/ *adjective, combining form*
● *adjective*
past tense, past participle of MAKE: *made in China*
● *combining form* **-made** (*used in adjectives*)

SEE ALSO: **custom-made, machine-~, ready-~, self-~, tailor-~**

made in the way, place, etc. mentioned: *well-made* ◊ *British-made steel*

ˌmade to 'measure *adjective* [usually before noun]
1 (especially about clothes) made specially to fit a particular person, place, etc: *made-to-measure suits*
2 made to solve a particular problem: *We will design a made-to-measure solution for your IT needs.*

ˌmade to 'order *adjective* [usually before noun]
made or produced specially for a particular customer, in the way that they require: *a producer of made-to-order computer chips*

ˌMadison 'Avenue /ˈmædɪsən/ *noun* [U]
used to refer to the US advertising industry: *She's a former Madison Avenue executive.* **NOTE** Madison Avenue is the street in New York City where many large advertising companies established their offices in the 1940s and 50s.

mag /mæg/ *noun* [C] (*informal*)
a magazine: *a new mag for travellers* ◊ *teen mags*

magalog /ˈmægəlɒg; *AmE* -lɔːg; -lɑːg/ *noun* [C]
(*Marketing*) a CATALOGUE (= a book that contains photographs and details of products that you can buy) that looks like a magazine and has articles to read in it: *Their magalog features products and editorial material of interest to young women.* **NOTE** Magalog is formed from the words **magazine** and **catalogue**.

magazine /ˌmægəˈziːn; *AmE* ˈmægəziːn/ *noun* [C]

SEE ALSO: **consumer magazine, trade magazine**

a type of large thin book with a paper cover that you can buy every week or month, containing articles, photographs, etc., often on a particular topic: *a women's/men's magazine* ◊ *a magazine* **aimed at/for** *elderly people* ◊ *a glossy fashion magazine*

⊕ *a* **monthly/quarterly/weekly** *magazine* ◆ *a* **colour/glossy** *magazine* ◆ *a* **business/fashion/lifestyle/music/specialist** *magazine* ◆ *a* **copy/** *an* **edition/issue** *of a magazine* ◆ *to* **launch/produce/publish/run** *a magazine* ◆ *to* **buy/get/subscribe to** *a magazine*

ˌmagic 'bullet *noun* [C, usually sing.]
(used especially in newspapers) a fast and effective solution to a serious problem: *There is no magic bullet to solve all our software problems.*

,magic 'circle noun [C, usually sing.] (BrE)
a small group of people or organizations that have a lot of influence and work together to help each other, but are not willing for other people to join them: *London's magic circle law firms* (= the small group of top firms)

magistrate /'mædʒɪstreɪt/ noun [C]
an official who acts as a judge, usually in the lowest courts of law: *to come up before the magistrates* ◇ *The magistrate ordered him to pay a fine.*

magnate /'mæɡneɪt/ noun [C]
a person who is rich, powerful and successful in business See note at BARON

mag,netic 'card noun [C]
a plastic card with a line of black material containing information on it

mag,netic 'disk = DISK (2)

mag,netic 'media noun [pl.; U]
(IT) the different methods that are used to store information for computers, for example plastic tape (**magnetic tape**), disks, etc.

mag,netic 'strip (also **mag,netic 'stripe**) noun [C]
a line of black material on a plastic card, containing information: *Your account details are stored on the magnetic strip.*

maid /meɪd/ noun [C]
a female servant in a house or hotel: *Should I tip the maid?* ◇ *The villas have a daily maid service.*

★ **mail** /meɪl/ noun, verb
● **noun** [U]

SEE ALSO: **certified mail, direct ~, electronic ~, flame ~, junk ~, registered ~, snail ~, surface ~**

1 (BrE also **post**) the official system used for sending and delivering letters, packages, etc: *The cheque is in the mail.* ◇ *Please return our copy of the contract by mail.* ◇ *a mail distribution centre*
→ AIRMAIL, VOICEMAIL
  O *express/first-class/second-class* mail • *internal/international* mail
2 (BrE also **post**) letters, packages, etc. that are sent and delivered: *Has the mail arrived?* ◇ *We received a cheque from them in the mail today.* ◇ *mail deliveries* ◇ *an item/a piece of mail* ◇ *The company has a licence to deliver bulk mail* (= letters, etc. sent in large numbers by businesses).
  O *to deliver/handle* mail • *to get/receive/send (out)* mail • *to answer/deal with/open/read* your mail • *incoming/outgoing* mail • *bulk/business/private* mail
3 messages that are sent or received on a computer: *Check regularly for new mail.* ◇ *incoming/outgoing* mail → EMAIL
● **verb** [+ obj]
1 mail sth (to sb/sth) | mail (sb) sth to send sth to sb using the POSTAL system: *We mail a new catalogue to our customers every year.* ◇ *We mail our customers a new catalogue every year.* ◇ *The company intends to mail 50 000 households in the area.*
2 mail sb | mail sth (to sb/sth) | mail (sb) sth to send a message to sb by email: *Please mail us at the following email address.* ◇ *Mail your order to the following email address.*
PHR V **,mail sth 'out** to send out a large number of letters, etc. at the same time: *The brochures were mailed out last week.* **SYN** SEND OUT → MAIL-OUT

'mail bomb noun [C]
an extremely large number of email messages that are sent to sb ▸ **'mail-bomb** verb [+ obj]

mailbox /'meɪlbɒks; AmE -bɑːks/ noun [C]
an area of a computer's memory where email messages for a particular user are stored: *They limit the size of your mailbox to 20MB.*

mailer /'meɪlə(r)/ noun [C] (AmE)

SEE ALSO: **self-mailer**

1 (AmE) = MAILING (2)
2 an envelope, a box, etc. for sending small things by mail: *makers of protective mailers*
3 a person or company that sends a letter, package, etc: *Costs are rising fast for bulk mailers.*
4 a program that sends email messages

mailing /'meɪlɪŋ/ noun
1 [U] the act of sending items by mail: *the mailing of invoices to customers* ◇ *Mailing costs have risen dramatically.* ◇ *a mailing address*
2 (AmE also **'mailer**) [C] an item that is sent by mail, especially an advertisement that is sent to a large number of people: *The service will be marketed through mailings to selected clients.* ◇ *a mass mailing*

'mailing list noun [C]
1 a list of the names and addresses of people who are regularly sent information, advertising material, etc. by an organization: *The company has 264 000 customers on its mailing list.*
2 a list of names and email addresses kept on your computer so that you can send a message to a number of people at the same time: *The software makes it easy to build a mailing list.*

'mail merge noun [U,C]
the process by which names and addresses are automatically added to a document on a computer, so that the same letter can be sent to many people
▸ **'mail-merge** verb [+ obj]: *a mail-merged document*

'mail ,order noun [U] (abbr **MO**)
a system of buying and selling goods through the mail: *We sell clothing by mail order.* ◇ *a mail-order business/company/retailer* ◇ *a mail-order catalogue*
▸ **'mail-order** verb [+ obj]: *These items can only be mail-ordered.*

'mail-out noun [C]
(Marketing) an act of sending an item of mail to a large number of people, especially by email → MAIL STH OUT at MAIL verb

'mail room = POST ROOM

mailshot /'meɪlʃɒt; AmE -ʃɑːt/ noun [C] (BrE)
(Marketing) an act of sending advertising or information to a large number of people at the same time by mail; an item sent in this way: *To be effective, a mailshot must be well targeted.*

mainframe /'meɪnfreɪm/ (also **,mainframe com'puter**) noun [C]
(IT) a large powerful computer, usually the centre of a network and shared by many users: *There has been a shift in IT from mainframes to servers.*
→ MICROCOMPUTER, MINICOMPUTER

,main 'market noun [sing.]
the part of the London Stock Exchange that deals with the shares of large valuable companies: *The company intends to move to the main market next month.*

,main 'office = HEAD OFFICE

mainstream /'meɪnstriːm/ noun, adjective
● **noun** the mainstream [sing.]
the main part of sth; the usual or normal way of doing or thinking about sth: *Sales has now come into the mainstream of business.*
● **adjective** [usually before noun]
normal or ordinary; used to describe organizations that provide goods and services for most people rather than for only a few: *Mainstream consumers still prefer the shopping mall to the Internet.* ◇ *mainstream companies/banks* → NICHE

mainstreaming /ˈmeɪnstriːmɪŋ/ *noun* [U]
(*HR*) the practice of considering the effect of all aspects of government and company policy on women as well as men, and on the equal rights of workers

'main street *noun* (*often* **Main Street**)
1 [C] the most important street in a small town in the US, where the shops/stores, banks, etc. are → HIGH STREET
2 [U] used to refer to small businesses in the US as a group: *Main Street companies that start small and stay small* → WALL STREET

★ **maintain** /meɪnˈteɪn/ *verb* [+ obj]
1 to make sth continue at the same level, standard, etc: *We will maintain prices at their current level for another six months.*
2 to keep a building, a machine, etc. in good condition by checking or repairing it regularly: *The equipment has been poorly maintained.*
3 to keep records and add new information when necessary: *The company maintains a record of all enquiries made.* → UPDATE

★ **maintenance** /ˈmeɪntənəns/ *noun* [U]

SEE ALSO: **total productive maintenance**

1 the act of keeping sth in good condition by checking or repairing it regularly: *We are responsible for the cleaning and maintenance of the building.* ◇ *building/car/road maintenance* ◇ *The maintenance work is done by an outside contractor.* ◇ *The plant is undergoing essential maintenance.*
[SYN] UPKEEP

○ *to* **carry out/do** *maintenance* • *day-to-day/ essential/planned/preventive/routine maintenance* • *sth* **needs/requires/undergoes** *maintenance* • *a maintenance* **agreement/contract/contractor** • *maintenance* **staff/work/workers**
2 the act of making a state or situation continue: *the maintenance of a high dividend* ◇ *price maintenance*
→ idiom at CARE *noun*

major /ˈmeɪdʒə(r)/ *adjective, noun*
● *adjective* [usually before noun]
very large or important: *major international companies* ◇ *the company's major shareholders* ◇ *They have encountered major problems.* ◇ *We see no need for a major change in strategy.* [OPP] MINOR
● *noun* [C, usually pl.]
a very large company in a particular industry: *The share prices of oil majors BP and Shell both rose.*

★ **majority** /məˈdʒɒrəti; *AmE* -ˈdʒɔːr-; -ˈdʒɑːr-/ *noun* (*plural* **majorities**)

SEE ALSO: **early majority, late majority**

1 [sing. with sing./pl. verb] the largest part of a group of people or things: *The vast majority of people interviewed said they were happy in their jobs.* ◇ *The majority was/were in favour of the proposal.* ◇ *Export orders now account for the majority of our sales.* ◇ *Women are* **in a/the majority** *in the Kenyan coffee and tea industries.* [OPP] MINORITY
2 [C] the number of votes by which one side in an election, a discussion, etc. wins: *The court decided by a majority of five to two to reject the claim.* ◇ *The resolution was carried by a huge majority.* ◇ *a majority vote/decision*
3 [sing.] (*usually used as an adjective*) used to describe a group of shares that is more than half of the total number of shares in a company, or sb who owns this amount: *They are seeking buyers for a majority stake in their Australian operation.* ◇ *a majority shareholder* ◇ *The group is* **majority-owned** *by Anglo American.* → MINORITY (2)

○ *a majority* **control/holding/investment/share/stake** • *a majority* **investor/owner/shareholder**

ma,jority 'interest *noun* [C, usually sing., U]
(*Finance*) a number of shares owned by a particular person or organization that is greater than half of a company's total shares: *They will retain majority interest, keeping 82% of the shares.* → CONTROLLING INTEREST, MINORITY INTEREST

★ **make** /meɪk/ *verb, noun*
● *verb* [+ obj] (**made, made** /meɪd/)
1 to create or prepare sth by combining materials or putting parts together: *to make a chip/device/ model* ◇ *to make cement/glass/paper* ◇ *It's the smallest computer the company has ever made.* ◇ *bags made from recycled plastic* ◇ *What is the shirt made of?*
2 to earn or gain money: *She makes around €80 000 a year in salary and bonuses.* ◇ *to make a profit/loss* ◇ *Some Internet retailers are struggling to make money.*
3 to elect or choose sb as sth: *She made him her assistant.* ◇ *He has been made chairman of the group.*
[IDM] [NOTE] Other idioms containing **make** are at the entries for the nouns, verbs or adjectives in the idioms, for example **make a killing** is at **killing**.
make 'good to become rich and successful **make sth 'good** to pay for, replace or repair sth that has been lost or damaged: *The tenant must make good any damage to the building.* **make sth 'good**; **make 'good on sth** to do sth that you have promised to do, pay back money that you owe, etc: *The company failed to make good on its promise to create more jobs.* **'make it**; **make it 'big** to be successful in your career or business: *companies wanting to make it big on the Internet*
[PHR V] ,**make sth 'out** to write out or complete a form or document: *He made out a cheque for €100.* ◇ *Invoices must be made out in triplicate.* ,**make 'up sth** [HELP] A noun comes after **up**, but a pronoun comes between the verb and **up**. **1** to form sth: *Older workers make up 18% of our staff.* → COMPRISE (2), MAKE-UP **2** to put sth together from several different things → MAKE-UP **3** to complete a number or an amount required: *We need one more person to make up the team.* **4** to replace sth that has been lost: *Can I leave early this afternoon and make up the time tomorrow?* **5** to prepare sth: *Can you make up my bill please?*
● *noun* [C]
the name or type of a machine, piece of equipment, etc. that is made by a particular company: *What make of car does she drive?* ◇ *There are so many different makes to choose from.* See note at BRAND
[IDM] **on the 'make** (*informal*) trying to get money or an advantage for yourself

makegood /ˈmeɪkɡʊd/ *noun* [C]
(*Marketing*) a free advertisement that a publishing company, TV station, etc. gives a company if they have made a mistake in the advertisement that the company paid for or if not as many people have seen it as they promised: *The advertiser must notify the account manager of any error or omission to be eligible for a makegood.*

,**make-or-'buy** *adjective*
(*Production*) used to describe a decision a company must make about whether to make sth itself or pay another company to make it for them: *You face a classic make-or-buy decision concerning software.* ◇ *the make-or-buy strategy for production components*

makeover /ˈmeɪkəʊvə(r)/; *AmE* -oʊ-/ *noun* [C,U]
the process of changing the impression sth gives to others: *Some of the stores will be relocated, the rest will be given a makeover.* ◇ *The corporate makeover is costing the company £20 m.*

★ **maker** /'meɪkə(r)/ *noun* [C]

SEE ALSO: decision-maker, market-~, moneymaker, order-~

a company that makes or produces sth; a person or a piece of equipment that makes sth: *an aircraft/a computer/soft drinks/steel maker* ◇ *the largest maker of computer disk-drives* ◇ *The competition between car makers is getting more intense.* ◇ *If it doesn't work, send it back to the maker.* ◇ *an electric coffee-maker*

,**make-to-'order** *noun* [U] (*abbr* **MTO**)
(*Production*) a system of manufacturing in which a product is only made when an order is received: *The manufacturing plant operates on a make-to-order basis.*

,**make-to-'stock** *noun* [U] (*abbr* **MTS**)
(*Production*) a system of manufacturing in which products are made and stored before orders are received

'**make-up** *noun* [sing.]
the different things, people, etc. that combine to form sth; the way in which they combine: *The make-up of their board of directors needs to change.* ◇ *the page make-up of a text* (= the way in which the words and pictures are arranged on a page)

'**make-work** *noun* [U] (*AmE*)
work that has little value but is given to people to keep them busy: *In some departments there is too much make-work.* ◇ *These are simply make-work schemes for accountants.*

maladministration /ˌmæləd.mɪnɪ'streɪʃn/ *noun* [U]
the fact of managing a business, an organization, an official process, etc. in a bad or dishonest way: *There were instances of maladministration during the course of the enquiry.*

malfunction /ˌmæl'fʌŋkʃn/ *noun, verb*
● *noun* [C,U]
(about a machine) a failure to work correctly: *A fire caused by an electrical malfunction.* ◇ *a computer malfunction*
● *verb* [no obj]
(about a machine) to fail to work correctly: *The bank's ATMs malfunctioned nationwide.* ◇ *malfunctioning computers*

mall /mɔːl/ (*BrE also* mæl/ = SHOPPING MALL

malpractice /ˌmæl'præktɪs/ *noun* [U,C]
careless, wrong or illegal behaviour while in a professional job: *The law firm is being sued for malpractice by the hotel group.* ◇ *investigations into financial malpractices*

man /mæn/ *verb* [+ obj] (-**nn**-)
(*HR*) to work at a place or be in charge of a place or a machine; to supply people to work somewhere: *The telephones are manned 24 hours a day.* ◇ *She mans the information desk at the store.* ▶ '**manning** *noun* [U]: *adjusting manning levels to shorter working hours*

★ **manage** /'mænɪdʒ/ *verb*
1 [+ obj *or* no obj] to control or be in charge of a business, an organization, a team of people, a project, etc.: *I have been managing 3 companies in the UK with around 200 employees.* ◇ *How many people do you manage?* ◇ *The firm manages $3 billion in investments.* ◇ *We need people who are good at managing.*
2 [+ obj] to use time, money, etc. in a sensible way: *She gave a presentation on managing time more effectively.* ◇ *a computer program that helps you manage data efficiently* ◇ *The service helps people to manage their finances.*

manageable /'mænɪdʒəbl/ *adjective*
possible to deal with or control: *The debt has been reduced to a more manageable level.*
OPP UNMANAGEABLE

,**managed e'conomy** *noun* [C]
(*Economics*) a system in which the government owns large parts of industry and sets prices for goods and services → COMMAND ECONOMY, MARKET ECONOMY

,**managed 'fund** *noun* [C]
(*Finance*) an amount of money that is given by an organization or many different investors to a company to invest for them, usually in shares and bonds: *Investors favoured managed funds over direct stock investing.*

,**managed 'hosting** *noun* [U]
(*IT*) a system in which the company that you pay to store your website and put it on the Internet (a **host**) also provides technical help with the HARDWARE and software

★ **management** /'mænɪdʒmənt/ *noun*

SEE ALSO: administrative management, asset ~, assets under ~, brand ~, cash ~, category ~, change ~, etc.

1 [U] the act of running and controlling a business or similar organization: *a career in management* ◇ *a management training course* ◇ *The report blames bad management.* ◇ *He is responsible for the day-to-day management of the firm.* ◇ *hotel management*
❍ *effective/good/solid/strong* management ◆ *bad/poor* management ◆ *day-to-day/general/overall/routine* management ◆ *a management* **company/consultancy** ◆ *management* **methods/practices/skills/styles/techniques**
2 [C with sing./pl. verb; U] the people who run and control a business or similar organization: *The management is/are considering closing the factory.* ◇ *The store is now **under new management**.* ◇ *My role is to act as a mediator between employees and management.* ◇ *Most managements are keen to avoid strikes.* ◇ *We have hired a new management team.*
❍ *junior/senior/top* management ◆ *a management* **committee/decision/meeting/team** ◆ *a layer/level/tier* of management
3 [U; C with sing./pl. verb] the act of running a particular part of a company's activities; the people who do this: *The critical skills in sales management are recruiting, selecting and hiring the best sales reps.* ◇ *a meeting between senior human resources management and employees' representatives*
❍ *data/inventory/sales/staff* management
4 [U] the process or skill of dealing with or controlling things or people: *poor management of people* ◇ *the management of the crisis in the company* ◇ *the waste management business*

'**management ac,counting** (*also* mana'gerial ac,counting) *noun* [U]
(*Accounting*) the process of collecting, analysing and presenting financial information about a company for managers to use in order to make decisions about company organization, future strategy, etc: *The management accounting team is involved in the annual budgetary and forecasting processes.*
▶ '**management ac,countant** (*also* mana'gerial ac,countant) *noun* [C]: *The Institute of Management Accountants (IMA)* '**management ac,counts** *noun* [pl.] → FINANCIAL ACCOUNTING

'**management ,audit** *noun* [C]
an examination of the way in which a company is organized and managed in order to identify areas that could be improved and to find any potential problems: *a management audit of the company's customer services* → AUDIT
▶ '**management ,auditing** *noun* [U]

'management board *noun* [C with sing./pl.verb]
a group of senior executives that are responsible for deciding on the way a company or an organization is managed: *She is a member of the management board.* ◇ *The management board meets/meet every month to review performance and to consider strategy.*

,management 'buy-in *noun* [C] (*abbr* **MBI**)
(*Finance*) a situation where a group of directors from outside a company buy more than 50% of its shares because they want to take over the management of the company: *A three-man management buy-in team took control of the company last year.*

,management 'buyout *noun* [C] (*abbr* **MBO**)
(*Finance*) a situation in which the senior managers gain control of a company or a particular part of it by buying all or most of its shares

,management by ex'ception *noun* [U] (*abbr* **MBE**)
(*HR*) a style of management in which the senior managers give those below them as much authority to control a project as possible and only become involved if there is a problem or an unusual situation (an **exception**)

,management by ob'jectives *noun* [U] (*abbr* **MBO**)
(*HR*) a style of management in which aims and goals are set for the staff in order to direct their work and measure how well they do it: *MBO is most applicable to those jobs which can be measured in numerical outputs.*

'management by 'walking a'round (*BrE also* **'management by 'walking a'bout**) *noun* [U] (*abbr* **MBWA**)
(*HR, informal*) a style of management in which the manager regularly makes informal visits to different departments to talk to staff and check on progress

'management com,mittee *noun* [C with sing./pl. verb]
1 a group of people who are elected to be responsible for deciding on the way a VOLUNTARY organization (= one that does not make a profit), a club, etc. is managed
2 a group of people who are responsible for deciding on the way a particular part of an organization or a particular activity or problem is managed, with less power than the MANAGEMENT BOARD

'management ,company *noun* [C]
a company that manages sth, such as property or investments, for different people or businesses: *an asset/property management company*

'management con,sultant *noun* [C]
a person that a company pays to advise them on how to improve the management and control of their company and its activities, how to deal with a particular problem, introduce changes, etc: *The management consultants are carrying out a review of the company's corporate strategy.*
See note at PROFESSION
▶ **'management con,sulting** *noun* [U]: *Businesses often use management consulting to improve strategy and tactics.* ◇ *a management consulting firm*

,management de'velopment *noun* [U]
(*HR*) the process of improving the skills of managers through training activities: *management development training for solicitors* ◇ *the International Institute for Management Development*

'management game = BUSINESS GAME

,management infor'mation ,system *noun* [C] (*abbr* **MIS**)
a computer system that is designed for business use

in order to supply information to managers from different departments of a company: *a Personnel Management Information System to promote the efficient use of personnel resources* ◇ *Several people were trained to handle MIS.*
→ DECISION SUPPORT SYSTEM

'management ,science *noun* [U] (*abbr* **MS**)
the study of the efficient and effective management of organizations, using ideas and techniques from mathematics, computing, science, etc. to understand how they work, to analyse problems and make decisions → OPERATIONS RESEARCH

,management suc'cession *noun* [U]
(*HR*) the act of sb taking over an important management position: *Management succession planning is an ongoing process of identifying and developing talent.*

,management 'summary = EXECUTIVE SUMMARY

'management team *noun* [C]
a group of people who work together to manage a company, a department, a project, etc: *We have built a strong management team for the company.*

★ **manager** /'mænɪdʒə(r)/ *noun* [C]

SEE ALSO: **account manager, brand ~, category ~, co-~, commercial ~, file ~, first-line ~,** etc.

a person who is in charge of running a business, a shop/store, a department of an organization, a project, etc: *Good managers know how to use the skills of the people who work under them.* ◇ *She's the manager of the accounts department.* ◇ *The assistant manager has been promoted to run the store.* ◇ *a meeting of senior managers* ◇ *regional sales managers* See note at BOSS
▶ **'managership** *noun* [U,C]: *She was offered the managership of the hotel.*

manageress /,mænɪdʒə'res/ *noun* [C] (*BrE old-fashioned*)
a woman who is in charge of a small business, for example, a shop/store, restaurant or hotel

managerial /,mænə'dʒɪəriəl; *AmE* -'dʒɪr-/ *adjective* [usually before noun]
connected with the work of a manager: *She was appointed for her managerial skills.* ◇ *He has a unique managerial style.* ◇ *decisions taken at managerial level*

mana'gerial ac,counting , mana'gerial ac,countant → MANAGEMENT ACCOUNTING

,managing 'agent *noun* [C]
a person or company that is paid to manage a property, an investment, etc. for the owner: *You will have to contact the owner's managing agent concerning changes to the property.*

,managing di'rector *noun* [C] (*especially BrE*) (*abbr* **MD**)
the member of a company's BOARD OF DIRECTORS who is responsible for running the business on a daily basis: *He joined the board as managing director in 2005.* ◇ *She has been appointed as a managing director of their European operations.* ◇ *the former chairman and managing director of the energy company in the UK* → CHIEF EXECUTIVE OFFICER

,managing 'underwriter (*also* **'book ,runner**) = LEAD MANAGER

mandate *noun, verb*
●*noun* /'mændeɪt/ [C]

SEE ALSO: **bank mandate**

1 (*formal*) an official order and instruction given to sb to perform a particular task: *Her mandate is to*

help the company perform at its peak. ◇ *The bank had no mandate to honour the cheque.*
2 a document that gives a bank or sb else the power to deal with your account: *Your new bank will ask you to sign a mandate enabling them to act on your behalf.*
●*verb* /'mændeɪt; ˌmæn'deɪt/ [+ obj] (*formal*) (*often be mandated*)
1 to order sb to do sth, to behave or vote in a particular way; to order that sth should happen in a particular way: *The number of days' vacation is not mandated by law.*
2 to give sb, especially a government or a committee, the authority to do sth: *The committee was mandated to draft a constitution.*

mandatory /'mændətəri; *AmE* -tɔːri; *BrE also* mæn'deɪtəri/ *adjective*
if a particular action is **mandatory** then you must do it, usually because it is required by law: *Retirement is mandatory for pilots at 60.* ◇ *It is mandatory for companies to change their auditors regularly.* ◇ *mandatory price cuts* ◇ *The meeting is mandatory.*

'mandatory con'vertible 'bond *noun* [C]
(*Finance*) a type of bond that a company issues that must be changed into shares in the company by a particular date

'man-hour *noun* [C, usually pl.]
the amount of work done by one person in one hour: *The team of 200 spent four years, a million man-hours and €35 million developing the new washing machine.* ◇ *Back injury caused by lifting or bending was the main cause of lost man-hours at the factory.*

manifest /'mænɪfest/ *noun* [C]
(*Transport*) a list of goods or passengers on a ship or an aircraft: *aircraft passenger manifests* ◇ *A cargo manifest must be submitted 24 hours before loading.*

★ **manipulate** /mə'nɪpjuleɪt/ *verb* [+ obj]
1 to control or influence sb/sth, often in a dishonest way so that they do not realize it: *Advertisers seem to be concerned with manipulating our attitudes.* ◇ *The managers manipulate borrowers into paying higher interest rates.*
2 to control or use sth in a skilful way: *to manipulate the gears and levers of a machine* ◇ *Computers are very efficient at manipulating information.*
3 to change or present information in a way that will deceive people: *The company committed fraud by manipulating its financial records.*
▶ **manipulation** /mə,nɪpju'leɪʃn/ *noun* [U,C]: *Advertising like this is a manipulation of the elderly.* ◇ *data manipulation* **manipulator** /mə'nɪpjuleɪtə(r)/ *noun* [C]

manoeuvre (*AmE spelling* **maneuver**) /mə'nuːvə(r)/ *noun, verb*
●*noun* [C]
a clever plan, action or movement that is used to give sb an advantage: *He managed to block the takeover with various legal manoeuvres.*
IDM **freedom of/room for ma'noeuvre; room to ma'noeuvre** the chance to change the way that sth happens and influence decisions that are made: *The company is heavily indebted and has little room for manoeuvre.*
●*verb* [+ obj or no obj]
to control or influence a situation in a skilful but sometimes dishonest way: *She manoeuvred her way to the top of the company.* ◇ *The deal follows months of manoeuvring by the company to gain control of the market.*

manpower /'mænpaʊə(r)/ *noun* [U]
the number of workers needed or available to do a

particular job: *a need for trained/skilled manpower* ◇ *a manpower shortage* ◇ *We don't have the manpower to stock the shelves, price and handle returns.*

,manpower 'planning *noun* [U]
(*HR*) the process of calculating the number of workers needed for a job, considering costs, skills, training needs, etc: *A manpower planning report recommended the reduction of the workforce.* ◇ *manpower planning software*

mantra /'mæntrə/ *noun* [C]
a word, phrase or sentence that is often repeated and that expresses an idea or a belief: *The company's mantra is 'No Excuses'.*

manual /'mænjuəl/ *adjective, noun*
●*adjective*
1 (used about work) involving using the hands or physical strength: *manual and non-manual workers*
◐ *manual* **jobs/labour/occupations/skills/work** ◆ *manual* **labourers/workers**
2 operated or controlled by hand rather than automatically or using electricity, etc: *a manual gearbox* ◇ *The camera has manual and automatic functions.* ◇ *The company has now transferred all its manual records onto computer.*
◐ *manual* **controls/processes/systems**
▶ **manually** /'mænjuəli/ *adverb*: *Final product packing is currently done manually.* ◇ *a manually operated machine*
●*noun* [C]

SEE ALSO: **training manual, operations ~, service ~**

a book that tells you how to do a task or how to operate sth, especially one that comes with a machine, etc: *Read the manual before you install the software.* → HANDBOOK
◐ *an instruction/a* **software/technical** *manual* ◆ *the* **owner's/user/user's** *manual*
IDM **on 'manual** not being operated automatically: *Leave the controls on manual.*

,manual 'handling *noun* [U]
any activity in which a person must use force to lift, carry, hold or move an object: *new legislation governing the manual handling of goods and materials* ◇ *manual handling injuries*

manufactory /ˌmænju'fæktri; -təri/ *noun* [C]
(*plural* **manufactories**)
used in the names of some companies that manufacture goods → FACTORY

★ **manufacture** /ˌmænju'fæktʃə(r)/ *verb, noun*
●*verb* [+ obj or no obj]
to make goods in large quantities from raw materials or parts, using machinery: *The plant manufactures 500 000 cars annually.* ◇ *They have a contract to manufacture one million TV sets.*
See note at PRODUCE
●*noun*
1 [U] the process of producing goods in large quantities: *the manufacture of microchips*
2 **manufactures** [pl.] goods that are manufactured: *a major importer of cotton manufactures*

★ **manufacturer** /ˌmænju'fæktʃərə(r)/ *noun* [C]

SEE ALSO: **original equipment manufacturer**

a person or company that produces goods in large quantities from raw materials or parts: *an auto/computer/drugs/steel manufacturer* ◇ *Always follow the manufacturer's instructions.* ◇ *Faulty goods should be returned to the manufacturers.* → MAKER, SUPPLIER, VENDOR

,manu'facturer's brand *noun* [C]
(*Marketing*) a brand that is owned by a manufacturer and has their name

SEE ALSO: **computer-integrated manufacturing, value-added manufacturing**

the business or industry of producing goods in large quantities in factories, using parts or raw materials: *Many jobs in manufacturing were lost during the recession.* ◇ *a new manufacturing plant* ◇ *a low-cost manufacturing strategy* ◇ *The manufacturing sector is starting to recover.*

ˌmanuˈfacturing base *noun* [C]
1 (*Economics*) (*also* inˈdustrial base) the part of the economy of a country or an area that is related to producing goods in large quantities in factories: *Finland's manufacturing base consists of the wood and paper industry, electronics, and other engineering.* ◇ *a strong/weak manufacturing base*
2 a place where a company has one or more factories that produce goods in large quantities: *The company has established its first manufacturing base in Europe.*

ˌmanufacturing inforˈmation ˌsystem *noun* [C] (*abbr* **MIS**)
(*Production*) a computer system that is designed to supply information to managers to help them organize production in an efficient way

ˌmanufacturing reˈsource ˌplanning *noun* [U] (*abbr* **MRP, MRPII**)
(*Production*) a type of software system that links together most aspects of a manufacturer's activities, such as engineering, ordering materials, controlling production, etc., designed to help the business manage and control its work most efficiently → FINITE CAPACITY SCHEDULING

map /mæp/ *verb, noun*
●*verb* [+ obj] (**-pp-**)
1 to discover or give information about sth, especially the way it is arranged or organized: *We used this software to map and manipulate the data.* ◇ *The team's job is mapping, analysing and improving our core systems.*
2 to match or link one or more items or qualities with those in a different group or area: *It isn't easy to understand your objectives and map them against possible jobs.* ◇ *Skills mapping is used to assign employees to specific tasks.*
PHR V ˈmap sth on/onto sth to link data, a group of qualities, items, etc. with their source, cause, position on a scale, etc: *I took the information and mapped it onto a graph.* ˌmap sth ˈout to plan or arrange sth in a careful or detailed way: *He has his career path clearly mapped out.*
●*noun*

SEE ALSO: **market map**

a drawing or plan of the earth's surface or part of it, showing countries, towns, rivers, etc: *a map of New Zealand* ◇ *an airline route map*
IDM put sb/sth on the ˈmap to make sb/sth famous or important: *The campaign has helped put the company on the map as a major fashion brand.*

★ **margin** /ˈmɑːdʒɪn/ *AmE* ˈmɑːrdʒən/ *noun, verb*
●*noun*

SEE ALSO: **gross profit margin, high-~, low-~, net ~, net profit ~, operating ~, operating profit ~, solvency ~**

1 (*Accounting*) [C,U] the difference between the cost of buying or producing sth and the price that it is sold for, calculated as a percentage of the selling price: *They make an 18% margin on the sale of each phone.* ◇ *Higher insurance and security costs had lowered the margin.* ◇ *There is so little margin right now that we cannot afford added expenses.* ◇ *high-margin products* **SYN** PROFIT MARGIN → GROSS MARGIN

❶ *a high/low/tight* margin • *to* **increase/make** *a margin*
2 [C] an extra amount of sth such as time, space, money, etc. that you include in order to make sure that sth is successful: *The calculation includes a safety margin to allow for price rises.* ◇ *The plan leaves us a slim margin for error.* → MARGIN OF ERROR
3 [C, usually sing.] the amount by which one quantity is greater or smaller than another: *The committee voted against the change by a margin of just five to four.* ◇ *Sales of children's clothing has outperformed other clothing by a considerable margin.*
❶ *a comfortable/considerable/narrow/wide* margin
4 (*Stock Exchange*) [C,U] money, shares, bonds, etc. that an investor must leave with a BROKER to cover any possible losses: *Brokers ask investors to cover daily price moves by depositing margin.* → MARGIN ACCOUNT
5 [C] the empty space at the side of a written or printed page or web page: *The software allows you to set the margins of the document.* ◇ *When the ads are at the margin they can be larger than top-of-page banners.*
6 [C] the part that is not included in the main part of a group, an organization or a situation: *Usually companies make changes at the margins rather than in their core business.* ◇ *Oil producers at the margin were driven out of business.*
7 (*HR*) [C, usually pl.] in Australia and New Zealand, an amount that is added to a basic wage, paid for special skill or responsibility
IDM on ˈmargin (*Stock Exchange*) if an investor buys shares, FUTURES, etc. on margin, they borrow money from their BROKER to pay for them, using their account as a guarantee: *You must have a minimum amount of cash or equity in your account to be allowed to trade on margin.*

┌─────────────────────────┐
│ **WHICH WORD?**   │
└─────────────────────────┘

margin/markup

Both words are used to describe the amount of money that a business makes from selling a product, but they are calculated in different ways:

• The **markup** is a percentage of how much it costs the business to produce the product. It is the amount by which this amount is increased to decide the price.

• The **margin** is a percentage of the amount that the product is sold for. It is the amount of the price which is profit for the seller.

If a store buys a product for $1 and sells it for $1.50, the markup is 50%, the margin is 33%.

●*verb* [+ obj]
(*Stock Exchange*) to buy, or allow sb to buy, shares, bonds, etc. with money borrowed using their account with the BROKER as a guarantee: *Some brokerages may decide not to margin certain stocks.*
▶ **marginable** /ˈmɑːdʒɪnəbl; *AmE* ˈmɑːrdʒən-/ *adjective*

ˈmargin acˌcount *noun* [C]
(*Stock Exchange*) an arrangement that an investor has with a BROKER in which the investor can borrow money for investments but must leave a particular amount of money, shares, etc. in their account (a **margin**): *Interest is charged on all margin accounts.*

★ **marginal** /ˈmɑːdʒɪnl; *AmE* ˈmɑːrdʒ-/ *adjective*
1 small and not having an important effect: *There has been a marginal improvement in retail sales.* ◇ *The difference between the two estimates is marginal.*

2 (*Economics*) [only before noun] connected with a single change in the level of an activity: *The company should increase the salary to the point where the marginal benefits equal the marginal cost.* → MARGINAL COST, MARGINAL PRODUCTIVITY, MARGINAL REVENUE

3 (*Economics*) that can hardly make enough money to cover the costs of production: *The bigger oil companies can spend money on marginal oil development.* ◇ *Marginal companies have been forced to leave the industry.*

4 not part of a main or an important group or system: *They have decided to expand their marginal brands.* ◇ *The business has been left with only marginal workers* (= for example, people who do not work regularly or all the time).

ˌmarginal ˈcost *noun* [C,U]
(*Economics*) the amount of extra money that a business must spend in order to increase its level of production or supply by one unit: *A business with extra capacity can produce extra units at low marginal cost.* → MARGINAL REVENUE

ˌmarginal ˈcosting (*also* ˌmarginal ˈpricing) *noun* [U]
(*Accounting*) a method of calculating the cost of a unit of a product that includes only the amount spent on producing it, such as the cost of materials or labour SYN VARIABLE COSTING

marginally /ˈmɑːdʒɪnəli; *AmE* ˈmɑːrdʒ-/ *adverb*
very slightly; not very much: *Profits rose marginally, from 3.9 to 4 million dollars.* ◇ *This figure is marginally above what we predicted.*

ˌmarginal producˈtivity *noun* [U]
(*Economics*) the extra amount that can be produced as a result of adding one unit of sth used in production

ˈmarginal proˈpensity to conˈsume *noun* [sing.] (*abbr* **MPC**)
(*Economics*) the relationship between a change in the money people have to spend and the change in the amount that they spend

ˈmarginal proˈpensity to imˈport *noun* [sing.] (*abbr* **MPM**)
(*Economics*) the relationship between a change in the total income of a country and the change in the amount that is spent on imported goods

ˈmarginal proˈpensity to ˈsave *noun* [sing.] (*abbr* **MPS**)
(*Economics*) the relationship between a change in the money people have to spend and the change in the amount that they save

ˌmarginal ˈrate (*also* ˈmarginal ˈrate of ˈtax, ˌmarginal ˈtax rate) *noun* [C]
(*Accounting*) a rate of tax that is paid on your next unit of income; the highest rate of tax that sb pays: *The government has promised to lower marginal rates.* ◇ *I've stopped doing freelance work as my marginal tax rate on it was more than 50%.*

ˌmarginal ˈrevenue *noun* [U,C]
(*Economics*) the amount of extra money that a business can earn by increasing its level of production or supply by one unit: *A firm will stop increasing its output when marginal revenue and marginal cost are equal.*

ˌmarginal ˈtax rate = MARGINAL RATE

ˈmargin call *noun* [C]
(*Stock Exchange*) a demand by a BROKER for an investor to add money, shares, etc. to their account because it has fallen below the amount that is allowed: *He was forced to sell some shares to cover a margin call.*

ˈmargin exˌpansion *noun* [U]
(*Accounting*) an increase in the amount of profit that a business makes from selling a product: *Sales growth and margin expansion remain strong.*

ˌmargin of ˈerror *noun* [C, usually sing.]
an amount that you allow when you calculate sth for the possibility that a number is not completely accurate: *The survey has a margin of error of 2.5%.*

ˌmargin of ˈsafety *noun* [C]
(*Accounting*) the difference between the quantity of goods or services that a business must sell in order to BREAK EVEN and the total quantity it expects to sell

marine /məˈriːn/ *adjective* [only before noun]
(often used in the names of companies) connected with ships or transporting goods by sea: *the marine industry* ◇ *The company produces both aeroplane and marine engines.* ◇ *Hyundai Merchant Marine, the Korean shipping company*

maˈrine inˌsurance *noun* [U]
insurance that pays for damage to ships or goods transported by ship: *It is important to take out adequate marine insurance when transporting goods by sea.*

ˌmarital ˈstatus *noun* [U]
(used especially on official forms) the fact of whether you are single, married, etc: *questions about age, sex and marital status*

maritime /ˈmærɪtaɪm/ *adjective*
connected with the sea or ships, especially in relation to trade: *maritime trade between continents* ◇ *the maritime industry/sector*

ˌmaritime ˈlaw *noun* [U,C]
the official rules that apply to ships and transporting goods or people by sea

mark /mɑːk; *AmE* mɑːrk/ *verb, noun*
● *verb* [+ obj]
1 mark A (with B) | mark B on A to write or draw words, a symbol, line, etc. on sth in order to give information about it: *We mark each packet with a sell-by date.* ◇ *Prices are marked on the goods.* ◇ *The envelope was marked 'Confidential'.*
2 (*Stock Exchange*) mark sth higher/lower (*usually* be marked) if shares are marked higher/lower, investors think they are worth more/less and so their value on the stock exchange increases/decreases: *Some investors marked the shares higher because the results showed an improvement.* ◇ *The airline was marked 4.7% lower.* → MARK STH DOWN (2), MARK STH UP (2)
IDM **mark ˈtime 1** to pass the time while you wait for sth more interesting: *I'm just marking time in this job—I'm hoping to get into journalism.* **2** if sth such as prices mark time, they stay at the same level although they may change soon: *The shares are marking time, as investors wait for next week's results.*
PHRV **ˌmark sth ˈdown 1** (*Commerce*) to lower the price of sth: *We've marked the price down from €49 to €29.* ◇ *marked-down items* OPP MARK STH UP → MARKDOWN **2** (*Stock Exchange*) (*usually* be marked down) if shares are marked down, their value on the stock exchange decreases: *The company saw its shares marked down 0.5 per cent* (= by investors on a stock exchange). OPP MARK STH UP → MARKDOWN **ˌmark sb ˈout as/for sth** to choose sb or to make people recognize sb as special in some way: *She was marked out for early promotion.* **ˌmark sth ˈup 1** (*Commerce*) to raise the price of sth: *We've marked the price up from €49 to €55.* OPP MARK STH DOWN → MARKUP **2** (*Stock Exchange*) (*usually* be marked up) if shares are marked up, their value on the stock exchange increases: *Share prices were marked up as soon as trading started.* OPP MARK STH DOWN **3** to mark or correct a text, etc., for example for printing → MARKUP

SEE ALSO: **check mark**

1 [C, usually sing.] a level or point that sth reaches that is thought to be important: *The price of oil has passed the $40-a-barrel mark.* ◇ *Unemployment remains below the four million mark.*
2 Mark [sing.] (followed by a number) a particular type or model of a machine or vehicle: *the Mark II engine*
IDM ,make your/a 'mark (on sth) to become famous and successful in a particular area: *The company made its mark with its online payment service.* → idiom at LINE *noun*

markdown /'mɑːkdaʊn; *AmE* 'mɑːrk-/ *noun* [C]
1 (*Commerce*) a reduction in the price of goods to encourage sales; an act of reducing prices: *a 20% markdown on many items* ◇ *Department stores have taken big markdowns to clear stock.*
O *big/heavy/steep markdowns (on sth)* ♦ *to introduce/make/offer a markdown*
2 (*Finance*) an amount of money earned by a dealer when buying shares, bonds, etc. from a customer, equal to the difference between the amount the dealer pays for the shares, bonds, etc. and the price at which they can sell them
3 (*Stock Exchange*) a reduction in the price of shares on the stock exchange: *The markdown in the price is unlikely to be regained quickly.*
OPP MARKUP

marked /mɑːkt; *AmE* mɑːrkt/ *adjective*
easy to see: *a marked increase in profits* ◇ *The company's results were in marked contrast to predictions.*
O *a marked decline/decrease/fall (in sth)* ♦ *a marked improvement/increase/recovery/rise (in sth)* ♦ *a marked deterioration/slowdown (in sth)* ♦ *a marked contrast/difference*
▸ **markedly** /'mɑːkɪdli; *AmE* 'mɑːrk-/ *adverb*: *This year's sales have risen markedly.*

marker /'mɑːkə(r); *AmE* 'mɑːrk-/ *noun*
1 [C, usually sing.] a sign that sth exists or that shows what it is like: *Price is not always an accurate marker of quality.*
2 [C, usually sing.] a standard for judging or deciding things: *The rate of inflation is widely used as a marker for pay deals.*
3 (*also* 'marker pen) [C] a pen with a soft thick tip
IDM put/lay/set down a/your 'marker (for sth) to show your position or opinion about sth; to show that you are committed to sth: *Peter has put down a marker for next year as the best time to launch the new product.*

★ **market** /'mɑːkɪt; *AmE* 'mɑːrk-/ *noun, verb*
● *noun*

SEE ALSO: **bear market, black ~, bull ~, buyer's ~, capital ~, cash ~, closed ~, etc.**

1 [sing.] business or trade; the amount of trade in a particular type of goods, services, investments, etc: *the world market in coffee* ◇ *the advertising/insurance/telecoms market* ◇ *the shares market* ◇ *The hardware market is severely depressed.* ◇ *The company performed well despite difficult market conditions.* → MARKET SHARE
O *to break into/enter/come into/go into the market* ♦ *to capture/dominate the market (in sth)* ♦ *the domestic/global/international/local/world market (in sth)* ♦ *an active/a booming/rising/steady/strong market* ♦ *a competitive/tough market* ♦ *a depressed/dull/falling/weak market* ♦ *market conditions/prices/rates*
2 [C] a particular area, country or section of the population that might buy goods or services: *We produce this version for the Japanese market.* ◇ *They hope to break into the teenage market.* ◇ *Our product is aimed at the corporate market.* ◇ *The Internet is opening up new markets for companies.* ◇ *The EU has become Chile's largest export market.*
O *to enter/find/open up/operate in/penetrate a market* ♦ *to break into/go into/move into a market* ♦ *the domestic/home/international/local market* ♦ *a developed/developing/growing/growth/mature market* ♦ *an important/a key/large/main market*
3 [C] a demand for a product; the number of people, businesses, etc. who buy it or want to buy it: *There is no longer a market for tin.* ◇ *Retailers have created a market for organic food.* ◇ *a slump in the global market for PCs*
O *to build/create a market* ♦ *a big/good/large/poor/small market (for sth)* ♦ *an expanding/a growing/shrinking market* ♦ *the annual/domestic/global/world/worldwide market for sth*
4 (*Economics*) [C] (*usually* the market [sing.]) an economic system in which the price of goods and services is affected by supply and demand rather than controlled by government: *Power supply cannot be left to the market.* ◇ *The market will decide if the TV station has any future.* ◇ *a crowded market* (= a situation where there are lots of competing products)
O *market-based/market-driven/market-led*
5 (*Finance*) [C] = FINANCIAL MARKET
6 (*Stock Exchange*) [C] = STOCK MARKET
7 [C] an occasion when people buy and sell goods; the open area or the building where they meet to do this: *a cattle/fish/fruit and vegetable/meat market* ◇ *We buy our vegetables at/in the market.* ◇ *The traders take their flowers to market early in the morning.* ◇ *Wednesday is market day.*
O *a covered/an indoor market* ♦ *an open-air/outdoor/a street market* ♦ *market stalls/traders*
8 [C] (*especially AmE*) a shop/store, especially one that sells food or one kind of goods: *There is a local mini-market only a short distance away.*
IDM be first, quick, etc. to 'market to be the first, be quick, etc. to get a product ready to sell: *Being first to market does not guarantee success.* **come to (the) 'market 1** (*Stock Exchange*) (about a company) to offer shares for sale on a stock exchange: *The retailer is planning to come to market next month.* **2** to be ready to start selling a new product: *Japanese carmakers are coming to the market with more efficient engines.* **corner the 'market (in/on sth)** to get control of the trade in a particular type of goods or services; to control the whole supply of sth: *They've cornered the market in silver.* ◇ *cornering the market on female engineering talent* **get, bring, etc. sth to 'market** to make a product ready to be sold: *They are too slow in getting their products to market.* ◇ *the high cost of bringing new drugs to market* **in the 'market for sth** interested in buying sth: *We're in the market for a new computer system.* **make a 'market** (*Stock Exchange*) (about a dealer) to be ready, willing and able to buy and sell particular shares: *The broker will make a market in the shares.* → MARKET-MAKER **on/onto the 'market** available for people to buy: *to put your house on the market* ◇ *It's one of the best laptops on the market.* ◇ *They are preparing to launch a mobile phone onto the UK market.* → idioms at PLAY *verb*, PRICE *verb*, SKIM
● *verb* [+ obj]
to advertise and offer a product for sale; to present sth in a particular way and make people want to buy it: *The company markets a range of clothing, mainly through independent stores.* ◇ *a drink marketed to 18 to 24 year-olds* ◇ *Many of these funds were marketed as low-risk.* → PROMOTE

marketable /'mɑːkɪtəbl; *AmE* 'mɑːrk-/ *adjective*
1 easy to sell; attractive to customers or employers: *We knew we had discovered a marketable technology.* ◇ *What can you do to make yourself more*

marketable to an employer? ◇ marketable goods/
products ◇ marketable qualifications/skills
2 (Finance) (about shares, bonds, etc.) that can be
bought and sold by investors: The company has $1.5
billion in cash and marketable securities on its books.
OPP NON-MARKETABLE
▶ **marketability** /ˌmɑːkɪtəˈbɪləti; AmE ˌmɑːrk-/
noun [U]: enhancing the marketability of your
products

ˌmarketable seˈcurity noun [C]
(Finance) a **security** (= a financial asset such as a
share or bond) that can be bought and sold: At the
end of the quarter, the group had cash and
marketable securities of $776 m.

ˌmarket ˈanalyst noun [C]
(Finance) a person who collects and analyses
information about a market, especially a stock
market

ˈmarket ˌbasket noun [C]
(Economics) a collection of different products that
consumers buy regularly; the price paid for them.
This is used to measure the COST OF LIVING: A
market basket of goods and services increased by only
1.8% last year.

ˌmarket capitaliˈzation (also ˌmarket ˈcap,
ˌcapitaliˈzation) noun [U,C]
(Stock Exchange) the total value of all a company's
shares, calculated by multiplying the number of
shares by their price on the stock exchange

ˌmarket ˈclearing price noun [C]
(Economics) the price at which the level of demand
equals the level of supply

ˌmarket concenˈtration noun [U]
(Economics) the situation when a small number of
companies control a large part of a market: There is
a high level of market concentration in the
information sector. → MARKET FRAGMENTATION

ˌmarket conˈtrol noun [U]
(Economics) the ability of buyers or sellers to affect
the price or quantity of goods or services

ˌmarket eˈconomy (also ˌfree-market
eˈconomy) noun [C]
(Economics) a system in which businesses manage
their own affairs and compete with each other and
people can choose what they buy: the move from a
centrally planned to a market economy ◇ Price
regulation is not consistent with a market economy.
→ COMMAND ECONOMY

marketeer /ˌmɑːkɪˈtɪə(r); AmE ˌmɑːrkəˈtɪr/ noun [C]

SEE ALSO: free marketeer

1 a person whose job involves getting people to
buy things: He is a skilled retailer and marketeer.
→ MARKETER
2 a person who is in favour of a particular system
of buying and selling

ˌmarket equiˈlibrium = EQUILIBRIUM

marketer /ˈmɑːkɪtə(r); AmE ˈmɑːrk-/ noun [C]
1 a specialist in marketing: the company's chief
marketer ◇ The marketer builds a relationship
between the brand and the customer.
2 a business that sells goods or services to the
public or that sells in a particular way: Forest Deli
is a distributor and marketer of tropical foods. ◇ a
business-to-business marketer

ˈmarket-ˌfacing adjective [usually before noun]
used to describe a business that gives special
attention to its customers and their needs: a
market-facing enterprise

ˌmarket ˈforces noun [pl.]
(Economics) things that affect the price of a product
or service or the quantity in which it is produced or
sold, for example the amount of raw materials
available or the number of customers: Market forces
have driven down the price of salmon. ◇ We believe
that foreign exchange rates should be left to market
forces (= rather than influenced by governments).

ˌmarket ˌfragmenˈtation noun [U]
(Economics) an increase in the number of different
groups of customers for a product or service or
different companies providing it → MARKET
CONCENTRATION

★ **marketing** /ˈmɑːkɪtɪŋ; AmE ˈmɑːrk-/ noun [U]

SEE ALSO: affiliate marketing, buzz ~, cooperative ~,
corporate ~, direct ~, drip ~, environmental ~, etc.

the activity of presenting, advertising and selling a
company's products in the best possible way: She
works in **sales and marketing**. ◇ Low-cost airlines
are known for their aggressive marketing. ◇ The
company invests heavily in the marketing of its
brands. ◇ a marketing campaign that targets
customers aged 20 to 30 ◇ to develop a marketing
plan for a new product
○ aggressive/clever/effective/successful marketing ◆
email/online/traditional marketing ◆ a marketing
campaign/plan/push/strategy ◆ the marketing
budget/spend ◆ a marketing director/manager/
officer

WHICH WORD?

marketing/advertising/promotion/
publicity/public relations

These words all describe ways in which companies
communicate with the public.

Marketing covers all the activities used to
encourage demand for products. The part of a
company responsible for these activities is usually
called the Marketing Department and a series of
activities planned for a product is a marketing
campaign.

Advertising and **promotion** are aspects of
marketing. **Advertising** involves paying for
advertisements, for example in newspapers or on
television. **Promotion** can include advertising as
well as other things, such as giving discounts or
free items in order to encourage sales.

A company receives **publicity** when it is
mentioned in news reports, magazine articles, etc.
Companies give out information so that the press
and public will take notice of their activities and
products.

Public relations is the activity of giving
information to the public that will create a good
impression of a company. The job of keeping good
public relations (= a good relationship with the
public) is often given to an independent public
relations firm that has experience in dealing with
journalists.

ˈmarketing board noun [C with sing./pl. verb]
an organization, usually created by the
government, that promotes and controls the sale of
an agricultural product such as grain, milk, etc: the
Pennsylvania Milk Marketing Board

ˌmarketing communiˈcations noun [U]

SEE ALSO: integrated marketing communications

(Marketing) all the ways in which a company gives
information about its products or services to
customers or possible customers, such as
advertising, events, SPONSORSHIP, etc: Direct mail

is an important part of the marketing communications mix. ◇ *He is director of worldwide marketing communications for the airline.*

'marketing ˌconcept *noun*
1 (*Marketing*) [C] an idea for a product and the way it should be sold and presented to the public: *to build/develop a marketing concept* ◇ *We need a strong marketing concept.* → SELLING CONCEPT
2 (*Economics*) **the marketing concept** [sing.] the theory that a company should concentrate on finding out what kinds of product customers want and then produce them rather than produce sth and then try to persuade the customer to buy it → PRODUCTION CONCEPT, SELLING CONCEPT

'marketing enˌvironment *noun* [C]
all the things that a company must consider when developing its marketing plans, such as people's incomes, the products of competitors, new technology, etc: *the impact of the Internet on today's marketing environment*

'marketing mix *noun* [C, usually sing.]
(*Marketing*) the main factors that influence a customer's decision to buy a particular product or service, which a business must consider when it is deciding how to advertise and sell its products: *You must develop the right marketing mix for your product.* → 4 Ps

ˌmarketing myˈopia /maɪˈəʊpiə; *AmE* -ˈoʊpiə/ *noun* [U]
(*Marketing*) the situation when a business focuses on its products rather than on the needs of the customers and so may miss changes in the market

'marketing orienˌtation = MARKET ORIENTATION

ˌmarketing reˈsearch = MARKET RESEARCH

ˌmarketing reˈsource ˌmanagement *noun* [U] (*abbr* **MRM**)
(*Marketing*) the use of computer software to organize, plan and improve a company's marketing

'marketing ˌservices *noun* [pl.; U]
(*Marketing*) activities connected with market research, advertising products and services, etc.; the department of a company that deals with this

ˌmarket inˈtelligence *noun* [U]
(*Marketing*) the process of collecting and analysing information about a market, such as information about industries, competitors, products and customers, that can help a company decide how to sell their goods

ˌmarket ˈleader *noun* [C]
(*Marketing*)
1 the company that sells the largest quantity of a particular kind of product: *We are the market leader in car insurance.* ◇ *We believe we are ready to challenge the market leaders.* ◇ *They are in second place behind market leader, Tesco plc.*
2 a product that is the most successful of its kind: *Our range of products includes 20 market leaders.*
▶ **ˌmarket ˈleadership** *noun* [U]: *The company has strengthened its market leadership in two key countries.* ◇ *to achieve/establish/win market leadership*

'market-ˌmaker (*also spelled* **market maker**, *especially in AmE*) *noun* [C] (*abbr* **MM**)
(*Stock Exchange*) a company or person that deals in shares, bonds, etc. and agrees to buy and sell particular shares at specific prices: *The investor buys through a broker who completes the transaction through a market-maker.* ◇ *A couple of market-makers were caught short of stock.*

'market map *noun* [C]
(*Marketing*) a diagram that shows the positions of brands in terms of the most important brand characteristics

'market ˌmechanism = PRICE MECHANISM

ˌmarket ˈniche *noun* [C]
(*Marketing*) a group of customers that a company's products are especially suitable for and which the company is seen as belonging to; a product, service or company that is different from or better than others in the same area: *The company has grown beyond its original market niche.* ◇ *The bank has created a market niche for itself in the commercial sector by focusing on project finance.* → MARKET SEGMENT, NICHE MARKET
● *to* **carve out/create/establish/spot** *a market niche*

'market ˌorder *noun* [C]
(*Stock Exchange*) an order to a dealer to buy or sell shares, bonds, etc. immediately at the current market price

'market orienˌtation (*also* **'marketing orienˌtation**) *noun* [C, usually sing., U]
(*Marketing*) the situation when a company focuses on what products customers need or want rather than on what they want to make: *The industry has been dominated by product orientation rather than market orientation.* ◇ *market orientation research*

ˌmarket parˈticipant *noun* [C]
(*Finance*) a person or company that buys or sells shares, bonds, etc: *Most market participants are either individuals or very small firms.*

ˌmarket peneˈtration *noun* [U]
(*Marketing*)
1 the number of buyers who have bought a particular type of product, or a particular company's product, compared with the total number of possible buyers: *The market penetration of mobile phones in Western Europe now stands at 78%.* ◇ *The company expects to end the year at 50% market penetration.*
● *to* **enhance/gain/increase** *market penetration*
2 the policy of trying to gain a larger share of an existing market, for example by changing the price of a product or advertising more, rather than changing the product itself: *Do we price for market penetration or cash generation?* ◇ *a market penetration strategy*

ˌmarket-peneˈtration ˌpricing *noun* [U]
(*Marketing*) the policy of trying to get a share of a market for a new brand or product by first offering it at a low price

★ **marketplace** /ˈmɑːkɪtpleɪs; *AmE* ˈmɑːrk-/ *noun*
1 **the marketplace** [sing.] the activity of competing with other companies to buy and sell goods, services, etc: *Companies must be able to survive in the marketplace.* ◇ *It's an online marketplace for small business products and services.* ◇ *How can we compete successfully in the global marketplace?* ◇ *the electronic/financial/media marketplace*
2 (*also* **ˌmarket ˈsquare**) [C] an open area in a town where a market is or was held

ˌmarket ˈprice (*also* **ˌmarket ˈvalue**) *noun* [C]
the price that a product or service will currently sell for: *The market price for gold has risen dramatically.* ◇ *Without a shift in demand and/or supply there will be no change in market price.* ◇ *Some customers are willing to pay above market prices for a top quality product.* → EQUILIBRIUM PRICE

ˌmarket ˈrate *noun* [sing.]
the usual price or rate for sth at a particular time: *We charge interest below the market rate on loans.* ◇ *Many small businesses cannot afford to pay market rates for legal services.* SYN GOING RATE

★ **ˌmarket reˈsearch** (*also* **ˌmarketing reˈsearch**) *noun* [U] (*abbr* **MR**)
the process of collecting and analysing information

about markets, competitors, customers' opinions and problems connected with advertising and selling goods and services: *They are doing market research* **on** *Brazil and other promising markets.* ◇ *She'd like a career in market research.* ◇ *a leading market research firm*
  ● *to* **carry out/do** *market research* • *a market research* **interview/questionnaire/survey** • *a market research* **company/firm/group**
  ▶ ˌmarket reˈsearcher *noun* [C]: *He used to work as a market researcher.* ◇ *the world's fourth largest market researcher*

ˌmarket ˈrisk = SYSTEMATIC RISK

ˌmarket ˈsector *noun* [C]
a part of a market such as a particular industry or group of customers: *The table presents a revenue breakdown by market sector.* ◇ *Key market sectors include IT, telecommunications, finance and insurance.* ◇ *You need to position yourself in your target market sector.* → SECTOR

ˌmarket ˈsegment *noun* [C]
(*Marketing*)
1 a group of possible customers who are similar in income, age, habits, etc: *Schools are a growing market segment.*
2 products produced for one particular group of customers: *Their strongest market segment is in small notebook computers.*
  → SEGMENT

ˌmarket ˌsegmenˈtation *noun* [U,C]
(*Marketing*) the act of dividing possible customers into groups according to their age, income, sex, class, etc.; one of these parts: *Market segmentation permits firms to tailor products for specific markets.*
  → SEGMENTATION

★ ˌmarket ˈshare *noun* [C,U]
(*Marketing*) the amount of sales of a particular type of product that a company has, compared with the total sales: *The company's US market share fell from 23.4% to 21.2%.* ◇ *Our market share increased in all segments.* ◇ *They hope to win market share from their competitors.* ◇ *They are using price-cutting to try to buy market share.* → VALUE SHARE
  ● *to* **boost/build/grow/increase** *market share* • *to* **gain/grab/take/win** *market share* • *to* **lose/ maintain** *market share*

ˌmarket-skimming ˈpricing = SKIMMING (1)

ˌmarket ˈsquare = MARKETPLACE (2)

ˌmarket ˈtest *noun* [C]
(*Marketing*) an experiment in which a product is made available in one or more areas to see if consumers like it and will buy it: *Products which do not meet consumer desires will fail the market test.*
  ▶ ˈmarket-test *verb* [+ obj]: *market-tested products* ˌmarket ˈtesting *noun* [U]

ˌmarket ˈvalue *noun* [C,U]
1 = MARKET PRICE
2 (*Accounting*) the value of an asset if it was sold at the current MARKET PRICE: *estimates of the market value of land for tax purposes*
3 (*Stock Exchange*) the total value of the shares of a particular company: *The company's market value has increased from $5 billion to $6 billion.*

ˈmarket weight (*also spelled* **marketweight**)
adjective
(*Stock Exchange*) if a collection of shares, bonds, etc. is **market weight** in a particular industry then you have the same proportion of these shares in your collection as the index that you are following: *The analysts rate the Telecommunication Services sector as 'market weight'* (= they think they will not do

especially well or badly and so investors should not buy more or less than the index). → OVERWEIGHT, UNDERWEIGHT

ˌmark-to-ˈmarket *noun* [U]
(*Finance*) (*usually used as an adjective*)
the practice of valuing shares, bonds and other investments at their current price rather than an earlier price or the price that was paid for them: *mark-to-market accounting*

markup /ˈmɑːkʌp; *AmE* ˈmɑːrk-/ *noun*
1 (*Commerce*) [C, usually sing.] an increase in the price of sth, usually one that is the difference between the cost of producing or buying sth and the price it is sold at, calculated as a percentage of the cost: *an average markup of 10%* ◇ *The selling price includes a 28% markup put on the goods by the retailer.* See note at MARGIN
2 (*IT*) [U] the symbols on a computer document that tell the computer how to organize the text on the computer screen or on the page when printed; the process of adding these symbols: *HTML (hypertext markup language) is the primary code used for web pages.*
  → MARK STH UP at MARK *verb*

marque /mɑːk; *AmE* mɑːrk/ *noun* [C]
a well-known make of a product, especially a car, that is expensive and fashionable: *the Porsche marque*

mart /mɑːt; *AmE* mɑːrt/ *noun* [C] (*especially AmE*)
a place where things are bought and sold: *a discount mart* ◇ *the world's No. 1 futures mart*
  → MARKET

ˈMaslow's ˈhierarchy of ˈneeds /ˈmæzləʊ; *AmE* -loʊ/ (*also* ˌhierarchy of ˈneeds) *noun* [sing.]
(*HR*) the theory, developed by Abraham Maslow, that people will feel satisfied and work best when they have everything that they require. These needs fall into several groups, which must be met in a particular order, starting with physical needs.

Maslow's hierarchy of needs

1. self-actualization needs
2. ego needs
3. social needs
4. security needs
5. physical needs

1. the need to achieve things for yourself
2. the need to be respected by others
3. the need to be loved and belong to a group
4. the need to feel safe
5. the need to eat, sleep, etc.

mass /mæs/ *adjective* [only before noun]

SEE ALSO: **critical mass**

affecting or involving a large number of people or things: *mass unemployment leading to mass bankruptcies*

ˌmass ˈadvertising *noun* [U]
(*Marketing*) advertising that tries to reach large numbers of people, especially by using newspapers, magazines, radio or television (the **mass media**): *We have redirected our marketing away from mass*

advertising towards our individual customers.
→ PRODUCT ADVERTISING

,mass customi'zation , -isation noun [U]
the ability to produce a product in large quantities
but also include small changes to meet the
demands of different customers: *Flexible
manufacturing systems allow for mass
customization.* ◇ *the mass customization of
computers* ▶ **,mass-'customize, -ise** verb [+ obj]

,mass 'marketing noun [U]
the activity of selling a product to as many people
as possible, for example by advertising through
newspapers, magazines, radio or television (**mass
media**): *mass marketing strategies/techniques* ◇ *the
mass marketing of health and welfare services*
→ NICHE MARKETING at NICHE MARKETER, TARGET
MARKETING at TARGET MARKET
▶ **,mass-'market** verb [+ obj] **,mass-'market**
adjective [only before noun]: *mass-market vehicles/
toiletries* ◇ *mass-market brands* **,mass 'marketer**
noun [C]: *a leading publisher and mass marketer of
software*

,mass 'media noun [pl.] (*usually* **the mass media**
[U with sing./pl. verb])
all the sources of information that are able to reach
large numbers of the public, such as TV, radio,
newspapers, etc: *We live in an era of mass media.* ◇
*The mass media have/has created new social
networks.* ◇ *the impact of mass media campaigns on
sales* → MEDIA

,mass 'merchant (*also* **,mass 'merchandiser**)
noun [C] (*especially AmE*)
(*Commerce*) a business or shop/store that buys and
sells a wide variety of products in very large
amounts: *mass merchants like Kmart and Target* ◇
discount mass-merchant retailers

,mass-pro'duce verb [+ obj]
to produce goods in large quantities, using
machinery: *CDs are cheap and easy to mass-produce.*
◇ *The toys were mass-produced in India.* ▶ **,mass-
pro'duced** *adjective*: *mass-produced goods* ◇ *the
first mass-produced computer for business use* **,mass-
pro'ducer** noun [C]: *It is difficult to compete with
the mass-producers.* **,mass pro'duction** noun [U]:
the mass production of consumer goods

,master 'franchise (*also* **,area 'franchise**) noun
[C]
(*Commerce*) a contract that gives one particular
person or company the right to develop a business
in a specific area or country for another company:
*We have signed a master franchise agreement with an
international corporation to develop stores in 8
African countries.* ▶ **,master franchi'see** (*also* **,area
franchi'see**) noun [C]: *We are looking for a master
franchisee to establish our transport company in
Denmark.*

masthead /'mɑːsthed; AmE 'mæst-/ noun [C]
1 the name of a newspaper at the top of the front
page
2 (*IT*) a box or an area at the top of a web page that
tells users what page they are on and may give the
name of the company and other information or
links

matching /'mætʃɪŋ/ noun [U]
(*Accounting*) the process of relating amounts of
money paid and received to the accounting period
in which they occur

material /mə'tɪəriəl; AmE -'tɪr-/ noun, adjective
● *noun* [C,U]

SEE ALSO: **bill of materials, collateral ~, direct ~,
raw ~**

1 a substance that things can be made from:
building materials (= bricks, sand, glass, etc.) ◇

recycled materials ◇ *They produce insulating
materials for the electrical industry.*
2 things that are needed in order to do a particular
activity: *cleaning/packaging materials*
3 written information, ideas, etc. used for a
particular purpose: *The company produces its own
training material.* ◇ *marketing/promotional
materials*
● *adjective*
1 connected with physical objects, money, etc: *He
must adapt to changes in his material circumstances.*
OPP NON-MATERIAL
2 important: *The deal will have a material impact
on our results.* ◇ *There are unlikely to be any
material changes in our strategy.*
▶ **materially** /mə'tɪəriəli; AmE -'tɪr-/ adverb

materiality /mə,tɪəri'æləti; AmE -,tɪr-/ noun [U]
(*Law*) the quality of being important or needing to
be considered: *The court will consider the
materiality of the evidence.*

ma,terial re'quirements ,planning noun
[U] (*abbr* **MRP**)
(*Production*) a process that uses computer programs
to organize the correct amounts of materials or
parts needed for particular levels of production and
the correct time for ordering them **NOTE** This is also
called 'material requirement planning' or 'materials
requirements planning'.

ma'terials ,buyer noun [C]
(*Production*) a person whose job is to choose
suppliers and buy the equipment or materials that
a company needs to produce sth **SYN** PURCHASING
OFFICER

ma'terials ,handling noun [U]
(*Production*) the process of loading, unloading and
moving raw materials and goods in a factory, using
machines: *The company plans to outsource materials
handling.* ◇ *materials handling equipment*

ma'ternity leave noun [U]
(*HR*) a period of time when a woman is allowed to
leave her job temporarily to have a baby: *She is on
maternity leave.* ◇ *You are entitled to 26 weeks' paid
maternity leave.* → PATERNITY LEAVE

ma'ternity pay noun [U]

SEE ALSO: **Statutory Maternity Pay**

(*HR*) money paid to a woman employee while she is
not working before and after the birth of a baby: *a
new agreement on maternity pay*

matrix /'meɪtrɪks/ noun [C] (*plural* **matrices**
/'meɪtrɪsiːz/)

SEE ALSO: **Ansoff matrix, Boston ~, growth-share ~,
salary ~**

a way of organizing a company or a project in
which people from different departments work
together and so each employee has two or more
managers in different departments: *Matrix
management relies on people reporting to both their*

matrix structure

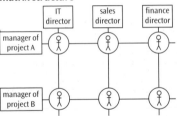

project and line managers. ◇ *We are a matrix* **organization**—*everybody knows what everyone else is doing.*

ˌmatters aˈrising *noun* [pl.]
used in a meeting to refer to sth connected with the last meeting that must be considered or dealt with: *Are there any matters arising?*

★ **mature** /məˈtʃʊə(r); -ˈtjʊə(r); *AmE* -ˈtʃʊr; -ˈtʊr/ *adjective, verb*
● *adjective*
1 (about an industry, a market or an economy) no longer growing very quickly and difficult for new companies to enter: *Software today is a mature, multi-billion-dollar industry.* ◇ *There are few opportunities for growth in a mature market.*
2 well developed and well established: *The technology is not yet mature enough for commercial use.* ◇ *a mature company*
3 (about a product, etc.) that has been produced, used, etc. for a long time and is now more difficult to sell or develop: *mature products near the end of their life cycles* ◇ *mature oil fields/wells* → PRODUCT LIFE CYCLE
● *verb* [no obj]
1 (*Finance; Insurance*) (about a bond, an insurance policy, etc.) to reach the date when it must be paid or paid back: *When the bonds mature, the principal invested will be repaid.* ◇ *She has a number of investments maturing at the end of the year.*
2 (about an industry, a market, etc.) to stop growing as fast as before and become difficult for a new company to enter: *Sales growth fell as our company and the market matured.* ◇ *Health club operators are finding themselves in a crowded and rapidly maturing sector of the market.*
3 to become more developed: *As companies mature and grow, they hire people for specific roles.* ◇ *The problems will be solved as the software matures.*
4 (about a product, etc.) to become more difficult to sell or develop as it has been produced or used for a long time: *maturing oil fields*

★ **maturity** /məˈtʃʊərəti; -ˈtjʊə-; *AmE* -ˈtʃʊr-; -ˈtʊr-/ *noun* (*plural* **maturities**)
1 (*Finance; Insurance*) [C,U] (*also* **reˈdemption date** [C]) the time when bonds, loans, insurance agreements, etc. must be repaid or paid; a bond, loan or insurance agreement that has reached this time: *You will receive a payout of $15 000 on maturity.* ◇ *Many investors want to keep securities until they reach maturity.* ◇ *bonds with maturities of 20 years* ◇ *The company has paid off more than $1.5 billion of maturities this year.* ◇ *They plan to extend the maturity dates of the notes by as much as three years.*
2 [U] when an industry, an economy, a market, etc. is fully developed and no longer growing very quickly: *The market for music, videos and books is reaching maturity.*
3 [U] the time when a product has been sold for a long time and is well known, but its sales are not increasing: *Income from the game has fallen as it has reached maturity in the market.*—Picture at PRODUCT LIFE CYCLE

maven /ˈmeɪvn/ *noun* [C] (*AmE*) (*informal*)
an expert in a particular subject: *Wall Street money mavens* ◇ *a business/design/marketing/software maven*

maverick /ˈmævərɪk/ *noun* [C]
a person who does not behave or think like everyone else, but who has independent, unusual opinions: *the ad industry's most famous mavericks*
▶ **ˈmaverick** *adjective* [only before noun]: *a maverick entrepreneur*

max /mæks/ *abbr, verb* (*informal*)
● *abbr*
1 (*also spelled* **max.**, *especially in AmE*) maximum: *max temperature 18°C*
2 at the most: *It'll cost $50 max.*
OPP MIN.
● *verb*
PHR V **ˌmax ˈout**; **ˌmax sth ˈout** (*AmE*) (*informal*) to reach the limit at which nothing more is possible: *I've maxed out my credit card.*

★ **maximize, -ise** /ˈmæksɪmaɪz/ *verb* [+ obj]
1 to increase sth as much as possible: *to maximize efficiency/profits/productivity/revenue* ◇ *The company has introduced new strategies to maximize performance.*
2 to make the best use of sth: *to maximize opportunities/resources* ◇ *You have to maximize your time.*
3 (*IT*) to make a window (= an area within a frame on a computer screen) larger: *Maximize the window to full screen.*
OPP MINIMIZE
▶ **maximization, -isation** /ˌmæksɪmaɪˈzeɪʃn; *AmE* -mə z-/ *noun* [U]

★ **maximum** /ˈmæksɪməm/ *adjective, noun* (*abbr* **max**)
● *adjective* [only before noun]
as large, fast, etc. as is possible; the most that is possible or allowed: *the maximum price/quantity/speed/temperature* ◇ *The maximum amount that we can pay is €250 000.* OPP MINIMUM
● *noun* [C, usually sing.] (*plural* **maximums** *or* **maxima** /ˈmæksɪmə/)
the greatest amount, size, speed, etc. that is possible, recorded or allowed: *They can charge a maximum of 12% interest.* ◇ *What is the absolute maximum you can afford to pay?* OPP MINIMUM

MB (*also spelled* **Mb**) = MEGABYTE

MBA /ˌem biː ˈeɪ/ *abbr* **Master of Business Administration** a university degree in subjects connected with managing businesses: *to do/have an MBA*

MBE /ˌem biː ˈiː/ = MANAGEMENT BY EXCEPTION

MBI /ˌem biː ˈaɪ/ = MANAGEMENT BUY-IN

MBO /ˌem biː ˈəʊ; *AmE* ˈoʊ/ (*also spelled* **MbO**) = MANAGEMENT BY OBJECTIVES, MANAGEMENT BUYOUT

MBS /ˌem biː ˈes/ = MORTGAGE-BACKED SECURITY

MBTI™ /ˌem biː tiː ˈaɪ/ = MYERS-BRIGGS TYPE INDICATOR

MBWA /ˌem biː dʌbljuː ˈeɪ/ = MANAGEMENT BY WALKING AROUND

Mbyte /ˈembaɪt/ = MEGABYTE

McJob /məkˈdʒɒb; *AmE* -ˈdʒɑːb/ *noun* [C] (*informal*) a job in a restaurant, supermarket, etc. with low wages and few benefits or chances of promotion

ˈm-ˌcommerce *noun* [U]
mobile commerce the buying and selling of products on the Internet by using mobile phones/cellphones and other WIRELESS (= without wires) technology: *Revenue from m-commerce is still low.* → E-COMMERCE

MD /ˌem ˈdiː/ = MANAGING DIRECTOR

meagre (*AmE spelling* **meager**) /ˈmiːɡə(r)/ *adjective* small in quantity and poor in quality: *Sales rose by a meagre 0.1%.*

mean /miːn/ *adjective, noun* (*Technical*)
● *adjective* [only before noun]
average: *The products had a mean price of €3.44.* ◇ *The earnings were well above the analysts' mean estimate of $3.08 per share.* ◇ *mean earnings/forecast/value*

● **noun** [C, usually sing.] (*also* **,arithmetic 'mean**)
the average calculated by adding together all the
numbers in a group, and dividing the total by the
number of numbers: *Wall Street analysts expect a
mean of 93 cents per share.* → MEDIAN See note at
AVERAGE

means /miːnz/ *noun* [pl.]
the money that a person has: *They currently do not
have the means to pay their bills.* ◇ *Many consumers
are living* **beyond their means** (= spending more
than they can afford).

'means test *noun* [C]
an official check of sb's wealth or income in order
to decide if they are poor enough to receive money
from the government, etc. for a particular purpose:
*In order to qualify for legal aid you must pass a
means test.* ▶ **'means-test** *verb* [+ obj] **'means-
testing** *noun* [U]

'means-,tested *adjective*
paid to sb according to the results of a **means test**:
means-tested benefits

measurable /'meʒərəbl/ *adjective*
1 that can be measured: *Each employee has
measurable goals.*
2 large enough to be noticed or to have a clear and
noticeable effect: *measurable improvements*
▶ **measurably** /'meʒərəbli/ *adverb*: *Working
conditions have changed measurably in the last ten
years.*

★ measure /'meʒə(r)/ *noun, verb*
● *noun*

SEE ALSO: **made to measure**

1 [C] a way of judging or measuring sth: *a measure
of US consumer confidence* ◇ *The consumer price
index is a key measure of inflation at the retail level.*
◇ *the standard industry measure* (= the one used by
most companies) SYN METRIC
❍ *a* **broad/common/good/key/reliable** *measure of sth
•* *a measure of* **demand/growth/inflation/
performance/sales**
2 [C,U] a unit used for stating the size, quantity or
degree of sth; a system or scale of these units:
weights and measures ◇ *dry/liquid measure*
3 [C] **measure(s) (to do sth)** an official action that
is done in order to achieve a particular aim: *Banks
are introducing measures to make it easier for
customers to change accounts.* ◇ *The factory in Wales
was closed down as an economy measure* (= to save
money).
❍ **austerity/cost-cutting/economy** *measures •*
**emergency/precautionary/preventive/safety/
security** *measures •* **drastic/effective/necessary/
tough** *measures •* **to adopt/introduce/take**
measures (to do sth)
● *verb*
1 [+ obj] to judge the importance, value or effect of
sth: *The data is used to measure economic growth.* ◇
*Assessments are an effective way of measuring staff
performance.* ◇ *It's difficult to measure the impact of
our ads.*
2 [+ obj] to find the size, quantity, etc. of sth in
standard units: *a device for measuring temperature*
◇ *Any type of data that could not be directly
measured was rejected.* ◇ *measuring equipment/
instruments*
3 [no obj] (*not used in the continuous tenses*) to be a
particular size, length, amount, etc: *The room
measures 4 metres by 6 metres.*
PHRV **'measure sb/sth against sb/sth** to
compare sb/sth with sb/sth: *The figures are not very
good when measured against those of our
competitors.* **,measure 'up (to sth/sb)** (*usually used
in negative sentences and questions*) to be as good,
successful, etc. as expected or needed:
Unfortunately, he just didn't measure up to the task.
◇ *The job failed to measure up to her expectations.*

measurement /'meʒəmənt; AmE 'meʒərm-/ *noun*

SEE ALSO: **work measurement**

1 [C] the size, length or amount of sth: *an inflation
measurement* ◇ *The exact measurements of the room
are 3 metres 20 by 2 metres 84.*
2 [U] the act or process of finding the size,
quantity or degree of sth: *Accurate measurement is
very important in science.* ◇ *measurement
equipment/instruments/tools*

mechanical /mə'kænɪkl/ *adjective*
1 connected with machines: *mechanical problems/
defects* ◇ *mechanical work/workers* ◇ *The breakdown
was due to a mechanical failure.* ◇ *We employed an
engineer to do the mechanical design.*
2 operated with power from an engine, a wheel,
etc: *a mechanical clock/device/system* ◇ *mechanical
parts*
▶ **mechanically** /mə'kænɪkli/ *adverb*: *a
mechanically powered vehicle*

me,chanical engi'neering *noun* [U]
the study of how machines are designed, built and
repaired: *She has a degree in mechanical
engineering.* ▶ **me,chanical engi'neer** *noun* [C]

★ mechanism /'mekənɪzəm/ *noun* [C]

SEE ALSO: **exchange rate mechanism, market ~,
price ~**

1 a method or system for achieving sth: *What
mechanisms are in place* **for** *dealing with
complaints?* ◇ *There is no legal mechanism* **to** *recover
the fees.* ◇ *Several factors can trigger the pricing
mechanism.*
❍ *a* **control/feedback/financial/funding** *mechanism •
to* **be/have/put** *a mechanism* **in place** *•* to **create/
set up/use** *a mechanism*
2 a set of moving parts in a machine that performs
a task: *a safety mechanism* ◇ *The door-locking
mechanism doesn't work.* → WORK *noun* (11)
❍ *a mechanism* **operates/works**

★ mechanize , -ise /'mekənaɪz/ *verb* [+ obj]
(*usually* **be mechanized**)
to change a process, so that the work is done by
machines rather than people: *Modern farming has
become highly mechanized.* ◇ *The production process
is fully mechanized.* SYN AUTOMATE
▶ **mechanization, -isation** /,mekənaɪ'zeɪʃn; AmE
-nə'z-/ *noun* [U]: *The mechanization of production
gave businesses control over work rates.*

med. *abbr* (*only used in written English*)
(especially for sizes of clothes) medium

media /'miːdiə/ *noun* **the media** [U with sing./pl.
verb]

SEE ALSO: **cross-media, magnetic ~, mass ~, mixed ~,
new ~, retail ~**

the main ways that large numbers of people receive
information and entertainment, that is television,
radio, newspapers and the Internet: *advertising* **in**
the media ◇ *The media was/were accused of
influencing the final decision.* ◇ *Details of the merger
will be announced at a media conference later today.*
◇ *The story generated widespread media* **coverage.**
❍ *the* **international/local/national** *media • the*
broadcast(ing)/digital/electronic/print/traditional
media • a media **business/company/giant/group/
empire**

'media ,agency *noun* [C]
a business that plans and buys space or time for
advertisements in newspapers, on TV, etc. on
behalf of other businesses

'media ,buying *noun* [U]
(*Marketing*) the activity of buying space in
newspapers, time during broadcasts, etc. for

advertisements: *The company has appointed an agent to handle its media buying.* ◇ *The group has won an $8 million media buying account for an airline* (= the job of buying space, etc. for its advertisements). → MEDIA PLANNING
▶ **'media ˌbuyer** *noun* [C]

median /'mi:diən/ *adjective, noun*
(*Technical*)
● *adjective* [only before noun]
having a value in the middle of a series of values: *The median age of the magazine's readership is 24.* ◇ *The median price is where half sell for more and half sell for less.*
● *noun* [C]
the middle value of a series of numbers arranged in order of size See note at AVERAGE

'media ˌplanning *noun* [U]
(*Marketing*) the activity of deciding how, where and how much to advertise sth and how much money to spend: *Our media planning is handled by our own marketing department.* → MEDIA BUYING
▶ **'media plan** *noun* [C]: *The media plan included the placement of ten TV commercials and five print ads.* **'media ˌplanner** *noun* [C]

mediate /'mi:dieɪt/ *verb*
1 [+ obj *or* no obj] to try to end a disagreement between two or more people or groups by talking to them and trying to find things that everyone can agree on: *An independent body was brought in to mediate between staff and management.* ◇ *He has been mediating in the dispute.* ◇ *the mediating role of middle management*
○ *to mediate (in)* **differences/disputes/negotiations/talks**
2 [+ obj] to succeed in finding a solution to a disagreement between people or groups: *They mediated a settlement which ended the strike.*
○ *to mediate a* **settlement/solution**
→ ARBITRATE

mediation /ˌmi:di'eɪʃn/ *noun* [U]
(*Law*) the process of trying to end a disagreement between two or more people or groups by sb who is not involved: *The pay dispute was settled through mediation.* → ARBITRATION

mediator /'mi:dieɪtə(r)/ *noun* [C]
a person or an organization that tries to get agreement between people or groups who disagree with each other: *Two independent mediators drew up a draft settlement.* ◇ *to act as (a) mediator in the negotiations* → ARBITRATOR

Medicaid /'medɪkeɪd/ *noun* [U]
in the US, the insurance system that provides medical care for poorer people

'medical cerˌtificate (*also* **'doctor's cerˌtificate,** *informal*) *noun* [C] (*both BrE*)
1 a statement by a doctor that sb has been ill and unable to work: *If you are absent for longer than five days, we may require you to produce a medical certificate.*
2 a statement by a doctor that sb is in good health and can do a particular job: *Pilots must hold a valid medical certificate.*

'medical inˌsurance (*also* **'medical ˌcover**) *noun* [U]
a type of insurance in which a person receives money to pay for medical treatment if they are ill/sick or injured, often provided by employers
SYN HEALTH INSURANCE

Medicare /'medɪkeə(r); *AmE* -ker/ *noun* [U]
1 in the US, the national insurance system that provides medical care for people over 65
2 in Australia and Canada, the national medical care system for everyone that is paid for by taxes

mediocre /ˌmi:di'əʊkə(r); *AmE* -'oʊkər/ *adjective*
not very good; of only average standard: *Their results last year were mediocre.* ◇ *The company is suffering from mediocre performance in many of its markets.* ◇ *mediocre managers*

medium /'mi:diəm/ *noun* [C] (*plural* **media** /'mi:diə/ *or* **mediums**)

SEE ALSO: display medium

1 a way of communicating information, etc. to people: *the medium of radio/television* ◇ *The Internet can be an effective advertising medium.* ◇ *Email is our preferred medium for communicating with clients.* ◇ *The ad campaign will run across all media.* **HELP** The plural in this meaning is usually **media**. → MASS MEDIA
○ *an* **effective/a good/powerful** *medium* • *an* **electronic/interactive/online** *medium* • *an* **outdoor/a print/traditional** *medium*
2 something that is used for a particular purpose: *Euros have been used as a medium of exchange since 1999.*

ˌmedium-'duty *adjective* [only before noun]
suitable for use in average, normal or slightly difficult conditions: *medium-duty trucks* ◇ *a medium-duty software program* → HEAVY-DUTY, LIGHT-DUTY

'medium-sized (*also* **'medium-size**) *adjective* [usually before noun]
of average size; between small and large: *medium-sized companies* → LARGE-SIZED, SMALL-SIZED

'medium-term *adjective* [only before noun]
1 used to describe a period of time that is a few weeks, months or years into the future: *The medium-term outlook is for lower oil prices.*
2 (*Finance*) used to describe sth such as a bond, contract, loan, etc. that lasts for a period of time in the middle between the shortest and the longest possible: *medium-term bonds such as the 5-year Japanese Government Bond*

★ **meet** /mi:t/ *verb, noun*
● *verb* (**met, met** /met/)
1 [+ obj *or* no obj] to come together formally in order to discuss sth: *The committee meets twice a month.* ◇ *We have agreed to meet their lawyers.* ◇ *The board met today to consider the offer.*
2 [+ obj] to do or satisfy what is needed or what sb asks for: *We expect to meet our target of opening 50 new stores by December.* ◇ *the importance of meeting customers' needs* ◇ *The design meets all applicable safety standards.* ◇ *Unless these conditions are met, we cannot proceed with the sale.* ◇ *I can't possibly meet that deadline.*
3 [+ obj] to pay sth: *The extra costs were met from our research budget.*
IDM **meet sb half'way** to reach an agreement with sb by giving them part of what they want: *Could you at least meet us halfway and do the work at a discount?* → idiom at END *noun*
PHRV **'meet with sb** to have a meeting with sb: *Management will meet with labor unions later this week.*
● *noun* [C] (*BrE*) (*informal*)
a meeting

★ **meeting** /'mi:tɪŋ/ *noun*

SEE ALSO: annual general meeting, annual ~, annual stockholders' ~, company ~, general ~, stop-work ~

1 [C] an occasion when people come together to discuss or decide sth: *They held a meeting to discuss the future of the firm.* ◇ *What time is the meeting?* ◇ *I have a meeting with my manager in an hour.* ◇ *a meeting between workers and management* ◇ *a meeting of shareholders* ◇ *a shareholder meeting* ◇ *Ms Keane is in a meeting at the moment—can I take a*

Ms Keane is in a meeting at the moment—can I take a message? ◊ (*informal*) *I'm stuck in meetings all week.* ◊ *You will need to book a meeting room.* See note at POSTPONE

◒ *to **arrange/call/have/hold/set up/organize** a meeting* ◆ *to **cancel/delay/put off/postpone** a meeting* ◆ *to **reschedule/schedule** a meeting* ◆ *to **take part in/attend** a meeting* ◆ *to **chair/conduct/run** a meeting* ◆ *an **emergency/a private/public/special/team** meeting*

2 the meeting [sing.] (*formal*) the people at a meeting: *The meeting voted to accept the pay offer.*

VOCABULARY BUILDING

Formal meetings

- the **chairperson** opens the meeting and gives the **apologies** of the people who are unable to attend
- the **minutes** of the previous meeting are approved
- the **agenda** for the meeting is agreed on
- **items** are added or taken off the agenda
- **motions** and **resolutions** are discussed and put to a **vote**
- a secretary **keeps/takes** minutes
- the chairperson asks if there is **any other business**
- the chairperson closes the meeting, or **adjourns** it to a later time

See note at ARRANGE

---

meg /meg/ = MEGABYTE

mega /ˈmegə/ *adjective* [usually before noun] (*informal*)
very large or impressive: *The company has focused on winning mega deals.* ▶ **mega** *adverb*: *They're mega rich.*

mega- /ˈmegə-/ *combining form* (*in nouns*)
1 very large or great: *a megastore* ◊ *Japan's four megabanks*
2 (*Technical*) (in units of measurement) one million: *a 500-megawatt electricity plant* ◊ *The chip runs at 510 megahertz.*
3 (*IT*) 1 048 576 (= 2^{20}): *a memory of 16 megabytes*

megabucks /ˈmegəbʌks/ *noun* [pl.] (*informal*)
a very large amount of money: *She earns megabucks.*

megabyte /ˈmegəbaɪt/ (*also* **meg**, *informal*) *noun* [C] (*abbr* **MB**, **Mbyte**)
(*IT*) a unit of computer memory, equal to 2^{20} (or 1 048 576) BYTES: *a 64-megabyte memory card* ◊ *510MB of memory*

meltdown /ˈmeltdaʊn/ *noun* [U,C]
a situation where sth fails or becomes weaker in a sudden and dramatic way: *The country is in economic meltdown.* ◊ *fears of a meltdown in consumer spending* ◊ *a meltdown on Wall Street* (= when the prices of US shares fall suddenly)

★member /ˈmembə(r)/ *noun* [C]

SEE ALSO: **charter member, founder ~, register of ~**

1 a person, a country or an organization that has joined a particular group or team: *The country is due to become a full member of the EU.* ◊ *a meeting of member countries* ◊ *We're recruiting eight new members of staff.* ◊ *The smaller the team, the faster the team members work.* OPP NON-MEMBER
◒ *board/committee/staff/team* members ◆ *a leading/new* member ◆ *an active/a full/permanent/voting* member
2 a person or company that owns part of a business organization, for example by buying some of its shares: *The company auditors are appointed by*

the members (= shareholders). ◊ *The stock exchange is owned by its member companies.*

membership /ˈmembəʃɪp; *AmE* -bərʃ-/ *noun*
1 [U,C] (*BrE*) **membership (of sth)** (*AmE*) **membership (in sth)** the state of being a member of a group, an organization, etc: *Who is eligible to apply for membership of the association?* ◊ *China was granted full membership of the WTO in 2001.* ◊ *The company offers free gym memberships to all employees.*
◒ *to apply for/qualify for/seek* membership (*of/in sth*) ◆ *to grant/offer/refuse (sb)* membership ◆ *a membership card/fee*
2 [C with sing./pl. verb] the members of a group, an organization, etc: *The membership votes/vote on the proposal this week.*
3 [C,U] the number of members in a group, an organization, etc: *Our society has a membership of two hundred.* ◊ *Union membership has fallen.*

★memo /ˈmeməʊ; *AmE* -moʊ/ *noun* [C] (*plural* **memos**) (*also* **memorandum**, *formal*)
an official note from one person to another or others in the same organization: *In a memo to employees, she explained the need to cut costs.*
◒ *a company/an internal/a staff* memo ◆ *to circulate/send/write* a memo

memorandum /ˌmeməˈrændəm/ *noun* [C] (*plural* **memoranda** /ˌmeməˈrændə/ *or* **memorandums**)
1 (*formal*) = MEMO
2 (*Law*) a record of a legal agreement which has not yet been formally prepared and signed: *The companies signed a memorandum to develop the product jointly, but the deal was never finalized.*
→ MEMORANDUM OF UNDERSTANDING
3 a proposal or report on a particular subject for a person, an organization, a committee, etc: *The group has issued an information memorandum on its publishing arm for potential buyers.*

memoˌrandum of associˈation *noun* [C] (*BrE*)
(*Law*) one of the legal documents that is created when a company is formed, that gives basic details about the company such as its name, address and the number and value of its shares SYN ARTICLES OF INCORPORATION → ARTICLES OF ASSOCIATION

memoˌrandum of underˈstanding *noun* [C] (*abbr* **MOU**)
(*Law*) a temporary written agreement between two companies, etc. that explains how they intend to do business with each other and what their relationship will be: *The two companies have signed a memorandum of understanding to share the costs of building a microchip plant.* → LETTER OF INTENT

memory /ˈmeməri/ *noun* (*plural* **memories**)

SEE ALSO: **virtual memory**

(*IT*)
1 [C,U] the part of a computer where information is stored; the amount of space in a computer for storing information: *Have you got enough memory available to run the program?* ◊ RAM, ROM
2 [U,C] (*used with other nouns*) a way in which information can be stored in a temporary or permanent form, for example on a disk or an electronic device: *Most digital cameras use flash memory.*

mend /mend/ *verb, noun*
● *verb* [+ obj]
1 (*BrE*) to repair sth that has been damaged or broken so that it can be used again: *Most of their business involves mending mobile phones.* ◊ (*figurative*) *They sought government funding to mend their broken balance sheet.*

2 to find a solution to a problem or disagreement: *She needs to mend relations with her staff.*
● *noun*
IDM **on the 'mend** (*informal*) improving after a period of difficulty: *We believe the US economy is on the mend.*

menial /'miːniəl/ *adjective*
used to describe work that is not skilled or important and is often boring or badly paid: *menial tasks/jobs*

menswear /'menzweə(r); AmE -wer/ *noun* [U]
(used especially in shops/stores) clothes for men
→ CHILDRENSWEAR, WOMENSWEAR

mentality /men'tæləti/ *noun* [C, usually sing.]
(*plural* **mentalities**)
the particular attitude or way of thinking of a person or group: *Retailers must develop a service mentality* (= the attitude that serving customers is very important). **SYN** MINDSET

mentee /ˌmen'tiː/ *noun* [C]
(*HR*) a person who receives advice and help from sb with more experience (a **mentor**) over a period of time: *In their first meeting with mentors, mentees talk about their career goals.*

mentor /'mentɔː(r)/ *noun, verb*
(*HR*)
● *noun* [C]
an experienced person who advises and helps sb with less experience over a period of time: *She is following advice from her mentor.* → MENTEE
● *verb* [+ obj]
to advise and help sb with less experience than yourself: *He brought Brown into the company, mentored him and chose him as his successor.*
▶ '**mentoring** *noun* [U]: *a mentoring programme*

menu /'menjuː/ *noun* [C]

SEE ALSO: **help menu**

(*IT*) a list of possible choices that are shown on a computer screen: *Use 'Save as' in/under the 'File' menu.* → DROP-DOWN

'**menu bar** *noun* [C]
(*IT*) a horizontal bar at the top of a computer screen that contains PULL-DOWN MENUS such as 'File', 'Find' and 'Help': *Click on 'tools' in the menu bar.*

the Merc /mɜːk; AmE mɜːrk/ *noun* [sing.]
an informal way of referring to the **Chicago Mercantile Exchange**, a market for trading FUTURES (= contracts to buy or sell a particular amount of sth in the future) that deals with financial and agricultural products

mercantile /'mɜːkəntaɪl; AmE 'mɜːrk-; -tiːl/ *adjective* (*formal*)
connected with trade and commercial affairs: *the development of Osaka as a mercantile city*

,**mercantile 'law** *noun* [U]
(*Law*) the collection of laws that deal with all aspects of business and trade, including contracts, buying, selling, storing and transporting goods, etc. **SYN** COMMERCIAL LAW

★ **merchandise** *noun, verb*
● *noun* /'mɜːtʃəndaɪs; -daɪz; AmE 'mɜːrtʃ-/ [U]
1 (*formal*) goods that are bought or sold; goods that are for sale in a shop/store: *The supermarket has expanded its range of non-food merchandise.* ◇ *attracting shoppers with discounted merchandise* ◇ *Wal-Mart, the general merchandise retailer*
2 things you can buy that are connected with or that advertise a particular event, organization, film/movie, etc: *official Olympic merchandise* ◇ *They have launched a new range of Star Wars merchandise, including toys.*

● *verb* (*also spelled* **merchandize**) /'mɜːtʃəndaɪz; AmE 'mɜːrtʃ-/ [+ obj] (*especially AmE*)
1 to buy and sell products for profit: *a plan to merchandise Mexican food products in grocery stores*
2 to encourage the sale of goods, especially by the way they are packaged and displayed in shops/stores: *We try to show our customers (the nation's retailers) the best ways to merchandise our products.*
▶ '**merchandiser** *noun* [C] (*especially AmE*): *The mass merchandisers have taken customers away from smaller clothes stores.* ◇ *Our merchandisers have big, bold ideas about how items should be displayed on our website.* **SYN** RETAILER

'**merchandise mix** *noun* [C, usually sing.]
(*especially AmE*)
(*Marketing*) the types and quantities of goods that a shop/store chooses to sell in order to encourage the greatest number of sales: *Our stores feature a merchandise mix of clothing, shoes and accessories for women.* ◇ *finding the right merchandise mix*

★ **merchandising** /'mɜːtʃəndaɪzɪŋ; AmE 'mɜːrtʃ-/ *noun* [U]

SEE ALSO: cross merchandising

1 (*especially AmE*) the activity of selling goods, or of trying to sell them, by advertising or displaying them: *The ad campaign will be supported by better merchandising and store design.* ◇ *She is their vice-president of merchandising.*
2 products connected with a popular film/movie, person or event; the process of selling these goods: *millions of pounds' worth of Batman merchandising* ◇ *They bought the merchandising rights to Winnie the Pooh.* ◇ *a drop in merchandising sales*

merchant /'mɜːtʃənt; AmE 'mɜːrtʃ-/ *noun, adjective*
● *noun* [C]

SEE ALSO: futures commission merchant, mass merchant

(*Commerce*)
1 a person or business that buys and sells goods in large quantities, especially one who imports and exports goods: *His father was a tea merchant.* ◇ *builders' merchants* (= businesses that sell supplies to the building trade)
2 (*especially AmE*) a business or person that sells goods directly to the public: *Online merchants also have to attract shoppers with bargains.* **SYN** RETAILER
3 a shop/store, etc. that has an arrangement with a bank so that it can accept payments by credit card: *Card issuers have been working with merchants to reduce the theft of credit-card numbers.* → MERCHANT ACCOUNT
● *adjective* [only before noun]
connected with the transport of goods by sea: *merchant ships/vessels* ◇ *The strike by dock workers brought merchant shipping to a halt.*

merchantable /'mɜːtʃəntəbl; AmE 'mɜːrtʃ-/ *adjective*
(*Law*) in a good enough condition to be sold: *Goods must be of merchantable quality.*

'**merchant ac,count** *noun* [C]
(*Commerce*) a type of bank account that allows a shop/store, etc. to accept payments made by credit card

,**merchant 'bank** *noun* [C] (*BrE*)
a bank that deals with large businesses, for example providing finance for trade with foreign companies, helping with the sales of shares or bonds, or giving advice on investments: *They appointed merchant bank Lazard to advise them on the takeover.* → INVESTMENT BANK
▶ ,**merchant 'banker** *noun* [C] ,**merchant 'banking** *noun* [U]

noun [C with sing./pl. verb]
a country's commercial ships and the people who
work on them

★ **merge** /mɜːdʒ; *AmE* mɜːrdʒ/ *verb* [+ obj *or* no obj]
merge (sth) (with/into) sth | **merge A with B** |
merge A and B (together) (used especially about
business organizations) to combine, or make two or
more organizations combine, to form a single
organization: *The companies are set to merge next
year.* ◇ *The bank merged with Swiss Bank Corp. in
1999 to form UBS.* ◇ *The sales and marketing
departments are being merged (together).* ◇ *The
newly merged company has its headquarters in Oslo.*
→ MAIL MERGE

'**merge/purge** (*also spelled* **merge-purge**) *noun*
[U,C]
the process of combining lists of names, addresses,
etc. (**merge**) and removing items from the
combined list that appear more than once (**purge**):
*Merge/purge is vital to avoid sending multiple
mailings to the same address or individual.* ◇ *merge/
purge software* ▸ '**merge/purge** *verb* [+ obj *or*
no obj]: *Your lists can be merge/purged at no extra
cost.*

★ **merger** /ˈmɜːdʒə(r); *AmE* ˈmɜːrdʒ-/ *noun* [C]

SEE ALSO: **horizontal merger, reverse ~, vertical ~**

(*Finance*) the act of joining two or more businesses
or organizations into one: *There is talk of a merger
between the two banks.* ◇ *Analysts expect the retailer
to seek a merger with a rival company.* ◇ *She works
in the* **mergers and acquisitions** *department of a
well-known investment bank.* → DEMERGER See note
at TAKEOVER
  ◐ to **plan/propose/seek** a merger ✦ to **agree (to)/
  approve/block/oppose** a merger ✦ a merger
  agreement/deal/plan/proposal ✦ merger
  negotiations/talks

'**merger ,partner** *noun* [C]
(*Finance*) a businesses or an organization that joins
with one or more other organizations in a **merger**:
*The company is committed to finding a North
American merger partner.*

merit /ˈmerɪt/ *noun* [U]
1 (*formal*) the quality of being good, true,
deserving reward, etc: *I want to get the job on
merit.* ◇ *The case against us is entirely without merit.*
2 (*HR*) used to describe increases in pay that relate
to how well, hard, etc. people work: *The company
successfully used merit pay to increase performance.*
◇ *Employees receive a merit rating every six months.*
  ◐ a merit **award/bonus/increase/raise/rise** ✦ merit
  pay

meritocracy /ˌmerɪˈtɒkrəsi; *AmE* -ˈtɑːk-/ *noun* [C]
(*plural* **meritocracies**)
an organization, an industry or a system where
people get power or money on the basis of their
ability: *The company is considered to be the ultimate
meritocracy, supporting talented people from all
walks of life.* ▸ **meritocratic** /ˌmerɪtəˈkrætɪk/
adjective: *a meritocratic organization*

message /ˈmesɪdʒ/ *noun, verb*
● *noun* [C]

SEE ALSO: **error message, text message**

1 a written or spoken piece of information, etc.
that you send to sb or leave for sb when you cannot
speak to them yourself: *There were no messages for
me at the hotel.* ◇ *I left a message on your answering
machine.* ◇ *Mr Lee isn't here at the moment. Can I
take a message?* ◇ *an email message* ◇ *a recorded
message*
  ◐ to **leave/record/send** a message
2 (*Marketing*) an important idea about a product,
brand, etc. that a company tries to communicate in

its advertising: *What is your marketing message?* ◇
*We are sending a strong message of quality to our
customers.*
  ◐ to **send (out)/deliver** a message
3 (*IT*) a piece of information produced
automatically by a computer program and shown
on a computer screen
4 (*AmE*) a television advertisement: *We'll be back
after the messages.*
● *verb* [+ obj]
to send a piece of information, an idea, a question,
etc. to sb, especially an email or a TEXT MESSAGE:
*She spent the morning messaging her friends instead
of working.* ◇ *I messaged the results to my boss.*

'**message board** *noun* [C]
(*IT*) a place on a website where you can leave
messages, information, advertisements, etc. for
other people to see: *I posted a question on the
message board.*

messaging /ˈmesɪdʒɪŋ/ *noun* [U]

SEE ALSO: **instant messaging**

the activity of sending a message or information to
sb, especially by email or TEXT MESSAGE: *an
electronic messaging system*

messenger /ˈmesɪndʒə(r)/ *noun* [C]
1 a person who gives a message to sb or who
delivers messages, letters, etc. to people as a job:
We sent the documents by messenger. ◇ *a bike
messenger*
2 (*IT*) a computer program that allows two or more
people to communicate over the Internet using
short written messages: *an instant messenger
program/service*

Messrs (*AmE spelling* **Messrs.**) /ˈmesəz; *AmE* -sərz/
abbr (*especially BrE*)
used as the plural of **Mr** before a list of names and
before names of businesses: *Messrs Clark, Brown
and Lee* ◇ *Messrs L Jones and Co*

meteoric /ˌmiːtiˈɒrɪk; *AmE* -ˈɔːr-; -ˈɑːr-/ *adjective*
achieving success very quickly: *a meteoric career* ◇
the meteoric rise of the low-cost airline ◇ *The
company enjoyed meteoric growth in the 1990s.*

meter /ˈmiːtə(r)/ *noun, verb*
● *noun* [C]

SEE ALSO: **people meter**

1 a device that measures and records the amount
of electricity, gas, water, time, etc. that you have
used, or the money you must pay: *The cab driver
left the meter running while he waited for us.* ◇ *a
coin-operated/pre-payment meter*
2 -**meter** (*used to form nouns*) a device for
measuring the thing mentioned: *speedometer*
● *verb* [+ obj]
to measure sth (for example how much gas,
electricity, etc. has been used) using a **meter**

★ **method** /ˈmeθəd/ *noun* [C]

SEE ALSO: **accrual method, critical incident ~, critical
path ~, declining balance ~, depreciation ~,
diminishing balance ~, double-declining balance ~,
etc.**

a particular way of doing sth: *We devised a new
method for measuring unemployment.* ◇ *Please
indicate your preferred method of payment.* ◇ *the
traditional methods of motivating employees* ◇ *The
industry has adopted faster and cheaper production
methods.*
  ◐ to **change/develop/devise/use** a method ✦
  conventional/traditional/unconventional methods
  ✦ **effective/good/preferred/reliable** methods

,me-'too *adjective* [only before noun]
(*Marketing, informal*) produced by a company in response to the success of a similar product sold by another company: *'Hello!' gave rise to a number of me-too publications.* ◇ *me-too products/marketing*
See note at COPY

metric /'metrɪk/ *noun, adjective*
●*noun* [C]
a system for measuring sth, especially how well a business is performing: *Earnings per customer is a key metric for our business.* ◇ *We establish metrics to track our progress on a project.* ◇ *Brand loyalty will not always be the defining metric of success.*
O *business/financial/performance/quality* metrics •
to **create/establish/track/use** metrics
●*adjective*
based on the system of measurements that uses the metre, kilogram, etc. as basic units: *metric measurements/sizes/units*

,metric 'ton (*also* **tonne**) *noun* [C]
a unit for measuring weight, equal to 1 000 kilograms

,mezzanine 'debt /'mezəni:n; 'metsə-/ *noun* [U]
(*Finance*) money that a business obtains from investors through MEZZANINE FINANCE

,mezzanine 'finance (*also* ,mezzanine 'financing) /'mezəni:n; 'metsə-/ *noun* [U]
(*Finance*) a way of providing funds for a business that involves lending money with a high rate of interest and often with the right to obtain shares in the business in the future: *Mezzanine finance carries more risk for the lender and is more expensive to the borrower than ordinary loans.* ◇ *a mezzanine finance provider*

mfg. *abbr* (*especially AmE*)
a short way of writing **manufacturing**, especially in the names of companies: *Honda of America Mfg. Inc.*

mgmt. *abbr* (*only used in written English*)
management

MICR /,em aɪ si: 'ɑ:(r); 'maɪkə(r)/ *abbr* **magnetic ink character recognition** a system in which words and numbers are printed on official documents such as cheques in special ink that can be read by an electronic device: *Banks use MICR technology to process cheques at high speed.*

micro /'maɪkrəʊ; *AmE* -kroʊ/ (*plural* **micros**) =
MICROCOMPUTER

micro- /'maɪkrəʊ; *AmE* -kroʊ/ *combining form*
1 (*in nouns, adjectives and adverbs*) small; on a small scale: *a microchip* ◇ *microlending* [OPP] MACRO•
2 (*in nouns*) used in units of measurement to mean one millionth: *a microlitre*

microcap /'maɪkrəʊkæp; *AmE* -kroʊ-/ *noun* [C]
(*especially AmE*)
(*Stock Exchange*) one of the smallest companies on the stock exchange, that have a very low total value of shares (**market capitalization**): *microcap stocks* ◇ *a microcap fund* (= one that invests in microcaps)
→ SMALL CAP

microchip /'maɪkrəʊtʃɪp; *AmE* -kroʊ-/ (*also* **chip**) *noun* [C]
(*IT*) a very small piece of a material that is used inside a computer, etc. in order to carry a complicated electronic CIRCUIT: *A small microchip is embedded in the card.* ◇ *a microchip designer/ maker/plant* ◇ *Intel, the world's biggest chip company*

microcomputer /'maɪkrəʊkəmpju:tə(r); *AmE* -kroʊ-/ (*also* '**micro**) *noun* [C]
(*IT*) a small computer that contains a
MICROPROCESSOR → MAINFRAME, MINICOMPUTER

microeconomics /,maɪkrəʊ,i:kə'nɒmɪks; -,ekə-; *AmE* ,maɪkroʊ,ekə'nɑ:m-/ *noun* [U]
(*Economics*) the branch of **economics** that studies individual markets or the decisions and choices made by individual businesses, families, etc. about spending or earning money, for example the choice to charge a particular price for goods
▶ ,**micro,eco'nomic** *adjective*

microelectronics /,maɪkrəʊɪ,lek'trɒnɪks; *AmE* -kroʊɪ,lek'trɑ:n-/ *noun* [U]
the design, production and use of very small electronic CIRCUITS: *the introduction of microelectronics in the twentieth century* ◇ *the microelectronics industry* ◇ *Sharp Microelectronics*
▶ ,**microe,lec'tronic** *adjective* [only before noun]

microengineering /,maɪkrəʊ,endʒɪ'nɪərɪŋ; *AmE* ,maɪkroʊ,endʒɪ'nɪrɪŋ/ *noun* [U]
engineering on a very small scale, often involving
MICROELECTRONICS

micromanage /'maɪkrəʊmænɪdʒ; *AmE* -kroʊ-/ *verb* [+ obj *or no obj*] (*especially AmE*)
to control every aspect and detail of a business, project, etc: *The board does not micromanage: it makes general recommendations.* ◇ *Entrepreneurs often micromanage their businesses.*
▶ '**micromanagement** *noun* [U] '**micromanager** *noun* [C]

microprocessor /,maɪkrəʊ'prəʊsesə(r); *AmE* -kroʊ'proʊ-/ *noun* [C]
(*IT*) a small unit of a computer that contains all the functions of the CENTRAL PROCESSING UNIT

microsite /'maɪkrəʊsaɪt; *AmE* -kroʊ-/ *noun* [C]
(*Marketing*) a small website that a business creates for a particular purpose, especially to advertise or sell a new product. The **microsite** has a different address from the business's main website, although the two may have links between them: *They are creating a microsite to promote their new game.*

mid- /mɪd/ *combining form* (*used in nouns and adjectives*)
in the middle of: *She is in her mid-thirties.* ◇ *The shop is holding a mid-season sale on Saturday.*

'**mid cap** *noun* [C]
(*Stock Exchange*) a company that has a medium total value of shares (**market capitalization**) on the stock exchange: *Among the mid caps, Selfridges* (= its share price) *was up 3.5%.* ◇ *an index of mid-cap stocks* → LARGE CAP, SMALL CAP

middle-'income *adjective* [only before noun]
earning an average amount of money; neither rich nor poor: *The tax cuts will not really help middle-income families.*
O *middle-income* **countries/earners/families/ households/workers**

middleman /'mɪdlmæn/ *noun* [C] (*plural* **middlemen** /-men/)
1 a person or company that buys goods or services from a supplier and sells them to sb else: *Buy direct from the manufacturer and cut out the middleman.*
2 a person or an organization who helps to arrange things between people who are unable or unwilling to deal with each other directly: *The broker acts as the middleman between buyers and sellers.* ◇ *The payments were made through a middleman.* [SYN] INTERMEDIARY

,middle 'management *noun* [U with sing./pl. verb]
the people who are in charge of small groups of people and departments within a business organization but who are not involved in making

important decisions that will affect the whole organization: *They have removed a layer of middle management.* ◇ *Middle management is/are often focussed on the daily demands of their job.*

▶ **,middle 'manager** *noun* [C]: *moves to give middle managers more authority* See note at BOSS

,middle 'market *noun* [sing.] (*usually* **the middle market**) the group of customers that are prepared to buy a product with an average price rather than the most or least expensive kind; trade in products with an average price: *We shifted our focus from luxury clothing to the middle market.* ◇ *They're a leader in the middle market.* ◇ *a service aimed at middle-market companies* → MIDMARKET

,middle-'ranking *adjective* [only before noun] having a responsible job or position, but not one of the most important: *middle-ranking executives*

midmarket (*also spelled* **mid-market**) /ˌmɪdˈmɑːkɪt; *AmE* -ˈmɑːrk-/ *adjective* [usually before noun]
(*Marketing*)
1 designed for or used by the group of customers that are prepared to buy a product with an average price rather than the most or least expensive kind: *They specialize in software for midmarket customers.* **O** *a midmarket brand/hotel/product/retailer*
2 used to describe people who are prepared to buy products or services with average prices: *midmarket customers*
→ DOWNMARKET, UPMARKET

,mid-'price (*also* ,**mid-'priced**) *adjective* [only before noun]
(about a product for sale) not very expensive and not very cheap: *Spending was strong in the group's mid-price product range.* ◇ *a chain of mid-priced department stores* (= that sell products in the middle price range) ▶ **,mid-'price** *noun* [U; sing.]

,mid-'range (*also spelled* **midrange**) *adjective* [only before noun]
1 (about a product for sale) not the cheapest or most expensive, not the best or worst, not the largest or smallest, etc: *mid-range computers* ◇ *to increase sales in the mid-range market*
2 (about a number, a value, etc.) not the highest or lowest; in the middle: *Low to mid-range scores should be cause for concern.*
▶ **'mid-range** (*also spelled* **midrange**) *noun* [U; sing.]

midsession (*also spelled* **mid-session**) /ˌmɪdˈseʃn/ *noun* [U; sing.]
(*Stock Exchange*) the middle of a period of trading on the stock exchange, usually around midday: *The euro was trading at $1.08 by midsession in New York.* ◇ *midsession trading*

,mid-'sized (*also* ,**mid-'size**) (*both especially AmE*) *adjective*
of average size, neither large nor small: *a mid-sized company*

midstream /ˌmɪdˈstriːm/ *adjective*
(*Economics*; *Production*) used to describe the middle stages in an industrial or commercial process: *Their midstream services division gathers and processes natural gas for marketing.* ◇ *a midstream energy company* → DOWNSTREAM, UPSTREAM

midtown /ˈmɪdtaʊn/ *noun* [C, usually sing.] (*AmE*)
the part of a city that is between the central business area and the outer parts: *a house in midtown* ◇ *midtown Manhattan* → DOWNTOWN

migrate /maɪˈɡreɪt; *AmE* ˈmaɪɡreɪt/ *verb*
1 [no obj] (about a lot of people) to move from one town, country, etc. in order to go and live and work in another: *Farmers migrated to the cities.*
2 [no obj] to move from one place to another: *Jobs and investment have continued to migrate abroad.*
3 (*Commerce*; *IT*) [+ obj or no obj] to change, or

cause sb/sth to change, from one service or technology to another: *Newspaper readers are migrating to the Internet.* ◇ *We are migrating customers to our new high-speed service.*
4 (*IT*) [+ obj] to move programs or HARDWARE from one computer system to another
▶ **migration** /maɪˈɡreɪʃn/ *noun* [U,C]: *labour migration from low to high-income countries* ◇ *a migration of customers to rival businesses*
migratory /ˈmaɪɡrətri; maɪˈɡreɪtəri; *AmE* ˈmaɪɡrətɔːri/ *adjective*

milage = MILEAGE

mile /maɪl/ *noun* [C]

SEE ALSO: **Air Miles™**, **Square mile**

a unit for measuring distance equal to 1 609 metres or 1 760 yards

mileage (*also spelled* **milage**) /ˈmaɪlɪdʒ/ *noun*
1 [U; C, usually sing.] the distance that a vehicle has travelled, measured in miles: *My annual mileage is about 20 000.* ◇ *The price of the car includes unlimited mileage, but not fuel.* ◇ *Where no public transport is available a mileage allowance* (= a payment based on the number of miles driven) *is paid.*
2 [C,U] the number of miles that a vehicle can travel using a particular amount of fuel: *The new model gets better mileage than a typical small car.*
3 [U] (*informal*) the amount of advantage or use that you can get from a particular event or situation: *There's still plenty of mileage left in our older products.*

milestone /ˈmaɪlstəʊn; *AmE* -stoʊn/ *noun* [C]
1 (*also* **milepost** /ˈmaɪlpəʊst; *AmE* -poʊst/, *especially in AmE*) a very important stage or event in the development of sth: *The company passed an important milestone yesterday, announcing its first profits.* ◇ *The appointment represents a milestone in her career.*
O *to pass/reach a milestone* • *sth marks/represents/signals a milestone*
2 a time in a project by which particular tasks should be completed: *Ideally, planning meetings should be linked to milestone dates.* ◇ *Milestones and deliverables are defined in the project plan.*
→ DELIVERABLE—Picture at PERT
O *to agree/define/set milestones*

'milestone ,payment *noun* [C]
a payment for completing a particular stage of a business project: *They earn milestone payments during the development phase plus a share of sales.*

milk /mɪlk/ *verb* [+ obj]
to obtain as much money, advantage, etc. for yourself as you can from a particular situation, especially in a dishonest way: *They haven't invested in the business but have milked it for all they can get.*

'milk round *noun* [C, usually sing.] (*also* **the milk round**) in the UK, a series of visits that large companies make each year to colleges and universities, to talk to students who are interested in working for them

mill /mɪl/ *noun, verb*
(*Manufacturing*)
● *noun* [C] (*often used with other nouns*)

SEE ALSO: **run-of-the-mill**

a factory that produces a particular type of material: *The company has decided to close its paper mills.* See note at FACTORY
O *a cotton/paper/steel/textile mill*
● *verb* [+ obj]
to cut or shape metal in a special machine: *machine-milled steel* ◇ *a milling machine*

milli- /'mɪli/ combining form (in nouns; used in units of measurement)
one thousandth: milligram ◇ millilitre ◇ millimetre

million /'mɪljən/ number (abbr m) **HELP** Million and **millions** are always used with a plural verb, except when an amount of money is mentioned.
1 1 000 000: an income of half a million ◇ tens of millions of euros ◇ The project will create millions of new jobs. ◇ a million-dollar contract **HELP** You say **a, one, two, several, etc. million** without a final 's' on 'million'. **Millions (of ...)** can be used if there is no number or quantity before it: Five million cars were sold last year. ◇ Two million (euros) was withdrawn from the account.
2 (informal) a very large amount: I still have a million things to do. ◇ She **made** her **millions** (= all her money) on property deals.

millionaire /ˌmɪljə'neə(r); AmE -'ner/ noun [C]
a person who has a million euros, dollars, etc. or more; a very rich person: a property millionaire ◇ a millionaire businessman ◇ They became millionaires from the deal.

min. abbr (only used in written English)
minimum: min. charge €2.50 ◇ min. 8MB RAM required **OPP** MAX.

mindset /'maɪndset/ noun [C, usually sing.]
a set of attitudes or fixed ideas that sb has and that are often difficult to change: the corporate mindset ◇ the mindset of the computer generation
SYN MENTALITY

mindshare /'maɪndʃeə(r); AmE -ʃer/ noun [U]
(Marketing) how aware consumers are of a particular product or brand, compared with other brands or products of the same type: If you want to gain market share you have to capture mindshare.
→ MARKET SHARE, SHARE OF MIND at SHARE noun

mine /maɪn/ noun, verb
● **noun** [C]

SEE ALSO: **gold mine**

a deep hole or holes under the ground where minerals such as coal, gold, etc. are dug → MINING
O a coal/gold/copper/diamond mine
● **verb** [+ obj or no obj]
to dig holes in the ground in order to find and obtain coal, diamonds, etc: Most uranium is mined in Canada, South Africa and Australia. ◇ The area has been mined for lead and silver.

miner /'maɪnə(r)/ noun [C]
a person who works in a mine taking out coal, gold, diamonds, etc.

mini- /'mɪni/ combining form (used in nouns)
small: minivan ◇ fears of a mini-recession ◇ a mini-recovery in the housing market

minicomputer /'mɪnikəmpjuːtə(r)/ noun [C]
(IT) a computer of medium size that is larger and faster than a personal computer

minimal /'mɪnɪməl/ adjective
very small in size or amount; as small as possible: The work was carried out at minimal cost. ◇ The purchase had a minimal effect on our earnings. ◇ The risks involved are minimal. ▶ 'minimally adverb: They were only minimally responsible for the delays.

minimarket /'mɪnimɑːkɪt; AmE -mɑːrk-/ noun [C]
a small supermarket or food shop/store

★ **minimize, -ise** /'mɪnɪmaɪz/ verb [+ obj]
1 to reduce sth, especially sth bad, to the lowest possible level: ways of minimizing costs/losses/risk
2 to make sth small, especially on a computer screen: Minimize any windows you have open.
OPP MAXIMIZE

★ **minimum** /'mɪnɪməm/ adjective, noun
● **adjective** [usually before noun] (abbr **min.**)
the smallest possible or allowed; extremely small: There's a minimum charge of 50¢. ◇ What's the minimum age for retirement? ◇ The body sets minimum standards for lawyers. ▶ 'minimum adverb: You'll need $300 minimum for travel expenses.
● **noun** [C, usually sing.] (plural **minima** /'mɪnɪmə/) (abbr **min.**)
the smallest amount or level that is possible, allowed or required: Job losses were **kept to a minimum**. ◇ Our salespeople receive a minimum of 16 weeks' training. **OPP** MAXIMUM

ˌminimum 'wage noun [sing.]
the lowest wage that an employer is allowed to pay by law: to introduce a national minimum wage ◇ a minimum wage policy

mining /'maɪnɪŋ/ noun [U]

SEE ALSO: **data mining**

the process of getting coal and other minerals from under the ground; the industry involved in this: Mining is prohibited in protected areas. ◇ WMC is one of Australia's oldest mining houses (= companies).
→ MINE
O coal/diamond/gold/tin mining • a mining company/engineer/group/house

minor /'maɪnə(r)/ adjective, noun
● **adjective** [usually before noun]
not very large, important or serious: We've had a few minor problems. ◇ There may be some minor changes to the plan. ◇ The company is a minor player in the car industry. **OPP** MAJOR
● **noun** [C]
a person who is under the age at which you legally become an adult and are responsible for your actions: Minors require the consent of their parents.

★ **minority** /maɪ'nɒrəti; AmE -'nɔːr-; -'nɑːr-/ noun (plural **minorities**)

SEE ALSO: **blocking minority**

1 [sing. with sing./pl. verb] the smaller part of a group; less than half of the people or things in a large group: Only a small minority of these businesses makes/make decent profits. ◇ There is a minority view that interest rates will fall. ◇ Those in favour of the scheme were **in a/the minority**. **OPP** MAJORITY
2 [sing.] (usually used as an adjective) used to describe a person or an organization that owns a smaller share of a business than the main owner, or the share of the business that they own: They hold a minority stake in the business. ◇ She paid €2 billion to buy out the minority investors and take full control of the company. → MAJORITY (3)
O a minority investor/owner/partner/shareholder • a minority holding/investment/share/stake

miˌnority 'interest noun
1 (Finance) [C] a number of shares owned by a particular person or organization that is less than the number owned by the CONTROLLING SHAREHOLDER: She sold her controlling shares but retained a minority interest in the company.
2 (Accounting) [C,U] in the financial records of a HOLDING COMPANY (= a company that controls other companies), an amount of profit, income, etc. that belongs to a person or an organization that owns a part of a company that it controls: Net profit before minority interests rose to €550 million.
→ MAJORITY INTEREST

mint /mɪnt/ noun, verb
● **noun**
1 [C] a place where money is made: the Royal Mint (= the one where British money is made)

2 a mint [sing.] (*informal*) a large amount of money: *He made a mint selling used cars.*

IDM **in mint con'dition** new or as good as new; in perfect condition

● *verb* [+ obj]
to make a coin from metal

minted /'mɪntɪd/ *adjective*
1 recently produced, invented, created, etc: *a newly minted dot-com* ◇ *They've just recruited a group of newly minted* (= recently qualified) *MBAs.*
2 (*informal*) very rich

minus /'maɪnəs/ *preposition, adjective, noun*
● *preposition*
1 used when one number or amount is being taken away from another: *$100 minus $92.50 gives you a gain of $7.50.* ◇ *The core rate of inflation is the consumer price index minus food and energy.*
SYN LESS
2 (*informal*) without sth that was there before: *We're going to be minus a car for a while.*
OPP PLUS → idiom at PLUS *prep.*
● *adjective*
1 used before a number to show that it is lower than zero: *a minus number* ◇ *Sales rose last month to $60 million from minus $24 million in June.*
2 making sth seem negative and less attractive or good: *What are the car's minus points?* ◇ *On the minus side, the job involves very long hours of work.*
● *noun* [C]
1 (*informal*) a negative quality; a disadvantage: *Let's consider the pluses and minuses of changing the system.*
2 (*also* **'minus sign**) the symbol (–), used in mathematics
OPP PLUS

'minus tick = DOWNTICK

★ **minute** /'mɪnɪt/ *noun, verb*
● *noun* **the minutes** [pl.]
a summary or record of what is said or decided at a formal meeting: *We have a secretary to take* (= write) *the minutes.* ◇ *The minutes of the meeting show that the issue had been discussed.* See note at MEETING

O *to keep/take* minutes ✦ *to agree/approve/read/sign* the minutes ✦ *to circulate/draw up/write up* the minutes

● *verb* [+ obj]
to write down something that is said at a meeting in the official record (**the minutes**): *I'd like that last remark to be minuted.*

'mirror site (*also* **mirror** /'mɪrə(r)/) *noun* [C]
(*IT*) a website which is a copy of another website but has a different address on the Internet. An organization may create a **mirror site** so that more people are able to visit and use a popular website: *If this site is slow, try our mirror site.* ◇ *This is the mirror site of the IMO homepage.*

MIS /ˌem aɪ 'es/ = MANAGEMENT INFORMATION SYSTEM, MANUFACTURING INFORMATION SYSTEM

misappropriate /ˌmɪsə'prəʊprieɪt; *AmE* -'proʊ-/ *verb* [+ obj] (*formal*)
to take sb else's money or property for yourself, especially when they have trusted you to take care of it: *She is accused of misappropriating money from the company's pension fund.* ◇ *The court found that the company had misappropriated trade secrets.*
→ APPROPRIATE
▶ **misappropriation** /ˌmɪsəˌprəʊpri'eɪʃn; *AmE* -ˌproʊ-/ *noun* [U]: *the misappropriation of company funds*

misc. *abbr*
a short way of writing **miscellaneous**

miscalculate /ˌmɪs'kælkjuleɪt/ *verb* [+ obj or no obj]
to make a mistake in calculating or judging an

amount, a situation, etc: *We miscalculated our financial targets for the year.* ▶ **miscalculation** /ˌmɪskælkju'leɪʃn/ *noun* [C,U]: *to make a miscalculation*

miscellaneous /ˌmɪsə'leɪniəs/ *adjective* [usually before noun]
consisting of many different kinds of things that are not connected and do not easily form a group: *She gave me some money to cover any miscellaneous expenses.*

misconduct /ˌmɪs'kɒndʌkt; *AmE* -'kɑːn-/ *noun* [U] (*formal*)
1 behaviour that is unacceptable, especially because it breaks the rules of a particular profession or job: *The committee charged her with professional misconduct.*
2 bad management of a company, etc: *misconduct of the company's financial affairs* ◇ *corporate misconduct*

misdirect /ˌmɪsdə'rekt; -daɪ'rekt/ *verb* [+ obj]
to send sb/sth in the wrong direction or to the wrong place: *Investors have been misdirected.* ◇ *misdirected mail* ▶ **misdirection** /ˌmɪsdə'rekʃn; -daɪ'rek-/ *noun* [U]

'misery ˌindex *noun* [C]
(*Economics*) a measure of the performance of an economy that considers the rate of unemployment and INFLATION (= the general rise in the price of goods and services over a period of time): *They found that the misery index for middle-income families had worsened by 13 points.*

mismanage /ˌmɪs'mænɪdʒ/ *verb* [+ obj]
to deal with or manage sth badly: *The department's budget was badly mismanaged.* ◇ *mismanaged companies* ▶ ˌmis'**management** *noun* [U]: *The agency is being accused of financial mismanagement.*

misrepresent /ˌmɪs,reprɪ'zent/ *verb* [+ obj]
to give information about sb/sth that is not true or complete so that other people have the wrong impression about them/it: *They were accused of misrepresenting the company's financial state.*
▶ **misrepresentation** /ˌmɪs,reprɪzen'teɪʃn/ *noun* [C,U]

ˌmis-'**sell** *verb* [+ obj]
to sell sth to sb that is not suitable for their needs, for example by not giving them all the information they need: *If the policy was mis-sold, the insurance company must be responsible.* ▶ ˌmis-'**sale** *noun* [C,U]: *the mis-sale of mortgage endowment and pension policies* ˌmis-'**selling** *noun* [U]: *the mis-selling of investment products*

mission /'mɪʃn/ *noun* [C]

SEE ALSO: **trade mission**

1 a particular purpose or aim that a company or an organization has: *Our mission is to become the country's leading supplier of business software.* ◇ *We need to stay focused on our core mission and values.*
→ MISSION STATEMENT
2 an important official job that a group of people is given to do, especially when they are sent to another country; the group of people who do this job: *a fact-finding mission* ◇ *The bank has sent a mission to Mexico.*
3 an important job that sb is given to do: *She has the tough mission of trying to save thousands of jobs.*

'mission creep *noun* [U]
the gradual addition of new work and duties to a project, or to the responsibilities of a group or department

ˌmission-'**critical** *adjective*
essential for an organization to function

successfully: *No one believes their mission-critical systems are going to fail.* ◇ *mission-critical employees/projects*

'mission ˌstatement *(also ˌstatement of 'purpose) noun* [C]

an official statement of the aims of a company or an organization: *The newly formed company does not yet have a mission statement.* ◇ *Our mission statement includes a strong commitment to the health and safety of our employees.* → VISION STATEMENT

❍ **to create/draft/write** a mission statement

misstate /ˌmɪsˈsteɪt/ *verb* [+ obj]

to write or say sth that is wrong or not accurate, especially in order to deceive sb: *They have misled investors by misstating or hiding expenses.*
▶ **misˈstatement** *noun* [C,U]: *accounting misstatements*

misuse *noun, verb*

● *noun* /ˌmɪsˈjuːs/ [U; C, usually sing.]
the act of using sth in a dishonest way or for the wrong purpose: *an investigation into the alleged misuse of company funds*

● *verb* /ˌmɪsˈjuːz/ [+ obj]
to use sth in the wrong way or for the wrong purpose: *It is clear that executives have been misusing company funds.* ◇ *People are worried about transmitting credit-card numbers on the Internet in case these are copied and misused.*

mitigate /ˈmɪtɪɡeɪt/ *verb* [+ obj]

to make sth less harmful, serious, dangerous, etc: *The bank uses several methods to mitigate risk.* ◇ *The company is trying to mitigate the effects of falling orders.* ◇ *He would have faced a prison sentence except for* **mitigating circumstances** (= that made his crime seem less serious).

mitigation /ˌmɪtɪˈɡeɪʃn/ *noun* [U]

a reduction in how unpleasant, serious or dangerous sth is: *Risk mitigation is all about taking actions that control risks.* ◇ *His lawyers are making a mitigation plea* (= to make his crime seem less serious).

IDM **in mitiˈgation** *(Law)* with the aim of making a crime seem less serious or easier to forgive: *In mitigation, I did discover and correct the mistake before there were any serious results.*

mix /mɪks/ *noun* [C, usually sing.]

SEE ALSO: **advertising mix, asset ~, business ~, investment ~, marketing ~, merchandise ~, product ~, sales ~**

1 a combination of different things or people: *The store sells a mix of frozen food and groceries.* ◇ *The company offered a $12 billion mix of cash and shares.* ◇ *We need to ensure we have the right skill mix.*
2 a situation, especially a difficult one, that has different things or people in it: *Business failure is tough enough without adding family trouble into the mix.*

mixed /mɪkst/ *adjective*

having both good and bad qualities or feelings: *The latest economic data is mixed.* ◇ *The plans met with a mixed reaction from the staff.*

ˌmixed eˈconomy *noun* [C]

(Economics) an economic system in a country in which some companies are owned by the state and some are private

ˌmixed 'media *noun* [U]

(Marketing) the use of different kinds of media for advertising, such as TV, radio, newspapers, etc: *More advertisers are using mixed media to get better results.* ◇ *a mixed-media campaign*

ml /mɪl/ *abbr* (usually used in written English)
millilitre: *25ml water*

MLM /ˌem el ˈem/ = MULTILEVEL MARKETING

MM /ˌem ˈem/ = MARKET-MAKER

mm *abbr* (only used in written English)
millimetre: *300mm chip manufacturing* ◇ *a 35mm camera*

MMS /ˌem em ˈes/ *noun* **Multimedia Messaging Service**

1 [U] a system for sending pictures, sounds and short written messages from one mobile phone/cellphone to another: *You will need to subscribe to MMS.*
2 [C] a message sent by **MMS**: *He sent me an MMS.*
→ EMS, SMS

mngmt *(also spelled* **mngmt.***) abbr (only used in written English)*
management

mngr *(also spelled* **mngr.***) abbr (only used in written English)*
manager

MO = MAIL ORDER, MONEY ORDER

mobile /ˈməʊbaɪl; *AmE* ˈmoʊbl/ *adjective, noun*

● *adjective*

SEE ALSO: **upwardly mobile**

1 [usually before noun] that is not fixed in one place and can be moved easily and quickly: *mobile equipment* ◇ *Capital, investment and talent are more mobile today than ever before.*
2 able to change your social class, your job or the place where you live easily: *a highly mobile workforce* (= people who can move easily from place to place)

● *noun* [C] *(BrE)* (often used in the names of companies) a mobile phone: *What's your mobile number?* ◇ *Call me on my mobile.* ◇ *Virgin Mobile*

❍ a mobile **business/company/maker/operator/user** • mobile **charges/handsets/networks/sales**

★ˌmobile 'phone *(also* **'mobile***) noun* [C] *(both BrE)*

a telephone that does not have wires and works by radio, that you can carry with you and use anywhere: *Please make sure all mobile phones are switched off.* ◇ *Europe's second largest mobile phone company* **SYN** CELLPHONE

ˌmobile 'worker *noun* [C]

(HR) an employee who does not have one fixed place of work but moves from place to place: *Some companies provide handheld computers for their mobile workers.* ▶ **ˌmobile 'working** *noun* [U]

mobility /məʊˈbɪləti; *AmE* moʊ-/ *noun* [U]

SEE ALSO: **labour mobility**

1 the ability to move easily from one place, social class or job to another: *French and Spanish companies particularly value mobility for senior managers.* ◇ *Limited* **upward mobility** (= moving towards a higher social position and becoming richer) *can lead to discontent among young people.*
2 the ability to move or travel around easily; the ability to be moved easily: *Someone with limited mobility may not be able to use a mouse.* ◇ *the mobility of capital*

moˌbility of 'labour *(AmE spelling ~ **labor**)*
= LABOUR MOBILITY

'mock-up *noun* [C]

a model or copy of sth, often the same size as the original object, that is used for testing, or for showing people what the real thing will look like: *Get back to me when you have a mock-up of your product.*

mode /məʊd; *AmE* moʊd/ *noun*
1 [C] a particular way of doing sth; a particular type of sth: *a mode of transport* ◇ *Please confirm the order and select mode of payment.*
2 [C,U] the way in which a piece of equipment is set to perform a particular task: *Switch the camera into the automatic mode.*
3 (*Technical*) [sing.] the value that appears most frequently in a series of numbers → MEAN, MEDIAN
See note at AVERAGE

★ **model** /ˈmɒdl; *AmE* ˈmɑːdl/ *noun, verb*
● *noun* [C]

SEE ALSO: **demo model, demonstration ~, pricing ~**

1 a particular design or type of product: *The latest models will be on display at the motor show.* ◇ *Prices are down on basic models.*
O *basic/cheaper/popular/standard* models • *luxury/more expensive* models • *current/the latest/new/old/previous* models • *to design/develop/make/produce* a model
2 a simple description of a system, used for explaining how sth works or calculating what might happen, etc: *business plans built on a variety of financial models* ◇ *The Bank has been working on a new forecasting model.*
O *an economic/a financial/mathematical/statistical model* • *a business/management/marketing/strategic* model
3 a copy of sth, usually smaller than the original object: *$3 million was spent on developing a* **working** *model of the device.* ◇ *The architect had produced a* **scale** *model of the proposed shopping complex.*
4 a particular system or way of doing sth that can be copied by other people: *Their independent gas and electricity market has provided a model for many other countries.*
● *verb* [+ obj] (-**ll**-, *AmE* -**l**-)
to create a copy of an activity, a situation, etc. so that you can study it before dealing with the real thing: *The program can model a typical home page for you.*

modem /ˈməʊdem; *AmE* ˈmoʊ-/ *noun* [C]
(*IT*) a device that connects one computer system to another using a telephone line so that data can be sent

moderate *adjective, verb*
● *adjective* /ˈmɒdərət; *AmE* ˈmɑːd-/
neither very good, large, etc. nor very bad, small, etc.; reasonable: *The retail sector expects moderate growth.* ◇ *Shares fell slightly on Tuesday in moderate trading.* ◇ *moderate wage demands* ▶ **moderately** /ˈmɒdərətli; *AmE* ˈmɑːd-/ *adverb*: *a moderately successful career* ◇ *Prices have risen only moderately so far this year.*
● *verb* /ˈmɒdəreɪt; *AmE* ˈmɑːd-/ [+ obj or no obj]
to become or make sth become less extreme, severe, etc: *We agreed to moderate our original demands.*

moderator /ˈmɒdəreɪtə(r); *AmE* ˈmɑːd-/ *noun* [C]
a person whose job is to help the two sides in a disagreement to reach an agreement → MEDIATOR

modernize, **-ise** /ˈmɒdənaɪz; *AmE* ˈmɑːdərn-/ *verb* [+ obj or no obj]
to make sth more modern by starting to use new equipment, ideas, etc: *The company is investing $9 million to modernize its factories.* ◇ *Unfortunately we lack the resources to modernize.* ▶ **modernization**, **-isation** /ˌmɒdənaɪˈzeɪʃn; *AmE* ˌmɑːdərnəˈz-/ *noun* [U]: *The company is focusing on the modernization of its existing systems.*

modest /ˈmɒdɪst; *AmE* ˈmɑːd-/ *adjective*
not very large, expensive, important, etc: *Tools are available at modest prices.* ◇ *He charges a relatively modest fee.* ◇ *We're only expecting a modest improvement in sales.* ▶ **modestly** *adverb*

★ **modify** /ˈmɒdɪfaɪ; *AmE* ˈmɑːd-/ *verb* [+ obj]
(**modifies, modifying, modified, modified**)
to change sth slightly, especially in order to make it more suitable for a particular purpose: *The software is modified for specific customers.* ◇ *We found it cheaper to modify existing equipment rather than buy new.* ◇ *They're planning to sell a modified version of their popular small car.* SYN ADAPT
▶ **modification** /ˌmɒdɪfɪˈkeɪʃn; *AmE* ˌmɑːd-/ *noun* [C,U]: *Considerable modification of the existing system is needed.* ◇ *It might be necessary to make a few slight modifications to the design.*

modular /ˈmɒdjələ(r); *AmE* ˈmɑːdʒə-/ *adjective*
1 consisting of separate parts or units that can be joined together: *modular software components* ◇ *modular shelving/furniture*
2 (*Manufacturing*) used to describe a system in which the parts or units of a car, machine, etc. are made separately by suppliers and then joined together by the manufacturer: *the auto industry's use of modular assemblies* ◇ *Modular production allows for mass customization.*

module /ˈmɒdjuːl; *AmE* ˈmɑːdʒuːl/ *noun* [C]
1 (*IT*) a unit of a computer system or program that has a particular function: *electronic control modules* ◇ *Companies can pick and choose the software modules that they need.*
2 one of a set of separate parts or units that go together to make a machine, a piece of furniture, etc.

mogul /ˈməʊgl; *AmE* ˈmoʊgl/ *noun* [C]
a very rich, important and powerful person: *a media mogul* See note at BARON

,mom-and-'pop *adjective* (*AmE*)
used to describe a small local shop/store or business that is often owned by a family: *The big chain stores can afford to sell goods for less than smaller mom-and-pop stores.* ◇ *mom-and-pop operations*

momentum /məˈmentəm; *AmE* moʊˈm-/ *noun* [U]
an energy or a force, particularly one that helps to increase or improve sth: *The economic recovery is gaining momentum.* ◇ *I'm afraid our sales team is beginning to lose momentum.*
O *to pick up/gain/gather/lose/maintain* momentum

monetarism /ˈmʌnɪtərɪzəm/ *noun* [U]
(*Economics*) the theory and policy that considers the best way to manage an economy and keep INFLATION low is by controlling the amount of money and credit that is available ▶ **'monetarist** *noun* [C] **'monetarist** *adjective*: *a monetarist economic policy*

★ **monetary** /ˈmʌnɪtri; *AmE* -teri/ *adjective* [only before noun]
1 connected with money or currencies: *Our society places a monetary value on labour.* ◇ *There are considerable monetary rewards in running a large company.*
2 (*Economics*) connected with the amount of money and credit that is available within a particular country or economy and the way this is controlled: *Pressure is also growing for further monetary easing by the central bank.* ◇ *The German economy required a bit of monetary stimulus* (= an increase in the supply of money).
O *monetary easing/expansion/growth/stability/tightening*

'monetary base *noun* [C, usually sing.]
(*Economics*) all the cash that is available within a particular economy including all the bills/notes and coins that are held by individuals and by banks **NOTE** In the UK, the **monetary base** is sometimes referred to as **M0**.

,monetary 'policy noun [C]
(*Economics*) the way in which a government or central bank controls the supply of money and credit in an economy: *Demand can be stimulated by the proper mix of fiscal and monetary policy.* ◇ *The European Central Bank is easing monetary policy.*
→ FISCAL POLICY
O *loose/tight* monetary policy • *to ease/loosen/tighten* monetary policy

'monetary ,system noun [C]
(*Economics*) the system that controls the supply and exchange of money within a country or between different countries: *There have been massive changes in the world's monetary system.* ◇ *the European/international monetary system*

'monetary ,unit noun [C]
(*Economics*) the standard form of currency in a country: *Has the euro become the monetary unit of the UK?* SYN UNIT OF CURRENCY

★ **money** /'mʌni/ noun

SEE ALSO: application money, broad ~, call ~, cheap ~, danger ~, dear ~, digital ~, etc.

1 [U] what you can use to buy and sell things and earn through your work, investments, sales, etc: *How much money is there in my account?* ◇ *I make more money in this job than in the last one.* ◇ *If the item is not satisfactory, you will get your money back.* ◇ *Factory automation systems can save you time and money.* ◇ *Smaller companies have found it difficult to borrow money to invest in assets.* ◇ *Foreign investors have poured money into US real estate.*
O *to earn/make/save/spend* money • *to borrow/lend/owe/raise* money • *to pour/pump/put* money *into sth*

2 [U] coins or paper notes: *I counted the money carefully.* ◇ *Where can I change my money into dollars?*

3 [U] a person's wealth including their property: *He lost all his money.*

4 (*Law*) **moneys** or **monies** [pl.] sums of money: *a statement of all monies paid into your account*
IDM **be, pour, throw, etc. money down the 'drain** to waste money: *It's a terrible idea—you'll just be pouring money down the drain.* **make 'money** to earn a lot of money; to make a profit: *I started my business because I wanted to make money.* ◇ *There's money to be made from tourism.* **make/lose money ,hand over 'fist** to make/lose money very fast and in large quantities **money 'talks** people who have a lot of money have more power and influence than others → idioms at COIN *verb*, GROW, LICENCE, THROW, TIME *noun*

,money at 'call noun [C]
(*Finance*) money which must be paid as soon as the lender demands it: *extremely liquid assets such as money at call*

'money at 'call and short 'notice noun [U]
(*Finance*) money which must be paid either as soon as the lender demands it, or within 14 days: *When banks are short of cash they will recall some of their money at call and short notice.*

,money-back guaran'tee noun [C]
(*Commerce*) a promise to return customers' money if they are not satisfied with a product or service: *Everything in our catalogue comes with a money-back guarantee.*

'money ,broker noun [C]
(*Finance*) a person or an organization that arranges loans between banks or other financial organizations for short periods of time

'money ,centre bank (*AmE spelling* ~ **center** ~) noun [C]
(*Finance*) in the US, a large bank that lends money to governments, large companies and other banks rather than to individual customers

'money fund = MONEY MARKET FUND

'money-,grubbing (*also* **'money-,grabbing**) adjective [only before noun] (*informal*)
trying to get a lot of money ▶ **'money-,grubber** (*also* **'money-,grabber**) noun [C]

'money ,laundering noun [U]
the act of moving money that has been obtained illegally into foreign bank accounts or legal businesses so that it is difficult for people to know where the money came from: *efforts to curb money laundering* ◇ *anti-money-laundering controls*
→ LAUNDER
▶ **'money ,launderer** noun [C]

moneylender /'mʌnilendə(r)/ noun [C]
(*Finance*) a person or an organization whose business is lending money, to be paid back with interest. Moneylenders are not part of the official banking system: *General Motors is a major moneylender, earning millions of dollars from making loans.*

'money ,loser noun [C]
a product, service, company, etc. that makes a loss rather than a profit: *Is electronic commerce a money-loser or a revenue generator for government?*
▶ **'money-,losing** adjective: *How do you turn a money-losing enterprise into a profitable business?*

moneymaker /'mʌnimeɪkə(r)/ noun [C]
1 a product, service, company, etc. that makes a large profit: *Tourism is still the big moneymaker here.*
→ MONEY-SPINNER
2 a person who is good at finding or creating opportunities to make money: *The paper is read by the City moneymakers and top investors.*
▶ **'moneymaking** adjective: *a moneymaking service* ◇ *moneymaking opportunities* **'moneymaking** noun [U]

'money ,management noun [U]
(*Finance*)
1 the activity of organizing the investments of a person, an organization or a financial institution so that they make as much profit as possible
SYN INVESTMENT MANAGEMENT
2 the activity of organizing income, savings, payments, etc. for yourself or on behalf of another person or company: *We can help you with debt problems and money management.*

'money ,manager noun [C]
a person who manages investments on behalf of a company or an individual: *If you like analyzing stock market trends, you could think about becoming a money manager.* SYN INVESTMENT MANAGER

'money ,market noun [C]
(*Finance*)
1 the activity of buying and selling short loans between banks and other financial institutions, for example in the form of CERTIFICATES OF DEPOSIT (= money borrowed by banks over short periods) or TREASURY BILLS (= money borrowed by governments over short periods); the banks and other institutions that are involved in this : *Cash was flowing out of the money market into the stock market.*
2 the buying and selling of foreign money: *The pound rose again on the money markets.*

'money ,market fund (*also* **'money fund**) noun [C]
(*Finance*) a type of fund that buys investments with a low risk, such as CERTIFICATES OF DEPOSIT (= money borrowed by banks over short periods) or

TREASURY BILLS (= money borrowed by a government over a short period), rather than shares

'money ,order (*abbr* MO) (*also* ,**postal 'money ,order**) (*BrE also* '**postal ,order**) *noun* [C]
an official document that you can buy at a bank or a post office and send to sb so that they can exchange it for money

'money-,spinner *noun* [C] (*BrE*) (*informal*)
a product, an idea, etc. that earns a lot of money: *A franchise can be a real money-spinner.* ▶ '**money-,spinning** *adjective*: *money-spinning Internet services*

'money su,pply (*also* '**money stock**) *noun* [sing; U]
(*Economics*) the total amount of money that exists in the economy of a country at a particular time: *The government has taken measures to control the money supply.* ◇ *An increase in money supply will not necessarily affect spending.* ◇ *The central bank cut inflation from 12.5% to 10.3% by tightening the money supply.* → Mo, M1, ETC.
🔾 to **control/increase/reduce/restrict** (the) money supply • a **growth/an increase** in (the) money supply

'money trans,mission *noun* [U]
(*Finance*) the process of moving money and making payments from one individual or organization to another, that is done by banks or other financial organizations: *Banks provide facilities such as money transmission and the provision of credit.*

'money ,wages *noun* [pl.]
(*Economics*) the amount of money sb is paid for the work they do, expressed only as a figure without considering what it can buy: *The increase in money wages still falls below the rate of inflation, so it represents a decrease in real wages.* → REAL WAGES

★ **monitor** /'mɒnɪtə(r); *AmE* 'mɑːn-/ *noun, verb*
● *noun* [C]
1 a screen that shows information from a computer: *a 17-inch, flat-screen monitor* ◇ *Flight boarding times are displayed on the overhead monitors.* → VDT, VDU—Picture at OFFICE
2 a person whose job is to check that sth is done fairly and honestly: *A court-appointed monitor had to approve the new CEO's pay package.*
● *verb* [+ obj]
to watch and check a process over a period of time in order to see how it develops and make any necessary changes: *This is a simpler system that requires fewer engineers to monitor it.* ◇ *The situation is being closely monitored.* ◇ *The software enables companies to monitor employees' Internet use.*

monopolist /məˈnɒpəlɪst; *AmE* məˈnɑːp-/ *noun* [C]
(*Economics*) a person or company that has a **monopoly**: *an alliance of media monopolists*

monopolistic /mə,nɒpəˈlɪstɪk; *AmE* mə,nɑːpə-/ *adjective*
(*Economics*) having or trying to get complete control over an industry, a market, etc: *monopolistic corporations* ◇ *The merger would give them a monopolistic position in the drugs market.*

★ **monopolize**, **-ise** /məˈnɒpəlaɪz; *AmE* məˈnɑːp-/ *verb* [+ obj]
(*Economics*) to have or take control of all or almost all of sth such as a market or an industry so that others are prevented from sharing it: *The companies were accused of attempting to monopolize the debit-card market.* ◇ *a salary structure in which a few top executives monopolize most of the benefits*
▶ **monopolization, -isation** /mə,nɒpəlaɪˈzeɪʃn; *AmE* mə,nɑːpələˈz-/ *noun* [U]

★ **monopoly** /məˈnɒpəli; *AmE* məˈnɑːp-/ *noun* [C] (*plural* **monopolies**)

SEE ALSO: bilateral monopoly, commercial ~, legal ~

1 (*Economics*) the complete control of trade in particular goods or the supply of a particular service; the type of goods or service that is controlled in this way: *They have a virtual monopoly in PC operating systems.* ◇ *Electricity, gas and water were considered to be natural monopolies.* ◇ *Health care has long been a public/state monopoly* (= owned and controlled by the government). ◇ *Ending the monopoly on letter deliveries would cost the company millions.*
🔾 to **create/extend/have** a monopoly • to **break (up)/end/lose** a monopoly
2 sth that is completely controlled or owned by one person or group, so that other people do not or cannot share it: *Managers do not have a monopoly on stress.* ◇ *The fight against corruption is not the monopoly of industrialized countries.*
🔾 to **have/hold** a monopoly

monopsony /məˈnɒpsəni; *AmE* məˈnɑːp-/ *noun* (*plural* **monopsonies**) (*Economics*)
1 [U] a situation where there is only one buyer in a particular market or where one buyer controls most of a market: *Monopsony is the equivalent on the buying side of a monopoly on the selling side.*
2 [C] a person or an organization that is the only buyer or the main buyer in a particular market: *The large wine makers were accused of being a monopsony, exercising huge buying power over grape growers.*
▶ **mo'nopsonist** *noun* [C]: *a monopsonist who is the sole buyer of labour in a local geographical market*

,**month-on-'month** *adjective, adverb*
compared with the same date one month earlier: *Consumer spending showed a 6% month-on-month drop in January.* ◇ *US retail sales numbers for October were unchanged month-on-month.* → idiom at YEAR

moonlight /'muːnlaɪt/ *verb* [no obj] (**moonlighted**, **moonlighted**)
to have a second job that you do secretly, usually without paying tax on the extra money that you earn: *He spent years moonlighting as a cab driver.*
▶ '**moonlighter** *noun* [C]: *Web design freelancers and moonlighters* '**moonlighting** *noun* [U]: *doing a bit of moonlighting*

'Moore's law /mɔːz; mʊəz; *AmE* mʊrz/ *noun* [sing.]
(*IT*) the theory that the possible power of computing doubles every 18 months

morale /məˈrɑːl; *AmE* -ˈræl/ *noun* [U]
the amount of confidence and enthusiasm, etc. that a person or a group has at a particular time: *ways of keeping employee morale high*
🔾 **high/low/poor** morale • to **boost/improve/raise** morale • to **damage/lower/undermine** morale

,**moral 'hazard** *noun* [U]
the situation where people or organizations are more likely to take risks because they are protected against the results, for example by insurance: *Government support for failing private-sector businesses has created moral hazard for private companies.*

,**moral 'rights** *noun* [pl.]
(*Law*) the rights of an author in relation to their work, for example the right for the work not to be changed in a way that damages the author's reputation

moratorium /ˌmɒrə'tɔːriəm; AmE ˌmɔːr-/ noun [C] (plural **moratoriums** or **moratoria** /-riə/)
1 a temporary stopping of an activity, especially by an official agreement: Money-saving plans include a six-month moratorium **on** all new projects.
○ to **end/impose/lift** a moratorium
2 (Law) a period of time during which an organization does not have to pay a debt or tax: A judge granted a six-month debt moratorium to the collapsed group. ◊ a three-year moratorium **on** new e-commerce taxes
○ a **debt/tax** moratorium

moribund /'mɒrɪbʌnd; AmE 'mɔːr-; 'mɑːr-/ adjective (formal)
no longer effective or active, and likely to fail or end soon: moribund state industries ◊ a year when capital spending has remained moribund

morph /mɔːf; AmE mɔːrf/ verb [+ obj or no obj] (informal)
1 to change into sth different: Our small company is morphing **into** a global business. ◊ rapidly morphing technology
2 (IT) to gradually change from one computer image into another: At different points in the game the cars morph **into** super-vehicles.
▶ **'morphing** noun [U]: The graphics give you highly complex morphing effects.

mor'tality ˌtables = LIFE TABLES

★ **mortgage** /'mɔːgɪdʒ; AmE 'mɔːrg-/ noun, verb
● **noun** [C] (also **'property loan**)

SEE ALSO: **endowment mortgage**

a legal agreement by which a bank or similar organization lends you money to buy a house, flat/apartment, etc. or land, and you pay the money back over a number of years; the sum of money that you borrow: Taking out a mortgage is a big financial commitment. ◊ You can save thousands in interest by paying off your mortgage early. ◊ Interest rates, and therefore mortgage repayments, are expected to rise next year. → HOME LOAN See note at LOAN
○ to **apply for/get/have/take out** a mortgage ◆ to **pay/pay off/repay** a mortgage ◆ mortgage **payments/repayments** ◆ mortgage **arrears**
● **verb** [+ obj]
to borrow money from a bank or similar organization, giving the bank the legal right to own your house or land if you do not pay back the money that you have borrowed: They financed the company by mortgaging their property.

ˌmortgage-backed se'curity noun [C] (abbr **MBS**)
(Finance) a type of investment that represents a share in a group of **mortgages** (= loans to individuals or businesses to buy property) and that receives income from the payments made by the borrowers

'mortgage bond noun [C]
(Finance) a safe type of investment which is protected by property or physical equipment that can be sold to pay the investor

mortgagee /ˌmɔːgɪ'dʒiː; AmE ˌmɔːrg-/ noun [C]
a person or an organization that lends money to people to buy property See note at EMPLOYER

'mortgage ˌfinance noun [U]
money lent to people or organizations to buy property: the demand for mortgage finance ◊ the mortgage finance giant, Freddie Mac

'mortgage ˌlender noun [C]
an organization such as a bank that lends money to people and businesses to buy property: Many mortgage lenders have cut their interest rates.

'mortgage ˌmarket noun [C]
(Finance)
1 (also **primary 'mortgage ˌmarket**) the activity of lending money to people and organizations to buy property; the banks and financial institutions that do this: Abbey has strengthened its share of the UK mortgage market.
2 (also **secondary 'mortgage ˌmarket**) the activity of buying and selling existing **mortgages**
→ MORTGAGE-BACKED SECURITY

'mortgage rate noun [C]
the rate of interest that banks and other lenders charge on loans that they give people to buy property: We can help you find the best mortgage rate.

mortgagor /'mɔːgɪdʒɔː(r); AmE 'mɔːrg-/ noun [C]
a person or company that borrows money to buy property: The term ends when the mortgagor has repaid the loan.

mothball /'mɒθbɔːl; AmE 'mɔːθ-/ verb [+ obj]
to stop using or developing a business or part of a business for a period of time: A slowdown forced the company to close or mothball several plants.
▶ **'mothballing** noun [U]: The plan will include the mothballing of research programs.

motherboard /'mʌðəbɔːd; AmE 'mʌðərbɔːrd/ noun [C]
(IT) the main board of a computer, containing all the sets of electrical connections that make up the computer's memory and power

motion /'məʊʃn; AmE 'moʊʃn/ noun [C]
a formal proposal that is discussed and voted on at a meeting: Shareholders tabled a motion to adjourn the meeting (= to stop it for a period of time). ◊ The motion was approved by a large majority. See note at MEETING
○ to **propose/put forward/table** a motion ◆ to **adopt/approve/carry/pass** a motion ◆ to **defeat/reject** a motion

★ **motivate** /'məʊtɪveɪt; AmE 'moʊ-/ verb [+ obj]
to make sb want to do sth, especially to work hard or try hard: She's very good at motivating her staff. ◊ These systems can motivate employees **to** become more productive. [OPP] DEMOTIVATE
▶ **'motivated** adjective: She is intelligent and highly motivated. **motivation** /ˌməʊtɪ'veɪʃn; AmE ˌmoʊ-/ noun [C,U]: Size was the main motivation for the merger. **motivational** /ˌməʊtɪ'veɪʃənl; AmE ˌmoʊ-/ adjective: motivational programs for employees

ˌmotivational re'search noun [U]
(Marketing) research that tries to discover the reasons behind consumers' decisions about which brands or products to buy

motivator /'məʊtɪveɪtə(r); AmE 'moʊ-/ noun [C]
1 something such as money that encourages people to work or try hard: His confidence in my abilities was a huge motivator.
2 a person who is good at encouraging others to work or try hard: A team leader has to be a teacher and a motivator.

'motor pool = CAR POOL

MOU /ˌem əʊ 'juː; AmE oʊ/ = MEMORANDUM OF UNDERSTANDING

mount /maʊnt/ verb [no obj]
to increase, often in a way that causes worry: Pressure is mounting for tax allowances on childcare. ◊ Mounting debts are adding to the company's problems.
[PHR V] **ˌmount 'up** to increase gradually in size and quantity: Meanwhile, my debts were mounting up.

mouse /maʊs/ noun [C] (plural **mouses** or **mice** /maɪs/)
1 a small device that you move and press with your hand in order to perform actions on a

computer screen: *You can sign up just by a click of the mouse.*—Picture at OFFICE
2 a way of referring to a very small company that can create no new jobs → ELEPHANT, GAZELLE

'mouse mat (*BrE*) (*AmE* **'mouse pad**) *noun* [C]
a small square, usually made of plastic, that is used as a surface for moving a computer **mouse** over—Picture at OFFICE

move /muːv/ *verb, noun*
● *verb*
1 [no obj] to change the place where you live or work or where sth is situated: *The company is moving to Madrid.* → RELOCATE
2 [+ obj] to make sb change from one job, department, etc. to another: *I'm being moved to the New York office.* ◇ *They moved her sideways* (= gave her a different job that was not at a higher level).
3 [no obj] (*used with an adverb or a preposition*) to make progress in the way or direction mentioned: *Share prices moved ahead today.* ◇ *The project is moving on steadily.*
4 [+ obj] to suggest sth formally so that it can be discussed and decided: *I move that a vote be taken.*
[SYN] PUT STH FORWARD
5 [+ obj *or* no obj] to be sold very quickly; to make sth be sold very quickly: *High street fashion is moving fast.* ◇ *Even heavier advertising failed to move the goods.*
▶ **'movement** *noun* [C,U]: *laws to allow free movement of goods and services* ◇ *There has been no movement in oil prices.* → idiom at TIME *noun*
[PHRV] **,move 'on (to sth) 1** to progress or start sth new, especially when this means forgetting the past: *It's time for me to move on and allow the company's new management team to do its job.* **2** to start discussing sth else: *Can we move on to the next item on the agenda?* **,move 'over to sth** to change to doing or using sth different
● *noun* [C]

SEE ALSO: **career move**

1 an action that you do or need to do to achieve sth: *The management have **made** no move **to** settle the strike.* ◇ *Selling the smaller stores was seen as a good move.*
2 a change in ideas, attitudes, or behaviour: *There was a move away from rail freight to transportation by road.*
3 an act of changing the place where you live or work, or where sth is situated: *What's the date of your move?* ◇ *The move from London to Manchester was a success for the business.*

mover /'muːvə(r)/ *noun* [C]

SEE ALSO: **first mover**

1 sth that changes its position, for example a company or currency that changes its position in a market: *The biggest upward mover in the index was Marks & Spencer.*
2 (*especially AmE*) = REMOVER
[IDM] **,movers and 'shakers** people with power in an important organization: *The movers and shakers of the media world were all present at the meeting.*

,moving 'average *noun* [C]
(*Technical*) the average price or value of sth such as shares over a particular period up to the present, for example the past 30 days: *Typically, when a stock price moves below its 50–100 day moving average, it's a bad sign.*

MPC /,em piː 'siː/ = MARGINAL PROPENSITY TO CONSUME

MPM /,em piː 'em/ = MARGINAL PROPENSITY TO IMPORT

MPS /,em piː 'es/ = MARGINAL PROPENSITY TO SAVE

MR /,em 'ɑː(r)/ = MARKET RESEARCH

MRM /,em ɑːr 'em/ = MARKETING RESOURCE MANAGEMENT

MRP /,em ɑː 'piː;/ *AmE* ɑːr/ = MATERIAL REQUIREMENTS PLANNING, MANUFACTURING RESOURCE PLANNING

MRPII (*also* MRP2) /,em ɑː piː 'tuː;/ *AmE* ɑːr/ = MANUFACTURING RESOURCE PLANNING

MS /,em 'es/ = MANAGEMENT SCIENCE

MSC /,em es 'siː/ *abbr* **Multimedia Super Corridor**
a small area in Malaysia where businesses connected with technology, computers, the Internet, television, etc. are offered special services and benefits

MSRP /,em es ɑː 'piː;/ *AmE* ɑːr/ *abbr*
(*Commerce*) **manufacturer's suggested retail price** the price at which the maker of a product suggests that it should be sold to customers in shops/stores: *The camera will be available in 2006 at an MSRP of $500.* [SYN] RRP, SRP

MTO /,em tiː 'əʊ;/ *AmE* 'oʊ/ = MAKE-TO-ORDER

MTS /,em tiː 'es/ = MAKE-TO-STOCK

multi- /'mʌlti/ *combining form* (*used in nouns and adjectives*)
more than one; many: *a multimillionaire* ◇ *multicoloured packaging* ◇ *the multibillion-dollar software industry*

multidisciplinary /,mʌlti'dɪsəplɪnəri; ,mʌlti,dɪsə'plɪnəri;* *AmE* -'dɪsəplənəri/ *adjective*
involving several different subjects of study or areas of activity: *a multidisciplinary team* ◇ *Our entry-level jobs are multidisciplinary.*

multilateral /,mʌlti'lætərəl/ *adjective*
in which three or more nations, companies, groups, etc. take part: *multilateral agreements on information technology* ◇ *a multilateral trading system* ▶ **multilaterally** /,mʌlti'lætrəli/ *adverb*

multi'level ,marketing (*abbr* MLM) (*also* **'network ,marketing**) *noun* [U]
a system of selling a company's products directly to consumers, in which you sell to people you know and persuade them to help you sell as well. They then persuade others. You usually get paid both for what you sell and for what the others sell.
→ PYRAMID SELLING

multimedia /,mʌlti'miːdiə/ *adjective* [only before noun]
1 (*IT*) using sound, pictures and film in addition to text on a screen: *Potter gave a powerful multimedia presentation.*
2 producing or selling several different types of media such as films/movies, books, or television programmes: *Stewart heads a multimedia company which produces magazines, TV shows, and merchandise.* ◇ *a multimedia empire*

multinational /,mʌlti'næʃnəl/ *adjective, noun*
● *adjective*
operating in or involving many countries: *multinational corporations/companies* ◇ *a national branch of a multinational organization* ◇ *They sent in a multinational team of auditors.*
● *noun* [C]
a company that operates in several different countries, especially a large and powerful company: *The country's industry is largely controlled by the multinationals.*

multipack /'mʌltipæk/ *noun* [C]
(*Marketing*) a set of several items of the same type, sold together in one pack: *A multipack of six fruit-flavoured yogurts costs $2.59.*

multiple /'mʌltɪpl/ *noun* [C]
1 (*Stock Exchange*) a number expressing the current market price of a particular share divided by the EARNINGS PER SHARE of the company: *Technology shares are still trading at high multiples.* → PRICE-EARNINGS RATIO
2 (*Commerce*) (*also* ,multiple 'store) (*both BrE*) a shop/store that is one of a series of shops/stores owned by the same company: *It's hard for us to compete against the big multiples.* SYN CHAIN STORE

,**multiple appli'cations** *noun* [pl.]
(*IT*) several different pieces of software running on a computer at the same time: *a way to reliably run multiple applications on a single Windows server*

,**multiple-'choice** *adjective*
used to describe questions that show several possible answers from which you must choose one: *a web-based multiple-choice test*

,**multiple 'pricing** *noun* [U]
(*Commerce*)
1 the practice of giving the same product a different price in different markets, in order to make the best profit
2 the practice of charging less for two or more units of an item bought together than the price of the units separately, in order to encourage people to buy more → BOGOF

,**multiple 'store** = MULTIPLE (2)

,**multiple tax'ation** *noun* [U]
(*Accounting*) a situation in which an amount of money is taxed more than once, for example by two different countries or authorities: *The President said that taxing stockholders on corporate dividends represented multiple taxation and was wrong.*

multiply /'mʌltɪplaɪ/ *verb* (**multiplies, multiplying, multiplied, multiplied**)
1 [+ obj] to add a number to itself a particular number of times: *This figure was calculated by multiplying the company's recent cash flow by 2.24.*
2 [+ obj *or no obj*] to increase or make sth increase very much in number or amount: *Over the past fifteen years, the number of private shareholders has multiplied.* ◇ *The company multiplied its outlets from 20 to 120.*

multiskilling /,mʌlti'skɪlɪŋ/ *noun* [U]
(*HR*) the fact that a person is trained in several different jobs which require different skills: *In the future there will be more flexible working and multiskilling.* → DIVISION OF LABOUR (1)

multitask /,mʌlti'tɑːsk; *AmE* 'mʌltitæsk/ *verb* [no obj]
1 (*IT*) to operate several programs at the same time: *It could run multiple large programs at once, and multitask even when I was online.*
2 to do several things at the same time: *Women seem to be able to multitask better than men.*

multitasking /,mʌlti'tɑːskɪŋ; *AmE* 'mʌltitæsk-/ *noun* [U]
1 (*IT*) the ability that a computer has to operate several programs at the same time: *It won't handle multitasking as well as some other hand-held computers, but it's much cheaper.*
2 the ability a person has to do several things at the same time: *We need a highly skilled workforce, able to take on multitasking.*

,**multi-'unit** *adjective* [only before noun]
(*Commerce*) consisting of or involving more than one shop/store or business unit: *the modern multi-unit business enterprise* ◇ *We are looking to hire a multi-unit manager for our successful franchise operation.*

,**multi-'user** *adjective* [only before noun]

1 (*IT*) able to be used by more than one person at the same time: *multi-user bulletin board software* ◇ *All mainframes are multi-user systems, but most PCs are not.*
2 (*Commerce*) used by many different customers or organizations: *We want the airport to be a multi-user facility rather than one used by a single airline.*

,**multi-'year** *adjective* [only before noun]
taking place over or including a period of several years: *Major US stock indexes tumbled to new multi-year lows.* ◇ *a multi-year restructuring plan*

muni /'mjuːni/ (*plural* **munis**) (*also* 'muni bond) = MUNICIPAL BOND

municipal /mjuː'nɪsɪpl/ *adjective, noun*
● *adjective* [only before noun]
1 connected with the local government of a town, city, or district: *municipal ownership of utilities* ◇ *municipal employees* ◇ *municipal debt*
2 (*Finance*) connected with MUNICIPAL BONDS
▶ **municipally** /mjuː'nɪsɪpli/ *adverb*
● *noun* [C]
(*Finance*) = MUNICIPAL BOND: *trading in municipals*

mu,nicipal 'bond (*also* **mu'nicipal**) (*also* '**muni**, *informal*) *noun* [C]
(*Finance*) a bond issued by a state or local government: *She was advised to invest in tax-friendly municipal bonds.*

municipality /mjuː,nɪsɪ'pæləti/ *noun* [C] (*plural* **municipalities**)
a town, city or district with its own local government; the group of officials who form the government: *Chongqing is a municipality in western China with 15m people.* ◇ *a spokesman for the building department of the municipality*

,**Murphy's 'Law** /,mɜːfiz 'lɔː; *AmE* ,mɜːrfiz/ *noun* [sing.]
the humorous idea that if anything can possibly go wrong, it will go wrong: *With any business, there are times when Murphy's Law takes over.*

mushroom /'mʌʃrʊm; -ruːm/ *verb* [no obj]
to rapidly grow or increase in number, especially when this is a bad thing: *We expect the market to mushroom in the next two years.* ◇ *Pre-tax losses for the six months to 31 October mushroomed to $264 000 from $69 000.* ◇ *mushrooming costs*

'**must-have** *adjective* [only before noun]
used to say that sth is so good, interesting, useful, fashionable, etc. that people will want to own it: *Web access will soon become a standard, must-have feature for mobile phones.*
● *a must-have* **accessory/feature/item/product**
▶ '**must-have** *noun* [C]: *These shoes are a definite must-have this summer.* ◇ *the latest trendy must-haves*

mutual /'mjuːtʃuəl/ *adjective*
(*Finance*) relating to a financial organization such as an insurance company that is a MUTUAL COMPANY: *a mutual life insurer* ◇ *mutual banks* ◇ *Many building societies are considering changing their mutual status to that of a plc.* ▶ '**mutual** *noun* [C] **mutuality** /,mjuːtʃu'æləti/ *noun* [U]: *He emphasized the society's commitment to mutuality.*

'**mutual ,company** *noun* [C]
(*Finance*) a type of financial organization such as an insurance company which has no shareholders but is owned by its members, with profits shared among them

'**mutual fund** = UNIT TRUST

,**Myers-Briggs 'Type ,Indicator™** /,maɪəz 'brɪgz; *AmE* ,maɪərz/ *noun* [C, usually sing.] (*abbr* **MBTI™**)
(*HR*) a set of questions that people answer about themselves to find out their strengths and the type of person that they are

,mystery 'shopper *noun* [C]
(*Marketing*) a person whose job is to visit or telephone a shop/store or other business pretending to be a customer, in order to get information on the quality of the service, the buildings, special features, etc: *A restaurant chain* employs mystery shoppers to secretly check on the quality of customer service. ▶ **,mystery 'shopping** *noun* [U]

N n

n/a *abbr* (*only used in written English*)
1 not applicable written on a form to show that you cannot answer a particular question because it does not affect you
2 (*Commerce*) **not available** written next to an item on a list, to show that the item is not available to buy

NACE /neɪs/ *abbr* **Nomenclature générale des Activités économiques dans les Communautés européennes** in the European Union, a system in which industries and services are given a code to show which type of economic activity they are involved in, for reference and research purposes **NOTE** This is a French phrase. → ISIC, NAICS

nagware /'næɡweə(r); AmE -wer/ *noun* [U]
(*IT*) software that repeatedly shows messages asking the user to do sth, such as pay to continue to use the product

NAICS /neɪks/ *abbr* **North American Industry Classification System** in the US, Canada and Mexico, a system in which industries and services are given a code to show which type of economic activity they are involved in, for reference and research purposes: *The NAICS code for 'Satellite Telecommunications' is 517410.* → ISIC, NACE

nail /neɪl/ *verb, noun*
● *verb* [+ obj] (*AmE*) (*informal*)
to achieve sth or do sth successfully: *The team had six weeks to nail that goal.* ◇ *They've just nailed the deal.*
PHRV **,nail sth 'down** to reach a definite agreement or decision, usually after a lot of discussion: *They met last month to nail down how much the company must pay.*
● *noun*
IDM **on the 'nail** (*BrE*) (*informal*) without delay: *They're good customers who always pay on the nail*

,naked de'benture *noun* [C]
(*Finance*) money that a company borrows that is not supported by particular assets that the company will lose if the loan is not repaid → UNSECURED

name /neɪm/ *noun, verb*
● *noun* [C]

SEE ALSO: **big name, brand ~, household ~, trade ~**

1 (*often used with another noun or an adjective to form an adjective*) a very well-known person, company, product, etc: *Vittorio Missoni, whose family is one of the biggest names in the Italian fashion industry* ◇ *big-name booksellers* ◇ *Sony became a household name around the world.* ◇ *brand-name goods*
2 (*Insurance*) one of the investors in the insurance company Lloyd's who promise their own money to pay claims and share in the profits or losses: *He was a name at Lloyd's.*
● *verb*
IDM **,name and 'shame** (*BrE*) to publish the names of people or organizations who have done sth wrong or illegal

'name-brand *adjective* [only before noun]
(*Commerce*; *Marketing*) used to describe goods that are marked with the name of a well-known product or manufacturer: *We sell name-brand clothing at great prices.* → OWN BRAND

nanosecond /'nænəʊsekənd; AmE 'nænoʊ-/ *noun* [C]
one billionth of a second: *an exchange of data that takes a few nanoseconds* ◇ *It only took me a nanosecond* (= a very short time) *to decide about the job.*

narrow /'nærəʊ; AmE -roʊ/ *adjective, verb*
● *adjective*
1 small: *a narrow majority* ◇ *a narrow sales rise of 0.5 per cent*
2 limited in variety or numbers: *The store sells only a narrow range of goods.*
● *verb* [+ obj or no obj]
to become less or smaller; to make sth become less or smaller: *The gap between short- and long-term interest rates is likely to narrow.* ◇ *The company saw its losses narrow in the third quarter.* ◇ *Exports to the US helped narrow Britain's trade gap.*
PHRV **,narrow sth 'down (to sth)** to reduce the number of possibilities or choices: *We have narrowed down the list to four candidates.*

,narrow 'market = THIN MARKET

'narrow ,money *noun* [U]
(*Economics*) a term used to refer to the part of a country's MONEY SUPPLY that is money in its more limited sense, meaning only cash and things that can be easily turned into cash **NOTE** This is known as **M1**. → BROAD MONEY

NASDAQ™ /'næzdæk/ *noun* [sing; U]
an electronic system for buying and selling shares, especially shares in particular companies that are not on an official stock exchange list, and giving price information about them: *Trading was light on NASDAQ.* ◇ *The NASDAQ gained over 4.4 per cent.* ◇ *Nasdaq-listed companies* **NOTE** NASDAQ was formed from the name 'National Association of Securities Dealers Automated Quotations'.

NASDAQ-100™ /,næzdæk wʌn 'hʌndrəd/ *noun* [sing.]
a list of 100 shares traded on the **NASDAQ**, chosen to give a guide to share prices in general

,national ac'count *noun*
1 (*Marketing*) [C] an important customer, usually a company, that does business with another company in many different parts of a country: *As a national account, your company will receive many benefits and cost savings.*
2 (*Economics*) [C, usually pl.] the financial records of a country: *It will be classed as a private sector company for the purposes of the national accounts.* ◇ *China's national accounts*

,national 'bank *noun* [C]
1 = CENTRAL BANK
2 in the US, a COMMERCIAL BANK that is officially approved by the government and is a member of the FEDERAL RESERVE SYSTEM

'national brand *noun* [C]
(*Marketing*) a **brand** of product that is available in

shops/stores in all areas of a country rather than one produced for a particular shop/store or area

,national 'debt noun [C, usually sing.]
(*Economics*) the total amount of money that the government of a country has borrowed and still owes: *a high/low level of national debt*

,National In'surance noun [U] (*abbr* **NI**)
in the UK, a system of payments that have to be made by employers and employees to provide help for people who are ill/sick, old or unemployed: *to pay National Insurance contributions*

★ **nationalize, -ise** /'næʃnəlaɪz/ verb [+ obj]
(*Economics*) to put an industry or a company under the control of the government, which becomes its owner: *The Kofuku Bank was nationalized in 1998.* ◇ *the country's nationalized electricity sector*
[OPP] PRIVATIZE
▶ **nationalization, -isation** /ˌnæʃnəlaɪˈzeɪʃn; *AmE* -lə'z-/ noun [U,C]: *the nationalization of the oil industry*

,National 'Market ,System noun [sing.] (*abbr* **NMS**)
a computer trading system for some shares, bonds, etc. in the US

,national 'product = GROSS NATIONAL PRODUCT

nationwide /ˌneɪʃn'waɪd/ adjective
happening or existing in all parts of a particular country: *a nationwide campaign* ◇ *the average nationwide price of petrol* ▶ **nation'wide** adverb: *The company has over 500 stores nationwide.*

natural /'nætʃrəl/ adjective
1 not made, caused or controlled by humans: *The country is rich in natural resources, particularly oil and iron ore.* ◇ *The company cut jobs by a natural process, rather than by redundancies.*
2 normal; as you would expect: *She was the natural choice for the job.*

,natural 'business year = ACCOUNTING YEAR

,natural 'gas noun [U]
gas that is found under the ground or the sea and that is used as a fuel: *power stations running on natural gas*

,natural re'source noun [C]
a supply of sth that exists naturally in a country and can be used, especially to create wealth: *Russia has abundant natural resources.* ◇ *Iron ore is the country's principal natural resource.*
❂ **abundant/limited/plentiful/scarce** natural resources ◆ to **deplete/exploit/use/waste** natural resources ◆ to **protect/safeguard** natural resources

,natural 'wastage (*also* **'wastage**) noun [U] (*both BrE*)
(*HR*) the process of reducing the number of people who are employed by an organization by, for example, not replacing people who leave their jobs: *There will be no job losses. Savings will be made through natural wastage.* [SYN] ATTRITION
→ REDUNDANCY

NAV /ˌen eɪ 'viː/ = NET ASSET VALUE

navigate /'nævɪgeɪt/ verb [+ obj or no obj]
1 to find your position and the direction you need to go in, for example by using a map
2 (*IT*) to find your way around on the Internet or on a particular website: *Their website is very easy to navigate.*
▶ **navigation** /ˌnævɪ'geɪʃn/ noun [U]: *an in-car navigation system*

,navi'gation bar noun [C]
(*IT*) an area along the top or one side of a web page

where you can click on items from a list (a **menu**) to go to other parts of the website

NAVPS /ˌen eɪ viː piː 'es/ = NET ASSET VALUE PER SHARE

NB /ˌen 'biː/ abbr
used in writing to say that the point that follows is very important: *NB Disconnect the power supply before removing the cover.* [NOTE] NB is the first letters of the Latin phrase 'nota bene', which means 'note well'.

NBV /ˌen biː 'viː/ = NET BOOK VALUE

NDPB /ˌen diː piː 'biː/ noun [C]
in the UK, an organization dealing with public matters, started and financed by the government, but working independently and with its own legal powers [SYN] QUANGO [NOTE] NDPB is formed from the first letters of the phrase 'non-departmental public body'.

'nearby de,livery = SPOT DELIVERY

'near-term adjective [usually before noun]
lasting a short time; lasting only for a short period of time in the future: *The near-term economic outlook is good.* ◇ *There is no indication of near-term improvement.* ◇ *near-term financial targets*
[SYN] SHORT-TERM [OPP] LONG-TERM

necktie /'nektaɪ/ = TIE noun (2)

need /niːd/ noun [C, usually pl.]
the things that sb requires in order to live in a comfortable way or achieve what they want: *Tailor your services to fit your customers' needs.* ◇ *We need to balance the needs of investors with those of the company.* ◇ *The aim of the project is to analyse our operational needs.* → WANT
❂ to **analyse/assess/determine/identify/understand** sb's needs ◆ to **address/fit/meet/serve/suit** sb's needs

★ **negative** /'negətɪv/ adjective, noun
● *adjective*
1 less than zero: *a negative trade balance*
2 bad or harmful: *The crisis had a negative effect on trade.*
3 without enthusiasm or support: *The response to our plans has been very negative.*
[OPP] POSITIVE
▶ **'negatively** adverb: *Some of the staff will be negatively affected by the change.*
● *noun* [C]
(*Technical*) the result of a test or an experiment that shows that a substance or condition is not present: *These tests sometimes produce false negatives.*
[OPP] POSITIVE

'negative cer'tificate of 'origin noun [C]
(*Trade*) a certificate that states that a product was not produced in a particular country that the buyer refuses to accept goods from

,negative 'inventory noun [U,C]
(*Production*) a situation when the number of items in the stock of a business appears to be less than zero, often as a result of a mistake in recording the movement of items

,negative 'territory noun [U]
often used in newspapers to describe a level that is below zero, or below the previous or expected level: *Share prices ended the day in negative territory.*

negligence /'neglɪdʒəns/ noun [U]
(*Law*) the failure to give enough care or attention to sb/sth that you are responsible for: *The injured workers are suing the company for negligence.*
▶ **'negligent** adjective: *The firm was found to be negligent in not ensuring that equipment was safe.*
'negligently adverb

negligible /'neglɪdʒəbl/ adjective
of very little importance or size and not worth

considering: *Growth in the industry last year was negligible.* ◇ *The drink was found to contain a negligible amount of fruit juice.*

negotiable /nɪˈɡəʊʃiəbl; *AmE* -ˈɡoʊ-/ *adjective*
1 that you can discuss or change before you make an agreement or a decision: *The terms of employment are negotiable.* ◇ *The price was not negotiable.*
2 (*Finance*) that you can exchange for money or give to another person in exchange for money: *€690 million in cash and negotiable securities* OPP NON-NEGOTIABLE

★ **negotiate** /nɪˈɡəʊʃieɪt; *AmE* -ˈɡoʊ-/ *verb*
1 [no obj] to try to reach an agreement by formal discussion: *We negotiated for more pay.* ◇ *The company is negotiating with its creditors.* ◇ *a strong negotiating position* ◇ *negotiating skills*
2 [+ obj] to arrange sth or agree to sth by formal discussion: *Bigger stores can negotiate better prices from suppliers.* ◇ *There's more to buying a business than negotiating a good deal.*
3 (*Finance*) [+ obj] to transfer sth such as a cheque or a bill to sb else in exchange for money: *The bill of exchange was negotiated several times.* ◇ *We are able to negotiate cheques payable in most currencies.*

negotiated /nɪˈɡəʊʃieɪtɪd; *AmE* -ˈɡoʊ-/ *adjective* [usually before noun]
that is the result of discussions: *The union is hoping for a negotiated solution to the problem before the strike is due to begin.*
◐ *a negotiated deal/fee/settlement/solution*

the neˈgotiating ˌtable *noun* [sing.]
used in newspapers to describe formal discussions to try to reach an agreement: *The two sides are not ready to sit down at the negotiating table to settle the dispute.*

★ **negotiation** /nɪˌɡəʊʃiˈeɪʃn; *AmE* -ˌɡoʊʃi-/ *noun*
1 [C, usually pl., U] formal discussions between people who are trying to reach an agreement: *They are beginning the next round of wage negotiations today.* ◇ *A contract is prepared in negotiation with our clients.* ◇ *The deal is still under negotiation.* ◇ *The price is not open to negotiation.*
◐ *to begin/enter (into)/open/resume/start negotiations* • *to break off/complete negotiations*
2 (*Finance*) [U] the process of transferring sth such as a cheque or a bill to sb else, who then becomes the legal owner
3 (*Finance*) [U] the process of changing a cheque into money: *There may be a €20 negotiation fee for each cheque.*

negotiator /nɪˈɡəʊʃieɪtə(r); *AmE* -ˈɡoʊʃi-/ *noun* [C]
a person who is involved in formal discussions that aim to reach an agreement, especially because it is their job: *the union's chief negotiator* ◇ *a skilled negotiator* ◇ *Europe's top trade negotiator*

neighbourhood (*AmE spelling* **neighborhood**) /ˈneɪbəhʊd; *AmE* -bər-/ *noun* [C]
1 a district or an area of a town; the people who live there: *Our store is in the commercial heart of the neighbourhood.* ◇ *Last year they opened 25 smaller neighborhood stores.*
2 the area that you are in or the area near a particular place: *The headquarters are located in the neighbourhood of Rome.* ◇ (*figurative*) *Our profit margins are in the neighbourhood of 7%.*

nepotism /ˈnepətɪzəm/ *noun* [U]
giving advantages to your own family if you are in a position of power, especially by giving them jobs

ˈnest egg *noun* [C, usually sing.] (*informal*)
an amount of money that sb has saved for the future: *After 20 years, the account had built into a nest egg of over $20 000.*

★ **net** /net/ *noun, adjective, verb*
● *noun*

SEE ALSO: **safety net**

1 the Net [sing.] = INTERNET
2 [C,U] (*AmE*) a net amount or weight: *The third quarter net was up 6%.*
● *adjective* (*BrE spelling also* **nett**)
1 (*Accounting*) [usually before noun] a net amount of money is the amount that remains when nothing more is to be taken away: *record net profits of £360 m* ◇ *The salary is €40 000 net of tax.* → GROSS
◐ *a net loss/profit/operating loss/operating profit* • *net earnings/income/proceeds/sales*
2 [only before noun] final, after all the important facts have been included: *The net result is that small shopkeepers are being forced out of business.*
▶ **net** *adverb*: *a salary of €50 000 net* ◇ *Interest on the investment will be paid net* (= tax will already have been taken away). → GROSS
● *verb* [+ obj] (**-tt-**)
1 to earn an amount of money as a profit after you have taken away some of it for tax, etc: *After paying all his debts, he netted $50 000.* → GROSS
2 to manage to obtain sth: *The deal netted over €200 000.*
PHR V **ˌnet sth ˈdown (to sth)**; **ˌnet ˈdown (to sth)** (*Finance*) to take sth away from an amount until only the net amount is left: *The $3 extra income per customer from the promotion nets down to $2.50 because it cost $.50 per customer.* **ˌnet ˈout/at/to sth** (*Accounting*) to produce an amount of money after some has been taken away for tax and other expenses: *They are offering $100 cashback, so the phone nets out at only $50.*

net 10 , net 30 *adverb*
(*Accounting, only used in written English*) used on an INVOICE to show that it must be paid within 10 (or 30) days

net 10 eom , net 30 eom (*also* net 10 prox, net 10th prox, net 30 prox, net 30th prox) *adverb*
(*Accounting, only used in written English*) used on an INVOICE to show that it must be paid on or before the 10th (or 30th) day of the next month
NOTE eom is a short way of writing 'end of month'. **Prox** is a short form of a Latin phrase that means 'next month': *Men's clothes are sold at net 30 eom.*

ˌnet ˈassets *noun* [pl.]
(*Accounting*) the value of a company's or person's total assets, minus their total LIABILITIES (= the money that they owe): *Capital Southwest reports net assets of $240.1 million.*

ˌnet ˈasset ˌvalue *noun* [U; sing.] (*abbr* NAV)
(*Accounting*)
1 the value of a company's assets calculated by taking its total LIABILITIES away from its total assets: *The fund now has a net asset value of $175 m.*
2 = NET ASSET VALUE PER SHARE

ˌnet ˈasset ˌvalue per ˈshare *noun* [U; sing.] (*abbr* NAVPS)
(*Accounting*) the value of a share in a company, calculated by taking its total LIABILITIES away from its total assets and dividing by the total number of shares: *The bank's net asset value per share fell by 4% to €3.64.*

ˌnet ˈbook ˌvalue *noun* [U; sing.] (*abbr* NBV)
(*Accounting*)
1 the current value of an asset or a set of assets in a company's financial records, calculated by taking the DEPRECIATION (= the decrease in value over a period of time) away from its original cost: *equipment with a net book value of $30 million*

2 the current value of a company shown in its financial records, which is the difference between its total assets after DEPRECIATION (= the decrease in value over a period of time) and its total LIABILITIES: *The company has a net book value of €100 000.* → SHAREHOLDER EQUITY

ˌnet ˈborrowings *noun* [pl.]
(*Accounting*) the total amount that a company has borrowed, minus the amount of assets it has that are in the form of money or that can easily be changed into money: *We have been able to cut our net borrowings by $125 million.*

Net-centric /ˌnet-ˈsentrɪk/ *adjective*
depending on or suited to the Internet: *Net-centric companies*

ˈNet ˌcommerce = INTERNET COMMERCE

ˈnet ˈcurrent ˈassets *noun* [pl.]
(*Accounting*) a company's CURRENT ASSETS minus its CURRENT LIABILITIES → WORKING CAPITAL

ˌnet exˈporter *noun* [C]
(*Economics*) used to describe a country that exports more than it imports: *The US is a net exporter of cotton.*

ˌnet imˈporter *noun* [C]
(*Economics*) used to describe a country that imports more than it exports: *Britain will soon be a net importer of oil and gas.*

netiquette /ˈnetɪket/ *noun* [U]
informal rules of behaviour for communicating with people over the Internet: *An important rule of netiquette is not to send an email when you are angry.*

ˌnet ˈlending *noun* [U]
(*Accounting*) the total amount of money that a bank lends in a particular period, minus amounts that have been paid back: *Total net lending to individuals increased by $8.7bn last month.*

ˌnet ˈmargin = OPERATING MARGIN

ˈnet ˈpresent ˈvalue *noun* [U,C] (*abbr* NPV)
(*Accounting*) the value of income from an investment calculated by taking the **present value** of money which will be received (**cash inflow**) minus the **present value** of money which will be paid out (**cash outflow**) **NOTE** If the **NPV** of an investment is positive it should be accepted; if it is negative it should be rejected. → DISCOUNTED CASH FLOW

ˌnet ˈprice *noun* [C]
the price that sb pays for goods or services after any reductions in price have been taken off and any tax has been added: *If the marked price is €100 and the discount is 5%, the net price is €95.*

ˌnet ˈprofit *noun* [C,U]
(*Accounting*) the money that you make in business or by selling things, after all costs, tax, interest, etc. have been taken off: *Subtracting the tax bill of $52 500, we are left with a net profit of $97 500.*

ˌnet ˈprofit ˌmargin = OPERATING MARGIN

ˈnet ˈrealizable ˈvalue *noun* [C,U] (*abbr* NRV)
(*Accounting*) the amount of money that will be received for an asset when it is sold, minus the costs involved in selling it: *Capital assets with a current net realizable value of less than $5 000 are considered minor items.*

ˌnet ˈrevenue *noun* [C,U]
(*Accounting*) the total amount of money received from sales of goods or services, minus the amount for goods returned by customers, etc: *On Thursday the coffee retailer reported a net revenue of $300 million for the last four weeks.* → NET SALES

ˌnet ˈsales *noun* [pl.]
(*Accounting*) the total value of goods and services sold, after an amount has been taken away for expenses such as transport, returned goods, reductions in price, etc: *Net sales were €12 million, an increase of 6% on the same period last year.* ◇ *The company recorded net sales of €166 million for the fourth quarter.* → GROSS SALES, NET REVENUE

ˈNet ˌsurfer *noun* [C]
a person who spends a lot of time using the Internet → SILVER SURFER

nett = NET *adj.*

ˈnet ˈtangible ˈassets *noun* [pl.] (*abbr* NTA)
(*Accounting*) the value of the physical assets that a company owns minus its CURRENT LIABILITIES (= debts that must be paid within a year)

ˌnet ˈton = SHORT TON

★ **network** /ˈnetwɜːk; *AmE* -wɜːrk/ *noun, verb*
● *noun* [C]

SEE ALSO: **fixed network, local area ~, run of ~, wide area ~**

1 a group of people, companies, etc. that exchange information or work together for a particular purpose: *a communications/distribution network*
2 (*IT*) a number of computers and other devices that are connected together so that equipment and information can be shared: *The office network allows users to share files and software, and to use a central printer.* → LAN, WAN
● *verb*
1 (*IT*) [+ obj] to connect a number of computers and other devices together so that equipment and information can be shared: *networked computer systems*
2 [no obj] to try to meet and talk to people who may be useful to you in your work: *Conferences are a good place to network.*

ˈnetwork aˌnalysis *noun* [C,U]
1 (*Economics; Production*) = CRITICAL PATH ANALYSIS
2 (*IT*) the process of recording the movements of information to and from a computer network: *Network analysis showed that staff were spending too much time browsing the Internet.*

networked /ˈnetwɜːkt; *AmE* -wɜːrkt/ *adjective*
1 used to describe a system in which different companies use technology to form a single system, in which they can work together to supply goods or services: *Networked companies manage a network of contract suppliers, manufacturers and distributors in order to deliver their products.* ◇ *the networked economy*
2 connected into a network: *We have 700 networked computer stations in this department.*

networker /ˈnetwɜːkə(r); *AmE* -wɜːrk-/ *noun* [C]
1 a person who works for a company from home or from another office using a computer network: *The company holds an annual conference for its networkers.*
2 a person who tries to meet and talk to people in order to make business contacts: *Being a natural networker helped her to build up her business.*

networking /ˈnetwɜːkɪŋ; *AmE* -wɜːrk-/ *noun* [U]
1 a system of meeting and talking to other people who may be useful or helpful to you in your work: *The key to good networking is the exchange of favours.* ◇ *networking events and meetings* ◇ *business networking groups*
2 (*IT*) a system of connecting a number of computers and other devices so that equipment and information can be shared: *computer/data networking* ◇ *the convenience of wireless networking* ◇ *networking equipment*

,net 'worth *noun* [U,C] (*also* **,owners' 'equity** [U]) (*Accounting*) a measure of the current financial value of a company, person, etc., calculated by taking CURRENT LIABILITIES (= debts that must be paid back within a short time) away from the total assets: *The average net worth of a household is €22 000.* ◇ *The company has a negative net worth and is still losing money.* ⌧ SHAREHOLDER FUNDS

net wt. *abbr*
a short way of writing **net weight**

,net 'yield *noun* [C,U]
(*Accounting*) the amount of profit an investment makes after taking off costs and taxes, expressed as a percentage of its value

newbie /'nju:bi; *AmE* 'nu:bi/ *noun* [C] (*informal*) a person who has just begun to use a computer, a particular program or the Internet: *This website offers technical advice to newbies.*

,new 'deal (*also spelled* **New Deal**) *noun* [sing.]
1 policies introduced by a government or an organization to help a region, group of people, etc. return to normal after a difficult period: *Under the New Deal, unemployed people will be offered six months' training with a company.*
2 **New Deal** the policies introduced in the US in the 1930s by President Roosevelt with the aim of helping the economy return to normal

the ,New E'conomy (*also spelled* **the new economy**) *noun* [sing.]
used to describe the economy that developed in the late 20th century, with industries based on very new technology and the use of the Internet to do business: *Ebay and Amazon are among the successes of the new economy.* ◇ *E-commerce is a major feature of many new-economy businesses.* → OLD ECONOMY

,new 'issue *noun* [C]
(*Stock Exchange*) a number of shares that are made available for investors to buy for the first time: *a new issue of 1.2 million ordinary shares* ◇ *The shares will be listed on the new issue market.*

'newly in'dustrialized 'country (*also* **'newly in'dustrializing 'country**) *noun* [C] (*abbr* **NIC**) (*Economics*) a country that did not have much industry previously, but where industries are now developing very fast: *Taiwan's economy has had one of the highest rates of growth among newly industrialized countries.*

,newly issued 'share = NEW SHARE
,newly issued 'stock = NEW STOCK
,new 'media *noun* [U]
(*IT*) ways in which large numbers of people can receive information and entertainment through computers: *new media industries who create content for the Internet*

,new 'money *noun* [U]
1 money that becomes available for use for the first time: *To prevent inflation, the government controls the flow of new money into the economy.*
2 wealth that has been gained recently; the people who have it: *It's new money that is buying property in this area these days.*

,new-'product *adjective* [only before noun]
used to describe activities related to developing and selling a new product: *new-product launches/ sales/teams*

,new-'product de,velopment *noun* [U] (*abbr* **NPD**)
(*Marketing*) the process by which a company changes ideas into new or improved products or services: *The extra investment will be used for*

marketing and new-product development. ◇ *a new-product development project/manager*

'news ,conference = PRESS CONFERENCE

newsgroup /'nju:zgru:p; *AmE* 'nu:z-/ *noun* [C]
an area of the Internet, with its own address, where people discuss a particular topic; the people who belong to this group: *An employee posted the complaint on an internal newsgroup.*

,new 'share (*also* **,newly issued 'share**) *noun* [C, usually pl.]
(*Stock Exchange*) a share that a company makes available for investors to buy for the first time: *There are several methods for determining the price of new shares for a stock market flotation.*

'news re,lease = PRESS RELEASE

,new 'stock (*also* **,newly issued 'stock**) *noun* [U,C]
(*Stock Exchange*) shares that a company makes available for investors to buy for the first time: *The company is issuing new stock to raise finance.* ◇ *The website recommends hot new stocks to investors.*

,next-'day *adjective* [only before noun]
used to refer to a service that is provided on the day after you order it: *guaranteed next-day delivery* → SAME-DAY

,next-gene'ration *adjective* [usually before noun]
used to describe a product that has been developed and improved using the latest technology, and that is much more advanced than the versions available until now: *next-generation mobile phones*

NGO /,en dʒi: 'əʊ; *AmE* 'oʊ/ *abbr* **non-governmental organization**, **non-government organization** an organization, such as a charity, that does not make a profit, is independent of government and business, and is formed for a particular purpose for the good of the public

NI /,en 'aɪ/ = NATIONAL INSURANCE
NIC /,en aɪ 'si:/ = NEWLY INDUSTRIALIZED COUNTRY
★ **niche** /niːʃ/ *noun* [C]

SEE ALSO: **market niche**

(*Marketing*) an opportunity to sell a particular type of product or service for which there is limited demand, but little or no competition: *They spotted a niche in the ice cream market for a high-quality, luxury product.* ◇ *To grow, the company needs to expand beyond its niche products.* ◇ *a small niche company* → MAINSTREAM
❍ *to* **carve (out)/create/look for/find/exploit/expand** *a niche*

'niche ,market *noun* [C]
(*Marketing*) a market in which there is little or no competition for a particular type of product or service, for which there is limited demand: *The company has carved out a strong niche market for its software.* ▶ **,niche 'marketer** *noun* [C]: *Niche marketers rely on customer loyalty.* **,niche 'marketing** *noun* [U]: *a niche marketing campaign*

nicher /'niːʃə(r)/ *noun* [C]
(*Marketing*) a **niche** company or product: *Nichers use different competitive strategies to mainstream companies.* ◇ *Most of their computer games are nichers.*

Nielsen™ /'niːlsən/ = NIELSEN RATING

,Nielsen/'NetRatings™ /,niːlsən 'netreɪtɪŋz/ *noun* [sing.]
a company that measures and analyses Internet use and provides information and advice to companies so that they can develop strategies for using the Internet

'Nielsen™ ,rating /'niːlsən/ (*also* **'Nielsen™**)
noun [C]
(*Marketing*) in the US, a measure of how many
people, and often what type of people, watch a
particular programme on television. The
information is used by companies who want to
advertise their products to a suitable audience, and
by television companies who set the price for
advertising in and around particular programmes:
The show scored a Nielsen rating of 2.9. ◇ *The
programme was cancelled following low Nielsen
ratings.*

'night de,pository = NIGHT SAFE

,night 'porter noun [C]
a person who looks after a hotel or an apartment
building at night

'night safe (*BrE*) (*AmE* **'night de,pository**) noun [C]
a box in the wall of a bank where companies, etc.
can deposit money when the bank is closed

NIH syndrome /,en aɪ 'eɪtʃ/ = NOT-INVENTED-
HERE SYNDROME

Nikkei™ /nɪ'keɪ/ noun (*usually* **the Nikkei**) [sing.]
1 used to refer to the **Nikkei Stock Average** or a
Nikkei Index: *On Tuesday, the Nikkei rose 19.25
points, or 0.23%, to close at 8 365.26 points.*
2 a financial and business newspaper in Japan that
publishes measures (**indexes**) of the share prices of
important companies

Nik,kei 'Index /nɪ'keɪ/ noun [sing.]
one of the measures of the share prices of the
companies that are traded on the Tokyo Stock
Exchange

Nik,kei 'Stock ,Average /nɪ'keɪ/ (*also* Nikkei
225 /nɪ,keɪ tu: tu: 'faɪv/) noun [sing.]
a measure of the share prices of the 225 most
important companies that are traded on the Tokyo
Stock Exchange

nil /nɪl/ noun [U]
nothing; zero: *Competition has reduced profit
margins to nil.* ◇ *The company reported nil growth in
like-for-like sales on last year.*

Nimby /'nɪmbi/ noun [C] (*plural* **Nimbys**)
a person who claims to be in favour of a new
development or project, but objects if it is too near
their home: *The Nimby lobby is slowing the
development of wind farms.* **NOTE** 'Nimby' is formed
from the first letters of the words 'not in my back
yard'.

NMS /,en em 'es/ = NATIONAL MARKET SYSTEM

NMW /,en em 'dʌblju:/ abbr **national minimum
wage** in the UK, used to refer to the lowest wage
that an employer is allowed to pay by law

No. (*also spelled* **no.**) abbr (*plural* **Nos, nos**) (*only used
in written English*)
number: *invoice No. 5370*
→ NUMBER noun (1)

,no-'brainer noun [C] (*informal*)
a question or problem that is so easy to answer or
solve that it needs no thought: *Setting up an email
marketing campaign is a real no-brainer.* ▶ **,no-
'brainer** adjective [only before noun]: *This software
is the no-brainer choice for anyone running a
network.*

node /nəʊd; *AmE* noʊd/ noun [C]
(*Technical*) a point at which two lines or systems
meet or cross: *a node in/of a network*

no-'frills adjective [only before noun]
including only the basic features, without anything
that is unnecessary, especially things added to

make sth more attractive or comfortable: *a no-frills
airline* ◇ *cheap, no-frills air travel*

noise /nɔɪz/ noun [U]
1 extra information, activity, etc. that is not what
is needed: *In all the noise of the Internet, I eventually
found something relevant.*
2 (*Technical*) extra electrical or electronic signals
that are not part of the signal that is being
broadcast or sent

,no-'load fund noun [C]
(*Finance*) a fund that does not charge investors a fee
when they put their money into it or take it out
→ BACK-END LOAD, FRONT-END LOAD

no,madic 'worker noun [C]
a person who moves from place to place in order to
get work

nominal /'nɒmɪnl; *AmE* 'nɑːm-/ adjective
1 being sth in name only, and not in reality: *He
remained in nominal control of the business for
another ten years.*
2 (about a sum of money) very small and much less
than the normal cost or change: *We only pay a
nominal rent for the office space.* ◇ *They bought the
company for a nominal €20.*
3 used to describe a size or quantity that is stated
on a product but may not be the exact size or
quantity
4 (*Economics*) used to describe a rate or other
figure that refers to current prices or numbers, but
has not been changed to consider the effects of
INFLATION: *5% nominal GDP growth* ◇ *Nominal
wages remain the same, while real wages* (= the
amount you can buy with this money) *are falling.*
→ REAL
▶ **'nominally** /'nɒmɪnəli; *AmE* 'nɑːm-/ adverb: *He
was nominally in charge of the company.*

,nominal 'capital (*also* **,nominal 'share ,capital**)
noun [U]
(*Accounting*) the value of all the shares issued by a
company which is equal to the total number of
shares multiplied by the price they were originally
sold for (the **par value**) **SYN** AUTHORIZED CAPITAL

,nominal 'damages noun [pl.]
(*Law*) a very small amount of money that is paid to
sb by the person, company, etc. that has done sth
wrong to them but has not caused them harm or
financial loss: *The court awarded the union nominal
damages of one euro.*

,nominal 'ledger = GENERAL LEDGER

,nominal 'price noun [C]
1 (*Accounting*) the money value of a product, raw
material, etc. without considering the effect of
INFLATION on this value: *Inflation reduced the real
price of our products by 15% before we were forced to
raise the nominal price.*
2 (*Finance*) = PAR
3 a very small amount of money that is paid for
sth, which is much less than the market price
would be: *They bought the company for the nominal
price of 1 cent a share.*
4 (*Finance*) (*also* **,nominal 'quotation**) the price
estimated for a share, COMMODITY, etc. that has
not yet been traded, and therefore has no market
price

,nominal 'share ,capital = NOMINAL CAPITAL

,nominal 'value = PAR

,nominal 'yield noun [C,U]
(*Finance*) the rate of interest that is paid on the
original value of a bond (**par**), without considering
the effect of INFLATION

nominate /'nɒmɪneɪt; *AmE* 'nɑːm-/ verb [+ obj]
1 to formally suggest that sb/sth should be chosen
for an important role, position, prize, etc: *Two of
their products have been nominated for the
'Innovation of the Year' award.*

2 to choose sb to do a particular job: *The state nominates the top two company posts.* ◇ *Franco Moretti has been nominated **as** the new Chief Executive.*

▶ **nomination** /ˌnɒmɪˈneɪʃn; *AmE* ˌnɑːm-/ *noun* [C,U]: *The closing date for nominations is 21 March.* ◇ *They opposed her nomination **to** the post of Deputy Director.*

nominator /ˈnɒmɪneɪtə(r); *AmE* ˈnɑːm-/ *noun* [C]
a person who suggests sb for a position, prize, etc.

nominee /ˌnɒmɪˈniː; *AmE* ˌnɑːm-/ *noun* [C]
1 a person who is suggested for a position, prize, etc.
2 a person, company, bank, etc. in whose name money is invested in a company or property, but who is not the real owner
3 (*Insurance*) a person who is named as the one to receive money if the insured person dies

ˌnon-acˈceptance *noun* [U]
the fact of not accepting sth OPP ACCEPTANCE

ˌnon-ˈaudit *adjective* [only before noun]
used to describe services other than AUDITING that a company pays an accountant to provide: *More than 50% of our income now comes from non-audit services.*

ˌnon-ˈcallable *adjective*
(*Finance*) used to describe a bond or other form of loan that the borrower may not pay back within the fixed time limit OPP CALLABLE

ˌnon-ˈcash *adjective* [only before noun]
not consisting of or involving money: *The school accepts non-cash gifts such as securities, personal property or real estate.*

ˌnon-comˈpliance *noun* [U] (*usually used in written English*)
the fact of failing or refusing to obey a rule: *There are penalties for non-compliance **with** the fire regulations.*

ˌnon-conˈtributory *adjective*
that you do not have to pay part of: *a non-contributory pension plan* (= that employees do not have to pay part of their salary into) OPP CONTRIBUTORY

ˌnon-ˈcore *adjective*
not the most important part of sth: *We cut overheads by outsourcing non-core activities.* OPP CORE
● *non-core* **activities/assets/business/operations**

ˌnon-current liaˈbilities *noun* [pl.]
(*Accounting*) debts that do not need to be paid until after a particular period of time, usually 12 months: *Our non-current liabilities of discontinued operations were €838 000.* SYN LONG-TERM LIABILITIES → CURRENT LIABILITY

ˌnon-deˈlivery *noun* [U]
the fact of sth not being delivered: *We sued our suppliers for non-delivery of goods.* ◇ *I got an email non-delivery message.*

ˌnon-disˈclosure *noun* [U]
(*Law*) the fact of keeping information secret: *The two companies signed a non-disclosure **agreement** in order to protect their confidential information.* ◇ *The company was fined for non-disclosure of earnings.* OPP DISCLOSURE

ˌnon-disˌtributable reˈserve = CAPITAL RESERVE (1)

ˌnon-ˈdurable *adjective*
that will not last for a long time: *non-durable timber/clothing* ◇ *Non-durable data is not saved when the Internet user disconnects.* OPP DURABLE

ˌnon-ˈdurable goods = CONSUMER NON-DURABLES

ˌnon-ˈdurables = CONSUMER NON-DURABLES

ˌnon-economic ˈdamages *noun* [pl.]
(*Law*) an amount of money that is paid to sb by the company, person, etc. who caused them harm or injury, even though they did not suffer financial loss: *The former employee was awarded €50 000 non-economic damages for pain suffered as a result of the accident.*

ˌnon-eˈxecutive *adjective*
used to describe sb who is not employed by a company but takes part in meetings of the BOARD OF DIRECTORS and gives independent advice: *She works for a television company in a non-executive role.* → EXECUTIVE *adj.* (2)
● *a non-executive* **board member/chairperson/officer** • *a non-executive* **committee/panel**

ˈnon-eˈxecutive diˈrector (*also* indeˌpendent diˈrector, ˌoutside diˈrector) *noun* [C]
a member of a company's BOARD OF DIRECTORS who is not employed by the company but takes part in meetings of the board and provides independent advice: *He was appointed as non-executive director in 2003.* ◇ *She claims that the role of the independent non-executive director is to challenge management.* → EXECUTIVE DIRECTOR
▶ **ˈnon-eˈxecutive diˈrectorship** *noun* [C]

ˌnon-ˈfarm *adjective* [usually before noun]
not connected with or including farming: *The government is developing policies to promote non-farm rural employment.* ◇ *the non-farm economy/sector*

nonfeasance /ˌnɒnˈfiːzəns; *AmE* ˌnɑːn-/ *noun* [U]
(*Law*) not doing sth that you must do according to an agreement or a law: *The construction company was penalized for nonfeasance after it failed to perform safety checks.*

ˌnon-ˈfood *adjective* [only before noun]
not being, or not connected with, food: *non-food crops/products*

ˌnon-inˈsurable = UNINSURABLE (2)

ˌnon-ˈlife *adjective*
(*Insurance*) used to describe insurance other than LIFE INSURANCE: *non-life insurance companies*

ˌnon-ˈmarketable *adjective*
(*Finance*) (about shares, bonds, etc.) that cannot be bought and sold by investors: *Only the government can redeem non-marketable government securities, which do not trade on secondary markets.* OPP MARKETABLE

ˌnon-maˈterial *adjective*
not consisting of physical objects or money: *Your non-material capital includes your knowledge and skills.* OPP MATERIAL

ˌnon-ˈmember *noun* [C]
a person, a country or an organization that has not joined a particular group: *The society's conference is open to non-members.* ◇ *Trading with EU members is harder for non-member countries.* OPP MEMBER

ˌnon-neˈgotiable *adjective*
1 fixed; that you cannot discuss or change before you make an agreement or a decision: *Some details of the contract are non-negotiable.* ◇ *a non-negotiable price*
2 (*Finance*) that you cannot exchange for money or give to another person in exchange for money: *non-negotiable securities* OPP NEGOTIABLE

ˌno-ˈnonsense *adjective* [only before noun]
simple and direct; only paying attention to important and necessary things: *a no-nonsense approach* ◇ *She is a tough, no-nonsense manager.*

,non-'payment *noun* [U]
failure to pay a debt, tax, rent, etc: *There has been a rise in the non-payment of loans.*

,non-per'forming *adjective*
(*Finance*) (about a loan) on which the borrower has not made a payment for a particular period of time: *The bank ran into trouble with non-performing loans.*

,non-pro'fessional *adjective*
1 doing sth out of interest rather than as a paid job: *computer applications aimed at non-professional programmers*
2 (*HR*) having a job that does not need a high level of education or special training: *non-professional staff*
→ PROFESSIONAL, UNPROFESSIONAL

,non-'profit (*AmE* spelling **nonprofit**) (*AmE also* **,not-for-'profit**) (*BrE also* **,non-'profit-,making**) *adjective*
(about an organization) that does not have the aim of making a profit: *an independent non-profit organization* ◇ *The centre is run on a non-profit basis.* → FOR-PROFIT

,non-re'course *adjective* [only before noun]
(*Finance*) used to describe a loan or debt where the lender only has the right to take back the asset that was bought with the loan if the money is not paid back, and cannot take any of the borrower's other assets

,non-re'curring *adjective*
(*Accounting*) happening only once in a particular period rather than repeatedly: *The loss included non-recurring items such as redundancy costs.*
→ RECURRING
○ *non-recurring* **charges/costs/items**

,non-re'fundable *adjective*
(*Commerce*) used to describe an amount of money that cannot be returned when you have paid it to sb: *a non-refundable deposit*

,non-re'newable *adjective*
1 that cannot be replaced after use: *non-renewable energy resources*
2 (*Law*) that cannot be continued or repeated for a further period after it has finished: *The contract is non-renewable.*
[OPP] RENEWABLE

,non-'resident *adjective, noun*
● *adjective*
(about a person or company) not living or situated permanently in a particular country, especially when this relates to tax: *non-resident holders of savings accounts* ◇ *You will be treated as non-resident for tax purposes.*
● *noun* [C]
1 a person who does not live permanently in a particular country or place: *sales of securities to non-residents*
2 a person not staying at a particular hotel: *The restaurant is open to non-residents.*
[OPP] RESIDENT

,non-resi'dential *adjective*
that is not used for people to live in: *The buildings in the area are mainly non-residential.*
[OPP] RESIDENTIAL

,non-'smoking (*also* **,no-'smoking**) *adjective*
[usually before noun]
(about a place) where you cannot smoke: *This is a non-smoking office.* ▶ **non-'smoking** (*also* **,no-'smoking**) *noun* [U]: *Non-smoking will soon be the norm for employees at work.*

,non-'standard *adjective*
1 not the usual size, type, etc: *paper of a non-standard size*
2 (*HR*) connected with work that is not FULL-TIME and permanent: *There has been a huge increase in non-standard types of work such as part-time jobs and self-employment.* ◇ *a non-standard contract*
[OPP] STANDARD

,non-tariff 'barrier *noun* [C] (*abbr* **NTB**)
(*Economics*) an official rule or policy, but not a tax, that a government uses to make it difficult for imports of particular goods to come into the country

,non-'taxable *adjective*
(*Accounting*) that you do not need to pay tax on: *non-taxable income* [OPP] TAXABLE

nontraditional (*also spelled* **non-traditional**)
/ˌnɒntrəˈdɪʃənl; *AmE* ˌnɑːn-/ *adjective*
(*HR*) different from the jobs or working arrangements that have usually been expected in the past: *women in nontraditional occupations such as construction* ◇ *Up to 40% of our employees work in nontraditional ways.*

,non-'transferable *adjective*
that cannot be given to or used by anyone else: *non-transferable tickets* ◇ *The option itself is non-transferable.* [OPP] TRANSFERABLE

,non-'union (*also* **,non-'unionized, -ised**, *less frequent*) *adjective* [usually before noun]
(*HR*)
1 not belonging to a trade/labor union: *non-union labour/workers*
2 (about a business, company, etc.) not accepting trade/labor unions or employing union members: *Many newly established firms are non-union.* ◇ *a non-union workplace*

,non-verbal communi'cation *noun* [U]
ways of making your thoughts and feelings known to other people that do not involve words or speech, for example by the position of your body

,non-'voting *adjective* [usually before noun]
(*Finance*) used to describe shares that do not give their owners the right to vote at shareholders' meetings: *non-voting shares/stock*

norm /nɔːm; *AmE* nɔːrm/ *noun*
1 (*often* **the norm**) [C, usually sing.] the usual or expected amount, number, situation, etc: *Spending on IT was about four per cent below the norm this quarter.* ◇ *profits far above industry norms*
○ *above/below* **the norm** ✦ *twice/double/ten times* **the norm** ✦ *to be/become* **the norm**
2 (*Technical*) [C] a required or agreed standard, amount, maximum, etc: *bringing the system in line with international norms*

nose /nəʊz; *AmE* noʊz/ *verb* [no obj] (*used with an adverb or a preposition*)
(about prices, values, etc.) to move gradually into a better position : *March futures nosed up 1.70 points.*
→ idiom at PAY *verb*

nosedive /ˈnəʊzdaɪv; *AmE* ˈnoʊz-/ *noun, verb*
● *noun* grammar [C]
a sudden steep fall or drop: *Sales continued their nosedive, sinking by 14 per cent.* ◇ *The markets could* **take** *a nosedive, destroying consumer confidence.*
● *verb* [no obj]
(about prices, costs, values, etc.) to fall suddenly and by a large amount: *The stock has nosedived from $20 a year ago to $2.*

,no-'show *noun* [C]
1 a customer who has reserved sth such as a restaurant table or plane seat but does not arrive to use it: *No-shows are a problem for hotel managers.*

2 an event that is expected to happen or arrive but does not: *With the inflation rise a no-show, the bank left interest rates unchanged.*

,no-'smoking = NON-SMOKING

,no-'strike *adjective* [only before noun]
(*HR*) in which workers promise not to have a strike: *The union refused to accept a no-strike deal.*

notary /'nəʊtəri; *AmE* 'noʊ-/ *noun* [C] (*plural* **notaries**) (*also* **,notary 'public,** *plural* **notaries public**)
(*Law*) a person, especially a lawyer, with official authority to watch a document being signed and make this document valid in law ▶ **notarial** /,nəʊ'teəriəl; *AmE* ,noʊ'ter-/ *adjective*: *notarial fees*

notch /nɒtʃ; *AmE* nɑ:tʃ/ *noun, verb*
●*noun* [C]
a level on a scale, often marking quality or achievement: *The bonds have been downgraded by one notch to AA.* ◇ *The quality of the food here has dropped a notch recently.*
●*verb* [+ obj] **notch sth (up)**
(used in newspapers) to achieve sth: *The managing directors have notched up 50 years with the company between them.* ◇ *Stocks have notched slight gains today.*

note /nəʊt; *AmE* noʊt/ *noun, verb*
●*noun* [C]

SEE ALSO: **advice note, bond ~, consignment ~, contract ~, convertible ~, cover ~, credit ~,** etc.

1 (*especially BrE*) (*AmE usually* **bill**) a piece of paper money: *a €50 note* ◇ *He counted out a pile of notes.* ◇ *We can only exchange notes and travellers' cheques.* SYN BANKNOTE
2 (*Finance*) a bond of a particular kind: *a 10-year note* (= that will be repaid after 10 years) ◇ *Treasury notes* (= notes issued by the US government)
3 a short piece of writing to tell sb sth or help them remember sth: *He wrote a note to his client.* ◇ *The notes in this column relate to unpaid invoices.*
→ NOTE TO THE ACCOUNTS
4 an official document that shows or proves sth: *If you are absent for more than 5 days you need a note from your doctor.* ◇ *a delivery note*
5 (*Finance*) = PROMISSORY NOTE
→ idiom at STRIKE *verb*
●*verb* [+ obj] (*formal*)
to notice or pay careful attention to sth: *Investors should note **that** income can fall as well as rise.* ◇ *When a company declares its sales, note the timing.*

notebook /'nəʊtbʊk; *AmE* 'noʊt-/ (*also* **,notebook com'puter, ,notebook P'C**) *noun* [C]
a very small computer that is easy to carry and use anywhere → LAPTOP

noteholder /'nəʊthəʊldə(r); *AmE* 'noʊthoʊldər/ *noun* [C] (*AmE*)
(*Finance*) a person or an organization that owns bonds (**notes**) in a company: *The management really wants the noteholders to agree to the deal.*

'note ,issue *noun* [C]
(*Economics*) a number of BANKNOTES (= pieces of paper money) that are made available at the same time; the value of these

,note 'payable *noun* [C]
(*Accounting*) a note relating to an amount of money that a company must pay

,note re'ceivable *noun* [C]
(*Accounting*) a note relating to an amount of money that a company is owed

,note to the ac'counts *noun* [C] (*plural* **notes to the accounts**)
(*Accounting*) extra information given in a company's financial records to explain particular items

,not-for-'profit = NON-PROFIT

notice /'nəʊtɪs; *AmE* 'noʊ-/ *noun*

SEE ALSO: **bankruptcy notice, deficiency ~, money at call and short ~, renewal ~**

1 [C] written or printed news or information, usually put in a public place: *posting notices on the firm's internal website* ◇ *legal notices*
2 [U] information or a warning given in advance of sth that is going to happen: *Prices may be altered without notice.* ◇ *The canteen will remain closed **until further notice*** (= until you are told that it is open again).
3 (*HR*) [U,C] a formal letter or statement saying that you will or must leave your job at the end of a particular period of time: *She has **handed in** her notice.* ◇ *They **gave** him two weeks' notice.* ◇ *500 workers have been issued with **redundancy notices.***
4 (*Property*) [U,C] a formal letter or statement saying that you will or must leave your home at the end of a particular period of time: *The agreement allows the tenant to give **notice to quit** before the end of the contract.* ◇ *Three families have received notices of eviction.*
IDM **put sb on 'notice** to give sb a formal warning about sth that is going to happen or is likely to happen: *Two retailers have been put on notice that they may face fines if they have been fixing the price of popular toys.* → idioms at SHORT *adj.*, SERVE

'notice ac,count = DEPOSIT ACCOUNT

noticeboard /'nəʊtɪsbɔːd; *AmE* 'noʊtɪsbɔːrd/ (*BrE*) (*also* **'bulletin board, board,** *AmE, BrE*) *noun* [C]
a board for putting notices on: *The details of the meeting will be put up on the noticeboard on Friday.*—Picture at OFFICE

,notice of de'ficiency (*also* **de'ficiency ,notice**) *noun* [C] (*often* **Notice of Deficiency**) (*all AmE*)
(*Accounting*) an official document that shows that sb owes more tax than they have shown on their tax forms

'notice ,period *noun* [C]
(*HR*) the period of time that there must be between sending or receiving a formal letter or statement saying that you will or must leave your job and when this happens: *He is on a six-month notice period and will stay until April.* ◇ *to work out a notice period*

★ notify /'nəʊtɪfaɪ; *AmE* 'noʊ-/ *verb* [+ obj] (**notifies, notifying, notified, notified**)
to formally or officially tell sb about sth, that sth is happening, etc: *You will be notified of any changes in the interest rate.* ◇ *If you are travelling with kids, notify the airline in advance.* SYN INFORM
▶ **notification** /,nəʊtɪfɪ'keɪʃn; *AmE* ,noʊ-/ *noun* [C,U]: *advance/formal notification*

,Not-Invented-'Here ,syndrome *noun* [sing.] (*abbr* **NIH syndrome**)
the way that companies or departments tend to reject or be suspicious of ideas, methods, systems, etc. that they have not developed themselves: *NIH syndrome causes programmers to waste a lot of time developing programs that could easily be bought.*

notional /'nəʊʃnl; *AmE* 'noʊ-/ *adjective*
used to describe a number or an amount that is estimated or guessed rather than real: *The company's shares are valued at a notional €7.50.*

nought /nɔːt/ *noun* [C,U] (*BrE*)
the number 0: *nought point one* (= written 0.1) SYN ZERO

novelty /'nɒvlti; *AmE* 'nɑːv-/ *noun* (*plural* **novelties**)
1 [C, usually pl.] a small cheap object that amuses or interests people, and is usually produced and

sold for only a short time: *They sell toys, books and novelties.*
2 [C] a thing or person that is interesting because it is new or unusual: *At the time, television was a novelty.*

'NOW ac,count /'naʊ/ *noun* [C]
Negotiable Order of Withdrawal account in the US, a type of bank account that pays interest

,**no-'win** *adjective* [only before noun]
a **no-win** situation, plan, etc. will end badly whatever you do: *Both sides were well aware that this was a no-win situation.*

no-,win no-'fee *phrase*
(*Law*) if a lawyer or a company works on a **no-win no-fee** basis, they agree to be paid only if the case is won

NPD /,en pi: 'di:/ = NEW-PRODUCT DEVELOPMENT

NPV /,en pi: 'vi:/ = NET PRESENT VALUE

NRV /,en ɑː 'viː/ AmE /-/ = NET REALIZABLE VALUE

n.s.f. (*also spelled* **NSF**) /,en es 'ef/ *abbr* (*especially AmE*)
(*Finance, usually used in written English*) **non-sufficient funds, not sufficient funds** used when there is not enough money in a bank account to pay a cheque that has been written **NOTE** **Insufficient funds** is also sometimes used to describe this.

NTA /,en ti: 'eɪ/ = NET TANGIBLE ASSETS

NTB /,en ti: 'bi:/ = NON-TARIFF BARRIER

,**nuclear 'option** *noun* [sing.]
an extreme solution to a problem, often one that many people would object to if it was used: *the nuclear option of declaring yourself bankrupt*

nudge /nʌdʒ/ *verb, noun*
● *verb* (*usually used with an adverb or a preposition*)
1 [+ obj *or* no obj] to reach a particular value or level; to make sth do this: *Profits are nudging $1 billion.* ◊ *The news has nudged shares down a few cents.*
2 [no obj] to move slightly up or down: *Japanese government bonds nudged higher yesterday.*
● *noun* [C, usually sing.]
1 a small action that encourages sth to happen: *The consensus is that the markets need a nudge.*
2 a small amount higher or lower: *The shares closed a nudge up at $1.27.* **SYN** FRACTION

,**null and 'void** *adjective* [not before noun]
(*Law*) having no legal force; not valid: *The contract was declared null and void.*

nullify /'nʌlɪfaɪ/ *verb* [+ obj] (**nullifies, nullifying, nullified, nullified**)
1 (*Law*) to make sth such as an agreement or order lose its legal force: *A court has nullified the ban on the proposed merger.* ◊ *The firm is taking legal action to nullify the $5 million compensation payment.* **SYN** INVALIDATE, VOID
2 (*formal*) to make sth lose its effect or power: *This tax will nullify efforts to revive the regional economy.*
▶ **nullification** /,nʌlɪfɪ'keɪʃn/ *noun* [U]

number /'nʌmbə(r)/ *noun, verb*
● *noun*

SEE ALSO: **bank identification number, box ~, DUNS™ ~, opposite ~, PIN ~, routing ~, serial ~**

1 [C] (*abbr* **No.**) (*often used with another noun*) a number used to identify sth or to communicate by telephone, etc: *Give me your number and I'll call you back.* ◊ *Please enter the number of the credit card you wish to use.* ◊ *My account number is 002345.*

○ *a credit-card/fax/registration/telephone number* ◦ *an account/invoice/order number*
2 [C] a quantity of people or things: *A large number of people have applied for the job.* ◊ *The number of companies working in this industry has increased dramatically.* ◊ *Passenger numbers have been falling.* ◊ *There are a number of* (= some) *questions I'd like to raise.* ◊ *People are buying environmentally friendly cars in increasing numbers.* **HELP** A plural verb is needed after *a/an* (*large, small, etc.*) *number of ...*.
○ *a large/limited/record/small number* ◦ *the total number* ◦ *a declining/dwindling/growing/an increasing number*
3 [C, usually pl.] an amount, used especially when talking about how a company or the economy is working: *October's numbers were hit by poor sales earlier in the year.* ◊ *The company posted worse-than-expected numbers.* **SYN** FIGURES
IDM **make the/your 'numbers** to achieve the figures that have been predicted: *Our salespeople are sure they will make their numbers.*
● *verb*
1 (*linking verb*) to make a particular number when added together: *Our sales force numbers 8 000.*
2 [+ obj] to give a number to sth as part of a series or list: *numbered receipts* ◊ *a numbering system*

'number ,cruncher (*also spelled* **number-cruncher**) *noun* [C] (*informal*)
1 used to describe a person whose job involves dealing with numbers and doing large calculations; an accountant
2 a computer or a computer program that can do calculations with large amounts of data in a short time
▶ **'number ,crunching** (*also spelled* **number-crunching**) *noun* [U]

,**numbered ac'count** *noun* [C]
a bank account that is identified by a number only, so that the name of the person who holds the account remains secret

,**number 'one** *noun* [U] (*informal*)
the most important or best person or thing: *We're number one in childrenswear.* ◊ *Saab is part of world number-one carmaker GM.* ◊ *My number-one priority is the future of this company.*

numerical /nju:'merɪkl; AmE nu:-/ (*also* **numeric** /nju:'merɪk; AmE nu:-/ *less frequent*) *adjective*
relating to numbers; expressed in numbers: *numerical data* ◊ *Each employee receives a numerical ranking within their department.*

nu,meric 'keypad *noun* [C]
a set of buttons on a computer keyboard that contain the numbers 0–9 and some symbols

NVQ /,en vi: 'kju:/ *abbr* **National Vocational Qualification** a British qualification that shows you have reached a particular level in the work that you do: *an NVQ level 3 in catering*

NYMEX /'naɪmeks/ *abbr*
1 **New York Mercantile Exchange** a very important market where FUTURES and OPTIONS for physical goods such as oil, related products and metals are bought and sold: *NYMEX crude oil futures fell more than one dollar yesterday.*
2 (*also* **'NYMEX di,vision**) the part of the New York Mercantile Exchange that deals with oil, related products and some rare metals (**precious metals**)
→ COMEX

NYSE /,en waɪ es 'i:/ *abbr* **New York Stock Exchange** one of the world's biggest stock markets, based in New York: *The stock was the most actively traded on the NYSE.* ◊ *The company did not meet the strict NYSE listing standards.*

O o

O&M /ˌəʊ ənd ˈem; *AmE* ˌoʊ/ = ORGANIZATION AND METHODS

oath /əʊθ; *AmE* oʊθ/ *noun* [C] (*plural* **oaths** /əʊðz; *AmE* oʊðz/)
a formal promise to do sth; a formal statement that sth is true: *Chief executives have to* **swear** *an oath certifying that accounts are accurate.*
IDM on/under ˈoath (*Law*) having promised to tell the truth in a court of law

OB /ˌəʊ ˈbiː; *AmE* ˌoʊ/ = ORGANIZATIONAL BEHAVIOUR

o/b *abbr* (*only used in written English*)
on or before used before a date to show that it is the last possible date when sth can be done: *Payment o/b 15 April 2006.*

★ **object** *noun, verb*
● *noun* /ˈɒbdʒɪkt; *AmE* ˈɑːbdʒekt; -dʒɪkt/ [C]
1 a thing that can be seen and touched: *The factory produces vases and small decorative objects.* ◇ *everyday objects such as cups and saucers*
2 an aim or a purpose: *Our object is to restore profitability.* ◇ *The object of the exercise is to ensure the efficient use of natural resources.*
● *verb* /əbˈdʒekt/ [no obj]
to say that you disagree with, disapprove of or oppose sth: *Many local people objected* **to** *the building of the new factory.* ◇ *If nobody objects, we'll postpone the meeting till next week.* ▶ **objection** /əbˈdʒekʃn/ *noun* [C]: *The main objection* **to** *the plan was that it would cost too much.* ◇ *No objections were raised at the time.* **obˈjector** *noun* [C]: *There were no objectors to the plan.*

★ **objective** /əbˈdʒektɪv/ *noun, adjective*
● *noun* [C]

SEE ALSO: **management by objectives**

details of what you are trying to achieve and when: *The main objective of this meeting is to give more information on our plans.* ◇ *You must set realistic* **aims and objectives** *for yourself.* ◇ *The company is likely to achieve its long-term strategic objective.* ◇ *My objective is to serve our clients better.* **SYN** GOAL
O *the* **key/main/primary/principal** *objective* ◆ **business/learning/performance/strategic** *objectives* ◆ *to* **agree/establish/set** *objectives* ◆ *to* **achieve/ meet/reach** *objectives* ◆ *to* **fail to meet/fall short of** (*your*) *objectives*
● *adjective*
not influenced by personal feelings or opinions; considering only facts: *an objective analysis/ assessment/report* ◇ *The important thing is to be objective when making decisions.* ▶ **obˈjectively** *adverb*: *It is difficult to examine your own performance objectively.* **objectivity** /ˌɒbdʒekˈtɪvəti; *AmE* ˌɑːb-/ *noun* [U]: *There were concerns about the audit's objectivity.*

obˌjective justifiˈcation *noun* [U,C]
(*HR*) in Europe, a legal reason that a company can use to show why it has to treat an employee in a different way from others

ˈobjects clause *noun* [C]
the part of a company's MEMORANDUM OF ASSOCIATION that states the aims and activities of the company: *Objects clauses can prevent companies from innovating and growing.*

obligate /ˈɒblɪgeɪt; *AmE* ˈɑːb-/ *verb* [+ obj] (*especially AmE*)
1 to make a person, company, etc. do sth, especially for moral or legal reasons: *Customers signed long-term contracts, obligating them to purchase a certain quantity of goods.* → OBLIGE
2 to state officially that a particular amount of money will be given for sth, for example to support a loan: *Before obligating corporate funds, check the background of the applicants thoroughly.*

obligated /ˈɒblɪgeɪtɪd; *AmE* ˈɑːb-/ *adjective* (*especially AmE*)
having a moral or legal duty to do sth: *I was not contractually obligated* **to** *stay the full five years in the post.* → OBLIGE

★ **obligation** /ˌɒblɪˈgeɪʃn; *AmE* ˌɑːb-/ *noun*

SEE ALSO: **tax obligation**

1 [C,U] a legal or moral duty to do sth: *The industry has an obligation* **to** *establish a pension scheme.* ◇ *He is* **under no obligation** *to reveal sales figures.* ◇ *We will send you an estimate for the work* **without** *obligation* (= you do not have to accept it).
2 obligations [pl.] something that a person or an organization has to do, because of a promise, a law or rule, etc: *The bank is unable to meet its financial obligations.* ◇ *We are committed to fulfilling our obligations to our creditors.*
O *to* **fulfil/meet** *your obligations* ◆ **contractual/ financial/legal/professional** *obligations*

obligatory /əˈblɪgətri; *AmE* -tɔːri/ *adjective* (*formal*)
that sb must do or have because of a law or rule: *It is obligatory for employees to wear protective clothing.* ◇ *obligatory health insurance*
SYN COMPULSORY

★ **oblige** /əˈblaɪdʒ/ *verb*
1 [+ obj] (*usually* **be obliged**) to make a person, company, etc. do sth, because it is the law or their duty: *The distributor is not obliged to pay for the goods if they don't sell them.* ◇ *Current EU law only obliges companies to publish results every six months.*
2 [+ obj *or* no obj] to help sb by doing what they ask or what they want: *Business travellers demand the best treatment and we are* **happy to oblige.**

OBM /ˌəʊ biː ˈem; *AmE* ˌoʊ/ = OPEN-BOOK MANAGEMENT

o.b.o. *abbr* (*especially AmE*) (*only used in written English*)
or best offer used in small advertisements to say that the person selling sth will accept a price that is slightly lower than the one they are asking: *For Sale: digital camera, $150 obo.* → O.N.O.

observer /əbˈzɜːvə(r); *AmE* -ˈzɜːrv-/ *noun* [C]
a person who watches and studies particular events, situations, etc. and is therefore considered to be an expert on them: *Many industry observers expect more job losses.*

obsolescence /ˌɒbsəˈlesns; *AmE* ˌɑːb-/ *noun* [U] (*formal*)
the state of becoming old-fashioned and no longer useful: *Mobile phones are an example not of* **planned** *obsolescence* (= designed not to last very long) *but instant obsolescence.* ◇ *products with* **built-in** *obsolescence* (= designed not to last long so that people will have to buy new ones) ▶ **ˌobsoˈlescent** *adjective*

obsolete /ˈɒbsəliːt; AmE ˌɑːbsəˈliːt/ adjective
no longer useful because sth new and better has been invented: obsolete technology ◇ Job skills can quickly become obsolete.

occupancy /ˈɒkjəpənsi; AmE ˈɑːk-/ noun [U]
1 (Commerce) the **occupancy** of a hotel, plane, etc. is the number of rooms, seats, etc. that are being used at any one time: Our room **occupancy rate is high**. ◇ Occupancy levels on short-haul flights have increased.
2 (formal) the fact of a building, room, piece of land, etc. being lived in or used: The offices will be ready for occupancy next month. → CERTIFICATE OF OCCUPANCY

occupant /ˈɒkjəpənt; AmE ˈɑːk-/ noun [C]
a person or an organization that lives in, works in or uses a particular house, building or room: The building's occupant is a major financial institution.
SYN OCCUPIER

occupation /ˌɒkjuˈpeɪʃn; AmE ˌɑːk-/ noun
1 [C] a job or profession: Please state your name, age and occupation below. ◇ What is your current occupation? ◇ high-risk/low-risk occupations
○ to **choose/follow/take up** an occupation
2 (formal) [U] the act of living in or using a building, room, piece of land, etc: The offices will be ready for occupation in June.

occupational /ˌɒkjuˈpeɪʃənl; AmE ˌɑːk-/ adjective
[only before noun]
connected with a person's job or profession: occupational health/injury/disease ◇ occupational medicine ◇ an occupational pension scheme
▶ occu'pationally adverb: occupationally induced disease

occupational 'hazard (also ,occupational 'risk) noun [C]
a risk or danger connected with a particular job: Back injuries are an occupational hazard for nurses.

occupational 'hygiene = INDUSTRIAL HYGIENE

occupational over'use ,syndrome = OOS

occupational psy'chology noun [U]
(especially BrE)
(HR) the study of how people behave at work and what influences their attitudes and behaviour → INDUSTRIAL AND ORGANIZATIONAL PSYCHOLOGY
▶ ,occupational psy'chologist noun [C]

occupational 'risk = OCCUPATIONAL HAZARD

occupier /ˈɒkjupaɪə(r); AmE ˈɑːk-/ noun [C]
a person who lives in, works in or uses a building, room, piece of land, etc: a letter addressed to 'The Occupiers' **SYN** OCCUPANT

★ **occupy** /ˈɒkjupaɪ; AmE ˈɑːk-/ verb [+ obj]
(**occupies, occupying, occupied, occupied**)
1 (formal) to live or work in a room, house or building: He occupies an office on the 12th floor.
2 to have an official job or position: Women now occupy 25 per cent of the senior posts in the company. **SYN** HOLD

OCR /ˌəʊ siː ˈɑː(r); AmE ˌoʊ/ = OPTICAL CHARACTER RECOGNITION

o/d abbr
(Finance) a short way of writing **overdraft** or **overdrawn** → DR

OECD /ˌəʊ iː siː ˈdiː; AmE ˌoʊ/ abbr **Organization for Economic Cooperation and Development**
an organization of thirty countries that produces economic information, helps governments decide the best economic policy and encourages trade

OEIC /ɔɪk/ abbr
(Finance) **open-ended investment company, open-end investment company** a company whose business is managing the money of its members by investing in a wide range of shares, bonds, etc. It sells or buys shares to meet the demand → UNIT TRUST

OEM /ˌəʊ iː ˈem; AmE ˌoʊ/ abbr **original equipment manufacturer** a company that buys equipment such as computers from a manufacturer in large quantities and then sells them under their own name. They may change the equipment first to make it suitable for a particular purpose or put different parts together to make a complete item. **NOTE** OEM is sometimes used to refer to a company that sells pieces of equipment to another company, which then uses them in other products that it sells under its own name.

off-'balance-sheet adjective [only before noun]
(Accounting) used to refer to items that a company does not show on its BALANCE SHEET (= the document that shows its financial state): The company has revealed $2.3 bn in off-balance sheet debts. ◇ He was asked what he knew of the company's off-balance sheet activities. **NOTE** Off-balance-sheet accounting is sometimes used as a way of hiding a company's problems or dishonest actions.

★ **offence** (AmE spelling **offense**) /əˈfens/ noun [C]
an act that is illegal or against the rules: Sending insulting emails is a disciplinary offence. ◇ It was not clear that he had committed an offence.
○ a **criminal/disciplinary/minor/serious** offence • to **commit** an offence

offender /əˈfendə(r)/ noun [C]
1 a person who commits a crime: The measures have allowed Customs to concentrate on **persistent offenders** (= people who commit many crimes).
2 a person or thing that does sth wrong: Businesses are losing billions through energy inefficiency, with London offices the worst offenders.

offending /əˈfendɪŋ/ adjective [only before noun]
1 (Law) guilty of a crime: The regulator may order offending companies to compensate thousands of investors.
2 causing people to feel upset or angry: The offending ads have been removed from the website.

offense /əˈfens/ = OFFENCE

offensive /əˈfensɪv/ adjective
rude in a way that makes people feel upset or angry: They were accused of sending emails with offensive content to other employees. ◇ Most of the complaints they receive are about offensive ads.

★ **offer** /ˈɒfə(r); AmE ˈɔːf-; ˈɑːf-/ verb, noun
● verb [+ obj]
1 offer sth (to sb) (for sth) | offer sb sth to say that you are willing to do sth for sb or give sth to sb: They decided to offer Ms Keen the job. ◇ They decided to offer the job to Ms Keen. ◇ He offered $4 000 for the car. ◇ Taylor offered him 500 dollars to do the work. ◇ The CEO has offered **to resign**.
2 to make sth available or to provide the opportunity for sth: The hotel offered excellent facilities for business people. ◇ The new shares will be offered at 66 cents each. ◇ The job didn't offer any prospects for promotion.
● noun [C]

SEE ALSO: **counter-offer, general ~, open ~, share ~, special ~, stock ~, tender ~, trial ~**

1 an act of saying that you are willing to do sth for sb or give sth to sb: She has received a firm job offer. ◇ You can't just turn down offers of work like that. ◇ the offer of a 3% pay rise ◇ an offer **to raise salaries**
○ to **make/receive/renew/withdraw** an offer • to

accept/decline/refuse/reject/turn down an offer ◆ *a job/pay* offer

2 an amount of money that sb is willing to pay for sth: *I've had an offer of $2 500 for the car.* ◇ *The offer has been withdrawn.* ◇ *Shareholders have voted to reject the $45-a-share offer.* ◇ *The original price was $3 000, but we're open to offers* (= willing to consider offers less than that). → O.N.O.

❂ to *make/receive/renew/withdraw* an offer ◆ to *accept/decline/refuse/reject/turn down* an offer ◆ to *improve/increase/raise* an offer ◆ *a cash/hostile/takeover* offer

3 a reduction in the normal price of sth, usually for a short period of time: *This offer is valid until the end of the month.* ◇ *They have an offer on sugar at the moment.* ◇ *bargain offers on home entertainment*

❂ *a bargain/free/an introductory* offer

4 an act of saying that sth is available for sale: *The offer closes on March 12th.*

IDM **on 'offer 1** that can be bought, used, etc: *The range of games on offer will appeal to all age groups.* **2** *(especially BrE)* on sale at a lower price than normal for a short period of time: *This software package is on offer this week.* **under 'offer** *(BrE)* if a house or other building is **under offer**, sb has agreed to buy it at a particular price

,offer by pros'pectus *noun* [C, usually sing.] (pl. **offers by prospectus**)
(Stock Exchange) an occasion when new shares are offered to the public with a written description of the aims, history and financial structure of the company: *The new share issue was made through an offer by prospectus.*

'offer ,document *noun* [C]
(Finance) a document that a company sends to the shareholders of a business that it wants to buy, giving details of the offer and why the shareholders should accept: *Shell is expected to post its offer document next week.*

offering /'ɒfərɪŋ; *AmE* 'ɔːf-; 'ɑːf-/ *noun* [C]

SEE ALSO: initial public offering, public ~, secondary ~, shelf ~

1 *(Commerce)* a product or service that a company offers for sale: *The store's non-food offerings have proved popular.* ◇ *The company has unveiled its latest offering.*
2 *(Stock Exchange)* an occasion when shares, bonds, etc. are offered for sale: *high-yield bond offerings* ◇ *The company is planning to raise capital through a share offering.*

'offering price = OFFER PRICE (2)

'offer price *noun* [C]
1 *(Finance)* the price that a buyer offers for shareholders' shares when taking over a company; the total price of all these shares: *Shareholders rejected the deal because they thought the offer price was too low.*
2 *(Stock Exchange)* *(also* **'offering price, 'asking price,** *less frequent)* the price at which a dealer offers shares, bonds, etc. for sale → BID PRICE

,offer to 'purchase = TAKEOVER BID

★ office /'ɒfɪs; *AmE* 'ɔːf-; 'ɑːf-/ *noun*

SEE ALSO: back office, front ~, head ~, home ~, land ~, main ~, patent ~, etc.

1 [C] a room, set of rooms or building where people work, usually sitting at desks: *The company is moving to new offices on the other side of town.* ◇ *We have offices in 19 countries.* ◇ *The bank expects to open a Hong Kong office next year.* ◇ *Are you going to the office today?* ◇ *an office manager*

❂ *a branch/local/an overseas/a regional* office ◆ to *close (down)/open/set up* an office ◆ office *jobs/work* ◆ office *staff/workers*

office workstation

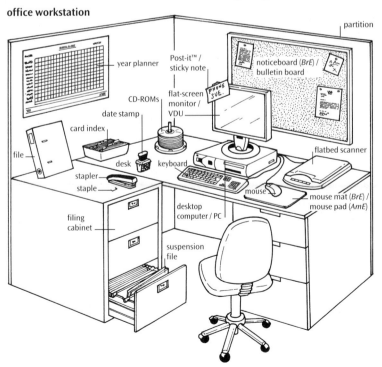

partition

year planner

Post-it™ / sticky note

noticeboard *(BrE)* / bulletin board

CD-ROMs

flat-screen monitor / VDU

date stamp

card index

file

desk

stapler

staple

keyboard

flatbed scanner

mouse

mouse mat *(BrE)* / mouse pad *(AmE)*

desktop computer / PC

filing cabinet

suspension file

2 [C] a room in which a particular person works, usually at a desk: *Is Ms Kent in her office?* ◇ *Some people have to share an office.* ◇ *office furniture* → OPEN-PLAN

O office **equipment/furniture/supplies**

3 [C] (*often used in compounds*) a room or building used for a particular purpose, especially to provide information or a service: *the local tourist office* ◇ *a tax office* ◇ *an employment office* ◇ *the company's sales office*

4 [U,C] an important position of authority, especially in government; the work and duties connected with this: *She has been disqualified from holding corporate office.* ◇ *The present government took office in 2005.*

O to **hold/leave/take** office • to be **in/out of** office • **corporate/executive/public** office

'office block (*BrE*) *noun* [C]
a large building that contains offices, usually belonging to more than one company: *high-rise office blocks*

'office boy, 'office girl *noun* [C] (*old-fashioned*)
a young person employed to do simple tasks in an office

'office hours *noun* [pl.]
the time when people in offices are normally working: *Our telephone lines are open during normal office hours.*

,office 'junior *noun* [C] (*old-fashioned*)
a person who has a low rank or status in an office

'office lady *noun* [C] (*abbr* OL)
in Japan, a woman employed to work in an office

,office ma'chinery *noun* [U]
equipment that is used in offices, such as telephones, computers, etc.

'Office of 'Fair 'Trading *noun* [sing.] (*abbr* OFT)
the government organization in the UK that makes sure that businesses trade honestly and do not cheat people: *The merger plan was referred to the Office of Fair Trading.*

'office park *noun* [C] (*AmE*)
an area of land designed and developed for a number of office buildings, often with attractive grounds and other buildings such as restaurants, health clubs, etc: *There are plans to build a high-tech office park.*

★officer /ˈɒfɪsə(r); *AmE* ˈɔːfɪsər; ˈɑːf-/ *noun* [C]

SEE ALSO: careers officer, chief executive ~, chief financial ~, chief information ~, chief operating ~, company ~, compliance ~, etc.

1 (often used in the titles of jobs) a person who has an important job in a company or an organization: *The officers of the company must act in the company's best interests.* ◇ *He was barred from serving as an officer or director of a public company.*
2 a person who is in a position of authority: *customs officers* ◇ *a public information officer*

'office space *noun* [U]
one or more empty offices; a place that can be used for offices: *Instead of working at home I'm going to rent office space.* ◇ *The building provides more than 500 000 square feet of office space.*

★official /əˈfɪʃl/ *adjective, noun*
● *adjective*
1 [usually before noun] agreed to, set, said, done, etc. by sb in authority, especially a government: *Official figures show that business investment fell by 12% in the third quarter.* ◇ *There is to be an official enquiry into the bank's collapse.* ◇ *The country's official language is Spanish.*

officer/official

An **officer** is a person with an important position in a company, often with particular legal responsibilities: *He signed the contract as an officer of the company rather than an individual.* The word is often used as part of job titles: *the chief financial officer*

The word **official** is often used in newspapers to describe a person who is acting as an official representative of their organization: *Company officials would not comment on the size of the contract.*

Official is also used to describe people who have positions of authority in government departments: *The goods were seized by customs officials.*

2 [only before noun] connected with a person's job, especially an important one: *official responsibilities* ◇ *His official title is director of research.* ◇ *She made the trip to New York in her official capacity.*
3 [only before noun] formal and attended by people in authority: *The plant's official opening is next week.* ◇ *an official reception*
OPP UNOFFICIAL
● *noun* [C]
a person who is in a position of authority in an organization or a government: *A senior official said the company had been considering a bid.* ◇ *Union officials have rejected the pay offer.*

of,ficial re'ceiver = RECEIVER (1)

of,ficial 'strike *noun* [C]
(*HR*) a strike that an accepted union organizes and approves of: *The dispute did not result in an official strike.* OPP UNOFFICIAL STRIKE

offline (*also spelled* **off-line**) /ɒfˈlaɪn; *AmE* ˌɑːf-; ˌɔːf-/ *adjective, adverb*
(*IT*) not directly controlled by or connected to a computer or the Internet: *We use online and offline media for recruiting.* ◇ *You can compose and read messages offline.* → ONLINE

offload /ˌɒfˈləʊd; *AmE* ˌɔːfˈloʊd; ˌɑːf-/ *verb* [+ obj]
to get rid of sth that you do not need by giving or selling it to sb else: *There were rumours that someone was trying to offload 2 m shares.* ◇ *The firm may offload much of its debt onto the newly-formed company.*

,off-'market *adjective* [only before noun]
involving the buying and selling of shares not through a stock market: *The shares have been acquired in an off-market transaction.* ► **,off-'market** *adverb*

,off-'peak *adjective* [only before noun]
used to describe a time that is less popular or busy, and things that happen or are used during that time which are therefore cheaper: *travelling at off-peak times* ◇ *off-peak flights/electricity* ◇ *The best deals are offered to off-peak users.* ► **,off-'peak** *adverb*

,off-'price *adjective* [only before noun] (*AmE*)
off-price shops/stores sell goods more cheaply than others: *an off-price store/retailer* SYN CUT-PRICE
► **,off-'price** *adverb*: *selling goods off-price*

'off ,season *noun* [sing.]
the time of year that is less busy in business and travel SYN LOW SEASON → HIGH SEASON ► **,off-'season** *adjective* [only before noun]: *off-season prices* **,off-'season** *adverb*

offset /'ɒfset; AmE 'ɔːf-; 'ɑːf-/ verb, noun
● *verb* [+ obj] (**offsetting, offset, offset**)
to use one cost or payment in order to reduce or
cancel the effect of another: *The sale had been offset*
against *costs.* ◇ *The job cuts will be partly offset by*
2 000 new posts.
● *noun* [C]
1 (*Accounting*) a cost or payment that is used to
reduce or cancel the effect of another: *corporation*
tax offsets
2 (*Law*) the right that enables sb to reduce a debt
that they owe to sb else because the other person
also owes them money

offshoot /'ɒfʃuːt; AmE 'ɔːf-; 'ɑːf-/ noun [C]
a small organization, business, etc. that develops
from a larger one: *The company is an offshoot of*
mass mobile phone marketer Nokia.

offshore /ˌɒf'ʃɔː(r); AmE ˌɔːf-; ˌɑːf-/ adjective, verb
● *adjective* [usually before noun]
1 (*Finance*) **offshore** accounts, investments, etc. are
kept in countries that have less strict laws and
lower taxes than most other countries: *Secret*
payments were made into offshore accounts.
  ● **offshore banks/banking/companies/funds/**
  investments
2 happening or based in a different country: *India*
has become the largest offshore supplier of software
to US organizations. [SYN] FOREIGN, OVERSEAS
3 connected with oil and gas production that takes
place in and under the sea: *Diamond Offshore is a*
Texas-based offshore drilling company.
  ▶ ˌoff'shore *adverb*
● *verb* [+ obj *or no obj*]
(*HR*) to move part of your company's operations to a
foreign country, for example to reduce the cost of
labour: *As many as 3.3 million jobs may be offshored*
in the next 15 years. → HOMESHORING
  ▶ ˌoff'shoring *noun* [U]: *Offshoring provides IT*
  services at a low cost.

ˌoff-'site *adjective, noun*
● *adjective* [usually before noun]
working or happening away from the main offices
of a business: *an off-site meeting* ◇ *off-site data*
storage ▶ ˌoff-'site *adverb*: *At any one time, 90% of*
employees are working off-site with clients.
● *noun* [C]'off-site
an occasion when a company takes its employees
away from the office, for example to discuss future
strategy: *He highlighted the improvements that*
resulted from the company's off-site. → ON-SITE

ˌoff-the-'books *adjective* [only before noun]
(*Accounting*) not officially recorded, in order to
avoid tax or deceive the authorities: *The company*
had massive off-the-books debts.

ˌoff-the-'job *adjective, adverb*
(*HR*) that happens away from the employee's place
of work: *off-the-job training* ◇ *Where do injuries*
occur off-the-job? → ON-THE-JOB

ˌoff-the-'peg (*BrE*) (*AmE* ˌoff-the-'rack) *adjective*
[only before noun]
of a standard type, design or size, rather than being
made for a particular person or situation: *The off-*
the-peg office supplier announced a series of new
deals. → TAILOR-MADE
  ▶ ˌoff the 'peg (*BrE*) (*AmE* ˌoff the 'rack) *adverb*

ˌoff-the-'shelf *adjective*
made to a standard design and available to buy and
use immediately: *off-the-shelf applications/*
components/software ▶ ˌoff the 'shelf *adverb*

ˌoff-the-'shelf ˌcompany = SHELF COMPANY

OFT /ˌəʊ ef 'tiː; AmE ˌoʊ/ = OFFICE OF FAIR TRADING

OHP /ˌəʊ eɪtʃ 'piː; AmE ˌoʊ/ = OVERHEAD
PROJECTOR

OHT /ˌəʊ eɪtʃ 'tiː; AmE ˌoʊ/ = TRANSPARENCY (3)

oil /ɔɪl/ noun, verb
● *noun* [U]
a thick liquid that is found in rock underground
and is used as fuel and to make parts of machines
move smoothly: *drilling for oil* ◇ *oil-exporting/oil-*
importing countries ◇ *engine oil* → idiom *at*
SQUEAKY
● *verb* [+ obj]
to put oil onto or into sth, for example a machine,
in order to protect it or make it work smoothly
[IDM] **oil the 'wheels** (*BrE*) (*AmE* **grease the 'wheels**)
to help sth to happen easily and without problems:
oiling the wheels of international finance

oilfield /'ɔɪlfiːld/ noun [C]
an area where oil is found in the ground or under
the sea

oilman /'ɔɪlmæn/ noun [C] (*plural* **oilmen** /-men/)
1 a man who owns an oil company
2 a man who works in the oil business

'oil ˌplatform (*also* pro'duction ˌplatform) *noun*
[C] (*both especially BrE*)
a large structure with equipment for getting oil
from under the sea

'oil rig *noun* [C]
a large structure with equipment for looking for oil
under the sea or under the ground

'oil well (*also* well) *noun* [C]
a hole made in the ground or under the sea to
obtain oil

OJT /ˌəʊ dʒeɪ 'tiː; AmE ˌoʊ/ = ON-THE-JOB
TRAINING (2)

OL /ˌəʊ 'el; AmE ˌoʊ/ = ORGANIZATIONAL LEARNING,
OFFICE LADY

the ˌOld E'conomy (*also spelled* **the old**
economy) *noun* [sing.]
an economy based on traditional industries and
businesses that lasted for a long time: *In many ways*
the new economy is the old economy transformed by
information and communication technologies.
→ NEW ECONOMY

'old-line *adjective* [only before noun] (*AmE*)
old-line businesses have been established for a
long time, have a good reputation and do things in
a traditional way: *an old-line Massachusetts shoe*
manufacturer

oligarchy /'ɒlɪɡɑːki; AmE 'ɑːləɡɑːrki/ noun [C]
(*plural* **oligarchies**)
a small group of people who control a business, an
organization, a country, etc. for a long time and are
unwilling to let other people share power; the
business, organization or country that they control:
They demanded that the 'self-perpetuating oligarchy'
of many boardrooms be opened up to a wider range
of people. ▶ 'oligarch *noun* [C]

oligopoly /ˌɒlɪ'ɡɒpəli; AmE ˌɑːlə'ɡɑːp-/ noun [C]
(*plural* **oligopolies**)
(*Economics*) the control of trade in particular goods
or the supply of a particular service by a small
group of companies; the type of goods or service
that is controlled in this way; the companies that
control the trade: *The North American market will*
ultimately turn into an oligopoly of five or six
companies. [NOTE] **Oligopoly** is formed from the
words **oligarchy** and **monopoly**.

OM /ˌəʊ 'em; AmE ˌoʊ/ = ORGANIZATION AND
METHODS

ombudsman /'ɒmbʊdzmən; -mæn; AmE 'ɑːm-/
noun [C] (*plural* **ombudsmen** /-mən/)
a government official whose job is to examine and
report on complaints made by members of the
public about the government, companies, etc: *The*

financial ombudsman is considering the complaints of about 280 investors.

,one-of-a-'kind *adjective* [usually before noun]
a **one-of-a-kind** product, service, company, etc. is the only one of its type that exists: *one-of-a-kind personal computers with powerful components*

,one-'off *adjective, noun*
●*adjective* [only before noun] (*BrE*) (*AmE* '**one-shot**) made or happening only once: *a one-off charge/cost/payment/profit* ◇ *one-off gains/losses*
●*noun* [C, usually sing.]
a thing that is made or that happens only once and not regularly: *Their improving performance is not just a one-off.*

,one-on-'one = ONE-TO-ONE

'one-shot = ONE-OFF *adj*

,one-size-fits-'all *adjective* [only before noun]
suitable for a wide range of situations, people or circumstances: *A one-size-fits-all approach to rewarding employees will not work.*

'one-stop *adjective* [only before noun] (*BrE*)
a **one-stop** shop/store or service offers a wide range of goods or services so that you only have to go to one place to buy or do everything you want: *Our agency is a one-stop shop for all your travel needs.*

'one-time (*AmE spelling* **onetime**) *adjective* [only before noun]
1 happening only once: *The package includes a one-time $300 tax cut.* ◇ *a one-time charge/cost/gain/loss* SYN ONE-OFF → EXCEPTIONAL
2 former: *Companies such as BP have been buying up one-time competitors.*

,one-to-'one (*especially BrE*) (*AmE usually* ,one-on-'one) *adjective* [usually before noun]
between two people only: *a one-to-one meeting* ◇ *one-on-one coaching*

,one-'way *adjective* [only before noun]
1 (*especially AmE*) = SINGLE *adj* (2)
2 operating in only one direction: *An ad should not be just one-way communication with customers.*

on-lend /ˌɒnˈlend; *AmE* ɑːn-; ɔːn-/ *verb* [+ obj] (**on-lent, on-lent** /-ˈlent/)
to lend money that you have borrowed from sb to sb else: *A company may need money for an investment or to on-lend to someone else.*
▶ '**on-,lending** *noun* [U]

★ **online** (*also spelled* **on-line**) /ˌɒnˈlaɪn; *AmE* ˌɑːn-; ˌɔːn-/ *adjective, adverb*
(II)
●*adjective*
(about a product or service) available on or done using the Internet or another computer network: *an online bank/retailer/database/bookstore* ◇ *Free delivery has increased online sales.* ◇ *a new online recruitment service for employers and job seekers* ◇ *The course combines classroom training with online learning.* → OFFLINE
●*adverb* (*also spelled* **on line**, *especially in AmE*)
using the Internet or a computer network: *The majority of small businesses now do their banking online.* ◇ *More and more businesses are going online to look for jobs.* → OFFLINE → idiom at LINE *noun*
❍ *to buy/come/go/sell/work online*

o.n.o. *abbr* (*especially BrE*) (*only used in written English*) **or nearest offer** used in small advertisements to show that sth may be sold at a lower price than the price that has been asked: *PC for sale: €700 o.n.o.* → O.B.O.

,on-'screen (*AmE spelling also* **onscreen**) *adjective* [only before noun]

1 appearing on the screen of a computer, television or cinema: *an on-screen logo/menu*
2 using a computer screen: *on-screen editing facilities*
▶ ,on-'screen *adverb*

onshore /ˈɒnʃɔː(r); *AmE* ˈɑːn-; ˈɔːn-/ *adjective* [usually before noun]
1 (*Finance*) **onshore** accounts, investments, etc. are kept in countries that have strict laws and normal levels of taxes: *The bank has 350 000 onshore and 25 000 offshore customers.*
2 happening or based within a particular country: *He is head of UK onshore business at the bank.*
3 relating to oil and gas production that takes place on land: *onshore oil and gas production*
▶ ,on'shore *adverb* → OFFSHORE

onside /ˌɒnˈsaɪd; *AmE* ˌɑːn-; ˌɔːn-/ *adverb*
IDM **bring/get/keep sb on'side** to get/keep sb's support: *Get your staff onside by asking for their suggestions for cutting costs.*

,on-'site *adjective*
1 working, based, or happening at the main offices of a business. *Only 1% of companies offer on-site daycare.* ◇ *on-site training/visits*
2 (*IT*) on a website: *To upload the program, just follow the on-site instructions.*
▶ ,on-'site *adverb*: *Most components are manufactured on-site.* → OFF-SITE

,on-the-'job *adjective, adverb*
(*HR*) that takes place within an employee's place of work: *The management programme included six weeks of classroom work and 14 months' on-the-job experience.* ◇ *Training is best carried out on-the-job.*
→ OFF-THE-JOB
❍ *on-the-job experience/learning* ● *on-the-job injuries/stress*

,on-the-job 'training *noun* [U]
(*HR*)
1 training that an employee receives while continuing to do their job, rather than by attending a course: *IT staff will be given on-the-job training in using the new software.*
2 (*abbr* **OJT**) training received while working for an employer for a fixed period of time in order to learn the particular skills needed in their job: *During your on-the-job training you will receive 50% of the full salary.* → APPRENTICESHIP

OOS /ˌəʊ əʊ 'es; *AmE* ˌoʊ oʊ/ *abbr* **occupational overuse syndrome** pain and swelling, especially in the arms and hands, caused by performing the same movement many times in a job or an activity SYN RSI

OPEC /'əʊpek; *AmE* 'oʊ-/ *noun* [sing.] **Organization for Petroleum Exporting Countries** an organization of countries that produce and sell oil, which controls the amount of oil produced in order to make sure that there is enough to meet needs, and to keep the price at a suitable level

★ **open** /'əʊpən; *AmE* 'oʊpən/ *adjective, verb, noun*
●*adjective*
1 [not usually before noun] if a shop/store, bank, business, etc. is **open**, it is ready for business and will admit customers or visitors: *We are open between 9 and 6.* OPP CLOSED
2 [not before noun] **open to sb** if a competition, building, etc. is **open** to particular people, those people can enter it: *The tender is open to both UK and international publishers.*
3 [not before noun] **open (to sb)** to be available and ready to use: *What options are open to us?* ◇ *We'll keep the job open for you until you can come back to work.*
4 **open to sth** (about a person) willing to listen to and think about new ideas: *They are open to offers for the high street business.*

5 (about a question) requiring sb to answer with an opinion rather than with 'yes' or 'no' SYN OPEN-ENDED

IDM **have/keep an ˌopen ˈmind (about/on sth)** to be willing to listen to or accept new ideas or suggestions

● *verb*
1 [+ obj *or no obj*] (about a shop/store, business, etc.) to start business for the day; to start business for the first time: *What time do the banks open?* ◇ *The company opened its doors for business a month ago.* → CLOSE DOWN, CLOSE STH DOWN at CLOSE
2 [+ obj] to start an activity or event: *to open a bank account*
3 [+ obj *or no obj*] to start a computer program or file so that you can use it on the screen
4 [no obj] if shares, currencies, etc. **open** at a particular price, they are worth that amount when people start trading them at the beginning of the day: *The group's shares opened down 6%.*
5 [+ obj *or no obj*] if a meeting **opens** or sb **opens** it, it starts: *Who is going to open the conference?*
6 [+ obj] to make it possible for goods, people, etc. to come through: *When did the country open its borders to Western business?*
OPP CLOSE

IDM **open ˈdoors for sb** to provide opportunities for sb to do sth and be successful: *A good CV/résumé will open doors for you.* **open the ˈfloodgates (to/ for sth); the floodgates ˈopen (to/for sth)** to start a process that is very difficult to stop: *If their case is successful it could open the floodgates to more damages claims against the industry.*

PHRV **ˌopen sth ˈup**; **ˌopen ˈup 1** to become or make sth possible, available or able to be reached: *The new catalogue will open up the market for our products.* ◇ *Exciting possibilities were opening up for her in the new job.* **2** to begin business for the day: *I open up the store for the day at around 8.30.* **3** to start a new business: *New banks are opening up all over town.* OPP CLOSE DOWN, CLOSE STH DOWN

● *noun* [sing.]
the beginning of the day of trading, especially on a stock exchange; the price of a share, currency, etc. at this time: *Stocks are set to rise at Friday's open.*
OPP CLOSE

O *a flat/low/weak open* • *a firm/high/strong open*

ˌopen acˈcount *noun* [C,U]
(*Commerce*) an arrangement with a shop/store or business to pay for goods or services at a later time: *To have an open account with us, you must first have your credit approved.*

ˌopen ˈbid *noun* [C]
(*Commerce*)
1 a situation where companies compete to be chosen to supply work or goods by offering a particular price. The price offered is not secret and the best offer is chosen: *The company won an open bid for the contract.* ◇ *an open-bid auction*
2 a bid that is not kept secret: *We purchased the building with an open bid of €200 000.*
→ CLOSED BID

ˌopen-book ˈmanagement *noun* [U] (*abbr* OBM)
(*HR*) a method of managing a company where all employees are given financial and other information about the company in order to encourage them to work as efficiently as possible

ˌopen ˈborder *noun* [C, usually pl.]
(*Trade*) the fact of goods and people being able to pass freely between countries: *an open border and free trade between the US and Mexico* ◇ *Local producers complain that the open borders policy has pushed down prices.*

ˌopen ˈcheque (*AmE spelling* ~ **check**) *noun* [C]
(*BrE only*)

1 (*also* ˌuncrossed ˈcheque) a cheque which can be exchanged for cash at the bank of the person who wrote it: *As anyone can cash an open cheque, it is not a secure means of payment.*
2 a cheque that has been signed but on which the amount of money has not yet been filled in: (*figurative*) *The research department were given an open cheque* (= unlimited money) *to develop the product.* SYN BLANK CHEQUE

ˌopen communiˈcation *noun* [U]
a situation where employees and managers can freely exchange information and ideas

ˌopen ˈcredit = REVOLVING CREDIT

ˌopen-ˈdoor ˌpolicy *noun* [C]
1 (*HR*) used to describe a style of management in which employees are encouraged to bring any problems directly to their managers **NOTE** Open-door refers to the idea that the manager's door is always open, not closed, so people can go in at any time.
2 (*Trade*) used to describe a situation in which imports or people can come into a country freely

ˌopen-ˈended *adjective*
1 (*especially BrE*) (*AmE usually* ˌopen-ˈend) without any limits, aims or dates fixed in advance: *an open-ended discussion* ◇ *The contract is open-ended.*
2 (*Finance*) (*also* ˌopen-ˈend, *especially in AmE*) (about a loan) allowing extra amounts to be borrowed at a later time, under the same conditions as the original loan: *The open-ended loan allows us to borrow money when we need it.* ◇ *an open-end credit account* → REVOLVING CREDIT
3 (*Finance*) (*usually* ˌopen-ˈend) used to describe a type of investment company that can issue and buy back shares at any time according to how many members it has, rather than having a fixed number of shares: *an open-ended fund/investment company* OPP CLOSED-END → UNIT TRUST
4 (*also* ˌopen-ˈend, *less frequent*) (*both especially AmE*) (about a question) requiring sb to answer with an opinion rather than with 'yes' or 'no' SYN OPEN

★ **opening** /ˈəʊpnɪŋ; *AmE* ˈoʊ-/ *noun, adjective*
● *noun*
1 [U,C] the act of starting business for the first time: *the opening of our branch in Hong Kong* ◇ *They are cutting back on new store openings.* OPP CLOSING
O *a formal/grand/an official opening*
2 [U,C] the act of starting business for the day, especially on a stock market; the price of shares at this time: *The FTSE 100 index is expected to rise sharply at Friday's opening.* ◇ *Wall Street's opening bell* ◇ *expectations of a weak opening on Wall Street* (= with low or falling prices) OPP CLOSING
O *a flat/higher/lower/strong/weak opening* • *the opening high/level/low/price*
3 [U] the state of being open: *Late opening of stores is common in Britain now.* OPP CLOSING
4 [sing.] = OPENING UP (1)
5 [C] a job that is available: *There are several openings in the sales department.* ◇ *a website listing job openings*
6 [C] a good opportunity for sb: *Winning the competition was the opening she needed for her career.*
● *adjective* [only before noun]
first; beginning: *the chairman's opening remarks* ◇ *the opening session of the conference* OPP CLOSING

ˌopening ˈbalance *noun* [C, usually sing.]
1 (*Accounting*) the **balance** that is shown in an account at the start of an accounting period: *The opening balance for April was minus $1 300.*
→ CLOSING BALANCE

2 the amount of money that must be placed in a bank account when it is opened: *The minimum opening balance is €2 000.*

'**opening hours** *noun* [pl.]
the time during which a shop/store, bank, etc. is open for business: *The store has extended its opening hours.* ◇ *longer opening hours*

'**opening stock** *(BrE)* *(AmE* be'ginning ,inventory) *noun* [U]
(Accounting) the amount of goods that a business holds at the start of a particular period of time; the value of these goods

,**opening 'up** *noun* [sing.]
1 *(also* '**opening**) the process of removing restrictions and making sth such as a market, jobs, land, etc. available to more people: *the opening up of the postal services market* **to** *competition* ◇ *the opening up of new opportunities for women in business*
2 the process of making sth ready for use: *the opening up of a new stretch of highway*

,**open 'learning** = DISTANCE LEARNING

,**open 'market** *noun* [C]
(Economics)
1 a market where anyone can buy and sell: *When the contract expired, the plant was forced to sell its electricity* **on** *the open market.*
2 used to refer to the situation when a country's central bank buys and sells government bonds, etc. in financial markets in order to control interest rates and the MONEY SUPPLY (= the total amount of money that exists in the economy of a country at a particular time)

,**open 'offer** *noun* [C]
(Finance) an offer that a company makes to its shareholders to buy new shares at a fixed price, usually lower than the current market price: *Salliss Cement has made an open offer to shareholders at €35 a share.*

,**open-'plan** *adjective*
used to describe an office where people sit at desks in an open area rather than in individual rooms

,**open po,sition** *noun* [sing.]
(Stock Exchange) a situation in which a dealer in shares, currencies, COMMODITIES (= products or raw materials such as grain, coffeee or metals), etc. is at risk if prices rise or fall: *An open position is vulnerable until it can be hedged or closed.*

,**open 'shop** *noun* [C]
(HR) a factory, business, etc. in which employees do not have to be members of a particular union: *In an open shop, a business can employ anybody it likes.* ◇ *Following the strike, the industry adopted an open-shop policy.* → CLOSED SHOP

,**open-'source** *adjective* [usually before noun]
(IT) used to describe computer programs that anybody can adapt for their own uses as the original SOURCE CODE is freely available: *open-source software*

,**open 'standard** *noun* [C,U]
(IT) (about computer equipment or software) a design that is available for everyone to use rather than one that belongs to a particular company: *Open standards are at the heart of e-business.*

★**operate** /'ɒpəreɪt; *AmE* 'ɑːp-/ *verb*
1 [+ obj] to use or control a machine or make it work: *You will be trained in how to operate this machinery.* ◇ *This software is needed to operate the computer.*
2 [no obj] (about machines, factories, etc.) to work in a particular way: *Most domestic freezers operate*

at below –18 °C. ◇ *The refinery is only operating at 50% capacity.* SYN FUNCTION
3 [no obj] (about a business, service, etc.) to be used or working; to work in a particular way or from a particular place: *A new late-night service is now operating.* ◇ *It has been operating* **as** *a commercial bank since 1993.* ◇ *The regulation operates in favour of small businesses.*
4 [+ obj] to manage or organize a system, service or business: *The airline operates flights to 25 countries.* ◇ *We operate 300 branches worldwide.*

'**operating ,assets** *noun* [pl.]
(Accounting) assets that a company uses to produce goods or services and run its business → WORKING CAPITAL

'**operating cost** *noun* [C, usually pl., U]
(Accounting)
1 the costs involved in the activities of a business or part of a business, such as supplies, small equipment, training, etc. → OVERHEADS
2 the costs involved in using a machine, a building, a vehicle, etc., such as the cost of electricity and repairs

'**operating ex,penditure** *(also* '**operating ex,pense**) *noun* [U]
(Accounting) the total costs involved in running a business, such as staff pay, electricity, materials, etc: *The airline reported operating expenditure of €106 million.*

'**operating ex,pense** *noun*
(Accounting)
1 [C, usually pl.] one of the costs involved in running a business, such as staff pay, electricity, materials, etc: *A lease payment on a building is deductible as an operating expense.*
2 [U] = OPERATING EXPENDITURE

'**operating ,income** *noun* [U]
(Accounting) the amount of money that a company makes from its normal business activities, calculated by taking OPERATING EXPENSES away from GROSS PROFIT: *Neogen reported a 30% increase in operating income.*

'**operating lease** *noun* [C]
(Finance) an arrangement by which a business pays to use a piece of equipment, a building, etc. for a period of time: *We offer a 24-month operating lease on all our computer systems.*

'**operating loss** *noun* [C]
(Accounting) the amount by which the cost of running a business during a particular period is greater than the money it makes: *An operating loss is expected for the fourth quarter.*

'**operating ,margin** *(also* ,**operating 'profit ,margin**, ,**net 'profit ,margin**, ,**net 'margin**) *noun* [C,U]
(Accounting) a measure of how efficiently a business is run and how successful its price levels are, calculated by dividing its OPERATING INCOME by its NET SALES: *Our operating margin is up 1% on last year.* → GROSS MARGIN

'**operating ,profit** *noun* [C,U]
(Accounting) the amount by which the money a business makes from its normal activities during a particular period is greater than the cost of running the business: *Nokia's operating profits rose by 8%.* → OPERATING INCOME

,**operating 'profit ,margin** = OPERATING MARGIN

'**operating ,strategy** *noun* [C]
the plan that a business follows in order to achieve its aims

'**operating ,system** *noun* [C] *(abbr* **OS**)
(IT) the main program on a computer, that controls how the computer works and allows other

programs to run: *All our computers use Windows XP as their operating system.*

★ **operation** /ˌɒpəˈreɪʃn; *AmE* ˌɑːp-/ *noun*

SEE ALSO: **holding operation**

1 [C] a business involving many parts: *a huge multinational operation* ◇ *Some smaller operations are having trouble getting funding.*
2 [C] the activity or work done in an area of business or industry: *the firm's banking operations overseas* ◇ *insurance/manufacturing/retail operations*
3 operations [pl.; U] the main activities that a business does to make money, for example buying and selling goods or services, or manufacturing products: *The company is seeking more funds to finance its operations.* ◇ *I've always worked in operations.*
4 [U,C] the process of working as a business: *We hope to break even in our fourth year of operation.* ◇ *The steelmaker suspended operations in 2001.*
5 [C,U] an act performed by a machine, especially a computer: *The whole operation is performed in less than three seconds.*
6 [U] the way that parts of a machine or a system work; the process of making sth work: *Regular servicing guarantees the smooth operation of the engine.*
7 [C] an organized activity that involves several people doing different things: *a security operation* IDM **come into ope'ration** to start working; to start having an effect: *The new rules come into operation next week.* **in ope'ration** working, being used or having an effect: *The system has been in operation for six months.* **put sth into ope'ration** to make sth start working; to start using sth: *It's time to put our plan into operation.*

operational /ˌɒpəˈreɪʃənl; *AmE* ˌɑːp-/ *adjective*
1 [usually before noun] connected with the way in which a business, machine, system, etc. works: *We have simplified many of our operational procedures.* ◇ *The catalogue describes the main operational features of each model.*
2 [not usually before noun] being used or ready to be used: *Our customer support centre is now fully operational.*
▶ **operationally**/ˌɒpəˈreɪʃənəli; *AmE* ˌɑːp-/ *adverb*: *The proposed system is not operationally viable (= would not work).*

ˌ**operational re'search** = OPERATIONS RESEARCH

ˌ**operation 'process chart** *noun* [C]
(*Production*) a diagram that shows the stages of a manufacturing process, and gives information about the time, people and parts needed at each stage

ˌ**ope'rations ˌmanagement** *noun* [U]
the process of managing the main activities that a business does to make money, for example buying and selling goods or services, or manufacturing products ▶ˌ**ope'rations ˌmanager** *noun* [C]

ˌ**ope'rations ˌmanual** *noun* [C]
(*HR*) a document that describes the systems and processes that a company or an organization uses to perform its activities: *Safety procedures are outlined in the operations manual.*

ˌ**operations re'search** (*also* ˌ**operational re'search**) *noun* [U] (*abbr* **OR**)
the use of scientific methods and technology to improve the way a business performs its main activities: *Companies undertake operations research to optimize their use of resources.*

operative /ˈɒpərətɪv; *AmE* ˈɑːp-/ *noun, adjective*
● *noun* [C]
a worker who performs a practical task for a company: *customer service/machine operatives*

● *adjective*
ready to be used; in use: *The new law will become operative on 5 July.* ◇ *Our online store is now fully operative.*

★ **operator** /ˈɒpəreɪtə(r); *AmE* ˈɑːp-/ *noun* [C]

SEE ALSO: **owner-operator, tour operator**

1 (*often used with another noun*) a person or company that runs a particular business: *a bus/ferry/train operator* ◇ *a telecoms operator* ◇ *the UK's second-largest port operator*
2 (*often used with another noun*) a person who operates equipment or machinery: *a computer/machine operator*
3 (*BrE also* **te'lephonist**) a person who works on the telephone SWITCHBOARD of a large company or organization: *Dial 100 for the operator.*

o'**pinion ˌleader** *noun* [C]
(*Marketing*) a person whose tastes and opinions are respected within a social group, and who therefore influences what people in that group buy: *Many marketing campaigns aim to identify and target opinion leaders.*

o'**pinion poll** = POLL

OPM /ˌəʊ piː ˈem; *AmE* ˌoʊ/ *abbr*
(*Accounting, informal*) **other people's money** used to describe money that a business uses or invests which it has borrowed or which it owes

opportunism /ˌɒpəˈtjuːnɪzəm; *AmE* ˌɑːpərˈtuː-/ *noun* [U]
the practice of taking any opportunities that appear, without thinking about the future result of doing so: *Business opportunism has resulted in poor quality products from companies who are only motivated by short-term profits.*

opportunist /ˌɒpəˈtjuːnɪst; *AmE* ˌɑːpərˈtuː-/ (*also* **opportunistic** /ˌɒpətjuːˈnɪstɪk; *AmE* ˌɑːpərtuːˈn-/) *adjective* [usually before noun]
making use of an opportunity, especially to get an advantage for yourself; not done in a planned way: *The group acquired the struggling company last year in an opportunist move.* ▶ **oppor'tunist** *noun* [C]: *This new market is very attractive to business opportunists.* **opportunistically** /ˌɒpətjuːˈnɪstɪkli; *AmE* ˌɑːpərtuːˈn-/ *adverb*

★ **opportunity** /ˌɒpəˈtjuːnəti; *AmE* ˌɑːpərˈtuː-/ *noun* [C,U] (*plural* **opportunities**)

SEE ALSO: **equal employment opportunity, equal opportunity**

a time when a particular situation makes it possible for you to do sth or achieve sth: *Which markets offer the greatest opportunity for growth?* ◇ *We aim to create opportunities for our employees to have contact with customers.* ◇ *The central bank may take the opportunity to raise interest rates.* ◇ *The offer was too good an opportunity to miss.* ◇ *exploring new business/market opportunities* ◇ *The Internet has created a* **window of opportunity** (= a period of time when the circumstances are right for doing sth) *for the online travel industry to grow.*
◆ *to* **create/offer/open up/present/provide** *opportunities* ◆ *to* **exploit/have/look for/see/seize/take** *an opportunity* ◆ *an opportunity* **arises/exists** ◆ **business/investment/market** *opportunities* ◆ **career/employment/job** *opportunities* ◆ *a* **lost/missed** *opportunity*

ˌ**oppor'tunity cost** *noun* [C,U]
(*Economics*) the value of sth that could be done, made, chosen, etc., that will be lost when a decision is made to do a particular thing: *The opportunity cost of expanding the Marketing Department is that Human Resources will have to be*

made smaller. **NOTE** **Opportunity cost** is an important part of the process of making decisions.

oppor‚tunity to 'see *noun* [C, usually pl.] (*abbr* **OTS**)

(*Marketing*) a measure of the number of times that possible customers might be expected to see a particular advertisement in a newspaper, on television, on a website, etc. during a particular period: *In our campaigns, average OTS reaches 10 or more per week.*

oppose /ə'pəʊz; *AmE* ə'poʊz/ *verb* [+ obj]
to disagree strongly with sb's plan, policy, etc. and try to change it or prevent it from succeeding: *Business leaders strongly oppose an increase in the minimum wage.* ◇ *The majority of shareholders have opposed the deal.*

‚opposite 'number *noun* [C]
a person who does the same job as you in another organization: *The CEO received an angry letter from his opposite number at a rival company.* See note at COLLEAGUE

‚optical 'character recog‚nition *noun* [U] (*abbr* **OCR**)
(*IT*) the process of using light to record printed information onto disks for use in a computer system: *an OCR scanner*

optimal /'ɒptɪməl; *AmE* 'ɑːp-/ *adjective*

SEE ALSO: **Pareto-optimal**

the best; the most likely to be successful: *We are improving the manufacturing system to achieve an optimal level of performance.* → OPTIMUM
● *an optimal **level/performance/strategy/way*** ◆ *optimal **conditions/effectiveness***

optimism /'ɒptɪmɪzəm; *AmE* 'ɑːp-/ *noun* [U]
optimism (**about/for/over sth**) a feeling that good things will happen and that sth will be successful; the tendency to have this feeling: *There are very real grounds for optimism.* ◇ *The CEO expressed cautious optimism about the company's financial future.* ◇ *Both orders and business optimism rose last month.* **OPP** PESSIMISM
● ***business/consumer/investor/market** optimism* ◆ *to be **brimming with/express/show** optimism* ◆ *to **boost/fuel/increase** optimism*
▸ **'optimist** *noun* [C] **optimistic** /‚ɒptɪ'mɪstɪk; *AmE* ‚ɑːp-/ *adjective* **optimistically** /‚ɒptɪ'mɪstɪkli; *AmE* ‚ɑːp-/ *adverb*

optimize , **-ise** /'ɒptɪmaɪz; *AmE* 'ɑːp-/ *verb* [+ obj]
to make sth as good as it can be; to use sth in the best possible way: *to optimize the use of resources* ◇ *We need to optimize the plant to improve efficiency.*
▸ **optimization**, **-isation** /‚ɒptɪmaɪ'zeɪʃn; *AmE* ‚ɑːptɪmə'z-/ *noun* [U]: *The strategy focuses on the optimization of the supply chain.*

optimum /'ɒptɪməm; *AmE* 'ɑːp-/ *adjective, noun*
● *adjective* [only before noun]
the best; the number, size, etc. that will produce the best possible results: *The optimum temperature setting for the machine is 70°C.* ◇ *What is the optimum team size?* → OPTIMAL
● *the optimum **level/price/range/size/temperature***
● *noun* [sing.] **the optimum**
the best possible result, set of conditions, etc: *The fruit is grown in plastic tunnels where conditions are close to the optimum.*

'opt-in *noun* [C] (*often used as an adjective*)
1 the act of choosing to be part of a system or an agreement
2 (*Marketing*) when the user of a company's website gives their email address so that they can be sent information about particular subjects, products or services

★ option /'ɒpʃn; *AmE* 'ɑːp-/ *noun*

SEE ALSO: **call option, currency ~, employee stock ~, index ~, nuclear ~, put ~, share ~, stock ~**

1 [C,U] **option** (**of doing sth/to do sth**) something that you can choose to have or do; the freedom to choose what you do: *There are various options open to us.* ◇ *Employees were given the option of working four days a week.* ◇ *Closing the factory is **not an option.*** ◇ *This particular model comes with a wide range of options* (= extra things that you can choose to have).
● *to **have/give sb/offer sb** an option* ◆ *to **choose/take** an option*
2 (*Finance*) [C] the right to buy or sell a fixed quantity of shares, currencies or COMMODITIES (= for example, grain, coffee, cotton or metals) for a particular price within a particular period or on a particular date: *The five directors earned more than $3 million through the sale of shares and options.* ◇ *She has an option to buy 100 000 shares.* ◇ *When does the option expire?*
● *to **buy/exercise/sell/trade/write** an option* ◆ *an options **contract*** ◆ *the options **exchange/market***
3 (*Finance*) [C] the right to buy sth or more of sth in the future: *We have an option **on** the land and will purchase it soon.* ◇ *The airline has bought 100 planes with an option **for** another 50.*
● *to **have/exercise/take (up)** an option*

optional /'ɒpʃənl; *AmE* 'ɑːp-/ *adjective*
that you can choose to do or have if you want to: *You must wear a shirt and tie, but jackets are optional.* ◇ *This model comes with a number of **optional extras*** (= things you can choose to have but which you will have to pay extra for).

'opt-out *noun* [C] (*often used as an adjective*)
the act of choosing not to be involved in an agreement: *The contract contains an opt-out clause.*
◇ *to seek an opt-out from an agreement*

OR /‚əʊ 'ɑː(r); *AmE* ‚oʊ/ = OPERATIONS RESEARCH

orchestrate /'ɔːkɪstreɪt; *AmE* 'ɔːrk-/ *verb* [+ obj]
to organize a complicated plan or event very carefully and sometimes secretly: *a carefully orchestrated publicity campaign*

★ order /'ɔːdə(r); *AmE* 'ɔːrd-/ *noun, verb*
● *noun*

SEE ALSO: **administration order, advance ~, back ~, banker's ~, bank ~, bankruptcy ~, build-to-~,** etc.

1 [C,U] a request to make, supply or send goods: *I would like to place an order **for** ten copies of this book.* ◇ *The company has just won an order to supply engines to a French business airline.* ◇ *We have firm orders worth $9 million.* ◇ *Domestic and export orders are growing.* ◇ *The machine parts are still **on order*** (= they have been ordered but have not yet been received). ◇ *These items can be made **to order*** (= produced especially for a particular customer).
● *to **place/put** in an order* ◆ *to **have/fill/fulfil/meet/process** an order* ◆ *to **cancel/get/lose/receive/win** an order* ◆ *a **bulk/cash/firm/large/small** order* ◆ *a **repeat** order*
2 [C] goods that are made, supplied or sent in response to a particular order: *The stationery order has arrived.* ◇ *Your order will be dispatched immediately.*
3 [C] an official instruction that is given by a court or similar authority: *The order required them to return to work within 80 days or face redundancy.* ◇ *The order was issued by the court last May.*
● *to **grant/issue/make/obtain/seek** an order* ◆ *to **lift/remove** an order* ◆ *to **appeal/comply with/execute/obey** an order*
4 [C] a formal written instruction for sb to be paid money or to do sth: *You can cash the order at any post office.*
IDM **in 'order** (about an official document) that

can be used because it is all correct and legal: *Check that your work permit is in order.* SYN VALID

in running/working 'order (especially about machines) working well: *The engine is now in perfect working order.* **of/in the order of …** (*BrE*) (*AmE* **on the order of …**) (*formal*) about sth; approximately sth: *She earns something in the order of €50 000 a year.* **order of 'business** the arrangement of subjects for discussion at a meeting SYN AGENDA **out of 'order 1** (about a machine etc.) not working correctly: *The phone is out of order.* **2** not arranged correctly or neatly: *I checked the files and some of the papers were out of order.* **3** (*formal*) not allowed by the rules of a formal meeting or debate: *His objection was ruled out of order.* → idioms at BULK *noun*, CALL *verb*

● *verb* [+ obj]
1 order (sb) sth | order sth (for sb) to ask for goods to be made, supplied or sent; to ask for a service to be provided: *These boots can be ordered direct from the manufacturer.* ◇ *You can order our product on the Internet.* ◇ *Shall I order you a cab?* ◇ *Shall I order a cab for you?*
2 to use your position of authority to tell sb to do sth or say that sth must happen: *The government has ordered an investigation into the accident.* ◇ *The company was ordered to pay compensation to its former employees.*
3 to organize or arrange sth: *The program orders the files according to their size.*
PHRV **,order sb a'bout/a'round** to keep telling sb what to do in a way that is annoying or unpleasant

'order book *noun* [C]
(*Commerce*; *Manufacturing*) a record kept by a business of the products it has agreed to supply to its customers, often used to show how well the business is doing: *We have an order book of over €2 million.* ◇ *a full/strong order book* ◇ *The forward order book stood at $5 million as of the end of December.*

'order form *noun* [C]
a document completed by customers when ordering goods: *For an instant quote, simply fill out the online order form.*

'order ,getter (*also* **'order-,maker**) *noun* [C]
(*Marketing*) a person whose job is to persuade new customers to place orders with a company and existing customers to buy more → ORDER TAKER

'order ,picking *noun* [U]
(*Production*) the process of taking the goods that a customer has ordered out of the place where they are stored: *highly automated order-picking systems*

'order point (*also* **re'order point**) *noun* [C]
(*Commerce*; *Production*) the time when an order is automatically made for more supplies of an item because the number has fallen below a particular level, considering future demand and the time it takes to deliver it: *If the order point is set at 10, an order is placed when the inventory level falls below 10.*

'order ,processing *noun* [U]
(*Commerce*; *Production*)
1 all the activities involved in dealing with customers' orders from receiving them to delivering the goods: *The turnaround time for order processing is usually under 24 hours.*
2 the activity of checking and recording every stage of a customer's order as it is dealt with: *Our order processing software is designed to help you control the flow of customer orders throughout your organization.*

'order ,taker *noun* [C]
(*Marketing*) the role that a salesperson performs when they take orders from customers who already use or wish to use the company but do not persuade people to buy → ORDER GETTER

ordinary /'ɔ:dnri; *AmE* 'ɔ:rdneri/ (*plural* **ordinaries**) = ORDINARY SHARE

,ordinary 'capital *noun* [U]
(*Finance*) the amount of a company's CAPITAL that is held in ORDINARY SHARES

,ordinary 'creditor *noun* [C]
(*Finance*) a company or person who will be paid money they are owed by a company that is BANKRUPT (= does not have enough money to pay its debts) only after everybody else except people who hold ORDINARY SHARES

,ordinary 'interest *noun* [U]
(*Finance*) interest that is calculated based on a year of 360 days instead of 365

,ordinary reso'lution *noun* [C]
a formal statement that is accepted by a simple majority of shareholders present at a general meeting of a company

,ordinary 'share (*also* **'ordinary**) (*both BrE*) (*also* **common 'share**, *especially in BrE*) *noun* [C]
(*Finance*) a share in a company that gives the owner the right to a DIVIDEND (= money paid to shareholders) according to how much profit the company has made, and usually the right to vote at meetings of shareholders: *The company plans to sell 6.2 million new ordinary shares.* → COMMON STOCK, EQUITY (2), PREFERENCE SHARE See note at SHARE

,ordinary 'stock = COMMON STOCK

organic /ɔ:'gænɪk; *AmE* ɔ:r'g-/ *adjective* [usually before noun]
1 used to describe the situation when a company develops its existing business rather than growing by buying other companies, etc: *The group announced plans for organic expansion and said it would open 830 new stores in 2007.* ◇ *Sales are up 6.3 per cent, driven by strong organic growth.* → INTERNAL (2)
○ *organic* **development/expansion/growth**
2 (about food, farming methods, etc.) produced or practised without using artificial chemicals: *organic cheese/milk/vegetables* ◇ *The share of agricultural land under organic farming has increased considerably in the last ten years.*
▶ **organically** /ɔ:'gænɪkli; *AmE* ɔ:r'g-/ *adverb*

organigram (*also spelled* **organogram**) /ɔ:'gænəgræm; *AmE* ɔ:r'gæn-/ *noun* [C]
a diagram that shows the structure of a company or an organization and the relationship between different jobs SYN ORGANIZATION CHART—Picture on page 380

★ **organization**, **-isation** /ˌɔ:gənaɪ'zeɪʃn; *AmE* ˌɔ:rgənə'z-/ *noun*

SEE ALSO: functional organization, International Labour ~, virtual ~

1 [C] a group of people who form a business or other group together in order to achieve a particular aim: *He's the president of a large international organization.* ◇ *the World Trade Organization* ◇ *The proposals were discussed at all levels of the organization.*
○ *a* **business/commercial/profit-making** *organization* • *a* **charitable/non-profit** *organization* • *a* **high-performance/large/small** *organization* • *to* **build/create/form/head/manage/run** *an organization* • *to* **join/leave** *an organization*
2 [U] the act of making arrangements or preparations for sth: *I leave most of the organization of these conferences to my assistant.* SYN PLANNING
○ **careful/efficient/poor/smooth** *organization* • *to* **lack/need/take** *organization*

3 [U] the way in which the different parts of sth are arranged: *The report studies the organization of labour within the company.* [SYN] STRUCTURE
▶ **organizational, -isational** /ˌɔːɡənaɪˈzeɪʃənl; AmE ˌɔːrɡənəˈz-/ *adjective* [only before noun]: *organizational change/structure* ◇ *organizational skills/ability*

organizational be'haviour (AmE spelling ~ **behavior**) *noun* [U] (*abbr* **OB**)
(HR) the study of the behaviour and attitudes of people within an organization and how they affect the way the organization works

organizational communi'cation = CORPORATE COMMUNICATION

organizational 'culture = CORPORATE CULTURE

organizational 'learning *noun* [U] (*abbr* **OL**)
(HR) the process in which people and groups within an organization continuously gain knowledge and develop skills, with the result that the organization can change and improve

organization and 'methods *noun* [U with sing./pl. verb] (*abbr* **OM, O&M**)
1 an analysis of the way an organization works and is arranged, and how it could be made more efficient: *organization and methods projects/studies*
2 the department in a company that does this

organi'zation chart *noun* [C]
a diagram that shows the structure of a company or an organization and the relationship between different jobs—Picture at ORGANIGRAM

organi'zation ,theory *noun* [U]
techniques for studying the structure, aims and strategies of organizations

★ **organize**, **-ise** /ˈɔːɡənaɪz; AmE ˈɔːrɡ-/ *verb*
1 [+ obj] to arrange for sth to happen or to be provided: *He organizes workshops on starting a business.* ◇ *The meetings were organized by different departments.* → RUN *verb* (2) See note at ARRANGE
2 [+ obj] to put or arrange things into a logical order or system: *Modern computers can organize large amounts of data very quickly.* ◇ *You should try and organize your time better.* ◇ *Sales information is organized by area.*
3 [+ obj *or* no obj] to form a union or a group of people with a shared aim: *the right of workers to organize themselves into unions*

organized, **-ised** /ˈɔːɡənaɪzd; AmE ˈɔːrɡ-/ *adjective*
1 arranged or planned in a particular way: *a well-organized office* ◇ *a badly organized event*
2 working well and in an efficient way: *This is one of the most organized companies I have ever worked with.* ◇ *She used to be such an organized person.*
3 [only before noun] involving large numbers of people who work together to do sth in a way that has been carefully planned: *an organized body of workers*

organized 'labour (AmE spelling ~ **labor**) *noun* [U]
employees who are members of a union

organizer, **-iser** /ˈɔːɡənaɪzə(r); AmE ˈɔːrɡ-/ *noun* [C]
1 a person who arranges for sth to happen or to be provided: *conference organizers* ◇ *She offered to be one of the organizers of the event.*
2 (IT) a very small computer that keeps information about people, what you have arranged to do, etc: *an electronic/a handheld organizer*
→ PERSONAL ORGANIZER See note at CALENDAR

organizing ,business *noun* [C]
a company that offers products and services to help people arrange their offices, their homes or their work in a tidy and efficient way; all the companies involved in this

organogram = ORGANIGRAM

-orientated /ˈɔːriənteɪtɪd/ = -ORIENTED

orientation /ˌɔːriənˈteɪʃn/ *noun*

SEE ALSO: **marketing orientation, market ~, product ~, sales ~**

1 [U,C] the type of aims or interests that an organization or a person has; the act of directing your aims towards a particular thing: *The business school is international in orientation.* ◇ *We want to hire people with a service orientation.* ◇ *Companies have been forced into a greater orientation to the market.*
2 (HR) [U] training or information that are given before starting a new job, course, etc: *New employees undergo a two-day orientation programme.*

-oriented /ˈɔːriəntɪd/ (BrE also **-orientated**)
combining form (used to form adjectives)
having the aim mentioned: *market-oriented* ◇ *profit-oriented* ◇ *relationship-oriented managers*

organigram

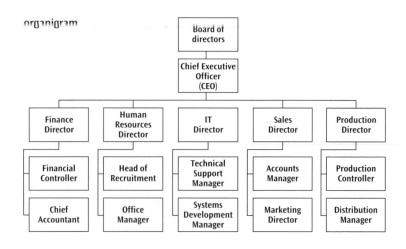

origin /'ɒrɪdʒɪn; AmE 'ɔːr-; 'ɑːr-/ noun [C,U]

SEE ALSO: **certificate of origin**

1 (also **'origins** [pl.]) the point from which sth starts; the cause of sth: *What is the origin of the name 'Coca-Cola'?* ◇ *The origins of the Internet go back to the 1950s.*
2 the place from which goods come: *We need to know the supplier, price and country of origin.* ◇ *Can you prove the origin of the goods?*
○ *the country/place/point of* origin

original /ə'rɪdʒənl/ noun [C]
a document from which copies are later made: *Send out the photocopies and keep the original.*

o,riginal e'quipment manu,facturer
= OEM

originate /ə'rɪdʒɪneɪt/ verb
1 [no obj] to start in a particular way or place, or at a particular time: *The business originated as a shoe shop, but now offers a full range of clothing.* ◇ *The program tells you where your emails originated.*
2 [+ obj] to create sth new: *They hired a consultant to help them originate new business.*
3 (Finance) [+ obj] to arrange a loan for sb, especially a loan for buying a home (**mortgage**): *The tiny six-employee operation originates mortgage loans for home buyers.*
▶ **o'riginator** noun [C]: *The originator of the virus was a student in the US.* ◇ *a loan/mortgage originator*

origination /ə,rɪdʒɪ'neɪʃn/ noun [U]
1 (Marketing) the process of finding or developing a new product or service to sell: *The first step in the origination of a product is to have an idea or a design.*
2 (Finance) the process of arranging a loan for a new customer: *mortgage origination* ◇ *origination fees/costs*
3 the process of preparing images or text so that they can be printed: *The origination process involves transferring the digital designs onto plastic film.*

OS /,əʊ 'es; AmE ,oʊ/ abbr
1 (IT) = OPERATING SYSTEM
2 (Commerce, only used in written English) (also spelled **O/S**) out of stock → STOCK noun (1)
3 (Accounting) (also spelled **O/S**) a short way to write **outstanding** in financial records
4 (Commerce, usually used in written English) (about clothes) outsize

oscillate /'ɒsɪleɪt; AmE 'ɑːs-/ verb [no obj]
1 to keep moving from one position to another and back again: *The cylinder oscillates to mix the liquids.*
2 to keep changing from one level or value to another and back again: *The dollar has been oscillating between 107 and 110 yen.* [SYN] SWING
▶ **oscillation** /,ɒsɪ'leɪʃn; AmE ,ɑːs-/ noun [C]: *the economy's oscillation between growth and recession*

OTC /,əʊ tiː 'siː; AmE ,oʊ/ = OVER-THE-COUNTER

OTE abbr (only used in written English)
(HR)
1 (BrE) **on-target earnings** used in advertisements to describe the pay that sb, especially a SALESPERSON, should be able to earn, including any extra pay for the amount of goods they sell
2 **ordinary time earnings** used especially in Australia and New Zealand to describe the total pay that employees receive in a particular period of time, not including pay for working after the normal hours

other /'ʌðə(r)/ adjective
(Accounting) used in financial records to describe amounts of money that are small enough not to be listed separately in specific named groups: *other current assets* ◇ *other long-term liabilities*

OTS /,əʊ tiː 'es; AmE ,oʊ/ = OPPORTUNITY TO SEE

ounce /aʊns/ noun [C] (abbr **oz**)
a unit for measuring weight, equal to 28.35 grams

oust /aʊst/ verb [+ obj]
(used especially in newspapers) to force sb out of a job or a position of power, especially in order to take their place: *He was ousted as chairman.* ◇ *The boss of the group was ousted from his job by fellow directors.* ◇ (figurative) *The new product may oust the market leader from its position.* ▶ **'ousting** noun [U]: *the ousting of the chief executive*

ouster /'aʊstə(r)/ noun [C, usually sing.] (AmE)
(often used in newspapers) the act of removing sb from a position of authority in order to put sb else in their place; the fact of being removed in this way: *the ouster of the board of directors* ◇ *shareholders seeking the CEO's ouster*

out /aʊt/ adjective, adverb

SEE ALSO: **clean-out, earn-~, face ~, first in, first ~, fold-~, last in, first ~, mail-~,** etc.

1 out (of sth) away from or not at work or home: *Mrs Kanu is out of the office this week.* ◇ *He isn't answering the phone—he must have gone out.*
2 available to buy for the first time: *The latest version will be out next month.*
3 (especially BrE) (informal) on strike: *The dockers stayed out for several months.*
4 not correct or exact; wrong: *The estimate was out by more than $2 million.*
5 (AmE) if a machine is **out**, it is not working
6 (informal) no longer fashionable: *This style of jacket is out now.*
7 out (of sth) used to show that sth/sb is removed from a place, job, etc: *Shareholders want the board out.*
[IDM] **out of 'line (with sb/sth)** different from sth: *Assets can get out of line with incomes.* ◇ *The fees are not out of line with the market.* **out of sth 1** used to show that sb does not have sth: *I was out of work for six months.* ◇ *We're out of printer paper—I'll order some more.* **2** from a particular number or set: *Nine out of ten people we asked said they would buy this product.* **out of the 'box** (about a system or device) not requiring much effort to prepare it for use: *The mouse can be used straight out of the box.* ◇ *The software is a complete out-of-the-box solution for document management.* → idiom at JURY

out- /aʊt/ prefix (in verbs)
greater, better, further, longer, etc: *outnumber* ◇ *outbid*

outage /'aʊtɪdʒ/ noun [C] (AmE)
a period of time when the supply of electricity, etc. is not working: *a power outage*

'out-,basket = OUT TRAY

outbid /,aʊt'bɪd/ verb [+ obj] (**outbidding, outbid, outbid**)
(Commerce; Finance) to offer more money than sb else in order to buy sth, for example at an AUCTION: *The German group outbid several others for a controlling share in the publisher.* ◇ *We were outbid on the contract.*

outbound /'aʊtbaʊnd/ adjective
travelling away from a place rather than arriving in it: *The strike will affect outbound flights only.* ◇ *The service department makes outbound calls from 9 a.m. and receives incoming calls 24 hours a day.* ◇ *outbound shipments* [OPP] INBOUND → INCOMING (2)

,outbound 'telemarketing noun [U]
(Marketing) selling goods or services by telephoning possible customers → INBOUND TELEMARKETING

outbox /'aʊtbɒks; AmE -bɑ:ks/ noun [C]
1 (IT) the place on a computer where new email messages that you write are stored before you send them
2 (also spelled **out-box**) (also '**out-**, **basket**) (all especially AmE) = OUT TRAY

★ **outcome** /'aʊtkʌm/ noun [C]
the result or effect of an action or event: We are waiting to hear the final outcome of the negotiations. ◇ We are confident of a successful outcome. ◇ helping teams to achieve their desired business outcomes

outdated /,aʊt'deɪtɪd/ adjective
no longer useful because of being old-fashioned: It is an outdated and inefficient system. → OUT OF DATE
○ outdated **equipment/laws/methods/practices/products**

,**outdoor 'advertising** (also ,out-of-home 'advertising) noun [U]
(Marketing) methods of advertising that are used in the open air, for example BILLBOARDS, signs, advertisements on the outside of buildings, on vehicles, etc.

outer /'aʊtə(r)/ noun [C]
(Commerce; Transport) a container in which goods already in boxes, bags, etc. are packed to be transported or displayed

outfit /'aʊtfɪt/ noun, verb
• noun
1 (informal) [C with sing./pl.verb] a group of people working together as an organization, a business, a team, etc: a market research outfit ◇ a 12-person outfit producing music software
2 [C] a set of clothes that you wear together, especially for a particular occasion or purpose: The sales team wear dark blue outfits.
• verb [+ obj] (-tt-) (especially AmE) (often be outfitted) to provide sb/sth with equipment or clothes for a special purpose: workstations outfitted with the latest technology [SYN] EQUIP
▶ '**outfitting** noun [U]

outflow /'aʊtfləʊ; AmE -floʊ/ noun [C]
1 the movement of a large amount of money, people, etc. out of a country, an area, a company or an organization: an outflow of cash from the group ◇ an outflow of skilled and professional people from the area
2 (HR) the way in which employees leave their jobs in an organization, for example, if they are dismissed, retire or stop work because there is no more work for them
[OPP] INFLOW

outgoing /,aʊt'gəʊɪŋ; AmE -'goʊ-/ adjective [only before noun]
1 leaving the position of responsibility mentioned: the outgoing chairman/board
2 going away from a particular place rather than arriving in it: This telephone should not be used for outgoing calls. ◇ outgoing flights
[OPP] INCOMING

outgoings /'aʊtgəʊɪŋz; AmE -goʊ-/ noun [pl.] (BrE)
the amount of money that a business or a person has to spend regularly, for example every month: Many small businesses are struggling to meet their outgoings. ◇ Their mortgage was 75% of their total outgoings. [OPP] INCOMINGS

outlay /'aʊtleɪ/ noun [C,U]
(Finance) the money that you have to spend in order to start a new project or to save yourself money or time later: The increase in sales quickly repaid the outlay **on** advertising. ◇ The new machines represent a total outlay of $1.5 million. → CAPITAL OUTLAY

○ **business/cash/financial** outlays • **a high/massive/small** outlay • **an initial/a total** outlay

outlet /'aʊtlet/ noun [C]

SEE ALSO: **factory outlet**

1 a shop/store or an organization that sells goods made by a particular company or of a particular type: The business has 34 retail outlets in this state alone.
○ **a convenience/fast food/gambling/retail/sales** outlet
2 (especially AmE) a shop/store that sells goods of a particular make at reduced prices: Nike outlets are supplied direct from the factory.
3 a way of making information or goods available to the public: a media/an Internet outlet

outline /'aʊtlaɪn/ verb, noun
• verb [+ obj]
to give a description of the main facts or points involved in sth: We outlined our proposals **to** the committee.
• noun [C]
1 a description of the main facts or points involved in sth: First I would like to give you a brief outline of our company's history. ◇ The report describes **in outline** the main findings of the research.
[SYN] OVERVIEW
○ to **do/give/make/publish/write** an outline (of sth) • **a brief/broad/rough/simple** outline • an outline **agreement/plan/proposal**
2 the line that goes around the edge of sth, showing its main shape but not the details: an outline map/sketch

★ **outlook** /'aʊtlʊk/ noun [C]
1 the probable future for sb/sth; what is likely to happen: The outlook **for** the financial industry is good. ◇ The study confirms a bleak outlook for the tech industry. ◇ the country's economic outlook
○ **a bright/an improving/upbeat** outlook • **a bleak/cautious/downbeat/gloomy/an uncertain** outlook • **a corporate/an earnings/economic/a financial** outlook
2 the way in which sb sees or judges sth: The credit rating agency revised its outlook **on** the bank from 'stable' to 'negative'.

,**out-of-'court** adjective [only before noun]
(Law) agreed or decided without going to a court of law: an out-of-court settlement

,**out of 'date** adjective
1 old-fashioned or without the most recent information and therefore no longer useful: These figures are very out of date. ◇ out-of-date technology → OUTDATED
2 no longer valid: This licence is out of date. → UP TO DATE

,**out-of-'favour** (AmE spelling ~ **favor**) adjective
not popular: out-of-favour businesses/stocks

,**out-of-home 'advertising** = OUTDOOR ADVERTISING

'**out-of-'house** adjective [only before noun]
working or happening outside a company or an organization: an out-of-house designer (= who works at home, for example) ▶ ,**out-of-'house** adverb: Less than 4% of our products are now made out-of-house. [OPP] IN-HOUSE

,**out-of-'pocket** adjective [only before noun]
1 used to describe costs that you pay directly yourself: Travelling and out-of-pocket expenses will be met by the firm.
2 (Insurance) (AmE) used to describe money that you pay for health care that is not covered by insurance
→ POCKET

,**out-of-'town** *adjective*
1 situated away from the centre of a town or city: *out-of-town superstores/sites*
2 coming from or happening in a different place: *an out-of-town client/trip*

,**out of 'work** *adjective, adverb*
unemployed: *How long have you been out of work?* ◇ *an out-of-work security guard* ◇ *The factory closed, putting 600 people out of work.* [SYN] UNEMPLOYED

outpace /ˌaʊtˈpeɪs/ *verb* [+ obj]
to go, improve, do sth, etc. faster than sb/sth: *Demand is outpacing production.* [SYN] OUTSTRIP

outperform /ˌaʊtpəˈfɔːm; *AmE* -pərˈfɔːrm/ *verb*
1 [+ obj] to achieve better results than sb/sth: *We have consistently outperformed our larger rivals.*
2 [+ obj *or no obj*] (about shares, bonds, etc.) to provide more profit than the average shares, bonds, etc. of a similar type: *These shares have been outperforming most of the market.* ◇ *The stock has been upgraded to 'outperform'.*
→ UNDERPERFORM
▶ **outperformance** /-pəˈfɔːməns; *AmE* -pərˈfɔːrməns/ *noun* [U]: *Most investors are looking for consistent outperformance.* ,**outper'former** *noun* [C]: *The stock is rated as a market outperformer.*

outplacement /ˈaʊtpleɪsmənt/ *noun* (*HR*)
1 [U,C] a service that a company offers to help people to find new jobs when the company can no longer employ them: *Employees who have been made redundant will be offered outplacement services.*
2 [C, usually sing.] a person that a company can no longer employ

outpost /ˈaʊtpəʊst; *AmE* -poʊst/ *noun* [C]
a small town or group of buildings in a lonely part of the country: *a remote outpost* ◇ (*figurative*) *He managed the New Zealand outpost of a large American bank.*

★ **output** /ˈaʊtpʊt/ *noun, verb*
● *noun* [U,C]
1 the amount of sth that a person, a machine, an organization or an industry produces: *Manufacturing output has risen by 8%.* ◇ *The larger workforce will increase the plant's annual output from 1.1 to 1.8 million tonnes.* ◇ *Greater efficiency leads to higher outputs.* ◇ *Output per worker hour has more than doubled in the third quarter of the year.* → INPUT See note at PRODUCE
○ *agricultural/economic/engineering/factory/ industrial/manufacturing* output ◆ *domestic/ global/national/regional/world* output ◆ *average/ overall/total* output ◆ *high/low/strong/weak* output ◆ *to boost/increase/lift/raise* output ◆ *to cut/ decrease/reduce* output ◆ *growing/improved/rising* output ◆ *dwindling/falling* output
2 (*IT*) the information, results, etc. produced by a computer: *data output* ◇ *an output device* → INPUT
3 (*Technical*) the power, energy, etc. produced by a piece of equipment: *an output of 100 watts*
4 a place where energy, power, information, etc. leaves a system: *Connect the cable to the output.*
● *verb* [+ obj] (**outputting, output, output**) *or* (**outputting, outputted, outputted**)
1 (*IT*) to supply or produce information, etc: *Computers can now output data much more quickly.*
2 (*Manufacturing*) to produce a quantity of goods: *We are capable of outputting goods in huge runs.*
→ INPUT

'**output tax** *noun* [C,U] (*BrE*)
(*Accounting*) the amount of tax (**VAT**) that a company adds to the price of its goods or services
→ INPUT TAX

outsell /ˌaʊtˈsel/ *verb* [+ obj] (**outsold, outsold** /-ˈsəʊld; *AmE* -ˈsoʊld/)
1 (about a product) to be sold in larger quantities than sth else: *Laptop computers may in the future outsell desktops.*
2 (about a company) to sell more products than another company: *Microsoft continues to outsell its competitors.*

,**outside di'rector** = NON-EXECUTIVE DIRECTOR

outsider /ˌaʊtˈsaɪdə(r)/ *noun* [C]
1 a person who is not part of a particular organization or profession: *The company brought in an outsider to assess its efficiency.* ◇ *They have decided to hire outsiders for some of the key positions.*
2 a person who is not accepted as a member of a society, group, etc: *The workforce still consider the new CEO an outsider.*

,**outside 'shareholder** *noun* [C]
any shareholder in a company who is not the shareholder that owns more than half of the company's shares: *Mr Malone is the largest outside shareholder in News Corp.*

,**outside 'worker** *noun* [C]
(*HR*) a person who works for a company but does not work in the offices, factory, etc. → INSIDE WORKER

outsize /ˈaʊtsaɪz/ (*also* **outsized** /ˈaʊtsaɪzd/) *adjective* [only before noun]
1 larger than the usual size: *These huge trucks deal with outsize cargo.* ◇ *People bought the investments hoping to make outsized returns on them.*
2 designed for larger people: *outsize clothing*

★ **outsourcing** /ˈaʊtsɔːsɪŋ; *AmE* -sɔːrs-/ *noun* [U]
(*HR*) the process of arranging for sb outside a company to produce goods or provide services for that company: *the outsourcing of catering* ◇ *cost savings from IT outsourcing* ◇ *outsourcing contracts/ deals* ▶ '**outsource** *verb* [+ obj *or no obj*]: *We outsource all our computing work.* → INSOURCING, SUBCONTRACT

outstanding /ˌaʊtˈstændɪŋ/ *adjective*

SEE ALSO: **shares outstanding**
---
1 (about payment, work, problems, etc.) not yet paid, done, solved, etc: *The money we received enabled us to pay off outstanding debts.* ◇ *The payment was still outstanding after 28 days.* ◇ *There are a number of outstanding questions about the timing of the changes.* → OVERDUE
2 extremely good; excellent: *This year's results have been outstanding.* ◇ *We plan to reward employees for outstanding performance.*

,**outstanding 'shares** (*also* ,**shares out'standing**) *noun* [pl.] (*also* ,**outstanding 'stock** [U])
(*Finance*) the number of a company's shares that are currently owned by investors → FLOAT *noun* (4), ISSUED CAPITAL

outstrip /ˌaʊtˈstrɪp/ *verb* [+ obj] (**-pp-**)
1 to become larger, more important, etc. than sb/ sth: *Demand is outstripping supply.* ◇ *Industrial production has risen 2.5%, outstripping forecasts of a 0.6% rise.* [SYN] OVERTAKE
2 to be faster, better or more successful than a competitor: *Their latest computer outstrips its rivals.*

'**out tray** (*also* '**out-,basket**, '**outbox**, *especially in AmE*) *noun* [C]
an open container in an office for letters or documents that are waiting to be sent out or passed to sb else : *I'll sign the reports and leave them in my out tray.* → IN TRAY

'out-turn (*also spelled* **outturn**, *especially in AmE*)
noun [U; C, *usually sing.*]
(*Finance*)
1 the amount of goods or money produced in a
particular period of time: *The out-turn for steel
production for 2004 was 1.2% higher than the
previous year.* SYN OUTPUT
2 (*BrE*) the amount of money spent by an
organization in a particular period → ACTUALS

outvote /ˌaʊt'vəʊt; *AmE* -'voʊt/ *verb* [+ obj] (*usually
be outvoted*)
to defeat sb/sth by winning a larger number of
votes: *His proposal was outvoted by 10 votes to 8.*

outward /'aʊtwəd; *AmE* -wərd/ *adjective* [only
before noun]
1 going away from a particular place, especially
one that you are going to return to: *the outward
journey*
2 away from the centre or a particular point: *The
regional government organizes outward trade
missions for local exporters.* ◇ *Managers need to
become more outward-looking.* OPP INWARD

ˌoutward in'vestment *noun* [U,C]
(*Finance*) investment made by one country or area
in another: *Outward investment by home-based
manufacturing firms has been mainly in Europe.*
→ INWARD INVESTMENT ▶ **ˌoutward in'vestor**
noun [C]

outwork /'aʊtwɜːk; *AmE* -wɜːrk/ *noun, verb*
(*HR*)
● *noun* [U] (*BrE*)
work that is done by people working outside the
factory or office, for example at home
▶ **'outworker** *noun* [C] (*BrE*)
● *verb*
1 [no obj] (*BrE*) to do **outwork** for a business
2 ˌout'work [+ obj] to work harder or faster than
other people
▶ **'outworking** *noun* [U]

overachieve /ˌəʊvərə'tʃiːv; *AmE* -oʊ-/ *verb* [+ obj
or no obj]
to do better than expected: *We overachieved our
targets.* ◇ *overachieving companies/leaders*
▶ **ˌovera'chievement** *noun* [U] , **ˌovera'chiever**
noun [C]: *He has recruited a team of young, talented
overachievers.*

overage /'əʊvərɪdʒ; *AmE* 'oʊ-/ *noun* [U,C] (*AmE*)
an amount of goods, money, etc. that is more than
is needed or expected: *Any cash shortage or overage
of funds must be reported.* SYN OVERSUPPLY
→ SURPLUS

overall *adjective, adverb, noun*
● *adjective* /ˌəʊvər'ɔːl; *AmE* ˌoʊ-/ [only before noun]
including all the things or people that are involved
in a particular situation; general: *the person with
overall responsibility for the project* ◇ *Despite some
problems, there has been an overall improvement.*
● *adverb* /ˌəʊvər'ɔːl; *AmE* ˌoʊ-/ including everything or
everyone; in total: *The company will invest $1.6
million overall in new equipment.*
● *noun* /'əʊvərɔːl; *AmE* 'oʊ-/ [C]
1 (*BrE*) a loose coat worn over other clothes to
protect them from dirt, etc: *All laboratory staff must
wear a white overall at all times.*
2 **overalls** (*BrE*) (*AmE* **'coveralls**) [pl.] a loose piece
of clothing like a shirt and trousers/pants in one
piece, made of heavy fabric and usually worn over
other clothing by workers doing dirty work: *The
mechanic was wearing a pair of blue overalls.*

overallotment /ˌəʊvərə'lɒtmənt; *AmE*
ˌoʊvərə'lɑːt-/ *noun* [U,C]
(*Finance*) a situation where people are allowed to
order more shares, bonds, etc. than are available,

as it is likely that some people will cancel their
order: *The debt sale has an overallotment of $75
million.* ▶ **ˌoveral'lot** *verb* [+ obj] (**-tt-**)

overbanked /ˌəʊvə'bæŋkt; *AmE* ˌoʊvər'b-/
adjective
used to describe a financial system in which there
are too many banks, which then cannot make much
money

overbook /ˌəʊvə'bʊk; *AmE* ˌoʊvər'bʊk/ *verb* [+ obj]
to sell more tickets on a plane or reserve more
rooms in a hotel than there are places or rooms
available: *These flights are usually overbooked by 10-
15 passengers.* ▶ **ˌover'booking** *noun* [U,C]: *New
regulations will limit the practice of overbooking.*

overborrow /ˌəʊvə'bɒrəʊ; *AmE* ˌoʊvər'bɑːroʊ/
verb [no obj]
to borrow more money than you are able to pay
back or pay interest on: *Business start-ups tend to
overborrow when interest rates are low.*
▶ **ˌover'borrowed** *adjective*: *Overborrowed
countries must slow their economies to reduce
imports.* **ˌover'borrowing** *noun* [U,C]

overbought /ˌəʊvə'bɔːt; *AmE* ˌoʊvər'b-/ *adjective*
(*Stock Exchange*) used to describe a situation when
the value of shares, a currency, etc. has risen too
high as too many people have been buying: *The
stock market is currently overbought.* ◇ *overbought
shares* → OVERBUY, OVERSOLD

overbuy /ˌəʊvə'baɪ; *AmE* ˌoʊvər'baɪ/ *verb* [+ obj *or
no obj*] (**overbought, overbought** /ˌəʊvə'bɔːt; *AmE*
ˌoʊvər'bɔːt/)
(*Commerce*) to buy too much of sth: *Our new stock
control system makes overbuying less likely.*
→ OVERBOUGHT

overcapacity /ˌəʊvəkə'pæsəti; *AmE* ˌoʊvərkə-/
noun [U; *sing.*]
(*Economics*) a situation in which an industry or a
factory cannot sell as much as it is designed to
produce: *Mounting overcapacity in the steel industry
is driving prices down.* → OVERSUPPLY

overcapitalized , **-ised** /ˌəʊvə'kæpɪtəlaɪzd; *AmE*
ˌoʊvər'k-/ *adjective*
(*Finance*) (about a business) having more money
(**capital**) than is reasonable for its business needs or
the amount of profit it is able to earn
OPP UNDERCAPITALIZED → CAPITALIZED

★ **overcharge** /ˌəʊvə'tʃɑːdʒ; *AmE* ˌoʊvər'tʃɑːrdʒ/
verb [+ obj *or no obj*]
to make sb pay too much for sth, often by mistake:
They have overcharged us for these parts. ◇ *The bank
was accused of overcharging customers by billions of
dollars each year.* ▶ **'overcharge** *noun* [C]: *Many of
the bills included overcharges or other errors.*
OPP UNDERCHARGE

★ **overdraft** /'əʊvədrɑːft; *AmE* 'oʊvərdræft/ (*also
ˌbank 'overdraft*) *noun* [C]
(*Finance*) the amount of money that you owe to a
bank when you have spent more money than is in
your bank account; an arrangement that allows
you to do this: *We have a €20 million overdraft with
the National Bank.* ◇ *There is a €50 fee for an
unauthorized overdraft.* ◇ *We need to renegotiate our
overdraft facility.* See note at LOAN
● *to* **apply for/arrange/extend/have** *an overdraft* ◆ *to*
pay off/run up *an overdraft* ◆ *an overdraft* **facility** ◆
an **agreed/authorized/unauthorized** *overdraft*

★ **overdraw** /ˌəʊvə'drɔː; *AmE* ˌoʊvər'drɔː/ *verb*
[+ obj] (**overdrew** /-'druː/ **overdrawn** /-'drɔːn/)
(*especially BrE*)
(*Finance*) to take more money out of your bank
account than is in it: *We have overdrawn our
account by €100 000.*

overdrawn /ˌəʊvə'drɔːn; *AmE* ˌoʊvər'd-/ *adjective*
[not usually before noun] (*abbr* **o/d, DR**)
(*Finance*) (about a company or person) having taken

more money out of a bank account than was in it: *The firm is €5 million overdrawn.* ◊ *The firm is overdrawn **by** €5 million.* ◊ *We are about to go overdrawn.* ◊ *Your balance is €305 DR.* → CREDIT

overdue /ˌəʊvəˈdjuː; *AmE* ˌoʊvərˈduː/ *adjective*
not paid, done, returned, etc. by the required or expected time: *Some of the payments are 90 days overdue.* ◊ *overdue payments* ◊ *These computers are overdue **for** updating.* → OUTSTANDING

overestimate *verb, noun*
● *verb* /ˌəʊvərˈestɪmeɪt; *AmE* ˌoʊ-/ [+ obj]
1 to think or guess that the amount, cost or size of sth is larger than it really is: *The firm failed because it overestimated sales and underestimated costs.*
2 to think sb is better, stronger, etc. than they really are: *Have we overestimated the competition?* ◊ *They overestimated his ability when they promoted him.*
[OPP] UNDERESTIMATE
▶ **overestimation** /ˌəʊvərestɪˈmeɪʃn; *AmE* ˌoʊ-/ *noun* [C,U]
● *noun* /ˌəʊvərˈestɪmət; *AmE* ˌoʊ-/ [C, usually sing.]
an estimate about the size, cost, etc. of sth that is too high: *Our projection of 200 000 sales turned out to be a massive overestimate.* [OPP] UNDERESTIMATE

overextended /ˌəʊvərɪkˈstendɪd; *AmE* ˌoʊ-/ *adjective* [not usually before noun]
1 (*Finance*) spending or borrowing more money than you can manage without risking problems: *Consumers are seriously overextended.* ◊ *overextended borrowers*
2 involved in more work or activities than you can manage: *Many company managers are severely overextended.* ◊ *The firm found itself overextended and unable to supply all its orders.*
▶ ˌover**ex'tend** *verb* [+ obj]: *The group overextended itself by purchasing a publishing company.*

overfunded /ˌəʊvəˈfʌndɪd; *AmE* ˌoʊvərˈf-/ *adjective*
(*Finance*) (about an organization, a project, etc.) having received more money than is necessary or than is allowed: *an overfunded company/plan*
[OPP] UNDERFUNDED
▶ ˌover'**fund** *verb* [+ obj], ˌover'**funding** *noun* [U]: *the overfunding of new companies*

overgeared /ˌəʊvəˈɡɪəd; *AmE* ˌoʊvərˈɡɪrd/ = OVER-LEVERAGED

overhang *noun, verb*
● *noun* /ˈəʊvəhæŋ; *AmE* ˈoʊvər-/ [C, usually sing.]

SEE ALSO: **debt overhang**

1 (*Commerce*) (*especially AmE*) the state of being extra to what is required; the things that are extra: *attempts to reduce the overhang **of** unsold goods* ◊ *We have a massive stock overhang **in** children's wear.*
2 (*Stock Exchange*) a large number of shares that have not been sold or which are held by an important shareholder, and which, if they were offered for sale all at the same time, would make prices fall: *The share overhang remains a worry for investors.*
● *verb* /ˌəʊvəˈhæŋ; *AmE* ˌoʊvərˈh-/ [+ obj] (**overhung**, **overhung** /-ˈhʌŋ/)
to have an influence and a negative effect on sth: *Soaring oil prices continue to overhang the stock market.*

overhaul *noun, verb*
● *noun* /ˈəʊvəhɔːl; *AmE* ˈoʊvər-/ [C]
an examination of a system, machine, etc., including making changes to it or doing repairs: *Our distribution system is in need of a major overhaul.* ◊ *The group has undertaken a strategic overhaul.*
⊙ *a complete/major/radical/sweeping overhaul* ◆ *to need/undergo an overhaul* ◆ *to carry out/plan an overhaul*

● *verb* /ˌəʊvəˈhɔːl; *AmE* ˌoʊvərˈh-/ [+ obj]
to examine every part of a system, machine, etc. and make any necessary changes or repairs: *We are working on a project to overhaul the IT system.*

overhead /ˈəʊvəhed; *AmE* ˈoʊvərhed/ *noun, adjective*
● *noun*

SEE ALSO: **direct overhead, indirect overhead**

1 (*Accounting*) (*especially AmE*) [U] = OVERHEADS
2 [C] a piece of transparent film with text, diagrams, etc. on, that is shown using an OVERHEAD PROJECTOR: *Good overheads can really improve a presentation.*
● *adjective* [only before noun]
(*Accounting*) connected with the general costs of running a business or an organization, for example paying for rent or electricity: *overhead costs/expenses* → OVERHEADS

ˌoverhead pro'jector (*abbr* OHP) (*also* pro'jector) *noun* [C]
a piece of equipment that sends (**projects**) an image onto a wall or screen so that many people can see it: *She used an overhead projector to show the statistics.*—Picture at PRESENTATION

★**overheads** /ˈəʊvəhedz; *AmE* ˈoʊvər-/ *noun* [pl.] (*especially BrE*) (*AmE usually* '**overhead** [U])
(*Accounting*) regular costs that you have when you are running a business or an organization, such as rent, electricity, wages, etc: *We may need to close branches to reduce our overheads.* ◊ *The company cut its overheads by €2.4 million by making 500 staff redundant.* → DIRECT OVERHEAD, INDIRECT OVERHEAD
⊙ *high/low overheads* ◆ *to cut/reduce overheads*

overheat /ˌəʊvəˈhiːt; *AmE* ˌoʊvərˈh-/ *verb* [+ obj or no obj]
(about an economy or a market) to be too active, with high demand causing prices to rise; to make an economy or a market too active: *The growth in consumption caused the economy to overheat.* ◊ *Higher interest rates would slow overheated consumer spending.* ▶ ˌover'**heating** *noun* [U]: *the danger of overheating in the property market*

overhype /ˌəʊvəˈhaɪp; *AmE* ˌoʊvərˈh-/ *verb* [+ obj] (*informal*)
to exaggerate the quality or the importance of sth: *Shareholders made, then lost, a fortune in overhyped Internet companies.* → HYPE

ˌover-in'vestment *noun* [U]
(*Finance*) the fact of more money being invested in sth than is needed: *Over-investment **in** steel production led to a fall in price.* [OPP] UNDER-INVESTMENT
▶ ˌover-in'**vest** *verb* [no obj]: *I think we are over-investing **in** promotion.* ˌover-in'**vested** *adjective*: *Employees were over-invested **in** company stock, and lost money when it failed.*

overissue /ˌəʊvərˈɪʃuː; *BrE also* ˌəʊvərˈɪsjuː; *AmE* ˌoʊvərˈɪʃuː/ *noun* [C,U]
1 (*Finance*) a situation where a company offers more new shares than it is allowed to offer
2 (*Economics*) a situation where too many new BANKNOTES are produced
▶ ˌover'**issue** *verb* [+ obj]

overlay /ˈəʊvəleɪ; *AmE* ˈoʊvərleɪ/ *noun* [C]
1 a transparent sheet with drawings, figures, etc. on it that can be placed on top of another sheet in order to change it
2 (*Marketing*) extra data from another organization that is added to a company's MAILING LIST (= a list of the names and addresses of people who are

regularly sent information or advertising material): *overlay data such as age, income or job*

overlend /ˌəʊvəˈlend; *AmE* ˌoʊvərˈl-/ *verb* [no obj] (**overlent, overlent** /-lent/)
(about a bank or financial organization) to lend too much money ▶ **over'lending** *noun* [U]

ˌover-'leveraged (*especially AmE*) (*BrE usually* ˌover'geared) *adjective*
(*Finance*) if a company, etc. is **over-leveraged**, it has borrowed too much money compared to the number of shares it has issued and may not be able to pay the interest on the loans: *A high debt-to-equity ratio indicates that a company is over-leveraged.* ▶ **over-'leverage** *verb* [+ obj]: *The firm had over-leveraged itself and was unable to service the debt.*

overload *verb, noun*
● *verb* /ˌəʊvəˈləʊd; *AmE* ˌoʊvərˈloʊd/ [+ obj]
1 to put too great a load on sth: *an overloaded truck*
2 to give sb/sth too much of sth: *He's overloaded with responsibilities.* ◇ *My voicemail's overloaded.*
3 to put too great a demand on an electrical system, a computer, etc., causing it to fail: *The lights went out because the system was overloaded.*
● *noun* /ˈəʊvələʊd; *AmE* ˈoʊvərloʊd/ [U; sing.]
too much of sth: *An Internet search can often result in information overload.* ◇ *An electrical overload caused the fuse to blow.* → WORK OVERLOAD

overmanned /ˌəʊvəˈmænd; *AmE* ˌoʊvərˈm-/ *adjective*
(*HR*) having more workers than are needed: *The industry is so overmanned that job cuts are inevitable.* **SYN** OVERSTAFFED **OPP** UNDERMANNED
▶ **over'manning** *noun* [U]

overnight *adverb, adjective, verb*
● *adverb* /ˌəʊvəˈnaɪt; *AmE* ˌoʊvərˈn-/
1 suddenly or quickly: *The company didn't become successful overnight.*
2 during or for the night: *I stayed overnight in Stockholm.*
3 (*Stock Exchange*) since trading ended the day before: *The US Nasdaq fell 2.4% overnight.*
● *adjective* /ˈəʊvənaɪt; *AmE* ˈoʊvərn-/ [only before noun]
1 happening suddenly or quickly: *The new range was an overnight success.*
2 happening during the night; for a night: *an overnight flight* ◇ *an overnight stay*
3 an **overnight** delivery of goods arrives the day after you order them: *Most of our products are available by overnight delivery.*
4 (*Stock Exchange*) happening since trading closed the day before: *an overnight fall on Wall Street*
5 (*Finance*) used to describe a loan that one bank makes to another for a very short period, for example one night: *Overnight loans are repayable within 24 hours.* ◇ *The central bank kept the overnight rate at 2.75%.*
● *verb* /ˈəʊvənaɪt; *AmE* ˈoʊvərn-/
1 [no obj] (*especially AmE*) (*used with an adverb or a preposition*) to stay for the night in a particular place: *We overnighted at the Grace Hotel.*
2 [+ obj] (*AmE*) to send or transport sth during the night so that it arrives the next day: *We overnight fresh fish to restaurants in New York.*

ˌover-opti'mistic *adjective*
1 too confident that sth will be successful: *I'm not over-optimistic about my chances of getting the job.*
2 too high: *The sales forecasts turned out to be over-optimistic.*

★ **overpay** /ˌəʊvəˈpeɪ; *AmE* ˌoʊvərˈp-/ *verb* (**overpaid, overpaid** /-ˈpeɪd/)
1 [+ obj] (*often* **be overpaid**) to pay sb too much; to pay sb more than their work is worth: *Many workers feel their bosses are overpaid for what they do.*
2 [+ obj *or* no obj] to pay too much for sth; to pay more than sth is worth: *Investors feared that the company had overpaid for recent acquisitions.* ◇ *I think I have been overpaying tax.*
OPP UNDERPAY → UNDERPAID
▶ **over'payment** *noun* [C,U]

overpriced /ˌəʊvəˈpraɪst; *AmE* ˌoʊvərˈp-/ *adjective*
too expensive; costing more than it is worth: *Their goods are high quality but overpriced.* ◇ *overpriced shares* **OPP** UNDERPRICED
▶ **over'price** *verb* [+ obj]

overprint /ˌəʊvəˈprɪnt; *AmE* ˌoʊvərˈp-/ *verb* [+ obj]
overprint A (**on B**) | **overprint B with A** to print sth on a document, etc. that already has printing on it

overproduction /ˌəʊvəprəˈdʌkʃən; *AmE* ˌoʊvərp-/ *noun* [U]
the fact that more goods, services, etc. are produced than was planned or than can be sold to make a profit: *Overproduction of oil has pushed the price down.* **OPP** UNDERPRODUCTION
▶ **overproduce** /ˌəʊvəprəˈdjuːs; *AmE* ˌoʊvərprəˈduːs/ *verb* [+ obj *or* no obj]: *Coffee growers have always had a tendency to overproduce.*
ˌoverpro'ducer *noun* [C]: *the biggest overproducers of oil*

ˌover-re'port (*AmE spelling* **overreport**) /ˌəʊvərɪˈpɔːt; *AmE* ˌoʊvərrɪˈpɔːrt/ *verb* [+ obj]
(*Accounting*) to say that you have earned, sold, etc. more than you actually have: *The company admitted over-reporting its sales for the first half of last year.* **OPP** UNDER-REPORT

override /ˌəʊvəˈraɪd; *AmE* ˌoʊvərˈr-/ *verb* [+ obj] (**overrode** /-ˈrəʊd; *AmE* -ˈroʊd/ **overridden** /-ˈrɪdn/)
1 to use your authority to reject sb's decision, order, etc: *The chairman overrode the committee's recommendation.* **SYN** OVERRULE
2 to be more important than sth: *Considerations of safety override all other concerns.* ◇ *Customer satisfaction is our overriding priority.*
3 to stop a process that happens automatically and control it yourself: *A special code is needed to override the time lock.*

ˌoverriding com'mission (*also* **overrider**) /ˌəʊvəˈraɪdə(r); *AmE* ˌoʊvərˈr-/ *noun* [C]
(*Marketing*) a payment earned by a manager of a company's office in another area or country, based on the business created by the agents in that office

overrule /ˌəʊvəˈruːl; *AmE* ˌoʊvərˈr-/ *verb* [+ obj]
to change a decision or reject an idea from a position of greater power: *The government overruled the decision to block the merger.* ◇ *One interviewer didn't want to give me the job, but the others overruled him.* **SYN** OVERRIDE

overrun *verb, noun*
● *verb* /ˌəʊvəˈrʌn; *AmE* ˌoʊvərˈr-/ [+ obj *or* no obj] (**overran** /-ˈræn/ **overrun**)
to take more time or money than was intended: *The project overran by a month.* ◇ *We overran the budget by 50%.*
● *noun* /ˈəʊvərʌn; *AmE* ˈoʊ-/ [C]
SEE ALSO: **cost overrun**
1 a situation when sth takes more time or money than planned: *The contractor is responsible for the cost of overruns in time or costs.*
2 (*AmE*) a quantity of sth produced that is extra or more than you need: *We will buy first-quality overruns.*

● **adjective**
connected with foreign countries, especially those that you have to cross the sea or ocean to get to: *overseas development/trade* ◇ *Japan is our biggest overseas market.* ◇ *Our overseas competitors have raised their prices.* → OFFSHORE

● **adverb**
to or in a foreign country, especially those that you have to cross the sea or ocean to get to: *to live/work/go overseas* ◇ *The product is sold both at home and overseas.*

oversee /ˌəʊvəˈsiː; AmE ˌoʊvərˈsiː/ verb [+ obj] (oversaw /-ˈsɔː/ overseen /-ˈsiːn/)
1 to watch sb/sth and make sure that a job or an activity is done correctly: *My job involves overseeing 120 employees and 600 contractors.* ◇ *A lawyer was appointed to oversee the break-up of the company.* SYN SUPERVISE
2 (*Finance*) to be responsible for the way an amount of money is invested: *an asset management fund that oversees $100 million*

overseer /ˈəʊvəsɪə(r); AmE ˈoʊvərsɪr/ noun [C]
1 a person or an organization that is responsible for making sure that a system is working as it should: *Webster served as an accounting overseer at a company facing fraud accusations.*
2 (*old-fashioned*) a person whose job is to make sure that other workers do their work

oversell /ˌəʊvəˈsel; AmE ˌoʊvərˈsel/ verb (oversold, oversold /ˌəʊvəˈsəʊld; AmE ˌoʊvərˈsoʊld/)
1 (*Commerce*) [+ obj] to sell too much or more of sth than is available: *The seats on the plane were oversold.*
2 (*Marketing*) [+ obj *or no obj*] to try to make sb buy more of sth than they need: *The group was accused of overselling insurance policies.*
3 [+ obj] to exaggerate the quality or importance of sth: *He has a tendency to oversell himself.* OPP UNDERSELL
▶ **over'selling** noun [U] → OVERSOLD

overshoot /ˌəʊvəˈʃuːt; AmE ˌoʊvərˈʃ-/ verb [+ obj *or no obj*] (overshot, overshot /-ˈʃɒt; AmE -ˈʃɑːt/)
to spend more money or to do more than you originally planned: *The department may overshoot its cash limit this year.* ◇ *We overshot our sales target by 20%.* OPP UNDERSHOOT
▶ **overshoot** /ˈəʊvəʃuːt; AmE ˈoʊvərʃ-/ noun [C]: *We need to avoid another big budget overshoot.*

oversight /ˈəʊvəsaɪt; AmE ˈoʊvərs-/ noun
1 [U] the state of being in charge of sb/sth: *The committee has oversight of finance and general policy.* ◇ (*AmE*) *Who was chosen to head the accounting oversight board?*
2 [C,U] the fact of making a mistake because you forget to do sth or you do not notice sth: *Due to an oversight, the company failed to register its shares in time.*

oversized /ˈəʊvəsaɪzd; AmE ˈoʊvərs-/ (*also* **'oversize**, *less frequent*) adjective
bigger than the normal size; too big: *You have to pay extra to send oversized packages.*

oversold /ˌəʊvəˈsəʊld; AmE ˌoʊvərˈsoʊld/ adjective (*Stock Exchange*) used to describe a situation when the value of shares, a currency, etc. has fallen too far as too many people have been selling: *A day of heavy losses left the market oversold.*
→ OVERBOUGHT, OVERSELL

overspend /ˌəʊvəˈspend; AmE ˌoʊvərˈs-/ verb [+ obj *or no obj*] (overspent, overspent /-spent/)
to spend too much money or more than you planned: *The company has overspent on marketing.* OPP UNDERSPEND

▶ **overspend** /ˈəʊvəspend; AmE ˈoʊvərs-/ noun [C, usually sing., U] (*especially BrE*): *We are still dealing with a €1 million overspend from last year.*
over'spending /ˌəʊvəˈspendɪŋ; AmE ˌoʊvərˈs-/ noun [U]: *The new president promised to end years of government overspending.*

overstaffed /ˌəʊvəˈstɑːft; AmE ˌoʊvərˈstæft/ adjective
(*HR*) (about a company, an office, etc.) having more workers than are needed: *The airline was heavily overstaffed.* SYN OVERMANNED OPP UNDERSTAFFED
▶ **over'staffing** noun [U]

overstate /ˌəʊvəˈsteɪt; AmE ˌoʊvərˈs-/ verb [+ obj] to say that sth is larger than it really is, especially an amount of money: *The company admitted it had overstated its revenues by $20 million.* OPP UNDERSTATE
▶ **overstatement** /ˈəʊvəsteɪtmənt; AmE ˈoʊvərs-/ noun [C,U]: *overstatement of profits*

overstock /ˌəʊvəˈstɒk; AmE ˌoʊvərˈstɑːk/ verb [+ obj *or no obj*] (*Commerce*) to buy or make more of sth than you need or can sell: *to overstock inventory* ◇ *The shop was overstocked with unsold goods.* ◇ *Since the new system was introduced, we no longer overstock on parts.* ▶ **overstock** /ˈəʊvəstɒk; AmE ˈoʊvərstɑːk/ noun [C,U]: *We have an overstock of summer clothing.* ◇ (*AmE*) *huge overstocks in clothing inventories* **over'stocking** noun [U]: *Our low prices are due to overstocking.*

overstretch /ˌəʊvəˈstretʃ; AmE ˌoʊvərˈs-/ verb [+ obj]
to make sb/sth do more than they are capable of; to do more than you are capable of: *The firm's mistake was to overstretch itself by expanding into Asia.* ◇ *Taking on another business may overstretch our management.* ▶ **over'stretched** adjective: *an overstretched budget* ◇ *overstretched services*

oversubscribed /ˌəʊvəsəbˈskraɪbd; AmE ˌoʊvərs-/ adjective
1 (*Finance*) if new shares, bonds, etc. are oversubscribed, too many people want to buy them: *The share issue was five times oversubscribed.*
2 (*Commerce*) if a service is oversubscribed, more people have the right to use it than is possible at the same time: *The ISP allows its dial-up Internet service to be oversubscribed by 20%.*
▶ **oversubscription** /ˌəʊvəsəbˈskrɪpʃn; AmE ˌoʊvərs-/ noun [U]: *The investment company announced a €4 million bond issue, with an oversubscription option of (= with the right to issue) a further €3 million.* ◇ *oversubscription of services*

oversupply /ˌəʊvəsəˈplaɪ; AmE ˌoʊvərs-/ noun, verb
● **noun** [U; C, usually sing.] (*plural* oversupplies)
more of sth than can be sold: *The steel industry is struggling due to oversupply.* ◇ *An oversupply of paper has led to a fall in price.*
● **verb** [+ obj *or no obj*] (oversupplies, oversupplying, oversupplied, oversupplied)
to provide sb/sth with more than they can use or sell: *Coffee is a heavily oversupplied market.* ◇ *Fruit growers have a tendency to oversupply.*

overtake /ˌəʊvəˈteɪk; AmE ˌoʊvərˈt-/ verb [+ obj] (overtook /-ˈtʊk/ overtaken /-ˈteɪkən/)
to become greater in number, amount or importance than sth else: *In the next century, nuclear energy could overtake oil as the main fuel.* ◇ *We mustn't let ourselves be overtaken by our competitors.* SYN OUTSTRIP

,over-the-'counter *adjective* [only before noun] (*abbr* **OTC**)
1 (*Finance*) used to describe investments, currencies, etc. that are traded between independent dealers rather than in an organized system such as a stock exchange: *over-the-counter shares/stock* ◇ *the over-the-counter derivatives market* ◇ *OTC markets* ◇ *In over-the-counter trading last Friday, the shares fell 25%.*
2 (about medicines) that can be bought without written permission from a doctor (a **prescription**): *Sales of over-the-counter medicines have increased 2%.*
▶ **,over the 'counter** *adverb* (*abbr* **OTC**): *Are these tablets available over the counter?* ◇ *The company's shares are traded over the counter on the NASDAQ system.*

★ **overtime** /'əʊvətaɪm; *AmE* 'oʊvərt-/ *noun* [U]
1 time that you spend working at your job after you have worked the normal hours: *Some employees were willing to work overtime at weekends.* ◇ *The union announced a ban on overtime.*
○ to **do/work** overtime • to **ban/cut** overtime • an overtime **ban**
2 the money that sb earns for doing **overtime**: *They pay $150 a day plus overtime.*
○ to **earn** overtime • to **pay** (sb) overtime • overtime **earnings/pay/payments**
3 extra time that a factory operates, especially to meet orders: *Several plants will* **work** *overtime next week.*

overtrade /,əʊvə'treɪd; *AmE* ,oʊvər't-/ *verb* [+ obj or no obj]
to do more business than you can afford; to produce or buy more of sth than you will be able to sell: *The market for women's magazines is badly overtraded.*

overtrading /,əʊvə'treɪdɪŋ; *AmE* ,oʊvər't-/ *noun* [U]
(*Finance*) a situation when a company has increased its business too quickly and does not have enough cash available to pay debts, wages and other expenses: *The company grew too fast, and cash-flow problems led to insolvency through overtrading.*

overturn /,əʊvə'tɜːn; *AmE* ,oʊvər'tɜːrn/ *verb* [+ obj]
(*Law*) to officially decide that a legal decision is not correct, and to make it no longer valid: *A court of appeal overturned the decision to ban the drug.*
○ to **overturn** a **ban/decision/patent/ruling/verdict**

overvalue /,əʊvə'vælju:; *AmE* ,oʊvər'v-/ *verb* [+ obj] (*often* be **overvalued**)
to fix the value of sth at a level that is too high: *The euro is estimated to be overvalued against the dollar by 10%.* ◇ *The shares are 25% overvalued.* ◇ *an overvalued exchange rate/stock* [OPP] UNDERVALUE

overview /'əʊvəvju:; *AmE* 'oʊvər-/ *noun* [C]
a general description of sth: *In this presentation I want to give you an overview of our schedule for the next year.* [SYN] OUTLINE → SURVEY
○ to **give/offer/present/provide** an overview (of sth) • a **broad/detailed/quick** overview

overweight /,əʊvə'weɪt; *AmE* ,oʊvər'w-/ *adjective*
(*Stock Exchange*) having more of a particular type of investment or asset in a collection than the index that you are following or than your usual position: *In our survey, 40% of investment fund managers said they were overweight* **in** *cash* (= are keeping more cash than usual because it is not a good time to invest in shares, bonds, etc.). ◇ *J.P. Morgan upgraded the company's investment rating to 'overweight' from 'neutral'.* [OPP] UNDERWEIGHT
→ MARKET WEIGHT

▶ ,**over'weight** *verb* [+ obj *or* no obj]

overwork /,əʊvə'wɜːk; *AmE* ,oʊvər'wɜːrk/ *verb, noun*
● *verb* [+ obj or no obj]
to work too hard; to make sb work too hard: *You look tired. Have you been overworking?* ◇ *The staff are grossly overworked.* ◇ *overworked executives*
● *noun* [U]
the fact of working too hard: *His illness was brought on by money worries and overwork.*

ovno *abbr* (*only used in written English*)
or very near offer used in private sales to say that the seller will accept a slightly lower price: *Desk for sale, €75 ovno.*

★ **owe** /əʊ; *AmE* oʊ/ *verb* [+ obj]
owe sth (to sb) (for sth) | **owe (sb) sth (for sth)** to have to pay sb for sth that you have already received or return money that you have borrowed: *We still owe €5 000 to the bank.* ◇ *We still owe the bank €5 000.* ◇ *How much do I owe you for the tickets?* ◇ *Nearly $1 billion is owed to foreign creditors.* ◇ (*figurative*) *I'm still owed three days' leave.*

owing /'əʊɪŋ; *AmE* 'oʊɪŋ/ *adjective* [not before noun] (*BrE*)
money that is **owing** has not been paid yet: *€500 is still owing on the loan.*

★ **own** /əʊn; *AmE* oʊn/ *adjective, verb*
● *adjective*
done or produced by and for yourself: *The store has launched its own product line of organic foods.*
→ idiom at BEAT
● *verb* [+ obj] (*not used in the continuous tenses*)
to have sth that belongs to you, especially because you have bought it: *80% of our customers own a personal computer.* ◇ *Pfizer owns the exclusive right to market the drug within the US.*

,**own 'brand** (*also* ,**own 'label**) *noun* [C] (*both BrE*)
(*Commerce; Marketing*) a product or group of products that a shop/store sells with its own name on rather than the name of the company that produced them: *Own brands account for less than 30 per cent of total packaged grocery sales.* ◇ *The company makes own-brand ice cream for the major supermarkets.* [SYN] HOUSE BRAND, STORE BRAND (*AmE*) → PRIVATE LABEL

-owned /əʊnd; *AmE* oʊnd/ *adjective* (*used to form adjectives*)
having the owner or type of owner mentioned: *state-owned/privately-owned/foreign-owned* ◇ *Japanese-owned companies in the US* ◇ *family-owned businesses* ◇ *The firm is majority-owned by France Telecom.*

★ **owner** /'əʊnə(r); *AmE* 'oʊ-/ *noun* [C]

SEE ALSO: **beneficial owner, part-~, process ~**

a person or an organization that owns sth: *the firm's owner* ◇ *The group is the owner of the largest shopping mall in the country.* ◇ *The current owners have spent $100 000 on modernizing the hotel.* ◇ *75% of business owners questioned were optimistic about the economy.*
[IDM] **at (the) owner's 'risk** used in formal notices to say that the owner of sth and not anyone else is responsible for any loss or damage: *Cars are parked at the owner's risk.* ◇ *Goods are carried at owner's risk* (= the owner must insure them).

,**owner of 'record** = SHAREHOLDER OF RECORD

,**owner-'operator** *noun* [C] (*AmE*)
a person who owns a lorry/truck and runs it as a business: *We are looking for owner-operators to join our fleet of trucks.*

,**owners' 'equity** = NET WORTH

SEE ALSO: common ownership, cross-media ~, cross-~, employee ~, fractional ~, part ~, partial ~, total cost of ~

the fact of owning sth; the legal right to own sth: *The restaurant is **under** new ownership.* ◇ *a growth in home ownership* ◇ *They have put in proposals to take **full** ownership of the company.* ◇ *Ownership of the land is currently being disputed.*

ownership in 'common = COMMON OWNERSHIP

own-price elas'ticity = ELASTICITY OF DEMAND

oz abbr (only used in written English)
ounce(s): *a 16 oz container*

P p

p (also spelled **p.**) abbr /piː/
1 penny; pence: *The shares closed 1p up at 25p.*
2 (only used in written English) (plural **pp.**) page: See p.135.

P2P (also spelled **p2p, P-to-P**) /ˌpiː tə ˈpiː/ adjective [only before noun]
(IT) **peer-to-peer** used to describe the situation when one computer can communicate with another directly, without using a central SERVER

P3 /ˌpiː ˈθriː/ = PUBLIC-PRIVATE PARTNERSHIP

P45 /ˌpiː ˌfɔːti ˈfaɪv; AmE ˌfɔːrti/ noun [C]
in the UK, a form that you receive from your employer when you stop working for them and that shows how much you earned in the job and how much tax you paid: *Within a few months, he was picking up his P45* (= he had lost his job).

PA /ˌpiː ˈeɪ/ = PERSONAL ASSISTANT, PUBLIC ADDRESS (SYSTEM)

p.a. /ˌpiː ˈeɪ/ abbr **per annum** per year; for each year: *Dividends are expected to be between 1.75% and 3.25% per annum.* NOTE Per annum is a Latin phrase.

PABX /ˌpiː eɪ biː ˈeks/ abbr **private automatic branch exchange** an automatic system for transferring telephone calls to the correct part of an organization

pace /peɪs/ noun, verb
● noun [C,U]
the speed at which sth happens or is done: *the slow pace of change* ◇ *Retail sales rose in January at their fastest pace in two years.* ◇ *How long will our workers keep up this pace?* ◇ *The pace of job losses is slowing now.* ◇ *The economy grew at a respectable 3.1 per cent pace.* → RATE
○ *a **brisk/fast/rapid/record** pace* ◆ *a **moderate/slow/sluggish/steady** pace* ◆ *to **increase/step up** the pace (of sth)* ◆ *to **change/slow** the pace (of sth)*
IDM **keep 'pace (with sth)** to happen, develop, or act at the same speed as sth else: *The company has not kept pace with its rivals.* **put sb/sth through their/its 'paces** to give sb/sth a number of tasks to perform so that you can judge what they/it can do: *The new system has been put through its paces.* **set the 'pace** to do sth at a particular speed or to a particular standard so that other people are then forced to copy it if they want to be successful: *His company has continued to set the pace with new technology and designs.* ◇ *They became the Footsie's best performer and set the pace for the rest of the sector.*
● verb [+ obj] **pace yourself** to work at the speed or level of activity that suits you best, so that you can continue without getting too tired: *She'll have to learn to pace herself in this job.*

the Pa,cific 'Rim noun [sing.]
the countries around the Pacific Ocean, especially countries in East Asia, considered as an economic group: *Pacific Rim countries/regions/markets*

★ **pack** /pæk/ verb, noun
● verb [+ obj]
pack sth (up) (in/into sth) to put goods into containers for delivery or sale: *The pottery was carefully packed into boxes.* ◇ *This is the least expensive way to pack and ship each order.* SYN PACKAGE
PHRV **pack sth 'in** (informal) to stop doing sth: *She decided to pack in her job.* **pack 'up; pack sth 'up** (BrE) (informal) to stop doing sth: *If things don't improve, we may as well pack up and go home.* ◇ *He packed up his job.*
● noun

SEE ALSO: blister pack, bubble ~, display ~, four-~, gift ~, in-~, multipack, six-~

1 [C] a container, usually a small one; a container and its contents: *a pack of cigarettes/gum* ◇ *You can buy the disks in packs of ten.* → PACKAGE, PACKET
2 [C] a set of documents or objects inside the same cover: *We've put together a pack which contains all the necessary information.* ◇ *an information pack* ◇ *a book and CD-ROM pack*
3 [C with sing./pl.verb] the people or things in a particular field or industry; the people or things that are not the leaders: *We pride ourselves on moving fast, staying ahead of the pack.* ◇ *Two of the supermarket chains are pulling away from the pack.*

★ **package** /ˈpækɪdʒ/ noun, verb
● noun [C]

SEE ALSO: compensation package, pay ~, remuneration ~, salary ~

1 (especially AmE) = PARCEL
2 (AmE) a box, bag, etc. in which things are wrapped or packed; the contents of a box, bag, etc: *Our system allows us to track each package.* ◇ *They cost $100 for a package of five.* → PACKET
3 (IT) a set of programs for a particular type of task which are supplied together: *an integrated software package* ◇ *an updated accounting package*
4 a set of products or services that are supplied together: *We put together the right package of services for each client.* ◇ *mobile phone packages for small- and medium-sized businesses*
5 a set of conditions, proposals, etc. that are offered and must be accepted together; the money involved in them: *They took a pay cut as part of a package of measures to save the company.* ◇ *His total benefits package exceeded $6 million.*
6 (informal) = PACKAGE HOLIDAY
● verb [+ obj]
1 **package sth (up)** to put goods into containers for delivery or sale: *We produce and package the drink here.* ◇ *The orders were already packaged up, ready to be sent.* ◇ *packaged teas/salads* ◇ *The camera comes attractively packaged as a gift set.* SYN PACK
2 to combine goods, services, etc. and provide them as a set: *The book is packaged with a workbook, CD and study guide.*

3 to present services, products, people, etc. in a particular way, especially in an attractive way: *an attempt to package news as entertainment*

'package deal *noun* [C]
an agreement to offer a number of things that must all be accepted together: *Customers can sign up to a package deal that includes unlimited local and national calls.*

'packaged goods *noun* [pl.]
goods, especially food and other things sold in supermarkets, which are already in boxes, bags or packages when customers choose them: *We've introduced more self-serve packaged goods. ◇ one of the UK's leading consumer packaged goods manufacturers*

'packaged ,holiday = PACKAGE HOLIDAY
,packaged 'software *noun* [U]
(*IT*) a computer program that is developed for sale to consumers or businesses, generally designed to appeal to more than a single customer: *There was no packaged software that we could buy that would do exactly what we wanted.*

'package ,holiday (*also* **'packaged ,holiday**) (*both BrE*) (*also* **'package tour,** *AmE, BrE*) (*also* **'package,** *AmE, BrE informal*) *noun* [C]
a holiday/vacation that is organized by a company at a price that includes the cost of travel, hotels, etc: *They went on a package holiday to Greece. ◇ a package holiday operator*

packager /ˈpækɪdʒə(r)/ *noun* [C]
a person, machine or company that packs or wraps products ready to be stored, transported or sold
→ PACKER

'package tour = PACKAGE HOLIDAY
★ packaging /ˈpækɪdʒɪŋ/ *noun* [U]

SEE ALSO: **blister packaging, bubble packaging**

1 the materials used to wrap or protect goods that are sold in shops/stores; the design of these materials: *a new type of packaging ◇ packaging materials ◇ Attractive packaging can help to sell products.*

○ *attractive/bright/fancy/glossy* packaging ◆ *paper/plastic/recyclable* packaging
2 the process of packing goods in containers or covers: *We outsource the packaging and distribution of our products.*
○ *a packaging* **company/group/plant** ◆ packaging **equipment/machinery**
3 the way that services, people or activities are presented; the way that makes them seem most attractive: *It's all about packaging.*
→ PACKING

packer /ˈpækə(r)/ *noun* [C]
a person, machine or company that puts food, goods, etc. into containers to be sold or sent to sb: *The firm is a medium-sized fruit and vegetable packer. ◇ The pickers deliver the completed orders to the packers, who wrap them ready for delivery.*
→ PACKAGER

packet /ˈpækɪt/ *noun* [C]

SEE ALSO: **pay packet, wage packet**

1 (*BrE*) a small container or covering for goods; the container or covering and its contents: *a packet of biscuits/cornflakes/cigarettes ◇ 'Is there any paper?' 'I've just opened a new packet.'* → PACK *noun,* PACKAGE *noun*
2 a small object wrapped in paper or put into a thick envelope so that it can be sent by mail, carried easily or given as a present: *Orders under 2 kg are sent as a small packet.*
3 (*AmE*) a set of documents or objects inside the same cover: *a packet of legal papers* [SYN] PACK
4 (*AmE*) = SACHET
5 (*IT*) a small amount of data that is separated from other data before being sent. The data is joined together again after it arrives: *packets of Internet data ◇ data packets*
[IDM] **cost, lose, make, etc. a 'packet** (*informal*) to cost, lose, etc. a very large amount of money: *They expect to make a packet over the next few years.*

packing /ˈpækɪŋ/ *noun* [U]

SEE ALSO: **postage and packing**

1 the act of packing goods for delivery or sale: *The system prints out labels for use in packing and shipping. ◇ meat received from the packing plant ◇ Returned items must be accompanied by the original packing slip.*

---

packaging

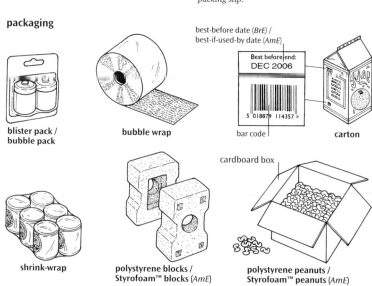

blister pack /
bubble pack

bubble wrap

best-before date (*BrE*) /
best-if-used-by date (*AmE*)

Best before end:
DEC 2006

5 018879 114357 >

bar code

carton

cardboard box

shrink-wrap

polystyrene blocks /
Styrofoam™ blocks (*AmE*)

polystyrene peanuts /
Styrofoam™ peanuts (*AmE*)

❶ *a packing* **factory/plant/station** • *a packing* **company/group**

2 material used for wrapping around delicate objects in order to protect them, especially before sending them somewhere (*BrE*): *The price includes* **postage and packing**. ◊ *Shredded paper is used as packing material.*
→ PACKAGING

pact /pækt/ *noun* [C]
an agreement or a promise to do sth: *the Kyoto Pact on cutting greenhouse gas emissions* ◊ *Chile has signed a free-trade pact with the EU.*

pad /pæd/ *noun, verb*
● *noun* [C]

SEE ALSO: **legal pad**

a number of sheets of paper fastened together along one edge: *a pad of paper* ◊ *a memo/writing/ sketch pad*
● *verb* [+ obj] (**-dd-**) (*AmE*)
to make an amount bigger, especially dishonestly: *Fashion accessories help to pad profit margins.*
PHR V ,**pad sth 'out** to make sth such as an article, seem longer or more impressive by adding things that are unnecessary: *The report was padded out with extracts from previous documents.*

,**padded 'envelope** *noun* [C]
an envelope with a layer of soft material in it, used for sending things that might break or tear easily
→ JIFFY

page /peɪdʒ/ *noun, verb*
● *noun* [C]

SEE ALSO: **full-page, half-~, home ~, landing ~, web ~**

1 (*abbr* **p**) one side or both sides of a sheet of paper in a book, magazine or newspaper: *It's on page 5.* ◊ *The report runs to (= is) 250 pages.* ◊ *The story was on the front page of The Wall Street Journal.*
2 a section of a newspaper or magazine that is used for a particular topic: *the business/financial pages of the newspaper* ◊ *We have doubled the number of ad pages in the magazine.*
3 a section of a website that can be shown on a computer screen at any one time: *the FT.com financial services page* ◊ *The page got a huge number of hits.*
4 the text on one side of a sheet of paper or on one section of an electronic document: *He had to scroll through page after page of sales data.*
5 a message that sb receives on a PAGER
IDM **be on the same 'page** (*especially AmE*) if two or more people or groups are **on the same page**, they work together and have the same goal: *Are the team members all on the same page about the project's goals?*
● *verb* [+ obj]
to call sb using a PAGER or by announcing their name in a public place such as an airport: *I had him paged.* ◊ *An engineer was paged immediately.*
PHR V ,**page 'through sth** to go from one page to another in a document or book, or on a computer screen: *After paging through hundreds of sites, we chose six.*

'**page break** *noun* [C]
a symbol on a computer screen that shows where a printer will start a new page in a typed document

'**page im,pression** = PAGE VIEW

pager /'peɪdʒə(r)/ *noun* [C]
a small electronic device that you carry around with you and that lets you know when sb is trying to contact you, by showing a message, making a sound, etc.

'**page ,traffic** *noun* [U]
the number of times that a web page is visited; the number of people who read a particular page in a

magazine, newspaper, etc: *FT.com achieved record page traffic.* → HIT *noun* (1)

'**page view** (*also* '**page im,pression**) *noun* [C]
(*Marketing*) one visit to a single web page: *The site has more than 7 million page views per day.* → HIT *noun* (1)

★ **paid** /peɪd/ *adjective*

SEE ALSO: **delivered duty paid, duty-~, low-~, post-~, reply ~**

1 [usually before noun] (about work, etc.) for which people receive money: *Neither of them is currently in paid employment.* ◊ *You are entitled to 20 days' paid leave/vacation a year.* ◊ *a well-paid job* ◊ *poorly/badly paid jobs*
2 [usually before noun] (about a person) receiving money for doing work: *Men still outnumber women in the paid workforce.* ◊ *well-paid bankers and accountants*
3 (*often used following a noun*) that has been paid: *postage paid* ◊ *a refund of taxes paid*
OPP UNPAID

,**paid-up 'capital** (*also* ,**paid-up 'share ,capital**) *noun* [U]
(*Finance*) the amount of money that has been received for shares that have been bought and paid for, rather than the money owed to a company from shares that have been bought but not paid for yet

,**paid-up 'policy** *noun* [C]
(*Insurance*) a LIFE INSURANCE agreement in which regular payments have stopped before the end of the agreement

,**paid-up 'share** *noun* [C]
(*Finance*) a share whose full value was paid at the time of issue

,**paid-up 'share ,capital** = PAID-UP CAPITAL

'**paint shop** *noun* [C]
the part of a factory in which goods are painted, especially in a car factory → BODY SHOP

pairing /'peərɪŋ; *AmE* 'per-/ *noun* [U,C]
two people or things that work together or are put together; the act of putting them together: *The pairing of espresso bars and booksellers* ◊ *The pairing of our two companies would be a great partnership and a great business.*

P & L /,piː ənd 'el/ = PROFIT AND LOSS ACCOUNT

pallet /'pælət/ *noun* [C]
a flat wooden frame used for storing and moving goods; the frame and its contents: *Each shelf contains two pallets and each pallet contains 60 bags.* → SKID—Picture at TRANSPORT

palm /pɑːm/ *verb* (*informal*)
PHR V ,**palm sth 'off (on/onto sb)**; ,**palm sb 'off (with sth)** to persuade sb to accept sth that has little value or that you do not want, especially by tricking them: *She's always palming the worst jobs off on her assistant.* ◊ *Make sure he doesn't try to palm you off with faulty goods.*

'**palm-size** (*also* '**palm-sized**) *adjective*
small enough to hold in your hand: *palm-size PCs* ◊ *a palm-sized pager*

palmtop /'pɑːmtɒp; *AmE* -tɑːp/ *noun* [C]
a small computer that you can hold in one hand: *a palmtop organizer*

p. and h. (*also spelled* **p. & h.**) /,piː ənd 'eɪtʃ/ *abbr* (*AmE*) **postage and handling** the cost of dealing with an order and sending the package by post

p. and p. *(also spelled* **p. & p.***)* /ˌpiː ən ˈpiː/ *abbr*
(*BrE*) **post(age) and packing** the cost of packing
and sending goods: *Add £2 for p. and p.* → S AND H

panel /ˈpænl/ *noun*

SEE ALSO: **consumer panel, customer ~, flat-~,
takeover ~**

1 [C with sing./pl. verb] a group of specialists
brought together to give their advice or opinion
about sth, discuss sth, decide on sth, investigate
sth, etc: *He was appointed to an advisory panel on
the issue of taxing Internet sales.* ◇ *The panel
recommended a new business park near the airport.*
◇ *She didn't get the job after a panel interview.*
  ○ *an* **advisory/interview/a selection** *panel* • *a panel of*
economists/experts/judges • *to* **appoint sb to/
assemble/set up** *a panel* • *the panel* **recommended/
ruled/said** *(that)* ...
2 [C with sing./pl. verb] a group of people used to
research or test sth: *Members of the audience panel
were asked to keep a diary of everything they
watched on TV.* ◇ *Our panel said they found the
website easy to use and appealing.*
3 (*Law*) (*also* **ˈjury ˌpanel**) [C] (*both especially AmE*)
= JURY
4 [C] a flat board in a vehicle or on a piece of
machinery where the controls and instruments are
fixed: *an instrument panel* ◇ *a control/display panel*

panellist (*AmE spelling* **panelist**) /ˈpænəlɪst/ *noun*
[C] (*BrE only*)
one of the group of people in a PANEL

ˈpanel truck *noun* [C] (*AmE*)
(*Transport*) a small van/truck with a space for
storing goods that can be reached from the driver's
seat, used for delivering goods, etc.

ˈpanel van *noun* [C]
(*Transport*) (*used mainly in Australian English*)
a small van/truck with doors at the back, used for
carrying goods, tools, etc.

ˌpan-Euroˈpean *adjective*
relating to, or affecting, the whole of Europe;
across the whole of Europe: *pan-European trading* ◇
Telecoms were stronger on the pan-European indices.

panic /ˈpænɪk/ *noun, verb*
● *noun* [U]
a state of great anxiety, in which decisions are
taken quickly, without careful thought: *There is no
sense of panic in the industry.* ◇ *The reports caused
renewed investor panic.* ◇ *There has been panic
buying at grocery stores* (= buying quickly without
careful thought in case the situation gets worse).
  ○ *an* **air/a sense/sign** *of panic* • *a* **state/wave** *of panic*
• *to* **cause/trigger** *panic* • *panic* **buying/selling** • *a
panic* **measure/move/reaction**
● *verb* [+ obj or no obj] (**-ck-**)
to be in a state of **panic**; to make sb be in this state:
The market was panicking. ◇ *The group's move has
panicked its competitors.* ◇ *Panicked investors are
withdrawing their money.*

paper /ˈpeɪpə(r)/ *noun*

SEE ALSO: **carbon paper, commercial ~, run of ~,
walking ~, working ~**

1 (*Finance*) [U] assets in the form of shares, BILLS
OF EXCHANGE, etc. rather than cash: *a bid made up
equally of cash and paper* ◇ *The yield on five-year
paper was up 8.1 basis points at 3.188 per cent.*
2 **papers** [pl.] documents: *a stack of work papers* ◇
Her desk was covered with books and papers.
3 **papers** [pl.] official documents that prove your
identity, give you permission to do sth, etc:
identification papers

4 [C] an article on a particular subject: *a
government consultation paper*
5 [C] a newspaper: *the New York papers* ◇ *the
Sunday papers* ◇ *It's the best business paper we have.*
  IDM **on ˈpaper 1** printed or written on paper,
rather than in electronic form **2** based on recorded
information, rather than on reality: *Centralization
saves money and increases efficiency—at least on
paper.* → idiom at WORTH *adj.*

ˈpaper-based *adjective*
1 using paper rather than electronic means: *a
paper-based billing* **system**
2 (*Finance*) involving payment in shares, rather
than in cash: *a paper-based deal*

ˌpaper ˈbid *noun* [C]
(*Finance*) an offer to buy a company, in which
payment would be in shares rather than in cash:
*Their 182¢-a-share offer was 23% higher than the
value of the rival paper bid.*

paperchase /ˈpeɪpətʃeɪs; *AmE* -pərtʃ-/ *noun* [C]
(*AmE*)
1 the fact of producing too much work on paper
2 a thorough search through books and
documents: *He spent a year on the paperchase that
uncovered the bank fraud.*

ˌpaper ˈcurrency = PAPER MONEY

ˌpaper ˈgain = PAPER PROFIT

paperless /ˈpeɪpələs; *AmE* -pərləs/ *adjective*
[usually before noun]
using computers, telephones, etc. rather than
paper, to store and send information: *the paperless
office* ◇ *a paperless data system*

ˌpaper ˈloss *noun* [C,U]
(*Accounting*) a loss in value which appears in your
accounts, but which may not exist in reality, for
example because an asset has become less
valuable: *They sold their stocks, turning paper losses
into real losses.* **OPP** PAPER PROFIT

ˌpaper ˈmoney (*also* **ˌpaper ˈcurrency**) *noun* [U]
money in the form of paper, not coins or cards

ˌpaper ˈprofit (*also* **ˌpaper ˈgain**) *noun* [C,U]
(*Accounting*) a profit that has been made but not
taken as real money yet, for example shares that
have risen in value but have not yet been sold
SYN BOOK PROFIT **OPP** PAPER LOSS

ˈpaper-ˌpusher *noun* [C] (*informal*)
a person whose job involves boring or unimportant
office work such as keeping records or writing a
great deal → PEN-PUSHER

ˈpaper trail *noun* [C, usually sing.] (*especially AmE*)
(*informal*)
a series of documents that show what you have
done or what has happened: *He established a paper
trail to show that they had links with the company.*

paperwork /ˈpeɪpəwɜːk; *AmE* ˈpeɪpərwɜːrk/
noun [U]
1 the documents needed or produced for sth: *How
quickly can you prepare the paperwork?*
  ○ *to* **complete/handle/prepare** *(the) paperwork*
2 the written work that is part of a job, such as
filling in forms or writing letters and reports: *I
spent the afternoon doing routine paperwork.*
  ○ *to* **deal with/do/get through** *(the) paperwork*

par /pɑː(r)/ *noun* [U] (*also* **ˌpar ˈvalue, ˌnominal
ˈvalue** [C,U]) (*also* **ˌnominal ˈprice** [C])

SEE ALSO: **above par, below par**

(*Finance*) the value given to a share when it is first
made available for sale, which may be greater or
smaller than the price paid for it: *The scheme offers
a range of securities priced to be purchased at par.* ◇
The bonds trade at less than 8% of par value. → FACE
VALUE

IDM below/under/sub 'par less well, good, etc. than is usual or expected: *Some key employees are performing below par.* ◇ *Performance is sub par.* **on a par with sb/sth** *(also* **on par with sb/sth**, *especially in AmE)* as good as usual or as good as it should be: *Prices in Germany are on a par with the UK.*

parachute /'pærəʃuːt/ *noun, verb*
• *noun* [C]

SEE ALSO: **golden parachute**

(HR) money or other benefits that you will receive if you lose your job; an agreement to receive this money or these benefits: *a parachute payment*
• *verb*
PHR V ,parachute sb 'in; ,parachute sb 'into sth *(usually* **be parachuted***)* to put sb from outside a company into a senior position in the company: *She was parachuted in last year to resolve the pensions crisis.*

'paradigm shift *noun* [C]
a very important and noticeable change in the way sth is done or thought about: *the need for a paradigm shift* ◇ *This is a fundamental paradigm shift in management.*

paralegal /ˌpærə'liːgl/ *noun* [C] *(AmE)*
an employee in a law firm who is trained to deal with some types of legal work, but who is not qualified as a lawyer

parallel /'pærəlel/ *adjective* [usually before noun]
1 *(Economics)* used to describe a system of buying and selling goods that happens outside the official system of the company that produces them. Goods are bought in one country and imported into another where they are sold at a lower price than the official price for that country: *parallel imports* ◇ *Parallel trade will lead to a reduction in price.*
→ GREY (1), GREY MARKET (2)
2 *(IT)* involving several computer operations at the same time: *parallel processing* **OPP** SERIAL

the ,parallel e'conomy = SHADOW ECONOMY
,parallel 'loan = BACK-TO-BACK LOAN
,parallel 'market *noun* [C]
(Economics) a separate market for goods and currencies that is different from a country's official money market, especially in countries where the official market is strictly controlled by government

paralyse *(AmE spelling* **paralyze***)* /'pærəlaɪz/ *verb* [+ obj]
to prevent sth from working normally: *The port is still paralysed by the lorry drivers' strike.*

parameter /pə'ræmɪtə(r)/ *noun* [C, usually pl.]
a target or limit which measures or controls an activity: *key performance parameters* ◇ *We had to work within the parameters that had already been established.*
○ *performance/price/risk* parameters ◆ *financial/ investment* parameters ◆ *to define/establish/set* parameters

parastatal /ˌpærə'steɪtl/ *adjective*
used to describe an organization, especially in some African countries, that has some political power and serves the state ▶ ,para'statal *noun* [C]

'par bond *noun* [C]
(Finance) a share, bond, etc. which is sold at the value it is given when it is first issued, rather than at a higher or lower price

parcel /'pɑːsl; *AmE* 'pɑːrsl/ *noun, verb*
• *noun* [C]
1 *(especially BrE)* *(AmE usually* **'package***)* something that is wrapped in paper or put into a thick envelope so that it can be sent by mail or carried easily: *There's a parcel and some letters for you.* ◇ *the parcel delivery business* ◇ *a parcel carrier*

2 a set of things, for example, a set of investments which are offered, bought or sold together: *parcels of shares* ◇ *the group's parcel of hotels* → BUNDLE
3 *(Property)* a piece of land: *The property was divided into 19 parcels.*
• *verb* [+ obj] **(-ll-,** *AmE* **-l-)**
parcel sth (up) to wrap sth and make it into a **parcel:** *She parcelled up the books to send.*
PHR V ,parcel sth 'off to transfer or get rid of a set of things: *They'll parcel off some of the stores to the other companies.* ,parcel sth 'out to divide things or arrange things in sets, and then offer or transfer them to other people or companies: *They will break up the company and parcel out bits to the other players in the sector.*

pare /peə(r); *AmE* per/ *verb* [+ obj]
pare sth (back/down) to gradually reduce the size or amount of sth: *The training budget has been pared to a minimum.* ◇ *a decision to pare down the workforce*

parent /'peərənt; *AmE* 'per-/ = PARENT COMPANY

pa,rental 'leave *noun* [U]
(HR)
1 time that the parent of a new baby is allowed to have away from work: *Men are entitled to four weeks' unpaid parental leave.*
2 in Europe and some other countries, time that a parent is allowed to have away from work to look after a child who is below a particular age

★ **'parent ,company** *(also* **'parent***) noun* [C]
(Finance) an organization that owns and controls another company: *a merger announcement between CRA and its parent company RTZ* ◇ *The share price of Reed International, parent of Reed Elsevier, rose 2¢.*
See note at HOLDING COMPANY

Pa'reto a,nalysis /pə'reɪtəʊ; -'riːt-; *AmE* -toʊ/ *noun* [C,U]
a method that allows you to identify the main causes of an effect, so that you know where you should aim most of your efforts, for example when dealing with a problem → 80/20 RULE

Pareto analysis

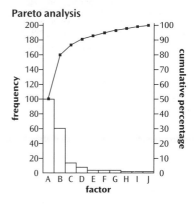

Pa,reto-'optimal /pə'reɪtəʊ; -'riːt-; *AmE* -toʊ/ *adjective*
(Economics) used to describe a situation, solution or result that is the best and most efficient possible, because any other situation would make things worse for at least one group

Pa'reto's ,principle *(also* **Pa'reto's law/rule***)* /pə'reɪtəʊz; -'riːt-; *AmE* -toʊz/ *noun* [sing.]
the theory that a small number or amount of sth always creates a large part of the results, problems, value, etc. associated with it: *Pareto's principle tells*

you that 80 per cent of your sales will come from 20 per cent of your sales staff. ◇ *applying Pareto's principle in management* SYN 80/20 RULE—Picture at PARETO ANALYSIS NOTE Pareto's original theory was that 20% of people in a society own 80% of the wealth.

the 'Paris Club *noun* [sing.]
the G10 group of countries, whose central banks meet and work together to support the international finance and currency system and who lend money to the IMF

parity /'pærəti/ *noun* (*plural* **parities**)

SEE ALSO: **fixed parity, purchasing power parity**

1 [U] the state of being equal, especially the state of having equal pay or status: *Part-time workers are demanding pay parity* **with** *full-time staff.* ◇ *The country is coming closer to economic parity with its neighbours.*
2 (*Economics*) [U,C] the situation when units of money of two different countries, or units of two different products, have equal value: *The dollar remained near parity* **with** *the euro.* ◇ *Gas was priced* **at** *parity with oil.*
3 (*Economics*) [C,U] the amount of a foreign currency that is the same as a particular amount of a country's own currency at an established rate of exchange: *a parity of 1.40 pesos to the dollar on the official market*

park /pɑːk; *AmE* pɑːrk/ *noun, verb*
● *noun* [C]

SEE ALSO: **business park, industrial ~, office ~, retail ~**

an area of land used for a particular purpose, especially for small businesses, office buildings, small factories, etc.
● *verb*
1 [+ obj *or* no obj] to leave a vehicle in a particular place for a period of time: *He had to pay one euro to park at the main train station.* ◇ *There is nowhere for customers to park their cars.*
2 (*Finance*) [+ obj] to leave money, shares, etc. with an organization for a period of time NOTE This may be illegal if it is a way for sb to hide the fact that they own sth: *investors looking for a safe haven to park their cash*
3 (*informal*) [+ obj] to decide to leave an idea or issue to be dealt with at a later meeting: *Let's park that until our next meeting.*

parking /'pɑːkɪŋ; *AmE* 'pɑːrk-/ *noun* [U]
1 the act of leaving a vehicle somewhere for a period of time: *Parking is not allowed here between 9 a.m. and 6 p.m.*
2 a space or an area for leaving vehicles: *There is free parking for customers.*

'Parkinson's law /'pɑːkɪnsənz; *AmE* 'pɑːrk-/ *noun* [U]
the humorous idea that work will always take as long as the time available for it

parlay /'pɑːleɪ; *AmE* 'pɑːrleɪ/ *verb*
PHRV **'parlay sth into sth** (*AmE*) to use or develop sth you have, such as money, a skill, an idea, etc. in order to get sth or make it more successful or valuable: *He was able to parlay his idea into a 70-employee company.*

part /pɑːt; *AmE* pɑːrt/ *noun, verb*
● *noun* [C]

SEE ALSO: **spare part**

a piece of a machine or structure: *They have difficulty getting parts for their ageing machinery.* ◇ *a manufacturer of aircraft parts*

IDM **take 'part (in sth)** to be involved in sth
SYN PARTICIPATE → idioms at PLAY *verb*, SUM *noun*
● *verb*
IDM **part 'company (with/from sb/sth)** to leave sb/sth; to end a relationship with sb: *The firm has parted company with its chairman* (= they asked him to leave).

,part de'livery (*also* ,part 'shipment) *noun* [C,U]
(*Commerce*) an order that has been only partly completed and delivered → PART ORDER

,part ex'change *noun* [U,C] (*BrE*)
a way of buying sth, such as a car, in which you give your old one as part of the payment for a more expensive one; the used item itself: *We'll take your old car* **in** *part exchange.* SYN TRADE-IN
▶ **,part-ex'change** *verb* [+ obj]

partial /'pɑːʃl; *AmE* 'pɑːrʃl/ *adjective*
not complete or whole: *a partial shutdown of the plant* ◇ *a partial sale/merger/payment* ◇ *They have introduced a partial retirement option.*

,partial ac'ceptance *noun* [U]
(*Finance*) the act of agreeing to pay part of the value of a BILL OF EXCHANGE (= a written order for sb to pay a particular amount of money at a particular time)

,partial equi'librium *noun* [U; sing.]
(*Economics*) a balance between supply and demand in one part of the economy

,partial 'loss (*also* 'average) *noun* [C,U]
(*Insurance*) a situation in which only part of a ship or its cargo is damaged and an insurance claim can be made for this

,partial 'ownership = PART OWNERSHIP

,partial 'payment = PART PAYMENT

participant /pɑː'tɪsɪpənt; *AmE* pɑːr't-/ *noun* [C]
a person who is taking part in an activity or event: *The course has attracted over 500 participants from different organizations.* → MARKET PARTICIPANT

★ participate /pɑː'tɪsɪpeɪt; *AmE* pɑːr't-/ *verb*
[no obj]
1 to take part in sth: *Employees are encouraged to participate* **in** *the running of the company.* ◇ *We as a country want to participate in global markets.* ◇ *You can redeem the tokens with any participating airline.*
2 (*Finance*) to receive part of an amount of money, for example part of the profits of a company you work for: *Workers had a right to participate* **in** *the profits of the company.*
▶ **participation** /pɑː,tɪsɪ'peɪʃn; *AmE* pɑːr,t-/ *noun* [U]: *employee participation in decision-making*

par,ticipating 'preference share (*also* par,ticipating pre'ferred share) *noun* [C, usually pl.] (*both BrE*) (*AmE* par,ticipating pre'ferred stock, par,ticipating 'preference stock** [U,C])
(*Finance*) a type of PREFERENCE SHARE (= share whose owner receives payments even when ordinary shareholders do not) which also allows the shareholder to receive DIVIDENDS and extra payments

participative /pɑː'tɪsɪpətɪv; *AmE* pɑːr't-/ *adjective*
involving several people who all take part in sth: *a participative approach to decision-making*

par,ticipative 'management *noun* [U]
(*HR*) a way of running a company in which employees who are not managers are involved in making important decisions: *We believe in participative management and employee involvement at all levels.* ◇ *Her participative management style has helped to build a strong team.*

particulars /pə'tɪkjələz; *AmE* pər'tɪkjələrz/ *noun* [pl.]
written information and details about a business, job, person, property, etc: *Application forms and*

partition /pɑːˈtɪʃn; *AmE* pɑːrˈt-/ *noun, verb*
● *noun* [C]
1 a thin wall or screen that separates one part of a large room from another: *an open-plan office with desks separated by low partitions*—Picture at OFFICE
2 (*IT*) one of a number of sections that a computer's memory or the place where information is stored can be divided into
● *verb* [+ obj] (*often* **be partitioned**)
to divide sth into two or more parts: *The room is partitioned into three sections.*
PHR V par‚tition sth ˈoff to separate one area, one part of a room, etc. from another with a wall or screen

‚partly-ˈowned *adjective*
used to describe a company that is owned partly by another larger company, and also has other owners: *The company sold 30 of its wholly- and partly-owned* **subsidiaries.**

‚partly paid ˈshares (*also* ‚partly paid-up ˈshares, con‚tributing ˈshares) *noun* [pl.] (*all especially BrE*) (*AmE usually* ‚partly paid ˈstock [U,C]) (*Finance*) shares for which the investor has paid only part of the price: *The second instalment is due on the partly paid shares.*

★ **partner** /ˈpɑːtnə(r); *AmE* ˈpɑːrt-/ *noun, verb*
● *noun* [C]

SEE ALSO: **active partner, general ~, merger ~, silent ~, sleeping ~, strategic ~, trading ~, working ~**
---
1 one of the people who starts a business by investing in it, and who shares the profits and the risks: *She founded the business in 2001, with Chris Smith, her friend and business partner.*
2 a member of a group of professional people who work together, own their business and share the profits of the business: *He is a partner at law firm Dewey Ballantine.* ◇ *a partner in an investment firm* ◇ *a junior/senior partner*
3 a company that works with another company in a particular area of business: *Nissan, the Japanese partner of French carmaker Renault* ◇ *Vivendi Universal is seeking investment partners.*
4 a country that has a political or economic agreement with another country: *The US is South Korea's biggest trading partner.*
● *verb* [+ obj *or no obj*]
partner sb | partner (up) with sb to be sb's **partner** in an investment or business project: *They considered partnering up with another company to buy the supermarket chain.* ◇ *He had partnered Mr Hobbs in many business deals.* ◇ *partnering strategies/skills*

★ **partnership** /ˈpɑːtnəʃɪp; *AmE* ˈpɑːrtnərʃɪp/ *noun*

SEE ALSO: **deed of partnership, general ~, limited ~, public-private ~**
---
1 [C,U] a relationship between people who own a business together and share the profits and risks; the state of having this relationship: *The brothers formed a successful partnership that ran several restaurants in the area.* ◇ *The office has been set up* **in partnership with** *FM Recruitment.* See note at COMPANY
❍ to **create/enter into/establish/form** a partnership ◆ to **go into/work in** partnership with sb ◆ to **dissolve** a partnership
2 [C] a business that is owned by a group of professional people who work together and share the profits; the state of being a member of this group: *a junior member of the partnership* ◇ *She was offered a partnership in the law firm.*
❍ to **establish/join/set up** a partnership

3 [C] a relationship between companies or organizations that work together: *The company has formed a partnership* **with** *a US airline to provide new routes.* ◇ *a partnership* **between** *unions and employers*
❍ to **create/enter into/establish/form** a partnership
4 [C] a relationship between countries that have a political or an economic agreement: *Canada, Japan and Brazil also joined the partnership.*

‚part ˈorder *noun* [C]
(*Commerce*) an order that has been only partly completed or delivered; an order for a smaller quantity than usual → PART DELIVERY

‚part-ˈowner *noun* [C]
(*Law*) one of two or more people or companies who own part of a business or a piece of property: *Anaconda, part-owner of one of Australia's biggest nickel mines* ▸ ‚part-ˈown *verb* [+ obj]

‚part ˈownership (*also* ‚partial ˈownership) *noun* [U]
(*Law*) the fact of owning part of a business or piece of property with one or more other people or companies: *An investor buys part ownership of a company in the form of shares.* ◇ *Both companies have part ownership* **in** *an electricity business.*

‚part ˈpayment (*also* ‚partial ˈpayment) *noun* [U,C]
the act of paying part of the total price of sth; the amount paid: *France Telecom issued 113 million shares* **in** *part payment for the company.* ◇ *The company's creditors have allowed it to make a part payment.*

‚part ˈshipment = PART DELIVERY

‚part-ˈtime *adjective, adverb* (*abbr* PT)
for only part of the day or week during which people normally work: *She's looking for a part-time job.* ◇ *to study* **on a part-time basis** ◇ *part-time workers* ◇ *I'm only part-time at the moment.* ◇ *Liz works part-time from 10 till 2.* → FULL-TIME

‚part-ˈtimer *noun* [C]
a person who works **part-time**: *Nearly a third of part-timers are in unskilled jobs.*

party /ˈpɑːti; *AmE* ˈpɑːrti/ *noun* [C] (*plural* **parties**)

SEE ALSO: **charter party, interested ~, related ~, third ~, working ~**
---
1 (*Law*) one of the people or groups of people involved in a legal agreement or dispute: *The contract can be terminated by either party.*
2 one of the people or organizations who are involved in doing sth together: *It is a complicated operation, with many parties involved.*

ˈparty plan *noun* [C]
(*Marketing*) a method of selling goods for the home or for personal use, in which people are invited to a party where they are shown examples of the goods: *Tupperware is one of the most well-known party-plan companies.*

‚par ˈvalue = PAR

Pascal (*also spelled* **PASCAL**) /ˈpæskl; ˌpæsˈkɑːl; *AmE* ˌpæsˈkæl/ *noun* [U]
(*IT*) a language that is used for writing programs for computer systems, and is often used to teach people to write programs

pass /pɑːs; *AmE* pæs/ *verb, noun*
● *verb* [+ obj]
1 to accept a proposal, law, etc. by voting: *The tax reform was passed by 360 votes to 280.*
2 to become greater than a particular total: *Unemployment has now passed* **the** *three million mark.*

3 to examine sb/sth and decide that they are/it is good enough or acceptable: *The committee has now passed the final bonus figures.* OPP FAIL

IDM **pass a 'dividend** (*Finance*) to pay no DIVIDEND (= a payment to shareholders) in a particular period of time: *The company announced it will have to pass its dividend as profits have been lower than expected.*

PHR V **,pass sth a'long (to sb)** (*especially AmE*) = PASS STH ON (TO SB) → PASS-ALONG **,pass sth 'off as sth** (*Law*) to dishonestly pretend that something is something different: *Cheaply made goods were passed off as designer clothes.* → PASSING OFF **,pass sth 'on (to sb)** (*also* **,pass sth a'long (to sb)**, **,pass sth 'through (to sb)**, *both especially in AmE*) to transfer sth, such as a higher or lower cost, to sb else: *Will the higher wage costs be absorbed or passed on?* ◇ *He believes the company can make savings it can pass along to its customers in lower prices.* SYN HAND STH ON **,pass 'over sb** to not give sb a promotion in a job, especially when they deserve it or think that they deserve it: *He was passed over in favour of a younger man.* HELP A noun must always follow *over* and *over*. but a pronoun comes between the verb and *over*. **,pass sth 'through (to sb)** (*especially AmE*) = PASS STH ON (TO SB) → PASS-THROUGH

● *noun* [C]

an official document or ticket that shows you have the right to enter or leave a place, to travel, etc: *Please show your visitor's pass at Reception.*

O *a press/security/visitor's pass* • *a boarding/parking pass* • *a one-day/temporary pass* • *to issue/produce/show your pass*

'**pass-a,long** *noun, adjective* (*AmE*)
● *noun* [C,U]
(*Economics*) = PASS-THROUGH
● *adjective* [only before noun]
(*Marketing*)
1 (*BrE* **,pass-'on**) used to describe people who read a newspaper or magazine after the person who has bought it: *Advertisers like this magazine because of the pass-along factor* (= the number of extra people who read each copy). ◇ *pass-on readership*
2 used to describe people who pass on an email message or a computer file: *The pass-along rate for an e-zine is much greater than for a web page.*
→ PASS STH ALONG at PASS *verb*, PASS STH ON at PASS *verb*

'**pass-along ,readers** = SECONDARY AUDIENCE (2)

passenger /'pæsɪndʒə(r)/ *noun* [C]
1 a person who is travelling in a car, bus, train, plane or ship and who is not working on it: *airline passengers* ◇ *The airline's last quarterly report showed that passenger numbers were down.*
→ TRANSIT PASSENGER
2 (*informal*) (*especially BrE*) a member of a group or team who does not do as much work as the others: *The firm cannot afford to carry passengers.*

,**passing 'off** *noun* [U]
(*Law*) the act of dishonestly leading customers to think that a product or service is associated with a particular company when it is not → PASS STH OFF AS STH at PASS *verb*

,**passing 'trade** *noun* [U]
(*Commerce*) customers who come into a shop/store or business because they are going past it and see it, rather than those who are regular customers: *The restaurant is out of town, and doesn't get much passing trade.*

passive /'pæsɪv/ *adjective*
(*Finance*)
1 used to describe shareholders who do not take part in any management decisions about the

company they invest in: *He agreed to be a passive investor and gave the company the cash that it needed to buy its first printing presses.*
2 used to describe a way of investing in which the investor buys a range of shares, bonds, etc. and allows their value to gradually increase as the market rises, rather than buying and selling shares often as the value changes: *Passive investing requires good initial research and patience.* ◇ *passive fund management*
→ ACTIVE

,**passive 'loss** *noun* [C]
(*Accounting*) a loss made through an activity in which you are not involved in an active way, for example renting property

,**pass-'on** = PASS-ALONG *adj.* (1)

'**passport con,trol** *noun* [U]
the place at an airport or port where an official checks your **passport** (= a document that identifies you and shows the country you belong to) before you enter or leave a country: *long queues at passport control*

'**pass-through** *noun* (*AmE*)
1 (*Economics*) [U,C] (*AmE also* '**pass-a,long**) the fact that sth such as a tax or a higher or lower price is transferred to customers: *There is a low degree of pass-through from exchange rates to import prices.* ◇ *price pass-through to end-users*
2 (*Finance*) [U,C] (*also* ,**pass-through se'curity** [C]) a type of investment in which investors lend money to home buyers or businesses through a bank or government agency, and the money paid back passes from the bank or agency back to investors: *Mortgage-backed certificates are the most common type of pass-through.*
→ PASS STH THROUGH (TO SB) at PASS *verb*

password /'pɑːswɜːd; *AmE* 'pæswɜːrd/ *noun* [C]
(*IT*) a series of letters and/or numbers that you need in order to be able to use a computer or computer system: *Enter your username and password.*
O *to enter/key (in)/type (in)/set/use* a password • *to change/forget/know your password*

,**past 'due** *adjective, adverb* (*AmE*)
after the date when a payment should have been made: *a message to remind the customer that a payment is past due* ◇ *They routinely pay invoices 90 days past due.*

paste /peɪst/ *verb* [+ obj *or no obj*]
to copy or move text into a document from another place or another document: *The editor lets you cut and paste text, photos and graphics into pages.*
→ idiom at CUT *verb*

★ **patent** /'pætnt; *BrE also* 'peɪtnt/ *noun, verb*
● *noun* [C,U]
a legal right to be the only person to make, use or sell a product or an invention; a document that proves this: *Edison took out a patent on the light bulb.* ◇ *Patents on some of their drugs will expire next year.* ◇ *The device was protected by patent.* ◇ *to file a patent application with the Patent Office* See note at COPYRIGHT
O *to apply for/file/obtain/take out* a patent • *to grant/issue/refuse* a patent • *a patent expires/lapses*
● *verb* [+ obj]
to obtain a **patent** for an invention or a process: *The technology was first patented in 2001.*
▶ '**patented** *adjective*: *patented technology*

patentable /'pætntəbl; *BrE also* 'peɪtənt-/ *adjective*
that it is possible to obtain a **patent** for: *For an invention to be patentable it must be new and useful.*

'**patent ,agent** *noun* [C]
a person who helps people or companies arrange **patents** for their product, invention, etc.

,patent ap'plied for = PATENT PENDING

,patent 'defect noun [C,U]
(*Law*) a fault in a product that is obvious enough to be noticed when you buy it: *The seller was not obliged to draw attention to the patent defects.*
→ LATENT DEFECT

patentee /ˌpætən'tiː; *BrE also* ˌpeɪt-/ noun [C]
a person or company that owns the **patent** for a product, an invention, etc.

'patent ,office noun [C]
(*Law*) a government office that deals with and gives **patents**: *the UK Patent Office*

,patent 'pending (*also* ,patent ap'plied for) phrase
words used on a product to show that the maker or seller has applied for a **patent**

'patent pro,tection noun [U]
laws that protect a person or company that has developed a new product, method, etc. from having it copied or used by others: *The drug's patent protection expires in 2009.*

'patent right noun [C, usually pl.]
the right to make or sell sth that is given to one particular person or company by a **patent**: *The company has lost patent rights for some of its top-selling drugs.*

paternalistic /pəˌtɜːnə'lɪstɪk; *AmE* -ˌtɜːrn-/ adjective
a **paternalistic** company is one in which people lower down in the organization are looked after very well but are not given much responsibility to make decisions: *paternalistic employers*

pa'ternity leave noun [U]
(*HR*) a period of time when the father of a new baby is allowed to be away from work: *to take paid paternity leave* → MATERNITY LEAVE

pa'ternity pay noun [U]
(*HR*) money paid to the father of a new baby while he is not working: *Paternity pay has recently been introduced.* → STATUTORY PATERNITY PAY

pathfinder /'pɑːθfaɪndə(r); *AmE* 'pæθ-/ noun [C]
a person, company, product, etc that finds or shows a new way of doing sth: *The company is a pathfinder in computer technology.*

'pathfinder pros,pectus (*AmE also* ,red 'herring, *informal*) noun [C]
(*Stock Exchange*) a document issued by a company that is going to sell shares for the first time, giving details of the company but no details of the price of the shares, etc. It is sent to people who might be interested in buying the shares.

patron /'peɪtrən/ noun [C]
1 (*Commerce, formal*) a customer of a particular shop/store, restaurant, theatre, etc: *The car park is for hotel patrons only.*
2 a person or company who gives money or support to an organization such as a charity: *a millionaire property developer and patron of the arts*

patronage /'pætrənɪdʒ; 'peɪt-/ noun [U]
1 (*Commerce*) the support that customers give to a business by spending money there: *a discount system that rewards customers for their continued patronage* ◊ *The restaurant's patronage declined by more than 70%.*
2 support, especially financial support, given to an organization such as a charity by an individual or a company: *her generous patronage of the arts*
3 a system by which an important person gives help or a job to sb in return for their support: *He is only still in his job because of the patronage of the company's controlling shareholder.*

patronize , -ise /'pætrənaɪz; *AmE also* 'peɪt-/ verb [+ obj]
1 (*Commerce*) to be a customer of a shop/store, restaurant, hotel etc: *The hotel is largely patronized by business travellers.*
2 to treat sb in a way that seems friendly but shows you do not think they are very intelligent, experienced, etc: *If you respect your customers, you don't patronize them by telling them what they want.*
3 to help a particular person, organization or activity by giving them money

pattern /'pætn; *AmE* -tərn/ noun, adjective
• noun [C]

SEE ALSO: career pattern

1 the way in which sth usually or repeatedly happens: *There is no set pattern for these meetings.* ◊ *Consumer spending follows a regular seasonal pattern.* ◊ *An up-and-down economic growth pattern is emerging.*
O a changing/familiar/predictable/set pattern • to establish/follow a pattern • a pattern develops/emerges
2 an excellent example to copy: *The store has set the pattern for others in customer service.*
→ idiom at HOLD verb
• adjective [only before noun] (*especially AmE*)
(*HR*) a **pattern** agreement, contract, etc. is based on other agreements or contracts with similar companies: *The local union has rejected the pattern agreement and are demanding their own contract.*

pave /peɪv/ verb
IDM ,pave the 'way for sth to create a situation in which sb will be able to do sth or sth can happen: *The changes helped pave the way for 12 new members to join the EU in 2004.*

pawn /pɔːn/ verb, noun
• verb [+ obj]
to leave an item with a person who lends money in exchange for it (**a pawnbroker**). If the money is paid back within an agreed period of time, the item is returned to the owner, but if not, the item can be sold: *Nobody would lend him money, so he pawned his gold watch.*
• noun
IDM in pawn if sth is **in pawn**, it has been **pawned**: *All her jewellery was in pawn.* **out of pawn** if you get or take sth **out of pawn**, you pay back the money you owe and get back the item that has been **pawned**

pawnbroker /'pɔːnbrəʊkə(r); *AmE* -broʊ-/ noun [C]
a person who lends money in exchange for items left with them. If the money is not paid back within an agreed period, the **pawnbroker** can sell the item.

pawnshop /'pɔːnʃɒp; *AmE* -ʃɑːp/ noun [C]
a **pawnbroker**'s shop

★ **pay** /peɪ/ verb, noun
• verb (paid, paid /peɪd/)
1 [+ obj or no obj] to give sb money for work, goods, services, etc: *How much are people willing to pay for your product?* ◊ *Are you paying in cash or by credit card?* ◊ *My company pays well* (= pays high salaries). ◊ *Last year they paid $16m in cash bonuses to staff.* ◊ *I'm paid $100 a day.* ◊ *She is paid by the hour.* ◊ *I don't pay you to sit around all day doing nothing!* ◊ *The service now has about 2.2 million paying customers.* → LOW-PAID, PREPAY
2 [+ obj] to give sb money that you owe them: *We don't have enough money to pay our bills.* ◊ *Have you paid her what you owe her?* ◊ *No dividend has been paid for several years.*

3 [no obj] (about a business, etc.) to produce a profit: *Training is a growth area—with the right skills you could* **make** *it* **pay.** ◇ *They have turned their website into a* **paying proposition.**
4 [+ obj *or* no obj] to result in some advantage or profit for sb: *It would probably pay you to hire an accountant.* ◇ *It* **pays to** *keep up to date with your work.*
IDM **pay 'dividends** to produce great advantages or profits: *He insisted that the money invested in e-commerce would pay dividends.* **pay for it'self** (about a new system, sth you have bought, etc.) to save as much money as it cost: *The software paid for itself within 90 days.* **pay its 'way** (about a business, etc.) to make enough money to pay what it costs to keep it going: *Our website is now paying its way.*
pay/spend over the 'odds (*BrE*) (*informal*) to pay more than you would normally expect: *The bank paid over the odds to get into the American market.*
pay through the 'nose (for sth) (*informal*) to pay much too much money for sth: *We paid through the nose for the repairs.* **pay your 'way** to pay for everything yourself without having to rely on anyone else's money: *She had to pay her way through college.*
PHRV **,pay sb 'back (sth); ,pay sth 'back (to sb)** to return money that you borrowed from sb: *I'll pay you back next week.* ◇ *You can pay back the loan over a period of three years.* → PAYBACK **,pay 'down sth** (*AmE*) (*Finance*) to reduce the amount of a debt by paying some of the money: *The money will be used to pay down their $2.4 bn debt.* → PAYDOWN **HELP** A noun follows **down** but a pronoun must come between the verb and **down.** **,pay sth 'down** (*Commerce*) to give an amount of money as the first payment for sth: *You can pay $200 down and the rest in 12 monthly instalments.* → DOWN PAYMENT **,pay sth 'in; ,pay sth 'into sth** to put money into a bank account: *I paid in a cheque this morning.* ◇ *I'd like to pay some money into my account.* **,pay sth 'off** (*informal*) (about a plan or an action) to be successful and bring good results: *Our efforts to improve quality and speed up delivery have paid off and profits have doubled.* → PAY-OFF **,pay sb 'off** to pay sb what they have earned and tell them to leave their job: *The crew were paid off as soon as the ship docked.* → PAY-OFF **,pay sth 'off** to finish paying money owed for sth: *We paid off our mortgage after fifteen years.* **,pay 'out; ,pay sth 'out** to pay a large amount of money for sth: *The company has paid out $1.5 bn in bonuses for the year.* → PAYOUT **,pay 'up** to pay all the money that you owe to sb, especially when you do not want to or when the payment is late: *I had a hard time getting the insurers to pay up.*
●*noun* [U]

SEE ALSO: at-risk pay, base ~, basic ~, call-in ~, callback ~, equal ~, hazard ~, etc.

the money that sb gets for doing regular work: *Her job is hard work, but the pay is good.* ◇ *workers* **on low pay** ◇ *a pay increase* ◇ (*BrE*) *a pay rise* ◇ (*AmE*) *a pay raise* ◇ *a 3% pay offer* ◇ *holiday/vacation pay* ◇ *Union leaders are campaigning for better* **pay and conditions.** ◇ *Some executives have agreed to 17% pay cuts.*
○ *to get/give (sb)/receive pay* • *good/high/low/poor pay* • *monthly/weekly pay* • *full/half pay*

★**payable** /ˈpeɪəbl/ *adjective* [not before noun]

SEE ALSO: accounts payable, bills ~, note ~

1 that must be paid or can be paid at a particular time or in a particular way: *The full fee is payable in advance.* ◇ *The dividend is payable on 7 March to shareholders as at 21 February.* ◇ *The price is payable in monthly instalments.*

2 when a cheque, etc. is made **payable to** sb, their name is written on it and they can pay it into their bank account: *Make your cheque payable to Next plc.*

payables /ˈpeɪəblz/ *noun* [pl.]
(*Accounting*) money that a company owes, for example loans to be paid back, services to be paid for, etc: *software to handle inventory, invoicing, and payables* ◇ *Managers need to keep control of payables.* → RECEIVABLES — Picture at WORKING CAPITAL

,payable to 'bearer *adjective*
(*Finance*) used to describe a cheque, a BILL OF EXCHANGE, etc. that can be signed by the person who holds it and paid to them

,payable to 'order *adjective*
(*Finance*) used to describe a cheque, a BILL OF EXCHANGE, etc. that must be paid to the person named on it

,Pay and 'File *noun* [U]
a way of paying tax in which a company or a person calculates the tax that they owe and pays it at the same time as they send their TAX RETURN (= a form with the details of what has been earned and spent)

,pay-as-you-'go *adjective* [only before noun]
connected with a system of paying for a service as you use it or paying costs as they happen, rather than paying one amount before or after, or fixed regular amounts: *pay-as-you-go phones* ◇ *a pay-as-you-go information service* ▶ **,pay as you 'go** *noun* [U]: *Pay as you go was introduced by the phone company this year.* → PREPAY

payback /ˈpeɪbæk/ *noun* [C,U]
1 (*Finance*) the profit that you receive on money that you have invested (especially when this is equal to the amount that you invested); the time that it takes to get your money back: *When you lend or invest money, you're hoping to get a payback.* ◇ *a 10-year payback*
2 the advantage or reward that sb receives for sth they have done; the act of paying sth back: *He feels his success is the* **payback for five years of hard work.** ◇ (*informal*) *It's* **payback time!** (= a person will have to suffer for what they have done)
→ PAY SB BACK (STH), PAY STH BACK (TO SB) at PAY *verb*

'payback ,period *noun* [C]
(*Accounting*)
1 the time it will take for the profit from a business project, an asset, etc. to be equal to the amount invested in it: *We estimate that the payback period for the new machinery will be two years.* **SYN** RECOVERY PERIOD
2 the amount of time over which a loan can be paid back: *The payback period expires on 20 May.*

'pay ,cable *noun* [U,C] (*AmE*)
a cable television service for which customers pay an amount of money each month: *to subscribe to pay cable*

'pay ,channel *noun* [C]
a television channel that you must pay for separately in order to watch it: *advertisers who target pay-channel viewers*

'pay cheque (*AmE spelling* **paycheck**) *noun* [C]
1 the cheque that you are given when your wages are paid to you: *They were given an IOU instead of a pay cheque.*
2 (*especially AmE*) a way of referring to the amount of money that you earn: *She earns a huge paycheck.*

'pay claim *noun* [C]
a demand by a group of workers for more pay: *Mineworkers were prepared to strike in support of their pay claim.*

,pay compara'bility *noun* [U]
(*HR*) similar systems of pay in different companies

payday /'peɪdeɪ/ *noun* [U,C]
1 the day on which you get your wages or salary: *Friday is payday.*
2 (*informal*) (*especially AmE*) a way of referring to an amount of money, especially money that can be won in a contest: *The way to get the biggest payday is to sell the business by auction.*

'pay determi,nation *noun* [U]
(*HR*) the process of setting rates of pay, including increases in pay

paydown /'peɪdaʊn/ *noun* [C] (*AmE*)
(*Finance*) a payment of part of an amount of money that has been borrowed → PAY STH DOWN at PAY *verb*

PAYE /,pi: eɪ waɪ 'i:/ *abbr* **pay as you earn** a British system of paying income tax in which money is taken from your wages by your employer and paid to the government

payee /,peɪ'i:/ *noun* [C]
(*Finance*) a person that money or a cheque is paid to: *The cheques were undated and had no payee's name.* → ACCOUNT PAYEE, PAYER

'pay ,envelope = PAY PACKET

payer /'peɪə(r)/ *noun* [C]
(*Finance*) a person or an organization that pays or has to pay for sth: *mortgage payers* ◇ *Part of her job is chasing up slow payers.*
○ *a bad/late/slow payer* ◆ *a fast/good payer* ◆ *dividend/fee/income tax/licence/mortgage payers*

,pay for per'formance = PERFORMANCE-RELATED PAY

'paying ,agent *noun* [C]
(*Finance*) a bank or other organization that makes payments to the holders of shares or bonds on behalf of the company that issues (= sells) the shares or bonds

'paying bank (*also* **'paying ,banker**) *noun* [C]
(*Finance*) the bank that is responsible for paying a cheque written by sb who has an account there

,paying-'in book *noun* [C] (*BrE*)
a set of PAYING-IN SLIPS fastened together inside a cover

,paying-'in slip *noun* [C] (*BrE*)
a printed form on which you record the amount of money, the date, etc. when you put money into your bank account SYN DEPOSIT SLIP

payload /'peɪləʊd; *AmE* -loʊd/ *noun* [C,U]
(*Transport*)
1 the passengers or goods on a ship or an aircraft for which payment is received: *The new ferries can carry 70% more payload* (= passengers and cars).
2 goods that a vehicle, such as a ship, a lorry/truck, or an aircraft, is carrying: *The ship was not carrying its usual payload of gravel or iron ore.*

paymaster /'peɪmɑːstə(r); *AmE* -mæs-/ *noun* [C]
1 a person or an organization that provides money for another person or organization and therefore controls them
2 an official who pays wages in the army or in a factory

★ payment /'peɪmənt/ *noun*

SEE ALSO: accelerated payment, balance of ~, debt ~, documents against ~, down ~, goodwill ~, interim ~, etc.

1 [U] the act of paying a person, paying a bill or debt, or of being paid: *We accept payment by cash, cheque, or credit/debit card.* ◇ *She demanded payment in advance for the work.* ◇ *There will be a penalty for late payment of invoices.* ◇ *an electronic*

payment system ◇ *Orders under €40 require payment with order.* OPP NON-PAYMENT
○ *to accept/receive/take* payment ◆ *to demand/refuse* payment ◆ *to defer/delay* payment ◆ *immediate/late/prompt* payment ◆ *full/part/partial* payment
2 [C] a sum of money paid or expected to be paid: *a cash payment* ◇ *He made a lump-sum payment of $12 000.* ◇ *We can calculate your monthly mortgage payments.*
○ *to accept/make/receive* a payment ◆ *to keep up/meet/miss* payments ◆ *cash/credit-card/electronic* payments ◆ *a bonus/lump-sum/one-off/single* payment ◆ *annual/monthly/regular* payments ◆ *dividend/interest/loan* payments

,payment by re'sults *noun* [U,C] (*abbr* **PBR**)
(*HR*) a system of paying people in which the amount of money they receive depends on the amount of work they do or the profits made

'pay-off (*AmE* spelling **payoff**) *noun* [C] (*informal*)
1 a payment of money to sb to persuade them to leave their job: *The fund manager left the company with a $1 million pay-off.*
2 the money you receive from an investment, etc: *The pay-off could be huge if the company succeeds in remaking itself.* → PAY OFF at PAY *verb*, PAY SB OFF at PAY *verb*
3 an advantage or a good result from sth: *The pay-off of the new system shows up in all stages of a project.*

payout /'peɪaʊt/ *noun* [C]
a large amount of money that is given to sb: *huge payouts to managers* ◇ *an insurance/a dividend payout* ◇ *The group's final dividend was 50¢, taking last year's payout to 85¢.* → PAY OUT, PAY STH OUT at PAY *verb*

'payout ,ratio *noun* [C]
(*Finance*) the proportion of a company's profits that it pays to its shareholders as DIVIDENDS: *Investors are seeking out companies with stable earnings and a high payout ratio.*

'pay ,package (*also* **'salary ,package**) (*also* **re,mune'ration ,package**, *formal*) *noun* [C]
(*HR*) the money that sb gets for doing their job, with other benefits that the company offers: *Your pay package will consist of cash and performance bonuses.* See note at SALARY

'pay ,packet (*also* **'wage ,packet**) (*both BrE*) (*AmE* **'pay ,envelope**) *noun* [C]
an envelope containing your wages; the amount sb earns: *Employees know what their bonus will be before they open their pay packets.* ◇ *The workforce is demanding larger pay packets.*

'pay-per- *combining form*
(*Marketing*) used to form adjectives describing a system in which people pay for a service as they use it: *pay-per-click advertising* ◇ *pay-per-use software* ◇ *television pay-per-play games*

'pay ,period *noun* [C] (*especially AmE*)
(*HR*) the amount of time for which a worker receives a regular payment: *Employees are required to submit timesheets for each pay period.*

,pay-per-'view *noun* [U]
a system of television broadcasting in which you pay an extra amount of money to watch a particular programme

payphone /'peɪfəʊn; *AmE* -foʊn/ *noun* [C]
a telephone, usually in a public place, that is operated using coins or a card

'pay re,straint = WAGE RESTRAINT

payroll /ˈpeɪrəʊl; AmE -roʊl/ noun
(Accounting; HR)
1 [C] a list of people employed by a company showing the amount of money to be paid to each of them: *We have 500 people on the payroll.* ◇ *a payroll assistant*
2 [C, usually sing.] the total amount paid in wages by a company: *The firm is growing fast with a monthly payroll of $1 million.*
3 [U] the activity of managing a company's **payroll**: *We are trying to improve our support services, including legal, human resources and payroll.* ◇ *the cost of payroll training*

payrolled /ˈpeɪrəʊld; AmE -roʊld/ adjective [usually before noun]
(HR) on the **payroll** of a company: *payrolled employees* ◇ *Do contractors make less money if they are payrolled?*

payrolling /ˈpeɪrəʊlɪŋ; AmE -roʊl-/ noun [U]
(HR) the situation when a company chooses staff, especially temporary staff, but asks an agency to employ them and organize their wages or salary

ˈpayroll tax noun [U,C]
(Economics) a tax that is based on the wages paid to employees and is paid either by employers or partly by employers and partly by employees: *a payroll tax to pay for an expanded health service*

ˈpay scale noun [C]
(HR)
1 the range of levels of pay that a person can receive in a particular job: *His promotion to the next degree of the pay scale gave him an extra €400 a month.*
2 the range of levels of pay that people receive in different jobs: *Within the industry, printers are at the top end of the pay scale.*
→ SALARY SCALE, WAGE SCALE

payslip /ˈpeɪslɪp/ (BrE) (AmE **ˈpay stub**) noun [C]
a piece of paper given to an employee that shows how much money they have been paid and how much has been taken away for tax, etc.

ˈpay spine noun [C] (BrE)
(HR) a series of fixed points between a lower and an upper limit that form the basis of a system of pay for groups of workers in some government organizations: *Progress on this six-point pay spine generally takes five years.*

ˈpay stub = PAYSLIP

ˈpay TˌV (also **ˈpay ˌtelevision**) noun [U]
a system of television broadcasting in which you pay extra money to watch particular television programmes or channels: *pay TV services/operators*
→ FREE TV

PBR /ˌpiː biː ˈɑː(r)/ = PAYMENT BY RESULTS

PBT /ˌpiː biː ˈtiː/ abbr (especially BrE)
(Accounting) **profit(s) before tax** the amount of profit that a company makes during a particular period, without taking away the tax that it owes: *PBT fell 28% to €4.5 million.*

PBX /ˌpiː biː ˈeks/ abbr **private branch exchange** a private telephone network used within offices or a company, in which there are a limited number of lines for making calls outside the company, which are shared

★ PC /ˌpiː ˈsiː/ abbr **personal computer** a small computer that is designed for one person to use at work or at home → DESKTOP COMPUTER, MICROCOMPUTER, MINICOMPUTER—Picture at OFFICE

PˈC card noun [C]
(IT) a device like a credit card in size that fits inside a small computer or a PC and is used for example to add memory or to make an Internet connection: *The PC card fits into a slot on the side of the notebook.*

pcm abbr (BrE) (only used in written English)
per calendar month used to show how much sb must pay each month, especially for rent: *Room available for single person, €600 pcm.*

pct. abbr (AmE)
a short way of writing **per cent**

PDA /ˌpiː diː ˈeɪ/ abbr
personal digital assistant a very small computer that is used for storing personal information and creating documents, and that may include other functions such as telephone, FAX, connection to the Internet, etc. See note at CALENDAR

PDF /ˌpiː diː ˈef/ (also **ˌPDˈF file**) abbr
(IT) **Portable Document Format** (used as a countable noun) a type of computer file that can contain words or pictures. It can be read using any system, can be sent from one computer to another, and will look the same on any computer: *I'll send it to you as a PDF.*

PDR /ˌpiː diː ˈɑː(r)/ = PRICE-DIVIDEND RATIO

ˌP/ˈD ˌratio /ˌpiː ˈdiː/ = PRICE-DIVIDEND RATIO

★ peak /piːk/ noun, verb, adjective
● **noun** [C, usually sing.]
a period of time when the level, value or rate of sth is at its highest; the best or most successful point: *Inflation is believed to have reached its peak.* ◇ *She's at the peak of her career.* ◇ *Economic growth moves through a cycle of peaks and troughs.*
[OPP] TROUGH—Picture at BUSINESS CYCLE
● *an all-time/a record peak* ◆ *above/below the peak* ◆ *to be at/hit/reach/rise to a peak*
● **verb** [no obj]
to reach the highest level or value: *Oil production peaked in the early 1980s.* ◇ *The price peaked at $22 per share.*
● **adjective** [only before noun]
1 used to describe the highest level of sth: *Property prices have reached peak levels.* ◇ *The machinery needs regular maintenance to operate at peak efficiency.* ◇ *She believed that a good night's sleep was the secret of peak performance.*
● *a peak level/rate/value* ◆ *peak efficiency/performance*
2 of a time when the greatest number of people are doing sth or using sth, and prices are often higher: *July and August are the peak season for travel in Europe.* ◇ *Phone calls are more expensive during peak times.* → OFF-PEAK
● *a peak period/season/time*

ˈpeak time (also **ˌpeak ˈviewing time**) = PRIME TIME

peanuts /ˈpiːnʌts/ noun [pl.] (informal)
a very small amount of money: *They employ a handful of people who work for peanuts.* ◇ *$80 000 is peanuts compared to what he used to earn.*

ˈpecking ˌorder noun [C, usually sing.]
the order of importance among the members of a group: *Junior officials are too far down the pecking order to influence decisions.*

peculation /ˌpekjəˈleɪʃn/ noun [U]
the act of taking sb else's money for yourself, especially when they have trusted you to take care of it: *He was charged with peculation of public funds.*

pecuniary /prˈkjuːniəri; AmE -ieri/ adjective
(Law) relating to or connected with money: *Damages were awarded for future pecuniary loss.*

peddle /'pedl/ verb [+ obj or no obj] (informal)
to try to sell goods, often by going from place to place: He used to design software and then peddle it to small businesses. ▶ **peddler** (BrE spelling also **pedlar**) noun [C]

peer /pɪə(r); AmE pɪr/ noun [C, usually pl.]

SEE ALSO: peer-to-peer

1 a company or product that is similar to others: The grocery chain has suffered as bigger peers have cut their prices. ◇ We are outperforming peer companies.
2 a person who is similar to you in age, social status, etc: She enjoys the respect of her peers. ◇ **Peer pressure** is strong among young people (= they want to be like other people of the same age).

peer ap'praisal = PEER REVIEW

'peer group noun [C]
1 a group of similar companies or products: a peer group of 13 global pharmaceutical companies
2 a group of people of the same age, social status, etc: The workforce was divided into peer groups based on their jobs.

peer re'view (also **peer ap'praisal**) noun [C,U]
(HR) a system of asking people who work with sb to give an opinion about them and their work: Everyone in the company undergoes peer review.

peer-to-'peer adjective [only before noun]
(IT) (about a computer system) in which each computer can act as a SERVER for the others, allowing data to be shared without the need for a central server: Peer-to-peer technology is used to exchange information between companies. → CLIENT-SERVER

peg /peg/ verb, noun
● verb [+ obj] (**-gg-**)
1 (Economics) to fix or keep prices, currencies, etc. at a particular level: Interest rates will be pegged at 4%. ◇ A decision had been taken to peg their currency **to** the dollar. → FREEZE verb (1) See note at CURRENCY
2 (informal) (AmE) to measure, consider or estimate sth at a particular amount: Unemployment was above the 400 000 level that economists peg **as** a weak labour market.
▶ **'pegging** noun [U]
● noun [C]

SEE ALSO: adjustable peg, crawling ~, currency ~, off-the-~, sliding ~

an arrangement to fix or keep prices, currencies, etc. at a particular level: The country has now abandoned its exchange rate peg to the dollar.

P/'E ,multiple → PRICE-EARNINGS RATIO

penalty /'penəlti/ noun [C] (plural **penalties**)
a sum of money to be paid by sb who breaks a rule or contract: The penalty **for** late payment of tax due is $100. ◇ You can withdraw money from the account at any time **without** penalty. ◇ The regulatory authorities have the power to impose financial penalties.
○ to impose/introduce a penalty ◆ to face/incur a penalty

'penalty clause noun [C]
(Law) part of a contract that states the amount of money to be paid by a person who breaks the contract: The purpose of the penalty clause is to ensure the building is completed on time.

pence /pens/ plural of PENNY (1)

pencil /'pensl/ verb (**-ll-**, AmE **-l-**)
PHRV **,pencil sb/sth 'in** to write down sb's name or details of an arrangement with them that you know might have to be changed later: We've pencilled in a meeting **for** Tuesday afternoon. ◇ The share sale has been pencilled in for April. See note at ARRANGE

'pencil-,pusher = PEN-PUSHER

pending /'pendɪŋ/ adjective, preposition (formal)
● adjective

SEE ALSO: patent pending

1 [not before noun] waiting to be decided or settled: Nine cases are still pending.
2 going to happen soon: A crisis is pending in the industry. ◇ Employees have been informed of the pending sale of the company.
● preposition
while waiting for sth to happen; until sth happens: He has been suspended pending the outcome of an internal enquiry.

penetrate /'penɪtreɪt/ verb [+ obj]
(Marketing) to start selling products or services in a new area or to a new group of customers: The research helps companies to identify and penetrate new markets. ◇ The chain has not yet penetrated our major cities.

penetration /,penɪ'treɪʃn/ noun [U]
(Marketing)
1 the extent to which a product or service is bought in a particular area or by a particular group of people: In South Korea, broadband penetration had reached 55%. ◇ We are developing a new strategy for achieving greater **market** penetration.
2 the sale of products or services in a new area or to a new group of customers: The campaign focuses on London, which is the target area for penetration.

,pene'tration ,pricing noun [U]
(Marketing) the activity of selling a new product at a low price for a short period in order to attract customers: Penetration pricing is used to build market share quickly.

penny /'peni/ noun [C] (plural **pennies** or **pence**)
HELP In sense 1 **pennies** is used to refer to the coins, and **pence** to refer to an amount of money. In sense 2, the plural is **pennies**.
1 (abbr **p**) a small British coin and unit of money. There are 100 PENCE in one pound (£1): That will be 45 pence, please. ◇ They cost 20p each. ◇ He had a few pennies in his pocket.
2 (AmE) a cent coin: Her change purse is full of pennies and nickels.
IDM every **'penny** all of the money: She's on a high salary but I'm sure she's worth every penny. **not a 'penny** no money at all: It didn't cost a penny.

'penny-,pinching adjective
unwilling to spend money on things: Thompson was well known for his penny-pinching approach to business. ▶ **'penny-,pincher** noun [C] **'penny-,pinching** noun [U]: The firm's penny-pinching is putting workers' lives at risk.

,penny 'share (BrE) (also **,penny 'stock**, AmE, BrE) noun [C]
(Stock Exchange) a share, usually in a small company, that has a very low price: Their business involves selling penny shares in struggling companies to amateur investors.

'pen-,pusher (especially BrE) (AmE usually **'pencil-,pusher**) noun [C] (informal)
a person with a boring job, especially in an office, that involves a lot of writing: We are trying to convert some of our clerical staff from pen-pushers to hands-on managers.

★ pension /'penʃn/ noun, verb
● noun [C]

SEE ALSO: personal pension, stakeholder pension

an amount of money paid regularly by a government or company to sb who is considered to be too old or too ill/sick to work: Our company offers good retirement pensions. ◇ She finds it difficult to live on her state pension. ◇ If you can

afford it, it may be a good idea to take out a private pension. ◇ *a disability/widow's pension*
→ RETIREMENT PLAN

○ *to draw/pay/receive a pension* • *an old-age/a retirement pension* • *a company/private/state pension* • *a basic/comfortable/generous/good/small pension*

● *verb*

PHR V ,**pension sb 'off** (*especially BrE*) (*usually be pensioned off*) to allow or force sb to retire and to pay them a **pension**: *He was pensioned off and his job given to a younger man.* ◇ (*figurative, informal*) *That PC of yours should have been pensioned off years ago.*

pensionable /'penʃənəbl/ *adjective*
1 giving sb the right to receive a pension: *an employee of pensionable age* ◇ *It was made clear that the employment was not pensionable.* ◇ *The amount of pension you receive is based on your total pensionable service.*
2 **pensionable** pay is the part of an employee's pay used for calculating how much pension they will receive: *Overtime payments are not pensionable.*

'**pension fund** *noun* [C]
an amount of money that is invested and then used to pay **pensions**: *There will be an investigation into the way the bank managed its pension fund.*

'**pension plan** (*BrE also* '**pension scheme**) (*AmE also* re'**tirement plan**) *noun* [C]
a system in which you, and usually your employer, pay money regularly into a PENSION FUND while you are employed. You are then paid a **pension** when you retire: *She has a good job, some savings and a pension plan.* ◇ *The union wants all workers to pay into company pension plans.* See note at SALARY.

,**pent-'up** *adjective* [only before noun]
not satisfied; not expressed: *Supply is restricted, creating constant pent-up demand.*

people /'pi:pl/ *noun* [pl.]
the men and women who work for a particular person or organization: *Our people are all highly trained.*

,**people-in'tensive** *adjective*
needing or employing a lot of people: *Producing cars is no longer as people-intensive as it was.* ◇ *Services is a people-intensive business.* → LABOUR-INTENSIVE

'**people ,meter** *noun* [C]
(*Marketing*) an electronic device used especially in the US that is attached to a television and used for recording who is watching and what they are watching

'**people skills** *noun* [pl.]
the ability to deal with people well: *Many candidates had good technology skills but poor people skills.*

,**peppercorn 'rent** *noun* [C] (*BrE*)
(*Law*; *Property*) a very low rent

★ **per** /pə(r)/ *or, in the strong form,* /pɜː(r)/ *preposition*
used to express the cost or amount of sth for each person, number used, distance travelled, etc: *Rooms cost £50 per person, per night.*
IDM '**as per sth** following sth that has been decided; according to sth: *The goods were delivered as per contract.* ◇ *We have carried out your instructions as per your letter.*

,**P/'E ,ratio** = PRICE-EARNINGS RATIO

per capita /,pə 'kæpɪtə; *AmE* ,pər/ *adjective*
for each person: *Per capita income rose sharply last year.* ▶ ,**per 'capita** *adverb*: *It publishes more books per capita than any other country.* **NOTE** Per capita is a Latin phrase.

per,**ceived 'value** *noun* [U]
(*Marketing*) how much a customer believes sth is worth compared with its price: *Consumers make decisions on the basis of price and perceived value.* ◇ *Items made of fine wood have a high perceived value.*

★ **per cent** (*AmE spelling usually* **percent**) /,pə 'sent; *AmE* ,pər/ *noun, adjective, adverb*
● *noun* (*plural* **per cent, percent**)
one part in every hundred: *Last year sales increased by 8 per cent.* ◇ *Fewer than 12 per cent of workers are union members.*
● *adjective, adverb*
in or for every hundred: *a 7 per cent rise in price* ◇ *They own a 16 per cent stake in the business.* ◇ *The company's shares fell 3 per cent yesterday.*

★ **percentage** /pə'sentɪdʒ; *AmE* pər's-/ *noun*
1 [C with sing./pl. verb; usually sing.] the number, amount or rate of sth, expressed as part of a total which is 100; a part or share of a whole: *The percentage of sales to Greece has risen.* ◇ *A high percentage of the female staff are part-time workers.* ◇ *The figure is expressed as a percentage.* ◇ *the percentage rise in the average salary* ◇ *Interest rates are expected to rise by one percentage point (= 1%).*
○ *a high/large/low/small percentage* • *to calculate/estimate a percentage* • *a percentage gain/growth/increase/loss/rise*
2 [C, usually sing.] a share of the profits of sth: *He gets a percentage for every car sold.*

GRAMMAR POINT

Expressing percentages

Percentages (= numbers of per cent) are written in words as twenty-five per cent and in figures as 25%.

If a percentage is used with an uncountable noun or a singular noun the verb is generally singular: *20% of their electricity is generated by wind power.*

If the noun is singular but represents a group of people, the verb is singular in *AmE* but in *BrE* it may be singular or plural: *Eighty per cent of the work force is/are against the strike.*

If the noun is plural, the verb is plural: *90% of our customers are under the age of 25.*

percentile /pə'sentaɪl; *AmE* pər's-/ *noun* [C]
(*Technical*) one of the 100 equal groups that a larger group of people can be divided into, according to their place on a scale measuring a particular value: *The 75th percentile represents the pay level higher than 75% of the wages reported.*

perception /pə'sepʃn; *AmE* pər's-/ *noun* [C,U]
an idea, a belief or an image you have as a result of how you see or understand sth: *This negative publicity will inevitably damage public perception of the company.* ◇ *testing the impact of packaging on product perceptions*

per diem /,pə 'di:em; *AmE* ,pər/ *noun, adjective* (*especially AmE*)
● *noun* [U,C]
money paid, for example to employees, for things they need to buy every day: *How do I find out how much per diem is allowable for my travel?*
● *adjective*
for each day: *The total for all meals in one day must not exceed the maximum per diem allowance.* **NOTE** Per diem is a Latin phrase meaning 'for each day'.

,**perfect compe'tition** *noun* [U]
(*Economics*) a situation in which there are enough buyers and sellers of a product, all with full information, to prevent prices being controlled by one person or organization: *Perfect competition*

provides a theoretical model for market efficiency.
→ IMPERFECT COMPETITION, MONOPOLY

★ **perform** /pə'fɔːm; *AmE* pər'fɔːrm/ *verb*
1 [+ obj] to do sth, such as a piece of work, task or duty: *She performs an important role in our organization.* ◇ *A computer can perform many tasks at once.*
2 [no obj] **perform well/badly/poorly** to produce a profit or loss: *The company has been performing badly in recent years.* ◇ *Britain's best-performing fund is to get a new manager.*
3 [no obj] **perform (well/badly/poorly)** to do sth, work or function well, badly or as expected: *The Chinese economy has been performing well.* ◇ *Poorly performing management teams will be replaced.* ◇ *It is supposed to be a high-growth business, but so far it has failed to perform.*

★ **performance** /pə'fɔːməns; *AmE* pər'fɔːrm-/ *noun*

SEE ALSO: high-performance, pay for performance

1 [C,U] how far a company or an investment makes a profit: *The group reported a strong performance (= a good profit) in its pharmaceuticals division.* ◇ *He criticized the recent poor performance of the company.*
○ a **good/solid/strong** performance • a **bad/ disappointing/flat/poor/weak** performance • **business/financial/operating/sales/trading** performance • to **boost/improve/measure** performance
2 [C,U] how well or badly you do sth; how well or badly sth works: *an assessment of your performance* ◇ *The new management techniques aim to improve performance.* ◇ *There is widespread dissatisfaction with the government's economic performance.*
○ **bad/good/impressive/satisfactory** performance • to **evaluate/improve/measure** performance
3 (*formal*) [U; sing.] the act or process of performing a task, an action, etc: *She has shown enthusiasm in the performance of her duties.*

per'formance ap,praisal = APPRAISAL (1)
per'formance as,sessment = APPRAISAL (1)
per'formance bond = CONTRACT BOND
per'formance evalu,ation = APPRAISAL (1)
per'formance fund = AGGRESSIVE GROWTH FUND
per'formance ,indicator *noun* [C]
a measure that shows how well or badly sth is working: *A new performance indicator is being introduced to measure the level of customer satisfaction.* ◇ *We can't compete with the bigger stores in sales, but we can beat them in growth rates, customer service and other performance indicators.*
→ METRIC *noun*, KEY PERFORMANCE INDICATOR

per'formance ,management *noun* [U]
the process of controlling the performance of employees, for example by setting goals for them, providing training and encouraging them to work as well as they can

per,formance-related 'pay (*abbr* PRP) (*BrE*) (*also* ,pay for per'formance, ,variable 'pay, *AmE, BrE*) *noun* [U]
(*HR*) an arrangement where the amount sb is paid depends on how well they do their job

per'formance re,view = APPRAISAL (1)

performer /pə'fɔːmə(r); *AmE* pər'fɔːrm-/ *noun* [C]
1 an investment or a business, considered from the point of view of how much profit it makes compared with the average shares, businesses, etc: *Toyota was the star performer with record annual profits.* ◇ *IT stocks are the worst performers this year.* ◇ *The shares have been downgraded to 'buy' from 'market performer'.*

○ an **average/a good/solid/star/strong/top** performer • a **bad/weak** performer
2 a person who works in the way mentioned: *Good performers can be rewarded with pay and promotion.*
○ **good/high/outstanding/star/top** performers • **bad/ low/poor** performers

peril /'perəl/ *noun* [C]
(*Insurance*) an event that can cause a financial loss, for example a fire or a storm: *The document lists the perils covered by your policy.* → RISK

★ **period** /'pɪəriəd; *AmE* 'pɪr-/ *noun* [C]

SEE ALSO: accounting period, cooling-off ~, pay ~, payback ~, recovery ~, reporting ~

a particular length of time: *You can repay the loan over a period of two years.* ◇ *Revenues were down 8% on the same period last year.* ◇ *The offer is available for a limited period only.* ◇ *This week is one of the busiest periods of the year.*

'period bill (*also* 'term bill) *noun* [C]
(*Finance*) a BILL OF EXCHANGE which will be paid at a particular time in the future

peripheral /pə'rɪfərəl/ *adjective, noun*
● *adjective*
1 not as important as the main aim, part, etc. of sth: *They are selling off their peripheral businesses.*
2 (*IT*) used to describe equipment that is connected to a computer: *a peripheral device*
● *noun* [C]
(*IT*) a piece of equipment that is connected to a computer: *USB ports are used for scanners and other peripherals.*

perishables /'perɪʃəblz/ (*also* ,perishable 'goods) *noun* [pl.]
types of food that decay or go bad quickly: *Perishables are transported in refrigerated vehicles.*

perk /pɜːk; *AmE* pɜːrk/ *noun, verb*
● *noun* (*also* 'perquisite, *formal*) [C, usually pl.]
(*HR*) something you receive as well as your wages for doing a particular job: *Perks offered by the firm include a car and free health insurance.* ◇ *There was a long-running dispute over executive perks.* See note at SALARY
● *verb*
PHRV ,perk 'up; ,perk sth 'up to increase, or to make sth increase, in value, etc: *Share prices had perked up slightly by close of trading.* ◇ *Our next task is to perk up sales in Europe.*

permanent /'pɜːmənənt; *AmE* 'pɜːrm-/ *adjective*
lasting or staying for a long time: *a permanent job* ◇ *permanent staff* ◇ *She will take over the job until a permanent replacement is found.* ◇ *You must register if you want to use the software on a permanent basis.* OPP TEMPORARY → REGULAR *adj.* (6)

permatemp /'pɜːmətemp; *AmE* 'pɜːrm-/ *noun* [C]
(*HR*)
1 a temporary worker who is employed many times by an organization as this is cheaper than having a permanent employee: *Some permatemp employees had worked for the company for 14 years.*
2 an agency that supplies temporary employees to an employer

★ **permission** /pə'mɪʃn; *AmE* pər'm-/ *noun*
1 [U] the act of allowing sb to do sth, especially when this is done by sb in a position of authority: *You must ask permission for all major expenditure.* ◇ *The trademark can't be used without permission.*
○ to **ask for/request/seek** permission • to **get/obtain/ receive** permission • to **give/grant** permission • to **deny/refuse** permission
2 (*Law*) [C, usually pl.] an official written statement allowing sb to do sth: *The publisher is responsible for*

obtaining the necessary permissions to reproduce illustrations.

per'mission ,marketing *noun* [U]
a method of advertising products and services to customers through the Internet in which they must first give their permission to receive advertising information

★ **permit** *noun, verb*
● *noun* /'pɜːmɪt; AmE 'pɜːrmɪt/ [C]

SEE ALSO: **building permit, construction ~, work ~**

an official document that gives sb the right to do sth, especially for a limited period of time: *They have been granted a permit to provide mobile phone services in the area.*
۞ *to apply for/grant (sb)/issue a permit*
● *verb* /pə'mɪt; AmE pər'm-/ (-tt-)
1 [+ obj] to allow sb to do sth or to allow sth to happen: *The government is unlikely to permit the merger of the two companies.* ◇ *Charities are not permitted to spend funds on political activities.*
2 [+ obj or no obj] to make sth possible: *The password permits access to all files on the network.* ◇ *Cash machines permit you to withdraw money at any time.*

per,petual 'inventory = CONTINUOUS INVENTORY

perquisite /'pɜːkwɪzɪt; AmE 'pɜːrk-/ = PERK

,per-'share *adjective* [only before noun]
(*Accounting*) used to describe the amount of income, profit, etc. that a company receives for each one of its shares: *On a per-share basis, earnings were down 3% at €1.73.*
۞ *per-share earnings/loss/profit/value*

personal /'pɜːsənl; AmE 'pɜːrs-/ *adjective*
1 belonging to or connected with an individual, not a company or an organization: *We want consumers to carry on spending but keep personal debt under control.*
2 intended for individuals, not companies or organizations: *Internet banks offered cheap personal loans to attract new customers.*
3 acting as an individual, not as a company or an organization: *The demand for credit from both corporate and personal customers remains high.*
4 connected with a particular person and not with their job or official position: *We will not disclose your personal information to other organizations.* ◇ *The letter was marked 'Personal'.*
→ PRIVATE

,personal 'action *noun* [C]
(*Law*) a type of court case in which sb tries to get money from sb who has caused them to suffer injury, damage, etc: *to bring a personal action against sb*

,personal al'lowance (*BrE*) (*AmE* ,**personal ex'emption**) *noun* [C]
the amount of money you are allowed to earn each year before you have to pay tax

,personal as'sistant *noun* [C] (*abbr* **PA**)
a person who works as a secretary or an assistant for one person: *the personal assistant to the Director*
→ EXECUTIVE SECRETARY

,personal 'care *noun* [U]
the activity of keeping your hair, skin and teeth clean and in good condition: *The new range of personal care products includes cosmetics, shampoos and foam baths.*

,personal 'cheque (*AmE spelling* ~ **check**) *noun* [C]
a cheque written by an individual using the money that they have in the bank

,personal 'contract *noun* [C]
(*HR*) a type of contract of employment that is designed for an individual employee rather than for groups of workers

,personal 'credit = CONSUMER CREDIT

'personal day *noun* [C]
(*HR*) in the US and other countries, a day that you are allowed to be away from work with pay for personal reasons: *My employer places no limit on sick or personal days.* ◇ *I took a personal day to attend my daughter's graduation.*
→ COMPASSIONATE LEAVE

,personal de'velopment *noun* [U]
(*HR*) the process of gaining the knowledge, skills and abilities you need: *The course will help you identify your development needs in your business context and produce a personal development plan in line with your goals.* [SYN] SELF-DEVELOPMENT

,personal ex'emption = PERSONAL ALLOWANCE

,personal 'finance *noun* [U]
the activity of managing the money belonging to an individual: *The website covers all areas of personal finance including investments, mortgages and taxes.*

,personal infor'mation ,manager *noun* [C]
(*abbr* **PIM**)
a computer program in which you write names, addresses, things you have to do, etc.

,personal 'injury *noun* [U]
(*Law*) physical injury to a person, rather than damage to property or to sb's reputation: *Industries such as construction and transport have been the worst hit by the increase in personal injury claims.*

personality /,pɜːsə'næləti; AmE ,pɜːrs-/ *noun*
(*plural* **personalities**)

SEE ALSO: **brand personality**

1 [C,U] the various aspects of a person's character that combine to make them different from other people: *She has a strong personality.* ◇ *There are likely to be personality clashes in any group of colleagues.*
2 [C] a famous person, especially one who works in entertainment or sport: *They decided to use a sports personality to help sell their products.*
3 (*Marketing*) [C,U] the qualities of a product or an organization that make it interesting and different: *Packaging should reflect and enhance the product's personality.* ◇ *What is the organization's corporate personality?*
4 (*Law*) [C,U] an organization which is considered in law to exist separately from the people who own it or run it and to have legal rights and duties

personalize, -ise /'pɜːsənəlaɪz; AmE 'pɜːrs-/ *verb* [+ obj]
1 (*usually* **be personalized**) to design or change sth so that it is suitable for the needs of a particular person: *The machines are personalized to meet our customers' needs.* ◇ *a highly personalized service*
2 to mark or change sth in some way to show that it belongs to a particular person: *By choosing your own ringtone, you can personalize your phone.*
▶ **personalization, -isation** /,pɜːsənəlaɪ'zeɪʃn; AmE ,pɜːrsənələ'z-/ *noun* [U]: *Website personalization means that the site caters to different users in different ways.*

,personal 'leave *noun* [U]
(*HR*) time that you are allowed away from work, with or without pay, for personal reasons: *You may take personal leave for education, an extended vacation or to deal with family problems.*

,personal lia'bility *noun* [U]
(*Law*) the legal responsibility that an individual has for injury or damage to sb/sth, or for the debts of a

company they own: *There are several ways to protect yourself from personal liability for business debts.*

,personal 'organizer *noun* [C]
a small file with loose sheets of paper in which you write down information, addresses, what you have arranged to do, etc.; a very small computer for the same purpose → FILOFAX™ See note at CALENDAR

,personal 'pension *noun* [C]
an arrangement in which you pay money regularly to an insurance company or a bank, etc. which invests the money and pays you a pension when you retire: *He puts $200 a month into a personal pension plan.*

,personal 'property (*also* **'personalty**, *less frequent*) *noun* [U]
(*Law*) the assets that sb has, such as money, shares, etc. except for land and buildings: *Personal property includes movable items such as vehicles and merchandise.*

,personal repre'sentative *noun* [C]
(*Law*) a person who is responsible for the assets of sb who has died

,personal 'selling *noun* [U]
(*Marketing*) the use of people who are trained to sell a company's goods or services to talk to and persuade a customer to buy sth: *Potential customers are reached through advertising and personal selling.*

,personal 'statement *noun* [C]
a written description of yourself, your education and working life, your abilities and your goals: *The personal statement is an important part of the application form for the job.*

personalty /'pɜːsənəlti/ = PERSONAL PROPERTY

★ personnel /ˌpɜːsə'nel; *AmE* ˌpɜːrs-/ *noun*
(*HR*)
1 [pl.] the people who work for an organization: *Key personnel will be appointed by March.* ◇ *The group is trying to cut personnel costs for low-margin products.*
○ **key/qualified/skilled/trained** personnel ◆ **marketing/sales/security/technical** personnel
2 [U with sing./pl. verb] the department in a company that deals with employing and training people: *She works in personnel.* ◇ *Personnel is/are currently reviewing pay scales.* **SYN** HUMAN RESOURCES
○ the personnel **chief/department/division/manager/officer**

,person-to-'person *adjective* [usually before noun]
1 happening between two or more people who deal directly with each other rather than through another person: *Technical support is offered on a person-to-person basis.*
2 (*AmE*) (about a telephone call) made by calling the OPERATOR and asking to speak to a particular person. If that person is not available, the call does not have to be paid for: *Person-to-person calls are charged at a higher rate.*

PERT chart

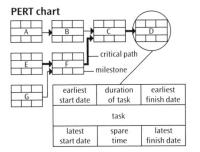

PERT /pɜːt; *AmE* pɜːrt/ *abbr*
(*Production*) **Project/Program/Performance Evaluation and Review Technique** a way of managing the tasks involved in a project and showing the order in which they should be completed and how much time is needed for each → CRITICAL PATH ANALYSIS

pessimism /'pesɪmɪzəm/ *noun* [U]
pessimism (**about/for/over sth**) a feeling that bad things will happen and that sth will not be successful; the tendency to have this feeling: *There is a mood of pessimism in the company about future job prospects.* **OPP** OPTIMISM
○ **business/economic/investor/market** pessimism ◆ **growing/increasing/widespread** pessimism ◆ a **mood/sense** of pessimism
▶ **'pessimist** *noun* [C] **pessimistic** /ˌpesɪ'mɪstɪk/ *adjective* **,pessi'mistically** *adverb* /ˌpesɪ'mɪstɪkli/

'PEST a,nalysis /pest/ (*also* **'STEP a,nalysis**) *noun* [C,U]
an examination of the political, economic, social and TECHNOLOGICAL aspects of the situation in which a company is operating to see how they will affect its products and markets: *Conduct a PEST analysis on the company and evaluate the strategies that it might pursue.*

'pester ,power *noun* [U] (*informal*)
the ability that children have to make their parents buy things, by repeatedly asking them until they agree

the 'Peter ,Principle /'piːtə(r)/ *noun* [sing.]
the theory that employees continue to be given a higher rank in an organization until finally they reach a position where they do not have the ability to do their jobs properly: *His promotion to the post of Marketing Director was a classic example of the Peter Principle.*

petition /pə'tɪʃn/ *noun* [C]
(*Law*) an official document asking a court of law to take a particular course of action: *One creditor has filed a petition for the company to be wound up.* → BANKRUPTCY PETITION

petrochemical /ˌpetrəʊ'kemɪkl; *AmE* ˌpetroʊ-/ *noun* [C]
any chemical substance obtained from PETROLEUM oil or natural gas: *The country's main exports are steel and petrochemicals.* ◇ *the petrochemical industry*

petrodollar /'petrəʊdɒlə(r); *AmE* 'petroʊdɑːlər/ *noun* [C]
(*Finance*) a unit of money that is used for calculating the money earned by countries that produce and sell oil: *An increase in oil prices raises the global supply of petrodollars.*

petroleum /pə'trəʊliəm; *AmE* -'troʊ-/ *noun* [U]
(often used in the names of companies) mineral oil that is found under the ground or the sea and is used to produce petrol/gas, etc: *the petroleum industry* ◇ *BP (British Petroleum)*

,petty 'cash *noun* [U]
a small amount of money kept in an office to pay small expenses: *Newspapers are paid for out of petty cash.*

pharma /'fɑːmə; *AmE* 'fɑːrmə/ *adjective, noun* (*informal*)
● *adjective* [only before noun]
pharmaceutical: *pharma companies*
● *noun* [U]
pharmaceutics

pharmaceutical /ˌfɑːməˈsuːtɪkl; -ˈsjuː-; AmE
ˌfɑːrməˈsuː-/ adjective, noun
• **adjective** [only before noun]
connected with making and selling drugs and
medicines: *She studied chemistry and then worked in
the pharmaceutical industry.*
• **noun** [C, usually pl.]
drugs or medicines: *Sales of pharmaceuticals used in
the treatment of HIV have increased rapidly.* ◇ *a
pharmaceuticals company* → BIOPHARMACEUTICAL

pharmaceutics /ˌfɑːməˈsuːtɪks; -ˈsjuː-; AmE
ˌfɑːrməˈsuː-/ noun [U]
the study and development of the production of
drugs and medicine

★ **phase** /feɪz/ noun, verb
• **noun** [C]
a stage in a process of change or development: *Our
company went through a phase of rapid expansion.* ◇
*Producing a quality product really starts in the design
phase.* ◇ *companies still in the start-up phase*
  O *the design/development/manufacturing phase* •
  the growth/start-up phase • *the early/final/initial/a
  late/new phase*
• **verb** [+ obj] (*usually* **be phased**)
to arrange to do sth gradually in stages over a
period of time: *The closure of regional offices was
phased over a two-year period.*
PHR V ˌphase sth **'down** to reduce sth gradually in
stages over a period of time: *We are phasing down
production of less profitable lines.* ˌphase sth **'in** to
introduce or start using sth gradually in stages over
a period of time: *The new tax will be phased in over
two years.* ˌphase sth **'out** to stop using sth
gradually in stages over a period of time: *Some
companies agreed to phase out the testing of
cosmetics on animals.*

phishing /ˈfɪʃɪŋ/ noun [U]
(*IT*) the activity of tricking people by getting them
to give their identity, bank account numbers, etc.
over the Internet or by email, and then using these
to steal money from them: *The most common form
of phishing is by email.* ◇ *The growth rate of phishing
scams jumped 52% in June.*

★ **phone** /fəʊn; AmE foʊn/ noun, verb
• **noun** [C,U]

SEE ALSO: **cellular phone, fixed ~, mobile ~**

a system for talking to sb else over long distances
using wires or radio; a machine used for this: *You
can get technical support **over the phone.*** ◇ *They
like to do business **by phone.*** ◇ *He's been **on the
phone** to his office for more than an hour.* ◇ *Her
phone must be switched off.*
• **verb** (*especially BrE*) (*BrE also* **ˌphone 'up**) [+ obj *or*
no obj]
to make a telephone call to sb: *You'll have to phone
her office to make an appointment.* ◇ *She phoned up
for a chat.* ◇ *Can I phone you back later?* ◇ *I'm
phoning about your ad in the paper.* **SYN** CALL
PHR V ˌphone **'in** to make a telephone call to the
place where you work: *Sarah phoned in to say she'd
be late.* ◇ *Three people have **phoned in sick** already
this morning.* ˌphone sth **'in** to make a telephone
call to the place where you work in order to give sb
some information

'phone book = TELEPHONE DIRECTORY
'phone call = CALL noun (1)
phonecard /ˈfəʊnkɑːd; AmE ˈfoʊnkɑːrd/ noun [C]
1 (*AmE*) a plastic card with an individual number
on it that allows you to use a telephone service, for
example to make international calls. The cost of the
call is charged to your account and you pay it later:
*Using a phonecard can be a very cost-effective way of
making calls abroad.*

2 (*especially BrE*) a plastic card that you can use in
some public telephones instead of money: *The first
phone was broken and the second took only
phonecards.* → CALLING CARD

photocopier /ˈfəʊtəʊkɒpiə(r); AmE ˈfoʊtoʊkɑːp-/
(*also* **copier**, *especially in AmE*) noun [C]
a machine that makes copies of documents, etc. by
photographing them: *The photocopier has run out of
paper.*

photocopy /ˈfəʊtəʊkɒpi; AmE ˈfoʊtoʊkɑːpi/ noun,
verb
• **noun** [C] (*plural* **photocopies**)
a copy of a document, etc. made by the action of
light on a specially treated surface: *Make as many
photocopies as you need.* → COPY noun (2)
• **verb** (**photocopies, photocopying, photocopied,
photocopied**)
1 [+ obj *or* no obj] to make a **photocopy** of sth: *Can
you get these photocopied for me by 5 o'clock?* ◇
photocopied documents ◇ *photocopying equipment/
facilities*
2 [no obj] **photocopy well/badly** (about printed
material) to produce a good/bad **photocopy**: *The
comments in pencil haven't photocopied very well.*
→ COPY verb (1)

physical /ˈfɪzɪkl/ adjective [only before noun]
1 (*IT*) existing in a form that can be seen or
touched, as opposed to electronic: *The website has
features that physical stores can't offer.* **OPP** VIRTUAL
2 (*Finance*) used to describe a product or a raw
material that can be bought and sold, or used, as
opposed to cash, shares or FUTURES: *Investors are
putting their money into physical assets such as gold
and property.* → TANGIBLE
  O *physical assets/commodities/goods*

ˌphysical 'capital noun [U]
(*Economics*) items such as land, factories, machinery
and materials that are used to produce goods and
provide services: *Our economy is no longer based on
the use of physical capital to produce material goods.*
→ HUMAN CAPITAL, SOCIAL CAPITAL

ˌphysical distri'bution noun [U]
(*Production*) the tasks involved in moving finished
goods from producers to consumers in the most
efficient way and in planning and controlling this:
*The physical distribution of products has two
primary aspects: transportation and storage.*

pick /pɪk/ verb [+ obj]

SEE ALSO: **cherry-pick**

(*Production*) to collect items that a customer has
ordered from the place where they are stored so
that the order can be packed and sent: *They claim
to be able to pick, pack and ship a large order in only
90 minutes.* ◇ **'picking** noun [U]: *You will be in
charge of ten **picking and packing** staff.* ◇ *a wireless
warehouse picking system*
IDM **pick up the 'bill/'tab (for sth)** (*informal*) to
pay for sth: *The company picked up the tab for his
hotel room.* → idiom at SLACK noun
PHR V ˌpick sth **'off** to take the best people or
things from a group and leave the rest: *Rival firms
are interested in picking off parts of the group.* ˌpick
sb/sth **'out** to choose sb/sth carefully from a group
of people or things: *She was picked out from dozens
of applicants for the job.* ˌpick **'up** to get better,
stronger, etc.; to improve: *In the last few weeks sales
have started to pick up.* → PICKUP ˌpick sth **'up**
(*informal*) to buy sth, especially cheaply or by
chance: *Investors have a chance to pick up some
bargains.*

picket /ˈpɪkɪt/ noun, verb
• **noun** [C]
a person or group of people who stand outside the
entrance to a building in order to protest about sth,
especially in order to stop people from entering a

factory, etc. during a strike; an occasion when this happens: *Five pickets were arrested by police.* ◇ *I was on picket duty at the time.* ◇ *a mass picket of the factory*
- **verb** [+ obj or no obj]
to stand outside somewhere such as your place of work to protest about sth or to try and persuade people to join a strike: *200 workers were picketing the factory.* ◇ *Striking workers picketed outside the gates.* ▶ **'picketer** *noun* [C] (*AmE*)

'picket line *noun* [C]
a line or group of **pickets**: *Fire crews refused to cross the picket line.*

pickup /'pɪkʌp/ *noun*
1 [C] an improvement: *Retailers are hoping for a pickup in consumer spending.* → PICK UP at PICK
2 (*Transport*) [C,U] an occasion when sth is collected: *Goods are delivered not later than noon on the day after pickup.*
3 (*also* **'pickup truck**) [C] a vehicle with low sides and no roof at the back used, for example, by farmers

pictogram /'pɪktə-græm/ *noun* [C]
a diagram that uses pictures to represent amounts or numbers of a particular thing: *This pictogram shows sales for the last three months.*

pictogram

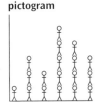

picture /'pɪktʃə(r)/ *noun*
1 [C, usually sing.] a description that gives you an idea of what sth is like: *The writer paints a gloomy picture of the economy.*
2 [sing.] **the picture** the general situation concerning sb/sth: *The overall picture for industry is encouraging.*
IDM **in/out of the 'picture** (*informal*) involved/not involved in a situation: *With our main competitors out of the picture, we have a good chance of winning the contract.* **put/keep sb in the 'picture** (*informal*) to give sb the information they need in order to understand a situation: *Just to put you in the picture—there have been a number of changes here recently.* → idiom at BIG

'piece rate *noun* [C]
(*HR*) an amount of money paid for each thing or amount of sth that a worker produces: *Slow workers on piece rates simply took home less pay.*

piecework /'pi:swɜːk; *AmE* -wɜːrk/ *noun* [U]
(*HR*) work that is paid for by the amount done and not by the hours worked: *Piecework payment systems can help boost productivity but may lower quality.* ▶ **'pieceworker** *noun* [C]

'pie chart (*also* **'pie graph**) *noun* [C]
a diagram consisting of a circle that is divided into parts to show the size of particular parts in relation to the whole: *Pie charts are often the simplest way to show statistics.*

pie chart

pigeonhole /'pɪdʒɪn-həʊl; *AmE* -hoʊl/ *verb, noun*
- **verb** [+ obj]
to decide that sb/sth belongs to a particular group or type, often without thinking deeply enough about it: *She never tried to pigeonhole her customers.* **SYN** CATEGORIZE
- **noun** [C]
1 one of a set of small boxes that are fixed on a wall and open at the front, used for putting letters,

messages, etc. in: *The letter had been put in the wrong pigeonhole.*
2 a group or type of people or things that sb/sth is put into, that is often too general, unfair or not correct: *Many clients want their advisers to fit into neat pigeonholes.* **SYN** CATEGORY

piggyback /'pɪgibæk/ *verb*
PHR V **'piggyback on/onto sth**; **'piggyback sth on/onto sth 1** to use a system that already exists as a basis for sth else: *Other search engines piggyback on one another to provide more complete results.* **2** to use a larger organization, etc. for your own advantage

pile /paɪl/ *noun* [C]
a large amount of money or debt: *The company is selling off assets in order to reduce its debt pile.* → CASH PILE

pilfer /'pɪlfə(r)/ *verb* [+ obj or no obj]
to steal things of little value or in small quantities, especially from the place where you work: *She regularly pilfered stamps and stationery from work.* ◇ *He was caught pilfering.* ▶ **pilferage** /'pɪlfərɪdʒ/ *noun* [U] (*formal*): *reducing the costs of theft and pilferage by employees* **'pilferer** *noun* [C] **'pilfering** *noun* [U]

pilot /'paɪlət/ *noun, verb, adjective*
- **noun** [C]

SEE ALSO: **automatic pilot**

1 a person who operates the controls of an aircraft, especially as a job: *a commercial/an airline pilot*
2 a person with special knowledge of a difficult area of water who guides ships through it
3 a single television programme that is made in order to find out if people will like it and want to watch further programmes
- **verb** [+ obj]
1 to fly an aircraft or guide a ship; to act as a **pilot**: *The plane was piloted by the instructor.*
2 **pilot sth (through sth)** to guide sb/sth somewhere, especially through a complicated place or system: *She has piloted the company through a period of successful growth.*
3 (*Marketing*) to test a new product, idea, etc. with a few people or in a small area before it is introduced everywhere: *We are considering piloting the software with small businesses in the London area.*
- **adjective** [only before noun]
done on a small scale in order to see if sth is successful enough to do on a large scale: *a pilot project/study/survey/test* ◇ *a pilot **episode** (= of a radio or television series)*

PIM /ˌpi: aɪ 'em/ = PERSONAL INFORMATION MANAGER

PIN /pɪn/ (*also* **'PIN ˌnumber**) *noun* [C] **personal identification number** a number given to you, for example by a bank, so that you can use a plastic card to take out money from a cash machine: *I've forgotten my PIN.* ◇ *Criminals are finding many ways to uncover clients' PINs.*

ping /pɪŋ/ *verb* [+ obj]
(*IT*)
1 to use an Internet program to test whether a computer you are trying to connect with is working properly
2 (*informal*) to send sb a type of electronic message similar to an email that appears on their screen as soon as it is sent (an **instant message**): *Employees can ping each other questions and requests.*
▶ **ping** *noun* [C] (*informal*): *An 'away message' tells other users that you're around, but not taking pings.*

ˌpink-ˈcollar *adjective* [only before noun] (*especially AmE*)
connected with jobs with low pay that are done mainly by women, for example in offices: *pink-collar workers* → BLUE-COLLAR, WHITE-COLLAR

ˈPink Sheetsᵀᴹ (*also spelled* **pink sheets**) *noun* [pl.]
(*Finance*) in the US, a list of the latest prices of OVER-THE-COUNTER shares (= shares that do not appear in an official stock exchange list), that is published every day: *The company's shares closed at 86 cents on the Pink Sheets.* → YELLOW SHEETS

ˌpink ˈslip *noun* [C] (*AmE*)
(*HR, informal*) a letter given to sb to say that they must leave their job: *About 20% of the workforce will soon receive pink slips.* ▶ **ˈpink-slip** *verb* [+ obj] (**-pp-**): *He was afraid he was going to be pink-slipped.*

ˈPIN ˌnumber = PIN

pioneer /ˌpaɪəˈnɪə(r); *AmE* -ˈnɪr/ *noun, verb*
● *noun* [C]
a person or an organization that is the first to develop a particular area of knowledge, type of product, etc. that other people or organizations then continue to develop: *He was one of the pioneers of wireless communications.* ◇ *Our company is a pioneer in the pharmaceutical field.*
● *verb* [+ obj]
when a person or an organization **pioneers** sth, they are one of the first to do, discover or use sth new

pioneering /ˌpaɪəˈnɪərɪŋ; *AmE* -ˈnɪr-/ *adjective* [usually before noun]
introducing ideas and methods that have never been used before: *They have played a pioneering role in the development of digital radio.* ◇ *pioneering research*

pipeline /ˈpaɪplaɪn/ *noun* [C]
a series of pipes that are usually underground and are used for carrying oil, gas, etc. over long distances
IDM **in the ˈpipeline** something that is **in the pipeline** is being discussed, planned or prepared and will happen or exist soon: *The company has a range of new products in the pipeline.*

piracy /ˈpaɪrəsi/ *noun* [U]
the act of making illegal copies of video tapes, computer programs, books, etc., in order to sell them: *a new way to deal with software piracy*

pirate /ˈpaɪrət/ *noun, verb*
● *noun* [C] (*often used as an adjective*)
a person who makes illegal copies of video tapes, computer programs, books, etc., in order to sell them: *pirate copies of CDs* ◇ *software pirates*
● *verb* [+ obj]
to copy and use or sell a product without permission and without having the right to do so: *pirated computer games* See note at COPY

pit /pɪt/ *noun* [C]
1 (*Stock Exchange*) (*AmE*) the area of a stock exchange or other EXCHANGE where a particular product is traded: *The futures contracts will be traded on-screen as well as in traditional pits.* → FLOOR
2 a coal mine: *planned pit closures*

pitch /pɪtʃ/ *noun, verb*
(*Commerce; Marketing*)
● *noun* [C, usually sing.]

SEE ALSO: **elevator pitch, sales pitch**

talk or arguments used by a person trying to sell things or persuade people to do sth: *an aggressive pitch* ◇ *Each company was given ten minutes to make its pitch for the contract.*
● *verb*
1 [+ obj] to set sth at a particular level: *They have pitched their prices too high.* ◇ *The takeover would be pitched at $4.6 billion.*
2 [+ obj] to aim or direct a product or service at a particular group of people: *The new software is being pitched at banks.* ◇ *The car is being pitched as a high-quality, low-cost alternative to local models.*
3 [+ obj *or* no obj] to try to persuade sb to buy sth, to give you sth or to make a business deal with you: *Improving your presentation skills will help you when pitching for business.*

pitfall /ˈpɪtfɔːl/ *noun* [C, usually pl.]
a danger or difficulty, especially one that is hidden or not obvious at first: *The article tells you how to avoid some of the pitfalls of online banking.* ◇ *Investors need to be aware of the potential pitfalls.*

pittance /ˈpɪtns/ *noun* [C, usually sing.]
a very small amount of money, especially paid to sb as wages: *They paid us a pittance and the working conditions were appalling.*

pivotal /ˈpɪvətl/ *adjective*
of great importance because other things depend on it: *The company plays a pivotal role in the local economy.*

pixel /ˈpɪksl/ *noun* [C]
(*IT*) any of the small individual areas on a computer screen, which together form the whole display

place /pleɪs/ *verb, noun*
● *verb* [+ obj]
1 to give instructions about sth or make a request for sth to happen: *Placing an ad in the local newspaper cost $250.* ◇ *As soon as customers place an order, they receive confirmation by email.*
2 to find a suitable job for sb: *The agency placed about 2 000 office workers last year.*
3 (*Finance*) to make new shares in a company available for sale to particular people or institutions: *The company will raise money by placing 20 million shares.* → PLACING
→ idiom at RECORD ˌnoun
● *noun* [C]
a building or an area used for a particular purpose: *The site acts as an online meeting place.* ◇ *He can usually be contacted at his place of work.*
IDM **be ˈgoing places** to be getting more and more successful in your life or career: *a young architect who's really going places* **in ˈplace** working or ready to work: *A deal on funding will be in place by June.*

placement /ˈpleɪsmənt/ *noun* [U,C]

SEE ALSO: **private placement, product placement**

1 the act of finding sb a suitable job or place to live: *a job placement service* ◇ *The recruiting agency handles mainly permanent placements.*
2 (*BrE*) (*AmE* **ˈpracticum**) a job, often as part of a course of study, where you get some experience of a particular kind of work: *The third year is spent on placement in selected companies.* ◇ *The program combines practicums with business and general studies courses.* ◇ *business students returning from work placements*
3 (*Finance*) (*AmE*) = PLACING

placing /ˈpleɪsɪŋ/ (*AmE also* **ˈplacement**) *noun* [C,U]
(*Finance*) an occasion when new shares in a company are made available for sale to particular individuals or institutions: *The deal will be partly funded through a share placing.* → PRIVATE PLACING

plaintiff /ˈpleɪntɪf/ *noun* [C]
(*Law*) a person who makes a formal complaint against sb in court → CLAIMANT (3), COMPLAINANT, DEFENDANT

★ **plan** /plæn/ *noun, verb*

● *noun* [C]

SEE ALSO: action plan, business ~, cafeteria ~, contingency ~, dividend reinvestment ~, employee share ownership ~, floor ~, etc.

1 a set of things to do in order to achieve sth: *They drew up a comprehensive plan **for** reducing costs.* ◇ *We've come up with a plan **to** save the business from collapse.*
2 an idea for doing or achieving sth in the future: *They are expected to announce plans **for** further factory closures.* ◇ *We have no plans **to** sell the business.*
3 (*Finance*) (*especially with other nouns*) a way of investing money or making payments: *The company offers a retirement **savings** plan for employees.* ◇ *The **payment** plan enables customers to pay for goods over a period of time.*
4 a detailed drawing of a machine, building, etc. that shows its size, shape and measurements: *The architect is **drawing up** plans for the new offices.*
5 a diagram that shows how sth will be arranged: *a floor plan* (= showing how furniture is arranged) ◇ *a seating plan*

● *verb* [+ obj or no obj] (**-nn-**)
1 to make detailed arrangements for sth you want to do in the future: *For a comfortable future, you need to plan ahead.* ◇ *A meeting has been planned for early next year.*
2 plan (on sth/on doing sth) to intend or expect to do sth: *The new owners are not planning any major changes in the near future.* ◇ *news of planned job cuts*
PHRV ,**plan sth 'out** to plan carefully and in detail sth that you are going to do in the future: *She has her career all planned out.*

Plan 'A *noun* [sing.]
the thing or things sb intends to do if everything happens as they expect

Plan 'B *noun* [sing.]
the thing or things sb intends to do if their first plan is not successful: *If Plan A fails, we'll go to Plan B.*

,**planned e'conomy** *noun* [C]
(*Economics*) an economic system that is controlled by the government rather than by the amount of goods available and the level of demand from customers: *This was the final stage in the transition from a planned economy to a market economy.*
→ COMMAND ECONOMY, MARKET ECONOMY

planner /'plænə(r)/ *noun* [C]
1 a person whose job is to plan the growth and development of a town: *a city/town/an urban planner*
2 a person who makes plans for a particular area of activity: *the country's top economic planner* ◇ *You should consult a tax planner before you sell any assets.*
3 a book, computer program, etc. that contains dates and is used for recording information, arranging meetings, etc.: *Use a wall planner to organize activities in your personal and professional life.* ◇ *a day/year planner*—Picture at OFFICE

★ **planning** /'plænɪŋ/ *noun* [U]

SEE ALSO: aggregate planning, enterprise resource ~, human resource ~, manpower ~, manufacturing resource ~, material requirements ~, media ~, etc.

1 the process of making plans for sth: *Organizing a conference requires a lot of careful planning.* ◇ *Consultants may be able to help with business planning.*
➊ *careful/detailed* planning ◆ *advance/forward* planning ◆ *business/financial* planning ◆ *to need/ require* planning
2 the control of the growth and development of towns and their buildings, roads, etc. so that they can be pleasant and convenient places for people to

live in: *Urban planning deals with the design of the built environment.*
➊ *city/town/urban* planning ◆ planning *approval/ consent/permission*

★ **plant** /plɑːnt; *AmE* plænt/ *noun*
1 [C] a factory or place where power is produced or an industrial process takes place: *Toyota has car assembly plants in the United States and Canada.* ◇ *It is Europe's most productive car plant.* See note at FACTORY
➊ *an assembly/a bottling/manufacturing/packing/ processing* plant ◆ *a car/chemical* plant
2 [U] large machinery that is used in industrial processes: *The company has been investing in new plant and equipment.* ◇ *specialists in plant hire*

plastic /'plæstɪk/ (*also* ,**plastic 'money**) *noun* [U]
(*informal*)
credit cards or other bank cards: *Do they take plastic?*

plateau /'plætəʊ; *AmE* plæ'toʊ/ *noun, verb*
● *noun* [C] (*plural* **plateaux** *or* **plateaus** /-təʊz; *AmE* -'toʊz/)
a time of little or no change after a period of growth or progress: *Inflation has reached a plateau.*
● *verb* [no obj] **plateau (out)** to stay at a steady level after a period of growth or progress: *Unemployment has at last plateaued out.* ◇ *Prices have pretty much plateaued for now.*

platform /'plætfɔːm; *AmE* -fɔːrm/ *noun* [C]

SEE ALSO: cross-platform

1 a basis on which sth can develop: *The deal will provide the company with a platform **for** long-term growth.*
2 (*IT*) the technical basis of a system, especially a computer or broadcasting system: *Versions of the software are available for Windows and Macintosh platforms.*
3 a raised structure standing in the sea, built by a company that is taking oil or gas from under the sea: *They deliver supplies to the offshore platforms of major oil companies.*

,**platform-'neutral** *adjective*
(*IT*) able to work on different technical systems: *The developers have a policy of producing platform-neutral applications.*

platinum /'plætɪnəm/ *noun* [U]
a very valuable silver-grey metal used in making expensive jewellery and in industry

play /pleɪ/ *verb, noun*
● *verb* [no obj] (*especially AmE*)
to have a particular effect on sb: *Providing good service plays well **with** customers.*
IDM **have money, time, etc. to 'play with** (*informal*) to have a particular amount of money, time, etc. for doing sth: *We don't have a lot of money to play with.* **play by sb's (own) 'rules** if sb **plays by their own rules** or makes other people **play by their rules** they set the conditions for doing business **play by the 'rules** to deal fairly and honestly with people: *They were a well-run company and played by all the rules, but still failed.* **play 'catch-up** (*especially AmE*) to try to be as good or successful as a competitor: *They are one of the biggest companies in the industry and we're always playing catch-up with them.* **play for high 'stakes** to be involved in an activity where you can lose a lot if it fails, but gain a lot if it is successful **play the ('stock) 'market** to buy and sell shares in order to make a quick profit: *Not all investors wish to take a risk by playing the market.* **play a (key, major,**

major, vital, etc.) 'part/'role to play (in sth) to be involved in sth and have an important effect on it: *She had played a key role in the growth of the business.* ◇ *Financial rewards play an important part in motivating staff.* play the 'system to use a set of rules that control sth in a way that gives you an advantage: *The developers are experts at playing the planning system.* play to your 'strengths to give your attention and effort to things that you do well; to give sb the opportunity to do this: *Each member of the team should have a task that plays to their strengths.*

PHRV ,play sth 'back to play telephone messages that have been recorded ,play sth 'down to try to make sth seem less important than it is: *They had made serious losses and were trying to play them down.* OPP PLAY STH UP 'play for sth to try to gain sth; to compete with sb for sth: *There is still 96% of the company to play for.* ,play 'out; ,play itself/themselves 'out to develop or end in a particular way: *Let's make a decision on this and see how it plays out.* ,play sth 'up to try to make sth seem more important than it is: *I played up my previous experience in the industry.* OPP PLAY STH DOWN

● *noun*

SEE ALSO: **Plug and Play, pure ~, role ~**

1 [U] the activity or operation of sth; the influence of sth on sth else: *the free play of market forces* ◇ *Unemployment figures have fallen but there may be seasonal factors at play.*
2 (*Stock Exchange, informal*) [C] an act of investing money in particular shares, bonds, etc: *Although the shares are not cheap, they are a defensive play that won't let you down.*

IDM bring/call sth into 'play to begin to use sth: *More funding will be brought into play.* come into 'play to begin to be used or to have an effect: *A number of factors come into play when you ask people to work together in groups.* in play if a company is **in play**, it can be bought by another company: *The company has been put in play as a takeover target.* make a 'play for sb/sth to try to obtain sth; to do things that are intended to produce a particular result: *She was making a play for the sales manager's job.*

playbook /'pleɪbʊk/ *noun* [C] (*AmE*)
a set of plans for achieving an aim: *The business plan serves as a playbook for everyone involved in the company.*

player /'pleɪə(r)/ *noun* [C]

SEE ALSO: **team player**

an important company or person involved in a particular area of business: *The company is a major player in the London property market.* ◇ *The new employee should be introduced to key players in the department.*
○ *a big/dominant/global/key/leading/major player* ● *a niche/small player*

'playing field *noun* [C, usually sing.]
(*Marketing*) used to describe a situation where people are competing with each other: *Do you have the skills necessary to perform on today's corporate playing field?* ◇ *The strength of the pound had tilted the playing field away from UK operations* (= made it more difficult for them to compete).
IDM a ,level 'playing field a situation where everyone has a fair and equal chance of succeeding: *The tariffs mean that Europe and the US are not competing on a level playing field.* ◇ *The aim of the changes is to create a level playing field for life assurance companies.* NOTE Variations of this idiom are also used: *Many people believe that technology can level the playing field. The government wants to*

ensure the playing field remains level. an ,uneven 'playing field a situation in which some competitors have an unfair advantage: *The proposed measure will create an uneven playing field among competing financial services.*

plc /ˌpiː el 'siː/ *abbr* (*BrE*)
1 (*usually used in written English*) (*also spelled* **PLC**) public limited company (used after the name of a company or business): *Lloyd's Bank plc* See note at LTD
2 (*Marketing*) **PLC** = PRODUCT LIFE CYCLE

pledge /pledʒ/ *verb, noun*
● *verb* [+ obj]
1 to formally promise to give or do sth: *Japan has pledged $100 million in aid.* ◇ *The CEO pledged that there would be no more job cuts.*
2 (*Law*) to leave sth valuable with sb to prove that you will pay back money that you owe: *The shares were pledged to the bank as security for loans.*
● *noun* [C]
1 a serious promise: *Management has given a pledge that there will be no job losses this year.* ◇ *Will the government honour its election pledge not to raise taxes?*
2 (*Law*) something valuable that you leave with sb to prove that you will pay back money that you owe: *The property is given as a pledge until the debt is paid.* ◇ *How can I redeem my pledge* (= pay back the loan and get the valuable item back)?

plenary /'pliːnəri/ *adjective, noun*
● *adjective* [only before noun]
(*about meetings, etc.*) to be attended by everyone who has the right to attend: *The new committee holds its first plenary session this week.*
● *noun* [C] (*plural* **plenaries**)
a **plenary** meeting: *The resolution will be put to a vote at the final plenary.*

'Plimsoll line (*also* 'Plimsoll mark) /'plɪmsəl/ = LOAD LINE

PLM /ˌpiː el 'em/ = PRODUCT LIFE CYCLE MANAGEMENT

plot /plɒt; *AmE* plɑːt/ *noun, verb*
● *noun* [C]
a piece of land that is used or intended for a special purpose: *The company invested $300 m, buying new plots of land for development.* ◇ *Building plots range in price from $246 500 to $440 000.*
● *verb* [+ obj] (-tt-)
1 to make a diagram or chart from some information: *The results of the survey are analysed and plotted on a chart.*
2 to mark points on a graph and draw a line or curve connecting them: *First, analyse the responses and plot them onto a graph.*

plough (*AmE spelling* **plow**) /plaʊ/ *verb*
PHRV ,plough sth 'back (into sth); ,plough sth back 'in to put money made as profit back into a business in order to improve it: *Surpluses will be ploughed back into the company to fund new projects.* ,plough sth 'into sth to invest a large amount of money in a company or project: *The company has ploughed an estimated $85 million into the online operation.*

plug /plʌg/ *verb, noun*
● *verb* [+ obj] (-gg-)
1 to provide sth that has been missing from a particular situation and is needed in order to improve it: *A cheaper range of products was introduced to plug the gap at the lower end of the market.*
2 (*Marketing*) to give praise or attention to a new product, book, CD, etc. in order to encourage people to buy it: *She came on the show to plug her latest album.* SYN PROMOTE
PHRV ,plug sth 'into sth (*IT*) to connect a

computer to a computer system: *All our computers are plugged into the main network.* **,plug 'into sth 1** (about a piece of electrical equipment) to be able to be connected to the main supply of electricity or to another piece of electrical equipment: *The modem plugs into the USB port on your laptop.* **2** to become involved with a particular activity or group of people: *The company has doubled its profits since plugging into lucrative overseas markets.*
● *noun* [C]
praise or attention given to a new product, book, CD, etc. in order to encourage people to buy it: *He managed to get in a plug for his new book.* → idiom at PULL *verb*

,Plug and 'Play™ *noun* [U]
(*IT*) a system which makes it possible for a user to connect a device such as a printer to a computer and use it immediately: *Newer machines feature plug-and-play capabilities.*

'plug-in *adjective*
1 able to be connected using a plug: *a plug-in kettle* **2** (*IT*) that can be added to a computer system so that it can do more things: *a plug-in graphics card*
▶ **'plug-in** *noun* [C] (*IT*): *a handheld with a dictionary plug-in* ◇ *downloading and installing plug-ins*

plummet /ˈplʌmɪt/ *verb* [no obj]
to fall suddenly and quickly from a high level or position: *Share prices plummeted to an all-time low.*
SYN PLUNGE See note at INCREASE
▶ **'plummet** *noun* [C, usually sing.]: *a plummet in pre-tax profits*

plunge /plʌndʒ/ *verb, noun*
● *verb* [no obj]
to decrease suddenly and quickly: *Share prices have plunged in recent months.* ◇ *The dollar plunged to its lowest level in six years.* **SYN** PLUMMET See note at INCREASE
PHRV **,plunge 'into sth; ,plunge sb/sth 'into sth** to experience sth unpleasant; to make sb/sth do this: *The country plunged deeper into recession.* ◇ *After losing the contract, the company was plunged into crisis.*
● *noun* [C, usually sing.]
a sudden decrease in an amount or the value of sth: *The group has announced a plunge in annual profits.* ◇ *This increase reversed an earlier price-plunge.* **SYN** DROP
IDM **take the 'plunge** (*informal*) to decide to do sth important or difficult, especially after thinking about it for a long time: *Even when you're ready to take the plunge, setting up a business is not easy.*

plus /plʌs/ *preposition, adjective, noun*
● *preposition*
1 used when the two numbers or amounts mentioned are being added together: *The book is available at $19.49 plus shipping.* ◇ *You pay back the original loan amount plus interest.* **2** as well as sth/sb; and also: *Give a description of your service or product plus information about who uses or buys it.*
OPP MINUS
IDM **plus or 'minus** used when the number mentioned may be more or less by a particular amount: *They expect to report earnings of $174 million, plus or minus $1 million.* ◇ *The margin of error was plus or minus three percentage points.*
● *adjective*
—————————————————————————
SEE ALSO: cost-plus
—————————————————————————
1 [only before noun] used to describe an aspect of sth that you consider to be a good thing: *The airline's safety record is a major plus **point**.* ◇ *On the plus side, all the staff are enthusiastic.* **OPP** MINUS

2 used after a number to show that the real number or amount is more than the one mentioned: *The profit from the sale of the factory is expected to be $22 million plus.*
● *noun* [C]
1 (*informal*) an advantage; a good thing: *If the software works with any type of computer, that's a big plus.* ◇ *One of the pluses of the job is being able to work from home.*
2 (*also* **'plus sign**) the symbol (+), used in mathematics: *He put a plus instead of a minus.*
OPP MINUS

'plus tick = UPTICK

ply /plaɪ/ *verb* [+ obj or no obj] (**plies, plying, plied, plied**)
to travel regularly along a particular route or between two particular places: *airlines plying transatlantic routes*
IDM **ply your 'trade** to do your work or business: *This is the restaurant where he plied his trade as a cook.*

PMI /ˌpiː em ˈaɪ/ *abbr*
(*Economics*) (*used as a singular noun*)
a measure of economic activity in the section of the economy that is concerned with the manufacture of goods, published every month: *A PMI over 50% means that manufacturing is expanding.* **NOTE** PMI is formed from the first letters of the words 'Purchasing Managers' Index'.

'P-note = PROMISSORY NOTE

PO /ˌpiː ˈəʊ; AmE ˈoʊ/ = POST OFFICE (2), POSTAL ORDER

POA /ˌpiː əʊ ˈeɪ; AmE oʊ/ = POINT OF ACTION

poach /pəʊtʃ; AmE poʊtʃ/ *verb* [+ obj]
to take and use staff, customers, etc. from another company in a dishonest or unfair way: *Several of our employees have been poached by a rival firm.* ◇ *The company poached the contract **from** their main rivals.* ▶ **'poaching** *noun* [U]: *the poaching of key personnel*

,P'O box (*also* **'post ,office box**) *noun* [C]
used as a kind of address, so that mail can be sent to a post office where it is kept until it is collected: *Mail your $100 deposit to PO Box 155, Irvington.*

pocket /ˈpɒkɪt; AmE ˈpɑːk-/ *noun, verb, adjective*
● *noun* [C, usually sing.]
the amount of money that a person, an organization or a government has available to spend: *London has hotels to suit every pocket.* ◇ *Employees pay for small items from their own pockets and then claim the money back.* **SYN** PURSE
IDM **,out of 'pocket** (*especially BrE*) having lost money as a result of sth: *The collapse of the company has left thousands of investors out of pocket.* → idioms at DEEP *adj.*, DIP *verb*, FILL, LINE *verb*, HAND *noun*
● *verb* [+ obj]
1 to earn or win an amount of money: *He pocketed a profit of $6 million from the deal.*
2 to take or keep sth, especially an amount of money, in an illegal or a dishonest way; to steal sth: *He regularly charges passengers more than the normal fare and pockets the difference.*
● *adjective* [only before noun]
—————————————————————————
SEE ALSO: out-of-pocket
—————————————————————————
used to describe sth that is very small or small enough to be put and carried in a pocket: *a pocket pager/organizer/dictionary* ◇ *You can use a pocket PC to send and receive email.* → POCKET-SIZED

'pocket change *noun* [U]
1 coins
2 a small amount of money: *Seven thousand dollars is not pocket change.*

'pocket-sized (*also* **'pocket-size**) *adjective*
small enough to fit into your pocket or to be carried easily: *a small pocket-sized recorder*

point /pɔɪnt/ *noun, verb*
● *noun*

SEE ALSO: action point, assembly ~, basis ~, break-even ~, breaking ~, bullet ~, gross rating ~, etc.

1 [C] a thing that sb says or writes giving their opinion or stating a fact: *She made several interesting points at the meeting.* ◊ *I take your point* (= understand and accept what you are saying).
○ to **make/raise** a point ◆ to **discuss/get across/prove** a point
2 (*usually* **the point**) [sing.] the main or most important idea in sth that is said or done: *The point is that unless we reduce costs we'll go bankrupt.* ◊ *I'll come straight to the point: we need more money.*
○ to **come to/get to the point** ◆ to **get/miss the point**
3 [U; sing.] the purpose or aim of sth: *What's the point of this memo?* ◊ *There's no point in throwing good money after bad.*
4 [C] a particular detail or fact: *The main points of the meeting were summarized in the minutes.* ◊ *a six-point survival guide for new managers*
○ the **main/finer** points (of sth)
5 [C] a particular quality or feature that sb/sth has: *He has some good points.* ◊ *One of the project's plus points is that it is very cheap.*
○ **good/strong/plus** points
6 [C] a particular time, stage or level: *At one point, the dollar fell to 128¢ to the euro.* ◊ *The negotiations have reached a critical point.*
○ a **high/low** point ◆ to **get to/reach** a point
7 (*Finance*) [C] a mark or unit on a scale of measurement, especially a financial index: *Blue chip stocks were up 87 points.* ◊ *The FTSE index closed down 144.51 points.* ◊ *Denmark's central bank cut its rates by half a point.*
○ to **drop/fall/increase/jump/rise** (by)… points
8 [C] a unit used to measure the quality of sb/sth: *Lending decisions are made on a points system.*
9 [C] a particular place or area: *I'll wait for you at the meeting point in the arrivals hall.* ◊ *Hamburg remains the focal point* (= the centre) *of our work.*
10 [C] a small dot that separates a whole number from the part that comes after it: *a decimal point* ◊ *2.6* (said: 'two point six')
IDM ,point of 'contact a place where you go or a person that you speak to when you are dealing with an organization: *The receptionist is the first point of contact most people have with the company.*
a ,point of de'parture 1 a place where a journey starts **2** an idea, a theory or an event that is used to start a discussion, an activity, etc.
● *verb* [+ obj or no obj]
to lead to or suggest a particular development or a logical way to continue an argument: *The evidence seems to point in that direction.*

pointer /'pɔɪntə(r)/ *noun* [C]
1 a sign that sth exists; a sign that shows how sth may develop in the future: *The index is seen as a pointer to the future performance of the economy.* ◊ *Results from the retail sector are key pointers to progress.*
2 (*informal*) a piece of advice: *Ask more experienced colleagues to give you a few pointers.* SYN TIP
3 a stick used to point to things on a map or picture on a wall, etc.
4 a small symbol, for example an arrow, that marks a point on a computer screen → CURSOR

,point of 'action *noun* [C] (*abbr* POA)
(*Marketing*) the place or time in a presentation, on a website, etc. when a possible customer has the opportunity and is encouraged to react and to do sth: *Too many choices at a point of action can stop possible customers going any further.*

,point of 'purchase *noun* [C] (*abbr* POP)
(*Commerce; Marketing*) the place where a product is bought: *The key to good marketing is not to bring the customer to the point of sale, but to put the point of purchase where it suits the customer.* ◊ *point-of-purchase displays/promotion* → EPOS, POINT OF SALE

,point-of-purchase 'advertising *noun* [U] (*abbr* POPA)
(*Marketing*) advertising at the place where a product is bought → POINT OF SALE

,point of 'sale *noun* [C] (*abbr* POS)
(*Commerce; Marketing*) the place where a product is sold: *More information on healthy foods should be provided at the point of sale.* ◊ *Reading product tags and checking credit are performed at the point of sale.* ◊ *point-of-sale advertising/displays* → POINT OF PURCHASE—Picture at STORE

,point of 'use *noun* [sing.]
the place where or the time when a product or a service is actually used: *Medical care is still free at the point of use.* ◊ *For the motor car, tax is levied at the point of use, rather than at the point of sale.*

poised /pɔɪzd/ *adjective* [not before noun]
completely ready for sth or to do sth: *The economy is poised for recovery.* ◊ *They are poised to make a takeover bid for their smaller rival.* SYN SET

,poisoned 'chalice *noun* [sing.] (*formal*)
a job or position that seems attractive at first but soon becomes very unpleasant: *The post of managing the company's aircraft division was seen by many as a poisoned chalice.*

,poison 'pill *noun* [C]
(*Finance, informal*) a form of defence used by a company when another company is trying to take control of it, in order to make itself less attractive, for example by selling some of its main assets: *The proposals would restrict companies' rights to use poison pills against hostile bids.*

★ **policy** /'pɒləsi; AmE 'pɑːl-/ *noun* (*plural* **policies**)

SEE ALSO: closed-door policy, credit ~, dear money ~, easy monetary ~, fiscal ~, insurance ~, monetary ~, etc.

1 [C,U] a plan of action agreed or chosen by a business, an organization or a political party: *The company has adopted a firm policy on shoplifting.* ◊ *We have to wear jeans on Fridays—it's company policy.* ◊ *the group's accounting policies* ◊ *Only senior management can take policy decisions.*
○ to **adopt/implement/introduce/pursue** a policy ◆ to **abandon/change/develop/discuss** (a) policy ◆ **economic/tax** policy
2 (*Insurance*) [C] a written statement of a contract of insurance: *Check the terms of the policy before you sign.*

policyholder /'pɒləsihəʊldə(r); AmE 'pɑːləsihoʊl-/ *noun* [C]
(*Insurance*) a person or group that holds a contract of insurance: *A travel insurance policyholder made a claim for thousands of dollars when his luggage was lost.*

'policy-,setting *adjective* [only before noun]
that decides on plans of action: *It is likely that the Bank will cut interest rates at its policy-setting meeting next week.* ◊ *a policy-setting board/committee*

politics /'pɒlətɪks; AmE 'pɑ:l-/ *noun* [U with sing./pl. verb]
matters concerned with getting or using power within a particular group or organization: *I don't want to get involved in office politics.*

poll /pəʊl; AmE poʊl/ *noun, verb*
● *noun* [C] (*also* o'**pinion poll**)
the process of questioning people who represent a larger group in order to get information about the general opinion: *A recent poll shows that 98% of dentists would recommend the product.* **SYN** SURVEY
➔ to **carry out/conduct/take** a poll ◆ a poll **indicates/ reveals/shows/suggests** sth
● *verb* [+ obj]
to ask a large number of members of the public what they think about sth: *Sixty per cent of those polled said they used the Internet to book flights.* ◇ *The survey polled 7 500 shoppers on Thursday.*

pollutant /pə'lu:tənt/ *noun* [C]
a dirty or harmful substance that makes land, air, water, etc. no longer pleasant or safe to use: *Chemical pollutants were found on the site.*

pollution /pə'lu:ʃn/ *noun* [U]
1 the process of making air, water, soil, etc. dirty; the state of being dirty: *We need stricter measures to reduce environmental pollution.* ◇ *The company denied responsibility for the pollution of local lakes and rivers.*
2 substances that make air, water, soil, etc. dirty: *A cloud of pollution hangs over the city.*

pol'lution ˌcredit = EMISSION CREDIT

polybag /ˌpɒli'bæg; AmE ˌpɑ:l-/ *noun* [C] (*informal*)
a bag made of strong thin clear plastic material (**polythene/polyethylene**), used for wrapping things

polystyrene /ˌpɒli'staɪri:n; AmE ˌpɑ:l-/ (*also* '**Styrofoam**™, *especially in AmE*) *noun* [U]
very light soft plastic that is usually white, used for packing goods or for making containers that prevent heat loss: *They have stopped using polystyrene 'peanuts' for packing shipments.* ◇ *polystyrene cups*—Picture at PACKAGING

'**Ponzi scheme** /'pɒnzi ski:m ; AmE 'pɑ:nzi/ *noun* [C] (*AmE*)
a plan for making money that involves encouraging people to invest by offering them a high rate of interest and using their money to pay earlier investors. When there are not enough new investors, people who have recently invested lose their money. **NOTE** Charles Ponzi organized the first scheme of this kind in the US in 1919.

pool /pu:l/ *noun, verb*
● *noun* [C]
SEE ALSO: **car pool, motor pool**

1 a supply of things or money that is shared by a group of people and can be used when needed: *Corporate clients gained access to huge pools of capital.* ◇ *a pool of cars used by the firm's sales force* ◇ *a pool car*
2 a group of people available for work: *The country has a large pool of cheap labour.* ◇ *There is a limited pool of people who have the right qualifications for the job.*
● *verb* [+ obj]
to collect money, information, etc. from different people so that it can be used by all of them: *As costs rise, departments are beginning to pool resources.* ◇ *Managers from the different divisions pooled ideas.*

POP /ˌpi: əʊ 'pi:; AmE oʊ/ = POINT OF PURCHASE

POPA /ˌpi: əʊ pi: 'eɪ; AmE oʊ/ = POINT-OF-PURCHASE ADVERTISING

ˌ**popular** '**price** *noun* [C]
a price that is liked because it is low: *We emphasize*

quality at popular prices. ➔ ˌ**popular** '**pricing** *noun* [U]

population /ˌpɒpju'leɪʃn; AmE ˌpɑ:p-/ *noun*
SEE ALSO: **floating population**

1 [C with sing./pl. verb; U] all the people who live in a particular area, city or country; the total number of people who live there: *One third of the world's population consumes two thirds of the world's resources.* ◇ *The city of Guangzhou has a population of over six million.* ◇ *An estimated twenty per cent of the population are unemployed.*
2 [C with sing./pl. verb] a particular group of people living in a particular area: *The textile industry employs a third of the working population.* ◇ *About six per cent of the adult population do not have a bank account.*

'**pop-ˌunder** *adjective, noun*
(*IT; Marketing*)
● *adjective* [only before noun]
appearing on a computer screen quickly to display an advertisement, etc. behind sth that you are looking at on the Internet: *pop-under ads*
● *noun* [C]
an advertisement that appears in a small window on your computer screen behind sth else that you are looking at: *Pop-unders can be used as part of your main Internet marketing mix.* → POP-UP

'**pop-up** *adjective, noun*
(*IT; Marketing*)
● *adjective* [only before noun]
appearing on a computer screen quickly to display a list of choices, an advertisement, etc. while you are working on another document: *Select the appropriate item from the pop-up menu.* ◇ *an effective way of blocking pop-up ads* → DROP-DOWN
● *noun* [C]
an advertisement that appears in a small window on your computer screen while you are looking at sth else: *The software automatically blocks annoying pop-ups.* → POP-UNDER

★ **port** /pɔ:t; AmE pɔ:rt/ *noun, verb*
● *noun*
SEE ALSO: **free port**

1 [C] a town or city with a harbour, especially one where ships load and unload goods: *Rotterdam is a major port.* ◇ *fishing ports*
2 [C,U] a place where ships load and unload goods or shelter from storms: *the largest deep-sea container port* ◇ *The ship spent four days in port.*
3 (*IT*) [C] a device on a computer where you can connect pieces of equipment such as a keyboard or a printer: *Your printer needs a port to connect to your PC.*
● *verb* [+ obj]
(*IT*) to move software from one computer to another one of a different type: *The software can be ported to an IBM RS/6000.*

portable /'pɔ:təbl; AmE 'pɔ:rt-/ *adjective, noun*
● *adjective*
1 that is easy to carry or to move: *Cellphones are easy to use, personal and portable.*
2 (about computer software) that can be used with different kinds of computers: *The software is highly portable over different computer platforms.*
3 a **portable** pension or loan is one that you can move to another company if you change jobs, banks, etc: *A portable pension gives you the flexibility you need to make career changes.*
▶ **portability** /ˌpɔ:tə'bɪləti; AmE ˌpɔ:rt-/ *noun* [U]
● *noun* [C]
a small type of machine that is easy to carry,

especially a computer or a television: *Apple has reduced the weight of its portables.*

portal /'pɔːtl; *AmE* 'pɔːrtl/ *noun* [C]
(*IT*) a website that is used as a link to the Internet, where information has been collected that will be useful to a person interested in particular kinds of things: *a business/news/shopping portal*

porter /'pɔːtə(r); *AmE* 'pɔːrt-/ *noun* [C]

SEE ALSO: **night porter**

1 a person whose job is carrying people's bags and other loads, especially at a railway station, an airport or in a hotel: *hotel porters*
2 (*BrE*) a person whose job is to be in charge of the entrance to a hotel, large building, etc: *The head porter will have staff ready to handle any luggage.*
→ CONCIERGE

'Porter's ge'neric 'strategies /'pɔːtəz; *AmE* 'pɔːrtərz/ *noun* [pl.]
(*Marketing*) the possible ways in which a business can achieve a strong position in a particular industry. These are: producing goods at a lower cost than competitors (**cost leadership strategy**), developing products that are different from other similar products and that customers value (**differentiation strategy**) or focusing on a small group of customers (**focus strategy**).

★ **portfolio** /pɔːt'fəʊliəʊ; *AmE* pɔːrt'foʊlioʊ/ *noun* [C] (*plural* **portfolios**)
1 (*Finance*) a set of investments owned by a particular person or organization: *The group has a property portfolio worth $2.4 billion.* ◇ *He gradually built up a portfolio of more than 1 000 stocks.*
⊙ *to build (up)/broaden/expand/have/hold a portfolio* • *a balanced/diversified/an international/a large/strong portfolio* • *a bond/an equity/investment/a share/stock portfolio* • *a loan/property portfolio*
2 (*Commerce*) the range of products or services offered by a particular company: *The company has a strong portfolio of retail brands.* ◇ *We needed to expand our product portfolio.*
⊙ *to build up/expand/have/offer a portfolio* • *a brand/business/product portfolio* • *a broad/strong/wide portfolio*

port,folio ca'reer *noun* [C]
(*HR*) a career that is based on building skills and knowledge in a series of different jobs rather than one based on increasingly senior jobs in one profession

port'folio ,manager *noun* [C]
(*Stock Exchange*) someone whose job is to control a group of investments with the aim of making the most profit with the least risk: *Many portfolio managers are showing an interest in technology stocks.* ◇ *a senior portfolio manager in the currency team* ▸ **port'folio ,management** *noun* [U]

portion /'pɔːʃn; *AmE* 'pɔːrʃn/ *noun* [C]
1 one part of sth larger: *He invested a substantial portion of his savings in the business.* ◇ *The division accounts for only a small portion of total sales.*
2 an amount of food that is large enough for one person: *The restaurant serves generous portions.* ◇ *They were specialists in individual **portion control** for the food-service industry.*

,**port of 'entry** *noun* [C] a place where people or goods can enter a country officially

POS /ˌpiː əʊ 'es; *AmE* oʊ/ = POINT OF SALE

★ **position** /pə'zɪʃn/ *noun, verb*
● *noun*

SEE ALSO: **bear position, cash ~, island ~, long ~, open ~, short ~, special ~**

1 [C] a job: *He held a senior position in a large company.* ◇ *I should like to apply for the position of Sales Director.* See note at JOB
⊙ *to advertise/fill/have/hold/take up a position*
2 [C,U] a person or an organization's level of importance or success when compared with others: *the company's dominant position in the world market* ◇ *They used their strong bargaining position to get a better deal.*
⊙ *to establish/gain/hold/strengthen/use a position* • *to be in a position of authority/power/strength*
3 [C, usually sing.] the situation that sb is in, especially when it affects what they can and cannot do: *The company's financial position is not certain.* ◇ *I'm afraid I'm not in a position to help you.* ◇ *The chairman's resignation has put the board in a difficult position.*
⊙ *to achieve/reach/strengthen/weaken a position*
4 (*Finance*) [C] the total amount of a particular share, bond, currency, etc. that a dealer or an investor owns, or has sold but needs to buy back in the future: *They plan to keep the fund's 275 000 share position steady for now.*
● *verb* [+ obj]
1 to put sth/sb in a particular position: *The company is uniquely positioned to compete in foreign markets.*
2 (*Marketing*) to advertise a product, service or company in a particular way in a particular part of the market so that it appears different from other products, services or companies: *The magazine has been positioned as an educational product.*

po'sition ,audit (*also* **po'sition re,view**) *noun* [C]
1 a thorough analysis of the current situation of an organization that is done in order to plan for the future
2 (*HR*) an analysis of exactly what is involved in a particular job with a company

positioning /pə'zɪʃnɪŋ/ *noun* [U]
(*Marketing*) the way a product, service or company is advertised in a particular part of the market so that it appears different from others; the way that people think about a product, service or company: *The market positioning of the two stores is very different.* ◇ *She suggested some changes in product positioning in order to attract the kind of customers we were looking for.*

po'sition re,view = POSITION AUDIT

★ **positive** /'pɒzətɪv; *AmE* 'pɑːz-/ *adjective, noun*
● *adjective*
1 greater than zero: *A positive amount indicates that there is money in the account.*
2 good or useful: *The news has had a positive effect on our finances.*
3 expressing agreement or support: *We've had a very positive response to the new product.*
OPP NEGATIVE
▸ **'positively** *adverb*
● *noun*
1 [C] the result of a test or an experiment that shows that a substance or condition is present
OPP NEGATIVE
2 [C,U] a good or useful quality or aspect: *We can take several positives from this experience.*

,**positive 'action** *noun* [U] (*BrE*)
anything that is done to give everyone the same chances of education or employment, especially by helping groups that are often treated unfairly because of their race, sex, etc. → AFFIRMATIVE ACTION, POSITIVE DISCRIMINATION

,**positive discrimi'nation** (*also* re,verse discrimi'nation) *noun* [U] (*BrE*)
the practice or policy of giving an advantage to people from groups that are often treated unfairly because of their race, sex, etc., for example by making sure that a particular number of jobs are given to people from these groups NOTE Positive

discrimination is illegal in some countries.
SYN AFFIRMATIVE ACTION (*AmE*) → POSITIVE ACTION

,positive-'sum game *noun* [C]
a situation in which both sides involved in a relationship or a piece of business gain an advantage: *a positive-sum relationship between people and technology* → ZERO-SUM GAME, WIN-WIN

,positive 'territory *noun* [U]
often used in newspapers to describe a level that is above zero, or above the previous or expected level: *Only five stocks ended the day in positive territory.*

possession /pə'zeʃn/ *noun*

SEE ALSO: immediate possession, vacant possession

1 [U] the state of having or owning sth: *If the loan is not repaid, the bank may take possession of the company's assets.*
2 [C, usually pl.] something that you own or have with you at a particular time: *Please remember to take your possessions with you.*

possessor /pə'zesə(r)/ *noun* [C] (*formal*)
a person who owns or has sth SYN OWNER

★**post** /pəʊst; *AmE* poʊst/ *noun, verb*
● *noun*

SEE ALSO: trading post

1 (*BrE*) (also **mail**, *AmE, BrE*) [U] the official system used for sending and delivering letters, packages, etc.: *I'll send the original to you by post.* ◇ *I'll put the information in the post to you tomorrow.* ◇ *My application got lost in the post.*
○ *first-class/second-class post* ♦ *internal/international post*
2 (*BrE*) (also **mail**, *AmE, BrE*) [U] letters, packages, etc. that are sent and delivered: *There was a lot of post this morning.* ◇ *Have you opened your post yet?*
○ *to deliver/handle post* ♦ *to get/receive/send (out) post* ♦ *to answer/deal with/open/read your post*
3 [U; sing.] (*BrE*) an occasion during the day when letters, etc. are collected or delivered: *The package came in this morning's post.*
○ *the first/last post* ♦ *to catch/miss the post*
4 [C] a job, especially an important one in a large organization: *He will leave his $300 000-a-year post this week.* ◇ *She has held the post for three years.* ◇ *We will be creating 15 new posts next year.* ◇ *The company has been unable to fill the post.* → idiom at RETURN *noun* See note at JOB
○ *a junior/senior/key/managerial post* ♦ *a full-time/part-time/permanent/temporary/vacant post* ♦ *to apply for/hold/leave/resign from/take up a post* ♦ *to appoint sb to/fill a post*
● *verb* [+ obj]
1 (*BrE*) (also **mail**, *AmE, BrE*) **post sth (off) (to sb)** | **post sb sth** to send a letter, etc. to sb by post/mail: *Have you posted off your order yet?* ◇ *Is it OK if I post the cheque to you next week?* ◇ *Is it OK if I post you the cheque next week?*
2 (*BrE*) (*AmE* **mail**) to put a letter, etc. into a public box (a **postbox**) to be sent: *Could you post this letter for me?*
3 (*usually* **be posted**) to send sb to a particular place for a period of time as part of their job: *She's been posted to Washington for two years.*
4 (*often* **be posted**) to put a notice, etc. in a public place so that people can see it: *A copy of the letter was posted on the noticeboard.*
5 (*IT*) to put information or a message on the Internet: *The results will be posted on the Internet tomorrow.*
6 (*especially AmE*) to announce sth publicly or officially, especially financial information or a warning: *The company posted a $1.1 billion loss.*
○ *to post a loss/gain* ♦ *to post earnings (of …)*
IDM **keep sb 'posted (about/on sth)** to regularly give sb the most recent information about sth and

how it is developing: *I'll keep you posted on his progress.*

post- /pəʊst; *AmE* poʊst/ *prefix* (*in adjectives, verbs, adverbs and nouns*)
after; later than: *post-tax income* ◇ *a post-conference meeting* ◇ *post-date*

postage /'pəʊstɪdʒ; *AmE* 'poʊ-/ *noun* [U]
the cost of sending a letter, etc. by post: *an increase in postage rates*

,postage and 'packing (*also* ,postage and 'packaging) (*both BrE*) (*AmE* ,postage and 'handling) *noun* [C]
the cost of wrapping an item and sending it by post: *price £30 + £5.50 postage and packing*

,postage 'paid *adjective* [usually before noun]
used to describe sth such as an envelope on which the company has already paid the cost of sending it by post: *Please use the postage-paid envelope enclosed to return the form to us.* ◇ *a postage-paid questionnaire/label* → BUSINESS REPLY SERVICE, REPLY PAID

'postage stamp = STAMP *noun* (1)

postal /'pəʊstl; *AmE* 'poʊstl/ *adjective* [only before noun]
connected with the official system for sending and delivering letters, etc.: *your full postal address* ◇ *the postal service/system*

'postal code = POSTCODE

,postal 'money ,order = MONEY ORDER

'postal ,order (*abbr* PO) = MONEY ORDER

postcode /'pəʊstkəʊd; *AmE* 'poʊstkoʊd/ (*also* 'postal code) (*both BrE*) (*AmE* 'zip code) *noun* [C]
a group of letters and/or numbers that are used as part of an address so that post/mail can be separated into groups and delivered more quickly: *postcode: CB11 3AD*

,post-'date (*AmE spelling usually* **postdate**) *verb* [+ obj]
1 to put a later date on a cheque or other document than the date at the time of writing, usually to delay payment: *I sent all the instalments together, as three post-dated cheques.*
2 (*BrE*) (*usually* **be post-dated**) to make sth, especially a payment, take effect from a later date: *Postal workers are getting a 5% post-dated pay rise.*
OPP BACKDATE

poster /'pəʊstə(r); *AmE* 'poʊ-/ *noun* [C]
a large notice, often with a picture on it, that is put in a public place to advertise sth: *The company put up posters to advertise its new product.*—Picture at STORE
○ *to display/put up/take down a poster* ♦ *to design/print a poster* ♦ *a poster advertisement/campaign*
IDM **'poster child/boy/girl** (*AmE*) a person or thing that is seen as representing a particular quality or activity: *The company has become the poster child for electronic commerce.* ◇ *He's the IT industry's poster boy for success.*

,post-'Fordism *noun* [U]
(*HR*) a term used to describe a method of management that aims to give workers a large amount of responsibility and freedom ▶ **,post-'Fordist** *adjective* **,post-'Fordist** *noun* [C]

,post-'free *adjective* [only before noun] (*BrE*)
used to describe sth that you can send by post without having to pay anything ▶ **,post-'free** *adverb*: *Information will be sent post-free to any interested readers.* → POST-PAID

posting /'pəʊstɪŋ; AmE 'poʊ-/ noun

SEE ALSO: **certificate of posting, cross-posting**

1 (HR) [C] an act of sending sb to a particular place for a period of time as part of their job: *an overseas posting ◇ a two-year posting in/to Athens*
2 (IT) [C] a message or information put on the Internet: *The newsgroup gathers postings on a particular topic and distributes them to the newsgroup's subscribers.*
3 (Accounting) [U,C] the activity of writing figures in a book where money paid and received is recorded (a **ledger**); the figures written: *transaction and payment posting ◇ identifying and correcting routine posting errors ◇ Interest is charged on credit from the date of posting.*

'Post-it™ (also **'Post-it™ note**) noun [C]
a small piece of coloured, sticky paper that you use for writing a note on, and that can be easily removed from where you put it—Picture at OFFICE

'post ˌoffice noun
1 [C] a place where you can buy stamps, send letters, etc: *Where's the main post office? ◇ post office branches ◇ a post office counter*
2 the Post Office [sing.] (abbr **PO**) the national organization in many countries that is responsible for collecting and delivering letters, etc: *He works for the Post Office.*

'post ˌoffice box = PO BOX

ˌpost-'paid (AmE spelling **postpaid**) adjective [only before noun]
that you can send free because the charge has already been paid: *a post-paid envelope* ▶ **ˌpost-'paid** (AmE spelling **postpaid**) adverb → POST-FREE

★ **postpone** /pə'spəʊn; AmE poʊ'spoʊn/ verb [+ obj]
to arrange for an event, etc. to take place at a later time or date: *We'll have to postpone the meeting until next week. ◇ They have agreed to postpone repayment of the loan to a future date. ◇ We have decided to postpone building a new store.*
OPP ADVANCE
▶ **post'ponement** noun [U,C]

VOCABULARY BUILDING

Changing a meeting

Changing to a later time

* *The talks have been **postponed** until 30 May.*
* *Can we **put off** the presentation for a week or two?*
* *The next board meeting has been **put back** by two weeks.*

Changing to an earlier time

* *We can **bring forward** the interview to tomorrow, if that suits you.*

Deciding not to have the meeting

* *I am sorry I had to **cancel** our appointment.*
* *The meeting with shareholders was **called off** at the last minute.*

See note at ARRANGE

'post room (BrE) (AmE **'mail room**) noun [C]
the department of a company that deals with sending and receiving mail

postscript /'pəʊstskrɪpt; AmE 'poʊst-/ noun [C]
1 an extra message that you add at the end of a letter after your signature → PS
2 something extra that is added to sth after it has finished: *HR plans are unfortunately treated as a postscript to the business planning process.*

potential /pə'tenʃl/ adjective, noun
● **adjective** [only before noun]
that can develop into sth or be developed in the future: *potential customers ◇ potential bidders/ buyers/investors ◇ the potential benefits of European integration* ▶ **potentially** /pə'tenʃəli/ adverb: *a potentially huge market*
● **noun** [U]
1 the possibility of sth happening or being developed or used: *The European marketplace offers excellent potential for increasing sales. ◇ The new service has huge market potential.*
2 qualities that exist and can be developed: *We try to help all our employees **realize their full potential**. ◇ This start-up has the potential **to** be a very successful company.*

POTS /pɒts; AmE pɑːts/ abbr
(IT) **plain old telephone service** used to describe a standard telephone service rather than a very fast one: *the POTS telephone network*

pound /paʊnd/ noun [C]
1 the unit of money in the UK and several other countries; £: *a ten-pound note ◇ Total losses were estimated at over three million pounds.*
2 [sing.] the value of the British pound compared with the value of the money of other countries: *The euro fell 1% against the pound. ◇ the strength/ weakness of the pound*
3 (abbr **lb**) a unit for measuring weight, equal to 0.454 of a kilogram: *This laptop weighs under 4 pounds.*

power /'paʊə(r)/ noun, verb, adjective
● **noun**

SEE ALSO: **bargaining power, buyer ~, buying ~, earning ~, pester ~, purchasing ~, spending ~, staying ~**

1 [U] the ability to control or influence people, things, events, etc: *The report said the banks had too much power **over** small businesses. ◇ She has the power **to** hire and fire. ◇ There is currently a **power struggle** over who will head up the company after the merger.*
2 [U] (used to form compound nouns) strength or influence in a particular area of activity: *the growing economic power of women consumers*
3 [C] a powerful country, organization or person that has a lot of influence: *world powers ◇ It has become one of the major powers in the world of IT.*
4 [U] energy that can be used to operate a machine, to make electricity, etc: *renewable energy sources such as hydro, wind and solar power*
5 [U] the public supply of electricity: *They've switched off the power. ◇ There was a power cut.*
6 [U] the ability of a machine, an engine, etc. to do work: *The new server breaks the record for computing power.*
● **verb** [+ obj]
to supply a machine or vehicle with the energy that makes it work: *The aircraft is powered by a jet engine. ◇ (figurative) Sales growth has been powered by new stores and a new image.*
PHR V **ˌpower sth 'up** to prepare a machine to start working by supplying it with electricity, etc: *I need to power up my laptop.*
● **adjective**
1 operated by a motor, electricity, etc: *power tools*
2 used to describe sth that shows you have an important position in a company

'power brand noun [C]
(Marketing) a very important and well-known brand, for example, one that has a large share of the market or that has been made and sold for a long time: *We have decided to focus on 15 power brands.*

-powered /'paʊəd; AmE 'paʊərd/ adjective (used in compounds)
using the type of energy mentioned: battery-powered toys ◇ hydrogen-powered cars

powerhouse /'paʊəhaʊs; AmE 'paʊərh-/ noun [C]
1 a group or an organization that has a lot of power: China has been described as an 'emerging economic powerhouse'. ◇ chief executive of a media powerhouse
2 a person who is very strong and full of energy: She's a powerhouse in the courtroom.

'power lunch noun [C]
an occasion when business is discussed or deals made during lunch: The restaurant was full of executives having power lunches.

'power nap noun [C]
a short sleep sb has while they are working in order to get back their energy: I took a quick power nap after lunch. ▶ **'power-nap** verb [no obj] (**-pp-**)

,power of at'torney (also ,letter of at'torney) noun [U,C] (plural powers of attorney, letters of attorney)
(Law) the right to act as the representative of sb in business or financial matters; a document that gives sb this right: The son had power of attorney over their father's business affairs.

PowerPoint™ /'paʊəpɔɪnt; AmE 'paʊər-/ noun [U]
a computer program produced by Microsoft™ for creating presentations for an audience: Are you doing your talk on PowerPoint? ◇ a PowerPoint presentation ▶ **'powerpoint** verb [+ obj]: All the other presentations were powerpointed, but I used a whiteboard.

'power ,station (also 'power plant) noun [C]
a building or group of buildings where electricity is produced

pp abbr (only used in written English)
1 (BrE spelling also **pp.**) pages: see pp 100–117
2 (BrE spelling also **p.p.**) used in front of a person's name when sb signs a business letter on his/her behalf: pp Tim Walker (= from Tim Walker, but signed by sb else because Tim Walker is away)
NOTE pp is now considered to mean 'on behalf of' and is usually written before the name of the person who has not signed the letter. It used to be written before the name of the person signing the letter and this is still done in some offices.

ppd abbr (only used in written English)
1 **prepaid** used to describe a service that you pay for before you receive or use it: ppd mobile phone/ cellphone customers
2 **post-paid**, **postpaid** marked on goods to show that POSTAGE is included in the price or has been paid by the sender: All CDs cost $12 ppd (US).

PPI /,pi: pi: 'aɪ/ = PRODUCER PRICE INDEX

ppm /,pi: pi: 'em/ abbr part(s) per million
1 (Technical) a measurement of how much of a substance a liquid or other substance contains: air with 50 ppm nitrogen dioxide
2 (Production) a measurement of how efficient a manufacturing process is, which records the number of DEFECTS (= faults in the way sth has been made) found in each million parts produced: We aim for a quality level of 3ppm in our production line.

PPP /,pi: pi: 'pi:/ = PURCHASING POWER PARITY, PUBLIC-PRIVATE PARTNERSHIP

★ **PR** /,pi: 'ɑ:(r)/ abbr
(Marketing)
1 **public relations** the business of giving the public information about a particular organization or person in order to create a good impression: She's in PR. ◇ The radio interview was a PR coup (=

---

success) for the company. ◇ Your website is a vital PR tool.
❶ a PR **agency/company/department/firm** ◆ a PR **consultant/executive/manager** ◆ **good/bad** PR
2 = PRESS RELATIONS

★ **practice** /'præktɪs/ noun, verb
● **noun**

SEE ALSO: best practice, fire ~, general ~, restrictive ~

1 [U] action rather than ideas: She's determined to put her new ideas **into** practice. ◇ The idea sounds fine in theory, but will it work **in** practice?
2 [U,C] a way of doing sth that is the usual or expected way in a particular organization or situation: guidelines for good practice ◇ a review of pay and working practices ◇ employment/labour practices
❶ **bad/good** practice ◆ **common/current/standard/ usual** practice ◆ **accounting/business/management** practices ◆ **employment/labour/working** practices ◆ to **adopt/follow/introduce/use** practices
3 [C] a thing that is done regularly; a habit or a custom: the German practice of giving workers a say in how their company is run
4 [U,C] the work or the business of some professional people such as doctors, dentists and lawyers; the place where they work: My solicitor is no longer in practice. ◇ a successful law practice
❶ a **dental/law/legal/medical** practice ◆ a **group/ private** practice ◆ to **go into/set up in** practice ◆ to **run/start** a practice ◆ to **join/leave** a practice
● **verb** (AmE) = PRACTISE

practiced = PRACTISED

practicing = PRACTISING

'practicing ,license = PRACTISING CERTIFICATE

practicum /'præktɪkəm/ = PLACEMENT (2)

★ **practise** (AmE spelling **practice**) /'præktɪs/ verb
1 [+ obj or no obj] to do an activity or train regularly so that you can improve your skill: I need to practise my French before my trip.
2 [+ obj] to do sth regularly as part of your normal behaviour: The company practises Total Quality Management.
3 [+ obj or no obj] to work as a doctor, lawyer, etc: There are over a thousand lawyers practising in the city. ◇ She practised **as** a barrister for many years.

practised (AmE spelling **practiced**) /'præktɪst/ adjective
good at doing sth because you have been doing it regularly: She is a practised negotiator. ◇ He has good ideas but he isn't practised **in** the art of marketing.

practising (AmE spelling **practicing**) /'præktɪsɪŋ/ adjective [only before noun]
taking an active part in a particular profession, etc: a practising lawyer

'practising cer,tificate (BrE) (AmE 'practicing ,license) noun [C]
an official document that proves that a professional person is qualified and has the right to work in their profession

practitioner /,præk'tɪʃənə(r)/ noun [C]

SEE ALSO: insolvency practitioner

1 a person who is qualified to work in a profession, especially medicine or law: a medical/legal practitioner ◇ the Institute of Practitioners in Advertising

2 a person who regularly does a particular activity or follows a particular theory: *enthusiastic practitioners of lean manufacturing*

pre- /priː/ *prefix (used in verbs, nouns and adjectives)*
before: *pretest ◇ precaution ◇ pre-tax*

,pre-addressed 'envelope *(also spelled* **preaddressed**, *especially in AmE) noun* [C]
an envelope with the address already printed on it that is sent with sth to make it easy to reply

,pre-ap'proach *(also spelled* **preapproach**, *especially in AmE) noun* [C,U]
(*Marketing*) the activities that a SALESPERSON does before they meet a possible customer: *What is the objective of your pre-approach? ◇ pre-approach planning*

pre,carious em'ployment *noun* [U]
(*HR*) the situation when sb is working on a temporary contract or has no guarantee that they will keep their job: *The gap between stable employees and those in precarious employment has been widening.*

precaution /prɪˈkɔːʃn/ *noun* [C, usually pl.]
something that is done in advance in order to prevent problems or to avoid danger: *safety precautions ◇ E-commerce companies have to take precautions against computer fraud. ◇ Run a virus check on a file before opening it as a precaution.*
▸ **precautionary** /prɪˈkɔːʃənri; AmE -neri/ *adjective: The bank has suspended its online banking service as a precautionary measure.*

precedence /ˈpresɪdəns/ *noun* [U]
the condition of being more important than sb/sth else and therefore coming or being dealt with first: *In the fashion industry, quality takes precedence over price. ◇ I give precedence to tasks that are important and urgent.* SYN PRIORITY

precedent /ˈpresɪdənt/ *noun* [C,U]
an official action or decision that has happened in the past and that is seen as an example or a rule to be followed in a similar situation later: *The judgement set a precedent for similar legal cases.*
♦ to **create/establish/provide/serve as/set** a precedent ◆ to **base sth on/follow** a precedent
▸ **precedential** /ˌpresəˈdenʃl/ *adjective: a precedential judgement*

precinct /ˈpriːsɪŋkt/ *noun* [C] (BrE)
a commercial area in a town where cars cannot go: *a shopping precinct ◇ a pedestrian precinct*

precipitous /prɪˈsɪpɪtəs/ *adjective*
1 sudden and great: *a precipitous fall in share price* ◆ *a precipitous decline/drop/fall/slide (in sth)*
2 done very quickly, without enough thought or care: *a precipitous decision*
▸ **pre'cipitously** *adverb: The dollar plunged precipitously.*

precis /ˈpreisiː/ *noun* [C,U] (*plural* **precis** /-siːz/)
a short version of a speech or a piece of writing that gives the main points or ideas: *The talk was a brief precis of the annual report.* SYN SUMMARY
♦ to **give/make/write** a precis
▸ **'precis** *verb* (**precises** /ˈpreisiːz/ **precising** /-siːɪŋ/ **precised, precised** /-siːd/) [+ obj]: *to precis a report*

precision /prɪˈsɪʒn/ *noun* [U]
the quality of being exact and accurate: *The saw must cut with great precision. ◇ precision instruments/tools*

pre,cision engi'neering *noun* [U]
the activity of designing and making machines, etc. containing parts that need to be made very accurately: *This camera is an excellent example of precision engineering.*

precondition /ˌpriːkənˈdɪʃn/ *noun* [C]
something that must happen or exist before sth else can exist or be done: *Structural reform is the precondition for strong recovery.*

predator /ˈpredətə(r)/ *noun* [C]
(used in newspapers) a company that uses weaker companies to its own advantage, for example by trying to buy them: *to protect domestic industry from foreign predators* → PREY *noun* (2)
▸ **predatory** /ˈpredətri; AmE -tɔːri/ *adjective*

,predatory 'lending *noun* [U]
(*Finance*) a situation where a financial organization lends money in an unfair or illegal way, for example to people who they know will probably not be able to pay back the debt ▸ **,predatory 'lender** *noun* [C]

,predatory 'pricing *(also* **,predatory 'price-cutting**) *noun* [U]
(*Economics*) a situation where a company makes its prices very low, even though this will lose money, so that other companies cannot compete and have to stop selling similar goods or services: *The airline was accused of predatory pricing. ◇ They have used predatory pricing to gain market share in the area.*
▸ **,predatory 'price** *noun* [C]

predecessor /ˈpriːdəsesə(r); AmE ˈpre-/ *noun* [C]
1 a person who did a job before sb else: *He blamed the company's problems on his predecessor.*
2 a thing, such as a machine, that has been followed or replaced by sth else: *This model is much faster than its predecessor.*

★ predict /prɪˈdɪkt/ *verb* [+ obj]
to say that sth will happen in the future: *Many analysts are predicting a rise in interest rates. ◇ It is impossible to predict what will happen. ◇ This new business is predicted to start producing revenue within a year.* SYN FORECAST

predictable /prɪˈdɪktəbl/ *adjective*
if sth is **predictable**, you know in advance that it will happen or what it will be like: *Sales of the new model followed a predictable pattern. ◇ Revenues have become less predictable.* OPP UNPREDICTABLE
▸ **predictability** /prɪˌdɪktəˈbɪləti/ *noun* [U]: *New forecasting methods have improved the predictability of our financial planning.* **predictably** /prɪˈdɪktəbli/ *adverb: Prices were predictably high.*

prediction /prɪˈdɪkʃn/ *noun* [C,U]
a statement that says what you think will happen; the act of making such a statement: *The sales figures confirmed our predictions. ◇ Not many people agree with the government's prediction that the economy will improve.*

pre-empt *(also spelled* **preempt**, *especially in AmE)* /priˈempt/ *verb* [+ obj]
1 to prevent sth from happening by taking action to stop it: *A good training course will pre-empt many problems. ◇ The CEO pre-empted criticism by resigning.*
2 to do or say sth before sb else does: *I do not want to pre-empt anything that the other speakers are going to say.*
▸ **pre-emptive** *(also spelled* **preemptive**, *especially in AmE)* /priˈemptɪv/ *adjective: Pre-emptive action is necessary to prevent inflation going out of control.*

pre-emption *(also spelled* **preemption**, *especially in AmE)* /priˈempʃn/ *noun* [U]
(*Law*) the opportunity given to one person or group to buy goods, shares, etc. before other people: *Existing shareholders will have pre-emption rights.*

pre-ˌemptive ˈright (also spelled **preemptive ~**, especially in AmE) noun [C]
(Law) the right that a shareholder has to buy shares that a company or another shareholder offers before they are offered to sb else

ˌpre-exˈceptional adjective [only before noun]
(Accounting) used to describe a company's profits that have been calculated without including unusual items of income or expenses: *pre-exceptional profits/earnings*

pref. abbr
(Finance, only used in written English) (used about a share) preference; preferred

★ preference /ˈprefrəns/ noun

SEE ALSO: consumer preference, liquidity preference

1 [U; sing.] a greater interest in or desire for sth/sb than sth/sb else: *It's a matter of **personal** preference.* ◇ *Investors are showing a strong preference **for** bonds rather than shares.*
2 [C] a thing that is liked better or best: *a study of consumer preferences*
IDM **give (a) preference to sb/sth** to treat sb/sth in a way that gives them an advantage over other people or things: *Preference will be given to candidates with some knowledge of Spanish.*

ˈpreference ˌcapital (also ˌpreference ˈshare ˌcapital) (both especially BrE) (AmE usually **preˌferred ˈcapital**) noun [U]
(Finance) money that is raised by a company selling PREFERENCE SHARES

ˈpreference ˌdividend (especially BrE) (AmE usually **preˌferred ˈdividend**) noun [C]
(Finance) the fixed DIVIDEND (= money paid to shareholders) that is paid to holders of PREFERENCE SHARES → ORDINARY DIVIDEND

ˈpreference share noun [C] (especially BrE) (AmE usually **preˌferred ˈstock** [U,C]) (also **preˌferred ˈshare** [C] BrE, AmE)

SEE ALSO: participating preference share

(Finance) a type of share in a company that gives the owner the right to receive regular fixed payments (**dividends**) but does not usually give them the right to vote at meetings of shareholders. People who hold them must be paid before owners of all other shares: *They plan to issue 500 million shares of common stock and 20 million shares of preferred stock.* See note at SHARE

ˌpreference ˈshare ˌcapital = PREFERENCE CAPITAL

preferential /ˌprefəˈrenʃl/ adjective [only before noun]
giving an advantage to a particular person or group: *Small sugar exporters are set to lose their preferential access to the EU.* ◇ *It was claimed that male employees were given preferential **treatment**.*

ˌpreferential ˈcreditor noun [C]
(Finance) a person or company whose debt must be paid before others if a business fails → PREFERRED (1)

preferred /prɪˈfɜːd; AmE -ˈfɜːrd/ adjective [only before noun]
(Finance)
1 a company's **preferred** investors are those who are paid first if the company has financial difficulties or fails: *The company intends to distribute new common stock to its old preferred shareholders.*
O *a preferred **creditor/investor/shareholder***
2 used to describe investments held by these investors or the money they receive from them: *Japan's largest banks want to raise capital by issuing preferred securities.*

preˌferred ˈcapital = PREFERENCE CAPITAL
preˌferred ˈdividend = PREFERENCE DIVIDEND
preˌferred ˈshare = PREFERENCE SHARE
preˌferred ˈstock = PREFERENCE SHARE
preˌferred ˈvendor (also preˌferred supˈplier, apˌproved ˈvendor) noun [C]
(Production) a business that has an agreement to supply another business with goods or services, or has met any necessary requirements: *a preferred vendor agreement*

prejudice /ˈpredʒudɪs/ noun, verb
● **noun** [U,C]
an unreasonable dislike of a person or group of people, especially when it is based on their race, religion, sex, etc: *There is little prejudice **against** workers from other EU states.* ◇ *a victim of **racial** prejudice* → WITHOUT PREJUDICE
● **verb** [+ obj]
1 to influence sb so that they have an unfair or unreasonable opinion about sb/sth: *Poor spelling or grammar in an email may prejudice the reader **against** you.*
2 to have a harmful effect on sth: *The threat of a long strike is prejudicing the future of the company.*
▶ **ˈprejudiced** adjective: *prejudiced opinions*

preliminary /prɪˈlɪmɪnəri; AmE -neri/ adjective
happening before a more important action or event: *The figures are preliminary results and will be confirmed by the company on 17 March.*

preˌliminary inˈjunction = INTERIM INJUNCTION

ˌpre-ˈmarket (also ˌpre-ˈopen) adjective [only before noun]
(Finance) pre-market trading takes place before the stock markets open officially: *The stock fell to $18.10 in pre-market trading.* ▶ **ˌpre-ˈmarket** adverb

premier /ˈpremiə(r); AmE prɪˈmɪr; -ˈmjɪr/ adjective [only before noun]
most important or successful: *Singapore is a premier business community.* ◇ *plans to develop and improve our premier product* ◇ *We want the site to be the premier customer service provider on the Web.*

premises /ˈpremɪsɪz/ noun [pl.]
the buildings and land that a business owns or uses: *We will soon need larger premises.* ◇ *business/commercial premises* ◇ *All the food is made **on the premises**.*

★ premium /ˈpriːmiəm/ noun, adjective
● **noun** [C]

SEE ALSO: insurance premium, share premium

1 (Insurance) an amount of money that you pay once or regularly for insurance: *We pay a monthly premium of $20.* ◇ *Health insurance premiums are rising rapidly.*
2 (Commerce) an extra payment added to the basic rate: *Customers are prepared to pay a premium for superior service.* ◇ *A premium of 10% is paid out after 20 years.*
3 (HR) (also **ˈpremium pay** [U]) extra money that is added to employees' basic pay for particular reasons, for example if they work at weekends or away from home
IDM **at a ˈpremium 1** if sth is **at a premium**, there is little of it available and it is difficult to get: *In big cities, parking is at a premium.* **2 at a premium (to sth)** (Finance) at a higher than normal price: *Their shares trade at a premium to most of*

their rivals. **put/place/set a premium on sb/sth** to think that sb/sth is particularly important or valuable: *The company places a high premium on creativity.*
● *adjective* [only before noun]
1 very high and higher than usual: *They are able to charge premium prices for their products.*
2 of high quality: *We are positioning the coffee as a premium product.* ◇ *premium brands*

'premium ,income *noun* [U]
(*Insurance*) the total amount of money that an insurance company gets from its customers

'premium pay = PREMIUM *noun* (3)

,pre-'open = PRE-MARKET

,pre-'owned *adjective* [usually before noun] (*AmE*) that has belonged to or been used by sb else before: *pre-owned homes/cars* [SYN] SECOND-HAND

,pre-'packaged (*AmE spelling* **prepackaged**) *adjective* [only before noun]
1 (*Commerce*) (*BrE also* **,pre-'packed**) **pre-packaged** goods, especially food, are wrapped before being sent to shops/stores to be sold: *pre-packaged bread*
2 (*Commerce*) **pre-packaged** services are sold as a whole rather than in separate parts: *Pre-packaged e-learning lessons for any part of the training programme are also available.*
3 (*Finance*) **pre-packaged** financial arrangements for a business that is in difficulty are agreed before the business is made officially BANKRUPT: *a pre-packaged bankruptcy plan*

prepaid /ˌpriːˈpeɪd/ *adjective* [usually before noun] (*abbr* **ppd**)
1 (*Commerce*) paid for in advance: *The prepaid cash card allows customers to order over the Web without a credit card.*
2 a **prepaid** envelope has already had the cost of posting paid: *Use a prepaid registered envelope.*
→ PREPAY

prepay /ˌpriːˈpeɪ/ *verb, adjective*
● *verb* (**prepaid, prepaid** /ˌpriːˈpeɪd/)
1 (*Commerce*) [+ obj *or no obj*] to pay for something before you get it or use it: *About 3.7 million customers prepay for their electricity.* ◇ *to prepay a bill*
2 (*Finance*) [+ obj] if you **prepay** a loan, you pay it back before you have to: *The company prepaid the remaining balance of its six-year term loan on Wednesday.*
▶ **prepayable** /ˌpriːˈpeɪəbl/ *adjective*
● *adjective* (*BrE*)
(*Commerce*) **prepay** goods and services are paid for before you get them or use them: *prepay phones*
→ PAY-AS-YOU-GO, PREPAID
▶ **'prepay** *noun* [U]: *Camera phones are still rather expensive on prepay.*

prepayment /ˌpriːˈpeɪmənt/ *noun* [C,U]
1 (*Commerce*) the act of paying for goods and services before you get them or use them; the amounts that you pay: *the prepayment of rent* ◇ *Customers can make prepayments electronically.*
2 (*Finance*) the act of paying the final amount of a loan before the date agreed: *a prepayment penalty*

★ **present** /prɪˈzent/ *verb* [+ obj]
1 to show or offer sth for other people to consider: *The business plan will be presented to the board on Thursday.* ◇ *You must excite people in the way you present your ideas.*
2 to give sb a cheque or bill that they should pay: *A cheque presented by Mr Jones was returned by the bank.* ◇ *We were presented with a huge bill for repairs.*

★ **presentation** /ˌprezn̩ˈteɪʃn; *AmE* ˌpriːzen-/ *noun*
1 [C] a talk or speech in which sth, especially a new product or idea, is shown or explained to a group of people; a meeting when this happens: *The sales manager will give a presentation on the new products.* ◇ *software for preparing slide presentations* ◇ *the company's annual results presentation*
● *to* **deliver/give/make/prepare** *a presentation* ♦ *a* **results/sales/strategy** *presentation*
2 [U] the way in which sth is offered, shown, explained, etc. to others: *Improving the product's presentation* (= the way it is wrapped, advertised, etc.) *should increase sales.* ◇ *They are very careful about both the content and the presentation of their accounts.*
3 (*formal*) [U] the act of presenting or giving sth to sb: *The money will be paid on presentation of a money order.*

presentation

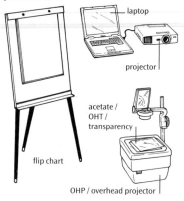

laptop

projector

acetate / OHT / transparency

flip chart

OHP / overhead projector

'present 'discounted 'value = PRESENT VALUE

presenteeism /ˌprezənˈtiːɪzəm/ *noun* [U]
(*HR*) staying longer at work than you need to, especially so that people will think you work very hard: *Most workers claim to suffer from a culture of presenteeism.* → ABSENTEEISM

,present 'value (*also* **'present 'discounted 'value**) *noun* [U,C] (*abbr* **PV**)
(*Accounting*) the value now of a particular amount of money that you expect to receive in the future, calculated by taking away the amount of interest likely to be earned on that amount between now and the future date [NOTE] Present value can be used to calculate how much money to invest now in order to receive a particular amount at a particular time in the future.

preset *verb, noun*
(*Technical*)
● *verb* /ˌpriːˈset/ [+ obj] (**presetting, preset, preset**) to set or adjust the controls of a piece of electronic equipment before it is used, so that it will work in a particular way: *The clock is preset in the factory to Greenwich Mean Time.*
● *noun* /ˈpriːset/ [C]
a control on a piece of electronic equipment that has been set or adjusted in a particular way before the equipment is used: *You cannot override the factory presets.*

★ **president** /ˈprezɪdənt/ (*also* **President**) *noun* [C]

SEE ALSO: **executive vice-president, vice-president**

1 (*also* **,company 'president**) (*both especially AmE*) the person who leads a company and is responsible

for deciding on policy, especially one who leads a group of people (**vice-presidents**) that manage different parts of it, usually under the authority of a CHIEF EXECUTIVE OFFICER: *She was named president and CEO of the company last week.*
→ CHAIRMAN (1)

✪ *to appoint sb (as)/make sb/name sb (as)/promote sb to president* ◆ *to be/become/retire as/serve as president*

NOTE In some companies the **president** is the same person as the **chief executive officer**.

2 (*especially AmE*) in some large companies, a person who is responsible for a part of the business: *AOL's president of/for technology* ◇ *Her new title will be President, Eastern Europe.*
3 the person in charge of some organizations, clubs, colleges, etc: *He was made President of the European Central Bank in 2003.*

press /pres/ *noun, verb*
● *noun*
1 (*often* **the Press**) [sing. with sing./pl. verb] newspapers and magazines, and the people who work on them: *The story was widely reported in the press.* ◇ *The press were invited to the launch of the new car.* ◇ *the financial press*
2 [U; sing.] the type or amount of reports that newspapers write about sb/sth: *The industry has received a lot of bad press.*
3 (*Manufacturing*) [C] a business that prints and publishes books: *Oxford University Press*
4 (*Manufacturing*) [C] a machine for printing books, newspapers, etc.; the process of printing them: *These prices are correct at the time of going to press* (= being printed).
● *verb*
1 [+ obj or no obj] to make strong efforts to persuade sb to do sth: *The unions are pressing for a 6% pay increase.* ◇ *The government is pressing airports to introduce new security systems.*
SYN PUSH FOR STH
2 [+ obj] to express or repeat sth with force: *She is still pressing her claim for compensation.*
PHRV **,press a'head/'on (with sth)** to continue doing sth even though it is difficult: *Management is determined to press on with efforts to return to profitability.*

'press ,agent *noun* [C]
a person whose job is to supply information and advertising material about a particular company, actor, etc. to newspapers, radio or television

'press communi,cations *noun* [pl.]
(*Marketing*) information or activities that are intended to make the media more aware of a product, service or company

'press ,conference (*especially BrE*) (*AmE usually* **'news ,conference**) *noun* [C]
a meeting at which sb talks to a group of journalists in order to answer their questions or to make an official statement: *The company held a press conference to announce its shutdown.*
→ BRIEFING (1)
✪ *to give/hold a press conference* ◆ *to tell a press conference sth*

'press kit *noun* [C]
(*Marketing*) a set of documents, photographs, etc. that advertise or give information about a particular product and are given to the media

'press ,office *noun* [C]
the office of a large organization that answers questions from journalists and provides them with information

'press ,officer *noun* [C]
a person who works for an organization answering questions from journalists about the organization and providing them with information

'press re,lations *noun* [U] (*abbr* **PR**)
(*Marketing*) the process of developing relationships with journalists and other people who work in the media in order to make a company or its products known to the public: *a press relations adviser to the company* ◇ *Public relations people may specialize in press relations, consumer PR or financial PR.*
→ PUBLIC RELATIONS

'press re,lease (*also* **'news re,lease**) (*also* **re'lease**, *less frequent*) *noun* [C]
an official statement made to journalists, etc. by a large organization: *The company issued a press release to end speculation about its future.*
✪ *to issue/publish/put out/write a press release*

'press ,secretary *noun* [C]
a person who works for an organization, especially a political organization, and gives information about them to the media

'pressure group *noun* [C]
a group of people who try to influence the government, people with power in organizations, and the opinions of ordinary people in order to achieve the action they want, for example a change in a law: *the environmental pressure group Greenpeace*

prestige /pre'stiːʒ/ *noun, adjective*
● *noun* [U]
the respect and admiration that sb/sth has because of their success, good quality, or social importance: *the prestige of British industry* ◇ *jobs with low prestige* ◇ *There is a lot of prestige attached to owning a car like this.*
✪ *occupational/social prestige* ◆ *low/high prestige* ◆ *to enjoy/gain/have/lack prestige*
● *adjective* [only before noun]
1 admired and respected because of looking important and expensive: *growing sales of prestige products* ◇ *a prestige waterfront office block*
SYN LUXURY
2 that brings respect and admiration; important: *a prestige job/project*

prestigious /pre'stɪdʒəs/ *adjective* [usually before noun]
respected and admired as very important or of very high quality: *It's a major coup for us to get such a prestigious contract.* ◇ *meetings with prestigious clients*

presumption /prɪ'zʌmpʃn/ *noun* [U,C]
(*Law*) the act of supposing that sth is true, although it has not yet been proved or is not certain: *Everyone is entitled to the presumption of innocence until they are proved to be guilty.*

,pre-'tax (*also spelled* **pretax**, *especially in AmE*) *adjective* [only before noun]
(*Accounting*) before tax has been taken away: *The company reported pre-tax profits of €182 million last year.* ◇ *At the pre-tax level, the group suffered losses of $450 million.*
✪ *pre-tax earnings/income/losses/profits*

pretest /ˌpriː'test/ *noun, verb*
● *noun* [C]
a test done on a product or an advertisement before it is made available or used, in order to make sure it is safe or effective
● *verb* [+ obj]
to test a product or an advertisement before making it available or using it, in order to make sure it is safe or effective: *The software had already been pretested.* ▶ **pre'testing** *noun* [U]

prevailing /prɪ'veɪlɪŋ/ *adjective* [only before noun]
existing or most common at a particular time: *the prevailing economic conditions* ◇ *Introductory rates*

on credit cards are likely to be lower than the 6% prevailing last year.

prevalent /ˈprevələnt/ *adjective*
that exists or is very common at a particular time or in a particular place: *This trend is most prevalent* **among** *larger companies.* ◇ *Price-cutting was especially prevalent* **in** *labour-intensive industries.*
▶ **prevalence** /ˈprevələns/ *noun* [U]: *the increasing prevalence of bankruptcy in the country*

ˌpre-ˈvet *verb* [+ obj *or no obj*] (-tt-) (*often* **be pre-vetted**)
the process of finding out information about sb/sth to see if they are suitable before using them/it: *a pre-vetted, or 'approved', contractor* ◇ *Our agency can supply your business with pre-vetted graduates.*
▶ ˌpre-ˈvetting *noun* [U]: *the pre-vetting of staff/advertising material*

preview /ˈpriːvjuː/ = PRINT PREVIEW

prey /preɪ/ *noun, verb*
● *noun* [U; sing.]
1 a person who is harmed or deceived by sb, especially for dishonest purposes: *Elderly people are* **easy prey** *for dishonest salesmen.*
2 (used especially in newspapers) a company that another company wants to buy, especially when the first company is weak or does not want to be bought: *The financial crisis may make the group prey to a bigger rival.* ◇ *The company was more used to being predator than prey.* **SYN** TARGET COMPANY → PREDATOR
IDM **be/fall ˈprey to sth** (*formal*) **1** to be harmed or affected by sth bad: *The rebuilding programme fell prey to cutbacks.* **2** (about a company) to be bought by another company: *Analysts believe that the business could fall prey to a US bidder.*
● *verb* [+ obj]
PHRV **ˈprey on/upon sb** to harm sb who is weaker than you, or make use of them in a dishonest way to get what you want: *lenders who prey on people with serious debt problems*

★ **price** /praɪs/ *noun, verb*
● *noun* [C,U]
SEE ALSO: after-hours price, asked ~, asking ~, ask ~, base ~, basic ~, best ~, etc.

the amount of money that you must pay for sth: *house/retail/oil/share prices* ◇ *He managed to get a good price for the car.* ◇ *Coffee prices have fallen by 15% this year.* ◇ *The store has put up the prices of many basic items.* ◇ *We plan to sell 10 000 units at a price of €15 each.* ◇ *The price charged to customers may be changed.* ◇ *Can you* **give me a price** *for the work* (= tell me how much you will charge)? ◇ *Shoppers are unwilling to pay* **full** *price for electrical goods.* ◇ *It's amazing how much computers have come down* **in** *price over the past few years.* → PRICE CUT See note at INCREASE
● *a competitive/high/low/reasonable price • falling/rising prices • to increase/put up/raise prices • to cut/lower/slash prices • price increases/reductions/rises*
IDM **at a ˈprice** costing a lot of money: *You can buy strawberries in England all year round, but at a price.* **put a ˈprice on sth** to say how much money sth valuable is worth: *They haven't yet put a price on the business.* → idiom at BALLPARK
● *verb* [+ obj]
1 (*Marketing*) (*usually* **be priced**) to fix the price of sth at a particular level: *The new model will be priced at $10 000–$15 000.* ◇ *These goods were priced too high.* ◇ *competitively priced PCs* ◇ *Imagine that bananas are priced* **off** (= in relation to) *apples.*
● *attractively/competitively/keenly priced • moderately/reasonably priced*

price/charge/commission/cost/fee/rate

These words are used to talk about the money that you pay for something.

Price is used about goods and other things that are traded in large numbers or amounts: *car/electricity/food/share prices* ◇ *the average selling price of a home*

Fee [C] and **charge** [C] are usually used about money that you pay for a service: *A service charge of 10% is added to the bill.* ◇ *legal/accounting fees*

Charge [U] can also be used about a product or service that is free: *The manual is available* **free of charge.** ◇ *There is* **no charge** *for delivery.*

Unlike a price, fee or charge, the **cost** of something is not advertised but needs to be calculated. It is the amount of money that you need to spend in order to buy, make, build or produce it: *The total cost of the building was several million euros more than budgeted.*

Rate is used when the price of the product or service is fixed according to its size, weight, length, etc.: *Our standard rate is $89 per night for a single room.*

Commission is money that is paid to an agent for selling something on behalf of somebody else. Although the commission comes from the money paid by the buyer, its size is decided between the seller and agent and is not always advertised.

2 (*Commerce*) **price sth (up)** to write or stick tickets on goods to show how much they cost: *I spent all day pricing tins of fruit.* ◇ *The clothes were sorted and priced up for sale.*
3 **price sth (up)** to compare the prices of different types of the same thing: *We priced various models before buying this one.*
IDM **price yourself/sth out of the ˈmarket** to charge such a high price for your goods, services, etc. that nobody wants to buy them: *Some restaurants in the city have priced themselves out of the market.*
PHRV ˌprice sth ˈin; ˌprice sth ˈinto sth (*Finance*) to include sth when you are fixing the price of an item, especially shares, bonds, etc: *Investors have fully priced in a small cut in interest rates.* ◇ *The bad news is already priced into the shares.*

ˈprice ˌceiling *noun* [C]
(*Economics*) a limit set by a government on the price of goods or services: *The government has lifted the price ceiling on petrol.* → CEILING

ˈprice compeˌtition *noun* [U]
(*Economics; Marketing*) a situation in which companies compete with each other to sell products by trying to keep their prices lower than the prices of similar goods and services produced by other companies: *There is intense price competition from the low-cost economies of the Far East.*

ˈprice conˌtrol *noun* [C, usually pl., U]
(*Economics*) limits that a government or an official organization puts on the amount companies can charge for goods and services: *If drug prices don't drop, the state could impose price controls.* ◇ *Any industry hit by price control will complain bitterly about it.*

ˈprice cut *noun* [C]
a reduction in the price of something: *Despite continuing price cuts, consumers are less willing to spend.* ▶ ˈprice-ˌcutting *noun* [U]: *The newspaper has lost sales following price-cutting by rivals.* ◇ *a price-cutting war*

'price discrimi,nation noun [U]
(*Economics*; *Marketing*) the practice of selling the same product to different types of customers at different prices

,price-'dividend ,ratio noun [C] (*abbr* **PDR, P/D ratio**)
(*Accounting*) the relationship between the present market price of the shares of a particular company and the DIVIDEND (= the money paid to shareholders) for the previous year, used to compare different companies

,price-'earnings ,ratio (*also* ,price-to-'earnings ,ratio) (*abbr* **P/E ratio**) (*also* ,price-'earnings ,multiple** *abbr* **P/E multiple**) noun [C]
(*Accounting*) the relationship between the present market price of shares in a particular company and the EARNINGS PER SHARE (= the amount of profit that the company earned in the previous year divided by the number of shares), used to analyse the company's performance over a period of time or compare it with others: *A high price-earnings ratio can mean that a company is growing fast.* ◇ *Its price-earnings ratio of about 27 is well below some of its competitors.* → MULTIPLE

'price ef,fect noun [C]
(*Economics*)
1 the way in which something that happens affects the prices of goods: *It is difficult to estimate the price effect of the merger.*
2 the way in which a change in the price of a product changes demand for that product

'price elas'ticity of de'mand (*also* ,price elas'ticity, ,own-price elas'ticity) = ELASTICITY OF DEMAND

'price-,fixing (*also* ,common 'pricing) noun [U]
(*Economics*) the practice of companies agreeing to sell the same goods for the same price, which is illegal in many countries → FIX *verb* (4)

'price ,index noun [C, usually sing.]

SEE ALSO: consumer price index, Producer Price Index, retail price index

(*Economics*) a figure that shows the change in the price of something over a period of time: *The government is to start publishing a new monthly house price index.*

,price-in'sensitive adjective
1 (*Economics*) if sales of goods and services are price-insensitive, the quantity does not change when prices go down or up
2 (*Marketing*) price-insensitive customers are not influenced by price when buying things
OPP PRICE-SENSITIVE

,price 'leader noun [C]
(*Marketing*) a business that is usually the first to reduce or increase prices, compared to other similar businesses: *As price leaders, whatever prices they charge for toys and games in their catalogue will be followed by the rest of the market.* → PRICE TAKER
▶ ,price 'leadership noun [U]

priceless /'praɪsləs/ adjective
extremely valuable or important: *Customer loyalty is a priceless asset.*

'price ,level noun [C]
(*Economics*) the average prices of goods and services in a country or an area at a particular time: *The overall price level has been stable or falling for the past few years.*

'price list noun [C]
(*Commerce*) a list of prices for goods or services that a business provides for its customers: *Web customers can see up-to-date price lists.*

'price ,mechanism (*also* 'market ,mechanism) noun [sing.]
(*Economics*) the way in which changes in prices influence the production of goods and services and those who receive them: *The market relies on the price mechanism to balance supply and demand.*

'price point noun [C]
(*Marketing*) the price that a product is sold for, chosen from a range of possible prices: *The product sells at an attractive price point.* ◇ *The snack has a price point similar to that of its chief competitor.*
❍ *a high/low price point*

'price range noun [C, usually sing.]
1 a group of prices that are close together, often within fixed limits: *There are a lot of choices for PCs in this price range.* ◇ *the higher/lower/middle price range*
2 (*Stock Exchange*) the price at which a share is offered for sale: *The group set a price range of $1.25 to $1.52 a share.*
3 the amount that a person can afford to pay for something: *The apartment was way out of my price range.*

'price ring = CARTEL

,price-'sensitive adjective
1 (*Economics*) if sales of goods and services are price-sensitive, the quantity sold increases or decreases when prices go down or up: *The computer industry is very price-sensitive.* OPP PRICE-INSENSITIVE
2 (*Marketing*) price-sensitive customers are influenced mainly by price when buying things: *Tight budgets are making customers more price-sensitive.* OPP PRICE-INSENSITIVE
3 (*Finance*) price-sensitive information could affect prices, especially share prices: *Companies have a legal duty to inform the market of price-sensitive information without delay.*
▶ ,price sensi'tivity noun [U]

'price sup,port noun [U]
(*Economics*) a system in which a government helps producers, especially farmers, by acting to stop the price of goods falling below a particular level

'price tag noun [C, usually sing.]
1 a label showing the price of an item that is for sale in a shop/store: *The price tag said $49.95.*
→ LABEL *noun* (1)
2 the cost of something, especially when this is high: *It's difficult to put a price tag on experience.* ◇ *The business is for sale with a price tag of more than $50 million.*

,price 'taker noun [C]
(*Economics*) a company or person that has little power or influence over the price at which sth sells → PRICE LEADER

,price-to-'earnings ,ratio = PRICE-EARNINGS RATIO

pricey (*also spelled* **pricy**) /'praɪsi/ adjective
(**pricier, priciest**) (*informal*)
expensive: *Consumers have cut purchases of pricier perfumes and make-up.* ◇ *At $1 000, the product is too pricey.* SYN DEAR

★ **pricing** /'praɪsɪŋ/ noun [U]

SEE ALSO: common pricing, dual ~, market-penetration ~, multiple ~, penetration ~, predatory ~, value ~, value-based ~

(*Commerce*; *Economics*) the prices that a company charges for its products or services; the act of deciding what they should be: *They are trying to win back customers with competitive pricing.* ◇ *The newspaper group is scaling back (= reducing) its*

aggressive pricing strategy. ◇ strong competition and pricing pressure in the personal computer market
○ **aggressive/competitive/fair/unfair** pricing • pricing **policies/practices/strategies** • a pricing **structure/system**

'pricing ,model noun [C]
(Commerce) a system that a company uses to decide what to charge for its products or services: We are going to revise our pricing model.

'pricing ,power noun [U]
(Economics) the effect that a change in the price of a company's products has on the quantity demanded: a time of low inflation and weak pricing power

pricy = PRICEY

primary /'praɪməri; AmE -meri/ adjective [usually before noun]
1 main; most important: Their primary business is life insurance. ◇ Our primary target is 20- to 35-year-olds. [SYN] PRIME
2 used to describe sth that is not caused by or based on sth else: the use of primary source materials
3 (Finance) relating to shares, bonds, etc. that are being sold for the first time: The primary bond market came back to life on Tuesday after a very quiet month.
→ SECONDARY

,primary 'action noun [U]
(HR) action such as stopping work that is taken by workers in a factory, company, etc. who are involved in a dispute with their employers
→ SECONDARY ACTION

,primary 'data noun [U]
(Marketing) information that a company collects itself, rather than getting it from other sources: For primary data, a marketing research organization is likely to be used. → SECONDARY DATA

,primary 'dealer noun [C]
(Economics) a financial institution that is allowed to deal directly with a country's central bank

,primary de'mand noun [U,C]
(Marketing) the desire of consumers for a type of product rather than for a particular brand
→ SELECTIVE DEMAND

'primary ,industry noun [U,C]
(Economics) industry that produces and collects things like crops, metals, raw materials, etc.
→ SECONDARY INDUSTRY, TERTIARY INDUSTRY

'primary ,market noun [C]
(Stock Exchange) the section of the money market where shares, bonds, etc. are sold for the first time: In the primary market, borrowing was once again concentrated in euros. → SECONDARY MARKET

,primary 'mortgage ,market = MORTGAGE MARKET (1)

,primary pro'duction noun [U]
(Economics) the production and collection of crops and raw materials, rather than making goods from them → SECONDARY PRODUCTION

the 'primary ,sector noun [sing.]
(Economics) the part of a country's economy that collects or produces crops, raw materials, etc.
→ SECONDARY SECTOR

prime /praɪm/ adjective, noun, verb
● adjective
1 main; most important: The care of the environment is of prime importance. [SYN] PRIMARY
2 of the best quality: prime office space ◇ The store has a prime position in the mall.

3 typical: Qantas is a **prime example** of a company that exceeded expectations.
● noun
[IDM] **above/below 'prime** (AmE) (Finance) an interest rate that is **above** or **below prime** is higher or lower than the PRIME RATE (= the lowest rate at which business customers can borrow from a bank)
● verb [+ obj]
[IDM] **prime the 'pump** to encourage the growth of sth such as a new business or a weak economy: The government needs to prime the economy's pump quickly. → PUMP-PRIMING

,prime con'tractor noun [C]
the **contractor** who has direct contact with the company that needs work done
→ SUBCONTRACTOR

,prime 'cost (also ,first 'cost) noun [C,U]
(Accounting) the cost of sth calculated by adding the cost of materials used to make it and the cost of paying sb to make it, but not including costs that are connected with running a business, such as rent and electricity (**overheads**) [SYN] DIRECT COST

'prime rate (also ,prime 'interest rate, ,prime 'lending rate) noun [C] (all especially AmE)
(Finance) the lowest interest rate at which businesses can borrow money from a bank: Some commercial banks have lowered their prime rate to 4.25%. [SYN] BASE RATE (BrE)

'prime time (BrE also ,peak time, ,peak 'viewing time) noun [U]
the time when the largest number of people are watching television or listening to the radio, usually the middle part of the evening: showing ads during prime-time broadcasts

principal /'prɪnsəpl/ noun, adjective
● noun
1 (Finance) [sing; U] an amount of money that is lent or invested to earn interest: You must make the required interest and principal payments.
2 (Law) [C] a person who is actually making a business deal or taking part in a legal case, rather than a person who is acting on their behalf
3 [C] an important manager or other person in an organization, who usually has legal responsibility for what the organization does: The company's three principals are women.
● adjective
1 most important; main: Tourist revenue is now our principal source of wealth. ◇ the principal markets for our products
2 (Finance) relating to an original amount of money that is lent or invested, rather than any interest: The total interest is now more than the principal amount.

,principal 'trading = PROPRIETARY TRADING

principle /'prɪnsəpl/ noun [C]

SEE ALSO: ability-to-pay principle, accounting ~, benefit ~, Pareto's ~, statement of ~

1 a law, rule or theory that sth is based on: The principles of banking have not changed much over the centuries.
2 a general or scientific law that explains how sth works or why sth happens: the principle that heat rises [SYN] LAW (5)
[IDM] **in 'principle 1** if sth can be done **in principle**, there is no reason why it should not be done although it has not been done yet: In principle, such loans have always been available.
2 in general but not in detail: The companies reached an agreement in principle last week.

● *verb*

1 [+ obj *or* no obj] to produce letters, pictures, etc. on paper using a machine that puts ink on the surface: *Do you want your address printed at the top of the letter?* ◇ *I'm printing a copy of the document for you.* ◇ *Click on the icon when you want to print.*

2 [+ obj] to produce books, newspapers, etc. by printing them in large quantities: *They printed 30 000 copies of the book.* ◇ *We design and print brochures and business cards.*

3 [+ obj] to publish sth in printed form: *Parts of the report were printed in several newspapers.*

4 [+ obj] to write without joining the letters together: *Print your name and address in the space provided.*

→ idioms at LICENCE, WORTH *adj.*

PHRV **,print sth 'off/'out** to produce a document or information from a computer in printed form: *I'll print off a copy of the letter for you.* → PRINTOUT

,print sth 'up to produce sth in printed form, especially quickly or in large quantities: *He printed up 200 000 catalogues for the new season.*

● *noun* [U]

SEE ALSO: **fine print, small print**

1 letters, words, numbers, etc. that have been printed onto paper: *The print quality of the new printer is superb.*

2 used to refer to the business of producing newspapers, magazines and books: *print and online media*

IDM **in 'print/,out of 'print** (about a book) still available/not available from the company that published it: *'Accounting for Growth' is still in print.*

'print ,advertising *noun* [U]

(*Marketing*) the act of using newspapers, magazines, etc. to advertise a company and its products; the advertisements that are used: *a 10% drop in print advertising* ▶ **'print ad** (*also* **'print ad,vertisement,** *formal*) *noun* [C]: *Print ads are expensive, so think carefully before using them.*

printer /'prɪntə(r)/ *noun* [C]

SEE ALSO: **dot matrix printer, laser printer**

1 a machine for printing on paper, especially one that is connected to a computer: *a colour printer*

2 a person or company whose job is printing books, etc.

printing /'prɪntɪŋ/ *noun*

1 [U] the activity of producing newspapers, books, etc. using machines that put words and pictures onto paper: *the printing trade/industry* ◇ *colour printing*

2 [C] the act of printing a number of copies of a book at one time: *None of his books has made it into a second printing.*

printout /'prɪntaʊt/ *noun* [C]

a page or set of pages with printing on it produced by a computer: *There is a printout of her daily schedule on her desk.* → READ-OUT, PRINT STH OFF/OUT at PRINT *verb*

'print ,preview (*also* **'preview**) *noun* [C,U]

(*IT*) a feature of some computer programs that allows you to see how a document or drawing will look when you print it

prior /'praɪə(r)/ *adjective* [only before noun]

1 happening or existing before sth else or before a particular time: *Sales grew 8% over the prior year to $20.3 bn.* ◇ *IBM said it had no prior knowledge of the matter.*

○ *prior* **approval/knowledge/notice** ◆ *the prior* **month/quarter/week/year** ◆ *a prior* **arrangement/engagement**

2 prior to (*formal*) before sth: *during the week prior to the meeting* ◇ *Prior to joining Kmart, East worked for the family firm.*

★ **prioritize** , **-ise** /praɪˈɒrətaɪz; *AmE* -ˈɔːr-; -ˈɑːr-/ *verb* [+ obj *or* no obj]

to put tasks, problems, etc. in order of importance, so that you can deal with the most important first: *Successful managers know how to prioritize.* ◇ *Use folders to prioritize your work.*

★ **priority** /praɪˈɒrəti; *AmE* -ˈɔːr-; -ˈɑːr-/ (*plural* **priorities**) *noun*

1 [C] something that you think is more important than other things and should be dealt with first: *Reducing costs is our top priority.* ◇ *The company made maintaining market share a priority.* ◇ *Financial security was high on his* **list of priorities**. ◇ *The deal has gone down the priority list of the company.*

○ *your* **first/main/number one/top** *priority* ◆ *a* **high/key/low** *priority*

2 [U] the most important place among various things that have to be done or among a group of people: *Preferred stock holders will be given priority.* ◇ *We give priority* **to** *training and customer service.* ◇ *The new project will take priority* **over** *other issues.* **SYN** PRECEDENCE

○ *to* **be given/have/take** *priority (over sth/sb)*

pri'ority claim *noun* [C]

(*Law*) a right that a company or person has to be paid money owed to them by a BANKRUPT company before others

privacy /'prɪvəsi; *AmE* 'praɪv-/ *noun* [U]

the right to keep some information private: *Searching employees' desks is a gross invasion of privacy.* ◇ *We must protect the privacy of individuals from companies that want to share sensitive information.* ◇ *Nearly all commercial websites now have a privacy policy.*

○ *to* **preserve/protect/respect** *sb's privacy* ◆ *to* **invade/violate** *sb's privacy* ◆ *an* **invasion** *of privacy* ◆ *privacy* **law/legislation/rules/policy**

★ **private** /'praɪvət/ *adjective*

1 [usually before noun] owned, managed or provided by an individual person or an independent company, rather than by the state: *a private law firm* ◇ *private medical insurance* ◇ *There is no shortage of private funding for biotechnology.* **OPP** PUBLIC → PRIVATE COMPANY

2 [usually before noun] working or acting for yourself rather than for the state or for an organization or a company: *A group of private investors got together to buy the company.* ◇ *As a private IT consultant he could earn ten times what he made as an employee.*

3 belonging to or for the use of a particular person or group; not for public use: *This car park is private.* ◇ *A number of their clients have their own private jets.* ◇ *The share documents were found among her private papers.* **OPP** PUBLIC

4 (*Commerce; Finance*) [only before noun] sold only to particular people or organizations; not offered to the public in general to buy: *a private sale of $1.25 billion of shares* **OPP** PUBLIC

5 intended for or involving a particular person or group of people; not for people in general to attend or know about: *The council held a private meeting this morning.* ◇ *The letter was marked 'Private'.* **OPP** PUBLIC

6 [usually before noun] not connected with your work or official position: *You should not make private calls from the office.* ◇ *She had some private business to attend to.* **SYN** PERSONAL

▶ **'privately** *adverb*: *One in three rented properties is privately owned.* ◇ *a privately funded organization* ◇ *Can we speak privately?*

IDM **go 'private; take a company 'private**

(*Finance*) if a company whose shares are sold on the stock market **goes private**, it becomes independent by buying back shares from shareholders; to make a company independent in this way: *a plan for the public utility companies to go private*

,private 'bank *noun* [C]
1 a bank that offers personal services in managing investments and assets to individuals and families with a lot of money
2 a bank that is not a member of a CLEARING HOUSE (= a central office through which banks pay each other money and exchange cheques)
3 a bank that is not owned by the state
▸ **,private 'banking** *noun* [U]

,private 'brand *noun* [C]
(*Commerce*; *Marketing*) a product sold by a particular supplier or shop/store with its own name on: *Most private brands of scotch, vodka, and gin are produced by well-known name-brand companies.* SYN HOUSE BRAND

,private 'company (*also* 'private 'limited 'company) *noun* [C] (*especially BrE*)
a business that may not offer its shares for sale to the public → PRIVATELY-HELD, PUBLIC COMPANY

,private corpo'ration *noun* [C] (*AmE*)
a business that may not offer its shares for sale to the public

,private 'enterprise *noun*
1 [U] the economic system in which industry or business is owned by individuals and independent companies and is not controlled by the government → FREE ENTERPRISE
2 [C] a business that is owned by individuals or other companies, not by the government → PUBLIC ENTERPRISE

,private 'equity *noun* [U]
(*Finance*) shares that are held by companies or investors in new or small companies whose shares are not available for the public to buy and sell on the stock market

,private 'income *noun* [U, C]
money that you receive from property or other sources, and do not earn by working: *He has a private income of several hundred thousand dollars a year.*

,private 'label *noun* [C] (*especially BrE*)
(*Commerce*; *Marketing*) a product or group of products that a shop/store or company sells with its own name on: *Private labels are usually slightly cheaper than brands.* ◇ *We provide private-label products for you to sell under your own name.*

,private 'law *noun* [U]
(*Law*) the part of the law that deals with the relationship between individuals and organizations, and not their relationship with the state

'private 'limited 'company = PRIVATE COMPANY

,privately-'held *adjective* [usually before noun]
(*Law*) used to describe a company whose shares may not be bought and sold by the public

,private 'placing (*BrE*) (*also* ,private 'placement, *AmE*, *BrE*) *noun* [C]
(*Finance*) when shares are sold directly to investors rather than to the public on the stock market

'private-'public 'partnership = PUBLIC-PRIVATE PARTNERSHIP

,private 'sale *noun* [C,U]
(*Commerce*; *Finance*) when sth such as property is sold by the owner directly to the buyer; when shares, etc. are offered for sale to only a few people and not to the public: *We bought the house by*

private sale. ◇ *raising capital through the private sale of equity*

,private 'sector *noun* [sing.]
(*Economics*) the part of a country's economy that is not under the direct control of the government, but is owned by individuals and independent companies: *salary increases in the private sector* ◇ *government medical laboratories working in collaboration with the private sector* ◇ *private-sector banks/organizations* → PUBLIC SECTOR

,private 'treaty *noun* [U,C]
(*Law*) an agreement to sell property or a valuable item between its owner and a buyer

privatize , -ise /'praɪvətaɪz/ *verb* [+ obj]
(*Economics*) to sell a business or an industry so that it is no longer owned and controlled by the government: *Air traffic control has been privatized.* ◇ *the decision to privatize the railways* ◇ *newly privatized companies* SYN DENATIONALIZE OPP NATIONALIZE
▸ **privatization, -isation** /ˌpraɪvətaɪˈzeɪʃn; *AmE* -təˈz-/ *noun* [U,C]: *the privatization of the water industry* ◇ *rail privatization*

privilege /'prɪvəlɪdʒ/ *noun*
1 [C,U] a special right or advantage that a particular person or group of people has: *countries which enjoy trade privileges with the United States* ◇ *Members of senior management have certain privileges.* ◇ *There is no executive privilege.*
2 (*Law*) [U] a special right that protects sb from being punished if they do or say a particular thing, or refuse to do or say a particular thing, because of their position: *He wants to force lawyers who find corporate wrongdoing to breach* (= break) *the attorney-client privilege* (= the right of a lawyer to say nothing about matters affecting their client).

privileged /'prɪvəlɪdʒd/ *adjective*
(*Law*) **privileged** information is known only to a few people and is legally protected so it does not have to be made public: *They had illegally profited from their access to privileged information.* SYN CONFIDENTIAL

privity /'prɪvəti/ *noun* [U,C] (*plural* **privities**)
(*Law*) a relationship between two people or groups that is accepted by law, for example the relationship between people who have signed a contract

prize /praɪz/ *noun, adjective*
● *noun* [C]
1 an award or amount of money that is given to a person who wins a competition, etc. or who does very good work: *The best slogan wins a prize.*
2 something very valuable or important that is difficult to obtain
● *adjective* [only before noun]
being a very good or valuable example of its kind: *This is a prize opportunity.* ◇ *If she leaves, the team will lose its prize asset.*

PRO /ˌpiː ɑːr ˈəʊ; *AmE* ˈoʊ/ *noun* [C] **public relations officer** a person whose job is to give the public information about an organization or a person in order to create a good impression

pro /prəʊ; *AmE* proʊ/ = PROFESSIONAL *noun*

pro- /prəʊ; *AmE* proʊ/ *prefix* (*in adjectives*)
in favour of; supporting: *pro-European* → ANTI-

proactive /ˌprəʊˈæktɪv; *AmE* ˌproʊ-/ *adjective*
controlling a situation by making things happen, rather than waiting for things to happen and then reacting to them: *The company has a proactive approach to recruiting.* ◇ *The agency, which currently acts in response to complaints, needs to become more proactive.* → REACTIVE
➊ *a proactive approach/policy/measure/role*
▸ **,pro'actively** *adverb*

methods of selling a company's products or services in which the company tries to find new ways of finding and attracting customers → REACTIVE MARKETING

probation /prə'beɪʃn; *AmE* proʊ-/ *noun* [U]

1 (*HR*) a time of training and testing when you start a new job to see if you are suitable for the work: *a period of probation*

2 a period of time during which a person or a company that has not been doing well must improve: *He said that management was **on** probation and some people may be dismissed.*

▸ **probationary** /prə'beɪʃnri; *AmE* proʊ'beɪʃəneri/ *adjective*: *a probationary period* **pro'bationer** *noun* [C]

probe /prəʊb; *AmE* proʊb/ *noun, verb*

● *noun* [C]

(used especially in newspapers) an investigation: *Investigators have launched a probe into the company's sales and marketing practices.*

● *verb* [+ obj *or no* obj]

to ask questions in order to find out secret or hidden information about sb/sth: *They have been probing more deeply into the way that teams work.*

probity /'prəʊbəti; *AmE* 'proʊ-/ *noun* [U] (*formal*) the quality of being completely honest: *financial probity*

'problem child *noun* [C]

1 something such as a product, business, or part of a business that is not very successful or causes particular difficulties for its makers or owners: *The UK subsidiary is turning out to be a problem child for its parent company.*

2 (*Marketing*) a product that only has a small share of the market in a market that is growing quickly: *Large investments will be needed for a problem child.* —Picture at BOSTON MATRIX

'problem-,solving *noun* [U]

the act of finding ways of dealing with problems: *developing problem-solving skills and strategies*

▸ **'problem-,solver** *noun* [C]

pro bono /,prəʊ 'bəʊnəʊ; *AmE* ,proʊ 'boʊnoʊ/ *adjective* [only before noun]

used to describe work that is done without charging a fee: *She agreed to take the case on a pro bono basis.* ▸ **,pro 'bono** *adverb*: *a lawyer who often works pro bono* **NOTE** Pro bono is a Latin phrase that means 'for the public good'.

procedural /prə'si:dʒərəl/ *adjective* connected with the way of doing sth, especially the correct or official way: *Many companies said they paid suppliers late because of procedural problems.* ◇ *The employer must comply with the procedural rules for a dismissal.*

★ **procedure** /prə'si:dʒə(r)/ *noun* [C,U]

SEE ALSO: disciplinary procedure, disputes ~, safety ~, standard operating ~

a way of doing sth, especially the usual or correct way: *Making a complaint is quite a simple procedure.* ◇ *You must follow the correct procedure **for** hiring staff.* ◇ *Policies and procedures are written down so that new workers can learn their jobs quickly.* ◇ *court/legal procedure*

● *to* **adopt/follow/review/use** *procedure(s)* • **accepted/established/normal/proper/standard** *procedure(s)* • **appeals/complaints/emergency** *procedures*

proceed /prə'si:d; *AmE* proʊ-/ *verb* [no obj]

to continue doing sth that has already been started; to continue being done: *Work is proceeding slowly.* ◇ *We are under pressure to proceed **with** this merger.* ◇ *The bank did not allow the transaction to*

proceed. ◇ *The industry will have to proceed carefully to avoid overexpansion.* → GO AHEAD at GO

PHRV **pro'ceed against sb** (*Law*) to start a court case against sb

proceeding /prə'si:dɪŋ/ *noun* [C, usually pl.] (*formal*)

a legal process which aims to settle a dispute or deal with a complaint: *We do not want to get involved in costly legal proceedings.* ◇ *a bankruptcy proceeding that lasted 45 days and cost the company about $750 000 in legal fees*

● **bankruptcy/divorce/extradition** *proceedings* • **legal** *proceedings*

proceeds /'prəʊsi:dz; *AmE* 'proʊ-/ *noun* [pl.] money that sb receives, for example when they sell sth; profits: *The sale proceeds will go directly to the company's creditors.* ◇ *She sold the patent and started a new business with the proceeds.* ◇ *proceeds **from** the sale of assets* See note at PROFIT

★ **process** /'prəʊses; *AmE* 'prɑ:ses; 'proʊ-/ *noun, verb*

● *noun* [C]

SEE ALSO: business process, four-colour process

1 a series of things that are done in order to achieve a particular result: *The whole purpose of the selection process is to pick the best person for the job.* ◇ *New workers are encouraged to observe interview sessions as part of the process of training.* ◇ *I'm afraid getting things changed will be a slow process.*

● *an* **approval/evaluation/inspection** *process* • *a* **consultation/decision-making/planning** *process* • *the* **hiring/selection** *process* • *to* **complete/finish/go through/start** *a process* • *to* **improve/speed up/ streamline** *a process*

2 a method used in industry for doing or making sth: *The manufacturing process involves the use of advanced technology.* ◇ *The company had developed a process **for** converting coal into petrol.*

● *an* **industrial/a manufacturing/production** *process* • *to* **improve/speed up/streamline/use** *a process*

IDM **be in the process of doing sth** to be continuing sth that you have started: *We sold one business and are in the process of selling another.* **in the 'process** while doing sth: *We improved the system and made substantial savings in the process.*

● *verb* [+ obj]

1 to treat raw material, food, etc. in order to change it, preserve it, etc: *They have signed a four billion euro contract to process nuclear waste.* ◇ *Bacteria were found in meat processed at the plant.* ◇ *The industry is working to reduce the levels of salt in processed food.*

2 to deal officially with a document, request, etc: *It will take a week for your application to be processed.* ◇ *The firm has cut the time it takes to process orders by 50%.*

3 (*IT*) to perform a series of operations on data in a computer: *The statisticians use computers to process large amounts of data.* ◇ *Database systems process and store information.* → DATA PROCESSING, WORD PROCESSING

▸ **'processing** *noun* [U]: *The food processing industry accounts for about a quarter of manufacturing jobs in Australia.* ◇ *a processing plant/facility* ◇ *computer processing power*

processor /'prəʊsesə(r); *AmE* 'prɑ:-; 'proʊ-/ *noun* [C]

SEE ALSO: word processor

1 a machine or business that processes things: *The company is the world's largest processor of freshwater fish.* ◇ *food/meat processors* ◇ *a chemicals/plastics processor*

2 (*IT*) the part of a computer that controls all the other parts of the system: *The industry focused on*

producing faster processors for PCs. [SYN] CENTRAL
PROCESSING UNIT → MICROPROCESSOR

'process ,owner noun [C]
the person who is responsible for a process in a
business, for how well it works and for improving it
→ BUSINESS PROCESS RE-ENGINEERING

procurement /prə'kjʊəmənt; AmE -'kjʊrm-/ noun
[U,C]

SEE ALSO: **e-procurement**

(Production) the process of obtaining supplies of
equipment or raw materials for an organization:
She has responsibility for the procurement of
equipment in the company. [SYN] PURCHASING

pro'curement ,officer = PURCHASING
OFFICER

★ **produce** verb, noun
● **verb** /prə'dju:s; AmE -'du:s/ [+ obj]

SEE ALSO: **mass-produce**

1 to make or grow things to be sold, especially in
large quantities: a factory that produces microchips
◇ The firm produces 25 million tons of steel a year. ◇
The sports shoes are produced in Indonesia, China
and Vietnam. ◇ Florida growers produced 42 million
boxes of grapefruit last year. → MANUFACTURE
2 to cause a particular result or effect: Price
increases have produced extra revenues for oil
exporters. ◇ The drug can produce serious side effects.
● **noun** /'prɒdju:s; AmE 'prɑ:du:s; 'proʊ-/ [U]
things that have been made or grown, especially
things connected with farming: The supermarket
buys produce from local farmers.

★ **producer** /prə'dju:sə(r); AmE -'du:-/ noun [C]

SEE ALSO: **integrated producer**

a person, a company or a country that grows or
makes food, goods or materials: The company is a
producer of industrial and electronic materials. ◇ It is
the world's largest packaging producer. ◇ They have
been losing business to lower-cost producers.
→ CONSUMER See note at SUPPLY CHAIN

pro,ducer 'price ,index (also spelled **Producer
Price Index**) noun [C] (abbr **PPI**)
(Economics) a set of figures showing the average
change in prices paid to producers and
manufacturers for goods over a period of time: The
producer price index is considered to be a reliable
indicator of inflation. → CONSUMER PRICE INDEX,
RETAIL PRICE INDEX

★ **product** /'prɒdʌkt; AmE 'prɑ:d-/ noun

SEE ALSO: **augmented product, by-~, commodity ~,
consumer ~, derivative ~, differentiated ~, end ~,**
etc.

1 [C,U] a thing that is manufactured, developed,
produced or grown, usually for sale: dairy/
electrical/pharmaceutical/software products ◇
investment in product development ◇ to launch a
new product onto the market ◇ We need new product
to sell (= a new range of products).
2 [C] a service that people can buy, especially a
way of investing or saving money: The bank is now
offering two new financial products. ◇ investment/
savings products
3 [C] (used with another noun) something that is
made from the thing mentioned: growing demand
for oil products ◇ paper/steel/wood products
4 [C] a thing produced during a natural, chemical
or industrial process: waste products
→ PRODUCE verb

'product ,advertising noun [U]
(Marketing) advertising that aims to make people
notice and want to buy a particular product: In

countries where the company has used product
advertising rather than brand advertising its market
share has fallen. → BRAND ADVERTISING, IMAGE
ADVERTISING, INSTITUTIONAL ADVERTISING

,product a'wareness noun [U]
(Marketing) to what extent people know about and
are interested in a company's products and their
main features: The survey shows that Internet ads
significantly increase product awareness. → BRAND
AWARENESS

'product base noun [C]
(Marketing) the range of goods produced or services
provided by a company: The company has a product
base of over sixty thousand software items.
● to **broaden/deepen/expand** the product base

'product ,category noun [C]
(Marketing) a general type of product: Every year or
so we add a new product category. ◇ Product
categories such as gifts, food and electronics have
been performing well.

,product de'velopment noun [U]
the process of designing, producing, and marketing
a new product: Investment in product development is
essential for the company's future growth.

,product di'version = DIVERSION (2)

,product engi'neer noun [C]
a person whose job is to develop new products for a
business and be responsible for the design,
manufacture and technical aspects of the products

'product ,family noun [C]
(Marketing; Production) a group of products made by
one manufacturer that are very similar in some
way: This printer is the latest addition to our product
family. ◇ The company now breaks down each order
by product family.

,product inno'vation noun
(Marketing)
1 [U] the process of improving an existing product
or creating a new and better product: Competition
between firms results in an increased emphasis on
product innovation.
2 [C] a product that is new or has been improved
in some way: Product innovations are introduced to
respond to changes in market demand.

VOCABULARY BUILDING

Production

● The plant **produces** 120 trucks a day.
● They **manufacture** chemicals.
● They **turn out** about 14 million televisions
annually.
● The agency is still **churning out** new ads.
● The new cars began **rolling off** the production line
in July.

★ **production** /prə'dʌkʃn/ noun [U]

SEE ALSO: **batch production, continuous ~, factor
of ~, flow ~, industrial ~, job ~, primary ~,**
secondary ~

1 the process of making goods or materials or
growing food, especially large quantities; the
department in a company that is responsible for
this: Production of the new aircraft will start next
month. ◇ The new computer will be in production by
the end of the year. ◇ We hope to go into production
(= start making our product) next year. ◇ That
model went out of production in 2004. ◇ The new
car has high production costs.
2 the quantity of goods, materials or food that is
produced: Production of saloon cars was up by 8%. ◇
a rise in car production ◇ It is important to monitor
production levels.

❍ *a decline/fall/increase/rise* in production
IDM **on production of sth** (*formal*) when you
show sth: *Discounts only on production of your
student ID card.*

pro'duction ˌconcept *noun* [sing.]
(*Economics*) the theory that consumers prefer
products that are easy to obtain and not expensive
and therefore companies should produce and
deliver goods as efficiently as possible
→ MARKETING CONCEPT, SELLING CONCEPT

pro'duction conˌtrol *noun* [U]
(*Production*) the activity of checking the process of
production to make sure that it is efficient: *the
application of computers to production control*
▶ **pro'duction conˌtroller** *noun* [C]

pro'duction line = ASSEMBLY LINE

pro'duction ˌmanager *noun* [C]
(*Production*) the person who is in charge of the
process of making goods or materials

pro'duction ˌplatform = OIL PLATFORM

★ **productive** /prə'dʌktɪv/ *adjective*
1 making goods or growing crops, especially in
large quantities: *highly productive workers* ◊
productive farming land ◊ *The new methods used in
factories are more productive but provide fewer jobs.*
2 doing or achieving a lot; producing a good
result: *We had a very productive meeting.* ◊
productive investments
[OPP] UNPRODUCTIVE
▶ **pro'ductively** *adverb*: *We have a responsibility to
ensure that the funds are used productively.*

★ **productivity** /ˌprɒdʌk'tɪvəti; *AmE* ˌprɑːd-;
ˌproʊd-/ *noun* [U]

SEE ALSO: **marginal productivity, resource
productivity**

the rate at which a worker, a company or a country
produces goods, and the amount produced,
compared with how much time, work and money is
needed to produce them: *Wage rates depend on
levels of productivity.* ◊ *Better training for workers
leads to greater productivity.* ◊ *Employees were
offered a monthly productivity bonus* (= extra
money for producing more goods).
❍ **high/low/lost** productivity • **to boost/improve/
increase/raise/reduce** productivity • a productivity
agreement/bonus • productivity **gains/growth/
improvement(s)**

productize, -ise /'prɒdʌktaɪz; *AmE* 'prɑːd-/ *verb*
[+ obj]
(*Marketing*) to present sth such as a process or a
service to customers by selling it like a product:
*Trainers want to figure out how to productize their
expertise and sell it.*

'product launch *noun* [C]
(*Marketing*)
1 the action of making a product available to
consumers for the first time: *Successful product
launches depend on creative promotional campaigns.*
2 an event at which a company presents a new
product

ˌproduct lia'bility *noun* [U]
(*Law*) the fact that a manufacturer or trader is
legally responsible for damage, injury or illness
caused by a product that is not working or not
made correctly

ˌproduct 'life ˌcycle *noun* [C] (*abbr* **PLC**)
(*Marketing*) the theory that sales of a product pass
through four stages: introduction, when there is a
gradual increase in sales; growth, when sales
increase rapidly; MATURITY, when sales increase
slowly; decline, when sales fall: *With personal
computers and software, the trend is toward shorter
and shorter product life cycles.*

product life cycle

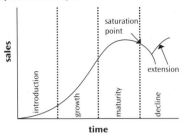

'product 'life cycle 'management *noun* [U]
(*abbr* **PLM**)
(*Marketing*) the job of organizing and directing the
work that is needed to get the most profit from a
product during the different stages of its life

'product line = PRODUCT RANGE

ˌproduct line 'manager = CATEGORY
MANAGER

'product line ˌstretching = LINE STRETCHING

'product ˌmanagement *noun* [U]
(*Marketing*) the process of planning and directing
the products that a company produces and the way
that they are sold

'product ˌmanager *noun* [C]
(*Marketing*) a person who is in charge of planning
and organizing the marketing of a particular brand
or product: *the product manager for Uncle Ben's Rice*

'product mix *noun* [C]
(*Marketing*) all the products and items that a
particular company offers for sale: *The management
plans to improve the stores and broaden the product
mix.*

'product orienˌtation *noun* [C, usually sing., U]
(*Marketing*) the situation when a company focuses
on the quality of the products that it makes, rather
than on what customers want to buy: *There has
been a major change from product orientation to
customer orientation.* → MARKET ORIENTATION,
SALES ORIENTATION
▶ **'product-ˌoriented** *adjective*: *The product-
oriented approach seeks or creates markets for
specific products.*

'product ˌplacement *noun* [C,U]
(*Marketing*) a type of advertising in which a
company pays to have one of its products appear in
a film/movie or television programme: *the practice
of product placement of cigarettes in the movies*

'product range (*also* **'product line**) *noun* [C]
a set of products of a particular type that are made
or sold by a company: *The company is trying to
widen its product range.* ◊ *The new car is seen as
filling a gap in the company's product range.*
❍ **to broaden/expand/increase/widen** the product
range

ˌproduct re'turn = RETURN *noun* (4)

ˌproduct substi'tution *noun* [U]
(*Marketing*)
1 when a company that has a contract to use or
provide particular products, uses different products
instead, especially ones that do not meet the
required standards
2 when consumers start to buy and use a related
but different product from the one they normally
buy and use; when producers start to offer a
different product

★ **profession** /prəˈfeʃn/ *noun*
  1 [C] a type of job that needs special training or skill, especially one that needs a high level of education: *She was at the very top of her profession.* ◇ *Public relations is one of the fastest-growing professions.* ◇ *He was an electrician **by profession**.* ◇ *What advice would you give to people entering the accounting profession?*
  ○ *to enter/go into/join* a profession • *the accountancy/accounting/legal/medical/teaching profession*
  2 the profession [sing. with sing./pl. verb] all the people who work in a particular type of profession: *The legal profession has/have always resisted change.*
  3 the professions [pl.] the traditional jobs that need a high level of education and training, such as being a doctor or a lawyer: *employment in industry and the professions*

VOCABULARY BUILDING

Members of professions

ENGINEERING AND CONSTRUCTION
● **architect** – designs buildings
● **engineer**
  — **electrical engineer** – designs electrical equipment
  — **civil engineer** – designs structures, roads, bridges, etc.
  — **mechanical engineer** – designs machines
● **quantity surveyor** (*BrE*) – calculates the time and materials needed to build sth

FINANCE
● **accountant** – keeps financial records
● **actuary** – calculates risks and payments for insurance companies
● **auditor** – checks that organizations keep proper financial records

LAW
● **attorney** – a US lawyer
● **solicitor** – a UK lawyer
● **barrister** – in the UK, represents people in the higher courts

MANAGEMENT
● **consultant** – an independent person who is paid to give advice
● **management consultant** – gives advice on how to improve companies

---

★ **professional** /prəˈfeʃənl/ *adjective, noun*
●*adjective*
  1 [only before noun] connected with a job that needs special training or skill, especially one that needs a high level of education: *an opportunity for professional development* ◇ *trade and professional associations* ◇ *He began his professional life as a lawyer.* ◇ *If it's a legal matter, you need to **seek** professional advice.*
  ○ professional *qualifications/skills/standards* • professional *advice/fees/help/services*
  2 (about people) having a job which needs special training and a high level of education: *busy professional couples with two incomes* ◇ *Most of the people on the course were professional women.*
  3 showing that sb is well trained and extremely skilled: *He dealt with the problem in a highly professional way.*
  4 suitable or appropriate for sb working in a particular profession: *professional conduct/misconduct* OPP UNPROFESSIONAL

  5 doing sth as a paid job rather than as a hobby: *Losses on the stock market have been common, both for individual and professional investors.*
  → NON-PROFESSIONAL
●*noun* [C] (*also* **pro**, *informal*)
  1 a person who does a job that needs special training and a high level of education: *You need a professional to sort out your finances.* ◇ *The cafe is a favourite with young professionals.* ◇ *a staff of over 500 IT professionals*
  ○ *a competent/dedicated/an experienced/ independent* professional
  2 a person who has a lot of skill and experience: *This was clearly a job for a real professional.*
  ○ *a real/true* professional

proˌfessional liaˈbility *noun* [U]
  (*Law*) the fact that sb such as a doctor, a lawyer, an accountant, etc. is legally responsible for any damage or harm that they cause by the way that they do their job

proficiency /prəˈfiʃnsi/ *noun* [U]
  the ability to do or use sth well because you have had training and practice: *developing technical proficiency* ◇ *You need to demonstrate a high level of proficiency **in** English.* ▶ **proficient** /prəˈfiʃnt/ *adjective*: *He's proficient **at** his job.* ◇ *She's proficient **in** several languages.*

★ **profile** /ˈprəʊfaɪl; AmE ˈproʊ-/ *noun, verb*
●*noun* [C]

SEE ALSO: age profile, consumer ~, customer ~, demographic ~, high-~, risk ~

  1 a description of sb/sth that gives useful information: *We built up a detailed profile of our customers and their requirements.*
  ○ *company/financial/personal* profiles • *to **build up/ develop** a profile*
  2 the general impression that sb/sth gives to the public and the amount of attention they receive: *They launched a campaign to raise the company's profile in Europe.* ◇ *His main value to the firm was his high public profile.* ◇ *She has **kept a low profile** (= tried not to attract attention) since details of the deal appeared in the press.*
  ○ *a **high/low** profile* • *a **corporate/public** profile* • *to **improve/raise** your profile*
●*verb* [+ obj]
  to give or write a description of sb/sth that gives the most important information: *His career is profiled in this month's journal.*

★ **profit** /ˈprɒfɪt; AmE ˈprɑːfɪt/ *noun, verb*
●*noun* [C,U]

SEE ALSO: accumulated profit, attributable ~, book ~, distributable ~, distributed ~, for-~, etc.

  the money that you make in business or by selling things, especially after paying the costs involved: *They reported a profit of $512 million.* ◇ *Profit **on** sales of the group's luxury brand have risen by 12%.* ◇ *The company made a profit last year.* ◇ *The transport operation has failed to **turn** (= make) a profit.* ◇ *The sale generated **record** profits.* ◇ *Profit from exports rose 7.3%.* ◇ *They should be able to sell **at a profit**.* ◇ *The agency is voluntary and not run **for profit**.* ◇ *The company said it would meet its profit forecast for the year.* OPP LOSS—Picture at BREAK-EVEN → idiom at TURN *verb*
  ○ *a **big/healthy/high/record/substantial** profit* • *a **low/modest/small** profit* • *an **annual**/a **first-quarter/full-year/half-year** profit* • *an **after-tax**/a **pre-tax/taxable** profit* • *a **drop/fall**/an **increase**/a **jump/rise** in profits* • *to **bring (in)/generate/make/ report/show** a profit*

Profits

- **profit** – *The company made a profit of €130 000.*
- **proceeds** (= the profits from a particular deal) – *The proceeds of the sale will be used to reduce debt.*
- **interest** – *Our savings account pays interest at 6.5% p.a.*
- **return, yield** (= used about investments) – *We estimate a net return of $41bn to shareholders.* ◇ *The bonds pay a high yield of 12%.*
- **surplus** (= more than what is needed or expected) – *The pension fund has a surplus of €48.8 m.* ◇ *The government reported a surplus of ¥3.1bn for January.*

● *verb* [+ obj or no obj] (*formal*)
to get money or sth useful from a situation; to be useful to sb or give them an advantage: *Banks profit from the interest they charge on loans.* ◇ *Small businesses are profiting from the new legislation.* ◇ *Many investors believe the development will profit them.*

★ **profitable** /ˈprɒfɪtəbl; *AmE* ˈprɑːf-/ *adjective*
1 that makes or is likely to make money: *a highly profitable business* ◇ *a profitable investment* ◇ *It is currently Japan's most profitable carmaker.*
2 that gives sb an advantage or a useful result: *The discussions were profitable and a possible solution was found.* ◇ *We had a very profitable meeting.*
[OPP] UNPROFITABLE
▶ **profitability** /ˌprɒfɪtəˈbɪləti; *AmE* ˌprɑːf-/ *noun* [U]: *We aim to increase profitability.* ◇ *The forecast showed lower levels of profitability.* **profitably** /ˈprɒfɪtəbli; *AmE* ˈprɑːf-/ *adverb*: to run a business profitably ◇ *The time was spent profitably.*

ˌ**profit and ˈloss acˌcount** (*also* ˌ**profit and ˈloss ˌstatement**) *noun* [C] (*abbr* **P & L**) (*all BrE*)
(*Accounting*) an official financial record that gives details of all a company's income and expenses for a particular period and shows if it has made a profit or a loss [SYN] EARNINGS REPORT

ˈ**profit ˌcentre** (*AmE spelling* ~ **center**) *noun* [C]
(*Accounting*) a part of a business that is responsible for its own income and for planning and controlling its expenses → COST CENTRE

profiteer /ˌprɒfɪˈtɪə(r); *AmE* ˌprɑːfəˈtɪr/ *noun* [C]
a person or an organization that makes a lot of money in an unfair way, for example by asking very high prices for things that are hard to get: *wartime profiteers* ▶ ˌ**profiˈteer** *verb* [no obj]: *Businesses who tried to profiteer from the new sales tax were fined.* ˌ**profiˈteering** *noun* [U]

ˈ**profit-ˌmaking** *adjective* [only before noun]
(about a product, an activity, or an organization) that does or is intended to make a profit: *a profit-making website* ◇ *The company's only profit-making operations are in the US and Canada.* [OPP] NON-PROFIT-MAKING
▶ ˈ**profit-ˌmaker** *noun* [C]: *a list of the top 50 profit-makers last year* ◇ *Not every car they sell is a profit-maker.*

ˈ**profit ˌmargin** *noun* [C]
(*Accounting*)
1 a percentage showing the relationship between the profit a company makes and the money that it obtains from sales (**revenue**) [NOTE] This is often seen as a sign of the general efficiency of the company: *The company showed a very disappointing profit margin of 0.4% of revenue.* ◇ *The most profitable department store had a pre-tax profit margin of 14.2% on sales of $9.3 billion.*
2 the difference between the cost of buying or producing sth and the price that it is sold for,

calculated as a percentage of the selling price [SYN] MARGIN

ˈ**profit ˌmotive** *noun* [sing.]
(*Economics*) the desire to make money, which is the reason that most businesses exist: *This is a business that trades for community benefit rather than from the profit motive.*

ˈ**profit-ˌsharing** (*also spelled* **profit sharing**) *noun* [U]
(*HR*) a system in which employees receive part of the profit the company has made, for example in one year, either in cash or as shares: *The company has set aside 5% of its pre-tax profits each year for employee profit-sharing.* ◇ *profit-sharing plans/schemes* ▶ ˈ**profit-share** *adjective* [only before noun]: *a profit-share scheme*

ˈ**profit squeeze** (*also* ˈ**profits squeeze**, *less frequent*) *noun* [C]
a situation in which profit becomes less over a period of time, because prices fall or costs increase

ˈ**profits ˌwarning** = PROFIT WARNING

ˈ**profit-ˌtaking** *noun* [U]
(*Finance*) the act of selling shares, bonds, etc. that have increased in value, in order to make a profit: *Profit-taking pushed coffee stocks lower.* ▶ ˈ**profit-ˌtaker** *noun* [C]

ˈ**profit ˌwarning** (*also* ˈ**profits ˌwarning**, *especially in BrE*) *noun* [C]
(*Finance*) a statement by a company that its profits will be lower than expected: *Shares fell after the company issued a profit warning.*
O *a shock/surprise profit warning*

pro forma /ˌprəʊ ˈfɔːmə; *AmE* ˌproʊ ˈfɔːrmə/ *adjective* [only before noun]
1 (about a document) prepared in order to show the usual way of doing sth or to provide a standard method: *a pro forma letter* ◇ *pro forma instructions*
2 (*Accounting*) used to describe a financial statement that is based on estimated or expected costs, income, etc. before the real figures are known: *a pro forma balance sheet*
▶ ˌ**pro ˈforma** *noun* [C]: *I enclose a pro forma for you to complete, sign and return.* [NOTE] **Pro forma** is a Latin phrase.

ˌ**pro forma ˈinvoice** *noun* [C]
(*Accounting*) a document that is sent before goods are supplied, for example to ask for payment from a new customer or to show prices that will be paid

★ **program** /ˈprəʊɡræm; *AmE* ˈproʊ-/ *noun, verb*
● *noun* [C]

SEE ALSO: application program, wellness program

1 (*IT*) (*also* com**ˈputer ˌprogram**) a set of instructions in code that control the operations or functions of a computer: *Load the program into the computer.*
O *to* **load/download/install/uninstall** *a program* ◆ *to* **run/design/develop/execute/use/write** *a program*
2 (*AmE*) = PROGRAMME
● *verb* (**-mm-**, *AmE also* **-m-**)
1 (*IT*) [+ obj or no obj] to give a computer, etc. a set of instructions to make it perform a particular task: *The company trained her to program.* ◇ *The printer can be programmed to handle any font.*
2 (*AmE*) = PROGRAMME

programmable /ˈprəʊɡræməbl; prəʊˈɡræm-; *AmE* ˈproʊ-; proʊˈɡ-/ *adjective*
(*IT*) (about a computer or other machine) able to accept instructions that control how it operates or functions: *programmable machine tools*

★ **programme** (*AmE spelling* **program**)
/ˈprəʊɡræm; *AmE* ˈproʊ-/ *noun, verb*
● *noun* [C]

SEE ALSO: **employee assistance programme,
employee referral programme**

1 a plan of things that will be done or included in
the development of sth: *a training programme for
new staff* ◇ *a programme of economic reform* ◇ *The
government's privatization programme has run into
trouble.* ◇ *We have recently launched a programme of
English classes for all junior managers.*
❍ *a building/development/research/training
programme* ◆ *to develop/finance/organize/plan/set
up a programme* ◆ *to carry out/initiate/launch a
programme*
2 something that people watch on television or
listen to on the radio: *news programmes*
❍ *to broadcast/do/make/show a programme (about/
on sth)* ◆ *to listen to/see/watch a programme*
→ PROGRAM
● *verb* [+ obj] (*usually* **be programmed**)
1 to plan for sth to happen, especially as part of a
series of planned events: *The project is programmed
for completion next month.*
2 to give a machine instructions to do a particular
task: *Robots can be programmed to do a variety of
jobs.*

programmer /ˈprəʊɡræmə(r); *AmE* ˈproʊ-/ (*also*
com,puter ˈprogrammer) *noun* [C]

SEE ALSO: **systems programmer**

(*IT*) a person whose job is to write computer
programs

ˈ**programme ,trading** (*AmE spelling*
program ~) *noun* [U]
(*Finance*) the automatic buying and selling of large
numbers of shares by computer when prices reach
a particular level

programming /ˈprəʊɡræmɪŋ; *AmE* ˈproʊ-/ *noun*
[U]
1 (*IT*) (*also* **com,puter ˈprogramming**) the process
of writing and testing programs for computers: *a
high level programming language* ◇ *a career in
computer programming*
2 the planning of which television or radio
programmes to broadcast: *Market forces do not
encourage quality programming.*

ˈ**programming ,language** = COMPUTER
LANGUAGE

ˈ**program ,trading** = PROGRAMME TRADING

progression /prəˈɡreʃn/ *noun* [C,U]

SEE ALSO: **salary progression**

the process of developing gradually from one stage
or state to another: *a steady progression from
family firm to multinational global corporation* ◇
opportunities for career progression

progressive /prəˈɡresɪv/ *adjective*
1 happening or developing steadily: *a progressive
reduction in the size of the workforce*
2 in favour of new ideas, modern methods and
change: *progressive employers*
3 (*Accounting; Economics*) used to describe a tax,
usually on income, in which people who earn more
money pay a higher rate or percentage of tax than
people who earn less money

ˈ**progress ,payment** *noun* [C]
a part of a larger payment, paid to a company when
they have completed a particular stage in a job: *A
progress payment clause is included in the contract.*

prohibit /prəˈhɪbɪt; *AmE also* proʊˈh-/ *verb* [+ obj]
prohibit sth | **prohibit sb from doing sth**
1 (*often* **be prohibited**) to stop sth from being done
or used, especially by law: *rules prohibiting the use
of certain additives in foods* ◇ *Retailers are no longer
prohibited from opening their stores on Sundays.*
2 to make sth impossible: *High set-up costs prohibit
many businesses from entering the industry.*

prohibition /ˌprəʊɪˈbɪʃn; *AmE* ˌproʊəˈb-/ *noun*
1 [U] the act of stopping sth being done or used,
especially by law: *the prohibition of imports of some
types of meat*
2 [C] a law or rule that stops sth being done or
used: *Some companies have a prohibition against/
on personal Internet and email use.*

prohibitive /prəˈhɪbətɪv; *AmE also* proʊˈh-/
adjective
1 (about a price or a cost) so high that it prevents
people from buying sth or doing sth: *the prohibitive
costs of entry into media ownership* ◇ *Three estimates
were received but the prices were prohibitive.* ◇ *a
prohibitive tax on imported cars*
2 preventing people from doing sth by law:
prohibitive legislation
▶ **pro'hibitively** *adverb*: *Car insurance can be
prohibitively expensive for young drivers.*

★ **project** *noun, verb*
● *noun* /ˈprɒdʒekt; *AmE* ˈprɑːdʒ-/ [C]

SEE ALSO: **capital project**

a planned piece of work, often involving many
people, that is designed to produce sth new, to
improve sth or to find information about sth: *to set
up a project to develop a new engine* ◇ *The company
has invested a lot in the water project.* ◇ *Our project
leader usually reviews our progress daily.*
❍ *an ambitious/a large/joint/major project* ◆ *a
building/construction/development/research
project* ◆ *to fund/launch/manage/run/set up a
project*
● *verb* [+ obj] /prəˈdʒekt/
1 (*usually* **be projected**) to estimate what the size,
cost or amount of sth will be in the future based on
what is happening now: *A growth rate of 4% is
projected for next year.* ◇ *The sales profits have been
projected to fall.* ◇ *The results have fallen 12% short
of this year's projected earnings.* SYN FORECAST
2 (*usually* **be projected**) to plan an activity, a
project, etc. for a time in the future: *The projected
merger will go ahead next year.*
3 to present sb/sth/yourself to other people in a
particular way, especially one that gives a good
impression: *They sought advice on how to project a
more positive image of their company.* ◇ *We need to
project ourselves better.*

ˌ**project engi'neer** *noun* [C]
a person with technical knowledge and
qualifications whose job is to arrange, organize and
control a project

ˌ**project 'finance** *noun* [U]
(*Finance*) the process of providing money for a large
project where the payment of the debt will come
from the project's own CASH FLOW ▶ **,project
'financing** *noun* [U]

projection /prəˈdʒekʃn/ *noun* [C, usually pl.]
an estimate or a statement of what figures,
amounts or events will be in the future, or what
they were in the past, based on what is happening
now: *Sales have exceeded our projections.* ◇
*Calculations are based on a projection of existing
trends.* ◇ *We have been making forward projections
as to the future profitability of the firm.*
❍ *budget/earnings/financial/growth/sales
projections* ◆ *gloomy/optimistic/rosy projections* ◆ *to
make/revise projections*

'project ,management *noun* [U]
the process of planning, organizing and controlling the tasks, costs, staff and resources of a project so that it is completed successfully in the most efficient way: *Financial planning and project management are key areas of the business.*
▶ **'project ,manager** *noun* [C]

projector /prə'dʒektə(r)/ = OVERHEAD PROJECTOR

PROLOG™ /'prəʊlɒg; *AmE* 'proʊlɔːg; -lɑːg/ *noun* [U]
(*IT*) a language for writing computer programs that is similar to a human language and used mainly in ARTIFICIAL INTELLIGENCE

PROM /ˌpiː ɑːr əʊ 'em; *AmE* oʊ/ *noun* [U]
(*IT*) **programmable read-only memory** a type of computer memory that can have information and instructions recorded on it once, after which the data cannot be removed

'promissory note (*also* note) *noun* [C] (*abbr* P-note)
(*Finance*) a signed document containing a promise to pay a stated amount of money on or before a particular date

promo /'prəʊməʊ; *AmE* 'proʊmoʊ/ *noun* [C] (*plural* promos)
(*Marketing, informal*) a video, film/movie, etc. intended to advertise a particular product: *a trade promo ◇ a promo video* NOTE Promo is a short form of 'promotion'.

★ **promote** /prə'məʊt; *AmE* -'moʊt/ *verb*
1 [+ obj] to help sth to happen or develop: *policies to promote competition in the industry*
2 (*Marketing*) [+ obj or no obj] to help sell a product, service, etc. or make it more popular by advertising it or offering it at a special price: *Promoting new products and getting them accepted in the marketplace is expensive. ◇ The area is being promoted as a tourist destination. ◇ The supermarket chain has been promoting aggressively.*
3 (*HR*) [+ obj] (*often* **be promoted**) to move sb to a more senior job in an organization: *She worked hard and was soon promoted. ◇ He has been promoted to assistant manager of the department.* SYN UPGRADE OPP DEMOTE
4 (*Finance*) [+ obj] to move a company to a higher position within a particular system, such as a stock exchange index: *The company's shares have been promoted to the FTSE All-Share index.* SYN UPGRADE OPP DEMOTE

promoter /prə'məʊtə(r); *AmE* -'moʊ-/ *noun* [C]
(*Marketing*)
1 a person or company that tries to persuade others about the value or importance of a product or service: *a leading promoter of goods made in Spain*
2 a person or company that organizes or provides money for an artistic performance or a sporting event: *concert/race promoters*

★ **promotion** /prə'məʊʃn; *AmE* -'moʊʃn/ *noun*

SEE ALSO: **cross-promotion, consumer ~, sales ~**

1 (*HR*) [U,C] a move to a more important job in a company or an organization: *Her promotion to Sales Manager took everyone by surprise. ◇ The new job is a promotion for him. ◇ a job with excellent promotion prospects* OPP DEMOTION
2 (*Marketing*) [U,C] activities done in order to increase the sales of a product or service; a set of advertisements done for a particular product or service: *Her job is mainly concerned with sales and promotion. ◇ We are doing a special promotion of French food.* See note at MARKETING
3 promotions [U with sing./pl. verb] the part of a company that is responsible for advertising products or services and increasing sales

promotional /prə'məʊʃənl; *AmE* -'moʊ-/ *adjective*
(*Marketing*) connected with advertising: *promotional material/activities/campaigns ◇ Promotional advertising informs the public of an item or a range of items in stock.*

prompt /prɒmpt; *AmE* prɑːmpt/ *adjective, noun, verb*
● *adjective*
1 done without delay: *Prompt payment would be appreciated. ◇ prompt action to stop falling sales*
2 (about a person) acting without delay; arriving at the right time: *Please be prompt when attending these meetings.* SYN PUNCTUAL
▶ **'promptly** *adverb*: *What happens if a buyer fails to pay an instalment promptly?* **'promptness** *noun* [U]: *the promptness of payments*
● *noun* [C]
(*IT*) a sign on a computer screen that shows that the computer has finished doing sth and is ready for more instructions
● *verb* [+ obj]
(*IT*) (about a computer) to ask the user for more instructions: *The program will prompt you to enter data where required.*

'prompt note *noun* [C]
(*Finance*) a letter sent to someone to remind them that their payment is due

'proof ,copy *noun* [C] (*also* proof [usually pl.])
(*Production*) a copy of the pages of a book, magazine or other printed material that a printer produces so that they can be checked and corrected before all the copies are printed

,proof of 'purchase *noun* [C,U]
(*Commerce*) a document that shows that you have bought and paid for sth: *We may refuse a refund if you do not have a receipt or other proof of purchase.* → RECEIPT

prop /prɒp; *AmE* prɑːp/ *verb*
PHRV **,prop sth 'up** to help or support sth that is having difficulties: *The government was accused of propping up declining industries.*

prop. = PROPRIETOR

propensity /prə'pensəti/ *noun* [C] (*plural* propensities) (*formal*)
a tendency to behave in a particular way or do particular things: *people's propensity to try to save tax ◇ a company's propensity for innovation*

★ **property** /'prɒpəti; *AmE* 'prɑːpərti/ *noun* (*plural* properties)

SEE ALSO: **intellectual property, personal property**

1 [U] a thing or things that are owned by sb; a possession or possessions: *You should take more care of your property. ◇ All information contained in this report is confidential and remains the property of the company.*
2 [U] land and buildings: *the property market ◇ She made a fortune from investing in property. ◇ The price of property has risen enormously.*
● **business/investment/residential** property • **to buy/ invest in/own/sell** property
3 [C] a building or buildings: *If you are trying to rent or buy an office property in London, click here. ◇ There are a lot of empty properties in the area. ◇ More people are looking for investment properties abroad.*
● **to buy/own/rent/sell** a property • **a business/an investment/a residential** property • **a hotel/an office/a retail** property

'property bond *noun* [C] (*BrE*)
(*Finance*) a bond sold by insurance companies, who invest the money in property

'property ,company (BrE) (AmE **'real estate ,company**) noun [C]
a company that buys, sells and rents buildings: *a property company specializing in industrial, warehouse and business space*

'property de,velopment noun
1 [U] the business of building new property or changing existing property: *property development projects* ◇ *The report looks at environmental issues in property development.*
2 [C] a place where new property has been built or is being built: *The business park is a new property development close to the airport.*
▶ **'property de,veloper** noun [C]: *He made his first fortune as a property developer.*

'property loan (AmE also **'real e,state loan**) = MORTGAGE

'property ,management (AmE also **'real estate ,management**) noun [U]
the business of making sure that sb's property remains in good condition, trying to get a good profit from land or buildings, helping people to rent a property to others, etc. ▶ **'property ,manager** (AmE also **'real estate ,manager**) noun [C]

the 'property ,market (AmE also **'real estate ,market**) noun [C, usually sing.]
the activity of buying and selling buildings and land: *trends in the property market* ◇ *to invest in the property market* ◇ *Cheap credit has fuelled the property market.*

'property ,register (also spelled **Property Register**) noun [C] (BrE)
1 a list where people can advertise their property for sale, or search for property to rent or buy
2 in the UK, an official list containing details about who owns buildings or land

'property tax noun [U,C]
tax that is paid on buildings or other things that you own, based on a percentage of their value

★ **proportion** /prə'pɔːʃn; AmE -'pɔːrʃn/ noun
1 [C, usually sing.] a part or share of a whole: *A significant proportion of the shares have been bought by overseas investors.* ◇ *The extra allowance is expressed as a proportion of your basic pay.* ◇ *The company employs men and women in roughly equal proportions.*
● *a high/large/low/significant/small* proportion ◆ *a* proportion *decreases/falls/grows/increases*
2 [U] the relationship of one thing to another in size, amount, etc: *The proportion of men to women in the workplace has changed dramatically over the years.* ◇ *Shareholders can buy new stock in proportion to the shares they own.* ◇ *The crime rate is in direct proportion to the unemployment rate* (= they are connected, so if one is high the other is also high). → RATIO
3 proportions [pl.] the measurements of sth; the size or shape of sth: *This method divides the task into more manageable proportions.* ◇ *The fall in share values is reaching crisis proportions.*
→ idiom at INVERSE

proportional /prə'pɔːʃənl; AmE -'pɔːrʃ-/ adjective
of an appropriate size, amount or degree in comparison with sth: *Salary is proportional to years of experience.* ◇ *to be directly/inversely proportional to sth* ▶ **pro'portionally** /prə'pɔːʃənəli; AmE -'pɔːrʃ-/ adverb: *Families with children spend proportionally less per person than families without children.*

pro,portional 'tax = FIXED TAX

proportionate /prə'pɔːʃənət; AmE -'pɔːrʃ-/ adjective
increasing or decreasing in size, amount or degree according to changes in sth else: *Increasing costs resulted in proportionate increases in prices.*
SYN PROPORTIONAL
▶ **pro'portionately** adverb: *Prices have risen but wages have not risen proportionately.*

★ **proposal** /prə'pəʊzl; AmE -'poʊzl/ noun
1 [C,U] a formal suggestion or plan; the act of making a suggestion: *Several companies submitted proposals for the project.* ◇ *Her sales proposal was extremely convincing.* ◇ *There have been protests against the government's proposal to raise the retirement age.* ◇ *They judged that the time was right for the proposal of new terms for the trade agreement.* See note at REPORT
● *to draw up/make/put forward/submit a proposal* ◆ *to accept/consider/discuss/reject a proposal*
2 (Insurance) [C] a written request for an insurance policy that involves giving information about yourself or your property on a printed form: *Insurance cover begins as soon as the proposal is accepted.* ◇ *a completed proposal form*

★ **propose** /prə'pəʊz; AmE -'poʊz/ verb [+ obj]
1 to suggest a plan, an idea, etc. for people to think about and decide on: *The union proposed changes to the regulations.* ◇ *She proposed that the product be withdrawn.* ◇ (BrE also) *She proposed that the product should be withdrawn.* ◇ *He proposed changing the name of the company.* ◇ *It was proposed to pay the money from public funds.* ◇ *The proposed changes will mean higher taxes for small businesses.*
2 to suggest sth at a formal meeting and ask people to vote on it: *I propose Tom Ellis for chairman.* → SECOND verb See note at MEETING
▶ **pro'poser** noun [C]

proposition /,prɒpə'zɪʃn; AmE ,prɑːp-/ noun [C]

SEE ALSO: **unique selling proposition**

a business idea or plan of action that is suggested: *I'd like to put a business proposition to you.* ◇ *He was trying to make it look like an attractive proposition.* ◇ *As an investment proposition the stock is a disaster.*
● *a business/commercial/financial proposition* ◆ *an attractive/a risky/viable proposition*

proprietary /prə'praɪətri; AmE -teri/ adjective
[usually before noun]
1 (about goods) made and sold by a particular company and protected by a REGISTERED TRADEMARK: *a proprietary brand/product* ◇ *Doctors often know drugs by their most common proprietary name.* ◇ *proprietary medicines* → GENERIC
2 used or owned by one particular company: *How much of the software's design is proprietary? ◇ Making proprietary information public would be damaging to the company.*
3 relating to an owner or to the fact of owning sth: *The company claims proprietary rights over the unique design.*

pro,prietary 'trading (also ,principal 'trading) noun [U]
(Stock Exchange) trading in shares, bonds, etc. by a financial institution on its own behalf rather than on behalf of its customers

proprietor /prə'praɪətə(r)/ noun [C] (abbr **prop.**)
1 the owner of a business, a hotel, land or buildings, etc: *Enquiries must be made to the proprietor.* ◇ *a national newspaper proprietor* ◇ *She is now the proprietor of her own electrical business.*
→ SOLE PROPRIETOR, SOLE PROPRIETORSHIP
2 (Law) the owner of a PATENT
▶ **proprietorship** /prə'praɪətəʃɪp; AmE -tərʃ-/ noun [U]

pro rata /ˌprəʊ ˈrɑːtə; AmE ˌproʊ-/ adjective
(about a payment or share of sth) calculated according to how much of sth has been used, the amount of work done, etc: *If costs go up, there will be a pro rata increase in prices.* ◇ *Leave entitlement is calculated on a pro rata basis, according to length of service.* ▶ **pro ˈrata** adverb: *Pay is €400 per week pro rata, according to hours worked.* **NOTE** Pro rata is a Latin phrase.

prorate /ˌprəʊˈreɪt; AmE ˌproʊ-/ verb [+ obj]
(*especially AmE*)
(*Accounting*) (*usually* **be prorated**) to divide a payment or share of sth according to how much of sth has been used, the amount of work done, etc: *Bills for less than a complete month's service will be prorated.* ◇ *Some people have agreed to work four days instead of five, on a prorated salary.*
▶ **proration** /ˌprəʊˈreɪʃn; AmE ˌproʊ-/ noun [U]

pros and cons /ˌprəʊz ən ˈkɒnz; AmE ˌproʊz ən ˈkɑːnz/ noun [pl.]
the advantages and disadvantages of sth: *We need to weigh up the pros and cons before deciding.*

prosecute /ˈprɒsɪkjuːt; AmE ˈprɑːs-/ verb [+ obj or no obj]
to officially accuse sb of a crime and try to prove it in court: *The company was prosecuted for breaching the Health and Safety Act.* ◇ *They said that strikers would be prosecuted.* ▶ **ˈprosecutor** noun [C]:
federal/state prosecutors.

prosecution /ˌprɒsɪˈkjuːʃn; AmE ˌprɑːs-/ noun
1 [C,U] the process of trying to prove in court that sb is guilty of a crime; the process of being officially accused of a crime in court: *The company paid the tax it owed in order to avoid prosecution.*
2 **the prosecution** [sing. with sing./pl. verb] a person or an organization that **prosecutes** sb in a court, together with the lawyers, etc: *She was a witness for the prosecution.*

prospect noun, verb
● noun /ˈprɒspekt; AmE ˈprɑːs-/

SEE ALSO: **key prospect**

1 [U; sing.] the possibility that sth will happen: *They had no business plan and no immediate prospect of generating any revenue.* ◇ *The figures suggest that an economic slowdown is **in prospect*** (= likely to happen).
2 [sing.] an idea of what might or will happen in the future: *Starting your own business is a daunting* (= frightening) *prospect.* ◇ *Faced with the prospect of being made redundant, staff agreed to a cut in pay.*
3 prospects [pl.] the chances of being successful in the future: *There were concerns about the company's financial prospects.* ◇ *Job prospects* (= the chances of getting a job) *are gloomy.*
4 [C] a person, company, etc. who is a possible customer: *We follow up the most likely prospects first.*
● verb /prəˈspekt; AmE ˈprɑːspekt/ [no obj]
to search an area for oil, minerals, gold, etc: *to prospect **for** oil* ◇ (*figurative*) *We'll go to the trade exhibition to prospect for business.* ▶ **prospector** /prəˈspektə(r); AmE ˈprɑːspektər/ noun [C]

prospective /prəˈspektɪv/ adjective [usually before noun]
1 expected to do sth or to become sth: *a prospective buyer/client* ◇ *On your résumé, give prospective employers examples of what you can do for them.* **SYN** POTENTIAL
2 expected or likely to happen: *to forecast the prospective yield of an asset/investment* ◇ *They are worried about prospective changes in the law.*

prospectus /prəˈspektəs/ noun [C]

SEE ALSO: **offer by prospectus, pathfinder prospectus**

1 a document that gives information about a company's shares before they are offered for sale: *40 000 people downloaded our prospectus, and 32 000 applied for shares.*
2 a small book that gives information about a new company or project, a college, etc: *The company has outlined its plans for expansion in its prospectus.*

prosper /ˈprɒspə(r); AmE ˈprɑːs-/ verb [no obj]
to develop in a successful way; to be successful, especially financially: *The business has overcome its early problems and is now prospering.* **SYN** THRIVE

prosperity /prɒˈsperəti; AmE prɑːˈs-/ noun [U]
the state of being successful, especially financially: *Our future prosperity depends on economic growth.*

prosperous /ˈprɒspərəs; AmE ˈprɑːs-/ adjective
rich and successful: *Farmers are more prosperous in the south of the country.* **SYN** AFFLUENT

prosumer /ˌprəʊˈsjuːmə(r); AmE ˌproʊˈsuːmər/ noun [C]
(*Marketing*)
1 a customer who wants very good quality technical products but cannot afford to buy professional equipment **NOTE** This is formed from the words 'professional' and 'consumer'.
2 a customer who becomes involved in the design and manufacture of products **NOTE** This is formed from the words 'producer' and 'consumer'.

★ **protect** /prəˈtekt/ verb

SEE ALSO: **write-protect**

1 [+ obj or no obj] **protect (sb/sth) (against/from sth)** to make sure that sb/sth is not harmed, injured, damaged, etc: *You should install software to protect your computer from viruses.* ◇ *The role of the board of directors is to protect the interests of shareholders.* ◇ *a password-protected website* (= one you can only visit if you know the right code)
2 [+ obj or no obj] **protect (sb/sth) (against sth)** to provide sb/sth with insurance against fire, injury, damage, etc: *Different types of policies protect against different risks.*
3 (*Economics*) [+ obj] to help an industry in your own country by taxing goods from other countries so that there is less competition: *Import restrictions were imposed to protect domestic industries.* ◇ *a protected industry*

★ **protection** /prəˈtekʃn/ noun [U]

SEE ALSO: **bankruptcy-law protection, bankruptcy ~, consumer ~, data ~, design ~, employment ~, investor ~,**

1 **protection (for/of sb/sth) (against/from sth)** the act of protecting sb/sth; the state of being protected: *The legislation gives workers legal protection against unfair dismissal.* ◇ *Computer users should ensure that their virus protection is up-to-date.*
2 (*Economics*) the system of helping an industry in your own country by taxing foreign goods: *The clothing and footwear industries benefit from trade protection.*
3 (*Insurance*) insurance against fire, injury, damage, etc: *Our policy offers complete protection against fire and theft.*

protectionism /prəˈtekʃənɪzəm/ noun [U]
(*Economics*) the principle or practice of protecting a country's own industry by taxing foreign goods: *The system of protectionism aims to preserve jobs.*
▶ **protectionist** /prəˈtekʃənɪst/ adjective: *The trade agreement will bring an end to protectionist measures in both countries.*

protective /prə'tektɪv/ *adjective*
1 [only before noun] providing or intended to provide protection: *protective gloves/goggles/headgear* ◇ *Workers should wear full protective clothing.*
2 (*Economics*) [usually before noun] intended to give an advantage to your own country's industry

,protective 'tariff *noun* [C]
(*Economics*) a tax on imported products that is intended to protect local businesses from foreign competition → REVENUE TARIFF

pro tem /,prəʊ 'tem; *AmE* ,proʊ-/ *adverb*
for now, but not permanently: *A new manager will be appointed pro tem.* ▸ **,pro 'tem** *adjective*: *A pro tem committee was formed.* **SYN** TEMPORARY
NOTE Pro tem is a short form of a Latin phrase, which means 'for now'.

protest *noun, verb*
● *noun* /'prəʊtest; *AmE* 'proʊ-/ [C,U]
the expression of strong disagreement with or opposition to sth; a statement or an action that shows this: *Workers organized a protest **against** proposed changes to their contracts.* ◇ *The director resigned **in protest** at the decision.* ◇ *The closure of the factory caused a **storm of protest**.* ◇ *The building work will go ahead, despite protests from local residents.*
○ *a huge/mass/nationwide/public* protest ◆ *a peaceful/violent* protest ◆ *a flood/wave of* protests ◆ *to* spark/trigger *a protest* ◆ *to* organize/stage/threaten *a protest*
● *verb* /prə'test; *AmE also* 'proʊ-/ [+ obj or no obj]
protest (about/against/at sth) to say or do sth to show that you disagree with or disapprove of sth, especially publicly: *Car workers went on strike to protest against job cuts.* ◇ *Small business groups have protested about the tax increases.* ◇ (*AmE*) *They fully intend to protest the decision.*

protocol /'prəʊtəkɒl; *AmE* 'proʊtəkɔːl; -kɑːl/ *noun*
1 (*IT*) [C] a set of rules that control the way data is sent between computers
2 [U,C] the rules for the correct way of behaving or of doing sth in a particular situation or organization: *What's the protocol for asking questions at these meetings?*

prototype /'prəʊtətaɪp; *AmE* 'proʊ-/ *noun* [C]
the first design of sth from which other forms are developed: *They designed and built a working prototype and then ran a series of tests.* ◇ *the prototype **of** a new online service*
○ *to* build/design/develop/test *a prototype* ◆ *a* physical/virtual/working *prototype*

★ **provide** /prə'vaɪd/ *verb* [+ obj]
1 provide sb (with sth) | provide sth (for sb) to give sth to sb or make it available for them to use: *Your website should provide the information that customers need.* ◇ *The bank has provided the company with a three-year loan.* **SYN** SUPPLY
2 (*Law*) **provide that** (about a law or rule) to state that sth will or must happen: *The final section provides that any work produced for the company is thereafter owned by the company.* **SYN** STIPULATE → PROVISION
PHR V **pro'vide against sth** (*formal*) to make preparations to deal with sth bad or unpleasant that might happen in the future: *You can take out insurance to provide against loss of income through sickness or accident.* **pro'vide for sth 1** to prepare to deal with sth that is going to happen or that might happen in the future, especially sth bad or unpleasant: *You should start saving now to provide for your retirement.* ◇ *This was a contingency (= an event) we had not provided for.* **2** (*Law*) (about a law, rule, etc.) to make it possible for sth to be done: *The*

agreement will provide for a possible extension of at least two years.

provident /'prɒvɪdənt; *AmE* 'prɑːv-/ *adjective*
often used in the names of organizations that help people plan for the future by saving money: *Friends Provident*

'provident fund *noun* [C]
a system in which you and your employer pay money regularly into an investment fund while you are employed. You are then paid a large sum of money when you retire or when you leave the company. → PENSION PLAN

★ **provider** /prə'vaɪdə(r)/ *noun* [C]

SEE ALSO: service provider

an organization that supplies sb with sth they need or want: *The company is Britain's biggest electricity provider.*

★ **provision** /prə'vɪʒn/ *noun, verb*
● *noun*

SEE ALSO: call provision, sunset ~, tax ~

1 (*Accounting*) [C,U] an amount of money that a company keeps for a particular purpose or to deal with possible problems or expenses in the future: *The bank has set aside extra provisions for bad loans.* ◇ *an increase in bad debt provision* **SYN** RESERVE
2 [U] the act of supplying sb with sth that they need or want: *The government is responsible for the provision of health care.* ◇ *the provision of broadband services for businesses*
3 (*Law*) [C] a condition or an arrangement in a legal document: *The contract is subject to the provisions of the Supply of Goods and Services Act.*
● *verb* [+ obj or no obj]
(*Accounting*) to keep an amount of money for a particular purpose, for example paying taxes: *The company had to provision $450m to fight a series of lawsuits.* ◇ *It is essential to provision **against** the possibility of non-payment.* → PROVISION
▸ **pro'visioning** *noun* [U]: *The bank has just increased its provisioning against bad loans.*

proviso /prə'vaɪzəʊ; *AmE* -zoʊ/ *noun* [C] (*plural* **provisos**)
a condition that must be accepted before an agreement can be made: *The committee has decided to approve the contract **with the proviso that** these amendments are made.* **SYN** PROVISION

proxy /'prɒksi; *AmE* 'prɑːksi/ *noun* (*plural* **proxies**)
1 [U] the authority that a shareholder gives to sb to vote on their behalf: *More than 53% of shareholders voted **by** proxy.* ◇ *All proxy votes must be received by 11 a.m. on Tuesday.*
2 [C,U] a person who has been given the authority to vote on behalf of a shareholder: *You may appoint a person to **act as** your proxy at the meeting by completing the attached form.*
3 (*formal*) [C] **proxy for sth** something that you use to represent sth else that you are trying to measure or calculate: *The company is seen by analysts as a proxy for the radio industry.*

'proxy fight (*also* **'proxy ,battle**) *noun* [C]
(*Finance*) a situation in which a company or a group that is planning to take control of a particular company tries to persuade the shareholders of that company to give them their authority to vote for new directors who will support their plans: *Mergers are even more difficult if they come as a result of a proxy fight.*

'proxy ,statement *noun* [C]
information that must be sent to shareholders before they give their authority to sb to vote on the company's plans

PRP /,piː ɑː 'piː; *AmE* ɑːr/ = PERFORMANCE-RELATED PAY

prudence /'pru:dns/ *noun* [U]
1 (*Accounting*) (*especially BrE*) (*AmE usually* con'servatism) the principle that a company's financial records must not make the company seem more valuable than it might be
2 care in making judgements and decisions; the practice of avoiding unnecessary risks: *We should have exercised more financial prudence.*

prudent /'pru:dnt/ *adjective*
1 sensible and careful when you make judgements and decisions; avoiding unnecessary risks: *a prudent businessman ◇ a prudent decision/ investment ◇ It might be more prudent to get a second opinion before going ahead.* OPP IMPRUDENT
2 (*Accounting*) taking care not to make a company seem more valuable in its financial records than it might be
▶ 'prudently *adverb*

PS /,pi: 'es/ *abbr* (*often used as a countable noun*)
an extra message that you add at the end of a letter or email, after your signature: *PS Could you send me your fax number again? ◇ She added a PS.* NOTE PS is a short form of the word 'postscript'. You can use PPS if there is a second PS.

PSBR /,pi: es bi: 'a:(r)/ = PUBLIC SECTOR BORROWING REQUIREMENT

PSV /,pi: es 'vi:/ = PUBLIC SERVICE VEHICLE

,psychic 'income *noun* [U]
(*HR*) satisfaction that you get from doing your job: *Although pay levels are low, I find the work interesting and feel valued by the company, so the psychic income is high.*

psychographics /,saɪkə'ɡræfɪks/ *noun* [U]
(*Marketing*) techniques for analysing the values, opinions and attitudes to life of a group of people, in order to understand the best way to advertise to them ▶ ,psycho'graphic *adjective* [only before noun]

psychological /,saɪkə'lɒdʒɪkl; *AmE* -'la:dʒ-/ *adjective* [usually before noun]
connected with a person's mind and the way in which it works: *Supermarkets use a range of psychological tricks to make customers buy more. ◇ $19.99 is an example of psychological pricing—people will be more willing to pay that than $20.*

,psychological 'test *noun* [C]
a type of test used to see if sb has the right skills, interests and personality for a particular job
▶ ,psychological 'testing *noun* [U]

psychometrics /,saɪkə'metrɪks/ *noun* [U]
techniques used for measuring mental abilities and processes ▶ ,psycho'metric *adjective* [only before noun]

,psychometric 'test *noun* [C]
(*HR*) any test that measures sb's mental abilities, personality, attitudes, etc., often used when choosing sb for a job: *Psychometric tests can help you decide what type of career you are suited to.*
▶ ,psychometric 'testing *noun* [U]: *The HR department uses psychometric testing as part of its selection process.*

PT /,pi: 'ti:/ = PART-TIME

P-to-P = P2P

Pty /,pi: ti: 'waɪ/ *abbr*
used in the names of some companies in Australia and South Africa See note at LTD

★ **public** /'pʌblɪk/ *adjective, noun*
● *adjective*
1 [only before noun] connected with ordinary people in society in general: *Levels of waste from the factory may be a danger to public health. ◇ Smoking in public places is already banned in some cities.*
2 [only before noun] provided, especially by the government, for the use of people in general: *a*

public education system ◇ public transport ◇ a public car park/telephone OPP PRIVATE → STATE
3 [only before noun] connected with the government and the services it provides: *The rail industry is no longer in public ownership. ◇ The government will put more public funds into the banking system.* SYN STATE OPP PRIVATE
4 (*Commerce; Finance*) sold or offered to people in general to buy: *investments and public offerings* OPP PRIVATE
5 known to people in general: *Details of the report have not yet been made public. ◇ This latest scandal has not done the company's public image any good.*
6 intended to be seen or heard by people in general: *a public apology/enquiry ◇ A public meeting will be held tomorrow evening.* OPP PRIVATE
7 where there are a lot of people who can see and hear you: *Can we talk somewhere a little less public?* OPP PRIVATE
▶ **publicly** /'pʌblɪkli/ *adverb*: *a publicly owned company ◇ This information is not publicly available.*
IDM **go 'public** (*Stock Exchange*) (about a company) to start selling shares on the stock exchange → idiom at COMPANY
● *noun* [sing. with sing./pl. verb]

SEE ALSO: general public

1 the public ordinary people in society in general: *The survey sample comprised 300 members of the public. ◇ The public has/have a right to know what is in the report.*
2 a group of people who share a particular interest or who are involved in the same activity: *the music listening public*

,public ac'count *noun* [C]
a bank account in which a national or local government holds money

,public ad'dress (,system) *noun* [C] (*abbr* PA)
an electronic system that is used to make music, voices, etc. louder so that they can be heard by everyone in a particular place or building

publication /,pʌblɪ'keɪʃn/ *noun*
1 [U,C] the act of printing a book, a magazine, etc. and making it available to the public; a book, a magazine, etc. that has been published: *The publication date of the catalogue is April 1st. ◇ specialist publications for engineers*
2 [U] the act of printing sth in a newspaper, report, etc. so that the public knows about it: *the publication of the company's annual results*

,public 'carrier = COMMON CARRIER

,public 'company (*also* ,publicly-owned 'company) *noun* [C] (*BrE*)
a company whose shares can be bought and sold on the stock market, etc. → PRIVATE COMPANY, PUBLICLY-HELD

,public corpo'ration *noun* [C]
1 (*AmE*) a company whose shares can be bought and sold on the stock market, etc: *A private company will require approval of the majority of its shareholders for a merger with a public corporation.*
2 a company that is owned and managed by the government

,public 'debt *noun* [U,C]
(*Economics*) the total amount of money owed by a national or local government: *The country has high private assets but higher public debts.*

,public de'posits *noun* [pl.]
(*Economics*) money held by national and local governments in bank accounts: *Atlanta's five largest banks receive more than a billion dollars in public deposits from local, state and federal governments.*

the ˌpublic doˈmain noun [sing.]
if sth is in the **public domain**, it is available for
everyone to look at, to know, etc: *They have made
the results of their research available in the public
domain.* ◇ *public domain software*

ˌpublic emˈployee noun [C]
a person who works for the government

ˌpublic ˈenterprise noun
1 [U] the development of businesses by the
government of a country rather than by the people:
the role of public enterprise in the economy
2 [C] a business that is owned by the government
rather than by individuals or other companies
→ PRIVATE ENTERPRISE

ˌpublic ˈholiday noun [C]
a day on which most of the shops/stores,
businesses and schools in a country are closed,
often to celebrate a particular event → BANK
HOLIDAY, LEGAL HOLIDAY

ˌpublic ˈissue noun [C,U]
(*Stock Exchange*) an occasion when a company
makes shares available for the public to buy for the
first time: *The shares were offered through public
issue.* SYN IPO

publicist /ˈpʌblɪsɪst/ noun [C]
(*Marketing*) a person whose job is to make sth, such
as a new product, a book or an event, known to the
public: *They have hired a publicist to promote the
brand in Europe.*

publicity /pʌbˈlɪsəti/ noun [U]
1 the attention that is given to sth/sb by
newspapers, television, etc: *The sackings have
attracted a lot of negative publicity to the company.* ◇
*The release of the report was timed to generate
maximum publicity.*
   ○ **adverse/bad/good/negative/unfavourable**
   publicity • to **attract/avoid/generate/get/receive/
   seek** publicity
2 (*Marketing*) the business of attracting the
attention of the public to sth/sb; the things that are
done to attract attention: *She works in publicity.* ◇
*There has been a lot of advance publicity for the
launch of this game.* ◇ *publicity material* See note at
MARKETING
   ○ *a publicity* **agent/budget/campaign/department/
   manager** • *publicity* **material/photos** • *to give sth
   publicity*

pubˈlicity stunt noun [C]
(*Marketing*) something that is done to attract
people's attention: *Fifty employees dressed as
tomatoes in a publicity stunt to advertise the new
sauce.*

publicize , **-ise** /ˈpʌblɪsaɪz/ verb [+ obj]
to make sth known to the public; to advertise sth:
*We use a range of promotional products to publicize
the brand.* ◇ *a* **highly/much/widely** *publicized
event*

ˌpublic ˈlaw noun [U]
(*Law*) the part of law that deals with the
relationship between the government of a country
and its people

ˌpublic liaˈbility noun [U]
(*Insurance*) when a company is responsible if a
member of the public or their property is harmed
by one of its products, while in one of its shops/
stores, etc: *public liability insurance* ◇ *a public
liability policy*

ˈpublic ˈlimited ˈcompany noun [C] (*abbr* **plc**)
in the UK and some other countries, a LIMITED
COMPANY whose shares are offered to the public
and are bought and sold on a stock exchange: *The*

firm was floated as a public limited company. See
note at LTD

ˌpublicly-ˈheld adjective [usually before noun]
(*Law*) used to describe a company whose shares can
be bought and sold by the public

ˌpublicly-owned ˈcompany = PUBLIC
COMPANY

ˌpublicly ˈtraded adjective
1 if a company is **publicly traded**, its shares are
sold to the public: *Most small businesses are
privately owned and not publicly traded.*
2 if shares are **publicly traded**, they are sold to
the public: *Smaller companies that do not issue
publicly traded shares are a vital part of the economy.*

ˌpublic ˈoffering noun [C,U]
(*Stock Exchange*) a number of shares, bonds, etc. that
are offered for sale to the public for the first time:
*The board of directors decided to conduct a public
offering of newly issued shares.* ◇ *a public offering of
3 million shares* ◇ *The company was privatized by
public offering.*

ˌpublic-ˈprivate adjective [only before noun]
used to describe a project or an arrangement in
which a government organization and a private
company both invest: *a public-private deal to build
new hospitals*

ˈpublic-ˈprivate ˈpartnership (*also* ˈprivate-
ˈpublic ˈpartnership) noun [C] (*abbr* **PPP, P3**)
an arrangement in which a government
organization and a private company invest in a
project and work together

★ **ˌpublic reˈlations** noun
1 [U] (*abbr* **PR**) the business of giving the public
information about a particular organization or
person in order to create a good impression: *She
works in public relations.* ◇ *The company organized a
public relations campaign to improve its image.*
   ○ *a public relations* **consultant/manager/officer/
   professional/specialist** • *a public relations* **agency/
   firm** • *a public relations* **campaign/exercise/
   operation/plan/strategy**
2 [pl.] the state of the relationship between an
organization and the public: *Sponsoring the local
team is good for public relations.* ◇ *We had to deal
with a public relations crisis.* See note at MARKETING
   ○ **bad/good** *public relations*

ˌpublic ˈsale noun [C]
(*Commerce*) an AUCTION of goods or property to the
public

the ˌpublic ˈsector noun [sing.]
(*Economics*) the part of the economy of a country
that is owned or controlled by the government:
careers in the public sector → PRIVATE SECTOR
   ○ *public sector* **employees/jobs/managers/
   organizations**

ˈpublic ˈsector ˈborrowing reˌquirement
noun [sing.] (*abbr* **PSBR**)
(*Economics*) the difference between the amount a
government spends and the income it receives from
taxes in a particular period, which it has to borrow

ˌpublic ˈservant noun [C]
a person who works in or for the government
→ CIVIL SERVANT

ˌpublic ˈservice noun
1 [C] a service such as transport or health care that
a government or an official organization provides
for people in general in a particular society: *to
improve public services in the area*
2 [U] the government and government
departments: *to work in public service* ◇ *public
service workers*
3 [C,U] something that is done to help people
rather than to make a profit: *to perform a public
service*

,public 'service ,vehicle *noun* [C] (*abbr* PSV)
a bus or large taxi that is used to carry members of the public, usually for money

,public 'spending *noun* [U]
the amount of money that is spent by a government or a government organization: *to increase/reduce public spending*

,public 'transport (*BrE*) (*AmE* **,public transpor'tation**) *noun* [U]
a system for carrying passengers from one place to another by road or rail: *to travel on/by public transport* ◊ *Most of us use public transport to get to work.*

,public 'warehouse *noun* [C]
a building where companies can pay to store goods and materials, usually for a short period of time
▶ **,public 'warehousing** *noun* [U]

,public 'works *noun* [pl.]
building work, such as that of hospitals, schools and roads, that is paid for by the government: *an ambitious programme of public works* ◊ *the city's public works director*

★ **publish** /'pʌblɪʃ/ *verb* [+ obj]
1 to produce a book, magazine, CD-ROM, etc. and sell it to the public: *Our catalogue is published in six languages.*
2 to print a letter, an article, etc. in a newspaper or magazine: *Volkswagen published a full-page ad in today's China Daily.*
3 to make sth available to the public on the Internet: *My business picked up after I published my own website.*
4 to make official information known to the public: *The report will be published on the Internet.*
▶ **'publishing** *noun* [U]: *He works in publishing.* ◊ *electronic publishing* → DESKTOP PUBLISHING

publisher /'pʌblɪʃə(r)/ *noun* [C]
a person or company that prepares and prints books, magazines, newspapers or electronic products and makes them available to the public: *Several publishers are competing in the same market.* ◊ *a leading publisher of college textbooks*

puff /pʌf/ *noun* [C,U] (*AmE also* **'puff piece** [C])
(*Marketing*) a short piece of writing that exaggerates the quality of a book, product, etc. and is used to advertise it: *His friend wrote a puff for the back cover of his book.*

pull /pʊl/ *verb, noun*
● *verb* [+ obj]
1 to cancel an event; to stop showing an advertisement, etc: *The company decided to pull the ad following complaints.*
2 to attract the interest or support of sb/sth: *The show pulled 6.3 million viewers.* ◊ *The special offers were pulling in shoppers.*
IDM **pull the 'plug on sth/sb** (*informal*) to put an end to sb's project, a plan, etc: *The company decided to pull the plug on its online store.* **pull sth/a ,rabbit out of the 'hat** (*informal*) to suddenly produce sth as a solution to a problem **pull 'strings (for sb)** (*AmE* **pull 'wires**) (*informal*) to use your influence in order to get an advantage for sb: *They say his father pulled strings for him.* **pull the 'strings** to control events or the actions of other people: *Although the founder of the company has retired, he is still pulling the strings.* **pull your 'weight** to work as hard as everyone else in a job, an activity, etc: *Some members of the team have not been pulling their weight.* **pull 'wires** (*AmE*) (*informal*) = PULL STRINGS (FOR SB)
PHRV **,pull a'head (of sb/sth)** to start to progress faster than sb/sth: *In terms of market share, Japanese firms are pulling ahead.* **,pull 'back (from sth)** to decide not to do sth that you were intending to do, because of possible problems **,pull sth 'in/ 'down** to earn the large amount of money

mentioned: *EMC's core software business pulled in $351 million last year.* **,pull sth 'off** (*informal*) to succeed in doing sth difficult: *We managed to pull off the deal.* **,pull 'out (of sth)** to move away from sth or stop being involved in it: *The project became so expensive that we had to pull out.* → WITHDRAW **,pull to'gether** to act, work, etc. together with other people in an organized way: *If we pull together, we can meet this deadline.*
● *noun*
1 [C, usually sing.] the fact of sth attracting you or having a strong effect on you: *The show is not the pull it once was.*
2 [U] power and influence over other people: *people who have a lot of pull with the media*

pullback /'pʊlbæk/ *noun* [C,U]
a situation where the price of sth suddenly changes after rising or falling steadily for a period of time: *Despite a recent pullback, oil shares are still performing well.*

'pull date = SELL-BY DATE

'pull-down = DROP-DOWN

'pull ,strategy *noun* [C]
(*Marketing*) a method of marketing that depends on spending a large amount of money on advertising, etc. in order to persuade consumers that they want to buy the product: *A good example of pull strategy is the television advertising of children's toys.* → PUSH STRATEGY

'pull ,system *noun* [C]
(*Production*) a system of production in which only the quantity of items needed are made, based on a signal of what has just been used or sold. This cuts costs by reducing the need for goods and materials to be stored, and reduces the time in which orders can be delivered: *We are cutting stock as we move towards a pull system defined by customer orders.* → KANBAN, PUSH SYSTEM

pulsing /'pʌlsɪŋ/ *noun* [U]
(*Marketing*) a pattern of advertising a product in which periods when there is little or no advertising and periods when there is a lot of advertising follow each other in a regular way → FLIGHTING

pump /pʌmp/ *verb*
1 [+ obj] to make water, air, gas, etc. flow in a particular direction by using a pump or sth that works like a pump: *The engine is used for pumping water out of the mine.*
2 [no obj] (about a liquid) to flow in a particular direction as if it is being forced by a pump
PHRV **pump sth 'into sth; ,pump sth 'in** to put a lot of money into sth: *The company has pumped millions into the advertising campaign.* **,pump sth 'out** to produce sth in large amounts: *The company pumps out hundreds of products every year.* **,pump sth 'up** to increase the amount, value or volume of sth: *The government is expected to pump up interest rates to slow down the economy.*

'pump price *noun* [C, usually sing.]
the price at which petrol/gas is sold to the public: *Tax accounts for about 6% of the pump price of a litre of petrol.*

'pump-,priming *noun* [U]
(*Economics*) a situation where the government invests money that it has borrowed in order to encourage economic activity: *The government has launched a major road-building scheme as part of its pump-priming exercise.* ▶ **'pump-prime** *verb* [+ obj or no obj] **'pump-,primer** *noun* [C]

punch /pʌntʃ/ *verb* [+ obj]
to make a hole in sth with a special tool or some

other sharp object: *to punch a time card* ◇ *The machine punches a row of holes in the metal sheet.*
PHRV ,punch 'in (*AmE*) = CLOCK IN/ON at CLOCK ,punch 'out (*AmE*) = CLOCK OUT/OFF at CLOCK

punctual /'pʌŋktʃuəl/ *adjective*
happening or doing sth at the arranged or correct time; not late: *She has been reliable and punctual.* ◇ *I want to make a punctual start at 9 o'clock.*
SYN PROMPT
▶ **punctuality** /,pʌŋktʃu'æləti/ *noun* [U]: *She insists on punctuality.* **punctually** /'pʌŋktʃuəli/ *adverb*: *They always pay punctually.*

pundit /'pʌndɪt/ *noun* [C] (*informal*)
a person who knows a lot about a particular subject and who often talks about it in public; an expert: *Few market pundits are prepared to predict the next move in share prices.*

punitive /'pjuːnɪtɪv/ *adjective*
1 intended as punishment: *During the dispute, the EU imposed punitive tariffs on US imports.*
→ RETALIATORY
2 very severe and that people find very difficult to pay: *punitive taxes*

,**punitive 'damages** (*also* e,xemplary 'damages) *noun* [pl.]
(*Law*) an amount of money that a court orders a person, company, etc. to pay as a punishment, rather than to pay for the harm or damage they have caused → COMPENSATORY DAMAGES

punter /'pʌntə(r)/ *noun* [C] (*informal*)
a person who buys or uses a particular product or service; a customer: *That restaurant's hoping its new menu will bring the punters in.*

★**purchase** /'pɜːtʃəs; *AmE* 'pɜːr-/ *noun, verb*
● *noun*

SEE ALSO: compulsory purchase, contract of ~, hire ~, offer to ~, point of ~

1 [U,C] the act or process of buying sth: *How many visitors to the store actually* **made a purchase**? ◇ *The company has just announced its €50 million purchase of the hotel.* ◇ *Keep your receipt as* **proof of purchase**. ◇ *I did not notice the defects at the time of purchase.* ◇ *We saved money by making a bulk purchase of 50 PCs.* ◇ *an employee share purchase plan*
● *a cash/credit/online purchase* • *big/big-ticket/ major/significant/small* purchases • *equipment/ house/share/stock* purchase
2 [C] something that you have bought: *There are several possible ways to pay for your purchases.* ◇ *If you are not satisfied with your purchase we will give you a full refund.*
● *verb* [+ obj] (*formal*)
to buy sth: *The equipment can be purchased from your local supplier.* ◇ *The group purchased the company for €6 million.*

'**purchase a,greement** (*also* 'sales a,greement, a,greement of 'sale) = CONTRACT OF PURCHASE

'**purchase ,invoice** *noun* [C]
a list of goods that have been bought, that a business receives from a supplier **SYN** BILL → SALES INVOICE

'**purchase ,ledger** (*also* 'bought ,ledger, *less frequent*) *noun* [C] (*all BrE*)
(*Accounting*) in a company's financial records, the group of accounts in which amounts owed to suppliers are recorded: *When you pay a supplier's bill, the payment is noted in the purchase ledger.*
SYN CREDITORS' LEDGER → ACCOUNTS PAYABLE, SALES LEDGER

'**purchase ,order** *noun* [C]
(*Commerce*) a formal document requesting the supply of goods or services, giving details of the goods, price, conditions of delivery and payment, etc: *Customers fax us their purchase orders and we send them the goods and an invoice.*

'**purchase price** *noun* [C]
(*Commerce*) the amount of money that sb actually pays for sth: *The purchase price was higher than early estimates of the value of the business.*
SYN BUYING PRICE → RRP

★**purchaser** /'pɜːtʃəsə(r); *AmE* 'pɜːrtʃ-/ *noun* [C] (*formal*)
a person who buys sth: *The agent's job is to find a purchaser for your property.* ◇ *They have been in negotiations with potential purchasers of the company.* **SYN** BUYER

'**purchase requi,sition** *noun* [C,U]
(*Commerce*) a formal document from one department in a company to the department that buys materials, equipment, etc., giving details of the goods and services they require: *The manager will check all purchase requisition forms and ensure they are countersigned.*

purchasing /'pɜːtʃəsɪŋ; *AmE* 'pɜːrtʃ-/ *noun* [U]
the activity of buying things that a company needs, such as materials, parts, equipment, services, etc.; the department that deals with this: *She has taken over responsibility for purchasing worldwide.* ◇ *All orders are sent to the purchasing manager for authorization.* **SYN** PROCUREMENT → PURCHASE, MATERIALS BUYER

'**purchasing ,officer** (*also* pro'curement ,officer) *noun* [C]
a person whose job is to choose suppliers and agree contracts with them to provide the equipment, materials or services that are used by a company **SYN** MATERIALS BUYER

'**purchasing ,power** (*also* 'spending ,power) *noun* [U]
1 the amount of money that a person or business has available to spend on goods and services: *Access to cheap imports raises the purchasing power of consumers in Japan and other countries.*
2 (*Economics*) the amount of goods and services that a currency can buy at a particular time: *The purchasing power of the dollar has dropped 10% since June.*
SYN BUYING POWER

'**purchasing power ,parity** *noun* (*abbr* PPP)
(*Economics*)
1 [U] the theory that the rate of exchange between two currencies adjusts so that eventually the cost of a range of goods and services will be the same in both countries: *According to the theory of purchasing power parity, market forces will equalize prices between countries.*
2 [U,C] a rate of exchange that is calculated for two currencies so that the amount paid for a range of goods and services in both countries is the same: *Purchasing power parity is useful for comparing living standards between countries.*

'**pure play** *noun* [C]
a company that is involved in only one type of business: *Some companies remained newspaper pure plays, while others went ahead and bought TV stations.* ◇ *They are the largest pure-play provider of financial services in Europe.*

purse /pɜːs; *AmE* pɜːrs/ *noun* [sing.]

SEE ALSO: electronic purse

the amount of money that is available to a person, an organization or a government to spend: *We pride*

ourselves on producing a car for every purse.
→ POCKET

IDM ,tighten/,loosen the 'purse strings to spend less/more money: *There is increasing pressure on the government to loosen the purse strings.* → idiom at HOLD *verb*

pursuant /pə'sjuːənt; *AmE* pər'suː-/ *adjective*
(*Law*) pursuant to sth according to or following sth, especially a rule or law: *A complaint was made pursuant to section 13 of the Act of 1987.*

pursue /pə'sjuː; *AmE* pər'suː/ *verb* [+ obj] (*formal*)
1 to do sth or try to achieve sth over a period of time: *She decided to pursue a career in law.* ◇ *He is leaving the company to pursue other interests.*
2 to continue to discuss or be involved in sth: *He told the seller he was no longer interested in pursuing the deal.*

purveyor /pə'veɪə(r); *AmE* pər'v-/ *noun* [C] (*formal*)
a person or company that supplies sth to people, especially food, services or information: *Brown and Son, purveyors of fine foods* ◇ *the leading purveyor of investment banking services* ▶ pur'vey *verb* [+ obj]

push /pʊʃ/ *verb, noun*
● *verb* [+ obj]
1 (*used with an adverb or preposition*) to affect sth so that it reaches a particular level or state: *The rise in interest rates will push prices up.* ◇ *Higher oil prices have pushed the economy into recession.*
2 (*informal*) to try hard to persuade people to buy sth: *It's up to the sales team to go out and push the product.*
3 to try hard to persuade people to accept an idea or argument: *No one pushed you* **to** *take the job, did they?*
4 to make sb or yourself work hard: *Jack should push himself a little harder.* ◇ *He had a reputation for pushing his teams to the limit.*
IDM be pushed for 'time (*informal*) to have too little time to do sth push the 'envelope (*especially AmE*) (*informal*) to do more than is usually considered possible: *The company has a reputation for pushing the envelope of computer technology.*
PHR V ,push a'head/'forward with sth to continue with a plan in a determined way: *The government is pushing ahead with the sale of state-owned enterprises.* ,push sth 'back to make the time or date of a meeting, etc. later than originally planned: *The launch of the campaign has been pushed back until next spring.* **SYN** POSTPONE 'push for sth; 'push sb for sth to repeatedly ask for sth or try to make sth happen because you think it is very important: *The pressure group is pushing for a ban on GM foods.* **SYN** PRESS ,push sb 'out to make sb leave an organization: *Richards was pushed out as president after about a year.* ,push sth 'out to produce sth in large quantities: *The factory pushes out up to 20 000 PCs each day.*
● *noun* [C]
a determined effort to achieve sth: *We are planning a major marketing push to promote our existing brands.*
IDM give sb/get the 'push (*BrE*) (*informal*) to dismiss sb; to be dismissed from your job: *They gave him the push after only six weeks.*

'push ,strategy *noun* [C]
(*Marketing*) a method of marketing that depends on persuading shop/store owners to make a product available and sell it to their customers: *Push strategies involve directing your communications to wholesalers and retailers.* → PULL STRATEGY

'push ,system *noun* [C]
(*Production*) a system of production in which more goods are made than are needed in order to have a BUFFER STOCK in case there is a sudden increase in demand → KANBAN, PULL SYSTEM

★ **put** /pʊt/ *verb, noun*
● *verb* (putting, put, put)
IDM put sb 'through it (*especially BrE*) (*informal*) to force sb to experience sth difficult or unpleasant: *They really put me through it* (= asked me difficult questions) *at the interview.* put sth/itself up for 'sale/'auction to make sth available to be bought: *No one wanted to buy the company when it put itself up for sale last year.* → idioms at ACTION *noun*, BLOCK *noun*, MARKER, RECORD *noun*
PHR V ,put yourself/sth a'cross/'over (to sb) to communicate your ideas, feelings, etc. successfully to sb: *She puts her ideas across very well.* ,put sth a'side (*also* ,put sth 'by, *especially in BrE*) to save money: *People are not putting enough money aside for when they retire.* 'put sth at sth to calculate sb/sth to be a particular age, weight, amount, etc: *The damage to the building is put at over $1 million.* ,put sth a'way to save money to spend later ,put sth 'back 1 to move sth to a later time or date: *The meeting has been put back to next week.* See note at POSTPONE 2 to cause sth to be delayed: *Poor trading figures put back our plans for expansion.* ,put sth 'by = PUT STH ASIDE ,put sth 'down 1 to pay part of the cost of sth: *House buyers need to put down a deposit of around 5%.* 2 to lower or reduce sth: *If demand is poor, you put your prices down, not up.* 3 to write sth; to make a note of sth: *The meeting's on the 22nd. Put it down in your diary.* ,put yourself/sb/sth 'forward to suggest yourself/sb as a candidate for a job or position: *Her name was put forward by the committee.* ,put sth 'forward to suggest sth for discussion: *None of the proposals put forward by the union has been accepted.* ,put sth 'in 1 to officially make a claim, request, etc: *The company has put in a claim for damages.* ◇ *They are reported to have put in an offer of $40 million.* **SYN** SUBMIT 2 (*also* ,put sth 'into sth) to spend a lot of time or work very hard at doing sth: *She often puts in twelve hours' work a day.* ◇ *Companies have to put considerable effort into protecting their computer systems.* 3 (*also* ,put sth 'into sth) to use or give money: *They put $80 000 of their own money into the business.* ,put 'in for sth (*especially BrE*) to officially ask for sth: *Perhaps I should put in for a rise.* ,put sth 'into sth = PUT STH IN (2,3) ,put sb 'off to cancel a meeting or an arrangement that you have made with sb: *It's too late to put them off now.* See note at POSTPONE ,put sth 'off to change sth to a later time or date: *The announcement was put off until the end of the week.* ,put sth 'on sth to add an amount of money or a tax to the cost of sth: *The tax would put an extra €70 on the price of a single ticket.* ,put sth 'out 1 to produce sth, especially for sale: *The plant puts out 500 new cars a week.* See note at PRODUCE 2 to give a job or task to a worker who is not your employee or to a company that is not part of your own group or organization: *A lot of the work is put out to freelancers.* ,put yourself/sb/sth 'over (to sb) = PUT YOURSELF/STH ACROSS (TO SB) ,put sth 'through to continue with and complete a plan or activity: *We managed to put the deal through.* ,put sb 'through (to sb/sth) to connect sb by telephone: *Could you put me through to the accounts department, please?* 'put sth to sb to offer a suggestion to sb so that they can accept or reject it: *Your proposal will be put to the board of directors.* ,put sth to'gether to create or prepare sth: *They put the report together in just two weeks.* ◇ *It takes a team of people to put together a campaign.* 'put sth towards sth to give money to pay part of the cost of sth: *Twenty per cent of the tax is put towards local environmental schemes.* ,put sth 'up 1 to raise or increase sth: *When they put up the rent, we had to find new premises.* 2 to provide or lend money: *The six investors each put up $105 000 to start the*

business. ◇ *A syndicate of banks put the money up.*
See note at FINANCE **3** to promise a particular asset
to sb who is lending you money if you do not pay
back the loan: *You may have to put up your home as
collateral.* **4** to fix sth in a place where it will be
seen: *to put up a poster/an ad* [SYN] DISPLAY
● *noun* [C]
(*Finance*) = PUT OPTION

'put ,option (*also* **put**) *noun* [C]
(*Finance*) a right to sell sth, such as a number of
shares in a company or a quantity of raw materials,
at a particular price within a fixed period or on a
particular date: *Put options are bought by investors
who expect market prices to fall.* ◇ *They announced
they would exercise their put option to sell their
11.5% stake in the German company.* → CALL OPTION
○ *to* **buy/exercise/hold/purchase/use** *a put option*

PV /ˌpiː ˈviː/ = PRESENT VALUE

p.w. *abbr* (*usually used in written English*)
per week for each week

pyramid /ˈpɪrəmɪd/ *noun* [C]
an organization or a system in which there are
fewer people at each level as you get near the top:
*There are not enough women at the top of the
corporate pyramid.* ▶ **pyramidal** /pɪˈræmɪdl/
adjective

'pyramid ,selling *noun* [U]
(*Commerce*) a way of selling things by encouraging
people to buy the right to sell a company's goods
and a particular amount of stock. They then sell the
right to sell the goods and a smaller amount of
stock to other people, who in turn sell to others and
so on: *With a pyramid selling scheme, recruiting
people is more important than selling goods.*
[NOTE] This system is illegal in some countries.

Q q

QA /ˌkjuː ˈeɪ/ = QUALITY ASSURANCE

QC /ˌkjuː ˈsiː/ = QUALITY CONTROL

QFD /ˌkjuː ef ˈdiː/ = Quality Function
Deployment

qtr *abbr*
a short way of writing **quarter** (a period of three
months)

★ qualification /ˌkwɒlɪfɪˈkeɪʃn; *AmE* ˌkwɑːl-/
noun

SEE ALSO: **bona fide occupational qualification**

1 [C, usually pl.] (*BrE*) an exam that you have passed
or a course of study that you have successfully
completed: *What qualifications do you have?* ◇ *In
this job, experience counts for more than* **paper**
qualifications.
○ *academic/educational/professional/technical/
vocational* qualifications ◆ *to* **acquire/gain/get/
obtain** qualifications ◆ *to* **have/hold** qualifications
2 [C] a skill or type of experience that you need for
a particular job or activity: *Previous managerial
experience is a necessary qualification for this job.*
3 [U] the fact of passing an exam, completing a
course of training or reaching the standard
necessary to do a job: *Students who do well on work
experience may be offered employment following
qualification.*

★ qualified /ˈkwɒlɪfaɪd; *AmE* ˈkwɑːl-/ *adjective*
1 having passed the exams or completed the
training necessary to do a particular job; having
the experience to do a particular job: *a list of
qualified candidates* ◇ *She's extremely* **well** *qualified*
for *the job.*
○ *a qualified* **accountant/electrician/lawyer,** *etc.* ◆
qualified **candidates/employees/staff/workers** ◆ *to
be* **fully/highly/suitably/well** *qualified*
2 [not before noun] having the practical knowledge
or skills to do sth: *I don't know much about careers
in accounting, so I don't feel qualified* **to** *advise you.*

,qualified o'pinion (*also* **,qualified re'port,** *less
frequent*) *noun* [C]
(*Accounting*) used to show that an AUDIT (= an
official examination of the financial records of a
company) is limited in some way, for example
because the information provided was not
complete or there is a problem [NOTE] The words
qualified opinion may be written on the front of

the report: *A qualified opinion may be issued when
the scope of the auditor's examination was restricted.*

★ qualify /ˈkwɒlɪfaɪ; *AmE* ˈkwɑːl-/ *verb* (**qualifies,
qualifying, qualified, qualified**)
1 [no obj] to reach the standard of ability or
knowledge needed to do a particular job, for
example by completing a course of study or passing
exams: *How long does it take to qualify?* ◇ *She
qualified* **as** *an accountant last year.*
2 [+ obj] to give sb the skills and knowledge they
need to do sth: *This training course will qualify you*
for *a better job.* ◇ *The test qualifies you* **to** *drive
heavy vehicles.*
3 [+ obj *or* no obj] to have or give sb the right to do
sth: *My credit card qualifies me* **for** *a discount at
some stores.* ◇ *Qualifying firms can reclaim 100% tax
relief on IT purchases.*

'qualifying ,period *noun* [C]
(*HR*) the length of time you must have been doing
sth in order to be entitled to a particular benefit:
*The qualifying period for parental leave is one year's
continuous employment.*

qualitative /ˈkwɒlɪtətɪv; *AmE* ˈkwɑːləteɪt-/
adjective [usually before noun]
1 considering sth by examining aspects that
cannot easily be measured or expressed as
numbers, such as opinions or attitudes: *qualitative
analysis/research*
2 involving a comparison based on quality: *There is
no qualitative difference between well-made local
computers and imported models.*
→ QUANTITATIVE

★ quality /ˈkwɒləti; *AmE* ˈkwɑːl-/ *noun, adjective*
● *noun* (*plural* **qualities**)

SEE ALSO: **credit quality, fair average quality**

1 [U,C] the standard of sth when it is compared to
other things like it; how good or bad sth is: *There
has been a decline in quality.* ◇ *We only sell goods of a
high quality* ◇ *When costs are cut, product quality
sometimes suffers.* ◇ *His job is to monitor quality and
ensure it is up to our high standards.* → QUALITY
CONTROL
○ *be of (a)* **good/high/top** *quality* ◆ **low/poor/varying**
quality ◆ *quality* **declines/improves/suffers**
2 [U] a high standard: *We aim to provide quality at
reasonable prices.* ◇ *The company has a reputation
for quality and value.*

3 [C] a thing that is part of a person's character, especially sth good: *He has leadership qualities.* ◇ *It's hard to find people with the right qualities for the job.*
4 [C] a feature or aspect of sth, often one that makes it different from sth else: *The quality that distinguishes our product from the competition is its lightness.*
● *adjective* [only before noun]
(used especially by people trying to sell goods or services) of a high standard: *We specialize in quality cars.* ◇ *We deliver a quality product with zero defects.*

'quality as,surance *noun* [U] (*abbr* **QA**)
(*Production*) the practice of managing every stage of the process of producing goods or providing services to make sure they are kept at the standard that the customer expects: *A national organization is needed to oversee quality assurance in training.*

'quality ,circle *noun* [C]
(*Production*) a small group of workers who meet regularly to propose solutions to problems related to work: *Quality circles have played an important role in the success of Japanese manufacturing companies.*

★ **'quality con,trol** *noun* [U] (*abbr* **QC**)
(*Production*) a system of keeping high standards in manufactured products by planning carefully, checking and making necessary improvements: *All our products are subject to strict quality control.*
▶ **'quality con,troller** *noun* [C]

'Quality 'Function De'ployment *noun* [U]
(*abbr* **QFD**)
(*Marketing*; *Production*) a method of creating products and services that involves basing design, development and delivery on what customers say they need: *Quality Function Deployment has helped to transform the way businesses plan new products.*

'quality ,management = TOTAL QUALITY MANAGEMENT

'Quality of 'Working 'Life (*especially BrE*) (*AmE usually* **'Quality of 'Work Life**) *phrase* (*abbr* **QWL**)
(*HR*) how happy and satisfied employees feel at work; techniques and methods designed to improve this

quango /ˈkwæŋgəʊ; *AmE* -goʊ/ *noun* [C] (*plural* **quangos**)
in the UK, an organization dealing with public matters, started and financed by the government, but working independently and with its own legal powers **SYN** NDPB → CHARITY **NOTE** The name **quango** is formed from the first letters of the phrase 'quasi-autonomous non-governmental organization'.

★ **quantify** /ˈkwɒntɪfaɪ; *AmE* ˈkwɑːn-/ *verb* [+ obj]
(**quantifies, quantifying, quantified, quantified**)
to describe or express sth as an amount or a number: *The risks associated with this venture are difficult to quantify.* ▶ **'quantifiable** *adjective*: *It is important to develop quantifiable goals that help you assess your progress.* **quantification** /ˌkwɒntɪfɪ-ˈkeɪʃn; *AmE* ˌkwɑːn-/ *noun* [U]

quantitative /ˈkwɒntɪtətɪv; *AmE* ˈkwɑːntəteɪt-/ *adjective*
1 considering sth by examining aspects that can be measured or expressed as numbers: *quantitative analysis/research* ◇ *a quantitative market research questionnaire*
2 involving a comparison based on quantity: *a quantitative change/difference*
→ QUALITATIVE

★ **quantity** /ˈkwɒntəti; *AmE* ˈkwɑːn-/ *noun* (*plural* **quantities**)

SEE ALSO: **bill of quantities, economic order ~, equilibrium ~**

1 [C,U] an amount or a number of sth: *The factory initially produced a small quantity of lamps and these sold quickly.* ◇ *Vast quantities of oil were found in northern Alaska.* ◇ *Materials are cheaper when bought **in large quantities**.* ◇ *Can the goods be supplied in sufficient quantity?*
O *huge/massive/vast* quantities ◆ *a large/small* quantity
2 [U] the measurement of sth by saying how much of it there is: *The data is limited in terms of both quality and quantity.*
3 [C,U] a large amount or number of sth: *We have a quantity of signed prints for sale.* ◇ *It was the first PC to be manufactured **in quantity**.*

'quantity sur,veyor *noun* [C] (*BrE*)
a person whose job is to calculate the quantity of materials needed for building sth, how much it will cost and how long it will take See note at PROFESSION ▶ **'quantity ,survey** *noun* [C]

quarantine /ˈkwɒrəntiːn; *AmE* ˈkwɔːr-; ˈkwɑːr-/ *noun* [U]
a period of time when an animal, a food product, etc. entering a country is kept away from others in order to prevent disease from spreading: *agricultural quarantine laws* ◇ (*figurative*) *Email messages from non-approved addresses will be placed in quarantine.* ▶ **'quarantine** *verb* [+ obj]

★ **quarter** /ˈkwɔːtə(r); *AmE* ˈkwɔːrt-/ *noun* [C]
(*Accounting*) a period of three months, used especially as a period for which bills are paid or a company's income is calculated: *Sales increased 20% in the third quarter.* ◇ *The rent is due at the end of each quarter.*
IDM ,quarter on 'quarter (*Accounting*) compared with the last quarter: *Sales rose 20% quarter on quarter.* → YEAR ON YEAR at YEAR

'quarter day *noun* [C] (*BrE*)
(*Finance*) the first day of a **quarter** (= a period of three months) on which payments must be made, for example at the stock exchange

quarterly /ˈkwɔːtəli; *AmE* ˈkwɔːrtərli/ *adjective, adverb, noun*
● *adjective* [only before noun]
1 relating to a period of three months: *quarterly earnings/income/profits* ◇ *This is an 80% reduction on the previous quarterly dividend.*
2 produced or happening every three months: *Managers attend quarterly planning meetings.*
● *adverb*
every three months: *We meet quarterly with our accountants.*
● *noun*
1 [C] a magazine, etc. published four times a year: *The magazine is a quarterly aimed at people working in advertising.*
2 (*Accounting*) **quarterlies** [pl.] in the US, the financial results that large companies publish every three months

'quarter point *noun* [C]
(*Finance*) one of four equal divisions of one per cent: *The bank has increased interest rates by a quarter point to 4 per cent.* ◇ *a quarter-point cut in interest rates*

quasi- /ˈkweɪzaɪ; -saɪ; ˈkwɑːzi/ *combining form* (*used in adjectives and nouns*)
1 partly; almost: *The car manufacturer had a quasi-monopoly position in the Italian market.*
2 that appears to be sth but is not really so: *The company chose a name with quasi-official overtones.*

quay /kiː/ *noun* [C]
(*Transport*) a platform in a harbour where boats come in to load, etc: *During the dockers' strike,*

thousands of containers piled up on the quays.
→ DELIVERED EX QUAY

★ **query** /'kwɪəri; AmE 'kwɪri/ *noun, verb*
● *noun* [C] (*plural* **queries**)
a question, especially one asking for information or expressing a doubt about sth: *Our staff will be happy to answer your queries.* ◇ *If you have a query about your insurance policy, contact our helpline.*
● *verb* [+ obj] (**queries, querying, queried, queried**)
to express doubts about sth: *Analysts queried whether the group would reach its financial targets.* ◇ *We queried the bill as it seemed far too high.*
[SYN] QUESTION

question /'kwestʃən/ *noun, verb*
● *noun*

SEE ALSO: **scaled question**

1 [C] a sentence, phrase or word that asks for information: *If something doesn't make sense, it's important to ask questions.* ◇ *Advisors are available to answer clients' questions.*
⊕ *to* **answer/ask** *a question*
2 [C] a matter that needs to be discussed or dealt with: *The report raises difficult questions about the company's environmental policies.* ◇ *The government will have to address the question of tax reform.*
[SYN] ISSUE
⊕ *to* **address/deal with/face/tackle** *a question* ◆ *to* **bring up/pose/raise** *a question* ◆ *a* **difficult/an important/a key** *question*
3 [U] doubt about sth: *His suitability for the job is open to question.*
[IDM] **bring/call/throw sth into 'question** to cause sth to become a matter for doubt and discussion: *Although he's very creative, his management skills have been called into question.* **in 'question 1** that is being discussed: *The amount in question is understood to be between $30m and $35m.* **2** in doubt; uncertain: *The stability of the economy remains in question.* **out of the 'question** impossible, not allowed and therefore not worth discussing: *Another strike is not out of the question.* **there is/was no 'question of (sth happening/sb doing sth)** there is/was no possibility of sth: *There is no question of the chief executive resigning.*
● *verb* [+ obj]
1 **question sb (about/on sth)** to ask sb questions about sth, especially officially: *Investigators have questioned the company's accountants.*
2 to have or express doubts or suspicions about sth: *Analysts questioned whether shareholders would benefit from the deal.*
[SYN] QUERY

questionable /'kwestʃənəbl/ *adjective*
1 that you have doubts about because you think it is not accurate or correct: *The government's assumptions about economic growth are highly questionable.*
2 likely to be dishonest or morally wrong: *He has denied all allegations of questionable accounting.*

questionnaire /ˌkwestʃə'neə(r); AmE -'ner/ *noun* [C]
a written list of questions that are answered by a number of people so that information can be collected from the answers: *We had to fill in a questionnaire about our spending habits.* ◇ *The market research company analysed the completed questionnaires.*
⊕ *to* **complete/fill in/fill out/reply to/respond to** *a questionnaire* ◆ *to* **analyse** *a questionnaire*

queue /kjuː/ *noun, verb*
● *noun* [C]

SEE ALSO: **dole queue**

1 (*BrE*) (*AmE* **line**) a line of people, cars, etc. waiting to do sth: *There were queues at all the check-outs.*
2 (*BrE*) (*AmE* **line**) a large number of people who want to do or have sth: *There will be a queue of buyers for the company.*
3 (*IT*) a list of jobs that a computer has to do in a particular order: *Your work is not printed immediately but is sent to the print queue.*
4 if your call is being held in a **queue**, a number of other calls will be dealt with before your call is answered: *Thank you for holding—your call is in a queue.*
[IDM] **at the front/back of the 'queue** among the first or the last people to do sth or have sth: *If a business goes bust, equity investors are at the back of the queue.*
● *verb* (**queuing** *or* **queueing**)
1 [no obj] (*BrE*) **queue (up) (for sth)** to wait in a line to do sth, buy sth, go somewhere, etc.; to be one of a large number of people who want to do sth: *Hundreds of shoppers queued from 2 a.m.*
2 (*IT*) [+ obj *or* no obj] to arrange jobs in a **queue**

'quick ,ratio (*also* ,**quick-'assets ,ratio**) = ACID-TEST RATIO

quiet /'kwaɪət/ *adjective* (**quieter, quietest**)
if business, trading, etc. is **quiet**, there is not much activity: *January and February tend to be quiet months.* ◇ *In the markets things were quiet.*

quit /kwɪt/ *verb* (**quitting, quit, quit,** *BrE also* **quitting, quitted, quitted**)
1 (*informal*) [+ obj *or* no obj] to leave your job, especially because you are angry or unhappy about sth: *What was the main reason you quit your previous job?* ◇ *He will quit* **as** *chief executive in May.* ◇ *Her decision to quit was completely unexpected.*
See note at RESIGN
2 [+ obj] to leave a place or an activity: *The company has said it will quit a number of markets.*
3 (*IT*) [+ obj] to close a computer program

quorum /'kwɔːrəm/ *noun* [sing.]
the smallest number of people who must be at a meeting before it can begin or decisions can be made ▶ **quorate** /'kwɔːrət/ *adjective*

quota /'kwəʊtə; AmE 'kwoʊtə/ *noun* [C]
1 (*Economics*) the limited number or amount of people or things that is officially allowed: *to introduce a strict import quota on grain* ◇ *export quotas* ◇ *a quota system for greenhouse gases*
⊕ *to* **impose/introduce/lift/set** *quotas* ◆ *to* **increase/raise/reduce** *a quota* ◆ *to* **comply with/exceed** *quotas*
2 a fixed amount of sth that sb can receive or must do; a fixed number of people that are expected or needed: *He never takes his full quota of holidays.* ◇ *Our sales quotas were not met last year.*
⊕ *to* **impose/introduce** *quotas* ◆ *to* **increase/raise/reduce** *a quota* ◆ *to* **achieve/fill/make/meet/reach** *a quota*

quotation /kwəʊ'teɪʃn; AmE kwoʊ-/ *noun* [C]

SEE ALSO: **application for quotation**

1 (*Commerce*) a statement of how much a particular piece of work will cost: *Price quotations may take weeks to receive.* See note at QUOTE
⊕ *to* **give(sb)/prepare/provide (sb with)/submit** *a quotation* ◆ *to* **accept/ask for/get** *a quotation*
2 (*Stock Exchange*) the price of a share on the stock market
3 (*Stock Exchange*) when a company's shares are accepted (**listed**) on a stock exchange and can be bought and sold: *The company does not have a full stock market quotation.*

★ quote /kwəʊt; AmE kwoʊt/ *verb, noun*

● *verb* [+ obj]
1 (*Commerce*) **quote sb sth** to tell a customer how much you will charge them for a job, service or product: *We were quoted a price of $9 a metre for 50 000 metres of material.*
2 (*Stock Exchange*) to record the name of a company on a stock exchange so that its shares can be bought and sold: *The company is quoted on the New York stock exchange.*
3 (*Finance*) to give the price of a share on a stock exchange or a currency: *Traders quoted the securities at about 70 cents on the dollar.*

┌─────────────────────────┐
│ **WHICH WORD?**   │
└─────────────────────────┘

quote/estimate/quotation

Before asking someone to do a piece of work, for example to repair a vehicle, it is usual to ask them to tell you how much they expect it to cost. They do this by giving you a written **estimate** or a **quotation/quote**.

A person giving a **quotation/quote** often agrees to limit their fee to the amount stated in it.

A person giving an **estimate** usually keeps the right to change their price if circumstances change, for example if the price of parts rises or the work takes longer than expected.

● *noun* [C]
(*Commerce*) a statement of how much money a particular piece of work will cost: *The first quote you get is rarely the most competitive.*

quoted /'kwəʊtɪd; AmE 'kwoʊt-/ *adjective*
(*Stock Exchange*) **quoted** shares are bought and sold on a stock exchange: *Trading in the Nasdaq-quoted stock was halted temporarily.* [SYN] LISTED
[OPP] UNQUOTED

,quoted 'company *noun* [C]
(*Stock Exchange*) a company whose shares are bought and sold on a stock exchange: *He is a director of a major **publicly quoted company**.*

QWL /ˌkjuː dʌbljuː 'el/ = QUALITY OF WORKING LIFE

R r

,race to the 'bottom *noun* [sing.]
the idea that economic competition will lead to lower standards, worse conditions for workers, and workers in some countries losing their jobs to lower-paid workers in other countries

rack /ræk/ *verb*
[PHR V] **,rack 'up sth** (*especially AmE*) to collect sth such as profits or losses, especially quickly or in large amounts: *The business racked up $205m in sales in its first year.* ◇ *It is not the only store that has racked up huge losses this year.*
[NOTE] A pronoun comes between the verb and **up**.
➊ *to rack up debt/gains/losses/sales*

racket /'rækɪt/ *noun* [C]
a dishonest or an illegal way of getting money

racketeer /ˌrækə'tɪə(r); AmE -'tɪr/ *noun* [C]
a person who makes money through dishonest or illegal activities ▶ **,racke'teering** *noun* [U]

'rack rate *noun* [C] (*especially AmE*)
the standard price of a hotel room

★ R&D (*also spelled* **R and D**) /ˌɑːr ən 'diː/ *abbr*
research and development (*used as an uncountable noun*)
1 work that examines new ideas and tries to develop new products and processes: *The company spends $5 billion a year on R&D.* ◇ *Our research and development budget has been cut.*
2 the department in a company that tries to develop new products and ideas and improve existing ones: *the chairman of research and development* ◇ *I work in the R&D division.*

radar /'reɪdɑː(r)/ *noun*
[IDM] **below/under the 'radar (screen)** if something is **below/under the radar**, people are not aware of it **on/off the 'radar (screen)** used to say that people are aware or not aware of sth, or are thinking or not thinking about it: *This sale was*

not even on our radar. ◇ *Gold is coming back onto investors' radar screens.*

raft /rɑːft; AmE ræft/ *noun* [C, usually sing.]
raft of sth a large number or amount of sth: *A raft of economic measures has been announced.*

rage /reɪdʒ/ *noun* [U] (*used with other nouns*)

SEE ALSO: **desk rage, work rage**

anger and violent behaviour caused by a particular situation: *a case of trolley rage in the supermarket*
➊ *air/computer/phone/road rage*
[IDM] **be all the 'rage** (*informal*) to be extremely fashionable and popular

raid /reɪd/ *noun* [C]

SEE ALSO: **bear raid, dawn raid**

(*Stock Exchange*) an occasion when a person or company unexpectedly tries to take control of another company by buying a large number of its shares: *In 1999 he made a successful raid on Telecom Italia.* ▶ **'raider** *noun* [C]

rail /reɪl/ *noun* [U]
railways/railroads as a means of transport: *The government wants to increase the amount of freight carried by rail.* ◇ *rail services/fares* ◇ *a rail link/network* ◇ *rail companies*

,rail con'signment note *noun* [C] (*abbr* **CIM**)
(*Transport*) a document that goes with goods that are sent by rail, stating that the company transporting them has received them in good condition

railway /'reɪlweɪ/ (*BrE*) (*AmE* **railroad** /'reɪlrəʊd; AmE -roʊd/) *noun* [C]
(*Transport*) a system of tracks, the trains that run on them, and the people and organization needed to

operate them: *This is one of Europe's busiest railways.* ◇ *a railway network/operator/system*

rainmaker /ˈreɪnmeɪkə(r)/ *noun* [C] (*especially AmE*)
a person who gets a lot of business and income for a company and makes it successful: *A good rainmaker can be invaluable to the bottom line of a business.*

★ **raise** /reɪz/ *verb, noun*
● *verb* [+ obj]
1 to increase the amount or level of sth: *to raise salaries/prices/taxes* ◇ *They raised their offer to $500.* ◇ *a campaign to raise awareness of the brand*
2 to bring or collect money together; to manage to get money for sth: *to raise a loan* ◇ *The bank has raised $2 billion to fund its expansion.* ◇ *They give new companies help in raising capital.*
3 to mention sth for people to discuss or for sb to deal with: *Analysts have raised concerns over the company's ability to survive.* ◇ *I'm glad you raised the subject of money.* **SYN** BRING UP
4 (*Accounting*) if you **raise** an INVOICE (= a bill for work or goods) you write out or print one or ask sb to do this: *Invoices are not raised where immediate payment is required.*
5 if you **raise** a call, you contact sb by telephone, email, etc. to ask for some help with a technical problem
→ idiom at ANTE
● *noun* [C] (*AmE*) = RISE *noun* (2)

rake /reɪk/ *verb*
IDM **rake sb over the 'coals** (*AmE*) = HAUL SB OVER THE COALS at HAUL *verb*
PHRV ,rake 'in sth (*informal*) to earn a lot of money, especially when it is done easily: *Between them, they were raking in $120 000 a year.* ◇ *The store's been raking it in in the last few weeks.*

★ **rally** /ˈræli/ *verb, noun*
● *verb* [no obj] (**rallies, rallying, rallied, rallied**)
(*Finance*) to rise in price after a period of falling prices or little activity: *The dollar rallied sharply on Tuesday.* ◇ *The company's shares had rallied slightly by the close of trading.*
● *noun* [C] (*plural* **rallies**)
a rise in prices after a period of falling prices or little activity: *They are confident that a market rally is around the corner.* ◇ *The market staged a late rally on Wednesday.*
○ *a market/price/stock rally* ◆ *a powerful/sharp/strong rally* ◆ *an early/a late rally* ◆ *to spark/stage/trigger a rally*

RAM /ræm/ *abbr*
(*IT*) **random-access memory** computer memory in which data can be changed or removed and can be looked at in any order: *32 megabytes of RAM*

ramp /ræmp/ *verb*
PHRV ,ramp 'up; ,ramp sth 'up to increase; to make sth increase in amount: *The manufacturer has ramped up production of this popular new model.* ◇ *Internet sales have been ramping up over the past year.*

rampant /ˈræmpənt/ *adjective*
(about sth bad) existing or spreading everywhere in a way that cannot be controlled: *Unemployment was rampant in Europe at that period.* ◇ *The government's policies were the cause of rampant inflation.*

RAN /ˌɑːr eɪ ˈen/ = REVENUE ANTICIPATION NOTE

random /ˈrændəm/ *adjective, noun*
● *adjective* [usually before noun]
done, chosen, etc. without sb thinking or deciding in advance what is going to happen, or without any regular pattern: *Create passwords using a random* assortment of letters, numbers and symbols. ◇ *The information is processed in a random order.*
▶ ˈrandomly *adverb*: *a survey of 2 000 randomly selected customers*
● *noun*
IDM at 'random without thinking or deciding in advance what is going to happen: *Select a customer at random each month to receive a special gift.*

,random 'sample *noun* [C]
(*Technical*) a number of people or things taken from a larger group using a process in which each person or thing has an equal chance of being chosen: *Questionnaires were sent to a random sample of 5 000 households.* ▶ ,random 'sampling *noun* [U,C]

★ **range** /reɪndʒ/ *noun, verb*
● *noun*
SEE ALSO: mid-range, price ~, product ~, top of the ~
1 [C, usually sing.] a variety of things of a particular type: *The hotel offers a wide range of facilities and services.* ◇ *The drugs are not approved until they have passed the full range of tests.*
2 [C] a set of products of a particular type: *The new range of hair products will be launched in July.* ◇ *The company has announced price cuts on its clothing ranges.* **SYN** LINE
3 [C, usually sing.] the limits between which sth varies: *Most of our customers are in the 18–30 age range.* ◇ *The budget increase will be in the range of 3 to 5%.*
● *verb* [no obj]
1 range from A to B | range between A and B to vary between two particular amounts, sizes, etc., including others between them: *Prices range from $20 to $50.* ◇ *The rate of tax ranges between 15% and 40%.*
2 range from A to B to include a variety of different things in addition to those mentioned: *There are hundreds of job advertisements, ranging from trainee to senior management positions.* ◇ *The company's products range from coffee to shampoo.*

rank /ræŋk/ *noun, verb*
● *noun*
1 [U,C] the position, especially a high position, that sb has in an organization: *He holds the rank of chief executive.* ◇ *Promotion will mean that I'm immediately above him in rank.* ◇ *Most of their management ranks were filled by business school graduates.* → RANKING
○ *a low/high/middle/top rank* ◆ *executive/junior/management/senior ranks*
2 [sing.] the position that sb/sth has in a list arranged according to quality or importance: *a business park of the first rank* ◇ *The new company will be in the top rank of financial institutions.*
○ *the first/second rank* ◆ *the bottom/top rank*
3 the ranks [pl.] the members of a particular group or organization: *joining the growing ranks of the unemployed* ◇ *Most of the candidates came from within the company's ranks.*
IDM break 'ranks if members of a group or an organization break ranks, they refuse to support the group
● *verb* [+ obj or no obj] (*not used in the continuous tenses*)
to give sb/sth a particular position on a scale according to quality, importance, success, etc.; to have a position of this kind: *The tasks have been ranked in order of difficulty.* ◇ *They rank among the top ten PC makers.* ◇ *a top-ranked business school* **SYN** RATE

the ,rank and 'file *noun* [sing. with sing./pl. verb]
the ordinary members of an organization, especially a trade union: *The rank and file have approved the union's proposals.* ◇ *the rank and file of the workforce* ◇ *rank-and-file members* ▶ ,rank-and-ˈfiler *noun* [C]

ranking /ˈræŋkɪŋ/ *noun, adjective*
● *noun*

SEE ALSO: **top ranking**

1 the rankings [pl.] an official list showing how good or important people or things are in relation to other similar people or things: *The company jumped from bottom place in last year's FT rankings to ninth this year.* ◇ *first place in the plant's productivity rankings*
2 [C] the position of sb/sth in this list: *Six companies have achieved a four-star ranking.*
3 [U] the action of giving a position in a list to sb/sth: *the annual ranking of fastest-growing companies*
● *adjective*

SEE ALSO: **high-ranking, middle-~, low-~**

1 (*especially AmE*) having a high or the highest rank in an organization, etc: *a meeting with our client's five ranking officers*
2 (*used in compounds*) having the particular rank mentioned: *lower- to middle-ranking staff*

ratchet /ˈrætʃɪt/ *verb*
PHRV ˌratchet sth ˈup/ˈdown; ˌratchet ˈup/ˈdown to make sth increase/decrease by small amounts; to increase/decrease by small amounts: *Overuse of credit cards has ratcheted up consumer debt.* ◇ *Year after year, prices have ratcheted up.*

★ **rate** /reɪt/ *noun, verb*
● *noun* [C]

SEE ALSO: **bank rate, base ~, basic ~, bill ~, cap ~, capitalization ~, capped-~**, etc.

1 a fixed amount of money that is charged or paid for sth: *advertising/insurance/postal rates* ◇ *a low hourly rate of pay* ◇ *We offer special reduced rates for students.* ◇ *the basic rate of tax* (= the lowest amount that is paid by everyone) ◇ *a business consultant whose normal rate is $200 per hour* ◇ *After 6 p.m. customers can make telephone calls at a cheaper rate.* See note at PRICE **NOTE** Rate is often used on its own to mean a particular kind of rate, such as 'exchange rate', 'interest rate', etc. *The targets for the year were based on a dollar/yen rate of 122 yen.*
○ *a cheap/competitive/low/reasonable rate* ◆ *a good/high rate* ◆ *a normal/reduced/special rate* ◆ *a fixed/flat/variable rate* ◆ *an annual/average/hourly/a weekly rate* ◆ *a drop/rise in the rate (of sth)* ◆ *to charge/fix/pay/set a rate (of …)*
2 a measurement of the speed at which sth happens: *Inflation is running at an annual rate of 4.5 to 5%.* ◇ *Some people wondered if the company could sustain its current rate of growth.* ◇ *The computer virus is spreading at an alarming rate.* ◇ *At the rate you work, you'll never finish!*
○ *a fast/slow/steady rate* ◆ *an alarming/a surprising rate* ◆ *to improve/increase/maintain/speed up a rate* ◆ *to cut/reduce/slow down a rate*
3 a measurement of the number of times sth happens or exists in a particular period: *Local businesses are closing at the rate of three a year.* ◇ *a high rate of unemployment* ◇ *a drop in the unemployment rate from 6% to 5.7%* ◇ *She makes about 100 sales calls a day, with a success rate of about 78%.*
○ *a high/low/rising/falling rate* ◆ *the annual/average/monthly/quarterly rate* ◆ *a drop/rise in the rate of sth* ◆ *a failure/success rate* ◆ *to improve/increase/maintain a rate* ◆ *to cut/reduce a rate*
● *verb*
1 [+ obj or no obj] rate sb/sth (as) sth | rate (as sth) (*not used in the continuous tenses*) to have, or think that sb/sth has, a particular level of quality, value, etc: *They rated him highly as a colleague.* ◇ *The ad campaign was rated a success.* ◇ *The software is highly rated for its ease of use.* ◇ *This rates as one of the best hotels I have been to.*

rating

2 [+ obj] (*usually* be rated) to place sb/sth in a particular position on a scale in relation to similar people or things: *The hotels were rated according to their price, comfort and quality of service.* ◇ *The company is currently rated number two in Europe.* ◇ *a top-rated programme* **SYN** RANK
3 (*Finance*) [+ obj] rate sth (as) sth to decide if shares, bonds, etc. are a good or bad investment because of the level of risk: *The analysts rate these shares a 'buy'.* ◇ *Triple-A rated bonds* ◇ *highly rated stocks*
○ *to rate sth (as) (a) buy/(a) hold/junk/(a) sell* ◆ *to rate sth (as) investment grade/Triple A*
4 [+ obj] to give a machine, a ship or an electrical device a number, mark, etc. according to how powerful it is, what it can do, etc: *The engine is rated 192 horsepower on regular gas.*

ˈrate card *noun* [C]
(*Marketing*) a list that shows how much it costs to advertise on television, in a particular newspaper, on a particular website, etc. and gives other important details

ˈrate-ˌcutting *noun* [U]
(*Economics*) the action of reducing the amount of money that people or businesses pay in interest on money that they borrow: *Further rate-cutting looks possible.* ◇ *a rate-cutting campaign*

ˌrate of depreciˈation = DEPRECIATION RATE
ˌrate of exˈchange = EXCHANGE RATE
ˌrate of ˈinterest = INTEREST RATE
ˌrate of reˈturn *noun* [C]

SEE ALSO: **internal rate of return**

(*Finance*) the amount of profit that an investment produces, expressed as a percentage of the amount invested: *The average rate of return on assets was 9.3%.* ◇ *It is better to invest in a company that offers a good rate of return.*
○ *a decent/good/high rate of return* ◆ *an average/a low/poor rate of return* ◆ *an expected/a guaranteed/projected rate of return* ◆ *to earn/generate/offer/provide a … rate of return*

ratify /ˈrætɪfaɪ/ *verb* [+ obj] (ratifies, ratifying, ratified, ratified)
to make an agreement officially valid by voting for or signing it: *The new wage agreement was ratified by union members in October.* ▸ **ratification** /ˌrætɪfɪˈkeɪʃn/ *noun* [U]

★ **rating** /ˈreɪtɪŋ/ *noun*

SEE ALSO: **AA rating, average audience ~, bond ~, buy ~, credit ~, debt ~, hold ~**, etc.

1 [C] a measurement of how good, popular, important, etc. sb/sth is, especially in relation to other people or things: *The publishers claim that the new magazine had an approval rating of 85% of all readers questioned.* ◇ *The directors were told how their skills were rated and how it compared to the average rating of all the other directors.*
○ *a high/low/poor/top rating* ◆ *to achieve/get/have/receive a rating* ◆ *to give sth a rating* ◆ *a rating climbs/falls/improves/rises*
2 (*Finance*) [C,U] = CREDIT RATING
3 (*Finance*) [C,U] a measurement of whether shares, bonds, etc. are a good or bad investment because of the level of risk: *Merrill Lynch has raised its rating on the stock to 'buy' from 'neutral'.*
○ *to have/put a rating on sth* ◆ *to raise/review/upgrade a rating* ◆ *to cut/downgrade/lower a rating*
4 ratings [pl.] a set of figures that show how many people watch or listen to a particular television or radio programme, used to show how popular a programme is: *The station is trying to improve*

ratings and increase advertising sales. ◇ *The show has gone up in the ratings.*

O *good/poor* ratings • *to get/have* ratings • *ratings decline/go up/go down/improve* • *a ratings battle/war*

5 (*Insurance*) (*also* **in'surance ,rating**) [C] a measurement of the risk involved in giving sb insurance, used to calculate how much they must pay: *This rating will apply until your next birthday.*

O *to calculate/have/receive a rating*

'rating ,agency (*also* **'ratings ,agency**) *noun* [C] (*Finance*) an organization that analyses how likely a company is to pay back the money that it owes and provides a score (**rating**) for this: *The ratings agencies say the AAA ratings of the insurance company are not likely to be downgraded.*

SYN CREDIT RATING AGENCY

'ratings point *noun* [C] (*Marketing*) a way of measuring the size of an audience for a television programme. One **ratings point** is one per cent of all the homes in a particular area watching a programme.

ratio /'reɪʃiəʊ; AmE -oʊ/ *noun* [C] (*plural* **ratios**)

SEE ALSO: **accounting ratio, acid-test ~, asset turnover ~, capital adequacy ~, capital ~, cash ~, cash-deposit ~,** etc.

the relationship between two groups of people, things or amounts of money that is represented by two numbers or a percentage showing how much larger one group is than the other: *Ten years ago, the ratio of employees to customers was about 1:10.* ◇ *the ratio of a company's share price to its earnings* ◇ *The ratio of public sector debt to GDP was 55% in January.* ◇ *The ratio of passengers to seats available has fallen.* ◇ *The bank has a high trainer-to-employee ratio.* → PROPORTION (2)

'ratio a,nalysis *noun* [C,U] (*Accounting*) the study of the relationships between various financial numbers or amounts, used to judge a company's financial condition: *Ratio analysis produces such measures as return on capital employed.*

rationale /ˌræʃə'nɑːl; AmE -'næl/ *noun* [C, usually sing.] (*formal*) the principles or reasons that explain a particular decision, course of action, etc: *The firm believes the strategic rationale for the deal is strong.* ◇ *The rationale behind the merger is clear.*

rationalize , -ise /'ræʃnəlaɪz/ *verb* [+ obj or no obj] to make changes to a business, an organization, etc. in order to make it more efficient, especially by spending less money: *If we rationalize production, will that mean redundancies?* ◇ *The move is an attempt to rationalize an industry suffering from excess capacity.* ▶ **rationalization, -isation** /ˌræʃnəlaɪ'zeɪʃn; AmE -lə'z-/ *noun* [U]: *The bank's rationalization programme has still not brought the expected savings.*

the 'rat race *noun* [sing.] (*informal*) the way of life of people living and working in a big city where everyone competes in an aggressive way to be more successful, earn more money, etc: *He decided it was time to quit the rat race.*

raw /rɔː/ *adjective* [usually before noun] **1** **raw** substances are in their natural state and have not yet been changed, used or made into sth else: *He imports the raw cotton from India.* ◇ *Raw steel production is at about two thirds of capacity.* **2** **raw** data has not yet been organized into a form in which it can easily be used or understood: *It should not be forgotten that this is raw data, not*

refined information. ◇ *The company decided to publish the raw earnings figures.*

IDM **a raw 'deal** the fact of sb being treated unfairly: *Older workers often get a raw deal.*

,raw ma'terial *noun* [C,U] a natural or basic substance that is used to make sth in an industrial process: *We have had problems with the supply of raw materials to the factory.* ◇ *The rise in oil prices has pushed up the cost of raw materials.* ◇ *The plant produces the raw material for making polyester fibre.*

RD = REFER TO DRAWER

RDO /ˌɑː diː 'əʊ; AmE ˌɑːr diː 'oʊ/ = ROSTERED DAY OFF

Re /reɪ/ *abbr* (*Insurance*) **Reinsurance** used in the names of companies: *Munich Re is the biggest reinsurer in the world.*

re /riː/ *preposition* concerning; used in business letters and notes to say what the letter or note is about: *Re your letter of 1 September...*

re- /riː/ *prefix* (*used in verbs and related nouns, adjectives and adverbs*) again: *rebrand* ◇ *re-engineer* ◇ *recycle*

★ **reach** /riːtʃ/ *verb, noun*
● *verb* [+ obj]
1 to increase to a particular level: *Consumer debt has reached record levels.* ◇ *Total sales for October reached $800 million.* ◇ *There are signs that interest rates have reached their peak.*
2 to be seen or heard by a particular group of people, especially when you want them to buy your products: *We asked ourselves: How can we reach urban women?* ◇ *Daily papers reach a mass audience.*
3 to communicate with sb, especially by telephone: *I tried to reach him all morning, but without success.*
4 to achieve a particular aim: *We have reached agreement with the unions on the new labour contract.* ◇ *The aim is to reach a final decision by August.*
● *noun*
1 [sing.] the number of people that can see or hear sth, buy a product, use a service, etc: *The company's reach never went beyond 1% of the country's PC market.* ◇ *The Internet can extend your customer reach in more ways than one.*
O *a global/an international/a massive/wide* reach • *to expand/extend/increase* your reach
2 **reaches** [pl.] particular sections of an organization, a system, etc: *An MBA degree is often a passport into the upper reaches of management.*
O *the higher/lower/upper* reaches of sth
IDM **beyond/out of sb's 'reach; beyond/out of (the) reach of sb** costing more than sb can afford: *Rising property prices have put an ordinary house beyond the reach of many buyers.* **within sb's 'reach; within (the) reach of sb** costing an amount that sb can afford: *Rising incomes are putting cars within the reach of many more families.*

react /ri'ækt/ *verb* [no obj]
1 if markets, share prices, etc. **react**, they start to rise or fall as a result of things that happen: *People are waiting to see how the markets react.*
O *to react favourably/quickly/sharply* • *to react badly/cautiously/negatively*
2 if people or organizations **react** to sth, they change or behave in a particular way in response to sth: *Bookings have fallen and several companies have reacted by cutting jobs.* ◇ *Business leaders have reacted angrily to the announcement.*
O *to react angrily/coolly/furiously* • *to react badly/favourably/negatively/positively/quickly*
▶ **reaction** /ri'ækʃn/ *noun* [C,U]: *The euro showed*

little reaction to the news that producer prices were down. ◇ There has been a mixed reaction **to** her appointment as director.

reactive /riˈæktɪv/ adjective
waiting for things to happen before acting, rather than controlling a situation by planning or by making things happen: *We are still taking a reactive approach to customer satisfaction, responding to complaints as they arise.* → PROACTIVE

reactive 'marketing noun [U]
methods of selling a company's goods and services that rely on possible customers contacting the company → PROACTIVE MARKETING

readership /ˈriːdəʃɪp; AmE -dərʃ-/ noun [C, usually sing., U]
the number or type of people who read a particular newspaper, magazine, etc., often compared to the number of people who buy it: *Readership of the paper increased by more than a quarter in the first six months of this year.* ◇ *They have succeeded in attracting a new young readership.* → CIRCULATION

'read out noun [C]
(IT) the display of information on a computer screen → PRINTOUT

re-'advertise verb [+ obj or no obj]
to advertise sth again, especially a job
▶ **re-ad'vertisement** noun [C]

read-'write adjective (abbr RW)
(IT) if a file, disk or memory is **read-write**, it allows you to make changes to data: *a CD-RW drive/disk*

ready-'made adjective [usually before noun]
1 made in standard types and sizes, rather than for an individual customer: *ready-made clothing/ curtains/suits*
2 prepared in advance so that you can use it or eat it immediately: *You can fill your fridge with ready-made meals.*

ready-to-'wear adjective
ready-to-wear clothes are made in standard types and sizes, rather than being made to fit an individual customer

real /riːl; BrE usually rɪəl/ adjective [only before noun]
(Economics) including the effects of INFLATION (= a general rise in the price of goods and services): *The economy grew by a real 0.6% in April.* ◇ *GNP contracted 1.2% in real terms in the last quarter.*
→ REAL WAGES
O real *costs/earnings/incomes/prices*

the ˌreal e'conomy noun [sing.]
(Economics) the parts of the economy that produce goods and services, rather than the parts involving buying and selling on the financial markets: *What threat do problems in the financial markets pose for the real economy?*

'real eˌstate noun [U] (especially AmE)
property in the form of land or buildings; the business of buying and selling this: *Many investors sold stock and put their money into real estate.* ◇ *The group also has interests in packaging and real estate.*
→ REALTY
O to *buy/develop/invest in/own/sell* real estate ♦ *commercial/residential/retail* real estate

'real estate ˌagent noun [C]
1 = ESTATE AGENT
2 in the US, a person who has official permission from a state to be an ESTATE AGENT and works for a REAL ESTATE BROKER
▶ **'real estate ˌagency** noun [C] = ESTATE AGENCY at ESTATE AGENT

'real estate ˌbroker noun [C] (AmE)
a person or business that is given official permission by a state to help people buy and sell

houses, other buildings, or land, and often employs REAL ESTATE AGENTS → ESTATE AGENT ▶ **'real estate ˌbrokerage** noun [C]: *a 45-person real estate brokerage*

'real estate ˌcompany = PROPERTY COMPANY

'real eˌstate loan = PROPERTY LOAN

'real estate ˌmanagement, **'real estate ˌmanager** = PROPERTY MANAGEMENT

the 'real estate ˌmarket = PROPERTY MARKET

ˌreal ex'change rate noun [C]
(Economics) the relation in value between one currency and another when it has been adjusted for differences in prices between the two countries: *Real exchange rates should remain more or less constant over time.*

realign /ˌriːəˈlaɪn/ verb [+ obj]
to change the way a business, an organization, etc. is organized in order to adapt it to a new situation: *We believe losses will decrease as we realign our business to the lower demand.* ▶ **ˌrea'lignment** noun [U,C]: *A major realignment of organizational structure is planned.*

realizable, **-isable** /ˈriːəlaɪzəbl; BrE also ˈrɪə-/ adjective [usually before noun]
1 (Accounting) **realizable** assets, investments, etc. can be sold quickly to make money available → NET REALIZABLE VALUE
2 possible to achieve or make happen: *Goals should be both real and realizable.*

★ **realize**, **-ise** /ˈriːəlaɪz; BrE also ˈrɪəl-/ verb [+ obj]
1 to be sold for a particular amount of money: *The paintings realized $2.5 million at auction.*
2 to make or lose a particular amount of money: *The company expects to realize a $3.0 million pretax gain in the third quarter.* ◇ *realized gains*
3 (Finance) **realize an asset** to sell things that you own, for example property, in order to get the money that you need for sth: *He realized other assets in order to subsidize the business.*
SYN LIQUIDATE
4 to achieve sth important that you very much want to do: *We encourage all staff to realize their full potential* (= be as successful as they are able to be).
▶ **realization**, **-isation** /ˌriːəlaɪˈzeɪʃn; ˌrɪəl-; AmE ˌriːələˈz-/ noun [U]: *the realization of potential*

ˌreal 'time noun [U]
(IT) used to describe the way in which a computer system can receive information and react to it immediately: *While people enter data, we're tracking their work* **in** *real time.* ◇ *Brokers use real-time data and news to make investment decisions.*

ˌreal-time 'company noun [C]
a company that uses the Internet and other technology so that they can react immediately to information or requests from customers and suppliers

Realtor™ /ˈriːəltə(r)/ = ESTATE AGENT

realty /ˈriːəlti/ noun [U] (AmE)
(often used in the names of companies) land or property: *Kimco Realty* → REAL ESTATE

ˌreal 'wages noun [pl.]
(Economics) a person's income measured by what it can buy rather than the money received, considering the effects of INFLATION: *Real wages fell through the 1990s.*

ream /riːm/ noun
1 reams [pl.] a large amount of writing or infor-mation: *The program can help you put in order the reams of data that a modern office has to deal with.*
2 (Technical) [C] five hundred sheets of paper

reap /riːp/ *verb* [+ obj]
(often used in newspapers) to obtain money or a benefit as a result of sth you have done: *Losses fell dramatically as the company began to reap the rewards of cost cuts.*
◊ *to reap benefits/gains/profits/rewards*

reasonable /ˈriːznəbl/ *adjective*
1 (about a price or the cost of sth) acceptable and appropriate; not too cheap and not too expensive: *He made us a reasonable offer for the goods.* ◊ *They offer high quality products at a reasonable price.*
2 fair, practical and sensible: *It is a reasonable request.* ◊ *It seems reasonable to expect growth in the range of 2.5%.* [OPP] UNREASONABLE
3 [usually before noun] fairly good, but not very good: *The sales results were reasonable* (= good enough).
▶ **'reasonableness** *noun* [U]: *The test is used to assess the reasonableness of a dismissal.*

rebadge /ˌriːˈbædʒ/ *verb*
(*Marketing*)
1 [+ obj] to buy a product or service from another company and sell it as your own: *They could import a small car and rebadge it.*
2 [+ obj *or no obj*] to change the name or symbol of a business or one of its products or services: *All the stores are being rebadged under the new corporate banner.*

rebate /ˈriːbeɪt/ *noun* [C]
1 (*Accounting*) an amount of money that is given back to you because you have paid too much: *You may qualify for a tax rebate.* → REFUND See note at REDUCTION
2 (*Commerce*) an amount of money that is taken off the cost of sth before you pay for it: *Customers were lured with a range of cash rebates, interest-free loans and other discounts.* [SYN] DISCOUNT → CASHBACK
▶ **'rebate** *verb* [+ obj]

reboot /ˌriːˈbuːt/ *verb* [+ obj *or no obj*]
(*IT*) if you **reboot** a computer or it **reboots**, you switch it off and then start it again immediately

rebound *verb, noun*
● *verb* /rɪˈbaʊnd/ [no obj]
to rise, increase or become more active again after a difficult period: *The bank's share price fell sharply to $26 in February, before rebounding to $36 on Thursday.* ◊ *We believe advertising is rebounding strongly.*
● *noun* /ˈriːbaʊnd/ [C]
a positive reaction that happens after sth negative: *Investors are looking for a rebound in the manufacturing sector.*
◊ *a quick/sharp/strong rebound ◊ a modest/slight rebound ◊ to report/show/stage a rebound*

★ **rebrand** /ˌriːˈbrænd/ *verb* [+ obj *or no obj*]
(*Marketing*) to change the image of a company or an organization, or of one of its products or services, for example by giving it a new name, advertising it in a different way, etc: *The group is rebranding its outlets as 'Game'.* ◊ *These companies are trusted and do not need to rebrand.* ▶ **rebrand** /ˈriːbrænd/ *noun* [sing.]: *a multi-million-dollar rebrand* ◊ *A creative agency has been appointed to work on the rebrand.* **ˌre'branding** *noun* [U; sing.]: *a rebranding exercise* ◊ *a $10 million rebranding*

rebuff /rɪˈbʌf/ *verb* [+ obj] (*formal*)
to refuse an offer, request or suggestion in a way that is unkind or not polite: *The bid was rebuffed by the board.* ▶ **re'buff** *noun* [C]

rebut /rɪˈbʌt/ *verb* [+ obj] (**-tt-**) (*formal*)
to say or prove that a statement or criticism is not true: *He was quick to rebut suggestions that the company might be sold.* ▶ **rebuttal** /rɪˈbʌtl/ *noun*

[C,U]: *The company put out a 26-page rebuttal of the claims.*

recall *verb, noun*
● *verb* /rɪˈkɔːl/ [+ obj]
1 (*Commerce*) to ask people to return a product they have bought, usually because there is sth wrong with it: *The company recalled 6.5 million of its tyres.* ◊ *recalled products* [SYN] CALL IN
2 (*not used in the continuous tenses*) to remember sth you have seen or heard: *Customers who have heard your message in a 60-second ad will recall it in a 10-second one.*
● *noun* /rɪˈkɔːl; ˈriːkɔːl/
1 (*Commerce*) [C] an official request for a product to be returned; the product itself: *Officials refused to put a cost on the recall, which affected 1.6 million vehicles.* ◊ *a series of product recalls*
◊ *to conduct/issue/order a recall*
2 [U] the ability to remember sth you have seen or heard: *After the ads appeared in June, brand recall surged 150%.*

recap /ˈriːkæp/ *verb* [+ obj *or no obj*] (**-pp-**)
to repeat or give a summary of what has already been said, decided, etc: *Let me just recap on what we've decided so far.* ▶ **'recap** *noun* [C]

recapitalize, **-ise** /ˌriːˈkæpɪtəlaɪz/ *verb* [+ obj *or no obj*]
(*Finance*) to put more capital into a business or change the way the capital is held: *The banks have been recapitalized with $33 billion in new funds.*
▶ **recapitalization**, **-isation** /ˌriːˌkæpɪtəlaɪˈzeɪʃn; *AmE* -ləˈz-/ *noun* [C,U]: *a recapitalization plan designed to help the firm cut its debt*

recd *abbr*
a short way of writing **received**

recede /rɪˈsiːd/ *verb* [no obj]
to become smaller, weaker, etc: *Expectations of an imminent cut in interest rates have receded* (= it is less likely). ◊ *Revenues have been put under pressure because the market in general is receding.*

★ **receipt** /rɪˈsiːt/ *noun, verb*
● *noun*

SEE ALSO: **debit receipt, delivery ~, depositary ~, depository ~, trust ~, warehouse ~**

1 (*also* **'sales slip**) [C] a piece of paper that shows that goods or services have been paid for: *Can I have a receipt, please?* ◊ *Make sure you keep all your receipts.* See note at INVOICE
◊ *to ask for/file/keep/need a receipt • to give sb/ issue/make out/sign a receipt • a credit-card/sales receipt*
2 (*Accounting*) **receipts** [pl.] money that a business, bank or government receives: *Receipts from tourism fell by about one third.* ◊ *The economic slowdown has reduced tax receipts.*
◊ *cash/export/tax receipts*
3 (*formal*) [U] the act of receiving sth, or the fact of sth having been received: *Businesses should acknowledge receipt of an order without delay.* ◊ *Items should be paid for within 14 days of receipt.* → PAYMENT
● *verb* [+ obj] (*often* **receipted**, *used as an adjective*)
1 to sign or mark a bill to say that it has been paid: *a receipted hotel bill*
2 to give a **receipt** for money or goods: *What is the procedure for receipting goods?*

receivable /rɪˈsiːvəbl/ *adjective* [not usually before noun]

SEE ALSO: **accounts receivable, bills ~, note ~**

(*Accounting*) for which money has not yet been received: *Net interest receivable fell from $22m to $12m.*

receivables /rɪˈsiːvəblz/ *noun* [pl.]
(*Accounting*) money that is owed to a business: *You*

receiver /rɪˈsiːvə(r)/ *noun* [C]

1 (*Law*) (*also* **ofˌficial reˈceiver**) a person who is chosen by a court to manage the financial affairs of a company that is BANKRUPT, to sell its assets in order to pay its debts, and to close it: *The receiver said he had the legal duty to obtain the best price for the business.* → idiom at CALL *verb*

2 the part of a telephone that you hold close to your mouth and ear: *The speaker connects easily to your telephone receiver.*

○ *to* **lift/pick up/put down** *the receiver*

receivership /rɪˈsiːvəʃɪp; *AmE* -vərʃ-/ *noun* [U,C]

(*Law*) a situation where the financial affairs of a company are being controlled by a **receiver**, because it has no money: *Five hundred jobs were lost last year when the company went into receivership.* ◇ *Her company has been in receivership for six months now.*

○ *be in/be placed in/go into* receivership

reˈceiving ˌorder *noun* [C]

(*Law*) in the UK, an order from a court placing a company in the control of a **receiver**

★**reception** /rɪˈsepʃn/ *noun*

1 [U] (*especially BrE*) the place inside the entrance of a hotel, an office building, etc. where guests or visitors go first when they arrive: *We arranged to meet in reception at 6.30.* ◇ *You can leave a message with reception.* ◇ (*AmE, BrE*) *She got a job on the reception desk.* → FRONT DESK

2 [C] a formal social occasion to welcome sb or celebrate sth: *a civic/an official reception* ◇ *We hosted a reception for 75 guests.*

3 [sing.] the type of welcome that people give to sb/sth: *The new products got a cool reception from customers.*

4 [U] the quality of radio, television and telephone signals that are broadcast: *My cellphone has poor reception outside the city.* ◇ *bad/good/poor reception*

★**receptionist** /rɪˈsepʃənɪst/ *noun* [C]

a person who works in a hotel, an office building, etc. answering the telephone and dealing with people when they arrive

★**recession** /rɪˈseʃn/ *noun* [C,U]

(*Economics*) a difficult period in the economy of a country or group of countries, when there is less trade and industrial activity than usual and more people are unemployed: *The economy is now officially in recession.* ◇ *The manufacturing sector is recovering slowly from last year's recession.*

→ DEPRESSION, DOUBLE DIP—Picture at BUSINESS CYCLE

○ *to* **be hit by/be in/enter/fall into/slip (back) into** *(a) recession* • *to* **emerge from/recover from** *a recession* • *(a)* **deep/prolonged/severe** *recession* • *(a)* **mild/shallow** *recession* • *(a)* **global/world** *recession*

recessionary /rɪˈseʃnri; *AmE* -neri/ *adjective* [usually before noun]

(*Economics*) likely to cause a **recession** or typical of one: *Recessionary pressures around the world have slowed sales growth and cut profits.*

recharge /ˌriːˈtʃɑːdʒ; *AmE* -ˈtʃɑːrdʒ/ *verb* [+ obj or no obj]

to fill a battery with electrical power; to be filled with electrical power: *You may need to recharge your phone every two days.* ▶ **reˈchargeable** *adjective*: *rechargeable batteries*

IDM **recharge your ˈbatteries** to get back your energy by resting for a while: *I need a week off work to recharge my batteries.*

recipient /rɪˈsɪpiənt/ *noun* [C] (*formal*)

a person who receives sth: *The country is one of the biggest recipients of foreign investment.* ◇ *email/loan recipients*

reciprocal /rɪˈsɪprəkl/ *adjective* [usually before noun]

involving two people or groups who agree to help each other or behave in the same way as each other: *In case of a disaster, we have a reciprocal arrangement with another firm that uses the same computing systems.* ◇ *reciprocal trade between the EU and Chile* ▶ **reciprocity** /ˌresɪˈprɒsəti; *AmE* -ˈprɑːs-/ *noun* [U]

reclaim /rɪˈkleɪm/ *verb* [+ obj]

1 to get back sth that has been taken from you, that you have lost or that is owed to you: *The company wants to expand and reclaim its markets.* ◇ *He should be able to reclaim his $500 deposit.*

2 to make land that is naturally too wet or too dry suitable to be built on, farmed, etc: *The airport is built on reclaimed land.*

3 to obtain materials from waste products so that they can be used again → RECYCLE

▶ **reclamation** /ˌrekləˈmeɪʃn/ *noun* [U]: *land reclamation*

★**recognition** /ˌrekəɡˈnɪʃn/ *noun* [U]

SEE ALSO: brand recognition, optical character ~, speech ~, voice ~

1 (*Marketing*) the fact of knowing what sth is when you see it: *You don't need to spend a lot of money to gain recognition of your products and services.* ◇ *They quickly realised the brand had little name recognition in the US.*

2 the ability of a machine to recognize sth: *voice recognition for computers and the Internet* ◇ *face recognition technology*

3 praise and rewards for the work that sb does: *She gained little recognition for her work.*

4 the act of accepting that sth exists, is true, or is official: *the recognition of trade unions*

→ RECOGNIZE

ˌrecogˈnition ˌtest *noun* [C]

(*Marketing*) a test that is done after an advertisement has been shown to find out how well sb can remember the advertisement

★**recognize** , **-ise** /ˈrekəɡnaɪz/ *verb* [+ obj] (*not used in the continuous tenses*)

1 to know what sth is when you see it or remember who sb is: *Not everyone recognizes a clever idea when they see it.* ◇ *The logo is becoming a nationally recognized brand.*

2 (*often* **be recognized**) to praise and reward people for the work that they do; to think of sb/sth as good or important: *Every team member is recognized for their efforts.* ◇ *Hirshberg is recognized as a truly great designer.*

3 to accept sth officially: *The company refused to recognize the union.* ◇ *recognized qualifications*

4 (*Accounting*) to put a particular figure on sth or to show sth in a particular way in a set of financial records: *Barnes and Noble recognized a pre-tax gain of $22.4m.*

5 if a machine **recognizes** sb/sth, it identifies them and reacts in the correct way: *The new CD players can recognize a variety of formats.*

→ RECOGNITION

★**recommend** /ˌrekəˈmend/ *verb* [+ obj]

1 to tell sb that they should do sth, especially because you have expert knowledge: *The report recommended an $11 pay increase.* ◇ *We recommend that our shareholders vote in favour of the proposal.*

2 to tell sb that sth is good and useful: *80% of dentists recommend this product.* ◇ *The new restaurant comes highly recommended* (= a lot of people have praised it).

3 to suggest sb for a particular job or task because you think they would do it well: *At the meeting, the board will recommend an auditor.*

★ **recommendation** /ˌrekəmən'deɪʃn/ *noun*
1 [C] a suggestion about the best thing to do, especially by sb with expert knowledge: *The review's recommendations could have a big impact on many boardrooms.* ◇ *Merrill Lynch cut its recommendation on the stock from 'buy' to 'neutral'.*
2 [U] the act of telling sb that sb or sth is good, useful, suitable, etc: *26% of non-executive directors are appointed on the recommendation of family or friends.*
3 [C] a product that sb says is good: *The book is one of this week's recommendations.*

recompense /'rekəmpens/ *noun, verb (formal)*
● *noun* [U; sing.]
money that is given to a person as payment or because they have suffered in some way: *For those who have lost their savings, recompense looks unlikely.* SYN COMPENSATION
● *verb* [+ obj]
to give sb money as payment or because they have suffered in some way SYN COMPENSATE

reconcile /'rekənsaɪl/ *verb* [+ obj]
(*Accounting*) to make one set of financial records or figures agree with another: *Reconciling bank statements and cash accounts took a long time.*
▶ **reconciliation** /ˌrekənsɪli'eɪʃn/ *noun* [U]

reconcili'ation ˌstatement *(also* **ˌreconcili'ation)** *noun* [C]
(*Accounting*) a document that explains the differences between two sets of accounts → BANK RECONCILIATION

reconfigure /ˌriːkən'fɪɡə(r); *AmE* -'fɪɡjər/ *verb* [+ obj]
(*IT; Technical*) to change the way that sth is organized or arranged, especially computer equipment or a program: *It took 60 days to reconfigure the network.* ◇ *The factory space is designed to be reconfigured easily.*
▶ **reconfiguration** /ˌriːkənfɪɡə'reɪʃn; *AmE* -fɪɡjə'r-/ *noun* [C,U]

reconnect /ˌriːkə'nekt/ *verb* [+ obj or no obj]
to make a connection again between people or things that had stopped being connected: *I had to disconnect the modem and reconnect the phone.* ◇ *Reconnecting with your old company may be a good career move.* ▶ **reconnection** /ˌriːkə'nekʃn/ *noun* [C,U]

reconstruct /ˌriːkən'strʌkt/ *verb* [+ obj]
to build or make again sth that has been damaged or that no longer exists: *The reconstructed plant now employs over 2 000 people.*

reconstruction /ˌriːkən'strʌkʃn/ *noun* [U]
1 the process of changing or improving the condition of sth or the way it works; the process of putting sth back into the state it was in before: *a reconstruction and development programme* ◇ *the economic reconstruction of the country*
2 the process of changing the way a company is organized, usually because it has financial problems: *The $4 billion reconstruction will hand control of the company to its bankers.*
→ RESTRUCTURE

★ **record** *noun, verb*
● *noun* /'rekɔːd; *AmE* 'rekərd/

SEE ALSO: **attendance record, employer of ~, holder of ~, owner of ~, shareholder of ~, stockholder of ~, track ~**

1 [C] a written account of sth that is kept so that it can be looked at and used in the future: *You should keep an accurate record of your expenses.* ◇ *You can update your records online.* ◇ *Our records show that you have been a customer here since 2001.* ◇ *It has been one of the worst years on record for the tourist industry.*
➊ to **keep/update** a record (of sth) • records **contain/ show/suggest** sth • **accounting/administrative/ financial/personnel/tax** records
2 [C] the best result or the highest or lowest level that has ever been reached: *UK consumers have set a new record for spending on credit cards.* ◇ *This year the company has enjoyed record sales.* ◇ *Shares reached a record low* (= the lowest level ever) *of 150 000 yen in October.*
➊ to **break/hit/hold/set** a record • a record **high/level/ low/number**
3 [sing.] the facts that are known about sb/sth's past behaviour, character, achievements, etc: *The airline has a good safety record.* ◇ *The company has a poor record on environmental issues.* ◇ *When it comes to quality, our record speaks for itself* (= shows our quality clearly).
➊ a **good/**an **impressive/**a **proven/strong** record • a **bad/poor** record • to **have/keep/maintain** a record
IDM **(just) for the 'record** used to show that you want what you are saying to be officially written down and remembered ˌoff the 'record if you tell sb sth **off the record**, it is not yet official and you do not want them to repeat it publicly **put/place sth on (the) 'record; be/go on (the) 'record (as saying ...)** to say sth publicly or officially so that it may be written down and repeated: *He didn't want to go on the record as either praising or criticizing the proposal.*
● *verb* /rɪ'kɔːd; *AmE* rɪ'kɔːrd/ [+ obj]
1 to keep a permanent account of facts or events by writing them down, storing them in a computer, etc: *You should record all your expenses during your trip.* ◇ *The accounts department has changed the ways in which foreign sales are recorded.* → LOG *verb* (1)
2 to show a particular amount of profit or loss, or a particular number of sth: *The bank recorded a net loss of €55 million for the year.* ◇ *The dollar recorded its eleventh drop in twelve days.*

'**record-ˌbreaking** *adjective* [only before noun]
bigger, better, etc. than has ever been done before: *The deal was said to be worth a record-breaking $80 million.* ◇ *There have been record-breaking sales figures in the last few months.*

'**record date** *noun* [C]
(*Finance*) the date when a shareholder must own shares in order to be able to vote at a meeting, receive a DIVIDEND (= money paid to shareholders), etc.

re,corded de'livery *(BrE)* *(AmE* **ˌcertified 'mail)** *noun* [U]
a method of sending mail in which the sender is given a note to say it has been posted and the person receiving it has to sign a form to say it has been delivered: *The original documents were sent by recorded delivery.* → REGISTERED MAIL

'**record-ˌkeeping** *noun* [U]
the job or process of storing documents, files, information, etc. in an office

recoup /rɪ'kuːp/ *verb* [+ obj]
to get back money that has been spent or lost: *The company could take seven years to recoup its investment.* ◇ *The dollar recouped early losses to edge higher against the euro.* SYN RECOVER

recourse /rɪ'kɔːs; *AmE* 'riːkɔːrs/ *noun*

SEE ALSO: **non-recourse, without recourse**

1 (*formal*) [U; sing.] the fact of using sth that can provide help in a difficult situation; the person or

thing that you use for help: *The business was stabilized **without recourse to** (= without using) external financing.*
2 (*Law*) [U] the legal right to claim money from sb for a loss, injury, etc. that they have caused: *You have no recourse **against** the seller if the goods are faulty.*

★ **recover** /rɪˈkʌvə(r)/ *verb*
1 [no obj] to improve and begin to return to a normal position or level after a period of difficulty: *The market is recovering from its 20-year low.* ◇ *She made two big mistakes and her business has never recovered.*
2 [+ obj] to get back money that has been spent or lost: *Investors have formed an action group to recover their lost money.* ◇ *The company has set itself the target of recovering its investment within five years.* [SYN] RECOUP
3 (*Law*) [+ obj] **recover costs/damages** to obtain money by a legal process because of loss or injury that you have suffered: *There have been delays in recovering damages from the supplier for faulty machines.*
4 [+ obj] to get oil, minerals, etc. from the ground

recoverable /rɪˈkʌvərəbl/ *adjective*
1 used to describe money that can be got back after it has been spent or lost: *Travel expenses will be recoverable from the company.* ◇ *Much of the cost of damage from the flooding will not be recoverable.* [OPP] IRRECOVERABLE
2 (*Law*) used to describe money that can be obtained by sb by a legal process, for example if they have been injured: *recoverable costs/damages*
3 **recoverable** oil, minerals, etc. can be taken from the ground: *Surveys have shown there could be about 100 million barrels of recoverable oil.*

recovery /rɪˈkʌvəri/ *noun* (*plural* **recoveries**)

SEE ALSO: **bad debt recovery, disaster recovery**

1 [U; C, usually sing.] the process of improving or becoming strong again: *There are no signs yet of an economic recovery.* ◇ *a recovery **in** consumer spending* ◇ *The company's recovery plan will be unveiled at a meeting in New York.*
2 [U] the process or fact of getting back sth, for example money that you are owed: *The country's poor legal system has proved to be an obstacle to debt recovery.*
3 [U] the process of obtaining oil, minerals, etc. from the ground

reˈcovery ˌperiod *noun* [C, usually sing.]
(*Accounting*) the time it will take for the profit produced by an asset to be equal to the amount invested in it [SYN] PAYBACK PERIOD

★ **recruit** /rɪˈkruːt/ *verb, noun*
● *verb*
1 (*HR*) [+ obj *or* no obj] to find new people to join a company or an organization: *We need to pay top salaries to recruit and retain the best people.* ◇ *200 new employees have been recruited.* ◇ *She's responsible for recruiting at all levels.* ◇ *a recruiting company* See note at EMPLOY
2 [+ obj] to persuade sb to do sth, especially to help you in some way: *We are trying to recruit new customers in the 16-20 age group.* ◇ *He recruited investors to fund the project.*
▶ **reˈcruiter** *noun* [C]
● *noun* [C]
(*HR*) a person who joins a company or an organization: *attempts to attract graduate recruits to the oil industry*

★ **recruitment** /rɪˈkruːtmənt/ *noun*

SEE ALSO: **e-recruitment**

1 (*HR*) [U] the act or the process of finding new people to join a company or an organization: *the*

recruitment of top executives ◇ *staff recruitment* ◇ *a recruitment company/agency*
2 (*HR*) [C] a person who has been chosen to join a company or an organization; an occasion when sb is chosen: *Twenty-one recruitments have been carried out so far this year, of which ten were new posts.*
3 [U] the act of persuading sb to do sth for you: *We are involved in the recruitment of people to take part in our market research.*

reˈcruitment fair = JOB FAIR

recuperate /rɪˈkuːpəreɪt/ *verb* (*formal*)
1 [no obj] to improve and begin to return to a normal position or level after a period of difficulty: *I expect the stock to recuperate in the long term.*
2 [+ obj] to get back money that has been spent or lost: *It said the state would recuperate its investment by 2011.* [SYN] RECOVER

recurring /rɪˈkɜːrɪŋ/ *adjective* [usually before noun] happening more than once, or a number of times: *Recurring revenues from services such as maintenance are growing.* → NON-RECURRING
● *recurring **costs/expenses/profit/revenue***

recycle /ˌriːˈsaɪkl/ *verb* [+ obj *or* no obj]
to put things that have already been used through special processes so that they can be used again: *The UK has a target of recycling 25% of all waste by 2006.* ◇ *envelopes made from recycled paper*
▶ **recyclable** /ˌriːˈsaɪkləbl/ *adjective*: *We use 100% recyclable packaging.* , **reˈcycling** *noun* [U]: *The UK lags far behind its European neighbours in recycling levels.* ◇ *a recycling business/plant*

red /red/ *noun*
[IDM] **be, remain, etc. in the ˈred; move into, return to, etc. the ˈred 1** to be operating at a loss; to be spending more than you earn: *The communications group is €70 billion in the red.* ◇ *My bank account is in the red this month.* **2** (*Stock Exchange*) if markets or shares are in **the red**, they are lower in value than they were previously: *Most shares dipped into the red yesterday although trade was light.*
[OPP] BE, REMAIN, ETC. IN THE BLACK, MOVE INTO, RETURN TO, ETC. THE BLACK → idiom at HAEMORRHAGE *verb*

ˌred-ˈcircling *noun* [U]
(*HR*) the situation when a job has been moved to a lower grade with a lower rate of pay, but the people who are already doing that work are still paid the old rate. New employees will be paid at the lower rate. ▶ **ˌred-ˈcircle** *verb* [+ obj]

redeem /rɪˈdiːm/ *verb* [+ obj]
1 (*Finance*) to pay back the full amount of money that you owe; to pay a debt: *There are fears the firm may lack funds to redeem its debt.* [SYN] PAY OFF
2 (*Finance*) to exchange shares, bonds, etc. for money: *The shares can be redeemed at any time after March 4.*
3 (*Commerce*) to exchange a VOUCHER (= a printed piece of paper that can be used instead of money to pay for sth) for goods or services: *The gift certificates can be redeemed at any of our hotels.*
4 to get back a valuable object from sb by paying them back the money you borrowed from them in exchange for the object → PAWN *verb*

redeemable /rɪˈdiːməbl/ *adjective*
1 (*Finance*) **redeemable** shares, bonds, etc. can be bought back for money by the company that issues (= sells) them: *The bonds are redeemable at their face value after five years.*
● *redeemable **securities/shares/stock***

2 (*Commerce*) able to be exchanged for goods, services or money: *The points you earn on your loyalty card are redeemable for gifts.*

redefine /ˌriːdɪˈfaɪn/ *verb* [+ obj]
to change the nature or limits of sth; to make people consider sth in a new way: *Technology is constantly redefining the nature of work.* ◇ *Some of the most demanding top jobs might have to change or be redefined.*
O *to redefine a* **brand/business/job/problem**
▸ **redefinition** /ˌriːdefɪˈnɪʃn/ *noun* [U,C]

redemption /rɪˈdempʃn/ *noun* [U,C]
(*Finance*)
1 an occasion when money invested in shares, bonds, etc. is paid back to the investor: *£52 billion in bond redemptions is due later this year.* ◇ *If you redeem your shares early, you may pay a redemption fee.*
2 the act of paying back a loan or MORTGAGE: *Mortgage customers should be clearly informed of penalties such as redemption charges.*

re'demption date = MATURITY (1)

re'demption yield *noun* [C]
(*Finance*) the amount of money that an investor will get back from a bond if it is kept until the end of its life (**maturity**), usually expressed as a percentage **SYN** YIELD TO MATURITY

redeploy /ˌriːdɪˈplɔɪ/ *verb* [+ obj] (*formal*)
1 (*HR*) to give employees a different job to do or move them to a different place of work: *The bank said it was working to redeploy staff in other roles.* **SYN** TRANSFER
2 (*Finance*) to use money or resources for a different purpose: *We are selling assets, leasing them back and redeploying the capital within the business.*
▸ **,rede'ployment** *noun* [U]: *the redeployment of staff/resources*

redesign /ˌriːdɪˈzaɪn/ *verb* [+ obj]
to design a product, service, system, etc. again in a different way: *The Seattle-based company has redesigned its logo.* ◇ *Engineers completely redesigned the way the car's body was manufactured.*
▸ **,rede'sign** *noun* [U,C]: *She recommended a complete redesign of the company's website.*

redevelop /ˌriːdɪˈveləp/ *verb* [+ obj]
(*Property*) to change an area by building new houses, roads, factories, etc: *The site will be redeveloped for mixed residential and business use.*
▸ **,rede'velopment** *noun* [U,C]: *New office and retail space will form part of the redevelopment.*

'red-eye (*also* **,red-eye 'flight**) *noun* [C, usually sing.] (*informal*)
a flight on a plane at night, on which you do not get enough sleep

,red 'herring = PATHFINDER PROSPECTUS

,red-'hot *adjective*
extremely strong, active, successful, etc: *Interest rate rises have failed to cool the red-hot housing market.*

,red 'ink *noun* [U] (*AmE*)
used to talk about a situation in which a business is losing a lot of money: *It was the company's third consecutive quarter of red ink.* ◇ *The health-care industry is bleeding red ink* (= losing a lot of money). **NOTE** In the past, red ink was used to show losses in financial records.

redirect /ˌriːdəˈrekt; -dɪ-; -daɪ-/ *verb* [+ obj]
1 to use money, resources, etc. in a different way or for a different purpose: *We redirected funds to a new marketing campaign.*

2 to send sth such as mail, phone calls, etc. to a different address: *You can have calls redirected to your mobile phone.* ◇ *Complaints are being redirected to the sales manager.*

★**redistribute** /ˌriːdɪˈstrɪbjuːt; ˌriːˈdɪs-/ *verb* [+ obj]
(*Economics*) to share money or resources in a different way: *Raising taxes will redistribute wealth more fairly.* ◇ *The amount of work is the same, but it has been redistributed among more people.*
▸ **redistribution** /ˌriːdɪstrɪˈbjuːʃn/ *noun* [U; sing.]

redistributive /ˌriːdɪˈstrɪbjətɪv/ *adjective* [usually before noun]
(*Economics*) **redistributive** policies or actions use a country's tax system to give a more equal share to poorer people: *Income tax generally has a redistributive effect.*

redline /ˈredlaɪn/ *verb* [+ obj] (*AmE*) (*informal*)
to refuse to provide loans, insurance or other financial services to people or businesses in particular areas: ▸ **'redlining** *noun* [U]: *It is claimed that the company knew about and tolerated redlining.*

redraft /ˌriːˈdrɑːft; *AmE* -ˈdræft/ *verb* [+ obj]
to write a document, a letter, etc. again in order to improve it or make changes: *He was asked to redraft his paper.* ▸ **redraft** /ˈriːdrɑːft; *AmE* -dræft/ *noun* [C]

redress *verb, noun*
● **verb** /rɪˈdres/ [+ obj] (*formal*)
to correct sth that is unfair or wrong: *They will attempt to redress the budget deficit next year.*
IDM **redress the 'balance** to make a situation equal or fair again
● **noun** /rɪˈdres; ˈriːdres/ [U]
(*Law*) a legal solution to a problem, especially sth that you should get for sth wrong that has happened to you or harm that you have suffered: *She is seeking legal redress for unfair dismissal.* **SYN** COMPENSATION, REMEDY

,red 'tape *noun* [U]
official rules that seem more complicated than is necessary and prevent things being done quickly: *The government said it would cut red tape to allow farmers to boost exports.* **SYN** BUREAUCRACY

★**reduce** /rɪˈdjuːs; *AmE* -ˈduːs/ *verb* [+ obj]
reduce sth (from sth) (to sth) | **reduce sth (by sth)**
to make sth less or smaller in price, quantity, size, etc: *The company has reduced costs and cut its workforce.* ◇ *Losses were reduced from €4.7m to €2.7m.* ◇ *The number of employees is likely to be reduced by 10%.* ◇ *You may be able to work reduced hours while your children are very young.* **SYN** CUT **OPP** INCREASE

re,ducing 'balance ,method (*also* de,clining 'balance ,method, di,minishing 'balance ,method) *noun* [sing.]
(*Accounting*) a way of reducing the value of (**depreciating**) an asset in a company's financial records in which the amount taken from the asset's value decreases each year. The value of the asset (its **book value**) is reduced by a fixed percentage each year. → DOUBLE-DECLINING BALANCE METHOD, STRAIGHT-LINE METHOD, SUM OF THE DIGITS METHOD—Picture at DEPRECIATION

★**reduction** /rɪˈdʌkʃn/ *noun*
1 [C,U] an act of making sth smaller or less; the state of being made smaller or less: *a $300 million reduction in costs* ◇ *There has been some reduction in unemployment.*
O *a* **drastic/significant/slight/substantial** *reduction* ◆ *to* **achieve/make/produce** *a reduction*
2 [C] the amount by which sth is made cheaper to buy: *There is a €100 reduction for a child sharing a room with two adults.* ◇ *price reductions*

● **big/huge/massive** reductions ◆ **to ask for/get/ receive** a reduction ◆ **to give/make/offer** a reduction

reduction/cashback/deduction/ discount/rebate/refund

Discount, **cashback**, **rebate** and **reduction** can all be used to describe an amount by which a price is reduced. Compare their use in the following examples:

- We offer a 10% **discount on** cash purchases.
- There's a €50 **reduction for** guests staying more than 7 nights.
- (BrE) You'll get 1% **cashback on** all purchases with your credit card (= the credit-card company will pay 1% of the bill into your account).
- (AmE) The computer sells for $900 **after rebate** (= after the discount is taken away).

A **refund** is not a reduction in price, but a return of the price or part of it: If not entirely satisfied, return the goods within 14 days for a full refund.

A **rebate** and **refund** can also be an amount that is paid back to you because you paid too much: a tax rebate/refund. A **deduction** is taken off the amount you owe before you pay it: You are allowed a tax deduction for money given to charity.

★ **redundancy** /rɪ'dʌndənsi/ noun [U,C] (plural **redundancies**) (BrE)

SEE ALSO: **collective redundancy**

(HR) a situation when a person loses their job because there is no more work available for them; jobs lost in this way: Thousands of factory workers are facing redundancy in the New Year. ◇ Workers will be offered €5 000 to take voluntary redundancy. ◇ There could be as many as 32 000 redundancies, 16% of the workforce. ◇ The employees are entitled to redundancy payments. ◇ 200 workers have been issued with redundancy notices. → LAY-OFF

● **to announce/avoid/make** redundancies ◆ **to accept/ face/take** redundancy ◆ **compulsory/forced/ involuntary/voluntary** redundancy/redundancies ◆ **large-scale/mass/sweeping** redundancies

★ **redundant** /rɪ'dʌndənt/ adjective (BrE)
(HR) without a job because your employer has no more work available for you: the cost of retraining redundant employees
IDM **be made re'dundant** to lose your job because your employer no longer has work for you: He was made redundant after 40 years with the same company. See note at DISMISS

,re-engi'neer (also spelled **reengineer**, especially in AmE) verb
1 [+ obj or no obj] to change the structure of a company or an organization in order to make it more efficient: He was hired to re-engineer the struggling company. ◇ The challenge is in re-engineering the way we do our business.
2 [+ obj] to change the way a product is made so that it works better: The car was re-engineered for the European market.
▶ ,re-engi'neering (also spelled **reengineering**, especially in AmE) noun [U]: a corporate re-engineering effort

,re-e'valuate (also spelled **reevaluate**, especially in AmE) verb [+ obj or no obj]
to think about sth again, especially in order to form a new opinion about it: We have been forced to re-evaluate our business strategies. ◇ My job has been re-evaluated and upgraded. ▶ ,re-evalu'ation (also spelled **reevaluation**, especially in AmE) noun [U]

re-export (also spelled **reexport**, especially in AmE) noun, verb
● **noun** /,riː'ekspɔːt; AmE -'ekspɔːrt/ [C, usually pl.]
(Trade) goods that are imported into a country and then exported, often without being changed at all: Drugs companies are clamping down on illegal re-exports of cut-price medicines.
● **verb** /,riːɪk'spɔːt; AmE -ɪk'spɔːrt/ [+ obj]
to import goods into a country and then export them, either in a different form or without changing them at all: Imported parts are assembled and then re-exported.
▶ **re-exportation** /,riːɪkspɔː'teɪʃn; AmE -ɪkspɔːr't-/ noun [U, C]

ref. abbr
a short way of writing **reference** (= a set of letters or numbers that identifies a person, letter, etc.): our ref. 3498

refer /rɪ'fɜː(r)/ verb (-rr-)
PHRV **re'fer to sb/sth (as sth)** to mention or speak about sb/sth: I refer to your letter of May 26th. ◇ I promised not to refer to the matter again. ◇ Those were the days when workers were referred to as 'hands'. **re'fer to sb/sth 1** to describe or be connected to sb/sth: The figures referred to data for the previous month. ◇ What does the term 'economic demand' refer to? **2** to look at sth or ask a person for information: She gave her 40-minute presentation without once referring to her notes. ◇ to refer to a dictionary **re'fer sb/sth to sb/sth** to send sb/sth to sb/sth for help, advice or a decision: All three bids will be referred to the competition commission.

referee /,refə'riː/ noun, verb
● **noun** [C]
1 (BrE) (also '**reference**, AmE, BrE) a person who gives information about your character and ability, usually in a letter, for example when you are applying for a job: Please give the names of three referees. ◇ Would you act as a referee for me?
2 a person who is asked to settle a disagreement: to act as a referee between the parties involved
3 a person who reads and checks the quality of a technical article before it is published
● **verb** [+ obj]
1 to help to settle disagreements between people or groups: The panel referees all takeover battles.
2 to read and check the quality of a technical article before it is published → REVIEW

reference /'refrəns/ noun, verb
● **noun** [C]

SEE ALSO: **bank reference, banker's ~, terms of ~**

1 (abbr **ref.**) a set of letters or numbers that identifies a person, letter, etc: Please quote reference ZK42. ◇ Put the **reference number** in the subject line of your email.
● **to give/quote** a reference number
2 a letter written by sb who knows you, giving information about your character and abilities, especially to a new employer: We will take up references after the interview. ◇ They always carry out in-depth **reference checks**.
● **to ask for/follow up/take up** references ◆ **to give (sb)/provide (sb with)/write (sb)** a reference
3 (especially AmE) = REFEREE noun (1)
IDM **in/with 'reference to** (formal, usually used in written English) used to say what you are talking or writing about: With reference to your letter of July 22 ...
● **verb** [+ obj]
to refer to sth; to provide sth with a **reference** number: Each order has a unique number and can be referenced at any time.

'reference group *noun* [C]
1 a group that gives advice to an organization, the government, etc. on a particular issue: *a marketing/ transport reference group*
2 (*Marketing*) a group that people compare themselves to and that influences their choices and opinions → CONSUMER GROUP (2)
3 (*Technical*) a group that another group is compared with when you are analysing data to study the effects of sth: *This low-income group is the baseline reference group in our model.* SYN CONTROL *noun* (6)

referral /rɪˈfɜːrəl/ *noun* [U,C]
the act of recommending sb or sth; a person or an organization that has been recommended: *positive/ negative referrals* ◇ *Employee referrals are their most useful recruiting method.*

re'ferral ˌmarketing = VIRAL MARKETING

re ˌfer to 'drawer *phrase* (*abbr* RD)
words written on a cheque when a bank refuses to pay it, usually because there is not enough money in the account

refinance /ˌriːˈfaɪnæns/ *verb* [+ obj or no obj]
(*Finance*) to borrow money, usually at a lower rate of interest, in order to pay a debt or loan: *Consumers can save money by refinancing mortgages at lower interest rates.* ▶ **re'financing** *noun* [U,C]: *debt/mortgage refinancing* ◇ *a refinancing deal/ package/proposal* → REFUNDING

refine /rɪˈfaɪn/ *verb* [+ obj]
1 to make a substance pure by taking other substances out of it: *The company refines crude oil from Venezuela.* ◇ *refined products*
2 to improve sth by making small changes to it: *The design has been refined.* ▶ **re'fining** *noun* [U]

refinery /rɪˈfaɪnəri/ *noun* [C] (*plural* **refineries**)
a factory where a substance such as oil is REFINED (= made pure)

refit /ˌriːˈfɪt/ *verb* [+ obj] (**-tt-**)
to repair equipment, furniture, machinery, etc. in a building, shop/store, ship, etc. or replace with new: *Stores will be refitted with wider aisles and better lighting.* ▶ **refit** /ˈriːfɪt/ *noun* [C]: *a programme of store refits*

reflate /ˌriːˈfleɪt/ *verb* [+ obj or no obj]
(*Economics*) if a government or a national bank **reflates** the economy it increases or brings back economic demand by lowering taxes, increasing government spending, lowering interest rates, etc: *The government will take steps to reflate the economy.* ◇ *Debt loads are reduced as the economy reflates.* → DEFLATE, INFLATE
▶ **reflation** /ˌriːˈfleɪʃn/ *noun* [U]: *global reflation* **reflationary** /ˌriːˈfleɪʃnri; *AmE* -neri/ *adjective*: *reflationary policies*

refocus /ˌriːˈfəʊkəs; *AmE* -ˈfoʊ-/ *verb* [+ obj or no obj] (**-s-** *or* **-ss-**)
to give your attention or effort to sth new or different: *A new CEO has been appointed to refocus the company.* ◇ *The business has cut jobs and refocused on core areas.*

★ **reform** /rɪˈfɔːm; *AmE* rɪˈfɔːrm/ *noun, verb*
● *noun* [U,C]
change that is made to an organization, law, social system, etc. in order to improve or correct it: *reform of the labour market* ◇ *much-needed reforms in the banking sector* ◇ *Businesses have welcomed the new tax reform bill.*
  ❍ *corporate/economic/financial/structural reform* ◆ *essential/far-reaching/fundamental/sweeping reforms* ◆ *to carry out/introduce reforms* ◆ *to call for/discuss/plan/propose reforms*

● *verb* [+ obj]
to improve a system, an organization, a law, etc. by making changes to it: *proposals to reform the tax system* ◇ *The law needs to be reformed.* ▶ **re'former** *noun* [C]

refresh /rɪˈfreʃ/ *verb* [+ obj or no obj]
(*IT*) to get the most recent information, for example on a website or Internet page: *Click here to refresh this document.* ◇ *The page refreshes automatically.*

re'fresher course (*also* **re'fresher**, *especially in AmE*) *noun* [C]
a short period of training to improve your skills or to teach you about new ideas and developments in your job

★ **refund** *noun, verb*
(*Accounting, Commerce*)
● *noun* /ˈriːfʌnd/ [C]
a sum of money that is paid back to you, especially because you paid too much or because you returned goods to a shop/store: *a tax refund* ◇ *Return the product to the place of purchase for a full refund.* See note at REDUCTION
  ❍ *to claim/demand/receive a refund* ◆ *to make/offer/ pay a refund*
● *verb* /rɪˈfʌnd/ [+ obj]
refund sth (to sb) | **refund sb sth** to give sb their money back, especially because they have paid too much or because they are not satisfied with sth they bought: *Tickets cannot be exchanged or money refunded.* ◇ *We will refund you your money in full.* SYN REIMBURSE
▶ **re'fundable** *adjective*: *a refundable deposit* ◇ *Tickets are not refundable.*

refunding /ˌriːˈfʌndɪŋ/ *noun* [C,U]
(*Finance*) the act of borrowing money, usually at a lower rate of interest, in order to pay a debt or loan SYN REFINANCING

refurbish /ˌriːˈfɜːbɪʃ; *AmE* -ˈfɜːrb-/ *verb* [+ obj]
to clean and decorate a building, an office, a shop/ store, etc. in order to make it more attractive or useful: *The store has been extensively refurbished.*
▶ **re'furbishment** *noun* [U,C]: *The hotel is closed for refurbishment.*

reg *abbr*
used as a short way of writing words such as **regular, regulation, registered**, etc.

regain /rɪˈɡeɪn/ *verb* [+ obj]
to get back sth you no longer have: *The government needs to regain control of the economy.* ◇ *We believe we are regaining our position in the local market.* ◇ *Oil companies have managed to regain lost ground* (= have started to be successful again).

regard /rɪˈɡɑːd; *AmE* rɪˈɡɑːrd/ *noun* [C]
regards [pl.]
used to send good wishes to sb at the end of a letter, or when asking sb to give your good wishes to another person who is not present: *With kind regards, Yours...*
IDM **in/with regard to sb/sth** (*formal*) (often used in letters, etc.) concerning sb/sth: *I am writing with regard to your application...*

regarding /rɪˈɡɑːdɪŋ; *AmE* -ˈɡɑːrd-/ *preposition*
(often used in letters, etc.) concerning sb/sth; about sb/sth: *I refer to my previous letter regarding your overdue payment...*

regd *abbr*
a short way of writing **registered**

★ **region** /ˈriːdʒən/ *noun* [C]
a large area of land such as a part of the world or one of the areas that a country is divided into: *The Kansai region contributes 19% of Japan's GDP.* ◇ *the economic downturn in the Asia-Pacific region*

IDM **in the region of** used when you are giving a number, price, etc. to show that it is not exact: *He earns somewhere in the region of €50 000.*
SYN APPROXIMATELY

★ **regional** /ˈriːdʒənl/ *adjective* [usually before noun]
1 used to describe a business or an organization that operates in a particular part of a country rather than the whole country: *one of Spain's biggest regional banks* ◇ *a regional airline/airport* (= one that operates within a country rather than between countries)
2 connected with a particular part of a country or of the world: *a regional newspaper* ◇ *The diagram represents our network at a local, regional and national level.* ◇ *a regional manager*
▶ **regionally** /ˈriːdʒənəli/ *adverb*: *regionally based television companies*

,**regional 'jet** *noun* [C]
(*Transport*) a small plane that is mainly used for local flights over short distances: *the fast-growing regional jet industry*

★ **register** /ˈredʒɪstə(r)/ *verb, noun*
● *verb*
1 [+ obj *or* no obj] to record your/sb's/sth's name on an official list: *to register a company/trademark/design* ◇ *Customers can register online.* ◇ *I've registered with an employment agency.* ◇ *Fund managers may need to register as investment advisers.* ◇ *More than 200 000 subscribers have registered for the service.*
2 [+ obj] to show or record an amount or measurement: *The stock exchange has registered huge losses this week.* ◇ *Food stores had a good year, registering a 5% increase in sales.*
3 [+ obj] to make your interest or opinion known officially: *At least four potential buyers have registered an interest.*
4 [+ obj] (*usually* **be registered**) to send sth by mail, paying extra money to protect it against loss or damage: *Can I register this, please?* ◇ *a registered letter*
● *noun* [C]

SEE ALSO: **cash register, companies ~, property ~, share ~, shareholders' ~, transfer ~**

1 an official list or record of names, items, etc.; a book that contains such a list: *a national register of qualified engineers* ◇ *They have compiled a full register of assets.* ◇ *Could you sign the hotel register please?*
○ *to* **compile/draw up** *a register* ◆ *to* **appear on/be on** *a register* ◆ *to be* **struck off/taken off** *a register*
2 (*Commerce*) (*AmE*) = CASH REGISTER
→ idiom at RING *verb*

registered /ˈredʒɪstəd; *AmE* -tərd/ *adjective* (*abbr* **reg, regd**)
1 included on a legal or an official record (**register**): *a registered bank/charity* ◇ *the website's registered users* ◇ *We currently have a million registered customers.*
2 (*Finance*) **registered bond/security/share/stock** that has the name and address of the owner on a central record kept by the company that issued the bond or by its agent

,**registered 'capital** *noun* [U]
(*Finance*) the maximum amount of money that a company is allowed to raise by selling shares
SYN AUTHORIZED CAPITAL

,**registered 'company** *noun* [C]
1 in the UK, a company that is on the COMPANIES REGISTER → INCORPORATED
2 (*Stock Exchange*) (*AmE*) a company that is on the official list of the SECURITIES AND EXCHANGE COMMISSION and is able to issue shares

,**registered 'mail** (*BrE also* ,**registered 'post**) *noun* [U]
a method of sending a letter or package in which the person sending it can claim money if it arrives late or is lost or damaged → RECORDED DELIVERY

,**registered 'office** *noun* [C]
(*Law*) in the UK, the official address of a company which is recorded on the COMPANIES REGISTER

,**registered 'post** = REGISTERED MAIL

,**registered 'trademark** *noun* [C]
(*Law*) the sign or name of a product, etc. that is officially recorded and protected so that nobody else can use it, shown by the symbol ®

,**register of 'companies** = COMPANIES REGISTER

'**register of di'rectors' 'interests** *noun* [sing.]
(*Law*) in the UK, an official record that provides information on the number of shares in the company that each director owns

,**register of 'members** = SHAREHOLDERS' REGISTER

,**register of 'transfers** = TRANSFER REGISTER

registrar /ˌredʒɪˈstrɑː(r); ˈredʒɪstrɑː(r)/ *noun* [C]
a person or an organization whose job is to keep official records

,**Registrar of 'Companies** *noun* [C, usually sing.]
the official who is responsible for recording information on all companies in the UK

registration /ˌredʒɪˈstreɪʃn/ *noun* [U,C] (*abbr* **reg**)

SEE ALSO: **shelf registration**

the act of making an official record of sth/sb; a document showing this information: *Online registration is quick and easy—just fill in your details and choose a password.* ◇ *New car registrations rose 13.1% to a record 195 637 in July.* ◇ *a registration fee/card/form*

regis'tration ,statement *noun* [C]
(*Stock Exchange*) in the US, a document that a company must give to the SECURITIES AND EXCHANGE COMMISSION before it can sell shares, containing financial information that will help investors to judge the value of the company: *to file a registration statement with the commission*

registry /ˈredʒɪstri/ *noun* [C] (*plural* **registries**)

SEE ALSO: **Companies Registry, Land registry**

a place or an organization where official information is kept: *The American Registry for Internet Numbers*

,**Registry of 'Companies** = COMPANIES REGISTRY

regressive /rɪˈɡresɪv/ *adjective*
1 becoming or making sth less advanced: *The policy has been condemned as a regressive step.*
2 (*Economics*) used to describe a tax such as sales tax that has less effect on people with a high income than on people with a low income: *Tariffs are a regressive tax on smaller firms and the poor.*
OPP PROGRESSIVE

re'gret ,letter = LETTER OF REGRET

regroup /ˌriːˈɡruːp/ *verb* [+ obj *or* no obj]
to organize a group, team, etc. in a new way so that it is more efficient and more competitive: *It is time for the financial services industry to refocus and regroup.* ▶ ,**re'grouping** *noun* [U,C]

regs /regz/ *noun* [pl.] (*informal*)
a short form of **regulations**: *rules and regs*

regular /'regjələ(r)/ *adjective, noun*
● *adjective*
1 frequent and usually happening at the same time each day, week, month, year, etc: *The sales division holds regular meetings to exchange information.* ◇ *The equipment is checked* **on a regular basis.** ◇ *Back up your work* **at regular intervals.** OPP IRREGULAR
2 [only before noun] (about a person) often going to the same place or using the same service: *We offer a special service to our regular customers.*
3 [only before noun] usual: *My regular duties include dealing with customer complaints.* ◇ *It's important to follow the regular procedure.*
4 (*Commerce*) (*especially AmE*) of a standard size or type; ordinary: *Regular or large fries?* ◇ *The price has gone up on regular unleaded gasoline.*
5 (*Stock Exchange*) during the usual hours of trading for the stock exchange: *Shares ended at $9.25 in regular NASDAQ trade on Monday.*
6 lasting for all the normal working hours of the week; working during all the normal working hours: *She couldn't find any regular employment.* ◇ *The company has been forced to cut 1 500 regular staff and 500 contract workers.* SYN FULL-TIME, PERMANENT
● *noun* [C] (*informal*)
a customer who often goes to a particular shop/store, pub, restaurant, etc: *He's one of our regulars.*

★ **regulate** /'regjuleɪt/ *verb* [+ obj]
to control sth by means of rules or laws: *The activities of credit companies are regulated by law.* ◇ *The industry is still allowed to regulate itself.* ◇ *a regulating authority* OPP DEREGULATE

regulation /ˌregju'leɪʃn/ *noun, adjective*
● *noun*

SEE ALSO: **building regulation**

1 [C, usually pl.] (*abbr* **reg**) an official rule made by a government or some other authority: *accounting/environmental/financial/safety regulations* ◇ *the rules and regulations of corporate life*
2 [U] controlling sth by means of rules: *the voluntary regulation of the press* OPP DEREGULATION
● *adjective* [only before noun]
that must be worn or used according to the official rules: *in regulation uniform*

★ **regulator** /'regjuleɪtə(r)/ *noun* [C]
1 a person or an organization that officially controls an area of business or industry and makes sure that it is operating fairly: *a banking/energy/financial/securities regulator*
2 a device that automatically controls sth such as speed, temperature or pressure

★ **regulatory** /'regjələtəri; *AmE* -tɔːri/ *adjective*
[usually before noun]

SEE ALSO: **self-regulatory**

having the power to control an area of business or industry and make sure that it is operating fairly: *The deal is subject to regulatory approval.* ◇ *The merger has now passed regulatory hurdles.*
● *a regulatory* **agency/authority/body** ◆ *a regulatory* **examination/investigation/review** ◆ *to get regulatory* **approval/clearance** ◆ *regulatory* **hurdles/obstacles**

regulatory 'filing *noun* [C]
an official document such as a financial statement that a company must send to the organization that controls its industry (**the regulator**): *regulatory filings to the Securities and Exchange Commission*

reimburse /ˌriːɪm'bɜːs; *AmE* -'bɜːrs/ *verb* [+ obj]
to pay back money to sb which they have spent or lost: *We will reimburse any expenses incurred.* ◇ *You will be reimbursed* **for** *any loss or damage caused by our company.* SYN REFUND
▶ ˌreim'bursement *noun* [U,C]

reimport /ˌriːɪm'pɔːt; *AmE* -'pɔːrt/ *verb* [+ obj]
1 (*Trade*) to bring back into a country finished goods made from materials that have been exported, or goods that have previously been exported: *A Japanese car company plans to reimport minivans made at a plant in Canada.*
2 (*IT*) **reimport sth into sth** to copy a file, data, etc. back into a program: *You can quickly reimport this data into any database.*
▶ **reimport** /riː'ɪmpɔːt; *AmE* -pɔːrt/ *noun* [C,U]
reimportation /ˌriːɪmpɔː'teɪʃn; *AmE* -pɔːr't-/ *noun* [U]

rein /reɪn/ *noun, verb*
● *noun* **the reins** [pl.]
the state of being in control or the leader of sth: *It was time to* **hand over the reins** *of power* (= to give control to sb else).
IDM **give/allow sb/sth free/full 'rein; give/allow free/full 'rein to sth** to give sb complete freedom of action; to allow a feeling to be expressed freely: *The designer was given free rein.* → idiom at TIGHT
● *verb*
PHR V ˌrein sb/sth 'back; ˌrein sth 'in to start to control sb/sth more strictly: *Consumers are starting to rein back spending.*

reinforce /ˌriːɪn'fɔːs; *AmE* -'fɔːrs/ *verb* [+ obj]
(*Technical*) to make a structure or material stronger, especially by adding another material to it: *The floor of the warehouse had to be reinforced.* ◇ *reinforced concrete*

reinstate /ˌriːɪn'steɪt/ *verb* [+ obj] **reinstate sb/sth (in/as sth)**
1 to give back a job or position that had been taken away from sb: *He was reinstated in his post.*
2 to return sth to its previous position or status: *The 40-hour week is unlikely to be reinstated.* SYN RESTORE
▶ ˌrein'statement *noun* [U,C]

reinsurance /ˌriːɪn'ʃɔːrəns; -'ʃʊər-; *AmE* -'ʃʊr-/ *noun* [U]
(*Insurance*) the practice of one insurance company buying insurance from another company in order to share the risk of large claims that their clients could make: *a reinsurance agreement* ▶ **reinsure** /ˌriːɪn'ʃɔː; -'ʃʊər; *AmE* -'ʃʊr/ *verb* [+ obj] **reinsurer** /ˌriːɪn'ʃɔːrə(r); -'ʃʊər-; *AmE* -'ʃʊr-/ *noun* [C]

reinvent /ˌriːɪn'vent/ *verb* [+ obj]
to present yourself/sth in a new form or with a new image: *The company is trying to reinvent itself* **as** *a retailer of casual clothing.* ▶ **reinvention** /ˌriːɪn'venʃn/ *noun* [C,U]
IDM **reinvent the 'wheel** to waste time creating sth that already exists and works well

reinvest /ˌriːɪn'vest/ *verb* [+ obj or no obj]
to put profits that have been made on an investment back into the same investment or into a new one: *Our profits might be reinvested* **in** *stores and products.* ◇ *It's better to reinvest in the corporation than pay out a dividend.*
▶ ˌrein'vestment *noun* [U,C]

reissue /ˌriː'ɪʃuː/ *verb* [+ obj]
to make a new supply or a different form of sth available: *The book was recently reissued in paperback.* ◇ *He feels that the government should start reissuing the 30-year Treasury bond.* ▶ ˌre'issue *noun* [C,U]

(*used as a countable noun*)
in the US, a company that invests in and manages property on behalf of a number of investors; a share issued (= sold) by one of these companies: *to invest in REITs*

★ **reject** *verb, noun*
● *verb* /rɪ'dʒekt/ [+ obj]
1 to refuse to accept or consider sth: *Our proposal was firmly rejected.* ◇ *Shareholders are likely to reject the $47-a-share offer.*
2 to refuse to accept sb for a job, position, etc: *I've been rejected by all the companies I applied to.*
3 to decide not to sell or use sth because its quality is not good enough: *Imperfect articles are rejected by our quality control.*
OPP ACCEPT
▶ **rejection** /rɪ'dʒekʃn/ *noun* [U,C]: *The rejection of the deal by 57% of the workers came as a surprise.* ◇ *I've got another rejection letter (= telling me I have not been given a job).*
● *noun* /'riːdʒekt/ [C]
something that cannot be used or sold because there is sth wrong with it: *factory rejects*

rejig /ˌriː'dʒɪɡ/ *verb* [+ obj] (**-gg-**) (*BrE*) (*AmE* **rejigger** /ˌriː'dʒɪɡə(r)/) (*informal*)
to make changes to sth; to arrange sth in a different way: *We can solve some of the problems by rejigging our assets.* ▶ **'rejig** *noun* [C]: *a management rejig*

rejuvenate /rɪ'dʒuːvəneɪt/ *verb* [+ obj]
to make sb/sth more confident, more successful, more exciting, etc: *Money alone can't rejuvenate an organization.* ◇ *a fresh, rejuvenated brand*
▶ **rejuvenation** /rɪˌdʒuːvə'neɪʃn/ *noun* [U; sing.]

rekey /ˌriː'kiː/ *verb* [+ obj]
to enter data, text, etc. into a computer again using a keyboard: *We spent hours rekeying all the data.*

relapse /rɪ'læps/ *verb* [no obj]
to go back into a previous condition or into a worse state after making an improvement: *The weak economic data suggest the US may relapse into recession.* ▶ **relapse** /rɪ'læps; 'riːlæps/ *noun* [C,U]: *The bad news has caused a relapse in world stock markets.*

relate /rɪ'leɪt/ *verb* [+ obj]
to show or make a connection between two or more things: *In the future, pay increases will be related to productivity.* ◇ *We use a database to relate products and pricing.* SYN CONNECT
PHR V **re'late to sth/sb** to be connected with sth/sb; to refer to sth/sb: *Both companies are pursuing legal action relating to the merger.*

related /rɪ'leɪtɪd/ *adjective*

SEE ALSO: **earnings-related, job-~, work-~**

connected with sth/sb in some way: *The corporation's problems are directly related to the poor economy.* ◇ *Salaries and related costs rose 17% last year.* ◇ *a media-related company*
→ PERFORMANCE-RELATED PAY
▶ **re'latedness** *noun* [U]

re,lated 'company *noun* [C]
a company that controls or is controlled by another company or is a member of a group of companies, especially an ASSOCIATE COMPANY → AFFILIATE *noun* See note at GROUP

re,lated 'party *noun* [C]
an individual, a company, etc. that has the ability to control or influence another organization: *Anyone who owns more than 50% of the stock qualifies as a related party.*

relations /rɪ'leɪʃnz/ *noun* [pl.]

SEE ALSO: **customer relations, employee ~, employment ~, human ~, industrial ~, investor ~, labour ~,** etc.

the way in which two people, groups or countries behave towards each other or deal with each other: *US-Europe relations* ◇ *We seek to improve relations with the unions.* ◇ *The relations between the two companies are still good.*

★ **relationship** /rɪ'leɪʃnʃɪp/ *noun* [C]

SEE ALSO: **customer relationship, employment relationship**

the way in which two people, groups or countries behave towards each other or deal with each other: *The company hopes to build relationships with customers.* ◇ *the relationship between brokers and the companies they represent* ◇ *I have established a good working relationship with my boss.*
❍ to **build/develop/establish/maintain** a relationship
• a **business/contractual/personal** relationship

re'lationship ,management = CUSTOMER RELATIONSHIP MANAGEMENT

re'lationship ,manager *noun* [C]
(*Marketing*) a person whose job is to develop and maintain the relationship between an organization and a customer → CUSTOMER RELATIONSHIP MANAGEMENT

re'lationship ,marketing *noun* [U]
(*Marketing*) marketing activities that concentrate on developing a good relationship with a customer which will last for a long time

relatively /'relətɪvli/ *adverb*
to a fairly large degree, especially in comparison to sth else: *The software is relatively cheap.* ◇ *We had relatively few applications for the job.*
IDM **'relatively speaking** (*used when you are comparing sth with all similar things*): *Relatively speaking, these jobs provide good salaries.*

relaunch /ˌriː'lɔːntʃ/ *verb* [+ obj]
(*Marketing*) to start or present sth again in a new or different way, especially a product for sale: *to relaunch a product* ◇ *The magazine was relaunched as a monthly to attract new readers.* ▶ **relaunch** /'riːlɔːntʃ/ *noun* [C]: *the relaunch of the magazine*

relax /rɪ'læks/ *verb* [+ obj]
to allow rules, laws, etc. to become less strict: *It's time to relax some of the rules on e-commerce.*

release /rɪ'liːs/ *verb, noun*
● *verb* [+ obj]
1 to make data, information, a report, etc. available to the public: *The central bank released its report on bad loans.* ◇ *The sales figures have not yet been released.*
2 to make a product, especially a film/movie or a CD, available to the public to buy: *The film will be released throughout the UK in April.* ◇ *They have released a new version of their award-winning game.*
3 to free sb from a duty, responsibility, contract, etc: *The new law released employers from their obligation to recognize unions.*
4 to make sth available that previously had not been allowed or had been used for another purpose: *They hope to release $1 bn cash by selling the car repair company.*
● *noun*

SEE ALSO: **block release, day ~, news ~**

1 [U; sing.] the act of making sth available to the public such as a new product or new information: *The release of the report was delayed.* ◇ *The new software is scheduled for release in January.*

2 [C] a product that is made available to the public to buy, especially a new CD or film/movie: *New releases often sell for around €14.*
3 [C] = PRESS RELEASE

reliable /rɪ'laɪəbl/ *adjective*
1 that you can trust or rely on: *We are looking for someone who is reliable and hard-working.* ◇ *a reliable machine*
2 that is likely to be correct or true: *They provide reliable information to investors.*
▶ **reliability** /rɪ,laɪə'bɪləti/ *noun* [U]: *The aircraft has an exceptional record of reliability.* ◇ *Some economists have questioned the reliability of the data.*

reliance /rɪ'laɪəns/ *noun* [U; sing.]
the state of needing a particular person or thing: *They want to reduce their heavy reliance on foreign capital.* ▶ **re'liant** *adjective*: *Businesses have become increasingly reliant on computers.*

relief /rɪ'liːf/ *noun*

SEE ALSO: tax relief

1 [U] if you are given **relief** from a debt, a payment, tax, etc. then you do not have to pay it or you pay it at a lower rate: *The organization is asking for relief from fuel tax.* ◇ *The bank has agreed to some interest relief on loan repayments.*
○ *to give/offer/provide relief ◆ to claim/gain/get/ receive relief ◆ to be eligible for/be entitled to/ qualify for relief*
2 [U] help given to a country or people after a war or natural disaster, etc: *emergency/flood relief*
○ *to give/provide/send relief ◆ a relief agency/ organization/worker*
3 [U] (*especially AmE*) financial help given by the government to people who need it: *state and federal relief funds* ◇ *relief for farmers whose crops have suffered from the hot weather* → BENEFIT *noun* (2)
4 [C with sing./pl. verb] (*often used as an adjective*) a person or group of people that replaces another when they have finished working for the day or when they are sick: *The relief crew comes on duty at 9 o'clock.* ◇ *relief drivers*

relieve /rɪ'liːv/ *verb* [+ obj]
to make a problem less serious: *Lower energy prices will relieve the pressure on household finances.*
PHR V **re'lieve sb of sth 1** to dismiss sb from a job, position, etc: *The manager was having trouble, so they decided to relieve him of his duties.* **2** to help sb by taking away a difficult task or problem: *The new secretary will relieve us of some of the paperwork.*

relocate /,riːləʊ'keɪt; AmE ,riː'loʊkeɪt/ *verb* [+ obj or no obj]
to move or to move sb/sth to a new place to work or operate: *The company relocated its head office to Stanford.* ◇ *The owner is selling because his partner has relocated.* ▶ **relocation** /,riːləʊ'keɪʃn; AmE ,riːloʊ-/ *noun* [U,C]: *a generous relocation package/ allowance* ◇ *business expansions and relocations*

remainder /rɪ'meɪndə(r)/ *noun, verb*
● *noun*
1 [sing.] the remaining amount of sth such as money, people, time, etc: *Two-thirds of the job cuts were in the US and the remainder in Europe.* ◇ *We expect order levels to improve for the remainder of the year.*
2 (*Commerce*) [C] a book, CD, etc. that is sold at a reduced price: *a bookstore for remainders and secondhand books*
● *verb* [+ obj]
(*Commerce*) (*usually* be remaindered)
to sell books, CDs, etc. at a reduced price, for example because there are too many left: *remaindered books and DVDs*

remarket /,riː'mɑːkɪt; AmE ,riː'mɑːrk-/ *verb* [+ obj or no obj]
1 (*Marketing*) to sell new or used things that were produced by or belonged to sb else: *The company buys and remarkets IT equipment that is nearly new.*
2 (*Finance*) to sell shares, bonds, etc. that are issued by another company or organization: *Goldman Sachs will remarket $75 million of these bonds.*
▶ **,re'marketer** *noun* [C] **,re'marketing** *noun* [U]

remedy /'remədi/ *noun, verb*
● *noun* [C] (*plural* remedies)
1 (*Law*) a legal solution to a problem or disagreement: *One legal remedy might be to sue the agency for breach of contract.* SYN REDRESS
2 a way of dealing with or improving an unpleasant or difficult situation: *There is no simple remedy for unemployment.*
● *verb* (remedies, remedying, remedied, remedied) [+ obj]
to correct or improve sth: *This situation is easily remedied.*

reminder /rɪ'maɪndə(r)/ *noun* [C]
a letter or note informing sb that they have not done sth such as paying a bill: *If an invoice is not paid within seven days, a reminder will be sent.* ◇ *a reminder email/invoice/letter*

remission /rɪ'mɪʃn/ *noun* [U,C]
1 (*formal*) an act of reducing or cancelling the amount of money that sb has to pay: *New businesses may qualify for tax remission.*
2 a period during which a bad situation improves although it is likely to become bad again: *With brief periods of remission, the insurance company has been in crisis ever since the early 1990s.*

remit *noun, verb* (*formal*)
● *noun* /'riːmɪt; rɪ'mɪt/ [C, usually sing.] (*BrE*)
the area of activity over which a particular person or group has authority, control or influence: *Such decisions are outside the remit of this committee.* ◇ *In future, staff recruitment will fall within the remit of the division manager.*
● *verb* /rɪ'mɪt/ [+ obj] (-tt-)
1 (*Finance*) to send money, etc. to a person or place: *using banks for remitting funds* ◇ *Payment will be remitted to you in full.* → REMITTANCE
2 to cancel or free sb from a debt, duty, punishment, etc: *to remit a fine*

remittance /rɪ'mɪtns/ *noun*
(*Accounting*; *Finance*, *formal*)
1 [C] a sum of money that is sent to sb: *Please return the completed form with your remittance.*
→ REMIT *verb* (1)
2 [U] the act of sending money to sb to pay for sth: *Remittance can be made by cheque or credit card.* ◇ *Enclose the remittance slip with your payment* (= a form with details of the payment, the customer's name, etc.).

remortgage /,riː'mɔːgɪdʒ; AmE -'mɔːrg-/ *verb* [+ obj or no obj]
to arrange a second MORTGAGE on your house or apartment, or to increase or change your first one: *They had to remortgage their home.* ▶ **,re'mortgage** *noun* [C,U]: *Loans for house purchases, excluding remortgages, were down 12%.* **,re'mortgaging** *noun* [U]: *Remortgaging accounted for 52% of all mortgage lending in July.*

remote /rɪ'məʊt; AmE rɪ'moʊt/ *adjective*
1 (*IT*) (about a computer system) that you can connect to from far away, using an electronic link: *The company has set up remote data centers in Dallas and Orlando.* ◇ *We are facing increasing demands for remote access from our branch offices, mobile workers and business partners.*
2 (*HR*) used to describe the situation when people work for a company from home by using a computer that is linked to the central office

computer system: *Remote working is mainly about cutting costs.* ◇ *remote workers*
▶ **re'motely** *adverb: You can access the extranet remotely.*

removal /rɪˈmuːvl/ *noun*
1 [U] the act of getting rid of sth or of taking sb/sth away: *the removal of trade barriers* ◇ *Investors welcomed the removal of the tax.*
2 (*HR*) [U] the act of dismissing sb from their job: *The crisis led to the removal of Mr Grant as chief executive.*
3 [C] (*BrE*) an act of taking furniture, etc. from one building to another: *home and office removals* ◇ *a removal company/firm*

remove /rɪˈmuːv/ *verb* [+ obj]
1 (*HR*) to dismiss sb from their position or job: *to be removed from office/power* ◇ *She was shocked by the decision to remove her.*
2 to get rid of sb/sth or to take sb/sth away: *to remove barriers/obstacles/objections/restrictions* ◇ *They want a clause removed from the contract.* ◇ *I asked to be removed from their mailing list.*

remover /rɪˈmuːvə(r)/ (*BrE*) (*also* **'mover**, *AmE, BrE*) *noun* [C, usually pl.]
a company that takes possessions to new offices or homes for people or organizations: *furniture removers*

remunerate /rɪˈmjuːnəreɪt/ *verb* [+ obj] (*formal*) (*usually* **be remunerated**)
to pay sb for work that they have done: *People are remunerated according to their productivity.* ◇ *Mr Davis was well remunerated for his work.*

remuneration /rɪˌmjuːnəˈreɪʃn/ *noun* [U,C] (*formal*)
an amount of money that is paid to sb for the work they have done: *Including pension contributions, his total remuneration for the year was €52 000.*

re,mune'ration ,package = PAY PACKAGE

remunerative /rɪˈmjuːnərətɪv/ *adjective* [usually before noun] (*formal*)
paying a lot of money: *remunerative work*

rename /ˌriːˈneɪm/ *verb* [+ obj]
to give sb/sth a new name: *Use a logical system when you rename your files.*

render /ˈrendə(r)/ *verb* [+ obj] (*formal*)
1 (*Accounting*) to present sth such as a bill, financial accounts, etc: *All departments must render accounts for audit.* ◇ *When the order ships, we will render an invoice for the amount due.*
2 to officially give a decision, judgement, etc. about sth: *Judge Parris rendered his decision.*
3 to provide help, a service, etc. to sb: *to render assistance* ◇ *The fees were charged for services rendered.*
4 (*IT*) to make a computer image appear like a real object: *3D-rendered images*
▶ **rendering** /ˈrendərɪŋ/ *noun* [U,C]: *a workshop on rendering*

renege /rɪˈniːɡ; rɪˈneɪɡ/ *verb* [no obj] (*formal*)
to break a promise, an agreement, etc: *to renege on a commitment/contract/deal* ◇ *She accused the company of reneging on its agreement.*

★ **renew** /rɪˈnjuː; *AmE* -ˈnuː/ *verb*
1 (*Commerce*) [+ obj or no obj] to make sth valid for a further period of time: *to renew a contract/licence/lease/loan* ◇ *He applied to have his membership renewed.*
2 to begin sth again after a pause or an interruption: *We have to renew our efforts to attract young graduates.*
3 [+ obj] to change sth that is old or damaged and replace it with sth new of the same kind: *Some of the wiring needs to be renewed.*

renewable /rɪˈnjuːəbl; *AmE* -ˈnuː-/ *adjective*
1 (*Commerce*) (about a contract, licence, loan, etc.) that can be made valid for a further period of time after it has finished: *a renewable lease* ◇ *The work permit is not renewable.*
2 (*Technical*) [usually before noun] (about energy, fuel, resources, etc.) that is replaced naturally or controlled carefully and can therefore be used without the risk of finishing it all: *renewable sources of energy such as wind and solar power*
OPP NON-RENEWABLE
▶ **re'newable** *noun* [C]: *The government has set targets for generating electricity by renewables.*

renewal /rɪˈnjuːəl; *AmE* -ˈnuːəl/ *noun* [U,C]
1 (*Commerce*) the act of making a contract, etc. valid for a further period of time after it has finished: *The insurance policy is coming up for renewal.* ◇ *software license renewals*
2 a situation in which sth is improved or made more successful: *economic renewal* ◇ *The new model is part of an ongoing product renewal.*

re'newal ,notice *noun* [C]
(*Commerce*) a warning given in advance that a contract is going to end and that you must make it valid for a further period of time if you want it to continue: *Your new premium is shown on your renewal notice.*

renminbi /ˈrenmɪnbi/ *noun* [C] (*plural* **renminbi**)
1 the renminbi [sing.] the money system of China
2 the unit of money in China (the **yuan**)

★ **renovate** /ˈrenəveɪt/ *verb* [+ obj]
(*Property*) to repair and decorate an old building, etc. so that it is in good condition again: *The offices are on the fifth floor of a renovated warehouse.*
▶ **renovation** /ˌrenəˈveɪʃn/ *noun* [U,C]: *buildings in need of renovation*

★ **rent** /rent/ *noun, verb*
● *noun* [U,C]
SEE ALSO: **peppercorn rent**
1 an amount of money that you pay regularly so that you can use a property, etc: *Office rents in London fell by 15%.* ◇ *The landlord has put the rent up again.* ◇ *Her company has saved at least €240 000 in rent.* → HIRE *noun*
○ *a fair/high/low* rent ◆ *to* **charge/pay** rent ◆ *to* **fall behind with/owe** rent
2 (*especially AmE*) = RENTAL (1)
IDM **for rent** (*especially AmE*) (especially on printed signs) available to rent: *offices and warehouses for rent*
● *verb*
1 [+ obj or no obj] to regularly pay money to sb so that you can use sth that they own, such as a property, a machine, etc: *rented accommodation* ◇ *She rents office space* **from** *a letting agency.*
2 [+ obj] **rent sth (out) (to sb)** to allow sb to use sth that you own in exchange for payment: *They rent office space to an IT company.* ◇ *She wants to rent out the top floor of the building.*
3 [+ obj] (*especially AmE*) to pay money to sb so that you can use sth for a short period of time: *We rented a car at the airport.* ◇ *Consumers spent $3.7 billion on renting DVDs.*
4 [no obj] (*AmE*) to be available for sb to use if they pay a particular amount of money: *The apartment rents for $600 a month.*
▶ **'renter** *noun* [C]: *a renter of industrial equipment* ◇ *It's a renter's market* (= rents are cheap at the moment). → HIRE, LEASE, LET

rental /'rentl/ noun

SEE ALSO: **list rental**

1 (also **rent**, especially in AmE) [U; C, usually sing.] the amount of money that you pay to use sth for a particular period of time: Telephone charges include line rental. ◇ The weekly rental is $59.99.
2 [U,C] the act of renting sth or an arrangement to rent sth: the rental of machinery and equipment ◇ the world's largest car rental company ◇ DVD rentals account for 20% of the company's revenues.
[SYN] HIRE
3 [C] (especially in AmE) a house, car, or piece of equipment that you can rent: 'Is this your own car?' 'No, it's a rental.'
→ HIRE

¹rental fleet noun [C]
a group of cars or other vehicles that are owned by a company and rented to customers

reopen /ˌriːˈəʊpən; AmE -ˈoʊ-/ verb
1 [+ obj or no obj] to open a shop/store, etc. again, or to be opened again, after being closed for a period of time: The market has reopened after the New Year break.
2 [+ obj or no obj] to deal with or begin sth again after a period of time; to start again after a period of time: Management have agreed to reopen talks with the union. ◇ The trial reopened on 6 March.
3 (Finance) [+ obj] in the US, to issue additional amounts of an existing bond, etc. with the same MATURITY date and rate of interest as the original
▶ **reopening** /ˌriːˈəʊpənɪŋ; AmE -ˈoʊ-/ noun [U; sing.]: the reopening of merger talks

reorder /ˌriːˈɔːdə(r); AmE -ˈɔːrd-/ verb [+ obj or no obj]
to ask sb to supply you with more of a product: Please quote this reference number when reordering stock. ▶ **reˈorder** noun [C]: You can place a reorder online.

reˈorder point = ORDER POINT

reorganization, **-isation** /riˌɔːɡənaɪˈzeɪʃn; AmE -ˌɔːrɡənəˈz-/ noun [U,C]
1 a change in the way in which sth is organized or done: The reorganization has freed up space in the warehouse. ◇ a plan for reorganization of the business
2 (Law) in the US, an official change in the way a company is organized because it has gone BANKRUPT: The company could be in bankruptcy reorganization for two years. ◇ He filed a **reorganization plan** with the bankruptcy court.

reorganize, **-ise** /riˈɔːɡənaɪz; AmE -ˈɔːrɡ-/ verb [+ obj or no obj]
to change the way in which sth is organized or done: The warehouse is to be reorganized. ◇ The steelmaker needs to reorganize and become more competitive.

rep /rep/ noun, verb (informal)
● noun [C]
1 (Marketing) = SALES REPRESENTATIVE
2 = REPRESENTATIVE noun (1,3)
● verb [+ obj or no obj] (-pp-)
to act as a SALES REPRESENTATIVE: At eighteen she was working for the family firm, repping on the road.

repackage /ˌriːˈpækɪdʒ/ verb [+ obj]
1 (Marketing) to put a product in a new container or cover so that people will want to buy it: They have renamed and repackaged one of their cleaning products.
2 to present sb or sth in a new way so that they will become more popular: The radio station has been repackaged to appeal to younger listeners. ◇ Milk could be repackaged as a designer drink.

★ **repair** /rɪˈpeə(r); AmE -ˈper/ verb, noun
● verb [+ obj]
to make sth that is broken or damaged in good condition again: A man came to repair the photocopier. ◇ Where can I **get/have** my car **repaired**?
● noun [C,U]

SEE ALSO: **credit repair, home ~, running ~**

an act of repairing sth: You will have to pay the cost of any repairs **to** the rental car. ◇ The **repair work** has now been completed. ◇ The fax machine had gone in for repair.
● to **carry out/complete/do/make** repairs ◆ **emergency/essential/extensive/major/minor** repairs
[IDM] **in good/bad reˈpair** (also **in a good/bad state of reˈpair**) in good or bad condition: Floors, stairs and passages must be kept in good repair.

repairer /rɪˈpeərə(r); AmE -ˈperər/ noun [C]
a company or a person that repairs things: a ship repairer ◇ auto repairers

repairman /rɪˈpeəmæn; AmE -ˈperm-/ noun [C] (plural **repairmen** /-men/)
a person whose job is to repair things: a TV repairman

reparation /ˌrepəˈreɪʃn/ noun [C, usually pl., U]
money that is paid to a person, company, or country for loss, damage, or suffering that has been caused to them: Punishment for offences can include reparations to the owners of damaged property.

repatriate /ˌriːˈpætrieɪt; AmE -ˈpeɪt-/ verb [+ obj]
(Finance) to send money or profits back to your own country: The agreement enables countries to repatriate their profits freely. ◇ repatriated earnings/funds ▶ **repatriation** /ˌriːˌpætriˈeɪʃn; AmE -ˌpeɪt-/ noun [C,U]

★ **repay** /rɪˈpeɪ/ verb [+ obj] (**repaid, repaid** /rɪˈpeɪd/)
to pay back money that you have borrowed; to pay back money that has been taken from a person or an organization: He sold shares in order to repay the loan early. ◇ Mortgage lenders sometimes agree to give you extra time to repay them. ◇ Decide how much you can afford to repay each month. ◇ When he left he had to repay the $5 000 bonus he had received.
● to repay a **debt/loan/mortgage**

repayable /rɪˈpeɪəbl/ adjective [not before noun]
(Finance) that must be paid or can be paid back at a particular time or in a particular way: The loan is repayable in 2010. ◇ repayable loans ◇ The loan is repayable in monthly instalments.

★ **repayment** /rɪˈpeɪmənt/ noun
1 [U] the act of paying back money that has been borrowed from a bank or other organization: The loan is due for repayment by the end of the year. ◇ There is a penalty for early repayment. ◇ The normal repayment period is five years. ◇ The sale of assets should raise $200 million towards debt repayment.
● to **be due for/claim/demand** repayment ◆ **debt/loan/mortgage** repayment ◆ **early/late** repayment
2 [C] a sum of money that is paid regularly to a bank or other organization as part of paying back a loan: Your monthly repayments will vary according to the lender's interest rate. ◇ people who were unable to meet their mortgage repayments
● to **keep up/make** repayments ◆ to **afford/meet** the repayments ◆ **monthly/weekly/yearly** repayments ◆ **capital/loan/mortgage/overdraft** repayments ◆ a **minimum** repayment

repeat /rɪˈpiːt/ noun [C]
an event that is very similar to sth that happened before: We don't expect a repeat of last year's sales gains. ◇ We all know that customer satisfaction equals **repeat business** (= when customers return to buy more products or services). ◇ This form is for

repeat orders (= for a further supply of the same goods) *only.* ◇ *repeat buyers/customers/visitors*

re,petitive 'strain ,injury *(also* re,petitive 'stress ,injury)* = RSI

★ replace /rɪˈpleɪs/ *verb* [+ obj]
1 to be used instead of something else: *The new design will eventually replace all existing models.* ◇ *Their currency has been replaced* **with** *the US dollar.*
2 to take a new job, or to put a new person in a job, instead of sb else: *Mr Hill replaces the outgoing Head of Communications.* ◇ *People leaving are not being replaced.* ◇ *She will be very difficult to replace.*
3 *(Commerce)* to change sth that is damaged, old, or does not work properly for sth new or better: *People aren't replacing their computers as often as manufacturers would like.*

replacement /rɪˈpleɪsmənt/ *noun*

SEE ALSO: **cost of replacement**

1 [C] a thing that replaces sth that is old, broken, not good enough, not available, etc: *Aluminium is becoming popular as a replacement* **for** *steel in cars.* ◇ *If you are not happy with any item, return it for a replacement or refund.*
2 [C] a person who replaces another person in an organization, for example by taking their job: *It won't be easy to find a replacement* **for** *Louisa.* ◇ *We have been forced to use replacement workers during the strike.*
3 [U] the act of replacing one thing with another, especially sth that is newer or better: *the replacement of old, inefficient electrical equipment* ◇ *Our PCs are due for replacement.* ◇ *replacement parts*

re'placement cost *(also* ,cost of re'placement, re'placement ,value)* noun* [U,C]
1 *(Accounting)* the cost of replacing an asset, calculated by considering the cost of buying or producing the same item today: *The cost of maintaining our computer systems is now higher than the replacement cost.* → CURRENT COST
2 *(Insurance)* the cost of replacing an item of property with a new one of the same type and quality

★ reply /rɪˈplaɪ/ *verb, noun*
● *verb* [+ obj *or no* obj] (**replies, replying, replied, replied**)
to say or write sth as an answer to sth that has been said or written to you: *I texted him about the meeting but he hasn't replied yet.* ◇ *Over a thousand people replied* **to** *the initial job advertisement.*
● *noun* [C,U] *(plural* **replies**)
something said, written, or done as an answer to sth: *All letters of complaint should receive a prompt reply.* ◇ *The next morning I had a reply* **to** *my email.*
● *get/have/receive* a reply • *give/make* a reply
IDM **in re'ply to** used to start a formal letter which is an answer to a letter that you have received: *In reply to your letter of 16 March, I regret to inform you that there are currently no vacancies within our company.*

re'ply card *noun* [C]
a printed card or piece of paper, or an electronic form, that a company provides for sb to reply to sth such as an offer, an invitation, or a survey: *The best method of cheap direct mail marketing is a sales letter and reply card.*

re,ply 'paid *noun* [U]
a service in which a company provides a card, envelope, etc. that a possible customer can use to send a reply. The customer does not have to use a stamp but the company pays only for the replies that are sent back to them: *Sign the form and send it back to us reply paid.* ◇ *a reply-paid card/envelope*
→ BUSINESS REPLY SERVICE, POSTAGE PAID

---

repo /ˈriːpəʊ; *AmE* -poʊ/ *noun, verb (informal)*
● *noun*

SEE ALSO: **reverse repo**

1 *(Finance)* [C] = REPURCHASE AGREEMENT
2 [U,C] the act of taking back property or goods from sb who has borrowed money to buy them and not paid it back; the property or goods taken: *specialists in debt recovery and repo* ◇ *House repos are down this year.* → REPOSSESSION
● *verb* [+ obj] = REPOSSESS

★ report /rɪˈpɔːt; *AmE* rɪˈpɔːrt/ *noun, verb*
● *noun* [C]

SEE ALSO: **annual report, audit ~, credit ~, direct ~, directors' ~, earnings ~, expense ~,** etc.

1 a spoken or written description of sth, usually for sb that needs particular information: *The department produces a monthly progress report.* ◇ *a confidential medical report* ◇ *The analysts' report valued the business at $1.4 billion.*
● *to* **prepare/present/produce/write** *a report*
2 an official document written by a group of people who have examined a particular situation or problem: *The committee will publish their report* **on** *the coal industry in a few weeks.* ◇ *Several people have disputed the report's findings.*
● *to* **call for/commission/issue/publish** *a report*
3 an account of an event that is published in a newspaper or broadcast on television or on the radio: *a special report* **on** *women in industry*
● *to* **compile/file/write** *a report* • *to* **broadcast/print/ publish** *a report* • **newspaper/press/radio/TV** *reports*
4 *(Accounting)* = ANNUAL REPORT
5 *(IT; Production)* a way of finding particular information, for example about costs, stock, etc., from information that is stored electronically; the information you get: *Some reports display information; others allow you to perform analyses.* ◇ *SAP reports*
● *to* **run** *a report* • *to* **download/use** *a report*
6 *(HR)* a person that a particular manager is responsible for: *How many reports do you have?*

WHICH WORD?

report/proposal

These words are used to describe two different types of documents.

A **report** gives information about something in the past or about something taking place at the moment: *a sales/training report.* It often contains suggestions about how a situation can be improved.

A **proposal** makes suggestions about something to be done in the future: *a proposal to build a new factory* ◇ *to draw up a proposal for a client.* A proposal tries to persuade the reader that its suggestions are right.

● *verb*
1 [+ obj *or no* obj] to make a public statement about a company's accounts and its profits and losses: *The company is expected to report record profits this year.* ◇ *The firm will report its end of year results next week.* ◇ *the first bank to report in the big banks' reporting season*
2 [+ obj *or no* obj] to give people information about a subject or an event: *The committee will report* **on** *its research next month.*
3 [+ obj *or no* obj] to present an account of an event in a newspaper, on television, etc: *The proposed*

merger has been reported in the financial press. ◇ *She reports on financial markets for CNBC.*
4 [no obj] to tell sb that you have arrived, for example for work or for a meeting with sb: *You should report for work at 7 a.m.* ◇ *All visitors must report to the reception desk on arrival.*
PHR V **re,port 'back** to return to a place, especially in order to work again: *Take an hour for lunch and report back at 2.* **re,port 'back (on sth) (to sb)** to give sb information about sth that they have asked you to find out about: *We will report back when we get the results.* ◇ *She reported back to us on the meetings she had attended.* **re'port to/into sb** (*HR*) (*not used in the continuous tenses*) if you **report to** a particular manager in an organization that you work for, they are officially responsible for your work and tell you what to do: *She has set up a group of five people who all report to her.*

reporting /rɪˈpɔːtɪŋ; *AmE* -ˈpɔːrt-/ *noun* [U]
1 the act of giving written or spoken information about sth, especially the financial position of an organization: *The data has helped us with the reporting of figures for non-payment.* → FINANCIAL REPORTING
2 (*HR*) the system in an organization of having managers who are officially responsible for the work of particular employees: *Structures of reporting within the company are to be changed.*

re'porting line *noun* [C, usually pl.]
(*HR*) a system in an organization of having managers who are officially responsible for the work of particular employees: *About 400 of the bank's 5 700 staff will be affected by the change in reporting lines.*

re'porting pay = CALL-IN PAY

re'porting ,period *noun* [C]
(*Accounting*) the period of time included in a report about sth such as the financial position of a company: *Total income in/during the reporting period was $3.5 million.*

reposition /ˌriːpəˈzɪʃn/ *verb* [+ obj]
(*Marketing*) to present a product in a new way so that it will attract more or different customers: *The parent company intend to reposition the brand as sportswear, rather than fashion.* ◇ *The bank is repositioning itself to focus on consumers and personal finance.* ▶ **repo'sitioning** *noun* [U]

repossess /ˌriːpəˈzes/ (*also* **'repro**) *verb* [+ obj] (*usually* **be repossessed**)
to take back property or goods from sb who has borrowed money to buy them but does not pay it back as agreed: *The mortgage company were threatening to repossess the house.* ◇ *Whatever assets of the firm are not repossessed will be sold.*

repossession /ˌriːpəˈzeʃn/ *noun*
1 [U,C] the act of **repossessing** property or goods: *borrowers who are in arrears and facing repossession* ◇ *a 42 per cent drop in house repossessions*
2 [C] something such as a house or car that has been repossessed: *a repossession sold at auction*

★ **represent** /ˌreprɪˈzent/ *verb*
1 [+ obj] to act or speak officially for a person, a group or an organization: *Mr Moline represented the Human Resources team at the meeting.* ◇ *Local businesses are well represented on the committee* (= there are a lot of people from them). ◇ *The union's role is to represent the interests of its members.*
2 [+ obj] (*not used in the continuous tenses*) to be a symbol of sth: *Each colour on the graph represents a different department.* ◇ *Our brand represents good design and high quality.*
3 (*linking verb*) (*not used in the continuous tenses*) to be sth: *This contract represents 20% of the company's annual revenue.* **SYN** CONSTITUTE

,re-pre'sent *verb* [+ obj]
to give, show or send a document again, especially a cheque, bill, etc. that has not been paid

representation /ˌreprɪzenˈteɪʃn/ *noun*
1 [U] the fact of having people who will speak or vote on your behalf in official situations; the people who speak for you, etc. in these circumstances: *We are particularly disappointed with our legal representation.* ◇ *76 votes were needed to approve union representation.*
2 [U,C] the act of presenting sb/sth in a particular way such as financial accounts; something that shows or describes sth: *She was accused of making false representations about the company's performance.*
3 **representations** [pl.] (*especially BrE*) formal statements made to sb in authority, especially in order to make your opinions known or to protest: *The association may make representations to the chief executive to try to resolve the situation.*

★ **representative** /ˌreprɪˈzentətɪv/ *noun*, *adjective*
● *noun* [C]

SEE ALSO: **personal representative, sales ~, trade ~, union ~**

1 (*also* **rep**, *informal*) a person who has been chosen to speak or vote for sb else or on behalf of a group: *Representatives of 31 countries attended the conference.* ◇ *Union reps said the proposals were unacceptable.*
2 (*Marketing*) = SALES REPRESENTATIVE
3 (*also* **rep**, *informal*) (*BrE also* **'holiday rep**, *informal*) an employee of a travel company who stays at a place where customers are on holiday/vacation and helps them with problems, organizes activities, etc.
● *adjective*
1 typical of a particular group of people: *Is a questionnaire answered by 500 people truly representative of the population as a whole?*
2 [usually before noun] containing or including examples of all the different types of people or things in a large group: *We interviewed a representative sample of health workers.*

reprice /ˌriːˈpraɪs/ *verb*
1 (*Commerce*) [+ obj] to change the price of sth: *Some of the older products have been repackaged and repriced.*
2 (*Finance*) [+ obj or no obj] to change the interest rate: *Lenders have already begun to reprice interest rates to reflect the change in the base rate.*

reprocess /ˌriːˈprəʊses; *AmE* -ˈprɑː-; -ˈprəʊ-/ *verb* [+ obj]
to treat waste material in order to change it or use it again: *Soda bottles contain only a few kinds of plastics and are relatively easy to reprocess.* ◇ *reprocessed fuel* ▶ **reprocessing** /ˌriːˈprəʊsesɪŋ; *AmE* -ˈprɑː-; -ˈprəʊ-/ *noun* [U]: *a nuclear reprocessing plant*

repudiate /rɪˈpjuːdieɪt/ *verb* [+ obj]
(*Law*) to refuse to pay a debt or do sth that a contract requires you to do: *The buyer is entitled to repudiate the contract and reject the goods.*
➊ *to repudiate a* **contract/debt/document**
▶ **repudiation** /rɪˌpjuːdiˈeɪʃn/ *noun* [C,U]

repurchase /ˌriːˈpɜːtʃəs; *AmE* -ˈpɜːrtʃəs/ *verb* [+ obj]
to buy sth back: *The aim is to repurchase the securities at a price that is lower than your selling price.* ▶ **re'purchase** *noun* [C]: *The stock price often increases when repurchases are announced.*

re'purchase a,greement (*also* ,**sale and re'purchase a,greement**) (*also* **'repo**, *informal*) *noun* [C]
(*Finance*) a way of raising money over a short period

in which sb sells shares, bonds, etc. and agrees to buy them back at a particular price at a later date: *With a repurchase agreement, sellers can get short-term funds without losing their shares.* → REVERSE REPURCHASE AGREEMENT

reputable /'repjətəbl/ *adjective*
that people consider to be honest and to provide a good service: *How can you be sure that you're buying from a reputable dealer?*

reputation /ˌrepju'teɪʃn/ *noun* [C,U]
the opinion that people have about what sb/sth is like, based on what has happened in the past: *The firm has a reputation **as** a good employer.* ◇ *They appointed a chairman with a reputation **for** being cautious.* ◇ *The company enjoys a world-wide reputation for quality of design.*
ℹ *to **build/develop/earn/gain/have** a reputation ♦ to **damage/dent/tarnish** sb's reputation ♦ a **good/growing/solid/strong** reputation ♦ a **bad/battered/poor** reputation*

★**request** /rɪ'kwest/ *noun, verb*
●*noun* [C]
the action of asking for sth formally and politely: *The bank is considering your request **for** a loan.* ◇ *He agreed to stay for another six months **at the request of** the company / **at the** company's **request**.* ◇ *Details of charges are available **on request**.*
ℹ *to **make/put in/submit** a request ♦ to **agree to/comply with/grant** a request ♦ to **refuse/reject/turn down** a request*
●*verb* [+ obj] (*formal*)
to ask for sth or ask sb to do sth in a polite or formal way: *They requested permission to build houses on the land.* ◇ *She wrote to the manufacturer requesting a copy of the document.* ◇ *You are requested **to** attend the next meeting.*

★**require** /rɪ'kwaɪə(r)/ *verb* [+ obj] (*formal*) (*not usually used in the continuous tenses*)
1 to make sb do or have sth, especially because it is necessary according to a particular law or set of rules: *Motorists are required by law to have insurance.* ◇ *Many vendors require payment by credit card.* ◇ *Output has fallen below the required level.*
2 to need sth: *The new equipment requires less maintenance.* ◇ *The launch of a new product requires careful thought and planning.*

★**requirement** /rɪ'kwaɪəmənt; *AmE* -'kwaɪərm-/ *noun*

SEE ALSO: **capital requirement, public sector borrowing ~, reserve ~**

1 [C] something that is needed or asked for by an authority: *There is no legal requirement **to** provide nutritional information on food packaging.* ◇ *In order to be listed on a stock exchange, the company must meet certain requirements.*
ℹ *to **fulfil/meet/satisfy** requirements ♦ to **impose/lay down/set (down/out)** requirements*
2 [C, usually pl.] something that sb/sth needs or wants: *a software package to meet your requirements* ◇ *Our immediate requirement is extra staff.* ◇ *These goods are **surplus to requirements** (= more than we need).*
ℹ *to **meet/satisfy/suit** requirements*

requisition /ˌrekwɪ'zɪʃn/ *noun, verb* (*formal*)
●*noun* [C,U]

SEE ALSO: **purchase requisition**

a formal, official written request for sth: *They carefully examined our requisitions for paper clips and notepads.* ◇ *Do you have a requisition number for these goods?*
●*verb* [+ obj]
to make a formal, official request or demand for sth: *They have enough support to requisition an emergency general meeting.*

rerate (*also spelled* **re-rate**) /ˌriː'reɪt/ *verb* [+ obj or no obj]
to make a judgement about the quality or value of sth again, especially the quality or value of a company or its shares: *The bond has been rerated upwards.* ▶ **re'rating** (*also spelled* **re-rating**) *noun* [C,U]: *The shares deserve a rerating.*

resale /'riːseɪl; ˌriː'seɪl/ *noun*
(*Commerce*)
1 [U] the sale to another person of sth that you have bought: *The nuts are packaged **for** resale by the big supermarket chains.* ◇ *This model is popular because it maintains its resale value.*
2 [C] something that has been bought in order to sell to sb else: *Resales account for about 80% of property transactions.*
▶ **resaleable** (*also spelled* **resalable**) /ˌriː'seɪləbl/ *adjective* → RESELL

★**reschedule** /ˌriː'ʃedjuːl; *AmE* ˌriː'skedʒuːl/ *verb* [+ obj]
1 (*Finance*) to arrange for sb to pay back money that they have borrowed at a later date than was originally agreed: *Repayments on the loan have been rescheduled over 20 years.*
ℹ *to reschedule a **debt/loan** ♦ to reschedule **payments/repayments***
2 to change the time at which sth has been arranged to happen, especially so that it takes place later: *The meeting has been rescheduled for next week.*
ℹ *to reschedule a **conference/delivery/meeting***
▶ **re'scheduling** *noun* [U]: *debt rescheduling*

rescind /rɪ'sɪnd/ *verb* [+ obj]
(*Law*) to officially state that a law, contract, decision, etc. is no longer valid: *If performance is unsatisfactory, the contract may be rescinded.*
SYN REVOKE

rescue /'reskjuː/ *noun, verb*
(*Finance*)
●*noun* [C,U]
an occasion when sb/sth is saved from a difficult financial situation: *She is a skilled negotiator and helped to secure the firm's rescue.* ◇ *A consortium has **come to the rescue** of the struggling company.* ◇ *It is likely that shareholders will give their approval to the rescue package.*
ℹ *a rescue **package/plan** ♦ a rescue **attempt/bid/deal***
●*verb* [+ obj]
to save sb/sth from a difficult financial situation: *A government loan helped rescue the airline.* ◇ *There is hope that exporters can rescue the economy **from** recession.*

★**research** *noun, verb*
●*noun* /rɪ'sɜːtʃ; 'riːsɜːtʃ; *AmE* 'riːsɜːrtʃ/ [U] (*also* **researches** [pl.])

SEE ALSO: **attitude research, audience ~, consumer market ~, consumer ~, credit ~, customer ~, desk ~,** etc.

a careful study of a subject, especially in order to discover new facts or information about it: *The company has invested a great deal in research.* ◇ *He has carried out extensive research **into/on** robotics.* ◇ *What have their researches shown?* ◇ *He is a research analyst in the field of mortgages.*
ℹ *to **carry out/conduct/do/undertake** research ♦ **detailed/extensive/in-depth** research ♦ research **proves/reveals/shows/suggests** sth ♦ a research **centre/laboratory/unit** ♦ a research **analyst/group/scientist/team/worker***
●*verb* /rɪ'sɜːtʃ; *AmE* -'sɜːrtʃ/ [+ obj or no obj]
research (into/in/on sth) to study sth carefully and try to discover new facts about it: *They're researching new product ideas.* ◇ *He has spent the*

last two years researching into how to improve the engine's performance. ▶ **re'searcher** noun [C]: She works as a researcher for ICI.

re,search and de'velopment = R&D

re'search ,manager noun [C]
1 a person at a company who is in charge of developing new products
2 a person in a financial organization who is in charge of studying investments to see how likely they are to make money: pensions/investment research managers

resell /ˌriːˈsel/ verb [+ obj] (**resold, resold** /ˌriːˈsəʊld; AmE -ˈsoʊld/)
(Commerce) to sell sth that you have bought: He resells the goods at a profit. ◇ Banks buy the stock directly and resell it **to** investors the next day.
→ RESALE

reseller /ˌriːˈselə(r)/ noun [C]

SEE ALSO: **value-added reseller**

(Commerce) a company that buys goods from manufacturers and sells them without making any changes to them: The computers are sold to the public by resellers and not by the manufacturer itself. ◇ the computer reseller market See note at SUPPLY CHAIN

reservation /ˌrezəˈveɪʃn; AmE -zərˈv-/ noun [C] an arrangement for a seat on a plane or train, a room in a hotel, etc. to be kept for you: I'll call the restaurant and **make** a reservation. → BOOKING

,reser'vation price noun [C]
(Economics) the lowest price that a seller will sell their product for or the highest price that a buyer will pay

★ **reserve** /rɪˈzɜːv; AmE rɪˈzɜːrv/ noun, verb
●noun

SEE ALSO: **bank** ~, **capital redemption** ~, **capital** ~, **capitalization of** ~, **contingency** ~, **distributable** ~, etc.

1 [C, usually pl.] a supply of sth that is available to be used in the future or when it is needed: large coal/gas/oil reserves ◇ The company has substantial reserves of capital. ◇ Soon the reserves of coal will be exhausted.
2 (Economics) **reserves** [pl.] the foreign currency, gold, etc. that is held by the central bank of a country: Russia's gold and foreign currency reserves were $84.6 billion. ◇ The euro will rival the dollar as the main currency for central bank reserves.
→ FOREIGN EXCHANGE RESERVES
3 (Accounting) [C, usually pl.] profits that a company has made and keeps as part of its CAPITAL and does not pay to shareholders: The company has cash reserves of $88 million. ◇ Their low reserves and large debts raised questions about their ability to survive.
→ CAPITAL RESERVE
4 (Accounting) [C] (especially AmE) money that is kept from a company's profits in order to deal with possible problems or expenses in the future: The purpose of the reserve was to respond to emergencies. ◇ The business will add $55 million in reserves to cover future lawsuits. SYN PROVISION → CAPITAL RESERVE
5 (Finance) [C, usually pl.] the amount of money that banks or similar institutions must keep to pay to customers when they ask for it. Most of this money is kept with the central bank. SYN BANK RESERVES
→ LEGAL RESERVE
6 (Commerce) [C] (BrE) = RESERVE PRICE
IDM **in re'serve** available to be used in the future or when needed: The money was being **kept** in reserve for their retirement.

●verb [+ obj]
1 to ask for a seat, table, room, etc. to be available for you or sb else at a future time: I'd like to reserve a table for three for eight o'clock. ◇ I reserved a ticket online. → BOOK
2 to keep sth so that it cannot be used by any other person or for any other reason: privileges normally reserved **for** executives ◇ The company said that it would reserve $3 million to cover legal costs.
3 to have or keep a particular power: The company **reserves the right** to check the way employees use the Internet and email. ◇ **All rights reserved** (= nobody else can publish or copy this material).
4 to not make a decision until you have all the evidence: I'd prefer to **reserve judgement** (= not make a decision) until I know all the facts.

re'serve bank = CENTRAL BANK

re'serve ,currency noun [C, usually sing.]
(Economics) a foreign currency that is kept by governments and central banks because it is strong and can be used for making international payments: The euro will become the reserve currency for some countries.

re'serve fund noun [C]
(Finance) the part of an income that is kept for a particular purpose or for unexpected expenses in the future: The board has been forced to run down its reserve funds. ◇ The surplus money is to be used to establish a reserve fund.

re'serve price (BrE also **re'serve**) (AmE also **'upset price**) noun [C]
(Commerce) the lowest price that a seller will accept for sth that is sold at AUCTION: The property was withdrawn after it failed to reach its reserve price.
→ RESERVATION PRICE

re'serve re,quirement (also **re'serve ,ratio**) noun [C] (especially AmE)
(Accounting) the percentage of their total assets that banks must keep in cash or in assets that can easily be exchanged for cash SYN CASH RATIO

reshape /ˌriːˈʃeɪp/ verb [+ obj]
to change the shape or structure of sth: The merger will reshape the drinks industry. ▶ **re'shaping** noun [U]: a radical reshaping of the business

reshuffle /ˌriːˈʃʌfl/ (also **'shuffle**, less frequent) verb [+ obj or no obj]
1 to change around the jobs that a group of people do: The company has reshuffled the management team.
2 to organize sth in a different way by giving new positions to the different items in a group: The index is reshuffled every quarter based on market values.
▶ **reshuffle** /ˈriːʃʌfl/ (also **,re'shuffling**) noun [C]: a boardroom reshuffle ◇ the latest quarterly reshuffle

resident /ˈrezɪdənt/ adjective, noun
●adjective
(about a person or company) living or situated permanently in a particular country, especially when this relates to tax: to be resident abroad/in the UK
●noun [C]
1 a person who lives permanently in a particular country or place, or who has their home there: a resident of the UK ◇ local residents
2 a person who is staying at a particular hotel: The restaurant is open to residents. OPP NON-RESIDENT

residential /ˌrezɪˈdenʃl/ adjective [usually before noun]
consisting of homes and houses rather than factories or offices; where people live: a quiet residential area ◇ We deliver electricity to 2.4 million residential and business customers in the UK.
OPP NON-RESIDENTIAL

residual /rɪˈzɪdjuəl; AmE -dʒu-/ adjective, noun
● **adjective** [only before noun]
1 (Accounting) (about money, income, etc.) still remaining after other costs such as tax have been taken away: *The company uses residual cash to fund other commercial activities.*
2 still remaining at the end of a process: *There are still a few residual problems with the computer program.*
● **noun**
(Accounting)
1 [C, usually pl.] = RESIDUAL VALUE
2 [C] the money that a company or person receives after particular costs are taken away: *For a corporation, the residual is corporate profits.*
3 [C, usually pl.] (especially AmE) = RESIDUAL INCOME (2)

reˌsidual ˈincome noun
(Accounting) [U,C]
1 the part of your income that remains after costs such as tax have been taken off: *Food is the major item to be paid for out of a family's residual income.*
2 (also **reˈsidual** [C, usually pl.]) (both especially AmE) money that sb such as a SALESPERSON continues to receive as a result of sth they have done, a customer they have gained, etc. without making any further effort: *A high reorder rate will increase your residual income.*

reˌsidual ˈvalue noun [C,U] (also **reˈsidual** [C])
(Accounting) the remaining value of sth after it has been used or when it is no longer useful: *After three years, the car's residual value is about 50.9% of its cost new.* ◇ *The company has changed the way it calculates residual values.*—Picture at DEPRECIATION

★ **resign** /rɪˈzaɪn/ verb [+ obj or no obj]
(HR) to officially tell sb that you are leaving your job, an organization, etc: *She resigned as manager after eight years.* ◇ *Two members resigned from the board in protest.* ◇ *He resigned his directorship last year.*

VOCABULARY BUILDING

Leaving a job

● She **resigned** as chairman following a dispute over company strategy.
● (informal) They wouldn't give me a raise, so I **quit**.
● Under company rules, men must **retire** at 65.
● He said he had **stepped down** to make way for someone younger.
● The chief executive and finance director **vacate** their posts next year.
● After 12 years in banking, he decided to **retrain** as a teacher.

★ **resignation** /ˌrezɪgˈneɪʃn/ noun
(HR)
1 [U,C] the act of officially giving up your job or position; the occasion when you do this: *a letter of resignation* ◇ *There were calls for her resignation from the board of directors.* ◇ *Further resignations are expected.*
❍ to **announce/call for/demand/expect** sb's **resignation**
2 [C] a letter, for example to your employers, to say that you are giving up your job or position: *We haven't received his resignation yet.*
❍ to **hand in/offer/tender** your resignation ◆ to **accept/reject** sb's resignation

resilient /rɪˈzɪliənt/ adjective
strong and able to recover quickly from difficulties, losses, problems, etc: *It is the world's most resilient and dynamic economy.* ◇ *The market has become very resilient to bad times.* ▶ **resilience** /rɪˈzɪliəns/ (also **resiliency** /rɪˈzɪliənsi/ less frequent) noun [U]: *the resilience of the US economy*

resistance /rɪˈzɪstəns/ noun [U; sing.]

SEE ALSO: **consumer resistance, customer ~, sales ~**

dislike of or opposition to a plan, an idea, etc.; refusal to accept sth: *The proposal has met with resistance.* ◇ *Resistance to change has nearly destroyed the industry.*

reskill /ˌriːˈskɪl/ verb [+ obj or no obj]
(HR) to learn new skills so that you can do a new job; to teach sb new skills: *The course is designed for employees who want to reskill.* ◇ *We need to reskill the IT team to become web services specialists.*
▶ ˌ**reˈskilling** noun [U]: *the growing need for reskilling of workers*

★ **resolution** /ˌrezəˈluːʃn/ noun

SEE ALSO: **dispute resolution, high-~, low-~, ordinary ~, special ~**

1 [C] a formal statement of an opinion that is decided on by a committee or a council, especially by means of a vote: *The board opposed the resolution.* ◇ *The shareholder resolutions were put to the vote.* See note at MEETING
❍ to **adopt/carry/oppose/pass/reject** a resolution ◆ a **draft/formal/special** resolution
2 [U; sing.] the act of solving or settling a problem, disagreement, etc: *Creditors are calling for a swift resolution to the crisis.* ◇ *It might be difficult to reach a resolution that's acceptable to everyone.*
❍ to **achieve/reach** a resolution ◆ to **call for/require** a resolution ◆ an **early/a final/quick/peaceful/swift** resolution
3 (IT) [U; sing.] the power of a computer screen, printer, etc. to give a clear image, depending on the size and number of dots that make up the image: *an LCD display with a resolution of 1 600 pixels by 1 200 pixels.*

★ **resolve** /rɪˈzɒlv; AmE rɪˈzɑːlv/ verb
1 [+ obj] to find an acceptable solution to a problem or difficulty: *to resolve a conflict/a crisis/an issue* ◇ *The company is trying to resolve a pay dispute.*
2 [no obj] to reach a decision by means of a formal vote: *The board has resolved to recommend the offer to shareholders.*

resort /rɪˈzɔːt; AmE rɪˈzɔːrt/ noun, verb
● **noun**

SEE ALSO: **lender of last resort**

1 [C] a place where a lot of people go on holiday/vacation: *seaside/beach/health/ski resorts*
2 [sing.] the **first/last/final resort** the first or last course of action that you should or can take in a particular situation: *We will only strike as a last resort, if all attempts to negotiate fail.* ◇ *The matter should be dealt with in the first resort by the line manager.*
● **verb**
PHR V **reˈsort to sth** to make use of sth, especially sth bad, as a way of achieving sth, often because there is no other possible solution: *We may have to resort to using untrained staff.*

★ **resource** /rɪˈsɔːs; -ˈzɔːs; AmE ˈriːsɔːrs; rɪˈsɔːrs/ noun, verb
● **noun** [C, usually pl.]

SEE ALSO: **natural resource**

1 a supply of sth such as money, labour, etc. that an organization or a person has and can use: *We do not have the resources (= money) to update our computer software.* ◇ *We need to allocate available resources more effectively.* ◇ *More companies are pooling resources (= each company is giving sth) in order to win big contracts.*
❍ to **have/lack** resources ◆ to **pool/share** resources ◆ to **allocate/manage/use** resources ◆ **capital/cash/**

financial/technical resources • *limited/scarce*
resources

2 (*Economics*) a supply of sth such as oil, gas, land,
minerals, etc. that a country has and can use,
especially to increase their wealth: *South Africa's
natural resources* ◇ *The priority was to develop fresh
water resources.*
➔ to **be rich in/have/lack** resources • to **develop/
manage/use** resources

● *verb* [+ obj] (*usually* **be resourced**)
to provide sth with the money, equipment, labour,
etc. that is needed: *You might be competing with
several other companies who are better resourced
than you.* ◇ *The IT department is **under-resourced***
(= does not have enough of sth such as money).

re'source allo,cation *noun* [U,C]
the way in which the resources of a company are
divided and given to different departments,
projects, etc.; the act of deciding this: *The review is
important to evaluate resource allocation.* ◇ *Resource
allocations will be made to projects on a yearly basis.*

re,source produc'tivity *noun* [U]
(*Economics*) the fact of producing more goods using
smaller amounts of raw materials and causing less
waste; ways of doing this: *improvements in resource
productivity*

respect /rɪˈspekt/ *noun*
IDM **in respect of sth** (*only used in written English*)
1 concerning: *A writ was served on the firm in
respect of their unpaid bill.* **2** in payment for sth:
money received in respect of overtime worked **with
respect to sth** (*only used in written English*)
concerning: *The two groups were similar with
respect to income and status.*

respond /rɪˈspɒnd; *AmE* rɪˈspɑːnd/ *verb* [no obj]
1 to give a spoken or written answer to sb/sth:
More than fifty people responded **to** *the
advertisement.* ◇ *We aim to respond to all email
enquiries within 24 hours.*
2 to react to sth that sb has said or done:
Customers responded positively **to** *the new
packaging.* ◇ *Profit margins are down and firms are
responding by looking for ways to reduce costs.*

respondent /rɪˈspɒndənt; *AmE* -ˈspɑːnd-/ *noun* [C]
1 (*Marketing*) a person who answers questions,
especially in a survey: *48% of respondents reported
sales higher than a year ago.*
2 (*Law*) in some legal cases, the person who is
accused of sth: *The respondent was ordered to pay
$1 500 dollars to his former wife.*

response /rɪˈspɒns; *AmE* rɪˈspɑːns/ *noun* [C,U]

SEE ALSO: **efficient consumer response**

1 a spoken or written answer: *We are evaluating all
the responses we have received.* ◇ *In response to
your enquiry...*
2 a reaction to sth that has happened or been said:
Shareholders gave a mixed response to the offer. ◇
*The product was developed in response to customer
demand.* ◇ *The ad campaigns did not generate an
immediate sales response* (= an increase in sales).

res'ponse rate *noun* [C]
(*Marketing*) the percentage of people who reply to a
message or an advertisement they are sent by
telephone, email, post/mail, etc: *The average
response rate per message was 40%.* ◇ *We sent out
over 1 000 letters, but the response rate has been low.*

res'ponse time *noun* [C,U]
the length of time that a person or system takes to
react to sth: *We try to maintain a set response time
for calls to our help desk.* ◇ *The new software has
reduced response time to less than 8 seconds for most
transactions.*

★**responsibility** /rɪˌspɒnsəˈbɪləti; *AmE* -ˌspɑːn-/
noun (*plural* **responsibilities**)

SEE ALSO: **corporate responsibility, corporate social
responsibility**

1 [U] **responsibility (for sth)** the duty of being in
charge of a particular activity, area, department,
etc: *The new sales manager will have responsibility
for the European market.* ◇ *She will assume
responsibility for managing the UK business.* ◇ *Each
worker takes responsibility for their own part of the
process.* ◇ *The job has a lot of responsibility.*
➔ to **assume/have/take** responsibility for sth • to
delegate/share responsibility for sth
2 **responsibilities** [pl.] the things that sb deals
with, manages or controls in their job: *I don't feel
ready to take on new responsibilities.* ◇ *comparing
key job responsibilities and skills*
➔ to **give up/have/take on** responsibilities • to **assign/
delegate** responsibilities • **day-to-day/heavy/
increased/key** responsibilities
3 [U; C, usually sing.] a duty to help or take care of
sb/sth because of your job, position, etc: *We have a
responsibility* **to** *our shareholders.* ◇ *She feels a
strong sense of responsibility* **towards** *her employees.*
4 [U] blame for sth bad that has happened: *The
bank refuses to accept responsibility* **for** *the mistake.*
➔ to **accept/assume/take** responsibility for sth

VOCABULARY BUILDING

Having responsibility

● to **be head of** *a department/division/an
organization/a project*
● to **head up** sth (*used about a department,
project or new business*): *We will recruit someone
to head up the venture.*
● to **be responsible for** sth (*used about a
department or job*): *She is responsible for
developing new products.*
● to **be in charge of/take charge of** *a division/
project/team*

See note at **BOSS**

★**responsible** /rɪˈspɒnsəbl; *AmE* -ˈspɑːn-/
adjective
1 having the job or duty of dealing with sb/sth, so
that it is your fault if sth goes wrong: *He was
responsible* **for** *the day-to-day management of the
bank.* ◇ *Mike is ultimately responsible if things go
wrong.* See note at **RESPONSIBILITY**
2 **responsible to sb** to have to report to sb/sth with
authority or sb that you work for and explain to
them what you have done: *As chief executive he is
responsible to the shareholders.*
3 [*usually before noun*] a **responsible** job or
position is an important one that needs sb that you
can trust and rely on: *Good students expect to have
responsible positions in industry as soon as they
graduate.*

WHICH WORD?

responsible/liable

If you are **responsible for** something, it is your
duty to look after it and you can be blamed if it
goes wrong: *Who was responsible for locking up the
shop?*

If you are **liable for** something, you are legally
responsible for paying the cost of it: *The partners
are liable for the debts of the firm.*

Responsible is only used as an adjective and not
as a noun:

● *I am responsible for sales and marketing.*
● ~~I am the responsible for sales and marketing.~~

responsive /rɪˈspɒnsɪv; AmE -ˈspɑːn-/ adjective
reacting quickly and in a positive way: *The Board is always responsive **to** the needs of shareholders.* ◇ *We aim to offer fast, responsive customer service.*
▸ **res'ponsively** adverb **res'ponsiveness** noun [U]: *improving responsiveness to customers' needs*

rest /rest/ verb
PHR V **'rest with sb (to do sth)** (*formal*) if a decision, action, etc. **rests with** sb, they have responsibility for it: *Responsibility for dealing with such issues rests with senior management.*

restart /ˌriːˈstɑːt; AmE -ˈstɑːrt/ verb [+ obj or no obj]
to start again; to make sth start again: *BP has restarted production on its wells in Alaska.* ◇ *Load the software and then restart your PC.*

restate /ˌriːˈsteɪt/ verb [+ obj]
(*Accounting*) if a company **restates** all or part of its financial results, it publishes them again with some differences, usually because of changes in the way sth is calculated: *The company said it would restate earnings due to accounting irregularities.* ◇ *Profits for the year were $7.4 million, compared with a restated $5.6 million for the previous year.*
○ *to restate **accounts/earnings/figures/profits/results***
▸ **ˌre'statement** noun [C,U]: *accounting/financial restatements*

restitution /ˌrestɪˈtjuːʃn; AmE -ˈtuː-/ noun [U]
(*formal*)
1 (*Law*) payment for some harm or wrong that sb has suffered: *He is seeking $100 million **in** restitution for small investors.*
○ *to **make/pay/seek** restitution*
2 the act of giving back sth that was lost or stolen to its owner
○ *to **claim/demand** restitution*

restock /ˌriːˈstɒk; AmE -ˈstɑːk/ verb [+ obj or no obj]
(*Commerce*; *Production*) to get new supplies to replace those that have been used or sold: *It makes no sense for sales clerks to leave customers while they restock shelves.* ◇ *The industry was restocking during the first half of the year.* ▸ **ˌre'stocking** noun [U]

restore /rɪˈstɔː(r)/ verb [+ obj]
1 to bring back a situation or feeling that existed before: *The proposals are aimed at restoring investor confidence.* ◇ *We have restored 60% of our regular service.*
2 **restore sb/sth to sth** to bring sth back to a former condition, place or position: *This modest rise in sales will not be enough to restore the industry to financial health.*
→ REINSTATE

restrain /rɪˈstreɪn/ verb [+ obj]
to stop sth that is growing or increasing from continuing to do so: *A weak economy and falling consumer confidence restrained spending.*

restraint /rɪˈstreɪnt/ noun
SEE ALSO: **pay restraint, voluntary export ~, wage ~**
1 [C] a rule or an agreement that limits what a person, group, country, etc. can do: *They claimed that the ban on the import and testing of GM crops is a restraint of trade.*
2 [U] the act of controlling or limiting sth because it is necessary or sensible to do so: *Employers continue to **exercise** restraint in pay increases.*
→ LIMITATION

restrict /rɪˈstrɪkt/ verb [+ obj]
1 to limit the size, amount or range of sth: *The company is accused of restricting competition.* ◇ *Private investors were restricted **to** just 35 shares each.* ◇ *The decline in trade was not restricted to Europe.*
2 to prevent sb from doing sth: *Insiders are restricted **from** selling their shares for a short period.*

▸ **re'stricted** adjective: *The restricted supply indicates that more price rises are to come.*

restriction /rɪˈstrɪkʃn/ noun
1 [C] a rule or law that limits what you can do or what can happen: *There should be fewer restrictions **on** trading, not more.* ◇ *There are no restrictions on the amount of money you can withdraw.*
○ *to **impose/place/put** restrictions **on** sth ◆ to **ease/lift/loosen/relax/remove** restrictions ◆ **banking/export/import/planning/price/trade** restrictions ◆ **tight/tough** restrictions*
2 [U] the act of limiting or controlling sth: *Restriction of supply will help support prices.*

restrictive /rɪˈstrɪktɪv/ adjective
tightly controlled by rules, in a way that prevents people from doing what they want: *Critics have branded the regulations as too restrictive.* ◇ *a period of restrictive shopping laws*

reˌstrictive 'practice noun [C, usually pl.] (*BrE*)
1 (*HR*) ways of working arranged by one group of workers that limit the freedom of other workers or employers in order to protect people's jobs: *an investigation into restrictive practices in the legal profession*
2 (*Economics*) (*also* **reˌstrictive 'trade ˌpractice, reˌstrictive 'business ˌpractice**) agreements between businesses in an industry or trade that limit or prevent free competition between businesses: *Some corporations engage in restrictive business practices.*

★ **restructure** /ˌriːˈstrʌktʃə(r)/ verb
1 [+ obj or no obj] to organize sth such as a company, an industry, etc. in a different way in order to make it more efficient: *The company has recently restructured, reducing the size of its stores and changing the product mix.*
2 (*Finance*) [+ obj] if a company with problems **restructures** its debts, it agrees with lenders to pay them in a different way from before: *Talks began in August to restructure $6.5 billion of debt.*
▸ **res'tructuring** noun [U; C, usually sing.]: *The group said it was about to embark on a major restructuring.* ◇ *a restructuring of debt* → DEBT RESTRUCTURING

re'structuring charge (*also* **re'structuring cost**) noun [C, usually pl.]
(*Accounting*)
1 the cost to a company, an industry, etc. of organizing itself in a different way in order to become more efficient: *They **took** a $26 million restructuring charge, mainly related to redundancy pay for staff.*
2 the amount that a company has to pay to organize its debts in a different way: *The firm had to pay restructuring charges of more than 350 m euros.*

★ **results** /rɪˈzʌlts/ noun [pl.]
SEE ALSO: **payment by results**
1 (*also* **fiˌnancial re'sults**) the profits and losses made by a company during a particular period; a report on this that a company prepares: *The company's end-of-year results were better than had been expected.* ◇ *Retailers have posted disappointing results for September.* ◇ *Sales results for this March are down by 15%.*
○ *to **announce/post/report** results ◆ **annual/first-half/first-quarter/full-year/quarterly** results ◆ **final/interim/preliminary** results ◆ **good/improved/solid/strong** results ◆ **disappointing/poor/weak** results*
2 things that are achieved successfully: *The project is beginning to show results.*
○ *to **achieve/bring/get/produce/show** results*

★ resume /rɪˈzuːm; *BrE also* -ˈzjuː-/ *verb* [+ obj *or* no obj] (*formal*)

if you **resume** an activity or if it **resumes**, it begins again or continues after an interruption: *European stock markets resumed trading after the three-day break.* ◇ *Car production has resumed at the plant.*
▶ **resumption** /rɪˈzʌmpʃn/ *noun* [sing; U]: *a possible resumption of merger talks*

résumé /ˈrezjumeɪ; *AmE* ˈrezəmeɪ/ *noun* [C] (*AmE*)

a written record of your education and employment, that you send when applying for a job: *Make sure your résumé is up to date.* [SYN] CV (*BrE*)

resurgence /rɪˈsɜːdʒəns; *AmE* -ˈsɜːrdʒ-/ *noun* [sing; U]

the return and growth of an activity that had stopped: *Recent economic data shows a resurgence in consumer confidence.* ◇ *There has been a resurgence of interest in health-related holidays.* [SYN] REVIVAL
▶ **reˈsurgent** *adjective* [usually before noun]

★ retail /ˈriːteɪl/ *noun, adjective, adverb, verb* (*Commerce*)

● *noun* [U]
the selling of goods to the public, especially through shops/stores: *On leaving college, she decided on a career in retail.* ◇ *The store combines food retail with home products.* → WHOLESALE

● *adjective* [only before noun]
connected with selling goods to the public, mainly through shops/stores: *department stores and other retail outlets* ◇ *Weekend work is usual in the retail trade.*
O *a retail* **business/chain/group** • *retail* **outlets/space/stores/units** • *retail* **consumers/customers** • *the retail* **market/sector/trade**

● *adverb*
being bought and sold to the public: *to buy/sell retail* (= in a shop/store)

● *verb*
1 [no obj] to be sold at a particular price: *The printer retails for $299.* ◇ *The shoe will retail at about $150.*
2 [+ obj] to sell goods to the public, usually in small quantities: *They had a family business manufacturing and retailing woollen goods.*

ˈretail ˌaudit = STORE AUDIT

ˈretail ˌbanking (*also* conˈsumer ˌbanking) *noun* [U]

the part of a bank's business that involves providing services to members of the public: *Retail banking accounts for 10 per cent of the bank's activity.* ◇ *the retail banking sector* → PRIVATE BANKING at PRIVATE BANK
▶ **ˈretail bank** *noun* [C]

ˌretail coˈoperative *noun* [C]

1 (*Finance*) = CONSUMER COOPERATIVE
2 (*Commerce*) (*also* ˌretailer coˈoperative) a group of RETAILERS who buy goods together in large quantities so that they can get lower prices

ˌretail deˈposits *noun* [pl.]

(*Finance*) small amounts of money that a bank's customers deposit in their accounts; money that local individuals or small businesses deposit: *The bank reported a 10% jump in retail deposits.* → CORE DEPOSITS

ˌretail distriˈbution *noun* [U]

(*Marketing*) the process of getting the goods that sb produces into shops/stores so that people will buy them; the shops/stores that sell a particular product: *a nationwide retail distribution system* ◇ *The product doesn't have general retail distribution.*

★ retailer /ˈriːteɪlə(r)/ *noun* [C]

SEE ALSO: general retailer

(*Commerce*) a business or a person that sells goods directly to the public: *There have been strong sales by the big retailers.* ◇ *clothing/electronics/food retailers* ◇ *a retailer of computer products* ◇ *The product is about to go on sale at a leading high-street retailer.* ◇ *Some retailers have decided not to stock the new product.* ◇ *the growth of online retailers*
→ WHOLESALER See note at SUPPLY CHAIN
O *a* **big/large/small** *retailer* • *a* **leading/major/top** *retailer* • *a* **high-street/an independent/a speciality** *retailer* • *an* **Internet/online/a mail-order** *retailer*

ˌretailer coˈoperative = RETAIL COOPERATIVE (2)

retailing /ˈriːteɪlɪŋ/ *noun* [U]

(*Commerce*) the business of selling goods to the public, especially through shops/stores: *career opportunities in retailing* ◇ *clothes/food/music retailing* ◇ *The management team have focused the company purely on retailing.*

ˌretail inˈvestment *noun* [U,C]

(*Finance*) investment that is made by an individual for themselves, rather than by an institution: *The shares have lost 78% of their value since the peak of the retail investment boom.* ▶ **ˌretail inˈvestor** *noun* [C]

ˈretail ˌmedia *noun* [U with sing./pl. verb]

(*Marketing*) ways of advertising products in shops/stores

ˈretail park *noun* [C]

a group of large shops/stores with a large car park, usually on the edge of a town or city: *a new out-of-town retail park*

ˈretail price *noun* [C]

(*Commerce*) the price that customers pay for goods in a shop/store: *The retail price of gasoline is up 8% since the start of the year.* → RRP, WHOLESALE PRICE

ˌretail ˈprice ˌindex *noun* [sing.] (*abbr* RPI)

(*Economics*) in the UK, a list of the prices of some ordinary goods and services which shows how much these prices change each month, used to measure the rate of INFLATION (= a general rise in the prices of goods and services over a period of time): *The UK Retail Price Index for November has risen by 0.1%.* [SYN] CONSUMER PRICE INDEX, COST-OF-LIVING INDEX

ˈretail sales *noun* [pl.]

sales to the public rather than to shops or businesses: *Retail sales fell for the second month in a row.*

ˈretail store ˌaudit = STORE AUDIT

ˌretail ˈtherapy *noun* [U]

shopping that is done in order to make yourself feel happier rather than because you need things

★ retain /rɪˈteɪn/ *verb* [+ obj] (*formal*)

1 to keep sth; to continue to have sth: *Many retailers cut prices to retain customers.* ◇ *Please retain your receipt.* ◇ *The deal allows him to retain control of the company.* [SYN] KEEP
2 (*HR*) if a company **retains** people, it continues to employ them: *You can't hire and retain good people without a good benefits package.* ◇ *After the company was restructured, the former management was retained.* [SYN] KEEP
3 to give regular payments or payments in advance to sb with special knowledge such as a lawyer so that they will do work for you: *The company has retained five law firms as well as other specialist firms.* ◇ *a retaining fee* → RETAINER

reˌtained ˈearnings (*also* reˌtained ˈprofits) *noun* [pl.]

(*Accounting*) the part of the profit made by a

company after tax has been paid that is invested in the company rather than being paid to shareholders as DIVIDENDS: *The vast majority of capital spending by companies is financed from retained earnings.* [SYN] UNDISTRIBUTED EARNINGS → SHAREHOLDER EQUITY

retainer /rɪ'teɪmə(r)/ *noun* [C,U]
an amount of money that is paid to sb to make sure they are available to do work when they are needed: *He received a monthly retainer of $6 000.* ◇ *The company has a labor lawyer **on retainer.*** → RETAIN (3)

retaliatory /rɪ'tæliətri; *AmE* -tɔːri/ *adjective*
intended to punish sb for sth they have done to harm you: *retaliatory action/tariffs* → PUNITIVE

retention /rɪ'tenʃn/ *noun*
1 (*HR*) [U] the ability of a company to keep its employees; the fact of this happening: *Call centres are looking at ways to improve recruitment and retention.* ◇ *Employee retention has improved dramatically.*
2 [U] the fact of keeping sb or sth: *The company was instructed to improve its document retention policy.*
3 (*Accounting*) **retentions** [pl.] part of the money that is owed to sb for work they have done that is not paid until the work is completed in a satisfactory way

rethink /ˌriː'θɪŋk/ *verb* [+ obj *or* no obj] (**rethought**, **rethought** /-'θɔːt/)
to think again about an idea, a plan, etc., especially in order to change it: *We need to rethink our whole business strategy.* ▶ **rethink** /'riːθɪŋk/ (*also* ˌre'thinking) *noun* [sing.]: *a radical rethink of our working practices*

retire /rɪ'taɪə(r)/ *verb*
1 (*HR*) [+ obj *or* no obj] to stop doing your job, especially because you have reached a particular age or because you are ill/sick; to tell sb they must stop doing their job: *She retired early because of ill health.* ◇ *He intends to retire **from** Lex at the end of the year.* ◇ *The company's official retiring age is 65.* ◇ *She was retired on medical grounds.* ◇ *the retiring chairman* See note at RESIGN
2 (*Law*) [no obj] if a JURY **retires**, it goes to a separate room to decide whether sb is guilty or not
3 (*Finance*) [+ obj] to pay a debt; to say that sb does not have to pay a debt: *They have retired $600 million of their $4 billion loan.*

retired /rɪ'taɪəd; *AmE* rɪ'taɪərd/ *adjective*
having retired from work: *retired executives* ◇ *I'm retired now.*

retiree /rɪˌtaɪə'riː/ *noun* [C] (*AmE*)
a person who has stopped working because of their age: *Retirees are talking about going back to work because their savings have disappeared.*

★**retirement** /rɪ'taɪəmənt; *AmE* -'taɪərm-/ *noun*

SEE ALSO: **compulsory retirement, debt ~, early ~**

1 (*HR*) [U,C] the fact of stopping work because you have reached a particular age; the time when you do this: *At 60, she was now approaching retirement.* ◇ *Susan is going to **take early retirement** (= retire before the usual age).* ◇ *retirement age* ◇ *a retirement pension*
⊕ **to approach/near/postpone** *retirement* ◆ *retirement* **age/date**
2 [U; sing.] the period of your life after you have stopped work at a particular age: *We all wish you a long and happy retirement.* ◇ *Up to a third of one's life could be spent **in** retirement.*
⊕ **to plan for/provide for/save for** *retirement* ◆ *retirement* **benefits/funds/income/savings**
3 (*Finance*) [U] the act of paying back loans completely: *costs for the early retirement of debt*

re'tirement plan = PENSION PLAN

retool /ˌriː'tuːl/ *verb*
1 (*Manufacturing*) [+ obj *or* no obj] to replace or change the machines or equipment in a factory so that it can produce new or better goods: *It will cost $1 billion to retool the plant.*
2 (*informal*) [+ obj] (*AmE*) to organize sth in a new or different way: *How should we retool our strategy?*
▶ ˌre'tooling *noun* [U; sing.]: *The plant won't require significant retooling for several years.*

retract /rɪ'trækt/ *verb* [+ obj *or* no obj]
1 to say that sth you have said earlier is not true or correct or that you did not mean it: *She declined to retract the comment.*
2 to become, or to make sth become, smaller in amount or value: *Corporate IT spending retracted last year.*
▶ **retraction** /rɪ'trækʃn/ *noun* [U,C]: *He issued a public retraction of his comments.* ◇ *the huge retraction of corporate investment*

retrain /ˌriː'treɪn/ *verb* [+ obj *or* no obj]
(*HR*) to learn, or to teach sb, a new type of work, a new skill, etc: *Staff have been retrained to use the new technology.* See note at RESIGN
▶ ˌre'training *noun* [U]: *Funds are available for worker retraining.*

retreat /rɪ'triːt/ *verb, noun*
● *verb* [no obj]
1 to lose value: *Shares retreated 4.4 per cent to $24.06*
2 to decide not to do or continue to do sth because the situation has become too difficult: *A spokesman said the group has retreated **from** its plan to launch 15 new stores.* ◇ *Why have they decided to retreat from retail?*
● *noun*
1 [C, usually sing.] an act of deciding not to do or continue to do sth because the situation has become too difficult: *A tactical retreat **from** e-commerce would be best for us.*
2 [sing; U] a fall or decline in value: *Investors are feeling the effects of the retreat in share prices.*
[IDM] **be in re'treat** to become weaker, smaller, less successful, etc: *The hi-tech sector was in retreat.*
go into re'treat to start to become less valuable or successful: *The Internet advertising business has gone into retreat.*

retrench /rɪ'trentʃ/ *verb*
1 (*formal*) [no obj] (about a business, government, etc.) to spend less money; to reduce costs: *The company is retrenching rather than expanding.*
2 (*HR*) [+ obj] to tell sb that they cannot continue working for you: *The plan is to retrench about 500 to 700 people.* [SYN] LAY OFF [NOTE] Retrench with this meaning is mainly used in Australia, New Zealand and South Africa. ▶ **re'trenchment** *noun* [U,C]: *Businesses have begun expanding after two years of retrenchment.* ◇ *Workers are demanding a retrenchment package.*

retrieval /rɪ'triːvl/ *noun* [U]

SEE ALSO: **information retrieval**

the process of getting back sth that has been lost, lent, etc.

retrieve /rɪ'triːv/ *verb* [+ obj]
1 (*IT*) to find and get back data or information that has been stored in the memory of a computer: *to retrieve information from the database* ◇ *to retrieve email/voicemail*
2 to get back sth that you have lost, lent, etc: *We will be exerting our right to retrieve our property.* ◇ *The company cannot retrieve millions of pounds owed to it.*

▶ **retrievable** /rɪ'triːvəbl/ *adjective*

retro- /'retrəʊ; *AmE* -troʊ/ *prefix*
back or backwards: *retrograde* ◇ *retrospectively*

retrospective /ˌretrə'spektɪv/ (*also* ˌretro'active /ˌretrəʊ'æktɪv; *AmE* -troʊ-/) *adjective*
(about a new law, rule, etc.) intended to take effect from a particular date in the past rather than from the present date: *retrospective pay awards* ◇ *retrospective legislation* ▶ˌretro'spectively (*also* ˌretro'actively) *adverb*: *The new rule will be applied retroactively.*

★ **return** /rɪ'tɜːn; *AmE* rɪ'tɜːrn/ *verb, noun*
● *verb* [+ obj]

SEE ALSO: **accounting rate of return, annual ~, diminishing ~, rate of ~, sale or ~, sales ~, tax ~, total shareholder ~**

1 (*Accounting; Finance*) to give or produce a particular amount of money as a profit or loss: *We have managed to return a profit in each of the past seven years.* ◇ *Bonds have returned 2.2% annually.* ◇ *My investments return a high rate of interest.* See note at PROFIT
2 (*Commerce*) to take or send a product back to the place it came from because you do not want it or because there is sth wrong with it: *We had to return the printer to the store because it was faulty.* ◇ *How do you process and store returned goods?* See note at EXCHANGE
3 to telephone or email sb who has telephoned or emailed you: *The support staff promise to return all calls within an hour.*
● *noun*
1 (*Accounting; Finance*) [U,C] the amount of profit or income that you get from a particular investment: *In the grocery business a 2% to 3% return on sales is considered healthy.* ◇ *Equities have produced higher returns than bonds.* ◇ *Shareholders are expecting to see some return from their investment.* → EARNINGS, YIELD
○ *a good/high/strong* return • *a low/modest/poor* return • *an annual/average* return • *a negative/positive* return • *to achieve/make* a return • *to deliver/produce/show/yield* a return
2 [C] an official report or statement that gives particular information about sth to an official body: *a VAT return* ◇ *The vendor must file a final sales return within ten days from the date of sale.*
○ *to do/file/make/submit* a return
3 (*Accounting*) [C] = TAX RETURN
4 (*Commerce*) (*also* ˌproduct re'turn) [C] goods that a customer has bought or ordered and then returned; the act of returning a product: *All returns must be packed in the original packaging.* ◇ *Product returns are accepted up to 90 days from date of invoice.*
5 [U] (*also* **re'turn key** [C]) the button that you press on a computer when you reach the end of an instruction, or to begin a new line: *To exit this option, press return.*
IDM **by re'turn (of 'post)** (*BrE*) using the next available post; as soon as possible: *Please reply by return of post.*

returnable /rɪ'tɜːnəbl; *AmE* -'tɜːrn-/ *adjective*
1 that can or must be given back after a period of time: *A returnable deposit is payable on arrival.* ◇ *The application form is returnable not later than 7th June.*
2 (about bottles, containers, etc.) that can be taken back to a shop/store in order to be used again

returner /rɪ'tɜːnə(r); *AmE* -'tɜːrn-/ *noun* [C] (*BrE*)
(*HR*) a person who goes back to work after not working for a long time: *women returners* ◇ *courses for adult returners*

re,turn on 'assets *noun* [U,C] (*abbr* ROA)
(*Accounting*) a measure that is used to see how well a company is using its assets to produce profits. It shows the profits for the year as a percentage of the recent total assets: *About 40 per cent of listed companies are set to earn a return on assets of below 1 per cent.*

re,turn on 'capital = RETURN ON CAPITAL EMPLOYED, RETURN ON INVESTMENT

re'turn on 'capital em'ployed (*abbr* ROCE)
(*also* re,turn on 'capital) *noun* [U,C]
(*Accounting*) a measure that is used to see how well a company is using the money invested in its activities to produce profits, often calculated by comparing the company's profits for the year before tax and interest are taken off with the value of its total assets minus its total debts: *The goal is to improve the company's return on capital employed to a range of 12 to 14 per cent over the next few years.*

re,turn on 'equity *noun* [U,C] (*abbr* ROE)
(*Accounting*) a measure used to see how much profit a company is producing compared to the value of its SHAREHOLDER EQUITY (= total assets minus all the money the company owes): *The firm failed to achieve its target of a 20% return on equity.*

re,turn on in'vestment (*abbr* ROI) (*also* re,turn on 'capital) *noun* [U,C]
(*Accounting*) a measure of how much profit an investment produces compared with the amount originally invested **NOTE** Return on investment is also sometimes used to describe figures such as **return on assets, return on capital employed,** and **return on equity.**

re,turn-to-'base *adjective* [usually before noun] (*abbr* RTB)
(*Commerce*) used to describe a GUARANTEE where the buyer must send the product back to where it came from in order to have it repaired or replaced: *The camera comes with a 12-month return-to-base warranty.*

revalue /ˌriː'væljuː/ *verb*
1 [+ obj] to estimate the value of sth again, especially giving it a higher value: *Investors revalued the group's assets.* ◇ *All overseas land and buildings will be revalued during the next two years.*
2 (*Finance*) [+ obj or no obj] to increase the value of a currency in relation to the money of other countries: *The yen is to be revalued.* ◇ *There is pressure for the country to revalue.* ◇ *The euro is being revalued against the dollar.* **OPP** DEVALUE See note at CURRENCY
▶ **revaluation** /ˌriːvæljuˈeɪʃn/ *noun* [U; C, usually sing.]: *Speculators are gambling on a revaluation of the yuan.*

revamp /ˌriː'væmp/ *verb* [+ obj]
to make changes to the form of sth in order to improve its appearance, how efficiently it works, etc: *He is revamping the company's web page.* ◇ *They plan to launch a revamped version of their product in France.* ▶ **revamp** /'riːvæmp/ *noun* [sing.]: *an ambitious revamp of its core business*

★ **revenue** /'revənjuː; *AmE* -nuː/ *noun*

SEE ALSO: **average revenue, Inland ~, marginal ~, sales ~**

1 [U] (*often* **revenues** [pl.]) the money that is received by a business usually from selling goods or services: *Revenue from local advertisers fell by 6%.* ◇ *The company has annual revenues of around £3 billion.* ◇ *They reported a three per cent increase in advertising revenue for the first half of the year.* ◇ *New products account for 40% of our total revenue.* See note at INCOME
○ *annual/full-year/quarterly* revenue • *expected/potential/projected* revenue • *to bring in/generate/*

produce/yield revenue • *to boost/grow/increase
revenue* • *to post/project/report revenues*
2 [U] (*often* **revenues** [pl.]) the money that is
received by the State from taxes: *Poor economic
growth will also hurt tax revenue.* ◇ *The law bans
foreign governments from using the courts to collect
lost revenues.* → INCOME
❿ *government/public/tax* revenue • *to collect/get/
lose/raise* revenue
3 the Revenue [sing.] = INLAND REVENUE

'revenue ac,count *noun* [C]
(*Accounting*) a record of all the money that a
company has earned and spent in its normal
business activities during a particular period
→ CAPITAL ACCOUNT (4)

,revenue antici'pation note (*abbr* RAN) (*also*
,tax antici'pation note) *noun* [C, usually pl.]
(*Finance*) in the US, a type of bond issued by a local
government that is paid back using money from
taxes and other income that the local government
expects to receive in the future

'revenue bond *noun* [C]
(*Finance*) in the US, a bond that is issued by a local
government in order to finance a public project
such as the building of a new hospital, bridge,
road, etc. The bond and interest payments are
taken from the profits made by the project once it is
completed.

,revenue ex'penditure *noun* [U] (*also* ,revenue
ex'pense [C,U]) (*abbr* revex)
(*Accounting*) money that is spent on the normal
activities of a business during a particular period
such as the cost of labour, materials, etc: *Apart
from the expected increase in staff costs, there was no
increase in revenue expenditure.* → CAPITAL
EXPENDITURE

,revenue re'serve *noun* [C, usually pl.]
(*Accounting*) profits that a company has made which
are kept so that they can be given to shareholders
through a DIVIDEND payment in years when profits
are low → CAPITAL RESERVE

'revenue stamp *noun* [C]
a stamp that is put on sth such as a packet of
cigarettes to show that a government tax has been
paid

'revenue stream (*also* ,stream of 'revenue, *less
frequent*) *noun* [C]
a source of income: *The firm is on the lookout for
new revenue streams.*

'revenue ,tariff *noun* [C]
(*Economics*) a tax on imported products that is
intended to raise money for the government rather
than protect local businesses from foreign
competition → PROTECTIVE TARIFF

reversal /rɪ'vɜːsl; *AmE* rɪ'vɜːrsl/ *noun*
1 [C,U] a change of sth so that it is the opposite of
what it was: *the reversal of a decision* ◇ *The
restructuring is a complete reversal in company
strategy.* ◇ *The latest fall in prices is a **reversal of
fortune** for these stocks.*
2 [C] a change from being successful to having
problems: *The company's financial problems were
only a temporary reversal.*

reverse /rɪ'vɜːs; *AmE* rɪ'vɜːrs/ *verb, noun, adjective*
● *verb* [+ obj]
1 to change sth to the opposite of what it was
before: *to reverse a procedure/process/trend* ◇ *The
company is battling to reverse the decline in sales.*
2 (*Law*) to change a previous decision, law, etc. to
the opposite of what it was: *The Court of Appeal
reversed the decision.* **SYN** REVOKE
3 **reverse the charges** (*BrE*) to make a telephone
call that will be paid for by the person you are
calling, not by you: *I want to reverse the charges,*

please. **NOTE** In American English, people **make a
collect call** or **call sb collect.**
● *noun*
1 [C] a change, especially a change from success to
failure: *Property values have suffered another
reverse.*
2 the reverse [sing.] the opposite of sth that has
been mentioned: *We seem to be consuming more,
but in fact the reverse is true.*
IDM **go/shift into re'verse**; **put/send sth into
re'verse** to start to happen or to make sth happen
in the opposite way: *After the announcement, the
shares went into reverse.*
● *adjective* [only before noun]
opposite to what has been mentioned: *The policy
had the reverse effect to what was intended.*

re,verse 'auction *noun* [C]
(*Commerce*) a type of **auction** in which prices go
down rather than up as suppliers compete for a
contract by offering to supply sth at a lower price
than their competitors: *The automaker recently tried
out an online reverse auction for tires.*

re,verse 'billing *noun* [U]
a method of payment on mobile phones/cellphones
in which the person receiving a message pays for it
rather than the person who sends it

re,verse-'charge *adjective*
a **reverse-charge** telephone call is paid for by the
person who receives the call, not by the person
who makes it ▶ **re,verse-'charge** *adverb*: *I didn't
have any money so I had to call reverse-charge.*

re,verse discrimi'nation = POSITIVE
DISCRIMINATION

re,verse engi'neering *noun* [U]
the copying of another company's product after
examining it in detail to find out how it is made

re,verse lo'gistics *noun* [U]
(*Production*) the process of handling and storing
products that have been returned by a customer or
sth that has been used and must now be thrown
away: *Reverse logistics is big business as so many
goods are returned for being faulty or unsuitable.*
▶ **re,verse lo'gistic** *adjective*: *reverse logistic
solutions*

re,verse 'merger (*also* re,verse 'takeover) *noun*
[C]
(*Finance*) a process in which a PRIVATE COMPANY
buys all or most of the shares in a PUBLIC COMPANY
so that it can issue shares and trade them on the
stock exchange

re,verse re'purchase a,greement (*also*
re,verse 'repo, *informal*) *noun* [C]
(*Finance*) an agreement to buy shares, bonds, etc.
from an investor and then sell them back at a
higher price at a later date

re,verse 'split (*BrE also* re,verse 'share split) (*AmE
also* re,verse 'stock split) *noun* [C]
(*Finance*) a reduction in the number of shares a
company trades without any reduction in the total
value of all the shares: *The company recently did a
1-for-20 reverse split* (= twenty old shares have
become one new share).

re,verse 'takeover *noun* [C]
(*Finance*)
1 the process in which a smaller company takes
control of a larger company
2 = REVERSE MERGER

reversion *noun, verb*
● *noun* /rɪ'vɜːʃn; *AmE* rɪ'vɜːrʒn/
1 (*Law*) [U,C] the legal return of sth to sb such as
land or property: *a reversion of rights from the
publisher back to the author*

2 [U; sing.] (*formal*) the act or process of returning to a former state or condition: *a steady reversion to normal conditions*

● *verb* (*also spelled* **re-version**) /ˌriːˈvɜːʃn; AmE ˌriːˈvɜːrʒn/ [+ obj] (*usually* **be reversioned**)
to make changes to sth such as a television programme, a film/movie, software, etc. in order to make it more suitable for a particular purpose or a particular market: *The Mac-only CD-ROM was reversioned for PC.*

revex *abbr*
(*Accounting*) a short way of writing **revenue expenditure**

★ **review** /rɪˈvjuː/ *noun, verb*
● *noun*

SEE ALSO: **peer review, performance review**

1 [U,C] a careful examination of sth, usually to see if any changes need to be made: *a pay/salary review* ◇ *They plan to carry out a review of this loss-making IT business.* ◇ *The terms of your contract are under review.*
ᴏ *to* **carry out/conduct/launch/undertake** *a review of sth* • *a* **financial/spending/strategic** *review* • *an* **independent/internal/**a **judicial** *review* • *a review* **body/date/panel**
2 [C] a report on a particular subject: *a review of customer complaints* ◇ *to publish a review of recent research*
3 [C] used in the names of magazines that deal with a particular subject or profession: *the Harvard Business Review*
● *verb* [+ obj]
to carefully examine or consider sth again, especially so that you can decide if it is necessary to make changes: *to review the evidence* ◇ *The board will review the situation later in the year.* ◇ *Staff performance is reviewed annually.*

★ **revise** /rɪˈvaɪz/ *verb* [+ obj]
to change sth such as a document or an estimate in order to correct or improve it: *We continually revise our procedures.* ◇ *Marketing budgets were revised downward.* ◇ *I'll prepare a revised estimate for you.* ◇ *a revised edition of a textbook*
ᴏ *to revise sth* **completely/slightly/thoroughly** • *to revise sth* **extensively/heavily** • *to revise sth* **downwards/higher/upwards** • *to revise sth* **down/up** • **downwardly/upwardly** *revised*
▶ **revision** /rɪˈvɪʒn/ *noun* [C,U]: *a downward/upward revision* ◇ *an earnings revision* ◇ *The system is in need of revision.*

revitalize, **-ise** /ˌriːˈvaɪtəlaɪz/ *verb* [+ obj]
to make sth stronger, more active or more healthy: *The local economy has been revitalized.*
▶ **revitalization**, **-isation** /ˌriːˌvaɪtəlaɪˈzeɪʃn; AmE -ləˈz-/ *noun* [U]: *the revitalization of the steel industry*

revive /rɪˈvaɪv/ *verb*
1 [+ obj *or no obj*] to become, or to make sb/sth become, strong and active again: *The economy is beginning to revive.* ◇ *The company has been struggling to revive falling sales.*
2 [+ obj] to bring sth back; to make sth start being used or done again: *She has been trying to revive the debate over equal pay.* ◇ *The poor trade figures have revived fears of higher interest rates.*
▶ **revival** /rɪˈvaɪvl/ *noun* [U,C]: *an economic revival* ◇ *the revival of trade*

revoke /rɪˈvəʊk; AmE -ˈvoʊk/ *verb* [+ obj]
to officially cancel sth such as a decision, licence, rule or a particular right to do sth: *The commission has the power to revoke a commercial licence.*
SYN RESCIND → REVERSE *verb* (2)
▶ **revocable** /ˈrevəkəbl/ *adjective* **revocation** /ˌrevəˈkeɪʃn/ *noun* [U,C]

revolution /ˌrevəˈluːʃn/ *noun* [C]
a great change in conditions, ways of working, beliefs, etc. that affects large numbers of people: *a cultural/social/technological revolution* ◇ *There has been a revolution in management thinking.*
▶ **revolutionary** /ˌrevəˈluːʃənəri; AmE -neri/ *adjective*: *a revolutionary idea* **revolutionize**, **-ise** /ˌrevəˈluːʃənaɪz/ *verb* [+ obj]: *The Internet is revolutionizing the way that consumers buy their travel.*

revolve /rɪˈvɒlv; AmE rɪˈvɑːlv/ *verb* [+ obj]
(*Finance*) if you **revolve** a debt you do not pay all of it back but carry the remaining debt into a new financial period: *about seven out of ten credit-card holders revolve their debt.*

re¸volving 'credit (*also* **¸open 'credit**) *noun* [U,C]
(*also* **re'volving 'line of 'credit, re¸volving 'loan** [C])
(*Finance*) an agreement with a bank, etc. in which sb is allowed to borrow up to a particular amount. If they pay back part of the loan they can then borrow more money up to the agreed limit: *Consumers cut back on their use of revolving credit last year by $3.9 billion.* ◇ *The company has negotiated a €500 million revolving credit facility.*

re¸volving 'door *noun* [sing.]
1 (*HR*) used to say that the person holding a particular job or position in an organization frequently changes: *The project had been in development for years, with a revolving door of managers attached to it.* ◇ *revolving-door leadership*
2 a place, an organization or a system where people come in and go out again quickly, often many times: *a revolving-door workplace* (= where people take jobs but leave after a short time)
3 used to talk about a situation in which the same events or problems keep happening: *revolving-door crime*

re'volving 'line of 'credit = REVOLVING CREDIT

re¸volving 'loan = REVOLVING CREDIT

★ **reward** /rɪˈwɔːd; AmE rɪˈwɔːrd/ *noun, verb*
● *noun* [C,U]
a thing that you are given or money that you receive for working hard, doing sth good, etc: *The firm offers financial rewards to motivate its employees.* ◇ *His success is the reward for years of hard work.* ◇ *The investment's high reward justifies the high risk.* ◇ *The reward system recognizes effort as well as achievement.*
ᴏ *a* **big/high/low/rich** *reward* • **cash/financial/material** *rewards* • *to* **earn/get/win** *a reward* • *to* **offer/provide** *a reward*
● *verb* [+ obj]
reward sb (**with sth**) (**for sth/for doing sth**) to give sth to sb because they have done sth good, worked hard, etc: *Managers were rewarded with cash bonuses for reaching their targets.*

rewarding /rɪˈwɔːdɪŋ; AmE -ˈwɔːrd-/ *adjective*
providing benefits such as a feeling of achievement, a lot of money, etc: *This job is not very financially rewarding* (= is not very well paid). ◇ *My time at the company has been enormously rewarding.*

rework /ˌriːˈwɜːk; AmE -ˈwɜːrk/ *verb* [+ obj]
to make changes to sth in order to improve it, correct it or make it more suitable: *We had to rework our forecasts for the coming year.* ◇ *new and reworked vehicles* ▶ **re'working** (*especially BrE*) (*AmE usually* **'rework**) *noun* [C,U]: *a radical reworking of the tax code*

RFID /ˌɑːr ef aɪ ˈdiː/ *abbr* **radio frequency ID**, **radio frequency identification** (*usually used as a countable noun*)
an electronic device used for identifying sth or for preventing products from being stolen

ride /raɪd/ verb, noun

●**verb** (**rode** /rəʊd; AmE roʊd/ **ridden** /'rɪdn/) [+ obj]
to deal with a difficult or dangerous situation and
survive without being harmed: *The fund has ridden
the bear market since last autumn's launch.* ◇ *She
rode the Internet boom.*

IDM **be riding for a 'fall** to be doing sth that
involves risks and that may end in disaster: *The
stock markets were riding for a fall.* **be riding 'high**
to be successful or very confident **ride (on) the
'coattails of sb/sth; ride sb's/sth's 'coattails** to
benefit from sb else's success: *We've been riding on
the coattails of the New York rally.* **ride a/the 'wave
of sth** to enjoy or be supported by the particular
situation or quality mentioned: *We've been riding
the wave of the Italian food craze.*

PHRV **'ride on sth 1** to be supported by or to
follow a particular situation or change: *Interest
rates on mortgage loans have been riding on an
uptrend.* **2** (*usually used in the continuous tenses*) to
depend on sth: *My whole future is riding on this
interview.* **ride sth 'out** to manage to survive a
difficult situation or time without having to make
great changes

●**noun** [C, usually sing.]
used to describe how easy or difficult a particular
process or period of time is for sb/sth: *a rocky/
smooth/wild ride* ◇ *Foreign exchange traders may not
give the peso such an easy ride.*

IDM **take sb for a 'ride** (*informal*) to cheat or trick
sb: *The taxpayer is being taken for a ride.* → FREE
RIDER

rider /'raɪdə(r)/ noun [C]

SEE ALSO: dispatch rider, free rider

1 (*Law*) an extra piece of information (**clause**) that
is added to a contract or an official document
2 (*Insurance*) extra information that is added to an
insurance agreement in order to include extra
items that are not mentioned in the standard
agreement; a form used to add this information:
*You can add a rider to a home insurance policy to
cover computer equipment.*

rig /rɪg/ verb, noun

●**verb** [+ obj] (**-gg-**) (*usually* **be rigged**)
1 to arrange or influence sth in a dishonest way in
order to get the result that you want: *The
commission is looking into allegations that the
company rigged energy prices.* ◇ *to rig the market* (=
to cause an artificial rise or fall in prices, in order to
make a profit) **SYN** FIX
2 rig sth (up) (with sth) to fit equipment
somewhere, sometimes secretly: *The lights had been
rigged (up) but not yet tested.*

●**noun** [C]
1 a large piece of equipment that is used for taking
oil or gas from the ground or the bottom of the sea:
a drilling rig → OIL RIG
2 (*AmE*) (*informal*) a large lorry/truck

rigging /'rɪgɪŋ/ noun [U]

the act of working to cause an artificial rise or fall
in prices, in order to make a profit: *The company
was accused of market rigging.*

right /raɪt/ noun, verb

●**noun**

SEE ALSO: ex-rights, grandfather ~, moral ~,
patent ~, pre-emptive ~, stock ~, voting ~

1 [C,U] a moral or legal claim to have or get sth or
to behave in a particular way: *The union has a right
to strike on this issue.* ◇ *There is no right of appeal
against the decision.* ◇ *They have fought hard for
equal rights.*
➕ civil/human/political *rights* • consumer/
employment/labour/ownership *rights*
2 rights [pl.] the legal authority to publish, sell,
show, etc. a particular work such as a book, film/
movie, etc: *He sold the rights for $2 million.* ◇ *all*

rights reserved (= protected or kept for the owners
of the book, film/movie, etc.) ◇ *The company bought
the US rights to distribute the drug.*
➕ broadcasting/distribution/licensing/marketing
rights
3 (*Finance*) [C, usually pl.] = STOCK RIGHT
●**verb** [+ obj]
to correct sth that is wrong or not in its normal
state: *Righting the economy will demand major cuts
in expenditure.*

right first 'time phrase

(*Production*) used to describe a system of
manufacturing that aims to produce products that
are perfect from the start rather than quickly
producing sth that will need to be corrected or
repaired later: *He ranked right first time as the main
priority over turnover.* ◇ *right-first-time silicon chips*
→ ZERO DEFECTS

right of first re'fusal noun [C,U] (also first

re'fusal, *informal* [U])
(*Law*) the right to decide whether to accept or
refuse sth before it is offered to others: *The
company has the right of first refusal to acquire any
shares put up for sale by Softbank.*

'rights issue noun [C]

(*Finance*) an occasion when new shares are offered
to existing shareholders, often at a lower price than
the current market price: *The company is seeking to
raise $2.5 bn through a rights issue.* ◇ *The rights
issue will consist of 68.4 m shares at 96¢ per share.*
→ STOCK RIGHT

rightsizing /'raɪtsaɪzɪŋ/ noun [U,C] (*especially AmE*)

1 (*HR*) the act of making a company a more
efficient size, usually by reducing the number of
employees and cutting costs: *The bank carried out a
rightsizing of its workforce by reducing staff by 15%.*
2 (*IT*) when an organization changes to a more
efficient computer system, usually by using a
smaller, cheaper system to do the same work: *the
rightsizing of systems*
→ DOWNSIZING at DOWNSIZE
▶ **'rightsize** verb [+ obj or no obj]: *The company has
rightsized and many workers have been made
redundant.*

'rights manager noun [C]

a person whose job is organizing contracts and fees
for buying, selling and using goods, ideas, designs,
etc. in another country or another medium

rigorous /'rɪgərəs/ adjective

1 done carefully and with a lot of attention to
detail: *a rigorous analysis*
2 demanding that particular rules, processes, etc.
are strictly followed: *The work failed to meet their
rigorous standards.*
▶ **'rigorously** adverb: *Supermarkets only earn a
profit by rigorously controlling costs.*

ring /rɪŋ/ verb, noun

●**verb** (**rang** /ræŋ/ **rung** /rʌŋ/)
1 [no obj] (about a telephone) to make a sound
because sb is trying to telephone you: *Will you
answer the telephone if it rings?*
2 (*BrE*) (*also* **call**, *AmE*, *BrE*) **ring sb/sth (up)** [+ obj or
no obj] to telephone sb: *I'm ringing about your
advertisement in the paper.* ◇ *He rang up a few of his
contacts.* **SYN** PHONE

IDM **ring off the 'hook** (*AmE*) (*usually used in the
continuous tenses*) (about a telephone) to ring a lot of
times **ring the 'register; ring the 'cash register**
to sell sth and make a profit

PHRV **ring a'round**, **ring a'round sb/sth** (*BrE*) =
RING ROUND/AROUND **ring 'back** (*BrE*) to
telephone sb again, for example because they were
not available when you called earlier: *She's in a
meeting—could you ring back later?* **ring sb 'back**

(BrE) to telephone sb again; to telephone sb who has telephoned you: *I'll check the files and ring you back.* ,**ring 'in** (BrE) to telephone the place where you work: *Mark rang in to say that he won't be in today.* ◇ *Two members of staff rang in sick at short notice.* ,**ring 'off** (BrE) to put down the telephone because you have finished speaking ,**ring 'round/ a'round** (also ,**ring 'round/a'round sb/sth**) (BrE) to telephone a number of people in order to organize sth or to get some information, etc: *You should ring round a few suppliers to get quotes.* ,**ring 'through (to sb)** (BrE) to make a telephone call to sb, especially within the same building: *Reception just rang through to say your visitor has arrived.* ,**ring sth 'up** to enter the cost of goods being bought in a shop/store on a CASH REGISTER: *The cashier had rung up one of the items twice.* ,**ring 'up sth** to record an amount of sales or profits in a particular period of time: *The company rang up sales of $166 million last year.*
● **noun** [C]
1 a group of people who are working together, especially in a secret or illegal activity: *organized crime rings* → PRICE RING
2 (Stock Exchange) an area of a stock exchange where a particular product is traded SYN PIT
IDM **give sb a 'ring** (BrE) (informal) to telephone sb: *I'll give you a ring when I have some more information.* → idiom at THROW

'**ring-fence** verb [+ obj] (BrE)
1 (Finance) to protect a particular amount of money so that it can only be used for a particular purpose: *a ring-fenced bank account*
2 to protect sth by putting restrictions on it so that it can only be used by particular people or for a particular purpose: *All employees can access the parts of the Intranet that are not ring-fenced.* ▶ '**ring fence** noun [C]: *The government has promised to put a ring fence around funding for education.*

rip /rɪp/ verb (-pp-)
PHRV ,**rip sb 'off** (informal) (often **be ripped off**) to cheat sb, for example by making them pay too much or by selling them sth of poor quality: *Consumers feel they are being ripped off by their phone companies.* → RIP-OFF

'**rip-off** noun (informal)
1 [C, usually sing.] sth that is not worth what you pay for it: *The taxi fare from the airport was a real rip-off.* ◇ *The company is accused of charging rip-off prices for its products.*
2 [C] a copy of sth, especially one that is less expensive or not as good as the original thing: *These are genuine designer jeans, not rip-offs.*
→ RIP SB OFF at RIP

'**ripple ef,fect** noun [C]
a situation in which an event or action has an effect on sth, which then has an effect on sth else: *His resignation will have a ripple effect on the whole department.*

rise /raɪz/ noun, verb
● **noun** [C]

SEE ALSO: **high-rise**

1 an increase in an amount, a number or a level: *The industry is feeling the effects of recent price rises.* ◇ *There has been a 10% rise in sales.* ◇ *Credit-card use is on the rise.*
● *a dramatic/rapid/sharp/steady/strong rise* ◆ *a modest/slight/small rise*
2 (BrE) (AmE **raise**) an increase in the money you are paid for the work you do: *I'm going to ask for a rise.* ◇ *She criticized the huge pay rises awarded to industry bosses.*
● **verb** (**rose** /rəʊz/ AmE rouz/ **risen** /'rɪzn/) [no obj]
to increase in amount, number or level: *The price of*

gas rose. ◇ *Gas rose in price.* ◇ *Sales have risen from €800 million to €3 billion.* ◇ *Production rose by 8%.* ◇ *a period of rising unemployment* See note at INCREASE
● *to rise dramatically/sharply/slightly/steadily* ◆ *to be expected to/be likely to/be set to rise*
PHRV '**rise to sth** to show that you are able to deal with an unexpected situation, problem, etc: *How will they rise to the challenge of increased competition?*

★ **risk** /rɪsk/ noun, verb
● **noun**

SEE ALSO: **all-risk, buyer ~, buyer's ~, carrier's ~, country ~, credit ~, currency ~**, etc.

1 [C,U] the possibility of sth bad happening at some time in the future: *Going into partnership allows us to share the financial risks.* ◇ *There is still a risk that the whole deal will fall through.* ◇ *Any business venture contains an element of risk.* ◇ *The high risk deters many investors.*
● *a big/great/high/low/small risk* ◆ *a growing/real/ serious risk (of sth)* ◆ *economic/financial/health/ personal/security risks* ◆ *to avoid/face/increase/ reduce risk* ◆ *the risks associated with/involved in/ posed by sth*
2 (Finance) [U] the possibility that an asset may rise or fall in value: *an investment with a high degree of risk* ◇ *These stocks are ideal for investors who do not want too much risk.*
● *to carry/take on risk* ◆ *high/low risk*
3 (Insurance) [C,U] the possibility of loss or damage, that sth is insured against: *The goods are insured against all risks.* ◇ *The policy offers protection against the risk of damage.*
● *to cover (for)/insure against/protect against (a) risk*
4 [C] **a good/bad/poor risk** a person or business considered from the point of view of whether they are likely to pay back money they borrow, have an accident, etc: *With five previous insurance claims, we're now seen as a bad risk.* ◇ *The business seemed a good risk and the bank approved the loan.*
IDM **at 'risk** in danger of being lost or damaged; in danger of losing sth or being injured: *Five thousand jobs are at risk.* ◇ *Taxpayers felt that their money was being put at risk.* **do sth at your ,own 'risk** to do sth even though you have been warned about the possible dangers and will have to take responsibility for anything bad that happens: *If you send a credit-card number by fax, you do so at your own risk.* → idioms at OWNER, RUN verb, TAKE verb
● **verb** [+ obj]
1 to put sth valuable or important in a dangerous situation, in which it could be lost or damaged: *She risked all her capital in the new business.* ◇ *He would not risk his reputation if he did not think he could get the deal.*
2 to be in a situation in which sth bad could happen to you: *Some manufacturing companies risked collapse.* ◇ *We risk losing our most experienced staff to other firms.*

'**risk a,nalysis** noun [C,U]
1 the process of identifying possible risks, developing ways of making their effects less serious, and sharing information about them: *The goal of risk analysis is to uncover potential problems.* → RISK ASSESSMENT, RISK MANAGEMENT
2 (Finance) a method of calculating how safe it is to lend money to a person, an organization or a country, or how safe an investment is: *Risk analysis provides a framework for assessing loan requests.*

'**risk ,arbitrage** noun [U]
(Finance) the practice of using differences in prices in a market to try to make a profit, for example by buying shares in a company that is being taken over and at the same time selling shares in the company that is taking it over

'risk as,sessment *noun* [C,U]
the part of the process of RISK ANALYSIS that involves identifying possible risks, calculating how likely they are to happen, and estimating what effects they might have and how serious they would be: *The financial crisis has underlined the need for better risk assessment.* → RISK MANAGEMENT

'risk a,verse *adjective*
unwilling to do sth if it is possible that sth bad could happen as a result: *We're operating in a market that is extremely risk averse.* ◇ *Risk-averse investors are more interested in property than stocks.*
▶ **'risk a,version** *noun* [U]

'risk ,capital = VENTURE CAPITAL

'risk ,management *noun* [U]
the part of the process of RISK ANALYSIS that involves developing and introducing plans for making the effects of risks less serious, especially the risk of losing money: *Investors should ask about the fund's provisions for risk management.* ◇ *the bank's risk management policies*

'risk ,profile *noun* [C]
(*Finance*)
1 an analysis of a possible investment that considers how likely it is to result in a loss: *The company has a high risk profile due to the level of its debts and plans to expand.*
2 the amount of risk that a person, bank, etc. has when they invest or lend money: *Banks are trying to improve their risk profile by reducing the number of loans they make.*
3 how likely a person or company is to pay back money that has been borrowed: *a credit-card holder's risk profile*

'risk-,taking *noun* [U]
the practice of doing things that involve risks in order to achieve sth: *The reward of high profits encourages risk-taking.* ▶ **'risk-,taker** *noun* [C]: *Successful businesses are built by risk-takers.*

risky /ˈrɪski/ *adjective* (**riskier, riskiest** HELP You can also use **more risky** and **most risky**.)
involving the possibility of sth bad happening: *Many analysts believe the shares are still a risky investment.* ▶ **riskiness** /ˈrɪskinəs/ *noun* [U]

★ **rival** /ˈraɪvl/ *noun, adjective, verb*
● *noun* [C]
a person, company, or thing that competes with another: *We fought off competition from dozens of rivals to win the contract.* ◇ *This new magazine is widely seen as a rival to the major news weekly.* ◇ *The two men are now rivals for a top job in broadcasting.* SYN COMPETITOR See note at COLLEAGUE
● *a bigger/larger/smaller* rival ◆ *your closest/main/nearest* rival(s)
● *adjective* [only before noun]
that competes with another person, company or thing: *A French group has launched a rival bid for the company.* ◇ *The airline has plans to take over a rival company.*
● *a rival bid/offer* ◆ *a rival business/company/firm/group/operator* ◆ *rival products/services/brands*
● *verb* [+ obj] (**-ll-**, *AmE also* **-l-**)
to be as good, impressive, etc. as sb/sth else: *This young company may soon be rivalling the market leaders.*

rivalry /ˈraɪvlri/ *noun* [C,U] (*plural* **rivalries**)
rivalry (with sb/sth) (for sth) | **rivalry (between A and B) (for sth)** a state in which two people, companies, etc. are competing for the same thing: *The rivalry between the two software companies will continue.* ◇ *Personal rivalries prevented the proposal from receiving the support it needed.*

ROA /ˌɑːr əʊ ˈeɪ; *AmE* oʊ/ = RETURN ON ASSETS

road /rəʊd; *AmE* roʊd/ *noun*
IDM **on the 'road** travelling, especially for long distances or periods of time: *She brought in a lot of sales but was spending four or five days a week on the road.*

,road con'signment note *noun* [C] (*abbr* **CMR**)
(*Transport*) a document that goes with goods that are sent by road, stating that the company that is transporting the goods has received them and that they are in good condition

'road ,haulage *noun* [U] (*BrE*)
(*Transport*) the business of transporting goods by road: *road haulage companies*

'road ,haulier *noun* [C] (*BrE*)
(*Transport*) a company that transports goods by road: *Increases in the price of diesel fuel will be difficult for road hauliers.*

roadshow (*also spelled* **road show**, *especially in AmE*) /ˈrəʊdʃəʊ; *AmE* ˈroʊdʃoʊ/ *noun* [C]
a series of events in different places to encourage people to invest in a company: *The bank is holding roadshows to promote the issue of additional shares.* ◇ *an investor roadshow*

roaming /ˈrəʊmɪŋ; *AmE* ˈroʊ-/ *noun* [U]
a system that allows you to use local services to connect your computer to the Internet or use your mobile phone/cellphone when you are travelling: *With global roaming, you can use your mobile almost anywhere you go.*

roar /rɔː(r)/ *verb* [no obj] (*usually used with an adverb or a preposition*)
to act or happen very quickly and in an impressive way: *Share prices have come roaring back* (= they have increased a lot very quickly). ◇ *Sales roared ahead in the second half of the year.*

roaring /ˈrɔːrɪŋ/ *adjective*
IDM **do a 'roaring trade (in sth)** (*informal*) to sell a lot of sth very quickly: *The coffee shops were doing a roaring trade.* **a roaring suc'cess** (*informal*) a very great success: *The advertising campaign has been a roaring success.*

ROB /ˌɑːr əʊ ˈbiː; *AmE* oʊ/ = RUN OF BOOK

robot /ˈrəʊbɒt; *AmE* ˈroʊbɑːt/ *noun* [C]
a machine used in manufacturing that can do some tasks that a human can do and works automatically or is controlled by a computer: *These cars are built by robots.*

ROC /ˌɑːr əʊ ˈsiː; *AmE* oʊ/ = RETURN ON CAPITAL

ROCE /ˌɑːr əʊ siː ˈiː; *AmE* oʊ/ = RETURN ON CAPITAL EMPLOYED

,rock 'bottom *noun* [U]
the lowest point or level that is possible: *The shares* (= their value) *have hit rock bottom.* ◇ *Interest rates are at rock bottom.* ▶ **,rock-'bottom** *adjective*: *rock-bottom interest rates/prices*

rocket /ˈrɒkɪt; *AmE* ˈrɑːkɪt/ *verb* [no obj]
to increase very quickly and suddenly: *Sales rocketed by 110%.* ◇ *The price of oil has rocketed (up) from $25 a barrel to $40.* ◇ *rocketing costs* See note at INCREASE

'rocket ,science *noun*
IDM **it's not 'rocket science** (*informal*) used to emphasize that sth is easy to do or understand: *Getting the right products in our stores isn't rocket science—it's common sense.*

ROE /ˌɑːr əʊ ˈiː; *AmE* oʊ/ = RETURN ON EQUITY

,rogue 'trader *noun* [C]
(*Stock Exchange*) a STOCKBROKER (= a person who buys and sells shares for other people) who acts

alone and takes a lot of risks, sometimes losing a lot of their company's money: *The bank revealed that a rogue trader had lost large sums of money in the currency markets.* ▶**,rogue 'trading** *noun* [U]

ROI /ˌɑːr əʊ 'aɪ; *AmE* oʊ/ = RETURN ON INVESTMENT

★ **role** /rəʊl; *AmE* roʊl/ *noun* [C]
the function or position that sb has in an organization, an industry, a group, etc: *Owners of a small businesses have to assume a number of different roles.* → idiom at PLAY *verb*

'role ,playing *noun* [U] (*also* **'role play** [C,U])
a learning activity that is often used in business training in which you behave in the way sb else would behave in a particular situation: *Role playing is a powerful learning tool.* ◇ *role-playing exercises* ▶**'role-play** *verb* [+ obj *or no obj*]

roll /rəʊl; *AmE* roʊl/ *verb*
IDM **roll up your 'sleeves** to start to work hard: *He was prepared to roll up his sleeves and work on the shop floor.* → idiom at HEAD *noun*
PHR V **,roll sth 'back** to reduce a tax, price, rate, etc., usually back to a previous level: *The policy is designed to roll back rising insurance rates.*
→ ROLLBACK **,roll 'in** (about money, orders, profits, etc.) to arrive or appear in large quantities: *The orders kept rolling in.* ◇ *The product was a huge success and the money rolled in.* **,roll 'off sth** (about a product) to be produced, usually in large numbers, in a factory: *By next year, 60 000 cars will be rolling off its assembly lines.* See note at PRODUCE **,roll 'out; ,roll sth 'out 1** to introduce a new product, service or technology by gradually making it available to more people; to become available in this way: *The new service is to be rolled out next year.* **2** to show a new aircraft or vehicle to the public for the first time; to be seen for the first time: *It will be the world's biggest passenger airline when it rolls out in 2006.* **,roll 'over; ,roll sth 'over** (*Finance*) if money that has been paid into a fund, an insurance plan, etc. and not spent **rolls over**, or you **roll it over**, it is included in a new fund: *The money rolls over each year.* → ROLLOVER **,roll sth 'over** (*Finance*) to take an old debt, loan, etc. and include the money that is owed in a new loan agreement: *to roll over €4.2 billion of debt* ◇ *The company will be finished if the bank refuses to roll over the loan for a second time.* → ROLLOVER **,roll sth 'up 1** to buy several smaller companies and then combine their operations in order to make a more efficient business: *Industry after industry is being rolled up into just a few giant companies.* → ROLL-UP
2 (*Finance*) if an amount of money, such as the interest on an investment, is **rolled up**, it is not paid regularly, but added to the investment and paid in one amount at the end of the period of the investment

rollback /'rəʊlbæk; *AmE* 'roʊl-/ *noun* [C, usually sing.] (*especially AmE*)
a return of prices, taxes, etc. to a previous state: *a rollback of the tax increases* → ROLL STH BACK at ROLL

'roller ,coaster *noun* [C]
a situation or period of time when the prices of shares, currencies, etc. keep going up and down very quickly and by a large amount : *the stock market roller coaster* ◇ *The company has had a roller-coaster year on the stock market* (= the price of its shares has kept moving up and down).

,rolling 'contract *noun* [C]
(*Commerce*) a contract for a particular period of time that continues to be made valid for further periods of time until one person in the agreement decides to end it: *He has signed a one-year rolling contract.* → FIXED TERM

,rolling 'launch = ROLL-OUT

'rolling stock *noun* [U]
(*Transport*)
1 the engines, trains, etc. that a railway/railroad company owns or can use: *Rolling stock costs rose last year.*
2 (*AmE*) the vehicles, trucks, etc. that a company that transports goods by road owns and can use

roll-,on roll-'off *adjective* [usually before noun] (*abbr* **ro-ro, RO/RO**) (*BrE*)
(*Transport*) (about a ship) designed so that cars, trucks, etc. can be driven directly onto it at one end and off it at the other: *a roll-on roll-off car ferry*

'roll-out (*AmE spelling also* **rollout**) *noun* [C,U] (*BrE also* **,rolling 'launch** [C])
(*Marketing*) an occasion when a company introduces or starts to use a new product, service or technology by gradually making it available to more people: *They will begin the roll-out of their new product next July.* ◇ *increased demand for broadband roll-out*

rollover /'rəʊləʊvə(r); *AmE* 'roʊloʊvər/ *noun* [C, usually sing.]
1 (*Finance*) the act of allowing an old loan or debt to continue into a new agreement with the same conditions: *a rollover loan/mortgage* ◇ *The country agreed a debt rollover with the IMF.*
2 (*Finance*) (*AmE*) a situation when money is moved from one investment to another, often without paying tax
3 (*IT*) (on web pages) an image that changes when the mouse goes over it; a technique for creating this image: *Javascript rollover buttons*
→ ROLL OVER, ROLL STH OVER at ROLL

'roll-up *noun* [C]
a situation where several smaller companies are bought and combined in order to make a more efficient business → ROLL STH UP at ROLL

ROM /rɒm; *AmE* rɑːm/ *noun* [U]
(*IT*) **read-only memory** a type of computer memory that contains information and instructions that are permanent and cannot be changed or removed → RAM, CD-ROM

RON /ˌɑːr əʊ 'en; *AmE* oʊ/ = RUN OF NETWORK

'room ,service *noun* [U]
a service provided in a hotel, by which people staying in the hotel can order food and drink to be brought to their rooms: *At the hotel there is 24-hour room service.* ◇ *He ordered coffee from room service.*

ROP /ˌɑːr əʊ 'piː; *AmE* oʊ/ = RUN OF PAPER, RUN OF PRESS, RUN OF PUBLICATION

ro-ro (*also spelled* **RO/RO**) /'rəʊ rəʊ; *AmE* 'roʊ roʊ/ = ROLL-ON ROLL-OFF

ROS /ˌɑːr əʊ 'es; *AmE* oʊ/ = RUN OF SITE

roster /'rɒstə(r); *AmE* 'rɑːs-/ *noun* [C]
1 a list of the names of people such as employees, customers, etc: *a roster of clients/customers/partners* ◇ *He has assembled an impressive client roster.*
2 a list of people's names and the jobs that they have to do at a particular time: *the* **duty** *roster*

,rostered day 'off *noun* [C] (*plural* **rostered days off**) (*abbr* **RDO**)
(*HR*) especially in Australia and New Zealand, an arrangement in which, every two or four weeks, employees receive an extra paid day when they do not have to work, if they work longer hours on the other days

rotate /rəʊ'teɪt; *AmE* 'roʊteɪt/ *verb* [+ obj *or no obj*]
if a job **rotates**, or if people **rotate** a job, they regularly change the job or regularly change who does the job: *The EU presidency rotates among the members.* ◇ *We rotate the night shift so no one has to*

do it all the time. ▶ **ro'tating** *adjective* [only before noun]: *a rotating presidency*

rotation /rəʊˈteɪʃn; AmE roʊ-/ noun [C,U]

SEE ALSO: job rotation

1 the act of regularly changing the person who does a particular job: *The meeting is chaired by all the members of the team* **in rotation.** ◇ *a five-year rotation of audit firms*
2 (*Stock Exchange*) = SECTOR ROTATION
▶ **rotational** /rəʊˈteɪʃənl; AmE roʊ-/ *adjective* [only before noun]

rough /rʌf/ adjective, noun, verb

● *adjective* (**rougher, roughest**)
1 not exact; not including all details: *a rough calculation/estimate of the cost* ◇ *I've got a **rough idea** of what it will look like.*
2 not finished or corrected: *a rough draft of a report*
▶ **'roughly** *adverb: Sales are up by roughly 10%.* ◇ *Roughly speaking, we receive about fifty new clients a week.*
● *noun* [C]
(*Technical*) the first version of a drawing or design that has been done quickly and without much detail: *Only the best of the roughs are shown to the editor.*
IDM in 'rough (*especially BrE*) if you write or draw sth **in rough**, you make a first version of it, not worrying too much about mistakes or details
● *verb*
PHRV ,rough sth 'out to draw or write sth without including all the details: *I've roughed out a few ideas.*

round /raʊnd/ adjective, noun, verb

● *adjective*
a **round** figure or amount is given as a whole number, usually one ending in 0 or 5: *It is 110 to the nearest round number.* ◇ *In round figures* (= not the exact amount)*, it will cost $1.5 million.*
● *noun* [C]

SEE ALSO: milk round

a group of events that are part of a longer series: *the latest round of meetings/trade talks* ◇ *a new round of job cuts/tax cuts* ◇ *He's through to the second round of interviews.*
● *verb*
PHRV ,round sth 'up/'down (to sth) to increase or decrease a number to the next highest or lowest whole number: *1 980 543 rounded up to 2 million* ◇ *The price increases were caused by shops rounding up to the nearest euro.*

rounding /ˈraʊndɪŋ/ noun [U]
the act of increasing or decreasing a number to the next highest or lowest whole number: *Numbers don't add up to 100% because of rounding.*

,round 'lot noun [C]
(*Stock Exchange*) the standard unit of trading on the stock market that often equals 100 shares: *A round lot for an issue under CDN$1 is 500.*

,round 'table noun [C, usually sing.]
a group of people that meet to discuss sth at a conference, etc.; the meeting or discussion that takes place: *a round table on energy strategies* ◇ *a round-table discussion*

,round 'trip noun [C,U]
a journey to a place and back again: *a 30-mile round trip to work* ◇ *a round trip between New York and Chicago*

route /ruːt; AmE also raʊt/ noun, verb

● *noun* [C]
1 a fixed way along which a bus, train, plane, etc. regularly travels or goods are regularly sent: *a bus/*plane/shipping route ◇ *The airline has 44 routes operating out of Heathrow.*
2 (*IT*) the path that a piece of information (a **packet**) takes when it is directed from one computer system to another
● *verb* [+ obj] (**routing** *or* **routeing, routed, routed**)
1 (*IT*) to direct information that is received from one computer system to another: *Email is routed through several servers before it reaches its final destination.* ◇ *a system that routes messages to the appropriate workers*
2 to send sb/sth by a particular route: *The goods were routed via Lyons.* ◇ *All calls are now routed to local call centres.*

Route 128 /,ruːt ,wʌn twenti 'eɪt/ noun [U]
in the US, an area in Massachusetts where there are many companies connected with the computer and electronics industries

routeing = ROUTING

router /ˈruːtə(r); AmE also 'raʊt-/ noun [C]
(*IT*) a device that directs data from one computer system to another in the shortest possible time: *a wireless router*

routine /ruːˈtiːn/ noun, adjective

● *noun*
1 [C,U] the things you usually do every day or at regular intervals and the way you normally do them: *Reporting to my line manager is part of my daily routine.* ◇ *We clean and repair the machines as a matter of routine.*
2 (*IT*) [C] a list of instructions that enable a computer to perform a particular task: *The program contains two assembly code routines.*
● *adjective*
1 [usually before noun] done as a normal part of a particular job, situation or process; ordinary and not unusual: *routine enquiries/questions/tests* ◇ *The fault was discovered during a routine test.*
2 ordinary and boring; the same every day: *The work is interesting at first but it soon becomes routine.*
▶ **rou'tinely** *adverb: Visitors are routinely checked as they enter the building.*

routing (BrE spelling also **routeing**) /ˈruːtɪŋ; AmE also 'raʊtɪŋ/ noun [U]

SEE ALSO: call routing

1 (*IT*) the process by which a piece of information (a **packet**) is directed from one computer system to another: *Internet/network routing* ◇ *routing hardware/software* ◇ *We are trying to get smarter routing on the network.*
2 the route that a particular plane, train, road, etc. takes; the decisions you make about this route: *Routing is extremely important in pipelines.*

'routing ,number = SORT CODE

royalty /ˈrɔɪəlti/ noun [C, usually pl.] (plural royalties)
(*Commerce*)
1 an amount of money that is paid for the right to use the property of another person, such as the owner of a COPYRIGHT or PATENT. A particular amount is paid each time their book, product, etc. is sold or their work performed: *She received $5 000* **in** *royalties.* ◇ *a 12% royalty on sales of the drug* ◇ *royalty fees/payments/rates/revenue*
2 an amount of money that is paid by an oil or mining company to the owner of the land that they are working on

RPI /,ɑː piː 'aɪ; AmE ,ɑːr/ = RETAIL PRICE INDEX

RRP /,ɑːr ɑː 'piː; AmE ,ɑːr ɑːr/ abbr (BrE)
(*Commerce*) **recommended retail price** the price at which the maker of a product suggests that it

should be sold to customers in shops/stores: *RRP €500; member's price €350.* [SYN] MSRP, SRP

RSI /ˌɑːr es ˈaɪ/ *abbr* **repetitive strain injury**, **repetitive stress injury** pain and swelling, especially in the arms and hands, caused by performing the same movement many times in a job or an activity: *The spread of computers in offices has led to a rise in cases of RSI.* [SYN] OOS

RSVP /ˌɑːr es viː ˈpiː/ *abbr*
written at the end of an invitation to ask sb to reply [NOTE] RSVP is formed from the first letters of a French phrase meaning 'Please reply'.

RTB /ˌɑː tiː ˈbiː; *AmE* ˌɑːr/ = RETURN-TO-BASE

ˌrubber ˈcheque (*AmE spelling* ~ **check**) *noun* [C] (*informal*)
a cheque that a bank does not accept because the person who wrote it does not have enough money in their account

ˌrubber ˈstamp *noun* [C]
1 a small tool that you hold in your hand and use for printing the date, the name of an organization, etc. on a document
2 a person or group that automatically gives approval to the actions or decisions of others: *The directors were accused of acting as a rubber stamp for the company's management.*
3 automatic approval that is given to sth: *The committee denied that they had provided a rubber stamp for the scheme.*

ˌrubber-ˈstamp *verb* [+ obj]
to give official approval for sth, especially without considering it carefully: *The board refused to rubber-stamp the plans.*

ruin /ˈruːɪn/ *noun, verb*
• *noun* [U]
the fact of having no money, of having lost your job, position, etc: *The company is facing financial ruin.* ◇ *The property crash led to his ruin.*
[IDM] **in ˈruins** destroyed or severely damaged: *Her career was in ruins.*
• *verb* [+ obj]
1 to damage sth so badly that it loses all its value, etc.; to spoil sth: *The tourist industry has ruined this area of natural beauty.*
2 to make sb/sth lose all their money, their position, etc: *The company was ruined by bad investments.* ◇ *The scandal ruined him.*

rule /ruːl/ *noun, verb*
• *noun* [C]

SEE ALSO: **80/20 rule, work-to-rule**
-----
1 an official statement of what may, must or must not be done in a particular situation: *It's **against** company rules to smoke in offices.* ◇ *the **rules and regulations** concerning safety equipment* ◇ *The deal was unusual, but didn't break any rules.*
○ *to **establish/make/set** rules* • *to **follow/obey/observe** the rules* • *to **breach/break/violate** a rule*
2 a measuring instrument with a straight edge
3 a thin straight line that has been drawn or printed: *Draw a rule under the table of figures.*
4 a statement of what you are advised to do in a particular situation: *There are no **hard and fast rules** (= fixed rules) for successful presentations.* ◇ *The first rule is to make eye contact with your customer.*
[IDM] **bend/stretch the ˈrules** to change the rules to suit a particular person or situation **the rules of the ˈgame** the standards of behaviour that most people accept or that actually operate in a particular area of life or business → idioms at PLAY *verb*, WORK *verb*

• *verb*
1 [+ obj *or* no obj] to give an official decision about sth: *The deal may be ruled illegal.* ◇ *The court ruled that the women were unfairly dismissed.* → RULING, OVERRULE
○ *to rule **against/in favour of/on** sth*
2 [+ obj] to draw a straight line using sth that has a firm straight edge: *Rule a line at the end of every piece of work.*
→ idiom at COURT *noun*
[PHR V] **ˌrule sb/sth ˈout 1** to state or decide that sth is not possible or that sb/sth is not suitable: *He would not rule out the possibility of a merger.* ◇ *The proposed solution was ruled out **as** too expensive.* ◇ *They ruled him out for the top job at the bank.* **2** to prevent sb from doing sth; to prevent sth from happening: *His age ruled him out **as** a possible candidate.*

ˈrule book *noun* [C] (*often* **the rule book** [sing.])
a set of rules that must be followed in a particular job, company or organization: *a new rule book for how deals should be done*

ruling /ˈruːlɪŋ/ *noun* [C]
an official decision made by sb in a position of authority, especially a judge: *The court will make its ruling on the case next week.* → RULE *verb*

★**run** /rʌn/ *verb, noun*
• *verb* (**running, ran** /ræn/ **run**)
1 [+ obj] to be in charge of a business, etc: *to run a hotel/factory/store* ◇ *He has no idea how to run a business.* ◇ *The shareholders want more say in how the company is run.* ◇ *We hired an agency to run our ad campaign.* ◇ *a badly/well-run company* ◇ *state-run industries*
2 [+ obj] to make a service, a course of study, etc. available to people: *Training courses are run by various organizations.* [SYN] ORGANIZE
3 [+ obj *or* no obj] (about a machine, a vehicle, a computer, software, etc.) to operate or work; to make sth do this: *The software is designed to run **on** different operating systems.* ◇ *Press this key to run the program.* ◇ *It's cheaper to keep the machines running than to turn them off.*
4 [no obj] (*used with a preposition or an adjective*) to be at or near a particular level: *Inflation was running **at** 26%.* ◇ *Sales have been running below last year's levels.* ◇ *Don't let the hard disk run **low on** space.* → RUN SHORT at RUN
5 [no obj] to operate or be valid for a particular period of time: *The contract will run for 5 years.* ◇ *The lease on the building only has a year left to run.*
6 [+ obj *or* no obj] to show or publish advertisements, stories, television programmes, etc.; to be shown or published: *The company is running a series of ads on national TV.* ◇ *The magazine will run more in-depth news.*
7 [+ obj] **run a deficit/surplus** to have or keep a debt/an extra amount of money: *The federal government is likely to run a surplus of $150 billion.*
8 [+ obj] **run a test/check (on sth)** to do a test/check on sth: *This program allows you to run tests on your PC to see how it performs.*
9 [+ obj] to own and use a vehicle or machine: *I can't afford to run a car on my salary.*
10 [no obj] (*used with an adverb or a preposition*) (*usually used in the continuous tenses*) to happen in the way mentioned or at the time mentioned: *The business is now running smoothly.* ◇ *None of the software projects ran according to schedule.*
[IDM] **run a/the ˈrisk of (doing) sth** to be or put yourself in a situation in which sth bad could happen to you: *Retailers run the risk of being left with goods they cannot sell.* **run ˈlate** (*used especially in the continuous tenses*) to do things after the time you planned: *I'm running late for the meeting.* **run out of ˈtime** to have no more time available: *They're running out of time to find a buyer.* **run ˈshort; run ˈshort (of sth)** if sth **runs short** or you

run short of sth there is very little left: *Time is running short.* ◇ *The business has run short of cash.*
run a tight 'ship to organize sth in a very efficient way, controlling other people very closely: *She was known for running a tight ship in her previous post.*
→ idioms at BRICK, CONTROL *noun*, FOOT *noun*, GROUND *noun*, UP *adj*

PHR V **,run back 'over sth** to discuss or consider sth again: *I'll run back over the procedure once again.* [SYN] REVIEW **,run sth 'by/'past sb** (*informal*) to show sb sth or tell sb about an idea in order to see their reaction to it. *Run that past me again.* **,run 'down**; **,run sth 'down 1** to lose power or stop working; to make sth do this: *The battery has run down.* **2** to gradually stop working or become smaller in size or number; to make sth do this: *British manufacturing industry has been running down for years.* ◇ *The company is running down its sales force.* → RUNDOWN **'run into sth 1** to experience difficulties, etc: *Be careful not to run into debt.* ◇ *to run into danger/difficulties/trouble* **2** to reach a particular level or amount: *Her income runs into six figures* (= more than $100 000, etc.). **,run sth 'off** to copy sth on a machine: *Could you run off twenty copies of the agenda?* → PHOTOCOPY **,run 'on** to continue without stopping; to continue longer than is necessary or expected: *The meeting will finish promptly—I don't want it to run on.* **,run 'out 1** if a supply of sth **runs out**, it is used up or finished: *The money has run out.* ◇ *Time is running out for the company to find a buyer.* **2** if an agreement or a document **runs out**, it becomes no longer valid [SYN] EXPIRE **,run 'out (of sth)** to use up or finish a supply of sth: *We ran out of fuel.* ◇ *The company could run out of cash.* **,run sth 'past sb** = RUN STH BY/PAST SB **,run 'through sth 1** to discuss, repeat or read sth quickly: *Could we run through your proposals once again?* **2** to use up or spend money carelessly **'run to sth** to be of a particular size or amount: *Building costs may run to $1 million.* **,run 'up** to increase: *Product prices have run up faster than expected.* **,run sth 'up** to allow a bill, debt, etc. to reach a large total: *The company ran up a debt of 26 billion euros.* ◇ *Some banks have run up huge losses.* **'run with sth** (*informal*) to accept or start to use a particular idea or method: *OK, let's run with Jan's suggestion.*

● *noun*

SEE ALSO: **bank run, bear ~, bull ~, cheque ~, long ~, long-~, short ~,** etc.

1 [C] a period when good or bad things happen; a series of successes or failures: *The company has enjoyed a run of good luck.* ◇ *We've had a run of negative results.*
2 (*Manufacturing*) [C] the amount of a product that a company decides to make at one time: *Our first production run was only 400 units.* ◇ *The print run of 6 000 copies soon sold out.*
3 (*Economics*) [C, usually sing.] **a run on the dollar, yen, etc.** a situation when many people suddenly sell a currency and the value of the money falls: *Analysts fear a possible run on the dollar.*
4 (*Commerce*) [C, usually sing.] **a run on sth** a situation when many people suddenly want to buy sth, often because they are afraid there may not be enough: *There has been a run on this particular model and we are now out of stock.*
5 (*Economics*) [C, usually sing.] **a run on a bank, etc.** a time when too many people want to take their money out of the banks at the same time, so the banks cannot pay them all: *The financial crisis started a run on the banks.* ◇ *measures to protect small banks from a run on deposits*
6 (*Finance*) [C, usually sing.] a situation when many people want to buy shares, bonds, property, etc. and prices go up: *The market had a tremendous run.*
→ idioms at LONG RUN, SHORT RUN

runaway /'rʌnəweɪ/ *adjective* [only before noun]
1 increasing at a very fast rate and not able to be controlled: *fighting runaway inflation* ◇ *The company is trying to cope with runaway demand for its product.*
○ *runaway* **costs/inflation/prices**
2 very successful: *The book was a runaway best-seller.* ◇ *Their new product has proved to be a runaway success.*
○ *a runaway* **best-seller/hit/success/winner**

rundown /'rʌndaʊn/ *noun* [C, usually sing.]
1 an explanation or a description of sth: *Can you give me a brief rundown* **on** *each of the applicants?*
2 (*BrE*) a reduction in the amount, size or activity of sth, especially a business: *300 jobs are being cut because of a rundown* **in** *repair work.* ◇ *a rundown of transport services* → RUN DOWN at RUN *verb*

,run-'down *adjective*
1 (about a buildings, place, machine, etc.) in very bad condition; that has not been taken care of: *The offices are in a run-down but central area.* ◇ *rebuilding run-down factories*
2 (about a business, etc.) not as busy or as active as it used to be: *run-down transport services*

rung /rʌŋ/ *noun* [C]
a level or position in an organization, a company, a system, etc: *Women are now moving up the rungs of the corporate ladder.* [NOTE] A **rung** is one of the bars that forms steps in a ladder. → LADDER

running /'rʌnɪŋ/ *noun* [U]
the running of sth the activity of managing or operating sth: *the* **day-to-day** *running of a business* ◇ *He's responsible for the smooth running of the factory.*
[IDM] **in/out of the 'running (for sth)** (*informal*) having some/no chance of succeeding or of achieving sth: *Only two companies are in the running for the contract.*

'running cost *noun* [C, usually pl.]
the amount of money it costs to operate a machine, vehicle, business, etc: *a reduction in annual running costs* ◇ *The factory has low running costs.*
→ OVERHEADS

,running re'pairs *noun* [pl.]
small things that you do to a vehicle, a machine, etc. to keep it working: *to make/carry out running repairs*

,running 'total *noun* [C, usually sing.]
the total number or amount of things, money, etc. that changes as you add each new item: *We try to* **keep** *a running total of how much we spend.*

,run of 'book *noun* [U] (*abbr* **ROB**)
(*Marketing*) when an advertisement is placed anywhere in a newspaper, magazine, etc. and the advertiser has not paid for a particular place: *run-of-book ads*

,run of 'network *noun* [U] (*abbr* **RON**)
(*Marketing*) when an advertisement is placed on pages on some or all websites in an advertising network and the advertiser has not paid for a particular place

,run of 'paper (*also* **,run of 'press, ,run of publi'cation**) *noun* [U] (*abbr* **ROP**)
(*Marketing*) when an advertisement is placed anywhere in a newspaper, magazine, etc. and the advertiser has not paid for a particular place: *All ads are placed on a run-of-paper basis.*

,run of 'site *noun* [U] (*abbr* **ROS**)
(*Marketing*) when an advertisement is placed anywhere on a website and the advertiser has not paid for a particular place

,run-of-the-'mill *adjective*
ordinary or standard, with no special or interesting
features: *It was a run-of-the-mill laptop.*

'run-time *noun* [U,C]
(*IT*)
1 the amount of time that a program takes to
perform a task
2 the time when a program performs a task

'run-up *noun* [C, usually sing.]
1 a period of time leading up to an important
event; the preparation for this: *an increase in
spending in the run-up **to** New Year*
2 (*also spelled* **runup**) an increase in prices that is
often sudden: *a sharp run-up in share prices* ◇ *The
market is due for a run-up.*
→ RUN UP at RUN *verb*

rural /'rʊərəl; *AmE* 'rʊrəl/ *adjective* [usually before
noun]
connected with or like the countryside: *rural areas*
◇ *rural communities* ◇ *the rural economy*

'rush hour *noun* [C, usually sing., U]
the time, usually twice a day, when the roads are
full of traffic and trains are crowded because
people are travelling to or from work: *Don't travel
in the rush hour/at rush hour.* ◇ *rush-hour traffic*

Russell 2000™ /ˌrʌsl tuː 'θaʊznd/ *noun* [sing.]
(*Stock Exchange*) a list of the average of the share
prices of 2 000 smaller companies in the US,
published by the Russell Company: *The Russell 2000
index, which tracks smaller company stocks, rose 4%.*

'rust belt (*also spelled* **Rust Belt**) *noun* [C, usually
sing.] (*especially AmE*)
an area where there are many old factories which
are closed or which no longer make much money

RW /ˌɑː 'dʌbljuː; *AmE* ˌɑːr/ = READ-WRITE

S s

S /es/ *abbr*
(especially for sizes of clothes) small: *S, M and L*
(= small, medium and large)

SA *noun* (*only used in written English*)
used in the name of some companies in French-
speaking and Spanish-speaking countries: *Renault
SA* See note at LTD

sabbatical /sə'bætɪkl/ *noun* [C,U]
a period of time when an employee is allowed to
stop their normal work in order to study or travel:
*He's **on** sabbatical.* ◇ *to take a six-month sabbatical* ◇
sabbatical leave

sabotage /'sæbətɑːʒ/ *verb, noun*
● *verb* [+ obj]
1 to damage or destroy sth deliberately to prevent
sb from using it or to protest about sth: *The main
electricity supply had been sabotaged.*
2 to prevent sth from being successful or being
achieved, usually deliberately: *The rise in interest
rates sabotaged any chance of the firm's recovery.*
● *noun* [U]
1 the act of doing deliberate damage to
equipment, transport, machines, etc. to prevent sb
from using them, or to protest about sth: *an act of
industrial sabotage* ◇ *They blamed the problems on
sabotage by strikers.*
2 the act of deliberately spoiling sth in order to
prevent it from being successful

sachet /'sæʃeɪ; *AmE* sæ'ʃeɪ/ (*BrE*) (*AmE* **'packet**)
noun [C]
a closed plastic or paper packet that contains a very
small amount of liquid or a powder: *a sachet of
shampoo/sugar*

sack /sæk/ *noun, verb*
● *noun*
1 [C] a large bag with no handles, made of strong
rough material or strong paper or plastic, used for
storing and carrying things in: *The rice is sold in
20kg sacks.*
2 (*AmE*) [C] a strong paper bag for carrying
shopping: *a grocery sack*
3 [C] the contents of a **sack**: *a sack of flour/
potatoes* ◇ (*AmE*) *a sack of groceries*
4 the sack [sing.] (*BrE*) (*informal*) being told by your
employer that you can no longer work for a
company, etc., usually because of sth that you have
done wrong: *She **got** the sack for being late every*

day. ◇ *After several arguments with his boss, he was
given the sack.* ◇ *Four hundred workers face the
sack.* SYN DISMISSAL
● *verb* [+ obj] (*BrE*) (*informal*)
to dismiss sb from a job: *The sales manager was
sacked after the results were announced.* ◇ *calls for
the sacking of the CEO* See note at DISMISS

saddle /'sædl/ *noun, verb*
● *noun*
IDM **in the 'saddle** (*informal*) in a position of
authority and control
● *verb*
PHR V **'saddle sb/yourself with sth** (*often be
saddled with sth*) to give sb/yourself an
unpleasant responsibility, task, debt, etc: *I've been
saddled with organizing the conference.* ◇ *The
company was saddled with debts of €20 million.*

sae (*also spelled* **SAE**) /ˌes eɪ 'iː/ *abbr* (*BrE*) **stamped
addressed envelope, self-addressed envelope**
(*used like a countable noun*)
an envelope on which you have written your name
and address and put a stamp so that sb else can use
it to send sth to you: *Please enclose an sae for your
test results.* → SASE

safe /seɪf/ *noun* [C]

SEE ALSO: **night safe**

a strong metal box or cupboard with a complicated
lock, used for storing valuable things in, for
example, money or jewels

'safe de,posit (*also* **'safety de,posit**) *noun* [U,C]
the action of putting important documents or
valuable items in a strong room or metal box, for
example in a bank, to keep them safe; a place that
offers this service: *items on safe deposit at the bank*
◇ *a safe-deposit box/vault* ◇ *The bank has a safe-
deposit service.*

,safe 'haven (*AmE also* **,safe 'harbor**) (*BrE spelling ~
harbour) *noun* [C]
a place where sb/sth can go to be safe from danger
or risk: *Many investors see gold as a safe haven for
their money.* ◇ *a safe-haven currency/stock*

safety /'seɪfti/ *noun* [U]

SEE ALSO: **health and safety, margin of safety**

1 the state of not being dangerous: *The plant has
been closed for safety checks.* ◇ *The factory was closed*

down **on safety grounds**. ◇ *The airline has an excellent safety* **record**.
O *to* **check/improve** *safety* • *fire/flight/food/product/road safety* • *a safety* **assessment/check/inspection** • *safety* **regulations/requirements/rules/standards** • *safety* **measures/procedures**
2 the state of being safe and protected from danger or harm: *The safety of the employees is the company's main concern.*
O **passenger/personal/public/worker** *safety* • *to* **ensure/guarantee** *safety*
3 used to describe sth designed to prevent injury or damage: *a manufacturer of industrial safety equipment*
O *safety* **devices/equipment/features/glasses**

'safety ,culture *noun* [U,C]
a way of working where the safety of employees is considered to be one of the most important things: *The company is promoting a safety culture among employees following a series of accidents.*

'safety de,posit = SAFE DEPOSIT

'safety net *noun* [C]
an arrangement that helps to prevent disaster if sth goes wrong: *a financial safety net* ◇ *Unemployment benefit provides a safety net for people who lose their jobs.*

'safety pro,cedure *noun* [C, usually pl.]
the way that sth must be done or a rule that must be followed in order to prevent accidents or other dangerous events from happening: *New safety procedures have been introduced to ensure that a similar accident never happens again.*
O **adequate/basic/inadequate/poor** *safety procedures* • *to* **follow/improve/tighten** *safety procedures*

'safety stock *noun* [U,C]
(*Production*) the smallest extra supply of goods, raw materials, etc. that a company tries to have at all times in case more than expected is ordered or new stock arrives late: *Companies that once kept months of safety stock now get by with days.* → BUFFER STOCK

'safety valve *noun* [C]
a device that lets out steam or pressure in a machine when it becomes too great

sag /sæg/ *verb* [no obj] (**-gg-**)
to become weaker or fewer: *This year, profits have sagged.* ◇ *sagging consumer confidence* ▶ **sag** *noun* [U; C, usually sing.]: *a sag in share prices*

S & L /,es ənd 'el/ *abbr* (*AmE*)
savings and loan association

salable, salability = SALEABLE

sa'lami ,slicing *noun* [U]
the act of removing sth gradually by small amounts at a time: *Local rail services have been withdrawn by a process of salami slicing.* ◇ *a salami-slicing style of management*

salaried /'sælərid/ *adjective*
1 (about a person) receiving a salary: *a salaried employee*
2 (about a job) for which a salary is paid: *a salaried position* ◇ *salaried employment*
→ WAGED

★salary /'sæləri/ *noun* [C] (*plural* **salaries**)
SEE ALSO: **base salary, basic salary**
money that employees receive for doing their job, especially professional employees or people working in an office, that is usually paid every month: *an annual salary of $40 000* ◇ *a 9% salary increase* ◇ *She's* **on** *a salary of €33 000.* ◇ *Starting salaries ranged between $23 000 and $28 000.*
→ WAGE
O *to* **earn/receive** *a salary* • *to* **cut/increase/pay** *a*

salary • *an* **annual/a monthly/starting** *salary (of ...)* • *an* **average/a big/competitive/high/low/modest** *salary*

VOCABULARY BUILDING

The benefits of a job

Money
● *We offer a starting* **salary** *of up to 70k.*
● *The minimum* **wage** *is set at $7.15 an hour.*
● *You will receive a basic salary plus* **commission** *on each sale.*
● *She gets a €2 000* **bonus** *on top of her salary.*
● *Many argue that the* **pay packages** *offered to top executives are excessive.*

Other benefits
● *Benefits include* **health insurance** *and a* **pension plan**.
● *Free meals are one of the* **perks** *of working in a restaurant.*
● *Jobseekers rated* **flexible hours** *as a better perk than a* **company car**.

---

salaryman /'sælərimæn/ *noun* [C] (*plural* **salarymen** /-men/)
a word used especially in Japan to refer to a man who has an ordinary job in an office: *the year-end exchange of gifts between salarymen and their superiors* **NOTE** **Salarywoman** is also used, but less often.

'salary ,matrix *noun* [C]
(*HR*) a chart with rows and columns that show the range of pay in a company, used to decide what increase in pay employees should receive

'salary ,package = PAY PACKAGE

'salary prog,ression = SALARY SCALE (1)

'salary scale *noun* [C]
(*HR*)
1 (*BrE also* **'salary prog,ression**) the range of levels of pay that a person can receive in a particular job within a company or an organization, especially when they are paid every month: *She was promoted to the next grade, where the salary scale was €28 500 to €37 000.*
2 the range of levels of pay that people receive in different jobs within a company or an organization, especially when they are paid every month: *They are only hiring people at the lower end of the salary scale.*
→ PAY SCALE, WAGE SCALE

★sale /seɪl/ *noun*
SEE ALSO: **agreement of sale, bill of ~, cash ~, clearance ~, closing-down ~, conditional ~, conditions of ~**, etc.

1 [U,C] an act or the process of selling sth: *regulations governing the sale of vitamins* ◇ *The sale of assets raised €100 000.* ◇ *She gets 10% commission on each sale.* ◇ *I haven't made a sale all week.*
O *to* **close/complete/lose/make** *a sale* • *a sale* **makes/raises**...
2 [C] an occasion when a shop/store sells its goods at a lower price than usual: *The sale starts on 28 December.* ◇ *the January sales* ◇ (*BrE*) *I bought a coat* **in the sales** (= the period when many shops are selling goods at lower prices). ◇ *sale items/goods*
O *an* **annual/end-of-season/a summer/winter** *sale* • *to* **have/hold** *a sale*
3 [C] an occasion when goods are sold, especially an AUCTION: *a contemporary art sale*
IDM **for 'sale** available to be bought: *The company*

is not for sale. ◇ *The group has **put** its book business up for sale.* ◇ *'for sale' signs on* **,sale 1** available to be bought, especially in a shop/store: *The latest model goes on sale next week.* **2** being offered at a reduced price: *All DVD players are on sale today and tomorrow only.*
→ SALES → idiom at PUT *verb*

saleable (*AmE spelling also* **salable**) /'seɪləbl/ *adjective*
1 that can be sold; good enough to be sold: *In order to be a saleable product, the vehicle would require further development.*
2 that sb will want to buy: *The company's hi-tech factory is its most saleable asset.*
▶ **saleability** (*AmE spelling also* **salability**) /ˌseɪləˈbɪləti/ *noun* [U]

,sale and 'leaseback *noun* [U]
(*Finance*) the process of selling a building, machinery, etc. to sb and then continuing to use it by renting it from the buyer: *The company is hoping to raise over €1 billion from the sale and leaseback of its 200 high-street stores.*

,sale and re'purchase a,greement = REPURCHASE AGREEMENT

,sale as 'seen *phrase*
(*Commerce*) if used goods are advertised as **sale as seen**, the buyer must examine them carefully as they are not offered with a promise that they are suitable or in good condition: *All used cars on this website are offered for sale as seen.* → SOLD AS SEEN

,sale by des'cription *phrase*
(*Commerce*) a situation in which a buyer cannot see goods for sale, but must rely on a description of the goods, for example on a label or packet: *As catalogues use sale by description, the law requires that their descriptions are accurate.*

,sale by 'sample *phrase*
(*Commerce*) a situation in which a buyer sees only a small amount or piece of sth before buying it and must assume that the quality of the rest will be the same: *Sale by sample allows stores to sell large quantities of goods without the need to store them.*

,sale or re'turn *phrase* (*BrE*) (*abbr* **S/R**)
(*Commerce*) if goods are supplied (on) **sale or return**, there is an agreement that any item that is not sold can be sent back without having to be paid for: *Our industrial products are available on sale or return for a period of up to two weeks.* ◇ *We can supply goods on a sale-or-return **basis***.

'sale price *noun* [C]
1 the price at which sth is offered for sale or is sold: *The sale price of the company is expected to be around €2 billion.*
2 a special low price that an item is sold at for a period of time when a shop/store reduces its prices: *The sale price was 20% lower than the list price.*

saleroom /'seɪlruːm; -rʊm/ (*BrE*) (*AmE* **'salesroom**) *noun* [C]
(*Commerce*) a room where goods are sold at an AUCTION

★ **sales** /seɪlz/ *noun*

SEE ALSO: after-sales, comparable-store ~, cost of ~, direct sale, field ~, gross ~, net ~, etc.

1 [pl.] the amount of goods or services sold: *Annual sales are up on last year.* ◇ *The company reported sales of $190 million.* ◇ *Retail sales fell by 2%.* ◇ *They hope to generate $500 million in sales.* ◇ *the sales figures for May*
❍ **annual/full-year/like-for-like/quarterly/total** *sales* ◆ **high/strong** *sales* ◆ **disappointing/flat/low/slow/**

sluggish/weak *sales* ◆ **global/international/ national** *sales* ◆ **to boost/generate** *sales* ◆ *a sales* **forecast/outlook** ◆ *sales* **growth/performance** ◆ *sales* **charts/quotas/targets**
2 [U] the business of selling things; the department of a company that is responsible for selling things: *One of the sales staff helped me to choose a gift.* ◇ *He works in sales.* ◇ *The sales meeting lasted for two hours.* ◇ *a big company with a large sales department*
❍ *a sales* **department/director/manager/staff/team** ◆ *sales* **presentations/techniques**
→ SALE

'sales ac,count *noun* [C]
1 (*Accounting*) a financial record in which total sales for cash or credit during a particular period are recorded
2 a company that is a customer of another company and buys goods or services from them

'sales a,greement = CONTRACT OF PURCHASE

'sales a,nalysis *noun* [C,U]
(*Marketing*) a detailed examination of a company's sales records in order to measure and improve its performance: *If you do a sales analysis of each of our stores, you'll find that those that are out-of-town have the highest sales.*

,sales and 'marketing *noun* [U]
the business of advertising and selling goods or services; the department of a company that is responsible for this: *They do the sales and marketing for a wide range of products.* ◇ *More than half the job losses will be in sales and marketing.*

'sales ,area *noun* [C]
1 (*Marketing*) (*also* **'sales ,territory**) an area, a part of a market or a group of products that a SALES REPRESENTATIVE or a team is responsible for: *My sales area covers eight states and 60 customers.*
❍ **to allocate/assign** *a sales area*
2 (*Commerce*) the part of a store where customers can buy things: *We have a retail sales area of more than 2 000 square feet.*

'sales as,sistant (*BrE*) (*AmE* **'sales clerk, clerk**) *noun* [C]
a person whose job is to serve customers in a shop/store SYN SHOP ASSISTANT

'sales ,budget *noun* [C]
(*Accounting*) a plan for a particular period of time of how much money a company is likely to receive from the sale of goods and services: *Our sales budget is 30% higher than last year.*

'sales cam,paign *noun* [C]
(*Marketing*) a series of planned activities that are intended to sell a particular product or increase sales of a product: *We are about to **launch** a sales campaign to highlight our new range of cameras.* ◇ *The aggressive sales campaign has nearly doubled their revenue.* → SALES DRIVE

'sales ,channel = CHANNEL *noun* (3)

'sales charge *noun* [C]
(*Finance*) a fee that you pay when you buy sth such as shares, bonds, insurance, etc. from a BROKER

'sales check = SALES SLIP

'sales clerk (*also spelled* **salesclerk**) = SALES ASSISTANT

'sales ,concept = SELLING CONCEPT

'sales ,conference *noun* [C]
(*Marketing*) an event at which members of a company's sales team from different offices meet to discuss and plan ways of selling the company's products

'sales drive *noun* [C]
(*Marketing*) an attempt to increase a company's
sales: *We have boosted business by 24% after a major
international sales drive.* → SALES CAMPAIGN

'sales engi,neer *noun* [C]
(*Marketing*) a SALESPERSON who has a good
technical knowledge of products and the market
and gives technical presentations

'sales ,figures *noun* [pl.]
the amount or value of goods or services that a
company has sold during a particular period: *Sales
figures for last year were disappointing.*
● *December/first-quarter/full-year/like-for-like/
monthly sales figures* • *good/solid/strong sales
figures* • *disappointing/inflated/poor/weak sales
figures*

'sales force *noun* [C with sing./pl. verb]
all the people who are involved in selling a
company's goods or services: *The Weldon Group has
a 6 000 strong sales force* (= with 6 000 people).

'sales ,history *noun* [C]
(*Marketing*) a record of how many of a particular
product have been sold since it was first produced

'sales in,centive *noun* [C]
(*Marketing*) a reward that is offered to SALESPEOPLE
to encourage them to sell more: *The company is
offering a two-day golf vacation as a sales incentive.*

'sales ,invoice *noun* [C]
(*Accounting*) a list of goods that have been sold, that
is given to the customer to show what they must
pay and when

'sales ,ledger *noun* [C] (*BrE*)
(*Accounting*) in a company's financial records, a
group of accounts that is used to record the
amounts owed by particular customers
→ ACCOUNTS RECEIVABLE, PURCHASE LEDGER

★ **salesman** /'seɪlzmən/, **saleswoman**
/'seɪlzwʊmən/ *noun* [C] (*plural* **salesmen** /-mən/
saleswomen /-wɪmɪn/)
a man or woman whose job is to sell goods, for
example, in a shop/store: *a car salesman* ◇ *an
insurance salesman* ◇ *one of the company's top
salesmen* → SALESPERSON See note at CHAIRMAN

salesmanship /'seɪlzmənʃɪp/ *noun* [U]
the methods and skills involved in selling things:
slick/aggressive/successful salesmanship

'sales mix *noun* [sing.]
(*Marketing*) the way that a company's total sales are
divided among all their products: *Sports cars are
likely to make up about 35% of our sales mix.* ◇ *If
you increase the price of an item with a high
percentage of the sales mix, your profits will increase
dramatically.*

'sales ,office *noun* [C]
a part of a company that sells a company's products
in a particular area: *Contact your local sales office
for a list of prices.*

'sales orien,tation *noun* [U]
(*Marketing*) used to describe a way of doing business
where a company competes mainly by developing
its methods for selling products, rather than by
producing better products or meeting customers'
needs better than other companies → MARKETING
ORIENTATION, PRODUCT ORIENTATION

★ **salesperson** /'seɪlzpɜ:sn; *AmE* -pɜ:rsn/ *noun* [C]
(*plural* **salespeople** /-pi:pl/)
(*Marketing*) a person whose job is to sell a company's
goods or services: *They have assembled a strong
team of salespeople.*

'sales pitch *noun* [C]
(*Marketing*) talk or arguments used by a person

trying to sell things: *This training course will help
you develop your sales pitch.* → PITCH

'sales pro,motion *noun* [U,C]
(*Marketing*) activities done in order to increase the
sales of a product or service: *We are **running** a sales
promotion in October with a 20% discount on our
camera phones.*

★ **'sales repre,sentative** (*also* **'sales rep, rep,**
informal) (*also* **,repre'sentative, 'trade
repre,sentative**) *noun* [C]
(*Marketing*) a person who sells a company's goods or
services by visiting possible customers, usually
receiving a COMMISSION on what they sell: *We now
have more than 200 sales representatives around the
country.* ◇ *She started her career as a sales rep and is
now a sales manager.* ◇ *You can request a sample or a
rep visit.* See note at AGENT

'sales re,sistance *noun* [U]
(*Marketing*) when someone is unwilling to buy a
product, especially as a result of aggressive selling
techniques: *Sales resistance is a direct result of a
salesperson's behaviour.* ◇ *tactics to overcome sales
resistance*

'sales re,turns *noun* [pl.]
(*Accounting*) goods that a customer has bought and
then returned: *We need to monitor sales returns to
find out why goods are being returned.* ◇ *the sales
returns account/book* → RETURN (4)

'sales ,revenue *noun* [U] (*also* **sales revenues**
[pl.]) (*especially AmE*)
(*Accounting*) the total income that a company
receives from sales of goods and services in a
particular period of time SYN TURNOVER (1)

salesroom /'seɪlzru:m; -rʊm/ = SALEROOM

'sales slip (*also* **'sales check**) = RECEIPT (1)

'sales sub,sidiary *noun* [C]
a company that is owned by a larger company
whose products it sells: *The company is to open a
sales subsidiary in Malaysia.*

'sales tax *noun* [U,C]
tax that must be paid on many goods and services
when you buy them: *The rate of sales tax in
Arkansas is 5.1%.* → VAT

'sales ,territory = SALES AREA (1)

'sales ,turnover *noun* [C, usually sing., U]
(*Accounting*) the total value of goods or services sold
by a company during a particular period of time:
*We expect to achieve a sales turnover of €300 million
in the coming financial year.*

'sales ,volume *noun* [C, usually sing., U]
(*Accounting*) the total number of units of a product
sold by a company during a particular period of
time: *The sales volume of BMW brand cars totalled
454 972 units for the six-month period.*

salvage /'sælvɪdʒ/ *verb, noun*
● *verb* [+ obj]
to save goods or a ship from being completely
destroyed in an accident or a disaster: *Goods worth
€4 million were salvaged from the warehouse
following the flood.*
● *noun* [U]
1 the act of saving goods or a ship from being
completely destroyed in an accident or a disaster:
*The salvage of the ship was made difficult by bad
weather.* ◇ *a salvage company/team/operation*
2 the things that are saved from a disaster or an
accident: *Some of the stock was only slightly
damaged and was sold as salvage.* ◇ (*figurative*) *hopes
of a salvage deal for the company*

'salvage ,value (*also* **'scrap ,value**) *noun* [C,U]
1 (*Accounting*) the value of an asset at the end of its useful life: *The delivery van was purchased for €40 000, and after five years will have a salvage value of approximately €5 000.*
2 (*Insurance*) the value of sth that has been damaged in an accident, etc., such as goods or a ship

'salvage yard *noun* [C] (*AmE*)
a place where old machines, cars, etc. are broken up so that the metal can be sold or used again

,same-'day *adjective* [only before noun]
used to refer to a service that is provided on the same day that you order it: *Most of our orders are for same-day delivery.* ◇ *a same-day printing service*
→ NEXT-DAY

,same-store 'sales (*also* **,comparable-store 'sales**) *noun* [pl.]
(*Accounting*) used to refer to the change in the value of sales in a company or group's stores compared to the same stores in the previous year, used as a way of measuring the performance of the company as a whole. Only stores that have been open for more than a year are included in the total: *Wal-Mart's July same-store sales were up 6%.* → LIKE-FOR-LIKE

★ **sample** /'sɑːmpl; *AmE* 'sæmpl/ *noun, verb*
● *noun* [C]

SEE ALSO: **random sample, sale by sample**

1 a small amount or example of sth that can be looked at or tried to see what it is like: *They are giving away free samples of shampoo in supermarkets.* ◇ *A book of fabric samples* ◇ *The website has useful sample letters and emails.*
● *to give away/offer/provide a sample* • *a fabric/product sample*
2 (*Technical*) a number of people or things taken from a larger group and used in tests to provide information about the group: *We did a telephone survey of a random sample of 1 000 workers.* ◇ *The drug was tested on a sample group of 24 people.*
● *a large/random/representative/small sample* • *to recruit/survey/use a sample*
3 (*Technical*) a small amount of a product that is looked at or tested in order to see what the rest is like: *A sample of parts are inspected for quality.* ◇ *A sample taken from the plant tested positive for the bacteria.*
● *to analyse/collect/provide/test a sample*
● *verb* [+ obj]
1 to try a small amount of sth to see what it is like; to experience sth for a short time to see what it is like: *Shoppers were sampling the perfumes.* ◇ *You can sample the service for two weeks.*
2 to question a group of people in order to find information about a larger group: *12% of the people sampled said they would be interested in the service.*
3 (*Technical*) to test a single item or a small amount of a product in order to see what the rest is like: *10 of the 29 sampled products failed one or more standard quality tests.*

sampler /'sɑːmplə(r); *AmE* 'sæm-/ *noun* [C]
a collection that contains typical examples of sth, so that people can try or experience them: *You can download a sampler of our designs from our website.*

sampling /'sɑːmplɪŋ; *AmE* 'sæm-/ *noun*

SEE ALSO: **acceptance sampling, activity ~, sequential ~, snowball ~, stratified ~, work ~**

1 (*Technical*) [U] the process of taking a sample: *statistical sampling of 2 000 customers*
2 [C] a small part, number or amount of sth that has been taken or chosen as a sample: *Here's a sampling of the price ranges we found.*

'sampling ,fraction *noun* [C]
(*Marketing*) the relationship between the part of a group that is chosen to take part in a survey and the size of the whole group: *We used a sampling fraction of 1 in 100.*

'sampling frame *noun* [C]
(*Marketing*) the list of people or things that form the group from which a sample is chosen: *The electoral register was used as a sampling frame.*

sanction /'sæŋkʃn/ *noun* [C, usually pl.]
an official order that limits trade, contact, etc. with a particular country, in order to make it do sth, such as obeying international law: *Trade sanctions were imposed against/on any country that refused to sign the agreement.* ◇ *The economic sanctions have been lifted.*
● *to apply/impose/lift sanctions* • *economic/financial/trade sanctions*

s and h (*also spelled* **s & h**) /,es ənd 'eɪtʃ/ =
SHIPPING AND HANDLING

'sandwich board *noun* [C]
(*Marketing*)
1 a pair of boards with advertisements on them that sb wears at the front and back of their body as they walk around in public
2 a wooden frame in two parts, joined at the top, that stands on the ground and has advertisements on each side

'sandwich course *noun* [C] (*BrE*)
a course of study which includes periods of study and periods of working in business or industry

S&P 500™ /,es ənd ,pi: faɪv 'hʌndrəd/ =
STANDARD AND POOR'S 500 INDEX

SARL /,es eɪ ɑːr 'el/ *abbr* (*only used in written English*)
used in the name of some companies in French-speaking countries: *KeeBoo SARL* See note at LTD

SASE /,es eɪ es 'iː/ *abbr* (*AmE*) **self-addressed stamped envelope** (*used like a countable noun*)
an envelope on which you have written your name and address and put a stamp so that sb else can use it to send sth to you: *Please enclose an SASE for your test results.* → SAE

satellite /'sætəlaɪt/ *noun* [C]
1 an electronic device that is sent into space, and is used for communicating by telephone, radio, television, etc. and for providing information: *We have linked all our offices by satellite.* ◇ *making a call to a satellite phone*
2 an organization, a town or a country that is controlled by and depends on another larger or more powerful one: *We have a satellite office in Hong Kong.*

satisfaction /,sætɪs'fækʃn/ *noun* [U]

SEE ALSO: **customer satisfaction, job satisfaction**

1 the good feeling that you have when you are happy with sth that you have done, that you have bought, that has happened, etc: *She had the satisfaction of seeing her book become a best-seller.* ◇ *He looked back on his career with great satisfaction.*
2 an acceptable way of dealing with a complaint, a debt, an injury, etc: *They agreed on a payment of $5 000 in full satisfaction of the debt.*

satisfactory /,sætɪs'fæktəri/ *adjective*
good enough for a particular purpose; acceptable: *A bonus will be paid on satisfactory completion of the contract.* ◇ *The law says that goods you buy must be 'of satisfactory quality' and free from defects.*

saturate /'sætʃəreɪt/ *verb* [+ obj]
(*Marketing*) (*often* **be saturated**)
to supply so much of a product in a particular market that few new customers can be found: *The*

mobile phone market is becoming saturated. ◇ *Japan's electronics industry began to saturate the world markets.* ▶ **saturation** /ˌsætʃə'reɪʃn/ *noun* [U]: *Sales of vending machines have fallen because of saturation of the market.* ◇ *The market for this product is reaching* **saturation point** (= a situation when few new buyers can be found). ◇ *Has broadband reached* **market saturation** *in North America?*—Picture at PRODUCT LIFE CYCLE

★ **save** /seɪv/ *verb*
1 [+ obj] to avoid wasting sth or using more than necessary: *We have installed new lighting to save energy costs.* ◇ *Book early and save €100!* ◇ *We'll take a cab to save time.*
2 [+ obj *or* no obj] **save (sth) (up) (for sth)** to keep money instead of spending it: *Workers are encouraged to save for their pension.* ◇ *Do you save regularly?* ◇ *I've been saving $200 a month for years.*
3 [+ obj *or* no obj] to make a computer keep work, for example by putting it on a disk: *Save the file* **to** *your hard drive.* ◇ *I've saved the file* **as** *a pdf.* ◇ *Don't forget to save regularly as you work.*
IDM **save (sb's) 'face** to avoid or help sb avoid embarrassment: *She was fired, but she saved face by telling everyone she'd resigned.* → idiom at LOSE → FACE-SAVING

saver /'seɪvə(r)/ *noun* [C]
1 a person who saves money and puts it in a bank, etc. for future use: *The increase in interest rates is good news for savers.*
2 (*often with another noun*) something that helps you spend less money or use less of the thing mentioned: *The program is easy to use and is a real time-saver.*

★ **saving** /'seɪvɪŋ/ *noun*

SEE ALSO: cost saving, face-~, labour-~

1 [C] an amount of sth such as time or money that you do not need to use or spend: *Buy three and make a saving of €5!* ◇ *With the new heating system we can make big savings on fuel bills.*
2 savings [pl.] money that you have saved, especially in a bank, etc: *He used his savings to start up his own company.*
3 (*Economics*) [U] the situation when income is greater than money spent; the process of spending less than income: *Consumers have not yet switched from consumption to saving.* ◇ *a drop in household saving*
4 -saving (*in adjectives*) that reduces the amount used of the thing mentioned; preventing waste of the thing mentioned: *energy-saving modifications* ◇ *time-saving devices*

'savings ac,count *noun* [C]
a bank account that receives interest on the money put into it

,savings and 'credit co,operative = CREDIT COOPERATIVE

,savings and 'loan associ,ation (*abbr* S & L) (*also* **,building and 'loan associ,ation**) (*both AmE*) *noun* [C]
an organization like a bank that issues shares to people who deposit money and lends the money to people who want to buy a home SYN THRIFT INSTITUTION → BUILDING SOCIETY

'savings bank *noun* [C]
a bank that pays interest on money you save in accounts but does not offer other services

savvy /'sævi/ *noun, adjective* (*informal*)
● *noun* [U]
practical knowledge or understanding of sth: *His business savvy comes from years of running his own company.*
● *adjective* (*informal*) (*especially AmE*)
having practical knowledge or understanding of

sth: *In business it helps if you are IT savvy.* ◇ *savvy shoppers/travelers*

SBU /ˌes biː 'juː/ = STRATEGIC BUSINESS UNIT

scab /skæb/ *noun* [C] (*informal*)
an offensive way of referring to a worker who refuses to join a strike or who works instead of sb on strike SYN BLACKLEG

scalable /'skeɪləbl/ *adjective*
(*IT*)
1 used to describe a computer, a network, software, etc. that can be adapted to meet greater needs in the future: *a scalable network/system*
2 designed to work on a large or small scale, according to needs: *scalable graphics*
▶ **scalability** /ˌskeɪlə'bɪləti/ *noun* [U]

scale /skeɪl/ *noun, verb*
● *noun*

SEE ALSO: diseconomy of scale, economy of ~, large-~, pay ~, salary ~, sliding ~, small-~, wage ~

1 [sing; U] the size or extent of sth, especially when compared with sth else: *The prototype was a success so we started producing it* **on a large scale**. ◇ *The sales figures revealed the full scale of the company's crisis.*
2 [C] a range of levels or numbers used for measuring sth: *a five-point pay scale* ◇ *The salary scale goes from €18 000 to €35 000.* ◇ *to evaluate performance on a scale from 1 to 10* ◇ *a scale of fees/ charges*
3 [C, usually sing.] the set of all the different levels of sth, from the lowest to the highest: *Small businesses make up 59% of industry in the region, while* **at the other end of the scale**, *2% employ over 500 people.*
4 [C,U] the relation between the actual size of sth and its size on a map, diagram or model that represents it: *a scale model/drawing* ◇ *a scale of 1:10 000* ◇ *These products are not pictured* **to** *scale* (= they appear bigger or smaller than in real life).
5 [C, usually pl.] an instrument for weighing people or things
● *verb* [+ obj]
(*Technical*) to change the size of sth: *Text can be scaled from 4 points to 108 points without any loss of quality.*
PHR V **,scale sth 'down** (*AmE also* **,scale sth 'back**) to reduce the number, size or extent of sth: *We are thinking of scaling down our training programmes next year.* ◇ *The IMF has scaled back its growth forecasts for the next decade.* ◇ *Smaller businesses are not scaled-down versions of larger ones.* **,scale sth 'up** to increase the number, size or extent of sth: *The call centre has been scaled up to handle over 10 000 calls a day.*

,scaled 'question *noun* [C]
(*Marketing*) a type of question that is used to get data on people's opinions, behaviour, etc., where a range of possible answers are shown and people choose the one that is closest to their own opinion, behaviour, etc. Each answer is represented by a number, for example 1,2,3,4,5, which shows its position in the range, so that people's answers can be easily compared and measured.

'scale e,conomy = ECONOMY OF SCALE

scalp /skælp/ *noun, verb*
● *noun* [C]
a symbol of the fact that sb has been defeated or punished: *The poor performance in recent months has now claimed the scalp of the firm's chief executive* (= he has lost his job).
● *verb* [+ obj]
to make a quick profit by buying tickets for

concerts, sports events, etc. and selling them for a much higher price

scalper /ˈskælpə(r)/ = TOUT *noun*

scam /skæm/ *noun* [C] (*informal*)
a clever and dishonest plan for making money: *Three people were found guilty of operating an insurance scam.*
O to *operate/pull/set up* a scam

scan /skæn/ *verb, noun*
• *verb* [+ obj]
1 (*Commerce*) to use a special machine (called a **scanner**) to read the information on a BAR CODE, etc: *In the warehouse we use hand-held scanners to scan the bar codes on the storage racks and parts.*
2 (*IT*) to change a document, picture, etc. into a form that can be stored or processed on a computer using a special machine (called a **scanner**): *All documents are scanned and stored digitally.*
3 to look quickly but not very carefully at a document, etc: *I scanned the list quickly for my name.* ◇ *scanning through the business pages*
▶ **scannable** /ˈskænəbl/ *adjective*
PHR V **scan sth 'into sth; ,scan sth 'in** (*IT*) to change a document, picture, etc. into a form that can be stored or processed on a computer, by using a special machine (a **scanner**): *Text and pictures can be scanned into the computer.*
• *noun*
1 (*IT*) [C] an image of sth produced on a computer screen by a special machine
2 [sing.] the act of looking quickly but not very carefully at a document, etc: *I just had time to have a quick scan of the report.*

scanner /ˈskænə(r)/ *noun* [C]

SEE ALSO: **flatbed scanner**

1 a device that uses a narrow line of strong light for reading the information on sth such as a credit card, BAR CODE, etc: *The identity cards are examined by an electronic scanner.* ◇ *Busy shoppers should check their price scanner receipts for errors.*—Picture at STORE
2 (*IT*) a machine for changing a document, picture, etc. into a form that can be stored or processed on a computer: *a document scanner*
—Picture at OFFICE

scarce /skeəs; AmE skers/ *adjective* (**scarcer, scarcest**)
if sth is **scarce**, there is not enough of it and it is only available in small quantities: *scarce resources* ◇ *Skilled engineers are becoming scarcer.* ▶ **scarcity** /ˈskeəsəti; AmE ˈskersəti/ *noun* [U,C] (*plural* **scarcities**): *a scarcity of resources/data*

'scarcity ,value *noun* [U,C]
(*Economics*) a situation where the price of sth rises because there is not enough of it available: *The price reflects the scarcity value of development land in the city.*

'scatter ,diagram
(*also* **'scatter chart, 'scatter graph, 'scatter plot**) (*also* **scattergram** /ˈskætəgræm; AmE -tərg-/) *noun* [C] a type of graph that shows the relationship between two values, numbers or quantities by creating a pattern of dots: *The scatter diagram clearly shows that heavier vehicles use fuel less efficiently.*

scatter diagram

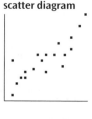

SCC /ˌes siː ˈsiː/ = SINGLE COLUMN CENTIMETRE

SCEM /ˌes siː iː ˈem/ = SUPPLY CHAIN EVENT MANAGEMENT

scenario /səˈnɑːriəʊ; AmE səˈnæriəʊ/ *noun* [C] (*plural* **scenarios**)
a description of how things might happen in the future: *Let me suggest a **possible** scenario.* ◇ *The **worst-case scenario** (= the worst possible thing that could happen) would be for the factory to close down.*

★ **schedule** /ˈʃedjuːl; AmE ˈskedʒuːl/ *noun, verb*
• *noun*

SEE ALSO: **aging schedule**

1 [C,U] a plan that lists all the work that you have to do and when you must do each thing: *I have a very busy schedule for the next few days.* ◇ *We're working to a tight schedule (= we have a lot of things to do in a short time).* ◇ *Let employees design their own work schedules.* ◇ *Work began **on schedule** (= at the planned time).*
O *a busy/full/heavy/hectic schedule* ♦ *a rigid/strict/tight schedule* ♦ *a production/training/work schedule* ♦ to *design/draw up/plan a schedule* ♦ to *have/keep to/work to a schedule* ♦ to *be/run ahead of schedule* ♦ to *be/fall/run/slip behind schedule*
2 [C] (*AmE*) a list showing what time particular events happen: *a bus/train schedule* SYN TIMETABLE
3 [C] a formal written list of things, for example prices, rates or conditions: *Our price schedule is printed in the enclosed document.*
4 (*Insurance*) [C] a list that describes what is covered by a particular insurance policy
• *verb* [+ obj]
1 (*especially* **be scheduled**) to arrange for sth to happen at a particular time: *The meeting is scheduled for Friday afternoon.* ◇ *The first scheduled event is a speech by the CEO.* ◇ *I'm scheduled to arrive in Milan at 10.15.* See note at ARRANGE
2 (*formal*) to include sth in an official list of things: *The substance has been scheduled as a poison.*
▶ **'scheduler** *noun* [C]: *programme schedulers*
'scheduling *noun* [U]: *Most manufacturers can offer scheduling options.*

scheme /skiːm/ *noun* [C]

SEE ALSO: **final salary pension scheme, Ponzi ~, small self-administered ~, suggestion ~**

1 (*BrE*) a plan or system for doing or organizing sth: *a training/insurance scheme* ◇ *a scheme for recycling plastic* ◇ *Most employees will pay less tax **under** the new scheme.* → PLAN *noun*
O to *design/devise/draw up/propose/introduce/operate a scheme*
2 a plan for getting money or some other advantage for yourself, especially one that involves deceiving other people: *an elaborate scheme to avoid taxes*

,scheme of ar'rangement *noun* [C] (*BrE*)
(*Law*) a legal arrangement that is reached between a company that is unable to pay all its debts and its CREDITORS and shareholders, in which the company will pay what it can

SCI /ˌes siː ˈaɪ/ = SINGLE COLUMN INCH

SCM /ˌes siː ˈem/ = SUPPLY CHAIN MANAGEMENT

scope /skəʊp; AmE skoʊp/ *noun* [U]
1 the opportunity or ability to do or achieve sth: *The group believes there is scope **for** up to 150 stores.* ◇ *The extra money will give us the scope to improve our facilities.* ◇ *Her job offers very little scope for promotion.* ◇ *First try to do something that is within your scope.* SYN POTENTIAL
2 the range of things that a subject, an organization, an activity, etc. deals with: *Our*

*powers are limited **in scope**. ◊ We have broadened the scope of our market research.*

,scorched-'earth ,policy *noun* [C]
(*Finance*) a situation in which a company makes itself less attractive in order to prevent sb else taking control of it. The company may, for example, sell its assets, or borrow money at a very high rate of interest. → POISON PILL

scrap /skræp/ *noun, verb*
● *noun* [U]
things that are not wanted or cannot be used for their original purpose: *The old vehicles were sold **for scrap*** (= so that any good parts could be used again). ◊ *scrap metal/iron ◊ a scrap merchant/dealer* (= a person who buys and sells scrap)
● *verb* [+ obj] (*-pp-*) (*often* **be scrapped**)
to cancel or get rid of sth that is no longer practical or useful: *Plans for a new staff restaurant have been scrapped.*

'scrap ,value = SALVAGE VALUE

scratch /skrætʃ/ *verb, noun*
● *verb*
IDM **'you scratch 'my back and 'I'll scratch 'yours** used to say that if sb helps you, you will help them, even if this is unfair to others
● *noun*
IDM **from 'scratch** without any previous preparation or knowledge: *The prototype was designed and built from scratch in just one month.*
(be/come) up to 'scratch; (bring sb/sth) up to 'scratch as good as sth/sb should be; satisfactory: *His work simply isn't up to scratch. ◊ Our products are good, but we need to bring our customer service up to scratch.*

screen /skri:n/ *noun, verb*
● *noun* [C]

SEE ALSO: **flat-screen, touch screen**

the flat surface at the front of a television, computer, mobile phone/cellphone, etc. on which you see pictures or information: *Move your cursor to the top of the screen. ◊ We have sold a lot of flat-screen TVs.*
● *verb* [+ obj]
1 (*HR*) to find out information about people who work or who want to work for you in order to make sure that they are suitable or that they can be trusted: *We screen all job candidates carefully.*
2 to check sth to see if it is safe or suitable to be used, seen, etc: *We use an antivirus program to screen attachments. ◊ Products are screened **for** their toxic effects.*
SYN VET
PHRV **,screen 'out sb/sth** if you **screen out** a person or a thing, you reject them/it: *Candidates are first interviewed informally over the telephone to screen out those that have no chance. ◊ The program screens out spam before it reaches your inbox.*
HELP A noun usually comes after **out**, but a pronoun comes between the verb and **out**.

'screen-based *adjective*
used to describe an activity that is done using a computer: *the change from floor-based to screen-based trading in futures ◊ screen-based advertising*

screening /'skri:nɪŋ/ *noun* [U]
the process of checking whether sb/sth is suitable: *All candidates undergo a day-long screening process. ◊ the screening of ideas*

'screening ,interview *noun* [C] (*AmE*)
(*HR*) a first short interview for a job, used to identify who is suitable for the company and who is not: *Screening interviews with students usually take place on campus, at conferences or at job fairs.*
→ CALLBACK, FLYBACK

'screen ,saver *noun* [C]
an image that appears on the computer screen when the computer has not been used for a particular amount of time, originally to stop the screen from being damaged; the program that does this

scrip /skrɪp/ *noun*
(*Finance*)
1 [C,U] one of a group of extra shares that a company gives to shareholders instead of a DIVIDEND; the set of shares given **SYN** SCRIP DIVIDEND → BONUS ISSUE
2 [C] a certificate showing that sb owns shares or bonds

'scrip ,dividend (*especially BrE*) (*AmE usually* 'stock ,dividend) *noun* [C]
(*Finance*) an amount of the profits that a company pays to shareholders in the form of new shares
SYN SCRIP

'scrip ,issue (*also* 'free ,issue) *noun* [C] (*BrE*)
(*Finance*) a situation in which a company uses its spare profits (**reserves**) to create new shares, which are then given free to the shareholders in proportion to the number of shares that they already own **SYN** BONUS ISSUE, CAPITALIZATION ISSUE

script /skrɪpt/ *noun, verb*
● *noun*
1 [C] words that are prepared for sb to say: *They are working on the script for the TV ad.*
2 (*IT*) [C,U] a list of instructions or a simple program for a computer; the language that is used to write these
● *verb* [+ obj] (*often* **be scripted**)
1 to prepare words for sb to say: *Call centre staff use scripted greetings when they answer the phone.*
2 (*IT*) to write computer **script**

scroll /skrəʊl; *AmE* skroʊl/ *verb* [+ obj or no obj]
(*IT*) (*often used with an adverb or a preposition*) to move text up or down on the screen of a computer, a mobile phone/cellphone, etc. so that you can read different parts of it: *Scroll down to the bottom of the document. ◊ I start every day by scrolling through my email.*

'scroll bar *noun* [C]
(*IT*) a strip at the edge of a computer screen that you use to **scroll** through a file with, using a mouse

'scroll key *noun* [C]
a key on a computer, a mobile phone/cellphone, etc. that allows you to **scroll** through information

scrutinize , -ise /'skru:tənaɪz/ *verb* [+ obj]
to look at or examine sth carefully: *Your business plan will be carefully scrutinized by the bankers.*

scrutiny /'skru:təni/ *noun* [U]
careful and thorough examination: *The bank's investment policy has **come under** close scrutiny from shareholders.*

SCSI /'skʌzi; 'seksi; ,es si: es 'aɪ/ *noun* [C,U]
(*IT*) **Small Computer System Interface** a system used for connecting a computer to another device

SD card /,es 'di: kɑːd; *AmE* kɑːrd/ *noun* [C]
(*IT*) **Secure Digital card** a very small card containing memory that can be used in electronic devices such as cameras, mobile phones/cellphones, etc.

seal /si:l/ *verb, noun*
● *verb* [+ obj]

SEE ALSO: **self-seal**

1 to close PACKAGING (= material used to wrap or protect goods) so that the contents cannot get out: *Heat is applied to seal the shrink-wrap.*
2 to close an envelope by sticking the edges of the opening together: *Make sure you've signed the form before sealing the envelope.*
3 to make sth definite and final, so that it cannot be changed or argued about: *They hope to seal the deal with a cash offer of €35 per share.*
→ idiom at SIGN *verb*
PHR V ˌseal sth 'in to prevent sth that is contained in sth else from escaping: *The food is frozen quickly to seal in the flavour.*
● *noun*
1 [C] a substance, strip of material, etc. used to fill a crack so that air, liquid, etc. cannot get in or out: *Make sure the seal is intact before closing the lid, or air will escape.*
2 [C] a piece of paper, metal, etc. that is placed across the opening of sth such as a letter, a box, etc. and which has to be broken before the letter or box can be opened
3 [C] an official design or mark, stamped on a document to show that it is genuine and carries the authority of a particular person or organization
4 [sing.] a thing that makes sth definite: *The CEO has given the project his seal of approval.*
IDM under 'seal (*Law, formal*) (about a document) that cannot be copied or made available to the public

ˌsealed 'bid *noun* [C]
a bid that is kept in a sealed envelope and therefore remains secret until all other bids have been received when they are opened all together: *Their sealed bid was less than the valuation.* ◇ *a sealed-bid auction*

SEAQ /ˈsiːæk/ *noun* [U]
(*Stock Exchange*) **Stock Exchange Automated Quotation System** a system used by the London Stock Exchange to show the latest prices of shares on computers around the world

searchable /ˈsɜːtʃəbl; *AmE* ˈsɜːrtʃ-/ *adjective*
(*IT*) that can be searched: *a searchable index of names and addresses* ◇ *a searchable database*

'search ˌengine *noun* [C]
(*IT*) a computer program that searches the Internet for information, especially by looking for documents containing a particular word or group of words

'search firm *noun* [C]
a company that provides the service of finding managers for other companies → HEADHUNT

ˌsearch unem'ployment = FRICTIONAL UNEMPLOYMENT

season /ˈsiːzn/ *noun* [C,U]

SEE ALSO: **dead season, high ~, low ~, off ~**

1 a period of time each year when a particular activity takes place or particular conditions exist: *The tourist season begins in May.* ◇ *Plane tickets are most expensive at the height of the season.*
● the holiday/tourist season ● the autumn/spring/ summer/winter season ● the earnings/reporting season
2 a period of time during one year when a particular style of clothes, hair, etc. is popular and fashionable: *This season's look is cool and feminine.*
IDM con'fessional ˌseason/ˌperiod (*especially AmE*) (*Stock Exchange*) a period of time during the year when companies warn that their profits will be lower than expected: *Investors fear the fourth-quarter confessional season will be worse than expected.* **in 'season** (about fruit or vegetables)

easily available and ready to eat because it is the right time of year for them: *Strawberries are now in season.* **out of 'season 1** at the times of year when few people go on holiday/vacation: *Hotels are cheaper out of season.* **2** (about fruit or vegetables) not easily available because it is not the right time of year for them

seasonal /ˈsiːzənl/ *adjective*
happening or needed during a particular season; varying with the seasons: *Farmers employ seasonal workers to pick fruit.* ◇ *seasonal variations in unemployment figures* ◇ *Click here for the hotel's seasonal rates.* ▸ **seasonally** /ˈsiːzənəli/ *adverb*: *The unemployment figures are seasonally adjusted* (= do not include the changes that always happen in different seasons).

ˌseasonal unem'ployment *noun* [U]
(*Economics*) a rise in the number of people who are not working at particular times of the year as a result of the jobs that can only be done at other times: *The tourist industry has high rates of seasonal unemployment.* → FRICTIONAL UNEMPLOYMENT, STRUCTURAL UNEMPLOYMENT

'season ˌticket *noun* [C]
a ticket that you can use many times within a particular period, for example on a regular train or bus journey, that costs less than paying separately each time: *an annual/a monthly season ticket* ◇ *a season ticket holder*

seat /siːt/ *noun* [C]

SEE ALSO: **hot seat**

1 an official position as a member of a committee, council, Parliament, etc: *The majority of seats on the board will be held by business representatives.* ◇ *Mr Isherwood took over the chairman's seat last year.*
2 (*Stock Exchange*) (*especially AmE*) if you have a **seat** on a stock exchange, you are a member of the exchange and are allowed to buy and sell shares: *There are currently 1 366 seats on the New York Stock Exchange.*
3 a place where you pay to sit on a plane, in a theatre, etc: *There are no seats left on that flight.* ◇ *You can book seats online.*
→ idioms at DRIVE *verb*, BACK

SEC /ˌes iː ˈsiː/ = SECURITIES AND EXCHANGE COMMISSION

Sec. (*AmE also* **Secy.**) *abbr*
a short way of writing **secretary**

second¹ /ˈsekənd/ *verb, noun*
● *verb* [+ obj]
to state officially at a meeting that you support another person's idea, suggestion, etc. so that it can be discussed and/or voted on: *Any proposal must be seconded by two other members.* → PROPOSE (2) See note at MEETING
▸ 'seconder *noun* [C]
● *noun*
(*Commerce*) [C, usually pl.]
an item that is sold at a lower price than usual because it is not perfect: *These shoes are slight seconds.*

second² /sɪˈkɒnd; *AmE* -ˈkɑːnd/ *verb* [+ obj]
(*especially BrE*)
(*HR*) (*usually* **be seconded**)
to send an employee to another department, office, etc. in order to do a different job for a short period of time: *Two of our engineers have been seconded to our factory in China.* ▸ se'condment *noun* [U,C]: *Mr Riba is currently on secondment overseas.*

secondary /ˈsekəndri; *AmE* -deri/ *adjective*
1 less important than sth else: *secondary airports* ◇ *Attractive design is of secondary importance to quality.*

2 used to describe sth that happens as a result of sth else: *Leather is a secondary product of farming goats.*
3 (*Finance*) used to describe the buying and selling of shares, bonds, etc. that already exist rather than new ones: *Secondary trading was at low levels.*
→ PRIMARY

▶ **secondarily** /ˈsekəndrəli; *AmE* ˌsekənˈderəli/ *adverb*: *Selling the company was primarily a personal decision and secondarily a business decision.*

secondary 'action *noun* [U]
(*HR*) action such as stopping work that is taken by workers in a factory, company, etc. that is not directly involved in a dispute in order to protest against employers in the factories or companies that are involved → PRIMARY ACTION

secondary 'audience *noun* [C]
(*Marketing*)
1 the people who are not the main people that your product, advertising, report or presentation is aimed at
2 (*also* 'pass-along ˌreaders [pl.]) people who read a particular newspaper or magazine but who do not buy it

secondary 'boycott *noun* [C]
a situation when people refuse to buy the goods of, or do services for, a company that is not directly involved in a dispute in order to persuade them not to do business with a company that is involved

secondary 'data *noun* [U]
(*Marketing*) information that was originally collected for a particular purpose and is then also used for another purpose or project: *Secondary data such as the results of public opinion polls and surveys are widely available on the Internet.*
→ PRIMARY DATA

'secondary ˌindustry *noun* [U,C]
(*Economics*) industry that uses raw materials to make goods to be sold or to make machines, etc. that are used to make goods → PRIMARY INDUSTRY, TERTIARY INDUSTRY

'secondary ˌmarket *noun* [C]
(*Stock Exchange*) a market in which investors buy and sell existing shares, bonds, etc. rather than new ones: *Some of the 30-year bonds have performed poorly in the secondary market.*
→ PRIMARY MARKET

secondary 'mortgage ˌmarket = MORTGAGE MARKET (2)

secondary 'offering *noun* [C]
(*Stock Exchange*) an occasion when an important shareholder or a group of important shareholders sells their shares in a company to the public

secondary 'picketing *noun* [U] (*BrE*)
the act of preventing workers who are not involved in a strike from working or supplying goods to the company where the strike is held **NOTE** This practice is now illegal in the UK.

secondary pro'duction *noun* [U]
(*Economics*) the process of manufacturing goods for sale from raw materials and the activity of building houses, bridges, roads, etc. → PRIMARY PRODUCTION

the 'secondary ˌsector *noun* [sing.]
(*Economics*) the part of a country's economy that manufactures goods for sale from raw materials. Sometimes construction, for example, building houses, bridges and roads, is also included.
→ PRIMARY SECTOR

second 'class *noun, adverb*
● *noun* [U]
1 a way of travelling on a train or ship that costs less and is less comfortable than FIRST CLASS
NOTE In the UK this is now usually called **standard class.**
2 in the UK, the class of mail that costs less and takes longer to arrive than FIRST CLASS: *second-class letters*
3 in the US, the system of sending newspapers and magazines by mail
● *adverb*
1 using the less expensive seats or accommodation in a train, ship, etc: *to travel second class*
2 by the slower and cheaper form of mail: *I never send important letters second class.*

second-geneˈration *adjective* [only before noun]
1 used to describe technology, a product, etc. that has been developed and improved since it first appeared: *Second-generation e-learning no longer just provides information, but instead forces the student to make choices and decisions.*
2 (*abbr* **2G**) used to describe mobile telephone networks without wires that were the first to use DIGITAL technology: *second-generation cellphones*

second 'half (*also* ˌfiscal second 'half, *especially in AmE*) *noun* [C, usually sing.]
1 (*Accounting*) the second six months of a company's FINANCIAL YEAR: *We had a disappointing second half.* ◇ *second-half results*
2 the period of six months between 1 July and 31 December: *The product will not be launched until the second half of 2007.*
→ FIRST HALF

second-'hand *adjective*
not new; owned by sb else before: *second-hand cars/books* **SYN** USED, PRE-OWNED (*AmE*)
▶ **second-'hand** *adverb*: *You can buy these cars cheaply second-hand.*

second 'section *noun* [sing.]
(*Stock Exchange*) the part of the Tokyo Stock Exchange on which the shares of the smaller and less successful companies are traded: *second-section companies/shares* → FIRST SECTION

second 'tier *noun* [C]
the second level of sth or a less important level than the first level: *He was promoted from the second tier of management to a top job.* ◇ *second-tier companies/stock* (= smaller, less important companies)

second-tier supˈplier *noun* [C]
(*Production*) a company that delivers raw materials or goods to a FIRST-TIER SUPPLIER, who will then make them ready for the customer and deliver them → FIRST-TIER SUPPLIER

secretarial /ˌsekrəˈteəriəl; *AmE* -ˈter-/ *adjective*
involving or connected with the work of a secretary: *secretarial work/qualifications*

★ **secretary** /ˈsekrətri; *AmE* -teri/ *noun* [C] (*plural* **secretaries**)

SEE ALSO: **company secretary, corporate ~, executive ~, press ~**

1 a person who works in an office, working for another person, dealing with letters and telephone calls, typing, keeping records, arranging meetings with people, etc: *a legal/medical secretary* ◇ *Please contact my secretary to make an appointment.*
2 = COMPANY SECRETARY

section /'sekʃn/ noun [C]

SEE ALSO: **first section, second section**

1 a department in a company, an organization, etc: *He's the director of the finance section.* ◇ *the section of the company dealing with customer services* [SYN] DIVISION
2 a separate part of a document, book, website, etc: *the business section of the newspaper*
3 (*Stock Exchange*) a group of companies on the Japanese stock markets: *The shares went up to €228 on the second section of the Tokyo Stock Exchange.*

★ **sector** /'sektə(r)/ noun [C]

SEE ALSO: **corporate sector, market ~, primary ~, private ~, public ~, secondary ~, tertiary ~, third ~**

(*Economics*) a particular area of activity or business; a part of a country's economy: *the banking/ business/financial/IT sector* ◇ *weak sectors of the economy* ◇ *service-sector jobs* (= in hotels, restaurants, etc.). ▶ **sectoral** /'sektərəl/ (*also* **sectorial** /sek'tɔːriəl/) adjective: *a sectoral study*

'sector ro,tation (*also* **ro'tation**) noun [C,U]
(*Stock Exchange*) the movement of money from one area of the market or **sector** to another: *a sector rotation from consumer and retail stocks to financials and technology*

★ **secure** /sɪ'kjʊə(r); AmE sə'kjʊr/ verb, adjective
● **verb** [+ obj]
1 (*formal*) **secure sth (for sb/sth)** | **secure sb sth** to obtain or achieve sth, especially when this means using a lot of effort: *He was unable to secure funding for the project.* ◇ *They have secured the contract to build the new retail and leisure complex.* ◇ *She secured herself a place at business school.*
2 (*Finance*) (*usually* **be secured**) to legally agree to give sb who lends you money particular property or goods if you do not pay the money back: *The loan was fully secured on/against properties the company owned.*
3 to protect sth and make it safe: ◇ *The investment will secure 577 jobs.*
● **adjective**
1 safe and likely to continue or be successful for a long time: *a secure job/income/investment* ◇ *The future of the company looks secure.*
2 safe and protected so that it cannot be harmed or affected by sth/sb: *Is your computer secure from virus attacks?* ◇ *a secure network/website* (= where private information cannot be seen by another person)

secured /sɪ'kjʊəd; AmE sə'kjʊrd/ adjective
(*Finance*; *Law*)
1 if a loan, debt, etc. is **secured**, the borrower agrees to give the lender particular property or goods if they do not pay the money back: *They have obtained a $1.4 billion secured loan from their bankers.*
➊ secured **credit/debt/lending/loans**
2 used to describe a person, company, etc. that lends money to sb on the agreement that if the borrower does not pay back the money they will give the lender particular property or goods: *In the case of bankruptcy, secured creditors must receive the equivalent of their secured claims.*
➊ secured **creditors/lenders**
[OPP] UNSECURED

the Se,curities and Ex'change Co,mmission noun [sing.] (*abbr* **SEC**)
in the US, a government organization that is responsible for controlling how shares, bonds, etc. are traded to make sure that this is done in an honest way in order to protect investors
→ FINANCIAL SERVICES AUTHORITY

the Se,curities and 'Futures Au,thority noun [sing.] (*abbr* **SFA**)
in the UK, an organization that controls the buying and selling of shares, bonds, etc. and protects investors, now part of the Financial Services Authority → FINANCIAL SERVICES AUTHORITY

se'curities ,market (*also* **se'curities ex,change**) noun [C]
(*Stock Exchange*) a place where shares, bonds, etc. are bought and sold; the business activity involved in this: *the NYSE, NASDAQ and other securities markets* → STOCK EXCHANGE

securitize , **-ise** /sɪ'kjʊərətaɪz; AmE sə'kjʊr-/ verb
[+ obj]
(*Finance*) to change a financial asset such as a loan into bonds that can be bought and sold in order to raise cash: *They plan to securitize $2.2 billion of commercial and industrial loans.* ▶ **securitization**, **-isation** /sɪ,kjʊərətaɪ'zeɪʃn; AmE sə,kjʊrətə'z-/ noun [U; C, usually sing.]: *mortgage securitization*

★ **security** /sɪ'kjʊərəti; AmE sə'kjʊr-/ noun (*plural* **securities**)

SEE ALSO: **convertible security, dated ~, employment ~, fixed-interest ~, government ~, job ~, mortgage-backed ~,** etc.

1 [U] the activities involved in protecting a country, building or person against attack, danger, etc: *airport/hotel security* ◇ *There will be round-the-clock security at the factory.*
➊ lax/strict/tight security • to improve/strengthen/ tighten security • a security **alert/check/system**
2 [U with sing./pl. verb] the department of a large company or organization that deals with the protection of its buildings, equipment and staff: *Security was/were called to the incident.* ◇ *the head of security*
3 [U] protection against sth bad that might happen in the future: *financial security* ◇ *Which type of investment offers the greatest security?*
➊ economic/financial security • to give (sb)/have/ offer (sb)/provide (sb with) security
4 (*Finance*; *Stock Exchange*) **securities** [pl.] a financial asset such as a share or bond; the certificate that shows you own this: *to buy high-yield securities* ◇ *Merrill Lynch is one of the world's biggest securities firms.* ◇ *the change from paper to electronic securities*
➊ to buy/hold/sell securities • to deal in/issue securities • a securities **business/company/dealer/ firm/house**
5 (*Finance*; *Law*) [U,C] a valuable item that you agree to give to sb if you are unable to pay back the money that you have borrowed from them: *His home and business are being held as security for the loan.* ◇ *Shares in the company were pledged as security against the loan.* → COLLATERAL
➊ to give/offer/pledge sth as security

se'curity de,posit noun [C]
(*Commerce*) a first amount of money that a seller asks a buyer to give them in case the buyer does not complete the business

se'curity guard noun [C]
a person whose job is to guard money, valuables, a building, etc: *He had a job as a night security guard.*

se,curity of em'ployment = EMPLOYMENT SECURITY

se'curity ,rating noun [C, usually sing.]
1 (*Finance*) a measurement of the risk involved in investing in a particular company: *The securities are triple-A rated, the highest form of security rating.*
→ CREDIT RATING
2 (*IT*) a measurement of how well a computer or computer system protects data from being read or

changed by sb without permission: *a computer network with a C2 security rating*
3 a measurement that shows if sth is safe or dangerous: *an airport with a low security rating*

Secy. = SEC.

seed /siːd/ *noun, verb*
● *noun*
1 (*Finance*) [U] **seed capital, money, etc.** money that is used to start a new business, project, etc. that will bring profits in the future: *There is enough seed money for 10 start-up firms.* ◇ *He raised only $150 000 in seed capital.* → SEEDCORN
O seed **capital/financing/funding/money**
2 (*Marketing*) (*also* '**decoy**) [C] a name that is added to a list of names and addresses of people who are sent advertising material, etc. in order to check how the list is being used
● *verb* [+ obj]
1 (*Finance*) to provide the money or other resources that are needed to start a new business, project, etc: *a venture capital company that seeds tech start-ups* ◇ *I've seeded the company with my own money.*
2 (*Marketing*) to add one or more names to a list of names and addresses of people who are sent advertising material, etc. in order to check how the list is being used

seedcorn (*also spelled* **seed corn**, *especially in AmE*) /ˈsiːdkɔːn; AmE -kɔːrn/ *noun* [U] (*especially BrE*) money, people, etc. that will bring success or profit in the future: *The work is seedcorn for a longer-term project.*

seek /siːk/ *verb* (**sought, sought** /sɔːt/) [+ obj] (*formal*)
(often used in newspapers) to try to obtain or achieve sth: *to seek funding for a project* ◇ *There has been a small rise in the number of people seeking work.* ▶ '**seeker** *noun* [C]: *job seekers' allowance*

★ segment *noun, verb*
● *noun* [C] /ˈseɡmənt/

SEE ALSO: **market segment**

1 a part or division of sth such as an economy, a market, a social group, a company's work, etc: *Small businesses are the fastest-growing segment of the economy.* ◇ *All six of our business segments grew this year.* ◇ *The company have launched two new cars into the lower-priced segment of the market.* ◇ *All segments of society should have access to the benefits of the Internet.*
O the **business/industrial/retail/services/technology** segment • the **energy/food/health-care/insurance** segment • **core/key/profitable/target** segments • the **low-priced/luxury/mid-priced** segment
2 a part or section of sth such as a chart: *The blue segment of the pie chart represents foreign sales.*
● *verb* /seɡˈment/ [+ obj or no obj] (*often* **be segmented**)
to divide sth into different parts; to divide into different parts: *Customers are segmented* **into** *4 basic groups.* ◇ *Market researchers often segment the population on the basis of age and social class.* ◇ *Our business is segmenting into three key areas.*

segmentation /ˌseɡmənˈteɪʃn/ *noun* [U,C]
the act of dividing sth into different parts; one of these parts: *Managers see segmentation as a tool to help marketing.* ◇ *the segmentation of work*
→ MARKET SEGMENTATION

seigniorage (*also spelled* **seignorage**) /ˈseɪnjərɪdʒ/ *noun* [U]
(*Economics*) the profit that is made by a government from issuing BANKNOTES, coins, etc.

seize /siːz/ *verb* [+ obj]
1 to take goods away from sb officially or legally: *The bank has the right to seize your assets if you fail to repay the loan.* ◇ *A large quantity of false credit cards was seized by the police.*
2 to take control of a place or situation, often very suddenly: *The company's bondholders could seize* **control** *of the business.*

seizure /ˈsiːʒə(r)/ *noun* [U,C]
the use of legal authority to take sth from sb; an amount of sth that is taken in this way: *the seizure of assets/funds* ◇ *Customs seizures are down by one half this year.*

select /sɪˈlekt/ *verb, adjective*
● *verb*
1 [+ obj *or no obj*] **select sb/sth (as/for sth)** | **select sb/sth (from sth)** to choose sb/sth from a group of people or things, usually according to a system: *Four candidates have been selected for interview.* ◇ *This model was selected as the best-value digital camera on the market.* ◇ *Customers can select from thousands of products.* ◇ *This service is available at selected stores only.*
2 (*IT*) [+ obj] to mark sth on a computer screen; to choose sth, especially from a list (**menu**): *Select 'New Mail' from the 'Send' menu.*
● *adjective* [only before noun]
carefully chosen as the best out of a larger group of people or things: *a select group of customers/investors* ◇ *Investors have been buying select technology stocks.*

selection /sɪˈlekʃn/ *noun*
1 [U] the process of choosing sb/sth from a group of people or things, usually according to a system: *There are guidelines for the selection of board members.* ◇ *He claims that the selection process was unfair.*
2 [C] a number of people or things that have been chosen from a larger group: *You can look through the catalogue, make a selection and pay online.*
3 [C] a collection of things from which sth can be chosen: *The showroom has a* **wide** *selection of cars.*
SYN CHOICE

selective /sɪˈlektɪv/ *adjective*
1 affecting or concerned with only a small number of people or things from a larger group: *selective price cuts* ◇ *a selective mailing*
2 careful about what or who you choose: *You will have to be selective about which information to include in the report.*
▶ se'**lectively** *adverb*: *The product will be selectively marketed in the US* (= only in some areas).
selectivity /sə,lekˈtɪvəti/ *noun* [U]

se,lective at'tention (*also* se,lective per'ception) *noun* [U]
(*Marketing*) a process in which consumers only notice or become aware of some pieces of information in an advertisement, etc.

se,lective de'mand *noun* [U,C]
(*Marketing*) the desire of consumers for a particular brand of product: *Advertising used to build selective demand for a brand by persuading customers that it offers the best quality for their money.* → PRIMARY DEMAND

se,lective distri'bution *noun* [U]
(*Marketing*) when a product is made available in a limited number of shops/stores, etc. in a particular area

se,lective per'ception = SELECTIVE ATTENTION

self /self/ *pronoun*
written on a cheque or other document to refer to the person who has signed

,self-actuali'zation, **-isation** noun [U]
(HR) the fact of using your skills and abilities and
achieving as much as you can possibly achieve—
Picture at MASLOW'S HIERARCHY OF NEEDS

,self-ad'dressed adjective
if an envelope is **self-addressed**, sb has written
their address on it → SAE, SASE

,self-ad'hesive adjective [usually before noun]
covered on one side with a sticky substance so that
it can be stuck to sth without using glue, etc.

,self-ap'praisal noun [U,C]
(HR) the process of judging your own work; your
opinion about your work: *Your manager may ask
you to conduct a self-appraisal before your
performance review.* **SYN** SELF-ASSESSMENT

,self-as'sessment noun [U,C]
1 a system of paying tax in which you calculate
yourself how much you should pay; a form with
this information: *If you are self-employed you have
to complete a self-assessment tax return.*
2 (HR) the process of judging your own work, skills,
strengths, etc.; your opinion about this:
*organizations engaging in self-assessment and
continuous improvement* **SYN** SELF-APPRAISAL

,self-cor'recting adjective [usually before noun]
if a system, machine, etc. is **self-correcting**, it
corrects or adjusts itself without outside help if it
begins to go wrong: *Economists believe that any
surplus of demand over supply will eventually be self-
correcting.* ▶ **,self-cor'rect** verb [no obj]: *In a market
economy, rising prices tend to self-correct.* **,self-
cor'rection** noun [U]

,self-'dealing noun [U]
(Law) when a person uses their influence in an
organization to make money for themselves rather
than the organization: *Shareholders have accused
the CEO of fraud and self-dealing.*

,self-de'velopment noun [U]
(HR) the process of gaining the knowledge, skills
and abilities you need: *Staff are encouraged to use
the library for professional self-development.*
SYN PERSONAL DEVELOPMENT

,self-di'rected adjective
not controlled by sb else; independent and making
your own decisions: *Workers in self-directed teams
are producing record numbers of new cars.* ◇ *self-
directed learning* → SELF-MANAGED

,self-em'ployed adjective
working for yourself and not employed by a
company, etc: *a self-employed designer* ◇ *If you are
self-employed you may need to hire an accountant.* ◇
retirement plans for the self-employed (= people
who are self-employed) ▶ **,self-em'ployment** noun
[U]

,self-'financing (also **,self-'financed**) adjective
a **self-financing** company, project, etc. produces
enough money to pay its own costs and does not
need financial support: *The research is largely self-
financing.* ◇ *The majority of new businesses are
completely self-financed.*

,self-'healing (also **,self-re'pairing**) adjective
(about a computer, material, etc.) able to make
changes to itself to correct a problem or limit or
repair damage without outside help

,self-'liquidating adjective
(Finance)
1 used to describe a debt or loan that buys sth that
will earn enough money to pay back the loan:
short-term, self-liquidating financing

2 used to describe a project, deal, etc. that makes
enough profit to pay for its costs: *The project will be
completely self-liquidating.* ◇ *a self-liquidating offer/
promotion* (= when the extra income received from
customers pays the cost of the special offer)

,self-'made adjective [usually before noun]
having become rich and successful through your
own hard work rather than having had money
given to you: *He was proud of the fact that he was a
self-made millionaire.*

,self-'mailer noun [C]
a printed sheet or card that is designed to be sent
without an envelope

,self-'managed adjective
making your own decisions and not receiving
instructions from sb else: *Work is distributed among
140 self-managed teams* (= that are responsible
for their own decisions and do not have a
manager). → SELF-DIRECTED
▶ **,self-'management** noun [U]: *She teaches career
self-management.*

,self-'powered adjective
used to describe sth that can produce its own
energy and does not need energy from another
source: *a fast-growing maker of self-powered radios
and flashlights*

,self-'regulating adjective
1 (also **,self-'regulatory** [usually before noun]) (about
an organization, a system, etc.) that is not
controlled by the government but decides on its
own rules and makes sure that they are obeyed:
The profession is largely self-regulating. ◇ *a self-
regulating organization* ◇ *A self-regulatory
organization (SRO) oversees the securities industry.*
2 (about a machine, system, etc.) that controls and
adjusts itself: *a self-regulating economy* ◇ *self-
regulating heating products*
▶ **,self-regu'lation** noun [U]: *The UK has developed
industry codes of self-regulation.*

,self-re'pairing = SELF-HEALING

,self-'seal adjective [usually before noun]
used to describe an envelope, etc. that will close
and stick when you press the two open edges
together

,self-'service adjective [usually before noun]
a **self-service** shop/store, restaurant, etc. is one in
which customers serve themselves and then pay for
the goods: *self-service check-in at the airport* ◇ *self-
service banking* ▶ **,self-'service** noun [U]: *The cafe
provides quick self-service at low prices.*

,self-'starter noun [C]
a person who is able to work on their own and
make their own decisions without needing anyone
to tell them what to do: *You'll need to be a self-
starter to work in this business.*

,self-suf'ficient adjective
able to do or produce everything that you need
without the help of other people: *The country is no
longer self-sufficient in oil.* ▶ **,self-suf'ficiency** noun
[U]

,self-sup'porting adjective
having enough money to be able to operate
without financial help from other people: *The
business will be self-supporting.*

,self-sus'taining adjective
able to continue in a successful way without
outside help: *The goal of any business is to be self-
sustaining.*

,self-'tender noun [C]
(Finance) when a company offers to buy back its
own shares from its shareholders, for example to
avoid sb else buying the company

★ **sell** /sel/ *verb, noun*

● *verb* (**sold, sold** /səʊld; *AmE* soʊld/)

SEE ALSO: **mis-sell**

1 [+ obj *or* no obj] **sell sth (to sb) (at/for sth)** | **sell sb sth (at/for sth)** | **sell (sth)** to give sth to sb in exchange for money: *The company has sold the hotel to private investors for $365 million.* ◇ *She sold him the car for $2 500.* ◇ *They sold the business at a profit/loss* (= they gained/lost money when they sold it). ◇ *The company expects to sell 300 000 cars a year.* ◇ *422 million mobile handsets were sold worldwide.* ◇ *Shareholders were advised not to sell.* → SHORT *adv.* (2), SALE
2 [+ obj] to offer sth for people to buy: *Most supermarkets sell a range of organic products.* ◇ *Do you sell stamps?* ◇ *This product is sold exclusively at one chain of stores.* → SALE
3 [+ obj *or* no obj] to be bought by people usually in the way or in the numbers mentioned; to be offered at the price mentioned: *DVD players now sell for only $80.* ◇ *The book sold well and was reprinted many times.* ◇ *The new design just didn't sell* (= nobody bought it). ◇ *The magazine sells 300 000 copies a week.*
4 [+ obj *or* no obj] to make people want to buy sth: *There's no doubt that advertising sells.* ◇ *It is quality not price that sells our products.* ◇ *These cars sell themselves* (= they are very easy to sell).
5 [+ obj] **sell sth/yourself (to sb)** to persuade sb that sth is a good idea, service, product, etc.; to persuade sb that you are the right person for a job, position, etc: *Now we have to try and sell the idea to management.* ◇ *You really have to sell yourself at a job interview.*
▶ **sellable** /ˈseləbl/ *adjective*: *sellable securities* ◇ *Prada's most sellable collection for years* (= easy to sell)
IDM **sell/go like hot 'cakes** to sell quickly or in great numbers → idiom at BULK *noun*
PHRV **,sell 'into sth; ,sell sth 'into sth** (*Finance*) to sell shares, bonds, etc. when the situation mentioned exists: *They were forced to sell into a falling market.* **,sell sth 'off 1** to sell all or part of an industry, a company, etc. often at a low price in order to get rid of it: *In the nineties most state-owned industries were sold off.* **2** to sell things cheaply because you want to get rid of them or because you need the money: *to sell off old stock* → SELL-OFF **,sell sth 'on** to sell to sb else sth that you have bought not long before: *We buy cars abroad and then sell them on to customers in the UK.* **,sell 'out (to sb/sth)** to sell your business or a part of your business: *The company eventually sold out to a multinational media group.* **,sell 'out; ,sell 'out of sth** (*Finance*) to sell particular shares, bonds, etc. that you own, often because they no longer seem to be a good investment: *The bad news prompted foreign investors to sell out of US stocks.* **,sell 'out; be ,sold 'out** to be all sold: *A hot product can sell out within 24 hours.* ◇ *The concert is completely sold out.* → SELL-OUT **,sell 'out (of sth); be ,sold 'out (of sth)** to have sold all the available items: *I'm sorry, we've sold out.* ◇ *Several online retailers have sold out of their stock of the software.* → SELL-OUT **,sell 'through** if items in a shop/store **sell through** they are sold to customers: *A really good guitar will sell through fast.* → SELL-THROUGH **,sell 'up; ,sell sth 'up** (*especially BrE*) to sell your home, possessions, business, etc., usually because you are leaving the country or retiring: *They plan to sell up and retire.*

● *noun*

SEE ALSO: **hard sell, soft sell**

1 [C] an act of selling sth or of trying to sell sth: *Every other TV commercial is a sell for a car.* ◇ *Luxury goods can be a **tough** sell* (= difficult to sell). → SALE

---

2 [C, usually sing.] an act of trying to persuade sb that sth is a good idea, product, service, etc: *Persuading the companies to be sponsors is going to be a **tough** sell* (= it will be difficult to persuade them). ◇ *Despite its benefits, the program isn't always an **easy** sell.*
3 (*Stock Exchange*) [U; sing.] = SELL RATING
4 (*Stock Exchange*) [C] = SELL ORDER

'sell-by date (*AmE also* **'pull date**) *noun* [C]
the date, printed on a container or package, that advises a shop/store how long it should offer a particular item of food or drink for sale. These items can usually be used after this date: *Is it safe to use a package of hot dogs when it is past its sell-by date?* See note at BEST-BEFORE DATE

★ **seller** /ˈselə(r)/ *noun* [C]

SEE ALSO: **best-seller**

1 a person or company that sells sth: *They are the largest retail seller of carpeting.* ◇ *a clothing/software/toy seller* ◇ *The online retailer will be the exclusive seller of the equipment.* ◇ *The law is intended to protect both the buyer and the seller.*
○ *a big/large/leading/top seller of sth*
2 a product that is sold in the amounts or the way mentioned: *The product remains a steady seller.* ◇ *The top sellers last month were toys and electronics.*
○ *a big/hot/large/strong/top seller*

,seller's 'market *noun* [C, usually sing.]
a situation in which people selling sth have an advantage, because there is not a lot of a particular item for sale, and prices can be kept high: *The shortage of homes is making it a seller's market.* ◇ *It's a seller's market for skilled workers.* **OPP** BUYER'S MARKET

selling /ˈselɪŋ/ *noun* [U]

SEE ALSO: **cross-selling, direct ~, forced ~, forward ~, hard ~, personal ~, pyramid ~,** etc.

1 the act of giving sb sth in exchange for money: *steady selling of shares* ◇ *A wave of panic selling drove the FTSE 100 index to its lowest level for five years.* ◇ *The holiday selling season proved disappointing.*
2 the job, skill, study, etc. of persuading people to buy things: *She began her career in selling.* ◇ *He used his selling skills in the software industry.* ◇ *The commission is investigating complaints about dishonest **doorstep** selling* (= going to sb's home and trying to persuade them to buy your product).
3 -selling used to describe a product that sells in the way mentioned: *the world's best-selling chocolate bar* ◇ *fast-selling goods* ◇ *a poor-selling product*

'selling ,concept (*also* **'sales ,concept**) *noun*
1 (*Marketing*) [C] an idea for the way to sell a product or products: *Salespeople will improve when they learn successful selling concepts.* ◇ *Their sales concept is 'a new experience every week'.* → MARKETING CONCEPT
2 (*Economics*) **the selling concept, the sales concept** [sing.] the approach to business that emphasizes persuading customers to buy products that you already have, sometimes in an aggressive way, rather than producing new ones that customers may want → MARKETING CONCEPT, PRODUCTION CONCEPT

'selling cost *noun* [C, usually pl.]
the amount that a company spends on advertising and selling a product: *Our selling costs amounted to 30% of sales.* ◇ *high/low selling costs*

'selling ,order = SELL ORDER

'selling point *noun* [C]
(*Marketing*) a feature of sth that makes people want to buy or use it: *The price is obviously one of the main selling points.* → USP

'selling price *noun* [C]
the price at which sth is sold: *a high/low selling price* ◇ *The average selling price of its products has fallen by about 12%.* → ASKING PRICE, COST PRICE

'sell limit ,order *noun* [C]
(*Stock Exchange*) an order to a BROKER to sell a number of shares, bonds, etc. at a particular price or higher → BUY LIMIT ORDER
○ *to execute/place* a sell limit order

'sell-off *noun* [C]
1 the sale of all or part of an industry, a company, etc., especially at a low price in order to get rid of it: *The firm has announced the sell-off of most of its American bus operation.* ◇ *a major sell-off of billions of dollars in assets* → SELL OFF at SELL *verb*
2 (*Finance*) (*especially AmE*) the sale of a large number of shares, bonds, etc., after which their value usually falls: *The sell-off in technology stocks may be slowing down.*

'sell ,order (*also* **sell**, **'selling ,order**) *noun* [C]
(*Stock Exchange*) an order to a BROKER to sell a number of shares, bonds, etc. → BUY ORDER

'sell-out *noun* [C, usually sing.]
a product that has sold very well so that there are none left; an event for which all the tickets have been sold: *The book was a sell-out.* ◇ *We had a sell-out season in December* (= we sold all our stock of many items). ◇ *a sell-out tour* → SELL OUT; SELL OUT (OF STH) at SELL *verb*

'sell ,rating *noun* [C] (*also* **sell** [U; sing.])
(*Stock Exchange*) a statement made by a bank, a dealer, etc. that investors should sell a particular company's shares: *Our analyst has put a sell rating on the stock .*
○ *to have/put* a sell rating on sth

'sell ,signal *noun* [C]
(*Stock Exchange*) a situation where the pattern of recent movements in a share price indicates that it is a good time to sell shares → BUY SIGNAL
○ *to generate/give* a sell signal

'sell-through *noun, adjective*
● *noun*
(*Marketing*)
1 [U,C] the number of items of a particular product that a shop/store manages to sell to customers compared to the number it bought to sell: *The average sell-through rate for these magazines is 35-38%.* ◇ *Wholesale sell-throughs improved compared to the previous six months.*
2 [C] an item, especially a video that you can buy rather than hire: *Sell-throughs of movie classics have increased.*
● *adjective* [only before noun]
(used about videos) available to buy rather than to hire: *sell-through titles* → SELL THROUGH at SELL

semi- /'semi/ *prefix* (*in adjectives and nouns*)
1 half; partly: *semicircular* ◇ *semi-professional* ◇ *semi-precious stones*
2 happening twice during the period mentioned: *semi-weekly meetings* (= twice a week) ◇ *a semi-annual review*

,semi-'durable *adjective*
(*Economics*; *Marketing*) (about goods such as clothes, furniture, etc.) not expected to last for more than a few years: *semi-durable fabrics* ◇ *Semi-durable products continue to show the best sales performance.* ▶ **,semi-'durable** *noun* [C, usually pl.]:

spending on semi-durables → DURABLE GOODS, NON-DURABLE GOODS

,semi-'finished *adjective*
partly made; ready to be made into a finished product: *semi-finished products/parts* ◇ *semi-finished steel*

seminar /'semɪnɑː(r)/ *noun* [C]
a meeting for discussion or training: *a one-day management seminar* → WEBINAR
○ *to conduct/hold/organize/run* a seminar ◆ *to attend/go to* a seminar ◆ *an all-day/a one-day/weekly*, etc. *seminar* ◆ *a business/management/training seminar*

,semi-'skilled *adjective* [usually before noun]
having some special training or qualifications, but less than skilled people: *a semi-skilled machine operator* ◇ *semi-skilled jobs* (= for people who have some special training)

,semi-structured 'interview *noun* [C]
(*Marketing*) an informal way of finding out the opinion of a person or a group of people in which the person asking the questions will ask some fixed questions but will also ask other questions that seem appropriate

send /send/ *verb* [+ obj] (**sent, sent** /sent/)
1 **send sth (to sb)** | **send sb sth** to make sth go or be taken to a place, especially by post/mail, email, etc: *to send a letter/package/cheque/fax/email* ◇ *She sent the letter by airmail.* ◇ *An email was sent to all the staff.* ◇ *All the staff were sent the email.*
2 to tell sb to go somewhere or to do sth; to arrange for sb to go somewhere: *Ed couldn't make it so they sent me instead.* ◇ *We are being sent on a training course next month.*
3 to make sth move quickly or suddenly; to make sb act quickly: *Analysts issued a positive report, sending shares 3 per cent higher.* ◇ *The news has sent investors hurrying to sell their stocks.*
PHR V **,send a'way (to sb) (for sth)** = SEND OFF (FOR STH) **,send sth 'back** to return sth to a place: *When it arrived, the computer was damaged, so we sent it back.* ◇ *How many people sent back the questionnaire?* **SYN** RETURN **,send sb 'in** to order sb to go to a place to deal with a difficult situation: *We sent Bob in to sort out the mess.* **,send sth 'in** to send sth by post/mail to a place where it will be dealt with: *Have you sent in your application yet?* **,send 'off (for sth)**; **,send a'way (to sb) (for sth)** to write to sb and ask them to send you sth by post/mail: *I've sent off for details of several jobs.* **,send sth 'off** to send sth to a place by post/mail: *I'm sending the files off to my boss tomorrow.* **,send sth 'on (to sb) 1** to send a letter, email, etc. that has been sent to you to sb else: *When I receive an invoice by email, I send it on to my secretary.* **SYN** FORWARD **2** to send a letter that has been sent to sb's old address to their new address: *Nobody sent on the mail to the new offices.* **SYN** FORWARD **3** to send sth from one place/person to another: *They arranged for the information to be sent on to us.* **,send sth 'out** to send sth to a lot of different people or places: *We have been sending out thousands of brochures.* ◇ *Have the invitations been sent out yet?* **SYN** MAIL OUT

sender /'sendə(r)/ *noun* [C]
a person who sends sth: *If undelivered, please return to sender.*

★ senior /'siːniə(r)/ *adjective, noun*
● *adjective*
1 [usually before noun] having a higher rank in an organization or a profession than others: *senior analysts/bankers/editors* ◇ *He is senior to me.* ◇ *The meeting should be chaired by the most senior person present.* ◇ *Senior management was/were involved in*

the decision. ◇ *She's senior partner at the law firm.*
See note at BOSS

O *a senior* **employee/executive/manager/official/**
vice-president • *senior* **management/staff** • *a senior*
associate/partner • *a senior* **position/post**

2 (*Finance*) used to describe a debt that must be
paid before all other debts have been paid if the
borrower has financial problems: *The company has
announced a $150 million senior note offering.*

O *senior* **debentures/debt/loans/notes** • *senior*
creditors/lenders

→ SENIORITY

● *noun* [C]
1 a person with a higher level of job or status than
others: *She felt unappreciated both by her colleagues
and her seniors.* OPP JUNIOR
2 (*especially AmE*) = SENIOR CITIZEN

,**senior 'citizen** (*also* '**senior**, *especially in AmE*)
noun [C]
an older person, especially sb over 65 years old
who has retired from work: *Senior citizens receive a
discount of 10%.*

seniority /ˌsiːniˈɒrəti; *AmE* -ˈɔːr-; -ˈɑːr-/ *noun* [U]
1 the fact of being older or of a higher rank than
others: *a position of seniority*
2 the rank that you have in a company because of
the length of time you have worked there: *a lawyer
with five years' seniority* ◇ *Should promotion be
based on merit or seniority?*

sensitive /ˈsensətɪv/ *adjective*

SEE ALSO: price-sensitive

1 sensitive (to sth) reacting quickly to sth or to
small changes: *Sales at larger stores are more
sensitive to changes in consumer spending.* ◇ *a
sensitive market* (= one that reacts very quickly to
changes or new information) ◇ *a sensitive scientific
instrument* ◇ *Your password is case-sensitive* (= you
must use the correct capital letters and small
letters).
2 (about information) not to be shared or given to
other people; secret: *hackers attempting to access
sensitive data*
3 aware of and able to understand other people
and their feelings: *The company is not being
sensitive to the needs of employees.*
▶ '**sensitively** *adverb*

sensitivity /ˌsensəˈtɪvəti/ *noun* [U]
1 the quality of reacting quickly to sth or to small
changes: *the sensitivity of economies to changes in
policy* ◇ *increased price sensitivity among consumers*
2 (about information) the quality of needing to be
kept secret and not shared with other people:
*Because of the high sensitivity of the data, high
security must be enforced.*
3 the ability to be aware of and understand other
people and their feelings: *developing sensitivity to
customers' needs*

sensi'tivity a,nalysis *noun* [C,U]
a study of how much a project, system, etc. would
be affected by a change in one of its elements, such
as sales, costs, etc: *A sensitivity analysis will show at
what point a project becomes economical.*

sentiment /ˈsentɪmənt/ *noun*

SEE ALSO: consumer sentiment

1 [U] a measure of how people, especially
investors or financial experts, feel about the
economy, especially about whether it will get
better: *a decline in business sentiment* ◇ *Sentiment in
the market was improved by some good results.* ◇
*Rising oil prices depressed sentiment among
consumers.* SYN CONFIDENCE → CONSUMER
CONFIDENCE

O **business/investor/market** *sentiment* • *to* **boost/**
improve/lift *sentiment* • *to* **damage/depress/hit/**

hurt/undermine *sentiment* • **bearish/bullish/**
positive/negative *sentiment*

2 [U,C] what a group of people feel or think about
sth: *Sentiment about the new CEO was very mixed.* ◇
*He said that the union should be doing more to help
them and other workers echoed this sentiment.*

separation /ˌsepəˈreɪʃn/ *noun* [U,C] (*AmE*)
(*HR*) when sb stops working for a company either
because they retire or because they lose their jobs:
*Most of the job losses will be through voluntary
separation.* ◇ *Ms Parks received a $4 million
separation package.*

sequential /sɪˈkwenʃl/ *adjective* (*formal*)
1 following in order of time or place; following in
a logical order: *Product development consists of four
sequential steps.* ◇ *sequential data processing*
2 (*Accounting*) compared with the most recent
similar accounting period: *There has been a slight
sequential decline in revenue.*
▶ **sequentially** /sɪˈkwenʃəli/ *adverb*: *data stored
sequentially on a computer* ◇ *Sales were 12 per cent
lower sequentially.*

se,quential 'sampling *noun* [U]
(*Technical*) a process of **sampling** (= taking a
number of people or things from a larger group in
order to provide information about the group) that
continues until enough data has been collected

sequester /sɪˈkwestə(r)/ *verb* [+ obj]
(*Law*)
1 to keep a group of people, especially a JURY
away from other people: *The jury will be sequestered
at a local hotel until they reach a verdict.*
2 = SEQUESTRATE

sequestrate /ˈsiːkwəstreɪt; sɪˈkwes-/ (*also*
se'quester) *verb* [+ obj]
(*Law*) to take control of sb's property or assets until
a debt has been paid: *In the event of such a ruling,
the court may sequestrate the stock.*
▶ **sequestration** /ˌsiːkwəˈstreɪʃn/ *noun* [U,C]
sequestrator /ˈsiːkwəstreɪtə(r)/ *noun* [C]

serial /ˈsɪəriəl; *AmE* ˈsɪr-/ *adjective*
1 (*IT*) sending data one unit (**bit**) at a time: *the
serial transmission of data* ◇ *You can download it to
your office computer using a serial cable.*
OPP PARALLEL (2)
2 (*Technical*) [usually before noun] arranged in a
series: *tasks carried out in serial order*
3 [only before noun] doing the same thing in the
same way several times: *Insurers claimed victory
after the conviction of a serial claimant.*
▶ **serially** /ˈsɪəriəli; *AmE* ˈsɪr-/ *adverb*

,**serial 'bonds** *noun* [pl.]
(*Finance*) a set of bonds that a company or local
government, etc. issues (= sells) that become due
for payment at regular times over a period of time

,**serial entrepre'neur** *noun* [C]
a person who creates several new companies,
usually selling each one before starting the next:
*He is a serial entrepreneur who started his first
business at the age of 18.*

'**serial ,number** *noun* [C]
a number put on a product in order to identify it:
*What is the model and serial number for your
printer?*

series /ˈsɪəriːz; *AmE* ˈsɪr-/ *noun* [C] (*plural* **series**)

SEE ALSO: time series

1 a range of similar products produced by one
company: *the BMW 3 series* ◇ *a new title in the
popular series of video games*

2 (*Finance*) a group of shares, bonds, etc. that have the same rules and guarantees about the rights of the owners, payment of interest, etc: *The company's shares are divided into Series A shares and Series B shares.* ◇ *A Series EE bond cannot be redeemed* (= exchanged for cash) *until 12 months after its issue date.* → CLASS (3)

3 several events or things of a similar kind that happen one after the other: *a series of meetings* ◇ *The share price has fallen sharply after a series of profit warnings.*

serve /sɜːv; *AmE* sɜːrv/ *verb*

1 [+ obj] to provide an area or a group of people with a product or service: *These firms serve local markets.* ◇ *The town is well served with buses and major road links.*

2 [+ obj] to deal with people, especially customers, and give them what they need: *We are looking for ways to serve our customers better and faster.* ◇ *The website will focus on serving* **the needs** *of small business customers.*

3 [+ obj *or* no obj] to give sb food or drink, for example at a restaurant: *Breakfast is served between 7 and 10 a.m.*

4 [+ obj *or* no obj] (*especially BrE*) to help a customer or sell them sth in a shop/store: *Are you being served?* ◇ *There was only one person serving behind the counter.*

5 [+ obj *or* no obj] to spend a period of time in a particular job, especially a senior one, or training for a job: *She served a one-year apprenticeship.* ◇ *He has served* **as** *chairman since 2004.*

6 (*Law*) [+ obj] to give sb an official document or instruction, especially one that orders them to appear in court: *to serve a writ/summons on sb* ◇ *to serve sb with a writ/summons*

IDM **serve 'notice (on/upon sb) (that …)** (*Law*) to officially inform sb, often in writing, that you will do sth or that they must do sth: *A landlord is required to serve notice on a tenant of a proposed rent increase.* → NOTICE (3,4)

PHRV ,serve sth 'out to continue working until a previously agreed period of time has been completed: *She will serve out her remaining term as a director.* ◇ (*BrE*) *They didn't want me to serve out my notice.*

server /'sɜːvə(r); *AmE* 'sɜːrv-/ (*also* 'file ,server) *noun* [C]

SEE ALSO: client-server, time-server

(*IT*) a computer program that controls or supplies information to several computers connected in a network; the main computer on which this program is run: *a server-based network*

'server farm *noun* [C]

(*IT*) a business that has a large number of SERVERS in one place that provide computer services for many different organizations

★ **service** /'sɜːvɪs; *AmE* 'sɜːrv-/ *noun, verb, adjective*

● *noun*

SEE ALSO: advisory service, answering ~, babysitting ~, business reply ~, civil ~, contract of ~, customer ~, etc.

1 [C,U] a business whose work involves doing sth for customers but not producing goods; the work that such a business does: *the development of new* **goods and services** ◇ *Smith's Catering Services* (= a company) *offers the best value.* ◇ *How much does the basic phone service cost?* ◇ *We can provide a home-delivery service.* ◇ *There has been considerable growth in the service sector* (= the part of the economy involved in this type of business). ◇ *a service industry*

● *to offer (sb)/provide (sb with) a service* ◆ *to expand/*

guarantee/improve a service ◆ *banking/financial/marketing/security/travel services*

2 [U] help and advice given to customers in hotels, restaurants, shops/stores and businesses: *The food was good but the service was very slow.* ◇ *10% will be added to your bill for service.* ◇ *We are committed to providing a high quality of service to all our clients.* ◇ *The training aims to improve service levels.* ◇ *We guarantee excellent service.*

● *to give (sb)/offer (sb)/provide (sb with) service* ◆ *efficient/excellent/good/quality/quick service* ◆ *bad/poor/slow service*

3 [C] a system that provides sth that the public needs, organized by the government or a private company: *the ambulance/bus/telephone service* ◇ *We want to provide a profitable postal service.*

● *to offer (sb)/provide (sb with) a service* ◆ *education/health/postal/social services* ◆ *an essential/a vital service*

4 [C] an organization or a company that provides sth for the public or does sth for the government: *a debt counselling service* ◇ *the diplomatic service*

5 [C, usually sing.] a system of regular buses, trains, planes, etc. that goes to a particular place; a bus, train, plane, etc. that regularly goes at a particular time: *There is now an air service to the island.* ◇ *The 10.15 service to Glasgow has been cancelled.*

● *to lay on/offer/provide a service* ◆ *to improve/operate/run a service* ◆ *to cancel/cut/suspend a service* ◆ *a fast/frequent/good/reliable service*

6 [U] the work that sb does for an organization, etc., especially when it continues for a long time or is admired very much: *She has just celebrated 25 years' service with the company.* ◇ *The employees have good* **conditions of service**.

7 [C, usually pl.] the particular skills or help that a person is able to offer: *You need the services* **of** *a good lawyer.* ◇ *He offered his services* **as** *a driver.*

8 [U] the use that you can get from a vehicle or machine; the state of being used: *That computer gave us very good service.*

9 [C] an examination of a vehicle or machine followed by any work that is necessary to keep it operating well: *I had taken the car to the garage for a service.* ◇ *a service engineer*

IDM **be of 'service (to sb)** (*formal*) to be useful or helpful: *Can I be of service to anyone?* → idiom at ENTER

● *verb* [+ obj]

1 (*Finance*) **service a debt/loan** to pay interest on money that has been borrowed: *The company can no longer service its debts.*

2 (*Finance*) **service a loan** to collect and manage the regular payments made to pay back a loan: *The mortgage providers service over 350 000 loans a year.* → LOAN SERVICING

3 (*formal*) to do sth for people or provide them with help or with sth they need, such as shops/stores, or a transport system: *The department services the international sales force.* ◇ *The city is serviced by six international airlines.* → SERVE

4 to examine a vehicle or machine and repair it if necessary so that it continues to work correctly: *We need to* **have** *the vans* **serviced**.

● *adjective* [only before noun]

used only by people who work in a building or who are delivering sth to a building: *a service elevator* ◇ *the service entrance* ▶ **'servicing** *noun* [U]: *debt servicing* ◇ *Like any other type of equipment, it requires regular servicing.*

'service a,greement = SERVICE CONTRACT

'service ,bureau *noun* [C]

(*IT*) a business that sells a variety of computing or printing services or allows people to pay to use their computers or printers

'service ,centre (*AmE spelling* ~ **center**) *noun* [C]

1 a place that checks or repairs machines and equipment and provides parts for them

2 a place (**garage**) where vehicles are repaired and where you can buy parts for vehicles

3 a place where a company provides help and information for customers who have bought or are using its products

'service ,charge *noun* [C]

1 a charge for work that sb does for you that is usually extra to the main bill: *A $5 service charge will be added to all orders under $100.* ◇ *There is a 2.75% service charge for processing credit-card payments.* → BANK CHARGE

2 (*BrE*) an amount of money that is added to a bill in a restaurant that goes to pay for the work of the staff: *An optional service charge of 12.5% will be added to your bill.*

3 an amount of money that is paid to the owner of an apartment building for services such as putting out rubbish/garbage, cleaning the stairs, etc.

'service ,contract (*also* **'service a,greement**) *noun* [C]

1 (*HR*) a formal agreement about employment made between a company and an employee, usually one with special conditions that is given to a senior manager, a director, etc. → CONTRACT OF EMPLOYMENT

2 an arrangement with a company in which the company will check and repair equipment for a fixed fee for a particular period of time: *The group has won $228 million of service contracts covering road, water and electricity.*

3 an agreement with a company providing mobile phone/cellphone services in which a customer pays a fixed fee each month for a particular period of time → PAY-AS-YOU-GO
→ EXTENDED WARRANTY

'service e,conomy *noun* [C, usually sing.]
(*Economics*) an economy in which most of the workers and businesses are involved in providing services rather than manufacturing or producing things; all the businesses in an economy that provide services: *the shift from a manufacturing to a service economy* ◇ *Hong Kong is regarded as a service economy.* ◇ *employment in the service economy*

'service ,handbook = SERVICE MANUAL

'service ,industry = TERTIARY INDUSTRY

,service level a'greement = SLA

'service ,manual (*also* **'service ,handbook**) *noun* [C]
a book that describes how to check and repair a vehicle or a machine

'service pack *noun* [C]
(*IT*) a set of additional software elements that corrects any errors in the software or makes improvements to it

'service pro,vider *noun* [C]
(*IT*) a business company that provides a service to customers, especially one that connects customers to the Internet → *an Internet service provider*

'service road (*AmE also* **'frontage road**) *noun* [C]
a small road that runs parallel to a main road, that you use to reach houses, shops/stores, etc.

,service 'sector = TERTIARY SECTOR

session /'seʃn/ *noun* [C]

SEE ALSO: **bull session**

1 (*Stock Exchange*) (*also* **'trading ,session**) a period of trading on the stock exchange, usually from when it opens to when it closes on a particular day: *a session of heavy trading* ◇ *The FTSE 100 fell for a third consecutive session.* ◇ *The stock hit a session*

high (= the highest price reached during that particular period).

2 a period of time that is spent doing a particular activity: *a training session run by the IT department* ◇ *The course is made up of 12 two-hour sessions.* ◇ *a brainstorming session*

3 a formal meeting or series of meetings: *In an* **extraordinary session** (= an unexpected or emergency meeting) *of the board, the directors approved the new appointments.* ◇ *The court is now* **in session**.

SET /ˌes iː 'tiː/ *abbr*
(*E-commerce*) **secure electronic transfer** a safe and private way of ordering goods and paying for them on the Internet

★**set** /set/ *verb, noun, adjective*
● *verb* [+ obj] (**setting, set, set**)

1 to arrange or fix sth; to decide on sth: *Shall we set a date for the meeting?* ◇ *We must be careful not to set the price too high.* SYN FIX

2 to fix sth so that others copy it or try to achieve it: *Their latest computer sets the* **standard** *for others to follow.*

3 to give sb a piece of work, a task, etc: *We set ourselves targets each month.* NOTE Idioms containing **set** are at the entries for the nouns or adjectives in the idioms, for example **set up shop** is at **shop**.

PHR V **,set sth a'gainst sth; ,set sth 'off against sth** (*Accounting*) to use one cost or payment, or one group of costs or payments, in order to cancel or reduce the effect of another: *to set capital costs off against tax* → OFFSET, SET-OFF **,set sth a'side 1** to save or keep money or time for a particular purpose: *Each month we set a certain amount aside for emergencies.* **2** (*Law*) to state that a decision made by a court is not legally valid **,set sth/sb 'back** to delay the progress of sth/sb by a particular time: *The delay in the shipment has set production back by two weeks.* → SETBACK **,set sb 'back sth** (*not used in the form* **be set back**) to cost sb a particular amount of money: *The repairs could set us back over €200 000.* **,set sth 'down** to give sth as a rule, principle, etc: *Building regulations are set down by the government.* **,set sth 'off 1** to start a process or series of events: *The incident set off a series of protests throughout the industry.* **2** to make an alarm start ringing **,set sth 'off against sth** (*Finance*) = SET STH AGAINST STH **,set sth 'out** to present ideas, facts, etc. in an organized way, in speech or writing: *He set out his objections to the plan.* **,set sb 'up** (*Finance*) to provide sb with the money that they need in order to do sth: *A bank loan helped to set him up in business.* **,set sth 'up 1** to make a piece of equipment or a machine ready for use: *It will take a month to set up the factory ready for production.* → SET-UP **2** to arrange for sth to happen: *We'll set up a meeting to discuss the issue.* → SET-UP See note at ARRANGE **3** to create or start a company, a business or an organization: *She left the company to set up her own business.* See note at FOUND **4** to start a process or a series of events: *The slump on Wall Street set up a chain reaction in stock markets around the world.* **,set (yourself) 'up (as sth)** to start a new business: *He left the company and set himself up as a consultant.* ◇ *She took out a bank loan and set up in business on her own.* ◇ *setting-up costs for small businesses* → SET-UP See note at FOUND

● *noun* [C]

SEE ALSO: **commercial set, skill set**

a group of similar things that belong together in some way: *a set of accounts/keys* ◇ *There are a whole set of factors behind the decision.*

● *adjective*
1 [usually before noun] planned or fixed: *Tasks are performed in a set order.* ◊ *Shipping costs are included in the set price.*
2 (used especially in newspapers) likely to do sth; ready for sth or to do sth: *Interest rates look set to rise again.*

setback /'setbæk/ *noun* [C]
1 a difficulty or problem that delays or prevents sth, or makes a situation worse: *We suffered a major setback when the new product failed safety tests.* ◊ *The delay in receiving parts was a temporary setback.*
→ SET STH/SB BACK at SET *verb*
O *a big/major/serious/temporary setback* • *to experience/recover from/suffer a setback*
2 (*Stock Exchange*) (used especially in newspapers) a fall in prices: *Canadian stock prices suffered a 6.7% setback in July.*
O *to experience/recover from/suffer a setback*

'set-off *noun* [C,U]
1 (*Accounting*) a cost or payment, or a group of costs or payments, that is used to cancel or reduce the effect of another
2 (*Law*) an occasion when sb reduces the amount that they owe sb else because the other person also owes them money
→ SET STH OFF AGAINST STH at SET *verb*

settle /'setl/ *verb*
1 [+ obj] to pay money that you owe: *Most of our customers settle their accounts on time.* ◊ *The media empire was broken up in order to settle the debts.*
2 [+ obj or no obj] to put an end to an argument or a disagreement: *The union want to hold talks with management to settle the dispute.* ◊ *The companies have now settled their differences following a dispute over contracts.* ◊ *There is pressure on the unions to settle.*
3 [+ obj] (*often* be settled) to decide or arrange sth finally: *So we'll travel on May 22nd. Is that settled then?*
4 [no obj] if prices, etc. settle, they stop rising or falling and stay the same for a period of time: *The price for crude oil has settled at $34.4 a barrel.*
5 [no obj] to sink slowly down: *The contents of this package may settle in transit.*
PHRV **'settle for sth** to accept sth that is not satisfactory but is the best that is available: *The union wanted a 5% pay increase, but had to settle for 3%.* **'settle on sth** to choose or make a decision about sth after thinking about it: *We haven't yet settled on a name for our new brand.* **,settle 'up (with sb)** to pay sb the money you owe them: *I'll pay for the meal and we'll settle up afterwards.*

★ settlement /'setlmənt/ *noun*

SEE ALSO: **Bank for International Settlements, cash settlement**

1 [C] an official agreement that ends an argument between two people or groups: *The management and unions have reached a settlement over new working conditions.* ◊ *An out-of-court settlement* (= an agreement that is made or money that is paid to stop sb going to court) *has been agreed in the dispute over the terms of the loan.*
O *to agree/negotiate/offer/reach a settlement* • *a financial/global/an industry-wide/a negotiated settlement* • *a pay/wage settlement*
2 [U] the action of reaching an agreement: *the settlement of a claim/dispute*
3 [U] the action of paying money that you owe: *We offer a reduced price for quick settlement.* ◊ *the settlement of a debt* ◊ *a cheque in settlement of a bill*

4 (*Finance*; *Stock Exchange*) [U] the action of paying money that you owe for investments, etc: *the settlement system for securities*

'settlement date (*also* 'settlement day) (*BrE also* 'settling day, *less frequent*) *noun* [C]
(*Finance*; *Stock Exchange*) the date by which shares, bonds, etc. must be paid for and must be passed to the buyer: *The settlement date for bonds is three business days after the trade is made.*

,set-top 'box (*also* box) *noun* [C]
a device that allows you to receive DIGITAL television and to use the Internet on your television set

'set-up (*also spelled* setup, *especially in AmE*) *noun*
1 [C, usually sing.] a way of organizing sth; a system: *I'm new here and I don't understand the set-up yet.*
2 [C, usually sing.] the act of starting a company or making an official arrangement: *This is a problem often faced by companies during the set-up phase.* ◊ *There are set-up costs involved in opening an account.*
3 [C] a business or an organization: *He now runs his own set-up.*
4 [C, usually sing., U] the act of preparing machines and organizing a system in a factory in order to make a particular product: *Set-up only takes a few minutes.* ◊ *The software helped us reduce our set-up times and so cut costs.*
5 [C] the equipment that is needed for a particular task or purpose: *a new recording set-up*
→ SET STH UP at SET *verb*

severally /'sevrəli/ *adverb*
(*Law or formal*)
separately: *The company's directors are jointly and severally responsible for paying debts* (= they are not responsible for only their own part of a debt).

severance /'sevərəns/ *noun* [sing; U]
1 (*HR*) the act of ending sb's contract of employment: *They are expected to lose 8 000 staff, mainly through early retirement and voluntary severance.* ◊ *All employees are entitled to severance pay.* → REDUNDANCY
O *severance packages/pay/payments/terms*
2 the act of ending a connection or relationship: *the severance of relations*

sew /səʊ; soʊ/ *verb* (**sewed, sewn** /səʊn; *AmE* soʊn/ *or* **sewed, sewed**)
PHRV **,sew sth 'up** (*informal*) **1** to arrange sth in a satisfactory way: *We need to sew up the deal today.*
2 to be in complete control of sth: *They seemed to have the computer games market sewn up.*

sexism /'seksɪzəm/ *noun* [U]
the unfair treatment of people, especially women, because of their sex; the attitude that causes this: *legislation designed to combat sexism in the work place* ▶ **'sexist** *noun* [C] **'sexist** *adjective*: *a sexist attitude/remark*

'sex ,typing *noun* [U]
the belief that particular behaviour is more typical of either men or women; the belief that particular roles or jobs are more suitable for either men or women: *The sex typing of jobs has become less rigid in recent years.*

SFA /,es ef 'eɪ/ *abbr*
1 = SECURITIES AND FUTURES AUTHORITY
2 **sales force automation** software that deals with the whole process of selling goods and services

sgd *abbr*
a short way of writing **signed**

shadow /'ʃædəʊ; *AmE* -doʊ/ *verb* [+ obj]
1 (*HR*) to be with sb who is doing a particular job, so that you can learn about it: *New employees shadow other members of the department as part of their training.*

2 to behave, move, etc. in the same way as sb/sth else: *The company's success has shadowed the rise in popularity of the Internet.*

the ˌshadow eˈconomy *(also* in ˌformal e'conomy, ˌparallel e'conomy) *noun* [sing.] *(Economics)* illegal work, trade or business activities that are done without the knowledge or approval of the government: *It is difficult to estimate the size of the shadow economy.* → BLACK ECONOMY

ˌshadow 'market *noun* [sing.] illegal trade in sth → BLACK MARKET

shady /'ʃeɪdi/ *adjective* (**shadier, shadiest**) seeming to be dishonest or illegal: *a shady businessman/deal*

shake /ʃeɪk/ *verb* [+ obj] (**shook** /ʃʊk/ **shaken** /'ʃeɪkən/)
shake hands (with sb) (on sth) | shake sb's hand to take sb's hand and move it up and down to say hello or to show that you agree about sth: *In many countries, people shake hands when they meet.* ◇ *We shook hands on the deal* (= to show that we had reached an agreement). → idiom at FAIR *adj.*
PHRV ˌshake 'down to begin to work well in a situation, especially a new one: *The new employees are shaking down well.* ◇ *How does the latest version of the software shake down?* → SHAKEDOWN **ˌshake on sth** to shake hands in order to show that sth has been agreed: *They shook on the deal.* ◇ *Let's shake on it.* **ˌshake sth 'up** to make important changes in an organization, a profession, etc. in order to make it more efficient: *The whole industry needs shaking up.* → SHAKE-UP

shakedown /'ʃeɪkdaʊn/ *noun* [C] *(AmE)* *(Manufacturing)* a test of a vehicle, piece of equipment, etc. to see if there are any problems before it is used generally → SHAKE DOWN at SHAKE

'shake-out *(also spelled* **shakeout**, *especially in AmE) noun* [C]
1 a big change that takes place in an industry, in which people lose their jobs and one or more competing companies may disappear: *Ebay survived the dotcom shake-out.*
2 = SHAKE-UP

'shake-up *(also spelled* **shakeup** *(also* 'shake-out) *noun* [C]
a situation in which a lot of changes are made to a company, an organization, etc. in order to improve the way in which it works: *a management shake-up* ◇ *Union leaders are calling for a major shake-up of the system.* ◇ *a shake-up in the mobile phone industry*

shaky /'ʃeɪki/ *adjective* (**shakier, shakiest**) not seeming very successful; likely to fail: *Business is looking shaky at the moment.* ◇ *Their legal claim is on shaky ground.*

shape /ʃeɪp/ *verb*
IDM shape ˌup or 'ship out *(AmE) (informal)* used to tell sb that if they do not improve, work harder, etc. they will have to leave their job, position, etc.
PHRV ˌshape 'up (as sth) 1 to develop in a particular way, especially in a good way: *Our plans are shaping up nicely* (= showing signs that they will be successful). ◇ *2006 is shaping up as a difficult year for the company.* **2** to improve your behaviour, work harder, etc: *If he doesn't shape up, he'll soon be out of a job.*

★share /ʃeə(r); *AmE* ʃer/ *noun, verb*
●*noun* [C]

SEE ALSO: A/B/C share, all-~, asset value per ~, authorized ~, B ~, brand ~, bonus ~, etc.

1 *(Finance)* any of the units of equal value into which a company is divided and sold to raise

money. People who own **shares** become owners of the company and receive part of the company's profits: *shares in British Airways* ◇ *The retailer will issue 24 million new shares worth ¥3 billion.* ◇ *Will this affect the value of my shares?* ◇ *allegations of illegal share dealings* See note at STOCK
❍ *to* **acquire/buy/have/hold/own/sell** shares • *to* **allocate/allot** shares • *to* **deal in/invest in/trade in** shares • *to* **float/issue** shares
2 one part of sth that is divided between two or more people, businesses, etc: *Next year we hope to have a bigger share of the market.* ◇ *Channel 5 had a 7.5% share of advertising revenue last year.*
❍ *a* **big/growing/an increased/a large/small** share
3 the part that sb has in a particular activity that involves several people: *Everybody on the team has done their share of the work.*
IDM ˌshare of 'mind *(Marketing)* how aware people are of a particular brand or product compared with other brands or products of the same type: *We are competing with each other to capture the largest share of mind.* → FRONT OF MIND at FRONT *noun*

┌─────────────────────┐
WHICH WORD?

share/stock
Either **shares** [plural] or **stock** [U] can be used to describe the amount of a company that a person owns or a company's value on the stock exchange. In this sense, **share** is more common in *BrE* and **stock** more common in *AmE*: *The bank holds 60% of the company's shares/stock.* ◇ *The publisher's stock rose to $27.87 a share.*

As a countable noun in both *BrE* and *AmE*, especially in the plural, **stock** can refer to the shares of a particular company or type of company: *the largest 500 stocks on the NYSE* ◇ *technology stocks.* **Share** is less commonly used in this way.

Share, not stock, is used when talking about a particular number of shares in both *BrE* and *AmE*: *a profit of $3.75 a share* ◇ *1.2 billion shares*

In *BrE*, the phrase **stocks and shares** means 'bonds and shares'. This meaning of **stock** is also found in other phrases: *a company's loan stock* ◇ *government stock.* The *AmE* expression for 'bonds and shares' is **stocks and bonds**.

See note at STOCK
└─────────────────────┘

●*verb*
1 [+ obj *or* no obj] to have or use sth at the same time as sb else: *I share an office with two other people.* → JOB-SHARING
2 [+ obj] **share sth (out)** to divide sth between two or more people: *Profits are shared out yearly.*

'share appliˌcation *(also* appliˌcation for 'shares) *noun* [C] *(both BrE)*
(Finance) a request to buy some of the shares that a company is issuing (= selling): *You will need to fill in the share application form.*

'share ˌbuyback *(BrE) (AmE* 'stock ˌbuyback) *noun* [C,U]
(Finance) a situation when a company buys its own shares from shareholders

'share ˌcapital *noun* [U] *(BrE)*

SEE ALSO: authorized share capital, issued share capital

(Finance) the money that investors put into a company when they buy shares, which the company uses to continue its activities → LOAN CAPITAL

'share cer,tificate (*BrE*) (*AmE* **'stock cer,tificate**) *noun* [C]
(*Finance*) a legal document that is given to a shareholder, containing details of the shares that they own: *Fewer companies are **issuing** paper share certificates these days.*

'share ,dividend *noun* [C]
(*Finance*)
1 = DIVIDEND
2 an amount of profits that a company pays to its shareholders in the form of shares rather than cash
→ SCRIP DIVIDEND

★ shareholder /'ʃeəhəʊldə(r); *AmE* 'ʃerhoʊ-/ (*especially BrE*) (*AmE usually* **'stockholder**) *noun* [C]

SEE ALSO: **controlling shareholder, outside shareholder**

(*Finance*) a person or group that owns shares in a company or business: *They are the biggest shareholder **in** EFM, with a 30% stake.* ◇ *a shareholders' meeting*
◐ *a big/large/leading/major/substantial shareholder* • *the controlling/main/principal shareholder*

,shareholder 'equity (*also* **,shareholders' 'equity**) (*both especially BrE*) (*AmE usually* **,stockholder 'equity**) *noun* [U]
(*Accounting*) the value of a company as shown in its financial records, which is its assets minus its LIABILITIES (= the money that it owes) SYN BOOK VALUE

'shareholder funds (*also* **'shareholders' funds**) *noun* [pl.] (*both BrE*)
(*Accounting*) the value of a company's assets minus its LIABILITIES. This legally belongs to its shareholders. SYN NET WORTH

,shareholder of 'record (*especially BrE*) (*AmE usually* **,stockholder of 'record**) (*also* **,holder of 'record**, **,owner of 'record**, *AmE, BrE*) *noun* [C]
the person, company, etc. that is in a company's records as a holder of shares. Only **shareholders of record** can receive DIVIDENDS and other payments.

,shareholders' 'equity = SHAREHOLDER EQUITY

'shareholders' funds = SHAREHOLDER FUNDS

,shareholders' 'register (*also* **'share ,register**, **,register of 'members**) (*all BrE*) *noun* [C]
(*Law*) a legal document that contains a list of all the people or companies that own shares in a business

,shareholder value (*especially BrE*) (*AmE usually* **,stockholder 'value**) *noun* [U,C]
the financial benefits that a company's shareholders have, in the form of DIVIDENDS and the value of their shares if they sell them: *We are committed to delivering long-term shareholder value through continued revenue and earnings growth.*

shareholding /'ʃeəhəʊldɪŋ; *AmE* 'ʃerhoʊ-/ (*especially BrE*) (*AmE usually* **'stockholding**) *noun*

SEE ALSO: **cross-shareholding**

(*Finance*)
1 [C] a share of the ownership of a company; the value of shares in a company that a particular shareholder owns: *The agency has a 21% shareholding **in** Telecall.* ◇ *The company's founder is to sell his controlling shareholding (= enough shares to give the owner more than 50% of votes in company meetings).* SYN HOLDING (2)
◐ *to acquire/build up/increase/reduce/sell your shareholding* • *a controlling/majority/minority shareholding*

2 [C, usually pl.] a number of shares that a company, fund, etc. owns as an asset: *details of the company's shareholdings at the end of last year*
→ HOLDING (1)

,share in'centive plan (*BrE*) (*AmE* **,stock in'centive plan**) *noun* [C] (*abbr* SIP)
(*Finance*; *HR*) a system in which a company gives its employees shares, or allows them to buy shares, so that when the company makes a profit they will receive part of it SYN EMPLOYEE SHARE OWNERSHIP PLAN

'share ,index (*BrE*) (*AmE* **'stock ,index**) *noun* [C]
(*Stock Exchange*) a list of the average price of a particular set of shares, that can be easily compared with the average price on a previous date and used to show whether the value of shares in general is rising or falling: *Japan's Nikkei share index was up 2% on the previous day.*

'share ,issue (*also* **'share ,offer**) (*both BrE*) (*AmE* **'stock ,issue**) *noun* [C]
(*Finance*) an occasion when a company offers a number of new shares for sale to existing shareholders or to other investors or members of the public; the shares that it offers: *The company plans to raise the necessary funds through a share issue.*

'share ,offer (*BrE*) (*AmE* **'stock ,offer**) *noun* [C]
(*Finance*)
1 = SHARE ISSUE
2 an occasion when a company tries to buy another company by offering its own shares rather than money: *Shareholders are more likely to vote in favour of a cash offer than a share offer.*

,share of 'voice *noun* [U; sing.] (*abbr* SOV)
(*Marketing*) the amount of money that one company spends on advertising a brand in a particular period compared with other companies selling similar products: *The banner will switch between four ads, giving each advertiser a 25% share of voice.*

'share ,option (*BrE*) (*AmE* **'stock ,option**) *noun* [C]
1 (*Finance*; *HR*) a right that is given to employees to buy shares in the company at a low price: *The company set up a share option for its employees.* ◇ *You will have to pay tax when you **exercise** a share option.* ◇ *a share option plan/scheme/package*
2 (*Finance*) a right, which can be bought and sold, to buy or sell shares in a company at a fixed price by or on a particular date

'share-out *noun* [C, usually sing.] (*BrE*)
an act of dividing sth between two or more people; the amount of sth that one person receives when it is divided → SHARE OUT at SHARE *verb*

shareowner /'ʃeərəʊnə(r); *AmE* 'ʃeroʊ-/ *noun* [C]
(*Finance*) a person or company that owns shares in a company or business SYN SHAREHOLDER

'share ,premium *noun* [C] (*BrE*)
(*Finance*) the difference between the value stated on shares that a company issues and the higher amount it receives for them

'share price (*BrE*) (*AmE* **'stock price**) *noun* [C]
(*Stock Exchange*) the price at which a company's shares are bought and sold at a particular time: *The company's share price has dropped by half since April.* ◇ *You can check the latest share prices at the Stock Exchange website.*

'share ,register = SHAREHOLDERS' REGISTER

,shares out'standing = OUTSTANDING SHARES

'share split *noun* [C] (*BrE*)
(*Finance*) an occasion when a company divides its SHARE CAPITAL into more shares in order to lower the price of each share. People who already have shares are given a number of new ones according

to how many they already hold: *The bank is planning a four-for-one share split.* **SYN** STOCK SPLIT → BONUS ISSUE, CAPITALIZATION ISSUE, SCRIP ISSUE, STOCK DIVIDEND

shareware /'ʃeəweə(r); *AmE* 'ʃerwer/ *noun* [U]
(*IT*) software that is available free for a user to test, after which they must pay if they wish to continue using it → FREEWARE

shark /ʃɑːk; *AmE* ʃɑːrk/ *noun* [C] (*informal*)

SEE ALSO: **loan shark**

1 a person who is dishonest in business, especially sb who gives bad advice and gets people to pay too much for sth
2 a company that tries to take over another company that does not want to be taken over

'shark re,pellent *noun* [U,C] (*especially AmE*) (*informal*)
action that a company takes to make it less attractive as the object of a takeover → POISON PILL

'shark ,watcher *noun* [C] (*especially AmE*) (*informal*)
a person or company whose job is to warn and help a company if sb has bought a lot of its shares and may try to take it over

sharp /ʃɑːp; *AmE* ʃɑːrp/ *adjective* (**sharper, sharpest**)
1 [usually before noun] (especially about a change in sth) sudden and rapid: *There was a sharp increase in sales in July.*
❍ *a sharp* **decline/drop/fall/increase/rise**
2 [usually before noun] (about people or their minds) quick to notice or understand things or to react: *He has a sharp business brain.* ◇ *She is known as a sharp negotiator.*
3 (about a person or their way of doing business) clever but possibly dishonest: *His lawyer is a sharp operator.* ◇ *The firm had to face some* **sharp practice** *from competing companies.*
▶ **'sharply** *adverb*: *Profits fell sharply following the takeover.* **'sharpness** *noun* [U,C]
IDM **the 'sharp end (of sth)** (*BrE*) (*informal*) the place or position of greatest difficulty or responsibility: *He started work at the sharp end of the business, as a salesman.*

shed /ʃed/ *verb, noun*
● *verb* [+ obj] (**shedding, shed, shed**) (*often used in newspapers*)
1 to get rid of sth that is no longer wanted: *The factory is shedding a large number of jobs.* ◇ *The company is trying to shed its old-fashioned image.*
2 (about shares) to lose value: *The steel company's shares shed 6%.*
● *noun* [C] (*BrE*)
a large industrial building used for working in or keeping equipment

sheet /ʃiːt/ *noun* [C]

SEE ALSO: **balance sheet, fact ~, off-balance-~, time ~**

1 a piece of paper for writing or printing on, etc., usually in a standard size: *a sheet of A4* ◇ *an information sheet*
2 a flat thin piece of any material, normally square or similar in shape: *a sheet of glass/steel* ◇ *sheet metal*
IDM **sing from the same 'hymn sheet/'song sheet** to show that you are in agreement with each other by saying the same things in public

'sheet feed *noun* [C]
a device that pushes pieces of paper into a printer separately

shelf /ʃelf/ *noun* [C] (*plural* **shelves** /ʃelvz/)

SEE ALSO: **off-the-shelf**

a flat board, made of wood, metal, glass, etc. fixed to the wall or forming part of a piece of furniture for things to be placed on: *The book I wanted was on the top shelf.* ◇ *supermarket shelves* ◇ *stores with well-stocked shelves* ◇ *She got a job stacking* (= filling) *shelves at the local supermarket.*
❍ *a* **high/low** *shelf* ● *the* **bottom/middle/top** *shelf* ● *to* **fill/refill/restock/stock** *the shelves*
IDM **fly/leap/walk off the 'shelves** to sell extremely well: *DVD players are flying off the shelves.* **off the 'shelf** that can be bought immediately and does not have to be specially designed or ordered: *We buy some software off the shelf and develop some ourselves.* ◇ *off-the-shelf software packages* → OFF-THE-PEG at PEG

'shelf ,company (*also* ,**off-the-'shelf ,company**) *noun* [C]
a company that has been formed but not used, so that it can be sold to sb who wants to start a company immediately or to give the impression that their company has existed for a few years

'shelf-,filler = SHELF-STACKER

'shelf life *noun* [C, usually sing.]
(*Commerce*)
1 the length of time that a product remains in good condition after it is made and can be sold: *Canned food usually has a shelf life of two years or more.* See note at BEST-BEFORE DATE
2 the length of time that people will buy a product after it is first available: *Software packages usually have a shelf life of around 18 months before they need updating.*

'shelf ,offering *noun* [C]
(*Finance*) in the US, an occasion when a company offers for sale some of the shares, bonds, etc. that have already been prepared in a SHELF REGISTRATION

'shelf regis,tration *noun* [C]
(*Finance*) in the US, an arrangement in which larger companies can get permission to issue (= sell) shares, bonds, etc. at some time within a two year period if they need money

'shelf space *noun* [U]
(*Commerce*) the amount of space that a shop/store has available on its shelves for products or for a particular product: *There is fierce competition for tight shelf space in supermarkets.* ◇ *The more powerful companies usually get most retail shelf space.*

'shelf-,stacker (*also* 'shelf-,filler) *noun* [C]
a person whose job is to fill shelves with goods to be sold, especially in a supermarket

'shelf ,talker (*also* 'shelf ,wobbler) *noun* [C]
(*Marketing, informal*) a printed advertisement that is hung over the edge of a shelf in a shop/store to make people notice a particular product
—Picture at STORE

shell /ʃel/ *noun, verb*
● *noun* [C]

SEE ALSO: **cash shell**

1 a structure that forms a hard outer frame: *the body shell of a car*
2 = SHELL COMPANY
● *verb*
PHRV ,**shell 'out (for sth)**; ,**shell sth 'out (for sth)** (*informal*) to pay a lot of money for sth: *Customers will have to shell out $200 for the latest upgrade to the software.* **SYN** FORK OUT

'shell ,company (*AmE also* **'shell corpo,ration**) (*also* **shell**, **'cash shell**, *BrE, AmE*) *noun* [C] a company that has been formed but does not really do any business, often for legal reasons. It can be used by its owners to do some business deals or sometimes to hide illegal activities.

shelve /ʃelv/ *verb* [+ obj] to decide not to continue with a plan, either for a short time or permanently: *We've shelved the plans to move office until next year.*

shelving /'ʃelvɪŋ/ *noun* [U] shelves; material for making shelves: *wooden shelving* ◇ *warehouse shelving*

'sheriff's sale *noun* [C] (*AmE*) (*Law*) an occasion when a court orders that sb's property should be sold to the public because they have not paid money that they owe

shift /ʃɪft/ *noun, verb*
● *noun*

SEE ALSO: **back shift, graveyard ~, paradigm ~, split ~, swing ~**

1 [C] a change in position or direction: *the shift from a manufacturing to a service economy* ◇ *There has been a fundamental shift in the way the firm manages its staff.* ◇ *Management needs to clarify the strategic shift.*
  ✪ *a dramatic/fundamental/huge/major/significant shift* ✦ *a policy/strategic/structural/technology shift* ✦ *a shift away from/from/to/towards sth*
2 (*HR*) [C] a period of time worked by a group of workers who start work as another group finishes: *to be on the day/night shift at the factory* ◇ *The salespeople work eight-hour shifts.* ◇ *Experienced staff will be working in shifts to ensure a good service.*
  ✪ *the day/early/evening/late/night shift* ✦ *to be on/do/work a shift* ✦ *to change shifts* ✦ *a shift manager/supervisor/worker*
3 (*HR*) [C with sing./pl. verb] the workers who work a particular **shift**: *What time does the day shift come on?* ◇ *The night shift has/have just come off duty.*
4 [C,U] (*also* **'shift key** [C]) a key on a computer keyboard that allows capital letters or a different set of characters to be keyed
● *verb*
1 (*informal*) [+ obj] to move sth from one position or place to another: *Can you help me shift these boxes?* ◇ *They are shifting 70% of their production to China.*
2 [no obj] (about a situation, an opinion, a policy, etc.) to change from one state, position, etc. to another: *Consumer tastes are constantly shifting.* ◇ *The balance of power has shifted away from workers to employers.*
3 [+ obj] to change your opinion of or your attitude towards sth; to change the way that you do sth: *We need to shift the emphasis away from speed towards efficiency.*
4 (*Commerce, informal*) [+ obj] to sell goods, especially goods that are difficult to sell: *They cut prices drastically to try and shift stock.* ◇ *250 000 of the devices have been shifted this year.*

shifting /'ʃɪftɪŋ/ *adjective* changing all the time: *Shifting costs force us to revise our prices constantly.*

'shift key = SHIFT *noun* (4)

shingle /'ʃɪŋɡl/ *noun* [C] (*AmE*) a sign outside a doctor's or lawyer's office that gives their name, etc.

★ **ship** /ʃɪp/ *noun, verb*
● *noun* [C]

SEE ALSO: **delivered ex ship, free alongside ~, trans-~**

a large boat that carries people or goods by sea: *The ship is moored in Genoa.* ◇ *a fleet of merchant ships* ◇ *cargo ships carrying food and manufacturing equipment* ◇ *Goods are placed on board ship by the seller at the port named in the contract.*
  ✪ *to load (sth onto)/unload (sth from) a ship* ✦ *a ship loads/unloads (sth)* ✦ *a cargo/container/factory/merchant ship*
  IDM **abandon/jump 'ship** to leave an organization suddenly or unexpectedly because you think it is going to fail: *Investors abandoned ship after the scandal.* → idiom at RUN *verb*
● *verb* (**-pp-**)
1 (*Transport*) [+ obj] to send or transport sth by ship: *We ship goods all over the world.*
2 (*Commerce; Transport*) [+ obj or no obj] to send goods by air, road or rail: *This product usually ships within 24 hours.* ◇ *Purchases can be shipped or collected from the store.* ◇ *The machine wasn't working so we had to ship it back for repair.*
3 (*Commerce*) [+ obj or no obj] to be available to be bought; to make sth available to be bought: *The software will be shipping next month.* ◇ *We continue to ship more computer systems than our rivals.*
→ idiom at SHAPE

shipbuilder /'ʃɪpbɪldə(r)/ *noun* [C] a person or company that builds ships
  ▶ **'shipbuilding** *noun* [U]: *the shipbuilding industry*

'ship date *noun* [C] (*Production*) the date on which goods must be sent to a customer: *If we miss the ship date the order will not arrive on time.*

★ **shipment** /'ʃɪpmənt/ *noun*

SEE ALSO: **drop shipment, part shipment**

(*Commerce; Transport*)
1 [C] a load of goods that are sent from one place to another: *We have sent a shipment of computers to Norway.* ◇ *Visit our website to track your shipment online.* SYN CONSIGNMENT
  ✪ *to deliver/send a shipment* ✦ *to accept/receive/sign for a shipment*
2 [U] the process of sending goods from one place to another: *The goods are ready for shipment.*
  ✪ *shipment charges/costs*

shipowner /'ʃɪpəʊnə(r)/; *AmE* -oʊ-/ *noun* [C] a person or company that owns a ship or ships

shipper /'ʃɪpə(r)/ *noun* [C] (*Transport*) a person or company that sends goods from one place to another by ship, air, road or rail: *The shipper will pay all transportation expenses to get the shipment to the foreign port.* ◇ *large/small shippers*

shipping /'ʃɪpɪŋ/ *noun* [U]

SEE ALSO: **drop shipping**

1 (*Commerce; Transport*) the activity of carrying goods from one place to another by ship or by air, road or rail: *The regulations that govern the shipping of dangerous materials are very detailed.* ◇ *We offer free shipping for orders over $99.*
  ✪ *a shipping company/group/line* ✦ *shipping charges/costs/rates* ✦ *a shipping clerk*
2 (*Transport*) ships in general or considered as a group: *The canal is open to shipping.* ◇ *daily shipping forecasts* (= of the weather at sea)

,shipping and 'forwarding ,agent *noun* [C] (*Transport*) a person or company that arranges for goods to be sent from one country to another by sea, air, rail or road, arranges insurance and prepares the necessary documents

,shipping and 'handling noun [U] (abbr **s and h**)
(*Commerce*; *Transport*) the packing and transport of
goods; the charge for this: *The poster is available for
$20 plus $4 shipping and handling.* ◇ *Add on s and h
charges.*

'shipping ,conference noun [C]
(*Transport*) an international group of companies
whose ships sail the same routes and who agree on
charges for cargo and passengers, and the
conditions in contracts

'shipping ,documents noun [pl.]
(*Trade*; *Transport*) the documents that are needed
when goods are sent from one country to another,
including, for example, A BILL OF LADING or an air
WAYBILL, an insurance certificate, a commercial
INVOICE, an export licence, etc.

'shipping note noun [C] (abbr **S/N**)
(*Transport*) a document prepared and signed by an
exporter when sending goods by sea, giving details
of the goods

shoot /ʃuːt/ verb [no obj] (**shot, shot** /ʃɒt; AmE ʃɑːt/)
1 (*used with an adverb or preposition*) to increase
very quickly: *Profits shot up 40% last year.* ◇ *The
dollar briefly shot above 120 yen.* See note at
INCREASE
2 (*used with an adverb or preposition*) to become
important, powerful, famous, etc. suddenly or
quickly: *They think he will shoot to the top of the
company.* ◇ *She shot to fame by building up the
company from nothing into a stock market star.*
→ OVERSHOOT, UNDERSHOOT
PHR V **'shoot for sth** (*AmE*) to try to achieve or get
sth, especially sth difficult: *We've been shooting for a
pay raise for months.*

VOCABULARY BUILDING

Types of shops/stores

- *They operate a chain of 24-hour* **convenience
stores.**
- *I went to the* **corner shop/store** *to buy a
newspaper.*
- *Many* **supermarkets** *have expanded their range of
non-food items.*
- *They were the first to launch the idea of a music*
superstore.
- *Independent stores have lost business to the out-
of-town* **hypermarkets.**

★ shop /ʃɒp; AmE ʃɑːp/ noun, verb
● noun [C]

SEE ALSO: **body shop, bucket ~, closed ~, corner ~,
duty-free ~, factory ~, gift ~,** etc.

1 (*especially BrE*) a building or part of a building
where you can buy goods or services: *Our prices are
up to 50% lower than high-street shops.* ◇ *The shop
offers a large array of leather goods.* ◇ *a chain of
electrical shops* ◇ *airport retail shops*—Picture at
STORE
● *a* **high-street/local** *shop* ◆ *to* **have/own/run/set up a**
shop ◆ *to* **close (down)/open (up)/shut (down)** *a*
shop ◆ *a shop* **closes (down)/opens (up)/shuts
(down)**
2 (*used especially with other nouns*) a place where
things are made or repaired, especially part of a
factory where a particular type of work is done: *a
repair shop* ◇ *a paint shop* (= where cars are
painted) **SYN** WORKSHOP
3 [usually sing.] (*BrE*) (*informal*) an act of going
shopping, especially for food and other items
needed in the house: *We do a weekly shop at the
supermarket.*
IDM **mind the 'shop** (*BrE*) (*AmE* **mind the 'store**) to
be in charge of sth for a short time while sb is
away: *Who's minding the store while she's away?* ,**set**

---

up 'shop to start a business: *The software company
intends to set up shop in China.* → idioms at SHUT
verb, TALK *verb*
● verb (**-pp-**)
1 [no obj] to buy things in shops/stores: *to shop for
food* ◇ *He likes to shop at the local market.*
2 **go shopping** [no obj] to spend time going to
shops/stores and looking for things to buy: *There
should be plenty of time to go shopping before we
leave New York.*
3 [+ obj] (*AmE*) to buy things at a particular shop/
store: *Thank you for shopping Land's End.*
4 [+ obj] (*AmE*) to try to sell sth such as a company
by talking about it to people who might buy it: *The
owner may not want it known that he is shopping the
company.*
PHR V **,shop a'round** to compare the quality or
prices of goods or services that are offered by
different shops/stores, companies, etc. so that you
can choose the best: *Shop around for the best deal.*

'shop as,sistant noun [C] (*BrE*)
a person whose job is to serve customers in a shop/
store **SYN** ASSISTANT, SALES ASSISTANT

shopfitting /'ʃɒpfɪtɪŋ; AmE 'ʃɑːp-/ noun [U]
the business of putting equipment and furniture
into shops/stores ▶ **'shopfitter** noun [C]

the ,shop 'floor noun [sing.]
1 the area in a factory where the goods are made
by the workers: *to work* **on** *the shop floor* ◇ *We need
to increase efficiency on the shop floor.*
2 (*HR*) the workers in a factory, not the managers:
*Most decisions about how work should be done are
taken in the office rather than on the shop floor* (=
by the workers).
▶ **'shop-floor** adjective [only before noun]: *shop-
floor productivity*

shopfront /'ʃɒpfrʌnt; AmE 'ʃɑːp-/ noun [C] (*BrE*)
1 the front of a shop, that people can see from the
street: *The company logo is on the shopfront.* ◇ *a
shopfront sign*
2 (*E-commerce*) (*also* ,**web 'shopfront**) a website that
a company uses to sell goods or services
→ STOREFRONT

shopkeeper /'ʃɒpkiːpə(r); AmE 'ʃɑːp-/ (*especially
BrE*) (*AmE usually* **'storekeeper**) noun [C]

SEE ALSO: **small shopkeeper**

a person who owns or manages a shop/store,
especially a small one

shoplifting /'ʃɒplɪftɪŋ; AmE 'ʃɑːp-/ noun [U]
the crime of stealing goods from a shop/store by
deliberately leaving without paying for them: *Most
stores don't raise prices to make up for losses due to
shoplifting.* ▶ **'shoplift** verb [+ obj or no obj]
'shoplifter noun [C]: *Shoplifters will be prosecuted.*

shopper /'ʃɒpə(r); AmE 'ʃɑːp-/ noun [C]

SEE ALSO: **mystery shopper**

a person who buys goods from shops/stores:
*Competition between stores can result in big savings
for shoppers.* ◇ *Last year the average shopper spent
$700 online.*
● **holiday/home/last-minute/online** *shoppers* ◆ *to*
attract/draw in/lure/woo *shoppers* ◆ *shoppers* **buy/
choose/look for/pay for** *sth*

shopping /'ʃɒpɪŋ; AmE 'ʃɑːp-/ noun [U]

SEE ALSO: **home shopping, window-shopping**

1 the activity of going to shops/stores and buying
things: *to go shopping* ◇ *to go on a shopping trip* ◇
(*BrE*) *to do the/your shopping* ◇ *This is the busiest*

shopping period of the year. ◇ *Click on the link to change or delete an item from your shopping cart.*

❍ *a shopping* **bag/basket/cart/trolley** ◆ **catalogue/ Internet/online** *shopping* ◆ *a shopping* **expedition/ spree/trip**

2 (*especially BrE*) the things that you have bought from shops/stores: *to put your shopping away*

'shopping bot (*also* **'shopping ˌagent**) *noun* [C]
(*E-commerce*) a piece of software that searches for products that are being sold on the Internet and compares prices

'shopping ˌcentre (*AmE spelling* ~ **center**) *noun* [C] (*especially BrE*)
a group of shops/stores built together, sometimes under one roof

'shopping goods (*also* **'shopping ˌproducts**) *noun* [pl.]
(*Commerce*) items that people do not buy very frequently, such as furniture and clothes, and like to compare in quality and price before they buy

'shopping list *noun* [C]
a list that you make of all the things that you need to buy when you go shopping: *The group has put the supermarket chain on its shopping list* (= it wants to buy the company).

'shopping mall (*also* **mall**) (*both especially AmE*) *noun* [C]
a large group of shops/stores, restaurants, etc. built together under one roof and closed to traffic

'shopping ˌproducts = SHOPPING GOODS

'shop-soiled (*BrE*) (*AmE* **'shopworn**) *adjective*
(*Commerce*) **shop-soiled** goods are dirty or not in good condition because they have been in a shop/ store for a long time: *a sale of shop-soiled goods at half price*

ˌshop 'steward *noun* [C] (*especially BrE*)
(*HR*) a person who is elected by members of a union in a factory or company to represent them in meetings with managers

shopworn /'ʃɒpwɔːn; *AmE* 'ʃɑːpwɔːrn/ = SHOP-SOILED

shore /ʃɔː(r)/ *verb*
PHRV **ˌshore sth 'up** to help to support sth that is weak or going to fail: *The company had to sell assets in order to shore up its balance sheet.* ◇ *The measures were aimed at shoring up the economy.*

★ short /ʃɔːt; *AmE* ʃɔːrt/ *adjective, adverb, verb*
● *adjective* **HELP** The forms **shorter** and **shortest** are not usually used in these meanings.
1 [not before noun] **short of sth** not having enough of sth: *She never seems to be short of cash!* ◇ *Many companies in the area are short of qualified workers.*
2 [not before noun] not easily available; not supplying as much as you need: *Time is getting short so we'd better start working.* ◇ *Cash is very short at the moment.*
3 (*informal*) **short on sth** lacking or not having enough of a particular quality: *The industry is short on good leadership.*
4 [not before noun] **short (of sth)** less than the number, amount, weight, etc. mentioned or needed: *I think we're still two people short* (= we need two more people) *on the project.* ◇ *The delivery was short by 540 pairs of shoes.*
5 **short (for sth)** being a shorter form of a name or word: *'Co' is short for 'company'.* ◇ *file transfer protocol, or FTP for short*
6 (*Finance*; *Stock Exchange*) relating to the situation when sb sells shares, currencies, etc. that they do

not yet own, in the hope that their price will fall and they will make a profit by buying them later at a lower price: *Investors who are* **short on stock** *will do well if prices continue to fall.* **OPP** LONG
IDM **at short 'notice** (*AmE also* **on short 'notice**); **at a moment's 'notice** not long in advance; without much warning or time for preparation: *The meeting was called at very short notice.* **in ˌshort sup'ply** if something is **in short supply** there is not enough of it available: *Good managers are in short supply at the moment.* **on short 'notice** (*especially AmE*) = AT SHORT NOTICE
→ idioms at RUN *verb*, SHORT RUN
● *adverb* **HELP** The forms **shorter** and **shortest** are not usually used in these meanings.
1 if you **go short of** or **run short of** sth, you do not have enough of it: *We're running short of stock so we'd better put in an order.*
2 (*Finance*; *Stock Exchange*) if you **sell** sth **short** or **go short** (on sth), you sell shares, currencies, etc. that you do not yet own, hoping that their price will fall and you will make a profit by buying them later at a lower price: *Investors who went short on stock made big profits when the share price fell.*
3 before the time expected or arranged: *I'm afraid I'm going to have to stop you short there, as time is running out.*
→ idiom at FALL *verb*
● *verb* [+ obj or no obj]
(*Finance*; *Stock Exchange*) to agree to sell shares, currencies, etc. that you do not yet own, in the hope that their price will fall and you will make a profit by buying them later at a lower price: *You have to be able to borrow shares to short them.*

★ shortage /'ʃɔːtɪdʒ; *AmE* 'ʃɔːrt-/ *noun* [C,U]
a situation when there is not enough of the people or things that are needed: *a shortage of funds/space* ◇ *There are serious labour shortages in some sectors.* ◇ *There was* **no shortage of** *candidates* (= there were a lot) *for the post.* **OPP** GLUT → SURPLUS
❍ *an* **acute/a chronic/critical/serious/severe** *shortage* ◆ *a* **cash/parts/supply** *shortage* ◆ **labour/skills/staff/ talent** *shortages* ◆ *to* **face/suffer** *a shortage* ◆ *to* **cause/create/lead to** *a shortage* ◆ *to* **combat/ease/ overcome/prevent** *a shortage*

ˌshort-'change *verb* [+ obj] (*often* **be short-changed**)
1 to give back less than the correct amount of money to sb who has paid for sth with more than the exact price: *I think I've been short-changed at the checkout.*
2 to treat sb unfairly by not giving them what they have earned or deserve: *Poor after-sales service can leave customers feeling short-changed.*

ˌshort 'covering *noun* [U]
(*Stock Exchange*) the process of sb borrowing or buying shares, bonds, etc. in order to replace the ones that they have sold or agreed to sell but did not own

shortfall /'ʃɔːtfɔːl; *AmE* 'ʃɔːrt-/ *noun* [C]
if there is a **shortfall in** sth, there is less of it than you need or expect: *They are selling assets to make up for a shortfall in profits.* ◇ *Several staff were made redundant to meet a shortfall of funds.* ◇ *The company is facing a $9.2 million shortfall.*
❍ *to* **compensate for/cover/make up/meet** *a shortfall* ◆ **capital/earnings/funding/profit/revenue** *shortfalls* ◆ *an* **order/a production/sales/supply** *shortfall* ◆ *a* **big/huge/large/significant/small** *shortfall*

shorthand /'ʃɔːthænd; *AmE* 'ʃɔːrt-/ *noun*
1 (*AmE also* **ste'nography**) [U] a quick way of writing using special signs or short forms of words, used especially to record what sb is saying: *Do you do shorthand?* ◇ *to take something down* **in** *shorthand*

2 [U,C] a shorter way of saying or referring to sth: *We want our brand name to be shorthand for a healthy lifestyle.*

short -'handed *adjective* [not usually before noun]
not having as many workers or people who can help as you need: *Can you do any extra shifts this week as we're short-handed?* SYN SHORT-STAFFED

shorthand 'typist *noun* [C] (*BrE*)
a person whose job is to write down what sb says using **shorthand**, then write it on a computer or type it SYN STENOGRAPHER (*AmE*)

'short-haul *adjective* [only before noun]
that involves transporting people or goods over short distances: *a short-haul airline/flight* ◇ *short-haul trucking* → LONG-HAUL

shorting /'ʃɔːtɪŋ; *AmE* 'ʃɔːrt-/ = SHORT SELLING

shortlist /'ʃɔːtlɪst; *AmE* 'ʃɔːrt-/ *noun, verb* (*HR*)
● *noun* (*AmE spelling also* **short list**) [C]
a small number of candidates for a job who have been chosen from all the people who applied: *We have narrowed the applicants down to a shortlist of four.* ◇ *to draw up a shortlist*
● *verb* (*AmE spelling also* **short-list**) [+ obj] (*usually be shortlisted*)
to put sb/sth on a **shortlist** for a job: *Candidates who are shortlisted for interview will be contacted by the end of the week.*

'short po,sition *noun* [C]
(*Finance; Stock Exchange*) a situation in which an investor sells or agrees to sell shares, currencies, etc. that he/she does not own yet, hoping that the price will fall and they will make a profit by buying them later at a lower price: *If you think the price will decline, you might want to take a short position in that stock.* ◇ *When the price falls, the bank will buy shares cheaply to cover its short position.* SYN BEAR POSITION → LONG POSITION

short-'range *adjective* [only before noun]
connected with a short period of time in the future: *short-range plans*

short 'run (*also* ,short 'term) *noun* [sing.]
(*Economics*) the period during which a business or an industry can change the quantity of some of the things that are needed in order to produce goods or services, but at least one is fixed → LONG RUN
IDM **in the 'short run; in the 'short term** concerning the immediate future: *In the short run, unemployment may fall.* ◇ *A deal is unlikely in the short term.*

'short-run = SHORT-TERM (1)

shorts /ʃɔːts; *AmE* ʃɔːrts/ *noun* [pl.]
(*Finance*)
1 investments such as bonds that are due to be paid back in a short time, usually less than five years
2 shares that a dealer has borrowed and sold but does not yet own
→ LONGS *noun*

short 'sale *noun* [C]
(*Finance; Stock Exchange*) when sb sells or agrees to sell shares, currencies, etc. that they do not own, hoping that the price will fall and they will make a profit by buying them later at a lower price

short 'selling (*also* 'shorting) *noun* [U]
(*Finance; Stock Exchange*) the act of selling or agreeing to sell shares, currencies, etc. that you do not yet own, hoping that the price will fall and you will make a profit by buying them later at a lower price: *Some stock is difficult to borrow for short-selling transactions.* ▸ **short 'seller** *noun* [C]

short-'staffed *adjective* [not usually before noun]
having fewer members of staff than you need or usually have: *We're short-staffed at the moment because a lot of staff are off sick.* SYN SHORT-HANDED → UNDERSTAFFED

short 'term = SHORT RUN

'short-term *adjective* [usually before noun]
1 (*also* 'short-run) lasting a short time; lasting only for a short period of time in the future: *Most of our staff are on short-term contracts.* ◇ *a short-term solution to a problem*
2 (*Finance*) (about money) that is borrowed, lent or invested for a short period of time, usually one year: *I have short-term loans with several banks.* SYN NEAR-TERM → LONG-TERM

short-'termism *noun* [U]
a way of thinking or planning that is concerned with the advantages or profits you could have now, rather than the effects in the future

short-term lia'bilities = CURRENT LIABILITY

short 'time *noun* [U] (*BrE*)
(*HR*) a situation in which workers work fewer hours than usual when there are not enough orders, materials, etc., so that they can keep their jobs: *Staff at the factory have been put on short time.* ◇ *They have avoided redundancies by introducing short-time working.*

short 'ton (*abbr* st.) (*also* ,net 'ton) (*both especially AmE*) *noun* [C]
a unit of weight equal to 907.18 kilograms or 2 000 pounds → LONG TON, TONNE

shovelware /'ʃʌvlweə(r); *AmE* -wer/ *noun* [U]
(*IT*) content that is taken from, for example, printed material, and put on a website as quickly as possible without changing it to suit the Internet

show /ʃəʊ; *AmE* ʃoʊ/ *noun* [C,U]

SEE ALSO: **dog and pony show, no-~, trade ~**

an occasion when people, businesses, etc. show and sell their goods and services: *a trade show* ◇ *the Paris auto show* ◇ *The latest computers will be on show at the exhibition.* → EXHIBITION, FAIR, ROADSHOW
IDM **show of 'hands** a way of voting in which people at a meeting raise their hands to show if they agree with sth or are against it: *Strike action was rejected by a show of hands.*

showcase /'ʃəʊkeɪs; *AmE* 'ʃoʊ-/ *noun*
1 [C, usually sing.] an event that presents sb's abilities or the good qualities of sth in an attractive way: *The exhibition is a showcase for talented designers.*
2 [C] a box with a glass top or sides that is used for showing objects in a shop/store, museum, etc.
▸ **'showcase** *verb* [+ obj]: *We use the website to showcase our new products.*

showroom /'ʃəʊruːm; -rʊm; *AmE* 'ʃoʊ-/ *noun* [C]
a large shop/store in which goods for sale, especially cars and electrical goods, are displayed: *a car showroom* ◇ *We want to keep buyers coming into our showrooms.*

shred /ʃred/ *verb* [+ obj] (-dd-)
to cut sth into small pieces: *We shred old documents (= in a machine) and recycle the paper.*

shredder /'ʃredə(r)/ *noun* [C]
a machine that destroys documents by cutting them into thin strips so that nobody can read what was printed or written on them

shrewd /'ʃruːd/ *adjective* (**shrewder, shrewdest**)
1 clever at understanding and making judgements about a situation: *He is a shrewd businessman.* ◇ *She has a shrewd business brain.*
2 showing good judgement and likely to be right: *a shrewd guess/move*
▶ **'shrewdly** *adverb* **'shrewdness** *noun* [U]

shrink /ʃrɪŋk/ *verb* [+ obj or no obj] (**shrank** /ʃræŋk/ **shrunk** /ʃrʌŋk/ *or* **shrunk, shrunk**)
to become or to make sth smaller in size or amount: *The market for this type of product is shrinking.* ◇ *The new system will shrink the size and cost of PCs.*

shrinkage /'ʃrɪŋkɪdʒ/ *noun* [U]
1 the process of becoming smaller in size; the amount by which sth becomes smaller: *the shrinkage of the export market* ◇ *These cotton shirts are oversized to allow for shrinkage.*
2 (*Commerce*) (*also* **'leakage**) the amount of goods that a business loses because they have been damaged, stolen, etc: *If they reduced waste and cut out shrinkage, the store could be very profitable.*

'shrink-wrap *verb* [+ obj]
to wrap sth tightly in a thin plastic covering: *Cans come shrink-wrapped in packs of six.* ◇ *shrink-wrapped software* (= standard software sold in boxes ready to use)—Picture at PACKAGING
▶ **'shrink-wrap** *noun* [U]: *The book and CD are packaged in shrink-wrap to keep them together.*
'shrink-,wrapping *noun* [U]: *Shrink-wrapping can be done in less than a second.*

SHRM /,es eɪtʃ ɑːr 'em/ = STRATEGIC HUMAN RESOURCE MANAGEMENT

shuffle /'ʃʌfl/ = RESHUFFLE

shut /ʃʌt/ *verb, adjective*
● *verb* [+ obj or no obj] (**shutting, shut, shut**)
1 when a shop/store, restaurant, etc. **shuts** or when sb **shuts** it, it stops being open for business and you cannot go into it: *We shut at six.*
2 when a business **shuts** or when sb **shuts** it, it stops operating as a business: *We have been forced to shut several factories.*
IDM **shut up 'shop** (*BrE*) (*informal*) to close a business permanently or to stop working for the day
PHRV **,shut 'down** (about a factory, shop/store, etc. or a machine) to stop opening for business; to stop working: *Sixty employees were laid off when the plant shut down.* → CLOSE, SHUTDOWN **,shut sth 'down** to stop a factory, shop/store, etc. from opening for business; to stop a machine from working → CLOSE, SHUTDOWN **,shut sth 'off** (about a machine, tool, etc.) to stop working: *The engines shut off automatically in an emergency.* **,shut sth 'off 1** to stop a machine, tool, etc. from working **2** to stop a supply of electricity, gas, etc. from flowing or reaching a place: *Always shut off the power before removing the machine's cover.*
● *adjective*
not open for business: *Is the bank shut?*

shutdown /'ʃʌtdaʊn/ *noun* [C,U]
1 the act of closing a factory or business: *The strike was a protest against factory shutdowns.* → CLOSE-DOWN
2 the act of stopping a computer or large machine from working: *My PC freezes on shutdown.* ◇ *Factory staff are trained in emergency shutdown procedures.*

shuttle /'ʃʌtl/ *noun* [C]
a plane, bus or train that travels regularly between two places: *I'm flying to Boston on the shuttle.* ◇ *a shuttle service*

SI /,es 'aɪ/ *abbr*
International System (used to describe units of measurement): *SI units such as the metre, the kilogramme and the second* **NOTE** **SI** are the first letters of the French phrase **Système International.**

SIBOR /'siːbɔː(r)/ *abbr* **Singapore Inter-Bank Offered Rate** the rate at which banks lend money to other banks in Singapore, which is used as a measure of LENDING RATES in Asia: *The interest margin ranges from 1.5% up to 3.5% above SIBOR.*

sick /sɪk/ *adjective*
1 ill: (*BrE*) *Peter has been off sick* (= away from work because he is ill) *for two weeks.* ◇ (*AmE*) *Peter has been out sick for a few days.* ◇ *Three people called in sick yesterday* (= telephoned to say they were not coming to work because they were ill).
2 (about an organization, a system, etc.) having serious problems: *a sick company/economy*

,sick 'building ,syndrome *noun* [U]
a set of physical conditions that are not caused by a known illness but seem to be caused by spending time in a particular building

'sick day *noun* [C]
(*HR*) a day when an employee does not work because they are ill/sick: *There is no limit to the number of sick days workers can take.*

sickie /'sɪki/ *noun* [C] (*BrE*) (*informal*)
a day when you say that you are ill/sick and cannot go to work when it is not really true
○ *to have/pull/take/throw a sickie*

'sick leave *noun* [U]
(*HR*) permission to be away from work because of illness; the period of time spent away from work: *to be on sick leave*

'sickness ,benefit *noun* [U,C] money paid by the government to people who are away from work because they are sick/ill → SICK PAY

'sick note (*BrE*) (*AmE* **ex'cuse**) *noun* [C]
(*HR*) a letter that an employee gets from a doctor to say that they are or have been too ill/sick to go to work: *If you are off work for more than three days you must provide a sick note.*

'sickout (*also spelled* **sick-out**) /'sɪkaʊt/ *noun* [C] (*AmE*)
(*HR*) an occasion when workers protest against sth by staying away from work and saying they are ill/sick when really they are not: *Bus drivers across the city are staging a sickout.*

'sick pay *noun* [U]
(*HR*) pay given to an employee who is away from work because of illness → SICKNESS BENEFIT

side /saɪd/ *noun* [C]
SEE ALSO: **demand side, supply side**

1 one of the two or more people or groups taking part in an argument, a discussion, etc: *We reached an agreement acceptable to all sides.* ◇ *The two sides announced a deal yesterday.* See note at COLLEAGUE
2 one of the opinions, attitudes or positions held by sb in a business arrangement, an argument, etc: *Are you sure they will keep their side of the bargain* (= do what they say they will do)?
3 (*informal*) a particular aspect of a job or a company's business: *He worked for them on the sales and marketing side.* ◇ *I'll take care of that side of things.*
4 one of the two parts of a financial account: *the credit/debit side*
→ idiom at SAFE *adj.*

sidebar /'saɪdbɑː(r)/ *noun* [C]
(*IT*) a narrow section on the left side of a web page

sideline /ˈsaɪdlaɪn/ *noun* [C]
an activity that sb does as well as their main
activity in order to earn extra money: *Making toys
started as a sideline, but now it is the company's
main source of income.*

SIG /sɪg/ *abbr*
(*IT*) **special interest group** a place in a computing
system, especially the Internet, where people can
discuss a particular subject and exchange
information about it → NEWSGROUP

'sig file *noun* [C]
(*IT, informal*) **signature file** a short personal
message that can be automatically added at the
end of emails showing who has sent it

'sight bill *noun* [C]
(*Finance*) a BILL OF EXCHANGE that must be paid
immediately

'sight de,posit (*also* **de'mand de,posit**) *noun* [C,
usually pl.]
(*Finance*) money that is kept in a bank on the basis
that it can be taken out at any time: *Banks once
offered no interest on sight deposits.* → TIME DEPOSIT

'sight draft *noun* [C]
(*Finance*) a **draft** (= a written order to a bank to pay
money to sb) that must be paid immediately

,sight un'seen *adverb*
(*Commerce*) if you buy sth **sight unseen**, you do not
have an opportunity to see it before you buy it:
*Many small businesses order their office furniture,
sight unseen, through catalogues.*

sign /saɪn/ *noun, verb*
● *noun* [C]
1 a piece of paper, wood, metal, etc. that has
writing or a picture on it that gives you
information, instructions, a warning, etc: *There is a
sign displaying the name of the company on the roof
of the building.* ◇ *flashing neon signs* ◇ *a sign board*
2 a mark used to represent sth: *a plus/minus sign
(+/−)* ◇ *a euro/dollar sign (€/$)*
● *verb* [+ obj or no obj]
to write your name on a document, letter, etc. to
show that you have written it, that you agree with
what it says, or that it is genuine: *Sign here, please.*
◇ *Sign your name here, please.* ◇ *You haven't signed
the letter.* ◇ *to sign a deal/contract/cheque*
IDM **signed and 'sealed**;**'signed, 'sealed and
de'livered** definite, because all the legal
documents have been signed **sign on the dotted
'line** (*informal*) to sign a document to show that
you have agreed to do sth or buy sth: *Always read the
small print before you sign on the dotted line.*
PHR V **'sign for sth** to sign a document to show
that you have received sth: *Who signed for the
package?* **,sign 'in/'out**; **,sign sb 'in/'out** to write
your name or the name of a guest when you arrive
at or leave an office: *All visitors must sign in on
arrival.* **,sign 'off**; **,sign sth 'off** to end a letter, etc:
I usually sign off an email with 'regards'. **,sign sth
'off** to give your formal approval to sth, by signing
your name: *The accounts have not yet been signed off
by the auditors.* **,sign 'off on sth** (*AmE*) (*informal*) to
express your approval of sth formally and
definitely: *Investors have finally signed off on the
deal.* **,sign 'on** (*BrE*) (*informal*) to sign a form stating
that you are unemployed so that you can receive
payment from the government **,sign 'on/'up**; **,sign
sb 'on/'up** to sign a form or contract which says
that you agree to work for sb, do a deal, etc.: *She
signed on as a customer-support officer.* ◇ *We have
signed on three major home builders as partners.*
sign 'out; **,sign sb 'out** → SIGN IN/OUT; SIGN SB
IN/OUT **,sign 'up (for sth)**; **,sign sb 'up (for sth)**
1 to arrange to receive or do sth: *Sign up for our*

---

monthly email newsletter. ◇ *I've signed up for an
accounting course.* ◇ *Shall I sign you up for the
workshop too?* **2** = SIGN ON/UP; SIGN SB ON/UP

signage /ˈsaɪnɪdʒ/ *noun* [U]
a sign or signs that advertise a product, show the
name of a shop/store, etc.

signatory /ˈsɪgnətri; *AmE* -tɔːri/ *noun* [C] (*plural*
signatories) (*formal*)
a person, a country or an organization that has
signed an official agreement: *The country is not
among the signatories to/of the Kyoto Protocol.*

signature /ˈsɪgnətʃə(r)/ *noun*

SEE ALSO: **digital signature, electronic ~, specimen ~**

1 [C] your name as you usually write it, for
example at the end of a letter: *Each payment
requires two signatures.* ◇ *The chairman put his
signature to the deal yesterday.*
2 [U] (*formal*) the act of signing sth: *Two copies of
the contract will be sent to you for signature.*
3 [C, usually sing.] a particular quality, product,
phrase, etc. that makes sth different from other
similar things and makes it easy to recognize: *The
simple design and bright colours became the
signature of all their products.* ◇ *the company's
signature shoes and bags*

'signature brand *noun* [C]
(*Marketing*)
1 a range of products that is the most famous thing
made by a particular company: *Sales of the
company's signature brand vacuum cleaners are up.*
2 a product or range of products that have the
name of a famous person on them: *Calvin Klein
signature brand sunglasses*

'signature loan *noun* [C]
(*Finance*) money that is lent to sb without any
SECURITY (= a valuable item that the person,
company, etc. that borrows the money will lose if
they cannot pay the money back) except that the
borrower signs a document → UNSECURED

'sign-up *noun*
1 [U] the act of saying that you want to join sth,
receive sth, etc. by adding your name to a list: *Go to
our sign-up page to subscribe to this service.* ◇ *a sign-
up fee*
2 [C] a person who adds their name to a list in
order to join sth, receive sth, etc: *new sign-ups for
digital TV*

,silent 'partner = SLEEPING PARTNER

silicon /ˈsɪlɪkən/ *noun* [U]
a chemical element that is used in making
TRANSISTORS and glass

,Silicon 'Alley *noun* [U]
an area of New York where many Internet
companies started in business in the 1990s

,silicon 'chip *noun* [C]
a very small piece of **silicon** used to carry a
complicated electronic CIRCUIT

,Silicon 'Valley *noun* [U]
an area in California where there are many
computer and HIGH TECHNOLOGY companies
NOTE Silicon Valley is often used to refer to other
similar areas or to the computer and electronics
industries in general. **Silicon**... is also often used in
a similar way, especially in newspapers: *Silicon Fen*
(an area in the UK around Cambridge).

,silver 'market = GREY MARKET (3)

,silver 'surfer noun [C] (informal)
an older person who spends a lot of time using the
Internet, usually used about people over the
age of 50

sim /sɪm/ noun [C] (informal)
a computer or video game that creates the feeling
of doing (**simulates**) an activity such as flying a
plane or managing a business: We use business sims
for management training. ◇ a flight sim
→ SIMULATION

'SIM card /sɪm/ noun [C]
a plastic card inside a mobile phone/cellphone that
stores personal information about the person using
the phone **NOTE** SIM is formed from the first
letters of 'subscriber identification module'.

,simple 'interest noun [U]
(Accounting) interest that is calculated only on the
original amount of money lent or borrowed, and
not on any interest that it has earned → COMPOUND
INTEREST

simulation /ˌsɪmjuˈleɪʃn/ noun [C,U]
a situation in which a particular set of conditions is
created artificially in order to study or experience
sth that could exist in reality: He showed us a
computer simulation of how the building will look. ◇
The simulation of negotiations is a vital part of
training. → SIM
▶ **simulate** /ˈsɪmjuleɪt/ verb [+ obj]: Role-playing is
a useful way of simulating calls from customers.

simul,taneous engi'neering =
CONCURRENT ENGINEERING

sincerely /sɪnˈsɪəli; AmE -ˈsɪrli/ adverb
IDM **Yours sincerely** (BrE) (AmE **Sincerely (yours)**)
used at the end of a formal letter before you sign
your name, when you have addressed sb by their
name → FAITHFULLY

sinecure /ˈsɪnɪkjʊə(r); ˈsaɪn-; AmE -kjʊr/ noun [C]
(formal)
a job that you are paid for even though it involves
little or no work

sine die /ˌsɪneɪ ˈdiːeɪ; ˌsaɪni ˈdaɪiː/ adverb
(Law or formal)
without a future date being arranged: The meeting
was **adjourned** (= stopped until a later date) sine
die. **NOTE** Sine die is a Latin phrase.

sine qua non /ˌsɪneɪ kwɑː ˈnəʊn; AmE ˈnoʊn/
noun [sing.] (formal)
something that is essential before you can achieve
sth else: A good knowledge of a second language is a
sine qua non for many positions. **NOTE** Sine qua
non is a Latin phrase.

single /ˈsɪŋgl/ adjective, noun
● adjective
1 only one: the European single currency, the euro
2 [only before noun] (BrE) (also **one-'way**, AmE, BrE)
a **single** ticket, etc. can be used for travelling to a
place but not back again → RETURN adj
● noun [C]
1 (BrE) a ticket that allows you to travel to a place
but not back again → RETURN noun
2 (AmE) a note/bill that is worth one dollar

,single column 'centimetre (AmE spelling ~
centimeter) noun [C] (abbr **SCC**)
a unit used for measuring advertising space in a
newspaper or magazine: €35 per single column
centimetre

,single column 'inch noun [C] (abbr **SCI**)
a unit used for measuring advertising space in a
newspaper or magazine

,single 'digits, **,single-'digit** = SINGLE FIGURES

,single-entry 'bookkeeping noun [U]
(Accounting) a way of keeping a company's financial
records, in which each amount spent, received, etc.
is recorded in only one account

,single 'figures (especially BrE) (AmE usually **,single
'digits**) noun [pl.]
a number that is less than ten: Inflation is down to
single figures. → DOUBLE FIGURES
▶ **,single-'figure** (especially BrE) (AmE usually **,single-
'digit**) adjective [only before noun]

,single-'handed adverb
on your own with nobody helping you: She ran the
company single-handed for years. ▶ **single-'handed**
adjective: her single-handed attempt to save the
company **single-'handedly** adverb: He single-
handedly kept the company going during the crisis.

,single 'market (also in,ternal 'market) noun [C,
usually sing.]
(Economics) a group of countries that have few or no
restrictions on the movement of goods, money and
people between the members of the group: the
European single market

'single 'minute ex'change of 'dies phrase
(abbr **SMED**)
(Production) a technique for reducing the time
needed to prepare a machine or a piece of
equipment for a new task

,single 'sourcing noun [U]
1 (Production) the practice of buying all of a
company's supplies of a particular item from one
supplier
2 (IT) the use of information stored in one file to
produce many different types of documents
▶ **,single-'source** verb [+ obj]: Most of our raw
materials are single-sourced.

,single 'tax noun [C]
(Economics) a system in which there is tax on only
one kind of thing, for example a tax on the value of
land

,single-'use /ˈjuːs/ adjective [only before noun]
made to be used once only: inexpensive single-use
cameras → DISPOSABLE

sink /sɪŋk/ verb (sank /sæŋk/ sunk /sʌŋk/) or, less
frequent (sunk, sunk)
1 [+ obj or no obj] if a ship **sinks** or sb/sth **sinks** it,
it is damaged and goes below the surface of the
sea: The tanker sank off the coast of Brittany.
2 [no obj] to decrease in amount, volume, strength,
etc: The pound has sunk to its lowest recorded level
against the dollar.
PHR V **,sink sth 'into sth** to spend a lot of money
on a business, for example in order to make money
from it in the future: We sank all our savings into the
venture.

'sinking fund noun [C]
(Finance) money that a company keeps and adds to
regularly in order to pay debts, pay for equipment,
etc. at a fixed date in the future: a machinery
sinking fund

'sin tax noun [C,U] (informal)
a tax on goods or services that many people
consider bad, for example cigarettes and alcohol

SIP /ˌes aɪ ˈpiː; sɪp/ = STRATEGIC INFLECTION POINT,
SHARE INCENTIVE PLAN, STOCK INCENTIVE PLAN

siphon (also spelled **syphon**) /ˈsaɪfn/ verb [+ obj]
(used with an adverb or a preposition)
1 to move a liquid from one container to another,
using a special tube (a **siphon**) and pressure from
the atmosphere: The waste liquid needs to be
siphoned **off**.

2 to remove money from one place and move it to another, especially dishonestly or illegally: *He had siphoned millions out of the fund and into his own bank accounts.*

SIS /ˌes aɪ ˈes/ = STRATEGIC INFORMATION SYSTEM

'sister ˌcompany *noun* [C]
a company that is part of the same group, with the same PARENT COMPANY: *This link will take you to our sister company's website.* See note at GROUP

'sit-down *noun* [C]
1 a strike or protest in which people sit down to block a road or the entrance to a building until people listen to their demands: *to hold/stage a sit-down*
2 a more formal meeting to discuss things, rather than a quick conversation: *to have a sit-down*
▶ **'sit-down** *adjective* [only before noun]: *a sit-down protest/strike* ◇ *Have a regular sit-down meeting with each member of your team.*

site /saɪt/ *noun, verb*
● *noun* [C]
SEE ALSO: anti-site, destination ~, mirror ~, off-~, on-~, run of ~
1 a place where sth has been or will be built: *We are looking at potential sites **for** the new factory.* ◇ *Hard hats must be worn **on site**.*
○ *a **good/prime/suitable** site* ◆ *a **possible/potential/proposed** site* ◆ *a **brownfield/greenfield/protected** site* ◆ *a **building/construction** site*
2 a place where a particular type of work takes place: *We will repair the machine **on site** if possible.* See note at FACTORY
○ *a **manufacturing/an industrial** site*
3 (*IT*) a place on the Internet where a company, an organization, etc. puts information: *Visit our site for details.* → WEBSITE
○ *to **access/browse/search/visit** a site* ◆ *to **build/create/design/host/set up** a site*
● *verb* [+ obj] (*often* be sited)
to build or place sth in a particular position: *The plant will be sited as close as possible to the port.*

'sit-in *noun* [C]
(*HR*) a protest in which a group of workers refuse to leave their place of work until people listen to their demands: *to hold/stage a sit-in*

situation /ˌsɪtʃuˈeɪʃn/ *noun* [C]
SEE ALSO: special situation
1 all the circumstances and things that are happening at a particular time and in a particular place: *the present economic/financial situation* ◇ *We need to analyse the market situation.* ◇ *Financially, the company is **in** a difficult situation.* ◇ *I'm in a **no-win** situation* (= whatever I do will be bad for me).
2 the kind of area or surroundings that a building or town has: *The hotel is in a beautiful situation.*
3 (*old-fashioned or only used in written English*) a job → SITUATIONS VACANT

situˌational 'interview *noun* [C]
(*HR*) a type of interview for a job in which sb is asked what they would do in particular situations. **Situational interviews** are used especially in cases where candidates do not have much work experience.

ˌsituˈation aˌnalysis (*also* ˌsituˈation ˌaudit) *noun* [U,C]
(*Marketing*) the first stage in the process of planning marketing, in which an organization collects information and examines its strengths and weaknesses, the opportunities it has and the threats it faces → SWOT

Situations 'Vacant *noun* [U] (*BrE*)
(*HR*) a section in a newspaper, on a website, etc., where jobs are advertised: *We'll put an ad in the Situations Vacant section.*

ˌSituations 'Wanted *noun* [U] (*BrE*)
(*HR*) a section in a newspaper, on a website, etc., where people who are looking for a job can advertise

'six-pack *noun* [C]
a set of six bottles or cans sold together, especially of beer

ˌsix 'sigma (*also spelled* **Six Sigma**) /ˈsɪgmə/ *noun* [U]
(*Production*) a system that aims to improve production processes so that almost all products are of perfect quality: *Since launching a six sigma quality program the company has saved an estimated ten million dollars.*

size /saɪz/ *noun, verb*
● *noun* [C]
SEE ALSO: economy-size, full-~, king-~, palm-~
1 one of a number of standard measurements in which clothes, shoes and other goods are made and sold: *What size do you **take?*** ◇ *The jacket is the wrong size.* ◇ *I need a bigger/smaller size.* ◇ *The T-shirts come in three sizes: small, medium and large.* ◇ *Our tents are available **in a range of sizes**.* ◇ *The glass can be cut **to size*** (= to the exact measurements) *for you.*
2 (in adjectives) (*also* **-sized**) having the size mentioned: *a medium-sized market* ◇ *a pocket-size camera* ◇ *a trial-size pack of coffee*
IDM **one size fits 'all 1** used to describe an item of clothing that can be worn by people of most sizes and shapes **2** used to describe a situation where one action, policy, solution, etc. is considered suitable for everybody: *One size does not fit all when it comes to life insurance.*
● *verb* [+ obj] (*usually* be sized)
SEE ALSO: giant-sized, large-sized, medium-sized, mid-sized, pocket-sized
1 to mark the size of sth; to give a size to sth: *The screws are sized in millimetres.*
2 to change the size of sth: *Windows can be sized according to how much space you have on your screen.*

skeleton /ˈskelɪtn/ *noun* [C]
1 the main structure that supports a building: *Only the concrete skeleton of the factory remained.*
2 (*used as an adjective*) used to describe the smallest number of people, things or parts that you need to do sth: *There will only be **a skeleton staff** on duty over the holiday.*

skid /skɪd/ *noun* [C] (*especially AmE*)
a raised wooden base onto which goods are loaded so that they can be easily moved or transported, especially by a FORKLIFT → PALLET—Picture at TRANSPORT

★ skill /skɪl/ *noun*
1 [U] the ability to do sth well: *The job requires skill and an eye for detail.* ◇ *She has managed her team **with** great skill.*
○ *to **need/require/take** skill* ◆ *to **have/lack** skill* (*at/in sth*) ◆ ***considerable/extraordinary/great** skill*
2 [C] a particular ability or type of ability, especially one that needs training and experience to do well: *young people wanting to learn a practical skill* ◇ *She had to develop a whole new set of skills when she changed jobs.* ◇ *There is a serious **skill shortage*** (= there are not enough people with

skills) *in the construction industry.* ◇ *The IT industry is very **skill-intensive*** (= requires a large number of skilled workers). → PEOPLE SKILLS

O *analytical/business/organizational/social skills* • *communication/interpersonal/management skills* • *computer/practical/technical skills* • *to have/ lack/possess skills* • *to acquire/develop/learn skills* • *to broaden/improve/sharpen/upgrade skills* • *to apply/use skills*

skilled /skɪld/ *adjective*

SEE ALSO: semi-skilled

1 having the ability, experience and knowledge to be able to do sth well: *a skilled engineer/negotiator* ◇ *She is **highly** skilled **at** dealing with difficult customers.* ◇ *All our staff are skilled **in** at least two languages.* ◇ *a shortage of **skilled labour*** (= workers who have had training in a skill)
2 (about a job) needing special abilities or training: *Furniture-making is very skilled work.*
OPP UNSKILLED

'skill set *noun* [C]
a range of skills: *We offer a skill set that covers all aspects of web-based programming and development.*

skim /skɪm/ *verb* [+ obj] (-mm-)
1 (*informal*) to steal small amounts of money frequently over a period of time: *She'd been skimming money from the store's accounts for years.*
2 (*informal*) to illegally copy information that is stored electronically on a credit card in order to use it without the owner's permission: *I think my credit card was skimmed at a gas station.*
IDM **skim the 'market** (*Marketing*) to set the price for a new product high at first in order to make as much profit as possible and then lower it gradually to attract more customers, for example when other companies create competition: *Some drug companies skim the market, so only the rich can afford to buy drugs.*
PHRV **,skim sth/sb 'off** to remove the most valuable part of sth for yourself, often in an unfair way: *Too many employers skim off profits while not paying their workers enough.*

skimming /'skɪmɪŋ/ *noun* [U]
1 (*Marketing*) (*also* **,market-skimming 'pricing**) the practice of setting the price for a new product high at first in order to make as much profit as possible and then lowering it gradually to attract more customers, for example when other companies create competition: *Price skimming is used when a company has a unique product.* → idiom at SKIM
2 (*Finance*, *informal*) the illegal practice of not telling the government about part of your profits in order to avoid paying tax
3 (*informal*) the illegal practice of copying information that is stored electronically on a credit card in order to use it without the owner's permission

skip /skɪp/ *noun* (*BrE*) (*AmE* **'Dumpster™**) [C]
a large open container for putting old bricks, rubbish/garbage, etc. in. The **skip** is then loaded on a lorry/truck and taken away.—Picture at TRANSPORT

skive /skaɪv/ *verb* [+ obj or no obj] (*BrE*) (*informal*)
skive (off) to avoid work by pretending to be ill/sick or leaving early: *Have you been skiving again?* ◇ *He skived off work for a day.* ▶ **'skiver** *noun* [C]

SKU /skjuː; ,es keɪ 'juː/ (*also* **'SKU ,number**) *noun* [C]
(*Commerce*) **stock-keeping unit** a number or a group of numbers and letters that is used to identify a particular product that a shop/store sells; a product that has its own number: *Options such as*

colour and size do not affect a product's SKU. ◇ *The company has launched over 50 new SKUs this year.*

'skunkworks (*also spelled* **skunk works**) /'skʌŋkwɜːks; *AmE* -wɜːrks/ *noun*
1 [C with sing./pl. verb] (*plural* **skunkworks**) a part of a company that has the freedom to develop new products without being closely controlled by the company: *Some of their best software has come from their skunkworks.*
2 [pl.] projects that this part of a company works on

,sky-'high *adjective*, *adverb*
extremely high; too high: *sky-high prices* ◇ *Executives' salaries have gone sky-high.*

skyrocket /'skaɪrɒkɪt; *AmE* -rɑːk-/ *verb* [no obj]
to go up very high and very fast: *Prices have skyrocketed in recent months.* See note at INCREASE

skyscraper /'skaɪskreɪpə(r)/ *noun* [C]
a very tall building in a city

SLA /,es el 'eɪ/ *abbr*
(*Commerce*; *IT*) **service level agreement** a written agreement between a supplier of a service and a customer that states what the supplier will provide, when it will be provided, the quality of what is provided, what it will cost, etc.

slack /slæk/ *adjective*, *noun*, *verb*
● *adjective* (**slacker**, **slackest**)
1 (about a business) not having many customers; not busy: *a slack period* ◇ *April is always slack.* ◇ *slack demand for cars*
2 (about a person) not putting enough care, attention or energy into sth and so not doing it well enough: *He's been very slack in his work lately.*
▶ **'slackly** *adverb* **'slackness** *noun* [U]
● *noun* [U]
people, money, time or space that a company is not using fully: *There's very little slack in the budget.*
IDM **pick/take up the 'slack** to do sth, supply sth, etc. that is needed but is not being done or supplied: *Her colleagues have to take up the slack when she is away from work.* ◇ *As desktop PC sales have fallen, laptops have taken up the slack.*
● *verb* [no obj]
to work less hard than you usually do or should do: *I usually work a nine-hour day but I've been slacking this week.*
PHRV **slack 'off (on sth)** to do sth more slowly or with less energy than before: *We have been slacking off on our customer service.*

slacken /'slækən/ *verb* [+ obj or no obj]
slacken (sth) (off) to gradually become, or to make sth become, slower, less active, etc: *We've been really busy, but things are starting to slacken off now.* ◇ *The rise in demand has slackened pace* (= slowed down) *slightly.* ▶ **slackening** /'slækənɪŋ/ [U]: *a slackening of demand for steel*

slash /slæʃ/ *verb*, *noun*
● *verb* [+ obj] (*often* **be slashed**)
(often used in newspapers) to reduce sth by a large amount: *to slash costs/prices* ◇ *The workforce has been slashed by half.*
● *noun* [C]
the symbol (/) used to show alternatives, as in 'lunch and/or dinner' and '4/5 people' and to write FRACTIONS, as in '3/4' → BACKSLASH, FORWARD SLASH

sleeper /'sliːpə(r)/ *noun* [C] (*especially AmE*) (*informal*)
a share or sth such as a book or film/movie that is not successful immediately but then is suddenly a success

'sleeper stock *noun* [C,U]
(*Stock Exchange*) shares in a company that have not done well but whose price may rise suddenly

,sleeping 'partner (*BrE*) (*AmE* **,silent 'partner**) *noun* [C]
a person who has invested money in a new company and has a right to a share of the profits but does not take part in managing it

slice /slaɪs/ *noun* [C] (*informal*)
a part or share of sth: *The two supermarkets have a 17% slice of the market.* ◇ *Pensioners have lost a large slice **of** their retirement cash.* → idiom at ACTION
➊ *a big/huge/large/small slice of sth*

slick /slɪk/ *adjective* (**slicker, slickest**)
   1 done in a way that is clever and efficient but is often not sincere or lacks important ideas: *a slick sales pitch* ◇ *Their presentation was slick and detailed.*
   2 (*about a person*) good at persuading people but probably not sincere: *a slick salesman*
   3 done quickly and with great skill; doing things in this way: *a slick deal*
   ▶ **'slickly** *adverb*: *a slickly produced advertisement*
   'slickness *noun* [U]

slide *verb, noun*
   ● *verb* [no obj] (**slid, slid** /slɪd/)
   1 slide (from …) (to …) to become gradually lower or of less value: *Sales have continued to slide.* ◇ *Shares slid to a 10-year low.* ◇ *Shares slid (by) 38¢.*
   2 to move gradually into a worse situation: *The industry has slid **into** decline.* ◇ *They were sliding **towards** bankruptcy.*
   ● *noun*
   1 [C, usually sing.] a change to a lower value or worse condition: *a downward slide in the price of oil* ◇ *Drastic action was needed to prevent a slide into recession.*
   ➊ *a downward/dramatic/sharp/steady/steep slide ◆ to halt/prevent/stop a slide*
   2 [C] a small piece of film held in a frame that can be shown on a screen when you shine a light through it: *a slide show/projector*
   3 [C] a single screen of information that is part of a presentation given using a computer: *Press F5 to run the slide show.*

,sliding 'peg = CRAWLING PEG

,sliding 'scale *noun* [C]
a system of taxes, wages, etc. in which amounts paid increase or decrease in relation to changes or differences in sth else: *a sliding scale of charges based on frequency of use* ◇ *Personal tax is calculated **on** a sliding scale.*

slim /slɪm/ *adjective, verb*
   ● *adjective* (**slimmer, slimmest**)
   1 very small; not as big as you would like: *Airlines run on very slim margins.* ◇ *The government has only a slim chance of meeting its economic targets.*
   2 (*about a business or an organization*) reduced to a smaller and more efficient size: *The deal will make us a smaller and slimmer company.*
   ● *verb* [+ obj *or* no obj] (**-mm-**)
   slim (sth) (down) to make a company or an organization smaller, usually in order to make it more efficient; to become smaller in this way: *The group is slimming its management board from eight to five members.* ◇ *The slimmed down company should break even this year.*

slip /slɪp/ *verb, noun*
   ● *verb* [no obj] (**-pp-**)
   1 to fall to a lower level; to become worse: *Online retail sales slipped **to** $17 billion.* ◇ *The Nikkei slipped 0.67%.* See note at INCREASE
   2 (*used with an adverb or a preposition*) to pass into a particular state or situation, especially a difficult or unpleasant one: *The manufacturing sector is*

---

*slipping **into** recession.* ◇ *We seem to have slipped behind schedule.*
   PHR V **slip 'up** (*informal*) to make a careless mistake: *The agency had slipped up badly.* → SLIP-UP
   ● *noun* [C]

SEE ALSO: compliments slip, deposit ~, paying-in ~, pink ~, sales ~

   1 an occasion when sth becomes worse or falls to a lower level: *a 0.6% slip in profits*
   2 a small piece of paper, especially one with sth printed on it: *a credit-card slip* ◇ *packing slips*
   3 a small, careless mistake: *There were a few slips in the calculations.*

slippage /'slɪpɪdʒ/ *noun* [U; C, usually sing.]
   1 a slight or gradual fall in the amount, value, etc. of sth: *A slippage **in** prices would be bad for the economy.*
   2 failure to achieve an aim or complete a task by a particular date or to a particular standard: *The smallest slippage could delay completion of the project.*
   3 (*Finance*) the difference between an amount that you have estimated and the actual amount

'slip-up *noun* [C]
a careless mistake: *management slip-ups* → SLIP UP at SLIP *verb*

slogan /'sləʊgən; *AmE* 'sloʊ-/ (*BrE also* **'strapline,** *less frequent*) *noun* [C]
(*Marketing*) a phrase or sentence that is easy to remember, used for example in advertising to attract people's attention and make them remember a product: *advertising slogans*
   SYN TAG LINE

slot /slɒt; *AmE* slɑːt/ *noun* [C]
   1 a time when something is arranged to happen, as part of a series of similar things; a position in a list: *The airline has agreed to give up take-off and landing slots at London's Heathrow.*
   2 a job, especially a senior one: *He stepped into the top slot at Dixons in September.*

slow /sləʊ; *AmE* sloʊ/ *adjective, verb*
   ● *adjective* (**slower, slowest**)
   1 not happening quickly: *The outlook is for continued slow growth in Brazil.* ◇ *Economic recovery is expected to be slow.*
   2 not very busy; containing little action: *Sales are slow* (= not many goods are being sold).
   3 slow to do sth | slow (in) doing sth not doing sth immediately; not happening immediately: *The industry has been slow to react.* ◇ *They were very slow paying me.*
   ▶ **'slowly** *adverb*: *Things are changing very slowly.*
   'slowness *noun* [U]: *seasonal slowness in the travel market*
   ● *adverb*
   IDM **go 'slow (on sth)** to show less enthusiasm for achieving sth: *The government is going slow on tax reforms.* → GO-SLOW
   ● *verb* [+ obj *or* no obj]
   slow (sth/sb) (down/up) to go at a slower speed; to be less active; to make sb/sth do this: *The market showed little sign of slowing down.* ◇ *Businesses are trying to slow the pace of job cuts.* ◇ *a slowing world economy*

★slowdown /'sləʊdaʊn; *AmE* 'sloʊ-/ *noun* [C, usually sing.]
   1 a reduction in speed or activity: *a slowdown **in** economic growth* ◇ *A sharp consumer slowdown may hit new car sales in the UK.*
   ➊ *a gradual/marked/rapid/sharp/slight slowdown ◆ a consumer/an economic slowdown ◆ a global/worldwide slowdown*
   2 (*HR*) (*AmE*) = GO-SLOW

sluggish /ˈslʌgɪʃ/ adjective
happening more slowly than is usual; not very active: *Sales of sports shoes are sluggish.* ◇ *A sluggish economy has weakened demand.* ▸ **ˈsluggishly** adverb **ˈsluggishness** noun [U]

★ **slump** /slʌmp/ noun, verb
● noun [C]
1 a sudden fall in sales, prices, etc: *a sharp slump in share prices* ◇ *The sales slump continues to hit retail stores.* [SYN] DECLINE
  ➋ *a slump in* **demand/prices/profits/sales/spending** • *a* **bad/deep/dramatic/prolonged/sharp** *slump*
2 (*Economics*) a period when a country's economy or a business is doing very badly: *The US slump appears to be over.* ◇ *Tourism is in a slump.* [OPP] BOOM—Picture at BUSINESS CYCLE
  ➋ *an* **economic/industry/a stock market** *slump* • *a* **bad/deep/global/prolonged** *slump*
● verb [no obj]
slump (from sth) (to sth) | **slump (by sth)** to fall in price, value etc. suddenly and by a large amount: *The share price slumped from more than £3 to £1.* ◇ *Sales in shopping centres slumped 35 per cent.* See note at INCREASE

ˈslush fund noun [C] (*also* **ˈslush ˌmoney** [U]) money that is kept secretly for making illegal payments

ˈsmall ad noun [C, usually pl.] (*BrE*) (*informal*) a small advertisement that you put in a newspaper, magazine, etc. or on an Internet site if you want to buy or sell sth, employ sb, etc. [SYN] CLASSIFIED AD

ˈsmall and ˈmedium-sized ˈenterprise noun [C] (*abbr* SME) a business that does not have a large number of employees or sell a large amount of goods and services, and is often run by a family [NOTE] Small or/to medium-sized enterprise is also used.

ˌsmall ˈbusiness noun [C,U] a business that has a small number of employees; these businesses in general: *Today there are more small businesses in Japan than ever before.* ◇ *a plan to encourage investment and promote small business*

ˈsmall cap noun [C] (*Stock Exchange*) a company that has a small total value of shares (**market capitalization**) on the stock exchange: *small caps that trade on the NYSE* ◇ *This will give a boost to small-cap share prices.* → LARGE CAP, MID CAP

ˌsmall ˈclaim noun [C] (*BrE*) (*Law*) a court case involving a small amount of money, especially one brought by a consumer over goods or services that are not satisfactory: *How do I make a small claim?* ◇ *They took their case to the small claims court.*

ˌsmall ˈcompany noun [C] a business that sells goods or services worth less than a fixed amount, has assets below a particular amount and/or has less than 50 employees: *lower corporation tax for small companies* ◇ *More than 1 million small companies are in the retail trade.*

ˌsmall inˈvestor noun [C] a person who invests small amounts of money: *At £27 a share, the stock has attracted more than 1.6 million small investors.*

the ˈsmall print (*especially BrE*) (*AmE usually* **ˈfine print**) noun [U] part of a document, especially a contract, that is printed in small type and may contain important information that is easy to miss: *Read all the small print before signing.*

ˌsmall-ˈscale adjective [usually before noun] (about an organization or activity) not large in size or extent; limited in what it does: *The plans include tax breaks for small-scale enterprises.* ◇ *a small-scale test/study* [OPP] LARGE-SCALE

ˈsmall self-adˈministered ˈscheme (*also* **ˈsmall self-adˈministered ˈpension scheme**) = SSAS

ˌsmall ˈshopkeeper noun [C] (*especially BrE*) a person who owns or manages a small shop/store: *Small shopkeepers find it hard to compete against large stores.*

ˈsmall-sized (*also* **ˈsmall-size**) adjective [usually before noun] small; smaller than medium and large: *small-sized companies* → LARGE-SIZED, MEDIUM-SIZED

ˌsmall ˈstock noun [C,U] (*Stock Exchange*) shares in a company that has only a small total value of shares on the stock exchange: *In November, small stocks gained 8%.* → SMALL CAP

ˈsmall talk noun [U] polite conversation about unimportant things: *At office parties, you often have to* **make** *small talk.*

SMART /smɑːt; *AmE* smɑːrt/ abbr (*HR*) **Specific, Measurable, Agreed, Realistic and Timed** used in a formal system of APPRAISAL to describe the aims that a business or an employee is trying to achieve [NOTE] Some companies use different words in the way they explain **SMART**, for example **Agreed** might be replaced by **Achievable**.

smart /smɑːt; *AmE* smɑːrt/ adjective [usually before noun] (**smarter, smartest**)
1 smart design, technology, etc. is very advanced and usually uses computers: *Smart phones can handle email.* [NOTE] Smarter, smartest are not used in this meaning.
2 intelligent; very clever in business matters: *Selling part of the group would be a smart business move.* ◇ *smart companies/investors*
3 (about clothes) clean, neat and often formal: *Our dress code is 'smart casual'.*

ˈsmart card noun [C] a small plastic card that contains information stored in electronic form: *The firm makes smart cards for mobile phones.* [SYN] CHIP CARD

smarten /ˈsmɑːtn; *AmE* ˈsmɑːrtn/ verb
[PHRV] **ˌsmarten sb/sth/yourself ˈup**; **ˌsmarten ˈup** (*especially BrE*) to make yourself, another person or a place look neater or more attractive: *The hotel has been smartened up by the new owners.*

the ˈsmart ˌmoney noun [U]
1 money that is invested or bet by people who have expert knowledge: *It seems the smart money is no longer in insurance* (= is no longer being invested in insurance companies).
2 used to say what people who know a lot think will happen: *The smart money says that real estate prices will fall steadily.*

smartphone /ˈsmɑːtfəʊn; *AmE* ˈsmɑːrtfoʊn/ noun [C] a mobile phone/cellphone that can take and send photographs, connect to the Internet, etc.

SME /ˌes em ˈiː/ = SMALL AND MEDIUM-SIZED ENTERPRISE

SMED /smed; ˌes em iː ˈdiː/ = SINGLE MINUTE EXCHANGE OF DIES

ˌsmoke and ˈmirrors noun [U] something that is deliberately intended to attract people's attention so that they will not notice sth else: *It looked like a piece of accounting smoke and mirrors.*

'smoke-free *adjective* [usually before noun]
smoke-free areas are areas where no one is
allowed to smoke: *The job is based in our modern
smoke-free offices in Oxford.*

smokestack /'sməʊkstæk; *AmE* 'smoʊk-/ *noun* [C]
a tall chimney that takes smoke away from
factories. **NOTE** Smokestack is often used to
describe industries that produce a lot of pollution
by burning coal: *efforts to shed manufacturing's
smokestack image* ◇ *Many countries are moving
away from traditional smokestack industries.*

SMP /ˌes em 'piː/ = STATUTORY MATERNITY PAY

SMS /ˌes em 'es/ *noun, verb*
● *noun*
1 [U] **short message service** a system for sending
short written messages from one mobile phone/
cellphone to another
2 [C] a message sent by **SMS**: *I'm trying to send an
SMS.* **SYN** TEXT MESSAGE → EMS, MMS
○ to **get/receive/send** an SMS
● *verb* [+ obj or no obj]
to send a message to sb by **SMS**: *If you have any
comments, just email or SMS.* ◇ *He SMSed me every
day.* **SYN** TEXT

smuggle /'smʌɡl/ *verb* [+ obj]
to take, bring or send goods or people secretly and
illegally into or out of a country: *Fake goods are
being smuggled into the EU.* ◇ *smuggled cigarettes*
► **smuggler** /'smʌɡlə(r)/ *noun* [C] **'smuggling**
noun [U]: *tobacco smuggling*

S/N = SHIPPING NOTE

'snail mail *noun* [U] (*informal*)
a humorous name for ordinary mail, used by
people who use email: *You can contact us by email,
phone, fax or even snail mail.*

snap /snæp/ *verb* [+ obj] (**-pp-**)
(used in newspapers) to break a pattern of rising or
falling prices: *The Nasdaq gained 4.3% last week to
snap a six-week losing streak.*
PHRV **snap 'back** if markets, currencies or prices
snap back, they recover quickly: *The dollar snapped
back almost immediately.* → SNAPBACK **,snap sb 'up**
to act quickly in order to employ a person: *He was
snapped up by a rival bank.* **,snap sth 'up** to buy sth
quickly, for example because it is cheap or you
think it will increase in value: *Shoppers have been
snapping up bargains at the New Year sales.* ◇ *Fund
managers snapped up the issue.*

snapback /'snæpbæk/ *noun* [C]
a situation when markets, currencies or prices are
recovering quickly: *We are seeing a snapback in car
sales.* → SNAP BACK at SNAP

sneakernet /'sniːkənet; *AmE* 'sniːkər-/ *noun* [U]
(*IT, informal*) used in a humorous way to talk about
the way in which electronic information is passed
from one computer to another by being physically
carried, stored on a disk, CD, etc.
NOTE Sneakernet is formed from the words
'sneaker' (= a type of informal shoe) and 'net' (=
network).

snip /snɪp/ *noun* [sing.] (*BrE*) (*informal*)
a thing that is cheap and good value: *The phone is a
snip at $50.* **SYN** BARGAIN

snow /snəʊ; *AmE* snoʊ/ *verb*
IDM be snowed 'under (with sth) to have more
work than you are able to deal with: *We're
completely snowed under at the moment.*

'snowball ,sampling *noun* [U]
(*Marketing*) a method of finding people to take part
in research by finding a few and then asking them
to find others ► **'snowball ,sample** *noun* [C]

soar /sɔː(r)/ *verb* [no obj]
if the value, amount or level of sth **soars**, it rises
very quickly: *Unemployment has soared to 18%.* ◇
Share prices soared. ◇ *Smaller companies are unable
to pay soaring insurance premiums.* See note at
INCREASE
○ to **be expected/continue** to soar ◆ soaring **costs/
prices/profits/sales**

Soc. /sɒk; *AmE* sɑːk/ *abbr* (*usually used in written
English*)
Society: *Coventry Building Soc.*

social /'səʊʃl; *AmE* 'soʊʃl/ *adjective* [only before
noun]
1 connected with society and the way it is
organized: *plans for social and economic reform*
2 connected with your position in society: *Official
figures show a clear link between life expectancy and
social class.*
3 connected with activities in which people meet
each other for pleasure: *Social events and training
days are arranged for all the staff.* ◇ *The job requires
good social skills* (= the ability to talk easily to
other people and do things in a group).

,social 'capital *noun* [U]
(*Economics; HR*) the people who work for a company
or live in a society, their knowledge and skills,
considered as an asset: *organizations rich in social
capital* → HUMAN CAPITAL

,social 'cost *noun* [C]
(*Economics*) the total cost of a business activity to a
business and to everyone in society or in a
particular area: *He said that industries should pay
the full social costs of polluting the environment.*

,social in'surance *noun* [U]
(*Economics*) a system in which people pay money to
the government when they are working and
receive payments from the government when they
are too old or ill/sick to work

socialism /'səʊʃəlɪzəm; *AmE* 'soʊ-/ *noun* [U]
a set of political and economic theories based on
the belief that everyone has an equal right to a
share of a country's wealth and that the
government should own and control the main
industries

socialist /'səʊʃəlɪst; *AmE* 'soʊ-/ *noun* [C]
1 a person who believes in SOCIALISM: *a committed
socialist*
2 a member of a political party that believes in
SOCIALISM
► **'socialist** *adjective* [usually before noun]: *socialist
economies/ideas*

,social 'market *noun* [C, usually sing.]
(*Economics*) an economic system based on a FREE
MARKET (= in which the price of goods is affected
by supply and demand and not controlled by the
government) but with help from the state for those
who are old, ill/sick, unemployed, etc: *a social
market economy*

,social se'curity *noun* [U]
1 (*BrE*) (*also* **'welfare**, *AmE*, *BrE*) money that the
government pays regularly to people who are poor,
ill/sick, unemployed, etc: *people living on social
security* ◇ *cuts in social security benefits*
○ to **apply for/be eligible for/claim** social security
2 (*AmE spelling usually* **,Social Se'curity**) (*abbr* **SS**) a
system in which people pay money to the
government when they are working and receive
payments from the government when they are too
old or ill/sick to work → NATIONAL INSURANCE
○ to **pay/pay into** social security ◆ social security
contributions/payments/tax

societal /səˈsaɪətl/ adjective [only before noun]
(Technical) connected with society and the way it is organized: *Before considering cutting jobs, executives should consider the personal and societal costs.* ◇ *societal marketing* (= that considers the health, happiness and safety of consumers and society)

★ **society** /səˈsaɪəti/ noun (plural **societies**)

SEE ALSO: **24-hour society, building ~, classification ~, consumer ~, credit ~**

1 [C] (abbr **Soc.**) (used especially in names) a group of people who join together for a particular purpose: *the Society of Motor Manufacturers and Traders* ◇ *the Royal Economic Society*
SYN ASSOCIATION
2 [U] people in general, living together in communities: *the roles of men and women in today's society*
3 [C,U] a particular community of people who share the same customs, laws etc: *modern industrial societies* ◇ *We live in a consumer society.*

soft /sɒft; AmE sɔːft/ adjective (**softer, softest**)
1 going down or likely to go down in price, value, amount, etc: *The dollar was softer against the euro.* ◇ *The company has been hurt by soft sales in its retail stores.* ◇ *The labour market remains soft.* **OPP** FIRM
2 (HR) [only before noun] **soft** skills are the abilities that people have to communicate well and work with other people: *soft skills such as communication and teamwork* **OPP** HARD

,**soft 'benefit** noun [C]
(HR) advantages and rewards that employees receive that are not money: *They are offering soft benefits, such as childcare services, to try to keep talented staff.*

,**soft com'modity** noun [C, usually pl.]
(Finance) goods other than metals that are traded in the COMMODITY MARKETS (= where raw materials, etc. are bought and sold), for example coffee, grains and sugar: *Trading in soft commodities like wheat and coffee is now back to normal.* ◇ *Soft commodity prices look set to rise.* **SYN** SOFTS → HARD COMMODITY

'**soft costs** noun [pl.]
(Accounting) money that is spent on items other than physical equipment, for example labour, transport, software, fees, etc. → HARD COSTS

,**soft 'currency** noun [C]
(Economics) money whose value often falls so is not easy to exchange for money from another country
→ HARD CURRENCY

,**soft 'data** noun [U]
information that cannot be measured or proved: *We also use soft data, such as customer satisfaction, to evaluate our performance.* → HARD DATA

soften /ˈsɒfn; AmE ˈsɔːfn/ verb
1 [no obj] if prices, markets or the economy **soften**, prices stay the same or start to fall: *Bond prices softened in early trading.*
2 [+ obj] to make sth less severe or unpleasant: *The company was unable to **soften the blow** of the job cuts.*
▸ '**softening** noun [sing; U]: *a softening of demand* ◇ *a softening in the labour market*

'**soft goods** noun [pl.]
(Commerce) goods made of cloth such as curtains, sheets, clothes, etc. → DRY GOODS

,**soft HR'M** /ˌeɪtʃ ɑːr 'em/ noun [U]
(HR) **soft human resources management** an approach to managing people that regards them as assets that must be looked after, trained and developed in order to get the best out of them
→ HARD HRM

,**soft 'landing** noun [C, usually sing.]
(Economics, informal) a situation in which the economy, or part of it, slows down gradually after a period when it has been growing rapidly, without causing problems such as unemployment: *The government is trying to engineer a soft landing for the economy.* → HARD LANDING

,**soft 'loan** noun [C]
(Finance) a loan that is made to a person or a country on conditions that are good for the borrower, such as a very low rate of interest, a long time to pay back the money, or the chance to pay it back in a SOFT CURRENCY → HARD LOAN

,**soft 'market** noun [C]
(Finance) a situation in which the prices of particular goods or services are falling because there are more people selling them than people wanting to buy them **SYN** BUYER'S MARKET

softs /sɒfts; AmE sɔːfts/ noun [pl.]
(Finance, informal) goods other than metals that are traded in the COMMODITY MARKETS (= where raw materials, etc. are bought and sold) **SYN** SOFT COMMODITY

,**soft 'sell** noun
(Marketing)
1 [sing; U] a way of selling sth to sb by persuading them gently rather than using pressure or aggressive methods: *The booklet is a soft sell of the company's products and services.* ◇ *using a soft-sell approach*
2 [sing.] (AmE) a product that is easy to sell: *The new toy is a soft sell.*
→ HARD SELL

,**soft 'selling** noun [U]
(Marketing) the activity of selling sth to sb by persuading them gently rather than using pressure or aggressive methods ▸ **soft-'selling** adjective [only before noun]

★ **software** /ˈsɒftweə(r); AmE ˈsɔːftwer/ noun [U]

SEE ALSO: **application software, packaged ~, third-party ~**

(IT) the programs, etc. used to operate a computer: *a marketing-and-sales software package* ◇ *Will the software run on my machine?* ◇ *designing software applications for business* See note at INFORMATION
O *accounting/business/financial/investment software* ◆ *to design/develop/write software* ◆ *download/install/load/run/use (a piece of) software* ◆ *a software company/developer/firm*

'**software engi,neer** noun [C]
a person whose job is writing computer programs
▸ '**software engi,neering** noun [U]

SOHO /ˈsəʊhəʊ; AmE ˈsoʊhoʊ/ abbr **small office/home office** a small business, especially one that is run from sb's home, or a person who works at home; a room in sb's home that is used as an office: *new software products for the rapidly growing SOHO market*

,**sold as 'seen** adjective
(Commerce) (about goods) offered for sale with no promise that they are suitable or in good condition: *Firms who buy sold-as-seen machinery are advised to test it thoroughly before use.* → SALE AS SEEN

sole /səʊl; AmE soʊl/ adjective [only before noun]
1 only: *The company is the sole supplier in many rural areas.*
2 belonging to one person or group; not shared: *I'm the sole owner of my business.* ◇ *She has sole responsibility for the project.*

,sole pro'prietorship noun [U,C] (especially AmE)
(Law) a business that is owned and run by one
person ▶ **,sole pro'prietor** noun [C] See note at
COMPANY

,sole 'trader noun [C] (especially BrE)
(Law) a person who owns and runs a business and is
the only person who is legally responsible for it:
The business is run on a sole trader basis. See note at
COMPANY

solicitor /sə'lɪsɪtə(r)/ noun [C] (BrE)

SEE ALSO: **trainee solicitor**

a lawyer who prepares legal documents, advises
people on legal matters and represents them in
some courts: *She's a senior partner in a firm of
solicitors.* See note at PROFESSION

solid /'sɒlɪd; AmE 'sɑːl-/ adjective
good and steady but not excellent or special: *solid
growth in retail sales* ◇ *a solid company with good
prospects*

★ solution /sə'luːʃn/ noun [C]
a way of solving a problem or dealing with a
difficult situation: *There's no simple solution **to** this
problem.* ◇ *They specialize in providing **software
solutions*** (= software that will deal with business
activities or processes) *for small businesses.*
❍ *a creative/an easy/a good/practical/simple
solution • a final/long-term/quick-fix solution •
business/financial solutions • to come up with/
find/look for/produce/propose a solution (to sth)*

solvency /'sɒlvənsi; AmE 'sɑːl-/ noun [U]
(Accounting) the state of not being in debt (= not
owing money): *There are serious doubts as to the
company's solvency.* ◇ *Some insurance companies are
struggling to meet solvency requirements.*
OPP INSOLVENCY → SOLVENT

'solvency ,margin noun [C]
(Accounting) the money that a business has in
addition to the amount that it needs to pay its usual
bills. It can be in the form of cash or assets that can
be sold easily to provide cash.

'solvency ,ratio noun [C]
(Accounting) a method used to calculate how safe a
company is and if it can pay all the money it owes

solvent /'sɒlvənt; AmE 'sɑːl-/ adjective
(Accounting)
1 a solvent company has more assets than
LIABILITIES (= money that it owes): *The figures
showed the company was solvent.*
2 having enough money to pay your debts
OPP INSOLVENT

SOP /ˌes əʊ 'piː; AmE oʊ/ = STATEMENT OF
PRINCIPLES, STANDARD OPERATING PROCEDURE

sort /sɔːt; AmE sɔːrt/ verb, noun
● *verb* [+ obj or no obj]
to arrange things in groups or in a particular order
according to their type: *sorting the mail* ◇ *The
computer sorts the words **into** alphabetical order.*
● *noun* [sing.]
(IT) the process by which a computer puts data into
a particular order: *to do a sort*

'sort code (BrE) (AmE **'routing ,number**) (BrE, AmE
also **bank identifi'cation ,number**, less frequent)
noun [C]
the set of numbers, found on a cheque, etc., that
identifies a particular bank: *Do you have your sort
code and account number?* **NOTE** In the UK, this is a
set of six numbers. In the US there are nine.

sound /saʊnd/ verb, adjective
● *verb* → idiom at STRIKE verb
PHR V **,sound sb 'out (about/on sth); ,sound sth
'out** to try to find out from sb what they think

---

about sth, often in an indirect way: *Did you sound
him out about working for us?*
● *adjective*
1 sensible; that you can rely on and that will
probably give good results: *Accurate data provides a
sound basis for making decisions.*
2 good and thorough: *Applicants should have a
sound knowledge of network software.*
3 in good condition; not damaged: *The building is
old, but sound.*

sour /'saʊə(r)/ verb [+ obj or no obj]
to change and become more difficult or less
pleasant or friendly; to make sth do this: *What will
happen if the economy sours?* ◇ *Weak job prospects
soured spirits.*
IDM **go/turn 'sour** to become unpleasant or bad;
to fail: *The deal started to go sour.*

source /sɔːs; AmE sɔːrs/ noun, verb
● *noun*
1 [C] a place, person or thing that you get sth
from: *renewable energy sources* ◇ *What is their main
source of income?* ◇ *These reports are a very useful
source of information.*
2 [C, usually pl.] a person, book or document that
provides information about sth: *According to an
industry source* (= sb working in the industry) *a
deal will soon be signed.*
IDM **at 'source** (Accounting) used to show that
money is taken from sb's income before they
receive it: *Income tax is normally **deducted** at
source.*
● *verb* [+ obj]
(Commerce; Production) (often **be sourced**)
to get materials, parts or products from a particular
place: *40% of the steel the company needs will be
sourced **from** abroad.*

'source code noun [U]
(IT) a computer program, written in the form of
text, that must be translated into MACHINE CODE
(= code that a computer can understand) before it
can be run on a computer

,source credi'bility noun [U]
(Marketing) how much people believe or trust a
person, an advertisement, etc: *Age, sex and accent
can all affect source credibility.*

sourcing /'sɔːsɪŋ; AmE 'sɔːrs-/ noun [U]

SEE ALSO: **dual sourcing**

(Commerce; Production) the activity of finding and
buying materials, parts or products, especially ones
that are used to make other goods: *Local sourcing of
parts has increased.* ◇ *single sourcing* (= buying from
a single supplier)

SOV /ˌes əʊ 'viː; AmE oʊ/ = SHARE OF VOICE

sovereign /'sɒvrɪn; AmE 'sɑːvrən/ adjective [only
before noun]
connected with a national government: *fixed-
interest high-quality sovereign debt such as US
Treasury bonds*

,sovereign 'risk = COUNTRY RISK

SpA /ˌes piː 'eɪ/ abbr
used in the names of some Italian companies:
Unicredito Italiano SpA See note at LTD

space /speɪs/ noun [U]

SEE ALSO: **incubator space, office ~, shelf ~**

an amount of an area or of a place that is empty or
available for use: *more than 500 000 square feet of
new factory floor space* ◇ *How much disk space will*

this take up?
O *disk/floor/storage space* • *to make/take up/use
space*

'space bar *noun* [C]
a bar on the keyboard of a computer that you press
to make a space between words

spam /spæm/ *noun* [U]

SEE ALSO: **anti-spam**

(*IT, informal*) advertising material sent by email to
large numbers of people who have not asked for it:
There are filters to block spam from your inbox. ◇
spam emails/advertisements → JUNK MAIL
▶ **spam** *verb* [+ obj or no obj] (-mm-) **'spammer**
noun [C]: *There are plans to make spammers pay a
fine for each item of junk mail they send.*
'spamming *noun* [U]

,span of con'trol *noun* [C]
(*HR*) the number of people that a manager is
responsible for: *a wide/broad/narrow span of
control* ◇ *There are now fewer layers of management
and an increased span of control.*

,spare 'part *noun* [C, usually pl.]
a new part that is bought and kept to replace an old
or broken part of a machine, vehicle, etc: *The
airline industry is a big market for our new engines,
spare parts and maintenance.* ◇ *spare parts makers*

spawn /spɔːn/ *verb* [+ obj]
to cause sth to develop or be produced, especially
quickly or in large numbers: *Silicon Valley is still
spawning new companies.*

SPC /ˌes piː ˈsiː/ = STATISTICAL PROCESS CONTROL

-speak /spiːk/ *combining form* (*in nouns*)
the language used by a particular group of people,
especially when this is difficult for other people to
understand: *business-speak* ◇ *management-speak*

speakerphone /ˈspiːkəfəʊn; AmE -ərfoʊn/ *noun* [C]
a telephone that you can use without holding it to
your ear: *a desktop speakerphone*

spearhead /ˈspɪəhed; AmE ˈspɪrhed/ *verb* [+ obj]
to begin or lead an activity or a change: *She was
appointed to spearhead a **campaign** to boost sales.*

spec /spek/ *noun, verb*
(*Manufacturing, informal*)
• *noun* [C] (*especially BrE*) (*AmE usually* **specs** [pl.])
1 a detailed description of a product, especially
the design and materials needed to produce it:
detailed design specs for a new product ◇ *engineering
specs*
2 the particular set of features that a machine or a
vehicle has: *Have you decided on the specs you want
for your PC?* ◇ *spec sheets*
[SYN] SPECIFICATION
• *verb* [+ obj] (-cc-) (*especially BrE*)
to design and make sth to a particular standard or
with particular features: *The camera is well specced
at the price.*

special /ˈspeʃl/ *adjective, noun*
• *adjective* [usually before noun]
1 not ordinary or usual: *special discounts on
multimedia equipment* ◇ *They are running a special
promotion at the moment.*
2 appointed or created for a particular purpose:
*The board has appointed a special committee to
consider the bids.*
• *noun* [C,U] (*especially AmE*) (*informal*)
a price for a particular product in a shop/store or
restaurant that is lower than usual: *There's a special
on garden products this week.* ◇ *Brazilian coffee is **on**
special.*

,special de'livery *noun* [U]
a service that delivers a letter or parcel/package
faster than usual: *to send a package **by** special
delivery* → EXPRESS *noun* (2)

,special 'dividend (*also* ,extra 'dividend)
noun [C]
(*Finance*) money or shares given to shareholders in
addition to the normal **dividend**, for example
because the company has made higher profits than
usual: *Shareholders will receive 76¢ in cash and a
5.5¢ special dividend.*

,special 'interest group (*also* ,special 'interest)
noun [C] (*especially AmE*)
a group of people or organizations who have the
same aims and often try to put pressure on the
government to achieve them

specialism /ˈspeʃəlɪzəm/ *noun* [C]
an area of business in which a person or company
has a lot of knowledge and experience: *Sales and
advertising are separate specialisms.* ◇ *Their
specialism is the finance of international trade.*
[SYN] SPECIALITY

★ **specialist** /ˈspeʃəlɪst/ *noun, adjective*
• *noun* [C]
a person or company that has a lot of knowledge
and experience in a particular area of business: *Ben
is a tax specialist with a major bank.* ◇ *a firm of
recruitment specialists*
• *adjective* [only before noun]
1 a **specialist** business operates in a particular
area of activity: *a specialist engineering firm* ◇
specialist shops/stores
2 involving or having a lot of knowledge and
experience in a particular subject: *specialist skills/
advice/training*

speciality /ˌspeʃiˈæləti/ (*BrE*) (*also* 'specialty, AmE,
BrE) *noun, adjective*
• *noun* [C] (*plural* **specialities**)
1 an area of business in which a person or
company has a lot of knowledge and experience:
Mergers and acquisitions are the firm's speciality. ◇
My speciality is European tax law. [SYN] SPECIALISM
2 a type of food or product that a restaurant or a
place is famous for because it is so good: *regional/
local specialities*
• *adjective*
1 **speciality** products are designed for a particular
purpose: *speciality chemicals* ◇ *a speciality glass
manufacturer* (= who makes glass for special
purposes)
2 a **speciality** shop/store sells a small range of
special or unusual products: *a speciality retailer*

★ **specialize** , **-ise** /ˈspeʃəlaɪz/ *verb* [no obj]
1 to be involved in one particular area of business:
*a firm that specializes **in** charter flights*
2 to become an expert in one particular area of
business: *She decided to specialize **in** media sales.*
▶ **specialization, -isation** /ˌspeʃəlaɪˈzeɪʃn; AmE
-ləˈz-/ *noun* [U,C]: *industrial specialization* ◇ *What is
your specialization?*

specialized , **-ised** /ˈspeʃəlaɪzd/ *adjective*
1 designed or developed for a particular purpose:
specialized software
2 expert in a particular area of business: *highly
specialized companies*

,special 'leave *noun* [U]
(*HR*) a period of time when an employee is allowed
to be away from work, either with or without pay,
because of personal or family circumstances

,special 'offer *noun* [C,U]
1 a product or service that is sold at less than its
usual price, to encourage people to buy it; the act
of offering goods or services in this way: *a special*

*offer **on** suits* ◊ *Selected cheeses are **on** special offer this week.*

2 an extra item that is given free or at a low cost with a product or service to encourage people to buy the product or service

ˌspecial poˈsition *noun* [C]
(*Marketing*) a particular advertising space in a newspaper or magazine that advertisers must pay more to use: *10% is added to the rate for a special position.*

ˌspecial resoˈlution *noun* [C]
a **resolution** (= a formal statement that people vote on) that must be accepted by 75% of shareholders: *The annual meeting will debate a special resolution on environmental policy.*
→ ORDINARY RESOLUTION

ˌspecial situˈation *noun* [C, usually pl.]
(*Finance*) a company that seems a good investment because its shares are likely to rise in value for a particular reason, for example because it is being taken over: *The company is developing a new product and is considered a special situation stock.*

specialty /ˈspeʃəlti/ (*plural* **specialties**) =
SPECIALITY

specific /spəˈsɪfɪk/ *adjective*
1 -**specific** (*used with a noun*) done, made, produced, etc. for the purpose or people mentioned; connected with the thing mentioned: *We have a full range of industry- and market-specific products.*
2 [usually before noun] (about a tax) calculated at a fixed amount for each unit of the goods, using number, weight or volume, rather than on the value of the goods: *In the UK, tobacco is taxed as a specific duty per unit of quantity.* → AD VALOREM
O specific **duty/tariff/tax**

★ specification /ˌspesɪfɪˈkeɪʃn/ *noun*

SEE ALSO: job specification

1 (*Manufacturing*) [C, usually pl., U] detailed information about how sth is or should be designed or made: *the technical specifications of the new model* (= of car) ◊ *These houses are built to a high specification.* ◊ *The part will perform exactly to specification* (= exactly as it is supposed to).
O design/product/technical specifications ♦ to **agree/change/set** specifications ♦ to **comply with/conform to/meet** specifications
2 (*Manufacturing*) [C] the particular set of features that a machine or a vehicle has: *The regulations for cabs cover age, roadworthiness and vehicle specifications.*
3 [C,U] an act of giving detailed information about what sb wants or expects from sth: *There was no clear specification of objectives.*
SYN SPEC

speˌcific ˈrisk = UNSYSTEMATIC RISK

★ specify /ˈspesɪfaɪ/ *verb* [+ obj] (**specifies, specifying, specified, specified**)
to state or explain sth, giving an exact measurement, time, exact instructions, etc: *The customer specifies a date and time for delivery.* ◊ *They were given options to buy shares at a specified price.* ◊ *The law specifies that the account cannot be held on behalf of another person.*

ˌspecimen ˈsignature *noun* [C]
an example of the way you write your name (your **signature**) that you give to a bank, etc. so that they can compare it with the way your name is signed on cheques and other documents

specs /speks/ = SPEC *noun*

speculate /ˈspekjuleɪt/ *verb* [no obj]
(*Finance*) to buy shares, property, goods, etc. hoping

---

to make a profit when you sell them, but with the risk of losing money: *Many small investors lost money speculating **on** the stock market.* ◊ *He made thousands (of dollars) speculating **in** property.*

★ speculation /ˌspekjuˈleɪʃn/ *noun* [U,C]
(*Finance*) the activity of buying shares, property, goods, etc. in the hope of making a profit when you sell them, but with the risk of losing money: *speculation **on** the currency markets* ◊ *There has often been a lot of speculation **in** the company's shares before they announce their results.*
O currency/financial/market/property speculation

speculative /ˈspekjələtɪv; *AmE also* ˈspekjəleɪtɪv/ *adjective*
1 (about a business activity) done in the hope of making a profit but involving the risk of losing money: *A lot of properties have been bought as a speculative investment.* ◊ *The shares have been the target of speculative buying.*
2 used to describe sb who does sth hoping to make a profit, but who risks losing money: *Speculative investors have been betting against the euro.* ◊ *selling of the yen by speculative traders*

ˌspeculative appliˈcation *noun* [C]
a request that you send to a company for a job, although they have not advertised one: *We welcome speculative applications from recent graduates.*

speculator /ˈspekjuleɪtə(r)/ *noun* [C]
(*Finance*) a person who buys and sells goods, property, currency or shares in a company in the hope of making a quick profit: *property/currency speculators*

ˈspeech recogˌnition *noun* [U]
(*IT*) the ability of a computer to understand spoken instructions: *speech recognition software* SYN VOICE RECOGNITION

speed /spiːd/ *noun*
IDM **up to ˈspeed (on sth)** (*informal*) **1** (about a person, company, etc.) performing at the rate or level that is expected: *She aims to get new employees up to speed as quickly as possible.* **2** having the most recent and accurate information or knowledge: *Are you up to speed yet on the latest developments?*

spellcheck (*AmE spelling* **spell-check, ˈspell check**) /ˈspeltʃek/ *noun, verb*
● *noun* [C]
1 an act of checking the spelling of text, using a computer program: *The whole text needs a spellcheck.*
2 = SPELLCHECKER
● *verb* [+ obj]
to use a computer program to check text to see if the spelling is correct

spellchecker (*AmE spelling* **spell-checker, spell checker**) /ˈspeltʃekə(r)/ (*also* **ˈspellcheck, ˈspelling ˌchecker**) *noun* [C]
1 a computer program that checks text to see if the spelling is correct: *Always use a spellchecker.*
2 a small computer that you can use to check spellings: *a handheld spellchecker*

★ spend /spend/ *verb, noun*
● *verb* [+ obj] (**spent, spent** /spent/)
1 to give money to pay for goods, services, etc: *Shoppers spent a total of $17.1 billion in April.* ◊ *Mobile phone companies have spent millions trying to win new customers.* ◊ *We have very little to spend **on** marketing.* ◊ *The company spends a fortune* (= a very large amount of money) *on salaries.*
2 to use time for a particular purpose; to pass time: *We spend a lot of time getting to know our customers.* ◊ *How much time did you spend **on** the*

report? ◇ *I've spent more than 10 years in marketing and sales.*
●*noun* [sing.] (*informal*)
the amount of money spent for a particular purpose or over a particular length of time: *a $2.5 million marketing spend* ◇ *The average spend on leisure activities rose slightly.*

★**spending** /'spendɪŋ/ *noun* [U]

SEE ALSO: **deficit spending, discretionary ~, public ~**

the amount of money that is spent by a person, a government or an organization: *Consumer spending rose by 4.5% over the year.* ◇ *a sharp drop in business spending on technology* ◇ *High street spending* (= the amount that shoppers spend in the main shops/stores in a town or city) *fell unexpectedly.*
❍ *business/consumer/corporate/government spending* • *spending drops/falls/increases/rises*

WHICH WORD?

spending/expenditure

Expenditure is generally used to describe money that you must spend, although you try to limit the amount, while **spending** is often seen more positively, as money you choose to spend. Compare:

● *All advertising expenditure must generate a return.*
● *We have aggressive plans for spending on advertising.*

'**spending ,money** *noun* [U]
money that you spend for your own pleasure or entertainment rather than on things you need

'**spending ,power** = PURCHASING POWER

spendthrift /'spendθrɪft/ *noun* [C]
a person who spends too much money or who wastes money ▶'**spendthrift** *adjective* [usually before noun]: *spendthrift consumer behaviour*

'**spider food** *noun* [U]
(*IT, informal*) words or phrases placed on a web page to attract SEARCH ENGINES (= computer programs that search the Internet for information)

spiff /spɪf/ *noun, verb (AmE) (informal)*
●*noun* [C] (*also spelled* **spif**)
a special reward that a SALESPERSON (= a person whose job is to sell goods) receives for selling a particular product: *Spiffs were offered for selling PCs that otherwise did not sell well.* **NOTE** Spiff/spif is formed from the first letters of 'sales promotion incentive fund'.
●*verb*
PHR V ,**spiff sth 'up** to improve sth by making it more attractive, more efficient, etc: *They have spiffed up the website with a new look and new features.* ◇ *spiffing up customer services*

spike /spaɪk/ *noun, verb*
●*noun* [C, usually sing.] (*especially AmE*) (*informal*)
(used especially in newspapers) a sudden large increase in sth: *a spike in oil prices*
●*verb* [no obj] (*especially AmE*)
(used especially in newspapers) to rise quickly and reach a high value: *The US dollar spiked to a three-month high.*

★**spin** /spɪn/ *verb* (**spinning, spun, spun** /spʌn/)
PHR V ,**spin 'off (from sth)**; ,**spin sth 'off (from sth)** to happen or to produce sth as a new or unexpected result of sth that already exists: *products spinning off from favourite books* → SPIN-OFF ,**spin sth 'off (from sth)** (*Finance*) (*usually be*

spun off) to form a new and independent company from part of an existing one by selling or giving new shares to shareholders: *The company was spun off from its parent group only last year.* → SPIN-OFF
,**spin 'out (of/from sth)**; ,**spin sth 'out (of/from sth)** (*Finance*) (*usually* be **spun out**) to form a new and independent company from part of an existing one by selling or giving new shares to shareholders: *The mobile phone business spun out of BT in 2001.* ◇ *a newly spun out company* → SPIN-OUT

spinner /'spɪnə(r)/ *noun* [C]

SEE ALSO: **money-spinner**

(*Marketing*) a piece of equipment that usually stands on the floor and can be turned in a circle, used in a shop/store for displaying items such as books—Picture at STORE

'**spin-off** (*AmE spelling also* **spinoff**) *noun* [C]
1 (*Finance*) (*also* '**spin-out**, *especially in AmE*) the act of forming a new, independent company from part of an existing one; a company formed in this way: *the proposed spin-off of the group's restaurants from its hotels* ◇ *The group expects three of its spin-offs to go public in the next two years.*
2 an unexpected but useful result of an activity that is designed to produce sth else: *commercial spin-offs from medical research*
3 a book, a film/movie, a television programme or an object that is based on a very successful book, film/movie or television series: *The magazine is a spin-off from the successful TV show.*

'**spin-out** *noun* [C] (*especially AmE*)
1 (*Finance*) a company that is formed to develop and use the results of research done at a university or college: *Cambridge has produced 120 spin-outs over the last ten years.*
2 = SPIN-OFF (1)

spiral /'spaɪrəl/ *noun, verb*
●*noun* [C]

SEE ALSO: **wage-price spiral**

a continuous harmful increase or decrease in sth, that gradually gets faster and faster: *a downward spiral in share prices* ◇ *measures to control an inflationary spiral* ◇ *Executive pay has continued its upward spiral.*
❍ *to continue/fall into/lead to/start a spiral* • *to halt/stop a spiral*
●*verb* [no obj] (-**ll**-, *AmE usually* -**l**-) (*usually used with an adverb or a preposition*)
to increase rapidly: *Prices are spiralling out of control.* ◇ *spiralling costs/debts*
PHR V ,**spiral 'down/'downwards** to decrease rapidly: *Their shares have continued to spiral downwards.*

★**split** /splɪt/ *verb, noun*
●*verb* (**splitting, split, split**)
1 [+ obj] **split sth (between sb/sth)** | **split sth (with sb)** to divide money, property, etc. into two or more parts and share it between different people: *The five executives will split $44 million between them.* ◇ *She split the proceeds of the sale with her children.*
2 [+ obj or no obj] **split (sth) (into sth)** to divide into two or more parts; to make sth do this: *The group will be split into four divisions.* ◇ *Companies were advised to split the role of chief executive and chairman.* → SPLIT UP, SPLIT STH UP
3 [+ obj or no obj] **split (sth) (from sth)** to leave a company or group and become an independent company; to make part of a company do this: *plans for the firm's European operations to split from the US business*
4 (*Finance*) [+ obj] if a company **splits** shares, it divides its capital into more shares so that each share has a lower value: *The company said it would split shares two-for-one.*

IDM **split sth 50-'50** to divide sth so that each person gets or pays half: *Social security costs are split 50-50 between employer and employee.* → SPLIT noun (1) **split the 'difference** (when discussing a price, etc.) to agree on an amount that is exactly half way between the two amounts that have been suggested: *They offered £2 000 and I wanted £2 500, so we agreed to split the difference.*

PHR V **,split 'up**; **,split sth 'up** to divide sth into two or more parts; to make sth do this: *Splitting up the group would have been impossible.* → SPLIT verb (2)
● *noun* [C]

SEE ALSO: **reverse split, share split**

1 a way of dividing sth: *a 50-50 split between shares and bonds* (= half shares and half bonds)
2 (*Finance*) = STOCK SPLIT

,split 'run *noun* [C]
(*Marketing*) a newspaper, magazine or web page which is produced in different versions, with different advertisements in each, usually in order to see how successful the advertising is: *split-run testing*

,split 'share *noun* [C]
(*Finance*) one of a number of new shares with a lower value that a group of shares has been divided into → SHARE SPLIT, SPLIT STOCK

,split 'shift *noun* [C]
(*HR*) two periods of work with a long break in between that sb works in a day: *Employees are occasionally required to work split shifts.*

,split 'stock *noun* [U]
(*Finance*) the new shares that a group of shares has been divided into in order to lower the price → SPLIT SHARE, STOCK SPLIT

spokesman /'spəʊksmən; *AmE* 'spoʊ-/, **spokeswoman** /'spəʊkswʊmən; *AmE* 'spoʊ-/ *noun* [C] (*plural* **spokesmen** /-mən/ **spokeswomen** /-wɪmɪn/)
a person who speaks on behalf of a group or an organization: *a spokeswoman for the union*

spokesperson /'spəʊkspɜːsn; *AmE* 'spoʊkspɜːrsn/ *noun* [C] (*plural* **spokespersons** or **spokespeople** /-piːpl/)
a person who speaks on behalf of a group or an organization: *A spokesperson for the company confirmed that it would be opening 20 new stores.*

★ sponsor /'spɒnsə(r); *AmE* 'spɑːn-/ *noun, verb*
● *noun* [C]
1 (*Marketing*) a person or a company that helps pay the costs of sth such as a special event, a sports team or a scientific project, usually in order to advertise their products: *They are the main sponsors of the conference.* ◇ *The club's sponsors appears on the shirt.* ◇ *The race organizers are trying to attract major sponsors.* See note at FINANCE
  ● *a big/major* sponsor ♦ *a commercial/corporate/an industrial/a private* sponsor
2 (*Marketing*) (*especially AmE*) a person or a business that pays for a radio or TV programme or part of a website by buying advertising time: *Click here to visit our sponsors.*
3 a person or company that supports sb by paying for their training or education
4 a person who agrees to be officially responsible for another person
● *verb* [+ obj]
1 (*Marketing*) to help pay for an event, a sports team, a scientific project, etc. usually as a way of advertising: *The company has sponsored the team for seven years.* ◇ *sports events sponsored by the tobacco industry* See note at FINANCE

2 (*Marketing*) to pay for a radio or TV programme or part of a website by buying advertising time
3 **sponsor sb (to do sth)** | **sponsor sth** to pay for some education or training for sb, especially an employee

sponsorship /'spɒnsəʃɪp; *AmE* 'spɑːnsərʃɪp/ *noun* [U,C]
(*Marketing*)
1 the act of providing money for a special event, a sports team, etc. in order to advertise products; the money that is provided: *corporate sponsorship of the arts* ◇ *Local companies have provided €2 million in sponsorship for the scholarships.* ◇ *a $50 million sponsorship deal* See note at FINANCE
2 the act of paying to advertise on all or most of a particular part of a website or a radio or TV station

'sporting goods (*also* **'sports goods**) *noun* [pl.]
clothes and equipment used for sport

spot /spɒt; *AmE* spɑːt/ *noun*

SEE ALSO: **hot spot**

1 (*Finance*) [sing.] (*used with nouns*) connected with a system of trading where goods are delivered and paid for immediately after sale: *He had made considerable losses on spot trades.* ◇ *Spot gas sales to Britain will rise next year.*
2 (*Marketing*) [C] a television advertisement: *a 30-second TV spot*
3 [C] a position in a competition: *The two firms are competing for top spot in the PC market.*

'spot ,advertising *noun* [U]
(*Marketing*)
1 advertising that is done using television or radio advertisements: *We offer a package to suit your business, whether you want spot advertising or to sponsor one of your popular features.*
2 advertising that is done in a particular place or area, not everywhere
▶ **'spot ad,vertisement** (*also* **'spot ad**, *informal*) *noun* [C]

'spot cash *noun* [U]
(*Commerce*) payment for goods that is made as soon as they are delivered: *We pay our suppliers spot cash.* ◇ *a spot cash payment*

,spot 'check *noun* [C]
a check that is made suddenly and without warning on a few things chosen from a group to see that everything is satisfactory: *An independent body was set up to carry out spot checks on companies' accounts.* ▶ **'spot-check** *verb* [+ obj]

'spot colour (*AmE* spelling ~ **color**) *noun* [C,U]
(*Marketing*) one colour that is used in a black-and-white advertisement to make people notice sth

'spot de,livery (*also* **'nearby de,livery**) *noun* [U,C]
(*Finance*; *Trade*) when goods are delivered and paid for immediately rather than in the future

,spot ex'change rate (*also* **'spot rate**) *noun* [C]
(*Finance*) the rate at which one currency can be exchanged for another currency at the present time rather than at a future date

'spot ,market (*also* **'cash ,market**) *noun* [C]
(*Finance*) the buying and selling of goods, currencies, etc. that are available to be delivered immediately: *Much of our steel is sold on the spot market, not through long-term contracts.* ◇ *spot market prices*

'spot price (also **'cash price**) noun [C]
(*Finance*) the price of sth that is available to be
delivered immediately, especially an amount of a
raw material, an agricultural product, etc. (a
commodity): *The spot price of gold rose to $408 an
ounce.* → FORWARD PRICE

'spot rate = SPOT EXCHANGE RATE

SPP /,es piː 'piː/ = STATUTORY PATERNITY PAY

★ **spread** /spred/ *verb, noun*
● *verb*
1 [+ obj] **spread sth (out) (over sth)** to separate sth
into parts and divide them between different times
or different people: *We attempted to spread the
workload evenly between the two departments.* ◇ *The
payments are spread over a year.* ◇ *We are
diversifying into new products in order to spread the
risk.*
2 [+ obj or no obj] to affect or make sth affect, be
known by, or used by more and more people: *The
virus spread across the world in hours.*
3 [+ obj or no obj] (*used with an adverb or a
preposition*) to cover, or make sth cover, a large
area: *Our stores are spread throughout the country.*
● *noun*
1 [U] an increase in the amount or number of sth
that there is, or in the area that is affected by sth:
the spread of wireless technology
2 [C, usually sing.] a range or variety of people or
things: *The conference will cover a broad spread of
topics.*
3 [sing.] the area that sth exists in or happens in:
*The company has a good spread of hotels in this
country.*
4 [C] two opposite pages in a newspaper or
magazine; an article or advertisement that covers
two opposite pages: *We charge $10 000 for a
double-page spread.*
5 (*Finance*) [C] the difference between two rates or
prices: *the spread between the list price and the
market price of the car*
6 (*Finance*) [C] the difference between the interest
rate that a bank pays for borrowing money and the
rate at which it is prepared to lend it
7 (*Finance*) = BID-OFFER SPREAD

★ **spreadsheet** /'spredʃiːt/ *noun* [C]
(*IT*) a computer program that is used, for example,
when doing financial or project planning. You enter
data in rows and columns and the program
calculates costs, etc. from it: *to store data in/on a
spreadsheet*
● *to create/fill in/update a spreadsheet*

springboard /'sprɪŋbɔːd; AmE -bɔːrd/ *noun*
[C, usually sing.]
something that helps you start to do or become sth:
*Her job as a sales assistant was a springboard to a
successful career in business.*

spruik /spruːk/ *verb* [+ obj or no obj] (*informal*)
to try to sell goods or services by talking to
members of the public: *She's travelling around
Australia, spruiking her new book.* **NOTE** Spruik is
used especially in Australia. ▶ **spruiker**
/'spruːkə(r)/ *noun* [C]

spurt /spɜːt; AmE spɜːrt/ *noun* [C]
a sudden increase in speed, effort, activity, etc. for
a short period of time: *There has been a spurt in
sales this month.* ◇ *If we put on a spurt we'll finish
this job today.* ▶ **spurt** *verb* [no obj]: *Shares in the
company spurted 5% late yesterday.*

sq. (also spelled **sq**, *especially in AmE*) *abbr*
(in writing measurements) square: *2 000 sq metres
of office space*

SQC /,es kjuː 'siː/ = STATISTICAL QUALITY CONTROL

squander /'skwɒndə(r); AmE 'skwɑːn-/ *verb* [+ obj]
to waste money, time, etc. in a stupid or careless
way: *They have squandered millions of euros on legal
battles.*

square /skweə(r); AmE skwer/ *adjective, noun, verb*
● *adjective*
1 used before a unit of measurement to express an
area equal to a square with sides of the length
mentioned: *Office rental is €290 per square metre.*
2 (*abbr* **sq.**) used after a number to give a
measurement of area: *We have about 15 000 square
metres of factory space.*
3 (*informal*) (**all**) **square** if two people are **square**,
neither of them owes money to the other: *Here's the
$50 I owed you—now we're square.*
● *noun* [C]

SEE ALSO: **market square**

the number obtained when you multiply a number
by itself: *The square of 7 is 49.*
IDM **back to square 'one** used to describe a
situation when you are forced to return to the
beginning of a project, task, etc., and have
therefore made no real progress: *The prototype
failed safety tests, and we were back to square one.*
● *verb* [+ obj]
1 **square sth (off)** to make sth have straight edges
and corners: *The rods are sharpened at one end and
squared off at the other.*
2 (*Stock Exchange*) to make the total number of
shares bought and sold equal: *Investors are
squaring their short positions and taking profits.*
PHRV **,square 'up 1** **square up (to sb/sth)** to face
a difficult situation and deal with it in a
determined way: *We must square up to the
challenges posed by the new regulations.* **2** **square
up (to sb/sth)** to face sb as if you are going to fight
them: *Small stores do not have the power to square
up to supermarkets.* **3** (*informal*) **square up (with
sb)** to pay sb the money you owe them **'square sth
with sth**; **'square with sth** to make two amounts,
facts, etc. agree with each other; to agree with
another amount, fact, etc: *squaring invoices with
purchase orders* **'square sth with sb** to ask
permission or check with sb that they approve of
what you want to do: *I should be able to come, but
I'll have to square it with my boss.*

,square cut 'folder *noun* [C]
a folded piece of thin brown card with one side
wider than the other, used for keeping loose papers
together, often in a FILING CABINET

the ,Square 'Mile *noun* [sing.] (*informal*)
a name used for the City of London where there are
many banks and financial businesses → CITY

squeaky /'skwiːki/ *adjective*
IDM **the squeaky wheel gets the 'grease/'oil**
(*AmE*) used to say that a customer, an employee,
etc. who complains a lot gets most attention

squeeze /skwiːz/ *verb, noun*
● *verb* [+ obj]
1 to strictly limit or reduce the amount of money
that sb/sth has or can use: *High interest rates have
squeezed the industry hard.* ◇ *We have had our
profits squeezed this year.*
2 to get as much as you can from sb/sth, usually
with difficulty: *The bank is trying to squeeze more
money out of us.*
IDM **,squeeze sb 'dry** to get as much money,
information, etc. out of sb as you can
PHRV **,squeeze sb/sth 'in** to give time to sb/sth,
although you are busy: *Can you squeeze in a short
meeting about three?* **,squeeze sb/sth 'out (of sth)**
to prevent sb/sth from continuing to do sth or be in
business: *Supermarkets are squeezing out small
shops.*

●**noun** [C, usually sing.]

SEE ALSO: **credit squeeze, profit squeeze**

a reduction in the amount of money, number of jobs, etc. available; a difficult situation caused by this: *The magazine industry is having problems, with smaller titles feeling the squeeze.*
❍ *a cash/job/pay squeeze ◆ a squeeze on credit/jobs/ manufacturing/pay/profits*

S/R = SALE OR RETURN

SRDS™ /ˌes ɑː diː 'es; *AmE* ɑːr/ = STANDARD RATE AND DATA SERVICE

SRP /ˌes ɑː 'piː; *AmE* ɑːr/ *abbr*
(*Commerce*) **suggested retail price** the price at which the maker of a product suggests that it should be sold to customers in shops/stores
SYN MSRP, RRP

SS /ˌes 'es/ = SOCIAL SECURITY (2)

SSAS /es ˌes eɪ 'es/ *abbr* **small self-administered scheme, small self-administered pension scheme** a PENSION FUND organized by the main shareholders of a small company

SSL /ˌes es 'el/ *abbr*
(*E-commerce*) **secure sockets layer** a safe and private way of making payments on the Internet

SSP /ˌes es 'piː/ = STATUTORY SICK PAY

St. *abbr* (*only used in written English*)
State: *Ohio St.*

st. *abbr* (*only used in written English*)
short ton

★**stability** /stə'bɪləti/ *noun* [U]

SEE ALSO: **job stability**

the quality or state of being steady and not changing in any way: *There are doubts about the firm's financial stability.* ◇ *measures to ensure stability in the oil market* → STABLE
❍ *economic/financial/price stability ◆ to create/give/ maintain/provide stability*

stabilize , -ise /'steɪbəlaɪz/ *verb* [+ obj *or* no obj]
to become, or to make sth become, steady and unlikely to change: *Demand seems to be stabilizing after the fall.* ◇ *government measures to stabilize prices* → STABLE
▶ **stabilization, -isation** /ˌsteɪbəlaɪ'zeɪʃn; *AmE* -lə'z-/ *noun* [U]: *stabilization in the job market*

★**stable** /'steɪbl/ *adjective*
firmly fixed; not likely to move, change or fail: *Imports have dropped but exports have remained stable.* ◇ *They promised better service and stable prices for the basic phone service.* SYN STEADY
▶ **stably** /'steɪbli/ *adverb* → STABILITY, STABILIZE

stack /stæk/ *noun, verb*
●**noun** [C]
1 a pile of sth, usually neatly arranged: *She keeps neat stacks of fashion magazines on her desk.*
2 (*informal*) (*especially BrE*) a large number or amount of sth; a lot of sth: *I lost a whole stack of files when my PC crashed.* ◇ *I've got stacks of work to do.*
3 (*IT*) a way of storing information in a computer in which the most recently stored item is the first to be RETRIEVED (= found or got back)
●**verb**
1 [+ obj *or* no obj] **stack (sth) (up)** to arrange objects neatly in a pile; to be arranged in this way: *The boxes are stacked up in the warehouse.* ◇ *These containers stack for easy transport.*
2 [+ obj] to fill sth with piles of things: *staff stacking shelves in the supermarket* → SHELF-STACKER
PHRV ˌstack 'up to keep increasing in quantity

---

523 | **stage**

until there is large pile, a long line, etc. waiting to be dealt with: *The work stacks up when you are away for a few days.* ˌstack 'up (against sb/sth) (*used especially in questions or negative sentences*) to compare with sb/sth else: *How does their latest model stack up against ours?* ◇ *Let's test them both and see how they stack up.*

★**staff** /stɑːf; *AmE* stæf/ *noun, verb*
●**noun** [C with sing./pl. verb; usually sing.]

SEE ALSO: **support staff**

all the people who work for a company or an organization: *We have a staff of 25.* ◇ *We have 25 people on the staff.* ◇ *She joined the staff in 2003.* ◇ *Five staff members were sent to London to set up the office.* ◇ *Our development staff are working on a new project.* ◇ *We want better communication between managers and staff.* ◇ *companies with small technical staffs* ◇ *They raised salaries in an effort to reduce staff turnover.* → WORKFORCE
❍ *full-time/part-time/permanent/temporary staff ◆ administrative/office/sales/technical staff ◆ to appoint/employ/hire/recruit/take on staff ◆ to cut/ dismiss/fire/lay off staff ◆ staff development/ meetings/training ◆ staff cuts/shortages/turnover ◆ the staff canteen/dining room/restaurant*

GRAMMAR POINT

Staff

In *BrE* **staff** can be singular or plural:
● (singular) *a staff of ten* (= a group of ten people)
● (plural) *I have ten staff working for me.*
If it is the subject of a verb, this verb is plural: *The staff in this shop are very helpful.*

In *AmE* **staff** can only be singular: *a staff of ten* (but not *ten staff*) *The staff in this store is very helpful.*

The plural form **staffs** is less frequent but is used in both *BrE* and *AmE* to refer to more than one group of people: *Companies have increased their sales staffs.*

●**verb** [+ obj] (*usually* **be staffed**)
to work in a company; to provide people to work in a company: *The design department is staffed by recent graduates.* ◇ *We are fully staffed at the moment.* → OVERSTAFFED, SHORT-STAFFED, UNDERSTAFFED
▶ **'staffing** *noun* [U]: *staffing levels*

'staff ˌagency = EMPLOYMENT AGENCY

'staff associˌation *noun* [C]
(*HR*) an organization, similar to a union, for employees of a company or for people who do the same job, where they can discuss matters or problems related to their work, pay, conditions, etc.

staffer /'stɑːfə(r); *AmE* 'stæfər/ *noun* [C] (*especially AmE*) (*informal*)
(used in newspapers) an employee, especially of a newspaper

★**stage** /steɪdʒ/ *noun, verb*
●**noun** [C]

SEE ALSO: **early-stage**

1 a period or state that sth passes through as it develops: *This technology is still in its early stages.* ◇ *The product is at the design stage.* ◇ *We have no plans to sell the company at this stage.* ◇ *The project has reached a critical stage.*
2 a separate part that a process, etc. is divided into: *They have completed the first stage of the cost-*

cutting process. ◇ We can take the argument one stage further. ◇ The pay increase will be introduced **in stages** (= not all at once). [SYN] STEP
● **verb** [+ obj]
1 to organize an event: Next year's conference will be staged in Parma.
● to stage a **conference/an event/exhibition**
2 to organize and take part in action that needs careful planning, especially as a public protest: Drivers staged a 24-hour strike in protest at the new regulations.
● to stage a **protest/stoppage/strike**
3 to make sth happen: After a poor six months, the company is staging a recovery.
● to stage a **comeback/rally/recovery**

'**stage-gate** adjective [only before noun]
(Marketing) used to describe a way of developing a new product where the process is divided into separate stages. At the end of each stage managers must make a decision about whether and how to continue.
● a stage-gate **model/process/review/system**

stagflation /stægˈfleɪʃn/ noun [U]
(Economics) an economic situation where there is high INFLATION (= rises in the general prices of goods and services) but no increase in the jobs that are available or in business activity
[NOTE] Stagflation is formed from the words 'stagnation' (see 'stagnate') and 'inflation'.

stagger /ˈstægə(r)/ verb [+ obj]
to arrange for events that would normally happen at the same time to start or happen at different times: We asked if we could stagger the payments. ◇ staggered working hours

stagnant /ˈstægnənt/ adjective
not developing, growing or changing: Companies are fighting for sales in a stagnant market. ◇ a stagnant economy

stagnate /stægˈneɪt; AmE ˈstægneɪt/ verb [no obj]
to stop developing or making progress: Demand has stagnated and profits are down. ▶ **stagnation** /stægˈneɪʃn/ noun [U]: a period of economic stagnation

★ **stake** /steɪk/ noun, verb
● **noun**

SEE ALSO: blocking stake

1 (Finance) [C, usually sing.] money that sb invests in a company: The group has a 40% stake in the airline. ◇ He paid £140 million for a 51% controlling stake in the brewery.
● a controlling/majority/minority stake (in sth) • to acquire/buy/sell/take a stake (in sth) • to cut/increase/raise/reduce your stake (in sth) • to have/hold/own a stake (in sth)
2 [C] something that you risk losing, especially money, when you try to predict the result of a race, etc. or when you are involved in an activity that can succeed or fail: How much was the stake (= how much did you bet)? ◇ When you start a new business, the stakes are high, but the rewards can be great.
3 [sing.] an important part or share in a business, plan, etc. that is important to you and that you want to be successful: The workers all have a personal stake in the wage negotiations.
[IDM] **at 'stake** that can be won or lost, depending on the success of a particular action: Hundreds of jobs are at stake if the firm doesn't win this contract. → idiom at PLAY verb
● **verb** [+ obj]
to risk money or sth important on the result of sth: The company is staking its future on the success of this product.

[IDM] **stake (out) a/your 'claim (to/for/on sth)** to say or show publicly that you think sth should be yours: By taking over its main competitor, the group has staked its claim to be the biggest high-street retailer.

stakeholder /ˈsteɪkhəʊldə(r); AmE -hoʊld-/ noun [C]
a person or group that is involved in and can be affected by a particular organization, project, system, etc., for example directors, employees, shareholders and customers: The scheme encourages workers to become stakeholders (= to buy shares) in their own companies.

'**stakeholder ,pension** noun [C]
in the UK, a pension that is intended mainly for people who do not have a company pension and is organized according to rules set by the government. The money people save is invested by private financial companies in order to provide them with a pension when they retire.

stall /stɔːl/ noun, verb
● **noun** [C]
a table or small shop that people sell things from, especially in a market: a market stall [SYN] STAND
● **verb**
1 [no obj] to try to avoid doing sth or answering a question so that you have more time: They are still stalling on the deal.
2 [+ obj or no obj] to stop growing or making progress; to cause sth to stop growing or making progress: The economy seems to be stalling. ◇ The high value of the dollar has stalled exports.

stallholder /ˈstɔːlhəʊldə(r); AmE -hoʊld-/ noun [C]
a person who owns or sells things from a stall in a market, etc.

stamp /stæmp/ noun, verb
● **noun** [C]

SEE ALSO: date stamp, revenue ~, rubber ~

1 (also '**postage stamp**, formal) a small piece of paper with a design on it that you buy and stick on an envelope or a parcel/package before you post it
2 a tool for printing the date or a design or mark onto a surface
3 a design or words made by stamping sth onto a surface: a passport with a visa stamp ◇ (figurative) The new drug has not yet received the official stamp of approval.
● **verb** [+ obj]

SEE ALSO: rubber-stamp

1 stamp A on B | stamp B with A (often be stamped) to print lettrs, words, a design etc onto sth using a special tool: The box was stamped with the maker's name. ◇ The envelope had 'Private' stamped on it.
2 (usually be stamped) to stick a stamp on a letter or package

'**stamp duty** (BrE) (AmE '**stamp tax**) noun [U]
a tax that must be paid when land, buildings or shares are sold. A stamp is fixed to the legal document to show that the tax has been paid.

stand /stænd/ verb, noun
● **verb** [no obj]
1 to be in a particular situation, position, etc: Our market share stands at about 23%. ◇ Where do you stand on (= what's your opinion of) this issue?
2 if an offer, a decision, etc., that you have made earlier stands, it is still valid: Their offer to buy the company still stands.
3 to be in a situation where you are likely to do sth: They stand to make a lot of money from this deal.
[IDM] ,**stand or 'fall by/on sth** to be successful or fail because of one particular thing: Fund managers

make decisions and stand or fall by the results. **stand**
'pat to stay the same and not change; to refuse to
change: *The unemployment rate stood pat at 4%.*
stand the test of 'time to prove to be successful,
popular, etc. over a long period of time → idiom at
GROUND *noun*
PHR V ,**stand 'by** to be ready for action: *We have an
IT engineer standing by in case the system crashes.*
→ STANDBY ,**stand 'down** to leave a job or position:
*Eric Marsh stood down **as** chairman after ten years.*
'**stand for sth** (*not used in the continuous tenses*) to
be short for or a symbol of sth: *What does RSI stand
for?* ,**stand 'in (for sb)** to take sb's place: *My boss
couldn't go to the conference so I stood in for her.*
SYN DEPUTIZE
● *noun* [C]
1 an attitude towards sth or an opinion that you
make clear to people: *We **take** a tough stand **on**
quality control.*
2 a table or a vertical structure that goods are sold
from, especially in the street or at a market: *a
hamburger/newspaper stand* SYN STALL
3 (*especially BrE*) a table or a vertical structure
where things are displayed or advertised, for
example at an exhibition: *a display/an exhibition
stand* ◇ *There will be two reps **manning** the stand at
all times during the conference.*
4 (*often used with another noun*) a piece of
equipment or furniture that you use for holding a
particular type of thing: *a literature stand* ◇ *an
umbrella stand* ◇ *a floor stand for a TV*
5 [usually sing.] = WITNESS BOX

'**stand-alone** *adjective* [only before noun]
that exists or functions on its own: *Their retail
branch is now run as a stand-alone company.* ◇ *The
software usually comes as part of a package,
although you can also buy a stand-alone version.*

★ **standard** /'stændəd; *AmE* -dərd/ *noun, adjective*
● *noun*

SEE ALSO: accounting standard, gold ~, international
labour ~, open ~, Trading ~

1 [C,U] a level of quality that is expected or
required: *When it first appeared, this vehicle set new
standards for safety.* ◇ *We offer the highest standards
of customer care.* ◇ *The standard of the applications
for the post is very low.* ◇ *falling standards of service*
O *to **establish/set** standards* ◆ *to **achieve/meet/reach**
a standard* ◆ *to **improve/raise** standards* ◆ *a **high/
low/minimum** standard*
2 [C] an official rule used when producing sth; a
unit of measurement that is officially used: *The
government aims to increase recycling by introducing
tougher industry standards.* ◇ *For measuring
shipments, the international standard is TEU.*
O *to **apply/enforce/set/tighten/use** a standard*
3 [C] something that most people who do a
particular job use: *The manual is the industry
standard for health and safety.* ◇ *The wages are low
by today's standards.*
● *adjective*
1 average or normal rather than having special or
unusual features: *A standard letter was sent to all
candidates.* ◇ *Our standard terms and conditions
apply to all our products.* ◇ *All these PCs come with
wireless keyboard and mouse **as standard**.*
2 [usually before noun] following a particular
standard that is set, for example, by an industry:
standard sizes of clothes ◇ *I couldn't open the file as it
wasn't in a standard format.*
3 [only before noun] used by most people who are
studying a particular subject: *This has become the
standard book on marketing.*
→ NON-STANDARD

'**Standard & 'Poor's '500 ,index** (*also spelled
Standard and Poor's ~*) /,stændəd ən 'pɔːz; *AmE*

,stændərd ən 'pɔːrz/ (*also* '**Standard and 'Poor's '500
'stock ,index**) *noun* [sing.] (*abbr* **S&P 500™**)
an average of the share prices of five hundred US
companies, used to measure changes in the US
market: *The broad Standard and Poor's 500 index
rose 6.8 points.*

,**standard 'costing** *noun* [U]
(*Accounting*) a method of calculating and controlling
the costs of producing goods by comparing the
usual or estimated costs and income with the
actual costs and income: *The standard costing
system is helpful in creating a budget for a project to
design, develop and manufacture a new product.*
▶ ,**standard 'cost** *noun* [C,U]

,**standard de'duction** *noun* [C,U]
in the US, a fixed percentage that most people take
from their income on a tax form before their tax is
calculated. They can choose to use this percentage
or list amounts separately if this total is higher.
→ ITEMIZE (2)

,**standard devi'ation** *noun* [C,U]
(*Technical*) the amount by which measurements for
members in a group vary from the average for the
group: *Our survey of 100 people showed that they
spent an average of £52 on books per year, with a
standard deviation of £12.* → MEAN, MODE, RANGE

,**standard-form 'contract** *noun* [C]
(*Law*) a contract that a seller or an employer, etc.
uses in the same form for many different cases

,**standard 'issue** *noun* [U]
1 something that is given to everybody who does a
particular job, works for a particular company, etc:
*Hand-held computers are becoming standard issue
for construction companies.* ◇ *the company's
standard-issue business card*
2 a typical example of sth that has no unusual
features: *standard-issue office furniture*

★ **standardize**, **-ise** /'stændədaɪz; *AmE* -dərd-/
verb [+ obj]
to make objects or activities of the same type have
the same features or qualities; to make sth
standard: *We have standardized our manufacturing
processes worldwide.* ◇ *standardized tests/systems*
▶ **standardization**, **-isation** /,stændədaɪ'zeɪʃn;
AmE -dərdə'z-/ *noun* [U]

,**standard of 'living** *noun* [C]
the amount of money and level of comfort that a
particular person or group has

,**standard 'operating pro,cedure** *noun*
[C,U] (*abbr* **SOP**)
the official or accepted way that particular things
are done in a company, an organization or an
industry

'**Standard 'Rate and 'Data ,Service™** *noun*
[sing.] (*abbr* **SRDS™**)
(*Marketing*) in the US, a book published every
month that contains information about all the
newspapers, magazines and other media that have
advertising, such as how many are sold, how much
they charge for advertising, etc. → BRITISH RATE
AND DATA

,**standard-'rated** *adjective*
used to describe goods or services on which a
normal level of a particular tax is charged: *Pet food
is standard-rated for VAT.* → ZERO-RATED

'**standard time** *noun* [U]
the official time of a country or an area

standby /'stændbaɪ/ noun, adjective
● *noun* [C] (*plural* **standbys**)
a thing or person that can always be used if needed, for example if sth/sb else is not available or if there is an emergency: *I have a laptop as a standby in case my computer crashes.*
IDM **on 'standby 1** ready to do sth immediately if needed or asked: *We are on standby to increase production if demand increases.* **2** ready to travel if a ticket becomes available → idiom at **FLY**
● *adjective*
1 ready to be used if needed: *Leave the PC in standby mode.*
2 (*Economics*) used to describe an arrangement by which a country can borrow extra money from the International Monetary Fund in an emergency: *a $16 billion standby agreement with the IMF*
3 a **standby** ticket for a flight, the theatre, etc. cannot be bought in advance and is only available a very short time before the plane leaves or the performance starts: *a standby ticket to New York*
→ **STAND BY** at **STAND** *verb*

'standby 'letter of 'credit noun [C]
(*Finance*) a written document that a bank can provide for a customer in which the bank agrees to pay a bill, pay back a loan, etc. if the customer does not do so

standing /'stændɪŋ/ adjective, noun
● *adjective* [only before noun]
existing or arranged without a time limit, not formed or made for a particular situation: *a standing committee ◇ We have a standing arrangement to share printing facilities.*
● *noun* [U]
1 the position or reputation of sb/sth within a group of people or in an organization: *You can take on extra projects to increase your standing in your company. ◇ efforts to improve the firm's weak financial standing* (= it does not have much money)
SYN STATUS → CREDIT STANDING
2 the period of time that sth has existed: *The company's head of many years' standing is J. Pack.*

,standing 'order noun (also **,banker's 'order**)
[C,U] (*both BrE*)
an instruction that you give to a bank to pay sb a fixed amount of money from your account on the same day each week, month, etc: *to set up a standing order ◇ to pay by standing order*

,standing room 'only phrase
(*Marketing*) a technique in which sb trying to sell a product or service suggests that the customer should buy immediately as they may not have another chance in the future because so many people want to buy it

standout /'stændaʊt/ noun (*especially AmE*)
(*Marketing, informal*)
1 [C] a thing or person that is very noticeable because they are better, more impressive, etc. than others: *Their new minidisc player is a standout. ◇ a standout product*
2 [U] the ability to be noticed very easily: *We are confident our products will achieve significant standout in a crowded market. ◇ standout tests/ features*

standstill /'stændstɪl/ noun [sing.]
a situation in which all activity or movement has stopped: *The economy is at a standstill. ◇ The strike could bring production to a standstill for 24 hours.*

'standstill a,greement noun [C]
(*Law*) a contract in which both sides agree to leave the current situation as it is for a period of time: *The company reached a standstill agreement with the bank to allow it more time to repay the debt.*

staple /'steɪpl/ adjective, noun, verb
● *adjective*
forming a basic, large or important part of sth: *The price of rice, fuel and other staple goods has risen considerably.*
● *noun* [C]
1 a small piece of wire that is used in a device (called a **stapler**) and is pushed through pieces of paper and bent over at the ends in order to fasten the pieces of paper together—Picture at **OFFICE**
2 (*Economics*) something that is produced by a country and is important for its economy: *Copper is a staple of the local economy.*
3 a large or important part of sth: *Business clients are the staple of luxury hotels* (= their main customers).
● *verb* [+ obj]
to attach pieces of paper together using a **staple** or **staples**: *Staple the invoice to the receipt. ◇ Staple the invoice and the receipt together.*

'staple gun noun [C]
a device for fixing paper to walls, etc. using **staples**

stapler /'steɪplə(r)/ noun [C]
a small device for putting **staples** into paper—Picture at **OFFICE**

star /stɑː(r)/ noun [C]
1 a mark that tells you how good sth is in sb's opinion: *This printer received a top rating of five stars from 'Your PC' magazine.*
2 a thing or person that is the best of a group: *The company has become the star of its sector.*
3 in the BOSTON MATRIX, a product that has a large market share in a market that is growing very quickly—Picture at **BOSTON MATRIX**

★ start /stɑːt; *AmE* stɑːrt/ verb, noun
● *verb*

SEE ALSO: **jump-start, kick-start**

1 [no obj] (*used with an adverb or a preposition*) to begin at a particular level: *Prices for the clothes start at about $100 and run into thousands.*
2 [+ obj *or* no obj] **start (sth/sb) (up)** to begin to exist; to make sth begin to exist: *There are a lot of small business starting up in the area. ◇ They decided to start a catering business.* → **START-UP**
See note at **FOUND**
3 [+ obj *or* no obj] **start (out/off) (sth) (as sth)** to begin in a particular way that changes later: *The company started out with just 10 employees.*
4 [+ obj *or* no obj] when you **start** a machine or a vehicle or it **starts**, it begins to operate: *Just press this button to start the scanner.*
→ idioms at **FIT** *noun*, **HEAD** *noun*
PHRV **start 'out 1** to begin to do sth, especially in business or work: *to start out in business* **2** to have a particular intention when you begin sth: *I started out to fix a bug but I ended up writing a new program.* **,start 'over** (*especially AmE*) to begin again: *I messed up the design so I had to start over.* **,start 'up; ,start sth 'up** to begin working, happening, etc.; to make sth do this: *My computer won't start up. ◇ Start up the engine.* → **START-UP**
● *noun*

SEE ALSO: **housing start**

1 [C, usually sing.] the point at which sth begins: *Things were looking bad at the start of the year. ◇ The meeting got off to a good/bad start* (= started well/badly).
2 [sing.] the act or process of beginning sth: *We'd better make a start on these accounts.*
3 [C, usually sing.] the opportunity that you are given to begin sth in a successful way: *The job gave him his start in publishing.*
4 [C, usually pl.] a business, project, etc. that has just begun: *Last year there were a large number of*

new business starts, and new business failures.
→ START-UP
→ idiom at HEAD *noun*

★ 'start-up (*also spelled* **startup**) *noun*
1 [U] the action or process of starting or making sth start: *They announced the start-up of a new pension scheme.* ◇ *On start-up, the computer asks for a password.*
2 [C] a new company: *This region has the highest level of business start-ups in the country.* → START *noun* (4)
▶ **'start-up** *adjective* [only before noun]: *The venture failed because of high start-up costs.* ◇ *a start-up company* → START UP, START STH UP at START *verb*

starve /stɑːv; *AmE* stɑːrv/ *verb*
PHRV **'starve sb/sth of sth** (*AmE also* **'starve sb/ sth for sth**) (*usually* be starved) to prevent sb/sth from having sth that they want or need: *The company has been starved of investment for several years.* ◇ *The firm was starved for cash when it started up.* → CASH-STARVED

★ state /steɪt/ *noun, adjective, verb*
● *noun*
1 [C, usually sing.] the good or bad conditions that exist in an economy, a market, an industry, etc. at a particular time: *a report on the state of the economy* ◇ *The latest figures reflect the dire state of the steel industry.* ◇ *Much of the world engineering industry is in a state of depression.*
O *a buoyant/healthy* state • *a depressed/dire/ gloomy/poor/precarious/weak* state
2 [C, usually sing.] the condition that a thing or person is in: *The safety report criticized the untidy state of the warehouse.* ◇ *The factory is in a poor state of repair.*
O *a good/healthy* state • *a bad/poor/run-down/ terrible/untidy* state
3 (*also* **State**) [C] a country considered as an organized political community controlled by one government: *European Union member states* ◇ *the Baltic States*
4 (*also* **State**) [C] (*abbr* **St.**) an organized political community forming part of a country: *the southern States of the US*
5 (*also* **the State**) [U; sing.] the government of a country: *people who are financially dependent on the state* ◇ *The airline is 53% state-owned.*
● *adjective* (*also* **State**) [only before noun]
1 controlled or provided by the government of a country: *Aer Lingus, the Irish state airline*
2 connected with a particular state of a country, especially in the US: *a state bank/tax*
● *verb* [+ obj]
1 to formally write or say sth, especially in a careful and clear way: *The facts are clearly stated in the report.*
2 (*usually used in written English*) (*usually* be stated) to fix or announce the details of sth, especially on a written document: *You must arrive at the time stated.* ◇ *The new CEO's stated aim is a 30% market share.*

,state 'benefit *noun* [U,C]
in the UK, money provided by the government to people who need financial help because they are unemployed, ill/sick, etc.

★ statement /'steɪtmənt/ *noun* [C]

SEE ALSO: **bank statement, completion ~, financial ~, income ~, mission ~, personal ~, profit and loss ~,** etc.

1 a printed record of money paid, received, etc: *You will receive a customer statement at the end of each month.* ◇ *My bank sends me monthly statements.*
2 something that you say or write that gives information or an opinion: *Some of the statements in the brochure are misleading.*

527 **stationery**

3 something that is written and then read in public or published in order to give a particular message: *The company issued a press statement announcing a 56% rise in profits.*

,statement of ac'count *noun* [C]
(*Accounting*) a list that a company sends to a customer giving details of the amounts of money still owed for goods or services and of the amounts already paid: *If you pay the balance on your monthly statement of account within 14 days, no interest will be payable.* See note at INVOICE

,statement of af'fairs *noun* [C]
(*Accounting*) a list that shows the assets and the debts (**liabilities**) of a company or person that has become or is about to become BANKRUPT

,statement of 'claim *noun* [C]
(*Law*) a written statement made by a person or company that is making a legal claim against sb, giving details of why they are doing so and what they would like to happen

,statement of 'earnings (*also* **'earnings ,statement**) *noun* [C] (*AmE*)
(*Accounting*) a record that a company publishes of its income and expenses for a particular period that shows if it has made a profit **SYN** EARNINGS REPORT

,statement of 'principles *noun* [C] (*abbr* **SOP**)
1 a statement in which a company or an organization describes its aims and beliefs: *The new CEO has introduced a five-point statement of principles.*
2 (*Accounting*) **Statement of Principles** an official set of rules for recording a company's finances

,statement of 'purpose = MISSION STATEMENT

,state of the 'art *adjective*
using the most modern techniques or methods; as good as it can be at the present time: *This computer is nothing special now, but five years ago it was state of the art.* ◇ *state-of-the-art equipment/technology*

statewide /'steɪtwaɪd/ *adjective, adverb*
happening or existing in all parts of a state of the US: *Unemployment here is higher than the statewide average of 6.4%.* ◇ *This year Nissan has held more than 30 job fairs statewide.*

static /'stætɪk/ *adjective*
not moving, changing or developing: *Sales were up 5% on last year, but pre-tax profits remained static at $13.5 million.* ◇ *Customers will not return to a website if the information is static.*

station /'steɪʃn/ *noun* [C]

SEE ALSO: **docking station, power station**

1 a place in a room where a particular worker does their job: *Please tidy your station and log out before leaving the lab.* ◇ *The production line consists of the assembly station, the test station and the packing station.* → WORKSTATION
2 a place where trains or buses stop: *a train/bus station*
3 a place or building where a special type of work is done or a service is organized and provided: *an agricultural research station* ◇ (*BrE*) *a petrol station* ◇ (*AmE*) *a gas station* ◇ *a first-aid station*
4 a radio or television company and the programmes it broadcasts: *a local radio/TV station*

stationery /'steɪʃənri; *AmE* -neri/ *noun* [U]
materials for writing and for using in an office, for example paper, pens and envelopes: *office stationery* ◇ *a stationery store* ◇ *We need to put the new logo on every piece of stationery.*

★**statistic** /stə'tɪstɪk/ *noun*
1 statistics (*also* **stats**, *informal*) [pl.] a collection of information shown in numbers: *economic/ employment/unemployment statistics* ◇ *Official statistics show that people in the north of the country are the highest earners.*
○ **current/monthly/new/official/recent** statistics • **accurate/gloomy/reliable/surprising** statistics • *to* **analyse/collect/prepare/produce/release** statistics • statistics **tell** sb/**indicate/prove/show/suggest** sth
2 statistics (*also* **stats**, *informal*) [U] the science of collecting and analysing **statistics**: *We're looking for someone with a background in statistics.*
3 [C] a piece of information shown in numbers: *The key statistic used to price TV ads is the number of viewers.*
○ *an* **important**/*a* **key/vital** statistic • *a* **simple/ startling/surprising** statistic • *to* **release/use** *a statistic*
▶ **statistical** /stə'tɪstɪkl/ *adjective*: *We then do a* **statistical analysis** *of the measurements we have taken.* **statistically** /stə'tɪstɪkli/ *adverb*: *The level of customer complaints was not* **statistically significant** (= there were too few to make a difference to the statistics).

sta,tistical 'process con,trol *noun* [U] (*abbr* SPC)
(*Production*) the use of STATISTICS to analyse data and to study a process continuously over a period of time in order to control its quality and how efficient it is

sta,tistical 'quality con,trol *noun* [U] (*abbr* SQC)
(*Production*) the use of STATISTICS to study data about processes and products in order to make sure that the quality of items produced always meets the required standard

statistician /ˌstætɪs'tɪʃn/ *noun* [C]
a person who works with or studies STATISTICS

stats /stæts/ = STATISTICS

status /'steɪtəs; *AmE also* 'stætəs/ *noun*

SEE ALSO: marital status

1 [U; C, usually sing.] the situation at a particular time: *The current status of orders suggests that sales will be slow.* ◇ *According to the* **status report**, *the work is 72% completed.*
2 [U; C, usually sing.] the legal or official position of a company, person, country, etc: *They changed the legal status of the firm from partnership to limited company.* ◇ *She described her employment status as 'freelance'.*
3 [U; C, usually sing.] the level or position of sb/sth in relation to others: *low status jobs* ◇ *Their credit rating has been downgraded to 'junk' status.*
→ STANDING *noun* (1)
4 [U] high rank or social position: *The job brings with it status and high income.* → STATUS SYMBOL

'status di,vide *noun* [C, usually sing.]
(*HR*) a difference in the way one group of employees is treated or considered compared with another group: *Employees at the company believe there is a status divide between office workers and factory workers.*

'status en,quiry (*also spelled* ~ **inquiry**, *especially in AmE*) *noun* [C] (*BrE only*)
a request made to a bank to give a report about whether a customer is likely to be able to pay back a loan, pay rent, etc.; the report that the bank gives
→ BANK REFERENCE

'status ,symbol *noun* [C]
something that a person has or owns that they

think shows their high social position and wealth: *These watches have become the latest status symbol among young professionals.*

statute /'stætʃuːt/ *noun*
1 [C,U] a law that is passed by a parliament, council, etc. and formally written down: *The duties of company directors are laid down* **by** *statute.*
2 [C] a formal rule of an organization or institution: *Shareholders rejected a proposed change in the company statutes.*

★**statutory** /'stætʃətri; *AmE* -tɔːri/ *adjective* [usually before noun]
fixed by law; that must be done by law: *Temporary workers now have the same statutory rights as permanent employees.* ◇ *The employers failed to carry out their statutory duties.* ◇ *the statutory retirement age*
○ statutory **duties/obligations/responsibilities/rights** • statutory **powers/procedures/requirements**
▶ **'statutorily** *adverb*

,statutory 'books *noun* [pl.]
(*Law*) a set of records that a company must keep by law, for example giving details of the directors, shareholders, what happens at meetings, etc.

,statutory 'company *noun* [C]
in the UK, a company that is formed by a government law to provide a public service, such as supplying gas or water

,Statutory Ma'ternity Pay *noun* [U] (*abbr* SMP)
(*HR*) in the UK, the amount of money that a working woman is legally allowed when she temporarily leaves work to have a baby, if she meets particular conditions

,Statutory Pa'ternity Pay *noun* [U] (*abbr* SPP)
(*HR*) in the UK, the amount of money that the father of a new baby is legally allowed when he takes time away from work, if he meets particular conditions

,statutory re'port *noun* [C]
(*Law*) a report that a company or an organization must publish by law, especially the annual financial report

,Statutory 'Sick Pay *noun* [U] (*abbr* SSP)
(*HR*) in the UK, money that an employer must pay for a period of time to an employee who is ill/sick

stay /steɪ/ *verb*
PHRV **stay 'on** to continue working, etc. somewhere for longer than expected or after other people have left: *He was due to retire but was persuaded to stay on for another year.* **,stay 'out** (about workers) to continue to be on strike → idiom at STRING OF

'stay-at-home *adjective* [only before noun]
a **stay-at-home** mother or father is one who stays at home to look after their children instead of going out to work

'staying ,power *noun* [U]
the ability to continue doing sth even when it becomes difficult: *Internet companies with staying power* (= that last longer than others)

STD /ˌes tiː 'diː/ *abbr* **subscriber trunk dialling** a system of making direct telephone calls over long distances

std. *abbr*
a short way of writing **standard**

steady /'stedi/ *adjective*, *verb*, *adverb*
● *adjective* (**steadier, steadiest**)
1 developing, growing, etc. gradually and in an even and regular way: *a steady increase/decline in sales* ◇ *five years of steady growth* ◇ *We're making slow but steady progress.*

2 not changing and not interrupted: *This product has provided us with a steady income for years.* ◇ *She has a steady job with a good salary.* ◇ *The unemployment rate is expected to remain steady at 6%.* [SYN] REGULAR, STABLE

● *verb* [+ obj or no obj] (**steadies, steadying, steadied, steadied**)
to stop changing and become regular again or stay at the same level; to make sth do this: *The yen steadied against the dollar.* ◇ *They took action to steady the business and build for the future.*

● *adverb*
in a way that is steady and does not change: *Their shares* **held** *steady at €1.5.*

steal /stiːl/ *verb, noun*
● *verb* [+ obj or no obj] (**stole** /stəʊl; *AmE* stoʊl/ **stolen** /ˈstəʊlən; *AmE* ˈstoʊ-/)
to take sth from a person, shop/store, etc. without permission and without intending to return it or pay for it: *He was accused of stealing $2.4 million from his own firm.* ◇ *I* **had** *my credit card* **stolen.** ◇ *(figurative)* *We need a product that will steal business from our competitors.*
[IDM] **steal a 'march (on sb)** (*not used in the passive*) to gain an advantage over sb by doing sth before them: *The company is looking for ways to steal a march on its European competitors.*
● *noun* [sing.] (*especially AmE*)
something that is for sale at an unexpectedly low price: *The stock was* **a steal** *at $2.20.*

'stealth ˌmarketing *noun* [U]
a method of advertising your products without letting people realize that you are trying to make them buy sth: *The stealth marketing campaign for the cellphone camera involved actors pretending to be tourists.*

steel /stiːl/ *noun* [U]
1 a strong hard metal that is made of a mixture of iron and CARBON: *The frame is made of steel.*
2 the industry that produces steel: *steel workers* ◇ *a steel mill/plant* ◇ *the steel industry*

steelmaker /ˈstiːlmeɪkə(r)/ *noun* [C]
a company that makes steel ▶ **'steelmaking** *noun* [U]: *the steelmaking business*

steelworks /ˈstiːlwɜːks; *AmE* -wɜːrks/ *noun* [C with sing./pl. verb] (*plural* **steelworks**)
a factory where steel is made

steep /stiːp/ *adjective* (**steeper, steepest**)
1 [usually before noun] (about a rise or fall in an amount) sudden and very big: *The steep decline in demand will cost jobs.* ◇ *a steep increase in prices* ◇ *the steepest drop in retail sales for five years*
2 (*informal*) (about a price or an expense) very high; too high: *the steep cost of hiring and training staff*
▶ **'steeply** *adverb*: *Labour costs are rising steeply.*

'steering comˌmittee (*also* **'steering group**) *noun* [C with sing./pl.verb]
a group of people who are not directly involved in a project, but who are responsible for such things as making sure that it fits with the company's policy and aims, and that each stage is completed within the agreed time and cost

stellar /ˈstelə(r)/ *adjective*
(often used in newspapers) excellent: *The company has achieved stellar growth.*

steno /ˈstenəʊ; *AmE* -noʊ/ (*plural* **stenos**) = STENOGRAPHER, STENOGRAPHY

stenographer /stəˈnɒɡrəfə(r); *AmE* -ˈnɑːɡ-/ (*also* **'steno,** *informal*) *noun* [C] (*both AmE*)
a person whose job is to write down what sb says,

using a quick system of signs or short forms of words, and then write it on a computer or type it [SYN] SHORTHAND TYPIST (*BrE*)

stenography /stəˈnɒɡrəfi; *AmE* -ˈnɑːɡ-/ (*also* **'steno**) = SHORTHAND

step /step/ *noun, verb*
● *noun* [C]
1 one of a series of things that you do in order to achieve sth or to solve a problem: *This year's sales are an important step* **towards** *achieving our goal of being market leader.* ◇ *We need to* **take** *steps to prevent this from happening again.*
2 one of a series of things that sb does or that happen, which forms part of a process: *The next phase of the plan takes automation a step further.* ◇ *I'll explain how to install the program* **step by step.** ◇ *a step-by-step approach to dealing with stress* [SYN] STAGE
[IDM] **in/out of 'step (with sb/sth)** thinking or doing sth in the same way as/in a different way from other people: *They have raised their prices in step with other airlines.* **keep 'step with sb/sth** to be aware of changes that are taking place and be ready to change too if necessary: *The company failed to keep step with key trends.* **one step a'head (of sb)** in a better position than sb: *This information will allow us to stay one step ahead of our competitors.*
● *verb* (**-pp-**)
[IDM] **step into the 'breach** to do sb's job or work when they are suddenly or unexpectedly unable to do it **step into sb's 'shoes** to continue a job or the work that sb else has started
[PHR V] **,step a'side/'down** to leave an important job or position and let sb else take your place: *James Nellist will step down as chairman at the end of this year.* See note at RESIGN **,step 'in** to help sb in a dispute or difficult situation: *The bank stepped in to rescue the company with a large loan.* **,step 'up sth** to increase the amount, speed, etc. of sth: *We need to step up production to increase stocks.* [HELP] A noun goes after **up**, but a pronoun goes between the verb and **up**.

'STEP aˌnalysis /step/ = PEST ANALYSIS

'step change *noun* [C, usually sing.]
a big change or improvement in sth: *There has been a step change in production levels—up 48%.*

'step-up *noun* [sing.]
an increase or improvement in sth: *a step-up in consumer spending*

★ sterling /ˈstɜːlɪŋ; *AmE* ˈstɜːrlɪŋ/ *noun* [U]
the money system of the UK, based on the pound: *the value of sterling* ◇ *We accept payment in US dollars or in pounds sterling.*

stevedore /ˈstiːvədɔː(r)/ (*also* **'longshoreman**) *noun* [C] (*both AmE*)
a person whose job is moving goods on and off ships [SYN] DOCKER (*BrE*) ▶ **'stevedore** *verb* [+ obj or no obj]

steward /ˈstjuːəd; *AmE* ˈstuːərd/ *noun* [C]

SEE ALSO: shop steward

1 a man whose job is to take care of passengers on a plane, train or ship
2 a person who helps to organize a large public event, for example, a race, public meeting, etc.

stewardess /ˌstjuːəˈdes; ˈstjuːə-; *AmE* ˈstuːərdəs/ *noun* [C]
1 (*old-fashioned*) a female FLIGHT ATTENDANT
2 a woman whose job is to take care of passengers on a train or ship

stewardship /ˈstjuːədʃɪp; AmE ˈstuːərd-/ noun [U]
the act of taking care of or managing sth, for example an organization, property or money: *The business has prospered **under** the stewardship of Mr Fain.*

stick /stɪk/ verb (**stuck, stuck** /stʌk/)
1 [+ obj or no obj] to fix sth to sth else, usually with a sticky substance; to become fixed to sth in this way: *He stuck a stamp on the envelope.*
2 [+ obj] (*used in the form* be stuck) to stay at the same level, value, etc.; to fail to improve: *Our annual sales are stuck at $200 000.*
3 [no obj] to stay at the same level, value, etc: *Unemployment is sticking at around 12%.*
IDM **stick to the/your ˈknitting** to continue to do what you know and what you can do well: *His success is based on staying close to his customers and sticking to his knitting.*

sticker /ˈstɪkə(r)/ noun [C]
a sticky label with information, a picture, etc. on it
▶ **ˈsticker** verb [+ obj]: *Which products need to be stickered **with** consumer information?*

ˈsticker price = LIST PRICE

ˈsticker shock noun [U]
an unpleasant feeling that you get when you see that sth is much more expensive than you expected

sticky /ˈstɪki/ adjective, noun
● *adjective* (**stickier, stickiest**)
1 (used about paper, labels, etc.) with glue on one side so that you can stick it to a surface
2 (*IT*) (used about a website) that makes people want to stay for longer than usual or visit more often: *Experts measure the attractiveness of pages by how sticky they are.* ◇ *We want to create a sticky site that sells.*
3 (*Economics*) (used about prices or wages) slow to change or react to change: *Inflation remains sticky (unchanged at 1.7% in November).*
▶ **ˈstickiness** noun [U]: *increasing a website's stickiness*
● *noun* [C] (*plural* **stickies**) (*also* **ˈsticky note**)
a small piece of sticky paper that you use for writing a note on, and that can be easily removed: *I put a sticky on my PC to remind me about the meeting.* **SYN** POST-IT—Picture at OFFICE

stiff /stɪf/ adjective, verb
● *adjective* (**stiffer, stiffest**)
1 more difficult or severe than usual: *We are facing stiff competition from cheap imports.*
2 (*informal*) (about a price, etc.) high or too high: *There's a stiff $30 entrance fee to the exhibition.*
3 firm and difficult to bend or move: *stiff cardboard* **SYN** INFLEXIBLE **OPP** FLEXIBLE
● *verb* [+ obj] (*AmE*) (*informal*)
stiff sb (on/for sth) to cheat sb or not pay them what you owe them or what they expect: *He claimed they had stiffed him on his fee.*

★ **stimulate** /ˈstɪmjuleɪt/ verb [+ obj]
1 to make sth develop or become more active: *Falling prices will stimulate demand for new phone services.*
2 to make sb interested and excited about sth: *Do you feel stimulated by your work?*
▶ **ˈstimulating** adjective: *I don't find the work very stimulating.* **stimulation** /ˌstɪmjuˈleɪʃn/ noun [U]: *I enjoy the mental stimulation of my job.* **stimulative** /ˈstɪmjuleɪtɪv/ adjective: *the stimulative effect of the tax cuts*

stimulus /ˈstɪmjələs/ noun [C, usually sing., U] (*plural* **stimuli** /-laɪ; -liː/) **a stimulus (to/for sth)** something that helps sb/sth to develop better or more quickly: *the use of interest rate policies as a stimulus **to** economic growth*

sting /stɪŋ/ verb (**stung, stung** /stʌŋ/) [+ obj] (*informal*)
1 to charge sb more money than expected: *We changed shipping companies after we got stung **for** a large bill.*
2 to make sb lose money: *Shareholders were stung by a sudden collapse in the share price.*

stipend /ˈstaɪpend/ noun [C] (*especially AmE*)
a fixed amount of money that is paid regularly to sb as wages or money to live on: *Board members receive a stipend of $1 000 for every meeting they attend.* ▶ **stipendiary** /staɪˈpendiəri; AmE -dieri/ adjective: *stipendiary training* (= you receive a fixed amount of money while you do it) ◇ *a stipendiary instructor* (= who is paid a fixed amount of money) **stiˈpendiary** noun [C] (*plural* **stipendiaries**)

stipulate /ˈstɪpjuleɪt/ verb [+ obj] (*formal*)
(in a contract, etc.) to state clearly that sth must be done, or how it must be done: *A delivery date is stipulated in the contract.* ◇ *The job advertisement stipulates **that** the applicant must have three years' experience.*
▶ **stipulation** /ˌstɪpjuˈleɪʃn/ noun [C,U]: *We offer a money back guarantee. The only stipulation is that we receive your request in writing.*

stk. (*also spelled* **STK**) abbr
a short way of writing **stock** (= goods or shares)

★ **stock** /stɒk; AmE staːk/ noun, verb, adjective
● *noun*

SEE ALSO: **all-stock, average ~, buffer ~, build-to-~, capital ~, closing ~, common ~,** etc.

1 (*Commerce; Production*) [U,C] the goods that a business has for sale at a particular time: *We have a fast turnover of stock.* ◇ *That particular model is not currently **in stock**.* ◇ *I'm afraid we're temporarily **out of stock**.* ◇ *We carry a large stock of office stationery.* **SYN** INVENTORY
○ *to buy (in)/order/replenish stock* ◆ *to carry/have/hold/keep stocks (of sth)* ◆ *to control/get rid of/reduce/run down/sell off stock*
2 (*Accounting; Production*) [U,C] (*especially BrE*) goods owned by a company, such as raw materials or parts, products being made and finished products: *Just-in-time manufacturing allows firms to reduce their stock levels and so cut storage costs.* ◇ *The value of unsold stock is shown as a current asset in the financial records.* **SYN** INVENTORY → STOCK-IN-TRADE
○ *to build (up)/maintain/order/replenish/store stock* ◆ *to control/get rid of/reduce/run down/sell (off) stock*
3 [C,U] a quantity of a particular raw material, product, supply, etc. that is available to be used if needed: *The US had its lowest stock of oil in ten years.* ◇ *global stocks of cereals/fossil fuels* ◇ *The government is to sell off surplus stocks of sugar.*
○ *to build up/maintain/replenish/store stock* ◆ *to control/reduce/run down/sell (off) stock*
4 (*Finance*) [U] (*especially AmE*) all the shares a company can make available; the value of those shares: *The value of the company's stock has risen by 80%.* ◇ *He owns 32% of the stock.* ◇ *He has 10 000 shares of the company's stock.* ◇ *The family holds almost all the B-class common stock.* **SYN** CAPITAL STOCK See note at INCREASE, SHARE
○ *to issue/have/hold/own stock*
5 (*Stock Exchange*) [C, usually pl., U] a number of shares in a company that one investor holds: *an investment portfolio with a mix of 60% stocks and 40% bonds and cash* ◇ *Investors should keep buying stocks.* ◇ *(AmE) to invest in **stocks and bonds*** ◇ *She sold her large **block of stock** in the company.*
See note at SHARE
○ *to buy/have/hold/invest in/sell stocks*

6 (*Stock Exchange*) [pl.] the shares of a particular company, type of company or industry: *blue-chip stocks* ◊ *Technology stocks are expected to gain at tomorrow's open.* See note at INCREASE, SHARE
☉ *to buy/hold/invest in/sell stocks*
7 (*Finance*) [U,C] (*BrE*) a type of bond with a fixed rate of interest that a government sells in order to borrow money: *to buy government stock/stocks* ◊ (*BrE*) *to invest in stocks and shares* → GOVERNMENT SECURITY
☉ *to buy/have/hold/invest in/sell (government) stock*
IDM **on the 'stocks** in the process of being made, built or prepared: *The new model is on the stocks and will go on sale in May.* → idiom at TAKE *verb*

VOCABULARY BUILDING

Types of stocks

Newspapers often use the word **stock** [C] to mean the shares of a particular company or industry that are traded on the stock exchange. For example, **manufacturing stocks** are the shares of companies who manufacture goods. Other examples include:

- **oil** stocks – companies that sell oil
- **tech** stocks – companies that sell computer technology
- **financial** stocks – banks and companies that provide financial advice
- **insurance** stocks – companies that sell insurance
- **defence** stocks – companies that sell weapons

Sometimes an **adjective** is used with stock to describe the nature of a company's or industry's shares as an investment:

- **defensive** stocks – companies that are safe investments, even if economic conditions are bad (*compare* **defence** stocks)
- **blue-chip** stocks – well-managed companies that are a safe investment
- **growth** stocks – companies that quickly increase in value
- **volatile** stocks – companies that quickly increase and decrease in value

---

● *verb* [+ obj]
1 (about a shop/store, etc.) to keep a supply of a particular type of goods to sell: *Do you stock green tea?* ◊ *We stock a wide range of camping equipment.*
2 (*often* **be stocked** (**with sth**)) to have a supply of sth ready to be used: *The shelves are fully stocked with fresh produce.* ◊ *a well-stocked bookstore*
PHR V **,stock 'up (on/with sth)** to buy a lot of sth so that you can use it later: *The weather has encouraged consumers to stock up on T-shirts and shorts.*
● *adjective* [only before noun]
usually available for sale in a shop/store: *stock sizes*

stockbroker /'stɒkbrəʊkə(r); *AmE* 'stɑːkbroʊ-/ (*also* **'broker**) *noun* [C]
(*Stock Exchange*) a person or an organization that buys and sells shares for other people

stockbrokerage /'stɒkbrəʊkərɪdʒ; *AmE* 'stɑːkbroʊ-/ *noun*
(*Stock Exchange*)
1 [C] an organization that buys and sells shares, bonds, etc. for other people: *He works for a stockbrokerage.*
2 [U] = STOCKBROKING

stockbroking /'stɒkbrəʊkɪŋ; *AmE* 'stɑːkbroʊ-/ (*also* **'stockbrokerage**) *noun* [U]
(*Stock Exchange*) the activity of buying and selling shares, bonds, etc. for other people as a business; the business of a STOCKBROKER: *a stockbroking business/firm* ◊ *a stockbrokerage firm*

'stock ,buyback = SHARE BUYBACK

'stock cer,tificate = SHARE CERTIFICATE

'stock ,company *noun* [C] (*AmE*)
a company owned by people who have shares in it

'stock con,trol (*also* **'stock ,management**) *noun* [U] (*both especially BrE*)
(*Commerce*; *Production*) the process of making sure that a suitable quantity of goods, materials or parts are stored and available at any time while keeping the costs of doing this as low as possible; the department in a company that is responsible for this process: *stock control software* ◊ *She works in stock control.* **SYN** INVENTORY CONTROL
▶ **'stock con,troller** (*also* **'stock ,manager**) *noun* [C]

'stock count *noun* [C] (*especially BrE*)
(*Accounting*) an act of checking how many items a shop/store or business has available for sale: *The stock count made at 10 a.m. was 140 units.* **SYN** INVENTORY COUNT

'stock ,dividend = SCRIP DIVIDEND

★ **'stock ex,change** *noun* [C, usually sing.] (*often* **Stock Exchange**) a place where shares in companies are bought and sold; all of the business activity involved in doing this: *The technology firm is to start trading on the London Stock Exchange next month.* ◊ *The company is expected to float* (= to sell its shares) *on the Australian Stock Exchange later this year.* ◊ *YTL is listed on the Malaysian Stock Exchange.* ◊ *a stock exchange listed company*
→ SECURITIES MARKET
☉ *the stock exchange **closes/opens*** ◆ *the stock exchange **falls/rallies/rises*** ◆ *a stock exchange **collapse/crash/slump***

stockholder /'stɒkhəʊldə(r); *AmE* 'stɑːkhoʊldər/ = SHAREHOLDER

,stockholder 'equity (*also* **,stockholders' 'equity**) = SHAREHOLDER EQUITY

,stockholder of 'record = SHAREHOLDER OF RECORD

,stockholders' 'equity = STOCKHOLDER EQUITY

,stockholder 'value = SHAREHOLDER VALUE

stockholding /'stɒkhəʊldɪŋ; *AmE* 'stɑːkhoʊldɪŋ/ = SHAREHOLDING

'stock in'centive ,plan = SHARE INCENTIVE PLAN

'stock ,index = SHARE INDEX

,stock in 'hand *noun* [U] (*BrE*)
(*Accounting*; *Commerce*) the materials, parts, finished products, etc. that a company holds ready to be used: *value of stock in hand at year end* **SYN** INVENTORY ON HAND

,stock-in-'trade *noun* [U]
1 (*Accounting*) (*also* **'trading stock**) the goods that a business owns at a particular time, including raw materials or parts, products being made and finished products **SYN** INVENTORY
→ STOCK *noun* (2)
2 the normal work of a business: *Convenience is their stock-in-trade.*

'stock ,issue (*also* **'stock ,offer**) = SHARE ISSUE

stockist /'stɒkɪst; *AmE* 'stɑːk-/ *noun* [C] (*BrE*)
a shop/store that regularly sells a particular type (**brand**) of product: *The new collection is available from stockists throughout the county.*

'stock-,keeping *noun* [U]
(*Commerce*; *Production*) the activity of checking that

a shop/store or business has the right amount of goods available to sell

stocklist /'stɒklɪst; AmE 'stɑːk-/ noun [C] (BrE) (Commerce) a list published by a company of the products that it has available for sale to the public, and their prices

'stock ˌmanagement, 'stock ˌmanager
= STOCK CONTROL

★ **'stock ˌmarket** (also 'market) noun [C] (usually the stock market) the business of buying and selling shares in companies and the place where this happens; a stock exchange: The company was **floated on** the stock market (= its shares were sold to the public) in 2004. ◇ to **invest in** the stock market ◇ It is the only company of its type to be **listed** on the stock market. ◇ Pension funds have been hit hard by falling stock markets. ◇ US investors suffered big losses in the stock market slump.
  ● the stock market **closes/opens** • the stock market **falls/rallies/rises** • a stock market **collapse/crash/slump**

'stock ˌoffer = SHARE OFFER

'stock ˌoption = SHARE OPTION

'stock-out (AmE spelling **stockout**) noun [C] (Commerce) a situation in which a company or shop/store has no more examples of a particular item available: We have been experiencing frequent stock-outs in our distribution network. ◇ We keep safety stock as a buffer against stock-outs.
  ● to **avoid/minimize/reduce (the number of)/prevent/protect against** stock-outs

'stock ˌpicking noun [U] (Stock Exchange) the activity of choosing which shares to buy, sell or hold

stockpile /'stɒkpaɪl; AmE 'stɑːk-/ noun, verb
● noun [C]
a large supply of sth, especially sth that is kept to be used in the future if necessary: a stockpile of rice and wheat ◇ an emergency oil stockpile ◇ stockpiles of unsold goods
● verb [+ obj]
to collect and keep a large supply of sth: Companies are stockpiling goods in case of a strike by dock workers.

'stock price = SHARE PRICE

'stock right (also **right**) noun [C, usually pl.] (Finance) a right that is offered to existing shareholders to buy more shares at a particular price by a particular date → RIGHTS ISSUE, STOCK WARRANT

stockroom /'stɒkruːm; -rʊm; AmE 'stɑːk-/ noun [C]
a room for storing things in a shop/store, an office, etc.

'stock split (also **split**) noun [C] (AmE) (Finance) an occasion when a company divides its SHARE CAPITAL into more shares in order to lower the price of each share. People who already have shares are given a number of new ones according to how many they already hold. [SYN] SHARE SPLIT

★ **stocktaking** /'stɒkteɪkɪŋ; AmE 'stɑːk-/ noun [U] (especially BrE) (Accounting) the process of making a list of all the goods or materials that a company, shop/store, etc. has stored and available for use or sale; the time when this is done: The warehouse is closed for stocktaking. ◇ We **do** the end-of-year stocktaking in March. → INVENTORY
  ▶ **'stocktake** noun [C] **'stocktaker** noun [C]

'stock ˌticker noun [C]
(Stock Exchange) an electronic display that shows the current price of shares

ˌstock 'turnover (also ˌstock 'turn) noun [C,U] (also ˌstock 'turnover ˌratio [C]) (all BrE) (Accounting) the relationship between the value of goods that a business sells in a particular period, usually 12 months, and the average value of the goods it has available to sell: We are aiming to increase our stock turnover three times. ◇ If this product does fewer than 12 stock turns a year, it is overstocked. [SYN] INVENTORY TURNOVER

ˌstock valu'ation noun [U,C]
(Accounting)
1 the process of calculating the value of all the goods, finished or not finished, and materials that a company, shop/store, etc. has stored and available for use or sale at the end of a particular period; the value that is calculated [SYN] INVENTORY VALUATION
2 the activity or process of calculating how much shares in a company are worth

stop /stɒp; AmE stɑːp/ verb, noun
● verb [+ obj] (-pp-)
1 to prevent money from being paid: We paid for the goods but **stopped the cheque** (= told the bank not to pay it) when they didn't arrive.
2 if you **stop** an account, you do not supply goods or services to a particular customer, usually because they have not paid for the goods and services they have received
[PHR V] **ˌstop 'by; ˌstop 'by sth** to make a short visit somewhere: Hundreds of people stop by the store for a browse at lunchtime. **ˌstop 'off** to make a short visit to a place while going somewhere else: I stopped off at the bank on my way home. **ˌstop 'over** to stay somewhere for a short time during a long journey: We stopped over in Paris on the way to Hong Kong. → STOPOVER
● noun

SEE ALSO: one-stop, tab stop

1 [C] an act of preventing money from being paid: You can **put a stop on** the cheque if the goods don't arrive.
2 [U,C] a situation when a business will no longer supply a customer with goods or services, usually because they have not paid for goods or services they have received: We have put your account **on stop**.

ˌstop-'go adjective [usually before noun]
1 used to describe sth that does not continue smoothly, but stops and starts: stop-go negotiations
2 (Economics) (BrE) used to describe the policy of first restricting and then encouraging economic activity and growth: the damaging stop-go economic cycle

stopover /'stɒpəʊvə(r); AmE 'stɑːpoʊ-/ (AmE also **'layover**) noun [C]
a short stay somewhere between two parts of a journey: We had a two-day stopover in Fiji on the way to Australia.

stoppage /'stɒpɪdʒ; AmE 'stɑːp-/ noun [C]
(HR) a situation in which people stop working as part of a protest or strike: The union has staged a number of 24-hour stoppages. ◇ work stoppages
  ● to **call/join/organize/stage** a stoppage

ˌstoppage in 'transit (also ˌstoppage in tran'situ /'trænzətuː; 'traensə-/) noun [U]
(Commerce) a situation in which a seller discovers that a buyer is unable to pay for goods which have already been sent out, and so stops them from being delivered

'stop-work ˌmeeting noun [C]
(HR) in Australia and New Zealand, a type of strike

in which workers stop their work in order to attend a meeting to discuss working conditions

★ **storage** /'stɔːrɪdʒ/ noun [U]

SEE ALSO: virtual storage

1 the process of keeping sth in a particular place until it is needed; the space where things can be kept: *The goods are **in** storage, waiting to be shipped.* ◇ *Just-in-time manufacturing reduces the need for storage space.* ◇ *The oil terminal has a storage capacity of 5 million barrels.*
○ *long-term/short-term* storage • *a storage depot/facility* • *a storage bin/box/container/tank/unit*
2 (*IT*) the process of keeping information on a computer; how it is kept: *data storage* ◇ *The hard disk has a storage capacity of 50 gigabytes.* ◇ *50 megabytes of storage space*
○ *computer/data/document/information* storage • storage *devices/hardware/media/software/units*

★ **store** /stɔː(r)/ noun, verb
● *noun*

SEE ALSO: chain store, consignment ~, convenience ~, corner ~, department ~, destination ~, discount ~, etc.

1 [C] a large shop that sells many different types of goods: *a big department store*
2 [C] (*especially AmE*) a shop, large or small: *a retail store* ◇ *a new clothing store* ◇ *Their online store offers services that a physical store cannot.* ◇ *Their latest album is **in the stores** (= available to buy) now.* ◇ *The latest version of the program will **hit** stores (= become available to buy) this week.*
3 stores [pl.] goods of a particular kind or for a particular purpose: *fuel/medical stores*
4 [C] (*often* stores [pl.]) a place where goods of a particular kind are kept: *a frozen food store*
→ WAREHOUSE
5 [C] a quantity or supply of sth that is available to use: *a store of information*
→ idiom at SHOP *noun*
● *verb* [+ obj]
1 to put sth somewhere and keep it there to use later: *The goods are stored in warehouses until a buyer is found.* ◇ *The stand was dismantled (= taken apart) and stored **away** until the next conference.*
2 (*IT*) to keep information or facts in a computer: *These portable drives store up to one gigabyte of data.*

,**store-and-'forward** *adjective* [only before noun]
(*IT*) using or relating to an electronic system in

---

which messages are collected in one place and then sent to another place

'**store ,audit** (*also* '**retail ,audit**, '**retail store ,audit**) *noun* [C]
(*Marketing*) the process of calculating how many of a particular product have been sold in different shops/stores

'**store brand** (*also* '**store ,label**) *noun* [C]
(*both AmE*)
(*Commerce*; *Marketing*) a product that a shop/store sells with its own name on: *lower-priced store brands* ◇ *store-brand soft drinks* **SYN** HOUSE BRAND, OWN BRAND (*BrE*)

'**store card** *noun* [C]
a plastic card that you can use to buy things in one particular shop/store and pay for them later

'**store de,tective** *noun* [C]
a person employed by a large shop/store to watch customers and make sure they do not steal goods

storefront /'stɔːfrʌnt; *AmE* 'stɔːrf-/ *noun* [C] (*AmE*)
1 the front of a shop/store, that people can see from the street
2 a room at the front of a shop/store: *They run their business from a small storefront.* ◇ *a storefront office*
3 (*E-commerce*) (*also* ,**web 'storefront**) a website that a company uses to sell goods or services: *Welcome to our online storefront.*
→ SHOPFRONT

storekeeper /'stɔːkiːpə(r); *AmE* 'stɔːrk-/
= SHOPKEEPER, STOREMAN

'**store ,label** = STORE BRAND

storeman /'stɔːmən; *AmE* 'stɔːr-/ *noun* [C] (*plural* **storemen** /-mən/) (*BrE*) (*also* '**storekeeper**, *AmE*, *BrE*)
a person in charge of the goods or materials stored in a shop/store, factory, etc.

storeroom /'stɔːruːm; -rʊm/ *noun* [C]
a room used for storing things

'**store ,traffic** *noun* [U]
(*Marketing*) the number of people who visit a shop/store: *Lower prices have helped to increase store traffic.*

storyboard /'stɔːribɔːd; *AmE* -bɔːrd/ *noun* [C]
(*Marketing*) a series of drawings or pictures that

---

store

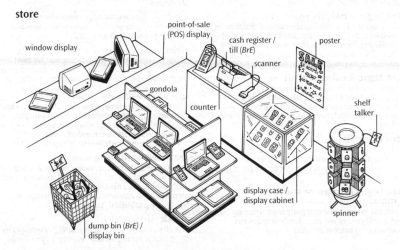

window display

point-of-sale (POS) display

cash register / till (*BrE*)

poster

scanner

gondola

counter

shelf talker

display case / display cabinet

spinner

dump bin (*BrE*) / display bin

show the outline of the story of a television advertisement, a film/movie, etc.

‚straight-'line ‚method *noun* [sing.]
(*Accounting*) a way of reducing the value of (**depreciating**) an asset in a company's financial records in which the value of the asset is reduced by the same amount each year. This amount is the difference between the original value of the asset and the final (**residual**) value, divided by a particular number of years. → DOUBLE-DECLINING BALANCE METHOD, REDUCING BALANCE METHOD, SUM OF THE DIGITS METHOD
—Picture at DEPRECIATION

‚straight 'rebuy *noun* [C]
(*Marketing*) when a person or a business orders exactly the same product again from the same supplier

stranglehold /'stræŋglhəʊld; *AmE* -hoʊld/ *noun* [sing.]
complete control over sth that makes it impossible to develop in a normal way: *The company has a complete stranglehold on the market.*

strapline /'stræplaɪn/ = SLOGAN

strapped /stræpt/ *adjective* (*informal*)
having little or not enough money: *a financially strapped airline* ◇ *Price competition has left many companies strapped for cash.* → CASH-STRAPPED

'strata ‚title *noun* [C]
(*Law*; *Property*) in Australia and some other countries, the legal right to own a part of a building, one of a group of homes, etc. and to use the shared areas

★ strategic /strə'tiːdʒɪk/ (*also* **strategical** /strə'tiːdʒɪkl/ *less frequent*) *adjective* [usually before noun]
related to a business's efforts to gain an advantage or achieve a particular purpose: *strategic goals/objectives* ◇ *The company faces key strategic challenges.* ◇ *The merger was a sound strategic move.* ◇ *By keeping the project secret they gained a strategic advantage.* ▶ **strategically** /strə'tiːdʒɪkli/ *adverb*: *a strategically important acquisition* ◇ *Their factories are strategically located near ports.*

stra‚tegic al'liance *noun* [C]
an arrangement in which companies work together in order to gain an advantage or achieve a particular purpose

stra‚tegic a'nalysis *noun* [U,C]
the process of examining the current situation of a company, its markets, the economy, etc. and of predicting future changes in order to develop a plan which will allow the company to gain as much advantage as possible

stra‚tegic 'business ‚unit *noun* [C] (*abbr* SBU)
a part of a business, for example a particular range of products or a division, that has its own customers and competitors and is allowed to operate more independently and develop business plans

stra‚tegic 'fit *noun* [sing.]
the extent to which an action that a company may take would help it achieve its aims: *We did a thorough strategic fit assessment before going ahead with the merger.*

stra'tegic 'human re'source ‚management *noun* [U] (*abbr* SHRM)
(*HR*) the process of a company organizing and using its employees in the way that best helps the company to achieve its aims

stra‚tegic 'industry *noun* [C]
an industry that is considered to be extremely important to the economy or the defence of a country or region: *The government is likely to raise tariff levels to protect strategic industries such as electronics.*

stra‚tegic in'flection point *noun* [C] (*abbr* SIP)
a time in the life of a business when it faces great changes, for example in technology or competition, and must change in order to continue to be successful

stra‚tegic infor'mation ‚system *noun* [C] (*abbr* SIS)
a computer system used in an organization to help it plan how to achieve a particular purpose or gain an advantage

stra‚tegic 'management *noun* [U]
the process of predicting the opportunities, difficulties, etc. that a company will have in the future and planning how the company can gain as much advantage as possible

stra‚tegic 'marketing *noun* [U]
the process of a company planning where and how to sell its products most effectively

stra‚tegic 'partner *noun* [C]
another company that a business works with in order to gain an advantage or achieve a particular aim ▶ **stra‚tegic 'partnering** *noun* [U]

stra‚tegic 'planning *noun* [U]
the activity of analysing the progress of a company or an organization and deciding what it must do in order to be successful in the future: *We use strategic planning to set long-term goals and short-term agendas.* ◇ *the director of strategic planning*

stra‚tegic 'value *noun* [U]
the benefits that a business would bring to another company if that company bought it: *They acquired their smaller competitor for the strategic value of increased market share.*

strategist /'strætədʒɪst/ *noun* [C]
1 a person whose job involves developing a plan which will allow the company to gain as much advantage as possible: *She's a market strategist at Morgan Stanley.*
2 a person who is good at analysing a situation and making plans: *He is known as a great strategist.*

★ strategy /'strætədʒi/ *noun* [C,U] (*plural* **strategies**)

SEE ALSO: **business strategy, competitive ~, competitor ~, corporate ~, extension ~, operating ~, Porter's generic strategies,** etc.

a plan that is intended to achieve a particular purpose; the process of planning sth: *We need to develop a global marketing strategy.* ◇ *basic pricing strategies* ◇ *He outlined his strategy for taking the business forward.* ◇ *a change/shift in strategy*
❍ to **build/develop/devise/formulate/plan** a strategy ♦ to **follow/implement/pursue** a strategy ♦ a **clear/coherent/good/successful/viable/winning** strategy ♦ a **basic/broad/core/general/an overall** strategy ♦ a **long-term/medium-term/short-term** strategy ♦ a strategy **consultant/director/group/team/unit**

‚stratified 'sampling *noun* [U]
(*Marketing*) a method of research in which people from different groups of the population are used in tests to find information about the whole population → RANDOM SAMPLING at RANDOM SAMPLE ▶ **‚stratified 'sample** *noun* [C]

streak /striːk/ *noun* [C]
a series of successes or failures: *The company has been on a winning streak recently.* ◇ *Wall Street*

stream /striːm/ noun [C]
a continuous flow of sth: *a steady stream of orders*
IDM **be, come, go on 'stream**; **bring sth on
'stream** to be in operation or available; to make sth
be in operation or available: *The new plant is
scheduled to come on stream in May of next year.*
→ INCOME STREAM

streamline /ˈstriːmlaɪn/ verb [+ obj]
1 to make a system, an organization, etc. work
better, especially in a way that saves money: *We
need to streamline the production process.* ◇ *A plan
was developed to streamline operations by cutting
staff and upgrading technology.*
2 (often **streamlined**, *used as an adjective*) to give
sth a smooth even shape so that it can move quickly
and easily through air or water: *The latest model
has a smoother, more streamlined design.*
▶ **'streamlining** noun [C,U]: *The airline needs to
undergo a major streamlining.*

stream of 'revenue = REVENUE STREAM

'street price noun [C] (*especially AmE*)
the price at which a product is sold in shops/stores:
*The radio goes on sale next month with an estimated
street price of about $100.* ◇ *Gasoline street prices
have jumped.* **SYN** RETAIL PRICE

★ **strength** /streŋθ/ noun

SEE ALSO: industrial-strength

1 [U] how strong a country's currency is in relation
to other countries' currencies: *the continuing
strength of the dollar against the yen* ◇ *The strength
of the currency is damaging exports.*
2 [U] the power and influence that sb/sth has: *The
new base will boost the airline's strength in Europe.* ◇
*to negotiate **from a position of strength*** ◇ *We will
focus on building brand strength.*
3 [C] a quality or an ability that a person or thing
has that gives them an advantage: *One of her main
strengths is her ability to cope with pressure.* ◇ *The
plan has both strengths and weaknesses.*
4 [U] the ability that sth has to resist force or hold
heavy weights without breaking or being damaged:
*Carbon fibre offers a superior strength to weight
ratio.*
5 [U] the number of people in a group, a team or
an organization: *The strength of the workforce is
about to be doubled from 3 000 to 6 000.* ◇ *The board
is now up to **full strength** (= with all the members
it needs).*
IDM **go from ,strength to 'strength** to become
more and more successful **on the strength of sth**
because sb has been influenced or persuaded by
sth: *I got the job on the strength of your
recommendation.* → idiom at PLAY verb

★ **strengthen** /ˈstreŋθn/ verb [+ obj or no obj]
to become stronger; to make sth/sb stronger: *This
week the yen has strengthened against the dollar.* ◇
plans to strengthen the euro ◇ *Their position in the
market has strengthened in recent months.* ◇ *The fall
in unemployment is a sign of a strengthening
economy.* See note at CURRENCY

stress /stres/ noun, verb
● **noun**

SEE ALSO: job stress

1 [U,C] pressure or worry caused by the problems
in sb's life or work: *The course teaches you to handle
workplace stress.* ◇ *She never escapes the stresses of
the CEO post completely.* ◇ *Can you make decisions
under stress?* ◇ *Increasing work pressure on staff is
leading to rising stress levels.* ◇ *the stresses and*

strains of running your own firm ◇ *stress-related
illnesses* ◇ *stress management* (= dealing with stress)
● *to **be under/experience/suffer (from)/have** stress ◆
executive/workplace stress ◆ to **cause/increase**
stress ◆ to **avoid/reduce/relieve/remove** stress ◆ to
cope with/deal with/handle/manage stress*
2 [U,C] pressure that is put on sth that can harm it
or cause problems: *Funding problems were placing
stress on the project.* ◇ *We cannot afford further
stresses to our balance sheet.*
● *to **place/put** stress on sth ◆ to **be under/put sth
under** stress ◆ **economic/financial/market** stress*
3 [U] special importance given to sth: *We need to
place more stress **on** attractive design.*
● *to **lay/place** stress on sth*
● **verb** [+ obj]
to emphasize a fact, an idea, etc: *She stressed the
importance of meeting the deadline.* ◇ *I must stress
that everything I've told you is in strict confidence.*

stressed /strest/ adjective
1 (*also* ,stressed 'out) [not before noun] too worried
and tired to be able to relax: *If I get too stressed out I
take a day's leave.*
2 that has a lot of pressure on it: *stressed market
conditions* ◇ *financially stressed companies*

stressful /ˈstresfl/ adjective
causing a lot of anxiety and worry: *I've had a very
stressful week.* → HIGH-PRESSURE
● *a stressful **job/lifestyle/situation/time***

'stress ,puppy noun [C] (*AmE*) (*informal*)
a person who enjoys stress but complains about it
all the time: *I seem to be getting along better with
the stress puppies now—they are a lot friendlier than
people in my last job.*

stretch /stretʃ/ verb, noun
● **verb**
1 [no obj] (*used in negative sentences and questions
about an amount of money*) to be enough to buy or
pay for sth: *Our budget won't stretch **to** a new server.*
2 [+ obj] to make money last longer or buy more
than planned: *tips for stretching your training
budget further* ◇ *The sale of the entertainment
division would clear the company's stretched balance
sheet.*
3 [+ obj] to make use of all your money, supplies,
time, etc. so that there is little or nothing left: *This
sudden rush of orders has stretched us **to the limit.*** ◇
*We can't take on any more work—we're **fully**
stretched as it is.*
4 [+ obj] to make use of all sb's skill, intelligence,
etc: *I enjoy my job because it stretches me.*
5 (*Marketing*) [+ obj] if a company **stretches** a
brand, they use a successful brand name to sell
new types of products or services: *stretching the
brand with new products and markets* → BRAND
STRETCHING
→ idiom at RULE noun
● **noun**
IDM **at full 'stretch** using as much energy as
possible, or the greatest possible amount of
supplies: *We have been working at full stretch.*

,strict lia'bility noun [U]
(*Law*) a situation where a person or company is
responsible for the harm or injury that their
actions, products, etc. cause, even though they did
not intend to cause the harm or had tried to act
carefully

strife /straɪf/ noun [U]
(used especially in newspapers) angry
disagreement between two groups of people: *The
industry has been hit by industrial strife* (= strikes)
in recent years.

★ **strike** /straɪk/ *noun, verb*

● *noun* [C]

SEE ALSO: **all-out strike, general ~, lightning ~, official ~, sympathetic ~, sympathy ~, unofficial ~**

(*HR*) a period of time when an organized group of employees of a company stops working because of a disagreement over pay or conditions: *the oil workers' strike* ◊ *a 48-hour strike by production workers* ◊ *Half the workers have gone on strike in protest against the pay cuts.* ◊ (*BrE*) *The workforce threatened to* **come out** *on strike.* ◊ *Catering staff in the company voted to* **take strike action.** ◊ *The union called a* **strike ballot** (= a vote for or against a strike) *of staff.*

● *to* **call (for)/have/hold** *a strike* ◆ *to* **be (out)/go on** *strike* ◆ *to* **call sb out** *on strike*

VOCABULARY BUILDING

Industrial disputes

- *No cars have been produced since the* **strike** *started.*
- *Management ordered a* **lockout**, *keeping thousands of workers from their jobs.*
- *The* **walkout** *by civil servants forced a number of government offices to close.*
- *Workers staged a* **go-slow/slowdown** *to protest against the introduction of new technology.*
- *The* **work-to-rule** *has included a refusal to work overtime.*

● *verb*

1 (*HR*) [no obj] to refuse to work, as a protest: *The union has voted to strike* **for** *a pay increase of 6%.* ◊ *Striking workers picketed the factory.*
2 [+ obj] to make an agreement with sb: *The budget airline has struck a $400 million deal to buy its low-cost rival.*

● *to* **strike an agreement/a bargain/contract/deal**
IDM **strike a 'balance (between A and B)** to manage to find a way of being fair to two opposing things: *You need to strike a balance between your work and your personal life.* **strike/sound a cautious, optimistic, etc. 'note/'tone; strike/ sound a note of 'caution, 'optimism, etc.** to express feelings or opinions of a particular kind: *The report struck a cautious note about prospects for the coming year.* **strike 'gold** to find or do sth that brings you a lot of success or money: *They struck gold with fat-free ice cream.* → idiom at **HARD** *adj.*
PHRV **,strike sb/sth 'off** to remove sb/sth's name from sth, such as the list of members of a professional group: *Harries was struck off as a director for ten years after receiving illegal payments.* **,strike 'out 1** to start being independent: *She decided to strike out on her own and form her own company.* **2** (*AmE*) to fail: *The company struck out the first time it tried to manufacture personal computers.*

'**strike-bound** *adjective*
that cannot function or move because of strikes: *strike-bound airports/passengers*

'**strike-,breaker** (*AmE spelling* **strikebreaker**) *noun* [C]
(*HR*) a person who continues working or is employed to work while others are on strike, and therefore makes the strike less successful: *They blamed the accidents on unqualified strike-breakers.*
▶ '**strike-,breaking** (*AmE spelling* **strikebreaking**) *noun* [U]

'**strike pay** *noun* [U]
(*HR*) money that a union pays to its members when they are on strike and not being paid by their company

'**strike price** = EXERCISE PRICE

striker /'straɪkə(r)/ *noun* [C]
(*HR*) a person who takes part in a strike: *The strikers plan to return to work on Thursday.*

'**striking price** = EXERCISE PRICE

stringent /'strɪndʒənt/ *adjective*
1 (about a law, rule, etc.) very strict and that must be obeyed: *stringent air-quality regulations* ◊ *Licences are only granted under the most stringent conditions.*
2 (about financial conditions) difficult and very strictly controlled because there is not much money: *stringent cost controls* ◊ *the government's stringent economic policies*
▶ **stringency** /'strɪndʒənsi/ *noun* [U]: *a period of financial stringency* **stringently** /'strɪndʒəntli/ *adverb*: *The rules are stringently enforced.*

strip /strɪp/ *verb, noun*
● *verb* [+ obj] (-pp-)
1 **strip sth from sb/sth | strip sb/sth of sth** to remove sth from sth/sb: *They were found guilty of stripping millions of dollars of assets from the company.* ◊ *Three of the company's directors were stripped of their posts after the scandal.*
→ ASSET-STRIPPING
2 (*Finance*) to remove the right to interest payments from a bond so that they can be sold separately from the bond: *A 10-year bond paying interest every 6 months could be stripped into 21 stripped bonds—one for each interest period plus the principal.*
PHRV **,strip sth a'way** to remove anything that is not necessary: *They are looking at ways of stripping away unnecessary regulation in the pensions industry.* **,strip 'down; ,strip sth 'down** to remove parts from sth in order to make it smaller, simpler, etc: *Many companies are stripping down* **to** *the essentials.* ◊ *We have stripped down the sales process to help cut costs.* **,strip sth 'down** to separate a machine, etc. into parts so that they can be cleaned or repaired: *The used computers are stripped down, cleaned, reassembled and sold.* **,strip sth 'out (of sth) 1** to remove or not include sth: *When South America is stripped out of the overall total, the sales figures are in fact quite good.* **2** (*BrE*) to take parts out of a machine so that they can be cleaned or repaired
● *noun* [C]

SEE ALSO: **magnetic strip**

1 (*AmE*) a street that has many shops/stores, restaurants, etc. along it: *Sunset Strip*
2 (*Finance*) the right to interest payments on a bond (the **coupon**) that is sold as a separate investment

'**strip mall** *noun* [C] (*AmE*)
a set of shops/stores, restaurants, etc. that are built together along a main road: *With a loan of $5 000 she opened one small retail women's clothing store in a strip mall in Chicago.*

★ **strong** /strɒŋ; *AmE* strɔːŋ/ *adjective* (**stronger** /-gə(r)/ **strongest** /-gɪst/)
1 (about a business or an industry) in a safe financial position: *Their catering business remained strong despite the recession.* ◊ *a strong balance sheet* ◊ *one of the strongest banks in Europe*
2 (about prices, an economy, etc.) having a value that is high or increasing: *The euro is getting stronger against the dollar.* ◊ *a stronger demand for powerful laptops* ◊ *strong growth in profits* ◊ *strong share prices* ◊ *The carmaker posted stronger-than-expected results.*

3 firmly established; difficult to defeat or destroy: *Building a strong brand brings many benefits.* ◇ *We are facing very strong competition in our market.* ◇ *The College has strong ties with business and industry.*
4 likely to succeed or happen: *There is a strong* **possibility** *that many businesses in the area will cease trading in the next 18 months.* ◇ *You're* **in a strong position** *to negotiate.*
5 having a lot of power or influence: *strong management*
6 good at sth: *Giving presentations is not my* **strong point** (= I am not very good at it).
7 used after numbers to show the size of a group: *The sales force will be 4 000 strong.* ◇ *our 2 500-strong workforce*
8 not easily broken or damaged; made well: *a strong cable/glue*
[OPP] WEAK
▶ **'strongly** *adverb*: *The business was performing strongly.* ◇ *Costs had risen more strongly than expected.* ◇ *The survey suggested happiness may be strongly linked to income.*
[IDM] **be 'strong on sth 1** to be good at sth: *The new PCs will be strong on graphics.* **2** to have a lot of sth: *The report was strong on criticism, but short on practical suggestions.* **be sb's 'strong suit** to be a subject that sb knows a lot about and does well: *Customer service is not their strong suit.*

strongbox /'strɒŋbɒks; *AmE* 'strɔːŋbɑːks/ *noun* [C]
a strong, usually metal, box for keeping valuable things in

strongroom /'strɒŋruːm; -rʊm; *AmE* 'strɔːŋ-/ *noun* [C]
a room, for example in a bank, with thick walls and a strong solid door, where valuable items are kept

structural /'strʌktʃərəl/ *adjective* [usually before noun]
connected with the way in which sth is built or organized: *The building had several structural defects.* ◇ *There have been structural changes in the industry.* ▶ **structurally** /'strʌktʃərəli/ *adverb*: *The building was found to be structurally unsound.*

ˌstructural aˈnalysis *noun* [U,C]
(*Technical*) a careful examination of sth to see how its parts function together: *structural analysis of a company/a chemical/a building* ◇ *structural analysis software for engineering departments*

ˌstructural ˈdeficit *noun* [C]
(*Economics*) the difference by which the amount of money a government would spend in average economic conditions is greater than the money it would receive → STRUCTURAL SURPLUS

ˌstructural engiˈneering *noun* [U]
the activity of applying scientific knowledge to the design and construction of buildings, bridges and other structures ▶ **ˌstructural engiˈneer** *noun* [C]

ˌstructural inˈflation *noun* [U]
(*Economics*) the rate at which the prices of goods and services in a particular country naturally rise because of the government's MONETARY POLICY (= its policy on controlling the supply of money and credit)

ˌstructural ˈsurplus *noun* [C]
(*Economics*) the difference by which the amount of money a government would spend in average economic conditions is less than the money it would receive → STRUCTURAL DEFICIT

ˌstructural unemˈployment *noun* [U]
(*Economics*) a reduction in the amount of paid work available as a result of a fall in demand for a product, changes in technology, etc. and not because of the temporary effects of the time of

year, particular events, etc. → FRICTIONAL UNEMPLOYMENT, SEASONAL UNEMPLOYMENT

★ **structure** /'strʌktʃə(r)/ *noun, verb*
● *noun*

SEE ALSO: **capital structure, career ~, corporate ~, cost ~, financial ~**

1 [U,C] the way in which the parts of sth are connected together, arranged or organized; a particular arrangement of parts: *changes in the structure of the company* ◇ *the airline's new fare structure* ◇ *The management plan to create a more flexible pay structure.*
2 [U,C] the state of being well organized or planned with all the parts linked together; a careful plan: *His presentation lacked structure.*
3 [C] a thing that is made of several parts, especially a building: *brick/wood/steel structures*
● *verb* [+ obj] (*usually* **be structured**)
to arrange or organize sth into a system or pattern: *The conference was structured* **around** *three key issues.* ◇ *We have a highly structured recruitment process.*

struggle /'strʌɡl/ *verb, noun*
● *verb* [no obj]
1 to have a lot of difficulties or problems while trying to achieve sth: *The manufacturing sector is struggling.* ◇ *The new CEO has the task of turning around the struggling company.*
2 to fight against sb/sth in order to prevent a bad situation or result: *The industry is struggling* **with** *weak demand.*
3 to compete with sb, especially in order to get sth: *The two products are struggling* **for** *market share in the desktop publishing sector.*
[PHRV] **ˌstruggle aˈlong/ˈon** to continue in spite of problems: *The business struggled along for some time before being shut down.*
● *noun*
1 [C] a hard fight in which people try to obtain or achieve sth, especially sth that sb else does not want them to have: *the struggle* **between** *start-ups and established companies* ◇ *He is engaged in a bitter struggle with his rival to get control of the company.*
2 [C] a fight to stop sth bad from happening: *the struggle* **against** *corruption*
3 [sing.] something that is difficult for sb to do or achieve: *It is a struggle to cope with such a heavy workload.*

stub /stʌb/ *noun* [C]

SEE ALSO: **pay stub**

the part of a cheque, ticket, etc. that you keep as a record when you give the other part to sb: *She saves all her bank statements and cheque stubs.*
[SYN] COUNTERFOIL
❍ *to* **complete/detach/tear off/fill in/keep/retain** *the stub*

study /'stʌdi/ *noun, verb*
● *noun* (*plural* **studies**)

SEE ALSO: **case study, feasibility ~, time-and-motion ~, tracking ~, work ~**

1 [U] the activity of learning: *Economics is the study of how we use limited resources to provide people with what they need and want.*
2 [C] a piece of research: *We are conducting a study of how people use our products.* ◇ *a market study produced by a well-known firm of market researchers*
❍ *to* **carry out/conduct/do/make/undertake** *a study*
3 **studies** [pl.] a particular person's learning activities: *I worked for a year before continuing my studies.*
❍ *to* **complete/continue/pursue** *your studies*

4 studies [U with sing./pl. verb] used in the names of some academic subjects: *I did Business Studies at university.*

O *to* **do/major in/specialize in**... *studies*

5 [U] the act of considering or examining sth in detail: *The proposal deserves careful study.*

● *verb* (**studies, studying, studied, studied**)

1 [+ obj *or* no obj] to spend time learning about a subject: *I've been studying English for fifteen years/ since I was twelve.* ◇ *I studied economics at Barcelona University.* ◇ *studying* **for** *a business qualification*

2 [+ obj] to examine sth carefully in order to understand it or find out sth: *We will study the proposals carefully before making a decision.* ◇ *The group are studying how men and women use different negotiation techniques.*

stump /stʌmp/ *verb*

PHR V ,**stump 'up (for sth)**; ,**stump 'up sth (for sth)** (*BrE*) (*informal*) (used especially in newspapers) to pay money for sth: *Investors could be asked to stump up as much as $1 billion.*

style /staɪl/ *noun*

1 [C,U] the particular way in which sth is done: *The two men have a very different style of doing business.* ◇ *She has an informal management style.* ◇ *differences in style*

O *a style of* **leadership/learning/management/work/ working**

2 [C] a particular design of sth, especially clothes: *Our sunglasses are designed in a wide variety of styles.*

stylus /ˈstaɪləs/ (*plural* **styluses** *or* **styli** /ˈstaɪlaɪ/) (*also* **ˈstylus pen**) *noun* [C]

(*IT*) a device like a pen that you can use to write text or draw an image on a special computer screen

Styrofoam™ /ˈstaɪrəfəʊm; *AmE* -foʊm/

= POLYSTYRENE

subagent /ˈsʌbeɪdʒənt/ *noun* [C]

a person or company who is paid to work for or represent an agent ▶ **subagency** /ˈsʌbeɪdʒənsi/ *noun* [C] (*plural* **subagencies**)

subcommittee /ˈsʌbkəmɪti/ *noun* [C with sing./pl. verb]

a group of people who are chosen to do a particular part of the work of a committee

subcomponent /ˈsʌbkəmpəʊnənt; *AmE* -poʊn-/ *noun* [C]

a part of one of the parts of sth

subcontract *verb, noun*

● *verb* /ˌsʌbkənˈtrækt; *AmE* ˌsʌbˈkɑːntrækt/ [+ obj] to pay a person or company to do some of the work that you have been given a contract to do: *We subcontracted the work* **to** *a small engineering firm.* ◇ *We subcontracted a small engineering firm to do the work.* ▶ **subcontracting** /ˌsʌbkənˈtræktɪŋ; *AmE* ˌsʌbˈkɑːntræktɪŋ/ *noun* [U]: *$160 million worth of subcontracting business*

● *noun* /ˌsʌbˈkɒntrækt; *AmE* -ˈkɑːn-/ [C]

a contract to do part of the work that has been given to another person or company: *More than £2 billion in subcontracts has been awarded to small businesses.*

subcontractor /ˌsʌbkənˈtræktə(r); *AmE* sʌbˈkɑːntræk-/ *noun* [C]

a person or company that does part of the work given to another person or company: *We work mainly as a subcontractor, supplying larger companies with machine parts.*

subdivision *noun*

1 /ˌsʌbdɪˈvɪʒn/ [U] the act of dividing a part of sth into smaller parts: *the subdivision of tasks*

2 /ˈsʌbdɪvɪʒn/ [C] one of the smaller parts into which a part of sth has been divided: *Supply chain management has four main subdivisions—logistics, purchasing, manufacturing and distribution.*

3 (*Property*) /ˈsʌbdɪvɪʒn/ [C] (*AmE*) an area of land that has been divided up for building houses on

subject /ˈsʌbdʒekt; -dʒɪkt/ *adjective* **subject to sth**

1 depending on sth in order to be completed or agreed: *The deal is subject to approval by shareholders.*

2 likely to be affected by sth, especially sth bad: *All flights today are subject to delay.* ◇ *All prices quoted here are subject to change.*

3 under the authority of sth: *As the company operates in Europe, it is subject to EU laws.*

ˈsubject line *noun* [C]

the words in the space at the top of an email that describe what the email is about: *Please put your reference number in the subject line.*

sub judice /ˌsʌb ˈdʒuːdəsi; -seɪ; -keɪ/ *adjective*

[not usually before noun]

(*Law*) if a legal case is **sub judice**, it is still being discussed in a court and it is therefore illegal for anyone to talk about it in newspapers, on the television, etc. **NOTE** Sub judice is a Latin phrase.

sublease /ˈsʌbliːs/ (*also* **ˈsublet**) *noun* [C]

(*Property*)

1 an agreement in which sb rents all or part of a property from sb who rents it from the owner: *good deals on sublease space*

2 an agreement in which sb who rents property from the owner rents all or part of it to sb else

▶ ,**sub'lease** /ˌsʌbˈliːs/ *verb* [+ obj *or* no obj]

= SUBLET *verb*

sublet /ˌsʌbˈlet/ *verb* [+ obj *or* no obj] (**subletting, sublet, sublet**) (*also* ,**sub'lease**)

(*Property*)

1 to rent to sb else all or part of a property that you rent from the owner: *They rented land from the government and sublet it* **to** *a hotel for car parking.*

2 to rent all or part of a property from sb that rents it from the owner: *They sublet office space at the airport* **from** *a major airline.*

▶ ,**sublet** /ˈsʌblet/ *noun* [C] = SUBLEASE *noun*

subliminal /ˌsʌbˈlɪmɪnl/ *adjective*

affecting your mind even though you are not aware of it: *subliminal advertising* (= that contains sounds or pictures you are not aware of)

★ **submit** /səbˈmɪt/ *verb* (**-tt-**)

1 [+ obj] to give a document, proposal, etc. to sb in authority so that they can study or consider it: *Completed projects must be submitted by 10 March.*

O *to submit an* **application/a plan/proposal/report** ◆ *to submit a* **bid/claim/an offer/a request**

2 [+ obj *or* no obj] to accept the authority or control of sb/sth; to agree to sth because of this: *The two sides have agreed to submit the dispute to arbitration.*

3 (*Law or formal*) [+ obj] to say or suggest sth ▶ **submission** /səbˈmɪʃn/ *noun* [U,C]: *When is the final date for the submission of proposals?*

suboptimal /ˌsʌbˈɒptɪməl; *AmE* -ˈɑːp-/ *adjective*

of less than the highest standard or quality: *There was a suboptimal performance of all the test shoes on wet surfaces.*

suboptimization , **-isation**

/ˌsʌbɒptɪmaɪˈzeɪʃn; *AmE* -ɑːptɪməˈz-/ *noun* [U]

a situation where individual parts of a business consider only the aims and benefits of their own departments, without considering other departments or the business as a whole

★ subordinate *adjective, noun, verb*

● *adjective* /sə'bɔːdɪnət; AmE -'bɔːrd-/
1 having less power or authority than sb else in a group or an organization: *The Project Manager is subordinate to the Product Manager.*
2 less important than sth else: *All other issues are subordinate to this one.*

● *noun* /sə'bɔːdɪnət; AmE -'bɔːrd-/ [C]
a person who has a position with less authority and power than sb else in an organization: *the relationship between subordinates and superiors*

● *verb* /sə'bɔːdɪneɪt; AmE -'bɔːrd-/ [+ obj]
to treat sth/sb as less important than sth/sb else: *Safety considerations were subordinated to commercial interests.*

subordinated /sə'bɔːdɪneɪtɪd; AmE -'bɔːrd-/
adjective [usually before noun]
(Finance) used to describe a debt that will only be paid after all other debts have been paid if the borrower has financial problems SYN JUNIOR
O subordinated *bonds/debentures/debt/notes*

subpar /ˌsʌb'pɑː(r)/ *adjective*
below an average or expected level: *subpar profit reports/performance*

subpoena /ˌsə'piːnə/ *noun, verb*
(Law)
● *noun* [C]
a written order for sb to attend a court as a WITNESS to give evidence or for documents to be brought as evidence: *He was served with a subpoena.*
● *verb* [+ obj]
to order sb to attend a court and give evidence as a WITNESS; to order documents to be brought to court as evidence: *The court has subpoenaed records from the company.*

subrogation /ˌsʌbrə'geɪʃn/ *noun* [U]
(Insurance) the right of an insurance company to claim back money it has paid out to sb from the person, company, etc. who caused the loss, damage or injury: *Relying on the subrogation clause in the policy, the insurer sued the negligent driver.*

★ subscribe /səb'skraɪb/ *verb* [no obj]
1 *(Stock Exchange)* to apply or agree to buy shares in a company: *Investors can register to subscribe to the share offer from today.* ◇ *subscribing for shares*
→ OVERSUBSCRIBED
2 *(Commerce)* to ask to receive, or to pay to receive, a service, regular copies of a magazine, etc: *Which journals do you subscribe to?* ◇ *Half a million people subscribe to their cable TV service.* ◇ *Subscribe to our free email newsletter.* → UNSUBSCRIBE

subscribed /səb'skraɪbd/ *adjective*
(Stock Exchange) used to describe how many new shares in a company have been applied for or bought: *The issue has now been fully subscribed.*
→ OVERSUBSCRIBED

sub,scribed 'capital = ISSUED CAPITAL

★ subscriber /səb'skraɪbə(r)/ *noun* [C]
1 *(Commerce)* a person who asks to receive, or who pays to receive, a service, regular copies of a magazine, etc: *subscribers to Newsweek/broadband services* ◇ *The digital channel has expanded its subscriber base to 2 million.* ◇ *the average revenue per subscriber*
2 *(Law)* a person who signs the MEMORANDUM OF ASSOCIATION for a new company and who joins with other members of the company in paying for a particular number of shares, appointing the first directors, etc.

★ subscription /səb'skrɪpʃn/ *noun* [C,U]
1 an amount of money that you pay to receive a service, regular copies of a magazine, etc.; the act of paying this money: *to take out a subscription to a*

trade magazine ◇ *an annual subscription of £500* ◇ *Copies are available by subscription.* ◇ *a subscription-based service*
O to buy/pay/take out *a subscription* • to cancel/renew *a subscription* • to charge *a subscription* • *a subscription charge/fee/price/rate*
2 *(Stock Exchange)* the act of applying for or agreeing to buy shares in a company: *Investors rescued the company by providing €23 million from a subscription for shares.* ◇ *The subscription list for the shares opens on Tuesday.*
O the subscription *list/price/period* • subscription *rights*

★ subsidiary /səb'sɪdiəri; AmE -dieri/ *adjective, noun*
● *adjective*
1 (about a company) owned or controlled by another company: *The company is selling off its subsidiary businesses.*
2 connected with sth but less important than it: *Apart from publishing, the company has several interesting subsidiary activities.*
● *noun* [C] (*plural* **subsidiaries**)
a company that is owned or controlled by another company: *Exis Power, a 58%-owned subsidiary of Exis Corp* → SALES SUBSIDIARY See note at GROUP

subsidize, **-ise** /'sʌbsɪdaɪz/ *verb* [+ obj]
to give money to sb or an organization to help pay for sth; to give a **subsidy**: *Their online service is subsidized by advertising.* ◇ *The company offered to subsidize anyone who came to work by bus or bicycle.*

subsidized, **-ised** /'sʌbsɪdaɪzd/ *adjective*
(about a price, a cost, etc.) reduced by a **subsidy**, usually from a government: *heavily subsidized imports from the EU* ◇ *Government employees can buy houses at a subsidized price.*

subsidy /'sʌbsədi/ *noun* [C,U] (*plural* **subsidies**)

SEE ALSO: **tax subsidy**

money that is paid by a government or an organization to reduce the costs of services or of producing goods so that their prices can be kept low: *a subsidy on petrol for transport companies* ◇ *public subsidy of aviation* ◇ *agricultural/farm/export subsidies* → SUBSIDIZE
O government/indirect/public/state *subsidies* • to get/qualify for/receive *a subsidy* • to give/grant/pay/provide *a subsidy*

subsistence /səb'sɪstəns/ *noun* [U]
the state of having just enough money or food to stay alive: *They work a 12-hour day for a subsistence wage* (= enough money to buy only the basic things you need).

sub'sistence al,lowance *noun* [C]
(especially BrE)
1 a small amount of money for food and other expenses that is paid to an employee who has to travel somewhere for their work
2 a small amount of money paid to a new employee from the money they will earn (an **advance**) so that they can live until they receive their first pay

,substance over 'form *phrase*
(Accounting) the important idea that a company's financial records should show what has actually happened, including what it actually owns or is owed, not just the legal form of pieces of business

'substitute goods *noun* [pl.]
(Economics) similar products or services for which an increase (or fall) in demand for one, due to a change in price, leads to a fall (or increase) in demand for the other

ˌsubstiˈtution efˌfect *noun* [sing.]
(*Economics*) the change in demand for a product or service that happens when its price changes relative to similar products or services → INCOME EFFECT

subtotal /'sʌbtəʊtl; *AmE* -toʊtl/ *noun* [C]
the total of a set of numbers which is then added to other totals to give a final number: *It is easy to calculate subtotals using the spreadsheet.*

subtract /səb'trækt/ *verb* [+ obj]
to take a number or an amount away from another number or amount: *To calculate overtime, subtract 40 from the total hours worked.* OPP ADD
→ TAKE (6)
▶ **subtraction** /səb'trækʃn/ *noun* [U,C]

suburb /'sʌbɜːb; *AmE* -bɜːrb/ *noun* [C]
an area where people live that is outside the centre of a city: *The factory is in a northern suburb of Paris.* ◇ *people who work in the city but live in the suburbs*

succession /sək'seʃn/ *noun*

SEE ALSO: management succession

1 [C, usually sing.] a number of things or people that follow each other in time or order; a series: *A succession of scandals have hit US companies recently.* ◇ *Interest rates have risen for the third month in succession.* ◇ *We lost four key members of staff in quick succession.*
2 (*HR*) [U] the act of taking over an official position or title; the right to take over an official position or title: *He became chairman in succession to Eric Marshall.*

sucˈcession ˌplanning *noun* [U]
(*HR*) the process of training and preparing employees in a company or an organization so that there will always be sb to replace a senior manager who leaves or retires ▶ **sucˈcession plan** *noun* [C]: *The CEO left before they could put a succession plan in place.*

successor /sək'sesə(r)/ *noun* [C]
a person or thing that comes after sb/sth else and takes their/its place: *Liam Cage is regarded as a potential successor to Chris Green as chief executive.*

succumb /sə'kʌm/ *verb* [no obj]
to fail to resist sth: *The company finally succumbed to a takeover bid.*

★ **sue** /suː; *BrE also* sjuː/ *verb* [+ obj *or* no obj]
to make a claim against sb in a court about sth that they have said or done to harm you: *The bank is being sued for $1 billion in damages by a group of angry investors.* ◇ *They threatened to sue if the work was not completed.*

sugˈgestion scheme *noun* [C]
(*HR*) a system in which employees, customers, etc. can give their ideas on how to improve aspects of a business: *You could earn yourself some money by putting forward your suggestions through our employee suggestion scheme.*

suit /suːt; *BrE also* sjuːt/ *noun* [C]
1 a set of clothes made of the same fabric, including a jacket and trousers/pants or a skirt: *a business suit* ◇ *a pinstripe suit*
2 (*informal*) [usually pl.] a person with an important job as a manager in a company or an organization, especially one thought of as being mainly concerned with financial matters or having a lot of influence: *We can leave the detailed negotiations to the suits.* → CREATIVE *noun*
3 = LAWSUIT
→ idiom at STRONG

suite /swiːt/ *noun* [C]

SEE ALSO: C-suite

1 a set of rooms, especially in a hotel or an office building: *a hotel/private suite* ◇ *a suite of rooms/offices* ◇ *questions being discussed in the company's executive suites* (=the offices of the top managers)
2 (*IT*) a set of related computer programs: *a suite of software development tools*

suitor /'suːtə(r); *BrE also* 'sjuː-/ *noun* [C]
a company that wants to buy another company: *They are under threat from a hostile suitor.*

★ **sum** /sʌm/ *noun, verb*
● *noun*

SEE ALSO: capital sum, lump sum

1 [C] an amount of money: *a large sum of money* ◇ *They paid a nominal sum of 1 cent per share.* ◇ *policies for savers with small sums to invest* ◇ *He was paid a six-figure sum* (= over 100 000 dollars, euros, etc.) *for joining the company.*
❍ *a considerable/large/significant/substantial sum* • *an enormous/a huge/vast sum* • *a modest/nominal/small sum*
2 [C, usually sing.] the number you get when you add two or more numbers together: *The sum of exports and imports rose by 5% in the first half of this year.*
❍ *to calculate/find/work out the sum (of sth)*
3 [C] a simple problem that involves calculating numbers: *I did a few sums in my head and decided it was a good price.* ◇ *If we've got our sums right, we should be profitable within six months.*
4 (*also* ˌsum ˈtotal) [sing.] all of sth: *The sum of all these small changes has had a huge effect on the industry.*
IDM **be greater/more than the ˌsum of its ˈparts** to be better or more effective as a group than you would think just by looking at the individual members of the group **in ˈsum** used to introduce a short statement of the main points of a discussion or speech
● *verb* (-mm-)
PHRV **ˌsum ˈup; ˌsum sth ˈup** to state the main points of sth in a short and clear form: *To sum up, there are three main ways of tackling the problem...* SYN SUMMARIZE → SUMMING-UP

ˌsum inˈsured (*also* ˌsum asˈsured) *noun* [C]
(*Insurance*) the maximum amount that a company will pay for a particular claim

summarize, **-ise** /'sʌməraɪz/ *verb* [+ obj *or* no obj]
to give the main points (a **summary**) of sth: *Can you summarize what was said in the meeting?* SYN SUM UP

★ **summary** /'sʌməri/ *noun, adjective*
● *noun* [C] (*plural* **summaries**)

SEE ALSO: executive summary, management summary

a short statement that gives only the main points of sth, not the details: *a two-page summary of the report* ◇ *The following is a summary of our conclusions.* → ABSTRACT
● *adjective* [only before noun]
1 giving only the main points of sth, not the details: *a summary financial statement*
2 done immediately, without paying attention to the normal process that should be followed: *a summary judgement* ◇ *Violence and theft may result in summary* (= instant) *dismissal.*
▶ **summarily** /'sʌmərəli; *AmE* sə'merəli/ *adverb*

ˌsumming-ˈup *noun* [C] (*plural* ˌsummings-ˈup)
1 (*Law*) a statement that the judge makes near the end of a trial in a court, in which he or she reminds the JURY about the evidence and the most

important points in the case before the JURY makes its decision
2 an occasion when sb states the main points of an argument, etc.

summons /'sʌmənz/ *noun, verb*
(*Law*)
● *noun* [C] (*plural* **summonses** /-zɪz/)
an order to appear in a court: *He received a summons to appear in court.*
● *verb* [+ obj]
to order sb to appear in a court: *He was summonsed to appear in court.*

,sum of the 'digits ,method (*also* ,sum of the ,years' 'digits ,method) *noun* [sing.] (*abbr* **SYD**)
(*Accounting*) a way of reducing the value of (**depreciating**) an asset in a company's financial records in which the amount taken from the asset's value decreases each year. The value of the asset (its **book value**) is reduced at a rate that gets smaller each year: *The sum of the digits method is used for assets that lose value rapidly in the first years of ownership, for example cars.* → DOUBLE-DECLINING BALANCE METHOD, REDUCING BALANCE METHOD, STRAIGHT-LINE METHOD

,sum 'total = SUM *noun* (4)

sundries /'sʌndriz/ *noun* [pl.]
various items, especially small ones, that are not important enough to be named separately: *You can claim up to £20 a day for sundries.*

sundry /'sʌndri/ *adjective* [only before noun]
various; not important enough to be named separately: *sundry expenses* ◇ *a sundry account* (= where items that do not belong in any another account are recorded)

,sundry 'debtor *noun* [C, usually pl.]
(*Accounting*) one of the companies or people who owe a relatively small amount of money to a company for services or goods usually not connected with the main work of the company: *sundry debtors accounts*

'sunk cost *noun* [C]
(*Accounting*) an amount of money that a company has already spent and cannot now get back: *a high level of sunk costs, such as all the network gear a phone company needs to serve customers*

'sunrise ,industry *noun* [C]
(*Economics*) a new growing industry, using new technology: *new sunrise industries like computers and telecommunications* ◇ *attempts to attract sunrise industries to the area* → SUNRISE INDUSTRY

'sunset clause = SUNSET PROVISION

'sunset ,industry *noun* [C]
(*Economics*) an old industry, using old technology, that has started to become less successful: *Shipbuilding is a classic sunset industry.* → SUNRISE INDUSTRY

'sunset pro,vision (*also* 'sunset clause) *noun* [C]
(*Law*) part of a law, rule, agreement, etc. that states that it will stop being effective on a particular date

sunshine /'sʌnʃaɪn/ *adjective* [only before noun]
(*especially AmE*)
used to describe laws, rules, etc. that are introduced to make government organizations do business in an open way, so that the public can attend meetings, etc. and check that nothing dishonest or illegal is happening: *The sunshine laws were introduced to curb corruption.* ◇ *a sunshine policy*

super- /'su:pə(r)/ *combining form*
1 (*in adjectives, adverbs and nouns*) extremely; more or better than normal: *super-advanced* ◇ *a super-fast aircraft* ◇ *a superstore*

2 (*in nouns and verbs*) above; over: *superstructure*

superannuation /,su:pər,ænju'eɪʃn/ *noun* [U]
(*especially BrE*)
(*HR*) a pension that you get, usually from your employer, when you retire and that you pay for while you are working; the money that you pay for this: *a superannuation fund/scheme*
O *to contribute to/pay/receive* superannuation

supercomputer /'su:pəkəmpju:tə(r); AmE 'su:pərk-/ *noun* [C]
(*IT*) one of the most powerful computers that exist at a particular time

superette /,su:pə'ret/ *noun* [C] (*AmE*)
a small supermarket

Superfund /'su:pəfʌnd; AmE 'su:pərf-/ *noun* [U; sing.]
in the US, a government system for finding and cleaning up places where dangerous waste has been thrown away: *The Environmental Protection Agency cleans up an average of 86 superfund sites a year.*

superhighway /,su:pə'haɪweɪ; AmE ,su:pər'h-/ = INFORMATION SUPERHIGHWAY

superintend /,su:pərɪn'tend/ *verb* [+ obj]
to be in charge of sth and make sure that everything is working, being done, etc. as it should be: *He superintended the building work.*
SYN SUPERVISE

superior /su:'pɪəriə(r); AmE su:'pɪr-/ *adjective, noun*
● *adjective*
1 better in quality than sb/sth else; greater than sb/sth else: *This model is technically superior **to** its competitors.* ◇ *investments with **vastly** superior returns*
2 (*used especially in advertisements*) of very good quality; better than other similar things: *We provide superior customer service.* ◇ *superior products*
3 higher in position, importance or rank: *He had the largest office for practical reasons, not because of his superior status.*
● *noun* [C]
a person of higher position, status or rank: *my immediate superior* (= the person immediately above me)

supermarket /'su:pəmɑːkɪt; AmE 'su:pərmɑːrkət/
(*AmE also* 'grocery store) *noun* [C]

SEE ALSO: financial supermarket

a shop/store that sells food, drinks and goods used in the home. People choose what they want from the shelves and pay for it as they leave (at the **checkouts**): *the UK's largest supermarket chain* ◇ *The new range will hit supermarket shelves* (= will go on sale) *next month.* See note at SHOP
O *a high-street/leading/major* supermarket ♦ *a* supermarket *chain/giant/group/operator/retailer* ♦ *supermarket aisles/checkouts/shelves/trolleys*

superstore /'su:pəstɔ:(r); AmE 'su:pərs-/ *noun* [C]
1 a very large supermarket that sells a wide variety of goods: *shopping at an out-of-town superstore*
O *an edge-of-town/out-of-town* superstore ♦ *a* superstore *chain/giant/group/operator/retailer*
2 a large shop/store that sells a wide variety of one type of goods, often at lower prices than normal See note at SHOP
O *a computer/DIY/an office/a toy/used-car* superstore ♦ *a discount* superstore ♦ *a superstore chain/giant/group/operator/retailer*

supertanker /ˈsuːpətæŋkə(r); *AmE* ˈsuːpərt-/ *noun* [C]
(*Transport*) a very large ship for carrying oil, etc.

supertax /ˈsuːpətæks; *AmE* ˈsuːpərt-/ *noun* [U,C]
(*especially BrE*)
an extra tax on sth that has already been taxed, especially a higher rate of tax that is paid by companies or people who earn more than a particular amount SYN SURTAX

★**supervise** /ˈsuːpəvaɪz; *AmE* ˈsuːpərv-/ *verb*
[+ obj or no obj]
to be in charge of sb/sth and make sure that everything is done correctly, safely, etc: *She supervised more than a thousand people in her last job.* ◇ *to supervise building work* ◇ *Trainees are closely supervised.* SYN OVERSEE
▶ **supervision** /ˌsuːpəˈvɪʒn; *AmE* ˌsuːpərˈv-/ *noun*
[U]: *The successful applicant will work **under the supervision of** our software development manager.*

supervisor /ˈsuːpəvaɪzə(r); *AmE* ˈsuːpərv-/ *noun* [C]
a person who is in charge of sb/sth and makes sure that everything is done correctly, safely, etc: *If you need to leave work early, speak to your supervisor first.* ◇ *my **immediate** supervisor* (= the person just above me) See note at BOSS

supervisory /ˌsuːpəˈvaɪzəri; *AmE* ˌsuːpərˈv-/ *adjective*
connected with the work of making sure that a job or an activity is done correctly, safely, etc: *She has a supervisory role on the project.*

ˈ**supervisory board** *noun* [C with sing./pl. verb]
in some countries, a group of directors who represent a company's shareholders, advising the directors who manage the company and checking that everything is done correctly: *The company's five-person **supervisory board** oversees strategy.*

ˌ**supervisory ˈmanagement** *noun* [U; C with sing./pl. verb]
(*HR*) the lowest level of managers in a company who are directly responsible for the work of a group of employees; the work that the managers do: *We offer personal development for all levels, from supervisory management to main board level.*
→ FIRST-LINE MANAGER

supplement *noun, verb*
●*noun* /ˈsʌplɪmənt/ [C]
1 a thing that is added to sth else to improve it or make it more complete: *Videoconferencing is a useful supplement to traditional meetings.*
2 an amount of money that you pay for an extra service or item: *There is a supplement of €30 per person for a single room.*
3 something that you eat in addition to what you usually eat, especially in order to stay healthy: *an online seller of vitamins and dietary supplements*
4 an extra section that comes with a newspaper or a book, report, etc: *a supplement to the main report*
→ COLOUR SUPPLEMENT
●*verb* /ˈsʌplɪment/ [+ obj]
to add sth to sth else in order to improve or make it more complete: *Employees' salaries are supplemented by performance bonuses.* ◇ *We supplement your training **with** team coaching.*

supplementary /ˌsʌplɪˈmentri/ (*AmE* **supplemental** /ˌsʌplɪˈmentl/) *adjective*
paid or provided in addition to sth else: *a supplementary charge/income* ◇ *A letter containing supplementary information was sent with the catalogue.* ◇ *supplemental payments made to workers in especially dangerous jobs*

★**supplier** /səˈplaɪə(r)/ *noun* [C]
SEE ALSO: first-tier supplier, second-tier supplier
1 a company that provides raw materials or pieces of equipment to companies that make goods; a company that provides finished goods, for example for other companies to sell to the public: *suppliers to the catering industry* ◇ *the world's largest supplier of mobile phones* ◇ *Boeing are the airline's **sole** (= only) supplier of aircraft.* ◇ *We have reduced our **supplier base** (= the number of companies that supply us) by half over the last year.* ◇ *a building supplier* (= a company that supplies materials for building) SYN VENDOR See note at SUPPLY CHAIN
◒ *a big/key/large/leading/major supplier*
2 a company that supplies gas, water or electricity: *a UK-based energy supplier* ◇ *a supplier of gas and power* ◇ *She claims that a third of households have switched suppliers* (= changed to another company) *in the last three years.*

supˈplier ˌrating = VENDOR RATING

★**supply** /səˈplaɪ/ *noun, verb*
●*noun* (*plural* **supplies**)
SEE ALSO: excess ~, money ~
1 [U] the act of providing sth or making it available to be used: *A delay in the supply of parts stopped work at the plant for a week.* ◇ *We need to streamline our supply network.* ◇ *It is vital for a manufacturer to have a reliable **supply base** (= a number of companies that supply materials, parts, etc.)*
2 [C, usually sing.] an amount of sth that is provided or available to be used: *Car manufacturers like to have a 64-day supply of vehicles.* ◇ *There is a plentiful supply of skilled labour.* ◇ *Up to 90% of the country's gas supplies will be imported by 2020.*
◒ *a dwindling/large/plentiful/small/steady supply (of sth)* • *to get/have/produce/provide/receive a supply* • *to boost/disrupt/increase/reduce a supply*
3 [U] the amount of sth that is offered for sale: *When demand for a product exceeds supply, it is usual for the price to go up.* ◇ *to match supply with demand* ◇ *The fall in steel prices is the result of a global supply glut (= a situation where there is too much steel available).* ◇ *The rise in oil prices has been driven by fears of a supply crunch (= a situation where there is not enough oil available).* → DEMAND *noun* (1), SUPPLY AND DEMAND
◒ *to exceed/match/outstrip supply* • *supply falls/increases* • *a supply crunch/glut/shortage/shortfall*
4 **supplies** [pl.] basic things that are needed for a particular purpose: *office supplies* ◇ *the nation's leading provider of medical supplies*
◒ *limited/plentiful/vital supplies* • *to lay in/provide supplies* • *supplies run low/run out/run short*
⚑ *ration of short ~ adj*
●*verb* [+ obj] (**supplies, supplying, supplied, supplied**)
1 to provide raw materials, equipment, etc. to companies, especially in large quantities; to provide goods or services: *The company supplies Daewoo **with** a range of equipment.* ◇ *We supply Internet-based services **to** big businesses in Europe.*
2 to provide sb/sth with sth that they need or want: *Can you supply a list of recent customers?* ◇ *Employees were supplied **with** home computers.*

supˌply and deˈmand *noun* [U]
(*Economics*) the relationship between the amount of goods or services that are available and the amount that people want to buy, especially when this controls prices: *Improvements to our distribution network allow us to maintain a better balance between supply and demand.* ◇ *the laws of supply and demand*
◒ *a balance/gap/an imbalance/a mismatch between supply and demand* • *to balance/match supply and demand*

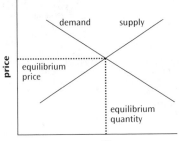

quantity

★ **sup'ply chain** *noun* [C]
(*Production*) the whole series of processes, companies, places, etc. that are involved in making and selling a product. The **supply chain** includes the supply of raw materials and parts and the processes of manufacturing, storing, transporting and selling the product to the customer: *every level/ point/stage in the supply chain* ◇ *We develop tools to help companies manage their supply chains.* ◇ *We have achieved a 5% reduction in supply-chain costs.* ◇ *This diagram represents the various **links in** the supply chain.* ◇ *The system allows us to monitor shipments as they move through the supply chain.*
→ DISTRIBUTION CHAIN
O *to **improve/optimize/overhaul/rationalize/ streamline** the supply chain • to **shorten/tighten** the supply chain • **along/down/in/through/up** the supply chain*

VOCABULARY BUILDING

The supply chain
Supplier/Vendor
(supplies materials and parts)
↓
Producer
(supplies finished goods)
↓
Distributors
— *wholesalers* (sell in large quantities)
— *retailers* (sell to the public)
— *resellers* (especially for computers and software)
↓
Customers
— *consumers*
— *businesses*

Note: The word **supplier** can be used to describe anyone in the chain who sells something to another person. So a distributor can refer to a producer as their supplier. In a similar way, anyone who buys from somebody earlier in the chain is their **customer**.

---

sup,ply chain e'vent ,management (*abbr* **SCEM**) (*also* **e'vent ,management**) *noun* [U]
(*Production*) a system for predicting, controlling and dealing with unexpected events in any part of the SUPPLY CHAIN, for example when customers order more of a product than usual: *They have developed a number of solutions* (= *pieces of software*) *for supply chain event management.*

sup'ply chain ,management *noun* [U] (*abbr* **SCM**)
(*Production*) the control of all the materials, money

and information in the whole series of processes involved in making, selling and delivering a product: *supply chain management software*

sup'ply price *noun* [C]
(*Economics*) the lowest price that sellers are willing to accept for providing a particular amount of a product or service: *The supply price usually goes up as demand increases.*

sup'ply side *noun* [sing.] (*usually* **the supply side**)
(*Economics*) the part of an economy that relates to the production and supply of goods and services: *attempts to strengthen the supply side of the economy to increase productivity* → DEMAND SIDE
▶ **sup'ply-side** *adjective* [only before noun]: *supply-side measures/policies* (= that try to increase the supply of goods and services and create jobs)
sup'ply-,sider *noun* [C]: *When the government increased taxes, supply-siders predicted an economic collapse.*

★ **support** /sə'pɔːt; *AmE* -'pɔːrt/ *verb, noun*
● *verb* [+ obj]
1 to help and encourage sb/sth by saying or showing that you agree with them/it: *If you raise it in the meeting, I'll support you.* ◇ *Managers and employees strongly supported the plan.*
2 to help sth/sb by giving it/them money: *Several major companies are supporting the project.*
3 to give or be ready to give help to sb/sth if they need it: *We will continue to support customers still using previous versions of the software.*
4 to prevent sth from failing; to help sth continue: *Oil prices are being supported by fears of a shortage.*
5 to help to show that sth is true or correct: *The decision cannot be supported by the data.*
6 (*IT*) (about a piece of computer software or equipment, etc.) to allow a particular type of software, equipment or data to be used with it: *The program supports HTML formatting.*
● *noun* [U]

SEE ALSO: **price support, technical ~, tech ~**

1 help and encouragement that you give to sb/sth by saying or showing that you agree with them/it: *support **for** union leaders* ◇ *There is strong support for the merger **from** shareholders.* ◇ *The restructuring program has the **full** support of employees.* ◇ *The CEO spoke **in support of** the proposal.*
O *broad/unanimous/widespread support • to give/ lend/offer/pledge/withdraw your support • to declare/express/indicate your support • to gain/ get/receive/secure/win support*
2 money that is given to sth/sb in order to help it/ them become successful: *A German media group provided €85 million in **financial support** to the firm.*
O *to give/provide support • to look for/receive/seek support*
3 help that is given to sb/sth or available if needed: *We are committed to providing the best after-sales support to customers.*
O *to offer/provide support*
4 the act of preventing sth from failing or helping sth to continue: *There will be no official support **for** the dollar until it has fallen further.*
O *to give/provide support*
5 evidence that helps to show that sth is true: *The statistics offer further support **for** our theory.*
O *to give/offer/provide support*

sup'port staff *noun* [C, usually sing.]
(*HR*) the people in a company who help it to operate, but who are not directly involved in the company's business: *The bank has had to lay off support staff, including computer programmers and*

translators. **HELP** In the singular, **support staff** is often used with a plural verb, especially in British English: *Our support staff is/are based in our London office.*

suppress /sə'pres/ *verb* [+ obj]
1 to prevent sth from growing or developing: *New anti-smoking laws have suppressed demand for tobacco.*
2 to prevent sth from being published or made known: *The company went to court to try to suppress the article.*

supranational /ˌsuːprəˈnæʃnəl/ *adjective*
involving more than one country: *supranational institutions such as the European Commission*

★**surcharge** /'sɜːtʃɑːdʒ; AmE 'sɜːrtʃɑːrdʒ/ *noun* [C]

SEE ALSO: **import surcharge**

an extra amount of money that you must pay in addition to the usual price: *The airline has imposed a surcharge on some routes to help pay for extra security.*
O to **add/impose** a surcharge ♦ to **pay** a surcharge
▶'**surcharge** *verb* [+ obj]

surf /sɜːf; AmE sɜːrf/ *verb* [+ obj or no obj]
to look at many different websites: *I was surfing the Web looking for exciting new products.*
O to surf **the Internet/Net/Web**
▶'**surfer** *noun* [C]: *The new service is for Internet surfers who use broadband.* → NET SURFER, SILVER SURFER '**surfing** *noun* [U]: *Cookies are files that contain personal Web surfing data.*

'**surface mail** *noun* [U]
letters, etc. carried by road, rail or sea, not by air: *to send sth (by) surface mail* → AIRMAIL, SNAIL MAIL

'**surface ˌtransport** *noun* [U]
1 the activity of carrying goods or of travelling by road, rail or sea, not by air: *See below for surface transport costs.*
2 vehicles that travel on roads, rail, or sea, not in the air: *Here is a map if you are arriving at the conference by surface transport.*

surge /sɜːdʒ; AmE sɜːrdʒ/ *verb, noun*
●*verb* [no obj]
to suddenly increase in value: *Share prices surged.* ◊ *Shares in the biotechnology company surged almost 12% yesterday.*
PHR V ˌsurge aˈhead to increase or improve quickly, by a large amount, and often more than other prices, companies, products, etc: *Demand for cellphones has surged ahead in Rwanda.*
●*noun* [C]
a sudden increase in the amount or number of sth; a large amount of sth: *a surge in consumer spending* ◊ *You need to protect your computer equipment from power surges.* → UPSURGE

surpass /sə'pɑːs; AmE sər'pæs/ *verb* [+ obj]
to be or do better than sth/sb: *Sales so far this year have surpassed expectations.*

★**surplus** /'sɜːpləs; AmE 'sɜːrp-/ *noun, adjective*
●*noun* [C,U]

SEE ALSO: **buyer's surplus, consumer ~, structural ~, trade ~**

1 an amount that is extra or more than you need: *a surplus of housing* ◊ *The area has large job surpluses, requiring 10 000 people to fill available posts.* ◊ *Skilled workers are in surplus in some regions.*
SYN GLUT **OPP** SHORTAGE
2 (*Accounting*; *Economics*) the amount by which money that a government or business receives is greater than the amount of money spent in a

particular period of time: *The country has a huge budget surplus as it is a large oil exporting nation.* ◊ *The balance of payments was in surplus last year* (= the value of exports was greater than the value of imports). ◊ *The final-salary pension plan still has a healthy surplus.* → DEFICIT See note at PROFIT
●*adjective*
more than is needed or used: *surplus cash/funds* ◊ *Surplus grain is being sold for export.* ◊ *These items are surplus to requirements* (= not needed). ◊ *The industry is suffering from surplus capacity* (= it can produce more than is needed) *across the world.*

surrender /sə'rendə(r)/ *verb, noun*
●*verb*
1 (*Insurance*) [+ obj] if you **surrender** a life insurance agreement you end it before its official end date and receive back part of the money you have paid: *People surrendering their policies early will now have a fifth of their money deducted.*
2 (*Finance*) [+ obj] (usually used in newspapers) if a share, an index, etc. **surrenders** a particular amount, its value falls by that amount: *The Nasdaq has surrendered 6% in the last two weeks.*
3 [+ obj or no obj] to give up sth when you are forced to or when it is difficult for you to continue: *They did not want to surrender control of key companies to foreign control.* ◊ *In June the vice-chairman surrendered to shareholder pressure and resigned.*
●*noun*
1 (*Insurance*) [C,U] an act of ending a life insurance agreement before its official end date: *The company plans to impose a 10% penalty on early policy surrenders.* ◊ *The surrender value* (= the amount you get when you end a policy) *of my policy has fallen again.*
O a surrender **charge/fee/penalty/value**
2 [U; sing.] an act of giving up sth when you are forced to or when it is difficult for you to continue: *Conditions included the surrender of her passport.*

surtax /'sɜːtæks; AmE 'sɜːrt-/ *noun* [U,C]
(*especially AmE*)
an extra tax on sth that has already been taxed, especially a higher rate of tax that is paid by companies or people who earn more than a particular amount: *They have imposed a 10% surtax on oil profits.* **SYN** SUPERTAX

★**survey** *noun, verb*
●*noun* /'sɜːveɪ; AmE 'sɜːrveɪ/ [C]
1 an investigation of the opinions, behaviour, etc. of a particular group of people, which is usually done by asking them questions: *The report is based on a survey of 5 000 households.* ◊ *We are conducting a survey into the attitudes of consumers to online shopping.* ◊ *The survey showed that 52 per cent of small firms think that the new law will seriously affect their business.* → POLL
O to **carry out/conduct/do** a survey ♦ to **participate in/respond to/take part in** a survey ♦ a survey **finds/indicates/reveals/shows sth**
2 a general study or description of sth: *The government has published a survey of safety conditions in factories.* → OVERVIEW
O to **carry out/commission/conduct/do** a survey ♦ to **issue/publish** a survey ♦ a survey **finds/indicates/reports/reveals/shows/underlines sth**
3 the act of examining and recording the measurements, features, etc. of an area of land or of a building: *An engineer conducted a structural survey of the factory.*
O to **carry out/do/make** a survey ♦ a **full/geological/structural/valuation** survey
●*verb* /sə'veɪ; AmE sər'veɪ/ [+ obj]
1 to investigate the opinions or behaviour of a group of people by asking them a series of questions: *87% of the 1 000 companies surveyed employ part-time staff.*

2 to study and give a general description of sth: *The websites of the major stores were surveyed to see how easy to use they were.*
3 to measure and record the features, etc. of an area of land or of a building: *Have the house surveyed before you decide whether to buy it.*

surveyor /səˈveɪə(r); *AmE* sərˈv-/ *noun* [C]

SEE ALSO: **quantity surveyor**

1 a person whose job is to examine and record the details of a piece of land
2 (*BrE*) (*AmE* **inˈspector**) a person whose job is to examine a building to make sure it is in good condition, usually done for sb who is thinking of buying it: *a surveyor's report* ◇ *A number of* **chartered surveyors** *reported a rise in the number of people planning to move house.*
3 (*BrE*) an official whose job is to check that sth is accurate, of good quality, etc: *the surveyor of public works*

suspend /səˈspend/ *verb* [+ obj]
1 to officially stop sth for a time; to prevent sth from being active, used, etc. for a time: *to suspend payments/talks* ◇ *Production has been suspended while safety checks are carried out.* ◇ *The shares were suspended from trading for an entire day.*
2 to delay sth; to arrange for sth to happen later than planned: *The introduction of the new system has been suspended until next year.*
3 (*HR*) (*usually* **be suspended**) to officially prevent sb from doing their job for a time: *He has been suspended on full pay while the complaint is investigated.* ◇ *Two more employees have been suspended from their jobs.*

susˈpense acˌcount *noun* [C]
(*Accounting*) a temporary account in which a company records items until they can be put into the correct or final account

suspension /səˈspenʃn/ *noun* [U,C]
1 (*HR*) the act of officially removing sb from their job for a period of time, usually as a punishment: *the temporary suspension of five employees*
2 the act of delaying sth for a period of time: *The incident led to the suspension of talks between union and management.* ◇ *a share trading suspension*

susˈpension file *noun* [C]
a file made of stiff card with metal edges that hangs in the drawer of a FILING CABINET—Picture at OFFICE

sustain /səˈsteɪn/ *verb* [+ obj]
1 to make sth continue for some time without becoming less: *a period of sustained economic growth* ◇ *a sustained period of falling prices* ◇ *We have enough cash to sustain the business for a year.*
2 to experience sth bad: *The company sustained massive losses.*
3 to provide evidence to support an opinion, a theory, etc: *The evidence is not detailed enough to sustain his argument.*
4 (*Law*) to decide that a claim, etc. is valid

★ sustainable /səˈsteɪnəbl/ *adjective*
1 that can continue or be continued for a long time: *sustainable increases in sales* ◇ *The company's growth rate is not sustainable.* ◇ *sustainable economic growth/recovery* ◇ *The goal of business strategy is to gain sustainable competitive advantage.*
2 involving the use of natural products and energy in a way that does not harm the environment: *the use of wind power as a source of sustainable* **energy**
▶ **sustainability** /səˌsteɪnəˈbɪləti/ *noun* [U]: *The report cast doubt on the sustainability of consumer spending.*

swamp /swɒmp; *AmE* swɑːmp/ *verb* [+ obj]
to make sb/sth have more of sth than they can deal with: *We are swamped* **with** *work at the moment.* ◇ *The market has been swamped* **by** *cheap imports.*

★ swap (*also spelled* **swop**) /swɒp; *AmE* swɑːp/ *verb, noun*
● **verb** (**-pp-**)
1 [+ obj] to give sth to sb and receive sth in exchange: *to swap ideas/information* **with** *colleagues*
2 [+ obj *or* no obj] **swap (sth/sb) (over/around/round)** to change places with sb; to change the place of two or more people or things, so that each one finishes where the other one was before: *The workers swap over when the shift finishes at 10.* ◇ *We swapped our desks around so I was nearer the door.* SYN SWITCH
3 [+ obj] to replace sth with sth else: *I'm swapping my car* **for** *a smaller model.* SYN SWITCH
● **noun** [C]

SEE ALSO: **debt-equity swap, debt-for-equity ~, debt ~, interest-rate ~**

1 an act of exchanging one person or thing for another: *Let's* **do a swap.** *You work Friday night and I'll do Saturday.*
2 (*Finance*) an exchange of different types of payments between two companies, for example payments in different currencies or with different interest rates
3 (*Finance*) an act of exchanging one investment or asset for another, instead of for money: *The company is negotiating a swap deal with bondholders.*

swatch /swɒtʃ; *AmE* swɑːtʃ/ *noun* [C]
a small piece of fabric used to show people what a larger piece would look or feel like

ˈsweat ˌequity *noun* [U] (*informal*)
the work, rather than money, that the owners of a new business invest in it and for which they receive shares in the business

sweatshop /ˈswetʃɒp; *AmE* -ʃɑːp/ *noun* [C]
a place where people work for low wages in poor conditions: *sweatshop labour/conditions*

sweeping /ˈswiːpɪŋ/ *adjective* [usually before noun]
having an important effect on a large part of sth: *Consumer groups are calling for sweeping* **changes** *in the European car market.*

the sweeps /swiːps/ *noun* [pl.] (*AmE*) (*informal*)
a time when television companies examine their programmes to find out which ones are the most popular, especially in order to calculate advertising rates: *Which news network will have the highest daytime viewership in the November sweeps?*

sweeten /ˈswiːtn/ *verb* [+ obj]
to make sth more pleasant or acceptable: *The supermarket has sweetened its offer* (= offered more money) *for its smaller competitor.*

sweetener /ˈswiːtnə(r)/ *noun* [C] (*informal*)
something that is given to sb in order to persuade them to do sth: *Staff were offered an extra day's holiday as a sweetener.* ◇ *He was accused of accepting sweeteners from suppliers.* → BRIBE

ˈsweetheart deal *noun* [C]
a private agreement between two groups or organizations which benefits one or both of them but is often unfair to other people who are involved: *Critics have accused the government of having a sweetheart deal with the airline.*

S.W.I.F.T. ™ /ˈswɪft/ *abbr* **Society for Worldwide Interbank Financial Telecommunciations** a computer network that allows member banks in all parts of the world to move money from one to another safely

swindle /ˈswɪndl/ *verb, noun*
● *verb* [+ obj]
to cheat sb in order to get sth, especially money, from them: *He swindled customers **out of** over 50 million dollars.* ▶ **'swindler** *noun* [C]
● *noun* [C, usually sing.]
a situation in which sb uses dishonest or illegal methods in order to get money from a company, another person, etc: *an insurance swindle*

swing /swɪŋ/ *verb, noun*
● *verb* (**swung, swung** /swʌŋ/)
1 [+ obj *or* no obj] to change or make sb/sth change from one level, situation, opinion, etc. to another: *Energy and food prices can swing widely from month to month.* ◇ *The company swung back into profit last year.*
2 [+ obj] to succeed in getting or achieving sth, sometimes in a slightly dishonest way: *Until a few years ago, only large companies could swing these deals.*
● *noun* [C]
a change from one level, situation or opinion to another; the amount by which sth changes: *The vote reflected a swing in favour of the euro.* ◇ *huge price swings*

'swing shift = BACK SHIFT

swipe /swaɪp/ *verb* [+ obj]
to pass a plastic card through a special machine that is able to read the information stored on it: *You just swipe a credit card and enter a password to use the system.*

'swipe card *noun* [C]
a special plastic card with information recorded on it which can be read by an electronic device: *Access to the building is by swipe card only.*

switch /swɪtʃ/ *noun, verb*
● *noun* [C]
SEE ALSO: **bait-and-switch**
1 a small device that you press or move up and down in order to turn a light or piece of electrical equipment on and off: *the on-off switch*
2 a change from one thing to another, especially when this is sudden and complete: *I've decided to* **make the switch** *from full-time to part-time work.* ◇ *a switch in/of policy* ◇ *a policy switch*
● *verb*
1 [+ obj *or* no obj] **switch (sth) (over) (from sth) (to sth)** | **switch (between A and B)** to change or make sth change from one thing to another: *We're in the process of switching over to a new system of invoicing.* ◇ *Press these two keys to switch between documents on screen.* ◇ *The meeting has been switched to next week.*
2 [+ obj] **switch sth (with sth)** | **switch sth (over/ around/round)** to exchange one thing for another: *I'll switch desks with you if you want to be near the window.* [SYN] SWAP
3 [+ obj *or* no obj] **switch (sth) (with sb)** | **switch (sth) (over/around/round)** to change jobs, work times, etc. with sb: *I managed to switch my shift with someone.* [SYN] SWAP
[PHR V] **,switch 'off/'on; ,switch sth 'off/'on** to turn a light, machine, etc. off/on by pressing a button or switch: *I forgot to switch off my computer.*

switchboard /ˈswɪtʃbɔːd; *AmE* -bɔːrd/ *noun* [C]
the central part of a telephone system used by a company, etc., where telephone calls are answered

and connected (**put through**) to the appropriate person or department; the people who work this equipment: *a switchboard operator* ◇ *Call the switchboard and ask for extension 410.*

swop = SWAP

SWOT /swɒt; *AmE* swɑːt/ *noun* [U]
a method used to study an organization and plan how it can change and grow, by analysing its strengths and weaknesses, the opportunities it has and the threats it faces: *A SWOT analysis is an effective way of analysing your company's potential.* [NOTE] SWOT is formed from the initial letters of 'strengths', 'weaknesses', 'opportunities' and 'threats'.

SYD /ˌes waɪ ˈdiː/ *abbr*
(*Accounting*) **sum of the year's digits** a short way of referring to the SUM OF THE DIGITS METHOD

symbol /ˈsɪmbl/ *noun* [C]
SEE ALSO: **status symbol**
1 a sign, number, letter, etc. that has a particular meaning: *The company uses a lion as its symbol.*
2 a company, a person, an object, an event, etc. that represents a more general quality or situation: *Fiat was a symbol of Italy's economic success.*
3 (*Stock Exchange*) = TICKER SYMBOL

,sympa'thetic strike = SYMPATHY STRIKE

sympathy /ˈsɪmpəθi/ *noun* [U;C, usually pl.] (*plural* **sympathies**)
the act of showing support for or approval of an idea, a cause, an organization, etc: *I have a lot of sympathy **with** what he has to say.*
[IDM] **in 'sympathy with sth** happening because sth else has happened: *Share prices slipped in sympathy with the German market.*

'sympathy strike (*also* **,sympa'thetic strike**, *less frequent*) *noun* [C]
(*HR*) an occasion when a group of workers stop work in order to show support for another group who have stopped work: *Train drivers staged a sympathy strike to show solidarity with the firefighters.*

symposium /sɪmˈpəʊziəm; *AmE* -ˈpoʊ-/ *noun* [C] (*plural* **symposia** /-ziə/ *or* **symposiums**)
a meeting at which experts have discussions about a particular subject: *an international symposium on change in the financial environment*

★ **syndicate** *noun, verb*
● *noun* /ˈsɪndɪkət/ [C]
(*Finance*) a group of people or companies who work together and help each other in order to achieve a particular aim: *a 24-strong syndicate of banks* ◇ *a 24-member banking syndicate* ◇ *An international syndicate is negotiating to buy the carmaker.*
● *verb* /ˈsɪndɪkeɪt/
1 (*Finance*) [+ obj] (*usually* **be syndicated**) to control or manage sth as a **syndicate**: *The bank syndicated the loan to five other banks to cut the risk.*
2 [+ obj *or* no obj] to form a **syndicate**: *syndicated lenders*
▶ **syndication** /ˌsɪndɪˈkeɪʃn/ *noun* [U]: *the syndication of loans*

syndicated /ˈsɪndɪkeɪtɪd/ *adjective* [only before noun]
(*Finance*) (about a loan) provided by a group of banks or investors (a **syndicate**)
O *a syndicated **credit facility/credit line/loan***

★ **synergy** /ˈsɪnədʒi; *AmE* -ərdʒi/ *noun* [C,U] (*plural* **synergies**)
the extra power, success, profits, etc. achieved by two or more groups, people, companies, etc. working together instead of on their own: *The combined companies aimed to achieve synergies of*

€300 m a year by 2006. ◇ We need to exploit the synergy **between** university research and commercial manufacture.

➊ to **achieve/create/deliver/generate** synergies ♦ **cost/ financial/operational** synergies ♦ **marketing/ merger** synergies ♦ synergy **benefits/savings**

▶ **synergistic** /ˌsɪnəˈdʒɪstɪk/ AmE -ərˈdʒ-/ adjective: a synergistic merger with another business ◇ synergistic relationships

synthesize , **-ise** /ˈsɪnθəsaɪz/ verb [+ obj]
1 to combine separate ideas, styles, pieces of information, etc: The results of all the research are synthesized in this document.
2 (Technical) to produce a substance by means of chemical or other processes: synthesized drugs
3 (Technical) to produce sound by electronic methods: a computer-synthesized voice

synthetic /sɪnˈθetɪk/ adjective, noun
● **adjective**
artificial; made by combining chemical substances rather than being produced naturally by plants or animals: skin products with no synthetic ingredients ◇ The new fabric bridges the gap between synthetic and natural materials. ▶ **synthetically** /sɪnˈθetɪkli/ adverb: synthetically produced drugs
● **noun** [C]
an artificial substance or material: cotton fabrics and synthetics

syphon = SIPHON

★ **system** /ˈsɪstəm/ noun [C]

SEE ALSO: **accelerated cost recovery system, accounting ~, banking ~, decision support ~, environmental management ~**, etc.

1 an organized set of ideas or theories, or a particular way of doing sth: They have introduced a new system **for** handling complaints. ◇ We are changing our system of recruitment. ◇ the tax system **2** a group of things, pieces of equipment, etc. that are connected or work together: an electronic trading system that connects investors and dealers ◇ a computer/transport system
→ idiom at PLAY verb

systematic /ˌsɪstəˈmætɪk/ adjective
done according to a system or plan, in a thorough, efficient or determined way: We need to handle customer feedback in a more systematic way.
➊ a systematic **analysis/approach/process**
▶ **systematically** /ˌsɪstəˈmætɪkli/ adverb: The information was systematically recorded and analysed.

ˌsystematic ˈrisk (also ˌmarket ˈrisk) noun [U,C]
(Finance) risk that affects the price of all investments of a particular type (shares, bonds, etc.), for example the possible effects of political or economic change → UNSYSTEMATIC RISK

systemic /sɪˈstemɪk; sɪˈstiːmɪk/ adjective
(Technical) affecting or connected with the whole of a system: The report identified systemic weaknesses in the network. ▶ **systemically** /sɪˈstemɪkli; sɪˈstiːm-/ adverb

sysˌtemic ˈrisk noun [U,C]
(Finance) risk that can cause serious problems for a whole system, especially the risk that a problem in one market can lead to very serious problems for the whole market: Where a bank is closed down there is also systemic risk.

ˈsystem ˌintegrator = INTEGRATOR (1)

ˈsystems ˌanalyst (also ˈsystems ˌarchitect, ˌbusiness ˈsystems ˌanalyst) noun [C]
(IT) a person whose job is to analyse the needs of a business company or an organization and then design processes for working efficiently using computer programs ⟨SYN⟩ COMPUTER ANALYST
▶ **ˈsystems aˌnalysis** (also ˈsystems ˌarchitecture, ˌbusiness ˈsystems aˌnalysis) noun [U]

ˈsystems ˌintegrator = INTEGRATOR (1)

ˈsystems ˌprogrammer noun [C]
(IT) a person who writes computer programs for a company's computer system

T t

t/a abbr (especially BrE) (only used in written English)
a short way of writing **trading as** in the name of a business, especially one owned by a SOLE TRADER: Jo Wilmot, t/a Jo's Supplies

tab /tæb/ noun, verb
● **noun** [C]
1 (informal) a bill for goods or services; the price or cost of sth: employers who pay the tab for business travel ◇ The tab for building the center was more than $450 million. ◇ Shareholders will have to **pick up the tab** (= pay the cost) for the failure of the company.
2 a record of the items ordered in a bar or restaurant: Can I put it on my tab?
3 a small piece of paper, fabric, metal, etc. attached to the edge of sth, that is used to give information about it or to help you find sth; a similar device on information shown on a computer screen: The website is well designed, with good use of colour-coded tabs.
4 = TAB STOP
● **verb** (-bb-)
1 [+ obj] to mark sth with a **tab**: tabbed pages
2 [+ obj] (especially AmE) to say that sb is suitable for a particular job or role or to describe them in a

particular way: He has been tabbed by many people as the next CEO.
3 [no obj] to use TAB STOPS

★ **table** /ˈteɪbl/ noun, verb
● **noun** [C]

SEE ALSO: **life tables, negotiating ~, round ~**

a list of facts or numbers arranged in a special order, usually in rows and columns: The table shows sales in each main market over the last five years.
⟨IDM⟩ **on the ˈtable 1** (BrE) (about a plan, suggestion, etc.) offered to people so that they can consider or discuss it: Management have put several new proposals on the table. **2** (especially AmE) (about a plan, suggestion, etc.) not going to be discussed or considered until a future date: The issue is on the table for future negotiations.
● **verb** [+ obj]
1 (BrE) to present sth formally for discussion: The firm tabled a motion to shareholders to reduce the number of board members.
2 (especially AmE) to leave an idea, a proposal, etc. to be discussed at a later date: They voted to table the proposal until the following meeting.

'tab stop (*also* **tab**) *noun* [C]
a fixed position in a line of a document that you are typing that shows where a piece of text or a column of figures, etc. will begin

tabular /'tæbjələ(r)/ *adjective* [usually before noun]
presented or arranged in rows and columns (a **table**): *tabular data* ◊ *The results are presented in tabular form.*

tabulate /'tæbjuleɪt/ *verb* [+ obj]
to arrange facts or figures in columns or lists so that they can be read easily: *December sales have not yet been tabulated.* ◊ *to tabulate results/complaints*
▶ **tabulation** /ˌtæbju'leɪʃn/ *noun* [U,C]

'T-ac,count *noun* [C]
(*Accounting*) a simple way of recording financial TRANSACTIONS, consisting of a DEBIT column and a credit column

T-account

Date	Item	Title	Amount
		CASH	
Jan	3 Bank	4 000	Jan 5 Purchases 2 500
	10 Sales	6 400	21 Wages 6 200
			21 Balance c/d 1 700
	Total →	10 400	10 400
	debit side		**credit side**

tachograph /'tækəgrɑːf; *AmE* -græf/ *noun* [C]
(*Transport*) a device that is used in vehicles such as large lorries/trucks and some types of buses to measure their speed, how far they have travelled and when the driver has stopped to rest

,tacit 'knowledge (*also* **im,plicit 'knowledge**) *noun* [U]
(*HR*) **tacit knowledge** is knowledge that sb gains from working in an organization and becoming familiar with the equipment, procedures, customers, etc: *Recent research has concluded that between 50% and 85% of the knowledge in an organization is tacit knowledge, i.e. only available through people.*
→ EXPLICIT KNOWLEDGE, KNOW-HOW

tack /tæk/ *verb*
PHR V ,**tack sth 'on**; ,**tack sth 'onto sth 1** to add sth to sth that is already there: *An update chapter has been tacked on at the end of the latest edition of the manual.* ■ (*Stock Exchange*) (*especially AmE*) if a share price **tacks on** an amount, it increases by that amount: *U.S. Electric tacked on 3 per cent to $20.95.*

tactic /'tæktɪk/ *noun* [C, usually pl.]
the particular method you use to achieve sth: *Their unusual marketing tactics have been successful.* ◊ *What strategies and tactics have they used to improve their operations?* ◊ *It's time to try a change of tactic.*

tactical /'tæktɪkl/ *adjective* [usually before noun]
1 connected with the particular method you use to achieve sth: *tactical discussions/planning* ◊ *His knowledge of the company gave him a tactical advantage in the negotiations.* ◊ *Telling your boss you were looking for a new job was a tactical error* (= it was the wrong thing to do).
2 carefully planned in order to achieve a particular aim: *Their decision to withdraw from the deal is seen as a tactical move to get a better price.*

tag /tæg/ *noun, verb*
● *noun* [C]
1 (*often used in compounds*) a small piece of paper,

fabric, plastic, etc. attached to sth to identify it or give information about it: *Employees are encouraged to wear name tags.* → LABEL *noun* (1), PRICE TAG, TICKET
2 (*Commerce*) an electronic device that is attached to sth so that it can be checked, for example to stop people stealing it: *security tags* ◊ *The tags can be used to show the presence and location of items.* → RFID
3 (*IT*) a set of letters or symbols that are put before and after a piece of text or data in order to identify it or show that it is to be treated in a particular way: *XML tags*
● *verb* [+ obj] (**-gg-**)
1 (*Commerce*) to fasten a **tag** onto sth: *All goods are electronically tagged.*
2 (*IT*) to add a set of letters or symbols to a piece of text or data in order to identify it or show that it is to be treated in a particular way

'tag line *noun* [C] (*especially AmE*)
(*Marketing*) a phrase or sentence that is easy to remember, used for example in advertising to attract people's attention and make them remember a product: *The company uses the tag line 'leaders in the lighting world'.* SYN SLOGAN

tailor /'teɪlə(r)/ *verb* [+ obj]
to make or adapt sth for a particular purpose, a particular person, etc: *We tailor our training courses to the client's needs.* ◊ *Advertising campaigns need to be tailored for different markets.*

,**tailor-'made** *adjective*
made for a particular purpose or person, and therefore very suitable: *tailor-made training* ◊ *The software can be tailor-made to fit your needs.* ◊ *She seems tailor-made for the job* (= perfectly suited for it).

★ **take** /teɪk/ *verb, noun*
● *verb* [+ obj] (**took** /tʊk/ **taken** /'teɪkən/)
1 to earn a particular amount of money by selling goods or services: *The store took $100 000 last week.* → TAKE STH IN (1)
2 to move sth/sb from one place, level, situation, etc. to another: *Her energy and talent took her to the top of her profession.*
3 (*used with an adverb or a preposition*) to remove sth/sb from somewhere: *The product has been taken off the market until safety tests have been done.* ◊ *The sign must be taken down.* ◊ *They have been taking market share away from their rivals.*
4 to get control of sth/sb: *Under the plan, creditors will take control of the company.* → CHARGE *noun* (4)
5 to choose, buy or rent sth: *I'll take the grey jacket.* ◊ *We took a room at the hotel for two nights.*
6 take A (away) from B | **take A away** (*not used in the continuous tenses*) to reduce one number by the value of another: *Take costs away from sales income and what is left is profit.* SYN SUBTRACT
7 (*not usually used in the continuous tenses or in the form* **be taken**) to accept or receive sth: *If they offer me the job, I'll take it.* ◊ *Does the hotel take credit cards?* ◊ *I'll take the call in my office.* ◊ *We took more than 1 000 orders last month.* ◊ *Workers were asked to take 4% pay cuts.*
IDM **have (got) what it 'takes** to have the quality, ability, etc. needed to be successful: *He doesn't have what it takes to lead such a large team.* **take ad'vantage of sth/sb** to make use of sth/sb well; to make use of an opportunity: *The company was slow to take full advantage of the opportunities presented by the Internet.* **take ad'vice (from sb)** to ask sb with special knowledge or skill for information or help in a difficult situation: *The company has taken advice from its accountants.* **take a 'bath** (*AmE*) (*slang*) to lose a lot of money, for example on a business agreement or an investment: *Big investors sold their shares before the*

take a 'bite out of sth to reduce sth by a large amount: *The costs of starting up the company took a €6 million bite out of earnings.* **take a 'dive** (*informal*) to suddenly get worse: *Profits really took a dive last year.* **take sth on 'board** to accept and understand an idea or a suggestion: *The idea that the company must modernize has now been taken on board.* **take a 'risk; take 'risks** to do sth even though you know that sth bad could happen as a result: *Every time we lend money, we are taking a risk that we won't be repaid.* ◇ *You must be willing to take risks to gain an advantage over competitors.* **take some 'doing** to be very difficult to do: *The new system will take some getting used to.* **take 'stock 1** (*Accounting*) (*especially AmE*) to count the items for sale in a shop/store → STOCKTAKING **2** to stop and think carefully about the way in which a particular situation is developing in order to decide what to do next: *We're meeting next week to take stock of progress to date.* **take time 'out (of/from sth) (to do sth)** to spend some time away from your usual work or activity in order to rest or do sth else instead: *When people don't take time out, they stop being productive.* **take a (heavy/terrible) 'toll (on sb/sth); take its/their 'toll (on sb/sth)** to have a bad effect on sb/sth; to cause a lot of damage, suffering, etc: *Falling stock markets have taken their toll.* **take a (dramatic, unexpected, etc.) 'turn (for the 'worse/'better)** to suddenly start getting worse/better: *Latest figures suggest that the economy is taking a turn for the better.*
→ idioms at ADVANTAGE, EFFECT, RIDE *noun*
PHR V **take sth a'part** to separate a machine, etc. into the different parts that it is made of **take sth 'back** if you take sth **back** to a shop/store, or if a shop/store **takes** sth **back**, you return sth that you have bought there, for example because it is the wrong size or does not work **take sth 'forward** to work with sth in order to develop it and make it successful: *We believe he is the right man to take this company forward.* **take sth 'in 1** (*especially AmE*) to earn a particular amount of money: *The business took in $9 million last year.* → TAKE *verb* (1) **2** to accept new people, etc: *The EU will take in more new members next year.* **take 'off 1** (about a product, an idea, etc.) to become successful or popular very quickly or suddenly: *The new magazine has really taken off.* ◇ *The company was formed in the early 1990s, before the technology boom took off.* **2** (about an aircraft, etc.) to leave the ground: *We took off an hour late.* **OPP** LAND → TAKE-OFF **take sth 'off** to have a period of time as a break from work: *I'm taking tomorrow off.* **take sb 'off sth** (*often* **be taken off sth**) to remove sb from sth such as a job, position, piece of equipment, etc: *200 staff have been taken off the project.* **take sth 'off sth** to remove an amount of money in order to reduce the total: *They have taken 10% off their prices in order to attract more customers.* **take sb 'on 1** to employ sb: *We have taken on 25 new staff this year.* ◇ *She was taken on as a trainee.* See note at EMPLOY **2** to compete or fight against sb: *After only a year, the company is already taking on established companies in the marketplace.* **take sth/sb 'on** to decide to do sth; to agree to be responsible for sth/sb: *This is the largest project we have ever taken on.* **take sth 'out** to obtain an official document or service: *to take out insurance/a loan* **take sth 'out (of sth)** to remove money from a bank account **take sth 'out of sth** to remove an amount of money from a larger amount, especially as a payment: *About 20% is taken out of salaries as tax.* **take 'over (from sb); take sth 'over (from sb)** to begin to have control of or responsibility for sth, especially in place of sb else: *Mazza will take over from Mudu as chairman.* ◇ *The factory was losing money when we took it over.* **take sth 'over** (*Finance*) to gain control of a company, especially by buying shares: *The supermarket chain was taken over by a rival.* ◇ *They have made an informal offer to take over the airline.* → TAKEOVER **take sth 'up 1** to start or begin sth such as a job: *She takes up her position as CEO next month.* **2** to accept sth that is offered or available: *He decided to take up the redundancy offer.* **take sth 'up with sb** to speak or write to sb about sth that they may be able to deal with or help you with: *She took up her complaint with the union.*

● *noun* [C, usually sing.] (*especially AmE*)

SEE ALSO: **tax take**

(*Accounting, informal*) the amount of money that is earned by a business during a particular period: *Last year's take totalled $10.2 million.* → TAKINGS
IDM **be on the 'take** (*informal*) to accept money from sb for helping them in a dishonest or an illegal way

'take-home pay *noun* [U]
the amount of money that you earn after you have paid tax, etc: *a small increase in take-home pay* ◇ *Take-home pay for retail workers seems to be about 33% of what workers in the car industry make.*

'take-off *noun* [U,C]
1 the moment at which an aircraft leaves the ground: *The plane is ready for take-off.*
OPP LANDING
2 the moment at which sth suddenly becomes very successful: *The local economy is poised for take-off.* ◇ *The company are hoping for a quick take-off for their latest phone.*
→ TAKE OFF at TAKE *verb*

take-or-'pay *adjective* [usually before noun]
(*Trade*) (about a contract) containing a condition that a company or person must pay a particular price for a particular amount of goods, especially gas or oil, even if they do not take or use that amount: *Under the take-or-pay contract, the country pays for a minimum quota of natural gas even if it does not demand it.*

'takeout ,financing *noun* [U]
(*Finance*) loans that are used to replace BRIDGING loans

★ takeover /ˈteɪkəʊvə(r); *AmE* -oʊ-/ *noun* [C,U]

SEE ALSO: **anti-takeover, reverse takeover**

(*Finance*) an act of taking control of a company by buying most of its shares: *The airline has announced details of the planned takeover of its rival.* ◇ *The bank is considered a potential takeover target.* ◇ *Were they right to reject the $3.5 bn takeover offer?* ◇ *The company eventually won a bitter takeover battle for Videotron with a $5 million bid.* See note on p 550.
● *a failed/successful/an unsuccessful takeover ◆ a rescue/an unsolicited takeover ◆ to accept/contest/reject a takeover ◆ an all-share/a cash takeover ◆ a takeover approach/attempt/battle/deal/offer ◆ a takeover candidate/target*

'takeover bid (*also* ,offer to 'purchase, *less frequent*) *noun* [C]

SEE ALSO: **conditional takeover bid, unconditional takeover bid**

(*Finance*) an offer made to the shareholders of a company to buy their shares at a particular price in order to gain control of the company: *They have launched a surprise $133 million takeover bid for the fitness group.* ◇ *The shareholders voted against acceptance of the takeover bid.*
● *to launch/make/mount/withdraw a takeover bid ◆ to accept/consider/defeat/reject a takeover bid ◆ a friendly/hostile/an unfriendly/unwelcome takeover bid*

MORE ABOUT

Takeovers and mergers

A **takeover** is when a company offers to buy all or most of the shares of another company. The company being bought may be bigger or smaller than the company offering to buy it, and the owners of both companies may or may not agree about the conditions of the sale. If they do agree, the takeover is **friendly**. If not, it becomes a **hostile takeover**.

A **merger** involves two companies of a similar size agreeing to join together and become a single company. This can involve a **takeover** in which one company buys the other's shares and pays for these with some of its own shares, or the owners of both companies can agree to exchange their shares for shares in a new company.

'takeover code *noun* [C]
(*Finance*) a set of rules that companies agree to follow, designed to make sure that **takeovers** take place in a fair way

'takeover ˌpanel *noun* [C]
(*Finance*) a group of people in the UK and some other countries who are given the job by the government of making sure that all **takeovers** obey the laws and rules that exist: *Takeover panel rules prohibit special deals with individual shareholders.*

taker /'teɪkə(r)/ *noun* [C, usually pl.]

SEE ALSO: **order taker, price taker**

1 (*often used with* **few**, **no**, **not many**, *etc.*) a person, company, etc. who is willing to accept sth that is offered: *The company has a price tag of around €800 million, but so far there are no takers.*
2 (*often used in compounds*) a person who takes or receives sth: *Salespeople are no longer just order takers.*

'take-up *noun* [U; sing.]
the rate at which people accept sth that is offered or made available to them: *high levels of broadband take-up* ◇ *a slow take-up of new TV services*
✪ high/low/poor/slow/widespread take-up (of sth)

takings /'teɪkɪŋz/ *noun* [pl.]
(*Accounting*) the amount of money that a business such as a shop/store, etc. receives from selling goods or services over a particular period of time: *Takings in the first half were €4.2 million.* ◇ *Takings are up on last year.* ◇ *She has gone to bank the day's takings.*

★talent /'tælənt/ *noun*
1 [C,U] a natural ability to do sth well: *He has a talent for finding the right words.* ◇ *She showed considerable talent as an organizer.*
2 [U,C] people or a person with a natural ability to do sth well: *They spend a lot of money on finding and recruiting top talent.* ◇ *She is one of our best talents.*

talk /tɔːk/ *verb, noun*
● *verb* [no obj]
to say things: *Can I talk to Mr Wong, please?* ◇ *He spent the morning talking with suppliers.* ◇ *Everybody's talking about the design of their new model.* ◇ *She's talking of retiring at the end of the year.*
IDM **be talking sth** used to emphasize an amount of money, how serious sth is, etc: *We're talking half a million dollars.* **talk 'shop** to talk about work with other people you work with, especially when

you are also with other people who are not connected with the work and not interested in it: *Let's not talk shop.* **talk the 'talk** (*informal*) to be able to talk in a confident way that makes people think you are an expert: *He could talk the talk, but he never actually achieved much.* ◇ *You can talk the talk, but can you walk the walk?* → WALK THE/YOUR TALK at WALK *verb*, WALK THE WALK at WALK *verb* **talk 'turkey** (*informal*) (*especially AmE*) to talk about sth honestly and directly
→ idioms at LANGUAGE, MONEY
PHR V **ˌtalk sth/sb 'down** to make sth/sb seem less important or successful than it really is: *You shouldn't talk down your own achievements.* **ˌtalk 'down to sb** to speak to sb as if they were less important or intelligent than you: *Don't talk down to your audience, even though you know more than they do.* **ˌtalk sb 'through sth** to describe or explain sth to sb so that they understand it: *Talk me through your plan.* **ˌtalk sth/sb 'up** to describe sb/sth in a way that makes them sound better than they really are: *The CEO was keen to talk up the benefits of the restructuring programme.*
● *noun*

SEE ALSO: **small talk**

1 talks [pl.] formal discussions between organizations or governments: *Talks between the airline and the union will begin today.*
✪ crisis/merger/pay/takeover/trade talks
2 [C] a speech or lecture on a particular subject: *He's giving a talk on e-publishing.*

'talking point *noun* [C]
1 a subject that is talked about or discussed by many people: *The company's disappointing results were the day's main talking point.*
2 (*AmE*) an item that sb will speak about at a meeting, often one that supports a particular argument: *He goes into meetings armed with talking points.*
3 (*AmE*) a new or special feature of a product that is used in advertising to interest people or persuade them to buy the product

'talking shop *noun* [C]
a place where there is a lot of discussion and argument but no action is taken

tall /tɔːl/ (**taller, tallest**) *adjective*
used to describe an organization where there are many levels between the top and the bottom: *There are more opportunities for promotion in a tall organization, but communications are not usually good.* → FLAT (4)

tally /'tæli/ *noun, verb*
● *noun* [C] (*plural* **tallies**)
a record of the number or amount of sth, especially one that you can keep adding to: *The final tally of job cuts this year is expected to be around 250 000.* ◇ *We keep a tally of the favourable comments that we receive.*
● *verb* (**tallies, tallying, tallied, tallied**)
1 [no obj] to be the same as or to match another set of figures, another person's account of sth, etc: *The specifications of the computer do not tally with the details in the brochure.*
2 [+ obj] to calculate the total number, cost, etc. of sth: *The estimates may turn out to be too low once the final figures are tallied.*

tamper /'tæmpə(r)/ *verb, combining form*
● *verb*
PHR V **'tamper with sth** to make changes to sth in a way that is not sensible and could damage it or make it dangerous: *It would be crazy to tamper with a successful formula.*
● *combining form*
used in adjectives to describe a device that is designed to prevent people from using, stealing, breaking, etc. sth: *The drug is sold in a tamper-*

proof container. ◊ an **anti-tamper** lock ◊ **tamper-evident** security labels (= ones which show if sb has tried to remove them or change them)

TAN /ˌti: eɪ 'en/ = TAX ANTICIPATION NOTE

tangible /'tændʒəbl/ adjective, noun
● **adjective** [usually before noun]
1 that can be clearly seen to exist: These figures provide tangible proof that the economy is recovering. ◊ We want tangible results.
O tangible **benefits/effects/improvements/progress/results** ◆ tangible **evidence/proof/signs**
2 that you can touch and feel: Prices of tangible goods are rising faster than services.
[OPP] INTANGIBLE
▶ **tangibly** /'tændʒəbli/ adverb
● **noun**
1 [C] a thing that exists physically and is not just an idea
2 (Accounting; Finance) [C] = TANGIBLE ASSET
3 (Finance) **tangibles** [pl.] physical things that you can invest in, rather than financial investments: There can be many problems in investing in tangibles like antiques. [OPP] INTANGIBLE

tangible 'asset (also **'tangible**) noun [C, usually pl.]

SEE ALSO: **net tangible assets**

(Accounting; Finance) a physical thing that is owned by a company or person, such as goods, machines, buildings and cash: Internet companies usually have few tangible assets. [OPP] INTANGIBLE ASSET

tangible ,net 'worth noun [U]
(Accounting) the total value of a company's TANGIBLE ASSETS minus its LIABILITIES

tank /tæŋk/ noun, verb
● **noun** [C]

SEE ALSO: **think tank**

1 a large container for holding liquid or gas
2 the contents of a tank or the amount it will hold
[IDM] **in the 'tank** (AmE) (Finance, informal) (about the price of shares, bonds, etc.) falling quickly: Technology stocks are doing well, but everything else is in the tank.
● **verb** [no obj] (AmE)
(Finance, informal) (about prices) to fall quickly: The company's shares tanked on Wall Street to a new low.

tanker /'tæŋkə(r)/ noun [C]
(Transport) a ship or lorry/truck that carries oil, gas or petrol in large quantities: an oil tanker ◊ a tanker driver

tap /tæp/ verb, noun
● **verb** (-pp-)
1 [+ obj or no obj] to make use of a source of energy, knowledge, money, etc. that already exists: We need to tap the expertise and skill of the people we already have. ◊ Some companies have tapped their shareholders for new cash. ◊ The new model will allow them to tap **into** a far larger market.
2 (AmE) [+ obj] (usually **be tapped**) to choose sb for a particular role or job: Bella Sands has been tapped **for** the top job.
[PHRV] **,tap sth 'in/'out** (informal) to put information, numbers, letters, etc. into a machine by pressing buttons: Tap in your PIN number.
● **noun** [C]
a device for controlling the flow of liquid or gas from a pipe or container: a gas tap ◊ (figurative) At first they had many investors, but now the money tap has been turned off.
[IDM] **on 'tap** (informal) **1** available to be used at any time: The new software means that we have the latest sales figures on tap. **2** (AmE) likely to happen at the planned time; planned and ready to happen:

The report is on tap **for** Friday. ◊ What's on tap for the week ahead?

'tape drive noun [C]
(IT) a device that is used for copying and storing information from a computer: It's a good idea to back up your data to a tape drive.

'tape ma,chine = TICKER (1)

tare /teə(r); AmE ter/ noun [U; sing.]
(Transport)
1 the weight of a container or vehicle that is used to transport goods, without its load: The maximum weight allowed on the roads is 20 tons including tare.
2 the weight of the materials used for wrapping and protecting goods

★ **target** /'tɑːgɪt; AmE 'tɑːrgɪt/ noun, verb
● **noun** [C]
1 a result that a business or an organization tries to achieve: The company has set an ambitious target of 20% sales growth. ◊ The group is likely to meet its earnings targets this year. ◊ We are still **on target** (= likely to reach our target) to achieve 12% growth this year. ◊ Production was well **below** target this year. ◊ The **target date** for the rollout is mid 2006.
O to **lower/set** a target ◆ to **exceed/meet/miss/reach** a target ◆ **earnings/financial/growth/performance/price/sales** targets
2 (Finance) a company that another more powerful company wants to buy: The company has become a possible target for Interbrew. ◊ They are seeking potential acquisition targets. [SYN] TARGET COMPANY
O an **acquisition/**a **takeover** target
3 (Finance; Marketing) the price at which a company or person aims to sell or buy sth: Deutsche Bank raised its target for the shares from €150 to €190. ◊ The **target price** for the model currently being developed is €3 500.
[IDM] **(be/make) an easy 'target (for sb/sth)** (to be) open to attack or not able to defend yourself: Is your computer system an easy target for hackers?
● **verb** [+ obj] (**targeting, targeted, targeted**)
1 **target sb/sth** | **target sth at/to sb/sth** (often be targeted at sb/sth) to try to have an effect on a particular group of people or a particular area: Their campaigns **specifically** target young people. ◊ a **carefully** targeted marketing campaign ◊ magazines targeted at teens [SYN] AIM
2 to choose to attack sb/sth or treat sb/sth in a particular way: The EU has published a list of products targeted **for** sanctions.

'target ,audience noun [C, usually sing.]
(Marketing) the group of people that an advertisement, a programme or a product is aimed at: the target audience **for** the new product ◊ We want to **reach** a target audience that's younger in age. → TARGET MARKET

'target ,buyers = TARGET MARKET

'target ,company noun [C]
(Finance) a company that another company wants to buy or get control of [SYN] TARGET

'target ,customers = TARGET MARKET

,Target Group 'Index noun [sing.] (abbr **TGI**)
(Marketing) a regular report, based on the answers to QUESTIONNAIRES (= lists of questions that are answered by many people), that provides information about the types of products and services, newspapers and TV programmes, for example, that are popular

'target ,market noun [C, usually sing.] (also **'target ,buyers**, **'target ,customers** [pl.])
(Marketing) the group of people that you want to sell your products to: Our target market **for** this

drink is teenagers. ◊ *We need to identify the target market.* → TARGET AUDIENCE
⊕ *to* **identify/know/reach** *your target market*
▶ **'target ,marketing** *noun* [U]

tariff /'tærɪf/ *noun* [C]

SEE ALSO: **protective tariff, revenue tariff**

1 (*Trade*) a tax that is paid on goods coming into or going out of a country: *New import tariffs have been imposed on a wide range of agricultural products.* ◊ *High tariff barriers protect domestic industry.*
⊕ *to* **impose/set** *a tariff* ✦ *to* **place** *a tariff* **on** *sth* ✦ *to* **abolish/eliminate/lift** *a tariff* ✦ **high/low/punitive** *tariffs* ✦ *tariff* **barriers/protection/walls**
2 (*Commerce*) a list of fixed prices that are charged by a company for a particular service, or by a hotel or restaurant for rooms, meals, etc: *a telephone tariff* ◊ *the hotel's daily/weekly tariff*

★ **task** /tɑːsk; *AmE* tæsk/ *noun* [C]
1 a piece of work that sb has to do: *Our first task is to set up a communications system.* ◊ *The new CEO faces an uphill task to prevent the company being taken over.* ◊ *Persuading staff to accept a pay cut will be* **no easy task** (= it will be difficult).
→ MULTITASKING (2)
⊕ *to* **carry out/complete/do/perform/undertake** *a task* ✦ *to* **give sb/set (sb)** *a task* ✦ *a* **big/crucial/an important/a time-consuming/an urgent** *task* ✦ *a* **challenging/daunting/difficult/hard/an impossible** *task*
2 (*IT*) an item of work which is processed by a computer as a single unit SYN JOB
→ MULTITASKING (1)
⊕ *to* **do/execute/perform** *a task*

'task force (*also* **'task group**) *noun* [C]
a group of people who are brought together to deal with a particular problem: *to chair a task force* **on** *renewable energy*
⊕ *to* **form/put together/set up** *a task force* ✦ *to* **chair/head/lead** *a task force*

'task-,oriented (*also* **'task-,orientated**, *especially in BrE less frequent*) *adjective*
1 used to describe a method of doing sth that is designed for a particular task rather than for all tasks
2 used to describe a style of management where performing tasks is the main aim rather than trying to improve how workers feel and relate to each other: *a task-oriented leadership style*

★ **tax** /tæks/ *noun, verb*
● *noun* [C,U]

SEE ALSO: **after-tax, capital gains ~, capital ~, consumption ~, corporate income ~, corporation ~, death ~,** etc.

money that you have to pay to the government so that it can pay for public services. People pay tax according to their income and businesses pay tax according to their profits. Tax is also often paid on goods and services: *They pay over €100 000 a year* **in** *tax.* ◊ *profits* **before/after** *tax* ◊ *They have put a tax* **on** *cigarettes.* ◊ *Has the tax been deducted from the interest?* ◊ *All menu prices are* **exclusive of** *tax.* ◊ *You must fill in and return your tax form by the end of September.* ◊ *The tax office demanded €200 000 in* **back** *taxes* (= taxes that are owed from a previous period).
⊕ **basic/basic-rate/high/higher-rate/low** *tax* ✦ *to* **introduce/impose/levy** *a tax* ✦ *to* **abolish/cut/lift/reduce/remove** *(a) tax* ✦ *to* **increase/put up/raise** *taxes* ✦ *to* **avoid/escape/evade** *tax* ✦ *tax* **cuts/increases** ✦ *a tax* **advisor/consultant** ✦ *a tax* **authority/office**

● *verb* [+ obj]
to put a tax on sb/sth; to make sb pay tax: *Shares in quoted companies are taxed* **at** *40%.* ◊ *You will be* taxed **on** *all your income.* ◊ *Companies are more* **heavily** *taxed in this country than in others.*

'tax a,batement *noun* [U]
an arrangement that allows a business to pay less tax than usual for a period of time: *Local governments often use tax abatement to attract new industry to the region.*

taxable /'tæksəbl/ *adjective*
(*Accounting*) (about money, etc.) that you have to pay tax on: *Car parking provided free at your workplace is not taxable.* OPP NON-TAXABLE
▶ **taxability** /,tæksə'bɪləti/ *noun* [U]: *The taxability of items used in manufacturing varies widely from state to state.*

'tax ac,counting *noun* [U]
the branch of accounting that prepares financial information so that tax can be calculated and aims to make sure that a company or person does not pay any more tax than necessary

'tax al,lowance (*especially BrE*) (*AmE usually* **'tax ex,emption**) *noun* [C,U]
an amount of money that you are allowed to earn or receive before you start paying tax
SYN ALLOWANCE (*BrE*) (2)

,tax antici'pation note = REVENUE
ANTICIPATION NOTE

'tax as,sessment *noun* [U,C]
the act of calculating how much tax sb must pay; the amount that has been calculated and that must be paid: *The tax assessment and tax collection process is now much easier to understand.* ◊ *appeals against tax assessments*

'tax as,sessor *noun* [C] (*especially AmE*)
a person whose job is to calculate how much tax sb has to pay → INSPECTOR OF TAXES

★ **taxation** /tæk'seɪʃn/ *noun* [U]

SEE ALSO: **deferred taxation, double ~, multiple ~**

1 money that has to be paid as taxes: *Low levels of taxation have attracted some big companies to the region.*
⊕ **excessive/heavy/high/low** *taxation* ✦ *to* **cut/lower/raise/reduce** *taxation*
2 the system or the act of collecting money by taxes: *Any profits made are exempt from taxation.* ◊ *changes in the taxation structure*
⊕ **company/corporate/general/local/personal** *taxation* ✦ **central/local** *taxation*
→ DIRECT TAXATION at DIRECT TAX

'tax a,voidance *noun* [U]
(*Accounting*) ways of paying only the smallest amount of tax that you legally have to: *tax avoidance plans/strategies* → TAX EVASION

'tax band *noun* [C] (*BrE*)
1 = TAX BRACKET
2 a range of properties of different values on which the same rate of tax must be paid

'tax base *noun* [C, usually sing.]
(*Economics*) all the things that tax is paid on in a particular country, region, etc: *The government chose to broaden the tax base rather than to raise rates.*
⊕ *to* **broaden/cut/protect/widen** *the tax base*

'tax bite *noun* [C] (*informal*)
the part of a particular amount of money that is taken as tax: *The change in the law will increase the tax bite on small companies.*

'tax ,bracket (*also* **'bracket**) (*BrE also* **'tax band**, *less frequent*) *noun* [C]

a range of different incomes on which the same rate of tax must be paid: *My salary increase means I'm now in the highest tax bracket.* ◇ *There were only two tax brackets—22% and 40%.*

'tax break *noun* [C] (*especially AmE*)

a special advantage or reduction in taxes that the government gives to particular people or organizations, often to encourage them to do particular things: *The government has introduced incentives such as tax breaks for companies that use environmentally-friendly technology.*
O *to give/offer/provide* tax breaks ◆ *to enjoy/get/ have/receive* a tax break

'tax ,credit *noun* [C,U]

a reduction in the amount of tax that you have to pay, which is allowed to companies or people in particular situations: *a research and development tax credit to boost business innovation*

'tax decla,ration *noun* [C]

(*Accounting*) a formal statement made by a company or person giving details of all the money they have received so that the amount of tax they have to pay can be calculated → TAX RETURN
O *to file/make/submit* a tax declaration

,tax-de'ductible *adjective*

(*Accounting*) (about an expense) that is allowed to be taken off the total amount of money earned or received before the amount of tax that must be paid is calculated: *Entertainment expenses are no longer tax-deductible.*

'tax de,duction *noun* [C]

(*Accounting*) an expense that is allowed to be taken off the total amount of money earned or received before the amount of tax that must be paid is calculated: *tax deductions for new equipment such as computers and machinery*
O *to claim/enjoy/get/take* a tax deduction

,tax-de'ferred *adjective* (*AmE*)

(*Accounting*) if an amount of money earned or received is **tax-deferred**, you pay tax on it at a later time than when you earn or receive it, for example after you retire: *a tax-deferred retirement/savings account*

'tax depreci,ation *noun* [U]

(*Accounting*) the total amount of money invested in new buildings, machinery, etc. that a company can take away from profits before calculating its tax → BOOK DEPRECIATION, CAPITAL ALLOWANCE

,tax-ef'ficient *adjective*

1 (*Accounting*) used to describe a way of organizing assets that allows a person or a company to pay the lowest possible amount of tax: *They established a tax-efficient structure for the acquisition and development of the company.*
2 (*Finance*) (*BrE*) used to describe an investment whose profits are taxed less than other investments: *A mortgage is one of the best tax-efficient investments you can have.* → TAX-FAVORED
▶ **,tax ef'ficiency** *noun* [U]: *The deal was structured for tax efficiency.*

'tax e,vasion *noun* [U]

(*Accounting*) the crime of deliberately not paying all the taxes that you should pay: *new rules aimed at fighting fraud and tax evasion*
O *to be accused of/charged with/found guilty of* tax evasion ◆ *to clamp down on/curb/fight* tax evasion
▶ **'tax e,vader** *noun* [C]: *a plan to stop tax evaders*
→ TAX AVOIDANCE

,tax ex'emption *noun*

(*Accounting*)
1 [U,C] (*BrE*) a situation in which a person or a company does not have to pay tax: *Competitors have challenged the company's tax exemption as unfair.*
2 [C] (*especially AmE*) = TAX ALLOWANCE

'tax ,exile *noun*

1 [C] a rich person who has left their own country and gone to live in a place where the taxes are lower: *Their success forced them to become tax exiles.*
2 [U] the situation when a rich person lives in another country as a **tax exile**: *He's now living in tax exile in Monaco.*

'tax-,favored (*BrE spelling* **~favoured**) *adjective* [usually before noun] (*AmE only*)

(*Finance*) used to describe an investment whose profits are taxed less than other investments: *tax-favored life insurance* → TAX-EFFICIENT

'tax form *noun* [C]

a document on which a company or person gives details of the amount of money that they have earned so that the government can calculate how much tax they have to pay: *Do I need to fill in a self-assessment tax form?* → TAX RETURN

,tax-'free *adjective*

(about money, goods, etc.) that you do not have to pay tax on: *Employees receive a tax-free lump sum on retirement.* ▶ **,tax-'free** *adverb*: *Employees can contribute up to €100 a month to pensions tax-free.*

'tax ,haven *noun* [C]

a place where taxes are low and where people choose to live or officially register their companies because taxes are higher in their own country: *a company based in an offshore tax haven*

'tax ,holiday *noun* [C]

(*Accounting*) a period during which a company does not have to pay tax or pays less tax: *New manufacturers should be given a five-year tax holiday to develop their products.*

'tax in,centive *noun* [C]

a reduction in tax that encourages companies or people to do sth: *The regional government is offering tax incentives to companies who move to the region.*

'tax in,spector = INSPECTOR OF TAXES

'tax ,invoice *noun* [C]

(*Accounting*) especially in Australia and New Zealand, a document that a business provides when it sells goods or services to another company, which gives details of the tax that has been paid

'tax lia,bility *noun*

(*Accounting*)
1 [C] the amount of tax that a company or person must pay: *The company now faces a $1.5 billion tax liability.* ◇ *I needed advice on how to minimize my tax liabilities.*
2 [U,C] the fact of having to pay tax on sth: *No tax liability arose from the sale of the company.*

'tax lien *noun* [C] (*AmE*)

(*Law*) the right of authorities who collect taxes to claim assets from a person or company if they do not pay tax: *The IRS filed a tax lien on the property to collect taxes owed by the sellers.*

'tax loss *noun* [C]

(*Accounting*)
1 a loss that a company makes which reduces the amount of tax it has to pay: *They sold the machinery for scrap and claimed a tax loss on it.*

2 a situation where a government receives less tax than it should because of illegal trading: *Software piracy resulted in an estimated tax loss of $62 million.*

taxman /ˈtæksmæn/ noun (plural **taxmen** /-men/) (*Accounting*)
1 [sing.] a way of referring to the government department that is responsible for collecting taxes: *Following its battle with the taxman, the company has been forced to pay almost a million euros in outstanding taxes.*
2 (*informal*) [C] (*especially BrE*) a person whose job is to collect taxes **SYN** INSPECTOR OF TAXES

'tax obli,gation noun [C]
the amount of tax that a person or a company owes: *Many people have to work out their own tax obligations.*

★ **taxpayer** /ˈtækspeɪə(r)/ noun [C]
a person who pays tax to the government, especially on the money that they earn: *Delaying the project will give more time for research and save taxpayers' money.*
○ *a basic-rate/higher-rate/standard-rate/top-rate taxpayer*

'tax pro,vision noun [C,U]
(*Accounting*) an amount of money that a company keeps in order to pay tax at the end of the year: *In the quarter just ended, the company made a $21 m tax provision.*

'tax rate noun [C]
the percentage of an amount of money or of the value of sth that has to be paid as tax: *Ireland's low corporate tax rate has attracted a number of manufacturers.*

'tax re,lief noun [U]
(*Accounting*) a reduction in the amount of tax you have to pay: *Small companies can claim tax relief on research and development expenditure.*
○ *to claim/gain/get tax relief • to be eligible for/be entitled to/qualify for tax relief • to give/offer/provide tax relief • to abolish/cut/end tax relief*

'tax re,turn (*also* re'turn) noun [C]
(*Accounting*) a statement of how much money a company or person has earned and their expenses, used by the government to calculate how much tax they have to pay; the form on which this statement is made: *a tax return for the year 2005–6* ◇ *Many companies file their corporate tax return online.*
→ TAX DECLARATION, TAX FORM
○ *to file/make/send in a tax return • to complete/do/fill in/fill out a tax return*

'tax sale noun [C] (*AmE*)
(*Law*) when a property is sold by a government because the owner has not paid their taxes

'tax ,shelter noun [C]
(*Accounting*) a way of using or investing money so that you can legally avoid paying tax on it: *Investors were taking advantage of a tax shelter in their retirement savings plans.* ▶ **'tax-,sheltered** adjective: *tax-sheltered savings plans*

'tax ,subsidy noun [C,U]
a reduction in the amount of tax that a company pays, given by the government for a particular purpose: *tax subsidies to encourage companies to create new jobs*

'tax take noun [C] (*especially AmE*) (*informal*)
the amount of money that is taken as tax: *The government will have to raise its tax take to pay for its public spending.* ◇ *a high tax take on earned income*

'tax ,threshold (*also* 'threshold, *less frequent*) noun [C]
the level of income above which a company or person starts to pay income tax: *The corporate tax threshold for small businesses is to be raised to €500 000.*

'tax year noun [C] (*especially BrE*)
(*Accounting*) the period of 12 months over which the taxes of a company or a person are calculated. In the UK it begins on 6 April; in the US, usually on 1 July. → FINANCIAL YEAR

t.b. (*also spelled* **TB**) /ˌtiː ˈbiː/ = TRIAL BALANCE

T.B.A /ˌtiː biː ˈeɪ/ abbr
(used in notices about events, etc.) to be arranged, to be announced, to be advised or, less often, to be agreed: *Meeting Tuesday 2.30, venue t.b.a.*

'T-bill = TREASURY BILL

'T-bond = TREASURY BOND

TCN /ˌtiː siː ˈen/ = THIRD-COUNTRY NATIONAL

TCO /ˌtiː siː ˈəʊ; *AmE* ˈoʊ/ = TOTAL COST OF OWNERSHIP

't-,commerce noun [U]
1 the buying and selling of products through INTERACTIVE television (= that allows information to be passed in both directions)
2 the buying and selling of products by telephone

★ **team** /tiːm/ noun, verb
● **noun** [C with sing./pl. verb]

SEE ALSO: management team

a group of people who work together: *a team leader/member* ◇ *a team meeting* ◇ *A team of experts has/have been called in to investigate.* ◇ *We met in the boss's office for a team briefing.* ◇ *We take a **team-based** approach to work.* ◇ *The success of this project has been a team effort.*
○ *the design/development/marketing/sales team • to build/form/recruit/train a team • to head (up)/lead/manage/run a team*
● **verb**
1 [no obj] **team (up) (with sb)** to join with another person or group in order to do sth together: *The two record companies teamed up to launch an online service.*
2 [+ obj] **team sb/sth (up) (with sb/sth)** to combine or match two or more things or people: *We teamed our head of design up with a freelance software engineer to work on the website.*

'team ,building noun [U]
the process of getting people to work together on a particular job: *Changes to production methods involved team building and creating a multi-skilled workforce.* ◇ *The roleplay enables us to look at candidates' team-building skills.* ◇ *team-building activities/exercises*

teaming /ˈtiːmɪŋ/ noun [U]
the practice of working as a team: *Good teaming increases both efficiency and morale.*

teammate /ˈtiːmmeɪt/ noun [C]
a person who works in the same team as yourself

,team 'player noun [C]
a person who is good at working as a member of a team: *Some of his colleagues have accused him of not being a team player.*

teamster /ˈtiːmstə(r)/ noun [C] (*AmE*)
a person whose job is driving a truck

teamwork /ˈtiːmwɜːk; *AmE* -wɜːrk/ noun [U]
the activity of working well together as a team: *Trust is essential for successful teamwork.*

teamworking /ˈtiːmwɜːkɪŋ; *AmE* -wɜːrk-/
noun [U]
(*HR*) a way of organizing work in which employees
work together in groups and are trained to do a
range of tasks: *He said that teamworking was still
new in the building industry.*

teaser /ˈtiːzə(r)/ *noun* [C]
(*Marketing*)
1 = TEASER AD
2 (*AmE*) an advertisement that offers sth free, such
as a gift or sample, to attract customers

'teaser ad (*also* **'teaser**) *noun* [C]
(*Marketing*) a short or strange advertisement that is
used to increase the public's interest in a product,
especially one that is not yet available. It does not
usually give the name of the product: *Retailers have
been **running** teaser ads this week in preparation for
tomorrow's launch.* ◇ *a teaser ad **for** an upcoming
concert* **NOTE** Teaser ads are usually followed by
normal advertising when the product becomes
available.

'teaser rate *noun* [C]
(*Marketing*) a low rate of interest that is offered for a
period of time to attract people to use a credit card
or arrange a loan

tech /tek/ *noun, adjective* (*informal*)
● *noun* [C, usually pl.] (*also* **'technical**)
(used especially in newspapers) a technology
company: *Techs were down last night on all
European stock markets.*
● *adjective* [only before noun]
──────────────────────────
SEE ALSO: **high-tech**, **low-tech**
──────────────────────────
technology; technological; technical: *tech
companies* ◇ *the tech sector*

'tech-ˌheavy (*also* **'tech-ˌladen**) *adjective* (*informal*)
(*also* **tech'nology-ˌheavy**)
(*Stock Exchange*) (about a stock market) including
mainly technology companies: *the tech-heavy
Nasdaq index*

techie (*also spelled* **techy**) /ˈteki/ *noun* [C] (*plural*
techies) (*informal*)
a person who knows a lot about or is very
interested in technology, especially computing: *the
company's group of bright young techies* ◇ *techie
jargon*

'tech-ˌladen = TECH-HEAVY

techMARK™ /ˈtekmɑːk; *AmE* -mɑːrk/ *noun*
[sing.]
(*Stock Exchange*) a group of technology companies
that have their own section on the London Stock
Exchange: *The FTSE TechMARK closed down 0.7%.*

technical /ˈteknɪkl/ *adjective, noun*
● *adjective*
1 connected with the practical use of machinery,
methods, etc: *The crash was caused by a technical
fault.* ◇ *Younger employees tend to have more
technical know-how than older ones.* ◇ *We have
experienced technical difficulties with our email
distribution list.*
☉ *a technical **fault/glitch/hitch** • a technical
breakthrough/difficulty • technical **capabilities/
developments***
2 connected with a particular subject and
therefore difficult to understand if you do not know
about that subject: *The manual contains too much
technical jargon.* ◇ *The guide is too technical for a
non-specialist.*
☉ *technical **jargon/language/terms***
3 connected with the exact details of official laws,
rules, etc: *The economic slowdown does not yet meet
the technical definition of a recession.* ◇ *The
shareholders have had two requests for an*

*extraordinary meeting turned down on technical
grounds.*
☉ *technical **grounds/reasons/rules***
▶ technically /ˈteknɪkli/ *adverb*: *It is not
technically possible to install the system in such a
small space.* ◇ *Although the practice is technically
illegal, it is still very common.*
● *noun*
1 (*Stock Exchange*) **technicals** [pl.] (*also* **ˌtechnical
ˈindicator** [C]) measurements, such as the price of
shares and the number that have been bought and
sold, that are used to predict what will happen to a
stock market in the future: *Technicals represent a
good picture of the present situation.* ◇ *I follow the
market technicals.* → FUNDAMENTALS, TECHNICAL
ANALYST
2 [C, usually pl.] = TECH *noun*

ˌtechnical ˈanalyst (*also* **'chartist**) *noun* [C]
(*Stock Exchange*) a person who studies investments
and uses charts, diagrams and computer programs
to analyse how the share prices of particular
companies have risen and fallen in the past. These
patterns are then used to see what might happen in
the future. **▶ ˌtechnical aˈnalysis** *noun* [U,C]

ˌtechnical efˈficiency *noun* [U]
(*Manufacturing; Production*) a situation in which a
machine or a business produces the highest
possible amount or quality of goods or services
with a particular amount of resources: *an analysis
of the technical efficiency of the UK steel industry*
[SYN] X-EFFICIENCY [OPP] TECHNICAL INEFFICIENCY

ˌtechnical ˈindicator = TECHNICAL *noun* (1)

ˌtechnical ˌinefˈficiency *noun* [U]
(*Manufacturing; Production*) a situation in which a
machine or a business could produce more or
better goods or services with a particular amount
of resources: *measuring the technical inefficiency of
farms* [SYN] X-INEFFICIENCY [OPP] TECHNICAL
EFFICIENCY

ˌtechnical supˈport (*also* **ˌtech supˈport**)
noun [U]
help from experts that is available to people who
use computers, machines, etc.; the department in
an organization that provides this: *We offer free
technical support for all users of our software.* ◇
*Don't install new software when the staff in technical
support may not be there to help you.*

technician /tekˈnɪʃn/ *noun* [C]
a person whose job is keeping a particular type of
equipment or machinery in good condition:
laboratory/computer technicians ◇ *a pool of skilled
technicians*

★ technological /ˌteknəˈlɒdʒɪkl; *AmE* -ˈlɑːdʒ-/
adjective
connected with the practical use of scientific
knowledge in industry: *technological advances in
manufacture* ◇ *They combine technological know-
how with high-quality manufacture.*
☉ *technological **capabilities/know-how/skills** •
technological **advances/breakthroughs/
developments/innovations/progress***
▶ technologically /ˌteknəˈlɒdʒɪkli; *AmE* -ˈlɑːdʒ-/
adverb: *technologically advanced*

★ technology /tekˈnɒlədʒi; *AmE* -ˈnɑːl-/ *noun*
(*plural* **technologies**)
──────────────────────────
SEE ALSO: **disruptive technology**, **high ~**,
information ~, **intermediate ~**
──────────────────────────
1 [U,C] scientific knowledge used in practical ways
in industry, for example in designing new
machines: *recent advances in medical technology* ◇
The company has just unveiled two promising new

digital technologies. ◇ **technology-based** products (= ones that are developed using the latest technology) ◇ a **technology-driven** company (= one that uses and relies on the latest technology) **2** [U] machinery or equipment designed using **technology**: *The company has invested in the latest technology.*
▶ **tech'nologist** noun [C]: *a food technologist*

tech'nology-,heavy = TECH-HEAVY

technophile /'teknəfaɪl; *BrE also* -nəʊf-/ noun [C]
a person who is very interested in new technology

technophobe /'teknəfəʊb; *BrE also* -nəʊf-; *AmE* -foʊb/ noun [C]
a person who does not like using new technology

,tech sup'port = TECHNICAL SUPPORT

techy = TECHIE

tel abbr
a short way of writing **telephone** before a telephone number: *tel: 556768*

telco /'telkəʊ; *AmE* -koʊ/ noun [C]
(used especially in newspapers) a TELECOMMUNICATIONS company: *Telcos were struggling to make money from broadband services.* → TELECOM

tele- /'teli/ combining form (used in nouns, verbs and adjectives)
1 over a long distance; far: *telecommunications* ◇ *teleworking*
2 connected with television: *teletext*
3 done using a telephone: *telesales*

telecast /'telikɑːst; *AmE* -kæst/ noun [C] (*especially AmE*)
a broadcast on television ▶ **telecast** verb [+ obj] (**telecast, telecast**) (*usually* **be telecast**): *The match will be telecast live to over 150 countries.* '**telecaster** noun [C]

telecentre (*AmE spelling* **telecenter**) /'telisentə(r)/ noun [C]
(*HR*) a building, usually in the country, filled with computer equipment so that people can work there instead of travelling to an office in a town or city → TELECOTTAGE, TELEWORKING

telecom /'telikɒm; *AmE* -kɑːm/ noun
1 [C] (often used in names) a telecommunications company: *France Telecom* → TELCO
2 [U] (*informal*) telecommunications: *telecom equipment/systems*

telecommunication /,telikə,mjuːnɪ'keɪʃn/ (*also* **telecom**, *informal*) noun [U]
telecommunications: *The company is to start selling telecommunication services to residential customers.* ◇ *a telecommunication expert*

★**telecommunications** /,telikə,mjuːnɪ'keɪʃnz/ (*also* **telecoms**, *informal*) noun [pl.; U]
the technology of sending messages over long distances by radio, telephone, television, SATELLITE, etc: *technological developments in telecommunications*
❶ *a telecommunications business/carrier/company/group/operator/provider* ◆ *the telecommunications industry/market/sector* ◆ *telecommunications equipment/technology* ◆ *a telecommunications infrastructure/link/network/system*

telecommuting /,telikə'mjuːtɪŋ/ noun [U]
the activity of working for a company from your home and communicating with your office, colleagues and customers by computer and telephone, etc. SYN TELEWORKING

▶ **,telecom'mute** verb [no obj] **,telecom'muter** noun [C]

telecoms /'telikɒmz; *AmE* -kɑːmz/
= TELECOMMUNICATIONS

teleconference /'telikɒnfərəns; *AmE* -kɑːn-/ noun [C]
a meeting, discussion, etc. between two or more people in different places, using telephones, television or computers to connect them: *Every two weeks, I dial into a teleconference with a group of other agents.*
❶ *to conduct/have/hold/participate in a teleconference*
▶ '**teleconferencing** noun [U] '**teleconference** verb [no obj]

telecottage /'telikɒtɪdʒ; *AmE* -kɑːt-/ noun [C] (*BrE*)
(*HR*) a building, usually in the country, filled with computer equipment for people who live in the area to use for work or pleasure → ELECTRONIC COTTAGE, TELECENTRE, TELEWORKING
▶ '**telecottaging** /,teli'kɒtɪdʒɪŋ; *AmE* -'kɑːt-/ noun [U]

telegram /'teligræm/ noun [C]
a message sent by TELEGRAPH, then printed and given to sb

telegraph /'teligrɑːf; *AmE* -græf/ noun [U]
a system for sending messages over long distances, using wires that carry electrical signals
▶ '**telegraph** verb [+ obj or no obj]

,tele'graphic 'transfer = WIRE TRANSFER

telemarketing /'telimɑːkɪtɪŋ; *AmE* -mɑːrk-/ (*also* '**telephone ,selling**) noun [U] (*BrE also* '**telesales** [U; pl.])

SEE ALSO: inbound telemarketing, outbound telemarketing

(*Marketing*) a method of selling goods and services and taking orders for sales by contacting possible customers by telephone → COLD-CALLING
▶ '**telemarketer** noun [C]

telematics /,teli'mætɪks/ noun [U]
(*IT*) the branch of INFORMATION TECHNOLOGY that deals with using computers to send information over long distances: *The company uses telematics to track the position of its vehicles at all times.*
▶ **,tele'matic** adjective **NOTE** The word **telematics** was formed from 'telecommunication' and 'informatics' (= the study of processes for storing and obtaining data electronically).

★**telephone** /'telifəʊn; *AmE* -foʊn/ noun, verb
● **noun** [C,U]

SEE ALSO: fixed telephone

a system for talking to sb else over long distances, using wires or radio; a machine used for this: *Could you answer my telephone if it rings, please?* ◇ *I need to make a **telephone call**.* ◇ *We negotiated the details over the/by telephone.* ◇ *Business travellers no longer need to spend time **on the telephone** arranging their trips.* SYN PHONE
❶ *a telephone company/carrier/operator* ◆ *a telephone line/network/system* ◆ *a telephone conference/conversation/interview/meeting/survey*
● **verb** [+ obj or no obj]
to speak to sb by telephone: *Please email or telephone for details.* ◇ *You can telephone your order 24 hours a day.* SYN CALL, PHONE

'**telephone di,rectory** (*also* '**telephone book**, '**phone book**) noun [C]
a book that lists the names, addresses and telephone numbers of people or businesses in a particular area: *to look up a number in the telephone directory*

'telephone ex,change (*also* ex'change)
noun [C]
equipment that connects telephone lines together so that people can make telephone calls to each other; the place where this is kept

'telephone ,selling = TELEMARKETING

telephonist /tə'lefənɪst/ = OPERATOR (3)

telephony /tə'lefəni/ noun [U]
the business or process of sending messages and signals by telephone: *a mobile telephony business* ◊ *The company offers Internet and telephony services.*
● *cable/fixed-line/mobile/voice/wireless* telephony ◆ *a telephony* **business/company/operator/provider**

telesales /'teliseɪlz/ = TELEMARKETING

teletext /'telitekst/ noun [U]
a service providing written news and information using television: *You can get the current exchange rate* **on** *teletext.*

'television ,rating noun [C] (*abbr* TVR)
(*Marketing*) the number of people who watch a particular programme on television, compared with the total number of people available to watch, used to measure how popular the programme is. One rating is one per cent: *The World Cup final had a record television rating of 48.3%.*

teleworking /'teliwɜːkɪŋ; AmE -wɜːrk-/ (*also* 'telework) noun [U]
(*HR*) the activity of working for a company from your home and communicating with your office and colleagues by computer and telephone, etc. either all or part of the time [SYN] TELECOMMUTING
▶ 'telework noun [U] 'telework verb [no obj]
'teleworker noun [C]

telex /'teleks/ noun
1 [U] an international system of communication in which messages are typed on a special machine and sent by the telephone system: *Applications should be made by fax or* **by** *telex.*
2 [C] a message sent or received by **telex**: *Several telexes arrived this morning.*
3 [C] (*informal*) a machine for sending or receiving telexes
▶ 'telex verb [+ obj or no obj]: *Can you telex the order today?*

teller /'telə(r)/ noun [C]
1 = BANK TELLER
2 a machine that pays out money automatically: *automatic teller machines* [SYN] ATM

temp /temp/ noun, verb
(*HR*)
● noun [C]
a temporary employee in an office: *We'll need to get in a temp while Anna's away.* ◊ *a temp agency*
[SYN] CASUAL
● verb [no obj] (*informal*)
to do a temporary job or a series of temporary jobs: *I've been temping for an employment agency.*

template /'templeɪt/ noun [C]
1 a thing that is used as a model for producing other similar examples: *This contract may be used as a template* **for** *future agreements.* ◊ *The program lets you set up a basic email template for orders.*
2 a shape cut out of a hard material, used as a model for producing exactly the same shape many times in another material

temporary /'temprəri; AmE -pəreri/ adjective
lasting or intended to last only for a short time; not permanent: *The canteen has been closed as a temporary measure while the problem is investigated.* ◊ *More than half the staff are temporary.* ◊ *workers on temporary contracts* [OPP] PERMANENT → TEMP

,temporary 'help ,agency noun [C]
(*HR*) a business that provides workers for other businesses for limited periods of time

ten /ten/ number
[IDM] **'tens of 'thousands/'millions/'billions (of sth)** used to refer to any large amount or number between ten thousand/million/billion and one hundred thousand/million/billion: *The company paid tens of thousands of dollars in bonuses last year.*

tenable /'tenəbl/ adjective
1 (about an opinion, a theory, a situation, etc.) easy to defend against attack or criticism: *Following the scandal, it was no longer tenable for him to stay on as CEO.*
2 (*HR*) (about a job, position, etc.) that can be held for a particular period of time: *The scholarship is tenable for up to three years.*

tenancy /'tenənsi/ noun (*plural* **tenancies**)
(*Law*; *Property*)
1 [C,U] the right to live or work in a building or on land that you rent: *a tenancy agreement* ◊ *They have taken over the tenancy of the building.*
● *to* **get/give up/take (over)/hold/surrender** *a tenancy* ◆ *to* **grant/offer/renew/terminate** *a tenancy*
2 [C] a period of time that you rent a house, land, etc. for: *a 12-month tenancy*
● *a* **life/fixed-term/long-term/short-term** *tenancy* ◆ *a tenancy* **expires/lapses**

tenant /'tenənt/ noun, verb
(*Law*; *Property*)
● noun [C]

SEE ALSO: **prime tenant, anchor tenant**

a person or company that pays rent for the use of a building, land, room, etc. to the person or company that owns it: *The shopping mall has 115 tenants.*
● verb [+ obj] (*usually* **be tenanted**)
to work or live in a place as a **tenant**: *a tenanted farm/pub*

,tenant at 'will noun [C] (*plural* **tenants at will**)
(*Law*) a **tenant** that can be forced to leave a property, piece of land, etc. without any warning

★ tender /'tendə(r)/ noun, verb
● noun [C,U]

SEE ALSO: **legal tender, self-tender**

1 (*Commerce*) a formal offer to supply goods or do work at a stated price: *We are inviting tenders* **for** *the provision of training courses for staff.* ◊ *A local firm submitted the lowest tender.* ◊ *Cleaning and laundry services have been* **put out to (competitive)** *tender.* [SYN] BID
● *to* **invite/request** *tenders* ◆ *to* **accept/announce/award/issue** *a tender* ◆ *to* **apply for/bid for/prepare/submit/win** *a tender*
2 (*Finance*) an offer to buy shares, etc. at a stated price: *The shares are being sold by tender.* ◊ *The group planned to buy back 10% of the company's stock at a tender price of $0.66-0.75 per share.*
● verb
1 (*Commerce*) [+ obj or no obj] to make a formal offer to supply goods or do work at a stated price: *Local firms were invited to tender* **for** *the project.* ◊ *competitive tendering*
2 (*Finance*) [no obj] to make a formal offer to buy shares, etc. at a stated price, especially in order to gain control of a company: *They are expected to tender* **for** *51% of the shares.*
3 (*Finance*) [+ obj] to make a formal offer to sell shares, etc. at a stated price: *85% of the common shareholders had tendered their shares in response to the $20-a-share offer.*

4 (*formal*) [+ obj] to offer money as payment: *The program reads the purchase price and the amount tendered and calculates the change.*
5 (*formal*) [+ obj] to offer or give sth to sb: *The CEO and the finance director tendered their resignations last Sunday.*
▶ **'tenderer** noun [C]: *Unsuccessful tenderers will be told why their bids failed.*

WHICH WORD?

tender/bid

If a business **bids** or **tenders** for work, they offer to do it for a particular price in competition with others: *The company is bidding for a Health Department contract.*

The offer itself, usually in the form of a document, is referred to as the **bid** or **tender**: *Tenders submitted after 31 October will not be accepted.*

Tender [U], not bid, is used to refer to the process of competing to do the work: *They put the contract out to tender.* ◇ *a tender application*

Bid, both as a noun and a verb, is also used in the context of an auction (= when people offer to buy sth in competition with each other): *They have invited bids for a 33% stake in the company.* ◇ *Decide how much you're prepared to pay before you start to bid.* Tender is not used with this meaning.

'tender ,offer noun [C]
(*Finance*)
1 an invitation to the existing shareholders of a particular company to sell some of their shares at a particular price either to the company itself or to another company: *The shares rose 20% after the company said it would return $6 m to shareholders via a tender offer at 50 cents a share.*
2 the act of offering to buy new shares at a particular price: *The Swiss entrepreneur made a tender offer for 15% of the company at €2.34 a share.*

tenner /'tenə(r)/ noun [C] (*informal*)
1 (*BrE*) £10 or a ten-pound note: *You can eat well here for under a tenner.*
2 (*AmE*) ten dollars

tenor /'tenə(r)/ noun [sing.]
(*Finance*) the length of time stated on a BILL OF EXCHANGE, etc. before it becomes due for payment: *the tenor of the bill* [SYN] TENOR

tentative /'tentətɪv/ adjective
1 (about an arrangement, agreement, etc.) not definite or certain because you may want to change it later: *The airline has reached a tentative agreement with its employees.* ◇ *There are tentative signs of recovery in the advertising market.*
2 not behaving with confidence; not done with confidence: *Consumers are no longer tentative about online shopping.*
▶ **'tentatively** adverb **'tentativeness** noun [U]

tenure /'tenjə(r)/ noun [U]

SEE ALSO: job tenure

1 the period of time when sb holds an important job: *The company's share price trebled under his tenure as Chief Executive.*
2 (*HR*) the right to stay permanently in your job, especially as a teacher at a university: *It's still extremely difficult to get tenure.* → LIFETIME EMPLOYMENT

3 (*Law*) the legal right to live in a house or use a piece of land: *When you rent a house here, you don't have security of tenure.*

tepid /'tepɪd/ adjective
(used especially in newspapers) lower in level, less successful, less good, etc. than expected: *A tepid economy is discouraging investors.* ◇ *The company's sales rose a tepid 0.4%.*

★ term /tɜːm; AmE tɜːrm/ noun, verb
● *noun*

SEE ALSO: fixed term, long-~, medium-~, near-~, short-~

1 [C] a word or phrase used as the name of sth, especially one connected with a particular type of language: *'Recovery' is a technical term for the period following a recession.*
✪ business/legal/scientific/technical terms
2 [C, usually sing.] a period of time for which sth lasts; a fixed or limited time: *If you hold the loan for the full term, you will pay more interest.* ◇ *During his second term as chairman, the company expanded into food and drink.* ◇ *a five-year term of office*
✪ a fixed/long/short term • a term runs out/ends/ expires
3 [sing.] the end of a particular period of time, especially one for which an agreement, etc. lasts: *The research programme will reach its term at the end of this month.*
4 (*Finance*) [sing.] the length of time stated on a BILL OF EXCHANGE, etc. before are due for payment: *the term of the bill* [SYN] TENOR
→ TERMS
[IDM] **in/over the 'long/'medium/'short/'far/ 'near term** used to describe what will happen a long, short, etc. time in the future: *The deal might be more expensive in the short term, but it would offer shareholders better value in the longer term.*
● *verb* [+ obj]
to use a particular name or word to describe sb/sth: *Management and union leaders held what was termed a 'crisis meeting'.*

'term as,surance (*BrE*) (also **'term in,surance**, *AmE, BrE*) noun [U]
a type of life insurance that only lasts for a fixed time and does not pay money if the insured person dies after that time

'term bill = PERIOD BILL

'term de,posit = TIME DEPOSIT

terminal /'tɜːmɪnl; AmE 'tɜːrm-/ noun, adjective
● *noun* [C]
1 a building or set of buildings at an airport where air passengers arrive and leave. A third terminal was opened last year.
2 (*IT*) a piece of equipment, usually consisting of a keyboard and a screen that joins the user to a central computer system: *Please switch off your computer terminal before leaving.*
● *adjective*
1 certain to get worse and come to an end: *The industry is in terminal decline.*
2 [only before noun] at the end of sth: *the terminal bonus on a policy*

'terminal ,market noun [C]
1 (*Finance*) a place where COMMODITIES, FUTURES, etc. are bought and sold that is in a trading centre such as London or New York rather than in the country where the goods are produced
→ COMMODITY EXCHANGE
2 (*Commerce*) (*AmE*) a central place, usually near an important town or city, where goods, especially agricultural goods, are brought from many different areas to be bought and sold

★ **terminate** /'tɜːmɪneɪt; *AmE* 'tɜːrm-/ *verb*
1 [+ obj *or* no obj] to end; to make sth end: *Your contract of employment terminates in May.* ◇ *The agreement was terminated immediately.*
2 (*HR*) [+ obj] (*especially AmE*) to remove sb from their job: *They had been terminating people in their fifties.* ◇ *terminated employees* See note at DISMISS

termination /ˌtɜːmɪ'neɪʃn; *AmE* ˌtɜːrm-/ *noun* [U,C]
1 the act of ending sth; the end of sth: *Failure to comply with these conditions will result in termination of the contract.*
2 (*HR*) (*especially AmE*) the act of removing sb from their job: *He sued the company for **wrongful termination**.* ◇ *Employees are entitled to receive either notice of termination or termination pay.*

ˌtermi'nation charge *noun* [C, usually pl.]
the fee for making a call to a mobile phone/cellphone from another system

'term in,surance = TERM ASSURANCE

'term ,loan *noun* [C]
(*Finance*) a loan for a fixed period of time, usually from a bank to a company, that is repaid in regular amounts: *The company has decided to cancel the $500 million three-year term loan.*

★ **terms** /tɜːmz; *AmE* tɜːrmz/ *noun* [pl.]

SEE ALSO: account terms, credit ~, easy ~, trade ~

1 the conditions that people offer, demand or accept when they make an agreement, an arrangement or a contract: *The Board has now agreed the terms of the deal.* ◇ *Under the terms of the agreement, their funding of the project will continue for some time.* ◇ *The **terms and conditions** of employment are changing.*
● *to accept/agree (on)/negotiate* terms ♦ *to give sb/offer/set* terms ♦ *attractive/better/favourable* terms
2 (*Commerce*) conditions that you agree to when you buy, sell, or pay for sth; a price or cost: *to buy sth on easy terms* (= paying for it over a long period) ◇ *attractive credit terms offered by car companies* ◇ *Our terms are 30 days* (= payment must be made in 30 days).
● *attractive/easy/favourable* terms ♦ *cash/payment/trade* terms
3 a way of saying sth or of expressing yourself: *I'll try to explain in simple terms.*
● *in broad/general/simple/strong* terms
→ TERM
IDM **be on good, friendly, bad, etc. 'terms (with sb)** to have a good, friendly, etc. relationship with sb: *I'm on **first-name** terms with my boss* (= we call each other by our first names). **in terms of sth; in ... terms** used to show what aspect of a subject you are talking about or how you are thinking about it: *Success is not just measured in financial terms.* **on your own 'terms; on sb's 'terms** according to the conditions that you or sb else decides: *I'll only take the job on my own terms.*
→ idiom at EQUAL

ˌterms of 'reference *noun* [pl.]
the limits that are set on what an official committee or report has been asked to do: *The matter, they decided, lay outside the commission's terms of reference.*

ˌterms of 'trade *noun* [pl.]
(*Economics*) the average price of a country's imports compared with the average price of its exports. If export prices rise faster than import prices, **terms of trade** are said to improve

terrestrial /tə'restriəl/ *adjective*
(used about television and broadcasting systems) operating on earth rather than from a SATELLITE: *terrestrial TV stations*

territory /'terətri; *AmE* -tɔːri/ *noun* [C,U] (*plural* **territories**)

SEE ALSO: negative territory, positive ~, sales ~

1 an area of a town, a country or the world that sb has responsibility for in their work: *Our representatives cover a very large territory.*
→ AREA (1)
2 an area of knowledge or activity: *Legal problems are Andy's territory* (= he deals with them). ◇ *This type of work is **uncharted territory*** (= completely new) *for us.* → AREA (3)

tertiary /'tɜːʃəri; *AmE* 'tɜːrʃieri; -ʃəri/ *adjective*
third in order, rank or importance: *Products and the manufacturing process seem to have priority, and marketing is only of tertiary importance.*
→ PRIMARY, SECONDARY

'tertiary ,industry (*also* 'service ,industry) *noun* [C,U]
(*Economics*) a business whose work involves doing sth for customers but not producing goods; these businesses as a group → PRIMARY INDUSTRY, SECONDARY INDUSTRY

'tertiary ,sector (*also* 'service ,sector) *noun* [sing.]
(*Economics*) the part of a country's economy that is connected with providing services rather than manufacturing or producing things

★ **test** /test/ *noun, verb*
● *noun* [C]

SEE ALSO: alpha test, aptitude ~, beta ~, blind ~, field-~, hall ~, market ~, means ~, psychological ~, psychometric ~, recognition ~

1 an experiment to discover whether or how well sth works, or to find out more information about it: *Market tests showed that €80 was too high a price.* ◇ *They demonstrated a test version of the software.* ◇ *I'll run a diagnostic test to see why the server keeps crashing.* ◇ *test engineers*
● *to conduct/do/perform/run* a test ♦ *a test proves/reveals/shows/suggests* sth
2 an examination of sb's knowledge or ability, consisting of questions for them to answer or activities for them to do: *All candidates must take an English test.*
● *to do/sit/take* a test ♦ *to fail/pass* a test
3 a situation or an event that shows how good, strong, etc. sb/sth is: *Sales of the latest model will be a key test of whether the company's change of image has worked.*
● *a big/crucial/good/key/tough* test ♦ *an important/the ultimate* test
IDM **put sb/sth to the 'test** to put sb/sth in a situation which will show what their true qualities are: *All of her negotiating talents were put to the test.*
→ idiom at STAND verb
● *verb*

SEE ALSO: beta-test

1 [+ obj] **test sth (out)** to use or try sth to find out how well it works or to find out more information about it: *Our products are not tested on animals.* ◇ *They opened a single store in Europe to test out the market.*
2 [+ obj *or* no obj] to examine sb's knowledge or ability by asking them questions or giving them activities to do: *Employees are tested on their customer service skills.*
3 [+ obj] to be difficult and therefore need all your ability, strength, etc: *Giving the presentation in France really tested my French.*
PHRV 'test for sth; 'test sth for sth to examine sth to see if a particular substance is present: *Has this software been tested for viruses?*

'test case noun [C]
(Law) a legal case or other situation whose result will be used as an example when decisions are being made on similar cases in the future: *The Italian group's bid will serve as a test case for the new takeover laws.*

'test deck noun [C]
(Technical) a small amount of data, material, etc. that is used as a basis for testing a project

'test drive noun [C]
an occasion when you drive a vehicle or use a piece of equipment, etc. to see how well it works and if you like it and want to buy it: *You can take the latest version of the software for a test drive if you download the 30-day trial.* ► **'test-drive** verb [+ obj]: *a chance to test-drive the newest cars*

tester /'testə(r)/ noun [C]
1 a person or thing that tests sth: *He started as a code tester for a software firm.* ◇ *The modem comes with a phone-line tester.*
2 a small amount of a product that you can try to see if you like it: *They are giving away thousands of perfume testers in their latest promotion.*

testimonial /ˌtestɪ'məʊniəl; AmE -'moʊ-/ noun [C]
1 (Marketing) a formal written statement about the quality of sth: *The catalogue is full of testimonials from satisfied customers.* ◇ *customer testimonials*
2 (HR) a formal written statement, often by a former employer, about sb's abilities, qualities and character: *She got a **glowing** testimonial from her former boss.* **SYN** RECOMMENDATION

★ **testing** /'testɪŋ/ noun [U]

SEE ALSO: concept testing, copy testing

the activity of trying or using sth in order to find sth out, see if it works, etc: *The product is still **in** testing and won't be available till next year.* ◇ *The project is **undergoing** testing.* ◇ *Consumer testing has shown that people like their washing to smell clean.*
◑ consumer/market testing ◆ to **carry out/do/ undertake** testing

'test ,market noun [C]
(Marketing) an area, a country, etc. where a product is sold in order to test it before it is sold in other places: *They ran television ads in two test markets to see if this was an appropriate way to advertise the product.* ◇ *several test-market cities* ► **'test-,market** verb [+ obj]: *The product is still being test-marketed.* **'test ,marketing** noun [U]: *Test marketing revealed that the product was too expensive.*

'test run noun [C]
(Marketing) an occasion when a product is tested: *We gave the software packages a test run.*
◑ to **give sth/conduct/do** a test run

tethered /'teðəd; AmE -ðərd/ adjective
attached to sth: *a keyboard tethered to a handheld computer by a cable* ◇ (figurative) *I couldn't do a job where I'm tethered **to** (= always working at) a computer.*

TEU /ˌti: i: 'juː/ abbr
(Transport) twenty-foot equivalent unit (used as a countable noun)
a standard container for transporting goods that is approximately six metres long: *a ship with a capacity of 6 000 TEU*

text /tekst/ noun, verb
● **noun**
1 [U] the words of a book, web page, etc., not the pictures, notes, etc: *The success of an ad may depend on how the text and the graphics are laid out.*

2 [U] any form of written material: *printed text* ◇ *The program converts scanned documents into **text files** that can be edited.*
3 [C] = TEXT MESSAGE
4 [C] the written form of a speech, an article, etc.
● **verb** (also **'text ,message**, less frequent) [+ obj or no obj]
text (sb) (sth) to send sb a written message using a mobile phone/cellphone: *Text me when you're on your way.* ◇ *I texted him the details.* **SYN** SMS
► **'texting** noun [U] = TEXT MESSAGING at TEXT MESSAGE

textile /'tekstaɪl/ noun
1 [C] any type of fabric made by weaving or knitting: *a factory producing a range of textiles* ◇ *the textile industry* ◇ *She works in textile design.*
◑ a textile business/maker/manufacturer/producer
2 textiles [pl.] the industry that makes fabric: *He got a job in textiles.*

'text ,message (also **text**) noun [C]
a short written message sent to sb using a mobile phone/cellphone **SYN** SMS
◑ to **get/receive/send** a text message
► **'text ,message** verb [+ obj or no obj] = TEXT verb
NOTE The verb **text** is usually used. **'text ,messaging** (also **'texting**, informal) noun [U]: *An estimated 70% of mobile phone owners use their phone for text messaging.* ◇ *text messaging services*

,text-to-'speech adjective [only before noun]
(IT) used to describe the technology that allows a computer to change data into spoken words: *text-to-speech software/programs* ► **,text-to-'speech** noun [U]: *You'll need to install text-to-speech to be able to listen to our e-books.*

TGI /ˌti: dʒi: 'aɪ/ = TARGET GROUP INDEX

'T-group (also **'training group**) noun [C]
(HR) a small group of people who meet, with a leader, and talk and think in order to improve their skills in dealing with people

theory /'θɪəri; AmE 'θɪri; 'θiːəri/ noun (plural **theories**)

SEE ALSO: expectancy theory, game ~, organization ~

1 [C,U] a formal set of ideas that is intended to explain why sth happens or exists: *Maslow's theory of human motivation* ◇ *the boom and bust theory of British economics*
2 [U,C] the principles on which a particular activity is based: *management theory* ◇ *the **theory and practice** of design*
3 [C] an opinion or idea that sb believes is true but may in fact be wrong: *The theory is that CEOs get rich only when shareholders get rich.*
IDM in **'theory** used to say that a particular statement is supposed to be true but may in fact be wrong: *In theory, these machines can last up to ten years.* ◇ *This all sounds fine in theory, but would it work in practice?*

,theory of con'straints noun [sing.] (abbr **TOC**)
(Production) a way of improving production by finding and improving the things or people that are limiting the amount or the speed of production

,Theory 'X /- 'eks/ noun [sing.]
(HR) a way of managing people based on the idea that most workers do not enjoy working for a company and do not want responsibility. They therefore need to be watched carefully, to receive a lot of instructions and be threatened with punishments.

,Theory 'Y /- 'waɪ/ noun [sing.]
(HR) a way of managing people based on the idea that most workers enjoy work and want responsibility. They should therefore be given

freedom to deal with difficult problems using their skill and imagination and be promised rewards.

Theory 'Z / - 'zed; AmE 'zi:/ noun [sing.]
(HR) a way of managing people, developed from Japanese styles of management. It is based on the idea that employees work best when they feel they are trusted and that they are an important part of the company.

therm /θɜːm; AmE θɜːrm/ noun [C]
(Technical) a unit of heat, used in the UK for measuring a gas supply

thin /θɪn/ adjective (**thinner, thinnest**)
(Finance) not very busy; with not much buying and selling: Bond prices were steady in thin trade on Tuesday. ◇ Market activity was much thinner than usual.

think /θɪŋk/ verb
IDM **think on your 'feet** to be able to think and react to things very quickly and effectively without any preparation **think out of/outside the 'box** to think in a new or different way in order to solve a problem: creative professionals who are paid to think outside the box ◇ We try to encourage out-of-the-box thinking. **think 'twice (about sth/about doing sth)** to think very carefully before you decide to do sth: You should think twice about employing someone you haven't met.
PHRV **think sth 'out** to consider or plan sth carefully: It's a very well thought out plan.

'think tank noun [C]
a group of experts who provide advice and ideas on political, social or economic issues ► **'think-tanker** (AmE spelling **think tanker**) noun [C]: think-tankers and businessmen

thin 'market (also ,narrow 'market) noun [C]
(Finance) a market in which there is not much buying and selling and small changes in supply or demand can have a great effect on the prices of shares, bonds, etc.

third-country 'national noun [C] (abbr TCN)
(HR) an employee of an international organization who does not come from the country in which the organization has its main base, or from the country in which they are working → HOST COUNTRY

third-gene'ration adjective [only before noun]
1 (abbr 3G) used to describe technology that has been developed to send data to mobile phones/cellphones, etc. at much higher speeds than were possible before: Third-generation technology allows you to download videos to a mobile phone.
2 used to describe any technology that is being developed that is more advanced than the earlier two stages

third line 'forcing noun [U]
(Economics) the illegal practice of a company refusing to allow a customer to have a product or service that they want unless they also buy sth that they do not want

third 'party noun, adjective
● *noun* [C]
(Insurance; Law or formal)
a company, an organization, a person, etc. that is involved in a situation in addition to the two main people or groups involved: The company might be bought back by its parent or sold to a third party. ◇ (BrE) **Third party, fire and theft** car insurance protects the victims of accidents and pays to repair or replace your car if it is stolen or damaged by fire.
● *adjective* [only before noun] **third-party**
1 (Law or formal) connected with a company, an organization, a person, etc. that is involved in a situation in addition to the two main people or groups involved: third-party suppliers ◇ The

materials that the company buys are checked for quality by independent third-party auditors.
2 (Insurance) connected with insurance that covers you if you injure sb or damage sb's property: All transport operators must be covered by third-party **liability**.

third-party inter'vention noun [U]
(HR) when an outside person or organization becomes involved in a dispute between employers and employees in order to try to end it

third-party 'software noun [U]
(IT) computer programs which add to the range of functions that existing programs can perform, that are developed or supplied by a different company from the one that develops or supplies the existing software: third-party plug-ins ◇ third-party software developers

the ,third 'sector noun [sing.]
(Economics) the part of the economy of a country that involves organizations that do not aim to make a profit and whose employees may work without being paid → PRIVATE SECTOR, THE PUBLIC SECTOR

the ,Third 'World noun [sing.]
a way of referring to the poor or developing countries of Africa, Asia and Latin America, which is sometimes considered offensive: the problem of third-world debt (= money owed to rich countries by poor countries) **NOTE** Developing countries is a more acceptable way of referring to these countries.

thirtysomething /'θɜːtisʌmθɪŋ; AmE 'θɜːrti-/ noun [C] (informal)
a person who is between thirty and thirty-nine years old: Their target market is thirtysomethings with no children. → TWENTYSOMETHING

thousand /'θaʊznd/ number (abbr K) (usually used with a plural verb)

SEE ALSO: cost per thousand

1 000 **HELP** You say a, one, two, etc. thousand without a final 's' on 'thousand'. **Thousands (of...)** can be used if there is no number or quantity before it. A plural verb is used unless the number refers to an amount of money, when a singular verb is used: ten thousand dollars ◇ One thousand jobs have been cut. ◇ Thousands of jobs have been cut. ◇ Twenty thousand dollars has been withdrawn from the account.

thrash /θraʃ/ verb
PHRV **thrash sth 'out** to discuss a situation or problem thoroughly in order to decide sth: The details have not been thrashed out yet.

three-'way adjective [only before noun]
involving three people, groups, processes or directions: a three-way bidding war for the grocery chain
● a three-way **battle/deal/merger/partnership**

threshold /'θreʃhəʊld; AmE -hoʊld/ noun [C]
(Accounting)
1 the level at which sth starts to happen, change or have an effect: Assets had fallen below a key threshold. ◇ Students will only pay back the loan once they have reached a particular pay threshold.
● a pay/salary/wage threshold
2 = TAX THRESHOLD

'threshold ef,fect noun [usually sing.]
1 (Marketing) the way in which advertising for a product has to reach a particular level before sales begin to increase

2 (*IT*) the way in which, as new technology, such as the phone, video recorder, etc. becomes familiar, people no longer think of it as technology

'threshold price *noun* [C]

(*Economics*) a minimum price that is set for a product: *Farmers are demanding that threshold prices be introduced for imported grain.*

thrift /θrɪft/ *noun*

1 [U] the habit of not spending too much money
2 [C] (*AmE*) = THRIFT INSTITUTION

'thrift insti,tution (*also* **thrift**) (*both AmE*) *noun* [C]

an organization like a bank that issues shares to people who deposit money and lends the money to people who want to buy a home SYN SAVINGS AND LOAN ASSOCIATION

thrive /θraɪv/ *verb* [no obj]

to become, and continue to be, successful, strong, healthy, etc: *The role of the government is to create an environment where small businesses can thrive.* SYN FLOURISH ▶ **'thriving** *adjective*

throughput /'θru:pʊt/ *noun* [U; C, usually sing.]

1 (*Production*) the amount of work that is done, or the number of people that are dealt with, in a particular period of time: *The improvements to the manufacturing process have increased throughput by 40%.* ◇ *the airports' combined passenger throughput* ◇ *The most impressive gain was in throughput time* (= the number of days needed to produce an order). See note at PRODUCE
2 (*IT*) the amount of data that passes through a piece of equipment or a system in a particular period of time: *The network will have to withstand high throughput.*

throw /θrəʊ; AmE θroʊ/ *verb* (**threw** /θru:/ **thrown** /θrəʊn; AmE θroʊn/)

IDM **throw the 'book at sb** (*informal*) to punish sb who has committed an offence as severely as possible **throw good money after 'bad** to spend more money on sth, when you have wasted a lot on it already: *The bank refused the company a further loan as it would be throwing good money after bad.* **throw your 'hat into the ring** to announce officially that you are going to compete in a competition, an election, etc: *He's thrown his hat into the ring for the chief executive's post.* **throw your 'money about/around** (*informal*) to spend money in a careless and obvious way **throw 'money at sth** to try to deal with a problem or improve a situation by spending money on it, when it would be better to deal with it in other ways **throw your 'weight about/around** (*informal*) to use your position of authority or power in an aggressive way in order to achieve what you want: *Although he's only got a few days left as chairman, he's still throwing his weight around.*
→ idioms at COURT *noun*, DEEP *adj.*, MONEY, QUESTION *noun*, WEIGHT *noun*
PHR V **,throw sth a'way 1** (*also* **,throw sth 'out**) to get rid of sth that you no longer want: *He threw away his laptop after three months and replaced it with a new one.* **2** to fail to make use of sth; to waste sth: *You must take the exam—you can't throw away all that work!* ◇ *to throw away a chance/an opportunity* → THROWAWAY **,throw sth 'in** to include sth with what you are selling or offering, without increasing the price: *Manufacturers may throw in benefits like training support.* **,throw sth 'out 1** = THROW STH AWAY (1) **2** to decide not to accept a proposal, an idea, etc: *A judge threw out a lawsuit that tried to stop the company building a telecom mast in the area.* **,throw sth 'up 1** to produce sth; to make people notice sth:

A Web search threw up a couple of useful pages. **2** to leave your job: *She threw up her job as a solicitor to become a writer.* **3** to build or make sth in a hurry: *People think you can just throw a website up and customers will find the answers to their questions.*

throwaway /'θrəʊəweɪ; AmE 'θroʊ-/ *adjective* [only before noun]

(about goods, etc.) produced cheaply and intended to be thrown away after use: *throwaway cameras* ◇ *We live in a throwaway society* (= a society in which things are not made to last a long time).
→ DISPOSABLE

,thumbs 'up/'down *noun* [sing.]

used to show that sth has been accepted/rejected or that it is a success/failure: *Shareholders gave a cautious thumbs up to the merger.* ◇ *The latest model has so far got the thumbs down from consumers.*

tick /tɪk/ *verb, noun*

● *verb* (*BrE*) (*AmE* **check**) [+ obj]

to put a mark (✓) next to an item on a list, an answer, etc., usually to show that it has been dealt with or is correct: *Tick this box if you do not wish us to send you information.*
IDM **have ,ticks in all the right 'boxes** (*informal*) to be doing the right things in order to achieve a particular result: *The company is making good progress in the health-care market, with ticks in all the right boxes.*
PHR V **,tick sb/sth 'off** (*BrE*) (*AmE* **,check sb/sth 'off**) to put a mark (✓) beside a name or an item on a list to show that sth has been dealt with: *It's a good idea to tick off the jobs on the list as you do them.* **,tick 'over** (*BrE*) (*usually used in the continuous tenses*) (about a business, a system, an activity, etc.) to keep working slowly without producing or achieving much: *Just keep things ticking over while I'm away.*

● *noun* [C]

SEE ALSO: **minus tick, plus tick**

1 (*BrE*) (*AmE* **'check mark, check**) a mark (✓) put beside a sum or an item on a list, usually to show that it has been checked or done or is correct: *I've put a tick against the things I've chosen.*
2 (*Finance*) (*also* **'tick point**) the smallest amount by which the price of shares, FUTURES (= contracts to buy or sell sth at a particular time in the future for a fixed price), etc. can change, often 0.01% of the NOMINAL VALUE: *The September gilt futures price closed 67 ticks up at 115.85.*
3 (*Finance*) an upward or downward movement in the price of a share, bond, COMMODITY, etc.
→ DOWNTICK, UPTICK

tickbox /'tɪkbɒks; AmE -bɑːks/ = CHECKBOX

ticker /'tɪkə(r)/ *noun* [C]

SEE ALSO: **stock ticker**

(*Stock Exchange*)
1 (*also* **'ticker-tape ma,chine, 'tape ma,chine**) a machine that prints data on a strip of paper, especially information about prices of shares on a stock market; an electronic device that shows information of this type: *5 million shares went through the stock exchange ticker late on Wednesday.* ◇ *a news ticker*
2 = TICKER SYMBOL

'ticker ,symbol (*also* **'ticker, 'symbol**) *noun* [C]

(*Stock Exchange*) especially in the US, a set of usually three or four letters that identifies a share, etc. on a stock exchange: *shares in Hewlett-Packard, trading under their ticker symbol 'HPQ'*

'ticker tape *noun* [C]
a strip of paper on which data is recorded by a
ticker; a similar strip on a computer screen: *A
ticker tape scrolls across the screen with breaking
news.*

'ticker-tape ma,chine = TICKER (1)

ticket /'tɪkɪt/ *noun, verb*
● *noun* [C]

SEE ALSO: **e-ticket, season ticket**

1 a printed piece of paper that gives you the right
to travel on a particular plane, train, etc. or to go
into a theatre, etc: *Many passengers still prefer paper
tickets to electronic ones.* ◇ *higher ticket prices*
O *to book/buy/reserve/sell* tickets ◆ *non-refundable/
one-way* tickets ◆ *bus/plane/theatre/train* tickets ◆
ticket *prices/sales* ◆ *a* ticket *agent/counter/
machine/office*
2 a label that is attached to sth in a shop/store
giving details of its price, size, etc: *This week you get
10% off the price on the ticket.* → LABEL, TAG
● *verb* [+ obj]
to produce and sell tickets for an event, a trip, etc.;
to give sb a ticket: *Passengers can now be ticketed
electronically.*

ticketing /'tɪkɪtɪŋ/ *noun* [U]
the process of producing and selling tickets:
ticketing systems → E-TICKETING

'ticket tout = TOUT *noun*

'tick point = TICK *noun* (2)

tie /taɪ/ *verb, noun*
● *verb* [+ obj] (**ties, tying, tied, tied**)
1 (*usually* **be tied**) to connect or link sb/sth closely
with sb/sth else: *Pay increases are tied* **to** *inflation.*
2 (*usually* **be tied**) to restrict sb and make them
unable to do everything they want to: *He was tied
to an unfair contract.*
IDM **tie the 'knot (with sb/sth)** (*informal*) (used
especially in newspapers) to join together with
sb/sth else in order to form a single business or
organization: *They are trying to tie the knot with a
rival company.* **NOTE** 'Tie the knot' is an informal
way of saying 'get married'.
PHRV **,tie 'in (with sth)** to match or agree with
sth: *The purchase of the magazine ties in with the
company's aim of raising its profile.* **,tie 'in (with
sth)**; **,tie sth 'in (with sth)** to link sth or be linked
to sth; to happen, or arrange for sth to happen, at
the same time as sth else: *A special magazine was
produced to tie in with the event.* → TIE-IN *noun* **,tie
sb 'into sth/sth** to restrict sb to a particular
situation, person, organization, etc: *They were tied
into an agreement to buy from particular suppliers.*
,tie sb 'up (*usually* **be tied up**) to keep sb busy so
that they have no time for other things: *I'm tied up
in a meeting until 3.* **,tie sth 'up 1** (*often* **be tied up**)
to invest money so that it is not easily available for
use: *He cannot retire as his money is all tied up in the
company.* **2** (*usually* **be tied up**) to connect or link
sth to sth else: *The brand's strength is tied up with
the image of the company's owner.* **3** to deal with all
the remaining details of sth: *We are hoping to tie up
the deal by tomorrow.* ◇ *I went to the office for an
hour to tie up some loose ends* (= finish remaining
small jobs). **4** to keep sth in use so that it cannot be
used for other things: *I was using the Internet, so the
phone line was tied up.* **,tie 'up with sb/sth** to be
linked to sth such as another company and work
together on sth: *Big insurance companies are
competing to tie up with banks.* → TIE-UP *noun*
● *noun* [C]
1 [usually pl.] a strong connection between people
or organizations: *The firm has close ties* **with** *a
Japanese corporation.*

2 (*AmE also* **'necktie**) a long narrow piece of fabric
worn around the neck, especially by men, with a
knot in front: *He always wears a* **suit and tie** *to
work.* ◇ *a collar and tie*

,tied 'agent *noun* [C]
(*Finance*; *Insurance*) a person who represents one
particular company and gives people advice only
about the products and services of that company
→ INDEPENDENT FINANCIAL ADVISER

,tied 'loan *noun* [C]
(*Economics*) money that is lent to one country by
another country on condition that it is spent on
goods or services from the country that provided
the money: *tied loans to developing countries*

'tie-in *noun* [C]
(*Commerce*; *Marketing*)
1 a product such as a book or toy that is connected
with a film/movie, television programme, etc: *tie-in
products to help market the movies*
2 the act of advertising or selling a product or
service that is closely related to the main product
or service being advertised or sold: *Selling nail
polish at the beauty salon is a great marketing tie-in.*
3 when two or more companies work together, for
example to try to sell their products: *a tie-in* **with**
an American satellite giant
4 (*especially AmE*) a way of selling sth in which two
or more products must be bought together; a
product that is sold in this way: *tie-in deals which
guaranteed they would buy more stock*
5 a contract or an agreement that limits what you
can do or makes you do sth for a fixed period of
time: *Business customers can rent software on a
monthly basis with no tie-in period.*
→ TIE IN (WITH STH), TIE STH IN (WITH STH) at TIE
verb

tier /tɪə(r); *AmE* tɪr/ *noun* [C]

SEE ALSO: **first tier, second ~, top-~, two-~**

1 one of several levels in an organization or a
system: *More women are reaching the top tier of
management.* ◇ *a two-tier pay structure*
2 one of several levels of quality: *a place in the top
tier of biotech companies*

,Tier '1 ,capital *noun* [U]
(*Finance*) the main part of a bank's funds that comes
from the money that shareholders have invested in
it and spare profits that it has kept **SYN** CORE
CAPITAL

'tie-up *noun* [C]
an agreement between two companies to join
together: *a tie-up* **between** *HNC and Arriba* ◇ *The
Japanese company is looking for a tie-up* **with** *a
European car manufacturer.* → TIE UP WITH SB/STH
at TIE *verb*

tiger /'taɪɡə(r)/ *noun* [C]

SEE ALSO: **Asian tiger**

(*Economics*) (used especially in newspapers) a
country whose economy is growing very fast:
Ireland's tiger economy is still expanding steadily.

tight /taɪt/ *adjective* (**tighter, tightest**)
1 (about time or money) difficult to manage,
because there is not enough: *We have a very tight
budget.* ◇ *I have a tight schedule today.*
2 very strict and firm: *We must continue to exercise
tight control over costs.* ◇ *There is a need for tighter
security on emails.*
IDM **keep a tight 'rein on sb/sth** to control sb/sth
carefully or strictly: *to keep a tight rein on costs/
expenses/spending* → idiom at RUN *verb*

tighten /'taɪtn/ *verb* [+ obj] **tighten sth (up)** to make sth become stricter; to increase control over sth: *The government is to tighten the rules on drug advertising.*

○ *to tighten* **policy/regulations/rules/security**
▶ **'tightening** *noun* [U; sing.] **(a) tightening (up) of** sth: *a tightening of safety standards*
IDM **tighten your 'belt** to spend less money because there is less available: *With price increases on most goods, everyone is having to tighten their belt.* → BELT-TIGHTENING → idiom at PURSE
PHRV **,tighten 'up (on sth)** to become stricter or more careful: *steps to tighten up on tax evasion*

,tight 'money *noun* [U]
(*Economics*) a situation when money is difficult to borrow and can only be borrowed at a high rate of interest: *Many small firms are feeling the impact of tight money and are being forced out of business.*
SYN DEAR MONEY

,tight 'money ,policy *noun* [C,U]
(*Economics*) a government policy of raising interest rates in order to make it more expensive to borrow money and so reduce the level of spending
SYN DEAR MONEY POLICY

tightrope /'taɪtrəʊp; *AmE* -roʊp/ *noun* [C, usually sing.]
a situation that involves a lot of difficulty and risk: *When setting prices, we are* **walking** *a tightrope* **between** *not making enough profit or not making enough sales.*

TIL /,ti: aɪ 'el / = TIME IN LIEU

till /tɪl/ *noun* [C]
1 (*BrE*) a machine used in shop/stores, restaurants, etc. that has a drawer for keeping money in, and that shows and records the amount of money received for each thing that is sold **SYN** CASH REGISTER—Picture at STORE
2 (*BrE*) the place where you pay for the things that you are buying in a large shop/store: *Please pay at the till.* ◇ *a long queue at the till* **SYN** CHECKOUT
3 (*especially AmE*) the drawer where the money is put in a CASH REGISTER
→ idiom at CATCH *verb*

timber /'tɪmbə(r)/ *noun* [U]
1 trees that are grown to be used in building or for making things: *the timber industry*
2 (*especially BrE*) (*AmE usually* **'lumber**) wood that is prepared for use in building, etc: *a timber merchant* (= a company that sells timber)

time /taɪm/ *noun, verb*
● *noun*

SEE ALSO: **closing time, comp ~, cycle ~, dead ~, double ~, drive ~, dwell ~,** etc.

1 [U] what is measured in minutes, hours, days, etc: *Revenue will increase* **over time** (= as time passes).
2 [U] the time shown on a clock: *The time is now half past ten.* ◇ *Look at the time! I didn't know it was so late.*
3 [U] the time in a particular part of the world: *Greenwich Mean Time* ◇ *We land at 6 o'clock* **local** *time.*
4 [U,C] the time when sth happens or when sth should happen: *Can we change the time of the meeting to 14.30?*
5 [U] an amount of time; the amount of time available to work, rest, etc: *I don't have much* **free/ spare** *time.* ◇ *She always* **makes time** *to meet new employees.* ◇ *It* **takes time** (= needs a long time) *to make changes.* ◇ *What a* **waste of time!** → TIME OFF

6 a time [sing.] a period of time, either long or short, during which you do sth or sth happens: *It would take a long time to redesign the layout.*
7 [C] an occasion when you do sth or sth happens: *How many times have you visited the factory?* ◇ *This* is **the first time** that *I've been to London.*
IDM **against 'time** if you do sth **against time**, you do it as fast as you can because you do not have much time: *We're working against time to get the project finished.* **ahead of/behind 'time** earlier/ later than was expected: *We finished three months ahead of time.* **all the 'time; the whole 'time**
1 during the whole of a particular period of time: *We are working on new products all the time.* **2** very often; repeatedly: *The photocopier breaks down all the time.* **at all 'times** always: *A hard hat must be worn at all times on site.* **at a 'time** separately or in groups of a particular number on each occasion: *We process the photographs in batches of several hundred at a time.* **in good 'time** early; with enough time so you are not in a hurry: *I made sure I arrived in good time for the interview.* **in 'time (for sth/to do sth)** not late; with enough time to be able to do sth: *Will we be in time for the six o'clock train?* ◇ *The division was sold just in time to save the company from bankruptcy.* **keep up/move with the 'times** to change and develop your ideas, way of working, etc. so that you do what is modern and what is expected **make up for lost 'time** to do sth quickly because you wish you had started it earlier or had worked more quickly: *The new company is so creative it will soon make up for lost time.* **,nine times out of 'ten;,ninety-nine times out of a 'hundred** used to say that sth is usually true or almost always happens **on 'time** at the correct time: *Nearly 90% of flights arrived on time.* ◇ *We have a good record for* **on-time delivery. time is 'money** time is valuable, and should not be wasted **the whole 'time** = ALL THE TIME → idioms at MARK *verb*, PUSH *verb*, RUN *verb*, STAND *verb*, TAKE *verb*
● *verb* [+ obj]
to arrange to do sth or arrange for sth to happen at a particular time: *'I hope we're not too early.' 'You couldn't have timed it better!'* ◇ *Publication of the report was timed* **to** *coincide with the annual conference.* → TIMING

'time ac,count = DEPOSIT ACCOUNT

,time and a 'half *noun* [U]
(*HR*) a rate of pay that is 50% more than the normal rate, which a worker gets for working outside normal hours: *You get time and a half if you work over 8 hours a day.* → DOUBLE TIME, OVERTIME

,time-and-'motion ,study *noun* [C]
a detailed study of how a person, a department, a company, etc. works, the results of which are used to find ways to make them/it more efficient
○ *to carry out/make/undertake* a time-and-motion study

'time card *noun* [C]
(*HR*) a card that is marked with the time when an employee arrives and leaves, usually by a machine (a **time clock**)

'time ,charter *noun* [C,U]
(*Transport*) the hire of ship or an aircraft and the people to operate it (the **crew**) for a fixed period of time

'time clock (*also* **'time re,corder**) *noun* [C]
(*HR*) a machine in a place of work, especially a factory, that records the exact times when employees arrive or leave by marking special cards (**time cards**)

'time de,posit (*also* **'term de,posit**) *noun* [C]
(*Finance*) a type of account at a bank or other

financial institution in which money is left for a fixed period of time with a fixed rate of interest

'time frame *noun* [C]
the length of time that is used or available for sth: *We expect to complete the project within a fairly short time frame.*

time in 'lieu = TIME OFF IN LIEU

timekeeping /'taɪmkiːpɪŋ/ *noun* [U]
a person's ability to arrive in time for things, especially work: *He was given a written warning for poor timekeeping.* ▶ **'timekeeper** *noun* [C]: *They are usually good timekeepers—they've never been late before.*

'time lag (*also* **lag**, **'time lapse**) *noun* [C]
the period of time between two connected events: *There is usually a time lag between invoicing a customer and getting paid.*

'time ˌlimit *noun* [C]
the length of time within which you must do or complete sth: *We have to set a time limit for the work.* ◇ *We don't want to put a time limit on the agreement.*
O *to **fix/set** a time limit (for sth)* • *to **impose/place/put** a time limit on sth* • *to **extend/relax** a time limit* • *to **go over/overrun** a time limit* • *the time limit **expires***

timeline /'taɪmlaɪn/ *noun* [C]
a line representing when the different stages of an event, a project, etc. took place or will take place: *The group has not yet set a timeline for the merger.* ◇ *There is still no timeline on the proposed job cuts.*

'time ˌmanagement *noun* [U]
the practice or skill of organizing your working time in the most efficient way

ˌtime 'off *noun* [U]
a period when you are away from work because you are ill/sick, taking a holiday/vacation, etc: *I need to take time off to study for my exam.*
O *to **ask for/get/have/take** (some) time off*

ˌtime off in 'lieu /luː; *BrE also* ljuː/ (*abbr* **TOIL**)
(*also* ˌtime in 'lieu *abbr* **TIL**) (*both BrE*) *noun* [U]
(*HR*) extra time away from work that employees can have if they have worked extra hours: *If they work on Saturdays, they expect time off in lieu during the week.* **SYN** COMP TIME (*AmE*) → OVERTIME

timeout /'taɪmaʊt/ *noun* [C]
(*IT*) an occasion when an action takes too long to be completed and is automatically cancelled: *We're losing too much time through server timeouts.*

'time rate *noun* [C]
(*HR*) an arrangement where people are paid for the number of hours they work rather than for the number of items they produce

'time reˌcorder = TIME CLOCK

times /taɪmz/ *noun* [pl.]
used in comparisons to show how much more, better, etc. sth is than sth else: *Today we're doing three **times as much** business as we were two years ago.* ◇ *Our marketing budget is three **times higher** than last year.*

timescale /'taɪmskeɪl/ *noun* [C]
the period of time that it takes for sth to happen or be completed: *What's the timescale for this project?* ◇ *We hope the negotiations will be completed within a six-month timescale.*

'time ˌseries *noun* [C]
(*Technical*) a series of values of a quantity obtained over a period of time, often with equal amounts of time between them: *You can use time series data to monitor sales trends over a period of years.*

'time-ˌserver *noun* [C]
used in a disapproving way to describe sb who does as little work as possible in their job because they are just waiting until they leave for another job or finish work completely ▶ **'time-ˌserving** *adjective*, *noun* [U]

'time sheet *noun* [C]
(*HR*) a piece of paper on which the number of hours that sb has worked is recorded: *Assistants' hours should be recorded on a time sheet and signed by their manager.*
O *to **complete/fill in/fill out/keep/submit** a time sheet*

timetable /'taɪmteɪbl/ *noun*, *verb*
• *noun* [C]
1 a plan of when you expect particular events to happen: *I have a busy timetable this week.* ◇ *We have **set out** a timetable for the opening of four new branches.*
O *a **detailed/firm/strict/tight** timetable* • *to **draw up/set** a timetable* • *to **keep to/stick to** a timetable*
2 a list showing what time particular events happen: *a bus/train timetable* (= when they arrive and leave)
→ SCHEDULE
• *verb* [+ obj] (*especially BrE*) (*usually* **be timetabled**)
to arrange for sth to take place at a particular time: *A discussion has been timetabled for next Monday.* ◇ *a timetabled meeting* **SYN** SCHEDULE
▶ **'timetabling** *noun* [U]

'time-ˌtested *adjective* [only before noun]
that has been used for a long time and has been proved to be successful: *'Two for the price of one' is a time-tested marketing idea.*

ˌtime to 'market *noun* [U; sing.] (*abbr* **TTM**)
(*Marketing*; *Production*) the amount of time from when a company starts to develop a new product until the product goes on sale: *Time to market is critical in the software industry.* ◇ *We are aiming to achieve advanced, reliable products and a fast time to market.*
O *to **cut/improve/reduce** time to market*

ˌtime ˌvalue of 'money *noun* [U]
(*Accounting*) the idea that the value of an amount of money received today is worth more than the same amount of money received in the future, as it can be invested to earn interest: *The time value of money means, in effect, that you lose money when customers take a long time to pay.*

'time zone *noun* [C]
one of the 24 areas that the world is divided into, each with its own time that is one hour earlier than that of the **time zone** immediately to the east

timing /'taɪmɪŋ/ *noun*
1 [U,C] the act of choosing when sth happens; a particular point or period of time when sth happens or is planned: *The timing of the announcement was calculated to take media attention away from the factory closures.*
2 [U] the skill of doing sth at exactly the right time: *The success of a new product depends to a large extent on good timing.*
→ TIME *verb*

tip /tɪp/ *noun*, *verb*
• *noun* [C]
1 a small piece of advice about sth practical or about what is likely to happen: *Can you give me any tips **for** dealing with a customer who won't pay?* ◇ *The book offers some tips **on** writing a good business plan.* ◇ *investment/share tips for 2006* (= the ones that are likely to do well)
O *to **give (sb)/offer (sb)/pass on** tips* • *to **get/pick up**/*

take/use tips • good/helpful/money-saving/
practical tips
2 a small amount of extra money that you give to
sb, for example sb who serves you in a restaurant:
We get rather poor tips on weeknights.
O *a generous/large/small tip* • *to give/leave (sb) a tip*
IDM **the tip of the 'iceberg** only a small part of a
much larger problem: *The fraud cases that are
discovered are only the tip of the iceberg.*
• *verb* (-pp-)
1 [+ obj] to say in advance that sb/sth will be
successful or that sth will happen: *She has been
tipped **as** a possible future chief executive.* ◇ *He was
widely tipped **for** the top job.* ◇ *Some analysts had
tipped shares of companies that were about to
collapse.* ◇ *They were accused of **share tipping**
for fees.*
2 [+ obj or no obj] to give sb an extra amount of
money to thank them for sth they have done for
you as part of their job: *The French always tip very
generously.* ◇ *How much should I tip?* ◇ *I tipped the
cab driver €2.*

TIR /ˌtiː aɪ ˈɑː(r)/ *abbr*
(*Transport*) **transport international routier** *or*
transports internationaux routiers an
organization that makes rules and sets standards
for international road transport in Europe: *600 000
or more trucks using the TIR system cross the borders
each year.* ◇ *The TIR carnet is a Customs control
document used for an international transit operation
of goods.* **NOTE** TIR is a short form of the French
phrase.

tirekicker = TYREKICKER

tissue /ˈtɪʃuː; *BrE also* ˈtɪsjuː/ (*also* ˌtissue **'paper**)
noun [U]
very thin paper used for wrapping and packing
things that break easily: *Gifts are wrapped in tissue
paper.*

titanium /tɪˈteɪniəm/ *noun* [U]
a strong light expensive metal: *titanium laptops*

title /ˈtaɪtl/ *noun*

SEE ALSO: **document of title, strata title**

1 [C] the name of a book, an article, etc.
2 [C] a particular book or magazine: *The company
publishes twenty new titles a year.*
3 [C] the name of a job: *My **job title** is 'Senior
Financial Analyst'.* ◇ *He handed over the CEO title to
his deputy.*
4 [C] a word in front of a person's name to show
their rank or profession, whether or not they are
married, etc: *Give your name and title* (= Mr, Miss,
Ms, Dr, etc.).
5 (*Law*) [U,C] the legal right to own sth, especially
land or property; the document that shows you
have this right: *Do you have **proof of title**?* ◇ *The
legal title **to** the shares is transferred to the buyer.*

'title deed *noun* [C, usually pl.]
(*Law*) a legal document proving that sb is the owner
of a particular piece of land, a particular house,
etc: *the title deeds **to** a property*

'title-ˌholder (*also spelled* **titleholder**) *noun* [C]
(*AmE*)
(*Law*) the legal owner of property

'title inˌflation *noun* [U]
(*HR*) the practice of giving an employee a more
important name to describe their job although the
job does not change

TLD /ˌtiː el ˈdiː/ = TOP-LEVEL DOMAIN

TM /ˌtiː ˈem/ *abbr*
a short form of the word TRADEMARK, shown by
the symbol ™

TNA /ˌtiː en ˈeɪ/ = TRAINING NEEDS ANALYSIS

TOC /ˌtiː əʊ ˈsiː; *AmE* oʊ/ = THEORY OF
CONSTRAINTS

to-do /təˈduː/ *adjective* [only before noun]
used to describe things that need to be done: *I have
a daily **to-do list** on my PC.*

toehold /ˈtəʊhəʊld; *AmE* ˈtoʊhoʊld/ *noun* [C]
a position in a place or an activity which you hope
will lead to more power or success: *The company is
hoping to establish a toehold in the American
market.*
O *to **establish/gain/get** a toehold*

TOIL /ˌtiː əʊ aɪ ˈel; *AmE* oʊ/ = TIME OFF IN LIEU

token /ˈtəʊkən; *AmE* ˈtoʊ-/ *noun, adjective*
• *noun* [C]
1 a piece of paper that you can collect when you
buy a particular product and then exchange for sth:
Collect six tokens and get a free T-shirt.
2 a round piece of metal or plastic used instead of
money to operate some machines or as a form of
payment: *a parking token* ◇ *Insert the token in the
machine.*
3 (*BrE*) a piece of paper that you pay for and that sb
can exchange for sth in a shop/store: *a book/gift
token*
4 something that is done, given, etc. as a symbol of
how strongly sb feels about sth: *Please accept this
small gift **as a token of** our gratitude for your hard
work.*
• *adjective* [only before noun]
1 involving very little effort or feeling and
intended only as a way of showing other people
that you think sb/sth is important, when really you
are not sincere: *The company made a token effort to
improve facilities for staff.*
2 done as a symbol: *a token one-hour strike* (= to
show that workers feel strongly about sth) ◇ *We
make a token* (= very small) *charge for this service.*

tokenism /ˈtəʊkənɪzəm; *AmE* ˈtoʊ-/ *noun* [U]
the fact of doing sth only in order to do what the
law requires or to satisfy a particular group of
people, but not in a way that is really sincere: *The
appointment of a woman to the previously all-male
board of directors could look like tokenism.* **NOTE** In
companies **tokenism** usually involves including a
few members of a particular group in an activity, or
moving them to a more senior position, only so that
the company will look as if it is behaving in a fair
way towards all its employees.
→ EQUAL OPPORTUNITY

'token ˌmoney *noun* [U]
(*Economics*) a system of notes and coins where the
value stated on them is much greater than the
value of the material they are made from

toll /təʊl; *AmE* toʊl/ *noun, verb*
• *noun*
1 [C] money that you pay to use a particular road,
bridge or area: *paying for parking or motorway tolls*
◇ *a toll road*
2 [C] (*AmE*) a charge for a telephone call that is
calculated at a higher rate than a local call: *toll calls*
3 [sing.] the amount of damage that sth causes: *the
emotional toll of running your own company*
→ idiom at TAKE *verb*
• *verb* [+ obj or no obj]
to charge for the use of a road, bridge, transport,
etc: *a new tolling scheme on a public road*

ˌtoll-'free *adjective* [usually before noun] (*AmE*)
(about a telephone number) that you do not have to
pay to call: *You can sign up for the service online or
by calling a toll-free number.* ◇ *toll-free technical*

support ► ˌtoll-ˈfree *adverb*: *Call toll-free on 0800 962872.*

ˈtolling aˌgreement *noun* [C]
(*Manufacturing*) an agreement to process a particular amount of a raw material at a particular factory: *The company produced 35 000 tonnes of refined copper under tolling agreements in the first half of the year.*

ton /tʌn/ *noun* [C] (*plural* **tons** *or* **ton**)

SEE ALSO: **American ton, long ~, metric ~, net ~, short ~**

1 a unit for measuring weight, in the UK 2 240 pounds or 1 016.04 kilograms (**long ton**) and in the US 2 000 pounds or 907.18 kilograms (**short ton**): *The plant turns out up to 630 000 tons of aluminium annually.*
2 a unit for measuring the size of a ship. One ton is equal to 100 CUBIC feet: *A 10 000-ton vessel can be unloaded in 10 hours.*

tone /təʊn; *AmE* toʊn/ *noun* [C]
a sound heard on a telephone line: (*BrE*) *the dialling tone* ◇ (*AmE*) *the dial tone* ◇ *Please leave your message after the tone.* → idiom at STRIKE *verb*

tonnage /ˈtʌnɪdʒ/ *noun* [U,C]
(*Transport*)
1 the size of a ship or the amount it can carry, expressed in TONS: *a large amount of new tonnage— 268 new ships this year alone*
2 the total amount that sth, especially cargo, weighs: *Rail freight tonnage along the route has dropped 20% in the last year.*

tonne /tʌn/ (*plural* **tonnes** *or* **tonne**) = METRIC TON

★ **tool** /tuːl/ *noun, verb*
● *noun* [C]

SEE ALSO: **machine tool**

1 an instrument that you hold in your hand and use for making things, repairing things, etc: *a cutting tool* ◇ *a tool kit* (= a set of tools in a box or bag) ◇ *power tools* (= using electricity)
2 a thing that helps you to do a job or to achieve sth: *research tools such as questionnaires* ◇ *The Internet has become a powerful business tool.*
✪ **business/decision-making/management/ marketing/sales** tools • *an* **essential/a key/ powerful/practical/useful** tool
3 a computer program that performs a particular function: *The program comes with standard tools such as dictionary, spellchecker and thesaurus.*
✪ **design/desktop publishing/interactive/online/ web-based** tools
IDM **the tools of your ˈtrade** the things that you need to do your job → idiom at DOWN *verb*
● *verb*
PHRV **ˌtool ˈup**; **ˌtool sb/sth ˈup** to get or provide sb/sth with the equipment that is necessary to do or produce sth: *They have invested heavily, tooling up to make the new model.*

toolbar /ˈtuːlbɑː(r)/ *noun* [C]
(*IT*) a line of symbols on a computer screen that show the different things that the computer can do when you click on one of them: *Click on the 'open file' icon on the toolbar.*

tooling /ˈtuːlɪŋ/ *noun* [U]
(*Manufacturing*) the activity or process of making special tools or machines for a factory; the tools themselves: *a supplier of machines and precision tooling for the can industry*

toolmaker /ˈtuːlmeɪkə(r)/ *noun* [C]
(*Manufacturing*) a person or business that makes tools and machines for the manufacturing industry

and keeps them in good condition ► **ˈtoolmaking** *noun* [U]

ˈtool shop *noun* [C]
(*Manufacturing*) the part of a factory where special tools and machines are made → MACHINE SHOP, WORKSHOP

top /tɒp; *AmE* tɑːp/ *noun, adjective, verb*
● *noun* [sing.]
the highest or most important position or rank: *He's at the top of his profession.* ◇ *She is determined to* **make it to the top** (= to be as successful as possible in her profession). ◇ *This decision came right from the top.*
IDM **at the top of the ˈtree** in the highest position or rank in a profession or career **come out on ˈtop** to win a contest or an argument: *He tends to come out on top in most boardroom disputes.* **from the top ˈdown** starting with the most important people in a company or an organization: *The company's focus, from the top down, is on the customer.* **OPP** FROM THE BOTTOM UP at BOTTOM → TOP-DOWN **get on ˈtop of sth** to manage to deal with or control sth: *We're struggling to get on top of all the work we've got.* **on ˈtop 1** in a leading position or in control: *Their investment in R&D has allowed them to stay on top.* **2** in addition: *It would cost around $900, with tax on top.* **on ˈtop of sth 1** in control of a situation; knowing about a situation: *You need to stay on top of technological changes.* **2** in addition to sth: *These job cuts come on top of the 500 redundancies already announced.* **ˌtop of ˈmind** (*Marketing*) = FRONT OF MIND at FRONT *noun*
● *adjective* [usually before noun]
highest in position, rank or degree: *My office is on the top floor.* ◇ *Prices at the top end of the market* (= the more expensive prices) *have fallen.* ◇ *The company announced changes in top management.* ◇ *We produce top-quality goods.*
IDM **ˌtop-ˈ10, ˌtop-ˈ100, etc.** (*also spelled* **top ten, top hundred, etc.**) among the ten best, most successful, etc. of a particular thing: *Most of the top-10 airlines were expected to report losses.*
● *verb* [+ obj] (**-pp-**)
1 to be higher than a particular amount: *Their market share topped 20% in May.*
2 to be in the highest position on a list because you are the most successful, important, etc: *The company again topped the list of best performers.*
3 to do or say sth that is better, more impressive, etc. than sth that sb else did or said: *I'm afraid the other company has topped your offer* (= offered more money).
PHRV **ˌtop ˈout (at sth)** if sth tops out at a particular price, speed, etc. it does not rise any higher: *Sales topped out at a record $10 billion.* **ˌtop sth ˈup** to increase the amount of sth to the level you want or need: *The group's cash flow will be topped up by the proceeds from the sale of its publishing business.*

ˌtop ˈbrass (*also* **brass**, *especially in AmE*) *noun* [sing. with sing./pl. verb] (*informal*)
the people who are in the most important positions in a company or an organization: *All the top brass was/were at the ceremony.* ◇ *The restructuring of the company will not affect the top brass.*

ˌtop ˈdog *noun* [C, usually sing.] (*informal*)
a person or group that is better than all the others, especially in a situation that involves competition: *He was top dog in the company before the merger.*

ˌtop ˈdollar *noun* [U] (*especially AmE*) (*informal*)
a high price; the highest price: *Companies will* **pay top dollar** *for same-day deliveries.*

,top-'down *adjective*
1 starting from or involving the people who have higher positions in an organization
○ top-down **decision-making/leadership/management/planning**
2 (about a plan, project, etc.) starting with a general idea to which details are added later
OPP BOTTOM-UP

,top-'end *adjective* [only before noun]
among the best, most expensive, etc. examples of sth: *Many people are upgrading their phones to top-end models.* ◇ *hotels catering for top-end business travellers* (= with most money to spend)

,top 'flight *noun* [C, usually sing.]
the best or most successful of a particular group: *They have kept their place in the market's top flight.*
► **,top-'flight** *adjective* [only before noun]: *We hired a top-flight sales force.*

,top-'grossing *adjective* [only before noun]
(about a product) that has earned more money than any other: *The drug is Glaxo's top-grossing product with sales of almost $2 billion.*

,top-'heavy *adjective*
(about an organization) having too many senior staff or managers compared with the number of workers: *The new CEO streamlined the company's top-heavy management structure.*

,top-'level *adjective* [only before noun]
involving the most important or best people in a company or an organization: *a top-level meeting* ◇ *top-level managers*

,top-level do'main *noun* [C] (*abbr* TLD)
(*IT*) the end of a name which identifies a website or a group of websites, for example '.com', '.org' or '.net'

,top 'line *noun* [sing.]
(*Accounting*) the amount of money that a company receives from sales: *We are hoping our new product will boost our top line.* SYN REVENUE
→ BOTTOM LINE
► **'top-line** *adjective* [only before noun]: *top-line growth/revenue/sales*

,top-'notch *adjective* [only before noun]
excellent; of the highest quality: *We must be prepared to pay for top-notch talent.* ◇ *They provide a top-notch service.*

,top-of-the-'line *adjective* [only before noun] (*AmE*)
used to describe the most expensive of a group of similar products: *a top-of-the-line DVD player*

,top of the 'range *noun* [C] (*BrE*)
the most expensive of a group of similar products: *This car is the top of the range.* ► **,top-of-the-'range** *adjective* [only before noun]: *The printer is a top-of-the-range model.*

topple /'topl; *AmE* 'ta:pl/ *verb* [+ obj]
to make sb lose their position of power

,top-'ranked *adjective* [only before noun]
considered to be the best or most popular of a number of similar things: *the top-ranked business schools* SYN TOP-RATED

,top 'ranking *noun* [C,U]
1 the highest or most important position in an organization, an industry, etc: *The airline has earned top ranking in customer-service measures.*
2 (*IT*) a high, or the highest, position in the list of websites given by a SEARCH ENGINE (= a computer program that searches the Internet for information): *ways to achieve a top ranking for your website*

► **,top-'ranking** *adjective* [only before noun]: *top-ranking executives in manufacturing* ◇ *We have a top-ranking website with new visitors every day.*

,top-'rated *adjective* [only before noun]
1 considered to be the best or most popular of a number of similar products or people: *the top-rated brand of soft drinks* ◇ *a top-rated media analyst*
SYN TOP-RANKED
2 that has received a high score for the measurement of a particular quality: *The top-rated bonds are known as 'investment grade', followed by 'high yield' and then by 'junk' bonds.*

,top-'selling *adjective* [only before noun]
(about a product) that has sold more than others

,top-'tier *adjective* [only before noun]
considered to be one of the best: *competing with top-tier companies in the printer and copier markets*

'top-up *noun* [C]
an extra amount of money that is added to the original amount so that there is enough: *pension-fund top-ups* ◇ *a top-up loan/payment*

'top-up card *noun* [C]
a card that allows you to make more calls from your mobile phone/cellphone to the value of the card or the money that you pay

torrid /'torɪd; *AmE* 'tɔːr-; 'taːr-/ *adjective* [usually before noun]
(often used in newspapers) very difficult: *a torrid period on the stock market*

tort /tɔːt; *AmE* tɔːrt/ *noun* [C,U]
(*Law*) something wrong that sb does to sb else that is not criminal, but that can lead to action in a civil court: *tort law* ◇ *the US tort system*

total /'təʊtl; *AmE* 'toʊtl/ *adjective, noun, verb*
● *adjective* [usually before noun]
1 being the amount or number after everyone or everything is counted or added together: *These latest redundancies bring the total number of job cuts to over 3 000.* ◇ *Total sales were up 2.3%.* ◇ *Medical products accounted for 61% of the company's total revenues.*
2 complete; including everything: *a total ban on tobacco advertising* ◇ *The venture was a total disaster.*
● *noun* [C]

SEE ALSO: grand total, running ~, sum ~

the amount you get when you add several numbers or amounts together; the final number of people or things when they have all been counted: *The chain has closed 170 out of a total of 420 stores.* ◇ *The bank employs a total of 80 000 staff.* ◇ *The bank employs 80 000 staff in total.* ◇ *The company posted a combined total of $2.4 billion in losses in the second and third quarters.*
● *verb* [+ obj] (-ll-, *AmE also* -l-)
1 to reach a particular total: *Imports totalled $1.4 billion last year.* ◇ *debts totalling around $4 billion*
2 to add up the numbers of sth/sb and get a total : *Daily balances are totalled at the bottom of the column.*
3 (*informal*) (*especially AmE*) to damage a car very badly, so that it is not worth repairing it → WRITE STH OFF at WRITE

'total 'cost of 'ownership *noun* [U] (*abbr* TCO)
(*Accounting*) a method of calculating the costs involved in buying and using a product or service which includes the cost of buying it and other costs such as ordering, delivering, keeping it in good condition, etc: *The new system will give customers improved software performance and a lower total cost of ownership.*

'total pro'ductive 'maintenance *noun* [U]
(*abbr* TPM)
(*Production*) a way of improving the way a factory's machines and equipment are used by continuously making sure that they are working as efficiently as possible

Total 'Quality 'Management (*also spelled* **total quality management**) (*abbr* TQM) (*also* **'quality management**) *noun* [U]
a system of management that considers that every employee in the organization is responsible for keeping the highest standards of work in every aspect of the company's work in order to meet the needs of the customers; the techniques used for controlling and checking quality: *Total Quality Management means that our customers can expect the highest quality service.* ◇ *to institute total quality management* ◇ *total quality management programmes/practices*

total 'shareholder re'turn *noun* [U,C] (*abbr* TSR)
(*Finance*) a measure of the profit gained from investing in the shares of a particular company over a fixed period of time, usually expressed as a percentage over one year: *The company's aim is to double total shareholder return every four years.*

touch /tʌtʃ/ *verb, noun*
● *verb* [+ obj]
1 to reach a particular level, etc: *Shares in the company touched a two-year low of €7.6.*
2 to put your hands or fingers on sth/sb: *Every time you touch a key, the computer voice tells you what command you have executed.*
3 to become connected with or work with a situation or person: *I didn't trust the company and refused to touch the deal.*
IDM **touch 'base (with sb)** (*informal*) to make contact with sb again: *She travels to Boston every other week to touch base with her home office.* **touch 'bottom** to reach the worst or lowest state: *Many analysts believe that the recession has now touched bottom.*
● *noun*

SEE ALSO: **high touch**
---

1 [C, usually sing.] an act of putting your hands or fingers on sth: *All this information is available at the touch of a button* (= by simply pressing a button).
2 [C] a small detail that is added to sth in order to improve it or make it complete: *I spent the morning putting the finishing touches to the report.*
IDM **be, get, keep, etc. in 'touch (with sb)** to communicate with sb, especially by writing to them or telephoning them: *I'll be in touch about the details next week.* **be, keep, etc. in 'touch (with sth)** to know what is happening in a particular subject or area: *It's vital to keep in touch with the latest innovations.*

'touch screen *noun* [C]
(*IT*) a computer screen which you touch with your finger or with a special pen (**stylus**) in particular places in order to give instructions to the computer: *a handheld with a touch screen and stylus* ◇ *touch-screen monitors/technology*

'touch-type *verb* [no obj]
to type without looking at the keys of the keyboard

tough 'love *noun* [U]
(*HR*)
1 used to describe decisions made by senior managers that benefit the organization but may not help the employees
2 used to describe the situation when managers make employees aware of the fact that they are not working well and make them responsible for

improving: *I received some tough love, but it was feedback I needed to hear.*

tough-'minded *adjective*
1 used to describe a person who makes firm decisions and does not easily change their mind: *tough-minded business leaders*
2 used to describe a decision, situation, etc. connected with this type of person: *a tough-minded strategy*

tour /tʊə(r); tɔː(r); *AmE* tʊr/ *noun* [C]
1 an act of walking around a place to look at it: *The CEO took the guests on a tour of the factory.*
2 a journey made for pleasure during which several different towns, countries, etc. are visited: *a two-week tour of Europe* → PACKAGE HOLIDAY

'tour company = TOUR OPERATOR

tourism /'tʊərɪzəm; 'tɔːr-; *AmE* 'tʊr-/ *noun* [U]
the business activity connected with providing accommodation, services and entertainment for people who are visiting a place for pleasure: *the tourism industry* ◇ ***mass/package** tourism* ◇ *The hotel chain has been badly hit by the slump in tourism.* ▶ **'tourist** *noun* [C]: *The hotel is very popular with foreign tourists.* ◇ *We usually travel tourist class* (= in the cheapest seats).

'tourist at'traction *noun* [C]
a place that is interesting and popular with people visiting an area for pleasure: *The London Eye is one of London's top tourist attractions.*

'tourist office (*also* **'tourist infor'mation office**) *noun* [C]
a place where you can get information about an area, interesting places to visit, accommodation, etc: *You can buy maps at the tourist information office.* **NOTE** This is also often called a **tourist information centre** (spelled **center** in American English) or just **tourist information**. ▶ **'tourist officer** (*also* **'tourist infor'mation officer**) *noun* [C]

'tour operator (*also* **'tour company**) *noun* [C]
a company that arranges visits to places for pleasure

tout /taʊt/ *verb, noun*
● *verb*
1 [+ obj] to try to persuade people that sb/sth is important or valuable by praising it/them: *She is being touted as the next head of the company.*
2 [+ obj or no obj] (*especially BrE*) to persuade people to buy your goods or services, especially by going to them and asking them directly: *Many attendees were at the conference to tout their latest products.* ◇ *companies publicly touting for investors*
● *noun* (*also* **'ticket tout**) (*both BrE*) (*AmE* **'scalper**) [C]
a person who buys tickets for concerts, sports events, etc. and then sells them to other people at a much higher price

toymaker /'tɔɪmeɪkə(r)/ *noun* [C]
a company that makes toys

To'yota Pro'duction System *noun* [sing.]
(*abbr* TPS)
(*Production*) a system of manufacturing developed by the Toyota Motor Corporation in Japan that aims to improve production by wasting as little time, money, etc. as possible and being able to change quickly to deal with new situations

TPM /ˌtiː piː 'em/ = TOTAL PRODUCTIVE MAINTENANCE

TPS /ˌtiː piː 'es/ = TOYOTA PRODUCTION SYSTEM

TQM /ˌtiː kjuː 'em/ = TOTAL QUALITY MANAGEMENT

trace

trace /treɪs/ *verb, noun*
(*Production*)
● *verb* [+ obj]
to follow the movements of materials, goods, stocks, etc. through a complete process: *These systems track and trace inventory through the supply chain.* ▶ **traceability** /ˌtreɪsəˈbɪləti/ *noun* [U]: ◇ *inventory traceability* **traceable** /ˈtreɪsəbl/ *adjective*
● *noun* [C, usually sing.]
the process of following the movements of materials, goods or stocks of items: *If only one of your boxes arrives, email us and we'll put a trace on the shipment.*

track /træk/ *noun, verb*
● *noun* [C]

SEE ALSO: **fast track, inside track**

a path or direction that sb/sth is moving in: *We want to improve morale and give all our employees a career track.*
IDM back on 'track going in the right direction again after a mistake, failure, etc: *The project had fallen behind schedule, but now it's back on track.* **be on 'track** to be doing the right thing in order to achieve a particular result: *The group is on track to achieve its ambitious growth targets.* **keep/lose 'track of sth/sb** to have/not have information about what is happening or where sth/sb is: *The new system keeps track of where each product is until it is sold.* **be on the right/wrong 'track** to be thinking or doing sth in the right/wrong way in order to achieve sth
● *verb*
1 [+ obj] to follow the progress or development of sth/sb: *The system for tracking sales needs updating.*
2 [+ obj or no obj] to move in a particular direction; to move in the same direction as sth: *Technology stocks were tracking higher.*
3 (*Production*) [+ obj] to follow the movements of goods and stocks of items: *Her job was processing orders, sending out invoices and tracking inventory.* ▶ **trackability** /ˌtrækəˈbɪləti/ *noun* [U]: *The system uses complex bar codes to provide complete trackability of each package.* **trackable** /ˈtrækəbl/ *adjective*

'tracker fund (*BrE*) (*also* **'index fund**, *AmE, BrE*) *noun* [C]
(*Finance*) a type of investment fund, consisting of some of the shares in a particular SHARE INDEX, whose value always follows the market

'tracking poll = TRACKING STUDY

'tracking stock *noun* [C,U]
(*Stock Exchange*) shares in one part of a company's activities that represent the value of that part rather than the company as a whole: *The group's wireless division trades as a tracking stock.*

'tracking ˌstudy (*also* **'tracking poll**) *noun* [C]
(*Marketing*) a study in which people are asked the same questions at different times, in order to find out how people's opinions, tastes, needs, etc. change over time: *We conducted a tracking study by phone to monitor awareness of our ads.*

'track ˌrecord *noun* [C]
all the past achievements, successes or failures of a person or an organization: *He has a proven track record in marketing.*
➕ *a good/poor/proven/strong track record*

tradable (*also spelled* **tradeable**) /ˈtreɪdəbl/ *adjective*
that you can easily buy and sell or exchange for money
➕ *tradable goods/securities/shares*

★ trade

★ **trade** /treɪd/ *noun, verb*
● *noun*

SEE ALSO: **balance of trade, fair ~, free ~, insider ~, invisible ~, passing ~, stock-in-~, terms of ~, visible ~**

1 [U] the activity of buying and selling or of exchanging goods or services between people or countries: *Trade between the two countries has increased.* ◇ *global trade in electronic equipment* ◇ *The US was accused of unfair trade practices.*
2 [C] a particular type of business: *It has been a bad year for the retail trade.* ◇ *the building/tourist trade*
3 **the trade** [sing. with sing./pl. verb] a particular area of business and the people or companies that are connected with it: *In the trade, this sort of computer is called a 'client-based system'.* ◇ *a trade magazine/journal*
4 [U] the amount of goods or services that you sell: *Trade was very good last month.* ◇ *Domestic companies are losing trade to foreign importers.*
5 [U,C] a job, especially one that involves working with your hands and that requires special training and skills: *He's a designer by trade.* ◇ *to learn a trade*
6 (*Stock Exchange*) [U; C, usually pl.] buying and selling on a stock exchange; one act of doing this: *The share price fell 30% in early afternoon trade.* ◇ *a 20% reduction in daily trades on the stock exchange*
→ idioms at PLY, ROARING

WHICH WORD?

trade/business/industry

These words are combined with many nouns to describe particular areas of commercial activity, but they tend to be used in different contexts.

Business is often used when talking about the activities of particular individuals or companies: *I always knew I wanted to work in the restaurant business.* ◇ *The company has returned to what it knows best: the car business.*

Industry is common when talking about the economy: *The country is trying to rebuild its oil industry.*

Trade is combined with only a small number of nouns. It is used especially about traditional types of business, for example: *the art/book trade* ◇ *the retail trade* (= running a shop/store, supermarket, etc.). It is also the word used when describing illegal forms of business: *the illegal diamonds/drugs trade*

See note at BUSINESS

● *verb*
1 [no obj] to buy and sell things: *companies that trade in agricultural products* ◇ *The euro has made it easier for European countries to trade with each other.*
2 [no obj] to exist and operate as a business or company: *The firm has now ceased trading.* ◇ *Rodine Limited now trades as Harvest Software.*
3 (*Stock Exchange*) [+ obj or no obj] to be bought and sold, or to buy and sell sth, on the stock exchange: *Shares were trading at half their usual value.*
4 [+ obj] to exchange sth that you have for sth that sb else has: *He earns a lot of money but I wouldn't trade places with him.*
PHR V 'trade at sth (*AmE*) to buy goods or shop at a particular store **ˌtrade 'down** to spend less money on things than you did before: *The survey showed that consumers are unwilling to trade down to cheaper cosmetics when times are hard.* **ˌtrade sth 'in (for sth)** to give sth you have used as part of the payment for sth new: *People can trade in their old PCs for the latest model.* **ˌtrade sth 'off** to balance two things or situations that are opposed to each other: *You sometimes need to trade price off against*

quality. → TRADE-OFF ,trade 'up **1** to sell sth in order to buy sth more expensive: *Many drivers are trading up to a four-wheel drive.* **2** to give sth you have used as part of the payment for sth more expensive

tradeable = TRADABLE

'trade ,advertising *noun* [U]
(*Marketing*) the act of making a product or service known to the people who will sell it to customers, rather than to the customers themselves

'trade a,greement (*also* com,mercial 'treaty) *noun* [C]
(*Economics*) an arrangement between two or more countries in which they agree to special conditions, for example lower prices and IMPORT DUTIES, when buying from and selling to each other: *a bilateral* (= between two countries) *trade agreement* ◇ *a multilateral* (= between three or more countries) *trade agreement*

'trade associ,ation *noun* [C]
(*Economics*) an organization for companies in the same industry, that provides advice, information and other services for its members: *the Mexican transport trade association, Canacar* ◇ *Intertanko, the trade association of independent tanker owners*
SYN INDUSTRY ASSOCIATION

'trade ,balance = BALANCE OF TRADE

'trade ,barrier *noun* [C]
(*Economics*) an action by a government that makes free trade between its own country and other countries more difficult or impossible NOTE Examples of **trade barriers** include TARIFFS, QUOTAS, EMBARGOES and SANCTIONS: *Under the agreement, member countries will remove trade barriers on industrial goods.* ◇ *Exports from developing countries face higher trade barriers than products from developed countries.* ◇ *Several countries agreed to lower trade barriers to their farm products.*
◑ to **create/erect/raise** trade barriers ◆ to **dismantle/ lower/reduce/remove** trade barriers

'trade bill (*also* com'mercial bill) *noun* [C]
(*Trade*) a BILL OF EXCHANGE that is used to pay for goods

'trade ,buyer *noun* [C]
(*Finance*) a company that buys another company, especially one in the same business: *If no trade buyer is found for the firm, it will be floated on the stock market.*

'trade ,counter *noun* [C] (*BrE*)
(*Commerce*) a part of a factory, WAREHOUSE or website where a business can buy goods at reduced prices

'trade ,credit *noun* [U,C]
(*Accounting*) an arrangement by which one company allows another company a period of time in which to pay for goods after it has received them

'trade ,creditor *noun* [C]
(*Accounting*) a company that has provided goods or services to another company but has not yet been paid

'trade ,cycle *noun* [C] (*especially BrE*)
(*Economics*) the usual pattern of a country's economy, with periods of success (**expansion**) and periods of difficulty (**contraction**) happening regularly one after another SYN BUSINESS CYCLE

'trade debt = BUSINESS DEBT

'trade ,deficit (*also* 'trade gap) *noun* [C, usually sing.]
(*Economics*) a situation in which the value of a country's imports is greater than the value of its

exports; the amount by which the two values are different: *a widening/worsening trade deficit* ◇ *The country posted a trade deficit of $1.5 billion in January.* → BALANCE OF PAYMENTS, BALANCE OF TRADE, TRADE SURPLUS
◑ to **post/run/suffer** a trade deficit ◆ to **cut/reduce** a trade deficit

'trade dele,gation *noun* [C]
a group of manufacturers or suppliers who visit another country in order to increase business with that country: *Canada sent a trade delegation to South Korea.*

,trade des'cription *noun* [C] (*BrE*)
(*Law*) something that describes all or some features of goods, for example their quantity, size, time or place of origin, method of manufacture, price, etc: *The firm was accused of false trade descriptions.*

,Trade Des'criptions Act *noun* [sing.]
in the UK, a law stating that all information given about goods must be true and clear: *The firm admitted making a false statement under the Trade Descriptions Act.*

,trade 'discount *noun* [C] (*also* 'trade terms [pl.])
(*Commerce*) an amount of money that is taken off the usual cost of goods or services when one company sells them to another company or business

'trade dis,pute *noun* [C]
1 (*HR*) a disagreement between employers and employees about pay, working conditions, etc.
SYN INDUSTRIAL DISPUTE
2 (*Economics*) a disagreement between countries or companies in different countries about trade

'trade exhi,bition = TRADE SHOW

'trade fair = TRADE SHOW

'trade ,figures *noun* [pl.]
(*Economics*) figures that show the value of a country's imports compared with the value of its exports: *The October trade figures show that the UK spent $2 bn more abroad than it received.*

'trade gap = TRADE DEFICIT

'trade-in *noun* [C,U]
a method of buying sth by giving a used item as part of the payment for a new one; the used item itself: *The company accepts trade-ins on desktop computers.* ◇ *the trade-in value of the old car*
SYN PART EXCHANGE (*BrE*)
▶ **'trade-in** *verb* [+ obj]

'trade maga,zine (*also* 'trade ,journal) *noun* [C]
a magazine that is published regularly and contains news and articles about a particular industry: *the trade magazine 'The Grocer'* ◇ *Ask your employees which trade journals they read.* → CONSUMER MAGAZINE

★ **trademark** /'treɪdmɑːk; *AmE* -mɑːrk/ *noun* [C]

SEE ALSO: **registered trademark**

1 (*abbr* **TM**) a name, symbol or design that a company uses for its products and that cannot be used by anyone else: *French law protects your trademark and logo.* ◇ *a registered trademark* ◇ *the rights of trademark holders* ◇ *The company was sued for trademark infringement* (= illegal use of another company's trademark). See note at COPYRIGHT
◑ **trademark holders/owners** ◆ trademark **infringements/violations**
2 a special way of behaving, dressing, etc. that is typical of sb and that makes them easily

recognized: *He was wearing his trademark white suit.*

▶ **'trademark** *verb* [+ obj]: *trademarked designs/names*

'trade ˌmission *noun* [C]
1 a group of government officials or business people who go to another country to encourage trade: *A British trade mission is to visit Ethiopia next month.*
2 an office of one country in another country which encourages trade between the two countries: *the Russian trade mission in Finland*

'trade name *noun* [C]
1 a name that is used by a particular company: *The company uses the trade name Marubeni in the US.*
2 a name that a company gives to a product: *The drug is sold under the trade name Lipitor.*
3 a word that is used for sth within a particular industry but is not well known outside the industry

'trade-off *noun* [C]
the act of balancing two things that are opposed to each other: *a trade-off between increased production and a reduction in quality* ◇ *The trade-off for better pay was less flexible working hours.*

'trade press *noun* [sing. with sing./pl. verb]
magazines and newspapers that are published for a particular industry: *The exhibition was advertised in the trade press.*

'trade price = WHOLESALE PRICE

★ **trader** /'treɪdə(r)/ *noun* [C]

SEE ALSO: **rogue trader, sole trader**

1 (*Commerce*) a person or company that buys things and sells them at a profit: *small market traders* ◇ *Plans for a new hypermarket have angered local traders.* ◇ *commodity traders*
2 (*Finance*; *Stock Exchange*) (*AmE*) = DEALER (2)

'trade repreˌsentative *noun* [C] (*abbr* **'trade rep**)
1 (*Marketing*) = SALES REPRESENTATIVE
2 a person or an organization that represents a country in matters relating to trade

'trade sale *noun* [C]
1 (*Commerce*) [usually pl.] sales that a company makes to another business rather than to the public
2 (*Finance*) when a company is sold to another company, usually in the same industry: *Shareholders are in favour of a trade sale to a large international company.*

ˌtrade 'secret *noun* [C]
a piece of information, for example the method of making a product, that a company does not want other companies to know: *The recipe for the drink is a closely guarded trade secret.*

'trade show (*also* **'trade exhiˌbition, 'trade fair**) *noun* [C]
(*Marketing*) an event at which many different companies producing related products show and sell their products → EXPO

tradesman /'treɪdzmən/, **tradeswoman** /'treɪdzwʊmən/ *noun* [C] (*plural* **tradesmen** /-mən/ **tradeswomen** /-wɪmɪn/)
1 a skilled person, especially one who makes or repairs sth: *tradesmen such as carpenters and electricians*
2 a person who buys and sells goods, especially on a small scale: *market tradesmen*
SYN TRADESPERSON

tradesperson /'treɪdzpɜːsn; *AmE* -pɜːrsn/ *noun* [C] (*plural* **tradespeople** /-piːpl/ *or, especially in formal use,* **tradespersons**)
1 a skilled person, especially one who makes or repairs sth
2 a person who buys and sells goods, especially on a small scale **NOTE** Tradespeople is usually used to talk about a group of men and women, or to avoid having to say 'tradesmen' or 'tradeswomen'. Tradesperson/tradespeople is also used in more formal language.

ˌtrades 'union = TRADE UNION

the ˌTrades Union 'Congress = TUC

ˌtrades 'unionist = TRADE UNIONIST

'trade ˌsurplus *noun* [C, usually sing.]
(*Economics*) a situation in which the value of a country's exports is greater than the value of its imports: *They have managed to maintain a large trade surplus.* ◇ *China posted a trade surplus of $2.2 billion in August.* OPP TRADE DEFICIT → BALANCE OF PAYMENTS, BALANCE OF TRADE

'trade terms = TRADE DISCOUNT

★ **ˌtrade 'union** (*also* **ˌtrades 'union**) (*both BrE only*) (*AmE* **ˌlabor ˌunion**) (*also* **'union,** *BrE, AmE*) *noun* [C]
an organization of workers, usually in a particular industry, that exists to protect their interests, improve conditions of work, etc: *a trade union representing car workers* ◇ *the trade union movement*
❍ to **belong to/form/set up/join** a trade union ◆ a trade union **activist/leader/member/official/representative**
▶ **ˌtrade 'unionism** *noun* [U]: *the history of trade unionism*

ˌtrade 'unionist (*also* **ˌtrades 'unionist,** *both BrE* **'unionist,** *AmE, BrE*) *noun* [C]
a member of a trade union

'trade war *noun* [C]
a disagreement between countries in which they take action to damage each other's trade: *The European Commission called for talks to try to avert a trade war with the US.*
❍ an **all-out/a bitter/damaging/fierce/full-scale** trade war

'trade-ˌweighted *adjective* [only before noun]
(*Economics*) that shows the value of a country's currency, compared with the currency of other countries that it trades with: *The dollar has fallen nearly 5% on a trade-weighted basis.* ◇ *Last year the dollar lost 9.6% of its value against a trade-weighted basket of currencies.*

★ **trading** /'treɪdɪŋ/ *noun* [U]

SEE ALSO: **day trading, emissions ~, fair ~, horse-~, insider ~, Office of Fair ~, principal ~,** etc.

1 the activity of buying and selling things: *Supermarkets everywhere reported excellent trading in the run-up to the holidays.* ◇ *The group has been badly hit by tough trading conditions.* ◇ *unfair trading practices* ◇ *oil/diamond trading* ◇ *new laws on Sunday trading* (= shops/stores being open on Sundays)
❍ **disappointing/excellent/illegal/poor/strong** trading ◆ **Internet/online** trading
2 (*Finance*; *Stock Exchange*) the activity of buying and selling shares, currencies, etc: *Shares worth $8 million changed hands during a day of hectic trading.* ◇ *When trading resumed the next day, the company's share price collapsed.* ◇ *fast electronic trading of futures*
❍ **busy/heavy/hectic/intensive/light/quiet** trading ◆ **commodity/currency/equity/share/stock** trading

'trading ac,count *noun* [C]
(*Accounting*) a statement of the money that a company has spent on making or buying goods and of the money received from selling those goods, so that the TRADING PROFIT can be calculated: *The trading account shows a profit of €85 205.*

'trading ,company *noun* [C]
(*Commerce*) a company that exists to buy and sell goods: *a textile trading company*

'trading es,tate = INDUSTRIAL ESTATE

'trading floor (*BrE also* **'dealing floor**) *noun*
[C, usually sing.]
(*Stock Exchange*) an area in a stock exchange where dealers meet each other and buy and sell shares: *The news of the rise in interest rates was greeted with shock on the trading floor.*

'trading loss (*also* ,**gross 'loss**) *noun* [C]
(*Accounting*) the amount by which money received from the sale of goods or services is less than the cost of producing or providing them. This is calculated before OVERHEADS, interest and tax is taken off: *Full-year results showed a substantial trading loss.* → TRADING PROFIT

'trading ,partner *noun* [C]
1 (*Economics; Trade*) a country or company that another country or company buys goods from or sells goods to: *Australia is New Zealand's largest trading partner.*
2 (*IT*) a company that is involved in exchanging electronic information with another company using EDI: *a small Hong Kong company that conducts e-business with more than 10 trading partners in the UK, Europe and Australasia*

'trading ,period = ACCOUNTING PERIOD

'trading post *noun* [C]
1 (*Trade*) a small place in an area that is a long way from any town, used as a centre for buying and selling goods (especially in N America in the past)
2 (*E-commerce*) a website where people can buy and sell things

'trading ,profit (*also* ,**gross 'profit**) *noun* [C]
(*Accounting*) the amount by which money received from the sale of goods or services is greater than the cost of producing or providing them. This is calculated before OVERHEADS, interest and tax are taken off: *The company reported a small trading profit in its second year.* → TRADING LOSS

'trading ,session = SESSION (1)

,Trading 'Standards *noun* [pl.; U]
(*Law*) in the UK, the process of making sure that laws protecting consumers are obeyed; the government department responsible for this: *Contact your local Trading Standards service for advice and information.* ◇ *a Trading Standards officer*

'trading stock = STOCK-IN TRADE (1)

traffic /'træfɪk/ *noun, verb*
● *noun* [U]

SEE ALSO: foot traffic, page ~, store ~

1 the vehicles that are on a road at a particular time: *I leave work early to avoid the rush-hour traffic.* ◇ *The road was built to ease traffic congestion in the city.*
● **heavy/light/rush-hour** *traffic*
2 the movement of ships, trains, aircraft, etc. along a particular route: *transatlantic traffic* ◇ *air traffic control/controllers*
● **air/rail/sea** *traffic* ▪ **domestic/international** *traffic*
3 the movement of people or goods from one place to another: *the traffic of goods between one country and another*

● **business/commuter/passenger** *traffic* ▪ *cargo/ container/freight* *traffic*
4 (*Marketing*) the number of people who come to a place or use a service in a particular period: *We used our website to **drive** traffic to our stores.*
● **customer/mall/shopper/walk-in** *traffic*
5 (*IT*) information that travels across a computer system in a particular period
● **data/email/Internet/network/voice** *traffic*
6 illegal trade in sth: *traffic **in** drugs*
● *verb* (-ck-)
PHRV **'traffic in sth** to buy and sell sth illegally
▶ **'trafficker** *noun* [C] **'trafficking** *noun* [U]: *the fight against human trafficking* (= illegally bringing people into a country)

trail /treɪl/ *verb, noun*
● *verb*
1 [+ obj or no obj] (*used especially in the continuous tenses*) to be less successful than other companies, people, etc: *Their sales are trailing **behind** other superstores.* ◇ *Our 24% market share is trailing our competitor's 41%.* ◇ *The UK trails **badly** when it comes to research and development spending on IT.*
2 [+ obj] to advertise a plan, product, film/movie, etc. in advance: *the company's **heavily/widely** trailed plans* ◇ *The revenues were slightly better than trailed.*
3 [+ obj] to follow behind sb/sth: *New business jet orders typically trail a recovery by nine to twelve months.*
PHRV **,trail 'off** (*especially BrE*) to gradually become less: *Income from advertising increased in the first half of the year, but then trailed off.*
● *noun* [C]

SEE ALSO: audit trail, paper trail

a series of marks that is left by sth as it moves and that shows where it has been (*figurative*): *She quit her job, **leaving** a trail of unfinished projects and unreturned phone calls behind her.*
IDM **be/go on the 'trail of sb/sth**; **be/go on the … trail** to be following or trying to find sb/sth: *Analysts expect the company to be on the acquisition trail next year.* **blaze a/the 'trail** to be the first to do or to discover sth that others follow: *Comet is blazing the jobs trail by creating 3 000 new jobs.*

trailblazer /'treɪlbleɪzə(r)/ *noun* [C]
a person or company that is the first to do or discover sth and so makes it possible for others to follow: *The company was a trailblazer in e-commerce in the 90s.* → BLAZE A/THE TRAIL at TRAIL *noun*

trailer /'treɪlə(r)/ *noun* [C]
1 (*Transport*) a truck, or a container with wheels, that is pulled by another vehicle: *The containers are lifted onto truck trailers for the last part of the journey.*
2 (*especially BrE*) a series of short scenes from a film/movie or television programme, shown in advance to advertise it

,trailing 'spouse *noun* [C]
a husband or wife who gives up their job in order to follow their wife or husband to a new place where they have found a job

★**train** /treɪn/ *verb, noun*
● *verb* (*often used as an adjective* **trained**)
1 [+ obj or no obj] to teach a person the skills for a particular job or activity; to be taught in this way: *The staff are fully trained **to** handle almost any situation.* ◇ *She trained **as** a lawyer before starting her own company.* ◇ *He felt he had been well trained **for** the job.* ◇ *highly trained sales personnel*
● *to be* **fully/highly/properly/well** *trained*

2 [+ obj] to develop a natural ability or quality so that it improves: *an alert mind and a trained eye*
● *noun* [C]

SEE ALSO: **gravy train**

a railway/railroad engine pulling a number of coaches/cars or trucks, taking people and goods from one place to another: *Britain's biggest train operator*
● *a commuter/passenger train* ◆ *a freight/goods train*

trainee /ˌtreɪˈniː/ *noun* [C]
(*HR*) a person who is being taught how to do a particular job: *a management/sales trainee* ◇ *a trainee manager/salesman/engineer* ◇ *They have plans to recruit up to 800 new trainees.*
▶ **traiˈneeship** *noun* [C]: *businesses offering graduate traineeships*

ˌtrainee soˈlicitor (*also* ˌarticled ˈclerk, *old-fashioned*) (*both BrE*) *noun* [C]
(*Law*) the title used for a person employed by a group of lawyers (a **law firm**) while he or she is being trained to become a qualified SOLICITOR

★ **training** /ˈtreɪnɪŋ/ *noun* [U]

SEE ALSO: **assertiveness training, computer-based ~, on-the-job ~, transfer of ~**

the process of learning the skills that you need to do a job: *New employees do a month's intensive training before starting.* ◇ *He had no formal training in design.* ◇ *You will receive in-house training throughout your first year.* ◇ *a training and development budget* See note at INFORMATION
● *to do/get/receive training* ◆ *to give/offer/provide training* ◆ *corporate/employee/staff/workforce training* ◆ *formal/hands-on/in-house training* ◆ *job/leadership/management/skills/vocational training* ◆ *a training centre/course/programme/session/workshop*

ˈtraining group = T-GROUP

ˈtraining ˌmanual *noun* [C]
a book, etc. that teaches you the skills necessary to do or use sth: *An online training manual is available for the software.*

ˈtraining needs aˌnalysis *noun* [C, usually sing., U] (*abbr* TNA)
(*HR*) a method of calculating what training is required to give a company's employees all the skills and knowledge that they need for the company to be successful
● *to carry out/do/perform/undertake a training needs analysis*

ˈtraining ˌtransfer = TRANSFER OF TRAINING

tranche /trɑːnʃ/ *noun* [C]
(*Finance*) a part of a loan, a payment, an investment or other large amount of money: *The first tranche of the fee will be paid when the contract is signed.*

transact /trænˈzækt/ *verb* [+ obj or no obj]
to do business with a person or an organization: *Manufacturers are getting used to transacting business online.* ◇ *People all over the world can now transact with one another instantaneously.*

★ **transaction** /trænˈzækʃn/ *noun*
1 [C] a piece of business that is done between people, especially an act of buying or selling: *financial transactions between companies* ◇ *an increase in online transactions*
● *a business/financial/property/share transaction* ◆ *to carry out/complete/conduct/do/make a transaction*

2 [U] the process of doing sth: *He broke the law by using a residential property for the transaction of business.*
▶ **transactional** /trænˈzækʃnl/ *adjective*

tranˈsactional ˈcosts = TRANSACTION COSTS

tranˌsactional ˈleadership *noun* [U]
(*HR*) a way of managing people by setting them clear tasks and rewarding them for good performance → TRANSFORMATIONAL LEADERSHIP

tranˈsaction ˌcosts (*also* tranˈsactional costs) *noun* [pl.]
(*Economics*) the amount of effort, time and money (not including the cost of buying sth) that it takes to arrange a piece of business: *the high transaction costs of buying property*

tranˈsaction ˌprocessing *noun* [U]
1 (*IT*) a type of computer system in which the computer responds immediately to a request made by a user. Each request is a **transaction**. → BATCH PROCESSING
2 (*Commerce*) a method of dealing with a piece of business: *Secure online transaction processing enables merchants to accept payment by credit card.*

tranˈsaction tax *noun* [C,U]
a tax that has to be paid when sth is bought or sold: *a 0.1% transaction tax on government bonds*

transcontinental /ˌtrænzˌkɒntɪˈnentl/ ; ˌtræns-; *AmE* -ˌkɑːn-/ *adjective*
crossing a continent: *transcontinental flights*

★ **transfer** *verb, noun*
● *verb* /trænsˈfɜː(r)/ (-**rr-**)
1 [+ obj or no obj] to move from one place to another; to move sth/sb from one place to another: *The containers are transferred to trains at the port.*
2 [+ obj or no obj] to pass money, shares, property, etc. from one owner to another; to pass money from one place to another: *Settlement is the process by which shares are transferred from seller to buyer.* ◇ *The money has now been transferred abroad.*
3 [+ obj or no obj] to move from one job, situation, etc. to another; to arrange for sb to move: *He's been transferred to Sales.*
4 [+ obj] to officially arrange for sth to belong to sb else or for sb else to control sth: *The functions of the firm's Milan branch will be transferred to its main office in Germany.*
5 [+ obj] to copy information, music, an idea, etc. from one method of recording or presenting it to another: *The digital images can then be transferred to/onto disk.*
6 [+ obj or no obj] to change from one vehicle to another when travelling: *The train was cancelled so we transferred to buses for the rest of the journey.*
7 [+ obj] to pass a telephone call to another telephone, person, etc: *I'm afraid that isn't my department. Let me transfer you.*
● *noun* /ˈtrænsfɜː(r)/ [U,C]

SEE ALSO: **bank transfer, book ~, cable ~, credit ~, deed of ~, file ~, telegraphic ~, etc.**

1 the act of moving sb/sth from one place, group or job to another; an occasion when this happens: *Technology is constantly making the transfer of information faster.* ◇ *the transfer of currency from one country to another* ◇ *I've applied for a transfer.*
2 an act of changing to a different place, vehicle or route when you are travelling: *Transfer from the airport to the hotel is included in the price.*

transferable /trænsˈfɜːrəbl/ *adjective*
that can be moved from one person, place or use to another: *The MBA equips the student with a range of transferable skills* (= skills that can be used in different jobs). ◇ *The licence is not transferable.*
OPP NON-TRANSFERABLE

'transfer deed (*also* ,deed of 'transfer) *noun* [C]
(*Law*) a legal document that shows that the owner
of shares or property has changed

transferee /ˌtrænsfɜːˈriː/ *noun* [C]
(*Law*) a person to whom property, shares, rights,
etc. are transferred See note at EMPLOYER

'transfer ,income (*also* 'transfer ,payment) *noun*
[C,U]
(*Economics*) money that is received from a
government in the form of pensions,
UNEMPLOYMENT BENEFIT, SUBSIDIES, etc., which
is not a payment for goods or services but comes
from taxes

,**transfer of 'training** (*also* 'training ,transfer,
less frequent) *noun* [U]
(*HR*) the practical use in your work of skills learned
in a training course

,**transfer of under'taking** *noun* [C,U]
(*Law*) the fact or process of a business passing from
one owner to another: *Employees' rights are
protected during a transfer of undertaking by an EU
regulation.*

transferor /ˌtrænsˈfɜːrə(r)/ *noun* [C]
(*Law*) a person who transfers property, shares,
rights, etc. to another person See note at
EMPLOYER

'transfer ,payment = TRANSFER INCOME

'transfer price *noun* [C]
(*Accounting*) the price at which part of a company
sells goods or services to another part of the
company ▶ **'transfer ,pricing** *noun* [U]

'transfer ,register (*also* ,register of 'transfers,
'transfer book, *less frequent*) *noun* [C]
(*Finance*) a book in which all movements of a
company's shares from one owner to another are
recorded

★ **transform** /trænsˈfɔːm; *AmE* -ˈfɔːrm/ *verb* [+ obj]
1 to completely change the character or
appearance of sth, especially so that it is better: *The
struggling company has been transformed into one
of the most successful in its field.* ◇ *The acquisition
will be a transforming deal for the company* (= one
that will bring new types of business).
2 to change the form of sth: *Photochemical
reactions transform the light into electrical impulses.*
▶ **transformation** /ˌtrænsfəˈmeɪʃn; *AmE* -fərˈm-/
noun [C,U]: *the company's transformation from
water utility to global media giant*
transformational /ˌtrænsfəˈmeɪʃənl; *AmE* -fərˈm-/
adjective → TRANSFORMATIVE

,**transfor,mational 'leadership** *noun* [U]
a way of managing people and change by making
them feel enthusiastic about their work and willing
to work hard for the company, and by providing a
personal example → TRANSACTIONAL LEADERSHIP

transformative /trænsˈfɔːmətɪv; *AmE* -ˈfɔːrm-/
adjective [usually before noun]
able to completely change and improve the
character of sth: *transformative deals that move
companies into new lines of business* → TRANSFORM

tranship, transhipment = TRANS-SHIP

transient /ˈtrænziənt; *AmE* ˈtrænʃənt/ *adjective*
1 continuing only for a short time: *The company's
recent growth is likely to be transient.*
2 staying or working in a place for only a short
time, before going to another place: *Shorter
contracts have meant an increasingly transient
workforce.*
▶ **'transience** /ˈtrænziəns; *AmE* ˈtrænʃ-/ *noun* [U]

transistor /trænˈzɪstə(r); *AmE* -ˈsɪst-/ *noun* [C]
a small electronic device used in computers, radios,
televisions, etc. for controlling an electric current
as it passes along a CIRCUIT

transit /ˈtrænzɪt; -sɪt/ *noun* [U]
SEE ALSO: **stoppage in transit**
1 (*Transport*) the process of being moved or carried
from one place to another: *The cost includes transit.*
◇ *goods damaged or lost in transit.*
2 the act of going through a place on the way to
somewhere else: *the transit lounge at Gatwick
airport* ◇ *a transit visa* (= one that allows a person
to pass through a country but not to stay there)
3 (*AmE*) a system for carrying people from one
place to another using vehicles: *the city's public
transit system* → TRANSPORT (1)

'transit ,passenger *noun* [C]
an air traveller who arrives at an airport and leaves
again on the same or another plane

translate /trænsˈleɪt; trænzˈleɪt/ *verb*
1 [+ obj *or* no obj] to change sth, or to be changed,
into a different form: *a system that translates Web
data into phone data* ◇ *translating customer desires
into competitive products* ◇ *I hope all this hard work
will translate into profits.*
2 [+ obj *or* no obj] to express the meaning of speech
or writing in a different language: *an Internet-based
service that translates email, web pages, etc. into 5
languages* ◇ *I'll need someone to translate for me.*
3 [no obj] to be changed from one language into
another: *The name 'Mitsubishi' translates as 'three
diamonds'.*

translation /trænsˈleɪʃn; trænzˈleɪʃn/ *noun*
1 [U] the process of changing sth into a different
form: *the translation of research into new products* ◇
*Excluding the impact of foreign currency
translation, net sales rose 2%.*
2 [C,U] a text or work that has been changed from
one language into another: *to make/do a
translation of a document*

translator /trænsˈleɪtə(r); trænzˈleɪtə(r)/ *noun* [C]
1 a person who translates writing or speech into a
different language, especially as a job
2 an electronic device that helps you to translate
into a different language: *an automatic translator*
→ INTERPRETER

transmission /trænsˈmɪʃn; trænzˈmɪʃn/ *noun*
SEE ALSO: **money transmission**
1 [U] the act or process of passing or sending sth
from one person, place or thing to another: *the
company that owns the UK's gas and electricity
transmission networks* ◇ *the transmission of
knowledge/diseases*
2 [U] the act or process of sending out an
electronic signal or message or of broadcasting a
radio or television programme: *the transmission of
data over the Internet* ◇ *The company has bought
transmission rights for the World Cup.*
3 [C] a radio or television message or broadcast

transmit /trænsˈmɪt; trænzˈmɪt/ *verb* (-tt-)
1 [+ obj *or* no obj] to send an electronic signal,
radio or television broadcast, etc: *The speed at
which data is transmitted over mobile phone
networks has increased dramatically.* ◇ *The server
then transmits an ad to the user's computer screen.*
2 [+ obj] to pass or send sth from one person, place
or thing to another: *Big banks control the way
money is transmitted around the system.*

transnational /ˌtrænzˈnæʃnəl; ˌtrænsˈnæʃnəl/ *adjective*

operating or existing in or between many different countries, without being based in any particular one

ᐅ transnational **companies/corporations/links/ relations**

★**transparency** /trænsˈpærənsi/ *noun* (*plural* **transparencies**)

1 [U] the quality of sth, such as glass, that allows you to see through it
2 [U] the fact of sth being easy to understand and not being secret: *Shareholders have called for more* transparency **in** *company dealings.*
3 (*also* '**acetate**, **OHT**) [C] writing or a picture printed on a piece of film that you can see through, that can be shown on a screen by shining light through the film: *She wrote the key points of her talk on* **overhead** *transparencies* (= shown using an OVERHEAD PROJECTOR).—Picture at PRESENTATION

transparent /trænsˈpærənt/ *adjective*
1 (of glass, plastic, etc.) allowing you to see through it
2 easy to understand and not secret: *a transparent and fair system of voting* ◇ *The company's strategy needs to be clear and transparent* **to** *shareholders.*

transport /ˈtrænspɔːt; *AmE* -spɔːrt/ *noun, verb*
●*noun* [U]

SEE ALSO: **public transport, surface transport**

1 (*especially BrE*) (*AmE usually* ,**transpor'tation**) a system for carrying people or goods from one place to another using vehicles: *to travel* **on/by** *public transport* ◇ *poor transport and distribution networks* ◇ *transport workers* → TRANSIT (3)

ᐅ **air/freight/passenger/rail/road** transport • transport **networks/infrastructure/links/systems** • a transport **company/firm/operator/service** • the transport **industry/sector** • a transport **plan/policy/ strategy**

2 (*BrE*) (*AmE* ,**transpor'tation**) a vehicle or method of travel: *Applicants must have their own transport.* ◇ *Will transport be provided?* ◇ *Transportation was provided from the hotel to the convention center.*
3 (*especially BrE*) (*AmE usually* ,**transpor'tation**) the activity or business of carrying goods from one place to another using lorries/trucks, trains, etc: *The goods were damaged during transport.* ◇ *controls on the transport of nuclear waste* ◇ *transportation costs*

●*verb* [+ obj]
to take sth/sb from one place to another in a vehicle: *The chemicals are transported by road to the processing plant.* ◇ *The airline transported over half a million passengers last year.*

transportable /trænˈspɔːtəbl; *AmE* -ˈspɔːrt-/ *adjective* [not usually before noun]
that can be carried or moved from one place to another: *These storage units are compact and easily transportable.*

transportation /ˌtrænspɔːˈteɪʃn; *AmE* -pɔːrt-/ = TRANSPORT *noun*

transporter /trænˈspɔːtə(r); *AmE* -ˈspɔːrt-/ *noun* [C]
1 a large vehicle used for carrying heavy objects, for example other vehicles: *a car transporter*
2 a company that moves goods from one place to another: *the country's largest gas transporter*

trans-ship (*also spelled* **tranship, transship**) /trænzˈʃɪp/ *verb* [+ obj] (-**pp**-)
to move goods from one ship or other form of transport to another: *80% of cargo arriving at the*

transport

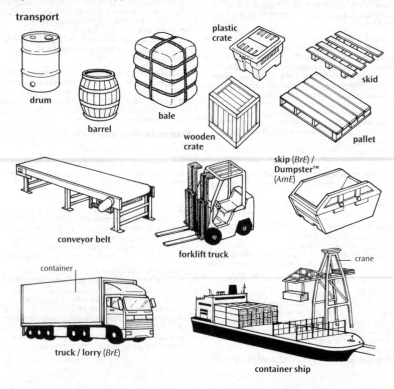

drum

barrel

bale

wooden crate

plastic crate

skid

pallet

conveyor belt

forklift truck

skip (BrE) / Dumpster™ (AmE)

crane

container

truck / lorry (BrE)

container ship

harbour is trans-shipped to other ports. ▸ **trans-'shipment** (*also spelled* **transhipment**, **transshipment**) *noun* [C,U]: *The port serves as a trans-shipment point for the region.*

travel /'trævl/ *verb, noun*

● *verb* [+ obj or no obj] (**-ll-**, *especially BrE, AmE usually* **-l-**)

1 to go from one place to another, especially over a long distance: *to travel abroad/overseas* ◇ *I travel a lot on business.* ◇ *He travels over 40 miles to work every day.*

2 to go or move at a particular speed, in a particular direction, or a particular distance: *These vehicles can travel at up to 240 kph.*

● *noun* [U]

the act or activity of travelling: *The post involves a considerable amount of foreign travel.* ◇ *Many companies are now cutting their travel expenses.* ◇ *Remember to take out* **travel insurance** *before leaving on your trip.*

O *air/car/rail* travel ◆ *domestic/foreign/ international/overseas* travel ◆ *business/corporate/ leisure* travel ◆ travel *budgets/costs/expenses* ◆ *the* travel *business/industry/market/sector* ◆ *a* travel *company/firm/operator*

'travel ,agency *noun* [C]

a company that arranges travel and/or accommodation for people going on a holiday/ vacation or journey

'travel ,agent *noun* [C]

1 a person or business whose job is to make arrangements for people wanting to travel, for example, buying tickets or arranging hotel rooms

2 **travel agent's** (*plural* **travel agents**) a shop/store where you can go to arrange a holiday/vacation, etc: *She works in a travel agent's.*

→ TOUR OPERATOR

traveler = TRAVELLER

'traveler's check = TRAVELLER'S CHEQUE

traveling = TRAVELLING

traveller (*AmE spelling usually* **traveler**) /'trævələ(r)/ *noun* [C]

SEE ALSO: commercial traveller

a person who is travelling or who often travels: *The airline is popular with business travellers.* ◇ *She's a frequent traveller to Belgium.*

→ SALES REPRESENTATIVE

'traveller's cheque (*AmE spelling* **traveler's check**) *noun* [C]

a cheque for a fixed amount, sold by a bank or TRAVEL AGENT that can be exchanged for cash in foreign countries

travelling (*AmE spelling usually* **traveling**) /'trævəlɪŋ/ *adjective, noun*

● *adjective* [only before noun]

1 going from place to place: *travelling salespeople*

2 used when you travel: *a small travelling bag*

● *noun* [U]

the act of travelling: *The job requires a lot of travelling.* ◇ *travelling expenses*

treasurer /'treʒərə(r)/ *noun* [C]

a person who is responsible for the money and accounts of an organization or a club: *She worked as assistant treasurer at/of a large oil company.* ◇ *The treasurer presented his report.*

O (*a*) *company/corporate/group* treasurer

Treasuries /'treʒəriz/ = TREASURY BOND

★ **treasury** /'treʒəri/ *noun* [sing. with sing./pl. verb]

the Treasury in the UK, the US and some other countries, the government department that controls public money: *the US treasury secretary* ◇

The Treasury expects GDP growth of 2.5 to 3 per cent this year.

'Treasury bill (*also* **'T-bill**) *noun* [C]

(*Finance*) in the UK and the US, a form of borrowing by the government for short periods of time, on which no interest is paid. **Treasury bills** are bought at less than their value.

'Treasury bond (*also* **'T-bond**) *noun* [C] (*also* **'Treasuries** [pl.])

(*Finance*) in the US, a bond issued by the government for a long period of time, that pays interest

'treasury ,management = CASH MANAGEMENT

'Treasury note *noun* [C, usually pl.]

(*Finance*) in the US, a form of government borrowing for between one and ten years, that pays interest

'treasury stock *noun* [U]

(*Finance*) shares that a company has issued but has bought back from public investors

treat /tri:t/ *verb* [+ obj]

1 to behave in a particular way towards sb/sth: *Treat your customers* **with** *respect in all circumstances.* ◇ *They felt they had been treated fairly by the disciplinary committee.* ◇ *The unions wanted pensions to be treated* **as** *deferred pay.*

2 to deal with or discuss sth in a particular way: *These optimistic forecasts should be treated* **with** *caution.*

3 to use a chemical substance or process to clean, protect, preserve, etc. sth: *wood treated* **with** *preservative*

treatment /'tri:tmənt/ *noun*

1 [U] a way of behaving towards or dealing with a person or thing: *The union is demanding equal treatment* **for** *agency and permanent staff.* ◇ *The bank is to change its treatment of bad debts.*

2 [U,C] a way of dealing with or discussing sth: *The book is an interesting treatment of how to measure employee success in the workplace.*

3 [U,C] a process by which sth is cleaned, protected, preserved, etc. with a chemical substance: *a sewage/water treatment plant*

treaty /'tri:ti/ *noun* [C] (*plural* **treaties**)

SEE ALSO: commercial treaty, private treaty

a formal agreement between two or more countries: *These fiscal measures are a clear breach of the EU treaty.* ◇ *They failed to fulfil their obligations* **under** *the treaty.*

★ **trend** /trend/ *noun* [C]

a general direction in which a situation is changing or developing: *There is a growing trend* **towards** *shorter contracts.* ◇ *current trends* **in** *advertising* ◇ *The success of this car* **set** *a trend for smaller vehicles* (= made them popular). ◇ *The company has* **bucked** (= been an exception to) *the trend for lower sales.* ◇ *Growth remains below the long-term trend.*

O *economic/political/social* trends ◆ *business/ industry/market/pricing/sales* trends ◆ *a downward/growing/negative/positive/rising/an upward* trend ◆ *current/future/long-term/recent* trends ◆ *a broad/clear/general/global* trend ◆ *to break with/reverse* a trend

▸ **trend** *verb* [no obj] (*especially AmE*): *Unemployment has been trending upwards.*

'trend line (*also spelled* **trendline**) *noun* [C]

the general direction in which sth is changing or developing, shown, for example, by a line on a chart connecting high or low points: *a downward sloping trend line on the Footsie*

trial /'traɪəl/ *noun, verb*

● *noun*

SEE ALSO: **blind trial, clinical ~, free ~**

1 [C] the process of testing the quality or performance of a product to see if it will be effective or successful: *The new drug is undergoing early-stage clinical trials.*

❍ **early-stage/initial/late-stage/mid-stage** trials ◆ **drug/safety** trials ◆ *to* **carry out/conduct/run/take part in/undergo** *trials*

2 [C,U] the process of using a product or service, employing a person, etc. for a short period before you make a decision about it or them: *You can* **give** *the service a trial before you make up your mind.* ◇ *The system was introduced* **on a trial basis** *for six months.* ◇ *She agreed to employ me for* **a trial period.** ◇ *We had the machine* **on trial** *for a week.*

3 [U,C] a formal examination of evidence in a court by a judge and often a JURY, to decide if sb accused of a crime is guilty or not: *The former CEO is to* **stand trial** *for fraud.*

❍ *to* **await/face/go on/stand** *trial* ◆ *to* **come to/go to** *trial*

● *verb* [+ obj] (-ll-, *BrE*, *AmE* -l-) (*especially BrE*)
to test the quality or performance of a product to see if it will be effective or successful: *They trialled the product* **with** *20 of their best customers.* ◇ *Only one in ten drugs which are trialled* **on** *humans makes it to the market.* ▶ **'trialling** *noun* [U]

'trial ,balance *noun* [C, usually sing.] (*abbr* **t.b.**)
(*Accounting*) a list of all the BALANCES in a company's accounts at a particular date, used to check that DEBITS and CREDITS are equal and that everything has been recorded accurately

'trial ,offer *noun* [C]
the opportunity to use a product or service free or at a low cost for a short period before you decide if you want to buy it: *Take up our trial offer and get three free issues of the magazine.* ◇ *trial offers of new software*

tribunal /traɪ'bjuːnl/ *noun* [C]
a type of court with the authority to deal with a particular problem or disagreement: *She took her case to a tribunal.* ◇ *Tribunal* **hearings** *are less formal than court sessions.*

❍ *an* **appeals/arbitration/employment/a disciplinary** *tribunal* ◆ *to* **bring sth before/go to/ refer sth to/take sb/sth to** *a tribunal*

trickle /'trɪkl/ *verb, noun*

● *verb* [no obj]
to go, or to make sth go, somewhere slowly or gradually: *Last month orders only trickled in.* ◇ *Investors are trickling back into the market after the long holiday.*

PHRV ,**trickle 'down** (especially about money) to spread from rich to poor people through the economic system of a country: *The rising costs are trickling down to millions of customers.* → TRICKLE-DOWN

● *noun* [C, usually sing.]
a small amount or number of sth, coming or going slowly: *There has been a steady trickle of redundancies over the last few months.* ◇ *The crisis has* **slowed** *exports* **to** *a trickle.*

'trickle-down *noun* [U]
1 (*Economics*) (in an economic system) the way in which the poorest people benefit as a result of the increasing wealth of the richest: *There has been no trickle-down of economic growth to the average family.*

2 used to describe a process where people at the bottom level of an organization or a system eventually start to have, do, etc. sth that people at a higher level had, did, etc. first: *Once the company improved its quality control, the* **trickle-down effect** *meant that its suppliers improved their quality too.*
→ TRICKLE DOWN at TRICKLE *verb*

trigger /'trɪgə(r)/ *noun, verb*

● *noun* [C, usually sing.]
something that is the cause of a particular reaction or development, especially a bad one: *The trigger* **for** *the strike was the closure of another factory.*

● *verb* [+ obj]
1 to make sth happen suddenly: *The release of the results triggered a sharp fall in the group's share price.*

2 to cause a device to start functioning: *Opening this door will trigger a security alarm.*

'trigger point *noun* [C]
a level or rate that is reached, or an event that happens, which causes action to be taken: *His frequent absence from work had reached the trigger point for formal action to be taken.*

trim /trɪm/ *verb* [+ obj] (-mm-)
to make sth smaller by cutting parts from it: (*figurative*) *20% of staff are to be trimmed by May.* ◇ *We must trim the training budget by €20 000.*

IDM **trim (the) 'fat** if a business **trims the fat**, it reduces or removes unnecessary expenses, for example by reducing the number of workers: *They have trimmed the fat out of their production process.*

trip /trɪp/ *noun* [C]

SEE ALSO: **business trip, round trip**

1 a journey to a place and back again for business or pleasure, or for a particular purpose: *Bill's away* **on** *a trip this week.* ◇ *I'm* **going on** *a three-day trip to China.*

2 a journey to or back from a place: *The truck was delayed on the* **return** *trip.* ◇ *the* **outward** *trip*

,**triple-'A** *adjective* (*abbr* **AAA**)
(*Finance*) used to describe a company that is considered one of the safest to lend money to: *The company lost its triple-A* **credit rating** *following its financial problems.*

'triple-,witching *noun* [U; sing.]
(*Stock Exchange, informal*) the situation that occurs on the third Friday of March, June, September and December when three types of FUTURES and OPTIONS reach the end of the time when they are valid: *triple-witching day/hour* → DOUBLE-WITCHING

triplicate /'trɪplɪkət/ *noun*
IDM **in 'triplicate 1** done three times: *Each sample was tested in triplicate.* **2** (about a document) copied twice, so that there are three copies in total: *Fill out the forms in triplicate.*
→ DUPLICATE

,**Trojan 'horse** /'trəʊdʒən; *AmE* 'troʊ-/ *noun* [C]
1 a person or thing that is used to deceive an enemy in order to achieve a secret purpose: *The move by supermarkets into banking is a Trojan horse. Banks may soon no longer exist.*

2 (*IT*) a computer program that seems to be helpful but that is, in fact, designed to destroy data, etc.

troll /trəʊl; *AmE* troʊl/ *verb* [+ obj or no obj] (*informal*)
1 to search for sth, especially on the Internet: *trolling Internet sites looking for information* ◇ *Many people troll* **for** *jobs in company time.*

2 (*Marketing*) to try to get new customers by telephoning or visiting people you do not know: *They were criticized for trolling for customers willing to sign on for legal services they might not need.*

'trophy wife *noun* [C] (*informal*)
a young attractive woman who is married to an older senior businessman and is thought of as sth that impresses other people and shows that the man is successful (a **trophy**)

troubled /ˈtrʌbld/ *adjective* [usually before noun]
(often used in newspapers) having a lot of problems: *Analysts expect the troubled company to be broken up or sold.* ◇ *Investors are not willing to take risks in these troubled times.*

troubleshoot /ˈtrʌblʃuːt/ *verb* [+ obj or no obj]
(**troubleshot, troubleshot** /ˈtrʌblʃɒt; *AmE* -ʃɑːt/)
1 to try to solve problems that sb/sth has: *She is responsible for troubleshooting problems with clients.*
2 (*IT*) to find and solve problems in a mechanical or an electronic system: *An IT consultant visits the company every Monday to troubleshoot.*
▶ **'troubleshooting** *noun* [U]

troubleshooter /ˈtrʌblʃuːtə(r)/ *noun* [C]
a person who helps to solve problems in a company or an organization

trough /trɒf; *AmE* trɔːf/ *noun, verb*
● *noun* [C]
a period of time when the level of sth is low, especially a time when a business or the economy is not growing: *The rate fell to a trough of 3% last year.* ◇ *The pension fund invested in bonds to avoid the peaks and troughs of the stock market.*
[OPP] PEAK—Picture at BUSINESS CYCLE
● *verb* [no obj]
if a price, a rate, a decrease, etc. **troughs** it reaches its lowest level: *Analysts believe that interest rates have troughed at 4%.* [OPP] PEAK

truck /trʌk/ *noun, verb*
● *noun* [C]

SEE ALSO: forklift truck, panel ~, pickup ~

1 a large motor vehicle for carrying heavy loads by road: *a ten-ton truck* [SYN] LORRY (*BrE*)—Picture at TRANSPORT
❍ *a commercial/delivery/heavy-duty/light/medium-duty/refrigerated truck*
2 (*BrE*) an open railway vehicle for carrying goods or animals
3 a vehicle that is open at the back, used for carrying goods, animals, etc.
4 a vehicle for carrying things, that is pulled or pushed by hand
● *verb* [+ obj]
to take sth somewhere by truck: *The goods are shipped to Oslo and from there trucked to Karasjok.*
▶ **'trucking** *noun* [U]: *trucking companies*

truckage /ˈtrʌkɪdʒ/ *noun* [U]
(*Transport*)
1 the movement of goods by road: *an international truckage company*
2 the charge made for this

truckload /ˈtrʌkləʊd; *AmE* -loʊd/ *noun* [C]
the amount of sb/sth that fills a truck (often used to express the fact that an amount is large): *20 truckloads of building materials*

,true and fair 'view *phrase*
(*Accounting*) in the UK, words that AUDITORS (= people who examine the accounts of a company) use to show that they have checked a company's accounts and think that they give accurate information about the company's financial state

trump /trʌmp/ *verb* [+ obj] (*informal*)
to beat another company's product or sth that another company does by producing sth or doing sth even better: *Ford hopes to trump its rivals with a new pickup truck.* ◇ *Their $55 million deal was trumped by a rival bidder.*

★ trust /trʌst/ *noun*

SEE ALSO: brains trust, breach of ~, business ~, deed of ~, discretionary ~, investment ~, living ~, unit ~

1 (*Finance*; *Law*) [C,U] an arrangement in which a group of people or an organization (the **trustees**) have legal control of money or property for another person or group of people (the **beneficiary/ beneficiaries**); an amount of money or property that is controlled in this way: *He set up a trust for his children.* ◇ *The money will be held in trust until she is 18.* ◇ *Our fees depend on the value of the trust.* ◇ *a bank's trust department*
2 (*Finance*) [C] an organization or a group of people that invests money that is given or lent to it: *Shareholders in a small number of trusts may lose virtually all of their capital.* ◇ *The money to set up these trusts is to be provided by local industries.* ◇ *a charitable trust* → INVESTMENT COMPANY
❍ *to create/establish/manage/set up* a trust ◆ *a trust board/manager*
3 (*Economics*) [C] (*especially AmE*) a group of companies that work together illegally to reduce competition: *antitrust laws*

trustbuster /ˈtrʌstbʌstə(r)/ *noun* [C] (*especially AmE*)
(*Law*) a person or an organization that works to prevent groups of companies from working together illegally ▶ **'trustbusting** *noun* [U]

'trust deed (*also* ,deed of 'trust, 'trust ,instrument) *noun* [C]
(*Law*) a legal document that creates a **trust**. It states the purpose of the trust, how it must be run and who the TRUSTEES and BENEFICIARIES are: *Under the terms of the trust deed, the trustees can decide how to invest any profit.*

★ trustee /trʌˈstiː/ *noun* [C]
(*Law*) a person or an organization that is responsible for managing money or property for another person or group of people: *The pension fund will continue to be managed by the board of trustees.* [SYN] FIDUCIARY → BENEFICIARY

trus,tee in 'bankruptcy *noun* [C]
(*Law*) a person chosen by a court to manage the affairs of a BANKRUPT company or person, sell its/ their property and pay its/their debts where possible

trusteeship /trʌˈstiːʃɪp/ *noun* [U,C]
(*Law*) the job of being a TRUSTEE; a situation where money or property is controlled by a TRUSTEE: *He has agreed to place his shares in a trusteeship for the next two years.*

'trust fund *noun* [C]
(*Finance*) money, property and other assets that are held for sb by an organization or a group of people: *The money from the sale of the products is put into a trust fund.*

'trust ,instrument = TRUST DEED

'trust re,ceipt *noun* [C]
(*Finance*) a document that is given to a bank by a company that has accepted goods but cannot pay for them at that time, to say that the bank owns the goods. The bank pays for the goods and the company pays back the money later, for example when the goods have been sold.

the ,Truth in 'Lending Act *noun* [sing.]
a law in the US that protects consumers by saying that companies who lend money must give full information about the cost of the loan and the annual rate of interest

TSR /ˌtiː es ˈɑː(r)/ = TOTAL SHAREHOLDER RETURN

TTM /,ti: ti: 'em/ = TIME TO MARKET

TUC /,ti: ju: 'si:/ *abbr* **Trades Union Congress** in the UK and some other countries, an organization to which many trade unions belong → AFL-CIO

tumble /'tʌmbl/ *verb* [no obj]
to fall rapidly in value or amount: *Shares tumbled 8 per cent to 460 yen.* ◇ *The euro tumbled **sharply** against the dollar yesterday.* ▶ **'tumble** *noun* [C]: *Shares in the troubled company **took** a sharp tumble yesterday.*

tune /tju:n; *AmE* tu:n/ *noun, verb*
● *noun*
IDM to the tune of sth
used to emphasize how much money sth has cost: *loans to the tune of $92 million* → idiom at CALL *verb*
● *verb* [+ obj]

SEE ALSO: **fine-tune**

1 tune sth (up) to adjust sth so that it works more efficiently: *We need to tune up our after-sales service.*
2 to prepare or adjust sth so that it is suitable for a particular situation: *Their products are **finely** tuned **to** their customers' needs.*

turbine /'tɜ:baɪn; *AmE* 'tɜ:rb-/ *noun* [C]
a machine or an engine that receives its power from a wheel that is turned by the pressure of water, air or gas

turn /tɜ:n; *AmE* tɜ:rn/ *verb, noun*
● *verb*
1 [+ obj *or* no obj] to change into a particular state; to make sth do this: *The loss has been turned **into** a profit.*
2 [no obj] to change and start going in a different direction: *After a good start, the markets turned lower.*
● *to turn **higher/lower/negative/positive***
IDM turn a (small, modest, $10 million, etc.) 'profit (*informal*) to make a profit in business: *Four years after she took over, the company had turned a profit.* **turn sth on its 'head** to make people think about sth in a completely different way; to change sth completely: *The magazine's low cover price has turned the usual pricing process on its head.* **turn sth to your ad'vantage** to use or change a bad situation so that it helps you: *The new manager aimed to turn the hotel's isolated position to its advantage.* **turn your 'back on sth** to reject sth/sb that you were previously connected with: *Investors are now turning their backs on Internet start-ups.* → idioms at ACTION, HOSTILE, SOUR
PHRV turn a'round/'round; ,turn sth a'round/'round if a business, an economy, etc. turns around or sb **turns** it **around**, it starts being successful after it has failed to be successful for a time: *The new management team turned the company around within 15 months.* → TURN-AROUND (2) **,turn sth a'round/'round** to do a piece of work that you have been given and return it: *They try to turn any repair around in 72 hours.* → TURNAROUND (1) **,turn 'down** to become weaker or less active, make less money, etc. → DOWNTURN, TURNDOWN **,turn sb/sth 'down** to reject or refuse to consider an offer, a proposal, etc. or the person who makes it: *The bank turned us down **for** a loan.* **,turn 'in sth** to achieve a particular performance, profit, etc: *The group had turned in a 21% increase in profits.* ◇ *Our UK division turned in a strong performance.* **,turn sb 'on (to sth)** to make sb become interested in sth or to use sth for the first time: *attempts to turn Internet users onto broadband* **,turn sth 'out** to produce sth/sb: *The firm turns out 75 000 bicycles a year.* See note at PRODUCE **,turn 'over sth** to do business worth a particular amount of money in a particular period

of time: *We turn over £3.5 million a year.*
→ TURNOVER (1) **,turn sth 'over** (*Commerce*) (about a shop/store) to sell goods and replace them: *A supermarket turns over its stock very quickly.*
→ TURNOVER (3) **,turn sth 'over to sb/sth** to give the control of sth to sb else: *He turned the business over to his daughter.*
● *noun* [C]

SEE ALSO: **inventory turn, out-~, stock ~**

1 a change in what is happening: *Analysts are predicting a turn in the economy.* ◇ *a downward turn in the company's fortunes*
2 (*Finance*) the difference between the buying and selling price of shares or other financial products; the profit that is made: *They were only interested in making a quick turn on the shares.*
→ idiom at TAKE *verb*

turnaround /'tɜ:nəraʊnd; *AmE* 'tɜ:rn-/ (*BrE also* **'turnround**) *noun* [C, usually sing.]
1 the amount of time it takes to do and return a piece of work that you have been given: *They guarantee a 2-day turnaround for small printing jobs.*
2 a situation in which sth changes from bad to good: *The past six months has seen a dramatic turnaround **in** the company's fortunes.*
3 the amount of time it takes to unload a ship or plane at the end of one journey and load it again for the next one
→ TURN AROUND at TURN *verb*

'turnaround ,management (*BrE also* **'turnround ~**) *noun* [U]
the act of making changes to a failing company in order to make it more successful; the study of this subject

turndown /'tɜ:ndaʊn; *AmE* 'tɜ:rn-/ *noun* [C]
1 a fall in the amount of business that is done; a time when the economy becomes weaker: *market turndowns* ◇ *We're in a turndown **in** the economy.* SYN DOWNTURN → TURN DOWN at TURN *verb*
2 a refusal; not being accepted for a job, position, etc. → TURN SB/STH DOWN at TURN *verb*

turnkey /'tɜ:nki:; *AmE* 'tɜ:rn-/ *adjective* [usually before noun]
1 (*IT*) used to describe a product or service, especially a computer system, that is supplied in a complete form, ready for the buyer to use: *turnkey systems*
2 (*Commerce*) used to describe a large project that one company designs, builds and provides equipment for on behalf of another, so that it is completely ready to use at the end of the contract: *We provide our clients with a complete **turnkey** operation.* ◇ *a turnkey contract to build an airport terminal*

★ **turnover** /'tɜ:nəʊvə(r); *AmE* 'tɜ:rnoʊ-/ *noun* [C, usually sing., U]

SEE ALSO: **asset turnover, capital ~, inventory ~, sales ~, stock ~**

1 (*Accounting*) the total value of goods or services sold by a company during a particular period of time: *The firm has an annual turnover of $75 million.* SYN SALES REVENUE
● *annual/daily/first-half/full-year/yearly turnover* ● *an **overall**/a **total/worldwide** turnover* ● *a **high/ low/strong** turnover*
2 (*HR*) the rate at which employees leave a company and are replaced by other people: *The factory has a high turnover of staff.* ◇ *plans to prevent avoidable turnover* ◇ *Our turnover rate last year was 3%.*
● *employee/labour/staff turnover* ● *a **high/low** turnover*

3 (*Accounting; Commerce*) the rate at which goods are sold in a shop/store and replaced by others: *Special offers help to ensure a fast turnover of stock.* ◊ *the stock turnover rate*
O *a fast/rapid* turnover
4 (*Stock Exchange*) the total value of the business done on a stock exchange during a particular period of time; the total number of shares bought and sold: *Market turnover was 2.6 billion shares.*
O *light/heavy* turnover

'turnover ,ratio *noun* [C, usually sing.]
(*Finance*) the relationship between the value of shares, bonds, etc. that a fund buys or sells in a particular period and the average total value that it holds during the period

'turnover tax *noun* [U; sing.]
(*Economics*) tax that a company pays on the money received from the sale of goods

turnround /'tɜːnraʊnd; *AmE* 'tɜːrn-/ = TURN-AROUND

'turnround ,management = TURNAROUND MANAGEMENT

TVR /,tiː viː 'ɑː(r)/ = TELEVISION RATING

twentysomething /'twentisʌmθɪŋ/ *noun* [C]
(*informal*)
a person who is between twenty and twenty-nine years old: *a staff of young, ambitious twentysomethings* → THIRTYSOMETHING

twisting /'twɪstɪŋ/ *noun* [U]
(*Insurance*) when an agent sells insurance to a customer based on a dishonest comparison of products

,two-'tier *adjective* [only before noun]
(about a system) having two levels: *a two-tier system of interest rates* ◊ *a two-tier workforce* (= where people are paid different rates for doing the same job) ◊ *They operate a two-tier structure with management and supervisory boards.*

,two-'way *adjective* [usually before noun]
1 moving in two different directions; allowing sth to move in two different directions: *two-way trade*
2 involving two people or groups: *a two-way battle for ownership of the company*

3 (about communication between people) with each person or side playing an equal role: *They maintain a two-way dialogue with their customers through their website.*

tycoon /taɪ'kuːn/ *noun* [C]
a person who is successful in business or industry and has become rich and powerful: *He is one of the world's wealthiest business tycoons.* See note at BARON
O *a business/media/an oil/a property* tycoon

type /taɪp/ *verb, noun*
● *verb* [+ obj or no obj]

SEE ALSO: **touch-type**

to write sth using the keyboard of a computer, etc: *I taught myself to type.* ◊ *I just need to type an email.* ◊ *Type the url into the address box.* → KEY
▶ **'typing** *noun* [U]: *typing errors* **'typist** *noun* [C]: *I'm quite a fast typist.*
PHR V ,type sth **'up** to type sth that was written by hand, often in the form of notes: *I haven't typed up the minutes of the meeting yet.*
● *noun* [U]

SEE ALSO: **display type**

letters that are printed or typed: *The warning is written in small type on the back of the packet.*

typeface /'taɪpfeɪs/ *noun* [C]
a set of letters, numbers, etc. of a particular design, used in printing: *The heading should be in a different typeface from the text.*

typescript /'taɪpskrɪpt/ *noun* [C,U]
a copy of a text or document that has been typed

typewritten /'taɪprɪtn/ *adjective*
written using the keyboard of a computer, etc: *The report is 20 typewritten pages long.*

tyrekicker (*also spelled* **tyre kicker** *in BrE*) (*AmE spelling* **tirekicker, tire kicker**) /'taɪəkɪkə(r); *AmE* 'taɪərkɪkər/ *noun* [C]
(*Marketing, informal*) a possible customer who asks a lot of questions about a product but never buys anything → idiom at KICK

U u

UK SIC /,juː keɪ ,es aɪ 'siː/ *abbr*
United Kingdom Standard Industrial Classification of economic activities in the UK, a system in which industries and services are given a code to show which type of economic activity they are involved in, for reference and research purposes → ISIC, NACE, NAICS

,ultimate con'sumer (*also* ,ultimate 'customer) *noun* [C]
(*Marketing*) the person who actually buys or uses a particular product: *The ultimate consumer pays considerably more than the manufacturing price.*
SYN END-USER

ultimatum /,ʌltɪ'meɪtəm/ *noun* [C] (*plural* **ultimatums** *or* **ultimata**)
a final warning to a person, group or country that if they do not do what you ask, you will take action against them: *The management issued an ultimatum to employees to accept the offer or risk redundancy.*

ultra vires /,ʌltrə 'vaɪriːz/ *adjective*
(*Law*) (about the action of a person, company or government) beyond legal or official powers: *an ultra vires transaction* ▶ **ultra 'vires** *adverb*: *The directors were judged to have acted ultra vires and therefore unlawfully.* **NOTE** Ultra vires is a Latin phrase.

u/m *abbr*
a short way of writing **undermentioned**

umbrella /ʌm'brelə/ *noun* [C]
a thing that contains many parts or elements: *There are 22 companies operating under the umbrella of SRC Holdings Corp.* ◊ *The Pakistan Tea Association is an umbrella organization for all importers.*
O *an umbrella brand/company/group/organization*

UMTS /,juː em tiː 'es/ *abbr*
Universal Mobile Telecommunications System
a system for sending information between mobile phones/cellphones: *UMTS licences/networks/services*

unac'counted for *adjective* [not before noun]
a thing that is **unaccounted for** is missing, for example from an account or an amount of money, and people cannot explain why: *$30 000 of the money is still unaccounted for.* → ACCOUNT FOR at ACCOUNT *verb* (2, 3)

unachievable /ˌʌnəˈtʃiːvəbl/ *adjective*
that you cannot manage to reach or obtain: *The sales targets proved unachievable.* OPP ACHIEVABLE

unadjusted /ˌʌnəˈdʒʌstɪd/ *adjective* [usually before noun]
(about data) that has not been changed to make it more suitable or more accurate: *the unadjusted unemployment figure* → ADJUST

unanimous /juˈnænɪməs/ *adjective*
1 if a decision or an opinion is **unanimous**, it is agreed or shared by everyone in a group: *a unanimous vote* ◇ *The decision was not unanimous.*
2 if a group of people are **unanimous**, they all agree about sth: *Local companies were unanimous in their backing for the project.*
▶ **u'nanimously** *adverb*

unaudited /ˌʌnˈɔːdɪtɪd/ *adjective*
(*Accounting*) (about financial accounts) that have not been examined by an AUDITOR: *half-yearly unaudited financial results* ◇ *They didn't want to do business with an unaudited company.* → AUDIT *verb* (1)
O *unaudited* **accounts/balance sheets/figures/results/statements**

unauthorized, **-ised** /ˌʌnˈɔːθəraɪzd/ *adjective*
without official permission: *Staff are issued with passwords to prevent unauthorized use of the computer system.* ◇ *She was sacked for making unauthorized payments to suppliers.* → AUTHORIZE
See note at COPY

unbalanced /ˌʌnˈbælənst/ *adjective* [usually before noun]
1 (*Accounting*) (in a set of financial accounts) where the total of the DEBITS is not equal to the total of the CREDITS, because a mistake has been made: *Unmatched records and unbalanced accounts are recorded in the report for action.*
2 (*Accounting*) (about a budget, etc.) where the money going out is greater than the money coming in: *The company has large financial reserves and so has never had an unbalanced budget.*
3 giving too much importance to one part or aspect of sth: *an unbalanced and inaccurate report* → BALANCE

unbundle /ˌʌnˈbʌndl/ *verb* [+ obj]
1 to divide a group of businesses into individual parts, especially in order to sell the less important parts: *The media group was unbundled following a year of heavy losses.* → DEMERGE, DIVERSIFY
2 (*Marketing*) to supply a product, a service or a piece of equipment separately and not with any other product or service: *The company decided to unbundle the Internet browser from its operating system.* OPP BUNDLE
▶ **un'bundling** *noun* [U,C]: *The deal prepared the way for the unbundling of the group's financial services division.*

uncalled 'capital *noun* [U]
(*Accounting*) the difference between the value of the shares that a company has issued and the amount that shareholders have paid for them so far

uncashed /ˌʌnˈkæʃt/ *adjective*
(about a cheque/check, etc.) that has not been exchanged for money → CASH *verb*

uncompetitive /ˌʌnkəmˈpetɪtɪv/ *adjective*
not cheaper or better than others and therefore not able to compete equally: *an uncompetitive industry* ◇ *uncompetitive prices* OPP COMPETITIVE

unconditional /ˌʌnkənˈdɪʃənl/ *adjective*
1 without any conditions or limits: *The new Financial Director has the unconditional support of the board.* ◇ *an unconditional offer* OPP CONDITIONAL
2 (*Finance*) [not usually before noun] if a TAKEOVER BID becomes **unconditional**, all the conditions, such as being accepted by most of the shareholders, have been met: *The offer will lapse if it does not become unconditional.* ◇ *The $3·5 bn takeover has now been declared unconditional.*
O *to* **become/be declared/go** *unconditional*
▶ **unconditionally** /ˌʌnkənˈdɪʃənəli/ *adverb*

unconditional 'takeover bid *noun* [C]
(*Finance*) an offer to buy any number of a company's shares at a particular price with no special conditions → CONDITIONAL TAKEOVER BID, UNCONDITIONAL (2)

unconsolidated /ˌʌnkənˈsɒlɪdeɪtɪd; *AmE* -ˈsɑːl-/ *adjective*
1 (*Accounting*) (about financial results, accounts, etc.) not combined into one set of figures: *unconsolidated accounts/balance sheets*
2 (about businesses, etc.) not joined into one group → CONSOLIDATE

uncontested /ˌʌnkənˈtestɪd/ *adjective*
without any opposition, argument or competition: *They have made an uncontested bid for the television company.* ◇ *These claims have not gone uncontested.*

uncrossed 'cheque (*AmE spelling* ~ **check**)
= OPEN CHEQUE

undated /ˌʌnˈdeɪtɪd/ *adjective*
1 without a date written on it: *an undated letter/cheque*
2 (*Finance*) (about an investment) that has no fixed date when it will be repaid: *undated bonds/securities/gilts*

underbid /ˌʌndəˈbɪd; *AmE* -dərˈb-/ *verb* [+ obj or no obj] (**underbidding, underbid, underbid**)
(*Commerce*) to make a lower **bid** than sb else, for example when trying to win a contract: *The agency started underbidding to win new work.*

undercapitalized, **-ised** /ˌʌndəˈkæpɪtəlaɪzd; *AmE* -dərˈk-/ *adjective*
(*Finance*) (about a business) not having enough money (**capital**) to be able to operate normally, pay debts and grow OPP OVERCAPITALIZED → CAPITALIZED

undercharge /ˌʌndəˈtʃɑːdʒ; *AmE* ˌʌndərˈtʃɑːrdʒ/ *verb* [+ obj or no obj]
to charge too little for sth, usually by mistake: *People have a tendency to undercharge when they start in business.* ◇ *Customers had been undercharged by $100.* ▶ **'undercharge** *noun* [C]: *an undercharge of $8 per meal* OPP OVERCHARGE

undercut /ˌʌndəˈkʌt; *AmE* -dərˈk-/ *verb* [+ obj] (**undercutting, undercut, undercut**)
1 to sell goods or services at a lower price than your competitors: *The bank says it will undercut rivals' rates and services.* ◇ *The scale of the company allows them to undercut prices.*
2 to make sth weaker or less likely to be effective: *Unions claim that the legislation undercuts workers' rights.*

underdeveloped /ˌʌndədɪˈveləpt; *AmE* -dərd-/ *adjective*
1 (about a country, society, etc.) having few industries and a low standard of living:

underdeveloped countries **NOTE** 'Developing countries' is now the usual term used.
2 not developed to a very high level or standard: *Telecommunications systems in the region remain underdeveloped.*
→ DEVELOPED, DEVELOPING, UNDEVELOPED
▸ ˌunderde'velopment *noun* [U]: *the underdevelopment of internal transport systems*

underemployed /ˌʌndərɪmˈplɔɪd/ *adjective*
not having enough work to do; not having work that makes full use of your skills and abilities: *When the contract ended the company was left with an office full of expensive, underemployed talent.*

underestimate *verb, noun*
● *verb* /ˌʌndərˈestɪmeɪt/ [+ obj]
1 to think or guess that the amount, cost or size of sth is smaller than it really is: *They grossly underestimated the costs involved.* ◇ *The scale of the challenge we face should not be underestimated.*
2 to not realize how good, strong, determined, etc. sb really is: *It would be unwise to underestimate our rivals.*
OPP OVERESTIMATE
▸ **underestimation** /ˌʌndərˌestɪˈmeɪʃn/ *noun* [C,U]: *a serious underestimation of the costs*
● *noun* /ˌʌndərˈestɪmət/ [C]
an estimate about the size, cost, etc. of sth that is too low: *The figure of €20 bn is probably a serious underestimate of the costs.*

underfunded /ˌʌndəˈfʌndɪd; AmE -dərˈf-/ *adjective*
(*Finance*) (about an organization, a project, etc.) not having as much money to spend as it needs: *The company's pension plan was underfunded by $2 million.* **OPP** OVERFUNDED
▸ ˌunderˈfunding *noun* [U]

the ˌunderground eˈconomy = BLACK ECONOMY

underinsured /ˌʌndərɪnˈʃɔːd; -ˈʃʊəd; AmE -ˈʃʊrd/ *adjective*
(*Insurance*)
1 (about a person) not having enough insurance: *an underinsured motorist* ◇ *attempts to increase health coverage for the underinsured*
2 (about a thing) insured for less than it is worth: *an underinsured vehicle*
▸ ˌunderinˈsurance *noun* [U]

ˌunder-inˈvestment *noun* [U]
(*Finance*) the fact of less money being invested in sth than is needed: *The chain of stores has suffered from years of under-investment.* ◇ *under-investment in plant and people* **OPP** OVER-INVESTMENT
▸ ˌunder-inˈvest *verb* [no obj]: *We have been under-investing in this brand.* ˌunder-inˈvested *adjective*: *Many funds are under-invested.*

★ **underlying** /ˌʌndəˈlaɪɪŋ; AmE -dərˈl-/ *adjective*
1 important in a situation but not always easily noticed or stated clearly: *The underlying assumption is that the amount of money available is limited.* ◇ *The underlying cause of the crisis was a lack of investment.*
2 (*Economics; Finance*) used to describe basic figures, rates, etc. excluding any special effect, event or payment: *Underlying sales growth rose 4.5%.* ◇ *an increase in underlying pre-tax profits*
3 (*Finance*) used to describe the items that particular types of investments are based on: *The value of derivatives depends on the value or change in value of an underlying security.* ◇ *underlying shares/stock/bonds/assets*

ˌunderlying inˈflation *noun* [U]
(*Economics*) the rate at which the prices of goods and services rise over a period of time, measured without considering prices that go up and down frequently, especially the costs of MORTGAGES:

Underlying inflation, which excludes food, energy and mortgage costs, rose by 0.1 per cent last month.
→ HEADLINE INFLATION

undermanned /ˌʌndəˈmænd; AmE -dərˈm-/ *adjective*
(*HR*) not having enough people working and therefore not able to function well: *The department is seriously undermanned.* **SYN** UNDERSTAFFED
OPP OVERMANNED
▸ ˌunderˈmanning *noun* [U]: *serious undermanning in maintenance and safety areas*

undermentioned /ˌʌndəˈmenʃənd; AmE -dərˈm-/ *adjective* (*only used in written English*) (*abbr* u/m)
used to refer to sth that appears below or in a later part of a document: *Applications are invited for the undermentioned vacancies.*

underpaid /ˌʌndəˈpeɪd; AmE -dərˈp-/ *adjective*
not paid enough for the work you do: *The maintenance staff are grossly underpaid.*
→ OVERPAY

★ **underpay** /ˌʌndəˈpeɪ; AmE -dərˈp-/ *verb* (**underpaid, underpaid** /-ˈpeɪd/)
1 [+ obj] (*often* be underpaid) to pay sb too little money, especially for their work: *They have a reputation for underpaying their female staff.* ◇ *I'm overworked and underpaid.*
2 [+ obj or no obj] to pay too little for sth; to pay less than sth is worth: *The acquirer has underpaid for the target firm.* ◇ *He received a fine for underpaying his taxes.*
OPP OVERPAY
▸ ˌunderˈpayment *noun* [C,U]

★ **underperform** /ˌʌndəpəˈfɔːm; AmE ˌʌndərpərˈfɔːrm/ *verb*
1 [+ obj or no obj] to not make as much money as expected or as sb/sth else: *The US branch of the bank has been underperforming.* ◇ *The company has underperformed its rivals for the last two years.* ◇ *underperforming companies/stores* ◇ *The stock has been downgraded to 'underperform'.* → IN-LINE
2 [no obj] to be less successful in your job than expected: *underperforming executives/managers*
→ OUTPERFORM
▸ **underperformance** /-pəˈfɔːməns; AmE -pərˈfɔːrməns/ *noun* [U] ˌunderperˈformer *noun* [C]: *The stock is rated as a market underperformer.*

underpin /ˌʌndəˈpɪn; AmE -dərˈp-/ *verb* [+ obj] (**-nn-**)
1 to provide a strong financial basis for sth: *The company's investment programme has been underpinned.*
2 to support or form the basis of an argument, a claim, etc: *The report is underpinned by extensive research.*

★ **underpriced** /ˌʌndəˈpraɪst; AmE ˌʌndərˈp-/ *adjective*
cheap; costing less than it is worth: *underpriced exports/stock* **OPP** OVERPRICED
▸ ˌunderˈprice *verb* [+ obj]

underproduction /ˌʌndəprəˈdʌkʃən; AmE ˌʌndərp-/ *noun* [U]
the fact that fewer goods, services, etc. are produced than are needed or than are planned: *Underproduction results in lost sales.*
OPP OVERPRODUCTION
▸ **underproduce** /ˌʌndəprəˈdjuːs; AmE ˌʌndərprəˈduːs/ *verb* [+ obj or no obj]: *Several countries have underproduced their oil quota.* ˌunderproˈducer *noun* [C]

ˌunder-reˈport (*AmE spelling* **underreport**) *verb* [+ obj]
(*Accounting*) to report or state a smaller amount of

money, etc. than the real amount, especially for dishonest reasons: *They devised a plan to under-report earnings by almost €100 million.* OPP OVER-REPORT → UNDERSTATE

undersell /ˌʌndə'sel; *AmE* -dər's-/ *verb* [+ obj] (**undersold, undersold** /-'səʊld; *AmE* -'soʊld/)
1 (*Commerce*) to sell goods or services at a lower price than your competitors: *They complain that foreign companies are underselling them.* ◇ *We are never undersold* (= our prices are the lowest).
2 (*Commerce*) to sell sth at a lower price than its real value: *They were underselling their computers to gain a share of the market.*
3 to make people think that sth is not as good or as interesting as it really is: *Don't undersell yourself at the interview.*
OPP OVERSELL
IDM never ˌknowingly underˈsold (*Commerce*) used by stores to advertise their policy of selling their products at lower prices than other stores. If you find the same product at a lower price somewhere else, the store will lower its own price to match.

undershoot /ˌʌndə'ʃuːt; *AmE* -dər'ʃ-/ *verb* [+ obj or no obj] (**undershot, undershot** /-'ʃɒt; *AmE* -'ʃɑːt/) to fail to reach a target: *We have undershot our sales targets for the last two years.* ◇ *Tax revenues undershot by $7 billion.* OPP OVERSHOOT
▶ **undershoot** /'ʌndəʃuːt; *AmE* 'ʌndər-/ *noun* [C]

the undersigned /ˌʌndə'saɪnd; *AmE* -dər's-/ *noun* [C] (*plural* **the undersigned**) (*only used in written English*)
the person who has signed that particular document: *We, the undersigned, agree to ...*

underspend /ˌʌndə'spend; *AmE* -dər's-/ *verb* [+ obj or no obj] (**underspent, underspent** /-spent/) to spend less than the amount that you can or should spend: *We have underspent our IT budget this year.* ◇ *For many years the government has underspent on public transport.* OPP OVERSPEND
▶ **underspend** /'ʌndəspend; *AmE* -dərs-/ *noun* [C, usually sing., U]: *The extra money comes from a £5 million underspend in another department.*
underspending /ˌʌndə'spendɪŋ; *AmE* ˌʌndərs-/ *noun* [U]

understaffed /ˌʌndə'stɑːft; *AmE* ˌʌndər'stæft/ *adjective*
(*HR*) (about a company, an office, etc.) not having enough people working and therefore not able to function well: *The office was seriously understaffed.* ◇ *understaffed hospitals* SYN UNDERMANNED
OPP OVERSTAFFED
▶ **underˈstaffing** *noun* [U]

understate /ˌʌndə'steɪt; *AmE* -dər's-/ *verb* [+ obj] (*Accounting*) to report a smaller amount of money, etc. than the real amount in official records: *The accounting methods used understated the company's liabilities.* OPP OVERSTATE → UNDERREPORT
▶ **understatement** /'ʌndəsteɪtmənt; *AmE* 'ʌndərs-/ *noun* [C,U]

undersubscribed /ˌʌndəsəb'skraɪbd; *AmE* -dərs-/ *adjective*
(*Finance*) (about a sale of shares, bonds, etc.) not having enough buyers: *The share issue was undersubscribed by 50%.* → OVERSUBSCRIBED

★ **undertake** /ˌʌndə'teɪk; *AmE* -dər't-/ *verb* (**undertook** /-'tʊk/ **undertaken** /-'teɪkən/)
1 [+ obj] to make yourself responsible for sth and start doing it: *The company is to undertake a major cost-cutting programme.* ◇ *to undertake a task/project* ◇ *No payment has been received for the work undertaken in July.*

◑ *to undertake a **programme/project/task*** ✦ *to undertake an **analysis/investigation**/a **study*** ✦ *to undertake **reforms/research/work***
2 [no obj] to agree or promise that you will do sth: *He undertook **to** finish the job by Friday.*

undertaking /ˌʌndə'teɪkɪŋ; *AmE* -dər't-/ *noun*

SEE ALSO: **transfer of undertaking**

1 [C] a task or project, especially one that is important and/or difficult: *To build a website to handle their worldwide sales was **no small** undertaking.*
◑ *an **enormous**/a **considerable/huge/major/massive** undertaking*
2 [C] a business: *Why do they keep pouring money into a failing commercial undertaking?*
3 [C,U] an agreement or a promise to do sth: *The company gave a written undertaking **to** compensate customers if there were serious delays.*
◑ *to **renege on/break/give/honour** an undertaking*

undervalue /ˌʌndə'væljuː; *AmE* -dər'v-/ *verb* [+ obj] (*usually* **be undervalued**)
1 to give sth a value that is less than its real value: *The currency is undervalued **against** the dollar.* OPP OVERVALUE
2 to not recognize sth/sb as being as good or as important as it/he/she, etc. really is: *She left the firm because she felt undervalued.*

underweight /ˌʌndə'weɪt; *AmE* -dər'w-/ *adjective* (*Stock Exchange*) having less of a particular type of investment or asset in a collection than the index that you are following or than your usual position: *The fund is currently underweight in both stocks.* OPP OVERWEIGHT → MARKETWEIGHT
▶ ˌunderˈweight *verb* [+ obj or no obj]

underwrite /ˌʌndə'raɪt/ *verb* [+ obj] (**underwrote** /ˌʌndə'rəʊt; *AmE* -'roʊt/ **underwritten** /ˌʌndə'rɪtn/)
1 (*Finance*) to agree to pay for an activity and accept financial responsibility for any losses it may make: *The money raised will enable the company to underwrite new business.*
2 (*Insurance*) to accept responsibility for an insurance policy so that money will be paid if loss or damage as stated in the policy happens: *to underwrite an insurance policy* ◇ *the company underwriting the risk*
3 (*Stock Exchange*) to agree to buy shares that are not bought by the public when new shares are offered for sale, at a fixed price and on a particular day: *As the rights issue is not **fully underwritten**, it is likely to fail if shares fall below 25 cents.* ◇ *an underwriting syndicate/group*
▶ **underwriting** /'ʌndəraɪtɪŋ/ *noun* [U]: *The insurance company sustained **underwriting losses** of over $2 billion.*

underwriter /'ʌndəraɪtə(r)/ *noun* [C]

SEE ALSO: **chartered life underwriter, insurance ~, lead ~, managing ~**

1 (*Insurance*) a person whose job is to estimate the risks involved in a particular activity, decide if it can be insured and how much sb must pay for insurance
2 (*Insurance*) (*also* **ˈwriter**) a person or an organization that **underwrites** insurance policies, especially for ships
3 (*Stock Exchange*) a bank or another organization that promises to buy the shares that are not sold when new shares are offered for sale

undeveloped /ˌʌndɪ'veləpt/ *adjective*
1 (about land) not used for farming, industry or building: *The north of the country is still relatively undeveloped.*

2 (about a country) not having modern industries, and with a low standard of living → DEVELOPING → UNDERDEVELOPED

undifferentiated /ˌʌndɪfəˈrenʃieɪtɪd/ *adjective*
(*Marketing*) used to describe products or services that are aimed at the largest number of people of all types: *undifferentiated products* ◇ *Undifferentiated marketing treats all customers and potential customers as identical.* → MASS MARKETING

undischarged 'bankrupt *noun* [C]
(*Law*) a person who has been officially stated to be BANKRUPT by a court but who has to keep paying back money and is not allowed to do business

undisclosed /ˌʌndɪsˈkləʊzd; *AmE* -ˈkloʊzd/ *adjective*
not made known or told to anyone: *The company sold its publishing arm for an undisclosed sum.*

undisˌtributable reˈserve = CAPITAL RESERVE (1)

undisˌtributed 'earnings (*also* ˌundisˌtributed 'profits) *noun* [pl.]
(*Accounting*) profits that are invested back into a company rather than paid to shareholders SYN RETAINED EARNINGS

undo /ʌnˈduː/ *verb* [+ obj] (**undoes** /ʌnˈdʌz/ **undid** /ʌnˈdɪd/ **undone** /ʌnˈdʌn/)
1 to cancel the effect of sth: *It's not too late to undo some of the damage.* ◇ *UNDO* (= an instruction on a computer that cancels the previous action)
2 to open sth that is fastened, tied or wrapped

undue /ʌnˈdjuː; *AmE* ˌʌnˈduː/ *adjective* [only before noun] (*formal*)
more than is thought to be reasonable or necessary: *The work should be carried out without undue delay.* ◇ *I don't want to put undue pressure on them.*
❍ undue *delay/influence/pressure/risk*

unearned 'income *noun* [U]
(*Accounting*) money that you receive but do not earn by working OPP EARNED INCOME

unease /ʌnˈiːz/ (*also* **uneasiness** /ʌnˈiːzinəs/) *noun* [U; sing.]
(used especially in newspapers) a feeling of worry about sth: *The country's economic difficulties are causing growing unease among observers.*

uneconomic /ˌʌniːkəˈnɒmɪk; ˌʌnek-; *AmE* -ˈnɑːm-/ *adjective*
1 using too much time or money, or too many materials, and therefore not likely to make a profit: *It would be uneconomic for us to employ more staff.* ◇ *ageing, uneconomic equipment* SYN UNECONOMICAL OPP ECONOMIC
2 not making a profit: *Prices have been fixed at uneconomic levels.* SYN UNPROFITABLE → ECONOMIC

uneconomical /ˌʌniːkəˈnɒmɪkl; ˌʌnek-; *AmE* -ˈnɑːm-/ *adjective*
using too much time or money, or too many materials, and therefore not likely to make a profit: *The old system was uneconomical to run.* SYN UNECONOMIC OPP ECONOMICAL
▸ **uneconomically** /ˌʌniːkəˈnɒmɪkli; ˌʌnek-; *AmE* -ˈnɑːm-/ *adverb*: *uneconomically low prices*

unemployable /ˌʌnɪmˈplɔɪəbl/ *adjective*
lacking the skills or qualities that you need to get a job OPP EMPLOYABLE

★ **unemployed** /ˌʌnɪmˈplɔɪd/ *adjective*
1 without a job although able to work: *How long have you been unemployed?* ◇ *an unemployed builder/engineer* ◇ *unemployed people/workers* SYN OUT OF WORK
2 the unemployed *noun* [pl.] people who are unemployed: *a programme to get the long-term*

unemployed back to work ◇ *The country now has four million unemployed.*
→ EMPLOYED, SELF-EMPLOYED

★ **unemployment** /ˌʌnɪmˈplɔɪmənt/ *noun* [U]
SEE ALSO: disguised unemployment, frictional ~, hidden ~, search ~, seasonal ~, structural ~
1 the fact of a number of people not having a job; the number of people without a job: *an area of high unemployment* ◇ *a rising/falling unemployment rate*
2 the state of not having a job: *people facing long-term unemployment*
→ EMPLOYMENT

unemˈployment ˌbenefit *noun* [U,C]
money paid by the government to sb who is unemployed: *to be on* (= receiving) *unemployment benefit* ◇ *the number of people claiming unemployment benefits*

unemˈployment compenˌsation *noun* [U] (*AmE*)
money that sb who has recently become unemployed receives regularly instead of their pay from a government or union plan: *The workers will receive unemployment compensation and extra unemployment benefits.*

unemˈployment inˌsurance *noun* [U]
a system where workers pay a regular amount of money, so that if they lose their job they receive a regular payment: *new unemployment insurance claims*

unemˈployment line = DOLE QUEUE

unethical /ʌnˈeθɪkl/ *adjective*
not morally correct or acceptable: *The company's actions were both illegal and unethical.* OPP ETHICAL
▸ **unethically** /ʌnˈeθɪkli/ *adverb*

unexpired /ˌʌnɪkˈspaɪəd; *AmE* -ˈspaɪərd/ *adjective* [usually before noun]
(about an agreement, a contract, etc) still valid and not yet having come to an end: *an unexpired lease/licence*

★ **unfair** /ˌʌnˈfeə(r); *AmE* -ˈfer/ *adjective*
not giving every group or person the same opportunity to do sth; not right or fair: *Steel makers face unfair competition from subsidized foreign producers.* ◇ *The new pension plans are unfair to older workers.* OPP FAIR
▸ **unˈfairly** *adverb*: *Some employees claim they were treated unfairly because they were disabled.*

unfair disˈmissal (*also* ˌwrongful disˈmissal) *noun* [U,C]
(*HR*) an occasion when sb is removed from their job without a good reason: *She is suing the company for unfair dismissal.* ◇ *He lost his claim for unfair dismissal against the company.*

unfavourable (*AmE spelling* **unfavorable**) /ʌnˈfeɪvərəbl/ *adjective*
1 (about conditions, situations, etc.) not good and likely to cause problems or make sth more difficult: *The company is delaying its share offer due to unfavourable market conditions.*
2 showing that you do not approve of or like sb/sth: *an unfavourable report* ◇ *The bank was affected by unfavourable comparisons with its main rival* (= its rival was said to be better). OPP FAVOURABLE
▸ **unˈfavourably** (*AmE spelling* **unfavorably**) *adverb*: *This year's results compare unfavourably with* (= are not as good as) *last year's.*

unˌfavourable 'balance (*AmE spelling* **unfavorable ~**) *noun* [C]
(*Accounting*) an amount of debt shown on an account SYN ADVERSE BALANCE → DEFICIT

un,favourable 'trade ,balance (also ,unfavourable ,balance of 'trade) (AmE spelling **unfavorable ~**) noun [sing.]
(Economics) a situation when a country spends more on imports than it earns from exports
[SYN] ADVERSE TRADE BALANCE

unfriendly /ʌnˈfrendli/ = HOSTILE

unfulfilled /ˌʌnfʊlˈfɪld/ adjective
that has not been completed, achieved or satisfied: They phoned customers with unfulfilled orders to explain the delays. → FULFIL
O an unfulfilled **contract/order** ✦ unfulfilled **expectations/potential/targets**

ungeared /ʌnˈɡɪəd; AmE -ˈɡɪrd/ adjective
(Finance) not using borrowed money; with no debt: ungeared investments ◇ an ungeared balance sheet

un,happy 'camper noun [C] (informal)
a customer, an employee, etc. who has complaints: The job satisfaction survey showed that there are some distinctly unhappy campers.

,uniform 'price ,auction = DUTCH AUCTION (2)

,unilateral 'contract noun [C]
(Law) an agreement in which only one side (person or company) promises to do sth or promises to do sth only if sb does a particular thing: An example of a unilateral contract is where you promise to pay a reward for somebody finding something.
→ BILATERAL CONTRACT

uninstalled /ˌʌnɪnˈstɔːld/ adjective (AmE)
(HR, informal) used to describe an employee who has been removed from their job (**fired**)

uninsurable /ˌʌnɪnˈʃɔːrəbl; -ˈʃʊər-; AmE -ˈʃʊr-/ adjective
(Insurance)
1 (about a thing or person) that cannot be insured: There is so much flooding here that houses are uninsurable.
2 (also ,non-in'surable) (about an event) that cannot be insured against because it is impossible to calculate possible losses exactly: Earthquakes are considered to be an **uninsurable risk**.
→ INSURABLE

uninsured /ˌʌnɪnˈʃɔːd; -ˈʃʊəd; AmE -ˈʃʊrd/ adjective
(Insurance)
1 (about a thing or person) that does not have insurance: an uninsured building/driver
2 (about an event) that is not insured against: uninsured losses

★ union /ˈjuːniən/ noun

SEE ALSO: company union, credit ~, customs ~, enterprise ~, European Monetary ~, European ~, general ~, etc.

1 [C] = TRADE UNION
2 [C] a group of states or countries that have the same central government or that agree to work together: the European Union
O to **create/dissolve/form/join** a union
3 [sing; U] the act of joining two or more things together; the state of being joined together: a discussion on economic and monetary union ◇ The website is a good example of the union of content and branding. ◇ the company's union **with** a big media empire

'union-,bashing noun [U]
(HR, informal) active or spoken opposition to trade/labor unions: union-bashing in the media

'union ,busting noun [U] (AmE)
(HR) the act or process of trying to stop trade/labor unions from having any power: Angry workers accused the company of union busting. ◇ union-busting activities

unionist /ˈjuːniənɪst/ = TRADE UNIONIST

unionize, -ise /ˈjuːniənaɪz/ verb [+ obj or no obj]
(HR) to organize people to become members of a trade union: a unionized workforce/industry
▶ **unionization, -isation** /ˌjuːniənaɪˈzeɪʃn; AmE -nəˈz-/ noun [U]: support for unionization efforts

,union repre'sentative noun [C]
(HR) a person who has been chosen to represent employees of a company who belong to a particular trade union: talks between union representatives and management

'union shop = CLOSED SHOP

unique /juˈniːk/ adjective
being the only one of its kind; very special or unusual: What is unique about your company? ◇ A unique feature of this gadget is the foldaway screen. ◇ The problems are not unique **to** that company.

u,nique 'selling propo,sition (also u,nique 'selling point) = USP

u,nique 'visitor noun [C]
(IT; Marketing) a person who visits a website in a particular period of time and can be identified, usually by the address of their computer, used as a measure of how popular the website is: The company claims more than 6 million daily hits and 800 000 unique visitors a month.

,unissued 'capital (also ,unissued 'share ,capital) noun [U]
(Finance) shares that a company can officially issue but has not yet issued

★ unit /ˈjuːnɪt/ noun [C]

SEE ALSO: accumulation unit, bargaining ~, central processing ~, decision-making ~, monetary ~, multi-~, strategic business ~

1 a single item of the type of product that a company sells: The game's selling price was $15 per unit. ◇ We expect to sell more than 100 000 units by the end of the year.
2 a part of a company that does a particular activity or that is not divided into smaller parts: Fiat's auto unit ◇ Six business units have been created.
3 a fixed quantity, etc. that is used as a standard measurement: a unit of time/length
4 (Finance) a single share, bond, etc: Shareholders are being asked to buy three new shares at 10¢ for each unit already owned.
5 a small machine that has a particular purpose or is part of a larger machine: the central processing unit of a computer
6 a building on an INDUSTRIAL ESTATE (= an area especially for factories): renting a unit on the industrial estate ◇ The workshop is in unit 20.

'unitary tax noun [C,U]
a form of CORPORATION TAX used in some states of the US, which calculates the amount a company must pay according to their total income, and not on their income in just one state

'unit cost noun [C, usually sing.]
(Accounting) the cost of producing, buying or providing one item: The more goods that are produced, the lower the unit cost. ◇ The department's PCs have a unit cost of $2 000 and a life expectancy of 3 years.

,unit-'linked *adjective*
(*Finance*) used to describe LIFE INSURANCE, etc. in which money is invested in a UNIT TRUST: *a unit-linked policy*

,unit of ac'count *noun* [C]
(*Accounting*; *Economics*)
1 money when it is used to measure the value of goods or services and to keep financial records
2 the standard system of money that is used in a particular country
3 a special system of money that is created only for accounting

,unit of 'currency *noun* [C]
(*Economics*) the money that is used in a particular country: *The unit of currency in Japan is the yen.* SYN MONETARY UNIT

'unit price *noun* [C]
(*Accounting*) the price of a single item: *We have ordered 50 000 boxes at a unit price of €0.12.*

'unit sales *noun* [pl.]
(*Marketing*) the number of items of a particular product that have been sold

'unit share *noun* [C]
(*Marketing*) the UNIT SALES of a particular product compared with the total sales of all similar products: *Our cordless phones have a unit share of 13% worldwide.*

,unit 'trust (*BrE*) (*AmE* **'mutual fund**) *noun* [C]
(*Finance*) an organization that manages a fund that is invested in a wide range of shares, bonds, etc. The fund is divided into small units which are bought and sold, usually by people who only invest a small amount of money: *Investing in a unit trust reduces risks for small investors.* ◇ *a unit trust company* → OPEN-ENDED (3)

universal /ˌjuːnɪˈvɜːsl; *AmE* -ˈvɜːrsl/ *adjective*
done by, involving, etc. all the people in the world or in a particular group: *The Harry Potter books have universal appeal* (= they are liked by all types of people in all places).

,universal 'bank *noun* [C]
a bank that combines INVESTMENT BANKING and COMMERCIAL BANKING ▶ **,universal 'banking** *noun* [U]

universe /ˈjuːnɪvɜːs; *AmE* -vɜːrs/ *noun* [sing.]
1 (*Marketing*) a complete group of people, companies, etc. that have the same features or qualities: *The assumed universe* (= number of possible readers) *for literary magazines is about 750 000.* SYN POPULATION
2 an area of activity; the people and companies involved in that activity: *a small but growing area of the investment universe* ◇ *the universe of companies considered socially responsible*

unladen /ˌʌnˈleɪdn/ *adjective* [usually before noun]
without a load: *unladen aircraft* ◇ *goods vehicles of an unladen weight exceeding 2 tonnes* OPP LADEN

unlawful /ʌnˈlɔːfl/ *adjective*
not allowed by law: *unlawful trading* OPP LAWFUL
▶ **unlawfully** /ʌnˈlɔːfəli/ *adverb*

unlicensed /ʌnˈlaɪsnst/ *adjective*
without a **licence** (= an official document that gives you permission to do or own sth): *unlicensed software/cabs* See note at COPY

unlimited /ʌnˈlɪmɪtɪd/ *adjective*
as much or as many as is possible; not limited in any way: *You can access the Internet for an unlimited number of hours.*

,un,limited 'company *noun* [C]
a company whose shareholders are responsible for all its debts if it fails → LIMITED COMPANY

,un,limited lia'bility *noun* [U]
the legal duty of the shareholders of an UNLIMITED COMPANY to pay all its debts → LIMITED LIABILITY

unlisted /ʌnˈlɪstɪd/ *adjective*
1 (*Finance*) (*also* **un'quoted**) not bought and sold on a stock exchange OPP LISTED
● *unlisted* **companies/securities/shares/stock**
2 (*especially AmE*) (about a telephone number) not listed in the public telephone book, at the request of the owner of the telephone. NOTE Telephone services will not give these numbers to people who ask for them. SYN EX-DIRECTORY

unload /ˌʌnˈləʊd; *AmE* ˌʌnˈloʊd/ *verb*
1 [+ obj *or* no obj] to remove things from a vehicle or ship after it has been taken somewhere: *It can take a whole day to unload a freighter.* ◇ *Several ships were waiting to unload.* OPP LOAD
2 [+ obj] to get rid of or sell sth, especially sth illegal or of bad quality: *They want to unload their shares at the right price.*

unlock /ˌʌnˈlɒk; *AmE* ˌʌnˈlɑːk/ *verb* [+ obj]
to allow sth to start being used that has existed but not been available for use: *The group is selling its publishing arm in an attempt to **unlock value** for shareholders.* ◇ *The deal with the USA will unlock billions of dollars of aid.*

unmanageable /ʌnˈmænɪdʒəbl/ *adjective*
difficult or impossible to control or deal with: *companies with unmanageable debt*

unmetered /ʌnˈmiːtəd; *AmE* -tərd/ *adjective*
(about the use of a service) not being measured, for example by a METER: *unmetered Internet access*

unmoved /ʌnˈmuːvd/ *adjective*
(about the value of sth) not having changed: *The FTSE 100 was unmoved for much of the day.*

unnerve /ʌnˈnɜːv; *AmE* -ˈnɜːrv/ *verb* [+ obj]
(often used in newspapers) to make sb feel nervous or lose confidence: *The poor results have unnerved investors.*

unofficial /ˌʌnəˈfɪʃl/ *adjective*
1 that does not have permission or approval from sb in authority: *Unofficial estimates put the figure at over 2 million.* ◇ *The unofficial exchange rate is 2 000 dinar to the dollar.*
2 that is not part of sb's business: *The Prime Minister is on an unofficial visit to Spain.*
OPP OFFICIAL
▶ **unofficially** /ˌʌnəˈfɪʃəli/ *adverb*

,unof,ficial 'strike *noun* [C]
(*HR*) a strike that does not have the approval or permission of an accepted trade union
OPP OFFICIAL STRIKE

unpaid /ˌʌnˈpeɪd/ *adjective*

SEE ALSO: delivered duty unpaid

1 (*Accounting*) not yet paid
● *unpaid* **bills/debts/fees/rent**
2 (about work, etc.) done or taken without payment: *unpaid work* ◇ *to take unpaid leave*
3 (about people) not receiving payment for work that they do: *unpaid volunteers*
OPP PAID

unpredictable /ˌʌnprɪˈdɪktəbl/ *adjective*
if a situation, an event, a price, etc. is **unpredictable** you cannot be sure what will happen because it changes a lot or depends on too many different things: *the unpredictable nature of oil prices* → PREDICTABLE
▶ **unpredictability** /ˌʌnprɪˌdɪktəˈbɪləti/ *noun* [U]
unpredictably /ˌʌnprɪˈdɪktəbli/ *adverb*

unproductive /ˌʌnprə'dʌktɪv/ *adjective*
not producing very much; not producing good
results: *an unproductive meeting* ◇ *unproductive use
of resources* OPP PRODUCTIVE

unprofessional /ˌʌnprə'feʃənl/ *adjective*
not reaching the standard expected in a particular
profession: *She was found guilty of unprofessional
conduct.* OPP PROFESSIONAL → NON-PROFESSIONAL
▶ **unprofessionally** /ˌʌnprə'feʃənəli/ *adverb*

unprofitable /ʌn'prɒfɪtəbl; *AmE* 'prɑːf-/ *adjective*
1 not making enough financial profit: *unprofitable
product lines* SYN UNECONOMIC
● unprofitable **businesses/companies/products/stores**
2 not bringing any advantage
OPP PROFITABLE
▶ **unprofitably** /ʌn'prɒfɪtəbli; *AmE* -'prɑːf-/ *adverb*:
*The company had been trading unprofitably for a
long time.*

unquoted /ˌʌn'kwəʊtɪd; *AmE* 'kwoʊt-/ =
UNLISTED (1)

unrealized , **-ised** /ʌn'riːəlaɪzd; *BrE also* -'rɪəl-/
adjective
1 not achieved or done
● unrealized **potential/projects**
2 (*Finance*) (about a profit, loss, etc.) that has been
made but not turned into real money yet: *The bank
has 400 billion yen in unrealized gains on its
investments* (= the investments have risen in value
but have not yet been sold).
● unrealized **capital gains/gains/losses/profits**

unreasonable /ʌn'riːznəbl/ *adjective*
not fair; expecting too much: *He claimed his boss
was making unreasonable demands.* ◇ *The fees they
charge are not unreasonable.* OPP REASONABLE

unrecoverable /ˌʌnrɪ'kʌvərəbl/ *adjective*
1 (about money that has been lent or lost) that you
will never be able to get back: *The bank lost $300 m
in unrecoverable loans.* OPP RECOVERABLE
2 (*IT*) (about information on a computer) that
cannot be found again: *an unrecoverable file*
3 (*IT*) (about an error in a computer program) that
cannot be corrected

unredeemed /ˌʌnrɪ'diːmd/ *adjective*
1 (*Finance*) if something given as SECURITY on a
loan is **unredeemed**, it can be kept by the person,
etc. who made the loan because the loan has not
been paid back: *He had a drawerful of unredeemed
pledges for loans he had made to students from his
personal funds.*
2 (*Commerce*) not exchanged for cash or goods: *She
has 35 000 unredeemed frequent-flier miles.*
→ REDEEM

unregulated /ʌn'regjuleɪtɪd/ *adjective*
not controlled by rules or laws: *a free, unregulated
market* → REGULATE

unreported 'income *noun* [U]
money that sb has earned and should pay tax on
but has not mentioned to the tax authorities

unscrupulous /ʌn'skruːpjələs/ *adjective*
without moral principles; not honest or fair:
unscrupulous companies/dealers/lenders ◇
unscrupulous practices/methods/tactics
▶ **un'scrupulously** *adverb* **un'scrupulousness**
noun [U]

unsecured /ˌʌnsɪ'kjʊəd; *AmE* -sə'kjʊrd/ *adjective*
(*Finance; Law*)
1 for a loan, debt, etc. is **unsecured**, there is no
SECURITY (= a valuable item that the person,
company, etc. that borrows the money will lose if
they do not pay the money back): *The new lending
company will offer unsecured loans to small
companies at an interest rate of 8–20%.*
● unsecured **credit/debt/lending/loans**
2 used to describe a person, company, etc. that has
lent money with no SECURITY
● unsecured **creditors/lenders**
OPP SECURED

unskilled /ˌʌn'skɪld/ *adjective*
1 (about a person) not having special skills or
training: *unskilled manual workers* ◇ *an unskilled
workforce*
2 (about a job) not needing special abilities or
training
OPP SKILLED

unsocial /ˌʌn'səʊʃl; *AmE* ˌʌn'soʊʃl/ *adjective* (*also*
unsociable /ʌn'səʊʃəbl; *AmE* -'soʊ-/ *less frequent*)
(*both BrE*)
outside the normal times of working: *Security staff
often have to work **unsocial hours**.*

unsold /ˌʌn'səʊld; *AmE* ˌʌn'soʊld/ *adjective*
not bought by anyone: *The store cut its prices to get
rid of unsold stock.* ◇ *10% of the company's shares
remain unsold.*

unsolicited /ˌʌnsə'lɪsɪtɪd/ *adjective*
not asked for and sometimes not wanted: *It is not
our policy to send unsolicited mail.* ◇ *The company
rejected an unsolicited takeover bid from an Italian
group.*
● unsolicited **calls/email/letters/mail** ◆ *an unsolicited*
approach/(takeover) bid/offer ◆ *unsolicited* **advice/
comments**

unsubscribe /ˌʌnsəb'skraɪb/ *verb* [+ obj or no obj]
(*IT*) **unsubscribe (from sth)** to remove your address
from an Internet MAILING LIST

★ **unsustainable** /ˌʌnsə'steɪnəbl/ *adjective*
that cannot continue or be continued for a long
time: *unsustainable levels of debt* ◇ *The decline in the
sector is the result of unsustainable growth over the
last few years.* OPP SUSTAINABLE

unsystematic 'risk (*also* **spe‚cific 'risk**)
noun [U]
(*Finance*) risk that affects the price of a particular
investment or a small number of shares, bonds,
etc., for example the possible effects of a strike in a
company or of a company going out of business
→ SYSTEMATIC RISK

untapped /ˌʌn'tæpt/ *adjective*
available but not yet used: *They regard Mexico as a
huge untapped market for their products.* ◇
*technology that creates energy from a previously
untapped source*
● untapped **demand/markets/opportunities/
potential/resources/talent**

unveil /ˌʌn'veɪl/ *verb* [+ obj]
(used especially in newspapers) to show or
introduce a new plan, product, etc. to the public for
the first time; to announce sth publicly: *The
supermarket chain has unveiled plans to create
10 000 jobs this year.*

unwind /ˌʌn'waɪnd/ *verb* (**unwound, unwound**
/ˌʌn'waʊnd/)
1 [+ obj or no obj] (used especially in newspapers)
to undo or change sth; to change or be undone:
*More than a third of the takeovers that had been
agreed are now being unwound.* ◇ *The price of oil,
which is still high, may start to unwind soon.*
2 (*Finance*) [+ obj] **unwind a long/short position** to
sell or buy shares, currencies, etc. in order to
gradually end the POSITION you are in
3 [no obj] to stop worrying or thinking about
problems and start to relax SYN WIND DOWN
▶ **un'wind** *noun* [C] **‚un'winding** *noun* [U]: *the
unwinding of our stake in the power company*

unzip /ˌʌnˈzɪp/ *verb* [+ obj] (**-pp-**)
(*IT*) to return computer files to their original size after they have been made smaller (**compressed**) [SYN] DECOMPRESS [OPP] ZIP

up /ʌp/ *adverb, adjective, verb, noun*
● *adverb*
to or at a higher level: *Prices are **well** up **on** last year's.* ◇ *Total sales were up **by** 7%.* [OPP] DOWN See note at INCREASE
[IDM] **up for sth 1** on offer for sth: *The house is up for sale.* **2** being considered for sth: *All the directors will be up for re-election next year.* **up to sth 1** as far as a particular number, level, etc: *The Human Resources Manager spends up to half her time interviewing.* **2** (*also* **up until sth**) not further or later than sth: *Up to now everything's been running smoothly.* **3** as high or as good as sth: *The production quality is not up to our usual standards.*
● *adjective* [not before noun]

SEE ALSO: **bottom-up, completely built-~, dial-~, hard ~, joined-~, pent-~, pop-~**

(*IT*) (of a computer system) working: *Our system should be up again by this afternoon.* [OPP] DOWN
[IDM] ˌup and ˈrunning (about a system, for example a computer system) working; being used: *It will be a lot easier when we have the database up and running.*
● *verb* [+ obj] (**-pp-**)
to increase the price or amount of sth: *The group upped its bid from $10 to $30 a share.* [SYN] RAISE
→ idiom at ANTE
● *noun*
[IDM] on the ˈup

SEE ALSO: **break-up, build-~, catch-~, clean-~, drive-~, follow-~, gross-~,** etc.

increasing or improving: *Business confidence is on the up.* **on the ˌup and ˈup** (*informal*) **1** (*BrE*) becoming more and more successful: *Their company is on the up and up.* **2** (*AmE*) = ON THE LEVEL at LEVEL *noun* ˌups and ˈdowns the mixture of good and bad things in a particular situation: *Every business has its ups and downs.*

upbeat /ˈʌpbiːt/ *adjective* (*informal*)
positive and enthusiastic; making you feel that the future will be good: *The company's founder was upbeat **about** its prospects.* ◇ *The presentation ended on an upbeat note.* [OPP] DOWNBEAT

UPC /ˌjuː piː ˈsiː/ *abbr*
(*Commerce*) **Universal Product Code** a pattern of thick and thin lines that is printed on things that you buy in a shop/store. It contains information that a computer can read. [SYN] BAR CODE

upcoming /ˈʌpkʌmɪŋ/ *adjective* [only before noun]
going to happen soon: *The website gives details of upcoming events.*

★ **update** /ˌʌpˈdeɪt/ *verb* [+ obj]
1 to make sth more modern by adding new parts, etc: *It's about time we updated our logo.* ◇ *updated software*
2 to give sb the most recent information about sth; to add the most recent information to sth: *I called the office to update them **on** the day's developments.* ◇ *Our records are regularly updated.*
▶ **update** /ˈʌpdeɪt/ *noun* [C]: *an update of the software* ◇ *to provide regular updates* ◇ *getting updates **on** travel information*

upfront /ˌʌpˈfrʌnt/ *adjective, adverb*
● *adjective*
1 (*Commerce*) [only before noun] paid in advance, before other payments are made: *There will be an upfront fee of 4%.*
❶ *an upfront **fee/payment***

2 not trying to hide what you think or do: *Investors are claiming that the company was not upfront **about** its financial problems.*
● *adverb* (*usually* **up front**)
as payment in advance: *We'll pay you half up front and the other half when you've finished the job.*

★ **upgrade** /ˌʌpˈɡreɪd/ *verb*
1 [+ obj *or* no obj] to make a piece of machinery, computer system, etc. more powerful and efficient; to start to use machinery or systems of this type: *We've just upgraded **to** the latest version of the operating system.* ◇ *upgraded computers*
2 (*Finance*) [+ obj] to give sth a higher grade, value or status: *The Bank has upgraded its rating on the stock **to** 'buy'.* ◇ *The company's credit rating has been upgraded* (= they are now considered to be more likely to pay their debts). [SYN] PROMOTE
3 (*HR*) [+ obj] to give sb a more important job; to make a job more important: *He's been upgraded **to** Head of Sales.* [SYN] PROMOTE
4 [+ obj *or* no obj] to give sb a better seat on a plane, room in a hotel, etc. than the one that they have paid for: *We were upgraded **to** business class.*
5 [+ obj] to improve the condition of a building, etc. in order to provide a better service: *The factory has been upgraded to meet current safety standards.*
▶ **upgrade** /ˈʌpɡreɪd/ *noun* [C]: *instructions for installing an upgrade to the existing system* ◇ *credit rating upgrades* ◇ *Frequent flyers qualify for a free upgrade.* **upgrading** /ˌʌpˈɡreɪdɪŋ/ *noun* [U,C]: *the upgrading of the firm's PCs* → DOWNGRADE

upkeep /ˈʌpkiːp/ *noun* [U]
the cost or process of keeping sth in good condition: *the upkeep of a **building/road*** [SYN] MAINTENANCE → KEEP STH UP at KEEP

uplift *noun, verb*
● *noun* /ˈʌplɪft/ [C]
(especially in newspapers) the fact of sth being raised or of sth increasing: *Figures out today show a 10% uplift **in** premiums from retail investment.* ◇ *a sales uplift of 18% over the year*
● *verb* /ˌʌpˈlɪft/ [+ obj] (*especially BrE*) (*formal*)
to collect passengers, luggage or goods: *Coaches may only set down or uplift passengers at these locations.*

★ **upload** *verb, noun*
(*IT*)
● *verb* /ˌʌpˈləʊd; AmE -ˈloʊd/ [+ obj *or* no obj]
to move data to a larger computer system from a smaller one; to be moved in this way: *You can upload an image directly from a digital camera.* [OPP] DOWNLOAD
● *noun* /ˈʌpləʊd; AmE -loʊd/
1 [U,C] the act or process of copying data from a smaller system to a larger one: *You can make future uploads easier if you tick the 'Save Password' box.*
2 [C] data copied from a smaller system to a larger one: *access other users' uploads*

upmarket /ˌʌpˈmɑːkɪt; AmE -ˈmɑːrk-/ (*AmE also* **ˈupscale**) *adjective* [usually before noun]
1 designed for or used by people who belong to a high social class; expensive and of good quality: *a maker of upmarket food products*
❶ *an upmarket **brand/hotel/product/restaurant/ store***
2 used to describe people who have more money and can afford expensive products and services: *upmarket customers* ◇ *an upmarket neighbourhood*
▶ ˌupˈmarket *adverb*: *The company has been forced to move upmarket.*
[OPP] DOWNMARKET

upscale /ˈʌpskeɪl/ = UPMARKET

upselling /'ʌpselɪŋ/ noun [U]
(*Marketing*) the technique of persuading customers to buy more products or a more expensive product than they originally intended ▸ **upsell** *verb* [no obj]

'upset price = RESERVE PRICE

upside /'ʌpsaɪd/ noun
1 (*Economics*; *Finance*) [sing; U] the possibility that sth will increase in price or value: *The shares have upside if the company focuses on increasing its customers in new markets.* ◇ *The plan involves high risks but also high **upside potential** (= opportunity for making high profits).*
2 (*Finance*) [sing; U] an increase in profits or share prices: *The deal should offer a 50% upside for shareholders.*
3 [sing.] the more positive aspect of a situation that is generally bad: *On the upside, this model does use less fuel than its competitors.*
OPP DOWNSIDE

upsize /'ʌpsaɪz/ verb [+ obj or no obj]
1 (*IT*) to move from a smaller computer system to a larger one: *There are good reasons to upsize to a larger system.* ◇ *an upsized database*
2 (*HR*) to increase the size of a company by employing more people: *28% of plants upsized and became more productive.*
▸ **'upsizing** noun [U]: *the upsizing of databases*
→ DOWNSIZE

upskill /'ʌpskɪl/ verb
(*HR*)
1 [+ obj or no obj] to teach sb new skills; to learn new skills: *The company has invested heavily in upskilling its workforce.* ◇ *a course for salespeople wanting to upskill in database management*
2 [+ obj] to change a job so that it needs more skills to do it: *upskilled tasks/jobs*
▸ **'upskilling** noun [U]: *the upskilling of the staff*

upstart /'ʌpstɑːt; AmE -stɑːrt/ noun [C]
a company or person that is new in a business, but may already be becoming important: *The company was bought by its upstart rival.* → START-UP

upstream /,ʌp'striːm/ adjective
(*Economics*; *Production*) at or connected with an early stage in an industrial or commercial process: *The company plans to expand its upstream business in oil and gas.*
◑ upstream **assets/businesses/earnings/operations**
▸ **,up'stream** *adverb*: *Manufacturers are looking both upstream and downstream to improve efficiency.* OPP DOWNSTREAM

upsurge /'ʌpsɜːdʒ; AmE -sɜːrdʒ/ noun [C, usually sing.]
a sudden large increase in sth: *a big upsurge in demand for new cars* → SURGE

upswing /'ʌpswɪŋ/ = UPTURN OPP DOWNSWING

uptick /'ʌptɪk/ (*also* **'plus tick**, *less frequent*) noun [C, usually sing.] (*both AmE*)
(*Economics*; *Finance*) a small increase in sth, especially in the price of shares: *The futures market is showing an uptick.* ◇ *an uptick in manufacturing activity* OPP DOWNTICK

uptime /'ʌptaɪm/ noun [U]
(*IT*) the period of time when a machine, especially a computer, is working and can be used: *We aim to achieve at least 99·96% uptime.* → DOWNTIME

,up to 'date adjective
1 having or including the most recent information: *Monthly meetings keep staff up to date **on/with** the latest developments.* ◇ *up-to-date records*
◑ up-to-date **figures/information/price lists/records**

2 modern; fashionable: *This technology is **bang up to date** (= completely modern).*
◑ up-to-date **equipment/methods/technology**

,up to the 'minute adjective [usually before noun]
1 having or including the most recent information: *The accounts must always be up to the minute.*
◑ up-to-the-minute **data/information/news/prices**
2 modern; fashionable: *up-to-the-minute designs*

uptrend /'ʌptrend/ noun [sing.] (*especially AmE*)
a situation in which business activity or performance increases or improves over a period of time: *The euro is on an uptrend.* OPP DOWNTREND

upturn /'ʌptɜːn; AmE -tɜːrn/ (*also* **'upswing**) noun [C, usually sing.]
a situation in which sth improves or increases over a period of time: *an upturn in trade* ◇ *The group's recent sales upturn may not last.* OPP DOWNTURN
◑ a dramatic/gradual/sharp/slight/sustained upturn

,upwardly 'mobile adjective
moving towards a higher social position, usually in which you become richer: *Their customers are mainly upwardly mobile people in their thirties and forties.* ▸ **,upward mo'bility** noun [U]

URL /,juː ɑːr 'el/ abbr
(*IT*) **uniform/universal resource locator** the address of a web page: *The URL is http:// www.oup.com.* SYN WEB ADDRESS

usability /,juːzə'bɪləti/ noun [U]
(*Marketing*) how easy sth is to use, especially a website: *She's a usability consultant at a London-based web company.* ◇ *This computer combines portability and usability in a sleek design.*

usance /'juːzəns/ noun [U; C, usually sing.]
(*Finance*) the time that is allowed for the payment of foreign BILLS OF EXCHANGE

USB /,juː es 'biː/ abbr
(*IT*) **universal serial bus** a device in a computer that allows other devices such as PRINTERS and SCANNERS to be connected to it: *The PC comes with two USB ports (= places where printers and other devices can be connected to the computer).*

'use-by date noun [C]
the date by which you must use some types of food or drink, printed on the container or package. It may not be safe to use the items after this date: *Throw away the milk—it's two days past its use-by date.* → EXPIRY DATE (3), SELL-BY DATE See note at BEST-BEFORE DATE

used /juːzd/ adjective [usually before noun]
that has belonged to or been used by sb else before: [illegible] OWNED (*AmE*), SECOND-HAND

,useful 'life noun [C, usually sing.]
(*Accounting*) the period of time that you can use an asset such as a machine or a vehicle before it is worth buying a new one to replace it: *This machinery has an estimated useful life of 80 000 running hours.* SYN ECONOMIC LIFE NOTE An asset is DEPRECIATED (reduced in value) over its **useful life**.

user /'juːzə(r)/ noun [C]

SEE ALSO: end-user, lead ~, multi-~

a person or thing that uses sth: *The software is too complicated for the average user.* ◇ *The system allows mobile phone users to see video clips.* ◇ *Financial services companies are heavy users of IT.*

'user fee noun [C] (*AmE*)
a tax on a service that is provided for the public: *The airport authority has proposed to raise user fees.*

,user-'friendly *adjective*
easy for people who are not experts to use and
understand: *The email feature has been made more
user-friendly.* ▶ **,user-'friendliness** *noun* [U]

username /'juːzəneɪm; *AmE* -zərn-/ *noun* [C]
(*IT*) the name you use in order to be able to use a
computer program or system: *Please enter your
username.*

USP /ˌjuː es 'piː/ *abbr*
(*Marketing*) **unique selling proposition** *or* **unique
selling point** (*less frequent*) a feature of a product
or service that makes it different from all others:
We need to create a USP for the product if it is to sell.
◇ *Many of the best slogans are simple statements of
USPs.*

★ utility /juː'tɪləti/ *noun* (*plural* **utilities**)
1 [C, usually pl.] a service provided for the public,
for example an electricity, water or gas supply: *the
administration of **public utilities***
2 [C] a company that provides a service for the
public, such as electricity, water or gas: *the world's
largest private electricity utility*
3 (*IT*) [C] a piece of computer software that
performs a particular task: *an anti-virus utility*

4 (*Economics*) [U] the amount of benefit or
satisfaction that sb gets from using a product or
service: *Water has high utility but low commercial
value.*

utilization, **-isation** /ˌjuːtəlaɪ'zeɪʃn; *AmE* -lə'z/
noun [U]
1 (*Production*) the relationship between the amount
that a factory, etc. produces and the amount that it
is designed to produce: *Industrial production fell 0.2
per cent and capacity utilization fell to 75.4 per cent.*
⊕ capacity/machine/plant utilization
2 the process of using sth, especially for a practical
purpose: *the utilization of equipment/knowledge*

,utmost good 'faith *phrase*
(*Insurance*) a basic condition of insurance in which
the person wishing to be insured must provide all
the necessary facts and information, even if they
are not asked for them

UW (*also spelled* **uw, U/W, U/w**) *abbr*
(*Insurance*) a short way of writing **underwriter**

V v

v (*AmE spelling* **v.**) *abbr*
a short way of writing **versus**

vacancy /'veɪkənsi/ *noun* [C] (*plural* **vacancies**)
1 (*HR*) a job that is available for sb to do: *We have a
vacancy **for** a designer.* ◇ *A vacancy has arisen **in** our
sales department.*
⊕ *a vacancy **arises/exists/occurs*** • *to **fill** a vacancy*
2 a room that is available in a hotel: *No vacancies*
(= on a sign).

'vacancy rate *noun* [C]
1 (*Property*) the percentage of buildings, offices,
etc. that are available to be sold or rented at a
particular time: *The office vacancy rate in the city
has risen to 15%.*
2 (*HR*) the percentage of jobs that are available to
be filled: *The high staff vacancy rate in the industry
is partly due to low levels of pay.*

vacant /'veɪkənt/ *adjective*
1 (*HR*) if a job in a company is **vacant**, nobody is
doing it and it is available for sb to take: *We are
having difficulty filling the vacant post.* ◇ *The job
becomes vacant in December.* ◇ *looking for a job in
the 'Situations Vacant' pages in the newspaper*
⊕ *a vacant **job/position/post/situation*** • *to **become/
be left/fall/remain** vacant*
2 empty; not being used: *They have bought a
vacant lot* (= piece of land) *to build a new
warehouse.* ◇ *The seat next to me was vacant.*
⊕ *a vacant **lot/property/room/seat*** • *to **become/be
left/remain** vacant*

,vacant pos'session *noun* [U] (*BrE*)
(*Property*) if a house, flat/apartment, etc. is offered
for sale with **vacant possession**, there will be no
one living in it when the sale is complete

vacate /və'keɪt; veɪ'k-; *AmE also* 'veɪkeɪt/ *verb*
[+ obj] (*formal*)
1 (*HR*) to leave a job, position of authority, etc. so
that it is available for sb else: *She has taken over the
role vacated by her boss.* See note at RESIGN
2 to leave a building, seat, etc., especially so that
sb else can use it: *Guests are requested to vacate
their rooms by noon on their day of departure.*

vacation /və'keɪʃn; veɪ'k-/ *noun*
1 [U,C] (*AmE*) a holiday or a period when people are
not working: *You look tired—you should **take** a
vacation.* ◇ *I'm **on** vacation next week.* ◇ *The job
includes four weeks' paid vacation.*
2 [C] in the UK, one of the periods of time when
universities or courts of law are closed; in the US,
one of the periods of time when schools, colleges,
universities or courts of law are closed: *students
looking for vacation work*
→ HOLIDAY

vacillate /'væsɪleɪt/ *verb* [no obj]
if a price, a currency, etc. **vacillates**, it goes up and
down frequently, but only by a small amount each
time: *the effect of vacillating oil prices*

'valet ,service /'væleɪ; 'vælɪt; *AmE also* vae'leɪ/
noun [C]
1 (*BrE*) a service provided by a hotel in which sb
cleans the clothes of the guests
2 a service which provides sb to park your car for
you when you arrive at a hotel, restaurant, etc.

★ valid /'vælɪd/ *adjective*
1 that is legally or officially acceptable: *a valid
passport* ◇ *They have a valid claim for compensation.*
◇ *The ticket is valid **for** three months.*
2 (*IT*) accepted by the system: *a valid
password* OPP INVALID
→ LEGITIMATE (2)
▶ **'validly** *adverb*: *The contract had been validly
drawn up.*

validate /'vælɪdeɪt/ *verb* [+ obj]
1 to check or prove that sth is accurate, true,
useful or of an acceptable standard: *The purchasing
manager validates all invoices.* ◇ *The product has
been validated against safety requirements.*
2 to make sth legally valid: *to validate a contract/
credit card*
OPP INVALIDATE
▶ **validation** /ˌvælɪ'deɪʃn/ *noun* [U,C]
OPP INVALIDATION at INVALIDATE

validity /vəˈlɪdəti/ *noun* [U]
the state of being legally or officially acceptable: *the period of validity of the agreement*

valuable /ˈvæljuəbl/ *adjective*
1 worth a lot of money: *Please leave valuable items in the hotel safe.* ◊ *We had to sell off valuable assets.*
2 very useful or important: *Her experience in Japan made her very valuable to the company.*
[OPP] WORTHLESS

valuables /ˈvæljuəblz/ *noun* [pl.]
things that are worth a lot of money, especially small personal things such as jewellery, cameras, etc: *Ordinary mail is not suitable for sending money or valuables through the post.*

valuation /ˌvæljuˈeɪʃn/ *noun* [C,U]

SEE ALSO: **inventory valuation, stock valuation**

1 (*Finance*) a professional judgement about how much money sth is worth; the estimated value of sth: *Surveyors carried out a valuation of the property.* ◊ *A valuation of almost $1 billion was put on the company.* ◊ *land valuation*
2 a judgement about how useful or important sth is; the estimated importance of sth: *She puts a high valuation on trust between colleagues.*

★ **value** /ˈvælju:/ *noun, adjective, verb*
● *noun*

SEE ALSO: **added value, agreed ~, assessed ~, asset ~, book ~, break-up ~, capital ~,** etc.

1 [U,C] how much sth is worth in money or other goods for which it can be exchanged: *Share values have fallen by 20% in the last year.* ◊ *Investments could increase in value by about 5% per year.* ◊ *Some people have put a value of $2 billion on the company.* ◊ *creating value for investors*
● to **decrease/drop/fall/halve** in value ◆ to **double/go up/increase/rise** in value ◆ the **current/long-term/ potential/present/short-term** value of sth ◆ a **high/ low** value ◆ to **place/put/set** a value on sth
2 [U] (*especially BrE*) how much sth is worth compared with its price: *Our printers represent excellent value when compared with similar products.* ◊ *Consumers are looking for the service that offers the best value for money.*
● **bad/excellent/good/poor** value ◆ to **give/offer/ provide/represent** value
3 values [pl.] beliefs about what is right and wrong and what is important in life: *The document lists the eight core values on which company policy is based.*
● **common/cultural/family/shared/social** values
● *adjective* [only before noun]
(about a product) produced and sold cheaply: *We have over a thousand items in our value range of toiletries.*
● *verb* [+ obj]
1 to decide how much money sth is worth: *The company has been valued at over €2 billion.*
2 to think that sb/sth is important: *I value him as a friend as well as a colleague.* ◊ *The metal is valued for its lightness and strength.* ◊ *valued customers/ employees*

ˌvalue ˈadded *noun, adjective*
● *noun* [U]
1 (*Economics*) the amount by which the value of a product increases at each stage of the production process, not including the cost of the basic materials: *In many rural areas, output per head and value added will be lower.* [SYN] ADDED VALUE
2 (*Marketing*) the extra value that a company adds to a basic product or service, for example by adding extra features, before it is sold to the consumer: *a*

comparison of consumer spending on goods with different amounts of value added [SYN] ADDED VALUE
3 (*Marketing*) the extra features that a product or service has that a customer is willing to pay more for
● *adjective* [only before noun] **value-added**
1 (*Marketing*) (about products) having extra features added to them that a customer is willing to pay more for: *standard lines such as wrapped white bread and value-added products such as wholemeal bread and crispbread*
2 (about a company) using raw materials or parts to produce products of much higher value
2 (about a company) offering extra or special services in a particular commercial area

ˌvalue-added ˌmanuˈfacturing *noun* [U]
the production of goods in which processes increase the value of the materials used and the price that they can be sold for: *high/low value-added manufacturing industries*

ˌvalue-added ˈreseller *noun* [C] (*abbr* VAR)
(*Commerce*) a company that adds extra features or improvements to another company's product or service, especially computers and software, before it is sold to the consumer

ˈvalue aˌnalysis *noun* [U,C]
(*Production*) a way of trying to reduce the cost of a product while keeping the same quality by examining all the things the product does for the customer and the production cost of each of these → VALUE ENGINEERING

ˈvalue-based ˌpricing = VALUE PRICING (1)

ˈvalue chain *noun* [C]
(*Marketing; Production*)
1 the series of stages involved in the design, manufacture, marketing and support of a product, each of which adds value to it: *She analysed a typical value chain for books, breaking the costs down into separate areas.*
2 a series of companies that includes the company that makes a product and those that add extra features to it before it is sold to the customer: *The company wishes to own more of the value chain.*

ˈvalued ˌpolicy *noun* [C]
(*Insurance*) a type of insurance policy in which the value of the items insured, and the amount that will be paid if a claim is made, is agreed in advance

ˈvalue engiˌneering *noun* [U]
(*Production*) the process of designing a product or service so that it gives as much value as possible to customers without unnecessary costs: *A value engineering exercise was carried out and some design changes were identified.* → VALUE ANALYSIS

ˌvalue for ˈmoney ˌaudit *noun* [C]
an official examination of the records of a charity or business that does not aim to make a profit in order to check that it is using the money that it spends in the best way

ˈvalue inˌvestor *noun* [C]
(*Finance*) an **investor** who buys shares that they believe are being traded at less than their real value and whose price will probably soon rise

ˈvalue ˌjudgement (*also spelled* ~ **judgment**, *especially in AmE*) *noun* [C,U]
a decision about how good or important sth is, based on personal opinions rather than facts

ˈvalue ˌpricing *noun* [U]
(*Marketing*)
1 (*also* ˈvalue-based ˌpricing) a way of deciding the price of a product based on its value to the customer rather than on the cost of producing it
2 the practice of selling a product at a lower price, while keeping its value to the customer the same

valuer /'vælju:ə(r)/ *noun* [C]
a person whose job is to estimate how much
property, land, etc. is worth: *The apartment was
sold at a price fixed by an independent valuer.*

'value share *noun* [C]
(*Marketing*) the share of a market that a particular
product has in terms of the money it makes: *Our
toothpaste's value share has improved from 48% to
50%.* → MARKET SHARE

'value-stream a,nalysis *noun* [U,C]
(*Production*) a method of analysing which parts of
the production process add to the value of the
product and which parts do not: *We carried out a
value-stream analysis of the plant in order to
eliminate waste and make our production leaner.*

vanilla /və'nɪlə/ *adjective* (*informal*)
ordinary; not special in any way: *Many customers
prefer plain vanilla cellphones.*

vapourware (*AmE spelling* **vaporware**)
/'veɪpəweə(r); AmE -pərwer/ *noun* [U]
(*IT, informal*) computer software that is being
advertised but is not yet available and may never
be developed and sold: *The technology is finally
moving from vapourware to product.*

VAR /,vi: eɪ 'ɑ:(r)/ = VALUE-ADDED RESELLER

★**variable** /'veəriəbl; AmE 'ver-; 'vær-/ *adjective,
noun*
● *adjective*
1 often changing; likely to change: *variable rates of
interest* ◇ *The images are of variable quality* (= some
are good, some bad).
2 able to be changed: *a tool with variable speed
control* ◇ *If you experience seasonal demand, variable
pricing might help* (= charging different prices at
different times).
→ ADJUSTABLE
● *noun* [C]
a situation, number or quantity that can vary or be
varied and affect a situation in different ways:
*Weather is one of the many variables that can affect
the profits of clothing companies.*

,variable 'budget *noun* [C]
(*Accounting*) an amount of money available to a
company, person, etc. that can be increased or
decreased as necessary

,variable 'cost *noun* [C]
(*Accounting*) an amount of money used to produce
goods that varies according to the quantity made:
Fuel consumption is a variable cost. ◇ *By cutting our
fixed costs we can concentrate on controlling our
variable costs.* → FIXED COST—Picture at COST

,variable 'costing (*also* di,rect 'costing) *noun* [U]
(*Accounting*) a method of calculating the cost of a
unit of a product that includes only costs that often
change, such as the cost of materials and workers
SYN MARGINAL COSTING

,variable 'pay = PERFORMANCE-RELATED PAY

variance /'veəriəns; AmE 'ver-; 'vær-/ *noun* [U,C]
1 (*formal*) the amount by which sth changes or is
different from sth else: *We test for any variance in
quality at all stages of production.*
2 (*Accounting*) the difference between the levels of
costs or income that have been planned for an
activity and the actual costs or income: *The
favourable variance of $700 000* (= we spent
$700 000 less than expected) *is mainly due to good
control of expenses.*
❍ *adverse/favourable/positive/unfavourable*
variance

★**variation** /,veəri'eɪʃn; AmE 'ver-/ *noun* [C,U]
a change, especially in the amount or level of sth; a
difference: *Results showed wide variations in the*

variance

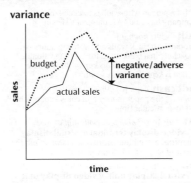

vehicle's performance under different conditions. ◇
*Interest rates offered by banks are subject to
variation.* ◇ *The new drinks are a variation on their
two best-selling products.*
❍ *considerable/marked/significant/substantial/wide*
variation(s) ● *minor/slight/small/subtle variation(s)*
● *regional/seasonal/year-to-year variation(s)*

varied /'veərid; AmE 'verid; 'vær-/ *adjective*
1 of many different types: *People's reasons for
leaving their jobs are varied.* ◇ *stores with low prices
and varied merchandise*
2 not staying the same, but changing often: *She's
had a varied career.*

variety /və'raɪəti/ *noun* (*plural* **varieties**)
1 [C] a type of a thing, for example a plant or
product, that is different from the others in the
same general group: *They sell seven varieties of
apple/apples.* ◇ *I've been buying the same variety of
toothpaste for years.*
2 [C, usually sing.] several different sorts of the
same thing: *We have a wide variety of models to
choose from.* ◇ *He resigned for a variety of reasons.*
3 [U] the quality of not being the same or not
doing the same thing all the time: *I like to have a lot
of variety in my work.*

va'riety store *noun* [C] (*AmE old-fashioned*)
a shop/store that sells a wide range of goods at low
prices

vary /'veəri; AmE 'veri; 'væri/ *verb* (**varying, varied,
varied**)
1 [no obj] (about a group of similar things) to be
different from each other in size, shape, etc:
Laptops vary considerably in size and weight. ◇ *We
introduced new methods with varying degrees of
success.*
2 [no obj] to change or be different according to the
situation: *Marketing methods vary with market size.*
◇ *A company's IT costs vary according to what type
of business it does.* ◇ *Prices vary widely depending on
where you live.*
3 [+ obj] to make changes to sth to make it slightly
different: *The job enables me to vary the hours I
work.*

★**VAT** /,vi: eɪ 'ti:; væt/ *noun* [U] **value added tax** a
tax that is added to the price of many goods and
services: *Prices include VAT.* ◇ *€85 + VAT*
→ SALES TAX

VATman /'vætmæn/ *noun* (*plural* **VATmen** /-men; -
mən/) (*informal*)
1 (*BrE*) **the VATman** [sing.] a way of referring to the
government department that is responsible for
collecting VAT: *It will soon be easier to deal with the
VATman and the Inland Revenue.*

2 [C] a person whose job is to check that a company has paid VAT: *the local VATman*

vault /vɔːlt/ *noun* [C]
a room with thick walls and a strong door, especially in a bank, used for keeping valuable things safe: *A complete backup of the computer system is kept in a secure vault.*

'vault cash *noun* [U] *(AmE)*
(Finance) the paper money and coins kept at a bank at any particular time

VDT /ˌviː diː ˈtiː/ *abbr (especially AmE)*
(IT) **video display terminal** *or* **visual display terminal** a computer MONITOR: *research into the effects of long-term VDT use* → VDU

VDU /ˌviː diː ˈjuː/ *abbr (especially BrE)*
(IT) **visual display unit** *or* **video display unit** a computer MONITOR: *Working at a VDU screen may be harder on the eyes than reading books.* ◇ *VDU operators* → VDT—Picture at OFFICE

vehicle /ˈviːəkl; *AmE also* ˈviːhɪkl/ *noun* [C]

SEE ALSO: **heavy goods vehicle, public service vehicle**

1 a car, bus, lorry/truck, etc: *The company is renewing its fleet of vehicles.*
○ *a commercial/delivery/(heavy) goods vehicle ◆ vehicle makers/manufacturers/producers ◆ to hire/lease a vehicle*
2 something that can be used as a way of achieving sth or to express your ideas or feelings : *The intranet provides a vehicle for teams to share information and knowledge.*

ve,locity of circu'lation *noun* [sing.]
(Economics) the average number of times that a unit of money is passed from person to person in an economy in a particular period of time: *The money supply has been rising rapidly with falling velocity of circulation over the last three years.*

vendee /ˌvenˈdiː/ *noun* [C]
(Law) a person who is buying a house or other property → BUYER See note at EMPLOYER

vender = VENDOR

vending /ˈvendɪŋ/ *noun* [U]
(Commerce) the activity of selling small items, especially food or drink, from a STALL or a machine: *Our vending service operates over 50 machines around the campus.*

'vending ma,chine *noun* [C]
a machine from which you can buy cigarettes, drinks, etc. by putting coins into it

★ vendor *(AmE spelling also* **vender**) /ˈvendə(r)/ *noun* [C] *(formal)*
1 *(Commerce)* a company or person that sells sth: *a software vendor* ◇ *street vendors*
2 *(Production)* a company that supplies raw materials or pieces of equipment to companies that make goods: *They have been chosen as preferred vendor for voice communications for the hotel group.* [SYN] SUPPLIER See note at SUPPLY CHAIN
3 *(Law)* a person who is selling a house or other property
→ SELLER See note at EMPLOYER

'vendor ,rating *(abbr* VR) *(also* sup'plier ,rating *abbr* SR) *noun* [U,C]
(Production) a system of recording and ranking how well a supplier does what they agree to do, the quality of the goods they supply, etc.; the score that they receive: *Vendor rating can help to raise the level*

of quality procedures throughout industry. ◇ *We were keen to get the highest vendor rating possible.*
○ *to get/give a vendor rating ◆ to carry out/undertake (a) vendor rating*

★ venture /ˈventʃə(r)/ *noun, verb*
● *noun* [C]

SEE ALSO: **joint venture**

a business project or activity, especially one that involves taking risks: *The publishing company was his first large business venture.* [SYN] ENTERPRISE
○ *a business/commercial/corporate/an Internet venture ◆ to create/form/set up/start a venture ◆ to invest in/finance/fund a venture*
● *verb*
1 [no obj] to go somewhere or become involved in sth even though it may be a risk to do so: *The restaurant chain is about to venture into the hotel business.*
2 [+ obj] to risk losing sth valuable or important if you are not successful at sth: *He ventured his financial security on the deal.*

'venture ,capital *(also* 'risk ,capital) *noun* [U]
(Finance) money that is invested in a new company to help it develop or expand, which may involve a lot of risk but can also bring good profits
○ *to attract/find/look for/raise/seek venture capital ◆ venture capital backing/funding ◆ a venture capital company/firm/group/investor*

'venture ,capitalist *noun* [C]
(Finance) a private investor or a financial business that invests money in new companies, which may involve a lot of risk and bring good profits: *to raise money from venture capitalists* → ANGEL INVESTOR

venue /ˈvenjuː/ *noun* [C]
a place where people meet for an organized event: *The hotel is a popular venue for conferences.*
○ *a concert/conference/an entertainment/exhibition/a sporting venue*

VER /ˌviː iː ˈɑː(r)/ = VOLUNTARY EXPORT RESTRAINT

verbal /ˈvɜːbl; *AmE* ˈvɜːrbl/ *adjective*
1 spoken, not written: *a verbal agreement* ◇ *She received a verbal warning from her manager when she arrived late again.*
2 relating to words: *The job applicant must have good verbal skills.*
▶ **'verbally** *adverb*: *The agreement cannot be terminated verbally.*

verdict /ˈvɜːdɪkt; *AmE* ˈvɜːrd-/ *noun* [C]
1 a decision that you make or an opinion that you give about sth, after you have tested it or considered it carefully: *We're still waiting for the Chairman to give his verdict on the designs.*
○ *to deliver/give/issue your verdict*
2 *(Law)* a decision that is made by a judge, a JURY, etc. in a court, stating if sb is considered guilty of a crime or of doing sth wrong or not: *The jury has already reached a verdict.*
○ *to reach/record/return a verdict*

,verification of 'assets *noun* [U]
(Accounting) the process of checking what buildings, machinery, vehicles, investments, etc. a company has and calculating their value

★ version /ˈvɜːʃn; -ʒn; *AmE* ˈvɜːrʒn/ *noun, verb*
● *noun* [C]

SEE ALSO: **demo version, demonstration version**

a form of sth that is slightly different from or newer than the original thing: *the latest version of the software package*
● *verb* [+ obj] *(often used as an adjective* **versioned**)
to create a new form of sth, especially computer software

versus /'vɜːsəs; AmE 'vɜːrsəs/ preposition (abbr **v, vs**)
  1 used to compare two different ideas, choices, etc: *We'll need to hire more people to finish the project quickly—it's time versus money.*
  2 (Law) used to show that two sides are against each other in a legal case: *in the case of the State versus Ford*

vertical /'vɜːtɪkl; AmE 'vɜːrt-/ adjective
  1 having a structure in which there are top, middle and bottom levels: *a vertical flow of communication*
  2 (about a line, etc.) going straight up or down from a level surface or from top to bottom in a picture, etc: *the vertical axis of the graph*
  → HORIZONTAL

vertical disinte'gration noun [U]
  (Economics) a situation where a company stops producing some goods or parts itself and starts to buy them from an outside supplier → VERTICAL INTEGRATION

vertical 'equity noun [U]
  (Economics) the principle that people with different characteristics should be treated in different ways, for example that the rate of tax people pay should vary according to their level of income
  → HORIZONTAL EQUITY

vertical inte'gration (also ˌvertical exˈpansion) noun [U] (also ˌvertical 'merger [C])
  (Economics) a situation where a company buys one of the companies which supplies it with goods or which buys goods from it: *The company moved one step closer to vertical integration after acquiring its distributors.* → BACKWARD INTEGRATION, FORWARD INTEGRATION, HORIZONTAL INTEGRATION, VERTICAL DISINTEGRATION—Picture at INTEGRATION

vertical 'loading noun [U]
  (HR) the fact of giving sb more responsibility in their job, more power to make decisions, etc: *Vertical loading challenges employees to grow in their jobs.* → HORIZONTAL LOADING, JOB ENRICHMENT

vertical 'merger = VERTICAL INTEGRATION

vertical segre'gation noun [U]
  (HR) used to describe a situation where some types of people, for example women, have less chance of getting jobs at a high level in a company, an industry, etc. → GLASS CEILING, HORIZONTAL SEGREGATION

vessel /'vesl/ noun [C]
  a large ship or boat
  ○ *an ocean-going/a sea-going vessel • a cargo/commercial/container/freight/merchant vessel*

vest /vest/ verb
  (Finance)
  1 [+ obj or no obj] (about shares in a company, especially ones given to employees) to come to the end of an agreed period after which their owner has the right to sell them: *The CEO's share option will vest/become vested after four years.*
  2 [no obj] to agree to keep your shares in a company for at least a particular period of time: *Even the founder of the company had to vest as a guarantee to investors.*
  PHR V **'vest in sb/sth** (Law) to be controlled by sb/sth legally: *In the case of bankruptcy, the property shall vest in the trustee.* **'vest sth in sb/sth**; **'vest sb with sth** (Law) (usually **be vested in/with**)
  1 to give sb the legal right or power to do sth: *Overall authority is vested in the Supreme Council.* ○ *The Supreme Council is vested with overall authority.*
  2 to make sb the legal owner of land or property

vested /'vestɪd/ adjective (AmE)
  (Law) (about an employee) having the right to receive a particular amount of benefits after working for a fixed number of years: *If you haven't worked for your employer long enough to be fully vested, you will not have a right to your full pension.*

ˌvested 'interest noun [C]
  1 a personal reason for wanting sth to happen, especially because you get some financial advantage from it: *The bank has a vested interest in seeing your business succeed.*
  2 a group of people who have a personal reason of this kind for wanting sth to happen: *The government will challenge the vested interests that control so much power.*

vesting /'vestɪŋ/ noun [U] (AmE)
  (Law) the process of an employee getting the right to receive full pension or other benefits

vet /vet/ verb [+ obj] (-tt-)
  SEE ALSO: pre-vet
  1 (HR) (especially BrE) to find out about a person's past life and career in order to decide if they are suitable for a particular job: *All candidates are carefully vetted for security reasons.*
  2 to examine sth carefully to make sure that it is correct, suitable, legal, etc: *The merger was allowed to go ahead after being carefully vetted.* ◇ *The document was vetted and approved by senior management.*
  SYN SCREEN
  ▸ **'vetting** noun [U]: *a rigorous vetting process*

veto /'viːtəʊ; AmE -toʊ/ noun, verb
  ● noun (plural **vetoes**)
  1 [C,U] the right to refuse to allow sth to be done, especially the right to stop a law from being passed or a decision from being taken: *The executive committee has a final veto on/over business decisions.* ◇ *The British government used its veto to block the proposal.* ◇ *to have the power/right of veto* ◇ *veto power/rights*
  2 [C] an occasion when sb refuses to allow sth to be done: *For months there was a veto on employing new staff.*
  ● verb [+ obj] (**vetoes, vetoing, vetoed, vetoed**)
  1 to stop sth from happening or being done by using your official authority (= by using your veto): *The takeover was vetoed by the European Commission.*
  2 to refuse to accept or do what sb has suggested: *The union vetoed the introduction of six-month contracts.*

viable /'vaɪəbl/ adjective
  that can be done, used, achieved, etc.; likely to be successful: *Meeting via the Internet is seen as a viable alternative to business travel.* ◇ *They could not get a large enough share of the market to make the business viable.*
  ○ *a viable alternative/option/proposition/solution • commercially/economically/financially viable*
  ▸ **viability** /ˌvaɪə'bɪləti/ noun [U]: *The Japanese firm is assessing the viability of opening a plant in France.* ◇ *There are doubts about the long-term viability of the business.*

viˌcarious liaˈbility noun [U]
  (Law) the fact of sb having legal responsibility for the actions of sb else, for example a company being responsible for the actions of its employees

vice- /vaɪs/ combining form (used in nouns and related adjectives)
  next in rank to sb and able to represent them or act for them: *Ruth Hawkin, vice-director of HPS group* ◇ *The chairman resigned and handed control to his vice-chairman.*

,vice-'president *noun* [C] (*especially AmE*) (*abbr* **VP**)

SEE ALSO: **executive vice-president**

a person in charge of a particular part of a company: *vice-president of marketing* ◇ *marketing vice-president*

videoconferencing /ˌvɪdiəʊ'kɒnfərənsɪŋ; *AmE* ˌvɪdioʊ'kɑːn-/ *noun* [U]
a system that enables people in different places to have a meeting by watching and listening to each other using computers, video cameras, etc: *Branch managers participate in meetings through videoconferencing.* ◇ *to use videoconferencing*
⊕ *videoconferencing* **equipment/software/systems/ technology**
▶ **'videoconference** *noun* [C,U]: *to hold a videoconference* ◇ *to talk to each other via videoconference*

videophone /'vɪdiəʊfəʊn; *AmE* -oʊfoʊn/ *noun* [C]
a type of telephone with a screen that allows you to see the person you are talking to

viewer /'vjuː.ə(r)/ *noun* [C]
1 a person watching television: *Advertisers know that the game will draw up to 100 million viewers.* ◇ *heavy/light viewers* (= people who watch television a lot/a little)
⊕ **television/TV** *viewers* ✦ *to* **attract/bring in/draw/ lure** *viewers*
2 a device or computer program that allows you to look at pictures: *a graphics viewer*

viewership /'vjuːəʃɪp; *AmE* 'vjuːər-/ *noun* [U]
the number of people who watch a particular programme or channel on television: *The network has lost 8% of its younger viewership.*

violate /'vaɪəleɪt/ *verb* [+ obj]
1 to go against or refuse to obey a law, an agreement, etc: *He was violating the company's rules about making personal phone calls.*
2 to disturb or not respect sb's peace, PRIVACY, etc.
▶ **violation** /ˌvaɪə'leɪʃn/ *noun* [U,C]: *To include the images on a website would be in violation of copyright restrictions.*

'viral ˌmarketing (*also* re'ferral ˌmarketing) *noun* [U]
(*Marketing*) a way of advertising and selling in which information about a company's products or services is spread by people telling other people or sending on emails **SYN** BUZZ MARKETING

★ virtual /'vɜːtʃuəl; *AmE* 'vɜːrtʃ-/ *adjective* [only before noun]
1 almost or very nearly the thing described, so that any slight difference is not important: *The company has a virtual monopoly in this area of trade.*
2 (*IT*) existing only on computer; using computers as the means of communication: *the success of the virtual bookstore* ◇ *We hold meetings that are part physical and part virtual—20 people are in the room and 40 in their offices.* ◇ *a virtual assistant/team/ worker* **OPP** PHYSICAL

,virtual 'memory (*also* ˌvirtual 'storage) *noun* [U]
(*IT*) a way of providing extra memory for a computer by moving data between the computer's memory and a disk

,virtual 'office *noun* [C]
(*HR*) a place for work that is not a physical building but consists of people working in different places, such as their homes, using computer equipment, telephones and other technology: *The three co-*

workers are thousands of miles apart, working in virtual offices.

,virtual organi'zation *noun* [C]
a group of companies, employees, suppliers, customers, etc. that work together using computer equipment, telephones and other technology in order to provide a service or a product

,virtual re'ality *noun* [U,C] (*abbr* **VR**)
(*IT*) images with sound of places, objects, etc., created by a computer, that appear to surround the person looking at them and seem almost real, often used for study or training purposes: *They use virtual reality systems to design and test building schemes.*

,virtual 'storage = VIRTUAL MEMORY

virus /'vaɪrəs/ *noun* [C]
(*IT*) instructions that are hidden inside a computer program and are designed to cause faults or destroy data: *The virus wiped everything off my hard disk.* ◇ *The software can detect over 500 different viruses.* ◇ *anti-virus software/virus detection software*
⊕ *a* **computer/software** *virus* ✦ *a virus* **alert/attack** ✦ *to* **detect/import/spot/spread** *a virus*

visibility /ˌvɪzə'bɪləti/ *noun* [U]
1 how easily sth/sb is seen or noticed by the public: *The advertisements were intended to increase the company's visibility in the marketplace.*
2 (*Accounting*) the fact that it is possible to see the activities and the financial state of a company from its accounts

,visible 'balance = BALANCE OF TRADE

,visible 'exports *noun* [pl.]
(*Economics*) goods, not services, that are sold to other countries → VISIBLES

,visible 'imports *noun* [pl.]
(*Economics*) goods, not services, that are bought from other countries → VISIBLES

visibles /'vɪzəblz/ *noun* [pl.]
(*Economics*) imports and exports that are goods not services → INVISIBLES, VISIBLE EXPORTS, VISIBLE IMPORTS

,visible 'trade *noun* [U]
(*Economics*) goods, not services, that are sold to or bought from other countries → INVISIBLE TRADE

vision /'vɪʒn/ *noun*
1 [C] an idea of how the future will be: *In her presentation she outlined her vision of how the market would change over the next few years.*
⊕ *a* **common/corporate/shared/strategic** *vision*
2 [U] the ability to think about or plan the future with great imagination and intelligence: *He had the clarity of vision to sell his Internet company before the market crashed.* ◇ *lack of vision*

visioning /'vɪʒənɪŋ/ *noun* [U]
the process of senior managers or directors thinking about and planning what they would like the future of their company or organization to be: *visioning exercises/workshops*

'vision ˌstatement *noun* [C]
an official statement of how a company or an organization would like to be in the future → MISSION STATEMENT

,visual 'aid *noun* [C, usually pl.]
a picture, video, etc. used in teaching or giving talks to help people to learn or understand sth

vocation /vəʊ'keɪʃn; *AmE* voʊ-/ *noun* [C]
a type of work or way of life that you believe is especially suitable for you: *Nursing is not just a job—it's a vocation.* ◇ *graphic designers and other*

people with a commercial vocation ◇ *He has a vocation for teaching.* See note at JOB

vocational /vəʊˈkeɪʃənl; *AmE* voʊ-/ *adjective*
connected with the skills, knowledge, etc. that you need to have in order to have in a particular job
❍ *vocational* **courses/education/guidance/ qualifications/training**

voicemail (*also spelled* **voice mail**) /ˈvɔɪsmeɪl/ *noun*
1 [U] an electronic system for storing telephone messages: *To reply to this message by voicemail, press 2.* ◇ *We have voicemail after business hours.*
2 [C,U] a message stored on this system: *If I'm not in my office, leave a voice mail.*

ˈvoice-ˌover *noun* [C]
(*Marketing*) information or comments in a television advertisement, etc. that are given by a person who is not seen on the screen: *She earns a lot of money doing voice-overs for TV commercials.*

ˈvoice recogˈnition *noun* [U]
(*IT*) a system that allows you to give a computer spoken instructions: *People who can't use a keyboard can use voice recognition for spoken commands.* SYN SPEECH RECOGNITION
❍ *voice-recognition* **programs/software/systems/ technology**

void /vɔɪd/ *adjective, verb*
● *adjective*
(*Law*) (about a contract, an agreement, etc.) not valid or legal: *The agreement was declared void.*
→ NULL AND VOID
● *verb* [+ obj]
(*Law*) to state officially that sth is no longer valid: *A decision was made to void the contract.*
SYN NULLIFY

voidable /ˈvɔɪdəbl/ *adjective*
(*Law*) (about a contract) that can be made no longer legally valid in particular circumstances, for example if one of the people or groups that sign the contract acts in a dishonest way: *The contract is voidable for fraud.*

vol. *abbr*
a short way of writing **volume**

volatile /ˈvɒlətaɪl; *AmE* ˈvɑːtl/ *adjective*
1 likely to change suddenly in value, state, etc: *Food prices are highly volatile* (= they rise or fall very suddenly). ◇ *UK carmakers saw record losses in a volatile market last year.* See note at STOCK
❍ *volatile* **markets/prices/shares/stock/trading**
2 (*Technical*) (about a substance) that changes quickly into a gas: *Petrol is a volatile substance.*
▶ **volatility** /ˌvɒləˈtɪləti; *AmE* ˌvɑːl-/ *noun* [U]: *the volatility of share prices* ◇ *market volatility*

★ volume /ˈvɒljuːm; *AmE* ˈvɑːl-; -jəm/ *noun*

SEE ALSO: high volume, sales volume

1 [U,C] the amount of space that an object or a substance fills; the amount of space that a container has: *Liquid fuels are sold by volume.* ◇ *The barrel has a volume of ten cubic metres.*
2 [C,U] the amount of sth: *The volume of trade between the two countries decreased last year.* ◇ *Sales have doubled in volume over the last two years.* ◇ *Volume sales increased by 15% last year.* ◇ *DVD equipment has sold in high volumes.*
❍ *an enormous/a* **high/low/huge/large/substantial** *volume (of sth)*
3 (*Stock Exchange*) [U,C] the total number of shares bought and sold on a stock exchange on a particular day: *an average daily trading volume of 100 000 shares*
❍ *(a)* **brisk/heavy/light/low/strong** *volume (of sth)*
IDM **in ˈvolume** in large quantities: *We're a small*

business and can't afford to buy supplies in volume. ◇ *the types of bikes that sell in volume*

ˈvolume ˌbusiness *noun* [U]
(*Commerce*) trade in very large quantities of goods: *We offer substantial discounts for volume business.*

ˈvolume ˌdiscount *noun* [C,U]
(*Commerce*) a reduction in the price of goods offered to sb who buys a large amount SYN BULK DISCOUNT

voluntary /ˈvɒləntri; *AmE* ˈvɑːlənteri/ *adjective*
1 done willingly, not because you are forced: *Where possible, redundancy should be on a voluntary basis.* ◇ *These pollution controls rely on voluntary action by business.* ◇ *to pay voluntary contributions into a pension fund*
OPP COMPULSORY, INVOLUNTARY
2 [usually before noun] (about work) done by people who choose to do it without being paid: *Large numbers of young people are involved in voluntary work in the community.*
3 (about a person or an organization) doing a job without wanting to be paid for it: *the voluntary sector* (= organizations which help people and which do not make a profit, for example charities)
❍ *voluntary* **groups/organizations/services** • *voluntary* **labour/workers**

ˌvoluntary arˈrangement *noun* [C] (*BrE*)
(*Law*) a legal arrangement made between a failing company and the people it owes money to (its **creditors**) to pay its debts and solve its financial problems without stopping doing business

ˌvoluntary ˈbankruptcy *noun* [U,C]
(*Law*) a situation in which a person or a company asks to be officially declared BANKRUPT

ˌvoluntary ˈexport reˌstraint (*abbr* VER) (*also* ˌvoluntary reˈstraint aˌgreement*) noun* [C]
(*Economics*) an agreement between two or more countries that limits the number of exports of particular goods that the exporting country can make to the importing country/countries

ˌvoluntary liquiˈdation *noun* [U,C] (*also* ˌvoluntary ˌwinding ˈup* [C,U])
(*Law*) a situation where a company's owners decide that it should stop doing business, sell its assets and pay its debts OPP COMPULSORY LIQUIDATION, INVOLUNTARY LIQUIDATION

ˌvoluntary reˈstraint aˌgreement =
VOLUNTARY EXPORT RESTRAINT

ˌvoluntary ˌwinding ˈup = VOLUNTARY LIQUIDATION

★ vote /vəʊt; *AmE* voʊt/ *noun, verb*
● *noun*

SEE ALSO: block vote, casting vote

1 [C] a formal choice that you make in an election or at a meeting in order to choose sb or decide sth: *There were 18 votes for and 12 against the motion.* ◇ *72% of the votes cast were in favour of a strike.*
2 [C] an occasion when a group of people vote on sth: *Let's take a vote on the issue.* ◇ *The issue was put to the vote.* See note at MEETING
❍ *to* **force/have/take** *a vote*
3 [C] the right to vote: *Only individual policyholders have a vote.*
4 [sing.] the total number of votes in an election: *She obtained 40% of the vote.*
● *verb*
1 [+ obj *or no obj*] to show formally by marking a paper, raising your hand, or using a special machine, etc. which person you want to win an election, or which plan or idea you support: *Let's listen to the arguments on both sides and then vote*

on it. ◇ Did you vote **for** or **against** her? ◇ Shareholders voted unanimously **in favour of** the merger.

● to vote **narrowly/overwhelmingly/unanimously against**, etc. sth

2 [+ obj] (usually **be voted**) to choose sb for a position or an award by voting: She was voted designer of the year in the sportswear sector.

3 [+ obj] to agree to give sb/yourself sth by voting: The directors have just voted themselves a huge pay increase.

PHR V ,vote sb/sth '**down** to reject or defeat sb/sth by voting for sb/sth else ,**vote sb 'in**; ,**vote sb 'into/'onto sth** to choose sb for a position or as a member of sth by voting: Castorri was voted in as CEO when he was only 32. ◇ She was voted onto the board of governors. ,**vote sb 'out**; ,**vote sb 'out of/ 'off sth** to dismiss sb from a position by voting: He was voted out of office. ,**vote sth 'through** to approve of sth by voting: Shareholders voted through an emergency issue of 2.3 billion new shares.

,**vote of 'confidence** noun [C, usually sing.]
1 an act that shows that people trust sb/sth: The appointment to CEO is a vote of confidence in her leadership abilities. ◇ Financial markets have **given** the new currency a vote of confidence (= its value on the markets has risen).
2 a formal vote to show whether people support a leader, a political party, an idea, etc: The prime minister resigned after the government lost a vote of confidence.

,**vote of no 'confidence** noun [C, usually sing.]
1 an act that shows that people do not trust sb/sth: Taking management of the company's property away from the directors amounts to a vote of no confidence in the board.
2 a formal vote to show that people do not support a leader, a political party, an idea, etc: He has narrowly survived a vote of no confidence.

'**voting rights** noun [pl.]
(Finance) the right of shareholders to vote at company meetings: The family owns 40% of the company's shares with 60% of the voting rights. ◇ Not all shareholders **exercise** their voting rights.

'**voting shares** noun [pl.] (BrE) (AmE '**voting stock** [U])
(Finance) shares that give the people who hold them the right to vote at company meetings: They hold 30% of the voting shares.

voucher /'vaʊtʃə(r)/ noun [C]

SEE ALSO: **gift voucher**

1 (BrE) a printed piece of paper that can be used instead of money to pay for sth, or that allows you to pay less than the usual price of sth: This discount voucher entitles you to 10% off your next purchase. ◇ vouchers for free flights
2 (Accounting) a document that shows that money has been paid for sth, or that explains why an amount has been recorded in a financial account: payment/receipt/sales vouchers See note at INVOICE

vouching /'vaʊtʃɪŋ/ noun [U]
(Accounting) the responsibility of an AUDITOR or an accountant to examine and approve all documents such as VOUCHERS and INVOICES when checking a company's financial records

'**voyage ,charter** noun [C,U]
(Transport) the hire of a ship or space on a ship for one or more journeys rather than for a fixed period of time: Up to twenty of their vessels are **on** voyage charter at any one time.

VP /,viː 'piː/ = VICE-PRESIDENT

VR /,viː 'ɑː(r)/ = VENDOR RATING, VIRTUAL REALITY

VRA /,viː ɑː(r) 'eɪ/ = VOLUNTARY RESTRAINT AGREEMENT

vs abbr
a short way of writing **versus**

W w

★ **wage** /weɪdʒ/ noun [sing.] (also **wages** [pl.])

SEE ALSO: **award wage, base ~, basic ~, fair ~, guaranteed ~, living ~, minimum ~, etc.**

a regular amount of money that you earn, usually every week, for work or services: wages of €700 a week ◇ Wages are paid on Fridays. ◇ You will receive a basic weekly wage of €500 plus bonuses. ◇ The union submitted a wage claim for a 9% rise. See note at SALARY

● an **average/a high/low/standard** wage ◆ an **after-tax/a gross/net/pre-tax** wage ◆ **hourly/regular/ weekly** wages ◆ to **earn/pay/receive** a wage ◆ to **increase/push up/raise** wages ◆ wages **go up/ increase/rise** ◆ wage **bargaining/negotiations/talks** ◆ a wage **agreement/claim/rise/settlement** ◆ a wage **cut/freeze/reduction**

'**wage bill** (also '**wages bill**, less frequent) noun [C]
the total amount of money that a company, an organization or an industry pays to its employees: The company lost $47 million as the wage bill trebled to $54 million.

waged /weɪdʒd/ adjective
1 (about a person) having regular paid work: waged workers
2 (about work) that you are paid for: waged work/ employment

3 the waged noun [pl.] people who have regular paid work: The cost is €40 for the waged and €25 for the unwaged.
→ SALARIED

'**wage diffe'rential** noun [C]
(Economics) the difference in rates of pay between groups of workers, especially the difference between workers with similar jobs in different industries, or between workers with different skills in the same industry: Wage differentials between large and small firms have widened. → EARNINGS DIFFERENTIAL, WAGE GAP

'**wage drift** noun [U]
(Economics) the situation when the average level of wages earned rises faster than the rates of pay that have been agreed at a national level: Wage drift consists of such things as overtime, bonuses and performance-related pay.

'**wage ,earner** noun [C]
a person who earns money, especially a person who works for **wages** (= is paid every week): There are three wage earners in the family.
● a **high/low/top** wage earner

'**wage gap** noun [C]
the difference in rates of pay between one group of

people and another: *the male-female wage gap* ◇ *The wage gap between CEOs and workers is much wider than it was ten years ago.* → WAGE DIFFERENTIAL
○ *the wage gap* **narrows/widens**

'wage in,flation *noun* [U]
(*Economics*) a general rise in the rates of pay in a particular industry, country, etc: *the aim of achieving falling unemployment and low wage inflation*

'wage ,packet = PAY PACKET

,wage-'price ,spiral *noun* [sing.]
(*Economics*) the idea that a general rise in prices causes levels of pay to rise, which then causes prices to rise again, and so on

,wage-'push in,flation *noun* [U]
(*Economics*) a rise in prices caused by a general rise in levels of pay that makes goods cost more to produce

'wage re,straint (*also* **'pay re,straint**) *noun* [U,C]
(*especially BrE*)
(*Economics*) the process of controlling the amount by which pay can rise: *dealing with high inflation through wage restraint*
○ *compulsory/voluntary* **wage restraint**

'wages bill = WAGE BILL

'wage scale *noun* [C]
(*HR*)
1 the range of levels of wages that a person can receive in a particular job: *The wage scale for an assistant chef is from €18 to €27 an hour.*
2 the range of levels of wages that people receive in different jobs: *cleaners, and others at the bottom end of the wage scale*
→ PAY SCALE, SALARY SCALE

'wages clerk *noun* [C]
a person whose job is to calculate and arrange payment for a company's employees

'wage slave *noun* [C] (*informal*)
a person who depends completely on the money they receive each week from their job, especially sb who has a boring or hard job

,wait-and-'see *adjective* [only before noun]
used to describe a situation where you wait to see what happens before making a decision: *We're taking a wait-and-see attitude to m-commerce.*

waive /weɪv/ *verb* [+ obj]
to choose not to demand sth in a particular case, even though you have a legal or official right to do so: *Lawyers working on the charity's behalf waived their fees.*
○ *to waive your* **claim/fee/right**

waiver /ˈweɪvə(r)/ *noun* [C]
(*Law*) a situation in which sb gives up a legal right or claim; an official document stating this: *A waiver of the licence fee may be made for educational events.* ◇ *The contract contained a* **waiver clause**, *stating that the company would not be sued if it failed to deliver on time.*
○ *to grant/obtain/seek/sign a waiver*

'wake-up call *noun* [C]
1 the service that hotels provide of telephoning guests to wake them up at the time they ask: *Could I have a wake-up call at 6?*
2 a sudden warning that you need to take action: *The shocking figures were a wake-up call to the sales team.*

walk /wɔːk/ *verb, noun*
● *verb*
IDM **walk off the 'job** (*AmE*) to stop working in

order to go on strike **walk the 'plank** (*informal*) to be forced to leave your job: *Their CEO has been made to walk the plank and hands in his resignation tomorrow.* **NOTE** In the past people on a ship were sometimes punished by being made to walk along a board placed over the side of the ship so that they fell into the sea.**,walk the/your 'talk** (*informal*) to start to do the things that you talk about: *Managers are walking the talk about encouraging new ideas.* → TALK THE TALK at TALK,**walk the 'walk** (*informal*) to do sth rather than just talk about ideas and plans for doing it: *They keep saying they're going to double sales, but now they need to walk the walk.* ◇ *Don't talk the talk unless you can walk the walk.* → TALK THE TALK at TALK, WALK THE/YOUR TALK
PHR V **,walk 'out** (*HR, informal*) to stop working in order to go on strike: *Workers walked out over the pay claim.* → WALKOUT ,**walk 'out (of sth)** to leave a meeting, etc. suddenly, especially in order to show your disapproval: *They walked out of the talks.* → WALKOUT ,**walk 'out (on sth)** to stop doing sth that you have agreed to do, before it is completed: *I never walk out on a job half done.*
● *noun*
IDM **a walk of 'life** a person's job or position in society: *She has friends from all walks of life.*

'walking ,papers *noun* [pl.] (*AmE*)
(*HR, informal*) the letter or notice dismissing sb from a job: *She's just been given her walking papers.*

walkout /ˈwɔːkaʊt/ *noun* [C]
1 a sudden strike by workers: *Workers at the factory staged a mass walkout in protest against an overtime ban.* See note at STRIKE
○ *to call/call off/hold/stage/threaten a walkout*
2 the act of suddenly leaving a meeting as a protest against sth: *There was a walkout by angry delegates.*

wall /wɔːl/ *noun*
IDM **go to the 'wall** if a company or an organization **goes to the wall**, it fails because of lack of money: *Many firms have gone to the wall in this recession.* → idioms at BRICK, HIT *verb* See note at BANKRUPT

wallchart /ˈwɔːltʃɑːt; *AmE* -tʃɑːrt/ *noun* [C]
a large piece of paper containing information that is put up on a wall, for example in an office, so that people can look at it

'Wall Street *noun* [U]
1 (*used without* **a** *or* **the**) the financial centre and stock exchange in New York City; the business that is carried out there: *Share prices fell on Wall Street today.* ◇ *people who work on Wall Street* ◇ *Wall Street responded quickly to the news.* See note at INCREASE
○ *Wall Street* **prices/shares/stocks** ◆ *Wall Street* **analysts/bankers/firms/traders** ◆ *Wall Street* **estimates/forecasts/gains/losses**
2 used to refer to large companies in the US as a group: *Foreign investors are pulling out of Wall Street and Main Street.* → MAIN STREET

WAN /wæn/ *abbr*
(*IT*) **wide area network** a number of computers and other devices that are far apart but are connected together so that equipment and information can be shared: *Gathering market information can be done over a WAN.* → LAN

want /wɒnt; *AmE* wɑːnt; wɔːnt/ *noun* [C, usually pl.]
something that you need or want: *Producers compete to satisfy the wants of customers.* → NEED

'want ad = CLASSIFIED AD

WAP /wæp/ *abbr*
(*IT*) **wireless application protocol** a standard system for sending information between HAND-HELD pieces of equipment and other electronic sources of information without using wires. It enables people, for example, to use a mobile phone/cellphone to look at the Internet: *WAP phones/technology*

war /wɔː(r)/ *noun* [C,U]

SEE ALSO: **trade war**

a situation in which there is aggressive competition between groups, companies, countries, etc. over a period of time: *a fierce price war between rival supermarkets* ◇ *It's time to declare war on the illegal use of copied programs.*
O *a bidding/price/sales war* • *to lose/wage/win a war*

'war chest *noun* [C]
(used in newspapers) an amount of money that a company or a government has available to spend on a particular plan, project, etc: *The group has a war chest of €50 billion available for acquisitions.*

ware /weə(r); *AmE* wer/ *noun*
1 [U; pl.] (*used in compounds*) objects used for the purpose or in the room mentioned: *ornamental ware* ◇ *kitchen wares* ◇ *a retailer of clothing and home wares*
2 [U; pl.] (*used in compounds*) objects made of the material or in the way or place mentioned: *ceramic ware* ◇ *a collection of local wares*
3 wares [pl.] things that sb is selling: *Agents can use the site to sell their wares over the Internet.*

★ warehouse /'weəhaʊs; *AmE* 'wer-/ *noun, verb*
● *noun* [C]

SEE ALSO: **bonded warehouse, Customs ~, data ~, discount ~, public ~**

a building where large quantities of goods are stored, especially before they are sent to shops/stores to be sold: *We have 30 000 square feet of warehouse space.*
● *verb* [+ obj]
to store goods in a **warehouse**: *It will be necessary to warehouse the surplus stock.* → AT WAREHOUSE, EX WAREHOUSE

'warehouse club *noun* [C] (*AmE*)
an organization that operates from a large store, usually outside a town, and sells goods cheaply in large amounts to customers who must pay to be members: *shopping at a discount warehouse club* → CASH AND CARRY

warehouseman /'weəhaʊsmən; *AmE* 'wer-/ (*plural* **warehousemen** /-mən/) (*also* **'warehouse ,keeper**) *noun* [C]
a person who works in, manages or owns a **warehouse**

,warehouse re'ceipt (*also* ,warehouse 'warrant, *less frequent*) *noun* [C]
(*Trade*) a document that proves that goods exist and shows where they are stored and who owns them. In financial markets it is often given to sb who buys goods instead of actually delivering the goods to them.

'warehouse store *noun* [C]
a large simple store that sells a limited variety of food and other items for the home very cheaply

,warehouse 'warrant = WAREHOUSE RECEIPT

warehousing /'weəhaʊzɪŋ; *AmE* 'wer-/ *noun* [U]
the fact or process of storing goods in a

warehouse: *warehousing costs* ◇ *automatic warehousing systems*

warning /'wɔːnɪŋ; *AmE* 'wɔːrn-/ *noun*

SEE ALSO: **health warning, profit warning**

1 [C,U] a statement, an event, etc. telling sb that sth bad or unpleasant is possible or might happen: *The instructions contain a clear warning about the dangers of working with electricity.* ◇ *They ignored warnings of increasing costs.*
O *a blunt/clear/dire/grim/stark warning* • *to give sb adequate/advance warning*
2 [C] a statement telling sb that they will be punished if they continue to behave in a particular way: *Employees must receive two written warnings before being dismissed.*
O *a final/formal/an official warning* • *an oral/a verbal/written warning*
▶ **'warning** *adjective* [only before noun]: *The poor results were warning signs of trouble ahead.* ◇ *Warning bells began to ring* (= it was a sign that sth was wrong) *when he wasn't invited to the meeting.*

warrant /'wɒrənt; *AmE* 'wɔːr-; 'wɑːr-/ *noun, verb*
● *noun* [C]

SEE ALSO: **dividend warrant, warehouse warrant**

1 (*Finance*) a type of investment that gives you the right to buy shares at a fixed price on or by a particular date: *the issue of warrants for equity shares* ◇ *Bondholders have been given warrants to buy the stock.*
2 (*Law*) a legal document that is signed by a judge and gives the police authority to do sth: *They issued a warrant for her arrest.* ◇ *an arrest warrant*
O *to apply for/get/issue a warrant*
● *verb* [+ obj]
(*Commerce; Law, formal*) (*usually* **be warranted**) to promise that a statement is true, or that sth is genuine or in good condition: *The goods are warranted to be in perfect condition on leaving the factory.*

warrantee /,wɒrən'tiː; *AmE* 'wɔːr-; 'wɑːr-/ *noun* [C]
(*Commerce; Law*) a person that a WARRANTY is given to See note at EMPLOYER

warrantor /'wɒrəntɔː(r); *AmE* 'wɔːr-; 'wɑːr-/ *noun* [C]
(*Commerce; Law*) a person or company that provides a WARRANTY See note at EMPLOYER

★ warranty /'wɒrənti; *AmE* 'wɔːr-; 'wɑːr-/ (*plural* **warranties**) *noun* [C,U]

SEE ALSO: **extended warranty**

(*Commerce; Law*) a written agreement in which a company selling sth promises to repair or replace it if there is a problem within a particular period of time: *The television comes with a full two-year warranty.* ◇ *Is the car still under warranty?*
SYN GUARANTEE → WARRANTEE, WARRANTOR

wastage /'weɪstɪdʒ/ *noun* [U]
1 the fact of losing or destroying sth, especially because it has been used or dealt with carelessly; the amount of sth that is wasted: *a new production technique aimed at minimizing wastage*
2 (*HR*) (*BrE*) = NATURAL WASTAGE

★ waste /weɪst/ *verb, noun, adjective*
● *verb* [+ obj]
1 to use more of sth than is necessary or useful: *We don't want to waste money on equipment that we won't use much.* ◇ *They are wasting their time trying to break into the US market.*
O *to waste energy/money/time*

2 (*usually* **be wasted**) to not make good or full use of sb/sth: *His talents are wasted in that job.* ◇ *It was a wasted opportunity.*

● *noun*
1 [U; sing.] the act of using sth in a careless or unnecessary way, so that it is lost or destroyed: *The report is critical of the department's waste of resources.*
2 [sing.] a situation in which it is not worth spending time, money, etc. on sth: *These meetings are a complete* **waste of time**.
3 [U] (*also* **wastes** [pl.]) materials that are no longer needed and are thrown away
☉ household/industrial/radioactive/toxic waste

● *adjective* [usually before noun]
no longer needed for a particular process and therefore thrown away: *Waste water is pumped from the factory into a nearby river.*

wasteful /'weɪstfl/ *adjective*
using more of sth such as money or resources than is necessary; not saving or keeping sth that could be used: *The whole process is wasteful and inefficient.* ◇ *a wasteful use of resources*

ˌwaste ˈproduct *noun* [C]
(*Manufacturing*) a useless material or substance that is produced while sth else is being made: *This acid is a waste product of the production of certain plastics.*
☉ to break down/dispose of/recycle/remove waste products

ˌwasting ˈasset *noun* [C]
(*Accounting*) a thing of value that a company owns that will only last or be useful for a fixed period of time, for example, a lease or a piece of equipment

watchdog /'wɒtʃdɒg; *AmE* 'wɑːtʃdɔːg; 'wɔːtʃ-/ *noun* [C]

SEE ALSO: **consumer watchdog**

a person or group of people whose job is to check that companies are not doing anything illegal and to protect people's rights: *A watchdog has warned that customers are facing rising water bills.*
☉ *a* **competition/financial/an industry/a pollution/safety** watchdog ◆ *a* **government/an independent/official** watchdog

ˌwatching ˈbrief *noun* [C]
the task of watching and reporting on the progress of sth on behalf of sb else: *The Network Manager has a watching brief on security issues.*
☉ to be given/have/keep/maintain a watching brief

ˈwatch list *noun* [C]
1 (*Finance*) a list of investments that are being studied very carefully because people think sth unusual or interesting will happen to them: *The website has a watch list of 50 companies that it predicts will do well this year.*
2 a list of people, companies, organizations, etc. that are being studied carefully because people think that they are doing sth dishonest or illegal: *a watch list of dishonest traders*

ˈwater ˌcooler *noun* [C]
1 a machine, for example in an office, that cools water and supplies it for drinking: *Go to the water cooler to catch up on office gossip.*
2 (*informal*) (*especially AmE*) (*used as an adjective*) used to describe any informal conversation among office workers of the type that takes place around the **water cooler**: *water-cooler chats/gossip*

watershed /'wɔːtəʃed; *AmE* 'wɔːtərʃed; 'wɑːt-/ *noun*
1 [C] an event or a period of time that marks an important change: *The 2005 pay agreement was a*

watershed **in** the relationship between the company and the unions.
2 [sing.] in the UK, the time before which programmes that are not considered suitable for children must not be shown on television: *A number of people complained that the advertisement was too violent and should not have been shown before the watershed.*

WATS /wɒts; *AmE* wɔːts/ *abbr* (*AmE*)
(*IT*) **Wide Area Telecommunications Service** a service that allows companies to make and receive large numbers of phone calls to and from places that are far away at a low cost

wave /weɪv/ *noun* [C]
1 a sudden increase in a particular activity or feeling: *The region is experiencing a wave of investment.*
2 (*Technical*) the form that some types of energy such as heat, sound, light, etc. take as they move
→ idiom at RIDE *verb*

waybill /'weɪbɪl/ *noun* [C] (*abbr* **WB**)
(*Transport*) a document that gives information about goods that are being transported, where they are going and who they must be delivered to

WB /ˌdʌblju: 'bi:/ = WAYBILL

WDV /ˌdʌblju: di: 'vi:/ = WRITTEN-DOWN VALUE

★ **weak** /wi:k/ *adjective* (**weaker**, **weakest**)
1 not very great: *a weak market share* ◇ *weak consumer spending* ◇ *weaker-than-expected results*
2 not financially strong or successful: *The clothing company was the weakest performer with a 25% drop in sales.*
3 (*about prices, markets, etc.*) moving towards a lower level; falling: *The industry is suffering from falling demand and weaker prices.* ◇ *The weak dollar has encouraged many foreigners to visit America.*
OPP STRONG
▶ **weakness** /'wi:knəs/ *noun* [U,C]: *the weakness of the pound against the dollar*

weaken /'wi:kən/ *verb* [+ obj *or no obj*]
1 to make sb/sth less strong or powerful; to become less strong or powerful: *The recession has weakened demand for luxury goods.*
2 to make a currency, market etc. move towards a lower level; to fall: *If the yen weakens it will help Japan's export sector.*
See note at CURRENCY

★ **wealth** /welθ/ *noun*
1 [U] a large amount of money, property, etc. that a person or country owns; how much money, etc. a person or a country has: *His personal wealth is estimated at $100 million.* ◇ *the country's diamond and mineral wealth* ◇ *The purpose of industry is to create wealth.* ◇ *The figures tell us nothing about the distribution of wealth in the population.*
☉ household/national/personal/private wealth ◆ **commercial/economic/financial/industrial** wealth ◆ **to create/distribute/generate/manage/redistribute** wealth ◆ wealth **creation/management**
2 [sing.] a large amount of sth worth having: *The new manager brings a* **great** *wealth of experience to the job.*
☉ *a wealth of* **detail/experience/information/talent**

ˈwealth efˌfect *noun* [sing.]
(*Economics*) an increase in the amount of money that consumers spend when the value of their investments and assets rises: *the wealth effect of rising house prices* ◇ *the* **negative** *wealth effect of recent stock market falls* (= people are spending less)

'wealth tax noun [U,C]
a tax that only very rich people have to pay

wealthy /'welθi/ adjective (**wealthier, wealthiest**)
1 rich; having a lot of money, possessions, resources, etc: *the world's wealthiest software company* ◇ *a relatively wealthy country*
2 the wealthy noun [pl.] people who are rich: *higher taxes for the wealthy*

wear /weə(r); AmE wer/ noun [U]

SEE ALSO: ready-to-wear

1 (*usually used in compounds*) used especially in shops/stores to describe clothes that have a particular purpose or occasion: *children's/ladies' wear* ◇ *menswear* ◇ *sportswear*
2 the fact of wearing sth: *casual clothes for everyday wear*
3 the amount or type of use that sth has over a period of time: *carpets that give years of wear*
4 the damage or loss of quality that is caused when sth has been used a lot: *The machines have to be checked regularly for signs of wear.*
IDM ,**wear and 'tear** the damage to objects, furniture, property, etc. that is the result of normal use: *The guarantee applies to manufacturing faults, not to normal wear and tear.*

wear out /'weəraʊt/ noun [U]
1 the process of sth becoming no longer useful or able to be used because it has been used for a long time: *research into wearout and failure in car engines*
2 (*Marketing*) the situation when an advertisement has been shown so many times that it is no longer useful as people are now bored or annoyed with it: *Advertising wearout can be avoided by varying the way in which the basic message is presented.*

,**weather 'working days** noun [pl.] (abbr WWD)
(*Transport*) days on which work can be done if the weather is good: *The contract allowed two weather working days for the ship to be unloaded.*

★**the Web** /web/ = WORLD WIDE WEB

'web ad,dress noun [C]
(*IT*) the address of a web page: *I must have typed in the wrong web address.* SYN URL

,**web-based 'seminar** = WEBINAR

webcast /'webkɑːst; AmE -kæst/ noun [C]
(*IT*) a live broadcast that is sent out on the Internet: *The event will be viewable via a webcast.* ▶ **'webcast** verb [+ obj] **'webcasting** noun [U]

'web de,sign noun [U]
(*IT*) the art or process of arranging the information in websites ▶ **'web de,signer** noun [C]: *He works as a web designer.*

'web de,velopment noun [U]
(*IT*) the art or process of making websites

'web-e,nabled adjective
(*IT*) designed to be used on the WORLD WIDE WEB; able to use the Internet for business: *web-enabled mobile phones*

'web ,hosting (*also spelled* **web-hosting**) noun [U]
(*IT*) the service of keeping websites on a SERVER so that they can be looked at by people using the Internet
❍ *a web-hosting business/company/group* • *web-hosting activities/services*

webinar /'webɪnɑː(r)/ (also ,web-based 'seminar) noun [C]
(*IT*) a meeting, talk, lesson, etc. that is broadcast on the Internet, in which the people taking part can talk to each other: *to participate/take part in a webinar*

'web log file noun [C]
(*IT*) a computer file that records information about the people that visit a website, the pages that they look at, any technical problems, etc.

webmaster (*also spelled* **Webmaster**)
/'webmɑːstə(r); AmE -mæs-/ noun [C]
(*IT*) a person who is responsible for particular pages of information on the World Wide Web

'web page noun [C]
(*IT*) a document that is connected to the WORLD WIDE WEB and that anyone with an Internet connection can see, usually forming part of a website → HOME PAGE

,**web 'shopfront** = SHOPFRONT (2)

★**website** (*also spelled* **web site**) /'websaɪt/ noun [C]
(*IT*) a place connected to the Internet, where a company, an organization, etc. puts information on the WORLD WIDE WEB: *Customers can visit our website to see the progress of their orders.* ◇ *Details of all our products are available on our website.* ◇ *Our website address is http://www.oup.com.*
❍ *to log into/log onto/look at/visit a website* • *to build/create/design/develop/make/set up a website* • *a company/an e-commerce/a group/an office website*

,**web 'storefront** = STOREFRONT (3)

webzine /'webziːn/ noun [C]
a magazine published on the Internet, not on paper: *a webzine for electronic computer users*

weekday /'wiːkdeɪ/ noun [C]
any day except Saturday or Sunday: *The service is only available on weekdays.* ▶ **'weekdays** adverb: *open weekdays from 9 a.m. to 6 p.m.*

weekend /,wiːk'end; AmE 'wiːkend/ noun [C]
1 Saturday and Sunday: *Have a good weekend!* ◇ (*BrE*) *The office is closed at the weekend.* ◇ (*especially AmE*) *The office is closed on the weekend.*
2 Saturday and Sunday, or a slightly longer period, as a holiday/vacation: *a weekend break*

WEF /,dʌblju: i: 'ef/ = WORLD ECONOMIC FORUM

weighbridge /'weɪbrɪdʒ/ noun [C]
a machine for weighing vehicles and their loads, usually with a platform that the vehicle is driven on to

weight /weɪt/ noun, verb
● **noun**
1 (*abbr* **wt**) [U,C] how heavy sb/sth is, which can be measured in, for example, kilograms or pounds: *It is about 70 kilos in weight.* ◇ *Bananas are sold by weight.* ◇ *This laptop has a weight of just 4 kilos.* ◇ *goods vehicles over 3.5 tonnes gross weight* (= including the vehicle and the contents) ◇ *Meat must be marked with its net weight, excluding packaging.*
2 [U] the fact of being heavy: *The pillars have to support the weight of the roof.*
3 [C] an object that is heavy: *Lifting heavy weights can damage your back.*
4 [C,U] a unit or system of units by which weight is measured: *tables of weights and measures* ◇ *imperial/metric weight*

5 [U] importance, influence or strength: *His opinion **carries weight** with the boss.*
IDM throw/put your weight behind sth to use all your influence and power to support sth: *The directors have thrown their weight behind the takeover bid.* → idioms at PULL *verb*, THROW
● *verb* [+ obj]
1 to give different values to things to show how important you think each of them is compared with the others: *The results of the survey were weighted to allow for variations in the sample.*
2 (*usually* **be weighted**) to arrange sth in such a way that a particular person or thing has an advantage or a disadvantage: *The proposal is heavily weighted **towards** smaller businesses.* ◇ *The new pay levels are weighted **against** part-time workers.*

,**weighted 'average** *noun* [C]
(*Technical*) an average value for a number of things that is calculated by first giving a value to each thing according to how important it is compared with others: *The Retail Price Index is a weighted average of the prices of a number of selected goods.*

,**weighted 'index** *noun* [C]
(*Economics*; *Finance*) an index (= a system that compares the level of prices, wages, etc. with those of a previous time) that considers the value of each item according to how important it is compared with others: *A price-weighted index counts changes in the prices of high-priced shares more than changes in the prices of low-priced shares.* ◇ *The Hang Seng Index is a capitalization-weighted index (= a company is given importance according to the value of all its shares).*

weighting /'weɪtɪŋ/ *noun*
1 (*HR*) [U] (*BrE*) extra money that you are paid for working in a particular area because it is expensive to live there: *She gets London weighting on top of her salary.* SYN ALLOWANCE
2 (*Technical*) [C,U] a value that you give to each of a number of things to show how important it is compared with the others: *Each of the factors is given a weighting on a scale of 1 to 10.*

'**weight note** *noun* [C]
(*Trade*) a document that says how much goods weigh when they are taken off a ship

welfare /'welfeə(r); *AmE* /welfer/ *noun* [U]
1 the general health, happiness and safety of a person, a country, etc: *They believe that international commerce is harmful to the welfare of developing countries.*
2 (*HR*) the physical and mental health of employees and practical help that is provided for people that need it: *an employee welfare plan*
3 practical or financial help that is provided, often by the government, for people that need it: *The state is still the main provider of welfare.* ◇ *a social welfare programme* ◇ *welfare services/work*
4 (*especially AmE*) = SOCIAL SECURITY (1)

'**welfare ,benefit** *noun* [C, usually pl., U] money that is given to people who are unemployed or who cannot work because they are ill/sick, or to their family if they die: *States may give welfare benefits to two-parent families where the main wage earner is unemployed.*

,**welfare to 'work** *noun* [U]
a government policy of helping unemployed people find work, for example by training them or by giving companies money to employ them
▶ ,**welfare-to-'work** *adjective* [only before noun]: *a welfare-to-work programme*

well /wel/ *noun* [C]
1 = OIL WELL

2 a deep hole in the ground from which people obtain water

'**wellness ,program** (*BrE spelling* ~ **programme**) *noun* [C] (*AmE only*)
(*HR*) benefits, activities or training that a company offers to improve and develop the physical and mental health of its employees

,**well 'off** *adjective* (**better off**)
1 having a lot of money; rich: *His family are very well off.* ◇ *tax reductions for the less well off*
2 in a good situation: *You'd be better off looking for a new job.*
3 having plenty of sth: *We're much better off **for** storage space in our new offices than in the old ones.*

,**well 'placed** *adjective*
in a good position or situation to be able to do sth: *The company is well placed to withstand the recession.*

'**wet goods** (*also* '**wet com,modities**) *noun* [pl.]
(*Trade*) liquids; goods from which water or other liquid may come out, for example, soap or fish: *containers for the transportation of wet goods*
→ DRY GOODS

'**wet lease** *noun* [U,C]
(*Transport*) an arrangement that allows a company to use another company's aircraft and the people who fly them for a period of time ▶ '**wet-lease** *verb* [+ obj] → DRY LEASE

wharf /wɔːf; *AmE* wɔːrf/ *noun* [C] (*plural* **wharves** /wɔːvz; *AmE* wɔːrvz/ *or* **wharfs**)
a flat structure built beside the sea or a river where boats can be tied up and goods unloaded: *a warehouse on the wharf*

wharfage /'wɔːfɪdʒ; *AmE* 'wɔːrf-/ *noun* [U]
(*Transport*)
1 a place at a **wharf** for loading, unloading or storing goods: *a harbour with two miles of wharfage*
2 a charge that is made for using this place: *paying wharfage charges*

wharfinger /'wɔːfɪndʒə(r); *AmE* 'wɔːrf-/ *noun* [C]
the person or company in charge of a **wharf**

,**what-'if** *noun* [C] (*informal*)
a situation or an event that might happen in the future and that you need to think about now: *We made a list of what-ifs to make sure we were prepared for anything.* ◇ *a what-if brainstorming session*

,**wheelchair ,access** *noun* [U]
a way of entering or leaving a place, a vehicle, etc. for sb who uses a chair with wheels (a **wheelchair**) because they cannot walk: *New regulations state that all cabs must have wheelchair access.*

,**wheeling and 'dealing** *noun* [U] (*informal*)
very complicated, sometimes dishonest, business deals: *A lot of wheeling and dealing is done over lunch.* ▶ ,**wheel and 'deal** *verb* [no obj] ,**wheeler-'dealer** (*also* ,**wheeler and 'dealer**) *noun* [C]: *He's the best wheeler-dealer in the business.*

'**whistle-,blower** *noun* [C]
(used especially in newspapers) a person who informs people in authority or the public that the company they work for is doing sth wrong or illegal ▶ '**whistle-,blowing** *noun* [U]

whiteboard /'waɪtbɔːd; *AmE* -bɔːrd/ *noun* [C]
1 a large board with a smooth white surface that you can write on with special pens when giving a talk, etc.

2 (*IT*) an area on a computer screen that several people at different computers can use to exchange information, often used in a TELECONFERENCE → INTERACTIVE WHITEBOARD

,**white-'collar** *adjective* [only before noun]
working in an office rather than in a factory, etc.; connected with work in offices: *white-collar workers* ◇ *a white-collar job* ◇ *white-collar crime* (= in which office workers steal from their companies) → BLUE-COLLAR, PINK-COLLAR

,**white 'elephant** *noun* [C, usually sing.]
a thing that is useless and no longer needed, although it may cost a lot of money to keep it: *The new office block has become an expensive white elephant.*

'**white goods** *noun* [pl.]
(*Commerce*) large pieces of electrical equipment in the home: *a manufacturer of washing machines and other white goods* → BROWN GOODS, GREY GOODS

,**white 'knight** *noun* [C]
(*Finance*) a person or an organization that rescues a company from being bought by another company at too low a price: *A white knight could come along and make a more friendly offer.* → BLACK KNIGHT, GREY KNIGHT

,**White 'Pages** *noun* [pl., U]
in the US and some other countries, the part of a telephone book that has white pages and gives a list of individuals and companies with their telephone numbers, arranged in alphabetical order. It has no advertising. → YELLOW PAGES

'**white sale** *noun* [C] (*especially AmE*)
(*Commerce*) an occasion when a shop/store sells goods at a much lower price than usual, originally a sale of sheets, cloths, etc. for the home (**linen**)

'**whizz-kid** (*AmE spelling usually* **whiz kid**) *noun* [C] (*informal*)
a person who is very good and successful at sth, especially at a young age
O *a computer/financial/technical whizz-kid*

,**whole-'life** *adjective* [only before noun]
(*Accounting; Insurance*) lasting until a person dies or until a product can no longer be used: *a whole-life insurance policy* (= one that pays a sum of money when the person insured dies) ◇ *The software calculates the whole-life cost of a vehicle.*
O *whole-life assurance/insurance/policies* ◆ *whole-life cost/costing*

★ **wholesale** /'həʊseɪl; *AmE* 'hoʊl-/ *noun, adjective, adverb, verb*
(*Commerce*)
● *noun* [U]
the buying and selling of goods in large quantities, especially to businesses, so that they can be sold again to make a profit: *I spent five years working in wholesale.* ◇ *The company has changed its focus from wholesale to retail.* → RETAIL
● *adjective* [only before noun]
connected with goods that are bought in large quantities and sold to businesses so that they can be sold again to make a profit: *the wholesale market* → RETAIL
O *a wholesale business/distributor/division/group* ◆ *wholesale goods/products/sales* ◆ *the wholesale market/sector/trade*
● *adverb*
being bought and sold in large quantities to be sold again to make a profit: *We buy the building materials wholesale.* → RETAIL

● *verb* [+ obj]
to sell goods in large quantities to businesses, so that they can be sold again to make a profit: *60% of the fruit is wholesaled.* ◇ *They import tea and wholesale it to retail stores.* → RETAIL
▶ '**wholesaling** *noun* [U]: *Their core business is the wholesaling of health-care products to pharmacists.* ◇ *a wholesaling business*

'**wholesale bank** *noun* [C]
a bank that provides services for other banks and large businesses and not to individual customers or small businesses ▶ ,**wholesale 'banking** *noun* [U]

,**wholesale co'operative** *noun* [C]
(*Commerce*) a **cooperative** that buys goods in large quantities to sell to the cooperatives that own it and to others

'**wholesale price** (*also* '**trade price**) *noun* [C]
(*Commerce*) the price that a RETAILER (= a business that sells goods to the public) pays for goods from a manufacturer or **wholesaler** → RETAIL PRICE

★ **wholesaler** /'həʊseɪlə(r); *AmE* 'hoʊl-/ *noun* [C]
(*Commerce*) a person or a business that buys goods in large quantities and sells them to businesses, so they can be sold again to make a profit: *fruit and vegetable wholesalers* → RETAILER
See note at SUPPLY CHAIN

,**wholly-'owned** *adjective*
used to describe a company whose shares are all owned by another company: *The company will become a wholly-owned subsidiary of Sun Life.*

,**wide area 'network** = WAN

widget /'wɪdʒɪt/ *noun* [C] (*informal*)
1 used to refer to any small device that you do not know the name of: *lots of different widgets to customize your car* ◇ *I had to pull some kind of widget to make the machine work.*
2 (*Manufacturing*) a product that does not exist, used as an example of the typical product of a manufacturer, especially when accounting or financial processes are being explained: *Calculate the total cost per widget.*

Wi-Fi /'waɪ faɪ/ *noun* [U]
(*IT*) technology without wires that allows several computers to share the same fast Internet connection in a small area such as an office, a shop or a home ▶ '**Wi-Fi** *adjective*: *Wi-Fi Internet access* **NOTE** Wi-Fi is a short form of **Wireless Fidelity.**
→ BLUETOOTH

'**wild card** *noun* [C]
1 a person or thing whose behaviour or effect is difficult to predict: *When it comes to making big changes in an organization, the wild card is the employees' ability to adapt to the new system.*
2 (*IT*) a symbol that has no meaning of its own and can represent any letter: *An asterisk is commonly used as a wild card.* ◇ *a wild-card search*

wildcat /'waɪldkæt/ *adjective, noun, verb* (*informal*)
● *adjective* [only before noun]
1 (*HR*) a wildcat strike happens suddenly and without the official support of a trade union: *4 000 workers may be fired unless they put a stop to wildcat strikes.* → LIGHTNING STRIKE
2 (about a business or project) that has not been carefully planned and that will probably not be successful; that does not follow normal standards and methods: *He made the mistake of putting his money into a wildcat scheme.* ◇ *wildcat stocks*
● *noun* [C]
1 (*AmE*) an oil or gas well (= a deep hole in the ground) made in an area where oil or gas has not yet been found: *The company expects ten wildcats to be drilled this year.*

2 a business or project that will probably not be financially successful
● *verb* [no obj] (*AmE*)
to look for oil where nobody has looked for it before: *They were wildcatting for oil in Texas.*
▶ **'wildcatter** *noun* [C]: *He was a wildcatter in the '60s in the oilfields of Wyoming.*

will /wɪl/ *noun, verb*
● *noun* [C]

SEE ALSO: **tenant at will**

a legal document that says what is to happen to sb's money and property after they die: *Have you made a will?* ◇ *My father left me the business in his will.*
● *verb* [no obj]
will sth (to sb) | **will sb sth** to formally give your property or possessions to sb after you have died, by means of a **will**

win /wɪn/ *verb, noun*
● *verb* (**winning, won, won** /wʌn/)
1 [+ obj *or* no obj] to be the most successful in a competition, race, battle, etc: *We seem to be winning the battle for the German market.*
2 [+ obj] to get sth as the result of a competition, race, etc: *The company has won a contract to build trucks for the army.* ◇ *Although we won several website awards, sales were disappointing.*
3 [+ obj] to achieve or get what you want, especially by your own efforts: *We won 250 000 new customers in the final quarter of last year.* ◇ *The two airlines have won approval for their planned merger.*
PHR V **win sb a'round/'over/'round (to sth)** to get sb's support or approval by persuading them that you are right: *Their latest model has so far failed to win over consumers.* **win sb/sth 'back** to get or have again sb/sth that you had before: *How can we win our customers back?*
● *noun* [C]
a victory in a competition, race, etc: *The order is an important win for the aircraft maker.*

wind /waɪnd/ *verb* (**wound, wound** /waʊnd/)
PHR V **wind 'down 1** (about a business, a piece of machinery, etc.) to go slowly and then stop: *The market is winding down ahead of the holidays.*
2 (about a person) to rest or relax after a period of activity or excitement: *I used to go online to wind down after a long day at work.* **SYN** UNWIND **wind sth 'down** to bring a business, an activity, etc. to an end gradually over a period of time: *The French bank is winding down its involvement in the joint venture.* **wind 'up; wind sth 'up** to bring sth such as a meeting or a speech to an end: *If we all agree, let's wind up the discussion.* **wind sth 'up** (*Law*) to stop running a business and close it completely: *The business will be wound up or sold.*
SYN LIQUIDATE → WINDING UP
See note at BANKRUPT

windfall /'wɪndfɔːl/ *noun* [C]
an amount of money that sb/sth wins or receives unexpectedly: *Shareholders got a windfall of $2 per share.* ◇ *Exporters have made windfall gains from the falling currency.*
○ *to get/have/receive a windfall • windfall gains/ profits*

'windfall tax *noun* [C]
a tax on profits that is paid once only, not every year: *The government imposed a windfall tax on some industries.*

wind farm /'wɪnd fɑːm; *AmE* -fɑːrm/ *noun* [C]
an area of land on which there are a lot of structures (**turbines**) for producing electricity from wind

winding up /ˌwaɪndɪŋ 'ʌp/ *noun* [U,C]

SEE ALSO: **voluntary winding up**

the process of closing a company, selling its assets and paying its debts: *The court ordered the winding up of the company.* **SYN** LIQUIDATION → WIND STH UP at WIND
○ *to vote for/order winding up • a winding-up order/ petition/sale • winding-up proceedings • winding up occurs/takes place*

window /'wɪndəʊ; *AmE* 'wɪndoʊ/ *noun* [C]

SEE ALSO: **discount window**

1 (*IT*) an area with a frame on a computer screen, in which a particular program is operating or in which information of a particular type is shown
○ *to click on/close/enlarge/minimize/move/open a window*
2 the glass at the front of a shop/store and the area behind it where goods are shown to the public: *I'd like one of the Swatch watches in the window.* ◇ *a window display*—Picture at STORE
3 a small area that you can see through: *The address must be clearly visible through the window of the envelope.*
4 a time when there is an opportunity to do sth, although it may not last long: (*informal*) *I think I can find a window to discuss the project with you.* ◇ *The months around graduation are a window of opportunity for companies to find good graduates.*

'window ,dressing *noun* [U]
1 the art of arranging goods in shop/store windows in an attractive way
2 the fact of doing, saying or presenting sth in a way that creates a good impression but does not show the real facts: *The reforms have been interpreted as window dressing.*
3 (*Stock Exchange*) trade on a stock market at the end of a FINANCIAL YEAR or part of a year that is intended to make a collection of investments look more successful: *With window dressing, professional investors drop losers from their portfolios and add winners.*

'window-,shopping *noun* [U]
the activity of looking at the goods in shop/store windows, usually without intending to buy anything: *to go window-shopping* ▶ **'window-shop** *verb* [no obj] (**-pp-**)

winner /'wɪnə(r)/ *noun*
1 [C] a person, team, etc. that wins a competition, race, etc: *The mobile phone boom created both winners and losers.* **OPP** LOSER
2 [C, usually sing.] a thing or person that is successful or likely to be successful: *The latest version of the software package is a winner.*

winning /'wɪnɪŋ/ *adjective*

SEE ALSO: **award-winning**

1 [only before noun] that wins or has won a competition, race, etc: *It took six months to develop a winning strategy.*
2 successful or likely to be successful: *The D500 looks like a winning product.*

win-'win *adjective*
used to describe a situation in which everybody involved gains sth: *A company spokesman described the pay agreement as a win-win solution.* → NO-WIN

WIP /ˌdʌbljuː aɪ 'piː/ = WORK IN PROGRESS

wipe /waɪp/ *verb*
PHR V **wipe sth 'off sth** to reduce the value of sth, especially shares: *Billions of pounds were wiped off*

share prices today. ,**wipe sth 'out** (*often* **be wiped out**) to destroy or remove sb/sth completely: *Last year's profits were virtually wiped out.*

wire /'waɪə(r)/ *noun, verb*
● *noun*
1 [U,C] metal in the form of a thin thread
2 [U,C] a piece of wire that is used to carry an electric current or signal: *telephone wires*
3 (*informal*) [U] (*AmE*) the system of sending messages by TELEGRAM; a TELEGRAPH
IDM **go, come, etc. (right) down to the 'wire** (*informal*) if you say that a situation goes **down to the wire**, you mean that the result will not be decided or known until the very end: *The pay negotiations went down to the wire, and a strike was narrowly avoided.* → idiom at PULL *verb*
● *verb* [+ obj]
1 **wire sth (up)** to connect a building, a piece of equipment, etc. to an electricity supply using wires: *The fire was caused by a wrongly wired plug.*
2 **wire sb/sth (up) (to sth)** to connect sb/sth to a piece of equipment, especially a computer system: *The government is aiming for all schools to be wired up to the Internet within five years.*
3 **wire sth (to sb)** | **wire sb sth** to send money from one bank to another using an electronic system: *We will wire the money to you today.*
4 (*AmE*) (*informal*) **wire sth (to sb)** | **wire sb sth** to send sb a TELEGRAM

wireless /'waɪələs; *AmE* 'waɪərləs/ *adjective*
SEE ALSO: **fixed wireless**
without wires; using radio signals rather than wires: *a wireless modem* ◇ *Professionals need secure wireless access to company data while away from the office.* ◇ *a wireless communications company*
▶ **'wirelessly** *adverb*: *to connect wirelessly to the Internet*

,**wireless 'Internet** (*also* ,**wireless 'Web**) *noun* [U; sing.]
(*IT*) a system that enables people to communicate with the Internet using a MOBILE PHONE or other device that is not connected to anything by wires → WAP

wireline /'waɪəlaɪn; *AmE* 'waɪərl-/ *adjective, noun*
● *adjective* [only before noun]
used to describe a system, a device or technology that uses telephone wires: *wireline communications/networks*
● *noun*
1 [C] a telephone wire
2 [U] technology that uses telephone wires: *Some telecoms companies only have wireline, others just have wireless.* → WIRELESS

'**wire ,service** *noun* [C] (*especially AmE*)
a company that sends news to newspapers, television stations, people's computers, etc.

,**wire 'transfer** (*also* ,**cable 'transfer**, ,**telegraphic 'transfer**) *noun* [C,U]
a quick way of moving money from one bank to another anywhere in the world by telephone, computer, etc. → EFTPOS

wiring /'waɪərɪŋ/ *noun* [U]
the system of electrical connections, cables and wires in a building, machine, etc: *The fire in the building was caused by faulty wiring.*

'**wish list** *noun* [C] (*informal*)
all the things that you would like to have, buy or do, or that you would like to happen: *Electronics and computer games are high on consumers' wish lists this year.*

withdraw /wɪð'drɔː; wɪθ'd-/ *verb* (**withdrew** /-'druː/ **withdrawn** /-'drɔːn/)
1 [+ obj] to take money out of a bank account, etc: *You can use the card to withdraw money from cashpoints all over the world.* **SYN** DRAW (1)
OPP DEPOSIT (1)
2 (*Commerce*) [+ obj] to stop giving or offering sth to sb: *The drug was withdrawn from sale after a number of people suffered serious side effects.*
3 [+ obj *or* no obj] to stop taking part in an activity or being a member of an organization; to stop sb/sth from doing these things: *There have been calls for Britain to withdraw from the EU.* **SYN** PULL OUT

withdrawal /wɪð'drɔːəl; wɪθ'd-/ *noun*
SEE ALSO: **in-service withdrawal**
1 [C,U] the act of taking an amount of money out of your bank account, a pension plan, etc.; the amount of money that you take out: *You can make withdrawals of up to €250 a day.* ◇ *There is no charge for cash withdrawals.* ◇ *There is a withdrawal penalty if you take your money out early.*
OPP DEPOSIT
2 (*Commerce*) [U,C] the act of moving or taking sth away or back: *the withdrawal of an offer* ◇ *the withdrawal of a product from the market* ◇ *The manufacturers found a fault and carried out a voluntary product withdrawal.* → RECALL
3 [U] the act of no longer taking part in sth or being a member of an organization: *the company's withdrawal from the merger agreement*

withhold /wɪð'həʊld; wɪθ'h-; *AmE* -'hoʊld/ *verb* [+ obj] (**withheld, withheld** /-'held/) (*formal*)
to refuse to give sth to sb: *They withheld payments as they were not satisfied with the quality of the goods.*

with'holding tax *noun* [C,U]
1 in the US, an amount of money that an employer takes out of sb's income as tax and pays directly to the government
2 an amount of money that a financial institution takes out of the interest or DIVIDENDS that sb earns on an investment and pays directly to the government

with,out en'gagement *adjective, adverb*
(*Commerce*) used to show that a seller has the right to change a stated price, delivery date, etc: *All prices quoted are without engagement.*

with,out 'prejudice *adjective, adverb*
(*Law*) words on a document that mean that the information it contains does not affect legal rights that already exist or any claim that sb has

with,out-'profit (*also* **with,out-'profits**) *adjective* (*BrE*)
(*Finance*; *Insurance*) used to describe an insurance policy or an investment where the amount paid does not include a share in the company's profits: *a without-profit policy* → WITH-PROFITS

with,out re'course *adjective, adverb*
(*Law*) words written on a BILL OF EXCHANGE that mean that money cannot be claimed from the person who prepared or sold it if the money is not paid

,**with-'profits** (*also* ,**with-'profit**) *adjective* (*BrE*)
(*Insurance*) used to describe a type of insurance or an investment where an amount of money related to the profits that the company has made is added each year to the amount you have invested or is paid separately: *You pay higher premiums on a with-profit policy than on a without-profit policy.*
→ WITHOUT-PROFIT

witness /ˈwɪtnəs/ *noun, verb*
● *noun* [C]
1 a person who gives evidence in a court: *a defence/prosecution witness* ◇ *She appeared as (a) witness for the defence/prosecution.*
➊ *to* **act as/appear as/be called as** *a* witness
2 a person who is present when an official document is signed and who also signs it to prove that they saw this happen: *She signed and dated the document* **in front of** *a witness.*
● *verb* [+ obj]
to be present when an official document is signed and sign it yourself to prove that you saw this happen: *A solicitor must be present to witness the signing of the document.*
➊ *to witness an* **agreement/a** *contract/signature*

'witness box (*BrE*) (*AmE* **'witness stand**) (*also* **stand**, *BrE*, *AmE*) *noun* [C]
the place in court where people stand to give evidence

wizard /ˈwɪzəd; *AmE* -ərd/ *noun* [C]
1 a person who is especially good at sth: *a computer/financial/publishing wizard*
2 (*IT*) a part of a computer program that helps the user do a complicated task by providing instructions or asking a series of simple questions: *The package uses a wizard to guide you through the testing process.*

wk *abbr* (*plural* **wks**) (*only used in written English*)
week

womenswear /ˈwɪmɪnzweə(r)/ *noun* [U]
(used especially in shops/stores) clothes for women: *There has been a big rise in womenswear sales.* → CHILDRENSWEAR, MENSWEAR

woo /wuː/ *verb* [+ obj]
(used especially in newspapers) to try to attract or get the support of a person, a group, an organization, etc: *The ads are an attempt to woo younger consumers.*

wording /ˈwɜːdɪŋ; *AmE* ˈwɜːrd-/ *noun* [U; C, usually sing.]
the words that are used in a piece of writing or speech, especially when they have been carefully chosen: *We can't agree on the wording of the document.*

,word of 'mouth *noun* [U]
the process of people telling each other about sth: *Most of our products are sold by word of mouth rather than by advertising.* ◇ *word-of-mouth marketing*

'word ,processing *noun* [U] (*abbr* **WP**)
the use of a computer to create, store and print a piece of text, usually typed in from a keyboard

'word ,processor *noun* [C] (*abbr* **WP**)
a computer that runs a WORD PROCESSING program and is usually used for writing letters, reports, etc.

,words and ,figures 'differ (*also* ,words and ,figures do not a'gree) *phrase* (*only used in written English*)
if a bank returns a cheque with the phrase **words and figures differ** written on it, it means that the amount written on the cheque in words is different from the amount written in figures SYN AMOUNTS DIFFER

★ **work** /wɜːk; *AmE* wɜːrk/ *verb, noun*
● *verb*
1 [no obj] to have a job: *Both my parents work.* ◇ *Do you work full-time or part-time?* ◇ *She works* **for** *an engineering company.* ◇ *He works* **as** *a programmer.*
2 [+ obj *or* no obj] to do sth that involves physical or mental effort, especially as part of your job:

You've been working too hard. Take a break. ◇ *My boss works very long hours.* ◇ *What project are you working* **on**? ◇ *We need to work* **at** *improving customer service.*
3 [no obj] to make efforts to achieve sth: *We're working hard* **to** *find a solution to the problem.*
4 [+ obj] to make yourself/sb work, especially very hard: *She works her staff hard and pays them well.*
5 [+ obj] to manage or operate sth in order to gain benefit from it: *Some of the sales reps have to work a very large area.*
6 [no obj] to function; to operate: *My phone isn't working.* ◇ *The new search engine works well.* ◇ *The article examines how companies work.*
7 [+ obj] to make a machine, device, etc. operate: *teaching customers how to work a VCR* ◇ *The machine is worked by wind power.*
8 [no obj] to have the result or effect that you want: *Our plan didn't work.* ◇ *The new informal meetings just aren't working.* ◇ *We think the new appraisal system works well.*
9 [no obj] to have a particular effect: *The fact that he is so young could work* **against** *him.* ◇ *The strength of the local currency worked* **in our favour**.
10 [+ obj *or* no obj] to move or pass to a particular place or state, usually gradually: *She* **worked her way** *from sales assistant to senior manager.*
IDM **'work it/things** (*informal*) to arrange sth in a particular way, especially by being clever: *I managed to work it so that I could have a day free for sightseeing.* **work to 'rule** to follow the rules of your job in a very strict way in order to cause delay, as a form of protest against your employer or your working conditions → WORK-TO-RULE → idioms at ADVANTAGE, GROUND *noun*, LONG
PHR V **,work 'out** to develop in a successful way: *My first job didn't work out.* **,work 'out (at sth)** if sth **works out** at sth, you calculate that it will be a particular amount: *That works out at almost $500.* ◇ *It would work out cheaper to fly.* **,work sth 'out**
1 to calculate an amount or the cost of sth: *We need to work out how much it will cost.* **2** to find the answer to sth; to solve sth: *I finally worked out what the problem was.* **3** to plan or think of sth: *Have you worked out the best way to do it?* FIGURE STH OUT **'work to sth** to follow a plan, TIMETABLE, etc: *to work to a budget* ◇ *We're working to a very tight deadline* (= we have little time in which to do the work). **'work towards sth** to try to reach or achieve a goal: *We're working towards a profit of $2 million this year.* **,work sth 'up** to spend time developing sth: *to work up a business plan*
● *noun*

SEE ALSO: assignment work, contingent ~, make-~, out of ~, welfare to ~

1 [U] the job that a person does: *I'm looking for work.* ◇ *I started work as soon as I left school.* ◇ (*BrE*) *Official figures show that the number of people* **in work** (= who have a job) *has risen by 65 000 this year.* ◇ *What* **line of work** *are you in* (= what type of work do you do)? SYN EMPLOYMENT
See note at JOB
➊ **full-time/part-time/permanent/regular/temporary** *work ◆* **paid/unpaid/voluntary** *work ◆* **badly paid/ well-paid** *work ◆ to* **find/get/look for/seek** *work ◆ to* **give up/go back to/return to/start** *work*
2 [U] (*used without* **the**) the place where you do your job: *I go to work at 8 a.m.* ◇ *She had to leave work early today.* ◇ *The new legislation concerns health and safety at work.*
➊ *to* **go to/leave** *work ◆ (be)* **at/off** *work*
3 [U] the duties that you have and the activities that you do as part of your job: *The accountant described his work to the sales staff.* ◇ *Do you enjoy your work?* ◇ *Power-plant work is hard, dangerous and often boring.* ◇ *Who handles the day-to-day work*

of the department? ◊ *What time do you finish work today?*
➊ *administrative/clerical/factory/office/secretarial* work ◆ *to do/produce/take on/undertake* work ◆ *to begin/finish/start/stop* work
4 [U] tasks that need to be done: *I have some work for you to do.* ◊ *Pressure of work forced him to cancel his trip.* ◊ *We have a lot of work on at the moment.*
➊ *to take on/do/have/undertake* work
5 [U] materials needed or used for doing work, especially books, papers, etc: *She often brings work home with her.*
6 [U] activity that uses physical strength or mental power in order to do or make sth: *She got her promotion through sheer hard work.* ◊ *We started work on the project two years ago.*
➊ *to carry out/put in* work ◆ *to complete/halt/start/ stop* work
7 [U] a thing or things that are produced as a result of work: *She did her best work before she was 30.* ◊ *His work is always faultless.* ◊ *The analysis is an impressive piece of work.*
➊ *bad/good/innovative/major/outstanding* work
8 [U] the result of an action; what is done by sb: *The report was the work of the company's production manager.*
9 works [pl.] *(often used with other nouns)* activities involving building or repairing sth: *engineering works* ◊ *roadworks*
10 works [C with sing./pl. verb] *(plural* **works***) (often used with other nouns)* a place where things are made or industrial processes are carried out: *an engineering works* ◊ *waterworks* See note at FACTORY
➊ *a cement/chemical/gas/steel* works ◆ *to open/close (down)/shut down a* works ◆ *the works close (down)/open* ◆ *the works canteen/foreman/ manager/supervisor*
11 the works [pl.] *(informal)* the moving parts of a machine, etc. SYN MECHANISM
IDM at 'work (on sth) busy doing sth: *Everybody is hard at work on the new project.* **get (down) to/set to 'work** to begin; to make a start **in the 'works** something that is **in the works** is being discussed, planned or prepared and will happen or exist soon → idioms at DIRTY, JOB *noun*, LIGHT

workaholic /ˈwɜːkəˈhɒlɪk; *AmE* ˈwɜːrkəˈhɔːlɪk; -ˈhɑːl-/ *noun* [C] *(informal)*
a person who works very hard and finds it difficult to stop working and do other things

workday /ˈwɜːkdeɪ; *AmE* ˈwɜːrk-/ = WORKING DAY

★ **worker** /ˈwɜːkə(r); *AmE* ˈwɜːrk-/ *noun* [C]

SEE ALSO: **assembly worker, co-~, contract ~, guest ~, inside ~, knowledge ~, mobile ~,** etc.

1 *(often used in compounds)* a person who works, especially one who does a particular kind of work: *The research showed that 40% of clerical workers suffer headaches and tiredness at work.* ◊ *The plant has 1 400 workers.* See note at CHAIRMAN
➊ *assembly-line/factory/farm/manufacturing/ production* workers ◆ *full-time/part-time/temp/ temporary* workers ◆ *agency/casual/freelance/self- employed* workers ◆ *blue-collar/manual/white- collar* workers ◆ *private-sector/public-sector* workers ◆ *semi-skilled/skilled/unskilled* workers
2 a person who is employed to do physical work rather than organizing things or managing people: *talks between workers and management* ◊ *profit- sharing and worker participation in decision-making*
3 *(usually after an adjective)* a person who works hard or who works in a particular way
➊ *a good/hard/productive/quick/steady* worker

---

worker di'rector *noun* [C]
(HR) an employee who has a place on the BOARD OF DIRECTORS (= the group of people who decide the policies of the company) to represent the ordinary workers

worker partici'pation = EMPLOYEE PARTICIPATION

workers' co'operative = COOPERATIVE

'work ex,perience *noun* [U]
1 the work or jobs that you have done in your life so far: *The salary will depend on your previous work experience and qualifications.*
2 a period of time that a young person, especially a student, spends working in a company as a form of training: *I did two weeks' work experience at a local radio station.* ◊ *a work experience placement*
→ INTERNSHIP at INTERN

workfare /ˈwɜːfeə(r); *AmE* ˈwɜːrkfer/ *noun* [U]
in the US, a system in which unemployed people have to do some work or training in order to get money for food, rent, etc. from the government: *to sign up for a workfare program* → WELFARE TO WORK

★ **workforce** *(also spelled* **work force***, especially in AmE)* /ˈwɜːkfɔːs; *AmE* ˈwɜːrkfɔːrs/ *noun* [C with sing./pl. verb]
1 all the people who work for a particular company, organization, etc: *The factory will have to lose half of its 1 000-strong workforce.* ◊ *Two-thirds of the workforce is/are women.* ◊ *The group plans to cut over 100 jobs, about 1% of its total workforce.* ◊ *Workforce planning is an ongoing process that influences all aspects of an organization.* SYN STAFF
➊ *the entire/total/worldwide* workforce
2 all the people in a country or an area who are available for work: *A quarter of the local workforce is/are unemployed.*
➊ *an educated/a skilled/trained* workforce
SYN LABOUR FORCE

working /ˈwɜːkɪŋ; *AmE* ˈwɜːrk-/ *adjective, noun*
● *adjective* [only before noun]

SEE ALSO: **hard-working**

1 having a job for which you are paid: *the working population* ◊ *a programme of tax cuts for* **working families** (= families where at least one person is employed) SYN EMPLOYED
2 connected with your job and the time you spend doing it: *poor working conditions* ◊ *long working hours* ◊ *I have a good working relationship with my boss.*
3 having a job that involves hard physical work rather than office work, studying, etc: *My father was an ordinary working man.*
4 a **working** breakfast or lunch is one at which you discuss business
5 used as a basis for work, discussion, etc. but likely to be changed or improved in the future: *The investigator now has a working hypothesis of what caused the accident.*
6 if you have a **working** knowledge of sth, you can use it at a basic level: *A working knowledge of Spanish would be useful.*
7 the **working** parts of a machine are the parts that move in order to make it function: *a working model*
→ idiom at ORDER *noun*
● *noun* [C] *(usually* **workings** [pl.]*)*

SEE ALSO: **collaborative working, flexible working**

the way in which a machine, a system, an organization, etc. works: *the internal workings of the company*

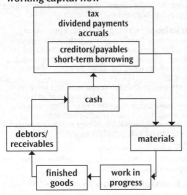

working 'capital (*also* ,circulating 'capital) *noun*
[U; sing.]
(*Accounting*) the money, stocks of goods, etc. that
are used to run a business, pay employees and
produce and sell more goods: *We may have to
reduce our working capital in order to pay off some
of the debts.* → NET CURRENT ASSETS

,**working 'day** *noun* [C] (*BrE*)
1 (*also* '**workday**, *AmE, BrE*) a day on which you
usually work or on which most people usually
work: *Sunday is a normal working day for me.* ◇
*Thousands of working days were lost through strikes
last year.* ◇ *Allow two working days* (= not Saturday
or Sunday) *for delivery.*
2 (*AmE* '**workday**) the part of a day during which
you work: *I spend most of my working day at my
desk.* ◇ *an 8-hour working day*

'**working group** (*BrE also* '**working ,party**)
noun [C]
a group of people given the task of studying a
subject and producing a report on it: *They set up a
working group on alternative sources of energy.* ◇
The working party will report in the spring.
○ *to **establish/form/set up** a working group* ✦ *to **head/
lead** a working group* ✦ *a working group **approves
sth/recommends sth/reports (on sth)*** ✦ *a working
group **looks at sth/meets/studies sth***

'**working hours** *noun* [pl.]
the time during the day when most people are at
work and when shop/stores and offices are open:
The call centre is staffed only during working hours.

,**working 'interest** *noun* [C]
a share in a property, especially one that produces
oil, gas, etc., that gives the owner the right to
develop it and to receive a share of the profits from
what is produced: *The company has a 50% working
interest in the oil field.*

,**working 'life** *noun* [C,U]
1 the part of a person's life that they spend
working: *He spent his whole working life in
publishing.*
2 the total amount of time that a machine, a
factory, etc., operates: *These parts will need to be
replaced several times during the machine's working
life.*

'**working ,paper** *noun*
1 [C] a report written by a group of people chosen
to study an aspect of law, education, health, etc.,
for people to discuss

2 working papers [pl.] in the US, an official
document that enables sb under 16 years old or
born outside the US to have a job

,**working 'partner** = ACTIVE PARTNER

'**working ,party** = WORKING GROUP

,**Working Time Di'rective** *noun* [sing.]
(*HR*) European Union rules, which have become law
in many member countries, that limit the number
of hours most employees can work to 48 a week,
and say how much rest and holiday/vacation they
should have

,**working 'week** (*AmE also* '**workweek**) *noun*
[sing.]
the total number of hours or days worked in a
week: *The working week will be reduced from 37 to
35 hours.*

,**work in 'progress** (*especially BrE*) (*AmE usually*
,**work in 'process**) *noun* [C,U] (*abbr* **WIP**)
1 (*Accounting*) products that are only partly
manufactured at the end of an accounting period,
valued at the cost of the materials, labour and
some regular costs (**overheads**): *There are three
levels of stock: raw materials, work in progress and
finished goods.*—Picture at WORKING CAPITAL
2 a piece of work that may be shown to people or
discussed with them but is not finished: *a work-in-
progress report*

,**work-life 'balance** (*also spelled* ,**work/life ~**)
(*also* ,**life-work 'balance**, *less frequent*) *noun*
[C, usually sing., U]
(*HR*) a situation when a person manages to spend
the right amount of time at work and on their
personal life: *She cut her working hours to improve
her work-life balance.*

★ **workload** /'wɜːkləʊd; *AmE* 'wɜːrkloʊd/ *noun* [C]
the amount of work that has to be done by a
particular person, organization or machine: *a
heavy workload* ◇ *We have taken on extra staff to
cope with the increased workload.*
○ *to **cut/ease/increase/reduce/share** a workload*

workman /'wɜːkmən; *AmE* 'wɜːrk-/ *noun* [C]
(*plural* **workmen** /-mən/)
1 a man who is employed to do physical work
2 (*used with an adjective*) a person who works in the
way mentioned: *a good/bad/poor workman*

workmanlike /'wɜːkmənlaɪk; *AmE* 'wɜːrk-/
adjective
done, made, etc. in a skilful and thorough way:
They've done a workmanlike job. ◇ *You agree to do
the work in a good and workmanlike manner.*

workmanship /'wɜːkmənʃɪp; *AmE* 'wɜːrk-/
noun [U]
the skill with which sb makes sth, especially when
this affects the way it looks or works: *Our buyers
insist on high standards of workmanship and
materials.* ◇ *A number of fatal accidents have been
caused by shoddy* (= bad) *workmanship.*
○ *bad/faulty/good/poor/shoddy workmanship*

'**work ,measurement** *noun* [U]
(*Production*) a system for calculating how long a
piece of work would take if done by an average
qualified or trained person

,**work 'overload** *noun* [U]
when a person has too much work: *Work overload is
one of the main causes of stress.*

'work ,permit *noun* [C]
an official document that gives a person the right
to work in a foreign country
○ to **issue/withdraw** a work permit • to **apply for/get/
have/receive/renew** a work permit

★ **workplace** /'wɜːkpleɪs; *AmE* 'wɜːrk-/ *noun*
[sing.] (*often* **the workplace**) the office, factory, etc.
where people work: *the introduction of new
technology into the workplace* ◇ *your first day in your
new workplace*

,workplace 'bargaining (*also* ,enterprise
'bargaining) *noun* [U]
(*HR*) discussions between employers and employees
about pay, conditions, rules, etc. in a particular
office, factory, etc. with the aim of reaching a
satisfactory agreement

,workplace 'learning *noun* [U]
1 an arrangement where students spend time in a
company in order to learn to use their knowledge
and skills in a real work situation
2 training or lessons that employees receive while
they are at work

,work psy'chology *noun* [U]
(*HR*) the study of how people behave at work and
what influences their attitudes and behaviour

'work rage *noun* [U] (*informal*)
a situation when an employee becomes extremely
angry because of sth that has happened at work:
Computers seem to be the main cause of work rage.

'work-re,lated *adjective*
connected with the work that you do: *He received
compensation for a work-related injury.* ◇ *I want to
talk to you about something that's not work-related.*
→ INDUSTRIAL (5)

workroom /'wɜːkruːm; -rʊm; *AmE* 'wɜːrk-/
noun [C]
a room in which work is done, especially work that
involves making things: *a small workroom at the
back of the shop*

works = WORK *noun* (9,10,11)

'work ,sampling *noun* [U]
1 (*Production*) (*also* **ac'tivity ,sampling**) a technique
of watching the activities of a group of people or
machines in a workplace at particular moments
over a period of time, in order to calculate how
much time is spent on each activity: *Work sampling
provides a measure of employee efficiency by showing
what proportion of the time is spent working.*
2 (*HR*) a method of finding out if a candidate for a
job has the necessary skills and abilities by asking
them to do a task that is an important part of the
job or by looking at examples of work that they
have already done

'works ,council *noun* [C with sing./pl.verb]
(*especially BrE*)
(*HR*) a group of employees who are elected to
represent all the employees at a factory, etc. and
meet with employers to discuss pay and conditions:
*The company is in negotiations with its works council
to close four plants.*

'work ,shadowing *noun* [U]
(*HR*) an arrangement that allows a student to find
out about a particular type of work by spending
some time with sb while they are doing their job
→ WORK EXPERIENCE

'work-,sharing = JOB-SHARING

worksheet /'wɜːkʃiːt; *AmE* 'wɜːrk-/ *noun* [C]
a piece of paper recording work that is being done
or that has been done

workshop /'wɜːkʃɒp; *AmE* 'wɜːrkʃɑːp/ *noun* [C]
1 a room or building in which things are made or
repaired using tools or machinery: *The leaflet gives
tips on safety in the workshop.* ◇ *Both our branches
have well-equipped workshop facilities.* → SHOP
noun (2)
2 a period of discussion and practical work on a
particular subject, in which a group of people share
their knowledge and experience: *They run a two-
day workshop on marketing techniques.*
○ to **conduct/do/hold/lead/organize/run** a workshop
• to **attend/take part in** a workshop

'work-shy *adjective* (*BrE*)
unwilling to work: *He refused to believe unemployed
people were work-shy and lazy.*

,work ,simplifi'cation *noun* [U; sing.]
(*Production*) the process of making tasks, for
example in manufacturing, as simple as possible so
that they can be completed quickly and costs can
be reduced

worksite /'wɜːksaɪt; *AmE* 'wɜːrk/ *noun* [C]
(*Manufacturing*) an area where a factory, etc. has
been built or where work is done: *Some workers are
sent for three months to our worksite in Germany.*

'works ,manager *noun* [C]
the person who is in charge of a factory and is
responsible for the work done, the people who
work there, etc.

workspace /'wɜːkspeɪs; *AmE* 'wɜːrk-/ *noun* [C,U]
1 an area that is designed for sb to work in: *The
team share a bright, open workspace.*
2 (*IT*) the area on a computer screen on which you
can work in a particular program; the way this is
arranged: *The program saves your workspace when
you shut down your computer.*

workstation /'wɜːksteɪʃn; *AmE* 'wɜːrk-/ *noun* [C]
1 the area where one person works, especially a
desk with a computer—Picture at OFFICE
2 (*IT*) a computer that is more powerful than a
personal computer and is used for very technical
work or design
3 (*IT*) a computer and a screen that are connected
to a central computer system and use data from
there
4 (*Production*) an area in a factory where a
particular process or task is done: *Parts arrive at the
next workstation 'just in time'.*

,work ,structuring *noun* [U]
1 (*HR*) the process of arranging important parts of
employees' jobs, such as their hours of work and
their duties, in the most efficient way
2 (*Production*) the process of arranging the steps in
making a product so that everything happens
quickly and efficiently

'work ,study *noun* [U] (*BrE*)
(*HR; Production*) a system of analysing the way work
is done in an organization in order to improve it:
*She advises companies on all aspects of work study,
efficiency and wages.* ◇ *a work-study officer*

'work-study *adjective* [only before noun] (*AmE*)
used to describe an arrangement that allows a
person to work part-time at the same time as
studying: *He graduated from college in a company
work-study program.*

,work-to-'rule (*especially BrE*) (*AmE usually* ,work-
to-'contract) *noun* [C, usually sing.]
(*HR*) a situation in which workers refuse to do any
work that is not in their contracts, in order to

protest about sth: *Union members voted for a work-to-rule.* → GO-SLOW See note at STRIKE
O *to begin/be on/call for/go on/stage/threaten/vote for a work-to-rule*

workwear /'wɜːkweə(r); *AmE* 'wɜːrkwer/ *noun* [U] (*AmE*)
clothes that are worn for work, especially to do MANUAL work

workweek /'wɜːkwiːk; *AmE* 'wɜːrk-/ = WORKING WEEK

the ˌWorld ˈBank *noun* [sing.]
a group of financial organizations, established in 1946 and linked with the United Nations, that provides loans for developing countries to help with their economic development: *The university was funded by a loan from the World Bank.*

the ˌWorld Ecoˌnomic ˈForum *noun* [sing.] (*abbr* **WEF**)
an international organization that works with politicians and leaders from business, education, etc. to encourage economic growth and social progress and does not aim to make a profit

the ˌWorld ˈTrade Organiˌzation *noun* [sing.] (*abbr* **WTO**)
an international organization, formed in 1995, that encourages and controls international trade and economic development

★ **worldwide** /'wɜːldwaɪd; *AmE* 'wɜːrld-/ *adjective* [usually before noun]
in or affecting all parts of the world: *an increase in worldwide sales* ◇ *powerful computers linked in a worldwide network* ◇ *worldwide economic slowdown* ▶ ˌworldˈwide *adverb*: *She travels worldwide as a consultant.*

★ **the ˌWorld Wide ˈWeb** (*also* **the Web**) *noun* [sing.] (*abbr* **WWW**)
(*IT*) a system for finding information on the Internet in which documents are connected to other documents using HYPERTEXT links: *to browse a site on the World Wide Web* → WEBSITE

ˌworst-perˈforming *adjective* [only before noun]
producing the worst results: *The group is to close over 100 of its worst-performing stores.*

★ **worth** /wɜːθ; *AmE* wɜːrθ/ *adjective, noun*
● *adjective* [not before noun] (*usually used like a preposition*)
1 having a value in money, etc: *The deal is worth about $28 million.* ◇ *How much is the information worth?* ◇ *My shares aren't worth much now.*
2 used to recommend the action mentioned because you think it may be useful, enjoyable, etc: *Their website is worth a look.* ◇ *This idea is well worth considering.*
3 important, good or enjoyable enough to make sb feel satisfied, especially when some difficulty or effort is involved: *I took a salary cut when I changed jobs, but it was worth it.*
IDM **not worth the paper it's ˈwritten/ˈprinted on** (*informal*) (used about an agreement or official document) having no value, especially legally, or because one of the people involved has no intention of doing what they said they would → idiom at JOB *noun*
● *noun* [U]

SEE ALSO: **comparable worth, high net ~, net ~, tangible net ~**

1 **ten dollars', €40, etc. worth of sth** an amount of sth that has the value mentioned: *$30 million worth of advertising space*
2 **a week's, month's, etc. worth of sth** an amount of sth that lasts a week, etc: *3 months' worth of stock*

3 the financial, practical or moral value of sb/sth: *a personal net worth of $10 million* ◇ *A good interview should enable candidates to show their worth* (= show how good they are).

worthless /'wɜːθləs; *AmE* 'wɜːrθ-/ *adjective*
having no practical or financial value: *The technology is practically worthless if people don't know how to use it.* ◇ *worthless currency/shares* **OPP** VALUABLE
▶ ˈworthlessness *noun* [U]

wow factor /'waʊ ˌfæktə(r)/ *noun* [C, usually sing.] (*Marketing*) the ability of a product to make people feel surprised and impressed when they see or use it for the first time: *Despite the addition of many new features, the latest model still lacks the wow factor.*

WP /ˌdʌbljuː 'piː/ = WORD PROCESSOR, WORD PROCESSING

wpm *abbr* (*only used in written English*)
words per minute, used to show how fast sb can type or do SHORTHAND: *My typing speed is 55 wpm.*

wrap /ræp/ *verb, noun*
● *verb* [+ obj] (-pp-) **wrap A (up) (in B)** | **wrap B round/around A** to cover sth completely in paper or other material: *All our products come wrapped in plastic, then securely packaged in a box.* ◇ *individually wrapped chocolates*
PHR V **ˌwrap sth ˈup** (*informal*) to complete sth such as an agreement or a meeting in a satisfactory way: *That just about wraps it up for today.*
● *noun* [U]

SEE ALSO: **bubble wrap, gift ~, shrink-~**

paper, plastic or other material that is used for wrapping things in: *a box covered with plastic wrap*
IDM **under 'wraps** (*informal*) being kept secret until some time in the future: *The development of the new machine was kept under wraps.*

wrapper /'ræpə(r)/ *noun* [C]
a piece of paper, plastic, etc. that is wrapped around sth, especially food, when you buy it in order to protect it and keep it clean: *a cellophane/plastic wrapper*

wrapping /'ræpɪŋ/ *noun* [U] (*also* **wrappings** [pl.])
paper, plastic, etc. used for covering sth in order to protect it: *wrapping paper/material*

wreck /rek/ *noun, verb*
● *verb* [+ obj]
to damage or destroy sth: *The union made an attempt to wreck the deal.*
● *noun* [C]
something that has been badly damaged or destroyed: *the wreck of a ship*

wreckage /'rekɪdʒ/ *noun* [U]
(often used in newspapers in a figurative way) the parts of a vehicle, building, etc. that remain after it has been badly damaged or destroyed: *They tried to salvage* (= save) *what they could from the wreckage of the bankrupt company.*

writ /rɪt/ *noun* [C]
(*Law*) a legal document from a court telling sb to do or not to do sth: *The company has been **served with** a writ **for** breach of contract.* ◇ *We intend to **issue** a writ **against** the newspaper.*

write /raɪt/ *verb* (**wrote** /rəʊt/ **written** /'rɪtn/)
1 [+ obj *or* no obj] to produce a document, an article or a piece of software: *We wrote a business plan for the new company.* ◇ *He writes **about/on***

business and social issues. ◇ She writes for the 'Times'. ◇ to write code/applications/software/ programs

2 [+ obj or no obj] to put a request or some information in a letter or an email and send it to sb: I am writing to inform you that your application has been accepted. ◇ I have written a memo to senior management. ◇ She sent them a letter of complaint but they didn't **write back**.

3 [+ obj] **write sth (out) (for sb)** | **write sb (out) sth** to complete a cheque or other form with the necessary information: I wrote (out) a cheque for €100. ◇ He wrote me a receipt.

4 (IT) [+ obj] **write sth to sth** to transfer or copy information from a computer's memory to sth that stores it in a more permanent form: to write data to a disk/file

→ idiom at WORTH adj.

PHR V ,write sth '**back** (Accounting) (usually **be written back**) to include an item in a company's accounts that had deliberately not been included before, when calculating the company's profits: The customer made a definite promise to pay, so the debt could now be written back. → WRITE-BACK ,**write sth 'down 1** to write sth on paper, especially in order to remember or record it: Write down all the specifications of your computer before phoning the help desk. **2** (Accounting) to reduce the value of an asset in a company's accounts: The company will write down the value of its property assets by $414 million. → WRITE-DOWN OPP WRITE STH UP ,**write sth 'off** (often **be written off**) **1** (Accounting) to reduce the value of an asset in a company's accounts over a period of time: Goodwill was written off over 5 years. ◇ The machinery was written off against profits (= the cost of the machinery was taken away from the profits, in order to pay less tax). SYN DEPRECIATE → AMORTIZE **2** (Accounting) to remove a debt from a company's accounts because the money cannot be collected; to remove an asset that has no value: The bank expects to write off bad loans (= loans made by the bank that were not paid back) of $8 billion. **3** (Insurance) (BrE) to accept that sth is so badly damaged that it cannot be repaired: The car was written off. → WRITE-OFF, TOTAL verb ,**write sth 'up 1** to record sth in writing in a full and complete form, often using notes that you made earlier: to write up the minutes of a meeting → WRITE-UP **2** (Accounting) (AmE) to increase the value of an asset in a company's accounts or give it a value that is too high → WRITE-UP OPP WRITE STH DOWN

'**write-back** noun [C,U]
(Accounting) a situation where money that had been kept to deal with a possible loss or expense is no longer needed; an amount of money entered in the profit side of financial records because of this: This credit represented a write-back of a provision made against a long-running court case.

'**write-down** noun [C,U]
(Accounting) a situation where an asset loses some value; an amount of money entered in the accounts because of this: The media group reported a €550 m write-down of its assets.

'**write-off** noun
1 (Accounting) [C,U] a situation where an asset loses some or all of its value; an amount of money entered in the financial records because of this: The company booked (= recorded in its accounts) a $2.7 billion write-off to cover goodwill and the

reduced value of assets. ◇ Last year's losses were due to bad debt write-offs.
2 (Finance) [C,U] a decision that a debt need not be paid back: countries qualifying for a debt write-off
3 [C] (BrE) a vehicle that has been so badly damaged in an accident that it is not worth spending money to repair it: I was OK, but the car was a write-off.

,**write-pro'tect** verb [+ obj]
(IT) to protect a computer file or disk so that its contents cannot be changed or removed
▶ ,**write-pro'tected** adjective

writer /'raɪtə(r)/ noun [C]
1 (Finance) a person or business that sells an OPTION contract
2 (Insurance) = UNDERWRITER (2)

'**write-up** noun [C,U]
1 (Accounting) a situation where the value of an asset increases; an amount of money entered in the accounts because of this
2 an article in a newspaper, magazine, etc. in which sb gives information and their opinion about a new product, book, etc: a clever write-up by an ad agency ◇ The site includes company write-ups.
3 an act of recording sth in a full and complete form: Do the write-ups of your books monthly.

,**writ of exe'cution** noun [C]
(Law) a legal document that makes sure that what has been decided by a court is done. For example, it may give the court the right to take and sell property from a person who has not paid a debt.

,**written-down 'value** = BOOK VALUE (1)

wrongful /'rɒŋfl; AmE 'rɔːŋ-/ adjective [usually before noun]
not fair, morally right or legal: fraud and other wrongful conduct

,**wrongful dis'missal** = UNFAIR DISMISSAL

wt abbr
a short way of writing **weight**: average net wt 120 g

Wtd. abbr
a short way of writing **warranted** to show that sth is guaranteed to be what it says it is: Wtd. 100% pure

WTO /,dʌblju: ,ti: 'əʊ; AmE 'oʊ/ = WORLD TRADE ORGANIZATION

wunderkind /'wʊndəkɪnd; AmE -dɑːrk-/ noun [C]
(plural **wunderkinder** /'wʊndəkɪndə(r); AmE -dɑːrk-/ or **wunderkinds**) (informal)
a person who is very successful at a young age: He is known as a wunderkind of investment banking. NOTE **Wunderkind** is a German word.

WWD /,dʌblju: ,dʌblju: 'di:/ = WEATHER WORKING DAYS

WWW /,dʌblju: dʌblju: 'dʌblju:/ (also spelled **www**) abbr
(IT) a short way of writing and saying World Wide Web, used in the addresses of websites: several useful WWW addresses ◇ www.oup.com

WYSIWYG /'wɪziwɪg/ abbr
(IT) **what you see is what you get** what you see on your computer screen is exactly the same as what will be printed or seen on other computers: a WYSIWYG display/editor ◇ WYSIWYG capabilities/ software

X x

xd (*also spelled* **XD**) /ˌeks ˈdiː/ = EX-DIVIDEND

x-efˈficiency *noun* [U]
the ability of a company to use the people, machines, etc. that it has in the best way in order to produce as much as possible quickly and at a low cost: *In order for a firm to achieve x-efficiency, staff motivation needs to be high.* SYN TECHNICAL EFFICIENCY OPP X-INEFFICIENCY
▸ **x-efˈficient** *adjective*

Xerox™ /ˈzɪərɒks; *AmE* ˈzɪrɑːks/ *noun* [U,C]
a process for producing copies of letters, documents, etc. using a special machine; a copy made using this process: *a Xerox machine* ◊ *She kept Xeroxes of all the letters.*

xerox /ˈzɪərɒks; *AmE* ˈzɪrɑːks/ *verb* [+ obj]
to make a copy of a letter, document, etc. by using **Xerox** or a similar process: *Could you xerox this letter please?* SYN PHOTOCOPY

x-inefˈficiency *noun* [U]
the amount by which a company does not use the people, machines, etc. that it has in the best way in order to produce as much as possible quickly and at a low cost: *The factory was found to have a 25% x-inefficiency.* SYN TECHNICAL INEFFICIENCY OPP X-EFFICIENCY
▸ **x-inefˈficient** *adjective*: *A lack of competition can make a company x-inefficient.*

xtn *abbr* (*only used in written English*)
extension: *call xtn 216*

Y y

yard /jɑːd; *AmE* jɑːrd/ *noun* [C]

SEE ALSO: **salvage yard**

1 (*usually with other nouns*) an area of land used for a special purpose or business: *a boat yard* ◊ *a freight yard*
2 (*abbr* **yd**) a unit for measuring length, equal to 3 feet or 0.9144 of a metre
IDM **the ˌwhole nine ˈyards** (*especially AmE*) (*informal*) everything; a situation that includes everything: *When I went out of business I lost everything—my house, the cars, the whole nine yards.*

yardstick /ˈjɑːdstɪk; *AmE* ˈjɑːrd-/ *noun* [C]
a standard used for judging how good or successful sth is: *GDP is not the only yardstick of economic success.*

yd *abbr* (*only used in written English*)
yard

year /jɪə(r); jɜː(r); *AmE* jɪr/ *noun* (*abbr* **yr**)

SEE ALSO: **accounting year, amount falling due after one ~, amount falling due within one ~, beginning of ~, calendar ~, end-of-~, financial ~,** etc.

1 [C] the period from 1 January to 31 December, that is 365 or 366 days, divided into 12 months: *The project ends early next year.* ◊ *The company has struggled in recent years.* ◊ *Recruiting is a non-stop, year-round activity* (= one that continues all year). ◊ *Investors had a difficult year in 2002.*
SYN CALENDAR YEAR
2 [C] a period of 12 months, measured from a particular time: *I started working here two years ago.* ◊ *The contract is worth $20 million a year.* ◊ *In the UK, the tax year runs from April to April.* ◊ *The share is down 45 cents from the year-ago period* (= compared with the same period a year ago). ◊ *year-earlier levels* (= levels at the same time the year before) → YEAR-TO-DATE
3 years [pl.] a long time: *They have been trying for years to break into the market.*
IDM **car, product, manager, etc. of the ˈyear** a thing or person that people decide is the best in a particular field in a particular year ˌ**year after ˈyear** every year for many years: *There were tax increases year after year.* ˌ**year by ˈyear** as the years pass; each year: *The company grew steadily year by year.* **year ˈin, year out** every year: *I've been buying the same brand of coffee year in, year out.* ˌ**year on ˈyear** (*Accounting*) (*used especially when talking about figures, prices, etc.*) compared with the figures, prices, etc. a year earlier: *Spending has increased year on year.* ◊ *a year-on-year increase in spending* ˌ**year over ˈyear** (*Accounting*) compared with the same period a year earlier: *Sales have declined 9% year over year.*

yearbook /ˈjɪəbʊk; *AmE* ˈjɪrbʊk/ *noun* [C]
a book published once a year, giving details of what happened the previous year in a particular company, country or area of activity

ˌ**year ˈend** (*AmE also* ˌ**year's ˈend**) *noun* [U; sing.]
1 the end of the FINANCIAL YEAR: *We will review our financial position at year end.* ◊ *We are on track to achieve our year-end targets.*
❍ **at/before/by (the) year end**
2 the end of December
→ END-OF-YEAR

year-ˈlong (*AmE spelling also* **yearlong**) *adjective*
[only before noun]
continuing for a whole year: *a year-long downward trend* ◊ *a year-long investigation/study*

yearly /ˈjɪəli; ˈjɜːli; *AmE* ˈjɪrli/ *adjective*

SEE ALSO: **half-yearly**

1 happening once a year or every year: *Pay is reviewed on a yearly basis.*
2 paid, valid or calculated for one year: *your yearly income*
▸ **ˈyearly** *adverb*: *The committee meets twice yearly.*

ˌ**year's ˈend** = YEAR END

ˌ**year to ˈdate** *noun* [sing.] (*abbr* **YTD**)
(*Accounting*) this year as far as today: *Our turnover has risen 50% in the year to date.* ▸ **year-to-ˈdate** *adjective, adverb*: *Year-to-date revenues are down 4%.* ◊ *The shares are up 15% year-to-date.*

,yellow 'book *noun* [C, usually sing.]
a book that contains all the necessary information
about a particular subject

,Yellow 'Pages™ *noun* [pl., U]
a book with yellow pages that gives a list of
companies and organizations and their telephone
numbers, arranged according to the type of
services they offer: *Look in the Yellow Pages to find
your nearest car hire firm.* → WHITE PAGES

'Yellow Sheets™ (*also spelled* **yellow sheets**)
noun [pl., U]
(*Finance*) in the US, a list of the latest prices of
bonds and other information about them, that is
published every day → PINK SHEETS

yen /jen/ *noun* (*plural* **yen**)
1 [C] the unit of money in Japan: *a net loss of
110 million yen*
2 the yen [sing.] the value of the **yen** compared
with the value of the money of other countries: *The
yen has fallen/risen against the dollar.*
See note at INCREASE

★ **yield** /jiːld/ *noun, verb*
● *noun* [C,U]

SEE ALSO: **current yield, dividend ~, earnings ~, high-
~, initial ~, net ~, nominal ~, running ~**

1 (*Finance*) the total amount of profits or income
that you get from an investment or from a business:
This will give a yield of 10% on your investment. ◇

*The dividend yield on the stock is too attractive to
miss.* See note at PROFIT
2 the total amount of sth that is produced: *a high
crop yield*
● *verb* [+ obj]
to produce or provide a profit, an income, a result,
a crop or a product: *Higher-rate bank deposit
accounts yield good returns.* ◇ *The oil field has
yielded over 3 million barrels.* ◇ *The research should
yield useful information.*

,yield to ma'turity *noun* [C] (*plural* **yields to
maturity**) (*abbr* **YTM**)
(*Finance*) the amount of money that an investor will
get from a bond if it is not paid back until the end
of its life (**maturity**), usually expressed as a
percentage SYN REDEMPTION YIELD

yours /jɔːz; *AmE* jɔrz; jɔːrz; jʊrz/ *pronoun* (*usually
Yours*) used, usually in phrases, at the end of a
letter before signing your name: (*BrE*) *Yours
sincerely/faithfully* ◇ (*AmE*) *Sincerely yours* ◇ (*AmE*)
Yours truly

yr (*AmE spelling usually* **yr.**) *abbr* (*only used in written
English*)
1 year
2 your

yrs (*AmE spelling usually* **yrs.**) *abbr* (*only used in
written English*)
1 years
2 Yrs a short way of writing **Yours** at the end of
letters

YTD /ˌwaɪ tiː 'diː/ = YEAR TO DATE

YTM /ˌwaɪ tiː 'em/ = YIELD TO MATURITY

Z z

ZBB /ˌzed biː 'biː; *AmE* ˌziː/ = ZERO-BASED
BUDGETING

zero /'zɪərəʊ; *AmE* 'zɪroʊ; 'ziː-/ *number, verb*
● *number* (*plural* **zeros** *or* **zeroes**)
1 (*especially AmE*) the number 0 SYN NOUGHT (*BrE*)
2 the lowest possible amount or level; nothing at
all: *I rated my chances of promotion as zero.* ◇ *The
economy recorded zero growth in November.*
● *verb* (**zeroes, zeroing, zeroed, zeroed**)
PHRV **,zero 'in on sb/sth** to fix all your attention
on the person or thing mentioned: *They zeroed in
on the key issues.*

,zero-based 'budgeting *noun* [U] (*abbr* **ZBB**)
(*Accounting*) a system of planning a company's
budget where each department is not
automatically given all the money it spent the
previous year, but instead must give reasons why it
needs all the money it is asking for: *We use zero-
based budgeting to control spending.*

,zero 'defects *noun* [pl.]
(*Production*) used to describe a system of quality
management which aims to make products that
contain almost no faults: *a strategy for achieving
zero defects in construction* ◇ *Our products are
manufactured to our zero-defects standard.* → RIGHT
FIRST TIME

,zero-'rated *adjective*
used to describe goods or services on which a
particular tax (**VAT**) is not charged: *These goods are
zero-rated for VAT.* → STANDARD-RATED
▶ **,zero-'rate** *verb* [+ obj], **,zero 'rating** *noun* [U]: *a
plan to abolish the zero rating of exports within
the EU*

,zero-'sum game *noun* [C]
a situation in which what is gained by one person
or group is lost by another person or group
→ POSITIVE-SUM GAME

zip /zɪp/ *verb* [+ obj] (**-pp-**)
(*IT*) **zip sth (up)** to make a computer file smaller in
order to send it or store it SYN COMPRESS
OPP UNZIP

'zip code (*also spelled* **ZIP**) = POSTCODE

'zip file *noun* [C]
(*IT*) a computer file that has been made smaller in
order to be sent or stored

★ **zone** /zəʊn; *AmE* zoʊn/ *noun, verb*
● *noun* [C]

SEE ALSO: **enterprise zone, foreign trade ~, free ~,
time ~**

1 an area or a region with a particular feature or
use: *an industrial zone* ◇ *the danger/safety zone*
2 one of the areas that a larger area is divided into
for the purpose of organization: *postal charges to
countries in zone 2*
● *verb* [+ obj] (*usually* **be zoned**)
1 to keep an area of land to be used for a
particular purpose: *The town centre was zoned for
office development.*
2 to divide an area of land into smaller areas
▶ **'zoning** *noun* [U]

'Z-score *noun* [C]
(*Finance*) a measure of how likely a business is to
fail: *A credit-strength test gave the company a Z-score
of 0, which indicated a 50% probability of
bankruptcy.*

Pronunciation and phonetic symbols

Phonetic symbols are used to show the pronunciation of single word headwords such as **ring** /rɪŋ/. They are also used for any unusual or difficult words that form part of a phrase (= a headword with two or more words) such as **Ansoff 'matrix** /'ænzɒf; AmE -zɔːf/. For most phrases, the pronunciation is not given but the typical stress of the phrase is marked (see below for **stress in phrases**).

Consonants

p	pen	/pen/
b	bad	/bæd/
t	tea	/tiː/
d	did	/dɪd/
k	cat	/kæt/
g	get	/get/
tʃ	chain	/tʃem/
dʒ	jam	/dʒæm/
f	fall	/fɔːl/
v	van	/væn/
θ	thin	/θɪn/
ð	this	/ðɪs/
s	see	/siː/
z	zoo	/zuː/
ʃ	shoe	/ʃuː/
ʒ	vision	/'vɪʒn/
h	hat	/hæt/
m	man	/mæn/
n	now	/naʊ/
ŋ	sing	/sɪŋ/
l	leg	/leg/
r	red	/red/
j	yes	/jes/
w	wet	/wet/

The symbol (r) indicates that British pronunciation will have /r/ only if a vowel sound follows directly at the beginning of the next word, as in **share offer**; otherwise the /r/ is omitted. For American English, all the /r/ sounds should be pronounced.

Vowels and diphthongs

iː	see	/siː/	
i	happy	/'hæpi/	
ɪ	sit	/sɪt/	
e	ten	/ten/	
æ	cat	/kæt/	
ɑː	father	/'fɑːðə(r)/	
ɒ	got	/gɒt/	(British English)
ɔː	saw	/sɔː/	
ʊ	put	/pʊt/	
u	actual	/'æktʃuəl/	
uː	too	/tuː/	
ʌ	cup	/kʌp/	
ɜː	fur	/fɜː(r)/	
ə	about	/ə'baʊt/	
eɪ	say	/seɪ/	
əʊ	go	/gəʊ/	(British English)
oʊ	go	/goʊ/	(American English)
aɪ	my	/maɪ/	
ɔɪ	boy	/bɔɪ/	
aʊ	now	/naʊ/	
ɪə	near	/nɪə(r)/	(British English)
eə	hair	/heə(r)/	(British English)
ʊə	pure	/pjʊə(r)/	(British English)

Stress

A *syllable* is part of a word that has one vowel sound and usually one or more consonants, for example *stock* has one syllable and *economics* has four syllables. When a syllable is *stressed* (= emphasized when speaking) it appears louder and longer than other syllables and can be noticed by changes in how high or low the voice is. The mark /'/ is placed before the syllable with the strongest stress (= *primary stress*). For example, in the word **moonlight** /'muːnlaɪt/ the first syllable is stressed while in **expense** /ɪk'spens/ the second syllable is stressed. Longer words with more than two syllables often have a *secondary stress* which is marked /ˌ/. The secondary stress is weaker than the primary stress, for example **integration** /ˌɪntɪ'greɪʃn/.

British English and American English

If there is a difference between British English and American English in the pronunciation of a word, then the British English form is usually given first with *AmE* written before the American pronunciation. For example:

quarterly /ˈkwɔːtəli; *AmE* ˈkwɔːrtərli/ .

If only part of a word is pronounced differently then only the part that is different is shown. Hyphens (-) represent the rest of the word. For example:

grocery /ˈɡrəʊsəri; *AmE* ˈɡroʊ-/

Derivatives

Derivatives are normally either the same as the headword or are formed by adding a suffix to the headword. They usually have the same pronunciation as the headword, plus the suffix if this is needed. Common suffixes include: *-ly* (/-li/), *-ness* (/-nəs/), etc. The pronunciation is not usually shown and only the stress of the derivative is marked. For example:

illicit /ɪˈlɪsɪt/ *adjective*
il'licitly *adverb*

However, if it is not clear how a derivative should be pronounced, then the pronunciation is shown:

statistic /stəˈtɪstɪk/ *noun*
statistical /stəˈtɪstɪkl/ *adjective*

Weak forms and strong forms

Certain very common words, such as **for, of** and **to** have a strong and a weak pronunciation depending on whether they are stressed or not. As an example, **for** can be pronounced /fɔː(r)/ (*stressed*) or /fə(r)/ (*unstressed*). When these words are used in phrases, such as ˌ**letter of** ˈ**credit** /ˌletər əv ˈkredɪt/ or **B-to-B** /ˌbiː tə ˈbiː/, they are not usually stressed and so the weak form is used.

Stress in phrases

A phrase will often have more than one stress. For example in ˌ**standard deviˈation** there are two stresses. When the phrase is said on its own, the stress on **deviˈation** is stronger so this is marked as the primary stress. Many examples with two important words, such as ˌ**systematic ˈrisk** and ˌ**carbon ˈcopy**, have a secondary stress followed by a primary stress.

Sometimes the main stress is not on the last word of a phrase. For example, in ˈ**press kit** the main stress is on **press**. Notice that **kit** is unmarked. Secondary stress is only marked *after* the primary stress when there is a word of two syllables or more, for example ˈ**press communiˌcations**.

The stress patterns we have given on phrases are the recommended ones, but you may occasionally hear others. For example, the stress may change when phrases are combined with other words. The main stress in the first phrase may move to the place of the secondary stress to avoid two stressed syllables being next to each other. For instance, ˌ**duty-ˈfree** has the main stress on **free**, but in the phrase ˌ**duty-free ˈshops** the stress on **free** is missing.

Longer phrases, with more than two important words, are generally shown with several primary stresses. In this case, the last primary stress should always be made the main stress. For example in ˈ**foreign diˈrect inˈvestment** there are three fairly equal stresses, but the main emphasis in pronunciation should come on **inˈvestment**.